Dalhuisen on International Commercial, Financial and Trade Law

D1808789

Jan Dalhuisen

Professor of Law, King's College London,
Visiting Professor at the University of California at Berkeley,
and the University of New South Wales, Sydney

·H A R T·
PUBLISHING

OXFORD AND PORTLAND OREGON
2004

Published in North America (US and Canada) by
Hart Publishing
c/o International Specialized Book Services
5804 NE Hassalo Street
Portland, Oregon
97213-3644
USA

Hart Publishing is a specialist legal publisher based in Oxford, England. To order
further copies of this book or to request a list of other publications please write to:

Hart Publishing, Salters Boatyard, Folly Bridge, Abingdon Rd, Oxford, OX1 4LB
Telephone: +44 (0)1865 245533 Fax: +44 (0)1865 794882
email: mail@hartpub.co.uk
WEBSITE: http//:www.hartpub.co.uk

British Library Cataloguing in Publication Data
Data Available

ISBN 1-84113-450-3 (paperback)

Typeset by Olympus Infotech Pvt Ltd, India, in Minion 10/12 pt
Printed and bound in Great Britain by
MPG Books Ltd, Bodmin, Cornwall

To my teachers and my students

DALHUISEN ON INTERNATIONAL COMMERCIAL, FINANCIAL AND TRADE LAW

The second edition of this uniquely wide-ranging work once again grapples with the dynamic and complex fields of law which make up the modern law of international commerce, finance and trade. As a guide for students and practitioners it is unrivalled.

The original structure has been retained, with an extensive introductory chapter dealing with the sources of the modern law in its comparative context, and modern efforts to develop uniform or harmonised law at international level (in the EU, Uncitral and Unidroit). Further chapters then deal with with contract in the Common and Civil Law, payments, movable tangible and intangible assets, and the concept of ownership and possession. Later chapters look at finance leases, repos, receivable financings and securitisations, the regulation of cross border financial services and investment banking practices. Litigation and procedural matters which are often by-passed in books dealing with substantive commercial law, are covered in chapters devoted to international jurisdiction, provisional measures, the recognition of foreign judgments and bankruptcy decrees, and, finally, international arbitration.

From the reviews of the first edition:

The essence of Dalhuisen's contribution is that it synthesizes and integrates diverse bodies of law into a coherent and accessible account ... remarkable in its scope and depth. It stands alone in its field not only due to its comprehensive coverage, but also its original methodology. Although it appears to be a weighty tome, in fact, in light of its scope, it is very concise. While providing a wealth of intensely practical information, its heart is highly conceptual and very ambitious. It is likely to become a classic text in its field.

Jane K Winn in the *American Journal of Comparative Law*

Dalhuisen's style is relaxed ... what he writes convinces without the need for an excess of references to sources...a highly valuable contribution to the legal literature. It adopts a useful, modern approach to teaching the young generation of lawyers how to deal with the increasing internationalisation of law. It is also helpful to the practising lawyer and to legislators.

Christina Hultmark Ramberg in the *Uniform Law Review/Revue de Droit Uniforme*

... this is a big book, with big themes and an author with the necessary experience to back them up. ... Full of insights as to the theories that underlie the rules governing contract, property and security, it is an important contribution to the law of international commerce and finance.

William Blair QC in *Law Quarterly Review*

Professor Jan Dalhuisen ... presents a very different case: that of a civilized and cultivated cosmopolitan legal scholar, with a keen sense of international commercial and financial practice, with an in-depth grounding in both comparative legal history and comparative law, combined with the ability to transcend conventional English black-letter law description with critical judgement towards institutional wisdom and intellectual fashions. ... a wide-ranging, historically and comparatively very deep and comprehensive commentary, but which is also very contemporary and forward-looking on many or most of the issues relevant in modern transnational commercial, contract and financial transactions...

Thomas Wälde in *International and Comparative Law Quarterly*

DALHUISEN ON INTERNATIONAL COMMERCIAL,
FINANCIAL AND TRADE LAW

Preface to the Second Edition

It is pleasing that so soon after the first edition, a second edition of this book became necessary. I have taken the opportunity to introduce a number of clarifications, remove unnecessary duplication (although I have not hesitated to repeat where cross-referencing seemed less opportune), and correct some mistakes. Teaching experience in the graduate programmes in which this book is mostly used suggested further that some parts of Chapters I, III and VI be rewritten. In respect of Chapter VI, that became necessary also because of the many new EU Directives in the financial area as part of the present EU Action Program aiming at a Single European Market for Financial Services and the looming impact of the Basel II Accord on the capital adequacy requirements for banks. The part on book-entry systems for investment securities in Chapter IV was also revisited. Important changes were also required because of the new texts of Articles 1 and 9 UCC in the USA, the revised Commercial Code and the new Financial Code in France, the amendments to the German Civil Code (BGB) in the area of contract law, the completion of the Mobile Equipment Convention of Unidroit and of the Receivable Finance Convention of Uncitral, and the entering into force of the EU Collateral Directive.

I am well aware that a book of this nature is a work in progress that can never be finished. The best that can be expected is to give interested readers, practitioners, academics and students up-to-date information and insights that may contribute to their better understanding of the forces that now shape international commercial and financial law and of the positive law that so emerges. The emphasis on finance derives here from the fact that it has become the modern motor of commercial law replacing to some considerable extent the more traditional sale of goods and trade or mercantile impetus.

The main aim of the book remains therefore the contribution to a more informed debate on the transforming forces in modern commerce and finance and the development of a view concerning their impact on the applicable law. This law is not here viewed as static but as a forward moving set of internationalised principles and rules that are largely articulated by participants themselves and draw widely from their practical needs, established ways of dealing, and best practices. It is submitted that only in this more *functional* manner the law in this area will be able to retain the necessary relevance in the distribution of risks and tasks between participants and in the solution of their disputes either in the ordinary courts or ever more often through international commercial arbitrations or other forms of ADR that are forced increasingly to ignore a more formal and purely domestic concept of law. In this connection it should not be forgotten that the law only provides one way of solving or avoiding disputes and can only effectively continue to do so if it remains convincing in its responses at the level of practicalities.

By attempting to understand and deal with this, in essence, dynamic nature of the law as it develops in the commercial and financial area at the international level as the new international law merchant or *Lex Mercatoria*, there results quite naturally a strong reconfirmation of party autonomy, its reach and evolution into practices, even in areas not traditionally at the free disposition of the parties (like in property law). Another important aspect is to determine how far this law must continue to respect and support domestic policies in international situations and how much parties, by choosing some other law, may affect such domestic policies. In practice, as far as the reach of party autonomy is concerned, the emphasis is increasingly on legal structuring that avoids the risk of having inappropriate or atavistic domestic (proprietary) laws or remote regulatory systems applied.

As to substance, one of the essences here is the abandonment of nineteenth-century concepts of contract and property law that are anthropomorphic (therefore centered on physical persons and assets and their relationships and dealings amongst themselves) and that often led to closed systems of rights but in more modern times also to a prescriptive approach particularly associated with consumer protection needs, especially in contract law with an important and on the whole undesirable, spill-over effect into the professional sphere. Barring overarching fundamental legal principles, including those aimed at the avoidance of fraud and other forms of manipulation and anti-competitive behaviour, and barring also relevant public policy limitations (emanating from states that may be justly deemed concerned in the particular international case), it seems to me that there are here, in dealings amongst professionals, few fundamental obstacles in terms of preordained balances of interests, abstract standards of behaviour, permanencies of legal systems, or the application of national laws. There are only practical needs.

In my view, the foremost task of academia in this area is to help adjust our traditional legal perceptions so as to respond to the new internationalised environment, its dynamics and needs, whilst indicating at the same time when, why and to what extent practical considerations of this nature may sometimes become exhausted. In commercial and financial law, such academic endeavour should thus hasten the adjustment of our more traditional notions of contract, property and tort in order better to capture modern realities and to achieve greater predictive value. In international commerce and finance, it implies finding or redefining legal concepts that may now transcend national borders and that may serve as yardsticks against which the positive law of a national or transnational type can be independently tested for its strengths and weaknesses. Any real success of academia in re-defining the basic legal structures (especially in contract and property) in the light of these modern needs in a less time- and place-determined manner could be of great importance. To (re)define these legal structures, legal history and comparative law may help, but the key is to find ones that can deal better with present-day realities and dynamics and articulate them into law.

Thus in contract, the old model of offer and acceptance, of consensus and bargain may be superseded by more modern notions of partnership in which we must distinguish between the pre-contractual, contractual or post-contractual phases, define the parties rights and duties in each of them, and accept evolving forms of dependency. It may impose objective standards of behaviour that transcend the will of the parties but may still work out differently for professionals as compared to others. Thus once a relationship is entered into, the future behaviour of the parties may no longer be considered merely a question of the original choice as everyone entering any type of relationship will know. Certainly in complex business dealings, reference to the parties' original intent becomes a nebulous concept. Justified reliance and, where appropriate, duties of care are likely to take its place. They can only be articulated on the basis of what the reasonable expectations of participants are in their various business environments, in international commerce and finance between well-informed professionals. They may on the other hand not need or expect much protection beyond what they have expressly negotiated and set as the applicable behavioural standard amongst themselves. In many countries of the civil law, notions of good faith in contract may underline and support this new approach.

In property law, especially regarding chattels and intangibles, the traditional (civil law) approach based on one integrated closed system of proprietary rights may no longer suffice either. To deal with the convulsions in the traditional domestic laws of property when becoming inadequate or even dysfunctional, eg to support the new financial structures that international business requires, more flexibility is needed and a more fractured set-up much more akin to that of equity (in common law terms) may become the better model. That set-up is in essence open, subject to a better protection of *bona fide* purchasers. It concerns especially the operation of floating charges, constructive trust and tracing notions, trusts, conditional and temporary ownership rights like repos and finance leases, assignments without notification, set-off and netting facilities, and the proprietary aspects of agency, all areas where civil law has had greater problems in coming to terms with modern life than common law (in its equity variant). New models, proto- or ideal types should thus enter the national and transnational commercial and financial law. They are likely to be the result of reinterpretation or re-characterisation in the light of a greater role for party autonomy even in property matters and of a broad acceptance of new practices or customs also in this area. In commerce and finance, these are now likely to be internationalized and to become embedded in the modern *lex mercatoria*.

In this vein, I have tried to develop a number of themes that were perhaps less obvious in the first edition. First, as a general proposition and on a more philosophical note, I do not believe that in the law's application it is entirely possible to separate the law that 'is' from the law that 'ought to be' and it may not even be desirable. The American 'realist' or more functional approaches in 'law and economics', 'law and sociology', and 'law and ethics' confirm this and more attention is therefore paid to them in this edition. This separation can, in any event, not easily be achieved when newer fact situations and practices present themselves all the time. To repeat, law in order to remain living and relevant must move with society serving its justified needs as best it can whilst promoting at least in our Western culture the ongoing objective of achieving order in a more just, peaceful and efficient manner. In a changing world, this law can in its formulation and application not be static or depend for its adjustment solely on national legislators or domestic precedent, certainly not in an international setting even if it must be hoped that its basic values are more permanent. It follows that the positive law (except where it remains absolutely settled) cannot always present a set of preconceived solutions, certainly not where it must now also deal with internationalisation or globalisation issues and from there with its own trans-nationalisation.

Whilst noting this, it should be acknowledged that the European legal culture of today, both on the European Continent and in England, remains largely positivist, formal and also nationalistic, at least in private law. It also remains perceived as essentially a given, even in an EU context which would appear to require a much more outward looking perspective and a willingness to transform. It would seem that the more unstable the private law by its very nature becomes in an uncertain and transforming world, the more there is (at least in Europe) a longing for certainty which is often expected still to result from a mathematical application of existing black letter law from domestic legal systems that are supposed to supply a solution for all eventualities, even in international cases. In this attitude, novelty is not considered a supreme evolutionary challenge but a disrupting factor.

In modern international commerce and finance, the desire for certainty has an obvious, more practical, root in a need for predictability in the division of tasks and the proper management of risk, but it can no longer be expected from a simple reliance on fixed domestic rules or traditions. These may in fact become major distorting and thereby destabilising forces themselves, around which parties must try to manage their risk and structure their deals often by opting for other more neutral and flexible laws to the extent they can do so, which could include an option for the *lex mercatoria*, although the room for manoeuvre will be limited, particularly in proprietary and public policy issues as already mentioned. Here more objective standards will have to develop, also at the international level.

This is all far removed from the more *realist* or functional attitude long since adopted in the USA which lives in constant search of a better law and accepts and has learnt to live with the unavoidable uncertainties whilst trying to limit and manage them with a much more incidental but also more modern approach. This is so even in proprietary law where equitable principles are developed further. That is reflected in the proprietary paragraphs of Articles 2 (sale of goods), 2A (finance leases), 4A (electronic payments), 8 (security entitlements) and 9 (secured transactions) UCC. They do not aspire to one proprietary system and are pragmatic in defining proprietary rights per subject or product. Naturally, given the unavoidable complications, especially in the last four Articles, there is here increasing emphasis on dealings and proprietary relationships between professionals only.

Even if, in order to retain its credibility, the law develops cautiously, develop it must and that development is now often fast in all its aspects, in Europe no less than elsewhere, all the more so in commerce and finance. Whatever the root cause, it is for us to spot the needs, articulate the trends, help formulate answers and define the legal structures to assist both the judicial and legislative functions in this process. I find it fascinating and of the greatest practical and intellectual interest to try to do so for private law now that it so clearly stands at the beginning of a new era of legal development leading to its trans-nationalisation in its response to the fundamental internationalisation or globalisation of all commerce and finance in the professional sphere.

One must thus accept that domestic legal systems and traditions no longer hold the key to the future development especially of commercial and financial law. They can no longer provide certainty that also guarantees adequate quality. A better understanding of risk and the way it can be handled and must be shared is more likely to do so. It is the international business community *itself* that through its reliance, restraint and practices holds this world together, therefore no longer in the first instance domestic laws, whatever their pretence. In international business, certainty must come foremost from the behavioural patterns of the participants themselves, their own discipline, and from the way they habitually handle risk, including the risk of a lesser reliance on domestic laws if proving wholly inappropriate or inadequate. It cannot or no longer come either from mere intellectualisation or abstract schemes resulting in more or less logical systems of law.

It follows that in identifying the new law, I am looking for what makes sense in the international business community and not necessarily for a common core in domestic laws. I also believe it largely a mistake to dwell here on (domestic) cultural patterns and divides. In any event, it is an established fact that in most countries many of the basic structures of private law were, at least in contract and property, always borrowed from other legal cultures, be they Roman or Byzantine for much of civil law, and Anglo-Saxon (therefore germanic) or feudal (therefore frankish) for much of the common law. But just as relevant is that these domestic laws of whatever origin were mostly recast by nineteenth century analysis and thinking which could not have a sufficient perspective nor realistic claim on future legal needs and developments. This is only to re-emphasise that the past or even what is done at present in various countries only proves of limited help and guidance for the future and that the present commercial and financial law structures must be constantly revisited, tested for their validity and effectiveness on the basis of ever and often rapidly evolving practicalities and needs, now more and more in an international context, and adjusted accordingly.

In this connection, I am also convinced that attempts at gathering the principles eg of modern contract law in the manner of the Unidroit Principles of International Commercial Contracts and of the Principles of European Contract Law have often been misguided. First, they are largely driven by a consumer ethos and remain trapped in an old-fashioned psychological and anthropomorphic notion of contract law and the protections it must bring. Second, they have no clear concept of what modern commerce and finance is, of what it needs legally to advance, and of how the law deals with dynamism. These sets of Principles were never demanded by practitioners and appear to be driven by misguided paternalism. The EU seems nevertheless determined to continue on this course. It is to be appreciated in this connection that a codification of this type is now only considered as an alternative, for parties to opt into. It is as such unlikely to make much of an impact. For it to be of any real value, there would appear to be a need for an entirely different mindset. This would be no less needed for any similar compilations of proprietary laws.[1] A practitioner's approach would be necessary in which intellectualisation would be the end, not the beginning of the process.

This is the way of the modern *lex mercatoria,* whose development as the modern transnational law of commerce and finance in this dynamic sense is here perceived as a matter of the autonomous evolution of *private* law within the international commercial and financial legal order. How this *lex mercatoria,* its development and the hierarchy of norms within it is to be known and articulated was largely the topic of the first edition, although the notion of legal orders itself receives further attention in this one.

In preparing the second edition, another more particular concern has been the already referred to evolution of state intervention in private law and the determination of the proper place and legal status of domestic *public* policies or governmental interests in international commerce and finance. The true issue here is to what extent these domestic public policies or interests remain relevant in the internationalisation of the commercial and financial flows and must be accepted and prevail over the *lex mercatoria* in civil litigation wherever initiated or in international commercial arbitrations. It could also be cast in terms of how the conflicts between the international commercial and financial legal order on the one hand and domestic legal orders on the other are to be resolved where governmental interests are involved.

There is no single or simple answer to this conundrum. Party autonomy cannot be the true solution, as indeed it is not in policy issues that arise in international commercial and financial order itself. As far as domestic public policies are concerned, obviously, the importance of the issues to be resolved relates, for the relevant domestic authorities, foremost to any conduct and resulting effect on their territory and more generally to the closeness of their policies with, or remoteness from the case if arising elsewhere (eg in the protection of nationals against foreign security frauds or anti-competitive abuse). It poses the important question to what extent such domestic policies or preferences are internationally justified and acceptable whilst the proportionality of the application of these policies in international cases may also need to be weighed.

At least in the American approach, there is, in this area, some return to seventeenth and eighteenth century Dutch *comity* thinking as introduced by Story in nineteenth century America. The Restatements reflect this in Restatement (Second) of Conflict of Laws, section 6 and in particular in Restatement (Third) of Foreign Relations, sections 402 and 403. There is some resonance of this in Article 7 of the EU Rome Convention on the Law Applicable to Contractual Obligations. In the USA, it fits well in the interest analysis now more generally adopted in conflicts cases. In this approach, there are no hard and fast rules and much depends on the facts and on more abstract notions of substantive justice and fairness. In view of the resulting discretionary undertones, the competency of courts and

---

[1] Only the Trust Law Principles so far developed appear to hold out some greater promise as may the Insolvency Principles of the World Bank and IMF.

international arbitrators (in terms of arbitrability) becomes, unavoidably, another matter of great importance. Again, a form of discretion in terms of a more modern contact approach or *forum non-conveniens* attitude is likely to redress excessive claims to jurisdiction.

Mutual respect between legal orders is an important issue. At least in this aspect, their cultural and sociological origins and contours may still play an important role. The *lex mercatoria* must thus at the same time be aware of overriding domestic public policy interests and develop a notion of legitimacy and of proper authority or jurisdiction of its own as well as of competing statist legal orders. The latter have to do the same in respect of the *lex mercatoria*.

In view of the foregoing, it may well be that an *international (commercial) court system* may be helpful in the further development and steadying of the *lex mercatoria* whilst better dealing with the discretionary elements within it and governmental interest or public policy issues encroaching on it. In some reviews of the first edition, this thought was considered far-fetched if not utopian. But it need not be and has already found important supporters. This support was originally confined to an international review court mainly in respect of international arbitral awards, but it is not too extreme to allow interested parties in civil proceedings or international arbitrations to seek binding opinions from such a court on *lex mercatoria* issues as well as on the proper recognition of governmental policies and interests in its application.

In this connection, it is not too far-fetched either to consider domestic civil courts themselves as being international courts when deciding such issues[2] whilst in a later stage their decisions might even become appealable to such an international court. It should in this connection usefully be remembered that, at least in the EU, domestic courts sit as European courts in EU matters and must seek binding guidance from the European Court of Justice whenever issues of European law remain unclear. It is true that where national courts sit as international courts in deciding public international law matters they do so as yet without a guidance possibility from the International Court of Justice. Nevertheless, the idea of international judicial co-operation under an international court in this manner is not unprecedented. Neither is it extraordinary.

Whilst completing this second edition, it is a privilege to record the help and encouragement of many. I should especially like to mention Professor William Blair QC, Professor Martin Krygier, Professor John Linarelli, Professor Thomas Waelde, Professor Philip Wood, and Professor Jane Winn; my colleagues at King's College: Professor Mads Andenas (Director of the British Institute of International and Comparative Law) and Professor Martin Hunter, my former students or co-teachers Dr Lodewijk van Setten LLM, Mr Mihael Jeklic LLM, Dr Luc Pittet LLM, and Mr Nick Tabatadze LLM, my PhD students Mr Sammy Chowdhurry LLM, Mr Jiabin Huang LLM (who also much concerned himself with the Index), Mr Ondrej Petr LLM, and Mr Hailiang Yu LLM.

Finally, I should like to thank the library staff in Berkeley for all their help and the Center of European Law at King's College London for its financial support which made it possible to engage the necessary research assistance.

Berkeley
March 2004

---

[2] So the English Court of Appeal in *Amin Rasheed Shipping Corporation v Kuwait Insurance Company* [1983] 1 WLR 241.

Preface to the First Edition

This book is written for students and younger researchers or practitioners who may be interested in a more conceptual approach to some of the basic themes of international commercial, financial and trade law. It contains the expanded texts of the lectures which I have given since 1990, first at the University of Utrecht and later at King's College in London, the University of California at Berkeley (Boalt Hall), and at the Institute of International Relations (MGIMO) in Moscow. They also reflect seminars I gave at Boston College in Boston, at the Asser Institute in The Hague, and in the Pallas Program of the University of Nymwegen, as well as guest lectures in the Universities of Edinburgh and Warsaw and at the Humboldt University in Berlin. All elaborated on the ideas first set out in my Inaugural Address at Utrecht in 1991. The research was concluded per 1 May 2000.

Whatever its size may suggest, the book is no more than an introduction and comment on modern international commercial, financial and trade law and its development as I have come to understand it at first as legal practitioner, later as investment banker, regulator, international arbitrator, and academic. It sums up most of what I have learned, how I see the law in the professional sphere developing and how to apply it. By concentrating my efforts entirely on the globalisation of the law for professionals, I have tried to take similar contributions of others a step further. Perhaps at this stage, this is no more than providing some direction and mapping out and condensing the field. I hope that the result will bene-fit the more ambitious students and make them better aware of the modern trends and the problems with which we struggle. Much more could have been said and many more useful sources and comments could have been included, especially those in other languages. I hope that I may be forgiven for not having done so. In a book in English with this limited objective, it could hardly have been otherwise. The amount of information it contains, cer-tainly also on civil law developments, is probably already excessive.

It is my view that the more specialised areas of the law must always be considered from the perspective of the broader legal requirements of the community the law serves and therefore be placed in the broader legal framework operating for that community. That is most certainly also true for commercial, financial and trade law. This community is here the international business community and the legal framework is here an internation-alised legal framework or order. The existence of the former is hardly contested in a globalised market place, but the existence of the latter is still debated. It is clear, however, that the globalisation has led to a receding impact of local restrictions on the cross-border flows of talent, goods, services, payment and captial and has resulted in a significant form of liberalisation which is doing away also with undue limitations imposed by domestic private laws. It leaves ample room for spontaneous law formation at a trans-national level leading to a form of 'privatisation' of modern business law within a legal order of its own. It is logical and only a historical repeat that these tendencies should be clearest in commerce and finance. It makes it in my view possible and all the more necessary to revisit the core legal themes of private law themselves, now in this international or trans-nationalised environment.

This is the key to the approach of this book. It opens in Chapter I with a discussion of the sources of this new trans-national private law and particularly with the types and hier-archy of norms which function in it and with their legitimacy. These norms derive prima-rily from fundamental legal principle, from party autonomy, from custom and industry practices, from uniform treaty law (in as far as we have it and countries have acceded to it), and from general principles. These general principles may be derived from uniform treaty law or may be articulated in comparative law studies and perhaps now also in modern compilations of these principles and in academic writings. Residually, the applicable norms may still come from domestic laws through the application of the traditional private international law rules.

The existence of different sources of modern commercial, financial and trade law and the hierarchy between the norms flowing from them is in my view the essence of the modern *lex mercatoria*. This new law merchant is clearly not yet a unitary system of transnational substantive rules and it may, depending on the subject, still have an important domestic law component. Yet, although the content and sources of this modern commercial, financial and trade law may sometimes remain uncomfortably opaque, we may increasingly rely on a communality of insights in the basic structures of private law to propel this law forward. We may therefore expect that in this hierarchy of norms the transnational substantive law component will continue to gain in importance at the expense of domestic notions. At least in professional dealings, they will eventually be overtaken altogether, even if for the time being many still consider sovereignty rather than different legal orders the true originator of public as well as private law.

The basic chapters II and IV try to conceptualise the law of contract and of movable property in this internationalised legal framework of principles and rules. In passing, they also explain important similarities and differences in civil and common law and between the laws of countries in each group. They attempt to formulate basic contractual and proprietary notions as substantive law concepts of international professional dealings. In my understanding of the practical needs of the international business community, in contract the result is a largely objective approach, geared to the needs of parties who are willing and able to take some risks and only seek limited protections beyond a fairly literal interpretation of the text of their contract. In agency, it means direct rights for the principal regardlessn of whether the agency is disclosed, undisclosed or indirect. For the law of movable property, it means for chattels an emphasis on the protection of physical possession mainly through extended tort actions rather than through ownership notions and proprietary actions. Title transfer would require a form of physical delivery also. Monetary claims are here treated like ordinary assets, not much different therefore from chattels, and their assignment acquires as a consequence much the same form as a transfer of negotiable instruments. It puts emphasis on their liquidity. Assignment restrictions and debtor's defences are as a conseqence not favoured.

For movable property generally, the modern developments may mean a more contractualised or open system of proprietary rights balanced by a better protection of outsiders both through a (in German terms) largely abstract system of title transfer and a fuller *bona fide* purchaser protection that extends also into intangible assets. Thus the duality of ownership rights, especially in conditional ownership structures as alternatives to secured transactions (which themselves require reconsideration at trans-national level) and in trust-like structures, are in this book generally encouraged, subject to this better third party protection. Even now, practical needs suggest in all these instances an alignment of common and civil law.

The discussion of the more traditional subjects of commercial law, like the law concerning the international sale of goods, documents of title and negotiable instruments, investment securities, and payments may be found in the later parts of chapters II and IV, and in chapter III. Here the law is not static either. Modern payment facilities much affect the way payments are made. Bills of exchange are much less important than they once were. Seawaybills are often replacing bills of lading. Shares and bonds are increasingly replaced by book-entry entitlements with an own (increasingly) internationalised ownership structure and depository regime. Registration systems have also been considered for documents of title like bills of lading, for secured interests in major capital assets that habitually move cross-border, and for international bulk assignments. It may be the way of the future even if I am doubtful of the immediate need and impact beyond the area of investment securities entitlements and probably bills of lading. In the meantime, modern financing relies much less on traditional secured transactions and chapter V deals with some of the major alternative funding instruments like finance leases, repurchase agreements and factoring of receivables and with their legal characterisation largely in terms of conditional transfers. Chapter VI deals with the regulatory aspects of the international financial service industry and the evolution of its supervision particularly in the EU. It required a fairly detailed description of the modern banking and securities business, of the operation of the financial markets and their trading and settlement systems, of the deregulation at national levels, and of the re-regulation in an international context.

Chapters on comparative company law, competition law, intellectual property law and administrative law should perhaps have been added, but any more would have overwhelmed the effort and certainly the student also. A final chapter on international jurisdiction, the nature and international reach of provisional measures and injunctive relief, the recognition of foreign judgments and bankruptcy decrees, and the role of international arbitration and other dispute resolution methods must wait. Also the underlying policies and the more substantive law aspects of insolvency and of restitution (especially in its proprietary aspects), which, as an undercurrent, are so strongly present in this book, need perhaps be better articulated and defined, but this must also await another effort.

I am aware of some repetition in the book, mainly for educational reasons but also because I meant the various chapters and even some of the sections to stand more or less on their own so that they could be used separately depending on the nature of the course or interest. In view of the educational nature of the book, I have often painted with a fairly broad brush, tried to avoid too many diversions, but could not always eliminate detail. Indeed, it seemed to me that in order to be meaningful, it was often necessary to give more than the obvious, but only in chapter V on the modern financial products did I present a fully footnoted text. I thought that these products could hardly be understood in their legal characterisations without providing more background. Moreover, information in English on the details of the civil law in this area is so scant that it seemed useful to include more than the minimum.

It will be clear from the foregoing that the book is unashamedly internationalist. I cannot see any other useful direction for the development of modern commercial, financial and trade law and certainly consider the nineteenth century Continental European nationalisation of private law, supported by the conflicts rules of those times, a modern day aberration, entirely inadequate for the modern business community, and out of date. We badly need new substantive rules to support international commerce and finance in their own trans-border dynamics. Even if at this stage, within the new *lex mercatoria,* only an own legal order with a hierarchy of norms can be identified, often still containing a large domestic law component, this hierarchy of norms provides nevertheless an important framework within which trans-national substantive rules can and will develop further. I believe that international business can better live with the unavoidable uncertainties inherent in this approach than with a blind application of some national laws that were never developed to facilitate it, are not seldom arbitrarily chosen by the courts, and are in any event often inadequate to guide modern developments in commerce and finance.

Even comparative law studies are here only modest instruments. It is important to know the differences — and I have given much attention to these differences although I would not like to exaggerate them, especially not between civil and common law, at least not in commercial and financial matters. Of course there are some important variations in style and attitudes especially towards legislation and industry practices or custom, but, as the book will amply show, the differences in positive law are sometimes as great between the countries of the civil law as they are between civil and common law countries. It is unwise to draw here sharp lines even if, especially in proprietary matters, there are clear differences in the basic concepts whilst the law of equity has produced in common law a number of legal structures and remedies not to the same extent explored in civil law.

The true importance of comparative law is probably mainly in determining demonstrable similarities in the positive laws as they may give rise to general principles to be applied within the new *lex mercatoria*. Where there are no such similarities, however, it should be appreciated that the development of the modern international commercial and financial law is hardly a question of finding some middle ground between domestic legal concepts. Modern efforts are often still made in that direction, particularly in the formulation of uniform treaty law and of international (contract) principles. It lacks credibility. Moreover, the rules so formulated are frequently derived from consumer law thinking which on that account alone may make them largely unsuitable for international trade and commerce. Yet, in the further development of international commercial and financial law, domestic laws and local legal scholarship can and should not be ignored. I have particularly considered the laws in Germany, England, France and the US in this connection, and sometimes also those of the Netherlands because they have the latest civil law codification. However, in commercial and financial law, the key is to formulate within the present *lex mercatoria* framework principles or rules in which the international practice better recognises itself and finds its justified needs accepted and reasonably protected.

In the business area, where the internationalisation of the law is most crucial, the approach should moreover be truly global and not merely regional or confined to associations of States like the EU. I suspect that in the next few years this will become particularly obvious for the electronic trading, clearing and settlement of investment securities and for the rights that can be established in them and in the protection of these rights. The divisive effect of the application of purely domestic laws in this area is unlikely to be tolerated any longer by the international business community in the absence of clear policy needs. Bills of lading, bills of exchange and other negotiable or semi- negotiable instruments should also regain there purely international status as the eurobonds already have. This will reinforce the trend. On the other hand, outside the professional area, I see at this moment much less need for trans-nationalisation of private law on any scale whether or not in an EU context. It may even be undesirable. That also applies to consumer law itself until e-commerce takes over altogether. It still seems some way off, although in the end it may well exercise the most decisive influence on the internationalisation of private law but in the consumer area more likely through governmental action than spontaneously.

Trans-national principles and rules are at this juncture especially formulated by international practitioners guiding the developing international practices on the basis of party autonomy, but there is at this moment also much room for the modern practices, the new rules and particularly for the principles underlying them to be articulated in a more coherent and less incidental or casuistic manner at academic level. In proprietary matters there is in any event a need for a more objective approach as third party effect cannot be left to party autonomy alone. Indeed, the development of trans-national private law depends at this stage much on legal reasoning and on application of principle, hence also the sometimes jurisprudential tenor of this book. That is unavoidable in the formative era of any new law that can hardly be imposed from above. It presents a particular opportunity for academics to help, provided they can rise above domestic dogma and positive law and avoid consumer law thinking.

In this process, academics must not only give critical attention to the autonomous transformation of the basic domestic contractual and proprietary notions into transnational ones, but also to the modern harmonisation efforts in the EU, Uncitral and Unidroit. In the absence of any clear direction and any consensus on method and content, I am not sure that these efforts always present the right way forward. It was already said that they are often the result of compromise between domestic concepts and of consumer law thinking. As far as uniform treaty laws are concerned, they present the additional problem that they remain at best partial codifications, are only binding in some countries and often difficult to adapt. In commerce and finance, perhaps the efforts of the ICC and, for financial products, of the ISDA and PSA/ISMA for the swap and repo master agreements, are more to the point, even if also only incidental. All require more in depth study for their proper formulation and functioning and sometimes simplification. The efforts in Unidroit and Uncitral may need a second generation to become more widely acceptable, as the Vienna Convention on the International Sale of Goods already is, whilst also in the US only the Second Restatements became truly authoritive. Still, these efforts constitute another important endeavour at formulating more and better trans-national law.

I hope that this book may be of some help also. I take great pleasure in the thought that this will be, no doubt, the very last commercial law book ever written with a substantial historical introduction. I needed it to show that the civil law idea of codification and national law as the only true source of modern civil and commercial law is mistaken. For most of our history decentralising and centralising tendencies in law creation and private and public rule making have operated side by side in commerce and finance. So they do in the present globalisation process of the law. The other thought that delights me is that this may be the first modern book that tries to resume the thread of the school of Grotius where is was left in the eighteenth Century. This is much preferred to the revival of the old *ius commune* or *pandektist* tradition as sometimes advocated. It could never result in anything more than a second coming of the BGB, now at European level. Notwithstanding the great merits of that codification, this is unfeasible if only because it is unlikely to bring together the civil and common law and it holds little message for modern business. Also it would tend to exclude the experiences and needs in the Americas and the Far East. In international commerce and finance this would seem untenable.

In any event, the result would be unduly retrospective and narrow. As the Dutch recodification effort has shown, the whole idea of codification in the civil law sense is itself probably largely out of date and unlikely to present an adequate and forward looking view of the law. The result is a trap in time. But perhaps the greatest objection would be the method of developing the law through mere de- or induction. I favour on the whole a more interdisciplinary approach to the formulation of the new law geared to the practical needs of the business community and, in business law, to economic objectives. Of course the result needs to be put in a form with which lawyers can work and the application of the new law cannot be let to extra-legal considerations alone. That still leaves much room, however, for practical and efficiency considerations. Yet I have not entered here greatly into the nature of the contributions other disciplines can make and have also avoided much of a law and economics analysis. It provides no panacea either and it seemed to me better to take one step at a time. I argue, however, for a large measure of flexibility and openness.

Amidst all these different currents, I must admit that I have found it difficult at times to keep a clear perspective myself and have often thought of abandoning the project. Only thanks to the encouragement of colleagues, assistants and students have I been able to complete it. I am particularly grateful to Professors CGJ (Robin) Morse, Anthony Guest,

David Hayton, Eva Lomnicka, and John Phillips (King's College London), Professor Sir Roy Goode (Oxford), Professors Herma Kay, Richard Buxbaum, David Caron, Jesse Choper, Robert Cooter, Mel Eisenberg, Jesse Fried, James Gordley, Andrew Guzman and Sanford Kadish (UC at Berkeley), Professor Wolfgang Fikentscher (Munich), Professors Axel Flessner and Christoph Paulus (Humboldt Berlin), Professor Peter van Schilfgaarde (Utrecht), Professor Walter van Gerven (Leuven), Professor George Gretton (Edinburgh), Professor Rick Verhagen (Nymwegen), Professor Philip Wood (Queen Mary and Westfield College), Professor Cynthia Lichtenstein (Boston College), Dr M Andenas (King's College London) and Dr M N Boon (Utrecht), who saved me from some perilous mistakes, my PhD students Dr LD van Setten, Dr V Lazic, Dr J-H Roever, my research assistants S Chowdhury LLM, Assessor, and J J Dalhuisen MA who also did much of the Index, and my former students Tom Hornbaker JD and Jan Schaefer LLM, Assessor. I am no less grateful to Lord Slynn, Lord Justice Schiemann and Lord Justice Mance for their interest. As ever, Mr T Reynolds in the Berkeley Law Library was of immense help. Must I also mention the patience of my family and the exasperation of my publisher?

  Whilst finishing this book, I cannot forget my teachers to whom I owe most if not all. I was extremely fortunate to have been educated by the very best, first in Amsterdam, then in Berkeley. Of my main guiding examples, unfortunately Professor Stefan A Riesenfeld at Berkeley did not live to see the publication of this book in which he took a keen interest until last year, but Professor Herman CF Schoordijk of Amsterdam is much alive. I can think of nothing more fitting than to dedicate this work to my teachers and my students.

Berkeley/London
May 2000

Contents

1 MODERN INTERNATIONAL COMMERCIAL AND FINANCIAL LAW AND ITS SOURCES

PART I NATIONAL AND TRANS-NATIONAL OR INTERNATIONAL COMMERCIAL AND FINANCIAL LAW

2   DOMESTIC CONTRACT LAWS, UNIFORM INTERNATIONAL CONTRACT LAW AND INTERNATIONAL CONTRACT LAW PRINCIPLES: INTERNATIONAL SALES AND CONTRACTUAL AGENCY

PART I   DOMESTIC CONTRACT LAWS

PART II   NEGOTIABLE DOCUMENTS OF TITLE AND
NEGOTIABLE INSTRUMENTS

PART III   INVESTMENT SECURITIES

PART II   MAJOR TYPES OF FINANCE SALES

6 FINANCIAL SERVICES, FINANCIAL RISK,
AND FINANCIAL REGULATION. INTERNATIONALISATION,
LIBERALISATION, AND RE-REGULATION OF CROSS-BORDER
FINANCIAL SERVICES IN THE EU AND WTO/GATS

PART I INTRODUCTION: FINANCIAL SERVICES ACTIVITIES,
SERVICE PROVIDERS AND FINANCIAL REGULATION

PART III   THE THIRD GENERATION OF EU DIRECTIVES COMPLETING
THE INTERNAL MARKET IN FINANCIAL SERVICES AND THE EU ACTION PLAN
FOR A SINGLE MARKET IN FINANCIAL SERVICES

Table of Cases

Table of Legislation

1

Modern International Commercial and Financial Law and its Sources

Part I National and Transnational or International Commercial and Financial Law or the Law concerning Professional Dealings

1.1 Introduction

1.1.1 The Meaning of Modern International Commercial and Financial Law

Commercial law, including financial and trade law, has long had a somewhat different meaning and place in civil and common law. This has first to do with the different attitudes in civil and common law towards legislation and systematic legal thinking. The evolution of the civil and common law systems and their differences will be discussed in much greater detail below in sections 1.2 and 1.3. Here it is sufficient to note that the codification ethos in civil law countries looks primarily for legislation and (often) assumes that private law, including commercial law, is one coherent national system that is essentially statutory, as such complete, explainable from within and capable of finding proper solutions under all circumstances on the basis of the statute and otherwise the code's own system and logic. It means that in civil law there is little room for other sources of law, like industry practices and custom. Instead, there is a natural tendency to look for legislative texts and to extrapolate existing legislation and its system even into areas that were never explicitly covered by them or are new. That is then done particularly through deductive and analogical reasoning.

It is true that in this system special areas of private law, including commercial law, are admitted to exist but they are considered *lex specialis* to the general system and are not perceived as independent from it. These specialised areas have therefore no separate place in the law and cannot evolve independently. Implicit in this approach is that social order and legal certainty are expected from a legislator, not therefore from the participants themselves or from their ways of operating. Another consequence is that all law is here in essence domestic, localised and territorial, or statist in nature. It means that the development of the law, even private law and within it of commercial law, is perceived as primarily an activity of the state and is as such centralised and nationalised. This is the nineteenth century inheritance of the civil law, often closely associated which the emergence of the modern state on the European Continent. In this approach, even for international transactions, a domestic law must be found. In that case, the most proper law is believed to result from the rules of private international law. International practices or custom in the sense of an overarching transnational law have no proper place in this system and are in any event not given any autonomy. It follows that in this approach commercial law is confined in its evolution and is even in its international operation and application in essence viewed as domestic.

This is at least to some extent different in common law that in its formation and further evolution was often helped, but never monopolised by legislation in a similar manner. Systematic thinking and the search for and application of one coherent system of private law is here not a major issue either, at least not traditionally. It leaves in principle room for other sources of law, in trade, commerce and finance especially for industry practices, therefore for the order that participants create amongst themselves. Particularly commercial law has as a consequence retained more of an own status and role in common law countries, even if (as we shall see) especially in England nationalism and a tightening grip of the common law itself have also impacted on a more decentralised approach to commercial law. The attitude remains nevertheless different.

Other differences derive from the coverage of commercial law. In common law countries, commercial law is traditionally associated with the sale and transportation of goods (which in English terms are tangible movable assets only) and with the related shipping, insurance and payment methods, therefore traditionally with the contract for the sale of goods and with specialised modern trade terms like Fob and Cif, with bills of lading, bills of exchange, promissory notes and other methods of payment. It includes the entire area, that is to say the contractual as well as proprietary aspects of the trade in goods, therefore also the transfer of ownership and any secured interests in these assets, e.g. to protect payment or raise finance, and the protection of *bona fide* purchasers. Thus in common law, the transfer of property in goods is seen as essentially a commercial law issue and not as a matter that is dealt with primarily by a general system of property law on which common law traditionally lays less stress anyway. It led to a tendency to treat the entire law of chattels and intangible assets as a distinct area within the common law. This more fractured approach to property law is also borne out by the operation of equitable proprietary interests as more incidental proprietary rights,[1] in commercial law especially relevant in the area of security interests in goods and in the assignments of payment claims or receivables.[2]

In civil law terms, the coverage of commercial law is traditionally different, much broader on the one hand and narrower on the other. It is broader in that it is not unusual e.g. to find company law and insolvency law and much of financial law covered by it, therefore also services — certainly in the French tradition. But it is narrower as this coverage is only partial and major topics in each commercial law area remain covered by the general law or system as just mentioned. This concerns particularly the proprietary aspects (like transfer of ownership in goods and investments and the creation of any security interests therein even if connected with the sale of goods), and their operation in a bankruptcy and brings with it the civil law restriction to only a small number of internally closely connected property rights. But it also concerns the general notions of contract law and of partnerships which in the commercial law area are in civil law equally derived from the general private law system.

When we turn to what may now perhaps be considered *international* commercial law or the new law merchant (*lex mercatoria*), we see that in as far as *coverage* is concerned the common law approach is the starting point. It means that the sale of goods is the essence as demonstrated eg by the 1980 Vienna Convention on the International Sale of Goods (CISG) and the other work of the United Nations Commission for International Trade Law (Uncitral), especially in the areas of bills of lading, negotiable instruments, payments, and receivable financing. Earlier it was shown also in the area of shipping and maritime law. It does not necessarily follow that the common law *method* became also prevalent in this type of international law, but there is a less structured approach and the attittude is bottom-up

---

[1] See for the notion of equity and its development in common law countries, s 1.2.11 *infra*.
[2] In England, commercial law as such is also referred to as trade law. There is a terminology issue here within the common law family. In the US eg, trade law is foremost associated with tariffs and international trade restrictions and agreements, now centered on the operation of the World Trade Organisation (WTO). The result is that trade law in English terms is private law and therefore more properly part of commercial and financial law, but it is in American terms rather public law or the result of governmental involvement and international arrangements between states meant to facilitate trade.

in the sense that commercial structures are first investigated whilst it is only subsequently decided what kind of legal support they need for their proper functioning. It is not dependent on a pre-existing legal system.

Whereas the sale of goods is thus also the major starting point of international commercial law, it is true that more recently financing and financial instruments have become an important area of it as well and are increasingly driving it. This is a most important change in direction. It suggests a broadening approach as to coverage but also a more incidental approach as to products. There is here some clear shift in emphasis partly because the old typical commercial law instruments like the bill of lading and negotiable instruments are loosing much of their importance in trading environments that are increasingly paperless and electronic and, especially for payments, closely connected with clearing, settlement and netting notions now more commonly the subject of financial law. Even domestically, the greater impact of modern finance on commercial law is increasingly clear, also in the civil law where it was always more apparent. In this connection, it may perhaps be noted that the drift of modern company law is both in common and civil law in the same financial (capital markets and corporate finance) direction. Relevant is here also that in as far as shares are concerned, the traditional bearer instruments are increasingly replaced by securities entitlements in paperless book-entry systems and are transferred no longer through physical delivery but rather through a system of debits and credits in securities accounts that resembles modern payment of money.

These developments explain the great interest in this book in the financial markets and their operation and in the creation of ever more sophisticated financial instruments and payment facilities internationally that have not only affected and internationalised the way capital is raised and payments are made but also the manner in which investments are held, transferred and protected. The internationalising tendencies in this area are based on autonomously creative forces which increasingly lead to a *transnational* financial law based on fundamental and general principles, industry practices, and party autonomy. That may even be so in areas traditionally considered the preserve of the objective law or of the legislator, like property law structures or the proprietary consequences of modern financial dealings. As we shall see, it is less objectionable where there is a strong protection of *bona fide* purchasers at the same time (as there always was in the common law approach in equity) which accommodates and balances greater party autonomy in this area. That is so even in modern financial transactions at the domestic level. Indeed, a more diverse and fractured system of proprietary rights, well known in the law of *equity* in common law countries as just mentioned, is evolving at domestic as well as international levels everywhere,[3] therefore with different proprietary notions for different areas of the law or for different

---

[3] As will be discussed more extensively in chapters IV and V, civil law has traditionally been opposed to an open system of proprietary rights and recognises only a limited number. It is the notion of the *numerus clausus* of proprietary rights. Common law in equity maintains in essence an open system important in modern financial terms especially in the law of chattels and intangibles. It means that third parties must in essence respect the rights so created and acquire the assets as transferees subject to these proprietary rights of others. In that (equitable) system, *bona fide* purchasers or assignees are, however, generally protected, but not the creditors of the transferor even where they rely in good faith on his outwards signs of creditworthiness. It is the idea of reliance on apparent ownership or *solvabilite apparente* which, as we shall see, is in decline everywhere as creditors' protection. In an open system of proprietary rights, *bona fide* creditors thus loose out against *bona fide* purchasers or even purchasers in the ordinary course of business who may not be *bona fide*. It is to protect the ordinary flow of assets better.

Creditors can then only defend through asking proprietary protection themselves in the form of security interests and conditional or temporary ownership rights so that they may figure in the ranking of proprietary rights in a debtor's assets, especially relevant in his bankruptcy. Since banks are the prime type of creditors, it is their own financial activities and the proprietary rights they wish to create in the process that are undermining the rights of common creditors of which they are themselves often the major ones. In fact, a bank in its lending activities must

(financial) products, be they the transfer of title in goods or investment securities, modern forms of (electronic) payment, securities entitlements and their transfer, the treatment of conditional and temporary ownership rights, of finance leases and repurchase agreements, the assignment of payment obligations especially in the context of receivable financing and securitisations, the development of security interests in the form of non-possessory floating charges, the notion of agency, the evolution of fiduciary duties, and the important principle of segregation of assets in formal or constructive trusts and the facility of tracing. In fact, the more incidental attitude to proprietary issues and the absence of systemic thinking in this area have long been supported by the different chapters or Articles of the Uniform Commercial Code (UCC) in the US which are particularly enlightening in these matters.

In truth, internationalisation or transnationalisation promoting these structures are now beginning to pervade all aspects of modern commercial and financial law and may even be considered a feature of all private law between *professionals*, therefore of *professional dealings* which should perhaps become the common denominator and true focus of study in this area rather than the more traditional commercial law. At least in these professional dealings the formation and operation of transnational law — therefore the de-nationalisation of the law in this area shedding its statist nature — may be considered the natural and unavoidable consequence of the internationalisation of the flows of persons, goods, services, capital and payments. It introducers at the same time legal structures particularly made for and refining these international dealings.

The law between professionals is then to be distinguished in particular from consumer law that remains by its very nature much more domestic and protection-oriented in national ways. That may have immediate consequences e.g. in the way concepts of reliance or good faith are applied in contract law as the protection they bring may be less proper and necessary or may play out very differently for professionals in their international dealings than for consumers in their protection needs at home. But, as just mentioned, there are also important proprietary consequences as it is becoming increasingly clear that in international commercial and financial transactions a unitary system of proprietary law (in a civil law sense) can hardly be maintained.

---

assume that debtors have all their assets encumbered in one form or another so that even the bank's own proprietary protections for new loans are likely to rank very low. That is the risk they take, in which connection they must also continue to accept that *bona fide* purchasers and purchasers in the ordinary course of business will always take precedence over them even as secured creditors and receive the assets free and clear regardless of the banks' charges. From that perspective, it makes not much difference whether they are secured or unsecured.

It follows that in a system of limited proprietary rights, common creditors are in principle better protected since only a few proprietary rights can be opposed to them and all the others are merely contractual or personal, that is only valid between the contracting parties. Since it is the major common creditors (banks) that wish it to be otherwise and are constantly pushing for a more open system, accepting in this regard the competition in new proprietary protections with other banks, it is hard to see what public interest is at stake in preventing this, all the more since *bona fide* purchasers remain protected any way (although depending on applicable law this might not yet be so for assignees of receivables and other intangible assets). In other words, if this is what the financial community wants, intent as it is on rebalancing the proprieytray protections amongst its own members, there is no overriding public policy notion against it. It may thus be seen that the opening up of the proprietary system is largely a competitive issue between banks themselves.

In this connection, it should be kept in mind that statistical evidence shows that unsecured creditors never get much anyway, not in a closed system of proprietary rights either. Statutory efforts to improve their lot by reducing the number of proprietary security rights and priorities, like in the new Dutch Civil Code of 1992, have not produced any tangible results. Proposals to give them a (small) fixed percentage of any bankrupt estate might achieve a better deal for them. It may be of relevance particularly for smaller unsuspecting consumer creditors but is unlikely to greatly figure in professional financial dealings. It is a policy issue that does not bear any direct relationship to the operation of a closed or open system of proprietary rights.

It could perhaps be said that what the good faith notion has done to the civil law of contract in making it adapt to modern realities, this type of transforming power must now come for proprietary structures from a development more akin to that of equity in common law. Although the good faith notion has indeed transformed much of the civil law of contract and is now also reflected in modern domestic codifications, so far much less has happened in property law, especially in the system-oriented civil law countries, as shown eg, in the 1992 new Dutch Civil Code (which incorporated the commercial law within it) and in the present redrafting of the French Commercial Code and in the drafting of a new French Financial Code (since 2000). The internationalising trends will here force the pace, eventually also domestically. The EU Collateral Directive of 2002 discussed more fully in chapter IV, Part III, may well give some indication of what is to come.

The increasing fracturing of a more systematic approach also in the proprietary area is undeniable even in civil law, and in this aspect at least, internationally the general attitude is becoming ever more like the one of the common law. Common law influence is also apparent in a greater reliance here on practices, custom and party autonomy. It is further promoted by the fact that it has always been more practitioner-oriented, is used to operating from case to case, is more sensitive to the facts or to the support of new business structures and their needs from a legal perspective (regardless of pre-existing legal notions) and generally more pragmatic. An important contributing factor is also that in the meantime, the English language has become the *lingua franca* of this world. Its legal terminology is naturally geared more to that of the common law than to any other. Its traditional lack of intellectual sophistication (although hardly any longer in the USA), gives it also a flexibility which the more systematic approach in civil law has often lost.

Altogether it is unavoidable that the emerging new international law mechant or *lex mercatoria* is less systematic. It is also less concrete and cannot avoid some flux, if only because it is still in its formative era. It is rather a way of thinking and presents an environment in which rules are foremost *guidelines*. Even domestically, this has increasingly become the case in respect of all black letter law, except perhaps in the few areas where the law remains absolutely settled. It is the unavoidable consequence of factual patterns becoming ever more diverse and of practical needs evolving ever more quickly. In the area of directory law (or default rules) where the legal system has a mere support function this may be more easily accepted but it is also unavoidable in areas where the law is mandatory like in property law, as already shown, or where public policy is at stake, like in the laws concerning consumer and investor's protection. Even domestically that is now much better understood in the context of so-called 'legal realism' in which ethical, economic, utilitarian and social factors are more readily accepted as independently changing the law.

It is a train of thought first articulated in the USA already in the 1930s as we shall see in section 1.2.13 below but that has been accepted (albeit often reluctantly) in one form or another everywhere, certainly also in countries that in the civil law codification tradition basically work with statutory text, like Germany, Austria and the Netherlands. It is part of a liberal interpretation attitude in respect of codified texts that could otherwise hardly be considered complete any longer and be operated as such. Besides the influx of custom and practices, this more liberal interpretation technique and attitude provides another (autonomous) source for adjustment and further development (or for the reliance on more general and universal principle) of the law. At the same time, it may suggest a more intellectual framework for the development of the modern transnationalised *law merchant*.

It raises the problem of a lack of certainty everywhere. In modern international transactions (given their ever greater frequency and value), this problem is aggravated by the fact that legal certainty can hardly come from domestic laws that were never meant for them. The traditional conflict rules of private international law come here to their useful end. In the absence of a proper supranational legislator and given the insufficiency of all black letter rules, we have to get used instead to the idea that the certainty that commercial (or more generally professional) law requires must in a modern internationalised environment increasingly come from the understanding, discipline, and practices of the participants themselves, helped by fundamental and more general legal principle that transcend domestic laws. As already observed before, this may entail a greater role also for party autonomy in proprietary matters. Even now this may already be shown (also in some civil law countries) in the area of receivables, their transfer, and the interests that may be created in them.

In international situations, this uncertainty may be compounded by the question in how far domestic mandatory laws or public policy may still impact on international transactions. It raises issues of relevant contact, conduct and effect that with present insights are only capable of resolution on a case by case basis. It depends therefore largely on an analysis of the facts and the circumstances of each case. It is the approach even now adopted in Artilce 7 of the EU Rome Convention of 1980 on the Law Applicable to Contactual Obligations and in the American Restatements.[4]

Some greater uncertainty is a fact of life in international transactions and is unavoidably increased by the ever greater internationalisation. It increases legal risk, which is not an ideal situation but seems inescapable. Yet it may be easier for the professional community to live with more uncertainty than with the wrong rules. At least it is a community that is used to taking and managing risks. Indeed, it appears that professionals can handle them helped by their ability to devise better structuring and protection schemes amongst themselves (which is the essence of much of the international lawyer's activity), by the international commercial arbitration practice in the case of disputes between them, and by their being better positioned to ask for help from states when needed in the form of supporting treaty law (or within the EU in the form of Directives or Regulations). Organisations like Uncitral and Unidroit may provide a useful supporting function in this connection as well. It is a situation that has in fact obtained in practice already for quite some time and has not led to disaster. It is unlikely to do so in the near future and this evolution should therefore be approached with confidence and imagination.

The formation, operation and application of the new transnational law or *lex mercatoria* in the professional sphere is the fundamental underlying theme of this book. In short, it is about how commercial law is escaping its present domestic grip and can be transformed better to support international transactions.

1.1.2   The Antecedents of Modern International Commercial Law in Civil and Common Law

To understand better why private law and commercial law in particular developed in the above indicated ways, therefore differently in civil and common law and what modern internationalisation to transcend these differences means, a brief historical note may be helpful at the outset. It leads into the origin of civil law and common law and their different attitudes to the sources of the law, especially after the era of the codification which for the civil law dates from the beginning of the nineteenth century. Only the succinctest

---

[4] Restatement (Second) of Conflict of Laws, s 6 and Restatement (Third) of Foreign Relations, ss 402 and 403.

of overviews can here be given, but it is hopefully sufficient to point the way. For those interested, greater detail will follow in section 1.2 below.

It is fair to say that in the history of the Western World, there only ever emerged two original systems of private law that attained some sophistication: that of the Romans and later that of the English. In Western Europe for a long time they operated each in their own area, and it may be said that the civil law, which is the progeny of the one, and the common law, which is the progeny of the other, still largely do so today.

Roman law may be considered history, but it had a second life as it was spontaneously (that is without supporting legislation) revived and became the received law in many important legal fields in much of the European Continent as of the twelfth century AD. This was at roughly the same time the common law started to develop in England. We refer to this revived Roman law as the *Ius Commune*, which was therefore the Roman law as resurrected in much of Western Europe (but not in England) in the latter part of the Middle Ages. It was internationalist and in its further evolution and application decentralist.

Not having been properly promulgated (for which in many areas statehood was at first not sufficiently developed), its binding force was often uncertain and there was much competing local law, a situation which on much of the European Continent continued until the nineteenth century. It created an environment in which commercial law and the commercial courts could also develop more or less autonomously. This was very different in England where the legislative and judicial functions were centralised around the crown from the beginning and competing laws and courts were ultimately absorbed in this central system, even if it became largely built on case-law. In England, this centralisation ultimately also affected the commercial law and the commercial courts and they were incorporated in the common law system by the eighteen century. It was a development completed under Chief Justice Coke, even if especially Lord Mansfield subsequently tried to evolve this commercial law alongside commercial practice but then always within the confines of the common law itself.

On the European Continent, the commercial law and the commercial courts continued to lead a more independent life longer, largely inspired by the needs of commerce, which, depending on the nature of the business, could take on an international or purely domestic flavour. Like earlier in England, this commercial law was *not* therefore necessarily uniform and could vary per market-place or activity. In any event, the law was not then territoral but could be personal (tribal), group related (in guilds), a transactional (in commerce). Here, it took until the nineteenth century for centralised legal systems of civil and commercial law to emerge together with a centralised court system and a purely territorial approach. This was done through *legislation*, as part of the Continental codification drive, therefore *per country*, with the consequence that first the independence and secondly, in relevant areas, the international flavour of commercial law and of the commercial courts also started to wane. The result of this codification drive was what we now call the civil law, laid down in separate codes per country which also incorporated the commercial law. One may see it as an early but profound example of the nationalisation of all laws which on the European Continent left little room for other legal sources than national statutes. These codes therefore had to absorb the commercial law as well which in this manner became exclusively domestic and an appendix to the general system of private law per country.

Commercial law therefore became nationalistic in both civil and common law but the difference between the English development and continental development was that on the European Continent it became part of one codified system of all private law, which was operated as one framework in which commercial law was merely *lex specialis* for certain clearly identified commercial situations. In the civil law approach, commercial law thus became not only national law but it was also seen as part of one coherent intellectual system of rules in which it had to fit and to which it became subservient. In that system, commercial law was *incidental* or even *exceptional*. In countries like Switzerland, Italy and the Netherlands, it was ultimately entirely absorbed by the civil codes.

It follows from this domestic statutory approach that the civil law family lost its unity and is now rather a legal family fractured along national borders with great differences between its adherents in the details of their laws. As statutory law, it is territorial and totally independent from the laws of other civil law countries. This became true for all private law but the consequences were apparent more particularly in commercial law which unavoidably lost its practice oriented and international flavour. Although, as we shall see, common law became also subject to nationalism taking commercial law with it, it never led to a similar nationalization of the private law by statute and there remained as a consequence more room for other legal sources, like the traditional case law, the rules of equity, and (international) custom (unless clearly abolished by statute). In any event, in common law there was never one systematic approach to the whole field of private law, not even per country. Thus commercial law continued to develop more freely and not as part of one system of private law (even if within the common law). As such it retained in common law more of an own character and independent coverage, which besides contractual aspects could thus also cover proprietary law, now in its typical commercial and financial configurations which do not necessarily recur in other parts of private law in similar ways.

The consequences were twofold. First, not being statutory in terms of a national coherent system of rules, the common law at least outside the area of statutory law (which became important also in common law countries — in the US even in commercial law as we shall see in its Uniform Commercial Code or UCC — but always continued to be perceived as exceptional and incidental), remained more internationalist. That is to say that in all countries where the common law is in force (broadly the whole English-speaking world), it still presents some unity and decisions rendered in one common law country may be and are often invoked in the others as good law and have at least persuasive force. This international character may remain of special importance in the commercial and financial areas. It is important even where, like in the US, the commercial law is now largely statutory as this so-called codification (in the UCC) remains of a very different nature compared to codifications in civil law countries.

Thus the UCC (in Section 1–103) is explicit in its intent to leave as much room as possible for custom and practices as independent legal sources. It is the consequence of the fact that private law legislation in common law is not meant to be systematic, exclusive, and all comprehensive. It leaves ample room for the binding nature of commercial practices also when internationalised. Moreover, the regular updating of the UCC, eg in the areas of trade terms and letters of credit, takes international developments and exigencies continuously into account. The second consequence is the structural flexibility that follows in this approach which does not depend on the unity of a system. American law may here even be less formal and more flexible than English law now is, at least in respect of commercial custom as we shall see.

Civil law on the other hand is per definition statutory, therefore nationalistic, system oriented, suspicious of all other sources of law, and unreceptive of any independence of commercial law. As a consequence, it lost all international coherence, both in and outside commercial law. What still binds civil law together and makes for a distinctive family of private law is a joint history and origin, a fairly common method looking for intellectual and logical coherence, and especially a statutory national approach which is perceived as producing a complete system of law assumed to cover all eventualities and to be capable of resolving all issues arising per country.[5] To repeat, it is in this systemic and in its exclusively statutory approach that we probably find the most fundamental difference with the common law or at least between the civil law and the common law as the latter operates in the US. But there is also a different undercurrent which has to do with the earlier noted sensitivity in common law to the facts and practical requirements, eg in business the support of new commercial and financial structures as they develop in which connection no general pre-existing system of law is presumed.

It should be understood in this connection that from the beginning of the codification, civil law countries started to legislate even in a facilitating or *directory* manner, notably in the law of contract. This example was later followed in England but through more incidental statutory law, like in the areas of the sale of goods and negotiable instruments. The consequence in civil law was that even such facilitating legislation was then often perceived as overruling other legal sources of which, in commercial law, custom and practices were the most important. Here again nationalism played a role and the idea that all law must ultimately emanate from the sovereign or be sanctioned by a state, a notion which, as we shall see, eventually also gained considerable authority in common law countries like England

[5] As far as civil law is concerned (as will be discussed in greater detail below), its history is thus largely Roman, its method is largely that of the natural law school of Grotius and his followers, and the nationalistic statutory approach is largely due to 19th century political imperatives and developments. Above, the Roman law and the common law were mentioned as the only truly original Western legal systems of private law. Whilst mentioning also the natural law school, a third development in Western Europe is suggested. It is for the proper understanding of the civil law and its development important and came out of the natural law concept of the Canon or Roman Catholic Church law, also as from the 12th century AD, but more in particular from the secularised version of it as developed as of the seventeenth century by Grotius and his successors, see section 1.2.7 below. See for important more reflective comments on this development, the classic treatise of Paul Koschaker, *Europa und das römische Recht* (1947, unchanged reprint in 1953) and Franz Wieacker, *Privatrechtsgeschichte der Neuzeit* (2nd edn 1967, unchanged reprint 1996).

This 17th-century natural law evolvement will be more fully discussed in s 1.2.6 *infra*. It considered the law based on fundamental ethical notions (which became secular rather than religious), on rationality, and even on efficiency considerations, and was as such sensitive to and guided by principle and extra-legal considerations. Most importantly, it became substantive rule oriented, deductive, and more systematic and intellectual in its development than Roman private law (which like common law was a patchwork, casuistic or inductive, at first largely directed towards procedural relief) or its *Ius Commune* derivative version had ever been. It was as a consequence less pragmatic, rather more abstract, never applied anywhere directly, but remained intimately connected with the rediscovery and spontaneous revival of this Roman law in Western Europe from the twelfth century onward. It developed largely at the intellectual level in the same region and took also much local law into account. This is eg, clear in the approach to the protection of *bona fide* purchasers of chattels, which it advocated but which was not a Roman law concept. It derived from commercial necessity as manifested in some local laws already. It remained *universalist* in that even in local law it looked for broader principle.

Because of its closeness to the *Ius Commune* and therefore to Roman law, the natural law movement may probably not be identified as having led to another entirely original new legal system as it did not effect a complete change. More importantly, it was not as such directly applied and often functioned in the manner of what would now be called soft law or a restatement, although much of the legal writings of those days was in that manner. Its crucial importance was in rendering possible the writing down of the private law in a coherent and systematic manner. Its formulation of substantive rules in this way became the basis for the later civil law codifications. They characterise the civil law of today and are based on this coherent systematic approach that in its codified form often pretends to a unified single system of (at least) private law per country. As such it shed any universalistic claim and became in the process also averse to other sources of law, like fundamental principle, rationality, custom, or notions of efficiency, and even to custom. In this respect, it became very unlike natural law which was soon seen as its enemy.

As already mentioned, this was an evolution absent from the common law. Although in that law there may also be an aversion to general principles (although much less so in the US today), statutory law was perceived as remaining exceptional and incidental and was in any event never meant to crowd out other legal sources, like the old common law, equity or custom, unless especially so provided in the relevant legislation. There was as a consequence no pretence to full statutory coverage either.

and then also covered private law, even though it did not automatically need to lead to a codification ethos, statutory law and a predeliction for system building.

In common law countries, efficiency probably plaid the more important role. In any event, nationalism never took a similar hold in private law in the US, perhaps because private law remained state law in that country, and was therefore on the one hand fractured per state, yet on the other also operated (more informally) as one system for the whole country. As already mentioned several times before, even when codified like in the UCC, this law remained essentially tolerant of other legal sources and never claimed completeness or exclusivity.

It follows that in common law there was never a systematic attempt at creating *one* system and at pushing out all other, non-statutory, sources of law. This type of statutory private law was foremost meant to be cleansing, facilitating and consolidating rather than to prevent alternative law from developing. Common law at least in private law is therefore less rule-oriented till this day. Where, like in the US, there is felt a modern need for more coherence like in the Restatements or even in codes like the Uniform Commercial Code, they are not of a similar comprehensive nature and there is never that overriding concern for the system or systematic interpretation in turn closely connected with what is now often called 'legal formalism', see more in particular in section 1.2.13 below. Again there is here no presumption of a pre-existing legal framework in which all subsequent legal developments must fit. It is the old common law approach.

The Continental European attitude was and remains thus based on a comprehensive systematic approach. In the nineteenth century codifications, there was at first also a strong utilitarian element, mainly to clear the slate of a myriad of regional or local laws and customs in order to provide a single national legal framework in which efficiency was believed promoted and transaction costs reduced. That was understandable in many respects but even then less opportune in commercial law that by its very nature depends much more on commercial practices which could be national but, in an international setting, also transnational, even if parties could normally deviate from the new national laws in matters that only concerned them, therefore in much of contract law. This organisational need of modern states as perceived on the European Continent soon started to lead an own life, however, and, in civil law, all law making was then increasingly considered the state's preserve on which in private law the codification notion of coherence, completeness, exclusivity and full coverage was superimposed. Even party autonomy was then often perceived as depending on state license also and so was the binding force of custom.

In this environment, even the derogating powers of parties in respect of directory statutory law became problematic and were often believed to be derived from state

---

It is clear that (secular) natural law, which was based on finding general and universal substantive law rules and principles, did not produce or support this idea of codification either which ultimately resulted in the final break with the Roman law tradition of the *Ius Commune* and in an even greater divergence from the approach of the common law. Rather, codification, even though it borrowed in its method much from the natural law approach, was a clearly separate nineteenth century Continental European political development connected with the emergence of the modern state in Western culture. In it, all law became statist, therefore a prime tool of the *raison d'etat* or public policy and potentially a prime organisational instrument of modern policy makers, who could thus use the law through legislation to further their objectives.

In the nineteenth century, the result may foremost have been institutional whilst its more activist and redistributive features became only apparent later. That became clear especially in the twentieth century's welfare state which resulted in *mandatory* regulation in all kind of areas and also affected private law eg in the areas of consumer and investor protection. As such, it should be realized that statutory law became no less frequent in common law. Yet it never claimed exclusivity, at least not in private law, unless absolutely mandatory.

authorization only, whilst all contracts, like all other legal structures, were believed to require a foundation in a national law as well, therefore dependent on statist fiat.[6]

In the process, respect for fundamental principle not contained in legislation faded whilst the autonomy of custom and practices if not also of the parties' intent was increasingly ignored. It is possible in this respect to refer to *state positivism* in the law creation with a considerable emphasis on written rules, therefore on so-called *black letter* laws, reduced to a logical system that was explained from within, therefore through literal interpretation or through logic, induction or deduction, or analogy. Yet in order to maintain its claim to completeness, codified law had in practice to be *liberally* construed, if necessary with the help of deduction or otherwise induction or analogy, and ultimately even through purposive or teleological interpretation through which also a reliance on general notions or principles became more palatable. Thus whatever its traditional positivist and statist approach, civil law in its application, although rule and system oriented, needs recourse to fundamental or more general principles to fill the gaps. Nevertheless, codification in this sense meant at the intellectual level the abandonment of the more casuistic and pragmatic approach of the Roman law and *Ius Commune*, which the traditional common law still largely shares with them.

Although that development was fundamentally different in the common law, nationalism was not alien to nineteenth century English thinking either in the sense that, as we already saw, all law, including case-law was then believed by many to emanate from the sovereign, whilst, with the advent of statutory law, state positivism also acquired an important place in it. As a consequence, the application of more fundamental, general or universal principles became no less problematic in common law, at least in England, but there was no exclusively statutory approach or a claim to full statutory coverage. The old common law, equity and custom thus continued to operate besides statutory law which was only considered dominant if it clearly meant to replace what came before or was mandatory, even if in England in modern times there developed an increasing unease with custom also, especially international custom, whilst after the eighteenth century all had to fit into the common law but not necessarily as one system, see more in particular section 1.2.11 below.

This confining attitude towards statutory law was further promoted by the common law's innate tradition of narrow rules (whether formulated in statute or deduced from case law) and holdings and by its predeliction for casuistry even in the interpretation of statutes. In it, literal and logical (syllogistic) interpretation methods prevailed in which on the basis of this narrow interpretation technique, factual situations were soon distinguished (rather than covered by extension or analogy as was the civil law approach). Further statutory law was then considered to be required to fill the gap should such a need be felt, whilst judges would not broaden the statute unless the result made no sense or could be seen to go against public perceptions.

---

[6] It is true that to some extent codification had already been an idea of the French Revolution and of the earlier Enlightenment with its notion of rationality. It expected from it predictability, equality and a better administration of justice. The codification notion of the early nineteenth century became in Continental Europe an instrument of public policy therefore of centralisation and nationalism rather than of rationalism with its universality. In civil law countries, it led to a dependence on *domestic statutory* law, which was the only law that states could dominate, and to a desire to incorporate all private law, including commercial law, into it. It destroyed the universalistic approach of both the *Ius Commune* and the natural law school whilst it attempted also to destroy other sources of law, especially fundamental overriding or more general principles (whether or not derived from natural law) and even custom, also in commerce, except to the extent fundamental notions were expressed in statutes (like some fundamental human rights and sometimes the notion of good faith) or custom was refered to in them or could be reduced to the will of the parties which itself was only thought to produce law in as far as statutes or the codifications would allow it.

1.1.3   The Impact of Civil and Common Law Traditions on the Modern Transnational Law Merchant and its Formation

The fact that in both the Roman Empire and England the judicial functions had always been more centralised made there a more gradual, *ad hoc* and fractured development of the substance of the law possible, which was perhaps also less politically inspired than the nineteenth century civil law on the European Continent. Roman law and common law did therefore not need an exclusive type of codification eliminating all other sources of the law. In the *Ius Commune*, it was virtually impossible as it covered many countries whilst there was no single legislator in control. It meant that it had to tolerate other sources of law besides it.

Although Roman law also experienced some kind of codification in the sixth century AD in Byzantium — the famous *Corpus Iuris Civilis* — it must be noted that the attitude was very different from that of the nineteenth century civil law codifications. In particular, natural law, the *ius gentium, ius honorarium* and custom remained valid as separate sources besides the Justinian codified law. The *Corpus Iuris* only feared in this connection the power of legal commentaries, see section 1.2.3 below. Again, it should be noted that where the term 'code' is sometimes also used in common law, like in the Uniform Commercial Code (UCC) in the USA, the attitude is also much different from the civil law approach and these codes do *not* aspire to be a codification in the civil law sense in terms of systematic unity and the pretense of full coverage. That is not to say that, like in the UCC, logic and systematical coherence have not been an important objective. In the UCC, a legislative technique of stating principle has also been used, much like in the civil law tradition, but as we saw other sources of law were (explicitly) not displaced (see Section 1–103 old and new), whilst its interpretation is liberal and not determined by systemic considerations, (Section 1–103, Section 1–102 old). This again is meant to leave ample room for custom and industry practices.

In this connection, it should further be re-emphasised that, whether or not statutory or customary, the *Ius Commune* as well as traditional common law always remained action-oriented, due in large parts to their origin in procedure and in the *practical* needs of litigants. As a system of substantive rules, they were, and common law at least in England still is, patchy, often incoherent even where it became supported by legislation and that is not felt as a handicap. Common law of this type remains still largely structured around the old writs or causes of action (or identified narrowly defined wrongs) in terms of procedural relief and can often hardly be fully understood without knowledge of them, although there has been much more streamlining in the US. In the process of formulating more precise substantive rules, it became unavoidable to take into account also different political priorities, cultural insights and social developments at the national level, so that even between common law countries in statutory law and rule formulation on the basis of case-law studies there is now substantial disparity in the private laws as well. But there is not the same emphasis on national systems and systematic reasoning as in civil law.

Another aspect of this emphasis on the system is that, in civil law, private law remains more of an intellectual exercise and academic subject than in common law, to which the fact that the Roman origin continued to require knowledge of the Roman law and therefore also of Latin well into the nineteenth century also contributed. Earlier, the *Ius Commune* revival and the natural law school had been more academic for much the same reason, the latter all the more so because of its rational approach, which the civil law of the codifications inherited. In the civil law, especially in the German tradition, the law is indeed considered a prime intellectual manifestation or in the German Civil Code or BGB a main

German cultural icon. As a consequence, much of the civil law until this day shows a double face: it is academic to nurse its system, to explain itself, and to propel it in concept and legislation, yet it must also be practical to have a meaning. There is considerable tension here and in modern times the systematic approach has proved increasingly to conflict with rapidly moving practicalities. The result is that the traditional civil law codification approach is increasingly discredited as a nineteenth century aberration and can at present also hardly serve as a realistic model for greater uniformity of private law in the Eureopean Union (or EU).

In England, on the other hand, an academic education in law was never necessary for the practice of the law (nor had it been in Rome where the law was, however, considered a highly intellectual exercise and its development a matter of great civic pride). Even today, it is still not so common amongst lawyers who are educated in practitioner-oriented legal courses after they have graduated from university in any subject of their choice (which need not be the law), although it has been said and can also be demonstrated that there is now an English inclination towards a more formal approach based on a logical or more systematical interpretation of black letter law and rules either derived from statute or otherwise from a rigid analysis of case law. This attitude finds support also in academia and in most of the modern legal text books in England.

That would mean some approximation with the traditional Continental European approach. It is very different from the modern approach in the USA, where the common law retains its pragmatic orientation at the practical level, even if modern codifications like the Uniform Commercial Code and the Restatements adhere to a much more conceptual drafting technique. But in the US, the interpretation is normative, not systematic, therefore in search of a truer meaning of the law as related to its impact in the situation, as will be discussed later in section 1.2.13 below. That is the essence of 'legal realism'. This may be largely due to (a) a more powerful judiciary (in its relationship to the legislature and executive branch of government) used to deal with policy issues and (b) to the development of a robust academic legal tradition without the same emphasis on systematic considerations. But there was early on also a greater sensitivity to social change. It is helped by the continuing acceptance of other sources of law so that a decentralised approach could be maintained and articulated. Extra-legal considerations in terms of the demands of morality, social peace and economic efficiency or utility find more easily expression in such an approach also. It follows that it becomes easier to deal with social and economic change in the further development of the law, also at the level of case-law, to accept this as a challenge, and to see the law as a dynamic, not a static force, and as a set of rules that must constantly be improved (not in the least by the judiciary) to achieve more palatable, fairer or more common sensical solutions. To retain credibility, legal reasoning and presentation become here key elements in the constant reformulation of the law in which black letter rules are indeed treated as no more than guidelines (unless absolutely mandatory assuming they are in that case precise and are then likely to be restrictively interpreted).

In periods of rapid change, systematic thinking cannot remain the ultimate objective in whatever system, all the more true in the development of the new transnational law merchant that must be practice oriented to acquire its full meaning. At the domestic level, this is now also clearly shown in civil law, especially in the need to use the concept of good faith to loosen the law of obligations and to adapt it to the realities of an ever faster moving world and in the fracturing of the (closed) system of proprietary rights in chattels and intangibles under the pressures of the modern financial structures which tend to maintain their own (disperse) notions of proprietary rights. This was already discussed in the previous section. Thus civil law is increasingly forced to allow a broad influx of beneficial, conditional, and temporary ownership rights concerning present and future assets especially in the context of financial transfers meant to raise and protect financing which are alien to its system of Roman law derived proprietary rights. This loosening up of the system, even of property law, is, beside the internationalisation or transnationalisation of modern financial law, a most important underlying theme of this entire book. The bankruptcy resistency and therefore the proprietary nature of these new financial instruments are here perceived to be at the heart of the modern developments in proprietary law which civil law codifications can no longer ignore. It is balanced by greater protections for *bona fide purchasers* or purchasers in the ordinary course of business but not so far by a greater protection of *bona fide* creditors of debtors who transfers these interests to others (except in the manner of a fraudulent conveyance therefore with the shared objective of depriving these creditors from the recovery facilities in the relevant assets).

In this connection, common law long had an advantage with its equitable proprietary rights, which gave it much more flexibility as most profoundly expressed in the law of trusts, but no less in other beneficial, conditional and temporary ownership rights in present or future assets, in notions of bulk transfers, asset substitution, and tracing or constructive trust, in the open system of proprietary rights (in equity) and the related and indispensable broad protection of *bona fide* purchasers in this context. Through equity — a facility civil law crucially missed — common law has long been comfortable with an unstructured approach to proprietary rights and with a lack of systemic coherence even in proprietary matters. Also here, the common law tradition remains essentially practical.

Another common law advantage is here that the commercial law is not systematically integrated in the rest of the common law, even if it is now considered part thereof. It allows for different legal structures including proprietary structures to operate in a commercial and financial setting. As already suggested in the previous section, in this modern commercial law, the law of finance has replaced trade law as the focus with a renewed interest in proprietary rights and their operation, much borrowed from equity and in any event not operated as one system. To abandon a systematic thinking and to become comfortable with flexibility also in property law poses a particular challenge to civil lawyers who, however, have already been forced to accept it in the law of obligations.

Contrary to what is often thought, the result of these developments is that the old Roman law can no longer always be so easily traced in modern civil law and change cannot be avoided. In fact, that was already so in the original drafting of the civil law codes. Whatever the desire of system creation and system thinking was, it became all the more true in the application and interpretation of these civil law codifications, starting with the great French one of 1804 (the *Code Civil*, or *Code Napoleon* or *Cc*) and ending with the great German codification of 1900 (the *Bürgerliche Gesetzbuch* or *BGB*). Increasingly also here, modern ethical, social and economic elements had to find expression in their application through case-law, more recently in a renewed judicial resort to more fundamental principle (especially through the good faith notion and normative interpretation techniques) never mind the system or the reliance on statute.

The codification method of formulating new substantive law largely came from the natural law school but it resisted its pretention to universal application and became territorial. In modern times there is an unavoidable revival of natural law notions in the search for new and better laws beyond national statutory law and its application. Hence the reliance on fundamental or more general principles. Natural law revival always stands at the beginning of new legal developments and it is no different at the present juncture, now that at least in commerce and finance we must find new contractual and proprietary structures and also deal with the internationalisation of the law at the same time. It must be expected that the Roman and Byzantine pedigree of civil law will thus be further diluted. It is also unavoidable that with the prevalence of common law (equity) notions in modern finance, helped by the development of the English language as *lingua franca* of all modern business, these notions will have to find a place in civil law so that its systematic thinking (at least in the professional sphere) will have to be substantially abandoned even in the law of property. But the major effect will at first be in the transnational commercial and financial law area, therefore in the new *lex mercatoria*. In the process, at least in commerce and finance, the emphasis on legislation and national laws as sole sources of the law will then fade.

That is not to say that the intellectualisation of the law will also finish — the American example which introduced it in the common law shows this very clearly, see section 1.2.13 below — but it cannot retain its grip if it is only meant to aid and sustain the present civil law systematic approach at national levels. Once this is understood, approximation between civil and common law at the international level, therefore especially in commerce and finance, may be anticipated. Again, it is unlikely that classic notions of (civil law) codifications can then be maintained or guide either, not even at EU level if only because the new law is not territorially confined but concerns all international commerce and finance, and second because there is no sufficient coherence in the modern developments which have in any event not fully crystallised. In such an environment, efficiency demands or considerations can no longer be met by or be expected from statutory intervention only.

Whatever the future development will be in this regard in civil law countries, to complete the picture of civil law codifications on a historical note, it may be said that at least the French *Code civil* always incorporated much local law and also allowed for the political desiderata of those revolutionary days. It was not therefore in its origin reflective of a static set of rules or order.[7] Nor was that local law even French. Rather it was frankish tribal law (*droit coutumier*), therefore germanic which until the end of the eighteenth century largely prevailed to the north of the river Loire. The Roman law that the *Code* incorporated (*droit écrit*), had until the codification mostly prevailed south of the Loire. As such, Roman law until this day remains in France especially important in the laws of property and obligations where it had retained a hold even in the *droit coutumier*.[8] This law also obtains in Belgium and Luxembourg, which virtually adopted the French Civil Code, as the Netherlands had done in a more amended form until 1992. In Spain, Italy and Portugal much of the French example is also followed, although especially Italy had always been more directly influenced by Roman law notions (it may have been different to the north, in Piedmont and Savoy), notwithstanding the fact that the Romans had largely been overwhelmed by Germanic (Lombard) tribes in Italy. So they had been in the rest of Southern and Western Europe in the fifth and sixth centuries AD, whilst the Iberian Peninsula was subsequently invaded by Islam, but there is no remaining influence. The French *Code Civil* was eventually also copied in much of Latin America, even in Louisiana and Quebec in North America, and in Japan.

In the modern codified civil law form, Roman law influence remained stronger in the substantive parts of the BGB in Germany, subsequently followed in Greece and with a great influence also on the Swiss Civil Code of 1912, itself copied in Turkey. The BGB also had an

---

[7] See more in particular s. 1.2.4 *infra*.

[8] It is true that in Germany and France, the feudal system also held sway during large parts of the Middle Ages, especially relevant for the law concerning real estate, but, unlike in England, it was completely eliminated at the time of the French Revolution (after 1789) and nothing of it was retained in the modern civil law codifications. See for this feudal law the *Libri Feudorum*, of Lombard origin, often attached to the medieval editions of the *Corpus Iuris*. They were important in Germany, but apparently less so in France which had its own feudal rules, see eg Molinaeus, *Commentarii in Consuetudines Principales*, Tit. 1 (*des Fiefs*).

important influence on the modern Japanese Civil Code that dates from about the same time (and whose original, wholly French-derived text, proved unacceptable). It had also much influence on the much later new Italian Code of 1943 and on the new Dutch Civil Code of 1992, which is the last in this line. It is also likely to still have an important impact on the revamping of the civil law in much of Eastern Europe.

English law, on the other hand, is in its origin Anglo-Saxon, therefore germanic and otherwise feudal until this day.[9] In its method, though not therefore in substance, it is much closer to Roman law than civil law now is as both English and Roman law originated in the law of procedure. The more ethical element came in common law originally in equity through the intervention of the Lord Chancellor's office, at first always a high clerical officer, and now more in particular through legislation, therefore, at least in England, on its face *less* through interpretation although references to natural justice are sometimes made in case-law.

The older germanic and feudal laws, as bases of the common law, as well as the law of equity migrated with it to the USA, Canada, Australia and New Zealand and remain important also in other Commonwealth countries including India and Nigeria. They still function there as a true common law for all, much more so than the civil law can now do for its adherents because of its exclusive statutory and therefore nationalistic nature. Together with the English language as the language of all modern commerce and finance, in international professional dealings, the common law now comes back at last also to its Continental frankish/germanic homelands, even if in this form it does not seem greatly welcomed there.

Whilst it is necessary to be aware of these different pedigrees and attitudes in civil and common law, the above is not meant to suggest that the practical differences between civil and common law are always great where commerce and finance are concerned. In fact, as a general proposition in similar Western-style economies, that would be unlikely. Especially in personal or movable property law and in the law of contract, the applicable law operates in fundamentally different ways with fundamentally different rules in commercial dealings only at the surface. Logic and environment suggest similarity in rights and duties and therefore also in the legal rules, favoured all the more so in a period of profound internationalisation. As we shall see in chapter 4, particularly in so far as proprietary interests are concerned, there are so far still substantial differences, however, certainly in the technical aspects of land law and in the concept of possession of which the student should be aware. Otherwise the main differences continue (as we already saw) especially in some typical (but extremely important) structures of the law of equity, therefore in trusts and agency, floating charges, tracing of assets and restitution concerning movable property, and in the assignment of claims. In the law of contract, the differences are already much smaller, as will be discussed in greater detail in chapter 2.

1.1.4   Civil and Common Law Notions of Commercial Law

In the previous sections, the different notions and coverage of commercial law in both the civil and common law system at the domestic level were already mentioned. This should be

---

[9] *Cf* also Koschaker, *supra* n 5, 212*ff*. English law, unlike Scottish law, thus avoided Roman law influence, although there were early attempts, notably by Henri Bracton in the thirteenth century, to let it appear otherwise, whilst until the late 19th century mainly Roman law was taught at the English universities, foremost in Oxford and Cambridge and later also in the London Colleges. Yet it never had much substantive impact except perhaps on the early Church law.

considered further. If one starts with looking at some civil law commercial codes, for example at the *Code de Commerce* (CdC) of 1807 (redrafted in 2000) in France and the *Handelsgesetzbuch* (HGB) of 1900 in Germany, and at some common law commercial codes like the Uniform Commercial Code (UCC) since 1962 in the USA, there is a considerable and obvious difference in *status* and *coverage*.

To repeat, codification is in itself a very different phenomenon in civil and common law even where the same term is used. This difference centers around the systematic approach (in civil law) and the acceptance of other sources of law (in common law), especially fundamental legal principles and custom and the different approach to the facts, as we saw. Civil law dislikes both fundamental principle and custom (unless they are incorporated by reference in the codes), but the common law traditionally encouraged custom, particularly in commerce as the UCC makes still very clear, Section 1–103, (Section 1–102 and 1–103 old). As regards the *coverage* of commercial law, which even differs markedly between the CdC in France and the HGB in Germany, it is in civil law always related to commerce, in which connection a notion of commerciality is used which may, as compared to common law, produce more limitations and the concept of commercial law may sometimes be narrower and more *service* oriented, although traditionally it may be broader in other respects and can sometimes (especially in France) also be concerned with commercial institutions like companies or with the liquidation of commercial activities through bankruptcy.

As was already mentioned in section 1.1.1 above, in common law, commercial law is more generally concerned with *all* aspects of the sale of goods, including transfer of title, transportation and payment. It used to be more *trade related* than service oriented. In this connection, goods are, in common law terminology, all tangible movable assets, like apples, pears, videos and cars, also called chattels. In this sense, the notion of commercial law was in common law narrower than in civil law, but it did, on the other hand, notably include the sales that are conducted between non-merchants or sales that are not commercial in nature. In fact, common law does not use a clear notion of commerciality at all and one finds under the heading of commercial law primarily all the law concerning the sale of goods in the widest sense. It covers then also the law concerning bills of lading and warehouse receipts, bills of exchange (or a little broader, negotiable instruments including also promissory notes), letters of credit, and in modern times the law concerning collections and fund transfers. Most importantly, one also finds here the title transfer in goods and therefore the *proprietary* aspects of a sale of movable property and the protection of *bona fide* purchasers of them (*cf* Section 2–401*ff* UCC), probably even the law of receivables, which are claims for unpaid sales proceeds, and their extinction through bank payment (Articles 4 and 4A UCC) or their transfer through assignment (*cf* Section 2–210 UCC). Security interests created in these assets may then also be considered covered by commercial law, certainly (but not only) to the extent that such interests are used in trade and commerce, like reservations of title and floating charges. This is indeed the case in the USA under Article 9 UCC, see chapter 5, section 1.6.

That would be very unusual in civil law countries. The sale of goods is in these countries basically governed by the civil, and not by the commercial codes. Although there might be some additional rules for the contractual aspects of commercial sales in these commercial codes, certainly the general proprietary (and security or collateral) aspects would be dealt with in the part of the civil codes dealing with the transfer of ownership and the creation of security interests generally. There are unlikely to be additional rules in this respect in the commercial codes of civil law countries. Payments, releases or assignments would also be considered part of the general private law and there would be nothing especially commercial about them.

It reconfirms a particular feature of the commercial law notion of civil law and its different status: it is *specialised* law, in principle for merchants or transactions between them, and even then substantially *lex specialis* and as such *never* separate from the mainstream private law as codified in the civil codes, and therefore never a fully separate branch of the law. As such, it contains only some additional, special and largely incidental rules for commerce and, to a lesser extent, finance but remains primarily covered by the civil codes. In civil law countries, commercial law does *not* therefore stand alone and is certainly not systematically independent.

The common law, on the other hand, being much less concerned with systematical considerations sees commercial law, especially where codified, much more like a different branch of the law altogether, although the earlier independence of the law merchant and of the commercial courts in England was eventually eliminated. This law and its court system were by the eighteenth century fully absorbed by the common law and its royal courts, the central pull of which could not be avoided even in commerce.

It means that, even though commercial law is often still referred to as a different branch of the law in common law, its rules are in essence often not much different from the ordinary rules either. They may always be invoked in support, but the subjects commercial law covers, especially the sale of goods, tend to be covered *in full*, therefore without obvious reliance on the rest of the law. As also in common law countries there is no longer an independent legal system for commercial law, this may now be considered a detail and the separate existence of commercial law within the common law has indeed also been questioned. Like in civil law it is thus often no more than an assortment of some different subjects; yet the emergence of financial law has reemphasised the different perspective and rules of commercial law, in the proprietary aspects greatly dependent, however, on the further evolution of the law of equity. That leads to even greater differences with the traditional civil law approach to commercial law.

The more important practical difference with the civil law approach remains, however, in the latter's already mentioned concept of codification and particularly in the role of custom, which in common law continues to be of prime importance as an independent source of law, also besides legislation, and may still have an overriding effect, particularly relevant in commerce. This is clearly expressed in Section 1–103(a)(2) (Section 1–102(2)(b) old) UCC in the USA, even if in modern times one finds it much less recognised in England, where market practices are often reduced to implied contractual terms and not otherwise accepted.[10] All the same, in common law, certain features of ordinary contract law like the notion of consideration never affected the transfer of negotiable instruments through endorsement. Also, contrary to the more normal *nemo dat* rule, *bona fide* purchasers or holders in due course of these instruments are generally protected. This type of protection finds generally better support in commercial law than in the rest of the common law (outside equity).

This being said, the significance of custom has, at least in England, been reduced by its relegation to implied term and been even further limited by the binding force of precedent in court decisions. It stultifies its further independent development. It may have been the unavoidable result of the commercial courts having lost their independence[11] even if practitioners in commerce and finance are less inclined to live by precedent and may see their

---

[10] See s 1.3.1. *infra* and chapter 2, s. 1.2.8.

[11] The old commercial courts and their laws were originally more particularly connected with fairs and ports where participants were peripatetic merchants and maritime transporters who required prompt justice to be enforced either against the person of the debtor or (particualrly in his absence) his goods if within the courts jurisdiction. In England, the origin of the commercial law and commercial courts was in the domestic staple markets and fairs, visited also by foreigners, and in the maritime activities of the Channel ports. The courts in the

practices evolve quite fast. It may force common law judges to distinguish cases more aggressively in commercial disputes in order to overcome the restraints of binding precedent. At least a greater dynamism in the development of the law appears here accepted.

It is true as already mentioned in the previous section, that in the late eighteenth century under Lord Mansfield as Chief Justice, building on the earlier work of Chief Justice Holt, some special commercial law was redeveloped in England, although then always within the common law.[12] This proved particularly important for negotiable

staple markets were the Staple Courts, which were statutory since 1354. Earlier, a Statute of Merchants (Acton Burnell) of 1283, in an effort to attract foreign traders to England, had promoted the speedy settlement of disputes between all merchants in England whilst an act of 1303 (Carta Mercatoria) had recognised the law merchant as an independent source of law, also exempted foreign traders from local taxes, and gave them the freedom to trade throughout England. At the local fairs there were Borough or Pie Powder Courts, all used for civil and criminal litigation between the participants in these markets. These Staple Courts consisted often of the Mayor and two constables or town merchants who could be foreign if a foreign merchant was involved. Often these Borough and Pie Powder Courts only operating during the fairs with a process "from hour to hour and day to day". Judges and juries of merchants were used to discover the applicable custom, although there were some written sources of the applicable commercial law also, such as the Red Book in Bristol and the Black Book of Admiralty in London. There were more in maritime law, notably the laws of Visby and the laws of Oleron, which is a small island off the French coast of Aquitaine, which were highly considered. Special maritime courts started to operate after 1360, at first competent mainly in criminal cases (piracy), later also in civil cases with emphasis on charters, ship mortgages, maritime insurance, bills of lading and the earlier forms of negotiable instruments like bills of exchange and cheques. To appear before these courts, the plaintiff had to prove the defendant a merchant and had to establish the applicability of commercial law or custom, but the presence of the defendant was not strictly speaking necessary as long as some of his goods were in the jurisdiction.

It should be noted that the law merchant was *not* as a consequence a uniform law in any sense and that its content varied with the markets and products covered and it could be very local, but the common outstanding feature was that both this law and the courts that administered it were autonomous. Others have noted as other common factors their customary character, summary jurisdiction, and spirit of equity and common sense that was not concerned with technicalities, see W Mitchell, *An Essay on the Early History of the Law Merchant* (Cambridge University Press, 1904). Jealousy by the common law courts especially originated in the Court of Admiralty in London. The common law judges eventually took the view that the older commercial and admiralty courts were only franchisal courts and could therefore be controlled by the common law courts. As a consequence, these older courts started to disappear, although they were never formally abolished, but after the middle of the 18th century only the Court of Tolzey in Bristol survived. The overriding influence of Sir Edward Coke is often mentioned in this connection. Eventually the requirements that the defendant had to be a merchant and that commercial law or custom was applicable disappeared. After 1765 the common law courts considered that "the law of merchants and the law of the land are the same: a witness cannot be admitted to prove the law of merchants": see *Pillans v Van Miero*, [1765] 97 ER 1035 [1765] 3 Burr 1663, 1669. This seems to have concluded the trend. However, the commercial law was for a long time poorly administered by the common law courts, the reason why eg the law of chattels remained underdeveloped.

The greater speed and flexibility of the older proceedings, not bogged down by procedural and evidential formalities, had fostered trade and proved especially important for foreigners and their protection. These benefits were lost when the commercial judges became common law judges with their chief experience in land and some tort law. It could not be avoided that the common law and its procedure then also started to take over. The result was that much commercial expertise and flexibility were lost in this part of the law. By the end of the 19th century the international connection was also largely lost and commercial law became a domestic affair also in England, a situation further promoted by the preponderant impact of British colonial trade.

[12] In *Pillans v Van Mierop* [1765] 97 ER 1035, [1765] 3 Burr 1663, Lord Mansfield indeed accepted that the rules of the law merchant had become part of the common law and were no longer autonomous custom. He also accepted the juridiction of the common law courts but added that the common law and its courts had to recognise the dynamics of international business so that "commercial law was to evolve alongside commercial practice". The law merchant as an independent legal order governing the legal relationship between merchants, had thereby ceased to exist and the national law maintained the international character of commerce only to a limited extent, more in the nature of courtesy or *comitas, cf also* C Schmitthoff, "International Business Law: A new law merchant", *Curr Law and Soc Probl* (1961) 129 at 138.

The difference may be highlighted by an earlier quote in *Sanders Bros v Maclean and Co* [1883] 11 QBD, 325, 343 in which Bowen LJ commented as follows: "[t]he practice of merchants … is not based on the supposition of possible fraud. The object of mercantile usage is to prevent the risk of insolvency, not of fraud; and anyone who attempts to follow and understand the Law Merchant will soon find himself lost, if he begins by assuming that instruments,[13] bills of lading, and (later) documentary sales, like the Fob and Cif sales, ship mortgages, the stoppage of goods in transit, and also in the concept of bailment, therefore in the protection of the physical possession of goods, in agency, partnership and joint ownership where commercial principle was closely followed. However, once having lost the autonomy of its courts, the commercial law never recovered a truly independent role in common law countries, and the same may now also be said for its modern branch of financial law. Yet it is not incidental or mere *lex specialis*, and it clearly covers whole areas of the common law in full. Nevertheless, the distinction between commercial and other private law is no longer fundamental in common law, except that no systematic unity is assumed. The distinction between law and equity, to be discussed in section 1.2.11 below, each with their own courts, became much more important and also cut through what may now still be considered commercial and modern financial law.

In the absence of any special role for custom, in civil law, there is also from that point of view less separateness of commercial law. There is in any event the already mentioned reversal of roles in the sense that in civil law the general private law system *always* provides the basis so that commercial law, however defined, is never self contained. The scope of commercial law is also more limited because the proprietary aspects hardly come under the commercial law as we saw. In other areas, however, this commercial law in a civil law sense may cover more ground. Thus it would not be unusual in civil law countries to find company law in the commercial code besides the more traditional commercial sales of goods (but only in their contractual aspects), negotiable instruments and transportation laws. Insurance law is often also included. In France, the banking and commodity exchange and stock exchange laws are traditionally also dealt with in the CdC. One may even find the bankruptcy laws in these commercial codes, especially in those countries which still follow the old French example of reserving bankruptcy largely to persons or entities engaged in commerce. It may now all be considered business law and may as such present an extended commercial law concept, even if in civil law, as we shall see, there are often, like in France and Germany, still some specific more *formal* criteria of commerciality that set commercial law in the legal sense apart.

In civil law countries — unlike these more general parts of commercial law — company, transportation, insurance and bankruptcy law, when considered part of commercial law, may be fully covered in the commercial codes and the status as *lex specialis* to the general civil law becomes as a consequence less obvious in these areas but it does not disappear. It does not make a difference in this connection that, technically speaking, company and bankruptcy laws are now often no longer part of the commercial codes in these countries but may be contained in separate statutes. They continue to be considered commercial if only applied to merchants and in any event part of a single system.

---

merchants conduct their business on the basis of attempting to insure themselves against fraudulent dealing. The contrary is the case. Credit, not distrust, is the basis of commercial dealings. Mercantile genius consists principally in knowing whom to trust and with whom to deal…".

Earlier, Gerard Malynes in *Consuetudo Vel Lex Mercatoria or The Ancient Law Merchant* (1622) had said that: "Every man knows that for manners and prescriptions, there is a great diversity amongst all nations: but for the Customs observed in the course of traffic and commerce, there is that sympathy, concordance and agreement, which may be said to be like condition to all people, diffused and spread by right reason, and instinct of nature consisting perpetually. And these Customs are properly those observations which Merchants maintain between themselves …. and this Law of Merchants hitherto observed in all countries, ought in regard of commerce, to be esteemed and held in reputation as the Law of the Twelve Tables was amongst the Romans. For herein you shall find everything built upon the foundations of Reason and Justice…".

[13] The first time the promissory note was declared a negotiable instrument in England was, however, already in 1680, in the case of *Sheldon v Hently*, [1681] 2 Show. 160, 89 ER 860.

In common law countries, special legal features in these areas are now more likely to derive from the fact that company and bankruptcy laws are part of the law of equity rather than commercial. As such they may particularly benefit from some greater judicial discretion and direction. Like in trust and tax laws, it re-confirms a flexibility that would otherwise have risked to be lost as these subjects are in common law countries traditionally considered outside the realm of commercial law proper. It is especially important in the area of modern financial instruments and their proprietary aspects.

Transportation and insurance law, more properly considered commercial law subjects, developed in common law in the trade between England and the European Continent and acquired some distinguishing features derived from that contact, in which there may still be some faint remnants of a Roman law orientation. As the common law mainly developed in connection with land law, there was here at first more room for the persuasive force of other law. In fact, the treatment of transportation and insurance as especially defined contract types was itself due to Continental influence as the common law traditionally does not define different types of contracts with each covered by a special contractual regime. In maritime law, there developed in this connection in England also the Continental concept of the ship master based on the *patria potestas* of Roman law. In common law, that no longer sets these contracts and maritime notions apart, however, as commercial law in a more Continental sense. In fact, in the nineteenth and twentieth centuries, these areas of the law developed more strongly in England as a trading nation than they did on the Continent.

In the absence of a clear *commerciality notion* or concept in the modern common law, there is no single overriding criterion that determines the coverage of the commercial law. Except for some of the specific rules already mentioned for special situations supported by custom, there are now hardly any particular consequences or special features in the law applied deriving from the commercial law qualification as such either. There are none in the type of courts before which commercial cases are brought, although, as in England, there may be commercial law divisions in the ordinary courts. In common law, it is now largely tradition or statutory convenience that determines whether a matter is considered part of commercial law.

Thus, in the USA, the modern Uniform Commercial Code, which dates from its third version of 1962, often revised thereafter, and which applies as uniform law (exceptionally) in all states of the USA (civil and commercial law being State matters),[14] covers negotiable instruments, bills of lading and warehouse receipts, and letters of credit besides the sale of

---

[14] It means that the UCC was promulgated separately in each state of the Union and that the text may still vary between states. Also amendments are not always introduced simultaneously in all States. Some have repealed part of it (especially Article 6 on Bulk Transfers). The UCC was itself a joint project of the American Law Institute and the National Conference of Commissioners on Uniform State Laws, started in 1942. The American Law Institute is a private body since 1923 devoted to the harmonisation of legal concepts among the various states of the USA, especially through producing Restatements of the law as it has done in various areas like torts, contracts, agency and (interstate) conflicts of law. They are non-binding but have nevertheless had a considerable impact on the further development of the law in the relevant areas and serve as guidelines also for the courts. The National Conference of Commissioners on Uniform State Laws, on the other hand, which has existed since the end of the 19th century, has drafted a number of Uniform Laws for adoption in the different states. The Uniform Commercial Code is by far the most important of these Uniform Laws and is now accepted (with certain modifications) in all 50 states of the Union.

The UCC uses the term "Article" in the sense of chapter or book. Each is divided in individual sections. Besides the chapter on sales (Article 2), there is the one on Bills of Exchange and similar types of payment instruments (Article 3), on Bank Deposits and Collections (Article 4), on Letters of Credit (Article 5), on Bulk Transfers (Article 6), on Documents of Title including Bills of Lading and Warehouse Receipts (Article 7), on Shares, Bonds and similar types of investment securities (Article 8), and on Secured Transactions (Article 9). Article 1 contains

goods. It also deals with secured transactions in movable property (including intangibles) and now even with finance (equipment) leases, which were eventually distinguished from secured transactions, and with payment systems and also investment securities. On the other hand, it does not cover transportation, either on land or by sea, nor the related insurance. Company law and bankruptcy were never part of commercial law in the common law sense. More importantly, non-merchants engaged in the sale of goods, using cheques and yielding security interests in their personal property are covered as much by the UCC as are merchants.

In civil law countries, which still have a separate commercial law, there is on the other hand usually a *more substantive* criterion of commerciality and therefore at least in theory a clearer view of what is commercial. In France, it is connected with the notion of the 'commercial act', in Germany with the notion of 'dealings with merchants'. These definitions form the intellectual basis of the coverage by the commercial codes of these countries as we shall see in the next section, but fundamental distinctions have become much less important there also, and the coverage by the commercial codes is in France and Germany often incidental as well if not erratic. Non-merchants in their dealings may sometimes be covered by them as well, like in writing cheques. No doubt, in France, the most important aspect is not the coverage by the commercial code itself but rather the jurisdiction of the commercial courts in commercial matters for merchants, still with lay judges and an accelerated procedure. These courts no longer exist in Germany. There are still commercial sections in the lower courts of that country, with some lay input, but they otherwise operate much like normal courts.

In view of the limited modern impact of the distinction between commercial and civil law, some civil law countries like the Netherlands, Switzerland and Italy have done away with it altogether. However, in the modern internationalised market-place, the distinction between professional and consumer dealings may have become more apt again, as we shall see in section 1.1.5, with the former essentially being covered by an internationalised legal regime or order and the latter remaining in essence subject to domestic laws.

1.1.5   The Development of a Separate Commercial Law in France and Germany

Obviously, if there is to be any true meaning in legally distinguishing between commercial matters and others, it must be in some special legal regime applying to merchants and the dealings between them. At the very least, the commercial law regime would have to be more informal and custom-oriented, if not also more international. No less important would be the competence of special courts to hear commercial cases in simplified proceedings. They would be more specialised, less formal and speedier. As we saw, in common law, the major difference is now in the role of commercial custom as an independent (but in England in practice often limited) source of law. There are no longer any autonomous courts. The UCC reflects, however, the accomodating approach to custom. In Section 1–103(a)(2) (Section 1–102(2)(b) old), it envisages that the Code for the areas it covers is liberally construed to promote its underlying purposes and policies, one of them being to permit the continued expansion of commercial practices through custom, usage and agreement of the parties. In Section 1–103 (new and old) it is further stated that the principles of law and

definitions. It is no exaggeration to say that Article 2 and especially Article 9 were at the time of their first publication (1952) original pieces of legislation. They were substantially introduced in the various states of the USA after 1962 and are regularly updated. Some new chapters have been added, particularly Article 2A on the Equipment Lease (a form of leasing) and Article 4A on Fund Transfers (payments).

equity, including the law merchant and the law relative to the capacity to contract, principal and agent, estoppel, fraud, misrepresentation, duress, coercion, mistake, bankruptcy, or other validating or invalidating cause, shall supplement the UCC, unless displaced by particular provisions of it.

The reference to (common) law, equity and custom as independent sources of law besides statutory law is in itself not exceptional in common law countries, as we already saw and as will be discussed more fully below. It is much less relevant in Art 9 UCC on secured transactions, but there is still an important difference in the UCC's attitude to its own liberal interpretation. As will be seen in section 1.2.12, in common law, at least in England, statutory law is itself normally restrictively interpreted so as to leave as much room as possible for law, equity and custom (always subject to precedent). The UCC, in asking on the other hand for a liberal interpretation of its texts, expressly abandons this attitude for the areas of the law it covers, although in a roundabout way it is mainly done to leave again more room for custom, which in this manner becomes integrated in the UCC. Codified civil law is, as will be discussed below in section 1.3.2, more used to such a liberal interpretation technique — it is dictated by the pretence that codes cover their subject matters fully — but a liberal resort to other sources of law, even to custom in the context of commercial law, is much more contentious.[15] The civil law courts remain here much more circumspect unless the codes or statutes themselves refer to these other sources.[16]

In summary, at the theoretical level, common and civil law countries differ particularly in respect of their attitude to custom in commercial law, although in England probably less than elsewhere in the common law world. It also affects the interpretation of commercial law, which remains in civil law systematic even if liberal. They differ also in the coverage and in commercial law being in civil law often *lex specialis* to the ordinary civil law and as such incidental (even though, in company, insurance and bankruptcy law, there may be a fairly full commercial law regime, as just mentioned). The most important practical difference, limited to France (and some countries like Belgium still following its lead), is the separate commercial court system. Finally, and a point still to be discussed in greater detail, there is the old definition of commerciality in France and Germany, from which the application of commercial law follows in a more specific manner.

At the end of the previous section it was already briefly stated that France looks in this connection at *acts of commerce* and Germany at the *status of merchant*. This German approach is often considered the more logical one, even in France, but in that country at the time of the codifications at the beginning of the nineteenth century it was not considered proper to create a special class of people — in this case merchants — with different rights, even if these rights did not imply privileges but perhaps only a less refined and sometimes harsher regime of enforcement. Nevertheless, to treat merchants differently was considered counter to the then new notion of equality. The result was that the basic French concept of commercial law became tied to commercial acts or 'actes de commerce'. There is

---

[15] In civil law, often an implied intention of the parties is assumed to make reference to custom palatable, in which connection the French are prone to make a subtle distinction and rather refer to *usages*, which are supposed to reflect such intent, whilst custom is not.
[16] If in civil law countries custom is accepted as normative, it is often only because of special statutory references to it, see in France eg the Law of 13 June 1866 concerning commercial usages, and the Law of 19 July 1928 concerning the relevance of usages in the decisions of employment disputes. See also Loussouarn, "The Relative Importance of Legislation, Custom, Doctrine, and Precedent in French Law", 18 *La L Rev* 235 (1958), see further s 1.3.1 *infra*. In Germany, *Section* 346 HGB, which refers to custom in commercial transaction, is considered such a provision and as such often viewed as no more than an elaboration of Section 157 of the German Civil Code or BGB, which allows references to good faith and custom in contractual interpretation, see also chapter 2, s 1.2.8.

no conceptual definition, however, and these acts are merely enumerated, *cf* Articles L 121–1 and L 110–1 (Articles 1 and 632 old) CdC. They concern mainly the purchase of assets for resale and the intermediary services rendered in this connection, the renting of property, manufacturing activity, transportation and banking business.

Even though the basis was therefore *not* the concept of *merchants or 'commercants'*, who are people or entities who habitually engage in commerce, the acts of commerce, as enumerated, are only covered by the CdC if they occur between merchants, except in as far as bills of exchange and cheques are concerned, which are commercial between all persons (except in a procedural sense). The result is in France therefore that merchants may not always be engaged in commercial acts as defined (even if they operate as merchants). On the other hand, persons not normally engaged in commerce may still engage in commercial acts but are not then covered in their activities by the CdC (except for bills of exchange and cheques). They are in any event sued in the ordinary courts.

In practice, in France the substantive law relevance of commercial acts is modest, even in the law of sales. The most important aspects of commercial sales are that testimonial evidence against commercial contracts is admitted unlike the situation under the Code Civil (Article 1341Cc).[17] Furthermore, under case-law,[18] registered mail notice rather than court action is sufficient to put a party to a commercial contract in default and to create the condition of the remedies of rescission of the contract and/or damages. Another point is that joint and several liability of commercial debtors is presumed in derogation from the rule of Article 1202 Cc. Since 1925, Article 631 CdC (old) provided further that agreements to arbitrate future disputes are valid and enforceable in matters in which the commercial courts are otherwise competent.

Tying the commercial law to acts of commerce (as enumerated) is often presented as the *objective* approach as distinguished from the *subjective* approach to commercial law, in France also referred to as the *droit réel v droit personnel* approach. This latter approach ties commercial law to the activities of merchants. France in essence opted for the objective approach (enumeration of the acts of commerce) as we saw with a subjective twist and limitation (in the indirect reference to these acts having to take place between merchants). In Germany it was the reverse: all merchants are in principle in their activity governed by the commercial code, but of course only for the activities that it covers. Here, the term 'merchant' remained largely undefined. In case law, there is an element of independence, of business activity, and of repetitiveness of the activity.

Thus in Germany, the coverage of the commercial code is primarily based on the activities of merchants as such (if both parties are merchants or at least the party making commitments), but only in the areas covered by the commercial code which in that country is also haphazard. Commercial law does not cover activities between merchants, which are not commercial in terms of that code. So, even in Germany, a definition of commercial acts (*Handelsgeschäfte*) comes in, although some activity is considered commercial *per se*. On the other hand, some commercial activity may also be engaged in by non-merchants, like the writing of cheques or the drawing of bills of exchange, which is now covered by a separate statute. Where in other instances non-merchants engage in commercial activity, it may still be covered by the commercial code, but this activity is then considered commercial only in a more generic or wider sense. In fact, many provisions of the HGB do not cover specific commercial matters at all and equally apply to non-merchants. The distinctions are therefore not so clean and clear in Germany either. Much is historical accident, not fully

---

[17] See also chapter 2, s 1.2.10.
[18] Cour de Cass *Req, 28 Oct 1903*, DP 1.14 (1904).

cleared up in 1897 when the present German civil and commercial codes were put into place. There are many German voices that argue for an abandonment of the distinction between civil and commercial law altogether.[19]

In Germany, the substantive law effect of commercial acts between merchants is thus also limited and incidental, not much different from France. Of particular interest is, however, that the transfer of a business activity implies the liability of the transferee for all its outstanding debt (Section 25 HGB). It is a much contested rule. Another interesting feature is that interest and fees are implied in business activity and need not expressly be agreed (Section 354 HGB).

The real problem in all this, in both France and Germany and in all countries that still maintain similar criteria for the application of commercial law, is that merchants are not only engaging in commercial activity but also in non-commercial acts. On the other hand, non-merchants also engage from time to time in commercial activities. The consequence is that neither the concept of merchant nor the concept of commercial activity can be defined exclusively in terms of the other. Hence the confusion. The other notable aspect of commercial law in France and Germany is the absence of any general reference to the impact of custom and industry practices even in commerce. As we saw, this is entirely in line with codification thinking that is suspicious of and uncomfortable with other sources of law and certainly also with a more internationalist approach.

In France, commercial law as a separate body of law remains more important than elsewhere because of the special court system. The French commercial law itself originated on two fronts: in the trade with England, through the ports of the Channel, leading to maritime and insurance law, and in the trade with Italy, through the fairs of Brie and Champagne, later moved to Lyons, in the East, leading to laws concerning transportation on land, bills of exchange, and bankruptcy laws.[20] These were codified in the *Réglements de la Place de Change de la Ville de Lyon* of 1667, largely copied in the first all-French commercial code (*Ordonnance de Commerce de Terre*) of 1673 promulgated by Louis XIV and amended in 1716 and 1739. It was the result of an initiative of minister Colbert who also ordered an *Ordonnance sur la Marine*, which was promulgated in 1681. They served as main sources for the French CdC of 1807. As a consequence, the French Commercial Code still maintains this distinction between land and sea transportation law (in Books I and II old), although maritime law is now the subject of many different statutes. In the meantime, company law was also put in a separate statute in 1966, bankruptcy in 1967, and banking in 1984. Many other provisions were repealed and de CdC is as a consequence much depleted but it notably still covers commercial intermediaries and exchanges, negotiable instruments, and the jurisdiction of the commercial courts. These subjects are, however, now being regrouped in the new French CdC of 2000.

As for the specialised commercial courts, in France, there are many commercial courts throughout the country. Their presidents are elected by the local business community and they have lay judges. These courts have their origin in an Edict of Charles IX of 1563, which established in Paris an elected lay commercial court to decide the smaller commercial cases. This set-up was subsequently copied in many provincial towns. The commercial courts hear the commercial cases, including matters of company and bankruptcy law regarding merchants. The proceedings are informal and geared to speed. Parties need not be represented by counsel. The system has worked well and had traditionally a good reputation, although it has not remained free from scandal and accusations of rigging in modern times.

---

[19] See CW Canaris, *Handelsrecht* (22nd ed. 1995), 8*ff, cf also* Karsten Schmidt, *Handelsrecht* (1999), 5.
[20] See for the history of French bankruptcy, 1 *Dalhuisen on International Insolvency and Bankruptcy* (1986), 1–60.

Belgium also has a system of commercial courts, but they were abandoned in the Netherlands. In that country, as well as earlier in Switzerland and Italy, there is no longer a separate commercial code either. Some of the content of the former commercial codes has been shifted to the civil codes or otherwise to separate statutes.

As regards the history of commercial law in Germany, there was enormous diversity in civil and commercial law between the different German States and Northern German (Hanseatic) towns well into the nineteenth century. After 1848, there was a Bill of Exchange Act as a uniform law, therefore promulgated per State and not at national level. From 1861, there was a General German Commercial Code, at first also as a uniform law, but it acquired federal status in the North German Bund in 1869 and became the all-German Commercial Code after Germany's unification in 1871. A commercial Supreme Court was established in Leipzig in 1871. After 1879 it was converted into the German Supreme Court or *Reichsgerichtshof* (now *Bundesgerichtshof*) and the separate commercial court system disappeared. Thus in Germany there are no longer special commercial courts but there are special commercial chambers within the courts. They deal with commercial cases pursuant to the *Gerichtsverfassungsgesetz* of 1877. In them, there are two lay judges, who need not be lawyers. They are appointed for a term of four years, which may be extended.

The German Commercial Code was adapted in 1897 at the time of the general German private law codification (*Bürgerliches Gesetzbuch* or BGB), without a fundamental re-orientation, and was then called the *Handelsgesetzbuch* or HGB. Both entered into force on 1 January 1900. In 1937, company law (the AG but not the GmbH) was put in a separate statute. In Germany, bankruptcy law had always been separate.[21]

1.1.6 Old and New Commercial and Financial Law: International Professional Law and the Revival of the International Law Merchant or Lex Mercatoria

In the previous sections, we saw that the contract for the sale of moveable tangible assets (or goods in a common law sense) is often considered at the hart of commercial law, certainly in common law but also in civil law, although in civil law there are only some limited special rules for it in the commercial codes which otherwise have a bias towards the commercial rendering of services and cover also other subjects like (sometimes) company, insurance and bankruptcy law. In any event, in civil law countries, the bulk of the law concerning sales, especially the proprietary aspect, is part of the civil codes (except for documents of title and negotiable instruments), which therefore also operate between merchants. Transportation contracts, sometimes even risk distribution through insurance contracts, are more closely connected with international sales and, in civil law, their legal regimes may therefore be more fully covered by the commercial codes, but in that case, they may also apply to non-merchants, as do the laws concerning cheques. The difference is that it does not give these non-merchants access to the commercial courts in countries like France that still have them.

---

[21] See for a history of German commercial law, Goldschmidt, "Universalgeschichte des Handelsrechts" in the 3rd edition of his *Handbuch des Handelsrechts* (1891). See for the 19th century discussions on the relationship between BGB and HGB, Raisch, *Die Abgrenzung des Handelsrechts vom bürgerlichen Recht als Kodifikationsproblem im 19 Jahrhundert* (1962). The first more theoretical treatises on commercial law appeared from the 16th and 17th centuries, notably in Italy: see Straccha, *Tractatus de Conturbatonibus sive Decoctoribus* (1553), and Casaregis, *Discursus Legales de Commercio* (1740). See for older French commercial law, J Savary (who largely drafted the *Ordonnance* of 1673), *Du Parfait Negociant*.

Professionality of the contracting parties is not a feature *per se* of traditional commercial law of this type, especially not in common law, but if, as in France and Germany, special commercial law rules are sometimes still applied to these contracts, it is because in essence they are concluded between merchants. Whatever the traditional differences between the French and German approaches in this respect discussed in the previous section, this suggests greater expertise, business contact and regular commercial activity for financial gain and therefore an activity between professionals or businessmen, even if sales may of course also be concluded between private persons under the normal private law rules, whilst cheques may be drawn by individuals under the commercial law rules.

For *domestic* activities, one may conclude, however, as many have, that the distinction between business (or professional) and private (or non-professional) activity as such has gradually become *less* important for the law. It is reflected in commercial law having become less significant as a different branch of the law everywhere, even if France still maintains a separate court system for commercial disputes. Some civil law countries, like Italy, Switzerland and the Netherlands have therefore abandoned any distinction and many writers in Germany argue for it. In modern times, domestically, special treatment has often become relevant, *not* for business partners, but rather for consumers or non-professionals in their dealings amongst each other and particularly with professionals. The result is that professionals and their dealings are again differently treated, although that is not by design on the basis of special commercial or customary considerations, but rather by default.

This may be relevant in the application of modern notions of good faith whilst determining the rights and duties of the parties to a contract, when expertise and reasonable expectations may be taken into account, *cf* in particular Sections 157 and 242 BGB in Germany. It was especially done for the protection of weaker parties and may be much less relevant for professional dealings, see more in particular chapter 2, section 1.3.5. In civil law, the good faith notion may thus result in the nature of the relationship of the parties and the legal effect thereof on their dealings becoming a distinctive feature, as it already did in common law, which did not need the good faith notion in this connection, see also chapter 2, section 1.1.

It was submitted before that more recently, financial rather than trade or mercantile law emphasises the special nature of modern commercial law and is introducing new notions not only of contract but also of proprietary law. This point was already made in section 1.1.1 above. In finance leases, repos, secured transactions including floating charges, and investment securities entitlements, new notions of proprietary rights emerge especially in civil law, alien therefore to its traditional thinking and its systematic unitary approach and regardless of the traditional closed nature of its proprietary system. In short (and much attention will be given to it later, especially in chapters 4 and 5), beneficial, temporary and conditional ownership rights in present and future replacement assets that were not unknown to common law, especially in its equity variant, must now also find a place in civil law. For the time being, that is unlikely to be done in a coherent systematical manner. It means that civil law must get used to a similar disperse notion of property as common law (especially in equity) has long been comfortable with. Commercial law is here the conduit. It is another reason why in both legal families under pressure of the internationalisation, commercial law regains its own place, not only therefore as a (prospective) transnationalised system of substantive law, but also as a system in which experimentation with new structures unavoidably most take place and can be separated from the rest of private law.

That the mercantile component recedes here from the center of commercial law is also related to the fact that the traditional paper based concept of ownership and transfer (like in bills of lading and negotiable instruments and investment securities) and the protection of *bona fide* purchasers or holders in due course need to be reformulated in an environment in which paperless trading must become the norm. In securities trading this is now clear in the emergence of security entitlements and securities accounts with inter-mediaries. The problems posed with regard to the legal chacterisation of the proprietary rights in such entitlements will be more fully discussed in chapters 4 and 5. Here it suffices to note that new proprietary structures must also be expected in the more traditional trade law aspects of commercial law where dematerialisation of proprietary rights may also become the norm (like in bits of lading or negotiable instruments). As will be discussed in greater detail below in section 3.2.2, these newer structures are largely meant to operate between professionals who are more likely for the time being to be able to deal with them and to fashion them. It reinforces at the same time the emphasis on professional dealings as the essence of all commercial law and of its separateness from the rest of the law. The necessary expansion of the *bona fide* purchaser approach at the same time makes that the reach of these new proprietary rights even if based on financial practices and party auton-omy will not become excessive.

In any event, special treatment of professionals has always remained more important in *international* dealings, of which the international sale of goods is perhaps still the best example even if financial dealings have eclipsed them in importance. International sales always presented a clear instance of a situation where extra risks and complications gave rise to a different regime. In a *technical sense,* international sales have indeed always been considered to be contracts between *professional* parties only, therefore between parties who are both knowledgeable in the area of their sale and its risks, are likely and able to make the special arrangements necessary in this connection and are aware of and able to develop *special industry practices* to this end, for which in international sales one should always be on the look-out, *cf* chapter 2, section 2.1.5. Also in the additional arrangements completing an international sale, like in transportation and insurance, one may see differences in treat-ment as compared to domestic dealings which may now also be more consumer influenced.

Much more obvious is the situation in connection with modern financial dealings, even domestically. If one takes the UCC as an example, it is clear that Article 2 on the sale of goods still maintains a more general notion of ownership and its transfer that also obtains between non-professionals (even if generally deemphasised), but in Article 2A on equip-ment leases and in Article 8 on the trading and holding of modern investment securities entitlements, the emphasis is increasingly on professional activities (of intermediaries and on the relationship of investors with them) and proprietary rights are only defined inci-dentally, that is for each structure specifically without any resort to general proprietary principles or a unitary system of proprietary rights. That is also true in Article 9 on secured transactions that in its new 1999 text also tends to address itself principally to professionals (therefore, excluding consumer transactions, *cf* for example, Section 9–109(d)(13)). In Article 4A (Section 4A–108) on electronic payment, consumers are explicitly excluded. They are also excluded in Article 5 from the practice of issuing letters of credit (Section 5–102 (9)(b)). It confirms the assumption that because of the specialized nature of these proprietary arrangements they cannot be handled or are less suitable or even dangerous for non-professionals.

The UCC, although not specifically written for international sales or even for modern financial structures, defines the notion of merchants and dealings between merchants in Section 2–104, but *only* in the context of the law of the sale of goods (and not as a broader concept like in France and Germany, see the previous section). It does not eliminate consumer sales from Article 2 UCC either, but has some special rules concerning merchants.[22] A merchant is here a person who normally deals in goods of the kind or otherwise holds himself out by his occupation as having knowledge or skill peculiar to the practices or goods involved in the transaction or to whom such knowledge or skill may be attributed by his employment of an agent or broker or other intermediary who by his occupation holds himself out as having such knowledge or skill. Dealings between merchants are transactions with respect to which both parties are chargeable with the knowledge and skills of merchants.

Unlike domestic sales, the subject of *international* sales in this sense is indeed not commonly thought to cover consumer sales at all or even sales of goods concerning which an otherwise professional party does not have special knowledge. To the extent an own pattern is developed, the international sale is further limited in scope in that, as a term of art, it is not believed to cover the sale of real estate, negotiable instruments, other documents of title, bonds and shares, or assignments of intangible property (like receivables) either. This is clearly reflected in the 1980 (Uncitral) Vienna Convention on the International Sale of Goods (Article 2). It gives a partial codification of the applicable directory law and is meant as a uniform law. As we shall see in chapter 2, section 2.3.1 it has been adopted by many countries, even if in practice often still excluded by the parties to these sales.

Other types of sales may of course also be the subject of international sales contracts, as may be consumer sales (which may require a whole set of other safeguards, increasingly important in cross-border internet transactions) and the rendering of connected cross-border services. However, they are not commonly included in a reference to international sales in a *technical* sense, which, as to subject matter, are therefore limited to tangible *movable assets sold between professionals located in different states*. In such sales, there are traditionally different rules as to delivery and passing of risk. In view of the distance, there may also result some special *duties of care* of the buyer to protect the goods upon arrival should disputes arise and goods be rejected. On the other hand, the seller might have a special duty of care if the buyer delays of taking delivery in order to preserve the assets, even if the risk has passed to the latter (eg upon tender of delivery), *cf* Article 85*ff* of the Vienna Convention. The subject of international sales will be dealt with more extensively in chapter 2.

In the meantime, separating out international professional dealings has become increasingly common in commerce, even outside finance. Sensitivity to the special nature of activities of *professionals* operating internationally is, eg, suggested in the 1995 Unidroit Principles of Contract Law. According to the Preamble, they apply only to international commercial contracts, a restriction not contained in the 1998 European (Lando) Principles of Contract Law, which also apply to consumers but are otherwise very similar. In the Unidroit Principles, internationality and commerciality are not defined but the idea is clear, even if many of the rules seem to come straight from domestic consumer laws, which explains the similarity with the European Principles. Both sets of Principles will be discussed in greater detail in chapter 2, section 1.6.

In arbitration laws, a special approach to international professional dealings is now also commonly taken. These laws may not only apply a special internationalised regime when

---

[22] In earlier proposals of Article 2 UCC, a broader distinction between consumer and professional sales was made, see also ZB Wiseman, "The Limits of Vision: Karl Llewellyn and the Merchant Rules", 100 *Harv LR*, 465. Article 2 UCC is therefore less professional oriented than originally planned, which reflects the reality that in domestic sales professional dealings have so far acquired fewer distinctive features. Consumers have in the meantime obtained special protection under broader consumer laws.

parties come from different countries but also when the subject matter is of an international nature or the arbitration takes place in an unrelated country, *cf* the French Decrees Nos. 80–345 and 81–500 and also Article 1(3) of the Uncitral Model Arbitration Law, now accepted in several common law countries, including some states of the USA, in Scotland and in some East European countries including Russia. This may lead to the application of some additional or different arbitration rules for professional dealings, especially providing (a) procedural flexibility in international cases, (b) discretion of the panel in the laws of evidences and in the private international law rules to be applied, and (c) a limitation of review by the domestic courts, either when the awards are challenged in the country where they are rendered (of their seat) or in the context of their recognition in other countries. It is the gist of the 1958 New York Convention on the Recognition and Enforcement of Foreign Arbitral Awards (Article 1.3) which allows states to limit the application of the Convention to such awards. Even if they do not do so, the common view is that on the one hand disputes between states on boundary and similar political issues are excluded and on the other hand also employment and family law issues except if incidental to the main dispute. The Convention limits itself in any event to international (or 'foreign') arbitral awards (Article 1.1). 'Foreign' means here enforcement in another territory than where the award is made.

Particularly in the international commercial arbitration context the 'internationality' and 'commerciality' notions acquire their full modern meaning and importance. They are closely connected and will together lift the dispute out of the local environment, thus focusing on a procedural and dispute solving approach that is devoid of local peculiarities and restraints and therefore better able to deal with the nature of professional dealings, their dynamics, and risk management features. As far as internationality is concerned, one may expect here major cross-border commercial and financial interests to be at stake which may derive from the fact that performance is in another country so that major assets must move between countries in the course of the performance or major services must be delivered cross-border or from the fact that the parties have their habitual residences in different countries. It follows that normally companies and not private individuals will be involved (certainly not consumers) and that the business in which the dispute arises is on some scale and that the interests to be defended are therefore considerable.

The more modern Uncitral Model Arbitration Law accepts that an arbitration is international when the parties (at the time of the conclusion of the arbitration agreement) have their places of business in different countries, or the place (or seat) of the arbitration or the place of (a substantial part) of the performance is outside the country of the parties. Parties may also expressly agree that the arbitration shall be international. As to 'commerciality' the Model Law states in a footnote to Article 1(1) that it should be given a wide interpretation so as to cover matters arising from all relationships of a commercial nature whether or not contractual. It then gives a number of non-exclusive examples. The idea is that all international business is covered.

Thus, at least in some important areas, the distinction between professional and other dealings has become more important, especially internationally.[23] A *more radical* approach altogether is the *distinction in general* between the *professional sphere* on the one hand and the *private or consumer sphere* on the other with emphasis therefore on the types of parties rather

---

[23] The notion of commerciality has also been defined in the context of sovereign immunity in terms of the distinctions between acts *de jure imperii* and *de jure gestionis,* but the aim is then to distinguish public and commercial acts of sovereigns and their agencies, not to distinguish between (international) commercial and other private law acts.

than on the nature of their dealings and the qualification of the one as essentially globalised and the other as remaining in essence domestic. Commercial law is then tied to all cross border flows of goods, services and money between professionals who increasingly conform to internationally established patterns. This is the preferred approach in this book and ties the new law to the emergence of a new legal order for professional dealings, see more in particular sections 1.4.3 and 1.4.4 below. The result in as far as the applicable law is concerned is the application of transnationalised legal concepts to their dealings, meant to support their practices and based on their legitimate needs, see more in particular section 1.5 below. Thus *professional dealings* are here considered to be the dealings in the international flows of goods, services and capital between individuals or entities that make it their business to do so, regularly engage in that activity, and are sufficiently expert in it. It may imply a less subtle legal attitude to these professionals who are used to dealing in risk. It may on the other hand also mean specialised proprietary structures that may not be used in other parts of private law.

In sales, it leads to the basic distinction between professional and consumer sales, with all of the first and the legal regime applicable to them being increasingly considered internationalised, even if on the occasion the relevant sale may not have any international aspects at all,[24] as in this approach it would be increasingly unrealistic to consider local professional dealings subject to different rules if they concern the same business. Economically speaking there is no longer a clear justification legally to treat professional dealings differently depending on the origin of the parties and their location in one or more countries. The result is a unitary approach for the professional sphere in which *internationality* needs no longer be defined. Arbitrary distinctions in this connection may thus be avoided.

In modern finance, it means special attention for specialised proprietary and bankruptcy resistent structures which at the same time are likely to also acquire a transnational status even when used purely domestically. In civil law, it will thus confer an altogether different status on modern commercial law locally — quite different therefore from what it is or means at present (as mere *lex specialis* of the existing national private law) — but much more importantly, both in civil and common law, it is the transnationalisation of this new commercial law as uniform contract and proprietary law that is truly going to matter.

The consequence of a transaction being in the professional sphere is therefore the increasing likelihood of it being taken out of a domestic law context altogether, both on the contractual and proprietary side. It will be governed by its own transnational legal concepts in a unifying transborder development, even if within that new law the contractual and especially the proprietary structures may not be perceived as forming one coherent or closed system of rights and obligations. That is precisely the area and challenge of the new *lex mercatoria*. The professional community is likely to be able to deal with that and devise the necessary protections and even make good use of the flexibility it entails. That has become the major task of lawyers in international commerce and finance. It suggests the operation of an altogether different *legal order of its own*, the emergence of own practices therein, the reduced impact of directory and even mandatory rules of a local nature on it, a lesser need to rebalance the relationship of the parties on the basis of (domestic) social considerations as professionals are on the whole well able to look after themselves, and in contract a less refined application of the basic legal protections in terms of disclosure, time to protest, undoing of transactions and the invocation of all kind of legal exceptions, like

---

[24] See for this unitary approach, JH Dalhuisen, *Wat is vreemd recht* [What is Foreign Law], Inaugural Address Utrecht (Kluwer, Deventer, 1991), 11.

force majeure, hardship or even negligent behaviour of the other party. Only the more explicit and obvious cases are then likely to be given relief, whilst proprietary protections become also *sui generis.*

To repeat, in this approach, the center of gravity of attention of commercial law shifts away from the traditional trade or mercantile laws, even if remaining an important subject, to international finance. Within this approach, certain subjects of a more fundamental nature stick out. In (a) contract, they may include (not merely in finance) the use of the concept of good faith and the normative approach to contract interpretation guided by international (business) standards and perceptions that may substantially limit the protections that may so be afforded, in (b) payments they may include notions of finality, and in (c) property they may include concepts of trusts, conditional and temporary ownership rights, bookentry entitlements for investment securities, a broad *bona fide* purchaser protection, bulktransfers (with or without full asset substitution), and floating charges, tracing, direct and especially indirect agency, set-off and netting, where again the normativeness fo remost derives from what is or has become normal and customary in the particular business concerned.

The final test of such newer (prospectively internationalised) proprietary structures is in *bankruptcy.* As so far bankruptcy laws remain purely domestic, this is likely to produce the greater problems exactly with internationalised property rights and structures of the just mentioned type. Earlier I have dealt extensively with international bankruptcy from the perspective of recognition and enforcement in other countries and the internationalisation of concepts that must take place in that connection.[25] In the meantime, international principles of bankruptcy are developing and are being written down.[26] Their usefulness will be limited if they do not manage to deal with precisely these types and their international use and acceptance.

The transnational approach suggests greater emphasis on the facts of the case, accepted practices, on the typical nature of the relationship and on the interests that need special protection rather than on a given functional rule of a traditional domestic type, even in bankruptcies, which rules, if existing, would then have to be reinterpreted in the light of these considerations. At this stage of the development of the new commercial law, it means a search both for the relevant structures *and* the relevant law in each particular case. It is therefore *not* a question of a system, which can only develop later. As was already mentioned before, this is a trend that may in fact also be observed domestically and is the essence of a more *normative or teleological* or (in American terms) more *realist* approach to the interpretation of the rights and duties of parties, at least under a contract. This more normative approach, favoured in the modern civil law of contract with its good faith notion (even if in legal scholarship often reduced to a mere extension of the system), will be discussed at some greater length in chapter II for contracts. As noted before, in proprietary matters, in civil law, the analysis of the development of new proprietary rights has hardly begun.

As the proprietary aspects may well present the greater conceptual problems in the development of this new transnational law in the commercial and financial (professional) area, they will be a special concern in this book, to which chapters IV and V testify.

---

[25] See 1 *Dalhuisen on International Insolvency and Bankruptcy* (1986), 3.266.3*ff.*
[26] See IMF, *Orderly & Effective Insolvency Procedures* (1999) and Worldbank, *Principles and Guidelines for Effective Insolvency and Creditors Rights Systems* May 2001, www.worldbank.org/iufa/ipg_eng.pdf. Unicitral in the meantime started work on a draft model insolvency law but has shifted to producing Guidelines, www.uncitral.org. See for another compilation, Koopman ao (eds). *Principles of European Insolvency Law* (2003).

Naturally, the absence of certainty, although unavoidable in all new developments, is the most glaring here. As a consequence, more than in the contractual aspects of international sales between professionals, where a distinct internationalised legal regime may start to operate more spontaneously, private international law establishing the applicability of a domestic law is likely to remain here in principle more relevant for the time being, especially in respect of the title transfer and the creation of security interests or conditional and beneficial ownership rights in sold assets to protect the financial product or the sales credit. Yet, particularly in these proprietary areas, private international law rules have always been uncertain, especially where assets move cross border or are intangible (like receivables), which is often the case in international sales or in international financial structures. If only for these reasons, transnational rules and ownership types with an own transfer and security interest regime must in any event evolve, but it is more generally promoted by the various typical international proprietary structures that are developing in international finance.

It should be noted that for negotiable instruments they always existed and they were recently informally developed also for newer negotiable financial interests, like those in eurobonds and modern book entry systems concerning investment securities. International property rights are also emerging in offshore drilling installations and mining rights, and in intellectual and industrial property and the beneficial, conditional, temporary and security intererests that can be established in them. These developments are of the greatest importance and will be further explored in Part III below and in chapter 4. Again, bankruptcy and the approaches of domestic bankruptcy laws in terms of their recognition of these international proprietary interests will present here the ultimate test.

1.1.7 International Commercial Arbitration and International Commercial Courts

As was already noted in the previous section, in international arbitrations, the internationalisation of modern commercial law is often more informally dealt with and there tends to be greater freedom for arbitrators in conducting the proceedings and in finding or developing the applicable transnational law and custom. They also have freedom in fashioning the rules of evidence and the applicable private international law rules wherever they may remain relevant. National courts should do the same but often hesitate. To support the new transnational law in the professional sphere, it would therefore not be a bad idea, nor too far-fetched a proprosition,[27] to set up an international court system for professional dealings operating in a similar manner as the commercial courts once did in regionally divided

---

[27] See for such a court to operate as appellate court in the supervision and recognition of arbitral awards internationally Mauro Rubino-Sammartano, *International Arbitration Law and Practice* (2001), 980. See further HM Holtzmann, "A Task for the 21st century: Creating a New International Court for resolving Disputes on the Enforceability of Arbitral Awards", and SM Schwebel, "The Creation and Operation of an International Court of Arbitral Awards", both in Martin Hunter a.o. (eds.), *The Internationalisation of International Arbitration*, The LCIA Centenary Conference (1995), at 109 and 115. The concern of these latter two authors is the recognition of foreign awards under the New York Convention of 1958 and the possible bias of local judges. The idea is to replace their involvement with that of an international court, which would acquire exclusive jurisdiction in the matter. Enforcement of recognition orders of such an international court would of course remain a domestic affair. It would be logical that such a court would also become solely competent for challenges or setting aside petitions, which are now normally brought in the domestic courts of the place of the arbitration. Other forms of ancillary proceedings could be added, like interim protection measures and compelling the attendance of witnesses, see also M Hunter, at 157. The proposal is important although more limited than what is proposed here, but the international court should be the same.

countries. Another possibility is to accept that domestic courts in commercial matters sit as international commercial courts. Judgments of these courts should then be universally enforceable, much as international arbitration awards are treated under the New York Convention of 1958 on the Recognition and Enforcement of Foreign Arbitral Awards or as *in rem* judgments are habitually enforced in admiralty world wide.

See for the idea of local courts operating as international courts in this connection, the English case of *Amin Rasheed Shipping Corporation v Kuwait Insurance Company*, [1983] 1 WLR 241 and 228. The case is especially of interest in view of the important cast of judges expressing their (minority) views in the lower courts with the House of Lords ultimately re-establishing orthodoxy. The facts in this case are not of great import. There was an insurance contract concerning an insurer in Kuwait, drafted much along the lines of the relevant standard English policy, yet without a choice of law and competent forum clause. There thus arose concern about the applicable law and about the jurisdiction of the English courts.

In the lower courts, Judge (as he then was) Bingham, [1982] 1 WLR 961, thought that the contract could be covered by an international regime inspired along English lines (although not so in this case), so that under the applicable English rules of international jurisdiction the competency of the English courts could be established on the basis of the application of English law. In the Court of Appeal, the Master of the Rolls Sir John Donaldson thought that English courts could have jurisdiction over an unwilling defendant because the English courts could in cases like these function as *international commercial courts* (emphasis added). In the House of Lords,[1984] 3 WLR 241, Lord Diplock thought, however, that contracts could not operate in a vacuum as they would then be only scraps of paper. International law was clearly considered vacuus in this connection and the implication was that only a domestic law could apply which in this case was eventually thought to be English law, a view supported by Lord Wilberforce. Lord Diplock further thought that English courts could not operate as international commercial courts and thus force themselves on unwilling defendants. Also for English jurisdiction in cases like these, there would have to be a solid basis, which could be, but needed not be, and was in this case *not* found to be in the application of English law, especially since in this case there was a Kuwaiti court available.

In a later unrelated case, *EI du Pont de Nemours v Agnew*, [1987] 2 Lloyd's Rep 585, Lord Bingham, then in the Court of Appeal, borrowed some of the "legal vacuum" language but seemed to leave open entirely the question whether that vacuum could be filled by international law, including international general principles or custom, whilst in the same year in the *Deutsche Schachtbau- und Tiefbohrgesellschaft* case, [1987] 3 WLR 1023, the Court of Appeal under Sir John Donaldson held unanimously that at least international arbitrators could rely for the applicable law on internationally accepted principles, thus accepting not only general principle as a source of law but allowing *international* principles and customs to operate in that connection also.

It is sometimes submitted that this could only be so in international arbitrations and that at least the Rome Convention on the Law Applicable to Contractual Obligations would not allow it, see *Dicey and Morris on the Conflict of Laws* (13th edn 2000), 1216, but in truth the text is inconclusive and the point seems never to have been considered. So much is clear, however, that, even in England, no true principle is any longer involved as it not conceivable that there is any fundamental difference between the applicable law in courts of law and in arbitrations, whilst, as far as the Rome Convention is concerned, it is a matter of interpretation on which there is much contrary opinion in the rest of Europe. In any event, where more substantive rules are introduced like in Articles 5, 6 and 7, more general principles of protection or balance are used. In the US, opinion moves also in the direction of accepting international principle as the applicable law, see eg DW Rivkin, "Enforceability of Arbitral Awards based on Lex Mercatoria", (1993) 9 *Arbitration International*, 67.

In connection with international arbitrations, the question has further arisen whether they themselves could operate in a legal vacuum, therefore, in this terminology, separate from a domestic law or legal system (or local arbitration act), often perceived to be the domestic law of the seat of the arbitration., see also A Redfern and M Hunter, *Law and Practice of International Commercial Arbitration* 3rd edn (1999), 77. ICSID arbitrations notably do not operate in a national arbitration framework. Again, the more proper issue would appear to be whether the vacuum may be filled in another manner, like by international law as law merchant (or common international arbitration standards). One thing is clear, there is in these international cases a close connection between the law applied and the status of the tribunal. If the law is international, it is not strange to assume that courts applying such law (be they national courts or arbitration panels) thereby acquire an international status as well. Thus when in *Amin Rasheed* there was a discussion of English law being applicable as common currency or *lingua franca*, this implied this internatiopnalisation of both the applicable law and the courts applying it. In certain areas, like letters of credit and guarantees, the ICC has facilitated this progress and subsequently captured the dynamics and evolution of these principles internationally, as we shall see, rather than merely borrowing or seeking some compromise with domestic orders. In articulating these international practices, their autonomous international status is highlighted at the same time.

Seen from this perspective, it was not at all so strange that the commercial courts in London in the minority opinion in Amin Rasheed were considered to operate as international commercial courts. Of course, commercial courts in other countries could then claim a similar status. It is not strange either that this may affect unwilling defendants if an adequate rule of jurisdiction could be formulated for these courts under international (customary)

The difference with international arbitrations is that there would be more stability in such a court system and also a facility for appeal. Such an international court system comprised of domestic courts sitting in international commercial cases (they could have some lay judges), could have a central highest international appeal court to test points of law. It could also supervise the challenging and recognition and execution of international arbitral awards. It would be an immensely important aid to the development of transnational commercial and financial law and is at this stage probably more important than codifying the transnational law itself, for which there is as yet no sufficient direction in practice and theory and no sufficient platform amongst legal practioners.[28]

There is some kind of example in the WIPO procedure concerning domain names conflicts. Under the classic rules of private international law great differences could here arise and forum shopping encouraged. The WIPO procedure allows everyone to ask on line to be entitled to use a domain name registered in the name of someone else. The WIPO will

law or on the basis of general principles. The jurisdictional limits would be found in a vibrant *forum non conveniens* approach in the courts asked to exercise this jurisdiction and in a broad concept of *lis pendens* in other international commercial courts subsequently petitioned and asked to intervene, or in an intelligent handling of subject-matter jurisdiction and comity requirements in the American manner, see s 2.2.6 *infra*.

One consequence often overlooked is that the ensuing judgment could then hardly be qualified as a domestic judgment either and be asked to be enforced as such. In fact, judgments of this nature should be enforced in the manner of arbitral awards under the New York Convention. Ideally, the Convention should be extended to them, in which connection the question of proper (judicial) jurisdiction would also have to be considered. Another idea would be to allow the parties to select the regime of the Convention for the international recognition of commercial judgments. In this context, it could certainly also be helpful, to create a superior international commercial court that could take final appeals in this type of cases. To be efficient, that would also require treaty law and could equally be embodied in an amendement to the New York Convention.

Note, however, in this connection also Judge Wilkey speaking for the majority in the Court of Appeals in the American *Laker* case, 731 F2d 909 (DC Circuit 1984), at the same time as the English judiciary in *Amin Rasheed*: "Despite the real obligations of courts to apply international law and foster comity, domestic courts do not sit as internationally constituted tribunals. Domestic courts are created by national constitutions and statutes to enforce primarily national laws. The courts of most developed nations follow international law to the extent it is not overriden by national law. Thus, courts inherently find it difficult neutrally to balance competing foreign interests". Note that this statement came within the explicit rejection of the balancing test of Para 403 of the *Restatement (Third) of the Foreign Relations Law* of the United States (1987), even though a reasonable link between forum and controversy was consired to be an important limitation on US jurisdiction. This Restatement was in preparation at the end is now more commonly accepted, *cf* the US Supreme Court in *Hartford Fire Insurance Co v California*, 509 US 764 (1993) in which both the majority and the dissent relied on it, see for a discussion more in particular, the dissent of Justice Scalia in that case. To the extent this Restatement is now accepted, it puts the status of the courts in dealing with international commercial cases also in a different light.

Note also that by using a forum selection clause, it is normally accepted (unless the forum selection would work out to be unfair or utterly unreasonable for one of the parties in the circumstances of a case) that parties may choose a court that balances the potentially involved governmental interests better or more neutrally, like an international commercial arbitration panel would do that has undoubtedly an international status, see also s 2.2.6 *infra*. To the extent national courts are increasingly willing to do the same, it is not illogical to impute to them a similar status. It would certainly seem fair to say that especially under the influence of much increased internationalisation and globalisation since 1984, matters have moved on.

It should also be noted in this connection that within the EU, domestic courts in EU matters sit as European courts subject to the guidance of the European Court of Justice from which prejudicial opinions may be and are frequently asked. The notion of national courts sitting as international courts is therefore by no means new. Another issue that could be raised in this connection is whether domestic courts would have to be more conservative in developing international law than internationl courts or international arbitrators would have to be. Of interest may be in this connection the observation of Lord Slynn in the first Pinochet case, [2000] 1 AC 61, which implied that the House of Lords in a case like this one did not sit as an international court and would therefore be more restricted in developing international law. The majority clearly did not see it this way although it did not argue the point explicitly, *cf.* also L Collins, "Foreign Relations and the Judiciary", *Int'l and Comp L Q,* 509 (2002) with reference to the Court of Appeal in Kuwait *Airways Corp v Iraqi Airways Co*, [2001] 3 WLR 1117, 1207 in which the further development of international law as to what was justiciable or not was also not impeded.

[28] Except perhaps in more limited areas, see for practioners input the Unidroit Mobile Equipment Convention of 2002, chapter 5, s 1.8.3 and the EU Financial Collateral Directive, chapter 4, s 3.2.4.

then appoint an arbitrator who decides within six weeks. If he finds in favour of the claimant, the respondent may appeal to the normal state courts to get his domain name back. At first these cases were decided on general principles and on those derived from national laws, but are now increasingly determined on the basis of the (transnationalised) case-law of these arbitrators themselves which can be accessed online.

As to the applicable law, rather than a system of hard and fast rules, in the formative era of this transnational commercial and financial law, a *hierarchy of different norms* is here the more likely answer, a hierarchy to be developed within the context of the a modern *lex mercatoria* and that starts with fundamental principle, mandatory custom and practices, mandatory uniform treaty, and subsequently concerns itself with party autonomy, directory practices and treaty law, and general principles. Much of the focus of this book will be on this hierarchy and the uniformity in the applicable law it brings in that manner. It will be further developed in sections 1.5.4 and 3.1.1 below. Much attention will in that context also be given to legal orders and their modern manifestation in a sociological as well as cultural sense, see section 1.4. Consequently, the statist view of law as an exclusively national creation and the role of private international law that seeks a solution in a domestic law for all international legal complications is here fundamentally re-evaluated and is to be preceded by a search for the applicable transnational law. Another important question in this connection will have to be how domestic public policy issues must be handled in the international commercial and financial legal order, see sections 1.4.3 and 2.2.6 below.

Before this development will be further discussed, it may be useful for those more in particular interested first to devote some extra time to the more traditional sources of private law in civil and common law countries and to the development of the codification approach and its significance in this regard. This will be the subject of section 1.2 and will explain more extensively the limited room traditionally left in civil law for the application of fundamental and more general principles and especially for custom. It will also seek to explain the attitudes in this regard in common law and the more modern American departures. In section 1.3, present common and civil law attitudes will be more fully compared. Subsequently in section 1.4, the discussion will move to the operation of international legal orders and the abandonment of exclusively statist and territorial view of modern law in favour of a more modern cultural, sociological, and economic approach to the sources of the law leading to a more universal approach (at least in international cases). In section 1.5, it will be followed by a discussion of the transnational commercial and financial legal order and of the interrelationship between the further development of domestic law (and public policy) and the transnational law in the new globalised market-place. This will lead to a first introduction to the concept and operation of the hierarchy of principles and norms in the modern *lex mercatoria*. It will amongst others identify the place of modern uniform treaty or model law, ICC and other restatements of industry practices, or private EU law (in as far as developed), and the residual function of private international law or conflicts law and therefore of domestic laws within this *lex mercatoria*. This approach will be further developed in Part III after the traditional conflicts of laws approach and its problems have been more fully analysed in Part II.

For the internationally oriented student interested in the development and operation of the different (commercial) legal systems, this broader excursion may also serve as an explanation for much of what may at first glance look unfamiliar or strange in other legal systems with which she or he will be confronted. Especially the different approaches in civil and common law to the sources of the law, the statist approach, and the different attitudes to other non-statist sources of laws should be better understood by all. For the next chapters the approach is to identify a number of legal structures, eg assignment in connection with receivable financing or other modern financial products like leases and repos, to highlight the intrinsic problems, then see what local laws have done with them, and ultimately consider the requirements of and developments in the international practice where party autonomy (therefore contractual clauses) are the beginning but broader practices may need to be demonstrated to underpin e.g. new proprietary structures which cannot be dependent on party autonomy alone but may for their status require a more objective base in the law, here the emerging transnational law or new law merchant, which follows in essence from the business community's concensus and ways of operating.

In a comparative sense (therefore in respect of the examples used as illustration and guidance or in identifying a uniform trend), I confine myself in this book largely to the laws of the major countries of common and civil law, therefore to the laws of England and the USA on the one side, and of France and Germany on the other. It is not done out of disrespect for any other, but not all can be covered and what is covered should, in my view, be covered in some considerabe depth to have meaning. It concerns here major industrial nations, the development of whose legal systems was of prime importance for the evolution of modern commercial and financial law. These legal systems, are also likely to provide the natural starting point for the globalised legal structures developing in the international commercial and financial sphere.

1.2   The Origin and Evolution of Civil and Common Law. The Sources of Private Law. Statist and Non-statist Views

1.2.1   *The Evolution of Modern Private Law and its Sources and their Importance for the Development of Modern International Commercial and Financial Law*

The development of modern international commercial and financial law as an autonomous transnational non-statist phenomenon may be better understood when some greater insight is acquired into the development of the sources of law and their autonomy in the course of time. Although we have become used to a view in which the law emanates from states — in civil law through codification, in common law of the English variety through the idea that all law emanates from the sovereign — it was not always thus and is a particular nineteenth century phenomenon that had already found important support amongst eighteenth century philosophers as we shall see and was connected with the emergence of the modern state. By then, in England it had already led to the absorption of the commercial (and church) law into the common law, but it is till this day not as completely integrated in the gereal body of private law as it is in civil law. It also did not mean legislation *per se*.

On the European Continent, the *Ius Commune* remained diversified longer and did not interfere with the commercial law as such. It therefore retained much greater independence, which it took the nineteenth century codifications to finish. This may have been an exceptional situation and the statist, therefore nationalistic view of commercial and financial law may abate and could even be coming to an end. In that sense, a situation more akin to the one that existed under the *Ius Commune* may revive. Room is thus created for the revival of a non-territorial *lex mercatoria*, albeit in a much updated form. This development will lay greater stress on the economic and social undercurrents of the law and on its in essence decentralised nature. That is a view of private law that has in the mean time received much attention in modern American academia, particularly in the 'law and economics' and 'law and sociology' variants of its 'legal realism', even if as yet American legal scholarship has not developed these notions much further in the context of the further evolution of international commercial and financial law. It is nevertheless necessary to also discuss these modern American attitudes briefly below, see section 1.2.13. But first the development of the legal systems and sources of law in Western Europe will be covered in some greater detail to set the scene.

1.2.2   The Early Roman Law Development

In the following pages only the barest overview can be given of the intellectual, cultural and social evolution of the law in the Western World. No more than a framework is intended so as to show in a comprehensive way what went before and to provide a ready platform for further investigation of what is to come in terms of transnational commercial and financial law or the modern law merchant or *lex mercatoria*.

Roman law was in the Western world the first legal system that truly developed into something that went beyond the basics and still has meaning today.[29] According to the writer Livy or Livius, Rome was founded in 754 BC and was at first under the leadership of Etruscan kings who could exercise all powers (or *imperium*) in this small community of probably no may more than 10,000 to 20,000 people. This *imperium* also included the judicial function. It was exercised on the basis of the leadership's insights, some customary law, edicts which the king had decreed, and some laws (*leges*), issued by popular acclaim through a people's assembly or *Comitia*, which later, when Rome became bigger, was subdivided in 30 groups or *curiae*. They each sent representatives and also provided military personnel for the defence of the City. Even then, there was already a Senate, which, however, could only give advice (*senatus consulta*).

This system continued after the last king, Tarquinius Superbus, was ousted in 509 BC following, according to the story, the outcry caused by his son Sextus who had raped the famous Lucretia who then killed herself. Henceforth, two consuls were appointed for a term of one year, during which they each exercised the *imperium* in full, including the judicial and legislative functions, although it became established that they were subject to the *leges* of the *Comitia*, which were considered higher than their *edicta*, whilst eventually the lower classes (*plebs*) obtained a veto right on all their activity through the *tribunus plebis* after they had threatened to leave Rome and create a separate city. It would have fatally undermined Rome's infrastructure and depleted the ranks of its footsoldiers.

The early Roman law is understood to have developed more properly from the law of the XII Tables (*lex duodecum tabularum*) of around 450 BC — which were lost when Rome was invaded in 390 BC. According to some, they never really existed. That is unlikely as there are so many precise references to them in the later literature. Reconstituted but fragmentary and often speculative texts have been produced since the sixteenth century; the most used version is the one by Schoell.[30] It clearly shows that the Tables contained the basic, largely administrative (but not organisational) rules and criminal laws of early Rome as well as the rules of procedure in force in those times.

---

[29] See for some still current studies, F de Zulueta, *The Institutes of Gaius* Part 1 (Oxford, 1946, reprint 1991), Part 2 (Oxford, 1953); Fritz Schulz, *History of Roman Legal Science* (Oxford, 1946) and earlier *Principles of Roman Law* (Oxford, 1936); B Nicholas, *An Introduction to Roman Law* (1962); David Daube, *Roman Law* (Edinburgh, 1969); W Kunkel, *Römische Rechtsgeschichte* (1964); M Kaser, *Römisches Privatrecht* (14th ed. 1986); WJ Zwalve, *Hoofdstukken uit de Geschiedenis van het Europese Privaatrecht* [Chapters on the History of European Private law] (Groningen, 1993). See for an English translation of the *Corpus Iuris* (Digests), Alan Watson, *Digests* (University of Pennsylvania, 1985).

[30] *Legis XII tabularum reliquiae* (1866).

According to the story, they were written down in order better to protect the *plebs* that had objected to the uncertainties in their lot and had managed to have the *imperium* transferred for one year to ten lawmakers (the so-called *decemviri de legibus scribundis*). They started to write up the laws but also to abuse their *imperium* and extend it in time. The consular system was firmly re-established after one of them, Appius Claudius, had set eyes on the beautiful Verginia and indirectly made her his slave. She was killed by her father to avenge her honour and to 're-establish her freedom'. Their legislative work was, however, enacted. This is all reported with some relish in the much later Digest Part of *the Corpus Iuris Civilis* of the Emperor Justinian (D.1.2.2.24).

According to Livy, the XII Tables were in their time considered the true source of public and private law (*fons omnis iuris publici atque privati*). They established early a number of very important principles. Legal equality was accepted, especially after the prohibition of marriages between the patriciate and the plebs was lifted. There was no primogeniture nor legal incapacity of women; no privileges remained in penal law; and no penalties were imposed without a judgment, even though they could still be harsh but the death penalty itself became subject to some important safeguards. Slavery apparently did not much exist in those early days in Rome, but not paying one's debts could lead to it but only by the sale of the debtor to the surrounding tribes. War could also lead to it and the institution of slavery is often thought to have had its real origin only amongst prisoners of war (*ius servitutis bello introductum*).

Soon there were interpretation questions concerning the XII Table laws. New actions (*legis actiones*) were increasingly deduced from them, but these were kept secret by the cast of priests that had started to occupy itself with the judicial function. This situation is also reported in the Digests, in an excerpt of the Enchiridion of Pomponius (D.1.2.2). A secretary, Gnaeus Flavius, let out the secret, however, for which the population greatly venerated him (D.1.2.2.7). The published practices showed an advanced interpretation technique in which the literal meaning of words had often been abandoned and the few original actions had been broadened to provide better protection, although there remained a great deal of formalism. The right formula had to be used and a mistake would lead to the loss of the case, which could not be restarted (D.1.2.2.6).

The importance of Flavius' action was that it opened the law and its enforcement to outsiders, therefore to lawyers outside the priestly circle, which had tried to monopolise the judicial function through secrecy. The legal actions so revealed are referred to in the Digests as the civil Flavian law (*ius civile Flavianum*), later on extended by Sextus Aelius as the Aelian civil law. Around the same time (367 BC), the *plebs* was allowed to appoint one of the consuls and the important office of the *praetor* was created. The latter also had the *imperium* and could therefore issue his own *edicta*, but was meant especially to focus on the judicial function by granting actions. Eighty years later under the *Lex Hortensia* of 286 BC, after further strike action by the *plebs*, they were allowed to create their own laws by plebiscites (*plebi scita*), which laws were subsequently given the status of *leges*, applicable to all (D.1.2.2.8).

The Roman law did not, however, principally develop through these *leges* or *plebicita* but rather through the office of the *praetor*, because by edict he was meant to and could add to the actions which derived from the XII tables or from the *leges* and *plebiscita* (D.1.2.2.10). His office was a high one, but lasted only for one year at the beginning of which he had to say which actions he would allow and he could not deviate from this programme (although he could extend it). The succeeding praetors would normally continue the previous practice, which led to a standard text. This became known as the *Edictum Perpetuum*, which was eventually firmly fixed. It was lost in history, but reconstrued by the German scholar Otto Lenel in the late nineteenth century (third and last edition 1927) and proved a greatly important document, also because large parts of it were later incorporated in the *Corpus Iuris*.

The praetors would not themselves adjudicate cases, but would in each instance indicate to parties the *action* on the basis of which they could argue before a privately appointed judge (*iudex privatus*), often supported by lawyers (*iuris consulti*), in the nature of a modern arbitration, the decision in which would be enforced. The praetors would also formulate *exceptions* if the basic claim was admitted but special circumstances were pleaded in defence. They could also issue so-called *interdicts* as orders or prohibitions in obvious cases, e.g. where there was unjustified appropriation of possession of someone else's goods. If litigation was necessary and the defendant did not want to submit to private judges, the praetor could declare him *indefensus*, so that he had lost his case, although he could reasonably object to the proposed judges. It all shows that, as the later English common law, the Roman law was essentially an *action-based* law and was developed accordingly. These actions were either *in rem*, if they meant to recuperate an asset, or *in personam*, if they sought to force some one to give or do something or to abstain.

The Edict and its interpretation subsequently created the so-called praetorian law or the *Ius Praetorium*, also called the *Ius Honorarium* (D.1.2.2.10). This *ius* was technically different from the *Ius Civile* which was the normal law prevailing amongst the Roman citizens. It was narrower, could be changed rapidly and was in principle only valid for one year. As a *decretum*, it was subject to the higher XII Tables, to the *leges* and to the *plebiscita*, which were themselves the real basis of the *Ius Civile*, for which the *Ius Honorarium* was only meant as support (D.1.1.7.1), but at times the praetor did not hesitate in his daily function of allowing or denying actions on the basis of his Edict to intervene and aid, supplement or amend the civil law on the basis of the public interest (*propter utilitatem publicam*). As such, he was effectively considered the living voice of the Roman civil law (*viva vox Iuris Civilis*, D.1.1.8). Also in this respect, there is a parallel with the later common law, where, in a wholly unrelated development, the Lord Chancellor could intervene in a similar manner through the law of equity, although, as it would seem, in a more restrained and incidental manner.

Eventually there was a special praetor appointed for foreigners (*perigrini*), the so-called *praetor perigrinus* operating alongside the *praetor urbanus* (D.1.2.2.28). It became necessary as foreigners did not benefit from the protection of the Roman *Ius Civile*, which was only intended for its citizens, but needed, in their relationship with Roman citizens and amongst each other when in Rome or its provinces, some protection too. In other respects they remained subject to their own laws, like in matters of marriage. In fact, the law was in those times considered *personal and not territorial*, each tribe having its own, as indeed the Roman citizens had in their *Ius Civile*. This protection element for the foreigners in Rome was provided by the *Ius Gentium*, further developed by the *praetor perigrinus* as the *Ius Civile* was by the *praetor urbanus*. This *Ius Gentium* could thus be part of the *Ius Honorarium* when formed by the praetor but applied in principle to different people.

The *Ius Gentium* was law that was considered primarily based on *natural reason* and as such considered common to all of mankind (*quod naturalis ratio inter homines constitutit*, D.1.1.9). It became therefore *also* applicable in dealings between Romans themselves as a supplementary law and was *not* then strictly personal any longer. It should as such be clearly distinguished from the law that later became the law between nations for which the term '*Ius Gentium*' is now used. For Roman citizens in Rome, it proved particularly important, because it developed, besides the *leges actiones*, a different form of proceeding allowing the plaintiff freely to describe in the complaint the relief required. That was the procedure *per formulam*, which subsequently became the normal way of starting civil legal proceedings by all.

Also in another respect the *Ius Gentium* proved crucial for Roman citizens. As it was much concerned with trade and commerce, it made the consensual contracts (*bona fidei iudicia*) of sale, rental, deposit and loan legally binding (D.2.14.7). In the *Ius Civile*, consensus itself had never been sufficient to create a contract. It gave binding force only to a small number of specially defined contract types and had for sales only developed a special type of formal transfer for certain assets (*mancipatio*).

The *Ius Gentium* was also the law covering slavery and the possibility to set slaves free (*manumissus*, D.1.1.4). It confirms indeed that slavery was originally only known in respect of or amongst the *perigrini*.

1.2.3   *The Classical Roman Law and the* Corpus Iuris Civilis

After a period of strife culminating in the murder of Julius Ceasar in 44 BC, his nephew Octavius assumed in the year 27 BC the consulate and *imperium* for life under the name of Augustus and at the same time the right of veto of the *tribunus plebis*. There was no more second consul. This is considered the beginning of the Roman Empire, although officially the Republic continued with all its laws and the Ocatavian succession was explained as a return to the old values. It started, however, an important new phase in Roman history, which also had an effect on its laws. The Senate substantially assumed the legislative function from the *Comitia*, which had become unwieldy (D.1.2.2.9). The *senatu consulta* thus acquired the force of law, but the Senate exerted in practice only a rubber stamping role. It meant that the *leges* were made subject to the *imperium* of the Emperor (*constitutiones principis*, D.1.4.1). Also the further development of the praetor's Edict came to an end and was by the middle of the second century AD overtaken by imperial constitutions. The procedure *per formulam* and the private nature of the proceedings were also abandoned, and by the third century, law suits were brought before imperial judges (*cognitio*). It is often thought that this centralisation fatally weakened the intellectual advance of the Roman law.

But first there developed a special class of lawyers, who could give official opinions (*responsa*), not unlike Queen's Counsels (QCs) in modern England. Some of them acquired an official status and their *responsa* the force of law (D.1.2.2.49). These lawyers were very highly regarded. The law was in Rome a matter of pride for its citizens and, with literature, seen as a most important intellectual and cultural manifestation. It is a selection of these *responsa*, especially of Papinianus, Ulpianus, Paulus and Gaius, that we largely find in the later Iustinian Digests as part of the *Corpus Iuris* to be discussed shortly, and which had earlier received some hierarchy if they conflicted (in the *Lex Citandi* of 426 AD). They became the true source of the classical Roman law and operated besides the imperial constitutions. It is generally considered that the Roman law development reached its highest point at this time, therefore, in the second century AD in Rome. It is more properly reflected in the legal treatise of that time by Gaius (the *Institutiones*), a copy of which was found in Palympsest in Verona in 1816.

The centralisation of the judicial function included a possibility of addressing questions directly to the Emperor who would answer in published *rescripta*. They did on the whole not aspire to the intellectual heights of the *responsa*. Many of them are still known and they illustrate the more mature period of the Roman law and a more political, verbose and often less precise style, especially since the Emperor Constantine the Great (306–37 AD) when there were sometimes also introduced more religious and ethical undertones (in a christianised Empire, especially in the East). There was also loss of effectiveness. True, all foreigners in the Empire became citizens after 212 AD, but many kept their own customary laws, leading to fragmentation. This is clear especially from the legal texts that were in modern times found in Egypt (the *papyri*).

With the extension of the Empire, it also became more vulnerable at the edges and more difficult to rule. In 330 AD, a second capital was created by the Emperor Constantine, who earlier introduced the freedom of religions. It was located in Byzantium (Constantinople, now Istambul). After Theodosius the Great (379–95 AD), who made the Christian church the state church (C.1.1.1), there were always two Emperors. They both had the *imperium* and therefore remained fully competent in the whole Empire, even if the one resided in Rome in the West and the other in Constantinople in the East. The constitutions were issued together, and when one died, the other was fully in charge and could block a succes- sor. The centre of the Empire, however, was gradually shifting eastwards.

After the end of the Roman Empire of the West in 476 AD following the attacks of the Vandals under Odoacer, the Emperor of the East automatically regained sole powers in all of the Empire, therefore also in the West, as these had never been surrendered. Odoacer accepted this and wanted to become an officer of the Empire or rather 'a patrician in charge of the diocese of Italy' under the Emperor Zeno, as indeed requested by the Roman Senate which declared the continuation of the imperial succession in the West inopportune and asked Zeno to re-establish unity. The Emperor, resuming full powers, refused to recognise Odoacer. Instead, he allowed the Ostrogoths under Theodoric to take over from the Vandals, but Theodoric became an independent ruler. Some of the Eastern Emperors, in particular Justinian (after 527 AD) later managed to re-establish an important presence in Italy, but this proved only temporary.

At first, the Germanic usurpers of Italy saw themselves, still mostly as kings, consuls or patricians under the Byzantine Emperor and were soon accepted as such. The structure of the old Empire remained also basically intact in Rome under the Senate but the West was *de facto* dominated by the newly established northern tribes: the Ostrogoths in Northern and Middle Italy, later followed there by the Lombards; the Visigoths in Southern France and even Spain; the Burgundians in the Rhone valley; the Francs in Northern France; the Saxons in Northern Germany, parts of the Netherlands, and eventually in England. The Empire of the West was in truth at an end. The official *imperium* of the Emperor of the East lasted, however, until the age of Charlemagne around 800 AD when this artificial situ- ation was ended and the Emperor of the East accepted a new Empire in the West (much later called the Holy Roman Empire), which became effectively a German empire until its demise in 1806. As we shall see, at least in name it considered itself a continuation of the Roman Empire, which was also important as regards the status of the Roman law.

It follows that after the fall of the Western Empire in 476 AD, the Roman law continued to develop only in the Empire of the East, in Byzantium, culminating in a kind of codifica- tion under the Emperor Justinian, which was achieved between 529 and 534 AD upon the direction of his minister Tribonianus and the law teachers Theophilus and Doretheus. This was the *Corpus Iuris Civilis*. It had been preceded by a Codex of Theodosius II of 438 AD meant to establish some order in the Constitutions and Rescripts of the Christian Emperors and earlier by private selections of them in the Codices of Gregorianus and Hermogenianus. The new *Corpus Iuris* was much more comprehensive. It signified the result of around 1,000 years of legal development and has rightly been identified as a mark of great civilisation even though some of the best work of the great *iuris consulti* might have missed out or may have been corrupted in the final texts.

The *Corpus Iuris* was not guided by a set of overriding legal principles, was not system- atic, recites scattered cases, opinions and statutory texts, and continues to reflect here a casuistic and fractured approach to the law. It even contains long historical tracts. Yet it had a number of underlying ideas and confirmed the notion that each free man was part of a society founded on respect for the law, that the state and not individuals would defend the person and his property, enforce binding contracts, and guard against wrongdoing, and that the state was one trained hierarchy of functionaries, including judges, who answered to the sovereign alone. Much of it is still fairly easily understandable. This is so also because until the twentieth century, the *Corpus Iuris* managed to retain legal force at least in some parts of Europe, especially in Germany, and was never completely forgotten. Even now, it has some residual importance in Scotland and especially in South Africa, although it is mainly followed there through the works of the seventeenth and eighteenth century Dutch writers like Voet, Vinnius, Huber, Groenewegen, Van Leeuwen and Van Bynckershoek.[31]

The *Corpus Iuris* consisted of four parts: the *Digests* or Pandects (50 books), the *Codex* (12 books), the *Institutes* (four books), and the *Novellae* which contained imperial decisions added later. As already mentioned, the Digests, which received the force of a constitution thereby eliminating all other opinions, contained a selection of the most important opinions (*iuris consulta*) of the great Roman lawyers on particular issues and also reflected through them much of the contents of the *Edictum Perpetuum*. These materials were to some extent categorised and harmonised into some coherence to eliminate contradictions or the resurrection of long-abolished practices. These textual changes are now called *interpolations* and have mostly been traced, but it could not be avoided that in this way older practices were connected with newer ones and made for imperfection and lack of coherence. The fiction was nevertheless that there was no contradiction in the Digest and that it presented a working system, although much of it might never have had much practical meaning. It was in Latin, whilst Byzantium spoke Greek. It could in any event be accessed only through experts.[32] Yet one still finds in the Digests the basics of the modern Continental European property law, including the notions of ownership, possession and holdership, and of contract law, which was, however, much less developed; so was the law of torts and unjust enrichment (restitution).

The Codex[33] contained the imperial constitutions and rescripts to the extent that they were still considered relevant. Those that were not, lost their force of law. Those included were not reissued. This meant that they retained their order in the sense that in the case of conflict, the newer prevailed over the older. Here we find for example some of the Roman laws of insolvency. The Novellae were added after the death of the Emperor in 575 AD and contained his newer constitutions. Constitutions of later Emperors were henceforth also called novellae, although not officially made part of the *Corpus Iuris*. They were in the Greek language.

The Institutes were a textbook made for students but also obtained the force of law and summarised and explained the basics of the law as it then stood, and followed in this

[31] In these countries, there was unavoidably much English influence, also on the law, but the differences with the common law are still significant, especially in property law but also in the binding force of contracts regardless of consideration, the possibility for third parties to derive benefits from a contract, the possibility of specific performance as a normal remedy in contract, the unitary law of torts based on the *Lex Aquilia*, etc. In trust, company and bankruptcy matters, these countries have substantially adopted common law (equity) notions, also clearly in commercial law. See for an early authoritive description of Scots law, James Dalrymple of Stair, *The Institutions of the Law of Scotland* (1681) and for a later one Bells, *Commentaries* (1820). The UK Parliament since the Act of Union has been empowered to enact legislation for all of the UK, but as far as the Scots are concerned only "if for the evident utility of the subjects within Scotland".

[32] See Koschaker, n. 5 *supra*, 128.

[33] The term 'codex' suggests a codification in the modern sense but means tree cork and became in fact the Latin word for a book with proper pages rather than a scroll.

respect very closely the earlier example of Gaius, who, as we saw, had written a similar book in the second century AD.

As already mentioned, the work was not based on any particular analysis or general principle. It is true that in the first Title of the Digests there are a number of more general remarks and even definitions. Thus, invoking Celsus, the law was considered the art of what is good and fair (*ius est ars boni et aequi*, D.1.1.1). Invoking Ulpianus, justice was considered a constant, unfailing disposition to give everyone his due (*iustitia est constans et perpetua voluntas ius suum cuique tribuendi*, D.1.1.10). It was added that the basic principles of the law were: to live upright, to injure no one and to give every one his due, whilst being learned in the law was to know what was just and unjust.

In D.1.1.1.2, public law was distinguished from private law as it was observed by Ulpianus that some things were good from the point of view of the state and others from the point of view of the individual. Thus, there were public and private interests in the law. Private law was considered to be deduced from natural law (which obtained between all living creatures, even therefore animals), from the *Ius Gentium* (which was the natural law applying to human beings, like the rights of parents over children, the right to repel violence and wrongs) and from the *Ius Civile* (which was the law for citizens of a particular state and could go beyond the *Ius Gentium* in more specific rules, which could be in writing or not). Then follows a definition of all three in D.1.1.1.3/4 and D.1.1.6/7, and subsequently also of the *Ius Honorarium* in D.1.1.8 and of the *Ius Gentium* again in D.1.1.9. These definitions, which struggle with the differences between ethics, laws and instincts, could hardly be perfect and had in any event not much consequence for the rest. Indeed in D.50.17.202 it was rightly said that all definitions in the law were dangerous (*omnis definitio in iure periculosa est*).

In classical times, the Roman law had been action-based as we saw in the previous section. It seems to have remained so, even though the litigation solely based on actions disappeared with the proceedings based on the *formulae*, later replaced by the *cognitio* proceedings in the imperial courts. No system of purely subjective rights based on more general rules followed. Thus, a contractual right could not be generally maintained and an action based on a particular type of recognised contract had to be brought. Only later, in the medieval studies of the Justinian law and particularly in those of the secular natural law school of Grotius did a more general concept of rules and rights emerge, see section 1.2.5 below.

In the *Constitutio Tanta*, by which the *Corpus Iuris* was promulgated, Justinian attributed the prompt accomplishment of this enormous task to the aid and grace of God, considered it sacred and an eternal oracle, and forbade any additions to it of any commentary (see Paragraph 29, but not of course of newer *novellae*; he could not and did not mean to bind his successors). In the case of doubt or need for supplementation, resort should be to the Emperor alone in the nature of the practice of the Rescripts. The *Corpus Iuris* was restated and revised in Greek under the Emperor Basil of Macedonia and his son Leo the Philosopher in the tenth century and was then called the *Basilica*. In fact, it had always been curious that the *Corpus Iuris* had been in Latin as it was directed at people who spoke Greek (as the West was already lost) and could therefore not read it. The reason was that the old Roman law had such prestige and legitimacy that at first nothing could detract from its texts whilst the language of the court administration remained latin at first.

The *Basilica* combined the relevant Digest, Codex and Novellae per subject matter, resulting in a single document of 60 books. The Latin text remained at first controlling, and was added in the margin (the *scholia*). After 1175, the Basilica was considered to have obtained the force of law and remained as such effective until the end of the Eastern Empire when it fell to the Turks in 1453 AD.

1.2.4 The Revival of the Roman Law in Western Europe: The Ius Commune

As was pointed out in the previous section, the fall of the Western Roman Empire in 476 AD led to a general decline in the influence of the Roman law and its legal institutions in Western Europe. It had in any event to make way for the new tribal or local laws, if it had not already done so, but it never disappeared completely. First, some territory in Italy remained for a considerable time under the influence of the Emperor of the East and in 554 AD the Emperor Justininan, through his *sanctio pragmatica*, declared the *Corpus Iuris* applicable even in Italy, which country was as such expressly mentioned (rather than the whole Empire of the West).

Secondly, the Frankish tribes in Northern France, the Burgundian tribe in the Rhone valley, the Visigoths in Southern France and in Spain, and the Longobards or Lombards in Northern Italy permitted the Romans and Gallo-Romans in their territory to retain their Roman laws and even codified these in so-called *Leges Romanae*. The best known of these was the *Lex Romana Visigothorum*, also called *Breviarium Alaricianum* or *Alarici* as it was compiled by their king Alaric II in Toulouse in 506 AD. It was particularly important as it included the *Codex Theodosianus*, which would otherwise have been lost, and also parts of the Institutes of Gaius, themselves only rediscovered in full in 1816. Then there was the *Lex Romana Burgundiorum* from their King Gundobad and the *Edictum Theodorici* from the Ostrogoth Theodoric in Italy, both from the beginning of the sixth century AD.

Thirdly, these tribes also codified their own laws in *Leges Barbarorum*, as they came to be called, which also showed some Roman law influence, although mainly concerned with criminal law. Of these, the *Lex Barbara Visigothorum* of the Visigoths (641–701) in Southern France and Spain (called there the *Fuero Juzgo*), the *Lex Ribuaria* of the Ribuaric Franks (around 700) and the *Leges Longobardorum* of the Lombards (seventh to ninth century starting with the *Edictum Rothari*) were the most important, but similar laws existed amongst the Frisians, Saxons, Bavarians and other Germanic tribes in Germany. Most important, the Salian Franks in Northern France as early as in the fifth century AD produced the *Lex Salica*. It is still known today for the heriditary nature of the kingdom it reposed in the male line only (LXII (5) or (6) depending on the known texts), although not coupled with a right of primogeniture as became the more modern variant.

These laws were based on the *personality principle*, which had also been the principle of Roman law. It meant that different tribes or citizenships in the *same* territory were governed by separate laws. In Rome, it had necessitated the development of the *Ius Gentium* for dealings with foreigners, eventually creating a supplementary natural or uniform law for all, whilst this personality principle was virtually abandoned when all inhabitants of the Roman empire were declared citizens in 212 AD. It did not drive out all local law, however. For this the Empire had by then become too big and diverse and, with the invasions of the newer tribes that did not wish to surrender their own laws, the personality principle revived, although in Italy the Lombards especially imposed some of their own laws also on others in their territory, as the other tribes must also have done for their organisational and more policy-oriented decrees.

In any event, intermarriage changed the tribal divides and rulers were naturally interested in the effect of their politically inspired measures amongst all who lived under their rule. Thus from the eighth century onwards, there are clear signs of territorial laws in the so-called *capitularia*, applicable to all in the various tribal territories, especially those of the Visigoths. These *capitularia* were mostly purely organisational but if touching upon private law they often showed Roman law influence, as had the *Leges Barbarorum* in these aspects. In private law, together they became the basis of what were later considered regional or local laws, especially in Northern France. They were there often referred to as customary law or the *droit coutumier*, later written up in regional or city law books, like the *Coutumes de Beauvais* at first[34] and later still in the most important sixteenth century *Coutumes de Paris*. These local laws were usually drafted by people who were also versed in Roman law. The Roman law itself, which remained more influential in the Southern Parts of France and in Spain and Italy, was then referred to as the *droit écrit*, but in the absence of any promulgation, it was only binding because of custom and therefore in reality only another kind of customary or at least traditional law.

The relationship between both local and Roman law was often tenuous as we shall see, especially in France. Yet it is clear that the decline in civilisation in general, although less so in Italy, southern France and Spain, and the lesser needs of trade and commerce led to a lesser degree of sophistication in the laws of most parts of Western Europe at that time. In fact, there may have remained little room for them until (as in earlier Roman times) the breakdown of the tribal system, the increase in private commercial dealings, the subsequent reinforcement of private property rights and of the right of individuals freely to enter into binding contracts, and the re-emergence of some stronger form of statehood with more centralised supervisory and enforcement powers.

In many parts of Europe, these developments did not take place much before the thirteenth and fourteenth centuries, and then often only in small regions or cities. Even the Empire of Charlemagne of around 800 AD did not provide such an environment and did not make much difference for the development of private law, although the administration of justice was improved through the reorganisation of the judiciary. Only when this Holy Roman Empire itself developed further did it start to favour the old Roman laws also, not only to confirm its own legitimacy but also to provide greater legal support and unity on the basis of a proven model. Even in Southern France for example, the *Breviarium Alarici* was for these last reasons pushed aside in favour of purer Roman law, but only after the twelfth century. So were the *Leges Romanae* in the Italian cities.

Thus at first there was not much need for the more sophisticated parts of the Roman law contained in the *Corpus Iuris*. In this situation, only some knowledge of the Codex and Novellae survived, which had always been more direct and simpler. The Institutes were not widely known in the absence of any legal education, and the Digests were lost altogether, but a copy of them was found in Pisa in the eleventh century (around 1050 AD). It led to a revival of the study of the Justinian Roman law, first in the new University of Bologna where the great Irnerius (in German often referred to as Wernerius) taught on the basis of it. This university was organised as an association of students, run by them. The legal studies became so popular that there were soon 10,000 students from all over Europe.[35]

It came at a time when society began to feel this need for better laws and there was an enormous impact, although at first only at academic levels, indeed to such an extent that Irnerius came to be called the *lucerna iuris*, the lantern of the law.[36] What the bible was for theology, the *Corpus Iuris* soon became for legal studies. Its influence on legal practice grew steadily, at first especially in the Church or *Canon* law, which had a limited coverage but a universal reach. It was imposed in the manner of modern legislation as, unlike the newly revived Roman Law, it was officially promulgated (by the Pope). This Canon law was

---

[34] In truth they were a reinterpretation by Philippe de Beaumanoir of local law in the Roman law manner as Bracton had done for English law in England around the same time, see n. 88 *infra*.

[35] The university was located in what was then part of the territory of the German Emperor, who supported this education as a unifying force. He provided special protection to foreign students and particularly broke with the rule that persons from the same region were jointly and severally liable for each other's debt.

[36] See Odefredus, *Lectura super digesto veteri* at D.1.1.6.

mainly concerned with typical organisational church matters and the law of marriage but eventually also covered some patrimonial law, especially the areas of church property and contracts. Parties could also agree to submit disputes to church courts when this canon law was applied or otherwise Roman law. Gradually, however, the old Roman law went outside this limited remit and entered everyday life more generally.

This resulted in what was later called the *Ius Commune* (a term derived from the definition of the *Ius Gentium* in D 1.1.19). This was therefore the Roman law as it was revived in Western Europe on the basis of these studies of the *Corpus Iuris*. As already mentioned, it was nowhere promulgated (except much earlier in some parts of Italy, in 554 AD, as we saw) and since there was in any event no single legislator (or any at all) competent to enact Roman law, it could not develop through legislation either. Its further development was thus largely left to legal scholars and to a lesser extent to educated judges. This was also a result of its more complicated character. Its force derived from its greater sophistication certainly in trade and commerce, from its status as the law of the Roman Empire, which was itself being revitalised by the German Emperors, from its unifying nature as there were bits and pieces of it everywhere (except in England outside the Canon law), and from the fact that, in an intellectual sense, it became to be considered the *ratio scripta* or the rational law, and as such an expression of the natural law supplementing all other law, if not also correcting it.

Hence the importance of the academic legal studies, which made this law in its further evolution largely the province of academics, who remained important also in the later civil law that was substantially derived from it, until in the twentieth century the civil law courts became more activist and started to take over. Its triumph was, however, by no means universal and certainly not immediate. In any event, this received Roman law or *Ius Commune* had to leave much room for domestic laws, which were often also not promulgated, but no less accepted in judge-made case-law.

The *Ius Commune* was in the end eclipsed by the natural law school and the subsequent civil law codifications of the nineteenth century. In the twentieth century, Roman law lost any remaining unifying tenor and became truly part of history except in certain smaller legal pockets like South Africa and Scotland, as already mentioned before.[37]

1.2.5   *The* Ius Commune *and Local Law*

The revival of the Roman law in Western Europe as from the eleventh century AD is a long story, which can only be recounted here in a nutshell. It is common to distinguish between a number of succeeding phases, which played themselves out in different countries and in somewhat different ways. The earliest school was that of the Glossators under Irnerius in Bologna, also active in Montpellier in France (Placentinus) and as far North as Oxford (Vacarius). Another famous name out of this school was Azo in Bologna, who wrote excerpts for students, especially of the Codex (*Summa Codicis*). Their method was otherwise to add remarks (*glossae*) in the margin of the *Corpus Iuris*, in which they would at first mainly give grammatical comments and explanations, make cross references, but later also indicate similarities and contradictions and identify those rules, mainly of a Roman organisational nature, which obviously no longer had much current application. These Glossators, as they became known, span the period from 1100–1250 AD and their work on the *Corpus Iuris* was selected and combined in the great glosse of Accursius, also at Bologna (*Glossa Ordinaria*).

---

[37] See text at n. 31 *supra*.

Their successors tended to elaborate further on these *glossae*, most notably a more critical group that flourished in Orléans in France between 1250 and 1350 AD, the so-called Ultramontani under De Revigny. How much of this early work had practical significance, except through Canon law and legal education, can only be guessed. The later followers mainly in Italy took a keener interest in the practical side and searched in the scholastic manner also for general principles. That allowed at the same time for an influx of the Christian morality as already more in particular embodied in the Canon law of those times with its divine or natural law, see also section 1.2.5 below. These commentators and practitioners are called the Post-glossators or Commentators and produced what came to be known as the *mos italicus*, of importance especially in the newly semi-independent cities of Northern Italy where oriental trade and local commerce started to thrive and where there was a corresponding need for better laws in a country that prided itself in any event on its Roman ancestry and where the Roman laws, especially the Codex of Justinian, had never completely lost their validity. In this school, which roughly spans the period between 1250 and 1500 AD, we find the great medieval Italian lawyers Bartolus and Baldus.

It is in this period that a better insight into more general rules and subjective rights under them emerged. It allowed for the beginning of more systematic thinking, which was further developed in the natural deductive law school of Grotius and perhaps a little earlier by Donellus, see section 1.2.5 below. Canon law and local law influence was probably conducive to it also. These Commentators no longer thought exclusively in terms of actions and procedural law, as Roman law had been apt to do even in its Justinian variant,[38] or inductively on the basis of existing actions and case-law.

The sixteenth century School of Bourges in France, also called the school of the Humanists, amongst whom were Donellus, Cuiacius and Antonius Faber, concerned itself more with the Justinian texts themselves and tried to discover the various interpolations from the more classical Roman law. It is also referred to as the *mos gallicus*. It was not interested in the *glossae* or the practical application of the Roman law and had a considerable influence on the seventeenth century Dutch School of Voet and Vinnius. They, however, never lost sight of the practice of the law. It can be said that the developments since Accursius were best summarised towards the end of the seventeenth century by the work of Voet (1647–1713) in this Dutch School, in his *Commentarius ad Pandectas*. It acquired a status similar to that of the *Glossa Ordinaria*.

The school of the *Usus Modernus Pandectarum* (Modern Use of the Pandects) from 1500–1800 AD, mainly in Germany, but also in Italy and Spain, was more a continuation of the *mos italicus* but it studied non-Roman sources as well. This School was represented by scholars like Carpzovius, Brunnemannus, Bachovius, the Hubers, Berlichius and Mevius. It is no chance that this later school was also the most practical in view of the increased practical needs. But the writings all tended to be in the nature of what we now call restatements and had only pursuasive force.

Again it should always be remembered that the Roman related laws were never promulgated. As a consequence, the theoretical basis for their application was always in some doubt and its force in relation to local law was uncertain.[39] It is true that the Digests themselves (D.1.1.9) stated that all nations made use partly of laws that were particular to them (in Roman terms the *Ius Civile*) and partly of such laws that were common to all (in

---

[38] See JE Scholtens, "Bartolus and his Doctrine of Subjective Rights", *Acta Juridica* (1958), 163. See for the reference to Donellus in this connection, R Feenstra, "Grotius en het Europese Privaatrecht" [Grotius and the European Private Law], (1996) 45 *Ars Aequi* 559.

[39] See Koschaker, n. 5 *supra*, 191.

Roman terms the *Ius Gentium*). In the Middle Ages, this was interpreted as meaning that the law common to all mankind was in fact the Roman law as it had come down through the *Corpus Iuris*. It was considered the *ratio scripta* or *ius commune omnium hominum* in the wording of D.1.1.9. Hence the term *Ius Commune*, which was then considered the written (Justinian) law or *lex scripta* (or in France the *droit ecrit*). It had, however, to accept that there was also a local law, under D.1.1.9 called *ius proprium*, which the *lex scripta* or Roman law could not ignore. It posed the question of the true relationship and priority. [40]

In D.1.3.32.1, there was a first complicating provision which said that custom could invalidate the law (*leges*) as it was simply a later demonstration of the people's will, see for custom also section 1.5.2 below. In the *Ius Commune*, this was believed not to apply, however, to new statutory law,[41] except perhaps city ordinances (or *statuta* in Northern Italy). It was, in this connection, clear that many of the organisational laws in the *Corpus Iuris* (contained largely in the last three books of the Codex) had lost their reason and force and were therefore of necessity superseded by newer local laws. It was even thought that the rule of D.1.3.32.1 could mean that the *lex scripta*, therefore Roman (private) law itself, was more generally set aside by local laws. Especially in Northern France, no distinction was in this connection made between custom and local statutory law (combined in the *droit coutumier*). On the other hand, Canon law, weary of pagan and secular influences, was inclined to reach the opposite conclusion and insisted that bad local law be always ignored.[42] That became the rule even outside the reach of the Canon law in most parts of Europe and was maintained also after the Reformation when in the protestant countries the Canon and Roman law were separated. What was more rational and reasonable therefore prevailed,[43] and that was normally considered to be the Roman law rule (*quidquid non agnoscit glossa, nec agnoscit curia*).

However, the *Ius Commune* itself eventually also became subject to the requirements of the *ratio* rather than being equated with it. We are then in the seventeenth to eighteenth centuries, when what was rational was separated from the Roman law, which thus no longer automatically qualified as the *ratio iuris*. That was the achievement of the *natural law school* of Grotius in Holland and more so of the *Vernunftrecht* of his followers Pufendorf and especially Wolf in Germany, see section 1.2.6 below. Only the later German Historical School in the nineteenth century, although accepting the systematic and deductive method of the rational natural law school, went back to Roman law itself from which it sought to deduce its legal system. Its adherents were therefore called *Pandectists*, see more in particular section 1.2.8 below.

---

[40] This was confirmed explicitly in the feudal law: see *Libri Feudorum* 2.1, and was also the position of the Canon law, *Decretum of Gratianus* (which contained an early compilation of the canon laws), *Distinctio* 1, which referred to the *ius naturalis* (meaning foremost biblical law as expressed by human beings, which could sometimes also be seen in the Roman law and was then higher law) besides the *mores* (meaning local customary law, which could technically also include the received Roman law, but was normally considered lower law).

[41] There was a problem in that originally the Emperor, who was German, was thought to have sole legislative authority over the Roman law and the power to amend it, and not eg the King of France. This issue was in the 14th century resolved in the sense that in this respect, in his own lands, a king was considered to have the status of the Emperor: *princeps imperator in regno suo* see Koschaker, n 5 *supra*, 141. It went closely together with the other maxim: *quod principi placuit vigorem legis habet*. It is the idea that the sovereign makes law.

[42] Canon law thus wished to reduce the pagan influences of the local or tribal laws as much as possible upon the argumentation of Decr, Dist 8 c 5 that saw Christ as the truth and therefore not custom, so that it had to give precedence to natural law, which could be Roman law as *ratio scripta*, although it was normally biblical law. The implication was in any event that the *ratio*, which was sooner associated with Roman law, prevailed over bad law: *parvum usum ratio vincat*, see also WJ Zwalve, n 29 *supra*, 46.

[43] See also Instruction Court of Holland, 20 Aug 1531, GPB II, 703, Art 81.

It should be clear from the above that the practical relationship between Roman and local law was not perceived in the same manner everywhere. As just mentioned, in France, it was clear that the kings wanted to promote the local law (*droit coutumier*), including their own decrees, at the expense of the Roman law (*droit écrit*) which they saw as the inimical imperial or German usurpers' law. This law was therefore considered applicable only if local law did not provide a solution. In Northern France, that is the part of France north of the Loire river, it largely disappeared and its study was even forbidden in the University of Paris as early as 1219 AD (officially by a Pope who was also not interested in furthering the imperial German pretenses at the time) until well into the seventeenth century, but in Southern France it always remained more powerful. Even in the North, as we saw, Roman law influence subsisted indirectly in the written-up *droit coutumier*, especially in property and contract law.

In Germany, the rule became the opposite, probably more as a consequence of the weakness of the Emperor than his strength. To counteract the effects of the lack of centralised power and the ensuing diversity in the various German regions, the Roman law acted there as unifier and became the preferred law, especially after the setting up of a central court for all of Germany, the *Reichskammergericht* of 1495 AD with its seat in Wetzlar, north of Frankfurt.[44] Before it, local laws had to be proven as a fact and, until they were, the Roman law prevailed as the law best known to the court. That was also the approach in Italy.

In Spain,[45] Alfonso X El Sabio between 1256 and 1265 compiled a code of law called the *Siete Partidas*, which was promulgated in 1348 and was a very full code in seven parts, as the title says, covering the laws in general, including a restatement of much organisational church law, governmental law, procedure and property, domestic relations, sales, succession, crimes and general principles. When it was promulgated (in the *Ordenamiento de Alcala*), it was made clear, however, at the same time that the royal decrees and local laws retained precedence. They were themselves much influenced, however, by Roman and Canon law, which was also used in their interpretation, and was studied with great intensity in Spain in the scholastic manner of the Commentators. Some of these studies, which showed great independence of mind, were also used by Grotius to build a rational natural law system in his *De Iure Belli ac Pacis*, as we shall see below.

There was another aspect. Even where local law prevailed, at least as long as it was reasonable, it was often interpreted in a restrictive way to leave as much room as possible for the Roman law. This approach was deduced by Bartolus from D.1.3.14, which required that all that was counter to the *ratio iuris* should not be extensively interpreted and should in any event not be considered a legal rule under D.1.3.15. In this vein, the reach of the Roman law was expanded by the Digests through analogous and extensive interpretation (D.1.3.12 and D.1.3.13). The result was that in the *Ius Commune* local law was often restrictively and Roman law extensively interpreted. Thus only when local law was clearly different, as was normally the case in personal and family law and sometimes in inheritance questions, the Roman law had no effect.

This approach nevertheless left room for the development of city laws especially in Northern Italy, like in Pisa, Bologna and Milan. It happened also elsewhere, especially in the trading cities of the Hansa in Northern Germany and the Baltic and later in towns like

---

[44] The German writer and philospher Goethe, *Dichtung und Wahrheit*, 3.12, reports, however, on its large business but very limited number of decisions: according to him, there were in 1772 20,000 cases pending of which the 17 judges managed to decide only 60.

[45] See for a general description of the laws of Spain in the Middle Ages, Von Rauchhaupt, *Geschichte der spanischen Gesetzesquellen von der Anfängen bis zur Gegenwart* (1923), Van Kleffens, *Hispanic Law until the End of the Middle Ages* (1968).

Antwerp, Rotterdam and Amsterdam. In the view of Bartolus, there was always room for such law as custom and city councils could even accelerate the pace in this connection through written city laws and regulations which were considered to have similar status (*paris potentiae*), although all such local law was to be restrictively interpreted in the face of Roman law on the subject so that as much room as possible was left for the uniform *Ius Commune* as a subsidiary source of law.

Again, in France, this analysis was not followed. Rather an opposite approach became accepted, supported by Molinaeus (1500–66), especially after the *Coutume* of Paris was published in 1510. This was liberally interpreted and the Roman law restrictively.[46] But, as we saw, there remained room for the Roman law, even in Northern France, particularly in the law concerning personal property and obligations, as was later also shown in these areas in the famous works of Domat and especially of Pothier, which eventually formed the basis for much of the *Code Civil* in these areas.[47]

As for these local laws, they were enforced in France by the so-called *parlements* of which the Parisian was the most important. These *parlements* were regional bodies which grew out of the *Curia Regis*. They therefore developed originally not as representations of the people, but as courts, in which the nobility and later also established lawyers (then called the *noblesse de robe*), exercised a judicial function often on a hereditary basis. Already in 1277 the *Parlement* of Paris was ordered by the King to apply local law before Roman law, whilst much at the same time, the study of Roman law was forbidden in Paris University by a Pope not anxious to promote German influences through Roman law as just mentioned. Eventually the *parlements* also obtained a legislative function when judges started to inter-pret the law by issuing general dispositions (*arrêts de règlements*).

In a later phase, they even acquired the power to promulgate the king's laws which had no force and would certainly not be enforced by these *parlements* without it (*droit d'enreg-istrement*). Both powers made the *parlements* considerable forces in the land, sometimes even directed against the king, and since Louis XIV, therefore since the later part of the sev-enteenth century, there was a constant struggle at least to suppress the promulgation powers of the *parlements* which effectively gave them a veto over the Royal laws and their applica-tion. However, only the French revolution managed to abolish the *parlements*, whilst the new French Civil Code of 1804 (Article 1) was quick to point out that laws entered into force only through promulgation by the sovereign and that there was also no longer any power for judges to decide by general disposition (Article 5).

1.2.6 *Natural Law and the Natural Law School: Grotius' De Iure Belli ac Pacis, its Approach and Impact*

As we saw, the Romans already used the notion of natural law. It has been an important source of law even since although its status is often much contested, more in particular by those who adopt a statist view to all law formation. According to the Digests (D.1.1.1.3), the Romans saw natural law in essence as instinct, the law that ruled between animals and people alike, expressing itself in the attraction between the sexes and the love of and care for one's offspring. *Ius Gentium* was the elaboration of it between human beings, expressed for example in the respect for one's parents and the acceptance of the gods and of the state (D.1.1.2.). It was the law that came naturally or that natural reason laid down

---

[46] See also the practical 18th-century treatise of Bourjon, *Le Droit Commun de la France et la Coutume de Paris Réduit en Principes.*
[47] See n 55 *infra.*

for mankind in general, largely, one assumes, based on rationality and common sense and, in the Roman vision, *not* always immutable, even though expressive of a certain intrinsic order (D.1.1.9). It is known that Cicero around 50 BC tried to build a code on it but it was mostly lost.

Cicero accepted that natural law in a broader rational sense came from nature, which he, saw as unchangeable. It is clear also from his other works (*De Legibus*) that he considered *pure reason* the true law, and as such part of all mankind. It was thought to result in a respect for freedom, equality and fairness as they were thought to have existed in the original and true human condition. These were considered the most precious social goods, best protected within a state, which was no less considered a product of nature in this rational sense.

This is the essence of the much older Greek philosophy of the Stoa, which was pantheistic and universalist or internationalist and saw the acceptance of this state of affairs as the highest human endeavour leading to harmony and happiness. In this view, states or organisations were not considered to play a different role from individuals and were subject to the same rational imperatives of freedom, equality and fairness. Morality acquired here a social function; impulsive and emotional behaviour was to be controlled. Evil was an aberration not compatible with true nature or reason, had to be fought and would eventually lose out. Seneca around 50 AD and the Emperor Marcus Aurelius around 160 AD were important other Roman followers of this philosophy.

There are here substantial differences with the other (older) great philosophy, that of Aristotle, which was less idealistic and perhaps more optimistic. It saw creation and achievement rather than self-control and endurance as the essence of human happiness and true virtue as keeping a balance between extremes like, for example, avarice and liberality. The highest emotional state was the intellectual one in which reason could change habits and bring them under control leading to balance and virtue, but not all could attain this state, even if it were better. The ethics of Aristotle are therefore less demanding and oppressive than those of the Stoa, but also less idealistic and universal. Law was here in essence a human creation, as was the state in which human beings were considered best able to develop. In this view, the state was seen as a local reality, not a universal condition or expression of pure reason. Natural law was limited to the law that ruled everywhere, which was basically the law of physics with its causality, independent from human judgment. Positive law involved such judgement and could therefore vary and lead to inequality and lack of freedom. That was the choice of a state or community and dictated by utility. Justice was what in such a state brought most happiness and balance. It depended on the environment and the situation. It had less of a moral underground.

There was agreement with the Stoa in so far that the world order was considered a given, subject to immutable or causal laws of nature. But in the Aristotelian view, men had freedom to deviate and make alternative arrangements in areas where the laws of strict causality did not obtain, for example in arranging one's personal and social life or for states to impose their own order (even if later, in the late Middle Ages, when these views became increasingly adopted, states of that type hardly existed). For the later Stoa, this was rather an aberration and demonstrated an improper use of abilities and a denial of nature, which was more fundamental in character.

These different considerations and attitudes naturally had an impact on the formulation and interpretation of laws but appear not to have had great significance in the distribution of justice and in the legislative activity in Roman times. It is true that in Ulpianus' definition of law in D.1.1.10 the accent is on giving every one his or her due, much in the tradition of the Stoa, but it did not carry any deeper message for the entire *Corpus Iuris*. However, at the time of the renewed study of the Roman law in the later part of the Middle

Ages, the situation was quite different. It was the time when the study of theology also took a great leap forward and imposed its own views also on the law.

In Greek and classical Roman times such a dominant religious force had never been present, at least not at the intellectual level. In the Middle Ages, the study both of the law and of theology became *scholastic*, in that it accepted the given authority of respectively the *Corpus Iuris* and the Bible, but — with the overriding authority of the Church at that time — the practice, if not also the study, of the law became subject to the theology of the Church, which in turn had been connected with philosophy, in particular with the works of Aristotle. It conditioned the attitude of Thomas Aquinas, the greatest thinker of those times, who also dealt with the law in his *Summa Theologica*. Once Thomism became the official line of the Catholic Church, it was bound to have an immediate impact on Canon law, which was naturally infused by church philosophy and morality, but eventually also on the rest of the law and particularly on legal studies.

In this approach, there were Divine and Human Laws. The first was either written law and then derived from the Bible (and its interpretation, mainly in the uncompromising North African manner of St Augustine) or it was Natural Law in the formulation of which humans as reasonable beings could participate. Biblical commands to love one's neighbour and to honour one's promises could thus be elaborated into a set of rules concerning inter-human relationships and into a law of contract and property. The Human Law was the rest, including the details of the Canon Law and the *Corpus Iuris* as well as the domestic laws. From early on it was considered that the will of the state could impose this Human Law, as the Pope imposed his will through Canon Law. The Divine Law was *always* superior, however, including its Natural Law because it was supposed to direct mankind towards its salvation. It meant that the law became subject to the Christian morality of those days as the higher norm and that the power to interpret these norms resided in the Church, at least in the more ethical or policy-oriented aspects of them.

Natural law thus became closely related to the biblical commandments of the Old and New Testament. As a consequence, this law had a universalistic pretence, as the Bible had. Under it, in the style of St Augustine, there was no basic freedom or equality, as there was none in the distribution of grace and salvation. In the style of Aristotle, in the human law uneven distribution of ownership or even slavery could thus be condoned on the basis of utility and a better balance within a state, although equity should guide it. Here one sees the beginning of *policy oriented* state laws and a root of the sovereignty concept, developed in Europe much later. Human law was subject to the natural law and in this manner an aid to the perfect Christian community. This was, incidentally, an improvement on the view of St Augustine, who had viewed the state and the laws as in essence evil or at least a response to it and therefore motivated by it. It was also a bow in the direction of the Stoa.

As far as Grotius (1585–1645) is concerned, it is easily possible to read almost anything into the works of so prolific and eclectic an author in many subjects during a long life. He was knowledgeable in theology, moral philosophy, history and the classics and knew the writers of his day. Yet he may be best understood as a lawyer. The essence of his legal thought, derived from the philosophy of the Stoa, was that the law was not limited in its effects by time and space. It did transcend borders and jurisdictions and depended for its force on basic principles which were universal and could be directly invoked regardless of their further clarification in a system of positive laws. Although these basic principles were immutable, they did not depend on divine inspiration but relied for their expression and implementations on rationality and utility in the affairs of this world. So the key was (a) principles, (b) rationality, (c) utility and (d) their relationship as fundamentals of the law and of legal systems.

This approach raised some important issues, notably the relationship between (a) principle and positive law, (b) the nature of substantive rights and their formulation (through deduction and systemic reasoning), and (c) the intervention of states in the law making process and the nature and impact of public policy or reasons of state per country and the status of fundamental or human rights in this connection. This last aspect will be further discussed in the next section.

Grotius' prime importance is that he had a quite different view of natural law from the one prevailing until his time. It began its secularisation. The essence of it, as explained in his main work: *De Iure Belli ac Pacis* of 1625,[48] was that all people had a similar inner understanding of what was good or bad and that this distinction, although of divine origin, was *rational* (I.1.10.1) and held as such true for all, even for God, who could not change it, and it would even hold true if God did not exist (I.1.10.5). This is probably the most provocative statement of the whole work, although it was not new. Its true message was that mankind had to strive for the good it knew and to subject its inclinations to this natural law and its principles of peace, freedom, equality and fairness which were understood to be universal. It led to a preference for the Greek philosophical school of the Stoa rather than for the school of Aristotle and Thomism that had dominated theology and the law until then. It was supported by mankind's presumed natural instinct for peaceful co-existence (*appetitus societatis, Prol* 6). It did not exclude the existence of divine law, but it was considered another form of positive law, which had to express the basic tenets of the natural law and not the other way around.

It allowed Grotius to separate the law (a) from the theology of St Augustine, (b) from the philosophy of Aristotle, (c) from Thomism, (d) from Canon law, and (e) from their influence on the Roman law revival. He did not abandon the old philosophy categorically, in fact praised Aristotle as philosopher (but not his work on ethics and the law, *Prol* 42, 43) and often cited Spanish scholastic writings.[49] Neither did he separate the law fundamentally from the teachings of Christianity itself or from its morality, or in fact from philosophy, only from the philosophical and theological views that had become traditional. The separation from the Roman law revival also did not entail its rejection but it allowed independent study and criticism.

The separation from theology altogether was achieved in this school by Pufendorf in Germany, who came 50 years later; the separation from philosophy and ultimately even from Roman law or the *Ius Commune* came in this school still later, through people like Wolf, who sought to build the law on the pure *ratio* as it was understood in the eighteenth century in Europe at the time of rationalism or *Enlightenment*.[50] That is the time of the *Vernunftrecht,* the logical-mathematical deduction or *mos geometricus* of the law. It achieved a degree of abstraction in rule formulation that was systematic but also became speculative, yet made codification in the modern civil law sense possible, although it was not its objective.

---

[48] This book exists in an English translation by FW Kelsey (Oxford, 1925) reprinted by WS Hein & Co, Inc, Buffalo, New York in 1995 and in a French translation of 1867 by Pradier Fodore, reprinted in 1999.

[49] It has become fashionable to emphasise the Spanish roots of the natural law school, and Grotius himself referred at times to the Spanish writers of the 16th century. See on these roots, Otto von Gierke, *Johannes Althusius und die Entwicklung der naturrechtlichen Staatstheorien* (3rd edn 1913), 157; J Kohler, *Die spanishen Naturrechtslehrer des 16 und 17 Jahrhunderts, Archiv für Rechts- und Wissenschaftsphilosophie* (1916/17) 10, 235, later especially also M Diesselhorst, *Die Lehre des Hugo Grotius vom Versprechen* (1959); F Wieacker, "Die vertragliche Obligation bei den Klassikern des Vernunftsrechts", in *Festschrift Hans Welzel zum 70 Geburtstag,* and R Feenstra, "L'Influence de la scolatisque espagnole sur Grotius en droit privé" in Grossi (edn), *La seconda scolastica nella formazione del diritto privato moderno,* (Milan, 1973) 377, and "Les Sources Espagnoles de la Pensée juridique de Grotius", in *Historia del Pensament Juridic, Festschrift Francisco Tomas y Valiente* (1999), 137.

[50] See Koschaker, n 5 *supra,* 249.

The practical effect was that, where the Augustinian/Aristotelian principle had sought to explain and accept human inequality, Grotius insisted on their equality, certainly before (natural) law. Thus the emphasis turned to peace, freedom, equality and fairness as it must have existed in mankind's original state. It led in essence to four key principles: (a) the principle of respect for others and their assets (*alieni abstinentia*), (b) the principle of respect for commitments voluntarily made (*pacta sunt servanda*, (c) the principle of repair of damages culpably inflicted on others (*damni culpa dati reparatio*), and (d) the principle that infringement of this natural law must be punished (*poena inter homines meritum*). The basic proposition was that these principles could be found in the study of the laws of all civilised peoples (I.1.12) and had to be carefully distinguished from positive law elaborations, therefore of subsequent detailed implementation.

These were therefore the guiding principles of his natural law, which was considered invariable, aprioristic but rational, much in the style of Cicero. All the rest, including the State, its organisation, the status of the individuals as free citizens, captives or even slaves, ownership and the way in which it was held did not belong to this natural law (or the principles deduced from it). Here the ideas of the Stoa were abandoned. They were only there to improve the human lot after mankind had lost its innocence, but they were not its ultimate state. It meant that by no means all subjective rights were an expression of natural law. Yet the key subjective rights (the *suum*) could be deduced from them and were (a) the right over oneself or the right to liberty, (b) the right over some others, like wife and children, (c) the right over one's property, and (d) the right to claim against others. Even so, the right to private property itself was *not* considered an original natural right but a human invention dependent on the human will which natural law could only protect in that manner (I.1.10.4 and 7).

Of the natural law, therefore of the innate distinction between good and evil and of the just mentioned basic rights and obligations resulting from it, the Old Testament's Ten Commandments were considered an important manifestation, so was the New Testament's Sermon on the Mount, and even the Roman law as *ratio scripta*, but only to the extent that they were rational, therefore distinctive of good and evil in the above sense. Rationality acquired here *independence* and was *not* or no longer considered inherent in any of these sets of laws. Where there was no such rationality, these laws could only be binding for those for whom they were made; therefore the Old Testament with its many derivative rules only for the Jews, the Roman laws only for the Romans, and the New Testament's commandments only for the Christians. They were positive laws for these groups of people.

The key message that followed was that the natural law was *not* monopolised by any of them, although Christians like Grotius himself would in a Christian society elaborate the positive laws in a Christian way and seek in that manner the fulfillment of the natural law ideals: peace, freedom, equality and fairness. There follows a strong ethical and irenic inclination, which, although in Grotius' case closely related to his protestant religion, needed not be religious. He thus argues (even contrary to the views of Cicero) that vows may not be broken, not even if made to criminals and tyrants, and that the requirements of good faith must also be maintained in respect of them. One must also not always insist on one's rights, certainly not on the right of war (not even in the case of self-defence), retrieval of possessions, enforcement of obligations, or in terms of justified punishment, and these should not be seen as typical Christian demands. In this approach, Roman law was often criticised,[51] for example in its requirement of delivery for the transfer of title in movable

---

[51] This has been called a Copernican revolution in the law: see JHA Lokin and WJ Zwalve, *Europese Codificatiegeschiedenis* [History of the Codification in Europe] (Groningen, 1992) 32. See also J Gordley, *The*

corporeal assets. Transfer at the time of the conclusion of the contract was thought more natural.

In Grotius' view, there was in essence only one law, one community of mankind, whilst the laws applicable between individuals were in essence the same as those between organisations and between nations. These were views already expressed by Seneca and Cicero, again in the tradition of the Stoa, although they had also received strong support in some scholastic writings, especially in Spain.

The natural law thus contained the fundamental universal principles of the law (*naturae principia*) but also the principles that could be deduced from them (*Prol* 8, 15, 39, 40). Importantly, there is, in this approach, a fundamental difference with the *Ius Gentium* which was based on *utility*, could be changed and appeared through *communis opinio* or common sense (*aliquis communis consensus, Prol* 40), even though in appearances there would not always be much difference. The *Ius Gentium* was, however, part of the changeable, voluntary law or *Ius Voluntarium*. In international relationships, it meant the law of contract or treaty, therefore the changeable law as distinguished from the basic principle or natural law. In this view, all national or domestic laws were subject to the natural law and to the principles deduced from it, *but also* to this *Ius Gentium* or common sense law, and this was true for the laws concerning individuals, organisations as well as states. It was typical for this approach that the *Ius Gentium* was *not* only interstate law, as it is now often considered. It had not been in Roman law either.

Grotius' approach allowed him to develop a substantially secular natural law in the abstract deductive manner, not only clearly distinguished from Canon law and its notion of natural law and Church morality, but ultimately also from Roman law itself, which became no more than an example of rational law. It allowed him to develop a rational, rule-based system on the strength of which individuals had *subjective* rights, in which he was supported by earlier works of Bartolus and Donellus[52] and of the Spanish neo-scholastics. This proved another vital departure and allowed for the subsequent systematization of especially the private law. His *Introduction to Roman-Dutch Law*,[53] published in 1631, but written (in Dutch) during his captivity around 1620, was the first major manifestation. It had a lesser impact than *De Iure Belli ac Pacis* (of around 1625) but is no less significant because of its greater detail in demonstrating Grotius' method and system.

In *De Iure Belli ac Pacis*, which deals with the law concerning war and peace, there are large tracts on private law, especially in Book 2 (Chapters 2–19) on the behaviour between individuals and contract as the basis for the behaviour and agreements amongst nations, which, as mentioned above, Grotius thought similar in the manner of the Stoa. The further elaboration of the private natural law on this basis was done by later writers, especially by Pufendorf in Germany,[54] Domat and Pothier in France[55] and by the German rationalists like Wolf.[56]

Although Roman law remained important for them at first, especially for Grotius and Pothier, the systematic approach and analysis of current laws and practices of whatever origin together with the gradual removal of the theological and philosophical overlay created a new freedom in legal analysis and produced a new direction. As we saw, the *ratio*

Philosophical Origins of Modern Contract Doctrine (1991), 112ff, for the (weak) relationship with the new (and later) ideas of Descartes, Hobbes and Locke.

[52] See n 38 *supra* and accompanying text.
[53] *Inleidinge tot de Romeins-Hollandsche Rechtsgeleerdheid* (trans RW Lee, 2nd edn Oxford, 1953).
[54] Samuel Pufendorf, *Ius naturale et gentium*.
[55] Jean Domat, *Les lois civiles dans leur ordre naturel*, and Robert-Joseph Pothier, *Traité des obligations*.
[56] Christian Wolf, *Ius naturae, methodo scientifica pertractum*.

iuris was no longer Roman law *per se* or in the later development not even natural law or solely to be deduced from both of them. It eventually became less a matter of natural or inborn law than of rationality in the modern sense (the new *Ius Gentium*). The ultimate result was complete secularisation and rationality as perceived in the age of nlightenment. The price was, however, the ever increasing differences on the details of the law, which in the end much discredited this school whose rational and internationalist aims, but not its systematic substantive rule orientation, were finally destroyed by the nineteenth century nationalism.

It did not therefore discredit its method which still stands out as having freed the study and development of the law from its historical (religious and phylosophical) clutches. In that respect, natural law revival stands at the beginning of any new age when a reassessment of fundamental principle and the deduction of new rules from new needs overtake the established order. In our day and age, it must as such provide for a new transnational law or *lex mercatoria* to facilitate the globalisation of trade, commerce and finance in order to break the grip of domestic laws by showing that there is legal principle and law outside it and which can overtake it. Even if there has always been some such source in new principle and in custom, and rational behaviour has always been the essence of most rules, at least in trade and commerce, the true challenge now is to create a more than incidental set of legally enforceable rights and obligations at global level as will be the subject of much of the rest of this chapter

The natural law school of Grotius was followed by the German Historical or Pandectist School of the nineteenth century, which is associated with von Savigny, Puchta and Windscheid and to a lesser extent with von Jehring. Although paying a great deal of lip service to nationality or *Volksgeist*, it accepted the intellectual scientific method of the natural law school but found its true inspiration in the Roman law rather than in more fiundamental principle. Regardless of much strife, both schools were mainly divided on the issue of universalism versus national law rather than on method. Whatever these differences, the natural law school of Grotius with its coherent and systemic drafting of rules had already opened the road to the modern codifications of civil law, first in France in 1804, then in Austria in 1811, whilst the Pandectist offshoot eventually led to the German Code of 1900 (the BGB). By that time, universalism had gone and all of them were at heart nationalistic.

In the meantime, the term 'natural law' easily gives rise to definitional problems. Basically it may mean religion-inspired law, human rights inspired law, or equitable or rational law. What all definitions have in common is the suggestion of a spontaneous source of law of a fundamental character and therefore built on more lasting principles, be they religion, ethics, human rights, social needs, equity, rationality, utility or perhaps simply commerce or common sense. In this connection, natural law should be distinguished from the other spontaneous legal source, which is custom. This source is practice-related and can therefore change much more rapidly.

Another achievement of the natural law school was perhaps its understanding that there is a fundamental difference between the abstractly formulated rule and the legal rules that are applied in each case and that in respect of the latter there is never a clear line between the law that *is* (*lex lata*) and the law that *should be* (*lex ferenda*), or between rule and guideline. There is, in other words, never an absolute pre-set system of precise norms (or black letter law) for each case, but in each instance the relevant norm must be found and articulated, no less than the relevant facts. In this articulation of the norm the configuration of these facts themselves plays an important role. In analysing and formulating the applicable norm, the method thus becomes inductive as well as deductive, see for a fuller discussion of these methods, section 1.3.2 below. From this point of view, the law is always moving and can never be entirely predetermined in a set of written rules. Or to put it in the terms of Cardozo: "Law never is, but is always about to be".[57]

On this point, there may be some convergence with the more inductive common law method, although it would not share the natural law school's relative comfort with applying general legal principle as distinguished from more precise rules, especially not when it comes to legislation. It is its partial origin in the natural law school that makes the present civil law comfortable with a more general approach in the formulation of rules and, in modern times even in contrast to its claim to exclusivity, also with broader notions of good faith in interpretation, from which new rules are now constantly deduced. This practice is sustained by its, on the whole, liberal (or teleological) approach to statutory interpretation, see more particularly sections 1.2.8 and 1.2.12 below, itself a consequence of the modern codification practice and its pretence that, through a system of general rules properly interpreted, it can cover all eventualities even if in this connection it does not traditionally like to rely on fundamental general principle if not contained in the relevant legislation or codification itself.

1.2.7.   Natural Law, Legal Principle and Positive Law: The Status of State Law in the Philosophies of Grotius, Hobbes, Locke, Kant and Hegel

As mentioned in the previous section, in the approach of Grotius (1585–1645) who wrote his major works when the devastating Thirty Years War was waged in Germany (from 1618–1848), the law was in essence universal, not therefore confined by time or space as it was rational, an approach supported by the philosophy of the Stoa which was the political correctness of seventeenth and eighteenth century thinking. However, already in the views of Grotius, the positive law could be more confined. This raised the status of local law, particularly of state law, which requires discussion of one other aspect of the natural law as perceived by Grotius. That is its relationship to the legislative powers of the modern state, which rose from the sixteenth century onwards. This may also be expressed in terms of the impact of public policy or the 'raison d' etat' on the law, its formation and its application. There arise here considerable tensions in Grotius' work and it is less clear cut in this aspect.

It is an important issue in the study of the relevant sources of law in national and internationalised legal orders. If states are given a crucial role or even a monopoly in law creation or if law creation can only take place within a domestic legal order, which is a closely related issue, there is in theory no place for law creation in any other legal order, the existence of which could even be denied. This became the drift of eighteenth- and nineteenth-century thinking and was connected with the emergence of the modern state as an organisational entity concerning itself with a multitude of facets of daily life. Ultimately this culminated in the modern welfare state, as such still balanced however, by notions of decentralisation, democracy, rule of law and human rights. That kind of state uses the law as a prime organisational tool. It is likely also to enter the formulation of private law rules, first in order to achieve unity of this law within its territory but secondly to update the system so as to promote efficiency and to reduce transaction costs. Fundamental principles, (international or other) custom and practices, and general core principles, which are in this book identified as vital autonomous sources of the new modern *lex mercatoria* in the international commercial and financial legal order, will then have to overcome for their effectiveness any

---

[57] See *Respectfully Quoted, A Dictionary of Quotations Requested from the Congressional Research Service of Congress* (1989), 191 (from a Yale lecture of 1921).

statist claims to exclusive law-making. Any international legal order will for its operation have to overcome statist barriers.

As we already saw, in Grotius' view, the state depended on the will of the people and was therefore a utilitarian construct not itself dictated by natural law, although natural law fundamentally supported all that was agreed. In that context, there were no fundamental or inalienable human rights and they could even be surrendered. In fact, there is in the approach of Grotius an implicit but full subjugation of individuals to the state in a kind of social contract through which state law (*ius civile*) may become superior to all other sources of law if so required by public policy or reasons of state. But it would have to be so intended.

In this approach, the state remained in principle subject to the fundamental natural law principles itself, but that was only so (a) barring the agreement of the subjects to the contrary in areas where natural law was not mandatory but permissory (*cf De Iure Belli ac Pacis* II,2.5), and (b) (even if mandatory) where the public interest required otherwise. In that case, there was no sanction against a state that behaved contrary to natural law (*cf De Iure belli ac Pacis* II.14.6.2).

Inalienable rights against a state emerged later in the philosophies of Locke and Rousseau. Only thereafter it became again possible to talk of value systems with a normativity that did not depend on states. It is clear in this connection that in the end Grotius' concept of natural law could not resist the increasing power of the modern state and allowed for the prevalence of domestic imperatives and therefore of national laws imposed in the public interest, however defined. Ultimately and somewhat surprisingly, there is here also no beginning of an overriding concept of the rule of law as the basis for the exercise of all power in conformity with natural law or, in modern terms, in accordance with an overriding value system in terms of human rights. But there was certainly the notion that the law for its validity did not depend on state sanction.

In fact, any restraining influence of universal natural law concepts increasingly disappeared after Grotius. This is clear in the work of Thomas Hobbes (1588–1679) in England, but also in that of Grotius' successor in the natural law school: the German writer Samuel Pufendorf (1632–94).[58] In Hobbes' view, rather than there being a natural instinct of people wherever they were or came from to live together in peace (*appetitus societatis*) in the style of Grotius, the human condition was considered to be one of all against all (*bellum omnium in omnes*).[59] To constrain the right of the strongest, people had to impose laws upon themselves. These became the sole sources of justice which could only operate within a state (after the natural condition had been abandonned).[60] There follows no less the construct of a social contract under which individuals in order to live in peace abandon their personal rights (except those to life and limb).

The accent shifts here entirely to the modern state, which becomes the source of all positive law, including even customary law. International law, as the law between states, has no autonomous place in this system either. In it, the sovereign does not owe obedience to its own laws and natural laws are at best a matter of conscience for the sovereign. They do not have a normativity of their own. Pufendorf follows in essence this reasoning also. Natural law has a meaning only if it has become positive law upon the order of the sovereign (VIII.9.5).

---

[58] *De Iure Naturae et Gentium*, Libro Octo.
[59] *De Cive I.12*, with the accent of each man being allowed to use his power as he will to preserve himself, *Leviathan*, chapter 14.
[60] *De Homine* X.5.

Whilst at the end of the seventeenth century, in England through John Locke,[61] the concept of inallienable rights against a sovereign emerged as a protection against the all powerful sovereign under the social contract, at that stage of jurisprudential thought, the effect was, however, mainly in private and criminal law, centred on notions of freedom or autonomy, equality and ownership. Even in Locke's case, this is all seen within the context of the modern state, which, on the basis of the public good, through legislation, may even affect the inalienable rights, although ultimately the people retain the supreme power to remove the legislature. Only in the teachings of Rousseau acquired these inalienable rights a human rights flavour and internationalist status, although in his view these rights were given back to the state so as to re-emerge as state protected private rights.

Immanuel Kant (1727–1804),[62] although accepting the existence of rational legal principles, did not give them any autonomous legal status either. All depended on their incorporation in positive law by a state which could ignore them. The rational legal principles (well distinguished from moral principles) were no more than guidelines and had no legal force of their own. The other dominant nineteenth century philosopher, Hegel,[63] confirmed this view in which law could be no more than positive law. It always had a local character since it depended for its force on a legislator and for its contents on the will of a people. Here enters an *irrational* element and nationalism starts to prevail which leads into the discussion of the nineteenth century German Historical School.

Whilst summarising the views of these thinkers on the sources of the positive law, it should of course be realised that they were foremost philosophers and not political theorists. They are therefore less explicit than modern thinkers would be. Nevertheless the drift in their ideas is clear and has undoubtedly to do with the emergence of the modern state in an increasingly nationalistic environment.

1.2.8   The German Historical or Romantic School

Before finally coming to the great nineteenth century codifications of civil law, the German Historical School of the nineteenth century, already mentioned in the previous section, must be discussed. It is also referred to as the school of the Pandectists. They preceded the German codification and prepared it. It was the school of FC von Savigny, Professor in Berlin since 1810. He rose to fame as the result of a pamphlet written in 1814,[64] in which he attacked in extravagant terms the suggestion of FJ Thibaut, Professor in Heidelberg, for an all-German civil code to counter the enormous diversities of laws in the diverse states within the Germany of those days (Germany being united only after 1870),[65] the desirabilitity of which could hardly be denied.

In the course of this diatribe, the French Code Civil of 1804 was also sharply criticised, even called a cancer that had spread into Germany (where it was in force in areas that had

---

[61] *Two Treaties of Civil Government* (1690).
[62] *Metaphysik der Sitten* (1797), 340, 341, trans Mary Gregor, *The Metaphysics of Morals*, 148 (Cambridge 1991).
[63] *Grundlinien der Philosophie des Rechts* (1821) Par 211*ff*, trans TM Knox, *Hegel's Philosophy of Right*, 136 (1967). It should be noted, however, that Hegel was no supporter of von Savigny and repeatedly rejected the teachings of the Historial School in the same book as atavistic, unworldly and ignorant of present day needs and interests, see also H Klenner, "Savigny's Research Program of the Historical School of Law and its Intellectual Impact in 19th Century Berlin", 37 *AJCL* (1989), 67, 77, who notes the conservative, mystical and even reactionary traits in the Historical School and in the work von Savigny in particular, in this respect thought to have been entirely in line with the Prussian politics of those days.
[64] *Vom Beruf unsrer Zeit für Gesetzgebung und Rechtswissenschaft* (1814).
[65] *Über die Notwendigkeit eines allgemeinen bürgerlichen Rechts für Deutschland* (1814).

been occupied by the French), in which context Savigny condemned its system as well as the works of Pothier on which it was partly based. Later (in the largely rewritten second edition of 1828 followed by a third one in 1840), he accepted the unfairness of this attack. His main thrust, which he did not later weaken, however, was against the natural law school, because of its abstractions, and especially its universalist pretensions and its perceived lack of respect for the historical development of peoples. The basic approach of the natural law school had in the meantime led to the *national* Prussian, French and Austrian codifications. Although they were undeniably expressions of individual state law and in that sense nationalistic, von Savigny considered them unscientific, by which he meant that they did not reflect the natural development of the laws of these countries. In this connection, he also showed a marked preference for a more flexible and dynamic concept of the law and became concerned about the static nature of legislation and codification in particular.

This suggested a practical down-to-earth approach instead, based on local laws and its dynamics, but the truth was that von Savigny was not at all a practitioner and was only interested in Roman law that he admired and this was not the *Ius Commune* version either[66] — it was probably considered too diverse[67] — but rather the classical Roman law in as far as it could be known, or otherwise the *Corpus Iuris*.[68] The rediscovery of the Institutes of Gaius in 1816 clearly helped in this connection. There were thus some glaring contradictions from the beginning. First, this effort was hardly germanic or nationalistic. Rather, the true aim appeared to be the formulation of a coherent national system of law derived from an analysis of the old Roman casuistry. Systemic thinking along national lines thus seemed to become the aim, which was therefore not to reconstruct the original texts. It lead to a second contradiction in that the intellectual and system building method of the natural law school method, which was so vividly rejected, was in this respect fully embraced and continued. The approach was here twofold. First, a general basic structure or general part of the (private) law was developed in which the development of the notions of subjective rights and legal act or *Rechtsgeschaft* and *Willenserklaerung* figure large. These general notions were thought to operate in all legal institutions, subsequently to be developed as a second tier in family, property, contract and tort law and be interpreted in the light of the essence of these institutions. Together they form the 'system' which was considered scientific and without which there was not supposed to be any correct legal reasoning at all. It led to a third contradiction in that legal dynamism was not considered to be able to operate outside it.

[66] To which he nevertheless devoted much of his earlier research published in his *Geschichte des römischen Rechts im Mittelalter* (1815–31) 6 vols.

[67] In fact, there was a significant break with the *Ius Commune* and its forward development, see H Coing, "German 'Pandektistik' in its Relationship to the Former 'Ius Commune'", 37 *AJCL* 9 (1989), noting in particular the retrogade attitude in respect of some of the major achievements of the *Ius Commune* like the unification of the law of contract, the abandonment of the distinction between *stipulatio* and the contracts *consensu*, the overcoming of the rule "*alteri stipulari non potest*" with the development of agency (which the Pandektists exceptionally accepted, however) and the third party beneficiary concept, the assignment of claims and the abandonment of the construction of the *procurator in rem suam*, the development of a general tort action based on an extended *actio legis Aquiliae*, and the transformation of the *actio de rem inverso* into an unjust enrichment action. Also commercial law concepts developed in the *Ius Commune* were ignored. They were left to a different branch of the law (so-called *Deutsches Privatrecht*) which created an academic attitude in the Pandektists that had little to do with the practice of the law and with subjects like company, patent and bankruptcy laws.

[68] To which he devoted his second big work, the *System des heutigen römischen Rechts* published in 8 vols between 1840 and 1849 supplemented by another 2 vols on *Obigationenrecht* in 1851 and 1852, but otherwise in the special parts never completed. It was translated into English but was hardly a treatise of Roman law nor of the use made of it in 19th-century Germany.

Since the required analysis and system, (and, more so, in von Savigny's view, the ability to create it) was lacking in Germany in the early nineteenth century, as there was no proper all-German legal science, in this view the moment for a German codification had not yet come. Systematic thinking and analysis and the creation of a proper German analytical ability to arrive at it therefore became von Savigny's programme, undertaken by himself and his students, amongst whom could be counted in particular Puchta (his successor in Berlin), Dernberg, Vangarow, and Windscheid (in Leipzig).[69] At the same time, the German Theodor Mommsen unravelled the Roman constitutional and criminal laws and sought nineteenth century conceptual inspiration in them for Germany. In the area of criminal law, codification had, however, already started in Germany, especially after 1813 in Bavaria through the work of Feuerbach, followed in 1851 by a new Prussian Criminal Code.

As just mentioned, it could not be avoided that in von Savigny's search for universal principles in the Roman law, on the one hand, the reference to Roman law seemed to contradict the national spirit or *Volksgeist* that was seen to be behind any proper legal system, whilst, on the other hand, the rejected method of the natural law school was adopted and practial dynamism was drowned in system thinking. Under Puchta, following Hegel, the *Volksgeist* idea soon became a belief in *national* law which was then translated into national legislation and therefore codification for a modern centralised and civil service-dominated state and judiciary. The *Volksgeist* thus started to concern form more than substance.[70] In such a state, the idea of the autonomy of private law was abandonned in favour of state formulation of the basic tenets of all law and individual rights and powers became less important. That was clear e.g. where in the absence of contractual detail, even statutory directory law became compelling. However, some basic human rights were guaranteed. That had been the achievement of the French Revolution and its *Déclaration des droits de l'homme (et du citoyen)*. It was the inheritance of John Locke. Yet they could not always be directly invoked and meant in any event little in private law. In the meantime, the more universal or pan-european spirit of the *Ius Commune* was lost.

This is the background of the all-German Codification of 1900. Especially after the unification of Germany in 1870, the need for such a national codification was ever more strongly felt and the systematic scientific basis for it, in the version of von Savigny who had died in 1861, was then considered to exist, although von Jehring had already criticised this intellectual exercise in favour of a much more practical (German) and much less academically abstract (Roman) approach.[71] Indeed, when the first drafts of the new Code (*Bürgerliches Gesetzbuch* or BGB) appeared, they were criticised for their dogmatic and high professorial tenor and for their lack of interest in social and practical problems. Nonetheless, after some minor revisions, the new Code entered into force in 1900. The new Commercial Code (*Handelsgesetzbuch* or HGB) of 1897, largely a recast of the Commercial Code of 1861 (see also section 1.1.4 above), entered into force at the same time.

---

[69] Of their books, Windscheid's commentary was the most important: *Lehrbuch des Pandektenrechts* that was reprinted even after the BGB and at that time updated by Kipp (in 1900 and lastly in 1906).

[70] The question thus was whether the *Volksgeist* was the national spirit (or perhaps an assortment of national spirits) that prevailed or rather the ordering techniques of a modern state that determined the shape of the new codified law? Was it therefore national custom oriented or was it state action driven? In other words, was the concern an immanent law (even if Roman) or was it about strategy and policy? Was the new law to be embedded in social cultures or values, in economic realities, or propelled by the raison d'etat or public policy? Or was it mainly an intellectual exercise — private law as icon of German legal thought and intellectual culture — or all of this and more? In the meantime, the Volksgeist itself appeared a romantic notion that proved to be largely anti-industrial, anti-capitalist, anti-big city, and in that context sometimes also anti-semitic.

[71] This was for von Jehring a conversion, as his earlier work, *Geist des römischen Rechts*, went in the opposite direction.

1.2.9 The Nineteenth-Century Civil Law Concept of National Codifications and the Role of Interpretation

As we saw, the abandonment of the procedural and often incidental nature of private rights under the *Ius Commune*, and the development of subjective rights under more general rules that were deduced from natural law principles, ratonalist notions and from case law or sometimes from local laws was a long process on the Continent of Western Europe. This law was only delivered from its Roman and later religious (Canon) law overtones through Grotius and his followers, and was then able to find its most articulate expression. It allowed for the creation of a legal system that was considered rational, in its basics universal, and intrinsically coherent, capable of being comprehensively written down and systematically explained. That was indeed the contribution of the natural law school and its Enlightenment variant. Although it became subsequently intertwined with nineteenth century nationalism, it provided the basic method and material for the modern civil law codifications, therefore for the French *Code Civil* of 1804, for the German BGB of 1900, and all the others.

The codification idea was itself not a natural law school idea. It was more properly product of the Enlightenment in the age of Voltaire. Other Enlightenment figures, like Montesquieu, had been less sure, and continued to see the law as a product of climate, soil, location, size of the region, its wealth etc., therefore as essentially regional and customary, *not* even as national in character. In fact, none saw it as a merely statist phenomenon, although the development of the notions of the modern state after the Peace of Westphalia in 1648 and the thinking of the modern philosophers of those days like Kant and Hegel clearly went in a direction in which public policy and the *raison d'etat* started to impinge on the development of the law as we saw.

The French Revolution in the *Déclaration des droits de l'homme* started to insist on a national codification of at least the criminal laws (Article 8) so that it would be the same for all residents (Article 6). From the first French Constitution of 1791, codification of the civil laws for all of France was also demanded. Still, it was not necessarily out of a nationalistic spirit but rather out of a desire for equality and certainty for all, also in private law. Only in the German Historical School did the nationalistic spirit (*Volksgeist*) take over and after Hegel and Puchta also the idea that it could only be expressed through legislation at the level of the state. In France, on the other hand, the codification was rather considered the expression of the general will of the people (*volonté générale*, Article 4 of the Declaration), a subtle difference perhaps.

The French and German Codes were not the only ones. The elaborate Prussian *Landrecht* of 1794, prepared by Karl Gottlieb Schwarz, who also called himself Svarez, had preceded the German Code in Prussia. It remained effective there until 1900 (and in some of its organisational and administrative law provisions even until the official end of the Prussian State in 1947). Austria produced a more important work in 1811, the *Allgemeines Bürgerliches Gesetzbuch* or ABGB, prepared by Franz Aloys von Zeiller and still in force today. In section 1.1.2, it was already mentioned how the French and German Codes' impact spread, whilst whole new Codes were introduced even in the twentieth century: in Switzerland (1912 prepared by Eugen Huber),[72] in Italy in 1942, in Portugal in 1967, and in the Netherlands as late as 1992. These latter four codes were much inspired by the German example, although the Portuguese one more indirectly through the Italian one. French

---

[72] The Law of Obligations was in fact already codified in 1883 and remained separate from the Code but was substantially amended in 1912.

influence substantially waned as a consequence, but it remains important, especially in Belgium and Luxembourg, and also in Spain and Latin America.

The Prussian *Landrecht* ('*Land*' in the sense of 'country', not of immovable property) was a Code of more than 19,000 articles, which also covered criminal law and much organisational, procedural and administrative law, and was indeed meant to contain all the law that was to be in force in all of Prussia at that time. Prussia itself spread from some possessions in the west, through the north into Berlin and its surroundings into the very east of Germany, to what is now Poland, whilst there were also some possessions in the south. In this large area, the *Landrecht* was only meant to replace the supplementary, mainly general Roman and Saxon laws, and as such became supplementary to local laws where in force. Only in some Prussian areas, where, at the beginning of the nineteenth century, French law had been introduced under French occupation and had abolished the local laws, did the *Landrecht* become the prime source of the law. On the other hand, in large areas that became Prussian only after 1815, French codified law continued into force until 1900, especially in the Rhineland.

The Prussian King, Frederick the Great, who ordered this early codification, had been wary of lawyers and of the poor state of the knowledge and administration of the laws in his scattered kingdom. He insisted on detail and thought that the judicial function could thus be reduced to the pure administration of the law. Hence the bulkiness, which was ultimately also disliked by him. It was all quite different from the later French approach in drafting the *Code civil*, where there was an effort to be concise, whilst the impossibility of covering every eventuality was understood and accepted from the beginning. It is an important insight in modern codification that is nevertheless often presumed to be complete (leading to and requiring a liberal interpretation approach). At first only private law was covered (1804), later on followed by a commercial code (1807), a penal code (1810), and procedural codes for the civil, commercial and criminal courts (1806 and 1810). A similarly concise approach was taken by the Austrians in their codification of 1811.

In France, it was the practitioner Portalis who ultimately managed to provide the necessary direction after four false starts under Cambaceres, later Consul together with Napoleon. Napoleon himself took an interest after 1800[73] although his true impact has never been properly established and was probably exagerated later. Portalis stressed that a code of this sort could not foresee everything but had to stick to the broader view and should not go into detail. That was the task of judges imbued with its general spirit. Unlike Justinian and Frederick the Great, there was here no fear of comment and interpretation, except if done through the courts by general disposition (as the old *parlements* had done in France, see section 1.2.5 above).

Although all three early Codes (Prussia, France and Austria) were in essence based on the method of the natural law school, as we saw, their status and approaches were quite different. The Prussian Code was intended to cover everything, did as a consequence not mean to leave much room for interpretation but was at first only a subsidiary source of law. The French and Austrian Civil Codes were on the other hand relatively short, were primary sources of law, stuck to the main topics and left the rest to interpretation, which consequently acquired a pivotal role. Only the Austrian Code in its Article 7 allowed in this connection for recourse to natural law if there was no precedent or other related statutes resolving the issue.

---

[73] The history of the new Cc is told by FA Fenet, *Receuil complet des travaux préparatoires du Code Civil* (1827), 15 Vols. The new commission of 1800 managed to make a proposal in four months (!) which was preceded by the famous *Discours préliminaire* of Portalis.

The French Code was in this respect considered *self-contained*. That proved an enormously important feature which at first seemed to follow from the explicit abolition of all customary local laws in Article 7 of the Introduction Statute. This came about after Cambaceres had at first insisted on the continuing relevance of those laws and of the Roman law if not conflicting with the new Code. One recognizes here the present statutory attitude in common countries in respect of case-law, equity and custom. In view of the great regional diversity in these laws in France at the time, others insisted, however, on their abolition. In fact, Portalis thought this abolition the most essential part of the whole project,[74] although in the discussions it had been observed that Roman law would always continue to have the persuasive force of the *raison écrite*.

The much later Swiss Civil Code has a well known special approach to its coverage in Article 1. It establishes that the Code answers all questions in the areas it covers but in the absence of a specific provision it allows judges to have regard to custom and otherwise formulate the rule as if they were legislators. This approach remains unique and the concept of civil law codification being self-contained remains in the minds of many in a conceptual sense one of its essential features.

Civil law thus cultivated the concept of codification in the sense of later statutory law having absolute precedence over all prior laws in the areas it meant to cover and of it being exclusive in those areas. It had or acquired the pretence, even in countries like Austria and Switzerland that had broader interpretation and supplementation provisions, of being, upon proper analysis, always *complete* in those areas and it was certainly not to be hindered by a lack of detail. However, only by moving interpretation to centre stage was it able to work with that fiction and this attitude. In fact, this approach suggests and implies a substantial measure of interpretational freedom for the judiciary, more so where the codification is less comprehensive and becomes older.

This is very different from the traditional common law approach to statutory interpretation as we shall see. It does not maintain an aura of completeness, leaves ample room for other legal sources (unless expressly curtailed) and tends towards a restrictive interpretation of statutory law in order to leave as much room as possible for these other sources. However, one finds a not dissimilar attitude in the USA at the level of the Constitution and its interpretation which therefore also practices a much freer interpretation technique. Yet the difference is that in civil law at least on its face systematic considerations prevail so that interpretation foremost entails a systematic search even if the result, like in the case of good faith case-law, may be more adventurous. Yet even then, legal scholarship sees it as its main task to readjust the system as such so that it can continue to be applied as a whole in the manner of a consistent set of rules in the belief that it can thus continue to yield the best answers to all questions.

This concept of (a) completeness is, together with (b) the systematic rule-based approach, (c) the statutory form, (d) the elimination of all other sources of law, and (e) the abolition of all prior rules and precedents, the *core* of the codification philosophy and therefore of the civil law, even if this idea of completeness and the refusal to accept other sources of law are by no means generally accepted, not even in civil law countries, to which, in their interpretation paragraphs, the Austrian and Swiss Codes always testified. In any event, as will be discussed more in detail in the next section, in the area of interpretation, adherence to the system often became a question of mere semantics when general principle, good faith notions, custom, and policy considerations connected with ethical, social and efficiency concerns entered the

---

[74] See Fenet, n.73 *supra*, XCII–XCIII.

interpretation and the issue became whether they were *separate* sources of the law or not. The need for considerable freedom of interpretation led to making use of them all, whether or not considered independent, regardless of how legal scholarship reacted.

However, there could still be a more technical aspect to it when it comes to the possibilities of appeal on points of law, which was originally often considered confined to an appeal of *statutory* interpretation only, in which context an appeal on points of law derived from other sources was not possible. This was the area of facts. Another view was that, if there were other sources of law to be considered, they could become relevant only if the statutory source was fully exhausted, assuming that moment could be truly determined.

On the narrower subject of codification proper — as may already be clear from the foregoing — modern civil law codes never had a pre-set content. Thus, some countries included in their codes company law and bankruptcy law but they could also be covered by different statutes. In this connection it should be appreciated, that the term 'code' itself means nothing and that all civil law private law statutes have a similar approach and status and are imbued with the same philosophy. The form is therefore not important and nothing should be read into the term 'code' itself. Although in civil law countries, the idea no doubt always was to cover substantially all of the civil and commercial law in comprehensive codes, it is ultimately a question of convenience whether they do or whether parts of it are enacted in separate statutes. The enactment procedure and requirements are no different and convenience is the reason that the contents of the various codes may differ considerably from country to country whilst some parts of the law are left to be covered by more specific statutes. The key is that they are in a codification country all systematically connected into one system of private law that in its purest version considered complete, exclusive as source of law, superseding all prior enactments, and to be explained from within a single rational framework that is to provide all answers.

France and Germany have Commercial Codes besides Civil Codes, but their contents differ greatly, see also section 1.1.4 above. On the other hand, Switzerland, Italy, and the Netherlands no longer have different Commercial Codes at all. They are substantially merged into the Civil Codes, although some of the more traditional content of the former Commercial Codes may now also be contained in separate statutes, like company and insurance laws.

Bankruptcy is another case in point: in most countries of the Continent, it started as part of the Commercial Codes, at least in countries that reserved this remedy for merchants, as France in essence still does. Yet even in France, bankruptcy law was taken out of the Commercial Code of 1806, so was company law, only reintegrated it in the new Commercial Code of 2000. In Germany, bankruptcy never was part of the Commercial Code and company law (in as far as the AG is concerned) is no longer; in the Netherlands, after the demise of the Commercial Code, company law was transferred to the Civil Code. In that country, bankruptcy law was part of the old Commercial Code at first, but had long been a separate statute (since 1896) and remains so after the new Civil Code became effective in 1992.

As has already been observed, the consequence of nationalism has been that civil law as we know it today is not one single law or even system. It stands for the codified private law obtaining on the European Continent as it has been *nationalised per country*. Decisions in one country have not even persuasive force in the others. Naturally, as a point of comparative law, the laws in other countries may be held up as examples, but that could also be the laws of non-civil law countries. Not even shared origin in Roman law and in natural law school thinking makes here a difference whilst general principle or custom also does not bind them closer together. In any event, they are in many civil law countries contested as independent sources of law.

As we saw, this situation is different between the countries of the Common Law, which still have a basic communality in their laws and have in that way remained closer.

1.2.10   Twentieth-Century Continental European Legal Thinking in Private Law: Begriffs- *and* Interessenjurisprudenz

In Continental Europe, in private law, legal thought in the twentieth century particularly concentrated on the question of interpretation and the validity first of systematic but subsequently more in particular also of extra-legal considerations in that context. The latter concern more in particular ethical, social and efficiency considerations or practicalities. In Germany, it led early to the theory of *Interressenjurisprudenz,* which accepted that such considerations when sufficiently pressing could be taken into account in the judicial function and adjudication practice as against that of the *Begriffsjurisprudenz* which in its interpretation technique foremost relied on the text of the law and its system. This is not to say that it was without merit as it managed further to develop in an intellectual manner large areas of the law and attained in case-law greater clarity especially in the law of property, but it became too restrictive. The *Interressenjurisprudenz* had its intellectual base in the later work of von Jhering[75] and received a more sociological expression in the so-called 'free law finding' movement (*Freirechtslehre*) often associated with the work of Hermann Kantorowicz[76] (a student of Max Weber) and Eugen Ehrlich.[77]

Whether this much freer attitude towards (statutory or code) interpretation was acceptable or not became in Germany an important issue even before the BGB was finally enacted in 1900. It never meant a free for all and only advocated greater flexibility to meet social needs, yet it sharply divided the followers of von Savigny who were likely to be more systematic in their approach, on the one hand, and those of von Jehring who were likely to be freer and more practical, on the other. The twentieth century development shows the ebbs and floods of these two approaches. By mid-century there appeared to be more freedom in this respect in legal writing than at the beginning and the end. Courts felt at first more restricted but towards the end of the century, there seemed to be greater flexibility in case-law than there was in German academic writing.

The more extrovert, socially oriented approach, one finds reflected in France in the (later) writings of François Geny, in those of Saleilles and of Léon Duguit (who in its extreme form only recognised social, not private rights) at the turn of the of the nineteenth century, later in that of Demogue, and in the Netherlands in the writings of Paul Scholten. It had a direct effect on interpretation techniques. Philosophically, this is the field of *hermaneutics*. In a more *methodological* sense, it concerns the explanation of texts and application of rules. In a more *ontological* sense, it concerns the intellectual power over this process but also the more conserving impact of culture, tradition, and habits or practices.[78] There is here obvious conflict in views concerning the intellectual makeability of society through legislation, its systematical application, and the balance of interests that is so maintained on the one hand, and the place of the autonomous transforming forces in society and their dynamic significance for the development of the law on the other. It may more in particular be reflected in case-law. In the one approach, reason and rationality are emphasised, in the other sociological, psychological and practial undercurrents. The resonance that statutory and case-law receive in society is here seen as the only legitimacy of both.

---

[75] See R von Jhering, *Scherz und Ernst in der Jurisprudenz* (1884) and *Der Zweck im Recht* (1887).
[76] *Der Kampf um die Rechtswissenschaft* (1906).
[77] *Grundlegung der Soziologie des Rechts* (1913).
[78] In this connection reference may also be made to H-G Gadamer, *Wahrheit und Methode* (1972).

Whatever the approach, a more ontological view readily leads to the insight that the purpose of the law is always extra-legal in that it serves practical, social, ethical or even economic or political objectives, and that the law therefore never stands alone or is an objective in itself. Except in areas where the law is clearly settled and becomes largely mechanical, like perhaps in conveyancing real estate and the following of traffic rules, rules thus become more like guidelines, in their application largely dependent on the configuration of the facts and on the ends the law is meant to serve. These objectives thus become important tools in the law's interpretation, also in private law. This suggest a *purposive* or *teleological* approach (in common law often still distinguished, the former one being the narrower). It is also called *normative*. It affects not only statutory texts but ultimately also contractual interpretation; it will not then be merely reduced to a textual analysis or to what parties may have meant in a psychological sense. What a reasonable person may have thought or what is fair, good faith requires, or what is socially acceptable and practiced may thus become equally normative. One sees here a clear connection with American 'realism' and its search for better law which will be discussed in section 1.2.13 below.[79]

Like in the US, legalism, classification or formalism is here abandoned, at least in respect of code interpretation (and probably even more so in respect of contractual interpretation). In its consequences, the approach is then likely to go beyond a mere liberal interpretation technique dictated by the notion of completeness of the codified system, which could still be largely systematic by using syllogism, deduction, even induction, or analogical interpretation techniques.[80] That has been the drift in the practice of the civil law for a long time, although it is unavoidable that there are moments when formalism or extreme systemic thinking return to some extent, as in the Netherlands subsequent to the enactment of new codes in 1992. As just mentioned, especially in present civil law legal scholarship, there remains indeed an important undercurrent that, even though forced to accept the liberal interpretation of the codes, foremost thinks in terms of its overall system and application. Although broader than the mere framework of the code, it is then just as closed to other arguments or ideas and wants to see all new developments explained in that systematic context and to be fitted into it.

This may in fact result in a similar narrowing of the perspective as pure code thinking once did. This tendency still favours black letter law and seeks particularly at the academic level to fit all case-law into the system even if its gradual adjustment to new situations is admitted. At the same time, this approach is likely to have a strong nationalistic/intellectual flavour that considers statutory law and the balance it aims to achieve as static and inviable, perfect standards regardless of the great systematic and other mistakes legislators might make and the opaqueness of the balances they might like to strike in which there is often unexpected and unanticipated effect and which are invariably and per definition subject to

---

[79] This connection seems obvious but was ultimately not accepted by Kantorowicz himself who saw the difference in the attitude towards the rule as a major intellectual divide, see "Some Rationalism about Realism", 43 *Yale LJ* 1240 (1934). Kantorowicz in short saw legal rules as abstract structures whilst he assumed that the common law lawyers could never consider them separate from facts. But in common law that would not be so for legislation (certainly not for constitutional principle in the US) and as far abstract rules deduced from case law are concerned they become, like all other rules, also in civil law only law in their application when the configuration of the facts and (in the normative, free law or realist approach) moral, social and efficiency arguments will also be discounted in the decision. One cannot escape the impression that Kantorowicz' emphasis had changed since his first book of 1906 and that he had become more interested in systematic thinking and abstraction in the meantime. See for a fuller discussion VG Curran, "Rethinking Hermann Kantorowicz: Free Law, American Legal Realism and the Legacy of Anti-Formalism", in A Riles (ed), *Rethinking the Masters of Comparative Law* (2001), 66.

[80] See s 1.2.12 *infra* for greater details of these various interpretation techniques.

immediate social challenge. There is no doubt, however, that this attitude remains a serious proposition in much of civil law and could still be considered the prevailing attitude in legal studies and education — perhaps an ongoing consequence of the age of Enlightenment and rationalism in civil law thinking. If in case-law and the practice of the law other ideas emerge, they are thus 'systematised' in a national system or otherwise ignored.

In studying case-law, the concern is not then the rationale of the decision but rather how it can be fitted into the system. Judges themselves will also be much concerned with that aspect in their reasoning even when forced to go beyond it in the substance of their decisions. There is certainly a tendency also in the judiciary to remain and to be seen as remaining system-conform in this sense. In Germany, this attitude is e.g. the one still favoured in the leading work on legal methodology of Karl Larenz.[81] The hope is that it contributes to certainty or at least predictability in the legal outcome. The downside is that it may lead to (a) rigidity and artificial and opaque reasoning leaving the real alternatives and options undiscussed, to (b) a lesser sensitivity to changing social and other needs, and to (c) an inability to appreciate the more policy oriented aspects of law formation or deal with autonomous undercurrents in it like the force of custom or internationalisation. They are then likely also to be ignored.

It follows that there is here little room for originality or renewal except through legislation but rather a fixation on the existing domestic (private) laws in the expectation that the system will continue to provide the right (and automatic) answers under all circumstances. *Legal certainty* and *predictability* are thus believed to be served, even though new cases multiply all the time, rules become antiquated, and factual situations diverse or unusual, whilst the systematic interpretation techniques (like inductive and analogical reasoning) may themselves prove entirely uncertain and unpredictable in their outcome. Historical and comparative research are in that approach commonly rejected. In civil law, there is here frequently a mood of denial, which may account for a present lack of spirit in Continental legal scholarship and the unease with new thought or ideas.[82] It is curious in a sense and seems a reversal of the more sociological and philosophical approaches that were much encouraged before World War II but that may have died with the pre-war generation of legal Continental European scholarship in the 1960s.[83]

Even though at the same time in private law the influx of good faith notions started in earnest, certainly in Germany and the Netherlands, it is noteworthy that it was largely product of case-law not of legal scholarship. It was forced on the courts which could no longer deal with modern practicalities within the established legal framework or system. Even in this area of good faith, needed to create greater flexibility and responsiveness to extra legal pressures, German scholarship has largely concentrated on following (not leading)

---

[81] *Methodenlehre der Rechtswissenschaft* (6th edn, 1991), 6, 437. See for the second (non historical) part (the student version, 3rd edn revised by CW Canaris 1995), 263.

[82] If one takes Germany as an example, there remained strong currents in other directions but they became more incidental, see eg J Koendgen, *Selbstbindung ohne Vertrag* (1981) and earlier J Esser, *Vorverstandnis und Methodenwahl* (1970), but it does no longer seem to affect the systematic tradition to which most modern PhDs, theses for professorships, handbooks, and articles testify. They all tend to be descriptive of the German rules and its system and of the way it operates and can be (better) used to cover eventualities. Indeed the German legal professorate is itself often considered a bar to renewal as it dominates the younger scholars. As a result, "law and economics" eg is rather studied in economics faculties.

[83] An exception may be found in the sociological oriented writings of Gunther Teubner, see eg "Breaking Frames: The Global Interplay of Legal and Social Systems", 45 *Am J Comp L* (1997); G Teubner edn, *Global Law without a State* (1997), in particular "Foreword: Legal Regimes of Global Non-state Actors" at p xiii–xvii, and "Global Bukowina": Legal Pluralism in the World Society' at p 3*ff*; and G Teubner ed, *Autopoietic Law: A New Approach to Law and Society* (1988). See in France also Laurent Cohen-Tanugi, *La metamorphose de la democracie* (1989) and *Le Droit dans l'etat* (1985).

developments whilst recreating from case-law some (legal) system through the classification of good faith functions (*Funktionskreise*) and by grouping cases (*Fallgrupen*)
in order to construct a so-called *inner system* of good faith (*Binnensystematik*), see also
Chapter 2, section 1.3.1. It reminds of the English academic attitude to cases, which likes to
line them up in a similar fashion (to produce rules in an inductive or deductive manner no
less to create some intellectual system in case-law even if less all consuming). It is somewhat unexpected that as a consequence the basic divide in private law may no longer be
between civil and common law but rather between formal and more informal, realist or
normative legal thinking.[84]

The more formal European approach with its continuing interest in black letter law, system building, technical analysis and systematic interpretation is thus capable of neutralising the civil law's basic attitude in which the phenomenon of codification itself requires a
liberal interpretation approach to maintain the credibility of its pretence to cover all, even
if, under the surface, the normative approach to interpretation is firmly established by the
courts as confirmed in the enormous expansion of the good faith concept, especially in
case-law in Germany and the Netherlands.

Another aspect of the more formal (academic) attitude is at least at the intellectual level
the continuing nationalism, even in an ever more open political system, in Europe personified by the EU. This constant search for rules within a (coherent) *national* legal system
expresses itself also in the European version of private international law, which remains
also typically domestic rule based. It hinders even comparative law, the normative
functional effect of which is denied if it goes against a national system and its order, even if
other law in sister states makes clearly better sense and is more representative of modern
thinking and practical needs. This attitude also hinders the research into law operating in
legal systems or orders other than national ones. As in such an attitude there was never
much room for the acceptance or application of more fundamental or universal legal principle, there is also little appreciation of internationalised custom and broader common or
general legal notions on which international commerce in a globalised market-place is
increasingly dependent.

Whilst it is clear that within the legal order of the EU e.g. (some) private law can be created at that level, see section 2.3.2 below, and also that there are other traces of private law
formation in other than stately legal orders, see section 1.4.5 below, it must be realised that
at least formally there is only limited EU jurisdiction to do so and renewal is not likely to
come from there. Only socio-economic factors creating new legal orders in commerce and
finance are likely to do this as will be discussed more extensively in section 1.4.

1.2.11   The Development of the Common Law

It is now time to come to the other great original legal system in Western Europe, that of
the English common law. It developed in a manner very similar to Roman law, i.e. as an
action-based law originating in the law of procedure.[85] This was favoured by the centralisation of the legal protection under the King almost from the beginning of the Norman
conquest of England after 1066 AD. This centralisation was in turn a natural consequence

---

[84] See on the increasing divide between English and American legal thinking along these lines PS Atiyah and
RS Summers, *Form and Substance in Anglo-Amrican Law; A Comparative Study of Legal Reasoning, Legal Theory,
and Legal Institutions* (1987).
[85] See for a full history of the English law, WS Holdsworth, *History of English Law* (1922–1956), 16 vols. The last
four vols. were edited by AL Goodhart and HG Hanbury.

of the feudal system with the Crown at its pinnacle. In this system of essentially landholding, royal protection was demanded and given in land and criminal matters, but was eventually expanded. The idea was that if the king agreed with the request for protection, he would issue the relevant order or *writ* to his sheriffs to take the necessary action.

This function was soon assumed by the royal *curia* with more regular procedures under which standardised writs or remedies (or indeed procedural relief) would be given provided the claimant could prove the basic facts on which the remedy was based. This *curia* was in the thirteenth century expanded into three royal courts in London (Common Pleas for normal private suits and supervision of the lower sheriff courts, King's Bench for politically oriented matters or appeals, and Exchequer for taxes), supplemented by travelling or 'itinerant justices' operating on the King's behalf. The highest court was (and still is) Parliament (now the House of Lords). Writs thus became commands to the relevant judges to call the defendants into their courts to resolve disputes of fact in connection with the relief provided under the writ. This function of issuing writs was later centralised in the office of the Lord Chancellor.

There was still old Anglo-Saxon and also newer feudal law on the basis of which disputes were resolved in the ancient communal and newer private (and feudal) seignorial or palatine courts for local tenants, but the issuing of writs leading to proceedings in the King's courts became more popular. At first, they largely depended on favour, but as we saw they soon developed into the formulation of certain, in fact quite narrow standard types of relief, which would be granted as of right and lead to redress if the judges found that the conditions for the relief existed whilst leaving the determination of the facts to a jury. These writs were subsequently written up and became accessible in the *register brevium* (a *breve* was another word for writ). The Royal courts became the normal venue for these suits, but they would by no means hear all types of complaints; it all depended on the writ. Thus the claimant had to find the right form of action without which he would fail and there were no broader substantive rights. The King, through his Chancellor, at first retained freedom to develop new writs, but this power was questioned after the basic English charter of the Magna Carta was agreed in 1215 and it was curtailed in the Second Statute of Westminster in 1285. The facility to expand became limited to actions in similar cases only (the writ *in consimili casu*). If there was doubt, the matter was referred to Parliament for statutory intervention.

It allowed a nucleus of more predictable law to develop whilst the writs evolved somewhat further and older ones were abandoned. It early brought *one national* law, although the centralisation was at that stage probably a more outstanding feature than nationality. This law was new, although of Anglo-Saxon or Germanic and often feudal origin. It is of interest that no external law, like Roman law, was necessary to achieve this unity in the law in England. The result was a true English development, which led to a distinctive legal system and culture that was largely procedural, basically practical, and evolved over a long time in a peaceful, constant, but also haphazard manner.

Eventually under this law, the Royal courts started to judge the 'fairness' of the old laws surviving outside this system, as was at the time also done on the European Continent (see section 1.2.5 above); subsequently they suppressed them. In the process, they also subsumed the commercial law or law merchant into the common law, which had until the sixteenth century been developed largely in trade with foreigners and had obtained some continental flavour, see more in particular section 1.1.2 above. This suppression also happened to Church law. As a consequence, from the seventeenth century, the merchant and ecclesiastical courts were merged with the Royal courts as the ancient Anglo-Saxon courts had been much earlier.

Although the common law was and is often presented as customary law of 'general immemorial usage', it originated rather in the writs and forms of action resulting in judge-made law that changed all the time. Decisions were published as from the thirteenth century in so-called Yearbooks, although judges would often invoke precedent on the basis of their memory and of what they had seen earlier in cases before them or remembered colleagues saying. The creation of the Inns of Court in which the practising lawyers — judges as well as advocates or barristers — would assemble and be educated was favourable to this development. Four of these Inns still exist today and all judges and barristers must be members. However, the system in which these precedents had to be followed only developed much later.

As after 1285 the king or his Chancellor were no longer free to formulate new writs, common law was slowed in its further development. It acquired a rigidity that eventually necessitated a supplementary approach. This emanated also (like the writs) from the King through the Lord Chancellor, but in a different system of law with its own court, which acted not on the basis of writs but rather of *subpoenas*. It sat without a jury whilst its practitioners were solicitors, although barristers later took over much of their court activity. This was the law of *equity*, administered by the Court of Chancery.

At first, the Chancellor was given discretion to decide in pressing cases according to his own conscience, but after the Chancellors became secular persons (starting with Thomas Moore in 1529), the discretion faded. As from the seventeenth century, the further development of equity became increasingly embedded in precedent, as the (common) law also was, and equity thus acquired a rigidity of its own. As a consequence, it remained incidental and never developed into a full system of more natural or equitable law. Although an independent system of rules, it could in any event not ignore the common law and was meant to follow, not to obstruct it and was as such only a reflection of the common law's imperfections. Nevertheless, it managed to fill a number of important gaps or shortcomings and also infused the old law with some more ethical notions, a more up-to-date set of values perhaps, and some greater sense of fairness which even now can lead to new forms of relief.

This shows similarity with the development of the praetorian law or *Ius Honorarium* by the praetor in ancient Rome, although there had already been some similar element in the original creation and expansion of the writs.[86] It was a facility the later development of the civil law missed. For more ethical flexibility, on the European Continent there had originally been the Canon law, but it had a limited reach and later there was the natural law school, but both proved in a number of areas less creative than equity was in England. The greatest practical differences between common and civil law today (apart from the former's more procedural attitude and feudal land law, and the latter' more systematic, codified and intellectual approach), are in as far as the law of property and obligations is concerned, exactly in the products of equity. They are in the future proprietary interests in personal property, equitable mortgages and (floating) charges, trusts, constructive trusts, tracing, unjust enrichment, agency, and equitable assignments.

Most importantly, in the area of remedies, equity developed the *injunctions* as (chancery) court orders to prevent rather than to indemnify harm after the fact. These court orders also have no true equivalent in civil law and are issued when it is 'just and equitable' to do so, which implies considerable judicial discretion. This greater judicial discretion is more generally found in all equitable matters and explains much of the judicial

---

[86] See also Buckland and Mc Nair, *Roman Law and Common Law* (2nd edn, 1952). See for the praetorian law s 1.2.2 *supra*.

activity in the law of trust and in company and bankruptcy law which are all creations of equity even if now largely developed within a statutory framework. Closely related to injunctions is the order for *specific performance*, which is also an equitable relief measure. It remains more incidental and dependent on the facts of the case, see more in particular in chapter 2, section 1.4.1.

As just mentioned, the development of the law of equity remained limited to certain areas and is patchy even in those areas. Like in the cases of trusts, companies and insolvency, there developed a more systematic approach only through legislation. Equity further used a number of *maxims* which tended to broaden its reach somewhat. Important ones are: 'equity looks to intent rather than to form', 'equity will not permit a statute to be made an instrument of fraud' or 'equity does not act in vain', etc. Others, however, rather limited it: 'he who comes to equity must come with clean hands' and 'equity follows the law' which suggest at least in principle (but certainly not always) a subordinate role.

The greater problems with equity resulted, however, from the duality in the courts. Points of law had to be dealt with in the King's courts, points of equity in the Court of Chancery. If points of law and equity were raised in the same case, the result was that the case would go backwards and forwards between both sets of courts. It caused endless delays and costs, as vividly told by Charles Dickens in his novel *Bleak House*. Only in the nineteenth century did this lead in England to the fusion of the courts of law and equity (in the Judicature Acts of 1871 and 1873) into one court system, although not strictly speaking to the merger of the two sets of courts or laws. The Court of Chancery is still competent in typically equity matters, like trusts, company and bankruptcy cases, and grants injunctions if such are just and equitable. The main importance of the reform was that points of equity can now also be raised before the courts of law and vice versa.

Of the old law courts, the King's (Queen's) Bench (which since 1970 has included an Admiralty and Commercial Court Division) and the Court of Chancery became Divisions (together with the Family Court) of what is now called the High Court of Justice in London, to which the itinerant justices, who normally come from the Queen's Bench, also belong.

The above history explains a number of important aspects of the English law and its legal system. As it is not intellectual or systematic, but rather practical and the result of gradual development, no great need is felt for complete clarity in the authorities and competencies of the courts and in the type of laws they administer. There was always some overlap of functions, which gradually separated but also came together again. Thus originally the King was supreme but delegated authority to the Lord Chancellor, appointed and discharged by him, first to issue writs upon which his courts would act and later to give equitable relief. Subsequently, the courts acquired virtual independence from the King, whilst also the Lord Chancellor as issuer of writs and later as equity judge became independent (but could be dismissed) in these functions, which were not merged, whilst the King could still issue amnesties or commute sentences.

Originally, the Lord Chancellor could streamline the procedures in the King's courts through the writs; later he could in equity also derogate from their powers. Although he could not do so officially as it was still said that 'equity followed the law', he could create a string of exceptions, e.g. fiduciary ownership types giving beneficiaries proprietary protection whilst respecting the ownership position at law. It is the origin of the law of trusts. Provisionally, he could also impose injunctions to order litigants to do certain things or refrain from doing them or he could issue an order or decree to comply with the law pending full litigation.[87]

---

[87] The Court of Chancery was a prerogative court set up by the King to achieve greater justice against the common law. When, however, he tried to set up another prerogative court to protect himself against the common law,

The 1873–75 Act established, however, that in the case of a conflict between law and equity the latter prevailed (subsection 11), but it should be realised in this connection that equity had by then lost its function of appealing to the judge's conscience and was formalised in a set of incidental rules. Inconsistencies remain notably in set-offs, tracing, compound interest, illegal contracts, limitation of actions and monetary remedies for wrongs. However, there seems no great urgency, at least not in England, to sort these inconsistencies out.

Through the existence of equity as distinguished from common law, common law may be referred to in the narrow sense of being the law different from equity and statutory law, but the term is also commonly used to distinguish it from the civil law. It then includes the other sources of English law. It is a confusing terminology of which the novice should be well aware.

1.2.12   The Common Law Approach to Scholarship, Precedent, Legislation and Statutory Interpretation

It was already observed in section 1.1.2 that Roman law never meant much in England, even though common law developed in similar ways. In the first four centuries AD, when England was part of the Roman Empire, Roman law must have been in force, but there were hardly any traces left of it. Henri Bracton had tried to show the seeming similarities between the early common law and Roman law in the thirteenth century,[88] but this proved an idle effort. In fact, although both sets of law were procedural in nature and developed in not dissimilar ways, Roman law was particularly incompatible with the germanic or anglo-saxon notion of seisin or physical possession, which dominated the law of chattels in England, and with the feudal law that dominated the law of real estate and put all ownership of land in the King subject to individual estates in land. The physical notion of possession or bailment in respect of chattels and the feudal system in respect of land still prevail in the common law to this day. Feudal law therefore still covers the most valuable class of assets. This law had also much influence on the common law of chattels, as in equity the proprietary interests in land were extended to them which is of particular interest for future interests in these assets. It concerns here in particular trusts, and conditional or temporary ownership forms. It results in a flexible and open system of proprietary rights in chattels and intangible assets of which there is no equivalent in civil law.

The practical nature of the common law never combined well with the much more intellectual and less procedural approach of the *Ius Commune*. In fact, in England there was not much academic interest in the law at all. Legal teaching at first took place in the Inns of Court but rapidly declined and this continued well into the eighteenth century. Besides law reports there were hardly authoritive legal texts. Only towards the latter part of the eighteenth century Blackstone (since 1758 the first Professor of Common Law in the newly created Vinerian Chair at Oxford) was able to write down the first commentary on *both* private and public law (including criminal law), as common law never developed or

which also administered public law writs to protect citizens (*habeas corpus*) or to give orders to officials (*mandamus*), the result, the so-called Star Chamber, became an important issue in the Civil War that ended in 1640, when it was removed and the principle (since Magna Charta of 1215) that the King operated under the common law and its courts was firmly re-established. In this struggle, the King at one time even considered adapting the Roman law and ousting the common law altogether.

[88] *De Legibus et Consuetudinibus Regni Angliae* (see also the edn by Twiss with a 19th-century English translation).

set much store by distinctions in this regard.[89] The Downing Chair of Law was founded in Cambridge in 1800 but like the Vinerian Chair in Oxford was unsuccesful in creating a proper law school as there were no degrees in Common Law. Until that time only Civil (in fact Roman or Roman related) Law was taught (by Regius Professors of Civil Law) in Oxford and Cambridge but hardly attracted any students. Modern law schools were established first at University College in London in 1826 and at King's College in London in 1831.

Only after a 1846 Select Committee of the House of Commons demanded a systematic instruction in the 'scientific and philosophical aspects' of the law and called for proper academic degrees in the (common) law, did things change but by 1900 there were still few law graduates and only about ten law schools. This number had risen by the 1970s to about 30 and are now around 75. Treatises and academic writings have multiplied also. They became significant much earlier in the USA, as we shall see in section 1.2.13 below. In England, well into the 1960s much that was taught in laws schools was taught by way of preparation for the solicitors exam and most law teaching remained part-time. Eminent law scholars were few (like Pollock, Anson and Dicey at Oxford and Maitland at Cambridge). Thus the status of legal scholarship remained subdued and opinions of the Bar (from whose ranks both judges and barristers still largely come) were much more important than scholarly findings. In fact, in England for a long time informally the rule obtained that only opinions of dead scholars could be used as authority.[90]

It is only in the last 35 years that English law schools have developed more broadly and that English judges and the Bar have become more receptive of legal scholarship which itself became more imaginative and ultimately also acquired some interest in sociology, economy and psychology, but it still retains, as we shall see, a broadly formal (or doctrinal)[91] bias, intent largely on making some sense out of disparate cases and statutory texts.

It was mentioned above that the common law eventually accepted the binding force of *precedent*, also referred to as the *stare decisis (et quieta non movere)* rule. It is often considered one of its basic traits but has been adhered to only since the end of the eighteenth century.[92] It ties a judge to his own decisions as well as to those of all his colleagues at the same or higher level, although only to the *ratio decidendi* of the decision, that is to the legal principle involved. Observations on the law with no particular relevance to the case (*obiter dicta*) have no such force. The *stare decisis* rule was never so rigorously followed in the USA, where there are far too many cases and the Supreme Court and lower *federal* courts are under the Constitution at times highly political bodies that must respond to quickly changing circumstances so that they could hardly be so bound. Yet within a State, in matters of State law, the lower state courts still follow their own precedents, subject to the decisions of the higher courts, but the Supreme Court of each state will overrule itself if necessary. Federal courts will apply the law of the state in which they sit, except in federal questions.

At least in England, the precedent rule also applies to equity, which as we saw became as a consequence just as rigid as the law, and strictly speaking it applied even to findings on customs and their existence. As already mentioned in section 1.1.2, this created

---

[89] *Commentaries on the Laws of England* (1773), 4 vols.
[90] See *Donoghue v Stevenson* [1932] AC 562 at 567.
[91] Note that in England and the US (in fact in the entire common law world) the term 'doctrinal' stands for the positive law and often for the more formal approach. That may be different in civil law, where it more generally refers back to legal doctrine or the results of academic thinking which suggests a more jurisprudential approach.
[92] It was, only formally recognised by the House of Lords in 1898 in *London Tramways v LCC* [1898] AC 375.

rigidity even in the application of customary (commercial) law and risked depriving it of the flexibility and movement that are inherent in it. Particularly in this commercial law area it now thrives perhaps less than one would expect.

In civil law, there was strictly speaking no similar need to follow precedent because of the codification of the law and its specific rules, which often pretended to contain the whole system of the law, but, of course, judges normally try to stick to a line and do not want to be erratic. Nor do they want to be inefficient. In that sense, civil law judges also accept the persuasive force of precedents, whilst in the absence of clear codified rules or in the case of very old ones, they may rely even more firmly on reforming precedent within their interpretational freedom. Scotland, even if often considered a civil law country, accepted the binding force of precedent more generally, again explicable in the absence of a codification of its Roman oriented laws.

Given the *stare decisis* rule in much of the common law and barring correcting statutory law, it proved more difficult to react to changing moral and social attitudes or to what was clearly wrong or superseded in the law and the *stare decisis* rule came as a consequence under pressure. Although it officially still prevails in England, in 1966 the Lord Chancellor announced that the House of Lords could henceforth overrule itself[93] but that was not to apply to lower courts.[94] The system in England is therefore now much as in the US under state law where lower courts can only distinguish cases on the basis of different facts (distinctions) or ignore what may be qualified as *obiter dicta*. Yet it always left considerable room for artful interpretation and the *stare decisis* rule probably never was what it is often reputed to be.

The idea is, nevertheless, that by following precedent in the absence of any general codification, the common law sustains itself in a similar rule-based manner, even though these rules are unwritten. It seeks in this way to promote predictability. Hence the frequent references to the rule in such or such a case. The crucial difference is, however, that these rules are not set in a coherent framework or applied systematically. There is no comprehensive effort to relate them to each other except in more academic writing. Statutory law, with the notable modern exception of the USA as shown in the Uniform Laws and in the US Bankruptcy Code, and perhaps also with the exception of nineteenth century commercial law statutes in England, does not have this as a primary aim either and remains therefore often a collection of incidental and disparate rules written for particular situations or covering particular concerns. There remains definitely a lesser urge to conceptualise in common law, although no longer in the USA.

At the beginning of the nineteenth century, therefore at the same time that the '*stare decisis*' rule became firmly established, Jeremy Bentham[95] started to argue in England in favour of codification, not on the basis of natural law, as developed in the school of Grotius, but rather on the basis of his well known utilitarian principle such that the legal system should also contribute to the greatest happiness of the greatest possible number. In his view, this required foremost an all-comprehensive body of laws, but this principle was

---

[93] *House of Lords Practice Declaration* [1966] 3 All ER 77.
[94] Notwithstanding Lord Denning's dissenting opinion in *Gallie v Lee* [1969] 1 All ER 1072.
[95] "Codification Proposals", in J Bentham, *Works* 4. As recent as 1974, Scarman LJ thought that the common law system had reached the end of the road, saw judges on the one hand as being duty bound to sometimes resist the will of Parliament, but argued on the other hand for the common law itself to move to a statutory basis as an exclusive source of law, see *English Law, the New Dimension* (Hamlyn Lecture, Sweet & Maxwell, London, 1974, 77. He wanted here also more than general principles, rather detailed rules. The Law Commission set up in 1965 was seen as the centre of this codification activity but it soon downgraded its ambitions to more piecemeal proposals for law reform.

also to be applied to each individual rule. Some of this has returned in the modern 'law and economics' movement in the USA. Although Bentham was principally opposed to the natural law school, in the practical elaboration of codes, his approach would have led to some similar rational deductive manner of rule formulation. It would also have been normal to expect some *universal* law to emerge from this utilitarian approach but it was eliminated through his surprising requirement of codification at the *national* level. Opposition to the codification idea, which never got much further, came in particular from Edmund Burke,[96] who did not believe that through legislation or otherwise one could or should overturn the fruits of the past. Bentham's disciple, J Austin[97] although a utaliterian, subsequently formulated the law as pure command of the sovereign leading to a strong form of positivism which in England has deep roots until today and is probably reflective of a nationalistic attitude that might have preceded Burke, Bentham and Austin, but which was typical nineteenth century and the common core in the teachings of them all.

In Burke's approach there was here an early vision of a *Volksgeist* in the development of the law, much as von Savigny would later propound in Germany. But there was none of the theoretical systematic approach to rule formulation on the basis of it, which von Savigny wanted as a first step to and a precondition of codification at national level which he ultimately favoured. In fact, it led in the civil law codifications to a revolutionary break with the past — with Roman as well as local laws, no matter how much lipservice was paid to them. Burke was here much more consistent in leaving the development of the law to natural (national) forces.

It meant that, after the Napoleonic times, English law was not overtaken by the codification ethos even though perhaps now also more nationalistic in the modern nineteenth century statist tradition. However, streamlining came to be necessary also in England and even there statutory law proved the only efficient way of doing it, but in England statutory law never claimed to cover the whole field as the civil law Codes tended to do and was essentially corrective or an expression of policy geared to particular situations or objectives (like consolidation or simplification). It remained in England only one source of law besides the old (common) law, equity and customary laws and only prevailed if it explicitly amended or abolished the earlier rules. Statutory law, at least in England, remains in that sense subsidiary and incidental even today.

In this vein, in England, the court system was nevertheless substantially modified and simplified by statute, first in the Common Law Procedure Act of 1854 and more fully in the Judicature Acts of 1871, 1873 and 1875. It also unified the procedural laws. As already mentioned, these acts also made it possible to invoke law and equity in all courts (section 25(11) of the Act of 1873). Moreover, they abolished the forms of action (or old writs) and allowed all lawsuits to start with a simple (writ of) summons which did not need to articulate a specific type of claim or cause of action but only its substance. However, in practice, the relief that could be obtained in this manner still corresponded to that available under the former forms of action. This was particularly clear in tort cases where the old forms became the modern torts. However, a more analytical approach became possible and in case-law eventually a broader tort of negligence was developed. In the mean the old torts became the intentional torts but were also expanded in types and coverage.

At the same time, important legislation was also introduced in other areas of substantive private law, also in the commercial area, like the Bills of Sales Acts 1854, 1866, 1882, 1890 and 1891, the Bills of Lading Act 1855 (Supplemented by the Carriage of Goods by

---

[96] *Reflections on the revolution in France* (1790, reprint Oxford University Press, Oxford, 1993).
[97] See John Austin, 2 *Lectures on Jurisprudence*, c XXXVII.

Sea Act (Cogsa) 1992), the Bills of Exchange Act 1882, the Factors Acts 1823, 1842, 1877 and 1889, the Partnership Act 1890, the Sale of Goods Act of 1893 (only replaced in 1979 by an amended version), the Maritime Insurance Act 1906, the Companies Acts, including the winding-up of companies, 1844, 1856, 1862, 1948, 1967, 1986 and 1989, and the Bankruptcy or (now) Insolvency Acts 1824, 1849, 1861, 1869, 1883, 1914, 1985 and 1986. In 1925, the whole law of real property was restated by statute in the Law of Property Act. Also in the area of torts and consumer protection, there is now much legislation. There is no doubt that even in private law it has become also more policy oriented, as indeed modern civil law statutes also are.

In particular the English Bills of Exchange Act 1882 and Sales of Goods Act 1893 have been lauded as great pieces of English (conceptual) legislation. They were drafted by Sir Mackenzie Chalmers. In the USA, the situation is hardly different. There the private law is still a matter for the different states of the Union, although they have obtained some uniformity in uniform laws prepared by the Commission for Uniform State Laws, of which the Uniform Commercial Code (UCC) is the broadest and by far the most important one, accepted in all states. It was substantially the product of the efforts of Professor Karl Llewellyn, who showed strong conceptual thinking, reflected at least in the original set-up. The result was an important reforming statute that did much more than restate the old law and reminds of the codification approach in Europe, very different therefore from the modern English approach to statutory law and its draftsmanship, which, except for the nineteenth century commercial law statutes already mentioned, remains directed to special situations and is casuistic in that sense.

In the USA at individual state level, there were since long some Civil Codes (the so-called Field Codes inspired by Benthamite thinking), for example in California in which much of the old common law is written up. However, their nature was substantially different from that of the European Codes in that they did not overrule the common law. In essence, they served only to facilitate access to that law.[98] Much more important are in the USA the just mentioned uniform laws of which the UCC is by far the most-important example, which are binding even though they leave room for the older sources of law unless especially overruled. In this aspect they are very different from the civil law codes and they also do not accept the same attitude to systematic thinking and interpretation.

There are further the modern Restatements in which various areas of the law are summarised (like contract, trust and agency) by the American Law Institute, a private institution created in 1923 by the American Bar Association which also co-operated in the drafting of the UCC. The uniform laws as well as the Restatements are regularly up-dated. Although the Restatements are not legislation and may not even have persuasive force, their unifying impact is considerable. Like the method in the UCC, the one in these Restatements is more directly intellectual, and reminds one in this aspect of the European codification ethos. There is no equivalent in England even though it has the Law Commission that suggest from time legislative improvements in the law, but rather on more specific issues.

Also in common law countries, legislation raises the question of *statutory interpretation*. In most of them, particularly in England, statutory law of this nature is essentially still seen as a foreign element in the development of the law and therefore *restrictively* interpreted, much as criminal laws are in civil law, and there remains therefore as much room as possible

---

[98] In fact, in 1888 the Californian Supreme Court in *Sharon v Sharon*, 75 Cal.1,13 (1888) declared that in instances where the Code was so confused and uncertain that it could be given no intelligible meaning, it could not be considered to have changed the common law. Already under its section 5, it was stated that the Code was substantially the same as prior law.

for law and equity. In any event, if the statutes do not clearly abolish older law, the relevant case-law can still be pleaded. In that sense all statutes in the area of the common law are in essence considered only a restatement, elaboration or correction of what went before, unless specifically stated otherwise.[99]

Hence the continued importance of case-law and the various law reports, which publish these cases. In this connection, it is well known that English judges remain particularly wary of teleological interpretation of statutes, more so than their modern American counterparts,[100] and will commonly also not consider the preparatory instruments as a guide to (historical) interpretation.[101] They still tend to a *literal* approach to statutory instruments, also of contracts as we shall see in the next chapter. Again, this is now very different in the US in the so-called *realist* approach or legal realism as we shall see shortly. In that approach, the Americans allow in appropriate cases clearly room for ethical, social and efficiency considerations. Even in their so-called codes like the UCC, they do not follow systematic reasoning either or at least do not see it as a bar to achieve social adjustments or economic ends.

This difference with the English is borne out by the English Interpretation Act of 1978 which was largely a restatement of the Interpretation Act of 1889, often considered a little precious and pedantic, even in England. The restrictive interpretation technique means in practice that the English legislator is required to be much more specific and precise than his civil law counterpart and that the drafting of statutes is often cumbersome and unduly detailed, geared to particular situations and problems. But it is also an attitude as contracts in common law tend to be equally verbose and elaborate reflecting no less specific situations and worries whilst risking to leave in this manner eventualities uncovered. In short, in traditional common law practice, contractual drafting is not conceptual either, rather more practical and often long. This can have advantages but particularly bad examples of this type of *statutory* drafting appeared between 1985 and 1987 in the English Insolvency, Companies and Financial Services Acts.

For the reason stated, the technique of drafting lucid legislation seems to have eluded the English, although the nineteenth century laws were often much more conceptual as we saw. So are the Uniform Commercial Code in the USA and the new English Arbitration Act of 1996 (which had the Uncitral Model Law for an example). They also had largely single draftsmen. Clearly, it does not always need to be this way.

In statutory interpretation, there is in any event in England a gradual change in favour of a more 'purposive approach' 'to promote the general legislative purpose of enactments', which eventually may also affect the drafting technique and there is a more flexible approach in contract interpretation as well.[102] Nevertheless, Lord Denning set the tone in the *Bulmer* case as follows:

> the draftsmen of our statutes have striven to express themselves with the utmost exactness. They have tried to foresee all possible circumstances that may arise and provide for them.

---

[99] More boldly, it was held in *Dr Bonham's Case*, 77 ER 646, 652 (1610) that if an Act of Parliament was against common law right and reason, common law would control it and adjudge it void. At least in England, that is not the practice. As Parliament cannot act *ultra vires*, the courts cannot annul statutes. However, in the US the judiciary can hold statutes unconstitutional ever since the famous case of *Marbury v Madison*, 1 Cranch 137, 2L Ed., 60 (1803). See for civil law the situation under the French Cc (Article 5) which does withhold that right from the courts expressly and is here illustrative for much of the rest of civil law, see also s. 1.2.5 *supra in fine*.

[100] See for the US also s. 1.2.13 *infra*.

[101] See Lord Denning, *The Discipline of the Law* (1979), 11*ff.* and his comments in *Bulmer v Bollinger* [1974] Ch 401.

[102] See for a number of recent House of Lord cases, Lord Hoffmann in *Investors Compensation Scheme Ltd v West Bromwich Building Societey* [1998] 1 WLR 896, 913 and *BCCI v Ali*, [2001] 2 WLR 749 in which a reasonable man approach was adopted but at least as a starting point the literal attitude towards statutory enactments remains largely in tact.

They have sacrificed style and simplicity. They have foregone brevity. They have become long and involved. In consequence the judges have followed suit. They interpret a statute as applying to the circumstances covered by the very words. They give them a literal interpretation. If the words of the statute do not cover a new situation — which was not foreseen — the judges hold that they have no power to fill the gap. To do so would be naked usurpation of the legislative function ... the gap must remain open until Parliament finds the time to fill it.

Thus statutes continue to be strictly interpreted in England, a rule, in fact, of long-standing validity (at least since 1343).[103] It allows more room for the old common law but there is clearly also a modern concern that the judiciary gets too close to legislative activity under the thin guise of interpretation.[104]

Under the influence of EU law, which, in the civil law tradition, is much more conceptual in its legislative approach, will also consider the preparatory work, and is used to and perhaps even based on the expectation of teleological interpretation, the attitude in the UK may in any event be affected, as was already discussed in the *Bulmer* case. It is unavoidable in the interpretation of EU Directives. It is nevertheless undeniable that in common law for the time being a restrictive attitude is still taken to the interpretation of statutes (unless they expressly instruct otherwise as the UCC did in Section 1–1–3) or legal theory dictates otherwise, as 'legal realism' now more generally does in the US, see section 1.2.13 below. On the positive side this means that there is at least ample room for the operation of law, equity and custom *besides* statute (as Section 1–103 (new and old) UCC also recognises).

1.2.13 Intellectualisation and Conceptualisation in Common Law. Modern American Academic Attitudes towards the Law and its Development: Legal Formalism and Realism. Post-realism or Legal Functionalism: The 'Law and ...' Movements

In the foregoing it was repeatedly said that the traditional common law tends to be practical and is not intellectual. It certainly never went through an intellectual phase as did the *Ius Commune* already at the time of Bartolus and Baldus and much more so in the natural law school of Grotius and Pufendorf or in the nineteenth century German Pandektist School. Even if modern civil law became ultimately dependent on positive state law or at least on *national* law (which could be case-law), all codification thinking was and remains basically intellectual and conceptual. It found as such no clear counterpart in common law, also not when statutory law started to become more prevalent, although in the US through the Uniform Laws and Restatements, intellectualisation and conceptualisation became much more common than elsewhere in the English speaking world.

Indeed, in the US in the twentieth century, a need came to be felt to study the law in a more academic and abstract fashion. It was promoted at first by the coming into being of major national law schools like those at Harvard, Yale, Columbia, Chicago and Berkeley and the requirement that all lawyers obtain an academic qualification in the law. At least in private law this American legal scholarship was at first closely related to the traditional search for *legal consistency* in rule patterns (whether derived from legislation or case-law), which was also the drift of the English academic approach and in fact no less common on the European Continent in the context of the early interpretation and elaboration of the codes.

---

[103] See also TFT Plucknett, *A Concise History of the Common Law* (1956), 333.
[104] See Lord Simonds in *Magor & St Mellons RDC v Newport Corp* [1952] AC 189, rebuffing Lord Denning on appeal.

This so-called *legal formalism* (an American term only invented later) was foremost intent on finding a more coherent system of rules which as we saw remains indeed much the direction of present English scholarship. It reminds as such to some extent of the rule-based codification attitude with its emphasis on intellectual coherence. It particularly looks for the logical thread in disparate case-law and even in statutory enactments and means to articulate the underlying consistency of the rules in a kind of system and to distinguish (new) cases on that basis. In codification countries, this consistency was largely assumed to exist in the codifications, although as explained in section 1.2.10 above, new case-law, even that concerning the good faith concept, often remains in Continental legal scholarship also typically so analysed. For the applications of the rules so found or recast, both, civil and common law emphasised as a starting point literal interpretation or otherwise the use of syllogism in which a black letter rule (which could also be derived from case-law) operated as the major and the facts of the case as the minor. For example: if every one must drive his or her vehicle on the right, that is the rule or the major. You happen to drive your car on the left, that is the fact or the minor. The result is a violation of the law (in this case this will often be criminal law narrowly interpreted anywhere, but it could also lead to an action in negligence).

Logic is here at the heart of the legal interpretation process in which the rule is taken as literally as possible (and historical interpretation is never and purposive interpretation only exceptionally accepted). It creates obvious problems where, in our example, the driver used a tricycle or bike which might not have been a 'vehicle' in a literal sense. Interpretation through *deductive* reasoning (in which the narrower lower category would be considered to cover a 'two wheeled non motorised vehicle') or, if that also failed, through *induction*[105] (in which the higher category is 'all that moves mechanically') or through analogy could then follow. It again reminds of the order civil law approach which is here reflected in the more formal variant of common law. The difference was in a greater reliance on the system as such in civil law.

Whatever the appearance, this type of interpretation was not necessarily objective and implied in fact much discretion. If it still did not work (in the sense that it did not yield a reasonable or sensible result), this type of formalism would have to be abandoned. Interpretation on the basis of the purpose of the rule or the policy behind it (*purposive* or *teleological* interpretation) would then appear unavoidable, assuming the purpose could be clearly distilled (which in the present example could be limitation of bodily harm), but was at first not favoured.

A still broader *normative* interpretation would take other pressing extra-legal consider-ations also into account, like broader ethical, social or efficiency notions and needs. In this context, the circumstances could also be considered. Perhaps the road was very wide, so

---

[105] This approach is also referred to as the technique *per genus proximum et differentia specifica*. It leads to a logical *Begriffspyramide* and is also in civil law a common method, especially in the analysis of case law. By taking extra-neous facts away, one may find the higher rule and by adding other ones, the lower rule for them. Thus looking at consumer and workers protection, one may conclude that the protection of weaker parties is the higher rule. Whilst adding in small investors, one may conclude that they are also protected under a lower rule concerning them, etc. Analogical interpretation might lead to a similar conclusion. So much seems clear, but considerable problems arise where eg civil delicts are thus compared with criminal acts, which tend to be much more narrowly defined, or where other legal structures that may at one level seem comparable but have in law a very different function, like eg security interests and conditional sales and transfers, see more in particular chapter 5, s. 1.1. The inductive method is therefore by no means objective and always dependent on structural characterisations and policy issues or objectives. In civil law, it may be restrained also in the sense that this inductive approach may be considered to have to fit within the overall system of the applicable code and will not then produce any rules which become too remote from the larger codified framework.

that a local traffic of cyclists and pedestrians in the other direction had developed on the side. Here custom and practices might come in. On the other hand, there may only have been a very narrow dirt road, where no normal traffic from either side could pass unhindered and where as a consequence talking of driving on the left or right does not make much sense. Here other arrangements must be made *ad hoc* to let traffic from different directions pass and practicalities take over from the law, except to the extent that both parties will have to show some spirit of co-operation and willingness to move on.

Again, it does not fit the formal legal approach but courts may be forced into it. As we saw in section 1.2.10 above, civil law courts in their liberal interpretation need of codes often more naturally incline to it, as has become particularly clear in their use of the good faith notion, even if present legal scholarship in civil law countries often prefers to reintegrate any such case-law into a system and does not seem to favour greater openness and a broader discussion of the alternatives *per se*. So formalism returns in legal writing, whilst judges also pay lip service to it and like to draft their decisions accordingly. Nonetheless, the whole development of the notion of good faith in civil law was largely their doing, therefore a judicial not a scholarly departure as we saw. It could be said that in the process the civil law courts have become more independent from legal scholarship than used to be the case. Although the civil law courts will continue their tradition and pay attention to more formal legal scholarship, the roles seem to be reversed, see also section 1.2.10 above. In England, scholarship never had much of a hold on the courts as we saw in the previous section. It was shown, however, that in that country they tend to argue no less formally and stick in any event to narrow findings and construct statutory law also narrowly unless the result is clearly unsatisfactory or public expectations have moved on.

Unlike in England, this more formal approach — in the US for case-law articulated especially by Langdell at Harvard in the late nineteenth century — did not long survive and yielded ultimately to a more normative approach. There the openly accepted political role of the US Supreme Court and of the federal circuit courts in particular helped to create a greater interest in extra-legal or policy objectives behind the law and eventually in legal concepts rather than in their black-letter manifestations.

Dissenting opinions make it possible to follow here the debates within the judiciary. Where such dissenting opinions are sometimes also given in Europe, it is clear that there is not the some leeway in the alternatives. Whether in England or on the Continent, the judiciary does not have a similarly strong constitutional position vis-à-vis parliament whilst in England there is also the binding force of precedent to consider. Judges have therefore fewer alternatives and like to be more circumspect. In this aspect, present thinking in England may be closer to that of the European Continent than to that in the US. As was already shown in the previous section, it shows that the common law tradition is not uniform and is in fact subject to a great divide.

In the more open normative approach, the search for *consistency* and legal certainty acquires another dimension. It is not the system or the existing black letter rules that are believed to guarantee them in a useful manner. Rather, in all decisions, the outcome is ultimately deemed to be determined by what in society or in the relevant communuity is considered right or normative which needs to be articulated per case. Particularly in areas where the law remains unsettled, rules, even if derived from statute, acquire the character largely of *guidelines*. It is very reminiscent of what was the approach of the free law movement in Germany, see section 1.2.10 above.

In the US, the Constitution is often considered complete in its arrangements and requires therefore a flexible approach to interpretation to be able to cover rapid changes in society. This is much reminescent of code interpretation in civil law, but without its systemic reasoning. *Ex facto ius creatur* is here the leading principle so that there can be a living law. Rather than to a system approach, it has led to a policy oriented attitude, although in the US the extent of the freedom of the courts in this connection and especially of the Supreme Court in respect of the Constitution remains a hotly debated political issue.

To avoid more argument than necessary, the US Constitution is often said to have in itself ample resources for the changing needs of successive generations.[106] Thus from early on, constitutional law was meant to define 'the whole American fabric',[107] in which connection the courts were thought to speak for the whole experience as a nation and to reinterpretate the Constitution on the basis of the prevailing American value system.[108] It helped that in its general norms, like the due process, interstate commerce, and full faith and credit clauses and in its bill of rights, a special overlay of fundamental principle was included in the constitution text itself and had legal effect of its own. It applies as a system of higher norms or values that are constantly re-balanced in the ongoing construction of a collective entity, which is intended to be — in the language of the Constitution — an 'ever more perfect Union'.

To this should be added the already mentioned American facility of the federal courts to overrule statutes if deemed unconstitutional. State courts will do so in respect of State statutes. They will be tested against the relevant State constitution, which is likely to contain similar principled language as the US Constitution.

This attitude had eventually an important impact on all legal interpretation, also that of state (private) laws and contracts. In the US, a liberal interpretation technique of statutes is now explicitly accepted in many fields of the law, in private law expressed particularly in Section 1–109 (1–102 old) UCC.[109] Similarly, in contract interpretation, mere deductive approaches or other forms of legal or logical formalism were increasingly rejected.[110] A more sociological approach in law application and interpretation became early apparent in the works of Oliver Wendell Holmes, the later Chief Justice, and of Roscoe Pound at Harvard in which social needs would be considered in determining legal issues. The new approach itself was further elaborated by Karl Llewellyn in what was since the 1930s called the American School of *legal realism*.[111]

Legal formalism is associated with the notion that law is rationality and that its rules make the administration of justice a mechanical activity. The law is here self-contained, whether or not encapsulated in codification notions and there is no outside goal. It assumes a social order of its own which is normative as such. The realists, on the other hand, had more difficulty in exactly defining thgeir method but basically looked at the law as it functioned in society (law in action) and at its operational sufficiency.[112] Extra legal

---

[106] See notably Felix Frankfurther, *Of Law and Life* (PB Kirkland (ed), 1965), 59.

[107] See John Marshall in *Marbury v Madison*, 5 US (1 Cranch) 137, 175 (1803).

[108] See Oliver Wendell Holmes in *Missouri v Holland*, 252 US 416, 433 (1920).

[109] ... "to promote its underlying purposes and policies", which was explained as to simplify, clarify and modernise the law governing commercial transactions, to achieve uniformity amongst the various states and to permit the continued expansion of commercial practices through custom, usage and agreement of the parties, see also s 1.1.2 *supra*. Here we see custom appear as an *alternative* and favoured source of law, as good faith (more timidly) now also is under the UCC, see also Chapter 2, s 1.3.1.

[110] See MA Eisenberg, "The Emergence of Dynamic Contract Law", 88 *Cal LR* (2000), 174. Here all axiomatic/deductive reasoning is shown to be abandoned and normative reasoning increasingly adopted, in which non-legal arguments will be considered and brought within the law and legal argument. Where they conflict, such a conflict will be resolved in the context of deciding the case.

[111] See for the many other supporters at the time, MJ Horwitz, *The Transformation of American Law 1870–1960; The Crisis of Legal Orthodoxy* (1992), 171.

[112] See for the modern views of formalism, B Leiter, "Positivism, Formalism, Realism", 99 *Colum LR* 1138 (1999). See for the classical texts on legal realism, Karl Llewellynn, "The Effect of Legal Institutions Upon Economics",

objectives and policy considerations became as a consequence much more important in the interpretation of the law. It assumed a general awareness of what was ethically, socially, and perhaps even from the point of view of utility and efficiency, more desirable. In its studies, the movement was fact oriented and empirical. It brought to an end the prevalence of literal and logical interpretation techniques in the application of the law. Although it favoured conceptual thinking in law formation, for which in private law there was German influence as may be shown in the UCC and also in the Restatements already mentioned, it did not adopt a systematical interpretation approach as civil lawyers tended to do, at least the system was not to thwart other more urgent considerations. It follows that in the US, the difference between *legal formalism* and a more policy oriented approach to the law and its application has long been understood. A lesser need was henceforth felt to apply rules in a logical and intrinsically consistent manner and black letter law as such lost much of its luster.

Legal realism is a development which has become ever more pronounced in American legal scholarship and law towards the end of the twentieth century, where courses in law and ethics, law and religion, law and sociology (Law and Society),[113] law and economics,[114] law and psychology, law and aesthetics, law and politics, law and culture (or critical legal studies), etc, are now common. It is also refered to as post-realism or functionalism resulting in the *'law and ....'* movements which have become popular with the result that black letter (or so-called doctrinal) law is increasingly disfavoured at least in legal scholarship and law teaching in the major American law schools. Legal scholarship has thus become more jurisprudental, much less profession oriented in nature. Its objective is rather the development of views that engender renewel and improvement of the law through intellectual analysis and forward looking instinct.

Especially in 'law and sociology', 'law and economics', and 'law and psychology', there is a simultaneous shift to more *empirical* research to prepare legislation and monitor its effects. Their proponents unite in wanting to fill a vacuum in which law making and application were mostly matters of opinion, experience, intuition or perhaps wishful thinking.[115] In the application of the law, empirical answers are particularly sought to the question of when and how non-legal considerations enter into the judicial decision making process thereby becoming legally normative and enforceable. In this connection, environmental

---

15 *Am Econ Rev*, 665 (1925); "A realistic Jurisprudence — The Next Step", 30 *Colum LR* 431 (1930); "Some Realism about Realism", 44 *Harv LR*, 1222 (1931); "The Normative, the Legal and The Law-Jobs: "The Problem of Juristic Method", 49 *Yale LJ*, 1355 (1940); and *The Bramble Bush: On our Law and its Study* (NY 1951).

[113] It is much associated with the work of Philip Selznick at Berkeley, see eg Ph Nonet and Ph Selznick, *Law and Society in Transition: Towards Responsive Law* (2nd edn, 2001) and Ph Selznick, *The Communautarian Persuasion* (2002) and earlier *The Moral Commonwealth* (1992).

[114] The law and economics movement tries in effect to rationalise the legal rules and their effect from the perspective of economic efficiency. In that connection, it is largely motivated by a concern for proper information supply and transaction cost. It is a more recent phenomenon, particularly derived from the economic thinking of von Hayek and the legal thinking of RA Posner, *Economic Analysis and the Law* (1973), see also WM Landes and RA Posner, "The Influence of Economics on Law: A Quantitative Study", 36 *J Law and Economics* (1993), 385, but it can be dated back to RH Coase, "The Problem of Social Cost", 3 *J Law and Economics* (1960), 1, and to G Calabresi, "Some Thoughts on Risk Distribution and the Law of Torts", 70 *Yale LJ* (1961), 499. The second generation is more interested in the internalisation of values, the motives for doing so and the application of economic modeling techniques to this process, see especially Robert Cooter, "Law and Unified Social Theory", 22 *Journal of Law and Society*, 50 (1995); "Three Effects of Social Norms on Law: Expression, Deterrence, and Internalisation" 79 *Oregon LR* 1 (2000); see also Cooter and Ulen, "*Law and Economics*", 3rd edn (1999). See at the more practical level further HN Butler, *Economic Analysis for Lawyers* (1998).

[115] It had its critics from the beginning, see RS Summers, *Instrumentalism and American Legal Theory* (1982), 115 with reference to the deadly bog of behaviorism.

justice and critical race theories (or critical or political legal studies more generally)[116] have added an ever stronger *political* dimension to legal theory which tends to go well beyond mere legal analysis of policy and action. Here there is much room for cultural considerations, national and other values or Burkean and *Volksgeist* notions, but also for (minority) group demands and for the notion that the law as it is cannot promote justice (or equality in a practical sense) without major (political) reforms.

In the wake of these developments, in the US, more traditional jurisprudential concerns about 'law as justice', 'law as order', and natural or positive law approaches seem to have receded into the background or are recast in a different mould. Where the positivist or black letter law approach has been substantially weakened, the search for the true justification behind the law has intensified. In this respect, there was always an idealistic and natural law undercurrent in American legal thinking probably connected with the strong ethical flavour of the constitutional principles. It means that in the US the law is hardly considered a product of the command of the state, although it may still be seen as embedded in a national recognition and acceptance process, therefore in *American* values and culture rather than in more universal principles. It may well be that a naturalism of American dimension is here impliedly assumed. Indeed, there is often little consideration of internationalism, universalism, or an acknowledgement that the American experience is part of a broader Western culture which is democratic and decentralist, subject to the rule of law, and mindful of basic human rights, even if in the twentieth century in the shaping of this more universal culture the Americans have largely taken over from Europe.[117]

In its application, it may well be that, at least at the academic level, the law as a rational system is increasingly mistrusted in the US. In the manner of Hume's skepticism and of some of the twentieth century Scandanavian scholars, contradictions and irrationalities in the law's aims are emphasized and accepted as unavoidable, even if the 'law and economics' movement tries to be more rational. The (a) lack of a unitary view of what justice is or of what the law needs to achieve in terms of social ordering, (b) questioning of value systems in favour of national or group cultures, race or gender, but also (c) influence of market forces and what are considered utilitarian preferences or rational choices, have had a considerable influence on modern legal studies in the US. They may so far have combined that ultimately the more extreme view is being heard that the law does not present an own system of values at all and therefore lacks autonomy.[118]

---

[116] The openly left wing aspirations of this movement, see eg Allan C Hutchinson (ed), *Critical Legal Studies* (1989), have contributed to an old fashioned rethoric seemingly leading to unnecessary isolation. It has tended to cloud its innovative approaches and to conceal the much broader relevance of many of its ideas. It can be seen as the politicised branch of modern legal thought in which rationality and a unitary approach to justice are particularly questioned, see especially the work of RM Unger at Harvard, eg his "Liberal Political Theory" in Allan C Hutchinson (ed), *supra*, 15.

[117] As far as these natural law undercurrents go, the work of Lon Fuller is clearly inspired by secular natural law, see *The Law in Quest of Itself* (1940). It laid much stress on the internal morality of the law (rather than rationality). The approach of J Rawls, *A Theory of Justice* (1971) and *Political Liberalism* (1996), in search of public policy justifications in the law, is very different but no less naturalistic. Others only advocate a *national* value system to underpin the law, which is not necessarily a conflicting proposition. It is sometimes even believed to be one of the insights of legal realism, see R Post, "The Challenge of Globalization to American Public Law Scholarship", 2 *Theoretical Inquiries in Law* (2001), 323. The idea here is that the legally relevant culture and values are primarily national and do not therefore have an anchor in the broader modern Western culture even if that produced our idea of the modern state, of democracy, rule of law, and protection of basic values in the first place. None rely, however, on mere positivism or the state's command to validate the law. Only in the American "law and economics" movement seems there to be a more natural understanding of the international dimensions and validity of the basic legal concepts, at least in commerce and finance, see eg RD Cooter, "Structural Adjudication and the New Law Merchant: A Model of Decentralised Law", 14 *International Review of Law and Economics* (1994), 215.

[118] RA Posner, "The Decline of Law as an Autonomous Discipline: 1962–1987", (1987) 100 *Harv L Rev* 761. Some care is appropriate here and semantics enter easily into the picture. The law as an own (philosophical) category,

Since the 1970s, the result has been a considerable *intellectualisation* of legal studies in the leading US law schools resulting in an immense flood of literature and debates that have produced valuable new insights but also serious criticism.[119]

Not all movements have retained their popularity and 'the law and society' and 'critical legal studies' are perhaps less favoured now than they once were. Especially the 'law and economics' school remains greatly popular as the more rational branch of modern legal thought that has attempted to translate and explain many legal structures in economic terms, whilst still valuing predictability and measuring the law's (economic) effects.[120] Nevertheless, it is no guide to legal reasoning nor to the law's application and remains therefore limited as a legal tool.

therefore subject to its own structure and normativity, never meant isolation and absolute separation from other categories, like the ethical, social and economic ones, very clear in the formulation of statutory law and regulation. They are closely connected and influence each other, how much so and in what manner (especially also in the application of the laws) is an obvious area of jurisprudential studies. It is clear that in times of great social and political movement and lack of consensus, there is greater tension but also a greater need (at least in an academic sense) for these categories to sustain and enlighten each other. That may well explain much of the "law and ..." movements in the US at present. That there is a lesser use for it in Europe at this time might be explained by a greater social consensus or coherence there (for the moment).

This may also be relevant in international commerical and financial law where, it could be argued, there is a greater consensus and therefore less need for political, moral or social adjustments to the evolving new law merchant. On the other hand, the emergence and autonomy of the international commercial and financial legal order — it will be argued — is itself a social phenomenon whilst utilitarian considerations will naturally also be of great importance in what is largely the elaboration of commercial and financial exigencies aand realities in the formation and application of this new law.

[119] See eg AA Leff, "Economic Analysis of Law: Some Realism about Nominalism" (1974) 60 *Virg LR* 451. Legal formalism is also not entirely abandoned and retains its supporters, see notably EJ Weinrib, "Legal Formalism: On the Immanent Rationality of Law", 97 *Yale LJ* 949,951 (1988). Here emphasis is put on the efforts of lawyers to find an intelligible order and apply it as such.

[120] This school has also different strands but the one associated with neo-classical economics is the more prevalent. Individual actors are here at the center of economic activity. They are assumed to act as rational beings, who maximize their own benefits and respond to prices and pay-offs whilst the aggregation of their choices is assumed to result in a variety of institutional frameworks that the law will sanction.

The general premise of "law and economics" is that all activities have a cost (including social costs or *externalities* that are not charged to those carrying out that activity like (often) pollution of the atmosphere) and that competing interests, like the need for clean air as against industrial activity require a trade-off that determines the acceptance and extent of these social costs. This trade-off is cast foremost in market or efficiency terms or as competition for scarse resources in terms of individual (rational) choices in which fault does not figure. Even if subsequently the law asks who is at fault in pollution matters or what legal justifications or excuses there may be, the efficiency question should first be posed as (in this view) the legal rule or result can (often) be explained in terms of a contribution to (or even being the product of) what was most efficient. What is efficient in this sense defies *a priori* analysis but depends in this approach on an investigation of the behaviour of individuals and how they respond to incentives to maximise their self interest. What happens here is that the pursuit of justice is cast foremost in terms of the pursuit of economic efficiency. In this approach economic ordering is considered the heart of the legal system.

Legal rights and markets are thus likely to interact in the sense that legal rights may be understood though the contribution they make to an efficient trade-off in the above terms (Coase). The law of torts can so be explained as a tool to contribute to the optimum level of accidents (Calabresi) in terms therefore of its contribution to efficiency (Coase). In terms of contract law, the contribution to efficiency (and reduction of transaction costs) may be even more obvious. Although the focus of the law shifts here from justice to efficiency considerations, it is also shown that the latter need not conflict as much with the former as could be assumed. As a (re)distributive concept, justice as a balancing of interests is not an economic concept. It is also argued that people are in fact worse off if distribution prevails over efficiency, see L Kaplow and Shavell, "Should Legal Rules Favour the Poor", 29 *J Legal Studies*, 821 (2000), questioned by J Waldron, "Locating Distribution", 32 *J Legal Studies*, 277 (2003).

The neo-classical strand lately focusses not only on the (aggregate) behaviour of individuals in the market, but also on what makes this behaviour more predictable, and on the development or evolution of the law in this connection and its contribution. This is sometimes also referred to as the second generation of "law and economics" and suggests a close connection with (mass) psychology. See for a good summary R Nobles, "Economic Analysis of Law" in Penner, Schiff, Nobles (eds), *Jurisprudence and Legal Theory*, 855 (2002).

The lack of clear direction is noticeable and there is so far less impact on the positive law than one might think although attention is sometimes paid to these newer approaches and ideas in case-law, especially in antitrust matters, in (draft) statutory law, and in newer Restatements. Rather, it could be argued that the intellectualisation of the legal studies in the US in this manner has contributed to a growing divide between academic legal thinking and legal practice in an environment in which the practical orientation of the living common law itself has hardly changed. In private law, one may see this lack of theoretical imput in particular in the regular amendements and revisions of the UCC. Even the further elaboration of the important federal bankruptcy statutes seems in the end not to have been greatly affected by newer thought.[121]

There is here a further complication in that the emphasis on policy may have shifted attention unduly to law making through legislators or to the courts in terms of *public* ordering. The essence of *private* law as a facilitating rather than mandatory force may thus become misunderstood, distorted or ignored. Governmental interests and their validity became early the theme of conflicts of laws in the US, see section 2.2.2 below, but also in the modern movements these seem to have become the major areas of concern, not only in the formulation but also interpretation of the law.[122]

At (a) the *legislative level*, absence of clear views on what the law is can more easily be accepted. Policy considerations will prevail here and decide what ought to be, although academic studies may help to show better ways. Lawyers have to accept this legislative outcome and are likely to be neutral, except if fundamental principles of a modern open society are ignored. The role of lawyers at the legislative level will mainly be in the drafting of statutes in such a way that they can apply them. To that extent a measure of systematic formalism is necessary, but there is at this level no true contradiction with realism.

For (b) the *interpretation* of these statutes or case-law, the absence of a unitary view on what the law is or should strive for may present greater problems. As we saw, American lawyers may now generally take a normative approach to interpretation and accept in that context extra-legal considerations in terms primarily of ethics, social needs, economic efficiency, or perhaps also environmental requirements, but they will in normal cases naturally be constrained in the application of these considerations if they are not in accordance with the drift of the positive law derived either from statute or precedent. It would seem that only in *pressing cases* could that be different.[123] Especially in comprehensive statutory

There is another more political strand in "Law and Economics" which concentrates on how law is made in the legislative process, therefore as a political tool. This is the area of public choice theory and political economics. This comes down to the personal interests and preferences of policy makers which are assumed to act much like other individuals and rationalise their preferences and maximise their self interests. The state is here not the subject of study (like in political science) but rather the politicians, civil servants, pressure group officials and the like. This strand of thought sees its origin in L Jaffee, "Law Making by Private Groups", 51 *Harv LR* 201 (1937) and later in JM Buchanan and G Tullock, *The Calculus of Consent* (1962). Its offspring is the so-called Chicago School which is empirical. Another variant is the one of "analytical politics". The idea is here to build formal (mathematical) models of collective decision taking, see eg A Schwartz and RE Scott, "The Politcal Economy of Private Legislatures", 143 *UPa LR* 595 (1994).

[121] See E Warren, "Bankruptcy policy making in an imperfect world", 92 *Michigan LR* 336 (1993), but *cf* also T Jackson, "Bankruptcy, Non-bankruptcy Entitlements, and the Creditors' Bargain", 91 *Yale LJ* 857 (1982), see also GE Brunstad, "Bankruptcy and the Problems of Economic Futility: A Theory on the Unique Role of Bankruptcy Law", 55 *The Business Lawyer*, 499 (2000).

[122] See for a critique, A Katz, "Taking Private Ordering Seriously", 144 *U Pen LR* 1745 (1996).

[123] As could be expected, in the US the discussion on interpretation itself is lively, see for a balanced view, M Stone, "Focussing the Law: What Legal Interpretation is Not" in Andrei Marmor, *Essays in Legal Philosophy* (Oxford, 1995). A plea for greater formalism at least in the interpretation of contracts between professionals is also being heard (not unlike the approach of this book), see eg RE Scott, "The Case for Formalism in Relational Contracts", 94 *Nw ULR* 847 (2000).

law, like in the US the UCC or Bankruptcy Code, tax laws, company laws, and federal procedure, a more coherent and systemic approach follows in any event from the statutory example. Yet other more technical considerations may also be valid in this context especially when the rule is ambiguous, increasingly out of date, or when it is unclear that it can apply to the facts of the case at all.

Lawyers of all eras will show respect to the positive law, whether statutory or case-law, and to the value system it represents. To that extent, they will accept the autonomy of the law and articulate its values even if the extra-legal purposes that the law serves and moral, social and/or economic values cannot always be ignored and may in pressing cases motivate judges to reformulate existing legal rules at least for the occasion. There can be little doubt that positive law is constantly re-formulated by judges for these reasons, not only in the USA — it is unavoidable especially in periods of rapid change — but it is likely to remain a cautious, searching process that is likely to lack behind these changes, even if the US legal scholarship appears at present much keener to close the gap or lead the way.

In (c) the *transactional practice*, the task of practising lawyers is again different. They will have to write down in a comprehensive and coherent manner the deal reached by their clients and the risk distribution inherent in it. This is logic and coherence or formalism in that sense. They will have an own role to play in assessing and distributing the legal risk, in international cases particularly in terms of the applicable law and jurisdiction. That is their contribution to legal certainty. As for the applicable law, this will also involve an assessment of context and extra-legal considerations that may become relevant in the application of the contract.

In international (or interstate) cases, that will be all the more difficult as these lawyers will also have to assess the possibitities of a contractual choice of law or jurisdiction. This requires a further assessment of what e.g. a contractual choice of law clause may mean in areas of the law that are not at the free disposition of the parties, usually those that have to do with third party rights, like property, collateral and bankruptcy issues, or with governmental policies of the states most concerned. A further assessment will here be necessary in respect of the applicability of the *lex mercatoria* and its meaning and content. As far as jurisdiction and alternatives go, the feasibility of arbitration or other alternative dispute resolution techniques will also have to be considered in that context. It is clear that legal formalism cannot be here much of a guide.

In (d) *legal scholarship* all is free. Here formalism or thinking in terms of systems and their application suggest a fixation with yesterday's rules. Yet it is not always useless, especially not in statutory interpretation where it may provide some help. Clearly, modern American academia goes beyond this and rather concentrates on the transforming forces in the law. In fact, it stimulates them with endless new ideas. It also takes a vivid interest in why and how rules are better accepted (or internalised). There is no less an interest in more epistimological issues like the meaning of fundamental principle, systematic thinking, the conditions for legal knowledge, and the use made of it. Legal education, at least in the best law schools, follows and is conceptual, free thinking, allowing for flexibility or pragmatism, and a more modern outlook, vocabulary, and articulation of the law.

If a more activist *judicial* approach seems to have become apparent all around, therefore certainly not only in the US, it is obviously motivated by the enormous social, cultural, scientific, demographic and ecological changes we see pressing upon us all. It is a matter of perception and study whether this is affecting the very nature of the law itself and its operation in society. Even if as a result the law were in modern times in essence seen as an empty shell, the next question would still be what should fill it on occasion and how? If extra-legal norms or demands must increasingly be taken into account as legally normative and thus binding, it still has to be asked which ones, when and to what extent? Or to put it another way, when do these norms become legally enforceable (thereby entering into the law)? That is, it is submitted, the true cause of the probing attitude of much modern American legal scholarship. Thus presented, this search is a function of the acceleration in social evolution. It has unavoidably led to disorientation, certainly also in the application of the law, which American legal scholarship reflects and has accepted as a challenge rather than an embarrasment.

Outside the US (except for Canada), these modern American ideas have not so far played a great role, even though noted,[124] also not the 'law and economics' school,[125] not even in *international* relationships of a private law nature and in the reformulation of substantive rules at that level, notably in international commercial and financial or business law. As a consequence, it has hardly figured in the development of the new international law merchant, although one would assume that it is in principle friendly to it as would be those legal currents that see group cultures and values as a determining factor in law formation, subject of course always to governmental interests, the extraterritorial validity of which would still have to be determined on their relevancy from case to case (barring treaty law or accepted international law concepts).

Many American commentators looking mainly at trade restrictions invoke here simply a liberal, market-oriented spirit aiming at the free movement of goods, services and capital. Where a form of re-regulation is necessary, they are likely to deprecate the notion of sovereignty so as to achieve a more proper balance between international and national legal orders or lower local or cultural organisms through notions similar to that of subsidiarity.[126] Others, however, may be less willing to look in the development of private law for transnational, therefore non-American norms, especially those American scholars who see the law in essence as a product of *national* values and cultures.

That the American ideas have not so far found great resonance in other parts of the common law world, let alone in the civil law world, especially not in private law, is not entirely surprising in view of their modest effect on the positive law in the USA so far, as already mentioned, whilst they tend in any event to be oriented more towards governmental interests and intervention, its policy, manner and desired or real impact.

In England, especially private law thinking remains largely dominated by the writings of Austin and later Hart,[127] based on a vivid positivism. Here we also find an intellectual justification for the *national* character of that law which leaves Parliament absolutely sovereign in its

---

[124] See eg Penner, Schiff, Nobles (eds), *Jurisprudence and Legal Theory* (Oxford 2002).

[125] See exceptionally RD Cooter, "Structural Adjudication and the New Law Merchant: A Model of Decentralised Law", 14 *Int'l Rev of Law and Economics* (1994), 215.

[126] See eg John H. Jackson, "International Economic Law: Reflections on the 'Boilerroom of International Relations'" (1995) 10 *Am U J Int'l L & Pol'y*, 595 and for a discussion D Kennedy, "The International Style in Postwar Law and Policy" (1995) 10 *Am U J Int'l L & Pol'y*, 671. They focus in that context mainly on the removal of tariffs and quantitative restrictions without a cost analysis *per se* and present in essence a pragmatic rather than a theoretical approach, especially in the issue of re-regulation at international level (primarily in WTO/GATT/GATS).

This approach is not concerned with methodology or deeper theoretical insights. See for a criticism on this point JP Trachtman, "John Jackson and the Founding of the World Trade Organisation: Empiricism, Theory and Institutional Imagination" (1999) 20 *Mich J Int'l L* 175 and earlier, RA Posner, "The Decline of Law as an Autonomous Discipline: 1962–1987" (1987) 100 *Harv L Rev* 761 also touching on the lack of interdisciplinary work in the area of international economic law and on the dominance of positivism and utopian ideals in that area. See for a more recent comment on this discussion M Koskennieni, "Letter to the Editors of the Symposium" (1999) 93 *Am J Int'l L* 351 suggesting that lawyers employ the tools of any method they find useful in a particular case and should not be guided by any one in particular.

[127] *The Concept of the Law* (1961, 2nd unchanged edn, 1994).

formation, although, as we saw, that does not rule out the further autonomous development of common law and equity *per se*. Other competent organisms of a national character (like judges on the basis of their professional practices) may contribute in the application of the law but there is no true place for non-national sources of law, not in truth for public international law either, and within England not even for custom or legal principle (which in this approach is seen as primitive law), let alone for an international law merchant. Legal formalism thrives in such an environment and is, as we saw, still largely the adopted method of much legal scholarship in the UK.

In England, the approach of Hart was fundamentally criticised by the American Ronald Dworkin,[128] his successor in Oxford, in whose views social and policy considerations play an important role and figure in legal principles. Fundamental criticism also followed from the writings of the American Rawls,[129] in which a search was made for the fundamental legal principles common to all civilised legal systems to arrive at a more objective and universal notion of fairness and justice in a modern redistributive social environment. The basic discretion and arbitrariness in rule making by the competent authorities is here questioned. However, in as far as legal theory is at all of interest in the development of English law, which remains largely practitioner dominated (especially by the Bar), the approach of Hart remains still the prevalent one and appears unavoidably nationalistic, insular and formalistic.

The conclusion of the foregoing is that in terms of the functioning of other than national legal orders and the sources of law in such orders — which is the prime concern of practitioners of the international law merchant and of this book — little progress has been made so far at the intellectual level, even in the new American realist schools although academic support is in common law countries at this moment more likely to come from American than from modern English academic thought in focussing on the cultural, sociological and economic undercurrents in the operation of other communities, like the international economic community of merchants and financiers that may exercise autonomous law making powers within its own area leading in commerce and finance to the development of the new international *lex mercatoria* as the law for that community. So far, the progress has probably been greater at the practical rather than at the intellectual level.

1.3 Civil and Common Law Compared. The Impact of Modern Regulatory and Mandatory Laws on Both. Public Policy and Governmental Interests

1.3.1 *The Relation between Statutory and Non-statutory Law in Civil and Common Law. Sources of Law: General Principles, Custom and Statutory Positivism*

Before going further into the operation of the new *lex mercatoria* or international law merchant, we may consider in greater detail the differences between civil and common law as they operate at present and which were already the subject of some discussion earlier and of the summary in sections 1.1.2 and 1.1.3. These differences are here more broadly considered, first from the perspective of the creation of new more international and universal commercial laws, their operation and the place they are likely to take beside

---

[128] *Taking Rights Seriously* (1977).
[129] J Rawls, *A Theory of Justice* (1971) and *Political Liberalism* (1996).

domestic laws. It poses amongst others the question which legal tradition is likely to be followed. It was already noted before that the way forward is likely to be more in the common law mould. That is so for linguistic reasons, but it is also so because of the greater flexibility in common law that in commercial and financial law especially derives from equity in proprietary matters and from a greater receptiveness in respect of practices and customs.

Another important factor is perhaps that the common law approach is much more used to moving from case to case or from one commercial structure to another and works on the basis of the facts and actual needs more than on the basis of broad rules captured in a pre-existing system to which all further rules must conform. The new law merchant that has no natural legislator (except to some extent in treaty law which is always likely to remain patchy) is more likely to develop in a similar way. Finally, common law was in its development not intellectual but pragmatic even if especially in the American UCC intellectualisation and intellectual coherence is much more apparent. It is, however, not an objective in itself and the facilitating nature of this type of law remains prevalent. A similar attitude may be expected in the law *lex mercatoria* as it concords more with the needs of commerce and finance than the systematic approach of the civil law which is primarily rule based. It is therefore often self-confining and withdraws too readily into intellectual reasoning on the basis of established rules in the formal legal tradition. Common law can also do so, especially in academic circles as we saw, but it tends to be to the detriment of a proper balancing of justified interests and may too easily lead to a disregard of the parties' needs and to a denial of the dictates of common sense which especially in commerce and finance are important driving forces and part of the dynamics of the international business world.

The significance of the discussion so far is in this connection the following. By the beginning of the nineteenth century, Continental private law had largely developed *spontaneously* to the point where it was able to formulate a large number of substantive legal rules on which individuals could base and claim their most important individual or subjective rights. They were no longer forced to rely on more narrowly defined causes or forms of action or enforcement rights, which could only be raised and obtained in a procedural context. In formulating substantive legal rules in this manner, it proved possible to connect them intellectually into a system that was internally coherent or could at least pretend that it was. This provided at the same time a clearer basis for interpretation, which was thus sustained by systematic considerations or analogy. It reduced its more subjective and historical elements. At least that was the idea. These rules themselves were drawn not only from Roman law casuistry but also from Canon and local laws or from more general principles seen as part of the natural law which itself had become secularised. Indeed this was the achievement of the natural law school. The emphasis thus shifted from an inductive to a deductive approach of rule finding and application.

In what was to become the civil law, it became thus possible to formulate general rules of contracts (which became generally binding) in terms of offer and acceptance, consensus and its defects, enforcement and excuses. It also became possible to arrive at a unified concept of negligence, and to develop a single system of property law based on internally connecting notions of ownership, possession and holdership which also allowed for other more limited, derivative proprietary rights to develop, like income and enjoyment rights through usufructs, easements and some types of long leases, and even security interests. These proprietary rights could be set apart from obligatory rights and the difference could be illustrated in relation to rights and duties of third parties in respect of the assets concerned, particularly in relation to the recovery rights of creditors of a bankrupt debtor in (constructive) possession of the assets, which would be postponed or be ranked in relation to the proprietary interests of others if they had some security or similar proprietary interest in the asset also. Another aspect was the free alienability of these *proprietary* income and enjoyment rights (therefore without consent of the owner). This did not apply to security interests, the proprietary nature of which was, as just mentioned, illustrated by their priority status in the secured asset and their ranking amongst each other according to the time of their creation (in principle).

The codification drive, in which on the European Continent legislation moved to centre stage, was a separate nineteenth century development. It needed the substantive rule formulation and subjective rights approach which were largely the achievement of the earlier secularised natural law school but was itself inspired by the evolution of the modern state in which the concept and formulation of a national law became a priority. It was meant to help consolidate these states and to support their central power, but it also intended to promote uniformity, equality and predictability in the exercise of their citizens' rights whilst doing away with antiquated, diverse and often regional rules. In these latter objectives one recognises the older ideals of the Enlightenment. It required a legislative drive which in due course also became an important vehicle perceived to support and even enhance the national social order and its economy. Thus legislation provided a ready and natural vehicle for reform, adaptation and greater efficiency. In the process, the idea of individualism and unchangeable natural law principles weakened unless they were more narrowly defined by statute as inalienable human rights. An overarching notion of statehood, national communities and national economies took over.

On the European Continent, positive law of a *nationalistic* nature thus became dominant whilst increasingly the only recognised true source of the law was the statute, even for law of a private nature that was not meant to be mandatory but rather directory. Another aspect of this development was that all legal structures like contracts and property rights were believed dependent on such law, therefore on state fiat. In this approach, the impact of custom and practices and even party of autonomy on the law was there by state authorisation only.

In *civil law*, the inclination of state law thus became to neutralise or push out other sources of private law. This affected first the old customary laws, but also fundamental or general principles of law whilst natural law notions became increasingly discredited. Even the international law merchant could not survive in that climate. Communities if not statist or state recognised were in their law-making capabilities also increasingly ignored. In that atmosphere, even new custom was accepted only if reduced to the parties' will as implied terms or made allowance for in statutes, which were thought to prevail over all earlier law in the same area, even if not directly conflicting.

In fact, the private law statutes started to exude the pretence of being all-embracing in the areas they meant to cover. The existence of gaps was then denied and all were considered complete on the basis of a proper interpretation of theses statutes themselves, whilst case-law acquired importance merely in that context. The other fiction was that solutions for all legal conflict would automatical follow the logical interpretation of this kind of law. Equality, consistency and legal certainty were in this manner considered guaranteed.

This became the attitude of the major civil law codifications (even if it became particularly stretched in interpretation, see section 1.3.2 below).[130] Although in civil law countries large areas of private law remained technically the subject of separate statutes, that did not make a difference as they were deemed to have the same status and approach. However,

---

[130] Koschaker, n. 5 *supra*, 279 attributed this attitude to 18th century thinkers like Wolf, but considered the idea abandoned in the free law finding movement of the earlier 20th century in Germany. See for the attitude of Portalis, s. 1.2.9 *supra*.

they never did cover, alone or together, all areas of private law and naturally could consider themselves complete only in the areas they did cover. Yet, there was an ethos that proper law and individual rights (and duties) could no longer legally exist in fields of both public and private law that were not covered by statutes, therefore by domestic legislation. All law thus became statist in nature. Even the human rights or the rights deduced from them were often thought to require a domestic statutory basis, mostly found in the national constitutions and could, as we saw, often not even be tested directly by the courts to overrule other statutory laws. It was not necessarily lack of concern, but in these countries parliament or the legislature were thought to be prevalent in these matters and have the last word rather than the courts.

The fundamental technical difference with common law is not, however, in the statutory nature of the private law or in its codification as such. As we saw, much private law is in common law countries now also contained in statutes. The basic differences are in (a) the civil law's *monopolisation* of the sources of the law by legislation, (b) in its claim to completeness, and (c) to systematic coherence. Common law never accepted the exclusivity of statutory law and always retained two other basic sources: (common) law and equity, and in fact also custom as a fourth source, see the key Sections 1–103 (a)(2) and (b) (1–102(2)(b) and 1–103 old) UCC in the USA already referred to several times above.

It means foremost that the common law does not have the civil law constraints as to the recognition of other sources of law and certainly does not give the same pre-eminence to statutory law. Even where, like in England it has at least in legal scholarship probably become no less black letter law oriented and systematic, this system is still less closed and there is greater acceptance of other sources of law (like equity and custom), even if in England the role of custom as an independent legal source is often questioned (although less in commercial law). In the US, that is much less problematic and there is there also the political role of the courts which allows more easily for alternatives motivated e.g. by ethical, social, cultural or economic considerations as was discussed more extensively in section 1.2.13 above in the context of the discussion of 'legal realism'.

This does not mean, however, that such an approach is *per se* less nationalistic. Thus, even though common law never accepted the primacy of statutory law — in fact interpreted it restrictively even when mandatory, as we saw, in order to leave as much room as possible for the other legal sources, especially equity and to a lesser extent custom — one may find amongst its practitioners and scholars, especially in England, no less a belief in the concept of national law to the extent that no law can exist beyond it, see for the theoretical base in the notion of sovereignty also section 1.2.12 above.[131] This view is not necessarily wary of principles and customary law (although it is in the English positivist variant which considers custom atavistic), as long as they are of a domestic nature, therefore in England English, and part of a *national* legal system. It follows that in this approach there is little room for international principle and practices as overarching and prevailing in cross-border activities. On this view, (national) judges will apply only a national law (although it could be that of other states under the rules of private international law or comity) and ignore all others.

This view is not uncommon in the US either, see also section 1.2.13 above, especially not in the more critical legal studies or sociological approaches, even though in that country there may be greater freedom in respect of legal rules or black letter law itself. Acceptance of fundamental and general principle is here much less of a problem, but there

---

[131] See eg Mustill, "Contemporary Problems in International Commercial Arbitration" 17 *Int Bus Law* 161*ff*, who even considered as absolutely void a contract in which transnational law is chosen as controlling.

is here often distinct nationalism also, in so far that they may for there acceptance be required to have been in or be attributable to the American notion of culture or its values.

The civil law's reliance on statutory law, its claim to exclusivity, completeness and especially systematic coherence, present the real theoretical differences with the common law, which has a direct bearing on the discussion following below on the sources of law in different legal orders. On the other hand, legal formalism or realism may divide very differently between common and civil law as we saw in section 1.2.13 and are forces known to both. There are of course other differences between common and civil law. It is clear, eg, that the common law was itself much more of a long historical accident. Especially in England, it is still largely casuistic and even statutory law tends to be directed towards special situations. Typical common law lawyers mostly look for more precise, narrowly drawn rules in legislation, to specific rules distilled from case-law whose holdings are narrowly construed, or otherwise to the case nearest to the present factual situation rather than to a more general rule except in modern legal scholarship that has, however, not yet attained the same high standing as in civil law and remains as we saw especially in England often formalistic and black letter rule construction oriented.

Common law also abandoned its action-oriented approach much later than civil law did and was in any event much slower in the formulation of substantive rules and subjective rights, although, through the *stare decisis* rule and statutory law, substantive rules are also actively formulated in common law. Here the difference with the civil law is that these rules are still not similarly connected or further developed within a (more or less) coherent system and do not pretend to be complete. Again they tend to be narrowly construed. It means that in common law individual decisions cannot always be so easily reconciled with the rest and there is certainly amongst the judges no primary concern with doing so, although again academic writing often gives a different impression and looks by its very nature for more coherence.

As mentioned before, there is here an important modern difference in emphasis between England and the US with legal teaching being much more conceptual in the US which also shows in modern American statutory draftmanship which has become much more intellectual and thus systematic. It was already observed in this connection that the UCC, even the federal Bankruptcy Code, and the Restatements read much more like civil law codes. Also in the US legal realism takes a greatly different view of interpretation and the role of policy objectives and extra-legal considerations therein,[132] see again the discussion in sections 1.2.12 and 1.2.13 above. On the other hand, in codification countries it may well be the case that in the development of tort law, systemic reasoning has become weaker so that in that area the approximation derives from deconceptualisation in civil law and from a more modern casuistic approach. In England, on the other hand, even in legislation, general principle remains disliked and mistrusted. Only the greatest judges like Lord Mansfield and Lord Denning looked for it.

Still, at least on its face, civil law remains more intellectual, conceptual, idea- and perhaps policy-driven, therefore also more activist, and, it could be argued, less stable but probably also more responsive to social change in its statutory approach and its systemic reasoning in case-law interpretations. Here again, the US seems to have moved closer to the civil law attitude but still depends more on liberal (non-systemic) interpretation techniques in case-law and on legal scholarship than on statute, even in its more policy and culturally oriented attitude to the law as now expressed in the 'law and …' movements. It never

---

[132] See for these important differences also PS Atiyah and RS Summers, *Form and Substance in Anglo-American Law: A Comparative Study of Legal Reasoning, Legal Theory and Legal Institutions* (London, Clarendon Press, 1987).

aspired to systematic unity or made systematic interpretation a priority, and its reliance on ethical, social and economic arguments in its interpretation technique is more open. Traditional common law was in any event always flexible in its move from case to case and especially in private law can be more practical than civil law. It has for example a very different and, through equity, a much more flexible open system of property law concerning chattels and intangible assets as we saw, allowing all kind of income and use rights and temporary and conditional ownership rights to operate, counter-balanced on the other hand by a much broader protection of *bona fide* purchasers or purchasers in the ordinary course of trade. It also has a very practical device in trust law and has a much more matter-of-fact attitude to possession and its protection. Agency, assignments, security interests, constructive trust, tracing and restitution are other areas where the common law (especially through equity) has shown greater originality in the past.

Yet all these differences, although especially in proprietary law of great importance, are relative and can be matters of detail compared to the just mentioned much more fundamental distinction that statutory law has essentially a different status and function in civil law. This is so even if in common law statutory texts are now often as pervasive in its coverage,[133] whilst in civil law case-law has gained enormously in importance, to which the whole development of the notion of good faith in contract law testifies. On the other hand, the important struggle between 'legal formalism' and 'legal realism' cuts through both systems and neither may be identified with either the one or the other system.

The exclusive civil law *legislative* attitude presents a uniquely nationalistic nineteenth century phenomenon, now often considered the ultimate democratic ideal, although, at first, this legislation was by no means always the result of a democratic process in the modern sense: the Prussian, French and Austrian Codes were certainly not so enacted. The exclusive statutory attitude did not find support in history either; to this extreme extent not even in the Justinian Codification, as we saw. The *Constitutio Tanta*, which introduced the *Corpus Iuris* in 533 AD, went in the same direction only by not allowing additional comment to emerge. Natural law, local laws and custom were never excluded as independent sources of the law, whilst the Justinian system, although meant to embrace in principle all the law,was not intrinsically sufficiently coherent to support completeness and exclusivity, which were in any event never claimed for it during the reception of this law in Europe(in the *Ius Commune*). It could not have been in view of the acknowledged attitude towards domestic laws (see section 1.2.4 above). The exclusivity of legislation as the sole source of private law was also entirely alien to Grotius' natural law school. To repeat, it was a unique nineteenth century political imperative connected with the centralisation of rule-making in the modern state, the need to do away with legal diversity, promote communities at the national level, update the law, and make it a vehicle of the objectives of modern statehood and its infrastructure, need for efficiency and cost reduction. It resulted in the complete nationalisation of all law on the European Continent.

It was already observed before that even in the countries of the codification, this exclusivity and completeness of statutory law was never universally accepted and often denied by some of the greatest jurists.[134] This may be easily demonstrated in the prevailing attitudes towards interpretation and supplementation, first of statutory law and later of contracts. In Germany, this became obvious in the free law-finding movement of the beginning of the twentieth century, see section 1.2.10 above. There were in any event always new policy or overriding social notions to be taken into account, even if this was still done

---

[133] See also K Zweigert & H Koetz, *An Introduction to Comparative Law* (3rd edn, 1997), 265.
[134] See for the Swiss attitude in Article 1 of its Civil Code, s 1.2.9 *supra*.

under the guise of interpretation of the prevailing codifications or similar statutory laws. As just mentioned, the thin basis of the exclusivity of statutory law became particularly clear in connection with the use of the good faith notion in civil law and the status of newly developing customary law and commercial practices, at least as directory, supporting or supplementing law: see more in particular chapter 2, section 1.3, and for custom also section 1.5.2 below. In the meantime, it could not be denied that even mandatory statutory law could become a dead letter or often had other than the intended effect and could at least in international cases not be considered in isolation but in pertinent instances had to be weighed against the interests of other states.

It is true that there was an argument that invoking good faith or custom was acceptable only when it was especially authorised by prevailing codified contract law (*cf* Sections 157 and 242 BGB in Germany and Articles 1134 and 1135 Cc in France for the interpretation and supplementation of contracts), but, at least in Germany, it became clear that good faith was a source of law that could impact also on company and even proprietary law or, as good morals (*bonnes mœurs*) or *gute Sitten*, even in the law of secured transactions that had no special provisions for it. New Dutch law (Article 3.12 CC) refers in this connection to generally recognised legal principles, the convictions living in the (Netherlands) population at large and the social and personal interests involved. The progressive impact of fundamental, human law-related rights is now increasingly recognised also in private law, therefore even between citizens.[135]

In a civilised society, it is increasingly understood that under the rule of law, modern states cannot and should not attempt to manipulate everything through legislation and that there is a limit to it, certainly also in private law. There is also a limit in the sense that not all can be comprehended by legislators and in practice legislation is often far behind as this type of legislative activity in which the political content is often small has no priority in the parliamantary agendas. When it is pushed through it is usually civil servant driven. Yet, the fact that modern codifications do still not easily tolerate fundamental legal principles to be applied, even if human rights related (unless itself allowed for in statutes), and to operate beside and over it, makes these codifications vulnerable to manipulation, especially in view of the extensive interpretation needs. These codes can be unprincipled, are often devoid of values and have, in a moral vacuum, certainly proven to be able to swing with any kind of regime, however objectionable, and support it.

It is submitted in this connection that fundamental and general principles as legal norms are not basically different from legal rules. Precision and detail is only a matter of degree. In fact, in the judicial practices broader principle will be narrowed to a more precise rule in individual cases on the basis of the facts whilst narrower rules will be broadened in the interpretation process on the basis of underlying principles at least if fairness or public policy require the rule to apply in the circumstances to related situations. It follows that in general it is not possible to say whether principle or rule produce the more predictable result or indeed in how far they can be distinguished, except in formal ways, in the sense of statutory or non-statutory principle.

In the USA, under the due process and similar clauses in the federal Constitution, the impact of fundamental principle had long been clearer, even in private law, at least in the elaboration and application of procedural and conflict of laws rules.[136] There is in fact also the all pervading reach of the Bill of Rights and the ability of the courts to declare statutes

---

[135] See in Germany eg CW Canaris, *Grundrechte und Privatrecht, eine Zwischenbilanz* (Berlin, 1998).
[136] See for modern conflicts law, s 2.1 *infra*.

unconstitutional. But also elsewhere, general principle could never be entirely ignored either. The law of tort and its development was always a reflection of what was considered anti-social, as such in many civil law countries still an extra-statutory norm which has nevertheless legal status. Bad behaviour may now also become legally relevant in environmental law, again as extra-statutory norm. So is (often) the notion of good government and the administrative law protection of citizens against government that derives from it.

In an EU context, the question of the *sources* of the private law has come up in the interpretation of private law conventions, like the Brussels Convention on Jurisdiction and the Enforcement of Judgments in Civil and Commercial Matters (the 1968 Brussels Convention)[137] now succeeded by Regulation and the proper implementation of the Directives touching on private law harmonisation, like those operating in the consumer area. The distinctive interpretation technique of the European Court of, for example, what is contractual or not, what is a consumer contract or an employment contract or not, what is a bankruptcy matter or not, and how requirements of good faith should be defined, is not based on national laws or on principles deduced from them, see also section 2.3.2 below. The European Court maintains its own normativity in this respect, which it finds in *European principles* and not necessarily in national laws. This attitude necessarily filters through into the national courts of Member States in the areas of private law subject to European law, which these national courts must uphold.

Public international law always recognised a wide variety of legal sources, culminating in Article 38(1) of the Statute of the International Court of Justice that refers to fundamental principles, contract and custom as major and independent sources of law.[138] On the other hand, in private law, any notion of exclusivity of domestic private law legislation bars the further development of the law in support of the internationalisation of business that goes by its own distinct rules and insists on internationally accepted standards and protections as we already saw. The diversity of the sources of law in modern commerce, the hierarchy of norms in its legal order, and the creation of substantive uniform rules within it remains therefore a difficult and sensitive subject that will be explored more fully in section 1.5 below.

1.3.2 Legal Attitudes in Civil and Common Law: The Role of Interpretation and the Attitude to Fact and Law-Finding

In the previous section, the main difference between common and civil law was identified in the attitude to private law legislation, more in particular in the exclusivity and systematical completeness the civil law codes (and related statutes) claim for themselves as sources of law. This pretence of exclusivity and completeness makes these Codes dependent for their credibility on liberal interpretation powers of judges and therefore often on considerable judicial freedom and inventiveness. Thus if a new type of contract became fashionable, its rules, if not determined by the parties in the contract, would technically speaking somehow have to be deduced from the general provisions concerning contracts in the applicable codes. Guidance would additionally be sought in the statutory provisions concerning special contract types that could be considered related when an exercise in making

---

[137] See the line of cases starting with European Court Case 12/76, *Tessili v Dunlop AG*. See for the EU good faith notion, chapter 2, s 1.3.4.
[138] See also Roy Goode on this divergence in attitude between public and (civil law) private law in the acceptance of different sources of law, in "Usage and its Reception in Transnational Commercial Law" [1997] *Int'l and Comp LQ* 1 and JH Dalhuisen, "International Law Aspects of Modern Financial Products" [1998] *EB LR* 281.

proper distinctions would follow but also in systematical and analogical interpretation. Thus one could ask whether directors of companies had an agreement with the company in the nature of employment contract or a contract for the provision of services or rather a contract of a *sui generis* type that had nevertheless some features of both.

This could allow case-law to produce over a period of time a whole system of new rules for that particular new contract. Another example may be found in the modern brokerage contract as an elaboration of the contract of agency. It takes longer to reach the appropriate level of modern investor protection against the broker and his practices and be less comprehensive than new legislation, but it is often the only way in the absence of much interest or a clear view from legislators. Thus it was unavoidable that in many civil law countries, much of the law of companies, partnerships and employment was developed in case-law and legal practice on the basis of only rudimentary code provisions, only subsequently aided by legislation.

The common law does not operate here very differently but would rely more in particular and more comfortably on case-law that would develop from situation to situation on the basis of the facts rather than of deductive anology in the application of rules. In fact, deeper differences with civil law have been spotted in this method of the common law and in its fact- and law-finding technique itself. It concerns here mainly its great reliance on facts and its more *casuistic and inductive* approach to law-finding, certainly in areas not covered by rules derived from precedent or statutory law, although even in England at present at least half of the cases are somehow statute interpretation-related (whilst case-law has, on the other hand, become much more important in civil law). There is here convergence of sorts, although, as we saw in section 1.2.12 above, in private law, statutory law never aspires to completeness in common law, whilst statutory interpretation remains a different matter in civil and common law and is, at least in England, still more literal, logical or syllogistic, and therefore less liberal and basically meant to resolve particular fact situations and not to defining a more general rule, see for the more literal, logical, and deductive or inductive interpretation techniques also section 1.2.13 above.

In England, statutory law is not conceptual either and the way of drafting statutes normally remains geared to special fact situations only and not to stating principle. Statutory interpretation accepts this and does not go beyond it. As far as case-law is concerned, whilst it is true that civil law now also greatly relies on it and therefore on precedent as well if only to provide stability to the interpretation of its codes, civil law never accepted the *stare decisis* rule. It is less necessary where the basic framework of rules is still formulated in a code supported by systemic reasoning. It remains nevertheless an important difference.

More importantly, it is true that in the method of fact- and law-finding itself, there remain some important differences. The civil law lawyer departs from a point where there is some given system of rules and principles and attempts to deduce further rules and principles from them and from the system itself to apply in the case before him. He will spot the relevant facts in the light of these rules and principles which provide for him a guide from the outset. The common law lawyer, on the other hand, will first look at the facts and will then ask himself what relevant rule can be found in precedents or in legislation that may be nearest or that otherwise may have application to the particular case.

In all rule formulation and certainly in statutory law, the traditional common law lawyer thus takes an *ad hoc* attitude and wants precise, fairly narrow rules and in statutes clear definitions, an attitude which the civil law lawyer is likely to adopt only in criminal cases. The civil law lawyer lives happily with greater abstractions and more general ideas. They quickly stake out the field for him, whilst the detail is left for later in any proceedings, that is for more precise interpretation on the basis of the facts. For the civil law lawyer, too precise a rule is often seen as an unnecessary limitation, giving rise to distorted interpretation, to incongruous results, and extra litigation costs.[139]

Much more can be made of this, and from the common law's emphasis on the facts closely tied to its trial practice (even in civil cases sometimes still before juries, especially in the USA where there is a constitutional right to them). This trial practice is indeed geared to fact finding and discovery to get all information first. In common law proceedings, it is as a procedural matter necessary to prevent any surprise in court (still considered to include a jury although in private law cases they are very rare outside the USA where there is a Constitutional right to a jury in all cases but it can be and is often waived for cost reasons). In this system, the court sits in only one session (which may go on for days, however). In civil law, further particulars may be sought and dealt with in subsequent meetings of the courts as and when they become necessary.

This difference is one of procedure, not necessarily one of substance, but the (often excessive) emphasis on fact finding remains a typical common law feature, not to the same extent shared in civil law. The civil law lawyer, on the basis of more abstract rules, seems to be able to distinguish sooner between facts that are or may become legally relevant and facts that are not. As a consequence, the civil law fact-finding operation tends to be less expensive and this is certainly an important reason why going to court in civil law countries is often much cheaper. This difference should not be exaggerated, especially not since the pre-ordained system of rules resulting in civil law from codification is often also patchy, out of date, and in any event frequently too unfocussed to be of immediate help so that the facts play a greater role (like in good faith situations and now also in much of the law of negligence). Yet the difference in cost is glaring, practical, and highly visible. This is aggravated in England by the multiplication of lawyers' functions and fees: those of solicitors, barristers and QCs in larger cases, whilst much of the rules of procedure and evidence is still determined by the jury tradition even if in private cases they are (in England) now hardly ever present.

Thus there clearly continues to be a different attitude to fact finding in civil and common law and to the guidance of the applicable law in finding the relevant facts early on. Common law is here thought to be primarily inductive on the basis of the facts and civil law deductive on the basis of its rules. Yet modern common and civil law are here often less far apart than may appear at first.[140] In civil law, the better rules and principles to be deduced from the codified system are in practice often also found on the basis of distinguishing rules and precedent in the light of the particular facts presented, much the same as in common law. Thus also in civil law, the key is often to construe in an *inductive* manner a broader rule from a narrower principle that may have emerged in a previous case. In common law, on the other hand, a more *deductive* approach looking for consistency amongst the rules that may be found in case-law and legislation also became apparent.

The main difference seems to be that in civil law the rules so found must still find additional support in the Code or its system or otherwise be cast in such a way that no conflict

---

[139] Here again, like in statutory interpretation, see s. 1.2.9 *supra*, exposure to European law may make a difference in English law, see C Schiemann, "The Application of General Principles of Community Law by English Courts" in M Andenas and F Jacobs, *European Community Law in the English Courts*, (1998) 136. See for important comments on the differences between common and civil law legal thinking also W Fikentscher, 2 *Methoden des Rechts* (1975). See for an incisive comment on the nature of the common law further, M Eisenberg, *The Nature of the Common Law* (1988).

[140] See for a classic essay in legal reasoning in respect of case law, statutory law and constitutional law in the US, which has retained its value until this day, EH Levi, *An Introduction to Legal Reasoning* (Univesrity of Chicago Press 1949, 1962). Here a sharp distinction between a deductive and inductive approach is questioned within the common law itself.

arises unless the relevant codified rules have clearly become a dead letter or have been interpreted away altogether. Common law is still more at ease with deviating cases or cases that do not fit very well in the greater scheme of things.

The modern teleological and normative interpretation approaches in either civil or common law, do not accept either that rules in order to be effective must be intrinsically consistent and that justice automatically results from a mechanical application of the written or otherwise established rules. They suggests a freer or more liberal attitude to interpretation, itself implied in the civil law approach to code interpretation as we saw, although subsequently often encapsulated in systemic reasoning. Civil law seems here to go through phases.

Interpretration seemed freer in the 1960s and 1970s, may be less so now at least in legal scholarship and in the lipservice cases always pay to the system. In countries with new codifications like the Netherlands, the systematic approach has certainly received some boost since 1992. In a freer approach, objectivity may be a less absolute objective as ethical, social, economic and other considerations enter the law, although it may be right that they should only do so in more pressing cases where one may assume substantial community support. Otherwise, these considerations could easily lead to conflicting results.

The practical differences are fairly obvious. Where in a codified system there may be only a limited number of proprietary rights, a freer, more practical and less systematic interpretation method may allow (exceptionally) for the development of newer proprietary interests if so demanded by commerce and financial practice. Indeed, this happened in Germany with the creation of the non-possessory security interest of the *Sicherungsübereignung* in chattels and in the development of the proprietary conditional ownership expectation in the reservation of title, leading to the concept of the *dingliche Anwartschaft*, see for these legal structures more particularly chapter 5, section 1.4.1. These were major case-law developments, upon a proper analysis going against the (closed proprietary) system of the BGB, even if often explained as developments *praeter legem*, therefore as being parallel to and therefore not truly in conflict with the existing system.[141] As another example, in common law, the movement to accept the binding nature of offers, therefore regardless of the consideration requirement that made them logically (on pure syllogism) unenforceable, may be abandoned between merchants on business grounds (as was indeed done in the UCC). Here we see extra-legal or economic considerations leading to profound legal adjustment in which a normative interpretation of a rule allows for the evolution of alternative legal structures.

In a similar manner, the concept of good faith or acceptable morals (*gute Sitten*) may be used in bankruptcy to deny proprietary execution rights or to readjust seniority and priorities against the rules laid down for them.[142] In the civil law of agency, the direct proprietary rights of principals in assets (goods or proceeds) the (undisclosed) agent buys or receives for them in his own name may also become more firmly established against the system. Constructive trust and tracing rights could even appear, all in aid of practical commercial and financial needs or, perhaps on a higher note, to prevent a windfall for others, notably creditors of the agent, who without this redress might become unjustly enriched in their own recovery possibilities. Conditional or temporary ownership rights may equally become more acceptable to underpin the safety of modern financial products, like finance leases and repurchase agreements. Acceptance of the concept of the formal trust in civil law

---

[141] See also JH Dalhuisen, "European Private Law: Moving From a Closed to an Open System of Proprietary Rights", 5 *Edinburgh LR* (2001), 1.
[142] See chapter 5, n. 147 and accompanying text.

may then not be far a way,[143] but again it should be realised that civil law presents no legal unity and different civil law countries may here take to very different attitudes.

Yet it may exactly be the benefit of a more systematic interpretation that no Pandora's box is opened and that at least some room for the traditional bankruptcy law principles and considerations is preserved, thus favouring the common creditors of a debtor over those who claim all kinds of proprietary interests and retrieval rights in his assets.

In the traditional common law, the teleological or normative interpretation technique is as such not favoured in civil and commercial matters and has hardly a place in the literal interpretation attitude to statutes, although it is much more important in the US, where, in legal realism, it now has a very firm base, see section 1.2.13 above. Modern Continental and American attitudes may more readily converge here and have also started to apply these techniques to contractual interpretation, even to the point of the Americans becoming comfortable with the good faith concept, see also chapter 2, section 1.3.2. Yet the inveterate germanic desire for systematisation, even in good faith case-law, was noted earlier, see section 1.2.10 above.

In England, there is now at least the *purposive* approach: see more in particular section 1.2.12 above, but it does not amount to a more fully normative approach. It is often distinguished from teleological interpretation. In contract interpretation, there is a stronger normative element in modern common law, however, also in England, in the notion of reliance, implied terms or distinctions between the character and nature of legal relationships, like between professional and non-professional dealings, as we shall see better in chapter 2. EU legislation and its interpretation force English judges more generally into teleological interpretation of European scripts. Even so, the idea that justice will follow automatically from a more technical application of statute and precedent remains more vivid in common law of the English variety and in modern civil law than it is at present in the US.[144]

As we saw, in the US under the influence of notably Holmes, Pound and Llewellyn, there emerged an increasing interest in the law as it functioned in society or the law in action and in its operational sufficiency. Social considerations and policy issues became as a consequence much more important in the interpretation of the law, in which constitutional interpretation techniques and needs started to show the way. It subsequently affected the interpretation of statutes more generally. It assumed a view of what was ethically, socially, and perhaps even from the point of view of utility, more desirable. Its effect showed early in the interpretation technique of the UCC (Section 1–103) and is in the USA increasingly important also in contract interpretation. Since the 1970s 'law and …' movements, a more empirical approach, and political studies and desiderata have joined legal scholarship, not only in drafting legislation but also in judicial interpretation. Legal scholarship has been greatly encouraged and intensified along these lines, see again more in particular section 1.2.13 above.

By way of summary, it may probably still be said, however, that, whilst putting the more recent US experiences to one side, common law continues to develop the law step by step on a case-by-case basis and remains in essence fact-oriented. Even if a more general rule is developed and identified, e.g. in statute, there is an inclination always to go back to a more restrictive and incidental approach by distinguishing situations in which the effect of the

---

[143] See also JH Dalhuisen, "Conditional Sales and Modern Financial Products", in A Hartkamp et al (eds), *Towards a European Civil Code*, (2nd edn, 1998), 525.
[144] See for these differences between the US and England, PS Atiyah and RS Summers, *Form and Substance in Anglo-American Law: A Comparative Study of Legal Reasoning, Legal Theory and Legal Institutions* (London, Clarendon Press, 1987).

general rule tends to be limited and a case-by-case approach is resumed. Thus in England, legislation in civil and commercial matters is still primarily considered to cover special situations only, and even if a more general rule is expounded, restrictive interpretation will see to it that a case-by-case attitude is soon resumed. That seems to be in the nature of the English lawyer.

This appears to be different in the USA where a more liberal and expansive approach to statutory interpretation is now often favoured, as borne out even in private law e.g. by the UCC and Bankruptcy Code, which are constantly updated, but no less in the experimentation in the Restatements. Thus in the USA, the treatment of statutory text, which themselves are more conceptual, is becoming more similar to that of the modern civil law approaches. This may well have been the lasting influence of the many German scholars that came to the USA to teach before and after the Second World War, although a more jurisprudential approach to the development of the law and a better appreciation of policy issues in that development was evident in the USA much earlier and already more typical for the American legal tradition. That was not similarly the case in England. The difference with the civil law is that it accepts systematical considereations as a help, but not as a bar. In this it is aided by a similar interpretation technique in respect of the US Constitution and related federal statutes including taxation laws.

It follows that in civil law and in the US, in twentieth century thinking, enormous attention has been given to interpretation and in that context especially to the role of (domestic) judges and their freedom, which is not similarly the case in England. In considering the freedom in the adjudicatory function, the attention unavoidably shifted to the sources of the applicable laws, how to find them, their interrelation and interpretation. It concerns here in essence the limits of legal positivism.

It may well be that under pressure of the internationalisation, the twenty-first century's concern will, as the next step, be the evolution, of other legal orders, to begin with the international commercial and financial legal order, each with an own law creating authority as distinguished from statist or other national legal orders. This will be the quit of the discussion in section 1.4 below. In this evolution, judges even if appointed by states would foremost seek to apply to each case the law emanating from the relevant legal order. Arbitrators would seek to do so all the more and might have here even greater freedom when especially appointed by persons operating within such orders (like the international commercial and financial one). It is the basis for all discussions on the revival of an international law merchant or *lex mercatoria*. All types of judges would have to determine the residual importance of statist laws, especially if mandatory, at least in respect of activities the conduct or effect of which would impact on the territory of the relevant state.

Finally, in civil and commercial matters, it should never be forgotten that the *practical* differences between the various legal systems are not always great, especially in Western culture where there is everywhere a similar combination of the rule of law with a neo capitalist economic and social system. As was already observed before, the greatest *practical* differences between common and civil law as far as commerce and finance is concerned are in the law of equity. This may be clearly seen in the development of fiduciary duties in trust, agency and company law. It may no less be seen in the laws of tracing, equitable liens and similar restitutionary claims, shifting liens, conditional and temporary ownership rights in chattels, and equitable assignments of intangibles.

Again there was in the development of equity much of a case-by-case approach and a dependence on the facts of each case. The result was only an incidental set of remedies which nevertheless tended to be more far reaching than would have been possible 'at law' in a less restrictive attitude to legal development and more flexibility. It meant that there was also less concern for clarity and certainty. Even in the USA, there is here not much of a rule formulating attitude either, except perhaps in a negative sense by cutting out (through case-law and statute) as many equitable proprietary interests as possible to preserve suffi- cient room for the operation of the Bankruptcy Code. Yet they always re-emerge. There is no true equivalent in civil law. In it, the use of the notion of good faith may only some- times point in a similar direction, see also chapter 2, sections 1.3.1 and 1.3.2, but it is mostly limited to contract law. Although as such more comprehensive and less incidental, it is (so far) also less revolutionary. In other parts of the civil law, there may be similar transform- ing forces at work but they are (as yet) not commonly identified as emanating from an equitable source. In commerce and finance, custom and practice must provide the base or otherwise party autonomy, although it is less appropriate especially where in proprietary matters rights of third parties are concerned.

1.3.3 Twentieth-Century Governmental Intervention in Private Law. Governmental Policies, Regulation and Mandatory Domestic Rules. The Effect of Globalisation and the Denationalisation of Private Law

In the previous section, reference was made to social pressures following great social changes, which force the adaptation of the prevailing legal norms, also in private law whether of the common or civil law variety. In either system the outstanding feature of twentieth century legislation has been that the law was not only streamlined especially in codification countries but became more generally imbued by policy considerations or was, in what became the modern welfare state especially after World War II, increasingly used as a public policy tool, even in areas traditionally considered the preserve of private law. It elevated the importance of statutory law further which did not leave the common law behind.

As a consequence, even private law acquired many more mandatory features than before. It was perhaps an unavoidable consequence of (a) the further consolidation of cen- tral government and national administrations in the nineteenth century, (b) the policy objectives of modern states even in capitalist systems, and (c) the acknowledgement that both government and capitalism had to come together to make the modern highly devel- oped and rich economies feasible after a period in which the statist approach had mostly been balanced by a liberal or *laissez faire* economic and social outlook. It disappeared under the pressures of economic shocks and, at least in Europe, of disastesous wars in the first half of the twentieth century. Subsequently, technical developments strengthened govern- ments' idea that they were perhaps better than autonomous market forces at creating the optimum economic and social conditions for a modern society in building and restructuring its infra-structure, actively redistributing wealth, and engaging in what came to be called more broadly 'social engineering'.

The effects of the industrial revolution on weaker parties, especially workers of all ages and both sexes, and the subsequent war and economic crisis measures after World War I had earlier led to increased state intervention. In the economic crisis of the 1930s, there followed the introduction of protectionist measures. It led to an increased division of mar- kets along national lines and, after the abandonment of the gold standard, around own currencies. It resulted in a large number of import and foreign exchange restrictions every- where. After World War II, the economic dangers inherent in this kind of nationalism were understood but budgetaire requirements and fiscal policies in strongly socialised market economies gave rise to new layers of regulation at domestic levels; it was all the easier as national currencies continued to remain isolated subject to national interest rate and currency policies and were, often as a matter of policy, not made freely convertible and transferable in order to allow for a more *dirigiste* nationalistic policy approach in economic and social affairs.

In many European countries, more governmental intervention resulted in this connection at first from national industrialisation policies or nationalisations and central planning objectives, which left whole areas of activity exclusively to state enterprises. Immediately after World War II, this was especially so in the areas of public utilities but was in many countries of Western Europe soon extended to other industries. Subsequently, modern welfare states required mutual insurance and support systems, e.g. in respect of unemployment and old age, to be organised at the national level. In other sectors price controls emerged because of chronic shortages, like in the rental of real estate. The organisation of a modern society with the need for an adequate infrastructure itself exerted many new pressures. Thus inner city and transportation policies and other infrastructure concerns, including health and education, created new areas where public or semi-public law started to impact on the rights and duties of private citizens and companies to operate. Yet the intervention on the basis of a perceived public interest could sharply differ per activity and country. It meant that even in the Western World govermental intervention was by no means uniform.

From a legal point of view, *regulation* is no more than governmental intervention through the law to achieve certain policy objectives. In discussing governmental policies and their implementation, this regulation is usually considered to be economic or social, therefore with an economic or social objective. Although this sounds like an administrative law intervention in terms of licensing and supervision, it may take very different forms. Thus competition policy may also figure under it and even interventions in private law, like the formulation of mandatory private law rules in the area of consumers' protection (notably under new laws concerning unfair contract, terms) or in the area of investors' protection (under the laws of agency or through issuers' disclosure and prospectus liability).

As just mentioned this all proved easier behind state borders, cut off from the international market-place and its management of resources. Unsurprisingly therefore, during large parts of the twentieth century, (domestic) governmental intervention was joined by a simultaneous and intentional control of the international flows of persons, goods, services and money. This had a deep impact on these flows, which at the beginning of the twentieth century had still been largely free worldwide. Whilst the immediate restrictive effects of World War II and the earlier economic depression abated, the emergence of the EEC (later EU) in Europe in 1958 meant to reopen the borders but it made at first only a modest impact. In reality, the 1970s and 1980s showed the high tides of governmental domestic intervention in peace time in Europe (the further cause being the 1970s oil shocks).

In the EU, it took until 1989 before the capital and money flows started to be fully liberated. Only the implementation of the Single European Act in 1992 liberated the goods and services sectors, although some services, like financial ones, had to be re-regulated, partly through harmonisation at European level. It will be dealt with extensively in chapter 6. The monetary union (like the single market foreseen and demanded from the beginning) was only completed after 1992, culminating in the Single Currency in 1999, in which not all Member States participated. In practice, there still continue some important restrictions on the free movement of persons and labour.

In this interventionist climate, private property did not remain as inviolable as it once seemed, contractual freedom in many areas proved more limited than had once been believed, and the freedom of movement of goods, services and money became (at first) more restricted than it had ever been. Modern society as a whole became more centralised and supervised at national levels, which had its effects, both on civil and common law, with wave upon wave of new legislation which also impacted on private law. Had the private law essentially been nationalised in the nineteenth century, the interventionist effect on it showed especially in the twentieth century.

Whatever the pros or cons of this development, it is a fact that the health and wealth of the Western European peoples were promptly restored after the disasters of the first half of the twentieth century. They continued to improve dramatically, regardless or perhaps because of continuing modern government intervention in all spheres of life. The role of modern states in providing a strong economic and social infrastructure internally and in promoting also some order in international economic affairs thus became well-established. This expanded role assumed that the more traditional liberal, democratic and economically decentralist outlook was not fundamentally impaired by a more interventionist or social-democratic stand and that it remained credible by putting emphasis on the essentially still limited nature of this intervention. Although coming at a high regulatory and tax cost, this type of state action became in fact associated with and typical for the richest countries that identified with this type of democratic evolution of the notion of the modern state.

Developments never move in one direction only. Gradually, doubts in terms of efficiency of management and capital, suspicion that the system led to stagnation, higher inflation and unemployment, and resentment of the tax consequences started to weigh on it and contributed to a mood of government re-evalutation and retrenchment. By the 1980's, domestically, privatisation and deregulation became political alternatives that could be discussed and put into practice. Regulation where still necessary, eg in privatised public utilities like rail, electricity and water, became itself the subject of discussions about its objectives and effectiveness and as a consequence less overbearing. Negotiation with affected parties on the details, reliance on forms of self-regulation (in whole or in part), no-action letters and plea-bargaining facilities became more common. The result was that by the turn of the twenty-first century, in modern open societies, there remained a widely accepted role for the modern state (apart from its traditional role in the internal and external security) but there also was a greater consensus that it had to concentrate on health, education and social services, and to some extent on road and rail infrastructure but even the continued acceptance of these remaining roles became more dependent on showing better results. In other areas, state intervention became still stronger, like in environmental matters.

The key point is that public concerns are no longer perceived as being static and requiring a pre-conceived model of governmental intervention and powers. They may change fundamentally over a generation constantly shifting the face of government in the process, but this also means, that, whilst regulation and full public ownership or management must justify themselves continuously, they cannot *a priori* be excluded from any particular field. Although the public will be concerned about power broking in public services, about their monopolies, about any resulting inefficiencies and stagnation, and more in particular about entrenched or immutable bureaucracies, there will also be room for re-nationalisation or re-regulation if private alternatives do not work.

There can be little doubt that in this more recent shift in regulatory outlook towards greater pragmatism, there is an *autonomous international* force at work which can no longer be ignored and has played a decisive countervailing role domestically. It is closely connected with the modern communication revolution which has itself led to a dramatic internationalisation of the flows of people, goods, services and money. This communication revolution, rather than a more liberal attitude domestically, re-activated the market mechanism, now at transnational or global levels and caused a spontaneous break down of national borders. It fundamentally challenged domestic isolation with its monopolies of regulatory power. The early emergence of the GATT and the EEC in Europe may have reflected the beginning of this after World War II, but it is now much more evident in the development of the successor organisations which thus became possible: WTO and EU. Their groundwork was only laid in the late 1980s.

It even led to a more fundamental reconsideration of concepts of national sovereignty. In Europe, within the EU, it made the completion of the Single Market and the Monetary Union, both early EEC objectives, possible. Eventually, even domestic currencies gave way to the Euro as an international currency. The EU itself, being the early product of this evolution and reformed as a framework for the next phase in this development in 1992 at Maastricht, is not immune to further modern worldwide influences either and is no less subject to these strong opening-up undercurrents (leading eg to important concessions in WTO), which, at least in the short term, seem to have been greatly beneficial to all.

Indeed, the result of international market forces appears so far to be greater discipline, less inflation, greater diversity, more competition, more choice, better quality, and lower prices at national levels. Especially in smaller countries, the idea that closed markets and nationalism could provide an adequate level of activity and wealth had to be abandonned. The renewed interest in more liberal social and economic values has on the other hand led to protests of minority groups, especially focussed on international agencies like the IMF and WTO. Clearly, the advance of market forces and their reforming or cleansing dynamics in the above manner are not welcome to all. They are sometimes thought not to square with democratic accountability either, which in this view is seen to be (best) exercised at national levels within complete state control. Any other autonomous and countervailing forces, especially those of the markets, are in this view suspect. That the statist approach had often proved to favour local cabals, reduce openness, promote manipulative practices, and to hold people back, is in this view readily discounted. Yet it can be compellingly argued that most countries of the world (and all the poorer ones) are foremost held back by their own governments, incapable or unwilling to slot properly into a more balanced international economic system that seems to provide the only real hope of creating greater health and wealth for all.

It is true that the corollary of the renewed openness and market-driven impulses has been a major reduction in the ability of national governments to regulate behind their borders and to keep a firm grip on their own economies and domestic markets for whatever purposes, but these governments have also learnt that restrictive domestic policies are likely to undermine growth in the modern world and that it is also easy to drive people, activity and money away. The fall of the communist model after 1989 reinforced this realisation and favoured openess and competitiveness further, thus re-enforcing a re-evaluation that had already started. Internally, it lend support to further deregulation and privatisation, much increased competition and governmental retreat to situations where the strong hand of centrally organising intermediary is more obviously needed. It meant renewed emphasis on the traditional governmental task of guaranteeing internal safety (with concerns for crime and terrorism rising) and a search for a better public/private balance in creating and providing a strong technical and social infrastructure to support private initiative whilst retaining sufficient social balance and coherence.

There is another important sequel. In this environment, domestic regulation, where still necessary, can often no longer be effectively organised in isolation and requires international co-operation. Financial regulation of banks and intermediaries is an example, at least within the EU, and will eventually also need attention in the WTO. In other respects, international financial co-operation has shifted to preventing sudden economic dislocation and (systemic) collapse and also to fighting financial irregularities and fraud. Issues of social cohesion and the environment may acquire also an international flavour.

It often means a shift from domestic over-regulation to a *lighter* or more flexible regulation at international level. Most importantly, it may leave more room for private law and private law structures of protection, like in financial services the law of agency for brokers and investment managers and disclosure liability of new issuers in the capital markets (rather than their licensing or supervision). It is in the international markets a natural consequence of greater dependence on international private initiative as the motor for economic activity and on international (rather than statist) frameworks to provide minimum legal and financial support. It is an expression of greater choice and more options all around which will continue as long as people perceive to prosper from it.

In the law, the emphasis of practical and academic interest shifts accordingly. Whereas at an academic level in the previous generation, for example, the accent was on the development of domestic administrative and tax laws and, in Western Europe, also on the institutional part of European Community law, the emphasis is in Western Europe now rather on the stimulation of the EU's internal market with its free flows of persons, services, goods and capital under a minimum of regulation (limited in a large part to the protection of consumers in cross-border trade and to proper concern for health and safety, and the stability of the monetary, fiscal and financial systems).

The sequel is the further development of the *private law transnationally for professional dealings*, at least within the EU, but more logically at the same time also between all major trading blocks. That favours the international law merchant or *lex mercatoria* revival. The biggest immediate challenge arising from the renewed importance of and interest in private law is indeed the question of its operation at transnational level to encourage cross-border trade, services and finance flows.[145] The more incidental work of Unidroit and Uncitral in this area as well as that of the more practice oriented International Chamber of Commerce (ICC) will be discussed throughout this book from this perspective. The study of general principles of contract and trust laws are other early signs of this new interest. The freedom to apply in international cases unwritten transnational principle and custom in national courts and in international arbitrations is another important feature of this modern tendency,[146] but it needs a broader intellectual *framework and method*, and an *understanding* of what is practically needed and how newly developing commercial and financial structures can best be legally understood and handled in view of past (local) experiences and new (international) market needs.

---

[145] See also J Basedow, "The Renascence of Uniform Law: European Contract Law and its Components" (1998) 18 *Legal Studies* 121.

[146] The LCIA and ICC Arbitration Rules in their newest form give arbitrators great freedom in the application of laws and the use therefore of transnational principle and practice: see Article 17 ICC Rules 1998 and Section 14(2) LCIA Rules 1998. French law (Article 1496 CCP) and Dutch law (Article 1054(2) CCP) now also allow for application of the *lex mercatoria*. The English Arbitration Act of 1996 (Section 46(3)) does not yet do so and follows here the Uncitral Model Law (Article 28) and Rules (Article 33) which refer to conflict of laws rules. Nevertheless even English law now upholds "internationally accepted principles of law governing contractual relations", at least it did do so in respect of an award rendered pursuant to an arbitration governed by Swiss arbitration law: *Deutsche Schachtbau- und Tiefbohrgesellschaft GmbH v Ras al-Kaimah National Oil Co* [1987] 3 WLR 1023. There was no contractual choice of law clause and Article 13(3) of the old ICC Rules was applicable which still referred to settlement of disputes through conflict of law rules. Even then, this requirement seemed no longer to exclude the application of general principles or the transnational law merchant or *lex mercatoria*.

It is probably true that the traditional divide between civil and common law and their methods is becoming here a side show, but it is in the discussions on the future direction still important to clearly understand the differences, especially in terms of systematic thinking and the attitude to alternative sources of law and their autonomy. Another matter to consider is whether we look here in essence at codification or at more informality (like restatements) and if it is to be codification whether that would be in the traditional civil law manner or more in the form of the American Uniform Commercial Code. Of particular interest in this connection will be the attitude within the EU (which itself has only limited competency in matters of private law formation). Will the EU states wish to go for their more traditional approach or opt for another? This will at least in part depend on whether they consider international commercial and financial law still a national/domestic matter albeit at EU level or a matter that affects also the broader international business community.

The civil law tradition here has conceptual thinking on its side, the ability to articulate concise rules and to effectuate sudden change. That has always been the true advantage of codification and the reason behind its generally strong impact and tendency to drive out all other (conflicting) sources of law. Common law has the English language, its flexibility and practical, step-by-step approach on its side and its willingness to consider custom and industry practices. In the US, the best of both approaches would appear combined in the UCC and the Restatements. Short of the creation of statehood and its paraphenalia at EU level, a traditional codification approach seems for the moment less likely in Europe and may in any event in its exclusive statutory attitude at least in commerce and finance be a thing of the past. Business does not need it and may well fear its intellectually imposing approach. Indeed, for the time being, commerce and finance may be better off with a new *lex mercatoria* for themselves, based on practical needs and principle for a broader community. It is the approach in this book and the elements of this law will be explored throughout.

A precondition may be the acceptance of the own transnational professional legal order with its own dynamism, rules that national judges and understanding must start learning to apply. It is an adaptation to a new environment that may be expected to take place within the next generation. It requires a different way of looking at the law which for this purpose needs to be captured in its international dynamics and in its interaction with domestic laws especially if reflecting policy and governmental interests (requiring an assessment at the same time of their international legitimacy in the case at hand). That is even now less of an issue or matter of bewilderment in international arbitrations. It will became less so even in domestic courts if they start understanding their international status in matters of international commerce and finance, as already discussed above at the end of section 1.1.7.

In this manner, the international market-place exerts its own force on the legal developments and the law and courts or international arbitration panels that reflect the new internationality of business. That is a *normal* consequence and evolution. The unavoidable result is a de-nationalisation of private law between professionals everywhere, therefore not only in civil law countries, although it may there be a more fundamental departure. It means a reversal of the nineteenth century nationalisation and the twentieth century publification tendencies in private law itself, which also emerged in non-codified legal systems. In this debate, no internationally oriented lawyer or any lawyer with an international business can truly remain neutral or disinterested. At this juncture, there is here a particular role for academic research and teaching to play. They should provide the insights and tools to facilitate the thought process concerning the evolution of this new law, its nature, operation and enforcement.

It allows this new development and the emerging new law merchant or *lex mercatoria* to be considered foremost from a cultural and sociological rather than from a nationalist or traditional common or civil law perspective. That will be the subject of the next sections.

1.4   Cultural, Sociological and Economic Undercurrents in the Formation of the Law. Legal Orders and their Manifestation

1.4.1   The Concept of Legal Orders

International commercial and financial law as an autonomous phenomenon and force presumes some legal environment or order in which it can emerge and operate. It could be said instead that law is what it is, therefore also the transnational law, but all law would seem to require some context. In this connection, the notion of legal orders may be useful. It is not new. States are prime examples but they are not the only ones. The notion of legal order is notably also used within the EU and denotes there an own (confederate) order separate from that of the Member States. Other non-statist legal orders may also be identified, as will be shown in section 1.4.5 below. Traditionally it was often assumed e.g. that the major churches had their own legal order of which church law was the result. Ecclesiastical courts could then exist and adjudicate this law or it could be adjudicated in the ordinary courts but always on the basis of church law.

In England in the eighteenth century, church law was subsumed in the common law and the ecclesiastical courts were absorbed by the common law courts. The same happened to the commercial law and commercial courts. Until that time, this commercial law or law merchant had also been independent as the expression of the legal order of the commercial and financial community of those days. Even later, there continued to be an own place for this type of law within the common law as there still is also for church law.

All communities form own sets of rules. For the present discussion, a key factor is to determine which of them have sufficient standing and autonomy to have their rules recognised and accepted in the ordinary courts or may even create their own courts, the decisions of which will be enforced by states either without or with a review of these decisions by the courts of such states. Only such communities could be considered proper legal orders.

The evolution of legal orders in this sense may be a *cultural* phenomenon, but it may also be seen as having its base more properly in *sociological* and *economic* realities. All seem to play a role but the criteria that actually distinguish communities in this sense, therefore communities with rule making powers amongst their members from mere communes that cannot be considered to have a similar standing (and are therefore not legal orders) are not clear cut. The competition with states, statist ambitions in this field, and states' desire for monopolies in legislation have since the nineteenth century obscured the underlying realities and tensions. In England, this friction already developed earlier. In the process, we lost much of our sense for legal diversity. Particularly in an international setting, freed therefore from direct state intervention and benefiting from legislative competiton between states, internationally organized communities may re-emerge as independent legal orders and re-exert their standing whilst challenging state monopolies in their law-making or law-sanctioning activities.

It is submitted that the international business community is a prime example of these communities and the re-emergence of a new international *lex mercatoria* is the natural result. The nineteenth century nationalisation and territorialisation of private law comes here to an end, especially therefore in the professional sphere. It was already observed before that there is here a return to some of the environment that obtained at the time of the *Ius Commune*, therefore to the Continental European approach that obtained in the seventeenth and eighteenth century or even before. This being said, it should be realized that the content of the new *lex mercatoria* can hardly bear comparision with the *Ius Commune* or the old *lex mercatoria* as developed in tandem with it.

The component parts of this new law merchant will be further discussed in section 1.5 and revolve around fundamental and general legal principles, industry practices, customs and party autonomy, not only in the law of obligations but also in the proprietary rights that are particularly propelled by the modern laws of international finance. A hierarchy of norms (or legal sources) is here assumed. In this part of the book, the prime objective is first to investigate (a) the notion of legal orders, (b) the manner of their modern manifestation, (c) the role of cultural, sociological and economic forces in this connection, and (d) the nature and outcome of the competition with state laws.

1.4.2   Law as Cultural Phenomenon

In section 1.2.8, reference was made to the people's spirit or *Volksgeist* in the formation of the law. It became an important consideration in Germany in the early nineteenth century in the formation of a new German private law that was meant to replace the more univeral (Roman law related) *Ius Commune* and the also more universal (ethics, rationality, and efficiency related) natural law tendencies that had also spread in Germany until that time.

The *Volksgeist* notion is associated with von Savigny and von Puchta, but was more properly an expression of the age of Romanticism[147] that followed the age of Enlightenment or Rationality. It led to nationalism even before Germany was unified in 1870. As such it had an early equivalent in England in the works of Edmund Burke, see section 1.2.12 above. In England, it soon translated into the Austinian view that all law emanated from the sovereign's command and was therefore statist even if not statutory. This Burkean view also had a sequence in the US where American values are now often considered to be the basis of the US legal system, see more in particular the discussion in section 2.1.13 above. Here we have a nationalism that is not necessarily statist in the sense that it does not require all law to emanate from a sovereign, but it still considers all law a typical domestic product or a *national* cultural manifestation. This then also applies to common law regardless of its common root in the laws of England.

In this manner an important *cultural* dimension in the formation of the law is noted,[148] often conveniently associated with nationality,[149] but *culture* whatever its precise

---

[147] A classic introduction to Romanticism and its contributions to modern thought and practice may be found in Isaiah Berlin, *The Roots of Romanticism* (Mellon Lectures 1965), edited by Henry Hardy (1999).

[148] Whilst discussing the effect of culture on the law, some idea of what law proper is would seem useful even if it has largely defied definition. As a mere *working hypothesis* it may be said that it concerns rules of action or conduct prescribed by controlling authority and having binding force, see *United States and Guarantee Company v Guenther*, 281 US 34 (1929). This begs the question, however, what 'controlling authority' and 'binding force' are and when they arise. Another way of defining law is as a body of *social* rules prescribing external conduct and considered justiciable, see H Kantorowics, *The Definition of the Law* (trans E Campbell 1958), 79. This puts emphasis on the close association between law and sociological forces more in particular discussed in the next section, but still begs the question what 'justiciable' is (as distinguished from moral dictates and social conventions). It suggests some state coercive power but does not explain when this must back up the rules of other (private) groups or associations or allows other (group) sanctions if the rules are not voluntarily complied with. Another important question is why law in this sense is usually complied with voluntarily without which it would collapse. What is the role of group culture in this connection and what is the connecting factor in terms of internalisation of its rules?

[149] In the writings of many, this seems to be axiomatic and often leads to a narrow nationalism in the law on the basis of cultural arguments, then seen as deep underlying national currents, perhaps in a mystical,

definition may as such as easily be associated with other important notions like religion (eg Christian, Islamic, or Buddhist cultures), regions (Asian, European, American or Western cultures), language (Anglo-American, Fench-speaking, or Russian cultures), or political/economic systems (Western democratic/capitalistic/ decentralised, or other more totalitarian cultures), or (more commonly) with aesthetic or intellectual endeavours (Aztec, Maya, Roman, Greek, Hellenistic, Renaissance or Barok cultures etc). In fact, culture itself is all that mankind achieves and is as such what it is. It is not nationalistic per definition and *only* obtains a more distinctive meaning when used in a clearly marked *narrower* sense (like a religious, ethnic, linguistic, nationalistic, political or artistic sense), particularly when it denotes some *mindset*.

But that requires at least one further building block. To provide a distinctive basis for the formation of legal normativity, culture as mindset must not only be strong but also requires *group cohesion* (amongst those of a similar mindset). In terms of law formation, culture should therefore be cast foremost in *sociological* terms, that is to say in the sense of community and its behaviour as a group. That suggests the close connection between cultural and sociological currents or forces when it comes to the law and its formation.[150] It would allow us to deduce from such a cultural mindset some predictability of behaviour, therefore some ways of doing that may be considered more deeply rooted, likely to recur within the group and capable of producing behavioural standards.

National culture is only one expression of culture in this sense and springs in terms of law formation often first to mind. It should be realised, however, that nationality may produce or be based on a rather weak kind of mindset. Other cultural strands may be much stronger and might from this cultural perspective have a much greater claim to and potential impact on the formation of the law (if seen as a cultural manifestation). Nevertheless, it is the group aspect that in modern times makes us look foremost at *national* cultures, therefore at states in terms of law formation, even if we can see that group cohesion along cultural lines needs not be associated with a state *per se* and may in fact much better be seen in other types of communities where the cultural base for the group may be much stronger — reference may in this respect be made eg to churches on one side of the spector or to the international business community on the other.

Thus even if for culture to count in this connection it cannot be merely a personal or individualistic experience but must show a close association with group trends so as to become relevant in the law-making process, that group needs not be a state *per se*. It could even be argued that it was rather unexpected that states came out on top. On the European Continent that was certainly not so in the times of the *Ius Commune*. It had to do with the fact that power ultimately became aggregated at state level. In other words, the state proved ultimately to be the more natural level at which power was to be monopolised. That became in Western Europe a typical nineteenth century development, in England perhaps a little earlier. It is true of course that there had been dominant regimes before but they had never had the physical means of communication and control to dominate society as a

---

irrational sense. This view tends to be highly romantic, see in this vein particular P Legrand, "Europeanisation and Convergence", in Paul Beaumont et al (eds) *Convergence and Divergence* in European Public Law, 225 (Oxford, Hart Publishing, 2002) and more soberly C Harlow, "Voices of Difference in a Plural Community", in the same vol, p 199 but *cf* also N Walker, "Culture, Democracy and the Convergence of Public Law: Some Scepticism about Scepticism", 257.

[150] The notion of culture and its definitions have perplexed many, see for a discussion GH Hartman, *The Fateful Question of Culture* (1997).

whole for any period of time. They could at best send an army or police force around from time to time or try to rule through a kind of feudal or similarly layered system.

In fact, in connection with the cultural impact of group formation on its rules and the position of states in this connection, another development should be noted. It is likely that, whatever the cultural base, group cultures of whatever type have become *less* strong in Western society. This is so first because Western society is itself likely to promote *diversity*. As a consequence, there may be different cultures of various sorts at work on the same territory which may easily compete within states and with other groupings. Especially where cultural diversity is promoted, national culture like all group cultures will be unavoidably weakened. But perhaps more importantly, Western culture itself suggests *individualism* and an open, thriving, forward-looking personal attitude based on experience and investigation, therefore on *experimentation*. That is likely to make people less conformist, often more tolerant and in any event more changeable but also harder to identify with group authenticity, especially at the state or national level. One could even say that the *lessening effect* of group cultures left room for the modern state and its growing power to impose its own laws on all within its territory.

Other strands of culture that are or have remained more traditional are likely to have a much more doctrinaire and unchangeable attitude. They may produce much closer knit communities showing much more coherence although they may at the same time lack adaptability because of the dictates of tradition or scripture. Nevertheless, it may be easier to find a much greater group sense and group normativity in such groups which are often of a religious nature representing religious cultures. Thus in a theocracy, law is likely to be foremost seen as part of a religious *all life* experience which dominates everything, also the rules of the group and of the nation.[151] We may think this atavistic, but it is not so very far removed from some Scandinavian philosophers who, in the last century, thought modern law hardly different from witchcraft.[152] In any event, religious, especially Christian values or overtones, were until quite recently a most obvious feature of Western values and laws as well.

Some introspectiveness of this nature would seem inherent in all types of cultures, but with greater individual mobility and more external information, all cultures are likely to loose at least some of their singularity and as a consequence also some of their particular mindset, behavioural predictability, and group cohesion. Modern Western civilisation is an important resultant example of this type of development as much greater individualism has emerged and is cultivated after group culture first moved away from a more tribal to a family environment, now often also abandonned.

This has led to a typical Western culture trait in which individuals are now foremost bound together in an *organisational* rather than in a cultural sense. That orginisation is the modern state.[153] Even if we still speak here of Western culture, it should be repeated that this is foremost a practical development that rather shows the *absence* of any particular cultural drive. Even if the result can be characterised as another culture (Western culture), it should be considered that in that kind of culture the identification with the group and

---

[151] It is of interest in this connection, however, that even the fundamentalist (universalist) Islam concept of the law of the shari'a could not avoid the influence of the state and its *raison d'etat* either, see for this development in the West in respect of the universalist natural law s. 1.2.6 *supra*. It substantially diluted it even if law formation by (Islamic) states was meant to be left only to god fearing rulers or Caliphs, aware of the divine commands, see also NJ Coulson, *A History of Islamic Law* (Edinburgh, 1964), 129.

[152] See the theories of A Hagerstrom, 1 *Der roemische Obligationsbegriff* (1927), 17 and of V Lundstedt, 1*Die Unwissenschaftlichkeit der Rechtswissrenschaft* (1936), 21.

[153] See also J Habermas, *The Structural Transformation of the Public Sphere* (trans Thomas Burger 1991).

therefore the group element is often weak. Its substantive effect on the substance of the law is therefore also weakened as that law like the group it serves becomes more *organisational,* depends on choices to be made in this connection, and is therefore *opportunistic, political or co-incidental* in nature.

It suggests that the modern close association between law formation and states is a demonstration of the fact that law has become *less* cultural and less continuous at the same time. There is a more versatile and less homogeneous mindset or group ethos behind the formation of modern law. For Western society, it underscores the need for a more sophisticated organisational infrastructure to hold modern states together. Culture alone can no longer do this and looses here at least an irrational or more romantic grip. It becomes more orderly, more modern and less forcefull at the same time.

It follows first that in Western society, politics and law as an organisational tool are likely to figure larger than in more traditional or static cultures and that the law that is produced is more variable, rather a policy tool, therefore a mechanism for remedial action, social change, and economic development much more than a typical cultural manifestation. Indeed through legislation, law became here an important instrument of public policy or the *raison d'etat* in which particularly *public* law, as the law that concerns itself with a state's organisation and objectives, acquires an enhanced status.

State intervention in private law and its formulation becomes here intent on streamlining, greater efficiency and lower costs in which connection the state is likely to provide in legislation models as directory law (with its default rules) and sometimes (like in property rights) mandatory law by way of protection against interfering outsiders. That is much behind a modern state's concern with statutory law for the whole or at least for the most important parts of private law. That is so not only in codification countries of the civil law but now also in common law countries, of which, in the US, the Uniform Commercial Code is an important example even if it does not aspire to exclusivity and systematical completeness as European Codes normally do. In civil law countries, on the other hand, this kind of statist private law is often given a higher status than more traditional customary law and a semblance of exclusivity.

If we call the resultant law still cultural, that is cultural in a Western sense. This type of culture is thus very dependent on a politicised system that is well organised and in which the law plays an enormous role as organisational tool. Group culture or a group mindset play here as a consequence lesser or more unpredictable roles. It is sometimes thought e.g. that respect for the law is the only thing that holds the US together and is as such the only real bond. That suggests survival instinct rather than any common underlying values, on very much of which there is not likely to be any consensus at all. No wonder the great interest in America in the law, how it can be accepted and transforms itself in that country in which a national culture plays a role only in the broadest sense of the word.

If we still speak of a common culture, here foremost a western culture, it is particular in that, without a strong group sentiment and regardless of its intrinsic individualism, it still manages to produce a set-up in which states and their governments can operate and provide added value to society as a whole without being able to become all dominant. As such these modern states appear foremost the expression of *societal energy* rather than of a communal mindset or culture, an energy which at the same time does not allow itself to be fully exhausted by and entirely absorbed in the modern state but competes with it to the likely advantage and the greater stability of both.

Such a state will thus have to allow room for more traditional communities and cultures that are able to maintain themselves within its territory in a sense of competition in which the lines of competency are never clearly drawn. Other legal orders operate in this margin, as will be the subject of the next section. This will be expressed (to some extent) in Constitutions or similar, which provide a legal framework guaranteeing some order and continuity but organisational instruments modern Western states in Western society are at the same time subject to a constant *redistribution of organisational power* (and wealth) between different individuals or groups. Whilst operating in this manner, they (have to) accept and promote the rule of all law whatever its legal source unless it offends public policy. Outside their sphere, especially in private law, modern states should as a consequence be decentralist, therefore foremost facilitators that respect individual and group autonomy unless the internal peace is challenged, efficiency is substantially threatened, or a need for redistribution of risks and reward is indicated. In that case, major public policy issues are at stake, which are likely to be balanced by popular feelings and human rights considerations rather than by cultural constraints.

In the private sphere, this type of decentralist, organisational, individualistic and rather a-cultural or culturally neutral Western 'culture' thus allows for organisational autonomy of parties, partnership and groups or communities, at least as long as others are not unduly affected and the public good is not unduly threatened in the state territory in question. It will also allow or even encourage cultural diversity in a religious, ethnic, linguistic or aesthetic sense as long as these cultures prove tollerant. Totalitarian tendencies are likely to be alien to this culture which invites others into it, whilst the rule of law and the concept of human rights underline basic respect for the private sphere.

It follows that, even where the modern state assumes a role in the formulation of private law through legislation, regulation will be limited — in business e.g. mainly directed at anticompetitive behaviour and other market abuses or undue interferences in other people's affairs or taking advantage. In other private areas, like in families, churches, and similar associations, or in partnerships and companies, state intervention should thus be directed against excess, like intolerance and fanaticism, subjugation of gender, or abuse of minorities. Again, only if a major public policy issue arises, should modern states intervene in these communities or in private relationships through mandatory laws. Even then they are subject to rule of law and human rights limitations. Where it otherwise devises rules for communities, they are likely to be merely directory and can thus be set aside by these parties, groups or individuals concerned.

One may take the argument one point further: whatever the claims of nationalism in this connection, it is important to note that these key notions of diversity, group autonomy, democracy, rule of law, and human rights are *not* themselves nationalistic in nature or belong to a national culture. At most, there is a much broader Western cultural aspect in which they are embedded or of which they are the expression, a broader attitude that is also concerned with efficiency and impatient with monopolies of whatever kind (except in respect of state enforcement power, itself considered subject to the rule of law). In its progress, Western culture relies here heavily on individual exertion but no less on self-restraint, tollerance, civic sense and participation at that individual level, on rationality and efficiency in an economic sense, and on flexibility and experimentation in an intellectual sense. Again, none of these are national cultural traits or preserves even though they may reflect them; they derive from a *broader* set of human experiences. To repeat also, culture is likely to loose here much of its more mystical, idiosyncratic and nationalistic features. In terms of diversity, cultural aspects of this type are likely in modern states to be preserved only in the manner of folklore.

It must be admitted that what has propelled this broader Western culture is particularly the *American experience*, which has become prevalent in the West in the twentieth century when Europe lost its grip through its internecine wars, its experimentation with totalitarian ideas, and its ultimate promotion of both fascism and communism, only demised through American intervention. The American experience to the extent here relevant would appear to be marked by at least *five basic characterisics* that confirm our perception of modern Western culture mainly as an organisational philosophy for a dynamic modern society.

First it is *secular*. This does not mean that it is anti-religious, but religion is considered a private matter and the US Constitution makes sure that it remains so, so that its divisive nature is not allowed to dominate public debate or enter the public domain unduly (unless prefaced by a reference to toleration tolerance). In fact, in this environment, fanaticism of whatever kind is not accepted but perceived as undemocratic and in that sense as culturally 'un-Western'.

Secondly, it reaches out and it is *outward looking* meaning that more extreme forms of nationalism and introspectiveness are not encourgaed. Narrow statism would seem here a contradiction as well, even if more conservative political forces, in the US as elsewhere, play with it from time to time, but they have their own experiences against them.

Thirdly, the American experience has a long *democratic tradition*, which separates, breaks down and fractures power as such and has close connections with the rule of law and human rights. It appreciates diversity and cultural competition and understands the notion of community and party autonomy. *Decentralisation* in an organisational sense is here an important feature. It steers particularly clear off the idea that modern wealth and well-being is largely due to a socio-economic infrastructure in which only the contribution of the state counts which would therefore be entitled to dominate all, at least within its own territory, and could take as much as it thinks it is entitled to or can get away with.

Fourthly, the American experience is determined by an all-absorbing and self-propelling *inquiry into nature and mankind*, its motive being the discovery of truth guided by experience and investigation. This was always the professed objective of academia but has acquired an altogether different dimension in the US. It leads to a respect for learning centred on the great American Universities and research institutions (with their related strong philanthropic support). As such, it transcends the cults of both Wall Street, Hollywood, or Silicon Valley which come a close second, thirdly and fourth and are in their own ways part of the same process of discovery. By looking for truth in nature and its processes, the American experience thus lives in the hope of a better or at least a more interesting world and in progress in that sense although it guarantees nothing.

There is a *fifth* feature of the American experience, in which it may be more truly unique, even within the West: *it does not seek to dominate* although it will forcefully defend itself against any physical threats. Instead, it desires to be emulated, to convince, and to involve all others to join the process. This is very different from many other cultures that have more often sought domination and find it natural to do so. That may still be the basic attitude in Western Europe, where the reflex often is to see the American experience not as an example but as a form of intrusion, imposition, or threat. In the US, there is instead an idealistic undercurrent that explains why the Americans are inclined to give others all the help and protection needed in order to rid themselves of wars and totalitarian philosophies. It does so even at the risk that ultimately others will compete with it in a political, military and also cultural sense (again unless they become a physical threat). That risk is accepted. Such acceptance may be unusual in other cultures.

How is modern law and its further evolution caught up in the dynamics of our present situation, this voyage of discovery, openness, and cultural demystification? Of course we have here the day to day practice of the law to consider. Much of it does not go beyond a 'practitioners' manual' or 'lawyers' toolbox' that can hardly be more than black letter law.

That is what in essence is now taught in European law schools, whether of civil or common law. This was discussed before and is intellectually only of modest interest. More important and more truly a subject of academic investigation is where the law is going, what the alternatives are, what the law may achieve in an ever evolving environment, society or civilisation, when and why it finds acceptance at group, national and international level, and how the focus may change in this respect over time. This is much the gist of modern American research in its major law schools, which have in this respect divided in the various ' law and …' directions discussed in section 1.2.13 above.

If in Western Society the law is now steeped in secular principle, therefore in some basic values of which human rights, the rule of law, and respect for individual[154] and group autonomy are indicative, and further in some rationality and utilitarian principles as more in particular advocated by the 'law and economics' school, this alone would suggest that local, national, or statist cultural content in this law will ultimately yield to more universal notions. It at least suggests that in Western society the basic tenets of the legal system have a foundation that is considerably broader than mere nationalism or statist activity. This would be so at least in business law or the law concerning professional dealings.

If it is true that the modern democratic state, like the modern decentralised social and economic structures through which individuals and groups or communities may exert their autonomy, all have a foundation in a broader Western culture which is *not* itself statist or nationalistic, it would suggests that, even if the law, its development and application have at the level of the positive law at present still an important anchor in the nation state and its organisation, that cannot be the whole story and need not be so *per se* or for ever. It follows that in our part of the world the law as a cultural phenomenon is (like the modern state) foremost Western and *only subsequently* national or cultural in any other sense and must then also be considered per group or in terms of party autonomy. At least that would seem a perfectly valid proposition to make.

Cultural simularity or an overarching Western culture shows here also in the structure of modern states itself operating along democratic lines which area everywhere very similar, in Western Europe often of recent origin, and now subject to further evolution within the European Union. It also shows because in its more practical aspects, the operation of states may change overnight depending on the prevailing political currents. Thus social and budgetary law will vary with each government and the impact of deep cultural undercurrents in this process or of pure nationalism seems highly exaggerated.

Whether or not nationalism and national culture still have a decisive meaning at least as far as private law is concerned, it should also be considered that much of it, at least in the law of property and contract, was seldom of a purely national (cultural) origin. It has much broader historical roots (Roman or Germanic) in virtually all its major aspects in whatever country, whilst in its newer aspects this law is likely to be technical, utilitarian, and meant to solve present day societal, commercial or financial problems which are seldom of a typical national nature (even if the urgency may be). In private law, it may thus be asked eg what the cultural or typical national aspect is of the notification requirement for a valid assignment in some countries, not demanded in others, whilst in 1992 the Dutch started to require it and in the same year the Belgians abandonned it. There is much like this in modern private law in which practicalities decide these issues rather than deeper considerations. Perhaps they never entered much into it.

---

[154] See the Preamble to the EU Treaty which refers to the Member States' "attachment to the principles of liberty, democracy and respect for human rights and fundamental freedoms and of the rule of law".

This may particularly be so for the entirety of commercial and financial law or all of the law concerning professional dealings, based as it is on practical needs and on the rationality of commerce and finance. In any event, at least in international commerce and finance it never found its cultural support in typical national considerations and even within modern states and their organisational structures there is hardly any true national principle or value in this type of law. Even if there was, there is ever less reason for there to be. One could still say (in civil law terms) that being part of the intellectual national system of private law presents some national value, but this system itself is largely contrived, often outdated, seldom capable of covering all realities, and, like any intellectual endeavour, in any event hardly culturally specific. To repeat: the new law merchant or *lex mercatoria* is more likely to find its reason in its own international environment and in the exigencies of its own legal order as an expression of the needs and logic that prevail in that transnational environment.

1.4.3   Sociological and Economic Considerations in the Law. The Competition with Mandatory State Laws or National Public Policies. States as Counterparties

In the previous section, for Western society, modern law as a typical statist or national cultural phenomenon (or both) was de-emphasised, except in the broadest sense. This may be especially clear in the case of commercial and financial law. Instead, the more pragmatic organisational aspect of modern law formation even at national levels was noted, whilst the sociological background of other sources of law was emphasised, therefore law's association with groups or communities and their functioning. The possibility of competition was also mentioned. As was suggested earlier, it is posited here that all law emanates in truth from *legal orders* which are community related and of which states are only one particular (even if at present the most important and powerful) example. If, as suggested in the previous section, societal energy is at the heart of all modern state formation, it will also sustain and create other communities within and beyond such states. Indeed that could be seen as the essence of all civil societies and their evolution. It is also at the heart of the recognition of the importance of diversity and gives it meaning.

The question then is which commununities function as legal orders, are therefore likely to produce their own law, and are entitled to have their laws recognised and respected by other legal systems or orders, therefore also by states, which might even have to give their sanction to it, much as they do to sister state laws and judgements subject to a number of conditions which should then be clarified. To put it in a different way: not every commune is a community in this sense and not all communities make law, but some do. Who count in this connection, who may as such compete with states and under what circumstances, where must we draw the line, and what are the rules of the game?

The notion of community in this sense could be left to state recognition but that would deny all autonomy of other orders and could not explain international legal orders. Alternatively, it could be intellectually attractive to attribute autonomy to them *all*, therefore to any grouping no matter how ephemeral and transient, at least to the extent *participation* could be considered to have been *consented* to. Party autonomy would then also present a legal order, in fact be at the heart of it. It is not that simple, however, not merely because it would make the setting aside or at least the challenge of state rules a seemingly casual affair, but more fundamentaly because the notion of participation itself presupposes other (*internal*) rules which determine when it counts, which rules are not necessarily of a consensual nature but concern the group or order (and its functioning) as a whole. They are likely to have a more objective status and a more independent origin which as such should be identifiable.[155]

Participation and consent are therefore not the sole determining factors for the autonomy of these legal orders and the law that results in them. Other criteria may have to be found to delineate the various legal orders and mark out the law that they produce. This would appear to concerns (a) the identification of the *relevant circle of participants in a given range of activities* or with a *particular purpose.* (b) There also has to be some sustaining *force or motive* like in international commerce and finance there is the modern international flows of professionals, goods, services and money, and the need for encouragement and adequate protection of the commercial or financial interests involved in these flows. (c) This force must be capable of not only identifying the group but must also be capable of producing and maintaining some infrastructure for it. (d) At least in (international) business, one would also expect some economic component in terms of efficiency, rationality, common sense, consistency and predictability, if not also some kind of morality in terms of honesty, transparency and accountability. (e) It also requires some consensus on the basic economic system which suggests a market approach in which states may nevertheless figure as important balancing actors.

This raises many fundamental issues. If we limit ourselves to international commerce and finance, the relevant circle of participants in a given range of activities are likely to be the professionals in those trades.[156] A more specific feature of the international and commercial

---

[155] Even contracts are embedded in and depend for their binding force on a broader legal set up that is not necessarily voluntary in all its aspects or depends on consent and participation alone. Even contracts may acquire a character of their own and bind participants regardless of their will. It is not impossible that within the group or order some rules acquire an (immanent) public order element and become absolutely mandatory in the order concerned. Although it is often thought that an important distinction between state and other legal orders is that the latter are voluntary and the former not, it is doubtful whether that is really so. At least it does not apply to all rules emanating from such orders. Although much of (private) law can be opted out of also within states, once operating in a group or state, some rules cannot be avoided. Not only stately orders have public policies. The rules under which it is determined whether internal laws are mandatory or not are unlikely to be voluntary either. There is here another, more immanent social ordering at work which responds to its own rules and determines their reach.

[156] Thus the 1980 Vienna Convention on the International Sale of Goods, in Article 1, whilst excluding consumer sales, clearly limits its scope to professional dealings. It could be considered extendable to all international transactions whether in goods, services or capital. The Unidroit Principles of Contract Law (1995) target such dealings for professionals more generally. In France, already in the 1930 the notion of 'international contract' was developed in this connection, for which gold (payment) clauses would be accepted and were upheld even though generally forbidden under domestic law, see also GR Delaume, *Law and practice of transnational contracts* (1988), 227.

An argument can be made that 'internationality' and 'professionality' have become inextricably linked in the sense that all professional dealings will come to conform to international standards even if they have in a particular case no international aspects, see s. 1.1.6 *supra.* The distinction is then between the international legal order which is professional and the domestic legal order which is for consumers.

This raises the issue not only of 'professionality' but also of 'internationality', a concept which has been explored more in particular in connection with international arbitrations. They occur when parties come from different countries, when the subject matter is of an international nature or the arbitration takes place in an unrelated country, see the French Decrees Nos. 80–345 and 81–500 and Article 1(3) of the Uncitral Model Arbitration Law.

The UCC in the US, although not written for international sales and not limited to dealings between professionals either, defines the notion of merchants and dealings between merchants in Section 2–104, therefore, *only* in the context of the law of the sale of goods (and not as a broader concept) and has some special rules for them. A merchant is here a person who normally deals in goods of the kind or otherwise holds himself out by his occupation as having knowledge or skill peculiar to the practices or goods involved in the transaction or to whom such knowledge or skill may be attributed by his employment of an agent or broker or other intermediary who by his occupation holds himself out as having such knowledge or skill. Dealings between merchants are transactions with respect to which both parties are chargeable with the knowledge and skills of merchants.

Regardless of the earlier proposals which suggested a broader distinction between consumer and professional sales, see also ZB Wiseman, "The Limits of Vision: Karl Llewellyn and the Merchant Rules", (1983) 100 *Harv. LR*, 465,

legal order may indeed be found in its foundation in the modern *free flow* of professionals, goods, services, capital and payments, the freeing of which has also been the main motive in the economic legal order of the EU and its internal market. These flows may also suggest a *connected* way of dealing or operating and an own pattern of legal rules which are certainly not confined to the EU and have no origin in domestic laws, can often not be satisfactorily explained by them but must be attributed to the operation of the international commercial and financial legal order itself.

As a practical matter, in these international flows, the dynamics are likely to be entirely different from the local ones. Local law is unlikely to have been developed for them and may be deficient or make no sense in international commercial transactions, e.g in its limitations on the protection of *bona fide* purchasers or in the type of proprietary and similar rights (like trust structures, assignment possibilities, security interests and floating charges, set-off facilities, agency relationships, and book-entry entitlements in respect of investment securitities) it allows to operate against third parties.[157]

In this connection, the view has authoritatively been expressed[158] that new law is constantly formed through the sectarian separation of communities. In this view, each legal order perceives itself as emerging out of something that itself is unlawful. *Separation* is here identified as a crucial constitutive element of new legal orders which may require in each case a normative mitosis or radical transformation of the perspective of a group or a new total life experience for a new legal order to emerge and qualify.

There follows the emphasis on *separateness, sustainability* and *prospectiveness* as group, on a *rule producing willingness and capacity,* and on *a capability* to hold the group as group together or at least to make it function better on the basis of their own rules. Mere communion is not enough and some (incipient) organisational structure will be required. The emphasis moves here to struggle and triumph, therefore to a revolutionary element in the creation of new legal orders, which essentially compete with the older ones. In line with this approach, in commerce and finance, the freeing of the international flows could then be seen as the fuse for the change of perspective in its participants and the establishment and operation of new (international and commercial) legal order between them.

Others[159] have put emphasis rather on how the new law can be found and identified and they have suggested that for international commercial law to arise and to count legally in the sense that states must accept it and back it up by coercive power (unless it has major public policy reasons not to do so), (a) the norms that arise in this specialised business community should be empirically identifiable, (b) the incentive structure that produces or internalises these norms should be capable of being analysed (by using game theory and the notion of equilibrium) in order to determine whether the norms empirically found are more than social convention or moral dictates and are experienced as binding, whilst (c) the *efficiency* (or public good effect) of the incentive structure should be measurable using analytical tools from economics to avoid harmful laws (like monopolistic practices, which will

---

Article 2 UCC is therefore less professional-oriented than could have been expected, which reflects the reality that in domestic sales professional dealings have so far acquired fewer distinctive features. It is consumers that have in the meantime obtained special protection under broader consumer laws.

[157] JH Dalhuisen, "European Private Law: Moving from a Closed to an Open System of Proprietary Rights", *Edinburgh LR* (2001), 1, *cf* also TW Merril and HE Smith, "Optimal Standardization in the Law of Property: The Numerus Clausus Principle", 110 *Yale LJ* 1 (2000).
[158] See R Cover, "Nomos and Narrative", 97 *Harv LR, 4 (1980)*, 31.
[159] RD Cooter, "Structural Adjudication and the New Law Merchant: A Model for Decentralisation", 14 *Intern. Rev. of Law and Economics*, 215 (1994).

therefore not be enforced). Here the emphasis shifts from struggle to *rationality, consistency and predictability*. In this connection, 'modernity' and the 'advanced nature' of the new legal system could themselves become issues in the context of their international validity and force.[160]

Similar objective criteria may also emerge from a rule of law test. It also assumes thresh-old standards of a more universal character and not mere state recognition. It is possible to refer here to a rule of law both in an institutional ('law of rules') and substantive ('set of values') sense. It is the common yardstick by which the exercise of power in Western soci-ety is more generally channelled, constrained and informed, not only at the national but also at the international level.[161] It could also play a significant role in the allocation of competencies between legal orders or in the acceptance by states of laws and decisions based on these competencies when rendered in other legal orders. The fact that there are here concepts at work that are more universal does *not* need to mean, however, that they are also static, immutably pre-determined by rationality, unchangeable values, or (meta-physical) truths (as natural law concepts are sometimes considered to be).

It is unlikely to go as far as to require high minded moral standards for legal orders to operate and be recognised even if in an ideal world this might be better. At least interna-tional business and its requirements present a more mundane and dynamic environment. Legal orders in order to function need not necessarily be democratic or be supported by more advanced values; it has never been a precondition for their operating at national levels.[162] However, international (or other) legal orders are not necessarily unaffected by such values.[163] It is quite obvious that in the acceptance of the validity of other legal orders and their laws and decisions elsewehere, and in the competition with statist legal orders, the accepted set of values (or the absence thereof) in non-statist legal orders may play a role, also in a more tolerant and secular Western environment.

There are clearly limits to what can be recognised and accepted as law from whatever legal order in any other legal order (certainly also that of states), although there may well have to be a large margin for any legal order to operate in its own ways, also within nation states, all the more so if there is acquiescence in the larger national or international com-munity. It is eg clear that the acceptance of rogue states may ultimately also affect the acceptance externally of their internal domestic legal order whatever its values and laws[164] and the same may go for other legal orders. The limits to what will be accepted by states

[160] In oil concessions, references to the law of all civilised nations etc used not to be uncommon, although now probably considered offensive whilst a reference to general principles is preferred, see also A Redfern and M Hunter, *Law and Practice of International commercial Arbitration* (3rd edn, 1999), 114. Nevertheless, in the international legal order as a newly emerging order, one would expect an attitude to problem solving that is less encumbered by the past even where concepts will be borrowed from domestic law in a comparative law search for better solutions.

[161] See M Krygier, "Rule of Law", in NJ Smelser and PB Bates (eds), 20 *International Encyclopedia of the Social and behavioral Sciences* (2001), 13403, and Ph Selznick, "Legal Cultures and the Rule of Law", in M Krygier, Adam Czarnota (eds), *The Rule of Law after Communism* (1999).

[162] J Habermas, *The Structural Transformation of the Public Sphere* (trans Thomas Burger 1991), 76, notes that the great codes in Europe were never democratically sanctioned but were subject all the same to some participation process which might have made them reflective of their times.

[163] In a Western sense, it would suggest the existence of more universal values that affect all legal orders oparating within it, their operation, and the legal force of their rules (even internally). The well-known example was the legal effectiveness in principle of the nazi laws within the German legal order or their voidness *ab initio* or their absolute voidness *per se* even within that order.

[164] On the other hand, the operation of competing international orders may be instrumental, at least on occasion, in containing local cabals even in democracies or indeed expose them to openness and better practices or in an economic sense to more rational decentralised approaches or privatisation. Globalisation has contributed in that

from legal orders operating within it, were discussed in the previous section in terms of democracy, rule of law, human rights, transparency and the like. It allows within Western society for a broader discussion of the values of other legal orders or the absence of such values in them, of the redistributive powers in or the unfairness of their system (as may be compounded by globalisation), and of any rightful or erroneous claims of the law in the international commercial and financial legal order to objectivity and formal effectiveness in supporting trade, commerce and finance.[165]

In subscribing to this approach, we should be helped by the fact that, at least for the economic benefits it brings, the present more or less decentralised, more or less democratic, more or less market supported socio-economic system finds some broad international support at least throughout the Western world and also in large parts of Asia. In the international commercial and financial order, the daily business of trade, commerce and finance is in any event less politically and culturally sensitive than larger labour and environmental issues or the much broader political issues with which G-8, WTO and IMF must grapple and which might then also have an effect in the international commercial and financial legal order, assuming some legal expression can be given to such an intervention in it. At the micro level in each legal order these broader considerations seldom play a major role. What e.g. is the value content of set-off, floating charges, constructive trusts, bookentry systems for investment securities and their operation, and the different rules that have developed in different countries in this regard? The details of these legal structures would often seem to be due to historical developments, coincidence, and especially justified needs. Even where legislators have spoken, the result is hardly more fundamental and the results normally limited to the insights and exigiencies of the day. The minimum required communality of values assumes a more immediate material meaning when decisions reached in the international commercial and financial legal order are asked to be enforced in a state legal order by inviting their coercive sanction.

Indeed, assuming for the moment that the relevant legal order can be found and its laws determined,[166] we still have the questions (a) when precisely a transaction may be deemed

sense to the demise of some inefficient government controls, to more choice, lower cost, perhaps lower inflation, more openness and diversity, a better informed public, less jingoism, more cooperation (whether in G-7, IMF or WTO). Nobody claims perfection, but what may be a-statist or a-nationalistic in the international order is not per definition anti-democratic, democracy offensive or devoid of modern Western values at the same time.

In the meantime much has been written on the democratic deficit of these organisations and also of the EU both in Europe and the US. The traditional view is that democratic control is best exercised at the level of the participating governments, therefore nationally. That was also the EU's original stance and is still the reason for the limited powers of the European Parliament. There is another problem here. The highly technical nature of much of the parliamentary discussions at the international level escapes the public and it is difficult therefore for an international parliament to profile itself, acquire credibility and inspire the masses. For the WTO similar arrangements are suggested but unlikely to work better. The alternative is greater openness in the negotiation processes and more reliance on public opinion and non-governmental organisations input besides that of local politicians. This raises the question of who may legitimately talk whilst it is not clear whether the results would be any better. In all these organisations there seems to be a bureaucratic phase that precedes further democratisation and seems to be necessary to get things off the ground. The EU is the best example but it is not different in WTO.

Of course if the international community was truly serious and willing in the matter, the democratisation process could easily be taken a step further. It is not beyond present day technical means to call an international 'constituante' in the election of which all citizens of the world could participate and which would devise a framework that at an institutional level could deal with globalisation issues democratically. But it would be a serious inroad into the remit of the nation state, seriously may undermine non-Western cultures, and also mean the *de iure* end of the influence of ngo's, reasons why this option may not gain much ground.

[165] Critical Legal Studies have eg always been sceptical of the objectivity and effectiveness of black letter law in pursuing social ordering, see for some in depth studies the anthology of AC Hutchinson (ed), *Critical Legal Studies* (Totowa, NJ, Rowman and Littlefield, 1989).

[166] It is to be noted in this connection that the alleged vagueness of the rules of the *lex mercatoria* have often been held as a conclusive argument against its existence, see most forcefully Mustill LJ, "The New Lex Mercatoria" in

to arise in that international legal order, (b) how the matter of competition with state legal orders is to be decided, and (c) what to do with enforcement. Here we may have to consider broader substantive law considerations even in more technical aspects but only when governmental interests or policies of the recognising state are apparent. In this connection, we also have to consider the issue of the attribution of competences between the various legal orders in what is in essence a *decentralist* or pluralist view of law-making which encourgages this competition and limits the facility of states to frustrate it. The proper concern is *not* here to find some *super* or *world* laws *per se*, but rather the identification of the more competent or pertinent legal order in respect of the particular actors or actions internationally the law of which would then prevail (even if this presupposes a broader view or framework of what law is and how it operates).

As to the first issue, modern conflict of laws rules may be a considerable help in determining the most appropriate order in which international professional activity takes place. Traditionally, they had the handicap that they were meant to indicate a state order only. In fact, that was the consequence of von Savigny's approach to these rules which date from the 19th-century era of state positivism and nationalism, see section 2.1.1 below.[167] Traditional conflicts' rules pointing to the application of state law only may, however, be helpful in a broader context and apply them to the laws of all legal orders rather than to those of state orders alone. It may show the way in terms of center of gravity of an activity, closest connection or, in contract matters, in terms of the legal order of the most characteristic obligation (as long as the applicable law is not merely defined with reference to the domestic laws at the residence of the party performing it), or in which the conduct and effect takes place. There is no need here to elaborate.

A more advanced view mentioned in section 1.1.6 above is that all professional business dealings are increasingly likely to operate in the international legal order even if they have no international connection on occasion, as it is ultimately unlikely that they retain different dynamics locally. In other words, they will increasingly aspire to similar legal standards. Such an evolution in thought would simplify the issue of finding the appropriate legal order greatly. Of course, if all the contacts were local, the impact of the pertinent national or statist public order requirements in respect of the transaction would more eagerly have to be accepted and there could remain an important difference in that respect.

As to the question of the interaction between legal orders and the competition between them,[168] the first practical question that arises is whether the international commercial and financial legal order may prevail over domestic law, also if the latter is mandatory, in respect of international transactions that have an effect in that particular state. International practices or even notions of international public order may underline the

---

M Bos and I Brownlie (eds), *Liber Amicorum Lord Wilberforce* (1987), 149 and "Contemporary Problems in International Commercial Arbitration" (1989) 17 *Int. Bus. L* 161. We shall see below in s 1.5 *infra* that these rules are by no means so vague and that a whole system of law will fairly easily emerge if one accepts the notion of different legal orders, takes principles also into account, and is willing to accept a hierarchy of norms in the international commercial and financial legal order.

[167] There was probably never much wrong with the idea that all legal relationships have a seat in a legal order as long as that could also be the international legal order or others that were not territorially defined and confined.
[168] Especially in the communitarian view, communities may claim moral primacy over (the notion of) states, see Ph Selznick, *The Communitarian Persuasion (2002)*, 64. Much earlier in French legal scholarship, G Gurvitch, *L'Idee du Droit Social* (1932), 84 and *Sociology of the Law* (1942) (with a Preface by Roscoe Pound), insisted on the internal sovereignty of all social groupings. They were even within nations considered to create their own law which limited that of states and was in this view in principle superior to it. See for a similar view of internal sovereignty, in The Netherlands, HJ van Eikema Hommes, *Hoofdlijnen der rechtssociologie en de materiele indeling van publiek- en privaatrecht* (1975).

fact that domestic rules are not or are no longer appropriately applicable in international cases, except if domestic considerations are of such urgency that they cannot be ignored by the international order, but this could only be considered from case to case on the basis of a balancing of interests. If there is such urgency, however, specific domestic policies may remain relevant and legitimate in an international context, as such to be respected even if not in accordance with the international trade practices which are likely to have a more liberal bias.

Examples are domestic import/export and foreign exchange restrictions, although these are generally of less importance today and lifted in most modern countries (unless in the context of trade embargos). It is a question of balancing in the manner of governmental interests in the US tradition of conflicts of laws (Restatement (Second) of Conflict of Laws Section 6) and foreign relation laws (Restatement (Third) of Foreign Relations Sections 402–3) or in the manner of Article 7 of the EU Rome Convention on the Law Applicable to Contractual Obligations, when not all elements of the case are connected with one country, see also section 2.2.6 below. In this context, the reach of policy-oriented *domestic* rules may become too remote or may be simply *excessive* in international terms or in a given situation and they may in such cases not apply at all, even in the absence of established international practices to the contrary.[169] The traditional example is here a state law that requires that foreign asset acquisition by its citizens be made subject to a license in their home country. Foreign countries are unlikely to let this requirement figure in the legality of the acquisition of real estate on their territory by such foreigners.

In this approach, if a domestic law is chosen by the parties as applicable to an international transaction, such a choice can first never go further than covering matters that are at the free disposition of parties and is therefore not likely to determine alone the applicable proprietary and regulatory regimes. Secondly, even where party autonomy prevails, such a choice of a domestic law cannot go beyond what makes sense in the international legal order and is always subject to the higher fundamental or other mandatory principles in that order preceding party autonomy. It does in any event not normally mean to include a preference for the public policy or regulatory rules of the domestic law so chosen. It may have no relevance in the particular international case at all through lack of sufficient contact with the chosen jurisdiction. It cannot be meant to undermine the essentials of the deal itself either, e.g. on the basis of purely domestic notions of the chosen law like 'consideration' or 'parole evidence' when say English law is chosen in a transaction that has nothing to do with England, if not at the same time in line with or confirming international standards which are unlikely to be derived from extraneous domestic (national or statist) laws alone. It could also be argued that any other rules could not have been in the contemplation of the parties. Acceptance of domestic policy issues is in any event always a matter of comity in the international legal order, of weighing therefore the relevant interests involved and of their relevance in view of the contacts of the case with the particular domestic legal order that claims the application of (mandatory) laws.

Where states operate as counterparties with international companies, they are likely to operate themselves in the international legal order, eg when granting oil and gas concessions

---

[169] Of course when all aspects of a transaction are in a particular country, the public policy rules of this state legal order will prevail. That may be so even if the transaction is international in nature as long as all its contacts are with one country only. That is clearly expressed in Article 2 of the 1980 EU Rome Convention on the Law Applicable to Contractual Obligations. If they are not, there arises the discretionary element as reflected in Article 7 of that Convention (in the context, however, of applying domestic laws only), even if it remains rule rather than interest oriented. The problem is in Europe usually identified as one of *règles d'application immediate*, see also s 2.2.6 *infra*.

whilst conceding at the same time a related foreign investment regime which will usually also include a stabilisation of the investment and taxation terms. Whilst entering in such agreements, states surrender their absolute monopoly of the rules governing investments on their territory and can no longer claim full autonomy but become subject to the rules of the international legal order in which they themselves then operate.

When creating a special investment climate under bilateral investment treaties (BITs), they may emerge as lawmakers in that order, whilst subjecting themselves to treaty law and to the investment rules they have set for themselves and foreign investors in that context. This treaty law itself may then be seen as part of the hierarchy of norms, therefore of the *lex mercatoria*, governing the operations of the international commercial and financial legal order.

This finally leaves the matter of enforcement. Here the assumption must be that in an integrating world amongst civil societies, the decisions rendered in one legal order are accepted in others subject to minimum requirements of due process and the rule of law as identified above. Indeed it is incumbent on all modern states to enforce the decisions rendered on the basis of the law of other legal orders operating within the Western cultural confines, subject to a scrutiny of procedural fairness and, in the law applied, of minimum standards only, while showing considerable restraint in upholding own public policy requirements in cases that are rightly arising in other legal orders. This is also the underlying theme in the 1958 New York Convention on the Recognition and Enforcement of Foreign Arbitral Awards, even if still wedded to the idea of national considerations only, restrained in the meantime by narrower notions of international public policy.[170] Even if an effect on public policy in the recognising state cannot be denied, such a restraint remains necessary unless the public policy interest of the recognising state is overwhelming.

In section 1.1.7 above, it was already suggested that in support the new transnational law in the professional sphere, it would not be a bad idea — or too far-fetched a proposal, to set up an international court system for professional dealings operating in a similar manner as the commercial courts once did in regionally divided countries. Their judgments should be universally enforceable, much as international arbitration awards now are under the New York Convention. The difference with international arbitrations would be the greater stability in the system and a facility for appeal. Such a system, which could have some lay judges, could have a central highest appeal court or highest court from which binding prejudicial opinions could be sought. This court might then also supervise the recognition and execution (or setting aside) of international arbitral awards or of domestic court judgments in international business cases. It could be an important aid to the development

---

[170] International public order requirements proper are well known from the international arbitration practice in the context of determining *arbitrability* issues and in connection with the recognition and enforcement of arbitral awards under the New York Convention, The Paris Court of Appeal dealt with the issue of arbitrability of public policy related issues (which are normally not considered arbitrable) in a judgment of March 29 1991, *Ste Ganz, Rev Arb* (1991), 478, 480 and held that, while international arbitrators determine their own jurisdiction including the matter of arbitrability, they could use an internationalised concept of public order, see J-P Ancel, "French Judical Attitudes Toward International Arbitration", 9 *Arb International* (1993), 121, see also V Lazic, *Insolvency Proceedings and Commercial Arbitration*, 149, 278 (1998). See for the public policy bar to recognition of arbitral awards under the New York Convention P Lalive, "Transnational (or Truly International) Public Policy and International Arbitration", in P Sanders (ed), *Comparative Arbitration Practice and Public Policy in Arbitration*, ICCA Congress Series no 3 (1987), 257. These are only two instances in which public policy plays a role at the international level. It may also in other instances and it would appear that there are eg also mandatory competition rules operating that may void contracts in that order. JH Dalhuisen, "The Arbitrability of Competition Issues", 11 *Arb International* (1995), 151. In the EU legal order there operate the competition rules of Articles 81 and 82 of the EC Treaty.

of transnational commercial and financial law. It is at this stage probably more important than codifying the transnational law itself, which, in the absence of sufficient direction in practice and theory and of a sufficient platform amongst legal practitioners, must be found in other ways, as shown in the next section.

At one stage the English commercial courts thought that they could operate as international commercial courts.[171] In view of what was said above, this is not as strange as it may sound. All courts applying international commercial law in international cases could be seen as operating in the international commercial and financial legal order, just like all courts in the EU are competent and obliged to apply EU law when appropriate and operate then as EU courts.

1.4.4   The International Commercial and Financial Legal Order and its Relevance: The Role of Legal Theory, Legal History and Comparative Law

International flows of goods, services and capital go in all kind of directions. In an open society it is not unlike water finding its ways to the seas. There are here inherent forces at work, whether or not considered organised by the invisible hand of market behaviour. They produce their own rules, which are connected with the inherent risk patterns and natural need for protection of the parties concerned. For them they are foremost dictated by logic and common sense in the relevant trade. Professional parties will elaborate on this in their contracts or otherwise impliedly rely on it. It forms the basis for the rules in the international commercial and financial legal order as discussed more extensively in the preceding section.

International sales are a case in point. There are obvious extra risks attached to the sale and transfer of assets internationally in terms of their transportation, proper delivery, quality and title for the buyer and payment for the seller. Without some clear rules in these regards it would require an excess of optimism to sell and send goods across the world. At the practical level handling agents are here a great help. They may be warehouse operators or carriers of the goods and will take the goods from the seller with the sole purpose of delivering them to the buyer. They have no own interest in the transaction except for their fee and the goods are therefore in independent and safe hands whilst having left the seller, who has lost control and can no longer interfere with the goods. That is an important safeguard for the buyer.

On the other hand, the seller will be concerned about the latter's payment and will not want the handling agents to deliver the goods to the buyer without such payment. These agents, when warehousing or transporting the goods, may issue warehouse receipts or bills of lading, without which the goods could not then be reclaimed. Possession of these documents therefore allows the buyer to claim the goods, but, for the protection of the seller, they will often be given to a bank, as another independent agent in this circuit, with the instruction not to release them to the buyer except against payment. That is the concept of (documentary) collection. It may even be that the bank (upon instructions of the buyer) will pay upon receipt of the bill of lading and becomes as such a guarantor of payment. That is the concept of the (documentary) letter of credit.

These structures do not derive from great legal thought but suggests themselves in the practicalities of international trade and are only further perfected to enhance that trade.

---

[171] *Amin Rasheed Shipping Corporation v Kuwait Insurance Company*, 1 WLR 241 228 (1983), see more in particular n 27 *supra*.

Bills of exchange had a similar origin and motivation. So had the protection of *bona fide* purchasers against others who could claim a better title to the goods (or documents) than the seller could. These rules develop all the time and are not restrained in their application by pre-existing black letter laws.[172] It is true that much nineteenth and twentieth centuries' codification in this area left that impression but it is not a correct reflection of the applicable commercial law and the way it evolves. Here the importance of custom or industry practices comes in and must be properly understood. By referring to them and their importance in this connection, we in fact underline more than anything else the dynamic nature of this law itself. It means that these customs and practices are not static and do not require for their validity long standing usage either. They can change overnight with the nature and logic of the business and so the law changes with them.

In suggests that in this area, perhaps more than anywhere else, *both* the *relevant* law and the *relevant* facts must always be found and articulated together per case. They are most closely related. The one cannot be found without the other and there can be no question here of a sharp separation between norm and fact, neither in the origin of the rule nor in its application or in the collection of the facts that may be considered legally relevant under it.

Even if commercial law remains in the perception of many still largely in the clutches of domestic legal systems, on the European Continent often in nineteenth century codified form, whilst even in England it lost its independence in the eighteenth century, it now reasserts its own nature at the international level, through the internationalisation and liberalisation of the commercial flows. However, it needs the help of legal theory, of legal history and comparative law to regain its proper place.

Legal theory proves its importance in all periods of great change and must provide a vision. That is the traditional task of jurisprudence in the US. It does not provide instant clarity. The American modern 'law and …' movements like 'law and morality', 'law and sociology', 'law and economics', 'law and psychology', 'law and aesthetics', etc. show great differences in emphasis, although they also demonstrate that in the evolution, explanation and application of the law external or non-legal considerations play an important role. When and how they do, remains obviously a matter of study, and how they can all be distinguished and connected is an epistemological question that has to do with the nature of our perceptions and the acquisition of our knowledge. These questions have received renewed interest especially in the major law schools in the US where the need for a better understanding of what is going on is acutely felt which has also led to more empirical research. It must be admitted, however, that this American jurisprudential interest has not yet been greatly extended to the study of the law creating forces in international legal orders, see further section 1.2.13 above.

It is nevertheless clear that legal theory has a particular contribution to make in our subject of globalisation of commerce and finance and of the effect this has on the applicable law.

---

[172] See also R. Goode, *Commercial Law* (2nd ed. 1995), 3*ff.* on the nature and sources of commercial law, see further his "Usage and its Reception in Transnational Commercial Law", 46 *Int'l & Comp LQ* (1997), 1. See more recently further Emmanuel Gaillard, "Transnational Law: A Legal System or a Method of Decision Making?", 17 *Arbitration International* (2001), 59, but *cf* also Pierre Mayer, "Reflections on the International Arbitrator's Duty to Apply the Law", 17 *Arbitration International* (2001), 235; LY Fortier, "The New, New *Lex Mercatoria*, or, Back to the Future", 17 *Arbitration International*, 121 (2001); ME Basile, JF Bestor, Dr Coquilette, C Donahue Jr, *Lex Mercatoria and Legal Pluralism: A Late Thirteenth Century Treatise and its Afterlife*, (The Ames Foundation, Cambridge 1998); H Mertens, "Lex Mercatoria: A Self-applying System Beyond National Law?", in G Teubner (Ed), *Global Law Without a State* (1997) 31; KP Berger, *The Creeping Codification of the Lex Mercatoria* (1999); Y Dezalay and B Garth, *Dealing in Virtue: International Commercial Arbitration and the Construction of a Transnational Legal Order* (University of Chicago Press, 1996).

More in particular this contribution may concern the concept and operation of distinct legal orders[173] that may be separated from or transcend national legal orders. As we saw in the preceding sections, they are not necessarily territorially defined, but may operate per class of activities or of persons, like amongst professionals in their business dealings. It suggests a more or less consistent set of rules per order, closely connected with its dynamics. They may be self-created in that order based, in the case of commerce and finance, on the innate or commercial logic and on common sense, whilst the rules could change very quickly depending on the change in the nature of the business. These rules are likeley to be articulated in many ways, through practitioners, think tanks, academics, ICC, Uncitral, Unidroit (in treaty or model laws or through general principles that may be deduced from them even if they are not incorporated in domestic laws).

Legal theory may thus help in the identification of the international commercial and financial legal order (as of any other), the various sources of the law in that order and their relationship and use. Practices and custom may thus be given their proper place whilst the impact of extra-legal considerations in the formation and application of the law may be better assessed. It may thus give a better and more coherent insight in the formulation and operation of the ensuing rules and in their ranking amongst each other. It is likely to show that black letter rules can hardly be more than guidance, no matter from which legal source they come. Legal theory may also be able to reconsider the status and impact of private international law and determine the proper residual role of domestic laws. It will also show that, although the necessary means of enforcement may still be through national courts, they may apply these new rules in professional dealings. Alternatively, enforcement could be through international arbitrations or other international *fora* (yet to be created), the rulings of which should be supported by all courts of modern commercial nations. It would be of prime interest to such nations (assuming they would want to continue to participate in the international flows of goods, services, capital and payments) that such support should be quickly and efficiently forthcoming.

Legal history is here also a help in showing that various sources of private law always operated side by side and that the attempted monopolisation of private law creation by modern states, particularly in civil law countries through legislation, is a recent phenomenon, was never entirely successful, and is probably an aberration.[174] It may also show that much in the law developed in a haphazard manner, was coincidental or transplanted from other legal systems. Indeed much of private law has no national root.

[173] Julius Stone, although a positivist in the Hart tradition, was concerned with legal orders, but since he concluded that law could not be defined, it was also impossible in his view to define legal orders but both could be described to some extent, see *Legal Systems and Lawyers' Reasoning* (1964), 178*ff*. Other modern writers mention legal orders or systems, but it is as such not yet a major area of study in modern legal thought. The concept has received some more attention in public international law, see recently also Neil MacCormick, *Questioning Sovereignty* (Oxford 1999), especially chapters 1 and 5 and certainly also in EU law, see the seminal European Court Cases 26/62, Feb 5 1962, *Van Gend & Loos* [1963] ECR 3; 6/64, July 16 1964 *Costa v ENEL* [1964] ECR 1203; 14/68 Feb. 13 1969 *Walt Wilhelm* [1969]ECR 1, and any current EU law handbook on the subject.

For the interaction in comparative law especially at EU level, see K Lenaerts, "Interlocking Legal Orders in the European Union and Comparative Law", 52 *Int'l & Comp LQ* (2003), 873, in which the nature of legal order itself was not, however, further discussed and was in essence perceived as statist but the emphasis was put on common denominators in the law of Member States as normative guidance for the ECJ, in which connection the reference in Article 228 (2) of the Treaty referring to 'general principles common to the laws of the Member States' should also be noted, not so far elaborated in a clear body of law, but it has reinforced notions of non-contractual liability under EU law of national and Community public authorities, see for example joined cases 83 and 94/76, 4,15 and 40/77, *HNL and Others v Council and Commission*, [1978] ECR 1209. A common vision of Member States may also underly state liability for non-implementation of community law, see joined cases C–6/90 and C–9/90, *Francovitch and Others*, [1991] ECR I–5357.

[174] See for a reconsideration of legal history and its role at least in common law research in the 20th Century, KJM Smith, "History's living legacy: an outline of 'modern' historiography of the common law", 21 *Legal Studies* (2001), 251.

Comparative law, finally, gives us a feel for our legal environment, provides us with a mirror and ideas at the practical level. More importantly, it may give us also an idea of general or core principles that could suggests an international normativity, as such potentially of great relevance in the hierarchy of norms within the modern *lex mercatoria*. But that could only be so if the commercial practice recognises itself in the result. That is the limit of comparative law in international trade and finance and also of the relevance of the sets of contract and other principles, like the European and Unidroit Principles of Contract Law, which are now proffered at the more academic level.

The comparison may be all the more subtle and valuable if the different legal orders from which the various rules hail are more fully understood and their own dynamics per order (and their limitations) better articulated. Traditional comparative law had little eye for these aspects and remained wedded largely to black letter laws and statist notions of the sources of law. This has come in for some considerable criticism[175] but it does not altogether do away with the usefulness and need of comparative law studies in a functional sense.[176] In fact, the conclusion of the discussion on legal culture in section 1.4.2 must be that at least in the West mythical or more mysterious origins of the law in a national psyche are replaced by greater openness and rationality. It can only be repeated in this connection that much present property and contract law is in its origin not nationalistic but rather Roman, germanic or feudal whilst, at least in commerce and finance, much modern law is practical, technical, and problem solving in ways that do not differ a great deal from country to country, except sometimes in the detail, where the differences seem often more coincidental than fundamental. Whereas in other areas of the law diversity may be of value and should be cherished, in international commerce and finance this is only disruptive and costly. The conclusion from section 1.4.3 must further be that in commerce and finance modern policy considerations play also a lesser role. Finally, where other cultures are involved that cannot accept Westerm standards in terms of the prevailing economic system and its flows, their practices can hardly be a model for anyone else in international commerce and finance.

In international commerce and finance, the emphasis in this connection may be usefully limited to the study of the living laws of the main modern trading nations (in this book limited mainly to the laws of England, France, Germany and the US) whilst, as just mentioned, the comparative results must always be tested for their usefulness in the light of the dynamics of the international flows of goods, services, capital and payments, the risks participants incur and the protections they need in that connection to the extent they cannot be negotiated. Comparative law beyond these limits may still have some academic value but no great practical meaning or authority.[177]

---

[175] See for a discussion of the critiques and a re-evaluation Anne Peters and Heiner Schwenke, "Comparative Law beyond Post Modernism", 49 *Int'l and Comp LQ* (2000), 800. See further also G Samuel, "Comparative law as a core subject", 21 *Legal Studies* (2001), 444.

[176] A more structuralist approach assumes on the other hand an immanent legal model against which national laws or even transnational law can be tested. This gives another meaning to comparative law which is not directly relevant in the context of this book. Whilst in this book a mere black letter approach is much avoided and the search for substantive transnational law formation is on, this is perceived as a probing attitude in which domestic laws are tested for their usefulness in an international context as they may be an expression of a potentially broader normativity in the dynamics and further development of modern international commerce and finance. In this connection, domestic laws may also usefully show at least the legal *issues* that need to be dealt with in the formulation of the *lex mercatoria* and for which the traditional solutions need also not *a priori* be rejected. Rather they must be retested for their validity in an internationalised context.

[177] Not much further attention can be given here to the aims of comparative law and its objectives. Some look for a common core (whilst rejecting any mythical search) like RB Schlesinger, "The Common Core of Legal Systems, An Emerging Subject of Comparative Law Study" in KA Nadelmann, AT von Meheren and JN Hazard (eds),

Above this was demonstrated *in international commerce* with international sales as an example. It may be of use to mention in this connection also a number of structures that require particular attention *in international finance* and where there is traditionally little communality. One may refer here to set-off and netting, assignments of receivables (or of contractual rights more generally, especially important in securitisations), floating charges, finance or conditional sales and reservations of title, trusts and constructive trusts, and to book-entry systems concerning investment securities entitlements. They will all receive a great deal of attention in the rest of this book with a view to the internationalisation of the evolving legal structures and practices concerning them.

1.4.5 The Operation of Different Legal Orders: Evolution of a Federal Commercial Law in the US, of Transnational Private Law Concepts in the EU, and of International Human Rights Law in the Council of Europe (European Court of Human Rights)

Ultimately it may be of some interest to look more carefully at the spontaneous evolution of commercial or other forms of private law in some easily identifiable different legal orders like the federal legal order in the US, the confederate legal order of the EU, and the international human rights order which the Council of Europe represents.

It was already mentioned several times that in the US private law remains in essence a matter of State law and that goes also for commercial law. As a consequence, the Uniform Commercial Code (UCC) is state law, based on unification of the law between States without any federal involvement (even though at an early stage in its preparation it was considered to make commercerical law federal law but this idea was not pursued). It was adapted in each State, often with some differences. That was so from the beginning. Further differences may arise where some States adopt amendements and others do not or only do so later, although the unity that the Code has brought is impressive and treasured. No State lightly goes here an own way and the courts, both federal and state courts, are also supportative of this uniformity in the interpretation process.

The foregoing would suggest that there is no room in the US for federal commercial law therefore for commercial law in the federal legal order but that is not strictly speaking so. First, specific provisions in the US Constitution may lead to it. Foremost there is original

XXth Century Comparative and Conflicts Laws. Legal Essays in Honor of Hessel E Yntema (1961), 65 *ff.* It leads to a search for universal, non-structural, fundamental principles common to all legal systems. In Zweigert-Koetz, *An Introduction to Comparative Law* (translation, Tony Weir 3rd ed. 1998), 40, there is even a presumption of similarity (*praesumptio simultudinis*), at least in the less politically driven areas of private law because the needs are very similar everywhere. However, it remains a fact that even in commerce and finance there are great differences especially in equity law concepts like trusts, beneficial ownership interets, conditional ownership rights, or security interests and floating charges where any common core becomes so general or superficial that it has hardly any distinctive or guiding meaning. See for a discussion in Germany also J Esser, *Grundsatz und Norm in der richterlichen Fortbildung des Privatrechts. Rechtsvergleichenden Beitraege zur Rechtsquellen- und Interpretationslehre*, (4th ed. 1990) where the emphasis is more in particular on the role of fundamental principles common to all legal systems in the further development of national laws, so also E Rabel, "International Tribunals for Private Matters", *The Arbitration Journal* (1948), 209. It should be noted that much of the search for common principles by these authors took' place in a somewhat different context and tends to be directed towards showing that the differences between common and civil law are not as great as sometimes assumed. In this book, the emphasis is foremost on legal issues that commonly arise in different legal systems, therefore on an inventory of problems that normally arise in more advanced economies in respect of certain legal structures, like eg security interest, conditional and beneficial ownership, or investment securities entitlements, rather than on common solutions, as these solutions are more likely to be dictated by the evolving needs of international commerce and finance itself than by examples in existing national laws.

federal power to legislate in the area of interstate commerce (Article II, Section 8, Clause 3). It forms the basis for the legislation in admiralty or maritime transport (like the Pomerene Act for bills of lading issued for transportation between the various States of the US, to foreign countries, US territories or the district of Columbia, see also chapter 4, section 2.1.5). Treaty law may provide another base, like the adoptation of the Brussels Convention incorporating the Hague Rules in the US Cogsa in 1936, see also chapter 4, section 2.1.10. The ratification by Congress of the Vienna Convention on the International Sale of Goods may provide another base in the area of international sales, although there may be foremost reliance here on direct effect under state law.

At one stage there was a broader, more general attempt made to create federal commercial law for all *interstate* commercial transactions. It was not unlike the creation of federal *jurisdisction* in cases where there was diversity of citizenship. However, this attempt failed; yet there remain some areas or pockets where federal commercial law is still important, even beyond specific federal statutes in this area or treaty law adopted by the US. Within the US, this move was early on accompanied by a similar de-nationalising process as we now see globally. It took (some) commercial law outside the State sphere proper, in which connection developing custom or the broader law merchant was instrumental. The important role of all commercial custom and therefore also of this kind was acknowledged in the UCC itself, in Section 1–103(a)(2) (1–102 (2)(b) old) to which reference has also already been made several times, even though here still by virtue of State law recognition and incorporation.

To understand this broader movement towards federalisation of commercial law within the US better, one has to take a step back and consider first the broader picture of the applicable law in *interstate* cases, either because of diversity of citizenship or because of the interstate nature of the subject-matter. Such cases arise in interstate commerce when e.g. contracts are concluded between persons from different States of the Union or the object of a sale must move from one State to another as part of the delivery process. They arise for similar reasons also outside the commercial areas in an environment where there was under the Constitution (Article III, Section 1) always a dual court system (State and federal), so that both types of courts (therefore also federal courts) could potentially deal with commercial issues.

Under the US Constitution, federal and diversity (of citizenship) cases were assigned to the federal courts but not cases with other interstate aspects. Even in federal and diversity cases, it left the possibility of federal courts still applying the procedural rules of the States in which they sat. This did not happen. At first, federal courts would only apply federal procedural rules in equity cases, but they now do so in all cases pursuant to the Federal Rules Enabling Act of 1934 and the Federal Rules of Civil Procedure that resulted from it (subsequently also used as the most important model for state procedural law reform leading to an important measure of harmonisation).

In federal diversity of citizenship cases, the issue similarly arose whether federal or state law applied to the merits (in terms of statutory, regulatory or case-law). If federal law was to apply that would have called for the development of a federal common and commercial law. However, in the important Erie case of 1938,[178] the applicable law was considered always to be state law in which the federal court sat (if necessary found through state conflict of laws rules, see eg Section 1–131 (1–105 old) UCC which refers

---

[178] *Erie v Tompkins*, 304 US 64 (1938). See in this connection especially WA Fletcher, "The General Common Law and Section 34 of the Judiary Act of 1789: The Example of Marine Insurance", 97 *Harvard L Rev* 1513 (1984).

in this connection to the law of the State that bears an appropriate relationship to the case).

For this restrictive attitude, there had always been a strong foundation in the Judiciary or Rules of Decision Act 1789 (Section 34) even though the US Supreme Court had at first tried to construe some substantive federal common law in areas not already covered by federal statutes. Since 1938 it is accepted that there is *no* federal common law as such (including federal commercial law) but that there are still pockets where there is some federal private law, especially in federal statutes and case-law pursuant to it and in some areas of commercial law and custom. Thus in marine insurance and the interpretation of the relevant policies, federal law was applied by the federal courts from early on followed later on by the law concerning negotiable instruments and interstate common carriers.[179]

There is an emphasis here on the interstate nature of commerce and the need to follow its ways and thus provide certainty beyond the confines of individual states. It may thus shift the law creating force to another more efficient legal order. That is a most important conclusion. Whilst in Erie the further development of a federal common law was halted in principle, it did not strictly speaking exclude the further development of federal commercial law under the commerce clause or pursuant to interstate custom or the law merchant. On the other hand, it cannot be overlooked that the UCC firmly re-established an efficient state law regime in much of the traditional areas of commercial law including negotiable instruments. Yet at least in specialised areas a federal commercial law applies, like for cheques drawn on the US Treasurer or in notes issued by the US. In this connection reference is indeed still made to a *federal law merchant*, which continues to develop separately from state law.[180] Similarly special federal statutes may concern bills of lading as we saw.

It will be of interest to see whether within the EU similar common notions will be allowed to develop especially in inter-community trade, in that case better considered in the context of the modern development of the international law merchant or *lex mercatoria*. For the EU proper, this is quite possible in areas where the EU has intervened through

---

[179] *Robinson v Commonwealth Ins Co*, 20 Fed Cas, 1002 (1838). A diversity case involving a bill of exchange in respect of the sale of land, title in which was subsequently disputed, was also held to be covered by federal law, *Swift v Tyson*, 41 US 1 (1842), in which Section 34 of the 1789 Act was not held to apply to questions of commercial law but only to the interpretation of local statutes and customs. With reference to Lord Mansfield in *Luke v Lyde*, 2 Burr R 883, 887, it was stated that the law of negotiable instruments was not the law of a single country. In *Western Union Telegraph Co v Call Publishing Co*, 181 US 92 (1901) the use of common information carriers was not believed subject to any state law either but in the absence of any federal statute rather to federal general common law, containing the general rules and principles deduced from the common law enforced in the different States.

[180] *Clearfield Trust Co v US*, 318 US 363 (1943). See for an important other instance of the further developmenmt, *Robinson v Commonwealth Ins Co*, 20 Fed Cas, 1002 (1838). A diversity case involving a bill of exchange in respect of the sale of land, title in which was subsequently disputed, was also held to be covered by federal law, *Swift v Tyson*, 41 US 1 (1842), in which Section 34 of the 1789 Act was not held to apply to questions of commercial law but only to the interpretation of local statutes and customs. With reference to Lord Mansfield in *Luke v Lyde*, 2 Burr R 883, 887, it was stated that the law of negotiable instruments was not the law of a single country. In *Western Union Telegraph Co v Call Publishing Co*, 181 US 92 (1901) the use of common information carriers was not believed subject to any state law either but in the absence of any federal statute rather to federal general common law, containing the general rules and principles deduced from the common law enforced in the different States, see also WA Fletcher, "The general common law and section 34 of the Judicature Act of 1789. The Example of Marine Insurance", 97 Haward LR (1984), 1513.

An important instance is thus the further development of the law merchant as such in interstate trade, *Southern Pacific Transportation Co v Commercial Metals Co*, 456 US 336 (1982). It shows clearly that there is room for such inter-state commercial law in the US. Typically federal matters are also lifted out off state law like a claim in respect of injuries caused to a federal soldier, *US v Standard Oil of Calfornia*, 332 US 301 (1947). The key is here the protection of uniquely federal interests and situations in which Congress has given the power to develop substantive law, see *Texas Industries v Radcliff Materials Inc*, 451 US 630 (1981).

Directives in specific private law matters, like in consumer law including the development of the concept of good faith in that context, see especially section 2.3.2 below and chapter 2 section 1.3.4 (for the good faith notion). Where EU levies or taxes must be reimbursed, some special EU rules of tort and unjust enrichment have also developed.[181]

In Europe, the European Court of Human Rights established by the Council of Europe (well to be distinguished from the EU European Court of Justice), in its jurisdiction under the European Convention on Human Rights of 1950 and its Protocols, has developed a notion of ownership independent from national laws in the context of ownership protection as a human right (pursuant to Article 1 of the First Protocol). This case-law is important and original as it seeks to develop and internationalised ownership concept.[182] Its main feataures are that no one may be deprived of his possessions except in the public interest but always subject to the conditions provided for by the general principles of international law (except that the payment of taxes or other contributions or penalties is not affected). There is therefore a need to define possession, interference and any justification thereof. The Court gives to the notion of possession in this context an *autonomous meaning* which is ownership- connected[183] but notably not limited to physical goods. There is here an emphasis on economic realities covering also beneficial rights.[184] From a jurisprudential point of view, the importance is indeed that possession, ownership or property need *not* be connected with a *national* legal order but may acquire an *internationalised* meaning in the international legal order the European Court of Human Rights represents and defends.

The evolution of *international* property rights will be further explored in section 3.2.2 below.

1.5   The Transnational Private Law amongst Professionals

1.5.1   *The Guiding Function of International Commercial and Financial Law. The New Legal Order in the Professional Sphere. The* Lex Mercatoria v Ius Commune *Approach*

In sections 1.1.6 and 1.3.3 above, the globalised commercial and financial legal order and the internationalisation or transnationalisation of the private law in the professional sector

---

[181] See also T Tridimas, *The General Principles of EU Law*, 313 (OUP 1999).
[182] See also Jan-Peter Loof et al (eds) *The right to property, The influence of Article 1 Protocol No 1 ECHR for several fields of domestic law* (Shaker Publishing, Masstricht, 2000).
[183] See *Marckx v Belgium*, ECHR June 13 1979, Series A, Vol 31, Par 63.
[184] See *Gasus Dosier und Foerderintechnik v Netherlands*, ECHR Feb 23 1995, Series A, Vol 306B par, 53. It can as such cover security interests of the tax authorities and others, reservation of title and other conditional ownership interests or limited proprietary rights. It also includes intellectual property rights and claims based on contract and tort. This is clear from the reference to 'valeur patrimoniale' or asset which suggests at the same time that the essence is right with a commercial value that can be sufficiently ascertained. It may as such cover goodwill or an existing clientele, see *Van Marle v Netherlands*, ECHR June 26 1986, Series A, Vol 101, Par 41 and later in *Iatridis v Greece*, ECHR March 25 1999 but not a mere expectancy (of an inheritance) or a right to receive property, see *Marckx v Belgium* cited in the pevious footnote. Yet a right to an inheritance of a deceased person may be claimable even if non-partioned, *Inze v Austria*, ECHR Dec 9 1987, Series A, Vol 126, Par 38 and *Mazurek v France*, ECHR, Feb. 1 2000. A disputed claim is not sufficiently established, but once adjudicated it is and a state against whom the claim was awarded can no longer annul the claim through legislation, see *Stran Greek Refineries v Greece*, ECHR Dec 9 1994, Series A, Vol 301B, Par 61. Even a claim in a prima facie case might be so protected, *Kitel v Poland*, ECHR Jan 17 1997, see also *Pressos Compania Naviera v Belgium*, ECHR Nov 20 1995, Series A, Vol 332, par 31.

were briefly discussed. This topic must now be revisited in the light of what was said above about the development of civil and common law, about the idea of codification and its effect on the development of alternative sources of the law, about the centralising and nationalistic tendencies in the formulation of laws at state level, about the cultural aspects of the law in a Western sense, and about the influence of group formation and the emergence of different legal orders, and especially about the application and impact of fundamental or more general legal principle and newly developing custom in the international commercial and financial legal order.[185]

The conclusions so far are that:

(a) The civil law of the codification is apt to adopt a statutory positivism, which drives out all sources of law except legislation. It is intolerant of fundamental or general legal principle and custom, except if the codes or other legislation specifically refer to them as they may do especially in the context of the reference to good faith (and sometimes custom) in the interpretation of contractual rights and obligations. Common law especially of the English variety does not like general principle either, especially not in legislation, mainly for practical reasons (such as giving too little guidance). It accepts besides statutory law, however, the common law and equity case-law and its further development as independent sources of law. It is also tolerant of developing customary law, although it tends to subject it, at least in England, to binding precedent which is a somewhat incongruous limitation whilst English law also views it as a mere implied condition. Common law interpretes statutory law restrictively to leave ample room for the other sources of the law, although statutory law has the power specifically to overrule them but aims in private law mostly at consolidation and the completion of legal developments and has as such mostly a facilitating function, that is to make the existing law work better.

(b) The civil law of the codification, although claiming full control over private law, accepts, however, that it cannot cover everything in detail and therefore allows for a liberal interpretation technique of statutory law, which is nevertheless considered complete and expected to cover all gaps and new developments. In modern times, civil law lawyers use in this connection mostly a teleological or normative interpretation technique. It looks at the aims and purposes of statutes and tries to find solutions on that basis. It often centres around the notion of good faith, particularly in contract. In countries like Germany, the good faith notion operates in all areas of the private law where there is interaction between parties, sometimes therefore even in proprietary law, eg in reshuffling preferences or priorities in execution sales.

(c) In common law in the absence of full codifications, following precedents creates a semblance of a similar order and the *stare decisis* policy backs this up. In civil law, on its face, such a policy is not necessary since the basic framework of rules is in place through codification, but in practice the older the codes and the more interpretational freedom is used by the courts, the more important established precedent becomes to provide predictability also in civil law. Although

---

[185] See for comments on the differences within the common law and particularly the differences between the English and American attitude which is thought often to be closer to the one of the civil law: RC van Caenegem, *Judges, Legislators and Professors* (1987). See for the differences between American and English legal thinking also, PS Atiyah and RS Summeres, *Form and Substance in Anglo-American Law* (1987).

common law case-law is in essence inductive in its rule formulation and civil law statutory interpretation deductive, in practice the facts of the case, their analysis, distinguishing them under the applicable precedent or statutory rules dominate in both legal systems. However, the civil law judge must somehow always find an anchor for his private law decisions in the codes or their systems or at least pay lip service to them. This is particularly clear in the practice of the *Cour de Cassation* in France. It is much less of a common law requirement, even in areas where there is statutory law.

(d)   There is also the point that common law tends to look first at facts and civil law rather at rules. It is important not to exaggerate this difference, but it seems to allow civil law to select and handle the facts more effectively, probably because the civil law lawyer has a given picture of the legal structure in mind that allows a more selective approach to the facts from the beginning, which may result also in substantial cost savings. Civil law also does not have the encumbrances of the old jury system and its effect on procedure and evidence which remain in common law too formal.

(e)   Another facet of this difference in approach is that common law will look at new commercial and financial structures in a pragmatic manner and support them legally on the basis of need rather than on the basis of fitting them into a pre-existing legal system to which all new rulers must conform.

(f)   Both in civil and in common law, there remains a strong current that all law, whether as a set of rules or of principles or whether from a sole statutory source or also coming from others, is nationalistic, therefore state-bound and cannot exist separate from sovereignty. This is contrary to both the history of common law which originally knew a separate (internationalist) law merchant with its own courts and to the history of the *Ius Commune*, the predecessor of the civil law. It is a nineteenth century idea, very much associated with the modern idea of centralised statehood. It never had a resonance in public international law, and can in Western Europe hardly be maintained in view of the human rights protections and the EU concept of the superiority of its own legal order and laws. Although in a technical sense, it could still be said that the application of human rights related notions and EU principles in private law depend on the national acceptance of the relevant underlying treaty law establishing their superiority, it has become clear (and accepted) that there are here different legal orders at work.

(g)   In the nineteenth century, the cultural aspect of the law was highlighted and used as an argument to nationalise the law, even private law, and see it as the expression of a national mindset. However, culture as such need not be nationalistic and can be broader based. The notion of modern statehood itself is founded in a broader Western culture which ultimately also determines the cultural context of the law as it now operates in Western countries, rather than national culture. In any event, modern culture is characterised by a lesser impact of mystical and atavistic notions or tribal roots and irrational subcurrents. Its individualism, openness, and search for rationality tend to go in another direction.

(h)   It was further argued that the cultural impact on the law requires a focus on a mindset that translates into authenticity of social groupings. In a more individualistic society this authenticity itself becomes more of a problem and requires the organisation of the modern state which in a Western sense is democratic, culturally *divers*, decentralist, respectful of the rule of law and of human rights, and tolerant in respect of other social groupings that may compete with it.

(i)   It was finally argued that in this atmosphere, different legal orders competing with states may exist and could acquire an autonomous law making function whilst they and the decisions reached under them would have to be respected in principle by states unless in respect of effects on their own territory there is a clear public policy consideration against this. State courts, if asked to, would also apply this law in matters concerning these groups and their members whilst all decisions under this law should be given state sanction when required, again subject to some basic minimum checks which will be public policy related.

(j)   We find here a cultural and sociological background to the operation of different legal orders. In this respect, the operation of the international commercial and financial legal order and its interaction with state legal orders is of prime importance.

It is one thing to apply laws within clearly defined borders or within clearly defined groups. As long as legal systems or orders do not habitually come into contact with each other they can operate in isolation. Well into the twentieth century, that was largely the situation with the exception of some legal orders (especially churches and other associations) operating within states. However, there was always an important view which assumed that these organisations could only operate by state fiat only. In commerce, even where transactions were crossing borders, it meant that some national law was habitually invoked to cover them. It was not always of great help as national law could sometimes not remotely cover the more modern ways of commerce or the more modern financial products developing internationally as we shall see throughout this book, quite apart from the question of which national law should in that case apply.

Private international law as we now know it is here the by-product of this nineteenth century attitude and purports to point to the applicability of the most appropriate national law in international cases, which for civil law countries largely means statutory law. It provides in theory a simple way to find the applicable domestic law, although the development of proper private international law or conflict rules themselves became increasingly complicated and the results often questionable and erratic, see section 2.1 below. In the meantime, the more curious aspect was that in civil law countries (except much later in Germany and Switzerland), these private international law rules were hardly based on codes or other forms of legislation, which contained few provisions in this respect. They developed in most countries completely independently from them on the basis of general principle, which was otherwise greatly mistrusted as a separate source of the law.

Instead, in the internationalised professional sphere, it proved often better to recognise the independence of international legal relationships and therefore of the international element itself in cross-border legal relationships and discount it in the *lex fori*, therefore still in a national law only. This became much the American approach as we shall see. Whilst cross-border transactions remained relatively few, the differences in approach, which did not necessarily produce different results, proved mostly acceptable but with the enormous increase in international trade, commerce and finance, this is less the case and the question of applying a national law *per se* and therefore the appropriateness of the applicable rule itself and of the adequacy of its contents is much more urgently posed.

As we saw, the more modern key issue is whether there now exists *a sufficiently independent international commercial and financial legal order in the professional sphere* in which legal relationships between parties operating in that order are or can be detached from a domestic environment and be subject to the legal principles and rules obtaining in that order. If so, and in the absence of much precedent for the time being, the further question is what these rules are and how they must be applied. Subsequently, the question arises how substantive rules in that order can be better developed. Is (a form of) codification in this order appropriate, or perhaps legislation (that is treaty law without any claim to exclusivity), or should fundamental and general principle combine with industry practices to arrive through case-law at a more developed system of substantive transnational rules?

It is indeed submitted that the independent professional commercial and financial order is now a sufficient reality for its own normativity to be accepted. It is even now expressed through fundamental principle, through more precise legal rules deduced from them or from comparative national law, through custom and practices formed in this order, and sometimes perhaps even through specific international public policy notions. There is also some uniform treaty law that must be assigned its place in the new legal order and might be further developed. It might even for transactions in non-Member States be indicative of more general principle operating in the international order as a whole, in which context comparative law, the Unidroit and European Principles of Contract Law, the Principles of Trust Law, etc may also play a role. In the further development of these rules, it is not only necessary to determine what their sources are and what the ranking of these various sources is, but it is also necessary to determine what the legitimate practical needs are and to formulate the transnational rules foremost on the basis of those needs. Restatements or sets of Principles gathered by academics as an expression of non-binding prevailing insights might here also help.

These rules should be seen as applicable to all private or public entities that are operating in the new legal order. National judges must in relevant cases take its normativity into account in the judicial process and the national authorities must attach their sanctions to the ensuing decisions. These authorities should also give their sanction to similar decisions from other jurisdictions or from arbitration panels which, pursuant either to domestic, treaty or international legal principle, are entitled to give full faith and credit, no matter how the applicable law is found and what it is. That must be left to those judges or arbiters who should learn to find and apply the new transnational law directly.

This leads into the discussion of the modern *lex mercatoria*, which will follow in section 1.5.4 below with a further elaboration in Part III. It requires a more utilitarian approach, but also more of a natural law attitude in which substantive rules are developed not only on the basis of practical need but also of fundamental principle. The relevant details can often be deduced from existing modern legal systems acting as models but would have to be responsive to the international context and reflect business circumstances and needs. In the civil law, that could mean a reversion to where we were at the beginning of the nineteenth century, therefore to the internationalist approach of those days as embodied in the pre-codification *Ius Commune*. This reversion would apply to the sources of law, not to the legal rules of those days which are largely superseded and must move forward.

It would indeed mean an acceptance of a multitude of sources of law operating through a *hierarchy of norms*. This is the first aspect of the modern *lex mercatoria* that will be explored more fully below. Indeed, it implies a return to pre-codification times in attitude but it could hardly be a return to the *Ius Commune* variant of the Roman law, which the natural law school had already abandoned,[186] or to the approach of the German

---

[186] One sees a different tenor in the work of Helmut Coing, *Europäisches Privatrecht* (1985–89), and of R Zimmermann, *The Law of Obligations: The Roman Foundations of the Civilian Tradition* (1990/1993). These authors look for a revival or at least continuation of the *Ius Commune*. They follow in this respect in the steps of

Pandectists which in Europe would suggest a reconstituted BGB now at European level. It would seem infeasible and undesirable if only because it is unlikely to be able to accommodate the common law and the requirements of the modern law merchant. In any event, the *Ius Commune* itself contained hardly any commercial and no financial law, which was much more recently developed. The new approach means much sooner the re-emergence of the natural law school method directed to modern international needs and to the development of new substantive rules and subjective rights in that context. It is the reason why in the foregoing so much attention was given to that school, its emergence, method and operation.

It may well be asked whether there is at this moment in time a sufficient number of lawyers who have the insight, vision and education to build a transnational professional law in this manner out of fundamental legal principle and general principles derived from the diversity of national laws (civil and commercial) and particularly industry practices legally to underpin international business in Europe and elsewhere. Is there a methodology and a sufficient unity in view to achieve transnational law on a more than incidental basis? Especially, is there a sufficient understanding of the dynamics of modern trade and finance and of the different perspectives of civil and common law and of their more fundamental differences to make some fusion possible?

If one looks at the efforts in Uncitral and Unidroit, one must doubt that there is at the moment any consensus on method and content. Also at EU level they are mostly lacking. At present, unity or uniformity is largely seen as a question of compromise between national legal rules and concepts. At least von Savigny had a method based on the analysis of a fairly neutral set of outside norms (the Roman law). The developers of the new *lex mercatoria* miss such a neutral model and need to be guided by the ever-changing dynamics and requirements of modern commerce and finance itself. Mere borrowing from existing civil or common law countries or finding some kind of compromise between their laws would hardly seem to be sufficient and an adequate response. Also the form this effort should take in terms of codification, uniform laws, model laws or restatement of principles is far from clear. These issues will be briefly revisited in section 1.5.5 below.

As far as practical need is concerned, it is even now possible to identify a number of issues, however, which will be further discussed in the following chapters. The dynamics of international trade and its need for adequate legal protection would probably mean that contracts in the professional sphere and conduct would be less based on traditional offer and acceptance or bargain and consideration notions. Reliance and conduct would be at the centre with a more tort oriented system of remedies. The new law, being the law between professionals, would be less concerned about pre- and post-contractual duties than is now more common in the consumer sphere. Although notions of good faith would play a role, contract interpretation amongst professionals would be fairly literal, but there should be ample room for custom and commercial practices. Agencies operating internationally may well acquire a different form, which for undisclosed or indirect agencies might lead to direct rights of the principal in assets bought even if the agent had acquired them in his own name.

Koschacker and Wieacker, n 5 *supra*, who wrote, however, for a different time. Their approach was rightly rejected by R Feenstra, 'The Development of European Private Law' in Miller and Zimmermann (eds), *The Civilian Tradition and Scots Law* (Berlin, Duncker and Humblot, 1997). Scotland and South Africa are often held up as an example in this connection but they have systems of law that substantially developed beyond their Roman and *Ius Commune* pasts. At least in commerce and finance, they may be some model in so far as they show a fusion between modern common and civil law notions and point to a future law in which commercial law is less systematic, more flexible and above all dependent on legal sources other than mere legislation.

As will be shown in chapters 4 and 5, in modern financings, conditional or temporary ownership rights would have to play a much larger role than at the moment in civil law countries as would the trust or trust-like structures. Segregation and tracing notions would have to be pursued. It suggests a more open and contractualised system of proprietary rights but also a better protection of third parties, both through a more abstract system of title transfer, discussed in chapter 4, and more extensive *bona fide* purchaser protection. In the area of secured transactions proper, there is a universal need for floating charges, equally with a more extensive third-party protection against the effects. In ownership questions, the emphasis should probably be on the protection of actual possession rather than on more abstract notions of ownership or constructive possession. Again this protection would essentially be in tort (rather than through proprietary actions). As far as monetary claims are concerned, they should essentially be considered ordinary assets and be treated and transferred much more like negotiable instruments in terms of transferability, defences of the debtor and *bona fide* third-party protection of the holder.

1.5.2   Spontaneous Sources of Law: Fundamental and General Legal Principle. Custom

In the foregoing, something has already been said about fundamental legal principle as a source of law. It came up especially in connection with the existence and status of natural law. In section 1.2.6 its origin was more extensively discussed and it appeared that Roman law, Canon law, the *Ius Commune*, and in modern codifications even the Austrian Civil Code of 1811, all accepted a more fundamental source of law besides the positive legal rules, which were often thought to have a more temporary character. Natural law became much less popular after the nineteenth century codifications when in the codification drive the legal force of fundamental principle operating besides statutory law became problematic in civil law. In the common law, especially of the English variety, principle was never very popular, particularly in legislation, but this was less a matter of principle than a matter of practice (sufficient guidance). In modern private law, at least the overriding impact of human rights principles even amongst citizens in their private law relationships is increasingly understood. Considerations of fairness or natural justice are often indirect references to them or to other more fundamental principles.

In the international legal order, these fundamental principles play a particular role and are likely to be the basis of the whole system of the law operating in that order. They are the basic notions of *pacta sunt servanda*, detrimental reliance and apparent authority, the acceptance and protection of ownership (or of the appearance thereof in others if occasioned by the rightful owner) and the possibility of transferring it to whomever one wants, the liability for one's own actions especially for substantial wrongdoings and possibly even for unjust enrichment, and the need for fair dealing, avoidance of fraud and market manipulation. It is the essence and basis of the law of contract, agency, property, tort and restitution.

In considering the nature of each relationship, there might also be fundamental fiduciary and disclosure duties or aspects of good faith or intrinsic logic to be considered, leading for example in the case of agency to postponement of the agent's interest if there is a conflict and in the case of a contract to an interpretation and completion of the rights and duties of the parties so as best to give effect to their envisaged relationship. Depending on the type of relationship between the parties (be they professional, evenly balanced or uneven in terms of power and information), they may require a measure of openness and disclosure and negotiation in good faith as pre-contractual duties. In matters of performance these principles may require due diligence and the necessary measure of co-operation. Trust, dependence and confidentiality may, depending on the situation, thus suggest other important legal principles: see further section 3.1.1 below.

In this connection, *fundamental* legal principle should be distinguished from *general* legal principle which can often be deduced from comparative research, that is from similarities in national laws. General principles show some consensus amongst domestic legal systems and may achieve a force of their own in the international legal order, always assuming that they reflect its basic needs and may be considered responsive to its dynamics.

As far as the other spontaneous source of law, which is *custom*, is concerned much has already been said in the foregoing about this source of law too. From the outset it should be re-emphasised that there is a difference between (a) custom operating as a separate source of law, (b) custom referred to in codifications or statutes when it does not operate autonomously, and (c) custom (or practices) operating as an implied contractual term when it operates by virtue of the parties' intent.

As we saw, the civil law of the codification is in principle hostile to custom as an independent source of law. Common law is friendly but reduces its impact by applying (at least in England) the *stare decisis* rule to it so that a finding of custom may at the same time deprive this law of the flexibility and adjusting facility that is its very essence. On the other hand, since it is by nature uncertain, it can often best be found in published decisions, although expert opinion is another important source of knowledge of custom. Both common and civil law systems in their more modern form see custom, in so far as it is accepted, often as part of a national law and of domestic attitudes. They have more difficulty with international custom as an independent self-propelling source of law that may override domestic laws (and customs). Both domestically and internationally, it has proved much easier to accept the force of custom, at least in contract, on the basis of an implied term or otherwise (in civil law) only when codes or statutes make a specific reference to it. That at least preserves the idea that the statute or code always remains superior and the ultimate source of the law.

Custom as an independent source of law has often been a problem for the legal mind, even before the time of the great codifications. To demonstrate it, much was said above on the relationship between customary law, statutory law and the Roman Law or *Ius Commune* as *lex scripta* before the nineteenth century when statutory law was still less relevant, see in particular section 1.2.5. In D.1.3.32.1 it was clearly stated that statutory law (*leges*) could be superseded by custom (*non-usus*), which was seen as the implied will of the people. There remained room for this view in the *Ius Commune*, especially in respect of city laws, like those of Northern Italy, which were in any event restrictively interpreted on the basis of D.1.3.14, which (in the view of Bartolus) implied that all that was counter to the *Ius Commune* as *ratio iuris* should have limited effect in order to leave as much room as possible for the unifying Roman law.

However, custom was unlikely to prevail over laws issued by sovereigns as the *Ius Commune* accepted that laws no longer emanated from the people's will but rather from the German (or Holy Roman) Emperor or from other local sovereigns, who were considered to have similar powers. This legislation was often liberally and extensively interpreted on the basis of D.1.3.12/13 as we saw for France in section 1.2.5 above and here custom (and the *Ius Commune*) lost out, even though statutory law and local custom often combined and were considered together like in the French *droit coutumier*. In that extended sense, D.1.3.32.1 was used in France (for political reasons) to support the dominance of the *droit coutumier* itself, even against the *lex scripta* or *Ius Commune* (but not the *leges* or statutes).

D.1.3.14/15/16 suggested on the other hand that the Digests and their *tenor rationis* were superior to custom, if not also to statutory law, and it became normal to interpret at least custom in the commercial sense in such a manner that it did not conflict with the *Ius Commune* or its *ratio scripta*. The Digests do not contain a clear definition of custom, but D.1.3.33 suggests a practice of long standing and does not seem to appreciate that practice implies change. D.1.3.34 even suggests case-law as the most certain source of knowledge concerning custom.

In later times, Hobbes and Bentham in England saw custom as an ill-expressed and ill-defined kind of law based on the inarticulate will of the people and only given effect to by the sovereign's tolerance. In similar positivist thinking, custom thus became indirectly a branch of statutory law. This was most certainly not the view of the natural law school of Grotius and his followers. It is also criticised by all those who take a more sociologiocal approach to the evolution and application of the law. It could at least be said that custom is as good an expression of the people's will as any other source of law including that emanating from legislatures even if in custom the will of the people expresses itself more in the following than in the creation. It is principally driven by practical needs and by what makes sense, at least in trade and finance.

Not all custom is legally the same. It is clear that some customs are no more than behavioural patterns or habits without legal significance, for example the canons of politeness and social intercourse. Others may acquire some legal effect but can be unilaterally abandoned by giving notice to the other party. If for example a broker normally gives certain commission discounts, clients may come to rely on them, all the more so if the habit becomes an industry practice when a legally enforceable rule may be the result. It prevails, however, only until the broker unilaterally (but explicitly) amends his terms. A custom proper is a practice which is universal in the trade or a relevant segment thereof and can as such not be unilaterally withdrawn or changed, and would require an industry shift or the other party's consent to be set aside in an individual case (except if mandatory). An important practical difference between a habit even if relied on and custom generally is that the burden of proof of their effectiveness is with the client in the first instance whilst in the latter case courts or arbitrators may accept and apply the rule *ex officio*.

Custom or trade or industry practices, which are not distinguished here, may be found in standard terms or even be reflected in *written* compilations, often of private bodies like the ICC (Incoterms and UCP), see for the status of these ICC practices also chapter 2, section 2.3.10. This may also apply to the Worldbank (IBRD) efforts in the area of international direct investment and their protection (Guidelines for Foreign Direct Investment). They may be regularly updated by these bodies and therefore abruptly changed without undermining their basic status of custom or objective law whereby these industry bodies may further elaborate on them without detracting from their customary status.

As just mentioned, in the interpretation of contracts and the determination of the rights and duties of the parties thereunder in civil law it became normal only to take custom into account (except as implied contractual term) if the codes specifically referred to it and, in contract, it then figures normally besides good faith notions in interpretation: see Article 1135 of the French Cc and Section 157 BGB in Germany. It is now mostly accepted that such good faith notions may in pressing cases also be used to adapt the contract. It is conceivable that in the normative or teleological interpretation method custom may sometimes play a similar corrective role, as Section 157 BGB in Germany clearly suggests, although parties may normally deviate from it when the clear provisions of the agreement prevail.[187] The new

---

[187] Mandatory customary private law is nevertheless rare, but custom in proprietary matters may be considered to be mandatory, as in the manner of transfer of negotiable instruments, where custom in England dispensed with the consideration requirement and accepted also *bona fide* purchaser protection. Internationally, the Hague-Visby

Dutch Civil Code in Article 6(2) always gives good faith a leading role and allows it to overrule, not only the wording of the contract, but also the effect of custom and equally of statutes impacting on the contract. This is a unique approach not followed anywhere else. It suggests that notions of good faith can be absolutely mandatory. In the USA, Section 1–302 (Section 1–103(3) old) UCC refers in this connection to parties still being able to set good faith standards amongst themselves unless they are not manifestly unreasonable.

Another question is whether custom may be subject to strong policy considerations as expressed in statutes. On its face that would seem so, but if a practice or custom continues notwithstanding contrary statutory law, it may be considered to have overturned it. There is much dead letter law, especially in older statutes, even in those that may have been intended as mandatory. In fact, many mandatory laws are undermined through widespread continuing old practices, like in health and safety standards. The fact that they are often not taken seriously and that local practices continue may fatally affect the status of these laws, even if invoked in the courts.

In the USA, Sections 2–202(a) and 2–208 UCC avoid the term 'custom' in the context of the sale of goods, but it is used in the general part, *cf* Section 1–103(a)(2) (Section 1–102(2)(b) old) where its overriding importance is made plain and accepted as we saw in section 1.1.2 above. The UCC rather refers to the course of business or usage of trade, at least in the context of the interpretation and supplementation of agreements for the sale of goods. They may not be invoked to contradict the express terms. Section 1–205 defines the usage of trade and also contains a statement as to the role of the course of dealing.

Under Section 1–303 (Section 1–205 old) UCC, trade usage is 'any practice or method of dealing having such regularity of observance in a place, vocation or trade as to justify an expectation that it will be observed with respect to the transaction in question'. A course of dealing 'is a sequence of previous conduct between parties to a particular transaction which is fairly regarded as establishing a common basis of understanding for interpreting their expressions and other conduct'. It is further stated that 'a course of dealing between the parties and any usage of trade in the vocation or trade in which they are engaged or of which they are or should be aware give particular meaning to and supplement or qualify terms of an agreement'.

In England, the emphasis remains in this connection often also on the implied term and presumed consent. As a consequence, custom may be considered subjective and has to be proven. It must then be more than a course of action habitually followed, has to have consistency and regularity, and must be recognised as binding by the parties.[188] It shows

---

Rules were often considered mandatory customary law also, long before they were generally adopted by the Brussels Bill of Lading Convention: see Haak, "Internationalism Above Freedom of Contract" in *Essays on International and Comparative Law in Honour of Judge Erades* (1983), 69. It is sometimes also suggested that international mandatory customary law overrides the jurisdiction of the *forum actoris* (of the plaintiff therefore), see Verheul, "The Forum Actoris and International Law" in the same *Essays in Honour of Judge Erades*, 196.

In proprietary matters, any custom thus has a mandatory flavour as property law with its *in rem* or third party effect depending on objective standards. Thus in the USA, under Article 9, which is subject to the underlying policy of the UCC to permit the continued expansion of commercial practices through custom, usage and agreement of the parties, (Section 1–103(a)(2) (Section 1–102(2)(b) old)), it has been held that a buyer in the ordinary course of business who is protected against contractual security interests under Section 9–320 Section 9–307(1) old), acquires this protection (where a down payment has been made) as soon as assets are set aside for him, therefore even before he acquires title, and the security interest of the financier of the seller's inventory is thereby dislodged: see *Daniel v Bank of Hayward*, 425 NW 2d 416 (1988). Commercial practice was invoked in this connection to support a fairer balance between the interests of the buyer in the ordinary course of business and the secured party. Little proof of the existence of such commercial practice or custom was presented in this case which also showed that the accepted practice in this respect could change overnight through case law which yielded here to academic writing and lower court findings.

[188] See *Product Brokers Co Ltd v Olympia Oil & Cake Co Ltd* [1916] 1 AC 314, 324. *cf* also *General Insurance Corp v Forsakringaktiebolaget Fennia Patria* [1983] QB 856.

sensitivity in English law to overruling the parties' stated intentions, especially in the professional sphere. The subjective approach appears to limit the effect of custom in proprietary matters. Yet in other contexts, objective custom is accepted. Thus the UCP and URC have found a status in England on the basis of custom current amongst banks and not as implied conditions between the parties.[189]

Sensitivity to accepted practices and custom is particularly important in international trade. Yet the Vienna Convention on the International Sale of Goods avoids any reference to custom and uses the terms 'usages' and 'practices' instead (Articles 4, 8 and 9). According to Article 9(1), the parties are bound by any usage to which they have agreed and by any practices which they have established between themselves. This is simply an extension of the contract and intent principles. It implies a subjective approach to custom. Article 9(2) tries to undo some of the impact by accepting as an implied condition all usages of which the parties knew or ought to have known and which in international trade are widely known to or regularly observed (but not merely widely operative) between the parties to contracts of the type involved in the particular trade concerned. It is not, strictly speaking, possible for the Convention to be conclusive in this matter as the force of international usages and practices may derive from other sources or from custom itself, especially if they operate generally, therefore also amongst other parties, as indeed the force of fundamental legal principle. This seems accepted in Article 4 of the Vienna Convention.

It is not uncommon for the construction of custom as an implied condition of a contract to be used to move from party intent to objective law. This has happened for example to the concept of good faith which in England remains largely an implied condition, whilst in Germany and the Netherlands it now constitutes an objective norm. Conflict rules in contract law were for a long time considered implied conditions as well, until it was found no longer appropriate that their status, and thereby the applicable law, was dependent wholly on the parties' intent whereupon these rules became accepted as objective norms. The reverse also happens: confidentiality has long been considered an essential feature of arbitrations, so much so that it was often not even mentioned in arbitration statutes or rules, but its status as objective norm to be respected by all is increasingly reduced to at best an implied condition and it is possibly now necessary to insert an express term in the arbitration clause for parties still to be able to rely on it. It might yet be different in alternative dispute resolution (ADR) proceedings see also section 3.2.4 below.

In conclusion, it would seem that there are four questions that merit special attention in connection with custom: (a) is custom subjective in the sense that it only applies if implicitly made part of the contract by the parties themselves and is it therefore merely an implied term, (b) can it also be objective and an independent source of law, (c) is it subject to any domestic or international policy constraints, including notions of good faith, especially if itself international, and (d) is it based on regularity or may it change over-night in view of rapidly changing trade or financial patterns and practices or taxation rules as they are the ultimate expression of what makes sense and is practicable?

1.5.3   Uniform Substantive Law as Alternative to Private International Law

Uniform substantive law may as treaty law also be an important source of transnational law. It is private law that may be agreed between different states and incorporated in their

---

[189] The UCP and UCR are collections of rules concerning documentary credits and collections compiled by the International Chamber of Commerce. Although they assume incorporation in contracts, this is not necessary, at least not in England: see *Harlow and Jones Ltd. v American Express Bank Ltd and Creditanstalt-Bankverein* [1990] 2 Lloyd's Rep. 343.

own legislation. As was already observed in the previous section, it may also have (at least persuasive) force as expression of general principles in other contexts, especially that of the *lex mercatoria* as will be discussed in the next section. It often covers only international transactions. That is certainly true for the uniform law concerning international sales, first agreed in the Hague Conventions in 1964 and later in the 1980 Uncitral or Vienna Convention on the International Sale of Goods. Much other work on uniform laws, both of Uncitral and of Unidroit, moves at the same level of international transactions. This need not, however, always be the case.

As we have seen, within the USA, there has long been uniform law between the various states — of which the UCC is the most important example — that does not concern itself only with interstate transactions. It is of course not international either and therefore here only of interest as a technique. This uniformity is adopted for *all* transactions the subject matter of which is covered by these uniform laws like the sale of goods. There is another difference: this American uniform law is prepared by private institutes and is not agreed between the various states of the USA. It is, however, incorporated in state law, but in the absence of an agreement amongst the states, this incorporation allows for variations in the text per state, of which there are some even in respect of the UCC. As far as suggested amendments are concerned, some states may also move quicker than others so that further disparities emerge, even if only temporarily. There may be further differences in interpretation. Nevertheless, in the USA there is on the whole a positive attitude towards uniform state law, particularly towards the UCC, and judges seek uniformity in its interpretation.

These two uniform law approaches (through treaty or parallel laws) are in principle also open to Member States of the EU if they want to organise themselves in that way, but within the EU there is also the possibility of harmonisation of private law through Directives in the limited areas where the EU has power to operate, which are even more limted in private law. They have been popular and important in the company law field but also in the consumer law area. They do not strictly speaking achieve unity, as the measures the EU proposes in this manner still need implementation in domestic laws which may result in considerable variations in the detail. The EU could impose strict uniformity by issuing Regulations but has so far not done so to achieve unity in private law, except in the area of recognition and enforcement of sister state judgments and bankrupticies. In the EU, the uniform law so created may only cover interstate (therefore international) transactions, but it is often broader.

Where uniform law is only meant to cover international transactions or other international legal relationships, there follows an approach to the applicable legal regime which is *fundamentally* different from the private international law or conflicts of law approach. The uniform substantive private (treaty) law (sometimes also called 'international private law' or 'transnational private law') tries to formulate a *joint* set of norms, therefore equal norms, between different countries for a particular subject, as Uncitral (partially) did in the 1980 Vienna Convention for the International Sale of Goods. The private international law approach, on the other hand, accepts conflicts of laws but tries to establish conflict of laws rules under which ultimately one of the connected *national* laws results as the most appropriate law to govern the case. In this connection, reference is sometimes made to the '*voie directe*' as against the '*voie indirecte*' approach to the law applicable to international legal relations.

The *voie directe* approach leads to the formulation of substantive transnational rules to be implemented through treaty law, either later or at the same time incorporated in the domestic laws of the treaty states, so that theoretically still only national law results.

This approach does not contemplate uniform parallel laws or a system of directives in state conglomerates like the EU. The *voie indirecte* approach, on the other hand, only leads to the formulation of some (conflict) rules as a conduit to reach the most appropriate domestic substantive rule, whereby the nature of the conduit rules in terms of purely national or transnational conflict of laws notions itself remains another issue. Normally, conflict rules are now considered purely national or domestic in nature and may as such differ considerably from country to country. They may themselves be unified, however, through treaty law, which is the objective of the Hague Conference. This Conference drafts uniform conflict laws, which should be clearly distinguished therefore from the just mentioned uniform substantive laws.

Uniform substantive laws as part of the *voie directe* approach create substantive law at a transnational level, even if they still rely on incorporation in domestic laws. The result may be imperfect transnational law in the sense that, in this manner, the operation of this law in an own transnational legal order is still not truly recognised or understood. As treaty law, it cannot go beyond the states that have accepted it and is always subject to its own rules concerning scope and applicability. This often implies great limitations. Even the 1980 Vienna Convention on the International Sale of Goods is only a very partial formulation of the law and applies only in certain circumstances. To the extent considered reflective of international practice, it may, however, have a wider reach within the *lex mercatoria* as example of general principle as we saw. Another problem is that, this type of law is hard to change as this would depend on the amendment of a treaty and it is therefore not flexible. It is an important other reason for the current unpopularity of the uniform treaty law approach. Moreover, it results so far mainly from academic compromise amongst domestic legal concepts, another reason it is less likely to catch the true dynamics and needs of the international professional sphere, not even in the relatively small areas where uniform law of this nature has so far been produced. There is often a great deal of complication and no clear message.

For all these reasons, the work of Uncitral and Unidroit in shaping uniform treaty law, see also section 1.4.5 above, has often lacked conviction and ratifications and its wider role in the *lex mercatoria* is therefore also limited.[190] In any event, they seldom mean to cover the whole field, so that references to conflict laws remain necessary for areas they do not. This is often even thought desirable in areas that are covered, should there be incompleteness. This is clear from the formula of Article 7 of the 1980 Vienna Sales Convention, which has become some kind of standard, see also chapter 2, sections 1.6.3, 1.6.4, 2.3.5, 2.3.6 and 2.3.7. Using conflict rules pointing to non-uniform domestic laws to fill the gaps in uniform law hardly squares with the codification idea and its concept of completeness (at least in the areas covered) and was therefore not adopted in the 1964 Hague Sales Conventions. Neither was the Article 7 language taken up in the 1995 Unidroit Contract Principles, but it re-appeared in the Finance Leasing and Factoring Conventions of Unidroit as it does in all Uncitral proposals and now also in the European Contract Principles. It can and does give rise to endless debate and confusion on the applicable law within the application of this uniform substantive law itself even in the definitions of the terms used. It tends to destroy completely what little uniform law these Conventions bring.

Only the 1980 Vienna Convention prepared by Uncitral has had some true success as uniform substantive treaty law. It is ratified by many states (even the USA, but not the UK), but is only a very partial codification of international sales law, often excluded by parties to

---

[190] See also Basedow, n. 145 *supra*, 257.

the contract. Uncitral's Model Arbitration Law has also been successful, not as treaty law but as a model for national laws, and was followed in many countries. Even where not followed, as in England, it has influenced modern arbitration law greatly, *cf* the English Arbitration Act 1996. The impact of Unicitral has otherwise been modest and Unidroit's impact has been more modest still. Whatever their merits, which will be discussed in chapter 5, its Finance Leasing and Factoring Conventions of 1988 now have a sufficient number of ratifications to be effective, but they are still few.

Uniform laws as part of the *voie indirecte*, notably the Private International Law Conventions of the Hague Conference, have had more success, especially in the area of family law, but also in trusts and agency, although again often with few ratifications. Beyond the efforts of the Hague Conference in this respect, the 1980 EU Rome Convention on the Law Applicable to Contractual Obligations has been one of the most successful conflicts conventions in modern times.

The uniform substantive and conflict of laws approaches are conceptually mutually exclusive, and to the extent both were embodied in treaty law from the 1950s onwards, they openly clashed when the Hague Conference at its seventh Session in 1951 and at its eighth Session in 1955 ultimately completed a private international law Convention on the Law Governing the International Sales of Goods.[191] The discussions continued thereafter in the sense that the Hague Conventions on the uniform law of sales were succeeded in 1980 by the Vienna Convention on the International Sale of Goods. The 1955 Hague private international law Convention on the Law Governing the International Sale of Goods was updated by a new text in 1986. Within the EU the 1980 Rome Convention on the Law applicable to Contractual Obligations also covers sales, but it goes beyond it.

In the Vienna Convention, there was an attempt at reconciling both approaches with as a result a substantial step backwards from an internationalist approach. Whilst the Hague Sales Convention more logically only relied on its general principles (Article 17) for its interpretation and supplementation, the later Vienna Convention as just mentioned retreated from the transnational uniform approach and allows in areas not expressly settled by it (but always within its scope, see Article 4), the applicability of private international law rules (Article 7(2)). The result is therefore ultimately the application of a domestic law in these areas, although only after consideration of the general principles on which the Convention is based (which are largely unclear and there is no longer any pretence at completeness of the uniform law in areas it covers), but apparently without further consideration of the international context of the sale, which is only mentioned in Article 7(1) in the context of interpretation, see for a discussion and critique more in particular chapter 2, sections 1.6.3.

In this approach, international custom is also given a limited function only, see Article 9, and is seen as an implied condition therefore ultimately dependent on the will of the parties. It is not therefore an objective norm of transnational law and, as significantly, neither is it an interpretation tool, see chapter 2, section 1.6.4.

As will be discussed more extensively in section 2.2.4 below, the evolution of the conflicts approach towards more substantive rules and general principles of fairness and common sense *itself* suggests a development towards *substantive* transnational standards which are

---

[191] Some of the animosity against uniform law at the time transpired in an important contribution of Professor Kurt H Nadelmann, "The Uniform Law on the International Sale of Goods: A Conflict of Laws Imbroglio", (1965) 74 *Yale Law Journal* 449, which also reproduces the negative opening statement on the uniform substantive law approach by the president of the Hague Conference Professor J Offerhaus from Amsterdam at the 10th Session of 1964.

result-oriented, at least in the professional sphere. It is this development within the modern *lex mercatoria* that has become the more significant now that the globalisation of the international market-place increasingly demands it. It is particularly relevant for international sales, regardless of what Articles 7 or 9 of the Vienna Convention provide, as they cannot rule on the effectiveness of other sources of law. In fact, it is becoming more obvious that the law of international sales should be considered from the perspective of the *lex mercatoria* and its hierarchy first, in which the Vienna Convention plays a role as a partial codification only (if applicable under its own terms or otherwise perhaps as an expression of general principles), rather than that any *lex mercatoria* notions must be fitted into the Vienna Convention and its methods of interpretation and supplementation.[192]

1.5.4   The Hierarchy of Norms in Modern International Commercial and Financial Law: The Role of Fundamental and General Principles, of Custom, Uniform Treaty Law, Comparative Domestic Law, and Private International Law

If one assumes an independent international legal order in which international commercial and financial transactions or perhaps all professional dealings are or may be operating and which is increasingly detached from domestic legal orders, the question becomes what law prevails in that order and how it must or can be found. It is clear that it is essentially built on fundamental and general principles, on custom and perhaps in some areas even on uniform treaty laws but may residually still use private international law rules pointing to a domestic legal system as well. The key then is the *hierarchy* between these various sources of law. That is the essence of the modern *lex mercatoria* approach in which substantive rules subsequently develop. The *lex mercatoria* will be discussed more extensively in Part III of this chapter, but may here be summarised as follows.

At the top there are a number of fundamental basic principles, more particularly discussed in section 3.1.1 below. First, is the notion of *pacta sunt servanda* establishing the binding force of promises. Closely connected are the detrimental reliance and apparent authority notions whilst there may also be principles of dependency, trust and confidence to be considered. Thirdly, there is the notion of ownership establishing the principle of exclusivity of property rights, the protection of the appearance of ownership, particularly in the possession of movables, the need for third parties in principle to respect these rights, and their transferability.[193] Fourthly, there is liability for the consequences of one's own actions, especially if clearly wrongful or leading to unjust enrichment; and fifthly there is the notion of fair dealing guarding in particular against fraud, market

---

[192] The *uniform* sales laws date from 1928 and came from Unidroit. They are associated with the name of the German Professor Ernst Rabel. The original idea for the project of uniform *conflicts* rules in the area of sales dated from the 6th Session of the Hague Conference in 1928 and is associated with the name of the French Professor Julliot de la Morandière. It led to a first draft in 1931. The Diplomatic Conference concerning the uniform sales laws immediately followed the 7th Session of the Hague Conference in 1951, which had the conflicts Convention in the area of sales as one of its main topics. Many of the same persons became involved in both projects notwithstanding the considerable difference in approach. The Hague Conference produced a final text on the *Law Governing the International Sale of Goods* in 1955. The *Uniform Sales Laws* were finally agreed in the Diplomatic Conference of 1964 which immediately preceded the 10th Session of the Hague Conference.

[193] This protection covers in fact all rights, even the contractual ones, as every claim has a proprietary side. It means that a claim derived from transnational law presupposes an ownership concept based on that law. In any event, proprietary structures are normally created by contract and follow from it. Between the parties themselves they remain largely contractual by nature. The difference is in the third party effect, often less relevant in chattels because of the fairly universal notion of the protection of the *bona fide* purchaser of goods. This is mostly different for proprietary rights in claims except with regard to equitable interests in common law.

manipulation including insider dealing and anticompetitive behaviour. There may here also be fundamental principles of environmental, safety and health protection.

There are more of these fundamental principles — human rights and European law tell us so — also in dealings between individuals, but these are not many in international trade and finance. All are in essence mandatory or *ius cogens* and form the basis of the whole system. They contain the essence of contract, agency, property, tort (negligence) and perhaps even restitution law.

In the details, one should *first* look for custom or practices of a *mandatory* nature, including proprietary protections. They are still rare but conceivable, especially in the area of financial products. That is clear from the development of negotiable instruments. It is in more modern times reconfirmed in the eurobond practices. Mandatory behavioural rules have undoubtedly developed internationally amongst the participants in the financial services industry as will also be discussed more in detail below. Here the views of the more sophisticated modern financial regulators may provide a further lead.[194]

Secondly, one should look for uniform substantive *treaty* law of a *mandatory* nature, at least to the extent that transactions are covered by them. This type of law may be limited to transactions between, and may only be applied by courts in, Contracting States. They are also rare,[195] but could in the area of financial regulation and market behaviour increasingly derive from standards set by the EU, BIS or other international organisations, like the WTO. In the proprietary aspects of assignments of receivables, Uncitral's work on receivable financing may here also prove important.

Thirdly, in contractual matters, one should subsequently look for the precise *contractual* terms, the force of which derives in this approach directly from the fundamental notion of *pacta sunt servanda*. Into this bracket also fit incorporated standard terms like, in finance, the ISDA swap master and the PSA/ISMA Global Master Repurchase Agreement.

Fourthly, one should look for directory customs or practices, like those for example that may prevail in the contractual aspects of underwriting, trading and settlement of eurobonds, now partly to be found under IPMA and ISMA rules or recommendations obtaining in that market, and one may similarly search for them in respect of other financial products. In this layer, we also find the UCP for letters of credit if incorporated in it.

Fifthly, one should look for uniform *treaty* rules of a *directory* nature like those of the Vienna Sales of Goods Convention, if and when applicable to the legal relationship in question. Again there are not many of these rules and their force may be limited to transactions between ratifying states or only bind courts in such states.[196]

Sixthly, one should look for *general principles* (to be distinguished from the fundamental or overriding principles or *ius cogens*) of the particular legal structures or relationships that may be considered common to leading civilised legal systems. Many of the more precise rules concerning contracts and personal property may be found here. In this sixth layer one should also look at the intrinsic logic of the transaction and at what good faith and common sense may require beyond the dictates of the fundamental principles or *ius cogens*. That certainly may also apply to proprietary structures, including the protection of the

---

[194] See for mandatory practices n. 187 *supra* and for the rules between the international capital markets participant s. 3.2.3 *infra*.

[195] An example is Article 12 of the 1980 Vienna Convention on the International Sale of Goods.

[196] It would be doubtful if the references to private international law in the manner of Article 7(2) of the Vienna Convention would carry much weight here. It was already suggested in the previous section that they would appear misconceived. Rather, the Uniform Law Conventions should, in the areas they cover, be considered as self-contained, perhaps like other pieces of codification, all the more so since they are drafted in the Continental style.

bona fide purchasers. Uniform treaty law may here be of further guidance even if under its own terms it is not applicable to the transaction in question for lack of an association with a Contracting State in the particular instance. Master Agreements or ICC rules, even if not incorporated in the contract, may also come in under this heading of general principle. So may uniform treaty law if not applicable under its own rules.

By now most of the missing parts of the *lex mercatoria* should have been filled out, but *ultimately*, if there is still no solution, one could apply a national law found through the most appropriate conflict of laws rules. Particularly in property matters, conflict of laws rules may still prove relevant in the formative period of the transnational *lex mercatoria* in the professional sphere. Here the *lex situs* traditionally prevails, but it creates particular problems for assets that move transborder and for intangible claims of which the location is much more difficult to identify, see also chapter 4, sections 1.8. and 1.9. In the hierarchy of norms explained here, there is in this application of domestic law through conflict of laws rules in any event a *discretionary* element; these rules are too *residual* in the hierarchy of norms to be always binding. As regards what conflict rules would be applicable, the Hague Conventions could give some leads, as could, in the EU, the 1980 Rome Convention in contractual matters, certainly for courts in countries that adopted them, but in this hierarchy of norms even they cannot provide the last word. That is expressed in the discretion which obtains here even in purely private law aspects, therefore even where no governmental interest is clearly at stake. It depends on whether the law so found has any message and whether it can reflect the dynamics of the situation.

Domestic law found in this manner may at first remain important, eg more in particular for secured transactions, except probably if they are created in assets that move transborder or are intangible or if they are created in internationalised assets, like aircraft and ships, but no less in eurobonds or other types of negotiable instruments or documents of title if used internationally. There are particular problems here with domestic rules governing non-possessory security interests including floating charges or shifting liens. This concerns *their type, coverage and ranking*. In a substantive transnationalised law sense, as to type and coverage, common law notions may increasingly show the way. As regards ranking, since it concerns here the world of professionals whilst small creditors are mostly out of it and *bona fide* purchasers of chattels in any event mostly protected against these charges, the substantive transnational rules could be fairly basic: the older go before the younger, the specific before the general, the contractual before those arising from the operation of the law, and purchase money security before loan security.

Publicising these charges may be a particular issue, but in view of the protection of *bona fide* purchasers of chattels, it is mostly an issue between creditors *inter se* and for non-possessory security rather a matter of disclosure duties and reliance on such disclosure (or the lack of it) in as far as professionals are concerned. We have to accept that, at least for movable property, proprietary and similar rights are by the very nature of the asset normally hidden. It is the main reason of course why *bona fide* purchasers of such assets are increasingly protected against hidden proprietary and security interests and why third party effect becomes less relevant in respect of them. The effectiveness of secured transactions in movables suffers from it and publication duties do not truly help because they are not commonly meant to deprive third parties from their *bona fide* purchaser protections. More attention is given to that aspect in connection with the American practice in chapter 5, section 1.6.2.

In any event, at the international level, secured loan financing is increasingly eclipsed by the use of other techniques, especially the sale and repurchase or conditional/finance sale (repos), as a funding alternative in finance leases, repos and factoring, see more particularly chapter 5. One of the reasons for this development must be that domestic notions and formalities, including publication requirements in connection with the creation of secured interests are avoided in this manner, although other problems arise, especially in the proprietary position and protection of the prospective owner of the assets and its creditors, as we shall see.

In the hierarchy of norms of the *lex mercatoria*, the impact of domestic *public* law rules also needs to be considered. Recognition of their extraterritorial effect is a matter of *comitas* and therefore an area of discretion of courts and arbitrators, not strictly speaking of the application of a conflicts rule at all, as Article 7 of the 1980 EU Rome Convention on the Law Applicable to Contractual Obligations clearly accepts. A proper balance must be struck here between domestic (and international) public policies if conflicting, except if there is a higher international consensus when we are back at the level of mandatory practices or uniform treaty law, therefore much higher in the hierarchy of norms. That is also the view in the US, see Restatement (Second) of Conflict of Laws, Section 6 and Restatement (Third) of Foreign Relations, Sections 402 and 403, see also section 2.2.6 below.

It follows that, in this hierarchy, domestic laws, *whether public or private*, are always applied with a measure of discretion depending on their relevance in each individual case, although they may remain very relevant for the time being in private law aspects when more general common principles are lacking.

In this hierarchy of norms, where reference is made to custom and practices, which are not distinguished in this book, see section 1.5.2 above, it means the normativity established in a particular trade or what is considered normal in that trade. Expert witnesses will explain or arbitrators will know what there is in this regard in terms of types of products and how the market in them works or how they are commonly provided and handled, and what is understood by these customs. Case-law may also increasingly help, especially domestic case-law that would be aware of the hierarchy of norms in this respect.

As for the law derived from international conventions — therefore uniform substantive private law in the commercial and financial area — one more point needs to be made. Naturally we should concern ourselves here mainly with conventions that are in force and are binding upon the parties, which often means that the underlying transaction is cross-border between persons in ratifying or Member States. As already mentioned several times before, even then they present a problem. Except within the EU, which boasts its own legal order, through incorporation this law may still be considered merely domestic and is often meant to be binding only on courts in ratifying states.

If international practices develop against these conventions or continue once these conventions, if contrary, are ratified, they must be respected as the higher norm, even in ratifying States. They can also override mandatory treaty law of this nature. The prevalence of international custom or practice will be made increasingly clear when conventions only reflect compromises between domestic legal orders and misunderstand the international dynamics and transactional patterns. In the hierarchy of norms, these international practices or customs are themselves only corrected by the fundamental requirements of the *ius cogens*, or if merely directory by the contract terms themselves.

As already observed before, in the hierarchy of norms, uniform treaty law that under its own terms does not apply to parties from non-contracting States may still be normative if sufficiently reflective of international practices. Draft uniform law conventions or conventions that remain insufficiently ratified may here also give clues as to the substantive law applicable in the international commercial and financial order and may have persuasive force but they should primarily be tested against the general principles and operate in that (sixth) class. The Contract Principles of Unidroit and the European Union should also be put in that class. Again much of these non-effective conventions and also the Principles are often too much of a compromise between all kinds of often purely domestic ideas and notions to be indicative or supportive of the prevailing international practice. At least in contract law, there is often also too much of a consumer law ethos in them, wholly inappropriate for the professional sphere. That will be discussed in greater detail in chapter II. It is of course the reason these Principles or Conventions often have so much difficulty in taking off. If they want to bring something new, they must show that the international practice embraces the novelty before it can become legally relevant, but it is not necessary in this connection that each and every party has (implicitly) accepted it.

It may be of interest briefly to consider at this stage the discussion of the impact of this hierarchy approach within the *lex mercatoria*, for example, for letters of credit. Naturally we have here the trade practices embodied in the UCP. It is of course possible that the UCP do not fully incorporate them or that new practices develop before the UCP text itself is adjusted, in which case these additional or newer practices obtain. Incorporation in the contract is not necessary as the UCP are now mostly considered customary, but if they are incorporated they achieve a higher ranking in the hierarchy of norms as just explained, and may well continue to prevail in that manner over newer directory custom and practices. That could be the true meaning and effect of incorporation. Now, the UCP concern only a partial codification, often they need supplementation. Again, one way is to go immediately to conflict of laws rules. Another is to explain the UCP rules first from the point of view of their own system and logic (as civil law codifications do), look at general principles commonly applied to them in the most important commercial countries, and only as a last resort apply a national law via conflict rules, in the manner as here explained, therefore on a discretionary basis only. It would seem to be the better approach.[197] It means that any domestic laws still applied became part of the transnational *Lex Mercatoria* and figure therein, therefore no longer as domestic laws.

1.5.5   Agents of International Convergence and Harmonisation: The Role of Unidroit, Uncitral, the ICC, The Hague Conference, the EU, and the American Law Institute and Commissioners on Uniform State Laws in the USA; and the Impact of the International Legal Practice and Scholarship

In the previous sections, reference was made several times to organisations like Uncitral and Unidroit as agents of international convergence and harmonisation of commercial and financial laws. Uncitral is the United Nations Commission on International Trade Law. It was created in December 1966 and has operated from Vienna since 1969. It has been particularly active in the area of the international sale of goods and prepared the 1980 Convention. The Uncitral Model Arbitration Law was also mentioned. Uncitral operates in many other areas generally through conventions, model laws, legal guides, and, in the area of arbitration, also through Rules and Notes.

Thus there are Uncitral Conventions on the International Sale of Goods, on the Limitation Periods in the International Sale of Goods, on International Bills of Exchange and International Promissory Notes, on the Carriage of Goods by Sea, and on Independent Guarantees and Standby Letters of Credit. The Convention on Receivable

---

[197] One may see an incipient recognition of this in Lord Denning's remarks in *Power Curber International Ltd v National Bank of Kuwait SAK* [1981] 3 ALL ER 607 in which it was said in connection with bank guarantees that courts should not interfere with them at the behest of the underlying parties nor recognise such interference by the courts of other countries. This would appear an expression of an underlying fundamental international principle.

Financing is the latest. There are Model Laws on International Commercial Arbitration, on Cross-border Insolvency, on Electronic Commerce, on the Procurement of Goods, on International Credit Transfers, and on Receivable Financing (to be discussed more extensively in chapter 4, section 1.9.3). There are Legal Guides on International Counter-trade Transactions, on Electronic Funds Transfers and on Drawing up International Contracts for the Construction of Industrial Works. Rules have been issued on Arbitration and Conciliation. As just mentioned, there are finally also Rules and Notes, like those on Organising Arbitral Proceedings.

Uncitral is directly run by the UN and operates under the General Assembly. Unidroit is the older organisation and is a left-over from the old League of Nations. It was not con-verted into a UN agency but re-established in Rome after World War II as an independent organisation. It has 56 Member States and operates under a Governing Council consisting of 25 members appointed by its General Assembly for five years. This General Assembly meets once every year to vote the budget. It also votes on the Work Programme proposed by the Governing Council which is in charge of policy, implemented by the Secretariat headed by the Secretary General. The President is appointed by the Italian Government and an *ex officio* member of the Governing Council. Unidroit is funded by Italy and other participating countries. There is a healthy competition with Uncitral, even some overlap, but the Uncitral remit is narrower and limited to trade law.

The main Unidroit project was originally the International Sales of Goods Convention, a project started in 1928 at the initiative of Professor Ernst Rabel from Germany, later at the University of Michigan at Ann Arbor. Because of the disfunctioning of Unidroit during and after World War II, the Dutch Government was asked by the United Nations to provide a venue for the continuation of this work which was completed in two diplomatic confer-ences in the Hague in 1951 and 1964. They resulted in the Hague Conventions on Uniform Law in the International Sale of Goods. The project was subsequently taken over by Uncitral, as we saw, resulting in the successor Vienna Convention of 1980. Important newer Unidroit Conventions are the one on International Financial Leasing, on Factoring, on Agency in the International Sale of Goods, on Stolen or Illegally Exported Cultural Objects, and on Mobile Equipment. The first two and last one will be discussed more extensively in chapter 5.

As may be seen, Uncitral has produced more results but in a narrower field as it is lim-ited to trade law. On an international scale, the International Chamber of Commerce in Paris (ICC) has been operative for years in the area of international trade. The Uniform Customs and Practice for Documentary Credits (UCP) have been in existence for letters of credit since 1933. Since 1956 there have also been Uniform Rules for Collections (URC). For guarantees, the ICC compiled two sets of uniform rules, the first being the Uniform Rules for Contract Guarantees of 1978 (URCG) and the second the Uniform Rules for Demand Guarantees of 1992 (URDG). The Incoterms have since 1936 covered the basic trade terms like Fob and Cif and now also many others. In the area of international sales, the ICC produced a Model International Sales Contract. These various rules and practices, which are very important, are deemed applicable by virtue of contractual incorporation or on the basis of custom only. They are not promulgated in any way. The significance of the ICC and its various committees in this respect is that these texts are very regularly updated. Outside organisations like Uncitral sometimes co-operate, as in the revisions of the UCP. These revisions do not always promote conceptual clarity and academic input is often missing, but they are at least up to date.

In the USA, the work of the National Conference of Commissioners on Uniform State Laws and of the American Law Institute on Restatements has already been mentioned several times.

It resulted from private initiatives, not supported by any agreement amongst the various states. The National Conference has drafted a number of Uniform Laws for adoption in the different states. The most important one is the UCC, which was (exceptionally) a joint project with the American Law Institute. Normally this Institute prepares only Restatements, which are non-binding, are not meant to achieve the force of legislation, but have nevertheless had a considerable impact on the further development of the law in the relevant areas and also serve as guidelines for the courts. They have a strong persuasive force.

The Uniform Commercial Code is now accepted (with certain modifications) in all 50 states of the Union. It was substantially conceived by Professor Karl Llewellyn (1893–1962) of Columbia University (later of University of Chicago) as Chief Reporter with the help particularly of Soia Mentschikoff as Associate Chief Reporter. Others also had a substantial input, like Professor Grant Gilmore of Yale on Article 9 concerning secured transactions. The UCC is regularly updated and a number of new chapters have also been added.[198]

The above institutes and organisations mainly aim at producing uniform substantive laws, either through treaty law, as parallel laws (in the USA), as models, or through guidance. As we saw, there has also been an attempt at drafting uniform conflict rules. This has long been the objective particularly of the Hague Conference on Private International Law, set up in 1893 under the leadership of Professor TMC Asser (1838–1913) from Amsterdam, who was later given the Nobel peace prize for his efforts (1912). This Conference produces draft treaties on private international law topics. It meets every few years on an irregular basis. Its approach is therefore notably *not* one of formulating uniform substantive laws. On the contrary, it is a proponent of the private international law approach to international transactions, looking for the application of a national law to apply to international transactions. It only seeks to formulate, through treaty law, common conflict principles in specific areas. In the business area, such conventions are not frequent but an important recent example is the Hague Convention on the Law Applicable to Dispositions of Securities held through Indirect Holding Systems, see more in particular chapter 4, section 3.2.2. The Conventions prepared by the Hague Conference are commonly referred to as Hague Conventions but should be clearly distinguished from the Hague Uniform Sales Conventions which produced uniform substantive sales law for goods. They were prepared at Diplomatic Conferences in The Hague in 1951 and 1964, as we saw. The Hague Conference was not involved in them.

Within the EU, some further efforts have been made in the area of unification of private international law rules of which the 1980 Rome Convention on the Law Applicable to Contractual Obligations is the most important, but more significant is that there is increasingly a call for uniform or at least harmonised substantive laws to be produced at EU level. They could amount to forms of codification. Especially for consumers, incidental measures have been taken through Directives,[199] which can only be issued in areas where the EU

---

[198] See n 14 *supra*.
[199] See Council Dir 76/207/EEC of 9 Feb 1976 [1976] OJ L39, on the implementation of the principle of equal treatment for men and women as regards access to employment, vocational training and promotion, and working conditions; Council Dir 85/374/EEC of 25 July 1985 [1985] OJ L210, on the approximation of the law of the Member States concerning liability for defective products; Council Dir 85/577/EEC of 20 Dec 1985 [1985] OJ L372, to protect the consumer in respect of contracts negotiated away from business premises; Council Dir 86/653/EEC of 18 Dec 1986 [1986] OJ L382, on the co-ordination of the Member States relating to self-employed commercial agents; Council Dir 87/102/EEC of 22 Dec 1986 [1987] OJ L42 later amended, for the approximation of the laws, regulations and administrative provisions of the Member States concerning consumer credit; Council Dir 90/314/EEC of 13 June 1990 [1990] OJ L158, on package travel, package holidays and package tours; Council Regulation 295/91 of 4 Feb 1991 [1991] OJ L36/5, establishing common rules for a denied-boarding compensation system in scheduled air transport; Council Dir 93/13/EEC of 5 Apr 1993 [1993] OJ L95/29, on unfair terms in consumer contracts; Directive 97/9/EC of the European Parliament and the Council of 20 May 1997 [1997]

has authority. They essentially present harmonisation efforts that need implementation at national levels, which still allows for considerable variation in the end result per Member State.

In the private law area, EU Directives have also been popular in the area of employment contracts and to achieve some harmonisation of company law. In the professional sector, they are otherwise much rarer but there is concern over late payments and in the Investment Services Directive (Article 11) there are also rules for conduct of investment business. Even these are mainly directed at consumer investor protection, but that is not clearly spelt out and most of the rules may therefore be equally applied to professional dealings. More recently the Finality Directive and Collateral Directive aim at uniformity in much narrower specialised fields in the financial area, see more in particular chapter 4, sections 3.2.2 and 3.2.4. Through Regulations, the EU could impose uniform law directly but in the private law area it has not so far done so. There is here, however, also the important issue of whether the EU has sufficient standing to legislate in the private law area, except where the issue is closely connected with the free movement of persons, goods, services and capital.²⁰⁰

In this context, more thought should here be given to the idea of legislation at transnational, especially at EU level. In real estate and the consumer areas, domestic laws should remain dominant. In the professional sphere, legislation seems premature as there is no method for it. The hierarchy of norms within the modern *lex mercatoria* may at present be more likely to respond to the true needs, at least in international business. It aims at a broader coverage worldwide. Much more important is that domestic courts should start to apply this hierarchy of norms. In section 1.1.7 above, it was argued that an international court system for professional dealings may well become desirable, especially if domestic courts remain reluctant to apply the *lex mercatoria* and its hierarchy of norms and do not co-operate in developing a body of case-law in this connection as international arbitrations to some extent already do. This court system should not be confined to the EU either and should take its lead perhaps from the international criminal courts that are now being established, see further also section 1.5.6 below.

For professionals, this seems a more important step than the more precise formulation of the *lex mercatoria* itself. The question should be asked, however, what the method should be if a more general codification effort were ever contemplated at EU level where

---

OJ L144/19, on the protection of purchasers in respect of certain aspects of contracts relating to the purchase on a time share basis; Directive 97/5EC of the European Parliament and of the Council of 27 Jan 1997 [1997] OJ L43/25, on cross-border credit transfers; Directive 97/7/EC of the European Parliament and of the Council of 20 May 1997 [1997] OJ L144/19, on the protection of consumers in respect of distance contracts; Council Regulation of 9 Oct 1997 [1997] OJ L285/1 on air carrier liability in the case of accidents; Directive 98/27/EC of the European Parliament and of the Council on injunctions for the protection of consumers' interests; Directive of 8 June 2000 [2000] OJ L 178 on Certain Legal Aspects of Electronic Commerce in the Internal Market.

See further also the proposals for a directive on the sale of consumer goods and associated guarantees [1995] OJ L307/8. In Oct 1998, a proposal (COM(1998)468 final) was also tabled for a directive of the European Parliament and of the Council concerning the distance marketing of consumer financial services, amending Council Dir 90/619/EEC and Dir 97/7/EC and 98/27/EC; see also the Green Paper: Financial Services — Meeting Consumers' Expectations, COM(96)209 final of 22 May 1996, and the Commission communication: Financial Services — Enhancing Consumer Confidence, COM(97)309 final of 26 June 1997. It raises the question of the interface between financial regulation and supervision and the contractual protection of long distance recipients of financial services. It concerns here conduct of business and product control.

A European Parliament and Council Dir 2000/35/EC. combating late payment in commercial transactions was approved on 29 June 2000. They often have transborder aspects. See for the Investment Services Directive, chapter 6, s 3.2.6.

²⁰⁰ See also n 279 *infra*.

there is an increasing interest in it as expressed by an EU Action Plan set in motion in February 2003. It is based on the idea that at least for contract a set of rules should be drafted which parties could opt into. The problem of this method was already raised in section 1.4.2 above. That method is by no means clear and should logically be established first. What rules should be contemplated; should they be practitioner- or scholar-oriented; would an approach based on some compromise between domestic notions really make sense? If so, should the professional and consumer rules be distinguished? Clearly, professional law can often be rougher and less detailed. What would be the status of other sources of law like fundamental principle, custom and perhaps good faith notions in commerce and finance? What should be the approach to interpretation? How far would regional variation still have a place?

Ideally, codification, if thought desirable for example to provide greater unity more quickly (assuming a true need could be established also for professional dealings), should be the end of a process rather than the beginning. It is in any event submitted that the approach should be very different from that adopted by the Historical School in Germany in the nineteenth century and should be practitioner-oriented, at least in the professional sphere, and it should be internationalist. There should never be an exclusively statutory approach. This law should develop for the entire international professional sector whose own separate legal order should be accepted. It naturally transcends a national attitude, but should also transcend a regional, even EU or Nafta, based approach.

So-called soft law through principles defined per topic is often seen as a first step to such codification, and we see them now arise in contract, trusts and even in secured transactions and insolvency. This activity is in the nature of the American Restatements and may be worthwhile provided the need for professionals and others, like consumers, are clearly distinguished. These principles depend for their effectiveness on clarity, inspiration and guidance rather than on detailed compilations of minuscule rules derived from often consumer oriented domestic laws, which at least in contract seems to have been the preferred approach so far. These contract principles, developed in two sets, one by Unidroit in 1995, and one with EU support in 1998, will be discussed in greater detail in chapter 2, section 1.6, together with the 1980 Vienna Sales Convention and the approach of Article 2 UCC in the USA.

1.5.6   *The Role of National Courts and of International Commercial Arbitration*

In the previous section, it was argued that domestic courts should directly apply the hierarchy of norms inherent in the *lex mercatoria* to professional disputes. If that remains problematic, an international commercial court system might be considered. As already suggested in sections 1.1.7 and 1.4.3, national courts could function in international commercial cases as international commercial courts in the international commercial and financial legal order. These courts should have the freedom to find the applicable *lex mercatoria* and where necessary balance then against governmental interests of the forum, or other states. It might not be a perfect solution as no perfect certainty could be attained in advance. It was observed before that perfect certainty has always remained elusive in the law in times of rapid change, even domestically, whilst governmental interest always serve as a distorting element in purely adjudicatory terms.

In any event, it would appear obvious that within the modern *lex mercatoria* and its hierarchy of norms, the search for better law or for what makes more sense in the circumstances is often to be preferred to the application of domestic rules that were never written for international transactions and are not seldom erratically applied under the modern rules of private international law. Especially in the commercial sphere used to taking some risk, the *lex mercatoria* or transnational approach is generally preferable and likely to lead to better results. As already discussed in section 1.4.3 above, it seems the only way the law can remain relevant for larger commercial or financial disputes. The resulting decisions should be enforceable wherever parties require them to be and all civilised nations and their courts should co-operate in the enforcement effort.[201]

This situation predominantly prevails for international commercial arbitrators. These may be conducted *ad hoc* or under existing arbitration rules. The most important of these rules are the Uncitral Rules, the ICC Arbitration Rules of the International Chamber of Commerce in Paris and the LCIA Rules of the London Court of International Arbitration. Under the latter two sets of rules, a whole organisation and administration of international arbitrations is provided. These sets are regularly updated; in both cases the last occasion was at the beginning of 1998. As far as the applicable law is concerned, they leave great flexibility to the arbitrators, *cf* Article 17 of the ICC Rules and Section 14(2) of the LCIA Rules and allow arbitrators to apply whatever rules of law they consider appropriate. This leaves ample room for the *lex mercatoria* and its hierarchy of norms. French arbitration law (Article 1496 CCP) and Dutch arbitration law (Article 1054 CCP) already allowed this earlier. The new English Arbitration Act continues to refer here rather to conflict of laws rules even if the arbitrators are free to determine which the appropriate conflict rule is (Section 46(3)). The English Arbitration Act follows in this respect the Uncitral Model Law (Article 28) which is also reflected in the Uncitral Rules (Article 33) and thus remains more restrictive.[202] The fact that the UK (unlike eg France and Switzerland) did not opt for a legislative split between domestic and international arbitrations may have retarded the development and the lack of distinction tends to limit the space for international commercial arbitration and to ignore its transnational nature.

International commercial arbitration is backed up by the New York Convention on the Recognition and Enforcement of Foreign Arbitral Awards of 1958 which (under certain minimum conditions) makes them enforceable in all participating States. They include all substantial trading nations. Such wide treaty support has notably been lacking for the international recognition and enforcement of ordinary judgments. Bilateral treaty law still remains here the most normal response and is still rare. In the USA amongst the various states, the Full Faith and Credit Clause of the Constitution at least guarantees the recognition of sister state judgments. In the EU, there is since 1968 the important Brussels Convention on Jurisdiction and the Enforcement of Judgments in Civil and Commercial

---

[201] There was an attempt in English case law to consider the English courts international commercial courts, rejected by the House of Lords, however: see *Amin Rasheed Shipping Corp v Kuwait Insurance Co*, [1984] AC 50, see also n 27 *supra*. The suggestion was that there was English jurisdiction over an unwilling defendant, without any other ground for it.

[202] Nevertheless even English case law upheld the application of 'internationally accepted principles of law governing contractual relations' in an award rendered pursuant to an arbitration governed by Swiss law, *Deutsche Schachtbau- und Tiefbohrgesellschaft mbH v Ras al-Khaimah National Oil Co*, [1987] 3 WLR 1023. There was no contractual conflict of laws clause and Article 13(3) of the old ICC Rules (1975/80), which still required settlement of the dispute through conflict of laws rules, was applicable. Such requirement thus seems no longer to exclude the application of general principles or of the law merchant (*lex mercatoria*), see also the Austrian Supreme Court (18 Nov 1982, 34 ICLQ, 727) and the French Cour de Cassation (XXIV ILOM 360, 1984)), in cases upholding the award in *Norsolor (Pabalk Ticaret Sirketi (Turkey) v Ugilor/Norsolor SA*, ICC Case 3131 (1979), one of the first awards making a direct reference to the *lex mercatoria* under Article 13(3) of the old ICC Rules. An award that is altogether detached from a *national arbitration* law may have greater difficulties to be recognised under the New York Convention, although upheld in the US: *Ministry of Defense of the Islamic Republic v Gould, Inc*, 887 F 2d 1357 (9th Cir 1989). In any event, this does not affect awards rendered on the basis of other than a national substantive law, see also AJ vd Berg, *The New York Arbitration Convention of 1958: Towards a Uniform Interpretation* (1981) 33.

Matters, now superseded by a Regulation in this area, followed by the very similar Lugano Convention which ties in most other Western European Countries.

Part II   The Nature, Status and Function of Private International Law

2.1   Modern Private International Law

2.1.1   *The Underlying Concept of Modern Private International Law: Party Autonomy*

For the reasons already explained in section 1.5.4 above, in this book, private international or conflicts law is relegated to a back seat in the hierarchy of norms of the *lex mercatoria,* although that does not make it irrelevant in areas where transnational law has not yet developed or is slow to do so. Even in those areas, the residual role of private international law would have to be tested, however, for its results. Thus the choice of a domestic law and the result thereunder would need to be evaluated in the light of business realities and the dynamics of international trade, commerce and finance. In fact, it was argued that in this manner the domistic laws so applied became part of the transnational law merchant. In the last generation, a more widespread unease with the more traditional methods and results of private international law had already become evident.[203] Nevertheless, it remains important to see what the traditional private international law is and what it meant to achieve.

The underlying concept of modern private international law is that all legal relationships have a basis (or *Sitz*) in a *national* law and are thus all domestic in nature, a view associated with the teachings of F von Savigny (1779–1861) in the German Historical School of the early nineteenth century.[204] He proceeded to formulate a set of (in his view) objective conflicts rules aimed at reaching *automatically* this national law in cases with international aspects, therefore in cases that could conceivably be covered by more than one (domestic) law. The great advantage of this approach was that the applicable law was in this way no longer dependent on the cooperation of or recognition by states (in terms of comity or otherwise) and could be applied without bias in favour or against any of them. The applicable law was thus considered neutral and not dependent on the outcome. It was always domestic and private international law had no longer any transnational substantive law element in it. As such, the new approach was an important by-product of the nineteenth century notion that all law was national and that there were no universal notions in it (and certainly also no international ones).

In this system, the conflict rules were in essence simple and few in number, the most important being the *lex rei sitae* or *lex situs* for proprietary issues, the *lex (locus) contractus* for contractual issues and the *lex loci delicti* for tort issues. These rules were not in themselves new, as we shall see in the next section, but, used in this manner they replaced earlier notions of *acquired* rights, which had been more interest- or fact- rather than rule-oriented, and *comitas,* which had been more concerned with the extraterritoriality of local rule patterns and the validity of their application to cases with foreign elements, in which connection the

---

[203] See for a dicussion eg FK Juenger, "Private International Law or International Private Law?", 5 *King's College LJ* (1994–95); "The UNIDROIT Principles of Commercial Contracts and Inter-American Contract Choice of Law", *Universidad Nacional Autonoma de Mexico — Universidad Panamericana* 229–236 (1998); "Conflict of Laws, Comparative Law and Civil Law: The Lex Mercatoria and Private International Law", 60 *La L Rev* 1133 (2000).
[204] *System des heutigen römischen Rechts* VIII, Nr 360, 108 (Berlin, 1849). See for this School, s 1.2.8 *supra.*

lex situs lex contractus, and *lex loci delicti* had served as subrules or guidelines but not as a set of hard and fast rules to determine conflicts of (domestic) laws. It was in essence a comity approach which left ample room for the consideration of state interests, but also for overriding notions of a more substantive law nature derived from rationality, logic or fairness and therefore from a more universal system of law as prevailed on the European Continent at that time. In view of a perceived greater subjective element in this approach, this was what von Savigny sought to avoid.

The modern proponents of uniform substantive (treaty) law and more recently the supporters of the transnational or *lex mercatoria* approach in trade and finance are more likely to insist that, in the international sphere, legal relationships are by their very nature *denationalised* and that application of a national law, even if the most proper one could be found, could be potentially inappropriate and distorting. On this view, a set of (often considered rough, automatic and neutral) hard and fast conflicts rules, like those just mentioned (*lex rei sitae, lex contractus, lex loci delicti* etc.) pointing to a particular domestic legal system as a whole is unlikely to deal with the problems arising from the international setting itself and therefore also unlikely to take properly into account the particular nature of the relationship between the parties as developing in that context and to balance properly the parties' legitimate interests at that level.

Other problems are in this view that private international law of this sort is unlikely to be able properly to take into account the legitimate interests of the parties' own states or those of any other state that might be directly concerned with the case and have some valid governmental interest in the implementation and enforcement of the parties' rights and duties as a matter of their own public policy, for example in the area of foreign exchange or in trade restrictions (still important in the arms trade and in the trade of forbidden substances). It could affect the validity of a contract (at least in the country of the prohibition and in its *fora*), which according to the applicable *lex contractus* (of another country) could otherwise be perfectly valid. Whether that validity would be upheld could in such cases still depend on the place where the case (eg for delivery) was brought. The court of such a place could not avoid to balance the various interests of the parties and of the governments involved for which there was no preset rule in private international law. It would seem therefore that the older comity approach which had left courts discretion in the application of foreign laws was dispensed with too soon or at least too radically.

There were also newer types of rules concerned with the protection of certain classes of interested private parties like consumers, workers, or small investors, the effectiveness of which could not solely depend on the old contacts approach, like the place of the contract or tort. We enter here the modern regulatory aspects of private law and their mandatory nature, for which in the case of conflicts the traditional private international law rules had no real answer either. In short, also in these areas of extra protection, which could be expressed in private law (like prospectus liability in the placement of new securities), there could be a problem in the search for the most appropriate rule in the case of conflict or in the impact of modern mandatory, public law-related domestic rules. Here again the Savignian private international law approach proved ill equipped to deal with the complications.

In other words, the *lex contractus* could result in the application of a domestic law (eg that of a foreign issuer of securities) which from the perspective of the law of the residence of an investor (the buyer) was wholly inadequate to protect him in terms of prospectus liability of the issuer and would create injustice for him. Similar problems could arise where foreign sellers sold goods to consumers in other countries that had a stricter regime of consumer protection but the law of which was unlikely to prevail on the basis of the *lex contractus* rule which more likely would make the law of the seller applicable.

In the traditional approach, it was thus difficult to take into account the special but lnevertheless justified interests of the harmed parties as recognised by their states. In other words, it was difficult to weigh the foreign element per case, as comity had once tried to do, in order to consider the different social or political setting in which the parties operated, and to honour the requirements of justice for all concerned in each instance.

In contractual interpretation, extra-legal elements of an ethical, social or efficiency nature could create similar problems where the *lex contractus* and the law of the persons involved differed greatly and were not able to use an internationalised concept either so that altogether justified expectations risked being ignored.

As far as public interests were concerned, which could even be meant to prevent the transaction like in the case of boycotts or tariff and foreign exchange restrictions, it was clear that in such situations — which increased dramatically through the rise of governmental intervention even in many aspects of private law — the Savigny model was hardly adequate, quite apart from the sceptical view that domestic private law was unlikely to be meant or to have been written for international cases which are in any event likely to have a different dynamic.

In its most extreme form, in this sceptical view, application of domestic private law could be seen as the truly alien and disturbing element in international transactions and the private law applicable to it. Rather, these transactions should be governed by their own internationalised rules.[205] Both, local directory (private) laws and all the more so national governmental intervention through such laws, for example to achieve some extra protection for certain individuals, especially weaker ones, like consumers, workers or smaller investors, or in the pursuit of their — state — objectives, like in trade or foreign exchange restrictions, are in this view no more than the expression of a declared interest. They may or may not be taken into account in international cases, which are all cases not solely or predominantly connected with the country in question. In this approach, not even a preponderant contact with one country or a balance of interest centering on that country could force the application of its laws, although it would be more likely if there was a reasonable governmental interest of that country at the same time.

Rather, the transnational law or *lex mercatoria*, whilst being *written* (in uniform substantive treaty law) should take these interests into account and decide on their relevance in the light of the nature and dynamics of the international transaction. The *unwritten* transnational law or *lex mercatoria* (that derived from fundamental principle, custom or general principle), whilst being applied (by the courts or in arbitrations), should consider and take into account these interests to the extent justified. In all these cases, the relevance of these policies would depend on the circumstances and ultimately remain a matter of appreciation per case. Only the resulting case law could subsequently lead to the formulation of clearer rules in respect of these outside interest whilst as between the parties the (hierarchy of the) *lex mercatoria* or their chosen rules would be presumed to prevail.

In this context, the role of *party autonomy* needs also to be discussed. That is the right to spell out the applicable legal regime or to choose a national system that appears more appropriate than the one resulting from the applicable conflict rules (or even the *lex mercatoria*, which in the view of many could now also be chosen to confirm its applicability). This freedom generally exists in matters at the free disposition of the parties, which are in essence those matters that raise no public interest or do not affect third parties (like proprietary rights). Even where a public policy matter of a particular state may be involved, such a choice may still be possible in favour of the law of the country which has the more obvious contacts with the case, but this may not avoid the need of weighing any conflicting governmental policies or interests to precede party autonomy.

When party autonomy is exerted to choose an applicable law, there is therefore always a question in how far it can opt out of the laws of the legal system or policy rules otherwise more properly applicable. Consumer protection might present a good case showing the limits. If a consumer is in his own country protected against unfair contract terms but buys products in a country that has no such rules or other rules in this respect, which might be less favourable to consumers, party autonomy chosing the law of the other country or of a third country might not be controlling in the matter and a more objective balancing of the policy issue may precede the application of the rule so chosen. It can only be repeated in this connection that in the absence of such a choice, the application of the traditional conflicts rule, like the *lex contractus* in the sense of the law of the place where the contract was concluded or had its centre of gravity or closest connection, might not (or no longer) decide the issue either.

Thus whilst opting for the law of a particular state, there is always the question of how far party autonomy goes and in how far parties may avoid the application of laws (especially of a public or semi-public regulatory or mandatory nature) less suitable to them. It may not mean the application of the mandatory or regulatory rules of that law so chosen either, especially not if the case has no real contacts with the country of that law. These public or semi-public law rules of that country are in such cases hardly likely to apply. E.g. assume an English and French resident agree to sell jute on the international market and make the law of India applicable which (assume) declares the selling of jute in the international markets outside its foreign exchange controls illegal. It is a prohibition unlikely to be upheld as the jute was already outside India and is not destined for it.

Nor may it mean the application of the more excentric provisions in the private law so chosen, like e.g. the application of the doctrine of consideration in a contract between a German and a Swiss made subject to English law. It could be seen as a structural or mandatory rule not applying to contracts not having any contact with England at all. Perhaps in that context parties could opt for English law, yet exclude at the same time its consideration doctrine. Should they not have done so (and it is most uncommon), the doctrine may still not be upheld in respect of them as they may not be deemed to have contemplated its application if leading to the non-existence of an agreement they clearly wanted.

2.1.2 Drawbacks of Conflict Rules

The approach of von Savigny, especially as later elaborated by his student Ludwig von Bar,[206] in fact nationalised all international legal relationships with reference to their seat in a certain jurisdiction. As such it was a typical product of nineteenth century nationalistic thinking in the German Historical School and supplemented the codification notion, although it was at first balanced by a liberal market approach and free movement of (most) goods, services and money so that the disturbing factor of governmental interest derived from trade and currency policies was not so likely to arise and the presumed neutrality of the new conflict rules could be upheld. In the absence of much other mandatory (regulatory) law at the time, it left also ample room for the parties to determine their own legal regime supplemented by any national law of their choice, although there were always

---

[206] L von Bar, *Das internationale Privat-und Strafrecht* (Hannover, 1862).

problems with the law of property which, whilst affecting third parties, could not be truly chosen by the parties.

Another area of doubt was that of the contractual infrastructure, covering eg validity questions. Parties could hardly determine the validity of their own contract, but it became accepted that they could chose any legal system in this respect (and not necessarily the ones objectively following under the conflict rules). Subsequenty there arrived the era of governmental intervention and its complications for this conflicts approach, whilst some relapse into comity seemed to be indicated. But even if no particular third party or governmental interest and policies were at stake or the parties had not made a choice, from the outset this approach to conflicts was based on some typical assumptions reflecting the times in which it was first proposed (and which changed). It also had to face a number of *technical* problems.

As already mentioned, the principal aim of the new method was to produce some *objective* clear-cut conflict rules from which the applicable law would automatically follow regardless of any outside interests in the outcome, notably of states. For this purpose, legal relationships were primarily understood in terms of their underlying legal *characterisation* as proprietary, contractual, delictual, corporate, procedural, etc. These characterisations themselves were perceived as essentially universal, intrinsically unchangeable and, even in the Historical School, probably independent from a state. The rules applicable to them could obviously still vary depending on the expression of these structures in local law, especially in the details. This gave rise to the conflicts in the first place, but that was originally not considered a great problem as the differences were in essence expected to be in the detail only and relatively few.

The new approach was therefore intended for a situation in which the perceived conflicts were considered fairly *insubstantial*. Moreover, the conflict rules and the adjustments they required to the application of the *lex fori* were believed to be *incidental*. Indeed, the conflict rules developed in this approach were few, some of which were already mentioned: the *lex rei sitae* for property issues, the *lex locus delicti commissi* for tort issues, the *lex locus contractus* for contract issues, the *lex societatis* for company issues, the *lex fori* or *locus actus* for procedural issues, etc. It was a *rule*- rather than interest-oriented method of conflict resolution, intended to drive out earlier notions of *acquired rights* and *comitas* in dealing with the more subjective notion of extraterritoriality of foreign laws in international relationships and cases.

The earlier comity approach had resulted from Dutch seventeenth century scholarship (Huber) and prevailed until the nineteenth century as a refinement of the earlier *statutist* approach. This earlier approach had been mainly concerned with the sphere of application or extraterritoriality of statutes or complexes of rules that governed certain situations or relationships: hence the personal statute for the law concerning the person and its capacity, the property statute concerning property and its status, etc. Under the personal statute, a person would take his own personal laws with him wherever he went. They determined his legal and marital status. Real estate would be governed by the law of its location as the propery statute and contract by the law of its formation, etc. The subsequent *acquired rights* and *comitas* approaches introduced here a substantial *discretionary* element as to the applicable law and were *fact*- or *issue-oriented*. There was no longer any automaticity.

That was meant to be avoided in the new approach advocated by von Savigny. Although it still used statutist and *comity* language in referring to the *lex rei sitae, lex contractus, lex locus delicti,* and later to the *lex societatis* in company law matters etc, the issue was no longer the determination of the extraterritorial effect of certain laws depending on the situation (or acquired rights) but rather their automatic application with reference to the seat of each legal relationship which was on all occasions to be found in a particular country. It was thus *relationship-oriented* and *nationalistic*. To identify the country of (the seat of) that relationship became the objective of the new approach.

Yet it became soon abundantly clear that even where a more precise conflicts rule was formulated in this manner, it might still not provide a solution or could remain ambiguous in its consequences. Thus the principle of the *lex contractus* had left open the question whether it was the law of the place where the contract is *concluded* (in any event problematic when parties came from different countries) or where it had to be *performed*. The reference to the *lex locus delicti commissi* left open the question whether the applicable law was the law of the place where the wrongful act was *committed* or where it had its *effects*. Thus under it, both French and Dutch law could be applicable in the case of the pollution of the Rhine river in France, causing serious damage downstream to horticulture in the Netherlands. The *lex societatis* which became later the conflicts rule concerning company law could mean the law of the country of *incorporation*, much the view in common law countries, Switzerland and the Netherlands, or the law of the country of the *main activity* of the company (*siege reel*), much the German and French approach. As for the *lex situs* rule, in proprietary matters concerning movables it was likely to resolve nothing as there arose problems mainly when in an international sale these assets had to move across borders, leaving a choice between the law of the country of *origin* and of *destination* in respect of the transfer of title, which both could lead to impractical results.

In proprietary matters, when assets moved between countries, the answer could much sooner be in the reasonable acceptance of the proprietary rights acquired at the original *situs* subject to a measure of adjustment to the equivalent interests (if any) in the country of destination to fit these rights into the latter's proprietary and, in the case of security interests, priority regime, see more particularly chapter 4, section 1.8. It is a variation on the old *acquired rights* theme and allows an unavoidable measure of discretion, which the conflicts system built on von Savigny's ideas had precisely sought to avoid. In other areas of property law it was even less clear how any one *national* law could deal with the differing complications that derive from the international setting of the case itself like in the bulk transfers of assets located in different countries when it is unlikely that one domestic legal system can satisfactorily cover this legal structure even in a contractual sense. The protection of debtors in various countries under bulk assignments equally does not appear to be capable of a solution by application of one single domestic rule (except for each debtor their own).

The situation became even more complicated where the basic structures themselves were not easily defined in terms of, for example, property, contract, tort, restitution, company, procedure etc. In tripartite relationships with contractual and proprietary aspects, like agency and trusts, but also in documents of title and negotiable instruments with their element of abstraction and independence and the own rights and obligations of the holders, there was often no obvious and certainly no single conflict rule that could point to a solution in a domestic law, see for assignments chapter 4, section 1.9.2. So it was for letters of credit or in assignments of monetary and other claims. Through so-called *depecage*, different conflicts rules had then to be devise for different aspects. Indeed, a complicated conflict of law structure is often invoked in these instances, even in Hague treaties, like in those on agency and trust, in practice often subjected to further corrections of the end result by the forum, which are then explained as yet other facets of conflict rules. The result thus proved often unsatisfactory and not transparent or predictable, even if the true problem was that the private international law or conflicts of laws approach did not take the underlying objective or logic and dynamics of the particular legal structure in its international context into account and refused to make them ultimately decisive.

No less important was subsequently the fact that the environment in which these conflict rules were meant to operate changed dramatically because of the much greater governmental intervention in private law in the twentieth century, already referred to in sections 1.3.3 and 2.1.1 above. It highlighted the difficulty of dealing within this conflicts' approach with a strongly increasing number of mandatory national policy rules which could differ greatly, particularly those concerning the protection of weaker parties, like workers, consumers and smaller investors rendering services or buying products or invest-ments in orther countries. They could also reflect particular state interests in international dealings expressed eg in foreign currency and trade limitations, specific use and licence requirements in respect of foreign products and services, or taxation or social security-related imposts on foereign trade. In these cases, a discretionary element (instead of an automatic conflicts rule) must of necessity be maintained when mandatory rules are invoked before the courts of other countries (as recognised in Article 7 EU Rome Convention of 1980 and in the notion of the *règles d'application immediate* or *Eingriffsnormen*).[207] It is an area of the law in the US more properly covered by Sec. 6 of the Restament (Second) Conflict of Laws (1971) for interstate conflicts and by Sections. 402 and 403 of the Restatement (Third) Foreign Relations Law (1986) for international conflicts, see more in particular section 2.2.6 below.

Again, this is reminiscent of the old *comity approach* (here limited, however, to rules with a clear public interest element to them), again precisely an approach which von Savigny's ideas had sought to avoid. As we shall see in section 2.2.2 below, much of the American conflicts' revolution has revolved around it and can be seen as a relapse into the older approach but also as a basis for internationalisation of the conflict of laws approach through the formulation of substantive rules of which in trade and commerce the *lex mercatoria* is an important part whilst for governmental interest balancing guide-lines and rules emerge. They may be even now relevant also in the more traditional approach in the area of statutory penalties and statutes of limitations which also have some clear public order overtones which in the case of conflict cannot satisfactorily be resolved through mere conflict rules either. In any event, the end result even under the application of the standard conflict rules (like the *lex situs, lex contractus* etc.) was always considered on its suitability and, if necessary, corrected on so-called *public order* grounds. The discretionary element was thus by no means lost and less progress was made through modern conflict rules than at first expected.

Thus we see that, at least in property matters, the old acquired rights theory was revived and, in public policy connected issues, the old comity approach, whilst public order always was allowed to function as a correction of the result of any conflict of laws rules. Whatever the objectives of the new approach, from the beginning the new conflict rules thus proved less clear-cut and less automatic than was suggested on their face. Moreover, discretion resulted in a number of other ways because of the imperfections of the conflict rules them-selves. The principal reasons can now be summarised as follows:

(a)   the notion of the seat of these legal relationships proved too narrow and the seat itself could be difficult to pin down;
(b)   the basic rules like the *lex contractus* and *lex locus delicti* or even *lex situs* proved multi-interpretable;

---

[207] In Europe, the direct application of mandatory rules (therefore without any reference to conflicts rules), especially those with a social or public policy objective, in this manner has in modern times been noted in partic-ular by Francescakis, Quelques précisions sur les lois d'application immédiate et leurs rapports avec les règles de

(c)   the legal structures to which they related could not always be so simply classified (as proprietary, contractual, delictual, etc.) and left considerable qualification problems especially between contract and tort;

(d)   the conflicts rules could be very different from country to country as they became purely domestic;

(e)   the increasing governmental intervention in private law reduced the scope for rules of private international law and left the impact of mandatory domestic laws of a public order nature unsettled, whilst

(f)   overriding ethical, social and economic considerations in normative interpretation techniques could in international transactions hardly be left to the domestic laws deemed applicable under the traditional conflict rules either.

So even in the Savignian approach, the notion of the *seat* of the legal relationship in a structural sense eventually shifted to the notion of its *centre of gravity* of the legal relationship in a non-structural sense,[208] whilst the automatic link between the applicable law and this presumed centre became the *closest connection*. All three (centre of gravity, relevant legal relationship and closest connection) were accepted to be poly-interpretable and subject to an appreciation per case resulting *de facto* in a measure of *discretion* for the courts. This was no less clearly the case in property issues where acquired rights retained a hold. So it was in determining which governmental interests were relevant in the case, where notions of comity resurfaced. The unavoidable result was that it started to make a difference which country assumed jurisdiction to resolve the issue. It raised the matter of adjudicatory jurisdiction where, at least in the English version, also a measure of *discretion* lurked further balanced by *forum (non) conveniens* notions.

A complicating factor was in this connection also that the resulting conflict rules were themselves increasingly viewed as rules of domestic law, notwithstanding the fact that von Savigny had considered them universal. As such they frequently failed to cover common ground and could in fact differ greatly, as became evident especially in areas where the method itself proved less clear, like in the definition of the closest relationship or connection. It presented a particular problem in international arbitrations where there is no natural *lex fori* and therefore also no naturally applicable set of conflict rules. This raised the question whether there were at least some common principles or standards of conflict of laws resolution to preserve the pretence of certainty, objectivity and unity of the system.

An obvious need to develop common conflicts rules consequently arose. However, even the development and formulation of these common rules, as promoted by the Hague Conference since 1893, see also section 1.4.5 above, and sometimes also in a bilateral or (more recently) EU context, remained marred by differences in view. The criteria used or proposed were often uncertain. Thus the Benelux Convention on Private International Law of 1951 (never ratified and withdrawn in 1976) referred for sales to the law of the country with the 'closest connection'. The Hague Convention of 1955 on the Law governing the International Sale of Goods (not to be confused with the Hague Conventions concerning the Uniform Laws on the International Sale of Goods of 1964) referred to the law

---

conflits de lois *Rev Crit de Droit International Privé* [1966] 17. Earlier, Pillet, *Principes de droit international privé*, (1903), 265, had already distinguished between the laws protecting private and social interests, the first protecting the individual against the state and the latter the state against the individual. They were respectively considered extraterritorial and territorial in nature.

[208] H Batiffol, *Les conflits de lois en matière de contrats* (1938), 3.

of the residence of the seller as the basic conflict rule in sales. The EU 1980 (Rome) Convention on the Law Applicable to Contractual Obligations returned to the notion of the 'closest connection', but presumed this to be the place of the residence of the party that must effect the most characteristic performance (Article 4(2)). It left substantial flexibility in the interpretation of this term with the additional facility to ignore the resulting law if it proved inappropriate (Article 4(5)). Article 8 of the new Hague Conference text of 1986, superseding the one of 1955, also uses the notion of the most characteristic performance. It leads mostly to the applicability of the law of the residence of the seller, but, unlike the Rome Convention, with a number of specific exceptions in favour of the law of the residence of the buyer.

It should perhaps also be noted that, notwithstanding von Savigny's emphasis on the independent nature of each legal relationship and regardless of some modern day relaxation, private international law still tends to use the legal relationship principally in terms of classification or qualification (as proprietary, contractual and tortuous and even then it may run into serious problems),[209] therefore as *formal* structures and not in terms of the specific needs and interests to be protected (including governmental interests) and the special requirements and dynamics of the situation. Lesser responsiveness to practical needs and objectives is therefore implied in this approach. That also concerns the *social* aspects of a case which may require a more incidental solution.

Locally this is often provided, at least in contractual matters, by the application of good faith notions, or through common sense and established practices in the commercial sphere. In an international professional context, however, these practical considerations and social needs may acquire an independent meaning which local laws can hardly discount. They may have a substantive law impact with which private international law can therefore also not adequately deal. For example, in international dealings, there may be much less need for good faith adjustments than local laws may assume, but it is not clear how choice of law rules aiming at finding the appropriate local law can deal with such an independent international requirement or rule.

Some of this is acknowledged and modern developments in Europe have led to some considerable amendment of the traditional conflicts approach. As we shall see the changes have been more fundamental in the US. It allows for example consumers and workers the protection of their own law as a matter of non-choice (of law), *cf* Articles 5 and 6 of the EU Rome Convention 1980 on the Law Applicable to Contractual Obligations, see also section 2.2.1 below, and gives maintenance creditors the benefit of the best rule for them, *cf* Articles 5 and 6 of the Hague Convention on Maintenance Obligations, see also section 2.2.1 below. More universal substantive principles of fairness and reasonableness are increasingly applied directly and the need for a sensible outcome is increasingly acknowledged. This is particularly so in the USA in interstate conflicts, see more in particular section 2.2.2 below. It may lead to new *substantive rules* at the international level, which therefore apply before the more traditional choice of law rules. The substantive law approach through uniform treaty law may be seen as another consequence of this insight, even if the result may still be only partial coverage and even then be unsatisfactory, see more particularly section 1.5.3 above.

In the end, in trade, commerce and finance, it is the *lex mercatoria* approach that provides the most flexible alternative, which is particularly inspired by the globalisation of the

---

[209] Eg whether particular aspects of a case tend to be contractual or tortious, or even proprietary, like the formalities and validity of bulk assignments including transborder receivables. See for the difficulties in this respect under Arts. 12(1) and 12(2) of the EU Rome Convention, chapter 4, s. 1.9.3 and chapter 5, s. 2.3.6.

markets in the professional sphere and the independent legal order there prevailing. Under it, the traditional conflict rules play only a residual role, see further section 1.5.4 above and section 3.2.5 below. What happened here is that the number of *substantive rules* have ballooned before conflict rules become necessary, thus reducing them to a lesser place although in areas where transnational law is not developing they may still have substantial impact assuming that the result makes sense in terms of the needs and dynamics of international commerce and finance. Within the *lex mercatoria* approach, fundamental principle, custom, general or common rules thus take precedence over private international law or conflict of laws rules in the hierarchy of norms which allows different sources of law to operate side by side. This approach of 'conflict removal' was identified early as unavoidable, even by conflict specialists, and is the essence of the modern development in conflicts resolution, at least in the law of property and obligations.[210] It requires, however, still a view on the treatment of governmental interests, a matter more broadly discussed in section 2.2.6 below.

2.2 The Modern European and US Approaches to Conflicts of Laws

2.2.1 *Refinement of the European Model*

As we saw, private international law or conflicts law as it developed in the nineteenth century tended to be rule-, not fact- or interest- and protection-oriented, and automatically assumed the appropriateness of the results derived from the application of its conflict principles and of the resulting applicable domestic law.

Further refinement proved necessary and even in the traditional European mould there is now everywhere an increasing search for a more refined private international law approach allowing for:

(a) the separation of the various aspects of a legal relationship (*dépeçage*) so that for different aspects different domestic laws may be appointed, see also Article 3 of the EU Rome Convention of 1980 on the Law Applicable to Contractual Obligations;

(b) reliance on concepts like the centre of gravity, closest connection and most characteristic obligation with the flexibility they provide, *cf* Article 4 of the EU Rome Convention;

(c) open or exception clauses allowing for the application of a different (domestic) law altogether if another law in the circumstances as a whole is more closely connected, *cf* Article 4(5) of the EU Rome Convention;

(d) more substantive rules, especially in the area of the protection of consumers and workers, see Articles 5 and 6 of the EU Rome Convention, allowing them the protection of their own law, even though still fashioned as a conflicts rule[211] whilst sometimes the most favourable rule may apply like in the case of Maintenance creditors under the Hague Convention on Maintenance Obligations;

---

[210] *Cf* KH Nadelmann, "Marginal Remarks on the New Trends in American Conflicts Law" (1963) 28 *Law and Contemp. Problems* 860, and G Kegel, "The Crisis of Conflict of Laws" (1964) 112 *Rec. Cours* 260.

[211] See also CGJ Morse, "Consumer Contracts, Employment Contracts and the Rome Convention" (1992) 41 *International and Comparative Law Quarterly* 1, and TM de Boer, "The EEC Contracts Convention and the Dutch Courts, A Methodological Perspective", (1990) 54 *RabelsZ* 24.

(e)   adjustments of the results eg in the case of the recognition of foreign proprietary rights and security interests in assets that move to other countries or figure in a bankruptcy elsewhere;

(f)   the abandonment of conflict rules altogether and the (discretionary) acceptance of (a degree of) extraterritoriality in the case of foreign public policy and similar mandatory rules (or *règles d'application immédiate*), see Article 7 of the EU Rome Convention; and finally

(g)   the result obtained under the conflicts rule generally proving appropriate, *cf* Article 8 of the 1992 Dutch draft of the Introductory Statute Law concerning Private International Law amended in 2002, discussed in section 2.2.4 below.

The end result has been a substantial refinement of the method of von Savigny and his successors. Even if the system remains based on a number of hard and fast rules, they are more flexible. Yet in essence the idea of the applicability of (an appropriate) *domestic* law to international dealings is fundamentally maintained.

It marks nevertheless the increased unease with the raditional conflicts approach, even in Europe, although not necessarily the acceptance of transnational law, even for the international professional sphere. Many still see the law anchored in sovereignty rather than in cultural, social and economic realities. Another consequence of this is that the approach remains in essence rule-based rather than interest- or fact-oriented.

2.2.2   *The Development in the USA*

In the USA, since the 1930s, the unease with the nineteenth century conflict rules led to a substantially different approach to interstate conflicts altogether. This example also tended to liberate the European attitude, but the flexibility it brought remained more limited in Europe. The new European attitude remains more hesitant and is basically cast along the propositions enumerated in the previous section which are substantially embodied in the 1980 EU Rome Convention on the Law Applicable to Contractual Obligations. In the US conflict rules have become no more than aides to achieving an acceptable result and have lost their hard and fast rule-oriented character. The end result need no longer be the application of a domestic law either. It could be an adaptation or mixture or rather an application of a more fundamental legal principle.

It is important to appreciate that the earlier developments in the USA towards flexibility took place against a somewhat different background. First, in the USA, the area for conflicts of laws is reduced through the existence of the common law, which, with the exception of Louisiana and some nineteenth century Spanish influence via Mexico in the southern and western states, essentially led to a fairly homogeneous system of civil and commercial law throughout the USA. Although the common law is unavoidably fractured by state intervention through statutory, policy-oriented, laws, eg in the area of product liability, this diversion may in modern times in other areas be counterbalanced, in commerce particularly by the UCC. Yet some divergence remains unavoidable because of the mandatory, protection- or own interest-inspired policy enactments (leading to specific governmental interests) of the various states. States may thus have very outspoken policies on insurance protections, on liability for passengers (guest statutes), and on environmental matters. On the other hand, much policy is exerted at the federal level so that policy issues are much more likely to figure as an issue on *international* conflict cases than in interstate conflict cases, like eg in competition matters, boycotts, embargos, etc.

Secondly, in the common law tradition, *no* sharp distinction is made between the public and private law aspects of such intervention. Putting the emphasis on the aspect of government intervention itself (whether in public or private law), this tends to reduce the area for true private conflicts of laws. They are often ignored except where they can be reduced to a difference in policy. In this manner, *all* conflicts of laws enter the ambit of what in Europe are called the *règles d'application immédiate*, see section 2.2.1(f) above, where for governmental action or mandatory laws a form of *comity* or judicial discretion also continues to rule in civil law countries.

In the USA, it tended to result in an interest-oriented approach across the board, even in the more traditional areas of private conflicts of laws like in contract, tort and property. It increased judicial discretion all around, highlighted the importance of (adjudicatory) jurisdiction (rules) and ultimately put particular emphasis on the *lex fori* and its interpretation techniques in accommodating foreign (sister state) interests, both of a public *and* private nature, which, as just mentioned, are in common law in any event never so clearly distinguished.

Section 6 of the *Restatement (Second) Conflict of Laws* (1971) reflects this state of affairs and introduces a very flexible conflicts rule which explicitly rejects any rigidity or automaticity. It allows a court to apply its own mandatory rules on choice of law in the absence of which a number of factors are provided for consideration. They centre on the needs of the interstate and international systems, the relevant policies of the forum, the relevant policies and interests of other states in the determination of the issue, the basic policies underlying the particular field of law, the certainty, predictability and uniformity of the result, and the ease in the determination of the law to be applied. In the USA, this approach to interstate conflicts is often distinguished from the one to international conflicts and the domestic attitude may not automatically be extended to the latter field, although it is unavoidable that the approach to international conflicts is becoming similar.[212]

In interstate conflicts, the accent is in fact primarily on a satisfactory solution with regard to the interests to be protected in the particular case in the light of all rules potentially applicable in order to achieve the application of 'the better law'.[213] It means a more *direct* and *substantive law* approach. One of the early leaders of this new movement (regardless of its many variants), Professor Brainerd Currie from Chicago,[214] who adopted an interest analysis, saw in it essentially a return to the true method of the common law and a denial of the continental European approach of von Savigny (although this German approach acquired and still has particular deep roots in England). The idea of clear conflicts rules as essential conduits to reach a domestic law is here abandoned. In interstate conflicts in the USA, applicable law may be reached by other means, either through a reinterpretation of the *lex fori* in the light of the foreign elements of the case or more directly formulated through reliance on general principles, especially of due process and fairness under the relevant provisions of the US Constitution. It is thus possible to weigh the various opposing interests independently of any particular conflicts or even domestic law. The search for objective, rule-oriented elements of conflict laws, so prevalent in the traditional European conflicts approach, is here increasingly abandoned.[215]

---

[212] See AA Ehrenzweig, *Private International Law, A Comparative Treatise on American International Conflicts Law, including the Law of Admiralty, General Part* (third printing, Leyden, 1974).
[213] A term particularly used by Robert Leflar, *American Conflicts of Law* (1977), 205.
[214] "The Verdict of Quiescent Years", in *Selected Essays on the Conflict of Laws* (1963), 627.
[215] See for an up to date case book DP Currie HH Kay L Kramer, *Conflict of Laws, Cases-Comments-Questions*, (6th ed. 2001).

Even though the Americans often continue to use private international law terminology, *cf* for example the reference to *the most significant relationship* both in Section 188 of the *Restatement (Second) Conflict of Laws* for *contracts* and in Section 145 *for torts* (both subject to the already mentioned Section 6, however), they thus often appear to resort ultimately to directly applied substantive principles of *reasonableness* and *fairness*. In this connection, the constitutional due process and full faith and credit clauses may provide a more specific base for these higher principles in certain cases. Under them, the arbitrary application of own state law and the rejection of the law of other states is unacceptable but a system of pure conflicts rules is discouraged at the same time. This attitude is further buttressed by the important facility to litigate in the federal courts in disputes where there is a diversity of citizenship (and a certain minimum amount at stake), even if state law remains in principle applicable.

The European criticism of the American approach still centres on the large judicial discretion and the supposed lack of predictability in that approach. It is also considered too dependent on the forum and its own laws, in turn leading to considerable dependence on the law of (adjudicatory) jurisdiction.[216] The lack of rules is clearly felt. This is somewhat strange in countries which often use a very flexible good faith approach in interpretational matters. Nevertheless, there is substantial approximation in practice between the European and American approaches, of which, as was shown, in Europe the EU Rome Convention is the clearest example and of which Article 8 of the previous Dutch proposals were the culmination, allowing the applicable law derived from the conflicts rules to be set aside if the result was inappropriate, see section 2.2.4 below.

There is in any event no doubt that the European conflicts approach — as indeed the general approaches under national laws, especially where imbued with the good faith ethos — is becoming much more sensitive to the nature of the parties' relationship, the interests to be protected and the nature and objectives of their deal in its (international) context, to the application of general principles of fairness, market and business requirements and practices, and of directly applicable substantive rules either of a mandatory or protection nature, although in this context use is often still made of pseudo-conflicts rules, like those allowing the fairest or most favourable domestic rule to prevail.

2.2.3   The Various Modern US Conflict Theories

As we saw in the previous section, in the USA in interstate conflicts, the accent has been increasingly on the evaluation, acceptance or rejection of so-called *governmental interests*, understandable because most differences in the applicable law derive in the USA from the legislative governmental intervention of the various states with clear policy objectives. This approach leads to a predominance of the *lex fori* if the forum State has a particular interest in the application of its law. If not, the law of the other interested state is applied and if there are more foreign states with an interest, the court may revert to its own law or apply the, in its view, superior law. Whether or not this leads to a balancing of these interests proper is contested. It would seem unavoidable but courts have been thought to be ill-suited for it.

---

[216] See notably Kegel (Cologne), "The Crisis of Conflict of Laws", 112 Rec Cours, 95 (Hague Lectures, 1966), and "Paternal Home and Dream Home: Traditional Conflict of Laws and the American Reformers," (1979) 27 *Am J Comp L* 615; De Nova (Pavia), "Historical and Comparative Introduction to Conflict of Laws," 118 Rec Cours, 443 (Hague Lectures 1966); Lalive (Geneva), "Tendances et méthodes en droit international privé," 155 Rec Cours, 1 (Hagues Lectures 1977); Vitta (Florence), "Cours general de droit international privé," 162 Rec Cours, 9 (Hague Lectures 1979).

This at least was the view of Professor Brainerd Currie of Chicago in which courts were never to apply another law except where there was a good reason for doing so under the rules just mentioned.[217] This rigidity is not generally followed.[218] There is here a strong element of a *lex fori* approach (or homeward trend), which returned in the USA in all the newer theories, most generally so in that of Professor Albert A Ehrenzweig of the University of California at Berkeley,[219] unless there were settled rules of choice that had worked satisfactorily, like the application of the *lex situs* in the proprietary aspects of assets that do not move. In this *lex fori* approach, the accent is not merely on governmental interests (and certainly not on the prevalence of rules), but the application of the *lex fori* in this sense becomes principally a matter of *interpretation* of the forum's laws aiming at the accommodation of *all* foreign elements of each case within it and therefore no less at the accounting for all foreign interests in the application of the domestic laws of the forum.

In this *lex fori* approach, the emphasis naturally shifts to the proper forum applying the proper (own) law of the forum, as may be adjusted (*lex propria in foro proprio*), with the resulting emphasis on proper jurisdiction rules based on substantial contacts, which itself suggest a discretionary element or at least some flexibility. Conflicts of laws in the traditional sense do not arise here. *All* foreign rules (even of private law) then operate like *règles d'application immédiate* in a European sense, in their application subject to the evaluation of their relevance by the forum as an expression of its own discretion and social policy.[220] In this way, we seem to be back entirely in the comity approach although with a more conscious effort to develop some rules, see also section 2.2.6 below. On this view, there is, however, only one possibly applicable law, which is the law found in this manner and tailored to the case.

In contract, it results in the application of the law that best supports its true meaning given its environment, but it could mean respect for performance and foreign exchange or investment restrictions in the country where the performance should take place, especially if that is the country of the forum, assuming the contract still made sense. If not, it could be at an end. In the case of a tort, it could mean respect for foreign limitations of liability, but the *lex fori*'s own views on a reasonable protection of victims and equitable distribution of unavoidable loss in the circumstances would ultimately prevail.

Under the influence of Professor Willis Reese of Columbia University, the *Restatement (Second) Conflict of Laws* (1971) adheres more to the 'centre of gravity' approach.[221] Earlier Professor David Cavers of Harvard had proposed a method with outright emphasis on the most satisfactory result through the interpretration of rules and policies,[222] but he allowed some principles of preference to develop and be taken into account, notably protecting weaker parties and party autonomy in contract.[223] The theory of Professor

---

[217] See his *Selected Essays*, n 214 *supra*, 119, 621. A governmental interest is here defined as a governmental policy and the concurrent existence of an appropriate relationship between the state having the policy and the transaction, the parties, or the litigation.

[218] Besides the aversion to balancing and the consequential preference for the *lex fori* in the case of conflict, there are two other important aspects to the interest analysis in the manner of Professor Currie. It is in this approach first necessary to determine the governmental interests as it may appear from numerous statutory texts and case law. This requires *purposive* interpretation and may introduce a considerable degree of uncertainty whilst the attribution of a purpose may become fictitious or unrealistic and may also lead to a special protection of forum residents, see eg Brilmayer, "Interest Amnalysis and the Myth of Legislative Intent", 78 *Mich L Rev* 392 (1980). In the process, other than state interests may easily be ignored. Closely related is the question whether there is a *true* or *false* conflict. The latter arises foremost when both 'conflicting' laws would yield the same result, see on this issue also D Cavers, *The Choice of Law Process*, 89 (1965).

[219] "The lex fori—Basic Rule of the Conflicts of Laws" (1960) 58 *Mich LR* 637.

[220] See Ehrenzweig, n 212 *supra*, 92*ff*.

[221] See also his "Conflict of Laws and the Restatement Second" (1963) 27 *Law and Contemp Probl* 679.

[222] See his "Critique of the Choice of Law Problem" (1933) 47 *Harv L Rev* 173.

[223] See *The Choice of Law Process* (1965).

Leflar (Choice-influencing Considerations or Factors) came close to an elaboration of this approach, although seemingly more receptive to foreign interests.[224] His choice of influencing factors were predictability of result, maintenance of the interstate or international order, simplification of the judicial task, advancement of the (own) state's governmental interests, and the application of the better rule of law requiring courts to undertake some more objective evaluation. Von Mehren and Trautman in their 'functional approach'[225] finally sought a balance or accommodation between the domestic interests and those individual and state interests which became relevant in multi-state situations. If such an accommodation failed, promotion of interstate activity, the parties' intent, or judicial economy and simplicity was to prevail.[226]

One could criticise all these theories and indeed no less the traditional approach of von Savigny to the conflicts of laws on the basis that they do not define any clear objective, except that in the American approach the forum's support of the own system and especially policy, whatever their merit, is often unashamedly clear, at least if there is some relevance in the case. Only in the approach of Leflar was this somewhat different but it lacked the elements of evaluation. Ultimately, these elements emerge in the application of *better or more just laws*, which implies a substantive law approach around a difficult value judgement that as a consequence often leads to the application of the forum law. It need not be so, however, or at least the forum law could be recast to take care of the foreign elements in the case. In that event, there could at least for commercial transactions also be an element of efficiency and cost to consider which is perhaps easier to evaluate. This approach may also be the more receptive to *lex mercatoria* considerations, therefore to broader considerations of substantive law,[227] although the *lex mercatoria* approach has received relatively little attention in the US so far.

The American approach to conflict of laws is certainly more sensitive to subtantive law considerations than the European approach, but it is true that the legal criteria remain often elusive although there is a large body of case-law. The notion that domestic laws may altogether be inappropriate to deal with international legal relationships remains here also under-explored.

Special problems result with the homeward approach in *international commercial arbitrations* that have no natural forum law and are therefore forced into balancing policies whether they like it or not. Here the Restatement (Second) Conflict of Laws and the Restatement (Third) Foreign Relations Laws may provide at least some guidenace, see also section 2.2.6 below.

2.2.4   The European Approach of Exception Clauses: Reasonable and Fair Solutions in the Dutch Proposals

In Europe, more in particular in civil law countries, the American approach has not gone unnoticed and its flexibility elicited a response, of which there is some tangible evidence in

---

[224] See his *American Conflicts of Law* (1977).

[225] *The Law of Multistate Problems* (1965), 304.

[226] See for a more recent discussion and evaluation of the American approaches in particular E Vitta of Florence, "The Impact in Europe of the American 'Conflicts Revolution" (1982) 30 *Am J Comp L* 1 and the important contributions of other authors in the same issue of that journal.

[227] *Cf* also F Juenger, *Choice of Law and Multi-state Justice*, 45, 190 (1993) who also notes the type of transaction and its requirements. Note also the approach of the UCC in Section 1–301 (1–105 old). It relies on a 'reasonable relationship' and allows parties to elect the law assuming that that relationship exists. In other areas, the contractual choice of law is explicitly limited or excluded like in Sections 1–301(f) and (g) (1–105(2) old). It concerns here more in particular the rights of creditors in sold goods (Section 2–402), leases (Sections 2A–105 and 106), bank deposits and collections (Section 4–102), funds transfers (Section 4A–507), letters of credit (Section 5–116), investment securities (Section 8–110) and the perfection provisons of Article 9, Section 9–301 through 9–307 (9–103 old).

the 1980 Rome Convention on the Law Applicable to Contractual Obligations, as we saw in section 2.2.1. Thus it refers in Article 4 to the applicability of the law of the country with the closest connection with the contract and presumes this to be the country in which the most characteristic performance takes place. It leaves room for another law, however, if the circumstances as a whole suggest that the contract is more closely connected with another country (Article 4(5)).[228]

In this connection, problems often arise when delivery and assembly of goods take place (by the seller) in the country of the buyer, whilst the seller's most characteristic performance is presumed to take place at his residence pointing to his own law as the most appropriate under Article 4(2). The problem can be particularly pressing in the construction industry where all kinds of local rules at the site may in any event prevail as semi-public or mandatory law. Use of selling agents in the other country may also complicate the picture but does not necessarily shift the balance of the contract towards the other party.[229] The problem of the place of the most characteristic performance or closest connection may also arise in connection with Article 5(1) of the 1968 Brussels Convention on Jurisdiction and the Enforcement of Judgments in Civil and Commercial Matters which ties jurisdiction in contractual matters to the place of performance of the contract rather than the residence of the performer, now replaced by Article 5(1) of the EU Regulation on Jurisdiction and the Recognition and Enforcement of Judgments in Civil and Commercial Matters of 2000, effective 1 March 2002.[230]

Thus the place of performance rather than the residence of the performer may sometimes be more relevant. Hence this technique of the exception clause. In statutory conflicts law, in tort, one sometimes sees similar corrections in respect of the *lex locus delicti* in favour of the law of the forum (usually that of the tortfeasor as defendant) if both parties to the accident, which took place elsewhere, are resident in the same country, see for example Article 45(3) of the Portuguese General Private International Law Statute of 1965 and also Article 31(2) of the Polish Private International Law statute of the same year. This may also result under the guise of the law of the forum (of the defendant) being always considered more closely connected, like under the open adjustment possibility of Article 15(1) of the Swiss Statute of 1987, not applicable, however, if the tortfeasor could have foreseen that the result of his action would be produced in another state (see Article 133(2)).

As already mentioned before, social considerations such as the protection of consumers and workers have given rise to the setting aside of traditional conflict rules altogether in favour of their own laws (Articles 5 and 6 of the Rome Convention). It may still be seen as a conflicts approach of sorts, but only in the sense that it ultimately points to a domestic law. In truth, it is an exception clause and there is really no choice of law here. Articles 5 and 6 of the Hague Convention on Maintenance Obligations give maintenance creditors the benefit of the best rule for them. They thus have a choice. This is not a proper choice of law or conflicts rule either but again an exception clause.

In the meantime, mandatory rules of other countries are increasingly considered on their own merits and may be given effect if the situation has a close connection with any such country having regard to their nature and purpose and to the consequences of their

---

[228] See for the first English application, *Bank of Baroda v Vysya Bank* [1994] 2 Lloyd's Rep 87 in a letter of credit case.

[229] See in the Netherlands, HR Sept 25 1992 [1992] NJ 750, which interprets Article 4(5) restrictively and in case of doubt finds for the presumption of Article 4(2). The Court of Appeal of Versailles was much more forthcoming in favour of a rebuttal of this presumption, see its decision of 6 Feb 1991 [1991] *Rev Crit de Dr Intern Privé* 745.

[230] See the Dutch case cited in n 229 *supra*, and further also *Dicey and Morris* on *the Conflict of Laws* (13th edn, 2000), rule 174, 1234.

application or non-application, see Article 7 of the Rome Convention. It should be noted that the UK and Germany availed themselves of the possibility to opt out of this clause. There is here discretion and no conflicts rule proper. It allows social and policy considerations to be taken into account directly, although Article 7 is still rule- and not interest- or result-oriented, see on this Article 7 further section 2.2.6 below.

Dutch law in its 1992 draft Introduction Statute to Private International Law (Article 8) extended the common public order exception to the application of a conflicts rule, and allowed considerations of reasonableness and fairness to affect the result. In this connection, it did not suggest the application of the law of any other country (with a closer connection), although according to some this was still implied. That would have reinforced a conflicts approach emphasising the applicability of some domestic law. The rule was more properly a sequel to Article 6. 2(2) of the new Dutch CC which submits all applicable law, be it statutory or customary, to the requirements of reasonableness and fairness and allows at least in the law of obligations the necessary corrections in the result as an autonomous function of the forum. This is closer to the modern American approach than may be found anywhere else in Europe and is to be welcomed.

For conflicts, this approach had as yet little support in Dutch private international law scholarship, which is still on the look out for clarity and certainty under some domestic rule. A new draft of 2002 was more modest and removed the references to reasonableness and fairness from the public order exception (Article 12). The notion of public order remained, however, undefined in this connection and may therefore still cover some fundamental legal principles maintained by the forum regardless of all conflicts law or theory. They may (but need not) derive from international agreements or EU legislation concerning eg market manipulation, money laundering, the protection of the environment or of cultural objects it is likely in such cases that the *lex fori* will be applied instead. This may still be done also when vital Dutch interests or convictions are challenged. Thus it would appear that within the public order exceptions, compelling Dutch notions of fairness and reasonableness may still be used to test the result of the application of conflict rules, even though this is no longer expressly stated. Again that is in line with the general approach of Article 6. 2(2) Dutch CC.

Objectives of clarity and certainty are unattainable in international transactions at this juncture if only because of the enormous increase in the movement of goods and modern services at global level where especially in finance and payments structures are used that are unfamiliar to many legal systems and because of the great and varying impact of policy and perhaps overriding reasonableness considerations for which a conflicts rule can hardly be given. Yet, notably the German Statute of 1986 and the Italian Statute of 1995 did not introduce similar flexibility. Also Article 15 of the Swiss law does not go so far and remains well within the proximity approach and traditional conflict of laws solutions. The ultimate question is nevertheless whether the application of any domestic law continues to be appropriate in international cases at all, especially if playing themselves out in the international professional sphere in manners and forms that have no domestic equivalent.

The corrections to the applicable law through exception clauses may not apply to situations where the parties have made a contractual choice of law, but there are even then exceptions in the case of consumer and workers contracts in order to protect the weaker party under Articles 5 and 6 of the EU Rome Convention. Moreover, it can only be repeated that a contractual choice of law is not always fully effective, certainly not in matters which are not at the free disposition of the parties to regulate amongst themselves, as is often also thought to be the case in proprietary matters in respect of any third party effect. In contractual matters, mandatory rules of a country with which all elements relevant to the situation are connected (at the time of the choice) cannot be set aside either (Article 3 of the Rome Convention). Also in tort matters the freedom to choose an applicable law is not always unrestricted: it is limited to the *lex fori* in Switzerland (Article 132). In Switzerland, the exception clauses do not apply to (the results of) the choice of a domestic law by the parties, see Article 15(2), but this is possible in the USA, see Section 187(a) of the Restatement (Second), and would also be possible under the proposed new Dutch approach when (internationalised) requirements of reasonableness and fairness would also apply to law (and forum) selection clauses.

Finally, corrections to the conflicts rules and applicable laws thereunder may result indirectly from *forum non conveniens* considerations to the applicable jurisdiction. However, this concept which is of Scottish origin and generally adopted in common law countries, remains alien to continental European thinking and does not figure in the Brussels and Lugano Conventions on Jurisdiction and Enforcement of Judgments in Civil and Commercial Matters either, nor in the 2002 EU Regulation replacing the Brussels Convention. It is proposed for a new European Regulation concerning the Jurisdiction and Enforcement of Judgments in Family and Succession Matters.

In domestic law, the *forum non conveniens* notion, where known, is sometimes restricted to a correction of the choice of jurisdiction by the parties, see Article 5(3) of the Swiss law of 1987, which allows rejection of the choice of Switzerland if neither party has a domicile, residence or establishment in that country. Article 429 of the Dutch CCP rejects the election if neither party has a sufficient contact with Dutch public order, whilst case-law requires an interest (which may exist if Dutch law is applicable, the Dutch language is used or a speciality of Dutch courts, like shipping matters in Rotterdam, is involved).[231] It could be seen as an expression of the *forum (non) conveniens* doctrine in continental terms. New Dutch legislative proposals concerning international jurisdiction confine themselves to the criterion of foreign parties being able to show an interest.

The European response to the modern American theories is significant but remains incidental and is thus often expressed in terms of corrections to the prevailing proximity rules by substituting another conflicts principle. Except for the Dutch proposals, a more open system based on the acceptability of the results remains exceptional and is not even now the law in the Netherlands or likely to be accepted there without further discussion.[232]

2.2.5 The Emphasis on the Facts rather than on the Rules: The Nature of the Relationship and of the Transaction. Modern Interpretation Techniques and the Effects of Internationalisation

The difference between the classical and more modern approaches to conflicts of laws is often dictated by temperament and practical experience. They pervade the approach to the

---

[231] See also HR 1 Feb 1985, NJ 698 (Piscator 1985).

[232] See for the subject of the exception clauses and *forum non conveniens* also the reports to the 14th International Congress of Comparative Law in Athens and especially the general report of D Kokkini-Iatridou, *Les Clauses d' Exception en Matière de Conflits de Lois et de Conflits de Jurisdiction* [Exception Clauses in Conflicts of Laws and Conflicts of Jurisdictions — or the Principle of Proximity] (Dordrecht, 1994), 3. The author proposes — with reference to JG Castel, "Commentaire sur certaines dispositions du Code civil du Québec se rapportant au droit international privé", [1992] *JDI* 630/2 — a second phase in the openness debate and, whilst criticising Article 8 of the Dutch proposals of 1992, suggests that exceptionally the traditional conflicts rules should not be applied if in all the circumstances it would be better to apply the law of another state, thus returning to the application of a particular domestic law with an emphasis on rules rather than on interests and results, the proximity notion being exceptionally abandoned, however. It is unlikely to be more satisfactory than the other exception clauses looking for better *domestic* laws to apply in international cases.

law generally but are of particular interest in the attitude to conflicts of laws and no less to the new law merchant or *lex mercatoria*. It basically concerns here:

(a)   a search for certainty in the behavioral patterns of the participants and peer group (and their transactional structuring) rather than in a set of hard and fast super-imposed rules of whatever nature,

(b)   a degree of suspicion towards artful rules that only provide an appearance of certainty but solve nothing,[233]

(c)   a level of comfort with and acceptance of a measure of uncertainty in respect of the applicable (black letter) law in order to facilitate

(d)   the search for better, fairer or more sensible and practical results, thus substituting a normativity of a different sort,

(e)   allowance in international cases for ethical, social, economic and environmental considerations to be taken into account which are not necessarily of a national character but respond to international values and international law (in which connection reference may also be made to the international public order).

There is always tension in these aspects in view of the facts of a case, the interests to be protected, the needs of the parties in this respect and the impact of public policy, thus between more positivist and teleological approaches, aggravated where the conflicts rules themselves, as in the traditional private international law, are often contrived or remain uncertain and contested like in the proprietary aspects of many modern financial transactions and set-off facilities.

It is nevertheless true that even practising lawyers often continue to rely on a domestic law (preferably their own) in a mistaken search for certainty and clarity in this manner. In this connection, they are often oblivious to the often limited or adverse impact of a contractual choice of a domestic law (even their own) which might prove entirely unsuitable in the circumstances. Eg, domestic good faith consideration may play out very differently in international transactions. It need also be established how far these clauses reach. It was already said that they can only affect issues that are truly at the free disposition of the parties to settle the way they chose. They cannot therefore concern proprietary issues that by their very nature involve third parties as competing interest holders or creditors of the transferor. It leaves in any event open the question of how far the idiosyncrasies of a domestic law, like for example the common law doctrine of consideration (see more in particular chapter 2, section 1.2.7), local concerns, like the protection of certain classes of minority groups or weaker parties, or typical domestic policy objectives like the protection of their own trade and currency (not allowing for example payment in any other), should, by choosing that particular law, extend to international cases in the professional sphere. Another question is whether more generally a domestic law chosen by the parties could set aside the mandatory rules of other countries more directly involved or introduce the regulatory rules of the laws so chosen to cases that have no relation to such regulation.

Why should eg the sale of drinking water in country X be made subject to the clean water provisions in country Y only because Y's laws have been chosen to apply by the

---

[233] See for the more convoluted results, even by conflict of laws standards, particularly the approach in tri-partite situations like agency, chapter 2, s 3.2, bills of lading, chapter 4, s 2.1.9, bills of exchange, chapter 4, s 2.2.10, and assignments, chapter 4, s 1.9.

parties? (a) To begin with, parties probably never realised or intended these restrictions of country Y to apply but were only concerned about the general contractual framework of the transaction. (b) Secondly, by chosing the law of another country, they do not nec-essarily opt out of the mandatory rules of the objectively applicable law (of country X) nor into those that have nothing to do with the case (the mandatory law of country Y). (c) In any event, the transfer of property (here drinking water) in country X would in any event be governed by the law of country X as being the law of the *situs* assuming the water was produced in country X and was not meant under the contract to be exported from it.

Many practitioners will not consider these issues at the time of the formation of the contract. It is against their instinct and it may mean that the contract might have to be handled by lawyers of other jurisdictions. The suitability of the chosen law is in any event difficult to judge by lawyers who are mainly educated in one legal system. Of course, the more the concept of transnational law or the modern *lex mercatoria* start to prevail, the quicker the monopoly of the lawyers whose legal system is somehow preferred in the case would disappear. The legal profession itself would then be opened up in the handling of international cases, which would no longer be exclusively subject to any party's domestic legal regime and rules.

Whatever the future development, there are always uncertainties in the application and interpretation of any rule, domestic or more internationalised, in the face of the factual patterns to be covered and the interests to be protected. This is not a typical problem of international cases, even if sometimes more apparent in them. In any event, the great increase in litigation also in civil and commercial matters domestically is clear evidence of the fact that even purely at the national level the search for certainty in the law has remained elusive. Needless to say, certainty is more difficult to achieve and to maintain in times of great change, as we have been experiencing during the last two generations, and is even in more stable times always relative. Most importantly, certainty in the applicable law most definitely does not automatically lead to the better result.

It is the proposition of this look that the only true certainty derives from the normativity that exists in the relevant community from time to time. But also rules evolve and espe-cially in the more contentious cases that tend to be litigated the outcome cannot be absolutely predicted. If that were possible they would not be brought. What is clear is that certainty cannot derive from yesterday's laws nor from rules from other legal orders (or nation states). The better result is likely to be obtained under the evolving rules of the legal order in which the transactions take place like, in trade and finance, the international com-mercial and financial legal order.

This realisation alone may more readily produce corrections to the *prima facie* applica-ble domestic law in international cases, at least in the professional sphere where parties are used to some uncertainty whilst often taking greater risks. In fact, they may make a busi-ness out of this uncertainty. That does not mean that they will not try to unbundle legal risks and protect against them in the structuring of their transactions. That is what trans-action lawyers largely do. It may prove more difficult in international cases, but there is nothing to prove that the present legal uncertainties especially at the international level are unmanageable. For professionals, in the case of disputes a more sensible solution is ulti-mately more valuable than the pretence of legal certainty. It can hardly be produced on the basis of the application of domestic laws that were never meant for international transac-tions. Indeed, in the professional sphere, corrections to any *prima facie* applicable domestic law (on the basis of the traditional conflicts rules) or its disapplication in the circumstances are likely to be based principally on what makes sense, whilst in the consumer sphere they are more likely to be geared to the vulnerability of the parties and then based on what is fairer in the circumstances of the case.

It was already pointed out that for professionals this basic approach might mean rougher justice with less rather than more refinement in the legal concepts or protections used. This was demonstrated in connection with good faith protection. It may sometimes even be true purely domestically. Thus the return of title in the goods upon default, even if the contract provides for it, may be deemed against the commercial flows. So may be under modern law any contractual restrictions on assignments of receivables. A lesser acceptance of specific performance may follow for altogether similar reasons. Sometimes there may be an extra reliance on the wording of an agreement or letter of credit, therefore on a more lit-eral interpretation, even in civil law countries that otherwise may rely on a more teleologi-cal or good faith approach. Thus for professional participants an emphasis on certainty returns here but then as industry practice rather than as a policy objective of the applicable law. In fact, a more teleological and normative interpretation may itself lead to this result as we shall see in chapter 2, section 1.3.5.

The emphasis is thus on the identification and (teleological and normative) interpre-tation of all legal rules and principles that are in varying degrees connected with the case and on the determination of their relevance in the circumstances. No rule or prin-ciple, whether purely domestic or not, has in this approach any absolute value or force whilst even the fundamental principles (or the *ius cogens*) are always subject to interpre-tation in the light of the circumstances of the case. The *facts of the case*, especially in terms of the nature of the relationship of the parties, the interests to be protected therein, and the particular dynamics and logic of each transaction, are thus likely to play the preponderant and ultimately decisive role. As already mentioned above, even extra-legal considerations may enter, as there may be ethical, social, economic and environmental aspects to consider, which are not nationalistic *per se* either. It will all enter into the ultimate determination of the applicability and choice of the available rules as a matter of interpretation. To put it in an extreme way: if a rule does not fit the facts, it will not apply as it cannot have been intended for them. Again, this may be more apparent where the reach of domestic rules through private international law rules is extended to also cover international situations for which they were never meant.

Emphasis on the nature of the relationship of the parties and its own requirements is certainly an aspect of the notion of good faith in civil law countries and has always been an aspect of the common law of contract, see also chapter 2, section 1.1.1. It points the way domestically but no less internationally and suggests different legal rules that might apply or existing rules that will need to be adapted to allow for the differences. Thus in interna-tional cases, one would expect quite naturally a special response, to begin with in interna-tional civil and commercial law cases, and an imaginative answer from the judiciary and especially from arbitrators to the parties' special needs, at least until more precise substan-tive transnational rules emerge in practice. That is the essence of the rapidly developing international law merchant or modern *lex mercatoria*, which is here perceived as in essence a hierarchy of norms amongst different sources of law that are all conceivably applicable, and amongst which domestic norms continue to figure but with different degrees of prominence depending on the facts of each case, whilst transnational law will increasingly emerge on the basis of fundamental legal principle, custom, to some extent uniform treaty law (or EU directives and the like), and otherwise common legal principles, see more in particular section 3.1.1 below.

2.2.6   The Issue of Public Policy or Governmental Interests and their Impact. The Notion of Comity and its Application. Competition between Transnational and State Laws

There can be little doubt that national govenmental policies have had an enormous impact on the development of the law in the twentieth century. They have not left private law untouched. This issue was already raised in more general terms in section 1.4.3 above. *Mandatory* private law thus increased as governments have often used private law to achieve their policy purposes eg in the protection of consumers and smaller investors. By using notions of fairness and good faith and by extending the negligence concepts, in contract eg in terms of pre-contractual and post-contractual duties, courts themselves have introduced mechanisms to broaden judicial policies. These are likely not only to further the demands for justice, social peace and perhaps also utilitarian principle and common sense notions, thus updating the living law, but may also coincide with and reinforce governmental policies. Furthermore, much public or administrative law spills over into the application and interpretation of private laws, eg when under competition or securities laws or under export restrictions contracts are invalidated.

In international cases, governmental interests present special problems which other legal orders and therefore also a *lex mercatoria* approach cannot avoid and must take into account when justified. This will especially be relevant in respect of international trade conducted in whole or in part upon the territory of the state or governments concernd. Although governments cannot in principle reach beyond their borders (nor interfere within their own borders in other legal orders without showing proper respect), their public policy rules cannot always be ignored elsewhere either, if only because their own courts may be asked to pass on situations that arose abroad (or in other domestic legal orders) but had an effect in the forum state and on which the forum government's policies could impact. Internationally, these situations arise in many different ways and may affect private parties in their dealings. Competition policy is again an important example. Can it be applied extraterritorially eg when non-residents organise a cartel to affect prices in the forum country eg in the US or in the EU?

This raises a number of important questions, first whether under the American or European competition laws, these laws extend under their own terms to actions abroad. This is often referred to as the issue of extraterritoriality, in the US also referred to as the question of *subject matter jurisdiction* or *jurisdiction to prescribe*. At least in the US, there is a presumption against exterritoriality of national laws but it depends first on the intent of the legislator and subsequently, in the application to foreign cases, also on the court's considerable discretion in these matters. This discretion is assumed by the (American) courts quite separately from the legislator's (presumed) intent and is based on *comity* which has fairness at its center. It is in such cases still mostly seen as a *national* rather than international concept although reference is in this connection now often made to moderation[234] and an awareness of the interests of others in which manner at least some attention is paid to international (public) law.[235] In this regard, Sections 402 and 403 Restatement

---

[234] See for this international law principle the *Barcelona Traction Case*, ICJ Rep 3 (1970).

[235] See for the extraterritorial application of competition laws in the US the line of cases starting with *United States v Aluminium Company of America (Alcoa)*, 148 Fed 2d 416 (1945) and *United States v Imperical Chemical Industries (ICI)* 105 F Supp 215 (1952). The creation of a (potentially fraudulent) worldwide patent network and its effect on the US may in this connection also be considered under its own tort and competition rules if restricting American plaintiffs activities, see *Mannington Mills Inc v Congoleum Corp*, 595 F2d 1287 (1979). What will be

(Third) Foreign Relations Law of the United States (1987) refer to reasonableness and set guidelines. They are of great interest, need to be carefully considered, and may also be indicative of a more international trend.

In Europe, reference is in this connection often made *to règles d'application immediate* in Article 7 of the 1980 EU Rome Convention on the Law Applicable to Contractual Obligations. Here the formulation of a conflict or private international law rule is preferred, even though it does not concern a private law matter. Under it, precedence is given to governmental policies when they are more obviously relevant, notably when there is (significant) conduct or effect on the territory of the state concerned. Here reference is sometimes also made to a so-called *unilateral* conflicts rule giving effect to public policy of forum states in such circumstances.[236]

As long as the same standards are not used everywhere, however, the outcome in terms of the applicable law and respect for the relevant governmental interest may at least to some extent depend on the location of the forum (or on forum selection by the parties or international arbitration being agreed, see below). That is still the present situation and raises important questions of *adjudicatory jurisdiction*, the question therefore whether the forum in the offended state has sufficient jurisdiction over the (alleged) foreign perpetrators. Here, at least in the US, constitutional considerations of due process, therefore of fairness, are additionally invoked to avoid excessive jurisdiction of the plaintiffs' chosen courts (preferably their own) even if this has not led to a set of clear rules of special jurisdiction over foreigners.[237] Mostly the types of activities are considered and the situation carefully explored for adequate contacts with the forum, but a hard and fast set of adjudicatory jurisdiction rules in respect of absent defendants has been increasingly abandoned as unworkable and is in any event not considered in accordance with due process.[238] This approach used in interstate cases, where there is no true discretion, is by extension also

---

considered in this connection is whether the ties with the foreign country are strong enough whilst ultimately the reasonableness may also be tested, see *Timberlane Lumber Co v Bank of America*, 549 F 2d 597 (1976), in which the relative effect on the US as compared to the effect on others was thought to be an issue and also whether there is another court readily available, see for a fuller discussion, and for the move from comity to legal guidelines or principles, also *Hartford Fire Insurance Co v California*, 509 US 764 (1993).

[236] See for a comparative study also GA Bermann, "Public Law in the Conflict of Laws", 34 (Supplement) *AJCL* (1986), 157.
[237] See the line of cases starting with *International Shoe Co v Washington*, 326 US 310 (1945) and *Helicopteros Nacionales de Colombia, SA v Hall*, 446 US 408 (1984).
[238] Thus importing goods or services *from* the US is unlikely to result in jurisdiction of the American courts, no matter how large the transnation is and it may even have some service element attached to it within the US. Obviously it is against the interest of US commerce to act otherwise and the State Department will seek to protect foreign buyers from American jurisdiction through *amicus curiae* briefs in the respective courts. Keeping a bank account in the US, taking out a loan there, or organising a letter of credit or other type of bank guarantee there is likely to be similarly considered. The more important issue is the importation of goods or services *into* the US and the extent to which this may create a business in the US.

That issue has been tested in numerous cases, particularly in product liability situations where various defending importers start cross claims for contribution against each other in the US (even through foreign themselves), on the basis of the original jurisdiction asserted by harmed American plaintiff, see eg *Asahi Metal Industry Co Ltd v Superior Court*, 480 US 102 (1987), *cf* also *Deutsch v West Coast Machinery Co*, 80 Wash 2d 707 (1972). Cross claims of this nature are unlikely to succeed for lack of sufficient presence in the US certainly in respect of component suppliers to the importers outside the US.

The issue of jurisdiction over importers into the US has also come up where foreign manufacturers like Volkswagen AG from Germany have tried to organise themselves in such a way that they are not coming on-shore in the US for jurisdictional purposes, their policy being that if there is to be litigation they wish to be sued in their own courts (for Volkswagen in Germany). Here concepts of agency, control or *de facto* amalgamation with the US sales organisations have been tried to establish jurisdiction of the American courts but generally not to much avail. Agency requires the American sales network to be able to legally bind the foreign manufacturer, a situation

used in international cases where it could be asked whether the discretion that comes with comity plays a more fundamental role or is perhaps the chief consideration (rather than constitutional due process).

In the UK,[239] the courts assume here broader discretion in a reflection of a more obvious comity approach which is in this area of international adjudicatory jurisdiction (on its face still) mostly avoided in the US. In Continental Europe, more traditional hard and fast rules attaching jurisdiction to the place of the tortuous effect or to other connecting factors are still being used[240] whilst the extraterritoriality issue will be seen as related so that no obvious distinction is (as yet) made between jurisdiction to adjudicate and jurisdiction to prescribe.

The acceptance of this approach under international law is stressed.[241] It shows a preference for a more certain, less discretionary approach in which potential unfairness may be less of a concern or a concern that is considered to be adequately dealt with in the prevailing hard and fast jurisdiction and conflict of laws rules (the latter always subject, however, to public order considerations).[242]

2.2.7 Practical Issures Concerning Conflicting Public Policies: Effect on the Lex Mercatoria *and the Importance of the Notion of* Forum non Conveniens

In practice, conflicts of public policies more in particular arise when eg anti-competitive activity is perfectly legal in the countries where it has been organised. The courts of the alleged perpetrators may in such cases not wish to pass on the offensive effect of the conduct elsewhere and may in any event not apply the foreign competition statutes. This may be a particular reason for the courts of (or chosen by) the aggrieved plaintiffs to take the case.[243] Similar issues have arisen in the enforcement of (American) securities legislation in respect of offensive acts abroad that affect American investors eg a securities fraud (according to American standards) on a foreign exchange or in a foreign issue of new securities.[244] But like in competition matters, *remoteness* is an important issue. Not all American investors in foreign markets can expect to be protected by the American securities laws in their own courts. There comes a moment that they are on their own and must sue in the place of the wrong under the laws of that place, although in situations of patent fraud the American laws may reach further.

that in these situations is much avoided. Control can only be alleged between parent and subsidiary, a situation also much avoided in this type of scheme, see *Delagi v Volkswagenwerk AF of Wolfsburg,* 29 NY 2d 426 (1972). Amalgamation may exist when foreign subsidiaries are newly set up and are not yet able to organize themselves, see *BulovaWatch Co, Inc v K Hattori & Co, Ltd,* 508 FSupp 1322 (1981). A forum selection clause in favour of a foreign court may also be sufficient to avoid jurisdiction of the American courts, see *Volkswagenwerk AG v Klippan, GmbH,* 611 P2d 498 (1980).

Whether the situation is different in respect of services and whether in that case, at least when unsolicited, jurisdiction of the American Courts is less likely to result, came up in *Landoil Resources Corp v Alexander & Alexander Services Inc,* 918 NYS 2d 739 (1990) in which the American insurance broker unsuccessfully sued a Loyds of London syndicate in New York in a cross claim for contribution.

[239] Para 6.20 UK Civil Procedure (Amendment) Rules 2000.

[240] See as main example Article 5 of the EU Regulation No 44/2001 on Jurisdiction and the Recognition and Enforcement of Judgments in Civil and Commercial Matters entered into force on March 1 2002 replacing the similar Brussels Convention of 1968.

[241] See *Alstrom v Commission* (Woodpulp case), European Court Case 89/85, ECR, 5193 (1988). In the EU it does not yet give rise to a balancing of competing interests.

[242] There is much increased awareness of the need for rules also in the US, see eg the concurring opinion of Judge Adams in *Mannington Mills* cited in n 235 *supra* but they are not necessarily the old rules.

[243] *Cf* House of Lords in *British Airways Board v Laker Airways Ltd* [1985] 3 WLR 413.

[244] See *Leasco Data Processing Equipment Corporation v Maxwell,* 468 F2d 1326 (1972).

More traditional situations are here questions of tariffs, import restrictions and boycotts and their effects on foreign contracts and on the delivery of goods thereunder if offensive to the forum state or any other. There is ample case-law in the US and also some in the UK on these matters.[245] Cases typically arise where a contract is asked to be enforced in another country (eg payment requested) but entails a trade that goes against tariffs (smuggling) or export restrictions (boycotts) in the first country and may as such be void under the law of that country which is likely to be the one most directly concerned (the export country). Especially if the boycott is directed against the forum country, however, it may not be enforced by that forum and the contract is more likely to be upheld (which may still give rise, however, to a *force majeure* excuse on the part of the exporter). Other instances may be where foreigners deal in real estate in another country which they are not entitled to do under the laws of their home country or for which they need a licence under those laws. In such cases, the courts in the countries where the property is located are unlikely to declare the ensuing contracts and property transfers void. They will consider the undisturbed functioning of their own real estate market a superior interest.

Issues like these may also arise in a more obvious private law setting as the following examples may show. State A protects consumers against oppressive contracts, but not State B where a resident of state A buys a car upon onerous conditions. What effect has the policy of State A on the contract? Pure conflicts laws would probably point to the law of State B where the transaction took place and the most characteristic obligation (delivery) was performed. But is the protection policy of State A entirely irrelevant especially when payment is claimed from the purchaser in State A? Again much may depend on whether the issue is litigated in State A or State B. The EU Rome Convention on the Law Applicable to Contractual Obligations has a special rule in this connection and allows in these situations a consumer (exceptionally) the protection of his own laws. A *substantive law* element, in this case the fairness of the outcome, thus slips into the equation. One could also call it an expression of the good faith notion at the international level.

Other more classical examples may be where a spouse under the law of her home country cannot give valid surety undertakings in respect of the business of her husband but is prevailed upon to do so in another country whilst that guarantee is subsequently sought to be enforced in the home country. There is an indication in all these protection cases that the domiciliary principle replaces notions of territoriality (therefore notions of the spacial effect of the law with which conflict of law rules are more traditionally concerned) in the name of fairness as a substantive law requirement. Other instances arise when under so-called guest statutes the liability in respect of the transport of passengers may be limited a extended in some countries. Conflict of laws results when an accident occurs in such a state but the passengers and driver are from other states whilst the car is also insured somewhere else.

At least in case-law in the US, the more traditional approach pointing to the law of the place of the wrong is no longer upheld in such cases[246] and any defense on the basis of a limitation of liability in the place of the wrong is no longer accepted, at least not when the passenger and driver are both from the same (other) state where the insurance policy is also held and the suit is brought. Here again one could see an overriding *substantive* law element of fairness and justice. In the US, it is more often expressed in a weighing of

---

[245] The base case is often still thought to be *Holman v Johnson* (Lord Mansfield) 98 ER 1120 (1775) formulating the so-called Revenue Rule. See for a more recent approach House of Lords in *Regazzione v KC Sethia* (1944) Ltd, [1958] AC 301 and in the US *Banco do Brasil, SA v AC Israel Commodity Comp Inc*, 12 NY 2d 371 239 (1963).
[246] See *Babcock v Jackson*, 240 NYS 2d 743 (1963) and *Tooker v Lopez*, 301 NYS 2d 519 (1969).

different policies in which the forum state policy tends to prevail or, under Sections 6, 145 and 188 Restatement (Second) Conflict of Laws (1971), the law of the most significant relationship which allows for a broad range of policies to be considered but may no less result in the application of forum law, see also sections 2.2.2 and 2.2.3 above. Hence again the importance of adjudicatory jurisdiction and the possibility of so-called forum shopping by plaintiffs to find the (for them) most convenient forum unless restrained from doing so under forum selection or arbitration clauses. The US is thus long used to an interest analysis in interstate conflicts and within that approach a weighing of policies of other nations can be easily accommodated. One could see Sections 402 and 403 of the Restatement (Third) Foreign Relations Law of the United States (1987) as a logical sequel to it.

It means that in the US prescriptive jurisdiction (and also act of state notions) are carved out of the more traditional conflict of laws approach and a different treatment is here given to governmental interests which easily fits into the interest analysis which in the US has also become common in private law conflicts (as public and private law issues are not as fundamentally distinguished as in civil law see more in particular section 2.2.2 above). It fits much less easily in the more conventional European conflict of laws approach which has been largely abandoned in the US, first in interstate cases but later also in international cases exactly because of the weight of these governmental or policy interests, which have long become evident also in private law cases, see more in particular section 2.2.4 above.

As already mentioned, in the 1980 EU Rome Convention on the Law Applicable to Contractual Obligations, Article 7 was introduced to cover this type of situation or at least the more traditional and more incidental onces associated with tariffs, boycotts and foreign exchange restrictions (even if the UK and Germany opted out of this clause as they were entitled to do under Article 22). It refers to mandatory laws, not directly to governmental or public policies and it is not clear how far there is a difference. Under Article 7(2), a forum may always apply its own mandatory rules irrespective of the law otherwise applicable to the case and regardless of any reasonable contact between the case and that law or between the case and the forum. That corresponds with the opening of Section 6 of the Restatement (Second) Conflict of Laws in the US. Under Article 7(1), such a court may, however, also give effect to the mandatory rules of other countries with which the situation has a close connection (if and in so far as under the law of the latter country those rules must be applied whatever the law otherwise applicable to the contract). In considering whether to give effect to these mandatory rules, regard must be made to their nature, purpose and the consequences of their application or non-application.

As just mentioned, Article 7(1) is often thought to be merely of an incidental nature and the corrections that are supposed to be made thereunder are then associated with tariff laws and the like although it will also have application in other cases. It raises the important issue of the *appropriateness* of applying these mandatory rules. In this connection, the proportionality and legitimacy of the underlying policies might have to be considered and tested from an international (law) perspective, therefore on the basis of internationalised substantive norms. So may be the question of *force majeure* that may arise in respect of a defendant who might thus be forced to perform a contract that he perhaps should not have concluded, and is invalid within his own jurisdiction (because of a boycott or other export restriction directed at the country of the plaintiff), but may still be upheld somewhere else.

It should be noted, however, that under Article 7(1) as drafted the interests of foreign countries or third parties are not as such mentioned and weighed nor is the question directly considered whether the mandatory rule might, internationally speaking, be exorbitant in the light of more general basic principles of international law. It is strictly speaking unclear whether Article 7(1) is itself an expression of *international* comity of which it has the appearance.

In terms of the *lex mercatoria* whilst operating in its own international order, it cannot be insensitive in its application to governmental or similar interests deriving from other, notably statist, legal orders (especially if a transaction is within or has, through conduct, effect or otherwise, a substantial contact with the territory of the state in question) and it will have to be considered from case-to-case to what extent the *lex mercatoria* and its application is to be overruled or adjusted on the basis of such interests when *sufficiently connected* with the case so that the consideration of such governmental interests if conflicting and their impact may be justified. Here the *comity approach* is again important and the tests under it of the relevance of these governmental interests in international cases. In this connection, for comity to be more credible it should be used as a concept of international and not domestic law, in which connection the balancing factors developed for example in American case-law as summarised in the Restatement (Third) Law of Foreign Relations may be of exemplary interest. Again, in the absence of a uniform approach, the issue of adjudicatory jurisdiction remains important as it will determine which courts (or arbitration panels) will be called upon to identify and, as the case may be, weigh the relevant interests.

In this connection the impact of forum selection and arbitration clauses should also be considered. Three American Supreme Court Cases are here of fundamental significance.[247] They broadly uphold forum selection and arbitration clauses in international cases even if bearing on American *public policy* issues, notably securities and anti-trust laws, but always subject to *forum non-conveniens* considerations in which the applicable substantive and procedural law normally do not figure,[248] but in which (the balance of) public policies may still play a role if these policies are *sufficiently strong.*[249]

It is for the party wanting to sue in another (American) forum to show that the selected forum or arbitration proceedings are inconvenient. The obvious advantage of a more neutral forum to consider the relevance of public policies is recognised in this regard and in *Scherk* it was specifically accepted that an arbitration clause "obviates the danger that a dispute under the agreement might be submitted to a forum hostile to the interests of one of the parties or unfamilar with the problem area involved". The advantage of avoiding in this way the jurisdiction of multiple competing *fora* was also noted. The risk that such proceedings may affect the application of public policy as embodied in securities laws of the US was clearly accepted. But it was pointed out in Mitsubishi (in footnote 19) that the combination with the selection by the parties of a foreign law could not suffice to block strong public policy claims. Recognition of the ensuing decisions would not pass the public policy test, at least not in the US.

Here may also enter the idea that the arbitration panel *itself* should adopt a *forum non conveniens* approach in respect of public policy related issues and, depending on the nature, decide to leave them to the ordinary courts to be decided in parallel proceedings. The phenomenology of the issue may also play a role. What antitrust violation is alleged; is it sufficiently incidental to the case even if not to the particular issue to be decided

---

[247] *The Bremen et al. v Zapata Off-shore Co*, 407 US 1 (1972), *Scherk v Alberto-Culver Co*, 417 US 506 (1974), and *Mitsubishi Motors Corp. v Soler Chrysler-Plymouth, Inc.*, 473 US 614 (1985).
[248] See *Piper Aircraft Co v Reyno*, 454 US 235 (1981) *and In Re Union Carbide Corp.* 809 F2d 195 (1987).
[249] See for a similar approach in England *Unterweser Reederei GmbH v Zapata Off-shore Company*, CA [1968] 2 Lloyd's L Rep 158.

(like contract validity)? Are the alleged perpetrators all subject to the arbitration clause, etc? In an intervening bankruptcy of one of the parties to an arbitration similar issues may arise eg in terms of proof of claim, suspension of enforcement rights, etc.[250]

It is therefore not so that these public policy issues have become irrelevant in international cases but the assumption of the American courts is that they may be competently handled elsewhere assuming that the foreign courts or international arbitrators will give them suffi- cient weight on the basis of the connection with the situation whilst more ordinary choice of law and conflict rules will *only* become relevant to point to the appropriate law in this respect *after* the issues of reasonableness and remoteness have been separately decided in respect of these governmental interests. This would also seem to be supported by modern case-law in the US[251] in which the law resulting as applicable under contractual choice of law clauses may be allowed to settle the issue, at least where a public policy protection is waived in this manner.

It would not appear helpful, to see this development as an instance of privatisation of public policy, the issues arising thereunder subsequently to be decided under the standard rules of private international law (which have in any event little to say on the law applicable in respect of public policy and were never developed for this complication). The ultimate consequence would then be that private parties could opt in and out of any public policy they wanted or disliked. They are unlikely to succeed.

The key is here to develop more *substantive* international rules to restrain the effects of domestic *public* policies and to determine when they must be given weight. These are issues of fairness, legitimate contact (through conductor effect) or remoteness, proportionality, legitimacy of the policy, etc. Domestic case-law and standards as those found in the US for- eign relations laws and in similar laws of other countries may serve as examples in this regard and show the way. In the *private* law aspects, substantive international or transna- tionalised rules would derive from the *lex mercatoria*.

It should be repeated that in civil law this type of discretion in the jurisdiction to pre- scribe and also *forum non-conveniens* considerations do not apply and that relevant arbi- tration and forum selection clauses are normally upheld as a matter of law, except that in as far as the latter are concerned national courts may not wish to put the resources necessary to hear cases that have no conceivable contact with the forum but for the forum selection at the disposal of foreign parties, see also section 2.2.4 *in fine* above. As far as the applicable law is concerned, in the traditional civil law approach, the tension between public policy handling and private international law rules has proved much less easy to resolve especially because of lack of flexibility also in this regard and the ingrained tendency to bring all under conflict of laws rules, therefore within the purview of private law.

As already mentioned, this is often done through the creation of a so-called *unilateral* conflicts rule, like the one of Article 7 of the EU Rome Convention. It allows the application of public policy when there is conduct or effect (as connecting factors) on the legislator's own territory, on its markets or when investors require the application of its own rules and may them require for the automatic application of the policy as *lex fori*. This has the appearance of a choice of law rule in the traditional sense but is in truth an accommoda- tion of governmental policy in terms of a hard and fast rule without the flexibility of the US approach in making comity considerations (including act of state considerations) precede the application of domestic policies in international cases.

---

[250] This may also affect bankruptcy issues, see V Lazics, *Insolvency Proceedings and Commercial Arbitration* (1998).
[251] See *Simula, Inc v Autoliv*, 175 F3d 716 (9th Circ 1999) and of the earlier Lloyd's cases see eg *Bonny v Lloyd's of London*, 3 F3d 156 (7th Circ 1993).

The important consequence of the American cases accepting forum selection and arbitraion clauses also in respect of public policy issues — which were motivated by the recognition that international trade had started to require these forum selection and arbitration clauses to be upheld — is that in as far as international arbitration is concerned the arbitrability notion has been greatly expanded. Was it formerly possible to say that public policy issues were not normally arbitrable and therefore had to be moved to the ordinary courts in duplicate or parallel proceedings even on a minor pretext of a competitive issue (so that arbitration panels would not enter into the consideration of governmental interests and their balancing if conflicting), this is now, at least from an American perspective, no longer the position. It signals a profound change in the nature of international commercial arbitration proceedings which has also had a resonance elsewhere,[252] even in the European Court of Justice.[253]

Even though arbitration panels may in such cases still be ousted by the appropriate state courts on the basis of *forum non conveniens* notions (at least in the US and probably the UK) at the beginning of the case (eg if a major antitrust case arises which may hardly be considered incidental to the litigated contract), awards may still ensue if the panel does not believe its task finished thereby. Under the New York Convention, such an award might then be challenged on the basis of public policy in the place where it was rendered and it would in any event be subject to a public policy test in the country where recognition is asked. This may still entail an important limitation of public policy issues being determined by arbitration panels. Another important question in this regard is whether this test itself is also subject to internationalisation, presenting therefore an objective international substantive law standard. One must assume that the trend is in that direction.

2.2.8   *Party Autonomy and Contractual Choice of Law*

In the foregoing paragraphs the parties' ability to choose the applicable law was already mentioned several times[254] and it was in that connection pointed out that such a choice itself, which normally means the choice of a domestic law but could also mean the choice of the *lex mercatoria*, may raise major questions especially when public policy issues are involved in the particular case. The first one is how far this choice goes, in which matters therefore such a choice may prevail. Obviously, it does not mean the application of the tax laws of the country whose laws have been chosen. It does also not mean the adaptation of its bankruptcy laws to determine the effect on the contract when either party is bankrupt.

---

[252] See in Switzerland *GSA v V SpA*, 118 Arrets du Tribunal Federal [AFT] II, 193 (April 28 1992), in which the Swiss courts held that an arbitration panel wrongly refused to apply the EU competition laws whilst determining the validity of the contract. See for a further discussion JH Dalhuisen, 'The Arbitrability of Competition Issues', 11 *Arb. International*, 151(1995).

[253] See the Benetton case, ECJ case C–126/97 (1998), in which it was held that the antitrust provisions of the EC Treaty (Article 81) were matters of public order that could first be raised in setting aside proceedings (the original agreement had not been properly notified to the EU antitrust authorities and was thus void), which in this case did not make a difference because of domestic procedural problems in the Netherlands which the ECJ did not remove. Procedural rules requiring *res judicata* effect of earlier decisions in the matter may therefore still stand. The ECJ did not strictly speaking decide whether arbitrators may or must apply anti trust rules *ex-officio* but it would appear that they may raise the matter in oral argument (so as to prevent a later setting aside procedure) and are not then necessarily exceeding their mandate.

[254] In England, the Privy Council in Vita *Food Products Inc v Unus Shipping Co Ltd* [1939] AC 277 expressly accepted that parties are free to choose a legal system to govern their contractual relationship subject to that choice not being contrary to public policy and it being *bona fide* and legal. That is a general principle of contractual freedom now also embodied in the EU in Article 2 of the 1980 Rome Convention of the Law Applicable to Contractual Obligations.

The competition laws of such a chosen legal system are not automatically activated in this manner either.

There are also obvious limits as to proprietary issues in respect of assets located elsewhere. There is no way in which a mortgage can be transfered in real estate in England in the French or German manner, no matter how much parties wish it (even if in an assignment of claims against foreign debtors, parties are sometimes thought to have more autonomy over the applicable law also in its proprietary consequences). Applicable public policy rules or mandatory provisions other than the ones already mentioned (in tax, bankruptcy and competition matters) can also not simply be discarded by party choice. Thus consumer protection will not cease simply by parties having selected a foreign law that does not provide any. What may also play a role is that a particular mandatory law so chosen may not have extraterritorial effect under its own terms, but that is not always decisive as eg tax, bankruptcy and competition laws (which are usually applied extra territorially) show. Even in contractual matters, especially in respect of the contractual infrastructure, parties may only achieve limited success by choosing a foreign law, e.g as to their own capacity and the legality of their actions. These are areas in which the objectively applicable law is also likely to speak much louder and is unlikely to tolerate its removal by party autonomy.

A contractual choice of law may then simply be ineffective. By choosing a foreign law, it remains therefore still a question of interpretation what this choice entails whilst the objectively applicable law is not necessarily discarded nor is the law which the parties have opted into necessarily adopted in its entirety. Courts and arbitrators will thus have to assess what a contractual choice of law means and in how far it must be ignored. Other issues already mentioned before arise when the effect of the contractual choice cannot have been reasonably intended by the parties, eg French and German contracting parties opting for the law of England under which their contract would have been void for lack of consideration, a concept probably not understood by either party, let alone its consequences for the validity of their contract (which they obviously wanted). Here the chosen law may give the wrong answer, but it could also not give any answer at all, not unlikely in respect of the more advanced modern financial instruments, or answers that are so antiquated as to be useless e.g in the areas of set-off and netting.

Of course, one could say that parties should have been wiser at the outset and it is true that choices of a legal regime are often made without much thought of the consequences. But that also suggests that they may not be intended and such a lack of intent may matter. The more natural answer in such cases would be to compare the result with that which would obtain under a *lex mercatoria* approach and see what makes more sense or is more just and reflective of the true needs of participants in the particular trade, unless international public policy is directed against it as the higher norm or a domestic public policy if it can be shown to still be relevant in the case. At least gaps in the applicable law are then likely to be filled by transnational law. It is a variation on the earlier rejection (in this book) of the (formal legal) notion that domestic laws are always complete in themselves. This may in some fashion still work at the domestic level but is unlikely to do so in international cases for which these laws were in any event never made.

In the *lex mercatoria* approach with the hierarchy of norms as advocated in this book, see section 3.1.1. below, party autonomy including the choice of a domestic law would in the international commercial and financial legal order in any event still be subject to the higher norms derived from the fundamental legal principles (including international public order requirements in terms of ethical, social, economic and environmental considerations as internationalised values, even if the details may have to be left to lower norms), mandatory customary law or industry practices (particularly relevant in the proprietary aspects of these transactions to the extent their emerging), and mandatory treaty law in as far as existing (including EU Regulations and Directives). Directory customs or practices even of an international nature could, on the other hand, still be overtaken by such a contractual choice of law assuming it is clear what parties intended. So would be any resort to general principles again unless there are clear gaps in the applicable law so chosen or if the result of such a choice of law would clearly be absurd in terms of the dynamics of international commerce and finance. The general principles may also acquire a higher status if theys implement fundamental principle or mandatory custom or treaty law.[255]

On the other hand, the choice of law clause may itself point in the direction of the *lex mercatoria*. Eg the construction contract of the Channel Tunnel provided that it was to be governed by ' the common principles of English and French Law, and in the absence of such common principles by such principles of international trade law as have been applied by national and international tribunals'. The Iranian Petroleum Agreement of 1954 referred to 'principles of law common to Iran and to the various countries to which the other partries belong and, failing that, by principles of law generally recognized by civilized nations, including such principles applied by international tribunals'. Under *ad hoc* exploration agreements with Lybia, the arbitrations that eventually also decided on the nationalisation issues were to be governed by the 'principles of law of Lybia common to the principles of international law and, in the absence of such common principles … then by and in accordance with the general principles of law as may have been applied by international tribunals'. Especially in the oil and gas industry there were many similar clauses. Thus the Aminoil Concession Agreement of 1979 made reference to ' the law of the Parties … determined by the Tribunal, having regard to the quality of the Parties, the transnational character of their relations and the principles of law and practice prevailing in the modern world'. Where such a choice of law is made, one must assume the fuller set of lex mercatoria norms and their hierarchy to apply.

On the basis of Articles 1, 3 and 7 of the 1980 Rome Convention on the Law Applicable to Contractual Obligations it is sometimes argued in Europe that a choice of law in respect of the *lex mercatoria* is not possible, in other words that the freedom to choose the applicable law must always result in the choice of a national law. The text of Articles 2 and 3(2) would appear to go in another direction. The point is in truth not at all considered by the Convention. The underlying idea is here that only statist laws count as laws whilst other legal sources cannot be considered, a view which must be considered out of date. Indeed the LCIA Arbitration Rules (Article 22(3), the ICC Arbitration Rules (Article 17(1)) and the ICSID Convention (Article 42(1)) make it perfectly clear that general principles may be considered in arbitrations. French Arbitration law (Article 1496 CCP) expressly sanctions the application of the *lex mercatoria* and there is now little doubt that arbitrators may apply it. They also may have greater freedom when determining the relevance of domestic public policy considerations per case. Yet the dichotomy that is here suggested between the application of the law by arbitrators and ordinary judges may not be welcome or convincing. In truth, ordinary judges should take a similar approach in international business dealings.

Where parties have not provided for any choice of law clause at all, in international cases the application of the *lex mercatoria* (and its hierarchy) would seem all the more indicated.

---

[255] In the Pyramids case, *SPP (Middle East Ltd) and South Pacific Projects v Egypt and EGOTRH*, [1988] LAR 309, 330, the ICC Tribunal held that even though Egyptian law was the proper law of the contract, it had to be construed so as to include principles of internatiuonal law and the domestic law could only be relied upon in at much as it did not contravene international principle.

International arbitrators in particular may be willing in such cases to directly apply transnational law rather than resort to choice of law considerations leading to the application of a domestic law. In any event, they are considered to have freedom in the choice of law rules they apply. Even if directly resorting to transnational law or the *lex mercatoria*, particularly in proprietary matters, there may not yet be sufficient international custom or practices to cover these aspects as was already pointed out several times (although in international finance this void may rapidly be filling up) so that some resort to domestic law and choice of law may be unavoidable even if the location may be so unclear that the application of the traditional *lex situs* rule to the transfer of movable assets may yield an unconvincing and disputable result (especially for chattels which must be exported as part of the deal or for intangible claims involving foreign debtors).

As was pointed out before, it may be the reason why the importance of party autonomy is increasing also in this area. This is incongruous as third party rights are at stake that cannot be settled by others in their contract but it may be unavoidable. It assumes at the same time an increase in *bona fide* purchasers' or *bona fide* assignees' protection at the transnational level also therefore for the assignees of intangible assets, which is at the moment less common in civil law. It may thus be shown that only by introducing such a new transnational rule increased party autonomy under transnational law may be able to function without great complications also in proprietary matters. *Bona fide* creditors of the transferor or assignor would, however, miss out. In international finance that is perhaps the trend as it has long been in domestic finance where only secured interests in the debtor's underlying assets that are transferred or assigned will better protect his creditors.

2.3   Interaction of Private International Law and Harmonised Law

2.3.1   *Private International Law and the Application of Uniform Law*

Uniform law in the traditional sense is treaty law, like the 1980 Uncitral Convention on the International Sale of Goods, and when incorporated by the Contracting States in their own law, it is normally applied automatically by their judges as *lex fori*, assuming of course that the uniform law under its own terms applies to the transaction or situation concerned. They may cover international transactions or situations only but need not be so limited. The relevant convention may include in this connection even a definition of what is considered international. Depending on the subject, it may limit the uniform law to international dealings but the relevant convention may also apply under its own terms to purely domestic situation or transactions.

If international dealings are covered, one could argue instead that there is always a preliminary question of private international law to be determined by the private international law rules of the courts of Contracting States so seized. They would in that manner decide which country's laws apply and only if those are of a country that is party to the relevant convention, would the application of uniform law follow. This is, however, mostly *not* the approach of the uniform laws themselves which tend to unilaterally determine the field of their application which, if they cover also international transactions, then prevails over otherwise applicable domestic private international law rules, at least in cases brought before the courts of Contracting States. In other words, uniform law is mostly considered to have direct effect at least in Contracting States (even if on the whole objected to by organisations like the Hague Conference on Private International Law)

The Vienna Convention on the International Sales of Goods, for example, applies automatically in Contracting States if both parties to the sale come from different Contracting States unless they have excluded the application of the Convention (Article 1(1)(a)). Only in *non-contracting* States would the applicable private international law first have to point to the application of the law of a Contracting State for the uniform law to apply, assuming that the other application (or scope) criteria are also met.

Another issue arises when uniform laws allow for differences in incorporation of that law. In that case, discrepancies between the incorporation texts may still give rise to the question of which state law prevails in the circumstances even amongst Contracting States. Such questions might also arise in the US where the Vienna Convention was ratified by Congress but the proper incorporation and interpretation remains a question of state law (which determines commercial law). In this context the question of the appropriate relationship will acquire relevance to determine which state law is applicable, see eg Section 1–301 (1–105 old) UCC.

2.3.2   The Situation with Regard to EU Directives of a Private Law Nature

In the EU under Directives affecting private law (for example, consumer law, product liability, and conduct of business and segregation issues in investment services), incorporation in domestic laws leaves much greater scope for differences as no uniform law but only harmonisation is the objective. Questions of applicable law may thus still arise between Member States regardless of the harmonisation effort, even if in the EU, as we shall see, the implementation and interpretation also locally needs to be conform to the wording and purpose of the relevant Directive. There is therefore a direct harmonising effect of these Directives under ultimate supervision of the European Court. Nevertheless, in the case of conflict, it will remain necessary to establish which domestic law applies. Again, under conventional private international law rules, this is likely to be a relationship matter.

That raises foremost the question whether the relevant Directive under its own terms applies to inter-state transactions or situations. The Directive may itself determine the applicability or reach of the law formulated therein. As in the case of uniform treaty law discussed in section 2.3.1 above, the Directive may apply to all transactions or situations within its scope, like in the case of consumer law, or only to interstate transactions, probably the situation in respect of the banking and investment services Directives. Often the Directives are not specific on their field of application and do not consider the issue at all. It then becomes a matter of interpretation what their field of application is and whether they cover the situation, especially if cross-border or even crossing into non-Member States. It follows that if they do *not* apply to cross border transactions, the normal rules of private international law would apply and would *not* be pre-empted by the Directive.

If the Directive does, however, apply or is deemed to apply (also) to interstate transactions, this must be considered a form of *direct* application which generally pre-empts the application of domestic conflict rules (again like in the case of uniform treaty law discussed in the previous section). In any event, the EU Rome Convention on the Law Applicable to Contractual Obligations is in that case postponed under its own terms (Article 20). If the Directive applies or is deemed to apply to typical inter-Member State situations, like the movement of workers to other Member States or to the selling of goods and services in other Member States, the rules of the Directive will then be invoked much like the uniform treaty law of the Vienna Convention between residents of Contracting States, assuming there are no material differences in the implementation.

The scope may be more difficult to determine in respect of transactions or situations with contacts in *third* countries, again especially where the Directive does not go into its scope at all. A field of application must be assumed to be inherent in all of them and, if not all elements of the case are connected with the EU, the field of application eg in respect of consumer law Directives might then have to be determined with reference to the domicile of the consumer being within the EU. Alternatively, as for the product liability Directive, the true issue may be whether the product is being marketed in the EU.

As just mentioned, within the EU, conflicts could still derive from differences in implementation in the various Member States even if the Directives were directly applicable to cross border traffic. Within the EU, conflicts would have to be resolved, however, foremost with reference to the Directive itself and its interpretation at EU level. That would most likely be the position of courts within the EU who could in the case of doubt also ask for an opinion of the European Court of Justice in Luxembourg. If the matter arose in the courts of non-Member States, however, the normal conflicts rules of these States would more likely be applied first in order to determine the applicable regime in the traditional conflicts of laws manner. If the choice was between two different implementations, the Directive's text itself would then less likely be considered in interpretational questions. Of course, the European Court would not then supervise the uniform interpretation either.

If mandatory EU law was involved in the Directives (like in consumer law), the courts in Member States would be particularly sensitive to it, even if the parties had attempted to contract out of the regime of the Directive altogether. The courts in non-Member States, on the other hand, would more likely use a measure of discretion in determining its impact as *règles d'application immediate* weighing the different governmental interests if conflicting.

If the transaction is in the international professional sphere, the applicable law would preferably be subject to the hierarchy of norms of the *lex mercatoria* amongst which these harmonised (domestic) rules could figure, whether or not the case was heard in a Member or non-Member State, although the harmonised rules would likely carry greater weight in Member State courts. Fundamental pinciples and mandatory custom and practices would then still prevail over these rules (like in the case of uniform treaty law) whilst they may be further implemented by directory practices, legal principles common in modern commercial nations and ultimately by national rules if everything else fails

The Amsterdam Treaty of 1998 amending the EC Treaty in Articles 61, 65, 67 contained a general reference to judicial co-operation and measures in the field of private international law in the EU in the context of the free movement of persons. A similar provision concerning judicial co-operation had already appeared in the earlier Maastricht Treaty in the context of the EU Third Pillar which concerns co-operation in the field of justice and home affairs (with its much more limited implementation facilities) and was not then related to the free movement of persons (Article K1(6)). It was also less specific. The EU can now operate in this field through Directives and Regulations in the First Pillar, but cannot bind the UK, Ireland and Denmark in this manner according to two special Protocols concerning these countries.

Through such future conflicts rules at EU level, it would be possible that at least for cases brought in courts within the EU any conflict of laws arising under Directives harmonising substantive laws in the Union are more generally resolved, but that is not the focus. Measures in the areas of recognition and enforcement of other Member States' judgments and even bankruptcy decrees have priority. There is also a project to extend the 1980 Rome Convention into the area of tort liability. Competition with the Hague Conference which aims at a wider audience will here unavoidably ensue. Still the determination (directly or indirectly) of the scope within these Directives themselves would be likely to continue to prevail over such conflicts rules, *cf* Article 20 of The Rome Convention already referred to.

The other question is which law applies in the case of a different implementation of EU Directives when it is clear that the Directive in principle covers the subject matter and is applicable. That remains relevant even if subsequently the competent court must seek a Directive-conform interpretation of the local implementation as it remains to be determined which implementation would in litigation be the *starting point* for the interpretation of the Directive itself. Assume that the case is brought in a court in the EU, it raises the question whether that court always starts with its own implementation as a matter of the application of its *lex fori* or whether the better starting law might not be the implementation in another Member State, eg the one of the State whose laws are more likely to be otherwise applicable in the case. That would still raise conflicts problems at that stage of the enquiry.

It is mostly assumed that the *lex fori* applies and that there is therefore no need for courts in EU countries to probe whether another implementation of the relevant Directive needs to be considered first. It would indeed seem the most efficient approach as the result ultimately should be the same. The implementation law of other countries will then only be relevant as a matter of interpretation but will still be invoked if there is a reasonable connection with the case. In international commercial arbitrations, the situation would be different as there is no *lex fori per se* and arbitrators would most likely start with the implementation law of the country most directly concerned or otherwise perhaps the one of the country of the defendant (if a Member State).

Jurisdictional issues remain here also important. The House of Lords has eg a much more literal interpretation technique in respect of domestic laws than say the Dutch Supreme Court and may therefore also have more difficulties in referring to the purpose of Directives although it should find comfort in this regard in the support of case-law of the European Court[256] or, if necessary when the issue is not yet clarified at EU level, the facility to refer the issue to it for a preliminary ruling (under Article 234, ex-Article 177 of the EC Treaty).

There are a number of more specific points to make. First there is the approach of the European Court itself which demands since 1984 a Directive conform interpretation of national implementation legislation. This is simply a result of the legal order of the EU which in the areas in which it operates is superior to domestic legal orders.[257] Domestic courts have here a support function in the system and operate therefore in relevant cases as European courts. An important issue remains, however, the relevance of domestic procedural limitations in the interpretation and the acceptance or rejection of these limitations by the European Court. The accepted objective here is an efficient and real protection which is non-discriminatory and allows the EU objective to prevail. Local procedural restrictions, although in principal respected may therefore not frustrate this process, eg in disallowing the testing of Directives in some specialised (provisional)

---

[256] So indeed in *Lister and Others v Forth Dry Dock and Engineering Co Ltd and Another*, [1989] 1ALL ER 1134 in which accordingly a purposive interpretation technique was adopted.
[257] See the seminal European Court Cases 26/62, Feb 5 1962, *Van Gend & Loos* [1963] ECR 3; 6/64, July 16 1964 *Costa v ENEL* [1964] ECR 1203; 14/68 Feb 13 1969 *Walt Wilhelm* [1969] ECR 1. A prerequirement is that the relevant rule of community law is meant to have direct effect in Member States. Even though Directives are not directly effective in Member States without domestic implementation, this general precedence of EU law provides the facility of direct application of Directives in the interpretation of domestic implementation laws, see European Court Case 14/83, April 10 1984 *Von Colsen and Kamann* [1984] ECR 1891. It leaves, however, a question whether this type of interpretation may in fact lead to the de facto adjustment of the implementation legislation if considered defective.

procedures or in rejecting punitive damages where the Directive's implementation would require it.[258]

Secondly, there is the untimely or faulty implementation which is strictly speaking not a mere interpretation issue. Direct effect may here be assumed provided the Directive is itself sufficiently precise. In this manner it may still operate vertically against the defaulting State, not *vice versa* and also not between citizens horizontally.[259] The Directive conform interpretation is there partly to remedy this and may be effective especially in the case of incomplete or defective implementation when it will acquire a correcting function. Another more draconic remedy, admitted in case-law since 1991, is state liability of the defaulting Member States that may thus become *directly* liable for any adverse consequences for citizens when the other two methods fail which may notably happen if a State is not otherwise directly liable under the relevant Directive when direct effect would be an adequate remedy. Domestic courts will thus be able to impose penalties on the defaulting State if a citizen misses a chance or a protection against others as a consequence.[260] Finally, there is the question of the power of domestic judges to invoke the relevant Directive autonomously, therefore without any of the parties having invoked it. This is in principle admitted if the EU rules are absolutely mandatory, assuming always that the local judge has the power to apply mandatory rules *sua sponte* under his own laws.[261]

A third point is that in interpreting EU Directives, the European Court is likely to use Europeanised concepts even in private law. These are therefore concepts that could be quite different from those which are known to local judges under domestic laws and that are used in the implementation legislation. The notion of good faith, relevant especially for the interpretation of the Consumer Directive, may be a case in point, see chapter 2, section 1.3.4. No less dramatic could be the interpretation of the client asset segregation requirement and agency duties in the field of investors' protection under Articles 10 and 11 of the Investment Services Directive. So far they may have received very inadequate implementation in several civil law countries, see chapter 6, section 3.2.6. It concerns here issues of tracing and constructive trust and of relative rights of principals after the disclosure of their interests in a bankruptcy of their broker/agent, see also chapter 2, section 3.1.6, chapter 4, section 1.4.3, and chapter 6, section 1.3.10. It could well be that in these types of cases the interpretation that will achieve the best customer protection overall will be chosen.

Part III   The Development of Transnational or International Commercial and Financial Law

3.1   The *Lex Mercatoria*, Interrelation with Private International Law

3.1.1   *The Concept of the Modern* Lex Mercatoria *as a Hierarchy of Norms*

To determine the law applicable to international commercial and financial transactions, the key question is whether there may exist or may be developing a whole pattern of transnational law in the professional sphere as an *own legal order*. It is the contention of

---

[258] See European Court Case C–261/95, July 10 1997 *Palmisani* [1997]ECR I–4025 and also W van Gerven, "Of Rights, Remedies and Procedures", *CMLRev.* (2000), 501.
[259] European Court Case C–91/92 July 14 1994 *Faccini Dor* [1994] ECR I–3325.
[260] European Court Cases C–6/90 and C–9/90, Nov. 19 1991 *Francovich* [1991] ECR I–5357.
[261] European Court Cases C–430/93 and C-431/93, Dec. 15 1995 *Van Schijndel* [1995] ECR I–4705.

this book that there is such a legal order operating in international trade and finance as a natural consequence of the globalisation of the international professional activities in these areas, see for the introduction of this theme section 1.4 above.

Originally it might have been thought logical to build the new *lex mercatoria* in that order around a nucleus of uniform treaty law as formulated for example in the area of international sale of goods by the 1964 Hague Conventions and subsequently in the 1980 Vienna Convention, in the area of transportation by sea in the 1924 Brussels Convention (the so-called Hague Rules later amended by the Hague-Visby Rules for bills of lading, especially in their transportation rather than proprietary aspects) or in the 1978 Uncitral Hamburg Rules, and in the area of bills of exchange and cheques by the 1930 and 1932 Geneva Conventions or the 1988 Uncitral Convention for International Bills of Exchange (and in several other areas by other Uncitral efforts like the one on the statute of limitations), see for the efforts at uniform law of both Uncitral and Unidroit more in particular section 1.5.5 above.

However, once the operation of the own international professional legal order is identified these Conventions cannot remain the nucleus of the new law. They are only one source of it. In any event, under their own terms, they are limited in reach and often apply only to residents of Contracting States, although they could also reflect more general principles. Other significant drawbacks of the uniform law were already spelt out above in section 1.5.3 and are connected with the limited and partial coverage of the area of the law they seek to unify and the difficulty to amend them.

As already suggested before in sections 2.2.5 and 1.5.4, the new transnational law would in fact primarily result from (a) the own nature of the relationship between the (professional) parties;[262] (b) their special interests, needs and protection requirements; (c) the nature and logic of their transactions and of the legal structures used therein; and (d) common sense.

Central is always an analysis of the *facts* of the transaction or the case, supported, in transactional matters by (a) the terms of the agreement, patterns of commerce already established between the parties and their usages; (b) customs or industry practices; (c) uniform treaty law to the extent formulated and applicable under its own terms; (d) common legal notions (for example of contract, tort or property) whether or not expressed in international conventions (like those just mentioned) or collections of principles (like those for contract law of the EU and Unidroit, see chapter 2, section 1.6).

The application of these rules should, always be *preceded* by the application of (e) the *fundamental legal principles* as *ius cogens* as the basis of the whole system, and any *mandatory* customary or uniform law (if applicable under its own terms) which tends to be closely connected with these fundamental principles.

If upon a proper analysis of the facts in the light of the norms that thus become applicable, there is still no solution, these norms would be finally *supplemented* by (f) the domestic law found under the traditional conflict of law rules. This domestic law would then residually function in the international legal order itself and be subject to it, so that its application would have a discretionary element as would have the application of any mandatory national laws and the result would have to be fitting.[263]

---

[262] See for this approach in the UK, Bingham LJ in *Interfoto v Stiletto* [1989] 1 QB 433, 439.

[263] In WA Bewes, *The Romance of the Law Merchant: An Introduction to the Study of International and Commercial Law* (1923, reprinted in 1986), 13, there is an interesting comment where it is explained that the *lex mercatoria* had its origins in the law of nations as it grew in a great degree out of transactions between different nations (but not necessarily by these nations). Private international law is here in its origin seen as a branch of the law of nations and closely connected with international private law or transnational law.

In section 1.5 above, the multiplicity of the sources of law and the *hierarchy* of the norms flowing therefrom was already identified as the essence of the modern *lex mercatoria* and will be further discussed in section 3.2 below.[264] The ranking was given as follows:

(a)   fundamental legal principle;
(b)   mandatory custom;
(c)   mandatory uniform treaty law (to the extent applicable under its own scope rules);
(d)   the contract (in contractual matters);
(e)   directory custom;
(f)   directory uniform treaty law (to the extent applicable under its own scope rules);
(g)   general principles largely derived from comparative law, uniform treaty law (even where not directly applicable or not sufficiently ratified), ICC Rules and the like, and
(h)   residually domestic laws found through conflict of law rules.

As to the *fundamental* legal notions or principles of private or transactional law which come first and form the basis of the whole system, they were also already briefly discussed in section 1.5.4 above and are particularly:

(a)   *pacta sunt servanda* as the essence of contract law;
(b)   the recognition, transferability and substantial protection of the notion of ownership as the essence of all property law, to be respected by all. It is a human rights related notion, see also Protocol 1, Article 1 of the 1950 European Convention on Human Rights and section 1.4.4 above, to be respected by governments and other citizens alike;
(c)   the liability for own action, especially
  (i)   if wrongful (certainly if the wrong is of a major nature) as the essence of tort law,
  (ii)   if leading to detrimental reliance on such action by others as another fundamental principal of contract law,
  (iii)   if resulting in principals creating the appearance of authority in others as an essential of the law of agency, or
  (iv)   if resulting in owners creating an appearance of ownership in others which is an additional fundamental principal in the law of ownership and at the heart of the protection of the *bona fide* purchaser.

There are other fundamental principles in terms of:

(d)   apparent authority and fiduciary principles in contract and in agency leading to special protections of counterparties, notably if weaker or in a position of dependence (including consumers against whole sales, workers against employers, individuals against the state, smaller investors against brokers), and to duties of disclosure and faithful implementation of one's obligations;
(e)   notions of unjust enrichment;

---

[264] See also JH Dalhuisen, *Wat is Vreemd Recht* [What is foreign law], Inaugural Address Utrecht (Kluwer, Deventer, 1991).

(f) respect for acquired or similar rights, traditionally particularly relevant to outlaw retroactive government intervention, but now also used to support owners of proprietary rights in assets that move to other countries;

(g) equality of treatment between creditors, shareholders and other classes of interested parties with similar rights unless they have postponed themselves.

Then there are the:

(h) fundamental procedural protections in terms of impartiality, proper jurisdiction, proper hearings and the possibility to mount an adequate defence, now often related to the more recent (and also internationalised) standards of human rights and basic protections, see Article 6 of the 1950 European Convention on Human Rights;

(i) the fundamental protections against fraud, sharp practices, excessive power, cartels, bribery and insider dealings or other forms of manipulation in market-related assets (also in their civil and commercial aspects) and against money laundering;

(j) finally there are also fundamental principles of environmental protection developing.

No doubt there are other fundamental principles, and the above list is not meant to be exhaustive. In commercial and financial law there are not many, however. The purpose here is only to show that fundamental legal principles are at the heart of all civilised modern legal systems, also in trade and finance. In modern law, especially of the codified variety, they are often hidden, but they come into their own again in the international legal order.

Some of these fundamental principles, if not all, are likely to be absolutely mandatory (*ius cogens*), also in civil and commercial matters, and might even in international sales adjust the balance between the parties, therefore on the basis often of social or public policy considerations (of that intenational legal order), although in the professional sphere this is less likely. They may increasingly be considered to have a universal reach at least in that order, as indeed they had in the natural law school, and may thus figure as fundamental internationalised concepts. They could be partly incorporated in an international concept of good faith or public order when called upon to adjust imbalances or prevent abuse.

The important point to note is here that the fundamental principle of protection between certain parties like professionals in certain types of deals, even if mandatory, may not result in the same protection between other (less professional) types of parties in the same or similar types of deals. Again, lesser protection and refinement of the law may result between professionals in commercial matters as an overriding requirement connected with the continuation of the normal commercial flows and the imperatives imposed on all participants in this respect. It may be connected with an international concept of good faith. It is in any event natural for the law to be sensitive to these differences in requirements which may also emerge in the form of implied conditions or industry custom or norm. This will be discussed more in detail in chapter 2. As a consequence, the impact of overriding fundamental principle will quite naturally still vary depending on the type of relationship and nature of the transaction and will in any event limit itself to the basic legal structures.

Thus fundamental principle may be supported and further directed by established *practices or custom*, which in their supporting role could also be *mandatory*. For example, where these practices or customs are property-connected, it is possible that they will prevail over contractual arrangements or a contractual choice of law, as in the proprietary aspects of international negotiable instruments like eurobonds, see also section 3.2.2 below. The same may be true in cases where an automatic return of title upon default is demanded in the contract. It may not prevail in the international legal order (except if couched in terns of a reservation of title). Also, a specific performance of sales agreements normally available in civil law might be deemed against the commercial flows and hence commercial practice or realities and common sense may rule out the possibility in international commerce. For foreign direct investments, codes of conduct are increasingly formulated on the basis of established practices and may present another set of mandatory rules. Wherever (international) practice or custom acquires such a mandatory aspect, it is likely that there is always a close connection with fundamental legal principle.

These internationalised practices in any event have supplementary force and, even if not mandatory in themselves, still pose the question whether they may prevail over domestic law, even if the latter is mandatory. International practices of this nature may indeed underline the fact that domestic rules are not or are no longer appropriately applicable in international cases, except if they are of considerable urgency, when the specific domestic policy may remain relevant and legitimate in the international commercial and financial legal order and as such be respected even if not in accordance with the international trade practices which increasingly have a liberal bias, see for the interaction with domestic mandatory or public policy laws section 2.2.6 above.

This can only be established on a case-by-case basis. Traditional examples are domestic import/export and foreign exchange restrictions, although these are generally of less importance today and lifted in most modern countries. More modern examples are in competition, securities and patent laws. It is a question of balancing in order to determine whether the reach of these policy-oriented domestic rules may be simply *excessive* in international terms or in a given situation and they may in such cases not apply at all, even in the absence of established international practices to the contrary.

If a domestic law is chosen as applicable to the transaction by the parties, even such a choice cannot go beyond what makes sense in the international legal order, and does not normally mean to include a preference for the mandatory rules of that law. Neither can it mean the exclusion of other domestic public policy laws that might be more relevant. It can in any event not be meant to undermine the essentials of the deal itself, except if there are very good reasons from the perspective of the international legal order (including its own public policies). They are unlikely to be derived from mandatory domestic laws alone. Acceptance of domestic restrictions is thus always a matter of comity for the international legal order, as indeed expressed in Article 7 of the 1980 Rome Convention on the Law Applicable to Contractual Obligations (in the context, however, of applying domestic laws only) and much better in Sections 402/403 of the American Restatement (Third) of Foreign Relations Law, see more in particular section 2.6.6 above.

International conventions with uniform law further supplement the fundamental principles and international custom, like those on sales, transportation and payment methods. They naturally supersede domestic laws in contracting States in the areas they cover even if the domestic law were mandatory, which means that a mandatory domestic rule may be replaced by a directory Convention rule. These Conventions contain so far only occasionally mandatory law (see Article 12 of the Vienna Convention on the international sale of goods). Even then it is unlikely that they prevail over fundamental legal principle or mandatory custom in the international legal order.

In all this, there are in contractual matters of course the *wording of the contract* and the intrinsic logic of the transaction itself to be considered, if necessary under standards of good faith, as already mentioned, although this is probably less relevant in the commercial sphere. Only fundamental legal principle, and mandatory international custom or mandatory uniform treaty law, to the extent existing, would prevail over it.

Common legal principles will have a further effect in defining in a directory manner international legal relationships where the contractual terms, fundamental principles, custom and treaty law fail or need further elaboration. They may be deduced from national laws if there is a wide consensus between them. If the applicable law is still not sufficiently established in this manner, domestic law may remain relevant as a matter of private international law or, if mandatory, as a matter of comity only, in both cases with a discretionary element, as already mentioned at the beginning of this section.

The result is the hierarchy of norms within the modern *lex mercatoria* earlier discussed in section 1.5.4 above, the details of which will be further explored in the following sections.

3.1.2   *The Major Protagonists of the* Lex Mercatoria *and Their Views: Legitimation*

The search for a better law based on these principles, practices and notions has culminated in the modern concept of transnational professional law (or international civil, commercial and financial law or new law merchant). In commercial transactions in the internationalised professional sphere, this law is now more often referred to as the (new) *lex mercatoria*, as we saw, a term in modern times particularly associated with Professor Berthold Goldman in France (1913–93), who in essence identified the new legal order based on industry custom and common legal notions, even if not using legal order terminology.[265]

The notion of the *lex mercatoria* or law merchant had existed between the Middle Ages and the seventeenth century, particularly in England, and was referred to in English case-law well into the nineteenth century, especially in connection with documents of title, and negotiable instruments, see also section 1.1.2 above. It was also mentioned in the English Sale of Goods Act of 1893, as it still is in Section 1–103 UCC in the USA where it remains good law, except if specifically overruled by the UCC. Yet there is here an important difference: the new *lex mercatoria* is at this stage in essence a hierarchy of diverse principles and norms whilst the old law merchant was a system of largely unwritten uniform customs and practices. Naturally the contents are very different from what they once were, in which connection it was observed earlier that this new law is likely to be driven as much by modern finance as by mercantile considerations.

Other authors like Professor Clive Schmitthoff in the UK were similarly sensitive to the new development, but took perhaps a somewhat more restrictive view and saw the new

---

[265] B Goldman, 'La lex mercatoria dans les contrats et l'arbitrage internationaux: realité et perspectives', *Clunet* (1979), 475; 'Lex Mercatoria', *Forum Internationale* no 3 (Kluwer 1983); 'The Applicable Law: General Principles of Law — Lex Mercatoria' in J Lew (ed), *Contemporary Problems in International Arbitration* (Queen Mary College London, 1986), 113, 'Lex Mercatoria and Arbitration: Discussion of the New Law Merchant', in TE Carbonneau (ed), *Transnational Juris Publications Inc*, New York (1990). The relative popularity of the *lex mercatoria* in France may be seen in the light of the earlier development of the notion of the 'international contract' operating under its own internationalised rules. It was particularly relevant for the validity of gold clauses which were upheld in these international contracts in the 1930s, see also chapter 3, n 3. In France the work of PH Fouchard should also be noted, see PH Fouchard, *l'Arbitrage Commercial International* (1965) and PH Fouchard, E Gaillard and B Goldman, *Traite de l'Arbitrage Commercial International* (1996) and Gaillard and Savage, *Fouchard, Gaillard and Goldman* on *International Commercial Arbitration* (1999). See more recently in France also Emmanuel Gaillard, "Transnational Law: A Legal System or a Method of Decision Making?" 17 *Arbitration International* (2001), 59, but *cf* also Pierre Mayer, 'Reflections on the International Arbitrator's Duty to Apply the Law', 17 *Arbitration International* (2001), 235. See further also the references in nn 172 and 203 above.

lex mercatoria primarily as an elaboration of domestic law,[266] whilst early protagonists like Professor Norbert Horn from Cologne,[267] Professor Ole Lando in Denmark,[268] Professor AF Lowenfeld in the USA,[269] and more recently Professor Roy Goode in Oxford[270] are largely pragmatic, but see for a more fundamental position in the USA in particular the work of Professor FK Juenger.[271] As we saw, this search for transnational law, especially in the professional sphere, is in essence a reaction against the nationalisation of all law in the nineteenth century, which ended the impact of the *Ius Commune* and the natural law approach on the European continent and saw law in terms of sovereignty which resulted in a nationalistic/territorial concept of the law, even if it was commercial. This nationalism also started to undermine the force of the common law as an universal system which became also increasingly subjected to and superseded by domestic statutory law and policy notions leading to substantial differences between the domestic laws even in common law countries like England and the USA.

From an academic point of view, there are here, as in the field of conflict laws *cf* section 2.1.1 above, in essence two schools of thought: the internationalist and domestic. Those who see a new legal order emerging are to be found in the internationalist camp. Others, in the positivist tradition, cannot see any legal order outside the context of a state. This does not prevent international considerations to be taken more directly into account in the interpretation of substantive domestic law, much as in the *lex fori* approach to interstate conflicts in the USA. The difference is, however, that in the latter approach, each country will ultimately go its own way and no true uniformity is likely to result as the unity in the international legal order is not recognised, certainly not as an own law creating force.[272]

The question of the legitimation of the modern *lex mercatoria*, therefore of the transnational law in the professional sphere as a spontaneously emerging own legal system, must nevertheless be posed and in this context also the question of the residual status of national law within the hierarchy of the new *lex mercatoria*, to be accepted in that context as a form of *comitas* if public policy issues are at stake or otherwise through the conflict

---

[266] It forestalled local criticism: see C Schmitthoff, *International Business Law: A New Law Merchant, Current Law and Social Problems* (University of Western Ontario, 1961), 129; 'International Trade Law and Private International Law' in *Vom deutschen zum europäischen Recht, 2 Festschrift Hans Doelle* (Tübingen, 1963), 261; "The Unification of the Law of International Trade," [1968] *J Bus Law*, 109. See for a compilation of his most important writings on the subject C Schmitthoff, *Select Essays on International Trade Law* (ed Chia-Jui Cheng, Kluwer, Dordrecht, 1988).

[267] N Horn, *Das Recht der internationalen Anleihen* (1972); N Horn, 'A Uniform Approach to Eurobond Agreements' 9 *L&Pol Int'l Bus* (1977), 753; N Horn, 'Uniformity and Diversity in the Law of International Commercial Contracts', in N Horn and C Schmitthoff, *The Transnational Law of International Commercial Transactions* (1982), 3ff.

[268] O Lando, 'The Lex Mercatoria in International Commercial Arbitration', (1985) 34 *Intern'l and Comp Law Q* 747. See for earlier reflections on the phenomenon also E Langen, *Studien zum internationalen Wirtschaftsrecht* (Munich, 1963) and P Kahn, *La Vente Commerciale Internationale* (Sirey, Paris, 1961) and 'Lex mercatoria et euro-obligation' in F Fabritius (ed.), *Law and International Trade, Festschrift C Schmitthoff* (Frankfurt 1973), 215.

[269] AF Lowenfeld, "Lex Mercatoria: an Arbitrator's View" 6 *Arb International* (1990), 133.

[270] R Goode, "Usage and its Reception in Transnational Commercial Law", 46 *Int'l & Comp L Q* (1997), 1.

[271] FK Juenger, "Conflict of Laws, Comparative Law and Civil Law: The Lex Mercatoria and Private International Law", 60 *La L Rev* 1133 (2000), see also n 203 *supra*. See for recent writers on the subject also nn 172, 203 and 265 *supra*.

[272] See further the analysis of F De Ly, *International Business Law and Lex Mercatoria* (Amsterdam, 1992). Mustill LJ in the UK has been particularly critical of the *lex mercatoria* as an own transnational legal system on the basis of his nationalistic views, wondering where this new law could come from: see 'The New Lex Mercatoria' in M Bos and I Brownlie (eds), *Liber Amicorum Lord Wilberforce* (1987), 149 and "Contemporary Problems in International Commercial Arbitration" (1989) 17 *Int Bus L* 161, criticised by AF Lowenfeld, *Lex Mercatoria*, n 269 *supra*, 123, who believes that the question where the law comes from could particularly be asked for all of the common law. See for a more recent overview also KP Berger, *The Creeping Codification of the Lex Mercatoria* (1999) who looks for more black letter law in the new *lex mercatoria* and collects these rules.

rules of private international law if the *lex mercatoria* does not provide a solution. As suggested throughout this book, the key is the acceptance (or rejection) of the own legal order of international trade, commerce and finance and within that order the formation of transnational commercial law based on fundamental legal principles as universal notions (*ius cogens*), providing the basic core of, and major protections not only in the international commercial and financial legal order but in all modern legal systems.[273]

The second feature is the acceptance (or rejection) of overriding international custom and the third the development of general more practical principles of international commercial and financial law. The relegation of domestic laws to residual status automatically follows from the acceptance of these three prime sources of transnational private law.

3.2   The Hierarchy of Norms: Elaboration

3.2.1   *Fundamental Legal Principle. Transnational Rules of Contract Formation and the Normative Interpretation Technique. Procedure*

The impact of fundamental legal principle appears transnationally first and foremost in contract formation and interpretation. The principle of *pacta sunt servanda* stands out as the basic norm for all contract law. Since the natural law school, it has often been associated with the concept of consensus between parties. It is unlikely, however, that professional contracts depend solely on consensus for their validity, certainly not in a psychological sense, if only because at least in business deals of some size the person who signs the agreement is unlikely to know much of its detail whilst no single person will have dealt with the various issues and the end drafting is often left to outside lawyers.

Fundamental legal principle in terms of liability for the justified reliance by the other party, and the objective requirements of trade or course of business, including a beginning of performance, may be equally important to establish the binding force of an agreement and subsequently its extent, and provide explanations, additions and, in extreme cases, possibly even corrections to the ultimate wording. In civil law terminology, this is all encapsulated in the concept of good faith or teleological interpretation of the contractual content, see also chapter 2, section 1.2.1. This would seem a logical approach in transnational law also. It is not then personal but mainly directed to the business sector. The result is often referred to as the *objective* or *normative* approach to intent and contract formation and interpretation which appears particularly to impose itself in the international professional sphere. In all circumstances, the objective approach fills in contractual gaps, and requires diligence and fair play in the performance.

It was already pointed one several times before that, although the objective or normative approach to contract formation and interpretation normally leads to more refinement, it may also lead to *less*, particularly in the professional sphere, therefore to defects in the consensus or to lack of clarity of the parties' intent carrying less weight. This was always the approach of commercial courts, which also had quicker procedures and lay (or peer group) input as they still have in France. As already suggested in section 3.1.1 above, it shows that even fundamental principle, like the binding force of the consensus or

---

[273] Goldman himself came to this realisation relatively late when he started to emphasise the fundamental principles besides his common legal notions (and industry practices) which were mainly derived from comparative law research into the different legal structures and terminologies, see 'Nouvelles réflexions sur la Lex Mercatoria' in *Etudes de droit international en l'honneur de Pierre Lalive* (Basle, 1993), 241.

obligations resulting from detrimental reliance on someone else's action, is not insensitive to commercial needs and in any event functions differently in different relationships and transactions.

The particular (commercial) nature of business relationships may also curtail special duties or remedies, like disclosure and co-operation duties in the pre-contractual or formation phase, limit protest periods, discourage transactions from being undone for lack of consensus or upon default especially in their proprietary aspects (although claims for damages may still be valid). Except in extreme cases like fraud, this special nature of the relationship of the parties may also restrict negligence or other misbehaviour arguments and *force majeure* exceptions to the more obvious cases, and limit rebalancing the contract in the case of hardship where parties are used to risk-taking and often make that their business, again excepting extreme cases. Even questions of capacity or *ultra vires* legal acts may not have the same importance and impact in the commercial sphere, see also section 3.2.3 below.

The objective or normative approach may, if the parties so intimate or if obvious from the circumstances, even mean a greater reliance on the *literal* wording of contracts in the professional sphere as the text of a contract often serves as a roadmap for performance by persons who were never present during the negotiations, assuming always that lack of clarity cannot so easily be invoked here by the party having done the drafting or having presented a standard text. The objective approach itself leads here paradoxically to greater reliance on the expressed will of the parties and will interpret the parties' duties strictly. On the other hand, a stricter attitude in agency cases may mean that an agency may be assumed sooner than might otherwise be the case. Apparent authority amongst professionals could even be assumed upon the mere declaration of the agent itself (for example, employees) if the principal has clearly taken that risk.

It must be admitted that in the Unidroit and European Contract Principles, there is as yet little appreciation of other sources of contractual rights and duties than the parties' intent, which may be relevant in interpreting their mutual rights and duties, see more extensively also chapter 2, section 1.6. Unlike the European Principles, the Unidroit Principles apply only to international commercial contracts (whatever they may be). Although both sets are very close, only the Unidroit Principles will therefore be considered in this context of international commercial and financial law. For contract formation, Article 3.2 seems to rely chiefly on consensus subject to reasonableness, established practices and fair dealing and the nature of the contract, but as implied terms only and not as more objective standard (Article 5.2), whilst Articles 1.6 and 4.1*ff* maintain a narrow concept of interpretation and supplementation. The wide and abstract notion of mistake in Articles 3.4*ff* also testifies to a doctrinaire attitude still closely connected with a psychological understanding of the consensus. In a similar vein, the notion of avoidance of the contract is broadly upheld, Article 3.17.

It is true, on the other hand, that Article 1.7 generally requires each party to act in accordance with good faith and fair dealings in international trade. However, there are no guidelines on its meaning nor any apparent sensitivity towards the circumstances of the case in terms of the nature of the relationship, the type of transaction and outside forces like market conditions. Nevertheless, good faith in this sense is considered a mandatory requirement, see Article 1.7(2), without any consideration whether its requirements are truly fundamental in the circumstances or of lesser urgency in commercial transactions. In the USA, Section 1–302 (1–102(3) old) of the UCC is notably more circumspect and allows parties to set the standards of good faith, diligence, reasonableness and care unless they are manifestly unreasonable.

It is of interest in this connection that in the Unidroit Principles, the impact of custom may be limited by unreasonableness (not good faith), Article 1.8, which precisely in the commercial sphere for which these Principles are collected may be less desirable. On the other hand, any deviation from statutory law or from the contractual terms on the basis of unreasonableness is not considered. This again suggests emphasis on the literal interpretation of abstract rules and of the parties' intent in subjective terms in the English tradition. There is a separate and broad notion of hardship in Article 6.2, whilst a subjective concept of *force majeure* is maintained in Article 7.1.7. Both may be more generous than business requires. Attendant negotiation duties are determined by the need to avoid bad faith without any guidance on what that may be in business relationships, which may require a narrower concept, Article 2.14, whilst co-operation duties at the performance stage are expressed in terms of reasonableness, Article 5.3. They thus also seem to be distinguished from the general duty of parties to act in good faith under Article 1.7 and are somewhat better described in Article 5.5. Parties appear able to deviate from them to the extent that these duties may be considered outside the ambit of Article 1.7, but it remains unclear when this may be the case.

The general attitude of rougher justice in the commercial sphere, even against more fundamental principles and the more traditional rules of contract law, in the interest of (a) the flow of commerce or (b) greater certainties if desired by the parties, may be demonstrated eg with reference to the status of *letters of intent* which are normally preludes to a contract. As intent or the lack of it is not the sole determining factor in establishing a legal relationship and detrimental reliance is in any event another fundamental principle, these letters may generally acquire some binding force between the parties if acted upon in good faith or even reasonably, which may imply a lesser requirement. In the professional sphere, there might be less need for this, however, as parties are left to their own devices to a greater extent and should not so readily rely on others, see also chapter II, section 1.3. Thus until there is a form of detrimental reliance or reasonable expectation justified in the circumstances, professional parties might not be bound in this manner.

The binding force of letters of intent is an area of the law closely related to negotiation duties in pre-contractual situations. Although no written documents indicating the state of the negotiations may exist, there may be duties to continue the discussions in good faith and an action if these duties are broken. Yet mere expectation of a favourable conclusion does not in itself give rise to legal rights.[274] Again the key is that the justification may be less obvious in commercial cases. Once there is such justified reliance, however, the other party may be forced to negotiate the full contract in line with the reasonable expectations, short of which there may be room for claiming damages against the party wrongfully terminating the negotiations, see also chapter 2, section 1.3.7. German and Dutch law are more categorical in the imposition of pre-contractual duties and hold that late withdrawal from negotiations may impose heavy contractual liability, including damages for *lost profits* under the contract, but probably always in the context of reliance on another improper cause to withdraw. It also suggests a lesser concern in the commercial and professional sphere, although as yet German and Dutch law are seldom so analysed.

These are also likely to be the considerations that could prove decisive and determine when adjustment of a contract or the continuation of negotiations to that effect can no

---

[274] See also the generally more conservative attitude taken by Lord Ackner in the UK in *Walford v Miles* [1992] 2 WLR, 174, in which at least in commerce a duty to negotiate in good faith was thought to be unworkable and inherently inconsistent with the position of a negotiating party, always it would seem as long as there was no detrimental reliance justified by the circumstances of the case.

longer be reasonably required and termination must follow, although it is conceivable that in the case of hardship the new terms need not be fully market-related and there could still be a discount or a longer term for gradual adjustment. Also a justified discontinuation of the negotiation upon hardship does not necessarily exclude claims for early termination damages, especially not if negotiations fail because there is clearly no longer any reasonable expectation of sufficient co-operation between the parties to make continuation a realistic option. Yet in the context of the *lex mercatoria* and its fundamental legal principles, pre-contractual duties, a duty to renegotiate or a duty to continue agreements beyond their termination date must not quickly be assumed and any damages payable upon discontinuation of such negotiations must be considered exceptional and limited to cases of obvious misbehaviour. The Unidroit Principles for International Commercial Contracts, do not appear to reflect international commercial practice in their support of these duties.

Fundamental legal principle has also to be considered in the context of procedure, certainly at the transnational level like in international arbitrations. It concerns here in particular the proper protection of respondents in the composition of the panel, their rights to a fair hearing, proper presentation of documents, and adequate time for a defence. Especially here, the operation of transnational fundamental legal principle can hardly be denied.

3.2.2   Fundamental Principles. The Notion of Transnational Ownership. A Fractured System of Proprietary Rights

From the enumeration of the fundamental legal principle in section 3.1.1 above it would appear that it implies a notion of ownership which reaches across borders. This has always been clear in the operation of negotiable instruments and documents of title which depended in their development on a transnational concept of property rights. In modern times, the eurobond presents another important example. Negotiable instruments are documents of title representing money claims, like bills of exchange and cheques. They developed as from the fourteenth century under 'merchant law' mainly for use in the international payment circuit. They obtained their present form during the first phase of the industrial revolution at the end of the eighteenth century.

Similarly, the bill of lading, which is a negotiable document of title representing goods (movable physical assets), developed from the end of the eighteenth century. This was closely connected with the evolution of the Cif contract, which was itself also considered covered by 'merchant law'. In England, modern writers still maintain this approach in the absence of statutory law.[275] International bonds as negotiable instruments have acquired a similar status and were as such revived in the eurobond market operating since the early 1960s.[276] Their replacement by securities entitlements in a book-entry system would not have appeared to change the internationality of these instruments and even if local law of the register is now widely thought applicable international custom still precedes the application of domestic law which is clear when adverse case-law is produced for similar domestic instruments.[277]

These instruments or documents of title, especially if made negotiable (by the insertion 'to order' or 'bearer'), thus acquired an independent proprietary status largely

---

[275] See eg R Goode, *Commercial Law* (2nd edn, 1995), 518.
[276] See for older English case law *Goodwin v Roberts* [1876] 1 AC 476 and *Picker v London and County Banking Co* (1887) 18 QBD 512 (CA), with emphasis on the financial community treating these instruments as negotiable regardless of domestic laws.
[277] It was therefore ignored in Belgium in relation to the operations of Euroclear, see also chapter 4, n 324.

demonstrated by an own manner of transfer, normally achieved through *physical delivery* (with endorsement if issued to order). This was so regardless of domestic laws even if they were used between nationals or residents from the same country. In further recognition of these instruments or documents operating under a separate law, in common law countries, the concept of consideration was never applied to their transfer either. There followed also an own protection of *bona fide* purchasers/holders notwithstanding '*nemo dat*' principles in domestic laws (important especially in common law countries). This extra protection was often applicable even in the case of a *bona fide* purchase from a thief — in modern times evidenced particularly by stolen banknotes. It follows that there is also an independent system of limited proprietary rights in these assets, but as in the case of pledges only in their most simple forms based on possession of the instrument (like a possessory pledge). Any more complicated non-possessory interests in them, for example under a floating charge, are for the time being likely to operate purely under an applicable domestic law.

For these instruments, there was also likely to be an independent approach to the question of the causal or abstract system of title transfer for these instruments, see chapter 4, section 1.5.6, and therefore to the proprietary consequences of an invalid transfer of the document, particularly relevant for eurobonds when mistakes were made in the delivery. One is likely to see here the bare (and *fundamental*) principles of (personal) property rights. In the international commercial and financial legal order, any refinement is likely to become a matter of international custom, uniform treaty law, or ultimately domestic laws. The (discretionary) application of conflicts of law within the *lex mercatoria* would be limited to these domestic refinements. In international cases where the basics of property law identified above now tend to reassert themselves, domestic refinements would be disregarded altogether if they concerned the core or contradicted the essence of the paper.

In bills of lading, we see similar principles of transfer through delivery, *bona fide* third party protection and possessory security operating, which cannot be violated by domestic laws without rendering them ineffective as documents of title, even purely domestically. In bills of lading as negotiable documents of title, the title transfer is delayed until the actual handing over of the document, which represents the underlying goods, see more in particular chapter 4, section 2.1. In countries like England and France where title in chattels normally transfers upon the mere conclusion of the sales agreement, this delay is considered implicit in Fob and Cif terms, even domestically, and a form of delivery is then accepted as an additional requirement. One may view this as a reversion to a more basic form of transfer of ownership based on delivery. This practice is confirmed in countries like Germany and the Netherlands, which traditionally require delivery for title transfer in all movables, but in these countries transfer of the document substitutes for delivery of the underlying assets where there is a document of title. Again, this is in recognition of international practice which local law cannot ignore in the creation of these documents. There are here clearly more fundamental principles at work supported by practical needs which may be (international) custom that could be considered mandatory in these aspects.

One should ask whether the recognition and further development of an independent transnational proprietary regime in this manner, based on fundamental legal principle and mandatory international custom, is also conceivable for assets other than negotiable instruments or documents of title, like commodities. It is difficult to see why not, at least for the more common aspects of property rights and their transfer. Especially coming from the English and possibly French approach to title transfer, it may be possible to let the parties' intent decide. However, publicity facilitates third party effect, like holdership and delivery for title transfer. They may be basic additional requirements or formalities also for the international transfers of goods, as they are for negotiable instruments and documents of title.

In this manner, title transfer in oil installations on the high seas is often achieved through transfer or delivery of certain documents like completion certificates even if such installations may be considered immovable. Exclusive access may be other objective requirements and outward signs of ownership in these situations.

Coming from countries like Germany and the Netherlands, which require delivery for title transfer, this would indeed seem normal, but in international situations of this sort the delivery requirement is also found in English contract models. Again, it relates clearly to a more basic model of ownership and its transfer, which puts emphasis on physical possession, user and disposition rights and their *physical* transfer and protection (rather than on more theoretical concepts of ownership and legal or constructive possession, well known in civil law, but not fundamental to the ownership concept). Protection of *bona fide* purchasers against *'nemo dat'* principles may equally follow in internationalised assets. Conditional title transfers in the international commercial sphere may at the same time allow for the creation of beneficial ownership rights and limited proprietary interests in them including (substitute) secured or fiduciary ownership interests. They may well approximate the common law trust construction at the same time. In line with common law, it renders proprietary rights more contractual in nature, which may well be the more modern trend everywhere, though always subject to the protection of *bona fide* purchasers. Nevertheless, the more intricate property rights and especially the non-possessory security rights may much longer remain the preserve of domestic law if only for lack of common features and easily understandable structures. Where common structures exist they may acquire international normativity on the basis of *general principle* which in such cases is likely to be *mandatory* (and as such move up in the hierarchy of norms).

Incipient transnational ownership rights have also been spotted in other areas like fishing and mining or drilling rights, in broadcasting and telecommunications and in intellectual and industrial property rights. The development of this concept under human rights notions was already noted in section 1.4.5 *in fine*. This evolution is of extreme importance as it concerns here often large investments and major capital goods or productive assets.[278]

The development and recognition of an internationalised concept of ownership along fundamental lines in this manner will facilitate at the same time the process of characterisation, recognition and adaptation of proprietary interests when assets are transferred to, surface or play a role in other countries with different legal systems, see for this recognition and adaptation process more in particular chapter 4, section 1.8.2.[279]

---

[278] Except to some extent in air and sea transport with the connected bills of lading and negotiable instruments, and now also in international finance, the notion of international property rights remains, however, unexplored, but it may be less unusual in the context of public international law and in intellectual property, see eg Churchill and Lowe, *The Law of the Sea* (3d ed. 1999); Ruggenkamp and others, *Energy Law in Europe* (2001) pars. 2.01ff; McCaffrey, *The Law of International Watercourses* (2001) chapter 5; Birnie and Boyle, *International Law and the Environment* (2nd ed. 2002), chapters 1, 5, 6, 7 and 10; Gillies and Marshall, *Telecommunications* (2nd ed. 2003) chapter 4; Tritton, *Intellectual Property in Europe* (2nd ed. 2002), chapters 2–6.

[279] It is in the meantime doubtful whether within the EU harmonisation of ownership concepts will be attempted in view of the text of Article 222 of the founding treaty (the Treaty of Rome of 1957), although in the area of security rights some early efforts were made, see chapter 5, n. 22, and in matters of patent law the EU has repeatedly been active, sanctioned by the European Court in Luxembourg, see Case C–350/91, *Spain v the Council* and earlier Case 30/90, *The Commission v The UK* [1992] ECR I-858. In these cases the Court held that Article 222 did not allow the Member States to legislate in the area of industrial and commercial property rights in ways which would impact on the free movement of goods. It seems that the Court is more favourably inclined towards extensions of these property rights in a transnational sense than to their limitation to purely domestic concepts. See further also the EU Settlement Finality Directive and Collateral Directive which touch on the status of payments and some security rights and finance sales like repos and on a number of bankruptcy aspects, also in connection with the netting principle, see chapter 3 ss. 1.2.6 and 1.3.5 and chapter 4, ss. 3.2.2 and 3.2.4.

To demonstrate the transnationalisation of the fundamental ownership concepts further, it may be of some interest to return to the modern eurobond. They have become the standard instrument of the largest capital market in the world. Imperceptibly transnational ownership notions were adopted for them in the last 40 years. For the most part, these bonds are subjected to a contractual choice of law for the proprietary regime, which is often English law, marked as such on the back of the instrument. The question is what this choice of law means in the circumstances. It is clear that a bearer instrument is normally intended, but it is unlikely that there is negotiability in the strict terms of Section 83 of the English Bill of Exchange Act 1882 because the conditions of the bond are not always sufficiently certain, especially not the payment which may be subject to all kinds of variations and conditions. This is counter to the concept of negotiable instruments under English (as under most other domestic) law.

However, in practice the contractual choice of law in proprietary aspects is not decisive. This is so first because of the third-party proprietary effect which cannot be freely created or conferred by choosing foreign laws. It may be possible or even necessary to rely here on more fundamental or common proprietary principles to determine the true status internationally of Eurobonds as negotiable bearer paper. This is in fact what happened as negotiability in these circumstances is always presumed, regardless of whatever English law may say on the matter, even though English domestic case-law happens to be accommodating.[280]

Although practices appear to be the decisive factor and are then likely to be international practices as it concerns here an internationalised instrument, the fact that these practices may be of recent origin could suggest that other considerations play a role as well and it is more likely that transnational ownership and transferability of this type are an expression of a more fundamental ownership concept or model that operates cross border and is the prototype of all ownership rights in movables, just as it operates for bills of exchange and bills of lading. Changeable demands of the market-place certainly play a role as well but could probably not prevail if there was no underlying property model in place.

Finally, it is not inconceivable that from a more fundamental ownership perspective, all monetary claims should be considered much like negotiable instruments and thus become transferable in similar ways through delivery of the collection right and power to give notice to the debtors. At the same time any transfer restrictions and debtors' defences against payment would be de-emphasised. It is the approach that is increasingly favoured in the USA, see Sections 2–210 and 9–406(d) (9–318 old) UCC and chapter 4, section 1.7.3.

As already observed in section 1.1.4 above, modern financial law is underlining the movement towards new proprietary rights in an international commercial (professional) context. The modern *lex mercatoria* serves here as a modern conduit to introduce them internationally, especially relevant where domestic law cannot accommodate them. That may be the case especially in civil law countries which normally practice a closed system of proprietary rights. Thus beneficial, conditional, and temporary ownership rights in present and future assets may be recognised in international commerce or professional dealings.

---

[280] It is often said that the negotiability of eurobonds derives from the force of market custom: see the older English cases on international bonds cited in n. 268 *supra* which relate to Russian and Prussian bonds, and further P Wood, *Law and Practice of International Finance* (London, 1980), 184. See also *Bechuanaland Exploration Co. v London Trading Bank* [1898] 2 QBD 658, in which it was accepted in connection with the negotiability of bearer bonds that 'the existence of usage has so often been proved and its convenience is so obvious that it might be taken now to be part of the law'. Modern case-law does not, however, exist confirming the point but in England it is still considered good law. See for the explicit reference in this connection to the custom of the mercantile world which may expressly be of recent origin, *Dicey and Morris on the Conflict of Laws* (13th ed. 2000), Rule 192, 1431.

Advanced forms of floating charges, bulk assignments and bulktransfers, repos and leases as conditional sales may thus become accepted, whilst domestic bankruptcy laws will learn to recognise these customary international financial structures. In common law, they found their expression foremost in equity. Civil law never had that facility but international commercial law may now serve to further develop these structures at the transnational level. It is a most important development, inspired also by the fact that traditional private international law has always had difficulties in dealing with intangible assets or assets that habitually move transborder whilst its reliance on domestic laws and their limitations is increasingly unlikely to lead to internationally acceptable solutions in the financial area.

Like in equity in common law countries, the new proprietary structures that will be so admitted or created are unlikely to present a unitary coherent ownership structure. Proprietary rights are more likely to be defined for each structure without regard to an underlying system which can only develop later. Common law countries have learnt to be comfortable with such a state of affairs which is maintained in modern statutory law in the US, notably the UCC. It may be more difficult for the civil law lawyers, but whatever their feelings and preoccupations may be, there is ample evidence from common law countries that a unitary systematic approach is not necessary, not even in proprietary rights. In fact, it may be argued that the absence of it has always been a great advantage in common law, especially in the further development of advances financial instruments and structures. The trust, constructive trust and tracing concepts are here perhaps the best demonstration, concepts without which modern financial products can hardly operate.

3.2.3 Mandatory Customs and Practices

The phenomenon of the law-creating force of custom and practices has given rise to much academic thought, with the possibility itself sometimes being doubted. It is the reason why a distinction between custom and trade practices is often maintained, see section 1.5.2 above. In modern civil law that has had much to do with the denial of sources of law other than statute, as we saw above. In this view, custom is objective law and to be avoided whilst trade practices are implied contractual terms and may as such be acceptable. This is not the approach of this book and seems particularly inappropriate in the international commercial sphere.

In this sphere, after the fundamental principles which are the basis of the whole system of the new law merchant or *lex mercatoria*, there follow in the hierarchy of the *lex mercatoria* the customs generally prevailing in each trade if considered mandatory, which is still rare, although the Hague-Visby rules are sometimes so defined where not already incorporated by statute.[281] Their being mandatory means in this instance that they need not be incorporated in the bill of lading or in any domestic law *per se*. Parties may, however, deviate from them, but they apply if one of them does not wish to do so. The more modern version of this customary law may be found in the Hamburg Rules prepared by Uncitral. True mandatory custom is more likely to emerge in non-contractual aspects or in contractual aspects that, like issues of validity, cannot be freely determined or changed by the parties. It is for international arbitrators and the courts when asked to rule on them, to acknowledge these international customs and practices. In the area of guidelines for foreign direct investment, there may be a transnational public policy element to custom which might thus also become mandatory.

---

[281] See Haak, 'Internationalism above Freedom of Contract' in *Essays on International and Comparative Law in Honour of Judge Erades*, 69.

In the elaboration of the rules of contract and property further mandatory rules of custom may develop, especially in the areas of legal capacity and contractual validity and its effects on the transfer of ownership or in the area of the return of title upon default already discussed above in connection with fundamental legal principle. They concern the infrastructure of the law of contract and property, and are as such not at the free disposition of the parties. These rules are more likely to be closely related to or an elaboration of the fundamental principles.

In section 3.2.2 above, it was already said that eurobonds are normally considered negotiable instruments on the basis of market forces or custom, although their status as international negotiable instruments might have more to do with the application of fundamental principles of property law which also allowed the development and operation of internationalised bills of exchange, later joined by bills of lading as internationalised negotiable documents of title. The primary concerns are the manner of transfer, the protection of *bona fide* purchasers and the creation of security and other more limited proprietary interests or conditional ownership rights in them. It is clear that custom here supports the operation of the fundamental proprietary concepts in their details and is then likely to acquire mandatory aspects.

Custom or practice may also surface in an entirely different manner, for example in certain presumptions, like, amongst professionals, the presumption of the capacity of the parties. As non-contractual matters, they then also acquire a mandatory flavour. At least in the international commercial sphere, typical legal capacity limitations derived from domestic law, even that of the residence of the party concerned, are increasingly ignored, although purely domestically they may remain of the greatest importance. This was shown in the cases concerning swaps entered into with municipal authorities in the UK.[282] In international commercial matters, local aspects of capacity, but also of illegality, nullity and collapse of title or voidable title, might well become less relevant. International trade and its flows may be considered an overriding concept between professionals in the business sphere. If this is the trend, it would concern here the applicability of mandatory customary rules in the legal infrastructure of international sales and transfers.

Mandatory custom may also affect the rules of adjudicatory jurisdiction. It has been said in this connection that international custom is now averse to jurisdiction being exercised by the court of the plaintiff (*forum actoris*) without any other supporting grounds for such jurisdiction.[283] This would be a further incidence of customary law acquiring a mandatory or fundamental flavour.

In connection with mandatory custom, it may also be of interest to look somewhat more closely at the operations of underwriters in the international bond markets (euromarket). The main concern here is to create a situation where the capital raising operation is in so far as possible detached from local elements especially in terms of tax, foreign exchange, syndication, underwriting or placement rules. To achieve this, the issuing company (often through a fully guaranteed financing subsidiary) may operate from a tax haven base so as to avoid withholding tax payments on interest. The foreign exchange restrictions on payment of interest and principal are likely to be minimised by the creation of paying agents in several countries providing a choice for the investor. Another measure to promote the detached nature of the instrument is the creation of an underwriting syndicate that operates from a country, like for example England, that does not hinder or regulate the

---

[282] As per Lord Ackner in *Hazell v London Borough of Hammersmith and Fulham and Others*, [1991] 1 All *ER* 545.
[283] See JP Verheul, 'The Forum Actoris and International Law' in *Essays on International and Comparative Law in Honour of Judge Erades* (The Hague, 1983), 196.

operation unduly and allows placement in other countries (although it may still limit the placement of eurobonds in the own currency in the own country). To have syndicate members in various countries promotes at the same time the international character of the syndication and placement.

These are practical measures an issuer can take to promote the internationality or transnationality of the negotiable instruments issued by him. The documentation surrounding the creation, nature and sale of these instruments like the subscription, underwriting and selling agreements, may as a consequence acquire a transnational flavour as well. It means that the choice of a domestic law in the documentation may not be controlling and could even be inappropriate as it may disturb the balance between all the elements of transnational law or the *lex mercatoria* to operate fully. In this connection, the Recommendations of the International Primary Market Association (IPMA) for the issuing activity and initial placement and the Rules of the International Security Market Association (ISMA, earlier the AIBD) have a natural role to play within the hierarchy of the transnational law. They may acquire mandatory aspect as well, although the former are officially not even binding between the members.

In the swap and repo markets, the ISDA Swap Master Agreements of 1987/1992 and the PSA/ISMA Global Master Repurchase Agreement of 1992/1995 might acquire a similar status of custom in the areas they cover, at least in the London and the New York markets where they operate. This may be particularly relevant for their close-out and netting principles. The status of contractual bilateral netting with its enhancements of the set-off principle and its inclusion of all swaps between the same parties, leading to a netting out of all positions in the case of default at the option of the non-defaulting party and *ipso facto* in the case of bankruptcy, could remain in doubt under local law.

This is particularly relevant in bankruptcy, because of the substantial impact of netting on the rights of other creditors whilst an indirect extended preference is created. Internationally, the acceptance of the set-off principle in this manner may well become customary if it is not already so and may then impose itself also on domestic bankruptcy laws. That is not to say that the netting principle would also be applied if the contract itself did not stipulate it. If it did, however, the result would be the acceptance of an international practice against domestic law principles (of a mandatory nature), giving custom here a public policy or mandatory aspect as well, especially when overruling local bankruptcy laws.

In the area of foreign direct investment, international agencies have attempted to define certain principles and set certain standards which may also be reflective of international practices or initiate them. Foreign direct investment is commonly defined as a long-term interest with an active management role in an enterprise or utility operating in a country other than that of the investor. Lesser developed countries saw here possibilities of abuse whilst investors held out for more protection. The first sentiment held sway in the later 1960s and 1970s and gave rise to the OECD Guidelines of 1976 (following the 1969 Andean Investment Code for the Latin American Region). They were not legally binding and often thought to represent the views of the richer countries only.

This led to an attempt (since 1977) to formulate a UN Code of Conduct for Transnational Enterprises which still remains at the drafting stage. In this climate, the World Bank (IBRD) tried to help as it had earlier taken a leading role in the formulation of the Convention on the Settlement of Investment Disputes between States and Nationals of Other States of 1965, presenting an institutional framework (through the International Center for the Settlement of Investment Disputes or ICSID) for disputes between foreign investors and home states through arbitration. Under it, the applicable law, in the absence of an agreement of the parties, is the law of the State that is party to the dispute, including its conflict rules and such rules of international law that may be applicable (Article 42). One may ask oneself whether this reference to international law includes the *lex mercatoria*.

The World Bank came up with its Guidelines on the Treatment of Foreign Direct Investment in 1992. They cover four areas ranging from admission, treatment and expropriation of foreign investments to the settlement of disputes in respect of them. They consist of general principles to guide governmental behaviour towards foreign investment and purport to reflect generally acceptable international standards for the promotion of foreign investment.[284] The Guidelines are based on an extensive study of current practices as reflected in international investment treaties, national investment codes, writings of international law experts and a host of arbitral awards mainly emanating from the ICC, ICSID and the Iran–US States Claims Tribunal. The Guidelines are extensive and, although no more than guidelines, their standard- and norm-creating effect has been noted which could lead to international custom.[285] It is not impossible that whilst becoming customary law they are mandatory at the same time. They may as such become serious compilations of compulsory international practices.

3.2.4 Mandatory Uniform Treaty Law, Contractual Provisions (Party Autonomy), Directory Trade Practices, Directory Uniform Treaty Law and Common Legal Notions

Following what was said in sections 1.5.4 and 3.1.1 above, in the context of the *lex mercatoria*, after (a) the fundamental legal principles and (b) the mandatory customs and practices, there applies (c) uniform treaty law to the extent applicable under its own rules and mandatory. Thereafter there are (d) in contractual matters the contractual provisions themselves. They are supplemented in descending order by (e) directory trade practices, (f) directory uniform treaty law (if applicable under its own terms), (g) common legal notions and, if all else fails, finally by (h) the private international law rules of the forum if the issue is not yet decided under the higher rules.

Mandatory uniform treaty law is rare, but *cf* Article 12 of the Vienna Convention was earlier mentioned as an example. It allows Contracting States to demand a writing for international sales agreements. If the Uncitral Receivable Finance Convention were to be adapted, there would be a great deal more of these mandatory provisions particularly in the formalities and proprietary aspects of international bulk assignments of receivables.

The contract itself may of course set important rules, but they can in principle only prevail in contractual matters and even then only in matters that are at the disposition of the parties which may not be the case as to their own legal capacity and in the matter of remedies, especially in the case of error or fraud. Also parties would not be able to address in their contract matters regarding third parties and especially not proprietary issues even if in matters of assignment there is a modern tendency to allow parties greater freedom at least in assignments with international aspects, see more in particular chapter 4, section 1.9.2. It will also be pointed out in chapter 4 section 1.2.1 and 1.3.7 that the civil law idea of a closed system of proprietary rights is increasingly under pressure. Conditional sales and

---

[284] See also the Report to the Development Committee on the Legal Framework for the Treatment of Foreign Investment (1992), 31 ILM 1368.

[285] See also I Brownlie, 'Legal Effects of Codes of Conduct for Multinational Enterprises; Commentary' in Norbert Horn (ed.), *Legal Problems of Codes of Conduct for Multinational Enterprises* (Deventer 1980), 41 and N Horn, 'Codes of Conduct for Multinational Enterprises and Transnational Lex Mercatoria' in the same publication (52).

transfers in particular are opening up and contractualising the proprietary system. A better protection of unsuspecting third parties (like *bona fide* purchasers) would appear to be the sequel.

Subsequently we have the directory customs and practices. Much was already said about them in section 1.5.2 and needs no repetition. It was already signalled there that as to these directory customs and practices, the status of the UCP, URC and Incoterms may be of special interest.The UCP are the Uniform Customs and Practice for Documentary Credits compiled by the International Chamber of Commerce since 1933, the latest version being from 1993. They are in the nature of a private codification of some of the most impor- tant rules concerning letters of credit and have obtained a worldwide acceptance. Even in countries like the US, where State law deals through Article 5 UCC with letters of credit, the latest amendments of Section 5–116(c) UCC assume derogation if the UCP is explic- itly made applicable to a letter of credit. The UCC and UCP thus became complemen- tary sources of law for letters of credit in the USA.[286] Nevertheless the status in law of the UCP has remained in doubt where the letter of credit does not contain a reference to them and the subject matter is not dealt with by an applicable statute. Many see them as international custom,[287] subject to regular adjustments by the ICC, and as such part of the objective international or transnational commercial law, even though the ICC is itself not a legislative body but only a compilator of international customs and practices in the process of which it also develops them further. Their status as international custom means that for their effectiveness they need no longer be incorporated in the text of the arrangements concerning the issuance of letters of credit or characterised as implied conditions.

It must be said, however, that the formulation of the UCP does not help here. In the 1974 version, Article 1 considered the UCP binding in all circumstances except if parties agreed otherwise. In 1983 the impression was created that the UCP were implied contract

---

[286] See also JF Dolan, *The Law of Letters of Credit, Commercial and Standby Credits* (1999) 4.06 [2][l].

[287] The idea of the UCP being transnational law is associated with the views of the Austrian F Eisemann, Director of the Legal Department of the ICC at the time, and was first proposed by him at a 1962 King's College London Colloquium, see *Le Credit Documentaire dans le Droit et dans la pratique* (Paris 1963), 4, an approach followed in England by C Schmitthoff, *The Source of the Law of International Trade* (London 1964), 15, although in his view always in the context of some national law, and later in France by Y Loussouarn and JD Bredin, *Droit du Commerce International* (Paris, 1969), 48. See similarly in Germany, N Horn, '*Die Entwicklung des internationalen Wirtschaftrechts durch Verhaltungsrichtlinien*', *Rabels Zeitschrift*, 423 (1980), 44. In France, their status as interna- tional custom is now well established, see J Puech, '*Modes de paiement in Lamy*', Transport Tôme II, No 324 (Paris 2000), see also Trib de Commerce Paris, March 8 1976, DMF, 558 (1976) and Cour de Cass, Oct 14 1981, JCP II. 19815 (1982) Note Gavalda and Stoufflet, see further B Goldman, 'Lex Mercatoria', in *Forum Internationale*, No 3 (Deventer Nov 1983), see for this approach also Cour de Cass, Nov 5 1991, Bull Civ, IV, no 328 (1992). It means that no reference to them is necessary in the documentation. In Belgium this approach was followed by the Tribunal de Commerce of Brussels, Nov 16 1978, 44 Rev de la Banque, 249 (1980). The German doctrine is uncer- tain, especially because of the written nature of the UCP and its regular adjustments which is seen there as con- trary to the notion of custom, see CW Canaris, *Bankvertragsrecht* (3rd edn, 1988) Part I, Rdn. 926.

In the Netherlands the Supreme Court has not so far fully accepted the UCP as objective law, see lastly HR, April 26 1985, NJ 607 (1985). The lower courts are divided. So are the writers with PL Wery, 'De autonomie van het Eenvormig Privaatrecht', 11 (Deventer 1971) and this author in favour, see JH Dalhuisen, 'Bankguarantees in International Trade', WPNR 6033, 52 (1992). English law does not require any incorporation in the documenta- tion, see *Harlow and Jones Ltd v American Express Bank Ltd and Creditanstalt-Bankverein*, 2 Lloyd's Rep, 343 (1990) concerning, however, the applicability of the ICC Uniform Rules for Collection (URC) which are much less well known, but nevertheless subscribed to by all banks in England; see for the UCP earlier Lord Denning in *Power Curber International Ltd v National Bank of Kuwait*, 2 Lloyd's Rep, 394 (1981) also with reference to the fact that all or practically all banks in the world subscribe to them, which seems the true criterion in the UK. See for the US, *Oriental Pacific (USA) Inc v Toronto Dominion Bank*, 357 NY 2d 957 (1974) in which the force of law the UCP was accepted 'to effect orderly and efficient banking procedures and the international commerce amongst nations'.

terms through the addition of a sentence requiring incorporation in the documentation. Since 1993, the UCP require incorporation in the documents and have deleted the earlier language of 1974, although there is a second sentence which suggest otherwise ('They are binding on all parties thereto, unless otherwise expressly stipulated in the credit'). This suggests a contradictory sentiment in the drafting. In any event their legal force as custom or other source of law cannot be pre-determined by the UCP themselves and is a matter of the objective law. The approach in case-law has therefore not changed. The Incoterms are similarly treated and often considered custom, at least in the commodity trade in Europe.

UCP, UCR and Incoterms are all partial codifications only and even if accepted as customary law do not cover the whole field and are in any event subject to interpretation and supplementation, like the partial uniform law contained in the Vienna Sales Convention is. The first rule here must be that they are to be explained on the basis of their international character and the general principles of these compilations themselves, but probably more important is to place them in the hierarchy of principles and rules constituting the *lex mercatoria* as here explained. That is to say that they are to be interpreted, explained and even superseded by the fundamental principles of law and any mandatory custom or treaty law (if any and applicable under its own terms). Thereafter there are to be considered the wording of the relevant contract itself, the notions of *bona fides* in the application of these contract terms, the logic and nature of the transaction, other (directory) custom, uniform directory treaty law like that of the Vienna Convention (especially relevant for the Incoterms), and common legal notions. Finally, if still no solution is found, there remains to be considered the choice of law rules identifying a national law, but only on a discretionary, result oriented basis,[288] whilst these domestic laws are thus transnationalised.

Another elaboration of directory customs and practices might be found in the confidentiality of arbitrations. It was said above that in international contractual matters the party autonomy determines in the first instance the applicable regime (unless there is other mandatory law or principle) supported by implied conditions and ultimately industry practices and uniform treaty law to the extent existing. The idea that knowledge of the parties may still be required in some legal systems for these practices to be taken into account, as also under Article 9 of the Vienna Convention, illustrates the ambivalence which exists towards custom in Civil Law, and a reluctance to part with the implied term approach. Yet one often sees here a progression from explicit contractual term to industry custom. It was said earlier, however, that the reverse may also happen and established custom may loose its autonomous status and acquire at best the status of implied term to be proven by the party relying on it or even looses that status and then requires for its continuous effect explicit agreement between the parties. The principle of confidentiality in arbitrations was given as an example.[289]

---

[288] See for this approach also MN Boon, *De Internationale Koop en het Documentair Accreditief ingevolge de UCP 1993* [The International Sale and the Documentary Letter of Credit under the UCP 1993], 7 and 425 (1998) and MN Boon, *Book review* of RA Schuetze, Das Dokumentenakkreditiv im Internationalen Handelsverkehr (1996) in *EBLR*, 331 (1998).

[289] The discussion in this respect was initiated by a decision of the High Court of Australia in *Esso/BHP v Plowman*, see 11 Int'l Arb. 235 (1995). The question of confidentiality of arbitrations often arises in the context of the joining of different but connected arbitrations when one of the parties objects because it may violate the privacy of the proceedings, see *Oxford Shipping Co v Nippon Yusen Kaisha*, 3 All E R 835 (1984) in which the confidentiality argument was upheld. It also arises where orders are issued to reveal particulars of other arbitrations, see *Dolling-Baker v Merret*, 1 WLR 1205 (1990), in which such orders were set aside, or where particulars are disclosed to reinsurance companies likely to be sued for recovery of the amount lost in the arbitration, *see Hassneh*

After customary rules and practices we have the rules of uniform treaty law but only in Contracting States and if applicable under their own terms. As we saw for the Vienna Convention on the International Sale of Goods, which is the most important example, normally these Conventions only present partial codifications. Only the Uncitral Receivable Financing Conventions appears to present a fuller regime of international bulk assignments but is in its proprietary aspects mandatory and therefore likely to be of much higher rank within the *lex mercatoria*.

Subsequently we have the general principles or common notions. These common notions may emerge eg in the area of offer and acceptance, duress, misrepresentation, negligence, liability without fault, proprietary rights, damage mitigation and computation, *force majeure* and hardship, *exceptio non adimpleti contractus* or anticipatory breach, set-off and other remedies including specific performance (*cf* also Article 28 of the Vienna Convention), statute of limitations, and the like, all forming the normal infrastructure of the law of contract. There are here also procedural questions like burden of proof, evidence and disclosure issues to be considered. These common notions may also be relevant outside the law of contract and procedure and concern in any event the whole law of obligations and movable property. These common notions are to be distinguished from the fundamental principles and are thus *not* part of the *ius cogens* in the above sense and therefore of a lower, non-overriding nature. They derive often from comparative law research in the sense that where similar rules are found in the domestic laws of the more advanced nations, they may enter into the *lex mercatoria* at this level assuming that they capture the dynamics of modern business. Rules of uniform treaty law may also be considered in this connection even outside Contracting States. UCP, UCR and Incoterms could also figure at this level if not already included at higher levels like the contractual one (if incorporated in the contract) or as directory custom or practice.

Contractual provisions in particular may be further supplemented by notions of good faith or intrinsic logic and common sense at this level of general principle. They are therefore *less than* fundamental principle or *ius cogens*, unless they are a reflection of it and are only then mandatory. Otherwise they are *less than* overriding requirements connected with the imperatives of the continuation of trade. They are then also less than mandatory or directory custom or uniform treaty law.

Insurance v Mew, 2 Lloyds Rep., 243 (1993), in which such disclosure was limited to the mere finding and the reasoning had to remain confidential.

In the 1995 Australian case *of Esso/BHP v Plowman*, it was the State of Victoria which wanted to find out certain information concerning cost, price, volume and revenue given to a gas utility by Esso in one arbitration in order for the State to use it in another. The High Court of Australia found no confidentiality rule (or custom) or even an implied term requiring the protection of the confidentiality. It only accepted the privacy of the hearings whilst documents compulsorily produced could not be used for any other purpose than the arbitration. Short of a specific confidentiality undertaking in the arbitration clause itself, it found no obligation of confidentiality and noted in this respect that the results of arbitrations are commonly divulged whilst witnesses could in any event not be held to secrecy. It was probably always clear that where a public interest was involved, like in disputes concerning the use of public property or possibly in consumer arbitrations, awards could be disclosed. However, it appears that the disclosure possibility now goes much further and may affect ordinary commercial arbitrations. Except in exceptional cases, confidentiality seems no longer guaranteed, at least not if the Australian case reflects modern thinking.

Thus of the original three main justifications of arbitration: speed, confidentiality and expert handling, at least confidentiality appears to have lapsed for all but the privacy of the hearing itself and the protection of confidential information presented therein. This may be because arbitrations have increasingly become pseudo-judicial proceedings. They also have lost much of their informal character. The awards are now also often published, at least by the ICC and ICSID, or in the Yearbook of Commercial Arbitration, even if in a sanitised form to render them more anonymous. In such procedures confidentiality has clearly taken a back seat. Alternative dispute resolution (ADR) may, on the other hand, have retained more informality and may as a consequence also enjoy greater secrecy protection.

3.2.5   Domestic Laws, Private International Law: Mandatory Provisions or Public Policy Issues

Finally there is domestic law and there are the private international law rules of the forum in this regard if the issue is not yet decided under the higher rules as just described. They are even then unlikely to be applied as hard and fast conflict rules, if as such still practised in the law of property and obligations.[290] As pointed out before in section 1.5.4 above, they are too residual in the whole hierarchy of norms here proposed to operate as hard and fast rules. However, they may indicate the closer contact and thus the domestic laws more in particular affected and to be considered, if only as expressions of domestic policy. It is possible to think here of the status of proprietary rights and particularly of the ranking of security interests in the country of destination of the goods or in a bankruptcy initiated in a third country.

This is far from the application of a system of hard and fast conflicts rules as the recognition of these rights elsewhere often entails adaptations if assets move to other countries or if their status needs to be assessed in a foreign bankruptcy of the owner/debtor, see the discussion in section 2.1.2 above. A simple reference to the (new) *lex situs* is then inadequate, if at all relevant. More fundamental overriding notions of acquired rights of beneficiaries or security interest holders play here an important role besides the practical question of how the recognising country can incorporate the foreign proprietary right into its own system to give it adequate protection. As a consequence, the conflict rules and their application will have to take into account other relevant considerations, the evaluation of which is, like in the case of governmental interests of a country affected by the case, never a matter of the application of one rule alone.

In international cases, the adjudicating court or arbitration panel will also have to decide what force, if any, it must still give to domestic public policies as contained in local rules, in the light of all applicable principles and other rules applicable in the context of the *lex mercatoria* in the manner as here explained, the relationship, interests and special deal features to be protected or respected. This matter was more fully discussed in section 2.2.6 above. There are unlikely to be many local policy issues considered relevant in international professional dealings, except in areas of abuse of monopoly power or arrangements in restraint of trade, insider dealing, bribery, money laundering or where there are environmental consequences. More traditionally there are also trade restrictions, currency limitations and tariff or taxation considerations to consider although less important now than they used to be. Globalisation and liberation of trade and finance make an important difference here. So does privatisation even locally.

As demonstrated in section 2.2.6 above, these local public policy considerations are more readily accepted if they are connected with or an expression of overriding fundamental principle and then no longer purely domestic in nature (although the elaboration is likely to be). This may even be so in the areas of consumer, retailer and worker protection.

3.3   Operation of the *Lex Mercatoria* and Objections to it

3.3.1   Operation of the Lex Mercatoria

It is submitted and the key message of this book that courts and arbitrators in international commercial and financial disputes may be better guided by the hierarchy of

---

[290] See for the more flexible American approach s 2.2.2 *supra*. See for the direct application of considerations of cogency and moral data even in conflict laws, either under the guise of public policy or natural law, AA Ehrenzweig, *op cit supra* n 212, 77*ff*.

norms under the modern *lex mercatoria* than by application of private international law rules (if at all clear which ones) pointing to some domestic law that is unlikely to be made for it.

An example may serve as illustration of the modern *lex mercatoria* approach: a contract for the sale (and exportation) of commodity type goods is concluded between two parties in different countries with the price expressed in the (soft) currency of the seller. According to the (mandatory) law of the country of the seller, this type of commodity sale requires a public auction in the country of the seller at which international buyers can only bid in hard currency.

Even short of the application of the formation rules of the Vienna Convention (which may or may not be applicable in this case depending foremost on whether the countries of seller and buyer are ratifying countries but, even if not applicable under its own terms, could still serve as a collection of general principles), the basic validity of the contract (not an issue itself covered by the Vienna Convention) as a moral imperative and practical requirement of all social and business intercourse is a given. It is fundamental (*pacta sunt servanda*) everywhere and certainly also in the international commercial and financial legal order in which this trade takes place. Its details could be worked out on the basis of notions common to all modern legal systems taking into account the special needs and features of dealings between professionals, always assuming the contract does not itself select an applicable law, the meaning of which needs in that case be further determined especially in respect of public policy interests of other states and of the international commercial and financial legal order itself. But its meaning would also have to be determined in terms of idiosyncracies of such a chosen domestic law especially in terms of contractual infra structure issues, which are not necessarily at the free disposition of the parties and may not fit international trade. Above, examples were given (if the laws of a common law country have been selected), eg the consideration requirement, the parole evidence rule, and in this particular case perhaps the notion that *ex turpe cause actio non oretur* meaning that if the transaction were declared illegal nothing might be retrieved by a buyer who had already made a down payment.

Even if for a transaction like the one here discussed between professionals in the international commercial and financial legal order, the prohibition in the country of the seller on dealing in this manner, therefore the policy of the country of the seller, cannot be ignored, it may figure in different ways and may have to be considered in terms of lack of legal capacity to contract, illegality of the transaction, or as a mere administrative measure (not affecting the sale itself). Common principles may be used to solve this characterisation problem — international arbitrators at least are likely to look here for a substantive (rather than conflict's) rule. The ultimate result will be further determined in the light of any overriding notions connected with the imperative of the continuation of international commerce, especially if the goods have already left the county even illegally, which would be the problem of the seller/exporter, as long as not aided and abetted by the buyer when fraud could be alleged in the performance of the contract when the seller's country interest may again become an item in the balancing of interests.

Thus, as to the effect of mandatory governmental or public policy rules concerning the sale and currency restrictions, arbitrators or foreign courts will naturally consider them in respect of commodities originating in the country of the seller and as a consequence may deem the contract void, but it depends on the circumstances and it is less likely if the relevant assets already went through the auction process once whilst invalidity or illegality is not at all likely if the commodities were acquired by the seller from elsewhere or were already abroad (even after illegal exportation at least as long as the buyer was not a party to the export itself).

The proprietary aspects and ownership rights of the buyer as well as any exceptions to the '*nemo dat*' rule (in respect of this acquisition or at least upon a resale abroad of the assets to third parties) might also be settled on the basis of fundamental legal principle. It may override notions of the continuation of international trade and common legal notions in terms of user and disposition rights, particularly in respect of tangible goods which have already moved out of the country. More complicated may be the creation of security rights or retention of title in the assets, but by using possessory pledges or conditional property rights instead, common ground may more readily be found facilitating the recognition process of such rights elsewhere (in domestic legal orders, eg in local bankruptcy proceedings).

3.3.2   Direct References to the Lex Mercatoria

In the meantime, because of the ambivalence on the subject and probably a lack of a clear idea what the modern *lex mercatoria* really is, direct references to the *lex mercatoria* remain rare and are on the whole also still avoided in arbitration statutes, whilst courts and arbitrators often prefer to use different terminology and like to limit theoretical controversy.[291] Equally, a contractual choice of law in favour of the *lex mercatoria* remains uncommon and has even been thought to render the contract void.[292] This must be considered an extreme view, in any event likely to be limited to the UK which remains more generally reluctant to accept what it considers extra-legal standards, sometimes, it would seem, even in international arbitrations. The possibility is in any event encouraged by the Unidroit and European Contract Principles.

Not choosing any (domestic) law may be a second best option. Courts or arbitrators will then decide the issues as they think fit on the basis of a multiplicity of norms, whether or not within the context of the hierarchy of norms of the modern *lex mercatoria*, especially if there are indications of the parties having been baffled by the problem of the applicable law. This is most likely to happen if there are a cluster of contracts involving performance in several countries whilst problems may only arise years after the signature of the contracts in circumstances and places that could hardly be foreseen.

There remains the question of enforceability of the award if based on general principles or on the *lex mercatoria* notion. It depends on the jurisdiction where enforcement is sought but many will allow it.[293]

Direct references to the *lex mercatoria* may be found in the Unidroit and EU Principles of Contract Law. They assume the Principles to be part of it if the *lex mercatoria* is made or deemed applicable to the contract, without, however, going into the hierarchy of norms of which they seem not to have any idea. The Principles are of course also binding if parties in their contract specifically so provide. They could also become customary.[294]

---

[291] But *cf* ICC Case No 3131, 26 Oct 1979 (Bernardo Cremades President) (1984) IX *Yearbook Commercial Arbitration*, 109.

[292] See Mustill LJ. "Contemporary Problems in International Commercial Arbitration" (1989) 17 *Int Bus L* 161*ff*.

[293] So did the Austrian Supreme Court ultimately on 18 Nov 1982 in the ICC Case No 3131, IX YB Com Arb 159 (1984), see also *AJ v D Berg, The New York Arbitration Convention of 1958* (Deventer, 1981), 29 who accepts the enforceability of a-national awards under the Convention provided the awards are themselves not detached from a national arbitration law. The English courts, after having consistently rejected awards based on equity until 1978, changed their attitude thereafter: *Eagle Star v Yuval* [1978] 1 Lloyd's Rep 357, see also DW Rivkin, "Enforceability of Arbitral Awards Based on Lex Mercatoria", 9 *Arbitration International*, 67 (1993).

[294] See for early comments on the Unidroit Principles the ICC Publication, *The Unidroit Principles for International Commercial Contracts: A New Lex Mercatoria?* (ICC Dossier of the Institute of International Business Law and Practice, 1995), see further chapter 2, s 1.6.

Even then their place amongst the other norms in the *lex mercatoria* would still have to be more properly established. In fact, international commercial custom is often identified with the *lex mercatoria* as such, but again it is submitted that this is too narrow a view as the *lex mercatoria* is truly the whole of transnational commercial law with its own hierarchy of norms.

The arbitration clause allowing arbitrators to decide *ex aequo et bono* does not necessarily mean a reference to the *lex mercatoria*. It appears to bind arbitrators to the fundamental principles but not necessarily to the other components of the *lex mercatoria* and suggests beyond these fundamental principles greater discretion, although mandatory rules of a national system that clearly affect the case might not be ignored and may still have to be given their due weight. Thus it appears incorrect to assume that the arbitrators finding *ex aequo et bono* state entirely outside the law, but they are not bound by the hierarchy of norms as they find them in the *lex mercatoria*. This may be different for *amiable compositeurs* who indeed have the duty to find a sensible solution in the manner they deem fit. They are likely to work out a compromise but, in doing so, even they may not be able to ignore duly applicable mandatory rules.

It is in any event necessary to determine under applicable contract law what parties intended arbiters to do, and what their role becomes if they are allowed to decide *ex aequo et bono* or as *amiable compositeurs*. This applicable contract law may in international commercial matters be the *lex mercatoria* itself.[295]

3.3.3 *Parties' Choice of a Domestic Law v the* Lex Mercatoria

It may be clear from the above that a contractual choice of a domestic law in international cases may profoundly upset the hierarchy and balance between the various principles and rules implied in the *lex mercatoria* as explained above and could prove a dangerous and unbalancing manœuvre. The true meaning of such a choice in favour of a domestic law is, in any event uncertain especially with regard to the application of mandatory rules of countries professing an interest in the case. It is also unclear in proprietary matters and in contract in matters of validity. They are not normally thought to be at the free disposition of the parties. In any event, fundamental principle and transnational mandatory custom is likely to supersede this contractual choice of a domestic law. Under Article 3 of the Rome Convention of 1980 on the Law Applicable to Contractual Obligations it could

---

[295] Article 28 of the 1985 Uncitral Model Law on International Commercial Arbitration allows the arbitrators to find *ex aequo et bono* or as *amiable compositeurs* (without definition of this concept) but only if the parties have expressly authorised them to do so. There is no reference to the *lex mercatoria* in this connection, but Article 28(4) allows the tribunal in all cases to decide in accordance with the terms of the contract and to take into account the usages of the trade applicable to the transaction. This is not dependent on the parties' authorisation and precedes any application of conflicts rules, Article 28(2), but may not cover the whole of the *lex mercatoria* as here explained. One must assume that in international cases the fundamental legal principles will always be applied if considered *ius cogens*, that international custom will also be applied (but not necessarily common legal principles), whilst the interpretation and supplementation of the contract increasingly acquire the status of an autonomous function, at least in international sales if the Vienna Convention applies.

French (Article 1496 CCP (new)) and Dutch (Article 1054 CCP) modern arbitration laws follow the Uncitral Model Law in international cases without clearly describing what is meant by the usages of the trade. The Dutch official comment at the time referred to the *lex mercatoria* in this context and allowed its application without discussing what it exactly was. The English 1996 Arbitration Bill in s. 46 copies to a large extent the Uncitral Model Law, but notably deletes the reference to the usages of the trade applicable to the transaction. It may mean that the parties would still have to authorise any other considerations to be taken into account than the ones resulting from the applicable law under the conflict of law rules the panel deems applicable. The ICSID Rules allow in Article 42 the application of international law in disputes between foreign investors and states in which the investments are made.

be asked whether parties may select the *lex mercatoria* to oust the provisions otherwise applicable under Article 4. This may be quite possible. In international arbitrations, the Rome Convention is in any event unlikely to compulsorily apply, see chapter 2, section 2.3.8.

Another matter is whether the *lex mercatoria* may be deemed impliedly applicable if no law is chosen by the parties or indeed whether the absence of such a choice (of a domestic law) must automatically mean application of the *lex mercatoria* in international cases. It would not appear problematic with regard to the application of fundamental legal principles as *ius cogens* and of mandatory customs. From this the application of the rest of the *lex mercatoria* would logically appear to follow.

3.3.4 Objections to the Lex Mercatoria *Approach*

The objections to the transnational or *lex mercatoria* approach, even in the manner of a hierarchy of norms as here explained, are both of a fundamental and practical nature. As we saw, fundamentally it is sometimes believed that no law can develop outside the framework of a state or that at least a state cannot provide a sanction for laws that are not essentially its own. In practice, the new approach is sometimes considered to provide too little legal certainty, a reproach very similar to that affecting the newer attitudes to conflict laws, see section 2.2 above. Also here the objections are likely to come down to questions of temperament and practical experience. The own dynamics of the law leading to its autonomous development at the international level are by no means new and were always recognised in public international law as confirmed in Article 38(1) of the Statute of the International Court of Justice. The recognition of the independent status of the *lex mercatoria* in the manner here explained is particularly relevant where the potentially applicable domestic laws result incomplete, old fashioned, fractured or have nothing to contribute at all when seen from the perspective of the globalisation of international trade — which is now taking place on a scale never seen before.

Unavoidably, there is less certainty as a result, as always at the beginning of new developments. The only certainty that appears to be on offer is that of domestic laws. That certainty may be of a very low quality, however, and must be weighed against the suitability of these laws which are not written or developed to co-ordinate and support new (now often internationalised) transactional patterns and needs, particularly amongst professionals, and against the uncertainty in the applicable conflict rules themselves.

In a dynamic legal environment, legal certainty also in the domestic variety is in any event always relative and can only be achieved when new ideas and notions sufficiently crystallise and are tested over time. Only then is it possible to consider to what extent the international community should more generally intervene through facilitating or correcting treaty law or codifications in that form. In the meantime, the development of new law in the international professional sphere is unavoidably haphazard and for the time being only a hierarchy of norms in the sense of the modern *lex mercatoria* can here provide some order. On the other hand, much is settled law worldwide and not really contentious at all. Disputes are always exceptional; in commerce it is in the interest of all to minimise them. Yet, especially in an area of proprietary rights and security interests in movables and intangibles, there may be a need for more international action. The evolution through case-law can be rapid but may ultimately result in confusion as the development in the USA has shown when notions of conditional sales developed under state law giving rise to the later consolidation in the UCC, Article 9, see chapter 5, section 1.6.3. But by then, the true needs had become apparent.

Particularly in contract, where most rules are in any event directory, the professional sphere used to risk taking is probably better able to deal with a degree of uncertainty associated with normal developments than with any certainty resulting from inappropriate (domestic) rules. In proprietary law, local rules like for instance those attempting the abolition of the *fiducia* in the proprietary law of the new Dutch Civil Code, see chapter 5, section 1.2.2, or the automatic conversion of conditional sales into security interests under Article 9 UCC in the USA, even in the case of financial leases and repurchase agreements, see chapter 5, section 1.6.2, and similar arbitrary interventions in a legal system, may in fact create unexpected uncertainties and obstacles, even domestically, only compounded internationally by the application of inflexible conflict rules, like those pointing to the *lex situs*, for example in the case of (a) assets located in the USA when used in international financings of the various modern types or (b) foreign assets shipped to the Netherlands with foreign conditional proprietary rights attached to them which no longer have an equivalent in that country.

In the professional commercial sphere, modern legal thinking requires a greater degree of imagination and, at least in the private law aspects, a willingness to think more in terms of legal guidance and peer group experience than in terms of clear-cut rules and a corrective legal framework. Domestic public policies should be tested in a comity approach based on models as provided in Article 7 of the EU Rome Convention on the Law Applicable to Contractual obligations and Sections 402/403 Restatement (Third) Foreign Relations Laws in the US. Only subsequently, can and will more precise legal concepts develop within the modern *lex mercatoria*.

Although this transnational law approach combined with a rejection of automatic conflicts rules is often believed novel since it was signalled particularly in France in the 1960s and 1970s by Professor Goldman, see section 3.1.2 above, it was in the Netherlands in fact already foreshadowed in the writings of Professor D. Josephus Jitta (1854–1924), the successor of Professor Asser as Chairman of the Hague Conference. This approach has also become much more understandable through the critical attitude in the USA towards interstate conflict rules since the 1930s, see section 2.2.2 above, even if in the USA the modern developments in conflict laws are not analysed in terms of a newly emerging international law but rather as interpretations of the own laws, if often in terms of overrridng substantive notions of justice whilst in public policy questions the trend is far more liberal and internationalist, see section 2.2.6 above.

The transnational approach is in tune with the greater freedom often assumed by arbitrators as to the applicable law in international commercial cases, both as to procedure, evidence, conflicts rules, public policy questions and the development of substantive transnational law.[296]

3.3.5 *Application and Enforcement of the* Lex Mercatoria

Finally, not much need be said any more on the application and actual enforcement of the *lex mercatoria*. The subject was already approached in section 1.1.6, 1.4.3 and 1.5.6 above and briefly revisited in section 3.3.2.[297] Its application will be a matter for the ordinary courts and international arbitrators. Their decisions or awards will be recognised elsewhere under treaty law or under the normal rules in each country and will be subsequently enforced.

---

[296] See also n 202 *supra* and accompanying text.
[297] See also n 292 *supra*.

In terms of the applicable law it means that substantive rules derived from the *lex mercatoria* hierarchy should precede the application of a domestic rule found through choice of law or private international law notions. Public policy considerations, especially those expressed by governments in domestic laws, should be tested in a comity manner subject to substantive international standards of balancing the relevant interests against each other and the requirements of international trade and commerce, a subject more extensively discussed in section 2.2.6 above.

State courts operating in international cases could be seen as agents of the international commercial and financial legal order, therefore as international commercial courts, as international commercial arbitration panels are and their decisions could be seen as rendered in that order subject to recognition if their enforcement in state legal orders is necessary under the normal rules which mostly depend on proper jurisdiction (in an international sense) having been exercised. In each country, there is further the normal public policy bar to such recognition which may be especially relevant if the rendering court or panel has not taken the public policy interest of the country in which recognition and enforcement is sought sufficiently into account. Here again, the use by the court or panel of international standards in weighing the different interests will help in the recognition and enforcement process whilst the public policy bar to such recognition in each country could also be considered increasingly to be subject to an international standard.

Again standards set under the 1958 New York convention in respect of international arbitrations, under the 1968 EU Brussels Convention now replaced by the EU Regulation on Jurisdiction and the Recognition and Enforcement of Judgments in Civil and Commercial Matters, and under the 1993 Draft Hague Convention on Jurisdiction and the Recognition of Judgments may provide important guidance even in situations where they do not directly apply.

It was argued in section 1.1.6 that a *central highest international appeal court* could be set up to guide the development of the *lex mercatoria*, the criteria for balancing governmental interests (or public policy) and also steer the public policy bar to international recognition and enforcement of commercial court decisions and arbitration panel's awards. It would be limited to findings or preliminary opinions on points of law only and as such would present a helpful and most significant development, not too far-fetched at all, and at this moment probably more important than codifying or rather restating the new international law merchant itself, for which the necessary method is unlikely to be sufficiently agreed and a sufficient insight in what is needed still lacking.[298]

---

[298] See for support of this idea especially n 27 *supra*.

2

Domestic Contract Laws, Uniform International Contract Law and International Contract Law Principles: International Sales and Contractual Agency

Part I   Domestic Contract Laws

1.1   Introduction

1.1.1   Modern Contract Law: Emphasis on Nature of the Parties or on Type of Contract?

In this chapter on contract law, the emphasis will be primarily on the formation of the contract, on its binding force, on its interpretation and supplementation (or construction) and the (limited) grounds for correction of its terms, on performance and the most current defences, on default and excuses, on remedies including specific performance (or real execution) and re-negotiation in appropriate cases, and on the privity of contract.

These aspects will be foremost discussed in the context of *the nature of the relationship* between the parties rather than of the type of contract they conclude. This broadly conforms to the common law attitude,[1] which looks in the application of each of these concepts at the type of parties that conclude or have concluded the contract. It is likely in this approach that amongst professionals a contract is concluded, performed or excused in a manner different from that obtaining in their relationship with consumers or between consumers amongst themselves. Closely connected with this is the development in common law of special fiduciary duties between parties in situations of trust, dependency and confidence. This also suggests different treatment depending on the nature of the relationship. In this connection, it should be noted that in civil law, on the other hand, the emphasis is traditionally on types of contracts, not on type of parties. This is an important difference. Only under the modern concept of good faith interpretation of the parties' rights and duties and the concept of abuse of rights, one may find greater sensitivity to relationship issues in civil law as well.

In civil law this has had an effect especially on the development of disclosure and negotiation duties, but civil law is still less likely to differentiate between the type of parties and remains on the whole more focussed on the type of contract concerned, like contracts for the sale of goods or rental agreements and the like. It remains in any event

---

[1] See Bingham LJ in *Interfoto Picture Library Ltd v Stiletto Visual Programmes Ltd* [1989] 1 QB 433, 439, in which it was held that particularly onerous or unusual conditions had to be brought to the special attention of the counterparty, that the conventional analysis of offer and acceptance was not followed in that case and that the English authorities looked instead at the nature of the transaction and the character of the parties to it to consider what was necessary to conclude to a binding contract. As common law is sensitive to the nature of relationships, it never proved necessary to develop a wholly separate administrative law either. Special norms for governmental behaviour are traditionally embedded within the common law of contract, tort, restitution and property itself.

much keener than common law to define these different contract types themselves and deal with different protection needs in that context.[2] It certainly also has overarching notions of contract like offer and acceptance, the notion of consensus, performance and excuses, but it is only now beginning to differentiate them according to the type of parties involved at that level.

Common law traditionally shows some interest in the type of contract only in commercial law, like in the sale of goods, transportation and insurance. One may detect here continental influence. The reason is that these contract types have their origin in the law merchant that was developed in England for trade with the Continent and showed some Roman law influence: see also chapter 1, section 1.1.4.

This is not the normal common law attitude, however. Taking the rental agreement as a ready example, in common law its basic characteristics are considered to be as much determined by the type of relationship — be they between professionals amongst themselves as in the renting of office and manufacturing space, between professionals and consumers or smaller companies, as in the renting of apartments and small offices, between local authorities and citizens, as in the renting of council flats, between companies and shareholders, as in the renting of group facilities, and between parents and children in the renting of housing bought for children — as by the nature of the rental itself in terms of a temporary transfer of user rights in tangible assets. And this attitude seems to be quite naturally also extended into the elaboration of the more general contract law concepts, as in the question when a contract is concluded, what kind of defenses may be used, and what kind of excuses are available, again more so, it would seem, than in civil law, even in its modern, good faith imbued, variety.

Accepting the vital impact of the nature of the relationship between the parties on their contractual rights and duties in this manner and following the discussion in the previous chapter, the emphasis in this chapter will mainly be on contracts in the *professional* sphere, therefore on contracts between professionals especially in international commerce and finance. They are entities of some size, making it their business to engage in commercial or or financial dealings amongst themselves. Smaller companies may form here an uneasy intermediary class which sometimes requires a treatment more akin to that of consumers but in other aspects they must be treated as professionals.

The general concepts of contract law will thus be considered particularly from the point of view of professional dealings. It may give rise to lesser refinement, and on occasion even to some rougher forms of justice. In countries like France, which still have commercial courts, it may also find expression in court proceedings. As for the types of contracts, two types will be analysed in particular towards the end of this chapter. They are the *sale of (movable) goods* and contractual forms of *agency (mandate)*. They will be considered as typical illustrations of relationship thinking where different rules prevail between professionals.

---

[2] See J Gordley, *The Philosophical Origins of Modern Contract Doctrine* (1991), 102 for the development towards different contract types in the natural law school of Grotius, see also *De Iure Belli ac Pacis*, Libri II, Cap. II, xii, 1–7, and subsequently in civil law. The contract types indentified in that school were partly based on Roman law distinctions and partly on Aristotelian notions of fairness supplementing the contractual terms and defining the parties' rights and duties. This approach was subsequently abandoned with the development of overriding notion of the parties' will and their autonomy in contract: see von Savigny, 3 *System des heutigen römischen Rechts*, III (1840), leading to different contractual types in the German Pandectist School of the 19th century, which, however, also borrowed from the French Code Civil of 1804 and from the earlier contractual distinctions of Domat and Pothier on which the French Civil Code was built and which had often been based on Roman law as developed by the earlier medieval writers in the *ius commune* and by the writers in the natural law school.

As far as the sale of goods is concerned, attention will in this connection be focussed on the international sale, which has always been a sale between professionals and is or should be structured accordingly, ie different from consumer sales, which are sales between professionals and consumers (or small companies) or between consumers amongst themselves. These consumer sales may of course also be international but are not commonly considered covered by a reference to international sales in this narrower professional sense. As far as contractual agency is concerned, especially in the financial services area, the distinction between wholesale and retail investors using agents or brokers has also become of overriding importance.

The significance of distinguishing not only in commerce but also in finance between professional dealings and dealings with consumers or other non-professional parties in this manner is in modern times further highlighted by the fact that professional contracts lend themselves increasingly to support by international or transnational legal principles and practices leading to the application of transnational law, often also referred to as the modern law merchant or *lex mercatoria*. In the previous chapter it was explained that this is a natural consequence of the globalisation of the market place and the cross-border nature of much international commercial and financial business which is normally conducted through professionals and is losing its typical domestic connections, also in law. For the independent legal order that is here created, the cultural and sociological forces that back it up, and the law that emerges in it, reference may also be made to the discussion in chapter 1, section 1.4.

In the international sale of goods, some uniform international sales law for professional dealings was already created through the 1980 Vienna Convention after an earlier attempt in the Hague Conventions of 1964. It provides only a very partial coverage of the subject matter. In other areas, uniform treaty law has remained even more incidental.[3] As we saw in the previous chapter, an informal but broader creation of trans-national law is now becoming apparent in the international professional sphere and is no longer centered around this uniform treaty law. On the other hand, it is not yet one coherent pattern of rules but rather a hierarchy of norms, in which, besides fundamental legal principle, the terms of the contract itself, custom or established practices, uniform treaty law, and general principle, even national law may still figure, although only residually, see chapter 1, sections 1.5 and 3.1.

Domestic laws may remain more particularly relevant for all non-professional dealings, therefore especially for dealings with consumers and employees, but also with smaller licensees, franchisees and distributors, even though within the EU there has been some harmonisation of the law in some of these areas.[4] Except on cross-border credit transfers

---

[3] See chapter 1, s 1.5.3.

[4] See Council Dir 76/207/EEC of 9 Feb 1976 [1976] OJ L39, on the implementation of the principle of equal treatment for men and women as regards access to employment, vocational training and promotion, and working condition; Council Dir 85/374/EEC of 25 July 1985 [1985] OJ L210, on the approximation of the laws of the Member States concerning liability for defective products; Council Dir 85/577/EEC of 20 Dec 1985 [1985] OJ L372, to protect the consumer in respect of contracts negotiated away from business premises; Council Dir 86/653/EEC of 18 Dec 1986 [1986] OJ L382, on the co-ordination of the Member States relating to self-employed commercial agents; Council Dir 87/102/EEC of 22 Dec 1986 [1987] OJ L42 later amended, for the approximation of the laws, regulations and administrative provisions of the Member States concerning consumer credit; Council Dir 90/314/EEC of 13 June 1990 [1990] OJ L158, on package travel, package holidays and package tours; Council Reg 295/91 of 4 Feb 1991 [1991] OJ L36/5, establishing common rules for a denied-boarding compensation system in scheduled air transport; Council Dir 93/13/EEC of 5 Apr 1993 [1993] OJ L95/29, on unfair terms in consumer contracts; Directive 97/9/EC of the European Parliament and the Council of 20 May 1997 [1997] OJ L144/19, on the protection of purchasers in respect of certain aspects of contracts relating to the purchase on a time share basis; Directive 97/5EC of the European Parliament and of the Council of 27 Jan 1997 [1997] OJ L43/25, on cross-border credit transfers; Directive 97/7/EC of the European

and in respect of distance selling of financial products to small investors, and in the liability of aircraft carriers for damage in the case of accidents, most of this effort on behalf of consumers, and to a lesser extent of workers, does not bear on cross-border activities and should arguably be left to local law, if only as a matter of subsidiarity. Long distance selling of consumer goods and the long distance marketing of consumer financial services are, however, appropriate EU concerns and may in fact benefit from harmonisation of the applicable laws.[5] Another important area where local laws remain dominant is in real estate dealings, even between professionals.

In this chapter, contract law will first be dealt with in a historical and comparative law context. Thereafter the more general concepts will be discussed before we move to the law of international sales and forms of contractual agency amongst professionals. As far as domestic contract law goes, it has been the subject of much comprehensive statutory intervention, on the European continent as part of national codifications, but in respect of the sale of movable property (goods) even in common law countries, like in England, where there is the Sale of Goods Act of 1979 (replacing a very similar earlier statute of 1893), also in force in Scotland. In the USA there are the *Restatements of Contract* and Article 2 of the Uniform Commercial Code (UCC) concerning the sale of goods, first prepared in 1951, with new texts in 1958 and 1962 and several later amendments.[6] It was introduced in all American states after 1964, albeit with some variations. As for agency, in civil law, domestic laws often remain rudimentary, especially in the case of indirect or undisclosed agency. That is different in common law. In the USA, there is in this connection the important *Restatement Second of Agency.*

Much of the discussion below will be based on an analysis of these domestic texts but attention will subsequently also be given to the uniform laws, for the professional sale of goods in particular to the 1980 Uncitral Vienna Convention on the Contracts for the International Sale of Goods (CISG) already mentioned, and for the more general part of contract law also to the 1995 Unidroit Principles for International Commercial Contracts and to the Principles of European Contract Law also first published in 1995 and substantially completed in 1998 although new chapters on special types of dealings are still added. Thus the latter also include a part on agency, in which connection the Unidroit Convention on Agency in the International Sale of Goods of 1983 (never sufficiently ratified) may provide some guidance as well.

Parliament and of the Council of 20 May 1997 [1997] OJ L144/19, on the protection of consumers in respect of distance contracts; Council Reg of 9 Oct 1997 [1997] OJ L285/1, on air carrier liability in the case of accidents; Directive 98/27/EC of the European Parliament and of the Council on injunctions for the protection of consumers' interests.

See further also the proposals for a Directive on the sale of consumer goods and associated guarantees [1995] OJ L307/8. In Oct 1998 a proposal (COM(1998)468 final) was also tabled for a Directive of the European Parliament and of the Council concerning the distance marketing of consumer financial services, amending Council Dir 90/619/EEC and Dirs 97/7/EC and 98/27/EC, see also the Green Paper: Financial Services—Meeting Consumers' Expectations, COM(96)209 final of 22 May 1996, and the Commission communication: *Financial Services — Enhancing Consumer Confidence*, COM(97)309 final of 26 June 1997. It raises the question of the interface between financial regulation and supervision and the contractual protection of long distance recipients of financial services. It concerns here conduct of business and product control.

A Proposal for a European Parliament and Council Directive combating late payment in commercial transactions was published in 1998 [1998] OJ C168/13. They often have transborder aspects. In fact when transborder they are likely to be all the more delayed. This proposal is of special interest because it contains a provision for the recognition of the reservation of title in other Member States (Article 4).

[5] See also chapter 6, s 3.4.8.
[6] See for the origin of the UCC, chapter 1, n 14.

1.1.2 Modern Contract Theory

The emphasis on the nature of (the relationship between) the parties and on the extra-contractual rights and duties that may derive from this relationship, all the more so in situations of dependency, is an important issue even if amongst professionals there may be a lesser concern for these extra-contractual considerations and a lesser acceptance of the consequent effect on party autonomy. Even then, more objective interpretation methods and the notion of reasonableness or the reasonable man standard may come in now that the psychological nature of eg consent is receding as in major contracts it is often unclear who was involved at the personal level.

A related aspect is the credit that must be given to the raising of expectations and any detrimental reliance on them by others. Often the way one party chooses to organise itself may give rise to expectations. It poses the question when such reliance becomes justified and binds the other. This will often depend on the circumstances. Thus the buying of a ticket on the bus and the purchase of groceries in a supermarket can often best be explained by reliance on the organisation that the seller of these service or the goods has put in place and the choice and selection power that is in this manner given to the buyer rather than in terms of offer and acceptance or of bargain and consensus. The way the seller has organised himself in these situations does not, eg, allow the ticket seller or cash attendant discretion in refusing resp. the travel service or the taking away of the groceries if the correct price is offered unless there are special reasons which the ticket seller or cash attendant would then have the burden of explaining.

Yet another aspect of modern contract law is the importance of the contractual purpose in determining the contract's effect, again quite regardless of what the original intent of the parties may or may not have been.

It is undeniable that these more objective considerations have started to play an ever greater role in modern contract law. The central importance of the notion of the parties' bargain or intent is consequently reduced when the contractual rights and duties are being determined. This became more obvious first in respect of weaker parties like workers and consumers who needed some more objective protections, but this current now operates perhaps more generally in the entire law of contract. It is indeed possible to detect here a trend and to move even further and put emphasis altogether on justified reliance, duties of care and co-operation, of disclosure, investigation and loyalty, and on the contractual purpose and consider them the basis or *essence* of modern contractual rights and obligations, only the details of which would then depend on the more special objectives the parties mean to achieve. In this approach, culpable breach of such expectations and duties would be the prime ground for actions for damages. It is clear that such actions are then more closely related to tort than to contract. Yet it remains important to distinguish here according to type of party and professionals may well have meant to be more litterally bound by the terms of their contract.

It is also useful to distinguish here further according to the contractual phase as these more objective considerations may play different roles at different contractual stages. Thus in the pre-contractual phase, there may be special disclosure duties. During the performance, there may be special co-operation duties and duties of care in that context. In what is sometimes called the post contractual phase, there may be re-negotiation duties. Again, these considerations may play out differently between professional parties.

Negatively, it can at least be said that modern contract theory tends to reject any single contract view or model or any single-value theory of contract, like mere offer and acceptance or consensus notions or the notion of party autonomy. Instead, it tends to accept multiple views, different contract models and values (that could even conflict) depending on the nature of the relationship and the type of their business. Thus professionals may rely more on party autonomy and consumers on more objective law protections against overbearing counter-parties. In the sale of a single physical asset like a bike, there may still be a clear personal offer and acceptance element plus traditional delivery against payment. But this model provides little elucidation in major long term construction or infrastructure contracts that know many parties and teams that do not speak with one voice and that are often barely aware of each other.

Particularly in such cases, modern contract theory may even reject the notion that a contract is promise based. At least traditional notions of offer and acceptance will play a more minor role. Also the idea of consensus might not then be what it once was. However, some initiative of a party must still set the contract in motion, even if it means no more than that the seller sets out his stall and the buyer approaches it and takes what is wanted. Modern contract theory accommodates that. In the main, it also continues to attempt to support the objectives of the parties, especially of professionals amongst themselves. On the whole it does not seek to introduce for them an own concept of behaviour, efficiency or value. Nor is modern contract necessarily based on pure rationality. Yet it does not take a psychological attitude either but assumes that the contract at least must make some sense and will in this connection take into account what is normal, including how people normally react and life's experiences. Whilst doing so, formalism is increasingly rejected. Even a written text is put in context and all legal reasoning concerning contract (interpretation and supplementation or even derogation) becomes substantive and normative in a legal sense.[7]

Purely professional dealings would thus continue to suggest an essential role for party autonomy. On the other hand, they highlight the shift from personal to institutional dealings. In this context, the traditional concepts of offer and acceptance and of agreement or consensus, which are all derived from situations in which individuals deal with each other, suffers a further blow and are increasingly replaced by agreements which are unlikely to have been negotiated by any individual in particular. It follows that signatories may have little or no knowledge of the content of these contracts, which may have been discussed by different departments per subject whilst outside lawyers may have had responsibility for the final text. Even in personalised consumer dealings, the traditional model (of offer and acceptance, exchange of promises etc) is increasingly strained as may be clear from the examples already given above in connection with buying goods in a supermarket or a ticket on a bus or when consumers submit to standard texts or pre-printed general conditions.

It follows that even in professional dealing, party autonomy unavoidably acquires a more abstract and objective meaning. Thus what was once cast in terms of the will of the parties and their intent, is now fashioned rather in terms of reasonable expectations in a more objective sense in which the whole set-up or organisation of the parties must be considered as much as the negotiation process itself. The important point to make here is, however, that the move towards objectivity in both professional and consumer dealings is of a different nature and has a different cause. But what is the same for both is that the emphasis on the nature of the parties and in that context on either professional autonomy or on consumer protection and the emergence of more objective rights and duties in that context for either group, leads in both cases to a more objective or *normative* interpretation of the rights and duties of the parties under a contractual framework.

Thus parties whilst entering or meaning to enter into a contractual relationship (like any other) enter at the same time into a situation which they no longer fully control. They are likely to face extra contractual duties especially in situations in which there is some

---

[7] *Cf* also MA Eisenberg, "The Emergence of Dynamic Contract Law", 88 *Cal LR* (2000), 1743, 1747.

dependency. In such situations their interests may shift to setting at least some standards of behaviour with which they both can live. This is the approach foreshadowed in Section 1–302(b)(1–102 old) UCC and it is a modern one.

The term 'normative' is here used *not* as referring to an ideal type or to ethical aspirations *per se*, as it usually is in the positivist tradition, but rather as referring to legally or objectively binding considerations or correctives which may have an extra-legal origin in moral, social, cultural or economic requirements. Normative or objective interpretation in this sense then also concerns the determination of the time as of which a contract comes into being or, perhaps better, as of which rights and duties are starting to emerge. It is more than merely purposive or teleological interpretation which looks for the purpose of the agreement in terms of its interpretation (although also important in this context). The normative interpretation suggests that under broader modern legal standards, there are likely to be different contractual phases in which not all contemplated rights and duties may as yet have acquired full legal status whilst, on the other hand, extraneous rights and duties, like those connected with disclosure, may start to impinge. It should be accepted in this connection that these broader legal standards may themselves conflict and need then be balanced in which again the contractual objective may only be one of the considerations.

The normative interpretation technique is as of necessity de-personalised in professional dealings and indeed relies more on notions of reasonable expectation and on the implementation and integration of what may be seen as extra-contractual duties. In countries like Germany, Austria, Switzerland and the Netherlands, the normative interpretation technique is now closely associated with the good faith concept in the interpretation and supplementation of contracts. In its extreme form, it may even lead to contractual adjustments on the basis of what may be considered fair and reasonable in objective terms or what may be required in a social sense or is morally accepted in an advanced society. In Germany in particular, that has long played a role also in the case of profound changes of circumstances as we shall see. Whether this is suitable in professional dealings is another matter which will be discussed further below. Whatever the view, it is again more than a purposive or teleological approach of interpretation which is tied to the manifested contractual purpose, even if it leads into the same direction.

This de-personification of contract law and the consequential downgrading of the traditional contract notions in terms of bargain and intent, conforms the already noted important development in which the nature of the relationship between the parties, the way they operate and the type of their deal become central elements. It must be accepted that parties who entered into a contractual relationship (as any other) thereby also accept extra-consensual duties although they may still be able to set standards in respect of them to the extent that they can foresee these duties emerging. They may thus face external ethical, social and efficiency standards in the implementation of their deal. It limits but needs not harm the notion of party autonomy even if it must be considered in more objective terms. The parties will retain the initiative and, in this approach, there may on the whole be less reason for judicial adjustment of contractual terms amongst professionals, although, as we saw, in civil law there is still a lesser inclination to take the nature of the parties and professionality into account, also in this connection. The result is that there is a danger particularly in civil law that notions of protection developed for consumers will also intrude on professional relationships.

In common law, the normative interpretation technique in the above sense is less well developed, at least in England, but it would be incorrect to say that it does not exist[8] and it

---

[8] See Lord Hoffmann in *ICS Ltd v West Bromwich BS*, 1 WLR, 896, 912 (1998) referring to the 'reasonable man approach', but also in *BCCI v Ali*, 2 WLR 735, 749 restating the principle of literal interpretation on the basis of a narrow view of the parties' intent, at least as a starting point.

is strong in the US,[9] see also chapter 1, sections 1.2.12, 1.2.13 and 1.3.2. Even if a more literal contractual interpretation technique is still favoured at least in England (following a similar attitude to statutory interpretation) and references to good faith are on the whole avoided, there is, as we saw, a much greater awareness of the impact of the nature of the relationship of the parties than in civil law. There is also traditional sensitivity for dependency considerations, as we also saw, even if in modern English law consumer protection is usually defined by statute. There is also acceptance of reliance notions in contract as we shall see. It is in the area of contract formation especially relevant if the reliance was detrimental. There is further a considerable reliance on implied terms, which are on the whole also objectively construed. Together, these newer concepts approximate the notion of good faith in civil law.

In this environment, the old terminology of contract law is becoming less and less satisfactory, both in civil and in common law. Perhaps the established contract model is out of date. In civil law, it centres on offer and acceptance within the notion of consensus as a shared contractual intent. It unavoidably suggests psychological overtones. To balance these, notions of *causa* were added from an early date and put emphasis on rationality and propriety, a role now often taken over by good faith. In common law, it was offer and acceptance in the context of an exchange of compatible declarations which must each have been seriously intended, but did not need to lead to a shared intent. It is therefore a more formal concept. As long as there was a bargain element and proper consideration (that is some *quid pro quo*), the contract was valid regardless of any consensus or even intent.

In this approach, there was also a formalised determination of the time as of which the contract was entered into and there remains less room for the different phases of the modern contract. As already mentioned, interpretation tended to be more literal, at least in England, supported by the parole evidence rule which would not allow earlier drafts and discussions to be taken into account in the interpretation of a contractual text either. Of course, if there was no such text, the situation would be different and the date and content of the contract would have to be determined by other means.

In the meantime it may indeed be asked whether the entire concept of offer and acceptance, developed relatively late in civil as well as in common law as we shall see, is still of great use in modern contract law. It is clear that consensus itself is becoming a more objective concept in civil law and the notion of bargain and consideration atavistic in common law. It is not difficult to demonstrate that in truth we have started to think in entirely different terms. These trends are important and here only summarised. They will be discussed in some greater detail below and where possible traced through comparative law.

1.1.3 The Challenge of E-Commerce

In the meantime E-commerce has become a fashionable subject, but it does not in itself present great new insights into the operation of contract law. In essence it merely adds a different layer of communication besides personal eye to eye contact, contact through the mail, by telephone, or by fax. It should not create truly new complications (eg as to when the contract is concluded, under which law, and with what kind of consumer protection), except where habitually documentation is required. The question is then whether an e-mail exchange complies with such a requirement as an exchange of faxes may now do. In common law terms, it becomes a statute of fraud matter. As we shall see, under it, even

[9] *Cf* also MA Eisenberg, *op cit* n 7 *supra*, 1747.

sales contracts for small values may still require a document. The more formal issue then is: what is a document in that sense?

Even in civil law, which tends to be more informal in this aspect (if parties so wish), sometimes a document remains required as eg in the case of gifts or in some countries for assignments of rights (receivables). That also raises the issue whether an e-mail or internet communication might be sufficient. There is the obvious related problem whether, when the law or parties require a document, an e-mail signature is sufficient. In this sense one must also ask whether an e-mail offer or acceptance or other instruction (like a payment instruction to a bank) may be considered to be sufficiently authentic to be recognised as legally valid. To aid and protect these communications, personal keys systems will of course help but all the same there remains the issue of what e-mail communications legally mean.

In e-commerce, types and recognition of signatures are therefore an important issue generally, more so where a document is required or used. The status of documents may all the more be an issue where they are considered negotiable instruments (like bills of exchange or cheques) or documents of title (like bills of lading). This will be discussed in chapter 4, section 2.3. In short, this negotiability is unlikely to attach to electronic imitations as the physical element remains the essence of these documents or instruments. In the capital markets, (electronic) book-entry systems often based on a centralised custody system of the underlying investment securities proved the answer. These underlying securities do not now much exist so that pure electronic trading has resulted. This development will be discussed also in chapter 4, section 3.1.4.

The subject of E-commerce may be broadened to include more generally the negotiation, confirmation and performance of commercial transactions by electronic means and then covers both the formation and implementation of the contractual relationship. The EU and international agencies like Uncitral have concerned themselves with these matters also. In the EU, the E-commerce Directive is a case in point. It is concerned with formalities. For the validation of electronic signatures there is another Directive.[10] The E-commerce Directive puts emphasis instead on the *free movement of the information society* between the Member States and the related services (rather than defining e-commerce itself). It concerns the legitimacy of all contracts concluded by electronic means. In this connection, e-mail and internet trading is considered synonymous.

In trans-border transactions problems may arise with the applicable law, with regulation and regulated industries (like financial services), and with protections of certain groups like consumers and workers. It may not require special rules. As to the applicable (contract) law, normally the law of the party that performs the most characteristic obligation will apply (Article 4.2 1980 EU Rome Convention on the Law Applicable to Contractual Obligations). Any regulation of the service provider will be determined by his domestic regime (as the service is in that respect normally located at his place, see the country of origin approach in Article 3 E-Commerce Directive), whilst consumers and workers may always invoke the protection of their own laws (Article 5(2) and 6(1) Rome Convention). The E-Commerce Directive does not mean to change the rules of private international law. There are no special consumer protection rules, nor would there appear a need.

Rather, the EU meant to eliminate legal uncertainties that may exist with regard to the extent to which Member States may control services originating from other Member State

---

[10] *Directive on Certain Legal Aspects of Electronic Commerce in the Internal Market*, 2000/13/EC, OJ L 178 (2000). Earlier, the EU passed a *Directive on a Community Framework for Electronic Signatures*, OJL 013 (2000). The WTO issued a *Declaration on Global Electronic Commerce* on May 20 1998. The OECD Council issued a *Recommendation Concerning Guidelines for Consumer Protection in the Electronic Commerce* in 1999. Uncitral concluded a *Model Law on Electronic Commerce* in 1996.

through the co-ordination of national laws and the clarification of a number of legal concepts. The idea was to make electronic contracts workable in all Member States. In this connection, the E-commerce Directive concentrates on five aspects of commercial dealing: (a) the conditions of establishment of the service provider (country of origin), (b) the requirements imposed on commercial communications, (c) the acceptance of electronic contracts and the way orders are placed, (d) the liability of intermediaries, and (e) the online enforcement mechanisms.

1.2 Formation and Interpretation or Construction of Contracts in Civil and Common Law

1.2.1 *The Role of Parties' Intent in Civil Law. The Normative or Teleological Interpretation Method. The Common Law Approach Compared*

Roman law did not have a general law of contract based on consent of the parties, although there was a class of contracts based on mere consensus (*obligationes consensu contractae*), of which the sale and the rental agreement were the most important. It was generally possible for two parties to commit themselves to each other, but if the result was not one of the contracts recognised by law (*ius civile*), there was only a moral commitment or *pactum nudum* which could not be enforced, although for some of them the *praetor* later gave an action.

The recognised contracts and some variations or extensions thereof are referred to in the Digests (D.2.14.7) which form part of the great Codification of the Roman Emperor Justinian in the sixth century AD in Byzantium (see chapter 1, section 1.2.3), but there was no rational system. Only the *Ius Commune*, which was the law developed on the West European Continent on the basis of this Roman law until the time of the European Codifications towards the nineteenth century,[11] managed to create a more coherent system based on the parties' intent and their consent. It was joined by the notion of *causa* insisting on the rationality and meaningfulness of the contract rather its form and formalities, as will be further discussed below.[12] This happened under the influence of commercial need (through the law merchant or *lex mercatoria* of those times) and ethical considerations (embodied in the church or Canon law).[13]

Especially in commerce, there was a growing need for parties to consider each others' promises binding and this could not remain limited — as in Roman law — to sales and rentals. Thus commercial need and Canon law combined to accommodate the imperative, both practical as well as moral, to keep promises and to support the binding force of all informal *commercial* contracts. On the West European Continent this was already achieved in the fourteenth century, at the time of the greatest jurists of those times, Bartolus and Baldus.[14] Roman law was reinterpreted to support this development which was later extended to *all* informal agreements, a development completed by the seventeenth century with the aid of local law.[15]

---

[11] See chapter 1, s 1.2.4.
[12] See s 1.2.6 *infra*.
[13] *Decretales* of Pope Gregory IX of 1234 in the *Liber Extra* added to the *Corpus Iuris Canonici*, Lib I, Tit XXXV, Cap I.
[14] Bartolus, *Commentaria* D.17.1.48.1; Baldus, *Commentaria in Decretales*, I *De Pactis*, Cap I, n 11. See for the development of the *ius commune* in Europe at that time, chapter 1, s 1.2.3.
[15] Seen as early as 1283 in the *Coutumes de Beauvais*, Cap 34, Articles 998*ff*: see further A Loysel, *Institutes coutumieres*, (Paris 3rd edn), 1611, no 342, who summed up the by then (17th century) completed development as

The natural law school of Grotius and Pufendorf[16] completed the theoretical structure of the law of contract based on consensus as we know it today in civil law.[17] It resulted in the general applicability of the famous maxim *pacta sunt servanda*, itself derived from the Canon law heading of the relevant chapter in the *Decretales* of Pope Gregory IX of 1234 which had been at the beginning of this development ('*Pacta quantumque nuda servanda sunt*'). Through the seventeenth century works of the French jurist Domat,[18] the consensus notion entered the French Codes after the other great French jurist, Pothier, had formulated the notion of offer and acceptance in that context in the eighteenth century,[19] although it must be said that the requirement of acceptance remained less clear when there was only one party committing itself.

French law still reflects this in Article 1108 of the *Code civile* (Cc) which only requires the party that gives an undertaking to consent. So does Section 516 of the BGB for gifts in Germany. More modern Codes, like the Dutch of 1992, always require acceptance in some form (Article 6.217(1) Cc). So do the Unidroit Principles (Articles 2.5 and 2.6), the European Principles in Article 2.206 being less clear. Under these modern rules, silence is not enough but acceptance may be by conduct. The idea seems to be that nobody should be bound or derive benefits against its will.

It does not solve the question of how far and for how long an offer remains open and as such binding. Civil law is divided on this issue to this day. German and Dutch law maintain that any offer remains open for a reasonable time and may during that time not be withdrawn by the offeror at will unless the offer itself allows for it. French law had no such rule but French case law increasingly accepts it: the offeror may withdraw but if he sets a certain period for acceptance or if a reasonable period for acceptance may be inferred from the circumstances and the offer is withdrawn within that period, the offeror may be liable to the offeree if he had wanted to accept and suffered damage as a result of the withdrawal.[20] In France, this liability may be based on tort rather than on contract.[21] In common law, which as we shall see does not adhere to the consensus idea of contract but rather to the notion of bargain or consideration in the sense of an exchange of formal unilateral promises, the offer itself remains non-binding, although statutory law in the USA now makes an exception for merchants if they spell this out in writing.[22] Importantly, detrimental reliance may also make a difference.

Another issue is the time of the acceptance. In civil law, it is normally considered the moment when the acceptance is received by the offeror.[23] Reliance on an offer may, however,

follows: '*on lie les boeufs par les cornes et les hommes par les paroles*' ['one ties cows together by their horns and people by their words']. See also R Feenstra and M Ashmann, *Contract, Aspecten van contractsvrijheid in historisch perspectief* [Contract, Aspects of the notion of contract and party autonomy in historical perspective] (1980), 1, 33.

[16] See chapter 1, s 1.2.6.
[17] See Grotius, *De Iure Belli ac Pacis*, Lib II, Cap XI, iv.1 (although emphasising the mutuality of promises rather than the consensus or even the process of offer and acceptance but *cf* also Cap XI, xiv and clearer in his *Inleidinge* or *Jurisprudence of Holland* (translation, Robert Warden Lee 1953) III.10, where he noted that by contract we mean a voluntary act whereby the one part promises something to the other with the intention that the other party should accept it and thereby acquires a right against the first party, *cf.* also Pufendorf, *De Iure Naturae et Gentium* 1674, Lib III, Cap IV, Sec 2. 7. But the idea that a promise is merely conditional until acceptance developed later and only in the 19th century was this development completed and were offer and acceptance made the key elements in the formation of contracts.
[18] *Les Lois Civiles dans leur Ordre Naturel, Livre I Introduction* (ed Paris, 1777).
[19] *Traité des Obligations*, no 4. The question of acceptance had already been raised by Bartolus, however, in connection with the use of agents: *Commentaria* D.15.4.1.2.
[20] See Cour de Cass, Civ, 10 May 1972 [1972] Bull.civ.III, 214.
[21] Ghestin, *Traité de Droit Civil, Les Obligations, Le Contrat: Formation* (2nd edn, 1988), 229*ff.*
[22] See Section 2–205 UCC for the sale of goods.
[23] See Section 130 BGB.

bring the moment forward. In common law, it is normally the moment the offeree dispatches the acceptance,[24] the postman being here considered the agent of the offeror. Detrimental reliance may sometimes move the date. The 1980 Vienna Convention on the International sale of Goods requires in Article 18(2), on the other hand, receipt by the offeror for the acceptance to become effective. That is also the approach of the Unidroit and European Principles of Contract Law. In all this it must be remembered that the offer and acceptance would only concern the major contractual conditions which must be more specifically agreed; all minor terms need not to be settled for the contract to be effective.

In both common and civil law, the principle of *formal* offer and acceptance still underlie the formation and validity of the ensuing contract and its performance, although the reliance notion or offer and acceptance through conduct is substantially developed in civil law and sometimes also used in common law, as we shall see. It may thus well be doubted whether the official offer and acceptance model remains realistic. At least in day-to-day life, contracts are entered into much more informally. In any event, in the context of performance, the determination of the rights and duties of the parties under the contract becomes the prime issue. This is principally a matter of *interpretation*, in which the offer and acceptance or conduct is only considered to the extent relevant in the circumstances of the case. It is now common to distinguish in this connection between a precontractual, contractual and post contractual phase of contract in all of which special rights and duties may more objectively emerge.

Roman law and the *Ius Commune* did not develop a coherent approach to interpretation, but the *Ius Commune* in the course of time abandoned the literal construction of the wording of the contract in favour of a more flexible interpretation, but still in a rather psychological or subjective manner with a bias towards a literal attitude to the wording of the agreement if expressed in writing.

The search for a more objective or normative interpretation of the parties' intent on the basis of practicability, reliance, reasonableness or even notions of fairness (which could adjust the parties' intent in extreme cases), or on the basis of profound moral, social and economic considerations, thus remained incomplete, even in the natural law school of Grotius and Pufendorf, which, however, started to focus on the role of the *'aequitas'* in this connection.[25] The interpretation of the parties' intent in the objective manner is more recent and, it was submitted, largely connected with the development of professional or inter-company rather than personal dealings, which stretched the psychological approach to interpretation, and with the greater impact of such arrangements on their surroundings or environment.[26] Hence more objective notions of reliance, mutual dependency, justified expectations etc. In labour and consumer dealings the normative interpretation technique acquired yet another impulse: the protection of weaker parties.

---

[24] Ever since *Adams v Lindsell*, 106 ER 250 (1918).

[25] See the text at n 2 *supra* and ss 1.2.1–2 *infra* for the supplementation of the parties' rights and duties by notions of fairness and also R Zimmermann, *The Law of Obligations* (Deventer, Boston, 1992) 548, 621*ff.* and 807.

[26] Since von Savigny, 3 *System des heutigen römischen Rechts* (1840), the role of the parties in the formation of their contract in Germany became connected with the doctrine of the juristic act or *Rechtsgeschäft* which covers all *voluntary* acts of individuals meant to create legal effects for them, thus also offers and acceptances, but no less eg the transfer of personal property and the writing of wills. All these juristic acts were made subject to similar techniques of interpretation in which the will was the central point, at first leading to a subjective interpretation of any declarations (*Willenserklärung*) made in the context of such acts. Modern civil law has made much of this concept as a more general legal category (itself again a sub-category of all legal acts, which are all acts with legal effect, whether voluntary or involuntary, or in German *Rechtshandlungen*) but this categorisation has proved of modest use, and has as such rightly been criticised: see K Zweigert & H Koetz, *An Introduction to Comparative Law* (2nd edn, 1987), 351 and (3rd edn, 1998), 146, and will not be further pursued here. As contracting always was the main example of a *Rechtsgeschäft*, it will be discussed as such and not as part of a bigger idea. The subjective interpretation technique was subsequently tempered first by a more literal interpretation based on declarations and later by a more normative approach to interpretation of the contractual rights and obligations of the parties.

All contracts need interpretation,[27] whether they are informally or formally expressed. The subject was itself already discussed more broadly in connection with statutes, see chapter 1, section 1.3.2. This is obvious in the case of informal agreements when there is no writing and there may be no more than inferences based on conduct, but even if there are declarations or there is a text, it may be said that words are by themselves not always clear and in any event derive their true meaning only from their context and, in the case of contracts, also from the environment in which a written contract is meant to operate. A complicating factor in this connection is that this context and environment are not always precisely determined and may easily change.

Nevertheless, contractual interpretation in this sense is often still seen as a search for the intent of the parties or otherwise for what they said. In the German academic tradition, the *will* of the parties is here contrasted with their *declaration(s)*; hence the *psychological* versus the *literal* interpretation of the contract, sometimes also referred to as the *subjective* versus the *objective* interpretation methods. Yet as the focus of interpretation, neither 'will' nor 'declaration' proved satisfactory.

In fact, they could often hardly be distinguished. In the subjective method, the wording of express agreements still had to be the starting point for interpretation whilst in cases of doubt or incompleteness, even in the literal interpretation method, there would still be a search for the parties' intent. Traditional common law shows this clearly: declarations are greatly important and often taken literally as we shall see, but in the case of doubt, ambiguity or contradiction or when there are gaps in the contract, the supposed intent or implied terms must often come to the rescue. It suggests an instant shift from the one extreme of the objective approach to the other extreme of the subjective approach.

In civil law there is here another important point to be made. The will or intent of the parties is not considered individually, but rather seen in the context of their consensus. This introduces itself a common or shared platform between the parties and some greater objectivity in the interpretation of their contract. Of great importance in this connection has been the evolution in civil law of the *teleological* and *normative* interpretation method. They were already discussed in connection with statutory interpretation in chapter 1, section 1.3.2 and in section 1.1.2 above in connection with modern contract theories.[28] In contract, it is still largely built on the notion of consensus in which, however, in civil law, the individual desires and aims of the parties are considered submerged to become detached *both* from their personal intent and their declarations. It leaves room, not for what was intended or declared by the one party, but rather for what the other party *reasonably could or should have understood*. This may then become a matter of reasonable reliance.

The teleological and normative interpretation techniques put intent and declaration in their context and also consider the circumstances in the sense of what is normal, practical, usual, makes sense, was justifiably or reasonably relied on (in terms of declarations, wording or conduct) and, sometimes (particularly in more extreme cases of contractual imbalance or hardship) goes further and depends on of what is basically fair and what the moral, social and economic setting of the contract requires.

Above, this was more broadly referred to as the normative approach. In a more abstract sense, it may also be said that these interpretation methods allow the norm to be tailored to the facts or allow for a selection of the facts that will relate them to the appropriate norm or that will result in the application of another norm or of an adjusted norm on the basis of what is in result more practical, normal or fair. The drawback is that it introduces

---

[27] So do statutes, the interpretation of which was discussed in chapter 1, ss 1.2.9 and 1.2.12.
[28] See chapter 1, ss 1.2.9 and 1.3.2.

a subjective element at the moment of judgment and relies therefore on the insight, experience, discipline and restraint of the judiciary.[29]

Although common law may often achieve a similar result by looking not only at the nature of the transaction but also at the nature of the relationship of the parties and any dependency or by implying contractual terms or by relying on custom or the ordinary course of business, whilst detrimental reliance has also become important, it continued, at least in England, with a more circumspect approach that may be partially connected with its failure early on to develop the consensus notion in contract. Although intent is now considered important also in traditional common law, it is mainly related to the *individual* promises of each party and their declarations and not directly to the contract itself or to a notion of consensus. The result is a less conceptual but sometimes also more practical approach to contract law.

In fact, it is in common law traditionally the exchange of formal declarations (or promises) which, *when sufficiently compatible*, form the basis of the contract within the common law notion of exchange, bargain or consideration, as we shall see, and there need strictly speaking not be a consensus or meeting of minds at all for a contract to be binding. It has led to a less comprehensive, often literal approach to interpretation (and a more incidental approach to remedies), in which even intent is not decisive whilst there is emphasis primarily on declarations.

It should be noted in this connection that both in civil and common law the term 'objective' is in the context of interpretation sometimes used in different ways: the literal interpretation of the declarations claims objectiveness. In the normative approach there is also objectiveness in the sense that psychological meaning of declarations is also no longer the aim whilst other more objective or reasonable considerations may be taken into account. The literal and normative approaches are here both contrasted with the psychological, subjective or 'will' approach. Both are in this sense objective but in very different ways.

In civil law, the *normative approach* to contract interpretation has achieved in essence *six* things:

(a)   it uses the consensus notion, abstracts it from the individual desires of the parties and will in that context not only consider declarations but also accept reliance on the actions or conduct of the other party if such is reasonable in the circumstances. It determines the resulting rights and duties and the moment as of which parties are bound accordingly.

(b)   it will at the same time put the contract in its context and look especially in the case of doubt or ambiguity at what the purpose was, what is practical and makes sense or is reasonable in the circumstances.

(c)   it may impose implementation duties, like duties of co-operation and loyalty, and will in extreme cases even correct or adjust the contract, also when the wording is clear and the intent not contested, especially when performance would lead to unconscionability or when there is a serious imbalance in the contract resulting from a difference in bargaining power or knowledge of the parties. Alternatively the notion of abuse of rights (*exceptio doli*) in asking strict performance may be used but amounts to the same thing. It may lead to the protection of weaker parties or even of professionals when a change of

---

[29] In s 1.1.2 *supra*, it was already explained that the term 'normative' is used here as legally normative or relevant, not in the sense of what is morally or otherwise desirable as is common in the positivist tradition. Extra-legal desiderata or objectives, like moral, cultural, sociological or economic objectives may thus enter into the law and be taken into account in its interpretation.

circumstances would create extreme hardship leading to re-negotiation duties in the post-contractual phase.

(d) in considering the broader environment in which the contract must operate, it may also consider the moral, social and economic context of the contract to avoid undesirable consequences, clearly in contracts with illicit purposes, in gaming contracts and contracts in restraint of trade. This may put added emphasis on the protection of the counter-party but sometimes even of third parties, for example when the contract is in restraint of trade, leads to market manipulation or has an adverse effect on the environment. It might be varied or abrogated (even punished) accordingly. When moral, social or economic considerations become sufficiently pressing in any particular situation they may also motivate more general relief or lead to relief on the basis of an abuse of rights by a counterparty insisting on strict performance.

(e) at the time of formation, in the pre-contractual phase, it may also impose information or disclosure duties and duties to (continue to) negotiate. Thus fundamental legal principles with their moral, social and economic imperatives may be considered, justifiable reliance may be honoured, disclosure and negotiating duties imposed, and abuse avoided.

(f) the normative approach to contract interpretation will in this connection also seek to take into account the nature of the professional or other relationship between the parties and any imbalance, their specific interest and the nature of their deal. This is an approach as yet less developed in civil law than in common law, as we saw. The consequence is that, whilst disclosure and negotiation duties may be imposed by law in the formation of the contract and a way may also be found to address extreme hardship caused by performance under changed circumstances in appropriate cases even leading to re-negotiation duties, the nature of the relationship of the parties will increasingly be taken into account to determine the effect on the parties' rights and duties in the circumstances. These newer concepts may therefore be less relevant in professional dealings which may also require a more litteral interpretation of the contractual terms.

Thus between professionals there are likely to be fewer disclosure and negotiation duties or reasons for contractual re-balancing or adjustment or re-negotiation duties, even in the case of hardship. The nature of the agreement may also be taken into account in this connection and a long-term construction agreement may sooner require re-negotiation and restructuring, a long-term sales agreement some adjustment of price. Capacity, negligent misrepresentation or mistake and minor irregularities may also be of lesser consequence between professionals, and that may be reflected in the normative or teleological approach to contract interpretation and the definition of the rights and duties of the parties.

In matters of interpretation or construction, common law remains more circumspect but will, as we already saw:

(a) firmly take into account the nature of the relationship of the parties rather than the specific type of contract of which it only developed special types in commercial law (the sale of goods the contract of carriage and the insurance contract),

(b) accept dependency as a source of extra rights and duties and sometimes also resort to reasonable reliance notions rather than continue to insist on an exchange of formal declarations and their compatibility in the consideration doctrine, and

(c) sometimes use implied conditions including those of reasonableness.

There is here some convergence with the modern, more normative or teleological approach of civil law. Weaker parties may thus be protected against contractual imbalances, but, particularly in England, it will not as willingly be accepted that the meaning of the declarations is ambiguous or that they are incomplete. Yet common law is on the whole practical, not inclined to a theoretical approach, although weary of pre-contractual disclosure and negotiation duties as such, particularly in the professional sphere, and certainly reluctant to adjust agreements, especially if clear on their face, except in relation to weaker parties like consumers, smaller companies and sometimes workers (statutory law has here also intervened) or (in the USA in the sale of goods) when there is unconscionability in the performance.

In practice, in these two areas of pre-contractual and post-contractual duties amongst professionals, one may find the greatest differences between the traditional common law and the modern civil law of contract. Another important difference is in the determination of the exact moment at which the contract arises. Lack of consideration plays a further differentiating role in a number of cases, notably in contractual amendments and releases and in the non-binding nature of offers, as we shall see. In some contracts, especially that of contractual agency, there are significant structural differences as well.

The evolution in the US needs increasingly to be considered separately from the traditional common law approach and shows great convergence with the more modern civil law attitude, even if it puts, in the traditional common law approach, greater emphasis on the nature of the relationship of the parties. It has fundamentally affected the limitations on enforceability derived from the consideration doctrine, sidelined the parole evidence rule, introduced past and present events as a factor in the interpretation of agreements, accepted limitations on expectancy damages, and started to introduce notions of good faith not only in the execution or performance phase but also (more timidly) in the negotiation phase.

1.2.2   The Civil Law Notion of Good Faith and its Modern Use in Interpretation

In the modern civil law of contract, use of the notion of *good faith* denotes the normative approach to interpretation, which is now also mostly followed in the interpretation of contract law statutes, see more in particular section 1.3 below.

Originally the notion of good faith found its fullest expression in Germany in Section 157 BGB which requires that contractual interpretation takes place on the basis of good faith with reference to normal commercial usage, see also Section 242 BGB. It appears here to ignore the more subjective approach to interpretation of all juristic acts of Section 133 BGB. New Dutch law in Article 3.35 CC states (for all juristic acts) that declarations of the other party may be accepted on their face if such is reasonable. Declarations may not then be negated by invoking lack of intent. Only for contracts does it add the references to good faith and custom in Article 6.248 CC.

It would be wrong to think, however, that there is complete unanimity between all civil law countries. The normative approach is most popular in Northern Europe, especially in Germany, the Netherlands, Switzerland and Austria but much less in Southern Europe, although French and Italian law is now moving in a similar direction. Especially pre-contractual duties and adjustment possibilities in extreme circumstances are more and more accepted everywhere in civil law, as we shall see.

The normative or good faith approach to contract concentrates on the definition of the rights and duties of the parties under the contract *in all its phases* and sees in its purest form a continuum between formation, binding force and performance of the contract and defines or (re)interprets the parties' rights and duties at each stage. Hence the pre-contractual disclosure and negotiation duties, the effect (in appropriate cases) of overriding legal principle in terms of moral, social and economic imperatives on the validity of the contract and the performance, the use of the abuse of rights notion in this context and sometimes the imposition of re-negotiation duties.

In this approach, the supplementation and, in extreme cases, adjustment of the contractual terms are also always matters of interpreting the true (legal) meaning of the contract in the sense of determining the rights and duties of the parties in the circumstances, given again their special position and interests as professional or other parties and the nature and manner of their commitments and structure of their deal. Thus there is no fundamental difference here between interpretation, supplementation and adjustment of the terms of the agreement. In its more outspoken form, in the normative, teleological or good faith approach, all is a matter of interpretation and determination of the true rights and obligations of the parties in the circumstances and the pre-contractual, formation, performance and post contractual phases of the contract are all considered integrated, although the rights and duties are likely to vary per phase.

As will be discussed more fully in section 1.3 below, the notion of good faith is often used better to relate the facts to the norm, that is in the selection and evaluation of the relevant facts and in the formulation of the relevant norm, and in that sense also has relevance outside the law of contract. Hence the emphasis on what is normal, practical and basically fair in the circumstances. This requires some judicial freedom, which is implied in all judicial activity. In contract where there is an emphasis on co-operation between the contracting parties, the notion of good faith is further used from the particular perspective of promoting that co-operation.

It is submitted that the modern normative, teleological or good faith approach also attempts to deal with the impact of large or standard contracts on their surroundings and caught the attention especially in that context. It here often concerns contracts used as *organisational tools* for large operators amongst themselves or for them to deal with a multitude of smaller parties through standard conditions. Hence sometimes the moral, social and economic considerations and the protection of weaker parties like workforces, consumers and smaller companies or even professionals, but for them only against severe hardship or unconscionability, especially if induced by an unforeseeable change of circumstances. It may be questionable whether the normative interpretation method may be stretched and further also to protect affected outsiders or 'stakeholders' more generally, although the protection of the environment may increasingly be an issue in the validity and interpretation of the contract. For damaged third parties it may find an equivalent in the law of torts and negligence.

In modern times, the normative approach has in civil law particularly served to propel the notion of contract from simple arrangements between individuals in terms of sale, rental or service into the modern arrangements of often great complexity and long duration between corporates or other legal entities in which the *personal dimension* has largely disappeared. There may instead be a whole organisation and infrastructure in place to perform the contract whilst these contracts operate in a broader social/economic context. For the parties the contract text then serves first as a division of risks and tasks but in duration contracts often also as a road map for other departments or successor individuals to those who were involved in the contract negotiations.

In these circumstances the personal element largely fades whilst the consensus of the parties must all the more be interpreted on the basis of what makes sense, is practical in the circumstances, and of what is reasonable or perhaps ultimately proves to be fair or makes sense. Again, what may be asked from parties on the basis of the contract may then be co-determined by the nature of their position as professionals or some other type of party, their special interests and the nature of their deal. In pressing cases moral, social and economic circumstances will also be considered.

As we saw at the end of the previous section, this force is also at work in common law, but, outside the US, it is unlikely to be referred to as good faith, normative or teleological interpretation. Note in particular that the old law of equity never had this bridging function. It was the result of an administrative facility on the part of the Lord Chancellor under which new rules were developed for particular situations, therefore only incidentally,[30] at first particularly in the law of property, through trusts or future interests in chattels. In contract, its role was always more limited but equity acquired great importance in particular situations, as in the development of the notion of mistake and other defences against the binding force of contracts and also in the possibility of specific performance. But equity was not an interpretational tool and only led to a limited number of different rules, therefore not merely to refinement and adjustment of existing rules or the incorporation of established practices. These rules of equity often became inflexible and were never suitable to a normative interpretation of the parties' rights and duties as developed in civil law countries like Germany, Switzerland, Austria and the Netherlands under the modern notion of good faith.

Although common law is keen to take into account the nature of the relationship of the parties, as we saw, it is probably fair to say that on the other hand, at least in England, it has been slower to adapt to the new professional contracts model and to considering the surroundings or environment in which such a contract must operate. Even between professionals, the exchange of individual desires in terms of formal declarations, remains the main basis for the binding force of their contract. Common law is in any event less concerned with consensus or a more objective or normative approach to interpretation on the basis of it. It seemingly still looks very much at the literal meaning of contractual texts but it has developed some other ways to determine the contractual contents mainly through implied conditions, as was noted in the previous section. As we saw, the nature of the relationship of the parties is also an important point and professionality may also become a greater issue in interpretation matters. Sometimes there is also the question of dependency and of reasonable or justifiable reliance.[31]

The differences may be greater in theory than in practice. At least in the US, a fundamental change in the contract model has been noted, particularly in its effect between professional parties. Where there is a practical difference (apart from the few typical consideration problems which will be discussed later), it is often because in civil law consumer or small companies' protection in the normative approach have sometimes inadvertently been applied also to professionals in their dealings amongst themselves. In civil law no sufficiently clear distinction is made. The reason is perhaps the pivotal role of smaller companies, which are here often caught in the middle. In fact, many of the modern protections under contract law were developed in that context in Germany. Common law, especially in England, is on the other land less inclined to protect professionals against themselves,

---

[30] See more particularly chapter 1, s 1.2.8.
[31] Bingham LJ in *Interfoto*, n 1 *supra*, 439 and 445, compared the civil law to the common law situation and saw the civil law notion of good faith in this respect as a principle of fair and open dealing. It would consider whether it is fair in all the circumstances to hold a counterparty bound to a specific contractual term. He noted that English law had no such overriding principle, but sometimes used equity in striking down unconscionable bargains, or statutory law to crack down on unacceptable standard terms or exemption clauses, or case law to distinguish according to the nature of the parties.

which is particularly clear in the disclosure, negotiation and implementation duties amongst professionals and in the adjustments of professional contracts or re-negotiation duties because of unconscionability.

To stick here to more consumer- or smaller companies-oriented attitudes seems a serious flaw in the civil law approach, a shortcoming reflected also in the Unidroit and European Principles. It was unnecessary since the normative approach allows for precisely such distinctions to be made as the more practical common law seems willing to make more readily, although in the UK the protection accorded to investors under the Financial Services Act of 1986 did not properly distinguish either between professional and consumer dealings as the protection given to small investors were also given to the larger. It was much critisised and this criticism is reflected in Article 11(3) of the EU Financial Services Directive that specifically allows for differentiation in protection levels amongst different classes of investors. This approach is now also adopted in the new Financial Services and Markets Act (2000) in the UK.

Especially in commercial matters, where parties tend to be more equal in expertise and power, more capable and ready to take risks, and are often rather precise in their written contracts, there may be less need or room for interpretational licence, something French commercial law and especially its courts always accepted.[32] Even if it is accepted that words can never be completely clear[33] and must derive their meaning from the context and the circumstances so that interpretation is always called for, it is also clear that many terms that were and are perfectly clear may subsequently be disliked by one of the parties, who also may feel that there was too little disclosure at the outset, even if the own enquiries were minimal. That is obviously not sufficient reason for adjustment of the contractual terms or for excuses of performance, certainly not between professionals, whether operating under common or civil law.[34]

It is sometimes said that the resulting new, more normative approach to the interpretation of the contractual rights and duties of the parties under a contract and more in particular the notion of good faith undermines the principle of party autonomy and deprives parties of a major tool to organise their own affairs in a predictable manner without outside interference, one of the essences of contracting certainly in the professional sphere. Contract as we knew it, it is argued, may be dead.[35] It pits a liberal nineteenth-century approach against a more social or *dirigiste* twentieth-century approach supported by considerable legislative and judicial intervention.

In this connection, the normative civil law attitude, which is often mirrored in the teleological or liberal interpretation of statutes, is often thought to be the result of a more consensual and less adversarial, more egalitarian and social approach in Germany, the Scandinavian countries, the Netherlands and Austria, particularly after the Second World

---

[32] See chapter 1, s 1.1.2.

[33] A notion also well known in the US, see Justice Traynor in *Pacific Gas & Electric v GW Thomas Drayage & Rigging Co*, 442 P2d 641 (Cal 1968).

[34] See also Lord Ackner in *Walford v Miles* [1992] 2 WLR 174.

[35] There are other reasons for this pessimism as well: see G Gilmore, *The Death of Contract* (Ohio State Univ Press, 1974), see also J Gordley, *The Philosophical Origins of Modern Contract Doctrine* (Clarendon Press, Butterworths, 1991), and in England, H Collins, *The Law of Contract* (3rd edn, 1997), 1ff. Another point to be made in this connection is that tort liability has to some considerable extent superseded contractual liability and defective performance often constitutes a tort with its more limited recourse, excluding recovery of future gains under the contract and other consequential damages. Also pre-contractual duties might give rise to tort rather than contractual liability as we shall see in sections 1.2.4 and 1.3.7 *infra*. Situations of dependency may themselves create fiduciary duties breach of which may in civil law give rise to tort rather than contractual liability: see also text at n 38 *infra*. Perhaps it could be said that, except in the contractual core, there is a return to tort rather than contractual protection with the attendant limitation on expectancy damages.

War, although it also became the approach in France and Southern Europe, even if less fundamentally anchored there in the concept of good faith. It is submitted, however, that it is as much the natural consequence of contract moving out of the sphere of personal private arrangements into the world of large professional dealings (or a multitude of dealings with individuals in similar positions), where through professional support or standard terms the personal element in the formation and enforcement of contracts becomes negligible and the environment in which the contract must operate much more important.

Whatever may be made of historical trends in this connection, as a general proposition, the view that contract as we once knew it exists no longer seems greatly exaggerated. In any event, the civil law normative approach to interpretation, whilst sometimes introducing moral, social, economic and practical considerations in the determination of the validity, content and enforcement of contracts in the interpretation, its reliance on extra-contractual duties of care especially in situations of dependency, and its sensitivity to honour reasonable expectations, does not mean to test *per se* — as some matter of high principle — the existence and meaning of a contract in the light of what is reasonable, normal, practical and sensible, or even fair.

It has always allowed parties to agree whatever they like, even if unreasonable, abnormal and impractical, or unfair, assuming it was clear what they wanted, there was a balance in power and knowledge, and the contract had no seriously unethical or otherwise illegal objective, or was obtained by fraud or undue influence, through serious misrepresentation or by mutual mistake, which would in any event invalidate it, as could the lack of sufficient disclosure at the time of the negotiations, at least if amounting to abuse.

It is the interpretation or construction question determining the extent of each party's rights and obligations under the contract which will first be discussed and compared for both the civil and common law systems in more detail. Thereafter there will be a special dicussion of some basic, contractual issues like capacity and formalities. A seperate section dealing in greater detail with the modern notion of good faith and its development in civil law will follow in section 1.3 below.

1.2.3 Consensus in Civil Law and its Normative Interpretation: Alternative Views

Consent in the civil law of contracts implies consensus and suggests congruent desires of the parties and a meeting of the minds concerning the contractual content and each party's contractual rights and obligations. When consensus becomes the basis of the rights and obligations of the parties, as it did in civil law, it is logical to look for the parties' *shared* intent in the interpretation of the contract and also extrapolate *this* intent or continues to supplement the agreement where the parties have not expressly covered their reciprocal rights and duties and left gaps, especially when the contract is rudimentary or of longer duration and may have to deal with circumstances not expressly covered by the agreement or which may have changed.

It was always clear that for their validity contracts could not depend merely on a consensus in a psychological sense. Between natural persons, there could too easily arise a later difference of view of what was meant undermining that kind of consensus. A more objective way of interpreting the consensus was thus always called for, short of concluding that most contracts might be void *ab initio* or could suffer from mistake virtually at the option of either party.

It was already pointed out before that in modern business dealings, it is all the clearer that the psychological approach to interpretation can hardly suffice, if only because the person who signs the agreement is unlikely to know much of its details and merely uses his authority or power of commitment, whilst no single person may have dealt with the various issues and the end drafting is often left to outside lawyers. It does not rule out literal inter-pretation of the parties' declarations but a purely subjective interpretation becomes more difficult. What some (succeeding) negotiators, who often operate in teams, really wanted is then not the decisive factor, even if it could be established on the basis of the text, but rather what reasonable expectations were raised on the other side and what that side could and did rely on or what must be considered to have made sense to both parties in the circumstances.

This is in fact true in both civil and common law, but each legal system gives a some-what different legal expression to these aspects of contracting and to the determination of the contractual rights and duties of the parties. Common law is largely unconcerned with deeper thought or systematic thinking and is always more *ad hoc* and practical but also more circumspect. In civil law, these considerations served to sideline the notion of con-sensus in a psychological sense. This allowed an easier route for interpretation to develop in cases of ambiguity or doubt and facilitated gap-filling in the contractual provisions without resort to an imaginary and often artificial parties' intent.

As we saw in the previous sections, in core civil law countries, the determination of the parties' rights and obligation in the various phases of the contract has in essence become a matter of *normative or teleological interpretation* in the sense of increasingly accepting *reliance* as the crucial notion of the time and content of the contractual undertaking and, in the case of doubt on the contractual content, also what is normal, practical or makes sense or what a reasonable man would do. The traditional offer and acceptance rationalisa-tion of the contract formation process here takes a step back. It brings contractual thinking closer to tort thinking and tends to limit the specific performance and damages notion at the same time to what was detrimentally relied upon or reasonably expected rather than to what may be objectively calculated on the basis of the other party's promises.

It is possible in this connection — a possibility already mentioned above in section 1.1.2 — to put emphasis altogether on duties of care, disclosure, cooperation and loyalty and consider them the essence of contract. Even the notion of privity and its exceptions may be better understood in this manner, e.g. in the aspect of respect for contracts between third parties or in the need for contracting parties to respect other people's rights. It again shows the closeness to tort remedies. One may thus also ask whether a lessor can object to the transfer of a lease as part of the transfer of a lessee's business. It would seem to require at least a reasonable interest before the contractual rights are exercised. The factual situation often dictates what parties must do regardless of the contractual framework and the rights deriving therefrom. Again abuse of rights in the nature of a delict presents itself.[36]

In this approach, even when there is no doubt about the meaning of the wording of the contract, it could still be adjusted according to what is fairer under the circumstances, especially when it concerns a weaker party or even when unconscionability results in the performance for stronger ones. Pre-contractual disclosure and negotiation duties could also result, whilst in the case of hardship in the performance it is equally possible that re-negotiation duties could be imposed. External moral, social or economic or competitive and even environmental considerations could in this approach affect the contractual con-tent. Again, in all of this, special regard must be had also to the nature of the relationship of the parties in terms of professionality or as consumers or workers, their special interests and the particular characteristics of the deal.

Yet in countries like France, there is, at least in the lower courts, still much emphasis on literal interpretation or otherwise on intent in a more psychological sense, not unlike in

---

[36] See also text following n 48 *infra*.

England, but according to the Cour de Cassation[37] the literal interpretation method can only be used as long as the relevant clauses are clear and precise. If the contract is ambiguous or incomplete, a freer attitude to interpretation may be adopted. Naturally, whether a contract is ambiguous or incomplete is itself a matter of interpretation.

Nevertheless, French law is here more timid and that certainly also affects the adjustment of contractual terms and even the development of pre-contractual disclosure duties. It is keener on the concept of the abuse of rights. Thus in the case of such abuse by employers, by parties invoking rescission rights, or by parties insisting on performance in the case of changed circumstances, the courts may come to the rescue and adjust the contractual obligations. Normally it concerns here instances of unequal bargaining power or the need to protect weaker parties. Increasingly, information and co-operation duties are also construed, although they may lead to actions only in tort.[38]

Common law remains here on its face more conservative whilst being keener on psychological intent, promises and expectations including expectation damages. Yet it may for supplementation rely on implied conditions, as we already saw, sometimes even of reasonableness and fairness and, as far as adjustment is concerned, will clearly distinguish on the basis of the nature of the relationship of the parties and protect the weaker party even against itself if necessary, although for consumer protection this is now often a matter of statutory law, as it is in fact also in many civil law countries. If necessary, it may also use the notion of reliance to better protect a counterparty as we shall see in the next section.

As was already mentioned in the previous section, in civil law countries, the notion of *good faith* is often used in this connection and a reference to it implies the normative or teleological approach to interpretation of the parties' intent and stands indeed for additional and amplifying support for the validity and meaning of the consensus of the parties. It also separates the serious from the non-binding friendly or family commitments, the moral from the immoral, the normal from the unconscionable, extortionate or manipulative.

In this sense, the normative approach may also subsume the illegality notion and even the *causa* element or rationality objective, see for this concept section 1.2.7 below, although it may still be true that sometimes the more subjective meaning of the parties is first determined and only thereafter adjusted for what good faith and the notion of *causa* may require. This is predominantly the Southern European approach and implies a two-step approach to interpretation. The continuum between formation, validity and performance of the contract and any excuses, considering them all matters of interpretation of the parties' rights and duties, is thus denied, but the result will normally be the same.

In practice, however, the normative interpretation of the parties' intent or objectives will lead to a deviation from the contract as the parties' roadmap, division of labour and risk only in exceptional situations, especially when:

(a)   reasonable expectations raised by the other party have been grossly deceived;
(b)   there is a lack of balance in bargaining power and information between the parties which highlights the social function of this approach by protecting weaker or dependent parties like consumers but also workers, licensees, franchisees or

---

[37] 14 Dec 1942 [1944] D.112. The French Cc contains some (antiquated) provisions on interpretation in Articles 1156*ff* which appear no longer of great relevance today although lip service continues to be paid to them.
[38] See more particularly also ss 1.3.4–7 *infra* on the effects on the *force majeure* requirement and on disclosure, negotiation and re-negotiation duties.

distributors or even performers under long-term musical agency agreements and is therefore less relevant in the professional sphere;

(c)   there results clear hardship which again might acquire a different meaning between commercial partners and between stronger and weaker parties;

(d)   fundamental legal principles are violated which are likely to be based on pressing moral, social and economic considerations and may then not merely lead to the reinterpretation or adjustment of the contractual terms but also to invalidity of the contract altogether.

Abuse of rights may also be pleaded in this connection in enforcement; it mostly amounts to the same thing. All these situations border in fact on wrongdoing and abuse in a modern sense, therefore also on tort liability. It is clear, however, that especially in the *professional* sphere things have got to be *pretty bad* before the courts will intervene. In civil law, the normative approach to intent allows here for the necessary flexibility and may thus adapt the contractual rights and duties, although probably less so amongst professionals. There has, however, been an undesirable inclination to extend the protection of consumers in this respect also to professionals as already mentioned in the previous section.

1.2.4   Intent in Common Law: Offer and Acceptance, the Notions of Consideration, Exchange or Bargain

Although the normative approach to interpretation remains less popular in England, in the USA wider notions of good faith did develop but did not extend as far or become conceptually as pervasive as in countries like Germany and the Netherlands, especially not with regards to the adaptation of the parties' rights and duties under a contract and the imposition of pre-contractual disclosure and negotiation or post-contractual re-negotiation duties, as will be discussed further in section 1.3.2 below.

As we saw, in common law the literal approach to declarations is, especially in England, often still preferred. This approach is supported by the old *parole evidence rule* which eliminates in the interpretation all contemporary or earlier evidence against any writing intended by the parties as a final expression of their agreement.[39] It finds a counterpart in the literal interpretation of statutory instruments,[40] but may be corrected by implying conditions. This is the preferred way of dealing with construction or interpretation in common law, which swings here from the objective literal approach to contractual declarations to the subjective or psychological approach in gap filling through implied terms, although they may be more objectively or normatively interpreted, especially when reasonableness, ways of dealing or custom is invoked. It has more recently also allowed 'reasonable man' considerations.[41] It is supplemented by a regard for the differences that may result from the nature of the relationship between the parties and type of deal or sometimes by reliance notions. Also here, common law may come closer to the normative or teleological interpretation of civil law than would at first appear. Especially weaker parties may be protected in this manner and the contract in respect of them may even be adjusted.

---

[39] See n 65 *infra*.
[40] See Lord Denning, *The Discipline of the Law* (1979), 11*ff* and his comments in *Bullmer v Bollinger* [1974] Ch 401 and chapter 1, s 1.2.9.
[41] See Lord Hoffmann in *Investors Compensation Scheme Ltd v West Bromwich Building Societey* [1998] 1WLR 896, 913 and *BCCI v Ali*, [2001] 2 WLR 749. The literal attitude towards statutory enactments is, however, largely in tact and remains also the starting point in contract.

The difference in emphasis between civil and common law with respect to consensus and the parties' intent in the formation and interpretation of contract has itself long been noted.[42] In common law, first there is no similar emphasis on consensus or a meeting of minds and the parties' intent relates rather to the individual promises they make. It retains as such a more subjective element. It is the abstract doctrine of consideration, which is the notion of exchange or bargain (or sometimes the notion of sufficient reason), that still provides the main basis for the validity of contracts in common law. Within it, the key is that as long as the exchanged declarations of the parties are sufficiently similar, there is a (bilateral or executory) contract. The mutual promises must be seriously meant,[43] but the emphasis remains on the exchange of compatible declarations and *not* on the intent of the parties individually or (even less) jointly in the sense of a consensus.

In fact, the importance of intent in the formation of the contract has in common law until modern times been denied altogether, even by important American writers like Williston,[44] and often it is still thought that there may be a contract even if there is no evidence of any positive intent of the parties at all to create a legal right and obligation, provided the formal prerequisites for the formation of the contract exist. This largely refers to the ritual of offer and acceptance, which terminology itself became in common law only current in the latter part of the nineteenth century. In common law, it put emphasis on the exchange of promises in the sense of formal declarations which must be intended by the parties making them but that goes for each one individually. Similarity or compatibility of mutual declarations and not of intent remains the true key to the contract in common law.

It squares with the consideration idea requiring a bargain or the exchange of a promise for a benefit to the promisor (or at least a detriment to the promisee). In a bilateral or executory contract, there will be such a promise and consideration on either side. In this approach, neither intent, nor, strictly speaking, even consideration is connected with the contract itself but rather with each parties' promise, the exchange of which (in a formal sense) results in the binding force of the commitments.

At the theoretical level, the central role of consideration or rather the exchange or bargain, if only between two individual formal promises, leads to a different approach to interpretation or construction as there is not necessarily a common platform between the parties, as there is in civil law. It is true that the term 'agreement' is sometimes used and presented as a condition for the existence and binding force of the contract, but it does not have the meaning of consensus as it has in civil law.[45] As a consequence, in the

---

[42] See Roscoe Pound, "Liberty of Contract", 18 *Yale LJ* 451 (1909). Note, however, also the emphasis on mutual promises rather than on consensus in the works of Grotius: see n. 17 *supra*. It tends to lead to a more psychological approach to contract interpretation.

[43] See *Dalrymple v Dalrymple* (1811) 2 Hag Con 54, 105.

[44] *Selection on Contracts* (1957), s 21. The highly esteemed American Judge Learned Hand once remarked that even 'if both parties severally declared that their meaning had been other than the natural meaning, [but] each declaration was similar, it would be irrelevant': *Eustis Mining* Co *v Beer, Sondheimer* & *Co*, 239 F 976 (1917). In his view it did not make the least difference whether a promisor actually intends the meaning which the law will impose on his words.

[45] See for the requirement of an agreement, eg GH Treitel, *The Law of Contract* (11th edn, 1999), chapter 2. In this sense it is probably also used in the USA in Section 2–204 UCC. On the other hand, in common law, a distinction is sometimes made between agreements and contracts, in the sense that agreements can be without consideration and are then not binding or exist only in equity (like in the context of the trust), whilst contracts are either under seal or based on consideration and as such always binding at law.

In the USA, the *Restatement (Second) of Contracts* of 1981 distinguishes between agreements and bargains (Section 3). A bargain requires an exchange of promises or an exchange of a promise and a performance. It includes barters. An agreement, on the other hand, is only the manifestation of a mutual assent, which may, or may not, result in legal consequences and may or may not be intended. In the USA, bargain is thus considered a narrower concept in the nature of a contract proper. A contract is in this connection a promise or a set of promises

interpretation or construction of contracts, common law remains more wedded to a literal interpretation of *each* party's declarations, although it must sometimes also use implied conditions. It is here less coherent than civil law, but often more practical.

In common law, the consideration notion played an important role in the development of modern contract law out of the law of torts. It provided by the middle of the eighteenth century a mechanism that developed the English law of contracts not under seal (sealed contracts had always been binding) from the idea of barter into a binding exchange of mere promises. It was done by requiring some balance in the exchange, at first even a measure of equivalence in the sense of there being some just bargain or price (*iustum pretium*).[46] In this connection it should not be forgotten that originally the English Royal courts were largely concerned with land matters only or with torts endangering the peace. Only gradually did other torts become actionable, ultimately even breaches of promises, but it took much longer to develop true contract actions. As in the law of chattels, where the proper proprietary defences remain in tort, see chapter 4, section 1.3.4, also in contract the remedies retain in common law a close affiliation with the law of torts from which they derive.

In this development, there was not much room for the parties' intent as the source for the binding force of contracts, at least not at first, although in the eighteenth century the Lord Chief Justice of the time, Lord Mansfield, accepted the seriously intended promise itself as the basis for contractual liability or 'honesty and rectitude' being itself sufficient consideration.[47] This could have opened the way for the Continental consensus and good faith interpretation approach to the binding force of contracts, but he was soon overruled.[48]

Yet after the eighteenth century, the exchange of mere promises could itself provide sufficient consideration,[49] in which context the notion of equivalency or a just price was abandoned and, as it seems, also the notion of reliance used earlier.[50] The development of the purely *executory* contract as a contract based on an exchange of (formal) promises was

for the breach of which the law gives a remedy or the performance of which the law in some way recognises as a duty (Section 1). An offer is the manifestation of willingness to enter into a bargain so made as to justify another person in understanding that his assent to that bargain is invited and will conclude it (Section 24). An acceptance is a manifestation of the assent to the terms of the offer made by the offeree in a manner invited or required by the offer. The acceptance may be made by the delivery of the required performance or the making of a counter promise. Acceptance by performance may operate as a counterpromise. The offer vests the recipient of the offer with the power to complete the manifestation of mutual consent by acceptance of the offer (Section 35).

[46] See Wooddeson, *A Systematical View of the Laws of England* (1792), 415. However, Holdsworth, 8 *History of English Law* (1926), 17, argues that courts never attempted to adjudicate upon the adequacy of consideration. Yet, until the development of the consideration approach, the writ of *indebitatus assumpsit* had provided protection for a contracting party only if it had relied on someone else's promise and performed, but was not given its *just* reward and suffered damage as a consequence. In this manner, the notions of promise, reliance and real loss became the essence of the action. The requirement of *real loss* subsequently developed into the consideration requirement that was thus considered necessary to create contractual liability of the other party and needed to be substantial if not equivalent to justify an action. Nominal loss was not sufficient. There was an echo of this in the development of the synallagmatic innominate contracts in civil law, which at first were thought to be actionable only by the party that had fully performed, see Zimmermann, n. 25 *supra*, 536.
[47] *Pillans v Van Mierop*, 97 Eng. Rep. 1035 (KB 1765), reversed in *Rann v Hughes*, 101 Eng. Rep. 1014 (KB 1778). Ever since, the doctrine of consideration has been upheld, importantly so in *Foakes v Beer* (1884) 9 App. Cas. 605 (HL), holding that a contract between a debtor and his creditor to forgive interest on a debt was unenforceable without proper consideration being given for the release. This is still good law.
[48] See Holdsworth, n. 46 *supra* at 45.
[49] Section 71 of the *Restatement (Second) of Contracts* of 1981 states: 'To constitute consideration, a performance or a return promise must be bargained for a performance or a return is bargained for if it sought by the promisor in exchange for his promise and is given by the promisee in exchange for that promise'.
[50] See Holdsworth, n. 46 *supra* at 2*ff*.

thus achieved in common law.[51] This came probably somewhat later than in civil law and this development may still not be fully concluded, in that it remains embedded in the consideration notion of exchange or bargain (although no longer of equivalence) rather than in that of agreement or consensus of the parties, even though, as we shall see, the practical limitations connected with the notion of consideration are virtually eliminated.

In fact, in common law, the more incidental approach to determining contractual rights and duties prevented any abstract theory of intent or consensus from developing.[52] This left room for other approaches to determine the validity of contract, like the notion of consideration with its formal exchange of promises. However, also in common law there has been a re-awakening of the *reliance notion* in modern times, and reasonable or justifiable and in particular detrimental reliance on the declaration or acts of the other party may now sometimes replace the emphasis on the exchange of formal promises and then also allows for a more normative approach to determining the rights and obligation of the parties, but in other cases the need for consideration by way of bargain or the exchange of formal promises subject to a more literal interpretation has by no means disappeared.

The re-awakening of the equitable *reliance notion or promissory estoppel* in common law may be traced back to developments in the USA where, since the 1930s, the importance of detrimental reliance on an offer (or promissory estoppel) has been stressed to create contractual rights and duties besides the exchange or bargain notion,[53] and is now widely accepted, sometimes in competition, more often as a supplement to the notion of an exchange of promises or consideration. Thus if there is a justified or reasonable reliance on an offer, the lack of consideration proper need no longer be a problem. To start hiring people or to begin a project in justifiable reliance on a promise of a construction contract or of adequate funding, may thus be sufficient. In England, Professor Atiyah has suggested that in order to assume the binding force of a contract, detrimental reliance or at least a beginning of performance is *always* the true key to the validity of the contract and necessary before any enforcement action can be based on it.[54] The promise based notion of contract is here abandoned altogether. The sequel is a normative attitude to contract formation and the determination of the contractual rights and duties.

This more radical proposition, which is tort related, could also lead to a curtailment of expectation damages in favour of restitutional or direct damages only. It has not found broad acceptance in common law, but could in a trans-national context prove useful. Certainly, if there has been detrimental reliance, even more so a beginning of performance in *justifiable* reliance on the declarations or actions of others, it may be right to assume a contractual bond. Still the offer itself continues to play an important role, also in the reliance doctrine, and can as such not be eliminated, but may now be more indirect or informal, whilst *formal* acceptance can then also be dispensed with. Thus the notion of consideration becomes less relevant and a more normative or teleological approach to contractual interpretation could follow even in common law, as it did for consensus in civil law.

---

[51] Thus Story considered the extent of the contractual obligation dependent upon the conveyance of individual desires; in the USA that was also the idea of Holmes. See Storey, *A Treatise of the Law of Contract not under Seal* (1844), 4, and Holmes, *The Common Law*, (1st edn, 1881, 58th printing), 293–94.

[52] See eg AG Chloros, "Comparative Aspects of the Intention to Create Legal Relations in Contract", 33 *Tul LR*, 606, 611 (1959).

[53] In the USA, the reliance doctrine may be traced to Full and Perdue, "The Reliance Interests in Contract Damages", 46 *Yale LJ*, 52, 373 (1936). The important case is *Hoffman v Red Owl Stores, Inc*, 26 Wis 2d 683, 133 NW 2d 267 (1965) allowing compensation for losses caused by reasonable reliance on the declarations made in the course of negotiations without an element of consideration or even unjust enrichment.

[54] "Contracts, Promises and the Law of Obligations", [1978] *LQR* 193.

1.2.5 The Practical Significance of the Consideration Requirement in Common Law

The more traditional notion of consideration is often thought to highlight and to give in common law expression to the dynamic role of contract and to the continuing ability of the contracting parties to signal their intentions and plan their business or life without (too much) interference on the grounds of other notions, principles or imperatives.[55] As everywhere else — certainly also in the civil law notion of consensus — this autonomy remains an important aspect of contracting, no less in contracts between professionals, but the initiative of the parties is not or no longer always the only source of the binding force of contracts and of their content. Nor are subsequently their rights and duties merely determined by party autonomy, see also the discussion in section 1.1.2 above.

Yet in common law, there survives the idea that only consideration matters,[56] even if merely an exchange of (new) formal promises (instead of the giving of an actual thing or the creation of an actual detriment to the promisee, which are the more traditional expressions of consideration in this sense), including the promise of payment, resulting in bilateral or executory contracts. The key is thus the exchange of commitments which may or may not prove to have been intended as long as the declarations of the parties are sufficiently similar and congruous in a formal sense. This remains the fundamental importance of the consideration notion in common law and a main conceptual difference with civil law, although practically speaking, in modern times, consideration itself is of little consequence and long since de-emphasised or to put it another way: normally it is there, why otherwise contract?

However, in practice, the requirement of consideration cannot be fully ignored. In common law it remains particularly relevant in that offers or options without consideration are not legally binding until validly accepted. The legal rule that an offer is already accepted upon dispatch (rather than upon receipt) of the acceptance and cannot be legally withdrawn thereafter may be seen as a practical effort to limit the effect of the consideration doctrine. So may the notion of reliance.

Other examples of the importance of consideration are in contractual amendments. Although they can now be freely entered into without giving additional consideration, that is not necessarily so if a discharge, release, rescission or novation is intended. When work is agreed to be performed against a certain price, any amendment of the price is also still likely to have no legal effect, even if an extra effort is required to complete an already agreed full project.[57] Surety contracts or guarantees may also fail for lack of consideration, so may contracts that impose only a unilateral obligation, like those that reward services after performance, whilst the debtor is given the option not to do so.

Contracts to perform a moral or religious duty, like refraining from smoking or going to church, may also fail for lack of consideration. Past consideration is also not sufficient for example where an annuity is promised for past services or as a reward for an heroic act after they have been rendered. Most of this is undesirable and modern case law may distinguish on the basis of particular circumstances. Commercial agency agreements were traditionally also thought to lack consideration, although it has been found in the commercial agent promoting the business. Also an oral promise to make a gift is not enforceable.

---

[55] See C Fried, *Contract as Promise: A Theory of Contractual Obligation* (1981). The emphasis is here on the self-binding nature of the promise rather than the bargain theory of contract. The key is intent.
[56] See also Unger, "Intent to Create Legal Relationships" (1956) *MLR*, 96.
[57] See also M Chen-Wishart, "Consideration: Practical Benefit and the Emperor's New Clothes" in Beatson and Friedmann, *Good Faith and Fault in Contract Law* (1995), 123.

Even a written promise is only valid if in deed form or supported by statute. This is perhaps more understandable. It is the same in most civil law countries on the basis of statutory law in order to avoid rashness, although in civil law a rash gift actually made will normally stand.

The more important point is perhaps that the notion of consideration wherever still an obstacle, no longer requires equivalence between the value of the mutual promises or a fair price as it is now entirely left to the parties to determine what is proper consideration and it can thus easily be provided. In the USA it is quite normal to enter into option contracts by paying (or promising to pay) one US dollar. Although the exchange must be serious and seriously meant, the value of the consideration given may thus be nominal (a peppercorn), but it may not be illusory or fictitious.

In any event, the requirement may altogether easily be circumvented by entering into a contract under seal which means no more than affixing a mark on the contract or writing on the contract that it is *under seal* and have it witnessed by two witnesses. The promise contained in such a contract must somehow be expressed, but the handing over of the document is normally considered sufficient in this connection. In the USA, in states like New York and California, this circumvention route was eventually blocked, though not in England (see also Section 2–202 UCC).

When an exchange of promises became adequate consideration so that the purely executory contract became possible, the result was that the consensus notion came in sight as Lord Mansfield had wished. Indeed, the UCC in the USA follows this line at least for the contract of the sale of goods with its emphasis on agreement between the parties but also on their conduct, including the beginning of performance, see Sections 2–204 and 2–206. This was achieved at the expense of consideration, the lack of which under Section 2–205 no longer stands in the way either of offers by merchants being binding if the offers have been stated in writing to remain open. Yet, even though Article 2 UCC in its formation provisions makes no longer reference to consideration (except indirectly in Section 2–205), the notion is not abandoned, only de-emphasised.

In England, the abolition of the consideration notion has been advocated since 1975 by the Law Commission (Working Paper No 61). The important thing to appreciate here is that it would do away with the inconveniences of the doctrine, but would not replace the notion of a formal exchange of promises or bargain with the Continental idea of a consensus or a meeting of minds leading to a more normative and comprehensive interpretation technique at the same time. In common law, the parties' intent continues to refer less to consensus, as it does in civil law, than to each party having been serious in its offer or acceptance.[58] As intent therefore relates only to the declaration aspect of the consideration notion, which in modern times is content with a seriously intended exchange, that would survive the abolition of the consideration requirement. Declarations would thus still remain the true focus of contract formation in common law, at least in common law countries other than the USA.

1.2.6 Contracts: Construction and Remedies in Common Law. The Parole Evidence Rule

As we saw, in common law, the ambivalence towards the notion of contractual intent has blocked a more conceptual approach of consensus and failures of consensus to develop. An important consequence is that there is no clear-cut approach to interpretation or construction

[58] See the leading textbook by GH Treitel, *The Law of Contract* (11th edn, 1999), chapter 2.

either. It remains more casuistic. Another consequence is that lack of disclosure, mistake, misrepresentation, abuse of power or undue influence, and fraud at the time of the conclusion of the agreement, may all affect the validity of a contract but, as this is not primarily perceived as a consensus problem as it is in civil law, the types of relief are more incidental as we shall see in section 1.4.2 below.

In fact, they are more in the nature of excuses for non-performance resulting in a fractured system of remedies largely depending on factual situations and may not even lead to voidness with automatic restitution or title return under a failed (sales) agreement. In any event, the scope of contract seems narrower in common law than it is in civil law, and remedies sought in connection with contractual dealings soon become tort-base as we saw, e.g. where there was detrimental reliance or misrepresentation. So it may sometimes be in France as we saw in section 1.2.3 above. Fair dealing ideas, on the other hand, easily lead to notions of unjust enrichment and restitution remedies.

So reliance and fair dealing can be and have been explained as giving rise to non-contractual, tort, or restitution protections, rather than to contractual remedies, therefore to remedies *not strictly belonging to the contractual order*, which in that view is limited to the old bargain approach or to the area of voluntary commitments which may, however, also cover implied conditions. It may make a difference to the amount of damages that may be recovered, especially any lost future profits under the (anticipated) contract. Thus expectation damages may become less normal or may be more readily curtailed.

As a consequence, not only the approach to interpretation but also the system of common law remedies is different from that in civil law. As just mentioned, they are more incidental and based on practical requirements of the instant case. It leaves room, however, for implied terms in the construction of the contract, traditionally availed of to make allowance for notions of *force majeure* or sometimes even of hardship in connection with changed circumstances in duration contracts.[59] This suggests, as already noted, a jump from the literal or objective approach connected with the wording of offer and acceptance, to the subjective approach of intent. The use of implied terms of reasonableness and fairness[60] may, on the other hand, move common law closer to what in civil law is the normative approach to the validity and interpretation of contracts.[61] So does the reliance notion which has in proper cases a similar effect. As we saw, common law is also comfortable with distinguishing between the nature of relationships which again may lead to a more normative approach to contract interpretation. Professionals are thus more likely to be held to the literal meaning of their deals than consumers or employees.

Certainly also in England, notions of protection of weaker parties, especially against onerous terms, gained ground early,[62] although it has in recent times mostly been left to statutory intervention to protect consumers.[63] Hence the Consumer Credit Act 1974, the Unfair Contract Terms Act of 1977, and the Financial Services Act of 1986 now superseded

---

[59] See *Taylor v Caldwell*, 3 B&S 826, 32 LJ, QB 164 (1863).

[60] See for English law *Bankline v Arthur Capel* [1918] AC 435 and *Metropolitan Water Board v Dick* [1918] AC 119.

[61] Their impact then still depends on interpretation with the same restrictions in common law as just mentioned. Implied terms do not therefore operate as a general counterbalance or independent source of contractual rights and duties or amount to a validity test of the contract, see *British Movietonews v London and District Cinema* [1951] 2 All ER 617, rejecting Lord Denning's broader approach in the Court of Appeal in this case, see [1950] 2 All ER 390, 395.

[62] See *Parker v Smith Eastern Railway Co* [1877] 2 CDP 416 and *Hood v Anchor Line (Henderson Brothers) Ltd* [1918] AC 837.

[63] See, however, also *J Spurling Ltd. v Bradshaw* [1956] 1 WLR 461; *Mc Cutcheon v David Mac Brayne Ltd* [1964] 1 WLR 128; *Thornton v Shoe Lane Parking Ltd* [1971] 2 QB 163 and *Interfoto Picture Library Ltd. v Stiletto Visual Programmes Ltd*, cited in n. 1 *supra*.

by the Financial Services and Markets Act 2000. In fact, consumer and investor protection has been a matter of statutory intervention in most countries, also in civil law, where the normative approach to interpretation could have dealt with it. This also applies to the use of standard terms in contract, except in Switzerland, where it is still satisfactorily dealt with under the general legal principles, including the normative approach to interpretation.

Yet there is no conceptual clarity in the common law approach to contractual interpretation or construction and, on its face, common law often still relies on the more literal meaning of the contractual terms and does not easily extend its coverage, as stated in England by Lord Reid:[64]

> There is no need to consider what the parties thought, or how reasonable men in their shoes would have dealt with the situation if they had foreseen it. The question is whether the contract they did make is, on its true construction, wide enough to apply to [a] new situation; if it is not, then it is at an end.

It leaves open the question what true construction is. There is here some room for flexibility. Yet the *parole evidence rule* underpins a restrictive attitude.[65] This attitude does not stand alone and, as already mentioned before, a similar attitude may be found in the literal interpretation of statutory instruments in England.

In common law, there seems also little room at the theoretical level for the introduction of more general *equitable* principles to balance the intent and the contractual autonomy, as the doctrine of consideration once might have done. Equity itself presents in the common law system a fairly precise set of incidental rules and is certainly not a general source of supplementary law, as good faith or reasonableness and fairness increasingly are in civil law. As discussed in chapter 1, section 1.2.11, equity is no general counterbalance or independent source of contractual rights and duties and does not amount to a validity test of the contract or a facilitator of the interpretation process.[66] Thus the normative approach to contract interpretation implying a balancing of intent by notions of good faith remains largely a civil law concept and finds its parallels in common law, not much in equity, and in any event more piecemeal, in the different ways here explained: implied terms, the nature of the relationship of the parties, dependency and sometimes reliance or the acceptance of extra-contractual duties.

The 1980 Vienna Convention on the International Sale of Goods does not take sides. It largely accepts the offer and acceptance language of common law but does not require consideration (or *causa*).[67] It allows offers to be withdrawn before an acceptance is dispatched

---

[64] In *Davis Contractors v Farnham* [1956] 2 All ER 145.

[65] The common law 'parole evidence rule', which is mostly seen as a rule of construction and not one of evidence, does not allow any contradictory contemporary or earlier evidence (and in the opinion of many, even later behaviour) against any writing intended by the parties as a final expression of their agreement, *cf.* also Section 2–202 UCC which retained the rule, but allows a course of dealing or usage or the consistent use of additional terms to be pleaded regardless. Some of this may in England derive from the *Karen Oltmann* case, [1976] 2 Lloyd's Law Reports. 708 (QB). Article 8 of the Vienna Convention on the International Sale of Goods contains an interpretation provision and allows not only statements but also conduct to be considered in determining the meaning of the contract according to their reasonable interpretation. Due consideration is thus given to all *relevant* circumstances of the case including the negotiations, practices and usages and any subsequent conduct of the parties. It is clear that Article 8 does not follow the parole evidence rule, cf also Article 2.1 Unidroit Contract Principles and Article 2.101(2) European Contract Principles which allows a contract to be proved by any means, including witnesses.

[66] See *British Movietonews v London and District Cinema* [1951] 2 All ER 617, rejecting Lord Denning's broader approach in the Court of Appeal decision in this case [1950] 2 All ER 390, 395.

[67] It refers to the process of offer and acceptance as formation. It requires in Article 14 that there is an intention on the part of the offeror to be bound by the acceptance but has no similar language for the offeree (Article 18). Wider questions of validity do not concern it and are not covered by the Convention (Article 4).

unless the offeree acted in reasonable reliance upon the offer but does not dwell on pre-contractual disclosure and negotiation duties (Article 16(2)). It does not go into the matter of contractual interpretation either, only the interpretation of the Convention itself, see Article 7, and for the approach of the Unidroit and European Principles, section 1.6.2 below.

1.2.7 The Common Law Notion of Consideration and the Civil Law Notion of Causa: *International Aspects*

As we saw, consideration is a typical common law concept, which requires some *quid pro quo*. It is based on the notion of bargain or exchange, although in modern times a mere return promise may be sufficient consideration and there is no longer any need for equivalence in value. Thus the value of consideration is entirely left up to the parties. It may be minimal but must be serious and not illusionary. As we saw, it may be particularly lacking in gifts, agency agreements or in contractual amendments aiming at releases, novation or a higher price for the same performance. As for contractual amendments, the contract now usually stands, see Section 2–209 UCC, whilst, when a price increase is promised for an already agreed performance, special circumstances may be invoked to reward any extra effort. Yet there can still be no rescission, release or novation without new consideration.

As mentioned before, there is also a consideration problem when past performance (for example of servants or rescuers) is rewarded after the fact with an annuity or other benefit. Modern case law may again attempt to distinguish depending on the circumstances if the result would be clearly unfair. Other examples of contracts without consideration may be those under which the counter-party gives up immaterial benefits, like drinking or smoking, or other habits for some reward, whilst moral or other edifying undertakings may also not be sufficient consideration (for example, going to church for a price). Such contracts remain then unenforceable and the obligation to do or abstain is not legally binding, whilst the reward promised need not by law be paid. These contracts are, however, now fairly readily accepted as binding in the USA.

The most glaring consequence of the consideration doctrine is that offers and options are not binding in common law, but the doctrine of detrimental reliance or promissory estoppel is likely to bring here some relief. This principle is also inserted in the Vienna Convention on the International Sale of Goods (Article 16(2)), therefore in non-consideration language. By statutory amendment, the situation was also changed in the USA for merchants in the case of a sale of goods and an offer expressed in writing to be open till a certain date, is now binding for the indicated period (Section 2–205 UCC).

However, in ordinary contract situations there is always some *quid pro quo* so that a consideration problem seldom arises. In practice, the requirement may be circumvented by entering the contract or its amendments under seal. It is, as we saw a simple operation, although some states in the USA, notably New York and California, now disallow it.

The Romanistic civil law notion of *causa* has several meanings (*cf* Articles 1108, 1131 and 1133 of the French Cc) but requires a contract essentially to make some sense, be rational, be seriously intended and have some meaning. It was meant to overcome formalism. It was also used to avoid contracts on the basis of impropriety. At certain times, it was even explained as requiring a reasonable *quid pro quo*.[68] It has lost much of its impact

---

[68] In this limited sense, the concept of *causa* could be traced back to Roman law. Under Justinian law, the vendor of land could require the return of the asset if it proved worth more than twice its price: D.4.44.2. This was the theory of the *laesio enormis*, later supported by Canon law. There is a remnant in Article 1118 French Cc, but most

under modern law. Both concepts (consideration and *causa*) are sometimes also invoked as objective standards to cure contractual excess and are in that respect not dissimilar either, but there are increasingly other tools available to make adjustments, like indeed the use of the good faith concept in civil law.

In civil law, the requirement of a *causa* was often considered obscure and has progressively been abandoned, at least in the sense of requiring the contract to make sense according to some objective standard, *cf* the new Dutch Civil Code and earlier in the BGB of 1900. The normative contract interpretation facility discussed above can cover the same ground, if necessary. In civil law, the notion is maintained only to avoid contracts which are clearly immoral or concern gambling, although more relaxed moral attitudes and the speculative element in many modern financial structures have led to less emphasis on *causa* restrictions even in this narrower sense, see for example Article 3.40 of the Dutch CC. In any event the Dutch CC no longer uses *causa* language but rather the notion of illegality. However, French law in particular maintains the notion of *causa* which therefore retains residual importance, possibly because the notion of good faith is still less pervasive in balancing the contractual intent in France.

The English were willing to give up the notion of consideration for international sales when ratifying the 1964 Hague Sales Conventions, which were the predecessors of the Vienna Convention on the International Law of Sales, and the USA was willing to do so whilst ratifying the 1980 Vienna Convention which does not have a consideration or *causa* requirement, as we saw. This is clearly the trend. The requirements of consideration or *causa* are also absent from the Unidroit Principles for International Commercial Contracts and European Contract Principles.[69] As we saw, in England, the abolition of the consideration requirement altogether was proposed by the Law Society in 1975.[70] As discussed above,[71] this does not necessarily mean, however, an abandonment of the idea of bargain or exchange in favour of the notion of consensus and a normative contract interpretation.

It may well be that in international transactions the requirements of consideration or *causa* have already lapsed altogether. The question of the significance of consideration in international transactions has more generally arisen where for example English law is made applicable through a contractual choice of law clause. It is now often believed that such a choice does not necessarily mean to introduce consideration notions any longer, if there are no other clear contacts with English or common law. The idea is that, through a contractual choice of law, parties cannot have meant to enter into an agreement that was never binding for lack of consideration.[72]

Finally, a brief word on the history of these concepts of consideration and *causa*, which, although often compared, had by no means the same significance. In England, the doctrine of consideration was first formulated within the development of the writ of *indebitatus*

---

normal contract types are no longer affected by it. Under Article 1448 Italian CC, there is also a possibility of setting certain contracts aside because of disproportionality, but there must be another element, like abuse or exploitation. That is also the gist of German case law under Section 138(2) BGB. See for the *causa* notion also the references in n 80 *infra*.

[69] It does not appear that it may be reintroduced through application of a national law pursuant to applicable conflict rules under Article 7(2) as a matter of gap-filling in the area of formation or outright as a matter not covered by the Convention at all.

[70] See also Lord Wright, "Ought the Doctrine of Consideration to be Abolished", 49 *Harv LR* (1936) 1225; AG Chloros, "The Doctrine of Consideration and the Reform of the Law of Contract" 17 *Int' and Comp LQ* (1968) 137; Horwitz, "History of Contract Laws", 87 *Harv LR* (1974) 917, and PS Atiyah, "Consideration: A Restatement" in *Essays on Contract* (1986), 179.

[71] See text preceding n 58 *supra*.

[72] See also O Lando, "The Lex Mercatoria in International Commercial Arbitration" 34 *Intern'l and Comp LQ* (1985) 747.

assumpsit, as we saw, and was used to propel the notion of contract out of its primitive phase of barter into its modern form of an exchange of promises for the future, therefore of a bilateral or *executory* contract.[73]

The notion of *causa* in civil law developed in the *ius commune* which under scholastic influence looked for a cause in all legal acts. The *causa* is believed to have been first formulated as a general contractual requirement in the fourteenth century by Baldus.[74] It was combined with his then new view on the binding effect of the consensus which was itself inspired by the requirements of the commercial practice and the Canon law as discussed above.[75] This notion of cause allowed the abolition of the formalities earlier thought necessary to prevent rashness. Instead, the *causa* required an objectively serious intention for contractual engagements to be binding, but it sometimes came also to be seen as requiring some balance of the parties' interest, as such not much different therefore from the consideration notion in common law.

Yet it should be remembered that in civil law the *causa* operated next to the consensus as an occasional corrective only, whilst, in common law, the much later notion of bargain and exchange within the consideration requirement became basic for the formation of all contracts (except if under seal) and could result in agreements without a clear consensus. Although the notion of the *causa* may well have had an early influence in England and probably contributed there to the consideration notion in its emphasis on circumstance, seriousness and reasons for a promise,[76] in civil law the notion of *causa* never acquired anything near the central role consideration did in common law and these two concepts should therefore not be equated as they often are in legal scholarship.

By the nineteenth century, the *causa* requirement was no longer considered necessary by German scholars who increasingly depended on will theories rather than on internal contractual logic or virtue. It was not retained in the German BGB of 1900, for that reason. It was rather superseded by the good faith notion in contract which was increasingly used to re-introduce normative and moral elements. Grotius had retained the notion of *causa*, requiring a reasonable cause.[77] In the France of the eighteenth century, it also remained popular.[78] From there it entered the French *Code Civil* (Articles 1108, 1131 and 1133) and continued to be strongly defended by more modern authors like Capitant.[79] French law requires the valid cause to remain existent all through the life of the contract. This was unlike case-law in the Netherlands based on similar provisions (before its new Code). They required a valid cause only at the time of the conclusion of the contract.[80] As was shown, corrections of this sort to the parties' intent are in civil law

---

[73] It was virtually abandoned by Lord Mansfield in the 18th century in favour of a much more Continental approach, as we already saw but it did not persist: see n 47 *supra*.

[74] *Commentarius Codicis* ad C 4.30.13, nn 22 and 23. D. 2.14.7.4 already mentioned the concept and proved a ready base for its further development.

[75] See s 1.2.1 *supra*.

[76] See AWB Simpson, *A History of the Common Law of Contracts. The Rise of the Action of Assumpsit* (1975), 199.

[77] *Inleiding tot de Hollandsche Rechts-geleerdheid* [Introduction to Roman Dutch Law], II.1.53. See for the development of the will notion in Germany, J Gordley, *The Philosophical Origins of Modern Contract Doctrine* (Clarendon Press, 1991), 162 *ff*. The great protagonist was von Savigny, 3 *System des heutigen römischen Rechts* (1840), 258 against R von Jhering, *Zweck im Recht* (3rd edn, 1898) who continued to emphasise the purposes for which people contract and the reasons the objective law enforces their commitments. L Duguit in France followed him: *Les transformations générales du droit privé depuis le Code Napoléon* (2nd edn, 1920), 72 and 97 and even denied the independent existence of subjective rights believing them to be entirely dependent on the social order.

[78] See Pothier, *Traité des Obligations*, no 42, who limited it to an 'honest cause'.

[79] *De la Cause des Obligations* (1928). Planiol, 2 *Traité Elémentaire de Droit Civil* (1949), 291 proved critical of the cause concept, however.

[80] See HR, 6 Jan 1922 [1922] NJ 265. The use of the *causa* notion in the sense of requiring a proper balance or just price was explicitly rejected in modern times by the Dutch Supreme Court in 1936: see HR, 13 Nov [1937]

now increasingly obtained through the notions of fairness and reasonableness or good faith in the context of the objective or normative interpretation method in countries like Germany and the Netherlands.

The fact that fairness notions are less accepted as correctives in common Law but also in some civil law countries may have favoured the survival of the consideration doctrine in countries of the common law and the *causa* notion in countries like France. In this connection it may also be noted that the notion of a just price has not completely been abandoned either and stages regular revivals, although in the end it has always proved an impractical criterion for contract validity or adjustment.[81] It is in any event no longer related to the *causa* or consideration requirements, but rather to general notions of good faith leading to contractual adjustment only in exceptional cases.

1.2.8   Custom and the Interpretation of Contracts

In the interpretation of contracts and the determination of the rights and duties of the parties thereunder, it is normal in civil law to take custom also into account. It then operates alongside good faith notions, at least according to Article 1135 of the French Cc and Section 157 of the BGB in Germany. In the normative or teleological interpretation method, both come together in any event (sometimes as extra statutory norms) to determine the contractual contents and the rights and duties of the parties, although in Germany a distinction is often still made between custom and normal commercial practice or usage as implied condition. The latter must be proven as fact. Custom or customary law need not be so proven and is an independent source of law to the extent that it can still function in civil law, see also chapter 1, section 1.3.1 where we saw that the status of custom has always been a problem in civil law after the nineteenth century codifications in view of the exclusivity aims of these codifications.[82] Hence the preference to rely here only on implied consent of the parties[83] or otherwise on statutory references to custom like the ones just mentioned in de French Cc and the German BGB. Sensitivity to accepted practices and custom is, however, particularly important in international trade. It is also a major cornerstone of the notion and operation of the *lex mercatoria* as was also more fully discussed in the previous chapter.[84]

Like in the case of good faith, it suggests an objective approach. We have therefore the text of the contract and what good faith and custom add to it. Other statutory provisions may of course equally add to the contract and then we have the extra statutory duties of care and disclosure and sometimes even of renegotiatuion in the post-contractual phase. Again, it suggests different rights and duties in different contractual phases and variations also according to the nature of the relationship of the parties and the factual circumstances

---

NJ 433. In the Netherlands, the cause notion was particularly criticised by the original designer of the new Civil Code: see EM Meijers, *Nieuwe Bijdragen omtrent de Leer der Consideration en Causa* [New Contributions to the Notions of Consideration and Causa], Verz W [Collected Works] (1955), III, 301, and does not appear in the new Civil Code, except in the context of an immoral cause: see Article 3.40 (but differently phrased). See for the causa notion also M Storme, "The Binding Character of Contracts, Cause and Consideration" in A Hartkamp et al. (eds), *Towards a European Civil Code* (1998), 239.

[81] See eg O Schachter, "Just Prices in World Markets", (1975) 69 *AJIL* 101.
[82] See also chapter 1, s 1.3.1.
[83] See also Articles 8 and 9 of the Vienna Convention on the International Sale of Goods. See for a comment chapter 1, s 1.5.2.
[84] See chapter 1, s 1.5.2.

of the case. Within the normative interpretation technique, the good faith notion may also refer to pressing moral, social or even efficiency considerations in the interpretation of the contract as other objective standards. Party autonomy or parties' intent finds here its limit in the interpretation process.

As we saw, in the normative interpretation method, good faith notions may in such pressing cases also be used to adapt the contract. Mandatory statutory law may always do so assuming that the contract is sufficiently connected with the mandatory rule in question. Custom may sometimes play a similar corrective role.[85]

1.2.9 Other Aspects of Contractual Validity: Capacity and Authority

Capacity is truly only an issue for natural persons who may be minors or otherwise incapacitated. In the professional sphere it should not have any relevance as legal, not natural persons normally operate there, although their *legal existence* itself will have to be verified. Directors or managers may operate outside their authority or *ultra vires,* but it has long been accepted that this is the risk of the company rather than of a counterparty acting in good faith. There is no need therefore for counter-parties to verify the powers of those who act for a company and they may depend on *apparent authority* if there are no obvious reasons to doubt that authority.

Thus in the EU already in the First Company Law Harmonisation Directive (68/151) of 1968, the so-called *ultra vires* doctrine was abolished. It has more recently raised its head, however, in England in dealings with local authorities. Swap contracts with them have been considered *ultra vires* in the sense that these authorities were not considered to be empowered to enter into speculative interest rate instruments or derivatives. These agreements were as a consequence voided and local authorities and municipalities were not required to pay up under them.[86]

In England, it subsequently gave rise to much litigation and many restitution claims where local authorities already had collected under these swaps. The argument of *ultra vires* was also used in the USA by Orange County in its suit against Merrill Lynch in connection with its own disastrous derivative losses in the 1990s. The pressure to protect local authorities in this manner may be understandable, but the use made of the capacity argument to undermine the apparent authority and justifiable reliance may be seriously questioned.

In trusts, the situation is so far different that one has to look at the powers and capacity of acting trustees, *not* in terms of what the trust deed allows them to do, which is irrelevant as they always act in their own name, but in terms of their own capacity as natural or legal persons.

Lack of capacity should be distinguished from lack of disposition rights or *authority* in that sense. The thief has legal capacity but no disposition rights in the stolen assets, in which he can therefore not transfer valid title. That goes for all non-owners of assets, although the buyer may be protected because of his *bona fides,* especially in respect of chattels in civil law. That will not normally cover lack of capacity, see more in particular chapter 4, section 1.5.1.

---

[85] See also chapter 1, s 1.5.2 for the reference to custom in Section 157 BGB in Germany, the sometimes mandatory nature of custom in international law, the overriding concept of good faith in Article 6(2) of the new Dutch CC (which gives it always the leading role and allows it in pressing cases to overrule the wording of the contract, custom and even statutory law), the UCC and English approaches.

[86] *Hazell v Hammersmith and Fulham London Borough Council and Others* [1991] 1 All ER 545.

1.2.10   Other Aspects of Contractual Validity: Formalities

As regards *formalities*, in France, Article 1341 CC requires all contracts with a value in excess of 50 French Francs to be expressed in writing. If such a writing does not exist, evidence of its existence by witnesses may not be given. A similar rule obtained in the Netherlands until 1923. It has a long history and may be traced back to Article 54 of the French *Ordonnance de Moulins* of 1566. It does not apply to commercial contracts. In *non-commercial* contracts its impact has been reduced in France by allowing a beginning of written evidence to be sufficient. Also tape recordings are now accepted as sufficient evidence of a contract with a value in excess of 50 French Francs. Most importantly, admission or recognition may overcome the impediment or, to put it differently, if the voidness for lack of form is not invoked, the agreement stands.

In common law countries, there is the Statute of Frauds requirement. The Act dates from 1677 and requires a written document in a number of cases. The most important are real estate contracts and guarantees or sureties. Only for these two does the Act remain in force in the UK. In these cases, lack of form does not void the transaction *per se* but makes it unenforceable at the request of either party. In the USA under Article 2 of the UCC (Section 2–201), the sale of goods must still be evidenced by a written document if in excess of US$500 in order for such a sale to be enforceable. Again, recognition or admission cures the defect in form. A similar formal requirement is not contained in the English Sale of Goods Act and it is also not a requirement under the Vienna Convention for the International Sale of Goods.

The requirement of a document for a sales contract in respect of real estate is fairly common and has now also been introduced in the Netherlands through its new Code in 1992. In Germany a notarised deed is necessary for the sale of land, Section 311b BGB, but a buyer may, if good faith so requires, prove the agreement by other means and may demand possession even without the form being observed. On the other hand, the seller may repossess the land for lack of form if good faith so dictates for him. It clearly depends on the circumstances.

The requirement of a written document guards against lightheartedness but may also lead to abuse as it allows sellers to accept higher offers before a written contract is signed. They commonly do so in real estate transactions in England (gazumping), increasing the uncertainty and cost for the buyer. Here the German system seems to render fairer results. It is true that in common law there is the doctrine of *part performance* under which a vendor may be forced to perform if he knows that the buyer is acting in reliance on his oral promises, but this does not prevent gazumping in England.

Other contracts that often require written form are assignments. This is so in the Netherlands and in France. Equitable assignments in England do not, and that goes for all assignments in the USA. In many countries, secured transactions in movables also require a written document. So in the Netherlands where they must also be registered (if not notarial). Third-party guarantees always require a document in Germany, see Section 766 BGB.

In all these cases there is therefore the question whether, in the absence of the proper written form, the contract may still be proven. Another question is whether recognition may overcome the absence of the proper form and how abuse is to be countered. As we saw, there is no single answer to these questions. The international lawyer needs, however, to be aware of the different possibilities.

1.2.11   Other Aspects of Contractual Validity: Definiteness

As to the requirement of *definiteness*, traditionally it may be said that most contract laws require some specificity as to its object. In sales agreements that translates into clarity on quantity, quality, price and place and time of delivery.

Under the UCC in the USA a contract for the sale of goods does not fail for lack of definiteness, however, if one or more of these terms are left open, as long as there is a reasonably certain basis for an appropriate remedy. The UCC requires as the minimum for the validity of a sales contract only agreement on quantity. It need not even be accurately stated but recovery is limited by what is said, whilst the price, time and place of payment or delivery, the general quality of the goods or any particular warranties may all be omitted, see Section 2–204(2) and also the Official Comment at Section 2–201.

Similarly the Vienna Convention on the International Sale of Goods insists in Article 14 only on some clarity as to quantity and price, at least the offer must be sufficiently definite in these respects, although as far as price is concerned, Article 55 gives some further guidance. Article 19(3) of the Vienna Convention also suggests other material elements, like payment, quality, place and time of delivery, but they need not be spelled out in the contract for it to be binding and for most of them the Convention gives additional (directory) rules.[87]

The question of definiteness may also arise in other types of contracts. Mortgage arrangements must often be precise as to what asset is secured for what type of debt. In assignments, the assigned debts may have to be described with sufficient precision. More generally, contracts for the sale of future assets (or for the creation of security interests therein) may be undermined when they are not certain to emerge, although this may impact more on the validity of any transfers thereunder.

1.3 The Civil Law Notion of Good Faith and the Common Law Alternatives of Implied Terms, Nature of the Relationship of the Parties, and Reliance

1.3.1 The Notion of Good Faith in Civil Law

In section 1.2.2, some considerable attention was already devoted to the emergence of the notion of good faith as a central theme in the civil law of contract, all the more so within the modern normative interpretation methods. It warrants a further in-depth discussion. This being said, it should be immediately added that, in the civil law of contract, good faith is still a much stronger concept in the countries of Northern Europe than it is in those of the South.

Technically, references to good faith may be found in civil law codes, in Germany especially in Sections 157 and 242 BGB (but reference may also be made in this connection to Sections 119, 157, 226, 819 BGB), in France in Articles 1134 and 1135 Cc, in Italy in Articles 1337, 1366 and 1375 CC, and in the Netherlands in Articles 6.2 and 6.248 CC. As we already saw, it is increasingly used as a general concept in the interpretation, supplementation and sometimes correction of the parties' intent or the clear wording of an agreement. It may also be used more widely in any interrelationship between natural or legal persons like in the law of companies and partnerships. But it is also used (also outside contract law) to

---

[87] The Vienna Convention does not itself deal with the subject of validity any further, see Article 4, and therefore does not concern itself either with the effects of incapacity, mistake, misrepresentation, undue influence, fraud and illegality on the existence of the sales contract. The consensus, the importance of the parties' intent, the subject of implied conditions, and the impact of their pre-contractual duties on the conclusion of the sales agreement are also not covered. The Convention does not deal with representation or agency powers and their proper use either; in fact it expressly removes undisclosed agency from its scope: see Article 1(2). The Unidroit Principles for International Commercial Contracts are more comprehensive and may eventually also cover agency relationships.

relate better the facts to the norm whilst selecting and reformulating both and may then also affect statutory interpretation.

In the formation of the contract itself, reliance plays in this approach a most important role. Article 1337 of the Italian CC specifically refers here to good faith requirements, whereas Section 317(2)(3) BGB (new) now clearly acknowledges mutual obligations in the pre-contractual phase, which, as we saw, increasingly implies pre-contractual (disclosure and negotiation) duties. Good faith is traditionally more especially important in the performance of contracts, particularly in relation to weaker parties but may be no less relevant in the formulation of excuses when for example *force majeure* or hardship is invoked or where demanding punctual performance would become unconscionable or an abuse of right. Good faith may also play a role in the avoidance of the contracts for reasons of misrepresentation or mistake. It may even lead to post-contractual re-negotiation duties. This was already discussed in greater detail in section 1.2.2 above and need not be repeated.

The starting point is that in all these countries contracts are interpreted and must be performed in good faith. Particularly in Germany, but no less so in Switzerland, Austria and the Netherlands, the requirement of good faith has, however, become an all-pervading notion applicable to all dealings between persons, although especially relevant in determining the rights and duties of the parties in contract law and then plays a role in the continuum of pre-contractual, formation, performance and post-contractual behaviour of the parties.

Indeed in the *normative* interpretation method, good faith and interpretation fundamentally mix. In this approach, whether a contract is formed and when, whether it is valid and enforceable, and against whom, and how gaps are to be filled or how the contract is to be performed are all matters of interpretation and construction of the rights and duties of the parties in the light of the good faith requirement in an atmosphere of contractual co-operation. Within this good faith approach, principles of a moral, economic or social nature, as well as practical or ordinary course of business considerations and requirements of reasonable care and expectation may filter through and, if sufficiently pressing, may even override any original intent of the parties or the wording of their agreement. Within the good faith approach, regard may also be had to the nature of the relationship between the parties in terms of dependence or professionality, their particular interests and expectation whilst the subject matter of their contract will also be considered. In this approach, the good faith duty soon spills over into the pre-contractual and post-contractual relationships as we saw.

Although all seem to accept the better protection of weaker or less informed parties and, in this connection, also some distinction on the basis of the nature of the relationship between the parties, in non-germanic civil law countries, in the area of contract, it remains less clear, however, how far the concept goes. French law is here traditionally more cautious than German law, which has now (in 2002) put concepts of pre-contractual (Sections 311(2) and (3) BGB) and other accessory duties extending to the post-contractual phase (Sections 280 and 241(2) BGB) as well as the adjustment of contractual terms (Section 313 BGB) on a statutory basis. Common law, particularly in England,[88] also takes a cautious view, as we saw, although it is now different in the US. Traditional common law emphasises the compatible declarations in the formation of the contract, which are fairly literally or objectively understood, but it will in the performance of the contract also accept implied terms and

---

[88] See also R Goode, 'The Concept of Good Faith in English Law', in Centro di studi e ricerche di diritto comparato e straniero, *Saggi, conferenze e seminariu*, no. 2 (Rome, 1992).

distinguish on the basis of the nature of the (professional or other) relationship of the parties, thus protecting especially the weaker ones. Increasingly it also accepts more normative, dependency and reliance notions in the formation of the contract. Thus it accepts sometimes also fiduciary co-operation and disclosure duties if only giving rise to tort claims rather than entering the area of contractual remedies.

In the Netherlands has the concept of good faith been elevated to a rank above custom and statutory law and may affect and correct the application of both at least in contract law (Article 6(2) CC). This was already mentioned in section 1.2.8 above. Although this is understandable in individual cases when major overriding principles of justice and fairness are involved — one could even say that overriding moral notions must in a modern society in the end always prevail — the Dutch approach is all the same a new and isolated departure. It is somewhat curious for a notion that is inherently so vague and, in many of its applications, not necessarily mandatory. Where it is not mandatory, it would seem to be perfectly capable of being overruled or contractually curtailed, at least in its consequences, especially by professional parties amongst themselves as for example in the USA is fully understood in Section 1–302(b) (1–102(3) old) of the UCC (which allows parties to set standards unless manifestly unreasonable). It would appear that for professionals, good faith notions can be mandatory only in exceptional cases and must even then be used with restraint. The Unidroit and European Principles of Contract Law in extolling the mandatory force of the good faith notion seems to suffer from a profound misconception, unsupported by any serious comparative law analysis of domestic laws in this field.[89]

All the same, in contract law, there are several reasons for the modern pre-eminence of good faith notions and ideas. The main problem identified before is that the old contract framework, based largely on the notion of a private deal between two individuals motivated by their psychological intent or will, no longer suffices in the corporate or governmental world of major contracts often negotiated in different parts by different people. Another issue was that when these contracts are concluded in standard form with large groups of people or multiple legal entities they also started to have a much greater impact on their environment so that there arose special protection needs for large groups of weaker parties like at first workers and later consumers, smaller counter-parties or smaller investors under financial service contracts. Yet it proved almost impossible to provide for a newer coherent set of contract rules or indeed for an updated contract model altogether.

The pressures are the same everywhere. In civil law, especially in Northern Europe, the stress thus caused in the system of contract law was largely absorbed by the notion of good faith in the formation and enforcement of contracts, although often, it must be admitted, in inarticulate ways. Thus the notion of reliance, special pre-contractual disclosure and negotiation duties, special performance duties in terms of co-operation and loyalty, the possibility of adjustment of contractual terms in extreme cases, and post-contractual renegotiation duties have developed alongside more precise abuse notions as well as (more timidly) a greater sense of differentiation according to the type of counterparty. Common law, which always put more emphasis on the relationship between the parties and would also allow for special duties in the case of dependency, needed, from that perspective, the notion of good faith much less, but it also had to find a way for contract interpretation to become more reflective of social needs. Here implied terms (of reasonableness) may be used. Also it cannot avoid the process of better relating the facts to the existing norms either, whilst the distance between them seems to widen constantly, even if in common law this tailoring function is not captured in good faith terms.

---

[89] See also s 1.3.3 *infra.*

The notion of good faith in its function of relating facts to the applicable norm and even in tailoring that norm to the facts (themselves being selected on the basis of their relevance in relation to the chosen norm) has not fundamentally changed over time, but as just mentioned the distance between fact and norm may now be greater and there may be much more to bridge. Further, different situations need to be distinguished for which new (derivative) patterns of norms may have to be identified. That is what the normative approach, with its sensitivity also to pressing ethical, social and economic considerations, in essence does. Particularly in the northern European civil law countries, the old good faith notion has thus been stretched to provide the cover and has, on the norm side, become a much more dynamic concept of destruction, change and regeneration of rules, whilst becoming on the factual side much more selective and discriminating of different situations. In the process, it has also served as the basis for more judicial discretion, at least in the details and has, even in civil law, ultimately confirmed the courts in their (informal) rule formulating role.

A simple example is the situation where I do some construction work on my house, employ some workmen and order some materials from third parties. When these arrive, they will have to be unloaded and given a place. From all persons present some form of co-operation may be required. What is customary, normal, practical and makes good sense in the circumstances will figure in the proper performance of each party, in which there may be implied duties of co-operation, even though in principle the contractual frameworks under which each person works may be formally unconnected. The *factual circumstances* dictate what is required of everyone in this respect and how the rules under which everyone is engaged will be tailored to match the situation in a reasonable or good faith manner and what in this connection will be considered acceptable conduct in which supplementary duties may also figure quite apart from the contract with each party which are unlikely to be formally connected. That is reflected in Section 241(2) BGB. It here concerns a basic judicial function and technique which is in fact applied everywhere, even if not so identified.

It may thus be seen that the modern notion of good faith is primarily used in civil law to obtain greater flexibility, both in restating the applicable norm and the relevant facts. It always was and essentially still is an interpretation tool, connecting fact and norm and tailoring both to each other, but it has become a much more dynamic legal concept (especially, but not only, when responding to pressing moral, social or economic considerations) in its gap filling and correcting role. As such it is at once a destructive and a regenerating or norm-renewing force.

Indeed, good faith has obtained a *multifaceted* nature. It shows as it is sometimes norm, sometimes fact.[90] It is sometimes judicial discretion and sometimes judicial limitation. It may be legal principle, sometimes a more precise legal rule. It is sometimes highest norm (if morally, socially or economically sufficiently pressing, and then mandatory), sometimes practical norm (if promoting good sense, co-operation and reasonable care, and is then directory). It is sometimes legal refinement and differentiation, sometimes generalisation and system building. It is sometimes rule formulation, at other times rule application selecting and weighing the relevant facts and defining the legal consequences (*Konkretisierung*). It is sometimes subjective, but mostly objective. It sometimes looks at the nature of legal

[90] The traditional sharp Kantian distinction between fact and norm, although from a logical point of view correct and sometimes still defended, see Larenz, *Methodenlehre der Rechtswissenschaft* (5th edn, 1983), 128, has under Wittgensteinian influence lost its hold and it is clear that what 'should be done' legally takes the place of what is done when widely considered appropriate in common law. It is also reflected in the maxim of equity: 'equity considers done what should be done'.

relationships of the parties and their special interests and sometimes at the nature of their deal and its particular features. At one time it sets rules for judicial decision making but provides at other times only judicial direction and guidance. It looks for fairness, particularly in consumer and small company cases, and for what makes sense and is practical, particularly in business cases. It is sometimes structure, but mostly movement. It is always inter-relational but probably more important in human relationships than in business dealings.

On the factual side, it is attention for the individual case and its own distinctive features. On the normative side it is a quest for modernisation, refinement and social awareness which may lead to modernised rules. The use of the good faith notions in contract law signals a quest for more objective criteria to determine the parties' rights and duties, and as such it presents a challenge to the nineteenth-century will theory and to the notion of each party's psychological intent. If thus favours depersonification of contract law and limits the traditional anthropomorphic idea of contract. So far, it must be said that in this connection the formulation of new rules has *not* always had much priority in case law or in legal scholarship in the Northern European countries of the civil law group. This is certainly the situation in Germany and the Netherlands, although in German doctrine there is some attempt at classification of functions (*Funktionkreise*), like interpretation, supplementation and correction of duties or adjustment in case of a profound change of circumstances, functions which are by no means new and are now expressed in specific provisions of the BGB: Sections 241(2), 280, 311(2)(3), 313.[91] Within these functions, there is a further effort to distinguish classes of cases (*Fallgrupen*), like, in the supplementation function, the development of pre-contractual and post-contractual rights and duties and of consumer or workers' rights (not necessarily, however, along the lines of altogether clear rules or new contract types), and, in the correction function, the emphasis on estoppel, abuse of rights, own co-operation duties, and on the manner in which the rights were acquired or are invoked like in the case of standard terms.

The Germans talk in this connection often of the inner system (*Binnensystematik*) of the good faith notion, referring in particular to the reliance notion, pre-contractual duties, normative interpretation, supplementation and correction techniques, the (continued) validity of the contract, the performance obligations and excuses of the parties, and, in appropriate cases, to their re-negotiation duties, all originally developed on the basis of the good faith notion. It may be a function of the German predelection for system building, where academia tries to reintegrate disparate case-law in their system, judges having become here *more inventive* and less formal than legal scholarship, see also chapter 1, section 1.2.10. There is no question of a different legal system as equity once was in Common Law, rather of an elaboration and refinement or a curtailment of existing

---

[91] See the major commentary of Palandt/Heinrichs, *Bürgerliches Gesetzbuch* (1997), at s 242, nos 2 and 13. The functions of good faith are commonly the ones identified in the interpretation, supplementation or correction of the contract, in the formulation of co-operation duties in the performance and of special disclosure and negotiation duties in the pre-and post-contractual phases. In the normative approach all are rolled into one continuum.

The first three functions appear already in the Digests, there in connection with the definition of the powers of the Roman praetor in contract law (D.1.1.7 Papinianus), see also F Wieacker, *Zur Rechtstheoretischen Präzisierung des sec 242, Recht und Staat in Geschichte und Gegenwart* (Tübingen, 1956), 20. *The fallgrupen* are created by following or distinguishing precedent. They identify so far more a method of judicial activity than clear rules. Only some clear notions developed as the abuse of rights (*exceptio doli*), the notion of clean hands, of own misbehaviour and of lack of co-operation. Also the loss of a right to performance became accepted if there were contrary conduct or declarations on which the other party could rely as an excuse. Another development was in the loss of rights whilst not timely invoking them (*Verwirkung*). All are of limited application. It is altogether not a large crop.

contractual or other legal rules or concepts (like the notion of estoppel or abuse of rights) and their application. This has led, however, to a greater emphasis on the facts of each case and, in appropriate cases, to a review of the moral, social or economic consequences of the enforcement of the contract.

The *multifaceted* nature of good faith both on the factual and the norm side and its sometimes high tone, as well as the flexibility and judicial discretion it suggests, have induced a sense of unease in many, also in civil law, and a feeling that there is perhaps too much judicial freedom to distinguish and declare cases a-typical, too much attention to the facts, too much consideration of the environment or setting of each case, too much concern for moral, social and economic principle, too much judicial creativity as to pre-contractual, performance and post-contractual duties, whilst the courts are sometimes believed to arrogate to themselves perhaps too much policy initiative, and too much directory or rule making power as a result of which party autonomy suffers.

Yet in practice, the courts have always had these powers. This was never found exceptional or fundamentally objectionable in common law (especially not in equity). In civil law, it necessarily followed from its own interpretation techniques and requirements, which meant to fill in all gaps in its codes that pretended to cover all. Yet it went against one particular aspect of the codification notion, especially against the idea that judges should only decide on the basis of clear rules enacted by the legislature, and therefore against the idea of the separation of powers. This certainly explains some of the continuing resistance to the good faith notion, also in civil law, at least at the theoretical level. More to the point is probably the unease with the inability or perhaps unwillingness of courts and legal scholarship in civil law countries to formulate more precise new (self-binding) contract rules and more generally with the lack of a proper definition of the role of the judiciary in a modern society, whose powers have been extended everywhere on the basis of practical need and expediency (in the absence of help from often confused and insufficiently responsive legislatures), but who, on the other hand, are believed to lack sufficient democratic legitimacy.

It appears that in truth there is in civil law more fundamentally a shift from norm to fact, therefore from emphasis on rules to emphasis on the circumstances of each case and the nature of the relationship between the parties in terms of professional, small company or consumer dealings. There is here some convergence with the more traditional common law approach, which never needed the good faith notion to emphasise the different nature of the relationship between parties in terms of professionality or the lack thereof. In civil law, the development of the good faith concept in the modern expanded sense can simply be seen as the unavoidable consequence of a much more diversified and often more indirect way of (contractually) committing oneself and to a much greater variety of interests than were ever considered by the Codes.

There can be little doubt that in the civil law of contract, the notion of good faith has proved a great source of creativity, flexibility and adjustment, even if, as in all cases in which legal formalism and inflexibility ultimately let go under pressure of fundamental principle, economic and social developments, or simply practical needs, the result has often been unstructured and predictability has unavoidably suffered. Hence the urge in civil law academic writings particularly in Germany to find some structure even in good faith notions and their application. But it is exactly the flexibility they bring that should be treasured and was their justification.

Indeed a vague rule (or as the Germans call it a *Generalklausel*) left to be implemented, resulting in some greater judicial discretion, may often be better than a wrong rule or no rule at all. Although on occasion it may have reduced *party autonomy* even in the commercial or professional sphere whenever good faith aspires to a mandatory impact, this seems so far not to have been of great consequence, whilst it could even be argued that good faith notions have allowed the true meaning of party autonomy to develop and better prevail. But the real danger, shown by the German example is that consumer protection notions spill over in the professional sphere as a consequence of a good faith notion that is thought to operate in the same way for all. It is true that in appropriate cases, there are now more objective criteria impacting on the parties' rights and duties, often inspired by a quest for social peace and justice, sometimes mandatorily, but a better contractual environment all around may in itself be an advantage for contracting parties and may provide them with more safety in their dealings. It is also likely to be more cost effective. On the other hand, there may be a lesser concern for and therefore impact of good faith in dealings amongst professionals where the good faith notion could even lead to rules that are more strictly enforced or to an approach in which the literal meaning of the wording of the contract has a greater impact.

As already mentioned, German and Dutch law increasingly tend to see all legal relationships as conditioned by good faith and as acquiring their specific legal meaning in that context.[92] In these countries, in contract law, the notion of good faith folds into the normative approach to the interpretation of the contract. It places emphasis not only on what the reasonable man will do but on occasion also on what he ought to do, when the notion of good faith may acquire a social, redistributive function, especially, as we saw, in relation to weaker parties, like consumers and workers or smaller licensees or franchisees, but sometimes also between the stronger ones if there was unforeseeable unconscionability in the consequences.

To elaborate particularly on the case of a change in circumstances as an example, under German case law, notions of good faith (or *Treu und Glauben*) applied to rebalance the contract in the case of a change of circumstances that is so severe that it leads to a collapse of the basis of the agreement (*Wegfall der Geschäftsgrundlage*), now codified in Section 313 BGB.[93] Also in the Netherlands, this is now so under statutory law, see Article 6.258 CC.

---

[92] In Germany, there has been an attempt at condensing the field by introducing special duties only for persons that are in some special relationship. The sensitivity to the nature of the relationship of the parties is here beginning to find some better expression (*Sonderverbindungen*): see K Larenz, *Lehrbuch des Schuldrechts, I Band Allgemeiner teil* (14th edn, 1987), 14, but recent codification of extra-contractual duties from the pre-contractual to the post-performance stages as well as of the possibility to adjust contractual terms in extreme circumstances does not differentitiate between the nature of the parties.

[93] In Germany, the situation became particularly acute after World War I with the inflation wave in the early 1920s. It was left to case law to sort things out. In two important cases the German Supreme Court allowed a revaluation (*Aufwertung*) of fixed contract prices, RGHZ 103, 328 (1922) and RGHZ 107, 78, 87–92 (1923). At the time, a whole doctrine of change of circumstances developed: see especially P Oertmann, *Die Geschäftsgrundlage, ein neuer Rechtsbegriff* (1921), and *Geschäftsgrundlage, 2 Handwörterbuch der Rechtswissenschaft* (1927). The concept was distinguished from that of *force majeure* under Section 275 BGB and was at first built on a set of tacit assumptions surrounding the contractual arrangements from the beginning (*Tatbestand*), in the tradition of implied conditions. That was subsequently considered too subjective and the concept of adjustment then became connected with the notion of good faith under Section 242 BGB and with the normative interpretation of contracts, see Larenz, *Vertrag und Unrecht* (1936), i, 164 and *Geschäftsgrundlage und Vertragserfüllung* (3rd ed. 1963), whilst the emphasis was put on the circumstances the continued existence of which is objectively necessary to achieve the contractual purpose, see also GH Roth, *Münchener Kommentar* (1985), II, Sec 242, no 465. Today it is codified in Section 313 BGB.

In a country like France similarly affected by the war, but less so by its aftermath, no such development took place, and French law remains strict, although many attempts were made to achieve a contractual adjustment on the basis of changed circumstances. Revalorisation was even refused concerning a price fixed in 1845, Cour de Cass, 15 Nov 1933, s 34.1.13 (1934). The French courts did not react differently after World War II: see Marty-Reynaud, *Droit Civil* (1962), 201. Except in administrative law cases, French courts will not go beyond the traditional *force majeure* excuses. In the Netherlands, the concepts of *causa* and *justum pretium* were at one time also proposed but rejected as the basis for adjustment by the Supreme Court, HR 13 Nov 1936 [1937] NJ 433 and in

In these countries, through case law, there were also developed broad disclosure and negotiation duties at the time of the contract formation, as we saw, whilst the notion of reliance became fundamental in the formation of the contract and the determination of the timing and scope of the parties' rights and duties.

In civil law not all domestic legal systems react the same, however. French law, in particular, notwithstanding the generality of the formula of Articles 1134 and 1135 Cc, remains more hesitant in its approach to good faith, even in the performance of the contract, and limits use of the concept as a corrective of the contractual terms to particular areas, like abuse of rights (*abus de droit*) by neighbours, by employers, by parties benefiting from rescission rights, or by parties insisting on performance upon a change of circumstances. Usually it concerns here instances of unequal bargaining power or the need to protect weaker parties or special co-operation and loyalty duties or distill sub-duties. They are all more recent developments. Increasingly there are also information duties accepted under this heading of good faith, however.[94]

French law on the whole still prefers to rely on other more specific concepts to define or redefine the parties' rights and duties, as indeed *abus de droit* but also *bonnes moeurs, fraude, erreur* or *enrichissement sans cause* or the notion of *causa* itself, or *impossibilité économique*, all rejected at the time, however, to redress the impact of changed circumstances, but often used instead of the broader good faith notion in other contexts.[95] Particularly the abuse notion seems to have been progressively developed in this connection, but has now also become more and more embedded in the good faith notion. An important point in this connection is that in France, good faith is still largely considered a subjective concept, even in contract law, aiming at honesty, co-operation and loyalty in a subjective sense.[96] On its face, there is therefore still little normative value in it, although a similar approach in the UCC in the USA (Section 1-201(a)(20) (1–201(19) old) UCC) has found a more objective and therefore normative direction regardless.

It is of interest that in the Netherlands, with a formula in their old Code (Articles 1374 and 1375 CC until 1992) directly derived from the French Civil Code, case law nevertheless started largely to follow the more liberal German attitude. It consequently adopted an objective meaning of good faith, eventually even as a corrective, not only to the contractual stipulations (of which adjustment in the case of a change of circumstances under Article 6.258 CC is a particular example), but (in the new Code since 1992) even to the applicable statutory law and the application of custom in contractual matters, as we saw, see Articles 6.2 and 6.248(2) CC respectively. In Article 3.12 CC there is also a statutory

---

this connection also the notion of mistake, HR 10 June 1932 [1933] NJ 5 and HR 11 Jan 1957 [1959] NJ 37. Revalorisation was also expressly rejected before the new Code, HR, 2 Jan 1931 [1931] NJ 274. In administrative cases, the situation could be different as in France.

In modern times it has not been uncommon in situations of war for special relief to be provided by statute, even in France, and special legislation was passed there on 21 Jan 1918 (*Loi Faillot*) which allowed contracts entered into before Aug 1 1914 to be terminated if causing damage to a party unforeseeable at the time of the conclusion of the agreement. A similar law was enacted on 1 July 1949 in respect of agreements entered into before 2 Sept 1939. Similarly in Germany, an act was passed on 26 Mar 1952 (*Vertragshilfegesetz*) concerning contracts entered into before 21 June 1948. These laws left the final decision to the judge and did not give criteria or guidance for adaptation or termination of the contract. Where no special statutory law came into being, however — and they were all limited in scope — the question was everywhere whether general legal principles could provide a basis for similar contract adaptation. Hence the importance of case law in this connection.

[94] See M Fabre-Magnan, "Duties of Disclosure and French Contract Law: Contribution to an Economic Analysis" in J Beatson and D Friedmann (eds), *Good Faith and Fault in Contract Law* (Oxford, 1995), 99.

[95] See Paniol-Ripert, 6 *Traité Pratique de Droit Civil Français* (1930), no 394, Demogue, 6 *Traité des Obligation en général* (1931), no 632, and Bonnecasse, *Précis de Droit Civil* (1933), no 134.

[96] See Loussouarn, "Rapport de synthèse" in *Travaux de l'Association Henri Capitant*, xliii, année 1992 (1994).

indication how the good faith notion is to be construed. It is necessary to take into account generally accepted legal principles, the legal views held in the Netherlands and the social and personal interests concerned in the case in question. In Germany, Sections 157 and 242 of the BGB refer in this connection only to commercial usage (*Verkehrssitte*) to which in Dutch case law reference is also often made (*rechtsverkeer*). However this seems to be confined to the just mentioned 'legal views' held in this connection in the Netherlands.

The French attitude needs some further attention because of its (on the surface) still deviant attitude within the civil law tradition which still tends to be followed in Latin civil law countries. As a consequence, even in Italy there is still much uncertainty about the impact of good faith notions in contract. There is also an old constitutional issue already, hinted at above. In France, as a reaction against the broad powers of the old French *Parlements* which acted as regional courts before the French Revolution (see chapter 1, section 1.2.5), Article 5 of the French Cc specifically abrogated any rule-making power of judges, whilst the law of 21 March 1804 introducing the new Code (Napoléon) in its Article 7 ruled out any other source of law, meaning especially regional custom but also equity or more fundamental legal principle. It is true that Article 1134 Cc required contracts to be performed in good faith, but already in 1808 it was made clear by the Cour de Cassation that the original intent of the parties could not be disregarded on the basis of good faith and that has been constantly confirmed.[97] Equity is not seen here as an independent source of law, although in other contexts it may be.[98]

Late Roman law nevertheless had already contained some pointers in the direction of greater flexibility in the *iudicia bona fidei* which left the judge some discretion in the enforcement of certain contractual obligations, notably those arising out of the limited number of consensual contracts that even then existed, like sales and rental agreements,[99] but there was certainly no general influx of notions of fairness. The *Ius Commune* eventually took to the view that all contracts were based on consensus and consequently allowed for *bona fide* enforcement, as we saw, but it did not develop a coherent concept of good faith in contract law, rather initially only the idea of the *causa* to balance contractual intent see section 1.2.7 above. A more coherent approach only followed in the natural law school of Grotius and Pufendorf, but the approach to contract interpretation and the precise determination of the parties' rights and duties in contract remained uncertain.

In countries of the Codification, therefore in most civil law countries, the concern about the rule-making power of judges remains a conceptual or even constitutional issue, highlighting the fact that judicial rule-making is considered at variance with the codification concept proper as was discussed in chapter 1. Only in Switzerland, under the well known Article 1 of its Civil Code, there is such a possibility if the law is silent. In most other countries, even a measure of discretion to allow for minor adjustments, to smooth out minor problems with the contractual implementation, does not fit the system. On the other hand, judges must fill the gaps and deal with lack of detail in the codes. There is here obvious tension. It is another reason why it is unlikely that the modern tide can be turned and why good faith as a dynamic, connecting and renewing force in the formation and application

---

[97] See *Conclusion Merlin* (1808), s 1.183 and in more modern times Cour de Cass, 2 Dec 1947, [1948] Gaz Pal I.36, although especially Geny and Demogue argued otherwise, see Demogue, 6 *Traité des Obligation en général* (1931), 9. This author is in many respect more modern than the more recent French writers.
[98] Thus the Cour de Cassation recognised the unjust enrichment action, which was not covered by the Code, on the basis of equity, see its decisions of 15 June 1892, [1892] D I. 596 and particularly 12 May 1914, [1918/19] s 1.41.
[99] See also M Kaser, 1 *Das römische Privatrecht* (1955), 181, 406 and P Stein, "Equitable Principles in Roman Law" in *Equity in the World's Legal Systems* (1973), 75, 80.

of contract law in particular is not likely to go away. Judges are in any event unlikely to restrict the room for manœuvre that in modern times is necessary for them to come to solutions in ever more uncharacteristic situations and more unusual cases.

In fact, there is in civil law countries at the practical level no longer a great objection to this. Although especially the French judiciary still maintains the fiction of pure rule application in often fairly short and tightly argued decisions, this change in perception of the judge's role persists and is likely to be tolerated in civil law as long as judges practise restraint and are seen to do so and can reasonably explain their actions in terms of rules, precedent or on the basis of different facts, whilst reasonable consistency is maintained and justice is seen to be done at a reasonable and affordable cost. Certainly, much faith is here put in the judiciary, its strength, traditions but also worldliness and ability to distinguish according to the parties' relationship and their type of deal. It puts a considerable burden on younger judges in lower courts, particularly in countries where being a judge is a professional career with less exposure to real life, as it mostly is in continental European countries.

1.3.2   Good Faith in Common Law. Alternatives. Equity and Fiduciary Duties Distinguished

English law does not use the concept of good faith in any general manner, but at best as an implied condition moderating intent and it is then often wrapped in terms of reasonableness or in what a reasonable man would do, although the concept is more independently acknowledged in insurance contracts (which are *uberimae fidei*). Here it is principally used, however, to protect the insurer and, through it, the scales are often loaded against the insured, as under it the insurer may repudiate a policy even on the basis of failure to disclose technically relevant but minor facts by the insured that would not have made any difference to the insurer's underwriting decision.[100]

The English attitude towards the good faith notion was criticised by Steyn LJ in his 1991 Royal Bank of Scotland law lecture at Oxford,[101] but excepting cases of 'fraud', which often lead to redress in tort, it is not likely that good (or bad) faith notions will be used as a general implementing, supplementing or correcting factor in respect of contractual terms in England, except through specific legislation, like in the Unfair Contract Terms Act of 1977 (or in implementing EU consumer law directives, not so far applicable, however, to insurance policies).

Although the common law notion of equity is sometimes equated by outsiders with the civil law good faith notion and development, this is substantially incorrect. Equity in this sense is not a general interpretative concept allowing for an influx of new ideas or even of general notions of fairness, see chapter 1, section 1.2.11. Equity adjustment is used by judges only as a last resort, except perhaps in areas entirely covered by it, like trusts, agency, company and bankruptcy law. The notions of equity are often entirely rigid, certainly also when used in contract law (as for example in the concept of rescission and specific performance) and its rules are always incidental. In civil law terms, it could often do with some good faith or normative flexibility. Upon a proper analysis, the renewing forces identified in the previous section in civil law in this connection with all their contradictions and ambivalences

---

[100] See *Container Transport Inc v Oceanus Mutual Underwriting* [1984] Lloyd's Rep 1, 47. See for a general and fundamental rejection of the notion of good faith at least in the commercial sphere, Lord Ackner in *Walford v Mile*, n 34 *infra*. See for an important contribution to the discussion on the subject in England, J Beatson and D Friedmann (eds), "Introduction: From "Classical" to Modern Contract Law", in *Good Faith and Fault in Contract Law* (Oxford, 1995), 3.

[101] *The Role of Good Faith and Fair Dealing in Contract Law: A Hair-Shirt Philosophy?*

operate equally in common law but are *not* called 'equity' and even less 'good faith'. As such they remain in essence unidentified, although it is clear that common law (equity) is more comfortable with rule-making powers of the judiciary.

As mentioned several times before, English law, instead of using the good faith concept, reflects more particularly on the nature of the relationship between the parties,[102] whilst it never defined so sharply the contractual types except sometimes in commercial law as in the case of the sale of goods and in insurance and carriage agreements, which derive from the old law merchant and continental influence. It accepts extra contractual duties easily especially in situations of dependency, even if tort liability rather than contractual liability may result. From these perspectives, there is therefore in common law less need for the good faith notion or something equivalent to provide greater flexibility. It sometimes also uses the reliance notion to determine the existence of the contract and the rights or duties of the parties thereunder, as we saw. It is also well known for its resort (sometimes) to implied terms of reasonableness.

Together this may well result in relief similar to what may be obtained under the civil law of contract within the notion of good faith, but there remains a bias in favour of more literal interpretation of contractual terms, as also demonstrated by the 'parole evidence' rule that will not allow extraneous evidence in the determination of the content of written documents. In common law it seems that the professional sphere is always left more to its own devices and less protected as the courts will not seek to interfere lightly in professional relationships, either in the formation or performance of the contract, as has already been more extensively discussed above.

As far as implied terms are concerned, the technique of gap filling is an old one, also in England,[103] although in common law, especially in the professional sphere, often still based on the presumed intention of the parties, but nevertheless construed in a more objective manner[104] and sometimes subjected to the requirement of reasonableness.[105] The implied terms could even concern the reasonableness and fairness of the deal itself.[106] Yet, especially in the professional sphere, there will be caution and restraint.

In terms of pre-contractual duties and a duty to negotiate in good faith, English law remains in the professional sphere equally reserved as long as no weaker party needs special protection. For redress in the case of reliance, it may limit itself to tort action notably excluding damages for lost profits as we saw.[107] In the USA, on the other hand, in the UCC under German influence, a general reference to good faith was inserted in Section 1–304 (1–203 old). It imposes an obligation of good faith in the performance or enforcement of every contract or duty under the UCC, but strictly speaking *not* in the formation. Interestingly, Section 1–201(a)(20) (1–201(19) old) UCC defines the concept. It means 'honesty in fact in the conduct or transactions concerned'. The 'in fact' language suggests a subjective approach ('empty head, pure heart'), but has gradually acquired a more normative or objective meaning. Indeed, Section 2–103(1)(b) UCC adds to the definition of the good faith requirement in a sale of goods between merchants 'the observance of reasonable commercial standards of fair dealing in the trade'. Section 1–302(b)

---

[102] See Bingham LJ in *Interfoto v Stiletto* [1989] 1 QB 433, 439.

[103] See *The Moorcock* (1889) 14 PD 64.

[104] *Hirji Mulji v Cheong SS Co* [1926] AC 497, 510.

[105] *Shell UK Ltd v Lostock Garages Ltd* [1976] 1 WLR 1187.

[106] *Bankline v Arthur Capel* [1918] AC 435 and *Metropolitan Waterboard v Dick* [1918] AC 119.

[107] See the probably too sweeping rejection of the notion of good faith by Lord Ackner in *Walford v Miles* [1992] 2 WLR 174 to avoid contractual liability for loss of profit. An action in negligence was allowed, however, to recover the costs of consultants hired in reliance on a deal.

(1–102(3) old) UCC allows variation of the provisions of the UCC by contract, but not of the obligations of good faith, diligence, reasonableness and care prescribed by it but the parties may set the standards by which the performance of these obligations is to be measured if such standards are not manifestly unreasonable. It shows that the concept is not completely mandatory.

There are more references to good faith in the UCC like for the sale of goods in Sections 2–603 and 2–615. It remains exceptional in the common law of contract, however, and is substantially statutory and even then, as in the UCC, incidental, as the many individual references to it testify. At least in the UCC, good faith does *not* cover pre-contractual duties or strictly speaking even gap-filling but *only* the performance or enforcement of the contract, here joined by a general provision on the unenforceability of *unconscionable clauses* in contracts for the sale of goods, see Section 2–302 UCC, particularly (but not only) relevant in sales to consumers.[108] On the other hand, in the USA, the non-binding Restatement (Second) of Contracts of 1981, Section 205, states more generally that every contract imposes upon each party a duty of good faith and fair dealing in its performance and its enforcement. This was followed in the 1990 revision of Section 3–103(a)(4) of the UCC which accepts the idea that good faith now also means the observance of reasonable commercial standards of fair dealing, but this is in connection with negotiable instruments only, whilst good faith remains here also a matter of performance and enforcement of the contract only.

It follows, nevertheless, that in the interpretation of intent, the normative approach is now increasingly followed in the USA. Australia and New Zealand also have abandoned the narrow common law approach in this area. More limited notions of foreseeability and reasonableness may, however, commonly be found in most legal systems as possible correctives to the parties' exposure in this connection when it comes to any assessment of damages even where the requirements of good faith are deemed violated.

The more restrictive English attitude may not be as strange as it sometimes seems, particularly to German lawyers. As already suggested, the restrictive English attitude is largely limited to the commercial and professional spheres where parties are capable of providing a clear direction in their dealings, are less dependent on each other, often willing to take more risks and can hire expert advice better to look after themselves, whilst in that sphere, even in civil law, the good faith notions may be applied more restrictively, which may also affect the interpretation of the wording of agreements and their adjustment, even in the case of hardship.

It was, however, observed earlier, in section 1.2.2 above, that civil law is often inclined to use consumer protection notions also in the professional sphere and does not always clearly distinguish the nature of the relationship of contractual parties. In the professional sphere, English law is clearer in its reluctance to adjust the risk and mostly limits itself to adjustments that can still be explained on the basis of an implied term. It often takes a similar approach to custom, as we saw, probably for the same reasons. English judges are thus unlikely to imply pre-contractual negotiation or post-contractual re-negotiation duties between businessmen, but negligence may still be alleged in order to recover actual costs

---

[108] See also EA Farnsworth, 'Good Faith in Contract Performance' in J Beatson and D Friedmann (eds) n 94 *supra*, 153. See for a case that could more readily be explained as covering a pre-contractual situation, *Teacher's Ins & Annuity Ass'n v Butler*, 626 F Supp 1229 (SDNY 1986) in which a developer refused to close a loan deal whilst objecting to a pre-payment fee in the closing documents. The court recognised a duty of good faith and fair dealing in every commercial transaction and found a breach of this duty on the basis of commercial practice which accepted pre-payment fees in loan agreements even if not normally included in a bank's commitment letter. The court rejected therefore the borrower's argument as a pretext for getting out of the deal taking also into account that the draft loan agreement had included the fee and that the problem had never been raised until the eve of closing. The case can, however, also be seen in the context of the performance pursuant to the commitment letter.

(of advisors or designers) made in reliance on the statement or behaviour of the other party at the time of formation of the contract, but notably not for future profits.

As was already said many times before, in common law, the main emphasis is on the type of *relationship*[109] and sometimes on *detrimental reliance*,[110] more than on the type of contract and the parties' intent, except through implied terms, which, however, themselves are sometimes explained in a more objective way. On these three scores, there is in any event some important convergence between common and civil law, even if the notion of good faith is seldom used in English law. They both allow the concern for the contractual environment and the protection of weaker parties like consumers and workers to be taken into account, even if in England this is now rather left to statute. In this connection it may be noted, however, that in the USA for example employees are not *per se* protected under employment contracts without a duration clause and courts have held them terminable at will.[111]

If the nature of the relationship is indeed an important key, then the notion of good faith easily allows for the necessary variation in civil law, even if its natural inclination is to assume different (or *sui generis*) contract types to achieve distinctive treatment. The application of good faith notions in civil law should in any event be carefully studied and analysed from the perspective of the distinct relationships in which it is invoked (professional or not) and of the de-formalisation of contract types.

As already suggested in the previous section, this is still too rarely done but if it were, it is very likely that many perceived differences between civil and common law in this area would vanish. The protection of weaker parties, the pre-contractual disclosure duties and duties to continue negotiations, and, when circumstances change, any duties to re-negotiate, would largely be limited to consumers. In these areas may be found the most important differences between the civil and common law of contract, but they largely disappear when the nature of the relationship between the parties is properly taken into account.

Finally, the common law fiduciary duties should be discussed and distinguished in this context. They are products of the law of equity closely related to trust-like structures, therefore to situations where people or entities operate for others, as is also the case in agency, partnership or in directorships of companies. But they may also emerge more generally in situations of dependency or discretion affecting others. In all cases, there has to be a fiduciary relationship before the fiduciary duties can emerge and they apply therefore only in special circumstances and present a narrower concept than good faith does in civil law, but in areas where they operate, they may impose a much more formidable regime. Thus these fiduciary duties can go beyond mere fairness and honesty as is clearly shown in the relationship between the investment broker and his client where they acquire a protection function for the latter, see more in particular section 3.1.4 below. The other difference is that the liability they create is perhaps closer to tort than contract liability.

1.3.3   Good Faith in the Unidroit and European Contract Principles

The Unidroit Contract Principles, which are limited to international *commercial* contracts, present in Article 1.7(2) a typical example of the use of consumer law or small companies' protection in the professional sphere. It renders good faith generally a mandatory concept,

---

[109] See *Interfoto Picture Library Ltd v Stiletto Visual Programmes Ltd*, n 1 *supra.*
[110] *Walford v Miles*, n 34 *supra.*
[111] *Brehany v Nordsstrom Inc*, 812 P 2d 49 (Utah 1991) and *Murphy v American Home Products Corp*, 448 NE 2d 86 (NY 1983).

without explaining its role and meaning, and makes it compulsorily applicable even where it would not seem to appeal to higher overriding values. This would be unacceptable to common law lawyers and should also be to those of the civil law. It is in its generality an inexplicable provision which does not appreciate the multi-faceted nature of the concept with its many diverse functions as explained above in section 1.3.1. It is certainly not only a norm. Article 1.7(2), followed by Article 1.201 of the European Principles (which also cover consumer transactions but do not make proper distinctions either), can hardly be perceived as an established principle of *commercial* contract law as it pretends to be.[112] It has no basis in nor is it supported by a proper comparative analysis of domestic laws.

On the other hand, the Unidroit Principles seek to distinguish good faith from reasonableness (Article 5.2) without, however, indicating the dividing line. The terminology is here quite unstable and what must in this connection be considered mandatory or not is therefore unclear, see more in particular the discussion in section 1.6.3 below.

1.3.4   EU Notion of Good Faith

It is of interest in this connection that also at the EU level the notion of good faith has appeared. In the Council Directive (93/13/EEC of 5 April 1993) on Unfair Consumer Contract Terms, there is an important reference to it. Under Article 3(1), terms of not individually negotiated contracts are considered unfair if, in violation of the requirements of good faith, they cause a significant imbalance in the parties' rights and obligations to the detriment of a consumer. The Preamble elaborates somewhat on the good faith notion, which under the Directive requires an overall evaluation of the interests involved, whilst, in making an assessment of good faith, particular regard must be had to the strength of the bargaining position of the parties, whether the consumer had a special inducement to agree to the terms and whether the goods or services were sold or supplied to the special order of the consumer.

Whilst using terms like these, EU law considers them in essence separate from the meaning they may have in the domestic law of the Member States. Comparative research may be done but is not decisive to find the Community meaning.[113] As good faith is in most Member States undefined and varies widely in its impact, as we saw, it will be of interest to see how the European Court will eventually interpret the concept. In the context of the Directive, it seems likely that it will put the emphasis on the imbalance and leave it at that. It means that, following the normative or teleological approach, maintaining a proper balance is seen as a substantive element of the good faith requirement itself and not as an additional requirement for protection under the Directive. What this bears

---

[112] The concept of good faith in contract should be distinguished from the concept of *bona fides* in the acquisition of assets, therefore in proprietary matters, also relevant with regard to charges in assets which a *bona fide* purchaser might be able to ignore upon a sale: see Section 9–320 (9–307 old) UCC. There it is a question of knowledge. That is also relevant for the concept of the holder in due course of bills of exchange or promissory notes. The question in that connection is whether the *bona fides* is of a more subjective or objective nature. In other words: may the buyer depend on his lack of knowledge or is what he should have known but did not find out also relevant? It is clear in this respect that where charges or liens are filed, omitting to check the register cannot excuse the buyer. He has constructive notice. Good faith or *bona fides* is in civil law also important in connection with acquisitive prescription. Here again there are important variations: German law requires the *bona fides* to hold during the whole prescription periods, Dutch law only at the beginning.
[113] See W van Gerven, "The ECJ Case-law as a Means of Unification of Private Law?" in A Hartkamp et al. (eds.), *Towards a European Civil Code* (2nd ed. 1998), 91 and 102.

out is the relationship oriented approach, giving the concept of good faith here a special meaning in consumer transactions.

This being said, the concern of the EU for consumers is probably excessive. One would have thought that consumer protection is a typical concern of Member States as consumer transactions are seldom cross-border. Also in view of the notion of subsidiarity, the EU concern in this area appears substantially misplaced. The exception is undoubtedly long distance selling of consumer goods and of financial services to the smaller and inexperienced investor in other EU countries and more recently Internet dealings.

Under EU law, the concept of good faith is also used in Articles 3(1) and 4(1) of the Directive on self-employed commercial agents. Under them, the principal and agent owe each other a duty of good faith, largely referring, one assumes, to the common law notion of fiduciary duties. In this regard, comparative research would probably find in favour of the more extensive protection notions developed under the common law of agency.

The good faith notion also surfaced in the case law of the European Court of Justice in interpreting the original version of Article 17 of the Brussels Convention on Jurisdiction and the Enforcement of Judgments in Civil and Commercial Matters which allowed agreements on jurisdiction to be effective, but there were problems in determining when there was such an agreement. In this context the European Court relied in its early case law on good faith notions, now more generally formulated in Article 17 in terms of practices and usages.

1.3.5 The Lesser Need for Legal Refinement in the Professional Sphere: Interpretation, Mistake, Gross Disparity and Disclosure Duties

Although it seems that the normative approach to contract interpretation normally leads to *more* refinement in the protection of the various types of parties, be they professionals or consumers, workers or private investors, it may in fact also lead to *less* refinement as was already noted several times before. In other words, even if text, context, history, nature of the parties and their expertise, nature of the kind of contract, or even their custom or good faith and (statutory or other) rules of (black letter) law are together taken into account, it need not lead to more protection. This may explain why when third parties become involved, as in trust-like security interest arrangements or in assignments, the relevant texts concerning these arrangments are in respect of these third parties explained more in the nature of statutory texts (which may, however, also be interpreted in normative manner). It may also explain the lesser interest in pre-contractual duties amongst professionals. This was also already mentioned several times before and it is of great significance. In the common law of the English variety, this result is more obvious and achieved on the basis of distinguishing between the different nature of all relationships.

Thus, when the professionalism (or absence thereof) of the parties is properly taken into account, as well as their interests and the nature of their deal, it may well be that technical defects in the consensus or lack of clarity of the parties' intent carry less weight, also under the good faith notion in modern civil law. It means that even the application of fundamental principle like the binding force of the consensus or detrimental reliance on someone else's action is not insensitive to commercial needs, and in any event may function differently in different relationships and transactions. Where professional parties have signed an agreement, they must be assumed to have accepted and understood what they signed and should not attempt to avoid liability on the basis of misunderstandings of which they took the risk. It may lead in principle to a more literal interpretation of their roadmap and the division of tasks and risks they envisaged in the contract.

As a consequence, the special (commercial) nature of business relationships may also curtail the notion of mistake, negligent misrepresentation or error and the possibility to avoid the contract on that basis. These notions will be discussed in more detail in section 1.4.2 below. Especially in their expectations, parties may well be deceived, but that may hardly be a ground for rescission amongst professionals if no expectation was raised by the counter-party beyond mere sales talk. Professionals normally have the ability and means themselves to investigate and this will be an important point.

To invoke mistake or error to avoid contractual liability is for them often less convincing and likely to be limited to the obvious, that is rather extreme, situations, therefore to *prima facie* cases. In other words, the risk is normally for the professional party making the mistake, except (perhaps) if both parties were mistaken or (more likely) the other party realised or should have realised that the first party was mistaken unless of course the mistake was silly and inexcusable in the first place. In a similar vein, claiming that an unacceptable gross imbalance existed in the terms at the time of the conclusion of the contract (whether understood or not) is less credible between professionals.

The professional nature of the (business) relationship may also curtail special duties of the counterparty like disclosure, information and co-operation duties in the pre-contractual or formation phase (or the notion of *culpa in contrahendo*). It may limit protest periods, affect the remedies and in this regard discourage transactions from being undone even upon default, especially in their proprietary aspects (for example when a sales agreement fails but the goods are already delivered) although personal claims for damages may still be valid, except in extreme cases like fraud when even title might revert, giving rise to a real remedy or replevin.

In commerce, reliance on special skills of the other party will normally be no excuse as it may be for consumers or weaker parties, when they depend on the advice of their professional counterparties.[114] For professionals, the law may also want to cut down endless minor arguments concerning misbehaviour, negligent performance and *force majeure* exceptions to the more obvious cases, and limit the re-balancing of the contract even in the case of commercial hardship as these parties are used to risk taking and often make it their business, again excepting extreme cases. In short, for the courts to intervene in the professional sphere, things must be pretty bad.

As just said, it may even mean a greater reliance on the *literal* wording of contracts in the professional sphere as the text of a contract often serves as a roadmap for performance by persons who were never present during the negotiations, assuming further that lack of clarity cannot so easily be invoked here by the party having done the drafting or having presented a standard text.

In business, a stricter attitude in agency cases may also mean that an agency might be more readily assumed than would otherwise be the case and that apparent authority amongst professionals could even be assumed upon the mere declaration of the agent himself (for example employees), certainly if the principal has clearly taken that risk.

It is of interest in this connection that the 1980 Vienna Convention on the International Sale of Goods does not go into questions of validity in this sense and therefore also not into the notions of mistake and error, or into pre-contractual disclosure and negotiation duties in the context of contract formation. As between professionals for which the Convention is written, this seems not unexpected.

There are also no provisions for contractual adjustment in the interpretation of the parties' rights and duties, although, as the whole subject of interpretation (except of the

---

[114] See eg Lord Denning in *Esso Petroleum v Mardon* [1976], 2 All ER 5, 16.

Convention itself) is not covered by the Convention, nothing special may be read in this omission. The *force majeure* exemption in Article 79 is, however, (for professionals too) widely drawn and could also be used to excuse performance in the case of a change of circumstances even if it does not give rise to unconscionable burdens. There is, however, no facility for adjustment or re-negotiation of the contractual terms. The Unidroit and European Principles of Contract Law go much further and will be discussed in section 1.6 below.

1.3.6 The Status of Commercial Letters of Intent

The general attitude of rougher justice which may flow from the normative approach in the commercial sphere, even against more fundamental principle and the more traditional rules of contract law, in the interest of (a) the flow of commerce or (b) the greater certainties in the division of risks and distribution of tasks if desired by the parties, is also relevant for the status of *letters of intent* which are normally preludes to a contract. As intent or the lack of it is not the sole determining factor in establishing a legal relationship and detrimental reliance is in any event another fundamental principle, these letters may increasingly acquire some binding force between the parties if acted upon in good faith or even reasonably, which may imply some lesser burden of proof. In the professional sphere, there may be less need for this, however, as parties are left to their own devices to a greater extent and should not so quickly rely on others. Thus until there is a form of detrimental reliance or reasonable expectation justified in the circumstances, parties may not be bound at all, and this reliance will in any case be less quickly assumed in the professional or commercial sphere.

1.3.7 Pre-contractual Negotiation and Post-contractual Implementation Duties of Professionals: Abuse of Rights

The binding force of letters of intent is an area of the law closely related to negotiation duties in pre-contractual situations.[115] Although no written documents indicating the state of the negotiations may exist, there may be duties to continue the discussions in good faith and an action if these duties are broken. Yet mere expectation of a favourable conclusion does not give legal rights: see also the generally more restrictive attitude taken by Lord Ackner in the UK in *Walford v Miles*,[116] in which at least in commerce a duty to negotiate in good faith was thought to be unworkable and deemed to be inherently inconsistent with the position of a negotiating party, always, it would seem, subject to there being no detrimental reliance justified by the circumstances of the case. Even if this reliance does not result in the binding force of the letter, it could still allow for some reclaiming of costs made in the pursuance of the contract as a matter of tort or restitution law.

Again the key is that the justification for protection may be less obvious in commercial or professional cases. Once justified reliance arises, however, even in common law the other party may be forced to negotiate the full contract in line with the reasonable expectations, short of which there may be room for claiming damages against the party wrongfully

---

[115] See on this subject also S van Erp, "The Pre-contractual Stage" in A Hartkamp et al (eds), *Towards a European Civil Code* (2nd edn, 1998), 201, who signals here a diverging rather than converging tendency between civil and common law.
[116] [1992] 2 WLR 174.

terminating the negotiations, including a claim for lost profits. If one takes the element of professionality into the equation, common and civil law may be less different here than is sometimes thought.

In other situations, the tort of negligence (for example to achieve reimbursement of immediate expenses made during negotiations in terms of fees for advisors hired in reliance on statements of the other party) or the construction of *collateral* contracts (for example, an implied contract to negotiate, or justified reliance on an undertaking not to negotiate with others) may still result in some pre-contractual duties in English law, whilst there may sometimes also be cause for restitution (unjust enrichment), as just mentioned, but again these solutions are incidental and there is no general concept of pre-contractual duties in English law. The tort then leads to damages for misrepresentation which indeed were granted in the *Walford* case[117] and need be clearly distinguished from a contractual damage claim based on detrimental reliance leading to the formation of a contract. The difference between contract remedies and the incidental tort remedies available is notably that in the latter cases the lost benefit of future performance (lost opportunities) cannot be claimed.

Collateral agreements of this nature may, however, still not be enforceable for (a) lack of certainty, (b) lack of consideration or (c) failure to specify a time limit, whilst even express or implied agreements to negotiate may fail on similar grounds.[118] Under English law, the process of negotiation itself is apparently not thought to be capable of creating its own (contractual) relationship, although the requirement of consideration may have been eased.[119] This, however, removes only one barrier to the acceptance of contractual remedies in the pre-contractual phase.

German and Dutch law are more categorical in the imposition of pre-contractual duties and hold that late withdrawal from negotiations may impose heavy contractual liability, including damages for *lost profits* under the contract,[120] but probably always in the context of justified reliance or another improper cause to withdraw, which would also suggest a lesser concern in the commercial and professional sphere, although as yet German and Dutch law are seldom so analysed.

In France, the duty to negotiate in good faith leads in essence to a negligence (tort) action until such time that the negotiations have entered a phase where there may be said to be a contract.[121] The consequence appears to be a tort action requiring fault or bad faith with a limitation of damages to those actually suffered, but excluding the loss of the deal.[122] In the professional sphere, it is in any event believed that there is less reason for this liability.[123]

---

[117] There is also Dutch case law making the distinction between the various phases of negotiation and the remedies for terminating them. In a first phase both parties may withdraw, in a second phase they may not, but there will be no more than the reimbursement of actual costs. Only in a third phase could there also be a claim for the loss of the deal, HR, 18 June 1982 [1983] NJ 723 (Plas/Valburg). The liability in the second phase is sometimes based in tort. There is as yet no case awarding damages for the lost opportunity. In Germany, there is one in a labour case, BAG, 7 June 1963 [1963] NJW 1843, which is probably a case of special labour protection and not one concerning a more general principle.

[118] See also *Courtney & Fairbairn Ltd v Tolaini Brothers (Hotels) Ltd* [1975] 1 WLR 297.

[119] In *Pitt v PHH Asset Management Ltd* [1994] 1 WLR 327 the consideration requirement was relaxed so as to accept the binding force of a promise inducing reliance during negotiations.

[120] HR 15 Nov 1957 [1958] NJ 67 and 15 Feb 1991 [1991] NJ 493, and Sections 311 (2)(3) and 241(2) BGB (new).

[121] See Cour de Cass 20 Mar 1972 [1973] JCP 2.17542.

[122] The Court of Appeal in Riom, 10 June 1992, PTD Civ 343 (1993) came to the much criticised conclusion that an action for missed opportunity was possible. There is no case-law from the Cour de Cassation.

[123] Ghestin, *La Formation du Contrat* (1993), n 330.

In the USA, there is still no general duty to negotiate in good faith or at least to continue negotiations in that manner once they have seriously started, *cf Restatement (Second) of Contracst*, Section 205. Also Section 1-304 (1-203 old) UCC does not extend to pre-contractual situations either. The courts are, however, divided.[124]

Also in the implementation of the contract, the duties of professionals amongst them-selves may be less obvious than their duties in respect of non-professional parties. This also affects the invocations of any abuse of rights. Thus also in civil law terms, the requirements of good faith implementation may be fewer and less onerous for professionals. Closer adherence to the wording of the contract may be appropriate, also under the good faith reference in Section 1-304 (1-203 old) UCC in the USA. This may also have an effect on the *force majeure* excuse and any post-contractual re-negotiation duties.

1.3.8 Force Majeure, Re-negotiation Duties and Hardship Adjustments in Professional Relationships

Reliance on other sources of contractual obligations besides pure intent (including implied terms) is relevant not only for pre-contractual duties but also for such concepts as conform delivery and *force majeure* or change of circumstances leading to an adapta-tion of the clear wording of agreements in appropriate cases. If in the case of a change of circumstances, a duty to renegotiate is to be assumed, the situation is probably not much different from one where parties may be required to continue to negotiate in a pre-contractual situation or to continue an agreement after its expiry if there is a clause to that effect without clear instructions.

In the professional sphere, such a duty to re-negotiate or a duty to continue agreements beyond their termination date must, however, not quickly be assumed and any damages payable upon discontinuation must also be considered exceptional and limited to cases where there is some obvious misbehaviour. The lack of any reference to such duties in the Vienna Convention on the International Sale of Goods bears this out, although the Unidroit and European Principles take a different view closely related probably to their consumer-oriented ethos. Severe imbalance or unconscionability in the performance caused by a fundamental change of circumstances is often believed to be the proper trigger, as now also in Section 313 BGB. This change of circumstances and its impact must have been unforeseeable. In this connection, it could be argued that such circumstances had to be in the future and that present or past circumstances could only be characterised as a miscalculation unless they had an unforeseeable future effect. Whether it is realistic to make this distinction is another matter.

Another important aspect is here that the unforeseeability may also lead to claims of mistake with its rescission remedies which are likely to be quite different. This could be rel-evant especially in respect of past and present circumstances not discounted in the con-tract because the affected party did not know of them. Again as discussed above in section 1.3.5 above, mistake leading to the avoidance of the contract should not quickly be assumed in the commercial sphere either and neither should the emergence of an unfore-seen gross imbalance. Professional parties carry and must cater for substantial risks.

Again, factors likely to be taken into account include (a) the relationship between the parties in terms of their professionalism, with potentially a lesser need for protection in commercial transactions between professionals, (b) their special interests and reasonable

---

[124] See EA Farnsworth, "Precontractual Liability and Preliminary Agreements: Fair Dealings and Failed Negotiations", 87 *Colum L Rev* 217 (1987).

expectations also taking into account the division of risks agreed between them, the frequency of their transactions, the incidents that have arisen in them like for example poor performance generally, lack of continued co-operation, credibility and creditworthiness, (c) the nature of the deal as for example good faith or reasonableness is likely to have a different connotation and lead to different types of adjustment in employment contracts and supply agreements. But there may here also be other factors to take into account like (d) outside circumstances such as the market price or the required quality or style of merchandise. They may on the one hand lead to up-grading demands on a supplier which he cannot reasonably meet. On the other hand, the buyer may not have the capability to market more sophisticated products so that continuation of the contract makes little sense as demand for old fashioned products fades.

These are likely to be considerations that could prove decisive and determine when adjustment of a contract or the continuation of negotiations to the effect can no longer be reasonably required and termination must follow, although it is conceivable that in the case of hardship (usually on costs or price) new terms need not be fully market-related and there could still be a discount or a phase out or phase in for gradual adjustment. In this vein, an altogether justified discontinuation of the negotiation upon hardship does not necessarily exclude claims for damages against the party defaulting in the circumstances, especially not if the re-negotiation fails because there is clearly no longer any reasonable expectation of sufficient co-operation between the parties to make continuation a realistic option.

1.4 Performance of the Contract, Defences, Default and Excuses, Termination

1.4.1 *Performance in Kind or Specific Performance*

A contract is made with a view to enforcement of its terms. When one of the parties is not performing, the question arises what must or can be done. Court action is the natural answer in all modern societies but what may or could courts be asked to do? Even if the plaintiff's claim is accepted, what should the relief granted be and how could the judgment be enforced? It is simplest in *money judgments*: normally there will be a possibility of attaching the defendant's goods and obtaining a sales order or execution sale allowing the successful plaintiff to set off his monetary claim against the proceeds of this sale. Such a money judgment is the obvious answer when the claim is for *payment* of goods or services delivered. But if the claim is for the delivery of the goods or services itself, there may not be a request for a money judgment (covering damages), but rather a demand for *performance*. This is referred to as *specific performance* in common law. When is there a right to it and how is it to be enforced against the defendant?

Of course, it should be noted that in this sense, money judgments always allow performance in kind in whatever legal system. In civil law, that is also mostly the case with *proprietary* claims. In common law, it is also normal to *revindicate* specific assets on the basis of ownership but revindication in this sense strictly speaking only applies in land law. A variation is the foreclosure of a mortgage. In the law of chattels, revindication is, in common law, much more incidental and often limited to situations of fraud (in a common law sense), where there is a specific right of immediate repossession (e.g. on the termination of a user's right or finance lease), or in the case of conditional ownership rights leading to a right to reclaim the asset upon the maturing of the condition or in the case of a so-called repossession of secured assets upon a default under (non-pressesory) secured lending, sometimes (like under Article 9 UCC in the USA) backed up by statute, see more in particular chapter 4, sections 1.2.4 and 1.3.4.

In common law, the term 'specific performance' is, however, mostly used in connection with performance in kind of *other* obligations, notably contractual obligations to give or to do. Common law and civil law especially differ on the right to performance in kind or specific performance of these other obligations. In common law, it has remained in principle exceptional; in civil law it is in principle the norm. In civil law, the facility of specific performance developed gradually. Pothier[125] allowed specific performance very clearly, yet the French Code Civil is generally silent on the possibility and its implementation, notwithstanding the text of Article 1142 CC (as against Articles 1184(2) and 1610 Cc). French legal practice has always been in favour of it.[126] In the Netherlands, the Civil Code of 1838, largely based on the French Civil Code, which had been in force in the Netherlands until that time, abandoned the idea of specific performance against its own Roman-Dutch roots and germanic principle, although in line with the older Roman law. The facility of specific performance was, however, reintroduced in the Netherlands by statute in 1932.[127]

When a judicial order for performance in kind is used, *penalties* of some sort are the only possibility of making it work. They may be physical, like imprisonment and appropriation of an asset through a bailiff, or monetary in the sense of fines enforced like money judgments. These fines may be of an administrative nature and then accrue to the state, or they may accrue to the successful plaintiff as an extra form of compensation. Treble or punitive or exemplary damages for the plaintiff are sometimes possible in the USA but not in pure contract cases. Rather they are connected with contracts in restraint of trade or with malice in tort.

More likely in common law is the remedy of *contempt of court* under which courts will only subsequently set administrative fines or may order imprisonment for an unwilling judgment debtor. The superior courts have here wide discretion. In France, courts have developed the *astreinte* instead which allows them to impose a monetary penalty on unwilling defendants and leaves them also wide discretion as to the circumstances in which this sanction will be imposed and as to the appropriate amount. The money will accrue to the plaintiff. That is also the situation in the Netherlands. In Germany, on the other hand, the penalty so imposed will be administrative and collected by the state.

Specific performance is often a messy remedy and courts are not everywhere keen to get deeply involved. It is the reason that the possibility of obtaining a court order for performance in kind remains exceptional in common law countries. S*pecific performance* is possible in equity, it is only restrictively granted particularly in England, and then mainly in situations where there is no reasonable alternative. Mostly there is, and granting monetary damages can often adequately deal with the situation. In any event, in practice, parties often prefer it to forcing an unwilling counterparty still to perform. Thus a monetary judgment for damages normally follows a default with its much easier execution possibilities. Because of the difficulties involved in executing performance orders, even in civil law, performance in kind, although the rule, is *in practice* also fairly

[125] *Traité des Obligations*, No 156.
[126] See earlier especially Demogue, 6 *Traité des obligations en général* (1932), No 139.
[127] See for the history also HFWD Fisher, *De Geschiedenis van de Reele Executie bij Koop* [History of Specific Performance in Sales] (Haarlem, 1934).

exceptional and indeed normally equally restricted to situations where it is the best and most efficient answer.

Thus, when a sales contract is for the delivery of some *commodity* at a certain price, the purchaser under the contract will often be happy to be released from his contract whilst claiming damages for the delay by the non-performing seller and for any higher price he may have to pay elsewhere. For him it will normally be the cleanest and most efficient solution. Often he will already have purchased the goods elsewhere anyway because of the needs of his production facilities or to cover his trading commitments. On the other hand, if he wants a unique object, his remedy will be performance in kind and if the defendant upon judgment still does not perform, a penalty may be the answer. Performance in kind is also normal for the enforcement of real estate sales contracts, even in common law, as we saw.

Equally, in the case of services, if they are commonly provided and can easily be substituted albeit at a higher price, substitution is the answer and only damages for delay and higher costs will be claimed from the defaulter. If the service is more specific, for example the execution of an architectural design, performance in kind may be necessary. But if this service is highly personal or depends on other factors like good spirit or proper inspiration, as in the case of the services of a barman or portrait painter, there is a limit to what can be asked in kind and such a judgment may not work, whatever penalty. Damages again appear the better remedy however unsatisfactory in the circumstances.

It must also be realised that if the period of performance has lapsed, performance may no longer be valuable, and damages will again become more appropriate. In fact, depending on how long it may take to obtain a judgment for performance in kind, performance may have lost its urgency or significance and conversion of such a judgment into a monetary equivalent may then also be called for. If performance requires the help of others over whom the defendant has insufficient power, like subcontractors, again damages are the likely answer. If performance is no longer possible at all, because the portrait painter is dead, naturally there can only be a claim for monetary damages against his estate.

German law is clear in always allowing performance in kind (Section 241(1) BGB), but in the elaboration in the German Code of Civil Procedure, it sets out a number of scenarios and indeed differentiates between a number of basic cases for claims other than monetary claims (Sections 883*ff* German CCP). Appropriation by a bailiff of a specific chattel owed under a judgement or execution title is dealt with in Section 883 of the CCP. If an act or service owed by the unwilling defendant may be performed by a third party, this defendant will have to pay the cost for such a third party, see Section 887 of the CCP. Sections 888 and 890 of the CCP allow for *penalties* if the defendant does not perform a specific act or service which cannot be performed by any third party or if he remains obstructive, whilst being ordered to refrain from doing something or to allow others to take some action. These penalties may be imprisonment or fines which, in Germany, go to the State. The result may also be the conversion of a judgement in kind into a monetary judgement.

In France, the Code is older and the regime less precise. Moreover, there are contradictions. Article 1184(2) Cc allows an order for performance in all bilateral contracts but Article 1142 suggest that all contracts to do or not to do resolve upon default in damage claims, apparently in order not to infringe anyone's freedom of action so that only contracts to give appear capable of a performance order in kind. However, case law has much refined this system. In any event, under Articles 1143 and 1144 Cc, the courts may give preliminary restraining orders or may order others to do the act on which the first party defaulted if the performance is sufficiently impersonal. The already mentioned *astreinte* backs up the system[128] as a penalty developed in case law serving both as an inducement to comply and a reward for the patient but exasperated plaintiff.

In common law, the combination of the contempt of court remedy and specific performance in equity results in a system which in practice is not far away from the German one. Damages are the normal rule, but if harm to the plaintiff cannot be adequately expressed in monetary terms, specific performance may be the answer unless it is too inconvenient or does not hold out a realistic prospect of success,[129] especially if it would require long judicial involvement. Traditionally, specific performance was thus reserved for situations where the performance was unique or for land contracts. As an equitable remedy there is always discretion, however, and it depends on the circumstances whether it will be granted with categories of cases developed much in line with the more precise German categorisation. As already mentioned, the remedy can in particular not be used to enforce a personal work commitment.

In the sale of goods, statutory law both in England and the USA allows more generally for specific performance in favour of the buyer, in England under Section 52 of the Sale of Goods Act provided the goods are specific and ascertained. As regards the seller's right to recover the price or force the buyer to take delivery, the English Act provides in Section 27 that the seller must deliver the goods and the buyer must accept and pay for them. Yet according to Sections 51 and 52, the buyer's normal remedies are limited to damages, although the court still has discretion to order specific performance. For commodity goods the remedy is normally not granted.

In the USA, in sales, specific performance is liberally allowed, therefore no longer only when damages are inadequate but rather when there are no clear circumstances that dictate otherwise. For specific performance under the law of the sale of goods, Section 2–716(1) UCC requires the goods to be unique but also allows for 'other proper circumstances' in which specific performance may be obtained. It provides for the seizure of the goods by the sheriff. This remedy remains, however, in the common law (equity) tradition also at the discretion of the judge who may provide other relief as he may deem just. For the seller, recovery of the sale price will normally be allowed except where the seller never managed to deliver the goods, in which case he must minimise the damage and make a reasonable effort to sell the goods to others.

Although common and civil law have greatly converged in the matter of performance remedies in kind, at the theoretical level, in civil law, the discretionary element is lacking whilst contempt proceedings proper do not exist and are replaced by forced executions (against a seller in a sale through the forced removal of the goods if in his possession) or by the setting of a penalty for each day of further delay.

The Vienna Convention on the Law of International Sales has a curious provision in this respect in Article 28. It refers here back to the *lex fori*, see for the details section 2.3.4 below.

1.4.2 Lack of Consensus or Defences to Performance: Invalidity and Rescission

In common law writing of the American variety, the subject of defences against the enforcement of contracts is usually dealt with immediately after the formation of the contract. In this connection, the question of lack of formalities, especially in terms of documentation

---

[128] See in modern times, Cour de Cass Civ 20 Oct 1959 [1959] D 537.
[129] *Ryan v Mutual Tontine Westminster Chambers Association* [1983] 1 chap 116.

(Statute of Frauds), lack of capacity, illegality, fraudulent or innocent misrepresentation, mistake, duress or undue influence, and unconscionability (in the USA) are usually mentioned. In common law, the courts (in equity) developed here patchwork system of remedies centering on *rescission* as a technical term which is geared to defences against a demand for performance. In civil law, fraud, duress or undue influence, misrepresentation and mistake are mostly connected with a lack of consensus and therefore result not only in some valid defence to a claim for performance but also in voidness or more likely in voidability of the contract at the option of the affected party as a natural consequence of the failure of consensus. Thus, in civil law, these are really formation questions rather than defences as performance issues.

In common law, the consequences of any of the defences are likely to be more complex and varied, although in principle all of them discharge the party concerned from its contractual duties. Specific performance, in any event never a right, is then not granted. The contract itself may have come to an end. The different situations in which this may happen and the manner in which it does, as well as the consequences, need, however, traditionally to be much more clearly distinguished than in civil law.

In common law, *illegality and invalidity* are often interchangeable notions. In civil law they are distinguished; the invalidity is normally connected with the lack of consensus and goes to the heart of the existence of the contract and illegality with a statutory prohibition or restraint. In common law, illegality or invalidity usually result from moral or public order consideration and do not refer to a legal (statutory) prohibition. They result in defences against a demand for performance. In civil law, the notion of an improper *causa* may be used to avoid these illicit contracts. In common law, illegality or invalidity may also result from other impediments such as anti-competitive clauses.

There is a particular common law aspect not found in civil law in the same manner in that common law adheres in the case of illegality or invalidity to the old rule *ex dolo malo* or *ex turpi causa non oritur actio*, meaning that no one can derive an action pursuant to his own misbehaviour. Under an illegal or invalid contract in the common law sense, it is therefore in principle impossible for the offending party to reclaim anything done or given under the contract. In particular, money advanced to achieve illegal ends or to finance crime will not be returned on the basis of the contract's invalidity, although even then proprietary rights may be reclaimed between the parties if they subsequently abandoned their illegal objective. If the invalidity is based on less urgent social or policy considerations, the rule may be relaxed. In any event, if only one party benefits, as when a contract is void because it was unduly restrictive of trade, the party suffering the disadvantage may be able to reclaim its outlay from the other.

In civil law, any reclaiming rights in these situations may be treated through the concept of unjust enrichment or restitution, *cf* in Germany Section 817 BGB and in the Netherlands (the more flexible) Article 6.211 CC (referring to reasonableness), and not, as in common law, as a matter of contract law.

As regards *misrepresentation*, in common law it can be *fraudulent, innocent* or (in England) *negligent*. The situation is also quite different from the one in civil law where it goes to the heart of the consensus. First 'representation' in this sense assumes in common law that certain declarations are made that are not part of the contract but on which there has been reliance at the time of formation. The difference is that where contractual terms are agreed, for example about quality and its specifications, any subsequent shortcoming would give rise to a *breach of contract* or default. The remedy for misrepresentation (unless fraudulent) is rather *'rescission'* of the contract. To repeat: it is a technical term developed in equity. It implies avoidance of the contract at the option of the harmed party. It leads in sales to *voidable title*. If this defence is invoked, the consequences must be further considered, however, and it cannot simply be assumed that the contract is at an end, eg a watch is being sold according to the contract. It says nothing about the type. The seller says, however, that it is a Cartier watch. He genuinely believes so. Subsequently, after the sale, it transpires that it was a fake Cartier watch of which there are many. There is no breach of contract proper; the contract said nothing, but there was probably reliance. If so, rescission may be in order and the judge will decide what in the light of the circumstances the proper remedy is. It should be clear that much of innocent misrepresentation is in the realm of sales talk.

If misrepresentation is fraudulent, the matter is more serious and there may also be a tort (deceit) for which there must have been intent; if there was none, there may still be innocent misrepresentation. In England negligent misrepresentation holds some middle ground (since the Misrepresentation Act 1976) in that it puts the burden of innocent misrepresentation on the person having made the (mis)representation. Until such time, in *prima facie* cases intention to deceive is assumed. In common law, in all cases, the point of departure is always the position of the person who makes a representation, not of the victim, unlike in civil law where this is mostly only so in the case of clear fraud (*cf* Section 123 BGB in Germany, which in that case allows avoidance of the contract even if the damaged party was at fault whilst it is irrelevant whether the misrepresentation was caused by that party, although this is no longer so under new Dutch law, see Article 6.228 CC).

The differences are mainly in the remedy of rescission and its consequences. In the case of innocent misrepresentation, in common law, the possibility of rescission leading to a setting aside of the contract is limited. Even in the case of fraudulent misrepresentation, it is not automatically available but depends on the circumstances and a judicial order restoring the old situation will only be given if that is still possible. The *factual* situation is therefore decisive for the type and meaning of the remedy. If the delivered asset is consumed or a service already rendered on the basis of false premises, the rescission order will not be given. Damages may then be the only available alternative, again only as an equitable indemnity.

In equity, there is in any event always a measure of judicial discretion. Most importantly, movable property will not be restored to the damaged party if a *bona fide* third party buys from a person with voidable title. The *bona fide* party is protected, see Section 23 of the Sale of Goods Act in the UK and Section 2–403 of the UCC in the USA. In civil law, on the other hand, rescission is at the option of the harmed party and then likely to be fully effective, even in a proprietary sense. Thus property should return in principle, subject to the protection of *bona fide* purchasers of chattels only and therefore not of other assets, assuming that they acquired possession. In abstract systems of title transfer, like the German one, see also chapter 4, section 1.5.7, an automatic return of the assets is likely only in the case of fraud.

In other legal systems, the return possibility upon a failed *sales* agreement is also becoming less favoured, an issue that will be discussed in greater detail in section 2.1.10 below. In common law it seems exceptional and also limited to cases of pure fraud when an automatice return of the assets may be ordered in the nature of a specific performance remedy assuming the asset still exists, see also chapter 4, section 1.5.7.

As just mentioned, in common law the possibility of rescission is limited further if the misrepresentation is innocent, a situation in civil law usually referred to as 'error', which again in civil law goes to the consensus and voidability of the contract. Again, in common law, the circumstances of the case are decisive as to the consequences. The court will, however, always bar a request for specific performance of the contract and may always grant an equitable indemnity by way of damages if the effects of the contract cannot be undone.

The English term 'mistake' should in principle be clearly distinguished from innocent misrepresentation (or error in civil law), although there are borderline cases. It is a narrow concept and concerns here some mistake in the declarations of one of the parties at the time of the offer and acceptance rather than the making (fraudulently or innocently) of a misleading statement. The difference is subtle but important. A mistake in a declaration may follow when it is not properly understood, for example if a service is offered at a certain price, but VAT is not mentioned. Was it intended to be included or excluded? Especially in oral contracts, a mistake in this sense is easily made: for example both parties talk about 60 but one party means $60 per unit, while the other meant 60k for the whole lot and a misunderstanding may result which is nobody's fault. This is mistake in common law. If, on the other hand, a statement is made that a gold watch is offered that proves to be only imitation gold, then there is misrepresentation which may be fraudulent or negligent as discussed above. The key in mistake is that upon an objective reading of the situation the parties are not in agreement. It should upon an objective evaluation of the facts be clear that parties were talking about different things (whatever their intent which, in the traditional common law view, is not material in matters of formation of contract).

In civil law that is either fraud or error (which may be fraudulent or innocent misrepresentation in a common law sense). In fact, for mistake in this common law sense, civil law seems not to have an own term. It is usually distinguished from error or seen as a special instance of it. Whilst in civil law misrepresentation or fraud and error normally lead to forms of voidability at the affected party's request, in common law, mistake leads in principle to a void contract at law and any property transferred reverts. The risk of appreciation or depreciation is in the meantime with the seller. Even if the contract still stands at law, equity may all the same give a rescission remedy depending on the circumstances and may in any event refuse specific performance of the contract. Certain forms of mistake are considered less fundamental, however, and lead only to voidability. It is often difficult to draw precise lines. Unilateral mistake, a mistake not involving the other party, will seldom give rise to a rescission of the contract; it may be the mistaken party's own fault. He thought that he was offering a gold plated watch, but in the event it was pure gold.[130]

American law is often simpler here than English law. So is civil law in so far as it readily accepts lack of consensus as excuses in the case of fraud or error (fraudulent or innocent misrepresentation), and will ask which party should reasonably bear the risk in the case of a mistake. Civil law looks at consensus and the will of the parties and its defects. Common law needs the special category of defences to create protection against a claim for performance. In civil law, the normative or teleological interpretation technique may still find a valid contract, however, if the mistake was not attributable to the other party. As already suggested in section 1.3.4 above, professionals in particular may not have here much of a defence. Their mistakes should normally be their own problem. In any event, the fact that mere expectations were disappointed is not enough. *Caveat emptor* is the basic rule in sales. On the other hand, if parties have been clearly talking about different things, there may not be a contract. A mistake in this sense could be tantamount to a rejection of an offer and would result in voidness of the contract or rather in no contract at all.

Some forms of mistake (those as to the subject matter) may in civil law lead to the contract not having a proper object with avoidance on that basis, like in the case of a reference to the ship '*Peerless*' of which there were two at the time, with the one party meaning the

---

one and the other party the other.[131] Also in other respects, different characterisations may lead to different results: there is mistake and voidness in common law if there is a misunderstanding about the contracting counter-party; in civil law this is error, leading only to voidability.

In common law, mistake may also concern the possibility of performing the contract, which may be left to the impossibility or *force majeure* defence in civil law. Yet a contract that may be objectively incapable of being performed from the beginning may also be absolutely void in civil law, or only be considered valid as the basis for claims for damages, *cf* Section 311a BGB in Germany. This does not, however, obtain in cases where an estimate of cost is given which is subsequently overrun. The impossibility to perform for the agreed price does not discharge the debtor, even if it was foreseeable from the beginning and the creditor must have known about it.

Duress and *undue influence* may provide further defences. In a common law sense, duress is often physical. Civil law sees duress chiefly as psychological or economic pressure and it prevents the conclusion of a valid agreement for lack of consensus. In common law (equity), this is primarily covered by economic duress[132] or undue influence, which is not limited to abuse of a position of trust or of circumstances as it often is in civil law. Whether there was unacceptable pressure exerted in the circumstances or resulting from the circumstances depends on the facts. Avoidance is the normal remedy in common law (equity), supplemented by the rescission possibility in appropriate cases. In modern civil law, avoidance is also the rule rather than voidness, see Article 1117 Cc in France, Article 3.44 CC in the Netherlands and Section 123(1) BGB in Germany.

The Vienna Convention on the International Law of Sales excludes matters of validity in this sense from its scope (Article 4). That covers, in the context of that Convention, all matters relating to consensus and its failures. Therefore the impact of illegality, misrepresentation, mistake and duress or undue influence is not covered by the International Sales Convention.

1.4.3 The Significance of Promises, Conditions and Warranties in Connection with Performance in Common Law: Representations and Covenants

In common law, the contract is, as we saw, in essence based on an exchange of (formal) promises in the consideration context. They must be sufficiently congruous to lead to a contract. The mutual undertakings of the parties form the *terms* of the contract. The essential terms are in England called *conditions*, the non-essential ones *warranties*. The idea behind conditions is that their non-performance automatically discharges the other party (for example from payment) who may still have a claim for damages. *Force majeure* cannot be pleaded by the first party. Warranties are different and non-compliance with them does not excuse the other party. The distinction between conditions and warranties remains a matter of interpretation.

---

[131] *Rafflers v Wichelhaus* (1864) 2 HC 906. See for a discussion of mistake under common law also HG Beale, *Chitty on Contracts* (1999), 5.001 in England, and *Restatement (Second) of Contracts* (1979), Section 379 in the USA.

[132] See Mocatta J in *Northern Ocean Shipping Co Ltd v Hyundai Construction Co Ltd* [1978] 3 All ER 1170. In the USA, the concept is much more readily used than in England, see also Comment to Section 176 of the *Restatement (Second) of Contracts* (1979); see also *Centric v Morrison-Knudsen Co*, 731 P 2d 411 (1986). In the USA there is a preference for expanding the duress notion at the expense of the notion of undue influence. Economic duress should be distinguished from unconscionability which lies in the performance of the contract, not in its formation.

Performance of the major contractual terms by the other party is always a constructive or implied condition of payment. Performance as such thus becomes a condition of the contract, here of the payment duty. In the US, conditions are used in that sense. Americans thus look at conditionality of the contract or at what conditions the contract rather than at conditions in the English sense (which are certain contractual terms, *not* as such conditionalities), although the English conditions as terms of the contract are at the same time likely to condition the performance or promise of the other party. Indeed, in the American sense, failure of a condition (which may arise from the other party's failure to perform essential parts of the contract) discharges the promissor. Contractual conditions may in this sense be precedent, concurrent or subsequent. They can be express or constructive. Promises, which are duties to give, to do or not to do, may thus be varied by the implied conditions attached to them which may excuse or condition their performance.

Whether there is a failure of condition in this sense is also a matter of interpretation. Thus payment is conditional on the other party's performance, which, in this reasoning, is a condition precedent to the payment debtor's own performance, but it is a matter of construction which terms are conditions precedent in this sense. The performance itself may also be conditioned. An interesting example may be in the delivery of a certain quantity of goods before a certain date. Is the time element a promise to the buyer or was it also a condition of the contract? If it is the latter, the promissor is discharged if he cannot deliver by the appointed date. He operated only on a best effort basis. Normally, however, his failure leads to late delivery and to a situation of breach of an essential contract term for which there is no excuse. In either case, the other party is excused from payment as the main term of the contract is not performed, which was a condition of the payment performance.

The Vienna Convention in Article 25 here uses the notion of fundamental breach. It is defined as any breach that results in such detriment as substantially to deprive a party of what it was entitled to expect under the contract unless the party in breach did not foresee and a reasonable person of the same kind in the same circumstances would not have foreseen such a result.[133]

In civil law, default if considered sufficiently serious is often[134] also construed as a rescinding condition of the contract, *cf* Article 1184 of the French Cc, also referred to as the *lex commissoria*, but the common law of contract makes more of it and there is here a basic difference in emphasis, although again in practice the differences are not always great as will be further discussed below in the context of 'breach'. In common law, all substantial terms are or give rise to conditions. In civil law, this translates in a *guarantee* of performance, the absence of the *force majeure* defence (except if especially inserted), and the repudiation of the contract and discharge of the other party upon breach, whatever the reason. It means that in a common law sense, all contractual terms of civil law are warranties and not conditions unless especially reinforced by a guarantee.

It follows that in civil law, breaches are sanctioned only when there is sufficient consensus and the promissor can be blamed for non-performance, unless there was a guarantee. A situation of *force majeure* (or possibly of changed circumstances) is therefore normally sufficient excuse in all cases. If he is not to blame, the other party defends with an exception

---

[133] The concept of fundamental breach was earlier used in a different context in the UK: exoneration or exemption clauses, especially in respect of contractual liability towards consumers, were not considered effective if there was a fundamental breach by the other party seeking to discharge itself through such clauses. Scepticism of the House of Lords in *Suisse Atlantique v NV Rotterdamse Kolen Centrale* [1967] 1 AC 361 required intervention of the legislator to protect notably consumers against standard terms and led to the Supply of Goods (Implied Terms) Act 1973 and later to the Unfair Contract Terms Act 1977.

[134] Cour de Cass 24 Jan 1939, Gaz Pal 1. 5866.

against any claim to perform on his part. *Only* when he has given special undertakings like a guarantee of quality or of conform delivery in sales is a situation similar to that in common law achieved. Payment is, however, considered especially guaranteed in this sense and cannot be excused on the basis of impossibility or force majeure and can always be exacted if the other party has properly performed.

In England, breach of a condition allows the affected party to repudiate the contract. Warranties do not justify such action. In the USA, where the distinction between condition and warranties is not used in a similar manner, there is for repudiation of the contract a need for breach of a substantial term of the contract (the 'fundamental breach' of the Vienna Convention). Such terms condition the contract so that it amounts to a similar distinction and is in all cases a matter of construction or interpretation of the contract. Damages are still possible without repudiation and it is the normal remedy for breach of warranty in England. In that case, the mutual obligations of the parties remain in place. If the contract is already substantially performed, repudiation is in any event no longer a practical option. In England one speaks in that case of an automatic conversion of conditions into warranties or also of *ex post facto* warranties.

In this connection, it may also be useful briefly to discuss the relationship between *conditions precedent, representations and warranties*, and *covenants*, particularly common in *financial documentation* governed by English or American (state) law. *Conditions precedent* in this context normally require that certain documents are produced by a prospective borrower, like incorporation documents, board resolutions approving the deal, the consent of the competent authorities, legal opinions on the validity of the contract, etc. Other conditions may be that on the closing date there is no evidence of default and that the representation and warranties made are all correct. In banking facilities, the impact of these conditions as essential terms has not always been clear: do they inhibit the contract or the drawing down of any loan facility thereunder? Mostly the contract is held valid, so that at least the fees payable under it can be claimed.

Representations and warranties in this context concern the *creditworthiness* of the prospective borrower. There may here be some overlap with conditions precedent as we saw in the case of default, whilst the representations and warranties themselves may be declared conditions precedent. Examples might be the truthfulness of financial statements, absence of major events affecting the borrower's credit, like major lawsuits or other contingent liabilities, or the absence of any material default up to and including the closing date. Parent and subsidiary companies may be included.

Representations and warranties are in finance concerned with the past; *covenants* with the future. Under them, prospective borrowers promise to refrain from certain actions, maintain certain financial ratios, official consents, and provide financial or other information on a regular basis. They may not be able to take on other debt (the *pari passu* or negative pledge clause), nor dispose of certain assets or engage in a merger.

Breach of any of the representations and warranties or covenants will allow the lender to refuse any (further) draw down and to call any outstanding loan principle plus accrued interest immediately (at its option). This is *acceleration*. Any further loan commitment may then equally be withdrawn. The default clause will usually spell this all out in detail.

1.4.4   Default or Breach and Damages

In section 1.4.1, the question of performance was black or white. Either one does or one does not perform and in the latter case the question of a performance order in kind or payment of damages presents itself. In section 1.4.2 a number of common defences were identified which could protect against a claim for performance, like misrepresentation and mistake. In section 1.4.3 the conditions of performance were discussed. They could further excuse the promissor. Non-performance by the promissee in an essential part of the deal is the commonest of these excuses.

The defences and excuses leave wide open the question of the burden or *consequences* for the parties of the endangered or aborted deal. When the contract ends or may be ended by one of the parties in the circumstances, there will be cause for damages especially in the case of fraud and misrepresentation. But also where the counter-party may be excused his own performance, there may still be some room for a claim by him for expenses and the loss of the deal, especially if the first party has not performed and is to blame. If the performance was conditioned by an external factor, like, in a sale, by the timely supply of the goods to the seller, there will be no cause for a damage claim by either party.

The liability for default, whatever the defences or excuses, is apportioned in civil law primarily on the basis of who was *most* to blame. If it is the debtor, he is liable for damages whilst the creditor may terminate the contract (Sections 280 and 323 BGB). If it was the creditor himself, for example for lack of co-operation, he bears the burden and may still have to perform. In such a case, the debtor may also consider himself liberated whilst still being able to claim damages performance (Sections 275, 323(6) and (2) BGB). If neither party is to blame, both are free in principle (Sections 275 and 326(1) BGB) and both suffer the loss of the deal and their expenses. That may be so in the case of mutual mistake. It may also be so when one of the parties is in a recognised *force majeure* situation and cannot perform for that reason. *Force majeure* in civil law should therefore be seen foremost in the context of who is to blame.

Breach as a term of art concerns itself not only with indefensible or inexcusable part-performance or non-performance or with defective performance but also with impossibility, impracticability, frustration or *force majeure* and changed circumstances as excuses, or otherwise with the determination of damages or, if still possible or relevant, with any performance in kind or specific performance which may be accompanied by penalties ordered by the courts.

In Germany, the BGB originally considered in this connection only the situation of impossibility to perform (Section 306 BGB) or any late performance (Sections 284*ff* BGB), in which case a specific time limit (*Nachfrist*) had to be set by the creditor for performance (if not considered implied) before default could give rise to breach proper and a claim for damages. Case law, however, recognised the limitations in this system and accepted certain implied guarantees allowing for an immediate claim for breach. It was also available as a defence if the innocent party could not reasonably be expected to continue performance itself.

German law has now adopted a universal notion of breach of contract (Section 280(1) (new) BGB). Primarily it covers total or partial impossibility to perform and late performance. In the context of typified contracts, such as a sale, the breach of specific duties under such a contract may give rights to rescission resulting in a claim for damages. But also the breach of quasi-contractual duties in the pre-contractual stage as well as the amendment of the contractual terms in extremely changed circumstances are now covered in the BGB and may also result in damages.

This is also the French system for bilateral contracts (Article 1184 Cc), where, however, court action is always necessary to set the contract aside. That used to be the situation in the Netherlands also but no longer under its new Code. On the matter of guarantees or conditions, modern civil law converges with common law as already explained above in the previous section. German law and that of France and the common law all allow for the combination of repudiation or rescission and damages.

The nature of the contract and its aims have an impact on the remedies for breach. Even within one contract type, the set of remedies can be very detailed. That was traditionally so for the sale of goods under common law. The Hague Sales Conventions of 1964, which preceded the Vienna Sales Convention of 1980, showed this. In the USA, the UCC for the sale of goods simplified the structure of remedies considerably. Yet there remain the distinctions between the remedies of the buyer and the seller, although either may first ask for assurances, which, if not adequate, may give the party concerned a right to repudiate within 30 days.

In the UCC, the rest of the remedies are further subdivided, especially for the buyer, who may in the case of non-conformity with the quality requirements reject and send the goods back after notice with reasons, in which connection the seller may send specific instructions on how the goods are to be returned. The buyer may also retain the goods but claim damages for non-conformity. After the goods are accepted, they may still be returned or damages claimed in respect of them by a revocation of the acceptance of the goods if defects that were difficult to discover emerge and/or a seller's promised repairs are not timely executed. A buyer may also organise *cover* and thus replace the goods with others and claim his extra cost after a reasonable delay. If there is no cover, he may claim the difference between the agreed price and the market price at the time he learnt of the breach. If the goods are unique, specific performance is possible. Reasonably foreseeable consequential damages and the incidental damages attached to enforcement of the contract may be claimed subject to appropriate mitigation.

The seller under a failed agreement for the sale of goods may under the UCC stop manufacturing and shipment, retake or replevy the goods as a proprietary remedy (but only if the buyer becomes bankrupt within ten days of delivery), resell the goods if not yet delivered upon notice to the buyer who will be liable for any difference in price if lower; alternatively he may claim the difference between the contract and the market price at the time and place of delivery if lower. If there is a loss of volume although the price is the same, there may still be a claim for loss of profit. Specific performance will be granted to the seller only if the goods cannot readily be resold to anyone else, especially relevant if they were uniquely made for the buyer.

The Vienna Convention also has an elaborate system of remedies, although much simplified from those of the Hague Conventions. It deals with performance and default only in its *in personam* consequences, that is to say that it deals neither with the transfer of title nor its return upon default. The remedies under the Convention are basically specific performance if the lex fori allows it, as we already saw, or avoidance of the contract but only if the breach is *fundamental*, with the possibility always of claiming damages depending on the circumstances. Technically speaking, the Vienna Convention, like the UCC, abandons the English notion of (express or constructive) 'conditions', traditionally distinguished from warranties as a matter of interpretation. Instead, the Vienna Convention adopts the concept of fundamental breach with the possibility of avoiding or rescinding the contract in that case (only), see Articles 49 and 64. Fundamental breach is, however, only loosely defined (Articles 25 and 26) and remains, like negligence elsewhere, a matter of determination per case in view of all the circumstances.[135] See for further details of the system of remedies under the Convention, section 2.3.4 below.

---

[135] See, for the concept of fundamental breach in England, n 133 *supra*.

1.4.5   Excuses

The subject of excuses like *force majeure* and change of circumstances was already briefly discussed in section 1.3.7 in the context of the normative interpretation of contracts and the re-negotiation duties it may imply or impose. This is a difficult subject. It concerns principally the definition and applicability of the excuses but also the consequences in terms of a temporary or permanent release of the party required to perform. In appropriate cases, it may also concern the adaptation of the contract or the re-allocation of the risk, especially in the case of a significant change of circumstances imposing unforeseeable excessive burdens, usually referred to as *unconscionability* in the USA.

It was noted above that as regards the applicability of the concept of *force majeure*, in common law of the English variety, it did not excuse the performance of contractual conditions which are considered the essential terms. In a civil law sense, a guarantee of performance is implied. Non-performance would then always discharge the other party, unless there was a special *force majeure* or changed circumstances clause added in the agreement itself. As we saw, in civil law, such a guarantee is now sometimes also implied, but this remains more exceptional. Therefore, in civil law the concept of *force majeure* operates much more broadly and alleviates blame, which is at the heart of a claim for performance or damages (or both) in civil law as we saw.

The Vienna Convention did not follow the system of implied guarantees which even in common law presented an interpretation issue through which the effect could be much reduced. Article 79 states that a party is not liable for a failure to perform *any* of its obligations if it can prove that the failure was due to an impediment beyond its control provided that it could not reasonably have taken the impediment into account at the time of the conclusion of the contract or could have avoided or overcome it or its consequences. This is a flexible provision but Article 79(5) provides that nothing in Article 79 prevents either party from exercising any rights under the Convention other than claiming damages. Rights to avoid the contract upon a fundamental breach or to ask for repairs are thus not impaired. The Convention does *not* contain any special provisions allowing for an adaptation of the contractual terms.

In the case of *sales*, there is here also the *passing of risk* concept, which will be more fully discussed in sections 2.1.8 and 2.1.9 below. It concerns the risk to the sold goods during a limited time frame, normally the time between the conclusion of the sales agreement and the delivery of the assets, even though this time frame may be extended or shortened in special circumstances as will be discussed later. It means that during this time, the party bearing the risk (normally a seller still in possession) must repair or replace the goods if damaged through no fault of the buyer, regardless therefore of the seller's *force majeure*. Naturally the buyer then remains liable for payment of the full price. An alternative for the seller may be to offer a reduction in price. Here again, one could construe an implied guarantee of performance on the part of the seller that would, during the period that he carries the risk, not be excused by his *force majeure*.

Force majeure concerns a special instance of the distribution of risk of unforeseen circumstances and commonly leads to a discharge of both parties, except for the special rule of the passing of risk in sales agreements as just mentioned or when there was a(n implied) guarantee of performance. Moreover, certain *force majeure* situations never count as an excuse, like an inability to pay (where a guarantee may be deemed implied, except perhaps as to failure in the payment systems) or mostly the inability to perform for personal (health) reasons. This is a separate issue. Even if there is a proper excuse, the party unable to perform suffers loss. The effects of the loss of the deal may also affect the other party who may, however, find a ready substitute whilst reclaiming any payments already made and not making any further ones.

Thus, without a passing of risk rule in sales contracts, or implied guarantees of performance in other contracts, or instances of *force majeure* that do not count as a proper excuse, *force majeure* will discharge *both* parties in principle and will then allow the chips to fall where they fall if neither party is at fault. The debtor does not need to perform but also loses payment and his profit and expenses, although he may be able to reclaim whatever he already delivered (unless there is a special clause in the contract making other provisions). The creditor loses the benefit of the (rest of the) bargain and his own costs and expenses, although he may be able to reclaim pre-payments (unless the contract has made other provisions). Whether that is always fair is another matter. There could be good reasons for *adaptation* of the contract rather than for a release with ultimate termination.

Legal facilities or requirements of adaptation can be seen as expanding the *allocation of risk* concept. They may especially be provided in situations where there is an unforeseen change of circumstances other than *force majeure* proper. Here the condition is often that the readjustment relief will be granted only if without it an *excessive burden* would result for the party seeking the relief, in which connection it may be useful to distinguish between professional and other parties as already suggested earlier. We are then entering the area of hardship. What changed circumstances would qualify and what is excessive in this respect and whether the events or the consequences needed to be unforeseeable are matters of further definition.

In the following sections, the definition of *force majeure* and of hardship relief due to changed circumstances as well as contractual relief clauses in this connection will be further explored.

1.4.6   The Definition of the Concept of Force Majeure. *Frustration and Economic Impossibility. Development in Civil and Common Law*

It was said in the previous section that, in the context of default, *force majeure* is a special form of a change of circumstances and particularly concentrates on a failure to perform due to intervening circumstances which are (a) *beyond the control* of the party liable to perform, (b) *not foreseeable* by him at the time of the conclusion of the contract or were discounted therein, and (c) *not subsequently preventable* or capable of being confined in their consequences. It may, like lack of co-operation of the other party (*mora creditoris*), be only partial and its relative importance will in that case have to be assessed with regard to all the circumstances so that some claims may remain effective. In civil law, *force majeure* is a condition which lifts the blame for non-performance, which is itself at the heart of any claim for performance and/or damages. Only when guarantees of performance are given may *force majeure* excuses become irrelevant. They generally also are in respect of payment obligations or personal circumstances preventing performance. In common law, force majeure is generally irrelevant in respect of the essential terms (or, in England, conditions) of the contract, unless a specific *force majeure* clause is added in the contract.

Pure *acts of god* or *theft* are likely to create absolute barriers to delivery for a seller in terms of *absolute impossibility* rather than *force majeure.* Even so, it may not always be relevant as an excuse, for example if it concerns a manufacturer finding his manufacturing facility substantially intact after fire or if he has ready access to a market of replacement goods so that he can still limit the consequences. However, if under these circumstances performance becomes much more difficult, the excuse of *force majeure* may still be allowed. It could be seen as the more *subjective* (or economic) rather than a more absolute use of the concept of impossibility. In civil law the notion of *force majeure* was further developed especially within the normative interpretation method, which tends to consider more in detail the circumstances and facts of each case and might be more lenient to the weaker than to the professional defaulter. The force majeure and good faith concepts thus become connected.

In the objective or absolute approach, *force majeure* may equate with impossibility. In this view, it is irrelevant whether a performance becomes more difficult or disadvantageous than originally thought. Only absolutely unforeseeable impossibility to perform will discharge the debtor and, as we just saw, not even always, especially not if there is an alternative. In the more normative approach, on the other hand, the debtor need only do what may reasonably be expected of him in the circumstances. It could then even excuse non-payment (of a temporary nature but not a debtor's insolvency), illness of the party that must perform, or non-performance for other personal reasons.

Most legal systems accept some form of the normative or more subjective view — in common law the use of the term impracticability (normally of an economic nature) instead of impossibility in Section 2–615 UCC reflects this — but there is disagreement on how far this should go and what risks in terms of personal circumstances or even economic hardship remain with the debtor. No system adheres here fully to the subjective approach which in its most extreme form would make contractual performance entirely uncertain and a personal affair.

In the case of services depending on the debtor, even personal elements like incapacity may count as objective or absolute *force majeure*, like the portrait painter whose hand is damaged. Yet the portrait painter claiming lack of inspiration may have a harder time escaping liability. In other situations, personal circumstances may be totally irrelevant and illness or lack of money may not excuse anyone from delivering the goods under a sales agreement or paying for them (although payment system problems may). The personal aspects or impediments are then considered the risk of the directly affected party or may be considered discounted in the contract so that they cannot serve as an excuse. Again, when guarantees are given, *force majeure* may no longer play a role at all, as we saw, even in the normative civil law approach. So it is with conditions in English law where they are not balanced by a specific contractual *force majeure* clause, see also section 1.4.3 above.

A special aspect of the problem arises where there is no physical impossibility to perform but the *commercial object* or purpose of a contract becomes *frustrated*. The famous English Coronation cases provide the traditional examples: because of the postponement of the ceremony in 1901, all kind of seating and viewing arrangements along the route of the procession lost their purpose and an excuse was allowed.[136] How far this doctrine of *frustration* goes has always remained a matter of debate in England and also the remedies: excuse of performance or in suitable cases adaptation of the contract (to for example another date or another price, or to a different quality for a different price, etc)?

The *same* circumstances may create a *force majeure* situation in one contract but not in another even if they are closely related. The destruction of a mode of transport may not excuse the seller bound to deliver Cif and he may have to look for an alternative at his own cost. Yet under the contract of affreightment, the carrier is likely to be excused because of impossibility if the destruction of the ship was not due to his fault or negligence.

In section 1.3.8 above, the sometimes close connection with mistake was highlighted, especially where it concerns circumstances already existing at the time of the conclusion of the agreement and which could have been known. It was also argued in that section that

---

[136] *Krell v Henry* [1903] 2 KB 740.

mistake or a genuinely unforeseeable change of circumstance should not readily be accepted as an excuse for performance between professionals, let alone as creating a re-negotiation duty, which, even if imposed, should not easily lead to damages claims if the re-negotiation fails.

As far as terminology is concerned, *force majeure* is, as we saw, sometimes distinguished from absolute impossibility, but that is not always the case and it may be referred to also as impossibility or, more flexibly, as impracticability, especially in the USA. In common law, there is also frustration (of purpose as we saw). They all identify different roots of a similar problem or excuse. The term 'frustration' is sometimes used more precisely in the sense of longer term economic hardship due to changed circumstances and then suggests an adaptation of the contract rather than providing an excuse for non-performance. It is in such cases more in particular defined with emphasis on an unforeseen and not preventable event causing an excessive economic burden or unconscionability for the party liable to perform.

The Vienna Convention confirms in Article 79 the *force majeure* elements as discussed in the previous section but uses the term 'exemption'. Indeed, it considers *force majeure* an excuse for non-performance and ties it, as we saw, to an impediment beyond (a) the control of the party concerned, that could not (b) reasonably have been taken into account at the time of the conclusion of the contract and (c) could not reasonably have been avoided or overcome. It is thus clear that it does not require absolute impossibility to perform, yet it does not say how far it goes on the route to personal excuses and economic hardship. As already mentioned, the consequence is only the waiver of damage claims, assuming the *force majeure* concerns the whole performance (Article 79(5)), and there is no adaptation facility, which therefore depends on the provisions to that effect in the contract itself.

In the Vienna Convention, the concept of *force majeure* is accepted as an independent legal concept and is not considered to depend on an implied condition of the contract (although certain waivers may be deemed implied or certain risks considered discounted in the contract). This conforms to the modern civil law approach, see Article 1148 Cc in France and Section 275(2) BGB in Germany.

In common law, it took much longer for a *force majeure* concept to develop as an independent legal excuse beyond special contractual provisions and definitions. In England, the courts had rejected the notion for all contractual conditions in *Paradine v Jane*[137] in the absence of a contractual clause to that effect. This case also stressed the literal meaning of the terms (conditions) and disallowed any adverse testimony if the text of the contract was clear (the parole evidence rule, see section 1.2.5 above). It required the tenant of a house to make the agreed repairs, also of a house that had been 'burnt by lightning or thrown down by enemies', so that not even absolute impossibility or acts of god were considered a sufficient excuse (always short of a contractual *force majeure* clause). It took a long time before this strict rule was watered down by creating exceptions through implying terms of reasonableness.[138] *Force majeure* thus became to some extent a question of contractual interpretation and therefore of the parties' implied intent not to demand performance under the circumstances, but references to the (implied) intent of the parties in this manner remain controversial and are limited.[139]

Although (even in the absence of a contractual clause) *force majeure* may now provide an excuse, also in the case of economic impossibility or, in exceptional cases, when the

---

[137] 82 ER 897 (1647).
[138] See *Taylor v Caldwell*, 3 B&C 826 (1863), LJ 32 QB 164.
[139] See Lord Reid in *Davis Contractors v Farnham* [1956] 2 All ER 145 and for the role of intent in common law generally, s. 1.2.5 *supra*.

purpose of the contract is frustrated as in the Coronation cases, mentioned above, there is no adaptation facility implied under common law, except where there is statutory law to that effect, as provided in a limited way in the UK in the 1943 Law Reform (Frustrated Contracts) Act.

In this common law tradition, even Section 2–615 UCC in the USA continues to style the *force majeure* exception as an implied (here statutory) condition or basic assumption (of practicability) on which the contract was made and therefore as an excuse in appropriate circumstances. Good faith compliance with governmental regulation may also lead to a valid excuse under the UCC. Again being only excuses, neither results in an adjustment of the agreement without a particular clause to the effect in the agreement itself.

In France, *force majeure* still primarily concerns the old acts of god or *casus fortuitus* or *vis extraria*, as explicitly referred to in Articles 1147 and 1148 of the French Cc, including also governmental interference (*fait du prince*). Thus in France, the excuse of *force majeure* still requires an unforeseeable and irresistible event totally unconnected with the party that must perform, therefore absolute impossibility. This approach is now mostly thought too severe, however, and restricted to so-called *result contracts*. These are contracts where a certain result is the objective, like sales agreements for the timely delivery of conform goods, contracts of affreightment, rental agreements and building contracts. Clearly in modern terms there is here some guarantee deemed implied which makes a stricter approach to *force majeure* better understandable.

1.4.7   Unforeseen Circumstances and the Balance of the Contract: Hardship

It is clear that not every unforeseen or unavoidable change of circumstances can give rise to a *force majeure* excuse, let alone to re-negotiation duties. Even in the more normative or subjective approach in civil law, this is so when the defences concern payment of money or become too personal or the type of commitment does not allow it or may limit it, for example where the debtor accepted the risk, where a guarantee of performance is given or implied or, in France, where there is a result contract. Economic hardship itself is not necessarily an excuse either, especially not if it could have been reasonably foreseen or taken into account at the time of the conclusion of the contract. If it results from undiscountable fundamentally changed circumstances, there may, however, be some relief. The question then is what kind of hardship is necessary to qualify. This is all a matter of interpretation even under the flexible *force majeure* or 'exemption' formula of Article 79 of the Vienna Convention on the International Sale of Goods.

As we saw, this formula is broad and general in the subjective tradition. Whether it also covers unforeseeable changes of circumstances leading to economic hardship must be doubted. As a matter in principle dealt with in the Convention, guidance may have to be sought from its general (underlying) principles and as a last resort from the domestic law most directly concerned under the applicable conflicts of laws rule, see Article 7(2). This may also apply to the consequences in terms of adjustment or termination of the contract, not covered in the Vienna Convention itself. As the Convention does not consider adaptation, termination may, however, be considered more normal (in the absence of course of an explicit adaptation facility in the contract).

The question what should be done is also relevant when the interests of the parties unavoidably start to diverge in the course of the life span of a (longer term) contract. Following a progressive change in circumstances, there may easily result a *de facto* discontinuation of the co-operation on which full performance often depends *without* there being a clear situation of default or *force majeure* or even great economic duress. In such circumstances, the normal co-operation to make contracts work might start to falter. In this connection reference is often made to the contractual balance becoming disturbed for which the traditional excuses may not be the proper answer. The balance itself might require redressing which may lead to adaptation needs *short of* a situation of true *force majeure* or economic hardship. The proper answer might not then be a discharge of either party but rather a renegotiation of the contract.

In medieval law, there developed in this respect the notion of the *clausula rebus sic stantibus* or the implied condition that circumstances would not change and the will of the parties was considered conditioned thereby.[140] In a general way, the *clausula* goes back to the writings of Baldus in the fourteenth century,[141] and the doctrine remained popular until the nineteenth century when the parties' intent became more sacrosanct,[142] although in the Netherlands the *clausula* approach was never entirely accepted before 1806 and abandoned thereafter. It provided an alternative excuse to *force majeure*, often with another type of definition and an implied adjustment facility of the contractual terms. It operated on the basis of what in modern law would probably be considered *good faith* principles.

In cases of imbalance, at least one of the parties may strive for a solution through contractual re-negotiations and amendment. The question then is whether or when there may be grounds (and which ones) to rebalance the contract through forced re-negotiations and judicial intervention, with or without some form of damages being awarded, either as (partial) indemnification or as penalty for lack of co-operation, if the parties themselves cannot find a solution. The judges would then probably also have the option of early termination without awarding (some) damages. In purely professional situations, the parties themselves must here come to a solution. A judge or arbitrator may give some guidance but it is not for him to re-write the contract. That should only be done *in extremis*, and even then only when it is likely to work.

The essence is always the readjustment of the risk of unforeseen intervening events — not therefore to redress pure miscalculation, which is the risk of the party having made it. Redress is here meant to allow for some excusable lack of imagination at the outset or the impossibility of quantifying the risk at the time the contract was concluded, or for the impact of the turn of events, for example excessive market movements in the price of the relevant base materials. This may or may not result in a true *force majeure* situation at the same time. It is more likely under the subjective approach in the manner as adopted by the Vienna Convention, which refers to what could have been reasonably foreseen at the time of the conclusion and was not preventable or could have been overcome later.

As just mentioned, the trigger mechanism may be differently formulated, but is often geared to economic hardship as a balancing requirement. In the common law operating with the implied condition of practicability, the concepts of *force majeure* and frustration in this sense may indeed be less distinguishable, leading only to excuses or in extreme cases to termination but less readily to the adaptation of the contract. In any event, judicial restraint is necessary in professional dealings.

The modern variants of hardship, economic impossibility or impracticability with a re-balancing or re-floating of the contract, are novel departures, although they were not fully unknown in the *Ius Commune*, as we already saw for the *clausula*, but they became ultimately unfashionable. In modern times, the problem has particularly arisen in times of

---

[140] See also R Feenstra, 'Impossibilitas and Clausula Rebus Sic Stantibus' in *Festschrift Daube Noster* (1974), 81.
[141] *Commentaria ad* D.12.4.8.
[142] See the Prussian *Allgemeines Landrecht* I, 5 s. 378 (1794); Fritze, 'Clausula Rebus Sic Stantibus' (1900) 17 *Archiv für bürgerliches Recht* 20.

war and emergency, usually coupled with high inflation. It has not been uncommon in such situations for relief to be provided by statute. In France, special legislation was passed on 21 January 1918 (*Loi Faillot*) which allowed contracts entered into before 1 August 1914 to be terminated if causing damage to a party that was unforseeable at the time of the conclusion of the agreement. A similar law was enacted on 1 July 1949 in respect of agreements entered into before 2 September 1939. Similarly in Germany, an act was passed on 26 March 1952 (*Vertragshilfegesetz*) concerning contracts entered into before 21 June 1948.

These laws left the final decision to the judge and did not give criteria or guidance for adaptation or termination. Where no special statutory law came into being, however — and they were all limited in scope — the question was everywhere whether general legal principles could provide a basis for similar contract adaptation. Different legal systems reacted very differently, often as a result of the depth of the economic distress, with German law being most flexible but the law in other major countries remaining more rigid. The liberal German case-law approach was discussed within the context of the discussion of good faith in section 1.3.1 above and led to the notion of *Wegfall de Geschäftsgrundlage*, now codified in Section 313 (new) BGB (and it is not therefore treated as an instance of *force majeure* adjustment). It was first based on a disturbance of contractual balance and seen as an implied condition; later on it developed in a more objective sense under the German notion of good faith.[143] Under the new Dutch Code, the idea of adjustment in the case of changed circumstances is statutory and embodied in Article 6.258 CC.

In common law, there is, as we saw, more restraint, although in principle the theory of implied conditions, also used in the case of *force majeure*, could be extended to allow contractual adaptation or rescission, but it is not done, even though the *force majeure* concept itself is broadened into economic impossibility in exceptional cases as we saw in the Coronation cases. In England it was held in *Chandler v Webster*,[144] that the risk of changed circumstances lies where it falls, and this was only reversed in *Fibrosa v Fairburn*,[145] but it is still said that the doctrine of frustration has the effect of declaring on which party some unanticipated risks lie, not of altering where they lie. It remains a matter of interpretation of implied terms therefore, with its limitations in common law. Proper relief would often require an adjustment of that risk and may then not be forthcoming.

In England, the issue remains essentially unresolved with the English courts becoming less rather than more co-operative.[146] Businesses seem on the whole to be able to live with this restraint and might on balance prefer it to the uncertainty another attitude might bring, although hardship clauses may sometimes be included in the contract and are then indicative of a clear-cut attitude. In the USA, the situation seems in fact not much different. The lesser need for these facilities in the professional sector, except in exceptional cases, was already discussed above in section 1.3.7.

1.4.8   Modern Legislative Approaches to a Change in Circumstances: Contractual Hardship Clauses

Adaptation or rescission because of changed circumstances, beyond the narrow road of *force majeure* as contractual excuse, raise issues of judicial power and its basis in the light of the party autonomy and the parties' intent as expressed in the agreement. The issue was in

---

[143] See also n 93 *supra*.
[144] [1904] 1 KB 493.
[145] [1943] AC 32.
[146] See GH Treitel, *The Law of Contract* (London, 10th edn, 1999), 807.

its generality already raised in section 1.3.8 above. The authority to change this intent retroactively must be found either in the contract itself or in special provisions of the applicable law or in general legal or interpretative principle. The last solution was originally adopted in Germany through case-law in the 1920s, as we saw above in section 1.3.1, first by relying on implied conditions, then more fundamentally through concepts of good faith, now resulting in Section 313 BGB.

The statutory solution was also chosen in the new Dutch Civil Code, Article 6.258, tying the relief for unforeseen changed circumstances to the unreasonableness of the counter-party in insisting on the unchanged continuation of the contract and allowing the judge to terminate the agreement in whole or in part or to adapt it, in line with older case-law that enunciated, however, more particularly the principle of unconscionability.[147] The Dutch code allows the court to change the contract or to terminate it in whole or in part. It seems not to envisage re-negotiation duties as such but rather a judicial decision of some sort. If the contract has lost all purpose, termination seems to be appropriate.

The reason is probably that academic writing has not been greatly productive in analysing what the proper adaptation technique should be and how any re-negotiations should be conducted. It is clear that in essence the parties' original intent is asked to be set aside on good faith grounds, however expressed. Yet what fairness requires is unavoidably geared to individual factual situations which may be the main reason clear guidelines appear to fail here. Rabel saw the multiplicity of obligations as the major obstacle to formulating general principles of adjustment.[148] Corbin[149] stated: '[w]e cannot lay down one simple and all controlling rule. The problem is that of allocating in the most generally satisfactory way the risks of harm and disappointment that result from supervening events.' Meijers[150] formulated some general characteristics: the change in circumstances must have been unforeseeable, must be of an exceptional nature, beyond the ordinary risk incurred in a contract, must render performance excessively onerous and the change should not be due to the fault of one of the parties.

These characteristics do not go much beyond the normal subjective *force majeure* definition balanced by the emphasis on the excessive burden and do not give an indication of how any adaptation of the contract should be conducted. This emphasis on excessiveness also figures in the European and Unidroit Principles, but now less so in the new Dutch and German Civil Code. None gives the judge any guidance on his authority to terminate or adapt the agreement.

Where emphasis is put on an excessive burden or unconscionability, which seems appropriate at least in the professional sphere, some regard must be had to the overall financial position of the party invoking the re-negotiations rather than to the contractual situation itself. As such, there may be in descending order a need for (a) a dramatic economic disadvantage overall, for example a likely bankruptcy as a result of performance, or (b) a loss situation for the business as a whole for some time or at least in the line of business concerned with the contract. Of course this situation should derive from performance of the relevant contract. A loss or lesser profit than expected under the contract could by itself hardly qualify as hardship.

---

[147] HR 19 May 1967 [1967] NJ 261.
[148] *Das Recht des Warenkaufs* (1936), i, 157.
[149] *Contracts* (1951), s. 1322 at 256.
[150] 'La Force Obligatoire des Contrats et ses Modifications dans les Droits Modernes', *Rapport, Actes du Congrès International de Droit Privé* (Rome, 1950), I, 99 at 111, 112.

The principle of adaptation — less important in individual sales but potentially of great importance in long term supply and construction agreements — raises the practical issue of what a judge can do in the circumstances as he is hardly the proper authority to rewrite the contract. It seems that the parties of necessity must be heavily involved in re-floating their contract so as to provide a realistic future for it. This might require interim judicial measures, for example as to whether re-negotiation is called for, or even some immediate payments as part damages to provide survival relief. It appears, however, that, especially in the professional sphere, the re-balancing effort must remain exceptional and, failing this (upon a *bona fide* effort which in the commercial sphere may be limited) performance or otherwise termination (with or without damages depending on the degree of *force majeure*) must be the normal remedy.

It is not uncommon to find a more specific trigger mechanism in the form of a proper *hardship clause* inserted in the contract itself. Such a clause is likely to set some parameters for re-negotiation and its objectives. In the process, it might limit the judge's intervention to specific questions of discord, for example on the existence of the conditions triggering the re-negotiations, on damage claims up to the moment the burden became intolerable if the performance was interrupted earlier, on disagreements on the new price which could be resolved by a reference to *normal market* prices, on new specifications which again could be resolved with reference to the *normal* standard to be expected for the price to be charged, whilst duration or place of work or delivery might be changed and the reasonable *normal* effects on costs be taken into account.

Most significantly, however, the introduction of a hardship clause itself indicates that parties did not mean to be bound under all circumstances. The *force majeure* excuses themselves might be expanded thereby as the more important risks of a change of circumstances were clearly not discounted in the contract. This being the case, *bona fide* disagreement in the re-negotiations may be considered a sign of parties not wanting to continue and may be *prima facie* ground for discharge and termination of the agreement, which could, however, still allow for payment of (some) damages. This appears to be the fundamental difference between reliance on a contractual clause and on a statutory provision in this area.

As suggested earlier, the situation is probably not much different from the one where parties are required to continue to negotiate in a pre-contractual situation or on the continuation of an agreement after its expiry if there is a clause to that effect. As mentioned in section 1.3.7 above, in such a case (a) the relationship between the parties in terms of professionality, their special interests, reasonable expectations, the frequency of their transactions and the incidents that have occurred in them, for example poor past performance or lack of co-operation, credibility and creditworthiness, (b) the nature of the deal (in the sense that a rental agreement will require different adaptations from a supply agreement), and (c) outside circumstances such as the market price or the required quality or style, may prove decisive and determine when continuation of the negotiations can no longer be reasonably required and termination must follow. In any event negotiations cannot drag on for ever.

An overriding consideration may be that in the commercial sphere parties on the one hand may have to carry more risk in terms of a change of circumstances, thus not being able to invoke this relief easily, whilst on the other hand, once there is qualifying hardship, they may be sooner discharged from their *bona fide* re-negotiation. It is also possible that in the case of hardship adjustments, the market conditions are not fully determinative, whilst adjustment may be spaced over a longer period which may not be necessary or relevant in pre-contractual negotiations or in negotiations for a continuation of expiring agreements if the contract itself calls for them.

1.5   Privity of Contract

1.5.1   *Privity of Contract or Third Party Rights and Duties under a Contract*

The extent to which third parties may derive rights from a contract between other parties or may even incur duties or a liability thereunder, without themselves becoming formal parties to the contract, has greatly exercised legal minds, especially in common law, where the subject is normally referred to as 'privity of contract' and is often raised in the context of the notion of proper consideration. It tended to leave third party beneficiaries unprotected if they had not given any consideration. In civil law, the issue is more commonly raised in the context of the discussion of *in rem* and *in personam* rights, therefore in the context of the more theoretical discussion on the nature of and distinction between proprietary and obligatory rights. The first ones have per definition third-party effect and the latter not. Yet even where contractual provisions work against third parties, like in many countries still a contractual assignment prohibition that may thus operate against an assignee who is unaware of it and void the assignment, there is not truly a proprietary right created although one could say that there was a proprietary effect of the prohibition. There is only a deviation from the party autonomy principle and the idea that personal rights cannot be enforced by or against others. It may therefore be said that neither the original common law approach nor civil law approach lead to great enlightenment.

Naturally, the basic contractual rule everywhere is that a contract cannot confer rights or impose duties on any person other than those that are party to it (unless leading to a proprietary disposition which is then covered by the law of property and not by the contract). This has, however, become too simplistic a view and there are a number of situations in which a contract has an effect on outsiders, which may be both on the rights and obligation or duty side, although it is more common on the former. That does not mean that these outsiders thereby automatically become parties to the contract. Indeed, one of the *major issues* in this area is whether or when they become thereby subject to the contract in their relationship with (one of) the contract parties, even if this may concern only some aspects of that contract. In the case of third-party beneficiaries under a contractual clause by which parties give a benefit to an outsider, this is quite common, assuming the beneficiary becomes aware of the benefit (and assuming consideration is given or can be construed to have been given in common law). Parties can create in this manner rights for others, but it is much more difficult also to create duties for outsiders unless very closely related to the benefit (as eg a duty to arbitrate under the contract in the case of a dispute). Thus outsiders may become *indirect* contract parties at least in some aspects and *contractual* actions could result between them and the direct contract parties on the basis of a contract that they did not conclude.

Short of such a relationship, there could still be tort or proprietary actions which direct contract parties might have against outsiders in connection with their contract. Outsiders may thus have duties in respect of contracts that they have not concluded. That is *not* then a matter under the contract itself. It concerns here especially the right of contract parties not to have the contract interfered with by others and to have any transfer of assets or rendering of services pursuant to the contract respected by all the world, at least as long as they do not interference with the rights of others. On the other hand, if a third party is adversely affected by a contract, it may equally be able to defend itself in tort against the contract parties or invoke the illegality of their agreement and (sometimes) ask for punitive damages like in the case of contracts in restraint of trade and for the effect they have on others.

It is clear in this connection that generally, the existence of all contracts must be accepted as *a fact* and third parties are not free to interfere with them or undermine them at will in order to undo them to their own or somebody else's advantage. So there is a negative duty on all third parties in respect of any contract (as indeed there is in respect of any asset or property right). This also applies to supply agreements with competitors, even if concluded in defiance of a contractual obligation of the supplier *vis-à-vis* the complaining party not to do so. One could also say that in this respect the rights of a party under a contract are proprietary to him and must as such be respected by all. Again, it is not a duty governed by the contract itself.

In a similar manner, it is also possible to argue that, if under a contract one of the parties (the reimbursing party) has agreed (or is forced) to reimburse any extra costs of the other party and any outsider increases these costs, for example whilst defaulting in his supply duties to the other party, the latter may be liable in tort to the reimbursing party whilst breaching his supply obligations to the other. As default in one relationship may have serious consequences in another, this could more generally give rise to a direct action: if A does not deliver specialty goods to B, B may default under his resale contract with C. This does not normally give C a direct action under the contract against A. He may not have a tort action against A either, but B may still be able to seek recourse against A for any damages he must pay C under his resale contract with C. As a consequence, A may at least indirectly derive a liability (in tort) from the contract between B and C as a consequence of his destabilising behaviour.

The key is that in these cases, the duties of third parties are *not* of a contractual nature, even though it is the existence of the contract between others that creates their duties, which are duties to respect these contracts, not to interfere with them, or to make their performance under them more difficult or more expensive.

At the start of this section, reference was already made to proprietary rights and the way contracts change them although the change itself is unlikely to be a proprietary matter. This may need further exploring. It is very clear e.g. that contracts which transfer proprietary rights, like sales agreements, also acquire third-party effect in their consequences, especially those under legal regimes like the French and English that do not require further acts, like delivery, for the transfer of title in chattels. This also applies to situations in which intangible assets like claims are transferred or rather assigned, when the assignee may defend his new right against all the world, often even before notification of the debtor. It means that everyone has to respect the new situation as to his ownership of the claim.

This is no less a situation in which contractual results must be respected by others, but as already mentioned, it is not the contractual aspects that matter here but rather the proprietary consequences. Therefore, the contract parties do not in that case act or defend on the basis of the contractual terms, but rather on the basis of a proprietary action or in tort and the duties of the third parties are again not contractual in nature. That may be different, however, for restrictive covenants connected with the use of property, especially land. Particularly in common law, they may affect any subsequent third party transferee of the property, even though the latter was never a party to it. Here, the counter-party will act or defend against the new owner on the basis of the old contract. New owners thus become parties to the old covenants and take over the contractual duties *in their capacity* of new owners, therefore even without their consent.

In civil law terms, it could be said that *these* contracts acquire as a consequence (some) *in rem* or proprietary effect in the sense that the beneficiary may maintain his right under it against any succeeding owner in the property (any third party therefore in this particular capacity, even if not against all the world). In civil law, this is likely to be more difficult if the covenants are not expressed as *in rem* servitutes, the civil law equivalents of the common law easements. These are of a special type and limited by the relevant civil law codes. In some civil law countries, mere contractual covenants may now be entered into land registers as well, thereby acquiring (some similar) *in rem* or third party effect. Even without such registration, under modern civil law, a new owner may sometimes be considered to commit a tort whilst ignoring the contractual commitments made by his predecessor in respect of the property, at least if he knew of the covenants before he bought. But again, this would *not* be an action directly based on the contract.

Better known in this connection in civil law is the rule that new owners have to respect at least existing leases or tenancies in the property (*cf* Section 566 BGB), therefore also if they were not original parties to the relevant contracts. Also here they acquire obligations under pre-existing contracts as third-party successors in the property, therefore in their capacity as (new) owners.[151] Although the old contract has here effect against third parties, it is only against this special class of them (succeeding owners in their capacity as owners). The effect is that beneficiaries are given a right to the *status quo* in their contractual arrangements concerning property in which the owner has changed. The French often speak here of *obligations propter rem*; others call them qualitative obligations. As new owners voluntarily enter into the property, one could argue that they implicitly accept this state of affairs and therefore enter the lease contracts as willing parties. However, they would also be bound if they knew nothing of these leases. An important aspect here is that the previous owners are *discharged* and do therefore not even remain guarantors of the new owners obligations as lessor and this even without any consent of the lessee. Another aspect is that not only rights, but also duties under an pre-existing contract are here transferred to someone who was never a party to it nor agreed to become one.

In these cases of restrictive covenants, leases and ground rents, one may explain the situation by the need to promote the liquidity (transferability) of real estate. If the old owners were to be held to the existing covenants and leases whilst the new owners could ignore them, it would be impossible for owners to sell their rented buildings or any property in respect of which they had given some covenant before terminating all these leases and covenants as they would lose control over the proper performance of these contracts by the owner after a sale. Such termination would depend on co-operation of the beneficiaries, who would thus obtain a blocking vote. This would obviously be undesirable.

New house owners must usually also respect certain implied duties concerning neighbours, even if they did not know of them at the time of the sale. Here there is no contractual relationship, however, and the enforcement action of neighbours will be in tort. So it is in respect of retention rights which succeeding owners of an asset seek to ignore. If they do, there may be a special type of recourse for the retentor which may be proprietary or in tort.

The class of successor-owners presents *one important and clear cluster* of situations in which the contract itself is extended to others (rather than that tort actions are engendered

---

[151] It should be noted that more generally legal successors like heirs or shareholders upon dissolution of companies automatically succeed in the duties (and rights) of the heir or former company and thereby become party to all their contracts (as well as in their proprietary and other rights and duties). This is an aspect of third-party rights and duties that will not be further discussed here.

by it), here primarily the *obligation* side of these contracts (although in the case of rental agreements also the benefits), a circumstance of course discounted in the purchase price of the asset. It may also be a benefit as a good existing lease agreement may enhance an asset's value. Sometimes, one may also acquire a benefit or *right* from a transaction between other parties. This presents *another cluster* of situations where indirect contract parties emerge. A good example is a beneficiary under a trust arrangement in common law. In a transfer between settlor and trustee, such third-party rights commonly arise, even in a proprietary sense, and the beneficiary may subsequently defend his rights against most classes of third parties in the nature of all equitable interests on the basis of the trust deed to which he was unlikely to have been a party. It concerns here in particular the trustees, their creditors and even their successors in interest who knew of the beneficiary's prior rights or did acquire the interest for free. In trust situations there is no need for consideration on the part of the beneficiary or trustee for the benefit or right to pass.

To this same cluster belong situations already mentioned above when, also in civil law, contract parties agree to give more directly a benefit to a third-party. This possibility was already mentioned and the term *third-party beneficiaries* is commonly used. Consent or acceptance by the third-party is often not necessary for these rights *to vest* and to be invoked by the beneficiary, although there could be a rejection. Consideration may be required for him to benefit as was long the case in England. The *donnee beneficiary* thus has a problem. More normal is that one of the contract parties wants the other to pay the beneficiary in lieu of himself because he owes the beneficiary something on account of another arrangement. That becomes the justification and the consideration in cases like these. Economically there is likely to be a three partite arrangement that is legally expressed in this manner (therefore under two separate agreements under one of which there is a third-party beneficiary who is connected in another relationship with the creditor under the first agreement). One may note that in these cases a form of acceptance by the beneficiary of his substitute payment in this manner may become a natural issue. Hence the facility to refuse third-party benefits.

The rights so granted to third parties are likely to remain purely contractual, which means that they can be maintained against the original parties only: in life insurance e.g. the existence of third-party beneficiaries has long been accepted and once their interest vests under the terms of the policy, they can maintain it against the insurance company and the original parties can no longer change that unless the policy itself says so. In this case, there is unlikely to be a consideration requirement in common law; practice forbids it. Similarly, bank guarantees are often arranged for the benefit of third parties, as in letters of credit, and give them a direct right against the issuing bank. If they are issued in irrevocable form, they cannot be withdrawn. Here the consideration will derive from the whole of the arrangement which, *economically* speaking, is also likely to be tripartite. Child maintenance clauses are common in marriage contracts and divorce settlements and may give children equally direct rights against the paying parent. Consideration is here the parental obligation. Exemption clauses exonerating parties *vis-à-vis* each other from any adverse consequences of their performance under a contract or from any tort liability might be invoked by servants or subcontractors to exonerate them as well. They thus become third-party beneficiaries even without clear prior acceptance of that position and again without consideration.

These are all situations where the original parties are unlikely to be able to change the benefit because they impliedly agreed not to do so, even without the beneficiary knowing of it (at first), or otherwise after him having explicitly or indirectly accepted the benefit. If the third-party did know from the outset, it could be argued that it became a direct, rather than indirect, party to the agreement. But in all cases, the rights of the beneficiary are pre-set and governed by the contract concluded by others; the terms directly relating to the benefit are applicable to him but he will not have had a say in them. That could also include some closely related duties. In this connection, the duty to arbitrate in the case of conflict was already mentioned if there is such a clause under the contract or if there are any conditions to the benefit arising. Otherwise duties cannot be imposed on other persons. Only benefits can be given in this manner.

These third party rights may still be distinguished according to whether they need acceptance by the third-party beneficiary to bring them into the contract or not. This would seem to be unnecessary e.g. in the case of child support. It always seems possible to repudiate them, however. As already mentioned, these situations of third party benefit might be further distinguished into those under which the grantor owed the beneficiary something and those in which there was a question of a pure gift (the donnee beneficiary), under common law a distinction closely connected with the doctrine of consideration. Also in civil law, there may be certain formalities to make such a pure gift an enforceable benefit for the third-party.

The third-party benefit may also imply the split off of a proprietary interest in favour of a third-party. This is more like the trust situation, therefore the case of a trust beneficiary. The question here is whether, *outside* the area of pure trust, a form of acceptance is necessary for the proprietary right of the third-party to become maintainable against everyone else. The key in these cases is therefore not only contractual protection of the right so granted against the original parties to the transaction, but there may also be a proprietary protection against all others, which means that the beneficiary for the defense of his rights may no longer be dependent on the help of the original parties. In common law, there would likely be a consideration requirement in this kind of situation as well.

A *third cluster* of situations in which an outsider may become an indirect party to an agreement is presented in situations where there are *closely related* agreements. In modern finance leases, it is normal for example to expect that the lessee has certain direct installation and repair rights against the supplier of the goods under the latter's contract with the lessor who is often no more than the financier who ordered the goods upon the lessee's instructions and specifications. In these situations, the lessee may also incur some direct duties under the supply agreement, for example the duty to give access to and co-operate with the supplier. This is now very much the theme of Article 2A UCC in the USA, an approach also adopted in the Unidroit (Ottawa) Convention on International Financial Leasing of 1988, see also chapter 5, section 2.3.

In parallel loan agreements, where there is cross lending, or in a similar grouping of contracts, default under the one loan agreement may also impact on the other, especially as parties are likely to know of the existence of both, often concluded between the same parties or their subsidiaries. The contract may of course especially provide for it, but if forgotten, it may still be so. In financial swap arrangements, similarly, the two legs of the swap are now mostly considered irretrievably connected or integrated, particularly important for the acceleration and set-off possibilities and may thus impact on each other. Swap Master Agreements go further and connect also other swaps between the same parties in terms of close out netting upon a default (or cross default) concerning one of them, see also chapter 6, section 1.4.6. In repos, one may also find Repo Master Agreements which similarly connect repos between the same parties, see chapter 5, section 2.2.5. But here the connections are contractually induced and may not be assumed.

In this cluster may also be found co-operation duties where people work together e.g. on the same building site under different contracts. They are bound together by a joint objective, but their contracts may become indirectly related in that they concern the same project. In situations like these, the practicalities will often require them to help each other, at least in minor things. One may ask whether in these cases lack of co-operation is a breach of contractual duty (and under which contract) or rather a tort. In a normative contractual interpretation it is likely to be the former in respect of the contract under which each party works as the breach of their contract derives from not helping others in the performance of their contractual duties. It could be argued that these co-operation duties were indirectly accepted in the original contracts or that sharing burdens in respect of the same project was implied. Thus in Germany third parties may acquire quasi-contractual rights under a contract to which they are neither party nor expressly a beneficiary if they are found sufficiently close to the contract from its pre- to post- contractual phases, *cf* Section 311(3) (new) BGB.

Undisclosed or indirect agency presents a *fourth cluster* where someone (here the principal) becomes a party to a contract concluded between others. The position is more than the one of the third-party beneficiary in that the agent may drop out as party altogether. Thus in common law, upon disclosure the principal becomes the direct party, see more in particular section 3.1.5 below. A principal may in this way have to accept the contracts concluded by its agent with others, even if the agent acted outside his authority. In this cluster may also be placed a carrier, who must accept that any succeeding holder of the bill of lading may require performance under the contract of carriage even though there was never express consent by the carrier to the transfer of the bill (quite apart from the proprietary consequences of the bill of lading as a document of title). Similarly, a drawee who has accepted a bill of exchange will have to pay any succeeding holder of the bill without a direct contractual relationship.

In a similar vein, any debtor will normally have to pay the assignee of his debt upon notice (if not increasing his burdens). We are concerned here with situations in which the third-party (respectively the principal, carrier, drawee and debtor) incurs (performance or co-operation) *duties* under a contract concluded between others. Again, the essential point is that the third-party duties so obtained or incurred are in each instance in principle governed by the *contractual* regime created by the parties to the original contract to which the third-party is not itself directly a party but has exposed itself to this risk.

It is submitted that the situations in which third party rights or duties may arise in connection with or under a contract (therefore the four clusters mentioned above) do not differ greatly between civil and common law countries. They are on the whole exceptional and derive from *obvious practical needs*, although certain problems, like the one concerning proper consideration, are not likely to arise in civil law countries. On the other hand, in the approach to proprietary protection and protection of covenants in land against third parties (successors), the common law is less formal than the civil law and shows greater flexibility. This is also true in the protection of mere possessory rights like bailment under which the bailee could be considered a beneficiary who may defend his physical possession against all the world, even against the bailor subject to the latter's contractual reclaiming rights. In common law this may allow proprietary effect to flow more readily from contractual stipulations concerning property.

In purely contractual matters, the problems connected with third-party rights and duties are, however, hardly different in either system. There are no general rules in either. It is clear that both the *normative or reliance* approach to interpretation may more readily explain the rights or even duties of third parties under a pre-existing contract between others. Modern civil law may be more inclined to it but has not produced greatly new insights or the identification of new or more precise clusters either. This approach is, nevertheless, likely to put more emphasis on co-operation, investigation and disclosure or loyalty duties depending on the situation and the nature of the relationship between the parties. In that context third party rights and duties may also emerge but it may tend towards tort liability and in this approach it may be more difficult to explain the extension of the contractual regime to others.

1.5.2 Development of Contractual Third-Party Rights and Duties in Civil Law

As we saw, traditionally in civil law, the concern for third-party rights and duties under a contract is closely connected with the distinction between the law of property and the law of obligations. Roman law did not maintain a clear conceptual distinction between *in personam* and *in rem* rights, although it accorded different actions (*in personam* or *in rem*) from which a difference between proprietary and other rights could be deduced.

Equally Roman law did not maintain a conceptual approach to third party beneficiary rights or third party duties under a contract. Unlike under modern civil law, see for example Section 328 BGB in Germany, it was not possible for parties to a contract to make a stipulation in favour of a third-party (the *stipulatio alteri*) giving the latter any enforceable rights under the contract or otherwise, *cf* Inst II.9.5. The contractual bond was too formal and too ritually created for it to cover also outsiders and, in the equally rigid system of Roman law actions, there was no clear form of redress. In fact, for most contracts there was no action, let alone for third parties' rights under them.

Later when formality receded and more contract types became enforceable, the rule against third party benefits and duties acquired a material law significance and was as such incorporated in the Justinian Codification (D.45.1.38.17). Through a penalty clause in the contract, at least the party agreeing to transfer a benefit to a third party could be pressurised into performance. It was also possible to make a stipulation in favour of the contract party together with a beneficiary. The latter had no independent action in these circumstances, but payment to him would absolve the party committed to giving the benefit. As formulated in C.8.54.3, the Emperors eventually started to protect gifts to third parties that had to be passed on according to the terms of the original contract. A right of the debtor to redeem, stipulated by the pledgee in an execution sale with a third party, also became enforceable, C.13.7.13.

Yet that was all the *Ius Commune* in its further development of the Roman law on the subject had to go by.[152] The Dutch seventeenth century writers were the first to abandon the Roman law constraints, especially in the natural law school approach of Grotius, who saw the impossibility of stipulating in favour of others as against nature.[153] Here the emphasis was on the autonomy of the parties' intent, but it became necessary for the beneficiary to accept the benefit before he could enforce the stipulation in his favour, although such an acceptance could be implied until any outright rejection.

This rejection could naturally come about if the third-party beneficiary did not want to accept a replacement for whatever the contract party negotiating the benefit for him might have owed him, which would normally have been the reason to negotiate the third-party benefit in the first place. Others, notably Pothier, stuck, however, to the original maxim (*alteri stipulari non potest*).[154]

The French Civil Code of 1804 in this respect followed Pothier and retained therefore a restrictive attitude to third party benefits, see Article 1165 Cc, except (following late

---

[152] See also R Zimmermann, *The Law of Obligations* (South Africa/Deventer/Boston, 1990), 41.
[153] *De Iure Belli ac Pacis*, II, Cap XI, s. 18.
[154] *Traité des Obligations*, No 54*ff*.

Roman law) if it concerned a condition of the performance one had negotiated for oneself or if it concerned a gift that one was making to someone else (Article 1121 Cc). The benefit could not be revoked once the beneficiary had declared his intention to profit from it. However, French case law has widened the first exception and assumes that there is also a benefit for the party negotiating the concession if it derives some moral profit from the transaction[155] and allows the third-party in that case to claim directly under the contract.

German law in Sections 328 and 311(3) BGB allows third-party benefit in general, although still expressing in Section 241 BGB the more general principle that contracts bind only the parties thereto. This principle is no longer generally so stated in the new Dutch Civil Code (but may still be inferred from Articles 6.213, 6.248 and 6.261 CC), and third-party benefits may be freely granted, see Article 6.253 CC.[156] In the Netherlands, acceptance (not mere notice) is now necessary, however, and until such time the benefit may be withdrawn. In the case of a gift, acceptance is presumed as soon as the beneficiary has knowledge of it and does not immediately reject it. Modern Dutch law reverts here to the approach of Grotius, but the question is in how far this acceptance must be explicit and what the situation was before it. German law in Section 333 BGB allows the beneficiary to reject the benefit which is retroactive to the time of the conclusion of the agreement providing for it; explicit or presumed acceptance is not necessary.[157] This is now also the French approach.[158] It means that the third-party right dates and is enforceable from the moment of the conclusion of the contract under which it is granted.

Third-party duties result commonly for principals from the acts of unauthorised agents, for lessees under supply agreements between third parties and the lessor concerning the leased assets, for debtors upon an assignment, for drawees of bills of exchange upon their transfer to subsequent holders, and for carriers upon transfers of the bill of lading: see the previous section. More difficult are situations under exemption or exoneration clauses, not so much if used by subcontractors or employees of the one contract party as a defence against the other, see Article 6.257 Dutch CC (not accepted in France, however),[159] but rather if used as defenses *against* third parties who claim. This is allowed in Germany and the Netherlands, but only under certain circumstances. We are concerned here with situations in which the conduct of the third-party or his relationship to the contract party may give rise to the defence.[160]

Article 6.110 of the European Contract Principles contain a clause which allows a third party beneficiary to benefit from a contract giving him a direct action, but the promissee may deprive him of it unless there has been *notice* to him that his right has become irrevocable or the third party has accepted the benefit.

1.5.3 The Situation in Common Law and the Changes in the USA and England

In common law of the English variety, the doctrine of privity disallowing any third party beneficiary to claim under the contract was connected with the doctrine of consideration

---

[155] See J Ghestin, *Traité de Droit civil, Les obligations* (Paris, 1992), nos 835*ff.*
[156] See further B Kortmann and D Faber, "Contract and Third Parties" in Hartkamp et al (eds), *Towards a European Civil Code, Ars Aequi Libri* (Nijmegen/Dordrecht/Boston/London 1994), 237.
[157] See further Heinrichs, *Münchener Kommentar zum Bürgerlichen Gesetzbuch*, Band 2, Schuldrecht, Allgemeiner teil, 2 Auflage (1985), 1,003*ff.*
[158] See Ghestin, n 147 *supra*, nos 843, 853.
[159] See Cour de Cass, 21 June 1988 [1988] Semaine Juridique, (ed) G, II.21125.
[160] See for Germany RGH, 25 Nov 1911, RGHZ 77, 317 (1911) and for the Netherlands HR 12 Jan 1979 [1979] NJ 362.

but was in its strictest form of relatively recent origin and was formulated by Lord Haldane in *Dunlop Pneumatic Tyre Co v Selfridge & Co* in 1915.[161] It has always remained contested, particularly by Lord Denning,[162] but was reconfirmed by the House of Lords in *Scruttons Ltd v Midland Silicones Ltd.*[163] In its most rigid form, it has proved inconvenient and is not followed in the USA. Even in the UK, there are many exceptions. The negative effects are now reduced through statute.

There were in England as exceptions the situations of the principal having to accept the contracts concluded by his unauthorised or undisclosed agents, see also section 3.1.5 below, and of debtors under assignments, drawees under bills of exchange and carriers under bills of lading having to accept the transfer of receivables, bills of exchange and bills of lading and perform towards other parties unknown to them. English law also construed situations of semi-contract or ancillary or collateral contracts where third parties, notably subcontractors of the counterparty, were deemed to have entered into a contractual relationship with the other (first) contracting party, notably if they had given certain assurances of quality to the counter-party on which the first party subsequently relied. The same approach is likely to be taken where a person buys goods from a dealer who was given a guarantee by a manufacturer.

This approach was also likely to prevail in hire-purchase and finance leases when finance companies were interposed between the supplier and the customer (hire-purchaser or lessee). Any undertakings of the supplier to the finance company or lessor could then still be relied upon by the customer.[164] Payment by credit card could also involve a *collateral* agreement between shopkeeper and credit card company leading to payment services and giving the shopkeeper a direct action against the card company without a direct contractual relationship. It here concerns all cases in which third parties incur *duties* under a contract to which they are not (directly) a party.

Collateral agreements were thus a most important tool for diluting the adverse effects of the privity doctrine in England. Consideration could, however, still be a problem. In the cases mentioned, the consideration derived from the underlying relationship between the contracting parties. It could also imply reliance on the additional services like in the case of a lessee who would rely on the quality undertaking of the contract between his lessor and the supplier of the leased equipment. This could be sufficient to sustain also the collateral agreement as it could be said that there was here a detriment to the party seeking to invoke the collateral agreement or a benefit to the subcontractor or supplier: see *Shanklin Pier v Detel Products Ltd* as the classic case.[165]

Equally having a car repaired in a garage appointed by the insurance company could still give rise to a direct action against the garage by the car owner even though he did not pay or arrange anything but only left his car there in reliance on proper repairs (*Charnock v Liverpool Corporation.*[166]) Naturally, the subcontractor or supplier, therefore the defendants in these collateral cases, ought to be well aware of the relationship between the main contractors and intend to play a role therein.[167]

Where in a contractual relationship between A and B there were benefits (rather than duties as in the above cases) for third parties, the question of consideration played no less

---

[161] [1915] AC 847.
[162] See *Smith and Snipes Hall Farm Ltd v River Douglas Catchment Board* [1949] 2 KB 500 and *Drive Yourself Hire Co (London) Ltd v Strutt* [1954] 1 QB 250.
[163] [1962] AC 446.
[164] See also GH Treitel, *The Law of Contract*, (London, 10th Ed. 1999), 541.
[165] [1951] 2 KB 854, 856.
[166] [1968] 1 WLR 1498.
[167] See *Independent Broadcasting Authority v EMI Electronics* [1980] 14 Build. LR 1.

a role. As we already saw, it a true gift were meant, the beneficiary was unlikely to be able to claim for want of consideration. That is also true in the USA, where the beneficiary is then called a 'donnee beneficiary'. If the benefit is meant, however, for C to fulfil an obligation A has towards him, there is obviously no gift and sufficient consideration may be assumed. In England C would still not have a contractual right to claim the benefit from B, not even if he agreed to the substitute performance. It was an important difference with the situation on the Continent and in the USA, only recently remedied by legislation.

Naturally, the party negotiating the third-party benefit can always insist on perform-ance, even specifically, so that the third-party will receive the benefit unless refused, but this does not give the beneficiary an own right. Also the first party may claim damages if the counterparty does not perform towards the beneficiary, but only for himself and not for the beneficiary. It seems that these damages may sometimes include the beneficiary's loss, although case law is not consistent on this point.[168] If the promissor performs and gives the third-party his benefit, there is, however, under English case-law still a possibility that any successor to the promissee, like his bankruptcy trustee, may still consider it a ben-efit for the promissee to be held by the beneficiary in trust for him. Yet there are cases of some urgency in which it has been held that the promissor performs to the promissee as trustee for the beneficiary,[169] who thereby obtains an enforceable action but in equity and not under the contract directly. Also exemption or exoneration clauses may provide exam-ples of situations where there may be a truly enforceable third-party benefit, also in England, either by using the notion of an implied contract or agency.[170]

Besides the situations where a third party may owe a duty under an assignment or other type of transfer agreement or under collateral agreements, this is all to say that even in England the doctrine of privity, like everywhere else, was less well established than it may have seemed at first, notwithstanding its appearance of perfect logic. The English Law Revision Commission as early as 1937 demanded reform and proposed a general formula much like that adopted in Germany and now also in the Netherlands making third-party benefits under a contract generally enforceable.

Legislation has now been passed in England to bring this about (the Contracts (Rights of Third Parties) Act 1999), following a Law Commission Report of 1996. It gives the third-party beneficiary the same right to enforce the contract as if it were a party to it. It also means that it may rely on a contractual term excluding or limiting its liability. The new law does not concern third-party *obligations* except where construed as conditions for the exer-cise of their third-party rights. The beneficiary is made explicitly subject to any arbitration clause. Established case law remains effective in this area. When the third-party right has crystallised (usually upon communication), it can no longer be revoked by the parties unless they reserve that right or any right of amendment (which may also be exercised if there is a need and the whereabouts of the beneficiary cannot be established or when the beneficiary lacks legal capacity).

The situation in the USA has long been different since the leading New York case of *Lawrence v Fox,*[171] in an important instance of an outright third party benefit, provided there was always consideration to support the benefit which may exclude the donee-ben-eficiary or any other who does not have a kind of relationship with the promissee that makes the benefit likely in the sense that the promissee has some interest. We are concerned

---

[168] See Treitel, n. 164 *supra*, 549.
[169] See *Les Affrêteurs Réunis Société v Walford* [1919] AC 801.
[170] See Treitel, n. 164 *supra*, 577.
[171] 20 NY 268 (1859), see also *Restatement (Second) of Contracts*, Section 302.

here with mostly substitute performance by a debtor asking someone else to perform. This is a promise which is enforceable by the creditor-beneficiary under the contract once the benefit vests, which will normally be the case upon acceptance of the substitution by the beneficiary or even when the beneficiary hears of the benefit. But the promissee may also insist on the original performance, whilst the beneficiary may no less be able to sue under the contract to receive his benefit.

1.6 The Unidroit and European Principles of Contract Law: Vienna Convention and UCC Compared

1.6.1 The Applicability, Reach, and the Directory or Mandatory Nature of the Principles

The Unidroit Principles for International Commercial Contracts were issued in 1995.[172] According to their Preamble, they set forth general rules for *international commercial*

---

[172] For a rough comparative guide, the following references to the Vienna Convention (VC), Unidroit Principles (UP), European Principles (EP) and Article 2 UCC (UCC), as divided per subject, may be useful:

   Offer and acceptance (formation): Articles 14 and 18 VC; Articles 2.2 and 2.6 UP; Articles 2.101, 2.201, 2.204, and 2.205 EP; Sections 2–204(1) and 2–206 UCC;
   Bargain, consideration and causa: Article 14 and Article 29(1) VC; Article 3.2 UP; Article 2.101 (end) EP; Sections 2–205 and 2–209 UCC;
   Reliance or conduct: Articles 16(2)(b) and18(1) VC; Articles 2.1, 2.4(2)(b) , 2.6, and 4.2 UP; Articles 2.102, 2.202(3)(c), 2.204(1) , and 6.101(1) EP; Section 2–206(2) UCC;
   Definiteness: Article 14 VC; Article 2.2 UP; Articles 2.103 and 2–201 (1)(b)EP; Section 2–204(3) UCC;
   Capacity, legality and validity: Article 4VC; Article 3.1 UP; and Article .4.101 EP;
   Formalities, parole evidence: Articles 11, 12, and 24 VC; Article 1.2 UP; Article 2.101(2) EP; Sections 2–201 and 2–202 UCC;
   Binding nature of offer: Article 16 VC; Article 2.4 UP; Article 2.202 EP; Section 2–205 UCC;
   Time of contract: Article 18(2) VC; Article 2.6(2) UP; Article 2.205 EP; Section 2–204(2) UCC;
   Specific performance: Article 28 VC, Article 7.2.2 UP, Article 9.102 EP, 2–716(1) UCC;
   Defences and failure of consensus: Articles 3.5, 3.6, 3.8 and 3.9 UP, 4.103(1)(a)(ii), 4.104, 4.107 and 4.108 EP;
   Excuses and force majeure: Article 79 VC, Article 7.1.7 UP and Article 8.108 EP;
   Privity: Article 6.110 (third party beneficiary) EP;
   Pre-contractual and post-contractual duties: Articles 2.15 and 6.2.1 UP UP; and Arts 2.301 and 6.111 EP;
   Interpretation: Articles 7 (1) (of the Convention), 8 VC (only of statements of the parties), Articles 1.6 (of Principles) and 4.1 UP (of common intention), Articles 1.106 (of the Principles) and 5.101 EP (of common intention), Sections 1–102 (of the Code) and 2–301ff. (of sales contracts) UCC;
   Concept of good faith: Article7 VC (only in interpretation of Convention); Articles 1.6 (not in interpretation of Principles), 1.7 (mandatory concept), 2.15 (negotiations in bad faith), 4.8 (supplying omitted term in the contract) and Article 5.2 (implied contractual condition) UP; Articles 1.106 (only in interpretation of the Principles), 1.102 (mandatory concept), 5.101(g) (interpretation of contract) and 6.102 (implied contractual term) EP; Section 1–103 (1–102 (3) old) (mandatory concept and contractual standards), Section 1–304 (1–203 old) (enforcement of duty or contract), Section 2–302 (unconscionability only for sale of goods), Section 1–201(20) (1–201(19) old) (subjective definition) and Section 2–103(1) (b) (between merchants in the sale of goods) UCC;
   Fundamental principles and mandatory rules: Article 12 VC; Articles 1.3, 1.4, 1.7, 3.19, 2.14 (probably), 2.19 (probably), 5.3 (probably) 6.2 (probably), 7.1.6 (probably), and 7.4.13 (probably) UP; Articles 1.102(2), 1.103, 1.104, 1.201, 2.301 (probably), 4.110 (probably), and 6.111 (probably) EP; Sections 2–203 (probably), 1–103 (1–102(3) old) (for good faith) and 2–303 (rejecting mandatory rules in principle) UCC;
   Party autonomy: Article 6 VC; Articles 1.1 and 1.5 UP; Articles 1.102 EP; Sections 1–103 (1–102 (3)and (4) old) and 1–303(e) (1–205(4) old) UCC;
   Custom and practices: Articles 4.7.2 (not in supplementation of Convention), and 9 (custom) VC; Articles 1.6(2) (not in supplementation of Principles), 1.8 (custom and practices), 4..3(b) and

contracts. Neither internationality nor commerciality is defined, but the use of these notions may imply a reference to the international commercial legal order. This idea is not pursued, however, even if it finds some further support in Article 1.6 on interpretation. The same definitional problems arise here as in international commercial arbitrations, see also chapter 1, section 1.1.5 and more generally where the international commercial and financial legal order needs defining.

Although these principles are referred to as the Unidroit Principles, they derive from this no special status in law. They are no more than product of a Unidroit committee and as such have at best persuasive power in terms of a restatement or as soft law. Their authority is hardly in their academic pedigree and content, and their legitimacy if any can only derive from their reflection of international fundamental principles or from the ability of the international legal practice to recognise itself in them and to accept their guidance, see also section 1.6.8 below. To put it more crudely, short of them reflecting fundamental legal principle and mandatory international practice, only the market place can decide their ultimate fate. Ordinarily therefore, international trade and commerce have themselves here the last word.

In this vein and according to the Preamble, the Principles are indeed more properly meant to apply only when parties have expressly agreed to them but also (still according to the Preamble) if their contract is to be governed by 'general principles, the *lex mercatoria* or the like'. Again, whether there is authority to so decree is another matter, which will further depend on these Principles being reflective of international commercial practice. If there is such authority, it might also cover situations where parties have not agreed on any (domestic) law at all (and is then at the detriment of private international law notions).

In the Preamble, it is further suggested that the Principles may also provide a solution when it is impossible to determine the relevant rule under a domestic law deemed applicable in the case. This would seem to refer to gaps in that law, but not to atavitic domestic laws being superseded. It is further hoped that the Principles may also serve as a model for national or international legislators. They are also seen as interpreting and supplementing uniform law instruments in which connection the Vienna Convention on the International Sale of Goods of 1980 particularly springs to mind. It is clear on the other hand that there is no concept here of different autonomous sources of law and their relationship amongst each other in the modern *lex mercatoria* approach as explored in chapter 1.

The Unidroit Principles do not mean to restrict the application of any *mandatory* rule of a national, international or supranational origin that may apply in a case in accordance with the rules of private international law (Article 1.4). It is apparently not considered that these mandatory rules strictly speaking apply more directly as *regles d'application immediate* (*cf* also Article 7 Rome Convention on the Law Applicable to Contractual Obligations). On the other hand, it is considered that there are mandatory rules in the Principles themselves which may therefore not be excluded by the parties, although the

(f) (interpretation of contracts), 5.2(b) (implied term) UP; Articles 1–106(2) (not in supplementation of the Principles), 1.105 (custom and practices), and 5.102(f) (interpretation of contracts) EP; Sections 1–103 (supplementation of the Code including law merchant), 1–103 (1–102(2)(b) old), 1–205, 2–202(a) and 2–208 (custom and practices) UCC;

General principles: Articles 7(2) (supplementation of Convention) VC; Article1.6 (supplementation of Principles) UP; Article1.106(2) (supplementation of Principles);

Private international law: Articles1.1 (sphere of application), 7.2 (supplementation of Convention), and 28 (specific performance VC; Articles 1.4 (in connection with mandatory rules) UP; Articles 1.103 (in connection with mandatory rules) and 1.106(2) (supplementation of the Principles) EP; Article 1–301 (1–105 old) (territorial application of Code) UCC.

Principles themselves may be (Article 1.5). This would seem incongruous. The most important rule that cannot be excluded in this connection is the one containing the duty to act in accordance with good faith and fair dealing in international trade (Article 1.7(2), see for another mandatory rule Article 3.19 on validity). There is neither a definition of good faith or fair dealings nor of international trade in this connection, see also section 1.6.3 below. In any event, it ignores the multi-faceted nature of the concept of good faith and creates other obvious problems where reference is sometimes made to related notions like acting in bad faith, resorting to manifestly unreasonable behaviour, taking excessive advantage, or reasonableness.

There is here some overreach as draftsmen of Principles like these, whatever their authority, hardly have power to declare certain principles mandatory and determine their scope unless they derive indeed from fundamental legal principle or come from the commercial practice itself of which Principles like these can be the conduit and expression but to which such draftsmen cannot add.

Whilst it is clear that in the approach to the *lex mercatoria* as proposed in this book, *fundamental* legal principle cannot be set aside by parties to a contract and that there is some *ius cogens* also in international trade, they concern fundamentals like the binding force of agreements itself (*pacta sunt servanda*), the liability for one's own actions and probably some other fundamental principles (like standards of care in the case of dependency) discussed in greater detail in the previous chapter of this book. It was concluded there that at least in the professional sphere, there are few, if any, fundamental principles concerning the *contents* of the deal. The approach of the Principles is here unspecific and derives from consumer law which is more in particular concerned with *content* and may test it on the basis of fairness. That criterion would in any case be far too broad and lacks normativity in professional dealings.

A censorious approach of this nature — if that is meant by the reference to a mandatory notion of good faith — is in its generality largely untenable in international commercial transactions. If nothing else, it could imply judicial control which professional parties should always be able to limit or exclude, all the more so in international cases, except in *exceptional* circumstances, where fundamental (international) principle is at work and perhaps also when gross unfairness or unconscionability results (*cf* also Section 1–302 or 1–102(3) (old) UCC in the USA which even then allows parties to at least set standards unless manifestly unreasonable) or more clearly if fraudulent or monopolistic or abusive tactics have been used. However, in such cases, there would likely be other means of setting the contract aside or limiting or changing the performance duties. Outside this area of gross misbehaviour of one of them (or proper, and not self serving, public policy considerations assuming they emanate from a legal order that has a sufficiently close relationship with the case), professional parties should be able to redistribute the burdens, risks and financial consequences of their dealings in the way they see fit. The construction of good faith as a mandatory concept is here unhelpful and generally misleading except if parties are allowed at least to set standards in the American way (unless manifest unreasonableness results).

An example may help: if one European airline company buys airliners in the US for a dollar amount during a time that the dollar depreciates, it may obtain a very great benefit, which could well result in a reduction of 30 per cent of the price in terms of its base currency (the Euro). The American supplier may not suffer greatly because its costs are in dollars and neither party may complain. It may be very different for another competing European airline company that may have bought similar airliners in Europe in Euros. It may thus be incurring an enormous long term disadvantage compared to the first airline company, its European competitor. Yet it cannot complain or request a renegotiation of its European supplier. It was a risk it accepted and which could have gone the other way (through wise currency protection the exposures may still be curtailed). There is therefore no point in this airline company complaining to its European supplier about the disadvantageous deal, even if the result might be its bankruptcy. Rebalancing, notions of fairness or of good faith seem to have here hardly a place and could not provide an objective standard for readjusting or valuing these deals. Any other attitude could entail the bankruptcy of the European supplier.

When contracts are here cast foremost in terms of risk management, it means that the risk of the dollar dropping was taken by the second airline company and when it went out of hand it had to accept the consequences of its misjudgement just as investors must accept to consequences of markets moving against them. That is what risk is all about. If contractually risks shift between parties, it normally means that they had a different perception of the future evolution of these risks, which is reflected in the price and structure of their deals. Subsequently, they will have to live with the consequences and cannot invoke notions of reasonableness, fairness or good faith that redress the outcome.

In this case there was a relative disadvantage resulting from two unrelated deals, but the situation is not fundamentally different when, within one deal, currency risk is transferred to the other party by eg choosing a different currency. If, eg, the European deal had been done in dollars, the second airline company would have retained its competitive position at the expense of the European supplier whose costbase would have been in Euros and who might as a consequence be facing bankruptcy. Why should that make a difference? There is no reason why reasonableness, fairness or good faith should here redress the outcome either. There is certainly nothing mandatory about it. It is submitted that there is also no identifiable social or cultural consensus that might dictate otherwise. In any event, what is fair or reasonable in situations like these and what good faith might require is often wholly unclear. Informed people are likely to differ here to such an extent that no underlying norm can be identified unless the situation is truly excessive. Even then, the remedy may not at all be plain.

In any event, in terms of social consensus, the perspective ought to be that of the international commercial and financial legal order and not that of a national or domestic consensus which soon leads into mystical nationalistic considerations (of innate social balance) that can hardly have any relevance as to how international commerce and finance develops and that may in any event only have a weak contact with the case in hand. As a minimum, it would then be necessary to show that such domestic considerations are sufficiently relevant or connected to impact on the international flows. Usually a domestic redistributive urge is at the heart of these considerations and not seldom also a domestic regulatory mode in which the underlying thought is that national communities and especially their governments (including their legislators) always know best also in international cases, even if in the particular country there is no informed opinion whatever on what might be needed to rebalance international forces nor any demonstrable expertise in the field. Although the great commercial benefits of internationalisation may only too willingly assumed, they are then intellectually denied whilst market forces become a bogus mantra which somehow have to be fought by what are seen as high minded domestic cultures but which in truth only too easily represent narrow provincialism based on irrational fears and ignorance. The proper alternative would be to close one's borders altogether and stay at home.

Even if the way risk is divided has in modern contract theory itself a more objective flavour in that it can no longer always be fully explained by intent in terms of a psychological reshuffle or balancing act as we saw in section 1.1.2 above, it remains nevertheless a fact that parties can exert their initiative and cut their business cake by contract in many different ways and that should be respected except if there are exceptional factors at play or if (relevant) public policies of sufficiently connected states or *international* public order requirements themselves demand otherwise. The introduction of a mandatory concept of good faith is here misleading and does not operate as such except at the margin, therefore in excessive situations only.

This is never to deny that under modern contract law elements other than the mere desire of the parties may have to be weighed in the final decision. Above in section 1.3, much was made of these factors, like conduct and reliance, nature of the relationship, forms of dependency etc, external circumstances (including cooperation in the performance of related contracts) whilst also the purpose of the agreement itself will enter into its application. It followed that in the modern approach to contract, notions of offer and acceptance as deliberate acts, eg, may fade in favour of notions of conduct and reliance with the consequence that several phases in contract formation and performance might be distinguished (the pre-contractual, contractual and post- contractual situations) in each of which different types of duties may arise whilst the types of obligations that so result derive more objectively from a normative and teleological interpretation. It is also true that the interpretation methods so used are often identified with the notion of good faith, but it does not go so far that professional parties substantially loose control. In any event, in international commercial and financial dealings, these newer concepts and interpretation techniques transcend narrow domestic notions of balance or social needs — assuming they could be sufficiently identified — and unavoidably acquire an international or transnational flavour.

There may also be other, more independent outside considerations in terms of public morality, social peace and efficiency to consider in contractual cases, but again, in international dealings, they are likely to acquire an international flavour. They may then also be referred to as international public policy which could indeed be mandatory as such and could be cast in terms of good faith notions. But secondly and as was already pointed out before, in professional dealings these considerations may be less important in affecting or determining the relationship and parties could agree to ignore them, at least to some considerable extent, or determine their own standards. Again, referring here to mandatory notions seems incorrect or at best only partially reflective of the law.

Finally, above in section 1.3.1, the multi-faceted nature of the good faith notion was already noted. As it can be so many things, the idea that the notion is mandatory *per se* becomes all the more problematic. Thus not only a censorious attitude going to content may be questioned, but where good faith is more structural e.g. when used to more closely relate the facts to the rules (whilst restating the most relevant rule in that context), this suggest an adjudicatory technique which leaves more discretion to judges and arbitrators but hardly a mandatory concept.

In the European Principles, another instance of mandatory rules are the rules concerning the validity of the agreement, that is those on fraud, threat and gross disparity. In view of what has just been said about exceptional situations, their mandatory nature may be less surprising. Here the approach is at least more subtle. Thus the rules on the binding force of the mere agreement, initial impossibility and mistake may be varied by the parties (Article 3.19). In truth, these rules concerning validity are fundamental (in as far as they refer back to the notion of *pacta sunt servanda* as the basis of the whole contractual structure) and otherwise structural (rather than mandatory) and it seems possible at least for parties to make further arrangements in respect of the consequences of all of them. By opting for another legal system altogether parties have in any event traditionally been able to circumvent them if less suitable and this will be no less the case under the Principles (Article 1.5). In any event, in professional dealings, questions of innocent misrepresentation, mistake and gross disparity should not so soon arise, see also section 1.3.5 above, and it might be questioned in this connection why gross disparity (or at least its definition) may not also be left to the arrangements by or the definitions of *professional* parties themselves. Instead we see here again the impact of a consumer law mentality.

In the case of hardship due to intervening unforeseeable, unavoidable and undiscounted circumstances, re-negotiations may be sought under these Principles as soon as the contractual equilibrium is disturbed, whilst there need not even be severe financial consequences (Article 6.2). This is also hard to understand for professional dealings. One may wonder whether this rule is also considered mandatory. Again this could at most be so in manifest cases. These are all personal dealings or consumer concerns. In a similar vein, surprising (standard) terms must be expressly accepted (Article 2.19), whilst Articles 7.1.6 and 7.4.13 limit the parties' freedom with respect to exemption clauses and agreements to pay fixed sums for non-performance. These rules also seem to be mandatory even amongst professionals. The question is why? Who needs protection here against what?

Pointing in another direction may, however, be the absence in the Principles of notions of capacity (not specifically covered, see Article 3.1). They may indeed be less relevant in the professional sphere. It is a typical issue for personal dealings. The attitude of the draftsmen appears otherwise to remain anthropomorphic throughout, see also Articles 4.1(1) and 4.2(1), that means tied to personal dealings only.

In these Principles, there are no pre-contractual disclosure and negotiation duties *per se*, which one would indeed not immediately expect in commercial contract principles, but Article 2.14 makes a party liable for damages in the case of negotiations in bad faith. Bad faith is undefined but introduces a subjective element and seems a mandatory rule as well. One instance is highlighted: one party entering into or continuing negotiations intending not to make an agreement. This can happen when this party wants to prevent the counterparty dealing with competitors or seeks confidential or proprietary information. This would border on the fraudulent for which the more proper remedy may be in tort. Concern here seems fair enough; yet more generally between professionals the negotiating behaviour must have been very bad indeed, again bordering on the fraudulent, before liability of any sort can result. This is not obvious from Article 2.14 although the reference to bad faith rather than lack of good faith may suggest a higher threshold for liability. Again, one must question the authority of the draftsmen of the Principles to state on mandatory rules unless they are demonstrably reflective of fundamental principle or international commercial practice.

More traditional notions geared to contracts between individuals in the sense of their psychological intent (*cf* Article 4.1(1) and Article 4.2(1), only thereafter balanced by more objective notions of reasonableness, see Article 4.1(2) and Article 4.2(2)), or with consumers and their protection rather than with professional dealings thus seem to prevail throughout and the Unidroit Principles cannot therefore be presumed always to reflect the international *commercial* practice. If they do not, they cannot have much meaning. For all their focus on commercial contracts, the risk-taking dynamics of international trade and commerce seem to have eluded them and hardly find a reflection in them. This is all the more evident from Article 1.8 that deals with usages and practices themselves. They are still seen as implied terms in a psychological sense balanced by a reasonableness test, itself not elaborated, and again inappropriate in business matters, especially, it would seem, whilst testing the content of commercial practice. Except for this reasonableness requirement, this approach is derived from the Vienna Convention on the International Sale of Goods (Article 9). Again, the normative approach to the parties' contractual rights and obligations itself may suggest less concern for professionals and their dealings or practices, the suitability or reasonableness of which are hardly for a court to test.

It cannot be avoided that this consumer-oriented attitude seriously undermines the credibility of the Unidroit Principles. They present principally an academic effort on the basis of a trade-off in domestic theoretical thought concerning consumer or small business protection steeped in the tradition of black letter rules and a more modern ethos of governmental intervention. To repeat, for any effort of this nature to succeed, it must be conducted from the point of view of fundamental principle and practical need, internationally more in particular from the perspective of the law merchant or *lex mercatoria* or the law that prevails in that sphere between professionals. Consumer law should be separated out and remain for the time-being a domestic concern except perhaps for long distance cross-border selling and providing of services, especially in the sale of goods and in investment services to smaller investors elsewhere. Here there will have to be a balance or trade-off between the laws of the service provider and of the service receiver and their relative protections, particularly relevant in modern e-commerce cross border. These important retail aspects are different from those in professional dealings and generally outside the scope of this book (except in investment services as discussed in greater detail in chapter 6).

The same consumer-oriented attitude is adopted by the Principles of European Contract law published between 1995 and 1998 and still in the process of being supplemented. Here it is more understandable as they also apply to consumer transactions, but it means that the confusion between (international) business transactions and (domestic) private dealings is built into these Principles themselves, no less undermining their credibility as their true relevance only arises in *international* dealings which are likely to be primarily professional. Again, the rules concerning international dealings find their ultimate justification in their reflection of internationalised fundamental principle and industry practices, the rules concerning consumer contracts in domestic public policy. This being the case, an academic effort looking for a uniform framework is not likely to command any authority *per se* whilst ignoring in this manner the differences deriving from the nature of the relationship between the parties and the variations in the rights and duties of the parties that they imply.

That in *neither* set of Principles the needs and requirements of commerce are fundamentally evaluated is proven by the fact that they are largely the same. There are, however, a number of important differences in the details. First, there is a fundamental difference in their interpretation or supplementation, as we shall see. Furthermore, according to Article 1.101 (not here in a Preamble, like in the Unidroit Principles), the European Principles are meant to be applied as general rules of contract law in the European Communities when parties have agreed to their application or when they have agreed that their contract is to be governed by 'general principles of law, the *lex mercatoria* or the like', or when they have not chosen any system of law to govern their contract or when the applicable law does not provide a rule.

It is clear that the draftsmen see these European Principles primarily as a precursor of a European Code of Contract Law, if largely perceived as a set of rules that must be opted into and do not automatically apply. That seems indeed the present perception and is the objective at EU level as apparent from the EU Action Plan in this connection of 12 Feb 2003. But it leaves the important question why in business, even when used as *lex mercatoria*, it should be perceived as EU law. It would appear incongruous and not helpful to the international professional community and its perceptions of transnational laws with a worldwide reach.

Unless specifically incorporated in their contract, the reference to the European Communities in the European Principles raises other questions and could mean a reference to the EU legal order in which case, for the applicability of the European Principles, both parties would seem to have to be resident in the European Union in order to be subject to it (just like the Unidroit Principles could only apply to participants in the international commercial legal order). If so, that would seems to exclude the application of the Unidroit Principles (wherever different) in the EU. If, on the other hand, at least one of the (commercial) parties is not from the EU that would seem to give precedence to the Unidroit Principles. If, however, the European Principles were to be considered in the nature of an EU contract code, they could be relevant to outsiders under the traditional rules of private international law or compete as transnational law with the Unidroit Principles (where different) which could, however, claim to be a truer expression of the *lex mercatoria* since they are not limited in their territorial reach and more obviously written for the international business community.

The European Principles maintain a system similar to the Unidroit Principles in respect of their exclusion by the parties and to the derogation by them from its provisions, which derogation again may not affect any mandatory rule (Article 1.102(2)). In this connection, they also track the language of the Unidroit Principles on good faith and fair dealing and on the parties' mandatory duties in this respect (Article 1.201). The European Principles, which, as just mentioned, also cover consumer contracts, are narrower in that they do not refer here to international trade. These Principles are not therefore set in a similar manner in an international context (but only an EU one) regardless of the earlier reference to the *lex mercatoria*. As regards mandatory law, more generally, the European Principles also follow the Unidroit Principles in letting all mandatory rules of national, supranational and international law prevail pursuant to the relevant rules of private international law, again without considering the possibility of their direct applicability and more objective standards of appropriateness or justice (Article 1.103). There is a further refinement in that, when applicable law so allows, parties may set its mandatory rules aside by opting for the Principles, which goes without saying.

As regards the impact of custom, the European Principles again follow in Article 1.105 the Unidroit Principles relying on implied terms subject to reasonableness, although the text may be slightly more objective. A new element introduced by the European Principles (Article 1.302) is the definition of the requirement of reasonableness itself (also for other purposes) which refers to good faith and also takes into account the nature and purposes of the contract, the circumstances of the case and the usages and practices of the trade and profession involved, but notably not the nature of the relationship of the parties. It makes the test of reasonableness in the case of custom both circular and censorious. It only confirms that in these Principles *no* fundamental distinction is made between consumer and professional dealings. Although the circularity is curious, the reference to usages and practices in the definition of reasonableness in Article 1.302 may suggest a more objective source of law, therefore no longer merely implied terms.

Article 1.305, describing imputed knowledge of the parties, remains substantially based on personal dealings and again modern business dealings seem not to figure. In matters of capacity (Article 4.101), mistake and misrepresentation (Article 4.103), pre-contractual duties (Article 2.301, though cast in more objective terms), individual negotiation of unfair contract terms (Article 4.110), pre- and post-contractual re-negotiation duties (Articles 2.301(2) and 6.111), the approaches of the Unidroit Convention are substantially followed. Again they are as such essentially derived from non-professional dealings, except that in the European Principles absence of good faith already creates liability for broken-off negotiations whilst unconscionability of performance ('excessively onerous') is required for re-negotiation duties to arise. This may be a more severe test than that of the Unidroit Principles which refers to the contract equilibrium being fundamentally altered. One would have expected the stricter test in these latter Principles which only cover commercial dealings. Mistake cannot be invoked as an excuse if the mistake was inexcusable or the invoking party assumed the risks or if in the circumstances they should be borne by it (Article 4.103(2)). The Unidroit Principles prevent a party from invoking mistake only in the event of its own gross negligence or when it took the risk (Article 3.5(2)).

The European Principles are also a little more subtle in the mandatory nature of the validity provisions: only the remedies for fraud, threats, excessive benefit and the right to avoid an unfair term not individually negotiated may not be excluded; remedies for mistake and incorrect information may be except if contrary to good faith and fair dealing (Article 4.118). In the professional sphere one would have expected the possibility of exclusion also for excessive benefit and the right to avoid unfair terms not individually negotiated.

1.6.2 *Approach to Contract Formation: Capacity, Formalities and Specificity*

Generally in the area of formation, the Vienna Convention, both sets of Principles, and the UCC should be studied especially in terms of matching declarations of offer and acceptance or of the consensus notion; bargain, consideration and *causa*; dispatch and receipt of offers and acceptances, the importance of reliance and conduct in this connection, definiteness of the offer, the binding nature of the offer, time of contract; formalities and parole evidence; unilateral contract and cash sales; implied conditions, disclosure, (re)negotiation and co-operation duties. Attention to the nature of the agreement and especially to the difference in the relationship between the parties are other matters to be considered; the latter in particular remains much neglected in both sets of Principles. Subsequently there is the matter of interpretation and the role of good faith and custom, even in the formation of the contract.

In both sets of Principles, in the offer and acceptance language, the consequence of them being in essence still perceived as anthropomorphic acts based on personal dealings is that there continues to appear an inclination towards old fashioned 'will' theories. Both sets of Principles closely follow each other in this regard and are clearly inspired by the compromises reached within the formation rules of Part II of the 1980 Vienna Convention on the International Sale of Goods (Articles 14 and 18) and in the earlier Hague Sales Conventions concluded more than a generation ago in language that dated already from the 1930s.

The European Principles include some General Provisions in this regard which clearly base the binding force of the contract on the intent of the parties to be so bound and on there being a sufficient agreement between them (Article 2.101). According to Article 2.102, the intention to be legally bound may, however, be determined from statements or from conduct as reasonably understood by the other party. In the latest stage of the drafting of the Unidroit Principles, there was added Article 2.1 also allowing a contract to be concluded by conduct sufficient to show agreement. Both sets of Principles are also of interest in that, whilst avoiding consensus language as the Vienna Convention also does, Article 5.101 of the European Principles and Article 4.1 Unidroit Principles on interpretation of the contract refer to the *common* intention of the parties as the interpretational base. Here arises the civil law notion of consensus as common platform of the rights and obligations of the parties under a contract.

The Vienna Convention (Articles 14 and 29(1)) and both sets of Principles (Article 3.2 Unidroit Principles and 2-101 European Principles) all reject implicitly the notion of consideration in a common law sense and also of *causa* in a civil law sense (more clearly Article 3.2 of the Unidroit Principles). As regards offer and acceptance, the Vienna Convention (Articles 14, and 18) largely assumed the common law terminology and concepts of offer and acceptance except that acceptance, *if not by conduct* or in the manner as indicated *by established practices* between the parties, is effective only upon receipt by the offeror (see Artcicle 18(2) following Section 130 BGB), even if by mail, therefore rather than upon dispatch, which is the traditional common law rule (motivated at least to some extent by the need to lock in consideration as early as possible and reduce the incidence of non-binding offers).

The Principles, respectively in Article 2.6(2) UP and Article 2.205(1), follow this approach, allowing also for acceptance by other conduct reaching the offeror (Articles 2.1UP and 2.102 EP). The offer itself is effective when it reaches the offeree (Article 15 Vienna Convention and Article 2.3(1), a rule not found necessary to repeat in the European Principles, but may be revoked until acceptance unless reasonably relied upon, see Article 16 (2) Vienna Convention, Article 2.4 (2)(b) Unidroit Principles and Article 2.202 (3)(c) European Principles. It shows that, unlike in civil law, offers are not binding *per se*, not even for a reasonable period except if so stated or when there has been reasonable reliance (like in the case of subcontractors' quotes enabling a main contractor to make a final offer). That is also the approach of the UCC (Section 2-205). A reply that states or implies additional or different terms materially altering the terms of the offer is a rejection and counter-offer. Both sets require an offer to indicate the intention of the offeror to be bound (respectively Articles 2.2 and 2.103).

Like the UCC in the USA for the sale of goods, the Vienna Convention dispensed for formation purposes with the traditional common law distinction between unilateral and bilateral contracts, the first ones being for their effect dependent on full performance (and notice thereof instead of mere acceptance) like in offers to the public (if not an invitation to treat) and (normally) in offers for services. So do the Principles.

Under the Vienna Convention for the International Sale of Goods, an offer must be sufficiently definite but needs to specify only the essentials of the contract needed to be agreed, which meant quantity (the goods) and price (Article 14(1), although even for price (if not expressly fixed) Article 55 gives further rules. Additional terms which did not materially change the offer did not result in a rejection or counter-offer but, if bearing on price, payments, quality, quantity, place and time of delivery, parties' liability, or settlement of disputes, they were considered material *per se* and therefore in the nature of a counter-offer (Article 19(3)). This looks like a list of fundamental clauses or conditions in an English law sense, even if only the one on quantity (and price) must be specificly expressed in the contract. Article 2.14 Unidroit and Article 2.103 European Principles, which cover not only sales contracts, do not require minimum terms. They rely on more definiteness, see Article 2.2 UP and Article 2.201(1)(b)/Article 2-103(1)(a) EP.

Both sets of Principles although covering all types of contracts are in formation matters altogether greatly inspired by the Vienna Convention. Both sets of Principles (unlike the Vienna Convention) also contain language on the negotiations. If broken off contrary to good faith and fair dealings (Article 2.301 of the European Principles) or in bad faith (Article 2.15 of the Unidroit Principles which may suggest a more subjective approach but also a higher threshold), the party breaking off the negotiations may become liable for the other party's loss. The measure of damages is not specified and it is unclear whether they also cover the consequential damages of the loss of the deal (lost opportunities).

In the Principles, there is no need for documentation (Article 1.2 of the Unidroit Principles and Article 2.101(2) of the European Principles). The Vienna Convention has in Article 11 a similar provision but left this matter ultimately to the Contracting States which could make a contrary declaration (Article 12) as the USA has done. There is no parole evidence rule. The UCC continues to require documentation for sales contracts in excess of $500 and has shifted the parole evidence rule, see Sections 2–201/202. On capacity all are silent.

Finally one should consider how the system of the Vienna Convention and especially of both sets of Principles might apply to some *common formation complications*, like to cash sales especially for consumers, to the nature of the contractual obligations that derive from reliance on conduct, to the meaning of a signature under an agreement, to the impact of good faith on the formation of the contract and the disclosure and investigation duties in that context, to the duties of care and subsequently to the co-operation duties of the parties in the various phases of the contract.

1.6.3 Notions of Good Faith and Reasonableness: Interpretation and Supplementation of the Principles and Contracts thereunder

As we already saw in section 1.6.1, the Unidroit Principles for International Commercial Contracts in Article 1.7 require each party to act in accordance with good faith and fair dealing in international trade and view this as a mandatory rule. This was already questioned several times, as these concepts are themselves undefined and unclear and would in any event justify mandatory application only if referring to fundamental legal principle like the binding force of agreements, if reflected in commercial practice (eg in proprietary questions), or if based on industry practices or overriding moral or social concerns in an international context. Certainly amongst professionals there should not be a check on the contents of their dealings if they do not want this (except if there was manifest unreasonableness, especially if bordering on fraud or an abuse of a dominant position). Any other attitude reflects a consumer approach. During the discussions on the Hague Conventions, which preceded the Vienna Convention, this point was discussed and the idea of mandatory law expressly rejected.[173]

The concept of good faith does not play a role in the interpretation of the Unidroit Principles themselves, see Article 1.6, unlike the European Principles (Article 1.106) which copy the Vienna Convention in this respect (Article 7) as will be discussed shortly. The Unidroit Principles' interpretation is based on their international character and their purposes including the need to promote uniformity in their application. It was already noted before that this would appear to imply a clear reference to an international commercial legal order. Interpretation of the *contract* on the other hand is on the basis of intent or according to what a reasonable man would find in the same circumstances (Article 4.1). This seems weaker than the reference to good faith and fair dealing in international trade which is to guide in a mandatory fashion the parties' conduct under the contract according to Article 1.7 as we saw.[174] The relationship between both Articles remains unclear.

---

[173] See s 2.3.2 *infra*.

[174] The Comment 1 on Article 1.7 Unidroit Principles states that the clear intent is that the parties' behaviour throughout the life cycle of the contract, including the negotiation process, must conform to good faith and fair dealing. No standard is being set; unlike the UCC (except if resulting in manifest unreasonableness), the standard is not left to the parties, Section 1–302 (Section 1–102(3) old) UCC. It is considered to be objective. Only the reference to 'fair dealing' may be explained as referring to business practices in international trade, see MJ Bonnell,

Article 4.3 gives a list of the relevant circumstances to be considered in the interpretation of a contract: preliminary negotiations, practices established between the parties, their conduct after the conclusion of the contract, its nature and purpose, the meaning commonly given to terms and expressions in the trade concerned and usages. Clearly the parole evidence role and the narrower common law approach are here abandonned.

Supplementation of the Unidroit Principles themselves is done on the basis of their underlying general principles (Article 1.6). This follows the earlier Hague Conventions example and suggests the civil law approach in respect of codification, based on the notion of completeness followed by liberal interpretation. The reference to 'general principles' appears to mean here no more than that the Principles are to be explained from within as a self-contained system. Supplementation of the *contract*, on the other hand is done by supplying the term appropriate in the circumstances which depends on the intention of the parties, the nature and purpose of the contract, good faith (without any guidance on its meaning in this context either), and reasonableness (also without such guidance), Article 4.8. Here (in supplementation of the contract only) the good faith notion is explicitly used and in that case on top of the reasonable man approach. No reference is made in this connection to fair dealing in international trade.

Furthermore, contractual terms are deemed implied if they stem from the nature and the purpose of the contract, from practices established between the parties, from good faith and fair dealing and from reasonableness (Article 5.2). Fair dealing is here used for the first time in the context of interpretation and supplementation. It is easy to see that the terminology is unstable. As already mentioned in the previous section, not complying with negotiation duties may lead to a claim for bad faith (Article 2.15).

There are many other concepts in the Unidroit Principles said to be based on or derived from the principle of good faith, like those in Article 2.4(2)(b) (revocation of the offer), Article 2.16 (duty of confidentiality), Article 2.17 (written modifications clause), Article 4.2(2) (interpretation of statements and other conduct), Article 5.2 (implied obligations), Article 5.3 (co-operation between the parties), Article 5.8 (contract for an indefinite period), Article 7.1.2 (interference by the other party), and Article 7.1.7 (*force majeure*).[175] This is no doubt true and there is an abundance of references to reasonableness and similar requirements as well, see Article 1.8 (on usages), Article 2.20 (on surprising terms), Article 3.8 (on fraud), Article 3.9 (on threat), Article 3.10 (on gross disparity), Article 4.6 (adopting the *contra preferentem* rule), Article 4.8 (supplying an omitted term), Article 5.2 (adding an implied obligation), Article 7.1.6 (on exemption clauses) and Article 7.4.13 (on agreed sums for non-performance). In other Articles, a reference is made to a reasonable person (Article 5.4.2) whilst Articles 5.6 and 5.7 speak of a reasonable quality of performance and a reasonable price if neither are sufficiently determined by the contract.

An International Restatement of Contract Law (1997), 138, see also KP Berger, *The Creeping Codification of the Lex Mercatoria* (1999), 168. As is argued here, these ideas should have been clearly expressed in the Principles themselves. Apparently the notion of good faith does not result in any restraint in the case of professional dealings. Obviously in the socio-economic environment in which multinationals operate allowance must be made for variations in size, skill and standards of practice, see also Berger at 138. The Principles should have expressed this and clearly have allowed the parties to define standards rather than putting emphasis on the mandatory nature of good faith and fair dealings which between professionals only obtains in extreme circumstances. In conclusion, there seems not to be a proper balance between these concepts and parties freedom to contract. The idea seems to be to police unfairness because 'business people may have different levels of education and technical skills' (*sic!*) and are 'no less likely than the rest of humanity to yield to the temptation to exploit the weaknesses or needs of others', see Bonnell, at 151.

[175] See also MJ Bonell, An International Restatement of Contract Law (2nd ed. 1997) 136*ff.*

It begs the question whether all of these provisions also have a mandatory flavour, either in the nature of good faith and fair dealing of Article 1.7 or in the context of the mandatory validity provision of Article 3.19. It does not seem so[176] as it would make the Principles useless. When more specific rules are formulated, their relation to or origin in the mandatory good faith principle might thus have to be be ignored and most of these rules should therefore be considered directory,[177] except (in the context of these Principles) those on surprising (standard) terms that must be expressly accepted by the offeree (Article 2.19), and those that limit the parties' freedom with respect to exemption clauses and agreements to pay fixed sums for non-performance (Articles 7.1.6 and 7.4.13). As already said, even this much is less understandable for dealings between professionals unless in situations where the use of standard terms and exemption clauses borders on the manifestly unreasonable.

More generally, the term 'unreasonableness' appears to have a meaning somewhat different from lack of 'good faith'. Generally, it is sometimes seen as the objective element of good faith but mostly suggests a lower standard. As we saw, such a lower standard may still affect the applicable usages and practices, see Article 1.8(2), but not apparently the impact of the contract itself, although insisting on performance could be against good faith under Article 1.7. Supplementation of the contract may be done on the basis of good faith notions (Article 4.8) but co-operation duties at the performance stage are expressed in terms of reasonableness (Article 5.3). These co-operation duties, as further detailed in Article 5.5, thus appear different from those to which Article 1.7 refers and to be of a lower non-mandatory nature, although they may conceivably rise to the level of Article 1.7 if sufficiently pressing. Only in the case of hardship is there the option of adjustment of the contract (Article 6.2.3) in which context the doubtful concept of the contractual equilibrium and its re-establishment is used rather than good faith or reasonableness adjustments. What seems to be missing all through is a clear idea of what good faith and reasonableness are. They are undefined but related, yet clearly not the same.

Whilst the impact of custom may thus be limited by unreasonableness, any deviation from statutory law or from the contractual terms on the basis of unreasonableness is not considered. This suggests an emphasis on the literal interpretation of abstract rules and of the parties' intent in subjective terms in the English tradition.

There is, however, a special notion of hardship in Article 6.2, as we saw, whilst the more traditional concept of *force majeure* is maintained in Article 7.1.7. As just mentioned, the first in particular may be more liberal than business requires.

Negotiation duties pursuant to *force majeure* (Article 7.1.7) and hardship (Article 6.2) are determined by the need to avoid bad faith without any guidance on what that may be in business relationships which may require a narrower concept, Article 2.14, but co-operation duties at the performance stage are expressed in terms of reasonableness, Article 5.3. Again it suggests a difference with the general duty of parties to act in good faith under Article 1.7. These duties are somewhat better described in Article 5.5. Parties appear able to deviate from them to the extent these duties may be considered outside the ambit of Article 1.7, but again it remains unclear when this may be the case.

---

[176] See *ibid*, 149. See also Lando and Beal, (eds) *The principles of European contract law*. Prepared by the Commission on European Contract Law (1995).

[177] Article 5.3 setting forth the parties' duty to co-operate' does not expressly refer to the duty of good faith and fair dealing, but here the Comment makes the connection and it is suggested that such a duty lurks behind the requirement of co-operation. It would make the duty mandatory. It remains therefore a question of interpretation when these various provisions should still be considered mandatory, see also B Kozolchyk, "The Unidroit Principles as a Model for the Unification of the Best Contractual Practice in the Americas", 46 *Am J Comp L* (1998), 151, 154, 173, who appears somewhat naïve in his references to objective standards of brotherly care.

As for the Principles of European Contract Law, they consider the promotion of good faith and fair dealing principally in the interpretation of the Principles themselves, besides the need to respect their purposes and to promote uniformity in their application (Article 1.106). Here there is a considerable difference with the Unidroit Principles, the European Principles following the exemple of the Vienna Convention (Article 7), although a reference to internationality is missing (in the case of interpretation), probably motivated by the European character of these Principles. Good faith and fair dealing do not play a role in the supplementation of the European Principles which is based on the general ideas underlying them, failing which the rules of private international law are applied, which the Unidroit Principles do not accept either. Again, the European Principles track here the Vienna Convention that became subject to a curious compromise in its Article 7, see also sections 2.3.5 and 2.3.6 below. Contracts, as distinguished from the European Principles themselves, are interpreted according to good faith (Article 5.101(3)(g)); that is now fairly standard as we saw, even in the USA (although the Unidroit Principles do not refer to it in this context), but in the interpretation of statutory instruments or treaties this is unusual or at least was unusual as the Vienna Convention is now often (and uncritically) copied. It is true that it had a place in the Vienna Convention of 1961 on Treaty Law, but this dealt with contracts between states in which context a reference to good faith was more understandable.

In using the term good faith in this context, it could mean that generally the normative and teleological attitude to interpretation is adopted in both the Vienna Convention and European Principles and that would make good sense (see also the reference to 'purposes' in this connection). Much more serious is the reference to private international law in the supplementation of the European Principles, also absent from the Unidroit Principles which followed the Hague Conventions in this respect. It is likely to destroy any usefulness the European Principles may have as in each issue of their supplementation (and interpretation, as the two can hardly be distinguished as recognised in the case of contracts where interpretation and supplementation is no longer distinguished) debate on domestic laws may ensue. Again, this may be understandable in consumer law where the Principles themselves are hardly needed as it remains essentially a domestic law concern. For professional dealings, the reference to private international law may no longer be acceptable and should be seen as contrary to the whole notion of international principles unless properly preceded by the other sources of transnational law forming the substance of the modern *lex mercatoria*, see chapter 1, sections 1.5.4 and 3.1.1.

As already mentioned several times before, the European Principles more generally require each party to exercise its rights and perform its duties in accordance with good faith and fair dealing, which, like in the case of the Unidroit Principles, are seen as mandatory requirements (Article 1.102). They remain, as in the Unidroit Principles, undefined whilst the measure of urgency necessary to make the concept of good faith mandatory remains unclear. In the Comment on the European Principles, it is said that the purpose is to enforce community standards of decency, fairness and reasonableness in commercial transactions. It is by no means clear what such standards could be and how relevant they are in professional dealings. At least parties should be able to exclude them or set their own standards. To repeat, in commerce, this type of concern can only be relevant to the extent fundamental principle, manifest unreasonableness or public policy (to the externt relevant in the case) is involved. Again, as the European Principles also cover consumer dealings, the mandatory nature of good faith and fair dealing in this sense is more understandable but proper distinctions should have been introduced here for professional dealings.

As regards the interpretation of contracts, in chapter 5 of the European Principles, the first thing to observe is that the distinction between interpretation and supplementation is abandoned. This seems to be an improvement. On the other hand, reference is made to the common intention of the parties which prevails over the wording of the contract. Although the implied reference to the consensus notion must be welcomed, the clear preference for intent over the declaration is much less convincing, although of course if both parties agree that they meant a whale rather than a cod as they stated, one would assume an implied amendment.

If there is a difference in view, however, and one of the parties knew of the other party's interpretation but did not interject, then the view of the other party prevails. Only if no intention in this psychological sense can be established does there follow an interpretation according to what reasonable persons in the same circumstances would think (Article 5.101). So the psychological interpretation precedes a more normative one: see also Article 4.1(1) of the Unidroit Principles. Both the Unidroit Principles (Article 5.1) and the European Principles (Article 6.102) operate here also with implied obligations.

Article 5.102 of the European Principles states the points that must be specifically considered in interpreting (and supplementing) the contract when the psychological approach is exhausted: the circumstances in which it was concluded, the conduct of the parties, the nature of the contract, similar clauses and practices established between them, the meaning commonly accepted in their trade, usages, and finally good faith and fair dealing, but not, interestingly, the nature of their relationship in terms of professionality or experience. This compares to Article 4.2 of the Unidroit Principles mentioned above, which, however, only applies to interpretation and not to supplementation (*cf* also Article 4.8).

The European Principles in Article 1.202 provide for a duty to co-operate similar to that in the Unidroit Principles (Article 5.3), whilst there is, unlike in the Unidroit Principles (but *cf* its Article 5.3 *io* 5.5), in Article 1.302 a definition of reasonableness (see also section 1.6.1 above) referring to what persons acting in good faith and in the same situation would consider reasonable in view of the nature and purpose of the contract, the circumstances of the case and the usages of the trades and professions involved (here taken in a more objective manner), but notably not in view of the nature of the relationship between the parties in terms of professionality and expertise. Good faith thus also co-determines reasonableness but is itself *not* defined, although, as just mentioned, there is some indication in the comment. It is no less clear in the European Principles than in the Unidroit Principles when considerations of reasonableness may be mandatory or could be deviated from by the parties, but on its face at least it would appear that reasonableness and good faith considerations are not quite the same.

As regards the use of the terminology of good faith and reasonableness in the European Principles, there are the reference to good faith in the interpretation of the Principles and the contracts thereunder, in connection with the definition of reasonableness as just mentioned, in the negotiation duties in Article 2.301, as a bar to the exclusion of the remedy for mistake and fair dealing (Article 4.118), and as implied term (Article 6.102). There are references to unreasonableness notably in connection with the invocation of usages and practices in Article 1.105, and in connection with a unilateral determination of price by one of the parties or by a third person in Articles 6.105 and 6.106, see further also Articles 6.109, 6.111(2)(b) and (3).

It is noteworthy in this connection that reasonableness is not considered an implied term as good faith may be (Article 6.102) and as it was in the Unidroit Principles (Article 5.2). In the adaptation of a contract upon a change of circumstances making performance excessively onerous, the parties must distribute the loss in a just and equitable manner (Article 6.111(3)(b)), introducing yet another terminology as indeed the Unidroit Principles do in this connection also.

It follows that particularly in the Unidroit Principles for International Commercial Contracts there is as yet little appreciation of other sources of contractual rights and duties than the parties' intent which may help interpret their mutual rights and duties. Even reliance itself is not a concept much favoured but transpires in Article 16 (2)(b) Vienna Convention, Article 2.4 (2)(b) Unidroit Principles and Article 2.202 (1)(c) of the European Principles but only in connection with the possibility to revoke an offer, although conduct is more frequently used (Article 18(1) Vienna Convention, Articles 2.1 and 2.6 European Principles, Articles 2-102 and 2-204(1) European Principles and Section 2-206(2) UCC). Article 3.2 of the Unidroit Principles seems to depend chiefly on the mere agreement of the parties, whatever may be meant by it, subject to reasonableness, established practices and fair dealing and the nature of the contract, but as implied terms only and not as more objective standards (Article 5.2), whilst Articles 1.6 and 4.1*ff*. also maintain a narrow concept of interpretation and supplementation. The broad and abstract notion of mistake in Articles 3.4*ff* also testifies to a doctrinaire attitude closely connected with a psychological concept of consensus (although itself not expressly used). In a similar vein, the notion of avoidance of the contract and restitution is for commerce probably too broadly upheld, Article 3.17.

Generally, the European Principles follow the Unidroit Principles, although there may be minor shifts to a more teleological approach as in the interpretation of the Principles themselves and in the interpretation of the contracts under them and there is sometimes more subtlety in the detail. The different approach in both sets of Principles to the interpretation and supplementation of the Principles themselves as distinguished from the interpretation and supplementation of the contracts governed by them is itself of interest but not entirely logical. It seems to be more coincidental than properly thought through.

1.6.4   The Impact of Custom

The Vienna Convention (Article 9) and both sets of Principles (respectively Articles 1.8 and 1.105) are unanimous in allowing the effect of custom only if parties have incorporated them in their contract or as an implied term if they are widely known and regularly observed in the trade concerned. This is borne out by Article 5.2 of the Unidroit Principles, not repeated in Article 6.102 of the European Principles, which use in Article 1.105(2) somewhat more robust language in the sense that parties are bound by any usage which would be considered generally applicable by persons in the same position as the parties.

As already mentioned in the previous sections, both sets of Principles require application of custom (or rather usages and practices as they put it) not to be unreasonable. It was already questioned before whether that is appropriate in the professional sphere unless understood in the same way as contract rules must be applied in good faith and there should be no correction of the result on the basis of reasonableness or fairness unless perhaps in extreme cases. Again a test of content is only appropriate in the consumer sphere.

In section 1.2.7, it was already suggested that in international sales the effect of custom as an independent source of law could not ultimately be determined by the Vienna Convention (which does not have the reasonableness requirement) or the Principles, as what is concerned here is the autonomous judicial function of determining what the relevant sources of the law are and which rules apply and prevail, especially in international relationships where there is not one dominant source of law. In that connection, the question of custom and the interpretation of contracts was already discussed more broadly and also the impact of public policy considerations on it.

In Germany, the effect of custom is most closely connected to the objective good faith interpretation requirement. In that context, custom could rise to a mandatory level although this is rare and parties are normally able to deviate and make alternative arrangements and the clear language of the contract will normally prevail over it. On the other hand, customs or usages are sensitive to public policy considerations (not mere reasonableness) but if they maintain themselves internationally regardless of any adverse public policies, they prevail over them.

1.6.5   *Consensus and its Failure: Defences and the Question of Continued Validity*

In the previous sections it was established that the Unidroit and European Principles do not openly favour the civil law consensus notion even if in the Unidroit Principles there may be some reference to it in Article 3.2 and still more in the European Principles in Article 5.101. The common law notions of consideration and matching individual promises are, however, not followed either. From this there flows a more conceptual approach to the defences and excuses and to remedies.

Thus the common law fragmented case law and equity approach is here substantially abandoned, see for this approach section 1.4.4 above, in favour of the civil law concept of validity which concerns itself mainly with the binding force of the agreements absent failures of consensus or common intent and with the subsequent avoidance or rescission of the contract. In civil law, invalidity in this sense tends to be retroactive so that the effects of the contract will be undone. This is (mostly) not the case, however, when a contract is rescinded on the basis of non-performance (rather than invalidity). Delivered assets will then be returned only to the extent feasible. This problem of replevin will be more extensively discussed in connection with a default in international sales in section 2.1.10 below.The Vienna Convention according to its Article 4 is not concerned with validity in this sense at all.

Both sets of Principles exclude from consideration only matters of immorality and illegality (respectively Articles 3.1 and 4.101 or invalidity in the common law sense). They explicitly concern themselves, however, with civil law validity concepts in terms of initial impossibility (respectively Articles 3.3 and 4.102), mistake (respectively Articles 3.4 and 3.5 and 4.103), error (Article 3.6, essentially equated with mistake and covered by it in the European Principles in Article 4.104), fraud (respectively Articles 3.8 and 4.107), threat (respectively Articles 3.9 and 4.108), and gross disparity (respectively Articles 3.10 and 4.109). Mistake is used here as a generic term. Error as a neutral term is covered in Articles 3.5 and 3.6 Unidroit Principles and in Article 4.103 (1)(a)(iii) European Principles. Inaccuracy is mentioned in Article 4.104 European principles. The concept of fraud appears to put emphasis on what the fraudster did or intended to do. All lead to voidability in the civil law manner. Avoidance (in whole or in part, see respectively Articles 3.16 UP and 4.116 EP) is thus the normal remedy in all cases leaving therefore the initiative to the adversely affected party even in the case of fraud and threat, so that there is no voidness *per se.* The common law rescision notion with its broad inherent judicial discretionary element does not here operate.

The affected party may always confirm the arrangement (respectively Articles 3.12 UP and 4.114 EP) or, in the case of mistake and gross disparity, also seek adaptation of the contract (respectively. Articles 3.10 and 3.13 and 4.105 and 4.109(2)). Avoidance may be accompanied by a claim for restitution and damages (respectively Articles 3.17 and 3.18 and 4.115 and 4.117). These provisions are considered mandatory, except that in the European Principles the remedies for mistake or incorrect information may be excluded unless the exclusion is contrary to good faith and fair dealing (see respectively Articles 3.20 and 4.118(2)).

Of particular interest are the questions of innocent misrepresentation and mistake which were earlier identified as requiring lesser concern in professional dealings. The concepts are combined in both sets of Principles but the European Principles seem to deal better with the issue of professionality. As already mentioned in section 1.6.1 above, under the European Principles, mistake cannot be invoked as an excuse if the invoking party assumed the risks or if in the circumstances they should be borne by this party (Article 4.103(2)(b)). This language also appears in Article 3.5(2)(b) Unidroit Principles, but the latter prevent a party from invoking mistake in the event of its own gross negligence (Article 3.5(2)(a)). The European Principles refer here to inexcusable mistake in Article 4.103(1)(a)(ii). There is also a reference to good faith which would suggest a normative approach. Article 3.5 Unidroit Principles refers instead to a reasonable person and reasonable commercial standards, probably a lower test which could be the consequence of its concern with business dealings only.

The common law notions of duress and undue influence may have found a place under 'threat' in Article 3.9 Unidroit Principles and Article 4.108 European Principles.

1.6.6   *Performance, Default and* Force Majeure *Excuses: Hardship*

Both sets of Principles follow the civil law rule that specific performance is the normal remedy where there is no voluntary performance except when it imposes unreasonable burdens or the performance is of a highly personal nature (respectively Articles 7.2.2 and 9.102, see also section 1.4.1 above). It does not preclude damages whilst in bilateral agreements the other party may also withhold performance until the first party starts or continues to perform (respectively Articles 7.1.3 and 7.2.5 and 9.103 and 9.201). Under the Unidroit Principles, penalties may be imposed for the benefit of the aggrieved party unless the mandatory law of the forum dictates otherwise (Article 7.2.4). It was noted before that the Vienna Convention refers back to the *lex fori* (Article 28) on this point.

Besides this option of specific performance, whether or not combined with damages and/or the temporary withholding of own performance, the aggrieved party has the further option of terminating the contract or, in some cases, price reduction. Naturally, if the contract requires only a best effort, these remedies will not be available (the French distinction between *obligation de résultat* and *obligation de moyens*). On the other hand, where a guarantee is given or implied, even the *force majeure* excuse may not excuse the debtor. Payment is as such virtually never excused either, as we saw in section 1.4.6 above. Both sets of Principles distinguish between fundamental and other breaches leading to a differentiation in remedies.[178]

As regards *force majeure*, the Vienna Convention ties it to a performance impediment beyond the control of the party that must perform and which could not have been reasonably foreseen or could have been avoided or overcome (Article 79) as was already discussed above in section 1.4.5. The European Contract Law Principles (Article 8.108) use the same formula, as do the Unidroit Principles in Article 7.1.7.

In Article 6.111 of the European Principles and Articles 6.2.2*ff* of the Unidroit Principles, there is (unlike in the Vienna Convention) also a hardship clause which in the

---

[178] See also O Lando, 'Non-performance (Breach) of Contracts' in A Hartkamp et al (eds), *Towards a European Civil Code* (2nd edn, 1998), 333.

European Principles is tied to the performance becoming excessively onerous and in the Unidroit Principles only to a fundamental alteration of the equilibrium of the contract. It may require re-negotiation and, failing these, judicial intervention to terminate or adapt the agreement, with (in the European Principles) the possibility of awarding damages against the party refusing to negotiate or breaking the negotiations off in bad faith.

It is of interest that under neither set of Principles regard need be had to the overall financial position of the party invoking the renegotiations but only to the contractual situation itself. As such, there appears no need for a dramatic economic impact overall (for example a likely bankruptcy of the party involved upon his performance) or a loss situation for the business as a whole for some time or at least in the line of business concerned with the contract. There need not even be a distinct loss situation (for some time) under the contract itself, so that there may in fact not be any hardship at all. Under the Unidroit Principles it would seem that less profit than expected might already qualify as hardship. So even though excessive burdens or a profound unbalancing of the original contract may well be the trigger, upon closer inspection in terms of the effect on the overall business and financial state of affairs of the debtor, they could be insignificant. Again, asking for re-negotiation under these circumstances would seem less appropriate in the commercial sphere.

1.6.7 Privity of Contract

As already mentioned in section 1.5.2 above, Article 6.110 of the European Principles contain a clause which allows a third party beneficiary to benefit from a contract giving him a direct action, but the promisee may deprive him of it unless there has been notice to him that his right has become irrevocable or the third party has accepted the benefit.

1.6.8 The Nature and Impact of the Principles

Both sets of Principles are largely reflective of domestic laws and the result of comparative research in these laws and where different are in essence a trade-off between them. It is doubtful whether as such they can automatically be deemed to reflect international practices and can support professional operations for which they are intended. The European Principles are also meant for consumer transactions without making any distinctions. At least in the pre- and post-contractual duties, the disclosure and re-negotiation duties and the concepts of mistake and *force majeure*, one would have expected a more restrained approach for professional dealings. It would have been better if a clear reference had been made here to the nature of the relationship of the parties in terms of professional or other dealings.

Although the term 'Principles' is used, what has in fact emerged are two sets of restatements of very precise sets of rules. It may be doubted whether this is needed at this moment. Indeed, principles rather than details would seem greatly preferable at so early a stage of the development of transnational law. They should be intended to identify the main issue and provide key clarifications. Case-law or arbitral awards should then be given a chance to develop the notions further on the basis of practical experience and need.

Probably the most important reservations arise, however, from the fact that both sets are largely reflective of the protection needs in what became the consumer or small companies sphere and that the notions developed in that context are now paraded as reflective of international practice. That is hardly appropriate. Particularly the notion of good faith and reasonableness and their treatment in the 'Principles' lack proper insight in the multifaceted and true nature of this concept and is plainly confused if not wrong altogether. The meager place allotted to custom or practices is another indication that the dynamics and needs of business were poorly understood.

There results a lack of clarity in method and objective. Comparative law resulting in a trade off between domestic concepts is in itself *never sufficient* to produce trans-national law, which is not per definition the result of such an approach. Although comparative law may enlighten, it is in essence internationally directionless even if there is full agreement in the main legal systems. For Principles of this nature to have any real effect, they must for their credibility show both direction and inspiration, be clear, concise and flexible, whilst the international practice, dynamics and needs must be recognisable in them and be seen to be properly advanced unless there are clear reasons for it to be otherwise. Thus new ways must be shown, old ways discarded and above all a view of the dynamics and needs of the trade presented. It is this element that is so far largely missing in these contract principles and this is bound to limit their impact.

But there are two other inhibiting features. The first one is the absence of any insight in how different underlying notions and aims of the Principles relate to each other. Indeed, especially in the interpretation clauses concerning the Principles themselves, reference is being made to their international character, purpose and the need to promote uniformity and sometimes good faith. In the supplementation rules there appear references to general principles and private international law. Custom and practices play a more minor role as do implied terms. Through all of this the concept of mandatory laws is also interjected. Yet in neither set of Principles (nor in the Vienna Convention) these notions, which may even suggest the existence of a transnational legal order that drives them all, are related to each other and put in context. There seems to be no great understanding of the internationalisation process itself and how it is taking shape (nor indeed of what moves domestic laws). Thus where in the European Principles in supplementation private international law pointing to a domestic regime *follows* the application of general principles (or 'ideas'), this order seems to be stood on its head in Articles 1.101(3)(b) and 1.101(4) under which domestic laws would seem to come first.

The other point is the authority of the draftsmen, already briefly raised in section 1.6.1 above. To create law there has to be some authority. In established domestic legal orders the proper authority emanates foremost from the legislators and from the courts. Informal creation by participants themselves is known in customs and practices (which are not here distinguished). Indeed these participants have the power to change them overnight if the logic of their business changes. Legal scholarship and writings might be another informal source. In that sense, draftsmen of Principles also have a role to play and may equally have some authority, but it cannot affect or expand on what fundamental principle and practice dictates.

Thus although informal legal sources are naturally important in more informal legal orders like the international commercial one, and in the formulation of the relevant rules scholarship may certainly play a role, that role is necessarily a modest one. Draftsmen of principles may be guided here by a communality of insights known from comparative law studies, but must for their credibility be driven much more by custom and practices, rationality and perhaps efficiency and common sense considerations in so far as they can have an insight in them. Within these confines, they may even find structural rules of contract and property (or trusts) that are semi-mandatory. Outside these confines, they could hardly have any authority at all and could certainly not decree rules (certainly not in a mandatory manner) which business as such does not accept as reflecting its practices or legitimate needs. They can also not decree how mandatory rules of a domestic nature or from other legal orders play a role in the international commercial legal order. They can at best point to how case-law and treaties have tried to deal with these matters.

A last point that may merit some attention in this context is the notion of soft law. The Principles are often characterised as such. It means that they are not black letter law but at best guidelines probably in the same manner as the Restatements in the US are. They would as such only have persuasive force. On the other hand, they clearly aspire to being positive law in certain circumstances. This is clear from the definition of their purpose and scope in which context they are not only considered capable of incorporation into contracts but also of being an expression of the *lex mercatoria* itself when reference to it is made. They might also apply when no domestic contract law is chosen or when it proves impossible to establish the relevant domestic law.

Indeed, principles of this nature could as general principles figure within the *lex mercatoria* as perceived in this book and thus find a place within its hierarchy of norms as positive law. As such they would *not* be merely soft law or guidelines but living law; again, the principles figuring as such would depend for such authority on their being truly reflective of international practices and customs or, perhaps, on their being based on efficiency and common sense considerations in the particular business concerned amongst parties of similar expertise. Of course, it means that in each international case not only the relevant facts but also the relevant (*lex mercatoria*) norm has to be established and proven, although the relevant court or arbitration panel may be knowledgeable in this type of law as well and even been selected for that knowledge, which they could then use. Parties may not, however, rely on it and would be wise clearly to argue their case both in fact and in (*lex mercatoria*) law under all circumstances.

1.7 Directory and Mandatory Rules of Contract

1.7.1 *Directory and Mandatory Contract Rules in Domestic Laws*

Finally, it may useful to revisit briefly the notion of mandatory and directory rules in contract law and put it in a broader context. Rightly, contract law is considered the primary preserve of party autonomy. Parties are mostly free to deal with each other in the way they wish and there is normally no great governmental or judicial interest to interfere with their expressed wishes. In their contracts, parties may therefore normally arrange or rearrange their affairs and risks in the manner they want. Lawyers will handle the legal risk and will structure the deal accordingly in which connection they may avail themselves of the normally applicable legal rules or opt out of them, a facility (and its limitations) already discussed in chapter 1, section. 2.2.7. Some more was said about risk distribution in section 1.6.1 above.

In the case of the sale of a piece of equipment, parties thus normally determine the time and place of delivery, the quality the seller guarantees, and the liability of either party for deterioration of the asset pending delivery. If there is a default, they can agree the consequences in advance, even define what qualifies as default and what will be considered *force majeure*. They also may agree some hardship clause aiming at a form of re-negotiations when the circumstances under which they must perform change dramatically and therewith the division of risk agreed under the original contract. Domestcially, the normally applicable national laws may also provide some rules in these areas but they are likely to apply only when the parties have not agreed otherwise and they are therefore *directory*.

It may be more difficult for them to reach agreement in the contract on the preliminary rules of contract formation. Of interest are here foremost the traditional rules of offer and acceptance, the notion of consensus (in civil law) and their failure as in the case of mistake, fraud or abuse. It concerns here rules of the contractual infrastructure and the question of validity. Rules of the applicable objective law are likely to carry much more weight in this area, simply because parties cannot regulate everything in the contract nor can independently determine the validity in law of what they do. There is also a limit to the powers they can exert e.g. in matters of their own capacity and the legality of their actions. Thus the binding force of their agreement or the absence thereof is not entirely within their control. The normally applicable law might not be indifferent either as to the consequences of un-co-operative behaviour, of manipulation, for example, of market prices, or of ways of curtailing competition. Such rules might then become mandatory so that alternative stipulations in the contract would have no effect.

It is a matter of interpretation which rules of the objectively applicable law must be considered mandatory in this sense unless especially stated as such by the competent legislator. Here enters public policy and especially in international cases we shall have to determine which states may reasonably exert a public policy interest in the transaction so that their manadatory public policy rules may impinge on the deal. Naturally, ordinary courts will be inclined to stick to the *lex fori* in this connection but in arbitrations where there is no natural *lex fori* the situation may be different. It is the area of the law covered in Europe by Article 7 of the 1980 Rome Convention on the Law Applicable to Contractual Obligations. In the US we have the Restatement (Second) of Conflict of Laws (Section 6) and Restatement (Third) of Foreign Relations (Sections 402 and 403). These issues were more extensively discussed in chapter 1, sections 2.2.6 and 2.2.7.

Domestically, these policy rules are normally developed through legislation but may also result under case-law. Thus the notion of good faith was used to create case law concerning disclosure duties at the time of the creation of the contract or re-negotiation duties in cases of hardship. Depending on the case and especially on the type of relationship between the parties, they may suggest a mandatory element. One sees that element especially in the case law protection of weaker parties, therefore in consumer law and labour law and in the protection of smaller companies against bigger ones. Purely domestically much of this became the subject of mandatory statute law but that need not be so. Again, it concerns here public policy issues. They may play out quite differently in different types of relationships and the resulting rules may not always be absolutely mandatory e.g. in professional dealings as we saw. Even if they are in principle, parties might still be able to set at least some standards except if they turn out to be manifestly unreasonable. That at least is the American approach in commerce.

As was pointed out before, the law of property may present another mandatory facet. The sale of an asset between two parties may be seen as a purely contractual event, but when it comes to the transfer of ownership, this affects third parties who will have to respect the new situation. Thus the proprietary effect of a sale cannot be wholly determined by the parties alone, not even in the way they relate to each other when for example the contract is invalid and the *bona fide* buyer of chattels may still be protected. When a possessory and even more so a non-possessory security interest is given to a party, the sale of the asset to a third party may not affect that security unless that third party was *bona fide* and obtained possession, at least in civil law, but in that law the *bona fide* assignee is never protected and the rule only applies to chattels.

Thus the rules in this respect also have some mandatory flavour and parties between themselves cannot deviate from them or devise their own at any third party's expense. That at least was always the principle. They may, however, by contract be able to postpone the time of the transfer of ownership, for example in a reservation of title. Yet again, inconnected *bona fide* purchasers of the asset may be protected. In common law countries, they may even be able to vary the modality, that is they may impose a delivery requirement for example in the sale of chattels where it is not a statutory requirement (as in England), or delete it where it is (as under uniform law in the US). In civil law, in countries where a delivery requirement exists for title to pass, as in Germany and the Netherlands, parties cannot eliminate it, although delivery may be constructive only, but where it does not exist, as in France, parties may impose it. Internationally, it is not impossible that newer proprietary rights will be developed on the basis of market practices especially in finance. This suggest a greater imput of party autonomy and that seems to become an important trend.

Specific governmental interests traditionally added to the number of mandatory rules in contract law. Import and export restrictions and currency considerations were often at the heart of them. In modern trading nations, they have largely disappeared, as have any investment, production and sales restrictions under national economic plans. Through modern privatisation drives, special rules for contracts with state companies have equally dwindled in importance and number in many countries. Even where nationalised industries continue to operate, they often make use of normal private contract notions and no special rules are then likely to obtain for them.

Some more direct forms of state supervision may survive especially where in practice these industries or service providers continue to operate as monopolies, like water, electricity and sometimes communications and postal companies, or provide a typical public service such as national health and education. It is likely to result in a prohibition on refusing to sell the relevant products or services and there may also be some price controls. Even when privatised, these services are thus likely still to be regulated. So, traditionally, are the financial services for their conduct of business and the products they sell (besides their licensing requirements and prudential supervision of financial institutions themselves). There may indeed be a considerable governmental interest in the type of mortgage, securities and insurance products brought to the market and the way in which they are sold and advertised, especially to retail or smaller customers. Not complying with the mandatory rules in this respect may allow the buyer to disown the bargain or claim damages if it goes wrong.

The most important areas for mandatory rules are, however, in public safety, health and morality.

1.7.2 Treatment of Directory and Mandatory Contract Rules in Private International Law

As a matter of private international law, it is clear that parties can opt out of the applicable *directory* rules by choosing another legal system. They can apparently even opt out of a whole contractual system, its mandatory rules included. Thus an Italian seller and a French buyer may opt for English law in respect of goods that are produced in Italy, sold between them and that require delivery under the contract in France. As a result, all directory rules will be English in principle, but it is not immediately clear how far this goes. English law may cover all issues of validity and also those concerning the impact of good faith, which as we saw may sometimes acquire a mandatory flavour, although less soon in England. This might be the whole purpose of choosing English law which would then apply also to disclosure duties, the details of offer and acceptance, the rules concerning mistake, fraud or abuse.

So, party autonomy as apparent in contractual choice of law clauses may affect the entire contractual regime, also any mandatory and infrastructure rules of the traditional law of contracts. Usually a foreign contractual regime is here chosen in its entirety, although it is conceivable to choose different legal regimes in respect of different contractual aspects or define them in the contract themselves (eg in *force majeure* clauses) but especially in as far as the contractual infra-structure is concerned, it may be difficult to develop separate rules in the contract. It may also hardly be feasible to vary them contractually (eg the rules concerning consent and its meaning in civil law and offer and acceptance in common law). It could even be considered that the parties' freedom of choice does not go that far. It may mean that even though these rules are not absolutely mandatory, they can only be set aside by the parties choosing the law of some other country as a whole (a perhaps by choosing the *lex mercatoria*) and not by devising individual different rules themselves.

On the other hand, party autonomy is not likely to be able to settle capacity questions and issues of legality, including competition issues. They cannot so be excluded. Would on the other hand the choice of English law also include the mandatory regulatory rules of that law, even if they have nothing to do with the case or could hardly have been contemplated by the parties? Typically English health legislation would seem irrelevant for a sale of medical products between a French and Italian company under English law. Would even the English doctrine of consideration be adhered to? This could hardly have been in the contemplation of the parties if its should lead to the invalidity of the contract e.g. in the case of lack of consideration in respect of contractual amendements, releases or novations, and it is therefore unlikely even if internationally the concept still meant something which is probably no longer the case, see section 1.2.6 above.

Proprietary rules can hardly be devised by the parties either, as we saw in the previous section, and since they affect third parties, their mandatory nature cannot be much affected by the choice of another law either. The normal rule is that the place where the assets are located is decisive for the applicable proprietary law *(lex situs)*, assuming of course that that place can be established (which is not so easy in the case of intangible claims), and has some permanence, which may not be so obvious in the case of ships or aircraft. The latter are often considered to be located at the place of their registration which may not apply, however, to their engines and to other pieces of detachable equipment.

Claims are considered to be located at either the place of the creditor or the place of the debtor. The European Bankruptcy Regulation in Article 2(g) has a preference for the latter, the Uncitral 2001 Receivables Convention in Article 22 has a preference for the former. The different purposes of the rule may explain the differences in attitude. In some countries, the law of the underlying claim is deemed to be applicable even as to its proprietary regime, therefore in matters of the ownership and transfer of the claim. There is support for this view in England, Germany, the Netherlands and also in France, as we shall see more precisely in chapter 4, section 1.9.2. The consequence is that a choice of law by the parties in the underlying claim could determine the proprietary regime concerning it. This is exceptional in proprietary matters and hardly entirely satisfactory as far as third party rights are concerned.

Administrative rules concerning contracts are more normally seen as mandatory rules proper. In the 1980 Rome Convention on the Law Applicable to Contractual Obligations (so far applicable in 11 of the 15 EU countries), which will be discussed in more detail below in section 2.3.8 below, a contractual choice of law cannot circumvent these rules where all other elements relevant to the situation at the time of the choice are connected with one country only (Article 3(3)). Under Article 7, a court in a ratifying EU State may apply the mandatory law of another legal system with which the situation has a close connection in the light of its nature and purpose and the consequences of its application or non-application. It concerns here no conflict rule proper but foreign *règles d'application immediate,* but under Article 7(2) this court may always apply its own mandatory rules whatever the law applicable to the contract.

Under this Convention, there are special rules for consumer and labour contracts (Articles 5 and 6), the essence of which is that a consumer cannot be deprived of his home protections through a choice of law. In the EU Second Life and Non-Life Directives, there is similar language protecting policy holders against extraneous choice of law clauses in the policy.

The conclusion must be that a contractual choice of law in favour of some domestic law often leaves doubt on what is included in terms of mandatory rules of the chosen law and also about the continuing applicability of the mandatory rules that without such a choice would apply. It remains largely a question of interpretation and good sense.

1.7.3   Mandatory Uniform International Contract Rules

In the field of consumer law, we saw in section 1.1.1 that the EU has taken some steps and issued a number of Directives. As long as no cross-border activity was involved, this approach at EU level was questioned there and is in any event still incidental. Although within its social programme there is EU interest also in labour law protection, this has so far not given rise to a similar array of EU directives. Also in the insurance area, there are few.[179] The Rome Convention and the Insurance Directives were in this connection only concerned with a contractual choice of law deviating from mandatory domestic rules but did not set any such rules themselves.

In the 1980 Vienna Convention on the International Sale of Goods, which will be discussed in more detail in s 2.3.1 below, there is only one provision of a mandatory nature (Article 12 *io* 96) concerning the offer, acceptance, modification and termination being required to be made in writing if Contracting States opt for this rule. Earlier the Hague Diplomatic Conference of 1951 concerning the uniform sales law had explicitly rejected a more *dirigiste* approach, see s 2.3.2 below.

More serious are the mandatory elements in the European and Unidroit Contract Principles even though these Principles have no binding status. In them, particularly the notion of good faith is viewed as mandatory. It is not defined and its mandatory nature must depend on what one considers to fall under it. In its generality, this part of the Principles must be considered inept and inappropriate, leaving much doubt over its meaning, see more in particular sections 1.6.1 and 1.6.3 above. More understandable is that in the Unidroit Principles the rules concerning the validity of the agreement are considered (semi) mandatory, that is those on fraud, threat or gross disparity but not those on the binding force of agreements, initial impossibility or mistake. The European Principles follow a similar line.

1.7.4   The Effect of the Freedom of Movement and the Freedom of Establishment on the Application of Domestic Mandatory Rules

Especially in the EU, the effect of domestic mandatory rules which cannot directly be reduced to public policy, security and health concerns has been greatly reduced if hindering the free movement of goods and services and the right of establishment (*cf* Article 43, Article 46(2)), and Article 49). Important case-law of the European Court of Justice

---

[179] See n. 3 *supra.*

following *Dassonville* and *Cassis de Dijon* has stressed the great importance of the free movement of goods and later also of services and the right of establishment at the expense of domestic regulation except if justified by the general good: see more in particular chapter 6, section 3.1.3. This has also impacted on industries that are traditionally regulated, like the financial services industry, where a system has been found to divide home and host country supervision: see more in particular chapter 6, section 3.1.1, the latter being largely limited to the conduct of business and product control in the consumer area.

The result is an attack on all kinds of domestic mandatory laws, especially where hindering intra-Community trade. In respect of cross-border flows, it leads to deregulation at domestic level unless a need for it can be clearly shown and is accepted as valid from an EU perspective. That is the concept of the general good. It may in the case of financial services be backed up by more extensive harmonisation at EU level which itself is often conducive to more focussed regulation. In the EU, this deregulation is not primarily a matter of great conviction but simply the result of greatly diverging national laws which inhibits transborder traffic through very different concepts of the public good which clearly vary too sharply between Member States for them to be all credible. There is often no line, so that de-regulation is the least offensive approach unless specific interests need to be demonstrably protected. That is then the focus for re-regulation through the EU in a more harmonised fashion in which such regulation looses its purely domestic flavour. Much of the traditional regulation was in any event historical and needed reconsideration.

Part II   The Contract for the International Sale of Goods

2.1   The Main Aspects of the International Sale of Goods

2.1.1   Introduction

One of the most important contracts in international commerce remains undoubtedly the international sale of goods, that is to say the contract for the sale of tangible movable assets or chattels, which is the meaning of 'goods' in common law. The sale, whether domestic or international, is the principal means of effecting a transfer of ownership or title, which transfer may, however, also be achieved in other ways, for example through an exchange or a gift. The *price* or monetary element is here the main distinguishing feature and in the case of the transfer of title through a sale, one party, the seller or vendor, normally promises to deliver a *specific* good or a specified *quantity* of (generic) goods to the other party, the buyer, for an agreed *price*. Agreement on the sold asset or on quantity in the case of commodities and on price is therefore the minimum one expects to find in a sales agreement.

In *international* sales this approach is confirmed in Article 14 of the Vienna Convention on the International Sale of Goods which is the leading text covering international sales, to be discussed more fully below in section 2.2 and which was already mentioned several times before.[180] It is only a partial codification and limits itself mainly to the aspects of

---

[180] The Vienna Convention referred to in this context is the UN Convention on Contracts for the International Sale of Goods concluded in Vienna under the auspices of the United Nations Commission on International Trade Law (Uncitral) on 11 Apr.1980, also referred to as CISG. The most authoritive commentary is by J Honnold, *Uniform Law for International Sales* (Kluwer Law and Taxation, Deventer/Netherlands, 2nd ed. 1990), with the English text of the 1978 draft Convention and its predecessors (The Hague Conventions of 1964) attached.

quality, quantity, price and payment, place and time of delivery, passing of risk, default, *force majeure* (exemption) and remedies, therefore mostly to sales aspects that are normally covered in the contract itself (see also the list in Article 19(3)). It concerns itself therefore mainly with default rules or directory law.

The Vienna Convention notably does not cover most aspects that cannot be so easily covered in the contract itself but that are matters of objective law or of the contractual legal infrastructure, like the binding force of the agreement and its defects or defenses (in cases of mistake and the like) or other aspects of validity (Article 4) and any disclosure, negotiation and special performance duties. Here the Unidroit and European Contract Law Principles may acquire additional significance.

The Vienna Convention does, however, cover the offer and acceptance (referred to as 'formation' in Part II), but not any proprietary consequences of the sale (Article 4). The passing of title itself, the manner in which this is done and the moment at which the buyer becomes the new owner are therefore not covered by the Convention either. Many domestic sales laws, especially in countries that require delivery for the title transfer to be complete, do not do so either. This may require some further explanation.

As the object of a sales agreement is the transfer of ownership or title, it would not be illogical to expect parties to cover this aspect in the contract. It is certainly normal for them to specify the time and place of *physical* delivery. The title transfer itself is, however, a *proprietary* issue affecting third parties who will have to respect it in order to make it effective. The law is not likely to leave this aspect — therefore the questions whether, how and when the ownership transfers — to the parties to the sales agreement alone. This most important issue will be discussed more fully in chapter 4, but suffice it to say here that countries like Germany and the Netherlands, following Roman law in this respect, require besides a sales agreement also delivery of possession for ownership to pass, therefore in principle a certain physical form and publicity to achieve the transfer of title. Without it, ownership cannot pass in these countries.

The law of other countries like France (at least for the transfer of title in goods) and notably the traditional common law, at least of England, is here less formal, does not require delivery for the transfer of chattels, and allows parties to at least determine the moment of the transfer freely. Under these laws, the timing is as a rule the moment of the conclusion of the sales contract, but it may be deferred by common consent. In this approach, the moment of the transfer of title may in any event contractually determined by the parties independently of any act of delivery. Yet, at least in France and in countries like Italy following its example in this respect, this is so only because the relevant property law so determines and there is no true party autonomy in the creation of proprietary rights in this manner. Common law is here more flexible and also leaves the modalities of the title transfer to the parties.

As a consequence, even in countries like France, the proprietary consequences of the sale do not strictly speaking flow from the sales contract itself. Whether or not the transfer of title follows remains there also a matter of the objective law, no less so than in countries requiring delivery even if the moment is a different one and may be postponed. Only common law maintains here a degree of party autonomy. These considerable differences in the law of title transfer in the various countries were the reason the 1980 Vienna Convention explicitly excluded the proprietary aspects of the sale from its scope (Article 4(2)), following the example of the 1964 Hague Sales Conventions that preceded it, so that the domestic law resulting in international cases from the applicable private international law rules still determines this issue.

These rules normally refer to the *lex situs*, that is the law of the location of the sold assets which may still create problems in international sales when the contract requires transportation of the goods across border. In that case, the laws of the country of origin and of the country of destination may both qualify as applicable, raising a number of problems discussed in more detail in chapter 4. The internationalisation of the ownership concept in movables may well provide another angle to this problem and impose its own transnationalised ownership concept not impacted upon by domestic rules, as used to be the case with negotiable instruments. This aspect will also be more fully discussed in chapter 4, section 1.8.

As far as the sales agreement itself is concerned, both domestically and internationally, the quantity and price are thus the minimum terms one expects the parties to cover rather than the title transfer itself, but the agreement is also likely to cover other aspects of the sale and notably to describe the quality of the goods with or without some warranties. The contract may further specify the time and place of the passing of the risk in terms of liability for unavoidable loss or damage occurring before completion of the transfer of possession or conceivably even payment, the latter especially if there is a reservation of title. Then there are the time, place, currency and manner of the payment. Commonly the sales contract will also detail some excuses, like *force majeure*, frustration or economic impossibility or hardship, the latter especially where the sale is connected with a long term supply contract as is common in the construction industry and may need adjustment in the case of unforeseen circumstances, see also section 1.4.7 above.

The contract may also include some special provisions or protections in the case of default, for example a liquidated damages clause, particularly if damages are difficult to assess, a method usually upheld if the agreed amounts do not prove disproportionate. It may also make provisions for termination of the contract upon a substantial default (or fundamental breach in the terms of Article 25 of the Vienna Convention) and in the case of non-payment by the buyer it may even attempt to provide for an automatic return of title to the seller if under applicable law it has already passed to the buyer.

2.1.2   The Minimum Requirements of the Sales Agreement: Special Features and Risks of International Sales

As we saw, it is not uncommon to introduce special description and protection clauses into the sales contract, the latter sometimes even to secure a return of title and consequently of the asset upon non-payment, or to define the damages in the case of default or reduce judicial involvement in the early termination or adjustment of the agreement in other ways. This should be seen against a background in which the minimum contractual terms necessary for the sales agreement to be binding are steadily reduced. As already mentioned in the previous section, they now centre on the identification and quantity of the goods sold, the price, and the intention to transfer ownership, as confirmed for international sales in Article 14 of the Vienna Convention.

Yet in modern sales agreements, at least those of the international type, even the price need no longer be fully settled, see for example Article 55 of the Vienna Convention,[181] whilst the intention to transfer ownership may be considered implied. Absence of these and other obvious sales terms, like a description of quality, does not then render the

---

[181] Even under French law according to which the price had to be determined by the parties (Article 1591 Cc) and could not be left to be determined by one of the parties which would have rendered the contract subject to a potestative condition, as such a cause for the invalidity of the contract, Article 1174 Cc on objective price standards may now be applied to the relevant party's decision which could allow the contract to be implemented: see Cour de Cass, 1 Dec 1995 [1996] JCP 22.565.

contract void, and these terms may in such cases be derived from the general law of sales. The applicable law is in such cases likely to apply *objective*, often market-related, 'normal' or customary standards to fill in the gaps, which standards may be further elaborated in *applicable codifications* or other statutory instruments, *accepted practices, case law* or *legal writings*. They are thus supplementary or *directory* in nature and indeed apply only if the parties have made no further arrangements themselves.

These standards may also support the notion that the seller ordinarily sells from his place of business or manufacturing plant (*ex* works) at which point title (upon proper delivery in countries which retain this requirement for title transfer) and, more particularly the risk are likely to pass. As a consequence, at least in *domestic* sales, no provision on the division of labour and cost in terms of organising transportation and insurance is normally found in the law of sales, which means that the buyer usually makes his own arrangements, except perhaps in larger countries where substantial distances may have to be covered. This is likely to be different in *international* sales which acquire distinctive features as transportation and insurance become substantive issues whilst additional risks, organisational problems and payment complications may be encountered, so that this type of sales contract can no longer be seen in isolation but must be considered part of a whole cluster of arrangements without which an international sale cannot be truly meaningful or effective. This is reflected in the Vienna Convention even if the definition of internationality of sales agreements in the Vienna Convention is not directly related to the need for these additional services (which are more directly connected with the physical transfer of the assets trans-border), but rather to the parties residing in different countries (Article 1). This may be appropriate and sufficient in the contractual aspects of the sale which are the primary concern of the Vienna Convention.

In international sales, the law must respond, nevertheless, to a different factual situation with its own risks and protection needs which makes it difficult to consider the international sale in isolation as is usually possible for sales domestically. These sales are likely to raise special difficulties and face special risks related to the *cross-border* movement of the assets to be sold, the coverage of longer distances and dealings with foreign buyers and their payment. They require therefore additional arrangements, most obviously in terms of *transportation, insurance* and *payment* protection.

This is so even though, from a strictly legal point of view, international sales are normally still considered sales 'ex works' if nothing else is intimated by the parties in the contract. Indeed, this remains the residual rule even internationally, also under the Vienna Sales Convention (Article 31(c)). It follows that payment remains in principle also required at the place of the seller upon delivery unless otherwise agreed so that sales credit and payment in the country of the buyer continue to be considered exceptional features, see Articles 57 and 58. This is all in the domestic sale tradition.

One may ask whether this perspective is still appropriate. As just mentioned, the greater distances to be covered normally require special arrangements for transportation and insurance as they create their own perils. As payment is usually against delivery elsewhere long after the sale, this implies sales credit and often foreign payment which creates further risks that may have to be minimised through forms of personal (letters of credit) or real (reservation of title) security to achieve adequate protection.

There may be other *complications*, like the formalities to attend to at borders (and the delays they may create) and *risks*, like those connected with proper custody and care and the use of third parties in this connection. It all suggests a more elaborate scenario to be set out between the parties with clear instructions on what each of them will do or organise to be done by others since these details cannot habitually be left to the greater informality and co-operative spirit that may prevail in the performance phase between parties to a sale purely domestically, aided if necessary by their own (informal) domestic dispute-settlement arrangements or courts.

To this may be added the likelihood of sharper conflicts in international sales because of the often greater value of the merchandise and the higher cost of handling whilst parties may be less well known to each other and at any rate likely to be in different countries. As a consequence, the international sales contract is apt not only to be encapsulated in a number of ancillary arrangements in respect of transport, insurance and payment, but is often also more formal, precise and comprehensive and likely to be more *fully documented.*

In sum, the *most important risks* implicit in international sales chiefly lie with the increased difficulties in delivery (*transport* risk), the protection of the goods and their continuing good quality (*quality* risk), or payment (*credit* risk), but there may also be problems for the parties in the arrangement details on the spot (*completion or management* risk) and access to the judicial process and clarity concerning the applicable rules in the case of difficulties (*legal* risk) in view of the differences in jurisdiction and the greater uncertainties as to the applicable law and its meaning, not always curable by contractual forum or applicable law selections which may indeed serve only to make matters worse.

Traditionally, parties could also be exposed to tariffs or other import or even export restrictions. They have become much less important after the various GATT liberalisation rounds. Parties remain, however, exposed to potential upheaval in the other party's country or in those through which the goods must pass (*political* risk), which may leave the seller or sometimes also the buyer largely unprotected with regard to payment or proper delivery. Another kind of political risk derives from subsequent governmental interference in the deal, the most common being the refusal of foreign currency to the buyer in order to make the required payment under the contract (*country risk*), but there may also be legitimate health and safety concerns or more politically inspired other import restrictions. If there is a delay in payment as a consequence of all these complications, there may also be extra *currency* risk for the party who contracted in a foreign currency. The unforeseen delays also highlight the illiquidity attaching to goods in transit, which means that they must be financed and may tie up capital longer than anticipated (*funding or liquidity* risk), subjecting them at the same time to the effects of adverse price fluctuations (*price* risk).[182]

2.1.3   Legal Risk in International Sales

For lawyers, legal risk is of primary concern in international sales, that is to say at the time of the conclusion of the deal there is the need for them to provide a roadmap for performance, certainly in contracts of longer duration, to minimise misunderstanding between the parties on the interpretation, and to gain some insight into the types of legal issues that may arise later and in their possible solutions. It highlights the concern for the capacity and authority of the parties to contract and for the validity and legality of their agreement from the outset. But, especially in international sales, there may also be public policy issues and concern for the ancillary arrangements, especially in transportation, insurance and payment. In case parties should not be able to clear any differences that may arise subsequently, it raises also the question of the eventual access to the judicial process, therefore questions of jurisdiction, available remedies and the applicable law.

---

[182] See n.172 *supra* for a quick guide to the corresponding and supplemetary provisions in the Unidroit and European Contract Pprinciples and in Article 2 UCC.

Here the contract may steer the parties into the direction of certain courts or international arbitration panels and their procedures and elect the application of a chosen law.

Political risk may be closely connected with legal risk and then particularly derives from governmental intervention after the deal has been concluded (to be distinguished from the more obvious political risks like public disturbances and revolutions) either through legislative or administrative action when the legal status or effect thereof remains to be determined, like new health and safety standards. The contract itself may make the continued validity of the agreement dependent on the absence of such intervention. Nevertheless, the same governmental action may seek to abrogate such a clause.

In an international context, the relevance of foreign law, the level of knowledge thereof as well as the legal impact of foreign governmental action and foreign adjudicatory jurisdiction need to be especially considered in terms of foreign trade and payment restrictions and the measures that may be taken in advance to avoid or minimise any adverse effect by structuring the deal differently, for example directing it through different countries or including rebalancing or termination clauses in the agreement and guard over their continued validity.

Much can be done in terms of early clarification by writing full agreements setting out as much of the deal as possible in the documentation. It avoids reliance on unknown or unfamiliar directory rules of its own or other legal systems that may become involved. Standardisation of international contract types may help here too. In any event, the long form contracts in the common law style are normal in international commerce for these reasons. Yet they cannot foresee every complication — in fact they often foresee and contain a list of complications that have arisen in other types of situations handled by the law firms in charge of the final documentation, sometimes without much likely relevance to the present deal. This historical burden often makes these agreements longer than they should be, over-complex and costly, whilst they still cannot cover every eventuality. Nevertheless they are often better and less risky than the short forms which prevailed in the continental European tradition, now increasingly abandoned in international sales.

To provide clarity in the legal aspects, in these contracts a choice of a domestic law and choice of forum clause is common. In chapter 1, it was already said that the certainty that may so be expected could be of low quality and undesirable in its consequences and may in any event be illusory. First it locks the contract into a domestic law which may be poorly suited to cover the international dynamics of the deal. Secondly, it leaves unresolved the question of how far mandatory policy rules of other countries connected with the deal may be avoided or such rules of the chosen system prevail, even if they have no connection with the case. This is particularly relevant as these policy rules usually derive from the need to police certain deals in the country formulating them but may have no relevance for these deals if executed elsewhere: see for these problems more in particular section 1.7.2 above.

Equally the choice of a forum may result in jurisdiction in countries that have little relation with the case, may therefore not take it and there may in any event be hardly any assets in that country so that recognition and execution elsewhere become necessary, leading to further proceedings and cost. It may prevent action in the most suitable forum from the point of view of a creditor. A non-exclusive jurisdictions election clause may eliminate the danger of the appointed court not taking the case but does not prevent the other problems. Applicable law and jurisdiction clauses may thus increase the risks and need to be considered with the greatest care, probably more so than is at present usually the case.

Where no law is chosen by the parties, traditional private international law rules may obtain in the absence of uniform law, like the 1980 Vienna Convention on International

Sales of Goods, but these rules may be increasingly artificial and uncertain themselves, another subject of chapter 1. They may also show great gaps. International principle and custom, may in any event prevail over them. In fact, the preponderance of whatever domestic laws may prove ever more objectionable in international transactions and the proper law may more suitably be the trans-national *lex mercatoria*, which could now perhaps also be chosen by the parties. Again this was the subject of chapter 1. It may also affect the title and its transfer. Legal fragmentation and globalisation of markets do not go together and the markets themselves no longer accept this legal fragmentation and enforce change whilst creating their own legal frameworks. Rather than looking for a particular domestic law to apply, modern parties must learn to work with the *modern lex mercatoria* instead and its hierarchy of norms in a globalised professional legal order.

Domestic or foreign *governmental* action or interests when the execution of the contract is required outside its jurisdiction may have little impact, but as a matter of extraterritoriality of governmental policy this will remain a matter of appreciation by the competent court asked to rule on it as a question of comity (*règles d'application immédiate*, see Article 7 of the 1980 EU Rome Convention on the Law Applicable to Contractual Obligations, see more in particular chapter 1, sections 2.2.6 and 2.2.7 and also sections 2.3.7 ad 2.3.8 below), always assuming that its own public policy does not oppose such extraterritoriality in the first place. International arbitration panels will no less be forces to balance conflicting governmental interests.

Even if there is a close connection, some parties may still be able to ignore the relevant foreign governmental action, for example creditors may well recover from asset of a foreign debtor within their own jurisdiction or in a third country even if the foreign government of the debtor freezes all his payments or only allows payments in the domestic (weak or unconvertible) currency.

In any event, also where the performance is likely to be closely related to the foreign country concerned, internationally there may be increasingly an issue concerning the retroactive effect of governmental action or its administrative legality and the proportionality of its actions.

Written *legal opinions* are now often required by the parties from their lawyers to assess these and other legal risks at the time of the conclusion of the contract. They may also address questions of legal capacity and the authority of the parties, the proper formation, validity and legality of their contract and in this connection also make an assessment of the applicable laws. They may also pronounce on the effectiveness and risks of any choice of law and choice of forum clauses or omission thereof and may also point out the risks resulting under existing or anticipated intervening foreign governmental action under legislative and administrative processes elsewhere that may attempt to affect the deal. The closer the legal risk comes to political risk, the more the legal opinions are likely to be tentative or inconclusive.

2.1.4   Special Arrangements to Cover the Risks in International Sales

As a consequence of the additional complications and risks, in international sales some specific arrangements will normally have to be made at the more practical level with carriers, warehouses, insurance companies, and bankers in terms of transportation, warehousing and safekeeping before or after transportation, insurance, funding, payment or related security or guarantees (like letters of credit), whilst an easy facility to on-sell the goods may become very valuable to reduce liquidity risk, which may be created through the *issue of negotiable* documents, most notably a bill of lading.

The international sales contract will be concerned with all these aspects in terms of (a) who will make the necessary arrangements, (b) who bears the costs and (c) what else can be done in the circumstances to reduce risk or how best the risks can be shared in the balance of the contractual stipulations, as by their very nature not all risks (for example legal risk) can always be insured against.

The key is to appreciate that the various risks may be separately considered and dealt with in different ways according to their nature. Each of the parties will attempt to reduce its risks through these arrangements. This is done through what is now commonly called the *unbundling of risks*. Market conditions and bargaining power will normally determine the success of either party in this regard if they mean to transfer the burden and cost, for example of transportation, insurance and payment protection, on to the other.

Under the contract, the risk of safe arrival and deterioration of the goods whilst in transit will normally remain with the seller until delivery (quality risk), see Articles 66*ff* Vienna Convention. It means that it would be the seller's concern and cost to insure these, although the contract may always provide otherwise. For the transportation risk, the seller may be able to put this burden also on the buyer and it depends therefore on the sales contract who must make the transport arrangements and who pays, in which connection the best known terms are Cif (cost insurance freight) or Fob (free on board). The payment risk may be covered by modern bank guarantees, especially letters of credit, the cost of which are normally carried by the buyer, who also makes the necessary arrangements (subject to the seller's approval). He may, however, try to have some of these costs discounted in the sales price.

In this manner, the quality and transportation risks are likely to be *separated* from the payment or credit risk, especially under the terms of a letter of credit, which is usually made subject to the handing over of the documents (bill of lading if issued) *only*, therefore only to proof that the goods were properly shipped but not to their safe and unspoilt arrival.

Payment under a letter of credit thus supersedes for the time being the implied conditionality of all sales agreements under which conform delivery would be a normal condition of payment, but this payment under a letter of credit is subject to argument later and to possible litigation, which may lead to a return of the price in whole or in part. That does not, however, affect the paying bank under the letter of credit, which is reimbursed by the debtor separately. What we are concerned with here is re-payment in whole or in part to the debtor/buyer himself.

The letter of credit therefore has, in first instance, the effect of transfering the payment or credit risk of the buyer to a bank that is likely to have a much better credit standing and has no defences connected with the sale. Thus, the bank will make the payment regardless of the quality of the goods and their safe arrival. It receives a fee for doing so and will have an arrangement for reimbursement with the buyer, but the payment to the seller will not be conditional on either. The letter of credit derives its true importance from this *double* independence (from the contract between seller and buyer and the arrangement between buyer and bank) and further from the fact that it will normally lead to payment at the place of the seller. It will be more fully discussed in chapter 3.

Yet, even under letters of credit, the buyer may be able to insist on a certificate of quality or conform delivery upon arrival of the goods before the bank may pay on his behalf, which obviously makes the letter of credit much less attractive to the seller. It is a facility much discouraged in the modern practices. On the other hand, the bank in the letter of credit could require that the buyer default before it will pay. This is equally unattractive to the seller and therefore also discouraged in modern letters of credit.

As suggested above, payment or credit risk may also be safeguarded against by the seller retaining a proprietary interest in the assets, particularly through a rescission clause or a reservation of title, but in international sales they are likely to be less effective after the goods have sailed, first because the legal status of these clauses may be less clear elsewhere raising difficult choice of law problems and doubts over their effect, see section 2.1.2 above, whilst furthermore practical problems connected with custody and disposal and extra cost unavoidably result if title returns in goods that are in foreign lands.

As regards the other risks, political risk may be insured against or divided between the parties depending on the place where the interference occurs (in the place of the seller or buyer or during transit). As with quality, it is likely to be entirely separated from payment when payment is guaranteed by a bank under a letter of credit, which means that the bank will pay on the agreed day regardless of the safe arrival under the circumstances or of whatever payment impediment is subsequently imposed on the buyer through government action.

As just mentioned, the liquidity risk may be mitigated by the seller whilst negotiating the bill of lading for early payment, often part of the letter of credit arrangement under which payment may be made immediately upon loading and turnover of the bill of lading to the bank, long therefore before arrival of the goods. It will imply a discount on the purchase price. Another common method for the seller to obtain early cash is to assign the receivable to a bank (or factoring company) or to discount (upon acceptance) a bill of exchange drawn on the buyer, a technique now outdated in most countries, except where the assignment of the receivable is not well developed as an alternative, for example in countries where prior notification is still a requirement of the validity of such assignments, as used to be the case in France and Belgium under Article 1690 Cc and as now has become the case in the Netherlands under Article 3.94 CC (new), particularly inhibiting bulk assignments of future receivables.[183]

Another reason for the unpopularity of the bill of exchange in international transactions is that payment will often follow at the place of the drawee or buyer as only his bank will discount, which leaves the creditor/drawer with the foreign exchange and political risk if he wishes to convert the proceeds into his own currency and transfer these to his own residence. As already mentioned above, the letter of credit tends to remedy these problems as the paying bank will normally be in the country of the seller.

2.1.5   *International Sales as Contracts between Professionals: Applicable Law*

The extra risks and complications outlined above mean that international sales in a *technical sense* are normally considered to be contracts between *professional* (merchant) parties only, therefore between parties who are both knowledgeable in the area of their sale and its risks, likely and able to make the special arrangements necessary in this connection and aware of *special industry practices* to this end. One should always look out for these practices. Also in the additional arrangements completing an international sale, as in transportation, insurance and payment aspects, participants and their lawyers must develop extra sensitivity towards these practices. This is probably true in the case of all professional dealings.

Unlike in domestic sales, the subject of international sales is thus not commonly thought to cover consumer sales or even sales of goods of which an otherwise professional party does not have special knowledge. This is expressed in the Vienna Convention only in

---

[183] See more particularly chapter 3 *infra*. It does not mean that the bill of exchange practice is reviving in the Netherlands.

a negative manner in the sense that consumer sales are excluded from its scope. To the extent that a distinctive pattern was developed, the international sale is further limited in scope in that, as term of art, it is not believed to cover the sale of real estate, negotiable instruments, other documents of title, bonds and shares, or assignments of intangible property (like receivables). This is all reflected in the Vienna Convention (Article 2).

These types of sales may of course also be the subject of international sales contracts, as indeed consumer sales, transfers of receivables and the rendering of cross-border services may be, but they are not commonly deemed to be included in a reference to international sales, which as to subject matter are therefore limited to tangible *movable assets sold between professionals* and therefore limited to the commercial or professional sphere.

As for the definition of an international sale, the feature of cross-border delivery appears to be the principal aspect of these sales as *commonly* understood or even as understood in the narrower technical sense as *sales contracts concerning movables between professional parties*. Yet this aspect is *not* directly relevant in purely *contractual* terms. As in the Vienna Convention (Article 1), the internationality of the (sales) contract is in the *contractual* aspects normally tied to the contracting parties residing in different countries and *not* to the cross-border movement of the assets.[184] This is different in the *proprietary* aspects.

As we already saw, these proprietary aspects are excluded from the Vienna Convention (Article 4(2)), which limits the requirement of delivery to a duty only to hand over the assets physically. It means that the Vienna Convention may apply even if there is no border crossing of the sold goods at all as long as both parties are in different countries.

Delivery even in the limited physical sense of the Convention is likely, however, to include some special duties of the seller in terms of transportation and insurance, usually to an agreed loading point and these aspects are covered by the Vienna Sales Convention, cf Articles 31 and 32. From this point, the buyer will arrange further shipment and insurance (usually pursuant to a Fob term), although he may in this respect also rely on the seller (the Cif term). It depends on the contract and therefore on the will of the parties which term is used in this respect. These terms may have some further effect on the time and place of the passing of the risk (but not directly of title), see more in particular section 2.3.9 below.

In view of the distance, there may also result some special *duty of care* of the buyer to protect the goods upon arrival, should disputes arise and goods be rejected. On the other hand, the seller may have a special duty of care to preserve the assets if the buyer delays in taking delivery, even if the risk has passed to the latter (for example upon tender of delivery), cf Article 85ff of the Vienna Convention.

It should be pointed out that there are other possible approaches to internationality in international sales, even in their contractual aspect. Indeed, in France, early on, a legally relevant criterion closer to the ordinary meaning of 'internationality' depending on goods and payments crossing borders in opposite directions was used to preserve the validity of gold clauses, often illegal under applicable national law at the time. In the late 1920s and early 1930s, an exception was thus made for this type of clause in international sales as so defined.[185]

---

[184] Article 1 effectively refers to the place of business of each party rather than its residence. A similar criterion is usually followed in conflict conventions concerning sales, cf Article 1(1) of the Hague Private International Law Convention on International Sales of 1955 and Article 1 of its successor of 1986, but cf also Article 1(a) of both Hague Uniform Sales Conventions of 1964.

[185] See Cour de Cass, 27 May 1927, D.1928.25, followed in several other cases regardless of the applicable domestic law under the relevant conflicts rule, see also Y Loussouarn and JD Bredin, *Droit du Commerce International* (1969), 617.

In arbitration laws, a similar approach to internationality may be taken, not only applying therefore a special internationalised regime when parties come from different countries but also when the subject-matter is of an international nature or the arbitration takes place in an unrelated country, *cf* French Decrees n 80–345 and n 81–500 and also Article 1(3) of the Uncitral Model Arbitration Law, now accepted in several common law countries, including some states of the USA, in Scotland and in some east European countries including Russia. This may then lead to the application of some additional or different arbitration rules, especially providing for procedural flexibility in international cases and a limitation of review by the domestic courts, either when challenged or in the context of recognition.

Another approach altogether is the distinction between the professional sphere on the one hand and the private or consumer sphere on the other, and the application of transnationalised concepts to the former and local concepts to the latter. In sales, it leads to the basic distinction between commercial and consumer sales, with all of the first increasingly internationalised even if the relevant sale may not have any international aspects at all.[186] There is here no need to define internationality and the unity of the system is maintained at a transnational level and any arbitrary distinctions are thus avoided as economically there is no clear justification for treating such deals differently depending on the origin of the parties. As explained in chapter 1, this is the approach preferred in this book in which therefore internationality is a function of and included in commerciality or professionality.

Public enterprises should not be considered automatically excluded from the international commercial or professional sphere, although, depending on their activity, they may still enjoy a measure of sovereign immunity in their international dealings. Short of this, their public function might still affect the relationship with the counterparty which may be coloured thereby. This is a situation which cannot be entirely ignored, even in international dealings. In fact, each relationship is coloured by its own nature and the interests reflected therein. It was already said in section 1.1.1 above that common law is particularly sensitive to it but the law everywhere is ultimately always likely to recognise this. It is domestically particularly visible in the operation of administrative law for public functions and services. In international relationships, the emphasis is likely to be more on their particular commercial features and needs. This may also be reflected in the sales agreements with public bodies elsewhere and in the interpretation of these agreements, therefore also in international sales.

To repeat what was already said in chapter 1, section 3.1.1, the consequences of a transaction being in the internationalised professional sphere is (a) the increasing likelihood of the existence of trans-national legal concepts in a unifying transborder development suggesting the existence of a distinct legal order (under a new *lex mercatoria*, see more in particular in the previous chapter), (b) the impact of fundamental legal principle and the emergence of own practices therein, (c) the reduced impact of directory and even mandatory rules of a local nature, (d) a lesser need to rebalance the relationship on the basis of social considerations as professional parties are on the whole well able to look after themselves, and (e) a less refined application of the basic legal protections in terms of disclosure, time to protest, undoing of transactions and the invocation of all kinds of legal exceptions, like *force majeure*, hardship or even negligent behaviour of the other party. Only in the more explicit and obvious cases is relief likely to be granted.

In international sales, it may even imply an own distinct ownership concept and ownership transfer regime.

---

[186] See for this unitary approach, chapter 1, section 1.1.6.

2.1.6 Currency and Payments in International Sales: Free Convertibility and Transferability of Money

In international sales, a price is likely to be stated in whatever (foreign) *currency* the parties may choose. In domestic sales, on the other hand, a foreign currency election is exceptional and used to give some problems as it was often thought that the contract in such terms should be qualified as an exchange rather than a sale, although not in all legal systems the differences are great. In international sales this is not in itself an issue but concern shifts to the agreed currency (of payment) being *fully convertible and freely transferable*, see also chapter 3, section 1.1.4.

The key is that payment is made in the agreed (hard) currency and then not out of accounts blocked by government action. Also the seller should be concerned that payment is not automatically converted by applicable (mandatory) law, usually that of the buyer/payor, into the latter's (often non-transferable and weak) domestic currency. It raises the question of the effect of such a mandatory rule on international sales contracts: see Article 7 of the 1980 Rome Convention and section 2.3.8 below, under which there may remain doubt. The risk is that the agreed currency is not then put at the free disposal of the seller.

It puts the debtor in default of proper payment, although possibly under the protection of his own law. With the general liberalisation of exchange controls (in respect of both capital movements and current payments) in most trading nations, this has become less of an issue. Modern payment methods, especially irrevocable confirmed letters of credit payable in freely convertible and transferable currency in the seller's country, also help, and this was always an important reason for the popularity of letters of credit. Banks then take over the currency risk which they are often better able to handle, if only through informal clearing and set off, often in the context of special arrangements with the relevant central banks.

In this connection, it is possible that the international sales contract itself uses two different currencies, one, the *currency of account*, to denote the real obligation of the buyer and another, the *currency of payment*, which is usually that of the buyer and is then to be adjusted if the exchange rate changes between both of them. This gives the seller at least some protection.[187]

When it comes to judgments from the national courts, even in common law countries like England, these may now be expressed in foreign currencies.[188] The modern emphasis is on what would produce better justice or on what most accurately reflects the plaintiff's loss under the circumstances. Recognition of foreign judgments by another domestic system may also extend to the foreign currency of the original judgment, at least if properly related to the underlying claim. However, the point is not universally settled, and conversion sometimes still takes place.[189]

Any devaluation loss may be claimable if the debtor is unwilling to pay and causes delays during which devaluations take place.[190] In Germany, it appears that the currency is respected, even in proceedings for recognition of foreign judgments, but may in the course

---

[187] See also CM Schmitthoff, *Export Trade, The Law and Practice of International Trade* (9th edn, 1990), 224. One of the most authoritative treatises on the subject is by FA Mann, *The Legal Aspects of Money* (Clarendon Press, Oxford, 4th edn, 1982).

[188] *Cf* for the UK, *Miliangos v George Frank (Textiles) Ltd* [1975] 3 All ER 801, reversing earlier English case-law in the matter.

[189] *Cf* in France Tribunal de la Seine, 18 Dec 1967, G.P. 2.108 (1968).

[190] *Cf* for the Netherlands, HR, 8 Dec 1972 [1973] NJ 377.

of enforcement be converted into the local currency at the option of the debtor: Section 244 BGB. The exchange rate prevailing in the place of payment as at the original payment date is then controlling, foreign exchange losses resulting from pending enforcement being in principle for the account of the creditor.[191]

The question of payments in foreign currency and operation foreign exchange restrictions and the developments under the IMF rules and within the EU[192] will be discussed in greater detail in chapter 3.[193]

2.1.7   The Transfer of Title in International Sales

There is strictly speaking no distinct concept of transfer of title in international sales except where the international law merchant has come to fruition as might be said of international documents of title and negotiable instruments and may also be said in respect of eurobonds. In the previous chapter we also saw that the European Human Rights Court in Strasbourg developed a distinct internationalised ownership concept as well. This internationalisation even of ownership notions was more extensively discussed in chapter 1, section 3.2.2, and is of the greatest interest. Normally, however, the applicable domestic law continues to determine the issue of how and whether title has been transferred. In international sales, this law is in principle the *lex situs* of the asset. It is the general proprietary conflicts rule, but in international sales under which goods are likely to move from one country to another, the applicable law could under that rule still be the law of either the country of origin or that of the country of destination.

This issue will be explained in greater detail in chapter 4 where the different domestic attitudes to the transfer of title and its formalities will be discussed. As far as private international law is concerned, a sale and transfer completed in the country in which the asset is situated at that time will most likely be accepted in the country the asset moves to. If pursuant to the original law further formalities are to be performed in the country of destination necessary to make title pass, the situation will be reviewed upon the arrival of the goods in the new country.

This requires some further explanation. In section 2.1.1. above, it was already mentioned that there are in essence two types of systems for title transfer. In the first, the title in goods passes immediately upon the conclusion of the sales contract. That is the French and English system. In other countries there is the necessity of delivery as an additional requirement for title transfer. This is the German and Dutch system and also the one adopted in the USA under Article 2 UCC (unless parties have made other arrangements).

Problems arise when goods are sold in France for delivery to a German buyer in Germany, see more in detail in chapter 4, section 1.8. In France (the country of origin), the sale is complete, in Germany (the country of destination) it is not. The most favoured approach is that if the goods are with the seller in France, the French *lex situs* applies and the goods will be deemed to have left the estate of the seller and belong to the buyer immediately upon the conclusion of the sales contract. This will also be accepted in Germany. So when the goods arrive there, they will be considered to belong already to the buyer even short of delivery. In a bankruptcy of both buyer and seller, the goods will rightfully belong to the German estate.

---

[191] *Cf* OLG Cologne, 2 Feb. 1971 (1971), 47 NJW 2128, although for equitable reasons some adjustments may follow if actual damage can be proven: see Oertman, *Kommentar zum BGB*, s. 244, Anm.3.
[192] See especially Council Directive 88/361 EEC [1988] OJ L178 effective as of July 1990 (in Ireland and Spain as of 1992 and in Greece and Portugal as of 1995), see also chapter VI, s. 2.4.6.
[193] See for the combating of late payments in the EU, COM(1998)126 final, OJ C168.

If, on the other hand, the sale is between a German seller and a French buyer whilst the goods are with the German seller at the time of the sales contract, no title passes until delivery to the buyer in France and the goods continue to belong to the German estate until such time. French law could still consider title in the goods to have passed under French law immediately upon their arrival in France, so technically speaking even before delivery to the French buyer there, but this is not normally considered to be the case.

Other problems may arise in connection with the reservation of title in goods thus sold, especially between countries that have a different attitude towards this sales protection device, as indeed Germany and France did before 1980 when a reservation of title was not valid in a French bankruptcy, whilst France even now adopts a more restricted concept of a reservation of title, especially in the extension of the protection into replacement goods and proceeds and in the entitlement to overvalue see more in particular chapter 5, sections 1.3.5 and 1.4.1. Here again the rule applies in principle that if the reservation of title is properly established in the country of origin of the goods, the country of destiny will respect it. If the original country does not, the reservation of title could still attach upon arrival of the asset in the latter country, if it accepts the device.

On the other hand, even if properly created, the proprietary interest may still be transformed upon arrival in the country of destiny, for example into a more limited proprietary right or into a security interest as the nearest equivalent, as is the case when a good moves between Germany and France or indeed between Germany and the USA where the reservation of title is a security interest and may in capital goods fail altogether for lack of registration if a finance statement is not filed under Article 9 UCC in the USA. It follows that goods subject to such an interest moving from the USA to Germany may benefit from an upgrade and become a full blown proprietary interest in Germany subject to appropriation by an unpaid seller and to his right to retain any overvalue which would have been denied him in the USA.

2.1.8 Conform Delivery and the Passing of Risk in International Sales

Another subject that needs some particular attention in sales of the domestic as well as international type is the non-conform delivery, the liability for deterioration or loss of the goods in transit, and the passing of risk. In consumer (domestic) sales there may be more refined features in this connection than in professional (international) sales.

As regards the required quality standard, parties are likely to be specific, but if not the common law rule is along the lines of *merchantability* the essence of which is that the asset must be fit for the purposes for which it is ordinarily used and as such safe, *cf* also Sections 31–15 of the UK Sales of Goods Act and Section 2–134(2)(c) UCC. This, as we shall see, is also the rule of the Vienna Convention (Article 35(2)(a)), a more general warranty having been thought to be incompatible with the international commercial practice. Civil law still looks more at the intrinsic qualities of an asset. It is traditionally based on the notion of speciality assets rather than commodities, but at least for commodities it has moved also to a more extrinsic merchantability standard. This is important as more and more goods are of the commodity type.

Even then, the seller is also responsible for the goods' fitness for any particular purpose if the buyer relies on the seller's skill and judgement in this respect, provided this is known to the latter. Naturally, the goods must also be fit for any particular purpose expressly or impliedly made known to the seller at the time of the conclusion of the contract, see Article 35(2)(b), *cf* also Section 2-315 UCC. As part of the conform delivery, they must also be properly packaged in the manner usual for such goods which may mean having regard to their disclosed destination and known mode of transport, Article 35(2)(d).

The seller is thus responsible for these standards or any other agreed by the parties, except where he cannot deliver them for reasons of *force majeure* assuming there were no express or implied guarantees. Thus even if the seller is in a *force majeure* situation, he may still be responsible for the consequences if the risk is allotted to him (except probably for consequential damages). As discussed in section 1.4.3 above, this is quite normal for common law and a guarantee of fitness is deemed implied when the quality standard is seen as a condition of the sales agreement. It is a matter of interpretation, although any such implied guarantee could still be counter-balanced by an explicit *force majeure* clause in the contract. In civil law the position is the reverse. Normally, the *force majeure* defence is perfectly good, except where a guarantee is given which could be implied. In civil law, in the normative approach it is indeed becoming a matter of interpretation whether there may be an implicit guarantee. Differences are here likely to emerge between professional and consumer sales, in the sense that these guarantees are sooner deemed to exist *vis-à-vis* consumers.

In Germany, fitness for the agreed purpose upon delivery is a primary duty under the contract (*Hauptleistungspflicht*), *cf* Section 433 BGB). Only in the case of guarantees, see also Section 460 BGB in Germany, it must normally be assumed that the seller means to remain liable during the guarantee period whether or not the non-conformity was due to his fault or negligence. It normally implies a facility for the buyer also to claim consequential damages and ignore his early inspection duties.

On the other hand, even if there are special quality undertakings, other factors, like the buyer's non-compliance with his own investigation duties, any waiver of inspection or acceptance by him, might still affect his recovery possibility and could shorten the risk period for the seller. Impossibility of inspection and hidden defects that could not be discovered in time may further extend this period for the seller. Defences based on mistake or misrepresentation at the outset may also become relevant for him in this connection. Much depends on the factual situation and it is often difficult to draw clear lines in advance.

In sales law, this touches on another aspect which concerns the moment at which *risk passes*. This is the risk of the deterioration of the goods between the time of the sale and the delivery of the asset, assuming that this deterioration is not caused by either party. Thus the question becomes exactly when the risk in this sense passes from seller to buyer in the case of *force majeure* in respect of the conform delivery duty as this *force majeure* is not a proper excuse as long as the risk in this sense has not passed.

Under modern law, this is now normally at the moment the *physical* possession passes regardless of whether title has already passed before or passes later. It means that before such moment, the seller is still liable for conform delivery regardless of *force majeure* as he is still considered to have the risk. This moment may be further delayed if the seller has given special undertakings or guarantees or if the buyer could not reasonably exercise his inspection rights. If hidden defects are discovered later of which the buyer could not have been or become reasonably aware upon delivery, there may still be default on the part of the seller so that the passing of risk issue loses its relevance. Parties may always agree another moment for the passing of the risk between them or divide these risks in another manner.

The passing of the risk in this sense also covers theft or acts of god (*casus fortuitus*), like fire, flood or earthquake affecting the goods before physical delivery, or the unexpected reduction in the value of goods, most often seen in perishable products like foods and vegetables whilst still in the hands of the seller. If the losses are attributable to one of the parties, the passing of risk has *no* relevance and the party concerned will be liable for the consequences *vis-à-vis* the other, except where he could not reasonably prevent it or the risk was discounted in the contract, and may rely on the notion of *force majeure*, see on the notion in the sense of *vis maior* and the more subjective theory, including impracticability or economic impossibility, section 1.4.6 above.

The passing of the risk also does not play a role if the situation gives rise to other types of redress as in the case of mistake or innocent misrepresentation, for example if there was no sufficient disclosure at the outset, with or without the seller being directly to blame, although in the latter case there may be further redress beyond the voidness or avoidance of the agreement. Actions based on illegality, avoidability, or nullity of the contract after its execution are not affected by the risk allocation either and render it also irrelevant.

There are therefore other important concepts that may play a role in this context, even if closely related to non-conformity, especially if there was some misunderstanding about the quality requirements in the first place. In international sales under the Vienna Convention, the concept of non-conformity might itself include the concept of mistake as to the qualities of a sold good (Article 35(2)), so that the non-conformity remedies of the Convention apply, including the rule concerning the passing of risk throughout, rather than domestic notions of mistake or misrepresentation, which, in the absence of the coverage of these subjects in the Convention, might otherwise supplement it under applicable rules of private international law (Article 7(2) Vienna Convention).

2.1.9   The Passing of Risk in Civil and Common Law

Traditionally, the law, in the absence of a contractual provision dealing with the passing of risk, tended to let the 'chips fall where they fell'. Thus the *actual owner, whether old or new, in possession or not*, was the most likely party to have to accept the consequences of whatever was happening to the goods as long as no-one else could be blamed (*'res perit domino'*). It was therefore the owner who bore the risk of *force majeure*. It meant that in sales the passing of risk depended on the moment of title transfer under applicable law. This is still in essence the situation in France and England, at least for speciality or identified goods.

It is implied under traditional French and English law (where title transfers at the moment of the conclusion of the sales contract), that the new owner (the buyer) had the risk regardless of possession pending delivery (*periculum emptoris*), which is also expressed in the maxim '*caveat emptor*', see in France Article 1138 Cc and in England Section 20(1) of the Sale of Goods Act 1979. It meant in Germany and the Netherlands (which traditionally require delivery for title transfer), that until (legal) delivery, the old owner (the seller) had the risk (*periculum venditoris*).

However, in Germany and the Netherlands it is now the *physical* delivery that determines the transfer of the risk regardless of whether the transfer of title follows (which it normally does): see in Germany Section 446 BGB and in the Netherlands Article 7.10 CC, see also Section 2–509(3) UCC in the USA that abandoned the common law approach and now accepts the German approach in the absence of breach and, according to the Official Comment, intentionally shifted away from the earlier property approach in this connection. Only Dutch law under its *old* Code had a system where the risk was for the buyer whilst title would only pass to him upon delivery of the good. This approach was considered justified on the theory that the seller should be able and keen to deliver immediately and, if he did not do so, the buyer was believed to have had some interest in the delay.

Thus the modern variation on this theme is to attach the consequences of unavoidable loss or damages to *actual* (not legal or constructive) possession (or tender of delivery in this sense) rather than to ownership itself. It follows from the realisation that the physical holder of the goods is in the best position to know what is happening to them, look after them and insure them. In a commodity environment the necessary setting aside will in any event not take place sooner than the moment of physical delivery, and the completion of the (conform) performance usually follows at the same time. Thus the seller in possession normally retains the risk pending delivery, even if title has already passed as is normal under French and common law (although the UCC now favours the passing of title upon delivery also if there is no contrary stipulation in the contract, see Section 2–401 UCC). It also proved the logical approach in the Vienna Convention in the absence of a uniform provision on the passing of title in international sales (Article 69).

The buyer *without* physical possession is thus becoming better protected against the early passing of risk everywhere even if acquiring ownership at the time of the sales agreement (wherever such a system obtains), but as mentioned in the previous section, there are further refinements, and he may be longer protected, especially when there are implied guarantees whilst in the case of hidden defects the transfer of the risk may be further postponed or lifted as there may be a situation of default. The buyer has here information and inspection duties, balanced, however, by the duties of the seller in this regard and his information duties. Here again it follows that professional sellers are more vulnerable in consumer sales than in sales to other professionals. In respect of consumers, it could even be said that a situation of *force majeure* of the seller in respect of the required quality of commodity goods is increasingly unlikely to arise because of his own technological capabilities and investigation facilities. This may be different in the sale of specialty capital goods, either manufactured for or resold to other professionals.

Yet upon physical delivery, the buyer must promptly inspect and protest as he accepts full responsibility thereafter, assuming the seller has met his own (disclosure and other) duties at the time of the conclusion of the agreement and still barring undiscoverable hidden defects, again particularly in consumer cases, and certain safety defects under product liability statutes, or if the buyer has a guarantee, always assuming that the contract is not voidable or void for other reasons, like mistake as to the quality of the goods or misrepresentation upon a lack of full disclosure when, as mentioned before, the passing of risk has no relevance but the question of restitution and damages may still present problems.

In the foregoing, some references were already made to domestic laws concerning the passing of risk, see more in particular Article 1138 Cc in France, Section 446 BGB in Germany, Article 7.10 CC in the Netherlands, Section 20(1) of the Sale of Goods Act in the UK and Section 2–509(2) UCC in the USA. Although all use the concept of the passing of risk, they often select, as we saw, different moments and may also maintain different definitions of *force majeure* and different approaches to the subject of non-conform delivery and to its consequences in terms of the various actions that may be used, often for historical reasons.

The approaches of common law based on developing case law are the most flexible with their emphasis within their concept of *conform delivery* on merchantability, common standards and investigation and disclosure duties, but still restrained by the early transfer of risk (immediately upon the conclusion of the sales agreement, now abandoned under the UCC in the USA), and tempered by a case by case approach which allows for little conceptualisation and drawing of lines.

French codified law is on the other hand still based on intrinsic qualities of speciality assets. It assumes the risk for these goods to transfer with the title immediately upon the conclusion of the sales agreement, but it had to make considerable adjustment through case law to allow for a more modern attitude towards the later passing of risk in commoditised products. Even in Germany under its Code of 1900, the emphasis remained on speciality assets with their own intrinsic quality expectations, even though the risk was allowed to pass later. The emphasis was thus less on common standards of the sort or on contractual definition or exclusion and on information rights and duties or on disclosure to determine whether there was a breach in the first place.

The Roman law concerning the sale of goods and the passing of the risk in them had been fairly simple. It assumed that virtually all sales concerned speciality goods, in which the risk passed immediately upon the agreed sale, thus '*periculum emptoris*' (D 18.6.8pr.). However, this was not the case if the price had not yet been fixed or if the goods were not yet identified, if the sale was conditional or suspended, if there remained a choice between various performance duties, or if the buyer had to approve the goods: see Inst. 3.23.3, D 18.6.8 pr., D 6.19.1.13.12 or D 47.2.14 pr. In those cases, the risk could not pass before the final price was determined (*pretium certum*) which was seen as a substantive protection for the buyer and assumed a sufficient individualisation upon counting, weighing or measuring.

At first, knowledge of hidden defects was necessary to redress the instant transfer of risk which was considered to come close to a situation of fraud, but ultimately the knowledge of the seller became irrelevant and the recourse for the buyer in the case of hidden defects was the rescission of the sales agreement with a return of goods and price (*actio redhibitoria* of D 21.1.38pr. and the *actio quanti minoris* of D 44.2.25.1), limited in their effect, however, by a short statute of limitations. This is essentially still the system of the French Cc (Article 1644), which at least in professional sales assumes that the seller always had knowledge of the defects. Except for the timing of the risk transfer, it is also the system of the BGB (Section 437).[194]

In France, the law in this area traditionally centres on ordinary default, hidden defects (*vices cachées*, Articles 1641ff Cc), and mistake (*erreur*, Article 1109 Cc), each with a different set of consequences, redress, statutes of limitations and actions.[195] The action for default including non-conform delivery is subject to the ordinary defences including *force majeure*, taking into account, however, the regime for the passing of risk of Article 1138 Cc which puts it at the moment of the conclusion of the sales contract. As just mentioned, this passing of the risk is amended in the case of hidden defects on the presumption that at least the professional seller knew of the defects.[196] For commodities, the Cour de Cassation increasingly shifts the transfer of the risk, however, to the moment of identification which is likely to be the moment of delivery.[197]

For identified goods, the early transfer of the risk leaves little room for an action by the buyer for deterioration or loss of the asset but the risk transfer may also in modern French law be postponed, amended or restricted by investigation, information and custody duties of the seller in possession on the basis of which a default action may still be brought by the buyer also in the case of speciality goods rendering the passing of risk rule irrelevant. There may be no *force majeure* proper so that the early transfer of risk to the buyer has no meaning. It allows for a wide range of remedies, including specific performance, replacement and repair, rescission, damages or price reduction or combinations.

The hidden defects action arises commonly after the passing of risk and upon delivery. Although it presumes that the seller is to blame for the state of goods, the redress is (also in

---

[194] See further Windscheid/Kipp, 2 *Lehrbuch des Pandektenrechts* (Frankfurt am Main, 1906), 660; M Kaser, *Römisches Privatrecht* (14th edn, 1986), 193; F de Zulueta, *The Roman Law of Sale* (Oxford, 1945), 31; and R Zimmermann, *The Law of Obligations* (South Africa, Deventer, Boston 1990), 281.

[195] See J Ghestin, Conformite et garanties dans la vente (Produits mobiliers) (Paris, 1983).

[196] See Cour de Cass 30 Oct 1962 [1962] Bull Civ I 457 and 27 Nov 1972 [1972], Bull Civ IV.282.

[197] See Cour de Cass 8 July 1981 [1981] Bull Civ IV 316.

France) still limited to the *actio redhibitoria* or *actio quanti minoris*, see Article 1644 Cc and there is also a much shorter prescription period which starts running, however, only from the moment of discovery. Mistake leads, on the other hand, to voidness of the agreement when the transfer of risk does not play a role.

Which course of action is best taken depends on the circumstances and probably on the type of information that became or was available at the beginning of the transaction and there is not necessarily a free choice for the buyer. Misinformation or lack of detail may even lead to the remedy of mistake and then affects the existence of the agreement itself, especially if the seller was not volunteering the information and the buyer was not in a position to ask for it because it fell outside a normal enquiry, yet proved to be wholy relevant.

The burden of proof remains, however, on the buyer and under modern case law he will in this context have to explain what conformity meant, relying in this respect on intrinsic qualities, qualities of the sort or the contractually agreed quality, and what he did himself in terms of making his own enquiries or conducting his own inspection at the time of the sale and especially at the time of delivery. Only then will it transpire whether there was mistake, default or a relevant hidden defect.

In Germany, the starting point was also the individual asset with its own intrinsic qualities but the development has equally been in the direction of commodity-type assets that have at best a standard quality of the sort which is normally further described in the contract so that the contractual quality clause and the seller's disclosure and buyer's investigation duties are often determining the (non-)conform delivery issues.[198] German law does no longer distinguish between a default action (Sections 323*ff* BGB) and an action for defects as a matter of principle, but the former is not available upon *force majeure* even if the seller still has the risk, which is the case in Germany until the *physical* delivery of the asset, Section 446 BGB.

Under Section 437 BGB the consequences may vary and are based on the old *actiones redhibitoria* and *quanti minoris*, but not apparently in a limitative way: replacement, repair, price reduction, damages or even a return of asset and price may all be possible.

An action for mistake voiding the sales agreement altogether may also be available if there is an erroneous declaration of the seller (*Irrtum* of Section 119 BGB). There is not only an important difference (voidness) in the consequences, but also a different statute of limitations: for mistake it is ten years, see Section 121 BGB, but for a default action under Section 323 BGB it is three years (Section 195 BGB) and for the action pursuant to Sections 437*ff* it is only two years after delivery except again in the case of fraud, see Section 438(3) BGB when it is three years (Section 195 BGB).

In the Netherlands under its old law, the situation developed in such a way that for commodities the general default provisions were applicable even if the seller had the excuse of *force majeure* as long as he had the risk, which passed, however, immediately at the time of the sale agreement (even though title only passed upon delivery unless the goods were not properly set aside, when the title and risk only passed upon that event). The more limited rules for hidden defects derived from the French Cc were applied only to specialty goods.

The new Code postpones the transfer of risk until the physical delivery, Article 7.10 CC, and gives the normal rescission facility to the non-defaulting party — particularly relevant if there is non-conform delivery — in all cases in which the seller still has the risk, regardless of any excuse of *force majeure*, see Articles 6.265 and 7.17 CC. It is an action for the

---

[198] See Section 434 BGB.

buyer and allows him not to pay the price or insist on a reduction. Alternatively the buyer may insist on full performance through replacement or repair.

The new Code allows the buyer always to invoke his right to rescission of the sales agreement or replacement of the asset upon non-conform delivery or a later discovery of defects which could not be detected before and not apparent upon inspection following delivery (assuming the buyer did not waive all his rights by failing to inspect), see Article 7.10(3) CC. This may be particularly relevant in the case of hidden defects and additional guarantees. If there is a fault on the seller's behalf, the allocation of risk to the buyer after delivery is irrelevant and damages may be claimable by the buyer as well as the rescission which will discharge him from his own payment duty.

English law, on the other hand, depends principally on the contractual terms and their definition of quality and the (implied) designation thereof by the parties as condition or warranty which determines in the first instance the effects of default in terms of repairs and damages only or in terms of a rescission also. This being said, the Sale of Goods Act also contains statutory provisions concerning quality with implied terms of merchantability and fitness, as we saw, see Sections 13–15, whilst the objective law provisions concerning mistake or innocent misrepresentation may provide an additional remedy.

In the case of *non-conform delivery*, the passing of the risk plays as elsewhere a role and according to Section 20(1) takes place at the moment when ownership passes which is normally at the moment of the sale agreement, hence *'caveat emptor'*, even though the concept of *force majeure* is not a common law excuse and must be seen as limited to certain acts of god, like fire, floods etc., and for the rest depends on whether the quality term must be viewed as a condition or warranty. In the first case there is in principle no *force majeure* excuse as we saw in section 1.4.3 above, although this may be balanced by an express *force majeure* clause or sometimes even implied conditions.

If the goods have not yet been set aside to fulfil the contract, the passing of risk is always postponed, however, except where the buyer was dilatory or uncooperative in this process, see Section 20(2).[199] Also the insurance duty or possibility increasingly plays a role and, since the shopkeepers or custodians are usually in the best position to insure, it may mean that the risk in undelivered specific goods may still remain with them.

The preliminary question whether there was non-conform delivery depends on its definition. It will normally relate back to the contract but, failing this, Sections 13–15 of the Sale of Goods Act give alternative rules implying normal or *merchantable quality and fitness* for the intended purposes which in fact also redress the *'caveat emptor'* rule by holding a seller liable to these standards whatever happened to the asset. In the nature of a condition, he will not be performing fully without meeting them for whatever reason. Yet it does not discharge the buyer from making proper inquiries at the time of the conclusion of the sale agreement and properly inspect the goods at his earliest convenience and certainly upon delivery. If the breach is substantial and indeed concerns a condition, the buyer will be able to repudiate the agreement or reject the goods, if not already accepted after full inspection barring hidden defects; there is also the possibility of rescission for innocent misrepresentation or mistake.[200] If there is fault, an action for damages may follow.

In the USA Sections 2–314/5 UCC deal with implied warranties of merchantability and fitness and Section 2–509(3) with the passing of risk. Section 2–510 makes clear that, where there is a breach, the transfer of the risk is postponed until the breach is cured. It also allows

---

[199] *Sterns Ltd v Vickers Ltd* [1923] 1 KB 78.
[200] See *Goldsmith v Rodgers* [1962] 2 Lloyd's Rep. 249 and for the various remedies further also PS Atiyah and J Adams, *Sale of Goods* (9th ed. 1995), 185.

for any revocation of acceptance. The system in the USA has thus clearly moved on from the British notion of '*caveat emptor*' and accepts that the risk now passes only upon physical delivery. The old common law distinction between conditions and warranties is no longer fundamental in the UCC either. It has its own system of actions and concept of *force majeure*. If the risk has passed to the buyer, he is not likely to be able to do a great deal if he has accepted the goods, except where there are hidden defects which could not be discovered upon acceptance or if there are guarantees outstanding.

2.1.10   Proprietary Sale Price Protection in Civil and Common Law

Sale price protection is an important issue in sales, whether of the domestic or international type and is particularly connected with a buyer's failure to pay the price. The issue then quickly becomes what rights the seller still has in the goods even upon delivery to the buyer.

   Where a sales contract attempts to state the manner of termination upon default, it is likely to include a rescission of the agreement with a discharge of the non-defaulting party without resort to the courts, which is otherwise still required in some countries like France (Article 1184 Cc), where as a consequence the rescission of the sales agreement and the discharge of the non-defaulting party may remain dependent upon court approval. The modern trend is, however, to accept rescission (or avoidance) upon mere notice of default by the non-defaulting party. It is confirmed for international sales law in Articles 49 and 64 of the Vienna Convention provided the default was significant or 'fundamental' in the terms of Article 25 of the Vienna Convention, *cf* also Article 6.265 of the new Dutch CC. It makes the sale itself conditional upon full performance by the buyer.

   The precise meaning and effect of this rescission (or avoidance in Vienna Convention terms) upon default is, however, often not immediately clear, even under domestic law, especially not the effect on the title of the delivered goods and the (possible) retroactivity of the rescission and its significance. This is also true for the Vienna Convention, which does not cover these aspects, as it does not deal with the proprietary issues of the sale (Article 4(2)). A specific clause in the contract may attempt to clarify the issue, but, like the title transfer itself, it depends on the applicable domestic law (which in international sales results from the applicable private international law rules) or from the objective transnational law for *lex mercatoria* supporters), whether these are matters that may be left to the will of the parties or whether mandatory rules must be applied in this connection superseding such a clause. A most important question in all sales is therefore whether any contractual clause trying to clarify and further develop these aspects can have any (proprietary) effect amplifying the applicable (domestic) law (or setting out the *lex mercatoria* position) if not itself providing such redress. The reservation of title clause is the most important example.

   The issue of the automatic return of title and the so-called proprietary or *in rem* effect of the rescission of the sales contract is an issue that arises in all domestic sales laws and is particularly important in a bankruptcy of the defaulting buyer as it may give the seller revindication rights allowing him to ignore the common creditors. Even if the applicable *lex situs* allows this result in principle, it is still possible that the applicable bankruptcy law may not accept it, like Section 365(e) of the US Bankruptcy Code of 1978 as amended, or maintains exceptions, like in France under the theory of apparent solvency. This bankruptcy law could be different from the *lex situs* as it will normally be the bankruptcy law of the bankruptcy forum itself which under applicable jurisdiction rules may be in another country.

   This means that, if the appearance of credit worthiness is created by a creditor/seller leaving the debtor in possession of his assets, other creditors who relied in good faith on the appearance of solvency (so created) may be protected and may as a consequence be able to ignore the seller's proprietary claims. It is in fact an instance of the protection of *bona fide* creditors against hidden property interests, as such the equivalent of the *bona fide* purchaser protection in the case of movables. Yet where it may be said that the *bona fide* purchaser protection is constantly extended, it seems that the protection of the *bona fide* creditor in this manner is in decline. An example is in France the acceptance of the reservation of title in bankruptcy since 1980[201] and in England the elimination of the comparable doctrine of reputed ownership in the Insolvency Acts of 1985/6.[202]

[201] For unpaid sellers in a bankruptcy of the buyer, the inhibiting factor for the actual return of the asset is not the impossibility of the seller to retransfer title itself, which is likely to be automatic in the France system where title transfer does not depend on delivery (always assuming the goods are not converted or comingled in the meantime). This results in that country logically from its system which does not require delivery for title transfer but only the conclusion of the sales agreement (Article 1583 Cc) or its rescission which can be reinforced by a specific rescission clause (*clause résolutoire*) in the contract under Article 1584 Cc avoiding at the same time any need for judicial intervention and a supporting judgment under Article 1184 Cc.

Rather, the problem is the possession of the goods by the bankrupt debtor as this is likely to inhibit their *physical* return (delivery), see also Cour de Cass, 17 Mar. 1975 [1975] D.S.553. This practical impediment is then used to support their inclusion in the buyer's bankrupt estate as a way to support any reliance on the appearance of enhanced creditworthiness (*solvabilité apparente*) of the buyer by other creditors except if the seller has a *published* security right (*nantissement*), which will, however, usually require an execution sale and not allow automatic repossession. This approach is only taken in bankruptcy of the buyer and not in individual executions against him, see Cour de Cass., 24 June 1845 [1845] D.1.309.

It means on the other hand that in France, even in bankruptcy, goods not in the actual possession of the debtor are returnable, especially those still in transit. They are returnable also if the rescission of the contract took place or the action to this effect was initiated before the bankruptcy or at least if the demand for the return of the assets had been manifested before the adjudication, *cf* Cour de Cassation, 3 May 1935 [1935] D.H.313 and 7 July 1975 [1976] D.S.70. Similar restrictions apply to the statutory reclaiming rights under Article 2102(4) Cc: see also Articles 115, 116 and 118 French Bankruptcy Act 1985.

A more general exception is now made in France, if these rights were supported by a reservation of title since the 1980 amendment of the French Bankruptcy Act of 1967 in force at the time (Articles 59 and 65), superseded by Articles 115 and 121 of the French Bankruptcy Act 1985: see also Ripert-Roblot, 2 Droit Commercial, (16trh ed. 2000), nos. 3142, 3148*ff*. The reservation of title was further reinforced by the 1994 amendments to the French Bankruptcy Act (Article 59 of Law 94–475 of 10 June), meaning to preserve and extend the seller's protection if the assets in which title was reserved are subsequently converted or comingled by the buyer. It allows a revindication for the seller provided the goods are not irreparably damaged thereby. See also Sections L 621–117 and L 621-122 CCom.

[202] England (but not the USA) had the similar notion of reputed ownership in personal bankruptcy, especially in respect of commercial property held with the consent of the true owners by a debtor being a natural person who carried on business, see Section 38 of the UK Bankruptcy Act 1914: see also *Re Sharpe* [1980] 1 All ER 198. The notion was abandoned in the Insolvency Act of 1986 (Section 283), earlier implicitly by Section 235(3) *io.* Sched. 10, Part III of the Insolvency Act 1985, but may continue to be relevant in other common law countries except in the USA where it was never relevant. It could be rebutted only by notoriety and defeated any proprietary claim derived from a situation of default and rescission of a sales contract (for breach of a condition) with or without reservation of title, except possibly in the case of fraud or if the reservation of title was registered as a bill of sale, which is often treated as a security instrument, although leading to a form of appropriation in the manner of a conditional sale. See for the effect on the reservation of title also, I Fletcher, *The Law of Insolvency* (2nd edn. 1996), 217.

In England, the notion of reputed ownership did not have an application in corporate insolvency, *cf.* for the reservation of title, *Vaessen v Romalpa* [1976] 1 WLR 677, also not if the goods were converted into others, provided the charge was specifically meant to cover these goods, *cf. Borden (UK) Ltd v Scottish Timber* [1979] 3 WLR 672. For its continued validity, it had to be registered under the Companies Act for the case of shifting into replacement goods or if intended to attach to a multitude of unspecified goods so that a floating charge could result or when the reservation of title was meant to also protect other debt, *cf Independent Automatic Sales v Knowles and Foster* [1962] 1 WLR 974 and for more details chapter 4. The strong position of the holder of chattels in common law should also be noted in this connection and the lack of proprietary protection for the owner which still has an effect in the bankruptcy of the holder (bailee) and may thus still affect the effectiveness of the reservation of title in England: see further chapter 4. The return of chattels under these circumstances is in the discretion of the courts. Damages remain the more normal remedy, which is of little use in a bankruptcy of the defaulting party.

In Germany particularly, there is the problem of the power of the bankrupt to retransfer the asset, as in that country all transfers require a special act of (re)delivery. As a consequence, a return of title cannot be automatic (see for its so-called abstract system of title transfer also chapter 4, section 1.5.6). This is again particularly important in the bankruptcy of the buyer who is then no longer capable of executing such a retransfer, even if he would want to co-operate, the exception in Germany being the reservation of title.[203]

Reorganisation-oriented bankruptcy laws may on the other hand postpone any unilateral action of the seller in this regard, see for France Articles 33 and 47 of the Bankruptcy Act 1985 and further Section 362 of the US Bankruptcy Code. The Dutch Bankruptcy Act, even though not so oriented, allows now a two months delay of all individual execution action upon bankruptcy (Article 63a(1)).

The conditionality of the title transfer upon full compliance by the buyer (as distinguished from the implied conditionality of the sales contract itself) does not always depend on a relevant clause in the contract (*lex commissoria expressa*),[204] but may sometimes be implicit in the applicable law and then results upon a default under the sales agreement from the operation of that law itself (*lex commissoria tacita*), as is still the case in France (Articles 1184, 1610 and 1654 Cc) and as used to be the case under the former Dutch Civil Code (Article 1302 CC old, but *cf* Article 6.269 CC new).[205]

---

[203] In countries like Germany, upon non-payment, even the reservation of title could thus fail to lead to an automatic return of title as it requires, strictly speaking, still a form of retransfer of possession and there remained as a consequence a risk that the asset could not be returned in an insolvency of the buyer, as the defaulting buyer could be considered to have lost the facility or capacity to do so because of his intervening bankruptcy. Also in Germany, contractual rescission clauses requiring the return of the goods are indeed denied validity in bankruptcy, see Section 26 of the Bankruptcy Act (*Konkursordnung* 1877) replaced by Section 103(2) of the Insolvency Act 1999, introduced at the time as a uniform rule for all of Germany before the new Civil Code in 1900. Reservation of title is, however, exceptionally assumed to be valid in a German bankruptcy and may lead to a revindication against the bankrupt estate on the basis of Section 455 BGB io. Section 43 of the Bankruptcy Act 1877 now Section 47 of the Insolvency Act 1999, see also BGH, 1 July 1970, 54 BGHZ 214, 218 (1970).

[204] Even in France and in countries following its lead, there is still a problem in bankruptcy not only with rescission as just mentioned but more generally with the *in rem* effect of conditions although in principle accepted, an acceptance which in bankruptcy may now well be limited to failed sales agreements, however, as under Article 117 of the French Bankruptcy Act 1985 conditions can generally no longer mature after bankruptcy, see also Ripert-Roblot, 2 *Droit Commercial* (16th edn, 1992), no 3158. Yet the *lex commissoria tacita* still leads in France to the automatic return of title to the goods upon default, certainly if for its effect no co-operation of the bankrupt is required, although in the case of *solvabilité apparente*, the reclaiming possibility will be impaired.

Another way of looking at *contractual* conditions of this nature under French law is that the title transfer pursuant to it, rather than being rescinded upon default, is postponed in derogation from the principle of Article 1583 Cc which states the basic French rule that title passes immediately upon the conclusion of the sales contract but pursuant to Article 1138 Cc, which suggest that a delay can be agreed. This at least appears to be the way the French often look at the reservation of title, see also chapter 5, s 1.3.4, leaving the seller with the risk of the loss of the goods in the meantime but probably with a stronger position over all, especially valuable in a bankruptcy of the buyer in possession, see Ghestin/Desche, *Traité des Contrats, la Vente* (1990), No 600 and Cour de Cass, 20 Nov 1979 [1980] 33 Revue Trim de Droit Commercial 43, Note Breitenstein. In other words, payment is then a condition precedent for the title transfer rather than that non-payment is a condition subsequent under which the title transfer is undone.

[205] In a technical legal sense, there are good reasons to consider all contractual rights to an automatic return of title upon a default by the buyer under a sales agreement as an expression or extension of the *lex commissoria* of D.41.4.2.3 (later on forbidden in Roman law, see C.8.34.3 pr, at least if leading to appropriation under a secured transaction) and therefore as an indication of the conditionality of the sale. This is the approach obtaining in many countries, also for a reservation of title, as confirmed by Articles 3.84(4) and 3.92 of the new Dutch CC, *cf* also Section 449 BGB in Germany, although in England and according to some authority in France, the reservation of title is considered a delayed rather than a conditional sale. Under the Uniform Commercial Code (Article 9) in the USA, the reservation of title is now entirely equated with a security (Sections 9–102(2) and 9–202), like all conditional sales of movable assets in that country, as is the contractual retention right, see Sections 2–401(2) and 2–505 UCC, but not the statutory reclaiming right of Section 2–702 UCC.

The difference is that if a reservation of title is viewed as a security interest in this manner, there is no longer a right for the seller to reclaim the asset and an execution sale followed by a turnover of any excess value to the

Even then the true meaning of the proprietary effect of the rescission of the sales agreement (which could also result from other causes like illegality, mistake, misrepresentation or fraud or from the fulfillment of specific contractual conditions to the effect) could still be in doubt upon a subsequent bankruptcy of the transferee when delivery had already taken place, in France again particularly because of notion of the enhanced appearance of credit-worthiness or reputed ownership of the buyer.

Dutch law traditionally went furthest in the protection of the seller under these circumstances as it rendered the title return automatic without any restrictions derived from notions of apparent ownership, but this automaticity following a rescission of the sales agreement upon default even in a bankruptcy of the buyer in possession is now superseded by the new Dutch Civil Code (Article 6.269 CC) unless there is a specific contractual clause agreed and inserted to the effect in the sales agreement, see Articles 3.38 and 3.84(4) CC. Only in that case does it now lead to a revindication right of the asset allowing the seller to disregard the interests of other creditors even in a bankruptcy of the buyer.[206]

The seller may have or create other remedies, especially if still in possession and may, for example, be able to rely on a statutory lien as retentor, particularly in countries where the transfer of title normally occurs at the time of the conclusion of the sales contract. This is the situation in common law where as a consequence the title normally transfers before delivery but the unpaid seller in possession remains protected by a retention right (unless otherwise agreed), see Section 41 of the Sale of Goods Act 1979 for the situation in England, *cf.* also Section 2–703(a) UCC in the USA. In France, where title in tangible movable assets also transfers upon the conclusion of the sales agreement, the unpaid seller still in possession has similar rights and cannot be forced to hand over his assets before payment either, unless otherwise agreed, see Articles 1612 and 1613 Cc.

This statutory retention right is often seen in France as an expression of the *exceptio non adimpleti contractus*, therefore of the right to withhold performance under a reciprocal agreement if the other party is not performing even though not formulated as a general principle in the French Civil Code, as it is in Germany (Section 322 BGB) and now also in the Netherlands (Article 6.262 CC). In these latter two countries, where in any event delivery

---

buyer must follow upon default (Section 9–311). For the reservation of title, French case law seems to go into the same direction, see chapter 5, s. 1.3.4. Wherever the reservation of title is considered a security right, any *in rem* conditionality of the title transfer has disappeared. See for the differences between conditional sales and secured transactions more in general chapter 5, s. 1.7.

[206] An important aspect of the automatic return is the question whether it completely obliterates the transaction and is therefore *retroactive* or whether the return, even if automatic, only operates for the future. New Dutch law accepts that the *lex commissoria tacita*, therefore the statutory rescission of the sales agreement upon a significant default is no longer retroactive, see Articles 6.265 and 6.269 CC, from which it is concluded that it has therefore no proprietary effect either, although as a consequence of the rescission the parties must still reimburse each other for the adverse effects of the contract whilst existing in as far as possible. The express conditionality inserted in a sales agreement has, as mentioned before, still *in rem* or proprietary effect under Dutch law, leading to a revindication right even in a bankruptcy of the seller (*lex commissoria expressa* of Article 3.84(4) CC), although not retroactive either and neither is the title return under a reservation of title upon non-payment by the buyer, see Article 3.38(2) CC.

It means that, although title automatically retransfers, the effects of the earlier transfer cannot be fully negated. A good example is the retransfer of shares on which the conditional owner exercised his voting rights. The automatic retransfer does not then affect the earlier decisions taken but dividends received will have to be reimbursed as parties must put each other in a position as if the transfer had never taken place. The reclaiming right of Article 7.39 of the Dutch CC is also *in rem* but not retroactive either. It does not mean, however, that the acquirer of the goods from the interim owner is fully protected and his *bona fides* are required for the transfer to stand. It suggests that the acquirer should not reasonably have expected that a reclaiming right could be exercised, see Article 7.42 CC. Only a void agreement, e.g. for lack of consensus or a defective consensus in the case of fraud or misrepresentation, will lead to a return of title with full retroactivity, see Articles 3.53, 6.203, 3.84(1) and 5.2 CC.

is required for title transfer, the unpaid seller still in possession may try to rely both on his continuing title in the goods or on this exception connected with his continuing holder-ship of the asset if title has already past through a constructive delivery, then called the delivery *constituto possessorio* also in a bankruptcy of the buyer if the bankruptcy trustee does not offer full payment.

The retention right may sometimes go further in its impact than a mere exception to the performance duty of the seller as under modern law it may give priority status in any execution proceeds of the asset, as under Article 3.292 of the new Dutch CC. The seller's lien or retention right in the UK does not strictly speaking give a similar right and does not imply a power of sale but upon notice to the buyer there is a right to resell the goods to others free and clear under Section 48 of the Sale of Goods Act in the UK. In the USA, Section 2–706 UCC equally allows the resale to a *bona fide* third party and also makes clear that the defaulting seller is *not* entitled to any overvalue.

The retention right is not otherwise in the nature of re-transfering title, certainly not to the seller, not even in countries where title passes immediately upon the mere conclusion of the sales agreement or in countries where delivery is required but this has taken place by the seller (exceptionally) providing constructive delivery only leaving the seller as the phys-ical holder or custodian of the asset.

Even in countries where there is no automatic retention right for the unpaid seller in possession of the goods, it may still be possible to agree in the sales contract to such a reten-tion right. Yet the status of these contractual retention rights must remain in doubt in these countries especially as to their proprietary and preferential status. It is in any event no fore-gone conclusion that the rules concerning the statutory retention right automatically apply to any contractual retention right so created as well.

In the USA they convert automatically into security interests, for example where the bill of lading is retained by the seller, see Section 2–505 UCC. Elsewhere they may also be con-sidered possessory pledges subject to the formalities applicable to the creation of these rights, especially if an execution facility or power of sale is foreseen.

Also in the case of the (contractual) retention right, there is therefore the question whether it could facilitate the (automatic) return of title upon default and how (as a form of appropriation or otherwise), especially relevant in countries where title re-transfer does not automatically result from the rescission of the failed sales agreement or even from an express contractual clause to the effect. As mentioned above, the statutory retention right is unlikely to imply a re-transfer of title and any contractual clause to the effect would be unlikely to create an automatic title return in countries which do not allow this pursuant to a contractual term.

In the USA, there is, however, a statutory reclaiming or appropriation right for ten days after receipt of the goods if bought on credit whilst the buyer was insolvent, Section 2–702 UCC, a right since 1978 also recognised in bankruptcy, Section 546(c) of the US Bankruptcy Code. Another example of a statutory reclaiming right is in Section 2–401(4) UCC under which title re-vests (automatically) in the seller upon a rejection or other refusal by the buyer to receive or retain the goods, whether or not justified, or upon a justi-fied revocation of an acceptance.

In the USA cash sales give in any event an implicit lien recognised under Section 2–507(2) UCC, which lien is, according to the Official Comment, in the nature of a reclaiming right and not a security. In fact, a special statutory reclaiming right operative during a limited period after title transfer also exists in France under Article 2102(4) Cc, although interpreted there not as a revindication right but as a return of the legal retention right of the seller under Articles 1612 and 1613 Cc. Unlike the French statutory rescission right (Article 1184 Cc), this French statutory reclaiming right may exceptionally be exercised upon *mere* notice and is especially important if the goods are still in transit, although title remains strictly speaking with the buyer until the official rescission of the sales agreement. In the Netherlands, on the other hand, the brief statutory reclaiming right upon default during six weeks upon the due date, referred to in Articles 7. 39*ff* CC, is in the nature of a true revindication right and implies a return of title if this right is invoked.

As we have seen, conditionality with an automatic return of title and revindication right of the asset upon default, even in bankruptcy, may in many countries be more specifically achieved through a contractual reservation of title clause, especially in countries like Germany that do not otherwise accept any automatic return under the *lex commissoria*, even if specifically inserted in the sales agreement. There is no automatic re-transfer of title upon a major default in England either, where the reservation of title also overcomes this difficulty for the seller who has lost possession, although in that country the reservation of title is mostly seen as a delayed, rather than a conditional title, transfer.

In France, where the automatic title return upon rescission of the sale agreement because of default may be in doubt in the bankruptcy of a buyer in possession if the creditor has created the appearance of greater creditworthiness in the debtor, the status of the reservation of title was clarified in this respect in an important amendment to the French Bankruptcy Act in 1980, maintained in the new French bankruptcy Act of 1985 (Articles 115 and 121) and reinforced in 1994 (Article 59 of the Law of 10 June).

In the USA, where contractual clauses to the effect are unlikely to be effective in bankruptcy, see Section 365(e) of the US Bankruptcy Code, the reservation of title is known but no longer treated as a special condition reinforcing the automatic return of full title in the case of default. Like any contractual retention right, it is automatically converted into a security right requiring an execution sale and the return of any excess value to the buyer, thus excluding any automatic return of title or appropriation right, see 9–102(2) (old) UCC.

In conclusion, the more specialised default remedies either of a statutory or contractual nature aiming at *in rem* or proprietary protection whilst leaving the unpaid seller with, and especially without, possession with some power in the sold assets even if title is already transferred, present a number of well known problems and may not always result in an automatic return of the asset, especially not upon a bankruptcy of the buyer/debtor in possession when it matters most. As was already mentioned, in international sales, the Vienna Convention does not deal with the proprietary recourse actions of the seller at all (Articles 62*ff*) as a consequence of its lack of coverage of proprietary issues (Article 4).

Because of the (bankruptcy) complications in the case of reclaiming title upon a default in a sales agreement, *personal* security in the form of a bank guarantee may be more certain in result than rescission (clauses) or even a reservation of title or statutory reclaiming rights, especially upon shipment of the goods to a new *situs*. This may in any event change the availability and status of these remedies, which also applies to other types of security interests that may have been created by the seller in the sold assets, see also section 2.1.7 above. From a practical point of view, the resulting need for the seller in *international* sales to retrieve the assets or sell them to alternative buyers in foreign or distant places of destination or conduct an execution sale there create their own problems, costs and risks. Retention rights, be they statutory or merely contractual, by their very nature restrain any subsequent commercial activity in the goods.

Certainly in international sales, *bank guarantees* may therefore be more effective, whilst they also leave the benefits of the transaction intact and avoid the problems associated with the actual retrieval, custody and return of the goods after transportation to the buyer in another country. The international sales contract thus often requires some form of bank guarantee instead. Domestic sales contracts may also do so, but as it is more costly, the reservation of title where accepted is more normal domestically as it is much cheaper and simpler to arrange, there being no third party like a bank involved. The most common type of these bank guarantees is the modern *letter of credit*. Through the Uniform Customs and Practice for Documentary Credits formulated by the International Chamber of Commerce in Paris, it is receiving uniform use and application worldwide, also reflected in Article 5 UCC which can still not be said of the proprietary rights.

From the point of view of increasing their effectiveness, creating greater uniformity internationally in the return of title upon rescission because of default or in *in rem* securities supporting payment may well be desirable and a justified objective of the modern *lex mercatoria*, but even full harmonisation would not relieve the practical problems and inconveniences associated with the retrieval or execution, especially in foreign destinations.

2.2   The Role of Intermediaries and Documents in International Sales

2.2.1   *The Safe Harbour Function: Agents and Documents of Title*

The fact that international sales take some time and involve intermediaries unavoidably creates special complications, dangers and costs but clearly also *opportunities*. As it often requires the goods to be handled by third parties as *agents* who have *no other interest* than to be compensated for their services, this results by itself in some safe harbour for the goods whilst in transit and provides some safeguard against manipulation by either party during the period between the conclusion of the sale and the ultimate delivery of the goods.

It may also introduce flexibility in the resale possibilities and payment arrangements. Particularly the issue of *bills of lading* or *warehouse receipts* traditionally allows for an easy transfer possibility of the rights in the underlying goods with reasonable certainty that delivery would not be complicated by retention or other rights of the original seller because he has lost physical possession. The bill of lading itself and its proprietary function will be discussed more extensively in chapter 4.

Bills of lading also allowed for an early, simple and safe payment facility tied to the mere presentation of these documents by the seller, certifying the handing over of the goods to a carrier. It gave the buyer reasonable certainty that he would receive the goods without complication upon presentation of the bill to the carrier which allowed him to pay when the bill was presented to him. Any disputes on quality and safe arrival were then separately and independently argued out. Indeed 'pay first, argue later' is rightly the underlying maxim of all effective payment schemes based on presentation of shipping documents long before the development of the letter of credit which also operates on this basis.

This framework of basic and practical protections still remains in place today and banks may further facilitate the process by providing so-called collection facilities under which they receive the documents for the buyer whilst making at the same time the payment to the seller: see for these arrangements further chapter 3. As already suggested above, especially through documentary letters of credit tied to the bill of lading where transportation by ship takes place, the payment risk may be further reduced for the seller not in possession. Under it, an intermediary bank will accept the payment obligation and make payment usually in the country of the seller upon presentation of the documents, that is normally upon proof of loading.

In this manner, the credit, quality and political risk may all be mitigated for the seller, who may be assured of the sale price, whatever occurs during transportation to the country of the buyer and whatever payment restrictions may be imposed on him, as long as the seller has properly delivered the goods at the loading point and handed over the documents. As a consequence, the risk of safe arrival and the political risk will in the first instance be for the buyer, but this is always subject to any later recovery by him on the basis of the contractual remedies (like those for non-conform delivery subject to pleas of *force majeure* or hardship).

If, on the other hand, a buyer has been able to insert a condition in the payment arrangement to the effect that he or his bank need not pay until a proper certificate of arrival and quality has been presented, the seller will in the first instance remain liable for the quality and political risk affecting any arrival of the goods. The payment protection will then be much less effective and valuable to him.

Whatever arrangement is chosen in this connection, it will be free from the actual or physical possession of the goods by either party and any possibility of manipulation of the goods on the basis of such possession, for example by a seller who may want to hide the poor original quality of his goods or by a buyer who upon a change in market price would prefer not to receive the goods and might wish to take advantage of any political or other outside interference with the assets or the payment arrangements to that effect.

It must be assumed that in the meantime the intermediary will independently do whatever he can to protect and save the assets in his possession from whatever risk may occur and not use these risks and their management to the advantage of either party to the sale and handle, protect and deliver the goods as best as he can in accordance with the prearranged instructions. Banks will equally have an interest in making proper payment regardless of the circumstances concerning the buyer. There is thus a measure of neutrality inserted in the handling of the assets and the payment in this manner on which parties often depend.

In this way, liquidity risk may also be reduced as through negotiating the bill of lading, the goods may pass safely through further sales without the possibility of the seller or buyer holding the goods back for reasons of their own, as the matter is in first instance between the carrier or the warehouse and the last holder of the bill. This provides liquidity for whoever has the documents including seller or buyer: the seller in possession of the documents in order to obtain early payment upon presentation, the buyer upon gaining possession of them to resell or pledge the documents and receive payment or an advance in this manner. This flexibility makes the parties at the same time less vulnerable to price and currency changes during transportation and may reduce their funding costs.

2.2.2 The Use of Agents: Their Position

The basic pattern of international sales just described based on extensive use of intermediaries, although expensive, has served international commerce for a long time and still provides the basic framework. The position of these intermediaries is in the first instance determined by the contractual arrangements under which they operate, for example a warehousing or transportation agreement or a letter of credit.

However, these contracts may imply further powers: the warehousing or transportation agreement may give the warehouse or the carrier the right to hand over the goods to a third-party/buyer upon presentation of the warehouse receipt or bill of lading, thus at the same time completing the delivery duty of the seller which, in systems requiring delivery for the transfer of title, may pass full ownership. Alternatively the warehouse or carrier may be seen as the agent of the buyer so that the delivery and title transfer are completed when the goods are handed over to them. Under a letter of credit, the payment by the bank will discharge the buyer's payment obligation under the sale agreement at the same time.

What happens here is that intermediaries effect *legal acts* or obtain discharges for either seller or buyer as the case may be (under the contract between them to which the intermediary is not itself a party) to complete a sale without achieving any benefit or incurring any duties of their own. This is the essence of agency and is supplemental to and needs to be well distinguished from the underlying contract obligations between the seller and the buyer (in which the intermediary, although not a party, may play a role as representative of either of them).

Here operates the principle of *independence or abstraction* as the effects of the agency are determined by principles of the objective law rather than by the underlying sales contract or even the contract between principal and agent. Although this latter contract sets the agency in motion, the effect on others may be different from what this contract envisages or prescribes. There is here a risk for the party making use of an agent as others may rely on it and need not check the underlying arrangements and may not be affected by them. Thus a warehouse owner may not be empowered to hand over the goods to the buyer before payment, but if he does the buyer may retain possession certainly if he did not know of the condition (assuming no warehouse receipts were involved).

It is clear that not every intermediary is an agent in this sense, although the term 'agent' is often so used. In a legal sense, the key is that the agent initiates or completes a *legal* act or obtains a discharge for others. There is here an *internal* and *external* relationship, a relationship between principal and agent therefore and between the agent and a third party. The contract of carriage between the seller and the carrier is purely limited to the relationship between both of them and is therefore internal. Yet it may have an external effect in that the carrier operating for the seller may effect a legal act with the buyer on behalf of the seller under the original sales agreement between both of them, for example the act of delivery achieving at the same time the title transfer. That is the external aspect.

If there was a bill of lading or a warehouse receipt, however, the buyer in acquiring the bill or receipt will already have this title as the delivery of the bill of lading or receipt to him will substitute for the delivery of the goods. In that case the carrier or warehouse is unlikely to operate as agent in the transfer of title. They will only provide the buyer with the physical possession of the goods which may not itself be considered a legal act. Yet by delivering the goods in this sense, he still discharges a contractual duty for the seller, effects a discharge for him and may in this aspect still be considered an agent.

Agency relationships may also allow intermediaries to choose a counter-party and contract with it on its principal's behalf. In this way, selling or buying agents may be appointed to find buyers or sellers. In shipping, a shipping agent may thus be asked to make the necessary shipping arrangements with whomever and on the terms he thinks best. The *del credere* agent may have a function in the arrangement whilst accepting for himself the credit or payment risk in connection with the counter-parties he so chooses.

The agency agreements and the roles of the various parties affected will be more extensively discussed in Part III of this chapter.

2.2.3 The Use of Negotiable Documents of Title: Bills of Lading and Warehouse Receipts

As there are likely to be intermediaries in the shipping and warehousing arrangements, some document may emerge, if only as *receipts*, like the *bill of lading* or *warehouse receipt* originally were, when a seller physically delivered his goods at the appointed place, like the ship's rail or the warehouse, and receives these documents in return. These documents may develop into so-called documents of title, incorporating the goods into the document. It allows full use to be made of the intermediaries' safe harbour function and they may subsequently provide great flexibility in any resale and payment arrangements if they become negotiable. This is done by expressing them to bearer or order. Regardless of the whereabouts of the goods and their ultimate arrival in the place of destination, the issue of this type of document thus creates a simple method of handing over the (rights to the) goods to third parties who may claim these assets as owners upon their arrival against presentations of the documents. It promotes liquidity in international sales. See for the details of bills of lading as documents of title, chapter 4, section 2.1.

It also allows them to be handed over to the buyer against payment. This re-establishes a simultaneity in the performance of both parties (allowing payment to be made against delivery of the document) which is otherwise lost when the goods are shipped for delivery (seller's performance) whilst payment is in principle only upon arrival (buyer's performance). It provides protection for either party in a sale: upon tendering the documents the seller receives (immediate or early) payment and the buyer, now in possession of the bill of lading (either directly or through his bank) will collect the goods upon arrival and is no longer dependent on the co-operation of the buyer in this aspect. They can argue over the details, especially the safe arrival, quality and its effect on the price later.

As mentioned before 'pay first, argue later' is rightly the underlying principle of most effective payment schemes. Technically it still puts the buyer in the weaker position as he does not know whether the goods will arrive in good condition, but at least he can be sure that the goods are in independent professional hands and are not likely to be manipulated or held back as they are already with independent third parties. Intermediary banks may here provide further services, either in a collection arrangement in which they receive the documents and pay the seller on the buyer's behalf or, like in letters of credit, by accepting a payment obligation of their own in this respect, often in the country of the seller.

2.2.4 Documents of Title in Payment Schemes: Bills of Lading

On the payment side, the intervention of intermediaries holding the goods against the issue of documents of title like *bills of lading*, may thus give the seller additional security as he is unlikely to hand the documents issued by these intermediaries over to the buyer or his agent before proper payment arrangements are made. This is so even under Fob or Cif terms which will be discussed below in section 2.3.9, in the first case because even though the buyer arranges the transportation the seller when receiving the bill of lading upon loading is here at best his agent in possession of the bill; in the second case it is because the Cif term itself requires the documents to be handed over to the seller as part of the transaction, the seller being in charge of the transportation.

Especially in legal systems requiring a form of delivery for title to pass, title in the assets may thus effectively be reserved in an indirect manner[207] by a seller retaining the

---

[207] Explicitly so Section 2–505 UCC in the USA.

bill of lading as the goods cannot be handed over by the carrier to the buyer without the relevant documents being produced by him. Even if delivery is not required for title transfer which in such systems usually follows immediately when the sale is agreed, a contractual requirement that a bill of lading be issued is usually explained as meaning to postpone the title transfer until that moment. In the USA, the UCC explicitly recognises that the seller retains a proprietary interest in the goods if he retains the bill for payment (Section 2–401). In this system, if payment against documents is agreed, the bill of lading issued to the seller gives him a security right in the underlying assets. The issue of the document nevertheless allows the sale itself to go forward and the goods to sail (and even title itself to be transferred when the bill of lading is given to the seller as agent for the buyer) regardless of these seller protection aspects and the use that is made of the bill in this connection.

The existence of the bill of lading also allows for variation in the sense that it may be placed in the hands of further intermediaries, notably banks, especially in *collection schemes* under which banks achieve as agents the direct exchange of the bill against the purchase money which they will collect, see more in particular chapter 3. Under these schemes, the banks may also assume an autonomous function and *guarantee* payment upon presentation to them of the documents by the seller (therefore regardless of the creditworthiness of the buyer and always independent from the safe arrival and proper quality of the goods).

This is the essence of the *documentary letter of credit,* already mentioned too, see for the details also chapter 3. Upon such payment, the paying bank may itself acquire *vis-à-vis* the buyer a retention or security right in the bill of lading to achieve reimbursement by the buyer if no other arrangements are in place (for example, the buyer may have put the bank in funds or his current account may be debited or if necessary may be allowed to operate with a deficit for the time being).

The bank may thus be considered a *bona fide* holder of the bill of lading in its own right, and the bill then acquires the status of a negotiated document of title under which the bank is the presumed owner or pledgee of the goods.

Retaining the bill of lading under these circumstances has a significance in the possessory aspect as delivery of the goods to the buyer cannot take place before he has received the bill of lading from his bank.

2.2.5 *The Use of Negotiable Instruments: Bills of Exchange*

Documents of title in the payment circuit may not only concern the security aspect, but the payment itself may also be incorporated in a document of title. When concerning money, they are usually called *instruments,* which, like bills of lading, may also become negotiable by adding the words 'to order' to the beneficiary/payee[208] or by making the instrument payable to bearer fence the term: 'negotiable instruments'. They are mostly of two types: they may contain an instruction from the creditor to the debtor, as in the case of a *bill of exchange,* to pay to a named person (payee) or his order or to bearer, or they may contain a payment promise by the debtor himself, as in the case of a *promissory note,* in which the debtor promises to pay to someone named in the note or his order or to bearer, see for bills of exchange more particularly chapter 3. Promissory notes therefore circulate at the initiative of the debtor, bills of exchange at the initiative of the creditor.

---

[208] In the UK under the Bills of Exchange Act 1882, even if the words 'to order' are missing, the bill is so interpreted, see Section 8(4), but not so in the USA or on the European continent.

Although both types of instruments are in principle to order or bearer, bearer bills of exchange are uncommon on the European continent, see for example, Section 1 of the German Bills of Exchange Act 1933 (*Wechselgesetz*), and are even declared void under the Geneva Convention of 1930. Order paper may, however, be converted into bearer paper by an endorsement in blank by the holder.[209] Conversely, bearer paper can be made into order paper through endorsement to an identified person by the holder.

We will be concerned here only with bills of exchange, often also called drafts, which are the more important in international trade; promissory notes remain particularly common within the USA. Under bills of exchange, the creditor or drawer giving the payment instruction to a third party beneficiary or payee is likely also to incur a liability towards him. The beneficiary/payee is likely to be a third party to whom the creditor owes something and issuing a bill of exchange and handing it to the payee then becomes another way of paying this party and amounts to a form of assignment of the claim. The payee may, however, also be the seller's own bank which then collects in this manner as agent for the drawer. The payee may even be the seller/drawer himself.

When negotiated to *bona fide* third parties, these instruments acquire, like bills of lading, a status independent from the underlying claim and its validity and in fact render (unlike bills of lading) all signatories including endorsers liable for payment to the holder in the manner of the guarantor's note marked to himself as beneficiary/payee, by discounting the bill of exchange or selling the promissory note to a bank, which will normally be the buyer's bank, which is the only one familiar with the latter's credit, unless the bill of exchange is avalised, that is (in civil law terms) guaranteed by another bank.

Discounting (time) bills of exchange is a traditional way of obtaining early cash regardless of the arrival of the goods or their quality upon arrival and the agreed sales credit period. It means in fact that the drawer, if himself marked as the payee/beneficiary on the bill of exchange and after having obtained acceptance of the bill by the drawee, sells it to a bank who then becomes the holder and will present the bill of exchange to the drawee on the due date. It will apply a discount for the loss of interest until the due date, taking into account also the creditworthiness of the drawee/debtor. It may also charge an additional fee for the service.

The drawback of this substitute form of payment in international commerce is that since normally only a bank which knows the drawee/debtor under a bill of exchange will discount it, the discounting normally leads to payment in the country of the buyer upon the presentation of the bill of exchange to him (except if it specifies payment in the country of the seller which is exceptional or if it is avalised by a bank in the country of the seller). The letter of credit on the other hand normally achieves payment upon presentation of the documents by the seller to a paying bank in his *own* country. It has as a consequence become more common. It may be combined, however, with a bill of exchange and then allows the beneficiary of the letter of credit to draw a bill of exchange on the bank liable to pay under the letter of credit and, in the acceptance credit, even demand acceptance of the bill in order to create an early discount facility if the letter of credit is not immediately payable upon presentation of the documents.

The bill of lading and the bill of exchange may also be connected more directly in the sense that the bill of lading may be surrendered by the seller to the buyer against the latter's acceptance of a bill of exchange drawn on him which may subsequently be discounted by the seller. This is the *documentary bill of exchange*. In collection arrangements

---

[209] This used not to be possible in France before the law of 8 Feb. 1922.

a bank collecting for the seller may also be required to draw (as agent for the seller) a bill of exchange on the buyer and obtain acceptance by the latter before the documents are released.

The details of bills of exchange will be discussed more fully in chapter 4, section 2.2. Their importance has declined in modern times largely because of the direct involvement of guaranteeing and collecting banks in the payment circuit. These banks effectively make the payment directly to the seller through the banking system, see chapter 3. As an assignment substitute, instructing the drawee to pay a third party payee, bills of exchange have been eclipsed by the modern assignment facilitated in most modern countries by the abolition of the notice requirement to the debtor for the assignment to be effective. This facilitates at the same time more flexible forms of receivable financing (see chapter 5) and has rendered the discounting of bills of exchange to raise financing less efficient.

2.3   The Uniform International Sales Laws

2.3.1   Origin and Scope

International sales have been the subject of uniform treaty law, first in the Hague Conventions of 1964, which separated the formation of the contract from the more substantive parts of the law of sales, and subsequently in the already much mentioned Vienna Convention on Contracts for the International Sale of Goods (CISG) of 1980. It is practically speaking the successor to the Hague Conventions and combines both areas in one document.

It may be helpful at this stage to relate some of the history of the Vienna Convention. It was prepared by Uncitral, the UN Commission on International Trade Law established on 17 December 1966 and operating from Vienna since 1969, see also chapter 1, section 1.5.5.

But the idea of a uniform sales law originally emerged in Unidroit (Institute International pour l'Unification du Droit Privé or The International Institute for the Unification of Private Law) set up in Rome in 1926 under the authority of the League of Nations. In 1928 Professor Ernst Rabel from Berlin, later at the University of Michigan in Ann Arbor, proposed a project on international sales which led to a first draft in 1935 whilst his own book, *Das Recht des Warenkaufs*, first appeared in 1936. The project met considerable opposition, especially in the field of offer and acceptance (where common law maintained a much more formal structure).

Since 1939, there were as a consequence two projects, one on formation: *Loi Uniforme sur la Formation des Contrats de Vente Internationale des Objets Mobiliers Corporels (LUF)* or the Uniform Law on the Formation of Contracts for the International Sale of Goods (ULFIS) and another on the international sale itself: *Loi Uniforme sur la Vente Internationale des Objets Mobiliers Corporels (LUVI)* or the Uniform Law on the International Sale of Goods (ULIS). They were agreed at the Hague Diplomatic Conferences of 1951 and 1964 which, however, was attended by only a small number of countries, and they were only ratified by a few states, often with reservations (the UK, for example, required that the parties themselves made the Conventions applicable to their contract, which was never done).

Because of their limited support, the Hague Conventions were increasingly seen as not fully representative of the views of the world community at large and especially not of the need of less developed countries. Once Uncitral adopted the project, it moved quickly and on a much broader front of participants. It presented a first draft on international sales in 1978 and was able to conclude the matter at a Diplomatic Conference in Vienna in 1980 attended by 62 states, which approved the final text after five weeks of deliberations.

The Vienna Convention is the successor to the Hague Conventions and tracks much of their language. In chapter 1, section 1.5.5, the tribulations of Unidroit after World War II were already explained. When it was re-established, the sales project was in the hands of an independent Hague Diplomatic Conference which completed the project after conferences in 1951 and 1964. From there it moved to Uncitral which, as a UN agency, was thought to be the more proper forum likely to obtain the most ratifications.[210]

In the Hague Conventions of 1964, there was no definition of what an international sale was. They limited themselves, however, to the sale of goods as tangible, movable objects. The Vienna Convention does not contain a definition either but notably does not apply to the sale of consumer goods, auctions, execution sales, sales of investment securities and other negotiable instruments or money market transactions, sales of ships or aircraft and sales of electricity (Article 2). The civil or commercial nature of the sale is otherwise not considered (Article 1(3)). For the Convention to apply, parties must either have their place of business in different Contracting States or the applicable private international law should point to the law of a Contracting State for the Convention to apply (Article 1(1)), always assuming that both parties come from different States which in that case need not be Contracting States. If a party has more than one place of business, for example, if it operates through branches in different countries, the place of business with the closest relationship to the contract and its performance counts. If a party has no place of business, the habitual residence will be taken as relevant, Article 10.

The inference is that only cross-border sales between professionals are considered. The Hague Conventions indeed required cross-border movement of goods, but this criterion is now abandoned. It may be more appropriate where proprietary aspects are also considered, which has not so far been the case in the sales conventions. The Vienna Convention is as a consequence applicable even if no assets cross borders. This is in line with its purely contractual scope.

One thus sees a number of elements of international sales implied, *cf* more in particular section 2.1.2 above, without (for purposes of the uniform law) any single determining factor, although the emphasis is (for contractual purposes) on the different location of the parties, whilst as to substance, the emphasis is on the sale of movable tangible assets between professionals, which assets or parties need *not* themselves move cross-border. The system of the Vienna Convention is still based on delivery 'ex works', *cf* Article 31(c), so that again from a proprietary point of view, there may not be any international (cross-border) aspect at all.

The other main differences between the Hague and Vienna Conventions are in a narrower concept of uniform law under the Vienna Convention. It notably allows the application of conflict rules where the Convention itself is silent (but only after applying its general principles, Article 7(2)), see also section 2.3.7 below. Here the internationalist approach of the Hague Conventions is abandoned, see more in particular section 2.3.5 below. The Vienna Convention in its Article 9 is even more restrictive in its recognition of custom as source of law, apparently in order better to protect the unwary in international trade.

---

[210] The International Sales of Goods Convention had been Unidroit's major project. After it was re-established it diversified into other areas: see more particularly chapter 1, s. 1.5.5.

The Vienna Convention generally means to protect the buyer and therefore never accepts automatic termination upon breach, even if fundamental (Articles 61 and 64), gives the defaulter some possibilities to remedy his failure of performance even after delivery (Article 48), especially if the price is paid (Articles 63 and 64(2)), only accepts suspension (and no avoidance) of the contract if there are good reasons for fearing that the buyer will not pay (Article 71), allows avoidance in the case of anticipatory breach only upon notice of the intention to invoke this remedy (Article 72(2)), enhances the buyer's rights unilaterally to reduce the price upon (alleged) non-conform delivery (Article 50, often seen as an excessive right), allows inspection by the buyer within a short period after delivery rather than promptly (Article 38(1)), refers in the absence of a price to the market conditions rather than to prices generally charged by the seller (Article 55), and restricts implied usages to those agreed or established between the parties (Article 9), as they were otherwise considered to favour the strong. The notice periods are generally more flexible than in the Hague Conventions and the Vienna Convention never requires prompt answers.

Finally, there are a number of important simplifications, especially in the remedies. The Hague Sales Conventions had distinguished between five categories of performance, each with their own type of remedy in the case of default. It resulted in artificial distinctions and unnecessary complications. Also the concept of delivery was simplified and reduced to its physical aspects and to a number of obligations of buyer and seller in this respect (Articles 31 and 60), whilst the passing of risk was no longer immediately tied to it (Articles 66*ff*), although the principle that the risk passes upon physical delivery remains unchanged.

As already mentioned above, the Vienna Convention does not apply to consumer sales, the supply of services, auctions, the sale of securities and ships or aircraft (Articles 2 and 3). Even then, the Vienna Convention contains only a *partial* codification of the law of sales as it relates to the formation of the sale contract and the rights and obligations of parties thereunder, Article 4 (although this is a very broad formula), but notably not to questions of validity of the contract (therefore in questions of sufficient consensus and the defects therein) and custom, and to the property aspect of sold goods, including the title transfer. In fact, from the subjects covered it is clear that the scope is even more limited as it avoids all general contractual aspects except for offer and acceptance or formation (in Part II). Areas not covered by the Vienna Convention (and earlier the Hague Conventions) are therefore notably: (a) consent or lack thereof or the usual defences against binding force in the case of fraud, coercion or duress, abuse of power or undue influence at the time of formation, mistake or misrepresentation, and its consequences, in civil law often referred to as matters of validity, which then also cover questions of avoidance and nullity for other reasons like illegal purposes, (b) capacity and proper authority, including agency, or the consequences of lack thereof, (c) pre-contractual rights and duties, (d) enforcement or abuse of rights obtained under the contract including any re-negotiation duties in the case of hardship or gross imbalances, (e) the transfer of title, its manner and time and the property rights created thereby, and (f) prescription (the Uncitral Convention of 1974 on the Limitation Period in the International Sale of Goods suggests a period of four years). By special provision (Article 5), the Vienna Convention, does not apply to seller's liability for death or personal injury caused by his goods either.

The areas not covered by the Convention thus largely relate to the general part of the law of contract or to property aspects, especially the transfer of title pursuant to the contract. What we are mainly concerned with here is therefore the typical contractual infrastructure like questions of capacity, binding force or consensus and the interpretation of the contract, defences and excuses, pre- and post-contractual duties, and the proprietary consequences of a sale, aspects not likely to be covered in the contract itself either, certainly not if not themselves of a contractual nature, like the transfer and ownership aspects. Because these aspects cannot or are not normally covered in the contract itself, a Convention also covering these areas would have been much more important.

For the contractual infrastructure, the Unidroit and EU Contract Principles are now attempting to cover some of this, see section 1.6 above, and may, whatever their strengths or weaknesses, from that point of view become more important, although they are not meant as a binding set of rules. In fact, the Vienna Convention (with the important exception of its provisions on formation relating largely to offer and acceptance) covers particularly those aspects which parties are themselves likely to cover in the contract, like quality, quantity, price, place and time of delivery, default and the *in personam* remedies including the concept of *force majeure* and the passing of risk. Parties may certainly continue to do so (Article 6). It obviously reduces the importance of the Convention even further. Because of unfamilarity with its operations or effects and some peculiarities as the excessive power of the buyer unilaterally to adjust the purchase price under Article 50, many standard industry contacts exclude the application of the Convention altogether. In any event, it mainly centres on some aspects of offer and acceptance (Part II), on the time and place of delivery (Articles 31 and 33), conform (physical) delivery (Article 35), transfer of risk (Article 69(1)), payment (Article 57), default (Articles 45 and 61), damages (Article 74), *force majeure* (Article 79) and a duty of care for seller or buyer if something goes wrong in the implementation of the contract in order to protect the goods (Articles 85 and 86). The Vienna Convention is as a consequence of modest help and primarily meant to provide solutions when the contract, standard terms or industry usages (see Article 9) do not provide sufficient guidance themselves, which is usually only the case in oral contracts. They must be considered rare in international dealings.

The USA and all EU countries, except the UK, have ratified the Vienna Convention. The UK was represented on the Uncitral working group at the time but remains one of the most important commercial nations that have not so far accepted the Convention, although it ratified the earlier Hague Sales Conventions (but with the reservation that parties had to make a reference to it in their contract). The principal reason for the UK's abstention so far may be the one stated by the Law Society of England and Wales concerned about the diminishing role that might result for English law within the international trade arena.[211] Its own sales law for goods or movable tangible assets remains basically the one of 1893 updated in 1979 and may be doubted ever to have set a pattern in international sales, except within the British Commonwealth Article 2 of the UCC was more influential and emerged in draft very much at the same time as the Hague Conventions. The Vienna Convention is still different in a number of important aspects, notably in the absence of the concept of consideration and in the introduction of good faith notions in the interpretation and of general principles in the supplementation of the Convention itself which may suggest a more teleological or normative interpretation of the legal text. These would certainly be new features in countries like the UK, although less so in commercial law in the USA (see Section 1–103 1–102 (old) UCC which allows a liberal interpretation of the statutory text).

---

[211] See the Law Society of England and Wales, Law Reform Committee of the Council, 1980, *Convention on Contracts for the International Sale of Goods* (1981). The Department of Trade and Industry, *United Nations Convention on Contracts for the International Sale of Goods: A Consultative Document* (June 1989) was more neutral and did not express a clear preference.

In sum, in the more flexible approach to interpretation and in its detail, the USA with its Article 2 of the UCC is closer to the Convention and the USA has therefore not shown a similar resistance and ratified. Unification makes some sense as a system of different domestic sales laws creates considerable cost in terms of legal advice, creates some risks on its own, and may well slow down transactions. It increases uncertainty. Moreover, there result considerable uncertainties and undesirable consequences from the applicable choice of law rules or even from a contractual choice of a domestic law, see further chapter 1, section 1.5.1. Most importantly, domestic laws tend to ignore the character and dynamics of international sales; see more in particular chapter 1 for the development of a transnational legal order and *lex mercatoria* to accomodate modern needs.

Application of the Vienna Convention alone will not guarantee uniformity as it covers the subject of international sales only partially and notably not the aspect of the transfer of ownership which is the true objective of all sales contracts. In any event, there will remain diversity in its interpretation and certainly in its supplementation where, for the one, reference is made to the widely varying good faith notion and, for the other, to private international law rules, see more in particular sections 2.3.6 and 2.3.7 below.

It is submitted that uniform treaty law can only flourish and its true meaning can only become apparent within the context of this nature the hierarchy of norms of the whole *lex mercatoria.*

2.3.2   The System of the Vienna Convention: Directory or Mandatory Rules

The question was raised at the time whether provisions of the Hague Sales Conventions could be of a mandatory instead of a directory nature, especially important as to whether they could in whole or in part be set aside by the parties. Article 6 of the Vienna Convention, following Article 3 of the Hague Sales Convention, is unambiguous on the subject and allows parties to deviate from any of its terms, except where the domestic law of a party with its place of business in a Contracting State requires a written form for the contract of sale, its modification or termination, provided that the relevant Contracting State has insisted on maintaining this principle in international sales upon a special declaration to the effect (Articles 12 and 96), as the USA has done.

Earlier, an argument developed at the Hague Diplomatic Conference of 1951 to the effect that international trade required some basic mandatory rules on the structure of the international sales agreement, notably to avoid improper practices. This never became the accepted view, which remains based on the classical (civil law) notion of contracts in essence depending on the will of the parties in formation, coverage and interpretation, although corrections would be conceivable on the basis of fundamental legal principles or of mandatory custom. They may then be identified as overriding *ius cogens* in the context of the *lex mercatoria*, see chapter 1, section 1.5.2. In international sales, these overriding principles should be of an international nature and domestic considerations should not enter into them — they could at most be a bar to enforcement of such decisions in domestic recognition and execution proceedings. Under domestic law, these overriding principles may sometimes be covered by the concept of good faith or abuse of rights notions, especially in legal systems like the German and Dutch, where in pressing cases they may equally amend the contract and its implementation, see more in particular section 1.3.1 above.

The liberal attitude of the Convention towards full party autonomy was made uncontroversial because of its limited scope. The Unidroit and European Contract Principles which cover contract law more generally seem to adopt here a fundamentally different attitude, therefore not limited to acceptance of overriding international fundamental principles alone. That was identified in section 1.6.1 as largely the result of a personal dealing and consumer-oriented approach, even where these Principles (especially the Unidroit ones) mean to operate only in the international business sphere. It is bound to undermine the credibility of these Principles in international trade, see also the discussion in section 1.6.3 above.

2.3.3 Applicability of the Vienna Convention

The Vienna Convention only applies to the sale of goods or chattels as tangible movable assets between parties whose places of business are in different States. According to Article 1(1), for the Convention to apply, the further requirement is that either the parties must have their places of business in *contracting* States or the applicable private international law must point to the law of a contracting State, although contracting States may opt out of this latter provision (Article 95), as the USA has done.

If a party has more than one place of business (for example, branches in several countries), the relevant place of business for the purposes of the Convention is the one which has the closest relationship to the contract and its performance, having regard to the circumstances known to or contemplated by the parties at any time before or at the conclusion of the contract (Article 10(a)). If a party does not have a place of business, like most private persons, the habitual residence is the relevant place in terms of the Convention (Article 10(b)). The Convention appears to consider it exceptional that they should engage in international sales of the type covered by it although these sales are not strictly speaking excluded, provided they are not consumer sales.

For the Convention to apply it is thus not necessary for the courts in Contracting States first to determine which law is applicable in order subsequently to determine whether that law has incorporated the Convention for sales of the types covered by it. This is the approach only in the courts of non-contracting States. Courts *in* Contracting States must apply the Convention as *lex fori* if the conditions of Article 1 are fulfilled, that is particularly when the parties come from two Contracting States. The appropriateness of applying the international sales law is then automatically assumed.

Thus only if the parties are not both from Contracting States is there a more traditional conflicts rule inserted and the Convention then only applies if the forum's conflicts rules lead to the applicability of the law of a Contracting State (although under Article 95 Contracting States may opt out of this provision). In finding that the law of a Contracting State is applicable, courts would only subsequently apply the other applicability tests of the Convention, that is that parties came at least from different states and that in essence only non-consumer sales are covered (unless these conditions are waived by the parties), see further also chapter 1, section 2.3.1.

Thus, the Convention may under its applicability rules affect residents from non-contracting States in respect of whom the law of a Contracting State must be considered applicable under Article 1(1)(b) *provided always* that the parties come from different States even if not member States (which is logical as there is no reason to apply an international sales law in domestic situations). A contractual choice of law referring to the law of a Contracting State may in this way also achieve applicability of the Convention as a matter of the conflict laws of the forum in or outside Contracting States. It may be safer in such a case, however, to refer to the Convention explicitly, certainly if the law of the country chosen has itself opted to exclude Article 1(1)(b), as the USA has done.

Article 6, on the other hand, allows the parties expressly to exclude application even if they both come from a Contracting State or risk the applicability of the Convention under the prevailing conflict rules. A choice of law in favour of a country that has not ratified the Convention must mean its exclusion. On the other hand, a contractual choice of law making reference to the Convention would mean its applicability even if the parties came from the same State. In that case the diversity requirement of Article 1(1) must be deemed waived. This may make sense if the goods are to be shipped from other countries and the parties, although from the same country, wish the provisions of the Convention concerning quality, quantity, price, allocation of risk and default to apply. As was already mentioned, total exclusion of the Convention is still quite common between commercial parties because of some of the vagaries and eccentricities of the Convention or general unfamiliarity with it.

The result of the application provisions of the Convention is that a German and a Dutch resident, both coming from Contracting States, but the latter being on a visit to Germany, would be selling to and buying from each other under the Vienna Convention, except if the goods were bought for personal, family or household use (unless the seller did not realise that this was the case: see Article 2(2)). According to Article 1(2), this is also not so if the fact that the parties have their places of business in different countries does not appear from the contract or from any dealings between them.

This could be more particularly the case if there was an undisclosed foreign principal represented by an agent resident or with his place of residence in the same country as the other party. In any event, the buying of a loaf of bread by the Dutchman whilst on holiday in Germany would as a consumer transaction not be covered by the Vienna Convention, although according to Article 1(3) neither the nationality of the parties nor the civil or commercial nature of the contract is relevant in this connection. The buying of a combi-car thus probably would.

If, on the other hand, the buyer were an Englishman (therefore someone from a Non-contracting State) on a visit in Germany, the Convention would still be applied by the German courts if called upon to decide any litigation arising from the sale (assuming they had jurisdiction) as the parties would have their habitual residences in different States (although not Contracting States) whilst under Article 1.1(b) the Convention would apply as a matter of German law, this being the law of the seller who under Article 4 of the EU Rome Convention on the Law Applicable to Contractual Obligations performs the most characteristic obligation.

Should a case arise in England, then the Vienna Convention might still apply if German law were considered applicable to the transaction by the English courts, which would be likely in the circumstances as the UK is a party to the Rome Convention and would therefore be likely to apply German contract law. In that case the English courts would not apply the Convention as part of their *lex fori* but only as a matter of German law under the applicable conflicts rule.

In this system, the location of the asset or any requirement of delivery in another country is irrelevant. This is a consequence of the property aspects and the transfer of title itself not being overed by the Convention (see Article 4). As we saw, the earlier Hague Conventions still required this cross-border movement of the asset even though it did not cover proprietary aspects either, but this approach is now abandoned.

2.3.4   The Sales Law of the Vienna Convention

As already mentioned several times before, the Vienna Convention contains only a partial codification of the international sales law. In the following, its major topics, most of which were already highlighted before, will be briefly revisited.

As regards offer and acceptance, the Convention largely adopts common law terminology, concepts and practices, except that the acceptance (if not by conduct or in the manner as indicated by established practice between the parties) is effective upon receipt only, even if by mail, rather than upon dispatch, as is the normal common law rule (Article 18(2)). Like the UCC in the USA, the Convention further dispenses with the traditional common law distinction between unilateral and bilateral contracts, the first being under traditional common law for their effect dependent on full performance (and notice thereof to the other party, instead of mere acceptance), as in offers to the public (if not an invitation to treat) and normally in offers for services, not here relevant.

On the other hand, unlike the situation in civil law, offers are not binding *per se*, even for a reasonable time (Article 16). Here traditional common law continues to prevail, except where the offer states otherwise (which was not even then binding under common law without consideration, but between merchants now also possible under the UCC in the USA (Section 2–205)), or has been reasonably relied upon (like subcontractors' quotations enabling a main contractor to make a final offer). Common law requires detrimental reliance, which may be a stricter requirement. Offers must be sufficiently definite, but they are considered to be so if they fix or make provision for the determination of quantity and price, see Article 14(1), although strictly speaking even that much is not necessary if the offer is otherwise sufficiently definite. Article 55 makes further provisions for price so that in fact quantity is the only term parties must at least generally agree on.

This is also the approach of the UCC in the USA, which requires as the minimum for validity of a sales contract the agreement on quantity. It need not even be accurately stated but recovery is limited by what is said, whilst the price, time and place of payment or delivery, the general quality of the goods or any particular warranties may all be omitted (see Official Comment at Section 2–201). Under the Convention, additional terms, which do not materially change the offer, do not result in a rejection or counter offer, but if bearing on price, payments, quality, quantity, place and time of delivery, party's liability or settlement of disputes, they are considered material *per se* (Article 19(3)).

The Convention does away both with the requirement of consideration and *causa* (*cf* Articles 14 and 29(1)) in the formation. In this respect it also follows the earlier Hague Sales Conventions. Thus under the Vienna Convention, there is no search for a more objective criterion to make promises legally binding besides the mere intention of the parties. In the continental European tradition, any excesses are curbed only by notions of good faith or public policy, but these notions remain underdeveloped in the Vienna Convention. The good faith notion is only mentioned in Article 7(1) in the context of the interpretation of the Convention itself and has here supposedly a different meaning and may more properly stand for teleological or normative interpretation, as we shall see.

The absence of the requirement of consideration or *causa* in the Convention (and also in the Unidroit Principles for International Commercial Contracts) does not appear to mean that it may itself be reintroduced through application of a national law pursuant to applicable conflicts rules under Article 7(2) as a matter of gap-filling in the area of formation or outright as a matter not covered by the Convention at all. It may well be that in international transactions these requirements (of consideration or *causa*) have lapsed altogether, see also section 1.2.6 above.

Articles 31 and 33 deal with the time and place of the delivery. The normal delivery place remains 'ex works', that is at the seller's place of business, except where the sales contract involves a carriage of goods, therefore a transportation arrangement, when the seller must hand over the goods to the first carrier. If the goods are known to be in a warehouse or particular place of manufacture, they must be put at the buyer's disposal at that place.

The time is a reasonable time after conclusion of the contract, which means in fact that the ground rule is immediate delivery at the option of the buyer to be reasonably exercised.

The Convention thus concerns itself only with delivery in a *physical* and not a *legal* sense. As just mentioned, in essence goods are still put at the disposal of the buyer 'ex works'. The transfer of risk occurs at the same time, although strictly speaking it is at the moment the buyer takes over the goods (Article 69(1)), which could be later. In trade terms, like Fob and Cif, parties often agree, however, to a different regime altogether, see section 2.3.9 below. As proprietary aspects are not dealt with in the Convention, delivery must not be considered here in terms of transferring legal or constructive possession as a precondition for the passing of title in countries which require delivery for title transfer. They may in any event sometimes require mere legal or constructive delivery and therefore use a somewhat different concept of possession in this connection, see more particularly chapter 4.

As regards price and payment, although Article 14 of the Vienna Convention requires the price to be sufficiently definite, according to Article 55, the price if not established in the contract is the price generally charged at the time of the conclusion of the contract for such goods sold under comparable circumstances. Payment must take place at the place of seller (Article 57), unlike notably under French law (insisting on the place of the debtor, Article 1247(3) Cc) and the time is upon delivery (Article 58), all unless agreed otherwise.[212] The European and Unidroit Principles also require payment at the place of the creditor.

In Articles 28, 46 and 62, the Vienna Convention deals with specific performance, see also section 1.4.1 above. Subject to the provisions of the *lex fori* in this manner, the Convention in Article 46 allows the buyer specific performance unless it has resorted to another remedy. In the case of non-conform delivery, substitute goods may only be claimed if there has been a fundamental breach, otherwise the normal remedy is repair. Article 62 gives the seller a more unrestrained right to request payment or force the buyer to take delivery or perform his other duties unless he has chosen another remedy.

As regards other remedies, see section 1.4.4 above. To repeat, Article 47 gives the buyer the facility to set extra time (*Nachfrist*) for performance by the seller and Article 63 gives a similar facility to the seller to solicit performance by the buyer. The importance of this facility is in its consequences: if the defaulting party does not use the facility, the other party has a right to avoid the contract and thereby terminate his own performance duty, whether or not the breach was itself fundamental. It is then treated as such: see Articles 49(1)(b) and 64(1)(b).

As regards the default remedies of rescission and damages, the key is that, under Articles 49 and 64, a party can ask for a rescission of the contract upon default by the other party, but in the case of fundamental breach only (see for the definition Articles 25 and 26) or if he has set an additional time for performance and the other party has not taken advantage of it. It does not require judicial intervention and discharges the creditor (either seller or buyer as the case may be) from his own obligations and does not rule out any claim for damages under Articles 74 to 77. These may include a loss of profit, incidental (for example,

---

[212] It is clear that the Vienna Convention does not adhere to the principle of a price certain for the validity of the contract, as Roman law had required (the *pretium certum*, also of importance for the transfer of risk) and as French law in its wake still does, see Article 1591Cc, but the Cour de Cass. in a decision of 1 Dec. 1995 [1996] JCP 22.565, allowed the price to be unilaterally established if subject to objective criteria, like for telephone companies a generally applicable telephone charging scale. Article 1591Cc is now merely seen as a protection against abuse by the seller. German and new Dutch law do not retain the idea of a fixed price and, like the Vienna Convention, allow the determination of the price later with reference to objective, often market–related standards.

enforcement cost) and often consequential damages, but they cannot exceed the loss foreseeable by the defaulting party at the time of the conclusion of the contract. This is the common law approach, which maintains here a more difficult criterion than civil law which ties the foreseeability commonly to the moment the default occurs.

Article 50 contains a special and much criticised remedy in the case of non-conform delivery and allows the buyer unilaterally to reduce the price with the reduction in value of the asset. It does not require judicial intervention to establish whether the delivery was indeed non-conform and what the appropriate reduction is. Article 50 is a combination of the *actio quanti minoris* and the *exceptio non adimpleti contractus* except that there is neither an action nor an exception but rather an independent right on the part of the buyer unilaterally to reduce the price upon his allegation of non-conform delivery. It shifts the burden of litigation to the seller. This has given rise to considerable criticism but was asked for by developing countries which felt that their buyers were better protected in this manner. It is an important reason, however, why the application of the Vienna Convention is often excluded by contract. Where the non-conform delivery was due to *force majeure* whilst the seller was still at risk, he will, however, be excused from paying damages, see Article 79.

As to default, under the Convention, parties may also act in anticipation of a breach to preserve their positions (the anticipatory breach of Articles 71–73) and it is possible to suspend their own performance by giving notice thereof to the other party, provided the deficiency in the ability to perform or in the credit worthiness of the other party is serious or is in preparation for performance or in the performance itself. If it results in adequate reassurances of performance, the party giving the notice must continue his own performance.

The Vienna Convention deals with performance and default only in their *in personam* consequences, that is to say it deals neither with the transfer of title nor its return upon default or upon rescission or avoidance: see for the various options under domestic laws in this latter respect, section 2.1.10 above. The remedies under the Convention are basically specific performance or avoidance of the contract (if the breach is fundamental) with the possibility of always claiming damages depending on the circumstances. As we saw, by way of preventive remedies, the Convention also allows action, if a breach is expected (anticipatory breach), or preventive action, which may mean not performing any further oneself. This is particularly relevant in bilateral contracts (the *exceptio non adimpleti contractus*).

Technically speaking, the Vienna Convention, like the UCC, abandons the common law notion of (express or constructive) 'conditions', traditionally distinguished from warranties as a matter of interpretation. The express conditions could be related to the occurrence of an outside event or be a specific term of the deal, for example the specified quality or delivery date. Constructive conditions were those implied, for example a substantial default by the one party, which would condition the performance of the other and release him. As explained in section 1.4.3 above, in common law, technically conditions were considered so material that when remaining unsatisfied, the contractual obligation of the other party did not ripen unless there was a failure to co-operate or a waiver. In this way common law created a method of releasing the non-defaulting party without rescinding the agreement, which it found difficult to do.

Conditions thus automatically discharged a promisor without resort to the notion of breach proper and any right to cure, whilst there could still be a right to damages. Warranties did not have the same status, although they naturally could also be breached. The Vienna Convention adopts instead the concept of fundamental breach and speaks of the possibility to avoid or rescind the contract in that case (only): see Articles 49 and 64. Fundamental breach is only loosely defined (Article 25) and remains, like negligence, a matter of determination per case in view of all the circumstances.

The subject of *force majeure* is always a difficult one and concerns first the definition of *force majeure* but also its consequences in terms of a temporary or permanent release of the party required to perform, adaptation of the contract or allocation of the risk: see also section 1.4.5 above.

The Vienna Convention in Article 79 states that a party is not liable for a failure to perform any of his obligations if he proves that the failure was due to an impediment beyond his control and that he could not reasonably be expected to have taken the impediment into account at the time of the conclusion of the contract or to have avoided or overcome it or its consequences.

This is a wide definition, but Article 79(5) further says that nothing in Article 79 prevents either party from exercising any rights under the Convention other than claiming damages. Rights to avoid the contract as a result of fundamental breach or to ask for repairs are thus not impaired whilst avoidance may lead to restitution, but only if that is still possible (if not, avoidance may not be secant, Article 82). It means the return of all that has been supplied under the contract, but not as proprietary remedy with which the Convention does not deal.

The Convention does not contain any special provisions allowing for an adaptation of the contractual terms in the case of hardship due to change of circumstances or otherwise.

As regards the passing of risk of deteriorating or lost goods and its relationship to the concept of *force majeure*, above in sections 2.1.8 and 2.1.9, the basic rules were explained. In summary these were the following:

(a) In a sale, it is the legal owner or, more recently, the physical holder of the goods who must accept whatever happens to the goods in his possession after the conclusion of the sales agreement and before delivery if damage or loss is not caused by anyone in particular. If he is the seller, he is not therefore discharged from his conform delivery duty by force majeure (but he might from other ancillary obligations like servicing the goods).

(b) On the other hand, the seller, if no longer the holder, is no longer liable for any damage subsequently affecting the goods without his fault and is entitled to full payment. He is also excused from any remaining duties in respect of the goods, like a service obligation, in the case of force majeure on his part but might not be able to request payment for the performance of these duties either. This is only different if guarantees of performance have been given.

(c) The seller's own knowledge of dangers or investigation duties in the quality especially of goods which he did not himself manufacture may undermine his claims to *force majeure* concerning the state of the goods and therefore his reliance on the passing of the risk upon delivery. Defences of the buyer based on mistake or misrepresentation may then also be valid.

(d) The buyer upon delivery may still be protected even if the seller is not to blame for the deterioration in quality, if the buyer did not have a chance to inspect the goods properly, if there were hidden defects, or if he benefited from an express or implied guarantee (which may also imply a lesser investigation duty upon receipt) so that the risk is still not for him and has therefore not passed.

(e) If goods (as well as the payments made) may be returned upon non-conformity, not discoverable at the time of delivery (even if due to force majeure but also for other reasons like mistake, illegality, etc.), the seller may have to accept the goods in the state in which they then are (except if grossly mishandled by the buyer) and still may have the duty to provide new ones at his own expense, repair the old ones to their specified quality, reduce the price or abandon a claim for payment altogether and return all payments already made. So his risk may be increased by the ordinary wear and tear or any (complete) loss of the goods in the meantime (for reasons of force majeure affecting the buyer in possession).

(f) The seller, whilst having the risk but not being able to perform the quality requirements due to force majeure and therefore still being liable for repair or replacement or the loss of the sale price or for a price reduction, does not need to reimburse the buyer for the loss of the bargain or consequential damages except if he did not disclose known dangers whilst not insuring them properly either.

Thus under the *modern* law of sales, unless the contract states otherwise, the risk in this sense normally passes between seller and buyer when the buyer takes over the goods, or if he does not do so in good time, from the moment the goods were put at his disposal. This is also the approach of the Vienna Convention, *cf* Article 69. If intermediaries are used, for example in a Fob or Cif sale, the risk usually passes on loading to the first carrier: see also Article 67 Vienna Convention. For goods in transit, the risk passes upon conclusion of the contract (Article 68). Carrier and transit risk is thus now normally for the buyer. The Convention does *not*, however, deal directly with the other subtleties of the passing of risk, as just summarised, nor with its fluid character, but many of the exceptions and refinements may result under its other provisions.

As the Convention does not consider the question of the passing of title and whether or when it has passed, the passing of risk (Articles 66*ff*) acquires for goods a more particular significance. As the ownership question often takes care of itself (resulting under the applicable domestic laws either from the contract or from any subsequent delivery which will in any event be required as a matter of contract performance) and is mostly settled under the applicable law and not by contract, the passing of the risk is often of more immediate concern to the parties (as is its physical delivery) and can always be determined by contract.

As already mentioned in section 2.1.8 above, in international sales under the Vienna Convention, the concept of non-conformity might itself include the concept of mistake (not itself covered by the Convention) as to the qualities of a sold good (Article 35(2)), so that the non-conformity remedies of the Convention apply throughout, including the rule concerning the passing of risk, rather than domestic notions of mistake or misrepresentation, which, in the absence of the coverage of these subjects in the Convention, might otherwise supplement it under applicable rules of private international law (therefore without regard to Article 7(2)).

2.3.5 Supplementation and Interpretation of the Vienna Convention

Questions concerning matters governed by the Convention must be settled in conformity with the general principles on which the Convention is based and only in the absence thereof pursuant to the national law resulting from the applicable private international law rules. At least so says Article 7(2). These questions are in essence all matters concerning the rights and obligations arising from the sales agreement, *cf* also Article 4 of the Vienna Convention, including the *in personam* remedies and excuses, but notably *not* matters of validity and the proprietary and enforcement aspects of the sales agreement.

This reference to private international law as the last resort was notably absent from the Hague Conventions, *cf* Article 2 of the Hague Sales Convention, which only accepted conflict references in specific cases, Articles 16, 38(4) and 89. The Hague Conventions did also not distinguish between interpretation and supplementation and Article 17 of the Sales Convention required all matters in principle covered by the Convention to be generally decided in conformity with the general principles on which it was based, thus the first part of the Vienna formula on both supplementation and interpretation of the Conventions. This is in accordance with the general civil law approach to codification which assumes completeness in the areas of the law it covers. Gap filling or supplementation then becomes a matter of interpretation. In the area of uniform law, there is the added argument that this approach allows for a liberal interpretation of that law and of its scope. This approach is therefore in essence uniform law friendly and internationalist.

In areas *not* covered by the Hague Sales Conventions, conflict of law notions remained naturally applicable, but it was often felt that even in areas that the Conventions did cover this was unavoidable when its general principles were not sufficiently developed. This became the view of the Vienna Convention, at least in the case of supplementation or gap-filling of the Convention. It undermines the reference to general principles itself, which in a codification sense do not strictly need to be identified. There is here an important shift in the nature of the argument and in the Vienna Convention the codification notion and its uniform law friendly attitude seem abandoned. The general principles to which reference is made in Article 7(2) are now probably only the general principles on which the Convention is based in a narrower, more literal sense.

As regards these general principles, in this narrower, non-interpretational or non-judicial sense, it is indeed often unclear what they are and any party invoking them must then prove them on the basis of its own analysis.[213] They are in that case notably *not* the fundamental principles of the law in the sense of the *ius cogens, customary practices* or the general principles common to most commercial legal systems discussed earlier in chapter 1 as part of the hierarchy of the *lex mercatoria*.

Any impact of the fundamental or more general principles of the *lex mercatoria* is not excluded thereby, however. Their effect depends on the applicability of other sources of the law which the Vienna Convention (and earlier the Hague Conventions) could not regulate, as was more fully explained in chapter 1, section 1.5.2. It is, nevertheless, of interest that Article 7(2) of the Convention does not even make a reference to (international) custom or usage in this connection as one would have expected. This is reserved for the supplementation of the *parties' agreement* (and not of the Convention itself) in Article 9, and then only in a limited manner, see the next section. Even so, the validity of custom or usages is not ultimately governed by the Convention itself either, as recognised in Article 4.

It is in any event more normal to talk about supplementation (and interpretation) in the context of the sales agreement itself, with which the Convention does not generally deal. This *contractual* interpretation and supplementation is only more indirectly covered

---

[213] These principles must be distilled from the underlying approach of the Convention in its material provisions, which is not easy. Honnold, *supra* n. 180, 129*ff.* sees a general principle of reliance (on conduct), e.g on oral representations made after the contract was concluded (Articles 16(2)(b), 29(2) and 47), disclosure (Articles 19(2), 21(2), 26, 39(1), 48(2), 65, 68, 71(3), 72(2), 79(4) and 88), and of mitigation of damages (Articles 77, 85 and 86). He suggest nevertheless caution and restraint in invoking these general principles now that the reference to private international law has been added and that matters of pure interpretation have been separated out in Article 7(1). Case law so far collected by Uncitral and regularly published in their *Case Law on Uncitral Texts* has not shed a great deal of light on these general principles either. Another issue is what the matters governed by the Convention are. Although in general the excluded areas are clear from Article 4, and the coverage as a partial codification is quite limited, it must be assumed that in cases of amplification of the Convention, e.g. in the area of the passing of risk, underlying principles of liability must first be distilled and expanded to cover any gap pursuant to Article 7(2) before a domestic law can be invoked.

by the Convention, as the reference to the rights and duties of the parties in Article 4 makes clear. Articles 8 and 9, limited to the meaning of statements, conduct and usages, are only relevant in that context (see more in particular section 2.3.6 below).

There is here an element of confusion in the Convention between convention and contract interpretation, as there is in the distinction between interpretation and supplementation more generally (even if only of the Convention itself), which cannot be clearly separated, certainly not in the traditional civil law attitude to code interpretation. Again, whatever Article 7(2) of the Convention tries to do in terms of its own supplementation, the norms applicable to international sales and their hierarchy cannot be solely determined by the Vienna Convention itself, even in the areas covered by it.

Thus the failure in Article 7(2) of the Convention to refer (before the rules of private international law) to its own international character (and implicitly to international custom or usage) and to the need for uniformity, as it does in Article 7(1) in the context of interpretation — where therefore (correctly, it is submitted) a distinct legal order is suggested — has no ultimate relevance in this regard and these considerations may intervene anyway, also in Article 7(2). It suggests the relevance of sources of law extraneous to the Convention itself, to which the Convention may be subordinated (both in supplementation and interpretation). In fact, they can only properly be taken care of within the hierarchy of norms of the *lex mercatoria*, as explained in chapter 1, in which the uniform sales laws must also find their place. The omission of a reference to these other norms in the Convention is nevertheless unexpected and leaves it incomplete.[214] This can only be understood from the point of view of a general wariness of codification and general principle in common law, of custom in civil law, and more generally by an unclear view of the international law merchant and its operation among the draftsmen of the Convention.

As compared to the Hague Conventions, the Vienna Convention lost the internationalist approach in the process, but this cannot prevent it from having to operate in the context of all other norms applicable to the international sale of goods. When it comes to supplementation or gap filling, in the internationalist *lex mercatoria* approach, transnationalised notions of good faith also play a role in the supplementation, even if in the Convention only mentioned in Article 7(1) in connection with its interpretation (as distinguished from supplementation). This is so certainly where good faith appeals to fundamental principle but also if appealing only to more common legal principles. In respect of the Convention, the reference to good faith has a distinct meaning and means in effect teleological or normative interpretation (and supplementation) of the text. Thus the literal approach to statutes, treaties and contractual terms, normally adopted by the UK and towards which there may also be a bias in the Vienna Convention (certainly more so than in the Hague Sales Conventions), is somewhat relaxed, also for supplementation.

In the context of supplementation of the Convention, Article 7(2) refers in addition to general principles to the rules of private international law. It was already suggested earlier that this reference to private international law is itself careless and can easily destroy what little progress is made through the Convention in terms of uniformity. It narrows in any event the scope of the uniform law. It may even apply to the terminology used in the Convention. Where the Convention relies on the rules of private international law, as it does also in determining its scope in Article 1.1(b), for international sales cases pending in EU courts this means the rules of the 1980 Rome Convention on the Law Applicable to Contractual Obligations, see section 2.3.7 below.

---

[214] See for the law merchant impact more fully section 2.4 *infra.*

Again, the reference to private international law and therefore to domestic law to supplement the Convention can only be properly understood in the context of the hierarchy of norms within the law merchant or *lex mercatoria* concerning international sales, where it has the lowest rank and its application is discretionary, see also chapter 1, section 1.5.4. In a proper internationalist approach, the appropriate reference for both supplementation and interpretation of the Convention and of the sales agreements concluded under it should have been to the text of the Convention itself, its international character, its general principles, the need for uniformity in its application, and to international practice and custom. The observance of good faith could be added but is in international trade more an issue of interpretation (and supplementation) of the contracts concluded under the Convention.

Only in respect of its interpretation in Article 7(1) does the Convention refer more specifically to the need to consider its international character, to promote uniformity in its application and even to the observance of good faith in international trade. The latter reference did not exist in the Hague Sales Convention either, which also in this aspect relied on its general principles (Article 17).

The references to internationality and uniformity, albeit only in the context of interpretation, suggest at least that the Convention operates in a distinct legal order and that its provisions are autonomous, although this does not prevent consultation of domestic legislation, case law and doctrine by way of guidance. Guidance may of course also be obtained from the history of the Hague and Vienna Conventions and their application and now perhaps also from the EU and Unidroit Contract Principles. The reference to good faith is more complex. Again, it is used in connection with the interpretation of the Convention only, and not directly in connection with the interpretation of the relevant sales agreement, its terms and enforcement. It was a strange compromise but may not make a great deal of difference.[215] As already suggested before, it would appear to confirm a teleological or normative interpretation approach to the Convention itself and therefore a more objective or normative interpretation. It would also cover fundamental legal principle, custom and even general principles common to most modern legal systems and certainly also the own system of the Convention, even though these are concepts more specifically referred to only in connection with supplementation of the Convention under Article 7(2).

Because of the vagaries of the notion of good faith, its true significance under the Convention could, technically speaking, ultimately still remain a question of determination under a national law pursuant to Article 7(2), notwithstanding the reference to the requirement of uniformity in the application of the Convention under Article 7(1) and the reference to 'international trade' which indeed suggest a distinct set of norms. Wildly different good faith notions from domestic law could in this manner be introduced through the conflict rules. This route should not be chosen and good faith should indeed be seen here as a distinct internationalised concept, even if domestic interpretations are still likely to impact because of the general outlook and attitudes of judges groomed in their national systems of law.

It follows that whilst it is likely that the Vienna Convention itself in its approach to interpretation and supplementation maintains much respect for literal meanings and probably even a psychological attitude to contractual intent, borne out in the interpretation provision of Article 8 in respect of statements by the parties, this is not necessarily

---

[215] The reference to good faith interpretation of international conventions may well have its origin in the Vienna Convention on the Law of Treaties of 1969, Article 31, but it concerns here the regime of *agreements* between states, in which connection the reference to good faith seems much more traditional.

the end of the story. It might reflect the prevailing attitudes even in civil law during the formative period of the Convention, which was largely in the first half of the twentieth century, and also common law input. Strictly speaking, the objective or normative approaches to interpretation of both the wording of the Convention and the sale contract were probably never substantially considered. However, it must be seen as implicit in the good faith interpretation provision that came in with the Vienna Convention,[216] which may otherwise have narrowed the interpretational freedoms inherent in the language of the Hague Conventions. In this respect, the Vienna Convention may yet show some balance, even if it moved in a confusing way with a confusing terminology. However, it took a great step backwards when reducing the impact of general principles and relying on private international law, be it only within its (undefined) concept of supplementation. Again, putting the uniform law in its place in the *lex mercatoria* hierarchy of norms is here the proper answer.

The formula of Article 7 of the Vienna Convention may (unfortunately) be found in all Uncitral Conventions. It may also be found in the European Contract Principles (Article 1.106). It is even in the Unidroit Leasing and Factoring Conventions, where the reference to good faith may be entirely inappropriate as they also cover proprietary matters. It is not, however, the approach of the Unidroit Principles (Article 1.6), which revert here to the approach of the Hague Sales Conventions and seem therefore more favourably disposed towards internationalisation. Both sets of Contract Principles also contain elaborate sections on the interpretation of contracts, see section 1.6.3 above.

2.3.6 The Interpretation of International Sales Contracts under the Vienna Convention: Meaning of Conduct and Custom

In the previous section it was explained that the Vienna Convention does not deal in any general manner with the interpretation (and supplementation) of the sales contracts governed by it in Article 7. It only deals with interpretation and supplementation of the Convention itself. The contractual interpretation and supplementation is an issue that in principle seems to be covered by the Convention, however, in view of the reference in Article 4 to the rights and obligations of the parties arising from the sales contracts. The coverage of these rights and obligations by the Convention must imply interpretation and supplementation, if at all distinguishable. This is supported by the fact that in Articles 8 and 9 there follow more precise interpretation rules, albeit only limited to parties' statements and conduct and to the impact of usages.

There is in this context no reference to good faith and the interpretation rules must still be found through the supplementation rule of Article 7(2) with its reference to the general principles on which the Convention is based, which are few in this connection, and to the law applicable by virtue of private international law. It is likely to introduce here major variations by its indirect reference to national notions of gap filling and within that context to good faith and usages. With respect to the interpretation and supplementation of the Convention itself this might be avoided, as discussed in the previous section, by virtue of its place within the *lex mercatoria* hierarchy of norms or on the basis even of its own provisions. However, there could be more doubt with respect to the contractual interpretation and supplementation, although the *lex mercatoria* should equally apply to them.

---

[216] See for the English literal and purposive approaches to statutory interpretation, chapter 1, s 1.2.9.

Article 8 contains a distinct contract interpretation provision of some sort. Under it, the parties' statements and conduct are to be interpreted according to their true intent, at least to the extent that the other party knew or could not have been unaware of what it was. It ties interpretation principally to psychological intent and the parties' will, but if it cannot be determined whether the other party knew or could have known of the true intent, it allows a reasonable understanding. In determining intent or reasonable understanding in this context, due consideration must be given to all *relevant* circumstances of the case including the negotiations, practices and usages and any subsequent conduct of the parties, taking into account perhaps also the internationality and commerciality of the transaction and the professionality of the parties.

For a start, it is clear that Article 8 does do away with the common law 'parole evidence rule' which did not allow any contradictory contemporary or earlier evidence against any writing intended by the parties as a final expression of their agreement, *cf* also Section 2–202 UCC and section 1.2.6 above. A similar rule also exists in France for non-commercial contracts in excess of 50 francs: see Article 1341 Cc. Any express statement, however, that earlier evidence is not to be used would naturally be upheld under Article 6.

Article 9 deals with usages in terms of contract interpretation. It has been mentioned before that the Convention remains ambivalent on the issue of custom, much more so than Article 9 of the earlier Hague Sales Convention, as implicitly accepted in its Article 4. Sensitivity to accepted practices and custom was earlier identified as being particularly important in international trade, see chapter 1, section 1.5.2. Much international trade law developed on the basis of it. It is a major cornerstone of the notion and operation of the *lex mercatoria*. Strictly speaking, the Vienna Convention avoids any reference to custom and uses the terms 'usages' and 'practices' instead (Articles 4, 8 and 9). This is in the civil law tradition of suspicion of custom as an independent source of law. Thus, according to Article 9(1), the parties are bound by any usage to which they have agreed and by any practices which they have established between themselves. This is simply an extension of the contract and intent principles at the expense of custom as an own source of law. It implies a subjective approach to custom.

Article 9(2) tries to soften some of the impact by accepting as an implied condition all usages of which the parties knew or ought to have known and which in international trade are widely known or regularly observed (but not merely widely operative) between the parties to contracts of the type involved in the particular trade concerned. The Unidroit Principles maintain only the latter requirement (Article 1.8), come as such closer to Article 9(2) of the Hague Sales Convention, and do not therefore require that the usuages were known or should have been known by the parties concerned, as long as they are widely known and regularly observed. The Unidroit Principles are thus somewhat less restrictive (although they introduce a reasonableness test). Article 1.105(2) of the European Principles may even go a little further in stating that parties are bound by any usage which would be considered generally applicable by persons in the same position as the parties (also subject to a reasonableness test).

Article 9 of the Vienna Convention was meant to protect unsuspecting parties, although the need for it appears less obvious in the professional sphere in which international sales as defined in the Convention usually operate. As already submitted several times before, it is not strictly speaking possible for the Convention to be entirely conclusive in this matter as the force of international usages and practices may derive from other sources or from custom itself. This is in fact implicitly recognised in Article 4(a) which excludes the matter of validity of any usage from the scope of the Convention.

The exclusion of usages in Article 4 has been explained as leaving the determination of this issue (as one not covered by the Convention and therefore not subject to its Article 7(2) on supplementation) to applicable domestic law including the validity of these usages itself. It follows that all usages would be seen as essentially a domestic law phenomenon and that considerations of domestic public policy (or good faith like in the Netherlands) may prevail over them.

To the extent custom is viewed as a contractual term, as it essentially is in the Vienna Convention, rather than objective law, local public order considerations could all the more be able to override it. Where, however, it is agreed that the force of usage cannot be fully determined by the Convention itself, nor indeed the impact of the *lex mercatoria* more generally, it is likely that there is not only custom outside Article 9 but also that this custom could be international. This could be so especially where within the context of the *lex mercatoria*, it impacts on international sales. It would as such only be subject to public policy imperatives operating in the international legal order in which there are few and which, if they exist, are more likely to be expressed in fundamental (mandatory) *international* legal principle or public order requirement.

2.3.7 Supplementation of the Vienna Convention: Private International Law and the Rome Convention on the Law Applicable to Contractual Obligations

As mentioned before, in international sales, the 1980 EU Rome Convention on the Law Applicable to Contractual Obligations must, now the Vienna Convention is becoming widely accepted, increasingly be seen as a sequel to it within the EU in areas the law of the sale of goods the Vienna Convention does not cover (Article 4) or as a matter of supplementation or gap-filling even in those aspects that it does cover, but in that case only after the general principles on which the Convention is based have been considered (Article 7(2)). It should be realised of course that the scope of the Rome Convention is much wider than sales and embraces all situations where judges in the EU are confronted with a choice between the contractual obligations laws of different countries, whichever (also if non-EU).

The Rome Convention may also play a preliminary function in the context of the Vienna Convention in that under Article 1(1)(b) of the latter, its applicability may result from choice of law rules pointing to the law of a Contracting State. Under the European Principles, but not the Unidroit Principles, it also may play a role in the supplementation of these Principles (Article 1.106).

However, as noted in chapter 1, section 1.5.4 above, it should always be borne in mind that the application of both the Vienna Convention and the Rome Convention must be seen in the context of the application of the *lex mercatoria* as a whole with its own hierarchy of norms in which fundamental principle, international custom, uniform law, and common legal notions are likely to precede the search for a domestic law through conflicts rules, see for a summary also section 2.4 below.

The Rome Convention which dates from 1980, coincidentally from the same year as the Vienna Convention, is now ratified by all older EU Member States but operates for a period of ten years only, although it is renewed tacitly for five year periods thereafter if there has been no denunciation (Article 30). Although often viewed as an EU Convention, this is strictly speaking not the case as it is not based on the EEC founding treaty. Even though concluded between Member States, only a limited number needed to ratify for the Convention to become effective. New EU Members need not accede to the Convention, although in 1980 the view was expressed in a Joint Declaration that they should be encouraged to do so.

This situation is very different from the (unrelated) Brussels Convention of 1968 on Jurisdiction and Enforcement of Judgments in Civil and Commercial Matters which was based on Article 220 of the EEC Treaty and is in force between all Members for an unlimited duration and must be accepted by any new Members (and since 2002 replaced by an EU Regulation to the same effect). The consequence of the Rome Convention not being based on the EEC Treaty is that conflicts rules more directly based thereon prevail (Article 20). So far, they only exist in the area of insurance under the Insurance Directives, but there is no conflict here as the Rome Convention does not apply in insurance matters when the risk is in the EU. At one stage, EU private international law rules were also contemplated in the area of employment which could have caused a more acute conflict.[217]

Another consequence of the Rome Convention not being an EC Convention is that matters of interpretation are not referable to the European Court of Justice in Luxembourg (in fact even the Brussels Convention only made this possible by a special Protocol of 1971). Although two Protocols to the Rome Convention were signed in 1988 to allow an appeal from the highest courts in each Member State to the European Court in order to obtain the necessary prejudicial decisions in interpretation matters (without a duty as there is in the 1971 Protocol), ratification by all parties seems unlikely as some, like the UK, do not see interpretation of the Convention as a European Court matter.

The Convention according to Article 21 does not prejudice any other conflicts conventions to which Contracting States were already or may become a party. In the latter case consultation with the other Contracting States is necessary, however (Article 24). The most important examples are likely to be in the Hague Private International Law Conventions like those on the Law Applicable to the International Sale of Goods of 1955 and its successor of 1986 (not to be confused with the Hague Uniform Sales laws of 1964). One could also think of the Hague Conventions on the Law Applicable to Agency of 1978 and on the Law Applicable to Trusts and their Recognition of 1985. However, the Rome Convention itself excludes the coverage of agency and trusts.

The applicability of the Rome Convention is dependent on a forum in a Contracting State being faced with a choice between the laws of different countries which need not be EU States (Article 1), although the Convention does not spell out when this may legitimately be the case. It is left to the forum seised to decide. The Convention may apply even within one country with different legal systems like the UK.

It is important to realise from the way the Rome Convention is structured that it does not apply by virtue of the law of a Member State being made applicable to the underlying contract. For example if English law is made applicable to a contract between two Swiss parties, the conflicts rules of the Convention do not automatically apply (as Article 15, which excludes *renvoi*, confirms). Its application depends on a case subsequently being brought in a Member State. It is even doubtful whether the Convention would apply in an international arbitration with its seat in a Member State as an international arbitration is often thought subject to its own conflicts rules which are not necessarily derived from the place of the tribunal. That would not prevent the application of the rules of the Convention as a model or as general principles of conflicts laws which may be thought to apply in international cases but that would not then be a consequence of the applicability of the Convention itself.

---

[217] Others have appeared in the 1998 Settlement Finality Directive (Article 9(2)), 98/26/EC [1998] OJ L166 and the 2002 Financial Collateral Directive (2002/47/EC, OJ L168) with respect to security interests in securities that are recorded in a book entry system, and in the 2000 Directive combating late payment in commercial transactions (Article 4, 2000/35/EC, OJ L200) with respect to reservations of title. All are, however in the proprietary area and therefore out of the scope of the Rome Convention.

The Rome Convention does not apply in status matters, family matters (relationship and property aspects), negotiable instruments, typical company matters (like creation, capacity, organisation and winding-up), arbitration, agency and trust matters and in matters of evidence and procedure (Article 1(2)). Again, the *lex fori* seems to determine the true meaning of these exceptions. Proprietary matters are not covered by the Rome Convention, even if they follow from a contractual disposition as in the case of sales. This also appears to apply to assignments, although Article 12, especially in its second paragraph, has left some doubt in the matter, see more in particular chapter 5, section 2.3.6. Also Article 10(1)(c) suggests that the consequences of any breach are covered by the law resulting as applicable under the Convention but, in the case of a sale or exchange, that would be unlikely in the proprietary effects of an avoidance of the contract or in any enforcement aspects.

There is a special rule for insurance in that the Rome Convention does apply to reinsurance but not to ordinary insurance policies if the risk covered is located in a Member State.[218] If the risk is outside the EU the policy may indicate the applicable law subject always to an appreciation of the foreign mandatory rules (if any) under Article 7 of the Rome Convention, especially in consumer cases when there is the added protection of Article 5.[219]

2.3.8 The Main Rules of the Rome Convention on the Law Applicable to Contractual Obligations

There are two basic rules in the Rome Convention. *First* there is the law chosen by the parties, for the whole or part of the contract (Article 3). This choice must be expressed or appear with reasonable certainty from the terms of the contract or the circumstances and can thus not be purely implied as is possible under German conflicts law. The Convention does not limit this contractual choice of law to situations at the disposition of the parties and provides only that if all the elements relevant to the situation at the time of choice are connected with one country, the contractual choice of law may not prejudice the application of the mandatory rules of that country (Article 3(3)). What is to be considered mandatory in this regard remains undefined. There are bound to be considerable differences of view (even within the country concerned) on this point and on the true relevance of such rules in international cases.

The *second* rule is that in the absence of a contractual choice of law clause, the law of the country with the closest connection to the contract applies and Article 4 allows in this respect different applicable laws for severable parts of the contract. There is a rebuttable presumption that the law with the closest connection is the law of the place of the residence of the party which must perform the most characteristic obligation under

---

[218] Each judge must use his own internal law to determine where the risk is located: Article 1(3). The Second EU Non-Life Directive of 1988 (Article 7) and the Second Life Directive of 1990 (Article 4), maintain distinct systems when the risk is within the EU. They are inspired by respect for the mandatory contract rules of the Member States where the risk is situated for (mass) non-life policies and of the Member States of the commitment for life policies. These rules are explicitly not harmonised so as to protect the beneficiaries of mass non-life and life policies under their own law. The importance of the conflicts rules of the Insurance Directives is that the insurance policy may set aside these rules only if the applicable law allows it, which for this purpose is itself tied to the habitual residence of the beneficiary. If there is no chosen law in the policy, it is this law which is in any event presumed to apply. It means that only insurance products allowed in the country of the beneficiary may be sold into that country and are to be structured in accordance with that law. From this point of view there is no free circulation of insurance products even though the rendering of insurance services has been liberated in the EU.

[219] If there is no such choice of law, the Rome Convention relies, under its general rule of the characteristic obligations, on the law of the place of the insurer rather than of the place of the risk which is the more traditional approach. There is no rule for a situation in which the policy covers risks in and outside the EU at the same time, e.g. in the case of a fire insurance in respect of premises of a single party insured in the USA and the UK.

the contract (or, if severable, under the part of the contract in question), provided that this characteristic obligation can be determined (Article 4(2) and (5)). The residence in this sense is the habitual one for individuals and the place of the central administration for bodies corporate, except if the contract is entered into in the course of that party's trade or profession, when residence for this purpose is connected to the principal place of business of the party performing the characteristic obligation (Article 4(2)).

Clearly, the reference to the characteristic obligation itself introduces an aspect of considerable uncertainty. Article 4(3) and (4) maintains some special rules in matters of real estate and the carriage of goods, which, like the earlier presumption, is always subject to be disregarded if it appears from the circumstances as a whole that the contract is more closely connected with another country (Article 4(5)). In real estate matters the closest connection is presumed to be with the country where the property is located. For the carriage of goods the closest connection is presumed to be with the country of the carrier, at least if this is also the country of the place of loading or discharge or of the principal place of business of the consignor (shipper). No rule is given if none of these combinations obtains and it may well be that in that case Article 4(1) and (2) apply before Article 4(5).

Special rules also apply to consumer contracts (Article 5), which are contracts regarding the supply of goods or products to a person outside his trade or profession, *cf.* also Article 2(a) of the Vienna Convention and Article 13 of the 1968 EC Convention on Jurisdiction and the Enforcement of Judgments in Civil and Commercial Matters. The consumer will retain the protection of the mandatory rules of the country of his habitual residence in the case of cold-calling by the (foreign) seller in that country or when the latter induces the consumer to travel to his own for the purpose of making him buy. It means that if a consumer knowingly concludes a contract outside his own country without any special inducement by the seller, he loses the protection of his own mandatory rules. A contractual choice of law is not effective against these principles, nor is the general rule referring to the law of the closest connection (Article 5(2) and (3)).

For individual employment contracts, the law of the country in which the employee habitually carries out his work is believed to be the proper one and a contractual choice of law cannot be effective against the mandatory rules of the country protecting him either (Article 6). It will normally lead to applicability of the law of the place of residence of the employee or alternatively to that of the place where he was engaged if he does not habitually carry out his work in any one country, *cf* also Articles 5(1) and 17 in fine EEX for the assumption of jurisdiction in employment matters.[220]

One may thus see that through contractual choice of law, through the references to the circumstances as a whole in determining the applicable law under Article 4, and through the special protections for consumers and employees, the traditional conflicts approach of hard and fast rules determining the applicability of a legal system regardless of effect and consequence is in a number of aspects amended, although the basic concepts largely remain the same and national law is still assumed to provide an answer to all internationalised contract problems, always subject to the general escape of public policy, provided there is manifest incompatibility with the law resulting under the Convention, *cf.* Article 16. It introduces a subjective element which is in fact also the case wherever rebuttable presumptions are now used in the Convention. See for the discussion of the broader aspects of the conflicts and transnational approaches more in particular chapter 1, section 2.2.1.

---

[220] See for a comment also CGJ Morse, "Consumer Contracts, Employment Contracts and the Rome Convention" 41(1992) *International and Comparative Law Quarterly* 1.

There are a number of specific references to mandatory rules in the Convention: see Articles 3(3), 5(2), 6(3) and 9(6). Article 7(1) contains a special rule on the treatment of a specific type of mandatory rule which could be defined as governmental intervention in the law formation process which cannot be displaced by parties subject to this intervention, even by choosing another law. When application of the law of one country results under the Convention, effect may be given (this is thus discretionary) to this type of mandatory rule of another with which the situation has a close connection in so far as these rules must be applied to the contract under the laws of this latter country. This does not prevent there being varying views in that country itself on the mandatory nature of these laws. The appropriateness of applying them in international situations is here a different matter altogether and may depend also on proportionality and legitimacy of *force majeure* seen from an international perspective.

Article 7(1) only states that regard must be had to the nature and purpose of these rules and to the consequences of their application or non-application. Ratifying states may opt out of this clause (Article 22) as the UK and Germany have done. It nevertheless leaves the problem of what to do with foreign mandatory rules asserted in the case. Note, however, that even under Article 7(1) as now drafted, the interests of other parties and countries are not necessarily considered nor is the question whether the foreign rule, internationally speaking, might be exorbitant in the light of more general basic principles. The Convention remains here also purely rule-oriented. There is no balancing of different governmental interests when conflicting.

These matters are also not considered under Article 7(2) which allows the forum to apply its own mandatory rules at all times and in all circumstances apparently no matter whether the case in hand has any connection with them. The language of Article 3(3) that all elements of the case must be connected with the country of the forum is not repeated. No special interest of the forum state is apparently required at all for the application of its rules.

As mentioned above, the application of the rules of any other country may always be refused on the basis of public policy (Article 16) if there is manifest incompatibility. In fact, it is rare for courts to give precedence to foreign mandatory rules. This facility was in modern times particularly formulated in the Netherlands.[221] It suggested a bilateralism which even in the Netherlands in practice did not result in much precedence being given to foreign mandatory rules.[222] There is apparently a clear bias for a system not to be unduly disrupted by foreign political imperatives and for mandatory rules of the forum always to prevail. It underlines the importance of the rules of jurisdiction and of any obligatory recognition and enforcement of the ensuing judgment elsewhere, as under the EU Brussels Convention of 1968, now superseded by the Regulation of 2002.

In this connection, the wider problems associated with a contractual choice of law must also be considered. First, in some countries like France there is still a need for some contact between the law chosen and the contract, a concern on the whole more common in the case of a contractual choice of jurisdiction. In any event, the legal aspect concerned must be at the free disposition of the parties, and thus be purely directory.

Indeed, the facility to choose the applicable law is traditionally marred by the operation of mandatory rules, either of the law one attempts to opt out of or of the law one opts into, see chapter 1, sections 2.2.6, 2.2.7 and 2.2.8. Under a contractual choice of law clause, there

---

[221] See the *Alnati* case, HR, 13 May 1966 [1967] NJ 3 in which it was said that 'in respect of a contract … it is possible that a foreign state has such an interest in the application of its own mandatory rules … that Dutch courts must consider this interest and may have to give precedence to such rules and ignore the law chosen by the parties in their contract'.

[222] see also *Arnhold Karberg & Co. v Blythe, Green, Jourdain & Co* [1915] 2 KB 379, 388.

is bound to remain uncertainty on both accounts, and it is often unclear what the choice of law intends or can achieve in this respect and what its true effect may be, the more so as the definition and intended impact of national mandatory rules may itself be uncertain and vary from situation to situation. Within one country 'ordre public' rules, and modern administrative provisions are normally considered absolutely mandatory, but this is less clear, for example, in property and conveyancing law, status, capacity and other family law matters, company law, bankruptcy and attachments, prescription or procedural laws and concepts. Consequently, it is not always clear either which of these are at the free disposition of the parties and when they may be discarded by consent. The opting-in equally presents uncertainties. It is, nevertheless, common to establish the contractual legal framework through a choice of law clause, notably with regard to formation (offer and acceptance) and validity (consensus and its defects), all matters that cannot be covered in the contract itself and are therefore in that sense not at the free disposition of the parties either.

This all seems quite normal, yet foreigners opting for the application of English law to their contract may not mean to opt for the English rules of consideration or exemption (exoneration) clauses or other instances of investors or consumer protection or generally into any rule deeming the contract itself void or against public policy an health, safety a environmental founds unless there are other contacts with the UK, as application of such rules could never have been in the contemplation of the professional parties as between them. It was already mooted before that international contracts, the restrictions flowing from the consideration requirement may have lapsed altogether. Under the circumstances, a contractual election of English law may also not include the parole evidence rule. One could argue in this connection that the consideration and parole evidence rules have certainly no mandatory impact as part of a chosen contract law, if the case itself has no other major contacts with the law so chosen, see also the discussion in section 1.2.6 above.

In relation to the Vienna Convention, the opting for the law of a non-contracting State would imply the exclusion of the Convention even if both parties came from Contracting States. Opting into the law of a Contracting State implies on the other hand the application of the Convention even in respect of parties from non-contracting States and also of the rules of such States in areas not covered by the Convention, assuming always that such can be considered the intent of the parties and it cannot go further than what makes sense in the circumstances.

A contractual choice of law normally does not have an effect on the proprietary objectives or consequences of a contract. Thus in a sales contract, it is unlikely to determine the law under which the title will transfer. Here the *lex situs* of the asset acquires mandatory overtones. Yet especially in financial instruments like eurobonds the choice of law by issuers made and reflected on the document is sometimes thought also to govern this aspect, the mode of transfer of ownership, protection of *bona fide* purchasers, and the types of security interests that can be created in them and the formalities to be observed in this connection, although the final word is here more likely to be with custom or market practices, see also chapter 1, section 3.2.1.

It is true that the lack of clarity as to the precise whereabouts of these instruments may make the *lex situs* notion unworkable (as it may be in the case of transient assets like ships and aeroplanes). The consequence is thus rather the application of trans-national concepts instead of those of a chosen domestic legal system. Because of their third party impact, proprietary rights seem to need an objective basis in law, which is unlikely to be provided by the choice of parties to a sales contract or of issuers of securities. Modern registration systems creating security entitlements, may deem the *situs* for these purposes to be at the place of the enlargements, see also chapter 4, 3.2.2.

Although in the absence of a contractual choice of law rule, the Rome Convention is unlikely to apply in the proprietary aspects of international transactions as it only seeks out the law applicable to contractual obligations, especially in the case of assignments (Article 11), there is much different opinion and here again contractual freedom to appoint the relevant property law is often advocated, see chapter 5, section 2.3.6.

The contractual choice of law is also not normally meant to include the private international law rules of the law of the country so chosen, *cf* also Article 15 of the Rome Convention. International arbitrations have no *lex fori per se* and are not normally thought to be bound by any particular conflicts rule, no matter what law is chosen by the parties to cover the contract or in which country the panel sits. As already mentioned in the previous section this also applies to the rules of the Rome Convention which may, however, still serve as a model.

The ultimate danger is of course that the selection of a domestic law may be entirely unsuitable or does not lead to any solution at all, not only in proprietary matters if at variance with the *lex situs*. In terms of the *lex mercatoria*, the domestic law so chosen would, however, like any other domestic law resulting from conflicts rules, come low in the hierarchy of norms, see chapter 1, section 1.4.4, so that its possible harm would be limited. Where in international cases the *lex mercatoria* concept may increasingly be relied upon, at least in international commercial arbitrations, a good case may be made for not making any domestic law applicable at all. It could easily be a confusing and disturbing factor.

Another traditional complication of a contractual choice of law is the treatment of any changes in the law so chosen. If such changes signify the normal progression in that law, they may apply, but if there is a clear deviation of the chosen pattern, the changes in the directory rules of the legal system made applicable might not.

2.3.9 The Vienna Convention and the Different Trade Terms in International Sales

As mentioned before, important derogation from the Vienna Convention (or even its total exclusion) and also from national sales law where applicable (leaving aside the problem of the application of national mandatory rules, for example in currency and money transfer matters or in trade restrictions), may result from contract or established trade practices (Articles 6 and 9). They may also supplement the regime of the Vienna Convention and any other applicable sales law.

Wherever such terms derogate or supplement, the Convention and its supplementation provision of Article 7(2) no longer apply, for example under trade terms in the area of the passing of risk (Articles 66*ff*). There are in particular some established trade terms in this respect. Of these, the Fob (free on board port of shipment or loading), F&S (free alongside), Cif (cost insurance freight port of destination or unloading) and C&F (cost and freight) are the most important.

What they all have in common is that they divide the responsibilities for the handling of the goods and allocate certain costs and risks between seller and buyer, differently according to the means of transportation used and according to the stage of the transfer process. Thus, at one end of the spectrum is the term 'ex works' under which the only responsibility of the seller is to hand over the goods to the buyer or his agent at his own place of business, whilst all risks and expenses connected with the goods and their handling are thereafter for the account of the buyer who must also get himself properly organised. At the other end is the term 'free delivered' under which the seller must make and pay for all arrangements necessary to get the goods to the buyer and has all the risks connected with the goods and their transportation in the meantime.

The Fob (free on board) term dates from the early eighteenth century and the Cif (cost, insurance, freight) term from the late eighteenth century, each the product of their own situation: the Fob term was logical when the buyer or his agent sailed with the ship or sent his own and concluded sales contracts on the way and supervised the loading of the goods. Even now it means that the buyer nominates the ship and makes all necessary arrangements for transportation and insurance. The Cif condition on the other hand resulted when regular shipping lines were established and the buyer either depended on the seller to make the necessary transportation arrangement or, more likely, the seller availed himself of the opportunity to ship his own goods before any sale and received a bill of lading which he could negotiate later once a proper buyer was found. This gave him a great advantage as he could thus sell his goods Cif, whilst they were already sailing or even upon their arrival, directly in the international markets, thus eliminating his dependence on the visiting buyer. It is now by far the most important trade term.

Even where goods are already sold, the Cif term means that the seller is still in charge of the transportation and insurance arrangements. It is often thought that the Fob term is appropriate both in purely domestic and international sales and does not produce a bill of lading, whilst the Cif term always denotes an export transaction with carriage to an overseas destination and always produces a bill of lading. But there may also be a bill of lading under Fob terms. The difference is that under the Fob term the seller will collect it upon loading as receipt on behalf of the buyer, who is in charge of the transportation arrangements. He must as soon as possible send it to the buyer and is here subject to the latter's instruction. Under the Cif term, the seller collects the bill for himself and is under a duty to tender the documents to the buyer only as part of the sale. This buyer may in any event emerge later. In either case, the handing over of the documents may be affected and delayed as part of the payment arrangements, see more in particular section 2.2.4 above which is likely also to affect the transfer of title in the underlying goods especially relevant in countries like France and England, where in a sale of goods title normally passes upon the conclusion of the sales agreement. In these countries, use of Fob or Cif terms may itself indicate postponement and make the transfer dependent on the handing over of the bill of lading.

There is a modern variant of the Fob term under which the seller undertakes to arrange the shipment on the buyer's behalf and at his cost. In fact, this variant is so widely used that it is sometimes thought to be the more normal Fob arrangement. Under it, it remains in essence the buyer's duty, however, to nominate the vessel, but the seller may be given full powers to do so as an agent acting for the buyer whilst providing additional services to the buyer in terms of collecting the shipping documents and putting these at the buyer's disposal. As he will not pay for the freight, the bill of lading will reflect this and state 'freight collect' (instead of the more usual 'freight paid' under Cif).

The sales contract will specify these services as it is clear that they will not result from the use of the Fob trade term itself. This type of Fob deal is particularly common in established relationships, where it is often standard practice, but less prudent in incidental arrangements as the seller/debtor remains in possession of the shipping documents and remains therefore in a very strong position *vis-à-vis* his buyer, especially if a bearer bill of lading is issued which is a negotiable document of title.

A Cif sale is sometimes considered a sale of documents rather than a sale of the underlying goods.[223] Tendering documents is then the essential duty of the seller. If so

---

[223] *Arnhold Karberg & Co v Blythe, Green, Jourdain & Co* [1915] 2 KB 379, 388.

tendered (together with the insurance policy and invoice), the buyer must pay (if it was agreed to take place upon tendering), regardless of the situation concerning the underlying goods. They may even be lost or may never have been properly loaded. For the payment obligation to mature upon the tender of the bill of lading, the bill of lading itself should be an on-board bill of lading, see also chapter 4, section 2.1.1. It means that the goods must have passed the ship's rail and mere delivery of the goods by the seller at a dock warehouse of the carrier or even at its rail is not sufficient for this type of bill of lading to be issued. However, even with an on-board bill, the goods if shipped in bulk may not yet have been apportioned to the contract, so that title in them cannot strictly speaking pass despite the existence of a negotiable bill of lading. This may give rise to all kind of complications and actions but it does not excuse the buyer from payment upon the tendering of the documents.

In this arrangement, the documents may be rejected upon tendering if inaccurate on their face (especially relevant under letters of credit). This right must be clearly distinguished from the right to reject the goods, which is unconnected and can only be exercised after landing, claiming and examining them when they are found not to be in conformity with the contract. If the bill is used to obtain early payment, for example upon tendering of the documents, any rejection of the goods later may of course still give rise to an adjustment of the sales price and reimbursements but does not affect the original payment and its validity itself.

In this connection, the situation concerning the transfer of title, although *not* covered by the trade terms themselves, is of interest especially in systems which require delivery for title transfer. The reason for the trade terms not traditionally covering the title and its transfer is the considerable differences in the various laws on when title may pass and the mandatory rules in this respect in many legal systems. In systems passing title upon the mere conclusion of the sales agreement (unless postponed), like the English and French, title passes immediately as we saw. In systems that require delivery for title transfer, like the German and Dutch, the seller must as a minimum put the goods at the disposal of the carrier, see for this system chapter 4, section 2.1.3.

Under a Fob clause, it is common to view the carrier as the agent for the buyer who nominated the vessel and the title passes in systems requiring delivery therefore normally at the ship's rail. If a bill of lading is also issued, title may only pass upon the handing over off the bill, relevant especially if used in the context of a letter of credit. Under a Cif clause, it is also conceivable to view the carrier as an agent for the buyer, even though the buyer strictly speaking does not nominate the vessel and may not yet exist. In this approach, the delivery to the buyer may also be considered to have taken place at the ship's rail, which may complete the title transfer at the same time, provided always that the goods are identifiable (the more likely civil law approach) or have been properly appropriated to the contract (the more likely common law approach). It is, however, more likely that under a Cif sale, title is considered passed only if the documents have been tendered to the buyer and, upon any negotiation of the bill, title will only be considered to have passed further when the bill is handed over (plus endorsement if to order). Intent acquires here a special role.

Indeed in systems in which title transfers upon the mere conclusion of the sales agreement, the bill of lading only has significance if the title transfer is deemed to be postponed until tendering or delivering the bill of lading and this then depends entirely on the intent of the original parties. Under Fob and Cif terms, this intent may, however, be deemed implied, at least if the bill of lading is intended also to play a role in payment protection schemes. Otherwise, especially under Fob terms, the title is usually considered passed when the goods pass the ship's rail, as we saw. This may even be the case in France under the Cif term, although in England the tendering of the documents seems to be the moment, see also chapter 4, section 2.1.4.

Further delay will result, however, if the underlying goods have not yet been identified or set aside to the contract or if title in them has been reserved pending payment, no matter the tendering, delivering or negotiating of the bill of lading. If the goods have not yet been sold, but are simply shipped by the owner with a view to a later sale, the seller/shipper naturally remains the owner and also has the bill of lading. That sale may still be Cif (and this is normal for shipped goods) even though the loading has already taken place (on a ship nominated and paid for by the seller as in an ordinary Cif sale). It is also common to on-sell goods Cif even though in that case shipped by a previous seller who paid for the transportation.

As regards the *passing of risk*, the trade terms tend to be specific on the subject and especially in Fob and Cif terms the passing of the risk always takes place at the moment the goods pass the ship's rail and is thus entirely independent from the transfer of title or of legal possession. Thus the physical act terminating the seller's control of the goods constitutes at the same time the moment the risk in the goods passes: see for the concept of the passing of risk further section 2.1.9 above. If under a Cif contract the sale happens after the goods are already afloat, the passing of risk will be *retroactive* to the moment of loading.

2.3.10 The Incoterms, Their Status and Relation to the UCC and Vienna Convention

In Europe, the most important trade terms like the Fob and Cif terms have been compiled and restated by the International Chamber of Commerce since 1936, in the so-called Incoterms, the last edition being of 1 January 2000. They also cover a considerable number of other trade terms like 'ex works', 'free on rail', 'free on truck', 'arrival or ex ship', 'ex quay', 'delivered at frontier' or 'delivered duty paid' (DDP), etc. The Incoterms are sometimes still thought not by themselves to have the force of law. They may, however, have acquired the status of industry custom but not necessarily in all circumstances and detail, as may be seen shortly. At an early stage it was proposed to add them to the Hague Sales Conventions but it was not pursued. In the USA the Fob, Fas,Cif, C&F and 'free delivery, ex ship' terms have been codified under domestic law in Article 2 UCC, but not the others. The trade terms are seldom codified in other domestic laws.

One has to be aware of some differences between the USA and European practices in this field, especially relevant for the Fob term which in the USA allows reference to a destination rather then to a port of loading, a practice now also seen in Europe, for example where pipelines are used, and then implies free delivery to the designated destination point, although the risk may pass sooner.

As already mentioned, in essence these terms all aim at a certain division of labour and costs in terms of physical delivery, transportation and insurance. They also bear on the place of the transfer of risk (normally at the port of loading) and insist on notice (including procurement of the invoice), require the parties to keep each other properly advised on what is happening and, under the Cif terms, demand tender of a transportation document (bill of lading) and insurance policy to the buyer.

It is not uncommon in this connection to refer to 'C' terms, 'F' terms and 'D' terms: in 'C' or 'F' terms, risk passes at loading, in 'D' terms (like DDP) upon unloading, whilst the difference between 'C' and 'F' terms is in the liability for the cost of transport and insurance. Also under the Incoterms, the proprietary consequences remain an area for the applicable national law, if not of some advanced notion of the *lex mercatoria*, under which one must normally assume that after delivery to the ship's rail, the buyer is owner, the carrier his agent and the possession of the bill of lading the proof. It acquires then the status of transnational paper operating under its own rules, just as negotiable instruments of title largely do.

Whenever specifically referred to in a contract, the Incoterms are automatically incorporated and may then derogate from the Vienna Convention or from national law where otherwise applicable. But it is still necessary in this respect to determine their precise meaning where they lack detail. This may be decided on the basis of general principles or may itself entail references to a national law under the private international law reference of Article 7(2) of the Vienna Convention. Under the Hague Sales Convention, Article 9(3), the interpretation of terms was to conform to their usual meaning in the trade concerned. This is now less clear as this particular sub-section was not retained in the Vienna Convention.

This is all the more problematic where the Incoterms have not been made explicitly applicable to the contract. The question has arisen whether in this context the Incoterms, if not expressly made applicable to Fob and Cif references, at least in Europe, may be deemed to apply customarily. The Incoterms themselves (*cf* their 1990 Foreword) suggest that they must be included in the contract to apply, but this cannot be decisive as to their status as custom or usage. As already discussed in section 2.3.6 above, the Vienna Convention in Article 9 requires that a usage is, or ought to have been, known to the parties and must also be widely known in the trade concerned. Even though this can also not be ultimately decisive as to the true impact of international custom, it may well apply to the Incoterms in the *commodity* trade in Europe. In any event, one may expect the courts and commercial arbitrators to look to the Incoterms for lack of any better guide when the relevant sales terms are used in a contract without definition or reference to the Incoterms, even if they are not considered custom.

As a minimum, the Incoterms may thus have some explanatory, supporting or pursuasive effect and serve as guides, especially when there is no substantial statutory or case law explaining these trade terms in the jurisdiction identified by the conflicts rules as providing the applicable national law. Especially in the UK such a body of case law exists but that remains exceptional.[224] Even then, it is likely that the (English) courts will have regard to the need for uniformity in the interpretation of these terms and domestic precedent should not determine all issues, which in the UK is also the approach taken to the interpretation of the Hague (Visby) Rules.[225] Where the law of a state of the USA would be applicable under the pertinent conflicts rules, the UCC would be applied instead to the extent that it covers the relevant terms. Again the interpretation elsewhere cannot even then be fully ignored and international practice remains relevant, all the more so for the terms not defined in the UCC, in which connection the Incoterms may be of prime importance even in the USA.

It finally leaves the question whether conflicts may arise between the meaning of the established trade terms, whether or not supported by the Incoterms, and the Vienna Convention, in which case the trade terms prevail, assuming their meaning is clear. In this connection the Incoterms figure either if explicitly made applicable or as custom. Yet conflict will be rare. As a start, the need to deliver the goods to the carrier under both Fob and Cif terms is fully compatible with the provisions of Articles 30 and 31 of the Vienna Convention. Article 34 requires documents to be tendered at the time and place and in the form as required by the contract.

---

[224] See C Schmitthoff, *The Law and Practice of International trade* (9th edn, 1990), 9*ff*.
[225] See *Stag Line v Foscolo Mango & Co Ltd* [1932] AC 328.

The trade terms will be specific in these aspects and then supplement this provision. As regards the passing of risk, the Vienna Convention (Article 67(1)) again accepts the established trade term practice of the risk passing when the goods are handed over to the carrier (except in 'D' terms). Where the trade terms (indirectly) bear on or refer to other aspects of substantive law, they should prevail as contractual terms but will be amplified by the Vienna Convention, unless clearly meant to operate otherwise. An example may exist in Article 67(2) requiring for the passing of risk the clear identification of the goods, which may not strictly be necessary under the trade terms which would then prevail. There may also be some doubts: for example the Fob terms do not involve a carriage of goods proper so that the references to the handing-over point and the passing of risk in Articles 31 and 67 of the Convention may not, strictly speaking, apply. Even so, the Incoterms themselves clarify these aspects as if there was a carriage of goods.

Earlier, the packaging duty under Fob terms to which Article 35(1) of the Vienna Convention makes a reference, existed probably only until the place of loading was reached, in derogation from Article 35(2)(d), but a further duty now appears implied under the Fob terms as restated in the 1990 version (Comment 9).

2.3.11   *The Vienna Convention and the ICC Model International Sale Contract*

The Vienna Convention is only a partial codification of the international sales law. As we saw, it has its own rules of supplementation in the areas it covers in principle. They are all best explained in the context of the *lex mercatoria* with its hierarchy of norms, see sections 2.3.5 and 2.3.6 above. Also the Unidroit and European Principles may supplement them within that context. Within the ICC, an effort has further been made to produce a Model International Sale Contract which is divided into two parts: (a) specific conditions setting out terms that are special to particular contracts of sale and (b) general conditions setting out standard terms common to all contracts incorporating the ICC General Conditions of sale. Both the special and general conditions concern manufactured goods intended for resale when the purchaser is not a consumer and the contract is an independent transaction rather than part of a long-term supply arrangement. The model contract is subject to the Vienna Convention (if not excluded) but its general conditions serve in practice as an amplification of rules of the Vienna Convention. The specific conditions on the other hand contain an easy checklist of the basic deal terms. The trade terms used are as defined in the Incoterms (except as otherwise agreed).

2.4   **The Law Merchant Concerning International Sales**

As explained more fully in chapter 1 and in sections 2.3.5 and 2.3.6 above, within the international law merchant or *lex mercatoria* and its hierarchy of norms, the Convention has its own place as written uniform law, always subject to its own applicability rules. In this hierarchy of norms affecting international sales, the Vienna Convention and the general principles on which it is based are themselves not of the highest order and may be eclipsed by fundamental international mandatory principle as *ius cogens* and even by customary law, certainly if mandatory, which in sales must be rare, but also if directory if it maintains itself regardless of the impact of the Convention, which itself may of course be overridden by the contractual terms. This all has a place in the context of the Convention's interpretation or supplementation, regardless of the more muddled Article 7 of the Convention itself and is more particularly relevant in eventually determining the rights and duties of the parties under their sales agreement. Thus the terms of the relevant contract itself will precede the terms of the Convention, but the Convention will itself precede the application of common legal principles (not of a fundamental nature) which may, however, still supplement it even if not directly underlying the Convention itself. Where the Convention under its own terms does not apply it may still figure as a model as part of general principles. These general principles may also increasingly be found in international sets of Principles like the Unidroit and the European Contract Principles in so far as they are properly focussed on professional dealings. In this legal order, the conflict of law rules and the ensuing application of a domestic law come as the lowest set of rules which only apply when under all higher norms no solution is found, regardless of what Article 7(2) says. Even then, the conflict rules are so subsidiary that judges have discretion as to the application of the laws so suggested. That is also so with regard to mandatory domestic rules and its impact on international sales contracts (*règles d'application immédiate*), see further chapter 1, sections 2.2.6, 2.2.7 and 2.2.8.

In this approach, the contract itself, its interpretation and supplementation and the determination of the rights and duties thereunder are thus subject to a range of norms with their own hierarchy: *ius cogens*, mandatory custom (if existing), mandatory treaty law (if existing), the terms of the contract, directory custom, directory treaty law, general legal principles, and finally domestic laws appointed under the prevailing conflict rules.

In this hierarchy, the Vienna Convention, the Incoterms, the Unidroit and European Principles, and Rome Convention will each play a role in their allotted places as written norms. They will each be subject to their own applicability rules and their own rules concerning their interpretation and implementation in which, however, the norms from other layers of the law merchant also figure and override their effect if higher.

Except for the *ius cogens*, they cannot say anything much about their own rank in this connection. All are a source of law in their own right whose relationship is given by the dictates of the *ius cogens* as translated through international practice. In this connection, a reference to good faith and usage in the contractual interpretation of international (sales) agreements is often a reference to these other extra-contractual norms which besides the internal contractual elements, like the wording of the agreement, the intent of the parties, their conduct, nature and purpose of their contract, and the nature of their relationship, co-determine the contractual rights and duties under which they operate *vis-à-vis* each other.

The details of this approach were explained in chapter 1 and need not be here repeated. The key is the diversity in the sources of the applicable law and their hierarchy.

Part III   Agency

3.1   The General Notion of Agency

3.1.1   *The Use of Agents: Their Position*

The basic pattern of international sales as explained in the previous part of this chapter is based on an extensive use of intermediaries. Although expensive, this has served international commerce very well for a long time and still provides the basic framework for international sales. In fact, it was shown that the use of third parties handling the goods and payments as independent and professional intermediaries is a key element in making international sales possible on any kind of scale. In this connection they may act as mere service providers but also as agents, which means that in the exercise of their function as intermediary they fulfill legal acts for others. This has a long history and is very common as we shall see. But intermediaries and their functions have acquired an entirely different dimension in modern payments, security entitlement systems and clearing systems. These intermediaries may have an autonomous function in these systems, where they may be the subject of special service contracts or become counterparties. This will be discussed more extensively in chapters 3 and 4. The agency function becomes here less obvious and needs in any event no longer be combined with services.

The position of intermediaries is thus foremost determined by the contractual arrangements under which they operate, for example a warehousing or transportation agreement in the handling of goods by third parties or a letter of credit in the handling of payments by banks. These contracts might imply special powers and that may become the area of agency: the warehousing or transportation agreement may give the warehouse or the carrier the right to hand over the goods to a buyer. It may complete the delivery duty of the seller at the same time, which in systems requiring delivery for the transfer of title passes full ownership. Here the warehouse may become an agent for the seller in that it accomplished legal acts for him. Alternatively, the warehouse or carrier may be the agent of the buyer so that the delivery and title transfer are completed when the goods are handed over by the seller to them. If a warehouse receipt or bill of lading is issued, the transfer of the warehouse receipt or bill of lading to the buyer may itself pass title and the warehouse or carrier do *not* then fulfil this intermediary role in the delivery process and will *not* be agents in that aspect.

Under a letter of credit, the bank has an independent payment obligation but the payment by the bank will discharge the buyer's payment obligation under the sales agreement at the same time and the seller will have no further claim for payment on the buyer. Here again, there is an intermediary who completes performance for someone else, in this case the buyer who will have arranged this facility as part of his performance under the original sales agreement requiring the letter of credit. Again the paying bank may be seen as the agent for the buyer in fulfilling and extinguishing his payment obligation to the seller.

What happens in these cases is therefore that intermediaries effect *legal* acts or obtain discharges for either seller or buyer as the case may be to complete the sale without achieving any benefit themselves (except a right to be paid for their services) or incurring any duties of their own. This is the essence of agency and is often supplementary to and needs to be clearly distinguished from the underlying contractual obligations of the intermediary *vis-à-vis* his client or customer. An agent relates to a third party whilst committing, benefiting or releasing his client (or principal) *vis-à-vis* that party.

Often agency functions are *embedded* in or result from other relationships as in carrier agreements or in letters of credit, as we just saw, or in service agreements but they may of course also be more direct and figure as the main objective of a contractual relationship. This is likely to happen where a power of attorney is given which could even be *unilaterally* arranged so that there may not be an underlying contractual relationship proper, and therefore *no duty* but only a right to act as agent. If the attorney acts, however, there are likely also to be duties and there may then be an implied acceptance of the task. In brokerage, on the other hand, there is a clear *contractual agency*: the broker is required to buy or sell assets, especially commodities or investment securities, on behalf of his client, often on specified conditions in terms of volume, quality, time and price.

Again, agency is only the result of the brokerage arrangement, which may also produce other rights and duties, but unlike in the embedded cases of agency just mentioned, it is more at the centre of it and may be surrounded by special duties often referred to as *fiduciary duties* which may become especially elaborated for that type of agency. In all cases, agency is to be distinguished from the underlying contract. An important theoretical issue in this connection is whether agency is always *unilateral* or may also be considered *bilateral*. Between agent and principal this is important as to the special duties that the agent may owe the principal and that may not all derive from the underlying contract alone. This is clear for the fiduciary duties under common law which will be discussed shortly. The agency is more likely to be truly unilateral in as far as the third-party is concerned but that may not be an important issue.

Instead of the term 'agent' or 'agency', under civil law the term 'representative' with 'power of representation' or 'authority' is often used. These types of agents, operating as pure middlemen earning a commission but not incurring an own liability or taking any risk, must in turn be clearly distinguished from those who are sometimes also called agents but in fact deal for their own account, like sole distributors, some franchising agents and licensees. Securities brokers whilst dealing from their own inventories are no longer agents for their clients either. Neither are central counterparties in clearing systems. It is thus clear that not every intermediary is an agent in the sense of achieving legal acts or obtaining a discharge for someone else, although the term 'agent' is often used for *all* intermediaries. Legally this is not appropriate and proper distinctions should be made.

Agency relationships often allow intermediaries to choose a counter-party. In this way, selling or buying agents may be appointed to find buyers or sellers and contract with them on their principal's behalf. In shipping, a shipping agent may thus be asked to make the necessary shipping arrangements with whomever and on the terms he thinks best. Investment securities brokers are usually given similar facilities whilst in discretionary accounts they may also decide on the investment transactions and price. In commercial trade, it is even possible for a less sophisticated or infrequent international seller or buyer to leave the selling or buying of his goods and all supplementary arrangements to agents. These agents may (for an additional fee) even take all the risks and become legal owners of the goods for the time being (in common law perhaps in the nature of constructive trustees only). It is the traditional function of a so-called *confirming house*. In civil law, there are so-called the *del credere* agents who accept at least the credit or payment risk in their transactions, incurring thereby their own liability under the agency.

In this way, businesses may also appoint *general* agents or representatives to conduct their entire business in other countries even by way of establishments. They may appear to act in their own name but may still do so only for the account and risk of the principal. Their role is usually perfectly understood by the general public. The contract or applicable law may curtail these general agencies or powers, however, to acts of general management only and exclude from them any powers to dispose of the principal's assets except in the ordinary course of the business considering the purpose for which the powers were given, *cf* also Article 3.62 of the Dutch CC, unless of course specifically provided otherwise. Dutch law is used here as being to some extent representative of the modern civil law thinking on agency, since it is the most recent statutory expression of agency law on the European continent, although not necessarily the most enlightened. In its earlier drafts it had an influence on the Unidroit Agency Convention of 1983 and through it also on the European Contract Principles which now has a special paragraph on agency (Articles 3.301*ff*). As we shall see, these texts tend to prolong the possibility of misuse that is inherent in the civil law concept of *indirect* agency where the agent acts *in his own name* even though for the risk of his principal. In civil law, it tends to give the agent too much of an independent position, not sufficiently balanced by fiduciary duties towards his principal and by tracing powers of the latter. It may be the cause of serious abuse.

In a legal sense, the key to agency is always that an agent *initiates or completes a legal act or obtains a discharge for others* and does not (normally) incur liabilities or acquire rights of his own. Generally, there are *three* relationships which require attention in this connection: (a) the one between principal and agent which is at the origin of the ensuing transaction or legal act (like delivery) with the third-party (or the *internal* relationship), (b) the relationship between the agent and the third-party which achieves the transaction or other legal act (this relationship is likely to have *no* independent meaning, at least in disclosed agencies as the agent has no own position or rights and duties and will fall out of the transaction), and (c) the relationship between the principal and the third-party which results from the transaction or other legal act (the *external* relationship) and which in a fully disclosed agency is likely to be the same as the one between the agent and the third-party.

The following may serve as an example of the internal and external relationship: the contract of carriage between the seller and the carrier is purely limited to the relationship between both of them and is therefore internal. Yet it may have an external effect in that the carrier operating for the seller may effect a legal act with the buyer for the seller, like the act of delivery achieving the title transfer under laws which require delivery as a condition. That is the external aspect leading in the end to a direct delivery between the seller (principal) and the buyer (third-party). In brokerage functions, the contract between the broker and his client is the internal relationship. The relationship which the broker creates between his client and the counter-party is the external relationship. The broker does *not* create his own contractual relationship with that counter-party unless, in civil law, he acts in his own name or, in common law, he does not disclose the agency. At least in common law, disclosure will create the external relationship automatically. In that case, the broker is in principle discharged but may as we shall see still function as *guarantor* if the third party relied on his credit worthiness whilst entering the transaction unbeknown of the principal's interest.

In the external relationship, the party who is at the origin of the agency (here the seller) is thus commonly called the 'principal' and the other the 'third party' (here the buyer), whilst the intermediary is the 'agent'. In all these cases, there operates the principle of *independence or abstraction* as the effects of the agency, especially on third parties (therefore the external relationship) are mainly determined by principles of the *objective* law rather than of the underlying contract between the principal and his agent (or the limitations of internal relationship), although this underlying contract usually sets the agency in motion. The third party effect may thus be different from what the contract (the internal relationship) envisaged or prescribed. There is a risk for the party making use of an agent (the principal) as others ('third parties') may rely on this agency and need not check the underlying arrangements (the internal relationship) and are not necessarily affected by them. In other words, in modern agency, the third party may assume *apparent* authority. The principal takes that risk. As may be seen, the issue of independence is directly related to that of the authority of the agent and its possible extension under the notion of apparent authority. Not all legal systems may take here the same approach and especially in Germany it is more common to distinguish depending on how much the third-party could know of the agency. It is indeed useful in this connection to consider that the independence relates to the principal and the appearance of authority to the third-party's perception, but it may also be said that the one (apparent authority) presupposes the other (independence).

As just mentioned, the situation may be somewhat different if the agent acts in his own name (in civil law: indirect agency) or when the agency is not disclosed at all (in common law: undisclosed agency). In that case, the third-party may not know of the agency and sees the undisclosed agent as his true counter-party with fullest authority. In such cases the agent may acquire an own liability for performance and may even become jointly and severally liable with his principal *vis-à-vis* the third-party upon disclosure of the agency, as will be discussed more extensively in section 3.1.5 below. Another issue is what rights the undisclosed or indirect principal obtains in the assets which the agent may so acquire and what the effect is of a later disclosure of the agency on these (proprietary) rights. Particularly in this area (as in the area of fiduciary duties) there are important conceptual differences between civil and common law.

3.1.2   The Role of the Agent: Explicit and Apparent Authority

The position of the agent and his contractual or other rights and duties, including his fiduciary duties *vis-à-vis* his principal or client under common law, need to be considered in more detail. Whilst dealing with third parties on his client's behalf, in common law the agent must particularly avoid conflicts of interest between him and his client, see more in particular section 3.1.3 below. Also the contractual rights and duties of the principal and of any third-party with whom the principal deals through agents must be considered. Finally, the proprietary rights created through an agent need further investigation, especially if he is undisclosed or deals in his own name. The law in this respect is better developed in common law than it is in civil law, especially so in the fiduciary duties of the agent and the protection of his client against him and in the contractual and proprietary aspects, see section 3.1.6. This is a particular contribution of the law of 'equity' in common law legal systems.

As may already be clear from what was said in the previous section, the first observation to make is that the term 'agent' is often very loosely used. In commercial terms, it may be no more than a person who renders certain services for someone else. In a *legal* sense, the term has a specific meaning and assumes that this person acquires and exercises *power or authority* or obtains sufficient *control* to represent and if necessary to bind his principal *vis-à-vis* third parties and *vice versa* in the arrangements he makes on the principal's behalf. In these arrangements, he may have been given greater or lesser powers and freedom by his principal or client (in the internal relationship). Particularly in the choice of the third-party and sometimes even in the types of deals to be concluded with him, the agent may be allowed, however, (and may have been particularly chosen) to exercise a certain discretion depending on his expertise for which he will be rewarded accordingly. An investment securities broker will indeed normally have freedom to choose the counter-party in a traditional investment securities transaction. He is unlikely to ever disclose him as there is no need. Whilst acting through a broker of the counter-party, he may not even know who it is. He may even have been given the right to initiate these deals in a discretionary account, so that he is free to engage in continuous transactions which he finds of benefit for his principal. As expert he may, on the other hand, also acquire a position as protector of the principal whom he may have to guide through complicated transactions and must warn against the consequences of what he (the agent) may be doing.

Whatever the amount of discretion, the essence of agency may be summarised as follows:

(a)   The agent creates direct legal relationships between the principal and the third party whilst not normally incurring any liability himself (although doing so jointly with the principal or even severally does not need to distract from the existence of an agency). In fact, in common law the separate liability of the agent may be a question of the internal relationship between principal and agent and the arrangements they have made between themselves in this connection, therefore of mere intent. On the other hand, the agent's liability *vis-à-vis* the third party may also arise from the circumstances, particularly in the operation of an undisclosed agent on whom the third-party relied as counterparty.

(b)   The second aspect is that the rights the agent obtains, duties he performs or liabilities he incurs for his principal may be of any nature: they can be contractual or pre-contractual (if he negotiates only) but may also involve the transfer of title or the creation of other proprietary rights. Even tortious behaviour of an agent may so be attributed to a principal.

(c)   The third aspect is that under the notion of abstraction or independence, the agent's powers are not necessarily limited by the terms of his arrangements with the principal (the internal relationship) but the third-party may be able to rely on the appearance of authority or on apparent authority and need not check into the underlying relationship and any restrictions in it on the agency. As we already saw, that is the risk of the principal who uses agents.

(d)   The fourth aspect is that, although the principal has this risk, special protections are developed to avoid conflicts of interest between the agent and his principal, particularly relevant in undisclosed or indirect agencies. They may easily arise when the agent also operates for his own account in the same goods and only a limited number of them are available at a lower price. Here enters the idea of postponement of the agent, a notion particularly alive in common law and part of the *fiduciary duties* developed under that law.

Thus, although the principal sets the agency in motion and controls it to that extent, he must accept what the third-party makes of it but relies in this respect on the agents loyalty and care. There may be other such duties. In common law, they are particularly well developed and imply very substantial safeguards, also for investors.

The broad facility to use intermediaries as agents in this way was developed in medieval law but faced problems as late as the nineteenth century, even in England. Roman law had disallowed the concept in contractual matters as it generally considered contractual ties highly personal and not capable of being created through agents, certainly if counterparties were chosen by the agent at will,[226] a notion only fully abandoned by the natural law school of Grotius and his followers.[227]

Under Roman law it was, however, possible to use intermediaries to acquire property.[228] It suggests that the underlying contract could also be concluded by the agent, who was, however, thought in that case only to render a service (*mandatum*) and was not allowed any discretion. More problematic was the position of the undisclosed agent acquiring property in D.41.1.59, under which the decisive point was considered to be the *animus domini* (intent) or lack thereof in the agent, of which there had to be some manifestation. The result was that in case of doubt, the agent would acquire the property for himself. This at least was the interpretation of Bartolus.[229]

Agency or the power of representation or authority to bind a principal can now derive from or be implicit in many types of contracts, as we have already seen. It can also derive

---

[226] D.45.1.38.17 and D.45.1.26.2.
[227] *De Iure Belli ac Pacis*, Lib II, Cap XI, s 18. Grotius depersonalised the contractual bond except where clearly highly personal.
[228] See D.41.1.13 pr.
[229] *Commentarii in Primam Digesti Novi Partem ad* D.39.5.13. The Dutch Supreme Court in a decision of 1624 went further and accepted that the principal acquired the property (possession and ownership) directly on the basis of his agreement with the agent whether or not the agency was disclosed: see J Coren, *In Supremo Senatu Hollandiae*, XXV (Amsterdam, 1661).

from the mere operation of the law as in corporate, matrimonial and parental matters and in the vicarious liability under tort law, although common law does *not* operate a generalised agency concept as civil law is more apt to do in its notion of representation. Thus parents are not automatically the representatives of their children under common law.

The most obvious contract giving rise to agency is the pure (commercial) agency agreement or mandate agreement in civil law. But it may no less result from an employment or service contract or from any other contract meant to transfer this kind of facility or authority. In international sales it may, as we saw, be implicit in a transportation agreement pursuant to which the carrier is allowed to hand the goods over to a buyer thus completing the delivery, and in the arrangements concerning the documentary letter of credit under which a bank operates as an independent payor but also as agent for both parties liberating them under the contract by receiving the shipping document (for the buyer) in exchange for payment (to the seller).

To repeat, the internal relationship is not decisive for the extent of the agency. For a direct agency to operate, the *perception* of the third party is the essence and there need be no more than the appearance of an agency through declarations or conduct of the principal allowing third parties reasonably to rely on the power of representation or agency and claim a contract with the principal, see for example Article 3.61(2) of the Dutch CC (called agency by estoppel or *apparent* or ostensible agency or authority in common law). The third party has no investigation duty in this respect beyond the obvious. The agent who clearly exceeds his authority is naturally liable to his principal but it has no further effect on the innocent third-party dealing with the principal through the latter's agent. It is often less clear whether the principal may similarly invoke the third party's reliance to invoke a binding contract himself in those circumstances.

This notion of reliance is closely connected with (a) the *principle of publicity*, which underlies the normal form of agency under which the principal is disclosed by the agent in the transactions he concludes on the former's behalf, *cf* also Article 3.66 of the Dutch CC, and (b) the normative *theory of contract* on the other, see for this latter point also Section 8 of the Comment, *Restatement Second Agency* in the USA and what was said about the normative approach to contract in section 1.2.1 above.

It is important to appreciate that the normative approach acts here in the first instance in the relationship between the principal and agent (the internal relationship) upon which the third party subsequently relies in terms of the agent's authority. In the normative approach, reliance on the declarations and conduct of the principal is reduced to what is normal for the third-party to assume and expect under the circumstances, for example in respect of employees of a corporation, in which connection the conduct and declarations of the agent *himself* rather than those of the principal may even become controlling.[230] It thus depends on the setting and circumstances. There is here a strong analogy with the vicarious liability of the employer. Use of a company's signals like titles, letterheads, visiting cards and premises, lack of proper supervision and an unclear organisational structure may all lead to a situation in which a third-party may assume the agency and need not make further inquiries, although this may still remain exceptional.[231]

Where modern agencies continue to operate in commerce, they are normally de-personalised by large commercial entities which make agency their professional business, like shipping agents and investment banks as securities brokers and investment managers. It tends to support the notion of independence: the third-party relies on the agent and his

---

[230] See in the Netherlands HR, 27 Nov 1992 [1993] NJ 287.
[231] See also the English case of *First Energy UK Ltd v Hungarian International Bank Ltd* [1993] 2 Lloyd's Rep 194.

arrangements and need not fear the effects of any principal disowning the agent if he justly relied on the agency. Commercial practice also requires it. It is possible that the seniority and standing of the agent in relation to the principal also play a role. As a consequence, the professional agent may sooner have apparent authority *vis-à-vis* third parties in some matters than in others. It is difficult to generalise and the facts will be decisive.

3.1.3   The Notion of Independence, Apparent Authority and Agencies of Necessity

Whatever the (contractual or other) source of the authority to bind the principal and third party may be, we saw that this authority is subsequently likely to acquire an existence of its own and is in any event exercised according to its own rules not necessarily derived from the internal relationship between principal and agent, be it a contract or the appearance thereof or a unilateral act like the granting of a power of attorney, but rather from general legal principles. Creating power or authority in this sense is therefore often seen as a separate *unilateral* act of the principal addressed to a third party (even though this party is not necessarily identified by the principal but might be chosen by the agent), but it should be considered that as far as the agent is concerned it is likely to still be bilateral in respect of the principal and entail special duties which may not be derived from the underlying contract but rather from the agency concept itself.

Any underlying contract or the appearance thereof or a truly unilateral power of attorney (which gives a right but cannot impose a duty to act as agent until accepted and cannot therefore limit the attorney's own freedom to compete) is in this view only a way to bring the power of the agent into being which itself results, however, independently under the operation of the law. It is an approach borne out by the new Dutch Civil Code, Article 3.61. It also supports the notion in as far as the third party is concerned, that apparent authority is *always* the key (although the independence is its base, even if it relates primarily to the principal and the appearance of authority to the third party) while the agreement between principal and agent is not truly decisive as far as the third party is concerned. Thus legally relevant is only what the principal (or sometimes even the agent) either directly or indirectly intimates (by conduct) to the third party, not what the internal arrangements between principal and agent are.

This principle of *apparent authority* combined with the principle of *abstraction or independence* leads to the distinction between the internal and external aspect of the authority or power, a distinction first formulated in Germany by P Laband.[232] In common law, a similar approach was taken by Corbin.[233] There is therefore congruity between common and civil law in this most important aspect and there is clearly a common core in common and civil law inspired by similar practical needs, even if the law of agency remains better developed in common law as far as the fiduciary duties are concerned, whilst there also remain important differences in the undisclosed or indirect agency concept.[234]

---

[232] "Die Stellvertreter bei dem Abschluß von Rechtsgeschäften nach dem allgemeinen Handelsgesetzbuch", 10 Zeitschrift für das gesammte Handelsrecht (1866), 183*ff*.

[233] "Comment", 34 *Yale Law Journal* 788 at 794 (1925).

[234] See for comparative analyses especially the works of W Müller-Freienfels in Germany, *Stellvertretungsregelungen in Einheit und Vielfalt, Rechtsvergleichende Studien zur Stellvertretung* (Frankfurt, 1982), and also K Zweigert and H Kötz, 2 *Einführung in die Rechtsvergleichung* (Tübingen, 3rd edn, 1996), translated into English by T Weir, *Introduction to Comparative Law* (Oxford, 3rd edn,1998), 431. See for English law the treatise of FMB Reynolds, *Bowstead on Agency* (16th edn, 1995), and for US law, *Restatement (Second) of Agency* and DA DeMott, *Fiduciary Obligation, Agency and Partnership: Duties in Ongoing Business Relationships* (1991). See further Fridman's *Law of Agency* (7th edn, 1996).

That there is such a common core is in itself not surprising as it is often said that the notion of agency came into English law through continental commercial practices. The differences in fiduciary duties and in the consequences of undisclosed agency are probably connected with subsequent developments in common law in which agency became closely related to the trust whilst in equity agency and trustee duties became comparable, although they are by no means the same as we shall see.

The principles of abstraction or independence and of reliance on apparent authority allow for a more extensive role of the agent when the need arises, therefore regardless of any contractual stipulations about authority between principal and agent, if at all explicit and however confining. There may even be an *agency of necessity* in common law terms or a *negotiorum gestio* in civil law terms supplementing the consensual agency and taking over.

One could even consider it implicit or supplemental to all agency relationships, in this connection sometimes also referred to as *inherent* authority provided of course always that the agent acts reasonably. The very purpose of delegated authority is to avoid constant recourse by third parties to the principals.[235] Again, the result is that once a principal gets an agency going, he must realise and accept that it may create its own momentum and he cannot hide behind the internal relationship and the limitations he may have set therein on the agent's activity. The operations of the agent are for his risk whatever comes of it, *assuming* that the third party acts reasonably in his reliance whilst the agent, at least in common law, must comply with his fiduciary duties *vis-à-vis* the principal and support him as best he can, postponing his own interests, even if not doing so does not affect the third-party.

Not all legal systems go equally far in the aspect of independence. Particularly the idea of Laband that the third-party may depend on the authority even ignoring the restrictions agreed between the principal and agent or the defects in their contractual relationship *of which he knew* is often not accepted in modern legal systems like the Dutch and German. It follows that, where the agent holds himself out in that capacity but acts without proper authority whilst no apparent authority can be deduced from the circumstances and an agency of necessity does not exist either, there is no agency and the so-called agent is personally and exclusively liable to the third-party, certainly if the principal disowns the arrangements the agent made, even if there was *no* negligence on the latter's part, *cf* also Article 3.70 of the new Dutch CC.

The modern idea is that, besides the power bestowed by the principal as signaled to the third party and whatever necessity will subsequently require, the agent independently warrants his authority as well, a concept in common law long known in the context of undisclosed agency. This may mean that if the principal cannot perform that part of the transaction that went beyond the authority given in the internal relationship the misguided agent might still be liable to the third-party for the excess. Of course, even if there was no apparent authority or agency of necessity, the principal may always ratify the acts of the unauthorised agent and thus potentially discharge him. This ratification is commonly considered retroactive, see Article 3.69 of the Dutch CC.

3.1.4 *The Consequences of Agency: Conflicts of Interests, Rights and Duties of the Agent*

To repeat, the notion of independence suggests that lack of consent in and defences derived from the internal relationship between the principal and the agent normally have no

---

[235] See Learned Hand J in the American case of *Kidd v Thomas A Edison*, 239 F 405 (1917).

consequence in the external relationship between the principal and the third-party, at least if the latter did not know of them at the time he contracted. The notion of independence is also likely to lead to special rules in the area of set-off, *excluding* the direct or disclosed agent (and his own rights and obligations *vis-à-vis* the third party) from the process. Also in matters of retention rights of the third-party/seller *vis-à-vis* the principal/buyer, the relationship with the disclosed principal/buyer, and not with the agent, is likely to determine their extent. In the aspect of good faith when acquiring personal property from an unauthorised third party, even the good faith of the disclosed agent may be imputed to the principal.

The normal consequence of the agency is that the direct or disclosed principal is directly bound towards the third party (and *vice versa*) under any contract that the agent concludes or receives and acquires *cq* cedes directly any proprietary right that may accrue or be divested through his agent, whilst the agent himself does not normally acquire any rights or incurs any duties in this respect. He is entitled to a fee from the principal for his services and must perform his duties as well as he can. In common law these are of a contractual but additionally also of a *fiduciary* nature. Especially in investment brokerage they may be reinforced by statutory law.

The fiduciary duties in common law are of an equitable nature and require the agent to protect his principal's interest, avoid any conflicts with his own by postponing these, and observe the necessary discretion, often summarised as the duties of *care, loyalty and confidentiality*. They are of particular interest when the agent acts as a broker for several principals, and more so if he also deals for his own account at the same time. They are all the more important in undisclosed or indirect agencies where the agent is given some discretion. Civil law is notably less well developed in this area of potential conflicts and often continues to allow the agent, when he acts in his own name whilst the agency remains undisclosed, to possibly benefit from the transaction under circumstances which remain generally undefined, a situation which must be considered unsatisfactory.

The common law fiduciary duties are particularly important in trusts,[236] therefore in the relationship between the trustees and the beneficiaries who largely depend on their trustees and are vulnerable to abuse. They are not contractual in nature but may supplement certain types of contracts where there is a dependency relationship.[237] The common law technique of literal interpretation of contracts and its reluctance to imply terms or accept good faith notions here presented problems. Thus these fiduciary duties were introduced into the relationship between principals and agents, solicitors and clients, companies and directors, probably employers and employees.[238] There could be added the relationship between guardians and wards, executors and legatees, and each partner in its relationship to a partnership as a whole. The key is that these fiduciary duties may impose duties of care which are higher than normal and may require the fiduciary (here the agent) to act with greater care than he would use in his own dealings.[239]

These fiduciary duties are, however, gradually being introduced also in civil law, at least in investment securities brokerage, through Article 11 of the EU Investment Services Directive effective in all EU countries as of the end of 1993, see chapter 6, section 3.2.6.

---

[236] See for the beginning of this development *Keech v Sandford*, 25 ER 223 (1726).
[237] Not any situation of dependency or confidence gives rise to fiduciary duties, however, and the key is that the fiduciary undertakes to act in the interest of another person who is entitled to expect that the beneficiary will only act in his interest. Acting merely for the account of someone else is notably not sufficient.
[238] See the Australian case of *Hospital Products Ltd v United States Surgical Corporation* (1984) 156 CLR 41, 96–7.
[239] See Cardozo J in the US case of *Meinhard v Salmon*, 249 NY 458 (1928); see also *Restatement (Second) of Agency*, Section 387 and Comment.

They cannot be captured entirely by the good faith notion, although the elaboration of the information and performance duties in contract may be developed in the same direction and will probably be used as the context in which the fiduciary duties will be received in civil law. It would limit them to application in contractual situations only, may not so quickly highlight the extra effort that is required and may be hindered by the fact that they could be given relevance in *all* contractual situations and as such be diluted, unless the typical nature of each relationship between contractual parties is better understood, as was advocated for civil law in section 1.2.1 above. This is implicit in common law.

Certainly, also in common law some fiduciary relationships are more intense than others. The facts are very important.[240] Fiduciary duties co-exist with contractual duties but seem to be always overriding. Compared to the American notion of good faith in sales contracts under the UCC or in the *Restatement Second Contracts*, see section 1.3.2 above, the fiduciary duties are always objective requirements, whilst the fiduciary can never act in his own interest (without full disclosure assuming even then that there is a ready alternative for the principal) which contract parties naturally may do. Good faith in this sense usually requires parties to take into account only each other's justified interests and it seeks a balance after the contract has been concluded. Under fiduciary duties, on the other hand, the interest of the beneficiary always prevails over that of the fiduciary.[241] Under it, even pre-contractual disclosure duties (for example of conflicting interests) may arise in the formation of the internal relationship, which under concepts of good faith might be less pronounced as is still likely to be the case in common law, even where the good faith notion is accepted in the performance, like under Article 2 UCC in the USA. Another point is that because of the overriding nature of fiduciary duties, they are not easily excluded, diminished or varied by contractual stipulation, although parties in the internal relation may define some standards. The liability they give rise to is more comparable to the one in tort.

3.1.5 Undisclosed and Indirect Agencies

There may still be some form of agency even if it is not disclosed at all, whilst no indication is given or conduct established by the principal either leading to reliance by the third-party on apparent authority of an agent. Certain agents, like brokers or commission agents ('*commissionairs*' in civil law) who buy or sell goods for a principal may act in *their own name* upon the *undisclosed* instructions of others who give them possession of their goods or access to their accounts.

Particularly in civil law, this often gives rise to difficult questions about the relationship (if any) between the third-party and the principal under these circumstances. The question then arises whether there was any agency at all. In common law, a form of privity is clearly assumed between the undisclosed principal and the third party, thus establishing an agency relationship. The justification of agency in these cases is that consideration moved from the principal and not from the agent who is therefore not a proper party to the agreement. One thus sees a particular example of common law laying stress on the exchange or bargain principle rather than on the parties' intent or 'will', see section 1.2.4 above.[242]

However, even in common law, it is an exception to the traditionally strict rule of privity, see section 1.5.3 above, and the relationship between the undisclosed principal and the

---

[240] See Frankfurter J in the American Supreme Court case of *SEC v Cheney Corp* 318 US 80, 85 (1942).
[241] See also the Canadian Supreme Court case of *Cansons Enterprises Ltd v Boughton & Co* (1991) 85 DLR (4th) 129, 154.
[242] See also W Müller-Freienfels, "The Undisclosed Principal" (1953) 16 *MLR* 299.

third party is therefore sometimes viewed as arising only through the operation of the law, all the less therefore a contractual construction. A condition may be that the third party does not have any reasonable interest in the identity or nature of his counter-party, just like the debtor in the case of assignments. He normally will have such an interest, however, if the undisclosed agent has performance duties towards him.

In common law, the undisclosed agent must have had the intention to act for the principal in each instance and the contract between principal and agent should not have excluded that possibility.[243] The main difference with the normal agency is that, at least until disclosure, the agent will be liable *together* with the principal towards the third party as a natural protection for the latter (even though the agent did not provide any consideration) and does not even automatically drop out after disclosure if the third party has a continuing interest in him being so bound.[244] Through disclosure of the agency, the principal becomes in any event directly entitled to the *benefits* of the agency in common law and also becomes directly liable to the third-party, but such a disclosure does not automatically put the principal fully in the shoes of the agent. At least as far as the liabilities of the agent towards him are concerned, the third-party may be able to object to any transfer, not only because he may not want to release the agent because he does not trust the credit of the principal but also when it is inconvenient for him to deal directly with certain types of principals like private clients in investment securities transactions, e.g. because they are not connected to settlement systems necessary to make and complete share transfers in a safe and efficient manner.

In the meantime, it remains somewhat unclear, even under common law (because it never distinguishes sharply between contractual and proprietary aspects), whether title to any goods obtained under the undisclosed agency automatically passes through to the principal; it would seem logical, certainly upon disclosure of the agency (as a way to directly claim the benefit). There will in any event be a recovery possibility for the principal against the undisclosed agent in the internal relationship. It will also cover moneys received by the undisclosed agent from the third-party, at least if sufficiently set aside. Claims of the agent on the third party (eg for the delivery of shares or sales proceeds) will also belong to the principal who may pursue them in his own name upon disclosure unless again the third party has an interest in the agent exclusively pursuing them. This will be rare.

In common law (depending on the perceived *intention* of the parties), the construction of a trust may alternatively allow the benefits to accrue to the principal as beneficiary. The principal in that case does *not* become the counter-party, however, nor does he incur liability directly (and has no action against the third party, nor the third party against him). The exceptions to the '*nemo dat*' rule are also different when the agent acts as (constructive) trustee in this manner, in which capacity he may legally transfer title in the assets to *bona fide* purchaser for adequate consideration, thus defeating the principal's interest, see for these exceptions also chapter 4, section 1.4.4.

In fact, in common law it is entirely possible to appoint a trustee instead of an undisclosed agent to handle, sell or buy some goods and it may not always be clear whether an intermediary is appointed an agent or a trustee, although in the securities brokerage industry, the trust characterisation is uncommon and not easily presumed to have been intended, even in discretionary portfolios, although there may still be a constructive trust for tracing purposes. The differences are material in the sense as just mentioned. Even if there is a mere agency, the connection with the trust remains close, however, as particularly

---

[243] See also Bowstead-Reynolds, n 234 *supra*, 414*ff*.
[244] See for a leading case (Privy Council) in this area, *Siu Yin Kwan v Eastern Insurance Co Ltd*, [1994] 2 WLR 370.

expressed in the fiduciary duties which also affect the undisclosed agent and in the direct interests of the undisclosed principal, even if stronger in the agency than in the trust construction, where he has only the rights of a beneficiary.

This is all much less clear in civil law where reference is often made to *indirect agency or indirect representation* in this connection rather than to undisclosed agency when an agent acts *in his own name*. There is an important difference. Indeed, the indirect agency of civil law lays particular stress on the agent having acted *in his own name* rather than on the lack of disclosure. This type of agency may therefore also exist if the third party knows that there must be a principal or if the principal is even known to him, although this will normally not be the case.

In civil law, the agency idea remains much more embryonic in these circumstances. The problem is that the concept of the will or intent of the parties, developed in the nineteenth century, did not easily allow for the formation of a contract between two parties unaware of each other. Common law puts, as we saw, the emphasis here rather on the concept of the 'bargain' (and the movement of consideration). As a consequence, the agent acting in his own name is as such in civil law considered primarily responsible for the deal and the principal may not be given a direct interest, the corollary being that he has no direct liability to the third party either. In fact, the trust construction in common law comes closer to this civil law idea of indirect agency than the undisclosed agency with the important difference, however, that the common law undisclosed principal has in such cases still the rights and protections of a trust beneficiary and the advantage of the benefits being separated from the person of his trustee whilst in civil law he has (in principle) only a personal claim on his agent for the benefits which are not then considered separated.

3.1.6 The Civil Law Indirect Agency. The Relationship between the Principal and Third Party. Customers' Assets

Although acting in one's own name even though as undisclosed agent does not in civil law create on its face a direct relationship between the principal and the third-party, this has never been a satisfactory situation and, under practical pressures, some direct tie between the principal and the third party is often assumed, especially in Germany and Switzerland, if the third-party has no special interest in the identity and nature of the principal, when, unlike in common law, the agent may be considered discharged. This is the case for cash purchases of little value. But also where a person acts as an agent without disclosing the particular principal (open agency in Germany), a direct relationship between the principal and the third party may be established if the identity of the former does not matter to the latter. This is very much the normal situation in investment securities brokerage when the third party knows that there is an agency and therefore a principal even if undisclosed. Again there is the analogy with the debtor under an assignment and with the depersonalisation of contracts generally which is at the heart of the notion of agency ever since Grotius insisted on it.[245] Another reason for this approach may be the realisation that the indirect agent acts only upon the initiative and is always subject to the control of the principal even if the third party may not know this but could suspect it.

---

[245] See further for Germany KH Schramm, *Münchener Kommentar zum Bürgerlichen Gesetzbuch*, Vol 1, *Allgemeiner Teil*, (3rd edn, 1993) Fünfter Titel, s 164, nos 42*ff* and Section 392(2) of the German Commercial Code. It does not extend to the obligatory rights, see Section 392(1) HGB. See for Switzerland, Article 401 of the Code of Obligations.

The consequence is that the principal may usually claim the title to goods obtained for him by the agent *assuming* it has passed from the third party and is sufficiently identified. Yet in Germany the situation is again more complicated, at least in the proprietary aspects of agency as under German law the acquisition of title depends not only on a contract and delivery (of legal possession) but also on the agreement to deliver (*Einigung*), see chapter 4 section 1.5.6, the agent playing a role under all three. As delivery of physical possession is considered a factual matter in Germany, there is a special problem here in cases where it is required as agency under German law is limited to legal acts (*Rechtsgeschäfte*). Also the *Einigung* suggest a transfer to the undisclosed agent personally (Section 164 BGB).

In Germany, it is possible and common, however, to include in the contract between principal and agent, therefore in the internal relationship, a clause under which the agent commits to acquire legal title and to accompany this with an anticipated intent to transfer the asset to the principal, even though neither is declared at the moment of the actual acquisition of property by the agent to the third party. Here we see indeed some emphasis on the internal relationship itself and the question of control. If the transfer remains nevertheless defective from the principal's point of view, it may still be perfected later to what the agency contract originally required, see Section 181 BGB.[246] Another aspect may be that the third-party must have some awareness of the agency even though he does not need to know the principal. In security brokerage this requirement will normally be in place as end investors using brokers are aware of the fact they they usually do not operate for their own account (although in modern securities dealings large brokers often deal from own inventory or bookentry entitlements at best market prices, when in truth they have stopped being agents and the issue of title passing through them to the principal no longer arises).

In France, the situation is also less clear but in the case of use of commission agents the third-party upon disclosure may be able to hold both principal and agent liable whilst at least any property rights accrue directly to the principal.[247] In the Netherlands, on the other hand, there is still no direct tie admitted between principal and third-party in indirect agencies. However, property rights accrue to the principal if passed to the agent, but merely on the basis of the internal relationship, Article 3.110 CC, provided the agent holds the assets in question for the principal, the internal relationship is specific on this point, and the acquisition is the direct result thereof. Because of the apparent lack of an external relationship proper, it remains less clear in this connection whether the third-party may equally receive title directly from the undisclosed principal assuming the property has passed to the agent. There may also be a problem with moneys held for clients.

However that may be, the principal appears at least protected in his proprietary rights against his agent if the latter has executed the transaction with the third-party but not yet with his principal, at least as far as any *tangible* assets the agent has so acquired are concerned. This is particularly relevant in the agent's bankruptcy. As just mentioned, it may not, however, apply to money the agent received (for which Dutch case law may, however, give some protection if sufficiently separated out in a client account as we shall see).

---

[246] See also German Supreme Court, 11 June 1920, 99 RGZ, 208 (1920).
[247] See in this vein Jurisclasseur Commercial Facs. 7A (No. 76), 360 (No 120) and 365 (No 20). See in France for an early plea for a direct link upon disclosure between principal and third party (in both the proprietary and obligatory aspects) B Starck, "Les rappports du commettant et du commissionairs avec les tiers", in *Le contrat de commission* (Ed. Hamel), 163 (Paris 1949), but this approach was not followed, see Ripert/Roblot, 2 *Traite de Droit Commercial*, 682 (2000). In Belgium there was support from W van Gerven, Algemeen Deel, 494–497 (1969) and L Somont, "Le Probleme de representation dans le contrat de commission sur marchandises", *JCB*, 129 (1956) . Belgian case law accepts the proprietary link but not the obligatory link, see also Cour de Cass. Belge, Dec. 9 1999, Pas. I, 1669 (1999), see for a criticism, E Dirix, *Festscchrift Jacques Herbots*, 97 (2002).

Importantly it does not extend to any contractual rights which the agent still has against the third-party either, particularly for delivery or payment in a transaction which is not yet in the stage of performance. In Germany creditors of the undisclosed agent have full recourse to all assets acquired by the undisclosed agent. Only if the undisclosed agent acted as *Kommissionar* any contractual obligation of the third party against the agent will not be available for attachment by the agent's creditors, Section 392(2) HGB, but some protection of the principal may be achieved by anticipated transfer from the agent to himself, as we saw. Title may as a rule not shoot through, however, but will remain with the agent as shortly as possible. It must be remembered that this only applies to truly undisclosed agency and not to open agency when a direct link between principal and third-party is established.

Similarly, in the case of default or bankruptcy of the undisclosed agent, under new Dutch law, the principal may appropriate these contractual rights (if not highly personal), including the right to any damages or repairs, see Articles 7.420 and 421 CC (in the context of the contract of mandate but also applicable outside it, see Article 7.424 CC). He may do so by the mere declaration of his interest to both the agent and the third-party. The third party left in limbo by the agent but discovering the agency has similar rights against the principal in the case of a default or bankruptcy of the agent.

This facility is often in Dutch interpreted as a *statutory assignment*. However, it leaves important questions of set-off, retention rights and *bona fides* protections unresolved. The consequence seems to be that the principal's rights may still be curtailed by counterclaims the third-party may have had against the bankrupt agent. Equally, it could be asked whether any other defences (or retention rights) the third-party had against the agent continue against the principal. Another point is whether any good faith status of the indirect agent may also accrue to the principal in these circumstances. The complication of the transaction still being in a clearing process in which outsiders cannot normally intervene is also not considered. Another problem may be presented here if securities are held for clients with a custodian in a custody account in the broker's name, or through a book-entry system to the extent it is characterised as creating only contractual rights against a custodian (even though that is now increasingly uncommon, see chapter 4, Part III). Does the principal enter into these rights directly upon a bankruptcy of the broker as well?

It would have been more logical to extend the principle of Article 3.110 of the Dutch CC (that title to physical assets already received by the agent always shoots through to the principal) also to any contractual claims the agent has received for the principal against a third party and *vice versa*. It is a typical civil law problem not to characterise claims as assets but it would have substantially approximated the common and civil law notions of undisclosed and indirect agency and would have been better than the statutory assignment construction and yield a more modern result.

This being said, common law too is not without sensitivity as to the defences of the third-party in an undisclosed agency[248] that becomes disclosed after the agent has acted. As we saw, in general, the possibility that the agent drops out of the transaction is restricted when the third party relied on him personally or on the defenses like set-offs assuming they were contemplated and discounted in the deal he struck with the undisclosed agent but not those arising fortuitously or from later transactions. This is especially relevant in

---

[248] In a disclosed agency, there is no set-off unless the principal agrees or when there is a regular relationship between agent and third-party and a current account relationship between them, all the more so where individual principals are not disclosed as is common in investment securities brokerage, see also P Wood, *English and International Set-off* (1989), 996.

investment brokerage transactions when the third-party knows that normally there is an agency and a principal involved and does therefore not have these defences.[249] Yet, as in disclosed agencies, there is an exception when there is a regular current account relationship between agent and third party or when the agent deals for several clients (principals) and possibly also for himself at the same time short of immediate allocation (pooling).

The text of Articles 7.420 and 7.421 of the Dutch CC is largely derived from the Unidroit Agency Convention of 1983 (not yet in force because the necessary ten ratifications are still missing, the Netherlands being one of the ratifying powers so far), itself the product of Dutch input at the time. In its Article 13(2) it proposes this system as a compromise between common and civil law.[250] It gives the Dutch implementation some wider importance. This approach has also appeared in Articles 3.301*ff* of the European Contract Principles. Because it leaves major unresolved issues, it seems unsuitable, particularly for the commodity and investment securities brokerage business when, whilst dealing with brokers, the existence of an agency must in any event be assumed.

In the meantime, the notion of segregation of clients' accounts and customers' moneys (or other pooled client assets), although still in the name of the indirect agent, is a broader civil law problem but increasingly respected, even in Dutch case-law but also by no means completely. This is particularly important as to any moneys a bankrupt agent acting in his own name has received for his client(s). The situation under Belgian and French law as to segregated (pooled) assets including money still in the name of the agent seems not much clearer.[251]

---

[249] Especially in the USA the cases are unanimous in holding that there can be no set-off where the third party should know or suspect that there is a principal: *Branham v Fullmer*, 181 NW 2d 36 (1970). The third party is also not discharged from payment if he pays the agent in such circumstances unless in good faith: see *Fradey v Hyland*, 37 Fed 49 (1888), although the *Restatement (Second) of Agency* (Section 208) follows the English rule which does not even accept good faith payments, criticised by Bowsted-Reynolds, n 244 *supra*, 439 and not in accordance with business practice in investment securities brokerage. Upon disclosure, payment to the agent is the risk of the principal who could, however, instruct the third party not to pay to the agent, although in the security brokerage business the loss of the option may be deemed implied, at least in retail business.

[250] See [1983] *Uniform Law Review* 164*ff* and for a defence of the compromise (and its implicit disadvantages), AS Hartkamp, "Indirect Representation According to the Principles of European Contract Law, the Unidroit Agency Convention and the Dutch Civil Code" in *Festschrift Drobnig* (1998), 45. This approach has been fundamentally challenged by LD van Setten, *De Commissionair in Effecten* [The Investment Securities Broker], Diss (Utrecht, 1998), in favour of a pure agency construction which he sees in any event as the underlying idea of Articles 7.420 and 7.421 of the Dutch CC. Indeed, the better view is that this limited Dutch statutory system through which the principal may receive direct rights against the third-party in an indirect agency is in truth based on and derived from the agency notion itself and the assignment characterisation and its limitations are then illogical. Indirect agency should therefore be interpreted as a form of agency like the undisclosed agency is in common law. Especially the set-off complication would then be reduced to more normal proportions.

In Dutch legal scholarship from before the introduction of the new Civil Code, a far-reaching *automatic* recognition of the undisclosed principal's position had already been suggested by P van Schilfgaarde, *Toerekening van Rechtshandelingen* [Attribution of Legal Acts] (Diss Groningen 1969), as long as the agent meant to operate for the principal and the third-party had no particular interest in the agent as his counter-party, whilst the principal was sufficiently solvent. In this view, the agent upon disclosure became a mere guarantor of contractual obligations entered into by him much along common law lines, whilst the property acquired by the agency was always directly obtained by the principal. Van Setten follows this reasoning but takes a more radical stand, which would unite common and civil law concepts also in this area of agency.

[251] See HR 3 Feb 1984 [1984] NJ 752 but new Dutch case-law is more restrictive and limits segregation to situations of statutory separation, HR June 13 2003 RvdW nr 108 July 2 2003 and 6541 WPNR (2003). There remained, in any event important problems also in this area: see E Dirix and RD Vriesendorp (eds), *Inzake Kwaliteit* [The Client Account](1998). In Continental legal writing, the difference between agency and trust is little understood and in as far as client money and assets are concerned, the preference seems to be for trust structures, even though they have hardly any basis in civil law. In the meantime, the (indirect) agency concept which is much better known and much more suitable to be further developed in the sense of pure agency, see previous n., remains in this sense neglected and underdeveloped. It would give the principal a legal position *vis-à-vis* the third party however, which he does not have in a trust construction where he is a mere beneficiary subject to the rules in this connection.

The particular problems arising in connection with indirect agency in the investment services industry are discussed more fully in chapter 6 section 1.3.8. Another problem that arises in particular in this industry derives from the fact that undisclosed agencies are unlikely ever to create a direct relationship between a principal and a third party. But also open agency may be problematic if the principal is not even known to the agent or as yet non-existent. Thus, where brokers act upon instructions of investor advisors who do not disclose their own principals to the agent, no direct relationship between them and the third-party may come into existence, in fact not even under common law either. When intermediaries act for principals in a pooled manner leaving allocations of sales and purchases to them until later, it does not seem that an agency can operate either, at least not before the allocation, and the agency is then dependent on the agent's expressed intention about who will get what.

3.1.7   *The Economic Importance of Modern Agency*

The major differences between the common law of agency and the civil law of representation are thus likely to be in the areas of the undisclosed agent and of the conflicts of interests. The undisclosed agent, like any other acting *in his own name*, has in civil law greater independence *vis-à-vis* his principal and is traditionally more likely to be allowed to compete with him, although in modern securities' and investors' protection laws duties and restraints similar to those long known in the common law of agency are gradually being introduced following the EU Investment Services Directive, see chapter 6, sections 1.3.9, 1.3.10 and 3.2.6. Civil law countries have, however, had great difficulty in faithfully adopting the Directive in this regard. It would in truth have required a rewriting of the law of agency for investment transactions. In common law these fiduciary duties tend to be reinforced in the investment area under modern statutes like the UK Financial Services Act of 1986, replaced by the Financial Services and Markets Act of 2000, and much earlier under the Securities Exchange Act 1934 and its many amendments in the USA.

Agents of these various kinds are frequent in commercial business because of the distances or different specialities involved. Modern communications have often made it possible to dispense, however, with their services, thereby reducing cost, also in international sales, all depending on the sophistication and staff of the principal. As a consequence, by far the most important manifestation of agency is now in the area of investment services or commodity dealings through brokers, therefore in the area of undisclosed and open agencies where there are at the same time the greatest differences between common and civil law. But the implied or embedded agencies in transportation and payment arrangements remain important also. Another area where agency remains common is in the factoring of receivables for collection purposes only. New Dutch law makes clear that the creditor may give the collector exclusive rights in this respect, which does not, however, prevent debtors unaware of this exclusivity to pay the original creditor and receive a discharge, *cf* Article 7.423 CC. The true factor collects, however, in his own name and for his own account and is not an agent at all, see more in particular chapter 5, sections 2.3.1*ff*.

3.2   **International Aspects of Agency**

3.2.1   *Private International Law Aspects of Agency*

Finally, it may be of interest to mention briefly the private international law issues in agency. Early on, there was an English rule making even the disclosed agent liable for the obligations of a foreign principal, who in turn could not be sued or sue in England himself. Being foreign is now only one factor in determining whether the parties had meant the principal to be directly and exclusively liable by contract between them.[252] In the USA there has always been an unwillingness to recognise foreign general powers.[253] Beyond these simple and incidental rules, there has never been much consensus about the treatment of agency internationally.

As was pointed out before, in agency there are in essence three relationships which require attention: the one between principal and agent which is at the origin of the ensuing transaction or other legal act (like delivery) with the third-party (or the internal relationship), the relationship between the agent and the third-party which achieves the transaction or other legal act (but this relationship is likely to have no independent meaning, at least not in disclosed agencies), and the relationship between the principal and the third party which results from the transaction or other legal act (the external relationship). All three may conceivably be covered by different laws. Another aspect to consider is whether the granting of the authority itself as a legal act separate from, although initiated by, the underlying contract between agent and principal but based on the latter's declarations or conduct, is not itself subject to a distinct set of legal rules. That appears to be the better view and is a natural consequence of the notion of independence.

If one sees the declarations or conduct of the principal as the main factor in the creation of the agency to the extent disclosed, then his law would, from a private international law point of view, be of primary importance, at least in the *creation* of the authority. It is also possible, however, to refer in this respect to the law of the third party who relies on these declarations or this conduct, although it may leave the principal at the mercy of (the law of) any third party the agent may choose (if given that discretion). This may be his risk. Whatever law may thus apply to the creation of the agency, the agency is likely to depend for its *effect* on the law of the country where it is invoked. What we are concerned with here is the *recognition* of the authority conferred and the binding force of the obligations between principal and third party (and the elimination of the agent as a party) and any proprietary effect.

The law of the place where the effect is invoked will normally be the law of the country of either principal or third-party, at least as to them being bound under the relationship created by the agent (if the principal makes the allegation it is therefore normally the law of the third party and *vice versa*), including possibly their conflicts laws, but it is likely to be the law of the *situs* of the assets if it concerns the proprietary effects of the agency. The question of the discharge of the agent and the implementation of his (fiduciary) duties would more properly be a question of the law of his country. This is a particular manifestation of the *lex loci actus* which is normally associated with the place where the agent acts, intended to act or has his business.

Set-offs and retention rights or other defences would not apply to the agent if he properly drops out of the arrangement under his own law as is likely in a disclosed agency. If he does not, his law may have to be considered in these areas. *Bona fide* acquisition of chattels by the agent for his principal, likely to be possible in civil law countries may as to the determination of the *bona fides* also be a matter of the law of the place of the agent or otherwise of the location of the relevant chattels. These seem the most common sense and expedient solutions. It would appear to remove this aspect of (undisclosed or indirect) agency from the contractual choice of law by the principal and agent, logical if the authority and its

---

[252] *Teheran-Europe Co. Ltd v ST Belton (Tractors) Ltd* [1968] 2 QB 545.
[253] See *Von Wedel v McGrath*, 180 F 2d 716 (1950).

operation are seen as a question of the objective law as it affects third parties. It would also concern the nature of the fiduciary duties and the liability or discharge of the agent both *vis-à-vis* the principal and particularly the third party.

Another approach altogether would be to consider the agency internationalised when principal and third party are in different countries and view the legal nature of the agency and its independence, at least in international commerce and finance between professionals, as transnationalised concepts in that case under the notion of the *lex mercatoria* subject principally to its own principles and logic, see for the *lex mercatoria* and the hierarchy of norms more generally chapter 1, section 1.1.5.

According to the pre-eminent author in this field, Ernst Rabel,[254] virtually every type of conflict solution had even then (by 1929) been proposed, including applicability of (a) the law of the underlying agency contract or internal relationship, particularly in legal systems not accepting the notion of independence, (b) the law of the place of the agent, easy to verify and particularly relevant if agents act as general representatives or as establishments of the principal in other countries and are subject to local customs, but it presents problems where both parties use agents from different countries, and (c) the law of the main contract or relationship created between principal and third party itself. It achieves unity in the applicable legal regime, including the duties of disclosure in the pre-contractual phase, but is also problematic as the main contract is established only after the agency is already in being and the law applicable to it may itself remain uncertain. This latter point is also an argument against applying the law of the internal relationship, which, if ascertainable, may moreover be entirely extraneous to the third party. The great diversity of approaches continues to this day.[255]

In fact, tripartite arrangements are particularly difficult structures in private international law and can very seldom be covered by reference to one domestic law. The multitude of domestic laws that may become applicable to the various aspects of such arrangements often present a picture of considerable complication and arbitrariness.

3.2.2 Treaty Law Concerning the Law Applicable to Agency

It is to be noted in this connection that Article 1(2)(f) of the EU Convention on the Law Applicable to Contractual Obligations (The Rome Convention of 1980) excludes from its scope the question whether an agent is able to bind a principal. It does not mean that the purely internal relationship between principal and agent and the contract between principal and third party are also excluded. The Hague Convention on the Law Applicable to Agency of 14 March 1978 on the other hand more in particular concerns itself with the role of the agent *vis-à-vis* the third party and his authority to bind the principal (and the third party to each other). It entered into force in 1992 between France, Argentina and Portugal, joined later in the same year by the Netherlands. It is valid for a period of five years and is automatically renewed for States that have not denounced it (Article 26).

It refers to *international* agencies which term remains itself undefined (Article 1). One must assume that the Convention is to be applied by any forum in a Contracting State confronted with a serious conflict of laws problem in this area. Agency itself is not properly defined either and problems of characterisation are likely to arise especially in the area of undisclosed or indirect agencies and alternative trusts: Article 1 considers anyone an agent

---

[254] *Vertretungsmacht für obligatorische Rechtsgeschäfte* (1929) 3 RabelsZ 807.
[255] See for the various alternatives and their supporters, HLE Verhagen, *Agency in International Law* (TMC Asser Institute, The Hague, 1995), 66*ff.*

who has the authority to act, acts or purports to act on behalf of a third person (the principal) in dealing with a third party. The fact that formally the agent acts in his own name is not apparently in itself material for the (dis)application of the Convention. Indirect agency in a civil law sense may thus be covered, although it is a very different thing, at least in civil law. The characterisation may itself well be based on *transnational or internationally common* notions of agency. However this may be, it leaves considerable uncertainty about what kind of agencies are covered.

The serious lack of clarity of the Convention on its own scope suggests that the concept of agency and the issues arising in an international context were insufficiently mapped out and studied for a comprehensive consensus on the applicable law to arise, even if one accepts that Conventions of this type are unavoidably based on compromise between domestic concepts and insights as long as transnational law notions have not superseded the conflict of law approach in this area. Agencies operating in the family, corporate and perhaps also in the banking and securities (the securities broker or 'commissionair') areas do not seem to fit.

Proprietary aspects like the direct acquisition of tangible assets by the third party if the agent, even if undisclosed or indirect, acquires them and the good faith acquisition of movables by an agent, the consequences of set-off and retention rights are not considered. According to the official Report, the exclusion of proprietary matters is self-evident, but it is somewhat surprising that the Convention itself does not make that plain as it is a most important issue.

One must thus assume that the Convention concentrates on the contractual aspects of the more current forms of consensual agency only. This being the case, it would have been normal to include a measure of flexibility in the applicable law if the formulae of the Convention proved inadequate in the great variety of factual situations, types of agency, and agency issues that may present themselves from time to time along the lines of Article 4(5) of the Rome Convention, an idea expressly rejected, however, by the Hague Conference at the time in the interest of quickly and easily ascertaining the applicable law. Yet this cannot be the only objective of treaty law of this kind. It also needs to make some sense.

As a consequence of this approach, Article 11 introduces the principle of the *lex locus actus* as a hard and fast conflicts rule making the law of the state of the business establishment of the agent at the time of acting applicable to his role, except that the law of the state in which the agent acted (if a country other than his own) applies if the principal or third party has its business establishment there or if the agent has acted at an exchange or auction or has no business establishment at all (which suggest that he is not a professional). There is no flexibility nor any distinction made here between creation and effect, *cf* also Article 6 for the internal effects (although the existence and effect of the authority referred to in Article 8 hardly seem an internal matter).

The system of the Convention is unitary in principle and the agency is thus supposed always to operate under the law of the (professional) agent. This is therefore the law of the one party (the agent), who legally is meant to drop out of the transaction altogether, whilst the acts of the principal and of the third party relying on the agency are at least as important as the acts of the agent himself. Unavoidably, the agent will often act either at the place of business of the principal or third party, when under the Convention exceptionally their law applies (except when it is through telephone, fax or mail, see Article 13). The Convention further accepts a contractual choice of law by agent and principal to be binding, certainly less appropriate in the proprietary, set-off and retention aspects which, as just mentioned, are, however, not believed covered by the Convention. This choice is effective on the third party only with his consent (Article 14).

Whatever the merits of this overall approach may be, the applicability of the law of the agent would normally appear appropriate as to his direct liability towards the third party under the agency (if any), because this is likely to be the law of the most characteristic obligation. It may also be appropriate as to his liability towards the principal under his (fiduciary) duties in the exercise of his functions, *cf* also Article 8c. A more difficult problem is presented in this respect by the undisclosed agency, especially in the securities area, when the principal as a private investor may need protection against the agent under his own mandatory law. Upon the analogy of Article 5 of the Rome Convention, these protections might then prevail, or otherwise perhaps the most favourable rule for a consumer investor. Article 16 leaves greater discretion relying on a significant connection. The public policy bar may further be used to curb the undesirable effects of the choice of law rules (Article 17).

A good argument can be made that undisclosed agencies are not covered by the Hague Agency Convention at all if under the law of their creation they only have an internal relationship, which could still include, however, automatic *in rem* transfers to the principal of any tangible assets the agent acquires for him, if acceptable to the *lex situs*, and any reimbursements of his cost by the principal. Naturally the internal relationship should then be covered by its own law, rather than by the rules of the Convention which for the internal effect of true agencies (where a direct relationship between the principal and the third party is created) in Articles 5 and 6 refers to the law chosen by the principal and his agent and otherwise imposes the law of the agent. The Hague Agency Convention should then apply only where the undisclosed agency has some automatic external effect, as under common law or in countries like Germany and Switzerland when the third party has no reasonable adverse interest. Proprietary aspects would in any event not be covered.[256]

It would probably have been better if undisclosed or indirect agencies, especially those in the securities area, had been expressly excluded from the scope of the Hague Agency Convention which does not seem to concern itself greatly with fiduciary duties (only in Article 8c), investors' protection and proprietary aspects either, all issues of particular importance in this area. The Convention allows Contracting States not to apply the Convention to banking transactions (Article 18), but this appears not to cover the securities business, except, according to the Official Report, the underwriting activities in the (primary) international markets. The banking exemption appears to exclude, however, agencies in connection with documentary letters of credit and bank guarantees.

An exemption may also be made for insurance and the exercise of public functions, but no other (Article 18). Portugal has invoked all exemptions, the Netherlands only the insurance exemption, France and Argentina none at all. The Convention itself excludes the shipmaster's agency (Article 2*f*), which is often thought to be covered by the law of the flag.

3.2.3 *The* Lex Mercatoria *and Agency*

Instead of attempting to develop internationally acceptable private international law principles pointing to the application of a domestic law of agency whenever an agency operates across borders, it may be more useful and efficient to look at agency in an international and professional context as a distinct structure dominated by its own intrinsic purpose and logic and further develop the common principles which may be found in this connection in domestic laws in order to interpret and supplement the agency structure and always

---

[256] See, however, also Verhagen, nn 255, 152, 161, *supra*, insisting on the general inclusion of the undisclosed agency in the scope of the Convention, but presumably not for the proprietary aspects.

subject to fundamental legal notions which in the case of agency may have a particular meaning as *ius cogens* where a principal creates the appearance of authority in others and in respect of fiduciary duties of the agent, see also chapter 1, section 1.4.4. In this approach a domestic law selected on the basis of the prevailing conflict of law rules would only be applicable as a last resort.

In the area of agency, the principles so developed would largely build on the common law notion of agency which is farther advanced in the development of fiduciary duties, the notion of tracing also in undisclosed agencies, and in the limitation of defences of the third party if the agency is not disclosed but if this party must realise that there normally is one, as in securities brokerage. The proposals contained in the European Principles of Contract Law do not appear adequate here and sufficiently mindful of the practical requirements either, at least when intermediaries are used in the securities and commodity trades, see more in particular section 3.1.6 above, also for the Unidroit Agency Convention of 1983, So for not sufficiently ratified.

The civil law concept of indirect representation when an agent operates in his own name, albeit for the risk and account of someone else, is an unsuitable concept and has shown to leave far too much power to the intermediary not properly balanced by fiduciary duties of the intermediary and tracing powers for the principal, even if modern civil law tries to improve the situation and find some compromise with the common law (undisclosed) ageny notions. The result is rather more confusion.

3.2.4   The EU Commercial Agent Directive

On 18 December 1986, the EU issued a Council Directive on the co-ordination of the laws of the Member States relating to self-employed commercial agents[257] now incorporated in the law of all Member States. It applies only to intermediaries in the *purchase and sale* of tangible assets and contains a set of harmonised, largely *mandatory* rules covering in those situations the relationship between principal and agent only. The essence is the latter's protection against the former. It is, strictly speaking, *not* concerned with the legal consequences of agency at all and particularly not its third party aspect or even the fiduciary duties of the agent towards his principal. As such, it does not truly have a place in the present discussion but may play a role in international sales in terms of the contractual relationship between commercial agents and the entity appointing them. It concerns here in essence the service aspect of agency.

The Directive is limited to those acting in the name and for the account of others in disclosed agencies. It aims at the protection of the agent against the principal and covers basically the duties of the principal towards the agent, the agent's rewards, the extent of the agent's own liability under the transaction, the termination of the agency agreement, the compensation regime and limits on a non-competition provision after termination.

The harmonisation effort in the EU largely eliminates conflicts of laws for agencies operating in the EU in the areas covered by the Directive except where protection is given under national laws in excess of those of the Directive. If there are non-EU elements in the agency, the law applicable to the agent's protection will still have to be established in accordance with the normal conflict of laws rules of the forum (including those of the Hague Agency Convention in France, Portugal and the Netherlands, if the case is brought in those countries, which normally refers to the applicability of the law of the agent).

---

[257] [1986] OJ L382/17.

The mandatory nature of the minimum rules of the Directive mean that these rules cannot easily be set aside by the law thus considered applicable to the agency if not respecting these rules, even if the agency contract is concluded between a non-EU based principal and agent, as long as the agent is operating or the agency has an effect in the EU. Particularly a choice of law by the principal and agent to opt out of these protections by selecting a law which does not incorporate them might not be effective under the circumstances. This is the likely result under Article 16 of the Hague Agency Convention in those EU Member States having ratified it. For those EU members who did not ratify this Convention, in a more general fashion the same result would appear to follow under Article 7 of the Rome Convention.

The key is therefore the contact between the agency and an EU country and the competence of courts in the EU. The analogy with employment contracts presents itself, commonly disallowing a contractual choice of law, *cf* for cases brought within the EU also Article 6 of the Rome Convention. In this connection an argument can be made, however, that the EU mandatory rules do not apply if a *professional* agent expressly agreed to another, for him less favourable regime whilst it is to be noted that most agents in the international sphere must be considered professionals. Where the agency operates outside the EU, the situation may be less clear, even if both, principal and agent, are based in the EU. The courts, certainly if outside the EU, are then likely to exercise their own discretion depending on the extent of the remaining contacts with the EU or the protection under their own *lex fori* if the agency operates in their jurisdiction.

Finally, the distinction between an agent and sole distributor who operates in his own name and for his own account is often blurred. Sometimes the seller sets the price and takes back any unsold goods so that the risk for the sole distributor is much reduced. In other cases of agency, the (*del credere*) agent may take at least the credit risk of the third-party so that he has a substantial exposure under the agency and does not drop out completely even if the agency is disclosed.

Regardless of the distribution of risks and the name in which the agent *formally* acts (either in the negotiation or conclusion of deals and the EU Directive rightly does not make a distinction between these two activities), for proper agency, the key is always whether direct ties are created between principal and third parties or not, which may also be the result of mere negotiation as pre-contractual activity, and not whether the agent has fully dropped out. If there is no privity created, there is no agency proper. It does not mean that the protection of the agent as envisaged by the Directive cannot be extended to sole distributors and similar operators. Often that will be fair as they tend to fulfil a similar role in the promotion of the seller's business and implementation legislation in the various EU countries might take that into account. This goes well beyond the scope of the EU Directive and its limited notion of agency as a service.

3

International Payments, Payment Systems and Mistaken Payments

Part I   The Notion and Modalities of Payment

1.1   Payment and Ways and Means of Payment

1.1.1   What is Payment?

All acts of performance are a kind of payment in the sense of giving satisfaction, but payment in the more technical sense is associated with the fulfillment or extinction of pre-existing *monetary* obligations, which are obligations reduced to money as expressed in the unit of account of the relevant currency.

Monetary obligations normally result as a reward, eg from the selling of an asset or the rendering of a service. They may also result from funding operations like the granting of a loan and the later repayment of principal. In that case, they result from a credit transaction and are no reward, but the interest payment on the loan is. As a funding transaction, a loan is a form of credit but should as such be clearly distinguished from other forms of credit, which, as in the case of a later payment for goods, merely postpone the maturity or payment date of monetary obligations and do not create new ones. Until the payment date, the claim is then simply immature.

All these monetary or payment obligations result in payments when performed. It should be noted in this connection that depositing money with a bank is not payment proper as it is not meant to extinguish a pre-existing monetary obligation, but repayment of a deposit is payment in a legal sense.

Money judgments or money awards are other types of monetary obligations. In contractual cases, they usually mean to confirm and reinforce existing monetary obligations but may add an *involuntary* damages element to them. Tort claims are also involuntary claims in which monetary damages are usually the key element and the resulting money judgment the real source of the recovery right and payment obligation.

As just mentioned, monetary claims may be *mature* or *immature*. In the former case, payment may be demanded immediately. In the latter case, there is a credit element and a maturity date before which the money is not due, even if the monetary claim undoubtedly exists. Thus granting credit upon a sale or upon the rendering of a service results in a delayed payment obligation and therefore a later maturity date of an existing monetary claim. A payment obligation may also be *contingent*, that means that it is as yet non-existent or only potentially existing and depending for its emergence upon a later event. A claim for monetary damages will thus be contingent as it depends upon a favourable judgment. A (secondary) guarantee results in a claim only upon default. The sales price for next year's harvest will be contingent on there being such a harvest, etc. Contingent payment obligations may have a maturity date (at which interest may accrue on them assuming the contingency is lifted), but they are not payable before the condition is fulfilled and are in any event immature until the agreed payment date.

Payment is the way these monetary obligations are fulfilled and extinguished once they become firm and mature. It can be achieved in several ways:

(a) *in cash* in the agreed currency or in the currency of any judgment or award by handing over coins or banknotes of that currency. Notes are in this connection promissory notes issued by a bank (now mostly the central bank of the currency);[1]

(b) *through a bank transfer* where money assumes the form of a transferable money claim on a bank in the agreed currency and the payee receives the immediate and unconditional disposition rights in the money claim so transferred. It will normally entail the substitution of a money claim of the payor on his bank by a money claim of the payee on his bank (assuming both payor and payee do not bank at the same bank);

(c) *through a set-off* which means that the payment obligation is extinguished (in whole or in part) through the settlement of a counterclaim of the debtor (which normally must also be monetary, in the same currency and mature) on his creditor;

(d) *through novation* which is the replacement of the payment obligation by another obligation (which may be a new payment obligation between the same parties or a tripartite agreement under which some one else will make the payment to the creditor in the same or another currency, like in the case of the negotiation of a promissory note or bill of exchange, which is now much less common), or

(e) *through a release* by the creditor by way of a gift or similar type of contractual arrangement.

Payment is normally achieved through *voluntary* performance of the payment obligation (even if a money judgment) in one of the first two ways, therefore in cash or through a bank transfer, but may also be enforced (therefore be *involuntary*) through court action leading to an attachment and execution sale of a sufficient number of the debtor's assets and a set-off of the proceeds against the payment obligation with a return of any overvalue to the debtor. This is also the sequel of monetary judgment claims if not voluntarily settled. Thus the set-off is a key element of all *involuntary* payments, but it is also a normal way of payment outside enforcement action. In most modern legal systems it is considered a unilateral right of a debtor with a counterclaim. In cash and bank payments, the debtor normally takes the initiative. That is also in the set-off, but a novation requires the cooperation of all parties. A release on the other hand is entirely dependent on the creditor and is a unilateral act on his part.

Payment proper — in cash, through a bank transfer, by set-off, novation, or through a release by the creditor — should be clearly distinguished from a *payment promise, payment instruction or tender to pay* in any particular form, like signing a cheque, drawing a bill of exchange in favour of a payee, issuing a promissory note (as distinguished from handing

---

[1] Technically speaking, it is also possible for the payment to be made through the transfer of assets other than money, eg through the transfer of chattels other than coins or banknotes. This possibility is not considered here any further and would make the payment subject to the formalities concerning the proper transfer of such an asset. However, it points up the fact that payment in cash is also a transfer of assets in its own right and payment through a bank transfer no less so as it is a transfer of (part of) a bank balance of a payor to a payee, as we shall see below.

over a bank note) or a letter of credit. These are *not* payments themselves, but only actions eventually leading to payment in the above sense of extinguishing a payment obligation when the creditor has received a monetary payment thereunder, unless of course by contract these actions themselves are accepted as full payment. This is not likely in the case of the writing of a cheque which depends for its effectiveness on sufficient debtor funds being in place in the bank on which the debtor drew the cheque which can only be determined at that time. Nor is the endorsement of a bill of exchange likely to be accepted as payment as its effectiveness depends foremost on the acceptance and creditworthiness of the drawee. However, it is possible that the issuance of a letter of credit is accepted as full payment in a sales contract and extinguishes the debtor's payment obligation; so may be the issuance of a promissory note of a bank to the creditor (or his order).

Payment in cash is now largely limited to smaller consumer transactions, especially minor cash sales, or to payment for minor services. In commerce, it has become exceptional and is no longer assumed to be the normal manner of payment. In these transactions, payment is normally through *a bank transfer* initiated by a(n electronic) payment instruction of the debtor/payor, and, if nothing more is being said, the payor may be assumed to have a right to pay in that manner and be liberated upon such payment once completed. It means that if in commerce a cash payment is still required by the payee, it should be clearly agreed, although, unless specifically stipulated otherwise, the payor may still retain the option to pay in cash under his own law, at least if the payment is in his own country and in the currency of that country. That may be the consequence of this currency being legal tender. The debtor may have here more rights and more options than the creditor.

Payment through set-off depends on the existence of a counterclaim which must normally also be *monetary, mature* and in the *same currency*. In some countries, it also requires some *connexity* between both claims although all these requirements may be waivable by the parties in advance. These aspects will be discussed in greater detail in section 1.3 below. A set-off outside bankruptcy is under modern law normally *not* automatic and must be properly notified to the creditor/payee if the debtor/payor wishes to use this form of payment, but the creditor's consent is *not* required and there is therefore no creditor's veto right. Rather, it suggests that parties may vary the netting conditions as they often do in modern netting arrangements. Under applicable law, they may even be able to expand the scope of the set-off to include non-mature claims and claims in other currencies or lift other restrictions (like the one of connexity), see section 1.3.3 below.

Payment by novation is on the other hand exceptional and involves the termination of the old obligation in exchange for a new one. This cannot be done without the creditor's consent and is often a tripartite agreement under which a third-party undertakes to pay in lieu of the debtor. In that case, it leads to debtor substitution. It usually comes about because the first debtor has a claim on the second debtor which is settled in this manner (but only with creditor's consent). It is *not* a form of assignment, which means creditor substitution, does not require the other party's (debtor's) consent, and does not extinguish the existing payment obligation, see for the difference more in particular chapter 4, section 1.7.5.

Payment by set-off and payment by novation may be combined in *novation netting*: see for this important facility, especially in interest rate swaps, section 1.3.3 below. Payment by novation will not be discussed further here.

A *payment through a release* by the creditor will also not be discussed any further. It should be distinguished from a payment through novation as nothing is put in the place of the payment obligation proper. In common law, both may be so similar that the concept of consideration (see chapter 2, section 1.2.4) is a problem in either and a novation or a release may not therefore be binding except if arranged in a special form (by deed).

A payment in whichever of the above-distinguished ways is effective — therefore may be considered to have extinguished the payment obligation of the debtor — only if it achieves a full discharge of the latter. For this to happen, it first needs to be *complete* and *unconditional*. It must also be legally made. Completeness is normally easily verifiable in cash payments. In the case of a bank transfer, the payment is notably not complete and therefore not fully effective

(a)   when it is subject to a later value date (except if agreed) or release notice of the debtor,
(b)   when it does not give the creditor full disposal rights of the money (therefore an unconditional credit in his own account),
(c)   when it does not allow the payee to receive interest on the money, and
(d)   (in an international setting) when there is no full convertibility and transfer-ability of the (foreign) currency, unless that risk was clearly taken by the payee.

The result of a defective payment is a default if the due date has passed. Other require-ments of a valid payment are:

(a)   The payment must in principle emanate from the payor or be made by an authorised person on his behalf. Thus an unauthorised payment by someone else may not be payment of the relevant monetary claim, nice as it may be, without the debtor's acknowledgement,
(b)   the payment must be clearly identified in relation to its underlying cause. Thus leaving some cash may not be adequate payment,
(c)   as a corollary, the creditor/payee, or someone acting on his behalf with proper authority (usually his bank), may have to accept the payment for it to become final and to extinguish the debt. It is another reason why the mere tender of pay-ment is not sufficient to achieve liberating effect for the debtor and therefore proper payment, although the acceptance can be implied even if cash is left on the doorstep and not promptly returned or when a bank transfer is not promptly protested. Depending on the circumstances, the debtor/payor may even be seen as agent for the creditor/payee in the aspect of the acceptance of the payment. In any event, it would seem that the consent may not be unreasonably withheld,
(d)   in this vein and further depending on the agreement, the simple implementa-tion of the agreed payment steps could be considered to achieve full payment regardless of any further act of acceptance on the part of the creditor. As already mentioned, even the handing over of a cheque or acceptance of a bill of exchange could then suffice as full payment and discharge the debtor, provided the contract is clear on this.

It is obvious that there is here a more *subjective* or *objective* view of payment possible and it is necessary always to distinguish between the relationship giving rise to the payment obli-gation, the various ways of payment, and the formalities in this connection, and the act of payment itself in the nature of extinguishing a monetary claim whilst fully liberating the debtor.

The relationship giving rise to the payment obligation will usually dictate how payment is to be achieved and may therefore define the method of payment and the requirements in terms of a release, but all of the various payment methods also have *extra-contractual* aspects and requirements. Thus the payment in cash or through a bank transfer involves a *transfer of assets* between payor and payee and this transfer is in principle subject to the normal legal requirements of transfer which will depend under applicable law on the nature of the asset like coins, bank notes or bank balances. Payment through set-off, novation or a release is no less subject to further extra-contractual legal requirements concerning these various legal structures.

Thus the different methods of payment each have their own legal form and may foremost require *capacity* and *intent* of the parties to the relevant transfers, set-offs, novations or releases. In the case of payment in cash or through a bank transfer, there may also be delivery requirements, at least in countries that require it for the transfer of title in chattels and also impose the condition of proper acceptance. Especially in causal systems of title tranfers, see chapter 4, section 1.5.6, that makes these ways of payment all to some extent vulnerable and there could be situations in which the relevant form of payment would not succeed or could be undone for lack of capacity or intent on either side. This is *not* greatly desirable and below it will have to be considered how these ordinary legal requirements may be subject to some *modification* and *limitation* in connection with payments. This concerns the important issue of *finality*.

To repeat, when a proper tender of payment in one of these forms as well as an acceptance of the payment is necessary (in principle) for a valid payment in the sense of extinguishing the payment obligation, this implies as a minimum that for an effective discharge of the debtor there may be further legal requirements in terms of proper legal capacity and the intention of obtaining or granting the release (the *animus solvendi*). There may also have to be sufficient disposition in the case of a transfer of cash or bank transfer. In civil law of the German variety, this is the same as saying that payment in its various stages is a *juristic or legal act* on behalf of both the payor and payee even if the precise requirements may have to be distinguished for the various ways of payment and the various stages.

It might be and is sometimes argued, however, that, at least in the case of a cash payment, the acceptance is primarily physical and could result from the mere handing over of cash, accomplishing at the same time both the transfer and the liberating payment. This handing over and its acceptance could then be considered mere *acts in fact*, or factual acts which do not have any particular legal requirements (although the underlying real agreement or delivery still has). It is a way of promoting finality. Even the instruction and acceptance of a bank transfer could still be so construed, as we shall see, but it may be more strained. This would perhaps be a more normal way of arguing in countries that have an abstract system of title transfer, like Germany, see again chapter 4, section 1.5.6. Also it may be easier to argue in the case of an electronic transfer of book-entry entitlements in respect of investment securities than it is in respect of bank transfers under which banks transfer their own balances, see also chapter 4, section 3.1.6 for this difference.

Where a set-off is considered an automatic form of payment, as it is at least in bankruptcy of one of the parties to it, see section 1.3.1 below, it could also be seen as an act in fact that might at the same time lead to a liberating payment, but not where an election must be made and notice must be given by the payor which is now the more common approach outside bankruptcy. In a novation, payment could never be seen as a mere act in fact. Neither could it be in a voluntary release by the creditor. Thus the concept of a juristic or legal act, whether or not relevant in cash payments, is likely to be relevant with ever greater urgency in the non-cash forms of payment, therefore in bank transfers, set-offs, novations and releases by the creditor. It raises the question whether the liberating effect itself could ever be a mere factual consequence of the implementation of the payment steps without further legal requirements in terms of capacity, intent (and disposition rights for transfers).

The disadvantages of a liberating payment being itself a legal act may be substantially diluted by de-emphasising the capacity requirement at least in payments between professionals, by an objective interpretation of the co-operation rights and duties of payor and payee, by an abstract system of transfer, and by the assumption of full payment when all payment steps agreed by the parties have been taken by the debtor. Even so, the question remains how far capacity and intent (or the lack of it) may still affect the validity of the various alternative payment steps themselves (in terms of cash or bank transfers, set-offs, novations and releases). This aspect, which may show a greater civil law than common law concern (even if in common law these issues cannot truly be avoided either) will be discussed more in particular in connection with payment through a bank transfer in section 1.2.2 below.

1.1.2   The Notion of Money as Unit of Account or Unit of Payment; Money as Store of Value

In all payments of monetary obligations figures the importance of money.[2] In payment in cash or through a bank transfer, money figures both as *unit of account* and as *unit of payment*. In the set-off, novation or creditor's release, it only figures as unit of account.

Money as *unit of account* identifies the currency of the monetary obligation and the amount of money owed as expressed in that currency. Thus a unit of account figures in all types of payment, but money as *unit of payment* figures only if it effectively changes hands. That is therefore only relevant for cash payments and payments through a bank transfer, which is, technically speaking, the substitution (by the payor) of a claim on his bank for a claim on the payee's bank (if a different bank) in favour of the payee.

Particularly important aspects of money as *unit of payment* (and therefore not relevant in set-offs, novations and creditor's releases) are that:

(a)   the creditor must accept the payment in the agreed currency;
(b)   the origin of the money is irrelevant whether it is in the form of coins, of promissory notes of (central) banks, or of bank balances;
(c)   even if the money was originally stolen, this has no effect on the payment once the origin of relevant money can no longer be identified. This is normally the case when it becomes irreversibly commingled with other money of the payor of the same currency, either physically or in his bank account.

As already mentioned in the previous section, there remain in respect of all payments in principle all the normal transfer requirements in terms of capacity of the parties and an underlying intent. Only in respect of units of payment they are joined by the requirement of actual delivery at least in countries that require it for the transfer of title in chattels and notes and disposition rights in the case of transfers of cash or bank transfers.

Money is, besides a unit of account and a unit of payment, also a *store of value*. Under the old gold standard, the emphasis was principally on this aspect of money, which was not difficult to grasp as it meant gold. In that system, paper money was always convertible into it. Thus a (central) bank issuing banknotes promised to pay gold upon their presentation against a fixed exchange rate. In that system, the unit of account indicated how much gold

---

[2] See for the nature of money in a legal sense, the classic treatise by FA Mann, *The Legal Aspects of Money* (4th edn, 1984).

was to be given in payment of a monetary obligation. If currencies rather than gold were used, it would indicate how many notes in the indicated currency were required to achieve payment in full. In truth, it was not of great interest in which currency the notes as units of accounts were expressed, like dollars, sterling, marks or francs as long as central banks strove to maintain the intrinsic (gold) value of their notes, which they normally did (although they could devalue the currency in relation to gold). Being all convertible into gold, they were in fact interchangeable with each other on the basis of gold at a fixed rate.

The use of money in the payment circuit, therefore as unit of payment, would automatically follow and was like an exchange of one inherent value against another. There was no major risk here for the payee, even if he contracted for payment in a foreign currency, as long as all were convertible into gold and into each other at a fixed rate.

1.1.3   Paper Currencies and Modern Currency Election Clauses

The situation changed when money lost its intrinsic value after the abandonment of the gold standard by most countries in the 1930s. Its value could, depending on the currency, henceforth be politically adjusted and practically evaporate (through inflation). Modern paper money has no more than a statutory value base and has thereby acquired the form of a *national* currency without any objective value. It can be devalued against other currencies at will or be allowed to float against other currencies which is now the more normal situation. It is only accepted in payment because of a mandatory statutory requirement that at least in the country of the currency it should be so. There is no good reason why it should be accepted as such anywhere else except where parties have expressly agreed to it. As promissory note, it now means no more than that the central bank issuing the currency will upon presentation of the note provide another note in the same currency. Outside its own borders, the foreign exchange rates may change dramatically from day to day. This may make payment in foreign currency much more speculative as far as value is concerned. In the modern system of paper money, money thus lost its intrinsic value and as a consequence also its international status.

Especially where there are large differences between in- and outgoing payments in the country of the particular currency as a consequence of trade imbalances leading to serious payment outflows (not compensated for by capital inflows), the value of the currency will fluctuate considerably in the international markets. If these imbalances become structural, as they are in many developing countries and as they were even in many developed countries after World War II, a restrictive foreign exchange regime — therefore a regime that does not allow for the free convertibility and transferability of the own currency by the own citizens (as payors) — often is the sequel of such artificial or paper currencies. It thus becomes a *soft* currency. If in such situations foreign currency was agreed as unit of payment, it might not be automatically available to a payor either who could not then be allowed to obtain such foreign exchange freely in the foreign exchange market or from its own central bank in exchange for the own currency.

Such a restrictive foreign exchange regime preventing a free outflow of currency or of foreign currency reserves, may at the same time reduce imports (which in such situations often also become subject to prior official approvals, tariffs or quota systems). In most of the developed world, these foreign exchange limitations and import restrictions are now gone. That is for foreign exchange so at least between all EU Members (since 1988) and now also between the EU, the USA and Japan, although there may still be some trade barriers, even between these major economic powers (but substantially no longer within the EU).

They have been or are gradually dismantled in GATT/GATS/WTO, see also chapter 6, section 2.1.

Naturally, in a system of artificial currencies, there is a much greater importance attached to the currency chosen by the parties for payment and there also results a more fundamental distinction between the currency of account and the currency of payment if they are not the same. Clearly in international sales to preserve value in this system, (a) currency election clauses may become desirable under which the parties choose a strong currency for payment. As we just saw, in a restrictive foreign exchange regime of the *payor*, such clauses may not be effective as the payor may not be able to obtain the necessary strong currency on the due date. In that case, (b) foreign parties may agree a specific strong currency of account (a more stable currency therefore, usually the US dollar), different from the currency of payment, which will be the weaker currency of the payor, the only one that may effectively be used for payment). Payment would then be made in whatever number of units of the weaker currency of payment it would take on the date of payment to correspond to the amount stated in the currency of account and the exchange rate would be determined by the foreign exchange market on the payment day. The result is that the payee still ends up with non-convertible and non-transferable currency in the country of the payor, but at least he will have more of it and will have avoided the devaluation risk so far.

In international contracts, which are contracts between parties from different countries under which goods and services (normally) move, such clauses became quite common. In this connection a *gold clause* might also be used, at least as unit of account. Such clauses, even if forbidden for local transactions, were often upheld for international contracts, even if governed by that same local law. At least that was the situation in France after it left the gold standard in the 1930s.[3]

Currency election or gold clauses thus became quite common in international contracts before and after World War II and were more palatable if such an election was only made in respect of the unit of account. In domestic contracts it remained exceptional. Some thought that such (domestic) foreign currency contracts had to be re-characterised and became in the case of a sale in fact an exchange of two types of goods rather than a sale against payment even though the difference was not in all legal systems very great.

The risk of ending up with substantial balances in local currencies in the country of the payor which could not be exported or converted without approval of the country of the payor was, however, undesirable for parties which had no substantial payment requirements in that country. Hence prior agreement for such conversion and transfer was normally sought from the relevant authorities in the payor country. Even if letters of credit (see sections 2.1.6 *ff* below) under which foreign payments would be made (in the country of the seller/payee) were issued, the buyer/payor would normally require his government's or central bank's approval before they were arranged.

1.1.4   Freely Convertible and Transferable Currency

The principal concern of the payee in a system of artificial currencies is therefore that the currency of ultimate payment, whatever it is and however it is calculated (where there is a difference between the currency of account and the currency of payment), is *fully convertible*

---

[3] This was the gist of the French gold clause cases: see also GR Delaume, *Transnational Contracts* (1989), 119. In France it led to the development of the theory of the 'international contract' which in that country also became important in the attitude towards arbitration clauses.

and freely transferable. Convertibility means in this connection that the authorities in the country of payment will allow the conversion of the proceeds into a different (harder) currency if required. But the payee needs also to be certain that the proceeds (even if freely convertible) may be transferred to wherever he directs them (normally his own country). That is transferability. It usually goes together with convertibility but need not. Thus, if the currency of payment is not that of the debtor, the creditor will *not only* be concerned that the necessary currency is available to the payor on the date of payment, *but also* that there is free transferability to the place of the creditor or to any other he may indicate, assuming that the agreed currency is in principle available and as hard currency also convertible. Otherwise, the money might still have to be held in blocked accounts or could itself come from blocked accounts and remain as such embargoed, subject therefore to investment restrictions and the restrictions in the use these moneys in further payments (by the creditor).

So, even the transferability of harder convertible currency may still be curtailed by some countries, mostly in respect of residents but sometimes even in respect of foreign holders of such currency. Where there are restrictions in respect of both convertibility and transferability, different procedures and approvals may apply to lift them. In practice, the question of convertibility and transferability has lost a great deal of importance with the freeing up of currencies and their movement in the last two decades. Euros, Sterling, the US, Canadian, Australian and New Zealand dollar, as well as the Yen, are now all freely convertible and transferable *per se* (although one can never be absolutely sure that this will continue, especially important for long term agreements). Most other currencies have followed suit.

As already mentioned at the end of the previous section, the dangers to convertibility and especially transferability were traditionally alleviated through the use of confirmed letters of credit payable in freely convertible and transferable currency (often US dollars or the currency of the seller) in the country of the seller, see for the details sections 2.1.6*ff* below. Confirming banks in that country would often assume the currency (convertibility and transferability) risks which they could often handle better than their clients (sellers), if only through informal clearing and set-off facilities, frequently in the context of special arrangements with their own central banks as currency regulators or otherwise only with their approval from case to case.

By choosing a country of payment that does not restrict access to convertible currency and does not limit its transfer, parties may aim at a similar form of protection. However, if the country of the payor subsequently imposed mandatory restrictions disallowing the payor to make the relevant payments elsewhere, there would obviously still be a problem, especially if the payor did not have the relevant currency available in the agreed country of payment and was dependent on his own central bank to allow the transfer of adequate funds. Even if the payor had these funds available in the foreign place of payment, the limitations of his home country in this connection could still affect him or be used by him as an excuse. In that case, the courts in the agreed country of payment (assuming they had jurisdiction, to be determined for example pursuant to an attachment of the relevant funds by the payee) would have to consider the extraterritorial effect of these restrictions. Article 7 of the 1980 Rome Convention on the Law Applicable to Contractual Obligations (see chapter 2, section 2.3.8), gives the courts in the EU discretion depending on the closeness of the connection of the payment with the country of the payor and the effects of the application or dis-application of the relevant mandatory rules. There is here a balancing of interests and a determination of which policy must prevail, see also chapter 1, section 2.2.6.

In this connection, the International Monetary Fund (IMF) rules were also important and still are in countries that have not made their currencies fully convertible and transferable.

Under the Bretton Woods Agreements of 1944, which set up the IMF system, there is a distinction between current payments and capital transfers. The IMF rules concern themselves with payments in this connection (Article XXX-d of the IMF Articles of Agreement) and are self executing or directly effective. For current payments in respect of the delivery of goods and the rendering of services cross-border, governmental payment limitations are in principle forbidden (Article VIII-2-a), except for those members that claim an exception under the transitory arrangements of Article XIV. The number of these so-called Article XIV countries has steadily declined and accordingly the number of Article VIII countries has increased. Convertibility in this context means the right of the (foreign) seller when paid in the currency of the buyer to use the proceeds freely in settlement of current payment obligations in that currency, or to demand conversion into its own currency (through intervention of their own central bank with the central bank of the currency concerned). The free convertibility for payment purposes in this manner does not mean that there may not be supervision, if only to guard against disguised capital transfers in countries still limiting them or against the possession and circulation of foreign currency. There is a way of challenging these limitations on their legality before the relevant national courts pursuant to Article VIII-2-b since the IMF rules in this area are directly effective in Member States.

Before the full liberalisation of the foreign exchange regime in the European Union (EU), the EU had a farther reaching foreign exchange regime operating between its Members as a consequence of its freedom of movement of goods, services, payments and capital. It was effectively superseded (especially as to capital movements and payments by a 1988 Directive which since 1990 has eliminated virtually all foreign exchange restrictions (in respect of both capital transfers and payments), also in respect of nonmember countries, see more in particular chapter 6, section 2.4.6. This full liberalisation occurred after a period in which, on the basis of the directly effective Article 106(1) of the original founding Treaty (of Rome of 1958), only current payments were considered liberalised and merely as a sequel of the ongoing liberalisation in the movement of persons, goods, services and capital. Even then, it was only achieved in the currency of the Member State in which the creditor or beneficiary resided. Agreed payments in the currency of the debtor were therefore not necessarily free. Capital transfers were not liberalised at all as the relevant Article 67 of the Treaty (concerning the freedom of capital movements) was not considered directly effective in this respect without further implementing legislation.

The 1988 Directive was by its very nature directly applicable to all Member States and covered all movements of money, whether for capital transfers or current transactions, all at the prevailing exchange rate for the latter. It ruled out two tier foreign exchange markets in the process. Between those EU countries that accepted the Euro, the foreign exchange risk has completely disappeared in this connection.

1.1.5   *The Different Ways and Means of Payment: Pull and Push Systems*

It cannot be repeated often enough that promising payment, writing a cheque, giving a payment instruction to the bank, or even tendering payment is not the same as payment unless the relevant contract directly or indirectly so provides which may however, become a matter of interpretation. Normally, the writing of a cheque, the drawing or even acceptance of a bill of exchange in favour of a payee, the issuing of a promissory note or even a letter of credit, a credit card imprint, let alone the giving of a payment (or giro) instruction by the debtor to its bank, are not in themselves payment as long as they do not effectively result in the necessary cash or bank transfers extinguishing the relevant payment obligation itself. A key issue is therefore to determine when this has happened and that is often less clear than it may seem to be.

Thus in bank transfers, a cheque, credit card imprint or bank (giro) instruction directed by a debtor to his bank do not in themselves implement and extinguish the original promise to pay money. If acted upon by the bank, it could technically be considered to substitute (*vis-à-vis* the creditor) a promise of the bank for the original payment promise of the debtor (which could thereby be considered extinguished), although legally this is normally not considered to be the proper analysis (probably for lack of creditor's consent to what in effect would be debtor substitution). Under applicable law, the payment may be deemed concluded only by the crediting of the payee's account in his own bank. A direct debit should be similarly considered and even a credit card imprint, once accepted by the debtor's bank, produces no greater effect. The possible substitution or at least the meaning of the instruction being followed up in the payment circuit will be discussed more in detail below in section 1.2.

Payment instructions to banks technically vary, and this affects the initiative in the chain of transfers. It may lead to some legal differences. If by cheque, the initial instruction to the banking system will be given by the payee/creditor, who will normally send the cheque he received from his payor/debtor to his *own* bank which will present it (through the clearing) to the payor's bank (if a different bank) on which the cheque was drawn. It is sometimes thought, however, that the initiative of the creditor's bank will rather give rise to the interbank transfer described in greater detail below in section 1.2 at the initiative of the *creditor's bank* as a *'pull'* system of payment, based on a chain of *debit transfers*. This is also thought to result from direct debit instructions of the debtor which are usually also handled (or 'pulled') by the creditor's bank. Bank giro instructions or credit card imprints, on the other hand, give rise to a *'push'* system of payment (or *credit transfers*) because payment is then initiated by the *debtor's bank*.

Modern law may maintain somewhat different approaches in respect of either system. The 1989 Article 4A UCC in the USA and the 1992 Uncitral Model Law on Credit Transfers *only* cover the credit or 'push' systems and exclude more generally consumer payments of any kind (section 4A-108 UCC). In the USA, consumer transfers are mostly covered by the Federal Consumer Protection Act and their electronic banking by the federal Electronic Fund Transfer Act (EFTA) and Fed Regulation E. Article 4 UCC on the other hand covers the handling of cheques in the payment system and assumes here a pull mechanism or debit transfer system whilst ignoring that these cheques are usually presented by the creditor's bank to the debtor's bank that will subsequently push the funds through the system (if it still owes something after the clearing). The reason is one of convenience. The creditor may not have an account at the debtor's bank on which the cheque was drawn but may want his account to be credited rather than to receive cash. His own bank will normally handle the matter as a special service.

The terminology is in any event confusing. It would appear that there are in fact never debit transfers, not therefore in a 'pull' system either unless specially authorised by statute. Without such authorisation, debits being obligations cannot easily be transferred or pushed up through the banking system from the creditor's bank to the debtor's bank. A debit transfer system would suggest that the creditor's bank upon (provisionally) crediting its client's account, seeks reimbursement from the debtor's bank by debiting that bank (or any intermediary bank in the payment circuit). Legally, this would require a system of consents between the banks involved as nobody can be forced into a reimbursement or assume a debit function against its will. Failing a statutory base, this need for consent(s) complicates this system. It is, nevertheless, the system suggested by Article 4 UCC in the case of payments by cheque in the US which as a consequence envisages a series of provisional debits through the banking system up to the debtor's bank whilst a (provisional) credit to the creditor precedes the debit to the debtor (and is therefore strictly speaking not 'payment' as it is not complete and does not unconditionally give the creditor the free disposition of the money). In a 'push' system or system of credit transfers, a debit to the payor will precede the credit to the payee and it is the debtor's bank that subsequently *credits* other banks. Here at least no consents are necessary as only credits are transferred or these consents may be implied.

1.1.6 Cash Payments and the Bank Transfer Option in Commerce and Finance: The Notions of Independence or Abstraction and Finality

Cash payments are the simplest and oldest form of payment. They do not create great practical problems except that they are unwieldy in large amounts. They remain particularly common in consumer sales and in the payment for small services but have become unusual in commerce and finance. As already mentioned above in section 1.1.1, commercial payors must now be deemed always to have the option to pay through a bank transfer unless otherwise specifically required by the contract giving rise to the payment. They may also retain the right to make cash payment in their own country but only if the agreed currency is of that country and performs the role of legal tender. Even so, the contract may still indicate in which bank the payee wants to receive payment when cash payment must be deemed excluded. Commercial cash payments are now unlikely. Not only is the unwieldiness a problem, but cash payment in larger amounts may in modern times also give rise to investigations into the origin of the cash in the context of money-laundering prevention and are also from that point of view undesirable. The same applies to making large cash deposits or other large cash payments to banks.

On the other hand, where the payor has under current practices the option and wants to pay through a bank transfer, he may, as we already saw and as will be more extensively discussed below, not only need some kind of legal acceptance from the payee before the payment is complete but he is also dependant on the co-operation of the payee in the identification of the latter's bank account. As payees seldom have a good reason to withhold co-operation in this regard and insist on cash payment instead, problems are now rare in this connection but it is obviously wise to provide in the contract for the precise payment details. They may also appear from the invoice or may be known to the payor from prior business contacts.

Without some specific instructions or established practices, it is risky to pay into *any* bank account of the payee, who may hold them for very different purposes in different countries with different banks. Prompt notice to the payee indicating when and where a bank payment was made may in such circumstances still be considered a precondition for a full release of the payor/debtor.

As was already mentioned in section 1.1.1 above, even in cash payments there may be the question of the capacity and intent of either party to make or receive a payment with the subsequent release of the debtor, which may also imply disposition rights in the cash or bank balance transferred. Also, even in cash payments, there are extra-contractual aspects in the legal transfer of the cash itself and in the need for legal delivery in some legal systems. They raise themselves issues of capacity and intent and even legal formalities, although in business or professional dealings the former tend to be de-emphasised, see chapter 2 section 1.2.9, whilst the latter will acquire an objective meaning. There is also the question of acceptance, even if, depending on the circumstances, the debtor may here operate as agent for the creditor (whilst keeping the cash apart). At the level of the discharge, capacity and intent of the creditor may play a further role. In cash payments, it is not unusual to find (implied) amended rules so that at least the mere handing over of the cash in itself may be deemed to constitute a legal transfer, sufficient acceptance, and a full discharge of the debtor at the same time. Capacity and intent issues are then irrelevant whilst this type of payment is considered *factual* in principle (and therefore *not* a legal act, subject to its own legal requirements). This is much more difficult in bank transfers as was already noted above and as we shall see below. It is even more difficult in the other forms of payment.

To repeat, *minimising* these legal requirements for the transfer of payments and their liberating effect is an important legal issue in this connection and closely related to the important issue of *finality*. It is not useful that bank instructions and their effect remain uncertain and too much in abeyances. Whatever the direct requirements of capacity and intent may be, at least the system of instructions should not be disturbed by problems in the relationship (a) between creditor and debtor or (b) between them and their respective banks. This is the notion of *independence* or *abstraction* of payment instructions which has therefore a dual character. It means that if mistakes or invalid transfers are made between creditor and debtor, this will require new sets of instructions and no earlier payments through the banking system should automatically be deemed reversed.

That may still be different between the entities or banks *directly* involved in a mistake between them like in the case eg of a wrong booking (too much or too little or to the wrong account etc), which may give rise to an automatic (right to) adjustment between them within the confines of the (interbank) payment system that they operate, although it is unlikely to undo any further transfers in the chain that already took place. In any event, it could amount to a system of debit transfers for which authorisation would be required in every part of the chain.

1.2 Payment through Bank Transfers

1.2.1 The Nature of Bank Accounts, the Current Account and its Use in the Payment Circuit

The legal aspects of bank transfers remain in many legal systems unsettled. In most countries, the development of the law in this area was left to case-law. However, as was already noted, in the USA, Article 4 UCC and, more recently, also Article 4A UCC, which is devoted to electronic bank transfers, deal more extensively with the legal issues arising in this connection and with the position and duties of payor, payee and intermediary banks.

For payment through bank transfers, it is necessary to look more closely at (a) the nature of a bank account and its use in the payment circuit, (b) the intermediary banks that may become involved when payor and payee have accounts in different banks, and (c) the types of instructions that these banks require and at their validity and effect.

A banking relationship usually starts with the opening of a current or checking account and the depositing of some money into it. Legally this money becomes the property of the bank and the depositor will have no more than a contractual right to its restitution. The deposit should under prevailing rules entitle the depositor to take his money back when he needs it (if it is a demand deposit) and to participate in the payment system organised by the banks to the extent of the positive balance in the account. In most legal systems, there is a right in principle to such a checking account and to participation in the payment system in this manner and such an account can normally not be refused without cause (which may be in a bad credit record) or terminated at will short of (impending) default. However, for the account to be maintained, there will normally have to be some (nominal) positive balance at all times and the bank charges must be paid.[4] This being said, the right to a bank account is increasingly considered a fundamental right but there is also a practical governmental interest in even the poor having bank accounts so that at least social security benefits can be properly and timely paid in this manner.

This type of current account does not entitle the client to much more, notably not to a cheque book or credit card or to interest on the balance or to any kind of overdraft or other banking facilities in terms of loans or mortgages. These are all separate transactions even though they may become integrated in the overall banking relationship, certainly in terms of the banking lien or the netting off of all positions in the case of a default under any of these transactions or even in another relationship (under cross default clauses). This integration is likely to take place through the current account which is in any event likely to be credited with all income on special deposits and debited with all interest payments that must be made on outstanding long term loans as well as on any overdraft in the current account itself and by any credit card charges. This type of banking relationship and its integrated nature is more fully discussed in chapter 6, section 1.2.8.

As just mentioned, upon depositing money into a bank account, even if this is done in cash, the depositor (current account or deposit account holder) retains no more than *a personal claim* against his bank. The depositor is therefore no longer the legal owner of the money, *not even* together with all other depositors. For his creditors, this personal claim of an account holder against its bank remains, of course, an ordinary asset from which they may recover their own claims on the account holder through suitable legal process (garnishment of the bank). In a bankruptcy of the account holder, the creditors would therefore have direct recovery rights against the bank for the balance, but in a bankruptcy of the bank, they are only competing creditors of the bank itself, just like their debtor as the bank's client would have been.

There may be other parties interested in the account besides the creditors of the account holder. In fact, the bank account may become separated from the account holder and his estate, e.g. if it can be proven that the balance concerns proceeds belonging to others altogether and is not (substantially) commingled with moneys of the account holder himself. That is the situation with *client accounts*. In common law, there might also be tracing rights of a third party, for example when the account holder sold assets belonging to the third party and deposited the proceeds in his own account. The third-party is here likely to allege a (remedial constructive) trust in his favour for which the account holder is merely the trustee.

---

[4] There is longstanding case law to the effect in the US, see *Elliott v Capital City State Bank*, 103 NW 777 (1905) and *Grants Pass & Josephine Bank v City of Grants Pass*, 28 P 2d 879 (1934). The emphasis is on the bank's discretion subject, however, to applicable banking laws. The only obligation was the repayment of demand deposits, now probably followed by an obligation to accept payment instructions to the limit of any positive balance in the account. Consumer law is likely to be more specific, see in the US the Federal Consumer Protection Act and for electronic banking by the federal Electronic Fund Transfer Act (EFTA) and Fed. Regulation E. In Canada, the right to a bank account has more recently been cast in terms of a human right, Canadian Human rights Act, RSC 1985, c. H-6. In France under Article 58 of the Banking Act of 1984, the Central Bank may force a bank under its supervision to open an account for persons who cannot do so on their own but the kind of services that may be so obtained are naturally very limited and only cover deposits, incoming payments and cash withdrawals. There is not even a right to a cheque book, let alone a credit card. The liberal way credit cards are distributed, especially in the USA, may, however, give any account holder some kind of right in this regard.

Again, whosoever may claim interests in a particular bank account held in whomever's name, it should always be realised that the funds deposited with a bank are never properly the property of the account holder, his substitutes, or co-account holders. They belong to the bank alone, subject to personal (contractual) claims only of the various interest holders (even if they result from their proprietary claims against the account holder). This is quite different from a deposit made for a house purchase with a real estate agent or as down payment on the purchase of a car. These latter deposits should remain segregated from the agent or car dealer's own money and the client should retain a proprietary interest in them. The same goes for a deposit account with an investment broker or fund manager or a custody account with a custodian of investment securities in book-entry systems, see chapter 4, sections 3.1.3*ff.* Even if there is commingling with funds of others, there may result in that case a co-ownership right against the fund manager or custodian and interest holders remain in principle proprietary claimants. Mere personal claims may arise here only when the assets are commingled with those of the agent or custodian itself and more especially if they are used or substituted by him for other assets to such an extent that the original assets can no longer be identified. This danger may be greatest in respect of fungible assets like money and most types of investment securities which the agent or custodian may use as if they were his own, although strictly speaking it does not rule out co-ownership with the agent or custodian itself. One of the virtues of modern book-entry systems is that they attempt to overcome this commingling problem at least for investment securities.[5]

Obviously a bank would not normally accept payment instructions from a client if there is no sufficient money in the account unless there is also an agreed overdraft facility. On the other hand, as any deposit is converted in a claim against the bank, payment through a bank transfer is in essence always a transfer of (part of) a personal claim to (deposited) money only and never the transfer of a proprietary right in the balance of a bank account. To make a bank transfer, the payor/debtor instructs his bank for example, by a cheque, a bank giro instruction (which could be electronic) or by an imprint on a credit card slip to transfer a sum of money out of the balance of his account with his bank to the account of the payee/creditor, either at the same bank or at another bank through what amounts to a *push or credit transfer* system of payment, see for push and pull systems or credit and debit transfers also section 1.1.5 above.

In a push system the debtor's bank has the initiative. If both payor and payee have accounts at this bank, the payor/debtor's personal claim on his bank is upon his instruction *converted* by his bank into a personal claim of the payee on this bank and the payor's bank balance reduced and the payee's balance increased accordingly. In the latter case (another bank), the payor's bank, after debiting the payor's account, instructs the payee's bank to debit its own (payor's bank) account at that bank for the relevant amount in favour of the payee's account. If the payor's bank does not hold an account at the bank of the payee, an intermediary bank will be used at which both banks have an account.

That will normally be their central bank, assuming both banks are from the same country and the payment is in the local currency. If they do not come from the same country or payment is not made in the local currency, *a corresponding bank* at which both have an account or similar arrangement in the currency of the payment may be used to make payments or otherwise the foreign central bank of this currency if both the debtor's bank and creditor's bank (or more likely their branches in the relevant countries) hold accounts with it.

---

[5] See more in particular chapter 4, Part III.

In the case where intermediary banks are used for payment in this manner, it could be said that the bank of the payor takes over the payment obligation of the latter upon acceptance of the instruction and the debiting of the account. Equally, whilst itself instructing other banks, there would be further substitutions. Economically, this is what happens but *legally* the key is to determine whether the payor and the various banks in the chain are considered to have made payment and are discharged upon acceptance of their instructions or whether their payment obligations are only fulfilled when the creditor/payee is ultimately credited in his account with his own bank. That is now the more likely view. That also raises the question whether the payor and the intermediary banks have a joint and several payment liability in the meantime.

1.2.2   When is a Bank Payment Made? The Question of Acceptance and the Liberating Effect of the Payment. Finality

The question when in a bank transfer the payment to the payee is made is particularly relevant to determine (a) whether there is a late (or default in) payment, and (b) whether (in an intervening bankruptcy of either party to the transaction) the money has left the estate of the payor and belongs to the payee. The key is then to determine whether the payment through the bank, therefore the transfer of a personal right to payment of the payor against his bank to his payee (either at the same or at any other bank indicated by the payee), has been completed.

As already mentioned before, the promise of the payor's/debtor's bank to make payment, manifested by the acceptance of the instruction or at the latest by the debiting of the account of the payor/debtor, could be considered the essence of the payment through a bank transfer. This promise of the payor's/debtor's bank could then be seen as *replacing* the original payment duty of the payor/debtor. The acceptance of the instruction which creates this substitution could even be deemed automatic if the bank was put in sufficient funds by the payee so that there is a sufficient balance in his bank account. There could still be a question here whether there must be a *net* balance, that is a balance after all liabilities of the customer to his bank are deducted. Normally the balance means here a sufficient balance in the current account at the time the payment instruction is given and the bank will arrange payment accordingly unless it fears for the overall position of its client.

The payment obligation of the payor could therefore be deemed performed as soon as he gives proper instructions to his bank and has sufficient money in his bank account. This could even be so if this substitution is not itself necessarily concluding the payment transaction as far as the payee is concerned. This would then discharge the payor/debtor *as of that moment* and therefore accomplish his payment immediately. Consequently, there are here *two* approaches possible: either the payment is completed upon acceptance of the instruction by the payor bank or otherwise only upon crediting the client account by the payee bank.

One may see here the beginning of an important distinction between the payment instruction and the payment itself. Although the one may have been completed, the other may not. It is now *mostly held* that the payment is only completed if the payee can freely dispose of the money, therefore when it has been credited to his account. The other approach leads to debtor substitution and has the difficulty that it would only work if the substitution was made independent from the consent of the creditor which in a case of debtor substitution would normally be necessary, although the payee/creditor could still be considered to have implicitly agreed to it. A variation of this approach would be to assume here an assignment of the debtor's claim on his bank to the creditor. Again, also that type of debtor substitution would be dependent on the creditor's consent which is not normally apparent and is difficult to imply.

Whatever the approach in this connection under applicable law, in a bank transfer the promise by the payor's bank to be involved in the payment process will subsequently be implemented by (a) crediting the account of the payee if held at the same bank, or by (b) this bank using its own balance at the bank of the payee/creditor, or otherwise by (c) this bank using its balance at another (corresponding) bank, where both (the bank of the payor and the bank of the payee) have an account. The result is or should be that the account of the payee/creditor is ultimately unconditionally credited by his own bank for the amount. Only then is the full payment cycle complete as far as the payee is concerned and could from his perspective the release of the debtor/payee follow, resulting in liberating effect and extinction of the monetary obligation proper.

If other banks must be used in this process, the promise or acceptance of the payor's/debtor's bank to pay for the payor/debtor after the debiting of its account in its own books, needs a similar promise or acceptance to act in substitution by any intermediary bank used and ultimately by the creditor's bank which must also credit the payee's account and give him notice thereof for the payment transaction to be completed. It assumes that the payee's bank has a duty to credit the creditor's account when making the credit entry in its own accounts. Again, the payment is only complete upon such crediting, which must be unconditional, not subject to a later value date, allow interest to accrue for the payee and be in international payments in the agreed currency (transferable and convertible unless otherwise agreed).

The true reasons for the difference in view as to when the payment occurs has to do with real life. Naturally, the payor/debtor is likely to consider his payment duty fulfilled by his payment instruction to his bank and the payment completed in this manner (assuming always that the payor had sufficient funds in his bank). He can do no more. From the payee/creditor's point of view, it is naturally rather the duty or promise of his own bank and more in particular the implementation through the crediting of his own account that matters, and that will be the moment of payment for it. It shows that payor and payee may have here very different perceptions of the moment of payment. The law must decide. That goes therefore not only to the question when the payment must be deemed to have been made under the chosen payment method but also to the question whether the payment so made amounts to a liberating payment. The question is therefore whether for such a liberating payment not only the manner of payment and its validity must be considered (here the bank transfer), but also the liberation itself as a separate legal act. Mostly, applicable law will decide in favour of the creditor. It means that the debtor is liable *vis-à-vis* the creditor for the payment circuit and any delays that result for the creditor in it.

It was already said that the precise manner and moment of extinguishing the monetary obligation and therefore of full payment could further depend on the type of agreement that payor and payee have explicitly or implicitly reached between them. That could indicate the moment of the payment instruction of the payor or even when he signed a cheque and handed it over to the payee. It could also depend on the customs of their trade. That may be relevant if the payor avails himself of the payment option through a bank transfer based on commercial practice (whilst the contract is silent on how the payment should be made).[6] Again, in that case, payment is only likely to have taken place at the moment the creditor

---

[6] The acceptance of payment should be distinguished from the acceptance of the payment method. The acceptance of the payment method through a bank transfer may, as we saw in s. 1.1.6 *supra*, simply derive from the modern commercial practice which gives the payor the option.

was credited in his own account. In the case of non-contractual monetary obligations it may also be this latter moment. Obviously, the applicable law may look here for a uniform rule, which is now also the latter. To repeat, it is fairly increasingly assumed that the moment of payment in the case of a bank transfer is *always* the unconditional crediting of the payor's account in his own bank, unless there is an agreement that states or may be explained otherwise and providing further that all other requirements for a liberating payment are met.

As already mentioned in section 1.1.1 above, this may further require capacity and intent on the part of the instructing payor as the instruction is some form of legal *acceptance* by the payee, in the case of a bank transfer not only to conclude the bank transfer but also to achieve a liberating payment. This acceptance would then be considered yet another 'juristic or legal act' which requires for its validity also capacity and intent. In fact, similar requirements then apply to all intermediary instructions in the banking system for the intermediary banks, both for the validity of these instructions and for their substitution in the payment obligation and release. Payment in this manner would then be likely to be characterised as a *bilateral* legal act or series of bilateral legal acts. It may, however, also be possible to characterise payment and payment instructions as *unilateral* acts on the part of the payor or instructing banks only, assuming always that there are sufficient funds. Acceptance in a legal sense might then not be necessary, at least not for the various steps in the banking circuit, but payment would still be a juristic act (even if only unilateral) with its requirement of capacity and intent for each step, and it would likely remain a bilateral legal act *at the level of* the *liberating* effect which might require the *animus solvendi* on both sides.

Even though the requirement of capacity might be downgraded in international commerce, see chapter 2, section 1.2.9, and intent should always be seen in objective and not in subjective or psychological terms, see chapter 2, section 1.2.1, whilst in abstract systems of title transfer, see chapter 4, section 1.5.6, any (money) transfer after it is made may less easily be undone for reason of failure of intent, the characterisation of the payment transfer as a legal act could still be considered unduly complicated. Instead, it may also possible to characterise a bank transfer as merely an *act in fact*, like some do in the case of a cash payment, see also section 1.1.6 above, in order to avoid problems with the legal effectiveness and finality of the payment. It was already mentioned in section 1.1.1 above, however, that whilst moving away from cash payments towards the alternative payment forms, the characterisation of the various methods of payment as a legal act becomes virtually unavoidable and is certainly indicated in the case of a novation and a contractual release. Also for the liberating effect, it would seem unavoidable that the act of payment itself must be characterised as some kind of legal act, even if it follows mostly automatically from the implementation of the indicated payment method.

There may be legitimate controversy in this area and this is only to alert the reader to the different views. There is unanimity, however, that the effectiveness of payments should not be unduly undermined by subtle legal reasoning, both at the level of the payment method used and especially not at the level of the liberating effect. This may be a view that could also be important in the context of the development of the *lex mercatoria* for international payments. The best way forward is probably to *deem a liberating payment implied* if the agreed method of payment (or the bank payment option on the basis of industry practice, relevant also if the debt is not contractual) is fully implemented. It connects payment method and liberating effect very closely. In that approach, the question of acceptance by the payee is becoming entirely objective: he is deemed to have accepted the payment and to have conceded its liberating effect if he has the money, either in his bank account or in cash (or has been given notice of set-off or agreed to a novation or gave a release). In bank transfers, it could be as soon as the payee's bank is credited. It means that the payee takes the risk of late payment to him by his *own* bank. This bank could also be seen as agent for the payee which leads to a similar result. Payment could even be accepted to have taken place earlier if that follows from the payment clause in the contract giving rise to the payment, which could even accept the payor's payment instruction or handing over of a cheque as the decisive element and moment of the release.

In this approach, the various methods of payment used could of course still be questioned later on the basis of lack of capacity or intent, but, at least in the professional sphere, the requirement of capacity should in any event be de-emphasised and the requirement of intent explained in a strictly normative objective manner. Nevertheless, if the payment method proved invalid, the liberating effect of the payment would also lapse.[7] That could give rise to automatic retransfers, a possibility on the whole thought undesirable and destructive of a properly operating payment system. It is against the notion of finality. That is not to say that corrections should not be made, but it should require new correcting instructions and they should not be automatic as this would create too much uncertainty and confusion and undermine unduly the notion of finality. As already observed before, it should at most obtain between two parties that are directly connected, like between two intermediary banks giving rise to the elimination of obvious mistakes between them without affecting the rest of the chain. It could also obtain between a payor and his bank or between a payee and his bank, but it could *not* affect and automatically undo any other steps taken in *the payment chain*.

For the intermediate steps, it helps in bank transfers that banks having received payment instructions are now normally deemed to have accepted them if there is a sufficient balance in the account of their instructing client. It *limits* the accepting banks' facility to amend such a debit or withdraw it, and may be considered to create the legal links in the payment chain already referred to. Acting upon instructions may thus prevent any instructed bank in the chain to withdraw from the payment or recall it. Once acted upon in this manner, the person or bank giving the instruction may also not be able to withdraw or vary it unilaterally. In the USA, Section 4A–209 UCC deals precisely with this point in electronic payments.

In the USA, this duty to follow instructions is thus clearly accepted. Without a specific agreement to the contrary, the debtor's bank must accept any payment order from its client if in funds. In other words, there is involuntary substitution as long as the bank maintains a current account with its client. All banks in the payment system follow the same rule. In this situation, the whole chain of transfers is no longer dependent on any specific acceptance. It reinforces the payment system through bank transfers and ultimately enables the payee's bank to credit the payee's account with the required amount.

Again, it should be realised, however, that the promise or obligation of each successor in the chain to act on the instruction of the predecessor in this manner is not strictly speaking

---

[7] See in Germany, K Lahrenz, *Lehrbuch des Schuldrechts, Band I, Allgemeiner Teil* (14th edn, 1987), 237. Payment in Germany is often not considered a legal act subject to the requirements of capacity and intent. It means that if payment is made in the agreed manner it cannot be undermined by legal considerations and a liberating payment will follow regardless of the parties' intent and proper acceptance. But if the payment itself requires further acts, as in the case of a bank transfer, the situation might be more complicated and the solution may be that, even though further legal acts are required, the requirement of capacity and intent are largely ignored in the tendering, instructing and accepting of payments, as they now appear to be ignored under statutory law in the USA. See for the situation in the UK also *Momm v Barcleys Bank International Ltd* [1977] QB 790 and R Goode, *Commercial Law* (2nd edn, 1995), 513.

an undertaking towards the payee, perhaps not even in the case of his own bank. It means that there is here *no joint or several liability*. The payee may be no more than a *third-party beneficiary* of these undertakings, unless each bank should be seen as the agent of the successor bank in the payment chain and ultimately of the payee, a less common view. In fact, even the crediting of the payee's bank by a central or correspondent bank, in the way explained in the previous section, seems not itself to create the obligation of the payee's bank to credit the payee's account and the payee has then no automatic right to this credit either. This is an issue quite separate from the receipt of the funds by the payee's bank.

Section 4A–405 UCC in the USA introduces here another important statutory clarification and sees the obligation created by the acceptance of the money by the payee's bank as being for the benefit of the creditor. In this approach, the creditor's bank's duty to credit the creditor's account does not necessarily derive from the creditor's bank's acceptance of the instruction of the prior bank in the chain, but is statutory. Article 4A is also specific in determining (a) the other duties of participants in the payment circuit, (b) to whom they are owed, (c) the time at which each bank involved is deemed to have accepted its duties in this connection, and (d) until when any acceptance of instructions can be revoked or how it can be made conditional (notably upon receiving adequate funds).

In most other countries there may still be considerable doubt in these aspects as the subject remains mostly covered by case law only.

1.2.3   The Legal Characterisation of Bank Transfer Payments: Assignment, Novation or Independent Legal Status

Payment through a bank transfer is ordinarily *not* viewed as an assignment by the payor/debtor of his claim on his bank, even if both payor and payee have accounts at the same bank. The reason is the lack of clear approval by the payee/assignee. Although the approval or acceptance could be implied through an agency construction in which the receiving bank accepts on behalf of its client/payee, the characterisation of the transfer as an assignment is uncommon, if only to avoid the inherent assignment formalities. From a practical point of view, the assignment analogy is especially avoided as unsuitable in legal systems that subject it for its validity to documentation and notification, see for these requirements more in particular chapter 4, section 1.7.1. The assignment route can be specifically chosen by the parties in their contract if they see a need to do so and the payee bank would then likely act as agent for the assignee/payee, but again it appears uncommon.

Other legal issues may arise in a bank transfer in the nature of the payment obligation itself under which (if other banks become involved) the payee receives a (new) claim on its own bank instead of the (old) claim of the payor on the latter's bank. This looks like novation. This characterisation is normally also avoided, however. Here again the lack of clear approval of the payee is often cited as preventing novation, but as in the assignment construction, consent could easily be deemed implied. It would, however, change the nature of all payments by way of bank transfers. Still, payment may be made in the form of a novation if parties so choose, but again this is exceptional.

If the payment instructions through the banking system were an assignment or novation, it would become absolutely unavoidable for these payments to become juristic or legal acts subject to the legal requirement for it in terms of proper offer and acceptance, capacity and intent. Even where these two characterisations are commonly avoided and the payment through a bank transfer is now mostly considered to have its *own (sui generis) legal nature*, it still requires the payment transfer to be characterised as bilateral or unilateral legal acts or as acts in fact, or as a series of acts in this connection and the rules to be defined. The options were discussed in the previous sections.

The *sui generis* character of the payment transfer must be clearly understood and defined in *both* the obligatory and proprietary aspects. It allows the issues of capacity and intent, of payment instruction, acceptance and moment of payment, of finality, and of the proprietary aspects of the transfer to be approached and determined independently, therefore separate from the more conventional notions of obligatory and proprietary law. This may be of particular importance in civil law with its on the whole unitary systematical approach per country and could indicate at the same time a proprietary transfer and structure outside its closed system of proprietary rights. In common law, this is less of an issue. Article 4A UCC thus maintains an approach that foremost serves participants in the payment process, defines the proprietary aspects accordingly, and is not systematically concerned.

1.2.4　Modern Electronic Payment Systems. Clearing. Fedwire, CHIPS and CHAPS. Gross and Net Payment Systems. International Banktransfers (SWIFT)

Modern developments have made electronic payment systems possible.[8] In these systems, orders will be given by telephone or through electronic means, in a push system first by the debtor to his bank (these instructions or orders are themselves mostly not considered elements of the electronic system) and subsequently interbank which is the key modern communication element. The interbank orders are then no longer paper-based but are *paperless* and may as such be *on-line* or *off-line*. The on-line orders concern individual payments, usually of large amounts, conveyed through special telecommunication lines between the banks, which are in immediate and continuous communication for payment purposes. The on-line method achieves instantaneous debiting and crediting of the relevant accounts and thereby immediate payment. There is here no clearing but a *gross settlement system*. Only such a system can be real time.

Off-line orders, on the other hand, may be stored in magnetic form and netted out in a clearing system between the member banks. The result is a *net settlement system*, which will be all the more effective if it is multilateral, therefore between as many banks as possible. It results in later payment and usually requires a number of (settlement) days, often three, although same day settlement is becoming more and more an option. Settlement will then take place at the end of each business day. That is the way of the near future. It is an important development in terms of efficiency and cost, but it also reduces appreciably the settlement risk for the participants in the system as we shall see. It is the essence of modern clearing systems.

Indeed, many modern countries now have both (a) their own paperless on-line wholesale fund transfer and gross settlement systems, (b) an off-line net settlement or clearing system. Apart from these two new systems, they are likely to continue for the time being also a paper-based clearing system for cheques and sometimes a special bank giro payment instructions clearing for retail customers.

In the USA, the most important on-line electronic system is *Fedwire* which maintains therefore a gross settlement system. It operates between the 12 US Federal Reserve Banks for the benefit of those banks holding accounts at the Federal Reserve. In the USA, CHIPS (Clearing House Interbank Payment System) maintains the off-line net settlement system. In the UK, there is CHAPS (Clearing House Automatic Payment System). CHIPS and

---

[8] See for a fuller discussion of the systems and issues, B Geva, *Bank Collections and Payment Transactions, A Comparative Legal Analysis* (Oxford, 2001).

CHAPS have also proved useful for (domestic) payments in which foreign banks are involved. They operate on a net basis, include a multilateral clearing system, except that in CHAPS large value transfers may now also be settled gross on a real time basis through the Bank of England (provided it is put in funds) to limit day-time exposure.

In the EU, there is also a Euro clearing and settlement service (Euro-1) operated by the Euro Banking Association (EBA) as a privately owned multilateral cross-border net payment system providing same day value and receiving its messages through SWIFT (the UK is connected through CHAPS-Euro). It may not mean a great deal as smaller trans-border transactions remain relatively few. Larger payments normally go through real time gross payment systems for which in the EU there now is TARGET operated through the European System of Central Banks (ESCB). The present EU concern is not so much with these systems or with the setting up of one pan-European clearing house (which could also make domestic transfers cheaper through greater netting facilities), but rather with the cost of smaller bank transfers cross-border for retail where the Transparency Directive now at least insists on proper disclosure of the charges. As of July 2003, these charges are supervised.

To demonstrate the clearing methods: under CHIPS eg, once a day the settling participants are given a settlement report indicating their net debit or credit positions. They reflect the net positions on the basis of all payments made to or received from the other participants during the day. If the net debtor does not have sufficient funds in its reserve account with the system it will draw down balances or lines of credit held at other banks or at the Federal Reserve as central bank so as to clear the deficit. This is also done daily and there should be no overnight debt positions in the system. Payments processed during the day are finally settled only when a participant has cleared any debit position.

This means that if banks receive payments during the day whilst making funds available to their customers, they incur the risk that the settlement will not take place because the bank from which the funds came may have a debit balance at the end of the day. There is here a *liquidity risk* to the system which may turn into a *credit risk* in the case of the intervening insolvency of a bank that has a net debit position. There may also be *systemic risk* in the sense that the default of one bank may affect the settlement capability of others. To prevent this from happening in *multilateral net settlement systems,* there are certain risk control mechanisms possible which center on (a) the prior screening of all participants, (b) bilateral credit limits, restricting between two participants the volume of payments received to those of the payments sent (or allowing only a limited overshoot), and (c) limits on net debt positions (which requires monitoring during the day).

Defaults in settlement by members of the clearing may lead to *recasts* and *unwinds.* In a recast, the defaulting parties' payments (received and sent) are deleted from the settlement whilst the net positions of the other participants are re-calculated. An unwind undoes the entire netting and requires participants to settle all positions individually. It may create liquidity and even systemic risk problems as it removes the netting benefits from all participants. It may expose them to large gross settlements on which they did not count and for which they may not have the required liquidity. To avoid such a situation, members of the system may well guarantee the operation of the system in advance, effectively taking over the defaulting party's settlement obligations. To avoid liquidity problems for one of them, they may then also provide mutual lines of credit. There may even be some collateral in the case of weaker members to facilitate the obtaining of overnight funds by them. If the costs of support are not retrievable from the defaulting member, the participants may operate a pre-agreed cost sharing formula system.

Clearing of this nature is a form of *settlement netting,* see for this type of netting, which may also imply a *novation netting,* section 1.3.3 below, when all positions are transferred to the clearing agent and a new total position arises in respect of him for each participant. In fact, attempts are made to introduce the concept of continuous (novation) netting in clearing systems that have a longer cycle so that at least in theory there is always one netted outstanding amount between one participant and all the others. It is meant to better protect against any participant becoming insolvent during the clearing period.

In this connection, it should be appreciated that so far netting systems of this nature still practice decentralised controls under which each participant remains subject to the risks deriving from the behaviour of other participants. As just mentioned, it is conceivable to centralise this risk control. In such systems, a central body or counterparty (CCP) takes over all contracts and become the party to each transaction engaged in by participants with each other. This is now common in the futures and options markets, where the market organisation itself provides this facility and operates therefore a centralised clearing, see more in particular chapter 6, section 1.4.4.

This type of centralised risk control in which the counterpart 'buys' all payment obligations and becomes liable for payment of all of them is not so far common in payment clearing systems. Even though central banks are sometimes called central counterparties in these clearing systems, it does *not* mean that they take the full clearing and settlement risk. They only act as agents for the system to make or receive each participant's settlement balance. Settlement means here the making of the final (netted) payments *after* clearing.

The benefits of clearing in terms of liquidity and cost of payment netting may be demonstrated in a simple example. If Bank A receives daily 100 payments from 50 banks each, all for US$100 and makes 50 payments to 100 banks for US$100 per payment, it is clear that in a *gross* settlement there will be 10,000 payments (5,000 to and 5,000 by bank A) of US$100 each for a total of US$1,000,000. It has an ultimate nil net effect on Bank A as its total incoming and outgoing payments balance. Yet in principle (short of a clearing system), all payments must be made and liquidity must be provided for each of them by the paying bank during the day with the costs of the payments and the liquidity to be provided and the credit exposure to each of the counter parties that must pay to Bank A. This is different in a clearing or *net* settlement system.

In a *bilateral* netting system, Bank A and each other member would only net out the payments they made or received between each other. Assuming that the 100 payments from each of the 50 banks to Bank A were balanced by 50 payments made by Bank A to each of them, all payments being for US$100, the effect would be that only 50 payments would be made by each of these banks to Bank A. It would reduce the total payments by 2,500 and halve the net exposure of Bank A to each of these banks. In a full *multilateral* netting system, no payments would be made by and to Bank A at all, even if the 100 banks paying to A were all different from the 50 banks A must pay, provided they were all part of the same system. All payments of Bank A would be re-directed to satisfy the other banks. If a net overall payment had to be paid by or to Bank A taking them all together, this would be paid to or be received from the *operator* of the system as *common agent* for the system. As just mentioned, this is sometimes already called the central counter-party but that is strictly speaking confusing as the common agent does not act as central assignee.

A simpler example may demonstrate the same point: if, in full multilateral netting, A owes B 70 units, whilst B owes A 40 units and C 20 units whilst C owes A 20 units, there would be only one payment (instead of four) under which A would pay B 10 units.[9]

---

[9] See for CHAPS also Goode, n 7 *supra*, 505, and for CHIPS, HS Scott and PA Wellons, *International Finance* (8th edn, New York, 2001), 616. See in respect of payment systems also the work of the BIS Committee on Payment

In the above SWIFT was mentioned. This is the Society of Worldwide Interbank Financial Telecommunication. It is not a clearing system but an international *communication* system between member banks who own the system which is operated worldwide. Based in Brussels and operating under Belgium law, it provides in its current SWIFT II form a central switch system linking banks all over the world. There are two slice processors, one in the Netherlands and the other in the US, functioning as independent networks linking access points which exist in each country and to which local banks are connected. Thus, each message first goes to a domestic access point and from thereon onto the international circuit from where it is directed to the access point in the receiving bank's country.

International payments often involve foreign exchange transactions requiring the deliveries of two different currencies between the same counter-parties. As there may be different currency and therefore time zone's involved, the payments may not be concurrent which creates a special form of settlement risk, also called *Herstatt risk*. This risk was first identified when the Herstatt Bank in Cologne went bankrupt in 1972 during banking hours. Some of those who already had delivered DM to Herstatt in Germany were still awaiting US dollars in return from Herstatt in New York whilst the bank went out of business. This is a major risk in foreign exchange transactions of which each link will normally be settled through the settlement systems of the country of the currency. They are separate and operate in different time zones. US dollars will therefore normally be the last to settle during the day. These technical aspects prevent simultaneity in practice or delivery against payment (DVP). A multi-currency net settlement system through a single counterparty linked to central banks may eventually be the answer.

1.2.5   The Risks in the Modern Payment Systems: Payment Mistakes and Restitution

All payment systems based on bank transfers contain certain risks for the participants. The payment may be delayed in the system so that the debtor may enter a situation of default whilst the creditor is out of pocket and starts claiming damages. This may in turn expose any dilatory bank in the system to claims for damages, at least if there was an (implicit) acceptance of the instruction through the debiting of the instructor's account or a standing agreement with the customer to follow his instructions. Such an agreement is now probably implicit in all current accounts, as we saw, and creates a duty for the instructed bank, although only to the extent that the instructor is in funds as no bank is required to extend credit unless there is an (overdraft) agreement to the effect. It illustrates nevertheless the *liquidity* risk inherent in the system.

There is of course also ordinary counter-party or *credit risk* connected with one of the intermediary banks going bankrupt during the clearing and settlement process. It was already mentioned in the previous section when recasts and unwinds were discussed. So was *systemic risk* which may follow and affect also the other banks in the system, although mutual guarantees may protect it. *Herstatt risk* is a special form of counter-party risk and has also already been mentioned. It is typical for foreign exchange transactions. *Legal risk* is connected with the uncertain status of the instructions, of the duties of the various players in the system, of the legal requirements of money transfers and of the liberating effect of payment. To provide here more clarity internationally, Uncitral drafted a Model Law on

---

and Settlement Systems of Jan 2001, which also includes a useful Glossary of the terms used in payment and settlement systems .

International Credit Transfers structured very much along the lines of Article 4A UCC. It has had some following in domestic laws but was nowhere adopted as such. There is also a Uncitral Legal Guide on Electronic Fund Transfers. In the EU the Settlement Finality Directive has dealt with a number of issues, but only those that are more typical for trans-actions with the European Central Bank. This Directive is nevertheless important and will be briefly discussed in the next section.

A net settlement system does not reduce these risks *per se*. In fact, it may spread credit and liquidity risk by holding up payments to all banks if one of them defaults, hence the drive to reduce the number of settlement days. On the other hand there needs to be some period to allow the gathering of enough payment instructions to make the effort worth it. Only the introduction of central counter-parties, see the previous section, which would become the 'buyer' of every claim for payment and the 'seller' of every claim to payment in a centralised risk control system in the nature as now operating for the clearing and settle-ment of market traded derivative transactions, see chapter 6, section 1.4.4, would achieve substantial counter-party risk reduction.

Another risk in this connection is that instructions are revoked or payments are sought to be undone. For a proper bank transfer system to work, the key is to prevent both the instructing debtor and its bank (and any bank down the chain to and including the credi-tor's bank) from revoking instructions and thereby unilaterally undoing the payment once set in motion. This is important when the original debtor all of a sudden fears that he may not receive counter-value (for example, in the foreign exchange markets) because of an intervening bankruptcy of the counter-party and seeks to rescind his original instruction. Another complication may be that in the chain, the accounts used are in sufficient credit but that the overall position of the instructing bank *vis-à-vis* the bank that it instructs is negative so that unexpected delays may result.

It may, on the other hand, also be that the debtor's instruction was simply erroneous as he never owed the indicated creditor anything and he may seek no more than a correction. Again once the banking system is properly instructed and the payment set into motion, such a recall of the instruction would not appear to be a possibility. More frequent is the misplacement of decimal points in the instruction so that much larger amounts are being paid than were due. This goes to the aspect of intent. The mistake may be due to the payor, but may also be internal in the instructing banks. The payor's bank or the intermediary banks may catch fright after having acted on such an erroneous instruction. Again, once the payment has been set in motion there would not seem a way to correct. The creditor/payee has in any event a legitimate interest in knowing that his payment through the chain of instructions is safe once the necessary initial instructions have been given by his debtor and have been followed up. From this perspective, he is likely to maintain that the payment was his, once the mechanism for payment was activated.

Indeed, modern systems are likely to provide that a payor's bank cannot adjust the account of its client once debited, having discharged its own obligation to proceed with the payment and the same would go for intermediary banks once they have followed up instructions. General banking conditions might still change this, however, at least in the case of an *obvious mistake* of the bank itself, and the German banking conditions (number 8), which each banking client is supposed to have accepted, contain language to that effect. It does not mean, however, the reversal of payments or instructions received from clients or other banks in situations in which the bank accepted a mistaken instruction and acted upon it. These entities would have to start an action for recovery against the relevant account holder in the case of a mistake, probably on the basis of unjust enrichment. Above in section 1.1.6, it was already said that the adjustments that banks may thus make are likely to be limited to those concerning mistakes between themselves within the interbank payment system, but it cannot have an effect on transactions elsewhere in the chain.

Indeed, in the UK, restitutionary claims are normally based on unjust enrichment and are often divided in personal and proprietary claims depending on whether a constructive trust results from tracing proceeds of goods wrongfully sold or from failure to account for proceeds. If there is such a trust, the action is considered proprietary. If not, the action is personal. Restitutionary claims for misdirected funds by banks appear to be personal and unilateral adjustments to instructing customers' accounts do not appear possible once the payment process has started. In the USA, for professionals, Sections 4A–204 and 205 UCC deal with refunds of *unauthorised* and *erroneous* payment orders. The idea is here also that corrections to the payment orders once accepted are exceptional.

Article 4A UCC also deals with *fraud* problems in the sense that payment instructions may be fraudulently given to the detriment of third-party accounts but for the benefit of the instructing parties, see Section 4A–204. The question here is what kind of precautions the debtor's bank needs to take to protect its client. Section 4A–207 deals with non-existing or unidentifiable beneficiaries. The issue is here one of due diligence in trying to identify the real beneficiary. For consumers these issues are dealt with under the federal Electronic Funds Transfer Act and Regulation E that implements it.

1.2.6 Finality, Independence or Abstraction and the EU Settlement Finality Directive

In the foregoing, the great importance of the finality of payment was already highlighted. It has several aspects. First (a) there is the element of independence or abstraction, making the payment itself an act separate from the relationship out of which it arises. Thus if a sale is void, the connected payment once set into motion through the banking system is not thereby invalidated. This notion of independence also arises in connection with the transfer of negotiable instruments, in letters of credit, and in assignments. (b) Another aspect of finality in payments is the minimising of the elements of capacity and intent in the rendering of instructions and in the acceptance of the payment. (c) There are further the severe limitations on the revocation or amendment of instructions. (d) Finally, there is often also the impact of any intervening bankruptcy of one of the participants in the system to consider, especially in respect of the on-going capacity of the instructing party or the avoidance of any earlier instructions that could be deemed preferential. In the EU, this is the subject of the Settlement Finality Directive of 1998 (Arts 3(1) and 3(2)) and was meant to reduce the liquidity risk particularly in transactions with the European Central Bank (but was given a wider scope in most EU countries in the implementing legislation).

1.3   Set-off as Method of Payment: Netting

1.3.1   Legal Nature and Characterisation

Set-off is an alternative way of extinguishing a debt and therefore an alternative manner of fulfilling a payment obligation, therefore of payment. It is also possible to see it as a cross-assignment or as a cross-surrender of claims. It could even be seen as a novation. These characterisations are less desirable as they suggest particular formalities or consents and deprive the set-off of its important feature of unilaterality or automaticity. The unilaterality is an obvious advantage to a debtor. The automaticity is of particular value in a bankruptcy of one of the parties, which could otherwise undermine the effectiveness of the set-off as even a unilateral set-off election might not be effective against a bankrupt estate if made after the start of the bankruptcy.

A set-off concerns the following. If A owes money to B, but B at the same time owes money to A, it is only logical, convenient and efficient that the party owing the larger sum merely pays the difference. To the extent that the claim is eliminated, there results a *mutual* payment. Convenience has long given rise to a right and sometimes even to an obligation to off-set mutual monetary claims and settle them in this manner. As just mentioned, the facility is particularly important in the bankruptcy of one of the parties as the set-off generally allows the non-bankrupt party to reduce its own competing claim by any amount it owes the bankrupt debtor so that this party will be a competing creditor only for the excess indebtedness (if any). It gives the non-bankrupt party a preference to the extent of his own debt because this party recovers fully from the bankrupt estate to the extent of its own claim and it is no longer a competing creditor for that amount.

In bankruptcy, commonly payment through set-off is not only considered a right of the creditor, who is at the same time a debtor of the estate, but also a duty of the trustee or, putting it differently, is *automatic* or happens *ipso facto*, that is *without* any election by the non-bankrupt party. As just noted, such an election would risk being no longer effective in a bankruptcy of the other party, as the opening of insolvency proceedings tends to freeze the bankrupt estate and the exercise of all personal rights against it. It puts the legal effect of notices or elections of any sort against it in doubt.

One of the traditional issues in the set-off is therefore the question of its automaticity, and in this respect the law outside bankruptcy and in bankruptcy may be different within one legal system, as is indeed the case in England, Germany and the Netherlands. In England outside bankruptcy,[10] the set-off must be especially invoked which in that case can only be done in litigation and therefore requires judicial sanction *except* if both claims were closely connected, which means that they must arise out of the same legal relationship, or parties have agreed otherwise in advance. The set-off is here a *procedural* tool, a convenient way to settle accounts, or a defense. In France, on the other hand, the Cc accepts the automaticity of the set-off even outside bankruptcy (Article 1289*ff* Cc). That is also still the situation in Italy but now less common. The new Dutch Civil Code deviates in this respect from French law, which it used to follow, see Article 6.127 CC and is now much like Section 388 BGB in Germany. Outside bankruptcy, both legal systems require the notification of the party availing itself of the benefit. The difference with the common law approach, in which, as just mentioned, the set-off is procedural, is that upon notification the set-off is *retroactive* to the time the set-off possibility arose.

The importance of the election or notification requirement is that it suggests that the set-off is a legal act and thereby subject to party autonomy. It means that parties need not avail themselves of it and in their contracts they may make other arrangements, imposing additional requirements or excluding the facility altogether. Most importantly, it may also mean that they could extend the facility. Under new Dutch law, this freedom may be limited in consumer contracts, see Articles 6.236(f) and 6.237(g) CC. A limiting aspect may also be that such notification as a juristic or legal act requires capacity and intention of the party giving it and perhaps also of the party subject to it in the manner of an acceptance. It must in this sense be legally valid and becomes as a consequence vulnerable to defects which in turn may affect the finality of the payment. It is exactly to avoid the complications in this

---

[10] See for a discussion *Stein v Blake* [1995] 2 WLR 710.

connection in bankruptcy, that the automaticity is retained in bankruptcy situations and that outside it, just as in the case of other types of payment, the impact of the requirements of capacity and intent tend to be construed in a restrictive manner in order to promote the finality of the inherent cross payments.

The notification or election requirement is in any event inappropriate for a set-off in bankruptcy as it would likely lead to a disallowance of the set-off altogether since no valid notice can be given against the estate (or received by the bankrupt) unless allowed by the relevant bankruptcy act. Hence the automaticity. Another important consequence of the automaticity of the set-off in bankruptcy or its mandatory nature is that it cuts out prospects of 'cherry picking' by a bankruptcy trustee attempting to cash in the estate's claim whilst not settling the counterclaim and leaving the creditor as *pro rata* common creditor for his entire claim. The set-off facility in bankruptcy is therefore a special case of disallowing such cherry picking. An expanded netting clause may do the same but the avoidance of cherry picking in this manner is not a general bankruptcy principle, see chapter 5, section 1.1.6, and cannot necessarily be relied upon for more than the relevant bankruptcy act allows. It will thus depend on whether these expanded clauses are valid in bankruptcy.

Indeed in bankruptcy the set-off may be of a more precise and more limited nature, see Article 53 of the Dutch Bankruptcy Act and Section 95 of the German Insolvency Act. At least it raises the question in how far a contractually extended set-off (eg through netting clauses) could operate in bankruptcy *ipso facto*. In England, on the other hand, there is a broader set-off facility in bankruptcy, as we just saw (even if probably still narrower than in Germany) but the special and precise provisions in bankruptcy may still mean that except for special statutory sanctioning, any extension of the set-off concept in contractual (netting) clauses may be ineffectual in bankruptcy and that is an important issue, not only in England. It would throw into doubt the role of party autonomy in this context, reason why contractual netting clauses have attracted much interest and required amendment of bankruptcy statutes notably in the USA and France. Elsewhere, like in Germany and the Netherlands, it may be assumed that under modern practice these extended set-off or netting clauses are accepted in bankruptcy. In England, this may well depend on the nature and characterisation of the netting clause in terms of settlement, novation or close-out netting as will be discussed in greater detail in section 1.3.4 below. To avoid the constraints of the set-off especially in bankruptcy, there is even a desire to perceive or construe netting as an alternative to the set-off, especially through the devise of novation netting. It is a question of characterisation and may create novation problems instead and still raise the question of its effectiveness upon a bankruptcy of one of the parties.

1.3.2   Eligibility

Set-off is a way of payment, but not all claims may be eligible for payment through a set-off. Problems arise here when (a) claims are highly personal, like those for alimony, child support and often also for wages, and the payor of these moneys may not be able to reduce its payments by off-setting counter-claims. Other questions that commonly arise in the context of the set-off are (b) whether both debts must be connected, in other words must arise out of the same contract or legal relationship (which could be a tort when there may be a duty for the tort victim to contribute in the case of negligence). As already mentioned, this is the element of connexity. It was traditionally more particularly required in common law (outside bankruptcy or other litigation), except where there was a contractual provision doing away with the requirement, and it is in countries like Belgium and Luxembourg still necessary in a bankruptcy set-off. They still follow the French tradition in this respect, now abandoned in France itself in the case of contractual netting clauses, as we shall see below in section 1.3.4. Belgian and Luxembourg law in this aspect may be relevant especially in repo dealings of investment securities held in Euroclear or Cedel.

The set-off normally only applies to (c) monetary claims, although French law traditionally also allows a set-off between obligations to deliver goods of the same sort (Article 1291 Cc). That facility has now become more widespread and is of importance particularly for investment securities trading and clearing. It was, however, also interpreted to mean that even in monetary claims the set-off was only possible if it was in the same currency. Another set-off issue is (d) whether both debts must be mature, also a traditional requirement of French law, see Article 1291 Cc, so that future or contingent debts, including un-adjudicated claims or claims for damages, could not qualify for a set-off against a mature claim.

The consequence is that if the creditor's claim is mature but the debtor's claim is not, the former must pay even if he has no expectation of payment by the latter, a reason why bankruptcy law is here again often more lenient than non-bankruptcy law. It follows from the principle that in bankruptcy all claims against the bankrupt mature immediately. It may still leave problems with contingent debt. In many common law countries, the set-off of contingent debts of the bankrupt, including damages, is, however, also allowed in bankruptcy, provided they are provable in the sense of being capable of reasonable estimation under applicable bankruptcy law. It may still exclude tort claims (in England, but not in the USA and Canada), but normally not damages for breach of contract, promise or trust, which will then be reasonably assessed. In England there is the additional problem that Bankruptcy Rules 4.86 and 12.3(1) only assess the contingent debts of the bankrupt in this manner but not the ones of the solvent party, which may therefore remain excluded from the set-off.

Finally, (e) the question of retroactivity arises. It is a more complicated aspect that has an impact in many ways. In the case of full retroactivity of the set-off, it could be argued that interest payments cease on both claims from the date they become capable of set-off, even if the election (in systems requiring it) is only made later. It would also fix the date for conversion if one of the debts was in a foreign currency (unless other provisions were made between the parties). To the extent debts are retroactively set-off, there would be no default and therefore no repudiation possibility or penalty as at the date the set-off became possible. Any intervening insolvency restricting the set-off would also have no effect. Article 3.129 of the new Dutch CC specifically allows the retroactivity, see also Section 389 BGB in Germany. In the French system of an automatic set-off (even outside bankruptcy), the retroactivity would appear to be implicit as we saw. English law traditionally did not have it but it can be negotiated.

A special problem arises in respect of client accounts. Brokers or lawyers who maintain them for their clients may be tempted to set-off their claims for services against these accounts. It should be realised, however, that (in a modern legal system) these accounts do not belong to the broker or lawyer but that their client is the owner of the moneys which intermediaries only administer (in the manner of trustees). No mutuality in claims should therefore be expected or one could also say that the claim on the broker or lawyer is only administrative (for the release of the money and not monetary in nature). It does not leave the broker or lawyer without redress. They may be able to claim a lien in the account or request an attachment but that means that recourse will be obtained only under the rules pertaining to liens or attachments and not (although more convenient) under a set-off.

1.3.3   Contractual Adaptations of the Set-off: Settlement, Novation and Close-out Netting

In countries that subject the set-off concept to notification and thereby a large degree of party autonomy, parties may in principle correct and expand the concept by contract, relevant particularly in the aspect of connexity, acceleration of maturity, set-off of non-monetary obligations or of obligations in different currencies, and of retroactivity. Thus, in such a system, parties in their agreements could elaborate and for example delete the connexity requirement where in principle upheld outside bankruptcy, as is the case in the UK. In this way, they could also abandon the need for a court order in the absence of connexity to achieve the set-off of other debts, allow acceleration of immature debt, include contingent debt, and provide for the set-off of other than monetary claims or of monetary claims in different currencies. In the latter three cases, it would require valuation or translation formulae to make the set-off possible without further argument. Retroactivity could also be negotiated. The shaping of the set-off principle in this manner may in fact give rise to (netting) structures, that become separate from the set-off in the traditional sense.

Clearly, these variations on the set-off principle are likely to curry more favour in countries which allow parties a say in the set-off method than in those where the set-off is always automatic, even outside bankruptcy. The issue is particularly relevant for the status of the so-called netting agreements in bankruptcy. They are agreements expanding on the set-off facility and have become particularly important in *financial derivatives* (like swaps) and *repos*, see sections 1.3.4 and 1.3.5 below.

Common law here makes further distinctions and, at least in England, there is an effort in legal writings to differentiate between (a) settlement netting, (b) netting by novation and (c) close out netting.[11] *Settlement netting* is in this connection the netting of monetary obligations in the same currency whether or not connected (or of goods of the same sort as in the set-off of non-monetary obligations like those to deliver fungible assets like bonds and shares of the same type deliverable on the same day, sometimes also called position netting, delivery netting or payment netting). In England, it is particularly used to avoid the connexity problem outside bankruptcy, but it is also commonly used to deal with maturity and currency differences. It takes place only at the moment of payment or delivery, which raises the issue of its effectiveness in bankruptcy although it can be made retroactive. It is likely to be less effective in multilateral facilities like in clearing situations before settlement dates. In any event, mutuality and connexity are often considered bilateral in nature. Whether before the physical netting and payment through the clearing agencies there is still a set-off possibility in the case of an intervening bankruptcy of a participant in the system may then remain a matter to be determined under the ordinarily applicable bankruptcy laws.

The notion of retroactivity may acquire here a special meaning. Other structures have been tried, especially *netting by novation*. This is any netting in which parties agree to substitute a single net payment for two cross-claims, normally as soon as the relevant accounting entries have been made, even if payment is deferred until an agreed payment or settlement date. It is sometimes also called obligation netting and the relevant netting agreements may be very different in different situations. It often assumes a *continuing* process in which each new transaction is automatically consolidated with the earlier ones. In a bilateral manner, this may be the case in swap and foreign exchange transactions to produce single outstanding

---

[11] See R Derham, "Set-off and Netting of Foreign Exchange Contracts in the Liquidation of a Counterparty — Part II: Netting" [1991], *JBL* 536 and The Law of *Set-off* (3rd edn, 2002).

balances to be settled (and further consolidated for any other transactions) at the settlement date. The result is a running score. In a multilateral way, novation netting is often considered to happen in a clearing system that has a single counter-party and it suggests an immediate transfer of all claims on it in exchange for a net right or obligation in respect of each member of the system. The netting takes place here only at the level of the central counterparty and the novation itself could be seen as not being part of the clearing (which is multilateral) but rather the prelude to it. It should be noted in this regard that the clearing and single counter-party facility usually go together, like in derivative exchanges, but they should be clearly distinguished and may give rise to different types of netting.

Close-out netting is a netting that becomes operative only upon a default or other close-out event by a counter-party. It is also called default netting, open contract netting or replacement contract netting. It nets in a bilateral netting *all* outstanding positions between both parties as at the moment of default or upon another agreed close out event and *accelerates* or matures all outstanding obligations. It may be found especially in swap dealings and repos and is commonly provided for in the swap and repo master agreements. In a multilateral close-out netting, other parties are also roped in, see also sections 1.3.4 and 1.3.5 below.

These various distinctions between the types of netting were foremost inspired by the typical limitations of common law in respect of the set-off (notably in England) and may be much less relevant in other legal systems. Thus in Germany, no contractual enhancement would appear necessary to obtain a broad netting of mutual claims (if mature and in the same currency) as (unlike in England) the issue of connexity does not arise, not even outside bankruptcy where a court order is also not necessary. Much of the English effort in this connection is therefore centred on creating a form of contractual dependency of claims in bilateral netting but no less so in multilateral netting schemes by interjecting a single party who may assume all rights and obligations of the participants in the system and net them out, first bilaterally and then amongst all participants in a clearing system thus creating one debt or credit (possibly in the nature of a novation netting) for each member of the system in respect of claims accruing during an agreed period.[12]

In clearing systems without such a central counterparty, there may still result a netting but more likely only on a provisional basis as a book-keeping effort (therefore in the nature of a settlement netting) subject to all participants ultimately being able and willing to pay whatever is due by them. This is also called a net-settlement system. In countries like England, it has the disadvantage that it may be affected by a bankruptcy of one of the members who is thereby no longer able to perform. In any event, it is not complete before all have paid. Hence the ideas of retroactivity and novation netting, even at this multilateral

---

[12] When novation netting is combined with a clearing function, it is also referred to as 'novation and substitution'. This is even conceivable for swaps and would lead to a swap clearing facility, which is now being offered by the London Clearing House. The result is a swap exchange. An example of it may be found for foreign exchange transactions in the multilateral netting facility between a number of banks in the Exchange Clearing House Organisation Ltd. (ECHO), operating in London since 1995. The idea is that ECHO is inserted in all foreign exchange transactions between the member banks in the same way as an exchange is in futures and option dealings, see more in particular chapter 6, s. 1.4.4. In the case of the bankruptcy of any bank in the system, ECHO is the counter-party and the other banks will not directly be affected. ECHO nets all outstanding positions so that there remains one contract. If under it ECHO is the creditor and remains in whole or in part unpaid, the other member banks must support it according to a certain formula. To protect ECHO further, strict limits are imposed on the total outstanding with any bank and additional security may be requested in terms of margin. For swaps, the idea obtained early support from ISDA, see s. 1.3.5 *infra*, but as it would also give weaker swap parties ready access to the market and deprive the stronger banks of their credit rating advantage, it was not implemented at the time. ECHO is followed by a similar system in New York called Multinet.

level. Again there may be a lesser need in countries like Germany and the Netherlands, where upon the notification the set-off is immediately effective. Even then, novation netting may still be more efficient. Besides in single counter-party clearing systems, novation netting is also common in foreign exchange settlements when parties agree that their payment obligations to each other are netted out continuously and replaced by the resulting net amount payable by the net debtor to the net creditor. Particularly under master or frame agreements, it results in a running score (or at least that is the intention).

A special and more obvious form of novation netting may be found in contracts for differences when, as in modern interest rate swaps,[13] (theoretical) cash flows are netted out

---

[13] Swaps of cash flows have become greatly popular as financial tools. They allow flexibility to investors and borrowers who may in this way swap their investment income or borrowing cost, therefore their incoming or outgoing cash flows, for others with other interest rate structures or in other currencies to protect themselves against undesirable movements in interest or currency rates. Thus an investor receiving income out of fixed rate bonds may wish to receive a floating interest rate income stream when he expects interest rates to go up. A borrower with a fixed rate interest stream may want to change to floating if he expects interest rates to go down. That could result in an interest rate swap. Similarly when investments are in a currency which is expected to depreciate, the investor may want to choose another currency; the borrower will do so if he expects an appreciation. This is a currency swap.

The investor would thus receive another income stream in terms of interest or currency (or both) in what would be called (additionally) an asset or income swap, therefore an interest rate or currency swap on the asset side of his balance sheet. A borrower would pay out another interest rate or currency stream (or both) in what is called a liability swap, therefore a swap on the liability side of his balance sheet. The swap markets, now maintained by the major banks as market makers or providers of these facilities, allows great flexibility and will be more extensively discussed in chapter 6, s. 1.4.6.

The original technique was that cash flows were literally exchanged, which could take the form of a cross assignment in the case of an asset swap and a cross delegation of payment duties in a liability swap. Technically speaking this could raise all assignment problems in terms of notification, better rights of other assignees, payment re-direction and defenses of the debtors in asset or income swaps. In a liability swap there would in any event be the question of consent of the lender (or bond holders) to the delegation of the payment duty. Moreover there were differing views on the nature of this cross-assignment. Was it a (conditional) sale/repurchase, an exchange or a lend/borrow exercise? This could have an effect on the type of settlement at the end of the swap period if the value of both streams had diverted.

The legal status of these swaps was thus subject to considerable uncertainty and could in any event involve third parties either as payors or as receivers of a cash flow which was swapped. Where the cash flows derived from a large portfolio of borrowers or was payable to a large number of lenders, like bond holders, it could involve many parties. This was obviously undesirable as speed was often the essence of these transactions, even if in asset swaps the partners would normally own the underlying instruments out of which the cash flow would arise, which, if negotiable, they could also exchange. If to bearer, it would avoid any notification needs, but such an exchange of the underlying instruments was costly and could involve considerable market risk. It meant that the original physical cash flow exchanges were often only suitable within groups of companies or banking organisations when one subsidiary swapped certain assets with their income streams to others. In a liability swap, the exchange of the underlying proceeds of a public borrowing was more common but would not affect the payment duty of the borrower to his original bond holders and not avoid their approval of the delegation of such duty to a swap partner. The borrower thus normally continued to pay interest and principal to his public bond holders and the swap would be structured differently.

In fact, the modern idea of netting created here a new situation and produced a new financial instrument. By no longer exchanging incoming or outgoing cash flows but only paying the net difference between the value of the cash flows at regular intervals, the swap became a different instrument altogether and a contract for differences in which third parties were no longer involved. All parties would continue to receive or pay the original flows from or to the relevant counter-parties but amongst themselves they would have a netting formula. Cash flows were thus only theoretically exchanged to arrive at their net differences in value at certain dates. Such swaps became in this manner speculative interest rate or currency rate related market instruments that could be used to hedge an existing position or create an open position. The fact that the parties retained their original position *vis-à-vis* third parties and created an additional one between themselves split their market risk. It added, however, to their credit risk.

It is still possible that parties wish to receive the relevant cash flows, if only to fulfill their own payment obligations and such situations remain common. In such cases, the question of the legal characterisation of the cash flow swap remains relevant.

Swaps as contracts for differences can be seen as transferable, or at least the benefits thereunder. Their essence is, however, that, depending on market conditions, they may go in or out of the money, that is in or out of profit

on a bilateral basis at specific dates and the resulting benefit or loss constitutes the true obligation between the parties. Probably, the set-off has lost here its character as a means of payment altogether and the netting constitutes here the essence of a new financial instrument. The normal rules of set-off (and their limitations) would not then apply. It could be said that, unlike in situations where there were still back to back agreements, there is here only a contract for differences. Clearly, not every netting implies a set-off in the strictly legal sense of a form of payment.

It will be clear that whether there is novation netting or not may be a key issue, especially in a bankruptcy of the counter-party, and is often a question of contract interpretation. One indication already mentioned may be in the actual booking practices of the parties. In other words, it may depend on whether the transactions are immediately booked in a netted way. That may create problems where the novation netting is perceived as a continuing process. To be effective in bankruptcy, it would then have to precede it whilst balances are continuously notified (although payment may still be postponed) and could notably not result from an extended set-off facility in such a bankruptcy unless it may also be deemed retroactive.[14] Another danger is that in the nature of a novation there are extra requirements in terms of capacity and consent of the parties. The greater danger is that it may not exceed the set-off facility in bankruptcy, at least not for balances that have not yet been notified. Hence the simultaneous effort to distinguish novation netting as an altogether different facility, but this may be more difficult where payments are effectively netted out.

Novation netting most certainly is not implied in every set-off even if there is a resultant net obligation. That may be simply an accounting matter. Even a multilateral netting need not be more than that so that in truth no new obligations emerge. As a consequence, also settlement need not go beyond it, although of course any relevant novation netting agreement needs itself for its validity also capacity and sufficient consent, but not then the set-off under it when it comes.

Novation netting may play an especially important role in a multilateral close-out netting (as it could in settlement netting) and is not even for bilateral close-out netting always considered a truly different category of netting. Again, its particular objective is to prevent the effect of any intervening bankruptcy and a situation of *cherry picking* in which the non-bankrupt party is asked to perform but the bankrupt party will only do so if there is a benefit for his estate. If properly effectuated before a bankruptcy, such a novated close-out netting is thought to be especially bankruptcy effective and may then exceed the set-off facility assuming such would not be against public policy. As a contractual tool to create or enhance connexity or dependency, it may also make the relevant netting more acceptable in bankruptcy, especially important in countries which limit the bankruptcy set-off to situations where there is connexity. It in fact seems that, more generally, contractual set-off

---

for either party. Thus one party may be a winner on one date but a loser on another, therefore be a creditor one day and a debtor the other, the benefit being contingent on market movements in the values of the underlying cash flows. More logical than assigning the benefit of a swap to a buyer of the position would therefore be to assign the entire contractual position, including the possibility that the contract could turn negative. Without the consent of the other swap partner, which defeats much of the attraction of the transfer, this could raise the question whether the assignor was fully discharged. The assignment of swap contracts in this manner in what is often called the secondary swap market has as a consequence remained underdeveloped. If a party wants to protect its profit under a swap or limit its loss, thus if it wants to neutralise its exposure, it has proved easier to enter into the opposite swap position through a new swap contract, in this manner locking in any gain or loss. It means, however, a doubling of the contracts and extra (credit) exposure to yet another party that might default. For banks it means the need for more (risk) capital to be set and retained against that exposure.

[14] See *British Eagle International Airlines Ltd. v Compagnie Nationale Air France* [1975] 2 All ER 390.

enhancements (therefore going beyond the automatic bankruptcy set-off facility under applicable bankruptcy law) are always more likely to be accepted in bankruptcy when clear connexity of the claims or conditionality of the contracts out of which they arise can be demonstrated or contractually created. Novation may also help in this connection. That could be the true importance of novation netting in the context of a settlement or close out.

1.3.4   Use of Contractual Netting Clauses: Contractual Netting and Bankruptcy

Contractual netting clauses have in recent years particularly developed for swaps and repos in terms of a novation close out netting, although (depending on the precise contractual terms) probably in a somewhat different way as in swaps there may be emphasis more on novation netting and in repos more on close-out netting. The modern swap contracts may make use of the netting concepts basically in three different ways. As mentioned in the previous section, (a) in most modern interest swap structures, there is now an inherent netting of both cash flows, leading to the swaps' modern form of a contract for differences with payment only of the difference between two *theoretical* cash flows on certain agreed dates. There is here novation netting entered into at the beginning of the transaction. It is its essence so that most swaps now no longer involve any exchange of physical cash flows or of the underlying assets or liabilities out of which the cash flows arise either, which each would have given rise to settlement or close out netting.

Importantly it means that there is here no longer a true set-off therefore and no need to net the amounts out on the payment or close-out dates, although this is what modern swap documentation is still likely to want to achieve for *other types* of swaps, like (b) currency swaps where the underlying assets are still likely to be exchanged and (c) in respect of whole swap portfolios between the same parties in a bilateral netting. Especially in the latter case, this is done by means of integrating all swap aspects on the appointed day which may in close-out netting be upon acceleration. As was explained above, that does not strictly speaking need to mean novation netting, even if this is the preferred route of the banking industry especially in bankruptcy situations for the reasons explained above.

In achieving these results, swap documentation uses a number of concepts, like those of *integration, conditionality* and *acceleration* which under applicable law may be deemed implied but are here made explicit to clarify the situation for countries, like England, where it is less clear whether they are implicit. It is relevant if the entity against which the set-off is invoked resides in such a country. As may be seen from the previous discussion, these concepts are especially put to the test in bankruptcy for which they are primarily devised. Again, one aspect of this is a single swap position; something different may be the integration of all swaps between the same parties in a single balance. Multilateral netting and clearing may be yet another situation.

The aim is always to expand the netting facility, thereby minimising risk for the bankrupt's counterparty (often a bank) in such a manner that it can survive the scrutiny of any applicable bankruptcy law which may use a narrower set-off concept itself and avoid at the same time the impression of further legal acts having to be performed upon bankruptcy which could no less interfere with the effectiveness of the set-off. We enter here the area of risk management. There is further uncertainty also because the applicable bankruptcy law may not always be easy to predict, as it depends on the place where the proceedings are opened, which could be in several countries or at least in a country away from the swap partner in trouble.

On the other hand, in practice, any resulting bankruptcy law limitation may not always be effective against a bankrupt swap partner if it has its centre of affairs elsewhere, therefore not in the country where the bankruptcy was opened and whose bankruptcy law applies (whilst not itself making amends for the foreign situation). In the context of a recognition of such foreign bankruptcy proceedings if at all admitted in the country of the relevant swap party, the bankrupt swap party might still be subjected to its own law for any effects of the netting on the swap. Thus the bankruptcy law concerning a branch may limit the effect of netting clauses but that need not necessarily affect the recovery from the company itself if headquartered elsewhere. In terms of bankruptcy law policies, the limit is usually that no extra preference is created for the non-bankrupt party at the expense of the other creditors. As suggested above, by introducing integration and conditionality notions creating contractual connexity, the acceptance of a broader set-off may become more readily acceptable, even in bankruptcy. That is certainly the aim of the modern swap documentation, which for this reason may even prefer to avoid the set-off characterisation altogether. Another aim is to reduce the capital adequacy requirements for financial institutions as their swap risks become more limited because of the netting facility, see for this aspect also chapter 6, section 2.5.3. Yet it remains true all the same that extra preferences are created which may offend applicable bankruptcy laws. That is the danger.

In this connection, it may greatly help if the applicable (bankruptcy) law itself is willing to consider the principle of integration of the swap contract (regardless of contractual clauses to the effect). It is thus conceivable that the applicable law itself groups certain contracts together and makes them mutually dependent. It is against the notion of privity of contract, but this notion is not as absolute as it is sometimes considered to be in common law countries, see chapter 2, section 1.5.3. In the financial area, the modern example is the finance lease under which the supply agreement of the goods to the lessor/owner often creates certain rights and obligations in the lessee as user of the goods and normally the instigator of the deal. Article 2A UCC in the USA expresses this approach quite clearly and it is also taken up in the Unidroit Convention on International Finance Leasing. Economic interdependence may thus sometimes have a sequel in law and may even create trilateral relationships. Other examples are subcontracting, reinsurance, and chain sales.[15]

Parallel loan agreements and indeed swaps may present further examples in the financial services industry. Integration of the contracts on the basis of economic reality may here be all the easier as the integration of contracts does not (directly) involve third parties and is on a bilateral basis only. The effect is likely to be felt in the formation, performance and especially termination of the arrangement. There may be interdependence at all three levels. Definitions, interpretation and applicable law may then also become mutually connected. It is likely, however, that there must also be some more objective cause for the integration and interdependence in such cases, which may have to be found in economic realities. The importance of the integration, conditionality and acceleration language in modern swap agreements in the context of the contractual close-out and netting provisions may thus be enhanced when there are also signs of more objective interdependence. If so, these concepts could then even be considered to have been implicitly included in the contract by the parties. All in all, the real impact of netting clauses in bankruptcy is likely to be dependent on a generally receptive attitude of the applicable law to the concept of contract grouping and integration in the case of economic interdependence.

Thus modern contractual netting clauses are likely to attempt to tie all swap deals between the same parties together. This is *bilateral close-out netting*. It is very much the objective of the ISDA Swap Master Agreements, see chapter 6, section 1.4.6 and

---

[15] See in France where there is a special academic interest in the subject of economically connected contracts, B Teyssie, *Les groupes de contrats* (LGDJ, Paris, 1975). See for swaps also P Goris (Diss. Louvain, 1992), Swaps, 177*ff.*

section 1.3.5 below. In each swap and between the various swaps, this may require a system of valuations which depends on conversion formulae for foreign exchange and non-monetary exposures as the redelivery of bonds or other repurchase or retransfer duties under the scheme, especially important if underlying assets or liabilities are also exchanged. To make all obligations co-terminous under the acceleration clause, there may have to be further adjustments in the relative values. The contractual acceleration, close-out and netting are increasingly typical if a default occurs in any financial dealings between the same parties (which need not be confined to their swap transactions), especially if banks. They may also result between the parties if one of them defaults in his relationship with any third party pursuant to a *cross-default* clause. The netting itself could even be agreed between a group of active swap parties. This is *multilateral close-out netting* and operates quite apart from a pooling in a clearing and settlement system.

The intention is that *aggregation, contractual close-out* or *bilateral netting* results in one amount either owed or owned. Such termination through acceleration is at the option of the non-defaulting party which may alternatively wish to take the risk of continuation, not uncommon in the case of minor defaults outside a bankruptcy situation. The end result in a close-out is payment of one sum either way, that is either to the defaulting or to the non-defaulting party which however, was only a competing claim for this amount. Yet as it is only a net amount, in a bankruptcy of the counter-party it is likely to work out much better than a situation in which the non-bankrupt party is payor (in full) under all swaps where the bankrupt party is in the money, but receives the *pro rata* distribution dividend only in each swap where he himself is a beneficiary.

There has always been some opinion that in bilateral netting the non-defaulting party would not need to pay any defaulter or the bankrupt party anything where the latter were in the money, and this is because of the notion that nobody should profit from his own default. This is the so-called '*one way payment*' or walk-away facility, well accepted in English law in the case of a contingent instead of a vested profit. It may also be contained in a standard clause in a swap. On the other hand, when termination follows for reasons other than default, any benefit is often claimable under the contract by the non-petitioning party in whole or in part, but not by the petitioning party. Thus under the contract there is often a termination option for parties in the case of new tax or regulatory burdens or in the case of intervening illegality or impossibility, leading to a so-called '*limited two-way payment*' which can also be incorporated in standard documentation. The full two-way payment happens when payments are made to whomsoever is in the money (either in each swap or in bilateral netting overall). It is the more normal situation and also the ISDA approach. Walk-away clauses are increasingly criticised and have now been deleted from standard swap documentation. One reason for this is that they may further endanger bilateral netting schemes in bankruptcy. Another similar type of netting of values may be found in Repo Master Agreements, see chapter 5, section 2.2.4.

As mentioned above, *ipso facto* termination combined with a contractual acceleration and aggregation clause in close-out netting as foreseen in the modern swap documentation may not be acceptable under the set-off provisions of all bankruptcy laws. This could notably have been expected under French and US law, which, with their reorganisation-oriented insolvency laws, do in any event not accept the acceleration and automatic termination of contracts pending the decision on the continuation of the business, see Article 37 of the French Bankruptcy Act 1985 and Section 365 of the US Bankruptcy Code 1978. It has motivated bankruptcy law amendments in both countries to exempt swap netting, in France under Law No 93–1444 of 31 December 1993 for swaps now covered by Article L 431–7 of its Monetary and Financial Code of 2000, see also chapter 5, section 1.3.3), in the US under

Sections 559 and 560 Bankruptcy Act respectively for repos and for swaps. In Germany, there is now Section 94 of the Insolvency Act 1999, see also section 1.3.5 below. This is unlike the situation in the Netherlands that (still) has liquidation-oriented insolvency laws. Also in England, the acceleration is not impeded in this manner. In other countries, the fact that acceleration is possible in bankruptcy may *not* mean either that the other contractual set-off enhancements are also automatically acceptable under applicable bankruptcy law. Thus in Australia, Section 16 of the Payment System and Netting Act 1998 provides a broader exception.

1.3.5   *The ISDA Swap and Derivatives Master Agreements. Swap and Repo Netting. The Notion of Conditionality and the 'Flawed Asset' as an Alternative to the Set-off. The EU Collateral Directive*

To ease the problems with close-out netting, particularly in bankruptcy, the aggregation principle has been pursued through the use of master agreements under which particularly in swaps all swap dealings between the same parties are deemed integrated into one contract. Once signed between two parties, all their swap dealings are thus meant to be covered by it and any new swaps are integrated into this system through standard telex confirmations.[16] This integration is certainly the prime objective of the International Swap Dealers Association which produced in this connection in 1987 an industry standard agreement, the ISDA Swap Master Agreement, in the latest version extended to all derivatives. There were always two such Masters, the Rate Swap Master for interest rate swaps and the Rate and Currency Swap Master for both interest rate and currency swaps. The latter is the more common outside the USA and usually the one referred to. It was amended in 1989 and 1992 to cover also other derivative products and became a multi-product master agreement, recast as the Swaps and Derivatives Master Agreement in 2002 to better deal with distressed counter-parties and markets following the problems in the Asian markets in the late 1990s. In particular the close-out provisions were reconsidered. *Force majeure* and acts of state affecting payment or compliance with other material provisions are notably not to upset the close-out and its effectiveness and present a new termination event or event of default.

The Schedule allows parties a number of different options in the various swap aspects and provides flexibility. Cross-border swaps are also covered; for US counter-parties a special schedule is adopted. The Swaps and Derivatives Master is subject to New York law, although English law may alternatively be made applicable to the Rate and Currency Swap Master. It does not seem to prevent parties from choosing any other law, but it is not common. However, the impact in bankruptcy remains unavoidably subject to the applicable bankruptcy law.

Both Swap Masters are very similar in approach and in much of their detail. The more common Swap and Derivative Master is of immense importance and lends itself to extension to other products because of its generic nature. It attempts to expand the notion of integration to all swaps between the same parties (Section 1(c)), although it still makes exceptions: in the case of certain termination events, like a change in tax law, only certain swaps may be affected. Parties may also reserve the right to lift certain swaps out of the

---

[16] There are other important industry standard master agreements like the 2000 TBMA/ISMA Global Master Repurchase Agreement, the Overseas Securities Lender's Agreement, the International Currency Options Market Terms (ICOM) and the International Foreign Exchange Master Agreement (IEFMA).

totality and either terminate them or transfer them separately, whilst only specific swaps may be guaranteed by outsiders, like parent companies, and not the totality.

Section 2(c) contains the netting clause proper and refers to one transaction in the same currency. It may be extended to other transactions payable on the same date in the same currency. It is in the nature of a novation netting for interest rate swaps leading to a contract for differences, but it may be broader and also include exchanges of principal although through the schedule specific swaps may be excepted from it. Acceleration is provided for in Section 6 which includes a reference to a single payment obligation (in Section 6(c)) and a payments clause (in Section 6(e)) leading to the close out netting with the necessary valuation formulae(see for the calculations also Section 9(h)(ii)).

The aim is clear and the approach assumes that a contract with a chosen domestic law can govern an international financial transaction in all its aspects and even aggregate all such transactions between two parties for bankruptcy purposes. In practice, this may prove not to be fully effective, especially as regards aggregation and netting. The status thereof in bankruptcy may remain unclear or contested as the aim is to claim an enhanced (set-off) right at the expense of other creditors. Nevertheless, established *market practices* based on the universal acceptance of the principle of set-off itself may increasingly underpin the contractual netting concept internationally, also in its enhancement of the set-off principle, at least outside bankruptcy. In bankruptcy, it appears that there must still be some innate connexity on which to build, which may, well however, be found in economic interdependence, at least in as far as all aspects of one swap transaction are concerned, see also the discussion in the previous section. The increasingly customary nature of the ISDA rules, especially of the Swaps and Derivatives Master, may also help the status of contractual netting in bankruptcy everywhere.[17]

The netting facility under repo agreements is similar and discussed in greater detail in chapter 5, section 2.2. It may in this connection be of some interest to compare swap and repo netting in one particular aspect: the notion of a 'flawed asset'. It has been used to underline the status and characterisation of the ISDA swap master as an *alternative* to set-off, therefore as a facility that is not constrained in bankruptcy by any limitations that may be inherent in an (automatic) bankruptcy set-off. Indeed, Section 2(a)(iii) makes it clear that the Swap Master is based on conditionality and not on traditional notions of set-off. Whether it succeeds or can ever succeed in this objective is another matter where mutual

---

[17] For banks and other financial institutions that are subject to regulation, one of the regulatory requirements is usually that they maintain certain minimum capital adequacy standards under which all their outstanding liabilities are weighted and protected by the capital of the institution according to certain formulae more extensively discussed in chapter 6, s. 2.5.2ff. In this respect it is of the greatest importance for these institutions that their liabilities may be netted out as it will reduced their need of capital and thereby their cost. Naturally, if in a swap only their outgoing cash flow is counted as a liability without any set-off of a related incoming flow, the need for capital will rise dramatically. Also if in a swap hedge, both positions are counted separately, it will create extra capital cost in terms of credit risk but also market risk. On the other hand, if the whole swap book may be netted, at least for market risk purposes, this will be greatly beneficial. If all swaps may be set off between two parties in a full bilateral netting, the credit risk is still more reduced which will save further capital.

International regulators have been careful in accepting the netting concept for capital adequacy purposes without further discussion. Originally, they accepted novation netting only on the basis of the 1988 Basle Accord but have gradually allowed bilateral close out netting, see chapter 6, s. 2.5.5, provided there results a single obligation between the parties and the financial institution concerned obtains legal opinions confirming that the netting agreement is enforceable under the law (a) of the jurisdiction of the counterparty, (b) its acting branch if situated elsewhere and (c) of the relevant netting agreement. This could mean three legal opinions at some considerable cost. In Apr. 1996 the BIS allowed reinterpretation of the Basle Accord to facilitate multilateral netting, but only for foreign exchange contracts as is now operated interbank in London for members of ECHO: see n. 13 *supra*.

payments are concerned. The 'flawed asset' theory which is based on the conditionality assumes in this connection that a flawed asset is created that disappears upon an event of default and is then automatically replaced by the early termination amount. The conditionality works, however, best in respect of a single swap. The integration of different payment obligations into one single amount upon default and acceleration may not be so conditioned and public policy may still prevent the extension or avoidance of the set-off under applicable bankruptcy law (unless amended to the effect). In other words, there may be a limit to what may be expected from netting clauses whether or not encapsulated in novation in view of the mandatory provisions of bankruptcy law and the limit to party autonomy in this regard.

Preferences cannot be created at will and although novation may be a form of payment it might not be possible to use it to avoid and amend the bankruptcy set-off provisions without proper authorisation of the relevant bankruptcy statute. Indeed the fall back position would always appear to be the relevant set-off provisions of the applicable bankruptcy statutes except in situations where there is a true contract for differences and therefore a new financial instrument created. Otherwise, there would appear a need for statutory clarification as was obtained in the US, France, Germany, Switzerland and Australia, but somewhat surprisingly not deemed necessary in England and the Netherlands. In these countries, there may be a greater willingness to depend on international practice or consensus in this regard.

The EU Collateral Directive envisages here a special close-out netting facility that must be considered bankruptcy resistant, see also chapter 4, section 3.2.4. The idea is that financial transactions that are conditional or temporary like repos and securities lending or move in and out of the money like swaps, futures and option and maintain collateral requirements to back up the resulting retransfer or payment obligations are subject to a (statutory) bilateral close-out and netting of all payment and delivery rights and duties in each EU country. Collateral is a broad and undefined concept that may entail security, title transfers or margin accounts. For the Directive, the key is the untrammeled facility to realise any security interest in or to appropriate the relevant assets (in the case of a title transfer) or margin, all to the extent these assets are in possession of the non-defaulting party, and net out all delivery and payment obligations in a final close-out upon an event of default. Another aspect is that the assets serving as collateral (and being of the fungible type) may be used by the possessor in exchange of an obligation to replace them in accordance with or at the end of the collateral arrangements. Local bankruptcy laws that impede these facilities or require statutory delays are made ineffective for these types of financial transactions.

1.3.6 The Evolution of the Set-off Principle

It is hardly useful here to start with history. The Roman law of set-off or the *compensatio* remained incidental. It was a procedural device depending therefore on the type of procedure in which it was invoked. In the more common of them, the *iudicia bonae fidei*, there was judicial discretion (except in the case of bankers or bankruptcy). For it to be given, there was a need for connexity but it did not matter what type of performances were set-off as in litigation all types were reduced to money, see also Gaius 4.61*ff.* The Justinian compilation (C.4.31.14) remained confused in the matter.[18] The *ius commune* concentrated at first mainly on the nature of the set-off as an instrument of party autonomy expressed in

---

[18] See also Inst. 4.6.30 and R Zimmermann, *The Law of Obligations* (1990), 760.

the requirement of notice, or, alternatively, on its automaticity or *ipso facto* nature. The first approach is generally speaking the German one which is believed to have had its origins in the writings of Azo.[19] The other approach roughly embodied in French law and in many bankruptcy statutes also had its origin in the writings of the thirteenth century glossators. Opinion remained divided in the Dutch seventeenth century school of Voet and others and still is in South Africa. In modern civil law, Section 388 BGB in Germany stands at the one end, Article 1289 Cc in France at the other.

Common law presents a mixed picture. With its rigid set of original actions, it could not easily accommodate the set-off.[20] At first, it depended mostly on statutory law in set-off statutes. In *Green v Farmer*,[21] Lord Mansfield summarised the position and, whatever natural equity said, held that at law apart from statutory relief, each party had to continue to recover separately in separate actions. Outside bankruptcy or other statutory law, the impact of the will of the parties is now accepted, however, allowing contractual set-off. Without such a clause, which is often deemed implied on very slight grounds, there are still problems in England, however. The set-off is then normal only between claims which are connected, that is have their origin in the same contract or legal relationship. In the set-off as a self-help measure based on connexity, one of the claims may be unliquidated, however. This is often referred to as an equitable set-off.

Otherwise the common law set-off is, barring contractual stipulation, a procedural device which can only be invoked in the manner of a defense in litigation as a way of settling accounts and depends therefore on a court order. It thus has no meaning outside it, except where specifically induced by contract or in the case of connexity. It means that a payment of the difference is normally *not* sufficient payment in England. Moreover, even in litigation there is only a set-off of mature claims, except again in equity, but it is then by its very nature subject to a measure of discretion of the courts.[22]

In insolvency, the situation is very different in the UK. The set-off is then automatic or *ipso facto* but it does not then go any further than allowed by statute or the bankruptcy rules: see Section 323 of the Insolvency Act 1986 and for company liquidation, Insolvency Rule 4.90 (1986); see also Section 382 and Rule 13.12. Under them, it is also immaterial whether the debts are present or future.[23] It may still be doubtful whether contractual enhancements of the netting principle are effective in bankruptcy in the UK, but at least an acceleration clause survives bankruptcy.[24] In the UK, the trustee's option to repudiate contracts under Section 175(2) of the Insolvency Act 1986 does not appear to prevent contractually agreed acceleration in bankruptcy either, but there remains doubt about the validity of other contractual enhancements of the set-off principle.[25] Further expansion of the

---

[19] *Summa Codicis, Lib IV, De Compensationibus Rubrica.*

[20] See "Comment, Automatic Extinction of Cross-Demands: Compensatio from Rome to California," 53 *Cal LR* 224 (1965).

[21] 98 ER 154 (KB 1768).

[22] See for terminology and further comment also the important comparative study by PR Wood, *English and International Set-off* (London, Sweet and Maxwell, 1989).

[23] See *Stein v Blake* [1995] 2 WLR 710.

[24] See *Shipton, Anderson & Co (1927) Ltd v Micks Lambert & Co* [1936] 2 All ER 1032.

[25] In the UK contractual netting appears accepted only as long as it does not give better rights, that is better than those provided by Bankruptcy Rule 4.90 (1986), *cf Carreras Rothmans Ltd v Freeman Matthew Treasure Ltd* [1985] 1 Ch 207 and also R Detham, "Set-off and Netting, in the Liquidation of a Counterparty" [1991] *JBL* 463, 541 and his *The Law of Set-off* (3rd edn, Oxford 2003). See further the Paper of the British Bankers Association of 13 Aug 1993, BBA Circular 93 (56) on the validity of bilateral close out netting under English law: see also the guidance note of the City of London Financial Law Panel on Netting of Counterparty Exposure of 19 Nov 1993, BBA Circular 93 (82).

set-off facility in bankruptcy may still be considered to violate the principle of equality of the unsecured creditors expressed in Section 107 of the Insolvency Act 1986.[26]

Documentation commonly tries to increase the chances of acceptance, however. In close-out netting, it seeks to make it effective as at the date of the close-out event as defined, which may well be before the bankruptcy petition. It may also introduce the notion that parties accepted this type of net payment as from the beginning of the contract, whilst sometimes defining it in terms of novation of the claims into one net obligation of the net debtor as off that moment. Modern law also avoids penalties, like one-way or limited two-way payments to make this set-off more palatable.

In the USA, the set-off outside bankruptcy is a matter of state law. In most states, particularly in New York, the set-off is no longer merely a defense in litigation and generally does not depend upon a court order. The early non-bankruptcy case was *Green v Darling*,[27] in which Justice Story allowed the set-off only in the case of connexity. It is now generally a self-help remedy, at least for banks. It developed as such in a more general way particularly through the bank current account practice (where it stopped in England except in situations of connexity).[28] The claims must be mature,[29] if only upon acceleration under a contractual clause to the effect.[30] In (federal) bankruptcy, Section 553 of the Bankruptcy Code applies. It is not an original grant of bankruptcy set-off rights but it limits the reach of the set-off under state laws if exercised within 90 days before the petition. The automatic stay provision of Section 362 also applies against the set-off (Section 362(a)(7)) whilst Section 365(e) renders contractual acceleration clauses ineffectual in bankruptcy, although through amendments of the Bankruptcy Code relief against it was given in repo and swap situations (see Section 559 for repos and Section 560 for swaps).[31]

In Germany, the set-off is at the request of the party invoking it and is outside bankruptcy not *ipso facto*: see Section 388 BGB. It has two purposes.[32] It is (a) a settlement, payment or discharge of mutual debt, and (b) a self-help measure for the notifying creditor, giving him in fact a preference. It has been viewed in this connection as a charge back or a lien on debt. The debts must be mutual and mature, homogenous, therefore of the same sort, enforceable, therefore not time barred, but may apparently be in different currencies. In bankruptcy, the trustee operates under the BGB provisions but the creditor has special facilities under Sections 94 and 96 of the 1999 Insolvency Act (formerly Section 54 of the German Bankruptcy Act (KO)): in bankruptcy the claims to be set-off need not yet be mature or unconditional and the claims need not be homogenous, in which case estimated monetary values are used.[33] Both claims must be due and payable before the proceeding started or at least the claim of the creditor must become payable before the claim of the bankrupt (except that instructions into systems governed by the EU Finality Directive are subject to the same day rule). Contractual modifications or enhancements of the set-off

---

[26] See *Carreras Rothmans Limited v Freeman Mathew Treasure Ltd* [1985] 1 Ch 207.
[27] 10 Fed Cas 1141 (DRI 1828).
[28] See *Otto v Lincoln Savings Bank*, 51 NYS 2nd 561 (1944).
[29] See *Jordan v National Shoe and Leather Bank*, 74 NY 467 (1878).
[30] See also PM Mortimer, "The Law of Set-off in New York", *International Financial Law Review*, 24 (May 1983).
[31] In the USA, netting is now allowed in the context of settlement payments, also accepted in the UK under the Companies Act 1989 but there limited to transactions executed on recognised exchanges, whilst a statutory amendment of 1990 in the USA now more generally allows the integration and acceleration in the case of standard swaps: see Sections 101 and 560 of the US Bankruptcy Code (and similar provisions in the laws covering institutions like banks, insurance companies and the like not subject to the US Bankruptcy Code).
[32] See BGH, 24 Nov 1954 [1955], NJW 339.
[33] See Jaeger, *Konkursordnung*. (8th edn, 1958), Section 54.

principle are not necessarily upheld in bankruptcy, certainly not any contractual exclusion of the benefit.[34] Section 104(2) of the 1999 Insolvency Act elaborates on the close-out netting of financial transactions under master agreements and specifically accepts the conversion of the outstanding obligations between the parties into a single claim, for which Section 104(3) gives a calculation method.

In France the system essentially remains one of *ipso facto* set-off, both in and outside bankruptcy with the narrowing concept of connexity in the latter case for debts that mature only after bankruptcy.[35] Bank account set-offs are probably also allowed in a bankruptcy of the client. Under modern French bankruptcy law since 1985, see Article 37, there is also a stay of acceleration clauses, although since amending bankruptcy legislation by the Law No 93–1444 of 31 December 1993, now replaced by Article L 431–7 of the Monetary and Financial Code of 2000, the situation has been clarified in the case of swap contracts. French law now allows contractual netting in these cases even in bankruptcy, provided it is covered by a master agreement or *convention cadre* using generally accepted principles, whilst one of the parties must be a bank or other financial, insurance or brokerage institution.

Although the integration and acceleration through master agreements have now been accepted at least in the USA and in France in this connection, they may still not be accepted in other countries.[36] Like all contractual set-off enhancements, acceleration is in general more vulnerable in the case of a full bilateral netting than in the context of integration and damages calculation within each particular swap as it is likely to give the greater benefit to the non-bankrupt party at the expense of the other creditors of the bankrupt. As suggested before, conditionality and connexity creating contract language may help, but appears to need some base in economic reality, and thus can only be an expression and reinforcement of a more objective principle.

Part II   International Payments

2.1   International Payment Arrangements to Minimise Payment Risk

2.1.1   *Cross-border Payments and their Risks*

In international trade, payment and payment protections acquire a special significance because there are greater payment risks. There is primarily the risk of the far away debtor not

---

[34] See BGH, 6 July 1978 [1981] NJW 2244.

[35] See Ripert/Roblot, 2 *Droit Commercial* (16th edn, 2000), nos 2842, 3039 and 3217.

[36] In Switzerland, there was considerable doubt, see M Affentranger and U Schenker, "Swiss Law puts Master Agreement in Question," *International Financial Law Review* 35 (Jan 1995), now alleviated by a change in the Swiss bankruptcy act. In Ireland, special legislation was also introduced through the Netting of Financial Contracts Act 1995: see R Molony and J Lawless, "Irish Legislation Validates Close-out Netting," *International Financial Law Review* 15 (Sept 1995). See for the history of the amending legislation in the USA, SK Henderson and JAM Price, *Currency and Interest Rate Swaps* (1988), 144*ff.* Under prior law the contractual integration created only a presumption which could be defeated when there remained too many individual elements of the different trans-actions. In this connection, the addition of new swaps and the termination or transfer and thereby elimination of others remained a problem. Differences in currencies were also problematic, so that different masters per currency were not uncommon. Other authors emphasised, however, the existence of material circumstances favouring the integration concept. In their view, an interrelationship was to be assumed when there was the same contractual framework, a close-out netting clause for all, a consolidated credit risk approach, mirror swaps or

being able or willing to pay. This *credit* (or *counter-party*) *risk* is inherent in all transactions, but internationally it is greater as the credit worthiness of the counter-party and its willingness to pay may be much more difficult to gauge. In any event, the supplier of goods or services will on the whole be in a poorer position than he would be locally to remain informed until the payment day. A special aspect of this counter-party risk is the foreign debtor refusing to accept the goods or documents themselves for reasons which may not be easy to ascertain, but have, whatever the excuse, in practice often to do with the goods no longer being needed or the buyer having spotted a better deal somewhere else. It naturally leads also to a refusal to make the necessary payments.

Another risk is in disputes, real or contrived, concerning the quality of the goods upon arrival which could hold up the payment indefinitely. The need of transportation unavoidably implies risks in terms of safe arrival and (deteriorating) quality of the goods, often referred to as *quality or manufacturing* but may also be viewed as another form of *credit* or *counter-party risk* where the foreign buyer proves unusually quarrelsome and is intent on price reductions or likes to take advantage of a more complicated situation than would follow purely locally. The fact that litigation would most likely have to be conducted in the foreign country is in itself of course of some help to the debtor, if only because of the practical difficulty that the creditor may encounter in terms of cost and communication.

When payments are made in the country of the buyer, either in his own currency or in any other, there is in a restricted foreign exchange regime also the question of free convertibility and transferability of the currency. They present great risks to the seller already discussed in section 1.1.4 above. A seller may want some safeguards in this connection in terms of depreciating values but more so in terms of proper payment in convertible and transferable currency. To guard against depreciation he may use a different unit of account in the contract, see section 1.1.3 above, or may otherwise organise some currency hedge in his own country. It is likely to be costly. To guard against the convertibility and transferability of the payment proceeds, he may demand a letter of credit with payment in his own country, as we shall see. It is also likely to be costly and for its effectiveness the debtor who opens these letters may still require prior authorisation of his own authorities.

There are other risks inherent in international trade, like the *country risk and political risk*. They are closely related to the convertibility and transferability risks. Country risk has to do with the country of the debtor no longer being able to provide the necessary foreign exchange when the price is expressed in other than the local currency, even though it was originally promised. It may also be in such disarray as no longer to be organised to supply timely the necessary currency for the debtor to make international payments, even though the debtor himself may be perfectly willing to do so and is in a position to provide the necessary local currency to buy the foreign exchange at prevailing rates. Political risk is narrower and arises, for example, where a country no longer allows the free convertibility and transferability of the agreed price as a matter of policy or interferes in the transaction in other ways through legal action. It may also affect any intermediary bank in the country concerned, when used in the payment process, for example under a collection or letter of credit, although it may have a special position and more leverage than its clients or greater set-off possibilities allowing it still to arrange the necessary payments to the foreign seller (at a price).

---

swap hedges, etc, see DP Cunningham and WP Rodgers Jr, 'The Status of Swap Agreements in Bankruptcy' in WP Rodgers Jr (ed), *Interest Rates and Currency Swaps* (1989), 229. This reasoning was somewhat circular but nevertheless taken seriously.

There are also related risks, for example delays in local settlement (and authorisation) practices, often referred to as *settlement risk* but often connected with country risk when any promised convertibility and transferability of the payment proceeds are not forthcoming. See for these various risks also chapter 2, section 2.1.2.

2.1.2   Payment in Open Account

In international sales transactions, like in domestic ones, parties may agree a *payment in open account*. In that case, the seller ships the goods and sends the invoice together with the other documents to the buyer, who is invited to pay the agreed amount on the appointed date into the account indicated by the seller. It provides the seller no payment protection at all and is therefore limited to transactions involving small amounts or to situations where the seller/creditor has no doubts about the credit worthiness and/or the willingness of his debtor/buyer to pay. It assumes that the parties are well known to each other and this mode of payment is then very efficient. It is also the cheapest and often the quickest and simplest way to proceed, and therefore an attractive one. It results in a simple bank transfer, facilitated by the progressive liberalisation of current payments cross-border and the ease and speed with which these payments can now be made through modern international payments systems like Swift and CHAPS which avoid funds being tied up in the banking system (without earning interest for the parties) for very long. They also reduce settlement complications at the same time. The details of such bank payments were discussed above.

Nevertheless there is no protection against credit risk. If the need for such protection arises, some may be provided in the contract itself, for example through a reservation of title, but that does not force the buyer to accept the goods and may not prove to be effective when the goods are shipped to another country, see for the private international law aspects chapter 4, section 1.8, or when the goods have been commingled with or converted into others. Moreover, upon shipment their precise location may be unknown and any reclaiming of the goods may present considerable problems as will their subsequent resale in a foreign environment for which the seller may not be sufficiently prepared and/or equipped. Even if the seller succeeds in retrieving the assets, he may have to appoint an agent or incur other costs in storage, whilst the risk of loss of, or damage to, the goods in practice reverts to him (if not also in law).

Similar contractual protection may derive from the seller being allowed to retain the bill of lading until payment, but it also does not help where the buyer does not want the goods any longer, so that there is only an unsecured damages claim, neither does it alleviate the risk of loss or damage and disposal elsewhere. Where title or documents are retained, there is also no protection against country or political risk after the goods have left the country of the seller.

A particular feature of international sales is that the buyer is unlikely to agree to any forms of payment (except down payments in the case of the supply for large capital goods) that aim at payment (or at least acceptance of a bill of exchange) before the goods are out of the *control* of the seller. This also applies to any bill of lading or warehouse receipt issued to the seller in respect of them as these documents embody the goods, see for these documents of title more in detail chapter 4, section 2.1. That is understandable but naturally, the seller is equally unlikely to surrender the goods or the documents to the buyer without payment or unconditional and watertight assurances to the effect. There is here an inherent deadlock situation in all sales, made worse in international sales because of the need for transportation and the impossibility of simultaneity in surrender of the goods and their payment. Unavoidably there is a different time and place for the seller physically to surrender his asset and for the buyer to take it and pay for it. It also means extra risks in transportation and deterioration of the quality of the goods. This complicates payment further in the sense that the seller will be all the more reluctant to send the goods before payment and the buyer to pay before receipt.

There is an obvious need in all sales for the parties simultaneously to hand over the goods (or to documents representing them) and the money (or to achieve any other form of unconditional payment at the same time), or at least to approximate such a situation in order to reduce the counter-party risks for both. Whilst as just mentioned, in international sales this will be typically lacking, a form of simultaneity may be reinstated in this connection by the use of intermediaries or agents through whose hands the goods and the payments are likely to pass. These intermediaries are the carriers and warehouse operators in respect of the goods and they are the banks in as far as payments are concerned. The intermediation of banks in particular has allowed here the creation of some schemes to approximate some simultaneity. Of these, the *collection* arrangements and *letters of credit* are the most common. In both, the bill of lading is likely to play a significant role and will be handed over through the banking system in return for payment.

In a collection, a bank established in the country of the buyer will collect the money from the buyer as agent for the seller (or his bank) after having been put (usually) in possession of the bill of lading by the seller (or his bank). Under a letter of credit, the issuing bank (or its agent in the country of the seller) will pay the seller in his own country after the seller has produced the bill of lading which he will have received when he shipped the goods and put them in the hands of the carrier as independent third-party in this respect. If transportation is by road similar schemes can be devised. It is, however, easiest and most common to discuss the structures on the basis of the carriage of the goods by sea and that will be the approach of this book also.

Naturally, payment protection is also important where no goods are involved or no transportation needs to take place under an international contract, for example because the goods are already on location or the contract concerns only services. For those situations payment protections are much less well developed, although letters of credit are perfectly feasible in those cases also. Obviously, the documents to be presented cannot then be bills of lading but they can be certificates of independent parties that the goods or services in question have been delivered (whatever their quality).

2.1.3 Ways to Reduce Payment Risk

It is thus clear that through lack of contact and/or information, the creditor in international transactions is likely to incur a considerable payment exposure (short of special precautions) and may as a minimum suffer substantial payment delays and loss of interest income on the payment proceeds as a consequence. Administrative expenses may also be incurred in chasing the debtor and his payment intermediaries. At worst there will be no payment at all.

In international trade, originally the *bill of exchange* played a role in the reduction of the payment risk for the seller. Later on, collection arrangements and letters of credit were developed, as we saw. The bill of exchange has only modest effectiveness in this connection as it depends on acceptance by the debtor, which can mostly not be compelled, and does not even then protect against the debtor's insolvency (or counter-party risk). This will be discussed in the next few sections. Moreover, any collection is normally in the country of the debtor, so that the creditor also retains the transfer risk. As the goods are normally delivered before the payment date, they are gone. On the other hand, nothing in this arrangement compels the debtor to accept the goods if he does not want them any longer. Whatever the motive and justifications, this will lead by itself to non-payment.

Collection arrangements, which will be subsequently discussed, provide a protection based on the retention of the bill of lading by intermediary banks in the collection process. It gives some protection through the inherent retention of the goods, but collections of this nature still lead to payment in the country of the debtor with the attendant transfer risks. They do not guard against a buyer being no longer interested in the goods either. Only the *letter of credit* may amount to a payment guarantee in the country of the creditor, regardless of whether or not the goods have safely arrived or whether or not the buyer wants them any longer. That is to be sorted out later whilst the creditor at least has the money. Letters of credit are therefore usually preferred by the seller. They are costly, however, and even though the cost is normally borne by the buyer, this way of payment affects the competitiveness of the seller who may be forced indirectly to contribute by lowering the price. Instead of letters of credit which are in fact a type of bank guarantee, banks may also give some more direct guarantees. These payment protection measures will also be discussed in the next sections.

2.1.4   Ways to Reduce Payment Risk: The Accepted Bill of Exchange

As just mentioned, bills of exchange are the traditional method of reducing payment risk. Their creation and legal status as negotiable instruments are more extensively discussed in chapter 4, section 2.2. Here the only issue is how they may reduce payment risk. They may do so when they are accepted by the buyer. Only time bills can be so accepted and may at the same time allow the creditor (drawer of the bill) to sell these accepted bills to (or rather discount them with) a so-called discount bank (which specialises in this form of financing) so as to obtain ready money regardless of the maturity date of the bill. In that case, a discount will be applied to the nominal amount of the bill to allow for its later maturity and also for the collection risk of the bank.

The signature of the buyer on a time bill of exchange expressing his *acceptance*, provides some extra safeguard for payment as dishonouring an accepted draft is generally considered a most serious matter and likely seriously to affect the credit standing and therefore borrowing power of a debtor/accepting drawee. However, a buyer need not normally accept a bill of exchange. Even if under the contract he must, or where in countries like in the Netherlands and France, there may be a statutory obligation for the buyer to accept a bill of exchange, see chapter 4, section 2.2.2, this obligation is no substitute for the acceptance itself, which would still have to be enforced through the courts. In any event, acceptance does not protect against the credit risk, including the bankruptcy of the buyer/debtor/drawee.

If discounted to a bank or sold to a third party without recourse to the seller/drawer of the bill of exchange (if possible under applicable law), the accepted bill of exchange may prove a way of obtaining early payment in a credit sale transaction which has a delayed payment. As just mentioned, there will be a discount for interest until maturity and another one for credit or collection risk. Discounting or negotiating the accepted bill transfers the credit risk from the seller to the next holder of the bill, here the discounting bank. It may be difficult to find a bank that will discount the bill of exchange. It is likely that only the house bank of the buyer in his home country will do so as it has enough knowledge of the debtor who is likely to be dependent on his bank for other services. It will leave the seller with cash in the house bank's country (normally therefore the country of the buyer) so that the seller retains the foreign exchange and country risks. A bill guaranteed (avalised) by a bank without recourse to the seller and payable in the latter's home country would help, but few banks except again the house bank of the buyer may be willing to do so. It is unlikely to co-operate as it puts the risk of proper and timely payment in the required (convertible and transferable) currency fully on this bank, minimised only to the extent the debtor has put it in the required funds or has provided other forms of security or comfort. As this will normally exactly be the problem in the relationship between the seller and buyer/debtor, it will not be any less so between a buyer/debtor and the avalising bank. In any event, for all these reasons such an aval would be costly.

2.1.5   Ways to Reduce Payment Risk: Collection Arrangements

Under a collection, the seller (principal) normally requests his own bank (the *remitting bank*) to turn over the documents relating to the goods (normally a bill of lading issued by the carrier) to a bank in the country of the buyer (the *collecting bank*). Thus it is here the seller/creditor who organises this payment facility. The collecting bank will be acting as the agent of the remitting bank and collect from the buyer through the buyer's bank (the *presenting bank*) the money agreed in the contract of sale. It will do so against the handing over of the bill of lading to the presenting bank. Normally, the collecting bank will receive either money or a bill of exchange accepted by the presenting bank. The function of the collecting and presenting bank may be combined. Obviously this type of collection will have been discussed between buyer and seller beforehand and be agreed amongst them.

The ICC 'Uniform Rules for Collections' (URC) 1995, which are usually applicable in these situations as we shall see, prescribe that all documents sent for collection must be accompanied by a collection instruction from the seller to the remitting bank giving complete and precise details. The remitting bank has to act upon this instruction. It will also indicate what it is subsequently to do with the money or bill of exchange it so receives. This bank will provide its services in this respect for a fee, which incorporates also the fees of the other banks involved in the scheme. They have no interest of their own or exposure in the transaction as there are no guarantees. Besides the fees, they may also earn a foreign exchange spread upon conversion of the money into another currency or an interest rate spread on any discounting of the bill of exchange or on any deposit of the proceeds made with them in the meantime.

The URC assume that the seller puts the instructing bank in possession of the documents, normally a bill of lading in order to organise the collection.[37] It will include instructions to deliver these documents to the buyer (the presenting bank), in which connection three methods of collection may be indicated. They are usually reflected in the contract of sale itself:

(a)   Cash against documents or CAD: in that case, the documents relating to the goods are delivered (to the presenting bank) against cash (to the seller) or a bank transfer, that is upon presentation by the seller's bank (the remitting bank) of the bill of lading as soon as possible after the loading of the goods sold. It means immediate transfer of the documents against immediate payment.

(b)   Documents against acceptance (of a bill of exchange) or D/A: in that case, the documents related to the goods, as well as a bill of exchange drawn on the

---

[37] See for the collecting bank, Article 3(a)(iii), and for the presenting bank, Article 3(a)(iv) URC.

buyer's bank (the presenting bank), are delivered to that bank as soon as possible after loading. The bill of exchange will be presented for acceptance and will demand payment at an agreed maturity date (acceptance is strictly speaking not payment itself). It means payment (for the seller) later, so that the seller retains a credit risk. The accepted bill of exchange may be discounted (without recourse as a 'forfait')[38] in which case the credit risk is transferred to the discounting bank. This will often be the presenting bank itself.

(c)   Documents against payment (often of a sight bill of exchange) or D/P: in that case the documents related to the goods are delivered (to the presenting bank) only after the payment in cash of a sight bill of exchange (to the seller) on an agreed later date. D/P is thus documents (for the buyer) against cash (for the seller) later. It results in a deferred payment.

Of these three collection schemes, the CAD term is obviously the best for the seller as it effects, through the banks, a simultaneous exchange of payment against documents (allowing the buyer to transfer these or collect the goods), normally immediately upon loading. It will accordingly eliminate the risk of the buyer refusing the goods upon arrival and thus also payment. But as payment takes place in the country of the buyer there are still the convertibility and transfer risks and the related country and political risk. The remitting, collecting and presenting banks guarantee nothing in this connection.

The D/A always involves credit and is only of real help to the seller if he can discount the accepted bill of exchange without recourse. If he has this opportunity, the D/A provides for the seller protection very similar to CAD, although the discounting will impose extra costs. If the discounting facility is not available, D/A will normally be acceptable to the seller only if the buyer is well known to him as he still has the credit risk, assuming further that there is no undue convertibility, transferability, country or political risk. The credit risk may also be overcome through an aval of the presenting bank. D/A gives the buyer the chance of immediate disposal of the goods and some credit and is therefore generally more favourable to him, although he may have to carry the cost of any aval or guarantee the forfaiting.

D/P is the most risky for the seller as, depending on its terms, it may allow for the simultaneous exchange of documents and payment only towards the end of the transaction when the goods have already arrived. The danger is that the buyer may refuse acceptance of the goods, show no interest in the bill of lading at all, and will not pay. There are also still the convertibility, transferability, country and political risks. Some refinement is therefore not uncommon through additional instructions which may require, for example acceptance of a bill of exchange forthwith even though presentation for payment will take place only much later at the agreed time and place. It then resembles the D/A without putting the goods (or documents) at the disposition of the debtor. It makes the arrangement more favourable to the seller.

The drawback of all these collections remains the dependence of the seller on the creditworthiness of his debtor/buyer, and especially under D/P and D/A the later payment when the goods are already in transit and cannot easily be retrieved without making additional cost. Then there is the payment in the country of the debtor with the attendant convertibility, transferability, country and political risk exposure. Even the CAD, which like all

---

[38] See for 'forfaiting' more in particular CM Schmitthoff, *The Law and Practice of International Trade* (10th ed. 2000), 233. The forfaiter usually agrees to this only if the payment is secured by a third party, here often the buyer.

other arrangements is usually executed in the country of the buyer, retains thus an element of uncertainty. Only the facility to discount accepted bills of exchange in the seller's country without recourse (*a forfait*) may constitute full protection in this regard (or an aval by a bank in the seller's own country) but may not be easily obtainable and in any event is likely to carry a high price.

2.1.6   Ways to Reduce Payment Risk: Letters of Credit.
The Different Banks Involved

A better and now more common way to avoid payment risk has evolved in the letter of credit. This is an undertaking of a bank (the issuing bank) which commits to pay the seller (beneficiary) a sum of money (usually the sales price) or to accept a bill of exchange (drawn on itself and usually with the seller/drawer as payee) upon the delivery of certain specified documents, usually including the bill of lading, assuming they are regular on their face. Although the issuing bank will subsequently hand over these documents to the buyer (applicant), who has normally arranged and requested the letter of credit (as condition of the sales agreement) and by whom it will ultimately be reimbursed, the payment to the seller (beneficiary) is *not dependent* on it. Nor is it affected by any problem that may arise in the relationship between the buyer/applicant and the issuing bank or even in the original relationship between the buyer/debtor and the seller/creditor. That is for them to sort out later. The payment obligation of the bank is thus an *independent* obligation.

Whilst a collection is organised by the creditor/seller at his expense and is effected at the place of the debtor/buyer, the letter of credit is requested by the debtor/buyer from a bank as provided for in the contract of sale. The costs are in principle also for the buyer (although they may be partially discounted in the sales price) whilst payment will normally be arranged in the country of the seller. That is besides the independence the great attraction of the letter of credit for the latter. The reason an issuing bank is willing to give an undertaking of this nature (for a fee) is normally that it knows the buyer/debtor who instructs it well. Naturally, it takes a risk as to its own reimbursement by the buyer, but it is likely to have a lot of business with its client under which it regularly receives money on its behalf. Alternatively, it may have been put into funds by the latter or been given other types of security or comfort. As the bank is likely to become holder of the bill of lading upon payment of the seller, this may also give it a retention facility as added security for reimbursement by the buyer.

For the issuing bank, the situation may not be fundamentally different from an aval given for payment to the seller directly in his own country. As mentioned before, an aval is a bank guarantee supporting an accepted bill of exchange drawn by the seller on the buyer, but there is an important difference in that the aval is mostly considered a secondary obligation only. This means that the creditor (holder) can invoke it only if the drawee/debtor defaults on his payment. This is not so for the letter of credit, under which the bank has a *primary* obligation and is required to pay (or accept a bill of exchange) as soon as the relevant documents are presented to it and found to be in order. That means that the issuing bank must pay if the documents are on their face in compliance with the terms and conditions of the letter of credit. Although this primary payment obligation of the bank does not, strictly speaking, substitute for the payment obligation of the buyer/debtor it will be normally the bank that pays but the buyer is not released and may still be required by the seller to pay if the bank somehow does not or cannot do so (for example, because the documents are not in order or because the bank is bankrupt). The buyer remains therefore a primary responsible debtor, at least in such cases. That is only exceptionally relevant, however, and not the normal method of payment once a letter of credit is issued as the letter of credit is likely to give the seller a more creditworthy debtor than the buyer and more efficient access to the money. Through it, the credit and other payment risks are all shifted to the bank which is the principal benefit of the letter of credit and its rationale.

As just mentioned, there is here not only an *independent* but also a *primary* obligation of the bank issuing the letter of credit which is only subject to the documents being found in order. The issuing bank still acts as agent for the buyer (and therefore not in all aspects independent from him), however, in effecting through its payment a release for the buyer under the sales contract. It has on the other hand an independent duty *vis-à-vis* the buyer to provide him with the documents.

The ICC restated the most common rules concerning the letter of credit in its Uniform Customs and Practice for Documentary Credits or UCP, for the first time in 1933, with the latest text issued in 1993. The UCP contain only a *partial* codification, like all ICC Rules. They are without official status but they have great authority. Upon request, the ICC Commission on Banking Technique and Practice also gives interpretations. Like the ICC Uniform Rules for Collections or UCR, they have developed their own terminology. The revised Article 5 UCC in the USA tracks this UCP system: see its Comment 1.

The UCP apply only to *documentary* letters of credit, therefore only to letters of credit that are payable upon the presentation of specified documents. This normally concerns the bill of lading but there could be others.

The *key provisions* of the UCP define the various banks involved and their duties, like those of

(a)   the issuing bank,
(b)   the instructing bank and correspondent issuer,
(c)   the advising bank,
(d)   the nominated bank, and
(e)   the confirming bank.

They also define the various kinds of credits, like

(a)   the sight credit,
(b)   the deferred payment credit,
(c)   the acceptance credit, and
(d)   the negotiation credit.

Indeed, in documentary letters of credit of this sort, there are in international situations normally a number of banks involved. The chain normally starts in the country of the buyer/debtor who organises the facility and ends in the country of the seller/creditor who will want to receive the money in his own country mainly to avoid counter-party, transfer and country risk. The *issuing bank* is in this connection the bank that is asked by the buyer/debtor to issue the letter of credit. That is normally its own bank in its own country (assuming it is acceptable to the seller) but it can be another bank, for example when the buyer's own bank does not provide this kind of service. The buyer's own bank can then limit its role to that of an *instructing bank*. In relation to the instructing bank, the issuing bank is then the *correspondent issuer*.

The issuing bank will sign the letter of credit and send it to the seller/beneficiary but it may use an *advising bank* in the country of the seller to advise the issuing of the letter of credit. It gives the seller the comfort of the originality of the signatures (as there are many falsified letters of credit in circulation). Under Article 7 UCP, the advising bank has to ascertain with reasonable care the apparent authenticity of the letter of credit. In the USA under Section 5-107 UCC it also assumes an obligation for the accuracy of its own statements in this connection, but (at least in the USA) there is no duty of timely transmission.[39]

The issuing bank may further appoint a *nominated bank* in the country of the seller. This bank will examine the documents presented by the seller and, if they are in compliance with the terms of the credit, it will take them up against payment or against acceptance of a bill of exchange drawn by the seller: see Article 10(b)(c) and (d) UCP. This nominated bank is usually the advising bank but need not be the same: for example, the advising bank may be the house bank of the seller/creditor but the nominated bank may be the branch of the issuing bank in the country of the seller. For these purposes branches are usually considered independent entities.

The examination of the documents is a very sensitive task. The documents may be falsified but the more common problem is that they are not strictly speaking in compliance with the terms and conditions of the letter of credit: Articles 13 and 14 UCP. Especially if quality certificates are required, they may not be in the precise form. Shipping documents may not be made out to the proper entities (but rather to agents). Especially invoices establishing the sale price are often not in the required form or may slightly deviate in amount. Many deviations are small and do not matter but they may nevertheless require consultation with the issuing bank and subsequently with the buyer to prevent any danger to the reimbursement of the issuing bank by the buyer and of the nominated bank by the issuing bank.

The compliance of the documentation is determined by international standard banking practices as reflected in the UCP, not necessarily an easy criterion, but the ICC Banking Commission may help in the interpretation. Section 5-109(2) (old) UCC used to require that the documents were examined with care leading to immediate reimbursement by the applicant, but the UCC did not define the necessary standard. The new Section 5-108(e) UCC refers to standard practices of financial institutions that regularly issue letters of credit. The UCP refers to *international* practices in this respect, the UCC probably still to national standards. In any event, standards per branch are ignored[40] because it was considered quite impossible to know the customs of thousands of trades for whose dealings letters of credit may be issued. Article 13(b) UCP sets a seven banking days time limit for the examination, but the bank cannot use more than reasonable time, even within that time limit. The reasonable time and the time limit concern the examination activities of all the banks involved *together* and they are not a time frame for each bank involved, as there may be the issuing and nominated bank.

In international transactions, the duty to examine the documents is normally delegated to a nominated bank appointed by the issuing bank. It does not, however, discharge the issuing bank from its own duty in this regard *vis-à-vis* the buyer/applicant of the credit. As already mentioned, normally, the nominated bank is also authorised to take up the documents from the seller against payment under a sight credit. It may also be authorised to do so against acceptance of a bill of exchange on behalf of the issuing bank. This is called an *acceptance credit*. In such a case, the nominated bank may also be called the *paying bank*,

---

[39] *Sound of Market Street, Inc v Continental Bank International,* 819 F 2d 384 (1987).
[40] See the English case of *JH Rayner & Co v Hambro's Bank Ltd* [1943] 1 KB 37.

respectively *the accepting bank*. If the nominated bank is required to negotiate the bill of exchange at the same time, it may also be called the *negotiating bank*.

If the documents are not found to be in compliance with the letter of credit, the nominated bank has a duty to refuse payment, Article 14(b) UCP. It will then give notice stating all discrepancies to the seller/beneficiary within seven days of receipt of the documents, Article 14(d)(i) and (h) UCP, and should return the documents to the beneficiary (or the bank acting for him in the collection). If the documents appear on their face in compliance with the terms of the letter of credit, the nominated bank will pay or accept a bill of exchange as the case may be. It will turn over the documents to the issuing bank, which is bound to reimburse the nominated bank provided it also finds the documents on their face in compliance with the credit: see Article 14(a)(i) and (h) UCP.

In this process, neither the advising bank nor the nominated bank accepts liability. They are only operating as agents for the issuing bank subject to its instructions, see also Article 10(c) UCP,[41] although the agency notion should be seen here primarily as operating within the context of the letter of credit. As already mentioned, the advising bank may at a later stage also become the nominated bank as it is rare for more than one bank to be involved in the country of the seller.

The situation is *very different* when the issuing bank appoints a *confirming bank* in the country of the seller/beneficiary. It is a normal request of the latter when the issuing bank is elsewhere. The confirming bank takes an independent undertaking under the letter of credit, see Article 9(b) UCP, and is often inserted to make absolutely sure that the seller may depend on payment in his own country. It gives the seller/beneficiary at the same time extra security because the issuing bank is not discharged. If there is a confirming bank in the country of the seller, it is normal for it to be the advising bank in the first instance and/or later also the nominated bank. If there is a payment obligation and a bill of exchange to negotiate, the nominated bank must also negotiate the bill of exchange on behalf of the issuing bank without recourse to the drawer or holder in order to provide for the necessary payment. The confirming bank is *sometimes* considered the agent of the issuing bank,[42] which is not necessarily inconsistent with the language of the UCP. It may be doubted, however, and in any event this agency would be of a very different nature from that of the advising bank and the nominated bank. Under Article 18 UCP, the issuing bank is notably not liable for any negligence or misconduct of the confirming bank.

There may yet be another bank, to wit a bank engaged in a *silent confirmation*, but such a bank operates at the request of the seller who pays for the benefit and this arrangement is quite separate from the letter of credit itself and not covered by the UCP.

On the seller's side there may be another set of banks involved. The seller can use a bank, usually his own house bank, to hand the documents over to the nominated bank at the counter of which the letter of credit will be available for payment or acceptance (or negotiation). It is not a relationship covered by the UCP either, but rather by the Uniform Rules for Collections (URC), see section 2.1.5 above. Under the URC, this bank will be the *remitting bank* (to which the documents are remitted by the seller for collection). It may still use *a collecting bank*, which may in turn use a *presenting bank*.

When the nominated bank takes up the documents against payment or acceptance (or negotiation of a bill of exchange), the issuing bank must reimburse it, Articles 10 and 14(a)(i) UCP. The issuing bank may in this connection use *a reimbursing bank*, Article 19 UCP, useful in particular when the currency of the credit is neither that of the issuing bank

---

[41] See in the USA, *Bamberger Polymers International Bank Corp v Citibank NA*, 477 NYS 2d 931 (1983).
[42] See in England *The Bank of Baroda v The Vysya Bank Ltd* [1994] 2 Lloyd's Rep 87.

nor of the nominated bank. The issuing bank carries here also the transfer risk. Special complications may arise in the case of the bankruptcy of the issuing bank. The paying bank may not then reclaim the money from the beneficiary.[43]

2.1.7 The Types of Letters of Credit

A letter of credit must clearly indicate whether it is available by *sight payment*, by *deferred payment*, by *acceptance* or by *negotiation*: see Articles 10(a) *io* 2 (i), (ii) and (iii) *io* 9 (a)(i), (h), (iii) and (iv) UCP. The most convenient letter of credit for the seller is the one available *at sight* upon presentation of the documents by a bank in his own country, because the proceeds thereof are then at the immediate disposal of the seller.

There are many other ways, however. In a *deferred payment credit*, the issuing bank undertakes to pay after a period of time. Nonetheless, it assures the seller that payment will be made on the due date. In the *acceptance credit*, the seller must draw a time bill of exchange on a specific bank (which can be the issuing bank, the confirming bank or another bank). After the documents have been found to be in compliance with the letter of credit, the drawee bank will accept the bill of exchange, by which it confirms to the seller/payee a commitment to pay on the maturity. In respect of the bank, the acceptance credit allows the buyer a grace period, giving him the documents and therefore the disposition rights over the goods, whilst he will be charged with the draft amount only upon maturity. It does not prevent the seller or a third-party payee to discount the draft (usually with the accepting bank), if they want ready cash, which protects them fully assuming they may discount without recourse. The acceptance of a draft by the nominated bank acting on behalf of the issuing bank can be affected by a mistake, however. This may present a valid excuse for the issuing bank not to pay the beneficiary, but it will not affect any third party holder in due course of the bill.

In a *negotiation credit*, the bill drawn on a bank indicated in the letter of credit is available for negotiation with a bank either designated in the letter of credit, when there *is a limited negotiable credit*, or to be chosen by the beneficiary, when there is *a freely negotiable credit*. If a negotiating bank is appointed, it has to give value for the bill of exchange (and/or the documents, see Article 10(b)(ii)), but only conditionally, that is depending on whether the issuing or confirming bank will subsequently reimburse the negotiating bank interposed by them. The bill of exchange (and/or documents) is (are) thus conditionally sold to the negotiating bank for immediate cash. This negotiation results in a *provisional* payment only, which may be recovered from the beneficiary if the issuing or confirming bank does not reimburse the negotiating bank.[44]

The drawing of a bill of exchange under both an acceptance credit and a negotiation credit will be in the interest of the seller as it gives him the chance to obtain ready cash by

---

[43] This will be different in the case of negotiation. Admittedly, there is no recourse to the seller but it is accepted that a negotiating bank will only pay provisionally subject to its reimbursement by the issuing bank. Thus the negotiating bank takes up the documents or a bill drawn on the issuing bank by the seller to his own or someone else's order, and pays the seller for the documents or the bill of exchange conditional upon reimbursement by the issuing bank.

[44] This system is not immediately clear from the UCP, but see Decision (1975–79) of the ICC Banking Commission, ICC Publication No 37 1, R. 6, 18 (meeting 11 Oct 1976), see also Articles 9(a)(iv) and (b)(iv) UCP 1993. It suggests that the negotiating bank does not negotiate without recourse, unless it is at the same time the issuing bank or the confirming bank, when recourse is excluded. Thus it is obviously better for the seller always to negotiate with the issuing bank or the confirming bank. If there is *'a freely negotiable credit'*, this is what he will do. In continental European countries, the drawer/beneficiary cannot exclude recourse against himself. This is different in England and the USA.

discounting the instrument. Under an acceptance credit, he will receive payment in this manner unconditionally (assuming he may do so without recourse), but under a negotiation credit, only conditionally, therefore depending upon reimbursement of the issuing bank (Articles 14(a) *io* 19).

2.1.8   *The Documents Required under a Documentary Letter of Credit*

In the previous sections reference was made to documents. In documentary letters of credit, presentation of certain documents is a condition for payment. They are mostly assumed to be shipping documents like the bill of lading or a sea waybill, but they may also be insurance documents or invoices. In fact all may be required in the case of a sale of goods. Only an invoice may suffice in the case of services.

Less common, although not infrequent are quality, quantity, weight or origin certificates or customs papers. There may also be a combination. The UCP discourages conditions if not reduced to the presentation of a specific quality or health certificate certifying the on-spec quality of the products upon arrival: see Article 13(c). In particular, quality requirements destroy much of the purpose of the letter of credit, which seeks to achieve payment regardless of any dispute on quality or even an official certificate that all is well. It does not exclude the possibility, however, that the seller has to provide a special bank guarantee to cover any shortcoming in quality. One sees here a system of guarantee and counter-guarantee developing, in each case for different risks.

The UCP in Articles 23–38 distinguish between four types of documents:

(a)   the transport documents, which may be the marine/ocean bills of lading (Article 23), a non-negotiable sea waybill (Article 24), charterparty bills of lading covering a time or voyage charter of a ship which normally implies an agreement for the carriage of the goods (Article 25), multimodal transport documents which are used for different modes of transport (for example, ship, aircraft or truck) and derive their name from the Unctad or UN Convention on International Multimodal Transport of Goods and the Unctad/ICC Rules for Multimodal Transport of 1991 in countries that adopted the Convention, *cf* also the ICC Uniform Rules for a Combined Transport Document 1991 (Article 26), air transport documents (Article 27), road, rail and inland waterway transport documents (Article 28), courier service documents and post receipts (Article 29), and transport documents issued by freight forwarders (Article 30);

(b)   the insurance documents as proof of the appropriate insurance safeguarding the quality whilst in transit and the safe arrival of the goods unless otherwise stipulated in the letter of credit (Articles 34–36);

(c)   the invoices which on their face must be issued by the beneficiary in the name of the applicant but need not be signed, but the amount may not exceed the amount permitted by the letter of credit (Article 37); and finally

(d)   a category of other documents, like warehouse receipts, certificates of origin, weight, quality or health or custom papers, the latter either being furnished by the seller, like packing lists, or issued by an independent third-party, like certificates of origin, when the name of the certifier needs to be checked if indicated in the credit (Article 38). If there is a need for the beneficiary to draw a bill of exchange, this will also be covered by Article 38 UCP, but in that case also by Article 9(a)/(b) UCP.

2.1.9   The Right of Reimbursement of the Issuing Bank under a Letter of Credit

The issuing bank is bound to reimburse the nominated bank which has paid or accepted or negotiated a draft. The issuing bank thereafter looks for reimbursement to the applicant/buyer/debtor. When the applicant fails to reimburse and there is no special security for the issuing bank, the question arises what the issuing bank may do.

When the issuing bank is also the house bank of the applicant, it may be able to set off its claim for reimbursement against the current account balance of its client which is likely to be used by the applicant for normal collection purposes.

Failing timely reimbursement, the issuing bank may also have a retention right to the documents in its possession and therefore to the underlying goods. A negotiable document, for example a bill of lading made out to bearer (that is, that there is no named consignee) acts as a document of title. This is important where an issuing bank is forced to look for security. Under a document issued to bearer (or endorsed in blank), the bank in possession of the document can reach the goods. If made out to the buyer or his order, this would require an endorsement by the buyer to the issuing bank. If the buyer is not willing to do so, the document may still be retained by the issuing bank until reimbursement. Even if the document is non-negotiable, the issuing bank could still be marked as the consignee. American law may in these cases assume a perfected security interest on the basis of possession: see Section 9–312 (Section 9–304 old) UCC.[45] This would require an execution. A retention right may also imply possibility, at least in modern systems of retention like the Dutch one.

If the documents are made out to bearer or to order with blank endorsement, that facilitates also execution if allowed under the applicable law of retention (the *lex situs* of the documents). If the document is made out to the order of the seller with endorsement to the issuing bank that implies also an easy execution possibility. If, however, the buyer is indicated in the document, an execution sale of the document may be unfeasible,[46] but the retention right may still be valuable as a means of pressure because the document is necessary for the buyer to reclaim the goods. This is even so in the case of a sea waybill, see for these various documents chapter 4, section 2.3.1.

In the USA and England, the issuing bank may also benefit from a trust receipt. However, this protection must be specifically agreed between the issuing bank and the buyer and is more particularly used when the applicant/buyer needs the documents to on-sell the goods which will enable and require him to reimburse the issuing bank out of the proceeds he receives upon the resale. These trust receipts have also become common in the Netherlands and Germany (*Treuhandschein*). Under it, the buyer keeps the documents, goods and proceeds in trust for the issuing bank. In civil law countries, it may remain doubtful, however, whether the goods and proceeds, if not clearly kept separate, represent

---

[45] The prevailing view is that an issuing bank that pays the seller against the documents is, in as far as the documents are concerned, only an agent for the buyer, see eg Gavalda-Stoufflet, *Droit de la Banque* (1974), 734; J Hartmann, *Der Akkreditiv-Eroeffnungsauftrag* (1974), 93. The UCP are silent as they do not deal with proprietary issues. It means that the issuing bank has no ownership rights in the documents *even if* they are made out to bearer or endorsed in blank or to the issuing bank (although *bona fide* purchasers of the bill of lading from the issuing bank may then be protected). If the bill of lading is in the name of the buyer, the issuing bank is unlikely to have any proprietary right in it at all. The consequence is that the buyer is the owner of the goods at the time the issuing bank or its agent bank takes up the documents against payment. That does not, however, rule out a retention right of the issuing bank in these documents which under some laws may be construed as a security interest at the same time.

[46] Section 9–601 (a) (2) (Section 9–501 old) UCC gives the creditor alternatively the right to proceed against the goods covered by a document of title.

assets that are sufficiently segregated from the applicant's estate and are reclaimable by the issuing bank, particularly in the applicant's bankruptcy.

2.1.10 The Letter of Credit as Independent and Primary Obligation: Legal Nature of Letters of Credit. The 'Pay First, Argue Later' Notion

The letter of credit is in fact neither a letter nor a credit,[47] but rather an independent payment obligation of the issuer as we already saw in section 2.1.6 above. This payment obligation is meant to be *independent* of the underlying contracts. It is therefore not tied to any defense emanating from either (a) the relationship between the seller and the buyer giving rise to the payment, when, for example, the goods do not meet the quality requirements of the underlying sale, or (b) the relationship between the buyer and the issuing bank out of which the letter of credit in favour of the seller arose, when, for example, the buyer goes bankrupt and is unlikely to be able to reimburse the issuing bank. This *double independence* of the undertaking of the issuing bank is one of the keys to the whole scheme (besides the payment in the country of the seller), see Articles 3 and 4 UCP and Section 5–103 (d) (new) UCC, as contrasted with the so-called *accessory* guarantee, of which the surety is the main example, and which stands or falls with the validity of the underlying contract it guarantees (but, on the other hand, remains attached to the obligation to pay even if transferred to others).

The other aspect of the letter of credit is that it contains a so-called *primary* undertaking of the bank. If the documents are in compliance with the credit, the nominated bank must pay regardless of whether the seller has demanded payment from the buyer first and has refused tro do so. In fact, in international transactions, the seller will normally only request payment from the bank as it will give him the proceeds in his own country and save him considerable collection and administration costs. Again this is unlike the surety. Under it, enforcement must first be sought against the main debtor and the guarantor is only held liable for any shortfall. Under this type of secondary undertaking, whatever is required in terms of enforcement may be unclear as it may vary from a single letter requesting payment to a default judgment. In such cases, it is a matter for the guarantee or for the law to define the trigger mechanism. This is not an issue in letters of credit.

The practices developed for the letter of credit in the succeeding versions of the UCP over many years aim at preventing any uncertainty in these aspects of independence and primary liability and any confusion about what is required. In Europe, domestic practices have attempted to restructure the surety in the form of an independent and primary obligation in a similar manner through standard documentation developed by banks. Only the efforts within the ICC have managed to give these attempts the required unity of purpose and standing so that a truly new type of protection could be developed. We shall revert to this in the context of independent guarantees in section 2.1.13 below. Like in the case of letters of credit, the independence and primary nature of guarantees find their true support in the *international law merchant* for which now room is often made in national laws, usually through case-law but sometimes also through codification, as in the UCC in the USA. In that country, the notion of independence of guarantees did not evolve from the indemnity contract, with which banks were not allowed to concern themselves, but was

---

[47] The term derives from the former practice of banks that issued their traveling clients with letters (of credit) requesting correspondent banks in the country to which these clients were traveling to provide them with cash upon request.

more directly derived from the established letter of credit practice which developed separately in its own right.

In an economic sense, the letter of credit may be seen as a tri-partite structure under which a bank acting on the instructions of the buyer undertakes to pay the seller. There are therefore at least two contracts: the sale between the seller and the buyer and the instruction to issue a letter of credit from the buyer to the issuing bank. The payment commitment contained in the letter of credit itself creates yet another legal relationship, now between the issuing bank and the seller. In a legal sense, however, the letter of credit itself is *not* a tripartite arrangement even if it results from a tripartite structure. It is an undertaking of a bank to the seller only, even if instructed by the buyer, and is entirely independent of the two underlying contracts giving rise to it.

In countries like Germany and the Netherlands which find it difficult to accept under local law the unilateral binding nature of such a payment commitment, a kind of acceptance by the seller is mostly thought necessary so that a contract comes into being between the bank and the beneficiary supporting the bank's obligation. Internationally, such an attitude is not useful and may give rise to the applicability of very different contract models in terms of offer and acceptance and consideration requirements. It is not favourable to international letters of credit and their independence. If the contract construction is used, however, it is best to view the bank as agent for the beneficiary in the acceptance of the commitment which is therefore instantaneous and does not depend on a further act of the beneficiary. In any event, there is no possibility for the bank of withdrawing or varying the letter of credit before acceptance by notice to the seller/beneficiary. The seller is not even a true third-party beneficiary under the agreement between the buyer and the bank (in any event as a concept not accepted in this connection in English law), although it has some attractions. Under it the beneficiary has a vested third-party beneficiary interest once the letter of credit is received by it and kept. In common law terms, the consideration or justification is found in the entire arrangement.

Once the undertaking is in place, which means signing and handing over the letter of credit to the beneficiary or its agent, it is binding and cannot be withdrawn, unless perhaps there was a mistake in the sense that the contract between seller and buyer never required a letter of credit. It would in any event be an abuse of right by the seller then to invoke it. If on the other hand the sale proves invalid or is voided, this does not affect the agreement between the buyer/applicant and the issuing bank or the letter of credit itself. In fact, the letter of credit can best be seen as an *irrevocably binding unilateral* commitment of the issuing bank towards the beneficiary (*unless* expressly made revocable). The true justification lies in commercial necessity rather than in any particular domestic legal constructions. As so often in commercial law, they have here a facilitating function only.

As was already noted before, where payment is promised by the bank pursuant to the letter of credit, it does not replace the payment obligation under the sale. There is therefore *no* payment substitution agreement. In fact, the issuing of a letter of credit itself is no payment at all. Only an alternative payment duty is provided, under which the payment itself is subject to proper tender and acceptance especially if the payment is ultimately made through a bank transfer, see also section 1.2.3 above. The letter of credit does not properly suspend the payment obligation of the buyer either, although there may be some doubt on this point. In any event, the buyer remains additionally liable and the seller still has an action for payment against the buyer if the issuing (or confirming) bank does not pay. This may happen either because the documents are not in order or the bank is bankrupt. The normal way of payment is, however, through the letter of credit. As mentioned earlier, that is so because there may be fewer collection costs and the payment will be safeguarded in this manner in the country of the seller.

Payment pursuant to a letter of credit aims at immediate payment (or the acceptance of a bill of exchange by a paying bank) regardless of any defenses or disputes between seller and buyer (or buyer and the issuing bank). That is the consequence of the independence notion, which makes payment under a letter of credit only dependent on the presentation of the proper documents. It results for buyer and seller in a situation of *'pay first, argue later'*. That is the essence of all good payment protections. This maxim relies on the fact that, even when, for example, the seller has defaulted on or has committed a breach of the contract of sale (for example, by delivering off-spec material), the issuing bank (or its agent, the nominating bank) must pay and will normally already have done so before the goods have reached the buyer and breach is discovered, e.g. in the case of the supply of faulty material. Thus upon default, which the buyer is likely to discover only when he takes delivery of the goods from the carrier, he will have to start an action against the seller for recovery in whole or in part of the money paid by the issuing bank (and likely to have been debited to buyer's account with it). This action will be based on a breach of the sale contract.

Since payment has been made, the result is that the litigation burden substantially shifts to the buyer. Under a letter of credit the calling for a quality certificate as part of the documents to be delivered to the bank before payment is made may reduce the room for later argument in this connection considerably but it also substantially defeats the attraction of the letter of credit for the seller. In independent bank guarantees on the other hand, 'pay first, argue later' is not always the objective. They may replace the original obligation upon default altogether, whilst payment under it could then be final by way of liquidated damages. That is often the case in performance bonds. Where the guarantee replaces an attachment to preserve the goods pending litigation, there is also no question of paying first and arguing later.

The slogan 'pay first, argue later', although popular in this context is no legal maxim and no particular legal consequences flow from it. It is a state of affairs, which results from all payments being agreed to be made against documents without inspection of the goods. The expression refers more in particular to the double abstraction or full independence of the undertaking of the bank towards the beneficiary. As such it signifies a most important aspect of a letter of credit and often also of independent guarantees (see for these more in particular section 2.1.13 below).

2.1.11   Non-performance under Letters of Credit: The Exception of 'Fraud'

As we saw, under a documentary letter of credit, the issuing bank has an unconditional obligation to pay the seller upon presentation of the required documents (assuming they are in order). No defenses may be presented on the basis of the underlying sales contract giving rise to the payment or on the basis of defects in the relationship between the buyer and the issuing bank giving rise to the letter of credit. There may still be some question, however, on the validity of and payment duty under the letter of credit when it was issued by mistake in which case the seller may not be able to rely on it, as we saw in the previous section. The issuing bank (or its agent, the nominating bank) is also not required to pay under the letter of credit when there has been 'fraud' by the seller.

The 'fraud' exception is important and much talked about in the literature, although in practice seldom relevant. It remains mostly undefined but is limited to situations when eg there is *prima facie* irregularity on the part of the seller, or when the documents presented by him or on his behalf look obviously forged. Non-payment then serves the paying bank as protection against any charges of conspiracy to defraud the buyer/debtor. The UCP as partial restatement of the rules do not cover the fraud exception. The UCC in the USA mentions the concept in Section 5–109 (a), again without any definition. It depends on the circumstances and the courts are likely to assume here some discretion, but it is clear that a *prima facie* case must be presented. In other words, the situation must be pretty bad and the need for redress obvious. It should be noted in this connection that a holder in due course of a bill of exchange drawn under a letter of credit is always protected whatever the 'fraud'.

The issuing bank is entitled to refuse payment only when the 'fraud' is proven. Normally there will therefore be a need for a court order. The refusal to pay can never result from a buyer's complaint concerning the performance of the underlying (sales or other) contract. The buyer can protect himself against defective products by requiring presentation of further documents in the letter of credit, for example one that verifies quantity and quality by an independent expert, as we saw, even though it is none too common. It is costly and in any event detracts substantially from the efficiency of the letter of credit as it may give rise to problems (and delays) at the start. It will reduce the chance of argument later but also of payment first. It is also possible (and more likely) that the buyer as part of the original deal will require a (primary or secondary) bank guarantee from the seller to match the letter of credit and cover the eventuality of poor quality after payment pursuant to a letter of credit. The result is two guarantees: one in favour of each party but for different risks. The letter of credit guarantees payment by the buyer and the bank guarantee guarantees conform delivery by the seller which will be an issue to be settled later. In that sense the guarantee does not detract from the letter of credit.

In politically sensitive situations, for example when governments embargo trade as happened between the USA and Iran and Iraq, the issuing bank (in the USA) still had to pay the seller (here in Iran or Iraq) regardless of the non-delivery (because of the embargo) but were, nevertheless, put under great pressure not to do so by the US government and were thus tempted to refuse to reimburse any confirming bank in Iran and Iraq for any payments it made to the seller in these countries. Avoiding any impression of conniving with the enemy may then be invoked as excuse by the issuing bank but should not be accepted. In other words, political risk is no excuse for non-payment. It is certainly no part of the 'fraud' exception either.

The seller may sometimes have to refrain from invoking the letter of credit but equally only in exceptional circumstances, often also referred to as situations of 'fraud' (although this could also happen if the credit was issued by mistake, as we saw) which for him are not normally defined either, but frequently connected with known deficiencies in the assets as produced by him. In fact, it might in such situations be much easier for the interested ultimate debtor (buyer) to restrain the beneficiary from asking payment from the issuing bank than to restrain the bank from making it. The seller may notably be considered to be abusing his rights under a letter of credit or guarantee when he has knowingly provided rubbish or where he has already been satisfied through a properly notified set-off or agreed to a substantial reduction in price and still seeks full payment on the basis of the letter of credit. It may well be that civil law notions of good faith (*gutte Sitten* or *Treu und Glauben*) may be more lenient in this area to the buyer/debtor than common law traditionally is. International custom should adjust the attitudes in this aspect and lead to a more uniform approach, which could incorporate the stricter common law attitude, which itself may well result from the nature of the commercial or professional relationship. It is better to refer here to the developing own standards of international trade or transnational law.

2.1.12   *Transferable Letters of Credit and Back-to-Back Letters of Credit*

Where a seller obtains goods from a supplier, he may agree with his buyer that the letter of credit shall be transferable to pay the supplier. However, a letter of credit can be transferred only if it is expressly designated as 'transferable' by the issuing bank. In that case, the seller (the so-called first beneficiary) may request the bank authorised to pay (the transferring bank), to accept or to negotiate the credit to make the 'transferable credit' available to the supplier (the second beneficiary). It leads to direct payment of the supplier under the letter of credit.

The 'transferable credit' can only be transferred on the same terms, but the name of the seller can be substituted for that of the buyer in order to protect his interests whilst the amount of the letter of credit, the unit prices stated therein, the expiry date, the last day for presentation of the documents and the period for shipment may be reduced or curtailed. In the required documentation, the seller has the right to substitute his own invoice(s) to the buyer for that of his supplier. The letter of credit will remain good for payment of the rest (the seller's profit) to the seller. The UCP allow only one such transfer. Naturally, the proceeds of a letter of credit may themselves be assigned by the seller but that does not amount to a transfer of the letter of credit itself.

The seller may in this connection also apply for a back to back letter of credit in favour of his supplier under which a new letter of credit is issued on the basis of an already existing, non-transferable letter of credit. Amount, duration and required documents or other imposed conditions will be exactly the same, although the second letter of credit will be legally entirely independent of the first and not conditional upon its effectiveness. It allows a seller to use the credit organised by his buyer (the first credit) to support a letter of credit which he needs to arrange for the benefit of his own supplier (the second letter of credit). The documents will be directed by the supplier to activate the first letter of credit under which payment will be directed towards the issuing or confirming bank under the second letter of credit. This will trigger its payment to the supplier.

2.1.13   *Ways to Reduce Payment Risks: Autonomous Guarantees.*
           Examples. Standby Letters of Credit

The bank guarantee appears frequently in international trade. Although the letter of credit implies a primary bank guarantee as we saw, it has developed in its own way and it is better to distinguish it form other such guarantees. It is true that the seller may want a guarantee from a bank for the eventuality that a buyer does not want to pay and the (documentary) letter of credit is a variation on that theme. But there may be other reasons or needs, not directly related to payment or the counter-party risk in this connection. As already noted in the previous section, a buyer who has to provide the seller with a letter of credit may still demand from the seller a bank guarantee to secure the conformity or quality of the delivered goods. A bank, in providing such a guarantee, undertakes to compensate financially the creditor/beneficiary for any default in the performance of the obligations of the debtor/applicant.

A guarantee of this sort will generally be 'autonomous'. It means that the guarantee (like the letter of credit) is independent of the principal contract between the creditor and the debtor and from the relationship between the debtor and the guarantor. Although it guarantees the seller's performance under the principal contract, it is thus separated from the contract itself and it will narrowly define the obligations to be guaranteed. Any valid excuse that the seller may have had for non-performance will then not be accepted as a defense against payment under the guarantee. Again, that would have to be argued out later.

There are other, more common forms of autonomous guarantees. The performance guarantee or performance bond is a most important example. It serves as a security for the correct performance of the underlying contract by the debtor, for example in the construction industry. Also here, the guarantee may balance the letter of credit: the first may protect the party who orders a project against poor workmanship. The second will protect the seller or construction company against non-payment. The performance guarantee will, cover only a small percentage of the value of the sale or the project whilst the letter of credit or a sequence of letters of credit may cover the entire price of the project. It may also be that the performance guarantee constitutes the liquidated amount of damages that can be claimed for non-performance by the construction company in this connection, especially if it has not even started the project and will not continue with it. It does not void letters of credit already opened to pay for the construction but they may contain language that covers the cancellation possibility.

The tender guarantee or bid bond is another example of an autonomous guarantee. It protects the instigator of a public tender and covers the risk that the bidder who was awarded the contract may ultimately not sign it or not provide the required performance bond.

The maintenance guarantee or maintenance bond is usually also drafted as an autonomous guarantee and serves to secure the supplier's undertaking for maintenance of the equipment.

The autonomous guarantee is thus independent. It will normally also be a *primary* obligation, therefore not dependent on an earlier call by the creditor on the debtor and a default of payment in that relationship. As in the case of a letter of credit, it means that the guaranteeing bank will normally pay the price or amount guaranteed directly to the creditor and must seek to recover the amount so paid from the debtor.

At the other end of the scale of the autonomous guarantee as independent and primary obligation, is the (bank) *surety* as an *accessory* and *secondary* obligation. It allows defenses in the underlying relationships to be a bar to effective payment and also requires the debtor to be in default of payment to the creditor. It is still used, especially where a parent company guarantees the performance of a subsidiary. An advantage for the creditor may be that a surety transfers with the debt and therefore remains in place for any assignee.

In between these two types of guarantees, there are all kinds of other bank guarantees, as for example the aval on a bill of exchange, mostly considered an independent but secondary guarantee. All types may have further conditions attached to them. In view of these differences, it is always necessary to ascertain exactly the quality of a guarantee in terms of (a) its independence, (b) its primary or secondary status, and (c) its conditions, like the presentation of documents (which may simply be a written request for payment under the guarantee) or evidence of performance of the parties to the underlying agreement (which may be a quality or completion certificate). The *first demand guarantee* denotes in this connection and independent and primary guarantee payable upon first demand of the creditor, with this first demand in writing being the *only* condition or document required for the payment obligation of the guarantor to mature.

Confusion on these key points in the drafting remains all too common and may prove fatal for the effectiveness of bank guarantees. In letters of credit, it is less likely as there is now sufficient standardisation supported by the UCP, but it is not impossible when confused language is being used. Where a judgment in the underlying obligation against the buyer is a prerequisite, it is to be noted that a bank guarantee thereby automatically becomes accessory and secondary, thus a surety, no matter what other wording may have been used in the document. A similar situation results if a letter of credit is made dependent on a default judgment against the buyer. The UCP will then no longer (fully) apply.

The *standby letter of credit* was developed in the USA when banks could not guarantee obligations of others and act as sureties. Traditionally this activity was left to insurance and bonding companies, but banks could always issue an independent guarantee in the manner of a letter of credit. They were thus allowed to accept an undertaking in this respect. Outside the payment circuit, these independent guarantees were then called *standby letters of credit*. The term is confusing but was imposed by expediency. The difference with a letter of credit is in the default condition. It is irrelevant in the letter of credit but triggers the standby letter of credit. This does not, however, undermine its independence from the underlying contract the performance of which is guaranteed, and is therefore not subject to its defenses. There is a further difference in the presentation of documents which in the case of a standby letter of credit may be no more than a unilateral written declaration of default by the seller/beneficiary. Since 1983 standby letters of credit as payment guarantees are (in principle) covered by the UCP. They tend to be cheaper as they require much less involvement of the bank. Technically they could be made fully documentary but may then still be considered different from the normal documentary letters of credit because of the default condition.

2.1.14   The Law and/or Rules Applicable to Collections, Letters of Credit and Bank Guarantees. The ICC Rules and their Status. The Lex Mercatoria

The ICC has issued Uniform Rules for Collections (URC) since 1956 with new versions in 1967, 1978 and 1995 (ICC Publication 522). They require, according to Article I(a), incorporation in the collection agreement.

Since 1933, the ICC has issued for documentary letters of credit the Uniform Customs and Practice for Documentary Credits (UCP). They were last revised in 1993 (ICC Publication 500). As we saw, the key principle of independence is expressed in Article 3 UCP and the primary nature of the undertaking in Article 9 UCP. As we also saw, the UCP particularly concern themselves with the roles of the various banks used in the scheme, with the various types of letters of credit, with the role of the documents and with the use of bills of exchange in the context of letters of credit. They particularly fail to cover the principle of fraud, which is (without clear definition) mentioned in the USA in Section 5–109 UCC, at least in respect of the payment obligation of the issuing and confirming banks. In other areas not covered, or in deviations from the rules, much depends on the wording of the letter of credit itself. It is important that this wording generally conforms to the UCP terminology so as to avoid unnecessary confusion.

In chapter 1, section 3.2.4, the role of the URC and especially the UCP within the *lex mercatoria* was discussed as directory custom and practice. Even though both set of rules assume for their application the incorporation of the rules in the respective contracts creating the collection or letter of credit facility and the facility itself, it is not the sole manner in which these rules may become relevant and they may also or even more likely apply as custom or industry practices. It is in fact best to assume the applicability of an autonomous legal system in and around the URC and especially the UCP within the *lex mercatoria*. This clarifies at the same time the question which law applies when the URC or UCP do not elaborate. In the manner of Article 7(2) of the Vienna Convention on the International Sale of Goods, it would in any event be normal to look first at the general principles on which the URC and UCP are based and only subsequently at domestic laws resulting under the applicable rules of private international law. It is the thesis of this book that besides custom and contract, the other rules of the *lex mercatoria* as elaborated in the hierarchy of norms, especially mandatory fundamental principle and directory general principles also precede the application of domestic laws rendering private international law appointing a domestic law as applicable only residually relevant as the lowest ranking rule within the *lex mercatoria* hierarchy. Where private international law rules are still important, they may within the EU derive from the Rome Convention on the Law Applicable to Contractual Obligations of 1980 but in the countries which have ratified it in agency aspects also from the Hague Convention on the Law Applicable to Agency of 1978, which, as the more special law, would prevail over the Rome Convention in countries like France and the Netherlands that ratified both, see also chapter 2, section 3.2.2.

For guarantees, the ICC has compiled two sets of uniform rules. The first, the Uniform Rules for Contract Guarantees of 1978 (URCG), is meant to cover the tender bond, performance and repayment guarantees. It has not been successful because it requires a prior judgment or arbitral award and is therefore little more than the traditional surety and is not therefore considered an independent primary obligation of the bank. This goes against industry practice. The second set, the Uniform Rules for Demand Guarantees of 1992 (URDG), covers the first demand and other types of documentary guarantees as independent, primary obligations (see Articles 2(b) and 20). It is meant to replace the first set which has, however, not been withdrawn and covers in any event a narrower field. Because of this discordant approach the URCG has probably no place within the *lex mercatoria*. The URDG that are reflective of market practice have such a place, much in the same way as the URC and UCP.

The standby letter of credit, being a special form of bank guarantee, is not covered by the URDG, but by the UCP (since 1983), even though large parts of the UCP (titles D, E and F) are not directly relevant to it since it is often not documentary. It could even be argued that standby letters of credit are covered by both when the URDG are incorporated and the UCP function as custom. This may be undesirable and coverage of standby letters of credit by the UCP is an historical accident. They fit better under the URGD. The main reason for the confusion is that, in the American view, the similarity between the (American) standby letter of credit and the (European) first demand guarantee was not at first fully understood in terms of the similar approach to the independent and primary status of the payment obligation and also the possibility for these guarantees to operate in the payment circuit beside the letter of credit. It must be admitted that there was also some confusion in Europe especially in the first aspect, probably because the independent payment guarantee developed there out of the surety.

Comparative research especially of case law showed the similarities between the standby letter of credit and independent bank guarantee which is increasingly accepted. As already noted, it suggests that standby letters of credit are better covered by the URDG only, except that the status and sophistication of these rules are not yet comparable to those of the UCP.

1.2.15 The Uncitral Convention on International Guarantees and the World Bank Standard Conditions

Uncitral drafted a Convention on International Guarantees and Standby Letters of Credit in 1995. It covers the guarantee and the standby letter of credit in similar terms and has achieved an important convergence of view between the American and European traditions. The Convention is intended to receive treaty status and will as such be of a different order from the ICC Rules. It will largely convert the ICC rules into (uniform) law. It makes adaptation to new practices much more difficult, however, as that would require a formal amendment to the Convention. Parties from Contracting States who were opting for the ICC Rules, the UCP or UDRG, instead would have to exclude the applicability of the Uncitral Convention in doing so. Even if not contractually incorporated in the standby letter of credit or the bankguarantee, at least the UCP might still prevail over the Convention as customary law. It would be a difficult question to resolve should the Convention be widely adopted, but it follows automatically from the hierarchy of norms in the *lex mercatoria* (in which the UCP is the higher norm) here advocated.

The World Bank (IBRD) also operates some standard conditions in this area under its General Conditions — applicable to loan and guarantee agreements of the World Bank (1980) and under its Guidelines for Procurement Under World Bank Loans and IDA Credits (1977). Their status as custom within the *lex mercatoria* may be in greater doubt but they are likely to have persuasive influence outside the area of their immediate application.

2.2   International Set-offs

2.2.1   *The Law Applicable to Set-offs and Contractual Netting*

As we saw in section 1.3.1 above, common differences in the approaches to set-off may be found in the nature of the set-off, which may give rise to netting agreements either to widen the set-off or to avoid it and its limitations altogether. The set-off may be (a) a remedy to be invoked by the parties outside bankruptcy when they may be able to invoke it either generally upon giving notice (like in Germany and the Netherlands) or only as a defense in litigation (as in England, unless there is connexity or an agreement to the contrary). In these countries, the set-off is in essence subject to party autonomy including the right of the parties to expand the notion in the context of bilateral or even multilateral netting agreements. The alternative is to view the set-off (b) as an *ipso facto* or automatic facility as in France generally and elsewhere in bankruptcy only. A key issue here is whether by agreement the *ipso facto* set-off can be expanded or avoided by alternative netting agreements. This may be more difficult when mutual payments are involved.

Other differences may arise in (a) the eligibility of the payment obligations that may be reduced by set-off, (b) the questions of the maturity of both claims, (c) their being liquidated to money, (d) their being in the same currency, and (e) the question of the retroactivity in legal systems that require notification by the party invoking the set-off. Another difference may arise (f) in the set-off possibility of time-barred counter claims. Most importantly, (g) the applicable bankruptcy law may not be receptive to any expansion of the set-off concept by contractual netting arrangements, when it may matter most.

Conflict rules in matters of set-off have not been the subject of much study, but there is no consensus and different suggestions have been made. The *lex fori* approach is a common one and leaves the decision to the law of the country in which the adjudicating court sits. In a bankruptcy that is probably most understandable even if the debtor and the claimants are outside the bankruptcy jurisdiction. It introduces clearly an objective element and the set-off does not then appear to be capable of being governed by a contractual choice of law either. Outside bankruptcy, this approach is perhaps understandable in countries where the set-off requires a judicial decree as is necessary in England (except where there is sufficient connexity) or is always *ipso facto* as in France. This approach may also be justified by the indirect preferential nature of the set-off.

The *lex fori* approach is sometimes advocated in the Netherlands[48] and has understandably also found support in England.[49] A cumulative application of the set-off requirements under the laws of both claims to be set off is another option if they are covered by different laws. These laws may be chosen by the parties which introduces a subjective element. It is more particularly the French approach,[50] but it is sometimes also favoured in the Netherlands.[51] Finally, it is not uncommon to see an approach under which a debtor invoking a set-off (therefore a counterclaim) in his defense, can only do so under the law of the first claim. This is the German[52] and Swiss[53] approach in which the applicable law therefore depends on the party first invoking the set-off (as it is always the law of the other party's claim). Since the law so applicable may be a law chosen by the parties to their contract, there is here also a subjective element.

It is an approach sometimes believed supported by Article 10(1)(d) of the 1980 EU Rome Convention on the Law Applicable to Contractual Obligations: see for this Convention chapter 2, section 2.3.7. It provides that the law applicable to a contract under the Convention also applies to the various ways of extinguishing obligations. Yet, even though the set-off is a means of payment, therefore a particular means of extinguishing a monetary obligation, it need not necessarily be characterised as a way of extinguishing obligations under Article 10 of the Rome Convention and could equally be viewed as a surrender of claims or as an accounting devise.[54] In a contract for differences depending on novation netting, it is even questionable whether the set-off is a way of payment of underlying claims at all. Rather there is a new financial instrument as we saw in section 1.3.3 above. In the approach opting for the applicability of the law of the claim against which the set-off is invoked (as a defense), an exception is commonly made for the case of bankruptcy when the applicable bankruptcy law is thought to determine the set-off right. This is then a variation of the *lex fori* approach.

2.2.2 The Law Applicable to Novation Netting and Swap Transfers

In swaps in particular, the essence is often a contractual netting arrangement that acquires a distinct character and is likely to be subject to its own (contractual) rules. Novation netting

---

[48] The *lex fori* approach finds support in the lower courts in the Netherlands: see Crt Alkmaar, 7 Nov 1985, NIPR, no 213 (1986) and was perhaps logical when all set-off was *ipso facto* as was the case in the Netherlands before 1992 (in the French tradition).

[49] It is to be noted that English law is undecided: see Dicey and Morris on *The Conflict of Laws* (13th edn, 2000), Rule 17, 168.

[50] See for the French cumulative approach, Batiffol/Lagarde, *Droit international privé* (1983), ii, no 614. There are several variations on this theme in France and it is sometimes believed that the details of the set-off in terms of calculation and the effects depend on the law applicable to each claim: see P Mayer, *Droit international privé*, (1983), no 732.

[51] See Crt Arnhem, 19 Dec 1991, NIPR nr 107 (1992).

[52] See BGH, 11 July 1985 [1985] NJW 2897, and earlier 38 BGHZ 254 (1962), see further D Martiny, *Münchener Kommentar zum Bürgerlichen Gesetzbuch* (1990), EGBGB, Section 32, Rn 37. In a bankruptcy, however, the *lex fori concursus* is preferred: see BGH, 11 July 1985, cited *supra*; see also H Hanish, Report for Germany in I Fletcher (ed), *Cross Border Insolvency* (1992), 111.

[53] See Article 148(2) of its Private International Law Act referring to the law applicable to the claim against which the set-off is invoked as a defence. See also L Pittet, *La competence du juge et de l'arbitre en matiere de compensation: etude de droit interne et international* (2001).

[54] As regards the applicability of Article 10(1)(d) of the Rome Convention, opinion is divided. In Germany, it is applied only if both claims are governed by the same law: see J Kropholler, *Internationales Privatrecht* (1994), 426. In the Netherlands, its general applicability to set-off outside bankruptcy has been advocated by RIVF Bertrams, 'Set-off in Private International Law' in K Boele-Woelki (ed), *Comparability and Evaluation, Essays in Honour of Dimitri Kokkini-Iatridou* (1994), 153.

producing the modern swap as a contract for differences has in fact resulted in a separate financial product in this manner.[55] It is not properly a set-off issue. As for these contracts for differences, there is something to be said for the applicability of the law of the place of payment if parties have not chosen another law in their contract. However, it would make the applicable law dependent on whether a party was in the money, which could change from one payment date to another. It may be compatible, however, with the *lex fori* approach assuming that any litigation will normally take place at the place of the debtor (for the time being) under the swap. Applicability of the law of the claim against which a counterclaim is being set off as a defense is here in any event entirely beside the point as the netting is the essence of the contract, takes place *ipso facto*, and is not meant to be used as a defense or to create a preference. In fact, there is here no settlement or payment of underlying claims at all and no set-off either. This makes it more likely that in a bankruptcy of one of the parties this type of a swap will be considered a purely contractual matter.

If there is no new financial instrument intended (as a contract for differences) but merely the integration of all aspects of one swap transaction and the netting out of all payments thereunder in a bilateral manner, the situation may be very different regardless of any attempt at integration, conditionality and novation netting. Its implementation is still a matter of contract law in which connection it would be equally unlikely that the law applicable to any particular aspect of the transaction would prevail if the parties had not chosen the applicable law. Again the applicable law could be that of the place of the net payment but it could also be the *lex fori*. This is particularly understandable in a default or bankruptcy situation, more so when a full bilateral close out netting follows, which is in any event usually structured as an *ipso facto* set-off of all claims between the two parties. The question of characterisation in terms of settlement or novation netting and the status of the latter in such a bankruptcy would then also be matters for the *lex fori concursus*. Whether in a full multilateral netting in the context of clearing systems, this would be different is yet another matter. Applicability of the law applicable to the system would in such cases be another possibility and would be attractive as the system could not then be disturbed by different bankruptcy laws that may impinge on one of the members.

Yet at least in bilateral close out netting, the *lex fori (concursus)* is not unlikely to apply (when there is a bankruptcy situation) regardless of what parties may have agreed in their contract or (swap) documentation, as preferences are intended to be created at the expense of other creditors, the acceptability of which would appear to be determinable only under more objective standards. In any event, the law of the main claim could not possibly function as controlling as there are many claims and the whole objective is to arrive at one amount regardless of which party goes bankrupt or invokes the set-off.

It should be noted on the other hand that in this respect the ISDA Swap Master Agreements, see section 1.3.5 above, may well have acquired their own international status superseding in reality the domestic law declared applicable by the parties (usually English or New York law) or any domestic mandatory law resulting under conflict of laws rules. The true issue is in how far that also obtains in bankruptcy situations where the *lex fori concursus* may still be considered ultimately to control the effect of the netting agreement, especially where it means to give the non-bankrupt party a preference at the expense of

---

[55] In s. 1.3.3 *supra*, it was noted that especially modern swaps make use of the netting concept and this at three levels: (a) the level of the exchange of cash flows where there is in essence a contract for differences with settlement on agreed dates during the swap period, (b) the level of all related transactions in one swap including any exchanges of underlying assets out of which the cash flows arise, (c) at the level of the close out netting when all swaps between two parties are netted out through bilateral netting (there could at this stage even be multilateral netting. It is quite conceivable that the law applicable to netting is different in each instance.

other creditors of the bankrupt. Yet even the applicable domestic bankruptcy laws may increasingly have to accept the ISDA netting arrangements as an expression of the international market practice or custom in the context of the hierarchy of norms of the modern *lex mercatoria*, see also chapter 1, section 3.2.3. They could thus amount to mandatory practice or customary law binding also on bankruptcy courts.

The BIS has also become involved whilst allowing netting in banks for capital adequacy purposes, see chapter 6, section 2.5.5. It allows bilateral swap netting if the country of the residence of the counter-party (or of its place of incorporation) and of the branch through which the bank acted as well as the law applicable to the swap accept the close-out netting principle. Legal opinions have to be produced to the effect and the dependence on national laws should be noted. As yet, there is here no internationalised concept at work.

The *transfer* of swaps may also follow an *own* distinct pattern. It requires the consent of the other party to the swap and may well result itself in a novation. These complications are the reason why swaps are usually not transferred but rather hedged or unwound. If there is nevertheless a transfer, the law selected by the parties[56] is usually believed to be able to cover the novation in all its aspects (if it is not assumed that distinct international practices prevail here as well). It is logical as termination of the old agreement (or an amendment short of a novation) would also be covered by such chosen law and any new agreement would be subject to the parties' choice also, at least in the aspects at the free disposition of the parties. In EU countries, the 1980 Rome Convention on the Law Applicable to Contractual Obligations would determine the applicable law in the contractual aspects of the swap transfer. It is either the law chosen by the parties or otherwise the law with the closest connection, which is presumed to be that of the party that must perform the most characteristic obligation. In a swap, it is not easy to determine, however, which party in an exchange of cash flows performs the most characteristic obligation. There is something to be said for the law of the party that must pay but under a swap this party is likely to change at different payment dates.

Whatever the applicable law, it covers according to Article 10 of the Rome Convention the interpretation, the performance, the consequences of breach, including the assessment of damages, the various ways of extinguishing obligations and the consequences of nullity. It appears that (under the Convention) it does not cover, however, questions concerning proper capacity (although it may cover the consequences of the lack thereof) and any proprietary matters such as the tracing of proceeds, exchange of underlying assets, etc., should that become necessary as part of a swap transfer even if itself only considered a novation. Under the Convention it may thus remain questionable whether the law of the novation can also deal with these aspects.

Part III   Money Laundering

3.1   Techniques and Remedies

3.1.1   Objectives and Mechanisms

Ultimately, as far as payments are concerned, the question of laundering illicitly obtained proceeds (often cash) through the international banking system has created some considerable

---

[56] See in the Netherlands, HR, 19 May 1989 [1990] NJ 745.

interest in view of the large amounts of money involved in drug trafficking and other offences, notably terrorist activity and similar types of serious crime. The amounts involved are difficult to estimate but the IMF in 2001 believed the amounts to be in the region of $500 billion — 1.5 trillion dollar equivalent per year or 1.5 per cent — 4.5 per cent of gross world product. The objective of money laundering is to make illicit acquired proceeds appear legal by making them indistinguishable from others in the banking system. Traditionally the concern was foremost with cash derived from drug trafficking and it would be of the greatest interest for money launderers to let any cash obtained through these and other illegal activities (like international prostitution, pornography and immigration rings) ultimately surface in an account in a first class bank so as to create the impression of respectability and achieve free circulation and participation of these proceeds in the international money, capital and investment flows. One key to combat this practice is therefore for banks always to be able to establish where cash came from and to refuse it if its origin or the persons or entities attempting to make the deposits are suspect, or if intermediaries (especially little known banks or investment management companies in poorly regulated countries) are knowingly used to push this money into the international banking system. Banks should always be aware and able to reveal the principals whilst records should be kept to identify all deposit entries (the 'know your customer' principle).

There are usually several phases in the process of money laundering.[57] An obvious one is cash deposits being made with suspect banks in their local currencies. From there they may be moved to somewhat better banks in probably a better known country upon conversion of the money into the currency of that country. The money launderer may also attempt to buy assets (bearer shares, long-term bearer bonds or real estate) and pay from his local account either into the anonymity of a broker's account or through privileged lawyers' or other professionals' accounts. Part of this process is always to confuse the trail by engaging in numerous interim transfers and transactions (so-called *layering*) and commingling dirty with clean money.

The fight against this type of money laundering has been greatly complicated by the large sums of US dollars cash floating around in Eastern Europe and other countries as common currency in a cash society. Thus a criminal cash hoard in US dollars might be shipped to Russia, converted there in local currency through organisations of cash operators and converters and be invested in the Russian manufacturing or mining industry with readily exportable products. These products may be sold several times to confuse the trail. Ultimately they may be bought by a London shelf company of the original money launderers and then sold in the international markets for hard currency paid by the buyers into the bank accounts of the sellers in first class London banks. The question for the London banks is whether or when they must intervene and how they can do so not knowing the background story. Even if they did, would they be obliged to refuse the payment or report it, now that the payment is totally clean, coming from a *bona fide* buyer in the market who pays through the banking system from his own funds that are entirely legal? It is a fact that the illegal money entered the system once the Russian interest was bought and should have been checked at that time. If that was not done for whatever reason it may not be reasonable to require action from the banks down the chain on the basis of later suspicions. The approach in most countries is now that banks must report all suspicious transfers. It discharges them from further action and it is then up to the regulators

---

[57] See also P Alldridge, *Money Laundering Law* (2003).

to pursue the investigation and take the appropriate measures, but it leaves the burden of determining what is suspect largely with the banking system. Many countries maintain a simple rule to the effect that cash deposits above a certain amount must be reported *per se*. In other countries bank transfers by foreigners above a certain amount must be accompanied by information about the original instructing party and the recipient as well as their bank.

The problem is not one of cash alone, however, and money laundering need no longer to concern only cash and its entering into the banking system. It may also concern ordinary bank payments in respect of illegal activities, therefore the use of money already in the system to promote or pay for crimes. Here again, it is for banks to make sure that the accounts held with them are not used for this type of activities. Knowing the principals and keeping records has here also become a key control function of banks. Related to this category are amounts already held by criminal groupings and terrorist organisations in reputable banks and the simple holding of these funds by these organisations in the banking system may be objectionable as such. Not all of the money may be tainted and some may be legally obtained. It may even be used for legal activities. Here the idea is rather to prevent these organisations from using the banking system at all and to have their balances confiscated. This goes beyond money laundering proper and must be seen in the context of international crime prevention as such and the war against organised crime and international terrorism.

The definition of the relevant crimes is a key legal aspect of the fight against money laundering. Narcotics syndicates, later drug trafficking, illegal immigration rings, and prostitution and child abuse organisations spring immediately to mind. The prime relevance is that the proceeds of such crimes may become traceable through the banking system, in which connection banks have acquired special investigation and information duties and bank secrecy duties are lifted. This may be reasonable in respect of major crimes but an important development in this connection has been the increasing governmental concern with more minor crimes especially tax evasion. It may involve parking altogether legal income streams abroad (on which subsequently no tax is being paid) or depositing black economy proceeds in foreign bank accounts, the origin and purpose of which can hardly be known or only be evaluated with the benefit of hindsight. This may nevertheless entail an important further infringement of traditional bank secrecy provisions. Thus reporting of suspicions in respect of much broader crime categories or even in respect of potential crimes not only puts a major further burden on banks in terms of attention and good judgment but also forces upon them a further breach of their fiduciary duties to their customers, especially their duty of secrecy for ever less compelling or vaguer reasons. Whether this is wise is another matter by broadening the scope of the offence of money laundering in this manner, it may unduly encumber and undermine the money laundering combating efforts themselves.

3.1.2.   Why Action? Remedies and the Objectives of Combating Money Laundering

Money laundering is considered a major new crime. It requires international action as without it some countries may wish to benefit from the investment streams it engenders (whatever their origin) which other countries are trying to prevent at a high cost to them. How it works in all its diverse manners, what the total amounts involved are, to what extent money laundering distorts payments and investment streams is much less clear as is its effect on the operation of the capital markets. Its impact may be less than sometimes claimed, especially by the organisations involved in combating money laundering and there may be a fashionable element in it.[58] Nevertheless, preventing it is an important objective if only in the context of combating organised crime which is now largely drug, immigration and terrorist related. Confronting organised crime at the international level including terrorism has probably become the true aim whilst the distortion in money and investment streams and its effect on the capital markets are secondary, although the market and regulatory concern with clean money and a clean banking system are real, especially for the major international capital centres, which do not wish to become tainted.

It could be said that combating money laundering is now only one way (albeit important) to counter the larger threat of organised crime of all sorts at the international level. The actual measures to prevent money laundering or to combat it effectively center on the role of banks as informants, on the cooperation of other intermediaries like brokers and similar agents or lawyers, and on confiscation or forfeiture. The co-operation and information duty of banks and other intermediaries is a substantial deviation from the traditional notion of confidentiality and secrecy in client dealings and not only puts a considerable administrative burden on these intermediaries but also requires a great deal of sound judgment on their part. The confiscation notion focuses on disgorging the benefits of illicit activity so that no one can benefit from major crimes as defined for these purposes and is as such new in many countries, although there was always some (often limited) room for it in homicide cases. Rather, in most countries, punishment was traditionally seen as a separate issue, leading to prison sentences or to fines whilst confiscation was not an automatic sequel. It could leave criminals with substantial gains, an issue now increasingly addressed. Confiscation might raise further legal issues, however, especially the question who would be entitled to the money. At least the traditional distinction between criminal and civil law is here blurred. The manner in which the confiscation is done may also need some review under human rights principles, but the concept is sound and is now often also found in insider dealing cases.

In the case of (suspected) terrorist accounts or of the accounts of erstwhile dictators, the remedies may also involve freezes of these accounts and in the case of dictators the eventual turn over to the states from which these dictators have been driven. Like in the case of terrorists, the status of these accounts can often only be determined with the benefit of hindsight and not when the deposits are being made.

As for terrorism itself, the situation appears profoundly changed after the attacks in the US in 2001, leading to a political environment in which the borderline between military and police action has been blurred whilst at the international level this type of criminal activity may acquire the status of acts of war leading to military intervention and international sanctions, rather than to extradition, trial and punishment of individuals within the more traditional frame work of the criminal systems of nations states. International organised crime gangs with related or other objectives may increasingly meet similar responses. Again, the prime issue is here no longer one of money laundering proper although international terrorism and other organised crime often have close connections with arms dealings, drug trafficking, and illegal immigration.

Even in respect of money laundering itself, the internationalisation of the effort to combat it has led to the notion of the nation state as the prime mover in criminal law being abandoned.

---

[58] See for a critical review P van Duyne, "Money Laundering: Pavlov's Dog and Beyond", 37 *Howard Journal of Criminal Justice* (1998), 359.

3.2   International Action

3.2.1   *The Group of Ten, the Council of Europe, and the United Nations*

Globalisation has made money laundering a particularly difficult problem that can no longer be dealt with at the national level alone. Above it was already pointed out that criminal law of the national variety is reaching its limits in its effectiveness. Moreover, organised crime and especially terrorism has now acquired forms that can hardly be combated by the traditional criminal law methods. International co-operation at the criminal, political and now also military level appears increasingly necessary to have adequate effect, in which connection the measures against money laundering constitute only one of the tactics used.

Since 1980 when the Council of Europe first issued certain recommendations in the field of money laundering, the subject of money laundering has increasingly received the attention of international bodies. The banking supervisory authorities of the Group of Ten (within the BIS) adopted a declaration of principles in 1988 whilst the Group of Seven of the most developed countries at its Paris Summit in 1989 instituted a financial action task-force on the subject, the Financial Action Task Force or FATF. It now covers 29 so-called FATF countries. It issued 40 recommendations so far. They have no binding effect as such but have had a great deal of influence. The key is customer identification, mandatory suspicious activity reporting and due diligence by banks. A major objective is further to include also non-banking entities in the drive against money laundering, like lawyers, accountants and other professional advisers. One of its (informal) sanctions is to blacklist countries thus excluding them from the international banking circuit. Especially tax haven countries like the Bahamas, Liechtenstein, The Cayman Islands and Panama have been so targeted and did adjust their ways. On the other hand, many Eastern European countries remain a major problem. In fact, the involvement (whether active or passive) of the City of London has also often been mentioned. On the other hand, in many countries including the US the 'know your customer' and reporting rules have been questioned in the context of a concern for privacy. In this connection it should be considered that the operation of offshore tax havens is not in itself offensive and the question is in how far banks in those havens must guess the motives of the moneys deposited with them, especially if they come to them through payment instructions from reputable international banks. In 1996 the FATF asked for the offenses to be extended to all serious crimes and in 1999 it asked for the inclusion also of tax evasion.

In the meantime, the United Nations adopted a (Vienna) Convention against Illicit Traffic in Narcotic Drugs and Psychotropic Substances in 1988.[59] It defined a number of drug trafficking related crimes, lifted bank secrecy in respect of them, and required domestic laws to incorporate the concept of confiscation. By 1994 it had been adopted by 148 and the European Community.[60] It was followed more generally in relation to all criminal

---

[59] Earlier the fight was mainly against opium, see the International Opium Convention of the Hague of 1912. In 1939, there followed the Convention for the Suppression of the Illicit Trafic in Dangerous Drugs. It first introduced the concept of confiscation. In 1964, the UN followed with the Convention of Narcotic Drugs. The 1939 Convention was expanded to synthetic drugs by the 1971 UN Convention on Psychotropic Substances. These earlier Conventions covered production and dissimination. The 1988 UN Convention covered the money laundering aspect.

[60] In 1993, the UN set up a model law facility on Money Laundering, Confiscation and International Co-operation in relation to Drugs. A Global Program against Money Laundering was set up in 1997 under the Office for Drug Control and Crime Prevention as a means to further technical co-operation and preventive action. The financing of terrorism was condemned immediately after the terrorist attacks on the US in Sept. 2001.

activity (as to be determined by individual States) by a Council of Europe Convention on laundering, tracing, seizure and confiscation of proceeds of crime in 1990, which acquired the required number of ratifications (three) in 1993 (the UK, the Netherlands and Switzerland). It is now ratified by most FATF countries. It should be recalled in this connection that the Council of Europe has two particular features that make it important in this field. First, it has criminal jurisdiction (even though it cannot bind its members) which the EU generally misses (except if intimately connected with the free flow of persons, goods, services and money). Secondly, it has amongst its members the Eastern European countries and former members of the Soviet Union even in Asia, all countries which may be used for money laundering purposes. The prime importance of this Convention is that it goes beyond drug trafficking.[61] It requires co-operation between the signatories in the investigation and confiscation of proceeds. The Council of Europe has an active implementation program and issues papers on best practices in the combating of fraud, drugs and organised crime.

3.2.2   The EU

Finally, on 10 June 1991 the EU issued a Directive on the prevention of the use of the financial system for the purpose of money laundering in connection with all criminal activity whether or not in a Member State or elsewhere aiming through a separate declaration also at a system of (domestic) criminal sanctions in each EU country.[62] Although it has no general criminal jurisdiction it is agreed that it may assume[63] powers in this field if the free flows of persons, goods, services, capital and payments are affected and the stated motive for EU action in this field was indeed the protection of the integrity of the financial system at large in the Community.

The Directive itself elaborates rules on combating the offence by imposing on financial institutions special duties of *identification* (of their customers, Article 3) and of *investigation* (like tracing, disclosure and reporting of suspicious money movements (which remain undefined, Article 6). These financial institutions must avoid any notice to customers (Article 8) and maintain internal procedures in this respect (Article 11). To this end, bank secrecy obligations (statutory or contractual) are lifted and special protection is given to reporting financial institutions and persons therein against liability for wrongful disclosure (Article 9). It is clear that within this framework financial institutions within the EU are forced to undertake their own identification and investigation role in aid of criminal prosecutions, an onerous and sensitive task. Other professionals (like lawyers and auditors) may also be included through the implementing legislation, as the UK has done. A Contact Committee is set up at EU level to co-ordinate the approach of the authorities in this matter (Article 13).

Laundering of drug money is the main target of the Directive, but as Member States may add the holding of proceeds of other offences, notably those connected with terrorist activities, the coverage of the implementing legislation may be wider in each EU country.

---

[61] A Counsel of Europe Criminal Law Convention of Corruption has additional money laundering provisions in this area.

[62] It followed an earlier resolution of the European Parliament of 1986, see on the history also KD Magliveras, 'Money Laundering and the European Communities', in J Norton (ed), *Banks: Fraud and Crime* (1994), 171.

[63] Under the so-called Third Pillar there are further powers based on additional Conventions between Member States that deal with fraud and corruption. There is an Action Plan in this connection which has been first to suggest that the major enemy is now organised crime.

Most, like the UK, include proceeds of any serious crime such as fraud, theft or extortion. It is not yet the intention to cover the proceeds of all crimes generally, including those connected with taxation and black market operations, although France has gone that way. Indeed, this EU system of forced bank co-operation in criminal prosecutions may serve as a model eventually to attack the so-called black money circuit more generally. As already observed before, that may well undermine the credibility of the entire policy, which would thus become a tax collection tool.

It is necessary in this connection to define the policy objectives clearly, all the more so because of the criminal nature of the charges. Is it illegal cash entering the banking system, is it money already in the system but transferred in respect of illegal transactions, is it the criminal record of the recipients itself, and is, in terms of criminal activity, tax evasion or the suspicion of it through black market transactions or the diversion of income streams to other countries included? Other obvious questions are to what extent banks can reasonably and efficiently be used or relied upon as enforcement agencies and in how far bank secrecy is to be lifted. It should be noted that so far the objectives in this connection may remain quite unclear or some kind of mixture.

The developments since 1991 centered first on the implementation in which connection there were two Commission Reports which notably asked for central reporting units and the inclusion of lawyers. The European Parliament responded to the first report with a 21 point resolution calling notably for the extension to the proceeds of all organised crime. A main problem was that in each Member State the reporting of banks to the authorities acquired a domestic form which inhibited the exchange of information as the status of these so-called Financial Intelligence Units could be quite different and be e.g. part of the police, of the judiciary, independent or an administrative body.[64] The problem was especially the exchange of information with non-state bodies. In 1996 a common definition was agreed and a certification procedure which gave access to a central internet and e-mail system of information exchange.

A Second Money Laundering Directive was finally agreed in November 2001 when under pressure of the terrorist attacks in the US the stumbling block of including lawyers in the investigation and reporting process was removed. It amended the First Directive and extended the coverage to all drug trafficking offenses of the Vienna Convention, organised crime, serious frauds, corruption, and any offence which may generate substantial proceeds and which is punishable by severe imprisonment under the criminal law of the relevant Member State.

---

[64] See for the operation of these Units also G Stessens, Money Laundering: A New International Law Enforcement Model (2000), 143ff. and V Mitsilegas, 'New Forms of Transnational Policing: The Emergence of Financial Intelligence Units in the European Union and the Challenge for Human Rights', 3 *Journal of Money Laundering Control* (1998), 147.

4

Ownership, Possession and Limited, Future, Conditional or Temporary Legal or Equitable Proprietary Rights in Chattels and Intangibles

Part I   Laws of Movable Property

1.1   Proprietary Laws in Common and Civil Law

1.1.1   Types of Assets

Chattels are tangible movable assets, like cars, machinery, other equipment, clothes, foodstuffs or utensils, in common law often also referred to as '*goods*'. This terminology will be used here. 'Goods' do not therefore cover *all* assets, as is the case in most civil law countries, and notably not land and intangibles. Intangibles are movable assets that have no appearance and cannot physically be held. The most common example of an intangible asset is a claim, which, if it is monetary and results from a sale, is often called a receivable or account receivable or in the USA sometimes simply an account, but there are of course many other types of claims in contract, tort or unjust enrichment (restitution). They are all personal, which means that they can be maintained only against the counterparty. In most civil law countries, a claim may also be purely proprietary, like a revindication, which can therefore be maintained against all the world. Intellectual and industrial property rights, like copyrights and patents, also fall into the category of intangible assets, but are proprietary. We shall not here be further concerned with them.

This Part will deal mainly with the law of chattels or goods and intangible assets or claims, their legal characteristics, protection and transfer, either in full or by way of a security interest or another more limited proprietary right, like usufruct or life interest, or in trust. The transfer may also be conditional or temporary. The law concerning these assets will first be dealt with in a comparative context but subsequently also in the context of private international and transnational law. Chapter V will deal more extensively with these assets when used in the context of financing.

Claims may sometimes be incorporated in documents and are then often treated as chattels. This is so with claims for the retrieval of goods when incorporated in *documents of title*, like bills of lading or warehouse receipts, which are *negotiable* if issued to bearer or order. Monetary claims or claims for payment may also be incorporated in documents, such as bills of exchange or promissory notes. If issued to bearer or order they are usually referred to as *negotiable instruments*, which are, therefore, documents of title concerning monetary claims and are then also treated more like chattels. These documents and instruments will be discussed in Part II of this chapter.

In the capital markets, promissory notes are called 'bonds' when representing loan principal. 'Shares', the other type of capital market instruments, represent participation entitlements in companies including rights to vote, to dividends, liquidation proceeds and information concernig the issuer, and were traditionally also issued in negotiable (bearer or order) form and then often also treated more like chattels. Bonds and shares (or equities or stocks) are together usually referred to as (investment) securities, to be distinguished from securities that result from secured transactions as ways to secure an indebtedness. In modern times, investment securities have often abandoned their traditional negotiable form, are often dematerialised and held through book entry systems organised by custodians. The proprietary structure concerning them has as a consequence become more uncertain. They will be dealt with in Part III of this chapter.

The way in which this chapter will proceed for the civil law is by describing the intellectual model of proprietary interests on which property law is in essence based in *all* civil law countries. This has the advantage of presenting a framework that is not dependent on that of any particular civil law country. It allows the law of the different civil law countries to be contrasted with this model, which itself may be seen as an abstraction as such nowhere fully implemented. Yet it is useful to come to grips with the considerable differences which exist even between the major civil law countries in the details of their proprietary systems. It also allows a ready contrast with the common law approach.

This civil law system of property law is in principle unitary; it means to cover all types of assets under one proprietary concept, which concentrates on the abstract notions of ownership, possession and holdership of the various recognised proprietary rights, largely regardless of the type of asset. The common law system is, on the other hand, more down to earth and practical, largely built around the physical holding (or *seisin*) of an asset but also more incidental in the elaboration of the details. In common law, possession in this physical sense is especially relevant for chattels. Intangibles fit uneasily into the common law approach and tend to have their own proprietary regime in which contractual, tort and restitution claims may be further distinguished. For land, there is a different common law proprietary regime altogether that remains in most common law countries feudal in origin. As a consequence, there is no unitary proprietary system in common law and the rules tend to be different depending on the type of asset. Only chattels and intangibles will be considered here.

1.1.2   Chattels and Intangibles, Land

Chattels or goods and intangibles or claims are in common law together referred to as *personal property* or personalty and sometimes as movable property (the latter being the normal civil law expression). In common law, tangible movable assets (chattels or goods) are also called *choses in possession*, and intangibles *choses in action*.[1] Both are distinguished from *real property* or immovable property or realty, which is land and the buildings on it. There may here be some confusion, as in common law (like in civil law) there is some movable property that is considered realty, like chattels affixed to immovable property, and (more typical for common law) some immovable property that is treated as a chattel. These are the *chattels real*, which are estates in land (or ownership of land) for a limited number of years only, more properly called leaseholds or leases.

In common law, the distinction between real and personal property in this sense is associated with the distinction between real and personal actions. The first exist in respect of land and the latter in respect of chattels and intangible assets. This is fundamentally different in civil law where real actions are proprietary and personal actions are obligatory.[2] In common law, chattels real can only be defended in 'personal actions' as the proprietary right in them

---

[1] So W Blackstone, 2 *Commentaries on the Laws of England* (1773), 384, 389.
[2] The terms 'realty' and 'personalty' derived in common law from the Roman *actiones in rem* and *in personam*. In civil law, as we shall see, these Roman law actions were developed into the substantive law distinction between proprietary and obligatory rights or rights *in re* (or sometimes *in rem*) and rights *ad rem* or *in personam* through

(the *seisin*) is still considered to be with the owner or lessor. Leases are therefore considered personal property. These are finer points, however, that should not confuse the general picture. In both civil and common law, the normal distinction is between land, movable tangible assets, and intangible assets. The difference is that civil law strives towards one proprietary regime for all types of assets, whilst in common law there is in essence proprietary system in respect of each of them, for chattels under commercial law.

In order for assets to be the object of proprietary rights in a private law sense, everywhere they must have a certain *economical value* and *specificity* in the sense that they are at least *identifiable*. Things that have no value or only sentimental value can hardly be the object of ownership. The love one feels for someone even if of the highest value to the lover cannot legally be owned. It is often said that in this sense the most important things in life are free. They are not of a particular proprietary interest in a legal sense, although in another context one may defend one's honour or good name, whatever their commercial value. Yet, even whilst claiming damages, purely sentimental values are unlikely to be greatly taken into account. In a similar vein, the air one breathes is free and cannot as such be owned until it is captured and set aside. One sees here the relationship between value and specificity. They seem to come first. On the other hand, in modern times, there are also intangible rights that have acquired value only because the law has given them legal status, in particular industrial and intellectual property rights. What one owns and how one owns it, whether the property can be privately owned or only publicly or communally are other important (legal) issues which do not distract, however, from the two essential features of ownership in terms of economic value (particularly in terms of user, enjoyment and income rights) and specificity. It is of course quite true that in this connection the extent of the property right and its modalities are socially determined and are not given in themselves. Crucial as that insight is, it is not here the key element.[3]

Specificity *makes* that we can speak of owning a certain car and not cars generally, even though, as we shall see, legally we refer here to our ownership right in the car. From a legal point of view that is all we have. It is asserted *vis-à-vis* others, and not in fact in the car itself although it is exerted in respect of the car. Especially in civil law, the physical aspects

the writings of Bartolus, Grotius and Vinnius: see R Feenstra, 'Real Rights and their Classification in the 17th Century' (1982) *Juridical Review*, republished in R Feenstra, *Legal Scholarship and Doctrines of Private Law, 13th–18th Centuries* (Variorum, 1996): see also his *Ius in Re*, Presentation, University of Ghent, 1978.

In common law, these Roman law actions led to an entirely different emphasis on the type of asset to be defended: land was defended by actions *in rem* and became as a consequence called real property, and chattels were defended by personal actions and were then called personal property. This 'personal action' to retrieve chattels was subsequently superseded by the old tort actions and true proprietary actions remained only possible in land law. It highlights an essential point in the common law of chattels in that the plaintiff does not have an absolute right to reclaim the asset but must mention its value and be satisfied with the payment of its value at the discretion of the defendant unless it is absolutely unique. In common law, the distinction between real and personal actions is therefore *within* the law of property and *not* between this law and the law of obligations, as became the civil law approach. See for the early common law development in this direction, the 13th-century English author Bracton, *De Legibus et Consuetudinibus Regni Angliae* (ed Woodbine, Yale, 1922), f 102 and (ed Twiss, with English translation) (1879), ii, 133.

[3] In common law the more philosophical aspects of this discussion received scant attention for a long time but see more recently C Rotherham, *Proprietary Remedies in Context* (Oxford, Hart, 2002), JW Harris, Property and Justice (Oxford University Press, 1996), earlier (with strong civil law background) AM Honoré, 'Ownership' in AG Guest (ed), *Oxford Essays in Jurisprudence* (Oxford University Press, 1961), 161, and J Waldron, *The Right to Private Property* (Oxford University Press, 1987). See earlier in the US, WN Hohfeld, *Fundamental Legal Conceptions as Applied in Judicial Reasoning* (Yale University Press, 1919) which remains significant and more recently JE Penner, "The Bundle of Rights' Picture of Property", (1996), 43 *UCLA L Rev* 711, and *The Idea of Property in Law* (Oxford University Press 1997). Much of the common law discussion will be familiar ground for civil law lawyers who are used to theoretical thought in their more intellectual approach to property rights.

are (in law) in any event less important, except in the aspect of specificity. This does not at first appear a great problem in respect of chattels, rather more so in respect of intangible claims, but even they can be properly described and identified, often with reference to the debtor. In respect of both categories of assets, there may be a greater problem with *future* chattels or intangibles and the (prospective ownership in them). In this connection (in German terminology), assets may be absolutely future, meaning that they are not at present existing, like next year's crop or future claims for payment, or they may be relatively future in the sense that they do exist but are not yet owned or otherwise possessed or used by the party who wants to dispose or otherwise transact in respect of them.

Another point to make here is that in all assets, the issue is not normally the specificity or identification *per se*, but rather the disposition possibility and right in them for which specificity or at least identification would appear to be a precondition. Again, it is a problem often associated with the transfer or disposition of future assets. Even then, there is normally no problem on the contractual side: future assets can always be disposed of by contract regardless of their present or future state, as long as they can be reasonably described (so that the contract has a proper object), but for a transfer they must be sufficiently set aside or identified. That is clearer in legal systems that require delivery of the asset for title transfer, like Germany and the Netherlands (even if this delivery need not be strictly physical, as we shall see), but it is so even in systems that do not require delivery for ownership transfer, like France, Italy and England, where the transfer of future assets cannot merely be constructive (non-physical) either.

Then there are the assets that appear in *bulk*, like libraries, inventories, portfolios of receivables and the like. In this case also, the true issue is whether these assets can be transferred, or better whether they are sufficiently specific to have any owner-, possessor- or user-rights in them transferred in bulk, and how. In the case of (existing) bulk assets, the more precise question is whether they can be legally transferred (into ownership or a security interest) in *one* legal act, for example with reference to a certain (enclosed) place, or whether each part must still be individually transferred. The true issue is here whether ownership in bulk can exist at all. If so, there must be some way of transferring it as such.

These problems will be discussed in greater detail below. Suffice it to say here that domestic laws may take different attitudes in the definition of chattels and intangibles and the specificity required to allow proprietary interests in them to operate and be transferred, especially when the assets are not physical, unspecific, future, or exist in bulk. The divide is here not necessarily between common and civil law whilst even within one legal system the requirements may be different for ownership and more limited proprietary rights like security interests. They may not even always be clear.

Thus in the most recent codified system, which is the Dutch one under its new Civil Code of 1992, receivables in order to be transferred must be identifiable, but even here the exact requirements sometimes remain unclear and are in any event not statutorily defined. In respect of claims, identification is foremost done with respect to an identified debtor, but this leaves a problem with respect to the proprietary status of future claims. Nevertheless, a sufficiently described claim on a certain debtor (even if only future) may be the object of ownership and may be transferred as such (through an assignment), but for secured interests to vest in it, the contract (or other legal relationship) out of which the claim arises must also be in existence. This may be more restrictive. French law has similar requirements for both the transfer and creation of security interests in receivables, as we shall see, but German and English law are more relaxed especially important when in floating charges replacement goods are deemed included with a rank as of the original date of the security.

For bulk transfers or assignments, similarly great differences may exist. Some laws may be much more flexible than others and allow the transfer of a multitude of assets in one transaction with reference to a certain place or in the case of a multitude of receivables with reference to one debtor and include any replacement goods. New Dutch law remains here still uncertain in the identification requirements in the case of transfers in bulk and has not managed to define the concept.[4] In the case of assignments, it has, moreover, introduced a notification requirement for their validity. In practice, this rules out any bulk assignment, although an exception is made for the creation of a security interest in receivables although the collection right and the collections do not even then accrue to the security assignee before the notification. In the meantime, in countries like Belgium and in financing arrangements between professionals also in France, the requirement of notification for the validity of assignments was recently deleted, exactly to make these bulk assignments possible, see chapter V, sections 1.2.1 and 1.3.5. Recent Dutch proposals mean to delete the notification requirement only introduced in 1992 also. English and German law were always more flexible, also in this area, as we shall see.

Before proceeding, another broader issue should be discussed.

1.1.3   *Proprietary Aspects. Claims*

The intangible right itself may require here some further thought. As mentioned above, the most common example is a monetary claim or receivable. This is in civil law terminology a personal right against another that can only be enforced through a personal or *in personam* action. That is the *internal* aspect. However, it is at the same time *also* an asset with likely economic value and as such it can be the object of an ownership right just like any other asset and can be defended against all the world, therefore against all intruders, in principle through the same proprietary or *in rem* actions. That is the *external* aspect. In this connection, one could say that it is hardly possible to steal a claim, but one can induce a debtor to redirect the interest payments and the ultimate repayment of principal, amounting to a similar act of appropriation. Thus a personal claim on a debtor is at the same time a piece of property of the creditor who can as such dispose of it and defend his (property) rights in it against all others in the manner of any other proprietary right.

The nature of the asset means, however, that the disposal is often effected in a different way (through assignment) and may be subject to different formalities, perhaps notification to the debtor. It depends on the applicable law of assignment. Also the defence of the proprietary rights in claims may be organised differently and there are unlikely to be revindication rights or possessory actions as we have in civil law in respect of chattels. The normal defence will be in tort (which conforms to common law where all defenses of proprietary rights in respect of movable property are in tort). The fact that in civil law there are no possessory proprietary actions in respect of intangible assets may seem inconsistent, but no system is perfect and especially the proprietary regime in intangibles developed in a haphazard way, even in civil law, and may still not be considered complete. It will be more extensively discussed in section 1.7 below.

Thus not all assets are similarly treated in the details of their transfer and protection, even in civil law, which nevertheless strives for a uniform proprietary regime for all types of assets, therefore for one regime of ownership and of the other more limited proprietary

[4] See SCJJ Kortmann and NED Faber, 'Bepaaldheidsvereiste by cessie en verpanding' [Specificity requirement for assignments and security transfers of claims] (1998) *WPNR* 6324, and 'Een streng bepaaldheidsvereiste: geldend recht of "Wishful Thinking"' [A strict specificity requirement: positive law or wishful thinking] (1999) *WPNR* 6374.

rights that may coexist with it and are derived from it. The modern approach is indeed to appreciate the proprietary aspect of claims (in fact of all rights) and see them as assets like any other,[5] although again Dutch law in its new Code of 1992 is hesitant, avoids the use of the term 'ownership' in respect of intangibles, speaks rather of disposition rights (Article 3.84(1) CC) and restricts the limited proprietary rights, except for the usufruct and the security interests, to immovable and tangible movable assets only (Article 3.1 CC). Curiously, it does not define the most complete right that one can have in a claim at all. However, it is clear that the ownership concept is implicit also for claims. They can as such be transferred (through assignment) whilst they are also subject to possession (in the abstract civil law sense, as we shall see) and acquisitive prescription and even holdership notions. There is no proprietary or possessory action for intangibles, however. There is no *bona fide* purchaser protection either and, as just mentioned, the protection is in tort only (*cf* Article 3.125 CC).

Dutch law still presents here some half-way house. It is clearly influenced by German Pandectist thinking and codified law which since 1900 in Sections 90 and 903*ff.* BGB only deal with the idea of ownership in respect of physical assets. It was thought to be closer to the everyday use of the ownership concept.[6] French law, following the teaching of Gaius, never made that distinction, neither did earlier Dutch law in which things could be tangible (corporeal) or intangible (incorporeal).[7] That was also the view of Grotius.[8] Legal doctrine remains divided on the subject;[9] it would seem unnecessarily so.

On a proper analysis, it must be admitted, however, that there remains some difference between ownership of chattels and that of intangibles, but this difference is perhaps primarily one of ordinary speech. For all tangible assets, the law has always identified the ownership right with the object of the right itself, therefore with the asset. Hence rights in things or *iura in re*. Thus we normally speak of owning a piece of land or a car and not of having an ownership right in land or in a car, although it is different for life estates or, in civil law, usufructs or other more limited proprietary rights in tangible assets. However that may be, proprietary rights are often thought to be rights in things as opposed to obligatory rights which are rights against persons, even though they could also be rights to (acquire) a thing (*iura ad rem*). Strictly speaking, that does not seem to be correct. Rights have a meaning only against other natural or legal persons, even if they are asserted in respect of certain

---

[5] The Germans use here the notion of *Vermögen*, the French of *patrimoine*. There is no good English legal term for it. It is best to refer to *assets* in this connection. The discussion on what is an asset in this sense and how it can best be protected is for intangible claims not entirely alien to common law either: see the line of cases starting with *Lumley v Gye*, 2 E&B 216 (1853). They show that the violation of a (contractual) right itself may lead to a tort action to protect the right as if it were an asset or piece of property: see further Lord Mcnaghten in *Quinn v Leathem* [1901] AC 495, 510 stating: 'it is a violation of a legal right to interfere with contractual relations recognised by law if there be no sufficient justification for the interference'.

[6] See H Dernburg, *System des Römischen Rechts* (8th ed. 1911) I, 319 (Sokolowski) and Windscheid, *Lehrbuch des Pandektenrechts* (9th edn, 1906) I, 856 (Kipp).

[7] See Gaius, *Institutes*, 2, 12–14, repeated in the Justinian *Institutes*, 2, 2.1–3, but intangible assets were not at that time commonly considered objects of proprietary rights because there was nothing like a *traditio* in respect of them, and therefore no technique of transferring them or creating acquisitive prescription in them: see also s 1.7.1 *infra*.

[8] See Grotius, *Inleidinge tot de Hollandsche Rechts-geleerdheid* (Introduction to Roman Dutch Law), II.1.9.

[9] In German law there is, however, a possibility of substituting the delivery requirement by an assignment of the retrieval claim in chattels leading to a transfer of ownership which in Germany does not require notification to or co-operation of the holder: see Section 398 BGB. Thus assets under third parties may be transferred by assigning the reclaiming right, see Sections 931 and 870 BGB (which is limited to the transfer of legal possession but also implies a transfer of the underlying contract with the third party), but they may also be transferred through delivery of possession under Section 930 BGB at the option of a seller without physical possession of the asset (the *traditio longa manu*).

assets. The key is not that proprietary rights represent rights in things (*iura in re*), whether or not tangible, but that they can be maintained against *all* (the world) and therefore imply rights that can be maintained against others than the person from whom they were obtained without there being any special legal relationship with them (until someone violates the proprietary right). Obligatory rights on the other hand can only be maintained against a *specific* counter-party. To speak of rights in an asset is in this connection legally meaningless and confusing. Ordinary speech is here better left to one side. Legally, we should always think of having *rights* against other persons, whether or not these rights concern assets, and whether or not in the case of assets they concern tangibles or intangible assets like obligatory rights.

Thus all rights are intangible, whether or not they are proprietary; only the objects of rights may be tangible or intangible. For intangibles, like claims or receivables, but also user, enjoyment or income rights in other assets, the identification of the ownership right with the object is indeed more difficult, but this should not disturb us, as it should now be clear that this is, at least in civil law, legally largely irrelevant. What is more important is that it seems to make their protection more complicated as there are no clear indices or manifestations of ownership or possession in these assets. Yet again, in civil law, ownership (as the expression of a proprietary right to an asset), possession (as the expression of the will to hold the right for oneself), or even holdership/detention (as the expression of the will to hold the right for another, subject to own user or similar rights to the asset) can in truth all exist without a physical element, as we shall see. The protections or defences given in connection with each of them do not depend on it either: see more in particular sections 1.2.2 and 1.2.4 below.

These concepts of ownership, possession and holdership provide in civil law the main bases for proprietary protection rather than the physical element itself. This is in general terms different in common law. The civil law approach is here fundamentally more intellectual and abstract. In it, the physical holding of an asset has no legal meaning itself but needs to be legally characterised first in terms of the relevant underlying *proprietary* right, like ownership, usufruct, servitudes, some long leases, security interests etc., and subsequently in terms of ownership, possession or holdership of the type of proprietary right in question. It is another fundamental aspect of civil law that *both* these proprietary rights and the way in which they can be legally expressed and protected are *limited*.

The essence is, as we shall see, to appreciate that in this system there are only certain underlying proprietary rights and equally only certain forms of expression and protection of these rights. In this matrix, we have the ownership right as the most absolute right to an asset whether tangible or intangible and the ownership expression of it (or the assertion of the right itself), as we have for other proprietary rights, like usufuct and security interests. In civil law, these proprietary rights may also be expressed through possession (the will to hold the right for oneself as if one were the owner) or holdership (the will to hold for another, subject to own user right), giving rise to different actions in each case.

Our language and terminology are here often imperfect, and when we speak in this connection of the ownership right and of ownership in terms of legal protection, we use two different types of ownership notions: the one being its expression, protection and enforcement and the other being the proprietary right itself. It is easier to speak here of the ownership of a usufruct right. In civil law, transfer is often through delivery of possession only, which in this system means only the demonstration of the end of the will to hold the right for oneself. This may or may not be through the physical handing over of the asset and the delivery of possession may in this sense be purely constructive (non-physical) when a declaration may suffice, for example when assets are under third parties (the *traditio longa manu*). In some countries, like France and Italy, the mere sales agreement is sufficient expression of the will no longer to hold the right to an asset for oneself. Even holdership can in this system be non-physical as there may be subholders. All is expressed as a question of intent and rights (and obligations) and *not* in physical terms.

In civil law, it is therefore correct to view ownership of an asset in terms of ownership of a right, in fact of the fullest right in it. In this approach, it is not at all impossible to view ownership in property as a bundle of intangible proprietary rights that may be subdivided in the limited proprietary rights like usufructs, certain types of long leases or security interests, under which certain income, user or enjoyment rights may be split off by the owner in favour of others who thereby acquire more limited proprietary rights in other people's assets (*iura in re aliena*) and may defend them against all the world as owner, possessor or holder of that (sub) right. But in civil law, the composition of this bundle of rights is preordained and parties may (in principle) not split off proprietary rights at random. To repeat, in this approach, *all* legal rights are intangible, including the right of ownership itself, even in tangible assets. This does not rule out that the object of these rights in terms of land, chattels or intangibles may still impact on the details of these rights, their protection and transfer.

Thus in civil law, the transfer of ownership rights in chattels is not through assignment as it is in the case of intangible assets.[10] *Bona fide* purchasers of chattels are (mostly) considered the full owners, but a similar rule does not exist for intangible assets (and also not for land). Proprietary rights in intangible assets therefore still seem to have some important different features, but, except for the protection of *bona fide* purchasers, they are less fundamental than they may appear at first: where under applicable law no delivery is required for the transfer of title in chattels or notification of the assignment of a claim to the debtor as a condition of its validity, there is no difference as the transfer of ownership in either type of asset would be through the conclusion of the transfer agreement only. This is now Belgian law.

As we shall see, it is less easy to summarise the common law in this repect. Whilst physical possession plays an important role in the protection of the physical holder of the asset, delivery of possession is no requirement for the transfer of ownership of chattels in England. They transfer through the mere sales agreement (unless otherwise agreed). Intangible assets are transferred through assignment without notification (at least in equity). In the USA under Article 2 UCC delivery of possession is necessary for the transfer of title in chattels (unless the parties agree otherwise). For assigments generally there are considerable differences between the various states in the formalities but for the assignment of receivables there is now a special regime under Article 9 UCC.

1.1.4   The Importance of the Law of Chattels and Intangibles. The Physical and Anthropomorphic Approach to Property Rights. Modern Developments. The Effect of Financial Law and New Financial Structures

As mentioned before, we shall be concerned in this chapter mainly with the proprietary law concerning chattels and intangibles or, in common law terms, with personal property,

---

[10] In German law there is, however, a possibility of substituting the delivery requirement by an assignment of the retrieval claim in chattels leading to a transfer of ownership which in Germany does not require notification to or co-operation of the holder: see Section 398 BGB. Thus assets under third parties may be transferred by assigning the reclaiming right, see Sections 931 and 870 BGB (which is limited to the transfer of legal possession but also implies a transfer of the underlying contract with the third party), but they may also be transferred through delivery of possession under Section 930 BGB at the option of a seller without physical possession of the asset (the *traditio longa manu*)10.

including documents of title, negotiable instruments and investment securities, and not with immovables. It is true that at least in common law, the emphasis in so far as proprietary rights are concerned has traditionally been on the law of real estate and its development. That is also reflected in legal education. As long as real estate was the traditional store of value, this is to some extent understandable. It was true that well into the twentieth century the total value of chattels was modest. In a cash society, receivables were also not major assets. Documents of title and negotiable instruments were mostly commercial law specialities, whilst investment securities were few in number and not widely held.

However, with the enormous increase of wealth in private hands and with the development of the consumer society in which large corporations became active, the total value of tangible movable assets and intangible claims, especially receivables, and of investment securities, has increased many fold. It now probably matches land values, even if real estate remains often the largest asset of an individal. Consequently, the law of property concerning chattels and intangibles has also become of much greater importance, including the law of modern financial instruments or structures based on these assets. Investment securities are now most important investment instruments, widely held. One need think further only of the modern non-possessory security interests like floating charges in manufacturing equipment, inventory and receivables, purchase money protection through reservation of title of goods, and of modern financing structures like finance leases, repurchase agreements and factoring that all take chattels or receivables as their base. The law of personal property remains nevertheless little studied in common law and remains largely nineteenth century in its thinking in civil law, a situation that requires urgent reversal.

Land law is of relatively little interest in international commerce and finance. From an *international business law* perspective, conflicts of laws do not habitually arise in connection with it either, as immovable assets are unlikely to have a great impact outside their own country. Succession apart, only where they are the subject of sales agreements under a foreign law or when they are used as security under foreign loans may some problems arise, mainly concerning the manner, formalities and moment of transfer of ownership or perfection of the security interests. From a *comparative law* perspective, the feudal nature of real property in common law makes land law so different from the modern civil law in this area that comparing is hardly instructive, but even between countries with fairly similar land law systems, like those of the civil law, comparative analysis is not greatly valuable in the law of immovable assets.

In this chapter, the law of real property will be referred to only where it was used as a model for the development of the law of property concerning chattels and intangibles. In common law, the trust concept was, for example, borrowed from land law and then also applied to chattels and intangible assets. So are the future or conditional and temporary ownership interests, which, as we shall see, appear as equitable interests in chattels. Otherwise, the law of chattels and also of intangibles was in common law mainly developed as part of the commercial law, more in particular in connection with sales of goods and the transfer of ownership in them. In common law countries, this commercial law is in itself, however, no longer a different type of law, as we saw in chapter I yet it has probably retained a more specialised character than in civil law. It also covers a broader field, including title and bailment notions and related proprietary structures. As we saw, that is uncommon in civil law.

Although land law was at one time also feudal on the European Continent, the law of chattels and intangibles was not affected. In fact, the feudal features of land law were abandoned early and modern civil law now largely maintains a unitary system of property law which covers all types of assets along the Roman law model as further developed, even though with some additional rules per type of asset. It became the system of the modern civil law codifications. New elements were the modern land registration facilities which made for a number of important changes in the area of transfer of ownership and the creation of other rights in immovables. For chattels there followed also the extensive protection of *bona fide* purchasers, whilst the modern law of assignments was a new addition for intangibles. In common law, the situation is still very different. It was already said that there are different proprietary regimes for each type of assets, different therefore for land, chattels and intangibles, whilst intangible claims may be further divided into contractual, tort and restitution claims. The basic land law notions still derive in common law from the feudal system with its particular estates in land, although in England, the feudal system itself was already abolished in 1660, earlier therefore than in most other parts of Europe.

   As just mentioned, in England, the feudal concepts continued in land law as a historical accident. Land law is thus still based on the notion that the Crown is owner of all land. That is now merely a fiction; there is only a residual effect when there are no heirs when the Crown takes the land by so-called *escheat* rather than as ultimate heir and successor. Yet in a technical sense, private ownership in land still does not officially exist in England. Much earlier, the notion of *seisin* or physical possession had, however, allowed private rights in land to develop based on its occupation and use. Subsequently, these rights acquired a measure of independence and ultimately became as good as ownership rights. Thus private interests in land acquired a kind of entitlement status, but the ensuing system of various estates in land (like the fee simple, the life interests and the estate for years or leasehold) and the conditional or future interest, like the reversionary interests and remainders (either vested or contingent depending on the conditions attached), prevented a more conceptual ownership concept from developing and led to an incidental approach even with respect to the various interests that can now be created in land. It was as such not suitable for chattels and intangibles, even if the law concerning them borrowed from land law especially in respect of conditional, temporary and beneficial (trust) ownership interests in them.

   This notion of *seisin* or physical possession in a common law sense was itself germanic or saxon in origin ('*gewere*') and apparently came to England via the Low Countries in the sixth and seventh centuries,[11] when the earlier Roman law completely disappeared. It also prevailed in France ('*saisine*'), even for chattels, at least until the later reintroduction of Roman ideas through the reception of Roman law. It became in England the basis of the law also for chattels, although an ownership notion for chattels could independently have developed but it remains weak to this day. Although the term 'seisin' is now no longer used in the context of chattels, it played a substantial role in the development of the notion of bailment or physical possession which in common law is at the heart of the proprietary protection of chattels, rather than the ownership concept as we shall see.[12] For intangibles, there was no such basic notion at all and the common law concerning these assets remained as a consequence even more underdeveloped and subsequently mainly evolved in equity. In England, the feudal land law concepts were updated by statute in 1925 when all future interests in land became equitable and therefore subject to the protection of the *bona fide* purchaser of the legal interests. The old law still applies under state law in the USA (except in Louisiana).

---

[11] Informally, the notion found its expression in Article 3.125 of the so-called Saxon Mirror (*Sachsenspiegel*), a collection of Saxon laws by Eike von Repgau dating from the 13th century.
[12] See FW Maitland, 'The Seisin of Chattels' (1885) 1 *Law Quarterly Review* 324 and 'The Mystery of the Seisin' (1886) 2 *Law Quarterly Review* 481.

Statutory rules concerning the sale of chattels or goods, including the transfer of ownership in them in a statutory manner, started to appear in England through the Sale of Goods Act 1893 (updated in 1979). In the USA, similarly, some aspects of the proprietary law concerning chattels derive from statute, especially in the sale of goods, now through Article 2 UCC, accepted (with some minor modifications) in all states of the USA. Thus these ownership aspects became part of the law of sales or commercial law as understood in these countries and largely statutory. It is a further indication of the absence of any unitary law of property in these countries.

Whatever the progress in the law of property may have been, it has everywhere retained a *physical* and *anthropomorphic* aspect, aspects therefore that human beings can see and physically handle. It derives from the law of property's origin in an agricultural society where land was all and as far as chattels were concerned, the interest went to cattle, a few beasts of burden, and some tools. Money was largely absent in such a society and much interchange was in the form of barter. Such a society thinks in a physical manner and sees all property in relationship to individuals (even if tribal). Thus the emphasis is on what is mine, not primarily on how I exert my rights in respect of the property *vis-à-vis* others. It easily leads to an absolute notion of ownership. In such an environment, there is also little room for monetary or other claims as economic valuables or of property as a more abstract concept like ownership of future assets or entitlements. Our continuing difficulties with assignments of claims and the transfer of future assets are a reminder of this earlier state of affairs, but it is also apparent in the identification requirement for assets for them to be capable of being owned and transferred (which impedes the bulk transfer or assignment in particular), in the types of proprietary rights that are commonly accepted, in the perception of possession and holdership being physical concepts, of delivery as a physical act (which the ensuing difficulties in the transfer of future assets and intangibles). The anthropomorphic nature of the concept of ownership is closely related, first in determining what is mine in a personal sense but also in relating the requirement of sufficient disposition rights in assets, necessary to dispose of them, (often) to (a form of) personal capacity of which it is then thought that it cannot be irrevocably surrendered in respect of assets that do not yet exist in the ownership of the disposing party.

Although land law retains the center stage in common law, at least in equity in terms of future and temporary interests and beneficial ownership rights, the law of property has become less physical or anthropomorphic and as a consequence more flexible as reflected also in the absence of a *numerus clausus* of proprietary rights, the concepts of trust and agency, and in the notion of floating charges and bulk transfers and assignments with automatic replacement facilities in respect of future assets and tracing possibilities. Especially the law of assignments was thus able to develop further. Transfers of future assets and the automatic shift of title to the transferee as soon as the assets emerged in the (constructive) possession of the transferor became also possible. The shooting-through of title of an agent acting in his own name to the principal upon disclosure of the agency is another facet of a less physical and anthropomorphic approach to property in modern common law. As 'equity' was a facility that passed civil law by, civil law is especially deficient in these areas. Yet in other areas like in the notions of seisin and possession, the protection of *bona fide* purchasers as a general concept, common law remains at least as atavistic as civil law.

The requirements of modern financial law are now making further demands on the system, especially in civil law. Structures long developed in common law through 'equity' can no longer be dispensed with on the European Continent. It is the thesis of this book that this is becoming particularly clear in the professional dealings of a financial nature which are becoming the center of modern commercial law or the new *lex mercatoria*, that must be perceived as an expression of a new legal order, therefore separate from the traditional domestic laws in this regards. This new law functions at the same time as a conduit for these newer proprietary rights and structures which derive therefore from international practice. As such, their status is to be respected also in domestic laws, especially in domestic bankruptcy laws.

Because of these modern demands and pressures, everywhere, the modern law of property is starting to lack simplicity in its intellectual base. At this juncture it may no longer be capable of presenting a unitary system, at least not in finance, not even domestically. To maintain the semblance of such a system creates even now great stress particularly in civil law countries as the new Dutch Civil Code has shown (which is particularly weak in its approach to modern assignments, security interests, agency notions and newer interests as conditional and temporary ownership rights and security entitlements, bulk transfers and assignments and substitution possibilities involving future assets). Modern property law is on the one hand up against the haphazard way in which especially in common law it was put together (in 'equity') and on the other hand against the narrow physical and anthropomorphic notions of ownership in civil law and no less 'at law' in common law. It appears difficult to cut through this by devising a coherent new intellectual framework. In fact, one may hardly hope that in its details modern property law can retain intellectual rigour. One key element is here the recognition that all proprietary interests are at the same time also intangible rights and as such intellectual concepts which have nothing physical to it even if the object of that right may be physical. It makes it much easier to understand what is happening to these rights and the way they operate and change.

Because of a lack of insight in this state of affairs, over the last fifty years, the general or formal law of property has not moved a great deal in either system. There hangs a veil of intellectual impotence and practical foreboding over proprietary law in both the civil and common law. In this situation, in the US under the UCC, the response has been simply to ignore property law as a general structure and reach for *ad hoc* solutions. This is clear from Article 2A on equipment leases, from Article 4A on payment transfers, from Article 8 on security entitlements, and from Article 9 on secured transactions.[13] In civil law, in the law of contract, the infusion of good faith and reliance principles has removed at least to some extent a subjective anthropomorphic attitude and replaced it with a more objective a-physical/a-psychological, normative approach, but a similar development has not so far happened in property law. This is not to suggest that good faith notions should be introduced in property law in a similar manner, although they have at least a function in the way property rights are exercised and in the protection of *bona fide* purchasers.

Putting emphasis on the nature of the particular proprietary right *as intangible right* and on how it is exercised makes it certainly easier to deal with any redistributive character of property law and to understand the rebalancing of proprietary interests in modern case law.[14] It makes it perhaps also easier to understand how ethical, social and efficiency considerations enter into the development of modern property law, illustrating no less than in the law of obligations its in essence dynamic character, although in property law these dynamics are not necessarily the same as in the law of obligations.

A more abstract or normative approach of another type would appear necessary in property law in order to facilitate its further development in response to modern needs. It concerns here not so much the way these rights are exercised, but rather how they are

---

[13] Cf. JH Sommer, 'A Law of Financial Accounts: Modern Payment and Securities Transfer Law', 53 (1998) *The Business Lawyer*, 1181.
[14] See on this subject in England also C Rotherham, *Proprietary Remedies in Context* (Hart, 2002).

transformed or expanded. In finance, further dynamism arises in this connection from the nature of the financial instruments and structures themselves and from their further evolution. Here again, the particular nature of the proprietary right *as right* must be put at the center of the investigation rather than physical notions of the holding of assets (in terms primarily of 'mine and dine') and the types of these assets themselves which to a large extent are immaterial.[15] As just mentioned, particular illustrations of this trend may be found in the US in the creation of security entitlements in Article 8 (see Section 8-503 and the Official Comment) and equipment lease interests of lessor and lessee in Article 2A UCC (see Sections 2A-301/7).

No less important are in this connection the increasing impact of *party autonomy* on property law and its indirect redistributive effect. In recent times, that impact has become apparent especially in private international law where the transfer regime concerning assignment and book-entry entitlements for securities is now often left to the parties' contractual choice of law. In this respect reference may be made to the interpretation of Articles 12 and 13 of the 1980 EU Rome Convention on the Law Applicable to Contractual Obligations, see also section 1.9.3 below, and to Article 4.1 of the 2002 Hague Convention on the Law Applicable to Certain Rights in Respect of Securities held with an Intermediary, *cf* also Section 8–110 (e) UCC, and section 3.2.2 below. In a similar vein, Article 5 of the 1985 Hague Convention on the Law Applicable to Trusts allows the settlor to determine the law applicable to the trust regardless of the *situs* of the trust assets. Even domestically, the use of temporary and conditional ownership rights unavoidably leads to new forms of ownership rights the content of which is more fundamentally determined by the parties as a function of how they formulate the condition or the time element, also in modern civil law even if in this respect also it remains embryonic, see section 1.6 below.

Comparative law is not here the determining element even if the common law approach to equitable proprietary rights may be of great help, see also section 1.3.7 below. It is a question rather of capturing the requirements of a dynamic foreward moving process. Social and cultural differences are here not of great importance either, although they may play a role in the way proprietary rights of whatever type are exercised especially in respect of weaker parties. A more dynamic approach to proprietary rights, which even in civil law will ultimately force open its traditionally closed system (or '*numerus clausus*'), has the disadvantage of apparent instability, but it must be asked whether the stability the old regime suggests is not dysfunctional and therefore a risk management liability. Stability in a modern sense, therefore in a dynamic environment, must foremost come from the participants and the way they commonly handle risk and structure their deals. It must therefore come from the structures they create themselves and from the manner in which they are used. In this area, there is no normativity beyond it. The law ultimately is there to serve the interests of the participants in this process unless there are clear public policy reasons why it should be otherwise. This support is in proprietary matters the prime concern of modern commercial and financial law, especially in an international context.

---

[15] That is not to say that the type of asset should fully lose its importance, but the divide between real and personal property may well do. The nature of assets remains important, eg in floating charges in respect of equipment, inventory and receivables. It remains also important to the extent assets are meant to trade when purchaser protection may be normal even in respect of known charges in the asset or to the extent they are meant to serve as collateral as receivables now normally do which again would allow assignees to ignore charges or transfer restrictions in them, trends that have indeed found a more modern expression in the UCC in the US (*cf* Sections 9-329 (9-307 old) and 9-406 (9-318(4) old)). On the other hand, the distinction between types of assets should be much less important for the protection of *bona fide* purchasers which in a modern system should be protected regardless of the type of asset, be they chattels or claims (and not only in equity).

1.2   The Types of Proprietary Rights in Civil Law

1.2.1   *The Nature and Limited Number of the Traditional Proprietary Rights in Civil Law: The* Numerus Clausus *Notion*

In civil law, there is the right of ownership as the most complete right, best expressed by Article 544 of the French Cc. Derived therefrom are a number of limited proprietary rights like usufructs, in some countries certain forms of long leases, easements or servitudes like rights of way — the latter two being normally only in real estate — and security interests, like mortgages in land and pledges or more modern non-possessory security interests in chattels and intangibles. In principle no other proprietary rights can be created in civil law. In this system of proprietary right, which was first identified in the *ius commune*,[16] it is a debated issue how far possession (the will to hold the proprietary right in an asset for one-self) or even mere holdership or detention (the will to hold the proprietary right in an asset for another subject to one's own user rights) of these assets may also be considered proprietary rights.[17] As we shall see below in section 1.2.2, unlike the approach of the old Austrian and former Dutch Civil Codes in the case of possession, it is better not to consider them so but only to see them as ways in which proprietary rights (all of them) may manifest themselves and be best protected.

As already mentioned above in section 1.1.3, it is in this connection useful to talk also of ownership as one of the three possible expressions of each proprietary right itself (ownership, possession and holdership). The ownership notion used in this way is not then a proprietary right either, even when used in respect of the proprietary ownership right itself. In civil law, legal possession is the ownership right's appearance or shadow. Ownership and legal possession in this sense usually go together here and are normally not distinct. Thus the owner (of a proprietary right) in civil law will also be the possessor (of that right), as he means to hold the right for himself as if he were the owner (which he normally is), but whilst in civil law there can only be one owner of a right, there can be more possessors. The most obvious situation is that of the thief, who is not an owner but, upon physically taking the asset for himself, becomes a possessor besides the owner, even if the loss of control in the owner technically weakens his possession, but it does not do so in a legal sense and he will keep his possessory remedies. Holdership on the other hand presents a split. The holder does not mean to hold for himself but rather for someone else. One cannot be legal possessor and holder at the same time because one cannot hold at the same time for oneself and another. Again there can be various holders of an asset through sub-holderships.

It is true that German law at the theoretical level presents a somewhat different picture, which at first glance may confuse. Although in earlier drafts of the BGB the above system was maintained, in the end, following criticism from Von Jehring,[18] Section 854(1) BGB

---

[16] The identification of the limited number of proprietary rights was first achieved by Heinrich Hahn at the University of Helmstedt in Germany in 1639: see also R Feenstra, 'Real Rights and their Classification in the 17th Century: the Role of Heinrich Hahn and Gerhard Feltmann' in R Feenstra, *Legal Scholarship and Doctrines of Private Law*, 13th–18th Centuries (Variorum, 1996). This contribution was first published in *The Juridical Review* in honour of Professor Sir Thomas B Smith (1982): see also R Feenstra, *Ius in Re*, Presentation, University of Ghent 1978; see also no 52 *infra* and accompanying text.

[17] See Section 308 of the Austrian CC of 1811 and Article 584 of the old Dutch CC of 1838; *cf* also the more general Article 543 of the French Cc of 1804 which does not give a list, whilst the new Dutch CC of 1992 in Article 3.81 refers only to the proprietary rights allowed by statute and does not enumerate them. In the German BGB there is no list either, nor even a reference to the closed system of the proprietary rights. It was considered implicit in its system.

[18] *Der Besitzwill¹e* (Jena, 1889), 212. See for a resonnance in the Netherlands, n 29 *infra*.

seems to base possession on the physical holding of the asset in the nature of the old *gewere* or seisin notion. Yet the concept of legal possessor was not abandoned: see Section 872 BGB. This is the *Eigenbesitzer* (the one who holds for himself), the other is legal holder or *Fremdbesitzer* (who holds for another). If the *Eigenbesitzer* or *Fremdbesitzer* has the property physically, he is the *unmittelbare* (immediate or direct) *Besitzer* (see Section 854), otherwise the *mittelbare* (constructive, intermediate or indirect) *Besitzer* (see Section 868). The *Fremdbesitzer* is normally *unmittelbar* (with physical possession) but even he can be *mittelbar* if there is a contractual subletting involved.[19]

This system is curious because it tries to steer some middle course between old Saxon and Roman law, the one being based on physical realities, the other on abstract rights. The advantage is that it gives the mere holder possessory rights and thereby proprietary protection, but systematic confusion unavoidably results where the legal possessor involuntarily loses the physical possession, as in the case of theft, when in Germany legal possession ends but the possessory actions remain (Section 861). Also the transfer of title becomes in this manner systematically more complicated as delivery of possession seems to suggest a physical act. This is problematic where the buyer already has the asset in his physical possession, when the second sentence of Section 929 indeed deletes the requirement of delivery altogether (the *traditio brevi manu*), or where the asset remains with the seller when only a retrieval right is created in the buyer (the *constitutum possessorium* of Section 930), or where the asset is in the hand of a third party when an assignment of the retrieval right is necessary (the *traditio longa manu* of Section 931 BGB).

In common law, on the other hand, we have ownership and physical possession or bailment as the only proprietary rights at law, which operate as two distinct interests or titles, at least in chattels. Bailment is often distinguished from possession in this sense as it tends to denote a voluntary transfer of possession for a more limited period of time, but its chartacteristics are otherwise the same. In equity, on the other hand, the types of proprietary interests that may be created are in this system limitless. This may be seen in particular in the rights of trust beneficiaries and future interest holders. Rather than limiting the number of proprietary rights, common law limits their effect and does not uphold these equitable rights against *bona fide* third parties who acquire a legal interest (ownership or bailment) in these assets for value. So, in common law, the proprietary system is in principle open and proprietary rights can be created freely by contract (in equity), but the corollary is much better protection for *bona fide* purchasers, even in respect of assets other than chattels. This is an important and understandable trade-off which does not operate at law, therefore not against ownership and possession, except where so provided by statute as in the Sale of Goods Act in the UK, see for this '*nemo dat*' rule more in particular section 1.5.9 below.

At least at the more theoretical level, common and civil law here present great differences and even where the terms are the same, like ownership and possession and the student must understand that their meaning is quite distinct: common law has a much weaker notion of ownership in chattels, allows (unlike civil law) multiple ownership rights in them, and sees possession, which in common law is the physical holding, as a concept from which a stronger *prima facie* protection is derived and which hardly allows of multiple possessors of the same asset (as civil law is used to). In this sense, the physical aspects of assets are much less important in civil law as we already saw. As a theoretical concept it is in that

---

[19] In Germany, the relationship between the immediate or constructive possessors and holders or between holders is called the *Besitzmittlungverhältnis* and may derive from proprietary as well as contractual dispositions, like respectively in the case of usufructs and rental agreements.

law in its purest form mostly insignificant, except (often) in the case of protection of *bona fide* purchasers of chattels and in the specificity requirement for proprietary rights in assets to operate. To this may be added that *prima facie* the existing physical situation concerning the assets is always protected as a matter of social peace. In this sense, the physical possessor (even if merely a holder) is assumed to be the legal possessor and owner. This is an important and necessary policy preference but it does not make possession in civil law the same central issue as it is in common law.

In proprietary matters, even as to ownership, common law does not have typical proprietary actions but the proper protection is through tort actions which do not rely on absolute but rather on relative rights, that is on the relatively stronger or better right, than on the strongest (in fact the absolute) right as civil law is apt to do in its proprietary protections, especially of ownership. The concept of relativity or priority is in this connection also not unknown in civil law, especially in the notion of possession and holdership, as we shall see in section 1.2.5 below for the case of multiple possessors or holders when the older rights normally prevail as they do in the ranking of security interests. There is here definitely a different emphasis from that in common law.

As already mentioned above, in proprietary matters, civil law in essence follows Roman law, although the conceptual framework deduced from it is much more recent and was developed in the *ius commune,* that is the Roman law as it further evolved after its reception in most of Western Europe from the twelfth century onwards, and, in the proprietary system, especially by the natural law school of Grotius and Pufendorf in the seventeenth and eighteenth centuries after an initial period in which the law on the Continent often also used for land feudal notions subject to the notion of seisin or *gewere,* which was at first also used for chattels. The law concerning chattels was then much closer to what is still the English proprietary system for these assets, especially in the notion of bailment.[20]

But this approach was gradually abandoned in favour of the reception of Roman law, also in this area (and eventually also for land), and further elaboration of the Roman law ideas followed by the German Pandectists in the nineteenth century when an un-united Germany still depended for a large part on received Roman law. Elsewhere in Europe, codifications had already been enacted, mostly along the lines of the French model of 1804. The German Civil Code (BGB) which followed in 1900 only on its surface changed this approach somewhat, as we just saw. If within the EU a more uniform framework for the law of chattels and intangibles were ever considered, a more fundamental choice must be made here: is it to be the abstract Roman approach or, for chattels, the more physical old germanic approach which is still that of the common law. A middle course seems impossible here as the faint-hearted German approach demonstrates. The old germanic approach may ultimately well carry the day and prove to be the real bridge between civil and common law in this area.

In the civil law theoretical system of proprietary rights, ownership as the most complete right can be split by contract into derivative proprietary rights, peeled off from the whole like an onion. In German law it is probably more precise to say that the key is not the contract but rather the disposition (or *Verfügung*) by the owner in which no other person may be involved and which may follow from the operation of the law. They behave thereafter as independent proprietary rights until their end, when they collapse back into

---

[20] See also WJ Zwalve, *Hoofdstukken uit de Geschiedenis van het Europese privaatrecht, vol 1 Inleiding en zakenrecht,* [Chapters from the History of European Private Law, vol 1 Introduction and Property Law] (1993), 81.

the ownership right. A disposition itself is not normally sufficient, however, to bring about these limited proprietary rights, their transfer or split. First, as already mentioned several times, there are only a limited number of proprietary rights that can be so created. Moreover, except in countries like France and Italy for chattels (but not even there in respect of pledges), forms of delivery of the right in the asset are further required to bring them about, even though this delivery (of possession in the civil law abstract sense) may only be constructive.

The more limited proprietary rights that can so be created are the already mentioned usufructs, certain long leases, servitudes and security interests that are all absolute, proprietary or *in rem* rights. Like ownership, they can therefore be defended against *the entire world*. This means that all others must abstain from interfering with them. To repeat what has already been said before, these limited proprietary rights may in turn be owned, possessed or held. The other aspect of the proprietary nature of these limited rights is that, like ownership, they can be transferred (often, however, only together with the asset as in the case of a servitude and in the case of a pledge or mortgage only with the indebtedness they insure) *without* the consent of anybody else, including notably the owner (of the ownership right) or any physical holder of the asset (even though the latter may have to be notified to protect the new situation). This confirms their independent proprietary status.

In civil law, these derivative rights automatically re-integrate into the ownership right upon the end of their term, which ownership right thus becomes full again whilst the (then) owner reacquires his full rights, without any additional transfer requirements. This is often referred to as the *elasticity* of the civil law ownership concept. It has as such no clear equivalent in common law. It does *not* mean, however, that these more limited proprietary rights during their period of existence have an inferior or dependent existence. They operate independently beside the ownership right and *vis-à-vis* each other, much as they do in common law, and are defended separately until the end of their term. As such they must be respected by all, including the owner, even though he is the older interest holder, because he granted them. The younger (proprietary) interest holders naturally take subject to them. The independence of these rights and their transferability in principle also means that they may themselves be encumbered by security interests or made subject to usufructs so that it is conceivable to create layers of different proprietary rights in one asset. In this way, it is possible to have an ownership right, a usufruct and a security interest in the usufruct, all in the same asset at the same time, but for different interest holders.

Because of their third party effect, civil law *limits* proprietary rights in number, as just mentioned. This is so even in countries like France where the delivery requirement for the transfer of ownership and for the creation and transfer of the other more limited proprietary rights (except pledges) was deleted in the Civil Code of 1804 so that this transfer is achieved through the mere contract ('*par l'effet des obligations*': Article 711 Cc). This could suggest that parties may have more freedom to create whatever proprietary right they like with full third party effect. It was earlier indeed than? the attitude of the French Cour de Cassation, never overruled, but it is not truly the modern French approach.[21] The limitation of the proprietary rights everywhere in civil law has a public order aspect in the sense that it is believed that two parties cannot privately decide which of the rights they create

---

[21] See for the original approach, Cour de Cassation, 13 Feb 1834, s 1.205 (1834), but see for the modern attitude, J Ghestin and B Desche, *Traité des Contrats, La Vente* (1991), no 612.

have third party effect. This limitation finds an important mirror in the prerequisite of publicity in the sense that private rights that are advertised or known to others are more likely to be given proprietary protection, but in civil law publicity itself has *never* been sufficient to create proprietary effect. So a rental under a publicised rental agreement does not acquire any better proprietary protection *per se* than one under an unpublicised rental agreement.

The normal means of publicity are the land registers for proprietary rights in immovable property and physical possession in the case of chattels; hence the requirement of delivery of possession in the case of title transfer, even if (later) only constructive and entirely deleted in countries like France. Thus for these rights to be established, publication or the taking of possession may be converted into other requirements or even deleted altogether — it depends on local laws.

In this sense, the opposite of these proprietary or absolute (*in re(m)*) rights are the personal or relative rights (*ad rem* or *in personam*), like the rights derived from contract to receive an asset or some other performance, damages claims derived from the commission of a tort or unjust enrichment claims.[22] These personal claims can only be maintained against the debtor, although, as we already saw, in terms of them being also an asset of the creditor, they can as such still be defended against all the world. The difference between *in re(m)* or proprietary rights and *ad rem* or personal rights is fundamental in civil law and may be demonstrated in a right of way. In civil law, this can be granted as a proprietary right by way of a servitude in the manner the objective law allows, but it can also be granted by contract as a purely contractual right in the manner the parties wish. In the first case, the beneficiary can maintain his right of way as a proprietary right against all the world, therefore also against all succeeding owners of the land, even if they did not know of the servitude. On the other hand, if the right of way is merely contractual or personal, succeeding owners may ignore it. In that case, the beneficiary only has recourse, that is a damages action, against the original party who granted the right on the basis of his inability to protect the enjoyment where the right is withdrawn by succeeding buyers of the land.

In modern civil law one may see here some important approximation, however, between these extremes and it may be that the beneficiary who has only a contractual right can maintain it against succeeding owners of the land if they knew of the existence of his right at the time of their purchase. This may be all the more so if such a right, even though only contractual, could be registered in land registers and as such acquire publicity. One sees here the element of publicity sustaining rights against third parties, which at the theoretical level never used to be sufficient in the distinction between proprietary and personal rights. In civil law, publicity and knowledge may thus open up the closed proprietary system to some extent in certain circumstances. It remains, however, the subject of debate how far this can succeed, in fact no less so in common law where similar situations arise and the issue for a new owner always is what he may ignore in terms of earlier contractual

---

[22] The distinction is often traced to the Roman law distinction between real and personal actions (*actiones in rem* and *in personam*), but it is doubtful that this is correct as the situations giving rise to the *actiones in rem* are hardly the same as those that give rise to proprietary actions in modern civil law: see also R Feenstra, n 16 *supra* and G Pugliese, 'Diritti Reali', in *Enciclopedia del Diritto* (pub Milan 1964), XIV, 755*ff*. The distinction was only articulated in the later *ius commune*: see also the work of Hahn referred to in n 16 *supra*, particularly in the natural law school of Grotius and in the German 19th-century Pandectist school. Grotius in *De Iure Belli ac Pacis*, II, 3,19, 2 clearly started to distinguish *dominium* and *creditum*. In his *Inleidinge* (Introduction to Roman Dutch Law), II, 1, 58 he uses in the margin the terms *ius in rem* and *ius in personam* as the fundamental distinction and also incorporates amongst the real or proprietary rights the limited proprietary rights or *iura in re aliena*.

rights of others concerning the property. In common law, because of its less conceptual approach, it may even be more difficult to determine and may largely depend on the type of situation.[23]

In any event, there are also in civil law certain so-called qualitative obligations that will run with an asset and can be enforced against any subsequent owner regardless of the latter's knowledge or any publication. They are especially rights of neighbours and tenants in real estate. In France they are often referred to as rights *propter rem*. These may concern an expanding class of rights that may be maintained against any owner of land or buildings and may again include rights of way, even if not expressed as a servitude but generaly known.[24]

We shall come across other instances below where, due to practical considerations, the civil law proprietary system is not as closed as once used to be thought. This is particularly so in the area of security interests where new non-possessory securities have been created in Germany. It is also true in the area of conditional sales and proprietary rights used in financing, where there arise at the theoretical level considerable problems in civil law. Where holdership is protected in a proprietary (possessory) manner, as it is in Germany, the underlying contractual claims (as in the case of custody, rental, etc) may also acquire a proprietary aspect for the holder, even if he merely holds pursuant to a contractual right, as in the case of a rental, rather than to a proprietary right, as in the case of a usufruct or pledge.

1.2.2   The Way Proprietary Rights are Expressed and Protected in Civil Law: The Notions of Ownership, Possession and Holdership or Detention; Constructive Possession and Holdership

The existence of the derivative or limited proprietary rights and the restrictions on their number are the first major features of the civil law of property, whatever the modern intrusions and doubts. Besides the five or six limited proprietary rights that are so authorised (mostly by statutory law or in legal doctrine), there is, as a second basic feature, in each civil law country the expression of these rights and the appearance or shadow of them. The assertion of the various proprietary rights themselves is a matter of invoking their *ownership*. The shadow of them is *possession* in civil law terms: the will to hold the proprietary right in an asset for oneself as if one were the owner. This is also the position of the thief but one can also hold a right in a *bona fide* manner, for example pursuant to a void sale agreement. Then there is the *holdership* by third parties: the will to hold the proprietary right for someone else subject to one's own user right. This is the situation in rental agreements, but holdership may also result from the limited proprietary rights, like a

---

[23] See in England, *Tulk v Moxhay*, 2 Ph 774 (1848) and its aftermath, especially in respect of covenants that run with land (like licences to pass) and goods (like leases in aircraft): see *Bristol Airport Plc v Powdrill* [1990] Ch 774 and also S Gleeson, *Personal Property Law* (1997), 21. It is clear that such covenants when known to a buyer cannot be ignored, certainly if characterised as equitable interests. In the case of land, they may still prevail even if unknown to a buyer if they are considered to run with the land, which is usually the case if they are part of a development plan and are meant, eg to maintain the residential nature of the development, when there may also be deemed to be constructive notice. They are especially enforced as such in the USA. Even in chattels, covenants that restrict their resale have long been upheld in France, see Cour de Cass, 20 Apr 1858, D.1.154 (1858). It requires that the original seller, buyer or a third party has a justified interest and that the restriction is limited in time, see Cour de Cass 24 Jan 1899, D.1.535 (1900); 23 Mar 1903, D.1.337 (1903); and 18 Mar 1903, D.1.126 (1905). The defendant need not have had knowledge of the original covenant, but in the case of chattels his *bona fides* means that he is considered full owner and need not return the asset.

[24] See more in particular chapter II, s 1.5.1 on privity of contract.

usufruct or pledge. One holds these rights for oneself (therefore as owner and possessor of those rights) but in relation to the owner one is a holder of his proprietary right. The owner remains also the legal possessor of the asset, but only in respect of his residual ownership rights upon the end of the usufruct.

There is in this system a confusing element already alluded to in section 1.1.3 above. All proprietary rights, including full ownership, appear in civil law in three ways: the assertion of the proprietary right itself, also called the exertion of the ownership of that right. Then there are the possession and holdership of that right (to the relevant asset). It means that in respect of the proprietary ownership right itself, we speak in the exertion of this right of owning the ownership right. It came to the surface earlier and it is not elegant, but the idea behind it is sound and is what truly counts. To avoid confusion we could also refer to the assertion of the proprietary right itself. More important is that there are here two quite different concepts of ownership at work: the expressional and proprietary. They are quite different and subject to different rules. The expressional type of ownership operates in respect of all limited proprietary rights, as do possession and holdership. This shows that ownership, possession and holdership in this sense are *not* in themselves proprietary rights and should not as such be confused with the underlying proprietary rights that they express. It is true that when the idea of the limited number of proprietary rights was first developed in the *ius commune* of the seventeenth century, possession was seen as one of these rights,[25] but the modern answer, at least in German doctrine, is that it is not, and the less so holdership. In a civil law context that seems to be the correct view.

In the case of the proprietary ownership right, owning that right means the assertion of the right itself, as it would in the case of a usufruct or pledge. In this connection one normally finds in civil law a special proprietary action at least for the exertion of the ownership right. That is the *revindicatio* of Roman law. Possession means the control (or *corpus*) of the relevant proprietary right in the asset (either directly or indirectly) with the intent to hold it as owner (the *animus domini*) or, better perhaps, exerting the underlying proprietary right in the asset as if one were the owner of that right. In the case of the usufruct, long lease, servitude or security interest, possession means therefore exerting these rights and using the assets thereunder as if one were the rightful beneficiary, therefore the owner of these rights in an expressional sense. More generally, reference is in this connection also made to the *animus possedendi*, which may therefore exist in respect of each proprietary right. In a perfect system, there would follow a special possessory action irrespective of the underlying proprietary right. In Roman law, that was the *actio Publiciana*.

As already mentioned in section 1.1.3, ownership and possession in this sense can also exist in relation to the proprietary rights to intangibles or claims, which rights are assets of the creditor, therefore the object of proprietary rights, even though there may not exist revindication and possessory actions in respect of them, whilst these rights are only protected in tort. Naturally, possession is here never physical, as legally it never needs to be in civil law. It is all to say that obligatory rights are assets. Proprietary rights are rights *in* assets (iura in re) and in that sense not assets themselves.

In civil law, in the case of tangible property, the physical part of the possession can be transferred to others, the *holders* or *detentors*, who hold the asset (mostly physically, although there may also be sub-holders) but only according to a special relationship with the possessor, who does thereby *not* lose his legal possession proper. This is the situation in the case of a warehouse or custody arrangement or a borrowing or hire purchase

---

[25] See for the reference in the Austrian and old Dutch Civil Code, n 17 *supra*.

agreement with the owner. It is better to say, however, that the holder then holds the proprietary right to the asset subject to own user rights. Holdership in this sense need not therefore be physical and may also exist in respect of intangible assets, as in the case of a collection agent to whom receivables are transferred for collection purposes only.

The key is that these holdership arrangements and the surrender of the asset thereunder do in civil law *not* disturb the legal possession of the asset under the relevant proprietary right which would merely become *constructive* (or in German *mittelbar*), although the holders acquire an own position *vis à vis* third parties that they can defend. They do not normally do so through an own type of action, but only in tort, yet in countries like Germany in the case of chattels in a possessory manner, subject always to the better rights of the owner and legal possessor. Holdership in that sense can only be disturbed if the holder subsequently manifests the desire to hold as owner (or beneficiary of limited proprietary rights) for himself, thereby acquiring the *animus possedendi*. The result is *two* legal possessors, of which the older has the stronger right. Again, in this system there can only be one real owner, but there could be more than one possessor and even more than one holder of the same right to an asset if one also keeps the possibility of sub-letting in mind, an example where holdership can become purely non-physical or constructive (or *mittelbar*) itself.

It is also of interest to see how ownership, possession and holdership in this sense are acquired and surrendered. The transfer of *ownership* results here from the proper transfer of the underlying proprietary right which includes surrender of legal possession by the previous owner, either directly as a requirement of the transfer of title through delivery of possession in this sense of the asset, or indirectly, as in the case of chattels, in countries like France and Italy, through the signing of the sales agreement. In civil law, the transfer of ownership may of course also result from *bona fide* purchases in the case of chattels or from acquisitive prescription for all types of assets. Transfer of legal *possession* of the relevant proprietary right to the asset will go with it. Possession may also be created spontaneously and autonomously through physical appropriation of the right, as in the case of theft, when an additional possessor starts operating, possession itself not having been transfered. It may also result from invalid transfer agreements when ownership proper is not passed. In Germany, legal possession of chattels not in the physical possession of the owner may pass through assignment of the retrieval right, as we saw (Section 870 BGB). Transfer of *holdership* on the other hand results from contracts meaning to establish it, like rental agreements.

To repeat: the limited number of proprietary rights in civil law each manifest themselves as (a) the full right in the sense of ownership of that right (even the ownership right itself), (b) the possession of that right, or (c) the holdership or detention of that right. That is therefore so for ownership as the most complete right but also for the derivative limited proprietary rights like usufructs, security interests and the others. As we shall see below in greater detail in section 1.2.4, from the type of manifestation in civil law follows the system of protection of these rights and the gradations of that protection. As just mentioned, in this system, ownership and legal possession are most closely related and normally go together, therefore the right to own and to hold for oneself. The owner is in this system always the possessor, except in the rare cases in which a holder becomes owner unknown to himself, for example as heir or in situations where an owner/possessor converted himself into a holder through a contract with a third party that was void.

In civil law, the full proprietary right and its possession (in this sense of holding as if one were the true owner) will thus be fully separated only in exceptional cases like theft or embezzlement or when the asset is lost and found by someone else who subsequently wants to hold it for himself, or perhaps when the underlying arrangement, by which the ownership or a limited proprietary right was transferred, was avoided, like a sales contract for lack of capacity or consensus, or because it was void by law or rescinded upon non-payment. Lack of disposition rights may equally cause this separation, although in that case the *bona fide* purchaser of chattels who acquires physical possession is now protected in most civil law countries. It means that the erstwhile owner loses all rights including his (legal) possession and the younger possessor who also physically holds the asset (or is in a situation in which at least the erstwhile owner was without it) becomes the owner.

Thus in this system, ownership of a proprietary right and holding it for oneself (possession) are normally the same. *Legal* holdership/detention on the other hand is fundamentally separate from possession as one cannot hold the same proprietary right for oneself and for another at the same time (although one could say that the beneficiary of a usufruct holds the usufruct for himself but the asset for the owner). In this system, the *physical* holding can, as we saw, be *unmittelbar* with the legal possessor or a legal holder or, as far as the latter is concerned, even with a sub-holder and is also for chattels *not* a prerequisite for the concept of possession or even of holdership itself, strictly speaking also not in Germany where it may always be *mittelbar* or indirect or constructive but some element of *control* is always required. The consequence of this system is that the legal possessor, even though physically surrendering the asset, does *not* necessarily lose his possessory status but may retain the benefits, actions and defences accorded to the possessor. The legal holder is in most civil law countries not protected in a similar manner and is therefore more vulnerable to a loss of the physical holding of the asset, except notably under German law. For its retrieval he only has a tort action and in the meantime depends on the owner or legal possessor of the underlying proprietary right if the asset has reached third parties, whom the legal holder could not reach in tort. Again it is important to appreciate that the holder, whilst losing the asset involuntarily, thereby does not lose his status as legal holder or its connected protections.

The benefits of legal possession in this sense, even if the possessor does not physically hold the asset, are (a) the possessory protections which the possessor in the legal sense can raise against any physical holder of the asset including a holder/detentor (after the end of the contract creating the holdership), against the thief who stole the asset from him, or against the thief's holder, and against any finder, whilst (b) any acquisitive prescription running in favour of the legal possessor is not interrupted either unless legal possession is voluntarily surrendered. In Germany similar protection exists for the holder in respect of subholders, thieves or finders and their holders but there is no acquisitive prescription for the holder or *Fremdbesitzer* unless he changes his position to legal possessor or *Eigenbesitzer*. This is just like in other civil law countries.

1.2.3   *The Acquisitive Prescription and its Importance in Civil Law. Procedural and Substantive Law Aspects. Acquisitive Prescription and the Protection of Bona Fide Purchasers*

In civil law, the acquisitive prescription is of prime importance as it allows any owner to prove his proprietary right in an *absolute*, exclusive or ownership manner, which is the basis of his protection as owner of the right. It results from *bona fide* legal possession, which in this context acquires a central place. The acquisitive prescription function, connected with possession in this sense, derives in civil law from the notion that in the end the law will always follow the appearance of the right and applies therefore to *all* proprietary rights, assuming therefore that there is no *mala fides*. This is the practical need but the notion of legal possession is used to achieve it. Acquisitive prescription should be clearly distinguished from the operation of the statute of limitations. This does not require *bona fides*. Thus even the retrieval action against a thief will eventually be time barred (usually after 30 years) but that does not make the thief technically the owner (although that result is often accepted under more modern law).

We already saw in the previous section that ownership, usufructs, easements or servitudes and security interests may all be defended on the basis of legal possession of these rights, but also on the basis of their ownership, proven in turn with reference to the required time of *bona fide* legal possession, that is through acquisitive prescription. In fact, acquisitive prescription was, as we saw, at the origin of the Roman notion of possession. Wherever there is a reference to possession in a civil law sense it must be assumed that there is also a possibility of acquisitive prescription if this possesion was *bona fide*, which itself may be presumed. Where there is a problem with this possession in respect of intangible assets, as there is in Germany, the acquisitive prescription possibility may also be in doubt.

In the case of tangible movable assets, the acquisitive prescription is now mostly attached to three years of *bona fide* possession in the civil law sense and 30 years for intangibles and immovables (10 years for all *bona fide* acquisitions of other assets under the new Dutch Civil Code, Article 3.99). In Germany it is 10 years under Section 937 I BGB which only applies to chattels. In principle, acquisitive prescription arises in favour of any legal possessor, therefore in favour of anyone (a) who wants to hold the proprietary right to the asset for himself, (b) has control of the asset, even if only through a holder or detentor, or did not surrender it voluntarily (in the case of theft or loss), and (c) is *bona fide*, made all the easier as this *bona fides* is presumed.[26] The *bona fide* purchaser does not need to have himself acquired the asset pursuant to a valid cause (usually pursuant to a contract of sale or exchange) or from a person with proper capacity and disposition rights, again as long as he is not aware of any such defects in his purchase. In this system, the *mala fide* possessor can never acquire ownership through acquisitive prescription, but when the actions against him run out, usually after 30 years (although this may be shorter under modern law), he is the *de facto* owner and, in some civil law countries, modern law may even give him ownership status.

The *bona fide possessio* for a number of years thus covers *all* defects in the acquisition of the relevant proprietary right to assets including any invalidity of the underlying contract where required for the transfer, and any lack of capacity to transact in the transferor or any lack of disposition rights in him. That is the general rule. It is true that under modern civil law, in most countries, in the case of chattels (only), the *bona fide* acquisition is now *immediate*, but only in the case of lack of disposition rights in the seller. What concern us here are any defects earlier in the chain of ownership of which the buyer is not aware, provided he himself has at least a valid contract (which assumes capacity and legality), paid good value and (in most countries) obtained *physical* possession. In countries like Germany, invalidity of the contract itself does not inhibit the transfer *per se*, which is seen as a separate legal act (*dingliche Einigung*) so that acquisitive prescription may play a lesser role, as we shall see below in section 1.5.7.

In France, the acquisition may even be immediate if there was no valid contract, assuming the buyer was not aware of this and not himself causing the invalidity, for example in

---

[26] Still there are some important differences. In countries like Germany (Section 937(2) BGB) following canon law and the teachings of Bartolus based thereon, the *bona fides* of the buyer must subsist during the whole prescription period. This was not the Roman law (C.7.31.1) and is not required in France (Article 2269 Cc) and in Dutch law (Article 3.118 CC) where the *bona fides* is relevant only at the moment of acquisition.

the case of lack of capacity to contract in the transferor or in the case of illegality.[27] This immediate acquisition notwithstanding, these defects are often expressed in terms of an immediate or acquisitive prescription of nil years. Because of its more limited scope, in Germany and in the Netherlands under modern law, the *bona fide* purchaser protection is rather seen as another way in which property is instantly acquired. As we shall see, the immediate protection of *bona fide* acquisition of chattels in this manner came in order to protect the ordinary flow of goods and derived from the practices in the commercial centres of Italy and the Netherlands, but later became a more general rule, first in France in the seventeenth century: see section 1.5.8 below. It spread from there through most of the civil law, as an alternative to acquisitive prescription (which, unlike in France for chattels, was mostly not instantaneous).

Under later Roman law, it appears that the acquisitive prescription foremost protected the *bona fide* buyer who had technically acquired the asset in the wrong manner, that is without the proper formalities under the various methods of transfer designated under Roman law, but was otherwise difficult to invoke.[28] Acquisitive prescription was thus originally substantive, therefore another way of acquiring full ownership as it now again is in Germany and the Netherlands. Only later on its function became largely procedural in that invoking the prescription became the traditional way of *proving* and asserting ownership. As such it remains still important in civil law where an *absolute* rather than a better right has to be proven in ownership claims.

1.2.4   The Proprietary Defences in Civil Law

To repeat, in civil law there is besides the ownership of each proprietary right its appearance or shadow in the form of legal possession from which detention or holdership may be further split off. This triptych is particularly important from the point of view of the protection of proprietary rights. For each manifestation, there is in principle a different defence in civil law. They all lead to forms of *specific performance*, as money judgments also do: see for this concept more in general chapter II, section 1.4.1. This idea of specific performance is in proprietary matters (in fact in all non-monetary claims) more limited in common law, as we shall see in section 1.3.4 below.

In bankruptcy, proprietary rights and their protection acquire a special meaning as they may give the beneficiary the right to ignore the bankruptcy and claim his interest directly from the bankruptcy trustee outside the distribution process. In bankruptcy, the general concept is that the debtor is liable with his entire estate for all his debts (see Article 2093 Cc: '*les biens du débiteur sont le gage commun de ses créanciers*'), but this implies respect

---

[27] Normally, if advertised (except in the case of under-age children), there would be constructive notice of such incapacity, but only, it appears, if so advertised in the country of the buyer.

[28] The main problem for a wider use was in the *res furtivae* (Inst. 2.6.2) which could not be obtained through acquisitive prescription. They were goods that were once stolen or embezzled or even goods that were earlier in the ownership chain transferred without a valid contract (Inst. 4.1.6). They could never be retained, therefore, even by a *bona fide* possessor who himself had obtained the asset under a valid contract. These were at the same time impediments of the possessory action, the *actio Publiciana*: see D.6.2.7.16–17. The prescription therefore in most cases did not protect against lack of disposition rights or capacity for which in modern times it is primarily meant. So it could rarely be invoked against the real owner (see also D.6.2.16–17), but it could still be of use against other possessors. D.6.1.24 notes, however, that the normal and easiest way for the owner or possessor to retrieve the property was through the use of the possessory interdicts which allowed recovery on the basis of an action in tort but would be effective only against the depossessor and not against his successors in interest. The owner would also have the *actio furti* which was a tort action later available to holders who were disseised but liable to return the goods to the owner (Inst. 4.1.13). However, it only led to payment of damages.

for all existing proprietary or priority rights of others in the debtor's estate's assets. Normally, a judgment creditor will proceed upon judgment (if not voluntarily complied with) to attachment of the goods of the debtor, if necessary to a general attachment through bankruptcy proceedings. In principle he will share equally with all other creditors in his collections (if not himself a secured creditor or lien holder) and will not have a preference in respect of the proceeds of attached assets. He will normally also have to respect all third party proprietary rights in these assets including earlier conventional or statutory security interests or liens.

It is true that judicial liens may in some countries support monetary judgments (especially in the USA under state law) and also lead to proprietary interests of competing creditors and repossession rights in respect of the assets to which these liens attach but this is exceptional. In most civil law countries, there are no judicial liens giving priority status (except the judgment lien in real estate under French law, the *hypothèque judiciaire* of Article 2123 of the French Cc). Only in Germany, do attachment liens still yield priority (see Sections 804, 867 and 930 of the German CCP of 1877). This is the old germanic rule which also prevailed in the Netherlands until codification, when the French sharing approach was adopted. The preference for the attaching creditor is, however, also accepted in many states of the USA. It gives the attaching creditor a preference in the proceeds of the attached assets, always subject to senior proprietary interests. This attachment lien does not extend to the creditor who opens bankruptcy proceedings.

Full ownership rights of third parties in assets under the debtor are the clearest example of an exceptional status in bankruptcy. They will be reclaimed by their rightful owners, also in common law, although theories of apparent ownership of the debtor may still distract from their rights, especially if they voluntarily surrendered possession to the debtor. To what extent third parties may claim here indeed better rights, especially if their proprietary rights are less than full ownership rights, as, for example, under a non-possessory reservation of title or other appropriation rights upon default or under a floating charge, is an important theme throughout this book. It is rightly a matter of great practical but also intellectual concern. Especially in a bankruptcy of the holder of the assets, the result cannot in general be predicted and also depends greatly on the special provisions of the applicable bankruptcy laws, which may change the normal rules.

It is necessary first to explore the main rules of proprietary protection before the complications can be properly understood. In civil law, the *ground rule* for the protection of proprietary rights in assets, no matter who is holding them for the time being and whether or not this holder is bankrupt, is still derived from the Roman law of ownership, possession and holdership. In it, the holder was *presumed* to be the possessor and the possessor the owner, therefore even the mere holder or detentor of the asset was presumed owner and had as such certain protections. Indeed in the new Dutch law, Article 3.109 CC still expresses the presumption that the holder is also the legal possessor and Article 3.119 that the legal possessor is the owner. This is principally a requirement of the civil peace and in this respect anyone in *physical* possession who is interrupted in the enjoyment or use of it has a tort action against his detractors to re-establish his enjoyment or user rights if illegally taken away: see for example Article 3.125(3) of the Dutch CC. It might, however only lead to a claim for damages, and a measure of negligence or fault needs to be established. It is nevertheless an important facility and another instance where physical possession is relevant, also in civil law, but only in a negative or defensive sense and there is here no more than a *personal* retrieval action (and no proprietary protection) which would not go far in the bankruptcy of the tortfeasor. However, in Germany there is not only a personal retrieval right in tort for holders/possessors/owners but also a proprietary/possessory action for repossession: Section 861 BGB, in principle also valid in a bankruptcy of the wrongful possessor: Section 47 of the Bankruptcy Act (InsO).

In traditional civil law, the legal possessor has a much stronger defence than the tort action of any holder. He derives this better protection from his ownership. So if the physical holder of an asset proves not to be a mere detentor who holds under an arrangement with the legal possessor, but is the legal possessor himself who wants to hold as owner, he has better protection and can operate against third parties. He can in this way also back up the involuntarily dispossessed holder and re-establish the asset in him even if in the meantime it has been transferred to third parties who could not be reached in tort. In the case of theft, exceptionally he may even pursue the action against *bona fide* purchasers for value with actual possession (in the case of chattels). Only acquisitive prescription would protect them; therefore in this sense only a number of years of *bona fide* possession.

This possessory action was in Roman law the *actio Publiciana*, whilst the owner himself had the *revindicatio*, the strongest proprietary action of all, but not easy to bring because ownership had to be proven, often difficult where the prescriptive acquisition possibilities were still limited: see the previous section. The *actio Publiciana* was given to any possessor whose acquisitive prescription period was still running as if it had been completed. In later times, it became the possessor as pretended owner who would 'borrow' the revindication action, now backed up by a better developed system of acquisitive prescription to support the ownership claim, but it was more limited in time and always subject to the better possessory rights of others, that is, older possessors of the same good, or the owner. This is still the approach of the new Dutch law (Article 3.125 CC, *cf* also Article 2279 Cc in France). In Germany there is much greater emphasis on the proprietary action or *revindicatio*: see Sections 985*ff* BGB. The advantage is that it awards permanent protection as opposed to the temporary protection of the possessory action based on the involuntary loss of possession only.

The possessory action nevertheless allows the recovery of the asset, even out of the bankruptcy of the defendant, and if necessary also from holders who refuse to return the goods or from any others in physical possession without a better right to it. When ownership and possession are not in the same hand (the normal example being the situation of theft, or when goods are lost and found by someone else, or when the underlying arrangement under which ownership is obtained proves to be void), the owner, who, strictly speaking, never lost his legal possession, is faced with a competing possessor but revindicates the asset from the pretended owner, as possession is always subject to the better right of the lawful owner and/or older possessor.

One may thus conclude that in modern civil law, the legal possessor has his own proprietary action even if possession is not itself a proprietary right. It is only another way in which a proprietary right is manifested and protected besides the right itself. Holdership has mostly not acquired a proprietary defence in this sense, although there are those who have argued for giving holders or detentors similar protections subject, however, to the better rights of other holders, of sub-holderships, and of legal possessors and owners.[29] Indeed, in Germany under the BGB since 1900, both legal possession in the above sense

---

[29] In the Netherlands, especially by HCF Schoordijk, 'Enige opmerkingen ober de bescherming van bezitters en houders [Some observations on the protection of possessors and holders] 1984' in *Assembled Works* (1991), 447, invoking in support the English rather than the German approach. Similar views had been expressed earlier by JC Naber, 'Het onredelijke der bezitsbescherming' [The unreasonableness of the protection of possession], *Tijdschrift voor Privaatrecht, Notariaat en Fiscaalrecht* (1902), III, 161. The only protection he proposed was that

and holdership are brought under a more generic notion of possession, as we saw, and both are as such protected (Sections 861 and 862 BGB), although they are subsequently still distinguished in their own and third party possession (*unmittelbarer* and *mittelbarer Besitz*). This system leads to a stronger protection of the mere holder and makes any underlying contractual rights of the holder stronger. They acquire absolute characteristics (as holdership under limited proprietary rights has) but again it does not make detention itself a proprietary right.

The key is always to appreciate the nature and status of the different proprietary actions in civil law. First, they are not found in the law of obligations (tort) but in the law of property and should be clearly distinguished, although the holder/detentor (except in Germany) and the owner of a claim normally only defend in tort. Proprietary actions can be used by the owner, the mere possessor (non-owner, whatever his pretence) and, in Germany, also by the holder against anyone improperly in the physical possession of the goods, wherever they may be or however they may have been acquired by the latter (in Germany the possessory action is, however, limited to the dispossessor and subsequent *mala fide* possessors or holders). This does not affect any older limited proprietary right or the *bona fide* purchaser of chattels in physical possession, who is in civil law now mostly protected unless he acquired from a thief (or his successor), and any beneficiary of acquisitive prescription. For each, the ownership, possession or holdership action, there are different requirements. For the full right (ownership) to be so defended, its absolute nature must be established. This is done through reliance on acquisitive prescription in which the notion of legal possession plays a crucial role, as we saw in the previous section. The legal possessor only asserts his better right, *cf* Article 3.125(2) Dutch CC. So does the holder if given proprietary protection.

1.2.5 The Civil Law Relativity or Priority Principle in Respect of Proprietary Rights: The Difference with the Relativity of Obligatory Rights

A final observation may be appropriate and helpful on the civil law notion of proprietary or absolute rights.[30] It was explained earlier that civil law maintains a limited number of absolute proprietary rights, in which system ownership operates as the fullest right and the others (like usufructs, some long leases, servitudes and security interests) operate as

---

of the better right, much in the English tradition: see later also JC van Oven, *De bezitsbescherming en hare functies* [The protection of possession and its functions], Diss, Amsterdam (1905), 199*ff*. Modern French law in Article 2282 Cc as amended in 1977 appears to give holders similar strong rights. Yet the French Civil Code, having abandoned the requirement of delivery for title transfer, is less concerned with the notion of possession and therefore also detention and their protection. It also abandoned the *actio Publiciana* as a special possessory protection. This lack of interest is also reflected in French legal treatises on the subject.

It may be of some interest in this connection to consider the position of Grotius. In s II.3.4 of his *Inleidinge tot de Hollandsche Rechtsgeleerdheid* [Introduction to Roman Dutch Law] of 1631, he characterises ownership as the right to be re-established in physical possession (regardless of whether the present possessor was *bona fide* and acquired the property for value). The key emphasis is here also on possession or user rights. Its protection was considered a basic natural right, although in *De Iure Belli ac Pacis*, II.2 and 3, Grotius emphasisied the common nature of property and denied that individual ownership itself had a basis in natural law. It was only a matter of positive law, which meant that states could intrude on ownership rights through legislation (perhaps to protect *bona fide* purchasers).

[30] It is of course a well known fact that under modern law no proprietary right is ever absolute and that social policies impact on all of them or, as the German Constitution expresses it: 'ownership creates social duties' (Section 14(2)). These duties are of a political nature and vary from time to time and from place to place. They will not be discussed here any further as they are not essential to the basic concepts here explained.

derivative rights. Although these rights in relation to the fullest right (ownership) may be more limited, they are not inferior to it during the period of their existence and no less absolute. There is no relativity here at all, but even the proprietary rights, however absolute in nature in that they can be maintained against all the world, are relative *vis-à-vis* each other. This follows exactly from their absolute nature itself in the sense that the older right always prevails over the younger. There is therefore a ranking among the various absolute rights according to time or seniority but not as between the various types on the basis of relative importance as the bigger or smaller right. Thus an older usufruct will always prevail over a later ownership right in the asset. It will naturally also prevail over the former owner who granted it, assuming the grant itself was not defective (when *bona fides* of the grantee may still be a protection in the case of chattels whilst acquisitive prescription will ultimately extinguish any defects).

There are two consequences: first the owner of a proprietary right who did not voluntarily cede it can normally pursue this right in the asset wherever it is, against whomever else pretends to be the owner of that right, or however the latter acquired it (except if there was a *bona fide* purchase of chattels or acquisitive prescription). This is called in French the *droit de suite*. It is based on the absolute nature of all proprietary rights, from which follows at the same time the just mentioned principle of relativity or priority, in that in principle the older proprietary right of whatever type is always the better, as it can be maintained against any younger proprietary pretences of whatever nature in the same asset, therefore including a younger ownership claim (if not backed up by *bona fide* acquisition in the case of chattels or in respect of all assets by acquisitive prescription). In the case of security interests this results in the *droit de préférence*.

In this connection the maxim '*prior tempore potior iure*' ('first in time first in right') is often used, very clear in the case of senior and junior mortgages in real estate, but the concept applies more generally and this relativity or priority manifests itself also where several possessors of the same proprietary right surface (or holders where proprietary possession also attaches to holdership). Proprietary or tort actions against thieves or finders will cut through this system.

However, in civil law, the older possessory right may be defeated in favour of a younger with physical possession if it can be proven that the older possessor was not the true owner or rightful beneficiary of the proprietary right, as in the case of a thief who lost physical posession. This is another instance in which physical possession matters in civil law. It means that the younger possessor, who can claim this so-called *ius tertii*, may be able to hang on to the asset, except that in the case of involuntary surrender by the thief, he still has an action against any younger possessor who stole the asset from him. Only if the younger possessor was not a tortfeasor in this sense and all the more so if he was *bona fide* (with a valid contract), would he be fully protected as such. In Germany, on the other hand, the older possessor prevails and a reference to the *ius tertii* is not permitted. Only in the *revindicatio* may the defendant prove that the plaintiff is not the true owner. It is a normal consequence of the German emphasis on the revindication rather than on possessory actions.

In a similar vein, a retentor or beneficiary of a possessory lien, for example a repairer of a watch, may retain the asset until payment as if he had a proprietary right and protect this even against older possessors. Also in the law of secured transactions there may be deviations from the principle that the older right prevails. Sometimes it is the younger more specific interest that prevails over the older more general, as we shall see below in the context of floating charges. Thus a younger purchase money security interest or reservation of title in favour of a more recent supplier of an asset may defeat the older charge over a whole business.

It is sometimes said [31] that where no delivery is required for ownership transfer in chattels, as in France upon a sale, there is a form of relativity (at least in chattels) of the ownership itself as upon a double sale the *bona fide* purchaser who acquires *physical* possession, even if he was the later buyer, acquires full title. Physical delivery is important here to establish the ownership *vis-à-vis* third parties. It suggests one ownership between the original parties and a different one *vis-à-vis* others, so that there results a duality or relativity of the ownership concept. This view is now abandoned as in truth it concerns here only a case of the *bona fide* purchaser protection. There is no duality or relativity as the *bona fide* purchaser has obtained all rights to the asset and the rightful (first) owner has lost all upon physical delivery, whilst before this moment the first buyer has all and the second buyer none. We will revert to this in the context of the discussion of double sales in section 1.5.2 below. Also the UK Sale of Goods Act 1979 has as a heading above Section 16 the '[t]ransfer of property between seller and buyer'. This is meaningless, however, as between two parties rights are always contractual. Proprietary status only arises in connection with third parties, here primarily the creditors of sellers and buyers in the question to whose estate the asset sold legally belongs.

Although the relativity of proprietary rights — in the sense of better rights rather than absolute rights to prevail — is more a common law concept than a civil law one, as we shall see, it is thus not unknown to civil law either, especially in the ranking of security interests. It is in fact basic to all property law. It should be clearly distinguished, however, from the other type of relativity more commonly referred to in civil law in the context of the distinction between proprietary and personal rights. In that context the proprietary rights are absolute as they work against all the world and the personal rights are relative as they work only against the debtor.

Common law distinguishes here less clearly. Not only does it not have a limitation of (equitable) proprietary rights, their definition and impact are also less clear. This may make a difference in the bankruptcy of a holder (bailee) of the asset who is not the owner or when the asset is alienated by a holder to third parties and the owner wants to retrieve it. In common law, the owner has in principle only a personal retrieval right against the bankrupt physical possessor or bailee.[32] Under civil law, on the other hand, the owner will

---

[31] See for a summary U Drobnig, 'Transfer of Property' in A Hartkamp et al (eds), *Towards a European Civil Code* (1994), 353.

[32] He would have to prove his stronger right to possession against the trustee in order to regain the asset. It might be based on a right to immediate repossession: see n 38 *infra*. There might also be some tracing rights suggesting an unjust enrichment or restitution remedy.

It is of interest that this problem is not a regular topic in treatises on bankruptcy in the UK: see eg the leading book by IF Fletcher, *The Law of Insolvency* (1996), 187*ff*, 206 and 217. Section 283(1) of the UK Insolvency Act, vests all property belonging to the bankrupt in the bankruptcy trustee. Section 436 defining the bankrupt's property does not mention possession, but that does not mean that mere possession of a bankrupt bailee has no relevance in his bankruptcy and is not included in the estate. The estate certainly also includes the equitable interests of the bankrupt debtor.

Short of real remedies which in the case of chattels are limited to situations where there are charges or security interests in the property, there is only a personal right to the return of the property (sometimes also referred to as a resale). Also the unpaid seller has no revindication right but must prove his better right in the circumstances which may not result in retrieval in a bankruptcy. The law in Scotland may well be different because of its Roman law origin and revindication rights in chattels. In the USA, Section 541(a) of the Bankruptcy Code includes in the estate all legal and equitable interests of the debtor and Section 522 defines what is exempt. It seems to cover possession but subject to the better rights of others. Whether such better rights may always be asserted against the bankruptcy trustee of a bailee may well remain doubtful.

The position of the trustee in bankruptcy is reinforced in the USA as he is given the status of lien creditor and *bona fide* purchaser of the bankrupt's assets, but at least property held under expired leases is not part of the estate: see Section 541(b)(2) of the Bankruptcy Code. See for special reclaiming rights in bankruptcy in the USA also chapter II, s 2.1.10 and n 132 *infra*.

in principle use his proprietary action to retrieve the asset. If the bankrupt has a limited proprietary right in it, like a usufruct, this will be respected and valued and could be the subject of an execution sale in which the usufruct is sold for its remaining period (but always subject to the owner's right). If there were personal rights of the bankrupt in the property, like contractual user rights, the rules concerning continuation or repudiation would apply, as in the case of all other contractual rights of a bankrupt.

Moreover, in respect of chattels, there is in common law never an absolute right to recover the asset; the defendant may pay damages instead, a discretion in England now vested in the courts. Even where chattels are sold conditionally or where the title transfer is delayed as in a retention of title, their retrieval from a defaulting buyer in possession may also be problematic, especially in the latter's bankruptcy.[33] Maybe the interest of the seller in the sold but unpaid asset must be characterised here as a constructive trust. Where in civil law, the owner's rights may be cut off because of the protection of a third party who is a *bona fide* purchaser in the case of chattels (therefore not to protect a buyer who is default-ing), common law may rely here more on notions of third party possession which must be physical (in principle) but need not then be *bona fide*, although under statutory law (excep-tionally) *bona fide* purchasers may obtain an extra protection also in common law. This may be seen under the Sale of Goods Act in the UK and in Article 2 of the UCC in the USA: see more in particular section 1.5.8. below.

1.3   The Types of Proprietary Rights in Common Law: The Practical Differences with Civil Law

1.3.1   *Legal and Equitable Interests in Chattels*

We must now contrast the common law of personal property, in particular of chattels, with the civil law approach as explained above, and then decide what differences there are in practice and evaluate any approximation which there is or is likely to be between the two systems. In common law, the law of personal property is little studied. The focus has always been on land, as it is considered to have the greater economic value even though in the modern industrial and consumer society this may no longer be so. The fact that personal property tends to have a shorter lifespan, usually loses its value promptly, and turns over quickly is another reason that traditionally in common law it has not inspired much com-prehensive legal thought. In any event, common law, being practitioners' law, is interested in solutions rather than in concepts and has never looked for a coherent system of legal rules for chattels and intangibles. It is not interested in the more theoretical aspects of this law either. As, however, in modern times the value and importance of chattels in terms of industrial equipment and stocks, of commercial receivables, and of consumer holdings or investment securities is very considerable, the law of chattels and intangibles has become much more relevant, if only from the point of view of their financing and the security that they can provide in this connection. As a consequence, the law in this area can no longer be ignored, in common law either.

---

[33] G Lightman and G Moss, *The Law of Receivers of Companies* (1986), 140 observe that even upon a reservation of title, once the seller has parted with possession, he has normally no satisfactory statutory remedy if the buyer becomes insolvent and defaults. R Goode, *Commercial Law* (2nd edn, 1995), 420 suggests that exceptionally in the case of the sale of goods upon rescission of the contract for reasons of default the title revests in the seller, although not retrospectively, but the effect in bankruptcy of the buyer in possession remains unclear.

In common law, the law of ownership in chattels or goods is usually considered in the context of the transfer of title, therefore mostly in sales. As such it is traditionally considered part of the commercial law in England and the USA and within it principally an issue of the law of contract (and not of property). Even then, this is not the complete picture as the protection of the owner is part of the law of torts. Possession itself is a different issue altogether, and if voluntarily separated from ownership is for chattels covered by the law of bailment and was developed, not within the law of sales but rather in connection with lending and letting arrangements or custodial functions, often still under commercial law. Thus in common law there is for chattels and intangibles no comprehensive system of proprietary rights and their protection. In all of this, as was observed before, there is not even a unitary approach to proprietary issues, as common law differentiates here according to the nature of the asset. There are as a consequence very substantial differences between the proprietary aspects of real estate, chattels and intangibles.

It is clear that common law never developed a system of proprietary rights in the manner in which civil law did under the influence of Roman law and the *ius commune*. In fact, it did not even develop a clear conceptual distinction between proprietary and obligatory rights. Although modern common law writers use the distinction between rights *in re* which are proprietary and rights *ad re* or *in personam* which are obligatory as a useful tool to express concepts which in one form or another must also exist in common law,[34] one should be careful not to assume from this usage of civil law terminology that common law has developed in a similar manner and now clearly distinguishes between proprietary and obligatory rights. Nothing would be further from the truth. It is not to say, of course, that proprietary rights and obligatory rights do not exist in separation in common law but they are not considered in their fundamental difference. Common law was and is protection oriented and still looks primarily at the available remedies and remains less interested in substantive rights, abstract rules and concepts, or a property system and its functioning. It is largely indifferent to it.

In this connection the maxims '*ubi remedium, ibi ius*' and 'remedies precede rights' are commonly used and still hold true in common law as in fact they also did in Roman law. But, as we saw earlier,[35] Roman law had here an effect on common law very different from that on civil law. The distinction between the old Roman *in rem* and *in personam* actions on which the civil law developments were subsequently based led in common law at first to a split between the types of assets that could be the object of proprietary rights (the distinction between realty and personalty) rather than to a distinction between proprietary and obligatory rights, as was the later civil law development, of which it can now be safely said that the right comes before the remedy. In such a system, the distinction between proprietary rights and obligatory rights can develop and even become fundamental. That did not happen in common law.

What was on the other hand a common law development was the emergence of *equity* as an additional support in the area of remedies where the common law itself proved inadequate. In the law of property, equity became of importance in the area of land law where certain uses that were not within the traditional common law system of estates (like custody arrangements in the case of absentee landlords) became protected in respect of beneficiaries, but only in equity, even though it offered less than full proprietary status to them. Yet it protected against custodians who did not want to return the property and against

---

[34] See eg R Goode, *Commercial Law* (2nd edn, 1995), 28.
[35] See n 2 *supra*.

their alienation of the land to persons who were familiar with the arrangements. After the Statute of Uses of 1535 that sought to outlaw the protection of these uses, ways were found to strengthen them under the new name of 'trusts'. These trusts could subsequently also operate in chattels. Both, the specific estates and other equitable rights, especially future interests as developed in land law, were later introduced into the law of chattels also. They were then all considered equitable even if they did not operate behind a trust.

Equity in this sense, although based on the King's conscience (through his Chancellor in the Court of Chancery, in England, now the Chancery Division of the High Court) at first offered only incidental protection. It subsequently developed a limited set of rules in certain areas, like equitable interests in assets including trusts and future interests, assignments of proprietary rights in intangibles, client protection in agency, and equitable liens. Only in the law of trusts, bankruptcy and companies is there a fuller equity system, now mostly supported by statute. As explained in chapter I, section 1.2.8, equity is *not* a system that allows a general influx of good faith and reasonableness notions into common law. In fact, unlike modern civil law of the northern European variety, common law is on the whole averse to such an approach (although it was introduced by statute in the law of the sale of goods in Article 2 of the American UCC, see chapter II, section 1.3), even though equitable principles may also be invoked in the courts of law like the Queen's Bench Division of the High Court in London since the Judicature Acts of 1873 and 1875.

Yet in the recognition of equitable interests in chattels and intangibles the common law goes much further than the civil law good faith ever did, although in some countries of the civil law good faith is becoming more influential also in proprietary matters, but so far only at the edges, in the manner proprietary rights are excised or possibly abused: see chapter II, section 1.3.1. Thus the good faith notion remains largely confined to the law of contract or to other situations where rights are excised against others in which connection some standard of care may now be implied.

The *first* major difference with the civil law is, however, that common law distinguishes between ownership and possession (or bailment) as the only interests in chattels at law. They operate side by side and are both indivisible (for chattels, not for land). Unlike in civil law, possession of chattels is a proprietary right governed by the law of bailment (which is sometimes seen, however, as a particular form of possession of a temporary and voluntary nature only). It is often stronger than the ownership right itself, at least when the owner has voluntarily parted with physical possession. It means that at law there are no limited proprietary rights at all in chattels. This possession in the common law sense is based on the physical holding of the assets once surrendered by the owner and is not a derivative right.

Equity subsequently developed the equitable interests in chattels, which in civil law terminology could be more properly considered examples of limited proprietary interests. But as a *second* major difference with civil law they are unlimited in number and their content depends on the parties creating them, although it can be said that they all concern user, enjoyment or income rights, therefore economic interests in these assets. It shows the importance of the contractual aspect in proprietary matters in common law under which economic interests may be freely split off. Although it leads to protection for the beneficiary only in tort, this is in fact in common law no different for ownership and possession — a *third* fundamental difference with civil law — and the equitable interests should therefore be seen as no less proprietary in nature. But they can be defended only against certain types of third parties, notably against successors in the legal interests who had knowledge of the equitable ones or did not acquire the assets for value. As we shall see, these beneficial interests may therefore not be defended against all the world, but only against certain successors in interest (and the trustees themselves). They concern mainly people who knew of the relationship or acquired a legal interest for less than adequate value. Nevertheless there is here clearly a third party effect, and only *bona fide* purchasers are protected.

The result is in civil law terms a largely *open* system of proprietary rights, a *third* major difference between the common and civil law of chattels. The insistence on better rather than on absolute rights and the absence of an absolute right to the return of the assets if the underlying contract fails and is terminated, with payment of the value instead, are yet others. As just mentioned, the common law allowed proprietary rights similar to those in land to operate also in chattels, like the trust and future estates. Indeed, in a trust, common law allows the power over the asset to be legally separated from the economic interests, but equitable rights need not operate behind a trust only. In equity, different interests in time may operate side by side, like equitable interests for years and life interests. They may be joined by conditional interests and the resulting reversionary interest or remainders.

In *intangible* assets like claims, in common law the ownership notion hardly ever developed at law at all and the transfer of these rights (through assignment) was also most restricted: see section 1.7.2 below. Here again equity developed its own facilitating rules of ownership and transfer, quite different from those in chattels and real estate. The concept of trusts and future interests in chattels will be discussed in section 1.4 below. Here we are only concerned with the main lines of the law of chattels in common law.

1.3.2 *Ownership and Possession of Chattels in Common Law*

Whilst common law also operates with the notions of 'ownership' and 'possession', legally they have a meaning which is quite distinct from those of their civil law equivalents. Ownership is a weak concept in common law even for chattels, whilst it never developed for private parties in land[36] and had (at law) no meaning for intangible assets. For chattels, the common law emphasis is on possession in a physical sense, therefore quite different from civil law, where this notion is based on the wish to hold the asset as owner or beneficiary of any of the recognised proprietary rights (the *animus domini* or *possedendi*) and on control of the asset (the *corpus*) but not physical holding *per se*. Possession in this civil law sense will often be constructive and is, as we saw, in essence the manifestation of all proprietary rights and as such an important basis for their protection, and leads (if in good faith) to acquisitive prescription, in turn the easiest way to prove and defend ownership as absolute right. As a consequence, it is usually combined with ownership, whilst the asset itself may be with a mere holder. The civil law notion of possession is theoretical and conceptual. On the other hand, in common law, ownership and possession must each be seen as separate proprietary rights, at least when physical possession is separated from ownership, as it is in the case of bailment.

Thus possession is here not the mere manifestation of an underlying proprietary right but is itself a proprietary right. It is in principle physical (*seisin*) as it results from the physical handing over of an asset by the owner, which particularly happens in the case of custody, hire-purchase, lending or a pledge. They are the most common forms of bailment or possession in this sense, although there are forms of custody that are sometimes

---

[36] At least for chattels, the common and civil law notions of ownership could have developed along similar Roman law lines. For common law this was attempted early on by Bracton, *De Legibus et Consuetudinibus Regni Angliae*: see n 2 *supra*. Their original similarity derived, however, rather from the germanic concepts of '*gewere*' or 'seisin', later abandoned in civil law under Roman law influences, as we saw in s 1.2.1 *supra*.

not considered bailment, for example when representatives, employees or servants handle the owner's goods. In those cases, a form of constructive possession (for the owner) emerges even in common law.[37] As we shall see in section 1.3.5, there are some other instances of constructive possession in common law, but they are all exceptional.

Bailment results from a voluntary split between ownership and possession on the part of the owner and has therefore largely a contractual arrangement at its origin. However, it remains clear that bailment itself does not derive from contract but rather from the physical handing over of possession and confers a distinct status. In this connection, it should be realised that bailment existed long before a system of (underlying) contracts (of custody, hire etc.) properly evolved in common law and bailment may as a consequence sometimes exist even without a valid contract (for example, in the case of custody without consideration).

Bailment may be usefully compared to a delivery of assets in trust: see also section 1.4.4 below. From this analogy there may derive some special (fiduciary) duties of the bailee which are more clearly formulated in common law than those of a holder *vis-à-vis* the owner/possessor in civil law. Nevertheless, in all cases where under a contract possession in this sense is transferred, the contractual rights so created for the beneficiary acquire in civil law terminology proprietary effect, which suggests an opening up of the proprietary system even at law. The contractual position of the owner and the strong position of the possessor in such cases mean in common law, however, that the owner has often not much more than a contractual retrieval right, except when the arrangement comes to an end or is interrupted. In those cases, there may be a right to *immediate repossession*[38] which may therefore lead to another form of constructive possession in common law, but is probably better characterised as a retrieval right only. Normally the bailee has the better defence position and will also act against third parties even if he is not liable to the bailor for the loss of or damage to the asset within his duties of care.[39] The bailor can only act in respect of third parties at the end of the bailment or when he acquires a right to immediate repossession. It is true, however, that the position of the owner in modern common law is here gradually reinforced.

There is in England also a concept of '*constructive delivery*' in cases in which possession must be delivered. That is no longer important for the sale of goods in England but it remains necessary for gifts and bailments, including the creation of a pledge. Delivery of constructive possession is in those cases relevant when the goods effectively remain with another bailee. This bailee must consent to the title transfer as a matter of '*attornment*', acknowledged in Sections 28 and 29 of the Sale of Goods Act. It is an exceptional situation, and constructive delivery has only limited importance in common law, very unlike

---

[37] In civil law there would be no possession in this case at all as the possession would be imputed to the principal.
[38] Against the bailee, the owner traditionally could defend himself only on the basis of his personal contract right (of rental, hire, custody or borrowing). He had no direct action against third parties either, even against any thief of his goods under a bailee, except through the latter or if he had an *immediate right to repossession*: *United States of America and Republic of France v Dolfus Mieg & Cie SA and Bank of England* [1952] 1 All ER 572, 584. In that case he could also recover damages or repairs in respect of his goods. Even then, this was in the nature of a tort action, true revindication rights in England existing merely in connection with real estate, whilst traditionally the defendant always had the option to pay damages instead of returning the asset. Naturally any recovery of damages from a third party by a bailee in excess of his own interest in the asset was kept in constructive trust for the bailor. The right of immediate repossession is now also presumed to exist if the bailee defaults under his contract with the bailor: see *North Central Wagon and Finance Company v Graham* [1950] 1 All ER 780.
[39] See Sir Richard Henn Collins in *The Winkfield* [1900–1903] All ER 346 in 1902, confirming much older law: '[a]s between the bailee and a stranger, possession gives title — and that is not a limited interest, but absolute and complete ownership'.

in civil law. It was always less likely in the manner of the *constitutum possessorium* of Roman law, under which the seller kept the asset as holder. It became for the sale of chattels in any event irrelevant in England when the requirement of delivery lapsed in the nineteenth century: see also section 1.5.2 below. The idea of constructive delivery was also supported under the Statute of Frauds of 1677, which guarded against undocumented non-possessory interests in tangible assets. Under it possession could replace the requirement of a document, again relevant mainly in respect of goods with custodians and bailees, when constructive delivery (subject to attornment) was sufficient: see for the Statute of Frauds also chapter V, section 1.5.2.

When in common law it is stated that both ownership and possession are indivisible, it means that they cannot be cut down by contract. It is in this connection also often said that both owner and possessor have title, therefore the one has the ownership title and the other the possessory title, which is often as good if not better, although other authors use the term 'title' only in connection with ownership.[40] Ownership is in this context considered to be indefeasible. It means that it cannot be destroyed by the separation of possession. It is in this sense the stronger right, but not always the easier to defend. Possession itself cannot survive its own transfer but moves on, leaving the erstwhile possessor with no proprietary right at all, although in the case of an involuntary dispossession he may still have a strong retrieval right as being the older (erstwhile) possessor. It could be seen as yet another instance of constructive possession, but it is probably better to consider it equally as a retrieval right (in tort) which may also exist against third parties unaware of the original dispossession and who obtained the assets lawfully.[41] Even if defended on the basis of a better possessory right, it should always be borne in mind that under common law, in chattels, the defendant always had the option to pay the reasonable value instead, a discretion in England now vested in the courts.

1.3.3 Equitable Proprietary Interests in Chattels

In the common law of personal property, limited or derivative proprietary rights can only be (contractually) created in equity. Even then, it may be better not to consider them as truly split off from the ownership right itself, which only operates at law. These more limited rights have their origin in equity and operate in chattels quite independently from the legal interests of ownership and possession, although they may overlap, for example when a trust beneficiary also obtains the possession of the asset to enjoy the benefit fully. Prime examples are future interests like (sometimes) those of a buyer under a promise to sell or those under temporary or conditional title transfers, those of the original mortgagor under a chattel mortgage (the equity of redemption), and those of the beneficial interest under a trust.[42]

These equitable interests are interests freely created by the parties and as good as proprietary rights *except* that they are extinguished by a transfer of title by the legal owner or possessor to a *bona fide* purchaser for value. It was already said above that this is a trade off and allows the common law system to accept an unlimited number of equitable

---

[40] The common law terminology is not stable in this connection. R Goode, *Commercial Law* (2nd edn, 1995), 46, gives both the owner and possessor a title. S Gleeson, *Personal Property Law* (1997), 25 on the other hand, refers to title only in connection with ownership. Another difference in terminology concerns 'possession'. Some, like Professor Goode, use it interchangeably with bailment. Others like Mr Gleeson, distinguish between the two.
[41] See *Clayton v Le Roy* [1911] 2 KB 1031, and earlier Lord Mansfield in *Cooper v Chitty*, 1 Burr 20 KB (1756).
[42] See also S Worthington, *Proprietary Interests in Commercial Transactions* (1996).

proprietary rights whilst limiting their effect to those third parties that know of them. When *equitable* proprietary rights are transferred in this manner, no delivery of possession is necessary for the protection of the *bona fide* purchaser. It is required only when *possessory* rights are so transferred, which may at the same time superimpose a bailment, for example when the beneficiary obtains the use and enjoyment of certain physical assets put in trust. For Continental lawyers, it will be of further interest that this *bona fide* purchaser protection against equitable interests also applies to land and intangible assets. It is a general principle of equitable protection, all the more interesting at law there is only exceptionally such a *bona fide* purchaser protection outside this area and is then mainly derived from statute: see also section 1.5.8 below. This protection of *bona fide* purchasers with respect to equitable interests is conducive to the acceptance in principle of the operation of equitable interests in a proprietary fashion because third parties are in this manner unlikely to be seriously affected. It is the common law answer to the unbridled creation of proprietary (equitable) rights, where civil law limits them in number.

It could be said that, strictly speaking, in common law the protection of equitable proprietary interests in this manner is itself not proprietary, but rather based on the bad faith of the buyer of the legal interests and the beneficiary's (tort) action to protect his interest. Nevertheless, the result is similar to a proprietary action as it may also be brought against any successor of such interest holders if themselves aware of the equitable interest. Where it is believed that the equitable interest is in truth nothing more than the splitting off of an economic interest in the asset, which interests became in this manner protected, they may increasingly find an equivalent in civil law, for example in situations where an asset has been sold and has been paid for but has not been delivered in a system where delivery is required for title transfer. It is possible to assume in such cases that in the intervening bankruptcy of the seller, the buyer is protected in a proprietary manner. This would be equivalent to the protection of an equitable interest in common law and we could see here the notion of a constructive trust operating in civil law. In civil law terms, the protection would then be proprietary rather than in tort, but the practical difference is not great, as even in common law these (tort) actions can be maintained against a bankrupt (wrongful) title holder and are as such (in a civil law sense) more proprietary than personal in nature.

In the common law systems, the result of these equitable rights is an ownership type and division that primarily functions between the parties to the original transaction. This has led some to conclude that they are closer to a contractual arrangement, although they may be defended in tort against certain classes of third party/successors of the legal interest holder, as we saw, which is in the nature of a proprietary action. Also, as between creditors of the trustee and the beneficiary, the ownership characterisation is important, as the creditors' recovery right in the assets in the case of the bankruptcy of either party (or both) cannot be varied by bankruptcy trustees repudiating the arrangements as if they were only contractual. It is therefore best to consider the relationship between both parties (the legal and equitable owners), and therefore also between their creditors as fixed in a proprietary manner.

1.3.4   The Common Law System of Proprietary Defences: Tort Actions Based on Better Rather Than Absolute Rights

Another general feature of the common law system, already briefly mentioned above, is that the emphasis is traditionally on the types of protection of one's rights rather than on the nature of these rights themselves. It tends to be the opposite of the civil law (but not of the Roman law) approach and also applies to ownership and its protection, which in common law in the case of chattels may be weak. In proprietary matters, the common law emphasis is, as we saw, on the protection of physical possession rather than on ownership, the origin of which is in the ancient notion of *seisin*, in French *saisine* or in German *gewere*. These notions, which also obtained in continental Europe before the reception of Roman law, are derived from the old germanic or Saxon approach. In real estate, the notion of seisin eventually allowed the development of interests in land in England. They became almost as strong as ownership rights, which in the feudal system remained, strictly speaking, vested in the Crown. In the common law of personal property, where the ownership notion could have developed independently, it continued to emphasise the overriding importance of physical possession and its protection at the expense of ownership.

This possessory protection is traditionally obtained through the old actions in trespass, detinue, conversion, trover or replevin. Although these actions are tort actions, they are quite different from the modern tort of negligence or the civil law tort action, which is a purely personal action. Although in common law the negligence action may also serve to protect the affected possessor, the special feature of the old possessory torts is that in civil law terms they have a proprietary effect, as they allow the asset to be pursued in the hands of anyone with a lesser right to it (especially in detinue). In England much of this protection has now become statutory. Even so, under common law there never was an absolute right to retrieve personal property. As such there are no revindicatory actions; they exist only in land law. Thus even under the old tort action of trespass against goods, the defendant always had the option to return the monetary value of the asset instead. In England since 1854 the courts have acquired here discretion under statutory law. This discretion naturally weakens the position of the dispossessed plaintiff and of any owner (if different) in the bankruptcy of the wrongful possessor.

In this system, anyone who has voluntarily surrendered possession, including the owner, is in a weak position. Thus an owner who allows possession to arise in his asset by surrendering it to a custodian, hire purchaser or a pledgee as security — all forms of bailment — will no longer have proprietary protection against them as he has lost possession and he cannot rely on his ownership for a similar protection instead. He has in principle only a personal action under his contract with the bailee and hardly any possibility at all of reaching the transferees or one who steals from his bailee. Although it is a generic term, the concept of bailment does not necessarily operate here in a completely identical fashion in the various situations in which it arises. Nevertheless, it leaves in all instances the owner or bailor in a weak position.

Thus in the bankruptcy of the bailee, the bailor cannot simply rely on his ownership right and retrieve the asset (subject to any payments for shortened use, as would be the civil law approach), but the bailment must be unwound first in the bankruptcy. Moreover, in the case of an involuntary dispossession of the bailee, it is in essence the latter who has the right and possibility to retrieve the asset, very different therefore from the situation in civil law where (except under modern German law) the owner (and legal possessor in a civil law sense) is the more likely party to pursue the asset and protect the dispossessed holder who has a personal retrieval action against the tortfeasor only and none against the latter's successor in interest. Only at the end of the bailment when the bailor obtains a right to *immediate repossession*,[43] which he may also acquire during the bailment when its

---

[43] See *North Central Wagon and Finance Co v Graham* [1950] 1 All ER 780, and *United States of America and Republic of France v Dolfus Mieg & Cie and Bank of England* [1952] 1 All ER 572, 584. See also n 38 *supra*. See for

essential terms are violated by the bailee, may the bailor have the possibility of defending his rights against third parties directly himself. In the meantime, even when the bailee goes bankrupt, the owner/bailor may not have a true retrieval right against him or his transferees at all. Constructive trust notions might help him here, but his proprietary rights are not clear-cut. It is true, of course, that in civil law the bankruptcy trustee of a holder of the asset may also elect to continue the agreement, for example in the case of the rental of equipment until the end of the agreed period whilst offering security for payment of the rentals. But at the end of the rental, the question of the proprietary protection of the owner will arise as a separate issue in common law, which is unlikely to be the case in civil law. Custody agreements may be here a case in point. Can the bankruptcy trustee elect to continue them and what are the rights of the owners for the assets to be handed over? Similar problems may arise where a bankrupt agent has client assets in his possession.

For chattels, the emphasis in common law is thus on physical possession, more than in civil law, which looks in the first place at ownership or otherwise at possession in the more theoretical civil law sense. Where in civil law physical possession is only sometimes pivotal (as in the protection of *bona fide* purchasers), possession itself is primarily a manifestation of ownership and may also be constructive. In the Roman law triptych of ownership, possession and holdership, holdership presumes possession and possession presumes ownership. In common law it is the physical holding which presumes ownership.

In fact, in common law the concept of ownership in connection with chattels is not further developed at all and is not the core of the system; that is physical possession. The proprietary actions and defences derive from it, and in the defence of the asset the owner hardly plays a role. Whilst in civil law ownership is the fullest right, in a common law context, for chattels, the ownership notion is often seen as no more than what remains, taking into account the position of the physical possessor and the equitable interest holders.[44] There is therefore no absolute or fullest right and ownership itself is easily undermined through bailments. In civil law physical possession by third parties may also lead to strong rights but this requires good faith as to the existence of the true owner. That is the difference. One may also say that whilst in civil law there is only one owner whilst there may be many possessors, in common law there may be many owners who rank according to the strength of their ownership rights but there is likely to be only one possession. It does not mean that in common law possession based on physical holding is a better right than ownership — the possessor takes subject to this right — but technically speaking he has the more effective protection.[45] It has, however, also a weak feature in that once the physical holding of the asset is lost, it is at an end, although, if involuntarily so, still with a retrieval right based on a better right, although always subject to the plaintiff being awarded only damages.

Consequently, the following picture results. In common law, if O as owner has allowed P to take physical possession, both are considered to have a title in the property. O's title is ownership. Being the best, it is indefeasible, which means that it can survive someone else taking physical possession; P's title is possession or bailment.[46] It is subordinate to that of

---

the right to immediate repossession upon the voidness of the transfer in a sale contract induced by fraud in the USA, *Moore Equipment Co v Halferty* 980 SW 2d 578 (1998). See for the lack of protection of *bona fide* purchasers in that case n 132 *infra*. See for the failure of arguments based on ostensible ownership in those cases n 32 *supra*. See for this notion in England and the USA more particularly chapter V, nn 85 and 164.

[44] See R Goode, *Commercial Law* (2nd edn, 1995), 35 and AP Bell, *Modern Law of Personal Property* (1989), chapter 4.
[45] See for the concept of possession in common law also DR Harris, 'The Concept of Possession in English Law' in A Guest (ed), *Oxford Essays in Jurisprudence* (1961), 69 and further Bell, n 44 *supra*, chapter 3.
[46] See n 39 *supra*, although the proprietary protection of the bailor was subsequently enhanced at least when he has a right to immediate repossession: see n 34 *supra* and accompanying text.

O but protected in contract against him during the time of the bailment and is also good against anyone else, including someone who takes possession from P against the latter's will. This latter person is then the possessor but has lesser or younger rights than P, whilst both must accept that O has the best right, even if he cannot reclaim his asset from P except on contractual grounds. Being indefeasible, O's right acquires, in civil law terms, some absolute features, but without possession (if voluntarily surrendered) it is difficult to defend against third parties including the bailee or his thief.

In this system, the thief T of P is possessor (but not, strictly speaking, bailee, bailment being limited to a voluntary transfer of possession) and protected against anybody else except his victim P, who continues to have a reclaiming right.[47] That is also the position of the happy finder F of an asset of which it is clear and admitted that he is not the owner. Any third party who takes the asset from T or F involuntarily and wants to retain the assets on the basis that T or F is not the owner will be thwarted by T or F's better (older) proprietary right. Possession of this sort needs to have some *animus*, as in the case of bailees, thieves or finders, but for its protection it needs not be the will to hold for oneself as if one were the owner, therefore it needs not be the *animus domini* or *possedendi* in a civil sense. Only, under modern statutory law in England, any possessors following T or F may invoke P or O's better right (*ius tertii*) by way of defence against them and may prevail in this manner if P or O intervenes and supports them.

In civil law, it would always be possible and indeed normal for any defendant to invoke the owner's right as a defence against anyone else claiming such ownership.[48] Even in a conflict between two possessors, possessor and holder or between holder and sub-holder, the ownership concept could thus intervene. It may favour the person in *actual* possession, even if a legal possessor could claim an older right without being the owner unless the actual possessor stole the asset, when there is still a tort action for the older possessor. The traditional common law approach is not interested in any such absolute rights but rather in relative rights, although through statutory adjustment in common law there is here now some approximation.[49]

On the other hand, modern civil law is not always insensitive to the relativity concept, so much part of common law, either, as we already saw in section 1.2.5 above. Where possessors in a civil law sense defend themselves in a proprietary fashion or holders are given similar possessory actions, their right must also yield to the better possessory or holdership rights of others and in any event to that of the owner. In fact, as between various proprietary rights the principle of priority, as we saw, introduces itself a form of relativity, certainly also in civil law where there can be only one owner but several possessors and holders.

1.3.5 Constructive Possession in Common Law. The Absence of Acquisitive Prescription. Statutes of Limitation

In common law, the instances of *constructive* possession are exceptional and in fact only an expedient, used when, as in the case of the owner at the end of a bailment, a void may exist as to the reclaiming rights against third parties: see section 1.3.2 above. In this vein, it can

---

[47] Already since 1722, see *Amory v Delamirie* [1558–1774] All ER 121. The action is in tort (trespass). See also *Clayton v Le Roy* [1911] 2 KB 1031.
[48] See s 1.2.5 *supra*.
[49] Under modern English law, bailees may invoke the rights of the true owner as a defence: see Section 8(1) of the Torts (Interference with Goods) Act 1977 (the *ius tertii* of civil law: see s 1.2.5 *infra*).

Dalhuisen on International Commercial, Financial and Trade Law

also be said that the bailee who loses his possession involuntarily retains it in a constructive sense, giving him an action for recovery. In these cases it may be better not to use the term 'constructive possession' at all as it concerns here only the ability to sue for the recovery of possession. There are other cases. Thus for purposes of UK insolvency law, the lessee remains the possessor *vis-à-vis* the lessor even if the assets have been transferred to a sub-lessee, at least for purposes of any stay of proceedings, which thus also affects a head lessee without actual possession.[50] There is further a limited notion of possession without physical holdership where representatives, employees or servants manage assets, as already mentioned above.

It is clear that common law never developed a more abstract notion of possession. Common law is in this connection not concerned with acquisitive prescription either or with the procedural or evidential function of possession, which contributed much to the development of the civil law approach: see section 1.2.3 above. There are statutes of limitations in common law and actions prescribe like anywhere else (tort actions mostly in six years and others after 30 years), but that is different from the concept of acquisitive prescription by a *bona fide* acquirer who becomes owner. In civil law it is a way in which ownership is acquired but beyond that especially a procedural tool to prove ownership.

Although originally in England delivery of possession was necessary for the transfer of title in chattels, that approach is now abandoned: see section 1.5.2 below, but it is still the rule in the USA, subject to the parties' right to agree otherwise. It always means *physical* possession (see Section 2–401(2) UCC) and the concept of constructive possession was not developed in this context either. Common law clearly has had less need to distinguish between legal possession and physical holdership or between constructive and actual possession. Whether one holds for oneself or for someone else does not make any fundamental difference as far as protection goes. Neither is it necessary for the holder ever to rely for his defence on the owner, which is the traditional civil law approach. As mentioned earlier, only in modern German law did we see a similar move towards possessory protection for the holder going back to the older germanic or Saxon notion of '*gewere*'. Nevertheless this does not truly affect the role of possession within the general Roman law structure of German ownership law: see section 1.2.1 above.

1.3.6 Practical Difference between the Common and Civil Law Approaches to Proprietary Rights in Chattels

What is the practical difference that results from the different attitudes of civil and common law in the area of proprietary rights in personal property? How serious is it? Functionally there is no great difference. The real issue in the case of chattels is always the entitlement to the user, enjoyment and income rights in the asset. In either system they can be created and transferred freely but their legal manifestation and protection are distinct, and when emerging out of proprietary rights they are limited in number in civil law. The differences manifest themselves therefore in (a) the open nature of the proprietary system in common law made possible by the proprietary protection of the equitable interests that may be freely created, (b) the emphasis on physical possession in common law, (c) the defense through tort actions based on the relative strength of the proprietary, possessory or equitable rights rather than on absolute rights, and (d) the

---

[50] *Re Atlantic Computer Systems Plc* [1990] BCC 859.

lack of specific performance: the plaintiff does not have an automatic right to retrieve the asset but may have to be content with its economic value.

The most important practical difference is in the relatively weak position of the owner in the common law of chattels when he loses his possession voluntarily. It leaves him with limited powers to recover the asset, the bailee being henceforth in the driver's seat. The main effects may be seen in situations where the bailee has transferred the property to someone else without the owner's consent and in a bankruptcy of the bailee. The first case is clear but may be remedied if the owner obtains an immediate right to repossession upon a breach of contract. The relative position of the owner *vis-à-vis* the bankrupt bailee or possessor is a less regular topic of discussion in bankruptcy treatises, even in the context of the definition of the bankrupt's estate. Is the possession of the non-owner part of his bankrupt estate and what are the retrieval possibilities of the owner?

As we saw,[51] Section 436 of the UK Insolvency Act 1986, whilst defining the bankrupt's property, does not mention his possessory interests. Neither are equitable interests mentioned, but they must be included. As far as possession goes, it seems clear that even a seller under a reservation of title who surrendered possession has a weak position in the bankruptcy of his defaulting debtor and his retrieval right cannot be presumed even though he is not paid. It has been suggested that exceptionally upon a rescission of the contract in these circumstances title re-vests in the seller, but the effect in the intervening bankruptcy of the buyer remains unclear. As in the case of a failed sale agreement because of mistake or fraud, the buyer in possession could be considered the constructive trustee for the seller, and as such the seller may acquire a proprietary retrieval right as beneficiary under such a trust. At least this could be a respectable American view. Yet when there are no clear security interests or charges proper, the retrieval possibility upon bankruptcy of the possessor may be in doubt.

In the USA, under Article 9 UCC, reservations of title are treated as security interests and no longer result in a retrieval right (which under earlier law was conceded), only in a disposition and set-off of the proceeds against the debt (sales price). As far as other instances go in which possession by a bankrupt may play a role, as in the case of a bankrupt custodian, Section 541(a) of the US Bankruptcy Code 1978 includes in the estate all legal and equitable interests of the debtor. It seems to cover possession or bailment as a legal interest, always subject to the better rights of others including the owner. Whether such rights can be asserted against the trustee in the bankruptcy of the bailee may be in doubt, but property held under an expired lease must be returned: Section 541(b)(2). In the USA the position of the trustee under modern bankruptcy law has been reinforced, as he has been given the position and status of a *bona fide* purchaser, so that he is protected against equitable interests and retrieval rights in his (possessory) title. It is only to demonstrate that common law itself does not present a clear-cut system of proprietary and contractual rights and in bankruptcy the situation is likely to be less transparent than in civil law.

The other major practical difference results from the proprietary protection of equitable interests, at least against third parties who acquire the legal interest in the knowledge of the equitable rights or those who, even though they are in good faith, acquired the legal interest without paying value. At a theoretical level, it means the common law practises an open proprietary system. Also in a bailment itself, there are hints of it: where possession is surrendered pursuant to an underlying contract of custody, hire etc, these underlying

---

[51] See n 32 *supra.*

contractual rights to the user, enjoyment and income rights acquire proprietary protection. It may thus be seen that common law is generally more generous in the proprietary protection of such rights of the beneficiary, either through the equitable ownership notions or through bailment. It limits at the same time the rights of the owner and his creditors in the bankruptcy of these beneficiaries.

1.3.7 Approximation of the Common and Civil Law Systems of Proprietary Law in Chattels. User, Enjoyment and Income Rights. The Unifying Impact of Modern Financial Structures

In the previous section four major differences were mentioned between the common law and civil law concerning chattels, and it may be of interests to see whether at least at the theoretical level there is some approximation. It could be said that civil law is opening up its proprietary system, which was traditionally firmly closed, by (a) introducing conditional ownership rights, (b) (perhaps) giving (as in Germany) possessory protection also to mere holders/detentors of chattels, thereby reinforcing their position under a contract pursuant to which they acquired the asset, (c) more generously protecting economic interests (the example given was the protection of the buyer who paid but had not yet received the asset in a system that requires delivery for title transfer), and (d) adding to or varying (as we shall see in section 1.6.3 below) the preferential rights of secured and similar creditors in certain cases.

As regards the strong position of possession in a physical sense in common law, also in civil law mere physical possession sometimes gives a special protection. As we saw this is primarily so in the sense that the law everywhere respects the *status quo* and does not accept a free-for-all. Holders are therefore assumed to be possessors and possessors owners and may themselves *prima facie* defend as such (even if, in some countries, only in tort). Another point is that for proprietary rights to vest, also in civil law they must be properly identified, which in the case of chattels means properly set aside in a physical manner. In civil law physical possession is often also relevant for *bona fide* purchasers of chattels who may ignore all interests in them of which they do not know. Another instance is the right of a *bona fide* physical possessor to invoke in his protection the *ius tertii* against an older legal possessor/non-owner. Physical possession is, however, in civil law relevant only in exceptional cases, and generally possession can be constructive and is only a legal concept, even if the basis for a strong protection. In this system, the physical holding of an asset means nothing in itself (except for a *bona fide* purchaser) and first needs to be characterised in law in order to determine its significance in terms of the underlying proprietary right or contract on the basis of which it is held whilst in terms of its defence the issue of ownership, possession and holdership arises as explained above.

It should be noted that in common law in the defence of possession, the *bona fides* requirement does not play a role in this connection so that each physical holder of a chattel or bailee operates in principle with a proprietary right. In civil law there is here at best a presumption of ownership in the physical holder's favour whilst possession in the legal sense is no proprietary right at all.

The important result is nevertheless that in the case of chattels, both in common and civil law, parties in physical possession are normally protected in their user, enjoyment and income rights and operate as presumed owners, even if in common law this position may be reversed in favour of anyone with a better right, including the real owner who did not part with the property voluntarily. In civil law absolute ownership or other limited proprietary rights with revindication protection may still be asserted and also better possessory and possibly even holdership rights, except where there is a *bona fide* purchaser in the case of chattels. In this connection, there is in common law the '*nemo dat*' rule which does not allow full ownership right for a *bona fide* purchaser (not a mere *bona fide* possessor) even with physical possession, except in respect of equitable interests of others, when physical possession does not matter, or on the basis of statutory law, as in the case of the sale of goods both in England and the USA.

On the other hand, the concept of ownership is known to all legal systems and it is as such not conceivable that ownership in movable assets is in practice very different wherever these assets go (particularly important for ships, aeroplanes and cars or lorries). Yet the manner of the protection of such ownership against third parties claiming older rights or even younger more limited proprietary or contractual rights combined with (physical) possession (and also the manner of the transfer of ownership, as we shall see below in section 1.5) may still differ considerably. The key always seems to be the different role physical possession plays at the legal level.

However, if one shifts the emphasis from physical possession to private user, enjoyment and income rights, one may see a move in the direction of stronger protection of these economic interests everywhere and the concern about them may become tantamount to ownership concerns in a more legal sense, as happened earlier in English land law in the various estates in land, based on actual possession or seisin (although in the case of land divisible in time, which in common law could originally only be achieved for chattels through a bailment, later joined by equitable interests). The concept of protected possession in this sense of use, enjoyment and income of the assets seems to be the *ultimate key* to proprietary protection subject, of course, to the better rights of others. This seems to be closer to the present day common law system, especially in the development of equitable proprietary rights. As we saw, in civil law this protection of user, enjoyment and income rights is so far only achieved for the *bona fide* (physical) possessor of chattels who may, at the same time, as owner ignore *all* other user, enjoyment or income rights in them of others. On the other hand, in case law economic interests may also increasingly be defended through tort actions. One could see here convergence with common law, especially if the tort action in civil law could be used in these cases against third parties. As we saw in common law, these economic interests may also be expressed in equitable interests in a (limited) proprietary sense, again protected through (extended) tort actions (like all proprietary interests in common law on the basis of a better right, even against third parties).

There is here in common law definitely some greater and useful flexibility in the creation of proprietary rights, if only in equity. The introduction of proprietary protection for both parties in a conditional transfer mentioned above, like in the reservation of title, and which will be discussed more fully in section 1.6.3 below,[52] also in connection with finance leasing, repo financing and factoring, may in civil law open up the proprietary system in a similar way and may even lead to trust-like structures. This is an important development and a further example of convergence. It confirms a shift, even in civil law, to a greater contractualisation of the proprietary notions and the interests that may be so created,[53] and here again it

---

[52] See also chapter V, n 70 and for arguments in favour of a much more open system, JH Dalhuisen, 'European Private Law: Moving from a Closed to an Open System of Proprietary Rights', (2001) 5 *Edinburgh LR*, 1. See for proposals for a more fundamental modernisation of Dutch property law (concerning chattels and intangible assets), JH Dalhuisen, *Zekerheid in roerende zaken en rechten* [Security in Chattels and Intangible Assets], *Preadvies Vereeninging' Handelsrecht* (2003). See also s 1.1.4 *supra in fine*.

[53] See for German legal writing on this development in connection with trust-like structures, W Wiegand, 'Die Entwicklung des Sachenrechts im Verhältnis zum Schuldrecht,' [1990] *AcP* 190, 131*ff*. and his reference to the '*Obligatorisierung der dingliche Rechte*' or the 'contractualisation of proprietary rights'.

would not be unreasonable to expect another move in the direction of the common law, which would also indicate an extended *bona fide* purchaser protection. Commercial practice requires it. It is as yet unclear how far in civil law countries the objective law will yield and define more material criteria for proprietary protection of the new interests and also for the protection of *bona fide* third party successors in these interests, even if they concern assets other than chattels. This is the true key to the necessary opening up of the system of proprietary rights in civil law.

A modern civil law would also have to develop a more adequate protection method in terms of beneficial interests and fiduciary duties of the interest holders or trustees and of court intervention adequately to protect the beneficiaries. The concept that a split ownership may require extra court protections in this connection and an organisational structure is less well understood in civil law. Often the need is not greater than segregation and partition of these interests when constructive trust notions may suffice. That is notably the case of client assets held by custodians, especially if fungible and mixed with assets of other clients or even of the intermediary itself.

Segregation can also be achieved through company structures which may even in common law countries compete here with more formal trust structures, eg when special purpose vehicles are being set up or open-ended collective investment schemes or funds are organised. Foundations might also be used. Sometimes a contractual separation may be sufficient. The point is here that common law offers more choice in business transactions, which will ultimately also appeal to civil law practicitioners. For the purposes of this book, private or family trust are less important and probably a very different world. It is not certain that there is a great need for these vehicles in civil law that has another patrimonial culture between the older and younger generation. Moreover, the abuse often made of these family vehicles by trustees who may be very difficult to control does not recommend them except in a judicial environment in which judges are activitist and very willing to intervene on a provisional basis through injunctive relief, not itself a strong feature of the traditional civil law.

The approximation in proprietary structures between common and civil law may become more visible in international commerce as dual ownership structures start to emerge in the international capital markets. The existence of separate funds with a purpose, as *Sondervermögen* or *Treugut* became known in germanic law, has been noted earlier, and they are still alive particularly in Germany and Switzerland.[54] In France, in recent years there have been proposals (now stalled) to introduce a *fiducia* concept in this connection by statute (Article 2061 Cc): see more in particular section 1.4.5 below. In the meantime, the concept of the trust has also gained some favour in countries like Italy and the Netherlands that recognise foreign trusts pursuant to the 1985 Hague Convention on the Law Applicable to Trusts and their Recognition. They may even include assets in the recognising country: see also section 1.4 below.

On the other hand, the lack of conceptual clarity in common law as to the meaning of ownership and the overriding impact of the physical aspect of possession often give the law in this area an uncertain bias. Together with the lack of a clear division between proprietary and obligatory rights, it results in the position of the owner or equitable interest holders without physical possession being complicated and frequently unclear in the bankruptcy of the physical possessor or in situations in which the latter is depossessed by third parties. Also the law of segregation or constructive trust, tracking or tracing of client assets, although all notions well known in principle, may in practice not always be as clear in result as one might wish. Typical of equity law, much may depend on the circumstances

---

[54] See H Coing, *Die Treuhand kraft privaten Rechtsgeschäfts* (Beck, Munich, 1973) and s 1.4.5 *infra*.

and whether assets are still physically retrievable or on the extent they are. Thus here again, much is left to the exact facts of the case. It is the ultimate demonstration that, legally, the property concept in connection with chattels is still not fully stabilised in common law, even if one must accept that intellectual concepts can never fully cover day-to-day realities, not in civil law either and the greater flexibility shown in the law of equity can be valuable.

In section 1.1.4 above, reference was already made to the new developments which derive from the dynamic requirements of modern financial law as part of the new commercial law or international law merchant or *lex mercatoria*. It accelerates within that law the above signaled trends and develops new proprietary rights which in common law are more easily recognisable in 'equity'. The *lex mercatoria* serves here as a conduit whilst modern financial dealings have created the dynamic environment in which this acceleration takes place and in which it becomes indispensible. It introduces more broadly an open, albeit fractured system, of proprietary rights in which for each financial structure these rights are likely to be individually determined.

Thus, like in Article 2A UCC in the US there are likely to be special proprietary protections for equipment lessees as defined in that Article. For payments in Artcicle 4A UCC, there may be anticipated a special system of credit transfers and relevant transfer methods (or instructions). Like in Article 8 UCC special proprietary rights may be identified for security account or entitlement holders which amount largely to a segregation right *vis-à-vis* their intermediary but not to a pass through right in respect of the underlying securities. Again the mode of transfer of these rights is specific and can not be characterised in terms of either a traditional assignment or novation. In Article 9 UCC, the entire law of modern floating charges is recast in a singular manner that has nothing much to do with a unitary proprietary system even if there are many echos of more traditional equity law. It is nevertheless internationally pace-setting. As far as this fractured system of proprietary rights is concerned, it may also be recalled that even in Article 2 UCC on the sale of goods, the title transfer is treated as an Article 2 subject, it being ignored in as much as possible in favour of the concept of a transfer of risk.

Indeed risk and risk management is at the heart of these new proprietary concepts, particularly relevant in the context of financial dealings. It is not therefore surprising that they receive an ever greater attention in that context, that they operate in a special manner per financial structure and that approximation between civil and common law is most relevant and urgent in this area, even if it requires the special (and more limited) conduit of the *lex mercatoria* to achieve it. Thus only international or transnational law and its acceptance and recognition of general principles and custom is likely to further it as an expression of the autonomous and spontaneous law creating force of the international economic and financial legal order. Under it, trusts, beneficial ownerships, conditional and temporary transfers, bulk transfers and assignments even of future rights, floating charges including replacement assets, security entitlements and the way they can be used for financing, payments through credit transfers, finance leases, repos, all kind of forms of factoring and securitisations, should be foremost accepted as international structures that operate under their own transnational law and that leave domestic laws well behind. It is for us to articulate the applicable rules on the basis of the internationally established or developing practices in the context of the *lex mercatoria* and to accept for the time being that this cannot be done on the basis of a unitary, intellectually coherent system of proprietary rights in the traditional civil law manner. Nor is it in truth important. The prime question is what works and meets best the requirements on international finance for all concerned?

1.4 Trusts, Constructive Trusts, Tracking and Tracing. Agency. The Civil Law Response

1.4.1 *The Basic Features of the Common Law of Trust*

The obvious example of equitable proprietary rights in common law is provided by the trust. In a trust in its simplest form, there is a three party arrangement under which a settlor transfers assets to a trustee for the benefit of certain beneficiaries. The beneficiaries have no direct access to these assets, which are held and managed by the trustee and distributed by the latter to the beneficiaries in the manner set out in the trust deed. Under common law, both trustee and beneficiaries have proprietary rights in the trust assets which operate side by side, the one in law, the other in equity, both conveyed or granted by the settlor. These proprietary rights of the trustee and the beneficiaries are not seen as directly connected or dependent for their continued existence on the settlor or on each other, and were originally enforceable in different courts (the courts of law and the courts of equity). The right of the beneficiary is therefore not commonly considered split off from that of the trustee as legal owner, eventually being reintegrated in his ownership as a limited proprietary right or *ius in re aliena* in civil law terms would be (in this sense the civil law usufruct is perhaps most closely related). In common law the idea is that the beneficiaries have an altogether separate set of rights, proprietary and obligatory or fiduciary under the trust.

The trust concept has always caused confusion in the minds of civil law lawyers, unnecessarily so it would seem. It is often said that the split in the ownership structure, which is at the heart of the common law of trust with its legal and equitable owners, is unfamiliar to civil law thinking. Civil law is, however, entirely familiar with limited proprietary right: see also section 1.2.1 above. One of them, the usufruct, can be easily structured in a trust-like fashion when conveying a benefit for a number of years. It is sometimes seen as a temporary ownership right (*cf* Article 3. 85 new Dutch Civil Code). Through conditional ownership rights, even if remaining underdeveloped in civil law (but see also section 1.6.1 below), similar splits in ownership may be achieved more informally. In any event, also in civil law there are trust-like structures, even if they are more incidental. Often the *fideicommissum* of Roman law and its *fiducia* are thought to be closely related. As a consequence, there should be little place for civil lawyers' bafflement in matters of trusts.

The *fideicommis* of Roman law allowed a person to leave his property (by will) to heirs or legatees and impose on them a duty subsequently to dispose of the property through transfer or by will in a certain indicated manner. Thus one could leave certain property to a spouse with the obligation on her to leave it subsequently to the children and any testamentary dispositions by her to the contrary would then normally be considered void. The result was a limited ownership in the spouse that amounted to the right to take the fruits and income for life only.

In civil law countries these facilities often survive: see for example Section 2100 BGB in Germany. It creates forms of suspended interests or ownership and it may even lead to perpetuities. Other elaborate testamentary structures may also lead to situations more closely related to common law trusts, like in Germany the appointment of a testamentary executor (*Testamentsvollstrecker*) to watch over this arrangement. He is sometimes said to have a mandate *without* representation. That means that he is not an agent and the property he manages is not therefore part of his estate, even if held in his own name. This position is not dissimilar to that of a common law trustee in a testamentary trust. Also the new Dutch Civil Code accepts a similar structure (Article 4. 1066), but the emphasis is on management and the ownership is with the beneficiary even if it may be immobilised in respect of him and he cannot manage or dispose. Guardianships over minors are closely related, at least under German law,[55] and also lead as a minimum to a split between the ownership and disposal rights in the assets.

In other countries, notably the Netherlands (see Title 3.7 CC in respect of owners who create themselves separate management structures in their assets, which Title remained unwritten and is now abandoned), the law has not been able to formulate broader structures and concepts of this nature, exactly because they are deemed to be against the system. Civil law traditionally puts extreme emphasis on the name in which the assets are held and it does not like to recognise beneficiary ownership types except themselves taking the form of a limited proprietary right like the usufruct or possibly conditional ownership. The consequence is that these beneficial ownership rights commonly only have contractual status and can only be defended as such. This suggests at the same time that there is no proper segregation of the assets and those creditors of the legal owner have access to these goods.

In business, this creates special problems in fund management, custodial arrangements and nominee accounts, when separate company structures or foundations may have to be used. Contractually created preferences or priorities (short of security interests), in French called priviliges, may sometimes also help and may be more easily created or recognised in case law. In some countries, the difficulties led to special statutory intervention to achieve sufficient segregation for these types of activities. The segregation issue remains problematic in all civil law countries and also shows itself in undisclosed or indirect agency, assignments of trade receivables for collection purposes, in transfers of any other assets for management purposes, including investment management, in client accounts held in the intermediaries name, and in partnerships without legal personality. Again special statutes may try to deal with the situation especially the segregation issue upon a bankruptcy of the intermediary. Modern custodial arrangements for investment securities organised through book entry systems may thus by statute acquire sufficient segregation and introduce in that connection the notion of joint ownership of the beneficiaries. The traditional example is here Euroclear, which, however, may also be said to operate rather on the basis of market practice, see for greater detail section 3.1.4 below.

On the other hand, the Roman law *fiducia* had provided a somewhat broader framework covering various forms of custody, with split rights, although with a lesser proprietary protection for the beneficiaries than possible through the *fideicommis*.[56] In Germany, there is as a survivor the *fiduziarische Treuhand*, as we shall see. It is a structure that more generally compares to the modern trust, but again it is now mostly seen as a purely contractual arrangement and is therefore in its generality less developed, although modern statutory forms of it may be more pronounced, but they are again incidental. This remains the basic civil law position and is certainly also the drift of modern Dutch law (Article 3. 84(3) CC) which superseded the earlier much more friendly case law disposition towards it, see also chapter V, section 1.2.2. Even in Roman and old German law, which have both been claimed to be at the origin of the trust in a common law sense — a view abandoned in modern times[57] — the *fideicommis* and this type of *fiducia (cum amico)* only presented special solutions. Where these structures continue to exist in civil law, it is the same and they are mostly connected with testamentary dispositions, custodial situations, indirect

---

[55] See also Fratcher, 6 *Int Enc Comp Law* (1973), chapter 11, ss 127–28.

[56] Both the *fideicommis* and the *fiducia* were mentioned by Gaius, the latter in two forms: the *fiducia cum creditore* and the *fiducia cum amico*: see respectively Inst I, 248 and 260 and II, 60.

[57] See R Helmholtz and R Zimmermann (eds), *Itinera Fiduciae, Trust and Treuhand in Historical Perspective* (Berlin, 1998).

agencies, or otherwise with charitable foundations or the legal personality of public institutions. In the latter case they go well beyond what common law trusts mean to be as they are never legal persons in that sense.

More generally, it has long been recognised, however, that where persons gather money from the public for charitable purposes or from a group of people with a special objective, which may even be commercial, this money does not belong to the persons having collected it. Everywhere it must be set aside (as *Sondervermögen*) and is separated from the estates of those who collected it. Its distribution is governed by the professed purpose for which the money was collected. As such, these funds may have *no* owner in the typical civil law sense at all. It would seem the only way to satisfactorily deal with this situation. As soon as beneficiaries are determined by name, they acquire a proprietary interest in the collections, but even that does not necessarily give them the property rights in all the moneys collected or so set aside. It is clear on the other hand that the gatherers only have management and investment duties corresponding with the professed purposes of the funds. Yet they may make disposals, always within the advertised purpose for which the fund was set up. As such they behave at least externally as owners. These relationships are in civil law typically not further developed and civil law remains here rudimentary in what is in essence a trust. In the meantime, in common law the trust concept fully evolved as an independent structure and overarching *unitary* concept since at least the nineteenth century — with much older and also much more incidental earlier roots. The law concerning it is of major significance both in a business and family context.[58] The segregation is the key and uncontroversial.

Civil law may conceptually come close to the common law trust not only in charitable collections, however, but also in the conditional sale, which, in enlightened modern civil law thought, leads no less to suspended ownership rights and a duality in ownership between both parties to the transaction. One party has here an ownership right under a resolutive condition and the other under a suspensive condition.[59] The most obvious example is in the reservation of title, but there are many more: see section 1.6 below. It is not only the separateness of the fund but also this duality in ownership which counts in trusts, where trustees and beneficiaries have split ownership rights which may go beyond the limited ownership rights civil law commonly allows. In trust structures these split ownership rights are less likely to be of a conditional nature but they may be temporary, that is for a number of years only. Common law is more advanced in the acceptance of future or suspended interests which (at least in England) are equitable rights if created in personal property. They now often operate behind a trust but may be well distinguished from trust structures, also in common law. Conceptually there is therefore room in civil law for the notion of a split ownership but it remains a rudimentary concept. It results in segregation, however, but it notably misses the trust infrastructure in terms of management through trustees and also the tools to remedy any abuses.

As just mentioned, in civil law, trust-like needs especially emerged in charitable collections, testamentary dispositions concerning minors with suspended interests, in investment management, custodial arrangements and client accounts, and in indirect agencies where an agent operates in his own name for the account and risks of his client. Only the latter are of interest here. In all, it is best to view the client as the owner of the assets which

---

[58] In Germany, the Lawyers' Association (*Juristentag*) discussed a general *Treuhand* law giving beneficiaries a proprietary right at its meetings in 1912 and 1930, but no further attempts were made to develop a unitary trust concept in Germany.

[59] See also JH Dalhuisen, 'Conditional Sales and Modern Financial Products' in A Hartkamp *et al* (eds), *Towards a European Civil Code* (2nd edn, 1998), 525.

the manager/custodian or indirect agent holds or acquires for him (even in his own name), as indeed is mostly the case in custodial arrangements and undisclosed agencies of common law. The alternative in common law is a constructive trust, although it gives the client lesser rights, an issue for indirect agency discussed more extensively in chapter II, section 3.1.6. Even in civil law, these assets do not properly belong to the estate of the custodian or agent, although civil law has no proper means of expressing this in a more general manner or through a more general legal structure. Hence statutory law that must here often come to the rescue.

The foregoing suggests four essential points in connection with trusts or trust-like structures, both in common and civil law: (a) a fund or certain assets are unilaterally set aside for certain purposes which determine how they are to be treated for a time which may exceed the life of trustees, (b) there is a management structure,[60] which, unlike in contract, may leave considerable discretion to the managers (trustees) and cannot be eliminated by contract[61] but is subject to the courts having the right to remove trustees and to a system of fidiuciary duties,[62] (c) the assets do not belong outright to the managers, are segregated and not rightgfully part of their estate,[63] and (d) this is underpinned by a duality of ownership or at least by a split in the proprietary disposition rights between the managers and beneficiaries. Neither is the sole owner. Only together do they have full ownership rights but may not even then be able to make disposals as they please as the giver of the moneys or provider of the assets or the settlor in a trust may have intended these moneys or assets to be used or treated in a specific way, at least for some time. The managers or trustees will be duty bound to deal with them accordingly. The consequence is not only that these moneys or trust funds do not form part of the manager/trustee's estate but also not of the beneficiaries' estate (except for allocated benefits). They have no joint ownership of the goods either.

The separation of property in this sense does in common law *not* lead to legal personality of the trust. In this sense, the trust should be clearly distinguished from corporate entities or other legal entities in civil law, even if the charitable trust is much like a foundation in civil law, but it remains different in that it still lacks legal personality. This is an important issue. The consequence is that trustees are in the first instance always personally liable for all they do in the trust. Only if they act within their allotted powers are they released from liability and may recover their costs from the trust. This is precisely the opposite for directors/administrators of legal entities. Their actions are in principle attributed to the legal entity, and only if they demonstrably exceed their powers or ignore their duties may they be personally liable for their actions. What is therefore normal for trustees is exceptional for directors.

The 1985 Hague Convention on the Law Applicable to Trusts and on their Recognition attempts some sort of definition of trusts or similar structures (in common and civil law). It covers 'legal relationships created — *inter vivos* or on death — by a person, the settlor, when assets have been placed under the control of a trustee for the benefit of a beneficiary

---

[60] This is the idea of the 'patrimony plus office', see GL Gretton, 'Trusts without Equity', (2000), 49 *ICLQ* 599, 618.

[61] See D Hayton, 'The Irreducible Core Content of Trusteeship' in AJ Oakley (ed), *Trends in Contemporary Trust Law* (Oxford 1996), 47.

[62] See on this development and its draw backs also R Cooter and BJ Freedman, 'The Fiduciary Relationship: Its Economic Character and legal Consequences', (1991), 66 *NYUL Rev* 1045 and FH Easterbrook and DR Fischel, 'Contracts and Fiduciary Duty', (1993) 36 *Journal of Law and Economics*, 425.

[63] Asset partitioning is indeed seen as the most important commercial function of trusts by H Hansmann and R Kraakman, 'The Essential Role of Organisational Law', (2000), 110 *Yale LJ* 387. They note the the partitioning may be less perfect in trusts than in companies, because there may not be much physical separation of property in trusts which complicates the segregation.

or for a certain purpose'. There is here *no* limitation *per se* to the common law trust. Specific characteristics are that the assets constitute a separate fund and are not part of the trustee's own estate. Although the title to the trust assets stands in the name of the trustee, he has the power and duty to manage, employ or dispose of the assets in accordance with the terms of the trust and the special duties imposed upon him by law. This suggests some duality of ownership. He is accountable for the exercise of his powers and the performance of his duties.

The Principles of European Trust Law (Article I), see section 1.4.6 below, are more elaborate in this respect. They also concentrate on the settlor transferring assets to a trustee with the intention that they shall not form part of the latter's estate but are held for the benefit of the beneficiaries. These beneficiaries have personal or proprietary remedies against the trustees or even third parties to whom part of the trust fund has been wrongly transferred. In the very nature of definitions of a phenomenon of this sort, they all tend to be incomplete and therefore only partially satisfactory, but the idea is clear.

Abuse by trustees has always been endemic, especially in family trusts. As a consequence, in common law, a large array of *fiduciary duties* of trustees was built up by the courts to deal with it and the courts' equitable powers have always been used to the full to protect beneficiaries. The key duties are those of loyalty, care and confidentiality. The duty of loyalty in particular requires the trustee to postpone his own interest and not to compete with the trust fund for the better opportunities. The fact that these duties and powers do not to the same extent exist in civil law may be another reason why, besides structural and fitting-in difficulties, trust-like structures were never encouraged in civil law. In civil law, these duties can only now be more extensively developed within the modern notion of good faith, here used beyond its normal contractual sense. Even then, civil law courts are not used to the same kind of activist intervention as the common law courts of equity are in a preliminary or final manner through injunctions and similar relief, especially relevant in this area of trusts. As we saw in chapter II, section 3.1.4, similar problems of abuse have bedeviled indirect agency in civil law where these types of agents have often been prone to ignore their clients' vital interests and compete with them for the best deals. Fiduciary duties and activist judges are vital aspects of the law of trust and agency and are central to this part of the law in common law countries, but are not (yet) so in civil law.

It is clear that in common law, there is a detailed regime for trusts which still has no obvious parallel in civil law, whether or not the concept itself is now recognised and practiced. In particular, in common law, the transfer in trust has a distinct legal character. It is notably *not* the same as a sale giving the trustee and the beneficiary a contractual right to delivery (although in the case of real estate, a sales contract in land by itself transfers an equitable interest in the realty). It is *not* considered a contractual transaction at all and can exist without consideration. It is unilateral and cannot (in principle) be undone in the manner of a contract by agreement of all concerned. As already mentioned, both trustees and beneficiaries have proprietary rights against the settlor and third parties upon the establishment of the trust. The recovery rights of the beneficiaries against the trustee are often considered *in personam*, however, therefore rather contractual or more properly fiduciary in nature. They are not primarily proprietary, although as regards the creditors of the trustees there is a clear split in a proprietary sense (and recovery possibilities) and there is strictly speaking no direct obligatory bond between the trustees and the beneficiaries. It is possible to say, however, that the personal rights of the beneficiaries against the trustees were subsequently allowed to attach to the trust fund itself and gained as such proprietary status.

As regards third party effect, in common law, the rights of the trustee in the trust fund are protected at law as ownership, but there can be little doubt that the beneficiaries have proprietary protection rights against third parties also, which are therefore of a non-obligatory nature. However, they are strictly speaking not rights against all the world. Rather they are rights that can only be exercised against a more limited number of third parties. They are (a) the trustee (although the relationship with him could still be seen as personal or obligatory, but as just mentioned there is no direct bond between them), (b) his creditors and (c) transferees from the trustee who acquired his title with knowledge of the beneficial interests or did not pay good value. They are nevertheless rights maintainable against (some) third parties and in that sense clearly proprietary. In other words these rights can be maintained against others than the settlor and trustees. Only *bona fide* third parties that acquire trust assets from the trustee may ignore these beneficial interests. As we saw in section 1.3.3 above, this is the traditional way common law protects third parties against an unbridled proliferation of equitable proprietary rights. That does *not* make them less 'proprietary'. Also in civil law nobody would deny ownership rights because they may be undermined by *bona fide* purchases. It only means that third parties are better protected against the effect of unknown proprietary rights including equitable rights in the assets they acquire.

The separate existence of trust funds in this manner means that they are protected not only against the creditors of the trustee but also against those of the beneficiaries, except for the benefits themselves as defined in the trust deed. In the USA, in so-called spendthrift trusts, the beneficiary cannot even freely dispose of his benefit, which is then also shielded from his creditors. Whatever the additional terms, the key is that the trust assets themselves cannot be reached by either type of creditor whilst the trustee's legal rights under the trust can only be transferred subject to those of the beneficiary (except to *bona fide* purchasers for value). The beneficiary's own equitable rights under the trust can be freely transferred by him (without the trustee's consent), but not more than he has under the trust deed and applicable law. In the main, the beneficiary will be entitled to some future income stream, but he may also have the actual enjoyment and use of certain assets of which he will then acquire (equitable) possession. He may transfer these income rights (through assignment plus surrender) and also his possession to third parties that receive them, however, subject to the beneficiary's limitations in them. In common law, there is no *bona fide* purchaser protection here. There may be, strictly speaking, no bailment either, as the beneficiary holds the benefit in his own (equitable) right.[64]

Trusts, except if set up for charitable purposes, have a limited duration. This is not of importance for identified beneficiaries who are alive, but under the rule against perpetuities, *future* benefits under a trust must vest within a period of no more than a life in being plus 21 years. The same goes for all sequences of equitable future (or non-vested) interests. The life in being need not be specified and can be among a class of persons, for example all the descendants of George V or Franklin D Roosevelt living at the time of the creation of the trust (although in England that is no longer possible and 'lives in being' must now be drawn from a narrow group of people directly connected with the trust, like the settlor, certain beneficiaries or parents or grandparents of them or persons with an interest prior to the non-vested interest in question). The duration of the trust for vesting purposes is then the life of the longest survivor plus 21 years. In many states of the USA and as an option in England, a fixed number of years has by statute replaced the rule against perpetuities.

Although the trust is normally tri-partite between settlor, trustee and beneficiaries, the settlor may convert himself into a trustee of his own assets for the benefit of others.

---

[64] See for the relationship between trust and bailment s 1.4.4 *infra*.

The trustee and the beneficiary may in principle not be the same person. In that case, the legal and beneficial interests join so that the trust implodes. However, under modern law it may be possible for a settlor to create as trust in favour of himself as one of several beneficiaries and manage it as a trustee as long as the separateness of the trust fund itself is respected.

1.4.2   The Practical Significance of Trusts in Common Law Countries

Trusts are of immense practical significance in common law countries, to such an extent that they are in these countries a cultural phenomenon of which there is a general awareness not only amongst the legal class and the better off. They appear either formally or constructively all the time and may be used to create all kinds of beneficial interests. In England, the management of assets and the passing of property between generations were the traditional motive. Another point was the position of minors. In the absence of well developed rules on guardianship and given the uncertainty concerning parental rights of management, trusts were the obviuos vehicle for the management of the estate of minors if of some value. In modern times tax and business considerations will be no less important in the use of trust structures.

In business, the segregation issue will be dominant also in common law countries but may also be achieved informally through the emergence of constructive trusts. They may play a decisive role in client accounts, fund management and custody, and undisclosed agency. The common law flexibility presents here a great advantage over the civil law concern with systematic thinking. This being said, in business even in common law countries the alternatives of companies and contractual arrangements are also practiced, depending on the needs of the situation. It is mainly in these tax and business areas that the (constructive) trust alternative is also of interest for civil law countries, foremost to obtain segregation.[65] It may well be that in this connection the acceptance of the notion of constructive trust is more important than that of formal trusts. That type of segregation cannot be achieved by contract alone. [66]

Where special trust statutes exist, especially in jurisdictions that only have a limited common law tradition such as South Africa, Scotland and Quebec, the concept may be more rigid and less all-encompassing. This is, however, not always so and it would, for example, not seem to have affected the trust concept in the Channel Islands. Apart from the uses already mentioned, trusts are often also used to circumvent debilitating legal restrictions and thus acquire a facilitating function. In this vein, trusts are not only useful to manage tax liabilities but may also allow mortgage replacements under which the legal interest is transferred to a trust company for the benefit of a bank. This may avoid cumbersome and costly registration duties. Debtors may even transform themselves into trustees of their assets to hold them on trust for their creditors. It is a more flexible security arrangement, although in the USA in the case of personal property this structure is now converted into a security interest subject to the formalities of Article 9 UCC. They remain, however, important in the USA as mortgage substitutes. When covering a whole business

---

[65] See for these commercial uses also S Worthington, 'The Commercial Utility of the Trust Vehicle' in D J Hayton (ed), *Extending the Boundaries of Trusts and Similar Ring-Fenced Funds* (Kluwer, London, 2002) 135–62, see also HLE Verhagen, 'Ownership Based Fund Management in the Netherlands', in D J Hayton (ed), *Extending the Boundaries of Trusts and Similar Ring-Fenced Funds* (Kluwer, London, 2002), and D Hayton, 'The Development of the Trust Concept in Civil Law Jurisdictions', (2000) 8 *Journal of International Trust and Corporate Planning* 159, 178, J Langbein, 'The Secret Life of the Trust: The Trust as an Instrument of Commerce', (1997) 107 *Yale LJ* 165.
[66] This is often overlooked by those who believe that contract can achieve the same as trusts, see also JH Langbein, 'The Contractarian Basis of the Law of Trusts', (1995), 105 *Yale LJ* 625.

or a multiplicity of changing assets, trusts are often called indentures and may equally serve as security interests supporting a debt or debenture.

In deceased's estate planning, trusts play traditionally an important role and they are often of crucial importance as they allow a testator in testamentary trusts to make all kinds of arrangements for his heirs or legatees which may afford them additional protection as trusts may deprive the beneficiaries of an actual say and thereby keep the asset from the reach of their creditors (except for their immediate benefits). The trust may also include the heirs of the settlor in the beneficiary class in order to avoid the payment of estate duties upon the death of the settlor. The transfer in trust itself may, however, attract gift tax.

There are many other conceivable uses of the trust. It may be very useful where it replaces partnership or joint venture arrangements as it creates a different ownership and management structure, which may prove more neutral, although the intervention of trustees, who must be paid for their services, may be costly. It may even acquire the shape of a company in which the trust *res* functions as the capital, the trustees as the board and the beneficiaries as shareholders. It was not uncommon in the USA and combating these combines gave rise to the term anti-trust laws. Again, it is the flexibility that counts and the unitary legal concept that now prevails in common law whatever the use made of trusts, of which there is no equivalent in civil law.

1.4.3   Constructive Trusts, Tracking and Tracing, Resulting Trusts, Statutory Trusts and Charitable Trusts

The *constructive* trust is a much less formal structure. It results from the objective law (not normally statute under which, however, there may be further trusts of this nature) and is often closely associated with the unjust enrichment notion. It means that it is usually imposed on the parties regardless of their intent. In England, it is often considered to follow automatically in certain circumstances; it suggests a more institutional approach. In the USA there may be greater discretion for the judge and there is a close connection with the judicial granting of equitable liens; it suggests a more remedial approach. But again in all cases it is the segregation that it entails, confirms or brings that is the key. It is of great value in business and in common law countries particualrly operative in respect of client accounts or other client assets, relevant therefore in particular in the fund management and custody functions. It implies the facility of the beneficiary to track these assets and physically to recover them.

At least in common law countries other than England, the constructive trust tends to be remedial in this sense, rather than institutional, although a constructive trust may still arise as a substitute for the trust proper. In the remedial sense, the constructive trust is the formula through which the conscience of equity finds expression, especially in the USA.[67] It is there seen primarily as a means by which courts order defendants to relinquish property the retention of which would lead to their unjust enrichment. It results in an order to surrender the property and creates therefore a proprietary retrieval right, not normally obtainable under an unjust enrichment action. It shows the temporary nature of this type of trust where the analogy with the institutional trust ends. The remedial function arises particularly when title in an asset results in someone who should not have it, for example after rescission of a contract for mistake when there is voidable title. In that case, the erstwhile buyer may be considered a constructive trustee held to return the

---

[67] See Justice Cardozo in *Beatty v Guggenheim Exploration Co*, 225 NY 380, 386 (1919).

asset to the seller, although a similar result could be obtained by avoiding the transaction and returning the asset on that basis. The rescission itself is, however, an equitable remedy, leaving some discretion to the judge in the implementation of the remedy and the notion of constructive trust. The return of the asset is not automatic. As just mentioned, in England the constructive trust notion can be remedial also, as when an asset has been sold but the title transfer is delayed.

The application of constructive trust principles is therefore mostly incidental but the constructive trust arises all the time. Thus the thief and his successors may be seen as constructive trustees for the true owner pending the return of the property, which, as in the case of fraud, will normally be ordered. It should be realised that in common law even the thief may be seen as legal owner *vis-à-vis* all, subject only to the better right of the person from whom he stole the asset. In countries that use the notion of the constructive trust more liberally, like the US, there is here a difference between adverse possession (at law) and constructive trust (in equity) but they seem not always to be clearly distinguished and may supplement each other. The equitable principle includes fiduciary duties whilst handling the asset even during periods of adverse possession, which could also amount to bailment: see for the relationship between both section 1.4.4 below. An element of overlap arises as the adverse possessor (even the thief) acquires at the same time features of a trustee. Another example of a constructive trustee may be an agent who holds the assets he acquired for his principal as constructive trustee whilst the principal is the true owner at law. Technically there seems here to be some confusion of concepts as the beneficiary under the constructive trust is already the true owner at law (as in the case of a theft), but pending confirmation of this status, the assets are held in trust by the wrongful legal owner for the rightful owner, who has therefore also an equitable ownership which is as such protected.

A trustee who wrongly converts trust property will hold the replacement asset as constructive trustee for the trust. Here we have the beginnings of the concept of the *floating charge* in equity under which an equitable security interest automatically shifts into replacement goods and proceeds. These floating charges may even result from security interests or conditional sales created at law, like the reservation of title upon conversion of the asset. In the USA under Article 9 UCC, this concept has been reaffirmed and extended by statute (see for replacement goods, when it must be agreed, Section 9-204 (new and old) and for proceeds when it is automatic, Section 9-315(a)(1) (9-306(2) old) UCC).

It is called *tracing* in England. Elsewhere tracing and constructive trust are more closely related and the one often presumes the other. Tracing then acquires a broader meaning and allows the beneficiary under a constructive trust to follow his original interest into the hands of any third party who is not entitled to it. As this does not concern converted assets, probably the term tracking is better. All kinds of fiduciaries may thus be held responsible for assets they control but which effectively belong to others, either outright or as beneficiaries, and these goods may as such be tracked in equity. This is especially important if a remedy at law fails. That is also true in the shift of charges into replacement assets, but there are many other instances of tracing, especially in the USA.

Obviously, the notions of constructive trust, tracking and tracing are most acute in bankruptcy. There is no general theory in common law suggesting a clear approach, however, except perhaps for tracing under floating charges, and bankruptcy courts have always been reluctant to broaden the concepts. In bankruptcy they could easily take away what little there is otherwise left for unsecured creditors. Nevertheless, in urgent cases, the concepts of constructive trust, tracking and tracing remain potent, also in bankruptcy, and especially in the USA, the courts allow new preferences or charges to arise, or correct, perfect or substitute old charges when such is just and equitable, but only in extreme cases and reluctantly. As already mentioned, the term 'equitable lien' is also used in this connection and is closely related.

All constructive trust or tracing rights (but by no means all traking rights (which may also arise as a sequal to ordinary property rights) are equitable (even if deriving from legal rights) and are therefore all subject to *bona fide* purchaser protection. Thus any security interest in assets held by a constructive trustee and given by him for value to third parties who had no notice of the equitable interest prevails over the equitable owner.[68] This situation is the same as in an ordinary trust. Naturally there is also the problem of co-mingling with the constructive trustee's own assets.[69]

A *resulting* trust should be clearly distinguished from a constructive trust and is created if a transfer without adequate consideration is made whilst there is no intention to make a clear gift. The transferor is then presumed to have had the intention himself to become the beneficiary. Other instances of a resulting trust may arise where an express trust fails in whole or in part. The distinctive feature is that the presumed intent of the parties is given effect, but where a resulting trust is imposed by law as it sometimes is in England, there may be no appreciable difference from a constructive trust.

There are also *statutory* trusts of which the bankrupt estate is the prime example.

Charitable trusts are very similar to foundations in civil law and may under applicable law be unlimited in time. A practical difference is that the creator of a foundation normally retains power to vary the terms of the foundation, which would require a special power (of appointment) in trusts. If charitable trusts lose their objective when the charitable cause disappears, the objective may usually be varied by the courts to the nearest alternative. This may be more difficult in foundations. Another major difference is that charitable trusts have no legal personality and are in that sense not separate from the trustees.

1.4.4 Trust and Agency; Trust and Bailment

It is sometimes said that *agency* is to services what trusts are to goods. It means that in providing services, for example the purchase of goods for others, the agent has a responsibility in rendering this service whilst the beneficiaries are his principals or clients. Accordingly, the agent is under a fiduciary duty to them to do whatever is required under the agency agreement and under objective law to complete the transaction in a proper manner and postpone his own interests, much as a trustee has to do in respect of a trust fund. Different types of agents may have further duties in this respect, like security brokers, even if acting in their own name albeit for the risk and account of their clients, or commercial and collecting agents. In common law, brokers must obtain best prices for their clients and may not compete with them for business. The assets acquired are in the meantime held for the clients (as owners) in constructive trust to shield them and preserve them for their clients in brokers' bankruptcies. So where ownership rights become involved, agency and trusts naturally come together and agents become constructive trustees pending the assertion of full ownership rights by their clients if they do not acquire it directly under agency rules. Being a beneficary or an owner makes an important difference for the principal, however, in terms of his protection. As legal owner he must (in principle) respect any transfer by the

[68] See eg *Department of Natural Resources v Benjamin*, 40 Colo App 520, 587 P 2d 1207 (1976).
[69] See, for some incongruous results DMW Waters, 'The English Constructive Trust: A Look into the Future', (1966)19 *Van der Bilt LR* 1215.

agent to third parties. As beneficiary he may ignore them unless the third parties were bona fide purchasers for value.

Trusts and bailments also have overlaps.[70] When goods are stored with third parties and kept in their names, there could result either a (constructive) trust or a bailment. If there is a bailment, the bailee could still be agent at the same time. In any event, even in bailment, there may be fiduciary duties very akin to those of a trustee. Again, there could be an important difference in the protection of *bona fide* purchasers in these cases. If they acquire the assets for value, they may ignore the trust or agency and any beneficiaries (the original or true owners) of whom they had no knowledge. Tracking would be impossible. A pure bailor, on the other hand, has an interest at law, which results in a better title that cannot be ignored by his *bona fide* purchasers (except if there is a statutory rule to the effect as there commonly is in sale of goods statutes in common law). If there is an agency at the same time, however, there may be a constructive trust also. Constructive trusts may also operate in replacement assets in a converted bailment, in that case subject to the better rights of *bona fide* purchasers. In practice, courts may opt for a pragmatic approach and equalise the results of bailment and constructive trust in these circumstances.

1.4.5   Related Civil Law Structures

It was already mentioned in section 1.4.1 above, that also in civil law the idea of certain funds being set aside for certain purposes and therefore not belonging to the person holding them is well known. The best example is the proceeds of charitable collections. In statutory form, trusts may exist as testamentary structures, as we saw for Germany. The suspended or dual ownership rights that flow from them are in those cases accepted, at least in embryo. These dual rights are now better known in some other situations, especially in reservations of title or situations of a *fiducia cum creditore* or finance sale, which may all be considered to result in some forms of conditional sales and transfers. In modern financial arrangements, these conditional sales play an important role, also in civil law, as will be discussed more extensively in section 1.6 below. The duality of ownership is thus also known, at least in principle, in all legal systems, even if in civil law again not treated as a unitary concept or structure, especially not in the proprietary effect for both parties. In custody and agency there are needs for separation of assets even if held in the name of the custodian or agent implying also a duality or conditional ownership in them, if not an outright ownership of the client. In modern client accounts, if sufficiently segregated, again the question of joint ownership of the assets by the clients arises or of a constructive trust of the account holder in his favour pending distribution. So it is in fundmanagement, custody and in partnership forms without legal personality.

In legal commentaries trust like structures are becoming better known, also in civil law. Especially in Germany, the testamentary trust and the *fiduziarische Treuhand* have received particular attention in this connection, the latter mostly still being considered a contractual device only, which makes a vital difference in the bankruptcy of the *Treuhänder* or trustee handling the assets.[71] Special applications of the concept may be found in client

---

[70] See also U Venema, *Law en Equity* (Zwolle, Antwerp, 1990), 214 and R Goode, *Commercial Law*, (2nd edn, 1995), 258.

[71] See for an overview, S Grundmann, 'The Evolution of Trust and *Treuhand* in the 20th Century' in R Helmholtz and R Zimmermann (eds), *Itinera Fiduciae, Trust and Treuhand in Historical Perspective*, (Berlin, 1998), 469. See also S Grundmann, *Der Treuhandvertrag* (1997) and H Koetz, 'National Report for Germany' in DJ Hayton, SCJJ Kortmann and HLE Verhagen, *Principles of European Trust Law* (1999), 85.

and custody accounts, in investment management and indirect agency, where statute may, however, have reinforced the proprietary rights of the beneficiaries. The best example may be in the *Kapitalanlagegesellschaftgesetz* of 1970 aiming at better protection of investors against their investment managers or brokers.[72] In Germany, the security transfer or *Sicherungsübereignung* is often also mentioned as an example of a *fiducia cum creditore* as is the *Sicherungszession* for receivables. As just mentioned, they are, like a reservation of title, more likely to have features of a conditional sale and transfer but are now mostly considered a security interest only. The charitable trust or *Stiftung*, also often mentioned in this connection, is a legal person and has therefore fewer trust-like features.

We may review these structures in the light of the most obvious aspects of the common law trusts identified before: (a) the separation of the estate of the trustee and the trust, (b) the duality of ownership between trustee and beneficiaries, (c) the primary liability of the trustee for his actions in connection with the trust property and the absence of legal personality, (d) the fiduciary duties, (e) the non-contractual nature of the transfer in trust which also allows for constructive trusts, and (f) the management structure that the trust entails. In civil law, the greatest weakness remains in the lack of segregation and in the consequential lack of protection of the trust assets in the case of the bankruptcy of a *Treuhänder* and in the lack of refinement in the fiduciary duties. At least in Germany, the first shortcoming could perhaps be overcome by a more extensive application of the regime of the *Testamentsvollstrecker*.[73] As for fiduciary duties, some writers have concluded that a much fuller regime already operates today in Germany.[74] It would not bring constructive trust notions and segregation on that bais which in business is perhaps the more urgent concern.

In France and Italy, the situation is even less developed. The discussion often stops with the general observation that split ownership structures do not exist in these countries, but there is more perceptive and flexible modern thinking. In France it has led to renewed interest in the *fiducia* or *fiducie*.[75] To create a securities transfer it was always possible and practices particularly for receivables, see also chapter V, section 1.3.5 but a project dating from 1992 to generally recognise it has so far not been implemented (Articles 2062ff CC), mainly it is said because of the unclear tax implications. Even though it meant to result in segregated property (*patrimoine d'affectation*), it was to be created by contract and could not result from a unilateral act.

Especially the ratification of the Hague Convention by Italy may lead in that country to the acceptance of foreign trusts created to hold Italian assets.[76] This may also be the

---

[72] See for other incidental statutory examples more in particular Grundmann, n 71 *supra*, 28ff.

[73] See Koetz, n 71 *supra*, 109. Creditors of the trustee aware of the arrangement are generally thought not to be able to recover from the trust assets. Earlier the German Supreme Court had already held that they were not entitled to a windfall: RGZ 45, 80 (1900), but it later changed its mind and drew a distinction between assets coming from a settlor and those coming from third parties, the latter being no longer protected: RGZ 84, 214 (1914). Newer case law is, however, more generous when the creditors are or ought to have been aware of the arrangement: BGH [1954] NJW 190. Many authors have gone back to the earlier windfall avoiding rule: see H Coing, *The Treuhand kraft privaten Rechtsgeschäfts* (1973), 178 and Grundmann, n 71 *supra*, 315.

[74] See Grundmann, n 71 *supra*, 478ff.

[75] See especially C Grimaldi, La Fiducie: reflexions sur l'institution et l'avant-projet qui la consacre, Repertoire Defrenois 1991.897.

[76] See for France P Remy, 'National Report for France' in DJ Hayton, SCJJ Kortmann and HLE Verhagen, *Principles of European Trust Law* (1999), 131 and for Italy, M Lupoi and T Arrigo in *ibid*, 123. In France, the French Revolution meant to base all social structures on equality and consequently the law of 14 Nov 1792 abolished all feudal rights including the restrictions (*inter vivos and mortis causa*) on the disposal of property rights. Family settlements became suspect whilst interstate heirs (depending on their degree) could not be deprived from a slice of the inheritence (the *reserve heriditaire*). Thus the *fideicommis* was curtailed. On the other hand, the *fiducia* was not abolished.

situation in the Netherlands, where as we saw in section 1.4.1. The *fiducia* has been outlawed under its new Code, thus eliminating and important support for the trust concept. In Switzerland, the environment has long been more congenial but legally no more certain.[77] In Scotland, the split ownership concept inherent in trusts is not recognised. Neither is the separation between law and equity and the rights of the beneficiaries are habitually characterised as *in personam* or obligatory. The beneficiary is, however, protected on the basis of a separation of the trust assets to which the personal creditors of the trustee cannot lay claim.[78]

Constructive trusts and tracing as remedies in the context of unjust enrichment and of secured transactions upon conversion of the assets into replacement goods and proceeds do not appear as general concepts in civil law either. Through contract, in Germany a reservation of title or security interest can be extended into replacement assets: see more in particular chapter V, section 1.4.1 but new Dutch law is much more reticent, see chapter V, section 1.2.2 and the creation of new preferences in this manner is discouraged.

1.4.6   Private International Treaty Law and Trust Law Principles

At the more theoretical level, serious problems arise in modern civil law especially in the area of dual, conditional or temporary ownership rights and their protection. The duality that may result in the ownership concept, as particularly demonstrated in the modern reservation of title as a purchase price protection and in modern forms of financing like finance leases, repurchase agreements and factoring of receivables, and its consequences will be discussed more fully below in section 1.6. They are also present in trust structures, which are therefore also difficult to place in civil law. The key is the status of trust assets in a bankruptcy of the trustee. In this aspect, more sophisticated civil law countries like Germany and Scotland seem to have developed workable solutions in case law. The other practical aspect is in the fiduciary duties, which are a necessary sequel to all trust law. Here again, there is no easy civil law replacement, although it may be found in modern notions of good faith, in this connection extended outside contract law proper. Tracing and constructive trusts are other legal facilities not easily incorporated into civil law either.

The acceptance of the trust concept through treaty law (in terms of recognition of foreign trusts), is now possible under the 1985 Hague Convention on the Law Applicable to Trusts and their Recognition, ratified also by some civil law countries like Italy and the Netherlands, besides the UK (also for Jersey, Guernsey, the Isle of Man, Gibraltar, Bermuda, the British Virgin Islands, the Turks and Caicos Islands), Canada (but not for Toronto and

---

[77] See AE von Overbeck, 'National Report for Switzerland' in *ibid*, 105.
[78] On the other hand if the trust goes bankrupt, beneficiaries are entitled only to the residual assets in a distribution. See for Scotland recently, KGC Reid, 'National Report for Scotland' in *ibid*, 67, and G Gretton, 'Scotland: The Evolution of the Trusts in a Semi-Civilian System' in Helmholtz and Zimmermann (eds), *Itinera Fiduciae, Trust and Treuhand in Historical Perspective* (Berlin, 1998), 507.

Interestingly, Gretton cites the law of Quebec (Article 1261 Civil Code) in this connection: '[t]he trust property, consisting of the property transferred, constitutes a patrimony by appropriation, autonomous and distinct from that of the settlor, trustee or beneficiary, and in which none of them has any real right'. It comes close to the concept of separation and legal personality of which Gretton approves (at 508 n 7). It makes the discussion of beneficiaries' proprietary or personal rights in the assets irrelevant.

It should be noted in this connection also that in European Court Case C–294/92 *Webb v Webb* [1994] ECR I–1717 in which a father claimed a constructive trust in real estate of a son in France, this was not considered a real estate matter to be decided by French courts under the exclusive jurisdiction provisions of Article 16 of the Brussels Convention on Jurisdiction and the Enforcement of Judgments in Civil and Commercial Matters of 1968 (as amended). It left open the question whether there was here an issue concerning a proprietary right or merely an obligatory right of the father.

Quebec), Australia, Hong Kong and Malta. France, Luxembourg and the USA are so far only signatories. The Convention itself will be more fully discussed below in section 1.8. It covers express trusts and similar structures and its definition is therefore wide enough also to cover similar civil law arrangements if voluntarily created and evidenced in writing (Articles 2 and 3), therefore not constructive trust and tracing facilities.

For the application of the Convention, not only its definitional structure, briefly discussed in section 1.4.1 above, and the exceptions, are of importance but also the rules of international jurisdiction. They derive in Europe from the 1968 Brussels and the 1988 Lugano Conventions on Jurisdiction and the Enforcement of Judgments in Civil and Commercial Matters. These two treaties cover together the recognition and execution of civil and commercial judgments in most countries of Western Europe (with the exception of legal capacity, arbitration and bankruptcy related matters). They provide in that context common jurisdictional standards. Articles 17(4), 5(6) and 2 are important for trusts. Article 17 allows an election of jurisdiction by the parties in the trust instrument in any proceedings against a settlor, trustee or beneficiary, if relations between these persons or their rights or obligations under the trust are involved. In the absence of such an election, a settlor, trustee or beneficiary must be sued in the State in which the trust is domiciled (Article 5(6)). This is, at least in the UK, the State with which the trust has its closest and most real connections, but under Article 2 they may also be sued in their capacity of settlor, trustee or beneficiary in a Contracting State of which they are habitually resident.[79] In this manner the competent court acquires also jurisdiction over the trust which is not a separate entity.

This is not without problems. If a foreign trust recognised in a EU member state has a trustee there, whilst others may reside elsewhere, that resident trustee may be sued in the relevant EU country e.g. to account and provide other relevant information. If trustees are delinquent in their duties, a replacement could be demanded before the competent court in the EU country concerned. This may well be problematic as these courts will not have the tradition of acting as equity judges, may not have the power to issue injunctions, and may be generally reluctant to get involved as a common law court (of equity) would. They might even suggest that parties go to the court of the country under the law of which the trust operates. Even though the concept of forum non-conveniens is not well known in civil law countries, it may amount to a similar thing in these circumstances, even if in the country of the applicable law there may not be any settlor, trustee, or beneficiary.

That is indeed likely to be the case when the law of small Channel or Caribbean Islands is chosen. In that case the jurisdiction would also be exorbitant, based only upon a provision in local laws that jurisdiction attaches to the applicable law (which is for trust law not uncommon). In any event, in the absence of execution treaties with such countries, any decision is unlikely to be recognised elsewhere. It is also likely to create great delays and extra costs. It shows the danger in recognising foreign trusts and allowing them to operate without adequate powers and experience in the courts of the recognising country to deal with them.

One of the most important aspects of the Trust Convention is that it may serve as a catalyst in the development of the trust in civil law to the extent that civil law countries ratify it, which Italy and the Netherlands have done, even if it only means to recognise foreign trusts. At least in Italy, it seems to allow Italians to bring their Italian assets into foreign trusts that would be recognised in Italy. A similar facility may now exist in

---

[79] See for these jurisdictional aspects also n 244 *infra* and accompanying text.

the Netherlands.[80] Domestically, trust structures are increasingly accepted in civil law countries, as we saw, especially in inheritance matters but now also in custody and in the holding of client assets and moneys in indirect agencies.[81]

The Principles of European Trust Law were in the meantime developed at Nymwegen University.[82] They contain eight Articles, subdivided into a number of subclauses and summarise the essence of trust law without getting into great detail. As such they are greatly instructive, to the point, and seem to provide more direction than the European and Unidroit Principles of Contract Law, which are too detailed and elaborate, perhaps even contentious, as we saw in chapter II, section 1.6. The Trust Principles may provide the better approach and model for future efforts of this nature.

Article I defines the main characteristics. It establishes the ownership of the trustee, the segregation of the trust assets, the duty of the trustee to deal with these assets for the benefit of others (the beneficiaries) of whom the trustee may be one, the ownership rights of the beneficiaries, and the immunity of these assets from claims on the trustee, notably by his personal creditors. Subject to the terms of the trust, a beneficiary can make a disposition of his benefit and may seek enforcement of the terms of the trust (Article IV (4) and (5)).

In order to create the trust, the settlor must transfer the trust assets to the trustee with the intention of creating a segregated trust fund, although he may himself become the trustee by making this clear (Article II). He must be specific in his designation of the beneficiaries or must designate purposes. Excess trust assets are for the settlor or his successors (Article IV). The trust fund not only consists of the original assets and those subsequently added but also of the replacement assets. Except to the extent that the trust was created to contravene the laws protecting the settlor's creditors (spouse or heirs), only creditors (including beneficiaries) dealing with the trustee in his capacity as such may recover from the trust assets (Article III).

Beneficiaries have a right to information to protect their interest and the trustee must account to them (Article IV(3)). The trustee must exercise his rights as owner in accordance with the terms of the trust, must take reasonable care of the trust assets, keep them separate and protect them, maintain accurate accounts, act in the best interests of the beneficiaries and honestly, and avoid all conflicts of interests. He must personally make good any loss occasioned by his breach of trust and personally augment the trust fund by the amount of any profits made by him in such breach (Article V).

Courts may restrain trustees or remove them for breach of trust and order compensation. They may also declare particular assets of the trustee trust assets or regard them as security for satisfying his liability (Article VI). Third parties who obtain trust assets and are not protected as *bona fide* purchasers (including their successors who are not *bona fide* either) must make good the loss to the trust or may be ordered to hold the assets (or those into which they are converted) as part of the trust fund, therefore separate from their private patrimony (Article VII).

---

[80] It earlier tried to turn the tide against splits in ownership in its domestic law in Article 3.84(3) of the new CC: see more in particular chapter V, s 1.2.3. Ratification of the Hague Convention would more logically have to be accompanied by the creation of a similar facility in domestic law. Only France has been considering this. In the Netherlands, the legislator wanted more experience with the recognition regime first. The key will be the activist role of Dutch courts in respect of the operations of foreign trusts in the Netherlands, including the formulation and enforcement of the fiduciary duties of the (Dutch or foreign) trustees in such trusts.

[81] See chapter II, s 3.1.6.

[82] See D Hayton, 'The Developing European Dimension of Trust Law' [1999] *King's College L J* 48; M Lupoi, 'Trusts and Civilian Categories' in R Helmholtz and R Zimmermann (eds), *Itinera Fiduciae, Trust and Treuhand in Historical Perspective* (Berlin, 1998), 497 and Hayton, Kortmann and Verhagen, n 71 *supra*.

Beneficiaries may terminate the trust and distribute the trust fund between them, the terms of the trust notwithstanding, provided they are unanimous, have capacity and all interests are vested. The trust also terminates if all funds are distributed, if there are no beneficiaries or potential beneficiaries left, by virtue of the exercise of a power of termination, or upon the end of the permitted period of the trust when the trust fund must be distributed as soon as practicable in accordance with the terms of the trust. If there are excess funds they must be held for the benefit of the settlor or his successors (Article VIII).

1.5 The Transfer of Proprietary Rights in Chattels

1.5.1 *The Legal Requirements for a Transfer of Chattels*

Ever since the Roman jurist Gaius (Institutes 2.20), it is said that for a valid voluntary transfer of chattels there needs to be (a) a *disposition right* in the transferor (normally ownership), (b) a *valid cause* (normally a sales contract, gift or exchange), and (c) an *act of transfer* (delivery or contract). In this connection one may also refer to power, intent and formalities. A further requirement is often stated to be sufficient *identification* of the asset to be transferred.[83] It will have to be considered in this connection also to what extent the asset must physically exist in order for it to be legally transferable.

It is efficient first to explain the formalities, especially the requirement of delivery in some countries. Thereafter we will turn to the requirement of identification and existence, then to capacity, then to the contract, and finally to the disposition right. The last normally derives from ownership and it should be clearly distinguished from capacity. Capacity goes to the heart of both the validity of the contract and of the delivery (if considered a juridical or legal act as is likely to be the case in countries requiring it as a condition for the transfer of ownership). Yet even though capacity and disposition right must be clearly distinguished, they may sometimes be closely related in the sense that lack of capacity earlier in the chain of transfers may affect the ownership and therefore the disposition rights of a seller. In that sense both are connected. So may invalidity of a sales contract for other reasons earlier in the chain of transfers be connected with the disposition right.

The discussion will be particularly addressed from the perspective of failure of any of these requirements for a valid transfer and its effect on the buyer if already in the physical possession of the asset, especially if a chattel. May he keep it, or must he return it and, in the latter case, is the return of title automatic or does it require a separate act of retransfer? If so, it is unlikely to lead to the retrieval of the asset in the case of the intervening bankruptcy of the buyer. Here the importance of *bona fide* purchasers and acquisitive prescription also comes in. In civil law, the *bona fide* purchaser of chattels is mosty protected against the defects earlier in the chain but not normally against invalidity of his own purchase agreement and acquisition (through delivery, wherever required) for whatever reason. In civil law, only acquisitive prescription, which in the case of chattels could, however, be immediate could achieve this. If the purchaser was not *bona fide* as to the causes of the failure of his own purchase contract only, statutes of limitation would help. Only the latter relief is available in common law whether or not there was *bona fides*. It may take much longer.

---

[83] R Goode, *Commercial Law* (2nd ed. 1995), 55. It is deemed implicit also in laws that do not require delivery for the transfer of title, like the laws of England and France: see also J Ghestin and B Desche, *Traité des Contrats, La Vente* (1990) No 544, see also Article 1129 Cc.

Transfer of ownership is the prime objective of sales agreements, although it can also be achieved through exchange or barter. Succession is another way of acquiring property, as are acquisitive prescription in civil law and *bona fide* purchases under certain circumstances. We shall be concerned here mainly with sales of goods of physical movable assets (chattels). They provide the normal way of transferring ownership but *bona fide* acquisition is closely related. Whether title has effectively passed as a consequence of either of them is for the applicable law to decide. This will normally be the *lex situs* of the asset.

In connection with the ownership transfer, the word 'title' is often used, but it should be realised from the outset that it may be used here in different ways. In civil law, title is in this connection mostly considered the underlying sales contract whilst in common law it is the ownership that is being transferred. Here we shall use the English terminology so that 'title' refers to the proprietary right that is transferred. Title may sometimes also mean the document giving rise to enforcement action. In the present context, transfer of title means transfer of ownership.

1.5.2   The Formalities of a Sale: Contract or Delivery; Double Sales

The formalities of the transfer of ownership in chattels may concern the sales agreement itself and any additional requirements. The sales agreement concerning chattels may be informal and needs no writing (except in common law where a deed is required when there is no consideration, an unlikely event in a sale).[84] Any formalities that we need to be concerned about in this connection relate therefore to any specific requirements of the transfer of title. They mainly concern the requirement of delivery of the asset to complete the ownership transfer. There are four possibilities here.

The main distinction is between the law of countries that require delivery and those that do not for the transfer of title in chattels. Germany (Section 929 first sentence BGB), Switzerland, Austria, the Nordic countries, the Netherlands (Article 3.84(1) CC), and Spain are in the first category and all require an act of delivery for the passing of title in chattels. The law in these countries uses in this connection the notion of delivery of possession, which is more theoretical and allows this possession and its transfer to be constructive. This largely follows Roman law, which, however, in sales also required payment, as we shall see shortly.[85]

England (Sections 17 and 18 of the Sale of Goods Act 1979), France (Articles 711, 1138 and 1583 Cc),[86] Belgium, Luxembourg, Italy (Article 1376 CC), and Poland are in the second category and do not require it. The civil law countries in this category follow here the teachings of Grotius and Pufendorf from the natural law school, who started to deviate from the Roman law model in this aspect and found the transfer of ownership upon the mere conclusion of the sales contract more natural. Common law required delivery for title transfer in chattels well into the nineteenth century and case law in England only

---

[84] See for the Statute of Frauds requirements and its remnants in common law and for the requirements of Article 1341 Cc in France, more in particular chapter II, s 1.2.10. See for the remnants in the creation of security interests in the USA, Section 9-203(b)(3)(C) (9-203(1)(a) old) UCC.

[85] Inst 2.1.41: see also R Feenstra, *Reclame en Revindicatie* [Reclaiming Right and Revindication] (Dissertation, Amsterdam, 1949), 11*ff.*, and more recently R Zimmermann, *The Law of Obligations* (South Africa/Deventer/Boston, 1992), 273. The question whether credit was extended and whether this could be done indirectly by not insisting on payment became a much-discussed point in medieval law, most authors requiring an express credit agreement.

[86] According to Article 711 Cc property transfers '*par l'effet des obligations*' and according to Article 1583 '*dès qu'on a convenu de la chose et du prix*'.

started to change towards the end of it. This was eventually reflected in the first Sale of Goods Act of 1893, but parties may still decide otherwise. Thus the idea of delivery for title transfer in chattels is not as alien to common law as it would now often appear. In fact, in the USA there is still a preference for the old delivery rule. The UCC confirms this and states that the moment of transfer of title in chattels upon a sale is still (physical) delivery except if parties agree otherwise (Section 2-401).[87]

The situation in England and France, although very similar on its face, is not exactly the same. In common law, parties are entirely free in the manner and timing of the transfer. Only if they do not make a choice in their contract, does statutory law decide for them with a different result in England and the USA. Contractual freedom is here the basis. That is not so in France where there is, strictly speaking, no possibility of creating proprietary rights in private and parties cannot decide the modalities of the ownership transfer. The *Code civil* (Articles 1138 and 1583) determines here that it is normally at the time the contract of sale is concluded (provided the assets sold are sufficiently specific which raises the question of the transfer of title in future or generic goods). Parties may by common agreement postpone this moment to a later date by including a time limit or a condition. They could even choose the moment of delivery or of the payment of the price, as common in a reservation of title. This is a statutory exception, however, and there is a mandatory regime of title transfer in all civil law countries, whether they require delivery for title transfer or not.

As a consequence of this mandatory statutory legal regime, one finds in sales agreements under civil law normally little said on title transfer. In common law, on the other hand, title transfer figures as an important part of a sales agreement and will be elaborated by the parties. Common law is here in essence directory or dispositive. The consequence is therefore that in the approach which transfers title at the moment of the conclusion of the contract (in principle) there are still two different attitudes that should be clearly distinguished: the French and English approaches.[88] The latter is freer.[89] It also affects the types of proprietary interests that can be created, which in common law are not restricted by a *numerus clausus* but are subject to a much better *bona fide* purchaser protection in the case of equitable interests, as was already discussed in section 1.3.1 above.

This makes in fact for three approaches: the German, French and English ones. The fourth type of law in this area is the old Roman law, which for title transfer in chattels

---

[87] The UCC states, however, expressly in its Comment that it does not want to focus on the title transfer and seems to consider it secondary in a sale of goods. It is true that in practice, the passing of risk is often a more important issue and this can also be determined by the parties in the contract. Nevertheless, the question of title cannot be completely ignored, especially in the case of the bankruptcy of the seller who has not yet delivered or of a buyer in possession who has not yet paid.

[88] U Drobnig, '*Transfer of Property*' in A Hartkamp et al (eds), *Towards a European Civil Code* (Ars Aequi Libri, Nijmegen/Dordrecht, 1994), 345 does not make this distinction and sees as a consequence only two systems operating, one transferring title by virtue of the sales contract, the other upon delivery, so also M Waelbroeck, *Le transfert de la propriété dans la vente d'objets mobiliers corporels en droit comparé* (Dissertation, Brussels, 1961). In the view of this author it does not sufficiently reflect the different attitude towards the creation of *in rem* rights in countries like France and in the common law.

[89] In the common law approach parties may thus fundamentally opt for the moment, place and other modalities of title transfer and the nature of the proprietary right created, which choice may, however, sometimes be deemed implied, as in the Fob term in England, when full title is assumed to pass at the ship's rail: see *Carlos Federspiel & Co SA v Charles Twigg & Co Ltd* [1957] 1 Lloyd's Rep 240. In the case of a reservation of title it is deemed to be postponed until payment. Only in the absence of such an explicit or implicit determination by the parties, is there, at least in England, the objective law rule which fixes (full) title transfer in the case of a sale of chattels at the time of the conclusion of the contract. Thus under traditional common law the sole *intention* of the parties prevails as regards the time, method, nature and extent of the title transfer, only failing at the moment of the conclusion of the sales contract as of which full title is considered transferred.

through a sale required not only delivery but also payment. It still prevails in South Africa. It is not as curious as it may seem, as a similar result is obtained through a reservation of title, which postpones title transfer until payment. In this sense the Roman law system included a reservation of title in all sales agreements, which parties could, however, agree to disregard in their contract. In the USA, until the advent of the UCC, cash sales were also thought to be completed only upon payment. The UCC now gives a brief reclamation right instead, which is proprietary and also obtains in a buyer's bankruptcy (Section 2-702).

In systems that require delivery for title transfer, the delivery itself should be considered a legal act. That is in civil law indeed largely the attitude.[90] In this approach, *delivery* is a two-step structure. It implies the conclusion of a further legal agreement followed by the *factual* delivery of the asset or the actual handing over (unless it is already with the buyer or remains with the seller when there is constructive delivery which may itself be seen as the legal act). It means that there is a need for acceptance of delivery of this type and for capacity of both parties. In Germany as we shall see in section 1.5.6 below, this additional agreement is referred to as the *dingliche Einigung*, earlier called the *dinglicher Vertrag* by von Savigny who first formulated this approach.[91] It is important, however, not to apply the precise requirements of contract law to this type of agreement but rather the general rules concerning bilateral juridical acts which may be found in the general Part of the German BGB.

Although a distinction must be made between countries that require delivery for title transfer in chattels and those that do not, it must be stated that in both systems there are exceptions. Where normally delivery is necessary, as in Germany and the Netherlands, there are traditionally three situations where it is not required and they all come from Roman law. If ownership is meant to be transferred but the erstwhile owner reserves for himself some contractual user rights in the asset, for example a rental, therefore converts himself in civil law terms from an owner/possessor into a holder, it is not necessary for him first to hand over the asset to the buyer in order for it subsequently to be given back. The result is that in such cases the ownership transfers upon the mere agreement of the parties. This is the transfer *constituto possessorio* (Section 930 BGB). It is sometimes said in countries that follow the French system that does not require delivery that under this system all transfers are by statute *constituto possessorio* so that also the French system is based on the notion of delivery. It is not immediately clear what is gained by this insight.[92]

---

[90] Although title transfer was in England originally also achieved through the physical act of delivery and the receiver had to have some intention to receive the asset, it was done without the Roman law distinction of possession and holdership and the protections behind it, even though the Roman law *traditio* requirement with *animus possedendi* was at one time seen as compatible with this system. See in the 13th century, Bracton, *De Legibus et Consuetudinibus Regni Angliae*, f 38 b, (ed Woodbine, Yale 1922), ii, and (ed Twiss, (with English translation 1878), i, 305). This line was not pursued and the voluntary physical handing over of the asset remained the key to the system and resulted in either the transfer of full title or the creation of a bailment: see W Blackstone, *Commentaries on the Law of England* (1756), 452.

[91] 3 *System des heutigen römischen Rechts* (Berlin, 1840), Par 140 and 2 *Obligationenrecht* (Berlin 1853), 256*ff*. One may well ask whether in a system like that of the UCC where in the absence of a contractual provision to the contrary title also only passes upon delivery, Section 2-401(2), it is not then also a juridical act, although Section 2-401(2) insists on physical delivery. The importance is in the need for acceptance and capacity of the parties. The (independent) status of the juridical act itself may become an issue if the underlying contract fails, as we shall see s 1.5.6 *infra*. It is not an issue commonly discussed in common law, however. The insistence on physical delivery shows that the act of delivery itself is not a common law concern nor is the possibility that it might be constructive. Constructive delivery is only considered in connection with transfers to bailees or when goods are under a bailee in the context of attornment: see s 1.3.5 *supra*.

[92] In the continental tradition, if delivery is implied, it means an additional legal act which is itself subject to the requirements of capacity, legality etc. It allows for the idea of an *Einigung* and for a more abstract system of title transfer, even in France: see also s 1.5.6 *infra*.

Another situation, where in countries that require delivery it can be done by the mere agreement, is when the asset is already with the buyer who thus converts himself from holder into possessor/owner. That is the *traditio brevi manu* (which in Germany does not require any delivery of constructive possession as a further legal act as, in the German concept of possession, the buyer already has it: see section 1.2.1 above and Section 929 second sentence BGB). Finally, there is the *traditio longa manu* under which an asset that is under the control of a third party, for example in a warehouse, is transferred (Section 931 BGB). It may be seen as a variation of the *constitutum possessorium* as the third party is here only the holder for the seller whilst title transfers by him becoming the holder for the buyer (which in the *constitutum possessorium* applies to the seller himself). This change is achieved by the mere agreement of which the warehouse will be told. It is conceivable that such information is itself a constructive element of the transfer which is delayed until such time.

In these three cases there is *constructive* delivery only. Of course also in systems that do not require delivery these situations may arise, but they do not then solicit special attention because title will have passed upon the conclusion of the agreement anyway, unless delayed by agreement. There is, however, a special aspect in common law: when the asset is with a third party bailee, it cannot be transferred without notice to him (earlier it required his approval). This is the so-called *attornment* still found in Section 29(4) of the UK Sale of Goods Act 1979. In common law, constructive delivery also arises in those few instances where delivery matters, as in the case of making a gift. Yet in other cases where delivery is necessary, it mostly meant to be a physical requirement, as for example in the case of the requirement for delivery that still obtains in the sale of goods in the USA: see Section 2-401(2) UCC (unless parties agree otherwise).

On the other hand, delivery may still be material in countries that do not normally require it for title transfer in chattels. The traditional situation concerns the situation of a *double sale*. Thus Article 1141 of the French Cc (limited to chattels) states clearly that if an asset is sold twice, the second buyer will prevail if the asset is delivered to him provided he was *bona fide*, therefore without knowledge of the first sale. It is in fact a *lex specialis* to the more general protection of the *bona fide* purchasers under Article 2279 Cc and the delivery requirement, which is here physical, may be better explained in the context of this *bona fide* purchaser protection than as a condition for the title transfer itself. In England, Section 8 of the Factors Act (meant to cover the situation in which a seller of goods appoints a representative or factor to handle the sale) and Section 24 of the Sale of Goods Act also give the second buyer the stronger title upon physical delivery[93] but again only if he was without notice of the first sale, which means here actual knowledge.[94]

In the system where delivery is required for an ownership transfer, the seller remains, on the other hand, the owner upon the first sale as long as delivery does not follow. When he effects a delivery under the second sale the second buyer becomes the owner therefore, even if he was not *bona fide* and knew of the first sale. That is the difference between the English and French systems on the one hand and the German (Section 929(1) BGB) and Dutch systems (Article 3.90(2) CC) that require delivery for title transfer, on the other. It was already Roman law, which in any event did not know of the *bona fide* purchaser exception (C.3.32.15 pr). Ownership of the second buyer follows here simply from the fact that the seller retains the disposition rights in the asset and can still legally deliver.

---

[93] See *Pacific Motor Auctions Pty Ltd v Motor Credits Ltd* [1965] 2 All ER 105 and *Worcester Works Finance Ltd v Cooden Engineering Co Ltd* [1971] 3 All ER 708.
[94] See also *ibid* (*per* Lord Denning).

Naturally, the aggrieved first buyer has an action for damages against the seller for breach of contract, but this will not give him the asset. However, in modern law the first buyer may have a tort action against the second buyer if the latter took advantage to push the original buyer out of his deal. In countries like France, there may even be specific performance so that the first buyer can still collect the asset, especially important when scarce equipment is involved. Where, as in the three cases mentioned above, systems requiring delivery are satisfied with constructive delivery, any subsequent purchaser who acquires the goods physically is also likely to be protected, but this purchaser will only be able to claim this protection if it was *bona fide*, therefore only on the basis of the normal *bona fide* purchaser's protection in the case of chattels.

1.5.3   The Importance of Identification. Effect on the Transfer. Sales of Future Assets, Bulk Transfers, and De Facto Transfers of Title

Nowhere can title transfer if the goods sold are *not yet sufficiently identified* or set aside to the contract — not even therefore in countries like England and France, countries that do not require delivery for title transfers in chattels. In countries that require delivery, this act itself suggests it but delivery may be merely constructive and not physical, as in civil law in the three traditional cases mentioned in the previous section and already identified in Roman law. However, as in countries that do not normally require this delivery, there may in those cases be a problem with the title transfer in *unidentified* goods. The result is that, in either system, the moment of transfer may sometimes be less certain when goods are not yet sufficiently identified or set aside. In those instances, the asset transfers *as soon as it is clear* that it is sufficiently identified or as soon as it has been sufficiently set aside, either by the owner or his representative or warehouse.

This problem arises more in particular when *future assets* are sold, see Section 18(1) of the Sale of Goods Act in the UK.[95] They may physically exist but not yet in the ownership of the seller although eventually they may enter his ownership, like under a call option upon the exercise of which title may shoot through to the buyer of the goods if sufficiently identified. In German terminology, these goods are *relatively future*. When goods do not yet exist this can only happen when they emerge. They are *absolutely future*. Both conditions can go together, but not all absolutely future goods are also relatively future, eg when future goods automatically accrue to a seller, eg next year's harvest. In the UK, there is in both cases only an agreement to sell to which the Sale of Goods Act does not apply (*cf* section 5(3)). It means that title cannot pass under it until there is an appropriation to the contract. In truth, there is no problem with the sale itself, but the transfer of title cannot follow before the goods emerge in the ownership of the seller.[96] Transfer is then immediate to the buyer in systems that do not require delivery or where in systems that do require it exceptionally it was constructive.[97]

---

[95] This sale is to be distinguished from purely contingent sales contracts under which a seller may be discharged if he cannot deliver, see Section 5(2) of the Sale of Goods Act.

[96] It is a severe handicap for those who order these goods and are faced with a bankruptcy of the construction company: see *Sir James Laing & Sons Ltd v Barclay, Curle & Co Ltd* [1908], AC 35.

[97] See also Section 2-501 UCC in the USA and Article 1472 of the Italian CC and for France in similar vein, J Ghestin and B Desche, *Traité des Obligations I: Vente* (Paris, 1990), no 550, again stressing the need for some form of individualisation upon the coming into being of the asset and the similarity with the situation concerning unspecific goods. This being said, French law allows the transfer of future tangible assets, also as security: see Article 1130 Cc, but is much more restrictive of a transfer of future claims: see s 1.7.4 *infra*. For chattels, these authors assume that title passes automatically as soon as the goods emerge and are identified to the contract, although there is older French case law to the contrary still requiring delivery in that case, see Cour de Cass,

Where no delivery is necessary, whether in a system that normally requires it for title transfer or not, the transfer *in bulk* also requires a special identification with respect to the container or place in which the goods are held and that they are sufficiently separate. Until they are so identified, no title will transfer into them either. Where certain assets in a *multitude* of them are sold, again a sufficient setting aside or identification is necessary until ownership can transfer. Surrendering control may also be sufficient as it already was in Roman law (D.41.1.9.5/6). Often weighing and measuring may achieve it. There may be further problems if future or unspecific goods are included whilst the bulk transfer never provides a vehicle to circumvent the specificity requirements, which may present an important hurdle even in countries that do not require delivery for title transfer.[98]

The circumstances will decide when the transfer is complete in these situations, but notions of *'generality of goods'* or definitions of what *'bulks'* are may help and facilitate their transfers whilst they may also include a concept of *substitution* or automatic inclusion of replacement goods which are likely to be (absolutely) future. That is particularly relevant when floating charges are created as security interests in inventory and in whole portfolios of trade receivables, which without such a concept of replacement would require new transfers to the lenders (even if sufficiently identified in the contract from the start) each time such a replacement took place and would then also endanger the rank of the security in these replacements which, coming later, would then (normally) be lower. Under applicable law, it may be different in respect of relatively future goods and the situation may again be different for receivables, see also sections 1.6.7 and 1.7.4 below.

Again, where delivery is required, it would suggest that the problem of what can be transferred re-surfaces. To put it another way, where assets are not yet sufficiently existing and identified, delivery is not possible, at least in a physical sense. Where there is constructive delivery, however, as for example in a delivery *constitututo possessorio* of assets that are meant to remain with the seller or in a *traditio longa manu* of assets in the custody of third parties, as a minimum the physical setting aside will become necessary for the transfer of title. That would seem to exclude the sale and delivery of future goods, but, as will be discussed shortly in section 1.5.5, it is conceivable to assume a delivery under an *anticipated constitutum possessorium* of (future) goods that therefore remain under the seller. Here a physical and anthropomorphic concept of delivery has been abandoned and the transfer of ownership in such future goods is considered in a predominantly normative manner always assuming that the goods are sufficiently described and are identifiable upon their emergence in the ownership of the seller.

Finally, although the applicable national property law will normally pronounce on the issue of resulting ownership rights, tying it to the conclusion of a sale contract or to delivery, some ownership change is also bound to arise *de facto* — for example where commodities are *converted* into semi-finished products or goods are *comingled* so that title perforce transfers to others with physical possession or it may have to be shared so

---

28 Nov 1900 [1901] D.1.65. Completion of construction is also an element in France: see Article 1130(1) Cc and Cour de Cass 20 Mar 1872 [1872] D.1.140 and 14 Mar 1900 [1900], D.1.497 with the problem of determining when it takes place. In any event, there is here a physical element to perfecting the title, no different from in countries requiring delivery, *cf* also Article 3.97 of the Dutch Civil of the Code, although delivery itself is, strictly speaking, not necessary but it would be indicative of the emergence of the asset as a prelude to the title transfer.

[98] In the USA, Article 6 UCC provides a special regime concerning bulk transfers. Its aim is to avoid fraud by a debtor who sells his estate for too little or for any price and thereafter absconds. It provides therefore mainly a creditors' protection measure. It renders ineffective against creditors of the transferor any such transfer without a list of creditors and sufficient identification of the assets, see Section 6-104 UCC. In many states is has been repealed.

that a co-ownership structure or forms of beneficial ownership emerge as a result of physically handing over of the goods, whatever the more formal title transfer regime may be. That happens with client accounts of brokers who trade investment securies for their clients and may retain such accounts in their own name. The applicable law will recognise this state of affairs and elaborate on it as a separate way of acquiring ownership. *Accession* is of course another way of acquiring ownership based on factual considerations.

In relation to future goods and their possible transfer it is possible to elaborate on the above in terms of the *disposition right* of the seller and distinguish in that connection also between the sale and delivery of future assets on the one hand and the conditional and temporary sale of present (and future) assets on the other. In this connection it is useful to make a further distinction between physical and intangible assets, especially between chattels and claims. This will be further discussed in connection with the disposition right in section 1.5.5 below.

1.5.4 The Development of the Rules Concerning Delivery as a Formal Requirement of Title Transfer in Civil and Common Law

Above, it was said that in England originally title in goods passed only through their physical transfer. It had to do with the concept of *seisin* which, unlike on the Continent, was in England never superseded by the Roman law notion of possession and delivery which could both be constructive. There had, however, long been an exception if the transfer was by deed. Eventually a further exception was created if there was a sales contract, as now reflected in Section 17 of the Sale of Goods Act 1979, superseding the earlier (but virtually identical) text of 1893 in this respect.

Strictly speaking, in England and Scotland, (physical) possession does therefore no longer play a role in the context of title transfer in goods: see Section 2(1) of the Sale of Goods Act 1979 (except in instances, discussed in the previous section). If the seller remains in possession, in this system he becomes a retentor (see Section 41 of the Sale of Goods Act 1979) or a kind of bailee of the buyer, who, in line with what has been said about bailment before, would, as bailor, have a personal right to delivery against his seller. Upon payment, this personal right can convert into a proprietary right if the seller/bailee defaults (as an immediate right to repossession), therefore also valid in the latter's bankruptcy, provided always of course that there was no agreement for title to pass later. A remedial constructive trust in favour of the buyer who has paid is also conceivable: see about this alternative section 1.4.3 above.

In the USA, the subject of the sale of goods is now covered by Article 2 of the UCC. It allows title also to pass at the moment set by the parties in the sale contract but presumes that it only passes upon physical delivery if parties have not agreed on the matter: see Section 2-401(2). Article 2 UCC de-emphasises the aspect of title transfer, however, and it does not concentrate on the proprietary aspects which may therefore remain a source of disparity under state law. In fact, the common law is in this aspect still controlling, except where especially abolished: see Section 1-103 (new and old) UCC. Article 2 is particularly relevant in this connection for the protection of *bona fide* purchasers from buyers who do not have good title: see Section 2-403.[99]

---

[99] It abolished in this connection the consequences of the distinction between credit and cash sales for *bona fide* purchasers. In *credit sales* there is a voidable title upon the buyer's default. In *cash sales*, title is often not considered transferred at all until payment, resulting in a kind of implied reservation of title if possession has been transferred (or a retention right if it had not been). The common law in the USA was and is here confused about

In France, the concept of seisin or *saisine* had earlier also led to a system based on the protection of physical possession at the expense of the owner who had voluntarily parted with it just as under English and early German law: see section 1.1.4 above.[100] In this system the transfer of physical possession was also necessary for a transfer of ownership. Eventually the Roman law approach prevailed for movables,[101] with the resulting distinction between the positions of the owner, possessor and holder. It confirmed the requirement of delivery for title transfer. However, in as far as the transfer of title in movables was concerned, it became the practice in France early on to include in the sale agreement a clause (*'clause de desaisine'*) under which possession in the legal sense was immediately transferred to the new owner whilst the seller remained the holder for the time being subject to immediate demand by the buyer.[102] It was an instance therefore of a *traditio* or delivery of possession (in the Roman law sense) without a physical transfer (*solo animo*), or a transfer *constituto possessorio*. The result was at the same time a retention right for the seller at least until payment.[103]

The standardisation of the *clause de desaisine* established the practice of title transfer at the moment of the conclusion of the sales agreement, at least for movables. The natural law school, starting with Grotius in the early seventeenth century, independently concluded that the transfer of property at the time of the conclusion of the sales contract was more natural and closer to the will of the parties who should have the right to decide these issues.[104] In France, this view was in the late seventeenth century followed by Domat,[105] who believed that the *clause de desaisine* was always implied. From there the principle entered the French Civil Code of 1804, *cf* Articles 711, 1138 and 1583, although it was not without opposition,[106] whilst Article 1138 still uses the old concepts declaring that the *delivery* of the good is achieved through the mere agreement of the parties. In fact, it may be seen as implying a delivery *constituto possessorio* in all cases, a fiction finally abandonned in the Italian Civil Code of 1942 (Articles 1376 *io* 1470 CC). It would still imply a separate legal act. This facility does not extend in France to the creation of other proprietary rights in tangibles, like a pledge. It also does not extend to the assignment of receivables, which still requires notice (Article 1690 Cc: see for the 1981 amendment chapter V, section 1.3.5), or to immovable property. Yet unlike in England, it is not limited to sales

---

the moment of title transfer which in cash sales seems to be only upon payment, as under the old Roman law, which attitude received some early support in England: see W Blackstone, *Commentaries* 247 (who also wanted delivery); see also 3, S Williston, *Sales* (1948), s 342. The UCC does not change the law but protects *bona fide* third parties against the consequences of this confusion.

[100] This development dates already from the 13th century when an owner even without physical possession was increasingly given standing to defend his rights *in rem* under the influence of Roman law concepts which became prevalent with regard to chattels under the local customary laws. The rights of the physical holders were thereupon considered inferior to and derived from the owner. In this system, the holder no longer had an independent possessory action against third parties who interfered with his holdership and could at best defend in tort motivated by his own inability to fulfil his obligation to return the assets on the due date to the owner. This owner was, on the other hand, denied the action against the wrongdoer under Roman law as long as he could recover from the holder: see Justinian Inst 4.1.17(19).

[101] See also J Brissaud, *A History of French Private Law* (Boston, Mass, 1912), 300.

[102] See Article 278 *Coûtumes d' Orléans*, in *Nouveau Coûtumier Général* (ed Bourdot Paris, 1724), III.2.

[103] *Cf* for modern law Articles 1612 and 1613 Cc, now often explained as a consequence of the *exceptio non adimpleti contractus*, which, although not as such expressed in the Code is often held to be a general legal principle under French law: see also Ghestin and Desche, n 97 *supra*, No 695.

[104] See *De Iure ac Pacis* Lib.II, Cap.VI, s 2*ff*.

[105] *Les Lois Civils dans leur Ordre Naturel*, Livre I, Titre 2, No 8 (ed Paris, 1777).

[106] Amongst others from Pothier, *Oeuvres Complètes* (Paris, 1821), Vol 3, s 1 and *Oeuvres de Pothier*, Vol IX 299, *Traité du Droit de Propriété* (Paris, 1823), No 245.

and any other agreement transferring title in chattels, like an exchange or barter, also effects an immediate passing of title (in movables).

For movables, possession in a Roman law sense is thus by law transferred with the title at the time of the conclusion of the sales agreement (assuming no further conditions are added and the title transfer is not postponed). In this connection, the traditional concept of delivery (largely as a transfer of physical possession) has lost its importance in France, but, as in England, it retains its significance in the proper performance of the agreement as delivery will always be one of the main objectives of a sale. As we already saw, possession in a physical sense is still of major significance in the context of the protection of the *bona fide* possessors of chattels in civil law, a concept not inherent in Roman law: see section 1.5.9 below. Finally, possession retains its role also in the context of the title transfer in the case of double sales (where it is conceptually more a requirement of the *bona fide* purchaser protection) and the sale of non-specific and future goods: see sections 1.5.2 and 1.5.3 above.

Dutch law, even in its new Code of 1992, remains for tangible movables very close to the Roman law concepts of ownership, possession and holdership, also in its manner of title transfer through delivery: see Article 3.84(1) of the new CC. The same may be said for German law in its Civil Code (BGB of 1900): see Section 929, first sentence, for the requirement of delivery for title transfer, although in other respects farther removed from Roman law, especially in its attitude to holdership, see section 1.2.1 above. The notion of *gewere* or seisin has, however, long been abandonned and the transfer of *physical* possession is not therefore necessary for the transfer of title but delivery of possession in the more theoretical Roman law sense is a prerequisite and may be constructive, as in the special cases of the *constitutum possessorium* and the *traditiones brevi* and *longa manu*: see section 1.5.2 above.

1.5.5   *Legal Capacity and Disposition Right. Causes of Contractual Invalidity. Effect on the Title Transfer. Future, Conditional and Temporary Sales*

In sales, the issue of legal capacity arises in two ways. Everywhere it is required for the validity of a sales agreement, but it may also arise at the level of delivery in countries where it is a prerequisite for the transfer of title, in other words where this delivery itself implies a further legal or juridical act (the German *dingliche Einigung*). Capacity in this sense does not exist in minors or in wards of court. Absence of it makes the sale contract absolutely void even though it may still be cured if the guardians accept it or the courts so decide, which they will only do when there is a clear benefit. Equally in civil law countries requiring delivery for the title transfer, it appears to invalidate the delivery as a legal act except if ratified later.

In this connection, the issue arises whether lack of legal capacity in the sales contract, therefore invalidity of the resulting sales agreement, itself undermines the delivery, even if in the meantime the incapacity was lifted or if the delivery was effected by guardians or through the courts. It may amount to an act of ratification of the earlier sales agreement, yet if not so considered the question remains whether the delivery may still stand, an issue which will be discussed more in detail below in section 1.5.6. The Germans distinguish here between the *abstract* and *causal systems* of title transfer. In the first approach, which is the German one, delivery is considered a separate legal act, which is separated from the underlying sales agreement in as far as its effect on the transfer of title is concerned. It ignores any defects attached to the original sales agreement. The invalidity of the underlying agreement may give rise to a damages action but it cannot itself affect the transfer once completed. There is no revindication possibility of the asset on that basis. To undo the transfer, an unjust enrichment action must be brought aiming at the (*ex nunc*) return of the asset. This is never automatic in the abstract system.

In the causal system, the invalidity of the underlying sales agreement entails the *automatic* invalidity of the title transfer (*ex tunc*), even if at the time of the delivery there was sufficient capacity. It gives the seller a revindication right or *in rem* remedy. If in the meantime the buyer went bankrupt, it would allow the seller to reclaim the asset as owner. This would not be so in the abstract system.

Not merely lack of legal capacity may invalidate the underlying sales agreement and pose the question of the continued validity of the transfer. The contract may be invalid for other reasons, for example illegality, fraud, misrepresentation, error or mistake. Most importantly it may be avoided for reasons of default. Especially in that case, the question of the abstract versus the causal system is important. In a pure causal system, the seller of a bankrupt buyer would be able to reclaim his property upon such a rescission even in a bankruptcy of the buyer, also if the bankruptcy itself were the event of default that avoided the underlying sale agreement. That used indeed to be the system in the Netherlands under its old Code. It meant that in practice an implied condition of payment or a reservation of title was implied in each sales agreement. As we shall see in the next sections that extreme position has now been abandoned in the Netherlands.

Legal capacity issues should be clearly distinguished from the *disposition right*. That is the right to be able to transfer ownership of an asset or any other proprietary right in it. It is therefore not a general requirement for legal acts but arises in connection with the transfer of ownership (or more limited proprietary rights in the asset) only. Only the owner can make such a transfer or anyone authorised by him. Neither the possessor non-owner in a civil law sense nor the holder in civil law has sufficient disposition rights to transfer ownership in the asset, neither has a bailee in common law. They can at best transfer their own more limited interest, but never more than they have. Naturally, by contract they may sell all they want, but without proper disposition rights they cannot make the buyer the owner, even in countries that do not require delivery for the transfer of title proper. In countries that require delivery, they cannot deliver, in those that do not, they can simply not transfer. As of necessity the transfer needs therefore always to be distinguished from the contract, even if the moment of transfer derives from it.

In most civil law countries and under statutory law also in some common law countries, the exception is the *bona fide* purchaser in the case of chattels. Even if he acquires from someone without sufficient disposition rights, he may become full owner: see in more detail, section 1.5.8 below. The notion of the *bona fide* purchaser thus normally goes to the lack of disposition rights in the predecessor. Except in France, as we shall see in the next section, it does not go to the lack of capacity of the predecessor or to the lack or invalidity of an agreement with him. Lack of capacity or of a valid agreement for other reasons *earlier* in the chain of transfers would, however, result in the lack of disposition right in the seller, which would then not, in the case of chattels, affect the *bona fide* buyer.

The disposition right arises in a more specific manner in connection with the sale of *future assets*. Can they be sold and transferred, assuming that they can be sufficiently identified in the contract? Must they also exist and, if so, must they also have entered the ownership of the seller or can the seller transfer a mere *expectancy* and what would then be the legal nature of such a transfer. Here we also have to consider the difference with conditional or temporary sales and deliveries (in countries requiring delivery for the transfer of title even if only conditionally or temporarily).

Assuming the asset can be sufficiently described in the contract, it is mostly assumed that a future asset of the seller can be transferred immediately at least if it *exists* although not yet entered into the ownership of the seller (either through physical or constructive delivery). It is in German terms a question of *relatively future* assets. In the case of chattels existence in this sense is a *physical* requirement; an intangible claim sufficiently exists for these purposes if at least the relationship out of which the future claim arises has been created when it is also considered identifiable. In legal systems like the German which require delivery for the transfer of chattels, the disposition right may then be deemed sufficiently to exist and for chattels the transfer is completed through a so-called *anticipated constitutum possessorium* therefore constructively (in anticipation of the seller acquiring the asset). In Germany, for intangibles, the delivery is complete with the assignment and there is no anticipated delivery necessary (as no delivery is required for the transfer of intangible assets). As just mentioned, for being *relatively* future, here the relationship out of which the claims are likely to arise or another sufficient *Rechtsgrund* (legal basis) must exist which as part of a floating charge or an extended reservation of title might even be the *mere replacement*, see also section 1.7.4 below. In both cases (relatively future chattels or intangibles), an intervening bankruptcy of the seller should *not* affect the transfer. As soon as the asset emerges in the property of the seller or assignor it shoots through to the buyer or assignee. Nothing further is required from the seller or assignor in terms of transfer (delivery) and the transfer is complete.

Problems arise here more in particular when assets are *absolutely* future, therefore do not (as yet) exist at all at the time of the bankruptcy of the seller or assignor. Under German law, at least in the case of chattels, a further act of delivery may be required and such a transfer may then not be effective until the asset at least starts to exist, which should therefore happen before an intervening bankruptcy of the seller. In other words, there is not than a possibility of an anticipated transfer. It may still be different for intangible claims in Germany where no act of delivery is necessary (assuming the assignment happened before the bankruptcy). S 91 German Bankruptcy Act 1999 gives expression to this approach, although it could be argued that the distinction between absolutely and relatively future goods is artifical and unhelpful. In the Netherlands, there is a similar provision in the bankruptcy act (Article 35(2)) which, however, applies not only to absolutely future assets but also when goods do already exist but have not yet entered into the ownership of the seller and are therefore only relatively future at the moment of his bankruptcy.

As just mentioned, both in Germany and the Netherlands (but more so in the latter country) it is relevant in particular for *floating charges*, see also section 1.6.7, which may thus be cut down in bankruptcy for any replacement assets that emerge only after the bankruptcy of the transferor. This may also be relevant in the extended reservation of title which is a reservation of title that shifts into replacement goods. But in Germany, the creditor may get good title to replacement goods (whether absolutely or relatively future) when their inclusion was meant to be in exchange for other assets under the floating charge like those that were sold free and clear or, like in the case of receivables, were cashed in by the debtor. Absolute or relative existence might not then be relevant for future replacement goods. That would not now be under present Dutch law.

In these cases of *future* assets, the disposition right has been qualified as *conditional* leading at most to a conditional sale and transfer as such vulnerable in a bankruptcy of the seller although there seems nothing against a seller binding his disposition right in advance, the expression of which is in the case of chattels the *anticipated delivery constituto possessorio* (thus constructively, title shooting through whilst the asset is obtained by the seller). In the case of receivables, in countries where notification to debtors is required for the validity of an assignment, like legal assignments in England, non-financial assignments in France, and all assignments in the Netherlands (and unlike assignments in Germany and equitable assignments in common law), it may require an *anticipated notification* to the debtors, who must therefore be known which is a serious limitation although it could conceivably also be done retroactively (at least in the Netherlands).

The situation of conditionality of the transfer relating to the *future* nature of assets and the disposition right therein should be *sharply distinguished* from a situation where *existing* assets owned by a seller or assignor are transferred conditionally or temporarily, on which there is no restraint. In the first case, the conditionality is *objective*, in the nature of the future asset and the disposition right over it, cannot be helped and may (in the opinion of some or under the applicable bankruptcy laws) restrict the transfer possibility. In the case of existing assets, the conditionality is *subjective* or contractual and not related to the state of the asset. But also future assets can be conditionally or temporarily transferred, which would again raise the question of the effectiveness of such a transfer upon an intervening bankruptcy of the seller.

A potent example is the finance sale or sale of future assets for financing purposes, see more in particular section 1.6 below. When (eg as part of a bulk transfer like in the case of factoring of receivables) future assets (receivables) are conditionally or temporarily transferred to achieve such financing (instead of being transferred by way of a floating charge), the situation may be very different from the one just mentioned, since in those cases the asset was never meant to come fully into the ownership of the bankrupt seller (or assignor of receivables) in the first place and the (conditional) ownership part that was always meant for the financier is likely to accrue to him directly. At most, the bankrupt or his trustee act here as (undisclosed) agents for the financier in the title transfer whilst it will depend on the agreed condition who ultimately acquires the full ownership in the asset.

In other words, if the sale of the future asset to a financier was conditional upon him releasing full ownership to the debtor upon the latter timely tendering the repurchase price, it would be the bankrupt estate that would become the full owner upon such a payment. should such a payment not occur, it would be the financier who would ultimately have full ownership rights.

Note that these problems do not arise in the US at least not in the context of a floating charge which according to Section 9-204 UCC (both in the old and revised 1999 text) allows the inclusion of absolutely and relatively future assets. It makes no distinction in this regard. In England, the situation would appear to be the same, the idea being that upon acquisition the charge becomes effective. Note also, however, that in the UK the floating charge has a very low rank which derives only from the date of its crystallisation which normally is the date of default of the debtor. That is not so in the US. In any event, in the case of the sale of future assets in England the idea is that title shoots through to the buyer upon their acquisition by the seller (regardless of whether they were absolutely or relatively future at the time of the sale).

1.5.6 *The Transfer Agreement: The Abstract and Causal System of Ownership Transfer*

In section 1.5.1 above, it was pointed out that, in civil law, the transfer of ownership needs an underlying reason or cause which is normally found in a contract, particularly in a sales contract, but it could also be an exchange or even a gift if resulting in a contractual obligation. Here we shall concentrate on the sales contract. In civil law, it is often argued that in the change of ownership or in the creation of other proprietary rights, the contract is the

562   Dalhuisen on International Commercial, Financial and Trade Law

motivator and the vehicle that transforms. The transfer of title or of a limited proprietary right follows and establishes a new equilibrium or balance meaning to produce a continuous effect whilst the contract itself comes to an end through the performance. Thus obligatory rights mean change and proprietary rights mean continuity and achieve a new *status quo* meant to endure. The abstract theory of title transfer which was already mentioned in the previous section and which obtains especially in Germany does not change this basic truth but it de-emphasises the legal consequences of an invalid contract and therefore of an insufficient cause for the title transfer once delivery takes place. As we saw, there is no automatic return and revindication right but at most an action for unjust enrichment meant to retrieve the asset, which can hardly be initiated after a buyer's bankruptcy.

Everywhere, the underlying cause of the transfer of title, therefore normally a sales contract, should be valid, although the consequences of it not being so may differ. This brings us back to the lack of capacity, but at least in civil law there must also be a valid consensus or in common law at least a valid exchange of offer and acceptance and some valid bargain in view of the consideration requirement. It is also clear that mistake or misrepresentation, force or undue influence, or fraud may undermine the contract as much as a lack of capacity may do. Illegality may be another reason for failure of the underlying agreement. Lack of an object may be another, or in older civil law codifications also a lack of cause, a requirement often equated with consideration in common law, although technically speaking not requiring any *quid pro quo*: see also chapter II, section 1.2.7. It is not necessary further to elaborate on these contractual complications; that was done in chapter II. The only aspect that is significant here is that a contract may fail and we will have to determine what the immediate legal consequences are if title under it has already been transferred. What is the effect on the asset, especially if a delivery has already taken place or the transfer has been achieved in another manner (for example, through the simple conclusion of the sales agreement in France and England)?

A *special* reason for the failure of the underlying sales agreement may be *default* of payment. In such cases the underlying contract may be rescinded and comes to an end in that manner. If so, under older civil law, the contract was often considered avoided from its beginning (*ex tunc*) and was then thought never to have existed and title would automatically and retroactively revert as a consequence. That would be so even in the bankruptcy of the defaulting buyer. The rescission of the sales agreement becomes here a resolving condition of the title transfer and is then also referred to as the *lex commissoria (tacita)*, a concept first referred to in D.41.4.2.3 (but not so named). This seems in principle still to be the French and Spanish approach (with modern limitations in France as we shall see), was also that in the Netherlands until its new Code, but has long been abandoned in Germany and does not figure in the BGB or in the new Dutch Civil Code. In this newer German and Dutch approach, the parties must still undo any acts of performance rendered so far and the defaulting party in particular must co-operate in the return of the asset. Yet this requires a retransfer of the asset and there is no automatic return, at least in the case of a default followed by rescission of the sales agreement. It is also said that the effect is here *ex nunc*.

Where under modern law the rescission in the case of default only works from the moment it is invoked (*ex nunc*), its effect on the title transfer itself may thus be less strong.[107] That is indeed the German and new Dutch system which therefore only gives a

---

[107] This is in the Netherlands indeed deduced from the rescission being now *ex nunc* and there being no longer any retroactive title effect. See Articles 6.265 and 269 CC. It confines the operation of the full causal systems to situations in which the underlying agreement is invalid for lack of capacity, lack of consensus or

personal retrieval right which has no proprietary effect and will therefore not be much good in the bankruptcy of the buyer. Parties may, however, still achieve the proprietary effect if they insert a special clause to the effect even if such a clause would not create retroactivity either so that accrued rights and liabilities remain in place and may need to be unscrambled separately. This is the *lex commissoria expressa* of Article 3.84(4) of the Dutch CC. In Germany such a condition would also be possible but not be retroactive either (see Section 159 BGB). Thus lack of retroactivity does *not* necessarily exclude proprietary effect, even though that conclusion is often drawn.

Nevertheless the effect of rescission *ex nunc* or *ex tunc* traditionally plays an important role in the discussion on the effect of the failure of the sale agreement on a title transfer and shows one side of the problem, particularly related to a situation of default and rescission for that reason. It is to be noted that this discussion and the lack of an automatic return of title (*ex tunc*) is in the Netherlands confined to the situation of default (unless otherwise agreed). Beyond it, new Dutch law retains a causal system of title transfer. In Germany there is (virtually) always an abstract system (*ex nunc* effect only and no proprietary remedy), therefore also if the sale agreement fails for reasons other than default unless the transfer or real agreement itself fails, as in the case of fraud, incapacity and illegality pertaining to it.

In fact, another perspective on the abstract or causal system of title transfer is that of the delivery itself, particularly in countries that require it for title transfer. Indeed in civil law countries a distinction is here often drawn between countries where delivery itself (even if only constructive) is a requirement for the transfer and those in which it is not. It is in this context often concluded that, where no such delivery is required for title transfer, the automatic retransfer would follow more readily upon the rescission of the underlying sales agreement. This would be all the more true, of course, if in the case of a default, the rescission itself were also considered *ex tunc*.

However, as we shall see, the question of the impact of a failed sale agreement and the survival of the transfer arises no less in countries that do not require delivery for title transfer, like England and France, but it explains why the issue of automatic return (or not) is there not conducted in the same way. Nevertheless, also in these countries it is still necessary to determine the effect of the invalidity or rescission of the sale agreement on the transfer and a clear distinction should still be made in these countries between the contract and the transfer of title, which are only co-terminous. One could even maintain the delivery perspective if a delivery *constituto possessorio* (therefore a constructive delivery) were to be always implied in countries that do not openly require delivery for title transfer. It is an analysis sometimes advocated in France and Belgium.[108] It suggests an implied additional legal act of transfer, which indeed highlights the difference between the sale agreement and the transfer of title even in countries like France. Normally, however, one uses in these countries the concept of voidable or void title in this connection, rather than the concept of transfer or real agreement, and determines when voidness may lead to an automatic return of title.

The German system itself is considered the prime example of an abstract system which is in that country indeed largely tied to the delivery requirement or real agreement itself. In legal systems of this type, the title does not automatically return upon a void or rescinded

---

illegality: see Articles 3.53, 6.203, 3.84(1) and 5.2 CC which in such cases of voidness of the sale agreement allow the title to revert *ab initio* or retroactively.

[108] See also n 92 *supra* and accompanying text.

sale agreement, especially important in a bankruptcy of the buyer, although there may be some limited exceptions, especially in the case of fraud and also in the case of a reservation of title. In Germany, the independence of the delivery as a legal act and separate type of contract (the real agreement or *dingliche Einigung* or *dinglicher Vertrag*)[109] leads by itself to the conclusion that the failure of the underlying sale agreement will not affect the delivery. That would only be so if it could be argued that this *Einigung* was void at the same time, which is often considered the case in a situation of fraud which it is then thought to pervade the *dingliche Einigung* also (Section 123 BGB). In the case of a reservation of title, it really needs to be included in the *dingliche Einigung*, although it will normally be considered part of the latter if it was in the sales agreement until proven otherwise.[110] In fact, in Germany it is possible to introduce the reservation of title only at the *dingliche Einigung* stage, assuming it can be established that that was what parties intended at that moment. If the *dingliche Einigung* is so affected, the transfer is conditional and the reservation of title will be effective also in the bankruptcy of the buyer in Germany who has failed to pay.

It should be noted that in countries like the Netherlands, Switzerland and Austria that all have the requirement of delivery as a separate legal act (even if not all going as far as assuming the need for an *Einigung* in the German manner), the causal approach can only exist whilst assuming that the legal act of delivery is invalidated *at the same time* as the underlying sale agreement. It shows indeed that the delivery perspective need not lead to an abstract system *per se* and the characterisation of delivery as a separate legal act can coexist with a causal system.

In countries like England and the USA, there is largely an abstract approach even though *never* so analysed. It is fairly clear from case law and statutory instruments, as will be discussed in the next section. Once title has passed, the asset is unlikely to be returned if the underlying contract is void except for fraud, and certainly not if it is rescinded merely for reasons of default. The reason that this is so in common law is not the requirement of a delivery as a juridical act, even in the USA where delivery is mostly still required for title transfer in chattels (see Section 2-401(2) UCC). At law it is probably rather the physical possession of the buyer and his bankruptcy trustee and in equity the discretionary implementation of the rescission remedy. There is for personal property in any event no revindication remedy proper in common law. The fact that even in a bailment the courts have discretion in ordering the return of the asset or damages also suggests a more abstract approach.

More generally, the absence of a general rule protecting *bona fide* purchasers of chattels in common law may lead to a more abstract approach to preserve the *status quo*. The exception again is in the case of fraud. Thus if a buyer fraudulently obtains an asset from the seller, it is likely to be returned. It borders on theft when the real owner is always protected in a proprietary sense. In an abstract system this is an exception, in a causal system the rule.

In France, Belgium and Luxembourg, no delivery is required for title transfer either. The return of title therefore in principle seems automatic in the case of an invalidation of the sale agreement. As we saw, in the case of a default and rescission of a sale agreement, the *lex commissoria tacita* is indeed normally implied in these countries, also in a bankruptcy of the buyer. It suggests a causal system, but also here it does not automatically follow and, at least in France, there are significant corrections to any implied causal

---

[109] See also n 91 *supra* and accompanying text.
[110] See for reservation of title in Germany, BGH, 1 July 1970, 54 BGHZ, 214, 218 (1970).

approach. Thus for effect in bankruptcy, the return of the asset must have been requested before the bankruptcy occurred.[111] More generally, there is a difficulty in France with conditions maturing upon bankruptcy. The common creditors of the bankrupt may also be protected against any automatic retrieval right under the theory of the *solvabilité apparente.*

This exception to any causal approach in France has to do with the position of the creditors of the buyer in his bankruptcy. If it can be established that they relied on the outward signs of creditworthiness of the debtor/buyer caused or inflated by the seller putting the buyer in possession of unpaid assets, they may be protected and prevail over the retrieval rights of the seller. The asset will in that case remain part of the bankrupt estate. This theory of the *solvabilité apparente* even prevented a reservation of title being fully effective in bankruptcy in France until 1980 and in Belgium until 1998. In the meantime, the bankruptcy acts of both countries have been expressly amended to overcome this problem: see chapter V, section 1.3.4, but it demonstrates only that France does not have a full causal system.

In fact, on the basis of French case law, the buyer may also hold on to his asset regardless of the invalidity of the underlying sales agreement provided he is *bona fide* and the cause of the voidness of the agreement does not lie with him.[112] He is not therefore protected in the case of his own default, but he may be *bona fide* as to other causes, as in the case of mistake or lack of capacity of the other party, therefore in respect of causes arising on the side of the seller. Naturally, the concept of the protection of *bona fide* purchasers of chattels is known to most civil law countries, but normally only cures a lack of disposition rights in the seller, not the absence of a valid *ius* agreement between seller and buyer. Only in France and in countries following its lead, does it also cover the case of a failed sales agreement for reasons concerning the seller and as regards which the buyer is *bona fide.*

In most other countries, the *bona fide* purchaser concept does not bear on the validity of the sales agreement, only on the power of transfer or disposition right. It makes possible a delivery of what one does not have, provided the sales agreement is valid and both parties have sufficient capacity. The lack of a valid sales agreement between seller and buyer is relevant for others because it takes away the subsequent disposition rights of the buyer. The *bona fide* purchaser protection normally only means to cure that. In the causal system, the successor in interest of such a buyer is thus protected but not the buyer himself. Here the French system is different and *not* strictly speaking causal, but rather abstract.

The abstract system, which protects the transfer even if the underlying sale contract fails, is the *more common.* It sustains the ordinary flow of goods. Roman law in the Justinian compilation was contradictory but the *ius commune* adhered to the abstract system, as we shall see in the next section. It is logical in a legal environment in which *bona fide* purchasers of chattels are not yet protected. Conversely, one may say that the causal system can only operate when *bona fide* purchases from the buyer without a valid contract with the

---

[111] If the goods are already with the buyer, they can only be returned upon his bankruptcy if the seller has already started the revindication proceedings: see Article 117 French BA 1985; see also Ripert-Roblot, 2 *Droit Commercial* (16th edn, 2000), no 3158. A distinction is now made (since the new Bankruptcy Act of 1985) between a situation in which the sale was already rescinded before the bankruptcy and in which rescission was petitioned or intended but not yet granted. In that case, revindication is still possible but only if the rescission was for reasons other than default of payment of the purchase price. This is because of Article 47 of the French Bankruptcy Act which after bankruptcy generally suspends all actions for the rescission of contracts based on lack of payment of a sum of money. See in France for the *lex commissoria tacita,* Articles 1184, 1610 and 1654 Cc and for the *lex commissoria expressa* Article 1656 Cc.

[112] Cour de Cass (civ), 6 July 1886 [1887] D.I.25.

original seller are safe. It is therefore even now less suitable for transactions in real estate and in intangible assets. In the case of chattels, only in Spain do we see a causal approach *without* the full protection of *bona fide* purchasers, although Spanish authors, like the French, do not analyse the situation in this way.

Only smaller countries like the Netherlands, Switzerland and Austria knowingly adhere to a causal system (even if for real estate and intangibles the *bona fide* purchaser principle does not normally work),[113] although in all these countries there have also been other views. That is logical where these countries require delivery for the title transfer as a separate legal act which may technically make any defect in the underlying agreement irrelevant for the title transfer itself.

In fact, most countries now adhere to a more pragmatic approach and the German dogmatic distinction between abstract and causal may look increasingly dated, although it shows up a fundamental legal problem that appears in all legal systems, whether or not so identified. But in practice, there is never a clear choice or the consistent application of a choice in favour of either system. As already mentioned, the more extreme application of the causal system was abandoned in the Netherlands through the curtailment of the *lex commissoria tacita*. In other more causal countries, the causal system may not apply when the rescission of the agreement is invoked after the bankruptcy as the debtor is not supposed to be able to effect a retransfer under those circumstances and there turn of title is not then deemed automatic. There are signs of this in France. Moreover, French law adheres in bankruptcy, when it truly matters, to the notion of the *solvabilité apparente* protecting unsuspecting creditors of the bankrupt, as we saw, whilst the buyer is protected if in good faith as to the causes of the invalid contract. It all undermines the causal approach.

On the other hand, the abstract system often yields to a causal result in the case of fraud or of a reservation of title, as we saw in Germany, whilst the situation in England for reservation of title is still not fully clear.[114] Nevertheless, in Germany we see the fullest abstract approach. For chattels, this is combined with the protection of the *bona fide* purchaser. In a sense, this is a double protection, even though it follows that the *bona fide* purchaser protection in Germany covers only situations when the abstract system fails to sustain the transfer. The connection between the two was never fully considered in Germany when the BGB was enacted. It is, however, in line with the later *ius commune* under which the abstract approach prevailed whilst as from the seventeenth century in France and earlier in the trading cities of Northern Italy and the Netherlands the notion of the protection of *bona fide* purchasers of chattels also started to develop, see section 1.5.9 below.

1.5.7   The Origin of the Abstract and Causal Views of Title Transfer

The problem of the continuing validity of the title transfer regardless of the invalidity of the underlying sales contract and the opportunity of protecting the ordinary flow of goods it offered was identified early, especially in the *ius commune*. As mentioned in the previous section, it is now often cast in terms of the abstract versus causal system of title

---

[113] For real estate and receivables, where normally the protection of the *bona fide* purchaser is not operative, it is now especially introduced into the new Dutch Civil Code to allow the acquisition even though there was an invalid transfer earlier in the chain of transfers, an important and unique innovation: see Article 3.88 CC, which became necessary in a causal system where in any event the entries in the land register may not always be relied upon as being correct.

[114] See text preceding n 109 *supra* and accompanying text.

transfer. In South Africa, where the *ius commune* system still obtains, the issue has been of special interest, also because of the common law influence on the law.[115] Both the *ius commune* and the South African system that follows it are abstract, the later (Justinian) Roman law itself having been unclear on the subject. There is a famous contradiction between D 41.1.36 and D 12.1.18.

The reason for the confusion might have been in the different forms of transfers of property under classical Roman law, some of which, like the *mancipatio*, were clearly formal and therefore likely to have been abstract. Others may not have been.[116] From the *corpus iuris* it is not clear in which forms of property transfers the two contradicting Digests may have had their origin. It followed its customary practice of retaining old texts but adapting them to new or solely surviving structures, which could be different in nature. At the root of the *ius commune* discussion concerning the causal or abstract approach is the well known passage in the Institutes of Gaius (2.20) requiring for the transfer of title (a) delivery, pursuant to (b) a valid title and assuming (c) proper disposition rights of the owner. In connection with the requirement under (b), D.41.1.31 pr speaks of a *iusta causa*. The question was what this meant, whether it was a continuing requirement, and what its failure or absence meant for any completed transfer of title in goods, especially if based on delivery.

An imaginary or putative contract appeared sufficient. That was at least the view of the *Glossa Ordinaria*,[117] but a simulated contract was not good enough as in that case there was no will to transfer at all. The same was more generally true when the parties were not *ad idem*, that is to say that they never intended any transfer. This was particularly the case when the contract was induced by fraud, although even that was sometimes contested, but no longer since the seventeenth century Roman Dutch School.[118] In practice, when the asset was handed over, it was normally assumed that there had been sufficient intent to transfer it, as it was unlikely that there had been no reason at all for doing so.[119] The result was that the *abstract* will to transfer title was considered a substitute for the sales contract as *iusta causa traditionis*.

In modern times, Germany remains the most perfect example of the abstract system.[120] In this country, the approach of the *Glossa Ordinaria*, which, as a form of unjust enrichment, gave only a personal retrieval action to the seller only if a failure of the sale agreement became apparent after delivery, remained the prevailing one during the nineteenth century before the introduction of the new German Codes in 1900 and was retained. In the meantime, this abstract approach was underpinned by von Savigny's concept of the 'real' or *in rem* agreement for delivery as a legal and not merely a physical

---

[115] See JE Scholtens, 'Justa Causa Traditionis and Contracts Induced by Fraud' (1957) 74 *South African LJ* 280ff.

[116] But *cf* R Zimmermann, *The Law of Obligations* (1992), 271, who accepts without reservation the causal system for the Roman *traditio* in classical Roman times.

[117] As far as the Digests go, D.41.1.31 pr does not seem to require the absolute validity of the underlying contract whilst D.12.1.18 does. The *ius commune* did on the whole not require a valid contract for a transfer of title and a putative or imaginary title was sufficient as long as parties agreed that somehow title should pass: see in particular the well known reference in the *Glossa Ordinaria* of Accursius, *Iusta Causa* Ad D.41.1.3.1 pr, of which the sales agreement could be an indication or even proof but not conclusively so. The argument used was that since the delivery pursuant to a failed sales agreement was considered a form of undue performance, the action for the recovery of undue payments (the *condictio indebiti* of D.12.6.1.1) was applicable to retrieve the value. This was, however, only a personal action and not an *in rem* remedy like the *rei vindicatio*.

[118] See J Voet, *Commentarius ad Pandectas*, 4.3.3 and for further sources and comments, Scholtens, n 115 *supra*, at 284ff.

[119] See Vinnius, *Commentarius ad Inst* 2.1.40.10.

[120] See also Drobnig, *supra* n 88, 355.

act (*dinglicher Vertrag*),[121] in a legal system that continued to require delivery even if only constructive as a prerequisite for title transfer, as is still the case under the present German Civil Code. This view was supported by his pupil Windscheid who had much influence on the drafting of the new German Codes.[122] It thus entered into the BGB (Section 929) which as a consequence does not view the prior (sales) agreement as the immediate cause of the transfer but rather the will of the parties (*dingliche Einigung*) that ownership should transfer at the time of the delivery (of tangible assets). Yet even in this approach, incapacity, illegality or fraud may invalidate the will both in the underlying sales agreement and in the real agreement (or delivery as a legal act). Mistake, however, is much less likely to do so.

In this system, only the *dingliche Einigung* or the real agreement is causing the *in rem* or proprietary effect of the transfer. As we saw, it does not, strictly speaking, require the physical transfer which can be constructive (*Übergabesurrogat*). The physical delivery is in this approach no more than a factual event or condition of the sale agreement but not itself a further legal act. In legal terms, it is insignificant except in the context of enforcement of the sale agreement if it requires the physical transfer.

In this approach, the terms of the *dingliche Einigung* itself may be different from the original sale agreement and the delivery may therefore be made subject to extra (proprietary) conditions at the time the legal possession is transferred. As we have seen, of these conditions, the reservation of title is the most important. Only if it is part of the real agreement may it lead to automatic return of the full title in the bankruptcy of the defaulting buyer.[123] It may be difficult to prove but there is, as we saw, some presumption under German law that the real agreement (*dingliche Einigung*) is in the same terms as the underlying sale agreement and a reservation may be deemed implied if it is a term of the underlying sale agreement, although it may still be inserted at the time of the *dingliche Einigung* itself, even if contrary to the original sales agreement.[124]

The situation in France is even less clear. Under older French law, the approach of the *Glossa Ordinaria*, limiting the retrieval possibility to a personal action only (in modern terminology resulting in the abstract approach), was normally followed.[125] In modern French legal writing, the subject is of less interest, apparently since delivery is no longer required for title transfer in chattels under the *Code Civil*. In the previous section it was already said that that cannot in itself be decisive and French case law does indeed not suggest the automatic return if the acquirer was *bona fide* as to the causes of the contract failure and had physical possession. This is largely an expression of the *bona fide* purchaser protection rule in France (Article 2279 Cc), extended here also to operate between two parties to a sale confronted with the invalidity of their contract.[126]

To repeat, as the *bona fide* protection operates here not in respect of third parties but also for a party under an invalid agreement, this may be an indication of a more abstract approach to title transfer in France. It is also clear that in the bankruptcy of a defaulting buyer, the *lex commissoria* or automatic title return — which would otherwise normally follow in France where the mere sale agreement transfers title and its demise therefore annuls the transfer — is not always fully effective and rescission of the sale agreement

---

[121] See n 91 *supra* and accompanying text.
[122] See Windscheid/Kipp, 1 *Lehrbuch des Pandektenrechts* (ed Frankfurt am. Main, 1900), Paragraph 171(5) and Paragraph 172(16a).
[123] See n 109 *supra* and accompanying text.
[124] See BGH, 9 July 1975, 64 BGHZ 395 (1975).
[125] See Pothier, *Traité du Droit de Propriété* (Paris, 1823), No 228.
[126] The classical case is Cour de Cass (civ), 6 July 1886 [1887] D.I.25.

thereunder does not automatically produce a return of title if the claim does not predate the bankruptcy.[127] Also if the asset is already in the possession of the bankrupt it may have to stay there in view of the theory of reputed ownership or *solvabilité apparente*: see section 1.5.6 above.

As we also saw, in English law, similarly, the lack of the delivery requirement has not led to a causal system of title transfer. Again the situation is never discussed in these terms in English legal literature,[128] but case law seems to bear it out.[129] There may be reasons to think that under the Sales of Goods Act 1979 title reverts *ex nunc* in the case of irregularities in the sale agrement or its performance, but physical possession by a buyer would give him strong rights to the asset regardless of the fate of the underlying sale agreement, whilst in the case of rescission, there is no automatic right to a return of the property in equity (specific performance).

This has clear consequences in bankruptcy and may weaken the seller's proprietary position fatally. Only in the case of fraud would, under English law, the title appear to revert automatically and retroactively, at least if the fraud went to the heart of the title transfer.[130] In most other cases of invalidity of the sales agreement, the question therefore remains

---

[127] See n 111 *supra*.

[128] Except in the context of Roman law discussions, see for the UK, F Schulz, *Classical Roman Law*, (Clarendon Press, Oxford, 1951), 350 and F de Zulueta, *The Roman Law of Sale* (Clarendon Press, Oxford, 1945), 56.

[129] See for older English case law, Lord Cairns in *Cundy v Lindsay* (1878) 3 App Cas 459 at 464, opting for an abstract approach, although the House of Lords in this case of fraud accepted the return of title as there had never been any intention to contract with the person who had lied about his identity. The leading modern case (of the Privy Council) is here *Sajan Singh v Sardara Ali* [1960] 1 All ER 269 in which Lord Denning, with reference to *Scarfe v Morgan* [1835–42] All ER 43, held that the lack of a government permit to acquire a transport vehicle did not prevent the transfer of title between parties, who clearly meant that title should pass, no matter the illegality and consequent invalidity of the underlying sale agreement. It had transferred the property, even though under Malayan sales law the title had not passed at the moment the contract was concluded, as would have been the case if the contract had been valid. Less clear became the situation after *Belvoir Finance Co Ltd. v Stapleton* [1970] 3 All ER 664, where in a similar case of invalidity of the sale contract Lord Denning accepted the permanence of the transfer of title 'even where the transferee has not taken possession of the property, so long as title to it has passed'. Implementation, performance or physical transfer of the asset seemed not required. See more recently also *Dewar v Dewar* [1975] 2 All ER 728, in which a gift, accepted as a loan, was still considered a gift, no matter the clear disagreement on the underlying cause.

It is true that most of these cases seem to be more concerned with the transfer of title itself than with its undoing whilst the last case involves a gift situation or loan substitution. In *RV Ward v Bignall* [1967] 1 QB 534 it was said that upon both termination and rescission of a sales agreement title automatically revests in the seller. The seller, even if not in possession, may as a consequence make a valid sale to a new buyer, but whether the latter can reclaim the asset from the first buyer, particularly in the latter's bankruptcy, must be in doubt. R Goode, *Commercial Law* (2nd edn, 995), 420 makes a distinction between rescission and termination and reserves the first term for situations of voidable title in cases of misrepresentation, fraud and duress, and the last for major breaches and notes that title revests in the seller in both cases, although in the case of termination not retrospectively so that in that case accrued rights and liabilities are not affected. This revesting is seen as exceptional and typical for the sale of goods only. However, it remains unclear what physical possession of the buyer means, especially in his bankruptcy. In that case there may be no real i.e. proprietary remedy, but only a personal retrieval action for the owner except where there is a charge, lien or other type of security or equitable interest in the asset.

The problem is that English law does not systematically analyse the contractual remedies (see chapter II, s 1.4) from the retrieval or proprietary perspective. Whether the situation in a sale under the Sale of Goods Act 1979 could be fundamentally different from other situations in which a title transfer is invalid seems doubtful but again it is hard to say in the absence of a comprehensive approach to the subject.

Restitution remedies seem to be of no help. In common law, restitution actions are personal: see also *Westdeutsche Landesbank Girozentrale v Islington London Borough Council* [1992] 2 All ER 961. It had always been so in the *ius commune* and also in Germany. No constructive trust or other proprietary right was therefore allowed in the original moneys the Council of Islington had paid under a swap, a remedy which under common law is in itself not at all unusual in respect of cash payments (in this case complicated by the fact that the moneys had been comingled, however, although that does not need to prevent tracing).

[130] See *Car and Universal Finance Co Ltd v Caldwell* [1965] 1 QB 525 and *Cundy v Lindsay* cited in n 129 *supra*. Third parties who were *bona fide* purchasers of the asset whilst the original sale agreement was not yet voided are

whether the seller can prove a better right to the asset against the bankruptcy trustee of the buyer in possession and retrieve the asset, which seems doubtful under English law. Lack of specific performance and the strong position of the physical holder appear to make the English system in practice abstract. The clear exception, confirmed in Section 2-401(4) UCC in the USA, is the situation in which the buyer rejected or otherwise refused to receive or retain the goods upon a tender of delivery, whether or not justified or where there is a justified revocation of the acceptance. The UCC very clearly states that in such cases the re-vesting occurs by the operation of the law and is not a sale or resale. The exceptional nature of this remedy giving the seller retrieval rights confirms at the same time that normally they do not exist, certainly in a bankruptcy when the bankrupt is in possession.

Clearly, American law does not suggest the return of title either in the case of the failure of the underlying sale agreement and specifically disallows the effect of rescission clauses with title return in bankruptcy.[131] It can be seen as another confirmation of the basic approach, which, in German terms, is the abstract one.[132] In common law countries there may here also be a remnant of the reputed ownership notion and in any event a suspicion of hidden non-possessory proprietary interests. As in England, the situation is less clear in the USA when there is invalidity, illegality or fraud voiding the contract rather than a rescission upon mere default. In the USA, early case law suggested a return of title in these cases,[133] but state law then developed in the sense that in a credit sale invalidity, illegality, fraud or default led to a voidable title only and no automatic return if the voidness was invoked. In cash sales, title was not even considered to pass before payment.

in any event protected by the special provision of Section 23 of the Sale of Goods Act 1979, provided there was at least an intention between the original contracting parties to transfer title. It is an instance of *bona fide* purchaser protection under common law, which remains exceptional under common law which itself suggests a greater need for an abstract approach to title transfer.

[131] Confirmed in Section 365(e) of its Bankruptcy Code.

[132] See also G Gilmore, 1 *Security Interests in Personal Property* (1965), 63. It is indeed established case law in the USA that default in a credit sale does not automatically retransfer title: see *Frech v Lewis*, 218 Pa 141 (1907). There is only voidable title. A voidable title also results if a sale fails in the USA for reasons of invalidity, illegality or fraud: see Section 164 of the *Restatement Second of Contracts* (1997), but not if the sale contract is induced by the fraud of a third party who presents himself as an agent for a non-existing principal: see *Moore Equipment Co. v Halferty*, 980 SW 2d 578 (1998). In that case there is no contract at all and no voidable title either, but rather a void title. In a cash sale, title transfer was traditionally considered postponed until payment and no title had therefore passed either. As it implied some kind of reservation of title, it could still give the seller repossession rights. Under present law, that would be a security interest, however, which implies the immediate transfer of title to the buyer: see Section 9-109(a)(5) (9-102(2) old) UCC. The UCC largely abolished the distinction between credit and cash sales and title passes when parties want it or otherwise upon delivery: see Section 2-401(2) UCC. Good faith purchasers from a defaulting credit or cash buyer are now in both cases protected against what is considered voidable title provided there is (voluntary) physical delivery to them: Section 2-403(1)(c) UCC. It is an instance in which the UCC does not necessarily correct or clarify the former law, but neutralises its effect on outsiders, here by assuming voidable title in both cases.

In fact, between the parties, there are still remnants of a special regime for cash sales in Section 2-507(2) UCC, which now assumes all sales to be cash sales unless otherwise agreed. It still makes delivery a condition for payment (not of title transfer if parties want it to be otherwise) and payment itself a condition of the buyer's right to dispose of the goods, but according to the Official Comment, a reclaiming right results *only* if the buyer does not pay when requested. This right is in the nature of a lien and protected in as bankruptcy of the buyer: see *In the Matter of Mort*, 208 F Supp 309 (1962), but still subject to the right of *bona fide* purchasers and the bankruptcy trustees' lien under the Bankruptcy Code (if the request for payment is made after bankruptcy). Another instance of a reclaiming right results in the USA under Section 2-702 UCC for 10 days after delivery of goods in a credit sale whilst the buyer was insolvent, a right since 1978 also recognised in bankruptcy, see Section 546(c) of the US Bankruptcy Code. Again it is incidental and exceptional and does not denote any causality of the transfer. It is also subject to the right of *bona fide* purchasers: see Section 2-702(3) UCC which refers to Section 2-403 UCC.

[133] *Gifford v Ford*, 5 Vt 532 (1833).

As already pointed out in the previous section, it is clear that in practice most systems are hybrids: German law is abstract but not when there is invalidity, illegality or fraud if also going to the heart of the *dingliche Einigung*. Most systems are here causal although in the case of invalidity it could still be argued that no one should hide behind his or her own incapacity or invalidating behaviour (like misrepresentation or fraud) as a defence, certainly in the professional sphere when the other party is innocent. In the case of illegality it may depend on the policy objective behind it which may not always require the undoing of the transaction. French law is seemingly causal but does not always bear this out. Dutch law is said to be causal but now with considerable restrictions in default situations.[134]

The subject remains of importance especially between seller and buyer in the bankruptcy of the latter and generally for the transfer of *immovables* and especially *intangible* property, where the *bona fide* protection is not normally available to *bona fide* purchasers of these assets, except for intangibles embodied in negotiable instruments or by special statutory provision like the new Article 3.88 of the Dutch CC for transfers having failed earlier in a chain.[135] The causal system seems more normal and is in modern comparative legal writing sometimes preferred,[136] but it is not the system that prevails most. The hesitancy concerning the causal system, although seemingly more natural, is understandable as it creates uncertainty in the title. It may be more objectionable if the avoidance or rescission derives from later acts of the parties, notably from the default of the buyer in possession. This is particularly clear in the transfer of ownership of highly speculative assets meant to trade, like securities and commodities, when a whole subsequent pattern of (hedging) transactions may be organised and the underlying values may have changed completely. A personal action for damages may then be more appropriate than the return of title, even if the asset is still with the buyer, at least if the buyer has taken further action with regard to the asset or the protection of its value.

Another obvious situation where respect for the *status quo* may be preferred may present itself when a sale contract is declared void for policy reasons in the country of the seller (for example for breaking its foreign exchange restrictions), but the asset is already transferred in another country (or is real estate located elsewhere), when the *lex situs* may still validate the transfer (even if it maintains a causal approach), in order not to disrupt its own proprietary system too much.[137]

The principle of abstraction in title transfers is in the meantime well established and is apparent in many other areas of the law. It is inherent in agency and the concept of its independence under which the principal may become the owner of assets bought by the agent regardless of underlying restrictions on the agent's activity in the agency agreement. Negotiating a bill of lading or other documents of title and acceptance of a bill of exchange are also believed abstract. The principle of abstraction operates in a not dissimilar way in

---

[134] Whilst legal doctrine in the Netherlands often accepts the concept of the 'real' agreement: see HCF Schoordijk, *Vermogensrecht in het algemeen naar Boek 3 van het nieuwe B W* [The General Part of the Law of Property and Obligations according to Book 3 of the New Dutch Civil Code] (Deventer 1986), 254*ff*, it does not lead to an abstract system as the law negates its effects by generally rendering it void together with the underlying sale contract. It has been argued in the Netherlands, however, that there are situations where the sale agreement itself is valid, but the later real agreement not, another way of proving its own separate character, *cf. ibid.*, especially in cases where governments intervene to prevent delivery without declaring the contract itself illegal or in situations in which an impending bankrupt is forced to deliver pursuant to a sale agreement without wanting to do so or in any other in which excessive pressure is exerted to achieve performance of an existing agreement.

[135] See n 113 *supra*.

[136] See Drobnig, *supra* n 88, 359; see also F Ferrari, 'Vom Abstraktionsprinzip und Konsensualprinzip zum Traditionsprinzip' [1993] *Zeitschrift für Europäisches Privatrecht* 52.

[137] See in the Netherlands HR 12 Jan 1979 [1980] NJ 526.

the issue of bank guarantees and letters of credit. In bills of exchange the acceptance is independent of the drawer–drawee relation as well as drawer–payee, whilst the commitments under a bank guarantee or letter of credit are separated from both the underlying sales contract and the instruction by the buyer to the bank. It may well be that notification of an assignment to the debtor and his subsequent payment are equally abstract. It seems that the principle of abstraction appears everywhere where the ordinary course of business needs protection against the consequences of complications which have their origin in underlying relationships or their failure.

1.5.8   Disposition Rights: The 'Nemo Dat' Rule and the Protection of Bona Fide Purchasers

The disposition rights of the seller do not concern his capacity but his ability to transfer rights in the assets he tries to sell. As far as the contractual side of a sale is concerned, it is possible to sell anything, even assets which do not (yet) belong to the seller, but title cannot be legally transferred in them if the seller is not the owner. Similarly he cannot sell any other interest in the asset if he is not the beneficiary or 'owner' of the interest. Lack of disposition rights may also occur if the seller has the asset but there was a defect in an earlier transfer so that someone else is the true owner in civil law terms or has the better ownership right in common law terms.

Unlike capacity, the ability to dispose of an asset is a more factual than legal concept. In Germany it also plays at the level of the *dingliche Einigung* or real agreement. Failure of disposition right leads in principle to an invalid transfer even if delivery took place in systems that require it, whether abstract or causal. Lack of disposition rights impacts no less on the title in countries that do not require delivery for title transfers. Section 21 of the UK Sale of Goods Act 1979 clearly says so. It embodies *the 'nemo dat (quod non habet)'* rule of Roman law (D.50.17.54). Therefore nobody can in principle give more than he or she has which is as such an obvious statement. Where the real owner consented there is no problem. The seller is his representative in this aspect, although there may still be a question whether the consent should have been expressed to the seller or also to the buyer, as in the case of an undisclosed agency.

The law has not halted here but has over time developed the concept of the *bona fide* purchaser, at least in respect of chattels. It is one way of protecting the ordinary flow of goods, which is not served by uncertainty as to ownership and even less by assets going (physically) backwards and forwards between the parties. The acquisitive prescription in civil law and statutes of limitation in common law had a similar objective: see sections 1.2.3 and 1.3.5 above. The *instant* protection of the *bona fide* purchaser took these concepts one step further, at least in situations where the only defect was a lack of disposition rights in the seller because of the earlier events concerning the chattels sold. The justification for this protection of the *bona fide* purchaser is normally that the original owner voluntarily parted with the goods and put them with a bailee or holder in a common law sense who subsequently sold them. Naturally the seller is here at fault but the question is who is protected: either the old owner or the new one? In modern law, even in common law, which is in principle stricter and will allow only statutory exceptions to the 'nemo dat' rule, the balance shifts increasingly towards the new owner. In this approach a sale by an unauthorised person to whom the original owner voluntarily handed his goods is considered his risk. It is also possible to see this as a variation on the agency principle.

Modern law will increasingly protect the *bona fide* purchaser at least of chattels provided he obtained at least the *physical* possession of the goods. This physical requirement is less clear under the statutory exceptions in common law and also in German law in the case of a sale of goods under a holder (*longa manu*) or custodian when in Germany the real issue appears to be whether the seller lost all control rather than whether the buyer obtained physical possession: Section 934 BGB. In these cases, technically only the retrieval right on the basis of the relationship with the holder (the *Besitzmitlungsverhältnis*, see also section 1.2.1 above) is assigned under Section 870 BGB (although if there are no disposition rights proper in the seller this relationship is hardly likely to exist). The question is in Germany especially relevant in a reservation of title, when the conditional buyer sells the asset *constituto possessorio* to someone else (for example, his bank for security purposes) who sells-on through a tradition *longa manu* to a *bona fide* purchaser. Upon default of the first buyer under a reservation of title and in physical possession is the first seller or the last buyer protected? In the absence of physical possession of the latter, it should be the former, but that does not seem to be the solution of Section 934 BGB, which has as a consequence been criticised. Another aspect of the present German system is that whilst a *traditio constituto possessorio* of a non-owner to a *bona fide* purchaser fails under Section 933 BGB, it would succeed if the non-owner were to put the asset with a custodian or agent and subsequently deliver it *longa manu*.

The *bona fide* buyer must also have paid good value, although this value need not be commensurate whilst the requirement is altogether absent in the German abstract system. The other normal requirement is of course that the *bona fide* purchaser must be unaware of the disposition impediment of his seller. There are here different approaches. In some countries the criterion is less subjective than in others, the new Dutch law being here on one side of the scale (objective: see Article 3.11 CC, even implying an investigation duty) and the German BGB on the other (subjective: see Section 932(2) BGB). Dutch law refers in this connection specifically to the disposition rights, German law only to the ownership question, although in Section 366 HGB (Commercial Code) broadened to the disposition rights to protect commercial dealings.

The concept of the *bona fide* purchaser where it prevails is usually not confined to the transfer of a full ownership interest. Here one sees in civil law the connection with the acquisitive prescription based on *bona fide* possession in a civil law sense as the manifestation of *any* proprietary right. French law looks at the protection of the *bona fide* purchaser still very much from this perspective and assumes in that case an immediate acquisitive prescription or a prescription period of zero years. It cures not only the lack of disposition rights in the seller but *any* defect in the sale of chattels on the part of the seller as long as the buyer/possessor was *not aware* of any defect in the transfer when he concluded the transaction: see also section 1.5.6. It could even have dispensed with the physical element of possession, which for prescription was never necessary in Roman and civil law, but this is not the approach of Article 2279 Cc. It puts emphasis on the *possession réelle* rather than on the transfer itself. It is the meaning of the maxim '*en fait de meubles possession vaut titre*'.

Earlier French law had allowed the transaction to stand on the basis of the mere physical possession of the buyer. This was expressed in the maxim '*meubles n'ont pas de suite*' (or '*mobilia non habent sequelam*'). It still finds a resonance in the English bailment and the English buyer in possession has a strong position, even if his underlying contract is invalid, as we saw in section 1.3.2, and probably no less when there were no disposition rights, in the seller. It may be a reason why the *bona fide* purchaser protection under common law still does not need to operate as a general principle for chattels.

On the other hand, in common law, the applicable statute will sometimes allow all transfers *in the ordinary course of business* to stand, that is even without *bona fides* on the part of the buyer. This is so in particular where the law guards against security interests and does not want them to obstruct the ordinary flow of goods. An important example of this may be found in the USA under Section 9-320(a) (9-307(1) old) UCC.

It may be clear from the discussion in sections 1.5.6 and 1.5.7 above that the abstract system itself may provide protection for a purchaser as especially the lack of a valid contract earlier in the ownership chain is no longer relevant after delivery. Fraud and lack of disposition rights, as in the case of theft or of a holder, still do, except perhaps in sales conducted on open markets or at auctions. The abstract approach is in fact an older and less subtle way of achieving a result similar to the one under the *bona fide* purchaser rule (which came in later), by limiting the instances in which a lack of disposition rights in the seller could occur. There is no *bona fides* requirement.

It protects the buyer even against an invalid contract between him and the seller, in Germany subject to an unjust enrichment action only. In France, the extension of the *bona fide* protection to instances of a defective agreement leads to a result similar to that of the abstract system, but only if the buyer does not have knowledge of the invalidity of his contract nor himself gave rise to it. In most civil law countries, the need for this protection of the abstract approach to title transfer has now largely been achieved by the *bona fide* purchasers protection except for real estate and intangible assets acquisition (if not embodied in negotiable instruments) where the *bona fide* purchaser protection is still not commonly available, although in the former case land register entries may protect the buyer so that abstract protection appears to become less relevant.

1.5.9   Origin of the 'Nemo Dat' Rule and of the Principle of Bona Fide Purchaser Protection

Above in section 1.2.1, we saw that under the old germanic principles of property law, no clear distinction was made between ownership and possession. Under the prevailing notion of *gewere, seisin* or *saisine,* possession appeared the basic right, at least for chattels. It is still so in the common law of possession when possession in a physical sense is *voluntarily* surrendered by the owner, leaving him only in the position of a bailor with not much more than a personal action against the bailee for retrieval of the asset at the end of the bailment whilst the latter has all actions against third parties. In England, even in modern law, the bailor can retrieve the asset from them only if he has a right to immediate repossession in his relationship with the bailee. In this system, the bailor runs the risk of losing his reclaiming rights particularly in the bankruptcy of the physical holder of the asset. In the case of involuntary loss of the asset, the basic action of the owner is in principle still personal, in tort, but could reach third parties and is thus stronger, almost proprietary.

Under the old germanic law, there was a similar strong position for all physical possessors and the protection of all who acquired actual possession even *regardless of* their *bona fides.* One finds this expressed in the germanic maxim 'Hand muß Hand wahren'. It is clear that in such a system the protection of *bona fide* purchasers of a holder is less urgent, at least if they are in the physical possession of the asset.

In France, this same approach led originally to the old French maxim: '*meubles n'ont pas de suite*', in medieval Latin expressed as '*mobilia non habent sequelam*'. It also left any rightful owner with only a personal action against a holder of his assets if he voluntarily surrendered them. As regards the protection of title acquired from this holder and presumed owner, it was only later made dependent on notions of good faith of the acquirer. Except in France, probably as the consequence of its old tradition based on the *saisine,* it was often further refined in the sense that there also had to be a valid contract besides the acquisition from someone who had sufficient power over the asset effectively to deliver it but no sufficient legal disposition right. However, in this approach, acquisition from a thief would lead to full ownership (or lack of a retrieval action) only after a number of years, even if the purchaser was *bona fide* and obtained possession, except (in many countries) where the acquisition took place on a public market or at auction. As in England this often did not require good faith at all (as long as there was no bad faith).[138]

Roman law had not pursued the idea of the protection of the *bona fide* purchaser of movables and adhered strictly to the requirement of D.50.17.54 which formulated the so-called '*nemo plus (iuris ad alium transferre potest, quam ipse haberet)*' maxim of which the '*nemo dat (quod non habet)*' maxim is a simplified version. It meant that nobody could transfer more than he had and the receiver could therefore not receive more and have better rights than his predecessor. There only was one exception in Justinian law (C.7.37.2/3): in the case of execution sales by the tax authorities, the buyer was exceptionally protected. The concept of *bona fide* acquisition was itself known in Roman law, but it remained limited to acquisitive prescription, which was exceptional, as we saw. The idea of *bona fide* acquisition was later extended to beneficiaries of usufructs and to pledgees, but only in the sense that, if *bona fide*, they were given a tort action to defend against infringement by third parties and always in a non-exclusive way, as the true owner/legal possessor retained these actions also: see respectively D.9.2.11.10 and D.9.2.17. The pledgee could also transfer ownership in an execution sale, but this facility was considered based on the implied assent of the pledgor: see Inst 2.8.1 and D.41.1.46.

One of the keys to understanding the Roman system is that the mere holder (as distinguished from the legal possessor) who sold the asset became a thief and acquisition from him could therefore never result in ownership since it rendered the asset a *res furtiva*.[139] In such a system, the protection of the *bona fide* purchaser cannot develop. This was not a problem in the old germanic law except in respect of the true thief, but it remained a serious complication in the further development of Roman law in western Europe, which, as we saw, gradually overtook the germanic law of chattels from the thirteenth century onwards. In fact Spanish and Portuguese law remain to this day closer to the Roman notions in this regard, notwithstanding the general protection of the *bona fide* purchaser of movables with possession (and for value) developed under modern civil law in most leading civil law countries. They balance this by having very short acquisitive prescription periods.

Although the holder may often have misappropriated the assets, in the *ius commune*, this was gradually no longer considered theft in the Roman law sense, probably because the owner had for whatever reason voluntarily parted with the assets. The practice under older germanic law was here probably a facilitating argument. Acquisitive prescription of the asset sold by a holder thus became possible *provided* there was good faith and a valid contract with the seller/holder. Some city laws in Italy and the Netherlands had in the

---

[138] Another idea altogether was the option of the owner to retrieve the assets from the outsider upon payment of certain damages, usually the price the third party had paid or a part thereof, thus sharing the burden of any unauthorised sale. This idea also had a base in old germanic law and is often referred to as the *Lösungsrecht*: see R Feenstra, 'Revendication de Meubles et "Lösungsrecht" des Tiers Acquéreurs,' in *Collatio Iuris Romani, Etudes Dediées à Hans Ankum à l'Occasion de son 65e Anniversaire* (Amsterdam, 1995), 87. It has no equivalent in modern law.

[139] See for this concept and its consequences, n 28 *supra*.

meantime adopted similar approaches in the interest of continuing trade, often, however, without great clarity on the aspect of good faith acquisition.[140]

As we have seen, in France the original, maxim '*meubles n'ont pas de suite par hypothèque s'ils sont mis hors du pouvoir du débiteur sans fraude*' which suggested that all physical possession represented ownership in line with the concept of *saisine*, was eventually superseded by the requirement of *bona fide* possession under the maxim '*en fait de meubles possession vaut titre*'. Also in France, the requirements of trade contributed to this development,[141] but the Roman law of acquisitive prescription, which required *bona fides*, seems to have been the model. Although the newer maxim was originally only an evidence rule (*fonction probatoire*), it became gradually seen as an acquisition rule (*fonction acquisitive*).[142]

However, unlike under Roman law, no *iusta causa* was required for this acquisition in France. As a consequence, *bona fide* acquisition with physical possession from a mere holder always gave rise to the protection and to the passing of title in chattels, even if there was no valid sales agreement: see section 1.5.6 above. This is probably still a vestige of the old '*meubles n'ont pas de suite*' or *saisine* approach and also suggests some features of the abstract system of title transfer, as we saw, although the protection did not extend to the acquisition from the thief, which situation was clearly distinguished.[143]

In the German sphere, the Prussian Codes of 1794 followed the Roman law system rather than old germanic law in this area. The Austrian Civil Code (Section 367) of 1811 clearly introduced the notion of the protection of the *bona fide* purchaser of movables from a non-owner who had voluntarily been put in possession by the original owner. The protection was cast in terms of a defence against the original owner. In the German Civil Code of 1900 (Section 932 BGB), the protection is cast neither in these terms, nor as an acquisitive prescription as in France, but rather in terms of an independent way of acquiring possession and ownership. It requires as a consequence still a valid cause, but not necessarily a valid sales agreement and concentrates here on the *dingliche Einigung* as a sufficient *causa traditionis* in the German abstract approach to title transfer. It may not insist on physical possession in that context either and also allows constructive possession for the operation of the *bona fide* purchaser protection but only in the case of the *traditio longa manu*.[144]

---

[140] See also the later notes of Grotius on the laws of Amsterdam and Antwerp in his *Inleidinge tot de Hollandsche Rechts-geleerdheid* [Introduction to Roman-Dutch Law] in the Lund manuscript, (F Dovring, HFWD Fisher and EM Meijers, 2nd edn, 1965), 50–55. In II.3.5 Grotius adhered, however, to the general rule that protected the owner against *bona fide* possessors even if they acquired the chattels for value.

[141] In the 18th century, the '*sureté du commerce*' was invoked as argument for the extension of the protection in this manner by Bourjon, 6 *Le Droit Commun de la France et la Coûtume de Paris, Réduits en Principes*, Titre 8, chapter 3, s 4(18).

[142] This development was in particular reflected in the writings of Bourjon in the 18th century, 3 *Le Droit Commun de la France et la Coûtume de Paris, Réduits en Principes* (ed Paris 1770), Title 2, chapter 5 and Title 22, chapter 5 who fully deduced this acquisition principle from the prescription (reduced to zero years) and hence implied the *bona fides* requirement: see also WJ Zwalve, *Hoofdstukken uit de Geschiedenis van het Europees Privaatrecht* (Groningen, 1993), 95 and JA Ankum, *Actio Pauliana* (Zwolle, 1962), 273. From there the principle reached the French *Code Civile* of 1804, thus in the chapter concerning prescription (Article 2279).

[143] The French approach insists on *bona fides* at the time of acquisition and requires actual possession (here even in the context of acquisitive prescription) so that a mere acquisition pursuant to the conclusion of a sales agreement (the normal French rule) is not sufficient. It excepts the acquisition from the thief.

[144] Dutch law largely follows this German example, although its emphasis in terms of the *causa traditionis* is on the validity of the sale agreement itself in the causal tradition, rather than on the validty of the delivery as a legal act. It is less elaborate in discussing the various types of delivery in the context of *bona fide* purchaser protection, but excludes the acquisition *constituto possessorio* from the protection whilst it requires the acquirer to disclose his predecessor in order to benefit: see Article 3.88 new Dutch CC.

In England, the law of chattels, although still largely based on the germanic principle of seisin, unexpectedly did not develop a protection for the acquirer with physical possession buying movables from a non-owner. It is somewhat surprising that the common law in its basic approach is here closer to Roman law than most civil law countries now are. On the other hand, the old principle of protection of the possessor/bailee upon the voluntary surrender of the asset to the latter by the true owner makes him virtually the title holder (as possessor) against all the world. Also the true owner has only a weak personal claim against him. Even then, the defendant holder always had the choice either to return the asset or pay damages, a discretion which in England may now be exercised by the defendant at the discretion of the courts. The result is that the owner's position is enfeebled towards holder and even more so towards acquirers from the latter (except if the transfer to them creates a right to immediate repossession in the owner *vis-à-vis* the bailee), regardless of their good faith.

The English developments must be seen against this background, which may explain why *bona fide* purchaser protection might not have been so necessary and remains even now exceptional in principle in common law. The *'nemo dat'* rule is in England expressed in Section 21 of the Sale of Goods Act 1979 which Act formulates, however, a number of important exceptions, which take it (for the sale of goods only) close to the dominant civil law approach. The oldest exception was the purchase in markets overt (Section 22 old), which were certain market places and shops in the City of London. It required a weak form of *bona fides* of the buyer, rather absence of bad faith. It was an exception never introduced in the USA and now also abolished in the UK (since 1995). Then there is the more general protection of all persons in possession buying from sellers who were voluntarily entrusted with the goods by the original owner (Section 25). It approaches the wider protection for *bona fide* purchasers under civil law, under which the notion of voluntary loss of the physical possession of the asset often also plays a major role in the protection of the *bona fide* purchaser. Another important exception is in England the one caused by estoppel when the owner of the goods through his conduct is precluded from denying the seller's authority to sell. It leads in the same direction (Section 21).

Section 24 of the Sale of Goods Act 1979 further protects dispositions by a seller who has not yet delivered the assets to his buyer and concerns the question of the protection of the *bona fide* buyer in a second sale, for which English law, unlike legal systems in which title has not yet passed because of the lack of delivery, logically requires *bona fides*, as French law does in a similar situation. Then there is the protection of the *bona fide* buyer who bought and obtained possession before the seller's contract with his predecessor was voided for fraud or similar reasons: Section 23.[145] Section 25 protects the *bona fide* buyer from someone who himself bought the goods and received possession but not title (which normally follows the conclusion of a sale contract subject to any agreement to the contrary).[146] Section 9 *io* Section 2(1) of the English Factors Act 1889 similarly allows the commercial agent who handles assets of his principal with the latter's consent to make any kind of disposition in the ordinary course of his business, whilst any *bona fide* purchaser of the agent in possession is protected under these circumstances. Except where there is a second sale, there may not be the same insistence on actual possession of the acquirer

---

[145] This avoids any problems of retroactivity of the rescission or invalidation of the contract in the manner of the abstract system of title transfer, although the buyer must be *bona fide* as to the causes of the invalidity, very much like the situation in France.

[146] It produces a so-called agreement to sell rather than a sale agreement, only the latter of which immediately transfers ownership. The reservation of title is the prime example.

under these statutory exceptions, as civil law often requires, notwithstanding the common law's normal insistence on seisin for proprietary protection.

In the USA, the principle of *bona fide* purchaser protection also remains exceptional at law. However, it is increasingly accepted for goods but only if traded in the ordinary course of business. This exception also applies to security interests in those goods. Thus proprietary interests of third parties in goods that are normally sold in the ordinary course of business are ineffective against subsequent buyers, in the case of security interests even regardless of their good faith or more properly regardless of the filing of the security interest if the assets are sold in the ordinary course of business of the seller. In this connection Section 2-403(2) UCC elaborates on the entrusting notion in sales but only to a merchant who deals in the goods of that kind, probably without delivery. Section 9-320(a) (9-307(1) old) UCC elaborates on this protection against non-possessory security interests in chattels sold in the ordinary course of business, which protection is not conditional on any entrusting notion.[147]

Note, however, the definition of a buyer in the ordinary course of business under Section 1-201(a)(9) (1-201(9) old) UCC which itself requires that the buyer is in good faith and without knowledge that the sale to him was in violation of the ownership rights or security interests of a third party in the asset. He must also buy in the ordinary course of business from someone in the business of selling goods of that kind. The good faith requirement is not meant to undermine the concept of protection in the ordinary course of business under Article 9, however. In fact, it is confirmed in the Official Comment on Section 9-323 (9-307 old) that the third party buyer takes free even if he knows that there is a prior interest. He takes subject to it only if he knows that the sale was in violation of the underlying agreement between the seller and the original buyer or in violation of a security agreement, which term was not waived by words or conduct of the seller or secured party.[148] Special protections apply for good faith purchasers in the case of failed sales agreement because of default.[149]

In the USA, the concept of the protection of *bona fide* purchasers is normally tied to the concept of the purchase being for value. This is usually added in the statutory texts. It is less clear whether there has to be actual possession by the third party purchaser of the assets in order for him to be protected. Section 2-403(2) UCC does not require it in the case of a purchase in the ordinary course of business when the entrusting of the goods by the seller to a merchant appears sufficient, whilst the protection against secured interests under Section 9-320 (9-307 old) the possession of the *bona fide* purchaser is not relevant at all.[150] Only the seller with a voidable title must be in possession in order to be able to make a valid sale to a *bona fide* purchaser (which could also involve a security transfer) under Section 2-403(1).

---

[147] See for the classic study on the subject, G Gilmore, 'The Commercial Doctrine of Good Faith Purchase' (1954), 63 *Yale LJ* 1057 showing that the requirement of good faith itself became less and less demanding. In the USA, it may mean no more than an absence of *mala fides* whilst for a purchase in the ordinary course of business from a merchant dealing in the goods the *bona fides* may no longer be relevant altogether, at least after the goods have been entrusted to the other party. See for the problem of voidable title and the protection of Section 2-403(1) UCC, n 132 *supra*.

[148] See also JJ White and RS Summers, *Uniform Commercial Code* (4th edn, 1995), 881.

[149] See n 132 *supra*.

[150] See also *Tanbro Fabrics Corp v Deering Milliken Inc*, 39 NY 2d 632 and 19 UCC 385 (1976). See for the situation under Section 9-320(a) (9-307(1) old) UCC, very explicitly *Daniel v Bank of Hayward*, 425 NW rd 416 (1988). It may raise questions about any continuing interest of a debtor remaining in possession of the assets which could conceivably be sufficient for the continuation of the security interest under Section 9-203 (new and old) UCC. Section 9-203 (new and old) which does not require ownership of the debtor in order for him to give (and maintain) a security interest of a third party in his asset is here not helpful and could still give a foreclosing secured creditor some protection if unaware of an earlier sale (without a delivery of possession) in the ordinary course of

The concept of protection of third party purchasers being still exceptional in common law, it must be restrictively interpreted: see for the general ('*nemo dat*') rule in respect of sales of goods, Section 2-403(2) UCC first sentence, and in respect of security interests in personal property in the USA, Sections 9-201 (new and old) and 9-315(a)(1) (9-306(2) old) UCC. In this connection Section 9-320(a) (9-307(1) old) UCC adds that the exception in respect of buyers in the ordinary course of business is only in respect of security interests created in the sold asset by the seller (and not by any of his predecessors in the title).

Finally, in common law, there is the overriding trust law principle under which the trustee is able to transfer full title free of the beneficiary's interest to anyone who is unaware of the transfer in breach of trust, provided this is done for adequate consideration. This general principle of equity also applies outside the law of sales and to other than movable assets, but it should not be confused with the much more limited concept of the protection of *bona fide* purchasers against other than *equitable* proprietary interests in the property which are usually only statutory.

1.5.10 The Retention Right of the Seller in the Case of Default of the Buyer

In legal systems that normally transfer title in goods at the time of the conclusion of the sale agreement, as is now the rule in England and also in France and in many legal systems derived from French law, the seller is naturally extra vulnerable as he loses title even before delivery, let alone payment. It is normal therefore to construe both under English and French law a legal lien or retention right in the sold assets for the protection of the seller who has not yet physically delivered the goods and therefore remains in possession, although he has lost title. It means that in cash sales, the seller cannot be forced to deliver the goods before he is certain that he will receive payment. In legal systems, which do not require delivery of possessions for the transfer of title, it is another instance in which physical possession has an important meaning. The lack of it weakens the new owner's position considerably. In systems that require delivery for title transfer, like the German and Dutch systems, the seller remains the owner before delivery so that there is only a need for a retention right if there has been constructive delivery with the seller retaining the asset, as in a delivery *constituto possessorio*: see section 1.5.2 above.

Section 41 of the Sale of Goods Act 1979 in the UK states that the unpaid seller in possession is entitled to retain possession (the seller's *lien*) until payment even in the case of insolvency of the buyer, unless there are credit terms except where they have expired before delivery. In France this legal retention right (*droit de retention*) results under Articles 1612 and 1613 Cc and is reinforced by the legal reclaiming right of Article 2102(4) Cc during a short period after the sale when possession has been transferred but the buyer is in default of payment. It re-establishes the retention right and is therefore itself not in the nature of re-transfering title.

---

business. The civil law requirement of physical possession of the buyer in order for him to be protected presents a clearer picture but obviously also gives less protection. However, also in the USA, only physical possession would give the buyer in the ordinary course of business full protection.

In a situation where there was first an unauthorised sale plus delivery to a buyer who subsequently resold the goods in the ordinary course of his business to a *bona fide* purchaser after having given a security interest in the asset to a third party, the *bona fide* purchaser would defend against the original owner on the basis of the entrusting notion under Section 2-403 UCC and against the security holder on the base of a sale in the ordinary course of business (assuming the requirements for it were met) under Section 9-320(a) (9-307(1) old) UCC: see also White and Summers, n 148 *supra*, at ss 33–16, and *Gorden v Hamm*, 74 Cal.Rptr 2d 631 (1998).

In civil law, a lien or retention right does *not* automatically result from the mere possession by any creditor but normally depends on statute or the operation of the law, see for example Article 3.290 of the Dutch CC and Sections 273, 986 and 1000 BGB. It provides as such a strictly limited remedy and guards against proprietary action of the owner. It may also be agreed in the contract but does not then automatically follow the rules of the statutory liens. The contractual retention right may under applicable law equate to a possessory charge subject to the rules concerning the creation of such charges. That is the position in the USA. Even where statutory or contractual retention rights are operative, parties may of course still be able to rely on other remedies, of which the *exception non adimpleti contractus* is the most common. It may generally be used in all situations where mutual contracts remain executory and allows a non-defaulting party to suspend its own performance pending compliance by the other party. In a sale, it allows the seller to defend himself against the contractual delivery right of the buyer pending the latter's full performance and may allow a seller in possession to retain the asset until payment. In that case, it implies yet another kind of retention right (besides the statutory and contractual ones). Reference to that kind of retention right is in Germany made in Sections 273 and 320 BGB. In that case it protects against personal contract claims rather than proprietary actions.

In modern legal thinking, the *exceptio non adimpleti contractus* and the statutory retention right may both be considered examples of suspension or postponement rights, see for example Article 6.52 of the new Dutch Civil Code,[151] although the consequences are often very different. The retention right, even if resulting under the *exceptio non adimpleti contractus*, may have some proprietary and preferential aspects and has often become much more than a simple defence. It is likely to provide a first step in the return of title, especially in systems in which title transfers upon the mere conclusion of the sale agreement, as in France and England. Modern law may allow the retentor subsequently to dispose of the property in an execution sale in which he may satisfy his claim by priority out of the sale proceeds, but at least in civil law he is unlikely to be able to appropriate title in the asset under it.[152] Section 48 of the Sale of Goods Act 1979 in the UK on the other hand gives the seller a right to sell the asset to someone else which is a facility quite separate from the retention right.

For a retention right to operate, it is normally thought that there must be *reciprocity* of the obligations: see Section 273 BGB. The obligations must therefore exist between the same parties. There must further be some direct connection between the handling of the asset and the (resulting) claim, although it need not necessarily arise from the same contract but must come out of the same legal or economic relationship. At least that is so in

---

[151] In France, the retention right is now often also explained as a consequence of the *exceptio non adimpleti contractus*, which, although not as such expressed in the Code, is held to be a general principle under French law: see also Ghestin/B Desche, *Traite des Contrats, La Vente*, No 695 (1990).

[152] Apart from these retention rights for the unpaid seller still in physical possession, in most legal systems there are also retention rights for other types of creditors with actual possession (or possibly with possession through an employee, broker or custodian, but not through other holders or bailees, mere legal or constructive possession not being sufficient) of certain goods (if movable and being of some economic value) in some other precisely defined circumstances. The most common example is the retention right of the repairer in respect of the repair costs of the asset he holds. The carrier may also have certain retention rights in the goods he carries in respect of the freight price or loss averages. In the Netherlands, the security broker ('commissionair') has now also been given a retention right on the securities he holds for his clients. They are all incidental and specific and there is especially in Civil Law no general retention right for any physical possessor of goods in respect of any claim he may have against their owner. Special liens of this nature are sometimes also available in Common Law but equally only in certain situations, like for a private carrier, a warehouse, a bailee, a trustee, a lawyer, arbitrator and any general or special agent, see in the US, *Sheinman and Salita, Inc. v Paraskevas*, 22 Misc. 2d 436 (1959).

Germany where the retention right may now also be used for prior claims relating to the retained asset.[153] This principle of *connexity* is clearly expressed in Article 6.52 of the new Dutch CC, which covers all postponement actions, including the retention right, applicable unless connexity was explicitly not required: see Article 6.57 and Articles 3.290*ff* of the Dutch CC). The connexity may be more widely or more narrowly interpreted depending on the facts and on reasonableness in a contractual sense. The general course of dealing between the parties may here also be relevant: see also Article 6.52(2) of the Dutch CC. In Germany, in the case of a retention right under a mutual claim, a greater degree of connexity seems necessary: Section 320 BGB.

Another fairly general requirement of a retention right is that the claim of the retentor must be mature (except in commercial matters in Germany: see Section 369 HGB when the principle of connexity is also relaxed in that country) and for an amount of money, although the final determination of the total sum may have to await judgment. It means that non-monetary claims, like those for specific performance, may not be backed up by a retention right in the asset, but it may be possible to set off mutual claims for the same sorts of assets (likes stocks and shares). Moreover, the owner or holder (or bailee) must have ceded the asset voluntarily to the retentor or must have left it voluntarily with him, as in the case of a sale without transfer of physical possession. Appropriation of an asset will normally not give rise to a retention right.

It is increasingly accepted that the true owner need not be the contract party of the retentor who therefore even prevails over an owner or over the beneficiary of an older proprietary right, *cf* Article 3.291 of the Dutch CC. A related question is whether the retention right may be transferred with the debt it secures and is therefore an accessory right. This is often contested, certainly in Germany and the Netherlands (where the retention right remains clearly distinguished from a security interest), but believed possible in France (where as a consequence it acquires distinct features of a security interest).[154]

In common law, there is the possibility of a more *general* retention right, that is a retention right in a whole class of assets (for which in England the term 'lien' is usually reserved, unlike in the USA where this term primarily covers security interests, whether consensual, statutory or judicial). It considerably loosens the requirement of connexity. However, these general retention rights operate only for certain providers of services, particularly bankers and brokers.[155] They may then cover all outstanding debt between them and operate as security interests. The essence of such a *general lien* is that whatever good is surrendered to the rightful owner, the remainder will continue to serve for the rest of the owner's debt to the retentor. Any additions to the assets will serve as further security at the same time, whilst unsatisfied earlier obligations and future obligations are also covered. Although the instances of a general lien are limited in common law, commercial usage appears to add to them and have a greater impact in this area than under civil law which looks more towards statutory authorisation, even if broadened under the *exceptio non adimpleti contractus*.

If by contract certain present and future goods are designated for the purposes of a retention right, there is no question of illicit retention. Thus, in countries where no

---

[153] See OLG Düsseldorf, 27 Oct 1977 [1978] NJW 703.
[154] See F Derrida, *Encyclopédie Dalloz* (Paris, 1987), Rétention No 30. In a French bankruptcy of the debtor, the bankruptcy trustee may, however, demand the handing over of the asset but he must then cede a preference in the proceeds of an execution sale of the asset to the erstwhile retentor: see Article 60 of the French Bankruptcy Act 1985.
[155] See in England *Brandao v Barnett* (1846) 3 QBD 519.

general liens or general retention rights exist, banks may through their general conditions of business still claim a retention right covering all they have received or may receive on behalf of their client in order to protect any credit or other types of client indebtedness from being extended in the present, past or future. Even in civil law countries this may amount to a general retention right and the question then arises whether this contractual enhancement of the retention right does not exceed its normal use whilst creating or attempting to create a more general security interest at the same time. As already mentioned above, such liens if contractually created in individual assets might be considered possessory pledges and become subject to their rules. If they are in future assets of the debtor, they may be considered *floating* charges which may also be subject to certain formalities in terms of documentation and registration or publication at the risk of the retention right so extended becoming a voidable preference. There may also be problems with the identification requirement, especially under new Dutch law. In either case, the ranking may be affected in the process of characterisation and these retention rights or liens may therefore not necessarily have the highest priority. The resulting protection may even lack the nature of a charge in the asset altogether and become limited to a preference in the execution proceeds only, as is the case in a French bankruptcy.

The related question is always whether the retentor may appropriate or execute the property he holds under statutory or consensual liens or only has a right to retain the asset, of which the nuisance value is then the most important aspect. This used to be the situation in most countries under statutory retention rights, but is now abandoned in the new Dutch Civil Code in favour of an execution right with the highest priority, assuming the conditions of a pledge or charge are inapplicable (Article 3.292 CC). Prior judicial authorisation following attachment of the goods (under the retentor himself) is required. Thus, even the *statutory* retention right acquires here some features of a security interest and a right *in rem*. This is in civil law indeed the more modern tendency: see also Article 37 of the Swiss Bankruptcy Act, for statutory retention rights or liens not so far followed in common law. However, there may be a contractual or implied power of sale for the creditor/retentor, which would not be an execution proper but lead all the same to a preference for the selling retentor or lienee.

There remains in this connection the question whether upon a default under a sales agreement, the statutory retentors in countries like England and France, where title passes upon the conclusion of the sales agreement, may appropriate the title if not automatically returned to them upon a rescission of the sale agreement. It appears that where such a rescission is subject to judicial approval as in France (except if waived in the agreement itself), title cannot revert earlier on the basis of the statutory retention right of the seller alone.

In contractual retention rights whether of an individual or general nature, parties will often introduce special provisions covering default situations which may authorise appropriation or sales and recovery out of the proceeds. As already mentioned, the main question is here whether the retention right must be characterised as a pledge or charge as a consequence subject to their rules. Modern statutory retention rights are moving in the same direction.

The modern retention right is of a hybrid nature. It has clear proprietary aspects where it may lead to appropriation of title in sales when ownership has already been transferred but not yet the physical possession and there is a default in payment, or where it begins to function as a secured interest in the assets concerned. On the other hand, retention is clearly a matter of the law of obligations in terms of the determination of the reciprocal nature of the obligations and of the connexity between asset and claim, in which reasonableness and commercial reality will also play a role. It may also give no more than a contractual defence or exception. Where they are contractually created, they may even be seen as security substitutes or as ways to avoid the formalities normally attached to the former and may as such be curtailed or converted. A particular instance of this is the retention of a bill of lading in the USA: see Section 2–401 UCC, an attitude sometimes also favoured by English law. Statutory retention rights may acquire similar features.

1.6   Secured Transactions and Conditional Sales

1.6.1   *The Difference between Secured Transactions and Conditional Sales*

A person who has assets and needs money can do one of two things. He can sell his assets to obtain cash or he can try to take out a loan secured on these assets. Everyone would agree that these are two quite different funding operations. The obvious difference is that in the first case the person requiring the money will not only lose the ownership of his asset but also the user rights in it. This may not at all be convenient, hence the attraction of the secured loan in legal systems, which will become all the more attractive as an alternative if the security may be non-possessory. Yet a loan secured in this manner may be expensive, as the security is left with the debtor and therefore less safe, whilst in any event interest must be paid and much less than the real value of the asset may be obtained in financing. Naturally, the asset will still be lost in the case of default, although any overvalue on the security will be returned.

Thus an outright sale might be better after all. An alternative may be a sale with a right to repurchase the asset at a certain date against a pre-agreed price. This is the sale-repurchase structure under which the seller pending the repurchase may be able to retain the use of the asset. The economic value of this user right is likely to be added to the repurchase price, which may also contain a fee element. The seller is here more likely to obtain the full value of the asset. On the other hand, if he does not repurchase the asset on the appointed date, all interest in it may be lost, therefore also any right to any overvalue that may have been created in the meantime (for example in times of inflation or in the case of market related assets like investment securities that may have increased in value). Any decrease in value will be for the original seller who can only avoid this if he has an option and no duty to repurchase.

There are here immediately three issues to consider: first, how the repurchase right should be characterised; secondly how the sale and repurchase can be distinguished from a secured loan; and thirdly how either operates. These issues are discussed in much greater detail in chapter V and will only be summarised below.

1.6.2   *What are Sale-Repurchase Agreements or Finance Sales? The Characterisation Issue. Property-based and Security-based Funding*

As suggested in the previous section, the sale and repurchase agreement or repo presents itself principally in terms of (a) a (call) option for the original seller to repurchase the asset on a given date. In that sense, he has probably no more than a personal right to do so. This facility has long been known and was called the *pactum de retroemendo* under Justinian law (C.4.52.2), still existing in France as the *vente à remère* (Article 1659 Cc). However, the sale and repurchase could also be cast in terms of (b) a right *and duty* of the original seller to retrieve the asset on the appointed date. Finally, the sale-repurchase may be cast in terms of (c) a (put) option for the buyer. In Germany this is called an uncharacteristic (*unecht*) repo and will be of lesser interest in this context.

The arrangement under (b), therefore the one under which the seller has a right and duty to repurchase the asset on the agreed date, could be seen as a purely contractual arrangement but also as resulting in a conditional sale under which, upon a timely tender of the repurchase price, the asset would *automatically* revert to the original seller. The importance of this characterisation is first that in the bankruptcy of the buyer, the seller may still be able to repossess the asset and ignore the bankruptcy, at least in countries where in bankruptcy such repossession is not stayed pending liquidation or especially reorganisation proceedings, or where other considerations may prevail, like the notion of the *solvabilité apparente* in France, which protects the outward signs of creditworthiness, or more generally the impossibility under applicable law for conditions to mature against a debtor after his bankruptcy has been opened.[156] An important issue is therefore the reclaiming or appropriation right upon default. As we shall see, the importance of the characterisation makes itself felt particularly in reservations of title, which, at least in Germany and the Netherlands, are conditional sales. It is no less relevant, however, in the modern financing structures of the hire purchase, finance lease, investment securities repo, and the factoring of receivables.

How the conditional sale works in this context will be briefly explained below and in more detail in chapter V. At this stage it may suffice to look first at the *reservation of title*. Under it a seller sells and hands over the asset to a buyer who has not yet paid, whilst the seller retains title for himself. The conditional sale nature of this transaction, at least in Germany and the Netherlands, means that the seller retains a conditional title only, subject to the payment right (and duty) of the buyer who can make himself the full owner at any time. The buyer has a proprietary expectancy (*dingliche Anwartschaft*), as German case law confirms. It may, as we shall see, be better to accept that both seller and buyer have a kind of title, the seller under the resolving condition of the buyer's timely payment and the buyer under the suspending condition of his own performance. In a *hire purchase* there may be a very similar situation, except that the buyer is likely to pay in instalments, whilst at the end of all instalment payments title automatically passes to him.

In the *finance lease* it is not much different. The lessee orders the goods to his specifications from a supplier, but title is officially acquired by a finance company that leases the goods to the lessee against regular payments or installments. Depending on the arrangement, the end result may be either for the lessee to acquire after the last installment payment full title either automatically or at his option, which option could be for free or for some further payment. Alternatively all rights in the asset may revert to the lessor. It depends on the contractual arrangement. In some countries this latter solution is the more common, as in the USA, for reasons that will be explained later. In civil law countries, mostly there is an option for the lessee to become the full owner at the end, but in some countries it may be more normal for him automatically to become one. Especially in that case, the arrangement could be characterised as a conditional sale.

In the *repurchase agreement* of investment securities or repos, what happens is that an investor wishes to acquire bonds or shares for a short time and wants to finance this transaction by obtaining funds through a sale and repurchase of the same securities with a third party, usually a bank that is specialised in this kind of repo financing. In these repos, the seller will have accepted the *right and duty* to repurchase the investment securities at a certain date. Again the result may be characterised as a *conditional* sale under which the assets will automatically revert to the seller upon a tender of the repurchase price. This would introduce a *resolutive* condition in the transfer. It could also be seen as an *outright or unconditional* sale and conditional repurchase with an *automatic* retransfer under the *suspensive* condition of repayment. This legal characterisation may however be affected by any fungibility of the securities, as we shall see. In the factoring of receivables (when they arise), also called *receivable financing*, their transfer may be made conditional on the approval or collectability by the assignee/factor/funding provider and the receivables may be automatically returned when they are not approved or cannot be collected. They may also be so returned when the total of the collections by the factor reaches the amount he has provided in funding plus an element of reward.

Reservations of title and hire purchase agreements are sales protection devices. They do not provide funding as such but protect sales credit. Repos and factoring create funding and may also be referred to as *finance or title sales*. The finance lease is also often put in that category as it is a way of obtaining financing for capital goods. These finance sales all have in common that they are often based on conditional transfers of ownership in the underlying assets. They have become very important. Repos are used to finance large short-time investment positions in banks and run into billions of US dollars (equivalent) per day in the main financial centres. Factoring of receivables has become a normal way to finance trade credit and is closely related to the securitisation of portfolios of similar claims like those under credit cards or under mortgage arrangements. Finance leases are believed to cover at least one eighth of all financings of capital goods and are particularly popular in the aircraft industry. Real estate may equally be acquired on that basis.

The finance or conditional sales used in financings is in fact considerably older. Under common law, the traditional real estate mortgage has always been a conditional sale under which the party in need of financing sells his land upon the condition that he may repurchase it on the appointed date whilst returning the principal plus the agreed interest. The difference is that there is here a true loan rather than a finance sale, as demonstrated by the interest rate structure. However, upon default there is no true execution sale and the mortgagee becomes full owner. There is no return of overvalue either (although it may be agreed that the mortgagee keeps the overvalue as constructive trustee for the mortgagor) nor indeed need the mortgagor make good any undervalue. Yet the courts in equity devised a special protection (the *equity of redemption*) allowing the debtor to repurchase the asset by still offering payment of principal and interest during a certain time, until the mortgagee asked for foreclosure of this equity of redemption to obtain the full disposition rights in the asset. In common law, these mortgages could also exist in chattels and were then called chattel mortgages, which in England now require registration as bills of sale if used by private persons. In the USA, under state law, they were often also made subject to registration, lost their conditional sale features, and became more like ordinary security interests with disposition needs upon default. They have been superseded by Article 9 UCC.

Historically, the conditional sales are always used when secured interests are not available or become too restrictive. Thus in Germany and later also in the Netherlands, where in the nineteenth century the *non-possessory* chattel mortgages were outlawed (they had existed under Roman law and in the *ius commune*) and all security interests in chattels had to be possessory, the sale and repurchase were used to achieve a similar (*non-possessory*) result. It was an obvious way out when non-possessory security became a necessity in a more advanced industrial society, where equipment and inventory had to be used to support financing but could, as part of the business of the borrower, not be turned over to the financier. The same happened in the USA. It was the origin of the German *Sicherungsübereignung* and of the Dutch fiduciary transfer, both creations of case law, in Germany gradually transformed into a kind of security interest,[157] as also happened in the Netherlands (although in a different way) where it is now superseded by a statutory non-possessory pledge. Under the conditional sales, it became possible to transfer equipment and inventory whilst retaining the physical assets, although there is an important difference between both countries in the shift of the security in replacement assets or proceeds. It is not encouraged in the Netherlands but may be achieved by contract in Germany. In common law it followed always in equity on the analogy of the conversion of trust funds as a form of tracing.

Receivables became similarly transferable in what came to be called in Germany a *Sicherungszession*. In France, on the other hand, the funding arrangement through finance sales never became popular because conditional sales where handicapped in a bankruptcy of the buyer by the difficulty to reclaim them because of the general impossibility for conditions to mature in bankruptcy (except in pure sales) and in any event because of the notion of the *solvabilité apparente*, already discussed above in connection with the reservation of title: see section 1.5.6 above. In England, there was never a problem with non-possessory security and the English developed here also equitable floating charges as true security interests instead of building further on the conditional sale structure inherent in (chattel) mortgages. As these chattel mortgages were legal interests, they moreover had to be in *specific* assets whilst the automatic shift of the interest into replacement goods was more problematic than in equity, the reason floating (in equity) charges became more popular.

Their drawback is, however, that they provide a low priority as they crystallise only at the time of default, a complication eliminated under Article 9 UCC in the USA. Both in England and the USA, in the nature of a true security interest, they also require a form of disposition upon default with the return of overvalue and they need publication. The debtor remains responsible for any undervalue which results in an unsecured claim for the creditor. As an alternative, debtors may convert themselves into trustees for their assets and hold them for their creditors as beneficial owners. In the USA, this remains a traditional way of financing real estate. True conditional sales for financing purposes are also still possible under common law (although for chattels and intangibles no longer in the USA, as we shall see) and do not lead to the equity of redemption, at least if not clearly supporting a loan structure. Finance leases, repos and factoring fall into that category, although it should be added that they are seldom so analysed in England, where they are not, however, considered secured loans either. It is true that even the reservation of title is in England seen rather as a delayed than as a conditional sale and transfer, but in any event never as a security interest. Common law (except under statute in the UCC in the USA) is not inclined to go here behind the wishes of the parties.

1.6.3   *When are Finance Sales Converted into Secured Transactions?*

Secured transactions concern loans supported by security interests in the debtor's assets. In this sense, security interests are more in particular connected with loans, not directly

---

[157] In Germany, in the modern lending practice, banks normally do not allow automatic return of the asset to the borrower upon repayment but prefer to keep control of the asset subject to a contractual obligation to retransfer only.

with sales credit protection as reservation of title or hire purchases are. It is true that under the UCC in the USA security interests support any payment or performance of an obligation, see Section 1-201(a)35 (1-201(37) old) UCC. In that country reservations of title, conditional sales, finance leases and receivable financings are all converted into secured transactions if supporting such payments or the performance of other obligations, see Sections 1-201(a)35 (1-201(37) old), 9-109(a)5-6) (9-102(1)(a) and (2) old) UCC. The consequence is that the UCC subjects them all to the same formalities in terms of publication (except charges in consumer goods: Section 9-302 (new and old) UCC) and disposal upon default with the duty to return all overvalue to the debtor.

It is said that the UCC looks at economic realities in a *unitary functional approach*. This approach ignores the different risk and reward structures and the parties' choice in this connection and attempts to eliminate in particular true conditional sales with their appropriation possibility and release of the buyer in favour of a system under which overvalue is returned and the debtor remains liable for any shortfall. In the new Dutch Civil Code there is a not dissimilar resistance to funding alternatives. Security substitutes are given only contractual effect and therefore no rights against third parties (Article 3. 84(3) CC). There is no conversion into a security interest (subject to its formalities and safeguards) either. On the other hand, since securities are not defined, it is difficult to determine what true security substitutes are. The conditional sale seems not to be included, as under Article 3.84 (4) CC the proprietary effect of conditions is explicitly accepted in the Netherlands, although, as in the case of reservation of title, the new Code does not elaborate on the parties' rights thereunder and seems not to consider duality in ownership. It has left the status of the modern finance sales in considerable doubt and left it to be determined by case law. It does not give the lessee in a financial lease a proprietary interest, except where clearly so negotiated: see more in particular chapter V, section 1.2.3. The result is the opposite of the situation in the USA where the conversion into a security interest means that the lessee becomes the legal owner subject to a security interest for the lessor in the leased assets.

Elsewhere, no such approach has been taken and the distinction first between sales and loan credit is usually maintained so that sales credit protection like in reservations of title is not considered a security interest, whilst conditional or finance sales may present other funding techniques altogether, even if their characterisation (as conditional sales and what that means) may remain subject to (considerable) doubt. In this approach, security is connected with loan credit and security interests thus support loans which are advances of money subject to repayment (together with agreed interest). It is an agreed *interest rate structure* that is the essence of this type of funding. Without it there is no loan agreement, and without a loan agreement there can be no security interest, but if there is a loan in this sense, it is likely that any supporting structures will be characterised as secured transactions. Since sales credit is normally not a loan because there is no interest rate structure, reservations of title and hire purchases are not normally converted into a security interest. If there were such a structure, however, it would be normal to assume such a conversion. It would render them subject to the formalities of secured transactions in terms of creation and enforcement or foreclosure.

The case in point is the German *Sicherungsübereignung* and the former Dutch fiduciary sales, both developed in case law on the basis of conditional sales to allow funding assets with non-possessory protection. Since there is here a normal loan (with interest rate), it was logical to expect the conversion of these conditional sales into security interests and that is indeed what happened, especially in the Netherlands, whilst in Germany the position of the bank was further eroded as in a bankruptcy of the borrower it was given a preference only in the proceeds of a sale of the relevant assets rather than a separate repossession and execution right. However, if there is no such loan structure, as there may not be in finance leases, repos and other finance sales, one should assume that there is a conditional sale without any need for conversion. Such sales can indeed exist in Germany but it should immediately be added that the finance lease, repos and factoring are not readily so analysed in that country: see chapter V, section 1.4.3.

The distinguishing features are that *secured transactions* (a) create proprietary interests that go with the asset and that are (at least in civil law) accessory to the loan they support. It means that a sale of the asset will not extinguish the security interest in it (except if sold to a *bona fide* purchaser or purchaser in the ordinary course of business) and that an assignment of the secured claim will automatically entail the transfer of the security interest to the assignee. These security interests (b) require upon default a disposition, therefore normally some form of public sale, or a sale which may attain some objective value of the asset, and a return of the overvalue to the defaulting debtor. There is (c) also the question of the extension of the interest into replacement assets and proceeds to be considered and there may be (d) extra formalities, especially in terms of publication or turning over of possession. Finally, there are (e) the questions of ranking and (f) the separate repossession or execution right of the security interest holder in the nature of a self help remedy in the bankruptcy of the counterparty.

As far as the accessory issue is concerned, it receives traditionally more attention in civil than in common law. In civil law it is typical for secured interests but not for conditional sales and therefore not for reservations of title. The same is true for retention rights. That is to say that if an assignee of a claim (a sales receivable) wants the benefit of the reservation of title, it must be separately transferred to him by the assignor. In the case of a retention right, the asset must be transferred with the claim. This may be very important in factoring where, depending on its terms, the creditor through the assignment of the receivable may also be considered to have been paid so that the reservation of title or retention right lapses altogether and the buyer becomes the full owner. Only in France and probably also in Belgium under modern case law this is different in the case of a reservation of title which is now considered accessory to the receivable it supports: see chapter V, section 1.3.4. It shows French ambiguity as to the nature of the reservation of title and the security analogy is increasingly pursued in France, although so far an execution sale is not required but under case law any overvalue must be reimbursed to the debtor. It comes close to the situation in the USA where a disposition and repayment of any overvalue to the debtor is now required under Article 9 UCC also for a reservation of title.

It is indeed typical for security interests that the debt will be set off against the proceeds upon some objective disposition and that the overvalue will be returned to the debtor. In finance sales, on the other hand, in the case of default, there will be appropriation of the asset by the financier without any return of such overvalue. Against this, there are obvious benefits for the party requiring the funding: the funding may be larger, up to the full value of the asset, and it may be cheaper. It may be quicker as formalities may be avoided in terms of documentation, publication or special treatment, which goes especially for the repo of investment securities that may fit in the normal system of transfer and settlement of investment securities rather than needing special pledge registers. There may also be tax and accounting treatment differences. The result is a different risk and reward structure, which shows security-based and ownership-based funding as true alternatives. It also shows that conversion from the one into the other or the risk thereof can be greatly inconvenient to the parties who wanted another *risk and reward*.

Especially giving back the overvalue to the defaulter under the circumstances might be a very great disadvantage and an unexpected variation of the contractual balance reached between the parties or desired by their economic objectives. Where the interests shift into replacement goods, the overvalue possibility is greatly increased but other suppliers of commodities or spare parts may become involved as well and may have to be accommodated at the level of priorities. In that case, also in common law, one sees a change into a charge or security interest leading to a disposition upon default and a return of overvalue whilst the debtor remains liable for any undervalue to these secured creditors. Lack of formalities, especially publication of these charges (like other floating charges), may upon automatic conversion reduce the financiers interest to the lowest secured rank. On the other hand, where a conditional sale, including a reservation of title, does not shift into replacement goods and is limited to specific goods, a disposition seems improper and unnecessary.

Thus only where a clear loan or a floating charge results in that manner a disposition with a return of overvalue is to be expected, although in the USA, in chattels, the conditional sale is no longer an acceptable alternative, as we saw, even if it is in specific assets and parties opt for this structure.

As we saw, in civil law, this shifting of the security into replacement assets is in many countries problematic even for security interests, and that may be another reason why there remains more room for conditional sales in such countries. There are great differences here, however, with German law being liberal, and creditor and debtor may agree to this shifting. Dutch and French law are much less generous, which also applies to conditional sales like the reservation of title, which are not extended into replacement goods either. Then there are the formalities. In the case of a pledge, there is the old requirement of the transfer of physical possession in civil law and the creation of a bailment in common law. Constructive delivery is outlawed in this connection in most civil law countries. For non-possessory security, publication became an alternative for corporate floating charges in England and for most non-possessory security interests in chattels and intangibles in the USA (through the finance statement), but there is an important difference, already mentioned before. In England, the security interest of the floating charge only crystallises upon default and notably not upon filing so that the floating charge gives only a low priority right (just above that of the unsecured creditors). This is not so in the USA, where under Article 9 UCC the security is perfected as from the moment of filing. Only if filing is omitted (except for security interests in consumer goods that do not require it), is the ranking just above that of the unsecured creditors.

Civil law mostly still accepts that the non-possessory interests or charges in chattels and intangibles remain hidden but are nevertheless ranked as from the moment they are created. In Germany this is in bankruptcy clear for the *Sicherungsübereignung* and *Sicherungszession*. It was also true for the fiduciary transfer under former Dutch law, which is now replaced by a statutory facility that requires registration with a notary but only to identify the transaction and its timing. It is no publication facility. In France, there is no general facility allowing non-possessory security in chattels but they may exist in certain types or in a business (*fonds de commerce*) for which instances special publication facilities are imposed which are very different in nature. For non-possessory security interests, the formalities may thus vary considerably from country to country, in chattels especially in the aspect of publication. Conditional sales do not normally require any publication anywhere. That is clear for the reservation of title, although when it shifts into replacement goods so that it acquires features of a floating charge this may be in doubt in England if companies are the debtors. Conditional sales do not require other formalities either, like special documentation or registration requirements.

Then there is the ranking. In finance sales there is unlikely to be any, although it is conceivable that the seller sells the asset twice under a finance sale. It is certainly not unknown under the German *Sicherungsübereignung* but this is now largely treated as a non-possessory security interest, as we saw, which allows a ranking according to time. In true conditional sales, the seller can certainly sell his remaining interest or reversion in the asset, but that does *not* amount to a ranking amongst his succeeding buyers. Thus in a reservation of title, the second buyer risks automatically losing his interest if the first one pays the original seller because the reversionary interest is lost.

As far as the ranking of secured transactions is concerned, the first in time will be first in right although first publication or perfection may change the order. This ranking principle according to time follows in general from the nature of the proprietary right, which may be maintained against all the world, therefore also against younger interest holders. Hence the principle of relativity or priority, also called the *droit de préférence*, already discussed above in section 1.2.5, and expressed in the maxim: *prior tempore potior iure*. Yet specific interests may rank above general ones. Thus a younger reservation of title is likely to prevail over an older floating charge owned by someone else in the same asset (in England obtaining its rank in any event only from the moment of crystallisation). Possessory interests may always prevail over non-possessory ones. By security statute, further changes in the order may be imposed, which may also result from applicable bankruptcy laws.

Finally, there is the separate repossession or self-help remedy and execution right of the security interest holder to be considered. It follows in general terms from the fact that the security interest is a proprietary right that can be maintained and executed against all the world, from which also follows that it can be maintained against whoever owns and is in possession of the asset (except if it has a better, older right thereto). This is the *droit de suite* aspect of all proprietary rights already highlighted before. The repossession and execution right is expressed in Germany as the *Aussonderungsrecht*; it is typical for owners and for those who benefit from reservations of title. It is in Germany denied to security interest holders in bankruptcy if they do not have a possessory interest. But even a pledgee in possession conducts a normal execution sale, although outside the bankruptcy (but with a return of overvalue to the trustee), not therefore the beneficiary of the *Sicherungsübereigung* or the mortgagees of real property because they are not in possession. This is set to change to some extent with the implementation of the 2002 Financial Collateral Directive (foreseen in 2004). In the forthcoming Section 1259 BGB, the pledgee in possession under a commercial pledge of assets (with a market value) may upon bankruptcy not only execute his securities interest but also appropriate the asset if so agreed. This would amount to a true *Aussonderungsrecht*.

For the non-possessory security interest holders there is in Germany in bankruptcy only an *Absonderungsrecht*, that is a preference in the execution proceeds after a sale is conducted by the trustee. It is a typical German limitation, not often followed elsewhere. (Outside bankruptcy, the position is different and the status of the *Sicherungsübereignung* then depends much on the contractual terms. There is now no appropriation facility, however, except if expressly agreed.) In France there is a special class of statutory lien holders (*privilèges*) who also do not have a separate execution or repossession right.

Elsewhere, the repossession or self-help right of security interest holders is very important in a bankruptcy of the debtor, whether or not they have possession. It gives the security interest holder in principle the right to ignore the bankruptcy, claim the secured asset from the trustee, dispose of it, and set off the claim against the proceeds, whilst only the overvalue is returned. The initiative and timing are therefore with the secured creditor who also does not need to contribute to the costs of the estate. Those who do not have the repossession right will have to contribute, and as the cost of the estate normally have the highest rank, the collection of those who cannot repossess is thereby limited even if they rank higher than ordinary creditors.

Modern bankruptcy statutes may intrude on the repossession right to prevent a situation in which the secured creditors take most of the assets immediately, so that a reorganisation under modern reorganisation statutes becomes a practical impossibility. Thus Section 362 of the US Bankruptcy Code imposes a stay by law subject to the courts being able to vary the measure. It does not mean that the security is lost; its benefit is, however, suspended, but the self-help remedy may be reinstated if no adequate protection can be offered by the bankruptcy trustee. Security interest holders may also have to accept the immediate release of overvalue and accept alternative security interest if to the benefit of the estate, provided always that they remain adequately protected. They may now even be forced to co-operate in the reorganisation and their rights may be 'crammed down' under certain circumstances although they cannot be fully taken away from them against their will. Also the French Bankruptcy Act of 1985 includes the secured debtors in the proceedings, which are mainly meant, however, to provide a delay to facilitate a reorganisation. The new German Insolvency Act of 1999 goes in many respects in the direction of the American approach with its reorganisation ethos, but did not need these elaborate special stay provisions as there was never an *Aussonderungsrecht* for non-possessory security holders (including mortgagees) in Germany.

The repossession or self-help facility and separate position of the secured interest holders remains nevertheless an important feature of most secured transactions and continues to give them a special place also in modern bankruptcy statutes. It means that they may mostly still avoid sharing in the cost of the bankruptcy administration, can time their own recovery, and need not wait for the trustee and his distribution schedule, even if the repossession right may be stayed for some time pending the decision of reorganisation or liquidation. In addition, statute or case law may create statutory liens with preferential rights. They could give certain creditors repossession rights or only preferential rights in the proceeds of a bankruptcy liquidation. The difference is again in initiative, timing and sharing in the cost of the estate.

Tax authorities and wage earners are the best known beneficiaries of statutory liens of either type. They normally have a high statutory preference, in civil law mostly without their own repossession and execution right, however. Modern German bankruptcy law has done away with the tax preferences altogether. On the other hand, some individual creditors may also have preferential rights to the proceeds, like (often) the unpaid repairers of assets without a retention right. Since they have no repossession rights, they share in the cost of the administration and must wait for the trustee to start distribution. They have in Germany only an *Absonderungsrecht* or in France a *privilège*.

Conditional ownership rights as proprietary interest give in principle repossession rights, as we already saw when the condition (or term of time) matures. In bankruptcy, they may as such be maintained against the bankruptcy trustee assuming that, if the condition has not already matured in their favour, it may still do so and be effective *after* the bankruptcy. Even in Germany, reservation of title gives an *Aussonderungsrecht*. Whether conditions of this nature may still mature after bankruptcy is, as we saw, in many countries an important issue whilst in France the theory of the *solvabilité apparente* or of 'apparent ownership' may be a further bar to the recovery rights. In reorganisation-oriented bankruptcy statutes there is also likely to be a stay. Where conditional transfers have been converted into security interests because they support loans, they may be weakened further, like the German *Sicherungsübereignung*, by being treated as a preference so that the beneficiary of the right must share in the cost of the estate and can recover only after the trustee has liquidated the assets. Where the reservation of title is allowed to shift into replacement goods and proceeds, the end result may also be a degeneration of the proprietary interest of the seller into a preference or *Absonderungsrecht* only, as it is indeed in Germany.

1.6.4   The Operation of Finance Sales. Effect of the Conditionality of the Transfer. Proprietary Effect of Conditions. Duality of Ownership and of Possession in Civil Law. Openness of Proprietary Systems?

Security interests have a long history, and in the course of time their status and effect became accepted, more particularly so in civil law where the security interest as a proprietary right of the creditor became well established. The mortgage in real estate and the possessory and non-possessory pledges in chattels date from Roman law. The protection of the debtor through an arm's length sale of the asset to obtain objective values with the return of the overvalue to him was an early concern and led even before Justinian times to an outlawing of an appropriation clause (*lex commissoria*) in the pledge (C.8.34.3). It did not, however, outlaw the conditional sale itself as we saw, at least not the *pactum de retroemendo* of C.4.54.2 *Cf* also D.41.4.2.3.

Yet neither Roman law nor the *ius commune* elaborated much on the conditional ownership theme. Common law on the other hand stayed in its development of security interests much closer to the conditional sale and was always more relaxed about the possibility of appropriation upon default. This may be seen in the traditional mortgage. It was considered a conditional sale (even if in modern English law it can also be structured as a true security interest) resulting therefore in a full appropriation of title upon default, balanced only by the equity of redemption. In this approach, there was no return of overvalue *per se*; on the other hand if the lender sought to repossess the property, there was no need for the borrower to pay any undervalue either. This followed from the nature of the conditional sale itself, which became absolute upon default. Execution and supervised sale with a return of overvalue is a more specific aspect of recent American statutory law in this area, especially for chattels, as may be seen in Article 9 UCC (Sections 9-601*ff* (9-501 old)).[158]

In common law, the situation with respect to conditional or delayed title transfers leading to future interests is generally quite different from the situation in civil law. Common law has always accepted these conditional or future interests, also in chattels, although they were first developed in respect of land. Besides the fee simple, the life interests, and the estates for years or leaseholds, they arose early in common law. Especially upon a life estate, future interests like reversionary interests arose if the land was supposed to revert to the grantor or there could be remainders if it was to go to someone else, again either for life or in fee simple. The future interests were either vested in the beneficiary, that is to say subject to the passing of a term of time only, or contingent when a condition was attached. Traditionally, in a life estate, the normal condition was that at the end of the life interest the beneficiary of the remainder was alive. If not, the interest would revert to the grantor. Later any type of condition became possible, like the grant of an estate for as long as the asset served a particular purpose or for as long as the grantee behaved in a certain manner.

---

[158] See SA Riesenfeld, *Creditors' Remedies and Debtors' Protection* (3rd edn, 1979), 149.

In common law, these future interests exist beside the present interests, are fully transferable, and are not affected by statutes of limitation or, in civil law terms, extinctive prescription, although if not vested they (together) are curtailed in time under the statutes against perpetuities. They are not retroactive. It is not necessary in this context to elaborate further on what is not an easy subject in common law where the precise characterisation of these future interests (into reversions, remainders or executory interests, either vested or not) is often complicated and they are by no means all treated the same.

As just mentioned, these conditional and future interests subsequently became possible also in chattels even though then only in equity. It meant that the protection was largely based on an economic interest in the asset giving a limited proprietary right that could in particular *not* be maintained against *bona fide* purchasers of the legal interest or bailees. In England these future interests in chattels are now mainly hidden behind trust structures. They receive as such less attention. That may be different in the USA.

There is no proper equivalent for these future proprietary interests in civil law. In civil law, conditions and terms of time are well known, but their proprietary effect is unclear. In this connection, *conditions or contingencies* are uncertain events like payment in a sale under a reservation of title. The date at which the condition matures (or not) may be certain, but the event is not. If the event is certain, there is a *term of time*, eg when ownership is only transferred after a certain date, even though that date itself may be uncertain, eg death. The fact that a transfer is delayed until a certain date as in a reservation of title does *not* itself mean that it is not conditional. That is clear under German and Dutch law, although in France and England this seems not to be fully appreciated. The difference between conditions and terms of time is, however, on the whole not great in civil law, and it is therefore not normally necessary to distinguish sharply. Yet conditions may redirect title retroactively (although not now in Germany and the Netherlands with regard to the condition of payment in sales agreements, except where expressly so provided). Terms never have such retroactive effect. In the Netherlands under its new law (Article 3.85 CC), transfers for terms are (surprisingly) converted into usufructs, not, however, the conditional transfers.

In civil law, conditions and terms may be suspensive or resolutive. It is difficult to determine which they are. The reservation of title may be seen as a resolutive condition for the seller but could be characterised also as a suspending condition for the buyer at the same time (a step as yet not taken in most civil law countries). It is indeed best to see them as complementary. Consequently, the seller in a reservation of title has ownership or title under a resolutive condition, the buyer under a suspensive condition. The sequel is in civil law that the seller has resolutive possession and the buyer suspensive possession. As the buyer under a reservation of title is normally the holder of the asset in a civil law sense, one could further say that until payment he holds for the time being for another (the seller). Once payment is made, the scene changes of course completely as the condition is fulfilled and all the seller's conditional rights in the asset cease. The same goes for the buyer if he does not make timely payment but he remains holder for the seller until the asset is returned.

It may not matter much whether the one party has the suspensive or resolutive rights. Physical possession may matter more (in a reservation of title with the buyer) as it may give the possessor in that sense the income and user rights (or even an implied right to on-sell the property) which also suggests that he will be liable for the maintenance and harm caused to others (unless the contract says otherwise). The more important point, however, is that there results here even in civil law a duality in ownership and an independent right for each party to defend and transfer the conditional ownership and accompanying possession.

For the party not physically holding the asset, this transfer in countries where transfer of ownership or title requires delivery of possession could be achieved only through constructive delivery. It means for the seller under a reservation of title delivery through a transfer *longa manu* (which might under applicable law require notice to the buyer/holder as a constitutive requirement, see eg Article 3.115(3) Dutch Cc). It is also conceivable that the transfer of these conditional proprietary rights of a seller not in possession could take the form of an assignment, more likely the German approach (under which no notification of the debtor, here the original buyer under the reservation of title is required: Section 870 BGB). For the party holding the asset (here the buyer), delivery would be possible. If physical to a *bona fide* purchaser, the latter would in most civil law countries obtain full title, even if the title of the original buyer who is now selling would only be conditional. If the interest of the original seller under the reservation of title was disclosed, however, the purchaser from the buyer would obtain no more than the latter's interest. The purchaser from the original seller would never obtain more than the latter's interest (his conditional ownership right in the asset, probably transferred together with the assignment of the receivable) as in civil law the constructive nature of the delivery would in most countries not make this buyer a protected party even if *bona fide*.

The duality of ownership here discussed is largely accepted in Germany and probably also in the Netherlands, at least for reservations of title, but seems not so far more generally developed for other forms of conditional ownership. In the context of the reservation of title, the Germans speak here of the *dingliche Anwartschaft* of the buyer or the proprietary expectancy since a decision of the German Supreme Court in 1956.[159] It is an important development that pushes open the proprietary systems in civil law and gives parties considerable powers to divide ownership by contract in any way they want, always subject (in the case of chattels) to the protection of *bona fide* purchasers of the assets, in those countries that generally protect such purchasers. One could also say that the more third parties are protected, the more conditional sales may be likely to operate. The conceptual problem in civil law is therefore not truly the closed system of proprietary rights but the shortcomings in the protection of *bona fide* purchasers, especially of real estate and receivables. In common law, the law of equity protects third parties much better against hidden equitable proprietary interests. It may well be seen as the trade off in allowing their free creation.[160]

Where the duality of ownership in this manner forces itself through conditional ownership concepts also on civil law, it is finally necessary to determine the relationship between both owners and their respective rights in the asset, especially in cases of default but subsequently also in a bankruptcy of either (or both). It must be admitted that these aspects are not always clearly elaborated in common law either, although for the conditional sale and the reservation of title in the USA before the UCC became effective there developed extensive case law,[161] but much less in England.

The most pressing issues are the entitlement to income and capital gains and the liability for the loss of the asset and for the harm it may cause others, already briefly mentioned above. So is the transfer of each party's interests and the position of *bona fide* purchasers. Other issues are the possibility for each party to encumber its interest. Could the conditional ownership rights also concern future assets, and may they shift into replacement goods? What is the non-bankrupt party's position in a bankruptcy of a conditional owner

[159] See BGH, 22 Feb 1956, BGHZ 20, 88 (1956), see also chapter V, s 1.4.1.
[160] See also s 1.3.7 *supra*.
[161] See chapter V, s 1.7.3.

in possession? The question of what the effect is of an attachment of the asset on the other (non-possessory) party's rights in it seems related. It raises the issue of the relationship of this conditional owner *vis-à-vis* the secured and other creditors of the other conditional owner with possession of the asset. A reservation of title may eg give in principle the strongest status to the seller upon a default of the buyer but if the seller retakes the asset is it likely to be subject to any security interests the buyer has created in it in favour of others. This is certainly so if they are *bona fide* in those countries that protect *bona fide* purchasers of chattels. In those that do not, the question is whether the buyer under the reservation of title has sufficient title to make a disposal. If he could not transfer more than his own interest, that interest is at an end upon default. That could also mean the end of his purchaser's right.

1.6.5 Examples of Finance Sales: Finance Leases, Repos and Factoring. Finance Sales as Executory Contracts, Cherry Picking and Netting

In the foregoing a number of finance sales or ownership-based funding techniques were identified, like the finance lease, the repo of investment securities, and the factoring of receivables with particular emphasis on their characterisation in terms of options or conditional sales, of which the more traditional example is the reservation of title as is the hire-purchase. These are both, however, sales credit or sales price protection devices rather than schemes to raise financing, as is the case with repos, factoring of receivables and, although less obviously so, in finace leasing, although it should of course be borne in mind that in all cases there is credit provided, whether there is sales credit, loan financing through secured transactions or funding provided through conditional sales. They are more extensively discussed in chapter V.

Of the modern funding schemes, the finance lease is probably most developed in law, although in practice the finance repo and the factoring of receivables are probably no less important. The finance lease was the subject of early statutory law in France (*credit bail*) and other southern European countries. The finance repo was the subject of legislation in France (the *pension livrée* since 1993) and in Germany (Section 340b HGB). Special factoring or receivable financing statutes are less common so far, but both the finance lease and the factoring of receivables have caught the attention at the international level, the finance lease and factoring in Unidroit and receivable financing in Uncitral: see again for the details chapter V. Unidroit produced conventions in 1988 on the leasing of assets if moving transborder and on factoring of portfolios of receivables with debtors in various countries. The result was mostly a set of private international law rules. The 2001 Uncitral Receivable Financing Convention is more ambitious and attempts to provide a uniform law in the major aspects of receivable financing itself. The Unidroit Leasing Convention has obtained a small number of ratifications and has thus entered into force. So did the Factoring Convention more recently.

Finance leases should be distinguished from operational leases, which are mere contractual arrangements or rental agreements normally for the use of the assets for a shorter period. The finance lease itself has proprietary aspects and resembles more closely the reservation of title and probably even more the hire purchase, especially if it is an instalment arrangement under which the lessee eventually becomes the owner although he may have a mere option (possibly against further payment). Where he automatically becomes the owner or has a free option (which is more common), it appears that there is a conditional sale. This characterisation is sometimes avoided (especially in England) in order to eliminate the hire purchase analogy and the consumer protections of modern hire-purchase statutes which are inappropriate in the finance lease which is normally a professional financing tool. In the USA, the concern is rather to avoid the application of Article 9 UCC and therefore the conversion of the lease into a security interest making the lessee the immediate owner subject to a security interest of the lessor that needs to be properly filed. In Germany it seems that the finance lease remains characterised as a purely contractual arrangement for the lessee, although he may benefit from the general protection of a hire contract which can survive eg a sale of the asset by the lessor and in this manner probably also his bankruptcy. Dutch case law seems to go in similar directions.

In the repo of investment securities and more so in the old sale and repurchase agreement of which the German *Sicherungsübereignung* was an example and which in its conditional transfer form still seems a possibility if parties expressly so provide, there may be a purer instance of a conditional sale, although again it is not widely so analysed and for investment securities there is in any event a problem with the *fungible nature* of these securities so that not the same securities are likely to be returned but only the same quantity of the same sort, which may further undermine any proprietary claims of the seller. In new German and French law on these repos, their proprietary aspect is not covered and it remains a matter of characterisation. At least in Germany there is, as in the case of the lease, a disposition towards a purely contractual approach. It may mean that there is much less protection for the party acquiring the funding (the seller) than there is under a security interest. The simple tendering of the repurchase price may not then result in his full ownership.

In factoring of receivables, on the *contractual* side, there are *three* possibilities: it may be a mere administration and collection agreement under which the creditor leaves this part of his activity to an expert who can handle the receivables more efficiently, quickly and cheaply. There may also be a credit risk transfer to the factor, which means that the factor gives a guarantee of collection to the creditor. Finally there may be a funding operation under which the factor funds the receivable portfolio on a current basis. For true factoring there is always administration and collection and there must either be a guarantee arrangement or funding or both. Mere administration and collection are therefore best seen as a contract for services and not factoring proper. Factoring proper always implies a transfer of the receivables to the factor. This poses the problem of a bulk transfer and the inclusion of future receivables already discussed earlier.

As regards the transfer itself, therefore on the *proprietary* side, there are also *three* possibilities. The (bulk) transfer may be in full, it may be as security transfer only, or it may be a conditional transfer. Often it is conditional, at least as regards the individual claims: they may have to be approved by the factor, may have to be uncontested by the debtor, may not be affected by an insolvency of the debtor so that there is no credit risk for the factor at all. These are forms of *recourse factoring* in which all claims that do not comply with the conditions are then automatically returned. It only has the first and last contractual aspect just mentioned (or also a limited version of the second aspect). The most common form of factoring — the *old line* or *non-recourse* factoring — has all three contractual aspects and is on the proprietary side best characterised as a full sale and transfer of the receivables. See more in particular also the discussion in chapter V, section 2.3.1.

The alternative to finance sales having a proprietary aspect for both parties is to view them as purely contractual arrangements. As just mentioned that is not at all uncommon and seems to be the position especially in Germany for finance leases and repos. It means for the finance lease that the lessor remains the full owner of the lease assets whilst the lessee has only contractual (and perhaps some possessory) rights. In a repo, it suggests that the purchaser is the full owner and that the seller has no more than a personal retrieval right. In factoring, it would put the financier equally in the strongest position and the seller of the receivables could retrieve those rejected by him in a personal action only.

This is all pertinent especially in a bankruptcy of the financier when his counter-party may be in a weak position. In a long-term agreement like the finance lease for example, the lessee risks that the trustee of the bankrupt lessor (as finance company) may attempt to repudiate the contract as executory and retrieve the lease asset if beneficial to him. In the repo it could also mean that the bankrupt buyer/financier would insist on full performance of the agreement if the price of the securities had gone down but may wish to keep them even if the seller tendered the repurchase price on the due date if they had gone up. This is called the *cherry picking* option, which invariably results from the characterisation of finance sales as being merely contractual. In Germany and the Netherlands there is a difference in that agreements covering market quoted assets are automatically rescinded upon a bankruptcy of either party. Also rentals might be protected and (exceptionally) survive a sale of the asset, as is a common protection especially in real estate. It will all be discussed in greater detail in chapter V.

Where the finance sale is characterised as a mere contract, some relief may be obtained through netting. This is relevant only if there are sufficient positions either way between the same parties. It can only occur in repos where professional parties may be each others' financiers in different repo transactions between them. It requires a contractual expansion of the set-off concept to allow claims that are not all mature or even monetary or in the same currency. The contract will have to introduce here acceleration of maturities and related discount clauses, valuation clauses for non-monetary claims like the one for a return of the investment securities, and an exchange rate valuation if not all values are in the same currency. As it is not clear whether such expanded set-off clauses could be upheld in bankruptcy, some bankruptcy laws, like the ones in the US (upon amendment, see Section 559 of the US Bankruptcy Code) and the new German Insolvency Act (Section 104) especially so provide.

1.6.6 The Outward Signs of Security and Ownership-based Funding Interests. Possession or Filing. Attachment and Perfection of Security Interests under the UCC

To give effect to third party security interests or conditional ownership rights, some outward manifestation of the interest may be deemed desirable. The normal proprietary effects of security interests and conditional ownership rights are the right to pursue these interests or rights in the assets regardless of who owns them (allowing the debtor to transfer them regardless of any security interests or conditional ownership rights in them or any contrary stipulation in the security agreement itself, *cf* Sections 9-315(a)(1) (9-306(2) old) and 9-401 (9-311 old) UCC), the right to repossess the assets upon default (Section 9-503 UCC) and, in the case of a security interest, the priority in the distribution of the proceeds upon a disposition (Sections 9-609 (9-301 old), 9-339 (9-316 old) and 9-615*ff* (9-504 old) UCC).

In fact, for proprietary rights of any sort to emerge and be recognised in their third party effect, some outward sign of them is often required to warn and protect the public as it must accept and respect these rights and could only acquire the assets subject to them. The requirement of delivery for title transfer in chattels in most civil law countries and also under the older common law, see section 1.5.2 above, is often seen as an example of such a manifestation, here of title transfer. If there is no such sign, in modern legal systems the proprietary rights in the asset might be ignored and holders may be presumed the owners. As a consequence, *bona fide* purchasers of such holders tend to be protected if they acquire the physical possession of the property. At least that is the civil law rule in the case of chattels: see section 1.5.7 above. It defeats all prior proprietary interests in these assets of which the purchaser did or could not know.

As far as *real* property is concerned, modern public registration sitemaps, in which all proprietary interests in these assets are marked, allow (in most cases) for sufficient outward manifestation of rights in real estate. They must therefore be accepted by all and are not defeated by *bona fide* purchasers (in some countries unless the register is incorrect). In the case of chattels, it is physical possession that traditionally serves a similar purpose, but is only effective in that it allows others to presume that the holder is the owner. It is not and cannot in truth be indicative of any proprietary right proper and must, even in the common law of bailment, in any event yield to better rights, that is foremost to the rights of the real owner or other proprietary interest holders including those with security interests, unless *bona fides* protects the physical holder and makes him the owner free and clear of any other proprietary interests. In the case of intangible assets like monetary claims or receivables no outward sign of proprietary interests is easily conceivable at all, although a collection agent whilst collecting manifests power in the asset.

Indeed, for chattels and even more for intangible assets, the outward manifestation of lesser proprietary rights and certainly also of security interests (or conditional ownership rights supporting funding) in them is and has always been problematic. More generally, if a person holds these assets, in the case of chattels for example on the basis of contractual user rights or a proprietary usufruct, or in the case of intangibles as a collection agent, who can say what the real proprietary structure in these assets is? Only full title registration as in the case of land would resolve the issue but is totally unrealistic in view of the multitude of personal property items. Proprietary rights in personal property therefore normally remain secret unless they coincide with physical possession. This is only to some extent different in the common law in which physical possession is itself considered a proprietary right (bailment) and is more strongly protected, but even then highly defeasible by better rights: see section 1.3.2 above. In fact, to make commercial exploitation of chattels possible, the separation between ownership and physical possession is mostly a precondition and not in any way sinister or undesirable. The law must support that.

To minimise confusion, it has nevertheless not been uncommon for the applicable law to require in the case of security rights in personal property, especially chattels, (physical) possession for the validity of the interest. This was neither the Roman law nor *ius commune* system, however, which knew the non-possessory security interest (or hypothec) also in chattels and even a pledge with no more than constructive possession,[162] nor was

---

[162] In Roman law the security interests in assets developed as an alternative to personal security (through guarantees or sureties) and became preferred: see D 50.17.25. The oldest form was the *fiducia cum creditore* which was a conditional transfer or finance sale: see also s. 1.4.5 *supra* and for the development of the condition in the Roman law of property, chapter V, s 1.2.2, n 47. It was also used for non-funding purposes and then more a custody arrangement (the *fiducia cum amico*, see Gaius Inst. 2.60). In neither context, did clear fiduciary duties and reclaiming rights develop, a problem still apparent in the development of conditional or finance sales and custodial arrangements in civil law today: see s 1.4.5 *supra* and chapter II, ss 3.1.4 and 3.1.6. It is clear, however, that the *fiducia* allowed for a transfer with constructive delivery only and could therefore leave the physical possession with the former owner of the goods resulting in a non-possessory ownership right of the financier. It seems not to have been used to cover claims even when monetary: see for the limitations on their transfer in Roman law s 1.7.1 *infra*. The non-possessory nature of the fiducia was a risk for the new owner, but as *bona fide* purchasers of the former owner in possession were not protected under Roman law, which adhered to the *'nemo dat'* rule: see s 1.5.9 *supra*, legally that risk was limited. (*Note continues.*)

it that of the common law which accepted chattel mortgages (usually a conditional sale, however),[163] but it became progressively a requirement in the nineteenth century,

In the Justinian compilation, the notion of the *fiducia* was itself deleted but not the conditional sale as such. By that time there were, however, also security interests proper: see D 13.7.9.2. The difference was in the right to any overvalue in the assets upon default, which in the case of a security would belong to the defaulting debtor. These security interests were the hypothec (*hypotheca*) which was non-possessory and could be used both in respect of real estate and chattels. The pledge (*pignus*) was always possessory and the term was then also used in respect of land: see D 50.16.238.2. The basic difference in later Roman law was therefore in possession: see Inst 4.6.7 and D 13.7.1, but even where it was required, as in the case of the *pignus*, it could be constructive: see D.13.7.37, so that the difference between the *hypotheca* and the *pignus* was not always great: see also D 20.1.5.1, which acknowledged this state of affairs. It allowed for multiple transfers as security under which the oldest transferee was protected: see for the *prior tempore potior iure* rule, C 8.17.3 (whilst *bona fides* and/or possession of later interest holders was irrelevant), but an officially established security right (by a kind of deed or through witnesses) had a higher rank: see C 8.17.11.1.

By this time, also claims could be pledged. C 8.16.4 gave the lender the *actio utilis* (see n 181 *infra*) to collect. If the claim was monetary, the proceeds would be set off against the debt, but if the claim was for the delivery of goods, the security interest would shift into the assets upon their receipt by the borrower: see D 13.7.18. A closely related aspect was that future assets could be liberally included under the suspensive condition of their acquisition by the borrower: see D 20.1.16.7. C 8.16.4 suggests the possibility of general liens that could also include receivables and D 20.1.1. specifically mentions in this connection the inclusion of future assets, whether tangible or intangible. It amounted to the possibility of non-possessory floating charges that seem to have been very popular in later Roman times. They could be established through a hypothec but also through a constructive *pignus* as D 20.1.1 clearly states, and their priority would arise as at the time of the creation of the interest, not therefore of the later emergence of the assets so that later specific security interests in any of them in favour of other lenders would be subordinated. At least D 20.4.2 seems to suggest so and the idea also finds clear support in D 20.1.34.

In the *ius commune*, there was a tendency, especially in the natural law school, to limit the effect of the non-possessory interests to situations in which the asset was still with the debtor. In any event, upon a sale of the asset by him to a third party, the security interest came to an end, apparently even absent *bona fides* on the latter's part: see Grotius, Inleidinge 2.48.28, at least in the case of a hypothec. It seems not to have affected the constructive *pignus* which was popular, based on necessity and in Holland supported by the Supreme Court: see its decision of 13 Nov 1737 cited in Van Bynkershoek, *Observationes Tumultuariae* (ed Meijers 1962) IV, no 3051, but it disappeared in the 19th-century codifications under the influence of earlier French customary law: see n. 163 *infra*. The general (contractual) lien as floating charge became subject to the better right of later specific security interest holders: see Grotius, *Inleiding* 2.48.34 and was also in other aspects progressively reduced in effectiveness and equally disappeared in the 19th century codifications. On the other hand, some general (and special) statutory liens emerged (*pignora tacita*), some derived from Roman law, like the one for the tax man in C 8.14 (15). They sometimes prevailed over consensual liens. There also emerged preferences in proceeds without special repossession rights which would prevail over non-secured creditors but not over secured ones, unless so dictated by statute.

In this system, confusion could easily arise. An interesting countervailing feature was that already in later Roman law lack of disclosure on the part of the borrower of any liens against his assets was a criminal offence. This is the *stellionatus* of D 47.20.3.1.

[163] Customary law in France, which prevailed in its northern part (especially in Paris and surroundings) was unfavourably disposed to the Roman law system and required for security interests in chattels physical possession: see Article 170 of the *Coutume de Paris* (of 1510) which stated the famous maxim: '*meubles n'ont pas de suite par hypothèque, quand ils sont hors de la possession du débiteur*', from which later the general principle of protection of *bona fide* purchasers of chattels was deduced in France: see s. 1.5.9 *supra*. The non-possessory hypothec thus lost its significance for chattels but retained it for real estate and entered as such the *Code civil* (Article 2114 Cc). The principle of '*meubles n'ont pas de suite par hypothèque*' was retained in Article 2119 Cc, and the transfer of physical possession became a validity requirement: see Article 2076 Cc. In real estate there remains also a possibility of a possessory security interest with the use of the asset, called the *antichrèse* (Article 2072 Cc). It is uncommon. The floating charge had already been eliminated in the *Ordonnance de Commerce* of 1673 which in Article 8 required a document in which the collateral was clearly described. Article 2074 Cc retains that requirement, although in the commercial sphere a document itself is not necessary (*gage commercial*, Articles 91 and 109 *Code de Commerce*).

Only in the more recent *nantissement du fonds de commerce* established by the Law of 17 Mar 1909 (which also covered the sale of the fonds de commerce), now codified in Article L 142-1 to L 142-5 Code de Commerce is there a more limited floating charge facility, especially in respect of a business (which needs not to be incorporated) and its equipment. It is a peculiar French concept not defined in law, *cf.* also Article L 144 Code de Commerce for the lease of the fonds de commerce (replacing an earlier law of March 20 1956). It may also cover the receivables of the business but not its debt (therefore assets only). See further also F Lemeunire, Fonds de Commerce (2001). For receivables, the pledge became uncommon in France as it was doubtful whether it

especially on the European Continent and also in the USA.[164] Thus the old pledge became preferred and survived as the only type of security interest for chattels, as a possessory interest. The unavoidable separation between ownership and possession, also in this instance, protects the security interest holder in his proprietary or third party rights, which cannot be surreptitiously taken away from him. It leaves on the other hand the (better) interest of the owner and of other interest holders in the asset exposed. That is a trade-off for the owner who will normally be the beneficiary of this situation as a secured borrower.

Yet this method of providing security in respect of personal property is costly as it deprives the borrower/owner of the use of the asset in his business. It is the reason non-possessory security interests in personal property became a necessity after the industrial revolution, especially in respect of equipment, inventory and accounts receivable of a debtor, exactly to finance these assets themselves. This raised again the issue of their manifestation. In some countries, mainly of the civil law and notably in Germany, the non-possessory hidden liens of the *Sicherungsübereignung* became all the same accepted,

---

allowed collection by the lender. A conditional assignment became therefore the more common method of using receivables for funding purposes: see chapter V, s 1.3.5, also for the modern statutory amendments facilitating security transfers of receivables by eliminating the notice requirement. See for the development of the modern reservation of title in France, chapter V, s 1.3.4.

In Germany, the further development of the *ius commune* led in the 19th century also to the elimination of non-possessory security interests and floating charges in chattels which was borne out by Sections 14 and 43 of the first all-German Bankruptcy Act of 1877, enacted before the BGB which also accepted only one security interest in chattels which had to be possessory in which connection constructive possession was not sufficient: see Section 1205 BGB. In the meantime, even before the introduction of the BGB in 1900 the German courts had, however, accepted the principle of a conditional or finance sale in chattels (with mere constructive delivery of possession through a transfer *constituto possessorio*) in the so-called *Sicherungsübereignung* which subsequently developed in the direction of a non-possessory security interest. See for this development and for that of the related *Sicherungsabtretung* for receivables, more in particular chapter V, s 1.4.2 and for the development of the modern German reservation of title, chapter V, s 1.4.1.

[164] In England, the mortgage was a conditional sale: see chapter V, s 1.5.2 and could also exist in chattels when, however, registration with the courts became necessary in 1854 if used in the private (and not in the corporate) sphere. They were then called bills of sale. It also established priority in accordance with the time of registration, which was more generally meant to warn unsuspecting creditors, whilst at the same time protecting the debtor against hasty decisions in transferring assets to obtain funding. The conditional sale nature of the chattel mortgage was confirmed in *Ryall v Rolle*, 26 ER 107 (1749) with emphasis on the ownership status of the buyer and his risk of a reputed ownership of the seller if the goods were left with the latter. At first they could be structured as floating charges but that became progressively more difficult under statutory law and these floating charges subsequently developed in equity helped by the equitable tracing rights and shifts of charges into proceeds.

In English law the pledge was a proper security interest and possessory but limited to chattels. As English law was never strict in the physical possession requirement, constructive delivery could be sufficient. It may be difficult in such a situation to distinguish it from a chattel mortgage with its formal registration requirements (in the private sphere). The effect remains different, however. The differences are mainly in the disposition requirements, overvalue repayment or redemption facility and position of *bona fide* purchasers. In the case of a bill of sale, there is only an equity of redemption for the debtor upon default whilst *bona fide* purchasers of the creditor (even if not in possession) are likely to be protected against any equitable (redemption) interests of the debtor (even though in possession). In the case of a pledge, the debtor remains the owner and can reclaim his title from all purchasers of the creditor even if the latter is in possession. The sale or re-pledging of pledged assets by a debtor in possession is not likely to be subject to *bona fide* purchaser protection. The creditor/mortgagee will retain his rights, in which connection the publication of the interest provides an additional argument.

In the USA, the chattel mortgage as conditional sale was in the 19th century in many states superseded by state laws converting them into true security interests subject to registration. In that approach the pledge of chattels always required physical possession and there was a disposition upon default. The subsequent difficulties of creating floating charges were remedied in a number of different departures, depending on state law, partly based on conditional sales especially for reservations of title, partly on factoring acts which aimed at general contractual liens shifting into replacement equipment and particularly inventory and receivables, and partly on assignment statutes especially aimed at funding transfers of shifting portfolios of monetary claims. All are now superseded by Article 9 UCC: see for these US developments more in particular chapter V, ss 1.6.1 and 1.6.2.

although subject to *bona fide* purchaser protection of anyone acquiring title and physical possession in them, at least in the case of chattels. This *bona fide* protection against hidden liens did not exist in the case of receivables. Thus liens in them, although hidden, were perfectly valid against subsequent assignees of these assets, even if unaware of the earlier interests. Only in the USA did a *bona fide* protection of these assignees develop: see section 1.7.9 below. This was somewhat unexpected as it did not exist under common law in respect of chattels (and needed in that case statutory backing as was given in the USA in Article 2 UCC and in the UK in the Sale of Goods Act: see section 1.5.9 above).

There is a related problem in the *bona fide* protection of the security interest holder himself. May the lender rely on the outward signs of the debtor's personal property whilst creating the security interest and deem all included (if the security agreement is so formulated), even if the assets themselves belong to others? In respect of chattels this is indeed likely in civil law on similar grounds. In common law, this may be so by statutory disposition. Section 9-203(b)(2) (9-203(1)(c) old) UCC presents (indirectly) an example of this approach. Only if there is *mere possession*, is the debtor not supposed to have a sufficient interest in the property in his possession to transfer it to a lender as security.[165] One must assume that the lender as a type of purchaser must indeed be *bona fide*, although that idea is not clearly expressed in Article 9 UCC and does in any event not apply if the borrower has mere possession only (but voidable title is sufficient). But ownership in the borrower is not necessary. It exposes all those who have lent assets to a borrower or who have paid for inventory still in the latter's possession or gave any assets to a borrower subject to custodial interests (as agents or asset managers). Assets leased to a borrower may be included as well, although no longer if an equipment lease under Article 2A. The alternative of a special registration facility in respect of these assets to publicise and protect the position of the lessor and true owner was also specifically rejected.[166]

Unless clear exceptions are made, *appearance of ownership, apparent ownership* or *ostensible ownership* of a borrower seem here to be sufficient[167] resulting in a prospective windfall for the *bona fide* secured lender and a risk for anyone who leaves assets with a third party. This is curious in the sense that this notion of apparent ownership that works here in favour of *secured* creditors may under modern law not or no longer be sufficient

---

[165] Under case law concerning Article 9 UCC it is made clear that whilst a *pure* bailment may not create an interest that may be claimed by a secured lender of a bailee, any rights in the assets beyond mere possession will constitute a sufficient interest in the bailee/borrower and may be covered by a floating charge in favour of the lender under Section 9-203(b)(2) (9-203(1)(c) old) UCC. It is especially important when a customer or third party has supplied a bankrupt builder with materials which we may not therefore be able to retrieve: see also *Litwiller Machine and Manufacturing, Inc v NBD Alpena Bank*, 457 NW 2d 163 (1990). The UCC is here not interested in ownership rights even if mere possession is not good enough, *cf* also Section 9-112 (old) UCC (now omitted). The question is whether there are 'sufficient' rights which need not be strictly proprietary. The right of the bankrupt may be an entirely personal or contractual user right, which would still lead to the inclusion of the assets in his estate (assuming he has also physical possession). Generally, title (in the sense of ownership) itself is of relatively little significance under the entire UCC and deprecated, even in the sale of goods: see also Section 2-401 UCC (and this not only in respect of *bona fide* purchasers).

Ostensible ownership by the bankrupt may here be an additional argument and also the easy facility for the customer who provides materials to the construction company to protect himself by granting instead a loan with a purchase money security interest in the assets and filing a finance statement in respect of it: see *Kinetics Technology International Corp v Fourth National Bank of Tulsa*, 705 F 2d 396 (1983). However, it is curious that the apparent ownership approach is under modern law less likely to protect ordinary creditors or even statutory or judicial lien creditors: see also chapter V, s 1.3.2.

[166] Article 2A UCC made one exception in Section 2A-309. See further also CW Mooney Jr, 'The Mystery and Myth of "Ostensible Ownership" and Article 9 Filing: A Critique of Proposals to Extend Filing Requirements to Leases', (1988) 39 *Ala LR* 683.

[167] See for this notion also chapter V, s 1.3.2, n 85 and its demise in England in the Bankruptcy Act of 1986.

to protect ordinary, non-secured, *bona fide* creditors or even judicial or statutory lien creditors, at least no longer in the USA under applicable state law. Thus their reliance on the debtor's outward signs of wealth even if created by hidden non-possessory security holders leaving the debtor with their assets, works no longer in their favour, even if the secured interest holders themselves increasingly benefit from a similar protection.

In England and France, the notion of reputed ownership to protect *bona fide* ordinary creditors is also clearly on the wane. The acceptance of a reservation of title creating a hidden interest of the seller is here the most important example.[168] Security interest holders, even if hidden, are therefore better protected all the time unless their interests clearly arise from fraudulent conveyances.[169] Even in the USA in respect of personal property under Article 9 UCC, contractual or voluntary lien holders appear to have an extra protection derived from the apparent ownership of the borrower on top of their priority in the distribution of the disposition proceeds of the secured assets. Mere possession by a borrower is not enough, as we saw, but anything more seems to be, except where by statute exceptions are made. Hidden interests do not therefore in general stand in the way of voluntary liens in the USA and may easily be ignored by lenders secured on the assets in which these liens exist.

These security interests themselves, if non-possessory, are now mostly subject to a filing requirement in the USA, at least for their priority status. It is of interest in this connection to explore this US filing requirement and its meaning somewhat further, as it is often held out as a model. What does it do and what does it fail to achieve? Here we need to go into the meaning of *attachment* and *perfection* of the security interest in personal property under UCC law.

Under Section 9-201 (new and old)UCC a security agreement is valid immediately upon its conclusion and has third party effect. It works therefore against purchasers and other creditors. For this third party effect itself *no* filing or publication is necessary at all. No formalities are therefore imposed except that of a writing under Section 9-203(b)(2) (9-203(1)(a) old) UCC. This is unlike a full transfer of ownership under the law of the sale of goods where Section 2-401(2) still requires physical delivery unless parties agree otherwise. It is to be noted in this connection that public filing of a security interest does not replace the delivery of possession requirement in respect of the validity of the security interest, even for a pledge which may now also be validly created before possession is taken. The security interest attaches immediately and is under Sections 9-201 and 9-203 (9-203 old) UCC enforceable provided it is in writing, value is given and the debtor has a sufficient interest in the assets (which is any interest beyond mere possession, as just discussed).

The priority right is in consequence also immediately created. Sections 9-317, 9-102 and 9-323 (9-301 old) UCC reflect this. It suggests that there is an immediate priority in respect of all later attaching creditors and non-secured creditors. Only perfected voluntary security interests and statutory or judicial lien creditors prevail over it. As regards the latter, in bankruptcy, there is in particular the lien of the bankruptcy trustee to reckon with, which pushes the attached but non-perfected security interests automatically down. That is most important, but here a detail. The key is that the priority right of the secured creditor against non-secured creditors is attached upon the mere conclusion of

---

[168] See chapter V, s 1.3.4 for the situation in France and s 1.5.4 for the situation in England.
[169] This is the English approach since the famous *Twyne's case*, 76 ER 809 (1601), when a debtor transferred his assets to a friend whilst maintaining possession and all user and income rights. In modern bankruptcy laws, there have been added presumptions of fraud in transfers made between a certain period before bankruptcy (suspect period) but these presumptions are normally rebuttable. In civil law, this is the reach of the *actio revocatoria or Pauliana*.

the security agreement and that in principle it is also valid against purchasers of the asset (unless they purchase in the ordinary course of business or are *bona fide,* in which connection they do not have an investigation duty: Section 9-323 (9-307 old) UCC).

The publication/filing or perfection itself only establishes priority over later secured creditors under voluntary or statutory and judicial liens. That is all. The filing is limited to a finance statement. It only indicates in summary terms the type of collateral covered. It is important mainly as a warning to later secured lenders, but it also establishes clearly the time of the priority over other secured creditors and allows an advance filing system under which the loan and security may be agreed later and even the collateral may emerge later under an after acquired property clause (Section 9-204 (new and old) UCC), whilst the priority always relates back to the time of the filing of the finance statement. These last two aspects of the filing requirement are especially important. The *warning* function on the other hand is a means of giving the enquirers a rough idea, but any professional lender will have to make his own enquiries anyway, ask for detailed information from the borrower, and search its accounts.

In fact, the filing itself *does not guarantee anything,* especially not the existence or extent of the collateral, or the capacity of the debtor to dispose of it in this manner or indeed the existence of any valid security agreement at all. Thus the debtor may have void title, even if the security interest holder will be protected against a voidable title if he is unaware of it. The collateral may not exist at all, as in the case of future property, even though the lien will relate back to the date of filing as soon as it emerges whilst the contract to acquire the future goods may itself be pledged (as a 'general intangible' under Section 9-102 (9-106 old) UCC). Other assets of the debtor may be excluded because the debtor has insufficient interest as in the case of leased property under Article 2A. On the other hand, for other property in the possession of the debtor, even though not owned by him, there may be inclusion, as we saw. The filing has no special relevance in this connection. It also does not protect against statutory or judicial liens in the same assets which are not normally published or against any purchases in the ordinary course of business or *bona fide* purchases, which will be free and clear of the interest regardless of filing as there is no investigation or inspection duty on purchasers. Possessory interests of all kinds and purchase money security interests, at least in consumables, may also prevail over the filed interest if older, even though not filed themselves.

Although the filing guarantees nothing, it is relatively costly whilst the filing systems in many states are still cumbersome, the place of filing and investigation sometimes uncertain and could be in any one of several states where the debtor is engaged in business. The name of the debtor may have changed in the meantime or the debtor may have been subject to a merger or reorganisation. Also here the registers guarantee nothing. Most importantly, they do not allow for the filing of adverse interests of third parties (if not themselves secured creditors) in the property to protect them against later security interests.

The consequence is that the benefits of this filing system which is meant to establish an easy, simple and certain method of creating priorities are in practice much less obvious than they appear at first. Consequently there is much less of a model in the American example than would appear from its face. Scepticism has been expressed although no abolition suggested.[170] Filing was not foreseen in earlier drafts of Article 9 UCC.[171] In

---

[170] RT Nimmer, IM Hillinger and MG Hillinger, *Commercial Transactions: Secured Financing Cases, Materials, Problems* (1999), 144 suggest that Article 9 notice requirements have long outgrown their historical roots. In Europe the American system has been extensively studied, also with sceptical conclusions: see UH Schneider and J Miss, *US-Amerikanische Erfahrungen mit dem Abtretungsregister, Institut für deutsches und internationales Recht des Spar-, Giro- und Kreditwesens, Arbeitspapiere* (University of Mainz, Working Paper in English) 1998.
[171] See 1 G Gilmore, *Security Interests in Personal Property* (1965), s 15.1.

Europe not much need has been felt for a similar system, particularly not in Germany understandably so, it would seem. The 2002 EU Directive on Financial Collateral explicitly ignores all domestic filing requirements for the validity of security in, or conditional sales of stocks and shares (in dematerialised form).

Yet in an international context more than lip service is sometimes paid to it. As an alternative, some form of filing appears in the 2001 Uncitral Convention on Receivable Financing and it is also an important aspect of the 2001 Unidroit Mobile Equipment Convention. Filing as a substitute for possession remains an article of faith in many quarters. As *bona fide* purchasers are normally protected and have no investigation duties (except where security purchasers), the essence is (except in the Mobile Equipment Convention where it concerns specific high value items) to warn other creditors who should and will make their own inquiries. It is not immediately apparent what filing systems add here to justify their cost and expense even if access were easy and there was no confusion possible on where to look.

1.6.7   Floating Charges in Common and Civil Law. Extended Reservations of Title. The Concepts of Bulk Transfers, Asset Substitution and Tracing and the Inclusion of Future Assets. The Facility to Sell Goods Free and Clear

Article 9 UCC in the USA is rightly famous for the system of security it introduces and in particular for the broad facility of creating floating charges (a term not itself used in the text of the UCC although it is in the official comment) especially in respect of equipment, inventory and receivables (or accounts). It allows in this connection the inclusion of future replacement assets which may also be used to protect future debt, see Section 9-204 (in both the old and new text of 1999). In such cases, the charge may relate back to the date of the original filing. It is further note worthy that the concept of *absolutely* or *relatively* future goods, see also section 1.5.3 and 1.5.5 above, derived from German law does not play a restricting role. As long as the assets to be given as security can be reasonably described in the security agreement, there is no further requirement for their inclusion. For receivables there is thus also no need for the relationship from which they derive to already exist. The future credits that are secured in this manner do not need a basis in an already existing legal relationship either. Thus a bank may obtain security in all what the debtor has or will ever acquire (assuming these are the asset classes covered by Article 9 which include notably equipment, inventory and receivables) in respect of all that he may owe the bank for whatever reason, see for the US system further also the previous section and more in particular chapter V, section 1.6.

In England there is a similar broad system, in that country substantially based on case law, under which the rank, however, is determined not from the date of registration in company registers but from the date of crystallisation of the floating charge which is normally the date of default of the debtor. It is therefore a less potent security. As a consequence, it will include also a number of fixed charges which acquire in respect of specific assets (notably real estate) the rank as from the date they are established. What is decisive here is the matter of control over the asset — not always an easy criterium, see also chapter V, section 1.5.2.

The existence of floating charges is a test of the modernity of any security regime, not in the narrower English sense (proposed to be changed in that country also),[172] but rather in

---

[172] See Law Commission Paper no 164 of July 2002 in which an advanced filing system was proposed along American lines under which floating charges would acquire their rank as per the date of filing and would therefore move from lowest to (conceivably) highest rank.

the manner as now accepted in Artcle 9 UCC in the US. In countries like Germany and the Netherlands, the situation is greatly more complicated as a floating charge as such is not supported by statutory law and must be cobbled together on the basis of contractual clauses. In Germany, there are in this connection the so-called *Raumsicherungsvertrag* which allows for bulk transfers of assets within a certain space, the *Verarbeitungsklausel* which allows their conversion into other products in which the charge is then contractually extended, and the *Vorausabtretungsklausel* which allows for an anticipated assignment of all future claims from sales of the assets. In the Netherlands similar clauses are customary. They allow therefore in principle for the charge to be extended into replacement assets, see also chapter V, sections 1.4.1 and 1.2.2. It also plays a role when a reservation of title is extended into replacement goods when the additional question arises whether a floating charge results or a special type of conditional sale.

However, in the absence of more general provisions concerning bulk transfers, asset substitution and tracing in the civil codes of these countries, a particular problem arises with respect to *future assets* that are acquired by a bankruptcy debtor only after his bankruptcy, even though included in the charge and regardless of the earlier release of assets from the charge (e.g. upon the sale to third parties or upon collection of receivables) in exchange for which the charge was extended to the future replacement goods. This may entail a considerable windfall for the other creditors in a bankruptcy. One way to limit the damage is to deem any further releases invalid after default or bankruptcy so that the trustee cannot continue to deliver goods free and clear to prospective buyers, whilst the present charge over them 'chrystalises' and gives rise to execution remedies (or *Absonderung* in a German bankruptcy). Another is to limit the vulnerability of the transfer of future assets to those that are absolutely future, therefore to those that do not yet exist at all at the date of the bankruptcy, although in truth it may well be asked whether from a theoretical perspective there is any difference between assets that do not yet exist or that do exist but are not yet in the patrimony of the transferor.

Another possibility is to deem all *replacement* assets sufficiently identified and transferable *per se* even if still absolutely future at the time the security agreement was agreed. That would appear the German approach under S 91 of its Insolvency Act of 1999 under which the transfer of absolutely future assets would otherwise be vulnerable if they have not emerged before bankruptcy of the transferor. In the Netherlands, both the transfer (if only by way of security) in absolutely and relatively future assets is ineffective under Article 35(2) of the Bankruptcy Act. In this important aspect, there may be a difference with conditional sales in future assets which may not be so affected, see section 1.5.5 above *in fine*. See for the transfer of future goods more generally section 1.5.3 and 1.5.5 above for the transfer of future claims section 1.7.4 below.

In the context of a floating charge covering also *future* assets, one should as a minimum appreciate the vital importance and close connection between (a) the contractual description or identification possibilities to include them, (b) the possibility of an anticipated delivery of future assets whether or not absolutely or relatively future and their automatic transfer to the chargee when future goods emerge or (c) the concept of automatic replacement goods either as a valid description and identification or implicit in legal notions like (i) 'generality of goods or bulks' (ii) asset substitution, and (iii) tracing.

Another important aspect of the floating charge is the facility of the chargee to sell his goods free and clear of any charge. This is expressed in Section 9-320 UCC (formerly Section 9-307 UCC) for goods sold in the ordinary business. It depends therefore on the natrure of the assets. The *bona fides* of the buyer is not important in those cases. Elsewhere one may be able to say that there is an implied license to sell regardless of the charge. Thus if a manufacturer sells his inventory to a distributor under a reservation of title, the distributor will be able to sell free and clear. If the buyer of the distributor in order to purchase the goods needs financing and gives his financier a charge in the assets (even if they are still with the distributor but sufficiently identified), in a modern system that latter charge will prevail over the possessory rights or liens of the distributor and over any reservation of title of the original manufacturer. It is simply a function of the nature of the assets that must move and be sold and all that prevails over the rights of interestholders earlier in the chain. It is in the nature of bills of lading or warehouse receipts on which such interests are not marked (thereby becoming incorporated in the asset) even though the endossee might know about the charges.

1.6.8   *Uniform Security Law and Principles of Security Laws*

Some uniform treaty law is being developed in respect of secured transactions especially in the Unidroit Mobile Equipment Convention: see also chapter V, section 1.8.3. In respect of receivables, the Unidroit Factoring Convention of 1988 and the 2001 Uncitral Receivable Financing Convention are also relevant: see more in particular chapter V, section 2.3. The attempt to formulate some principles of security laws, especially by the EBRD, is briefly discussed in chapter V, sections 1.1.5 and its Model Law in 1.8.2: see further also section 1.8.4 below. Some early efforts were also made in the EU: see chapter V, section 1.1.5. The 1999 Settlement Finality and 2002 Financial Collateral Directives are more tangible examples, see also section 3.1.3 and 3.2.4 below

1.7   Proprietary Rights in Intangible Assets: Their Creation and Transfer

1.7.1   *Proprietary Rights in Intangible Assets and the Possibility and Method of their Transfer. The Meaning of Notification and the Situation in Double Assignments. The Civil Law Development.*

In section 1.1.3 above, the proprietary aspects of claims were already discussed and it was argued that claims, even though intangible, are ordinary assets like any other and should as such be proprietarily protected against third parties who must respect the owner (creditor)'s rights in them. It follows that they also serve as a basis for recovery of the creditor's own creditors, are in principle transferable, and can be given as security.[173] Yet, because of the dual nature of these assets in terms of the internal and external relationship, it took a long time for the law to create a system for the transfer of these rights without the consent of the debtor and to devise a means of proprietary protection, even in civil law.[174] In fact in

---

[173] See for this development even in common law SA Riesenfeld, *Creditors' Remedies and Debtors' Protection* (3rd edn, 1979), 215. See for an important overview of the laws of assignment in Europe, the US and Japan W Hadding and UH Schneider (eds), *Die Forderungsabtretung, insbesondere zur Kreditsicherung in ausländischen Rechtsordnungen* (Berlin, 1999).

[174] Under Roman law, for intangibles the problem seems to have arisen primarily because there was no possibility of a *traditio* or of a physical transfer of possession in the case of an assignment: see Gaius 2.38. As there was not something akin to a *traditio* or physical manifestation of a transfer in respect of them, intangibles were not believed capable of transfer and of acquisitive prescription and they were as a consequence not commonly considered the objects of property rights either: see also D 41.1.43.1 (Gaius), even though in Inst 2, 12–14

French law, assignments remained part of the law of contract, even under the *Code Civil* of 1804. Only in the German BGB of 1900, where the assignment figures in the General Part, did the transfer of intangible claims become a matter of property law.

Naturally, the internal (obligatory) relationship between creditor and debtor should not be confused with the external one, that is the relationship between the creditor and the entire world. The internal relationship is covered by the law of contract, tort or unjust enrichment, whatever the basis of the claim may be, and is therefore *in personam*, but the external one is a matter of the law of property and is *in rem*. Assets are thus not only real estate and chattels but also intangible claims and they are all subject to similar laws of property or proprietary interests. This was mostly well recognised in civil law which strives for one ownership concept in respect of all assets,[175] but there are still some differences, especially in the proprietary rights that can be created in these intangible assets and in the manner of their transfer and protection.

First, in civil law terms, real estate may be subject to all recognised limited proprietary rights of which the usufruct, the secured interests, servitudes and some long-term leases are, as we saw, the most common. For the creation and transfer of these rights and also the right of ownership itself, there are likely to be special publication rules now that most countries maintain a land register. For chattels, most limited proprietary rights are also available, although servitudes and long-term leases in respect of them may be less common. The transfer is either through contract or upon subsequent delivery of possession as previously explained. For intangible claims, the proprietary rights that may be created in them (besides full ownership) may be limited to the usufruct and the security interests as is now the Dutch system. In fact, this system does not speak of ownership of claims either and does also not refer to the most complete right in them. It refers only to disposition rights (Article 3.84(1) CC).

This approach is new in modern Dutch law and derived from the German example: see section 1.1.3.[176] It is mere semantics, however, because there is no doubt that the new Dutch Code and the German BGB treat claims also as assets, even though only implicitly.

Gaius clearly refers to intangibles as incorporeal assets: see also s 1.1.3 *supra*. Any transfer was therefore considered a contractual matter only, when there was the further problem of the personal nature of each relationship which was not considered changeable, even on the active side, by an act of the creditor alone: see Inst 3.13 and n 182 *infra*.

[175] Even in England, where the assignment of contractual claims is considered a contract matter and of tort claims a tort matter, intangible assets are not always only considered personal rights (contractual, tort or restitution rights). In *Fitzroy v Cave* [1905] 2 KB 364, 372 it was said that the Courts of Equity admitted that the assignee of a debt had title and the debt was considered a piece of property, an asset capable of being dealt with like any other. This remains, however, a difficult concept in common law where even for chattels the concept of ownership is often overtaken by that of physical possession: see s 1.3.2 *supra*, which has no equivalent in the case of intangibles. As far as the property nature of intangibles is concerned, in common law the emphasis is still on the integration of the proprietary regime of real estate and chattels and the fundamental difference in the type of proprietary protection between tangible and intangible assets remains.

In this fragmented system, the transfer of contractual claims is normally still considered a contractual matter and of tort claims a tort matter and is not discussed as part of the law of property, although in *Republica de Guatemala v Nunez* [1927] 1 KB 669, 697, it was held that it was wrong to consider the proprietary effect of the assignment dependent upon the existence of a prior valid contract to assign. Yet the line between the assignment as a purely contractual matter and a transfer of title remains also blurred, not helped by the general lack of a clear distinction between *in rem* and *in personam* rights in personal property.

There is no doubt, on the other hand, that claims are classified as personal property and that this status endures within the limits of the law especially in terms of transferability without the debtor's consent.

[176] New Dutch law appears here to take a retrograde step by splitting out the intangible assets (Article 3.1 CC) and formally restricting the concept of ownership (but not of possession and holdership) to tangible assets only: see Articles 5.1*ff* io Articles 3.107*ff* CC.

The new Dutch Code allows in this connection expressly for (legal) possession, which in civil law normally stands for ownership, and for acquisitive prescription (Article 3.99 CC). Presumably there is also holdership as in a collection arrangement. Nevertheless, there is no proprietary or possessory defence and the intangible claim as an asset can be defended only in tort against third parties that infringe the creditor's rights (Article 3.123 Dutch CC). This is the general attitude in civil law towards the protection of claims and brings it in line with common law in which all proprietary protection in personal property can only be achieved through tort actions, see section 1.3.4 above.[177]

As for the transfer of claims, this is done in a special way, through *assignment*. It may or may not require notification to the debtor but it now *never* requires his consent, which demonstrates the proprietary nature of the right in the claim. The same goes for the creation of limited proprietary rights in claims like a usufruct or secured interests. As regards the notification requirement of the debtor (but never his consent), this is traditionally a formal constitutive requirement in France, which also requires a formal document (although recognition of the assignment by the debtor is a substitute: see Article 1690 Cc, but it must be done through a notarial deed unless there is actual payment by the debtor to the assignee).[178] The consequence is that traditionally some outward manifestation is required for the transfer of claims in France. It is curious as a manifestation of physical transfer or delivery had been abandoned in France for the transfer of chattels in the Civil Code of 1804 under which delivery of possession was no longer necessary: see Article 1138 Cc and section 1.5.2 above. To facilitate bulk transfers of receivables for financing purposes, these formal requirements have now been abandoned in France since the amendments in 1981 by the *Loi Dailly*.[179] In Germany, they were never required under the BGB

---

[177] Everywhere there remain differences with the law of chattels, as in the exceptions to the *nemo dat* rule for *bona fide* purchasers (assignees), in civil law often not deemed applicable in the case of intangibles, although this may sometimes be different in common law: see text at n 189 *infra*. The contractual prohibition of a transfer also tends to be valid in the case of claims: see Section 399 BGB and BGH 14 Oct 1963, BGHZ 40, 156 in Germany and Article 3.83(2) CC in the Netherlands, whilst it has most certainly no *in rem* or third party effect in the case of chattels: see Section 137 BGB, Article 3. 83(3) Dutch CC and Section 9-401 (9-311 old) UCC. Statutory law in the USA is much more reluctant to give these contractual assignment prohibitions third party effect: see Sections 2-210 and 9-404*ff* (9-318 old) UCC and Section 1.7.2. *infra*. It is true that everywhere the assignment is still seen as a technique somewhat different from the title transfer of tangible assets, in terms of formalities and notification to the debtor. This is also likely to affect the creation of any security or conditional ownership rights in claims.

[178] French law remains closest to the Roman system of C 8.41.3 as elaborated in the *ius commune* requiring notification for the effect of the assignment on third parties, especially on the debtor, or the latter's recognition: see Article 1690 Cc. It did so under the influence of one of the leading French commentators at the time: see Pothier, *Nouveau Coutumier Général* (Paris, 1724) III, 1, and follows here a course very different from the one for chattels where Pothier's teachings requiring delivery of possession had been less successful and was abandonned in favour of the natural school approach which allowed title in chattels to pass through the mere sales agreement: see again s 1.5.4 *supra*.

The notification of Article 1690 Cc was originally of a very formal nature and needed to be given by an official judicial officer, whilst the alternative of recognition of the assignment by the debtor still requires an official (notarial) deed (*acte authentique*). In the case of a transfer for security purposes only, a public deed or at least the registration of an informal document was necessary except in the commercial sphere: see Article 2074 Cc as compared to Articles 91 and 109 *Code de Comm*. This system allowed, however, payment to the assignee even before notification in the context of the possibility of recognising the assignment, which in the case of payment needed not to be similarly formal: see Cour de Cass, 9 May 1864, D.1.190 (1864). France thus kept to the old *ius commune* built around official notification or formal recognition as repeatedly confirmed by the Cour de Cass: see the decisions of 20 June 1938, D.1.26 (1939) and 12 June 1985, Bull civ III. 95 (1985), notwithstanding serious criticism.

[179] See Law 81-1 of 2 Jan 1981 modified by the Banking Law of 24 Jan 1984 (Articles 61*ff*) and supplemented by Decree 81-862 of 9 Sept 1981, now codified in Articles L 313-23 to L 313-35 CMF. It provides for an alternative way of assignment for professionals to facilitate modern financing structures involving portfolios of receivables: see also Ripert/Roblot, 2 *Droit Commercial* (16th edn, 2000), nos 2428 *et seq*. It requires an official deed (*bordereau*) to

(Section 398) following in this respect late nineteenth-century German case law which had abandoned the *ius commune* approach in this connection.[180] Following late Roman law,[181] the *ius commune*[182] had required notice (or recognition or the start of a lawsuit by the assignee for recovery from the debtor). This is the origin of the approach of the Cc in France.

incorporate the receivables which may then be transferred to a credit institution providing advances on the basis of it. The necessity of notification to the debtors as a constitutive requirement of the transfer is abandoned for these types of assignment. Nevertheless the requirement of the *bordereau* remains restrictive and any further receivables need a new document which would appear not to allow the inclusion of future receivables in the transfer so that it is still not possible to assign whole cashflows derived from certain types of activity in this manner. Belgium has more radically and generally abandoned the notification requirement for assignments in Article 1690 of its own Cc in 1994.

The French amendment of 1984 allows the *bordereau* transfer technique now also to be used by way of guarantee and without any determination and payment of a price. It may lead to a security in the guise of a fiduciary transfer, which has been favoured in France since the Cour de Cass allowed it on 19 Aug 1849, D 1.273 (1849), see also chapter V, s 1.3.5. It made collection possible to reduce any advances given which were in this manner amortised. This collection possibility had remained uncertain where receivables were merely pledged under Article 2073 Cc. The fiduciary transfer still required individual notification of each creditor for its validity, however, which may now be avoided by using the *bordereau* transfer technique if the transfer is to banks.

[180] The approach of Voet, see n 182 *infra*, is at the root of the modern German system, see Section 398 BGB, after the older *ius commune* continued to be applied in this area in Germany during the 19th century: see Windscheid/Kipp, 2 *Lehrbuch des Pandektenrechts* (1900), No 331, until the decision of the RGH, 8 Mar 1881, RGHZ 4, 111 (1881). It allowed in a bankruptcy of the assignor the assignment to be operative as at its date and not as at the notification. This modern German approach still requires a special act of transfer or *Einigung* (which in the case of intangibles signifies at the same time the transfer of legal possession: see for the transfer of chattels more in particular s 1.5.2 *supra*) to complete the assignment. This fits in with the approach of Voet and this requirement was never equated in Germany with giving notice as a matter of publicity.

[181] In Roman law, because of the view that all contractual relationships were highly personal, see n 174 *supra*, creditor substitution could be achieved only through a *novation* which means through a new agreement requiring the debtor's consent: see Inst Gaius 2. 38 and 39. Commercially, this proved too restrictive and a kind of transfer possibility without consent was created by the creditor giving others a licence or power to collect, with the attendant rights to sue the debtor. This was the *procuratio in rem suam*, or the power for a third party to act and collect for his own benefit, for which he would have paid the creditor. It did not mean creditor substitution, however. First the debtor could still pay the original creditor. Moreover, the mandate by its very nature could always be terminated by the creditor and lapsed in any event upon the death of one of the parties (unless a lawsuit concerning the collection had become pending between the *procurator* and the debtor), although this could result in an action for recuperation of the consideration paid: see for these complications C 4.10.1 which gave a so-called *actio utilis* to ease the situation and allowed the *procurator* to continue his collection if the creditor had died in the meantime, see for the procedural details also Kaser, *Römisches Privatrecht* [Roman Private Law] (14th edn, 1986), 246.

The *actio utilis* became subsequently the vehicle to achieve a situation which became broadly similar to the modern assignment. This development was underpinned by the facility existing since the Emperor Antoninus Pius in the middle of the 2nd century to assign deceaseds' estates in their entirety: see D 2.14.16 pr and further C 4.10.2 and C 6.37.18. Eventually the *actio utilis* became available to all purchasers of claims even before a *procuratio* was given, C 8.41.3, and ultimately also to the heirs of a deceased assignee: see C 8.53.33 pr, but it never meant that the original creditor was fully substituted and he could still collect whilst the debtor could always make a liberating payment to him. The assignee could stop this under later law, however, by giving notice (*denuntiatio*), see C 8.41.3, and could in any event exert recovery rights against the collecting original creditor. Recognition by the debtor, payment, or the start of a lawsuit by the assignee would also suffice and signify sufficient knowledge on the part of the debtor. It was accepted that the debtor could make a liberating payment to the assignee even earlier. His right became exclusive, however, only after any of these actions. Until such time the assignor could still demand payment as well.

[182] The *ius commune* used the *actio utilis* of C 8. 41.3, see n 181 *supra*, as the basis for further development: see also WJ Zwalve, *Hoofdstukken uit de Geschiedenis van het Europese Privaatrecht, Inleiding en Zakenrecht* (Groningen, 1993), 280 but increasingly required notification as a precondition for the validity of the assignment. The consequence was that the assignee giving notice *first* and to whom the debtor paid obtained an advantage even if his assignment had been *later* and that until such time (or recognition or the start of a lawsuit by the assignee) the claim still belonged to the assignor whose creditors could garnish the debtor for payment to them. Some authors suggested therefore a return to the older Roman law in which the notice or recognition had not fulfilled a similar role (although the starting of the law suit had) whilst believing that the mere assignment should be sufficient to transfer the claim to the estate of the assignee. In this view, notice was only a matter of convenience allowing the

Modern German law requires neither a document nor notification as a condition for the validity of the assignment, but it requires a real transfer or *traditio* (or *Einigung*), as in the case of real estate and chattels, which is, however, believed implicit in the assignment agreement, unless clearly intended to be otherwise.[183] In this respect it is not common in Germany to distinguish between the agreement to assign, which is the sale of the claim, and the assignment agreement which is considered to complete the assignment as transfer. In the Netherlands, the requirement of a document was inherited from French law but it needed not be notarial and the French notification requirement was abandoned under the old code.[184] The requirement of a document remains in force under the new law, but surprisingly notification was reintroduced as a constitutive requirement of the assignment in the new Dutch Code of 1992. It is rightly criticised as it renders bulk assignments in principle impossible. Although for a security transfer this notification is not necessary, there is in that case a registration requirement with notaries which creates similar problems for bulk security transfers as the formalities still apply in respect of each transferred claim.[185]

The main reason for the Dutch switch was dogmatic. It was considered incongruous that there was a requirement for delivery for the transfer of chattels[186] but that claims were transferred by mere (written) agreement (although it probably implied a *traditio* at the same time in the German manner). As in France, notification is in this view considered a form of publicity, like delivery is for chattels, and manifestation of the proprietary right (rather than an expression of the real agreement) which is assumed to depend on it. Yet for chattels, delivery can be entirely constructive as we saw in section 1.2.2 above, whilst notification to the debtor is not publicity in respect of anybody else at all. In any event, it is doubtful whether publicity is indeed the heart of the proprietary right, as we saw above. At least in chattels, most of these rights are normally hidden. The only practical advantage of

debtor to pay to the assignee directly but was not a constitutive requirement for the transfer of the claim and assignees with earlier rights would in this view have an action for recovery against the collecting assignee with lesser rights, even if *bona fide*. This was the influential approach of the late 17th-century Dutch writer Voet, *Commentarius ad Pandectas*, 18.4.15*ff*, who invoked the customary law of his time.

In this system upon a double assignment, the first assignee would ultimately prevail whilst the asset would be part of this assignee's estate as at the moment of the assignment and not as at the moment of notification, although, until notice, the debtor, if *bona fide*, could still validly pay the former creditor/assignor, and upon notice by any assignee, he could safely pay the latter. In this manner the second assignee could prevail at first but would owe any collections made to the first assignee. Where notice is a constructive requirement of the assignment, the debtor may also pay the second assignee but the difference is that his knowledge of an earlier assignment attempt without notification is then irrelevant as it would not have led to the desired transfer, although new Dutch law, which now requires the notification for the validity of the assignment, may well have left some doubt in this aspect: see Article 6.34 CC.

An on the surface similar theory to that of Voet, leading to the full effect of the assignment as at the moment of the conclusion of the assignment agreement, was proposed by the 17th- and 18th-century natural law school: see Wolf, *Institutiones Juris Naturae et Gentium* (ed Halle, 1734), Par 338 which school had also argued that in the case of chattels the mere agreement should transfer the asset, an approach for movables accepted in France: see s 1.5.4 *supra*. There was, however, a difference with the approach of Voet who had still wanted a formal transfer in the sense of *traditio* so that the mere assignment agreement (or *pactum de cedendo*) was not sufficient but needed to be completed by a further transfer agreement (the *pactum cessionis*), even though they could and would normally be embodied in one document.

[183] See n 180 *supra*.
[184] As in Germany under the BGB of 1900 and following Voet, in the Netherlands under the old Code (until 1992) delivery of possession remained necessary for the transfer of chattels but not notification for the assignment.
[185] See Article 3.239 CC, which still raises the question whether the registration must be done for each receivable individually. In order to facilitate this registration possibility at least to some extent, the Dutch Supreme Court now allows computer lists of the assignor to be used to which reference may be made by identifying the first and the last assigned claim on the list, see HR, 14 Oct. 1994 [1995], NJ 447.
[186] Article 3. 94 CC.

the notification requirement is that it simplifies the situation if there has been a double assignment, as we shall see shortly.

For the assignment of intangibles, notification was even in England sometimes also seen as a substitute for delivery as originally required for the transfer of chattels:[187] see the famous case of *Dearle v Hall* of 1828,[188] although English law never went as far as to require it for the validity of the transfer itself. It only gave the assignee giving notice first priority in the collection by considering only his assignment to be properly completed or perfected (whilst further requiring the debtor to be in good faith whilst paying, but not strictly speaking the assignee whilst giving notice). It did not amount to making the notification an absolute condition of the validity of the transfer but it gave it crucial importance by preferring any assignment followed by notification even if there had been earlier ones without it.

Naturally where notification to the debtor is not a constitutive requirement for the validity of the assignment, it is still a practical requirement to make the debtor pay the new creditor. That is not then a requirement for the assignment itself but a question of implementation of the assignment, much like delivery is in systems that do not require it for title transfers in chattels. Without it, the debtor may still pay the former creditor/assignor and liberate himself in so doing. In this system, if the debtor pays a second assignee upon notification without knowledge of an earlier assignment, he is equally liberated and the only question that then results is whether the second assignee (whether or not aware of the first assignment) must surrender his collections to the first assignee who did not notify. It follows in systems that require notification for the validity of the assignment that only the notifying assignee is the true assignee. Even so, there could be several of them before payment when only the first notifying assignee appears to have the right to the claim, unless (perhaps) later ones manage to collect in good faith (when the debtor is likely to have been at fault in paying and may have to pay again).

This concerns the question whether a collecting *bona fide* (second) assignee of a claim without notice is protected and may keep the proceeds: see also section 1.7.9 below. The question is more likely to arise in systems which do not require notification for the validity of an assignment when the first assignee has the right but later assignees may give notice to the debtor first and may do so unaware of the earlier assignment. Protection of *bona fide* assignees is normally *not* part of civil law that generally protects only *bona fide* purchasers of chattels (on the basis of the outward manifestation of ownership of the transferor), but it may be different in common law and there are states in the USA, notably New York, that accept that *bona fide* collectors may retain their collections:[189] See also Section 342 of the *Restatement (Second) Contracts* (1981).

Other assignment problems arise where claims are highly personal, where according to the underlying contract they are not transferable, or where they are future claims or claims that are insufficiently specific. Another question is whether claims, especially receivables, can be transferred separately from the legal relationship out of which they arise, and if so whether and which *closely related rights* and especially *duties* are automatically transferred with them. Another issue is what happens to an assignee if the assignor and debtor change their contract affecting assigned (future) claims thereunder. Then there is the status of the defences, which the debtor may have had against the assignor and

---

[187] In England for chattels the requirement of delivery for title transfer upon a sale was abandonned during the 19th century: see Sections 17 and 18 of the Sale of Goods Act 1979 and also s 1.5.4 *supra*.
[188] 3 Rnss 1 (1828).
[189] See also n 194 *infra*.

their continuing efficacy when payment is requested by an assignee. This includes also the right of set-off which the debtor may have had against the assignor. These aspects will be discussed in greater detail below.

1.7.2   The Development in Common Law

Before going into greater detail, the common law of assignment justifies a closer look. The common law system, especially in England, struggled with the concept of assignment longer than the Continental legal systems did. In common law, the situation remained therefore more complicated than in civil law, although not when compared to Roman law. As under Roman law, claims were in common law at first hardly considered transferable as they were considered too personal in nature and could therefore be transferred only with the debtor's consent through a kind of novation. Later on, some power of collection could be given to a third party (the Roman *procuratio in rem suam* and the common law *assignatio* from which the term assignment is derived), but if disputes arose in respect of the assigned claim, the original creditor would still have to be involved. This type of arrangement also required documentation.[190] Equity on the other hand became willing to accept that claims were ordinary assets and it was therefore able to do away with both restraints. The equitable assignment thus became the normal way to transfer claims, but this was at first possible only if the assigned claims were themselves equitable (like restitution, corporate or tax claims).[191]

Although (in England) by statute the legal assignment was subsequently expanded, it still requires notification and documentation. Thus the equitable assignment continued to be used and as a consequence of the merger of law and equity it became also available for claims at law (like those in contract and tort, although notionally in these cases the name of the original creditor is still used in litigation).[192] This is the present situation in

---

[190] The creditor would give a written *power of attorney* to a third party to collect and an instruction or *assignatio* (hence the later term 'assignment') to the debtor to pay to the third party so appointed. Yet there remained a problem with these powers of collection, which were in principle revocable, and also with the facility to conduct lawsuits of someone else's for one's own benefit (it was considered against the law of maintenance which prohibited the intervention in lawsuits merely for one's own benefit without any other concern: see W Holdsworth, 7 *History of English Law* (1927), 534). Most importantly, the creditor/assignor was not released from the contract and would have to join any lawsuit by the assignee against the debtor who in any event could still pay him, although in the assignor's bankruptcy the debt was eventually believed to belong to the assignee (since 1787): see *Winch v Keeley*, 29 ER 1284. It also became possible for the debtor to agree to pay a third party at the request of his creditor. This is called *acknowledgement*, dispenses with any novation or assignment requirements and remains common: see *Shamia v Yoory* [1958] 1 QB 448.

[191] For *equitable* claims (as in tax, agency, partnership, company, trust, insolvency, and specific performance matters), equity did accept the ownership notion from an early date and rejected the restrictions on transferability as confirmed in *Fitzroy v Cave* [1905] 2 KB 364, 372. It did not require a document and notification as conditions for the validity of the assignment either: see also *Dearle v Hall*, 3 Russ. 1 (1828), although the first notifying assignee had the better right as only his assignment was deemed completed and his title *perfected*. There had to be adequate consideration: see *Glegg v Bromley* [1912] 3 KB 474, but any lack of it only affected the assignment between assignor and assignee and was not considered to affect the payment duty of the debtor to the assignee upon notification: see *Walker v Bradford Old Bank* (1884) 12 QBD 511. This is like an abstract approach in assignments: see also s. 1.5.6 *supra* for the case of a sale of chattels, and further *Republica de Guatemala v Nunez* [1927] 1 KB 669, 697, where it was held that the validity of the assignment did not depend on the existence of a prior valid contract to assign as far as the debtor was concerned.

[192] This was the consequence of the Judicature Act 1873 which merged law and equity, although even then not fully. Section 25(6) of the 1873 Act (now superseded by the similar Section 136 of the Law of Property Act 1925) instituted a statutory assignment facility requiring a document and notification for the assignment to be valid. This statutory assignment does *not* require consideration and gives the assignee power to discharge the debtor without the consent of the assignor. It requires an absolute assignment, therefore, not an assignment by way of charge or a conditional assignment, although it does not exclude the assignment of a mortgage: see *Tancred v*

England under which neither notification nor documentation is a formal or constitutive requirement for the (equitable) assignment of legal or equitable claims. Yet common law continues with a fractured system under which moreover contract claims are assigned under the law of contract, tort claims under the law of tort and restitution claims under the law of restitution, each with its own rules of assignability. In this connection, the assignability of tort claims may continue to present special problems because of their often personal and punitive nature. But even the assignability of contractual claims may present special issues, especially in the case of contractual assignment restrictions. This is in fact no different in civil law but it seems to be less disconcerted by it.

In the USA, the legal assignment seems to be entirely abandoned but in other aspects[193] the law amongst the various states remains divided especially in the meaning of notification.[194] Some states adhere here to the English equitable approach protecting

Delagoa Bay Co (1889) 23 QBD 239 as mortgages are not considered charges or limited interests: the whole interest of the mortgagee (or conditional buyer) is considered transfered in that case subject to a redemption right.

Nevertheless the statutory assignment remained cumbersome and the equitable assignment technique (still requiring consideration) therefore survived on the basis of the argument that the statute had not meant to destroy equitable assignments and that in the case of a conflict between law and equity the latter prevailed: see *Wm Brandt's Sons & Co v Dunlop Rubber* [1905] AC 454. The equitable assignment now covers claims at law as well, but still in a different way as upon the equitable assignment of claims at law, the assignor must still be involved in lawsuits of the assignee against the debtor: see *Durham Bros. v Robertson* [1898] 1 QB 765 and more recently *The Aiolos* [1983] 2 Lloyd's Rep. 25, 33. The reason is that technically legal title cannot be transferred in equity. Thus the assignor of a legal claim must be made party to the equitable assignee's lawsuit against the debtor. Only the assignee of an equitable claim may therefore sue in his own name as equity can pass full equitable claim. This technicality is now probably of little importance in the USA today. The assignor must also become involved in equitable claims if he retains an interest in the contract, e.g. when the assignment is only partial or limited, like for security purposes only, or is conditional: see *Durham Bros. v Robertson*, cited *supra*, which is logical as the assignor is not meant to be released.

As far as *tort* claims are concerned, under common law, traditionally their transfer was impeded by the impossibility to assign a right of action. Under modern law, the proceeds of such an action may, however, be assigned: see *Glegg v Bromley* [1912] 3 KB 474, and probably now also the action itself. At least actions for other types of damage are now assignable: see *Linden Gardens Trust Ltd v Lenesta Sludge Disposal Ltd and Others* and *St Martins Property Corporation Ltd and Another v Sir Robert Mc-Alpine & Sons Ltd*, [1993] 2 All ER 417 (1993), but an *assignment prohibition* in respect of the 'contract' as a whole is upheld and considered to affect the obligations as well as the rights, not only in respect of future performance under it but also in respect of payments and accrued rights of action thereunder. In fact it was held that there was no need for a market in choses in action. The Court of Appeal (*per* Kerr J) had allowed a split and ignored the prohibition in respect of payments and rights of action. See for more recent case law also *Don King Productions v Warren* [1999] 2 All ER 218 (CA) under which it was held that at least in an equitable assignment. There could still be a declaration of trust in favour of the assignee regardless of the assignment prohibition. It begs the question whether the assignee has a search duty.

[193] In the USA the law of assignment developed on the basis of the equitable assignment and did not inherit the old common law impediments: see also Cook, 'The Alienability of Choses in Action', (1916), 29 *Harv. LR* 818 but even in the USA the subject remained riddled with controversy primarily centring on the question whether the assignor's right has been fully extinguished or whether the assignee has only an irrevocable power of attorney to collect, albeit in his own name and not affected by his death or bankruptcy. The difference between law and equity played here a role; equity in the USA would accept that the assignee had a claim in his own right and did not need to rely on the power of attorney notion, but the courts at law never permitted the assignee to sue in his own name: see the NY case of *Wardell v Eden*, 2 Johns. Cass. 258 (1801), also stating, however, that an assignor had no more power over the judgment than a stranger. Only the name of the assignor had to be used, for which his consent was not required. Suing exclusively in the assignee's name was only made possible by statute and most states now have these enacted, superseded or amended by the UCC for sales contract claims and security assignments: see Section 2–210 and Section 9–406(d) (9–318(4) old), whilst in the USA the courts sitting in equity have largely renounced the jurisdiction once exercised in assignment cases: see *Hayward v Andrews*, 106 US 672 (1883).

The consequence is, nevertheless, that where there is no assignment statute operative, the assignee can still only sue in the name of the assignor although for his own benefit. However, in the other aspects of assignments, the equity approach usually prevails, including its ownership concept of claims and the absence of a need for notification in order for the assignment to be valid.

[194] Some states follow the English approach of *Dearle v Hall*, see n. 191 *supra*, giving the first notifying (perfecting) assignee the right; others give the first assignee the title regardless of notification, although in New York any

the assignee first giving notice; others give the first assignee the best right regardless of notification, whilst in New York traditionally the first assignee has the better right but any *bona fide* later assignee may retain his collections. All seem agreed, however, that notification is no requirement for the validity of the assignment itself. The *Restatement (Second) Contracts* in Section 342 gives the *bona fide* assignee the better right before notice. More important is the special assignment regime of Section 2-210 UCC for the assignment of sales receivables and Sections 9-406(d) (9-318 old) UCC for security assignments of all claims that may be assigned as security under Article 9 UCC. For assignments of monetary claims Article 9 UCC has in fact a special regime which allows for assignment without filing or notification unless it concerns substantial portfolios of receivables. In fact, every assignment of receivable is now treated similarly under state law in the USA unless it is done for collection purposes only.[195]

1.7.3   The Transferability of Claims and Contracts. Assignment of Rights and Delegation of Duties. The Debtor's Defences and the Impact of Contractual Restrictions on the Transfer

As regards the transfer of intangibles, the general rule is that only the asset side of a contractual arrangement may be assigned to third parties without the consent of the debtor and may then be separated out, in particular the payment rights, provided that no material extra burdens are created and the contract is not fundamentally changed thereby. This easy transfer possibility involving *creditor substitution* does normally not apply to any

---

later assignee who collects *in good faith* may retain the proceeds: see also *Salem Trust Co v Manufacturers' Finance Co*, 264 US 182 (1924) and *Corn Exchange NB & T Co v Klauder*, 318 US 434 (1943) and further Corbin, 4 *Contracts* (1951), s 902. Notification is, however, nowhere an absolute requirement for the validity of the assignment itself.

[195] Section 2-210(2) UCC provides for a special regime for assignments of sales receivables (although Article 2 does not generally deal with the sale and transfer of claims but only of goods: see Section 2-201 UCC). Except where the assignment materially changes the duties or increases materially the burden or risk of the other party (the debtor), the assignment is allowed. It also deals with the delegation of duties which equally does not need the consent of the counter-party except where there is a substantial interest in the performance of the original promissor whilst the transferor is not released without the consent of the counter-party, but like the counter-party he may also insist that the transferee performs. The rights and duties can be made non-transferable in the sales contract but a right to damages for breach of the whole sales contract or a right arising out of the assignor's due performance of his entire obligation under such a contract can be assigned despite agreement to the contrary.

The method of assignment of claims is not covered by Section 2-210 UCC and has its own regime under Article 9 UCC, even if not especially transferred for security purposes (unless transferred for collection alone), see Sections 9-102(a)(2), 9-109(a)(3), 9-309(2), 9-317(d), 9-403, 9-404ff, 9-501, 9-607, 9-615(e) , (see the corresponding old Sections 9-102(1)(b), 9-104(f), 9-106, 9-206(1), 9-301(1)(d), 9-302(1)(e), 9-306(5), 9-318(1)–(4), 9-401, 9-502 and 9-504(2)) UCC. These assignments under Article 9 do not only cover sales receivables, but may also cover others, like those for services, and even rights to damages under a contract, but they may not cover individual tort claims: see Section 9-106. They are not customarily used as commercial security, although it is conceivable that an insurance company assigns all claims in which it is or may be subrogated as security for an advance. Under the Revision becoming effective in 2001, the assignment of commercial tort claims will be covered.

Additional rules are to be found in Section 9-604ff (9-318) UCC. There are differences in approach between Section 2-210(2) and Section 9-318 UCC which go beyond the fact that in Article 2 only the transfer of sales contracts rights and duties is considered, whilst Article 9 UCC concerns the (security) assignment of all kinds of monetary claim, Section 2-210(2) UCC is much more willing to accept the transfer of duties with the rights except where this materially increases the burdens on the debtor or changes the duties: Section 9-406(5) (9-318(4) old) on the other hand seems even less disposed to accept assignment restrictions on receivables when assigned for security purposes. In any event, in the USA the splitting out of a receivable and its separation from the context out of which it arose seem less problematic under the UCC than under earlier common law, even if the assignment is only partial or limited for security or other purposes or merely conditional: see also G Gilmore, 2 *Security Interests in Personal Property* (1965), 1077ff.

transfer or delegation of contractual (or other) duties, thus not to *debtor substitution*, or to the liability side of the contract. The reason is obvious: except in the case of personal services, it is often immaterial for a *debtor* whether he performs to an assignor or assignee, especially clear in the case of a payment, but it is normally very relevant to a *creditor* who the person is who must perform (or pay) to him.

For the creditor there is in the case of payment a credit risk to be considered or a quality risk in the case of other duties owed him, which means that debtors cannot normally substitute themselves for others without the consent of the creditor (whilst creditors can normally substitute themselves for others without the consent of the debtor). As far as personal services are concerned, even creditor substitution is difficult as a personal service provider, like a servant, cannot normally be asked to provide his service to anyone whom the creditor might identify, except where that was part of the contract. In French (Latin) terminology the contract is *intuitu personae*, which is an implied condition in many service contracts. This personal aspect applies then to debtor and creditor alike.

The modern trend is to facilitate the splitting off and assignability of the asset side, particularly of a receivable, and one may conclude that monetary claims are now ordinarily assignable everywhere, but it is obvious that monetary claims that are highly personal rights remain unassignable, like claims for alimony or child support. Life insurance policies, future wages and pension payments may equally not be assignable. Social security benefits may also be in that category, as are more generally claims that are created with the person of the debtor in mind. Other claims may be considered inherently unassignable for other reasons. Future claims may be the classic example. Their assignability will be discussed in the next section.[196] Yet even then it remains to be seen how far the lack of assignability avoids the transfer altogether or only allows the debtor to ignore the assignment.

All in all, there is no doubt that the transfer of intangible claims remains generally more complicated than the transfer of chattels. First, the assignment of claims involves a third party, the debtor, at least to the extent that his performance must be redirected towards the assignee. To this end, notification must be given. In some countries, this notification became a prerequisite or formal requirement for a valid assignment, as we saw in the previous section. It is then often considered an act of publicity or even a delivery substitute believed necessary to create proprietary rights in an assignee. But in all cases notification is necessary if it is the intention of the assignor and assignee that henceforth the debtor pay the assignee. Obviously that must normally be the intention, but in security assignments, the assignor may not want debtors to know that he needs financing and the assignee may in that case be willing to let the assignor collect the receivables, the proceeds of which will then be held by the assignor for the assignee.

Another important aspect of the involvement of the debtor is that, if substantial extra burdens result for him, he may also be able to ignore the assignment, even upon notification, and refuse to pay the assignee. It means that in such cases an effective assignment would need his consent. One could think of a situation in which different places or countries of payment result upon an assignment or higher payment costs. There are also the *defences* against the claim the debtor may derive from his relationship with the assignor, including his set-off rights. The most important defence against payment is non-conform delivery in sales contracts[197] and as long as the quality of the delivered goods is not

---

[196] In Germany, rights of a company to payment by its shareholders of the unpaid part of the issue price of subscribed shares were also considered inherently unassignable: see n. 204 *infra*.

[197] It includes the benefits of the *exceptio non adimpleti contractus*. This is established in France through case law: see Cour de Cass., 29 June 1881, D.1.33 (1882), in Germany through Sections 404 and 407 BGB, again allowing all

improved there is likely to be a right to set off repair costs or damages.[198] Under present law, such defences usually remain effective against the assignee, although the contract out of which the assigned claims arise may in its assignment clause prevent the debtor raising any defences against assignees.[199] Otherwise, the internal relationship has an external effect in respect of assignees even if in the case of defences the assignor is unlikely to be released without the debtor's consent.

If there is an extra burden or detriment, the first question is whether it is sufficiently burdensome to be taken into account. The modern approach is that a debtor is bound to co-operate if the burden on him is not substantial. If it is, the next question is what the effect is on the assignment: (a) does it undo the assignment or may it be ignored by the debtor, (b) does it impose extra duties on the assignee to minimise the effects or are the defences maintained against him without necessarily discharging the assignor? It is clear that these consequences may vary, depending on the applicable law.

There further arises the question whether ancillary or accessory rights and closely related duties transfer with the assigned claim. To put it another way, how far can a right be separated from its context and separately assigned? Stepping back for the moment, the most obvious example of an intangible asset that may be assigned is the contractual right. In sales, this means especially the right of the buyer to receive the goods and of the seller to receive the payment (resulting in a receivable). In modern law, all these rights can be transferred through assignment, although receivables are the most common and likely assets to be so transferred because of their liquidity and easy separation possibility.

In bilateral contracts, as in sales and exchanges, rights are often balanced, however, by contractual liabilities or duties resulting in an interwoven contractual relationship in which these rights and benefits may not stand sufficiently alone to be individually assigned. Thus a buyer will indeed be entitled to receive the goods on the appointed date but that right, which is in principle assignable, may be subject to his duties in terms of collection of sworks or transportation, insurance and payment. They are unlikely to be automatically transferred with the right to delivery, but these related duties may make it more difficult to make an effective assignment without some consent of the seller who may not want to be confronted by an unknown or unreliable new counter-party, whilst the transfer of the whole contractual position is in any event likely to require such consent. On the other hand, although a receivable may be easiest to assign separately for a seller, even in that case

---

defences accruing to the debtor until he becomes aware of the assignment: see also Section 9-404 (9-318(1) old) UCC in the USA for security assignments. See for England *Ord v White*, 3 Beav 357 (1884). See for the Netherlands, Article 6. 145 CC under which all defences accruing until the notification can be maintained.

[198] The retention of the set-off facility upon an assignment against the assignee is commonly agreed: see for Germany, Section 406 BGB, which allows the set-off in respect of all claims which the debtor acquires against the assignor even after the assignment but before the debtor becomes aware of it. That is also the system of Section 9-404 (9-318(1) old) UCC in the USA for security assignments. In the Netherlands under its new system requiring notification for the validity of the transfer, all counterclaims until the notification can naturally be offset, as was earlier the case under the *ius commune*: see C.8.41.3. In England, the set-off right is at least good for claims arising out of the same contract whether they arise before or after the debtor has notice of the assignment, see *Graham v Johnson* (1869) LR 8 Eq. Other claims may be set off only if they arose before notice was given: see *Stephens v Venables*, 30 Beav 625 (1862). A problem is that for a set-off normally both claims need to be mature: see eg Article 1291 French Cc and Article 6.127 (2) Dutch CC. If the claim of either assignor or debtor was not mature before the assignment but mature thereafter, there is a question whether the debtor may still invoke the set-off against the assignee. It does not appear possible, but if the debtor waives his credit in anticipation of an assignment in order to render his claim against the assignor off-settable, he would appear to have that facility: see for France, Court of Appeal Paris, 8 Mar 1904, D.2.65 (1905), and for Germany Section 406 BGB.

[199] In the USA, Section 9-403 (9-206 old) UCC especially upholds these contractual limitations for security transfers of claims.

he is only entitled to receive the price subject to the defences of the buyer (against the seller) in terms of credit period and counterclaims or set-off rights in respect of the quality of the goods delivered, as we saw. The assignee cannot normally avoid these. As far as he is concerned, uncertainty about exposure may impede the assigment for him, but the more urgent question for the debtor is whether he may ignore the assignment under the circumstances or may at least hold the assignor additionally responsible.

The payment may also be subject to special procedures on the part of the creditor/ assignor or to an arbitration clause binding on him in the case of disputes. Generally, close relationships of this nature between the transferred right and supporting duties suggest a transfer of the duties, and even of closely connected rights (like security interests)[200] at the same time, as they may be considered integral parts of the assigned right. Closely connected duties are especially those that represent a precondition for the enjoyment of the right itself, for example the duty to make an advance payment before a right may be enjoyed.[201] The assignee will have to accept these preconditions, but that may still not be good enough for the debtor who may have reason to distrust an assignee whom he did not choose or approve of. This may impede the whole assignment as far as the debtor is concerned who may as a consequence be able to ignore it or at least to hold the assignor still responsible for any default of the assignee under these related duties.

Thus special burdens or exposure, defences and transfer of related duties may become practical impediments to the assignment of the receivable to protect a debtor with a justified interest or they may impact on any release of the assignor, whilst the assignee becomes additionally liable. They may no longer be a question of assignability and give rise to legal impediments. This is the more likely modern approach. Thus the right to additional deliveries under a purchase contract may be freely assignable, but only together with the duty to pay for them and without a full release in this regard from the assignor. Arbitration duties will similarly transfer. The absence of a release in this case is the consequence of the lack of consent of the debtor, even though the transfer of duties in this way, like the transfer of the payment obligation and of any related arbitration obligation, may also be in the interest of the debtor.

It always remains a question of interpretation of which rights and especially duties are so closely related as to be automatically transferred with a right, and there is here often an element of uncertainty. To avoid complications in this respect, parties may have excluded in their contract the assignment possibility altogether, but in modern law there may be a question how far these clauses are still enforceable and against whom: see in particular Sections 2-210 and 9-404*ff* (9-318 old) UCC in the USA.[202] Even if still enforceable in principle, again the precise consequence will have to be established. It may merely be a damages action for the debtor against the assignor whilst the assignment itself is increasingly likely to be enforceable by the assignee. The courts in the USA have been particularly impatient

---

[200] See for the accessory nature of the security interests more in particular, chapter V, n 3.

[201] The rights to mineral extraction subject to payments of royalties have, however, been found assignable without consent whilst imposing the royalty duty on the assignee: see the English line of cases on the subject starting with *Aspden v Seddon* (1876) 1 Ex D 496 see also *Tito v Waddell* [1977] chap 106, 302. It raises the issue whether the assignor is fully discharged in the process. It is likely that the debtor retains residual recourse against his original creditor unless explicitly released.

[202] In the USA Section 2-210(3) UCC presumes that a non-assignability clause only concerns the delegation of duties and not the assignment of rights except where the circumstances indicate otherwise. In any event, a right to damages for breach of the whole sale contract or a right arising out of the assignor's due performance of his entire obligation under a sale of goods agreement is always assignable despite agreement otherwise (Section 2-210(2) UCC). Section 9-406 (9-318 (4) old) UCC is even more liberal when receivables are assigned for security purposes, *cf* also n 182 *supra* and for the English approach nn 192 179 *supra*.

with contractual assignment restrictions.[203] However, German law in Section 399 BGB and Dutch law, even in its new Article 3.83(2) CC, still defend the older attitude: contractual limitations on the transfer have *in rem* effect and assignees cannot even invoke their *bona fides* in order for the assignment to be valid, except in situations in which the assignee could not have been aware of the restriction or was misled by the debtor because the restriction was for example not contained by the parties in the documentation on which the assignee relied: see Article 3.36 CC and for Germany Section 405 BGB.[204]

Another question is whether the debtor and assignor may change the underlying agreement after an assignment so as to deprive the assignee of a benefit. In the case of a security assignment in the USA, Section 9-405 (9-318(2) old) UCC makes such modifications effective if made in good faith and in accordance with reasonable commercial standards. The assignee will receive any benefit, but if harmed he may still have recourse against the assignor under the assignment agreement. This is also a radical approach, particularly relevant in the case of partial assignments only, as here in security assignments, therefore in situations when the contract at least partially continues between the original parties and only certain rights, the receivables, are normally cut out and assigned for special purposes only, whilst the assignor must continue to perform the rest of the contract. It may not have

---

[203] Although the debtor may thus often ignore the assignment in the case of a contractual prohibition in the underlying contract out of which the claim arises (unless great extra burdens arise), there may (a) be a complication if the debtor under a contractual assignment prohibition still pays. It seems to validate the assignment and perfect the transfer of the claim from assignor to assignee. Any further assignment by the assignee (or assignor) is then also free of the assignment restriction if the debtor has no demonstrable further interest in the limitation. Would it make a difference whether the transfer limitation were an outright prohibition of an assignment or required the debtor's consent only? The power to transfer is in the latter case not curtailed and upon an unauthorised assignment there may be recourse only against the assignor but not against a *bona fide* assignee. A further question is whether under such clauses the consent can be given conditionally and whether such a condition has automatic returning effect if breached. Another question may be whether the unauthorised assignment, although in principle valid, may void the underlying contract for fundamental breach. These issues remain little discussed but see earlier GC Grismore, 'Effect of a Restriction on Assignment in a Contract', 31 *Mich LR*, 299 (1933).

Under English law it is clear that if a contract is not assignable under its own terms, that does not mean that individual claims under it are not assignable either: see *Linden Garden Trust Ltd v Lenesta Sludge Disposal Ltd and Others* and *St Martins Property Corporation Ltd and Another v Sir Robert McAlpine & Sons Ltd*, n 192 *supra*.

[204] Illegality will of course void any assignment (Section 400 BGB). It can be inherent in the nature of the claim (Section 399 BGB) and be negotiated (Section 399 BGB). There may well be a difference in treatment if the restriction is inherent in the type of claim rather than negotiated by the parties. An example of the former is a claim of a company against its unpaid-up shareholders. In that case, the abstract nature of a transfer of title in Germany, see s 1.5.6 *supra*, may not allow the debtor to go behind the assignment and he may upon notification no longer be allowed to pay the assignor: see RGH, 23 Sept 1921, RGHZ 102, 385. The third party impact is thus lost upon assignment. It was never meant to protect the debtor in the first place and could thus hardly be invoked by him. In the case of a contractual restriction (to which he was a party), the debtor may ignore the assignment as the restriction is believed a debtor's right, not inherent in the claim but rather an integral part of it: see BGH, 14 Oct 1963, BGHZ 40, 156 (1963). It is even said that in such cases the assignment was ineffective *per se* so that the assignee has nothing at all. One might also say that the breach gives the debtor a defence, which he may be able to maintain against the assignee. As a consequence, this limitation is likely to work against third parties, therefore *in rem*. It is nevertheless exceptional that a contractual clause can have such effect against third parties. It is to be noted in this respect that contractual restrictions on the transfer of chattels are never considered to have *in rem* effect and cannot be opposed to buyers who did not know of them. In this aspect Section 137 BGB in Germany and Article 3.83(3) of the new Dutch CC are clear.

Even if contractual assignment restrictions may be opposed to unsuspecting assignees, it is not immediately clear to whose estate the claim belongs upon a forbidden assignment if the assignor goes bankrupt in the meantime: can his trustee invoke the invalidity of the assignment *vis-à-vis* the assignee or can only the debtor do so? Would the situation be different if the limitation or prohibition of the transfer were inherent in the claim and would the abstract or causal system of title transfer have any relevance in this respect in the relationship between assignor and assignee, as suggested by the first case cited above?

any wider application outside the area of security transfers, although again it is indicative of modern thinking in this area.[205]

The reason for the increasingly liberal attitude to the transfer of intangible rights, notably of receivables, is economic necessity as these assignments are often necessary to raise the funding that makes the extension of credit under the receivables possible in the first place. To repeat, the justification as far as the debtor is concerned is that the latter often has no reasonable interest in the identity of his creditor, although there may still be certain factors affecting and limiting the transfer possibility without debtor's consent, like (a) the close connection with (some of) the duties of the assignor under the contract, like a duty to pay in the case of the transfer of delivery rights, (b) any defences the debtor may have against payment in terms of poor quality of the delivered goods and any set-off of counterclaims, (c) any contractual limitations on the assignment (although under modern law no longer giving rise to an ineffective assignment), and (d) generally any resulting material extra burdens or risks on the debtor. Within reason, the debtor will have increasingly to accept, however, the inconvenience of assignments of rights others have against him as the ordinary flow of business requires it and his participation therein assumes here a certain flexibility which may even result in a co-operation duty. Only if unreasonable burdens or risks result may the modern debtor be able to ignore the assignment (and implicit transfer of related duties).[206]

Although the modern tendency is to favour the separation of the receivable or other monetary claims from their context (contract or other) in order to make them freely assignable, there may thus remain inherent limitations derived from the *in personam* nature of each claim or the internal relationship, even if assignability is now often encouraged by modern legislation and the courts, in the context of which contractual limitations of the transfer are increasingly unlikely to lead to nullity of the assignment. Thus, their *in rem* effect is increasingly disallowed.

Duties are generally less likely to be capable of being split out in this manner and being separately transferable, that is without consent of the counter-party. However, as just mentioned, closely related duties of a creditor are now primarily considered automatically to transfer with the claim without consent of the debtor but also without a release of the creditor/assignor. Yet modern law does not necessarily exclude a more general delegation of other duties by a debtor without consent either, unless there is a substantial demonstrable interest in having the original debtor perform or unless the duties themselves are materially changed as a result of the transfer and replacement of the debtor. The trade–off

---

[205] This was nevertheless held clear madness by Professor G Gilmore, *Security Interests in Personal Property* (1965), 1085. A comparison could, however, be made with the position of a third party beneficiary under a contract upon notice of his benefit, which benefit cannot normally be withdrawn after it has been signified to the beneficiary and even less so if he has accepted it. It is indeed entirely possible to organise a transfer of a partial benefit under a contract in this manner and avoid any restrictions or limitations inherent in assignments and the position of an assignee or third party beneficiary need not be very different. It is normally not thought to allow for any change between the original parties without consent of the beneficiary. This may be all the more reasonable because the debtor is aware of the beneficiary's interest as it was a term of the original contract. A similar situation arises when in an assignment there is some debtor involvement or acquiescence which may be explained as an amendment of the original agreement: see s 1.7.5 *infra*. Short of a novation, the assignee is then properly speaking the third party beneficiary of such an amendment, which cannot be varied or be undone without his consent either. It would suggest that a lender receiving security and a collection facility as a third party beneficiary may be in a better position than a lender receiving a security assignment of the same receivables. This is logical, as there is some debtor consent.

[206] Assignor and assignee could make special arrangements amongst themselves to ensure that no extra burdens arise for the debtor who under applicable law might otherwise be able to ignore the assignment even upon notification. As we saw in n 195 *supra*, Section 2-210(2) UCC in the USA requires the extra burdens, extra risks of performance, or changes in the debtor's duties to be material in order for the debtor to ignore the assignment.

in a more general delegation of duties is again that the debtor/transferor is likely to remain additionally liable for the performance and is not discharged. This is the system of Section 2-210 UCC in the USA. It completes the transformation from the old common law approach, in which rights were hardly assignable because of their personal nature, to a situation in which rights and duties, even those that are not directly related, are both ordinarily transferable. As a consequence, a contractual constraint in this respect may no longer be controlling. On the other hand, a delegation of duties remains subject to a guarantee of performance by the transferor.

Although contractual monetary claims, especially receivables, are the most likely objects of assignments, there are other types of rights, like tort claims or other claims like those for restitution, which usually stand more on their own and may then also be more readily separated from the legal relationship out of which they arise, leading to their assignability, although especially for tort claims it was long held that they were so highly personal by their very nature that they were not transferable, even as a mere claim for monetary damages. Especially in common law, there were other impediments, often of a procedural nature, whilst earlier, even in the case of contracts, the penalties that could be extracted by a dissatisfied creditor or victim could be such that the debtor could not be thought to be insensitive to the person of his creditor, which would serve as an impediment to assignment.

For the present discussion, the emphasis is on the contractual, tort and other damages claims, especially if monetary, and on their status, transfer and protection as ordinary assets of the creditors which increasingly de-emphasises their *personal* origin and nature for the purpose of facilitating their transfer without the debtor's consent. It even implies the disregard for contractual restrictions on assignments. It has become a business requirement, especially where these claims are used to raise financing.

1.7.4   The Assignability of Future Claims

The issue of inherent or statutory lack of assignability arises more in particular in respect of future claims where English and German law are the more liberal and French and even new Dutch law the more restrictive. Future claims are here defined as those not yet existing, not claims that do exist but have a future maturity date. The assignment of the latter should not be a problem (although under the English writ system they had no present value which could present further complications besides all other impediments attached to assignments in those early times) and the assignee cannot of course alter the maturity date.

The situation may be different in respect of future claims. The issue was already raised in section 1.5.5 above in connection with future chattels and in section 1.6.7 above in connection with floating charges. In fact, Roman law had been liberal (in those limited instances where an assignment was possible), see C 8.53.3, probably ever since a whole inheritance could be assigned, although there remained much controversy on this point in the *ius commune*. Eventually the discussion became connected with the need to give notification which was increasingly accepted as a constitutive requirement of an assignment,[207] unavoidably creating problems for future claims when the debtor might not even be known. German law, in abandoning the requirement of notification in the nineteenth century, freed itself from this constraint and the only German requirement is

---

[207] See n 182 *supra*.

in this connection that the claim be identifiable[208] at the time of the real agreement or *dingliche Einigung*, which agreement in the case of intangibles is implied and means transfer of legal possession at the same time, therefore at the time of the assignment agreement.

The most normal situation in which this type of assignment of future claims arises is under an extended reservation of title or in a floating charge.[209] In a(n extended) reservation of title, it means that all receivables connected with a resale of goods in which title is reserved by the supplier may be assigned to the latter at the time the reservation of title is made regardless of who the ultimate debtors will be and of the exact amount of the claims against them. German law proves indifferent to these two uncertainties.[210] The reference to the goods sold under a reservation of title and to all claims deriving therefrom upon a resale are considered sufficient identification of the claims and legal reason or *Rechtsgrund* for the transfer.[211] *Otherwise* these claims should at least be sufficiently identified with respect to the relationship out of which they are to arise. A more specific later assignment of them to a bank, even at the time of their emergence (upon the resale of the underlying goods), does in that case not take precedence. In a floating charge, it means that all future receivables in respect of inventory (to be) sold may automatically be included in the charge, although in a bankruptcy of the assignor it may still be important that at that time the receivables could at least be identified with reference to an underlying sales relationship out of which they are likely to emerge, see also section 1.5.5 above.

The English approach under equitable assignments, which do not require notification as a constitutive requirement, is very similar, yet the date of transfer may be different.[212] English law allows the assignment of all book debts due and owing or becoming due and owing during the continuation of a financing agreement. When future book debts are assigned, the subject matter of the assignment is considered capable of being identified only as and when *the book debts come into existence*, whether the description is restricted to a particular business or not. As in Germany, the later emergence of the claim does not suspend the assignment agreement, however, and the assignment is perfectly valid and effective as at the assignment date, but in England the proprietary right of the assignee (and any priority that comes with it) is only established as at the day the claim materialises. English law tends to distinguish here between assignments and agreements to assign as follows.

Money payable in the future under an existing contract is not considered future property and can be assigned. It is only a question of maturity, as just mentioned. If the contingency upon which a payment depends is essentially in the control of the assignee (for example his own performance) there is no problem with the assignment either.[213] If there is no control, it is still possible to assign a right to future income from a specific source.[214] But if there is not even such an identifiable source, the claim becomes wholly future and there is then only a contract to assign, which, if consideration is given, is perfectly valid, however, but the transfer under it only takes place as of the day the claim arises or control is established. However, equity, which regards as done that which ought to be

---

[208] See also BGH, 9 June 1960, BGHZ 32, 367 (1960).

[209] See chapter V, n 125.

[210] See BGH, 25 Oct 1952, BGHZ 7, 365 (1952).

[211] See also K Lahrenz, Schuldrecht, Allgemeiner Teil (14th edn, 1987), paragraph 34 III.

[212] See the leading case of *Tailby v Official Receiver* (1888) 13 AC 523 where the House of Lords followed *Holroyd v Marshall* (1862) 10 HL Cas 191 in which it had dealt with similar questions on the transfer of future chattels.

[213] *Hughes v Pump House Hotel Co Ltd* [1902] 2 KB 190.

[214] See *Shepherd v Commission of Taxation* [1966] ALR 969.

done will then *automatically* imply such a transfer (as an equitable assignment) without further formalities. An intervening bankruptcy of the assignor will therefore have no impeding effect on the transfer.[215] That would also appear to be the German situation even under Section 91 of its 1999 Insolvency Act. It is notably different in the Netherlands under Article 35(2) of its Bankruptcy Act, see also section 1.5.5 above.[216]

The situation in the USA is not everywhere the same, and in some states the policy of the courts appears more restrictive than in others, probably on the view that no one should commit too far out and mortgage the future or defeat the reasonable expectations for recovery of future creditors. However, the UCC under its Article 9 accepts for security assignments any description of the collateral, whether or not it is specific as long as it reasonably identifies what it describes: Section 9-110 UCC. The ethos of the Code (Section 9-204 UCC) is that for security transfers all future assets can be given for all future debt subject to publication (in the case of claims only if they account for a substantial part of the assignor's portfolio of claims) through the filing of a finance statement and one must therefore assume a liberal interpretation of any requirement of 'existence' of the debt. As regards the notification requirement, which is no constitutive requirement under the UCC, it must reasonably identify the rights assigned: see Section 9-406 (9-318(3) old) UCC, again without saying what this identification requires. The same applies to any security filings. As already pointed out before, in the USA all transfers of receivables and similar claims are now covered by Article 9 UCC whether or not a secured transaction is intended unless the assignment was for collection purposes only or clearly an incidental act.

On the other hand, French and Dutch law are more restrictive and require on the whole that the legal relationship out of which the claim arises must exist in order to make it assignable, although Dutch law under its new Code appears to leave some more room if the assignment is an outright transfer of title (Article 3.97 CC) but not in the case of an assignment for the purposes of security only (Article 3.239 CC).[217] In France, the restriction on the assignment of absolutely future claims has existed ever since the financial troubles of the writer Dumas and his attempt to assign his future copyrights of unwritten books to prevent his bankruptcy. These rights fell in his bankrupt estate regardless of the assignment for want of a debtor, that means for want of a contract out of which any

---

[215] *Cf Chityy on Contracts*, nos 20–028/20–032. The assignee's interest is therefore more than a mere matter of contract, even before the claim comes into existence.

[216] *Cf* also Article 5 (b) of the Unidroit Factoring Convention that also assumes the existence of the receivables before the transfer can be effective, see chapter V, s 2.3.7, but it is explicitly stated that there is no need for any new act of transfer. It may still depend, however, on the applicable *lex concursus* what the effect is in the case of an intervening bankruptcy of the assignor.

[217] Under pre-1992 law, this was a general requirement for all assignments, HR, 24 Oct 1980 [1981] NJ 265 and 25 Mar 1988 [1989] NJ 200.

For outright transfers of claims (but not for security transfers), Articles 3.84(2) and 3.97 CC now suggest greater flexibility by merely requiring that they are identifiable. At least the debtor must be known, a requirement reinforced by the need for notification to make the assignment valid. In this system it is conceivable that *all* claims against a particular debtor, whether they are present or future, may be assignable, which assignment would under the general rules of all assignments relate back to the date of the notification and not to the date of the emergence of the claim. This possibility could be limited, however, to all claims arising out of certain activities or derived from certain identified sources or any balance in a current account with a particular bank, but the requirement that the legal relationship out of which the claims arise is already in existence need not be fulfilled and the debtor remains here a potential debtor only, which cases where the contract out of which the claims arise is not yet in existence, seems not to impede the notification possibility itself.

The regime is likely to be stricter for security transfers, which impedes also the notification requirement. In that case, exceptionally, registration of the contract is possible as an alternative to notification but may also present identification problems. According to case law, this registration may be done by providing lists identifying the various claims arising which may be computer lists showing only the first and last entry: see HR, 14 Oct 1994 [1995] NJ 445. Yet it continues to require identification in principle of each and any claim.

benefit could arise.[218] Conversely, this meant that a theatre agreeing to assign future income even out of plays that did not yet exist or publishers agreeing to assign revenue out of books that had not yet been written could in this way transfer their future income if contracts with the (play)wrights were already in existence. It was not considered material in this connection that the benefit might not materialise. The restriction on assignability is material only for the writer who cannot assign the income if he has not yet got a contract for performance of his (future) plays or for the publishing of his (future) books.[219]

In France, where notification is traditionally required for the assignment to be valid (except under modern law in financing schemes with banks),[220] this approach stands to reason and is then very much connected with the debtor being known, even if the benefit that is being transfered could still be nil (for example if the plays or books were not produced). That is in itself not the determining factor. The difference in Germany is that the debtor need not be known at all, whilst the identity of the goods from the sale of which the claims may emerge or the identity of the source of the income will be sufficient. An author can therefore sell his future copyrights in Germany as long as they can be sufficiently described, even if in a subsequent bankruptcy of an assignee only those claims that arise out of a relationship existing before the bankruptcy may be considered sufficiently transferred.

Ultimately the question of the assignability of future claims mainly concerns the question into whose estate they fall if the assignor goes bankrupt in the meantime, first as between him and the assignee, but then also as between various assignees. Thus a reservation of title by a seller extended into the receivables may compete with a later factoring of the receivables to a bank, even if the receivables emerged later. It raises the question of retroactivity (or not) of their inclusion in the reservation of title. German law may here go further than English law. There is also the impact of the notification in countries that require it for the validity of the assignment which is likely to depend on the debtor being known at the time of the assignment. Countries with such notification requirements like France and the Netherlands have here a further impediment for the assignment of absolutely future claims.

1.7.5 *Assignment, Novation, Amendment, Subrogation and Subcontracting*

The use of the ownership concept to achieve a transfer of the active side of an agreement or the rights under it implies a *creditor substitution* under the original *in personam* relationship without the debtor's consent. The result is that the contractual relationship (or part of it) continues in force with another party or, to put it differently, that the debtor's contractual obligation is directed towards a new creditor without any other change in the contract, whilst the former creditor or assignor remains normally responsible for any duties he must still perform under the contract, perhaps even for those that are so closely related to the assigned rights that under modern law they transfer automatically with them, even if the assignor might then be able to insist that the assignee perform first. In that case the assignor becomes merely a *guarantor*. If the claim is secured by the debtor (on the latter's or somebody else's assets), this arrangement is also likely to remain undisturbed and the benefit of the security will in that case accrue to the new creditor/assignee, at least if there was a full assignment and not merely a security or conditional assignment.

---

[218] See Court of Appeal Paris, 31 Jan 1854, D.2.179 (1855).
[219] See also Court of Appeal Paris, 27 Nov 1854, D.2.253 (1856).
[220] See for the *Loi Dailly* and its aftermath n 179 *supra*.

Creditor substitution nevertheless means a fundamental change in the underlying legal relationship in terms of the counter-party (although not in terms of the applicable contractual or tort provisions), but can all the same be achieved without involvement of the debtor, in the example of a receivable therefore without consent of the buyer/payor of the price. It is the consequence of rights being treated as ordinary assets. As no consent is involved, this substitution is not normally perceived as an amendment of the contract either.

On the other hand, in unilateral *debtor* substitution and in those cases where unilateral *creditor* substitution may be more difficult because (a) the debtor retains an interest in the person of his creditor (especially likely in the case of him supplying personal services), or (b) there result material extra burdens or risks for the debtor as a consequence of the assignment, or (c) the whole contract is being transferred, the way of transferring the position of either party is likely to involve a degree of consent or acquiescence of the other party to the underlying agreement. The effect of this *consent* or acquiescence is itself troublesome. Does it mean the conclusion of a tripartite agreement introducing a new party and releasing the old one? That would be a *novation*.

A novation is a more circumstantial transaction as it terminates the earlier agreement and puts a new agreement with the new party (either as debtor or sometimes as creditor) in its place. It requires involvement of the counter-party and its actual co-operation and consent. The old contract and its supporting secured interests would lapse, as well as all defences thereunder (if not settled on that occasion) and any security interests supporting either party's obligations must be renegotiated if they are meant to continue in favour of the new creditor.

Novation is unattractive in these circumstances and has therefore become uncommon in civil law. New Dutch law no longer specifically deals with it (but see Articles 1449*ff* old CC, which may retain here residual importance). This novation may mean no more than a substitution of one of the parties with a release of the substituted one; it may also vary substantive terms of the agreement at the same time.

As an alternative, it is conceivable that the debtor's consent, for example to perform a personal service for another party, leads to no more than an amendment of the old contract allowing substitution of the old creditor. Its supporting arrangements may then remain in place, even though the old agreement may be changed at the same time to allow for the new situation, for example as regards the place where the service will be performed (now at the place of the new creditor or assignee). Thus it seems that creditor or even debtor substitution *with consent* need not always be novation but can lead to simple amendment of the contract between the original parties to which the assignee becomes a *third party beneficiary* for the rights and *third party debtor* for the connected obligations upon his acceptance.

Even then, the question could still arise whether the consent by way of amendment affects the defences of the debtor. It will often be a matter of interpretation on the basis of the circumstances — taking into account any implicit changes in the rights or duties of the parties and any implicit waivers — whether consent of the counter-party leads to (a) a mere creditor or debtor substitution, (b) a more fundamental change of the underlying contract (and what that means in terms of defences and supporting rights) especially in the case of some more explicit consent of the counter-party, or (c) a novation (when the old defences and supporting rights are all lost).

An important question in this connection is also whether the debtor's consent to creditor substitution may be achieved through mere *acknowledgement*, and, if so, how this affects his defences and supporting rights. It may at least in some legal systems substitute for a notification to the debtor,[221] whilst this alternative for notification may also result from recognition in France or possibly from mere payment or performance of any other duty of the debtor, the benefit of which was transfered by his obligee/creditor.[222] It could as such imply consent to mere creditor substitution but also give rise to an interpretation of the assignment in terms of amendment or novation.

The survival of supporting securities in the case of a mere substitution without consent or even upon consent in the case of a mere amendment of the contract or upon acknowledgement is a great advantage for the assignee whilst costs will be saved. The survival of the debtor's defences against the assignee may be an acceptable price to pay, as it is often in the assignee's interest that a novation is avoided and the liabilities will be discounted in the price paid for the receivable. For the assignor, however, there may remain a particular question whether, short of such a novation, he is fully discharged from any connected duties, as this is often unlikely to be explicit. Such a release would not necessarily be an indication of an amendment of the agreement or of a novation either, but may in common law lead to the requirement that adequate consideration is paid for this release to be effective and could then still mean an amendment or novation involving the debtor.

It may be the reason novations are more frequent in common law as they clarify the status of all parties so that the former creditor's release cannot be in doubt. In terms of consideration, the termination of the old agreement may be sufficient if the released creditor gives up some rights. It also removes any need for the assignor to be any further involved in lawsuits brought by the assignee against the debtor, in common law a particular remnant of the old controversies concerning assignments at law or in equity. However, even in civil law, novation remains often the only way out where a party wants to transfer all his duties at the same time and obtain a release, even if these duties are fairly closely related to assigned rights and may automatically transfer with them, or where a party wants to assign its entire relationship under a contract, at least when it also entails duties, which will normally be the case.

As far as *creditor* substitution is concerned, it may also be achieved through *subrogation*. Subrogation is commonly limited to situations where someone has actually paid somebody else's debt. The creditor is thereby satisfied whilst the payor steps into the position of the creditor so far as the debtor is concerned. Normally, this does not require the debtor's consent, even if under the same law an assignment may require it (to which it is closely related). The subrogated party retains the benefits of any securities but remains subject to the defences of the debtor. Subrogation is a limited concept, however, and not all payors may automatically demand subrogation. *Statutorily*, it often follows when a third party is forced to pay the debt either because he conceded a security interest in his assets to support someone else's debt or he conceded a guarantee or accepted an insurance contract. *Contractually*, it may arise when the debtor and a third party agree that the latter pay the debt to the creditor and does so with subsequent creditor's substitution. In new Dutch law, this type of subrogation is made subject to the requirement that the creditor at the moment of payment is made aware of this agreement (see Article 6.150 of the new Dutch CC).

In France, contractual subrogation has a much wider application. Under Articles 1249 and 1250 Cc, it does not require notice to the creditor if payment to him by a third party (who will be subrogated to the creditor's rights) is arranged by the debtor. Neither does it require notice to the debtor if payment by a third party is arranged by his creditor (as an

---

[221] See for this common law approach in England, n. 190 *supra*.
[222] See n. 178 *supra*.

assignment and also a pledge in receivables would require in France; see Articles 1690 and 2075 Cc). This third party payor will be subrogated to the rights of the original creditor. This kind of subrogation was before the *Loi Dailly* of 1981, which did away with the notice requirement in certain cases,[223] a useful substitute for assignments in France, and often still is to avoid the formalities and notification requirement of assignments. By contract, the transferor and transferee of the claim may thus agree that, upon payment of the nominal values of the outstanding debts by the transferee to the transferor, the former is subrogated to all the transferor's rights against his former debtor regardless of the latter's consent or notification. The debtor's defences remain intact. So do the security interests supporting the debt.

Subcontracting is a form of *debtor* substitution, which can usually not be achieved without the creditor's consent and cannot therefore by itself result in full substitution as the original debtor/contract party is not discharged, but it may not require full novation so that the original contract continues. It is better seen as an amendment, which may involve at the same time minor contractual adjustments to allow the new party to operate from his place of business. Often it will be clear from the start that a main contractor requires help in its performance of the agreement and the creditor's consent to the debtor substitution will then be implied if not already expressed in the agreement itself.

1.7.6   Different Types and Objectives of Assignments

The question of proprietary status of intangible assets will surface not only in the question whether and how intangible assets can be transferred but also in the question how the interests in intangible asset may be split up, often with strict transfer formalities (for example when creating security interests). The possibilities are similar to those in chattels and entail the possibilities[224] (a) of assigning outright or absolutely (b) of making a conditional assignment as may happen in receivable financings or factoring agreements concerning receivables, (c) of assigning by way of security or (d) of assigning in usufruct or temporary ownership, or (e) of assigning the residual rights or reverters and remainders of the assignor when previously less than a full transfer of ownership was made. There arise here issues of *formation, assignability* and *validity*, which are further complicated by the inherent limitations in civil law countries on the ways in which ownership rights may be split or be made conditional or temporary.

Common law was never averse to these splits in principle; see section 1.3.1 above, but at least in England the statutory (legal) assignment does not allow for the transfer of charges or conditional rights in this manner,[225] and English law must in this connection resort to equitable assignments. An imperfect statutory assignment may still be an equitable assignment at the same time. Equitable assignments concerning claims at law still would involve the assignor in legal proceedings. The assignor retains in any event a residual interest in security transfers. Most civil law systems practise here in principle a closed system of proprietary rights, see section 1.2.1 above, and may have particular difficulties with conditional assignments or fiduciary transfers of receivables from that point of view.

Where assignments concern monetary claims and create minor interests or charges, all in the end concerns the question who may exercise the collection right so that the

---

[223] See n 179 *supra* and accompanying text.
[224] See for English law *Durham Bros v Robertson* [1898] 1 QB 765 and more recently *The Balder London* [1980] 2 Lloyd's Rep 489.
[225] See n 192 *supra, cf* also the law of chattels.

order as between the various interests so created needs to be particularly considered in this context.

Thus it is clear that there is not only the possibility of the assignment itself to be considered but also the different objectives of assignments in terms of the rights being transfered thereby. Particularly for bulk assignments it is useful to distinguish from the outset between the various types of assignment. The outright assignment of a portfolio of receivables against a certain price is not uncommon in this connection. It leaves the assignee with the collection risk in exchange for which the assignor will normally be given a discount on the nominal value of the portfolio and a further one for interest if not all claims are mature and possibly yet another discount for the collection cost. Under such a scheme, all collections are for the assignee and he will have the autonomous right to pursue the debtors in the way he deems fit.

It may, however, also be that the portfolio is transferred only so as to allow the assignee to take all necessary collection action. In this arrangement, the collections are returned to the assignor who retains the credit risk of the portfolio and pays the assignee for his activities as collector. The assignor will then also determine what action the collector should take against defaulting debtors and is likely to bear the cost of such action. This is more properly called a collection arrangement and is also very common. Although the ownership is transferred for collection purposes whilst the assignee may technically become the owner of the claims, he acts here in fact as a *collection agent*.

The outright transfer and the collection agency (even if in practice often also done through an outright transfer to a collection agent) are two extremes. However, the portfolio may also be transfered for security purposes to support a loan, meaning that any receivables remaining after a certain amount is collected will automatically be retransferred to the assignor, as will any extra collections. Upon default there may be a disposition when any excess will equally be returned to the original assignor. In English law this is often referred to as a *collateral assignment*. The portfolio may also be transferred *conditionally* and it is likely that this arrangement is made in lieu of a loan amortised (together with interest) through the collections. However, if a portfolio of receivables is sold for a price but there is a specific interest rate agreed for the sum received, a loan structure is still likely to be assumed and any excess collections over and above the received sum and the interests must then be returned. In the USA, the outright sale of receivables in this manner is also considered covered by Article 9 UCC: see Section 9-109(a)(3) (9-102(1)(b) old). It is in line with its suspiscion of sales used for financing purposes (which are converted in secured transactions, see Section 9-1–2(a)(5–6) (9-102(2) old) UCC, except if for collection purposes only: see Section 9-019(d)(4–7) (9-104(f) old) UCC). Article 9, however, still makes some distinctions with the security assignment of receivables. Especially the disposition is not obligatory and the seller (debtor) is only entitled to any overvalue if the sale agreement so provides (see Sections 9-607and 9-608 (9-502(2) old) UCC).

A proper conditional sale of receivables is indeed likely to cover an arrangement with different or additional conditions concerning the risk in the portfolio and greater latitude as to the entitlement to overvalue and the reward structure. Especially where the arrangement puts the credit risk in the portfolio on the assignee, it is normal that he has certain (if not all) rights in any overvalue as compensation for this risk beside his normal reward. Article 9 UCC allows this. On the other hand, the arrangement may be such that those receivables which the debtors prove unwilling or unable to pay are automatically returned to the assignor. It leaves the assignor with the credit risk in the portfolio and allows the assignee to collect other receivables (if available) without the time and expense connected with legal action. This is often called recourse financing. It is less likely to leave the assignee with any overvalue in the portfolio, but there may be some special reward for his collection activities and naturally for his funding.

Apart from special statutory rules, the most material difference between the conditional sale and the security transfer of a portfolio of receivables is that (a) the former may leave the assignee with (part of) the overvalue depending on the nature and terms of the arrangement whilst in the case of a security arrangement, the collection must stop once the debt it secures (plus interest) is paid off. Another most important difference is that (b) in some countries like the Netherlands under its old law and still in France it was not believed possible for the assignee to collect receivables under a secured transaction at all and the creditor could merely hold the portfolio subject to an execution sale upon default or at best a set-off right at that time.[226] This restriction never applied in cases of a conditional transfer of the portfolio. There further exist (c) more obvious differences in documentation and other formalities, including sometimes publication or (in the Netherlands) registration requirements, at least if under a security transfer no notification to the individual debtors is being given. Another difference might be (d) in the assignability of the claims itself: new Dutch law requires for a (conditional) sale that the claims are identifiable and for future claims it may now be sufficient to refer to all claims on a certain debtor (Article 3.84(2)), as we saw, yet for an assignment by way of security it is necessary that the relationship out of which the claim arises is already in existence (see Articles 3.97 and 3.239 CC).

A further difference may be (e) in the right to invoke any security interests supporting the receivable itself, therefore of the accessory rights: in a sale this benefit is likely to be automatically transfered to the assignee, but in a security transfer of the portfolio it is possible that these accessory protections remain with the assignor who alone may institute alternative recovery proceedings against other assets of the debtor if the latter defaults. Finally, (f) in the case of chattels, the difference between conditional sales and security interests has been *more* fundamentally characterised as a difference in risk patterns: see more in particular section 1.6.3 above. This may play a lesser role in the case of intangibles where, at least if the assignment concerns monetary claims, all converts into collection rights (assuming that is also the case under applicable law when a mere security interest is transferred in the receivable) and there may therefore be less reason to dwell on the differences than in the case of chattels. Nevertheless the conditional sale allows for greater flexibility and parties' input. They may for example distribute the overvalue in the assigned portfolio very differently in exchange for other benefits like the allocation of the credit risk to the assignee in whole or in part. The reward structure is as a consequence also likely to be very different from that under a secured loan agreement where the prevailing interest rates will be used allowing for size, maturity and credit risk.

1.7.7   The Better Right of the Assignee. The Notion of Abstraction and Finality. The Comparison with Negotiable Instruments

From the discussion so far, the question arises whether and when under modern law the assignee may claim a better position *vis-à-vis* the debtor than the assignor had. It is a question of ignoring, in so far as the assignee is concerned, some of the rights and defences the debtor may have had against the assignor. It is clear that the assignee is

---

[226] See for former Dutch law Article 1200 CC and HR, 19 Jan. 1898, W 5666, and for France Article 2078(2) Cc. See for new Dutch law explicitly allowing the collection under secured transactions Article 3.246 CC.

receiving increasingly better treatment, especially against undisclosed and undiscoverable flaws in the assigned position, such as any undisclosed incompleteness in the documentation concerning an assigned claim if due to the debtor's oversight or to his lack of co-operation in not amending the text properly when alterations were agreed. A similar provision already existed in the German BGB of 1900 (Section 405 BGB) and was also introduced in new Dutch law (Article 3.36 CC).

There are therefore situations in which the (*bona fide*) assignee is in a better position *vis-à-vis* the debtor than the assignor. As yet it may not go so far as to allow the assignee to ignore assignment restrictions in the original contract or set-off rights and other defences of which the debtor was not or could not have been aware at the time of the assignment. Even in the case of a transfer restriction, it would reduce the debtor's rights in this respect to personal claims against the assignor only rather than affect the assignment itself. Especially in the modern bulk transfer of receivables to receive financing (to render possible the credit extended to the debtors in the first place), the assignee may be increasingly protected against the effects of limitations on assignments in the underlying agreements out of which the receivable arises. That is the direction in the USA. Also, in the USA, clauses in the underlying agreement not allowing the debtor to raise any defences against an assignee are common and favoured, at least in the context of creating security interests in receivables in the professional sphere.

The assignee is thus increasingly protected. However, even in the USA, set-off rights of debtors under the agreement between them and the assignor are likely still to be upheld against the assignee. Even transferability may suffer and defences accepted because of material extra burdens, but it may increasingly depend on how large they are, again especially important in bulk assignments and a reasonable co-operation duty of the debtor may be implied.

Where an assignment mostly aims at transferring the active or asset side of an *in personam* legal relationship only (primarily a contractual relationship and then more in particular a contractual monetary claim, normally the payment claim or receivable), any voluntary delegation of duties derived from the same contract or the automatic delegation of duties that is closely connected to the assigned rights may create another risk for the debtor. Allowing a delegation of duties without the debtor's consent is nevertheless also a feature of the modern American approach as now legislated for rights and duties arising under sales agreements in the USA (Section 2-210 UCC). As we saw, the trade–off is that it does not relieve the transferor and it is not allowed as long as the other party had a substantial interest in having his original promissor perform.

It was already noted that a delegation of duties may sometimes be automatic if they are closely related to the rights that are assigned. It may be in the interest of the debtor (and could be a concern of the assignee) for example the duty to arbitrate any differences, or the duty to make certain (royalty) payments being a condition for the enjoyment or continued existence of the right, or the duty to pay in the case of an assignment of delivery rights. There remains the crucial question in these cases how far the assignor is liberated. It may be a question of interpretation.

Another issue in this respect is the impact on the assignee of any later change in the contract made by the assignor and the debtor, which may reduce the assignee's rights. As we saw, in *this* aspect modern law in the USA may increasingly distract from the assignee's expectations and allow these amendments to affect him and his assigned claims if they are made in the ordinary course of business whilst the claims are assigned for security purposes only, but the question remains whether that should more generally become the rule in bulk assignments.

The essence is that because of modern economic requirements, which need increased assignment facilities without too many impediments, the extra burdens or risks resulting for the debtor as a consequence of the assignment may no longer give the debtor a sufficient excuse not to pay the assignee. They are in any event unlikely to avoid the assignment and the debtor will increasingly have to sort matters out with the assignor. In other words, the tendency is for the *internal* relationship to have less and less effect on the *external* relationship, which is in line with intangible claims being considered ordinary assets.

There is here an element of *abstraction* in an assignment under which the assignee may ignore unknown circumstances concerning the assigned claim. As a consequence, *payment obligations* will increasingly be allowed to be lifted out of existing contracts and assigned separately, at least if they are assigned in bulk. In that case there is less consideration for their context and the assignor's obligations under the underlying contract (unless closely related, when they will transfer with the claim), or for the debtor's set-off rights and defences except where material, and all without the debtor's consent. In this atmosphere, it is also likely that the assignee will be allowed increasingly to ignore a prohibition of the assignment under the original contract in respect of such monetary claims, at least if he was not made aware of it and an investigation duty may no longer be imputed in this respect. Especially in bulk assignments such an investigation duty would be unconscionable.

Naturally, the debtor would retain damages actions against the assignor in the internal relationship but neither would the assignment itself be affected, nor would the duty of the debtor to pay the full amount of the assigned claims. In the *commercial and professional* sphere, this may increasingly be seen as an ordinary risk of the debtor participating in business and requesting credit therein, thereby becoming an ordinary benefit for the professional assignor and a protection for the professional assignee, which in turn would enable the assignor to find more readily the financing he requires. It could even apply to assignees aware of the debtor's position if the receivable arises out of normal commercial or financial transactions. This appears the modern trend and is of great significance. It would end with the full *commoditisation* of receivables altogether.

In this connection it may also be considered that if the debtor had issued a note, the unimpeded transferability of the claim would have followed anyway. The modern trend appears to be that a negotiable document is no longer necessary to achieve the free assignability of a receivable regardless of the relationship out of which it arose, at least not if assigned for security purposes. It may be seen in this connection that the abstraction principle is rougher than the notion of *bona fides*, in that it does not depend for the protection of the assignee on what he knows or should find out in terms of the rights and duties of the debtor under his contract with the assignor.

It is on the other hand also conceivable that in the *consumer sphere* consumer protections may disallow certain assignments or impose some new restrictions. For example in mortgage banking, upon the assignment of floating rate mortgages, these mortgages could become subject to the interest rate structure of the assignee. It could be considered an unacceptable variation of the original contract, not achievable through an assignment without the debtor's consent, so that the interest rate structure of the assignor remains applicable.

1.7.8   *The Notion of Abstraction and the Liberating Effect of Payment by the Debtor*

In the previous section we discussed the better right of the (*bona fide*) assignee against the debtor and the notion of abstraction. On the other hand, upon an assignment, properly notified, the debtor may be able to pay an assignee and may not need to go behind the notice to look for those with better rights. Again good faith could play a role in this protection but, also here, this requirement may be weakened and it is conceivable that any notification that is on its face properly made would now protect a debtor. This is a further example of abstraction, here affecting the notification. For debtors, all resolves into the single question who has the collection right and whom he or she should pay (assuming the assignments concern monetary claims). Potential claimants are various assignees as full owners of the intangible assets, conditional owners, security holders or beneficiaries under a usufruct, their garnishing creditors or trustees in bankruptcy or those of the assignor for his reversions. They may all be in a position in which they are faced with the proprietary pretences of others and with the question how far they may ignore these, first by giving notice and requesting the debtor to pay and subsequently retaining any collections made. English law has traditionally resolved this issue by considering only the assignment completed or perfected upon notification to a *bona fide* debtor, which may introduce considerable uncertainty, as it all depends on the knowledge of the debtor and his investigation duties under the circumstances and still could leave open the question of the ultimate entitlement to the collection proceeds.[227]

There are various possibilities, however. It is clear that as long as there is no notification, the debtor may still pay the assignor, probably even if he knows of the assignment. However, his *bona fides* could be an issue. If notification is a prerequisite for the validity of the assignment, the debtor should know that only the first notification transfers the claim in a double assignment and he should therefore pay only the first notifying assignee. If before he makes payment, he receives several notifications claiming assignments by the original creditor, he still has a duty to pay the first notifying assignee. If he pays another, thinking that he has a better right (because his assignment contract was earlier) he may not be protected. At least he runs a risk and the question is how far his subjective *bona fides* protects him. What should he know about the intricacies of assignments anyway?

If the notification was not a requirement for a valid transfer, the first notifying assignee might not be the rightful assignee at all, but the debtor would in such a system not have an investigation duty and could pay. If in the meantime he received several notifications he would probably still be protected if he paid the first one and would in any event not have an investigation duty, but his good faith could be questioned if he paid the first notifying assignee but had subjective knowledge of an earlier assignment or made payment to a later notifying assignee. Problems derive here in any event from (a) the form of notice, (b) the person who can validly give it, (c) the order of notices when there have been competing assignments or, to complicate matters further, an assignee has re-assigned the claim to a succeeding assignee, (d) the relevance of *bona fides* of the debtor to paying upon notice or choosing between competing or further assignees with or without notice.[228]

---

[227] This is the famous rule in *Dearle v Hall*, see n. 191 *supra*. It can be criticised on several grounds: it undermines the equity assignment approach, which does in principle not rely on notification. It does not definitely settle the question who is entitled to any collection proceeds but allows junior assignees to prevail in the collection depending on the *bona fides* of the debtor which introduces considerable uncertainty and may induce the debtor to become passive if he is not sure of the existence of better rights of other assignees of whatever nature. In fact, where even lawyers fear to tread, see sect. 1.7.9 *infra*, it leaves the sorting out of the better right in the first instance to the unsuspecting debtor who is a total outsider as far as the assignments are concerned.

[228] The form of the notification may vary a great deal. In France where it is a constitutive element of the validity of the assignment, it requires under Article 1690 Cc notice by a judicial official (*huissier*) or through a notarial document, which greatly impeded assignments but had the advantage of raising the notification to an official level and assuring its status. It resulted in an implicit check on its being properly given whilst an assignment document was also required. Since the *Loi Dailly* of 1981 notification has no longer been required as a constitutive element

Any emphasis on the *bona fides* of the debtor whilst paying an assignee may put him in a difficult position if faced with several notices and should be avoided as it raises the question how much of an investigation into better rights he must conduct and what his *bona fides* requires. German case law is firm in that the debtor has no investigation duty and he is only not discharged if he has actual knowledge that the assignment has not taken place. It does not seem necessary for him to go into any suspicion of other assignments.[229] It thus appears that the first assignee who produces the assignment document to the debtor normally prevails, although other assignees may have better rights. What if they present them before payment? The debtor must pay the assignee if ordered to do so by the assignor and also if an assignee officially notifies him of the assignment (see Sections 409 and 410 BGB). He need then not worry about the various competing rights, and other assignees should require satisfaction either from the assignor or from the assignee knowing of their better rights.

Above, the English situation under *Dearle v Hall* was already mentioned with its emphasis on the *bona fides* of the debtor whilst paying. In the USA, Section 9-406(a) (9-318(3) old) UCC authorises the debtor to pay the assignor until notice. If requested by the debtor the assignee must furnish reasonable proof of his rights and unless he has done so the debtor may pay the assignor. As in England it may leave the debtor with a heavy burden, which could allow him to ignore the entire assignment or not pay anyone. A simpler system would be to require the assignor and assignee jointly to give the debtor notice or the assignee alone if authorised to do so on the assignor's behalf whilst producing the authorisation document or the assignment document itself. That would not prevent, however, multiple notifications.

A system that would require the debtor always to pay the first notifying assignee if his notice is regular on its face (regardless of a debtor's knowledge of other assignments and their ranking) would lead to greater simplification and be in line with the notion of abstraction. Any senior assignees or assignees alleging better rights would have to sort the matter out with the collecting assignee or with the assignor, either through tracing of the proceeds or recourse against the assignor if guilty of wrongful assignment. In this way, the debtor faces no extra burdens connected with his payment duty and the notification becomes an *abstract* payment instruction. If regular on its face, the debtor would never be required to go behind it. It would not be unlike paying an endorsee of a negotiable instrument like a bill of exchange or promissory note. For assignees, it would become a pure race situation, as in fact it already largely is where competition must be feared.

The abstract nature of the first notification, which would instruct and protect the debtor in this manner, would mirror the abstract nature of the assignment which sometimes gives

---

in bulk transfers supporting financing in the professional sphere, but in practice it is naturally still necessary to make the debtor pay the assignee but may then be informal. It raises, however, the question of whom the debtor can validly pay. In the Netherlands where it has become a constitutive requirement under its new Code, notice may be given by the assignor or assignee in any form. A document is required for the assignment itself but need not figure in the notification to the debtor. The latter may require, however, that the assignor provides him with an extract from the document, which appears to put the ultimate burden of the notification being properly given upon the debtor (Article 3.94(3) CC). In Germany, where notification is not a constitutive requirement and the assignment itself does not require a document (although the assignee may request one: Section 403 BGB), the emphasis is on the knowledge of the debtor, however acquired: see Section 407 BGB, and notification as such does not figure in the German Code. In the USA, in states where notice is required for a valid assignment (beyond those covered by the UCC), it may apparently be oral also: see *Fugatew v Carter County Bank*, 187 BR 221 (ED Tenn 1995). Knowledge by the debtor was considered sufficient.

[229] RGH, 19 Sept 1905, RGHZ 61, 245.

the assignee better rights against the debtor as discussed in the previous section. Both types of abstractions (of the first notification and of the assignment itself) provide greater clarity and may greatly facilitate the assignment practice and especially bulk transfers of monetary claims. In this vision, monetary claims are increasingly treated as negotiable instruments or semi-tangible assets.

Negotiable instruments like bills of exchange and promissory notes are normally considered to incorporate a claim fully and to separate it from the underlying legal relationship out of which it arises. The treatment of the claim is then largely like a chattel, therefore like a movable tangible asset and the transfer is not through assignment but through the handing over of the document if to bearer or through endorsement and handing over if to order, even in legal systems, like the French and English, that no longer require delivery for a transfer of title in chattels. In legal systems that protect *bona fide* purchasers of chattels, as most civil law countries now do, *bona fide* purchasers for value of this type of paper are protected against the claims of any senior transferees or other third parties as they may be the creditors of the transferors. They are then more properly called holders in due course. In common law a similar approach resulted under the law merchant.

A further consequence of this system is that the debtor who accepts a bill of exchange drawn on him or the debtor who issues a promissory note is considered to have surrendered all his defences against any subsequent buyer of the paper, at least if the latter was *bona fide*, that is unaware of these defences. The abstraction principle just mentioned separates the receivable from the underlying legal relationship out of which it arises. It is likely increasingly to limit the debtor in his defences, as we saw, and gives the assignee a better position as against him, although it is as yet unlikely to give the *bona fide* collecting assignee better rights *vis-à-vis* any senior assignee or protect him against any defective assignments earlier in a chain of assignments, although this is becoming the American approach as we shall see in the next section.

1.7.9   *The Ranking between Assignees, The* Nemo Dat *Rule in Assignments*

In the previous sections we saw that in the absence of a clear proprietary approach to claims, it took the law everywhere a long time to formulate a workable approach to the proprietary protection of claims, that is to the protection of the assignee against third parties, like other assignees claiming better rights. This issue is to be distinguished from the assignee's better rights against the debtor (compared to those of the assignor) under an assigned receivable and the liberating payment rights of the debtor upon an assignment, which were also discussed in the previous sections.

All raise issues of good faith protection but in different ways. In the case of the better right of the assignee against the debtor it is a matter of comparison with the position of the assignor, or more properly a question of the rights that the debtor may enforce against an assignee who is unaware of them. The protection of the debtor making a payment to an assignee may equally depend on his good faith, although that may ultimately also not be satisfactory, as we saw.

The protection amongst various assignees is of a different and more traditional nature and raises the question whether an assignee, having given notice to the debtor and having collected the money, may retain the proceeds if he collected in good faith, thus unaware of the better rights of any other assignee. This is an aspect of the *nemo dat* rule and of *bona fide* purchaser protection, related to the inability (in principle) of the assignor to transfer his claim more than once and is therefore a typical problem of double assignments.[230] Although often fraudulent, a second assignment of the same claim by the assignor does not need to be sinister in any way: the assignor may assign his claims first in a security transfer or in usufruct for some time and thereupon the remainder to another assignee. He may also make a conditional sale and assign the reverter to a junior assignee, so that a ranking may result. Normally this situation will be disclosed but in a bulk assignment of claims the remainders and reverters are likely to be included, or, to put it another way, the claims are implicitly assigned subject to any limited or better rights therein.

Better rights of others may not have been apparent to the assignee and the question then arises how far he is protected upon giving notice and collecting, assuming he gave good value for the assignment. The law in most countries does not allow *bona fide* purchaser protection to operate here, as its justification is normally based on the predecessor of the pretending owner having left him with indices or the appearance of ownership, typical in the case of chattels left with a bailee or holder. At least under civil law, the voluntary parting with the goods in these circumstances mostly disallows the real owner to invoke his own better rights against the *bona fide* purchasers for value and with a valid contract from the holder. The unauthorised sale is here considered the risk of the original owner. In the case of intangibles, the appearance of ownership of any unauthorised assignor is more difficult to maintain because of the lack of a physical manifestation of control on which the assignee might have relied and which may be imputed to the assignor's predecessor.

The exception to the *nemo dat* rule resulting in the protection of the *bona fide* assignees is therefore uncommon in the case of intangibles under civil law. Yet there is often a possibility under civil law of acquisitive prescription (but seemingly not in Germany) if someone other than the rightful owner starts collecting in good faith. It may suggest that there could also be room for a *bona fide* purchaser exception to the *nemo dat* rule but only after a certain time. Common law, which is on the whole less generous with *bona fide* purchaser protection even in the case of chattels, allows it under its general rule protecting such purchasers against earlier *equitable* proprietary rights, but otherwise only by statute.

Whether there is a further exception in common law in the case of double sales in intangibles seemed to remain until quite recently unresolved in English law. The case of *Dearle v Hall* gives the first notifying assignee the right to collect and the debtor may pay him if unaware of better rights but it does not say who has the ultimate right to the collection. It is now indeed the assignee who so collects *providing he is bona fide*, therefore unaware of earlier interests. That type of collection is then equated with perfection.[231] American law remains divided. The majority rule still appears to be that the first assignee is the rightful owner of the claim upon assignment, and this regardless of notification to the debtor,

---

[230] It may in this connection be asked whether for this protection the collecting assignee needed at least a valid agreement, much as in the case of the sale of chattels: see also s 1.5.6 *supra*. If there is no need for a valid contract, the protection of the collecting assignee may also result from the abstract system of title transfer when his *bona fides* is not relevant. This may be especially relevant in the case of intangibles where generally the *bona fide* purchaser protection does not obtain, even in systems that normally accept it for chattels as modern civil law does. See for indications of an abstract system in this respect in England, n 191 *supra*. In a causal system the collecting assignee is unprotected.

[231] See for *Dearle v Hall*, nn 191 and 227 *supra*. See for the *bona fides* requirement allowing the collecting younger assignee to retain his collections, which was only implicit in *Dearle v Hall*, *Rhodes v Allied Dunbar Pension Services Ltd* [1987] 1 WLR 1703. There is no investigation duty and acquiring knowledge of the earlier assignment after the second assignment but before notice is given thereunder is irrelevant for the entitlement to the collection, but if there is a registered charge, there may be constructive or implied notice, although this is not automatically so in England and in particular does not apply to any restrictive assignment covenants in a floating charge as they need no filing. (*Note continues.*)

although at least in New York a second assignee who manages to collect in good faith may retain the proceeds.[232] That is also the approach of the *Restatement (Second) Contracts* (Section 342). For security assignments, Section 9-406(a) (9-318(3) old) UCC fails to provide a fundamental rule, although Section 9-322(a) (9-312(5) old) UCC maintains for all filed security interests the priority of the first finance statement. Filings prevent junior assignees from retaining their collections. In this system, in the absence of filing, knowledge of earlier assignments is irrelevant for a collecting junior assignee.

Under the UCC, there is another aspect in that *all* assignments of claims (only accounts in the sense of Article 9) are covered by it, therefore also *ordinary sales* of such accounts (which exclude notably tort claims and bank deposits). This implies in principle a filing facility also in respect of such outright sales and priority for earlier assignees as per the date of filing of the finance statement concerning these sales or assignments. There is automatic perfection, however, for assignments of less than a substantial part of a debtor's receivables portfolio (Section 9-309(2) (9-302(1)(e) old) UCC). It is a somewhat curious departure in Article 9, more understandable in the case of chattel paper that was specially created as a collateral category to promote financing: see also chapter V, section 1.6.2. The implication is here that all sales of accounts are for financing purposes (pure collections are exempted under Section 9-109(d)(5) (9-104(f) old) UCC). The filing or automatic perfection here takes the place of notice to the debtor as a perfection method in respect of third parties. For attachment of the assignee's interest, Section 9-201 (new and old) UCC suggests that it takes place regardless of notice, therefore also in states that outside Article 9 require it for the validity of an assignment. That greatly facilitates bulk assignments. Disposition and a return of overvalue are here at the discretion of the parties (Section 9-6–8(b) (9-502(2) old). The effect on the ranking of assignees is that subsequent assignees, even if they collect in good faith, do so subject to the older interest and there is here no protection of *bona fide* assignees under Section 9-320(a) (9-307(1) old). Only good faith buyers of chattels subject to a security interest are protected (if buying in the ordinary course of interest from a merchant seller).

The conclusion is that the issue of the proper ranking as a proprietary matter is not always determined by the seniority of the assignment itself. There may conceivably be other factors: (a) notice to the debtor, at least in countries that see it as a requirement for the validity of the assignment, (b) *bona fides* of the paying debtor, at least in countries that see it as relevant in this connection, (c) *bona fides* of the assignee, at least in countries that allow some protection against the *nemo dat* rule in the case of assignments of claims, (d) filing, at least in countries that provide a filing facility in this connection, and (e) the type of rights transferred which may lead to a different regime for security transfers as distinct from outright transfers.

If the earlier assignment was a legal assignment, it would have required notice to be valid, and there would not appear a problem with a second assignee whose notice would then always be later, but what if the earlier assignment had already been notified (without collection) unknown to a later legal assignee? In that case, the priority of a *bona fide* legal assignee could follow from the general principle that earlier equitable interests of which the later legal purchaser is unaware may be ignored. Strictly speaking *Dearle v Hall* was not an expression of that principle as it concerned two equitable assignments. English courts prefer here, however, the rule in *Dearle v Hall*, upholding the right of the first *bona fide* collecting assignee in all cases: see *Pfeiffer GmbH v Arbuthnot Factors Ltd* [1988] 1 WLR 150 in which it was decided that for priority purposes the legal assignment is considered equitable. In this connection reference was made to Section 136(1) of the Law of Property Act 1925 making legal assignees 'subject to equities having priority over the right of the assignee'; but *cf.* also F Oditah, *Legal Aspects of Receivable Financing* (1991), 155*ff* challenging (with regret) this interpretation.

[232] See *Salem Trust Co v Manufacturer's Finance Co*, 264 US 182 (1924) and *Corn Exchange NB & T Co v Klauser*, 318 US 434 (1943); see also n 194 *supra* and accompanying text.

The subject is of great importance in receivable financing upon assignment of portfolios of claims and *bona fide* collections thereunder, when the question truly arises who may consider himself the owner of the collection right under the circumstances and therefore entitled to the proceeds upon payment by the debtor. The issue is also important for the creditors of the various assignees who may seek to recover these claims through garnishment. They are likely to prevail over creditors of an assignor if good value is paid for the assignment. Whether this is so regardless of notice in countries that require it for the validity of the assignment must, however, remain doubtful.[233]

1.7.10   *Contractual and Proprietary Aspects of Assignments. Mandatory Rules. Applicable Law and Party Autonomy*

The various complications of assignments as identified in the previous sections generally revolve around (a) the contractual requirements of the assignment and the formalities in terms of documentation and notice; (b) the assignability of the claims, especially in the case of future claims and contractual assignment prohibitions; (c) the question of the debtor's defences and extra burdens and his ability to ignore the assignment in certain cases; (d) the impact of multiple assignments, especially on the debtor in terms of his ability to make a liberating payment; (e) the kind of (limited, conditional or security) proprietary interests that may be assigned in claims (and any additional formalities that may be required in the case of security interests in terms of registration or publication); (f) the effect on the underlying agreement out of which the claim arises in terms of amendment or novation when some form of debtor involvement is necessary and the connected question of the preservation of any supporting securities; (g) the possibility for the original parties still to amend the underlying agreement; (h) the ranking between the various assignees and the entitlement to collect or to collections already made by any of them; and (i) enforcement against the debtor and the rights to accessory securities or to initiate alternative enforcement actions against the assets of the debtor in the case of his default, especially if the assignment was less than a full assignment and transferred a lesser interest in the claim.

In a private international law context, the characterisation of these issues as contractual or proprietary is of considerable importance as it may affect the law deemed applicable: see more in particular section 1.9 below. It is clear that some of these issues are purely contractual, such as the assignment agreement itself and the question of amendment or novation, but most have a proprietary flavour, like the question of assignability, including a prohibition clause, and its effect on the validity of the assignment and transfer. The same is true for the notification where it is a condition for the validity of an assignment. The type of proprietary right that can be created through an assignment is obviously also a proprietary issue, as are the rights of the various assignees in multiple assignments of the same claim by the same assignor *vis-à-vis* the debtor and amongst themselves. Even the question whether changes in the underlying contract between an assignor and a debtor could affect the assignee raises a third party issue.

An assignment is naturally an agreement which has, however, proprietary effect like any ordinary, conditional or security transfer. The contractual and property aspects of an assignment should never be confused. Neither should the law applying to the

---

[233] In the USA, there is an old Idaho case, thus from a state that required notification for validity, but nevertheless rejected the claims to the collection made by creditors of the assignor before notification: *Houtz v Daniels*, 211 Pac. 1088 (1922).

underlying relationship with the debtor out of which the claim arose alone determine the contractual or *a fortiori* the proprietary aspects of the assignment nor necessarily the debtor's position, rights, duties and protections upon the assignment. These proprietary and protection aspects are in any event non-contractual matters and a contractual choice of law might not cover them. This may also go for the formalities of the assignment in terms of documentation and notification or registration or publication, certainly in the case of security transfers. More properly what is at stake here is the issue of validity. Assignability, therefore the question whether, for example, future or highly personal or blocked claims may still be assigned, may not be an issue at the free disposition of the parties to an assignment either and can then also not solely be determined by the law they might have chosen to cover the assignment or the underlying claim being assigned.

Thus proprietary effect, formation, validity and assignability issues are more likely to be determined by objective or even mandatory rules. This is also likely to be the case with the determination of whether mere creditor substitution with or without amendment of the terms of the agreement took place or, upon the consent of the debtor, novation with the loss of any supporting personal or real securities. Mandatory rules are all the more likely to apply to the enforcement aspects, thus to the decision on what types of proprietary interests can be pursued, to the protection and ranking of various assignees *inter se* and the effect of the *nemo dat* rule in this connection, to the rights of creditors of either assignor or assignee to recover from these assets, and to the question who can sue the debtor and if necessary recover from his other assets. Again the comparison with chattels is illuminating here and there is no clear reason or necessity to view the situation very differently.

Again, it is unlikely that in these aspects the law covering the claim, which, if contractual, might have been chosen by the parties, can determine these issues. Even though, for example, it is often accepted that the parties to a contract can agree that claims under it cannot be assigned, that does not necessarily apply to all monetary claims arising out of it, at least under common law and certainly no longer in the USA. It must be doubtful whether parties choosing another law to apply to the assignment can opt out of these provisions if both are within the same jurisdiction. In civil law where the *in rem* effect of these restrictions is often upheld, the notion of abstraction is likely increasingly to limit their impact. If objective or mandatory rules are applicable here, the question arises which law is applicable in situations which have contacts with more than one country, an issue that will be discussed more fully in section 1.9 below.

1.7.11 *Special Assignment Issues: Warranties, Conditions and Default*

As regards warranties, there is in assignments principally the question of the existence and ownership of the claim or receivable. There may be problems with either if the claim is future or conditional. Future claims under existing contracts may be considered existing in some legal systems, notably in England, and any implicit or explicit warranty of existence would then appear honoured. Other legal systems might look here for further assurances and require that the claim has arisen. Conditions may make the claim future, except in England if the fulfilment is in the control of the assignor. Whether claims arising out of a certain source, for example the sale of assets in which title is reserved by the assignor, or from a particular line of business, or arising against a certain debtor are present or future remains here too a question of definition under the applicable law, closely related to the question of assignability.

Even existing unconditional claims may not properly belong to the assignor, for example if obtained through a chain of assignments one of which might have been defective. It raises the question of the effectiveness of the *nemo dat* rule for *bona fide* purchasers of claims and their collections may therefore belong to assignees with better rights. Of course any warranty of ownership will not then protect the title but will give the assignee only a personal action against the assignor for breach. A warranty may not put him in a much better position. In bulk assignments the breach of a warranty is likely to give the assignee the right to collect other receivables until the total number of permitted collections is reached.

A breach of the warranty may also lead to a rescission of the assignment or trigger other protections like a guarantee. In the case of a rescission on grounds other than lack of ownership of the assignor (when nothing will have passed to the assignee), the receivable may return to the assignor. More likely to trigger a return is any condition or warranty of solvency or payment on the part of the debtor. This is never an implicit condition but common in recourse financing (factoring). It will affect not the whole assignment but only the individual claims involving defaulting debtors. Default of the assignment agreement itself could operate as a condition, and in particular a (fundamental) breach by the assignee under a financing (bulk) assignment could give rise to the claim(s) reverting to the assignor, at least if that were the intention of the parties. It would be automatic in a causal system of title transfer; in an abstract system it would have to be established that parties did mean to annul the transfer under a resolutive condition.

In this connection any automatic return upon a default of the collecting assignee caused by his bankruptcy and its effect on the debtor having been given earlier notice of the assignment should also be considered, as well as his right or duty still to pay the assignee, the status of his *bona fides*, if relevant in this connection upon publication of the opening of the bankruptcy, and the possibility for the assignor to withdraw or change the notice in this type of situation.

1.7.12   Bankruptcy Aspects of Assignments

It may finally be useful briefly to consider the effects of a bankruptcy on an assignment, particularly in the case of an assignment of a whole portfolio of receivables or a bulk transfer, which is a normal technique to raise financing, also called factoring. As we saw, factoring may be a mere collection arrangement under which a factor collects for a creditor who lacks the skills or organisation to do so. It may also be a financing arrangement under which the factor buys the receivables outright, as a security or conditionally. In the latter case, the condition is likely to be that, when the collections have reached the sale price or any other agreed level, any excess receivables would automatically be returned to the assignor. The agreed total might allow part of the benefit of excess collections to be retained by the assignee as a reward for his activity and the risks he took, especially the credit risk of the portfolio. If he takes the full credit risk, the assignment or factoring is 'non-recourse'.

If there is 'recourse' financing this is likely to mean that the credit risk remains (substantially) with the assignor. This may be achieved by the assignor giving the assignee or factor a guarantee. More likely is that the arrangement allows the receivables concerning a defaulting debtor automatically to revert to the assignor so that the assignor deals with any collection difficulties whilst the assignee collects more of the claims left in the portfolio (if any). The arrangement may also be structured as a secured transaction under which the assignment backs up a loan or advance plus agreed interest which is meant to be amortised by the collections. The documentation and formalities are likely to be different from those in a conditional or recourse sale but in the case of receivables the difference between a conditional sale and a secured transaction is otherwise often small. This is certainly so in countries which allow collection and amortisation also under an assignment for security purposes which is now mostly accepted everywhere: see specifically Article 3.246 at the Dutch CC, *cf* also Section 9-607 (9-502 old) UCC in the USA (whilst in France there remains some doubt on this point). There remains an important difference in the entitlement to excess receivables and the collections thereunder, which in conditional sales may be left to the factor in whole or in part.

Whatever the precise arrangement in this regard, in the context of a discussion of the bankruptcy implications there are always three kinds of parties to consider: assignors or fund raisers, assignees or financiers, and debtors, who may all go bankrupt. As for the bankruptcy of (some of) the debtors, in large receivable financings there are always likely to be some and it does not usually disturb the arrangement a great deal. In non-recourse financing, the assignee will pursue the collection in the bankruptcy of the relevant debtor. In recourse financing, non-payment is likely to have a consequence in the relationship between the assignor and assignee, as the relevant receivable will automatically be returned to the assignor.

The effect of an intervening bankruptcy of the assignor or assignee must be considered in this connection, and one sees the situation best if both are bankrupt at the same time when it remains to be determined who gets what. Especially seen from the bankruptcy of the assignee, there are here a number of obvious questions:

(a) does the factoring agreement continue in force and may the trustee of the assignee continue to collect;

(b) do new receivables included in the original transfer as future claims still pass to the assignee's estate when they arise;

(c) upon full amortisation, do the remaining receivables automatically retransfer to the estate of the assignor regardless of the assignee's bankruptcy;

(d) in a recourse financing, do receivables that are not being paid by the debtor still revert to the assignor;

(e) if no notification was given (assuming it was not a constitutive requirement of the assignment itself) are any collections by the estate of the assignor still for the estate of the assignee and can the latter's trustee trace these payments;

(f) can notification still be given by the trustee of the assignee to redirect collections to him even ahead of other assignees, and can he still make the assignment effective in systems which see the notification as constitutive of the assignment itself and a condition for its validity;

(g) are stays or freezes of enforcement or executions under the applicable bankruptcy acts relevant here; and

(h) what is the situation as regards other assignees who may have better rights than the bankrupt assignee who is collecting? May they trace any collections?

There are undoubtedly other issues that may arise in bankruptcy, and in any event the solution will depend on the applicable bankruptcy law, usually the one at the residence or habitual place of business of the bankrupt, which, if both assignor and assignee are bankrupt whilst residing in different countries, may lead to conflict. Yet it may be possible to make some general observations on the effect of bankruptcy in the above mentioned aspects.

As far as the survival of the assignment itself is concerned, since the assignment does not seem to be an executory contract as it transfers only proprietary rights, it is not subject to the right of either trustee to terminate it and to any cherry picking. It may be recalled that an executory contract is a bilateral contract that is not yet fully executed by either party. In this case the assignor has received his money whilst the assignee is collecting the receivables up to a certain number, thereupon to return the remaining receivables to the assignor. Although there are many different types of arrangements possible, it seems that in essence nothing further is expected from the assignor and the contract is therefore no longer executory, even if it is not considered to transfer proprietary interests, although arguments to the contrary may be found in the treatment of repurchase agreements of investment securities which, although transferring proprietary interests, rightly or wrongly are often still treated as executory.

In any event, the collection under a conditional sale of a portfolio of receivables appears to survive, just as a security interest would survive if supporting a loan until the amount of principal and interest was collected.

The situation may be somewhat different as regards receivables which are committed to be transfered to the assignee but were future claims at the time of the assignment. Under applicable law, they may transfer only upon materialising. In this aspect, the assignment may still be considered executory, although there may be a technical problem in some countries in varying the qualification between old and new receivables. Drawing the line will in any event not always be easy and becomes a matter of the applicable law in international assignments. More in particular when these receivables result from the on-going business of the assignor after bankruptcy, transfer seems unlikely and inappropriate. Naturally, the trustee of the assignee would have a claim for damages for any discontinuation of the assignment agreement in this respect, but it would only be a competing claim in the assignor's bankruptcy and unlikely to be of great benefit.

The conditional nature of the transfer suggests that if collections reach the agreed amount, the remaining receivables are automatically retransfered to the assignor's estate regardless of the assignee's bankruptcy. This would clearly be the case if the receivables were transferred as a security interest only and there does not appear to be any reason to conclude differently in a conditional transfer. In a recourse financing, any receivables on which debtors are defaulting also seems to revert to the assignor even after the bankruptcy of the assignee if that was the parties' intention.

If no notification was given to the debtor(s), the bankrupt assignor's estate is still likely to collect but the assignee's trustee might be able to trace the proceeds at least in common law countries under equitable assignments, thus when that notification is not a constitutive requirement of the assignment itself. In civil law countries this tracing is much more difficult as a concept. Alternatively, the trustee of the assignee could attempt to give the notice and direct the collections to himself. One must assume that he is able to do so under a valid assignment. There is obviously a greater problem in countries like the Netherlands, France and under statutory assignments in England where the assignment itself is not valid (at least not as regards third parties) if no notification has been given, although in England it may still stand as an equitable assignment. It raises the question whether the trustee of the assignee could still give this notification upon a bankruptcy of the assignor to validate the assignment and allow the assets to move from the bankrupt to his own estate.

If under applicable law the assignor need not co-operate in such notification, and always assuming that the underlying assignment agreement is valid and subject to repudiation as an executory contract by the trustee of the assignor (the latter having fully performed), there does not seem to be any strong objection to the trustee of the assignee doing so.

Another situation arises if the assignee is in default under the assignment either before or as a consequence of the bankruptcy, for example where part of the collections must be turned over to the assignor. If the default is material it may void the assignment and the question again arises whether the receivable(s) automatically return(s) to the assignor. This may be more readily the case where such a return would not require any acts of co-operation of the assignee's trustee and thus be fully automatic. In abstract systems of title transfer, there would be no automaticity in the transfer except where clearly so intended. If there is automaticity, the further question arises whether the assignor may vary or with-draw any notification is already given to the debtor(s), whether in his own bankruptcy his trustee may do so and how this can be done. The question is always to which estate the assets belong in the circumstances and whose creditors benefit: those of the assignor or assignee.

Stays or freezes under applicable bankruptcy law, like the one under Section 362 of the US Bankruptcy Code, do not appear to impact on collections by the assignee's estate, but they normally have an effect on the completion or perfection of secured transactions or conditional sales. Yet there will be no effect if these are already in place, except that under security arrangements executions or forced disposals can no longer take place or continue in reorganisation oriented jurisdictions like the USA and now also France until the restrictions are lifted by the courts or by lapse of time. Collections of a cash flow under a bulk assignment, even if only for security purposes, are not so likely to be considered executions or dispositions in this context, however, and do not appear to be affected by freezes of this sort. The debtors simply continue to pay the assignee upon notification and can always liberate themselves by doing so, at least in jurisdictions where *bona fides*, or in this case knowledge of his bankruptcy and possible default under the assignment, are not relevant in this respect.

Finally, other assignees with better rights may assert them against the debtors. As discussed above, it seems, however, improper to put the burden of the determination of the better right wholly on the debtors and they should be able to pay the first notifying assignee, except where on its face this notification was clearly irregular. Better still would be a system under which the debtor would have to accept a duty to pay the assignee pursuant to a notification given by both assignor and assignee leading to a liberating payment *per se*. It means that assignees with better rights should trace the proceeds with the bankruptcy trustee of the collecting assignee in countries allowing such tracing but not bother the debtor. The alternative would be for them to garnish the debtor and let the courts determine the payment duty.

1.7.13 Uniform Rules Concerning Assignments

Important attempts to create some uniformity of rules for international assignments have been made by Unidroit in its Factoring Convention of 1988 and much more so by Uncitral in 2001 Convention on the Assignment of Receivables in International Trade. Attention is given to these Conventions and their uniform rules in chapter V, section 2.3.

The true importance of uniform law of this nature often shows itself in bankruptcy, here of the main performing parties, initially the assignor who must deliver the receivables and subsequently the debtor(s) who must pay the assignee(s). Bankruptcy is an important test of the usefulness of conventions of this nature, certainly if they are meant to protect modern financial practices. Mostly it can only be seen in bankruptcy whether one has got something better under uniform law than under domestic laws applicable pursuant to the rules of private international law. In this connection it should be taken into account also that the applicable bankruptcy laws may add their own views to those of the Convention and sometimes override non-bankruptcy law. This may also affect receivable financing.

For example, in a bankruptcy of the assignor, the true question is whether the receivables have left his patrimony and when, which is relevant especially for future receivables. Whether the bulk assignment may have been considered valid in bankruptcy at all may be another matter for the applicable bankruptcy law to consider. In particular if the bankruptcy is in the country of the assignor whilst this country is a Contracting State, the principles of the Convention are likely to have considerable weight and they may also be respected in a bankruptcy elsewhere if in these aspects the law of the assignor is deemed to prevail. The situation may be more difficult in the bankruptcy of a debtor. The proprietary interests which are allowed to operate or to be created under a convention of this sort, particularly if less than full ownership is conferred on the assignee, still have to be fitted into the priority ladder of the applicable bankruptcy law which is here more likely to have a distinct position. The *lex concursus* is moreover difficult to predict in advance. The place of the opening of the bankruptcy will normally depend on the location of the bankrupt debtor, who may be situated in various countries (through branches or more incidental activities), or on the location of the debtor's major assets.

However, in bulk assignments, bankruptcy of individual debtors is less relevant. There will always be some and a convention cannot by itself improve the credit quality of a portfolio of receivables, except where it creates certainty in the payment obligations of the debtors towards a (bulk) assignee. This is probably the crucial point, certainly in bulk assignments. In any event, a) in receivable financing it may be immensely helpful (even outside a bankruptcy situation), to have treaty law backing for the validity of a bulk assignment through one document or act of transfer. b) It should do away with any notification requirement as a precondition to the validity of the assignment for each individual claim). It will be similarly valuable to c) determine what future claims may be included in the bulk assignment and d) what type of interests can be created, e) to establish their order *inter se* at least *vis-à-vis* the debtor(s), and above all f) to force all debtors to pay the assignee upon notice specifying their duties in this respect. Even though in a bankruptcy of a debtor their rank cannot be fully pre-determined and not their priority *vis-à-vis* outsiders like other creditors of the debtor either (who might benefit from statutory liens or other protections), g) at least the relative priorities of the interests amongst various assignees can be established as far as the debtor is concerned.

This greater predictability particularly in terms of the validity of bulk assignments as such and the continuing payment duty of the debtors thereunder may also provide greater clarity upon a bankruptcy of either the assignor or assignee whatever bankruptcy law may be applicable.

1.8   Private International Law Aspects of Chattels

1.8.1   Application of the Lex Situs

In proprietary matters, the basic rule concerning the properly applicable law is the *lex situs* of the asset, at least for tangible assets. Their location is normally easily identifiable and the applicable law results from it. Selection and application of the *lex situs* in this manner may in fact not be a true choice of law rule at all but merely a statement of fact that solves nothing. A choice of law problem in a proprietary sense truly presents itself mainly when an asset moves across borders (although, as far as security interests are concerned, the issue of their proper place and law of filing may also arise when no asset moves but the owner is elsewhere). It raises the question whether the old or new *lex situs* applies. So in proprietary matters, the mere reference to the *lex situs* does not in itself produce any choice of law solution when it matters most, *viz.* when the asset moves. It leaves open the question whether the applicable law is the law of the *situs* of origin or of destination of the asset or how they may relate.

Proprietary rights must be assumed to be created pursuant to the *lex situs* of the *country of origin* of the asset, that is where it was at the time of the creation of the interest in the asset, but once the asset has moved to a new *situs* the conditions under which acceptance or recognition may follow elsewhere are those of the *lex situs* of the *country of destination*. Indeed, this recognition tends to centre primarily on the proprietary right having been properly *created* at the original *situs*. It means first that it must be created under the proprietary law of that place, even though it may be pursuant to a contract governed by the contract law of yet another country that may not know or accept the interest in its own law, or may even forbid it, as the *fiducia* is now forbidden (or at least cannot have proprietary effect) under new Dutch law. Secondly there should be *no adverse policy* in the recognising country. One must assume that no such adverse policy exists if there are the *same or equivalent* proprietary rights operating in the recognising country.[234] The key is thus to accept that in the case of conflicts in a proprietary sense, principally occasioned when assets move (therefore a typical problem for chattels), it is necessary to work at two levels: the proper creation of the interest in the country of origin and the proper recognition of the interest in the country of destination.

This means that if the interest is properly created under the law of the country where the asset was at the time of creation and the country of destination has a similar proprietary right under its own *lex situs*, the proprietary right created in the country of origin of the asset is likely to be accepted at the new *situs*. In the case of a full ownership right, this will normally be the case and recognition will be implied.[235] It seems to be a matter of the acceptance of acquired rights. Much more problematic may be the more limited ownership interests like usufructs or other temporary ownership rights, reservations of title or other conditional ownership rights, security rights or common law equitable interests like those of the beneficiary under (constructive) trusts.

On the other hand, when good value is given in the country of origin for the creation of these interests, it is difficult to see how these more a-typical acquired proprietary rights could be ignored elsewhere, although particularly their rank and status might still be affected in an execution against the asset. This is then primarily a question of the *lex executionis* or of the *lex concursus* in the case of bankruptcy opened or effective at the (new) *situs*.[236]

Another problem is that special formalities in terms of documentation and registration or publication may obtain at the new *situs* for the creation and maintenance of these rights. Even if a foreign security interest might have some equivalent under the *lex executionis* or *lex concursus*, it is unlikely that the formalities of this law have been observed at

---

[234] The problems in this connection are as yet little discussed, but see CGJ Morse, 'Retention of Title in English Private International Law' [1993] *Business Law Journal* 168, 174.

[235] This is so even if it concerns goods stolen at the original *situs*, subsequently transported and sold in another *situs* to *bona fide* purchasers and offered by them for resale in the original country, an example frequent in the art world: see in England, *Cammell v Sewell*, 5 H&N, 278 (1860) and *Winkworth v Christie, Manson and Woods Ltd*, [1980] Ch 496, see also Morse, *supra* n 234, 184.

[236] See also JH Dalhuisen, 'International Aspects of Secured Transactions and Finance Sales involving Movable and Intangible Property' in Kokkini/Grosheide (eds), *Molengrafica* (1994), 405, 430.

the creation stage. Recognition could then create an important disparity amongst creditors with similar interests in the recognising country. In other words, if charges in assets require registration in the country of execution and local creditors are subject to this rule under penalty of losing their security, foreign creditors without such registration duty in the country of origin but with an equivalent charge could seek to prevail without it. It will be a (public) policy question of the recognising court to what extent this discrepancy can and will be accepted. In this system, it cannot be denied or avoided that the recognising court exercises considerable discretion.

Even if full ownership rights rather than security interests or charges are involved, the creation aspect itself may still need some further consideration, which may be illustrated by an example. German law requires delivery for title transfer in goods, English law does not: see section 1.5.2 above. If as part of the sales agreement the asset must be delivered in the other country, the question arises whether the transfer of title will be under the law of the country of *origin* or of *destination*. Thus if a German and English resident conclude a sales contract in Germany concerning an asset in Germany that under the agreement must be delivered by the German seller to the English buyer in England, the question is when title passes and therefore what law applies to the title transfer. Is it the law of the country of origin or of destination? In line with what has just been said, one would expect the applicability of the law of the country where the asset is at the time of the conclusion of the sales agreement as to the time and manner of the creation of the ownership right, here German property law, requiring delivery.

It means that the asset upon arrival in England is still owned by the German seller whilst title transfers in England only upon the delivery (or possibly automatically upon arrival in England) and the asset remains part of the seller's estate until that moment should he go bankrupt in the meantime. In the reverse situation in which the contract had been concluded in respect of a chattel in England that was to be transported for delivery by the English seller to Germany, the goods upon arrival in Germany would already be owned by the German buyer, English law not requiring delivery for title transfer, and they would no longer be part of the English seller's estate in his intervening bankruptcy.

Where in this last case title has already transferred in the country of origin, this title transfer would be a matter of recognition in the country of destination, here Germany. In the circumstances, it is likely that German law would accept that the title transfer had already happened, as in the case of a transfer of the full title there is an obvious equivalent proprietary interest in Germany. The situation might be different, however, if only an equitable or limited ownership or security right had been created in this manner in England, for example under a trust which at the English *situs* of the asset could have been perfectly legally created by a German settlor, even pursuant to a German contract in favour of a German resident beneficiary in respect of an asset located in England. Yet the question of equivalence and public policy would arise in terms of recognition of this interest upon arrival of the goods for use by the German beneficiary in Germany, particularly if there arose a subsequent German bankruptcy of the settlor in which the proprietary interest of the beneficiary in the asset upon its arrival in Germany would have to be considered. Would it be respected in Germany where there is no clear equivalent? This may be much more doubtful. The beneficiary might have no more than a contractual claim to his benefit rather than a proprietary right.

In any event, the validity of the interest created at the *situs* of the asset depends on the law of the *situs* of the asset at the time of the conclusion of the agreement and *not* on where or under which law the agreement itself was concluded or operated. So, contractually, parties can agree any type of proprietary interest they want (perhaps even against the public policy requirement of a foreign law of contract under which they operate as long as the asset is elsewhere). Whether and when such a right attaches depends on the law of the *situs* of the asset at the moment of the conclusion of the agreement. If under this *lex situs* this can for example only take place upon delivery, then the title transfer will have to wait until that is done. It would mean applicability of the law of the country of destination if that is where the asset must be delivered (unless the goods are received through an agent in the country of origin or a third country). The formalities of delivery itself (or of the creation of other proprietary rights like securities) will also be governed by the law of that country.

In this vein it is also possible to create in one country under its contract law security interests in an asset that is located in another country, provided the formalities (if any) of that other country are complied with. If subsequently the asset were to move to the first country or to a third country, the security interest would be subject to the recognition process in that country and if the interest so created is not allowed in the recognising country or has no equivalent there, recognition is likely to be withheld or the interest may be varied to the nearest equivalent, whilst its ranking will be further determined by any formalities required in the recognising countries for the effectiveness of security interests of that sort.

There are many aspects of the operation of proprietary rights internationally when the asset moves, but the above pattern as to finding the applicable law remains the same. To highlight yet another variation, the following example may be of interest. Assume that two German residents conclude a sale agreement in Germany under which an asset in England is sold by the one to the other for transfer to Germany. As we saw, title in the asset would under the *lex situs* transfer immediately. Yet if the Germans had expressly agreed that title was to pass only upon delivery or if that followed from their relationship, for example in a Cif contract when title transfers on the tendering of the bill of lading by the seller to the buyer, the title transfer in England could under English law still be delayed pursuant to the intention of the parties. It may vary the normal rule of instant transfer under English law. In such cases the delay is still a matter of the English law of the original *lex situs* which allows it and not of German (contract or proprietary) law. One could of course argue that it was always the intention of the German parties that title should pass upon delivery, as they would not know any better, but English law as the law of the *situs* at the time of the conclusion of the agreement would probably require a clearer expression of the intention to delay title transfer under Sections 17 and 18 of the Sale of Goods Act, although in a Cif sale the delay may indeed be implied: see section 2.1.5 below. The question is whether the delay in title transfer until delivery in Germany subsequently makes German law applicable in the title transfer. That seems to be the result, as it can only take place when the asset arrives in Germany, therefore at the new *situs*.

If the German contract itself proved invalid, the result on the title transfer is again a question of the *lex situs*, and if the asset were still in England, English law would apply. As we saw, it maintains on the whole an abstract system except in the case of fraud and the title would therefore not automatically return to the seller in Germany, even less so in the case of a rescission of the sale agreement upon default: see also section 1.5.7 above. Rights of *bona fide* purchasers of an asset are also determined in the first instance by the law of the location of the asset at the time of the title transfer. Thus if the German seller of the English asset were not the owner, his German buyer could not rely on his *bona fides* under German law but only on the narrower concept of it under English law: see section 1.5.8 above. Had the asset been in the USA, where for chattels delivery is still required for title transfer (except where the parties agree otherwise), title transfer would only have taken place in Germany upon delivery there, and the German *bona fide* purchaser protection would in that case have prevailed, therefore the law of the new *situs* under which delivery took place.

A special complication presents itself if under the law of the old *situs* delivery could have been constructive, but for *bona fide* purchaser protection it would have had to be physical (therefore to the buyer in the country of destiny). The sale to the *bona fide* purchaser could therefore not be completed under the original *lex situs* and his protection must then be determined by the new *lex situs*, even if it did not itself require physical delivery for that protection. If on the other hand, the original *lex situs* did not have that requirement, the delivery would be complete under that law in respect of the foreign *bona fide* purchaser and his own law should recognise that, even if it maintained itself the physical delivery requirement for that protection, as the *bona fide* buyer would already be the owner of the goods upon their arrival in the country of the buyer. Of course, the picture could be blurred further by countries of transit when the asset is a *res in transitu*.

The discussion so far assumes that the question of ownership is always a matter of a national law and that no internationalised transnational forms of ownership exist or can develop. In the case of documents of title and negotiable instruments such as bills of lading and bills of exchange, these were originally of the transnational variety but substantially nationalised following the codifications in Europe at the beginning of the nineteenth century, although never fully satisfactorily so: see more in particular section 2.1.1 below for the bill of lading. The modern Eurobond as a bearer paper may be an example of a more compelling recent variant and expression of a transnationalised ownership concept in terms of a negotiable instrument: see chapter I, section 3.2.2. If the concept of transnational ownership is so (re-)established, there is no reason in principle why it should not start operating more broadly, therefore also in other types of assets that may be considered internationalised. There is in any event no reason why this concept should not be further explored. It would probably mean that the intention of the parties as expressed in their contractual arrangement and the law applicable thereto would acquire a greater significance in the proprietary aspects. This law could itself be the *lex mercatoria*, see section 1.8.5 below, as it always was for negotiable instruments and documents of title.

Although in an internationalised environment the creation of proprietary rights may be left more fully to the parties operating at an international level, the third party effect of the type of property rights so created cannot be left entirely to the will of the parties as it never was in purely domestic systems either, also not in common law where there is nevertheless much greater freedom in the creation of proprietary rights as we saw in section 1.3.1 above. Because of the third party effect, there is here a mandatory limiting element or public policy aspect often connected with the requirement of (some) publicity of the interest so created or of possession of the asset, either physically or possibly constructively. It is not to be excluded, however, that these mandatory rules and their publicity or possessory requirements are themselves becoming transnationalised. Fundamental legal principle of which ownership is an important aspect and supporting transnational custom may provide here the objective elements necessary to establish ownership at that level *vis-à-vis* third parties (and creditors of the interest holders so created): see more in particular chapter I, section 3.2.1. Again the trend is clear in negotiable instruments and most likely also for documents of title. Where monetary claims are increasingly commoditised and their free negotiability established regardless of contrary contractual clauses and defences, see section 1.7.7 above, the same could apply to them and there is no reason why chattels should then be exempt. It would also affect the manner of title transfer (or creation of other proprietary interests in the asset) and the protection of *bona fide* purchasers of these assets (or of unsuspecting creditors of an owner who conceded a security interest therein).

It is in fact somewhat unexpected that in international sales that require movement of the goods, the transfer of ownership, which is its real objective, still remains largely unsettled. The total value of the transborder trade in goods is estimated by the World Trade Organisation to have reached a US$ equivalent amount well beyond 5,000 billion, title in which thus remains largely unclear at least until the moment of physical delivery. The somewhat humbling conclusion for lawyers must be that this does on the whole not seem to matter a great deal or to present a substantial impediment to international trade. Neither seem the considerable vagaries of the international sales laws in their contractual aspects that remain even under the Vienna Convention (see chapter II, section 2.3) to present a great problem. It could on the other hand also be argued that the surge of international trade is now such that it no longer accepts domestic laws and concepts as an impediment to it and transforms the proprietary and other legal concepts if necessary at a transnational level. It is in any event entirely appropriate and indeed necessary to study the law in the commercial or professional sphere increasingly from this perspective. It was the subject of chapter I.

There is a particular reason why the international proprietary problems should not be exaggerated, however, at least in international sales without purchase money securities attached. In these sales, the accent is normally on the transfer of risk, the allocation of costs and income in connection with the asset and the place of the *physical* (not legal) delivery and the cost of transportation and insurance. These matters can all be decided in the contract and are not proprietary. It is the reason why in the USA the UCC in its Article 2 on the sale of goods no longer attaches great importance to the title transfer and seems to consider the concern about ownership largely a metaphysical urge. That is not entirely correct. The proprietary aspects still figure in respect of purchasers of the interest and creditors of the interest holders, especially in execution sales and bankruptcy, and may then figure very large. These remain exceptional events but require clarity in the proprietary aspects. Also buyers need to be clear about what they buy even though under the *lex situs* they may be protected if *bona fide* and in physical possession of the asset, which reduces their exposure.

Finally, it may be useful briefly to return to the question when conflicts arise. In the *proprietary sense* it was suggested that this is so primarily when assets move, although for security interests there may also be a question which place and law are relevant for their publication and registration or other formalities, therefore also if the assets in which they are created do not move.[237] The *lex situs* seems primarily involved but could point for publication of non-possessory security interests to the place of the owner who may be elsewhere. The formalities of creation would then be decided by the law of that place, although that might not ultimately be sufficient if the asset moves to a third country which has different formality requirements and becomes the place of execution. In a *contractual sense*, conflicts customarily arise only when the contracting parties are in different countries. In terms of *creditor action* against the asset, conflicts arise particularly when enforcement action is attempted from abroad, thus away from the *situs* of the assets.

---

[237] This matter has given rise to much thought in the USA in the UCC, revisited in the present (1998) revisions of Article 9. The emphasis is here for the formalities of the creation of non-possessory security interests on the law of the debtor/transferor of the security interests rather than on that of the *situs* of his assets given as security. That is clearer in the 1998 revision of Article 9 than in the older text: see Section 9-103 (old) and Section 9-301(1) (new).

As in a proprietary sense, conflicts arise mainly when the asset has to move under the contract, there results the interaction between the law of the place of origin and the place of destination as explained above. The result is that when both parties to a sale of goods reside in Germany but the asset must move to England under the contract, there is no contractual conflict but only a proprietary one. On the other hand, when parties are in different countries but the asset remains at the *situs*, there is no proprietary conflict of laws, only a contractual one. Execution is closely connected with the *situs*. In fact the applicability of the *lex situs* in proprietary matters is closely related to the execution possibility and normally coincides with the *lex executionis*.

Conflicts of law in matters of enforcement against the asset do not normally derive, however, from the movement of the asset (if it moves, the law of the new location always applies), but from any attempt to conduct enforcement proceedings from any place other than the *situs* whilst effect is wanted in that place. Again this is a question of recognition and public policy, which will on the whole not be favourable. Enforcement against an asset normally requires judicial intervention and the courts of the place of the asset are usually considered to have exclusive jurisdiction: see Article 16(5) of the 1968 Brussels Convention on Jurisdiction and the Enforcement of Judgments in Civil and Commercial Matters. Foreign enforcement decisions and preliminary attachments are unlikely to be recognised under the Convention and courts will apply their own law in matters of enforcement against assets within their jurisdiction. The principle of exclusive jurisdiction avoids conflicts of law in this area and emphasises the applicability of the *lex situs*.

In bankruptcy, the situation may seem somewhat different as a bankruptcy decree is likely under its own law to cover all assets of the bankrupt worldwide *regardless* of their *situs*, but for effectiveness at the *situs* it would still be dependent on recognition of this jurisdiction and public policy in the country where enforcement is sought. Modern law in many countries allows here increasing discretion for the judiciary. In order to facilitate it, the opening bankruptcy court may itself adapt its rules and take the foreign interests better into account. The effect of the bankruptcy on assets elsewhere and on the interests therein comes within the contemplation of the opening court if the interest holder is also a creditor of the estate and wishes to share in the bankruptcy proceeds. His foreign interest will then be given their proper place and any preferential separate execution at the *situs* may be discounted accordingly and affect the interest holder's share in the distribution of the bankruptcy proceeds.

Whether in this manner or through the recognition process, the result is that the foreign proprietary interests (like security interests or conditional ownership interests) are given their own status and ranking in the bankruptcy with adaptations of their original status if necessary.

1.8.2   The Notions of Equivalence and Adaptation; Conditional Ownership, Security and Retention Rights

Equivalency as a requirement for recognition is a legal criterion of dubious value. A reservation of title might for example exist in both the country of origin and that of destination but may still be very different. In France for example the right is of an accessory nature,[238] transfers therefore with the receivable (like a security right even though there

---

[238] Cour de Cassation, 15 Mar 1988, Bull civ IV, no 106.

is no execution), for example to a factoring company. The factoring company is the creditor for the assignment, so that the creditor/seller under the reservation of title has been satisfied without apparently the debtor/buyer obtaining full title as a consequence. In countries like the Netherlands, on the other hand, the reservation of title is a conditional ownership right not accessory to the underlying indebtedness.[239] It is likely to be lost in the case of an assignment of the receivable to a factoring company. It indirectly results in payment of the seller. This result may be avoided if the factoring is construed as a pure collection agreement only in which the factor is the agent of the seller and does not pay for the receivable assigned to him. In that case the assignment is made only to facilitate the collection process (giving the factor the facility to sue if he needs to).

In the USA, reservation of title, even if the term is used, is fully equated with a security interest to the point that it requires upon default an execution sale with reimbursement of any overvalue to the debtor, whilst in Europe an American reservation of title is more likely to be seen as a conditional sale. What looks the same is therefore legally often treated differently and may be subject to transformation. Thus even similar rights might be substantially transformed in the country of recognition upon movement of the asset. They may as such be upgraded or downgraded. Other security rights may be converted altogether into the nearest equivalent, for example a *typical* non-possessory security interest in a car created at its *situs* in France might be converted into the *general* German non-possessory security interest (*Sicherungsübereignung*) upon arrival of the French car in Germany.[240] Whether the reverse could be true for a German car moving to France without publication of the security interest there (Germany does not require such publication) is another matter. The result would be published and unpublished interests serving the same purpose operating side by side, a problem emerging in all cases upon recognition of foreign security rights, if the local equivalents require domestic publication or registration for their validity and ranking. Whatever the result, it is clear that the equivalence test cannot be taken at its face value.

As far as the formalities are concerned, an American reservation of title in a piece of professional equipment may easily be accepted in the Netherlands and may well allow the American seller to repossess the asset in the Netherlands upon shipment of the asset to that country, even though he could not have done so in his country of origin. A Dutch seller would certainly not have a similar repossession right in the USA when the relevant asset in which he had reserved title in the country of origin was subsequently shipped to a US port. Without having filed a finance statement in the USA, the Dutch seller of professional equipment may have lost his protection altogether upon shipment of his asset to that country (as only reservations of title in consumer goods do not need this type of publicity in the USA). It is likely to be an extra recognition requirement in the USA, which other countries might not similarly impose. For example although non-possessory pledges created in the Netherlands now require a form of registration, it does not exclude the recognition of foreign charges which are not registered in the Netherlands. It may help here that the registration in the Netherlands is not meant to achieve publicity but only determines the time of the grant of the security interest.

The key for recognition of foreign limited proprietary rights is thus in the adjustment and conversion of the foreign proprietary right as part of the determination of its status and rank in the recognising country upon movement of the asset to that country, at least if it concerns a foreign security or similar right, particularly relevant in an execution at

[239] HR 18 Jan 1994 [1994] RvdW 61.
[240] BGH, 20 Mar 1963, BGHZ 39, 173 (1963).

the new *situs*. Everywhere, the execution judge clearly has a measure of discretion in this regard. The solution is therefore not in a hard-and-fast conflicts rule. In that sense, reference to the *lex situs* of the country of origin or even of the recognising country may not mean a great deal. The question is whether the interest was properly created in the country of origin (whilst the asset was there) and to what extent it must be adjusted in the country where it is invoked (upon the asset moving to that country), which adjustment may even apply to the execution or bankruptcy laws of the recognising forum themselves, especially when making room for foreign security interests not known in the system of the country of origin.[241]

In the case of retention rights, as a matter of private international law, the *lex situs* will in principle also determine the proprietary aspects and any appropriation of title or conversion into a security right thereunder (and its rank upon execution) or any conversion into a mere preference to the execution proceeds. It should be recalled that in common law countries these retention rights are often statutory liens not giving rise to an execution facility. In civil law that was the same except under some more modern statutory law, like that of the Netherlands: see also section 1.5.10 above. When the retentor moves the asset to another country, the nature of the retention right may be affected in these aspects at the same time and there may then also arise questions of adaptation and adjustment in the same way as just mentioned for security interests in goods that are moved to other countries.

On the other hand, for retention rights the law applicable to the obligatory relationship between both parties may more properly determine the questions of reciprocity and connexity: see for these aspects of retention right also section 1.5.10 above. It is conceivable that purely contractual retention rights may be denied proprietary effect altogether if their proprietary status is not accepted by the law covering their creation, which will be the *lex situs* of the country of origin, even if the retentor moves the goods later to a *situs* whose law is more congenial to these rights. If properly created in the original country, they may still be upgraded whilst being adapted to and fitted into the system of the new *situs*, although originally merely contractual, provided that the law of the place of destination accepts proprietary effects of retention rights in its own system.

1.8.3 Trusts: The 1985 Hague Convention on the Law Applicable to Trusts and Their Recognition

In section 1.4, a basic outline of the common law trust was given. In cross-border situations the first question that usually arises is the status of the trustee in relation to the trust assets (his powers in them and their separateness from his own estate). Under the normal rules of private international law as explained above, the status of the trustee is normally fully accepted as well as his power over the goods if the trust was created in the

---

[241] Another example may throw some further light on the problem. A French reservation of title in a car after it has been moved to Belgium, where the law did not accept reservation of title to be effective in a Belgian bankruptcy until 1998, did as a consequence not have much effect in a subsequent bankruptcy of the buyer in Belgium even though properly created at its original *situs* and not rejected as such in the country of destination. It would have required the Belgian courts to make special room for it on the basis of the foreign properly acquired right (for value), which would seem unlikely: Commercial Court Brussels, 22 Mar 1988 [1989] RDCB 633, *cf* also Rigaux, *Droit International Privé II* (Brussels, 1979), no 1111. It would have such effect, nevertheless, if the car were subsequently moved to the Netherlands and a Dutch bankruptcy of the buyer would follow, as Dutch law accepts the consequences of the reservation of title fully under its own bankruptcy law: see further JH Dalhuisen, *International Insolvency and Bankruptcy* (New York 1986) 3–398*ff*.

country where the assets were at the time (which is unlikely, however, to be the case with off-shore trusts like those in the Channel Islands or in the Caribbean). The trustee may thus normally defend these assets and his title therein, also in a foreign bankruptcy, as he is considered the full owner for these purposes, even in countries that do not accept the trust notion. In that case, they will probably consider these assets part of the trustee's estate. If, however, the trust was a substitute security interest (an indenture under which a debtor/lender had transformed himself into a trustee holding the assets for the benefit of the lender), it is possible that in countries that do not have their own trust law the trust assets would still be considered part of the bankrupt estate of the settlor subject to a security interest of the beneficiary. This could be the nearest equivalent (see for this structure section 1.4.5. above), relevant especially if the assets were moved to the country of the bankruptcy, in which case the rank of the security interest would in any event also have to be determined. If they have not moved to that country, they may still be treated as security in the bankruptcy. However, the effect would be less likely to be accepted in the country of the assets where the trust in respect of them was created, even if the bankruptcy itself could be recognised in principle in that country.

More complicated is the question whether assets at the time of the creation of the trust located *outside* the country where the trust is created may also be included if the *lex situs* itself does not have the concept, quite apart from the question whether any trust so created could be recognised in the country of the assets concerned. This is the situation with off shore trusts which are often assumed to be able to cover such foreign assets, however. Yet there could be legitimate doubts in this aspect as the creation of proprietary rights normally follows the rules of the *lex situs*. This may be especially true in respect of real estate.

If on the other hand trust assets properly included are subsequently moved to a country that does not recognise trusts, the situation may be different and recognition may still be possible although it may imply adjustment of the interest to the nearest equivalent in the recognising country as just mentioned. As it is likely that in most civil law countries there is no such equivalent, the recognition itself may be in doubt. The result may be only a contractual enjoyment right for the beneficiaries, which they may lose in a bankruptcy of the trustees.

The Hague Convention on the Law Applicable to Trusts and on their Recognition of 1985 attempts to facilitate the recognition of foreign trusts and has so far been ratified by Australia, Italy, The United Kingdom (also for Jersey, Guernsey, the Isle of Man, Gibraltar, Bermuda, British Virgin Islands, Turks and Caicos Islands), Canada (but not for Toronto and Quebec), Malta, Hong Kong and The Netherlands, whilst France is also contemplating ratification. It is mainly a vehicle for recognising the typical common law trusts, although according to the Preamble[242] similar civil law structures are also covered, and amongst civil law countries Liechtenstein and Luxembourg in particular developed them:[243] see for approximations also section 1.4.6 above. France has also been considering for some time the introduction of a form of trust or *fiducia* in its own law, although in a more rudimentary form (see the proposed Article 2062*ff* Cc), which could also benefit from the recognition facilities of the Convention if showing the characteristics of Article 2.

---

[242] They show the characteristics of Article 2 under their own law (Article 5) if resulting as applicable under Articles 6–10. This suggests not a functional but rather a structural likeness: see also A Dyer and JHA van Loon, *Report on trusts and analogous institutions in Actes et Documents de la Quinzième Session of the Hague Conference* (1985), nr 13. Thus conditional ownership structures or foundations do not benefit from the recognition regime of the Convention.
[243] See for similar structures in other non-common law countries also *ibid*, nrs 33*ff*.

The approach of the Convention is to recognise trusts that are created according to the law applicable under the conflict rules of the Convention (Articles 6–10), *assuming that* such applicable law provides for trusts (Article 5). These will be recognised in their most salient aspects (Article 11) in Contracting States no matter whether the country of their creation is itself a Contracting State. Yet they will not necessarily be recognised in all their third party effects or against relevant mandatory rules. This depends on the law applicable pursuant to the conflict rules of the forum (see Article 15). Recognition may also be withheld if the trust assets are substantially connected with a country that does not recognise the trust in its own law (Article 13) or if there are serious tax avoidance problems (Article 19) or other public policy considerations against recognition (Article 18).

The Convention does not give a clear definition of trusts, even of the types it means to cover. Article 2 refers to a situation in which a settlor places assets under the control of a trustee for the benefit of a beneficiary or for a certain purpose. It further describes three characteristics: (a) the assets must constitute a separate fund and not be part of the trustee's own estate; (b) title to the trust assets must stand in the name of the trustee or in the name of another person on behalf of the trustee; and (c) the trustee must have the power and the duty, in respect of which he is accountable, to manage, employ or dispose of the assets in accordance with the terms of the trust and the special duties imposed on him by law. One sees therefore as essential elements the principle of separateness of the trust assets and the fiduciary duties of the trustee in respect of them.

One does *not* see here clearly the *in rem* protection of the beneficiaries and their rights to trace their interest in replacement goods or to follow them, but at least the latter rights result under Article 11 in the case of recognition. It implies the acceptance of the separate status of the trust assets, of the capacity of the trustee, and of the recovery rights of the beneficiary if the trustee has commingled the trust assets with his own or alienated them, assuming that the law applicable to the trust provides for these remedies. The rights of third party holders of the goods are determined according to the applicable law under the choice of law rules of the forum, which will normally be the *lex situs* of the assets, at least if tangible: see Article 11(d) and also Article 15(f).

The Convention applies only to trusts created voluntarily and evidenced in writing, which does not mean that writing is a constitutive requirement. They are principally the express trusts which may, however, also be testamentary and could in that case even cover the status, position and powers of an executor under a will if also appointed trustee to the property, and this regardless of whether probate has been granted in the country under the law of which the will was drafted or the executor operates. This is particularly relevant for any foreign assets of the deceased's estate and similar civil law structures are likely here to be covered.

Constructive trusts are *not* covered (except where Contracting States include them under Article 20) unless they result as ancillary to the trusts covered by the Convention, for example if *resulting* as a consequence of following the trust property under Article 11 or upon termination of the trust but before distribution of the assets. Even then, local law would appear to decide on the effect, see Article 11(d). That may exclude their remedial nature, see for the segregation concept also section 1.4.3 above. At least remedial constructive trusts (see section 1.4.3 above) would not appear to be covered or, if they were, their effect in terms of segregation would be determined by the law resulting from the applicable private international law rules (Article 11 d) which would in case of property most likely be the law of the situs of the asset. Statutory trusts like those concerning a bankrupt estate are always outside the scope of the Convention.

The Convention according to Article 4 does not cover preliminary issues relating, for example, to the validity of the transfer into trust itself or to the underlying testamentary, matrimonial or paternal dispositions, gifts, financial or other structures or security transfers in this regard. The trust is normally the result of such underlying relationships or objectives, the legality or validity of which may be an issue. This could happen for example in the case of lack of capacity, intent, or formalities, in the absence of consideration or because of fraudulent conveyance considerations or other restrictions on gifts or similar legal acts. These aspects are not covered by the Convention. It means that the applicable law according to the conflict rules of the forum will determine these issues, which may be all the more important when the trust covers assets outside its country of origin but is invoked in that country or in any other. This raises the question of jurisdiction in trust matters.[244]

Article 21 allows Contracting States to limit the application of the Convention to trusts the validity of which is governed by the law of Contracting States. So far this reservation has not been entered by any ratifying country. The basic idea is that all foreign trusts that qualify under Articles 5–10 are covered *regardless* of the country in which they were established or which law is applicable. The Convention is retroactive and applies to trusts regardless of the date on which they are created except where ratifying states enter a reservation, which so far none has done (Article 22).

The applicable law is determined by Articles 6 and 7. Especially the wide powers for the settlor to choose an applicable law are somewhat surprising and not normal in proprietary matters, certainly if the resulting regime is at variance with the law of the *situs* of (most of) the assets. It is not part of the traditional conflict rules concerning trusts either, although before the Convention the conflicts approach had been uncertain whilst literature on the subject was sparse.[245] However, Article 8 makes it clear that the applicable law resulting from this choice applies only to the validity of the trust, its construction, its effects and the administration of the trust, and it does not appear to cover the proprietary aspects: see also Article 11 *in fine* and Article 15. The choice of law by the settlor is also ineffective if the chosen law does not provide for the trusts or category of trusts involved (Article 6). This is itself somewhat surprising as in the previous sections it was maintained that the applicable contract law itself cannot determine the proprietary interests and cannot be a bar to their creation at the *situs* if that is what parties intended.

Article 7 gives a uniform conflicts rule in the absence of a choice by the settlor and opts in that case for the law with the closest connection when regard is to be had especially to (a) the place of administration; (b) the *situs* of the trust assets; (c) the place of residence or business of the trustee; and (d) the objects of the trust and the places where they are to be fulfilled. It is of interest that the language of Article 6 requiring that the applicable law so established provides for trusts is not repeated in Article 7. Again the applicable law so established does not cover the proprietary aspects (see Article 8).

In fact the applicable law resulting under Articles 6 and 7 governs only (a) the appointment, resignation and removal of the trustee and his capacity to act; (b) the rights and duties of trustees amongst themselves if there are more than one; (c) the right of the trustee to delegate his functions or the exercise of his powers, particularly relevant when he must manage the trust property; (d) the powers of the trustee to administer and dispose of the

---

[244] The rules of international jurisdiction in trust matters derive in Europe from the 1968 Brussels and the 1988 Lugano Conventions on Jurisdiction and the Enforcement of Judgments in Civil and Commercial Matters. They are important: see for the details sect. 1.4.6 *supra*.
[245] See for a more extensive comment, *Dicey & Morris, The Conflict of Laws* (London, 13th edn, 2000), 1087*ff*.

trust assets; (e) his powers of investment; (f) the restrictions on the duration of the trust (law against perpetuities) and on the accumulation of income; (g) the relationship between the trustee and the beneficiary including the trustee's personal liability to the beneficiary; (h) the variation and termination of the trust; (i) the distribution of the trust assets; and (j) the duty of the trustee to account for his administration.

Whilst it is thus clear that the law applicable pursuant to Articles 6 and 7 does *not* cover the proprietary aspects of the status of the trustee and the proprietary protections of the beneficiary's rights and his tracing facilities, at least the tracing powers are matters of recognition under Article 11. Whilst the Convention does not specifically mention the beneficiary's *in rem* protections, it is made clear that the trustee's own creditors cannot reach the trust assets (it is not made clear that the same applies to the beneficiary's creditors). Article 11 *in fine* and Article 15 state the rights of *bona fide* third parties who become holders of the assets and leave the determination of their rights to the law applicable according to the choice of law rules of the forum which, as far as tangible assets are concerned, will centre on the *lex situs*.

Article 11 deals with recognition of foreign trusts. The principle is that any trust created in accordance with the law specified in the Convention (under Articles 6 and 7) shall be recognised in Contracting States, and this without special proceedings. It allows the recognition of trusts in whatever assets, wherever located, even if this law is only applicable by virtue of the settlor's choice provided the trust construction is known and operates under that law (Article 6). This is a very liberal approach, balanced, however, not only by public policy considerations in the recognising country (Article 18) but also by the more elaborate provisions of Articles 13 and 15. Where the applicable law results from the more objective choice of law rule of Article 7, the same re-balancing is possible but probably less necessary.

The recognition according to Article 11 implies as a minimum that (a) the trust property constitutes a separate fund and (b) the trustee's capacity is recognised. The recognition also implies elaboration of these two principles, but only to the extent that the applicable law so provides and is then in particular likely to imply (a) the lack of recourse by the trustee's personal creditors against the trust assets; (b) the exclusion of the trust assets from the trustee's estate upon his insolvency; (c) the exclusion of the trust assets from the trustee's matrimonial property regime; and (d) the tracing rights of the beneficiary which is subject to the protection of *bona fide* holders if they are protected under the law applicable pursuant to the conflict rules of the forum in this aspect. Except for the tracing point, it is curious that the other three consequences of recognition are still made subject to the applicable law since, without them, a trust would hardly exist.

Article 13 limits recognition, however, if the trust (except for the choice of the applicable law, the place of administration and the habitual residence of the trustee) is more closely connected with States that do not have the trust in their own law. Article 15, moreover, accepts that the recognition of foreign trusts cannot go against applicable mandatory rules of the recognising country (expressed as not being able to go against the mandatory rules of the law applicable under the conflict rules of the forum). These rules may in particular (but not only) concern (a) the protection of minors and parties lacking capacity, (b) the personal and proprietary effects of marriage, (c) the succession rights especially with regard to the legal minimum distribution rights of relatives, (d) the transfer of title to property and security interests in property, (e) the protection of creditors in insolvency, and (f) the protection in other respects of third parties acting in good faith.

The Convention has a number of unavoidable weaknesses which may still be softened or remedied by the implementing legislation into domestic law. Thus Dutch implementing legislation allows its own mandatory rules concerning the transfer of title and of security interests and the protection of creditors in the case of insolvency (Article 15(d) and (e)) to be superseded by the recognition of foreign trusts even in respect of trust assets located in the Netherlands at the time of the creation of the trust. Article 15(d) and (e) could in fact have led to the substantial frustration of recognition in the Netherlands. Clearly the Dutch legislator meant to provide for a wide recognition possibility and any limitations are to be restrictively interpreted. In respect of trust assets located in the Netherlands, it means a deviation from the *lex situs* principle (except that in respect of real estate in the Netherlands the interest of the trust will require registration, *cf* also Article 12 of the Convention and Articles 3.17(1)(a) and 3.26 CC). A similar deviation from the *lex situs* is also increasingly common in the conflict rules concerning matrimonial property rights and in inheritance matters. It may also result from a more liberal recognition of foreign bankruptcies.

Although Dutch law itself has not chosen to introduce the trust domestically at the same time, it will not allow typical domestic considerations, even of a proprietary nature, or its own proprietary system (and the closed nature of its proprietary interests) to hinder the recognition of foreign trusts even in respect of Dutch assets. Its own explicit rejection of fiduciary ownership and substitute security rights under Article 3.84(3) CC, see chapter V, section 1.2.2, is also not seen as an impediment whilst it is expressly left to the Dutch courts to fit the foreign structure into the Dutch system of proprietary rights. The impression is given that the Dutch legislator, aware of the untenable aims of Article 3.84(3) in its new Civil Code of 1992, uses the recognition of foreign trusts with Dutch trust assets to rectify the situation to some extent.

Under the Convention, a close connection of the trust with a country other than the recognising one remains necessary for recognition. In this sense, the trust must be a truly foreign trust. A mere choice of law in favour of the law of a foreign country or the choice of a foreign trustee or a fictitious foreign place of administration is not sufficient to achieve foreignness, especially if there are substantial trust assets in the country where recognition is sought. It seems therefore likely that only trusts that substantially function outside the recognising country are capable of such recognition so that the trust assets in the recognising country may not be substantial or at least not a substantial part of the total trust assets. Unavoidably there remains here an element of doubt about where the line must be drawn. There is here some discretion for the recognising judge. The Dutch implementation statute in its favourable bias towards recognition may well have given the Dutch courts here greater freedom.[246]

1.8.4 Uniform Law Concerning the Proprietary Aspects of Chattels

Attempts at a uniform law regime especially in respect of secured transactions in chattels are being made by Unidroit in its 2001 Convention on International Interests in Mobile Equipment: see chapter V, section 1.8.3. There is an earlier Geneva Convention of 1948 on the International Recognition of Rights in Aircraft. It was widely adopted and was followed by an International Convention on Maritime Liens and Mortgages also concluded in Geneva (in 1993) but it met with less success. Together they concern aircraft and ships and accept the law of the country of registration of these assets as decisive for the security interests created in them. No substantive law is created here. There is also a 1926 Brussels

---

[246] For Italy, the liberal inclusion of domestic assets in foreign trusts has been advocated by Professor Lupoi, 'Trusts and Civilian Categories (Problems Spurred by Italian Domestic Trusts)' in R Helmholtz and R Zimmermann (eds), *Itinera Fiduciae, Trust and Treuhand in Historical Perspective* (Berlin, 1998), 507.

Convention on the Unification of Certain Rules Relating to Maritime Liens and Mortgages, followed by another one in 1967. These Conventions concern *substantive* law and have been widely incorporated into domestic laws, although often in quite different manners.

In 1994, the European Bank for Reconstruction and Development (EBRD) presented its Model Law on Secured Financing. It will be discussed in chapter V, section 1.8.2. The Unidroit Leasing Convention of 1988 will also be more extensively discussed in chapter V, section 2.1.5*ff.* Some efforts at harmonisation were also made within the EU: see chapter V, section 1.1.4.

The sum total of efforts in this area remains limited and they are geared to special areas of the law.

1.8.5   *The* Lex Mercatoria *Concerning Chattels*

In chapter I, section 3.2.2, the important development of the *lex mercatoria* in proprietary matters was discussed and especially the notion of transnational ownership in connection with negotiable instruments, documents of title, and the modern eurobond. For security interests in them, the key here is possession or control. There appears to be little room for more sophisticated non-possessory security interests under the *lex mercatoria* as it has developed so far. There may be much more room in it, however, for conditional sales and title transfers and that may be the more appropriate manner to organise chattel based funding under the *lex mercatoria*.

1.9   Private International Law Aspects of Assignments

1.9.1   *The Various Aspects of Assignments. Characterisation Issues.*
Mandatory Law

The international aspects of assignments are acquiring a particular importance in international financings based on bulk transfers of receivables with debtors in various countries, but they may be of interest also if the assignor and assignee are in different countries even though the debtors are not, for example when a creditor assigns a domestic portfolio of receivables to a foreign bank. Naturally they also arise in assignments of individual claims when assignor, assignee and/or the debtor are in different countries. The private international law aspects of assignments have until more recently not received a great deal of attention, even in the more traditional context of the assignment of one single claim, let alone in the newer context of bulk assignments or factoring of receivables. The discussion is here largely concentrated on the bulk assignment of receivables, therefore of monetary claims for payment of goods or services.

Where in the case of such a bulk assignment, the debtors are in different countries there is primarily the issue whether and under what law the bulk assignment is binding upon them. It raises questions of the proper law concerning the *formalities*, more especially documentation, or, if the assignment is meant to achieve a secured interest, possibly registration or publication. It also may raise questions concerning *validity*, which poses the further question whether the notification is a constitutive requirement for validity. Another question is the *moment of effectiveness* of the transfer (either at the time of the assignment or upon notification of each individual transfer if a constitutive requirement for the assignment).

Then there is the question of the *assignability* (particularly of highly personal claims, claims for services and claims in contractually blocked accounts) and in connection with assignability also the question of the assignment of *future* claims, of proper *identification* and the required *specificity*. Another assignability issue is the third party effect of any clauses in the underlying contract out of which the claims arise limiting the assignability. Closely related is the matter of the *defences* and counterclaims and whether and to what extent they can be raised against an assignee. Then there is the question of the *extra burdens or risks* the debtor may encounter as a result of an assignment for example in terms of a different place and method of payment or in terms of being sure that any payment to an assignee is liberating for the debtor. It raises the question of the *notification*, its form, manner and effect. Another well-known question is the effect of contractual amendments between debtor and assignor on any assigned (future) receivables. These are on the whole typical debtor protection issues.

In this connection, the applicable law will also have to determine whether the receivables can be fully separated from the underlying contract giving rise to it, to what extent related duties will be transferred automatically with the claims and whether the assignor may be considered discharged in respect of them. Another question will be whether the contract as a whole can be assigned or other duties under it delegated by the assignor and what the effect is on his liability. Does the assignor remain at least a guarantor? It raises also the question whether the assignment may imply an amendment or novation of the agreements out of which the claims arise, especially if there was a form of debtor's consent. Novation poses in this connection the further question of the continued validity of any supporting security.

More typical problems arise in the case of bulk assignments when any requirement of notification as a precondition for validity makes individual notification necessary, which destroys the possibility of one transfer in bulk whilst requirements of specificity or identification may in particular affect the inclusion of future debt and therefore the assignment of whole cash flows. As a form of financing is usually the objective of bulk assignments, the further question is whether the arrangement is a secured loan or may be characterised as a conditional sale and what kind of disposition is necessary upon default and who is entitled to the overvalue.

In all these instances, the applicable law will be relevant as these are hardly questions that can be determined by the parties in the assignment agreement itself. By choosing a particular legal system to apply, parties may, however, be able to influence the outcome. They can of course also try to be more specific in their contract and for example define the situations in which an assignment will be possible or agree that defences shall not be raised against assignees. The third party effect of assignment prohibition clauses may be in doubt, however, and therefore also the question whether the assignment itself can be affected by such clauses in so far as the assignee is concerned or whether the latter can derive rights from such clauses.

There are other, more typical third party or *proprietary issues*, like the power of the assignor to transfer title or other proprietary interests in the claim(s), the entitlement to the collection right amongst various assignees of the same claim and their ranking in the distribution of the proceeds and in this connection the effect of the *nemo dat* rule on a collecting assignee. The operation of the condition in a conditional transfer of receivables was already mentioned. There is also the effect to be considered of any default of the assignee under an assignment agreement on his interest in the assigned claims. The proprietary aspects normally lead to individual consideration of the situation in respect of each claim. That is unavoidable, even in bulk assignments. The same goes for *enforcement* issues against the debtor, which must also be considered for each assigned claim individually, including the question who (assignor or assignee) may sue the debtor if collection fails, especially relevant if the assignment was only a partial or security assignment, and who may invoke the protection of the accessory or supporting rights or securities if the interest transfered was itself only a limited proprietary interest like a security or usufruct, or who may recover from other assets of the debtor in the case of his default.

Also in these cases, assignor and assignee can hardly make provisions in the assignment contract itself and the applicable law will have to be established and is not automatically the law (made) applicable to the assignment agreement itself, whether or not chosen by the parties. It could also be the law of the underlying receivables, of the residence of the assignor or the residence of each debtor. Whatever the approach, which will be more extensively discussed in the next section, in these aspects there is a *mandatory* element and these matters are not normally considered to be at the free disposition of the parties and subject to their contractual choice of law.

The terms used or distinctions made in this connection are necessarily tentative, and concepts like validity, assignability, or protection of the debtor are poly-interpretable, although this is not always fully appreciated: see for example the use of the term '*assignability*' in Article 12 of the 1980 EU Rome Convention on the Law Applicable to Contractual Obligations. It could mean a reference not only to (a) the transferability of highly personal, future or blocked claims (and the validity of any contractual restraints on alienation in this connection), to their very existence as present or future rights or to the ability to split them out of the rest of the contract; but also (b) the type of proprietary right that might be created like a security interest, a conditional right, or usufruct, thus whether the claims are so assignable; (c) the modality of the transfer, thus whether the claims are assignable in bulk also in their proprietary aspects; (d) the protection of the debtor whose debt might not be transferable (as to him) if the assignment creates extra burdens for him; and (e) the position of various transferees or assignees *inter se* who might find that an earlier assigned claim was no longer validly assignable by the same assignor as regards them.

The reference to *validity*, often used in this connection (although not in Article 12), could imply a reference to (a) the validity of the assignment agreement itself including the documentation, (b) the formalities required for the assignment itself like notification (in some countries) or registration for certain security interests in these assets (if a constitutive requirement for the validity of such security interests), (c) the validity of proprietary interests created thereunder; or in the case of a bulk assignment (d) the possibility of a bulk transfer as such and to the type of interest created thereby (an outright transfer, a security interest, a conditional sale, or a collection arrangement), when individual notification of each assignment thereunder or identification of each claim to be assigned may create further impediments or even impossibilities of being included in the case of future debt.

Equally, the reference to the *protection of the debtor* also often used in this connection (although not so broadly in Article 12) may have many meanings. It may cover (a) his liberating payment in view of his vulnerability to creditors of the assignor as well as to other assignees (or their creditors) claiming better collection rights and who may attempt to recover from his other assets (in their own countries if more convenient) or invoke guarantees or execute security interests given by the debtor if he defaults as regards them, (b) the type of notice he may or must accept, (c) any need for his *bona fides* as regards better collection rights of others, or (d) the survival of his defences and his right to resist or ignore burdensome assignments.

References to *proprietary* interests (not made in Article 12) may mean references to (a) the types of interests that can be created or (b) the relative priorities of the various assignees of the same claim or (c) the rights of assignors pursuant to a default under the assignment or upon the fulfilment of the conditions leading to an (automatic) return of some or all receivables, but the reference to *enforcement* may cover similar ground.

Any reference to the *enforcement* (also not made in Article 12) could mean a reference to (a) the collection right of the assignee, (b) the relative rights of various assignees in this respect, (c) any rights of their creditors to garnish the debtor, or (d) any rights to execute under security interests granted by the debtor into his other assets or any other right to recover from such assets if the debtor refuses to pay.

It should be clear from the foregoing that use of the terms 'assignability', 'validity', 'protection of the debtor', 'proprietary aspects' or 'enforcement aspects' may lack precision and they may overlap. In private international law terms, the use of these terms and the legal characterisation it suggests are most important and may lead to different legal systems being made applicable in different aspects of assignments (in a process of so-called *dépéçage*) but is unsatisfactory as it is not clear what they cover. As a consequence, terms commonly used in this connection like 'validity', 'assignability' or 'protection of the debtor', cannot themselves determine the conflict rule and the applicable law without further analysis and are not sufficient characterisation in themselves.

Thus the effect of a German bulk transfer of present and future receivables, some of which arose subsequently in the Netherlands, was qualified by the Dutch lower courts as a matter of validity of the assignment to which the contractual law applicable to the assignment was deemed applicable in the manner of Article 12(1) of the Rome Convention, but the Supreme Court qualified it as a matter of assignability and applied the law of the underlying receivable on the basis of principles derived from Article 12(2) of the Rome Convention. There was no further investigation of contractual or rather proprietary and enforcement aspects of the assignment,[247] which were always unlikely to be covered by the Convention and in which aspects there might not have been a conflict issue in the case at all.

The proprietary and enforcement aspects are traditionally subjected to the *lex situs* of the asset, whilst, as non-obligatory matters, they cannot truly be considered covered by the Rome Convention as it deals only with the proper law of obligations, which is the internal aspects of claims. Many of the legal issues that arise here, especially the relationship with third parties like other assignees upon double assignments or subsequent assignments of different kinds of interests in the asset(s) and the protection of the debtor, are not at the free disposition of the parties. As a consequence, they cannot strictly speaking be the subject of their chosen law, be this the law of the assignment contract, of the underlying relationships out of which the claims rose, or any other. There are objective or mandatory rules.[248] This points to emphasis on the traditional *lex situs* approach instead. As we saw for chattels, conflicts in these aspects mainly arise when the asset moves, when there may be a question whether the law of the *situs* of origin or of the *situs* of destination applies. It will be submitted below that in the case of claims the asset moves and such a conflict arises mainly when the debtor moves his residence, which is exceptional.

Another important aspect here is the abstraction: see section 1.7.7 above. In modern thinking increasingly it lifts a monetary claim out of its own contractual or other context so that upon assignment new rules may apply in the assignee/debtor relationship which may supplement or even amend some of the aspects of the former relationship between the assignor/debtor out of which the claim arose, whilst also the aspect of the debtor's

---

[247] HR, 11 June 1993 [1993] NJ 776.
[248] See also P Lalive, *The Transfer of Chattels in the Conflict of Laws* (1955), 114.

protection may not be seen entirely in the light of fulfilling the old relationship after an assignment in terms of defences, assignment prohibitions and even the ranking of various assignees of the same claims. There are here *autonomous* rules at work, which are more properly those that derive from the place where the claim has its greatest impact or effect rather than from the underlying contractual law of the claim of the assignment, which might be chosen by the parties. It raises again the question of the proper *situs* or place of a claim, as its law would likely be the most appropriate to apply to the non-contractual aspects of an assignment.

In fact, rather than referring here to formation, validity, assignability and debtor's protection, if one wants more general conflicts rules to apply, the more useful distinction may be the one between contractual, debtor's protection and proprietary or enforcement aspects of assignments. The first (contractual) ones are covered either by the contractual law of the assignment itself or by the law of the original legal relationship giving rise to the assigned claim (and this relationship need not be contractual in nature), whether or not chosen by the parties themselves. Problems may arise here particularly in common law which does not so sharply distinguish between contractual and proprietary aspects, certainly in the case of intangibles, but a reference to the enforcement aspects as distinguished from the others may give similar results in that it puts emphasis on the law of the debtor in all aspects of the assignment that are not purely contractual.

As we saw, the Rome Convention in its Article 12 rather distinguishes between the validity and formation aspects (although these terms are not used as such) and assignability aspects. It makes the law of the assignment applicable to the validity (Article 12(1)) and the law of the underlying claim to the assignability (Article 12(2)), at least in the obligatory aspects. Strictly speaking, this does not cover proprietary and enforcement aspects at all, although this has become contested in case law. Under the Convention, the debtor's protection is governed by the law of the contract out of which the claims arise. This is contrary to any *lex situs* approach.

1.9.2   Current Approaches to Choice of Laws Issues in Assignments: The Situs of Debts

In Germany, established opinion remains that the law of the contract out of which the receivable arises determines its proprietary regime, transfer possibility and transfer method.[249] It virtually rules out bulk transfers *(Globalzession)* internationally, the reason German doctrine sometimes switches to applicability of the (proprietary) law of the assignor in that case.[250] In common law countries, this rule is often also accepted for global statutory assignments, like bankruptcy in respect of the transfer of the estate to the trustee in bankruptcy. It is unlikely to find universal support at the place of the account or receivable debtors, however. Yet also in France leading authors still opt for the law of the

---

[249] See Kegel, *Internationales Privatrecht* (6th edn, 1987), 478; C Von Bar, 'Abtretung und Legalzession im neuen deutschen Internationalen Privatrecht' [1989] *RabelsZ* 462 and Reithmann-Martiny, *Internationales Vertragsrecht* (5th edn, 1988), no 214ff, but *cf* also Kieninger, *infra*. However, the applicability of the law of the assignment in proprietary matters is supported in two German dissertations on the Rome Convention: see Keller, *Zessionsstatut im Lichte des Übereinkommens über das auf vertragliche Schüldverhältnisse anzuwendende Recht* (Munich, 1985), 145 and Kaiser, 'Verlängerter Eigentumsvorbehalt und Globalzession' [1986] *IPR* 219. Eva-Maria Kieninger, 'Das Statut der Forderungsabtretung in Verhältnis zu Dritten' [1998] 62 *RabelsZ*, 678 argues for the law of the residence of the assignor, which will normally follow if under the law of the assignment approach the assignor performs the most characteristic obligation, which is the delivery of the receivables in a bulk assignment.
[250] See Kegel, n 249 *supra* and Kieninger, n 249 *supra*.

underlying contract,[251] bulk transfers not having been of great interests because of the notification requirement before the *Loi Dailly* of 1991. In Switzerland, Article 105 of the Act on Private International Law of 1989 accepts the law chosen by assignor and assignee, but this law may not detrimentally affect the debtor except where he agrees to it. The normal rule is the applicability of the law of the place of the creditor or assignor, although it is not clear whether this also covers all protection and proprietary aspects. It is unlikely to cover enforcement. In the Netherlands there is no unity of view at all.[252]

---

[251] See Loussouarn-Bourel, *Droit International Privé* (3rd edn, 1988), nrs 424 and 425 and Batiffol-Lagarde, *Droit International Privé* (7th edn, 1983), nr 611.

[252] In recent Dutch case law, even in proprietary matters, sometimes the law of the underlying claim and in other cases the law of the assignment have been upheld as applicable following Article 12(1) and (2) of the 1980 Rome Convention on the Law Applicable to Contractual Obligations, even in proprietary aspects, rather than on the law of the debtor or that of the assignor. There are in the Netherlands three Supreme Court cases in this connection the last two of which have elicited considerable international interest: see HR 17 Apr 1964 [1965] NJ 23, HR, 11 June 1993 [1993] NJ 776 and HR, 16 May 1997 [1997] RvdW 126. See for a discussion of the first two cases, JH Dalhuisen, 'The Assignment of Claims in Dutch Private International Law', in *Festschrift Kokkini-Iatridou, Comparability and Evaluation* (Asser Institute, 1994) 183 and for the last one THD Struycken, 'The Proprietary Aspects of International Assignment of Debts and the Rome Convention, Article 12' [1998] *Lloyd's Maritime & Commercial Law Quarterly* 345 and Kieninger, n 249 *supra*, 678.

In 1964, with reference to the never ratified Benelux Uniform Private International Law Statute (Articles 17 and 21), the law governing the underlying claim was deemed applicable to their assignability and to the requirement and formalities of assignment when Indonesian subsidiaries assigned their claims on an Indonesian Bank to their Dutch parent for recovery out of the assets of the Bank located in the Netherlands, except that the law of the debtor was considered applicable to his protection (liberating payment) and to the protection of other third parties. In the proprietary aspects proper, as in the position of subsequent assignees, there was some suggestion at the time (in the opinion of the AG) that the law of the assignment applied. In this case, the assignments were deemed properly made under the applicable Indonesian law governing the claims (excluding the expropriation laws which were considered discriminatory) and recovery in the Netherlands was allowed against assets of the Indonesian Bank there, therefore regardless of a nationalisation decree concerning the assignors.

In 1993, the issue was a German *Globalabtretung* of future claims by a German supplier to his German bank. Later sale of the supplier of caravans to a Dutch customer resulted in the Dutch view in (future) receivables that under Dutch law could not have been validly assigned as, at the time of assignment, they were absolutely future. The buyers as a consequence refused to pay the German assignee bank. The problem was resolved by the Dutch Supreme Court with reference to Article 12 of the Rome Convention (although not yet in force at the time), and was ultimately identified as a problem of assignability under Article 12(2), therefore governed by the law of the underlying claim, rather than as an issue of the validity of the assignment (as the lower courts had found) covered by the law of the assignment under Article 12(1), although strictly speaking Article 12(1) does not refer to the validity requirements and formalities of the transfer, where in 1964 the HR had accepted the law of the underlying claim. In the end, the characterisation of the issue in terms of assignability rather than validity determined the issue and aligned the 1993 decision with the one of 1964.

In 1997, the issue was a *verlängerter Eigentumsvorbehalt* (a reservation of tile extending into the receivable) under which according to German law the sale of goods to a Dutch manufacturer who sold them on to an end-user resulted in a claim in which the original German supplier had a preferred position. Dutch law does not accept the *verlängerten Eigentumsvorbehalt* and the assignment of absolutely future claims it entails. It now also requires notification for such an assignment to be valid except where a security interest is created according to Dutch law whilst all alternative securities are invalid (Article 3(84(3))). The Dutch manufacturer went bankrupt and the question was to whom the end-user had to pay. This was resolved in favour of the German supplier with reference to the applicability of the law governing the assignment pursuant to Article 12(1) of the Rome Convention, therefore the law covering the validity of the assignment rather than the assignability under Article 12(2), which would have resulted in the applicability of the law of the underlying claim.

Who had the collection right, therefore to whom should the debtor pay, was the issue in both cases and is in truth a proprietary issue, according to most authors not covered by the Rome Convention. Not so, or no longer so, in the opinion of the Dutch Supreme Court, which applies Article 12 in proprietary matters, probably by way of analogy. Whether these proprietary issues are put under Article 12(1) as a question of validity of the assignment (as the HR did in 1997) or under Article 12(2) as a matter of assignability (as it did in 1993), both solutions seem to allow for party autonomy in the proprietary aspects of an assignment, either as a matter of party choice of law under the assignment agreement (Article 12(1)) or under the contract producing the assigned claim (assuming it was contractual). Dutch case law seems here to follow German law, which has always had difficulty in distinguishing between the proprietary and contractual side of assignments because it does not qualify claims as proper assets. Neither does modern Dutch law; see s 1.1.3 *supra*, although, as just mentioned, German law

In England, on the other hand, there is a preference, at least in matters of validity, for the applicability of the law of the assignment,[253] which may be chosen by the parties, whilst a clear distinction between the contractual and proprietary aspects is not made, so that this chosen law could also cover these aspects, although enforcement always seems to be covered by the law of the debtor. In this English approach, assignability and priorities are governed by the proper law of the assigned claim.[254] But an important more commercially oriented train of thought considers the law of the debtor applicable in these aspects.[255] In line with common law thinking which, as just mentioned, does not clearly distinguish the contractual and proprietary aspects of assignments, US law may also rely on the law of the assignment and party autonomy in this area. The place of the assignment to which reference is often made in this connection is for its determination itself dependent on the applicable law, however, and therefore not a useful departing point. In practice, it appears to be the place of the contract of assignment rather than the *situs* of the claim.[256] Yet there is at least in case law also much support for the law of the debtor in terms of the lex situs of the debt.[257] The UCC firmly opts, however, for the applicability of

looks to the law of the underlying contract rather than to the law of the assignment in this connection, although there is also some support for the law of the assignment: see n 223 *supra*.

On the other hand, the applicability in the proprietary aspects of the law of the underlying claim is defended in a more recent Dutch dissertation: see LFA Steffens, *Overgang van Vorderingen en Schulden in het Nederlandse Internationaal Privaatrecht* [Transfer of Claims and Liabilities in Dutch Private International Law] (1997) but in the Netherlands, RIVF Bertrams and HLE Verhagen preferred the law of the assignment: *Goederenrechtelijke Aspecten van de Internationale Cessie en Verpanding van Vorderingen op Naam* (1993), WPNR 6088, 261. THD Struycken, *supra*, prefers the law of the assignor. Dalhuisen, *supra* defends the applicability of the law of the debtor.

[253] See *Dicey and Morris on the Conflict of Laws* (13th edn, 2000), Rule 118 (24-054 and 24-061), 981 and 983, see also CGJ Morse, 'Retention of Title in English Private International Law', [1993] *Journal of Business Law* 168.

[254] Earlier the English Court of Appeal had suggested that there were at least five possible theories on the law governing the validity of the assignment alone: see *Republica de Guatemala v Nunez* [1927] 1KB 669.

[255] See R Goode, *Commercial Law* (2nd edn,1995), 1129 and Moshinsky, 'The Assignment of Debts in the Conflict of Laws' (1992) 109 *LQR* 613, except for bulk assignments which are thought covered by the law of the assignor), and Dalhuisen n 252 *supra*.

[256] See eg *Barbin v Moore*, 85 NH 362 (1932).

[257] The most important case in this connection is *Harris v Balk*, 198 US215 (1905), which has been overruled in other aspects, see *Shaffer v Heitner*, 433 US 186 (1977), but its debt situs holding remains unimpaired in matters of garnishment of the debt. In the USA there is, however, not one rule and the context needs to be considered. Thus in the UCC there is another rule in respect of secured transactions involving accounts (receivables), see Section 9-103. In *act of state* matters, the issue has acquired yet another setting and concerns the question whether a receivable may properly be considered expropriated within the jurisdiction of the expropriating authority so that its expropriation cannot be reviewed (because of respect for the foreign acts of state). The issue was litigated particularly in connection with claims of depositors on branches of foreign banks operating in Cuba that were expropriated whilst in addition some freezing orders were put on some deposits (of certain individuals whilst the foreign headoffices were asked to remit to Cuba sums equal to these liabilities, which they usually did). The question was whether in such cases the American headoffice still remained liable for repayment to the original depositor, see *Garcia v Chase Manhattan Bank, NA* 735 F2d 645 (1984) in which it was so held in the case of (non-negotiable) certificates of deposit in dollars seemingly guaranteed by the headofficie in the US and therefore deemed located at that officie in the US, therefore outside the reach of the act of state doctrine. In *Perez v Chase Manhatten Bank,* 61 NY 2d 460 (1984), it was found in a similar situation, however, that the debt was not exclusively payable in the US (there was no guarantee either) and the act of state doctrine was applied (so that no review of the expropriation took place). In the case of promissory notes in US $ and payable in the US but issued through a Costa Rica branch of an American bank put under a domestic (Costa Rica) order not to pay foreign currency notes to protect the local economy, it was believed on the other hand that since the notes were not wholly extinguished by the order, they could still be collected in the US where they were deemed located for this purpose, see *Allied Bank International v Banco Credito Agricola de Cartago*, 757 F2d 516 (1985) and the interest of Costa Rica to change the payment terms was not deemed sufficient to reach them. In *Alfred Dunhill of London v Republic of Cuba*, 425 US 682 (1976), receivables payable in New York were held to be located there, as a consequence still owned by the former owners of a nationalised Cuban cigar company and payable to them. In such cases it was assumed that the power to enforce payment depends on jurisdiction over the debtor, see also *Menendez v Saks*, 485 F2d 1355 (1973). In a similar vein, a bank that closes its foreign branch voluntarily (in Saigon before the collapse of

the law of the borrower/debtor who offers the receivables, therefore of the assignor (Section 9-301(1) (9-103(3)(b) old) UCC), at least in matters of perfection of security interests or transfers of receivables under Article 9 UCC and for its effects. This applies more generally also to goods that are mobile and are normally used in more than one jurisdiction (like aircraft). It is in line with the situation for chattels more generally where under the UCC the law of the debtor/transferor of the security interest is preferred above the *lex situs*: see Section 9-103 (1) and also section 1.8.1 above.

For the assigment of accounts receivable, the most important issues in the USA appear to be the conflicts arising in double assignments or in attachments of the assigned accounts, when the law of the assignor's business is sometimes held to be the most appropriate to apply.[258] As just mentioned, modern opinion especially amongst commercial lawyers makes a much sharper distinction between the contractual and non-contractual aspects of assignments and opts for the law of the debtor in the latter aspects.[259] They see

the old regime) retains the deposits on its book in the US, see *Vishipco Line v Chase Manhattan Bank, NA*, 660 F2d 854 (1981).

Vietnamese depositors (in local currency) who had placed deposits in branches of French banks in Saigon were not allowed to claim at the headoffices in France, however, French courts finding that under private international law these deposits were covered by Vietnamese law as the law of the place where the deposit was made and this law did not allow payment in French Francs equivalent abroad, see *Trib Gr Inst Paris*, March 8 1985, DS Inf Rap 346 (1985). This is another (private international law) way around a nationalisation or payment freeze order in which the public law element is deemed subsumed in the private law governing the case but the *situs* issue also arises. In the US, this approach is not unknown either, see *Wells Fargo Asia Ltd v Citibank, NA*, 852 F2d 657 (1990) in respect of a dollar deposit made in Manilla that could not be repaid there. Ultimately New York law was held applicable under which the headoffice of City Bank was held responsible for repayment as under this law a creditor may collect or enforce a judgement wherever he can obtain jurisdiction over his debtor.

In all these cases there is otherwise not much of the old banking rule that deposits are deemed to be made at the branch were the money is taken in and the account is held, meaning that without further arrangements it can only be withdrawn at that branch. This may be different for certificates of deposits when the deposit is not reflected in a deposit account balance in the bank but in the certificate itself. If it is negotiable it would represent the deposit itself which therefore would be located at the place of the holder. Note that in Garcia and Perez the certificates of deposit were *non-negotiable* so that it could be maintained that their *situs* was not that of the holder.

[258] See the authorative Comment, 67 *Yale LJ* 401, 418 (1958), but see also AA Ehrenzweig, *Conflict of Laws* (1962), 640 warning against a dogmatic approach in this area. In any event adequate protection of the debtor may dictate otherwise. Where the assignor continues to collect, the relevant receivables could still be considered included in his estate upon a bankruptcy of the assignor: *Benedict v Ratner*, 268 US 353 (1925), although not all state courts followed this. Garnisheeing creditors have been held protected by the law of the state of garnishment, likely to be that of the debtor's residence: *Lewis v Lawrence*, 30 Minn 244 (1883). The assignability issues including the effect of contractual limitations on the assignability are mostly held to be governed by the law of the underlying relationship out of which the claim arose, but policy considerations may supersede this approach, especially to support justified expectations of the debtor: *In re Poma's Will*, 192 NY Supp 2d 156 (1959). The matter of set-offs and defences has in the main been settled by statute preserving for the debtor all those arising until the date of notification, whilst his own courts would naturally protect him in collection suits when the *lex fori* includes such a statute, *cf.* also Section 2-210 and Section 9-404*ff* (9-318 old) UCC.

[259] See Goode, n 255 *supra*; Dalhuisen, n 252 *supra*; Anne Sinay-Cytermann, (1992) 81 *Rev crit dr internat privé 35*; Moshinsky, n 255 *supra*, although preferring the law of the assignor in the case of bulk assignments. See for support for the law of the debtor also *Re Helbert Wagg & Co Ltd's Claim* [1956] Ch 323 and C Schmitthoff, *The English Conflict of Laws* (3rd edn, 1954), 211. See for the early acceptance of the *lex situs* notion in this connection and of its close relationship to the place of enforcement, F von Savigny, *A Treatise on the Conflict of Laws and the Limits of their Operation in Respect of Place and Time* (translation of the original 1849 text by W Guthrie, 2nd edn, 1889), 366; see also the original view of AV Dicey, *A Digest of the Law of England with Reference to the Conflict of Laws* (1896), 533.

In more recent times AA Erenzweig accepted the law of the debtor in matters of his protection: see *Conflict of Laws* (1962), 641; *cf* also E Rabel, 3 *The Conflicts of Law, A Comparative Study* (1950), 424, 434; see in the USA from an early date *Moore v Robertson*, 17 NYS, 554 (1891). In the meantime, Article 2(g) of the new EU Bankruptcy Regulation defines the *situs* of a claim as the Contracting State in which the debtor has its main interest. This is a most important definition as the doubts on the principle of the *lex situs* applying in the proprietary and enforcement aspects of receivables usually derives from the difficulty in agreeing the proper *situs* of claims. See for the approach of Article 12 EU 1980 Rome Convention on the Law applicable to Contractual Obligations, more in particular section 1.9.3 *infra*.

it as a normal extension of the *lex situs* notion and emphasise the close relationship between proprietary and enforcement matters, the latter being normally also governed by the law of the debtor (except where enforcement is sought against his assets in other countries). Indeed, attachments and garnishments necessarily take place at the place of the asset, which in the case of claims translates into the place of the debtor. Modern case law confirms this tendency and it has often been held that a debt is situated where it is properly enforceable, thus normally at the place of the debtor.[260] In England, it does not strictly speaking rule out another place if payment is agreed, provided, however, there is an enforcement possibility in that place. If not, the *situs* of the claim is still at the debtor's residence, being always the residual enforcement place.[261] In fact, creating a contractual enforcement jurisdiction away from the place of the debtor does not change the location of the debt, which requires a more objective criterion. It suggests as proper *situs* of a debt the place where claims are *normally* enforceable, which is the place of the debtor (which only changes when he moves to another country with the related recharacterisation and adjustment problems especially if the assignment is conditional or for security purposes only).

It has also been argued that assets are located where they are controlled, which is therefore at the place of the owner or assignor.[262] This is clearly not always so in the case of chattels and need therefore also not be so in the case of intangible claims. It has nevertheless the attraction that in the case of a bulk transfer the law of the residence of the assignor would apply in the proprietary aspects rather than the law of the debtor, which would mean a different regime for each assigned receivable,[263] but there is perforce such a difference in regime when it comes to enforcement of the proprietary claims. The unity that may be so achieved exits therefore only on the surface and is artificial. Anyhow, bank accounts, whether in credit or debit, are normally deemed located in the place of the bank branch in which they are opened. Rights of claimants under non-negotiable share or bond certificates are usually deemed to be located at their register. It could be the same for bearer securities in book entry systems. Otherwise, negotiable instruments and documents of title are normally deemed located in the place of their physical whereabouts, which is with the debtor upon their presentation. It all points away from the place of the claimant to the place of the debtors or obligors under these arrangements and therefore not to the place of the assignors/creditors/obligees.

If the law of the debtor may be considered controlling in the proprietary and protection aspects of an assignment even if the assignor and assignee or one of them are resident elsewhere, one could say that in the proprietary, protection and enforcement aspects no true conflict of laws arises under an assignment as the intangible asset does not move (the debtor remaining in the same place). It is just like when a chattel is sold by two foreigners but remains in the same location. In this view, in an assignment conflicts normally arise only in the contractual aspects of the deal, therefore only when assignor and assignee are in different countries. This is probably the true reason why in international assignments the proprietary aspects receive so little attention. There is no true conflict in the proprietary and enforcement aspects except where the debtor himself moves to another country, which is unlikely!

---

[260] See the Privy Council in *Kwok Chi Leung Karl v Commissioner of Estate Duty* [1988] 1 WLR 1035; see also Article 2(g) of the Draft EU Bankruptcy Convention referred to in n. 259 *supra*.
[261] *Re Herbert Wagg & Co Ltd* [1956] Ch. 323.
[262] See T Struycken, n. 236 *supra*, 345 and Kieninger, n. 249 *supra*.
[263] See also the approach of Moshinsky and Kegel for bulk assignments: see respectively n. 255 and 249 *supra*.

Debtor substitution in the receivable would present a more realistic example if the new debtor were located in another country so that the claim would become enforceable elsewhere. It commonly requires the creditors' consent, but one would subsequently have to consider the new proprietary situation. This would be relevant more in particular if security interests in the claim were created in the original country when their recognition in the new country with the adaptations that may require could easily become an issue. Again, the key is here that conflict of laws in a proprietary or even in an enforcement sense are unlikely to be connected with an assignment of a claim.

1.9.3 Treaty Law Approaches to the Law Applicable to Assignments: The Choice of Law Provision of Article 12 of the Rome Convention and the Draft Uncitral Receivable Financing Convention

Article 12 of the Rome Convention on the Law Applicable to Contractual Obligations concluded between the EU members in 1980 provides as follows:

1.   The mutual obligations of assignor and assignee under a voluntary assignment of a right against another person ('the debtor') shall be governed by the law which under this Convention applies to the contract between the assignor and assignee.
2.   The law governing the right to which the assignment relates shall determine its assignability, the relationship between the assignee and the debtor, the conditions under which the assignment can be invoked against the debtor and any questions whether the debtor's obligations have been discharged.[264]

On its face it appears that the assignment itself in its contractual aspects is governed under Section 1 by the proper law of the assignment found pursuant to the general rules of the Convention (Articles 3 and 4). They focus on the choice of law of the parties and, failing such a choice, on the law with the closest connection, which is the law of the party performing the most characteristic obligation. One must assume that it is the assignor who performs that obligation as he must deliver the intangible, except perhaps in collection arrangements where it is the assignee who must administer and collect, usually for the benefit of the assignor. In other aspects, Section 2 suggests the applicability of the law of the underlying contract (or other legal relationship) out of which the claims arise. That applies in particular to the assignability, the relationship between assignee and debtor, the collection right against the debtor upon assignment, and the liberating payment of the debtor to the latter.

[264] It may in this connection be of interest to cite an earlier draft (then contained in Article 16): see 21 Am JCL, 589 (1973):

1.   Obligations between assignor and assignee of a debt shall be governed by the law applicable under Articles 2 to 8.
2.   The law governing the original debt determines whether the debt may be assigned; it also regulates the relationship between the assignee and the debtor and the conditions under which the assignment may be invoked against the debtor and third parties.'

The Official Report by Professors Giuliano and Lagarde suggest that the first section could have been drafted more simply as was at one stage proposed:

'...the assignment of a right by agreement shall be governed in relations between assignor and assignee by the law applicable to that agreement.'

It was already noted before that it is not clear whether and how the proprietary and enforcement aspects are covered by the Convention. It was also already noted above in passing that the term 'assignability' in Section 2 is not defined, see for its various meanings section 1.9.1 above.[265] Since the Convention applies only to contractual obligations the proprietary and enforcement aspects do not seem to be covered at all or can be covered only by analogy. Whether it is appropriate to cover also the area of the debtor's special duties pursuant to an assignment and his protection, which are not contractual either, may also be questioned. The letter of the Convention goes here in any event beyond the mere contractual; how far is not clear.

It should perhaps also be asked why, if Article 12 is mainly meant to cover contractual aspects, a rule different from the one under Section 1 was required so that in the contractual aspects of the assignment there is a different rule for the (formation and) validity aspects and for assignability which often overlap; it depends on the meaning of these concepts: see again the discussion in section 1.9.1. Yet subsequently to apply the law of the underlying claim also in the proprietary and enforcement aspects does not follow, if only because this law could then be chosen by the assignor and debtor in their original contract, which in proprietary and enforcement matters is normally considered inappropriate. These rules are normally mandatory. The effect of any contractual conflicts rules under the Convention should not automatically spill over in non-contractual aspects of the assignment, even if one must admit that common law never made sharp distinctions and civil law is sometimes still confused about the internal and external aspects of claims.

The Unidroit Convention on International Factoring of 1988 has uniform rules and no private international law rules. This is different for the Uncitral Receivable Financing Convention which in its present text (Articles 28*ff*) has a number of conflict rules supplementing its Article 8 that requires supplementation of the Convention on the basis of private international law rules unless the issue can be settled in conformity with the general principles on which the Convention is based. It is likely to lead to considerable problems and this requirement may well undermine the usefulness of the uniform regime as any doubt about its interpretation and meaning, which can not truly be separated from supplementation, may end in a search for local rules. This will not be aided by the fact that the conflicts rules of Articles 28*ff* are closely modelled on Article 12 of the Rome Convention. As a consequence, they leave similar questions about the applicable proprietary and enforcement rules, which under this Convention must be assumed to be covered, even if it is not clear how, except that as regards priority between assignees the law of the assignor is made applicable.

1.9.4   *Uniform Law Concerning Proprietary Rights in Intangibles*

The relevant texts here are the Unidroit Convention on Factoring and the 2001 Uncitral Convention on the Assignement of Receivables in International Trade, both already

---

[265] The undefined nature of the assignment aspects covered in Sections 1 and 2 unavoidably leads to confusion as was shown in the Dutch cases mentioned in n 252 *supra*. If Section 1 aims to cover the aspects of formation and validity of the assignment, it could also be thought to cover (a) the validity of the proprietary interests created, (b) the possibility of bulk assignments and (c) the interests created thereby. The term 'assignability' used in Section 2 could, however, also imply references to at least (a) the proprietary aspects (and the assignability of title), and (b) the types of proprietary rights that can be created (therefore the unbundling of the property right and the assignability as security, usufruct or by way of a conditional transfer). Assignability could also cover (c) the collection right *vis-à-vis* the debtor (or the lack of assignability *vis-à-vis* him because of extra burdens), and (d) the position of the various assignees *inter se* (or the lack of assignability *vis-à-vis* older ones).

referred to several times in the previous sections. They are important efforts and concern largely bulk assignments of receivables. They will be more extensively discussed in chapter V, section 2.3 including a discussion of what they consider to be international assignments for purposes of these Conventions.

1.9.5   *The* Lex Mercatoria *Concerning Bulk Assignments*

It is of course possible to take a much more transnational approach and allow transnational concepts to intrude into the non-contractual aspects of assignments, therefore in the aspects of debtor protection, in the proprietary and enforcement aspects, in questions of what types of assignments (including bulk assignments for whatever purpose) are possible and in what their effect is on the collection right of various assignees against the debtor. They may be derived from international Conventions like the Unidroit Factoring Convention and the 2001 Uncitral Receivables Convention, even in Non-contracting States. They could, however, also derive from fundamental legal principle or international custom: see more in particular chapter I, section 3.2.2. It would allow other than purely domestic proprietary rights to be created at the *situs* pursuant to whatever assignment agreement, international or not, and regardless of the otherwise applicable domestic law. This will facilitate international recognition when the debtor moves to another country or when the type of collection right so created needs enforcement against assets of the debtor in other countries (when there is no voluntary payment). In that case the question also arises who has the collection right and whether the debtor was right not to pay the assignee in view of his own defences or the better rights of other assignees.

The main example derives from negotiable instruments. The more the notion of abstraction is accepted in respect of the transfer of claims and they are as a consequence commoditised, the more like negotiable instruments or semi-chattels they become: see also section 1.7.7 above. That would also mean that they become more susceptible to transnational ownership and transfer facilities.

Part II   Negotiable Documents of Title and Negotiable Instruments

2.1   The Role of Documents

2.1.1   *Bills of Lading and Warehouse Receipts*

In the international sale of goods, there are often intermediaries in the shipping and warehousing arrangements. As a result, some document may emerge, if only as receipts, as the *bill of lading* and *warehouse receipt* originally were. The bill of lading was given when the seller physically delivered his goods to the carrrier at the ship's rail or in his warehouse. This is the *received for shipment* bill of lading. Once the goods were received on board, the bill would be stamped with the 'on board' stamp and become an *on board* bill of lading. It is this on board bill of lading that subsequently acquired the status of a document of title (if expressed to order or bearer), and that is normally referred to when we speak of a bill of lading. It testifies to the receipt of the goods on board rather than at the ship's rail or in the carrier's warehouse. This is an important difference. The seller will be given this document either in his own right under a Cif contract or as agent for the buyer in a Fob contract.[266] This document allows full use to be made of the intermediaries' safe harbour function, already referred to in chapter II, section 2.2.1.

The safe harbour function of intermediaries is crucial in international sales. It allows seller and buyer to make special delivery and payment arrangements whilst the goods are under the control of a third party (carrier or warehouse), out of the seller's reach and beyond his retention rights. In this system, the buyer may be given the documents (normally the on board bill of lading plus the insurance documents) mostly through the banking system, and thereby the reclaiming rights in the goods, against payment in the agreed manner only. In that system, the bank would objectively verify the documents and release the bill of lading only to the buyer upon his payment, so that he gains control only thereafter (whilst the goods may still be in transit). Thus the documents are given by the seller to the payee bank which collects the payment and is under a duty to release the documents thereafter (assuming the bank's charges have been paid).

It is inherent in this system that the payment cannot be threatened by a buyer in making all kinds of counterclaims on the basis of the quality of the goods upon delivery as this delivery can take place only after the payment is made and the documents are handed over, allowing the buyer to claim the goods. Subsequently, the mere presentation of the documents will assure him of the goods as the carrier or the warehouse is under an independent duty to hand them over upon the presentation of the documents (assuming that its charges have also been paid). It presents an added benefit to the buyer. Not only the reclaiming documents but also title transfers to him upon the documents being handed over to him after payment and there are no further delivery or other legal formalities in respect of the transfer of the underlying assets.

Retaining the bill of lading whilst the goods are *en route* and reach their destination re-establishes a simultaneity in the performance of both parties, now allowing payment to be made against delivery of the document rather than the goods themselves. It provides protection for either party in a sale: upon tendering the documents through the banking system, the seller receives (immediate) payment and the buyer is put in possession of the bill of lading and is able to collect the goods upon arrival without the co-operation of the seller in this aspect. Parties may still argue over the details later, especially the safe arrival and quality of the goods and any counterclaims and their effect on the price, but at least the seller has the money and the buyer the goods.[267]

This holdership of the goods by third parties or the safe harbour facility may subsequently also provide great flexibility in any resale arrangements. This resale itself may be greatly facilitated if the receipt documents can be considered to incorporate the underlying assets and become negotiable. In that case, the receipt documents are normally referred to as *documents of title*. These documents allow for the ownership transfer in the underlying goods through the transfer of the document itself. This is indeed the direction in which the on board bill of lading and warehouse receipt developed. The result is that regardless of the whereabouts of the goods and their ultimate arrival in the place of destination, the issue of this type of document achieves a simple method of handing over the (rights in the) goods to third parties. They may claim these assets as full owners against presentation of the documents without further formalities.

---

[266] See for Cif and Fob sales, chapter II, s 2.3.9.
[267] See for the 'pay first, argue later' nature of this payment also chapter II, s 2.2.3. See for collection arrangements and letters of credit more in particular chapter III, s 2.1.

As already discussed in chapter II, section 2.2.3, a (on board) bill of lading can be seen in this connection as:

(a) proof of the transportation or carriage arrangements (although as between the original shipper and the carrier their underlying transportation agreement may remain determining) and of the right to request performance and present claims and if necessary renegotiate the shipping arrangements;

(b) acknowledgement of receipt of the goods;

(c) expression of the shipper's presumed ownership or at least constructive possession of the goods and especially of his reclaiming right;

(d) confirmation of the apparent condition of the goods, that is their proper aspect and packaging; and

(e) a *negotiable document of title* creating a simple and speedy transfer facility of the goods through delivery of the document to bearer (or through endorsement plus delivery if made out to order).

In civil law, these features of the bill of lading are now normally confirmed in statutory codifications. Also in common law countries, like England and the USA, statutory law now normally covers them: see the Bills of Lading Act 1855 in England, supplemented by the Carriage of Goods by Sea Act of 1992, and Article 7 UCC for state law in the USA.

The transfer of the bill of lading as a negotiable document of title usually implies the transfer of the underlying transportation contract at the same time, or at least upon collection of the goods. This is so *both* in respect of the *rights* (of carriage) *and* the related *duties*, like payment of the freight and insurance, although this payment may already have taken place under a Cif term. As for an arbitration duty, this would however appear to require the arbitration clause to be included in the bill of lading and a reference to general trade conditions may not be sufficient. On the other hand, much against the normal rules of delegation of duties, see section 1.7.3 above, the transfer even implies a discharge of the *previous* holder of the bill by the carrier (unless it is the original party to the contract of carriage) without the need for the carrier's consent, provided always that these duties are clearly marked by the carrier on the bill of lading, as in the case of 'freight collect'. One could assume implied consent of the carrier. It makes the present holder and the original contract party the sole persons liable to pay the transportation cost.

Becoming a party to the contract of carriage in this manner reinforces on the other hand the position of the new holder of the bill of lading against the carrier. It also implies the assignment of the relevant insurance policies (without the insurer's consent, at least if the insurance policy itself is not a similarly transferable document when it needs to be transferred also).

Documents of title are proprietary instruments and the holder may be considered the *prima facie* owner of the underlying assets. The use of the term 'holder' is here different from that common in civil law where it means possession with the will to hold for someone else: see section 1.2.2 above. That is not here normally the case. The situation is, however, often more complex. In many countries, particularly England and France, title to the goods normally transfers at the mere conclusion of the sales agreement: see section 1.5.2 above. For a bill of lading to operate as a document of title in the above manner some intent to *delay* title transfer in the underlying goods until the presentation of the document must therefore be implied. This is in these countries indeed deemed to be the case under the Cif term and possibly also under the Fob term, certainly if payment against documents is agreed.

In countries like Germany and the Netherlands, the normal way to transfer title in chattels is through delivery of the goods themselves. For delivery through mere documents, the assets must be assumed to be incorporated in them, although in Germany delivery may also take place through an assignment of the reclaiming right against the carrier. It may also be deemed incorporated in the document, however, (this is a *traditio longa manu*, see section 1.2.2 above). In that case, the bill of lading may not be considered a document of title proper but rather a negotiable instrument.

In any event, there is an obvious complication with documents of title in all systems as the goods still maintain their own life and are by definition in the hands of someone other than the holder of the bill, like the carrier or the warehouse owner. The latter could still physically (even though probably improperly) dispose of these goods to, for example, a *bona fide* purchaser who might subsequently be protected, potentially leaving the holder of the bill of lading without any effective proprietary rights in the assets at all. In any event, it may still be necessary to determine when these documents are documents of title proper and what this exactly means.

Negotiability, on the other hand, is normally thought to result from the mere wording of the document itself: if it is issued to bearer or order, it is presumed to be negotiable, see for example Article 8.413 of the new Dutch CC, and then transfers either through physical delivery (if to bearer) or through endorsement (signature) and physical delivery (if to order).

Yet the holder, although *prima facie* entitled to the goods, will still have to prove its rightful holdership of the bill itself, if questioned, but may be able to do so on the basis of his *bona fide* acquisition of the bill for value. This may not be so in common law countries not normally accepting exceptions to the *nemo dat* rule (except by statute), although we are concerned here with an expression of the law merchant and not of a traditional common law principle. In any court, any prior rights of others in the underlying assets remain valid, no matter whether the bill of lading was acquired *bona fide*. Any holder of the document, if *bona fide* and having acquired the bill of lading for good value, may on the other hand be entitled to the underlying assets on the basis of the mere holding of the document. This is so at least in countries that require delivery for title transfer and also in countries that do not normally do so if the bill of lading was intended to postpone the delivery until the presentation of the document.

As regards later holders of the bill, in civil law they are likely to be owners of the goods *independently* of the original underlying arrangements with the carrier or the precise relationship with or between the previous owners of the assets or holder(s) of the documents. Any defects in the transfer of the assets or documents between them is then irrelevant, at least until proof of any better title in the goods is established, for example by *bona fide* purchasers for value of the assets who acquire possession in countries that protect them as such. Similar principles apply to the warehouse receipt, although its status in law is less clearly developed.

As a consequence, documents of title may give a better right to succeeding third party holders of the documents (and indirectly of the underlying assets) than to succeeding buyers of the underlying goods under ordinary sales agreements, at least in countries that do not protect *bona fide* purchasers of goods. The latter must submit to the better rights of third parties (except for the *traditio longa manu* in Germany). The *bona fide* holders of the bill may thus ignore all *personal* defenses of their predecessors, like default in payment by any of them. Depending on the applicable law, they may probably also ignore all *real* defences in terms of the consequences of theft (*cf* Section 7-507(2) UCC in the USA but differently Article 3.86(3)(b) of the new Dutch Civil Code), nullity, illegality and the like of any transfer in the chain of succeeding endorsements or deliveries of the documents. This is particularly interesting in legal systems which otherwise strictly adhere to the *nemo dat* rule as common law traditionally still does and which, as a consequence, do not generally protect the *bona fide* purchaser of the underlying goods themselves, even if acquired for value and with possession: see section 1.5.8 above. There thus results here a different treatment for *bona fide* holders of the bill, inspired by the old law merchant in which documents of title and negotiable instruments of this kind have their origin.

What this illustrates is that the special transfer and protection regime for documents of title is based on their *own* status, in essence independent from domestic law. This is so for all bearer and order paper. It is indicative of the continuing importance of *lex mercatoria* in this area and provides an important unifying theme, here clearly also operating in proprietary aspects: see more in particular chapter I, section 3.2.2. The more they are covered by typical domestic principles, the more they are likely to lose their status of documents of title, however, and become mere receipts. The simple replacement facility of the previous holder under the contracts of carriage and insurance, and particularly the transfer of the duties thereunder to the new holder without express consent of the carrier or insurer, would also be lost.

The protections of the holder of the bill of lading are not absolute, however, and often less extensive than those of the holder of a bill of exchange: see more in particular section 2.2.8 below, even though the protection against previous holders might be similar. This is so because the bill of lading cannot incorporate the tangible goods it represents as fully as the bill of exchange incorporates the underlying intangible claim to payment so that these goods are still likely to lead their own life separate from the bill of lading and may surface in the hands of a *bona fide* possessor for value, as we just saw. This may also occur under a bill of exchange but is less likely, and holders of claims, even if *bona fide*, are in any event less protected: see also section 1.7.9 above.

It means that in an international context the *situs* of the underlying goods will unavoidably remain relevant when bills of lading are presented. This is relevant when the underlying assets are moved to countries other than those in which the bill of lading was originally issued, all the more so if the transnational nature of the bill is not itself recognised. The physical whereabouts of the goods therefore remain always important.

However, the easy transfer possibility of the underlying goods, even in common law countries and in countries in the French tradition normally implied in a bill of lading under a Cif contract, greatly facilitates international trade. Although differences in its status in the different legal systems cannot be denied and holdership of a bill of lading never provides absolute protection of the rights in the underlying goods, in most circumstances the bill of lading provides adequate safeguards everywhere.

2.1.2   The Origin and Nature of the Bill of Lading and its Operation in the Proprietary Aspects of the Transfer of Goods

There is no unanimity internationally on the precise meaning and status of the bill of lading in its proprietary aspects. It once was undeniably an internationalised instrument that substantially operated under its own rules in the context of the law merchant but, like the bill of exchange, it became nationalised in the nineteenth-century era of the codifications or domestic legislation, although never fully so.

The pre-eminence of the bill of lading is closely connected with the development of the Cif term which became standard when regular shipping lines started to operate so that the carriage of the goods was no longer done by the parties themselves, which were now able to leave the goods for transportation with independent third parties like shipping companies.

This development dates from the end of the eighteenth century when the bill of lading was indeed considered based on the custom of merchants.[268] It acknowledged the negotiability of the bill of lading to order (or assign). In the 1805 English case of *Newson and Another v Thornton and Another*,[269] it was indeed confirmed that property could be transferred with the bill of lading, thus recognising its potential status as a document of title.

The principal divide in the views on the status of the bill of lading appears to be between countries that require delivery for title transfer, like Germany and the Netherlands, and those that normally do not, like England and France: see also section 1.5.2 above. The consequence is that in the first type of countries the bill of lading is normally considered primarily a document of title (if expressed to bearer or order). In these countries, it embodies the possession of and ownership in the underlying assets, which are in principle transferred with the delivery of the document only. Other ownership rights or more limited proprietary rights created in the underlying assets at the same time or later but not marked on the bill, like a reservation of title, might then be ignored by any *bona fide* holder of the bill upon negotiation (although *bona fide* purchasers of such rights may still be independently protected, especially if they acquire possession of the underlying assets). In this system, the holder of the bill may also be able to ignore any *earlier* proprietary rights in the underlying assets upon the *bona fide* acquisition for value of the bill.

In France and England, on the other hand, where title in chattels in principle transfers upon the conclusion of the sales agreement, the bill of lading can be a document of title only if parties have explicitly or implicitly postponed the title transfer to a later moment (presentation of the bill by the buyer). The nature of the bill of lading as a document of title then depends on the intention of seller and buyer, and any *bona fide* holder of the bill takes in principle subject to that intention and is accordingly at risk. In common law, the holder takes *also* subject to *earlier* proprietary rights of others in the underlying assets created *before* the issue of the bill of lading, even if he is a *bona fide* holder of the bill itself and unaware of these rights, as in common law the protection of *bona fide* purchasers does not generally apply to the purchasers of goods (because of the *nemo dat* rule: see section 1.5.8 above). It does to holdership of the bill of lading itself, but only as an expression of the rules of the law merchant in this field and this does not affect the rights granted earlier in the asset before a bill was issued, regardless of whether or not they are marked on it. This is confirmed in the USA where state law now accepts the presumption of the bill of lading being a document of title (in a system that normally requires delivery for title transfer in goods unless parties agree otherwise) but the *bona fide* holder still takes subject to any proprietary rights in the assets themselves established before the first negotiation: see more in particular section 2.1.5 below.

Use of the Fob or Cif term may itself imply the parties' intent to postpone the title transfer in France and in England, at least to the moment of loading at the ship's rail.[270] Especially under the cif term, under which the seller makes the transport arrangements, see also chapter II, section 2.3.9, there is normally a bill of lading that operates as a negotiable document of title transferring title to the goods each time the bill is transferred. In fact, under a cif term, the on-board bill of lading is normally *presumed* to be a document of title, also in England (when any other moment of title transfer indicated in the sales contract becomes irrelevant). However, this is always rebuttable whilst in any event the *first* transfer

---

[268] See in England the 1787 case of *Lickbarrow and Another v Mason and Others*, 2 TR 63.
[269] 6 East 17, with reference to the much earlier 1697 case of *Evans v Marlett*, 1 Ld Raym 271.
[270] See to this effect in England for the fob term *Carlos Federspiel & Co SA v Charles Twigg & Co Ltd* [1957] 1 Lloyd's Rep 240 and for the cif term *TD Bailey Son and Co v Ross T Smyth and Co Ltd* (1940) 56 TLR 825 and *The Future Express* [1993] 2 Lloyd's Rep 542.

(to the original buyer), if made at the time of loading, may still be considered to take place at that time and not therefore through the handing over of the bill of lading to the buyer.[271]

In a Fob sale (when the buyer traditionally organised the transportation in his own transport facilities: see again chapter II, section 2.3.9), there may also be a bill of lading, although it is not its essence. It may be collected by the seller but in this case as agent for the buyer who is in charge of transportation and as a consequence primarily entitled to the bill. In countries like England and France, the issue of a bill of lading is here less likely to be indicative of any creation of a document of title and could acknowledge a mere receipt of the goods. The presumption of a document of title is therefore less strong and not automatically accepted in England in Fob sales. That may be so even in countries like Germany and the Netherlands as title transfer under the Fob term is everywhere more typically at the ship's rail in which a bill of lading does not necessarily figure. If the bill is marked 'received for shipment' instead of 'on board', it is in any event only a receipt (and carriage agreement) and title will pass upon conclusion of the sales contract in France and England and upon delivery of the goods in Germany and the Netherlands (and not of the bill). As just mentioned, in England (but not under state law in the USA) and in France, the presumption under a Fob term is normally that the bill of lading (even if 'on board') is *not* a document of title at all, except where there is clear evidence to the contrary. There is such evidence if the seller is entitled to retain and present the document for payment when title transfer is deemed postponed until presentation of the bill of lading in that context.[272] It is sometimes said that a 'received for shipment' bill of lading is no more than a waybill, but that may be incorrect as the waybill testifies at least to the receipt of the goods on board.

It has been reported that in the North Sea oil trade title transfer is always deemed to be postponed until the handing over of the bill of lading to the buyer or its endorsement if to order, also in a Fob sale regardless of whether the sales contract specifies another moment of title, and even if the bill is not used to retain title pending payment. In fact, it is usually the oil terminal rather than the carrier that prepares the bill of lading (on its own terms) which is subsequently signed by the ship's master or an agent and handed to the first fob seller regardless of who arranged the transportation.[273] This may even lead to bills of lading circulating before the oil is loaded or produced. It is normal that in a chain of North Sea oil sales, the sales are Fob until the oil has been loaded, thereafter Cif, but it does not appear to make any difference to the (other) terms of the contract, and moment of title transfer which is always upon endorsement of the bill of lading.

2.1.3 The Status of the Bill of Lading in Legal Systems that Require Delivery for Title Transfer. Abstraction and the Conclusive Evidence Rule. The Situation in Germany and the Netherlands

In countries requiring delivery in the sense of surrendering possession in order to achieve a title transfer, which further assumes a valid contract and full disposition rights of the seller,

---

[271] See in France Cour de Cass, 11 June 1991, Bull des Transports et de la Logistique No 2443, 591 (1991), but it is in England more properly at the moment the bill of lading is tendered to the buyer: see *TD Bailey Son and Co v Ross T Smyth*, n 270 *supra*, and *The Glenroy* [1945] AC 124. It could still be later also in France, particularly when the first sale occurred later or when the original parties agreed to a payment against documents (or when the goods are appropriated to the contract later, or possibly when there is a reservation of title which in that case should be marked on the bill), *cf* in England also *Enichem Anic Spa and Others v Ampelos Shipping Co Ltd (the Delfini)* [1990] 1 Lloyd's Rep 252 and in France *Lamy Transports Maritimes (under the direction of Pierre Brunat)*, II No 219 (2000).

[272] See for France in particular, *ibid.*

[273] See RM Wiseman, 'Transaction Chains in North Sea Oil Cargoes' [1984] *Journal of Natural Resources Law* 134.

like Germany and the Netherlands, see section 1.5.1 above, the handing over of the bill of lading is perceived as a substitute delivery, *cf* Sections 363II and 650 of the German HGB and Article 8.417 of the New Dutch CC.

This assumes that the bill is negotiable and transferable to bearer or order. In that case, there is a presumption of full negotiability: see Article 8.413 Dutch CC (unless marked differently on the document).[274] In this system, regardless of the Cif and Fob term, holdership of a bill of lading always denotes *prima facie* possession of the goods and therefore ownership in civil law terms, at least for third party (*bona fide*) holders of the bill, until proven otherwise.

Under German law there is the further complication of the real agreement (or *dingliche Einigung*: see section 1.5.6 above) as German law (and also Dutch scholarship) sees the delivery not merely as a physical act but rather as a separate juridical act requiring the parties' intention to transfer the title in the underlying goods. This may create a particular difficulty and may complicate the holdership of the bill by a paying bank if it has not agreed the real status of the bill of lading with the beneficiary in respect of any ownership or security rights therein. It may thus be unclear whether the bank, whilst holding a bill of lading (to bearer or endorsed in blank which are the most common forms), has also received a proprietary right to the underlying assets.

In any event, even in systems like the Dutch and German, the presumption of ownership of the underlying assets is (a) not necessarily valid in relation to the immediately preceding holder of the bill, who may still have a better (proprietary) right to the assets. It depends primarily on how the bill was acquired. Amongst the original interested parties (like seller/shipper, carrier and buyer), the existence of the bill of lading may also have (b) little proprietary meaning, in the case of the buyer, even if he is aware of its existence, *as long as* the bill has not been handed over to a third party. This is commonly referred to as *negotiation*. The true proprietary effect of a bill of lading is therefore likely to become apparent only upon such negotiation. It also means that the carrier may no longer contest the terms of the bill of lading in respect of that third party. This is the conclusive evidence rule.

Until negotiation, the bill of lading is therefore not much more than a receipt. In all cases, (c) the goods still retain their own life and, if disposed of regardless of the bill of lading, *bona fide* third parties may still be protected and be able to ignore the bill of lading under the applicable law of the *situs* of the assets. Without negotiation, the bill of lading does not come into its own.

Another way of saying this is that it does not acquire sufficient *abstraction*, that is separation from the underlying situation between seller and buyer. It assumes that the new holder of the bill was *bona fide* as to any lack of disposition rights in his predecessor. In countries like England and France, there may not be abstraction even after negotiation if the bill of lading was never intended as a document of title. In Fob sales it may also be less likely in countries like Germany and the Netherlands as we saw.

The irrelevance of the bill of lading as a document of title between the original parties or the lack of abstraction more generally is particularly important in default situations after the bill has already been handed over to a buyer who has not paid. The existence of the bill does not then give him as holder any better right in the underlying assets and the unpaid seller is in that case perfectly capable of attaching the underlying goods (if not also the bill

---

[274] *Cf* also Article 1-b of the Hague Visby Rules and Article 15(2) of the Uncitral Hamburg Rules which suggest the same.

of lading), thus preventing the carrier delivering them to the buyer upon presentation of the bill. Mere notice to the carrier may well be sufficient in these circumstances and be considered adequate warning to the latter not to hand over the goods, all the more so, it seems, if a reservation of title exists and was marked on the bill. If the underlying agreement is subsequently rescinded because of a fundamental breach, or is suspended as a matter of anticipatory breach or as a consequence of the invocation of the *exceptio non-adimpleti contractus*, it may render any possessory or proprietary status of the document invalid at the same time. Article 71(2) of the 1980 Vienna Convention on the International Sale of Goods confirms this.

In any event, the buyer would be under the obligation to return the bill to the seller. Upon negotiation, however, the situation would be very different. Thus if the bill of lading has been negotiated by the buyer to a *bona fide* third party as the new holder, this implies that the seller has been paid, as he will normally not have allowed the buyer to obtain the bill of lading without such payment. If he has not been paid, he incurs a considerable risk as a result of his allowing a bill of lading to be issued to and negotiated by the buyer or on the latter's behalf. If the new holder is *bona fide*, this will allow him to ignore any prior proprietary interests not only in the bill but also in the underlying goods (unless in the hands of *bona fide* purchasers). For him, the incorporation of the underlying assets in the bill may operate as a double release.

Normally, in these systems requiring delivery for title transfer, when a bill of lading exists *and* has been negotiated (including presentation to a bank) whilst the goods are still with the carrier, the delivery is made through the handing over of the document (with endorsement if issued to order) to any subsequent holder who will only in this way receive possession of the goods and therefore presumed title, *cf* Article 8.441 of the Dutch CC (a similar rule does not, however, exist for the warehouse receipt under new Dutch law). If more than one bill of lading is issued, the first endorsee has the best right amongst any subsequent holders, assuming he can prove the time of his acquisition, can show he was *bona fide* and that he acquired the bill of lading for value: see also Article 8.460 of the new Dutch CC.[275]

2.1.4 The Status of the Bill of Lading in Legal Systems that Do Not Normally Require Delivery for Title Transfer: The Situation in France

In countries like France, delivery is not normally required for title transfer, and as a consequence the status of the bill of lading is likely to be different, which is also the case in England. For France, the relevant statute is Law 66-420 of 18 June 1966 on contracts of affreightment and maritime transport, as amended. It emphasises the nature of the document as presumption of proof of receipt of the goods whilst *upon negotiation* no evidence to the contrary may be presented (Article 18). It is logical that in a system like the French, which transfers title in goods '*par l'effet de l'obligation*' under Article 711 Cc, the accent is not on the document of title nature of the bill of lading. That is very clear in ordinary Fob sales, even if (as part of a payment scheme) they are deemed to delay title transfer until

---

[275] The existence of several bills of lading in respect of one cargo is, however, undesirable and when one of the bills of lading travels with the cargo in order for the buyer to be able to claim the goods immediately upon arrival to avoid the costs of delays, it may destroy any built-in payment protection for the seller. It is more common in respect of sea waybills, which are not documents of title. In the USA, Section 7-402 UCC makes the issuer liable for any damage caused to holders of duplicates not so marked, whilst the duplicate holder has no rights in the goods. Generally, performance under one bill of lading renders the others void (*cf* Article 8.413 Dutch CC).

loading. If in a Fob sale payment against documents is agreed, it is indeed assumed that title transfer is always delayed by common agreement of the parties under Articles 1583 *io* 1138 Cc and it is then thought that the transfer of title in the goods is effected only through the delivery of the bill of lading, which may in that case more properly be considered a document of title.[276]

Even under the Cif term, title transfer is in France normally still considered to take place at the moment of loading, at least between the original seller and buyer, if the sale is made at that moment. It is further postponed, however, if individualisation of the goods can only take place later or when payment against documents is agreed, when the accent is again on the delivery of the bill of lading as '*titre représentatif des marchandise*'.[277] It shows that as in England, the emphasis is in France in truth on the will or intention of the parties and the nature of the bill of lading as a negotiable document of title depends on it. It even means that in the case of a reservation of title by the seller not marked on the bill of lading, the bill may not acquire any proprietary effect at all. Upon default, the title is deemed to have remained with the seller and the bill of lading in the hands of the buyer may be null and void, at least in its proprietary aspects.[278] The key is whether this would also be so in respect of third parties who had acquired the bill upon negotiation and were *bona fide*, or whether for them it would depend on them also gaining actual possession of the goods, thus receiving title only as at that moment. It seems to follow but this remains unclear under French law.

2.1.5   Bills of Lading as Quasi-Negotiable Instruments in the UK; The Situation in the USA

In English law, the tenuous nature of the bill of lading as document of title is also obvious, as in that country title normally also transfers upon the signing of the sale agreement. But it can be postponed and in England, at least in Fob sales, title is supposed to have been agreed to pass at the ship's rail only. In a Cif sale, title probably only passes upon the tendering of the documents by the seller. Any later issuing of a bill of lading does not affect the title of the buyer if becoming title holder immediately under the sales contract, not even for a *bona fide* subsequent holder of the bill. The buyer is in that case the owner notwithstanding the existence of the bill of lading which does not then fulfil a function in the context of the transfer of title, even though its handing over may complete the delivery by providing access to the goods as a matter of performance under the contract. Other prior rights in the goods, like security interests, are equally not affected by the later issue of a bill of lading concerning these goods or even by its negotiation to a *bona fide* successor holder of the bill.

As in France, a particular problem presents itself in England when buyer and seller agree that ownership passes upon conclusion of the contract, but a bill of lading is issued later and payment is agreed to be against this document. Unlike in France, in England it is assumed in such cases that, since the bill of lading clearly was not intended to have a function in transferring the ownership in the underlying assets, ownership is not affected by it and is firmly established in the buyer. As the goods may not be physically delivered to the buyer without him presenting the bill of lading, there results only some kind of indirect

---

[276] See Lamy/Brunat, n 271 *supra*.
[277] See *ibid*, No 276.
[278] See Tribunal de Commerce de Nanterre, 31 Oct 1990, Bull des Transports et de la Logistique, 136 (1991).

retention right for the seller and his instructed bank, although the position of the buyer as title holder is all the stronger if somehow he obtains the goods from the carrier without the bill of lading: see for English case law the text below. This problem does not as easily arise for the bank in countries like Germany and the Netherlands, where both title and possession are being withheld until the buyer acquires the bill of lading, so that it is easier for the seller to negotiate the bill with the bank. In the USA where state law concerning bills of lading was completely revamped by statute, Section 2-401 UCC converts this type of retention into a security interest. English case law goes here in a similar direction.[279]

Thus under English law, the nature of the bill of lading as a negotiable document depends primarily on the underlying *intent* of the parties and the bill's status as document of title cannot generally be presumed.[280] This is not limited to bills of lading issued in the context of Cif sales only. The bill has in any event no function *per se* in the transfer of title and is mainly an instrument in terms of securing performance under the sales contract by giving the buyer access to the goods. In England, the holder of a bill of lading is also not considered free of equities which means that he cannot acquire better title than his predecessors, except where so provided under statute as was done in a limited way in Section 47(2) of the Sale of Goods Act 1979. Also its negotiability, if intended, must be practically possible, as demonstrated by the requirement that the assets it represents have been sufficiently set aside, *cf* Section 16 of the Sale of Goods Act 1979 and are not comingled (although in some other countries co-ownership may result). As a consequence, the bill of lading is often qualified in the UK as no more than a quasi-negotiable instrument and its status as a document of title should not be presumed in an Fob sale. Even in a Cif sale, it is clearly rebuttable.

In line with common law practice, the UCC in the USA explicitly recognises all legal and security interests in the goods obtained before the issue of the bill of lading including any granted by the mere operation of the contract (like a transfer of title without delivery, also possible in the USA), *cf* Section 7-503 UCC, yet it accepts the nature of the bill of lading as a document of title in respect of the underlying goods (if not fungible), but only upon its negotiation and thus not for the first holder (the shipper or his principal): Section 7-502(1) UCC. The more ready acceptance of bills of lading as documents of title may be connected with the fact that delivery is the normal moment of title transfer in the sale of goods in the USA except where parties agreed otherwise (see Section 2-401 UCC). The subsequent holder has a strong position, apparently even if the goods have been surrendered by the carrier to *bona fide* purchasers for value (who are as a general rule less protected under common law: see also Section 1.5.8 above) and whether or not the bill of lading was intended to be negotiated (except where marked as non-negotiable). Also serious defects in the chain of holders, even theft, fraud or other forms of misrepresentation, do not impair the rights of the present holder of the document, Section 7-502(2), provided he is *bona fide* and paid good value, Section 7-501 UCC, but always subject to the rights of others in the goods dating from before the first negotiation.

The situation in the USA is more complicated, however, as there is also a set of federal laws concerning bills of lading. It equally abandoned the English approach by means of the Pomerene Act of 1916 (as amended) which supplements the earlier Harter Act of 1893, which was more hesitant in defining the status of the bill. The 1916 Act applies

[279] *Cf The Parchim* [1918] AC 157.
[280] See also Carver, *Carriage by Sea* (13th edn, 1982), 1113, even though it may be clearly expressed in negotiable terms through the use of the term 'bearer' or 'order': see *Henderson v Comptoir d' Escompte de Paris*, LR 5PC 253 (1873).

(see 49 USCS Section 80102) when the bill is issued for transportation between the various states of the USA, to foreign countries or in the US territories and the District of Columbia. Federal law is therefore probably of greater importance in this area than the UCC which is pure state law applying to movement within a state only. Under Federal law, the bill is considered negotiable if made out to order and represents the title to the goods, see Section 80105(a)(1)(A), and (b). It operates as such for any holder who negotiated the bill in good faith and for value, but the proprietary rights to the goods the bill represents are always subject to the earlier rights of third parties obtained before the first negotiation. Here the general common law approach is followed under which *bona fide* purchasers are not protected (except where there is statutory law to the effect).

2.1.6 Consequences of the Different Attitudes to Documents of Title when Goods are Transferred to Transferees Other than through a Transfer of the Bill of Lading

In the German and Dutch systems a buyer without the bill of lading (pending payment) is in a vulnerable position. Any holder of the bill including the original seller may transfer or negotiate the bill to others, who, if *bona fide*, acquire proprietary rights in the underlying assets. This may even happen if the goods are constructively delivered to the buyer before a bill of lading is issued. However, if the buyer under these circumstances somehow manages to appropriate the goods and takes physical possession upon their arrival (which is not uncommon), his position may be enhanced even if he is aware of the bill of lading. The seller and his bank holding the bill for payment may then find their protection endangered, all the more so if the bill has not been negotiated at all.

The problem also exists in England and was identified early. Except in a Cif sale, the bill of lading has no *prima facie* title function but only plays a role in terms of (constructive) possession providing access to the goods as part of the seller' performance under the contract of sale (unless otherwise agreed). Indeed in *Bristol and West of England Bank v Midland Railway Company*,[281] goods were delivered by the carrier to the buyer before the bill of lading had been negotiated by the seller to his bank, which, upon receipt of the bill, found itself only left with a claim for damages against the carrier.

If a bill of lading has been negotiated to a third party including a bank or a pledgee, however, the original buyer of the goods upon receipt of them is unlikely to be so protected, if he is *aware* of the existence of the bill. At least in the Dutch and German systems, he would not receive title under the circumstances. If not so aware, protection could still result for the buyer in a situation in which the seller is obliged to deliver the goods to him at his place of business and uses a carrier that issues a bill of lading to the seller *without* the buyer's knowledge. If this carrier, aware of the contractual obligations of the seller, hands the goods over to the *bona fide* buyer without the bill of lading, the latter will be protected. In the English and French systems under which title is normally transferred upon conclusion of the sales agreement or in a Cif sale at the latest upon the tendering of the documents to the buyer (unless payment is against documents only, when it will be at that moment), the acquisition of possession of the goods under these circumstance is more generally likely to fully protect the buyer even regardless of his *bona fides*.

Another way of approaching this situation, more particularly so in England, is to say that in cases where a buyer is unaware of the shipping arrangement and receives the goods without knowledge of the existence of the bill of lading, the *intention* of the seller/shipper

---

[281] [1891] 2 QB 653. It was followed by a long line of cases, *cf* lastly *The Future Express* [1992] 2 Lloyd's Rep 79.

and carrier must have been that the bill of lading was no more than a receipt and not a document of title in the first place, even if expressed in such way as to make it negotiable. If the seller in possession of the bill nevertheless negotiated this bill of lading, the subsequent rightful holder of the bill would have no rights in the assets if transferred to the original buyer, although he would of course still have a personal action for damages against the original seller in respect of a double sale or wrongful conversion of possession and possibly against the carrier for having released the goods without the holder's authorisation as long as the carrier knew of any legitimate interest of the original seller/shipper that he should not do so. A similar system appears to prevail in France. The presumption of the bill being a document of title generally renders the intention irrelevant, however, in systems like that of the new Dutch Civil Code which also protects the *bona fide* holder of the bill against any further interests being created in the underlying assets by others, at least as long as they know of the existence of the bill of lading.[282]

2.1.7 The Transfer of Risk

The transfer of risk in the underlying assets is not related to the title transfer and therefore also not to the handing over of the bill of lading to the buyer. Under modern law, the risk is normally associated with the physical possession of the assets: see chapter II, section 2.1.9. More old-fashioned approaches, which still associate the risk with ownership, like French law, pass the risk with the title transfer, in which connection the status of the bill of lading as negotiable document of title may also be of importance.[283] The passing of the risk may be determined freely by the parties to the sales contract, and trade terms are likely to do so in which connection the Fob and Cif terms refer to a special risk distribution under which the risk passes upon loading regardless of the holdership of the bill. This is confirmed in the Incoterms: see chapter II, section 2.3.10.

2.1.8 The Named Bill of Lading and Sea-way Bills

There is no doubt that the named bill of lading (or straight bill of lading under the 1916 Pomerene Act in the US) in which the person entitled to the goods is specifically mentioned, can present problems as regards entitlement to the asset under it. It is not necessarily so that the person named in the bill has the exclusive rights to the assets, for example a bank may be named in the bill of lading (as consignee) under a letter of credit but it may still be no more than an agent, and upon reimbursement by the buyer it is in any event the latter who is entitled to the bill and to the goods. The bank would naturally be required to make the necessary arrangements. This could not be endorsement as these named bills are not truly endorsable (they are not to order). An assignment would therefore be the proper way of transferring the bank's rights under the bill. However, short of it, the buyer is not

---

[282] Thus in Germany and the Netherlands also the carrier or any other handling agent, naturally aware of the existence of the bill of lading, cannot claim a pledge or other contractually created security rights or lien in the assets they hold, not even under the contract of affreightment or storage, although commonly included in their standard conditions, e.g. in order to recover their costs by priority (although they may still benefit from statutory liens or priviliges, *cf* explicitly Sections 7-307/8 UCC in the USA for the carrier), because they cannot legitimately claim to have become the holder of the goods in their own right (they hold for the holder of the bill), without also obtaining or having retained at the same time the bill of lading (unless the bill of lading itself states on the pledge facility), *except* again, it seems, if the bill has not yet been negotiated by the original holder (a distinction implicit in the Netherlands, *cf* HR, 26 Nov 1993 [1993] RvdW 15.108). In countries like England, it follows from the fact that the bill of lading was never meant to be more than a receipt, except in cif sales, when, however, prior claims to the assets still survive.
[283] See Cour d'Appel Aix en Provence, 24 Oct 1980, Bull de Transports, No 186 (1980).

without proprietary rights, even without possession of the document, which has no proper document of title status. It means that the transportation contract is more likely to indicate who is entitled to receive the goods whilst the entitlement to them may also be proven in other ways. In any event, it would appear that any collection of the assets by the bank is in these circumstances only done as agent for the buyer and that the buyer is the rightful owner of the assets even if the agency remains undisclosed.

The named bill of lading is now often considered a sea-way bill. This is a document in principle in the nature of a receipt only and not a negotiable document of title. This is by implication now even statutory law in the US and the UK. It follows that there is no negotiability and that third parties obtaining the bill from the bank are not protected. It need not be presented to collect the assets. However, in countries where the named bill is not so 'degraded', its status remains ambivalent and it may still be necessary in order to claim the goods. This may be very inconvenient if it does not arrive on time or is still with the banks for payment under a letter of credit. That may also happen with ordinary bills of lading and can be a real problem, but they at least have the balancing advantage of being documents of title.

If a named bill is made out to the buyer, the bank holding it under a retention right pending reimbursement is in a weak position. It cannot dispose of the bill in an execution sale, not even in countries that allow it under a retention right, as the buyer (or its order) is marked as the rightful owner of the goods and is certainly no agent for the bank. This may also be a problem if the bill of lading is issued to order. There may, however, be specific statutory provisions to the contrary, see in this respect eg Section 9-601(a) (9-501(1) old) UCC in the US which in the case of an execution sale of documents of title allows either the document or the underlying goods to be reached in an execution sale.

The precise status of sea-way bills is in many countries still unclear except that (unless otherwise intended) it is not a document of title. The Comite Maritime International (CMI) issued in 1990 Uniform Rules for Sea-way Bills. Under them, only the sender of the goods may give instructions concerning them and the goods must be delivered to the addressee assuming reasonable identification, but both have a claim to them. As for the liability for the transportation, the rules are the same as if the sea-way bill were a bill of lading. The sea-way bill is furthermore assumed to describe the goods adequately and no proof to the contrary may be presented against the addressee who relies on the description in good faith. Here again there is a parallel with the rules for bills of lading. The way-bill is normally used in transportation to subsidiary companies within the same group or wherever the goods are not likely to be sold to others whilst being transported or when documents are not required in the payment circuit.

2.1.9   *Private International Law Aspects of Bills of Lading*

It may be of some interest to consider the private international law complication resulting from different attitudes concerning the status of the bill of lading as document of title and possessory instrument (or mere receipt). Is (a) the law of the place where the goods are claimed applicable or (b) perhaps the law of the underlying contractual transportation agreement or (c) the law applicable to the bill itself even if this law is chosen by the parties? (d) Could it be the law of the place where the bill of lading was issued or is held?

If it is the first, then it is likely that the nature of the bill changes and is adjusted depending on the location of the underlying goods, even if acquired rights are given some protection in principle, as in the case of the recognition and execution of foreign security rights in movables: see section 1.8.2 above. If it is the second or third, then it is conceivable that proprietary issues are decided by the parties' mere choice, not on the whole believed desirable or even possible in proprietary matters which by their very nature affect third parties. If it is the last, then foreign proprietary rules especially in respect of *bona fide* holders of the bill or of the assets could prevail at the final delivery point of the goods against the notion of the *lex situs*. In the Netherlands under the law of 18 March 1993, the liability of the carrier under the bill of lading is governed by the law of the place of discharge (Article 5).

If the bill of lading is considered a fully negotiable document of title subject to the law of its own location from time to time (*situs*), at least in the aspects of its negotiability, transfer and the validity of the title in the bill itself,[284] there still remains a problem in the relationship to the underlying assets. The location of the bill will in the case of presentation coincide with the place of the location of the goods upon unloading, so that there is only one *lex situs* in respect of both at that moment. It presents a clean solution, although in other situations the law of the location of the bill may profoundly affect the rights that can be exercised under the bill, for example if a bill conceived as a negotiable document of title in the place of issue is presented in England, the parties' intent may become relevant and affect any negotiation, or when a bill intended to be merely a receipt in England is subsequently negotiated and presented in another country where it may be a *prima facie* document of title.

The place of issue of the bill of lading will normally be the place of loading of the goods, although this function may now be centralised at the headquarters of shipping companies. If not, the law of the place of loading may be considered relevant, at least in respect of the continued capacity of the original seller/shipper to engage in further sales of the goods after any negotiation of the bill. In this respect, the law applicable to the first negotiation could also have relevance, again often thought to be the law of the location (for the time being) of the bill. As a minimum, it appears to be necessary for a bill in order to be given a fully negotiable and document of title status in another country to be at least *created* with such status at the place of its issue. If not, it would at best be a question of discretion of the recognising courts in the country of unloading (and of the bill if presented upon that occasion) to what extent its negotiability is accepted, quite apart from the common question of how it could be fitted in the proprietary system of the recognising country as document of title and affect the title in the underlying assets in competition with the proprietary rights of any other claimants in these goods. This process of recognition and adjustment seems similar to the one more commonly encountered in the recognition of foreign proprietary rights: see section 1.8.2 above.

2.1.10   Lex Mercatoria *and Uniform Treaty Law Concerning Bills of Lading*

Finally, it is possible to treat the bill of lading as what it originally was: a typical transnational document of title that was derived from the law merchant and substantially operates under its own principles and rules supplemented by treaty law. This is likely to be the more productive direction of modern research.

Whilst uniform treaty law has been produced in this area, this is far more the case in the transportation aspects of the bill of lading than on its status as a document of title. This

---

[284] See for the attitude in connection with bills of exchange, *Dicey and Morris on the Conflict of Laws*, (13th edn, 2000), 1432. Authority is scarce on the subject of the law applicable to documents of title *cf.* the single reference to bills of lading in *Dicey and Morris*, 1433: see, however, also Ehrenzweig, *Private International Law* (1974), 226 and E Rabel, *The Conflict of Laws* (2nd edn) 280*ff.*

status is therefore principally to be determined on the basis of the intrinsic purpose and logic of these documents themselves therefore on the basis of established practice subject to any requirements of the fundamental legal principles as *ius cogens* and further to be interpreted and supplemented on the basis of the principles common to domestic legislation in this area and only ultimately on the basis of the application of a national law if deemed applicable on the basis of the prevailing principles of private international law. This approach conforms to the hierarchy of norms which may be seen as the essence of the modern *lex mercatoria*: see more in particular chapter I, section 3.2.2. It is likely to emphasise their status of document of title at the expense of parties' intent.

As far as treaty law in the transportation aspects is concerned, in this connection the Hague, Hague-Visby and Hamburg Rules are relevant. The need for uniform law appeared first after World War I when the freedom of the parties to agree the transportation conditions left the carriers in practice great bargaining power to impose their conditions whilst there was often a great lack of clarity even on the transportation terms as printed on the bill of lading. In the USA, the federal Harter Act of 1893 had first achieved here some order and provided a mandatory infrastructure for the carriage of goods by sea (between different states of the USA) and achieved here a compromise between the conflicting interests of shippers and carriers. The USA pursued this policy internationally.

The International Law Association (ILA), which is a voluntary body of legal practitioners existing since 1873, took the initiative internationally. It led to the Hague Rules accepted by the ILA in 1921 in the Hague, amended and translated into French in 1922. They were the subject of a diplomatic conference in Brussels in 1923 leading to the Brussels Convention incorporating these Hague Rules in 1924. Under it, mandatory rules especially in the area of carrier liability were agreed for the period of the carriage of the goods (not for their handling by the carrier in the port of loading or discharge). It thus remained a very partial codification and only unified rules for bills of lading with regard to damage occurring between the time of loading and discharge (to hull cargo other than life animals), see Rule I(b)(c) and (e), whilst Rule III(8) stressed the mandatory character of the rules if embodying a prohibition or restriction rule. Choice of law or forum selection clauses likely to result in a limitation of the liability as determined by the Rules are now mostly ignored, at least by *fora* in the Contracting States, which, as in the case of the Netherlands, may sometimes assume jurisdiction themselves on the single ground that the cargo is destined for ports within their jurisdiction.

The Brussels Convention left Contracting States the choice of ratifying the Convention or incorporating its rules in national law, which incorporation took place in some countries in various succeeding steps (as in the Netherlands where this process was completed only in the 1950s). In the UK, the Carriage of Goods by Sea Act (UK Cogsa) incorporating the Hague Rules was adopted as early as in 1924. The US Cogsa dates from 1936. The result was the emergence of unavoidable differences between the various countries adopting the Rules. In particular, problems continued to arise in the determination of the carriers' liability and the validity of negligence clauses in bills of lading. An attempt at greater uniformity was made through amendments resulting in the Hague-Visby Rules agreed in Visby in 1967 upon the initiative of the Comité Maritime International (CMI), adopted by a diplomatic conference in Brussels in 1968, the relevant Protocol becoming effective in 1977. The Hague-Visby Rules notably increased the limits of the liability of the carrier. Since 1979 these limits are expressed in special drawing rights (SDRs) of the International Monetary Fund (IMF).

In the meantime, the character of the Hague and especially Hague-Visby Rules as customary law applicable regardless of their ratification and/or incorporation into local law even as mandatory rules was advocated.[285] They may also apply to transportation arrangements other than under bills of lading, like those under sea waybills or charterparties (if not already clarified under incorporation statutes).

The Hague-Visby Rules have been widely adopted: see for the UK the Cogsa 1971 replaced in 1992, for France a law of 1977, for the Netherlands a law of 1982. The US and Germany remain party to the old Hague Rules and have so far signed but not ratified the Hague-Visby Rules. Several countries like France extended the coverage to waybills. Pressure from less developed countries for greater carrier liability, especially in respect of servants and agents, also during handling in the port of loading and discharge and therefore not only during the carriage of the goods, led to the Hamburg Rules. They are an Uncitral compilation adopted at the diplomatic Conference in Hamburg in 1978 and became effective in 1992. They replaced the risk allocation of the Hague-Visby Rules in favour of a rebuttable presumption of liability of the carrier, which proved controversial. As a consequence, the Hamburg Rules have been ratified by only a number of smaller countries, amongst which is Austria. The USA and France signed but have not so far ratified them. Some East European and African countries have ratified without apparently repealing The Hague or Hague-Visby Rules to which they had become a party. It may give rise to conflicts.

As a consequence of all these developments, various countries may now apply the Hague Rules, Hague-Visby Rules, Hamburg Rules or their own rules (if not incorporating any of these rules). The Hague Rules are applicable to contracts of carriage covered by a bill of lading or any similar document of title in so far as such document relates to the carriage of goods by sea (Rule I(b)), assuming that the law of a Contracting State applies to the bill of lading. They do not apply to carriage covered by sea waybills or a charterparty under which no such document is issued (although some countries did extend their application to sea waybills). As just mentioned, the Hague Rules put emphasis on the transportation aspect and not on the documentary aspect of the bill. The bill of lading is in truth *prima facie* seen as only proof of receipt of the goods (see Rule III(4)) and there is notably no definition of the bill of lading itself.

According to Rule X, the Hague-Visby Rules apply to all carriage of goods by sea under a bill of lading (a) issued in a Contracting State, (b) concerning carriage from a port of loading in a Contracting State regardless of any other choice of law clause, and (c) in which a choice of law is made in favour of the law of a Contracting State. They continue to view the bill of lading as *prima facie* evidence of the receipt of the goods but no longer allow proof to the contrary upon negotiation (Rule III(4)). The Hamburg Rules define the bill of lading as a document of title if expressed as a negotiable instrument (Article 1(7)) and also apply to incoming carriage of goods by sea under a bill of lading.

It may thus be seen that the various Rules are not directly concerned with the bill of lading as negotiable document of title. The Hague-Visby Rules are the least controversial and therefore probably the best standard. They do not clearly state that the bill must be in writing or manually signed. The carrier must, however, issue a bill of lading upon the demand of the shipper, in which connection reference is made to documents and to information that must be supplied thereon: Rules III(3), V, VI, and X. Most incorporation laws require a document and in most countries there must be a hand-written signature.[286] The bill

---

[285] See WE Haak, 'Internationalism above Freedom of Contract' in *Essays on International and Comparative Law in Honour of Judge Erades* (The Hague, 1983), 69. See for the similar public order characterisation of the Hague-Visby Rules, W Tetley, *Marine Cargo Claims* (Montreal, 3rd ed. 1988), 944.

[286] See also AN Yiannopulos, 'Ocean Bills of Lading: Traditional Forms, Substitutes, and EDI Systems', *General Report XIVth International Congress of Comparative Law* (The Hague/London/Boston, 1995), 3.

of lading must also contain leading marks to identify the goods (see Rule III(3) of the Hague Rules).

2.2   Negotiable Instruments

2.2.1   *Bills of Exchange*

The bill of exchange or draft was used in the large European fairs as early as the fourteenth century AD to avoid the need for traders at these fairs to carry large amounts of cash (gold and silver). The Lombard banker present at these fairs would offer these traders the facility of receiving in their residence the cash they collected at these fairs through the banking system of those times. To this end, the Lombard banker would take the trader's cash and instruct its correspondent in the residence of the trader to make the necessary payment, and this instruction would be given to the trader who would present it to the correspondent bank in his own town upon his return. It became naturally also possible for buyers at these fairs to draw cash from the correspondents of their home banks present at the fairs, to which end they would carry an instruction of their own banks. The bankers operated amongst themselves a clearing system to reduce their own subsequent needs for sending cash to other places.

The bank instructions used in this connection were subsequently made negotiable and developed into the modern bill of exchange. The bills of exchange as negotiable instruments as we know them today date more properly from the end of the eighteenth century, when, in the earlier stages of the industrial revolution, trading and shipping of goods became more frequent and new payment methods had to be designed. In this context, the old drafts were re-fashioned to suit the new needs. Like the bills of lading, they then acquired their present legal form.[287]

The modern bill of exchange in its simplest form is no more than an *irrevocable instruction* (in writing) by a creditor to his debtor to pay his debt on the appointed date to the bearer of the bill or the person indicated by the creditor (who may be the creditor himself) on the bill or to that person's order. Normally the instruction is given by a seller (the *drawer*) to his buyer (the *drawee*) ordering him to pay whatever he owes the drawer to a third person/beneficiary (the *payee*). The reason for this payment to a third party will often be that the drawer[288] owes the payee something himself. It is then an alternative way of paying the payee and the bill of exchange operates in that case much like an assignment. The difference is that the drawer and the drawee upon acceptance of the draft lose any defences derived from their underlying relationship in respect of any subsequent holder of the bill. The survival of the defences against an assignor which may also be levelled against an assignee were identified in section 1.7.3 above as a major problem in assignments and a source of uncertainty to any assignee. These problems do not arise in respect of a payee who has accepted a bill of exchange once it is negotiated and, it was submitted, should arise less and less also in respect of receivables which are increasingly treated like instruments. Industry practice is likely to evolve in that way.

---

[287] In England, the modern development of the bill of exchange is associated with the name of Lord Mansfield: see also G Gilmore, 'Formalism and the Law of Negotiable Instruments', 13 *Creighton LR* 441, 446–50 (1979). It was a product of the law merchant but became incorporated into the common law, which in turn much affected its further development: see also chapter I, s 1.1.1 and JS Rogers, *The Early History of the Law of Bills and Notes* (Cambridge University Press, Cambridge, 1995).
[288] See for competing assignments s 2.2.8 *infra*.

A bill of exchange must be in *writing*, must be for a *sum certain* and payable on a *specific payment date*. There is no prescribed form or type of paper that must be used, and the instruction may be written on any material and in any manner as long as it is duly signed by the drawer. There must be a sum certain but this may include a specified interest rate (unless it is a floating rate).[289] The payment cannot be conditional or the sum payable otherwise vague. The bill of exchange must instruct the drawee to make immediate payment or payment at a later date. In the case of an instruction to make an immediate payment, we speak of a *sight draft or sight bill* which the drawee either refuses or pays upon presentation. In the case of a payment at a later date, we speak of a *time or term draft or bill* which the drawee either accepts or ignores upon presentation. The due date may be specified on the draft or may be expressed in a number of days after sight (that is after presentation) or after the date the bill of exchange was drawn.

The basic principle of a bill of exchange is that nobody is bound under it except those who have signed the bill itself — thus the drawer is always liable, a drawee if he has accepted the bill by putting his signature on it, and the payee only upon endorsement, which means the sale of the bill to someone else, as are all other endorsers. Anyone else who signed the bill will be considered to have done so as guarantor (or for aval in civil law terms).

Acceptance by the drawee is crucial but only for *time* bills (it is neither relevant nor possible for sight bills). Without it, a time bill has no value. Acceptance does *not* mean payment, but rather the commitment of the drawee to pay on the due date, of which his signature on the draft is his acknowledgement. An accepted time draft thus signifies not merely a special liability of the debtor upon negotiation of the instrument but it also signifies a benefit in terms of credit for the drawee. It means that during the period of the bill the seller cannot invoke default remedies like a reservation of title or other security given to protect the underlying indebtedness of the drawee. This is not novation, merely a postponement of payment probably already agreed in the sale contract and is otherwise an amendment thereto. The main significance of a time draft is, however, that it may be discounted with a bank for immediate payment, as already mentioned above. This implies a discount related to the prevailing interest rate to maturity taking into account also the creditworthiness of the drawee as ultimate debtor under a bill of exhange. As we saw, a sight draft cannot be accepted. It is either immediately paid or refused upon presentation. It can therefore not be discounted either. Technically, it may still be negotiated — that is, sold to whoever wants to buy it so that there may also be holders (in due course) of sight drafts, but in view of the lack of acceptance this is rare. The main relevance of sight drafts is in the order to pay a third party immediately, implying the drawee's discharge if he obeys the order and collects the sight draft as a result. If made out to the order of the drawer (as payee), possession of a sight draft gives the paying drawee written proof of his payment and release *vis-à-vis* his creditor/drawer as he becomes the rightful holder of the draft upon payment.

We see here a doubling of functions. This is common in bills of exchange. Thus in a *time* draft the drawer may be the payee at the same time (when the bill of exchange is to the own order or in German a *frassiert-eigener Wechsel*). This makes sense if the agreed payment takes place only later and the drawer wants a facility to receive immediate payment from a bank through discounting. This is a method of raising cash on bills of exchange that mature later. Banks will provide this facility at a discount. If the time draft is to bearer, it usually means that the drawer has the bill of exchange. He is then in the same position as if the draft had been to the own order.

[289] Except in Germany, see Section 5 of the *WechselGesetz* [Bill of Exchange Act] 1933.

The drawee and the payee of a time draft may also be the same. It means that the drawee is instructed by the drawer to pay to himself (or order) on the payment date. This makes sense if the drawer owes the drawee money at some date earlier than the bill's maturity and wants to give the drawee a facility to raise cash by discounting the bill upon his own acceptance. It is also possible that the payee is not the drawer/seller himself but rather his bank, which in this case is not a true third party but will collect as agent on the drawer's behalf in this manner. The drawer may also be the same as the drawee. This means that a drawer has drawn the bill of exchange on himself in favour of a payee. The draft is then treated as a promissory note (assuming the drawer had accepted the bill of exchange drawn on himself at the same time, therefore as a promise to pay the payee a sum certain upon demand or at a certain date).[290]

It may, however, also happen that a head office draws a draft on an establishment or branch of the company elsewhere, in which case it is less likely that a mere promissory note results. For purposes of the bill of exchange, the establishment may here be assumed to have sufficient independence, even though not itself a legal person separate from the company. The result is that the drawer and drawee are not the same. The payee is often, however, a third party or his order. The bill of exchange will be given to him and he will be the one to cash it by presenting it to the drawee on the indicated date as the true debtor under the bill. He may discount it earlier with a bank.

The terms 'to order' or 'to bearer' were used above. This is standard language in bills of exchange (as it is in documents of title) and denotes negotiability of the paper. It means that if proper language is used and the instrument is to a named payee or his order or to bearer, it will be negotiable and can be transferred by endorsement and delivery if to order, or by delivery only if the bill was to bearer. The result is that bills of exchange become *negotiable* instruments. It is true that in civil law the bill of exchange to bearer is discouraged, unlike in common law. Under the Geneva Conventions of 1930, see section 2.2.10 below, the bill of exchange to bearer is even considered void, but a similar result is achieved when the drawer draws a bill of exchange to his own order (making himself the payee), whilst endorsing the bill in blank. The pure bearer bill is considered negotiated when in third party hands. This is relevant for its status as an abstract obligation: see section 2.2.4 below.

Only the holder of the bill of exchange may request payment. When the holder is in good faith, he is called a holder *in due course* and may have a better right to ask payment than his predecessor as he takes free and clear of earlier defects in the chain of transfers of the document (but not of any in the transfer to himself). As such he may demand payment from anyone who has signed the bill, except from a drawer or any endorser who has put 'without recourse' next to his signature, or from any signatory indicating that he is signing only as agent or representative of others. Pure guarantors or avalists might also have a special status in this respect and might only be liable after other signatories are in default of their payment obligations (in which case the guarantee is only a secondary obligation).

As just mentioned, the holder in due course may ignore defences arising from irregularities earlier in the chain of transfers but also in the creation of the instrument unless apparent from its face. In demanding payment from the original payee, the drawer or the drawee, the holder in due course may thus also ignore all defences derived from the underlying relationships between drawer and drawee or drawer and payee. If any earlier endorser is asked to pay, he has recourse against any signatory before him (except a drawer or any endorser without recourse) but not after, so that ultimately the drawer and any drawee

---

[290] See also I Ronse, *Wissel en Orderbriefje* (1972), no. 144, 55.

who accepted the bill of exchange are liable under it *vis-à-vis* the payee and all his successors in interest.

2.2.2 Acceptance and Discounting of Time Drafts

The practical importance of bills of exchange is mainly in the possibility of discounting accepted time bills or drafts. There is on the whole no obligation for the drawee to accept a bill of exchange and thereby incur greater liability if the bill is discounted or otherwise negotiated to third party holders when he loses the defences he may have had against his creditor/drawer. However, in some countries there is a duty to accept, notably in France and the Netherlands. It has been a traditional feature of the Dutch law of bills of exchange in this connection that they must be accepted by the drawee if the seller/drawer has fully performed his obligations under the contract. That means in the case of a sale upon delivery of the goods: see Article 127 of the Dutch Commercial Code. A seller who remains unpaid at that moment may therefore draw a time draft on the buyer for payment to the payee (or himself) on the payment date, which bill of exchange the buyer must accept. It is nevertheless an onerous legal act on the buyer's part and the acceptance duty must be considered outdated and is certainly not required by the Geneva Conventions of 1930: see section 2.2.10 below. Belgium deleted the acceptance obligation from its own law (Article 8 of the Bill of Exchange Law of 1872 which had been thought to reflect comercial custom) in 1930 on the occasion of the incorparation of the Geneva Conventions into Belgian law. Of course, it is always possible that the sale agreement itself imposes a duty on the buyer to accept the bill of exchange drawn on him in respect of the sale price, but under Dutch law acceptance concerns a statutory right of the drawer under the stated circumstances. It does not, however, itself effect acceptance, and even a judgment ordering acceptance cannot take its place if the debtor remains unwilling (as it did at one time in Belgium). Specific performance action would be required.

In France, the acceptance duty dates only from 1938 (Decree of 2 May): see Article 124 of the French Commercial Code. The Cour de Cassation had earlier rejected the obligation,[291] but a 1938 amendment includes it to protect sales credit. As a sanction, a buyer refusing to accept loses his sales credit and the price becomes immediately due. The usefulness of the acceptance obligation is debated in France as the acceptance is required only upon full compliance by the seller and there may always be some doubt on that point. At least it is easy for the buyer to find excuses in the quality and delivery of the goods.[292] Also in France the contract itself may impose an acceptance obligation. More intriguing is whether commercial usage may also impose a duty to accept, as was earlier the Belgian view.[293]

The drawer whilst handing a time draft to the payee (after giving notice to the drawee) guarantees acceptance (except where he indicates otherwise on the bill). He also guarantees payment by the drawee. This liability cannot be excluded under the Geneva Conventions but it can be under common law: see section 2.2.3 below. Acceptance is a condition for the discounting of bills of exchange. Banks that make a business out of the discounting of time drafts become themselves the holders of the drafts they discount and they will present them to the drawees on the appointed dates. They incur therefore the credit risk of the drawee but they have recourse against anyone who has signed the bill of exchange as all signatories (except those who sign as disclosed agents or without recourse) are assumed to have guaranteed that

---

[291] 10 Apr 1878, D.78.1.289.
[292] See also Ripert/Roblot, 2 *Droit Commercial* (16th edn, 2000), nos 1986 *et seq.*
[293] This was earlier suggested in the leading Dutch treatise of Scheltema/Wiarda, *Wissel en Cheque Recht*, 285.

the drawee will have sufficient funds on the payment date. This concerns principally the drawer and payee.

2.2.3   The Persons Liable under a Bill of Exchange: Recourse

The persons liable under a bill of exchange are in principle all those whose signatures appear on the bill. They all function as guarantors of payment *vis-à-vis* the holder. They are principally the drawer and any endorsers, except for the latter if they signed 'without recourse'. As we saw, under Article 9(2) of the Geneva Convention, the drawer may not do so, but he may under common law: see Section 16 of the English Bills of Exchange Act 1882 and Sections 3-414 and 3-415 UCC in the USA. This is likely to complicate and change the chain of recourse.

Any special guarantors or avalists (in civil law terminology) may also have a lesser guarantee obligation. In some legal systems, they may not be considered primary guarantors, which means that others liable under the bill of exchange must first default before the avalist may be required to pay. The aval may be limited to non-payment by certain parties. The aval is often thought to be relevant for time drafts only. It is in any event unlikely to be given without acceptance of the draft by the drawee. In English law, these special types of guarantors are usually not distinguished from endorsers, although in terms of recourse they may still come later and are as such more properly considered quasi-endorsers which requires their place in the line of endorsers to be established.[294] If the signatories are without recourse (which would make no sense in the case of an aval) any discounting bank is likely to apply an extra discount for assuming the full credit risk.

The drawee himself becomes liable on the bill only through his own signature as token of his acceptance. Without it, the draft has value to holders only as a guarantee of acceptance and payment by the drawer (without defences derived from the underlying contract giving rise to the claim) or any endorsers (provided they have not signed without recourse). It is clear that a bearer draft is from the point of view of his protection less interesting to the holder as it will have only the signature of the drawer and of the drawee in the case of accepted term drafts. An advantage for the holder of a bearer draft is, however, that he cannot and need not show a continuous line of endorsements so that it is easier for him to establish that he is the proper holder.

An endorser against whom recourse is taken does not strictly speaking become a holder in due course as a consequence of his payment. He has recourse only against his predecessors and therefore not against all signatories of the bill of exchange. The idea is that, in terms of recourse, ultimately the original payee, and thereafter the drawer in that order, are reached. The drawee who has accepted is the principal obligee (as are any avalists if primary guarantors) and can in that position always be asked to pay. He is not therefore a recourse debtor who can only be reached in the order of endorsement. If the bill of exchange is not accepted, as in the case of the sight draft, the ultimate debtor is the drawer, who may, however, still be able to solicit payment from any guarantors of the bill and from the drawee but only as debtor under the original sales contract.

The bill need not be presented on the due date but the periods thereafter during which this may still be done are likely to be limited under applicable domestic laws.

It is of interest to note that under a bill of exchange endorsers become liable by adding their signature. They thus guarantee to their successors that the drawee will have sufficient

---

[294] See about this problem which will not be discussed here any further: R Goode, *Commercial Law* (2nd edn, 1995), 551.

funds upon presentation of the bill to him. No similar guarantee structure is implied in the endorsement of bills of lading and the endorser of such bills does not therefore guarantee in any way that the goods are with the carrier and are collectable upon presentation of the bill of lading.

2.2.4   The Principle of Independence or Abstraction

The key to the understanding of the bill of exchange is that as an 'instrument' embodying a claim (a) it is upon negotiation independent of the underlying creditor/debtor relationship between the drawer and drawee, (b) it has its own manner of transfer separate from domestic laws under which the transfer is achieved through the handing over of the paper (with endorsement if to order), and (c) it also has its own way of protecting *bona fide* holders for value (or 'holders in due course'). These principles all derive in origin from the law merchant rather than from national law (which has only introduced more refinement). Any national law not accepting these principles destroys thereby the essence of the bill of exchange. The principle of independence is particularly important in this connection and serves as a major support for the negotiability of bills of exchange, which in turn implies its own mode of transfer and protection of third parties. It makes the bill of exchange (like bills of lading) a proprietary instrument that cannot be directly fitted under the general rules of property of the applicable legal system. They continue to have their own separate status everywhere.

This notion of independence, which is also called the principle of abstraction of the bill of exchange, is not relevant as between the seller (drawer) and the buyer (drawee). Thus if the former retains the bill made out to his own order or to bearer (where possible) and presents it to the drawee on the due date, the ordinary defences as between them prevail even if the drawee has accepted the bill. There is an effect in so far that the burden of proof may shift to the drawee upon acceptance, as any drawer will in the first instance sue on the bill of exchange and not on the basis of the underlying relationship. The abstraction is particularly relevant, however, for any third party holder if he acquired the bill in good faith, and thus for the holder in due course.[295] It protects against all with whom the holder did not deal. Indeed, the 1990 Comment on the UCC (at Section 3-302) explains that the holder in due course doctrine applies only in cases where more than two parties are involved. The essence is that the holder in due course does not have to suffer the consequences of a defence of the obligor on the instrument that arose from an occurrence or relationship with a third party of which he did not know.

It means that in connection with payment of the purchase price in a sale, the drawer or a drawee, whilst being asked to pay on a sight or accepted time draft by a holder in due course, cannot invoke any defences derived from the underlying agreement between seller/drawer and buyer/drawee in order to refuse payment. They cannot reclaim any (full) payment made under those circumstances either. In this connection, it should be noted that the original payee is *not* strictly speaking a holder in due course and may therefore have a weaker position, at least under English law.[296] In his presentation of the bill to the drawer he may be faced with the defences derived from his own underlying relationship with the drawer giving rise to him becoming the payee in the first place. This may not apply

---

[295] See Section 17 of the German *WechselGesetz*, Article 121 of the French Commercial Code and Section 3-305 UCC in the USA.
[296] See *RE Jones Ltd v Waring & Gillow Ltd* [1926] AC 670.

in the case of his presenting the bill of exchange to the drawee. At least in England, he may also be able to claim the status of holder in due course *vis-à-vis* the drawer if he later renegotiated the draft and became an endorsee.[297]

Thus the underlying relationships are not superseded by the issue, acceptance or endorsement of a bill of exchange. In those relationships, the bill of exchange is only a means of achieving a payment and the transfer of the proceeds, no more. There is notably no novation but only an additional set of obligations created through the issue, acceptance or endorsement of the bill of exchange itself. In Swiss law, this is expressly so stated: see Article 116(2) OR.

2.2.5   The Holder in Due Course. Personal and Real Defences. Other Types of Holders

As we saw in the previous section, the holder in due course is strongly protected but he must make sure that the bill of exchange is not overdue, incomplete or irregular on its face. It also means that a bill to order must have a continuous line of endorsements. At least in common law, the holder in due course must have acquired the bill of exchange for value and, under all legal systems, in good faith as regards any prior defects in the chain of transfers. He should not have any notice of a previous dishonour. The transfer of the bill to himself will be subject to the normal rules, defences and exceptions in terms of capacity of the parties and validity of the contract. With this proviso it is, however, possible to say that holders in due course do not derive their rights from their predecessors but rather out of the documents themselves, which is a common feature of all negotiable instruments and documents of title.

As a consequence, subsequent holders in due course need not be concerned about defects in the issue, acceptance or negotiation, lack of capacity or any nullity or illegality of transfers earlier in the chain of which they did not know. However, there may be some differences in the various national laws in the area of these so-called defences. As in bills of lading, it is not uncommon to distinguish here between *personal* and *real* defences. Personal defences are those derived from the relationship between a plaintiff and a defendant in an action concerning a bill of exchange. They only operate between parties that entered direct relationships with each other and therefore not against endorsees. Real defences are based on the nature of the bill of exchange itself and concern defects in the instrument itself. Personal defences in an action between a drawer and drawee are likely to be based on their underlying sales agreement. Between succeeding holders they are likely to be based on any defects in the negotiation or discounting of the bill.

Personal defences do not affect the status of a bill of exchange itself but affect only the current holder of the bill. They concern his status as holder in due course, therefore the requirements of that status, like proper acquisition or otherwise his *bona fides* itself, or, in respect of the immediate predecessor, they concern the circumstances under which the holder acquired the bill of exchange. As already mentioned before, between drawer and drawee their underlying relationship may equally be invoked as a defence even if the bill has been accepted. As we saw, also *vis-à-vis* the payee, the drawer may have certain defences derived from their underlying relationship which gave rise to the drawing of the bill of exchange in the payee's favour in the first place. In any event, if the bill is not accepted or is dishonoured, the original relationship is re-established and it may always be sued upon between a drawer and drawee.

---

[297] See *Jade International Steel Stahl und Eisen GmbH & Co KG v Robert Nicholas (Steels) Ltd* [1978] QB 917.

Real defences concern the bill of exchange itself and its validity and may relate to forgery of signatures, alterations to the bill, nullity or illegality of the issue of the bill or transfers, but also to lack of capacity in drawing or transferring it earlier in the chain of transfers. They thus signify an irregularity in the creation of the bill of exchange itself or a break in the chain of title transfers. It is not strictly speaking true that these occurrences are always irrelevant to the holder in due course, at least in England,[298] but they may only be invoked as a defence by parties who became signatories of the bill *prior* to the irregularity. For them the (changed) bill of exchange (for example the amount), forged later signatures, or irregular transfers are not relevant at all and they may ignore them. But later signatories are considered new drawers or endorsers of the bill and cannot deny liability *vis-à-vis* subsequent holders of the bill of exchange on the grounds of earlier invalidity, irregularities or other real defences.

Common law often makes a further distinction amongst the types of holders and, besides the holder in due course, there may also operate the notion of the normal holder as distinguished from the mere holder. It is all a question of powers and defences and they become stronger for each type, the holder in due course having the strongest position. English law distinguishes in this connection between the holder, the holder for value, and the holder in due course,[299] who each have different defences. Continental law distinguishes only between the holder and the holder in due course.

2.2.6 Cheques

Cheques are very common in common law countries, also amongst professionals. They are simply sight drafts to order, drawn on one's bank ordering it to pay to a third party (payee or his order). They may also be issued and handed to a payee in blank, creating a bearer instrument until the holder fills in his own or somebody else's name. As a sight draft, a cheque cannot be accepted by the bank and the bank either pays the third party payee (usually debiting the current account of the drawee) upon presentation of the cheque by the payee or dishonours the cheque by simply refusing to pay the payee or his order. The bank will normally dishonour the cheque if there is insufficient balance in the drawer's account unless other arrangements were made in terms of overdrafts on the account. Negotiation has a meaning only in the sense that the cheque, if not crossed (a typical English practice that requires the cheque to be paid into the payee's own bank and not to him directly or to any one else as endorsee), may be transferred by the payee or his order or otherwise by any bearer to a third party who will subsequently present the cheque for payment to the bank with recourse on his predecessors and the drawer if no payment is received in this manner.

It is particularly important in this connection that, as between the drawer and payee, the cheque creates an independent payment obligation, even if, as in the case of bills of exchange, the payee is not truly a holder in due course and the drawer therefore still retains the personal defences against the payee derived from their relationship that gave rise to the issuing of the cheque in the first place. Nevertheless, if the bank does not pay, the payee may (at his option) still sue the drawer for payment on the cheque rather than on the

---

[298] See Section 24 of the Bill of Exchange Act 1882. On the Continent, the forgery may not distract from the right of *bona fide* purchasers of the bill: see Section 7 of the German Bills of Exchange Act 1933. This is also the situation in the USA: see Section 3-404 UCC. Theft of a bearer instrument may equally be irrelevant to the holder in due course, see Article 3.86(3)(b) of the new Dutch CC.

[299] See R Goode, *Commercial Law* (2nd edn, 1995), 536.

underlying contract or relationship. This is likely to be simpler, and writing a cheque therefore implies a risk for the person doing so.

2.2.7   Modern Use of Bills of Exchange and Cheques

The bill of exchange has lost much of its attraction in modern times, particularly in countries that have an easy way of assigning receivables as security, that is particularly in countries that do not require notification as a constitutive requirement for assignments. In countries that still do, as those in the French tradition used to do, see also section 1.7.1 above, this requirement could be avoided by drawing a bill of exchange in favour of the third party. As the bill of exchange is usually presented at the place of the debtor (drawee), the attendant country and political risks attached to the transfer of the proceeds meant that, in international transactions, it was eclipsed by the letter of credit: see for these letters of credit chapter III, section 2.1.6. They are normally payable in the country of the seller. A bill of exchange may, however, still be used in that context and is then often drawn as a domestic bill on a confirming bank in the home country of the seller.

In all cases, the chief advantage of a bill, if a time draft, remains that it allows for the facility of acceptance and subsequent discounting to obtain ready cash, which latter facility is not inherent in the letter of credit facility itself. It is in a sense in factoring of receivables, but the difficulty of a bulk assignment and the possibility of defences of the debtors under these receivables make straight discounting impossible. Hence the need to make receivables themselves more abstact undertakings.

In some countries, dishonouring an accepted draft by the drawee or failing to provide recourse by the other signatories may give rise to criminal penalties and is in any event considered a grave undermining of one's own credit standing. As a consequence, drafts still have some advantages, but in international trade their overriding importance has disappeared as other payment methods have become more popular, and modern communication facilities have allowed greater informality, especially between parties who are now in closer contact and better known to each other. One may also say that the risk inherent in international trade has been substantially reduced as a consequence of the modern communication facilities and the increased possibilities of following goods and payments from afar.

On the other hand, cheques continue to have extensive use in countries like England and the USA in the consumer sphere. They have been the subject of much attention and modern legislation to protect consumers better. Also the processing of thousands of cheques on a daily basis has required legislative action to make handling easier for the banks. Much of the modern legislation concerning negotiable instruments has been in this area without affecting the fundamental principles.

2.2.8   Bills of Exchange and Competing Assignments of the Underlying Claim

The problem of competition between a bill of exchange and an assignment of the underlying claim often presents itself in the factoring of a portfolio of receivables. It raises the question of the status of any bill of exchange drawn on a debtor by his creditor in favour of a third party payee, either before or after a bulk assignment of receivables to a factor or other financier. Especially where notice of the assignment to the debtor (drawee) is not necessary under applicable law for the assignment to be valid, any later notice to the drawee with a request for payment to the assignee may conflict with the debtor/drawee's earlier duty under an accepted bill of exchange to pay the payee or any holder in due course on the payment date. May the drawee refuse any notice and payment request of the assignee under the circumstances?

In principle, he may ignore any assignment materially detrimental or burdensome to him: see section 1.7.3 above, and may, if he has already honoured the bill, be able to refuse any payment to the assignee on that ground or as a defence under his original contract with the assignor/drawer out of which the claim arose in the first place. If the drawee has not yet accepted the time draft or if a sight draft is presented after payment to the assignee, he will naturally not accept or honour when requested to do so. Where there is an acceptance duty there may be a greater problem for the drawee. The drawee if forced to pay twice will probably have recourse against the drawer, not under the bill of exchange, but rather under the original contract or perhaps as a matter of unjust enrichment of the drawer.

On the analogy of the bill of lading, in common law countries, it may be possible to say that the holder of a draft is always subject to the rights of third parties in the underlying claim, in this case the assignee, at least if the assignment was made *before* the bill of exchange was drawn and accepted. Even in civil law countries, there is here no exception to the *nemo dat* rule in the case of the transfer of receivables. Their incorporation into a negotiable instrument is not therefore likely to protect the payee and his successors against earlier rights of others. It would mean that the right of the earlier assignee is always stronger than that of the later holder in due course of the bill of exchange and that the drawee may plead that right as a defence against the holders in due course whilst paying the assignee. It does not oblige the drawee to pay the assignee unconditionally, certainly if an endorsee has already been paid, and paying the assignee will entail double payment. If he must subsequently also pay the assignee, he may be able to recover from the earlier endorsee. He would certainly be able to recover any double payment from the drawer/assignor.

As the bill of exchange is only another method of payment, it could also be said that any later assignments affect the drawee equally, even if holders in due course may then be better protected. It means that they may be able to keep their collections even if the drawee is subsequently forced to pay to the assignee also. In that case he is more likely to recover any double payment from the drawer/assignor than from the holders in due course.

2.2.9 Position of the Holder in Due Course of a Bill of Exchange Compared to the Bona Fide Holder of a Bill of Lading

Because the bill of exchange is likely to incorporate the underlying claim more fully than the bill of lading can incorporate the underlying assets, the position of the holder in due course of a draft is likely to be stronger than that of the *bona fide* holder of a bill of lading who may easily face a situation in which the goods are in the hands of a third party (like handling agents) claiming rights in respect of them without being at the same time the holder of the bill of lading.

This problem with bills of lading was discussed in section 2.1.6 above. At least in common law countries like England, but also in civil law countries like France, the absence of the need for delivery to transfer title in the underlying assets makes the holder of the bill of lading extra vulnerable to alternative alienations or the vesting of security interests of others in the underlying assets. In any event, in these countries, the status of the bill of lading as negotiable document of title depends on the intention of the parties creating the instrument, and any holder of the document takes subject to that intent. This is less of a risk in countries like Germany and the Netherlands requiring delivery for title transfer, and the handing over of the documents will always be a good substitute regardless of intent, even if one cannot avoid the underlying assets still leading an independent life.

This is here also less of a danger in the case of bills of exchange which more truly incorporate the underlying asset and have their own more exclusive method of transfer and protection, also in common law,[300] although, as we saw in section 2.2.5 above, the defences of earlier endorsers cannot always be ignored by the holder in due course of a bill of exchange either, especially if derived from the face of the bill. As we saw in the previous section, bills of exchange also remain subject to the prior rights of others in the underlying claim. That is also true for bills of lading in common law countries. In countries like Germany and the Netherlands, on the other hand, the creation and negotiation of a document of title are likely to erase all earlier proprietary rights in the underlying assets in respect of *bona fide* holders of the document.

2.2.10 *Foreign Bills of Exchange: Private International Law Aspects*

Foreign bills of exchange have under domestic legislation sometimes a somewhat different status, as for example under the English Bills of Exchange Act 1882 (Section 4). They are in English law defined as bills of exchange drawn by non-residents or drawn on a person resident abroad *and* payable abroad, which normally (but not necessarily) follows. The main difference is that foreign bills of exchange, as distinguished from inland bills of exchange, must be formally protested upon dishonour by non-acceptance or non-payment (Section 5). It means that dishonour must not only be notified to the drawer and each endorser but must also be established formally by a notarial deed. This protest, which will be marked by the notary on the bill of exchange, is not necessary in England (unlike in other countries) for inland bills.

Also the interpretation of the endorsement abroad of a bill governed by English law is different (Section 72(2)). The Act further contains in Section 72 some detailed conflict of law rules dealing with validity, interpretation, the preconditions for the right to recourse, the effect of the bill of exchange, and discharge.[301]

It is quite clear that bills of exchange may be drawn by a seller in one country on a buyer in another, who is likely to accept the bill in his own country. This bill may be in favour of and handed to a payee in a third country and may be payable in a fourth. The bill of exchange itself may subsequently circulate in yet more countries and be delivered and endorsed in any of them. There are here four basic areas of conflict: (a) the creation of the bill of exchange in terms of formalities, capacity and validity; (b) any subsequent transfer in the same aspects; (c) the acceptance and the effect of the bill of exchange elsewhere when ultimately presented for payment to the drawee, but no less when presented for recourse by the holder to any signatory of the bill and the strength of any defences levelled in those situations against the presentation; and (d) any payment and discharge under the bill of exchange.

The basic rule, at least in England, is that the creation and transfer are complete when the instrument is delivered to the party concerned. That means, as far as the creation of the document is concerned, its handing over to the payee. For acceptance it means its return by the drawee (to the payee) and for transfer it means its delivery (upon endorsement if to order) to the subsequent holder. In each case it is considered that the law of the place of

---

[300] See also CM Schmitthoff, *The Law and Practice of International Trade* (9th edn, 1990), 573.
[301] See also Dicey and Morris, n 284 *supra*, 1431.

delivery (or receipt even though the delivery itself may be constructive, for example through an agent) applies to the relative legal act (creation, acceptance and transfer) in its formalities, capacity and validity. It is therefore not the law of the place of the signatures but rather the law of the place where the bill of exchange is sent after it.

The law applicable to these acts has therefore nothing to do with the law applicable to the underlying contract between the drawer and drawee, for example of sale giving rise to the drawing of the bill, or to the underlying contract between the drawer and payee giving rise to this type of benefit for the payee, or to any underlying contracts between succeeding holders giving rise to the transfer of the bill. The impact of conditions is another problem. Where in a *documentary* bill of exchange[302] acceptance is subject to a bill of lading being handed over and/or having been genuine, the effects of this conditionality are again determined by the law of the place of delivery of the bill upon acceptance and not by the law of the place where the condition was entered. Yet emphasis on the law of the place of delivery may not require full compliance with all its rules and especially not with typical domestic complications like stamp duty requirements in the UK. It only concerns rules which are of a typical bill of exchange nature and conform to its basic purposes.

Emphasis on the law of the place of delivery in these aspects of creation, acceptance and transfer, which are not strictly or, in any event, not only contractual, is logical from the point of view that the bill of exchange is likely to circulate in that place and must therefore exert the desired effect in that place. Even then, the law so held applicable is likely to relate only to the personal defences and upon negotiation of the bill of exchange it may no longer be relevant and other rules may apply. It nevertheless suggests a close relationship to the *lex situs* which more properly applies in the proprietary aspects of the bill of exchange as if it were a tangible movable asset. What concerns us here principally is the question whether the holder may be truly considered the owner of the bill of exchange even upon forgery or theft, particularly relevant to the holder in due course but also to pledgees. It also concerns the kind of (personal and real) defences that may be used against them if they present the bill for payment or for recourse.

In all instances upon circulation in other countries, it is likely that the new *lex situs* will adjust rights acquired earlier under a bill of exchange to its own system as a matter of adaptation but in a positive sense so as to respond best to the purposes for which bills of exchange are used. The law of the place of payment or recourse may well make further adjustments in this sense and will also have its own formal requirements as to the timeframe for payment. See for the adaptation technique particularly in proprietary aspects also section 1.8.2 above.

To demonstrate this approach, the examples of the effect elsewhere of an acceptance of a bearer draft, of a blank endorsement, or of any endorsement may be illuminating. That would be so especially in countries which allow a forced acceptance, like the Netherlands do not allow bearer bills, like most continental European countries, do not allow a blank endorsement as once was the case in France, or do not allow an endorsement if the bill is not expressed 'to order' as in the USA. It appears that whether an acceptance can be imposed would in this approach not depend on the law of the residence of the acceptor but rather of the payee, often the drawer. Whether effectively the courts in the country of the debtor would accept this is another matter as public policy may be involved. A German

---

[302] A documentary bill of exchange is a bill of exchange to which a bill of lading is attached. It is sent to the buyer of the goods together with the bill of exchange. The buyer may keep the bill of lading only if he accepts the bill of exchange if a time draft or honours the bill of exchange immediately if a sight draft. The drawee must return the bill of lading forthwith if he does not pay on the due date.

creditor could, however, draw a bearer bill on a drawee in Switzerland, payable in England if returned to the payee in that country. A blank endorsement, although invalid in the country of the endorsement, may be valid in the country of the endorsee upon delivery there and enforceable against the payee in a country, which also accepts blank endorsements. An endorsement of a bill to a named person only may be perfectly valid if delivered to the endorsee in a country which accepts such endorsements under its own law, like England.

The attitude in all these cases may be contrasted with the more traditional approach in conflicts laws which would as a minimum requirement insist on the act of which recognition elsewhere is sought being valid in its country of origin, but (except in the case of forced acceptances) it conforms to international standards concerning bills of exchange, a result here achieved by giving preponderant weight to the law of the country of delivery even in the creation of the instrument as a matter of adaptation. As suggested above there may be further adaptation at the place of endorsement or of payment or when the bill of exchange is being presented for recourse. Thus German bills of exchange, which under their own law cannot allow interest to be added to the amount payable, may be perfectly valid against a drawee outside Germany, notably upon presentation for payment in England. Set-off rights of the signatories if under applicable law qualified as a matter of discharge rather than as a personal remedy may be invoked against the holder in due course when payment is requested. Yet what the applicable law in this respect should be is less clear. There must be a bias against these set-offs, however. Lack of consideration in the country of origin or transfer for the various undertakings of the different parties becoming signatories and thereupon a kind of guarantor, is a typical common law complication, also, it is submitted, alien to the concept of bills of exchange (except perhaps as regards the position of holders in due course who are not signatories as long as they do not endorse the bill), and therefore unlikely to affect the bill of exchange if delivered elsewhere or presented for payment or recourse outside common law countries.

More complicated may be the question whether a choice of law by the parties may have a bearing on the applicable law, and in what aspects. The first requirement would be that it is indicated on the draft, which is not usual (it is much more common on bonds as promissory notes). Even so it could prevail in the aspects of form, possibly presentation and acceptance or in the contractual aspects of a transfer, but much less likely so in the aspects of validity of the creation and transfer of the instrument and especially in the proprietary aspects. There is legitimate doubt about the impact in these areas of a choice of law clause even if reflected on the bill of exchange.[303]

The second of the 1930 Geneva Conventions deals with certain aspects of conflicts of law concerning bills of exchange. The obligations of the drawee who has accepted are covered by the law of the place of payment (Article 4(1)). The form and other obligatory aspects are determined by the law of the place where the relevant signature was placed on the bill of exchange (Article 3).

Conflicts of law problems are difficult to resolve in all tripartite situations, as we saw in the case of agency and trusts: see chapter II, sections 3.2 and 1.8.3 above. It is also clear in respect of bills of lading: see section 2.1.9 above. There is no simple singular conflict rule conceivable which may cover all situations. This begs the question whether references to domestic laws in this fractured manner as a result of the application of private international law rules may be at all satisfactory or realistic or solve anything.

[303] See also Dicey and Morris, n 284 *supra*, 1425.

2.2.11 Uniform Treaty Law

Considerable differences developed in the law of negotiable instruments as a consequence of the various codifications in the nineteenth century (France in the *Code de Commerce* of 1808, Belgium in the Bill of Exchange Act of 1872, the Netherlands in the Commercial Code of 1838, the Germans in the *Allgemeine Deutsche Wechselordnung* of 1848, the English in the Bills of Exchange Act of 1882 and the Americans in the federal Negotiable Instruments Law of 1896, later followed by uniform state law in Article 3 UCC). The result was the emergence of basically three types of approaches: the French (including the Belgian and Dutch), the German (including Switzerland and Italy) and the Anglo-American. In the French group the bill of exchange was seen as the sale of the claim, therefore as an alternative to an assignment, which required the payee to give (or to have given) counter-value whilst another basic requirement was that the draft needed to be payable in a place different from the one in which it was drawn, although in the course of time both requirements were eroded in case law. The German group accentuated the abstract nature of the draft and tended to ignore the underlying relationships even between the original parties so that an underlying default did not affect the status of the bill of exchange as between them, whilst the Anglo-American group protected the holder in due course but withheld this protection to the parties to the bill of exchange. This proved the more sensible and viable approach.

For civil law countries, the differences were narrowed for bills of exchange in the Geneva Conventions of 1930 and for cheques in the Geneva Conventions of 1932, which were concluded upon the initiative of the League of Nations (in both fields as a set of three Conventions dealing respectively with certain material, conflict of law and stamp duty aspects). Although common law countries participated in the deliberations, they ignored the results whilst a number of South American countries signed but did not ratify (except Brazil). As a consequence, the Conventions became mainly European affairs, with the Scandinavian and Benelux countries, France, Germany, Italy, Portugal, Switzerland, Austria, Poland, Hungary and the Soviet Union as parties, although outside Europe, besides Brazil, Japan also ratified. The Conventions led, however, to different forms of incorporation into domestic law and allowed also certain deviations and reservations. Moreover, the incorporation legislation was differently interpreted.

Nevertheless, the Conventions introduced a substantial measure of unification of the law in the civil law countries in the areas of bills of exchange and cheques and were particularly important in redefining the status of the holder in due course, much along common law lines. As a consequence, there is now much greater uniformity in the material aspects of bills of exchange worldwide and the remaining differences between the civil and common law group are mainly in a number of technical issues: the civil law mostly does not accept a bearer draft and in some countries like France and the Netherlands the drawee may be forced to accept time drafts under certain circumstances.[304]

In the details, Uncitral in its Convention on International Bills of Exchange and International Promissory Notes of 1988 has attempted to narrow the differences between civil and common law concepts further for the so-called international bill of exchange which is defined as a bill of exchange which specifies in it two of the following five places as being

---

[304] See for a further discussion, also M Rowe, 'Bills of Exchange and Promissory Notes — Uses and Procedures in International Trade' in N Horn (ed), *Studies in Transnational Economic Law, Vol 6, The Law of International Trade and Finance* (Deventer, Boston, 1989), 243, with an Appendix B comparing the Geneva Convention with Article 3 UCC and the English Bills of Exchange Act.

in different countries: the place where the bill of exchange is drawn, the place indicated next to the signature of the drawer, of the drawee, and of the payee, or the place of payment, provided that for the Convention to apply either the place where the bill is drawn or the place of payment is in a Contracting State. It is an indication of the complex nature of this Convention, also in many of its other aspects. Following the UCC, it distinguishes between the holder and the protected holder and their various powers and defences in an extremely convoluted manner. The position of the various types of guarantors (avalists) and their defences also remains complex and can only be understood by tracing a large number of sections of the Convention. This lack of conceptual clarity is likely to prevent early ratifications.[305]

2.2.12   *The* Lex Mercatoria *Concerning Bills of Exchange*

In section 2.2.1 above, reference was made to the fact that the bill of exchange (like the bill of lading) is the product of the law merchant and that local legislation concerning it only developed later and cannot deny or contradict the basic nature of these negotiable instruments in terms of (a) the principle of independence, (b) the method of transfer, and (c) the protection of *bona fide* holders of the bill. There is here an independent legal regime and nowhere do the rules concerning bills of exchange follow completely from the general rules of the applicable law. They are unlikely to fit although since the nineteenth century many efforts have been made to 'nationalise' the bills of exchange and fit them into domestic legal regimes.

    Modern treaty law in order to be successful must reinforce the innate general principles governing bills of exchange, and it is desirable and efficient to continue to view these negotiable instruments as operating under their own transnational rules supplemented by treaty law to the extent existing and applicable. Certainly, if operating in international commerce, they should be brought under the various layers of law making up the hierarchy of norms of the *lex mercatoria*: see more in particular chapter I, section 3.1.1. It accepts that these instruments are best covered by their own customary law, as elaborated by treaty law to the extent existing and applicable under its own terms (and always subject to the fundamental legal principles or the *ius cogens* when relevant). Interpretation and supplementation should primarily take place on the basis of the intrinsic purpose and logic of these instruments themselves, the basic principles and rules concerning them, common principles developed for them in national laws and only ultimately through application of a domestic law selected on the basis of the applicable private international law rules.

2.3   The Dematerialisation of Documents of Title and Negotiable Instruments; Electronic Transfers

2.3.1   *The Traditional Use of Documents of Title and Negotiable Instruments. Their Inconveniences and Risks. Seaway Bills*

Documents of title, like bills of lading, and negotiable instruments, which are documents of title concerning money, like bills of exchange, have facilitated the international transfer of goods and payment in the manner described above. The use of them in payment or

---

[305] See for a discussion of the Uncitral Convention also H van Houtte, *The Law of International Trade* (1995) 337.

collection schemes was more extensively discussed in chapter III. Yet the need physically to handle them is cumbersome, largely because of the need for them to travel to the person who is entitled to them. Because of the increasing number of bills of lading in particular, there are also likely to be costly delays when, for example, they need to be checked before they can be handed over to the buyer, as in the case of documentary letters of credit, which were also discussed in greater detail in chapter III.

The consequence is that a buyer of goods may well receive the *bill of lading* (through the mail or otherwise) after the arrival of the goods. More time will be lost in the process of presentation to the carrier (or warehouse). This may cause serious delays for the carrier also, who is not authorised to release the goods to the buyer without the presentation of the document. The carrier thus incurs extra (demurrage) costs whilst the ship is held up. It may encourage neglect of the goods or even the handing over of the goods to the buyer without presentation of the bill of lading, often in exchange for an indemnity. This may be understandable but it undermines the effective use of the bill of lading as security in the payment circuit, which depends on the bill of lading being retained by the seller or his agent until payment. Allowing the bill of lading to travel with the goods instead of the seller retaining it for presentation to the bank is a common solution for avoiding these delays but its role as security instrument under letters of credit is then seriously diminished.

The need for the carrier to deliver the goods immediately upon arrival has given rise to the use of sea waybills instead of bills of lading. They are mere receipts and only sometimes reclaiming instruments, but are not negotiable. As a consequence, they do not have the status of documents of title and may not be necessary for taking delivery of the goods at all as, without a bill of lading being issued, the carrier may make delivery to anyone who can prove that he is entitled to the goods. Their lack of proprietary status allows them more easily to travel with the ship should their presentation still be required to reclaim the goods. The carrier who normally issues the bill of lading will know that there is none, so that he is safe to hand over the goods to the party entitled to them. Only in the US, the status of these sea waybills has been the subject of comprehensive legislation in 49 USCS Sections 80101*ff* (1994) as an amendement to the Pomerene Act of 1916.

The consequence of the status of these sea waybills is that there is no function proper for them in the payment circuit, as they cannot as such fulfil the function of a proprietary instrument for payment under letters of credit. Nevertheless, banks do sometimes accept them for documentary credit purposes when the waybill is given some reclaiming status. That was the aim of the Cargo Key Receipt System, developed in Sweden but all the dangers connected with the bill of lading travelling with the ship then re-emerge, plus the extra danger that the carrier may still issue bills of lading to others. Under the Hague Rules (Article 3.3) and the Hamburg Rules (Article 14) he must do so whenever the shipper (often but not always the seller or his agent) requests it. It renders the sea waybill ineffective as a reclaiming document at the same time.

Naturally, a shipper of the goods should only request a bill of lading when he is still in control of the sea waybill. However, in the case of less scrupulous or careless shippers a bill of lading issued under these circumstances may end up outside the payment circuit set up by the seller (even if the buyer makes the necessary arrangements with the issuing bank). It undermines any payment protection in terms of documentary letters of credit if based on the presentation of a waybill. In these circumstances, the seller may not be able to present a bill of lading for payment to the issuing bank and the buyer only has a void waybill upon his payment. In any event, if there is no bill of lading but only a sea waybill, the carrier may have to hand over the goods to someone claiming better rights. Still, presentation of the sea waybill may require the issuing bank to pay under the terms of the letter of credit.

The bank will not then have any proprietary leverage against a buyer who has not yet put the bank into funds. If he already has, the buyer will obtain the sea waybill from his bank but may not be able to retrieve the goods on the basis of it.

The danger that a bank may lose its recourse against the buyer in this manner has led to demands for indemnities by banks from sellers whilst making payment to them under a letter of credit if there is only a sea waybill. It defeats the whole purpose of documentary letters of credit, which are normally organised by buyers and meant to give sellers untrammelled payment expectancy. Even carriers may ask indemnities from buyers presenting sea waybills, certainly if they have issued bills of lading to the shipper or, if not, because others with better proprietary rights may, in the absence of any bill of lading, still claim better rights in the goods later.

The problem of indemnities has become endemic and is particularly felt in the oil industry.[306] In the absence of the presentation of a bill of lading upon arrival of the oil for whatever reason (which could be that longer credit has been given by the seller), in this industry indemnities have even been asked by the carriers from a seller (oil company) if arranging the transportation as the buyer may be less well known to the carriers. The result is that the sea waybill route has become ever less attractive to speed up delivery. No wonder that in this situation there has been a search for better and especially quicker ways of dealing with bills of lading proper, including their endorsement, through the use of the modern *electronic* filing, registration and communication facilities. They could at the same time shorten the time required to handle these documents by banks when presented to them by sellers under letters of credit.

The physical handling of *bills of exchange,* including their endorsement and the verification of the authenticity and order of signatures, may be equally slow. It may delay payments under letters of credit further and also payments through collection schemes if under them use is made of bills of exchange, which remains in both cases common: see also chapter III, section 2.1. Also here ways of electronic filing, registration and communication could help and it is logical that moves in this direction have been afoot in order also to achieve greater certainty, speed and efficiency for these instruments.

In the area of the identification and transfer of ownership in *shares and bonds,* there has been a particular need to reduce paperwork and facilitate the handling of a large number of sale transactions of millions of shares or bonds per day where physical handling of the instruments becomes an impossibility. Also here the solution must be found in the use of electronic identification of ownership and the recording of the transfers. Progress has probably been the most urgent and greatest in this area through the introduction of book entry systems, which will be discussed in greater detail in Part III below.

In modern times another concern has joined the extensive use of documents of title and negotiable instruments. It is the relatively simple possibility of fraudulent use of duplicate documents in the case of bills of lading or of falsification of the bill of lading itself to obtain goods or payment, respectively from a carrier or from a buyer/drawee or his bank, either by the fraudster or by a *bona fide* holder of fraudulently used duplicate documents or falsified documentation. These holders may be protected under duplicate documentation at the expense of the true beneficiary but will themselves be the victims if under falsified documentation there are no goods at all or the drawee indicated in a bill of exchange is non-existent. Falsifying documents is often a question of false signatures or of effacing or changing certain markings on the bill, like altering 'received for shipment' to 'shipped', so

---

[306] See FL de May, 'Bills of Lading Problems in the Oil Trade: Documentary Credit Aspects' [1984] *Journal of Natural Resources* 197.

as to convert a mere receipt into a document of title. Modern recording methods may allow here verification possibilities and therefore added protection for participants. The same may apply to shares and bonds.[307]

The electronic systems that may increasingly be used in this connection are computer to computer exchange of information systems, which rely on predetermined format methods. They are also referred to as *electronic data interchanges* or EDI, of which SWIFT is a most important application in the interbank payments and money transfer circuit. A similar system is conceivable to create electronic bills of lading. Electronic bills of exchange are also possible. For bonds and shares, book entry systems have been developed which are not exclusively based on EDI but which could also be helped by it. The modern practice here is that the bonds and shares are physically deposited with a custodian who maintains a register of ownership and changes in it, which changes may be electronically communicated to it: see section 3.1.3 below. For bills of lading, such an approach was at one stage proposed in the Seadocs Registry project of Chase Manhattan Bank in 1984 and may still be the simplest because it does not profoundly change the legal foundations of the system, but only introduces a custody system. It is superseded by the more recent Comité Maritime International (CMI) proposals for a more truly electronic bill of lading to be discussed shortly in section 2.3.2 below.

The best way forward may indeed be to look at the different industries and types of documents and to determine in respect of each of them the most appropriate or convenient approach. Within each area the emphasis will then be on international systems developed by the relevant industries themselves with their own set of rules of a transnational nature, just as the eurobond developed into a transnationalised instrument with its own transfer system and legal infrastructure, particularly aided by Euroclear and Clearstream: see also section 3.1.2 below and earlier chapter I, section 3.2.1.

The main *legal* issues in electronic data transfer systems of this sort are:

(a) the authenticity and evidentiary effect of signatures (upon leading and unloading) and documentation,

(b) access by the most directly concerned parties and their successor (including their banks and insurers to the extent they have a legitimate interest) to the electronically stored information without the facility to change it,

(c) negotiability as far as the electronic documents of title and instruments are concerned and the way this should be organised,

(d) the maintenance of the abstraction principle and of the exclusive evidence rule in respect of bona fide third parties who acquire the rights to the electronic document,

(e) the identification of the time of electronically created proprietary rights and of charges in them, of particular importance in enforcement,

(f) liability for faulty messages, communication failures and systems breakdown,

(g) applicability of the mandatory Hague-Visby Rules (which automatically follows if there is a bill of lading or similar document but might have to be stipulated if there is not),

---

[307] Another situation presents itself when the bill of lading indicates a lesser quantity (or different quality) than is actually shipped. In a cif sale this is a problem for the buyer who will have to prevail on the carrier to release the missing part; in an fob sale the seller will still be liable to provide the missing part to the buyer and will have to retrieve the goods from the carrier: see in England *Hindley & Co v East Indian Produce Co Ltd* 2 [1973] Lloyd's Rep. 515.

    (h)   the confidentiality of the system, and

    (i)   determination of the applicable proprietary law as the *lex situs* principle based
         on the location of the bill of lading loses its meaning.

Overriding *practical* issues are the expertise, stability and independence of the operators,
the costs of the systems and who must bear them.

2.3.2   *Electronic Systems and Their Importance in Replacing Transportation Documents*

Internally carriers of course use electronic means to maintain and amend their records of
loaded and unloaded goods, to achieve the best stowage and to advice their agents of dates
of arrival. However, in relation to their clients or third parties (like banks under documentary letters of credit or insurers), there is a practical limit which has to do with the lag status
of documents of title and their possible alternatives under electronically driven communication systems. It is the reason that so far electronic bills of lading have not developed, but
electronic data and communication systems have started to be used in some countries for
reporting sea waybill information especially to allow the buyer to obtain the goods even
without presenting the sea waybill in the port of destination.[308] An earlier experiment for
bills of lading concerned a kind of book entry system through the Sea Docs Registry, which
was a private venture of Chase Manhattan Bank going back to 1984, already referred to in
the previous section. Under it, the bank was to be the custodian of the bills of lading, maintain a register of ownership and any changes therein, which transfers could be achieved
electronically. The project failed because of lack of transparency in the cost structure but
probably also because there was a fear about confidentiality and the exclusive control of
the system by one bank.

    In the meantime, the Comité Maritime International (CMI) developed in 1990 Rules
for Electronic Bills of Lading. It allows the carrier to maintain the registry. The nature of
these rules is contractual, supposedly until they may be qualified as industry practice or
custom, like the Hague Rules and UCP now often are. The system is based on delivery of
the goods to the carrier who subsequently transmits a receipt message to the shipper's electronic address. It must contain the name of the shipper, the description of the goods, the
date and place of receipt, the carrier's terms and conditions or a reference thereto and the
'private key' to be used by the shipper in subsequent transmissions. This receipt message
must be confirmed by the shipper immediately upon receipt and is then the equivalent of
the traditional bill of lading whilst the private key makes endorsement possible.

    Any transfer instruction requires the *carrier* to send a new message with the same infor-
mation to the transferee who must accept the transfer. The new owner will thereupon
receive a new private key and the valid private key holder is the only one who can claim the
goods. This system may conceivably work but places a great burden on the carrier, his reliability and professionalism in these matters. It is the true weakness in the system. This may
also create additional liability. The resulting electronic bill of lading would be a creation
solely of the law merchant, which as yet may be considered an insufficient basis for its effectiveness. Transfer would in effect be through assignment of the instruction right which

---

[308] See also AN Yiannopulos, 'Ocean Bills of Lading: Traditional Forms, Substitutes, and EDI Systems', *General
Report XIVth International Congress of Comparative Law* (The Hague, 1995), 3.

could require additional formalities under applicable law. The acknowledgement by the carrier introduces here a uniform rule but it is less clear whether the assignor is entirely discharged as his duties may not sufficiently transfer at the same time. Electronic communication is through a number of 'private key'messages.

Although the CMI in these Rules showed an approach that could work, there was no sufficient confidence in the operational aspects, especially not in the ability of carriers to maintain proper systems and in their ready cooperation in the acknowledgement of transfers. Also the legal aspects were probably covered in too rudimentary a fashion and the international or customary (or uniform) status of the contractual arrangements on which the approach was based may still have been too uncertain or weak.

Other organisations have also dealt with the matter, if only collaterally. In 1993 the Uncitral EDI Working Group published Uniform Rules on the Legal Aspects of Electronic Data Interchange and Related Means of Trade Data Communication. They concern the exchange and storage of electronic data generally and do not take a product approach. It is not necessary, as they do not cover the substance of the transaction either. The Rules contain provisions to solve the problems connected with the requirement of a written document and signing under national laws and allow in this connection that the terms 'signing, 'writing' and 'original' also cover electronic documents and give them evidential effect. There is no provision on transferability of the underlying rights, however, which is an issue to be dealt with later. Until such time it seems that the Uncitral Rules have no special meaning for bills of lading and bills of exchange.

In 1996 there followed a Uncitral Model Law on Electronic Commerce. Artcicles 16 and 17 deal more in particular with commerce. Artcicle 16 contains a long list of actions to be taken by the parties concerned in the case of carriage of goods by sea. They may be of a practical, contractual or even proprietary nature (Article 16 (f)) and are as such split up and separately considered in terms of electronic communication and storage. Artcle 17 deals more in particular with transportation documents. It follows under this apporoach that they are in essence the result of a number of data messages, the legal status of which is no further defined. No proper, or at least legally reliable, substitutes of bills of lading therefore result.

The American Bar Association produced a Model Trading Partner Agreement in 1990 for EDI use in commercial sale transactions and communications, but as it is limited to the sale of goods, it has no significance for bills of lading or bills of exchange either. The International Chamber of Commerce adopted in 1987 Uniform Rules of Conduct for Interchange of Trade Data by Teletransmission (UNCID). They concern the transfer and receipt of messages in terms of identification of the parties, completeness, confidentiality and storage of data, but not in any way documents of title or their negotiability. Similar international or local standards have also been set for EDI by the UN (UN/Edifact) which particularly relate to the trade in goods and services and also covers a syntax and format for the recognition of shipping documents regardless of the hardware and software used. EDI Associations in countries like the UK, Australia and Canada have produced standard EDI agreements for use by commercial partners. The EU Commission also produced a model agreement in 1990 (TEDIS). None of them has any specific relevance for bills of lading or bills of exchange.

In the area of transferable documents of title, an English research institute, Marinade Ltd., prepared a more specific study for TEDIS (Mandate 1995). It led to a system called Bolero that became operative in 1999 as a commercial venture in which SWIFT also participates. It does not attempt to change the present processes used in international trade but to find the electronic equivalents, including that for the bill of lading where used. At the centre is a Rule Book between the members.[309] The succession is here by way of a form of novation that does not, however, entirely discharge predecessors whilst new holders carry on the obligations of the shipper in terms of disclosure (e.g. of dangerous substances) and timely unloading.[310]

The true solutions would, however, appear to be a central registration or bookentry system in the way as originally contemplated by Seadocs for which the operations in the international bond market through Euroclear and Cedel may well provide the best model. If this is now not the direction, one could consider the aspect of security for payment in isolation. If the whole field of the sale of goods and their transportation is to be considered, Uncitral may have to provide a better international legal infrastructure at international level even if its success in achieving treaty law is modest.

In the meantime the EU E-Commerce Directive in Article 9 imposed on Member States the duty to render the electronic conclusion of contracts possible. It will be of interest to see whether member States will also deem this an obligation to deal with transportation agreements and the documents issues in connection therewith.

2.3.3   The Situation with Regard to Bills of Exchange: Electronic Bank Transfers

As may appear from the previous section, so far there are also no specific EDI Rules concerning or producing electronic bills of exchange, although that might seems a normal sequel once electronic bills of lading are developed.

Electronic bank transfers may, however, substitute the payment functions of negotiable instruments and have already substantially reduced the use of (a) cheques drawn on bank to pay a foreign creditor which proved a lengthy process causing much payment delay and expense, (b) bankers' drafts purchased from the bank drawn on a bank in the country of the creditor which was quicker but costly as the own bank was guaranteeing the payment, and (c) telex transfers to achieve a foreign payment which depends on the foreign correspondent network of the bank and could still be costly.

It is this last method of electronic transfer which is refined by EDI (electronic data interchange). It should be distinguished from SWIFT which, although itself an EDI, is an *interbank* money transfer system. It is likely to be used in this connection as an alternative by the banks for interbank operations, see also chapter III, section 1.2.4.

These electronic bank transfers are no substitute for endorsement and negotiation or discounting of negotiable instruments. It must be admitted though that these facilities have lost much of their earlier attraction as the important ability to raise cash on them has now often been overtaken by receivable financing and related forms of factoring. Electronic transfers are in any event normally preferred by parties that habitually deal with each other and are cheaper: see for the modern use of negotiable instruments also section 2.2.7 above.

Yet in the context of letters of credit and collection schemes bills of exchange remain more common, as we also saw in chapter III. As in the case of bills of lading, the issue of negotiability requires a further facility in the electronic transfer process, which in the case of negotiable instruments has not yet received wide attention. One of the problems is that bills of exchange now mainly operate in international trade (connected to certain types of letters of credit) for which the international legal base remains weak whilst their status under the international law merchant may be further undermined by making them

---

[309] This system is described by R Caplehorn in Walden & Edgar (eds), *Crossborder Electronic Banking*, (2000) chapter IV.
[310] This follows the much criticized Section 3 of the UK Cogsa of 1992.

electronic. Largely the same legal problems arise here as in the case of electronic bills of lading, see section 2.3.1 above *in fine*.

Part III   Investment Securities

3.1   The Different Types of Shares and Bonds

3.1.1   Traditional Distinctions. Negotiable Instruments and Transferable Securities. Dematerialisation and Immobilisation. Securities Entitlements

Investment securities are capital market instruments issued and used to raise capital in that market. In chapter VI, section 1.3, the nature of investment will be more fully disclosed. Investment securities often imply a trading facility by being transferable so as to establish their liquidity, which is the facility to reduce them to money (through a sale) at any time. The most common types are bonds and shares. Bonds are promissory notes of an issuer, which may be a company or a government or governmental agency. Shares are rather participation certificates denoting ownership of the company issuing them. They are therefore more typically connected with the ownership and financing of corporations. The joint shareholders own the company and their shares give them typically rights to (a) dividends, (b) voting in shareholders' meetings, (c) any liquidation surplus, and (d) corporate information.

Shares and bonds come in several varieties. Shares (sometimes also referred to as equities or stocks) may be distinguished according to the dividend rights they give. Thus *ordinary* shareholders share the dividend *pro rata*, but *preferred* shareholders have a preferred right to dividends and they take therefore *before* the ordinary or common shareholders. Other classes of shareholders may have *extra* dividend rights which are often also preferred (the cumulative preferred shareholders). Shareholders may also be distinguished according to their voting rights and some classes may be given more voting rights than others. There might even be non-voting shareholders altogether.

Bonds come also in different types. There are *fixed* and *floating interest rate* bonds or notes. Notes are bonds which usually have a shorter maturity. As far as this maturity is concerned, there is short, medium and long term paper. Short term paper is also called a *money market* instrument and often comes in the form of commercial paper (CPs), issued by commercial companies, and of certificates of deposit (CD's), issued by banks. Medium term paper may take the form of medium term notes (MTNs). Long term paper may even take the form of perpetual bonds. In each instance, their precise terms, manner of issuing, and way of trading need to be carefully considered and could be very different.

There are also hybrids like bonds *convertible* into shares. There may also be *warrants*, which are a special type of options issued by a company at a certain price and allowing the owners to acquire new shares in that company at a specific issuing or striking price on a specific date in the future. Intermediaries holding a portfolio of these shares or options to acquire them sometimes also issue these warrants, therefore warrants in the shares of another company.

Investment securities that are intended to be traded were historically often issued as *negotiable capital market instruments*. They are *bearer* or *order* instruments and as such documents incorporating title in the securities, which title was transferred with the document. Their trading normally took and often still takes place on regular stock exchanges, but this trading could often also be informal and is for the more important issues now frequently conducted in the informal international (telephone) markets largely created by the large investment banks: see for greater details of the operations in these markets, of which the euromarkets are the most vivid example, chapter VI, section 1.3. In this process, international market practices may transform, change and even reinforce the status of these investment securities as negotiable instruments as happened in the case of eurobonds: see also chapter I, section 3.2.2.

As just mentioned, these investment securities as *negotiable instruments* could be to *bearer* or *order*, transferable respectively through handing over the document or through endorsement plus handing over. The bearer type of shares and bonds was the common type on the European Continent and was also preferred in the international capital markets as witnessed in particular by the traditional eurobond. Shares and bonds to order were uncommon in Europe, but not in the USA (if endorsed in blank, they become bearer securities). Under the company laws of the various states of the USA (which are not uniform), Memoranda and Articles of Association of corporations may vary the nature of the shares considerably. They could thus also be of the purely *register* type, like they are mostly also in England when negotiability is *not* implied, even though these shares are commonly still transferable but such a transfer depends on notification to and a change in a *share register* held at the company. A certificate could still be issued but again it would *not* be negotiable, only a record.

Consequently in the EU in order to cover all types, the broader notion of *transferable securities* is now often used in this connection (rather than that of negotiable instruments which is a term of art that represents a narrower class of transferable instruments), see also chapter VI, section 1.3.1. Mainly for regulatory purposes (including prospectus requirements in respect of public offerings), it no longer puts emphasis on negotiability *per se* but more generally on all forms of transfers and may also cover contractual rights, likes futures and options as long as they are transferable (often through formal derivative exchanges like LIFFE in London, which in truth provides a system for closing out contractual positions). (See chapter VI, section 1.3.7.) In the USA, Article 8 UCC, which presents perhaps the most important modern statutory instrument in this connection, deals with investment securities generally and was last updated in the Revision of 1994. It still reflects the traditional situation as regards the types of bearer and order securities or registered shares and follows the practices under state company laws. It does *not* therefore itself create new types of shares or bonds. Thus according to Section 8-102(a) (15), investment securities are obligations of an issuer or a share or other participation or interest in the issuer. They are represented by a security certificate in *bearer* or in *registered security certificate* form, or (only since the earlier 1977 Revision) by *uncertificated or dematerialised* securities, which are investment securities only marked in the books of the issuing company.

As already mentioned, in *bearer* form, securities transfer through *mere delivery* (Section 8-301(a)(1)). In the *registered security certificate* form, the owner is indicated on the certificate and in the US this type of security transfers also through delivery of the certificate but with *endorsement* to effect the name change (Section 8-301(a)(3). In the US, this certificate is therefore still negotiable, *viz* in the nature of an instrument to order, but the new owner may in addition have to be registered in books maintained to that effect by the issuer (Section 8-102(a)(13)) and may not be entitled to dividends or bond interest payments before that is done. Full negotiability of the certificate is thus lost (or at least affected). That is indeed all the more the normal situation in the UK, as we saw, where registered certificates and company share (and bond) registers are common. In the UK, the change in name on the certificate is normally only achieved through the registrar and *not* through endorsement. These English certificates are therefore non-negotiable *per se* and therefore not true share certificates at all. Only the shareholder's position in the books of the company is transferable and can only be transferred through adjustment of the register.

Transaferability (not negotiability) is achieved by the company having to accept the transfer instructions from the registered owner.

Securities of this type are *only* registered in books maintained for that purpose by or on behalf of the issuer and there is normally (except in the UK) *no* document at all.[311] They are fully *uncertificated or dematerialised*. In the US, many state company laws did not until recently provide for this type of share and they were only created in response to the 1977 Article 8 UCC Revision. These dematerialised securities thus transfer only through registration of the new holder in the company's register of which normally notice is sent in the same way the account holder receives notice of any changes in bank balances. Where they exist, these registers are thus indicative of the ownership of the securities (even if rebuttable) and any document issued is no more than proof of registration and is *not* then a negotiable instrument proper, as is in fact also the English situation, although (reissuance of some) share certificates (as a matter of record only) continue to play a role in the transfer of ownership in that country. It makes for a cumbersome transfer system that has all the disadvantages of shuffling paper and none of the advantages.

This registration facility leading to dematerialised shares (therefore to shares without a certificate proper as mere *intangible property rights*) should *not* be confused with the modern *book-entry* system. These create an *additional layer* of ownership rights, in the USA under Article 8 UCC, and presume a *depository function* under which the issuer places all securities with a depositary (or a small number of them) who thereby becomes legally the owner of the securities. This arrangement is combined with one under which a broker or other intermediary (in this connection also called *custodians*) in respect of their clients hold security entitlements against these depositories through a book-entry system. The idea is that these clients then hold entitlements against their intermediaries only, who in turn hold corresponding entitlements against the depository (or any intermediate custodians in the chain. It is thus quite normal for a French end investor who buys Dutch shares to have an entitlement against his French broker (say BNP), who has an entitlement against a Dutch broker (say ABN/Amro), who has an entitlement against a Dutch depository. It may also be that both BNP and ABN have a securities and bank account at Euroclear in Brussels

---

[311] Dematerialised securities should not be confused with fungible securities. Fungibility is connected with custodial arrangements, not with issuers. There is a parallel to the extent that in neither case is the investor entitled to specific securities, only to a similar number of the same sort. Dematerialised securities are intangible but still capable of identification by number which allows them to be part of a custody portfolio (on which entitlements might be based) and book entry system. These rights may not only be determined in numbers of shares but also in register numbers.

Fungibility of securities should also not be confused with fungibility of bank deposits. In the latter case there can only be a contractual claim against a bank and *pari passu* status of the depositor. In fungible securities, the investor has still a proprietary right but only to his *pro rata* part of a pool which will only convert into a purely contractual claim if the pool is no longer sufficiently segregated from the other property of the custodian.

The fact that securities may be dematerialised and thereby become intangible does not rule out that they are owned, albeit not in a physical sense. Just as one can own a claim, one can own the rights inherent in a share even if it is not physical. The same goes for a registered bond. In other words, the holder of a registered (and not a physical) bond has a different position than the owner of a monetary claim that is not embodied in a security or other type of negotiable instrument (like a bill of lading or promissory note), even if there is no longer a physical element. Although also the claimant with a monetary claim (or any other) has a proprietary interest in his claim, see s 1.1.3 *supra*, and the transfer in either case will be a kind of assignment, the manner will be different. So will be the position of *bona fide* purchasers and of pledgees or other security interest holders in dematerialised securities. The fallacy should be avoided that the registered investment security owner has only a personal claim on the register. In the case of book entry entitlements, it is more understandable to speak of a personal claim against the intermediary holding the securities, but in truth this is also confusing, as in that case there is also a co-ownership right in the pool of similar securities the intermediary holds. This is not to say that intermediaries were acting as agents for their clients but operating in their own name may, under civil law notions of indirect agency, not have ownership of the rights in the pool rather than their client. This is a different problem: see further section 3.1.5 *infra*.

where the positions are settled whilst Euroclear in turn has an entitlement against the Dutch depositary of government bonds (normally Negicef). If the French investor wanted German government bonds, a German broker (say Deutsche Bank) would become involved. Settlement could still be at Euroclear in Brussels, who would maintain a corresponding entitlement in respect of these German government bonds against Clearstream in Frankfurt, which is the normal depository in Germany.

A depository holding securities in this manner (as owner) leads to so-called *immoblisation*. It may go together with dematerialisation but that depends on how the ownership of the underlying securities is handled: either through negotiable (bearer) instruments when there is no dematerialisation or through registration in a shareholder (or bond) register when there is. The holdings through a depository in this manner usually come about at the request of the issuer who has therefore only one (or a limited number of selected) owner(s) of the securities to deal with which has considerable advantages for him in terms of costs. The depositories keep these securities per type and class in the form of pools in which the investors (or their brokers) as clients are therefore *entitlement holders* through a booking system that operates much like bank accounts in a bank.

Investors will thus have security accounts with their brokers, who have them with the depository (either directly or via subcustodians in a system of layers), much in the way a depositor has an account with a bank. Transfers are booked in a similar manner. But there is an important difference in that the securities intermediaries in respect of their clients do not become owners of the underlying securities as a bank becomes the owner of the deposits and each operator of a book-entry system in its layer may not dispose of its entitlement with the depository or other intermediaries as if it were his own (at least to the extent that the entitlement corresponds to its clients' investments and not his own).

The right of each entitlement holder is often understood (in civil law) in terms of a *pro rata* co-ownership of these underlying pools or (in common law) in terms of beneficiaries under a (constructive) trust arrangement in which only the depository is the legal owner of the shares, but in the nature of a trustee. All the rest, therefore all intermediaries and their end investor clients, have no more than beneficial ownership rights in the underlying shares, which consist of the right to coupons and repayment of principal in the case of bonds and in the case of shares to dividends, voting, liquidation proceeds and corporate information. These benefical ownership rights against the depository are in turn held through a tiered system of security entitlements, in which these beneficial rights may (in principle) only be exerted against the previous layer. It is possible to see here a double trust structure in the sense that in respect of the underlying beneficial ownership rights in each layer (therefore in each entitlement) the intermediary acts as trustee in respect of the entitlement holder in the next layer (who has therefore a beneficial right in respect of his intermediary) in what was itself never more than a number of beneficial rights against the depository.

Yet it should be understood that this is only an administrative arrangement. Although of the greatest importance in facilitating the modern holding and transfer of securities in an efficient and safe manner avoiding any confusion through compartimentalisation of the holding and transfer structure in this manner, it is nevertheless true that, even if in principle the entitlement can only be claimed against the immediate intermediary and certainly not directly against the depository or the issuer, it is undeniable that should all intermediaries somehow disappear, the end investors still have direct rights against the depository. On the other hand, if all end investors disappeared, the intermediaries would have no proper right against the issuer or depositary who would owe them nothing. It could also be said that as a consequence the entitlements of the intermediaries are not truly of the same order as those of the end investors who are the true beneficiaries. This also explains why (in a proper book-entry system) if an intermediary goes bankrupt, his entitlement in respect of his clients against the previous layer can be immediately redirected by his clients to such replacement intermediaries as they chose and that the bankruptcy trustee must give immediate co-operation to achieve this. In other words, the entitlement against the previous layer does not belong to the bankrupt estate (except for that part of which the bankrupt was himself the demonstrable end investor).

Although all end investors together are jointly entitled to all beneficial interests their joint intermediary holds for them through his own entitlement with the depository or other intermediary, the characterisation of their interest as common or joint property (as is usual in civil law) is less satisfactory. In the US, Article 8 UCC creates here a *sui generis* proprietary right as a package of a number of rights against an intermediary under which the investor *looses* direct access to the underlying securities (or entitlements higher up in the chain except if otherwise agreed), but, whatever the layers of holdings and regardless of any direct access to the issuer and depository, *retains* the exclusive right to the coupon and principal repayment in the case of bonds and to income or dividends in the case of shares and then also to the voting rights, any winding-up proceeds, and to corporate information. It is relevant in this connection that the 1994 Revision of Article 8 UCC in the US was foremost meant to facilitate the safe and efficient operation of the systems for clearance and settlement of investment securities in the USA and started to promote book-entry facilities in this sense in that context. It was not meant to change the basic structure of security holding to any other effect or diminish the rights of investors for more than absolutely necessary to achieve this limited objective.

It is important to realise that to achieve this objective, book entry systems of securities entitlements have in principle nothing much to do with the issuer and the way or form in which the securities are issued, but everything with the way the investment securities are subsequently held (first by the depository and thereafter through brokers or other custodians as intermediaries) and transferred in other layers. They will be discussed more fully in section 3.1.6 below. The result is that in a book entry system, the entitlement holder is a person identified only in the records of his immediate securities intermediary (rather than the issuing company), like a depository or more likely a broker (who in turn will have an account and entitlement with the depository). There may in fact be a whole *chain of intermediaries or sub-custodians* who hold entitlement rights only against the next intermediary or sub-custodian in the chain until the depository is reached who is the share- or bondholder proper as far as the issuer is concerned (*cf* Section 8-102(a)(7) UCC).

These entitlements thus operate at various levels. In such a system it is very likely that a smaller investor has an entitlement against his broker, who in turn has a corresponding entitlement against another custodian (pooling that of other clients in the same type of securities) who has an entitlement against the depository as the legal owner of the shares, either because the latter physically holds them (in the case of negotiable instruments) or because he is registered as such in the issuer's register (in the case of dematerialised securities). As just mentioned, one of the key questions in this respect is whether entitlement holders in the various layers automatically take the place of their intermediary in its bankruptcy, can request his replacement, or only have a competing claim against this intermediary. This goes to the heart of the legal characterisation of the 'entitlement' right. Indeed the complications deriving for the investor from a bankruptcy of the intermediary (broker or even depository) in book-entry systems are the main concerns in systems of this nature. Naturally they also arise outside a book-entry system where a broker holds client assets either directly or in a (pooled) client account. There are here important issues of *segregation* and tracing which may be easier handled in a book-entry system, see more in particular section 3.1.3 below.

In the USA, these entitlements come about and are treated and transferred in the manner described in Section 8-501 UCC. In a purchase of securities, the delivery of securities to a broker for the account of his purchasing client led traditionally to a form of ownership of the broker (who was acting in his own name but as indirect or undisclosed agent), from which subsequently his clients' entitlements resulted. Under applicable rules of agency, title could shoot through to the clients immediately assuming that the securities could as such be identified per client. In modern book-entry systems, as a consequence of a purchase, an entitlement will first be shifted in the previous layer of the chain from the broker of the seller to the broker of the buyer, as a consequence of which the broker for the buyer will create a client's entitlement *vis-à-vis* him. Similarly, in a sale, this entitlement will be transferred from the seller's entitlement with his broker to the buyer's entitlement with his broker through adjustments of both brokers' entitlements in the previous layer. This is becoming the normal system of holding and transferring investment securities, even in respect of bearer instruments (or in the US of registered certificates endorsed in blank, which are treated similarly: see Section 8-304 UCC) or in respect of dematerialised registered share certificates.

The consequence is that an entitlement holder has a security entitlement which means a *pro rata* interest (as defined) with other entitlement holders in all that the same intermediary holds in the particular class of shares or bonds, either in his own name or through his own entitlement in respect of other intermediaries, especially depositories (see Sections 8-503 and 8-504 UCC). It does not, however, include an ownership right in the underlying securities or entitlements but it means to respect an own right to income, voting, liquidation proceeds and corporate information. In the relationship between a broker and his clients, this is still coupled with *indirect agency* rules which remain relevant especially in respect of *unfinished* trades and under which automatic rights to entilments result for buyers in respect of whose purchases the broker's own entitlement is already adjusted. It should, however, be understood at the same time, that often a broker will simply supply his client out of his own inventory. It means that the purchase is no longer directly related to the broker finding another broker dealing for a seller. Nevertheless for the following it may still be instructive to see what happens in such cases which are in any event not academic for smaller brokers. It could be observed in this connection that in payment systems which at least as to transfer instructions operate in similar ways, the intermediary banks always 'supply' out of own inventory as they are truly the owner of all deposits for their clients and there is no separate chain of client moneys as there is in the case of client securities which do not (in principle) belong to the brokers.

In the case of book-entry entitlements, *pooling* is another essential feature of the arrangement and assumes *fungible* securities (even though it may not result in mere common property) so that there is no longer any right to receive securities (unless there is also a so-called *pass through* right to reach the depository). In common law terms, there is *no* bailment. It is likely to be backed up by some statutory law. This will notably require the intermediary to follow the entitlement holder's instructions even if he knows of adverse claims and the intermediary will not be liable in this connection for inappropriate *transfers* (Section 8-115 UCC). It is the notion of abstraction or independence also known from letters of credit and in negotiable instruments personified by the strong position of the holder in due course. It is extremely important and no book-entry system can operate effectively without such a rule. Systems would become paralysed if they had to assume the reversibility of payment instructions and payment transfers except between two intermediaries if a mistake has been made and the transfer has not yet involved others in the 'pipeline'. Again, security entitlement transfer instructions and transfers show here a close likeness to payment instructions, see chapter III, section 1.2.4, taking into account, however, always that in the case of securities the intermediary that operates a book-entry system is not the owner of the underlying rights and cannot dispose of them as if they were his own. He is at most a trustee and cannot use the underlying securities for his own benefit as a bank may use depositors' money for its own account since it has become the owner of the deposited money.

In this connection, an *entitlement order* is an instruction to transfer (or redeem) an investment security given by the client to its intermediary (Section 8-507 UCC). It retains the idea of transfer of negotiable instruments in so far that the transfer can only be challenged on very narrow grounds, as is also the case in payment systems. This is more properly an issue of *finality*, see also section 3.1.3 below. It lays stress on the system as one of communications and administrative entries only, from which proprietary consequences flow nonetheless but only to the extent specifically defined. Also here there is similarity with bank accounts and payment systems, demonstrated by the absence of bailment in either case, even if in the case of securities entitlements that does not lead to the intermediaries' ownership of the rights in the shares. This has an important consequence that unlike in the case of bank accounts (and earlier in many legal systems when client securities were irretrievably commingled with those of his broker), the client does not here assume the insolvency risk of the intermediary but retains (in principle) his *pro rata* entitlement in the latter's bankruptcy. There remains a risk in so far that even though the intermediary must retain sufficient assets against the entitlement, he may not do so in which case the pool and the *pro rata* shares of investors are diluted through the emergence of *bona* fide purchasers from a fraudulent intermediary.

In this connection, a distinction can be made in the sense that modern securities holdings represent *tiered systems* and modern bank account holdings *chained systems*. In the case of transfers, it means that there are in a tiered system no credit transfers through the system proper, therefore no push systems either. In chained systems that is different and modern payment is therefore normally achieved through a chain of transfers in a push or credit transfer system in which all intermediary banks are credited in order to push the credit on to the bank of the creditor, see more in particular chapter III, section 1.1.5. That can but need not happen in a tiered system of securities entitlements and transfers and securities entitlement transfers are in any event not dependent on the performance of upstream intermediaries. A security entitlement is created as soon as a broker undertakes to do so even if he fails to meet his asset-maintenance obligation and no underlying adjustments are made.[312] It reconfirms the usual practice for large brokers to only deal from their own inventory. Smaller brokers may act differently and still go through the chain. There may also be a chain when both end parties are identifiable as in the case of securities lending.

The pass-through right was just mentioned and is in fact a reminder and remnant of the earlier system. If share or bond certificates exist or are still issued by the issuer to the depository, in the US, the entitlement holders may still have a so-called *pass through right* and the intermediary must obtain the underlying certificates if the entitlement holders so request (Section 8-508 UCC unless they are only issued in bookentry form). In the meantime, the intermediary (either as owner or through the depositary) has a duty to collect payments, vote in accordance with the directions of the entitlement holders, and supply

---

[312] See for a clear expose also JH Sommer, "A Law of Financial Accounts: Modern Payment and Securities Transfer Law", (1998) 53 *The Business Lawyer*, 1181, 1203. The reason for the difference appears a practical one. Banks do not like to tier deposits which would lead them to hold balances with their corresponding banks larger than needed to run a payment system. That is not economical for them. It appears on the other hand cost effective for them to use higher-tier intermediaries to satisfy their asset-maintenance requirement.

them with the information the issuer must by law pass to investors (Sections 8-505 and 8-506 UCC). As already mentioned, depositories will be paid for that service as part of the custody fee they charge their clients.

To repeat, it shows a fundamental difference between the rights of intermediaries in the various layers and that of the end investor. The latter are the rightful beneficiaries of the dividends, liquidation proceeds, coupons and principal, as well as voting and information rights. It is true that in a modern book-entry system they may not normally any longer pursue these rights directly but through other layers and that their proprietary rights in that respect are severely curtailed (and mostly limited to segregation and the right to appoint another intermediary if their direct intermediary becomes insolvent or cannot handle the entitlement any longer for other reasons). But should all intermediaries some-how disappear (including the depository), it must be assumed that the end investors still have direct rights against the issuer.

3.1.2   Negotiability and Transferability of Investment Securities: Use of Securities Entitlements to Enhance Transferability

As mentioned in the previous section, shares and bonds were traditionally issued in certifi-cated form and were, at least on the European Continent, meant to be *negotiable instru-ments* in order to allow an investor to change his investments instantly. This was of course facilitated by regular securities exchanges which would centralise liquidity in respect of those issues which they listed. Negotiable instruments themselves denote a special, simpli-fied form of transfer in that all rights of the investor and obligations of the issuer are assumed to be incorparted in the document and transfer with it. As negotiable bearer or order instruments, they had as such a status that could not easily be altered in the Memorandum and Articles of Association of a company without depriving the shares and bonds of their negotiability at the same time. To put it differently, if there were limitations on the transfer in the Memorandum or Articles, they were unlikely to affect the instru-ments unless marked thereon. If so marked, these instruments would most likely no longer be negotiable instruments. This status as negotiable instruments derived from their legal roots in the old law merchant. It could be changed by domestic laws or the rules of the exchanges on which these instruments traded, but again in making such changes the nego-tiability of the instruments could be easily undermined and would then start to depend on these domestic laws themselves.

International off-exchange trading practices, as in the euro-market, could, on the other hand, enhance the status of investment securities as negotiable instruments in the tradi-tional sense. This proved especially relevant for eurobonds as bearer securities. Because many conditions could be printed on them in connection with payment of interest and principal, these bonds did often not qualify under local laws as bearer instruments, e.g. because no sum certain was due under them, not therefore either under those laws that were often made explicitly applicable to them by the issuer (often English or New York law). In such cases, international market practices were likely to prevail instead and imposed their own proprietary regime and notion of negotiability as if there was an instru-ment in that form (therefore expressed to bearer or order): see also chapter I, section 3.2.1. That international status now probably also extends to the book-entry entitlements created in them through Euroclear and Clearstream, which are the habitual depositories and clear-ing and settlement agencies in the euro-market. It suggests a transnational notion of trans-ferability and *bona fide* purchaser protection, even if no longer cast in terms of negotiable instruments. It should immediately be noted in this connection, however (as will be further explained below), that in the opinion of many the introduction of a book-entry system in this manner and the consequential acceptance of a new form of transferability has served to destroy the transnational character of eurobonds and their transfer and (like in the case of register securities) means the return to purely domestic laws. It is suggested that this is a short sighted and undesirable attitude.

It is true, as we saw in the previous section, that under purely domestic laws, register(ed) shares do not have the status of negotiable instruments (unless certified securities in the USA) and are therefore primarily domestic instruments. This allows further limitations on their transferability in the Memorandum or Articles of Association, by domestic company law, or local (stock exchange) regulation. In continental Europe, the more international bearer securities variety was normal but only in publicly quoted companies, therefore not in private companies, which are companies typically not quoted on stock exchanges, like GmbHs in Germany, Sarls in France and BVs in the Netherlands. These companies tend to have register(ed) shares only and normally restrict the transfer of their shares whilst commonly submitting them to first-refusal rights of other shareholders or to company approval. They never were negotiable instruments. Dematerialised investment securities have long existed in these situations but the difference from the modern dematerialised registered shares is that they were never meant freely to trade at all whilst their issuance was not directed to the public either.

Registered (non-certificated) shares, even if targeted to the public and made tradable, were thus always more domestic in nature and were therefore always more readily subject to domestic transfer restrictions. They are certainly less easy to handle in an international context when quoted on foreign exchanges or traded in internationalised informal telephone exchanges as they are subject to domestic registration requirements which may as a minimum raise formal, stylistic and linguistic problems in a transfer. In the US, on the other hand, the restrictions on transferability resulted mainly under private placement arrangements without SEC registration rather than from company law provisions. The shares if physically existing would then be *marked* as such. In the US, in the case of modern non-certificated registered shares, any transfer restrictions of this nature will be marked on the register.

As we saw, transfer of registered (non-certificated) shares, even if not restricted, is unlikely to be through a simple handing over of a document and endorsement. Legally, a type of *assignment* may be required, which may, besides registration as a constitutive requirement of such an assignment under local law, further depend on other formalities like specific documentation. It is on the whole not therefore useful to develop the assignment analogy further and apply its rules. Like in the case of payments it is better to assume here an own or *sui generis* way of transfer as expressed in company law. It may acquire yet another form if there are book-entry entitlements and become much more akin to payment through simply crediting and debiting secrity accounts (remaining differences were already highlighted in the previous section). Further restrictions or formalities may also result under rules of stock exchanges on which these investment securities are listed or, if unlisted, from local securities or company law (which on the European Continent for private limited companies may even necessitate notarial deeds for transfer and company approval whilst there may also be a right of first refusal for existing shareholders, as we saw).

Even if full transferability in dematerialised securities is maintained, local formalities in this respect may prove to be particularly destructive of share transfers if the shares are *internationally* traded, on foreign exchanges or in the international telephone markets. In the first case, the company concerned may, however, seek to maintain a special register in the relevant foreign country. This may (partially) lift the transfer out of the *lex societatis* of the issuing company at the same time and may create a different regime of transfer, which may imply fewer (or different) limitations on and formalities of the transfer. It could also allow for foreign pledges or similar security interests to arise in such securities. Alternatively, it may also be that the domestic share register is adapted to accept foreign types of transfer notices. The issuing company may favour either approach if it encourages its shares to be traded elsewhere. It may thus change the traditional way of notification or even its impact in the case of registered shares. It may for example be in a foreign language with different stipulations.

However, if a company seeks to complicate or limit the transfer of its shares under local law through a registration system, it should stay at home. This is indeed the normal situation for shares in private companies. However, especially if international capital-raising or trading is favoured in the formal foreign or informal international markets, the need is for a form of transnationalisation of the ownership transfer practices in respect of registered (non-certificated) shares and there will be a drive for uniformity in those markets, especially if they are themselves internationalised as the euro-market is. In any event, it is likely that the practices in this respect will ultimately be lifted beyond the legal patterns and limitations of transfer of the *lex societatis* and incorporation documents. It is for this reason that it is so important to retain the transnational nature of at least eurobonds even after they have entered book-entry systems like those of Euroclear and Clearstream and are now transferred accordingly. It is therefore not useful to relegate these transfers to matters of Belgian or Luxembourg law or to the law of any book-entry layer (of other intermediaries and brokers) between the end invester and depositories like Euroclear and Clearstream.

In fact, the use of *book-entry systems* may prove here especially useful and provide an opportunity. It could lift the transfer even of register shares beyond the domestic laws and limitations, all the more so therefore if these book-entry systems are themselves internationalised, as should be considered the case in particular with Euroclear and Clearstream, when the relevant investments are expressed in entitlements only. One could also say that, like in the case of the *traditional* negotiable bearer certificates, registered shares or book entry entitlements may, in the case of international trading, by themselves start conforming to an international or law merchant type of transferability which goes beyond its local statutory form. As already mentioned, we saw this happen with the eurobond as bearer security of a transnationalised type. It should be considered as reinforced when book-entry systems became common in that market and it may also happen when domestic shares are traded internationally in the form of book entry entitlements.

It is a most important development, which will impose itself further with the increase in international trading. The creation of book-entry entitlements as *internationalised* proprietary structures separated from the underlying securities and the nature in which they are held and transferred (through the intermediation of depositories) also promotes their transfer and the versatility in the type of other interests that may subsequently be created in them, like security interests, repos or conditional or temporary interests for financing purposes. The key is that through book-entries a different interest layer is created which may be internationalised *independently* and which is in any event separated from the underlying securities and *not* covered by the laws of those underlying securities. Through a book-entry ssystem, these domestic securities may thus become indirectly internationalised (by the same token they may become subject to the law of another country e.g. that of the place where a depository or intermediary/custodian is located if this is preferred, assuming that their law is sufficiently sophisticated to handle the new interests). This development will be discussed more fully below in section 3.2.2. In its ultimate phase, it may mean that domestic laws become irrelevant and conflict of laws' rules redundant in this area. They may in respect of international registers or book-entry systems also become fortuitous for lack of sufficient contact. This will also be discussed more fully in section 3.2.2 below. It would also allow for transnationalised notions of security interests or repos to attach to or operate in them.

Indeed, at least in respect of the *status* of securities entitlements and the *type* of proprietary interests that may be created through them or in them (like repos, conditional transfers, pledges, and the like) domestic laws so found applicable may not contain much guidance (they are likely to concentrate on the transfer only). International market practices may start here to prevail also, even domestically. This applies no less to the protection of *bona fide* purchasers and in the issue of *segregation* of the client's interest from that of its broker or other intermediaries, which in turn relates to the entitlement representing some proprietary interest in the underlying securities or to co-ownership rights in pools, or (in the worst case) merely to some contractual claim against the intermediary. Internationalisation is here a good development that creates uniformity on the basis of market requirements and reasonable expectations. It is the ultimate opportunity to provide certainty through uniformity.

Issuers if not actively promoting this internationalisation, will have to accept the results which are likely to be dictated by the interests of the international investors and not by the issuers or their legal systems. Through this *layering*, in reality (if not also legally), the nature and status of domestic securities may be transformed and the trading therein at the same time. That can be seen as the risk an issuer takes whilst encouraging international trading in its investment securities, whether through special share registers abroad or through depository arrangement coupled with book-entry systems. So far, this may be clearest for eurobonds but the same pressure applies to all investment securities or entitlements to them that are internationally traded with (or even without) the encouragement of the issuer.

3.1.3 The Risk Factors in the Holding and Transfer of Investment Securities: Bankruptcy Issues and Risk Reduction Techniques

Investment securities always carry the risk of the insolvency of the *issuers* but also the expectancy of their prosperity. These are risks and expectations that are probably the essence of these instruments and largely determine their value. The investors seek them out for this reason. As risk selection, not risk elimination, is here likely to be the concern, it will not be further discussed. A connected risk is that of liquidity. That is the risk that the security, although transferable, cannot be sold readily or even then only at a large discount or can only be bought at a large premium as there is no ready (official or unofficial) market in them. It is a reflection of the efficiency of markets, or rather of the lack of it, therefore of their inefficiency. That is also an aspect of investing proper but will not be further discussed here either.

More important for the present discussion are the *operational or collateral* risks, especially if of a legal nature, for the investor if not *physically holding* the investment securities himself (assuming that they are negotiable instruments) or if not himself registered as the owner in an immobilised system of securitites holdings. It concerns here depository arrangements or arrangememts with brokers who hold securities for their clients, now often resulting in book-entry systems and security entitlements as explained above in section 3.1.1.

One of these risks, which the investor will seek to minimise, is the *bankruptcy* of the depository or other intermediary (like brokers) with whom or in whose name the investment securities are kept and against whom the investor therefore has in modern terms an 'entitlement'. The issue arises in two different ways: (a) there was always the question who owns the investment held by a broker for his clients whilst going bankrupt, in which respect a distinction may usefully be made between situations in which the insolvent broker held (i) negotiable instruments directly for his client in his own possession, had them (ii) pooled in client accounts with a custodian, or was (iii) operating a book-entry system, and (b) the situation in respect of a broker who went bankrupt whilst transfers remained *unexecuted*, which concerned the further question of (i) the ownership of the securities (or securities entitlements) the delivery of which was already in the pipeline and coming to the bankrupt broker either as a netted number in a clearing system or more directly, (ii) the ownership of the rights to delivery of undelivered securities (or securities entitlements) upon a purchase, the settlement of which was not yet in the pipeline or clearing or of any moneys owed upon a sale. In the first case (under a) there are problems of ownership and commingling to be considered, in the latter case (under b) there are problems of ownership and agency.

In this connection, there arise (a) proprietary questions which have to do with the *nature of the holding of the investors* in terms of proprietary, co-ownership or beneficial (or similar) rights against intermediaries, (b) a number of special so-called *finality issues* which have to do with the power of the insolvent intermediary still to give transfer and settlement instructions, his (continued) functioning in the relevant clearing and settlement facility, the effect on his participation in the netting, and any retroactivity of the bankruptcy in this regard till the beginning of the day of the bankruptcy (which is a common bankruptcy rule and undermines all transactions in which the bankrupt was involved on the day of his bankruptcy), and (c) the question whether any transfer to clients under these circumstances is prejudicial or preferential in respect of the general creditors of the intermediary (but only if still considered the legal owner of the entitlements which he holds for his clients).

In the EU, the EU Settlement Finality Directive of 1999 seeks to deal especially with the problems under (b) and (c) and provides for a harmonised regime in the first instance meant to protect the position of the European Central Bank in its liquidity providing function to the banking system which is based on repo financing. Most EU countries have implemented the measure to apply more generally. It side-stepped intentionally the even more crucial issues under (a) which therefore remain unharmonised in the EU. A limited effort has been made in the Collateral Directive, however, to deal with (some) rights (in terms of securities or repos) that can be established over securities entitlements, see section 3.2.4 below, without, however, defining these entitlements and their nature themselves.

As just mentioned, in a bankruptcy of the broker holding securities for his clients, a distinction should first be made whether the broker holds these assets physically (in the case of negotiable instruments) or is registered as owner for them (in the case of registered or dematerialised securities). As a consequence of agency notions, it may now often be assumed that in the first case these securities are then owned by the clients, *assuming* that they can be clearly identified (therefore by the printed numbers in the case of bearer instruments or register entry, title shooting through as a consequence of disclosure (in common law) of the agency or on the basis of a special rule in respect of indirect agency in civil law. It may, however, also be that these securities are pooled with others. This may lead to forms of co-ownership, unless they are of the same sort and fungible when ownership might be deemed lost upon commingling so that the broker may result still as the true owner. Hence the serious problem of *commingling* and *segregation*. One way around this is the holding of the securities in *an omnibus client account* held by the broker (even in his own name but marked as client account) with a third party custodian (in the case of physical securities) assuming that under applicable law a kind of trust account is here construed. It reinforces *segregation* notions and avoids *commingling* with the broker's other assets; otherwise (therefore in the case of commingling and lack of segregation) *tracing* becomes the issue, a concept much less developed in civil law (where one may have to construe some form of co-ownership instead). It is also a serious issue when client moneys (even in client accounts) are reinvested by the intermediary in his own name.

In any event for the indicated reasons, the rights of investors in pooled accounts (even assuming sufficient segregation) remain under serious threat in the case of *fungible* securities in many legal systems, which in the worst scenarios may lead to no more than a personal right for delivery of shares of the same sort rather than a proprietary claim in the bankruptcy of the relevant intermediary or custodian. The result is that investors will get no more than the pro-rata share in a liquidation proceeds of their bankrupt brokers which they must share with all other creditors. The latter ones thus receive the benefit of the commingling confusion.

It would seem *inappropriate* as long as investors can still identify how many securities they contributed assuming the totals add up. In this aspect, a common property notion would seem a more appropriate answer also in the case of commingling of fungible securities with a sharing of any deficit like in the case of commingling of non-fungible assets in the sense of producing a new product from them. Otherwise trust notions, beneficial ownership and segregation are more appropriate characterisations for the investors' rights. These two proprietary approaches (co-ownership and trust) should be well distinguished.[313] From this perspective, book-entry systems are *a further step* in the development of pooled assets, where the rights of the investors in the underlying investment securities and the issue of pooling and segregation are *more fundamentally addressed*. Here the question of beneficial ownership and co-ownership rights of entitlement holders arises more directly and the possibility to move these rights simply to other brokers after a bankruptcy of the first one in the ordinary manner of shifting accounts.

The ideal is always that the business of the depository, broker or other intermediary should not impact on the business they do for their clients. Their personal creditors should therefore not obtain a windfall in having recovery or set-off rights in client assets. Notions of segregation or pooled ownership and constructive trust are here of great importance even if the latter remain underdeveloped in many countries of the civil law and may lead, even in common law, to uncertainties, especially where client and broker assets are practically commingled in such a way that they can no longer be clearly distinguished especially where proceeds have been reinvested in the broker's own name. As already mentioned, the fungible nature of investment securities themselves is here a different issue and is itself often seen as another bar to clear ownership rights of the clients. At least where in modern systems the emphasis is on client entitlements represented by book-entries with pooling arrangements based on the fungibility of assets,[314] the problem of investors' rights should be less of a conceptual issue in a system that legally separates clients' entitlements (and the underlying rights) more clearly from the intermediary's other assets and of the underlying securities and their nature. That clarification is in itself an important achievement of book-entry systems, more in particular in civil law countries.

The special risk and complication of the intermediary or broker going bankrupt whilst the transaction between client (principal) and the third party is *not completed* was already

---

[313] Notions of co-ownership prevail, however, always when there are too few underlying securities in a pooled arrangement so that the shortage must be divided pro-rata amongst the participants (pending a claim against the custodian for the missing securities).
[314] See also n 311 *supra*.

broached in chapter II, section 3.1.6 and will also be further discussed in chapter VI, section 1.3.9. It presents additional problems and more acutely raises (indirect) agency issues. It poses the question whether the rights to the assets received by the intermediary (whilst bankrupt) in his own name but for the account of the client (eg, by having his own entitlement *vis-à-vis* the depository already increased) shoot through to the latter, resulting in an automatic adjustment of the client's (segregated) entitlement with the broker. In civil law, this was likely in the case of *physical* securities only, but there may be much greater problems (except for statutory clarification) in the substitution of book-entry entitlements and for monetary claims. Attempts are likely to be made, however, to give the clients the benefits, possibly through some kind of legal assignment structure in respect of these uncompleted deals, especially if the end investor had already put his broker in funds. The same may go for the *pro rata* share of client bank accounts for proceeds received by bankrupt intermediaries upon a sale. In all these cases, there remain problems in respect of the set-off of non-related claims by the counterparty on the intermediary, see again chapter II, section 3.1.6.

As for security entitlements, a distinction may have to be made here between (a) the substitution itself, which once set into motion by the relevant instructions may well be completed under its own rules, (b) the reliance on general indirect agency notions, and (c) the operation of the clearing. The latter is *not* in itself considered to engender a transfer between the end-users but only a settlement technique achieved under the special rules of these facilities themselves.[315] It results, however, in one net number of securities (or security entitlements) coming to the relevant broker (even if bankrupt) subsequently to be unscrambled per client. But there remains (d) also the question of the rights under transactions that are to be settled *later* (and are therefore not yet in the process of being settled) and to the securities or moneys to be received thereunder where the bankrupt broker has acted in his own name. Do these rights to security entitlements or money also shoot through to the clients?

The above mentioned complications are increasingly likely to be resolved in a different way, however. Most larger brokers deliver securities (entitlements) from their inventory and credit their clients' securities accounts accordingly. They may therefore not at all go into the market to cover this credit or may do so only at a moment they consider more opportune. Yet for smaller brokers and those who do not regularly operate in the markets for their own account, the situation will be different and remains as described above.

Apart from these important ownership, settlement and clearing risks when intermediaries are or become insolvent, another risk for investors is that intermediaries will not collect and transfer to them timely any distribution on the investment securities, will not (timely) follow their instructions, for example to obtain and deliver the underlying security certificates (if this pass-through right still exists in a book entry system which may depend on there still being share certificates), will not timely make the necessary sales (or purchases) or create the required security interests in respect of his creditors. In the US, Article 8 UCC has special provisions in this connection, as we saw. For book-entry systems (and other pools of assets), there is also the risk that the pool is smaller than the sum total

---

[315] From a legal point of view, at the level of the book-entry holders, the substitution is likely to be some form of transfer under which the relationship between the seller and his broker as holder of the securities is replaced by one between the buyer and his broker. If the broker is the same, the substitution will be at the level of that broker alone. If there are different brokers involved (who are not dealing from their own accounts), their respective entitlements with a (joint) custodian up in the chain or at the depository will first be adjusted following by adjustments of the entitlements of their respective clients in their own books. This system of adjustment of book-entries has the appearance of a novation of the interest (although under applicable statutory law it may be handled differently). It is in the nature of administrative adjustments and should be distinguished from the trade between seller and buyer which concerns a transfer of a co-ownership or of a *pro rata* beneficial interest in an underlying unallocated pool of ownership rights and has therefore more the appearance of some assignment, although legally mostly not handled in that manner either, see further s 3.1.6 *infra*, and also s 3.1.1 *supra*.

of the entitlements through *mismanagement* (if not *fraud* or other misconduct) of the intermediary who is in charge but normally released from any liability for mere mismanagement in this connection. It is the simple result of the book-entry emerging when the broker accepts the transfer regardless of the broker meeting his asset-maintenance duty. There is not necessarily a chain of credit transfers like in the case of payment through bank transfers and such a chain of transfers is no condition for the emergence of the book-entry entilement of the purchaser in the books of his broker. (See also s 3.1.1 above.)

These risks are, however, not typical for book-entry systems but arise wherever investors' assets are handled by others (brokers or custodians), but tend to be more specifically dealt with in these newer immoblised systems of securities holdings.

There are other risks more typically connected with the *transfer* of securities or entitlements. They are essentially twofold. The first one is that the transaction will not close. That is the *settlement risk*, thus the risk that either the seller or buyer of the securities will not perform. The second risk is that, unknown to the buyer, the securities or entitlements did not legally belong to the seller because of *defects in his acquisition* or were *encumbered* and the question then is whether a *bona fide* purchaser of a security or security entitlement is protected. Legally the situation may be different here in respect of investments as negotiable instruments or book-entry entitlements. Again market practices may have something to say in this regard and the situation may be equalised in international securities trading.

The risk that the deal will not close because the counter-party or the broker *fails to perform* (for reasons other than bankruptcy) is real. In this connection, there is another closely related risk, which derives from *order mistakes*. It is therefore important that buy and sell orders can be immediately matched so that any mistakes or misunderstandings as regards number and class of investment securities are sorted out promptly and the necessary corrections made and that the deal does not close before that is done.

In the eurobond market, to minimise this risk, early on a system of delivery against payment (DVP) was developed, sometimes also referred to as cash against documents (CAD). It meant that if the buy and sell order did not match or the counter-party was not able to come up with the cash or securities, the transaction would not settle. The parties would be informed immediately and could take protection measures against any resulting market exposure for them. In this connection, the role of clearing and settlement intermediaries became very important. As third parties in this process, they would be neutral and verify the DVP and not close the transactions if the simultaneous exchange, which was the aim, could not take place. In the Euromarket, Euroclear and Clearstream (formerly Cedel) performed that function from an early date and it is an important part of their modern clearing and settlement function, only later joined by their immobilised depository functions and the simplified transfer system resulting from it through the adjustment of book-entries only (disposing of the need for any physical movement of investment securities).

3.1.4   Modern Clearing and Settlement Systems: Internationalisation

Technically, clearing and settlement organisations operate on a membership or participants' basis subject to a membership agreement or general conditions. [316] In the case of a transfer, the *modern clearing* systems themselves may guard against default by the broker,

---

[316] The following techniques are commonly used in this connection:

   (a)   a settlement agent or central depository system requires the participants to enter into bilateral relationships with the settlement agent under which that agent holds cash and securities accounts in

of which the central counterparty technique is the more advanced.[317] It implies a guarantee of the operation of the system by the counterparty who takes over all rights and obligations from the participants through a kind of novation and nets-off all obligations in terms of security transfers and payments.

In the case of Euroclear and Clearstream, the system has not yet developed so far but similar net calculations are being made on a daily basis. Members are the established underwriters, brokers and traders in the Euromarket.[318] In addition to their general conditions for membership,[319] these organisations have developed their own international practices. The regime under which they operate is substantially a book-entry system (either supported by the relevant bond certificates or, to save costs, now more likely by a global note which may eliminate the right to ask for certificates altogether).[320] Indeed, by introducing the book entry system, these organisations did away substantially with the physical aspects of bond trading in the manner that will be discussed in section 3.1.5 below.

Although technically still subject to a domestic legal regime, respectively that of Belgium and Luxembourg,[321] the manner of their operation in the Euromarket, the functioning of

> which interday debits and credits are netted on a bilateral basis between the settlement agent and the participant. The modern book-entry systems on which security entitlements are based are an important example of this system and function also between a broker and his clients (assuming that the broker operates a book-entry system);
>
> (b) a clearing house system which has two phases in the settlement process that involves in principle all participants. In the first one, the payment and/or delivery instructions are calculated and netted out between the participants for a period (say one day). Subsequently (either the same trading day or within an agreed period thereafter, say T+1 or T+2) any resulting balances are settled by payment or delivery to each participant. That is the system of settlement through Euroclear and Clearstream and most modern payment systems — see chapter III, s 1.2.4;
>
> (c) a central counter party (CCP) system allows all transactions to be conducted with the same counter-party through back to back transactions whilst this counter-party nets and closes out (either the same day or within an agreed period thereafter) all deals outstanding between it and any participant in its system. It is often exchange connected (especially in derivative exchanges) under which in the case of a transfer between two end-users who have matching trades, the exchange becomes technically the buyer to any potential seller and the seller to any potential buyer — see also chapter VI, s 1.4.4.

Earlier the DVP or 'delivery versus payment' was the standard settlement method at least in the Eurobond market based on a shortened settlement cycle. Within it there were several more specific techniques practised, see also the 'Delivery versus Payment in Securities Settlement Systems (1992)', Report of the Committee on Payment and Settlement Systems of the Central Banks of the Group of Ten Countries (CPSS) which distinguished between (a) real time gross settlement, which meant simultaneous *trade by trade* execution of the securities and of the payment transfers, (b) gross settlement over a time period in which the trade by trade approach is maintained but both the securities and payment streams result in debits and credits (often guaranteed by banks) that are netted at the very end of the cycle, and (c) net settlement in which all is simply netted out between participants at the end of the settlement period (still on the basis of simultaneity). The practical difference is in the liquidity requirements of the participants. Regardless of DVP, bankruptcy laws may still undermine the finality in the case of an intervening bankruptcy of one of the participants. This is the concern of finality legislation as in the EU's Settlement Finality Directive of 1998, see chapter III, s 1.2.6.

---

[317] See for Clearing also HF Minnerop 'Clearing Arrangement', (2003) 58 *The Business Lawyer*, 197.

[318] See for a description of them, R Goode, 'The Nature and Transfer of Rights in Dematerialised and Immobilised Securities' in F Oditah (ed), *The Future for the Global Securities Market* (1996), 107.

[319] The Terms and Conditions Governing Use of Euroclear and the Operating Procedures of the Euroclear System.

[320] Global notes are substitutes for certificates, not for registrations. They may be permanent, semi-permanent, or temporary. The permanent global note rules out any individual rights in the issue and the investor's relationship can therefore only be with the custodian. In a semi-permanent note, the investor still has an option to acquire certificates. Euroclear and Cedel have done away with this possibility. It means that a eurobond investor who wants to hold certificates cannot operate through Euroclear or Cedel. The temporary note is only held for a limited period until certificates are delivered. The global note as another way of avoiding materialisation (besides registration) is favoured by Euroclear and Cedel. It means that the traditional eurobond as bearer bond now only operates outside the Euroclear and Cedel system. Physical bonds outside this system are often preferred by small investors who personally collect the coupons to avoid taxes.

[321] See Belgian Royal Decree No 62 of 1967 (as amended) and the Grand-Ducal Decree of 1971 (as amended).

their book entry system,[322] the rights in the pools,[323] the manner of clearing, settlement and netting, the repo business in, and manners of pledging of the assets, even the nature of the eurobond itself at first as a transnationalised negotiable bearer instrument and later as a book-entry entitlement, the transferability of these book entry entitlements and the protection of *bona fide* purchasers, all became substantially subject to the practices of the euro-market and should as such be considered internationalised. It was already mentioned in the previous section: see further chapter I, sections 3.2.2., 3.2.3, and section 3.2.1 below. It should neutralise not only the legal problems derived from any *lex situs* as applicable law in respect of the underlying bonds or other investment securities (as this *situs* was always likely to be fortuitous, all the more so in respect of security entitlements which have no true location, and could in any event easily change), but also the problems connected with the location of the book-entry system itself which is no less fortuitous and in any event bears little relationship to the place of the transaction, which could hardly be controlled by the law of the location of that system. In any event, the question of that location itself is not without its problems.

Thus inappropriate *leges situs* concerning the proprietary aspects of eurobonds and their transfer (or even inappropriately chosen domestic laws to cover the instrument) and inappropriate or inadequate domestic (Belgium or Luxembourg) laws concerning the system could thus be neutralised or overcome by established *trans-national market practices*. At least in the euro-market, it allowed a system of transfer, *bona fide* purchaser protection, repos and pledges to develop in respect of euro-securities regardless of the laws of these two countries and sudden changes therein, *eg* through adverse case law (like the 1996 Tilman case in Belgium, see the next section).[324] The result is a much less legally risky and also much more predictable and cost effective system, although amongst legal scholars much lip service is still paid to private international law notion in this connection, unnecessarily as it would seem and as will be discussed further in section 3.2.3 below.

---

[322] Technically Euroclear and Cedel hold no physical custody but they have sub-custodians in the countries of the currencies of the issues which they therefore indirectly hold in an immobilised manner.

[323] Technically the Belgian Decree backing up the Euroclear system, see n 321 *supra*, does not state on the ownership rights of entitlement holders in the pools. Market practice considers the participants co-owners: see also the Euroclear Communication on 'Rights of participants in the Euroclear System in Securities held on their behalf in the System' of 4 Apr 1997.

[324] A shock resulted in this connection from the decision of the Belgian Supreme Court of 17 Oct 1996 (Sart-Tilman) [1995–96] RW 1395 Note Storme, ruling out the fiduciary or conditional transfer of assets in Belgium. It greatly increased the re-characterisation risk in respect of ownership based funding through Euroclear and raised the spectre of the need for the execution of a pledge agreement in all cases and the crediting of the investment securities to the special Pledge Account in Euroclear under Article 5 of the Royal Decree of 1967 pertaining to Euroclear, assuming Belgian law was applicable. The situation was remedied through new legislation of 15 July 1998 concerning 'amendments to certain legal provisions regarding financial instruments and securities clearing systems' (Article 30), [1998] *Moniteur Belge* 28.934. The better view is that the 1996 case was not relevant in the first place as market practice applies to eurosecurities and the way they are held and transfered through Euroclear. Belgium law at most applies residually.

The Belgian legislation of 1998 covered more than the operations in Euroclear but is limited to situations where the transferor is a bank or other financial institution or performs investment activities for its own account or for the account of third parties (or is a foreign company or institution with a similar status). In other words, it only applies to fund raising in the professional sphere (but can be done on behalf of customers).

The re-characterisation risk was eliminated in Luxembourg much earlier through the Grand Ducal Decree of 19 July 1983 on fiduciary agreements entered into by credit institutions, but the protection is limited to securities located in the Grand Duchy, which raises the issue of the location securities entered in a book entry system: see for the modern solutions (also in Euroclear and Cedel) the text at n 231 *supra*.

3.1.5   Book-Entry Systems for Shares and Bonds: Depository Receipts and The Develoments towards Dematerialisation and Immobilisation

In the foregoing, the modern book-entry system of holding and transferring securities was already mentioned briefly and it needs to be discussed more fully. Already in the late 1960s, the transfer of shares and bonds as negotiable instruments in the informal international eurobond market proved increasingly cumbersome because of the great volume of trans-actions that each time involved a great number of physical (bearer) certificates. It was one of the reasons for the creation of Euroclear and Clearstream (Cedel) as *centralised* custo-dial, clearing and settlement institutions through which order verification and matching, payment and delivery were to be directed.

Purely *domestically*, the creation of register(ed) shares and bonds, which did not need physically to exist, could have simplified the transfer system, based as it was on register entries and *dematerialised* securities. It could easily have allowed for electronic trading and settlement. However, as it was still normal (especially in England) also to issue some type of certificate even if not itself negotiable, this made the procedure for transfer no less cum-bersome than in the case of the transfer of ordinary share (bearer) certificates. It much later also proved the wrong environment for electronic trading. Internationally, the com-plication of registration in company registers itself which could be far away and could imply also domestic restrictions on the transfers of such registered shares (or bonds) often hampered that type of trading also as already mentioned in the previous sections.

In the USA, changes to Article 8 UCC in 1977 (Section 8-313) introduced the possibility of electronic transfers precisely by allowing a system of registration to develop in which certificates would be entirely abolished. It meant therefore complete dematerialisation. The idea was that in this manner electronic transmission systems could become efficient and settlement a matter between the various settlement departments of the intervening brokers and the companies' registers. In this system, individual shareholders would continue to appear as the shareholders on the companies' registers. It meant converting all shares into registered shares and doing away with their status as negotiable instruments altogether. Transferability was to be maintained only on the basis of these register entries, sharehold-ers instructions, and statutory backing.

In the event, this statutory initiative did not succeed but an alternative practitioners' approach developed in the USA through the use of the Depositary Trust Company which came into being as a result of the back office crisis in the nineteen-sixties caused by an excess of paper securities.. It did not rely on *dematerialisation* but rather on *immobilisation* of the securities. Unlike dematerialisation, immobilisation technically breaks the link between issuer and investor by introducing an extra layer of holding the securities. It became the key to the new system and was based on custody of the investment securities by a custodial com-pany that would be the legal owner (or sometimes called 'depository') of the underlying shares and maintain a book entry system as proof of its clients' entitlements to the securities, much in the same way as Euroclear and Clearstream (Cedel) had already started to do.

Thus the Depositary Trust Company was likely to hold substantially all the shares of an issuer forever and issue entitlements against it. Only the latter would change when investors traded. For US government bonds, a similar system was developed by the Federal Reserve (which is the Central Bank of the USA) as depository/custodian. It is this system that is now supported by the 1994 revision of Article 8 UCC. It has also become the domestic sys-tem in many European countries (like Germany and the Netherlands)[325] and was, as just

---

[325] In Germany under the Depotgesetz and in the Netherlands under the Wet Giraal Effectenverkeer (Wge).

mentioned, for eurobonds already introduced by Euroclear and Cedel.[326] The new English electronic transfer system (Crest), on the other hand, is not based on this custody or immobilisation approach but retains an approach under which shareholders (instead of their intermediaries) remain directly connected to the share register of each company but in an increasingly dematerialised way.

The immobilisation thus means a *tiered system* of holding securities. In it, the issuer will only deal with a limited number of depositories, who in turn deal with the brokers who have the end investors as their clients. This system is only truly efficient if it is permanent, which results when an issuer only issues a global note to a depository, or will only recognise one depository (or a small number of them) as shareholder (or bondholder). It may be semi-permanent when it still allows an end investor an option to obtain shares or bonds in his own name (the *'pass through'* right), which option technically still exiss in the Euromarkets and is also backed up by statute in the US assuming certificates are still issued, see Section 8-508 UCC. In fact, it does not give here an absolute right but only speaks of *eligible* entitlement holders and the pass-through right *may be excluded* by contract or by the nature of the way the securities are held (like in a book-entry system only).

In the case of immobilisation, there are in the client tier only entitlements (and not securities) that change hands upon trading, which is likely to be followed by settlement through modern clearing systems. In the depository tier, there is an unchanged owner of the corporate shares and bonds in as far as the company is concerned. All income flows and information supply are directed by the issuer to the depository who deals with its clients and will be paid by them for that service. Consequently, there is here an important cost saving element for issuers. Naturally, these clients could be intermediaries themselves like brokers who have in turn a system of client accounts under which their clients will have entitlements against them. As mentioned in the previous sections, in modern systems there is likely to be also pooling at that level in respect of fungible securities of the same type.

In the US, the new Article 8 UCC framework is based on a distinction between investment securities held *directly* by share- or bondholders and those held *indirectly* by intermediaries on behalf of their clients. Part 5 of Article 8 applies to this second type of holding. Under it, custodians may hold amongst their assets securities indirectly owned by their clients through a book entry system but also securities that are registered by or endorsed to the clients themselves (who could also be brokers holding these securities for clients). Again, dematerialisation is here less important than the immobilisation and the book entry system also works in respect of shares and bonds represented by certificates in the various layers.

In book-entry systems, the true or economic owners of the investment securities (the clients or end investors) thus receive an interest either directly or more likely through their brokers in the pool of the relevant type of securities deposited with a depository institution (in the US the term 'depositary' is also used). Changes are communicated between the settlement departments of the brokers and the depositary institution, which communication is increasingly electronic in EDI fashion. This electronic data interchange method was already discussed in section 2.3.2 above. It normally means that the brokers remain the sole entitlement holders *vis-à-vis* the depository institutions which cater for them as members, whilst their clients' entitlement will only be marked in the brokers' own books. Pooling results therefore at different levels. The nature of the entitlements and their protection will be more fully discussed in the next section.

---

[326] See also RD Guynn, 'Modernizing Securities Ownership, Transfer and Pledging Laws', (Section on Business Law, International Bar Association 1996).

It should be clearly understood and cannot be sufficiently repeated that (in the absence of a pass-through right) in such an immobilised system there is *no* alternative right of the investor (and his creditors) in the underlying securities. As already mentioned before, the book-entry facility acquires a special meaning if the underlying shares are not themselves freely transferable. In such cases, it provides for an indirect way of making them transferable. Book-entry systems may also provide a special transfer facility at the international level if transfers of the underlying registered shares require cumbersome registration in domestic corporate registers or are subject to other restrictions. That need not then be an issue in international trading as the depository as registered owner remains the same and only book entries change in a simplified manner as agreed between the depository and its clients or members.

This facilitating of international transfers was earlier often the objective of depositary receipts (DRs) which function in a similar two-tier manner (and which may themselves be negotiable instruments). They re-created, however, the logistical problems of their own transfer. They may themselves become subject to immobilised depository and book entry systems at the DR level. In these DR systems, there may also still be a facility to receive the underlying shares (the 'pass through' right). If not, there may be a particular problem with pledgees or similar security interest holders whose repossession right would then be limited to the DRs. The limitations on the pass through right resulted in Europe often from schemes organised by a company to prevent an unfriendly take-over of the underlying shares. This is still a common protection method in the Netherlands, although even there conversion by DR holders cannot be entirely excluded.

3.1.6   *The Legal Characterisation of Book-Entry Entitlements.*
The Manner and Consequences of their Transfer.
Transfer Instructions and the Notion of their Abstraction or Finality

Book-entry systems raise the question of the characterisation of the book-entry entitlement holders' rights. The essence of most of these systems is that the economic interest holders (the investors) no longer have negotiable securities or appear on a company register as shareholders. Assuming there is a pass-through right, they still have a claim against their intermediary either for delivery (through the chain) of negotiable securities or to be put on the register themselves. The right may, however, be no more than a direct share in their intermediaries' own entitlements in book-entry systems higher in the chain. More likely, in modern systems it may be excluded altogether. In any event, it cannot operate if there is no more than a permanent global note with a depository.

It is useful to make here some distinctions and also create some historical perspective:

(a)   The *pass-through* right was always a problem where the intermediary or broker acted in his own name (as undisclosed or indirect agent) for his clients in the acquisition of investment securities. Especially in civil law, the position of indirect agents is here problematic even upon disclosure. As already mentioned in section 3.1.3 above, it could be argued in such cases that under applicable law their clients never had more than personal reclaiming rights (rather than pass-through rights): see more in detail chapter II, section 3.1.6. This would be all the more a problem in the case of securities that are by their nature *fungible* and the identification of which therefore presents a problem. This is sometimes also refered to as the problem of *practical commingling*.

(b) To the extent client assets could be identified, however, a pass-through right in the sense that title shoots through directly to the investors, could be accepted under applicable notions of agency and a client account could also help (even in the case of fungible securities and moneys) as at least segregation of a pool was achieved. It left the rights against such a pool as a separate item. It presented most likely a combination of a trust situation and form of common or pooled property. Co-ownership would obtain amongst the pooled investors themselves (therefore internally), who were likely to have a beneficial segregated right against the broker (therefore externally). Especially in the case of moneys owed clients upon a sale, that segregation could only be achieved in such a pooled manner through separate client accounts.

(c) Another issue was here the rights to unsettled trades, therefore to moneys or to securities a (bankrupt) broker could still be owed in respect of unfinished transactions and that had not yet been delivered to him (before its bankruptcy). Above, a further distinction was made here between transactions the settlement of which was already in the pipeline and those in which there were mere settlement rights. It concerns here the segregation of those rights as against the bankrupt broker and the (beneficial) owership rights of clients in respect of these rights. [327]

(d) Even if the client could acquire in the above manner a direct right in the assets acquired by his intermediary in the latter's name, there could still be *legal commingling* with the broker's *own* assets resulting in renewed segregation issues in the case of a bankruptcy of the intermediary, again unless special arrangements backed up by law were made to especially protect client assets or accounts. If the assets were physically held by the broker, tracing would become necessary, also in respect of reinvestments of clients' moneys by the broker in his own name. Tracing is a limited concept, however, in civil law. If there is a client account in which the broker also holds some own assets, it may be easier to maintain the notion of pooling and co-ownership of the pool in which the broker then also participates for his share.

(e) Where investment securities are deposited with a third party *depository/custodian* and a book-entry system with security entitlements operates, these problems are likely to be more fundamentally addressed even in civil law. Especially the issue of segregation and the limited rights of brokers/depositories/custodians may then find statutory expression. It is *not* the same, therefore, as depositing money with a bank when all segregation is abandoned and only a personal contractual claim remains for the depositor who fundamentally becomes a

---

[327] That seems to be the new Dutch situation, where special arrangments had to be made for that situation in terms of some form of statutory assignment of such claims. The Dutch Supreme Court in a decision of 23 Sept 1994 [1996] NJ 461 characterised the entitlement to that kind of claim as no more than a personal right. It suggests that entitlements may be split according to the nature of the underlying asset. It is probably a consequence of the confusion in modern Dutch law about the ownership rights in intangible assets. Co-ownership rights in a pool which itself contains entitlements may not be so affected. The statutory bankruptcy provision (Article 33 Wge, see n 325 *supra*) leading to a division of the assets upon a bankruptcy of the custodian neutralises the worst consequences of this decision, but only applies to securities and entitlements in the pools, not to related claims for payment and settlement. The clients do not therefore under present Dutch law automatically stand in the place of their bankrupt broker *vis-à-vis* the custodian or third parties. It is another vivid illustration of why internationalised custody systems should not be seen to become involved in the vicissitudes and peculiarities of local laws with which they have only a fortuitous relationship through their location.

common creditor in a bankruptcy of the bank. At least for investment securities, the securities remain *separate* even if only as pools of entitlements of investments of different types and are at least in principle segregated from the assets (and liabilities) of the intermediary/depository/custodian leading to *pro rata* beneficial ownership right or some similar *sui generis* pooled proprietary or co-ownership right against the intermediary who has thus deposited client securities. It is in this connection not useful to speak of a personal right against the broker/depository/custodian to a co-ownership or beneficial ownership right in his pools. The key is that investors are classified as *pro rata* beneficial owners so that they could seek at least a separation of their assets as such regardless of the solvency or insolvency of the third party intermediary/broker/depository/custodian.[328]

(f)   The modern *book entry system* in respect of immobilised securities may thus be seen as a refinement of the pooled client account in which entitlements take the place of the underlying securities as a different layer of interests resulting in a new type of security in the form of an entitlement that embodies a proprietary right of clients, is (even regardless of the nature of the underlying securities) always *fungible* and operates under its own transfer regime (again regardless of whether the underlying securities are transferable and how they are transfered under their own rules). Indeed the pooling, beneficial or co-ownership (or similar proprietary) notions are now readily accepted in connection with this type of book-entry system. In the absence of trust notions, in civil law countries, statutes still underpin the structure with a pure *co-ownership* construction giving the entitlement holders at least a direct interest in the pool upon a bankruptcy of the intermediary operating a book-entry system and a right to move the account after a bankruptcy of the relevant intermediary (usually an end investor's broker) leading to similar adjustments in the bankrupt broker's entitlement with the depository or other custodians in the system of immoblised securities.

(g)   In the US, Article 8 UCC has a general regime and decides so at all levels of entitlement holdings (Section 8-508 UCC). The interest of investors is not truly defined in this connection and neither is therefore the exact nature of their proprietary right; rather a number of consequences are identified. [329] A joint beneficial ownership under a constructive trust is probably the English approach, also at all levels.[330] Here there is a more explicit reliance on the trust concept and the fiduciary relationship between legal owner (depository) and equitable owner or beneficiary (the entitlement holder), but it is easy to see that the approach of Article 8 UCC in the US is in reality no different.

(h)   It suggests, however, that the entitlement holder has less than a proprietary right but is still protected as beneficial owner except against *bona fide*

---

[328] Section 8-102 (a) (17) cmt 2 UCC reflects in this connection: "A security entitlement is both a package of personal rights against a securities intermediary and an interst in the property held by the securities intermediary". In Section 8-503 *cmt* 2 it is said that "A security entitlement is not a claim to a specific identifiable thing; it is a package of rights and interests that a person has against the person's securities intermediary and its property".

[329] It is an approach also used in Artcle 2A UCC in respect of the rights of equipment lessees and a consequence of the American attitude that is not interested in abstract or systemetically inter-connected ownership notions in chattels and intangible assets, to which in sales Article 2 UCC also testifies.

[330] See R Goode, *Legal Problems of Credit and Security* (3rd ed, 2003), 6–08, see also J Benjamin, *Interests in Securities* (2000).

purchasers of the same interest from the intermediary. A consequence of this approach is that in a bankruptcy of the intermediaries, the entitlement holders do not function as legal owners but must look for a replacement of the intermediary. In the case of the bankrupt depository, it also means that his entitlement holders have no right *vis-à-vis* issuers to become legal owners but must look for a replacement depository who will also need the approval of issuers.

(i) But it is certain that in book-entry systems entitlement holders no longer risk being mere general creditors of the intermediary, even if they have not timely claimed their pass-through right (Section 8-503(a) UCC) *if* still available. They are also not secured interest holders claiming a priority in the distribution of execution proceeds concerning the pools held by a bankrupt intermediary. Under Article 8 UCC, they are indeed treated in the manner of owners (even if on more careful analysis they may be no more than beneficial owners). There is segregation and pooling in principle resulting in an (undefined) *sui generis pro rata* proprietary right that puts emphasis (for shares) on the rights to dividend, voting, liquidation proceeds and corporate information. The intermediary is essentially passive and does not hold a sufficient interest to use the clients' entitlements as collateral for its own debt unless the entitlement holders have so agreed (Section 8-504(b) UCC). This is the issue of rehypothecation. In fact, only end investors can effect a transfer and may give others security interests in their entitlements under Sections 9-309, 312 and 314 and Section 9-327–29 (formerly Section 9-115) UCC (leading upon default to a repossession right of the entitlement including any pass-through right (if any) without the entitlement holder's consent).

(j) In this system, any *pass-through* right should always be clearly distinguished from the security entitlement itself and has become exceptional (therefore no longer inherent in the entitlement). It is in the nature of connecting the various custodial layers of securities and allows entitlement holders to ultimately take the depository's position *vis-à-vis* the issuer as owner of the shares but only in such systems which still allow it and where there are still individual certificates. It does not work therefore when there is only a global note.

(k) It should further be noted that even if there is no pass-through right so that end investors have no rights through the chain of layers, the entitlements of intermediaries are not truly of the same nature as those of end investors. They retain in principle only segegrated rights which (unlike banks in respect of their deposits) they cannot use for their own interests and ultimately hold for the end investors only. The same is true for the depository and ultimately for the issuer. It means that if for some reason all intermediaries disappear, the joint end investors would have rights against the depository and if the latter also disappeared they would have rights against the issuer. It also means that if all end investors would disappear, the intermediaries including the depository would have no rights against the issuer. Even though it is therefore possible to see the depository as legal owner of the securities and all the rest as beneficial owners (divided in different layers in which each entitlement holder could be seen as trustee of his entitlement for benefical owners in the next layer, whilst an entitlement holder in the next layer would not have any direct right against a previous layer), that is not to suggest that all entitlements are of the same order.

(l)   The entitlements of the intermediaries are in truth only in the nature of
      administrative holdings whilst only the end investor has an entitlement that
      gives him the right to all the benefits in terms therefore of dividend, voting
      rights, liquidation proceeds and corporate information in the case of shares
      and in terms of coupon payments and repayment of principal in the case of
      bonds. That also has an effect on the transfer in each layer, which in as far as
      intermediaries are concerned are best considered administrative acts whilst
      between the end investors as buyer and seller there is more of a true transfer in
      terms of delivery (through their brokers as agents), although this is now often
      superseded by brokers simply delivering to their buying clients from their own
      inventory or taking from their selling clients into their own inventory.

(m)   That may also have an effect on the legal conditions for the transfers if still
      through the various layers or tiers, the legal requirements for them in terms
      of capacity and agreements between the parties and the characterisation of
      these transfers in terms of assignment, novation or transfer *sui generis* and
      the manner in which these administrative adjustments of book-entry entitle-
      ments in the chain may be legally attacked as between intermediaries assum-
      ing that proper instructions have been given. Although it is probably true that
      the instructions and the right to give them are personal to entitlement hold-
      ers, that upon transfer entitlements are simply extinguished and newly cre-
      ated, and that the new entitlements therefore simply result from changes in
      the entitlement holdings, that does not mean that there has not been an
      underlying transfer of entitlement holdings between seller and buyer in a pro-
      prietary sense, although more clearly the case when brokers go into the mar-
      ket for their clients or when there are identifind end users like in the case of
      securities lending.

(n)   Like in payment systems, there may thus still be some kind of credit transfer
      through the system. However, the book entry adjustment promised by the bro-
      ker is not dependent on itself and may not concern balances owned by the
      intermediaries.

As a consequence, the tendency, at least in common law countries, is to consider all types of
entitlement holders in a *proprietary* manner, but to make subtle differences between intermediaries and end-investors and also distinguish payment instructions even if largely
treated in a similar manner.[331] That has at least four consequences for entitlement holders:

(a)   The essence of the entitlement is (in the case of shares) the right to dividend,
      voting, liquidation proceeds and corporate information whatever the underlying

---

[331] Among civil law countries, only German law has attempted to devise a full regime for security entitlements
within their civil law system of proprietary rights. It has been hard work and the result is hardly convincing. The
key text is the *Depotgesetz* (DepG) which has a history going back to 1937 and which allows for the holding of
fungible securities (*Sammelverwarung*), but the general law concerning custody is still derived from the BGB,
especially relevant for the proprietary and transfer aspects of securities, also in the form of entitlements.
Dematerialisation through global notes (*Sammelurkunde*) has in the meantime indeed become common in
Germany and allows for fast and effective clearing (*Effectengiroverkehr*) normally done through Clearstream
Banking Frankfurt that is the only German entity conforming to the requirements of the DepG in this respect (as
Wertpapiersammelbank), which is therefore the only German entity that may operate as depository. Section 1
DepG makes clear that this statute does not only apply to traditional custody of paper securities but also to dema-
terialised secuities entitlements or securities accounts (*Gutschriften in Wertpapierrechnung*). Regardless of the still

holding structure, but in the case of intermediaries these rights do not belong to them personally. It is perhaps best to see the end-investors always as the beneficial owners of these rights in each intermediate layer, even if they cannot claim them directly in respect of the previous layer. These rights are transferred through instructions by the end-investors or their (instructed) brokers, who may deal from their own inventory or alternatively in the case of a purchase first adjust their own entitlements with a common intermediary and subsequently their own client entitlements with them, or, in the case of a sale, first adjust the seller's entitlement with them and subsequently adjust their own entitlement with a common intermediary with the broker of the buyer, upon which the broker of the buyer will adjust the buyer's entitlement with him. However, unlike in the case of a bank transfer through a push or credit transfer system, the entitlement adjustment is never conditional upon such credit transfers through the system.

overriding structure and impact of the BGB, *leges specialese* have thus developed as some form of capital market law (*Kapitalmarktrecht*) besides the more traditional banking law and may deviate from the BGB norm. As much of this is professional dealing, further rules may be contained in the German Commercial Code (*Handelsgesetzbuch* or HGB) which may also override the BGB. The Banking Act or *Kreditwesengesetz* may also retain some relevance in this area, but the most important statute is the DepG. The Negotiable Instruments Act or *Wertpapierhandelsgesetz* has under its own terms no relevance for custody services in connection with securities trading. The special conditions for Securities Dealings (*Sonderbedingungen fuer Wertpapiergeschaefte*) normally used by all intermediaries are relevant here as an expression of party autonomy. Clearstream Frankfurt also uses a special set of business conditions of its own: the *Allgemeine Geschäftsbedingungen Clearstream Banking Aktiengesellschaft.*

The sum total of these various legal instruments may be summarised as follows. The first result is an a-typical contract with the securities intermediary under which there is a form of custody (*Verwahrung*, s 688BGB, which is not in itself compatible with fungibility) and service providing (*Dienstleistung*, Section 611 BGB) in which connection there may also be some rules about instructions (*Entgeltliche Geschäftsbesorgung*, Section 675 BGB). Intermediaries may engage subcustodians under the DepG (*Drittverwalter*). All act and hold the securities with subcustodians in their own name.

The problem in this system is (as elsewhere) with the ownership structure. The end-investor in a domestic context is the legal owner and must ultimately be marked as such through the chain nof intermediaries. The German challenge is to express this in terms of its traditional notions of possession or holdership. In this system the depository is considered no more than holder for the end investor (*unmittelebarer Allein und Fremdbesitzer*, Section 854 BGB). This holdership is based on an obligatory right under the custody agreement with subcustodians. The end-investor has no more than a mere contractual relationship with his broker or intermediary and can in this system of contractual rights reach the holder or issuer directly.

Yet a problem still arises, where the ultimate investment is not physically represented by paper. This problem already occurred in the past in respect of registered securities. Rights or mere claims of this nature are not protected in a possessory manner. Since 1940, and 1942, however, by statutory instrument (*Verordnung über die Verwaltung und Anschaffung von Rechtsschuldbuchforderungen* and *über die Behandlung von Anleihen des Deutschen Reichs*)) they are treated by legal fiction in the manner of paper securities and subject to similar proprietary protection. That is now also deemed the case in respect of depositories of dematerialised securities. Thus it is not Clearstream but the end-investor who under German law is considered the owner of the securities in this manner. Clearstream as depository has only a personal holder's right in the securities which belong to the investor who can protect himself through proprietary actions. It is even accepted that in this system the end investor has a pass-through right and may at least in principle physically demand their delivery. Of interest is in this regard that the fiction of paper is maintained to give the end-investor the semblance of ownership in the traditional sense. The rules of subletting are her analogously applied (Section 546(2) BGB). This is done to achieve a form of segregation from the estate of intermediaries.

The problem of re-characterisation of the investor's interest in a modern system of securities accounts does not therefore strictly arise in German law as the thinking remains paper and delivery based, even if this is now so by way of fiction only. It can, however, not be ignored that in modern systems this pass-through right is eliminated which must therefore be deemed contractually abandoned in German law. It is in any event not possible to exercise if there are no shares or only global notes and the continuing importance of the fiction must then be found in the segregation it effectuates between the property of the intermediary and his clients.

(b)   Like payments made through bank transfer instructions, the transfer so
      induced is neither an assignment nor novation proper but *sui generis*, subject
      to an own regime. Unless there are pass-through rights, the investors (or their
      creditors) never have any rights to the underlying securities themselves. On the
      other hand, the intermediaries have no right to them either or even to the ben-
      eficial rights in them and must hold their own entitlements with the other
      intermediaries or the depository as back up for the rights of the end-investors
      and they cannot freely dispose of them. They are entirely passive in that respect
      and must (even as the depository in respect of his ownership rights) wait for
      instructions from entitlement holders which can only be activated by end-
      investors. Subsequently, they must (even upon their own bankruptcy) co-operate
      to adjust their own entitlement (ultimately with the depository) if an end-investor
      buys or sells or decides to move his securities account to another intermediary
      with a book-entry system. It would appear that the proprietary right of the
      entitlement holder translates here in a form of segregation from the interme-
      diary's estate.

(c)   In such a bankruptcy situation, the entitlement holders will either be able to
      step into the shoes of their intermediary *vis-à-vis* higher intermediaries in the
      chain if the intermediary in question falls away or more likely be forced to shift
      their accounts to other intermediaries and the latter's bankruptcy trustee would
      have no blocking right. The rights of end investors are in this sense *proprietarily
      derivative* even if they are no legal owners of the underlying securities. This is a
      great advantage but also reconfirms that entitlement holders in the chain have
      no independent position and may for example not be *bona fide* holders *vis-à-vis*
      entitlement holders higher in the chain and not be able to exert a better right in
      respect of them than their predecessors. Also, they are not protected against
      these higher entitlement holders giving out new entitlements against the pool
      so that a shortfall results. That seems also the Euroclear view.[332] Thus in systems
      of this sort, much still depends on the honesty, management and professional-
      ism of the intermediaries. As between end-investors the situation may be dif-
      ferent but they cannot ignore the mistakes that have been made in the chain
      and they must jointly bear the consequences of false entitlements having been
      issues to *bona fide* end investors.

(d)   In this system, only end investors may create more limited proprietary rights
      (like security interests) in their entitlements, but only at the level of their most
      direct intermediary (who need not consent). Thus the entitlements may be
      encumbered and end investors may insist that their intermediaries will reflect
      this through the chain up to the depository. It would in any event entitle the
      pledgee to any pass-through rights if still existing. Naturally, if the different
      layers of entitlements are against intermediaries in different countries, this
      may create applicable law problems. At least in the euro-market, in claims
      against Euroclear and Clearstream (Cedel), that could be resolved in a unitary
      transnational manner under the prevailing practices in that market, as will be
      discussed in the next sections. It could, however, still give rise to pass-through
      problems at the level of the issuer, relevant in particular if the securities are in
      registered form and therefore in principle issued and transferred under local
      laws.

---

[332] See also n 323 *supra*. Again it is for the Euromarket itself to sort out what this means exactly.

It may be illustrative in this connection to compare the right of a security entitlement holder to an investor in an open-ended fund or, in UK terms, a collective investment scheme which (again in the UK) may be an (authorised) unit trust, an open ended investment company or a recognised overseas scheme (see Section 238 Financial Services and Markets Act 2000). Under unit trusts, the investor receives a unit in exchange for his investment. In an investment company he receives shares. In either instance he would be dependant on the winding up of the trust or company before he would receive physical shares (if existing). Otherwise his rights to these shares or the legal characterisation of his investment is also obscure. It is of course easy to say that he is either a beneficial owner under the trust or a shareholder of the investment company but that does not say much about the actual rights he has. In truth, it would appear that either the benefical owner or the shareholder in this kind of open-ended scheme can only expect money, either as dividends or as sale's proceeds. His expectation is therefore different from that of a security entitlement holder. The extra protection the investor in a fund has over a depositor in a bank is that he has more than a mere personal claim. He is also entitled (together with all other investors in the fund) to segregation of the investments from the estate of manager of the fund. In that respect the situation is similar to that of a securities entitlement holder *vis-à-vis* his intermediary.

Finally, in order to better understand the transfer instructions, the legal details of the tranfer of the entitlements in the different layers should be further considered in terms of its effects on the relationship and transfer between end-investors as buyers and sellers. This concerns the issue of *finality*.

A first remark concerns the nature of the instructions of the end investors (through their brokers). The receivers of instructions through the chain need not be concerned about who has originally set them in motion and for what reason (either a sale and purchase between end investors, which might itself be invalid or erroneous, or their desire to change brokers for whatever reasons). This is often referred to as the *abstract nature* of these instructions about which only the one of the immediately concerned entitlement holder need to be considered by the relevant intermediary or the depository and not the correctness or underlying causes for the change.[333] These considerations cannot therefore invalidate these instructions. Between two intermediaries who are thus adjusting an entitlement, there may of course also be mistakes in that e.g. the wrong accounts were debited or credited, they were debited or credited for too much or too little, there may have been double bookings, or there might have been no proper instruction altogether, all mistakes which may give rise to a later adjustment as between them but such adjustments would not be justified or proper on the basis of problems in the relationship between end-investors or between these end-investors and their brokers. Also in this manner transactions further down the chain could not be undone (without consent of the relevant intermediary).

A broader problem is in how far lack of intent, capacity or disposition rights between those directly involved in an adjustment of entitlements may still undermine it. Again it is a problem already encountered in electronic banking payments, see chapter III, section 1.2.2. Are these instructions normal legal acts or rather acts in fact? In the latter case, intent, capacity and disposition rights are irrelevant. This is the more desirable approach which may

---

[333] See also JH Sommer, 'A Law of Financial Accounts: Modern Payment and Securities Transfer Law', (1998), 53 *The Business Lawyer* 1183*ff.*

ultimately have to be achieved through statute. There may be a difference with bank transfers where in the payment system real balances owned by these banks are being transferred, which is often not the case in book-entry systems of securities. In the case of a sale and purchase of securities, all is simply directed towards identifying the new end investor or in the case of a change in broker by an end investor towards identifying the end-investor's proper entitlement. If somehow the relevant end investor is not happy with the result of all the bookings, that will be foremost a question of adjustment between him and his counterparty or his old and new broker and not (or only subsequently) between the various intermediaries amongst themselves which may require new instructions from the relevant end investors.

3.2 The Internationalisation of Custody and Settlement Systems and its Opportunities

3.2.1 *The Role of the Euromarket for Bonds and the Effect on International Share Trading. The Dominant Role of International Practices and the Bankruptcy Law Implications*

In the foregoing the effect of the internationalisation of the investment streams on the nature, status and trading of the underlying investment securities was already noted and can be summarised as follows:

(a)   the eurobond developed as a transnational negotiable instrument, detached from domestic laws even those chosen by the parties or made applicable to it by the issuer, and is subject to the practices of the international euromarket: see also chapter I, section 3.2.2;

(b)   there also developed in that market underwriting and trading practices now subject to the rules and recommendations of the IPMA and ISMA which are in the first instance explained and enforced by market practitioners on the basis of their practices: see also chapter I, section 3.2.3;

(c)   there further developed special clearing and settlement facilities which meant (i) verification of all trades in Euroclear or Clearstream (formerly Cedel) without which the transfer could not settle, (ii) a DVP method and moment of transfer, which is upon payment and not delivery, (iii) a clearing system for intermediaries which does not itself result in the transfer but makes the transfer process safer, quicker and less costly, (iv) the possibility of creating more limited proprietary rights in these instruments in terms of pledges, repos, bond-lending, and conditional transfers, and (v) the development of an own internationalised rule for the protection of *bona fide* purchasers;

(d)   subsequently there emerged in that market also custodial arrangements with immobilisation of the securities and a book-entry system as another practitioners' development with the entitlements based on their fungibility, transferability, manner of transfer or substitution, co-ownership or beneficial ownership and pass-through rights, the types of limited proprietary and security interests that could be created in them, the manner in which this was done, and their protection and enforcement,[334] all being determined and further developed by (euro) market practices;[335]

(e)   in the case of shares, these practices prevailed over the *lex situs* of the underlying securities, largely because of the fortuitous nature of the *situs* in respect of negotiable instruments, although in the case of a global note there may be some doubt on this point, and more so in respect of security entitlements, which in any event, as intangible assets, hardly have a location. In truth, these practices prevail because of their recognition by the international law merchant which leads to uniform treatment regardless of location;

(f)   these market practices also prevailed over the domestic laws of the place of the book-entry systems or over conflict rules pointing to other domestic laws in respect of them, *prima facie* also because of their fortuitous location but in truth more because domestic laws are often totally inadequate and inappropriate to apply in international transactions conducted away from the place of these systems;

(g)   these domestic laws have in any event very often an unclear view of the nature of the book-entry entitlement in terms of co-ownership or beneficial ownership right or proprietary right *sui generis*, which (if domestic laws were applicable) even for international entitlements could then change depending on the place of the custodian or intermediary operating the book-entry system. That would then also affect the type of other interests that could be created in them like repos and security interest or conditional ownership rights when these entitlements are used for financing;

(h)   international practices demonstrate the decisive influence of the investors and traders (rather than issuers) and the impact of their private arrangements with their custodians or other intermediaries that operate book-entry systems;

(i)   it also shows, however, that the proprietary protections and the proprietary rights that may so be created cannot ultimately be decided by private arrangements alone. For their third party effect, which is the essence of proprietary rights, international book-entry entitlements must be supported by market practices in order to be recognised and enforceable in the market as a whole and against all its participants;

---

[334] See for the complications of a purely local view of pass-through rights, M Dassesse, 'Taking Collateral over Euroclear Securities: a Belgian Pledge Too Far' [1999] *JIBL* 141. Whether there is a pass-through right of clients of Euroclear members in the latters' Euroclear entitlements is a question of Euroclear rules or Euromarket practices. It could not operate in favour of non-members of the system. If there is such a right in principle, any pledgees of the clients will receive the pass-through when they foreclose their pledges against the client. Whether this pass-through right itself, if it still exists, may also be encumbered in favour of the same pledgee is equally a question of Euroclear or Euromarket practices. The same would be true for the formalities of the creation and enforcement of such a pledge in the pass through right, which is a pledge in the underlying entitlement. If this is possible, the next question is whether there is then also a pass-through right in the underlying securities and whether that could be pledged. That is again a matter of Euroclear rules and Euromarket practices, but would also affect the issuer in the cases of registered securities (as distinct from bearer securities deposited with Euroclear) and could therefore in the case of shares become a matter of the internal rules of the issuer as expressed in his Articles of Association or his *lex societatis*. It is clear that one must distinguish here between the various layers at which entitlements and pass through rights work.
[335] This should avoid re-characterisation risk if re-characterisation is not common in that market and it is not. It is the risk that ownership-based funding is re-characterised as a security interest, relevant especially for repos. See for the distinction between ownership and security based funding in this connection chapter V, s 1.7. See for the proposed EU Financial Collateral Directive, s 3.2.4 *infra*.

(j) in this process, general conditions and operating practices formulated by the
     market itself become of great significance. There is therefore an important impact
     of party autonomy but only in the context of the operation of the market and its
     products as a whole; it also means that market practices may be fluid as they must
     instantly react to market realities and changes in those realities. Custom is here not
     static, as in truth it never can be if reflective of market practices;

(k) however, to the extent bona fide purchasers are protected, the third party aspect
     of these proprietary rights becomes less significant. It means that in a sophisti-
     cated system of entitlements where there is such protection, there is more
     room for party autonomy. That is indeed acknowledged in the US in Article 8
     (section 8-110(e)(1) UCC. Under domestic European laws on the other hand,
     bona fide purchasers of intangible assets are on the whole not protected. In
     such a system, party autonomy may be less appropriate.

The practice based legal system for eurobonds developed very effectively and rapidly in this
manner and allowed a market to emerge that was largely offshore, operated under its own
rules, and became the largest bond market in the world. The lack of rigidity has proved a
great advantage, much better than any illusory certainty that the application of domestic
rules could have brought, even if they had been tailored to this market. Flexible law is for
international markets and their participants always preferable to wrong or underdeveloped
mandatory laws — contrary to what is often said by these same practitioners — and certainty on the basis of applicable *domestic* laws can be of such a low quality that it is much
better to do without in favour of the force of international practices and their dynamics.
They have always been the essence of the euromarkets, in which, upon a proper analysis,
domestic laws are only used to the extent compatible with them.

The internationalisation of the bond market has also moved in the direction of covering
(domestic) *shares* that are substantially internationally traded. The situation in respect of
them is, however, more complicated. Traditionally, only as *bearer* instruments could they
be easily traded internationally. In respect of such bearer shares, Euroclear and Clearstream
could easily expand their custody and book-entry services guided by the established market practices of the euromarket as it did for bearer bonds. In fact, in connection with
Euronext it is doing so in a major way (for these bearer shares). *Register* shares for their
transfer and holding depend, on the other hand, on company registers subject to by-law
restrictions and applicable domestic laws and formalities. They further depend on the
back-up of local laws for their negotiability and transfer, which may contain limitation in
terms of transferability especially if not publicly quoted. They may in any event suffer from
transfer formalities under local company, regulatory or stock exchange rules.

For (domestic) shares, the internationalisation of their trading and transfer could therefore manifest itself in several different ways depending on the manner of their transferability:

(a) as just mentioned, *bearer* shares which may in principle be transferred by sim-
     ple delivery can easily follow the route of eurobonds. Euroclear and Clearstream
     are already important custodians, clearers and settlement agencies in respect of
     such shares covered by similar internationalised rules as just mentioned for
     eurobonds;[336]

---

[336] Immobilisation may be less complete for shares which are still largely traded and settled through domestic
stock exchanges and settlement agencies. These may practise similar book entry systems, but in the case of a
domestic variety are subject to domestic laws. In international trading the result may be a flow between these
bookentry systems and Euroclear and Clearstream.

(b) *register* shares are in principle domestic instruments operating under the *lex societatis* but may be quoted on foreign exchanges to enhance the investors' base. Foreign register facilities may then be set up by the issuer. It dilutes the impact of the *lex societatis* and any transfer requirements, restrictions or impediments it contains or supports, as already suggested in section 3.1.2 in connection with their transferability;

(c) it may also lead to *foreign* proprietary interests, like pledges and similar security interests or repos created in them subject to the laws and practices of the countries of these additional registers.[337] Another possibility is to broaden the registration facilities in the existing company register at the issuer's head office to allow for foreign notices;

(d) local or internationalised *book-entry* systems may further overcome these local impediments in respect of the transfer of *register* shares and create as we saw an *entitlement structure* in a *custody layer* (if internationalised subject to its own internationalised rules in the manner explained above), in which the trading effectively takes place on the basis of complete *fungibility* and *transferability* or *substitution* of the entitlements and a *full set-off* of reciprocal claims;

(e) such book-entry systems are now also common in respect of bearer shares. As we saw, it is unlikely that there is still a pass-through right in such systems. Their (international) tradability and transferability enhancing ability is particularly clear in respect of shares which remain more domestic by nature;

(f) these book-entry systems may be seen as a further elaboration of the use of depositary receipts (DPs) structures which presented a more cumbersome system in that they operated on the basis of the issuance of substitute certificates or register shares which still caused logistic transfer problems although they could in turn become subject to a book-entry and entitlement system themselves;

(g) book-entry entitlements may also be seen as an elaboration of the client accounts containing pooled shares which are fungible and would require the broker (if so requested by his client) only to deliver the required number of shares of the same sort. In a book-entry system this pooling notion is institutionalised and leads to a simple securities account for participants;

(h) substantial movement between international and domestic book-entry systems in respect of domestic shares (and more so the exercise of any pass-through rights in them) may still put the entitlement into a local direction, however. On the other hand, internationalisation of the trading facility suggests the further dilution of the impact of the *lex societatis* in favour of a more internationalised concept of transferability of the relevant register shares. Issuers encouraging these shares to be traded through internationalised book-entry systems enhance that development;

(i) it may also allow for foreign or internationalised types of pledges and similar security interests in them or repos and conditional sales that may have to be

---

[337] The details of attachments and perfection of these interests are not further discussed here, but all aim at possession whether actual or constructive (through registration in the relevant share register) in which case the term 'control' is often used. There is here no need for sophisticated filing systems, now customary in the USA and some other countries especially in respect of non-possessory security interests or floating charges. If the subject of such a floating charge, a separate marking on the securities or entitlement register would probably still be necessary in respect of internationally traded securities in order for these security interests and any pass through rights thereunder to be effective. It all comes down to constructive possession.

respected even when this type of interest holder exercises any pass-through rights directly against the shares at the place of the issuer as a consequence of these schemes. The co-operation of and encouragement by the issuer in foreign trading suggest this result;

(j)   in any event, there can be little doubt that *international* custody is the way forward if only because the professional custodians are themselves substantially internationalised and ever fewer in number. It means that book-entry systems are increasingly internationalised also and as a consequence ever more detached from local laws;

(k)   they may be and are normally settled through modern international settlement systems based on settlement netting, either through a settlement agent or central depository, clearing house or central counterparty type of system. Euroclear and Clearstream combine a custody function with that of a clearinghouse. There is no central counter-party, however, which is more normal in modern derivative exchanges where only contractual rights are traded, see also section 3.1.3 above.

Naturally, the question arises what all this may mean in the bankruptcy of one of the participants under the appliable bankruptcy laws. How do these internationalised rights fit? It is not possible to generalise, but a number of observations may be made:

(a)   the entitlement tier concerned is important. If a domestic broker with many domestic clients is declared bankrupt in his own country whilst in the bankrupt estate there are entitlements in a domestic or even an international book-entry system, domestic law may in the first instance determine whether these clients can step into the shoes of the broker in respect of the entitlement higher up in the chain of entitlements or (more likely) may transfer their accounts with the corresponding adjustments of the entitlements of the bankrupt broker higher up;

(b)   if the client or investor has no direct right to the entitlement of the broker in the next layer under applicable local bankruptcy or other laws, that need not be the end of it in respect of a *foreign* book-entry system *outside* the bankruptcy jurisdiction, in which respect there may be a further difference when the clients are also foreign;

(c)   it may also make a difference when the broker is himself outside the bankruptcy jurisdiction. The status of the clients (i) outside the country of the bankruptcy (ii) in respect of a book-entry entitlement of their broker with a custodian also outside the bankruptcy jurisdiction, whilst (iii) the broker himself may have been declared bankrupt being outside the bankruptcy jurisdiction, becomes first a matter of the bankruptcy's extraterritorial effect on that foreign book-entry system but secondly also of the acceptance by the law of that foreign book-entry system of the consequences of the application of the relevant bankruptcy laws;

(d)   the extraterritorial effect of bankruptcy is normally not accepted elsewhere except under treaty or uniform law. Such law is mostly non-existent, but was in the EU introduced through the Insolvency Regulation and similar Directives for the winding up of banks and insurance companies.[338] Even then, the foreign

---

[338] It should be noted in this respect that Belgium has a liberal recognition regime and is also the country with most bankruptcy conventions: see 1 JH Dalhuisen, *Dalhuisen on International Insolvency and Bankruptcy*, (1986), 3–162 which might be relevant to Euroclear if its book entry system were considered Belgian.

bankruptcy measure may not affect the legal (proprietary) rights and practices in the recognising Member State without an adjustment process;

(e) it could in this respect be argued that the propietary regime in respect of entitlements to assets of an internationalised clearing institution operating under its own practices would demand acceptance by the applicable bankruptcy law when extraterritorially applied;[339]

(f) in view of its international status, this may even be so if this institution was within the bankruptcy jurisdiction itself. Thus in a Belgian bankruptcy of a Belgian broker, the broker's Euroclear entitlements might be distributed to its domestic and foreign clients or, more likely, *pro rata* to their new brokers under the practices of distribution of entitlements within Euroclear and not pursuant to Belgian bankruptcy legislation if different. It would be very much clearer where there still is a pass-through right;

(g) ideally, the pools should unravel on the basis of segregation and co-ownership or beneficial ownership rights in the next layer and ultimately in the underlying shares or bonds. If there is no pass-through right against the issuer, the pool will simply be put *pro rata* with new intermediaries chosen by the investors and operating a book-entry system. If the custodian is bankrupt, there will have to be found a replacement custodian who will become the legal owner of the securities. The issuing company might have here a contractual veto;

(h) an important further complication may be in the type of right that is held by third parties in the entitlement. One may think here primarily of security interests, repos, or conditional or temporary transfers, when the entitlements are used for financing purposes. It creates a further layer (of a different type, however) whilst the interest holders may become the entitlement holders upon default of the original one;

(i) to what extent these rights will be accepted in a bankruptcy of the broker or custodian maintaining the book-entry system in another country will pose further legal questions connected with the recognition of such rights elsewhere (in which conection the internationalisation of these rights themselves may be a facilitating factor) or their possible adjustment by the bankruptcy court to establish their status and rank under the *lex concursus*;

(j) this highlights a particular problem in international cases of this sort which has to do which a *trebling* of the level of uncertainty: the characterisation of underlying entitlement may be legally uncertain in terms of the (proprietary) rights it confers; the types of security and similar interests that may be created in them and how this is done may as a consequence also be uncertain, whilst a third uncertainty results from the international status of such interests themselves;

(k) the variants are here further in the *lex concursus* and its competency in the case which will have to do with the entity that is bankrupt (the book-entry holder or the entitlement holder), the location of the bankrupt and whether the bankruptcy is opened at that location or elsewhere, whether in the latter case the bankruptcy can be recognised at the location of the bankrupt, and what such a

---

[339] In the case of Euroclear, it would mean that the bankruptcy of a non-Belgian participant would not prevent the clients of the foreign broker taking its place *vis-à-vis* Euroclear in Belgium whatever the foreign bankruptcy regime would say even upon recognition (in principle) of the foreign bankruptcy in Belgium. As Euroclear would not want these customers as participants, in practice it would mean that each customer's theoretical *pro rata* share would be transferred to the new or replacement intermediaries.

bankruptcy or recognition means in terms of security or other rights held by third parties/financiers in the entitlement.

The internationalisation of investment security transactions along the above lines is in full swing and a natural sequel of the globalisation of the markets in which domestic transfer restrictions and impediments are more rapidly felt to be excessive and outmoded and are likely to be overcome. In this evolution, the dependence on local legal peculiarities becomes atavistic and practictioners will do everything to circumvent them. The market itself is likely to lead here, enforce harmonisation on participants, and impose freer, easier and cheaper transferability. The new possibilities that internationalised book entry systems offer in this respect are likely to increase in importance as they provide not only a means of overcoming logistical problems but also domestic transfer restrictions and other local peculiarities internationally. It offers a great opportunity to do things better, free from inappropriate or even irrational domestic constraints, techniques and disabling or out-of-date structures. That is on the whole a healthy development and is likely to remove layers of unnecessary legal ballast and to allow legitimate market practices favouring the investment flows to flourish. Ultimately, the law follows here the commercial and financial needs and the justified requirements of the commercial and financial community which is substantially internationalised.

The emphasis thus falls on the reliability of the operators of international custody, settlement or corporate registration systems and their efficiency. These aspects have rightly become matters of international regulatory concern.[340]

However, at the present stage in this development, domestic contacts can by no means be entirely eliminated or wished away, as in the following situations:

(a) book-entry systems may remain entirely domestic like those that are connected with domestic exchanges and their settlement systems. Yet, they may easily be connected with other similar domestic book-entry systems in other countries, for example, for foreign shares traded on the exchanges of those countries. Traditional conflicts of laws are likely to arise in such situations. They may, however, also be relevant for international book-entry systems like Euroclear and Clearstream. If the latter hold (directly or indirectly) an entitlement through a domestic book entry system in another country, this entitlement is likely to have to conform to the domestic practices and laws in respect of them. If the domestic systems hold accounts with internationalised systems, they will on the other hand conform to international practices;

(b) another domestic aspect is the exercise of pass-through rights in respect of registered securities or indeed entitlements in domestic book entry systems. In the case of register securities it was already noted that if the issuer actively promotes the international trading of its registered securities it may allow or institute a foreign register to operate and may have to accept the consequences in negotiability, transfer formalities, limited proprietary rights that can be created in them and eventually also pass-through rights whilst losing the domestic restrictions

---

[340] See the Group of 30 Think Tank in its 1989 Recommendations, in 1993 followed by a Euroclear study entitled *Cross-Border Clearance, Settlement, and Custody: Beyond the G 30 Recommendations.* The G 30 Recommendations were themselves refined in 1995 by the International Society of Security Administrators (ISSA). As suggested above, this development driven by the globalisation of the markets suggests itself a transnationalisation of the applicable law in the sense of the new law merchant or *lex mercatoria* as will be further explored, see s 3.3.2 *infra*. These Recommendations are likely to play an important role within the *lex mercatoria*.

and limitations in this connection. The shares may alternatively be held by an international custodian in an international book-entry system;

(c) where brokers lower in the chain operate with clients, it is increasingly likely that they operate at the domestic level within a domestic legal framework. In such cases, even foreign clients seeking out a domestic broker could be deemed to have submitted to that local regime in terms of entitlement against the broker.

3.2.2 Law Applicable to International Investment Securities Transactions

In the discussion of the law applicable to these book entry systems, in legal writing, much relevance is still given to domestic laws and as a consequence also to the applicable conflict of laws rules.[341] It is often still believed to give the greater stability and certainty. This approach is then preferred not only in respect of clearly domestic custodial and book-entry arrangements but also in those that are clearly internationalised. In this connection, four possible conflict rules present themselves: the *lex situs* of the investment securities, the *lex societatis* of the issuer, the *lex loci actus* of the book entry-system, or the law chosen by the parties. All have their defenders. The differences in view are indicative of the considerable problems in this area and the undesirability of the domestic law approach, which, however, cannot always be avoided and remains in any event also the lowest ranking of rules within the *lex mercatoria* which will be summarised in the next section. Here these four possible conflict rules and their variants will be analysed:

(a) The *lex situs* makes the law of the location of underlying investment securities applicable to the proprietary rights established in them and to their transfer. It recommends itself traditionally in respect of negotiable instruments like bearer securities that are treated as chattels. Indeed, the *lex situs* has long been the preferred conflict rule for chattels. It was copied from the law of immovable property where it is on the whole clearly appropriate, see section 1.8 above. For chattels, it presents, however, the complication of their movement which would suggest at the same time a change in applicable law. In such cases, the problems connected with application of the law of the place of origin and place of destination (or both) were discussed in section 1.8.1 above. For assets that constantly move, the rule is clearly unsuitable. An alternative is then application of the law of the place of the owner, who, however, changes in the case of a transfer leaving the question what law applies to such a transfer if buyer and seller are in different countries.

For investment securities entilements, the *lex situs* is the natural rule only if they are negotiable instruments *immobilised* in a book entry system. Yet even then, as in the case of Euroclear and Clearstream, they are usually held by sub-custodians in the country of the issuer (in the case of shares) or currency (in the case of bonds). The disparity this would create in the law applicable to the different pools of shares at the level of an international book-entry system may make such a system unworkable.[342] Apart from this immobilisation aspect, for

---

[341] See eg H Kronke, 'Capital Markets and Conflict of Laws', 286 *Receuil des Cours* (Hague Ac of International Law 2000), 318 and earlier R Goode, 'The Nature and Transfer of Rights in Dematerialised and Immobilised Securities', in F Oditah (ed), *The Future for Global Securities Markets*, (1996) 107. See also JH Sommer, 'A Law of Financial Accounts: Modern Payment and Securities Transfer Law', (1998) 53 *The Business Lawyer*, 1181, 1206.

[342] See for this objection also Goode, n 318 *supra*, 134; see further J Benjamin, 'Immobilised Securities: Where are They?' [1996] *JIFBL* 85.

book-entries proper, as intangible entitlements, the *lex situs* would appear to hold no message at all;

(b)   The *lex societatis* or the law of the issuer is a variation on the *lex situs* feasible more in particular for securities registered in the books of an issuer (who could also be a government or governmental agency in the case of government bonds when this law corresponds with the law of the country or issuing agency). Again, the result is disparity in the applicable law at the level of an international book-entry system as the rules concerning the entitlements would depend on the location of the issuer of the underlying securities or even on the place of the register itself which may no longer be physical either;

(c)   The *lex situs* and *lex societatis* approaches may combine at the place of the custodian in immobilised securities systems, so that its law becomes applicable. This approach is sometimes referred to as the *paper-based* approach even though there may not be any paper around. It does not provide a single solution as there are likely to be different layers of entitlement holdings. More importantly, the location of the intermediary may be in doubt and could be considered that of its incorporation, registered office or place of operation or main activities;

(d)   To protect book-entry systems more generally, the applicability of the law of each register, sometimes also referred to as the *lex loci actus* or the *record-based* approach (therefore the law of the place where the changes are made or transfer is effected) has been proposed. This is therefore the place of the administration of the accounts or of the system (and not necessarily the place of the incorporation or main activities of the relevant intermediary, although that may be the backup rule). This is often considered a variation of the *paper-based* approach (which is itself a *lex situs* variant). It is the system called PRIMA (Place of the Relevant Intermediary Approach);

(e)   PRIMA was adopted for security interests in investment securities legally recorded on a register, account or centralised system located in a Member State of the EU in Article 9(2) of its Settlement Finality Directive which became effective in December 1999 and was meant to underpin the collateralised liquidity operations of the new European Central Bank (even if the precise language left something to be desired).[343] The approach was earlier adopted for

---

[343] European Parliament and Council Dir 98/26 of 19 May 1998. The concern for proper settlement systems was inspired by Article 18 of the Statute of the European System of Central Banks (ESCB) and of the European Central Bank (ECB), according to which the ESCB lending operations (as instrument of monetary policy) must be based on adequate collateral. Within that framework, adequate settlement procedures became a concern and as a consequence also the applicable law. The title ('Finality') derives from the need to achieve a prompt system of settlement that cannot be unwound or reversed. In that connection, the effects of a bankruptcy on a settlement system and its participants are also curtailed and any retroactivity of the adjudication abandoned: see Articles 6, 7, 8, and 9(1).

See for English case law on the applicable law, *Macmillan Inc v Bishopsgate Investment Trust Plc (No 3)* [1995] 3 All ER 747. The lower court rightly pointed out that the place of the transfer and the *lex situs* would almost always be the same but there may be a discrepancy if security interests are created in registered shares whilst trading and held in other countries. Is there a pass-through right under the foreign law or the *lex societatis*? What is the proper *lex situs*? In this case the confusion was increased because certificates were involved even though in the UK not negotiable instruments themselves. The lower court chose the law of the place where the transfer entry was to be made. The Court of Appeal referred in this context to the *lex situs*: [1996] 1 All ER 585. In this case, the result was the same. A better approach would have been to rely in this case on an internationalised concept of the good faith acquisition for value of transferable property, see also W Blair, 'Book Review' (2002),118 *Law Quarterly Review* 482 noting that ".....the financial players themselves continue to hanker after the certainty of reference to

Euroclear and Clearstream by the laws of Belgium and Luxembourg.[344] The applicability of the law of the first immediately involved securities intermediary (and its booking system) is also the residual rule in the US, see Article 8-110(b) and (e)(2) UCC. It is for security interests in investment securitities also the EU Directive on Financial Collateral of 2002 (Article 9), see more in particular section 3.2.4 below; [345]

(f) It left some open questions about the creation or enforcement of such collateralised rights and also whether the rule could apply to *internationalised* book entry systems within the EU which appears accepted. It seems a workable solution, but is difficult to operate at the last level of security interests in foreign investment securities and in any pass-through rights following from them. Pass-through rights would naturally have to concern themselves with the laws applicable to the securities or entitlements so reached;

(g) It should be noted that the applicable law found in this manner is based on a formalised notion of location that has nothing to do with the place of the transaction and the practices concerning them, much against the essence of all modern conflict rules. The result is therefore artificial and makes the financial transactions dependent on no matter how atavistic or under-developed the law so found may be;

(h) For international custodians like Euroclear and Clearsteam, their location is further entirely fortuitous and the application of Belgian or Luxembourg law as the law of the country of the book entry system seems for them coincidental at best. It would lead to the largest capital market (the Euromarkets) being substantially covered by Belgian or Luxembourg laws, which is incongruous;

(i) For the euromarkets and its instruments transnational law has in any event prevailed for a long time as we saw. In truth it applies its practices to the Euroclear and Clearstream book-entry systems if only at that level. In a proper *lex mercatoria* approach, these practices precede an application of domestic laws (and the application of conflict rules). In fact, when adverse case law appeared in Belgium in 1996,[346] it was quite rightly ignored;

a particular legal system". This underlies indeed the entire PRIMA approach, which is as such defensive and temporary in its (complete) reliance in this respect on domestic laws no matter how atavistic.

[344] See for Euroclear the Royal Decree No 62, Article 10 as amended in 1995; see for Cedel the Grand-Ducal Decree of 7 June 1996.

[345] There are problems in the formulation of the rule, however. Article 9(2) of the 1999 EU Settlement Finality Directive (which is limited to situations in which one of the parties is a financial institution) applies the law of the place of the register (considered the place of the administration of the account, which may leave some doubts on the location) to the type of security (collateral) interests that can be created in the entitlements (leaving some further doubts on whether this concerns the creation or only the execution of such a right) *without* providing a conflict's rule for characterising the legal nature of the entitlement itself. Indirectly it must be assumed that the characterisation of the underlying interests is a matter for the same law (although further confusion arises from Recital 21 which appears to suggest the operation of the *lex situs* of the underlying investment securities which is a difficult, even undesirable, concept in this connection). Article 9 of the 2002 EU Colleral Directive refers here to the country in which the relevant account is maintained and is more elaborate in identifying a number of specific issues as being covered by the law so made applicable, notably whether the entitlement holder's right is overridden or subordinated to security interests or conditional sales, the legal nature of any such rights, their creation and effect, the position of *bona fide* purchasers in this connection, and the execution of such interests. A problem remains the complication of the clearing in which there is only a net amount delivered to the receiving intermediary subject to unscrambling. One must assume it to be done under the law of the receiving intermediary.

[346] See n 324 *supra*.

(j)   With that important correction which suggests *priority* for international dynamics and harmonisation, PRIMA could, however, work well and would present the residual rule;

(k)   Short of it, PRIMA would, however, provide a low quality certainty that could easily go against the dynamic development of the international financial markets. It is exactly this dynamism and this willingness to shape their own rules that has always been the essence of these markets and of their prosperity. The conclusion must be that a formal conflicts rule that cannot accept this state of affairs could not successfully operate without a substantial unification of the laws at national levels. In the EU, an attempt at harmonised law is here being made in the Financial Collateral Directive discussed in section 3.2.4 below. It would reduce the need for any conflicts rule substantially, at least within the EU;

(l)   The consequence of the PRIMA approach is in any event that, since the location of brokers becomes determining for most (client) entitlements, the applicable law can be changed simply by moving to another broker in another country. Even for members of Euroclear and Clearstream, Belgium or Luxembourg law can be avoided by interjecting another broker, eg in a tax haven country or in a country of which the applicable law is deemed more favourable. That is significant in respect of security interests that may subsequently be created in the entitlements or any repo transactions or conditional or temporary sales;

(m)   The law chosen by the participants is a last possibility. On its face, it has little to recommend itself. In proprietary matters full party autonomy is not acceptable. There are, however, modern instances of it. In international assignments, some accept the application of the law of the claim in its proprietary aspects. That law could be determined by the parties. There is also some case law to that effect in Europe: see for a discussion also section 1.9.2 above. On the other hand, Section 8-110(e)(1) UCC suggests alternatively party autonomy for the proprietary law applicable to investment security entitlements,[347] even though it has been questioned.[348] Nevertheless, as we shall see, it is also the approach favoured with limitations in Article 4 of the 2002 Hague Convention on the Law Applicable to Certain Rights in Respect of Securities Held with an Intermediary;

(n)   This approach is less surprising in legal systems like that of the states of the US that are not used to a sharp distinction between the proprietary and contractual aspects, at least not in intangibles, in an environment moreover where between the various states the conflicts are also not likely to be so severe;

(o)   Party autonomy is also more understandable if set against industry practices which are largely determined by its members and often reflected through the general conditions of its system. Although contractual in origin, these general conditions may thus soon acquire the status of industry practice, and the line between contract and custom cannot always be sharply drawn. The emphasis should in any event always be on industry practice as *objective* law even if

[347] The normal rule is, however, the law of the securities intermediary (and his book entry system): see Article 8-110(b) and (e)(2) UCC.
[348] See R Goode, 'Securities Entitlements as Collateral and the Conflict of Laws', (Oxford Colloquium, 1 May 1998), 16.

started by contractual arrangements amongst members. These practices can of course be entirely domestic, but for international agencies like Euroclear and Clearstream they are international as such with a strong claim to prevail over domestic laws. In a proper *lex mercatoria* approach, these practices being proprietary in nature could not be deviated from by mere contract;

(p) In this connection, the easy choice of a more convenient law by interposing a broker in a more convenient country under PRIMA also shows that there is in practice no great fundamental inconvenience against party autonomy in this area. Contractual choice may avoid extra effort and cost. It would also allow non-members of Euroclear and Clearstream to opt for the law concerning these systems including their international practices. In this manner an underdeveloped law could also be avoided whilst doing business with a broker operating from a country with poor law. In short, *on practical grounds* much may be said for party autonomy in these matters assuming a strong protection of *bona fide* purchasers, a protection which in Europe only euromarket practices appear to give.

The PRIMA approach has so far the ascendency but is (in a refined manner) only the residual rule (Article 5) in the 2002 Hague Conference Convention on The Law Applicable to Certain Rights in Respect of Securities Held with an Intermediary, where party autonomy is preferred in the choice of the applicable law (Article 4(1)). This is an important variation and addition to the approaches of Article 9(2) of the EU Settlement Finality Directive and Article 9 of the EU Collateral Directive. It is also the UCC approach (Section 8-110(e). Unlike in the UCC there are, however, a number of safeguards. Foremost, the relevant intermediary must have an office in the country of which the law is chosen which handles the securities accounts. It is unclear why there is this limitation.

The result is that different intermediary accounts involved in a transfer of entitlements, will oparte to different regimes. The seller may have an intermediary with whom the account is held in one country and the buyer in another whilst their intermediaries have both an account with a custodian in a third country, e.g. Euroclear. Bookings will take place in all four accounts. The seller or more likely his broker may instruct the intermediary of the seller (if not the broker himself) to debit his securities (entitlement) account, following by a debit of the corresponding entitlement account of the intermediary at Euroclear. Subsequently Euroclear will credit the entitlements account of the intermediary for the buyer, who ultimately will reflect this credit in the securities entitlement account of the buyer held with this intermediary. Proceeds will move through bank accounts in the opposite direction in a similar manner. Three securities registers are involved in three different countries. It follows that the debiting in the country of the seller will be according to the law of the seller, the debiting and crediting in the accounts with Euroclear according to Belgian law and the crediting of the account of the buyer according to his law (unless otherwise agreed, assuming the Hague Convention is going to apply).

The Hague Convention is specific in referring in Article 2 (1) first to the crediting of a securities account. That is ultimately the most important booking as it establishes the new entitlement holder and his proprietary position *vis-à-vis* others. It further refers to the legal nature and effects against the intermediary and third parties of a disposition of securities held with an intermediary, to the requirements for perfection of other rights in the entitlements, to the question of priority of such collateral and other rights in the entitlements, to the execution of such interests, to the rights of *bona fide* purchasers in respect of intermediaries, and to the question whether a transfer extends to the rights to dividends, income or other distributions or to redemption sale or other proceeds.

Not all problems are resolved in this manner, however, especially not those that arise from the nature of the entitlement itself and its status in a bankruptcy of the intermediary/ultimate custodian. Thus regardless of a choice of law, it would appear that the exercise of voting rights and the collection of dividends is always according to the law of the register and is not therefore affected by a contractual choice of law. From a company law point of view, there is no other than the registered entitlement holder whomsoever the ultimate investor may be and whatever his agreement with his intermediary may say in terms of choice of law. In any event, under the applicable rules to each tier, different claimants may arise, but it would appear immaterial in as far as the voting or dividend reception is concerned in each tier. Only an internationalised system could prevent this from happening. Also a (uniform) internationalised approach will be necessary to determine absolutely the status of book-entry entitlements in a bankruptcy wherever opened so that entitlement holders may always move their accounts to another intermediary resulting in an automatic corresponding reduction of the entitlement of the bankrupt intermediary against higher intermediaries wherever operating. An internationalised system is also necessary to determine the position of collateral holders where again a contractual choice of law per layer in favour of a foreign collateral law and its rules of perfection or control may not prove effective, at least not when it comes to collection of dividends and the exercising of voting rights.

3.2.3 The Lex Mercatoria *concerning International Investment Securities Transactions*

In the above two separate developments were signalled, first the changing nature of securities holdings and their transfer and second their internationalisation, two developments that are not only simultaneous but also connected. On the nature of the entitlement and its transfer, in summary a number of final remarks can be made, which also relate to modern bank accounts and the way bank payments are made. In fact, in the secureties dealings increasingly both must be considered immediately connected. In any event, securities accounts are now handled in much the same way as bank accounts and both may be made subject to similar collateral arrangements.

One key is that in both, the type of right and its transfer are no longer primarily seen from the perspective of ownership rights in the traditional sense, therefore in terms of handling negotiable instruments in the capital sphere (shares and bonds) or in the payment sphere (cheques and bills of exchange), which has also fundamentally affected the traditional choice of law approach in this area and made it moot and therefore uncertain and inappropriate (quite apart from other problems that afflict modern conflict of laws approaches, either in terms of hard and fast rules pointing to underdeveloped domestic laws or in terms of interest analysis). Instead, there are entries or accounts that are intangible and administratively adjusted. In banking, bank accounts never denoted more than a personal right against the bank. For securities this remains different and modern securities accounts denote a *pro rata* share in a pool of fungible assets which has a *sui generis* proprietary character (that needs therefore to be further detailed and defined, centers on the notion of segregation, and does not necessarily flow from the general notions of traditional property law), whilst for both bank and security accounts transfers are mainly operated through sets of (electronic) instructions. Both, payments of this nature (at least in the securities business) and security transfers of this type are viewed largely as professional dealings especially in the aspect of finality of transfer instructions,[349] but also in the type of collateral, therefore in the type of security interest that can be created in them,[350] and in the way this is done which again is similar for bank and securities accounts and turns on a measure of control for the collateral taker. It can be expressed in terms of a possessory charge especially relevant for bank accounts or as a title transfer or repo especially relevant for securities entitlements.

In a modern *commercial* setting, simularities between bank and securities accounts and payments and securities transfers often outweigh the differences. Speed, reliability and finality have become key notions here, not proprietary or contractual characterisations.[351] Traditional conflict of law theories and approaches are a further disturbing factor. Modern commercial law must accept this and adjust and the modern *lex mercatoria* must reflect these fundamental changes. Thus where once the law of negotiable instruments dominated this field, it is now largely redundant and intermediaries and their relationship with their clients have filled the gap. This is not agency either, although until such time that the new developments are completed and fully understood and refined, there will be a residual need for agency notions when brokers still act for clients rather than deal from their own inventory or when clearing agents still operate systems for others rather than act as central counterparties.

As far as the applicable rules are concerned, in international transactions the discussion in the previous section brings us back to the internationalisation of the modern investment securities business and of its applicable laws. Again the application of the *lex mercatoria* as a hierarchy of norms quite naturally presents itself. Fundamental principle dictates the binding force of agreements concerning investment securities' holdings and transfers at that level and also operates an ownership concept, very clearly where the investment securities are negotiable instruments, like eurobonds, but in more modern times also where securities entitlements are created as pro rata shares of fungible pools, held in and transferred through international book-entry systems like that of Euroclear and Clearstream and are *pro rata* share of a fungible pool.

The way these entitlements are held, traded, settled and paid for, the type of proprietary interests that can be created in them including pledges and repo interests, the pass-through rights in the underlying securities, and the manner in which they can be exercised, will then all be determined in first instance by the proprietary regime and transfer practices

---

[349] A severe attitude to finality may well conflict with consumer interests. It is the reason that consumer payments were excluded from Article 4A UCC in the US, see chapter III, s. 1.1.5. They may not issue letters of credit under Article 5 (Section 5-102(a)(9))and the revised Artcilce 9 also focused increasingly on professional dealings whilst prohibiting consumers to grant security interests in their bank accounts (Section 9-109(d)(13) (new)).

[350] The former version of Artilce 9 prohibited security interests in bank accounts altogether (Section 9-104(1)) and had a special regime for collateral in securities accounts (Section 9-317) since the new Artcile 8 (under the old one of 1978, securities interests in securities could not be perfected through filing, see Section 8-321 (1) (old)). See for the new set-up Section 9-304 UCC and Section 8-110 UCC.

[351] A new form of formalism may arise here as was signalled for commercial law also in the law of contract, see chapter II, s. 1.3.5. Good faith notions, individual protections, anthropomorphic thinking in terms of transfers as legal acts of persons subject to capacity and disposition rights must all be seen in a commercial professional context and may as such be curtailed or ignored. Notions of abstraction or independence of each tier or layer replace here the equally formalistic proprietary notion of the holder in due course or the protection of *bona fide* possessor of earlier law. In the new system, third party protection means the ability to ignore earlier problems in a chain and independence from actions or failures in other tiers. On the other hand, holdings and transfers in this system cannot be seen without regard to the sytems themselves and its chains or tiers and ways of operation. The (unavoidable) inherent weakness is in fact the dependency of the clients on the intermediaries operating the system, on their honesty, management skills, and adequate infrastructure. In this world professionality is all. Regulatory supervision will help but can not prevent individual lapses.

operating in the international market place. In the details, international mandatory usages or practices, especially relevant in the proprietary aspects and their newer forms and in the aspect of finality of transfers and transfer instructions, follow in the hierarchy of norms. Mandatory uniform treaty law is here so far absent: the various Uncitral and Unidroit efforts in the area of contract and financial products do not cover investment securities, but the 2002 Hague Convention and the EU Financial Collateral Directive do. The next level in the hierarchy is the party autonomy concerning participation in the system, which, as mentioned in the previous section, is not in itself likely to affect the proprietary and transfer aspects, but, if incorporating or creating standard practices, will be reflective of or add to the higher international mandatory practices just referred to.

In the details, directory practices are the next phase in the hierarchy of norms but are not likely to contribute greatly to the proprietary aspects of internationally operating custody and book-entry systems which are not directory in nature. General principles of property law operating in this area in modern nations with similar domestic custody and book-entry systems may, however, produce further guidance. Finally, if still no solution is found, conflict of laws rules may indeed point to the law of a particular country which could well be the country of the system (PRIMA) or be determined by party autonomy (like under the 2002 Hague Convention and Article 8 UCC). Even then it will not automatically apply if the domestic rule is clearly contradictory, disfunctional, inadequate or antiquated. If on the other hand, domestic contacts clearly arise, as there may in the exercise of any remaining pass-through rights in respect of issuers or purely domestic custody and settlement organisations, it seems appropriate to consider the applicable domestic laws in greater detail and more directly.

Much depends in these matters on the behaviour and insight of judges or arbitrators, just as in the day-to-day running of clearing, settlement, custody and book-entry systems much depends on the integrity and professionalism of the operators. Few legal problems have arisen so far. It is unlikely that many will. Considerable protection derives from the fact that all participants are professionals and few go bankrupt. This has created the right climate for the continuous and imaginative expansion of market practices supporting the international securities markets and protecting all its participants in the most legally effective and cost efficient manner.

3.2.4   Uniform Law: The EU Financial Collateral Directive

In the meantime, under pressure from the financial services industry and with the Settlements Finality Directive in mind (which was particularly concerned with the collateralisation of liquidity supply to the banking system by the European Central Bank and harmonised the (bankruptcy) laws in EU countries in a number of so-called finality aspects),[352] the EU agreed a Financial Collateral Directive in 2001 to be implemented by 2004. It is a significant development which even though limited to financial collateral aims to introduce at EU level a modern collateral law, a project which has eluded all EU countries for personal property more generally at the national level.

The most important features of the Directive are:

(a)   There are simplified uniform rules for the creation, perfection and enforcement of collateral, which is here limited to *cash* and *investment securities* given to

---

[352] See s 3.1.6 *supra*.

support financial obligations. They must be expressed through bank accounts for moneys and in book-entry entitlements for securities;

(b)   All formalities are dispensed with in terms of registration or publication of collateral or in terms of an execution sale/ appropriation underbit. Only a document is required to record the collateral transaction. For the interest to attach, the simple marking of the (possessory) pledge or title transfer in the books of the intermediary indicating the pledgor's or seller's interest is sufficient. An execution sale may be informal subject to a commercial reasonableness test, important especially when selling to related entities. Provided there is a proper valuation formula, there may also be appropriation;

(c)   There is a sharp distinction between pledge and title transfer (or finance sale) leading to the enforcement through a sale in the former place and appropriation of full title in the latter case. Re-characterisation both at the time of perfection and enforcement are avoided. It is to be noted that non-possessory security is not being considered and constructive depossession is necessary in all cases. Bankruptcy stay provisions are suspended in respect of the enforcement, which is cast in terms of a pure self-help remedy;

(d)   In the case of a title transfer, there is a recognition of close-out netting arrangements (Article 7), particularly relevant for repos.

The Directive is mainly concerned with the narrower issues of collateral and notably omits any consideration of protection of *bona fide* purchasers and does not go into the nature of the underlying interests either. Therefore, the nature of the underlying securities and especially of securities entitlements is not considered and as a consequence also not the important segration and pooling issues. Here conflict of laws notions may remain paramount in which connection the Directive follows the Settlements Finality Directive and opts for PRIMA, therefore for the law of the most immediately concerned intermediary with whom the account is held. There are some clarifications, however, and in Article 9 a number of issues are clearly identified as being covered by the law of the register, notably whether the entitlement holder's right is over-ridden or subordinated to security interests or conditional sales, the legal nature of any such rights, their creation and effect, the position of *bona fide* purchasers in this connection, and the execution of such interests.

The problems with this approach were highlighted in section 3.2.2 above and the absence of any sensitivity to market practices and international custom in respect of book-entry systems remains here also an important oversight. Another problem in the Directive is that even for the uniform perfection regime, reference is still made to conflict rules whilst also local registration requirements remain applicable as long as they do not undermine the validity of the relevant security interest or title transfer. Ranking is also specifically left to the law so found to be applicable. It would of course still be subject to the applicable execution or bankruptcy rules. On the other hand, close-out netting agreements are fully recognised in line with the approach of the Settlement Finality Directive.

Three narrower problems have arisen. First, the Directive is limited to professional dealings with companies of considerable size. The financial services industry had asked for all financial dealings in the EU to be included. Private investors do not have the same facilities as to membership of clearing and settlement institutions and therefore also less options to choose a more convenient law by going to another broker. There are for them also problems of disclosure in connection with suitability rules. Second, the industry asked for the right to *top up* security through collecting margin in respect not only of market risk but also credit risk regardless of any bankruptcy avoidance provisions on the basis of preferential transfers.

This became accepted. The third issue is the possibility of *re-hypothication* of any collateral collected under a pledge arrangement which possibility was in the end also accepted if the original collateral agreement allows it, but the two agreements in respect of which collateral is given in this manner must be co-terminus so that both charges will come to an end at the same time.[353] If earlier different assets are returned under the subcharge, the original charge will retain its original rank in any replacement goods (even if absolutely future at the time of the original agreement).

---

[353] There were here some specific legal problems. In civil law, re-hypothecation is not favoured and the original pledgor can reclaim his pledge as a matter of ownership right once he has paid off his debt. There is no protection of a sub-pledgee on the basis of his *bona fides* if it concerns an interest in an entitlement (it would be different for bearer securities). In common law, the pledgee is a bailee who has sufficient power to give a further pledge over the property he has acquired as pledgee. The original owner cannot reclaim his interest until the re-hypothication is unwound. The problem does not arise where there is a finance (or conditional) sale when there is a sufficient ownership right to pledge the asset. This being the case, it was not illogical to allow it also in the case of a pledge of entitlememts.

5

Security and Ownership-Based Funding Techniques

Part I   Secured Transactions and Finance Sales

1.1   Civil and Common Law Approaches

1.1.1   *Secured Transactions*

It is a well-known fact that there are considerable differences in credit cultures from country to country, that is in the types of funding techniques and financial structures most commonly used. In recent years the internationalisation and globalisation of the markets have tended to reduce these differences by favouring new financial products that may have a more general application. Yet as long as the law in this area remains largely domestic, it is likely to reflect the historic differences and cramp the internationalisation style. The main reason is that funding arrangements often imply some form of propri-etary protection for the creditor involving assets of the debtor. Since under the tradi-tional private international law approach, the law of the *situs* of the assets applies to the proprietary interests to be created or maintained in them, the international financial practice is here still substantially dependent on local law. It must therefore work with the substantial differences local law presents, [1] or otherwise structure around them.

Traditionally, these differences were principally reflected in the types of *security interests* domestic laws allow financiers to create in their debtors' assets to support and protect their funding activities, in the formalities surrounding the creation of these security interests (like documentation, publication or the requirement of possession), in the types of present or future assets that may be included, in the type of past, present or future debt they can insure, in the protection of *bona fide* purchasers of the assets, and in the realisation of the protection (and priority) they offer in the case of default, especially in the bankruptcy of the debtor. It was therefore not only the law of secured transactions that needed to be con-sidered in these aspects but also the applicable bankruptcy law which could impair, sus-pend or delay the independent repossession and execution rights of the creditor or even cut down the security, especially in modern reorganisation proceedings.[2]

Modern financing may often depend on other types of protection, like conditional own-ership rights, resulting from conditional sales of assets by the party requiring funding, or from options in certain assets of that party. The whole development of non-possessory security in chattels during the last century depended on these conditional ownership types

---

[1] See for an overview J-H Roever, *Vergleichende Prinzipien dinglicher Sicherheiten* (1999); U Drobnig, 'Vergleichender Generalbericht,' in KF Kreuzer (ed), *Mobiliarsicherheiten, Vielfalt oder Einheit?* (1999)9, who also summarises a number of options to proceed to greater, harmonisation at EU level; see earlier U Drobnig, 'Legal Principles Governing Security Interest', Doc A/CN.9/131 and Annex in (1977) VII *Unicitral Yearbook* 171; see for the (limited) EU involvement also EM Kieninger, *Mobiliarsicherheiten im Europäische Binnenmarkt* (1996) and for a summary, EM Kieninger, 'Securities in Movable Property within the Common Market' (1996) 4 *European Review of Private Law* 41–66; see also PR Wood, *Comparative Law of Securities and Guarantees* (1995).
[2] See eg in the USA, text following n 19 *infra*.

and they always loom in the background, even now in the more modern financial products like finance lease and repurchase agreement, and re-emerge all the time, as will be demonstrated below. Even though it may be said that ownership concepts are more universal in this respect and perhaps more flexible than security concepts — the reason in modern international finance these structures are often more popular — there are still important domestic legal differences in the use and acceptance of these alternative structures as well. They also impact on the effectiveness of the financiers' protection obtained in this manner. At least in civil law countries, domestic law is here often much less settled than for secured transactions. This may prove an advantage of sorts and may provide some flexibility in financial structuring but, since under the traditional private international law approach the law of the *situs* of the asset applies also to these proprietary interests, the more modern international financial practices remain here also still dependent on local laws. They can therefore not ultimately ignore the substantial differences and uncertainties local laws present, unless they can make out a case for transnational law to apply. This may be easier in respect of intangible assets like receivables in receivable financing than in respect of tangible movable assets being the subject of finance leases and repos.

This chapter deals with these differences in the areas of secured transactions, conditional sales and proprietary options in movable or personal property, whether chattels or intangible assets. The issues were already briefly summarised in chapter IV, section 1.6. The key is to try to explain what they mean and how they might be better handled. Even now, there may be some convergence. Existing security interests may have a common origin, often in Roman law, or may have developed in parallel ways that may reduce the differences. Thus both in civil and common law, security interests

(a)　are normally proprietary in nature;

(b)　give as a consequence (in civil law terminology) an *in rem* or proprietary right in the assets to the creditor, which (subject to any rights of *bona fide* purchasers) the secured creditor can maintain against all the world, and therefore retains even if the owner sells the assets (whether or not in possession of the creditor). In French this is referred to as the *droit de suite*;

(c)　give as a further consequence priority to the oldest security interest holder in the asset, who may ignore all others, in French referred to as the *droit de préférence*;

(d)　allow the secured creditor to seize or repossess the asset upon the default of his debtor (if he has not already taken possession),[3] sell it and subsequently set off his claim against the proceeds whilst returning any overvalue to the defaulting debtor but retaining an unsecured claim on the debtor for any undervalue; and

(e)　are accessory to the debt and therefore benefit any assignee of the claim, whilst, on the other hand, they are automatically extinguished with the debt (upon payment).[4]

---

[3] The execution sale will in principle leave other secured interests (higher or lower) in the asset unaffected.

[4] In civil law, provision may be made to the contrary as is done in the German *Grundschuld* and the security need therefore not be accessory *per se*. The *Grundschuld* is a secured borrowing facility that survives the repayment of the debt and is transferable separately from it. The existence of this type of facility is marked in the land registers but the change of interest holder results from the transfer of the paper. It is also possible to embody both claim and accessory security in one document, as is common in asset-backed securities and may also be seen in so-called chattel paper in the USA under Section 9-102(a)(11) (Section 9-105(1)(b) old) UCC.

In common law, the accessory nature of security interests is less developed as a concept, see also nn 195 and 239 *infra*, and may need agreement of the parties or statutory support as was done for chattel paper in the UCC Section 9-102(a)(11) (Section 9-105(1)(b) old). For reservation of title and other types of conditional sales, the

Yet, as just mentioned, there remain considerable differences in the details, like formalities, possession or publication requirements, the types of assets and debt that can be covered, the potential shift of the security into replacement goods and proceeds, and in the type of disposition. Applicable bankruptcy laws may create further diversions whilst laws protecting *bona fide* purchasers may also undermine the effectiveness of the security interest, especially in chattels when sold to unsuspecting third parties, especially when this is done in the ordinary course of business of the debtor. In common law this remains exceptional but is now often provided by statute.

The further evolution of conditional ownership rights and related options — still very much underdeveloped in civil law — might show some welcome international harmonisation as an alternative rather than a substitute for secured transactions, even if there is less certainty about the direction. The evolution of these conditional or finance sales will be another main issue in the following discussion. They differ from security interests especially as they:

(a)   allow in the case of default appropriation of full ownership by the seller or finance provider who is therefore entitled to any overvalue in the asset whilst the buyer or fundraiser may be released from his debt if there is undervalue;

accessory nature is often rejected also in civil law (unless parties agree otherwise): see n 96 *infra* plus accompanying text. As in common law most security interests are derived from conditional sales (except for the possessory pledge in chattels), this may explain why in common law the accessory nature of secured interests is much less considered. It leaves the question what a security interest still means upon the assignment of the claim it insures without the simultaneous assignment of the security interest itself. The assignor may even be considered paid so that the security interest is at an end and the assignee continues with an unsecured claim. It would of course affect the value of the assigned claim and the proceeds the assignor is likely to receive. Section 340(2) *Restatement (Second) Contracts* (1981) assumes, however, that the assignor holds the collateral in constructive trust for the assignee. The Cal Civ Code Section 2874 accepts on the other hand that a security follows the debt it ensures.

The question of the accessory nature of security interests has never been problematic in civil law (at least if there was an assignment of the entire right and not merely a security or conditional assignment): see for the survival and shift of the accessory or supporting rights upon assignment Article 1692 of the *Code civil* (Cc) in France, Section 401 of the Bürgerlicheesetzbuch (BGB) in Germany, and Article 6.142 of the Civil Code (CC) in the Netherlands. In Roman law, the accessory nature of security interests was obviously maintained when the assignee at first only operated on the assignor's behalf even though for his own benefit: see C 4.10.6 and D 18.4.6, but was later extended to all assignees: see C 4.10.7. Forms of personal guarantees, like sureties (but not always bank guarantees like letters of credit), may be equally accessory or incidental to the main claim and may therefore also benefit assignees. In the USA, this possibility is sometimes also considered: see B Ryan, 'Letters of Credit Supporting Debt for Borrowed Money: The Standby as Backup', (1983) 100 *Banking Law Journal* 404.

In common law, where the assignor in the assignments of legal claims (as distinguished from equitable claims) may retain a function in the actions against any debtor, the survival of the supporting securities may equally not have been in doubt, but upon his release the situation was less clear. In the case of a novation, the supporting security would in any event be lost. However, even short of novation, the accessory nature of the security interest remains more problematic in common law than in civil law. In the USA, on the whole the response has been in favour of the accessory nature of the security interest. It is often seen as incidental to the debt and transferring with it: see AL Corbin, 4 *Corbin on Contracts* (1951), s 907 following *National Live Stock Bank v First Nat'l Bank of Genesoe*, 203 US 296 (106) and followed by *Brainerd & H Quarry Co v Brice*, 250 US 229 (1919): see for more recent case law also *Sinclair v Holt*, 88 Nev 97 (1972); *General Electric Credit Corp v Allegretti*, 515 NE 2d 721 (Ill App Ct 1987), and *JWD Inc v Fed Ins Co*, 806 SW 2d, 327 (1991). Section 9-206(1) (old) UCC (last sentence) made it clear that upon an assignment, the debtor may not raise the implicit transfer of the security interest to the assignee as a defence against its effectiveness. *Cf* also Section 9-403(b) (new).

As a consequence, the assignee may repossess the collateral without any further action of transfer of the interest to him being required: see also RA Anderson, *Anderson on the Uniform Commercial Code* (3rd ed, 1994), s 9-503: 43 and *Midland-Guardian Co v Hagin*, 370 So 2d, 25 (1979). However, in the case of notes where the security interest is not marked on the note itself (which is uncommon), the situation may be different, which would mean that, upon transfer, the security interest supporting the note may lapse. In chattel paper, the close connection between the claim and the security interest is recognised by statute: Section 9-102(a)(11) (Section 9-105(1)(b) old).

The automatic end of the security interest upon payment would in the USA appear to follow from Sections 9-203 and 9-513 (Section 9-404 old) UCC which make the security interest conditional on the existence of a secured obligation.

(b) are not accessory;
(c) present a duality of ownership under which each party's interest in the asset is in principle transferable, resulting in conditional or defeasible title for either; and
(d) depend for their effectiveness in bankruptcy on conditions (or equitable expectancies) being able to mature against a bankrupt at the same time or after his bankruptcy has been declared.

The reservation of title is the traditional example of a conditional sale, but the conditional sale figured large in the development of non-possessory security interests everywhere and is still most relevant for the modern finance lease and repo. It tends to re-emerge where the prevailing system of security interests becomes too confining. Again under modern law *bona fide purchasers* are likely to be protected against these interests if unpublicised. In France, this protection may also apply to *bona fide* unsecured creditors under the principle of the *solvabilité apparente* as will be more extensively discussed in section 1.3.2 below. In common law countries, in chattels, the interest of the conditional owner not in possession is likely to be characterised as an equitable interest which cannot be maintained against *bona fide* purchasers for value of the legal interest, even if in other assets than chattels: see chapter IV, section 1.5.8.

As far as secured transactions are concerned, the real estate mortgage and the possessory pledge in chattels are probably the best examples of traditional convergence. The real estate mortgage is indeed universally used, even though in common law it is rather perceived as a conditional sale (which makes an important difference upon default) — sometimes also embodied in a trust-like structure, especially in the USA, where the house owner becomes as a consequence the trustee of the dwelling house for the lender as beneficial owner. The mortgage is commonly associated with house financing, although no less relevant in commercial property funding. Its essential features are that the interest of the lender is in a specific well-defined existing asset and normally supports a loan with a fixed principal amount (although Continental banks as mortgagees often include all the mortgagor may owe them from time to time), but not necessarily with a fixed interest rate. There is usually a fixed maturity date.

The more specific feature of a real-estate mortgage is that it is *non-possessory*, which means that the secured asset is left with the debtor. This is unlike the traditional pledge which requires the creditor to take physical possession of the asset for the security interest to be valid. It seems the more natural situation, as it gives the creditor tangible protection in that he does not need to fear that other creditors may create similar interests in it, or that the asset may be hidden, abused or lost by the debtor. There will also be no need to search for and retrieve or repossess the asset in order to execute the interest in it upon default of the debtor. It follows that the possessory pledge became the more suitable security interest in chattels and that the mortgage became mostly associated with real estate security, at least in civil law. Even though non-possessory, it was then at least in an asset that could not be hidden or lost.

Nineteenth century law reflected these patterns in many countries, but the convergence in the area of the real estate mortgage and the chattel pledge is relatively recent and certainly not complete. First, in pre-codification law, especially in France, there was also a possessory charge or a vifgage (or *vivum vadium*) in respect of real estate which allowed the creditor to take the land and amortise the loan he gave (plus accrued interest) through the income received out of this land. The French *antichrèse* is the remnant (Article 2085 Cc) and the result was a possessory security interest in land with user and enjoyment rights for the creditor. In England, under a traditional real estate mortgage, this is still a possibility upon default.

On the other hand, Roman law and the *ius commune* — which is the pre-codification civil law built on it which prevailed in most parts of Western Europe until the nineteenth century — had been liberal in allowing the mortgage or hypothec as a non-possessory security interest also in movables. This remains the position in common law where even now the chattel mortgage subsists (in the nature of a conditional sale as we shall see) as a traditional non-possessory interest in chattels, although sometimes, as in England, it is subject to a publication requirement if used outside the commercial sector — and is then called a *bill of sale*. In the USA there was a break, however, and whilst chattel mortgages re-emerged later in the nineteenth century under state law, they were then likely to be non-possesory security interests rather than conditional sales and subject to publication requirements.

For security interests, in civil law, the emphasis fell increasingly on possession *or*, alternatively, on a system of publication if the security interest was non-possessory. Thus the creditor's position under the real estate mortgage became compulsorily reinforced and safeguarded against other (later) creditors and the owner and his successors in interest by requiring publication of the charge in land registers which were progressively created in the nineteenth century. Where such publication was not practically feasible (at the time), as is mostly the case with chattels and claims, non-possessory security interests were abolished altogether and the nineteenth century codifications eliminated them. The result was that nineteenth century civil law no longer encouraged hidden non-possessory proprietary rights like security interests or even usufructs (life interests) in chattels. In the meantime the full (unregistered) ownership right in chattels became almost universally weakened in civil law through the protection of the *bona fide* purchaser who legally acquired *physical* possession. In common law this applied at least to equitable interests.

In this approach, publicity was thus increasingly seen as the equivalent of possession, in the sense that it demonstrated *both* the creditor's or others' proprietary interests in respectively immovable and movable assets. In the case of security interests in intangibles, such as receivables, it was the notification given to the debtor that was subsequently equated with this publicity, and the lack of it tended equally to rule out the perfection of security interests in them, even in countries that did not normally require such notification for the assignment of intangibles itself.

1.1.2 Modern Non-possessory Security Interests in Personal Property and the Alternative of Finance Sales

In civil law, the consequence of the nineteenth century approach to security interests was that *non-possessory* security interests in chattels without publication (for which there was mostly no facility), such as chattel mortgages, and in intangibles without notification were outlawed during much of the nineteenth century.[5] Informal means of publication or simple knowledge of all concerned was not sufficient to reinstate them and make them effective against third parties. The continuing facility of non-possessory security in personal property in common law, at least in England, gave it here a relative advantage, if only in the

---

[5] See, for the earlier continental European approach based on Roman law and the changes at the beginning of the 19th century, also WJ Zwalve, *Hoofdstukken uit de geschiedenis van het Europese privaatrecht, 1 Inleiding en Zakenrecht* [Chapters from the History of the European Private Law, 1 Introduction and Property Law] (Groningen, 1993), 388.

nature of a conditional sale. The trust concept also helped in the development of newer equitable charges which at first derived from the principle that trusts could be used as a security device and would then also continue into replacement assets or proceeds. Similar equitable interests subsequently also resulted upon conditional sales at law of assets which were converted into finished products. It raised the spectre of considerable overvalue, which could now easily arise when other goods were incorporated. It posed at the same time the question of the position of other conditional owners of commodities or semi-finished products converted into the same end product. Various conditional owners were then likely to be pooled as interest holders and needed to share at the same level of preference. Here the idea of a disposition and recovery from proceeds with a return of overvalue came in, borrowed from the pledge. Proceeds upon a sale of the asset in the normal course of business of the debtor were similarly divided. In this situation the debtor continued to be liable for any undervalue and there was no release.

In the USA, chattel mortgages, reservations of title, conditional sales especially of equipment, factoring of inventory and receivables (or collection agreements), and trust receipts were meant to fill the void left by the absence of non-possessory security in chattels and receivables as ways to finance them. Trust receipts were in these connection pieces of paper signed by car dealers and given to their financiers. They evidenced the financiers' equitable or beneficial interests in the cars the dealers held in inventory and would induce the financiers to pay the car manufacturers for this stock.

The enormous diversity in security and related interests that were so made available in the USA in the case of chattels and intangibles early led to some uniform law, like the Conditional Sales Act and Trust Receipt Acts, but only the UCC in Article 9 achieved fundamental consolidation after 1962. The key was that all these interests, if meant to back up payment or other obligations, were converted into security interests proper. The conditional sale and its derivatives were technically abolished, as was the idea of appropriation of the asset in the case of default (with the release of the debtor and retention of any overvalue). But Article 9 went much further in its concept of floating liens. It allowed the automatic shift in replacement goods and proceeds, the inclusion of future assets, the protection of future debt, the filing or publication of these changes, and the relation back of the security to the date of filing even if given in respect of future debt: see section 1.6.2 below.

On the European continent, eventually the modern business requirements demanded also a return of non-possessory security in chattels and intangibles, even without publication or notification, first in order to be able to use inventory and equipment as collateral for loans to finance these assets themselves, and subsequently to use receivables in a similar manner to provide for their funding. As a consequence, at the end of the nineteenth century, case law started to allow these hidden non-possessory charges back in many civil law countries, but the result was also greater divergence and variation in detail, like between the German *Sicherungsübereignung* and the Dutch fiduciary sale or *fiducia*. They both started also as a form of conditional ownership by the financier of certain assets of the debtor, but this facility soon developed in Germany into the direction of a weak preference in the proceeds of an execution sale upon bankruptcy. In the Netherlands it evolved also into a security interest but was there much stronger and retained an independent execution or repossession right for the buyer, good also in a bankruptcy of the seller, as will be discussed more in detail below.[6]

---

[6] In Germany this meant in bankruptcy a shift from the stronger *Aussonderungsrecht* to the weaker *Absonderungsrecht*, therefore a loss of the proprietary status and execution right of the creditor in the asset. This is

>ᵀü

The next step was to allow these (hidden) charges to shift automatically into replacement assets and proceeds, a development by no means completed in civil law everywhere either, much easier to achieve for example through a contractual clause to the effect in Germany than in the Netherlands. Here again, common law maintained its traditional advantage through the equitable right of tracing of the interest into replacement goods and proceeds. It remains one of the more fundamental differences between civil and common law in this area. In the new Dutch Civil Code (CC) of 1992 ultimately, the non-possessory security interests in chattels and un-notified security interests in intangibles found a statutory basis. However, they remain to all intents and purposes still hidden charges, although subject to a registration requirement to clearly identify them and establish their date, but this is not a publication facility,[7] although it does do away with the former informality in this area. A shifting of the interests into replacement goods and proceeds is not part of the system and cannot easily be achieved by agreement between the parties either. In Germany, the important *Sicherungsübereignung* leading to the normal non-possessory security interest in chattels, remains completely informal, as does the extension to replacement goods and proceeds. It does not seem to give rise to major problems.

In England, floating charges (a term not found in the text of the UCC in the USA, but used in the Official Comment) on whole companies were developed in case law as at the end of the nineteenth century. They were introduced by statute in Scotland in 1961, although to a lesser extent absorbed in the prevailing credit culture there. They are *equitable* security interests (unlike mortgages and bills of sale, which are conditional sales resulting in *legal* interests). The idea of publication of non-possessory proprietary interests in chattels became an important feature of bills of sale in the personal sphere, but for professionals, English law only requires publication of charges on whole companies. They have a low priority as they take their rank only from the moment of crystallisation (and not publication) which is normally upon default. It means that they normally rank just above the unsecured creditors but below any other.

All this will be discussed in greater detail below. Here, the key point is that the funding practices even if international had to adjust to what domestic law would allow in terms of proprietary protection of the creditor, but also that this domestic law sometimes had to change to accommodate new financing needs. No doubt the internationalisation of the funding practices in the commercial sphere will pose increasing challenges to these domestic laws. One finds in new legal developments in this area always *two* important recurring features: first, the adjustments are initially mostly made through *case law* and, secondly, they are often achieved by using the technique of a *conditional sale* of the asset. The developments were, however, not always successful, especially not in France.

We already met the technique of the conditional transfer above in the English real estate and chattel mortgage and later in the American and German rediscovery of non-possessory security rights in chattels. It needs further explanation. The key is to appreciate that it is generally possible to raise cash promptly by either selling one's assets or taking out a loan on the security of them. These are two fundamentally different fund-raising techniques. Rather than conceding a security interest in certain assets to support a loan, these assets may thus also be sold to someone who would pay for them. It is the payment for the assets that provides in that case the liquidity rather than the granting of a loan. These alternatives,

unlike the situation in the Netherlands where in a bankruptcy of the debtor the creditor was able to claim or repossess and execute the asset himself but with a return of any overvalue: see also the text at nn 48 and 136 *infra*.

[7] In France during the 20th century there were some specific statutory non-possessory security interests created in certain types of chattels each with very different publication requirements and facilities: see the text to n 78 *infra*.

although obviously quite different, may become more similar, however, if the sale of assets in these circumstances is made conditional upon repayment of the purchase price by the seller/debtor to the financier at an agreed moment when the assets re-transfer to him. But these facilities do not become the same. This is so first because the financier would often not obtain possession and use of the relevant assets. This was a great advantage as long as non-possessory security in chattels remained impossible and was indeed mostly the motivation for conditional sales. Moreover, there was also a very different situation upon default or the failure to tender the repurchase price on the appointed date. It would allow the buyer to keep the assets without any need for an execution sale and return of the overvalue.

Indeed, at the end of the nineteenth century, this sale and repurchase technique became particularly favoured because it allowed the party in need of funding to raise money through the sale of equipment whilst retaining the physical possession and use of these assets. This was so in the USA but even in countries like Germany and the Netherlands, which required delivery of possession to complete the transfer. That was an obvious handicap but this delivery of possession could be entirely *constructive (constituto possessorio)* as we saw in chapter IV, section 1.2.2. The result was the German *Sicherungsübereignung* and the Dutch fiduciary sale based on the Roman *fiducia cum creditore*. In the absence of trust structures in civil law it was translated into a conditional sale and became the non-possessory alternative to the possessory pledge of chattels, as chattel mortgages, trust receipts and conditional sales had in the USA.

In this conditional sale/repurchase structure, the nature of the repurchase could still vary, however, giving rise to an important characterisation issue. There could be:

(a)   a retrieval right or (call) option for the seller, through repayment or tender of a pre-agreed price at a certain date, a facility already known in Roman Law in the *pactum de retroemendo* (of C.4.54.2)[8] and retained in French law as the *vente à remère* (Article 1659 CC);

(b)   a right *and* duty of the seller to repay the agreed price on the appointed date to the buyer (or at least tender the repayment price) conceivably leading to an automatic return of the asset,[9] as we may see in the modern repurchase agreement: the *automaticity* here is one of the most important issues to be determined and may produce an *in rem* or proprietary interest in the asset for the repurchaser, as no act of co-operation is necessary or expected from the other (possibly bankrupt) party; or

(c)   a right or (put) option for the buyer to return the asset for a predetermined price on an appointed date, a technique which the Germans call an uncharacteristic, un-authentic, or untrue (*unecht*) repurchase agreement.

As previously mentioned, the arrangement could lead to physical possession by either seller or buyer. However, the buyer would be able to recover or retain the assets in *full* ownership in the case of a failure by the seller to tender the repurchase price on time (whether as a right or duty) or to accept the goods when tendered by the buyer if exercising a put option.

---

[8] See nn 47, 80, 122 *infra*.
[9] This unilateral right to effectuate a proprietary change against a counterparty is in German law often referred to as a *Gestaltungsrecht* or *einseitiges Rechtsgeschaft*. It is typical for reclaiming rights in terms of repurchase rights under conditional sales. It also figures in the setting aside of voidable transactions, the refusal or acceptance of an inheritance. It is often thought that the claimant has here an unbridled right that cannot be abused. In any event the threshold for abuse would seem to be much higer. Another aspect is that creditors of the claimant cannot exercise it for him or only in extreme and obvious circumstances.

In civil law, he could possibly revindicate them as owner if not already in physical possession of the asset, or otherwise initiate a tort action for wrongful possession by the seller. On the other hand, especially if the buyer had possession, a seller could be entitled to revindicate the asset from the buyer upon tendering the repurchase price.

History shows that the contractual arrangements in this respect and the courts' sanction of the conditional sale started with the first possibility (the *pactum de retroemendo*) but tended to proceed to the second (the modern repurchase agreement). This is apparent in the *Sicherungsübereignung* (for chattels) and *Sicherungszession* (for receivables) in Germany and in the fiduciary sale in the Netherlands; both developed as conditional sales of chattels and receivables to raise financing. Subsequently, however, they acquired significant features of a secured transaction, as already mentioned, but not all repurchase agreements necessarily did so. Another significant aim of this study is to determine when they did.

Indeed, the subsequent development was that if there was a clear loan — that is a conditional sale with a repayment clause to which an *agreed interest rate structure* was added or with a clause requiring regular interest payments on the purchase price to the buyer during the repurchase period — the courts in both Germany and the Netherlands (although in different ways, especially in the manner the repossession and disposition was conducted) would start to apply the rules of secured transactions to these conditional sales. It principally meant that in the case of default there had to be an execution sale and a return of any overvalue to the seller, even if in Germany that was less clear for the *Sicherungsübereignung* outside a bankruptcy situation when, however, the lending contract was interpreted to demand it unless expressly agreed otherwise (a proper proprietary recharacterisation happens there only in bankruptcy). Also the proprietary interest became accessory to the debt and unaffected by either an assignment of the secured claim or a sale of the secured asset, another clear aspect of a secured transaction, although again in Germany only a contractual obligation of the financier to tranfer his interest is implied outside bankruptcy unless clearly stated otherwise.

The courts proved, however, less willing to convert these interests into a security if there was no interest rate structure attached to the deal and the mere agreeing to the seller paying a fee (often discounted in the repurchase price) for this facility was not considered the same thing. Thus true repurchase agreements (not therefore limited to investment securities for which the term 'repo' is more often used) could often be entered into instead and did not acquire the characterisation of secured loan financing. Upon default, there would as a consequence *not* be an execution sale with a return of overvalue to the debtor. The interest would *not* be accessory or survive an assignment of the claim or a proper sale of the asset. Instead of a disposition, the financier would appropriate the asset upon default and keep it including any overvalue. In fact, he might have become the unconditional or full owner automatically. On the other hand, full ownership would have reverted to the seller upon his timely tender of the repurchase price (whether or not accepted). The justification for this different approach is in a different risk and reward structure.

1.1.3 *The Importance of Modern Finance Sales: Characterisation Problems*

From the point of view of the party requiring financing, there can be clear reasons for the alternative type of funding presented by repurchase agreements in the sense just explained. First, in this manner this party may raise a larger amount of money, secured lending often being confined to only 80 per cent of the asset's value. Furthermore, a sale of the asset would often shorten the balance sheet whilst a secured loan would lengthen it. There could also be significant tax advantages.

Most importantly, conditional sales may present a cheaper alternative to secured loan financing. The other side of it is of course that in the case of a default in timely tendering of the repurchase price, there is likely to be appropriation of full title by the buyer without a return of any overvalue. That is the risk and trade-off. This overvalue is less likely to occur where 100 per cent of the commercial value of the asset is paid by the financier at the out-set as is normal. But even then, the price of the assets, particularly in modern investment securities, repos or during times of high inflation, could vary considerably during the repurchase period.

Here surfaces a different risk and reward structure in the sale and repurchase agreement as a conditional transfer compared to secured loan financing and hence a true funding alternative to the secured loan. The conditional sale's structure may be used particularly in the modern financing techniques of the investment securities *repos*, as we already saw, but no less in *finance leasing* and in *factoring*. These may all (depending on their precise terms) be considered examples of conditional sales producing their separate, specialised funding facilities. In this connection one may also speak of '*finance sales*'. They will be more fully discussed in Part II of this chapter.

In the meantime, the reservation of title and hire purchase as purchase money protec-tion structures also emerged and are in most countries (expressly so in the German and Dutch Civil Codes but not in the USA as we shall see) retained in the form of a conditional (or sometimes delayed) sale and may provide good clues as to how the conditionality of these finance sales and their effects on the title transfer should be handled in civil law. Nevertheless, there remains considerable confusion in the area of characterisation of these finance sales. Often it is argued that, economically speaking, finance sales are secured loans and that therefore all rules of secured lending and loan credit protection should be applied. This is on the whole undesirable as it ignores the basic economic differences in the struc-tures as expressed in the different risks and rewards.

It is, however, very much the statutory approach in the USA, even though American case law sometimes demurs. Under Article 9 UCC, conditional sales of chattels and intangibles are normally converted into secured transactions, see Section 9-102(1)(a) and (2) old. The new text in Section 9-109 is less explicited on the point. All the same, in the US, even the reservation of title is now characterised as a security interest subject to the disposition duties of the creditor in the case of default by his debtor who is entitled to any overvalue in the asset. The modern funding facilities through finance lease, repur-chase agreement and factoring have been similarly threatened, which for equipment leases has given rise to a new Article 2A being added to the UCC. Case law in the USA considers repos and certain forms of factoring or securitisations not affected by the conversion threat either.[10]

In the Netherlands, the new Civil Code of 1992 is no less weary of security substitutes. It outlaws them in principle by denying them any proprietary effect, thus not even convert-ing them into secured transactions. They must be so structured from the beginning. The Code fails to define, however, what these substitutes are (Article 3.84(3) CC), so there is no clear line. Nevertheless the status of modern finance sales has been questioned and it is now left to Dutch case law to sort matters out. Courts are trying to correct the situation in order to preserve these modern financing means which are in legal commentaries indeed increasingly identified as conditional sales.[11] At least the new Dutch Code did confirm the conditional sales nature of the reservation of title (Article 3.92 CC) and allows for pure

---

[10] See text to nn 207 and 210 *infra*.
[11] See text at n 64 *infra*.

conditional sales with proprietary effect in Article 3.84(4), without, however, defining the parties' interests under them.

The legal approach in other European countries, notably in England, has been to appreciate the different risk and reward structures in security — and ownership-based financing which results from their fundamental economic difference, and to apply the rules of secured lending (with their abhorrence of appropriation or forfeiture and a need for a disposition and a return of overvalue to the debtor) only in true loan situations. The rules of secured lending are therefore applied only if there is a clearly agreed interest rate structure, which is not normally so in finance sales or in the sale price protection schemes of reservation of title and hire purchase.

Of interest in this connection is the real estate mortgage in England (and also in the USA). The common law mortgage has always been a conditional sale. There is as a consequence appropriation of the asset by the lender upon default, but since the mortgage normally supports a loan with (normally) a clear interest rate structure, this appropriation right is balanced by the right or equity of redemption of the debtor.[12] It is meant to achieve a similar form of protection for the defaulting debtor as the disposition requirement of the asset does in secured lending in other countries leading to preserving the overvalue for the defaulting debtor. The equity of redemption gives the debtor/mortgagor additional time to recover full title and allows him thereby indirectly to retain the overvalue. The situation remains so far different that any undervalue can no longer be recovered if the financier chooses to obtain full ownership (foreclosure) when the sale becomes complete. On the other hand, where there is *no* true loan, as indicated by the absence of an agreed interest rate structure, the right of redemption is unlikely to apply. That is clear, at least in England, in the case of finance leasing, repurchase agreements and in the factoring of receivables, and certainly also in the reservation of title as purchase money security.

Yet the conditional sales approach is seldom fully developed for the modern finance sales, even in common law. Yet common law is on the whole entirely comfortable with conditional ownership, in equity also in chattels and receivables (although the UCC in the USA deviates here by statute from the established common law pattern for chattels and intangible assets as we already saw), but this has not led to a clearly defined type of ownership right. In common law, there may also be an important overlap with bailment, especially in finance leasing in which parties may relate to each other as bailor and bailee which gives another set of protections. It, however, also creates a separate set of complications.[13]

Nevertheless, as a basic proposition it remains justified and necessary *always* clearly to distinguish between security based and ownership based financing or funding techniques. Upon closer examination, it is indeed apparent that in modern finance the conditional sales technique inherent in ownership-based funding is often preferred, as is clear from the popularity of financing through repos, finance leases and factoring of receivables. These financing techniques are of enormous importance. The repos of investment securities amount to billions of US dollars (equivalent) per day and serve largely to fund the short term or speculative acquisition of investment securities by banks. Finance leases are thought to be used in more than 12 per cent of all equipment financing, whilst the factoring of receivables and their securitisation are no less significant.

Internationally, the conditional or finance sale presents a technique which may lead to a greater commonality in use and to better financier's protection as opposed to

---

[12] See text at n 163 *infra.*
[13] See also nn 27 and 199 *infra* plus accompanying text. See for the earlier attempts in case law to define the rights of both parties under a conditional sale in the USA nn 232*ff infra.*

secured transactions. These are now often too localised in their applications to be useful in international financial transactions, especially if chattels and intangible assets like receivables or other monetary claims are involved.[14] However, under more traditional private international law concepts, domestic law cannot easily be ignored where it concerns the creation of conditional sales in assets whose legal regime remains determined by the *lex situs*, even though for intangible assets the *situs* itself may be uncertain.

Yet there may be more room for convergence and harmonised interpretation in the area of finance sales than in the area of secured transactions. That must certainly be the hope. Most importantly, there may also be room for the acceptance of overriding structures which have become accepted and customary in international finance practices and could as such enter and be supported by the international law merchant or *lex mercatoria*, as more fully explained in chapter I of this book. Whether that may imply sufficient protection in bankruptcy still depends on the applicable bankruptcy law assuming that the assets are within reach of the bankruptcy court.

The fact that especially domestic civil law remains underdeveloped here may allow for greater flexibility. However, it follows from what has already been said that in the context of conditional sales there remains the risk that such sales are re-characterised as secured transactions rather than being accepted as true finance sales with their own proprietary regime that could be internationalised. The principle of the *lex situs* unavoidably favours a certain national law for chattels, although perhaps less so for receivables where party autonomy is more directly accepted. In any event, in ownership-based financing, the details of conditional ownership itself, and the rights of both seller and buyer under it, often remain problematic, even in common law: see section 1.5.2 below.

In civil law, there is the additional problem that the conditional proprietary rights of either party fit poorly in the system of recognised proprietary rights. In civil law, the types of proprietary rights are often considerably limited by statute for public policy reasons, as was discussed more fully in chapter IV, section 1.2.1. Even under the new Dutch Civil Code, it remains therefore unclear how conditional ownership rights, in principle recognised in Articles 3.92 and 3.84(4) CC, can be properly fitted into this (closed) system of proprietary rights (Article 3.81 CC).

1.1.4   Major Differences in the Domestic Laws on Proprietary Financial Protection and the Impact of Bankruptcy Laws

In view of the history and present day practices, it is clear that major differences still exist between the various legal systems in the area of modern secured transactions. This is so particularly in the types of assets that can be used as security (be it movable or immovable property) and in the need for possession, notification or publication. Other differences are in the need to identify the assets covered (and the possibility of including future assets), in the specification of protected debt and the protection of future advances, and especially in the shifting of the interest into replacement goods and proceeds.[15]

---

[14] In connection with international finance sales, it could be asked to what extent the 1980 Vienna Convention on the International Sale of Goods covers them in countries that have ratified this Convention. It was clearly not written for these types of sales but nevertheless may well apply to the liability for the goods and the risks in them, except if the goods are shares, bonds or other negotiable instruments, investment securities or claims when the Convention does not apply (Article 2).

[15] New Dutch security law is generally restrictive and puts considerable emphasis on the identification of the asset and the specificity of the debt at the time of the creation of the charge. It is in consequence not easy under new Dutch law to include future assets and future debt and create a true floating charge over an entire business.

Further differences arise particularly in respect of the newer non-possessory security interests in chattels and intangibles. As we saw, at first they tended to take the form of conditional sales but became largely treated as non-possessory security interests. The German *Sicherungsübereignung* still shows here some ambivalence especially outside a bankruptcy situation. A particular issue is here also the shifting of these modern interests into replacement goods and proceeds in order for them to become truly floating charges in a common law (equity) sense.

Ultimately, uncertainty developed everywhere in the treatment of modern finance sales like the investment securities repos, finance lease and factoring. This was primarily identified as a characterisation issue. There is a danger that these sales are converted into secured transactions, especially in the USA, or considered undesirable security substitutes as such deprived of proprietary effect, especially in the Netherlands, as was already discussed above and as will be covered in greater detail below.

Even if the notion of conditional or finance sales were everywhere accepted, also in their proprietary effect, there remains in particular the question of the position of either party under them, but there may here be more flexibility as compared to the situation for secured transactions. It may allow for a more common, practice-oriented, internationalised approach superimposed on domestic laws. It could be argued that this may lead to more uncertainty for participants, who are, however, usually professionals in specialised financing schemes and may be able to live with some uncertainty rather than with unsuitable alternatives like purely localised secured transactions and security interests. They often take here certain legal risks and are used to doing so, but it would undoubtedly be better for them if the position of conditional sales were clarified, especially at an international level, assuming that in principle they would be allowed to play a full role if parties so wished.

It should be noted that between the various countries in this area the type of interest may be the same on its face but the details may greatly differ. As we already saw, even the characterisation of the reservation of title may become problematic, also in the professional sphere. It is sometimes (as in the USA) considered a secured interest rather than a conditional ownership right of the seller and there is also the problem of its shift into replacement goods and proceeds which, where allowed, may in any event transform it into a type of charge or security interest. For the reservation of title, another key issue emerged concerning whether goods so sold could still be sold on by the debtor to third parties free from the seller's interest, especially if these third parties were buyers in good faith or in the ordinary course of the debtor's business. The same problems arise where non-possessory charges exist in inventory. Where this became possible, the compensation for the creditor was often that new inventory could automatically be covered by the existing charge which thus became floating, but, as previously mentioned, there remain even greater differences here.

They exist in a number of important aspects even between common law countries which all have similar security vehicles. Thus the priority of the floating charge in England dates only from the moment it attaches or crystallises, which occurs only at the moment of default. As a consequence these charges give the creditor a fairly low status — just above the common creditors. In the USA, under the UCC, shifting charges may, on the other

---

Whatever the policy objectives behind this approach — and they are not fully clear: see n 49 *infra* — it seems to give debtors less flexibility to use their (future) assets as security for other debt: see further also n 50 *infra* and accompanying text. But there is confusion. Absolutely future claims cannot be assigned, but a certain percentage of a securities portfolio may be even if that means a given and precise percentage of an uncertain quantity. In this sense, probably all of a certain class of present and future assets is transferable.

hand, date back to the moment of filing or publication and are thus much more potent. In fact in the USA, it is now possible to give virtually all one has or may possess as security for all one owes or may owe in the future with a rank as of the filing date (Section 9-204 (new and old) UCC).

There is also the aspect of the power given the creditors under the various schemes. In the UK, the implicit power of house banks, benefiting from floating charges covering future assets, to virtually monopolise the credit supply to clients subject to these charges and dictate future credit terms has come in for some serious criticism. Excess security normally results and is not easy to free up. In practice, this criticism may be less valid in the USA, as it is easier and common for debtors there to pay off their debts with the help of successor banks in a situation where there is much more competition between banks. The result is less risk that the debtor must eventually return to the first bank.[16] Under the US Bankruptcy Code (Section 364), the courts may in any event release excess security that may build up under this system.

Nevertheless, although Article 9 UCC is often admired in Europe (particularly in the aspect of its perfection and publication requirements), its sweeping approach to secured lending, the power it creates over debtors, its negative attitude towards conditional sales, reservation of title and modern financing techniques are, upon proper consideration, unlikely to find much favour elsewhere.

The result of the present differences in traditions and views on secured transactions and finance or other types of conditional sales is that even between close neighbours, like the Netherlands, Germany or Belgium, the differences in the secured or conditional ownership interests that can be created are striking. Belgium did not even accept the effectiveness of the reservation of title in bankruptcy until a change in the bankruptcy law in 1997 as French bankruptcy law did for France in 1980.[17] In the meantime, the fiduciary sale was outlawed by Belgian case law, although especially reinstated by statute for transactions conducted through the book entry system of Euroclear in Brussels.[18] In France, non-possessory security interests in chattels are limited to certain types of assets. As in the Netherlands, floating charges are discouraged. Much is done to leave more room for unsecured creditors. For the American observer this all seems old-fashioned and unsophisticated. Yet it is unclear whether in the final analysis it makes any difference to the development of the economy at large. It should in this respect never be forgotten that security and similar interests to protect funding are always last resorts. A good financier will never extend credit on the basis of it. He wants to see a proper cash flow that can support the payment of interest and principal in the case of a loan or a repurchase in the case of a conditional sale. Repossession is to him an admission of misjudgement and an undesirable ending although better than nothing.

Repossession raises the question of ranking, the effect of the security in an execution and the differences in the case of conditional sales.[19] It may well be that the applicable bankruptcy

---

[16] See for the UK the 1981 Cork Report and further JH Dalhuisen, 'The Conditional Sale is Alive and Well', in *Emerging Financial Markets and Secured Transactions, Economic International Development Law,* Vol VI, (Kluwer, The Hague /London/Boston, 1998), 83, 86.

[17] See text at n 88 *infra.*

[18] See also n 107 *infra* and chapter IV, n 324.

[19] The principles of ranking themselves may be summarised as follows: the older right prevails over the younger (*prior tempore potior iure*) except that the grantor of the right is always postponed although likely to be fully reinstated at the end of the term of the security right (if not executed). This priority amongst the grantees is the normal consequence of proprietary rights having an effect against all the world. The older interest holder may therefore ignore the younger. Any secured creditor may (in principle) execute subject to the other liens or similar interests although subject to the rights of *bona fide* purchasers (not so likely in a forced sale). Bankruptcy laws may sometimes

law may adopt independent policies here. Especially in the USA, policy adjustments to the security laws, which remain state law although for personal property unified through the Uniform Commercial Code, normally occur through the federal bankruptcy legislation. Also in civil law countries, the effect of bankruptcy legislation can be that certain types of creditors' protection, especially of the conditional sale type, like a reservation of title, may not be fully effective, as was the case earlier in France and Belgium.

On the other hand, most newer non-possessory security interests, developed in case law for chattels and intangibles, were generally given some status and rank under the prevailing bankruptcy laws, often also through case law. The consequence of this flexibility is nevertheless that even where security interests are quite similar in appearance and even in their effect in different countries, their treatment or ranking could still vary greatly in bankruptcy and would then depend on the applicable bankruptcy law, at least if the assets are within reach of the relevant bankruptcy court.

Naturally, creditors may also voluntarily postpone themselves; for example, lenders conceding subordinated loans. It is very common and normally not contentious, although the ranking of these postponed creditors amongst themselves may be a further issue. More importantly, postponement may also result from the operation of the applicable law. This is again particularly relevant in bankruptcy in respect of creditors who have taken an active part in the management of a bankrupt company, like directors/sole shareholders and provided loans. It is an instance of lifting the corporate veil or of equitable subordination,[20] also relevant for loans of unlimited partners.

In modern finance sales as true conditional sales under which the financiers may take other than pure credit risks and buy (outright or through options) certain forms of temporary or conditional co-ownership or partnership rights in an asset instead (thus providing the party needing financing with the required liquidity through payment of a purchase price), the concepts of the *par conditio creditorum* and of security may, as we shall see,

---

provide for a sale free and clear by the trustee (to realise overvalue) subject to the secured creditors being paid off according to their rank out of the proceeds (or being given alternative security), see Sections 363(b), (c) and (f) of the US Bankruptcy Code and Sections 15(2), (3) and (9) of the UK Insolvency Act (for administrations under the Act). Sometimes there may also be an implied right for the debtor to sell free and clear in the ordinary course of business as under a reservation of title or floating charge to protect the ordinary flow of his business.

Although 'first in time, first in right' is the basic rule, there are exceptions: purchase money may have the highest priority in order to safeguard the ordinary flow of goods. More specific charges are also likely to prevail over more general ones: therefore the later reservation of title is likely to prevail over an earlier charge over all the buyer's present and future assets. In England this follows from the crystallisation requirement in respect of floating charges. Possessory liens may be advantaged over non-possessory liens so that they may more readily entail their own execution right even in bankruptcy of the debtor and may therefore avoid the trustee's cost and will not be dependent on his action and timing. This is not so in Germany where there is for both only a right to a priority in the proceeds (*Absonderung* rather than *Aussonderung*). Other countries like the USA and the Netherlands both give rights to repossession and separate recovery. It may be different for statutory liens or (in France) *privilèges* which are usually non-possessory and lead only to a preference. Contractual liens prevail over such statutory ones even if older, although some statutory liens, like tax liens, may sometimes also be given the status of a contractual security interest, especially in the USA, when the older ones prevail over younger contractual liens. Statutory liens, especially general tax liens, may by statute also be given super priority status and then take priority also over all contractual liens and also more specific statutory liens which normally would have precedence.

It may be added that in this area of status and ranking and the rights derived therefrom, the various legal systems are by no means always clear, even in respect of purely domestic proprietary and similar rights. Especially the conflicts between the reservation of title, particularly when shifting to replacement goods and proceeds and floating charges or earlier security interests comprising also future assets of the debtor, may be substantial and have given rise to much litigation. It should also be considered that the set-off gives perforce the highest priority whilst retention rights in practice may force the other creditors, even if secured, to pay off the retentor in order to be able to recover any excess value in the retained assets. The status of contractual enhancements of the set-off and retention right may again be much less certain and give rise to many questions.

---

[20] *Cf* Section 510 US Bankruptcy Code.

become altogether irrelevant. These financiers may not have creditor status proper but rather ownership status for which they pay. It will have to be considered in this connection if, and to what extent, they postpone themselves in this manner to secured creditors in the same asset or to ordinary creditors of their counterparties in respect of their repossession rights in the asset.[21]

1.1.5   Harmonisation Attempts: Principles of Security Laws?

The great differences in security interests and the legal uncertainties in modern conditional or finance sales have troubled the more internationally oriented academic community. It is unclear whether these differences are a noticeable handicap to international trade, for example in terms of the status of the reservation of title when goods move across borders or in the treatment of general charges on inventory subsequently moved to other countries. There is at least no widespread evidence of it in the EU or in domestic case law, even for the reservation of title. The main reason is probably that these protections are likely to be lost anyway by the creditor upon the sale of these goods to *bona fide* third parties. They are often destined to be sold in this way. Another aspect, no doubt, is that security interests and conditional sale protections are meant only as a last resort. No funding would result at all if there were any prospect that the resulting proprietary protections would have to be invoked whilst bankruptcy remains a rare occurrence.

In modern, large scale, internationally promoted finance structures, the differences and uncertainties are nevertheless undesirable. The use of repos in foreign investment securities, of finance leases in aircraft that habitually move across borders, and of factoring of receivables involving foreign debtors is impeded by the present uncertainties. Again, in a time of few bankruptcies, this is less apparent and the problems remain substantially hidden, but that is not to say that they do not exist and inhibit funding.

Some international efforts are being made to alleviate the problems in this connection and in 1988 Unidroit cameup with Conventions on Finance Leasing and Factoring. They have had few ratifications so far. Uncitral produced a Convention on the Assignment of Receivables in International Trade (2001) and Unidroit a Convention on International Interests in Mobile Equipment (2001). Most of these efforts will be further discussed below but none has been greatly successful so far. They are good initial efforts, however, but are likely to require a great deal more thought and much more political will to make a true difference. Industry rather than academic support would also seem vital. The financial community is wary, so far, of these efforts. The reason is that the present texts could easily undermine the flexibility in the financial structuring it seeks to which uniform treaty law by its very nature cannot easily adjust.

As far as this flexibility is concerned, there is as yet little indication that in these international efforts the nature and importance of conditional or finance sales, as distinguished from secured transactions, are properly understood and their operation facilitated. It may be one reason why these efforts seem to become less rather than more popular. Short of international public policy considerations, they should facilitate, rather than curtail, the international funding practices and the flexibility they seek and need.

It is clear that at EU level the disparities have not caused great concern so far and it is unlikely that a serious attempt will soon be made to harmonise the securities interests if only in chattels and receivables, or that an attempt will be made to develop conditional or

---

[21] See text at n 243 *infra*.

finance sales in regional harmony.[22] The example of the USA, until the introduction of the UCC, has shown that great differences may long subsist here even after the unification of whole countries. There was a similar situation in Germany upon unification until the introduction of the BGB in 1900. In both the USA and Germany there was, however, a federal or national bankruptcy Act. Yet more recently, the EU has acted in its 2002 Directive on Financial Collateral. Significantly, it makes a fundamental difference between securities and finance sales in respect of investment securities of the book-entry entitlement type and dispenses in the process with any filing requirement in respect of the validity of the interests, see more in particular chapter IV, section 3.2.4.[23]

In the USA, the UCC unnecessarily narrowed the field in its unitary functional approach of Article 9. State law prevails in principle but the federal Bankruptcy Code developed some rules of its own for the various securities and other proprietary interests or liens and preferences arising under state law. The liens are divided into three types: the consensual, judicial and statutory liens. They need to support an allowed claim to retain their effect in bankruptcy (Section 506(d)). Execution of all of them may now be stayed pending reorganisation proceedings (Section 362(a)(5)) when interest only continues to

---

[22] Some efforts at harmonisation were made in the past, however: see also Drobnig, n 1 *supra*, at 32. As early as in the 1960s, there was a proposal from the banking industry to deal with the extraterritorial effect of non-possessory securities in movables based on recognition of these securities if properly created at the original *situs* of the asset and entered into a central EEC register. The EEC Commission at the time reacted positively but wanted national registers and the inclusion also of the reservation of title. The effort which became closely connected with the development of private international law rules for all patrimonial law was abandoned after the first expansion of the EEC in 1973, but a text was prepared: see Doc XI/466/73. The text was published by U Drobnig and R Goode, 'Security for Payment in Export and Import Transactions' in RM Goode and KR Simmonds (eds), *Commercial Operations in Europe* (Boston, Mass, 1978), 378–82. In 1980 there was another proposal (Doc III/872/80 unpublished) concerning the reservation of title only, now allowed to be effective EC-wide without registration, including the agreement to shift the lien into proceeds. The project was not pursued.

In the meantime, Drobnig in his report to Uncitral of 1977, n 1 *supra*, 226, stated that 'mere recommendations, even if emanating from an international organisation of the highest repute, will not command sufficient moral or other support for adoption by any sizeable number of States'. Although Uncitral subsequently concluded that unification of the law of security interests in goods was in all likelihood unattainable, after the emergence of the Unidroit Factoring Convention of 1988, it made its own attempt in the area of receivables in 2001: see for these two Conventions s 2.3 *infra* and for the Unidroit effort in the area of finance leases, s 2.1 *infra*. See for the Unidroit Convention in the area of mobile equipment, s 1.8.3 *infra*.

The latest effort was the introduction of one notion of reservation of title into the Directive 2000/35/EC of June 29 2000 combating late payment in commercial transactions, which also envisaged an accelerated collection procedure. It followed a Recommendation in this area of 12 May 1995, which did not contain a reference to reservations of title. Under the earlier proposals, [1998] OJ C 168/13, Member States, pursuant to Article 4(1), had to ensure that sellers retained their reservation of title in goods if they informed the buyers of it at the latest at the moment of delivery, but this could apparently be part of general sales conditions. In as far as the Directive did not cover aspects of the reservation of title, Member States had to define the effect, particularly the effect on third parties acting in good faith. It did not say which Member State was here competent in international sales (Article 4(3)) even though the measure was inspired by the problems raised in commercial transactions between Member States although not limited to them.

The final text was simplified and stated that Member States should provide in conformity with the applicable national provisions designated by private international law that the seller retains title to goods until they are fully paid for if a retention of title clause has been expressly agreed between the buyer and the seller before the delivery of the goods. Member States may adopt or retain provisions dealing with down payments already made by the debtor. As only payments of commercial transactions are considered in the Directive, the rules for reservation of title appear not to apply to sales to consumers although member States may of course extend these rules to them as well.

In the context of Directive 87/101 [1987] OJ L42 concerning consumer credit, Article 4(3), Article 7, and Annex I, 1 v and vi and 4 ii, give certain minimum protection to consumer debtors requiring in essence full disclosure of any security interests. It does not amount to any kind of harmonisation of these interests of the position of credit providers.

[23] See also the 1999 EU Settlement Finality Directive which touches on a number of bankruptcy aspects, see chapter IV, s 3.1.3.

accrue to the extent that there is overvalue in the collateral (Section 506(b)). The stay may be lifted (Section 362(d)) if there is no overvalue (or equity) for the debtor in the property and if it is not necessary in an effective reorganisation or otherwise for cause, including the lack of adequate protection (as defined in Section 361). The proper valuation methods have given rise to much debate and depend on the situation. The Bankruptcy Code is not specific and the bankruptcy courts assume here their traditional role and latitude as courts of equity.

Another immediate impact of bankruptcy on security interests results from the facility to remove excess security to allow the collateral to be used for new financings if not otherwise available during the evaluation period. Again there is the need for adequate protection, which may mean the offering of replacement security or even cash (Section 364(d)). It again raises the valuation question. In reorganisations, security interests may be converted and adjusted as part of the plan, although not taken away without the consent of the secured creditor (Sections 1129 and 1325). However, in the so-called 'cram down', a delay in payment may be imposed as long as the present value of these payments is not less than the secured claim. There are here other important valuation questions to be considered.

In the USA, security interests may sometimes also be avoided as fraudulent transfers under the Bankruptcy Code (Section 548). Although still expressed in the traditional common law language of hindering, delaying or defrauding common creditors, the purpose is to prevent the debtor from transferring valuable assets in exchange for less than adequate value if the transfer leaves insufficient assets to compensate honest creditors. The transfer may be to these creditors or to third parties and there must be fraudulent intent on the part of the debtor (although not necessarily on the part of the beneficiary). Security interests may also be avoided as preferential conveyances (Section 547). In that case, they must be given to existing creditors (in respect of antecedent debt) and may (just like payments) be voided even if given pursuant to an existing obligation. Since the new Bankruptcy Code of 1978, it no longer matters whether there was beneficiaries' knowledge or connivance and the avoidance now follows as a matter of strict liability. There is an exception for (Security) transfers in situations where new value is given or where payments are made in the ordinary course of business.

Liens may also be pushed down as unperfected liens pursuant to Section 544 (the strong arm statute), in fact explained as another way of avoiding them, or may be ignored on the basis that they are in exempt property (unless contractual: see Section 522(f)).

As already mentioned, in the USA, the federal Bankruptcy Code deals here with the policy issues and also with the treatment in bankruptcy of the newer financial products, like swaps and repos. Specific amendments were introduced for them, especially to allow netting (see Sections 556*ff*; see for netting generally chapter III, sections 1.3.3*ff*; for repo netting section 2.2.4 below; and for swap netting chapter VI, section 1.4.5). Common law rights under conditional sales do not prevent the assets to be part of the estate under Section 541 (subject to the possibility of their abandonment as burdensome assets under Section 554). The stay provisions also apply to them unless lifted when the assets can be repossessed.

Besides lien recognition, the Code also has its own system of priorities (Section 506) which give a high rank to administrative expenses which also include the cost of preserving and managing the estate (under Section 503(b)(1)(A)). The contribution of secured creditors is, however, limited to the cost of the estate in preserving and liquidating their collateral (Section 506(c)).

On the US analogy, it would be more normal to expect a uniform bankruptcy law in the EU than a uniform secured transactions law. If the new German Bankruptcy Act introduced in 1999 proves successful, it could serve as the most ready model. It deviates, however, in important aspects from the more common attitude which allows repossession of assets subject to security interests and it has also abolished many statutory liens, especially those in favour of the tax and social securities authorities. Whatever the model, uniform bankruptcy law appears a better approach than that of private international bankruptcy law, now enacted by EU Regulation in countries other than Denmark.[24] As such it is only concerned with a choice of jurisdiction and of domestic laws in the myriad of issues and conflict of law situations that are likely to arise in domestic bankruptcies with substantial trans-border aspects. It concerns therefore bankruptcies that mean to cover the activities and the assets of the debtor abroad. The EU now means to deal in this centralised manner with the interests of others in these activities or in these assets. Under the Regulation, the foreign bankruptcy trustee's position is accepted and recognised in the other countries that become so involved.

If bankruptcies with debtor activities and assets in other EU Member States become more frequent, a private international law Regulation of this nature is unlikely to be truly sufficient (and domestic private international law or conflict rules even less) as it can hardly satisfactorily cover all the different aspects of insolvency proceedings. If such cross-border bankruptcies do not become more frequent, then even a private international law approach, whatever the merits of the present Regulation, seems hardly worth the considerable effort.

If a uniform Bankruptcy Act is the true answer, it is likely that harmonisation or approximation of the security interests laws of the various countries and a joint approach to conditional sales will only follow in its wake. As earlier in the USA and Germany, it may well be that such a uniform bankruptcy law would create exactly the climate in which such approximation could properly take place. It would also require the financing alternatives, which are ownership based, like finance sales and the different proprietary interests that are embedded in them, to be more carefully considered.

In truth, the key issues in all this are *separation* and *priority*. In other words *when* may in a bankruptcy some other party lay proprietary claims to assets of the bankrupt and segregate them, that means repossess them from the bankruptcy trustee or retain them if already in possession, and claim these assets his own or *when* may a priority right in them be asserted in an execution and who may conduct it?

Separation of assets and differences in ranking as part of execution sales emerge all the time in both civil and common law. First, true owners of assets in the possession of the bankrupt may reclaim them subject to any temporary user rights they may have given the bankrupt before the bankruptcy. In this category may also figure sellers benefiting from a reservation of title in assets still with the bankrupt. In the realm of separation, in common law we also have the *constructive trust* facilities and the possibilities of equitable liens. They are often a sequel of unjust enrichment or restitution actions against the bankrupt: see also chapter IV, section 1.4.3. When precisely they arise and how far they go (especially into commingled or replacement goods) is less clear. Common law is here basically pragmatic, especially in equity although not necessarily generous; civil law is even more restrained.

In civil law, the notion of separation beyond clear forms of ownership of third parties is often connected with *joint or common ownership* and *legal personality* notions, as in the

---

[24] The EU efforts in this field have a long history and go back to 1968: see also JH Dalhuisen, 1 *Dalhuisen on International Bankruptcy and Insolvency* (1986), 3–165 and orinigally took the form of a draft treaty. An ultimate draft was presented on 23 Nov. 1995, and the final date for signature was put at 23 May 1996. Because of the failure of the UK to sign the project it lapsed but was revived and resulted in the Bankruptcy Regulation only excludeding Denmark.

case of the bankrupt estate itself. It may be considered owned by the creditors and as such separate from the person of the bankrupt or his trustee. In this manner, the community of property between spouses is also in the main considered separated from their own as is the deceased's estate from the estates of executors and of the heirs before distribution. Partnership types may lead to similar forms of separation of assets. Again there seems not to be a clear guiding principle in civil law, but it appears that mere commonality of property is not enough to lead to separation in this sense. There must be a special outside or policy reason why these properties are or come to be held in common and obtain not only an asset but also a liability and profit and loss structure. Even if there is separation in principle, there may still be problems when the assets are irreversibly commingled with the assets of the holders, managers or trustees of these separated properties. That is also a problem in common law (*cf* in the case of proceeds especially Section 9-306(4) UCC in the USA).

In *agency and guardian relationships*, the management and treatment of client assets and moneys, the handling of assets of minors or incapacitated persons create mixtures of proprietary rights everywhere with a need for ever stronger protection of the principals or beneficiaries, especially if the assets are officially in the name of the agent or guardian. This is a problem in common law habitually resolved through trust instructions. This is much more difficult in civil law. Everywhere tracing is a problem if assets are commingled. Even sufficiently separated client assets and accounts may still give rise to pooling problems amongst the various beneficiaries. Further problems arise where an agent or guardian exercises (personal) rights for clients or beneficiaries. Ideally, if an agent has entrusted client goods or moneys to others like custodians or banks, the principal should be able to step into the agent's shoes and claim ownership of the claims of the agent against the custodians or banks whenever he wishes to do so. That is again more likely to be possible in common law than in civil law: see also chapter II, section 3.1.6. In civil law it might depend on how clearly these assets were marked to belong to others.

Even in civil law, however, the proprietary retrieval concept increasingly surfaces where moneys have been improperly handled or misappropriated by asset managers and broking agents or are threatened by their bankruptcy. It shows a true need, also apparent where proprietary rights are allowed to shift into replacement goods and proceeds (tracing), a need, which in the law of obligations earlier lead everywhere, but particularly in civil law, to increased possibilities of specific performance.

More limited segregation rights result from secured transactions. They normally arise under contract or statute. To what extent segregation rights can be privately arranged beyond secured transactions is not always clear. In modern times, especially in civil law they are thought to depend on statutory authorisation, but new security rights and preferences have always developed in case law of which the German *Sicherungsübereignung* or non-possessory security in chattels is the best example. Thus case law tends to recognise new or better liens all the time and may also rearrange the priorities and adjust repossession rights.[25] Conditional transfers may, as we saw, also give reclaiming rights in the assets and their recognition is an important issue. It is clear that in modern financing the position of partner or conditional owner of the debtor's assets is often preferred by the financier to a position as secured creditor.

It is not uncommon in this connection to refer to the *unbundling* of the ownership right (or of the attached risks in an economic sense) in manners as agreed between the parties.

[25] See for the German *Sicherungsübereignung*, s 1.4.2 *infra*. See for recent Dutch case law extending preferences n 45 *infra*. See for the principles of priority n 19 *supra*.

In this sense one could also refer to the *contractualisation* of the ownership structure. The true question is how far the modalities can be left to the parties without depriving the resulting split rights of their proprietary status and from the attendant strong position in enforcement proceedings against the other party, which is likely to be primarily a question of the objective law rather than of contract. To the extent that contracting parties are allowed by the objective law or practice more freely to create proprietary rights in their assets — either through conditional sales and proprietary options leading to appropriation or through security interests with and execution sale and return of over value upon default — the effect of any new structures in this regard on third parties will have to be curtailed. Their protection needs to be reviewed and extended.

This will be so in respect of *bona fide* purchasers but not necessarily of *bona fide* creditors of either party. Whilst in the modern approaches the concept of the protection of *bona fide* purchasers tends to be extended all the time, the rights of *bona fide* unsecured creditors tend to be curtailed. This is shown in the steadily reducing impact of the concept of the 'solvabilité apparente' in France: see section 1.3.2 below. The exception is where (in civil law) creditors take out a security interest in chattels belonging to the debtor unaware of older interests (in which connection they are often considered *bona fide* purchasers as well). Also, creditors are everywhere protected against the debtor frittering away his assets to third parties or providing them with preferences. This is done under special law against fraudulent or preferential transfers as we already saw for US law (called *actio revocatoria* or *actio pauliana* in civil law), but only during short periods after such transfers.

Unbundling of the proprietary structure and of the connected risks is a technique with which common law is more familiar and comfortable than civil law by allowing an unlimited variety of equitable proprietary interests to operate in chattels subject to a broad protection of *bona fide* purchasers of the legal interest. This has probably to do with the fact that common law much less clearly distinguishes between contractual and proprietary rights than civil law. Civil law has a more systematic approach leading to an (in principle) closed system of proprietary rights and a loss of them if they are not cast in one of the few expressly allowed types, like security rights, usufructs and some forms of long leases: see more in particular chapter IV, section 1.2.1. In civil law, a more liberal approach is often considered to lead to an undesirable wild growth of security and similar interests, in turn detrimental to unsuspecting purchasers (who are protected only if *bona fide* in respect of chattels) and to common creditors, even if the latter may expect very little in a bankruptcy of the debtor. The standard secured interests normally erode their position completely. As a consequence, avoiding the newer forms of ownership-based funding would only reduce the funding choices for those who need money but it would not help unsecured creditors. Yet it is true that the more traditional bankruptcy notion of creditors' equality, often considered fundamental, although more so in civil than in common law with its less structured and more flexible system of proprietary rights and claims, is under renewed attack. It was probably always less fundamental than it seemed.

More choice for financiers and better protection of third parties is the answer, but with the present insight at least in Europe, the drive for European solutions is more likely to reduce them. There is, however, a tilt to more fundamental research. In 1996 the EBRD issued a set of general principles of a Modern Secured Transactions Law. They deal, however, only with the more traditional proprietary securities and execution rights that attach to monetary claims, therefore only with those arising in the context of loan financing and sale price protection. They underline the need for security to be able to be offered for present, past and future debt and to cover present and future assets including intangible rights and changing pools of assets with a possibility of shifting into proceeds and replacement goods with an effective execution facility.

Professor Drobnig in his contribution referred to in note 1 above, rejects for the EU the uniform UCC approach as politically unfeasible. He still limits his concerns to securities in assets that move across borders and discourages the creation of a single uniform European non-possessory security right as it would leave considerable differences in the manner in which it would be absorbed in each Member State. On the other hand, an obligatory recognition requirement of the various domestic securities also leaves absorption and transformation problems. It would still be necessary to determine for each Member State how foreign security interests are to be considered. In his view, it should be determined to what extent action needs to be taken in respect of loan credit security (like non-possessory securities in chattels or the similar *Sicherungsübereignung*) and sale price protection (like reservation of title). True needs should be decisive. The emphasis would at first probably be on the latter rather than the former.

It is not difficult to agree with much of these analyses, except that the alternative of and interest in ownership-based funding are completely ignored, particularly the international repo and receivable financing instruments. Also the indirect preferences resulting from the ever widening set-off, retention and tracing possibilities are largely overlooked. At least the conditional ownership concept has as a concept a much more international appeal. This being said, it may indeed be useful to agree the basic characteristics of the various modern security rights and ownership-based funding techniques to start with the reservation of title.

But the problems are not small, even for this most common sale price protection device. Is it in the specific sold asset only or can it shift into replacement goods and proceeds? Can it serve other debt? Is it an accessory right? Does it require execution with the return of overvalue to the buyer, or will it lead to appropriation of the asset by the seller without any return of overvalue? Is it a conditional sale? If so, what are the disposition rights of the buyer; what is the position of the buyer in a bankruptcy of the seller; are *bona fide* purchasers protected or even purchasers in the ordinary course of business; etc?

Still, it would be possible to outline the basic issues in the operation of the various security and conditional or finance sales rights, at least in chattels and intangible assets. Another issue altogether is the question of publicity of non-possessory rights of funding parties, its feasibility and true meaning as regards competing creditors and *bona fide* purchasers.

However, such efforts, even though useful, seem to miss the key point, which is to establish what international funding practice wants and can best deal with and how the necessary legal protections are best articulated, beginning with conditional or finance sale as an overarching and unifying legal structure.

1.1.6   Conditional and Temporary Ownership Transfers

Where true conditional or finance sales are used to raise financing, ownership in assets is conditionally transferred. The conditions may vary but are (at least in civil law countries) legally essentially of two types. They may either be suspensive conditions, also called conditions precedent or suspending conditions, or they may be resolutive or resolving conditions, also called conditions subsequent or rescinding conditions.

In the first case some form of ownership remains with the seller until a certain event occurs, for example payment of the sale price, when the buyer becomes full owner. This is often considered the essence of the reservation of title. In the second case, some form of title is transferred immediately, but made subject to a resolutive condition, such as non-payment. The reservation of title can also be expressed in this manner, but it is less common. All sales agreements may even be deemed to be subject to an implicit resolutive condition of proper payment. In civil law this facility is also referred to as the *lex commissoria.*

Indeed Dutch law before 1992 gave proprietary effect to this implied condition, and would automatically allow title to return to the seller upon default, even in a bankruptcy of the buyer in possession. This particular resolutive condition of ownership is also called the *lex commissoria tacita.* It still exists in France, although its effect is curtailed in bankruptcy, as we shall see in section 1.3.2 below. Even now such a condition has full proprietary effect under Dutch law, also in the bankruptcy of a defaulting seller, if explicitly inserted into the agreement; this is the *lex commissoria expressa* of Article 3.84(4) CC.[26] In Germany if intended to undo the proprietary transfer agreement (*Einigung*), it may also be effective.

Whether a condition of ownership transfer is qualified as resolving or suspending may not matter greatly. In any event, a resolving condition, negatively expressed, becomes a suspending condition and *vice versa.* It is more important to appreciate that the one is always the mirror of the other, so that the resolving condition for the one party is necessarily the suspending condition for the other. Thus in a reservation of title, payment may be seen as the suspending condition of the ownership of the buyer, but it is the resolving condition of the ownership of the seller. Under the *lex commissoria*, default or non-payment is the resolving condition for the buyer and the suspending condition for the seller in whom full ownership automatically revests in that case.

In the repurchase agreement, failure timely to tender the repurchase price may resolve the title in the seller and vest it absolutely in the buyer. On the other hand, the tender itself may vest full title absolutely in the seller (assuming there was not a mere option of retrieval). In a finance lease, it is the payment of the agreed instalments that resolves the title of the lessor and vests it in the lessee absolutely (assuming that was the agreement and there is no mere option for the lessee to acquire full title, whether or not against a further payment). In factoring, excess receivables, receivables that cannot be collected or were not approved by the factor, may be automatically returned when this becomes clear, a feat that would resolve the factor's title and re-vest the receivables absolutely in the seller.

As just mentioned, it may not make much difference in this connection which party has the resolving or suspended title, *provided* both have proprietary protection. Only if that is not so, and one party remains with only an obligatory reclaiming right (usually, it seems, the party with the suspended title, at least if it has not also physical possession), the situation is very different. If both parties have a proprietary right, there is still a question which party would incur the burdens and benefit of ownership. This is usually the party in physical possession which incurs as a consequence some special duties to look after the asset, and this party may then also collect the benefits attached to it, although the contract may provide otherwise. These rights and duties seem to relate to physical possession rather than to the nature of the interest being resolutive or suspended.

Whether it matters or not, it is often efficient to consider the party who is intended to obtain the ultimate full title as the party with the suspensive interest, the other with the resolving interest, but it will also depend on whether the condition is positively or negatively expressed and, as we shall see, possibly on the way the proprietary interest is manifested (ownership, possession or holdership), at least in civil law. Thus in a reservation of title and

---

[26] See for the situation in the Netherlands see the text at n 58 *infra* and in France the text at n 83 *infra.*

in a finance lease, it is respectively the buyer and lessee who normally are considered to have suspensive title. The ownership is therefore suspended as regards them, but resolving to the seller and lessor respectively. They therefore have resolving title. Under the *lex commissoria*, and in repos, the sellers normally appear to have the suspending title and the buyers the resolving one.

As just mentioned, much more important is whether both parties have a proprietary interest. This is only so if these conditions result in a *duality* in ownership: one party as owner under a resolutive condition and the other under a suspensive condition. This would then also apply in civil law to the connected concepts of legal or constructive possession, and of the holdership of the asset. Thus in civil law, the owner under a resolutive condition is also the legal possessor under that condition, whilst the other party has suspensive ownership and possession.

In a reservation of title situation, this means that the seller has the title and legal possession in a civil law sense under the resolutive condition of the buyer's payment; the buyer has the title and the legal possession under the suspending condition of his own payment. In the repo, the seller has the title and possession under the suspending condition of his tendering the repurchase price, and the purchaser under the resolutive condition of this tender. In the finance lease (unless otherwise agreed) the lessor has the title and possession under the resolutive condition of full payment of the instalments; the lessee under the suspending condition of his full payments. In factoring, the seller of the receivables may retain suspended title and possession in them, as the case may be, under the resolutive condition of the receivables being collectible or being approved by the factor. Also any transfer of receivables in excess of certain amounts may be suspended in a similar manner.

As regards the holdership of the assets, in civil law terms it appears that the party in actual possession (even if subject to a sub-holdership) has the resolutive holdership as for the time being he holds for another. Thus in a reservation of title and in a repo, it is the buyer in possession who has resolutive holdership until his payment. Where, in a conditional sale, the seller retains holdership of the asset (as in *Sicherungsübereignung* situations in Germany and under the old *fiduciary sale* in the Netherlands (now outlawed if still arranged as a pure conditional sale as we already saw), the seller would have resolutive holdership. If he repays the loan he will become full owner and possessor and his holdership will lapse. The unpaid seller still in possession upon a transfer *constituto possessorio*, has also a resolutive holdership. It may be possible to construe a suspensive holdership in the counterparty. It seems the normal complementary or mirror right but it is too fanciful.

Where there is a duality of ownership, the resolutive and suspensive interests in title and possession so created are for each party truly each other's complement and together constitute full ownership and possession in civil law terms. It follows that in the case of ownership and possession, the resolutive and suspending condition is in either case the same, but may coincide with the opposite condition in the holdership. Thus the seller in possession under a reservation of title may be considered an owner and possessor under a resolutive condition but a holder under a suspensive condition. In the case of a default, his right becomes full. If the buyer has the asset, which is the more normal situation, he has suspensive ownership and possessory rights but holds under the resolutive condition of his own payment. If he pays, the holdership disappears; if he does not it becomes unconditional.

In common law, the situation is somewhat different. It is on the whole comfortable with the notion of conditional title, but normally the distinction is not along the lines of the resolutive and suspensive title. In common law the (Roman law) triptych of ownership, legal possession and holdership is also unknown, and the normal proprietary structures in chattels are (a) ownership, (b) (physical) possession (often bailment), and (c) equitable interests like beneficial, future or conditional ownership rights: see more in detail chapter IV, section 1.3.

These equitable interests in chattels are generally borrowed from real property law and concern remainder, reversionary and executory interests. They need not be explained here any further, but do not fit well into the civil law terminology of suspending or resolutive conditions. They have their own typical formulations (in the sense of rights that last 'as long as', or given 'on the condition that', etc). They may become connected in chains of ownership and are all hidden interests that are not extinguished by statutes of limitation.

On the other hand, they may not be acquired through prescription (as is possible for all proprietary interests in civil law). They are all lost when the legal interest in the asset is transferred to *bona fide* purchasers for value even in the case of real estate and intangible assets like receivables. This is unlike the attitude to proprietary interests in civil law which are superseded only by the better right of *bona fide* purchasers of chattels (although in some countries like Germany *bona fide* purchasers of real estate may be protected, at least against mistakes in the real estate registers).

In sum, conditional ownership rights under common law are in a number of important aspects quite different from conditional proprietary interests in civil law. The notion is in essence not different, however, when in civil law both conditional owners of an asset are given proprietary status and protection in a duality of ownership. Indeed, in the case of chattels, future or conditional interests in the title are, in common law, not directly related to possession (in the common law sense), but have their own trust-like structure in which a duality of ownership is inherent. Yet the rules concerning physical possession or bailment may cut through this as under common law bailees, as physical possessors, may have a strong separate protection right, also *vis-à-vis* conditional title holders who obtain full title, even after the bailee's own conditional title has lapsed: see more in particular chapter IV, section 1.3.2.

So it is in essence in a bankruptcy of the bailee/ buyer even under a reservation of title, when a special exception had to be made so that the position of the seller could become properly protected. The argument here is that conditional sales giving possession to the buyer create more than a buyer's bailment, as a bailment itself always implies a return of the asset after its objectives have been met.[27] The opposite is the intention in a reservation of title, which may falter upon non-payment.

In civil law, the key question remains whether the duality in ownership, and therefore the proprietary interest of either party is accepted. In common law, there was never much of a conceptual approach in these matters. In civil law, this is somewhat different, as Sections 158–63 BGB show in Germany, but the proprietary protection of future interests remains embryonic. Where the proprietary interests of both partners under a conditional sale and title transfer become accepted, these interests become protected against claims of third parties, including those of the creditors of the other conditional owner. At the same time the interests of either party become freely transferable. At least this seems to have happened in civil law in the traditional reservation of title as a sale price protection tool. Case law and doctrine show this particularly in Germany and the Netherlands, as we shall see in the *dingliche Anwartschaft*,[28] but it is even in these countries as yet much less clear for finance sales like repos, finance leases and factoring.

[27] See nn 199 and 234 *infra* also for the tenuous position of the bailor in a bankruptcy of the bailee.
[28] See n 127 *infra*.

It may be useful to consider here for a moment also *temporary* or delayed transfers. In civil law, they are often distinguished from conditional transfers. It is true that temporary or delayed transfers may arise from contractually agreed time limits, but they may factually also result from conditions. The practical *effect* of contingencies or conditions and time-limits is, therefore, often the same in terms of temporary or delayed transfers, but the *trigger* is likely to be different. In contingencies, the event that triggers the transfer or return of full ownership (and therefore the temporary or delayed transfer) is *uncertain*, like payment in the case of a reservation of title or the tender of the repurchase price under a repurchase agreement. In a time limit, the event is *certain* and the title will transfer or revert at the agreed time, for example where title is given to A until a certain date, and thereafter to B, or reverts on that date to the original owner in full ownership, There is no true condition here.

Conditions on the title transfer may also result from the stipulation of certain uses; for example, title is given as long as a property can be used by grantees for a specific charitable purpose, but is meant to revert thereafter or is then transferred to other grantees for other purposes. In civil law terms, this would be a condition. It may thus cut short an interest which does not thereby become temporary but merely conditional.

This may seem simple enough, but conditions and time limits may be intertwined and confusion often results. Naturally, in the case of a contingency, the uncertain event may be related to a date certain on which it is tested whether the contingency has matured, such as on the agreed payment or repurchase date. That date itself could also be flexible, such as the moment of delivery or completion of a project. Even if the testing date is certain, the triggering event may still be uncertain and there is, therefore, still a conditional transfer, the (un)certainty of the event and not of the date being the crucial element.

On the other hand, in a term of time, the event may be certain, for example death, but the date uncertain. Still, there is no condition but a time limit and the result is therefore a temporary rather than a conditional ownership. Yet it may not all be as clear as it looks. In the repo, there is a temporary transfer if one emphasises the repurchase date, but there is a conditional transfer if one puts the emphasis on the tender of the repurchase price.

In common law, these contingencies and time limits are well known in the law of *future interests* and defeasible fees or titles but not distinguished in this manner. In civil law, these future interests resulting in temporary or delayed ownership may sometimes show some similarity to usufructs,[29] especially when there are time limits set to certain user and income rights. In civil law, it is clear that time limits may, like contingencies, be resolutive or suspensive of the title transfer and — it is submitted — often result in a duality of ownership.

In fact, the difference between conditional and temporary ownership is unlikely to have significant legal consequences in civil law (*cf* also Section 163 BGB). For the purposes of this study it is usually unnecessary to make a distinction between transfers subject to a condition or contingency and transfers subject to a time limit, and therefore between conditional and temporary or delayed ownership. Such a need arises only when, as under new Dutch law, a temporary transfer of an asset is re-characterised as and converted into a usufruct (Article 3.85 CC).[30] It must then be distinguished from a conditional transfer

---

[29] Although in a reservation of title there is always a contingency, and therefore no time limit, in countries like France and the UK, the reservation of title is often characterised as a delayed rather than a conditional title transfer, as is more common in Germany and the Netherlands: see nn 52, 97, 121 and 191 *infra* plus accompanying text. Reference is made here to no more than the effect of the condition which is indeed to delay the transfer, but the resulting title for the buyer is conditional and not temporary.

[30] Unlike pseudo-security interests which are, as we saw, not converted into real security interests but are deprived of their proprietary effect under Article 3.84(3) CC.

which is in principle allowed (unless as a security substitute as we already saw) and is not treated in the same way. In French law, there is the argument that in conditional sales, the return of ownership is retroactive, whilst this is not believed to be the case if the title is merely temporary and its return in that sense delayed.[31]

1.1.7 The Duality of Ownership in Finance Sales

As set out in section 1.1.1 above, in more modern, often internationalised, financing arrangements, ownership-based funding techniques through conditional sales have acquired great importance. They should not automatically be thought of as types of security-based funding, although, as already mentioned several times before and for reasons which will be explained more fully later, this is still the clear tendency in the USA. In the Netherlands, a proprietary or security interest may not be accepted for the financier in finance sales at all.

Lack of insight into the difference between the two and into their basic structure may present considerable risks for the financier, especially when his proprietary interest is by law converted into a security interest requiring an execution sale instead of appropriation. In the case of default it allows any overvalue to accrue to the defaulting party. This conversion, which is imperative under Article 9 UCC in the USA, deprives the financier of an important potential benefit, especially if the underlying asset has a market-related value like investment securities. In return for this benefit, he may have accepted a lower or different reward for this kind of funding.

In bankruptcy, especially under modern reorganisation statutes, further adverse consequences may follow in terms of a stay and possible dilution of the converted interest when considered a security. Even where this risk is not great, there is, at least in civil law, a considerable danger that the proprietary nature of the ownership-based funding structure and of the parties' interests thereunder may not be sufficiently recognised or, as in the Netherlands, might be denied altogether in the context of funding.

In such cases, the arrangement may also be recharacterised as an *executory* contract, giving the parties only contractual rights *vis-à-vis* each other whilst ownership will be allotted to only one of them (even though it may not be immediately clear which of the two parties this will be). This has certainly given rise to problems in finance leasing because, using this approach, the lessor may be assumed to have retained the full ownership of the asset.[32] On the other hand, in the USA the lessor has only a security interest making the lessee the owner, although in equipment leases under Article 2A UCC, as we shall see in section 1.6.2 below, the ownership issue is largely ignored. In repurchase agreements, it may, in this approach, be the seller who is the sole owner, although in repos of investment securities, it could be the buyer, (especially) if the assets are fungible securities and, in factoring, it is probably the factor. Therefore the financier appears to result mostly as the owner in this kind of reasoning that does not want to give both parties proprietary rights.

The immediate consequence is that this allows the trustee in a bankruptcy of this party to claim full ownership but repudiate the rest of the deal (considered purely contractual) if detrimental to the estate, whilst allowing the other party to present only a claim for damages as a common creditor who may have to surrender his rights in the asset, even if as finance lessee he has possession.

---

[31] See n 97 *infra*.
[32] See for the situation in the Netherlands the text at n 63 *infra*.

In a repo it would allow the bankruptcy trustee of the financier to keep the asset if it has increased in value and ignore the seller's claim to it and let him file for damages as ordinary creditor instead. If on the other hand he wants to rid himself of an asset that declined in value and prefers to collect the repurchase price, he will uphold the counter-party's duty to repurchase. In a finance lease, the bankruptcy trustee of a lessor would hold the lessee to the lease if beneficial to the bankrupt estate or otherwise reclaim the asset, leaving the lessee as a common creditor (although he might have some rental protection or a retention right for his damages). This is often referred to as the '*cherry picking*' option of the bankruptcy trustee and shows the lack of balance that follows where the proprietary status of *both* parties is not sufficiently recognised and the characterisation of the finance sale as an executory contract results.

Commercial logic and needs increasingly require the law to accept differentiation, to acknowledge the different requirements in this area, and the different risk and reward patterns established by the parties. They also demand adequate protection, which in finance sales (or property-based funding) should be proprietary in nature for either party. As explained before, particularly in civil law, such proprietary protection depends on a more liberal acceptance of the duality of the ownership concept and, to that extent, also on some opening up of the (civil law) system of proprietary rights. The key is greater freedom for the parties in this connection than is at present mostly in order for them to arrange the details of these (proprietary) rights and the protection they bring through the formulation of the conditions in their contract.

The internationalisation tendency in modern financial products acts here as a creative and, at the same time, unifying force. Generally, it does not seek to force the new financial structures into the prevailing domestic patterns of secured loans, which could deform the product and introduce vast differences in treatment, nor do they reduce them to executory contracts. The problem remains, however, that the conditional ownership structure intended to be created in ownership-based funding and the desired proprietary protection of either party thereunder do not necessarily correspond to those maintained or authorised by modern codifications, including the UCC in the USA.

The expectation, particularly of the party looking forward to gaining full ownership (in Germany referred to as *dingliche Anwartschaft*), thus of the party under a suspensive ownership title, may not so easily be protected in a proprietary manner and be transferable as such. Moreover, there is as yet little guidance on how the proprietary relationship between both parties in a conditional sale must be seen. In civil law, it leaves the proprietary status of the rights of either party under these modern conditional finance sales in some considerable doubt. It is urgent for legal doctrine and case law to fill in some of the gaps. There is significant case law from pre-UCC practice in the USA, especially in connection with the reservation of title.[33] Although superseded in the USA it remains conceptually highly relevant and illustrative and will be summarised in section 1.7.3 below. History has shown that not much other than confusion can be expected here from statutory law.

The proprietary relationship between both parties to a conditional sale and title transfer concerns primarily the balance between the rights of conditional owners of the same asset, but this has an immediate effect on the rights of their creditors and their position in a bankruptcy of the other party. In the USA, the conditional sale became popular in its

---

[33] See for some early attention to the subject in Germany, n 122 *infra* and in Roman law and France n 80 *infra*. See for the USA, Estrich, *The Law of Instalment Sales of Goods including Conditional Sales* (Little Brown, Boston, Mass, 1926) and the references to US case law in nn 232–42 *infra*.

own right at the end of the nineteenth century mainly to avoid equipment sold on credit being caught by after-acquired property clauses, previously entered into by the buyer and promising his lenders the inclusion of any future assets in the security granted for their loans. It became established that equipment delivered under a conditional sale could not be included in such security. Subsequently the conditional sale also became popular as a way to avoid registration and execution problems under chattel mortgage laws, or the effects of antiquated usury laws. Their popularity led to the formulation of a Uniform Conditional Sales Act in the USA in the 1920s.

It was not successful and the great diversity in attitudes amongst the courts in the various states of the USA was one of the causes of the entirely different approach in the present Article 9 UCC. Main issues were nevertheless extensively discussed and the old case law in the USA remains therefore revealing. It centred on:

(a) the creation of the interest;
(b) the qualification of the arrangement as dual ownership, bailment or an executory contract;
(c) the comparison between the position of the seller and buyer;
(d) the shifting of the interests into replacement goods;
(e) the rights to possession, capital gains and the liability for loss;
(f) the transfer of the interests of each party and the possibility of sub-encumbrances in each party's interest;
(g) the protection of *bona fide* purchasers from either party;
(h) the consequences of default of either party, the execution duty or appropriation right and the entitlement to overvalue;
(i) the position of the creditors of each party;
(j) the effect of attachment of each party's interest; and
(k) the position and ranking of each party in the other's bankruptcy.

These issues will be considered below in section 1.7.3. So far, civil law has had here little on offer because of its unfamiliarity with the duality of ownership concept. At this stage the prime issue in civil law is the extent to which applicable domestic law allows these new conditional ownership structures to operate and develop in a proprietary fashion for both parties. An immediately related issue is the effect of the internationalisation drive in terms of the application or disapplication of domestic norms (if restrictive) to these new internationalised financial and proprietary structures. The question is then reduced to the single issue of how the new patterns of funding and risk distribution, often internationally established, relate to local thinking, itself expressed:

(a) in terms of the mandatory law of secured transactions and sometimes in terms of conversion into a domestic security interest;
(b) at least in civil law in terms of the closed proprietary system; and
(c) in terms of the continued applicability of the *lex situs* of the underlying asset in these aspects (in any event problematic in the case of bulk assignments of intangible assets and their securitisation).[34]

---

[34] Receivable financing has become an issue for Uncitral: since its Report on the work of its 28th session, Official Records of the General Assembly, 50th Session, Supplement No 17 (A/50/17) (1995), paragraphs 374–81. In 2001 it resulted in a Convention on the Assignment of Receiveables in International Trade. See s 2.3.8 *infra*.

Any flexibility at international level in this regard, ie any acceptance of the transnationalisation of the ownership concepts for these purposes to allow conditional or dual ownership rights to operate fully cross-border in financial transactions, will unavoidably reverberate in the domestic markets and claim its effect on local legal practices. In fact, allowing the new methods and structures of funding to be internationally effective in the end will also mean accepting them domestically in purely local transactions, at least those between professionals who also operate in similar manners internationally.

1.1.8   Autonomous Transnational and Domestic Legal Developments in Third Party or Proprietary Effect of Contractual Clauses

In the meantime, a prime example of this type of autonomous transnational development and its overriding impact on domestic contract and proprietary laws is the operation of the eurobond market and its effect on:

(a)   the domestic issuing, underwriting and trading practices;
(b)   the proprietary status of the document (the eurobond), the manner and also the timing of transfer of ownership (which in CAD sales may well depend on payment) and the protections of *bona fide* purchasers; on
(c)   the (dis)application of traditional private international law rules or the possibility of contractual choice of law in the proprietary and protection questions;
(d)   the force of transnational practices, even in matters of ownership and its transfer and of proprietary status and protection; and on
(e)   the effect of this force in the connected book-entry and custody arrangements and their segregated status.

The effect on third parties of the new ownership-based financing structures developed at the international level is one of the foremost issues under applicable domestic law, but in fact no less under transnationalised concepts of law superseding or incorporating domestically the accepted internationalised practices in this regard. The internationalisation has always had a clear impact on proprietary matters, as is shown for negotiable instruments (like bills of exchange, eurobonds, euro-commercial paper, or certificates of deposit) and documents of title (like bills of lading and warehouse receipts), both first developed in the old law merchant: see further also the discussion in chapter I, section 3.2.2. It is even true for negotiable stocks and shares. But the details need still to be worked out and this includes security interests in, and conditional transfers of, these instruments created at the international level.

The emergence in the meantime of book-entry systems for stocks and shares, see also chapter IV, section 3.1.4 seems to de-emphasise the ownership rights of the interest holders and may again rekindle interest in domestic laws through the application of private international law rules pointing to applicability of the law of the country in which the register or book-entry system is organised. It would emphasise the differences and may make trading in these instruments dependent on a fortuitous domestic law that may be insufficient and totally unaware of the international dimension and requirements of the book entry systems. It is submitted therefore that this is not a desirable development.

In the meantime, it should be considered also that the third party effect is not even purely domestically necessarily always a problem of property law only. In fact, third party effect of contractual clauses is itself increasingly an issue and progressively accepted. It is usually confined to special situations, however, traditionally where qualitative obligations or, in French doctrine, rights *propter rem* or *obligations réelles* exist:[35] see more in particular chapter II, section 1.5.

Thus pre-existing covenants, rental agreements, ground-rent obligations or (access) duties owed to neighbours may have to be respected by succeeding owners in their capacity as owners. In financial arrangements, third party effect of some contractual clauses may be found in finance leasing where the lessee is often thought to derive (collateral) rights from the supply contract between the supplier and the lessor. These rights are emphasised by Article 2A UCC in the USA and by the Unidroit Convention on International Financial Leasing of 1988.[36] Particularly important in financial matters is also the status in bankruptcy of contractual enhancements of rescission, retention and set-off rights and their increasingly acknowledged preferential effect for the beneficiary to the detriment of competing creditors.[37] The recognition of contractual conditions affecting title in finance sales must increasingly be considered in a similar vein.

The ultimate step is the creation of (some) rights maintainable against all the world through mere contractual stipulation only. As mentioned above, in civil law this is, in a closed system of proprietary rights, normally thought to be countered by public policy considerations, protecting third parties including the creditors of the seller. It would require better protection for all kinds of *bona fide* outsiders (as under equitable principles in the common law). It is here of some interest that in countries not requiring delivery for ownership transfers in chattels, such as France, Belgium, Italy and England, proprietary rights (in chattels) are seemingly created by contract alone. The relevant contractual terms transferring property rights must be respected by all, without the added formality of delivery as a form of publication of the new relationship. Yet to the extent that these are civil law countries, it is now well established that only recognised proprietary rights can be created in this way and that also in these countries the full proprietary effect normally depends on delivery: see also chapter IV, section 1.2.1.

It appears, however, that greater party autonomy is becoming accepted in this area everywhere, even domestically, but at least in civil law it remains a matter for the objective law (which could, however, be case law) to decide how far the parties' wishes in this respect can be accommodated. Greater flexibility, wherever conceded, cannot mean that the parties' intention can always fully prevail, however, especially where third parties, including the creditors of the parties dividing the property, are involved and asked to respect the result. This is no less true in common law, even if the concepts, are less clear and there is more flexibility. Indeed, equitable proprietary rights may be freely created by contract, as we saw, but their effect is cut short, in that they cannot be maintained against *bona fide* third parties.

Even in civil law on this point, the objective law is not a given and the line is constantly being redrawn. In domestic law, new security-related interests emerged in case law, as in Germany the *Sicherungsübereignung* and earlier in the Netherlands the *fiducia cum creditore* or fiduciary sale as types of non-possessory charges in chattels and receivables. As we saw, they were in origin both conditional sales. In Germany there emerged subsequently the proprietary expectancy or *dingliche Anwartschaft* for the suspended owner in conditional sales.

---

[35] See in the Netherlands, J Eggens, *Over de verhouding van eigendom en verbintenis* [On the relationship between ownership and obligation], Royal Netherlands Academy of Arts and Sciences, Part 23–7 (1960) and for France, G Cornu, *Droit Civil, Les Biens* (5th ed, 1991), 321.
[36] See also JH Dalhuisen, 'The Unidroit Convention on International Financial Leasing' in Kokkini et al, *Eenvormig en Vergelijkend Privaatrecht* (1994)27, 45.
[37] See JH Dalhuisen, 'Conditional Sales and Modern Financial Products' in A Hartkamp et al, *Towards a European Civil Code* (2nd edn, Ars Aequi Libri, Nijmegen, 1998), 525.

Domestic systems are in any event increasingly faced with the need to accept unfamiliar foreign or international structures and consider the effect in their own systems. Even the more traditional security interests, if foreign, attached to assets arriving from abroad cannot always be assimilated and may require special treatment under rules of private international law, if not also more directly under rules of transnational law, therefore not only for new types of negotiable instruments. This amounts in itself to an opening up of the domestic proprietary systems.

The evolution of transnational proprietary concepts will have a further impact. This is especially clear in international dealings in investment securities, but issues of public policy, definition and the divide between finance sales and secured transactions (which may also be further developed internationally) will surface also at the level of other assets and also be settled in a more uniform manner. Much more thought will have to be given to this subject which, in civil law terminology, directly concerns the distinction between *in rem* and *in personam* or between proprietary and obligatory rights.

Quite apart from these fundamental questions conceivably limiting the new funding alternatives under domestic laws but transferring them to the international level where, from a legal point of view, they also remain to be further developed, it could still be intellectually satisfying, even at that international level to limit the possibilities and have a unitary system of secured, security related and other property-based funding transactions and credit protections, whatever the practitioners' needs.

Yet such a restrictive approach does not operate successfully anywhere, even in the USA, where the conditional sale including the reservation of title, trust deeds creating security interests, and the assignment of receivables including factoring for other than collection purposes are, in their unitary functional approach, all considered part of one system of secured transactions.[38]

The unity which is imposed here proved artificial and it became clear that the finance lease and the repurchase agreement hardly fit into this system. Special clarifications for the equipment lease became necessary which may now be found in Article 2A UCC: see also section 1.6 below. For the practical reasons already stated, it appears that financial structures cannot be confined in this manner.

The domestic systems remain, however, the starting point for any discussion of the new proprietary structures and the legal regime concerning them. They will therefore be considered first for a number of countries. Most important are the USA, England, Germany and France. The Dutch approach is also of some interests as it presents the latest effort to deal comprehensively with proprietary interests including secured transactions and it will therefore be discussed first.

1.2   The Situation in the Netherlands

1.2.1   Introduction: The New Civil Code of 1992

The Dutch system was recast in the new Dutch Civil Code of 1992. It created a special security right in movables and intangibles, the non-possessory pledge. It replaced the earlier

---

[38] See Section 1-201(35) (1-201(37) old), Section 9-19(a)(1) (9-102(1)(a) and (2) old) and Section 9-109(d)(4) (9-104(f) old) UCC; see also the text at n 201 *infra*. See for arguments in favour of a much more open system in civil law countries, JH Dalhuisen, 'European Private Law: Moving from a Closed to an Open System of Proprietary Rights', 5 *Edinburgh LR*, 1 (Sept 2001). See for proposals for a more fundamental modernisation of Dutch property law (concerning chattels and intangible assets), JH Dalhuisen, 'Zekerheid in roerende zaken en rechten' [Securitty in Chattels and Intangible Assets], *Preadvies Vereeninging' Handelsrecht* (2003).

fiduciary transfer which started as a conditional sale although it subsequently acquired most features of a secured transaction — not unexpected in a clear loan situation, as we already saw in section 1.1.1 above. The fiduciary sale and transfer was comparable to, although often stronger as a security right than the German *Sicherungsübereignung* or *Sicherungszession* as they developed.[39] All were based on case law development and created unpublished or hidden non-possessory proprietary interests in movables, ultimately more in the manner of a security interest than a conditional sale. There was, therefore, an execution sale upon default instead of appropriation of the asset by the creditor and a return of any overvalue to the debtor.

New Dutch law did not continue this development, but introduced instead a statutory non-possessory pledge in chattels and receivables. This change from a conditional sale type of protection to a true security interest was fundamental, although the Government repeatedly attempted to appease opponents by suggesting that no substantial change was meant,[40] which in the end had significant consequences for new case law that readopted some of the old ways.[41] The new pledge does not transfer to replacement goods or proceeds. This is left to *contractual* elaboration. Problems are here the shift in *future assets*. For the charge to attach (at the original rank) these goods must be included and sufficiently identifiable at that time. That has proved more problematic for trade receivables than for replacement goods. Other limitations in this connection are that the new Code does not have a general regime for creating charges in a *generality of assets*, thereby allowing for replacement of individual items with maintenance of the original charge, and has no general regime for the transfer of proprietary interests, including security rights, in *replacement assets*. There is no general concept of *tracing* either. It is thus difficult to create a meaningful *floating charge* and careful draftmanship is necessary to approximate it, see also section 1.2.2 below. Germans practice appears to have been given greater freedom.[42]

The new non-possessory pledge requires a notarial deed or registration with a registration office which is more common. This does not mean publication, and was therefore not introduced to warn subsequent lenders or the public but rather to establish the existence and time of the security right and thereby its rank.[43] As a consequence, this non-possessory charge remains, for all practical purposes, hidden.

Thus registration does not mean publication. For the assignment of receivables (and other claims) by way of security in this manner, registration meant that the substantive requirement of notification to the debtor of each receivable, now necessary for the validity of all other assignments and often equated with publicity, was lifted,[44] but the relationship

---

[39] See HR March 6 1970 (Pluvier) , NJ 433 (1970) and for Germany, see the text at n 131 *infra*.
[40] See Parliamentary History, Introduction Statute Book III, 1197 (Dutch text).
[41] See n 45 *infra*.
[42] See ss. 1.4.2 and 1.4.4 *infra*.
[43] See Article 3.237 CC for tangibles and Article 3.239 CC for intangibles.
[44] See for the notification requirement in the case of assignments Article 3.94(1), which as a constitutive requirement for the assignment is new in Dutch law. The notification requirement was introduced at a time when French law made an exception to this approach in order to facilitate the supply of credit amongst professionals and Belgian law abandoned the requirement altogether: *cf* Article 1690 of their respective Ccs as amended, in France by the so-called *Loi Dailly* of 2 Jan. 1981, reinforced on 24 Jan. 1984: see n 112 *infra*. and now codified in Article L 313–23 to L 313–35 *Code Monétaire et Financier*. This Dutch departure from earlier law, which hinders all bulk transfers and therefore in particular factoring of receivables and their securitisation, has been severely criticised: see HLE Verhagen, 'Het mededelingsvereiste by cessie' [The notification requirement for assignments], in SCJJ Kortmann et al. (eds.), *Onderneming en 5 Jaar Nieuw Burgerlijk Recht* (1997), 163. It must be considered a serious policy mistake. In 2003, statutory proposals to modify the requirement were introduced to accommodate the financial practice. It allows *all* assignment without notification to be valid if registered in the manner of securities transfers of intangible assets.

out of which the debt arises must exist so that (if properly described) the security can attach before the emergence of the debtor but the interest holder cannot get at the debtor before he emerges as for this under new Dutch law notification is necessary. It follows that within a security assignment lists of new debtors must be regularly provided and in respect of the debts the security assignment can only take place as of the transfer of these lists to the asignee.

Naturally the security assignee cannot collect before notification to the debtors is given as a practical matter but since under new law notification is a formal requirement for the validity of assignments, without it, the pledgor remains entitled to retain the proceeds, as confirmed in case law, albeit subject to a preferred claim of the assignee, whilst the account debtor is fully liberated upon payment to him.[45] The registration requirement for receivables immediately caused severe logistical difficulties as it seemed to be a requirement in respect of each assigned receivable and naturally caused special problems for bulk security assignments of future claims. It gave rise to yet another major Supreme Court case to remedy the shortcomings of the new law.[46]

1.2.2   Security Substitutes and Floating Charges: The Reservation of Title

It is not necessary to go into further detail here on the new Dutch law of the non-possessory pledge, except to say that this new type of security is more formal, restricted and circumscribed than its (fiduciary) predecessor was and which had no statutory base. It developed on the basis of case law from 1929[47] and subsequently applied security law

---

[45] See Article 3.246(1) CC for the collection right of the security assignee or pledgee which remained an issue under old law and led to the fiduciary assignment being preferred under old law, now in its generality deemed ineffective: see Article 3.84(3) CC. Under the old system of the fiduciary assignment, the assignee was the party entitled to the proceeds (even if he could not collect for lack of notification so that the assignor would normally do this), as the assignment was valid in all its aspects without notification. In this approach the assignee reclaimed the proceeds, probably as a matter of unjust enrichment from the collecting assignor.

  Under the new law, the Dutch Supreme Court has allowed an assignee/bank still to claim a preference in these collections (through a set-off of its claim against its client in respect of installment payments made to his account with it after his bankruptcy) on the basis that no change had been intended by the new Code, thus conceivably undermining the logic of the new system: see HR, 17 Feb 1995 [1996] *NJ* 471. Although this case confirms at the same time that the charge does not shift to the proceeds so collected (as the lower court had proposed on the basis of an analogous interpretation of Article 3.246(5) CC) and that payment extinguishes the receivable and the security for which it served, there is here nevertheless a form of tracing of the interest. The priority has no statutory base and is of an undetermined rank. It is clear, however, that especially the cost of the bankruptcy administration takes precedence over it.

[46] HR, 14 Oct 1994, [1994] *NJ* 447 in which is was decided that it was sufficient for the document to contain the necessary detail (even retroactively) to determine which claims were included. Officially organised computer lists could be used by referring to the first and last receivable, the total amount, and date and number of the relevant pages. Again reference was made by the Supreme Court to no change from earlier practice being intended by the new Code. Absolutely future claims cannot be included, but as soon as the relationship out of which they arise is known, they may be added: Articles 3.239 and 3.94/97 CC.

  There is a difference here with an outright or conditional transfer of claims which, pursuant to Article 3.84(2), may follow when they are sufficiently identifiable. They are when the debtor is definitely known: see A Hartkamp, *Compendium* (1990), No 104. This allows a full assignment eg of all claims against a certain debtor: see also Goverment Memorandum (MvA, PG Inv W 3, 1248). It would therefore appear that a security assignment is easier to achieve in at least some future claims. Even then for the proceeds to belong to the assignee, notice to an existing debtor is necessary. This notice may be given before hand but is not effective before the debtor becomes known. As a consequence, the difference with an outright assignment is not as important as it may seem at first hand. It became more important after the decision referred to in n 45 *supra*, which gave the assignee a preference in any collection by the assignor under these receivables.

[47] HR, 25 Jan 1929 [1929] *NJ* 616, and 21 June 1929 [1929] *NJ* 1096. Originally the practice was based on the repurchase option as codified in the old Civil Code (Articles 1555*ff*.) following the French *contrat de remère* (Articles 1659*ff* CC): see for the different developments of the Roman law principle of C 4.54.2, which was also

principles by analogy to the extent that that made sense.[48] This type of *fiducia* was explicitly abolished and can no longer be used as a security substitute either (Article 3.84(3) CC). The apparent reason for this was to preserve the closed nature of the Dutch proprietary system on which the fiduciary sale had intruded.[49] But it was no less indicative of a search for greater formality and precision which also emerged in the Dutch weariness of shifting liens and floating charges, or other forms of tracing.[50] Dutch law also continues to require that the assets set aside must be and remain sufficiently identifiable and that the claims secured thereon must themselves have a minimum of specificity (Article 3. 231 CC).

It is, therefore, not possible generally to create security for future loans and in *future* assets, certainly not with a priority from the registration date. As already mentioned in the previous section, *floating charges* are, therefore, not easily created either. Unlike in Germany,[51] purely contractual enhancements and extensions of the non-possessory security right appear limited in their effectiveness as they miss support in more general provisions concerning bulk transfers, asset substitution and tracing. Future replacement goods are therefore difficult to cover. Especially, there is a special bankruptcy law provision (Article 35 (2)) which since 1992 requires that all assets that enter into the ownership of a debtor after his bankruptcy, are part of his bankrupt estate, which affects all transfers, including security transfers, of both absolutely and relatively future assets, regardless of their transfer. It may be different if they are conditionally transfered, see also chapter IV, section 1.5.5. It is certainly a more restrictive approach than that adopted

---

the basis for the further development of the non-possessory security in movables in France and particularly Germany, nn 80 and 122 *infra* and accompanying text. For receivables, the fiduciary transfer was accepted following the decision of the Amsterdam Court of Appeal of 16 Apr 1931, W 12326 (1931), see also HR, 17 June 1960 [1962] *NJ* 60. An important advantage of it was that it gave the assignee the ability to collect which had remained doubtful under a pledge of receivables (a doubt relieved in the new Code which gives the pledgee this right explicitly: see Article 3.246 CC and n 45 *supra*).

[48] This analogy proved increasingly unsatisfactory, however: see HR, 13 Mar 1959 [1959] *NJ* 579, 6 Mar 1970 [1971] *NJ* 433, 7 Mar 1975 [1976] *NJ* 91, 3 Oct 1980 [1981] *NJ* 60, 18 Sept 1987 [1988] *NJ* 876 and 5 Nov 1993 [1994] *NJ* 258.

[49] See Parliamentary History, Introduction Statute Book II, 1197 (Dutch text) and also W Snijders (the draftsman of the present text of Article 3.84(3) CC), Minutes Meeting Vereeniging Handelsrecht on 10 Mar 1989, 73 and (showing some greater flexibility but also an overriding concern for unsecured creditors) on 27 Apr 1990, 65. It does not appear that the limitation of the secured creditor's rights was the primary concern at the time, although there was probably an implicit bias in the new Code to limit the various creditors' preferences.

[50] Although the shifting of proprietary rights to replacement goods is well known in the new Code (see eg Article 5.16 CC), it is not a general principle and does not apply in the case of the non-possessory pledge. According to yet another fundamental case, in the case of a reservation of title it is lost if the asset in which the ownership was reserved loses its own identity and independence: see HR, 27 Nov 1992 [1993] *NJ* 316. Only for commingled property or for property not submerging into another asset upon conversion, are there in the case of reservation of title the special rules of Articles 5.14(2), 5.15 and 5.16 CC allowing joint ownership, but it does not apply to non-possessory security interest holders. According to the Dutch Government Explanatory Memorandum (MvA II, PG3, 744), the non-possessory pledge may shift into replacement goods, as in the case of inventory, if such is expressly agreed, provided the pledgee accepts in the loan conditions that the assets may still be sold by the pledgor in possession free and clear of the charge. The new law itself does not elaborate and the charge, even if so agreed, might still be lost when the asset loses its identity and independence. See for the transfer of future receivables assuming they are identifiable and the different approach in security transfers n 46 *supra in fine*.

Tracing is as such also not part of Dutch law, yet in case law it is not altogether unknown: see n 45 *supra in fine*. See for a case in which a faulty payment to a bankruptcy trustee was recovered on the basis of notions of unjust enrichment of the creditors (assuming that the payment was made after the bankruptcy was opened), HR, 5 Sept 1997, [1998] *NJ*, 437, also HCF Schoordijk *Onverschuldigde betaling aan de faillissementscurator* [Mistaken Payment to the Bankruptcy Trustee], Final Lecture, University of Amsterdam, 1997, *cf* also his, ongegronde verrijking, zaaksvervanging [Tracing, constructive trust, unjust enrichment, conversion], Valedictory Address, Amsterdam, 1991.

[51] See for the more liberal German approach, the text at n 125 *infra*.

under common law in general, and by the UCC in the USA in particular, see also chapter IV, section 1.6.7.

The new Dutch Code also incorporates the *reservation of title*.[52] Here it presumes a conditional sale, although it does not spell out how this presumption is to be rebutted, what the alternatives are, or how the proprietary status of each party must be characterised. It is clear that the parties may opt for another construction and notably exclude or adapt the conditionality, although they will have to ask themselves whether by doing so they are not creating a non-possessory security interest in the process subject to the above mentioned formalities and limitations, short of which the arrangement may have no proprietary and priority effect at all.

The reservation of title, as the new Code perceives it, is not registered like non-possessory pledges or published in any way. It remains therefore a secret proprietary interest, is not considered accessory to a credit agreement (a point confirmed in recent case law, the accessory nature always being an indication that there is a security interest),[53] does not (according to equally recent case law) automatically extend into replacement goods or proceeds either, and cannot be extended to cover other debt than the purchase price.[54] There is no execution sale but rather appropriation of the asset by the seller upon default.[55] As the

---

[52] Article 3.92 CC.

[53] See HR, 18 Jan 1994, [1994] *RvdW* 61 confirming that the *fiducia* was not an accessory right under the old law, which was (*a fortiori*) always assumed for the reservation of title: see Parliamentary History Book 3, 1241 (Dutch text); see for the accessory nature of true security interests the text at n 4 *supra*. The lack of this accessory status for a reservation of title can be disadvantageous for a factor of receivables as assignee of the receivable. In doing so he may be deemed to have paid the seller for or on behalf of the purchaser so that the reservation in any event lapses, Article 3.92 CC: see for the different French approach n 101 *infra*. A subrogation if at all following might not help him much either: see RD Vriesendorp, 'Eigendomsvoorbehoud en overgang van de verzekerde vordering' [Reservation of Title and the Transfer of the Secured Claim], WPNR 6133, 293 (1994); the answer may be in structuring the factoring as a mere collection arrangement: see for factoring also n 69 *infra*.

[54] See n 50 *supra* for the shift to replacement goods and Article 3.92(2) for the impossibility of covering other debt. If the extension into replacement goods is agreed the question arises what kind of interest is created. It cannot be an extended reservation of title which is under statutory law limted to the sold asset. It is not a security interests either which would be subject to its formalities eg in terms of registration. It is likely therefore to be a conditional transfer.

[55] The lack of the accessory nature of the proprietary interest and the appropriation right are distinctive features of conditional sales: see s 1.1.1 *supra*, and distinguish them from security rights, which since late Roman law (C 8.34.3 forbidding the *lex commissoria*, that is the rescission and appropriation upon default), and early common law (strictly insisting on the right of redemption: see the text at n 170 *infra*) require some sale and the return of any excess value to the debtor as his basic protection: see also Article 3.235 of the Dutch CC. This protection is often seen as an important argument to avoid substitute securities (besides the closed nature of the proprietary system and the protection of the common creditors).

Yet the difference between situations in which the *lex commissoria* is allowed (like in the Netherlands notably upon a failed sales agreement, if so agreed: see n 58 *infra*) and true secured transactions was never defined in Roman or medieval law. In fact, Baldus at C 7.72.6 sometimes suggested that the *lex commissoria* was a pledge but also that it was a conditional ownership right (*pactum reservati dominii*). In notarial deeds of those times, both were often negotiated at the same time. Roman law had never considered the position of the reclaiming right in bankruptcy and medieval law had here no clear answer. According to writers like Straccha, in sale price protection schemes, the reclaiming right obtained only as long as the goods were not physically delivered to the buyer. This narrower interpretation became accepted in Germany, France and England, but not in the Netherlands.

The difference between a reservation of title and the *lex commissoria* is not great. The one is an express, the other mostly an implied, condition, although even the *lex commissoria* may also be express. In that case, the difference is probably only in the nature of the condition. The reservation of title is usually seen as a suspensive condition of ownership for the buyer, the *lex commissoria* as a resolutive condition. Even then, the difference is slight: see the discussion in s 1.1.6 *supra*. See for the situation in Germany, n 121 *infra*.

Generally, there was no great clarity in Roman law on the nature of conditions. In classical Roman law, the rescinding condition did not clearly figure, unlike the suspending condition or *condicio*, which was well known. The rescinding condition was, however, sometimes construed as a suspensive condition for the counterparty of which approach there are remnants in D 18.3.1: see also JA Ankum, 'De opschortende voorwaarde naar Romeins recht en volgens het Nederlandse Burgerlijk Wetboek' [The suspensive condition in Roman law and in the Dutch

sale agreement is rescinded as a consequence, it appears that any installments paid have to be returned to the buyer.[56] A similar construction applies to hire purchase.[57]

1.2.3 Conditional and Temporary Ownership: The Lex Commissoria

Dutch law goes much further, however, than merely presuming a conditional sale in the case of a reservation of title and generally recognises conditional and temporary ownership rights where transfers are made conditional (Article 3.84(4) CC). An important example is indeed the reservation of title but also the *lex commissoria expressa*.[58] They render owner-ship right subject to a suspensive or suspending condition (or condition precedent) or a resolutive or rescinding condition (or condition subsequent). This is the causal system of property transfer. Dutch law also seems to understand (in principle) that, in a proprietary

---

Civil Code] in *Historisch Vooruitzicht, BW-krant Jaarboek* (Arnhem, 1994), 19; and R Zimmermann, *The Law of Obligations: Roman Foundation of the Civilian Tradition* (Juta Capetown, 1990/1992), 716. In Justinian law, the rescinding condition was known and thought to have operated retroactively with proprietary or *in rem* effect: see D 6.1.41 and M Kaser, *Römisches Privatrecht* [Roman Private Law] (Beck, Munich, 14th edn, 1986), 198, although contested by Windscheid: see n 127 *infra in fine*.

[56] Rescission of a sales agreement upon default (contrary to annulment or nullity of the transaction: see Articles 3.53 and 6.203) now lacks *in rem* effect under new Dutch law (*lex comissoria tacita*): see Article 6.269 CC, except if specifically so provided by the parties, *cf* Article 3.84(4) CC (*lex commissoria expressa*) which proprietary effect is also implicit in the reservation of title, Article 3.92 CC, although in that case there is a suspensive rather than a resolutive condition in relation to the buyer. Even in the express condition, the rescission is no longer retroactive: Articles 3.38(2) and 6.22 CC. Parties must still put themselves as far as possible in a situation as if the contract had not arisen. This gives in principle rise to personal actions only, eg for reimbursement of instal-ments already paid and the return of the goods, unless the parties intended *in rem* effect when title may still automatically revert, giving revindication rights to the seller, but always subject to the rights of *bona fide* pur-chasers for value who acquired the asset from the buyer in the meantime: Article 3.86 CC. One may, however, deem the buyer to have a retention right in the goods until the instalments are repaid. The buyer could also negotiate a possessory pledge in the sales agreement for the recovery of any sums paid, but reasonable damages of the seller would have to be set-off.
    The idea is that retroactivity should not undermine any disposition and management acts. In this connection, it is sometimes said that conditional ownership is no more than a bet on the future, as such to be distinguished from trusts and usufructs where there is an intent to organise the future.
[57] See Article 7A.1576h CC, although as a consumer financing vehicle it is subject to considerable restrictions and in particular requires the financier to return any overvalue to the debtor in the case of the latter's default: *cf* Article 7A. 1576(t) CC.
[58] The most important example remains the express condition of payment in a sales agreement, therefore the *lex commissoria expressa*, reinforced in Articles 7.39*ff* CC, but Article 3.84(4) is not limited thereto and other express conditions may be inserted into finance sales in order to give them *in rem* or proprietary effect and avoid any doubt and characterisation issues in this connection. It is a consequence of the Dutch causal system of property transfer, see chapter IV, s 1.5.6. Even so Artcile 3.84(4) does not elaborate on the relative rights of both parties to a conditional sale. See for the comparison with the reservation of title, n 55 *supra*. There is also a statutory right to reclaim the unpaid asset for a short period, Article 7.39 BW. It may be seen as a statutory expression of the *lex commissoria expressa* implying a similar conditional ownership structure.
    The conditional ownership notion is not entirely new in Dutch codified law and appeared already in the Code Napoléon as adapted for the Kingdom of Holland which was briefly in force in the Netherlands from 1809 to 1811 (Article 443) and was, through the author of an earlier Dutch codification (Book II, Title 2, Part 1, Article 9 of Draft Van der Linden) probably directly derived from Pothier, *Traité du Droit de Domaine de Propriété, Partie I, Chapitre premier*, not followed in the French Code itself. See for the notion of duality of ownership in the Netherlands in particular HCF Schoordijk, 'De Eigendomsvoorbehoudclausule en het gewijzigde Ontwerp van wet (Boek 3 BW)' [The Reservation of Title and the Amended Proposal of Book 3 Draft new CC], WPNR 5148/9, 457 (1971): see for the history also PL Neve, *Eigendom in Staat van Ontbinding* [Ownership Dissolved], Valedictory Address, University of Nijmegen, 1998, see for further comments NED Faber, 'Levering van toekom-stige goederen en overdracht onder opschortende voorwaarde' [Delivery of future goods and transfer under a suspensive condition], in SCJJ Kortmann et al. (eds.), *Onderneming en 5 jaar Nieuw Burgerlijk Recht* (1997), 179 and WJ Zwalve, 'Temporary and Conditional Ownerships' in GE van Maanen and AJ van der Walt (eds), *Property Law on the Threshold of the 21st Century* (1996), 333.

sense, the one is necessarily the complement of the other. In other words, when the seller has an ownership interest subject to a rescinding condition, the buyer will have an ownership interest subject to a suspending condition in the same asset, so that together they hold the full ownership right.

What is not known, however, is what this duality in ownership truly means; how the owner under the condition subsequent and the owner under the condition precedent, in the same asset, relate to each other and to third parties.[59] Do they both have *in rem* or proprietary rights and are they both able to protect and transfer their respective rights in the asset accordingly? Has the future interest, the reversionary interest or any remainder, as the case may be, proprietary status? Logically it appears to follow as is, in principle, the case in common law,[60] but would this work, particularly in the details in legal systems like the Dutch that in principle require delivery of possession as a precondition for the transfer of ownership rights? Could there be a form of assignment instead?

Here again the new Code is largely silent. Article 3.91 CC requires the transfer of physical possession of the asset, as in the case of a reservation of title, to create suspensive interests, but it does not say how the remaining interest of the one party and the expectancy of the other may subsequently be transferred in view of the Dutch requirement of delivery. It seems logical that for the owner under a resolutive condition without physical possession (therefore the seller in a reservation of title) the transfer of his interest is completed by notice to the holder (like a transfer *longa manu*: see Article 3.115(3) CC) whilst the owner under a suspensive condition with physical possession (the buyer in a reservation of title) transfers this possession.

What is clear is that new Dutch law disapproves of security substitutes and has attempted to draw a line between them and true security interests. It is obvious that it has not been successful because no real criteria are being given.[61] There remain, however, the taste and history of an abhorrence of these substitutes in some quarters.[62] What could these be? They must be the fiduciary transfer but also similar types of conditional sales and ownership forms. Yet in explicitly disallowing the *in rem* effect of the former in Article 3.84(3) whilst accepting it for the latter in Article 3.84(4), the new Code has introduced a potential contradiction of major proportions. What is allowed, and what is not?

---

[59] See for the apparent confusion this has created in the Netherlands, SCJJ Kortmann, 'Eigendom onder voorwaarde' [Conditional Ownership], in *Quod Licet Liber Amicorum Professor WM Kleyn* (Deventer, 1992), 199*ff.*

[60] The tendency in the Netherlands is towards recognition of the proprietary or *in rem* nature of the expectancy, at least in the case of the reservation of title: *cf* for a commentary Asser-Mijnssen-van Velten, *Zakenrecht* [The Law of Property] (12th ed. 1994), nr 428. See for Germany, n 126 *infra* and for common law the text following n 155 *infra*.

[61] Article 3.84(3) CC provides: 'a juridical act which is intended to transfer property for purposes of security or which does not have the purpose of bringing the property into the patrimony of the acquirer, after transfer, does not constitute valid title for transfer of that property': see for this translation PPC Haanappel and E. Mackaay, *New Netherlands Civil Code (Property, Obligations and Special Contracts)* (Deventer, 1990), 49. Transfer into the patrimony of the acquirer has been explained as the property becoming subject to the recovery rights of the acquirer's creditors but the question is when that is the case: see also WH Heyman, 'De reikwijdte van het fiducia verbod' [The extent of the prohibition of the fiducia], WPNR 6119, 6 (1994). What the 'transfer for purposes of security' is has remained equally unclear. W Snijders (the author of the present Article 3.84(3) CC), n 49 *supra*, 81, and 65 (1990) refers to the facility to recover by priority, admits that the resolutive condition of default in a sales agreement is not a security, but otherwise shows concern about the appropriation aspects and the avoidance of the protection of the security laws against it, without giving any criteria, however, for when a transaction must be considered a secured transaction.

[62] It may be traced back to the original designer of the Code, Professor EM Meijers, who saw the *fiducia* in particular as an avoidance of the statutory requirements of security rights even though it had become generally accepted in case law and legal doctrine since 1929: see for references n 47 *supra* and further the Parliamentary History of Book III CC, 317 (Dutch Text).

In the crossfire, some of the most important modern financial products like the finance lease, the repurchase agreement and major types of factoring have been caught and their basis in new Dutch law is uncertain. The draftsmen of the new Code never considered them. Again the Supreme Court had to come to the rescue to address this oversight.[63] It decided that finance leases are transactions not affected by the prohibition of Article 3.84(3) CC, and in any event they are not secured transactions, even the leaseback, and that they have in principle proprietary effect, leaving the lessor with some ownership right. As long as obtaining mere finance or funding is *not* the sole objective of the arrangement, conditional transfers, even in finance, are apparently not outlawed. The link with loan financing was not made in this connection.

Although the Supreme Court concluded that the lessor had a proprietary right, in finding thus it also had to consider the residual proprietary rights of the lessee. It found that the future interest of the lessee was purely *in personam*, therefore obligatory or contractual, even though the latter has physical possession. It suggests that the lessor is the full, and not a conditional, owner. This was unexpected as the reservation of title and hire purchase, which are closely related, were already defined as conditional sales (by way of presumption) as we saw in the previous section.

It seems that this conclusion cannot be correct, which is immediately evident in the event of the bankruptcy of the lessor, when the lease is at risk of being nothing more than an executory contract, subject to repudiation by the lessor's trustee in bankruptcy, except if it were subject to rental protection under Article 7.1612 CC (old) which was written for other situations. Of course, there are already voices that would give the lessee at least the status of a pledgor (and therefore proprietary protection in that manner)[64] but what needs to be studied is the duality of ownership itself and not the pledge analogy, which was tried but never considered fully satisfactory under the old Dutch law of fiduciary ownership.[65]

The pledge analogy would, in any event, suggest that the lessee, not the lessor, was the real owner; exactly the opposite of what the Supreme Court held. It would give rise to the requirement of an execution sale, which the lessor certainly does not intend as it may cause greatly detrimental delays, and major complications in re-leasing the asset and in readjusting its funding. It would also require any overvalue to be paid to the defaulting party, which appears to be totally improper and, in any event, against the idea of a conditional sale as already demonstrated by the reservation of title where modern Dutch law does not require a disposition or execution sale either. As suggested above in section 1.1.1, that would only be justified if there were an entirely different risk and reward structure, as there is in a loan situation. Therefore, only if the finance lease is structured as a loan agreement, or at least as an interest-related instrument, could there be the question of a secured transaction and of the attendant protections in terms of execution sale and a return of any overvalue. This is exceptional, as the Supreme Court rightly accepted, even though without formulating any criteria for secured credit.

---

[63] HR, 19 May 1995 [1996] *NJB* 119.
[64] SCJJ Kortman and JJ van Hees, 'Van fudicia-fobie naar fiducia-filie' [From fiducia-phobia to fiducia-philia], WPNR 6187, 455 (1995), see also JJ van Hees, *Leasing*. Dissertation, 1997, 63*ff*, supporting clearly the duality of ownership concept for Dutch law and starting to develop some rules concerning the right of either party. The consequence in bankruptcy appears to be that in a bankruptcy of the lessor, the lessee may hold on to the asset (200), assuming (supposedly) that there is no executory contract. In a bankruptcy of the lessee, the lessor retrieves the asset (196), but it is argued that any overvalue belongs to the lessee's estate (184). This appears to be counter to the characterisation of the lease as a conditional sale in which the entitlement of the buyer to the overvalue is an essential feature.
[65] See for references n 48 *supra*.

It is unlikely that the new Code's treatment of temporary ownership rights as usufructs (rather than security interests) will prove any less artificial, except perhaps if there is a clearly fixed term, although, as elsewhere,[66] there may often be doubt about the line between a term (of time) and a condition: see section 1.1.6 above. Another approach has been to accept the Supreme Court's recent decision as meaning to qualify the sale/lease-back as a full title transfer to the lessor, subject to the personal user right of the lessee, whilst leaving room for the conditional sale but only if parties so agree specifically pursuant to Article 3.84(4) CC.[67] Although certainly not incompatible with the system of the new Code, it appears only to increase the confusion. One should say that such an agreement is implicit in all finance leases (as indeed in repurchase agreements and factoring arrangements going beyond mere collection) unless the contrary is agreed, as in the case of a clear loan structure.

The key issues in a finance lease are normally:

(a)   the relationship between the contemporaneous owner under the resolutive condition and the owner under the suspensive condition;

(b)   possibly the role of physical possession in that context; the effect on third parties acquiring the respective interests, with or without physical possession; and

(c)   the manner of transfer and protection of their respective present and future interests under the circumstances, as will be discussed more fully below.[68]

Without recognition of a proprietary interest for both parties under the arrangement, there appears to be no proper balance, certainly in the case of a bankruptcy of either. No doubt we shall hear more on these issues from the Dutch Supreme Court, also in connection with repurchase agreements and factoring. The status of these latter two funding techniques has not given rise to much fundamental legal thought in Dutch case law and legal doctrine so far, although their vulnerability under the new Dutch Code is well understood, for securities repos, however, mostly discussed in the context of the alternative and effectiveness of close-out netting.[69]

In line with what the Supreme Court held in connection with finance leasing, there need not be an illegal substitute security in repos and factoring either — at least if there were reasons to enter into repos or factoring other than the mere obtaining of loan financing — but the purchaser under the repo and the factor would become the true owners. Crucially, as in the case of finance leasing, it leaves, as it now stands, the conditionality and effect of the factoring and repurchase agreement in Dutch case law largely unexplained.

1.2.4   Open or Closed System of Proprietary Rights

The discussion concerning the conditional and temporary ownership rights goes to the heart of the proprietary system and the freedom of parties to create additional proprietary

---

[66] See eg for France, n 105 *infra* and accompanying text. See for the qualification of the term as a usufruct in new Dutch law, Article 3.85 CC. It should most certainly not apply to repos.

[67] See JB Vegter, WPNR 6190 and 6191 (1995) 'Het fiduciaverbod bij een financiele sale' [The prohibition of the fiducia and finance sales]. Although the appropriation right is acknowledged, some dispute has arisen whether overvalue must be returned to the defaulting lessee: see, for a strong defence of the appropriation right without the execution analogy requiring a return of the overvalue, AF Salomons, 'Nogmaals sale en leaseback' [Again the Sale and Leaseback], WPNR 6204 (1995). This must be the correct approach short of creating a security interest.

[68] See s 1.7 *infra*.

[69] See, however, for factoring the illuminating discussion by CA Knape, 'Factoring', WPNR 6141 (1994), see more recently also J Beuving, *Factoring*, Diss, 1996 and JH Dalhuisen, *Assignment of Receivables in the World of Modern Finance*, Dutch Report, International Academy of Comparative Law (AIDC), Bristol, 1998. (*Note continues.*)

rights or to split the property rights according to their needs and claim (a measure of) third-party effect for the result. The key issue is the ability to transfer these conditional rights as ownership rights to be respected by all, and, if necessary, to protect them as such against creditors of other interest holders in the same assets (always subject of course to the rights of *bona fide* purchasers of the asset for value in countries such as the Netherlands where they are so protected in the case of chattels).

Dutch law, as a matter of policy, limits this freedom like any other legal system, but by having alone raised this policy to the status of dogma,[70] it seems to lose all flexibility at the theoretical level. It uses an abstract concept to force and control all development rather than seeing the present statutory system as a point of departure, leaving room for new proprietary rights to emerge in practice, whilst accepting these at least to the extent that they evolve out of, or are closely connected to, the present system. This becomes increasingly necessary under the influence of the globalisation and transnationalisation of the modern financial products.[71] It is to be expected that at the practical level Dutch law will eventually accept this need.

Yet factoring if construed as a conditional sale may now offend against the prohibition of the *fiducia* in the new Code: see Article 3.84(3). Until the Supreme Court decides, its true nature is in doubt. The consequence, accepted in present Dutch factoring practices, is that the receivables are transfered as a pledge with notification to the debtor or otherwise as a registered pledge with the problem of collection by the assignee: see also n 45 *supra*. It creates all kinds of other problems like the need for the assignor to continue to carry the receivables on his balance sheet whilst any advance under the facility is likely to be considered a loan. Registration implies extra formalities, time loss and extra costs. The pledge approach also deviates from established European patterns of factoring.

Factoring has not been identified by new Dutch law as a definitive legal structure. Properly to determine its legal nature, it is primarily necessary to distinguish between the contractual and proprietary side. On the contractual side there are three possibilities: there may be administration and collection, a credit risk transfer which mean a guarantee by the factor, and/or a funding structure. If only one of these is present it is probably better not to speak of factoring. It seems to require a cocktail of at least two of these possibilities of which administration and collection is always one. For factoring proper there must also be a proprietary aspect, therefore a transfer of the receivables to the factor. Again here are three possibilities: an outright transfer, a conditional transfer and a security transfer. In view of the many conditions that are often attached to the transfer of the receivables (they may have to be approved, may not be able to exceed in total a certain limit per debtor, may not be contested, may — in recourse financing — not be affected by an insolvency of the debtor), this transfer is therefore usually conditional as to the individual claims. The transfer of those claims that do not prove to comply is then avoided and these claims are automatically returned to the assignor and belong to his estate in the case of a bankruptcy of the factor, although Beuving, at 73, requires an act of retransfer unless there is a clear condition under Article 3.84(4) CC. The most common form of factoring (the old line factoring) has all three contractual features and a conditional sale of the receivables depending on approvals and credit lines.

As for investment securities repos, their status in Dutch law remains equally in doubt and was also not covered by the new Code. They have become more important because they are used by the ECB as a means to provide liquidity to banks. See for a rare Dutch legal discussion, WAK Rank, 'Repo's en Repowet' [Repos and Repo-statute] in SCJJ Kortmann et al (eds), *Onderneming en Recht Part 13* (1998), 371. This author continues to qualify the repo (economically) as secured lending and considers the repo rate a form of interest. This is at the heart of the confusion and raises indeed the spectre of a prohibition under Article 3.84(3) CC. See also JH Dalhuisen, 'Conditional Sales and Modern Financial Products' in A Hartkamp et al (eds), *Towards a European Civil Code* (2nd edn, 1998), 525.

In the Netherlands a statutory amendment was proposed in 1998 to clarify the position of the securities repo under Article 3.84(3) CC, not as an exception or presumption, however, but rather as a question of mandatory interpretation, see Article 2 a of the Law concerning the Supervision of Transactions in Investment Securities (*Wet Toezicht effectenverkeer*). It seems therefore also to cover the situation when there is true loan financing and secured lending. The danger of repos being characterised as usufructs under Article 3.85 CC was not considered but must now be considered removed.

---

[70] Article 3.81 CC; see also the text at n 49 *supra*. See for arguments in favour of a much more open system, JH Dalhuisen, 'European Private Law: Moving from a Closed to an Open System of Proprietary Rights', 5 *Edinburgh LR*, 1 (Sept. 2001). See for proposals for a more fundamental modernisation of Dutch property law (concerning chattels and intangible assets), JH Dalhuisen, *Zekerheid in roerende zaken en rechten* [Security in Chattels and Intangible Assets], *Preadvies Vereeninging' Handelsrecht* (2003).

[71] See further JH Dalhuisen, *Wat is vreemd recht?* [What is foreign law], Inaugural Address, Utrecht (Deventer, 1992), 20.

This need to accept uncommon proprietary interests is, in fact, already well understood in the Netherlands. The recognition of foreign secured and other limited proprietary interests as acquired rights in goods that are moved to the Netherlands after these rights were perfected is unavoidable, as is the requirement to adapt and introduce them into the domestic system (regardless of the fact that Dutch formalities are unlikely to have been fulfilled for their creation and that they may in fact operate as a type of substitute security forbidden under Dutch law).[72] The ratification of the 1985 Hague Convention on the Law Applicable to Trusts and their Recognition, allowing recognition of foreign trusts even over domestic assets, will open up the domestic closed system of proprietary rights even further.[73]

It is clear that the acceptance in principle of future, conditional or contingent interests in new Dutch law will also do so (Article 3.84(4) CC). They may even approach the trust construction in splitting the economic from the legal interest for a particular time span or until certain conditions are fulfilled whilst giving these interests proprietary status. This is a development which, when properly identified and understood, may prove greatly beneficial to the approximation of common and civil law and may meet a considerable practical need in civil law countries, a situation even now increasingly accepted in the German *fiduziarische Treuhand*[74] and also considered for introduction in France, although it has been held up there for reconsideration because the tax implications have not as yet been fully evaluated:[75] see more in particular chapter IV, section 1.4.5.

Another factor in the opening up of the domestic closed system may be the appearance of notions of good faith and reasonableness in proprietary matters which may increasingly allow or amend revindication rights, require and impose the separation of pools of assets for the benefit of special classes of creditors or for other interested parties being given proprietary protection in this manner, create new security interests and especially preferences or statutory liens in cases where this is just and decide on ranking. In fact, in the Netherlands, Article 3.13(2) CC on the abuse of rights may already provide a statutory basis for the return of assets on the basis of reasonableness, for example, by a trustee in bankruptcy who acquired goods from a third party by mistake after the commencement of the proceedings.[76]

The preference by recent case law granted to the registered security assignee against the collecting assignor may in truth be another example of proprietary adjustments on the

---

[72] See also JH Dalhuisen, 'International Aspects of Secured Transactions and Finance Sales Involving Movable and Intangible Property' in Kokkini et al, *Eenvormig en Vergelijkend Privaatrecht* (Molengrafica 1994), 405, 423. For an interesting case in which a German expectancy (*Anwartschaft*) for the acquisition of real estate in the former East Germany resulting from the registration of the sales agreement was thought capable of being the subject of an attachment under its Dutch owner in the Netherlands: see Court of Appeal Amsterdam, 9 July 1991 [1994] NJ 79, [1992] NIPR 418. Note that under German law other types of expectancies, notably those resulting from conditional transfers, are not accepted for real property: see Section 925(2) BGB.

[73] From the Comments to the Introductory Statute, it is clear that the government intends to leave the fitting-in process to the judiciary, whilst limiting on purpose the possible public policy corrections to the recognition (Article 4): see also chapter IV, s 1.4.6, n 69 and s 1.8.3.

[74] Swiss law has similar facilities but does not allow the *fiducia* to create non-possessory securities in movables: see Artcile 717 ZGB, without the dividing line between securities and conditional sales being defined either. Article 717(2) seems to leave to the judge considerable discretion in this connection. The *Sicherungsübereigung* as non-possessory security became accepted in Switzerland *praeter legem*. It is strictly speaking considered in violation of Article 717, however: see D Zolb, *Berner Kommentar zum schweizerischen Privatrecht, Band IV, 2 Abteilung, 5 Teilband, Die beschränkten dinglichen Rechte; Das Fahrnispfand, 1 Unterteilband, Systematischer Teil und Art 884–887 ZGB* (2nd edn, 1982) N 568*ff*, 719*ff*.

[75] Projet Loi No 2583 of 20 Feb 1992 proposing a new Article 2062 CC: see also the text following n 110 *infra*.

[76] See n 50 *supra in fine*.

basis of reasonableness. The developments in this direction are necessarily timid but significant, and may follow the German example, as will be discussed below.[77] Increasingly, it may be expected that forms of tracing or constructive trust will also be accepted in Dutch law because it is often only fair that they should exist in order to prevent an unjust enrichment of a bankrupt's estate. Greater awareness and impact of foreign practices may introduce here an element of international convergence.

1.3 The Situation in France

1.3.1 *Introduction: The* Vente à Remère *and* Lex Commissoria

Generally in France, the situation is hardly clearer than elsewhere, with respect to the status of conditional sales and ownership rights, their use in financing and their relationship to secured transactions. There is a very fractured system of non-possessory security rights in certain movables which are called *nantissements*. They are based on a measure of publicity but with very different publication requirements depending on the nature of the asset.[78]

For the purposes of this book, the question is mainly how this system relates to conditional sales. In France, there is a repurchase agreement covered in the Code in the so-called

---

[77] See n 45 and the text at n 146 *infra*.

[78] The first non-possessory charge in chattels was the maritime lien created in 1874. The situation in France as regards non-possessory charges in movable property may briefly be summarised as follows. Goodwill may be pledged through the *nantissement de fonds de commerce* since a Law of 1 Mar 1898 replaced in 1909 and later amended: *cf* also Article 2075 Cc. Motion picture films may be mortgaged through a *nantissement des films cinématographiques* since a Law of 22 Feb 1944. They require registration in a special register.

Since a Law of 18 Jan 1951, there is a *nantissement d'outillage et matériel d'équipement* (machinery and accessories) registered in the local commercial courts but available only to the seller or lender of money for the purchase of the materials (as purchase money security) and not generally for other debt, present or future. If a notice plaque is put on the equipment, the secured creditor may pursue his interest if the goods are sold to third parties (removal of the plate is a criminal offence). The security prevails over any earlier mortgage in immovables to which the secured assets become affixed. Since the Law of 29 Dec 1934, there has been a further *nantissement* in favour of sellers of motor vehicles in the *gage du vendeur de véhicules automobiles*.

There was a further attempt to fill the gap traditionally left in France in the field of non-possessory security in movables by the pledging of *warrants* symbolising certain movable goods like the pledging of warehouse receipts (*magasin général*). This traditional warrant technique known since Decrees of 22 and 23 Mar 1848, several times amended, was consequently extended by statute to cover other situations: the *warrant agricole* of 18 July 1898, later amended for farmers' crops and equipment. The sold goods may be replaced by others under the security but for security purposes the equipment must remain in the farmer's possession. If the farm is leased, the owner who has a security for rent may oppose the warrant and must in any event be notified. The warrant is registered in the local courts. In the case of a fixture attached to mortgaged real estate, the dates of the respective registrations will determine the relative priorities. Material, equipment and furniture of hotels may also be incorporated in warrants and given as security under a Law of 8 Aug 1913, later amended, assuming the *fonds de commerce* has not already been pledged. Warrants are also possible for petroleum stocks under a law of 21 Apr 1932.

Of these non-possessory security interests, the charge on the ongoing business (*nantissement de fonds de commerce*) is conceptually the most important and may cover real property leases, industrial property rights, and the equipment of a business. But inventory and accounts are excluded and there is also no possibility of creating a floating charge in them because of the lack of certainty and identification which impedes a security transfer in them. See, for the situation regarding the pledging of receivables after the *Loi Dailly* of 1981, n 108 *infra*. See for the assignability of future receivables also chapter IV, s 1.7.4.

See, for a more recent discussion of the *gage automobile* following a decision of the Court of Appeal, Versailles, of 20 Sept 1995, G Wicker and P Gaubil, 'L'efficacité du gage automobile non inscrit' [1997] *Receuil Dalloz Chroniques* A–1.

In the case of non-possessory security interests in chattels, a form of registration is usually provided, but *bona fide* purchasers remain protected unless the interest was marked on the asset. It should be noted that in France the priority status of the security interests so created may be seriously restructured in a bankruptcy of the debtor granting the interests. All secured interests may be subject to some super priorities (*privilèges*) concerning wages of employees and the cost of the bankruptcy.

'*vente a remère*'.[79] It has a long history, was copied from the *corpus iuris*[80] and is cast in terms of an option for the seller to repurchase the asset (for a period of five years maximum). Has it effect *in rem*, that is to say, can it be maintained and enforced against a counter-party even in the latter's bankruptcy? Ghestin and Desche in their well known book on French contract law dwell on this point at some length.[81] They think probably not, although they also cite important authority to the contrary which views the situation as one of conditional ownership of the buyer which may be rescinded and under which the erstwhile seller has at least a conditional or suspended right which he may alienate, give as security or in usufruct.[82]

Even Ghestin and Desche construe this repurchase option, as a '*condition résolutoire*' of the sale which, in France, at least in the case of default of a sales agreement, traditionally had proprietary or *in rem* effect (*lex commissoria tacita*) and led to an automatic return of title without further steps being taken. This is now considered exceptional in bankruptcy, however, the general rule being that conditions can no longer mature upon the opening of bankruptcy proceedings. If the goods are already with the buyer, they can only be deemed returned to the seller if the latter has started reclaiming proceedings before bankruptcy.[83]

1.3.2   The Impact of the Notion of the 'Solvabilité Apparente'

The true impediment in France to a return of the asset upon the rescission of the sale agreement after the bankruptcy of a non-paying buyer in France or under a repurchase facility is that, if the debtor is in possession, other creditors of the buyer may have relied on the outward signs of his creditworthiness ('*solvabilité apparente*') (Article 2279 Cc). French law protects them, especially if these signs are created by a seller having delivered goods to the buyer and having left him in possession, no matter his reversionary interest or any rescission of a sale with a revindication right upon default.[84] The other creditors may thus ignore the reversion rights of the seller.

Strictly speaking, it does not rule out the proprietary effect of a condition but limits its effect in bankruptcy, and provides an important check on the proliferation of secret security or revindication rights in France. It was similar to the English notion of reputed

---

[79] Articles 1659*ff* Cc. It was copied in the Netherlands in the former CC (Article 1555*ff*) but not retained in the new Dutch Civil Code: see n 47 *supra* and for Germany n 122 *infra*.

[80] C.4.54.2 (*pactum de retroemendo*). It is formulated as a rescinding condition in Justinian law: see for this condition and its proprietary effect in Roman law also n 55 *supra*. If C 4.54.2 is not accorded proprietary effect, however, see s 1.3.2 *infra*, this is probably because there was only an option for the seller, no duty and therefore no automatic retransfer. In any event, Roman law never dealt with the effects of a bankruptcy.

[81] *Traité des Contrats, La Vente* (1990), 635.

[82] P Malaurie, *Encycl Dalloz*, Droit civil V, Vente (elem const), no 776.

[83] Article 117 French BA 1985: see also Ripert-Roblot, 2 *Droit Commercial* (16th edn, 2000), no 3158. A distinction is now made (since the new Bankruptcy Act of 1985) between a situation in which the sale was already rescinded before the bankruptcy and in which rescission was petitioned or intended but not yet granted. In that case, a revindication is still possible, but only if the rescission was for reasons other than default of payment of the purchase price. This is because of Article 47 of the French Bankruptcy Act which after bankruptcy generally suspends all actions for the rescission of contracts based on lack of payment of a sum of money. See in France for the *lex commissoria tacita*, Articles 1184, 1610 and 1654 Cc and for the *lex commissoria expressa* Article 1656 Cc.

[84] In France, this principle has been operative in the indicated manner since Cour de Cassation, 24 June 1845, D 1.309 (1845); see in Belgium for a similar attitude, Cour de Cass (Belge), 9 Feb 1933 [1933] I Pas, 103, as recent as Cour de Cass 22 Sept 1994 [1994–95] RW 1264 (note Dirix). The amendments to the French BA since 1980: see n 96 *infra*, make here a full exception for the reservation of title, *cf* also Artcile 101 of the new Belgian Bankruptcy Act of 8 Aug 1997. French law allows the transfer of future assets, also for security purposes: see Article 1130 Cc, but is restrictive as regards future claims and requires that at the moment of the assignments all conditions for their emergence are fulfilled. This is established case law since 1854: see Cour de Cass, 31 Jan 1854, D 2.179 (1855).

ownership, another example of protection of *bona fide* creditors. In England it was, however, applicable only in the personal bankruptcy of a debtor who engaged in commerce under his own name and it was not maintained in the Insolvency Acts of 1985 and 1986.[85]

Whatever its true nature, according to case law, the French repurchase option leads to a return of the asset without any further formality upon the option being exercised and there is no need for an act of retransfer.[86] This suggests itself some *in rem* effect and its effectiveness in a bankruptcy of the buyer, barring the effects of the '*solvabilité apparente*'. The option is traditionally clearly distinguished from a security right, except where a security is suggested by the facts surrounding the option. This is considered the case only when the original sales price was much lower than the reasonable value of the assets whilst they remained in the possession of the seller who paid an artificial rent similar to the prevailing interest rate. If this type of transaction is frequent between the same parties, its character as a *scam* secured transaction may be further enhanced with the consequence of nullity.[87]

The distinctive criteria between a security interest and repurchase option are thus not always sharp under French law, and it is clear that the repurchase option must sometimes be seen as a security interest with *in rem* effect (giving the buyer a non-possessory interest in the asset which must be released upon repayment of the purchase price or otherwise executed). Whether the conversion into a security is desirable or not, it at least suggests that there may be little fundamental objection to accepting (some) *in rem* effect in a situation where the option operates in the nature of a true condition. It is further generally accepted that the option itself may also be sold and transferred to third parties except where prohibited under the original sales agreement.

Thus there are many facets to this option under the '*vente à remère*'. French law, as well as the authors, remain unclear or divided about whether the result is a mere personal right of the seller to retake the asset upon the exercise of the option, as indeed suggested by the original passage in the Justininan Codex, which did not, however, deal with the effect in bankruptcy, or whether there may be some third party effect and a stronger position for the seller in the bankruptcy of the counterparty, as appears to be suggested by the qualification of the option as a '*condition résolutoire*' under French law and by the instant return of the title upon the option being exercised, that is without any act of retransfer or other formality.[88]

1.3.3   The Modern Repurchase Agreement or 'Pension Livrée'

In the modern French repurchase agreement or repo of investment securities, the return of the assets (mostly fungible investment securities) is indeed automatic upon the mere

---

[85] See Section 283 Insolvency Act 1986. See for the concept also *Ryall v Rolle*, 1 Atk 165 (1749) and *Re Sharpe* [1980] 1 All ER 198. It dates back to 1603 and was last repeated in Section 38(c) of the Bankruptcy Act of 1914. It did not apply to corporate bankruptcy which was covered by the winding up provisions of the Companies Act and it was never accepted in the USA, but hidden proprietary interests are sometimes still vulnerable in the USA especially in the context of the creation of security interests under Article 9 UCC: see also n 164 *infra*. The concept is now also under pressure, however, in France, especially in connection with the modern reservation of title: see n 98 *infra*.

[86] Cour de Cass, 24 Oct 1950 [1950] Bull civil 1, 155.

[87] Cour de Cass, 21 Mar 1938, D 2.57 (1938), earlier 11 Mar 1879, D 1.401 (1879).

[88] The concept of conditional ownership has itself long been known in French law: see Pothier, (1699–1772), *Traité du droit de domaine de propriété*, Part. I, *Chapitre premier*, although not elaborating on the concept. It did not, however, find its way into the *Code civil*, but it was always known in French legal writing: see, eg C Demolombe, *Cours de Code Napoleon, Tôme IX*, (1854), 489. Planiol and Ripert, *Traité pratique de droit civil français, Tôme III. Les biens* (1926), No 231–32 recognised for the first time the duality in conditional ownership

repayment of the advance, but it implies a right as well as a duty of the seller to repurchase. In France, this is called the '*pension livrée*' and was reinforced by statute at the end of 1993 for repos in the professional sphere.[89] It is now covered by Articles L 432-12 to L432-19 *Code Monetaire et Financier* (CMF). Neither its legal nature and the aspect of its conditionality, nor the consequences of a bankruptcy of the financier/buyer, are, however, clearly discussed in terms of proprietary or personal rights.

The new Law specified that the transaction is one of sale or assignment and that the financier/buyer may keep the investment securities (provided they have been delivered to him) if the original seller does not repay the price (and the original seller may keep the sales price if the financier/buyer does not return the investment securities).

The more interesting question is, however, whether in the case of the financier/buyer's bankruptcy, the seller of the investment securities may revindicate the assets by merely tendering payment of the repurchase price on the appointed date, a point which is especially relevant if the investment securities have increased in value. That would be a true indication of the conditionality of the sale and of any *in rem* effect. Other aspects to consider here are the impact of the fungible nature of most of the securities used in the repurchase transaction and of these securities often being held by third parties/ depositories. The first circumstance could weaken the seller's position, but the latter could strengthen it, as the assets, although fungible and only returnable as the same number of the same sort, may be sufficiently identifiable and separate.

The new Law in Article L 432-15 CMF still talks of a *retrocession*, which may suggest that there is no automaticity in the retransfer of title upon payment of the repurchase price but that an act of retransfer is necessary, which is somewhat unlikely in view of the practice under the *vente à remère*. Yet in a bankruptcy of the buyer/financier the complication with the French Bankruptcy Act (in that it does not generally allow conditions to mature after bankruptcy) would still have to be taken into account, whilst it could be questioned whether the exception for defaulted sales would apply in this type of financial transaction, especially since the buyer is in possession.[90] Also the residual effect of the theory of 'the appearance of creditworthiness' would have to be considered.

The new Law does not go into any of these aspects and the question of an *in rem* right of the original seller against the buyer does not seem to have arisen in the mind of the legislator. Yet this cannot be the end of the story, as the system of the Law of 1993 would give both seller and buyer an option to default without impunity if the price of

---

and the complementary nature of the ownership under a resolving and suspending condition: see more recently also H and L Mazeaud and F Chabas, *Leçons de droit civil, Tôme II*, 2nd Vol, *Biens: Droit de propriété et ses démembrements* (7th edn, 1989), 156.

[89] Articles 12*ff* of Law 93–1444 of 31, Dec 1995: see also S Moury and S Nalbantian, 'Repurchase Transaction in the Cross-border Arena' [1995] *International Finance Law Review* 15. Relevant is also Article 47*ter* of Law 83–1 of 3 Jan 1983 (originally introduced as Article 47*bis* to this Law amended through Law 92–868 of 10 July 1992) covering default by either party and allowing them in a cash against documents (CAD) sale of investment securities not to perform if the other party did not do so. This would apply to each individual leg of a repurchase agreement but would not cover the re-transfer obligation resulting from the prior sale.

More incidental provisions may also be found in Article 31(c) of Law 87–416 of 17 June 1987 relating to securities lending and Article 52 of Law 96–597 of 2 July 1996 relating to derivative transactions. They explicitly accept the finance sale for investment securities located in France provided the transaction is governed by a local, national or international framework agreement and one of the parties is in the business of rendering investment services. In stock lending transactions the transferee obtains (full) title to the (conditionally) transferred assets only in the event of default of the transferor. What the proprietary situation is in the meantime is unclear.

[90] As mentioned in n 83 *supra*, Article 117 of the French BA 1985 offers for rescinded sales agreements upon default an exception to this general principle of French bankruptcy law (Article 47) but only if the goods are not yet in the possession of the buyer or if the recovery action is initiated before bankruptcy.

the investment securities had respectively dropped or risen, so that there would be a premium on default.

Personal rights to damages obviously supplement this system, also to restrain so-called 'cherry-picking', a facility of the trustee of a bankrupt buyer who commonly has the option to repudiate contracts if merely executory and not resulting in proprietary rights. Yet personal actions for damages are unlikely to be of great benefit against a bankrupt financier and his trustee. As in the case of finance leases, discussed previously with reference to the Netherlands,[91] it appears that a proper balance between the two parties can only be established by accepting an *in rem* repossession right of the seller, at least if the investment securities were not fungible or if they were held by independent depositories who would hold others of the same sort in substitution.

Because of the uncertainty concerning this repossession right in a bankruptcy of the buyer and the proprietary status of the repo, the more common solution at present in France (as elsewhere) is to provide an extended set-off or netting right in standard repurchase agreements,[92] reducing the retransfer obligation to money on the basis of market rates, whilst including in the set-off all other repurchase transactions outstanding between the parties, and considering them matured so as to arrive at one total net amount either owed by or to the bankrupt.

No less than the *in rem* status of the conditional sale in bankruptcy, this netting facility remains in France uncertain in its effect, however, as it creates an expanded indirect preference. No special bankruptcy provisions exist as yet in France supporting this netting (as introduced specifically in the US Bankruptcy Code in 1990 and in the German Insolvency Act of 1994, effective 1999) as will be discussed more extensively below.[93] In any event, if there are not enough counterbalancing transactions between the parties, the netting is to little avail.

1.3.4   The Reservation of Title

The nature of the reservation of title in France may provide further clarification of the possible qualification of repurchase agreements (or finance sales) as conditional sales and should therefore also be considered. It was always valid in principle in France, which logically follows from the mere facility to postpone the transfer of title if the parties so agree until the moment of payment.[94] Whether or not the reservation of title could benefit from the exception to the rule that conditions could not mature after bankruptcy, it was still faced with the doctrine of the appearance of creditworthiness of the buyer. Therefore it was not considered effective in a French bankruptcy[95] until the amendment of the French Bankruptcy Act of 1967 in 1980, later reinforced in the French Bankruptcy Act of 1985.[96]

---

[91] See the text following n 63 *supra*.

[92] In France, the relevant master agreement is the one prepared by the French Banking Association (AFB) since 1987 and referred to as the *Conditions Générales pour les Opérations d'Echange de Devises ou de Conditions d'Intérêts* providing, for contractual close-out netting: see also EJ Nalbantian, 'France Sorts Out Netting Uncertainty' [1994] *International Financial Law Review* 34.

[93] See text at nn 141 and 225 *infra*.

[94] See Article 1584 Cc.

[95] See Cour de Cass, 21 July 1897, DP 1.269 (1898) and 28 Mar/22 Oct 1934, D 1.151 (1934).

[96] See Articles 59 and 65 of the French BA 1967 as amended in 1980, superseded by Articles 115 and 121 of the French BA 1985: see also Ripert-Roblot, n 83 *supra*, 3155, 3159*ff*. The reservation of title was further reinforced by the 1994 amendments to the French BA (Article 59 of Law 94–475 of 10 June). It means to preserve the right

In France, on the basis of this statutory law, the reservation of title is now mostly considered a conditional sale,[97] fully accepted in a bankruptcy of the buyer and leading to appropriation by the seller regardless of the maturing of the condition after bankruptcy and the notion of reputed ownership with its protection of the appearance of creditworthiness.[98] The Cour de Cassation sees it, however, as an accessory right to the debt.[99] As we already saw in section 1.1.1, this points in the direction of a security interest which is somewhat incongruous and certainly not the view elsewhere in Western Europe.[100] This accessory nature of the reservation of title is of special importance in factoring when payment of the seller by the factor would normally extinguish the reservation of title and vest full title in the buyer.[101]

It seems that the security analogy is increasingly pursued for the reservation of title in France, although it is clear that there is no execution sale whilst full title automatically reverts to the seller upon default, the sale agreement having lapsed. This remains indicative of a conditional sale resulting in *in rem* effect of the condition, now also supported in a bankruptcy of the buyer.

Yet so far, in France, there seems to be no clear opinion in favour of this conditionality leading to a split ownership right between seller and buyer as present and future owners.[102] Rather, in a reservation of title, the condition is mostly seen either as rescinding or suspending, and not as creating complementary forms of ownership for the seller and the buyer at the same time. Instead, there is much inconclusive thought focusing mainly on the retroactivity of the title transfer to the seller, or of any retransfer to the buyer and the liability for the risk of the loss of the asset.[103] As mentioned

in converted or commingled property. French law also accepts the shift into proceeds (real subrogation), Cour de Cass, 8 Mar 1988, *Bull IV,* nr 99 (1988), 20 June 1989, *D Jur* 431 (1989) and 15 Dec 1992, *Bull IV* nr 412 (1992).

[97] This still allows for several different qualifications. Is the contract conditional or rather the transfer of the title itself, and in either approach is the contract or title transfer suspended or subject to later rescission: see also Ghestin and Desche, n 81 *supra,* nn 588*ff.* It is equally possible to see the reservation of title as achieving no more than a delayed transfer: see n 103 *infra* and accompanying text, which appears also to be the prevailing view in England: see the text at n 191 *infra,* and might be typical for countries in which title transfers upon the mere conclusion of a sale agreement, therefore without the additional requirement of delivery.

[98] Earlier, the Cour de Cassation had consistently held that the reservation was valid but lacked effectiveness in bankruptcy for the reasons stated in a line of cases started on 21 July 1897, DP.1.269 (1898).

[99] Cour de Cassation, 15 Mar 1988, Bull Civ IV, 106 (1988).

[100] See for the Netherlands n 53 *supra,* for Germany n 120 *infra* and for England the text at n 195 *infra.* In the meantime, the French Cour de Cass now also holds that overvalue must be returned to the buyer upon his default, Cour de Cass, 5 Mar 1996, Bull IV, nr 72 (1996), without, however, the need for an execution sale.

[101] The effect in France is that a factor having paid the seller retains the benefit of the reservation of title at the same time, which is unlikely in systems like the Dutch that do not accept the ancillarity and must therefore structure their factoring schemes in which reservations of title play an important role more in the manner of collection arrangements: see n 53 *supra.*

[102] See, however, also the approach to conditionality more generally of the writers cited in n 88 *supra.*

[103] See for an overview, Ghestin and Desche, n 81 *supra,* nn 588*ff.* See for the risk of the loss of the asset pending full payment, Cour de Cassation, 20 Nov 1979, (1980) 33 Rev Trim de Droit Commercial, 43, Note D von Breitenstein, in which case the Cour de Cassation ultimately appeared to opt for a delayed title transfer approach (like the amendments of 1980). The view is that there is no transfer of title pending payment, nor a retransfer if payment does not follow. The contract itself is rescinded upon default so that nothing subsists except that physical possession remains to be reclaimed by the seller, if necessary through a proprietary action. This approach strengthened the seller's position as owner in an intervening bankruptcy of the buyer before 1980. A further consequence of this approach was that the seller pending payment remained liable as owner for the risk of loss of the asset. Earlier case law had considered the reservation of title a suspensive condition of the contract rather than of the title transfer: see the original case of the Cour de Cass, 21 July 1897, DP 1.272 (1898), withholding effectiveness to both the contract and the title transfer until payment, which was strange in view of the implementation of the sale agreement. If, on the other hand, upon default the transfer had been considered rescinded, either alone or together with the sales agreement, there would have been a title transfer to the buyer and a retransfer would have

above,[104] the reservation of title is sometimes also seen as no more than effectting a delayed transfer avoiding the problem of retroactivity, but it is agreed that parties may be able to define it in their contract as a conditional sale.[105]

1.3.5 Finance Sales: Transfer of Receivables, Loi Dailly *and* Tritisation (Fonds Communs de Créances)

In France, it seems that in modern writings there is no great inclination to see the conditionality of ownership as a wider concept. This is borne out by the discussion of repurchase agreements, the '*pension livrée*' legislation and the reservation of title. The subject is not much raised in the context of the finance lease either, whatever the legal qualification of the reservation of title, which is the closest related structure.[106]

Yet the conditional sale structure may be used to create a transfer of ownership in the nature of a fiduciary transfer[107] in the former Dutch sense or *Sicherungsübereignung* in the German sense, subject therefore to its lapse in the case of repayment of the sales price. It is uncommon, however, because of the same impediments which affected the reservation of title in bankruptcy before 1980 (and which may also affect the repurchase agreement) in terms of the impossibility (normally) for conditions to mature after the opening of the proceedings and of the reputed ownership theory. Moreover, the Cour de Cassation has insisted that appropriation in bankruptcy is unlawful under this type of transfer,[108] much as in Germany and earlier in the Netherlands, but this has *not* led to a transformation of

---

become necessary which, even though automatic, would have weakened the position of the seller in a bankruptcy of the buyer before 1980. The buyer would in that case have carried the risk of loss unless otherwise agreed.

[104] See n 97 *supra*.

[105] See Malaurie, n 82 *supra*, nn 766*ff* and Ghestin and Desche, *supra* n 81, no 600. Following Article 1179(1) Cc, in France it is thought that only where the transfer of title is conditional, and not merely delayed, is it retroactive to the moment of the sale unless the parties agree otherwise: see for this possibility Cour de Cass, 21 July 1958 [1958] II JCP 10843. In the approach of a delayed title transfer, the buyer may have no proprietary rights whatever: see for this conclusion Ghestin and Desche, *supra* n 81, no 603. On the other hand, in view of the 1958 precedent, it appears possible for the parties to declare the reservation of title to be a conditional sale rather than a delayed transfer, implying the retroactivity and probably also certain proprietary protections for the buyer at the same time.

[106] See, however, for a more modern reconsideration of title transfers for funding purposes, Cabrillac and Mouly, *Les suretés* (1997), no 527*ff*.

In France, the finance lease was regulated by Law 66-455 of 2 July 1966 on the *credit-bail*, now in Articles L313-7 to L313-11 CMF, which is inconclusive in the proprietary aspects. Some see leasing as a financing method without defining it further in terms of secured transaction or conditional sale whilst emphasising the *sui generis* nature of the arrangement instead: see P Cordier, Note under Cour de Cass, 9 Jan. 1990, [1990] Gaz. Pal. 127. Others seem to accept a security interest: G Marty, P Raynaud and P Jestaz, *Les Sûretés, La Publicité Foncière* (Sirey, Paris, 2nd edn, 1987), 335. There are also those who see a mere rental agreement: El Mokhtar Bey, Note [1987] JCP 20865, although later underlining the hybrid character of the lease in terms of sale, rental and option, see 'Des conséquences de la jurisprudence de la chambre mixte de la cour de cassation du 25 novembre 1990 sur la symbiotique du crédit-bail' [1992] *Gaz Pal*, 568; see also D Kokkini-Iatridu, 'Enkele Juridische Aspecten van de Financiele Leasing (Credit-Bail) in Frankrijk' [Some Legal Aspects of Finance Leasing (Credit-Bail) in France] in Kokkini-Iatridu et al, *Eenvormig en Vergelijkend Privaatrecht* (Molengrafica, 1994), 55, 77.

[107] The facility follows from Article 1584 CC. Recent Belgian case law, in the meantime, has rejected the fiduciary transfer, that is all transfers of ownership meant to produce a security interest: see Cour de Cass (Belge), 17 Oct 1996 [1995–96] RW 1395 (Note ME Storme). Reservation of title is believed not affected because the security of the return of title upon default is deemed inherent in any sales transaction. A similar attitude may be taken towards Belgian finance leasing which resembles in many regards the reservation of title: Cour de Cass (Belge), 27 Nov 1981 [1981–82] RW 2141. See for remedial legislation but only for clearing systems, including the operations in Euroclear, chapter IV, n 301.

[108] French law in Article 2078 Cc specifically rules out any arrangement to the contrary and the fiduciary sale has been so caught: Cour de Cass, 24 May 1933 [1934] *Rev Cr de Dr Intern'l Pr*, 142. It is also weary of scam transactions see text at n 87 *supra*. French law is also weary of scams in this connection, see text at n 87 *supra*.

this kind of sale into a general non-possessory security interest. It was not much of an issue in connection with the *'vente à remère'*,[109] and (as yet) the reservation of title, as we saw. The explicit introduction of the *fiducia* in the French Cc, as is still being considered,[110] would most probably reinforce the difference with secured transactions.

In the meantime, in the reservation of title, the focus is now on the suspension of the buyer's title pending his payment, giving the seller the stronger position in a bankruptcy of the buyer but also the risk of damage to or of loss of the asset. In the case of other conditional transfers, like the *fiducia*, the emphasis may be on the rescission of the buyer's title upon compliance with the terms of the agreement including the repayment of the price, giving the latter the stronger position in the case of a bankruptcy of the erstwhile seller, but also the risk of loss of the asset. Again, the prospective (possibly *in rem*) rights of the other party (in this case the fiduciary seller) are not much considered. Also here, the duality of ownership remains, for the time being, substantially unexplored in French legal thinking.

French law is much less averse to the conditional transfer of receivables, probably because in its traditional system it required notification, which was considered sufficient publicity. In any event the theory of the *'solvabilité apparente'* would not endanger its effectiveness as it typically relates to chattels. It dispenses with the formalities attached to pledging receivables which is also possible but requires an official document or the registration of an informal document, except if this *gage* is in the commercial sphere.[111]

The conditional transfer of receivables allows for better treatment in bankruptcy as the buyer may claim his ownership right and it avoids any dispute about his right to collect any proceeds (which in France remains disputed when receivables were merely pledged). Dispensing with the requirement of notification for professional financial transactions, already achieved through the *Loi Dailly*, and introducing the *fiducia* for movable assets as proposed but not pursued through a new Article 2062 Cc since 1992,[112] would eliminate

---

[109] See, however, also the text at n 83 *supra.*

[110] See also n 75 *supra* and accompanying text.

[111] See Article 2074 Cc as compared to Artciles 91 and 109 of the Code de Comm. The Cour de Cassation has allowed the fiduciary assignment ever since its early case of 19 Aug 1849, D 1.273 (1849), confirmed on 16 Jan 1923, D 1.177 (1923).

[112] See for the introduction of the *fiducia* Projet Loi No 2583 of 20 Feb 1992 and nn 75 and 110 *supra* plus accompanying text. See on the subject of the *fiducia cum creditore* in present French law also P Remy, 'National Report for France' in DJ Hayton, SCJJ Kortmann, HLE Verhagen, *Principles of European Trust Law* (1999), 131, 137.

The *Loi Dailly* of 2 Jan 1981 (Loi 81-1) was itself reinforced on 24 Jan 1984, and is now incorporated in Articles L 313-23 to L 313-35 CMF. In France, the assignment of receivables under it still requires an official document ('*bordereau*') to incorporate these receivables which are then transferred to the credit institution. It underlines the fact that no special facility was provided to include future receivables in the nature of a floating charge. Their transfer remains unfeasible because of the lack of proper identification, unless the contract out of which they arise is in existence: see also chapter IV, s 1.7.4. New Belgian law (Article 1690 Cc), doing away altogether with the notification as a constitutive requirement for assignments, does not have this restrictive requirement any longer but also does not provide for a facility to cover future receivables.

Earlier, the discounting of bills of exchange had been used in France to raise money on claims but required these bills to be drawn and accepted in order to be so used, which is cumbersome and costly. Another much used way was for financier and creditor to agree a contractual subrogation pursuant to Article 1249 Cc. Under it, the financier pays the receivable to the creditor and substitutes himself as the new creditor under the receivable which he must expressly receive at the same time together with all rights, causes of action, priorities and mortgages supporting the receivable.

This approach still remains common in France especially in factoring of receivables: see Lamy, *Droit du financement, Affacturage* (1996), 1344, 1347 but is not effective in respect of future claims and is in any event individualised per claim and dependent on actual payment of the face amount which creates problems with the discounts normally applied for collection, maturity and the taking over of credit risk. See for older literature on factoring in France, C Gavalda and J Stoufflet, 'Le contrat dit de "factoring"' [1966] *Sem Jur, Doctrine* 2044 and more recently also C Gavalda, 'Perspectives et réalités juridiques de la convention dite d'affacturage' [1989] *Sem Jur* 534, El M Bey, Les tiers dans la complexion de l'affacturage', [1994] *RJDA* 207.

the differences with the fiduciary transfer in movables. Yet again the fiduciary transfer of receivables itself appears not much explored in France in terms of a conditional transfer with a duality of ownership.

More recently, new legislation was introduced from 1988 onwards for securitisation (*titrisation*) through the creation or facilitation of *fonds communs de créances* (FCCs), now contained in Articles L 213-43 to L 214-49 CMF. It originally allowed banks and insurance companies, but since 1998 anyone, to securitise loans or receivables under these structures in which the institutional investor may invest. See for securitisation technique itself chapter VI, section 1.4.7. It was originally meant as a balance sheet tailoring device following the Basel agreements on capital adequacy: see chapter VI, section 2.5.2, but these schemes may now more generally be used. The funds do not have legal personality but have a management company as sole representative. This company may not engage in other activities and must be approved by the COB (*Commission de Bourse*).

As for the formalities, the law of 1988, as amended, borrows the *bordereau* approach of the *Loi Dailly*. The document incorporates the assigned debts and indicates the assignee/FCC. It is delivered by the originator to the management company of the scheme. There is no need for notification to the debtors. These FCCs may now cover any kind of receivable, present or future. The inclusion of future receivables is here an important departure and might mean a broadening of the present regime under the Cc. FCCs may borrow (even through subordinated loans) to enhance their credit or to cover their temporary liquidity needs. However, the type of investor who may invest in these FCCs is limited and individuals are notably excluded.

As in the case of the modern legislation on the *pension livrée*, there is no attempt at characterisation of the transfer of the loans/receivables to the FCCs as outright, conditional or security transfers. In any event, the assignment of future receivables may become vulnerable in a bankruptcy of the originator if payable after the bankruptcy has been opened, resulting in only an un-secured claim on the originator, even if the debtor is subsequently notified.

The end result is that in France, bulk assignments for factoring and securitisation purposes may be achieved in different ways, through outright assignments subject to notification or recognition, through subrogation, through fiduciary or security assignments subject to notification, through a transfer under the *Loi Dailly* (Aritcles L 313-23 to L 313-35 CMF) and, especially in securitisations, through a transfer to an FCC (Articles L 213-43 to L 214-49 CMF). In the latter two cases the transfer is by way of the transfer of a *bordereau* without notification to the debtors. Only for FCCs, future receivables may generally be included.

1.3.6 Open or Closed System of Proprietary Rights

French law also adheres to the notion that proprietary rights cannot be created freely by the parties to a transaction. However it is often thought that there may be greater flexibility under its system where ownership in chattels transfers through the will of the parties and not through another more objective act, like delivery of possession as under Dutch and German law.[113]

To facilitate securitisations (*titrisation*), a special law was passed in 1988 (Loi 88-1201 of 23 Dec 1988, amended by Loi 93-6 of 4 Jan 1993, Loi 93-1444 of 39 Dec 1993, Loi 96-597 of 2 July 1996 and Loi 98-546 of 2 July 1998) supported by Decree 89-158 of 9 Mar 1989 (amended by Decree 93-589 of 27 Mar 1993, Decree 97-919 of 6 Oct 1997 and Decree 98-1015 of 6 Nov 1998) on the so-called *fonds communs de créances* (FCCs), now in Articles L 213-43 to L 214-49 CMF.

[113] See U Drobnig, 'Transfer of Property' in Hartkamp et al n 37 *supra*, 345*ff* and accompanying text.

Parties are thus able to create conditional sales[114] but their power freely to create proprietary interests is limited,[115] although their freedom in this respect was originally fully upheld in proprietary matters.[116] More modern French doctrine relies for third party effect on a measure of publicity (which may include physical possession in the case of tangible assets and notification to the debtors in the case of receivables) or on public policy,[117] which is understandable and conforms to the situation elsewhere. French law implies a measure of flexibility, however, which may well go beyond the present more modern official Dutch position.[118]

1.4   The Situation in Germany

1.4.1   Introduction: The Development of the Reservation of Title and Conditional Transfers; Floating Charges

In Germany, the section of the Civil Code dealing with conditional transfers[119] has given rise to much contemplation. If one may follow the comments in the *Münchener Kommentar* by Saecker, Westermann and Quack,[120] the *reservation of title* is considered a conditional sale, borne out by the reference to it in the Civil Code. At least this is so in the case of doubt,[121] although like in the Netherlands it is not immediately clear what the alternative would be. It should be noted from the outset that in Germany the concept of the conditional transfer is caught up in the abstract system of title transfer: see also chapter IV, section 1.5.6. Under it the sales agreement and the subsequent transfer of title are in principle independent of each other. A conditional sale therefore does not result in a conditional transfer unless it is indicative of the intention also to transfer title conditionally as is the case in a reservation of title.

The *Sicherungsübereignung* also started out as a conditional sale and transfer but developed more in the direction of a security interest. However, it may still be expressly organised

---

[114] Article 1584 Cc. The corresponding Article 1138 Cc still uses the old concept of delivery and fixes it at the moment of the conclusion of the sales agreement but it is generally accepted that parties may postpone the transfer as they wish.

[115] See Ghestin and Desche, n 81 *supra*, nn 542 and 612.

[116] Cour de Cassation, 13 Feb 1834, s 1.205 (1834), see also chapter IV, n 16.

[117] Ghestin and Desche, *supra* n 81, no 612 and A Weill (1974) Les Biens, No 10.

[118] See F Terre and P Simler, *Droit Civil, Les Biens* (1998) No 41; see for the modern, more restrictive approach, the text at n 70 *supra*.

[119] Section 161 BGB. Note also s 158 BGB which allows title automatically to pass or revert upon the fulfilment of a condition, but that must be a condition of the transfer itself (of the so-called *dingliche Einigung* or real contract or *dinglicher Vertrag*: see also chapter IV, s 1.5.6) and not of the underlying contract, which itself can also be conditional but — in the so-called *abstract* German system of title transfer: see more in particular n 127 *infra* — that has no effect on the title transfer, except if, as in the reservation of title, it is deemed to affect also the act of transfer itself. This contrasts with the Dutch causal system: *cf* also n 58 *supra* and chapter IV, s 1.5.6.

[120] *Münchener Kommentar zum Bürgerlichen Gesetzbuch, Band 1, Allgemeiner Teil* (ss 1–240) by FJ Saecker (1993); *Band 3, Schuldrecht, Besonderer Teil, 1 Halbband* (s 433–651k), esp Rdn 42ff, by HP Westermann (1988); and *Band 4, Sachenrecht* (ss 854–1296) by F Quack (1986).

[121] Section 449 BGB. Any conditionality of the title transfer in a sale is in Germany normally explained as a reservation of title. The alternative is not obvious. One could construe an immediate transfer to the buyer subject to a resolutive condition, as the *lex commissoria* probably does in the Netherlands, see nn 55 and 58 *supra*. In Germany reference is made in this connection to *Bedingungszusammenhang*. It seems a German variation on the *exceptio non-adimpleti contractus*: see also chapter IV, s 1.5. 10, which itself would not lead to a return of title, certainly in an abstract system of title transfer. It results in another form of proprietary sales protection not subject to re-characterisation in bankruptcy either, but, as in the Netherlands, the difference with the reservation of title is not great. The *lex commissoria tacita* as an implied resolutive condition seems to be unknown in Germany. It concerns here always sales credit protection, not funding proper.

as a conditional sale and transfer, although now uncommon.[122] In the reservation of title, there is certainly no execution upon default but rather appropriation, giving rise to a reclaiming right for the seller in the bankruptcy of the buyer if the trustee does not want to retain the contract (and offers payment guarantees). The return of title is in that case sanctioned by the Bankruptcy Act[123] and automatic. It does not therefore require a formal retransfer of the title. This automatic return is therefore not considered impeded by the lack of authority of the debtor or the intervention of his trustee.

The reservation of title is not accessory to the claim for the purchase price unless it is otherwise agreed. It means that the benefit must be separately transferred, if not altogether extinguished, when the seller is paid off through the assignment of his claim. The assignor is considered to be under an obligation to transfer the benefit of reservation of title to the assignee, again unless the parties agreed otherwise.[124]

If so agreed the right of the seller under a reservation of title may be reinforced by the shift of the proprietary right into the manufactured end products and into the proceeds upon a sale if previously authorised. This is done through what is called a *verlaengerter Eigentumsvorbehalt* clause which may take various forms, although it may weaken the reservation of title to a mere preference upon conversion of the good in the nature of a *Sicherungsübereignun.*[125] An *erweiterter Eigentumsvorbehalt* extends the protection of the

---

[122] Before the entering into force of the German Civil Code in 1900 when received Roman law still prevailed in Germany, but after the introduction of the new Federal Bankruptcy Act of 1877, its original Section 14 eliminated the proprietary effect (and thereby the *in rem* and priority status) of both the (Roman law) pledge if delivered *constituto possessorio* (that is without physical possession) and the (Roman law) non-possessory hypothec in movables, therefore all securities in movables without actual possession of the security holder or his agent.

This conformed to the earlier trend under the new European codifications at the beginning of the 19th century: see also s 1.1.1 *supra*. To regain the necessary flexibility, German law then started to use the Roman law repurchase option of C 4.54.2 to create the *Sicherungsübereignung* (although the repurchase became an obligation and not merely an option): see also text at n 58 *supra* for the situation in The Netherlands and at nn 80 and 109 *supra* for the situation in France, in which latter country the development was more hesitant and the conditional sale of Article 1584 Cc provided another method, as Article 3.84(4) CC now does in the Netherlands.

The subsequent German development of the *Sicherungsübereignung* has, however, moved away from the concept of conditional ownership and it is mostly treated as an ordinary ownership transfer. Thus for tangible movables, the transfer takes place pursuant to Section 929*ff*, especially Section 930, which deals with the transfer *constituto possessorio*, even though in bankruptcy it is not now considered to result in more than a preference in the execution sale: see text at n 144 *infra*. For receivables, the rules concerning the assignment apply which in Germany do not require any notification to the debtor: see Section 398 BGB.

See, for the continuing possibility of the conditional ownership construction in the case of a *Sicherungsübereignung*, M Wolff, *Sachenrecht* (München, 1993), 299 and 310, but it has become uncommon except perhaps in true repurchase agreements. *Cf*, however, also text at n 148 *infra* for limiting considerations especially in connection with the appropriation right.

[123] Generally, in Germany, contractual rescission clauses requiring the return of the sold assets upon default are denied validity in bankruptcy: see Section 26 of the Bankruptcy Act 1877 and now Sections 103–5 of the Insolvency Act 1999. The old Act introduced here a uniform law for all of Germany before the introduction of the all German Civil Code in 1900. This approach did not apply if the goods had not yet reached the point of delivery to the transferee: see Section 44 of the old Bankruptcy Act, not retained in the new Insolvency Act of 1999. In that case they were likely to be after-acquired. This after acquired property was not considered part of the estate in a German bankruptcy: see Section 1 of the Bankruptcy Act, not retained in the new Act either.

Reservation of title as a contractual condition is *exceptionally* valid in a German bankruptcy. The condition as expressed in the sale agreement is commonly deemed implied in the transfer of title itself, therefore in the real agreement or *dinglicher Einigung*: see also n 119 *supra*. It leads to a revindication (*Aussonderungsrecht*) against the bankrupt estate: see Section 43 of the Bankruptcy Act, now Section 47 of the Insolvency Act if the bankruptcy trustee does not elect to continue the contract and give guarantees for payment under Section 17 of the Bankruptcy Act, now Section 103 of the Insolvency Act: see also BGH, 1 July 1970, 54 *BGHZ* 214 at 218.

[124] BGH, 5 May 1971, *BGHZ* 56,123 (1971). See for the situation in the Netherlands and France, nn 53 and 100 *supra* and for England the text at n 195 *infra*.

[125] See also n 145 *infra*. These facilities are first the so-called *Verarbeitungsklausel* leading to the sellers' joint ownership of processed, assembled or mixed goods, title to which is under Section 950 BGB normally acquired by the manufacturer except where otherwise agreed, as indeed it normally is in the *Verarbeitungsklausel*: see BGH,

reservation of title to other debts of the buyer to the seller and may be combined with the *verlaengerter Eigentumsvorbehalt*. In a bankruptcy of the buyer, it results in an *Absonderungsrecht* or mere preference in any execution proceeds upon default, much in the way of the *Sicherungsübereignung* (Section 51 Bankruptcy Act 1999). The *Aussonderung* or retrieval right in the bankruptcy of a buyer is limited to the sold asset not being timely paid for, see also the next section for these concepts. It is therefore lost in the other situations.

The right of the buyer pending full payment of the price has been clearly qualified as proprietary in case law.[126] It has led to a more extensive study of this type of contingent property right or proprietary expectancy, also called a *dingliche Anwartschaft*, and the resulting duality of the title under the circumstances.[127] The discussions on this subject are

28 June 1954, *BGHZ* 14, 117 (1954), although appropriation is not then thought possible upon default and the seller only has a priority right in the proceeds upon an execution sale allowing a distribution of the proceeds.

Then there is the *Vorausabtretungsklausel* leading to an advance assignment of the proceeds of any (future authorised) resale and allowing collection by the original seller, which is common where the original buyer needs to sell the goods in his ordinary business.

Together they are normally referred to as the vertical *verlängerter Eigentumsvorbehalt*. There is also a horizontal *verlängerter Eigentumsvorbehalt*, sometimes called a *Kontokorrentvorbehalt*, created through a so-called *Saldoklausel*, which creates a general reservation of title to all goods passing between seller and buyer and valid until all outstanding debt is paid. It also leads to a priority right in execution sales only and not to appropriation rights: see BGH [1971] NJW 799.

There could even be a *Konzernklausel* or *Konzernvorbehalt* under which all transactions with an entire group of companies could be subject to reservations of title until all outstanding debt was paid. To avoid excess security and excessive inroads into the room for manœuvre for the buyer, German case law tested these arrangements in the light of its requirement of good morals (*gute Sitten*): see also n 146 *infra* and accompanying text. They are forbidden since 1 Jan. 1999.

[126] The German Supreme Court originally only gave the buyer a personal right in the asset in which the seller had reserved title. This right could be transferred through assignment pursuant to the normal rules of Sections 398 and 413 BGB: see RGH, 4 Apr. 1933, *RGHZ* 140, 223 (1933). Even if the physical possession was transferred to the buyer pursuant to Section 929 BGB, the result would not have been different, except for the *bona fide* purchaser pursuant to Section 932 BGB.

Since 1956 the German Supreme Court has taken a different view and has held that the expectancy of the buyer is an *in rem* right. It allows its transfer without the consent of the original seller under the reservation of title as and in the manner of a proprietary right: see BGH, 22 Feb. 1956, *BGHZ* 20, 88 (1956) and it is now well established that a buyer may transfer this interest to a third party, even as security: see HP Westermann, n 120 *supra*, 148. As such it can be part of a *Sicherungsübereignung*: see for this facility the text below. Thus the third party transferee no longer receives from a person without the right to dispose and need therefore not rely on his *bona fides* and possession of the asset under Section 932 BGB. *Dingliche Einigung* (see n 127 *infra*) and *Übergabe* (delivery) of the expectancy are necessary pursuant to Section 929 BGB, the latter not being a problem where the transferor has actual possession. Naturally, acquisition of the full title, therefore of any right in excess of the expectancy will still depend for its full effect on the *bona fides* and the actual possession of the acquirer under the general rule of Sections 932*ff*. BGB, even if he buys in the ordinary course of business.

[127] L Raiser, *Dingliche Anwartschaften* (Tübingen, 1961). Also in Germany there are some voices which would give the seller under a reservation of title only a security interest: see e.g. Huebner, [1980] *NJW* 729, 735, which is not extended, however, to the right of the buyer under a *Sicherungsübereignung*: see for this facility text following n. 133 *infra*.

The idea of a duality of ownership resulting from the conditional title is only one further step in the discussion of the *Anwartschaft*. This discussion is on this point often fierce as implementation of the concept of duality affects the basic characteristics of German civil law with its sharp and fundamental separation of the law of obligations and law of property as demonstrated by the concept of abstraction. In Germany proprietary rights are in principle operating independently from their underlying (contractual) cause or origin, like a sales contract. In this system, the sale agreement must be considered separate from the title transfer itself which requires a further (implicit) agreement (*dingliche Einigung* or *dinglicher Vertrag*) and is not affected by the underlying intent of the parties unless also made part of the *dingliche Einigung* or transfer itself: see for this principle of abstraction also Drobnig, n 113 *supra*, 357.

An important impediment to the duality of ownership is the closed nature of the proprietary system and the impossibility of parties freely to create rights that can be maintained against third parties. They cannot create *iura extra commercium*: see text at n 149 *infra*. This is strictly speaking an issue separate from the abstraction principle and more fundamental to civil law.

sometimes thought somewhat metaphysical and there is still some resistance to the idea,[128] but the concept would appear to be real enough and firmly accepted as such.[129]

The floating charge has no base in statutory or case law and must be gathered together on the basis of contractual clauses. In Germany, the situation compares closely to the *verlaengerter* and *erweiterter Eigentumsvorbehalt* situation. There are in this connection the so-called *Raumsicherungsvertrag* which allows for bulk transfers of assets within a certain space, the *Verarbeitungsklausel* which allows their conversion into other products in which the charge is then contractually extended, and the *Vorausabtretungsklausel* which allows for an anticipated assignment of all future claims from sales of the assets. Section 91 of the German Bankruptcy Act of 1999 may interfere with the transfer of future or replacement assets in this connection. It would appear (at least in the case of receivables) to apply only to assets that remain absolutely future at the time of the intervening bankruptcy of the

Another complication derives from the abstraction principle which in Germany allows the valid on-sale of the asset and title transfer by the buyer to a third party even if the latter knew of the limited purposes for which or under which the asset was originally sold to the buyer: see RGH, 4 Apr. 1919, *RGHZ* 95, 244 (1919); see further chapter IV, s 1.5.6. Under German law, it is not normal for the conditionality of the contract transferring proprietary rights to have an impact on the title, although there are exceptions, notably in the reservation of title, when the conditionality in the contract is also deemed to affect the title transfer itself. It is clear that the title transfer can be conditional, but that is then determined at the time of the *dingliche Einigung* itself and not through the underlying sales agreement. In this vein, Section 158 BGB allows title automatically to pass or revert upon fulfilment of a condition but only if it is part of the *Einigung*. The concept of abstraction is of great importance to German law. It is in sharp (theoretical) contrast e.g. to Dutch law that accepts the proprietary impact of contractual conditions as a matter of principle: see Article 3.84(4) CC and text at n 58 *supra*. That is the causal system. As we already saw in chapter IV, s 1.5.7, the notion of abstraction is by no means a universal civil law principle but only a matter of policy.

See for the discussion of these aspects in connection with conditional ownership rights in Germany, J Rinnewitz, *Zur dogmatischen Struktur des Anwartschaftsrechts aus dem Eigentumsvorbehalt* (Diss., Göttingen, 1989), dealing also with the proprietary complimentary nature of the interests of both parties to a conditional title and the duality of legal possession that necessarily follows the duality of ownership. Here we also see the idea that the *Anwartschaft* is a more general notion (a *sui generis* proprietary right) that arises in all types of conditional ownership and therefore not only in a reservation of title. In fact *both* parties to a conditional sale have a proprietary expectancy, therefore in a reservation of title also the seller: that is the expectancy again to become the full owner if the buyer not pay.

German doctrine, even to the extent that it is favourable to the idea, seems to remain generally puzzled about how to treat the consequences and the proprietary flexibility that would seem to follow. See for doubts on the terminology, D Medicus, *Bürgerliches Recht* (18th ed. 1999), no. 456. In fact denying proprietary effect to the *resolutive* condition (of the seller but not the suspensive one of the buyer), accepted in Justinian law: see n 55 *supra*, started in Germany with Windscheid: see Windscheid-Kipp, 1 *Lehrbuch des Pandektenrechts* (8th ed. 1900), s 91, who contested the more current interpretation of Justinian law on this point. It seems a normal consequence of the abstraction principle that does not favour the conditionality of a sale unless incorporated in the *dingliche Einigung*. As we saw, Dutch law now follows in the case of a rescission of the contract for reason of default, except if there is a special clause inserted to the effect: see n 67 *supra*.

[128] M Wolff, *Sachenrecht* (1993) *Rdns 504ff* and 547b accepts the *in rem* expectancy for the buyer under a reservation of title but notably denies the *in rem* right for the lessee under a finance lease if not clearly expressed in the contract even if the lease is very similar to the reservation, except that mostly the lessee has the option rather than the automatic right to acquire full ownership upon payment of the last lease instalment. See for the repo and finance lease situation more in particular n 141 *infra*.

[129] The subject tends to be more fully explored in connection with Section 161 BGB which discusses the suspensive and rescinding conditions in the General Part of the BGB: see Saecker, n 120 *supra*, 1362, who supports for commercial reasons the need for transferability of the expectancy, but *cf* also M Wolff, *Bürgerliches Gesetzbuch, Band 1, Allgemeiner Teil* (1987), 1241, who does not dwell on the point in connection with Section 161 BGB which is often associated with the reservation of title but has a wider reach. German law is clear that conditions are not retroactive (Sections 158 and 159 BGB) and only take *in rem* effect as at the date of their fulfilment, although personal actions may lie to undo the other effects if necessary. Only if the condition went to the *dingliche Einigung* itself, as probably in the reservation of title, would the situation be different.

There have been many attempts at defining the essence of the *dingliche Anwartschaft*. Recurring themes are the degree of certainty in the expectancy of acquiring a full right, the specificity of this right, the absence of the transferee/debtor.[130] Like in the Netherlands, a conditional transfer in respect of future assets may protect the financier better, see also chapter IV section 1.5.5. In either case there would only be an *Absonderungsrecht* in a bankruptcy of the debtor.

1.4.2   Sicherungsübereignung *and Conditional Sales*

In Germany, besides the reservation of title (and *lex commissoria* or *Bedingungszusammen-hang*), the other main non-possessory proprietary protection right in tangibles is the *Sicherungsübereignung*. As mentioned in the previous section, it started very much in the nature of a fiduciary or conditional transfer, operating under case law since 1890.[131] It became the major (non-possessory) loan protection device in chattels and may shift into replacement goods and proceeds if so agreed. In the form of the *Sicherungszession* it may cover intangible assets, present or future. It was surprisingly not covered in its Civil Code of 1900. As a consequence, its nature and effects were never coherently considered at legislative level and it remains a device *praeter legem* based on customary law.[132]

need for any further formalities in acquiring the full right when the condition matures; and the possibility of disposing of the asset or *Anwartschaftsrecht* in it without the other party's consent. Marotzke, *Das Anwartschaftsrecht* (Berlin, 1977), 7 and 13 starts with the power to dispose of the asset. In his view, the expectant party cannot dispose of the underlying asset but only of the *dingliche Anwartschaftsrecht* in it: see also Staudiger, *Kommentar zum BGB* (Berlin, 1995) ss. 164–240, 271. It implies that the expectancy is a limited proprietary right. The right itself exists when there is such certainty about the expectancy that it only depends on the expectant himself or on time for his full proprietary right to mature. Raiser, *Dingliche Anwartschaften* (1961, 3–4), sees it as arising if most acts or formalities concerning the transfer have been performed but only some or a last one are still missing, like payment in a reservation of title. Rinnewitz, n 127 *supra*, 60 seems to combine both views and believes that the *Anwartschaftsrecht* exists when sufficient steps to the creation of the full proprietary right have been taken for its structure and the interest holder to be known and in existence (*konkretisiert*) and the acquisition of the full right may with sufficient probability be expected. In a similar vein's, C Liebl, Die dinglichen Anwartschaftrechte und ihre Behandlung in Konkurs', *Europäische Hochschulschriften* (Frankfurt am Main, 1990), 7 and 71.

The situation in a bankruptcy is particularly important as the *dingliche Anwartschaft* is only relevant if the expectancy in the underlying assets can mature in a bankruptcy of the counterparty and gives rise to a revindication action (*Aussonderungsrecht*) of the expecting party once the condition is fulfilled even if this occurs after bankruptcy. The Germans use here the term '*Konkursfestheit*' or bankruptcy resistency. It is the true test of the existence of a proprietary right. It is clear that in the case of a reservation of title there is no problem: see the case law referred to in n 126 *supra* and the new Section 107(1) of the German Insolvency Act 1999. This could still be considered exceptional and emphasis could be put instead on the bankrupt's lack of disposition rights and therefore inability to shift assets out of his estate.

Nevertheless if no more acts are required of the bankrupt counterparty or his trustee to make the other party the full owner, it can be convincingly argued that the conditional ownership right of the non-bankrupt party is always effective against the bankrupt estate when the condition matures, even if this is after the bankruptcy itself. It can also be said that in that case ownership passes to the non-bankrupt party by the force of law. Actual possession and use are not the determining factors here. Even if they are with the bankrupt, they can still be validly reclaimed by the non-bankrupt party on the basis of his matured ownership right. Section 103 of the German Insolvency Act containing the facility for the trustee to repudiate executory contracts is not relevant and Section 161 BGB does not appear to have relevance either where it refers to the interaction of a bankruptcy trustee and implies that neither party in a conditional sale (thus also not the seller under a reservation of title) has fully performed.

[130] See K Larenz, *Schuldrecht, Allgemeiner Teil*, Sec. 34 III (1987). The difference with chattels may be that in their case delivery is necessay which may not be deemed completed through an *anticipated constitutum possessorium*, see also chapter IV s 1.5.5. In Germany an assignment does not require any other formal steps.

[131] RGH, 2 June 1890; RGZ 2, 173 (1890); see also n 137 *infra*.

[132] The draftsmen of the BGB considered outlawing the transfer of title *constituto possessorio* (therefore the transfer which left physical possession with the seller or an agent, whilst transferring only the legal or constructive possession to the buyer) if this mode of transfer was intended to create a substitute security. This attempt did not succeed, however, as under the abstraction principle, see n 127 *supra*, the underlying intent is not considered directly relevant in the German law of title transfer: see for the German discussion at the time, 'Mugdan, Die gesammten Materialien zum BGB' [All the Materials concerning the BGB], I *Sachenrecht* [Property Law], (Berlin, 1899), 626.

It is still not a true security right, although the subsequent case law development clearly moved in that direction and subsequent transfers are possible which rank according to time.[133] The financier is still considered the buyer, however, and advances technically the purchase price to the seller rather than extending a loan to him, but the assets will be repurchased by the buyer on an agreed date against the original price plus an agreed interest rate. That clearly implies a conditional sale supporting a loan structure which, as suggested in section 1.1.1 above, would lead one to expect a conversion of the title transfer into a secured transaction. That is what has largely happened in Germany even if technically there remain some features of a conditional sale. In this structure, normally the seller will retain the assets for his own use and the delivery to the buyer will be *constituto possessorio*, that is constructive only.

It seems frequent, however, that the seller transfers title unconditionally to the buyer who, in that case, has only a personal duty to retransfer title upon repayment of the loan. In that case there is no conditional sale or security proper and the position of the seller in a bankruptcy of the buyer/financier would be weak and he would have no automatic repossession right. As he has the money, this will be a disadvantage only if the assets have increased in value. As in the case of equipment or even inventory that is seldom the case, this structure may in practice prove adequate for the parties.

If there is a proper conditional sale the *Sicherungsübereignung* results in the seller of the assets retaining an *in rem* right to retrieve his assets (or *dingliche Anwartschaft*) upon fulfilling his duty to offer repayment of the advance (plus interest) on the due date, which right is also effective in the event of a bankruptcy of the financier. It then results in a so-called *Aussonderungsrecht*.[134] The buyer/financier is not considered to have an appropriation right upon default of the seller, however (unless expressly so agreed) and must conduct an execution sale with a return of overvalue. He has in a bankruptcy of the seller only a preference in the sale proceeds of the assets, whatever was agreed, therefore only an *Absonderungsrecht*. In this respect the ownership right of the buyer/financier has become weak and debased.[135]

Thus compared to the seller under a reservation of title, who has, in German terminology, an *Aussonderungsrecht* from which the seller under a *Sicherungsübereignung* also benefits if he can offer the repayment amount, the buyer under a *Sicherungsübereignung* has at least in the bankruptcy of the seller a mere *Absonderungsrecht* that is a preferential right to the

---

[133] This is an important exception to the rule that no one may dispose twice of the same property, subject of course to the rights of *bona fide* purchasers of movable tangible assets. The second buyer need not be *bona fide* under the circumstances: see Quack, n 120 *supra*, 787. Another, probably better, way of looking at this problem is to recognise the proprietary expectancy of the seller (*dingliche Anwartschaft*) and his right to dispose of it even to (second) purchasers who are aware of the (first) fiduciary transfer.

[134] RGH, 23 Dec 1899, *RGHZ* 45, 80 (1899). References are often also made to RGH, 20 Mar 1919, *RGHZ* 79, 121 (1912); RGH, 10 Oct 1917, *RGHZ* 91, 12 (1917); and RGH, 5 Nov 1918, *RGHZ* 94, 305 (1918).

[135] RGH, 14 Oct 1927, *RGHZ* 118, 209 (1927) and 9 Apr 1929, *RGHZ* 124, 73 (1929). The term fiduciary transfer is here sometimes used but unlike under the pre-Justinian Roman law of the *fiducia*, the financier cannot rely on his ownership rights and ignore the bankruptcy of his counterparty. The thought appears to be that in a bankruptcy of the seller his repayment obligation becomes due whilst the ownership interest of the buyer lapses and is converted in a priority right: see also Section 27(2) of the German Reorganisation Act (*Vergleichsordnung* of 1935), now superseded. It is also said that the financier has a claim for repayment and should not therefore have ownership of the asset as well (*Problem der doppelten Befriedigung*). The true reason is probably the residual proprietary interest of the bankrupt seller. The resulting mere preference for the financier is in line with the situation prevailing under the received Roman law before 1900 under which the hypothec as a *non-possessory* security resulted only in a preference (*droit de préférence*) but not in a revindication right at the same time: see Zwalve, n 5 *supra*, 342, 394. It is also in line with the general modern German approach that in bankruptcy *all* security interests, whether possessory or not, lose their repossession and separate execution facilities in bankruptcy, see Section 51 Bankruptcy Act 1999.

sales proceeds of the asset.[136] In a bankruptcy of the seller, he is therefore dependent in timing on the bankruptcy trustee who is in charge of the asset and of his disposition and the buyer has no repossession and execution right. The buyer's right is mostly considered accessory to the advance, unless otherwise expressly agreed. This is also indicative of a lesser right than full ownership, in particular of a security right, which suggests that the ownership reverts automatically to the seller upon repayment.[137] It implies that the *seller* remains the true owner and that the asset still belongs to his estate, just like any owner who has conceded a security interest in them. It explains the seller's *Aussonderungsrecht* in a bankruptcy of the buyer. Duality of ownership, unlike in reservations of title, would not therefore seem to be the issue in the *Sicherungsübereignung* as it developed.

However, the fiduciary assignment or *Sicherungszession* of receivables allows for collection by the financier and amortisation of the advance in the manner of an owner, as if therefore a full assignment to the buyer had taken place, although any excess collection must be returned.[138]Most importantly, the buyer/financier in a *Sicherungsübereignung* or *Sicherungszession* may also legally on-sell or assign the assets. It may subject him to any claims for damages by the original owner, although they would not affect the title of purchasers/assignees. He thus appears to have full disposition rights and the conditional ownership rights (if any) of the seller do not figure here.

---

[136] See respectively Sections 43 and 48 of the old German Bankruptcy Act, now Sections 47 and 50 of the Insolvency Act 1999. In Germany *Aussonderung* is based on a full proprietary right in assets, that is ownership or any other proprietary right entitling the beneficiary to possession. Reservation of title is supposed to give the seller an *Aussonderungsrecht*, assuming it is also part of the *Einigung*. It leads to a self-help remedy. *Absonderung* is typical for security interests and signifies that the asset still belongs to the debtor's estate even though the creditor has a proprietary security interest in it. It means that there must be an execution sale and the secured creditor only has a preference in the proceeds. The trustee takes here the initiative in the sale if the interests are non-possessory (also therefore in the case of real estate mortgages). It applies also to the possessory pledge and only if the trustee is not entitled to take action remains the right to repossession and separate execution in tact: see Sections 50 and 173 of the German Insolvency Act 1999. Statutory liens are treated similarly but the liens of the tax and social security authorities have since 1999 no longer been effective in a German bankruptcy whilst the lien for the workforce is substituted by a state funded guarantee.

The distinction between *Aussonderung* and *Absonderung* is typical for German bankruptcy law (and not outside it). Most other countries make a distinction between self-help and non-self-help remedies in the case of secured transactions or statutory liens. If there is self-help, the secured creditor may in essence ignore a bankruptcy of the debtor as self-help means a right to repossession upon default. That is in most countries normal for possessory as well as non-possessory security interests. Non-self help remedies only give a preference in the proceeds of an execution, conducted by the trustee in the case of a bankruptcy of the debtor. It means that the creditor is dependent on the trustee in the timing and must also share in the expenses of the bankruptcy. In many countries in the French tradition, statutory liens are in that category and do not lead to self help. They are called *privilèges* rather than secured interests. In reorganisation-oriented bankruptcy statutes like those of the USA and now also of Germany and France, self-help remedies are mostly subject to a stay provision pending the decision on reorganisation or liquidation. It does not, however, make them mere privileges and the stay is only a temporary measure and may be lifted in certain circumstances especially when the asset is not needed in the reorganisation or depreciates fast.

[137] BGH, 23 Sept. 1981 [1981] NJW 275. There is criticism of this approach, and it has been suggested that even though the property re-transfers automatically to the seller upon payment, this does not imply the automatic transfer of the buyer's rights with the assignment of his repayment claim, but this may be agreed: see Quack, n. 120 *supra*, 778. The alternative to the accessory nature of the *Sicherungsübereignung* is to consider repayment a rescinding condition of the title transfer to the buyer, which was the Dutch approach before the new Code abolished the fiduciary transfer: see HR, 3 Oct. 1980 [1981] *NJ* 60 and the fiduciary transfer to the financier was never considered accessory: see n 53 *supra*. The German general banking conditions do not depend on automaticity but allow the banks to remain owners until they retransfer the title. The accessory nature of the *Sicherungsüberei-gung* is thus abrogated by agreement. One of the dangers was that in a bankruptcy of the bank the original seller loses his *in rem* status as a consequence and only retains a personal right to retrieval but this is countered by case law.

[138] The BGH accepts that the fiduciary assignment may be chosen merely to avoid the notification that would be required if the same receivables had been pledged: see BGH, 23 Sept. 1981, cited in n 137 *supra*, and for a similar attitude in France, the text at n 112 *supra*.

As a consequence, *bona fides* of the purchaser is not required in order to obtain full title, nor is the transfer of physical possession (which the buyer/financier could not have provided).[139] Both of those would be indispensable for the protection of the transferee if he had acquired the asset from an unauthorised person under the German exception to the *nemo dat* rule (section 932 BGB). The proper method of delivery by the buyer/financier is here *longa manu* by mere agreement without notice even to the original seller of the interest on the basis of sections 870 and 931 BGB, although it is also conceivable that German law opts for the assignment route instead.

From this perspective it is the *buyer/financier* who is considered to have full title, although, as we just saw, from other perspectives it is the seller/borrower. Thus there must be some duality in the ownership structure if the *Sicherungsübereignung* is not reduced to a mere secured transaction. Yet the hybrid character of the title remains here largely unexplored, contrary to the situation in the reservation of title, probably because the conditional sale analogy has been mostly lost in the *Sicherungsübereignung* which in practice operates in Germany as the principal non-possessory security interest in personal property.

1.4.3   Finance Sales

Perhaps a more general statement should be made here. The development of the reservation of title and much more so of the *Sicherungsübereignung* in Germany shows that great latitude is left to the parties. Except for the security interests covered by statute which, besides the statutory liens, are mainly the real estate mortgage and the possessory pledge, there is no preconceived framework or mandatory form for new financial products. They may in essence be freely created, although of course within the German system of proprietary rights and an, in principle, closed system of these rights. Thus the characterisation issue cannot be avoided and courts will intervene in case of doubt. They will interpret the parties' intentions and define their basic proprietary and other protections, but there is in all this in Germany probably some greater flexibility than in other civil law countries. It shows in the unstructured development of the *Sicherungsübereignung* and related floating charge. It may also show in the liberal set-off facilities for repos, see below. Besides the existing proprietary system, the concept of good morals or *gute Sitten*, forms the outside limit of the modern financial products and their status in law.

As was already pointed out in the last section, German law thus also allows the true conditional sale and transfer. It seems in principle all to depend on the parties' intention (in respect of the real agreement) and how they structure their deals. There are no functional bars, even though there may be objections to the right of a finance lessee or repo seller being characterised as a *dingliche Anwartschaft*, but it depends on the structure of the lease and type of repo. A mere option for the lessee to acquire full ownership upon payment of the last instalment might not be sufficient support for such a characterisation. The finance lease is therefore normally considered in its contractual aspects only. In true conditional sales, on the other hand, the protection of the sellers/fund raisers through execution sales and repayment of overvalue seems not to be one of the concerns. Appropriation of the asset is possible instead, except perhaps if there is a clear loan structure when the need for an execution sale and return of the overvalue is often deemed implied in the contract and when, as in the case of a *Sicherungsübereignung* there may only be an *Absonderungsrecht* in bankruptcy as we saw in the previous section, even if it may still

---

[139] *Cf* n 126 *supra in fine.*

be structured as a true conditional sale with an appropriation facility also effective in bankruptcy (*Aussonderung*).[140]

The repurchase agreement or *repo* for investment securities was the subject of new legislation in Germany in 1994: see Section 340b of the Commercial Code and Section 104 of the new Insolvency Act of the same year, effective only in 1999, but brought forward in this aspect in 1994. Proprietary aspects are virtually ignored. The practice has been to balance the contractual 'cherry-picking' approach in the bankruptcy of either party (which in the case of market-related securities under Section 18 of the old German Bankruptcy Act was already converted into an automatic termination) with a contractual netting facility. The validity of this netting facility is now endorsed by the new German Insolvency Act (see Section 104 for *Fixgeschäfte* and *Finanztermingeschäfte*).

As just mentioned, in Germany, finance leasing is normally also only considered in its contractual aspects. That is not to say that proprietary aspects do not exist in leases and repos, even if in Germany the intent of the parties determines the existence of a conditional transfer and title. But the problem remains what this means, although this is not much discussed in connection with finance leasing and the repo business.[141] Also in factoring of receivables there may be a characterisation risk. To avoid it, the transfer of the receivables is often structured in Germany as being complete and unconditional. It is then an outright sale. In that case the duality of ownership is not an issue, but in other forms of factoring, see section 2.3 below, it may be, even if they are purely domestic.

---

[140] See n 122 *supra in fine* and also nn 128 and 129 *supra* plus accompanying text. See for the good morals concern n 146 *infra* and accompanying text.

[141] See for the proprietary aspects also the references to M Wolff in nn 122 *supra in fine* and 128 *supra*. See, however, for the lack of an extensive discussion of the *Anwartschaft* notion in connection with conditional ownership in Germany n 127 *in fine* and n 129 *supra*, and this crucial notion does not figure in the discussion of the finance lease and repurchase agreement either. In the repurchase agreement of investment securities, the fungible nature of the securities may be a further hindrance to the recognition of the proprietary status for the seller, but he may rely on the general German facility to shift ownership rights into replacement goods if contractually agreed (the anticipatory *dingliche Einigung*). For the finance lease, the key would have to be the automatic shift of title to the lessee upon payment of the last instalment or at least the *in rem* option to acquire full ownership at that time without the payment of further consideration. Without such clauses the lease is purely contractual everywhere but in Germany probably also if there is only an option.

See for a more recent discussion of the repurchase agreement of investment securities in Germany, Krumnow, Sprissler, Bellavite-Hoeverman, Kemmer and Steinbruecker, *Rechnungslegung der Kreditinstitute* (Stuttgart, 1994), 75*ff*. Discussions of the tax complications seem more common than of the legal complications: see A Lohner, *Echte Pensionsgeschäfte, ihre ertragsteuerliche Behandlung und ihr Einsatz als Sachverhaltgestaltungen im Rahmen der Steurerplanung* (Frankfurt am Main, 1992); see also J Wagenmann, *Wertpapierpensionsgeschäfte: das Überlegene Refinanzierungsinstrument, Pfaffenweiler* (1991), 52–72 and further Waschbusch, 'Die Rechnungslegung der Kreditinstitute bei Pensionsgeschäfte. Zur Rechtslage nach Section 340b HGB' [1993] 3 *Betriebsberater* 172–79.

See for the netting aspects in Germany after the changes of 1994 U Bosch and S Hodges, 'German Legislation on Netting of Derivatives' [1995] *Butterworths Journal of International Banking and Financial Law* 304.

See for the various theories on the (contractual) nature of finance leasing PW Heermann, 'Grundprobleme beim, Finanzierungsleasing beweglicher Güter in Deutschland und den Vereinigten Staaten von Amerika' [1993] *ZVglRW* 362*ff*. highlighting the problem of the particularly tripartite nature of many of these arrangements; others see a credit agreement which is also the approach of Section 3 (2)(1) of the Consumer Credit Act (Verbraucherkreditgesetz or VerbrKG of 1 Jan 1991). The German Supreme Court (BGH) traditionally qualifies the finance lease as a rental agreement, *BGHZ* 71, 189, only more recently with some emphasis on the financial nature of the arrangement, *BGHZ* 95, 39, not seen as a fundamental shift; however, see F von Westphalen, 'Leasing als "sonstige Finanzierungshilfe" gemäss. 1 (2) VerbrKG' [1991] *ZIP* 639, 640 and SM Martinek, *Modere Vertragstypen, Band I: Leasing und Factoring* (München, 1991), 72. The former author explicitly maintains the BGH interpretation against the newer definition of the VerbrKG. The latter argues for a *sui generis* approach (at 86) with emphasis both on the financial and users' aspects. Others see a contract of a mixed nature with aspects of a credit-giving role and of a purchasing agent role for the lessor with payments of interest and a commission by the lessee: see CW Canaris, *Interessenlage, Grundprinzipien und Rechtsnatur des Finanzierungsleasing* (1990), 450*ff*.

1.4.4 Curbing Excess: Open or Closed System of Proprietary Rights

To summarise the situation for the more commonly discussed reservation of title and *Sicherungsübereignung*: in both cases, it is the seller/transferor in need of funding who mostly has the upper hand in a proprietary sense. The difference is that in the *Sicherungsübereignung*, he is not perceived to have much of a title for the time being,[142] even though he still has physical possession. The opposite is the case for the seller under a reservation of title, who has no physical possession but is deemed to retain ownership. Under German law *both* have an *in rem* retrieval right (or *Aussonderungsrecht*) in the bankruptcy of their counter-party.

In a reservation of title in Germany, the buyer has an *in rem* expectation (*dingliche Anwartschaft*). This appears less likely for the buyer/financier under a *Sicherungsübereignung*,[143] probably because his expectation of becoming full owner is so much less realistic than in the case of the buyer under a reservation of title and it is certainly not the intention. Yet if the *Sicherungsübereignung* is structured as a true conditional sale, he has that *Anwartschaftsrecht*. Even if it is not so structured, he may still resell the goods as owner. On the other hand, if there is no conditional sale structure, in a bankruptcy of the seller, the financier's property right will be converted into a mere preference in the proceeds of the asset. This was different under old Dutch law, where the buyer was thought to have a security right with a self-help facility, at least to the extent that made sense whilst the conditional sale concept was increasingly ignored.[144] It was logical in a situation where economically speaking there was loan financing and an interest rate agreed.

The *Sicherungsübereignung* is of great importance in Germany, particularly for the bulk transfer of present and future tangible assets and receivables, normally contractually supplemented by a similar right in converted assets or proceeds. As such, it may achieve a floating charge on future cash flows.[145] In terms of priority, an earlier reservation of title prevails over it as the seller in a *Sicherungsübereignung* (being the buyer under a reservation of title) does not have sufficient title to include the asset and is not transferring actual possession to the fiduciary buyer. This superiority of the earlier reservation of title does extend to any contractual shift into converted products and sales proceeds unless the clauses to this effect were agreed later than the conflicting *Sicherungsübereignung*, provided that the extended reservation of title does not result in excessive security which would be considered against good morals (*gute Sitten*). The concept is traditionally less

---

[142] *Cf* n 135 *supra*.

[143] The possibility of the seller having an expectancy (*Anwartschaft*) which may be subject to the recovery rights of his creditors has, however, been suggested: see Quack, n 120 *supra*, 781.

[144] See text at n 48 *supra*.

[145] The requirement of specificity nevertheless remains an impediment as it is necessary to force the bulk transfer in the established patterns of individual transfers which is more in particular problematic for future tangibles and receivables. The requirement of specificity is only (partly) overcome by the use of special constructions like the *Raumsicherungsvertrag* for tangible movable assets and the *Globalzession* for intangibles. For tangibles it allows them to be described with reference to a certain place or room *(Raum)*. Receivables may be sufficiently described with reference to certain debtors. For the transfer of future goods, the facility of the anticipated *constitutum possessorium* through a representative was created: see RGH, 11 June 1920, *RGHZ* 99, 208 (1920).

The assignment of future receivables was much facilitated as notification is not a constitutive requirement under German law and the claim itself need only be identifiable when it emerges: see BGH, 25 Oct 1952, *BGHZ* 7, 365 (1952), whilst the relationship out of which it arises need not exist (as Dutch law eg still requires, see n 46 *supra*). As in the case of an extended reservation of title, see n 125 *supra*, the *Verarbeitungsklausel* and the *Vorausabtretungsklausel* will attempt to cover situations of conversion of the assets in manufactured goods and of resale.

restrictive for reservation of title than for a conflicting *Sicherungsübereignung* which could be invalid for the same reasons.[146]

It is the German way of curbing charges, which in the case of a *Sicherungsübereignung* give a preference, in principle, as at the moment of the original agreement, even if it involves future debt and assets. Others, like the Dutch and the French, continue to insist on a greater measure of individualisation of the debt and the assets here, or require, in respect of the assignment of future claims for funding purposes, that the contract out of which they arise already exists. In any event, they limit more generally the possibility of the charge shifting into manufactured replacement goods and sales proceeds. French law also protects the appearance of creditworthiness, thus guarding against secret charges and revindication rights, in particular.[147]

In the USA, there is a possibility of avoiding early perfection at the expense of others on the basis of good faith, and equitable subordination under the Bankruptcy Code (Section 510) as we shall see in section 1.6 below. In Germany, the impact of the *gute Sitten* may exceptionally limit the reach of the *Sicherungsübereignung*. It could conceivably also limit any right of the parties to create a real conditional transfer instead especially in order to obtain an appropriation right in bankruptcy to circumvent creating a mere preference only and to gain also any overvalue, but, as just mentioned, there does not seem to be much concern on this point.[148] The intent of the parties dominates. The modern repurchase agreement in respect of investment securities could be characterised as an example of such a conditional sale and appropriation facility in a bankruptcy of the seller.

Finally, the German approach to the limitation of proprietary rights generally needs to be considered. The granting of *in rem* rights (or an *Anwartschaft*) to the buyer under a reservation of title, the construction of the *Sicherungsübereignung praeter legem* and its development in case law, the extension of the priority into converted assets and proceeds by mere contractual enhancement of the reservation of title or *Sicherungsübereignung*, the possibility of true conditional ownership with a dual ownership structure, and the modern German approach to the trust or *Treuhand*,[149] all suggest flexibility.[150] Even if parties may not directly change the possibilities here, it is generally accepted that customary law may.[151]

---

[146] BGH, 30 Apr. 1959, *BGHZ* 30, 149(1959), pursuant to Section 138(1) BGB: see earlier also RGH, 9 Apr. 1932, *RGHZ*136, 247 (1932). It may disallow the bank's older priority if the client would be forced to disclose it to his suppliers who may refuse to deal with him if their own extended reservation of title would be in danger. It may also be seen as an instance in which the specific assignment of the future sale proceeds (upon the condition of which the supplier is willing to allow the resale of his goods) prevails over any earlier general assignment of any present and future goods and receivables arising out of their on-sale. As a matter of policy, it is clear that suppliers receive here an extra protection at the expense of the bank in order not to interrupt the ordinary course of business.

[147] See for the Netherlands the text at n 50. *supra* and for France n 84 *supra* and accompanying text.

[148] See also Quack, n 120 *supra*, 90.

[149] See the text at n 74 *supra*.

[150] To this list may be added the *in rem* effect of a contractual prohibition of an assignment regardless of Section 137 BGB: see BGH, 14 Oct. 1963, *BGHZ* 40, 156 (1963), the German Supreme Court concluding that the prohibition was an innate part of the claim and not an addition or separate element thereof which would have been ineffective under Section 139 BGB.

[151] See Saecker, n 120 *supra*, 1363, who notes that Section 161 BGB does not decisively indicate that conditional ownership entails a split ownership right. In Germany the underlying agreement may be unconditional whilst the transfer is not: see BGH, 9 July 1975, *BGHZ* 64, 395 (1975). It goes back to the German concept of *dingliche Einigung* and the principle of abstraction: see also n 127 *supra*. It is also possible in a reservation of title so that this reservation may be introduced at the moment of the transfer only: see Westermann, n 120 *supra*, 125. As mentioned in n 58 *supra*, Dutch law does not follow this approach and sees the conditionality of the underlying agreement as the cause of the conditionality of the ownership, Articles 3.38 io 3.84(4) CC.

Compare the analysis of former US law in s 1.7 *infra* for the lack of elaboration of the position of both owners in a dual or conditional ownership situation in Germany.

Yet, for conditional sales the split ownership right and the resulting duality in the ownership still remain largely unexplained and the relative rights of both parties unanalysed.

Another important aspect of the modern devices, particularly the *Sicherungsübereignung*, is the application of the test of good morals (*gute Sitten*) to the use of the device and the determination of its rank when conflicts arise.[152] This also underlines the flexible public policy approach to third party effect. It may be an important application of the principle of good faith in proprietary matters.

1.5   The Situation in the UK

1.5.1   Introduction: Differences from Civil Law

There are a number of important aspects in which the common law is traditionally different from the continental civil law in the areas of law under discussion. In the USA, through Article 9 of the UCC, as we shall see, some convergence with the continental European tradition took place in the area of secured transactions in chattels and intangible assets, a development which left English law unaffected:

(a)   The essence is that common law — and this is also true in the USA, possibly even more so there — is used to future interests, not only in land but also in chattels, such interests having proprietary protection and being transferable as property rights. The reverters and remainders are the traditional types and the most important examples.

(b)   Furthermore, in England, the traditional mortgage, which like the Roman law hypothec may still be created in chattels as a non-possessory interest, entails a transfer of ownership subject to a duty of the transferor to repay the purchase price at a certain date. Upon such repayment, the ownership right automatically reverts, but with a right of redemption for him to do so later if he cannot repay in time. The common law mortgage (also in land) is not therefore a typical security interest but remains structured like a conditional sale with proprietary effect, resulting in an (*in rem*) reversion right for the seller or mortgagor. It is not uncommon either to see a trust construction emerge here under which trustees will hold the property for a certain purpose, in this case the return of the advance. The owner may even convert himself into a trustee for this purpose. Reference is often made in such situations to an equitable mortgage. Again, the result is some split ownership and not a security interest proper.

(c)   English law is relaxed about the possibility of appropriation of full title upon default which the conditional sale approach entails. This may give the ultimate owner a windfall if the asset increases in value, but he is also expected to release his defaulting counterparty if there is a shortfall. That is the other side of the conditional sale. There is no fundamental emphasis on an execution or supervised sale with a return of the overvalue, even under the equitable charges (see below) which are much more in the nature of a (non-possessory) pledge as true security interests. However, the courts will strictly enforce and favour the redemption right for chattel mortgages as well, even for an uncertain period.

---

[152] See n 146 *supra*.

This equity of redemption is not implied in other types of conditional sales, as in reservation of title and hire purchases and finance sales.

(d)   English law makes a fundamental distinction between (i) loan credit, (ii) sales credit, and (iii) finance sales. In this connection it distinguishes sharply between loan agreements and late payment agreements. The former commonly give rise to mortgage arrangements or secured transactions, the latter to protection through retention or reservation of title, or hire purchase arrangements. The mortgage is set up as a type of conditional transfer subject to the equity of redemption; and the reservation of title and the hire purchase are set up as delayed or other types of conditional title transfers without this equity. In this regard, English law is fairly flexible about the way parties go about their affairs and readily accepts that they may make alternative or substitute arrangements to avoid what they consider to be the undesirable legal consequences of any of them. As a consequence, if a conditional sale of chattels is preferred to raise money instead of taking out a loan on the security of the same assets (even if only to avoid a registration), then the law will not normally go behind the parties' intent and will not consider their structure illegal *per se* or a sham. Only if there is a mortgage to secure a loan, the equity of redemption cannot be circumvented.

(e)   In connection with secured transactions proper, common law, at least in England, requires neither a great deal of identification of the assets nor specification of the debt they secure. It is not averse either to secured interests shifting into manufactured goods and proceeds. In fact it normally assumes that they do, at least in all equitable charges except where otherwise agreed, an approach which is backed by the equitable notion of tracing. This is probably the most fundamental difference from the civil law approach. It is less certain whether this liberal attitude also applies to mortgages as borne out by bills of sale (which are registered chattel mortgages, see below), or whether it applies to other types of conditional sales, like reservation of title, without additional arrangements being made in the contract to the effect, which may themselves amount to the creation of bills of sale or security interests.

(f)   Even in respect of chattels and intangibles, non-possessory securities, including the chattel mortgage and the floating charge, are, under English law, subject to a wide ranging system of registration. Yet this system is fractured and different types of registrations may mean different things and may have different consequences. It does not apply to finance sales.

Scottish law has very different features and remains in essence based on received Roman law (*ius commune*). Even though it has accepted the floating charge by statute since 1961, and the reservation of title through case law, the latter is explicitly not as a security interest. Scottish law remains fundamentally opposed to any non-possessory security interest in chattels,[153] an attitude mostly respected by the House of Lords, which is also the supreme appeal court for Scotland.[154]

---

[153] *Cf* Voet, *Commentarius ad Pandectas*, 20.1.12, although not followed by the Dutch Supreme Court at the time, see HR, 13 Nov 1737, in Van Bynkershoek, IV *Observationes Timultariae*, (Haarlem 1962), [189–85]. The House of Lords in *North Western Bank v Poynter* [1895] AC 56, no 3051. All ER 754 allowed a certain relaxation if the pledgee returned the goods to the pledgor for certain limited purposes.

[154] See in particular *Armour and Others v Thyssen Edelstahlwerke AG* [1990] All ER 481.

1.5.2   Basic Features of Conditional or Split Ownership Interests. Equitable and Floating Charges. Open System of Proprietary Rights

It may be useful briefly to expand on the above mentioned features of the Common law as still operating in England. First the question of conditional or future interests, that is the issue of their proprietary effect, even if these interests are merely contingent. Common Law has long accepted these interests, provided that, if contingent, they do not go on too long together, hence the application of the law against perpetuities.[155] The main principles of the law of conditional or future interests were first developed in respect of land. Besides the fee simple, the life interests and the estates for years or leaseholds, there thus arose conditional or future interests like reversionary interests or remainders, either vested or contingent depending on the conditions attached.

However, these notions were mostly also made applicable to chattels even though then only equitable. This means that their protection is largely based on the exercise of power in or over the asset in an economic sense giving a more limited proprietary interest. These rights may be freely created, but their third party effect is limited, as *bona fide* purchasers from the title holder are protected. In England, these future interests in chattels are now mostly hidden in trust arrangements as the law is more specific in this area. Therefore, the subject of future interests in chattels receives less attention. This is different in the USA.

Therefore, the principal consequence of these rights being equitable is that *bona fide* purchasers of the legal interest in chattels are generally protected against these future or beneficial interests. Protection of *bona fide* third party purchasers is otherwise not generally available under common law but is, on the other hand, also available against future interests in intangibles (and land) which have no counterpart in civil law (except in some countries, like Germany, in respect of errors in land registers).

The approach of split, conditional or future interests in this manner, supported by a variety of actions, highlights at least for chattels an underlying concern of the common law with user, possession or retention rights and their duration. In this system better rights rather than absolute rights are the basis for proprietary protection. Physical possession (mostly in bailment)[156] or user rights are strongly protected, often more than ownership.

This contrasts with the Roman or civil law system of more abstract absolute rights in the property — rights maintainable against all the world in terms of ownership, of which legal possession is the appearance and holdership the physical expression: see for these concepts more in particular chapter IV, section 1.2.2. In civil law, physical holdership, legal possession and ownership are thus interconnected and allow for increasing levels of protection for the interest holder. Limited proprietary rights, like usufructs and secured interests, are, in this system, seen as derivatives of the ownership right which eventually submerge again in it when the entitlement lapses and allow themselves for ownership, legal possession and holdership of those limited rights. The importance of legal possession (besides its own protection) is the possibility of acquiring ownership on the basis of it through acquisitive prescription.

It shows the principal (theoretical) differences between the common and civil law of property, and especially the different function of possession. In truth, however, the concept

---

[155] See for England, the still classic treatise of FH Lawson, *Introduction to the Law of Property* (Oxford, 1958), 65*ff* and 134*ff*, revised in a second edition by Bernard Rudden. *Cf* S Worthington, *Proprietary Interests in Commercial Transactions* (1996).
[156] See chapter IV, s 1.3.2 and also n 199 *infra*.

of physical possession (of chattels) and its protection (usually through tort actions) is not very different in either system. In practice in civil law this crucial user facility also depends on better rather than on absolute rights, as is shown by the protection the *bona fide* purchaser of chattels who obtains physical possession: see further chapter IV, section 1.3.7.

It is clear that in civil law the proprietary protection against third parties is on the increase, and that non-owners in physical possession are normally able to protect their position against all parties except the true owners, as if they were the owners. Even the proprietary protection of mere physical holdership against third parties through possessory actions has been advocated in civil law and is indeed accepted in Germany.[157] It marks a return to the more Germanic concepts of possession, abandoned on the Continent since Grotius' return to Roman law thinking in this area, but still at the heart of the common law where there is no such concept as absolute title.[158] In any event, protection of holdership through tort actions is now largely accepted, also in civil law, and a holder is therefore no longer fully dependent on the owner for this protection.

The difference is that, in civil law (unlike in common law), such an action can only be brought against a tortfeasor and not against any third parties who in the meantime have obtained the asset from the latter (assuming that this person is not protected as a *bona fide* purchaser). Also in the event of the bankruptcy of the tortfeasor, the physical holder without proprietary protection has a weak position in civil law and may have to rely on the owner to re-establish his holdership. The possessor in common law may be better off here, although it should be remembered that in the case of chattels, common law allows no true revindication right. Moreover, at least in England, the courts may exercise discretion so that the wrongful possessor usually has an option to pay damages rather than return the asset.[159]

It remains true, however, that the common law of property operates a much more fractured system of proprietary rights and does not think systematically on the subject. However, notions of proprietary or third party effect, ownership and possession, their protection and transferability, priorities in the assets or proceeds in an execution or bankruptcy which are substantially elaborated in civil law are no less known to common law.

Yet, thinking in terms of a system of proprietary rights, and especially of a closed system, is alien to traditional common law, although it admits only two proprietary rights in chattels: ownership and possession (or bailment). But there are also the equitable rights in them, including those of trust beneficiaries, and the trust deed can cut the ownership and users' right in almost any way the settlor wants (except as curtailed in the statutes against perpetuities).

Thus, in common law, ownership can be split almost at will, subject to the rights of *bona fide* purchasers of the legal title only. The effect of terms and conditions, and the difference between them, is basic to this system. Reversions or remainders, if accruing to lives already

---

[157] See HCF Schoordijk, 'Enige opmerkingen over de bescherming van bezitters en houders' (1984) [Some observations on the protection of legal possessors and holders], in HCF Schoordijk, *Assorted Works* 447. It means that only someone who is holder pursuant to a contractual right may still defend this right as his asset or property right *vis-à-vis* third parties. The new Dutch Civil Code does not generally go this far but does award the retentor - that is the person who may retain the property for cause, e.g. because he has not been paid for the repairs — exceptionally this position: see Article 3.295 CC.

[158] See Lord Diplock in *Ocean Estates Ltd v Pinder*, [1969] 2 AC 19.

[159] In England this discretion to order specific relief was eventually vested in the courts in Section 78 of the Common Law Procedure Act 1854, now superseded by Section 3(2) of the Torts (Interference with Goods) Act 1977.

in being whilst not made dependent on the person of the beneficiary, are deemed subject to a term. All other future interests are subject to a condition. Neither is retroactive whilst the various resulting proprietary interests coexist with each other.[160]

This sets the scene for the discussion. The common law mortgage fits into this scenario in a particular manner. It is a transfer of ownership, therefore a transfer of title, and does not create a security interest in the transferee of either immovable or movable (including intangible) property, who will have advanced a sum of money against this transfer. This sum of money is likely to be related to the value of the asset although like a purchase price, therefore unlikely to represent this value in full. The sale is conditional and the asset will automatically reconvey to the transferor upon repayment of the advance and the agreed interest.[161] The transferor therefore retains a conditional or future interest in the asset. This interest is, in principle, transferable, for which common law does not even require transfer of possession.[162]

The conditional ownership right of the transferor or mortgagor is reinforced by his *right of redemption*. This gives him the possibility of reclaiming the asset upon offering full payment even after the term for repayment has expired and is not itself limited in time, at least for chattels, and will be granted as long as reasonable, whilst in normal circumstances the courts are greatly in favour of this right. There is thus no execution sale or repayment of any overvalue, although the transferee may cut the redemption possibility short to avoid undesirable uncertainty about the redemption possibility, by conducting a sale upon court order, under any contractual power of sale, or by asking the court for foreclosure,[163] which is here known as judicial appropriation[164] with a release of the debtor for any undervalue.

---

[160] It may be of some interest that in the USA the idea has been expressed that proprietary interests in goods are, under the UCC, specifically limited in order to promote the free flow of goods: see JF Dolan, 'The UCC Framework: Conveyancing Principles and Property Interests', 59 *Boston University Law Review* 828 (1979). The conveyance is considered similarly limited to produce only the allowed proprietary rights identified as title, the special property interest of 2 UCC, the security interest and the lien. To this could be added the special interests of lessor and lessee in an equipment lease under the new Article 2A UCC: see also L Harris, 'The Rights of Creditors under Article 2A', 39 *Alabama Law Review* (1988), 803. The basic conveyance principles are considered to be the *nemo dat* rule and its two exceptions: the protection of the *bona fide* purchaser and the purchaser in the ordinary course of business of someone entrusted with the goods by the original owner. In this connection, it was said that the acknowledged four property interests along with the three principles of conveyancing form the analytical framework of the entire Code.

[161] Interestingly, the common law mortgage was compared to the repurchase facility under Justininan Roman Law (C.4.54.2, see nn 80 and 122 *supra* and accompanying text) in the 1749 case of *Ryall v Rolle* [1558–1774] All ER 82, and notably not to the Roman hypothec which was not considered to give a similar property interest to the transferee.

[162] See Section 17 of the Sale of Goods Act 1979. It may also be construed as a sale of the equity of redemption: see text below and *Thomas v Searles* [1891] 2 QB 408. It may even be considered a second sale of the original full interest by a seller still in possession. In this latter case, the buyer's protection depends on his *bona fides*: see Section 24 of the Sales of Goods Act.

[163] Foreclosure allows title to vest in the transferee (or mortgagee) unconditionally. In both these cases of a judicial sale or a foreclosure, the surplus is appropriated by the transferee, which is the reason the courts may seek to delay them to allow for the redemption to take place and may give only a provisional authorisation (a decree nisi) setting a further redemption period for the mortgagor. On the other hand, if the mortgagee takes this route, the mortgagor is released from his debt should there be undervalue: see also RM Goode, *Commercial Law* (London, 2nd ed. 1995), 692. In a private sale conducted under a contractual power of sale, the mortgagee is bound to return any overvalue to subsequent and lower ranking mortgagees or to the mortgagor; alternatively he may, in the case of land, appoint a receiver to exploit the property using the income to pay off the mortgage: see Lawson, n 155 *supra*, 162.

[164] The transferee lacking possession was vulnerable to charges of reputed ownership of the transferor and could thereby be deprived of his appropriation rights in bankruptcy, a typical bankruptcy concept in personal bankruptcy now abandoned in England and never adopted in the USA: see n 85 *supra* plus accompanying text.

Earlier the Statute of Frauds of 1677 had tried to curb non-possessory interests in tangible assets by requiring writing. In this connection, constructive delivery is possible in respect of assets under third parties like custodians

The other feature of the mortgage is that it does not depend on actual possession. This distinguishes it from the pledge but relates it to equitable charges,[165] notably *floating charges*, which, like the pledge, are otherwise much more in the nature of a true security interest[166] with an implied power of sale upon default subject to the return of any over-value. Under common law though, the pledge as a possessory instrument may also be created through mere constructive possession, usually through the use of a third party bailee.[167] One of the key elements of the mortgage will thus be that the transferor remains in physical possession, although without power to dispose.

Under the Statute of Frauds of 1677, abolished in England in 1954, transfer of (constructive) possession was one way of creating a sale by way of a mortgage. The non-possessory mortgage is, however, more likely to be created by deed or, especially for

or bailees, but the transfer requires in those cases the consent of the holder. This is attornment: see *Farina v Home*, 153 ER 1124 (1846), retained in Section 29(4) of the Sale of Goods Act in the UK, even if for the transfer of chattels delivery is no longer required. In the USA, where it is, the old English case law remains relevant.

The legal suspicion of secret interests went back further to *Twyne's Case*, 76 ER 809 (1601) in which a debtor sold all his goods to one of his creditors but retained possession. In this case the Star Chamber accepted that this sale was not *bona fide* but was meant to defraud his other creditors. It is the origin of the law against fraudulent conveyances in common law which subsequently became statutory law, but the notion of apparent or reputed ownership did not completely disappear until the UK Insolvency Act of 1986: see n 81 *supra* and accompanying text.

In the USA, the reputed ownership notion was not introduced but the question of ostensible ownership remained an issue. Retrieval rights upon default in sales are discouraged in the USA, probably for these reasons: see chapter IV, s 1.5.7. Modern filing requirements for non-possessory security interests, especially under Article 9 UCC, have alleviated the problem in respect of such interests, but the other side of this filing is that non-filed proprietary interests in chattels may become subordinated, creating a windfall for any secured creditor under Article 9. See for this problem and the impact of filing, chapter IV, s 1.6.6.

[165] Equitable charges arise when a person *promises* to set aside certain goods for a particular purpose including the satisfaction of debt when a trust structure is deemed to have been created. They are always non-possessory. A particular asset may thus be designated to the discharge of the indebtedness, the debt being set off against the sale proceeds of the asset. The sale may result from the debtor's voluntary act, the execution of the contract if including a power of sale, or from a court order made upon the request of the chargee. The commonest and most all-embracing is the *floating charge* which may cover a whole business including real estate usually created by a contract called a debenture. Their importance is mainly derived from their shift to replacement goods and proceeds, so that money may be advanced on the security of future cash flow.

The technique has generally been upheld in case law since the end of the nineteenth century: see *Government Stock v Manila Rail* Co. [1897] AC 81; *Re Yorkshire Woolcombers Associations Ltd* [1903] 2 chap. 284 and *Illingworth v Houldsworth* [1904] AC 355. Their weakness is that these non-possessory charges do not crystallise into a fixed charge until default and it is only at that time that they derive their rank, which is therefore very low and may induce the chargee also to solicit fixed charges on individual assets, e.g. real estate, within the floating charge. They normally allow the chargee, usually a bank, to appoint an administrator to conduct its own type of liquidation outside bankruptcy. This is not traditionally considered an insolvency procedure as it involves only one creditor. See for the equitable mortgage n 169 *infra*.

The promise to set aside may create the charge. It implies that the chargee does *not* receive *control* of the assets. Should he do so, the charge would be fixed. Control or sufficient control is the difference between fixed and floating charges, which may not always be easy to distinguish. Control of the chargee leaves the chargor with less freedom to dispose of the asset. In this connection, a contractual requirement of consent to disposal may already imply sufficient control of the chargee. This may be sufficient also in receivable financing or securitisations and a contractual prohibition of any further assignments without the chargee's consent may thus create a fixed charge in the receivables.

It is to be noted that the Law Commission in its 2002 Consultation Paper No 164 on Registration of Security Interests: Company Charges and Property Other than Land, proposes and advance filing system along the lines of Article 9 UCC, see for the American system section 1.6.1 *infra* and for a critique chapter IV s 1.6.6. The main importance of the English proposal is in the ranking of floating charges which is proposed to relate back to the date of filing. Consequently the distinction between fixed and floating charges will disappear in the aspect of priority whilst the notion of cristallisation becomes irrelevant.

[166] The pledge, mostly in the form of a pawn, is for small debts regulated under the Pawnbrokers Acts 1872–1960 and otherwise follows common law principles.

[167] *Dublin City Distillery v Doherty* [1914] AC 823. This mere transfer *constituto possessorio* was particularly curtailed under continental European law: see the text at n 5 *supra*, but not in England. See for the Scottish law development n 154 *supra* with accompanying text.

movables or chattels, by 'some other note or memorandum'. Since 1854 it has for chattels required registration (with the Royal Courts of Justice in London) as a bill of sale under the Bills of Sale Act, unless it is given by corporations.[168] In fact, the Act covers any document giving someone other than the owner (except if corporate) a legal or equitable right to the goods, entitling that person to seize or take possession of the goods in certain circumstances. The term 'chattel mortgage' as distinguished from 'bills of sale' is now normally reserved for mortgages created in personal property in the corporate sphere by (constructive) delivery or in registered chattels, like ships and aircraft, or for mortgages.

An important consequence of the 1854 Act was that the transfer of the chattels into a non-possessory mortgage in the personal non-corporate sphere no longer takes place as an ordinary sale of goods under the Sale of Goods Act, but through a registered document (a bill of sale) under the Bills of Sale Act. This does not affect its character as a conditional sale and transfer[169] but it is relevant as the mortgagee under the Bills of Sale Act does not have the protection for the *bona fide* purchaser of Section 24 of the Sale of Goods Act. On the other hand, it means that the mortgagee is protected against later mortgagees of the same asset even if they are *bona fide* (regardless of the registration, as long as they are not aware of it; they are not assumed to have knowledge and do not have a search duty).

Appropriation or forfeiture upon default is a normal feature of the common law mortgage, which only became mitigated by the all-important equitable right of redemption, as equity was said to abhor forfeiture. It should be noted that in this respect common law did not have anything like the basic civil law principle of an execution sale, a supervised sale

---

[168] The original Act was of 1854–66 repealed by the Act of 1878 as amended in 1882, 1890, 1891. The effect of the Act has been severely to limit the use of the chattel mortgage as a non-possessory instrument in the personal sphere. It became a facility mainly solicited by all kinds of moneylenders and obtained a bad reputation until the Moneylenders Act of 1900, amended in 1927 and now largely repealed.

The Act made money lending other than through recognised banks subject to an annual licence and imposed strict conditions on moneylending contracts. The combined effect of both Acts (together with Section 4 of the amendment to the Bill of Sales Act of 1882 which imposed the requirement of specificity of the assets being set aside) was virtually to end floating charges in the private sphere. Combined with the reputed ownership doctrine, see nn 85 and 164 *supra*, they also discouraged reservations of title.

This led to greater emphasis on other types of conditional sales, especially on hire purchase, which under the Hire Purchase Act 1965 is virtually implied in all conditional sales if used to raise finance in the private sphere like any lease with an automatic right or option to acquire the full ownership of the asset after all instalments are paid. This latter Act particularly remedied the vulnerable position of the original transferor under a conditional sale of movables because of the protection of *bona fide* purchasers from the transferee under Section 9 of the Factors Act and Section 25(2) of the Sale of Goods Act by defining the transferee as a hirer rather than an owner which leaves *bona fide* purchasers from him unprotected. They must return the goods to the transferor or pay damages if the assets revert to the latter under the conditions set: see also *Wickham Holdings Ltd v Brooke House Motors Ltd*, [1967] 1 All ER 117. This rule does not apply in the motor trade and does not necessarily deprive the hire purchase of its nature of a conditional sale for other purposes.

[169] It was mentioned above in the text that the trust may also be used to create what is in essence an equitable mortgage under which the mortgagor may transform himself into a trustee and hold the asset for the benefit of the person or institution giving the advance. In England this is the normal way of achieving a mortgage in future goods or interests or of creating a second mortgage in the same asset, is in fact mortgaging a beneficial interest, the equity of redemption. The result is a weak right subject to the protection of *bona fide* purchasers of the goods even when actually obtained by the mortgagor: see *Joseph v Lyons* (1884) 15 QBD 280. In England the equitable character of this mortgage does not prevent it from being a bill of sale subject to registration (this registration does not itself deprive any bona fide purchaser from his protections, as there is no search duty).

This type of equitable mortgage is still very common in the USA for real estate, and remains in England a different way of achieving a similar result besides the creation of a mortgage often for 999 years as an estate in land and the charge by way of a legal mortgage under the Law of Property Act 1925. In the USA, the trustee conducts a sale upon default but the right of redemption (in those states that retain it instead of a public execution sale) is reinstituted upon any sale so conducted. It is only another way of splitting the ownership with a similar objective and notably does not create a security interest.

with a return of any excess value. The approach was only introduced into several US states by statute, and it subsequently became one of the main features of Article 9 UCC.[170] In civil law, the mortgagee has only a limited proprietary right. It is always subject to an execution sale and there is never any appropriation.[171]

In England, a similar attitude prevails for the pledge and for equitable charges, which are all in the nature of security interests (and not therefore conditional sales) although, as in Roman law,[172] the execution sale need not be judicially conducted or supervised. Any excess value is returned to the debtor. This does not strictly apply to the mortgage (which is subject to the equity of redemption), or to any other type of conditional sale,[173] and the pledge and the equitable charges may even be superseded by other arrangements in the contract. As already mentioned, in the case of the mortgage, the trade-off in England is that although the mortgagee may retain the overvalue, he surrenders any claim for undervalue if he chooses appropriation.[174]

1.5.3 The Distinction between Conditional Sales and Secured Transactions: Publication Requirements

This leads to discussion of the distinction between conditional sales and security interests. Professor Goode, in his well known book on commercial law, sees a fundamental difference under English law between loan and sales credit.[175] That English law makes this distinction is probably pragmatic and also eases the problems connected with the

---

[170] See for the civil law approach in the Netherlands, Article 3.248*ff* CC, in France, Article 2078 (first paragraph) Cc and in Germany, Sections 1234*ff* BGB. See for the situation in the USA, SA Riesenfeld, *Creditors' Remedies and Debtors' Protection* (3rd edn, 1979), 149.

[171] Under late Roman law, appropriation (and a clause to the effect in the contract) was strictly forbidden since a decree of the Emperor Constantine, repeated in C 8.34.3: see also n 55 *supra*. It remains the underlying attitude in civil law, although the clause (or *lex commissoria*) is effective in the case of a failed sale agreement in some countries, notably in the Netherlands at least as long as entered into by the parties as a contractual condition and is then also operative in the bankruptcy of the defaulting buyer leading to revindication rights. Other civil law countries do not go that far, however: see for the situation in France, Article 2078 (second paragraph) Cc and n 108 *supra*, in Germany Section 1229 BGB and n 123 *supra*.

[172] In Roman law, the principle of a supervised sale with the return of any excess value (*superfluum*) to the creditor only gradually developed and in this respect Roman law is closer to common law than to modern civil law. Originally, appropriation seems to have been the normal practice at least under the possessory pledge or *pignus*, unless there was a clause to the contrary (*pactum de vendendo*). Under Justinian law, such a clause was always deemed implicit, D 13.7.4, whilst a redemption right after the normal repayment period and sale could also be agreed, even allowing the debtor to retrieve the asset from the buyer at the latter's purchase price: see D 13.7.13 and also M Kaser, *Römisches Privatrecht* [Roman Private Law] (Munich, 14th edn, 1986), s 31, 146; see further F de Zulueta, *The Institutes of Gaius* (Oxford, 1953), Part II, 75.

Yet it left room for alternative arrangements short of the (later) forbidden appropriation: see n 171 *supra*. In the non-possessory security or in the earlier non-possessory fiduciary transfers, the situation may have been different as the creditor did not acquire possession so that appropriation would have been more difficult. Special sales provisions in the underlying agreement were then all the more appropriate and necessary.

[173] The question when any other type of conditional sale is created rather than a mortgage was the subject of the early case of *Becket v Towers Assets Co* [1891] 1 QB 1. One of the key elements appears to be that in the mortgage there is a duty to redeem rather than some option to repurchase under the conditions stated. Although the result may be the same upon the exercise of the option, the parties' intention decides whether there is a registrable mortgage (bill of sale) or any other type of conditional sale. A similar borderline issue to be decided on the basis of intent may arise between the pledge when subject to constructive delivery only and the (non-possessory) chattel mortgage as a bill of sale which requires registration: see *Sewell v Burdick* (1884) 10 AC 74. In fact, possession itself does not necessarily signify a pledge either but could also be part of a chattel mortgage or an equitable charge. Again it is the intention that is decisive and it is certainly not possible to be a pledgee, mortgagee and chargee at the same time: see Goode, n 163 *supra*, 666.

[174] See n 163 *supra*.

[175] See n 163 *supra*, 637, 646.

difference between charges and sale protection. It has been defined in a line of cases starting with *Re George Inglefield Ltd*[176] and ending for the time being with the Court of Appeal's decision in *Welsh Development Agency Ltd v Export Finance Co (Exfinco)*.[177]

A loan is a payment of money to a borrower, upon terms that the sum advanced together with the agreed interest will be repaid, mostly at a date certain. It may be supported by security in the debtor's assets. Bank loans and bank real estate mortgages, but also overdrafts, credit card and similar arrangements, fall into the category of loan credit. Credit sales, on the other hand, involve payment deferment which may take the form of a simple contractual concession, or part of wider schemes like installment sales or hire purchases; reservation of title arrangements are also likely to be in this class. There is normally no agreed interest-rate structure here and therefore no loan proper. However there may be a form of proprietary protection as in the case of a reservation of title.

The English courts have always considered both types of credit (loan and sales), as essentially different. Thus, legislation concerning lending (and usury) has never been applied to deferred payment arrangements, installment sales, hire purchases and reservation of title or other forms of purchase money arrangements and sales credit. This is also true for the application of the Bills of Sale Act. The natural progression from here is to conclude that only true loans can give rise to secured transactions proper with disposition duties and the return of overvalue to the debtor or to mortgage arrangements as conditional sales with the equity of redemption as the basic protection for lenders. These safeguards for the debtor do not apply to credit sales arrangements like reservation of title, which are also conditional, or to deferred sales, as there is no loan credit. The next step is to accept that all conditional sales of assets (like repurchase agreements and the sale-leaseback) do not have these safeguards for the conditional seller either, even those used to raise funding (which do not have a loan structure, as no agreed interest rate is being applied to the original sale proceeds given to the conditional seller). Conditional sales have other types of rewards and attractions for the parties. They are not considered to be secured loans and do not give the person receiving the funding the normal secured loan benefits in terms of a return of any overvalue or an equity of redemption upon default. Upon default, they lead to appropriation of full title by the conditional buyer, who is entitled to the overvalue as part of the deal.

Thus, deferred payment clauses may lead to property-based protection for the seller of the goods, like deferred and conditional sales, of which hire purchase and reservation of title could be considered prime examples. However, they do not normally lead to special protection for the defaulting debtor in terms of an execution sale and return of overvalue. Upon rescission of the underlying agreement because of default, there would be a personal action for the return of the installment payments only (after deduction of any claims for damages). The same applies to repurchase agreements and other types of conditional sales used to raise funding. Only in the mortgage, which, as explained above, developed in England as a conditional sale, is there a case for giving some special protection to the debtor as there is normally a loan structure. It may then be more readily (and rightly) equated with and treated as a security or charge than the reservation of title,[178] in which context the equity of redemption is appropriate.

---

[176] [1933] chap 1.
[177] BCC 270 (1992), see also F Oditah, 'Financing Trade Credit; *Welsh Development Agency v Exfino*' [1992] *Journal of Business Law* 541.
[178] See for the question when a reservation of title might be considered a charge, the text at n 194 *infra*.

The differences in the treatment of the resulting protection, in terms of security or ownership-based devices, does not prevent parties making use of ownership-based (instead of security-based) funding, even in situations which may have greater similarity with the granting of a loan. In fact, ownership-based funding may be used to avoid the limitations imposed on security-based funding, either by law or by contract. Thus when under a floating charge, receivables may not be allowed to be pledged any further, they may still be sold subject to a reversion when a sufficient amount is collected under them by the financier/buyer of the receivables. It is the essence of factoring, at least in this case, more properly considered a conditional sale.

Common law in England is *not* normally inclined to go behind the preference of the parties and re-characterise their arrangement. More generally, it will not deem a secured transaction, chattel mortgage or similar secured arrangement to have been created instead. Even if the clear intention may have been merely to avoid contractual restrictions or even registration under the Bills of Sale or Companies Act.[179]

The choice is usually considered a matter of business judgement between professional parties to be respected by the courts. Nothing else should be put in its place,[180] although even then there are limits and mere shams are avoided.[181] English law will thus accept that selling property to raise funds, even if subject to a repurchasing right or duty, is in essence different from raising a loan on the security of the same assets.

In the first case, there are likely to be fewer protections. Also, there is appropriation upon default without a possibility of redemption or other safeguards in terms of an execution sale and return of any overvalue to the seller. There is another agreed balance of benefits and costs, and the contract may elaborate on them without any dangers of re-characterisation of the structure as a secured loan situation. Only when there is an agreed interest reward (and not all types of other fees) besides the return of the principal is there by law also a return of any overvalue or an equity of redemption. In England, in the case of a foreclosure of this equity of redemption, the debtor is released if the assets have been reduced in market value in the meantime. It is the parties' choice and financier's risk.

In modern English case law, however, there is some evidence that for property-based protection not leading to the presumption of secured lending, a (registrable) bill of sale, or a company charge, the emphasis would have to be on the seller not retaining any proprietary interest in the property, in terms of an automatic reversion or any liability for the risks attached to owning the asset. Also the buyer would have to be able to sell on the goods and retain the profits for himself. A similar approach is taken in the USA.[182]

Thus, any automatic return of the (replacement) assets or of the payments received thereon (as in the case of shares or bonds) or any restrictions concerning sale-on would have to be separately agreed and construed. This would be necessary to avoid the sales being considered mere arrangements to curtail the equity of redemption or retain the overvalue, which would in truth suggest a chattel mortgage or charge.[183] However, to look

---

[179] This is quite established law: see *Olds Discount Co Ltd v John Playfair Ltd* [1938] 3 All ER 275 and *Chaw Yoong Hong v Choong Fah Rubber Manufactory* [1962] AC 209. Discounting of bills of exchange is also not considered loan financing in England: see *IRC v Rowntree and Co Ltd* [1948] 1 All ER 482. See for the avoidance of registration duties, *Re Watson* (1890) 25 QBD 27 and *Polsky v S&A Services* [1951] 1 All ER 185 and 1062. In England, the finance lease is not considered a conditional sale if there is no automatic transfer of title upon full performance of the lease agreement or an option to the effect at that time (without the payment of further consideration) and is then merely a bailment. In fact if there is an automatic transfer the finance lease is qualified as a conditional sale rather than a lease and if there is an option as a hire purchase: see Goode, n 163 *supra*, 776.

[180] See *Welsh Development Agency v Exfinco*, cited in n 177 supra.

[181] See *Re George Inglefield*, n 176 *supra*, 17.

[182] See text at n 212 *infra*.

[183] This was often considered the message from *Re George Inglefield Ltd*: see n 176 *supra*.

merely at the arrangements concerning the assets and their return does not appear to be in accordance with English law as it stands.[184] The whole of the transaction needs to be considered.

In this regard, it is fully accepted that a sale is not always a mercantile transaction but may be purely financial (as in the case of futures). Any reference to substance may mean a substance of a different sort.[185] Funds can thus be raised by way of a sale of the underlying assets without borrowing proper. But a reverter plus an agreed interest rate structure as compensation is likely to be indicative of a loan agreement. The arrangement may then be viewed as a (registrable) mortgage or equitable charge, subject to the formalities concerning their creation and the protections of the debtor in terms of the equity of redemption, or repayment of the overvalue.[186]

If, however, there is an agreed interest rate structure, it was submitted that a loan must be presumed, see section 1.1.1 above, and if a security exists even if clad in the form of a conditional sale, it is then likely to be re-qualified as a mortgage or equitable charge subject to its formalities and protections. Finance leases, repurchase agreements and factoring of receivables are therefore not normally secured lending for lack of such an agreed interest rate structure. They are sales of assets, albeit conditional.[187] English law is not likely to deem an interest rate structure if one has not been clearly agreed and other types of fees or charges are not equated with it.

Finally, it may be of interest to look at the various types of registration and their impact in England. There are many registers,[188] registration does not always mean the same thing and each type may attract its own priority regime. Only in respect of bills of sale does

---

[184] See for earlier case law, *Alderson v White*, 2 De G & J 97 (1858) whilst conditionality of ownership clearly does not always imply a security interest or charge, even in the case of a mortgage: see for the sale and repurchase (option) also *Manchester, Sheffield and Lincolnshire Railway Co v North Central Waggon Co* (1888) 13 App Cas 554 and for the sale and repurchase duty, *Lloyds & Scottish Finance Ltd v Cyril Lord Carpet Sales Ltd* (1979) 129 NLJ 366.

[185] *Clough Mill Ltd v Martin* [1985] 1 WLR 111; see much earlier the House of Lords in *McEntire v Crossley Brothers Ltd* [1895] AC 457 in which, with regard to the whole agreement, it was decided that a leasing transaction was a sale and not a registrable charge under the Bill of Sales Act. The use of the term 'security' is in this context not decisive either: see *Siebe Gorman & Co Ltd v Barclays Bank Ltd* [1979] 2 Lloyd's Rep 142.

[186] *Automobile Association (Canterbury) Inc v Australasian Secured Deposits Ltd* [1973] 1 NZLR 417.

[187] See for a further discussion, Goode, n 163 *supra*, 646*ff*. As far as the repurchase agreement of investment securities is concerned, also in England retrieval problems are in practice minimised through contractual netting clauses, the status of which in a bankruptcy of the buyer remained as elsewhere (see for Germany n 141 *supra* and for the USA the text at n 199 *infra*) in some doubt, however, as netting is accepted only if it does not give better rights under Section 323(2) of the Insolvency Act 1986 or for company liquidation under Insolvency Rule 4. 90 (1986), *cf* the *Carreras Rothman* case [1985] All ER 155 and also R Derham, 'Set-off and Netting in the Liquidation of a Counterparty', [1991] *Journal of Business Law* 463, 541 and further the paper of the British Bankers Association (BBA) of 13 Aug 1993 (Circular 93(56)) on the validity of bilateral close out and netting under English law: see also the guidance notice of the City of London Law Panel on Netting of Counterparty Exposure of 19 Nov 1993 (BBA Circular 93 (82)) and further J Walter, 'Close out Netting in English Law: Comfort at Last' [1995] *Butterworths Journal of International Banking and Finance Law*, 167*ff*.

Lord Hoffmann retraced the set-off concept and the *ipso facto* (or automatic) nature of the set-off in bankruptcy in *Stein v Blake* [1995] 2 WLR 710; see also his earlier judgment in *MS Fashions Ltd v BCCI* [1993] chap 425, and emphasised that in bankruptcy the set-off does not require the trustee or creditor to invoke or exercise it. Proof by the creditor is not necessary. Cross-claims therefore are extinct as at the date of bankruptcy and there is by law only a net balance either way. Any supporting charges disappear at the same time as the bankruptcy set-off provides its own form of security. It also includes future claims, claims certain or contingent, liquidated or not, payable or not. When future or contingent claims have become quantifiable since the bankruptcy, the amounts will be treated as having been due at the bankruptcy date, otherwise they are evaluated as under Insolvency Rule 4.86 if the claim is on the debtor. Contingent counterclaims on creditors are not so brought forward and are therefore outside the set-off. The result of the automatic set-of in these terms is that liquidators cannot cherry pick and keep claims outside a bankruptcy set-off.

[188] Goode, n 163 *supra*, 702, refers to 11 different registers for different types of consensual mortgages and charges. The bills of sales register, the companies register and the land register are the most important. See for the 2002 Law Commission proposals (Consultation Paper 164) n 165 *supra in fine*. They cover both floating charges and bills of sale.

non-registration lead to absolute nullity, even *inter partes*. In the other cases the effect of registration, like that of the company (floating) charge,[189] is mainly on the effectiveness of any subsequent outright sale or on the priorities, but as between various mortgagees and chargees registration may not even create the presumption of the absence of their *bona fides*.[190]

1.5.4   Reservation of Title

It is also necessary to give some attention to the recent development of the reservation of title in England. It was technically always possible as a delayed title transfer under Section 19 of the Sale of Goods Act 1979, and under Section 17 of its predecessor of 1893, in a system which in essence transfers title upon consent of the parties, but it was substantially introduced by case law in 1976.[191] In this connection reference is now normally made to *Romalpa* clauses. As elsewhere, the defining line between charges has also been raised in this connection.[192] It now seems well established that once title passes under an extended reservation of title to the buyer, who then retransfers replacement rights in them to the seller, for example upon conversion of the asset into manufactured goods or upon a sale into the proceeds, this may imply an equitable charge, which as such needs registration in the Companies Register.[193] Any agreed extension of the protection into proceeds is likely to be considered a registrable charge also if interest in the proceeds is meant to end only when all outstanding debts have been paid or if the proceeds are insufficient to pay the claims and a claim for the balance remains.[194] It is clear that such charges are not necessarily supporting loans but normally relate to sale credit which introduces an element of confusion.

The accessory nature of the interest, with the automatic shift of the protection to any succeeding owner of the claim it supports and the automatic release of the asset upon payment of the sale price, does not appear to play a similar fundamental role in common law to the one it does in civil law. It is not commonly seen as an essential element or an indication of a security interest as distinguished from a conditional sale. In recent case law, it may have played a role, however, in assuming a security interest if the accessory right was contractually introduced.[195] Indeed it may also be so in the civil law of conditional sales and

---

[189] See Section 298 of the Companies Act 1986.

[190] See also text following n 169 *supra*.

[191] *Aluminium Industrie Vaassen BV v Romalpa Aluminium Ltd*, [1976] 2 All ER 552. Arguments against the effect of the reservation of title on the basis of reputed ownership of the buyer in possession subsided and are even less relevant in England after deletion of the concept in the Insolvency Act of 1986: see n 85 *supra*.

[192] Almost from the beginning the *Romalpa* case gave rise to controversy as it also covered converted assets and proceeds. This requires specific stipulation, and is not considered automatic: see *Borden (UK) Ltd v Scottish Timber* [1979] 3 All ER 961, and would for its effectiveness have required registration under the Companies Act (Section 395) if intended to attach to a multitude of unspecified goods so that it may become a floating charge, whilst this would also seem to be necessary if the (extended) reservation of title is meant to cover debt other than the sales credit: see the Irish case of *Re Interview Ltd*, [1973] IR 382, except (probably) if it concerns identified assets in which title is reserved even in respect of sister-company debt.

Any right to pursue the protection into the balances of the buyer's accounts is also problematic, but the buyer is usually considered here an agent or bailee of the seller, at least as long as he is under a duty to separate the proceeds and accepts a fiduciary duty in connection with their distribution: see also *Chase Manhattan Bank v Israel British Bank* [1979] 3 All ER 1025, although it has now also been held that this fiduciary relationship may itself be indicative of a charge: see *Tatung (UK) Ltd v Galex Telesure Ltd*, (1989) 5 BCC 325, confirmed in *Compaq Computer Ltd v The Abercorn Group Ltd*, BCC 484 (1991). If registration is required it will in principle be necessary in respect of each individual sale: see *Independent Automatic Sales v Knowles & Foster*, 1 LR, 1974 (1962).

[193] See *Clough Mill Ltd v Martin*, n 185 *supra*.

[194] See n 189 *supra*.

[195] See *Compaq Computer Ltd v The Abercorn Group Ltd*, see n 189 *supra*. See for the situation in The Netherlands, France and Germany respectively nn 53, 99, and 124 *supra*. Instead of automaticity, common law appears to think

their operation then depends on the nature of the condition and such a contractually agreed accessory right would still not render the arrangement automatically a secured transaction.

In common law, a more distinctive element appears to be the automatic shift of the protection of a security or at least of an equitable charge[196] into replacement goods and proceeds. It does not normally happen in property-based funding where there seems to be a requirement of greater specificity of the asset and of the debt it supports, as there still is in the English chattel mortgage.[197]

1.5.5 Finance Sales

The English approach is not always fully clear about where the modern finance sales like repos, finance leases and receivable factoring can be placed. So far only a little has been said on the subject of the repos and finance leases.[198] How they fit in the English system as outlined above is hardly ever discussed in any detail.[199]

more in terms of the creditor being able to transfer his security with his underlying advance or claim if, and only if, so agreed between the parties: see Goode, n 163 *supra*, 693 and also n 4 *supra*.

[196] Equitable charges carry through to products and proceeds as a consequence of the equitable principle of tracing under which the chargee becomes the trustee for the chargor subject to the *bona fide* purchaser protection of the acquirer of the constructive trustee. If these replacement assets are subsequently commingled there is likely to be a form of co-ownership. The charge may be floating as to the replacement goods but can be fixed as to the proceeds if kept separate: see Goode, n 163 *supra*, 667 and 752*ff*.

[197] It raises principally the question of the inclusion of future assets. As at law for its effectiveness the mortgage required transfer of ownership and the pledge transfer of possession, there was obviously a problem with security in future assets or after-acquired property as a mere agreement to create these instruments was not sufficient to give effect to their operation and the emergence of the property in the hands of the mortgagor or chargor did not automatically extend the mortgage or charge to this property as some new disposition appeared necessary. Only equity could achieve the desired result as long as consideration had been paid and was not merely promised: *Rogers v Challis*, 27 Beav 175 (1859).

For the validity of these charges it is not necessary for the property to be exactly described as long as it is identifiable, and they may cover classes of assets: *Re Kelcey* [1899] 2 chap 530 and *Syrett v Egerton* [1957] 3 All ER 331. These equitable charges are not dependent on transfer of ownership or possession either. They cannot attach, however, before the asset is acquired by the chargor but the attachment is then automatic: *Holroyd v Marshal* (1862) 10 HL Cas, 191. In ths connection, property (or income) accruing under existing contracts is considered present: see *G&E Earle Ltd v Hemsworth RDC* (1928) 140 LT 69. On the other hand, a security cannot attach before the related advance is made and attachment will cease when the advance plus interest is paid off. Here again the notion of accessory right comes in: see Goode, n 163 *supra*, 742.

Whether or not the priority relates back to the original agreement or each advance thereunder is an important, albeit moot, point under English law: see Goode, n 163 *supra*, 686.

Existing requirements of the mortgage and the pledge in terms of ownership and possession were not so diluted, although the notion of constructive possession was helpful in the case of the pledge even at law: see n 167 *supra*. Thus the Bill of Sales Act requires specificity (1882 Amendment, Section 4) and conditional transfers of ownership as under a reservation of title are equally limited; anything more would create at best a registrable charge: see text at n 193 *supra*.

[198] See respectively nn 179 and 184 *supra*.

[199] As far as the finance lease and repo are concerned, there are no leading treatises and these structures are more likely to be discussed from an accounting and a tax perspective: see for finance leasing D Wainman, *Leasing* (1991), who sees leasing as a contract of bailment (1), therefore recognising at least the protections of possession and use by the lessee, but the legal aspects are further largely ignored.

In English law a distinction is often made between hire contracts, hire-purchases and conditional sales. A conditional sale in this narrower sense is usually confined to reservation of title, therefore to sales credit protection under which title is often thought to remain with the seller until the purchase price has been paid. It then differs from the hire purchase in that the hire-purchaser has an option and not an obligation to buy, see *Helby v Matthews* [1895] AC 471. A finance lease is seen as a bailment under which the lessee has the enjoyment and use of the asset but is distinguished from the conditional sale and the hire-purchase in that the lessee has neither option nor obligation to purchase the goods but must return them to the lessor when the bailment ends: see also Goode, n 163 *supra*, 776. The limited nature of the lessee's rights is inspired by the wish to avoid a hire-purchase situation to which all kind of mandatory rules would apply for the protection of the hirer. (*Note continues overleaf.*)

It appears, however, that the conditionality of the ownership in these finance sales would not present a basic problem under English law and that there is no great threat that finance sales could be equated with secured transactions as a consequence. What the effects are in a bankruptcy of either party remains, however, little discussed. At least in repos there is reliance on contractual close-out netting under standard repo documentation, which in England is the PSA/ISMA Global Master Repurchase Agreement. It may well be that lending of investment securities is different here and that the proprietary issues are more likely to surface in that context. In all these finance sales a proprietary or at least possessory element in the structure seems to be assumed, which tends to be protected. It appears that if the arrangement is only contractual there is no finance lease, repo or factoring proper.[200]

As the duality of ownership is no common law problem, it may be that no greater fundamental discussion is required, but in English law it leaves the relationship between both parties (and their creditors, especially in bankruptcy) in doubt. In the case of chattels, the law of bailment is likely to provide some further guidance. US law also showed that there remain here significant uncertainties.

1.6   The Situation in the USA

1.6.1   Introduction: The Approach of Article 9 UCC

In the USA, Article 9 UCC, which is with minor adjustments accepted in all states, operates a unitary system of security interests in chattels and intangible assets. It notably purports to convert reservations of title, conditional sales, trust deeds substituting securities, and assignments of receivables (other than for collection purposes) into security interests.

It is not possible to discuss at length here the concept of possession in common law: see more in particular chapter IV, s 1.3.2, but it implies the protection of the holder/user of assets who has a much more independent position than the holder under civil law and can defend it, if necessary even in a bankruptcy of the possessor. In fact it is the bailor who may have real difficulty in retrieving the asset in a bankruptcy of the bailee. As a consequence, in a bankruptcy of both the bailor and bailee, the creditors of the bailee may prove stronger than the creditors of the bailor. It is not ownership that is here necessarily decisive as would be the civil law attitude. Thus there is a form of proprietary protection (in civil law terms) for the bailee.

Even under a reservation of title, the position of the seller in a bankruptcy of the buyer in possession may for these reasons remain unclear, although it has been suggested that exceptionally full title revests here automatically in the seller who retains a reclaiming right: see Goode, n 163 *supra*, 420, see for the USA before the UCC n 234 *infra*. As between the bailee and a stranger, possession is considered to give title, and this is not seen as a limited interest but as absolute and complete, see *The Winkfield* [1900–03] All ER 346. It is therefore said that both bailor and bailee have title at the same time: the title of the bailor is indefeasible but difficult to defend against third parties; the title of the bailee is relative but may be defended by an action of the bailee.

It is an original action and not a sub-right, only reduced by the bailee's duties towards the bailor which are mainly contractual. When it comes to the return of the property, the courts traditionally have considerable discretion in the case of chattels, as it is seen as a form of specific relief giving the (wrongful) possessor normally the option to pay damages instead. True revindication rights exist under common law only in the case of real estate. Hire purchasers, lessees, pledgees and possessors under a conditional title transfer are all bailees in this sense and in a strong position especially since possession was voluntarily transferred by the owner. Again it should be emphasised that common law does not maintain a co-ordinated or integrated concept of title and possession or ownership and bailment. They stand side by side and cannot easily be reduced to each other as in the civil law approach.

See for factoring of receivables, FR Salinger, *Factoring* (3rd edn, 1999), who emphasises the practical aspects of factoring: see for a legal analysis of receivable financing more generally F Oditah, *Aspects of Receivables Financing* (1995). Under English law, factoring implies a sale of the receivables to the factor, subject to certain defined classes of receivables being returned under certain circumstances: see Goode, n 163 *supra*, 802. Whether this return is automatic also in a bankruptcy of the factor remains undiscussed.

---

[200] See for a fuller description of factoring in this connection s 2.3 *infra*.

Consequently, it treats them all as security interests, see Section 1-201(35) (1-201(37) old), Section 9-109(a) (9-102(1)(a) and (2) old) UCC.[201] It means that they are subject to its formalities, especially in terms of documentation to achieve the immediate effect against all (which is *attachment* which also assumes a sufficient interest of the debtor: Sections 9-201 and 9-203 (new and old), and its *perfection* requirement to establish the priority. Perfection usually depends on proper attachment and filing but there is no such filing requirement in respect of possessory security, non-possessory security in consumer goods, and incidental assignments of receivables. In these cases, the perfection is automatic upon attachment; see Sections 9-309 and 9-310 (9-302 old) UCC.

The conversion of conditional sales including reservations of title into security interests results from the functional approach of Article 9 UCC in which 'a security interest means an interest in personal property or fixtures which secures payment or performance of an obligation'.[202] Substance prevails here over form and all contractual creditor protection involving personal property is covered regardless of the type of indebtedness, like loan or sales credit, or other types of funding by way of conditional sale or assignment. One important aspect of this is the already mentioned application of the attachment and perfection regime to all. In addition, Section 9-601 (9-501 old) protects this approach by compulsorily requiring (generally) disposal of the affected assets in the case of default and the turning over of any surplus proceeds to the debtor.

Another dominant feature of the secured transaction regime of Article 9 UCC is the *advance* filing facility.[203] Under the filing requirement, an early finance statement can be filed against a debtor. The security will relate back to that date, even if the loan is given later, and its ranking or perfection will date from that date, see Section 9-308 (a) (9-302(1) old) and Section 9-322 (9-312(5) old). It was done to give negotiating parties time without fear for an intervening filing. The debtor can withdraw the filing at any time before attachment. No less important is in this connection that all the debtor has or shall have, (except future consumables, see Section 9-204(b) (9-204 (2) old)) may be so given as security, see Section 9-204 (a) (9-204(1) old)), even in respect of later debt, see Section 9-204 (c) (9-204(3) old). The priority still dates back to the date of the filing. This is the basic ethos of Article 9. It naturally gives money lenders a strong position, even if in modern times, there are certain consumer protections through the Federal Trade Commission Unfair Credit Practices Regulations, 16 CFR Sections 444.1(i) and 444.2. They concern especially wage assignments or non-possessory security interests in household goods (which are narrowly defined) other than purchase money security interests.

Much depends on the description of the collateral in the securities agreement and on its type. There are here no strict identification requirements (Section 9-203(b)(3)(A) (9-203(1)(a) old) but *cf* also Section 2-105(2) (new and old) which is stricter and may have some relevance in this connection, although Section 9-108 (9-110 old) accepts any description as specific if it reasonably identifies what is described).[204] As to types of assets, the UCC distinguishes primarily between equipment, inventory and accounts (or receivables). An important aspect of this distinction is that floating charges in

---

[201] The idea is that parties may agree whatever they like, but if their relationship may be qualified as a secured transaction, the pertinent Sections of Article 9 will apply, see further also Section 9–202 (new and old) which shows a similar indifference whether title is put in the secured party or in the debtor under the scheme. In this respect Article 9 appears mandatory: see also Section 9-601 (9-501 old).
[202] See Section 1-201(a)(35) (1-201(37) old).
[203] See for a critique of the American filing rquirement, chapter IV s 1.6.6 and for English proposals to follow this approach n 65 *supra in fine*.
[204] See for third party rights in assets left with the debtor, chapter IV, s 1.6.6, n 165.

inventory and accounts are presumed in the filing (finance statement) but not in equipment. There are further differences between these various classes of assets in the perfection method (Sections 9-308*ff* (9-302 old)), in the priorities (Section 324 (9-312(3) and (4) old)), in the manner of foreclosure (Sections 9-607 and 90608 (section 9-502 old)), and in the disposition upon a default (Section 9-609 (9-503 old)). One of the principles of the UCC is that all can be varied by agreement, see Section 1-302 (1-102(3) old), except as otherwise provided by the Code. That also applies to Article 9, but notably priority rights of third parties against unperfected liens cannot be challenged, see Section 9-317 (9-301 old), and the disposition provisions upon default cannot be varied (except as to manner if not manifestly unreasonable, Section 9-603 (9-501(3) old)). The obligation of good faith and reasonable care of Section 1-304 (1-203 old) also stands, but is subject to interpretation (see below). Debtor protection statutes must also be respected.

The liberal policy of Article 9 on the inclusion of future assets to cover future advances with the priority relating back to the filing of the relevant financing statement is accompanied by a facility for the security interest liberally to shift into replacement and commingled goods (Section 9-336 (9-315 old)) and into proceeds. In the latter case (since 1972 in most states) this now happens even without a special clause to the effect (Section 9-315(a) (9-306(2) old)). The result is an accommodating stance in respect of floating liens or charges. It is balanced by a strong protection for buyers of the secured assets. They are protected even if they are aware of the charge assuming that the goods are sold in the ordinary course of the debtor's business. They must therefore come out of inventory (Section 9-320(a) (9-307(1) old)) but the buyer remains unprotected if he knew of any resale restrictions in the security agreement (see Section 1-201(9) (new and old) which maintains a good faith requirement in this aspect only). The *bona fide* consumer buyer of consumables is equally protected (Section 9-302(b) (9-307(2) old)). It concerns sales between consumers. The good faith requirement is here purely subjective (the 'empty head, pure heart' test).

The protection of buyers under Section 9-320 (9-307 old) does not seem to depend on actual possession of the goods but does not apply to pledgees or chargees (even though they are also purchasers under Section 1-201(29) (1-201(32) old) but not buyers under Sections 9-320 and 9-323 (Section 9-307 old). *Bona fide* security holders *with possession* are protected against older perfected interests only in the case of chattel paper (which under Section 9-102(a)(11) (9-105(1)(b) old) means documented secured claims or lease income, used as collateral) and negotiable (or semi-negotiable) instruments: see Section 9-330 (9-308 old).

As regards the priorities, Sections 9-102(a)(52), 9-317 and 9-323 (9-301 old) and Sections 9-322, 9-323 and 9-324 (9-312 old) give the ranking for attached and perfected security interests respectively. The first are vulnerable especially to older statutory and all perfected liens. They rank in fact just above the unsecured creditors, see Sections 9-102(a)(52), 9-317 and 9-323 (9-301 old), but are in a bankruptcy pushed down to that level by the statutory lien of the trustee under the so-called strong-arm statute of Section 544 of the Bankruptcy Code. For perfected security interests, the essence is first in time (of filing or perfection, whichever is first), first in right (Section 9-322(d) (9-312(5)(a) old)), except for purchase money security and some other special situations.

The emphasis on filing rather than on perfection in this connection allows for the advance filing facility and the relation back of the priority to that date for filed security interests. By including a proper after-acquired property clause, it eliminates the need for further security agreements (which would still relate back to their date of filing) or filings. Although none can perfect before attachment (Section 9-308 (9-303 old)), which itself normally requires a document, the existence of the collateral, a sufficient right of the debtor therein, and the giving of value (Section 9-203 (new and old)), this does not undermine the ranking in the case of filing (assuming it properly mentions the collateral). Filing may thus also be relevant in respect of securities that are ordinarily perfected through delivery of possession. Few security interests may only perfect by taking possession. Examples are security interests in money or instruments.[205]

Another question is whether the secured creditor takes subject to unknown third party rights in the collateral. Above it was already said that he does not have the *bona fide* buyer protection, but except in the case of pure bailment and equipment leases, the creditor secured on these assets may ignore any such interests unknown to him; that is the risk of third parties that leave their assets in the possession of others. The debtor only needs to have a sufficient interest (Section 9-203(b)(2) (9-203(1) (c) old)).

It should be noted in this connection that filing of a security interest itself does not guarantee anything: it does not mean that the collateral exists or that there are no hidden proprietary rights in it (like bailors' and equipment leasors' rights). The filing statement itself may be very incomplete. In any event *bona fide* purchasers or purchasers in the ordinary course of business do not need to worry about any filings, have no investigation duty and may ignore the charge. In fact, the filing guarantees nothing and is only meant to warn subsequent lenders, who would in any even make their own investigation of the debtor's financial commitments.[206] It is an expensive warning system, which in many countries is found to be unnecessary and was not originally foreseen in Article 9 either. Its main merit is in establishing the date, and therefore (normally) the rank of the security interest. But this could also have been achieved through a (non-public) registration system at a fraction of the cost. It is clear that this type of filing system only serves to make the life of banks a little easier. It was the price for their support of Article 9 when it was first proposed.

The provisions of all security agreements under Article 9 are subject to good faith requirements (Section 1-304 (1-203 old)) and may not become unduly oppressive in themselves or in their enforcement. This is similar to the *gute Sitten* effect of German law: see section 1.4.4 above. The good faith adjustment under the UCC has been used to subordinate priorities created by filing creditors aware of competing unperfected interests and gaining an unfair advantage in the race for perfection.[207] This subordination facility

---

[205] An important instance where perfection rather than filing remains relevant is also in the priority over judicial lien creditors under Section 9-317(a)(2) (9-301(1)(b) old). This is changed in the 1999 Revision effective in 2001. It is also relevant for the lien of the bankruptcy trustee under Section 544 of the Bankruptcy Code, even though federal, but it will not affect the all-important federal tax lien under Sections 6321*ff* of the Federal Tax Lien Statute, which is generally interpreted as a judicial lien but has its own federal regime and definition of security interests that take precedence over it. It adopts in this connection much of the attachment language of Section 9-203(1)(a) old (now 9-203(b)) as a condition for priority (see Section 6323(h)(1) FTLS).

[206] See for a broader discussion of this aspect of publicity, chapter 4, s 1.6.6

[207] See for Germany n 146 *supra*. See in the US for a rare case, *General Ins Co v Lowry*, 412 F Supp 12 (1976) in which a lawyer charged with the delivery of shares to perfect a security interest in them for a third party retained them whilst later creating his own security interest in these shares through perfection based on his possession. We are interested here in equitable relief in narrowly defined circumstances, however. The impact of good faith notions in this area remains contested. It has long been held that 'in commercial transactions it does not in the end promote justice to seek strained interpretations in aid of those who do not protect themselves': see Judge Learned Hand in *James Baird Co v Gimbel Bros, Inc*, 64 F 2d 344, 46 (1933), see also Judge Easterbrook in *Kham & Nate's Shoes No 2 v First Bank of Whiting*, 908 F 2d 1351 (1990) denying any 'general duty of kindness' in lender/borrower relationships or, one must assume, between secured lenders *inter se*. Article 9 tends to be neutral in these matters but in the interpretation of the UCC, it cannot be avoided that its good faith notion is tested. Section 9-401(2) (old) presented a statutory example allowing a wrong filing made in good faith to be upheld against anyone who has knowledge of it. In view of the simplified filing requirements, this provision has been deleted in the 1999 Revision.

sometimes assumed by the courts has been criticised. In bankruptcy, Section 510 of the US Bankruptcy Code supports the principle of equitable subordination, but this is usually limited to special situations, for example, where sole shareholders are managing their company and claim back their loans ahead of other creditors. On the other hand, the Bankruptcy Code may affect perfected security interests more fundamentally, especially through the stay provision, the possibility of immediate removal of excess collateral, the precedence of the estate over unperfected liens, and the cram down in a reorganisation: see also section 1.1.3 above.

1.6.2   The Unitary Functional Approach and Finance Sales: Problem Areas in Article 9 UCC

It follows from the American unitary functional approach that conditional and similar contractually created ownership interests are automatically converted into secured interests if supporting payment or the performance of an obligation. One of the consequences is that if the interest is not filed, it will be reduced in rank to just above that of the common creditors and in bankruptcy to their level, as an attached but unperfected security interest, as we just saw. Other consequences are that upon default a disposition with a return of overvalue to the debtor must (in principle) follow. Moreover, in the latter's bankruptcy, there will be a stay whilst the security interest may be further curtailed.

In practice, however, it will still be necessary to decide whether a conditional interest of this sort is meant to 'secure payment or performance' or has a different purpose. So borderline issues arise in the functional approach, notwithstanding its search for economic realities. Lines must still be drawn, although this is mostly left to case law and therefore to the facts of each case. Apparently no great need has arisen to test the borderlines, except for leasing,[208] where a new Article 2A was eventually introduced into the UCC to make some distinctions. However, the legal status of investment securities repos has recently also attracted attention. There seems to be a fairly general consensus that they are not affected by Article 9, as we shall see, and they are not usually treated in that manner.

This is significant as it shows not only that the functional approach of Article 9 in its generality proved untenable for finance leases but also that it is not necessarily all-embracing in practice. The issue of a sale or a secured transaction has recently also arisen in securitisations where an income stream is used to raise new financing. If the buyer/financier (usually a special purpose vehicle or 'SPV' created to function as assignee) is guaranteed a certain return by the seller, a danger exists that the sale will not be considered complete but that the transaction will be re-characterised as a loan arrangement secured by the income stream.

To elaborate, in leasing the transaction may be characterised as a sale under Article 2, therefore, as 'the passing of title from the seller to the buyer for a price'; as an equipment lease under Article 2A, therefore, as 'the right to possession and use of goods for a term in return for consideration', or still as a security interest in the above terms.[209]

---

[208] The difference between finance leases and security interests is considered one of the most frequently litigated issues under the entire UCC: see J White and R Summers, *Uniform Commercial Code* (4th edn, 1996), 719.

[209] See respectively Section 2-106(1), Section 2A-103 and Section 9-109(a)(5) (9-102(2) old). Article 2A dates from 1987 and is now introduced in most States. The terminology remains confusing. Article 2A distinguishes between consumer leases, which are mere rental agreements, and finance leases which are equipment leases for much longer periods in which the lessee normally negotiates with the supplier directly and receives collateral rights under this agreement even though ultimately concluded with a lessor/financier. The line with Article 9 leases/secured transactions remains thin.

Terminology is not decisive and there is nothing in the word 'lease' itself to determine the characterisation issue.

Equally, a repurchase agreement, especially of investment securities, may be defined as a sale, a loan or, depending on the facts, as a secured transaction, although as already observed, the latter appears less common.[210] It could also be considered a mere contractual arrangement, but that would not explain the disposition rights of the repo buyer. A similar qualification problem affects factoring in the USA which may be a sale or a secured loan, even if not merely for collection purposes which the Code itself excludes from Article 9.[211] However, Section 9-109(a)(3) (9-102(1)(b) old) no longer makes any distinction and covers *all* assignments of accounts for whatever purpose, although the consequences in the filing requirement, Section 9-309(2) (9-302(1)(e) old) and the disposition regime, Section 9-607(c) (9-502(2) old) are alleviated. Filing is necessary only if a significant part of the debt portfolio is sold. Upon default, the assignee/financier has the choice of collecting or of selling the portfolio to a collection agent. If there was a security agreement overvalue must be returned but if there was an outright sale of receivables

In this book the term 'finance leases' is used as a more generic term for all leases that include a financing element, whether or not subsequently characterised as a secured transaction or a conditional sale under applicable law.

[210] See *Cohen v Army Moral Support Fund (In re Bevill, Breslett and Schulman Asset Management Corp)*, 67 BR 557 (1986) and *In the matter of Bevill, Breslett and Schulman Asset Management Corporation and S S Cohen v The Savings Building and Loan Company*, USCA 3rd Circuit, 896 Fed Rep 2d, 54 (1990). In these cases intention was considered decisive as to whether there was a security agreement or a sale and repurchase: see also *Jonas v Farmers Bros. Co (In re Comark)*, 145 BR 47, 53 (9th Cir, 1992), but the fungibility of the underlying assets was believed to have an undermining effect on proprietary claims, although it seems that if the assets are with a depository who will provide replacement goods, the fungibility issue may be less urgent. All now translates into entitlements, which could be shared or conditional. See for the new model for transfer and pledging of such securities and the priorities of owners and pledgees in them, Article 8 UCC 1994 Revision: see chapter IV, s 3.1.4.

However, case law may sometimes still be construed to be more generally adverse to true repurchase agreements: see *Lombard-Wall Inc v Columbus Bank & Trust Co*, No 82–B–11556 Bankr. SDNY 16 Sept 1982; *cf* also *In re Lombard-Wall*, 23 BR 165 (1982), which characterised repos as secured loans and led to the 1984 Bankruptcy Code amendments: see n 225 *infra*. See more recently still the US Supreme Court in *Nebraska Dept of Revenue v Loewenstein*, 115 S Ct 557 (1994), holding the same, but expressly limited this finding to taxation matters. It did not mean to interpret 'the Securities Exchange Act of 1934, the Bankruptcy Code or any other body of law'. It is often thought that the 1982, 1984 and 1990 amendments to the Bankruptcy Code especially dealing with repos in government and other securities (Sections 101(47), 741(7), 101(49), 555 and 559) and exempting the netting of these transactions from the stay provisions now indicate a different approach to repos whilst taking them outside Article 9 UCC.

It is generally agreed in the USA that the characterisation of repos as a secured transaction would be disastrous. It would lead to dispositions upon default and perhaps even to filing needs at the time of creation in view of the fungible nature of investment securities and therefore the tenuous nature of the possession by the financier. There would also be the danger of a stay and adjustment of the security: see MA Spielman, 'Whole Loan Repurchase Agreement', 4 *Com LJ* 476 (1994) and JL Schroeder, 'Repo Madness: The Characterisation of Repurchase Agreements under the Bankruptcy Code and the UCC', 46 *Syracuse LR* 999 (1996). However, where the repo price is clearly expressed in terms of the original purchase price plus an agreed interest rate, the repurchase seems to be re-characterised as a secured loan, also in the USA. It is submitted that that is correct and certainly in line with the approach of this book.

[211] Section 9-109 (d)(5) (9-104(f) old). See 1. G Gilmore, *Security Interests in Personal Propert* (1965), Sections 2.2–2.5 and 11.6–11.7 describing the philosophy behind the new rules concerning assignment of accounts in Article 9. Floating liens in them had historically met with much resistance culminating in the decision of the US Supreme Court in *Benedict v Ratner*, 268 US 353 (1925) in which the court struck down the assignment of present and future receivables as a fraudulent conveyance in view of the unfettered dominion and control of the assignor over the collateral and proceeds. The result was simply the imposition of more expensive formalities on the ongoing financing of accounts (and inventory), leading to daily remittances of all receivables and collections received even though they were immediately returned to the debtor to keep him funded. Many state laws tried to overcome the inconvenience: see also the Official Comment on Section 9-205 (new and old) UCC. It is still the situation in many European countries. Article 9 UCC effectively repealed *Benedict* by introducing Section 9-204 (new and old). But Article 9 goes further and brings all assignments of receivables within its reach, as will be discussed shortly below.

to the financier, overvalue is returned only when the agreement so provides. As just mentioned, the use of special purpose vehicles in securitisation may also have to be considered in this context, as may the effect of any ring-fencing and credit enhancement agreements, which are not normally considered by Article 9 either.[212]

Where there is a finance sale such as this rather than a secured transaction, it is likely to be conditional. It is an example of the typical common law tolerance towards splitting the ownership in ways the parties desire. But, as in other common law countries, in the USA it still poses the questions of:

(a)   the type of proprietary interest of either party and its protection as well as that of those who acquire rights in the assets from either of them, problem areas not explicitly considered in Article 2 UCC,[213] and

(b)   the borderline with secured transactions.

In any event, it is clear that there may be conditional sales or perhaps even reservations of title which may not be secured transactions under the Code, such as where the conditions are not financial at all. Yet not all financial conditions would make the conditional sale a secured transaction either. It all depends on the facts[214] in which the intention of the parties may also figure.[215]

---

[212] The guaranteeing of a certain income level by the seller independently of the yield of the underlying financial assets constituting the income stream must be considered a serious danger to securitisation and may convert the sale of the investment stream to the SPV into a secured loan. This is different from guaranteeing the existence of the income stream itself. It is submitted that also in the USA this danger is the greatest if a certain interest income is guaranteed in this manner: see the early case of *Home Bond Co v McChesney*, 239 US 568 (1916) and also G Gilmore, 1 *Security Interests in Personal Property* (1965), 47ff. Others refer to an economic return which may have to be measured, however, in similar terms: see PV Pantaleo, HS Edelman, FL Feldkamp, J Kravitt, W McNeill, TE Plank, KP Morrison, SL Schwarcz, P Shupack and B Zaretsky, 'Rethinking the Role of Recourse in the Sale of Financial Assets,' (1996) 52 *The Business Lawyer*, 159.

A similar danger exists in factoring and securitisations where any overvalue beyond a certain agreed amount of collections must be returned, especially when that amount is the sale price plus an agreed interest rate on it: see *In re Grand Union Co*, 219 F 353 (1914), but the return of uncollectable receivables at their face value was not sufficient to convert the sale into a secured loan: *Chase & Baker Co v National Trust & Credit Co*, 215 F 633 (1914). This is still good law also after the emergence of the UCC and shows that not all forms of receivable factoring are secured transactions, but modern case law suggests that the level of risk that remains with the seller is the determining factor and not so much the guaranteeing of a certain collection plus interest: see *Major's Furniture Mart, Inc v Castle Credit Corp*, 602 F 2d 538 (1979). This leads to uncertainty and has rightly been criticised: see Pantaleo et al., *supra*, where courts require that the risk of loss of the asset must be with the buyer, as in *In re Executive Growth Investment*, Inc 40 BR 417 (1984).

In a bankruptcy of the seller, the buyer (SPV) may then find that it is only a secured creditor whose collection rights may be stayed under Section 362 of the US Bankruptcy Code whilst the seller may retain any current collections under Section 363 and the security may even be diluted under Section 364 (in the latter two cases always subject to adequate protection of the buyer, however). This is always assuming that the buyer has properly filed the security interest. Without it he may have at best a position just above the unsecured creditors but below all others as his interest is attached but not perfected: see Section 9-322(a)(3) (9-312(5)(b) old) UCC.

[213] In this connection it should be noted that Article 9 abandoned the equitable interests or charges and therefore also the inherent protection of *bona fide* purchasers against these interests if undisclosed which required a new approach to the *nemo dat* rule, a subject beyond the scope of this chapter. It has led, however, to a liberal approach which allows *bona fide* purchasers in sales between consumer full protection and even non-*bona fide* purchasers of all goods except farm products if they are sold in the normal course of business of the party requiring the funding: see Sections 9-320 and 9-323 (9-307 old) UCC. The free flow of assets is thus normally not to be hindered by security interests, see for the details chapter IV, s 1.5.9.

[214] See for the emphasis on the facts of the case in particular in connection with leases; Section 1-201(a)(35) (1-201(37) old).

[215] See White and Summers, n 200 *supra*, 725 and the official Comment to Section 9-109 (9-102 old). The original text of Section 1-201(a)(35) (1-201(37) old) cryptically stated that 'whether a lease is intended as security is to be determined by the facts of each case'.

Article 9 has a tendency to buckle under its own sophistication. The uncertainty it leaves under its unitary functional approach in respect of major financial instruments like leases and repos is one aspect of it. No less curious in this respect is the treatment of assignments of accounts or receivables. All these assignments are covered by Article 9, whatever their purpose. Thus an outright assignment of a claim (rather than a security assignment) of the type covered by Article 9 is also governed by it. It is said in the Official Comment to Section 9-109(a)(3) (9-102(1)(b) old) that a sale of accounts is often so conducted that the distinction between a security transfer and a sale is blurred. Exceptions are made in some instances only when there is clearly no financing motive as in the case of a collection agreement, or when the assignment is part of the sale of a business, or when a payment right is assigned to someone who will perform the major obligation under the contract, or when the assignment is meant as payment for a pre-existing debt, Section 9-109(d)(7) (9-104(f) old).

In the case of other assignments of receivables (or accounts) covered by Article 9, the difference from a security assignment is, however, still fully recognised and there is, as we saw, no disposition and return of overvalue under Sections 9-607 and 608 (9-502 old) if the assignment does not secure indebtedness. Still, the collection rights are determined by perfection through filing (except if they are incidental when perfection may be automatic: Section 9-309(2) (9-302(1)(e) old) and not on the basis of the *bona fides* of the collecting assignee which is otherwise the more normal rule in the USA: see chapter IV, section 1.7.9. Notice to the debtor is no requirement of the validity of the assignments (or the attachment of the transfer), and the assignment of receivables becomes immediately effective in respect of third parties even in states that otherwise require notice to the debtor. It follows from Section 9-201 (new and old) UCC.

To introduce here some uniform rules is undoubtedly useful — and especially the abolition of the notice requirement for the validity of the assignments in some states promotes bulk assignments greatly — but to bring all assignments of receivables under Article 9 in this manner is an unusual departure as the ordinary sale of chattels could never be so treated. It brings all forms of receivable financing, factoring and perhaps even securitisations within the ambit of Article 9 (assuming they cover account receivable, chattel or realty paper, which are financial obligations insured by security interests in personal or real property) unless it can be demonstrated that there was no financial motive at all in the terms of Section 9-109(d)(5) (9-104(f) old) (as in pure collections).

Other areas where Article 9 in its elaboration may be self-defeating concern the very refined system of collateral distinctions, the coverage of the security interests, the identification requirements in the security agreement and (to a lesser extent) in finance statement, and the meaning of filing and the details thereof.

As to the collateral distinctions for chattels, in Section 9-102(44) (9-109 old) a distinction is made between consumer goods, farm products, inventory and equipment, and for intangibles in Sections 9-102 (9-105 old) and 9-102(2)(42) (9-106 old) between chattel paper (which embodies secured claims or lease payments), instruments, accounts and general intangibles. Other classes are documents and in the 1999 Revisions also commercial tort claims, deposit accounts, and letters of credit benefits. Different treatment arises especially in the area of perfection and priority of a security interest in these different types of collateral, which like everywhere else comes, however, always down to possessory and non-possessory security. The distinctions seem in this connection over-elaborate whilst overlap and the attendant confusion cannot always be avoided.

As regards the coverage of the security interests, they may under Section 9-203(b)(2) (9-203(1)(c) old) include all collateral in which the debtor has rights. These rights could be merely contractual or temporary. Whilst it is clear that mere possession of the collateral by the debtor is not sufficient, anything more could be given as security. It suggests a protection for any lien creditor in respect of any type of personal property in the debtor's possession, at least if the lien creditor is unaware of the earlier interests of others (is therefore a *bona fide* purchaser regardless of possession). It is a benefit of apparent or ostensible ownership no longer given to unsecured creditors or perhaps even statutory or judicial lien creditors under state law.[216] It creates problems particularly in the case of agents or brokers who need secured financing and have assets of others in their control or in the case of assets held by a debtor pursuant to a voidable title.

Other problems arise in the identification requirement under Section 9-108 (9-110 old) for security agreements and finance statements for which different requirements obtain, *cf* also Sections 9-502, 503 and 504 (9-402 old). They tend to undermine the ideal of Section 9-204 (new and old) aiming at a situation in which all present and future assets may be given for all present and future debt. In the security agreement, the identification requirement has given rise to problems where omnibus clauses are used which may become too generic whilst in addition the collateral description must also be an adequate reflection of the parties' intention. In the finance statement, the concern is now less with generic description and more with adequate warning of unsuspecting prospective creditors. The terminology of Article 9 need not strictly speaking be used in these documents, but courts still seem to use the descriptive requirements to limit the security granted and leave more room for new secured or old unsecured creditors. Overreaching of secured creditors is in this way countered.

Finally, it is clear that the finance statement and its filing themselves guarantee nothing in terms of the existence of the security, the collateral or the rights of the debtor therein whilst the security may in any event be undermined by later *bona fide* purchasers or buyers of the asset. The organisation of the various filing systems per state and the confusion that may arise about where to file or where to look with the probabilities of name changes, reorganisations or movement of debtors, makes the direct and indirect costs of filing and searches high. The present system does not eliminate uncertainty and any necessity for creditors to make their own enquiries into the collateral status and liabilities of the debtors. In the case of an advance filing, there may not result any security interest at all. The finance statement gives at most some warning. It clouds the title in the collateral for five years and any later filer must assume an inferior status: even if the security does not include after-acquired property any subsequent filing in respect of the same type of collateral will establish priority (not perfection) as at the original filing date. The true significance of filing is in the registration of the moment at which the priority arises for non-possessory security interests but that may be better and more cheaply achieved through an official stamping of the security agreement. It is of interest in this connection that a filing system was not originally contemplated for non-possessory security interests but only came in under pressure from the financial service industry.

In truth filing achieves a great deal less than may appear on the surface and as would be desirable for it to be truly meaningful. Outside the USA this filing system is nevertheless often admired.

1.6.3 Proprietary Characterisations

An analysis of the American case law would be most appropriate at this point to determine how the different financial interests in chattels may be distinguished in the light of Article 9

---

[216] See also n 85 *supra* for the bankruptcy context.

UCC, but it is beyond the scope of this chapter. In Article 2A, the Code gives some indication of what facts may be considered in the case of equipment leasing (in the USA also called finance leasing) but becomes so convoluted that clear guidance remains elusive. However, if the lessee has a future proprietary interest in the asset, such as when the lease is for its useful life, or when the lessee acquires full title at the end without further valuable consideration, see Section 1-201(a)(35) (1-201(37) old), the structure is likely to qualify as a secured loan agreement under Section 9-109 (9-102 old).[217]

The law treats the lessee in that case as an immediate owner subject to a security interest of the lessor, with the need of a disposition of the asset upon default by the lessee under the lease and a return of any overvalue. It is a potentially dangerous and often costly process for the lessor, unless a clear loan with an interest rate structure was always intended when this consequence would naturally follow.[218]

At the other end of the spectrum are the shorter term leases, at least shorter than for the economic life of the assets. If the lessee may terminate the arrangement at any time, there cannot be a finance lease at all. Pure rentals result which are merely contractual arrangements, but they are also possible in situations without a funding perspective. For consumers they are often called consumer leases. They will not be further considered in this context. The true area covered by Article 2A is between the rental agreement and secured transaction under Article 9. Most leases need therefore to be properly characterised. It does not appear that equipment leases are merely operational leases in a European sense, which are no more than contractual arrangements and come close to rental agreements. The equipment lessee is a funding technique in which the emphasis is mainly on the lessee receiving the collateral rights against the supplier of the equipment (even though officially ordered by the lessor): see Section 2A-103(1)(g). It also suggests that the lessee must pay the rental whatever the circumstances. The lessor becomes here passive (a mere financier).

Once there is an equipment lease, the lessee has more than purely contractual rights, however, although it is not fully clear whether he also has a proprietary status. Probably, the type of ownership created in a true equipment lease under Article 2A should not be seen as split between lessor and lessee in the manner of a conditional sale, however.[219] Indeed, any future interest of the lessee in the title may be construed as an indication of a

---

[217] Filing a finance statement may itself be indicative of parties considering their lease a secured transaction so that even preventive filing under Section 9-505 (9-408 old) is dangerous: see *Mann Inv Co v Columbia Nitrogen Corp*, 325 SE 2d 612 (1984).

[218] It should be noted here that the execution sale concept is now fully embraced by the UCC but is not as such part of the common law tradition: see also n 167 *supra* and accompanying text, although it became more common in the USA. The UCC in Sections 9-610*ff* (9-504 old) requires advance notice of any default action by the lessor and a commercially reasonable disposition of the asset followed by a handing over of any overvalue, provided that the lease is considered a secured transaction in the first place which will also require the filing of a financial statement as a way of perfecting the security and of protecting the lease against adverse third party interests, like those of purchasers and lien creditors or the bankruptcy trustee of the lessee: see Sections 9–309, 310 and 310 (9-302 old) *io* respectively Sections 9-320 and 323 (9-307 old), Section 9-317(a)(2) (9-301(1)(b) old and Section 9-102(a)(52) (9-301(3) old).

In the case of a lease under Article 2A, there is no filing or disposition duty. The disposition requirement itself is interpreted in a flexible manner and could in the case of a finance lease be another lease arrangement, possibly one under Article 2A. This was done on purpose and is a consequence of the interest of the lessor being outside Article 9. It means that whatever interest he still has in the asset amounts to a hidden proprietary interest which nevertheless may be asserted against all other later interest holders (as if it had been published).

[219] *Cf* also JB Vegter, 'The Distinction between True Leases and Secured Transactions under the Uniform Commercial Code,' in *Kokkini* et al, *Eenvormig en Vergelijkend Privaatrecht* (Molengrafica 1994), 163, 182, who also goes briefly into the different proprietary concepts and property forms on which the UCC focuses and the protection of the dual ownership of lessor and lessee. See further the Official Comment, ULA Vol. 1B, 775 which makes clear that the distinction between the lease as a conditional sale and the equipment lease was borrowed from the old Uniform Conditional Sales Act.

secured transaction, as just mentioned,[220] certainly if the conditions are financial. In any case, the new Article 2A does not elaborate on any duality in ownership, the transferability or possibility of attachment of the interests of either party, although in Section 2A-103(1) it qualifies the lessor's interest as 'residual'. It suggests some remaining interest, especially in a bankruptcy of the lessee, but is otherwise mainly reflective of the lessee's consuming powers in the asset.

That the position of the lessee itself is stronger than contractual[221] follows, however, from his protection as *bona fide* purchaser in two different ways: Section 2A-307 allows the lessee in the ordinary course of business to take the lease asset free of the charges as his fair expectation, whilst Section 2A-301 also protects the lessee against any *bona fide* purchaser of the assets. On the other hand, it is also clear that the lessor may still sell full title to others (subject to the lessee's interest) and has a reclaiming right in the case of default of the lessee.

However, in the latter's bankruptcy, this appropriation by the lessor seems to yield to the right of the bankruptcy trustee of the lessee to make an election to continue or reject the contract as long as it may still be considered executory.[222] It would also be subject to a stay of all unilateral action (subject to any relief from it under the special provisions of Section 362 of the Bankruptcy Code) whilst under Section 365(e) an early termination clause would not be effective. The equipment lease is usually treated in this way, even though the lessor may have fully performed. It is a further indication that the arrangement under Article 2A is not a conditional sale, but it must remain uncertain whether it is purely contractual. A special proprietary right for both parties has been advocated.[223] Bailment protection is also conceivable here for the lessee.[224]

Although it is clear that *other types* of conditional sales of movables and intangibles may also emerge outside Article 9, the true distinctive criteria may be even less clear, particularly in repurchase agreements of investment securities. It is somewhat surprising that in a jurisdiction as large and sophisticated as the USA, these issues seem little discussed.

In any event, to say that in the financial sphere all is in principle under Article 9 and that therefore the issue of characterisation does not normally arise is avoiding the issue. In the USA, policy adjustments are often left to the Bankruptcy Code as a federal statute so this Code also needs to be considered. Sections 555*ff* of this Code are particularly relevant here for repurchase agreements and the concept of netting, and now seem to have taken the

---

[220] SL Harris, 'The Interface between Articles 2A and 9', (1989) 22 *UCC Law Journal* 99*ff* suggests that leases are only secured transactions if structured as conditional sales. See for the traditional definition of a lease, *Undercofler v Whiteway Neon Ad Inc,* 152 SE Ed 616, 618 (1966) in which it was said that a lease is a contract by which one owning the property grants to another the right to possess, use and enjoy it for a specified period of time in exchange for periodic payment of a stipulated price, referred to as rent.

[221] See also comment in n 213 *supra.*

[222] The trustee of a bankrupt lessee has the right to assume or reject the lease as an executory contract under Section 365 of the Bankruptcy Code. Characterisation of the equipment lease as an executory contract means that the lessor does not have an automatic appropriation right in a bankruptcy of the lessee. Conversely in a bankruptcy of the lessor, the lessee has no automatic right to retain the goods either but is subject to the election by the lessor's bankruptcy trustee either to assume or reject the lease contract. In the meantime the concept of executory contract, that is a contract not fully performed by either party and therefore subject to the trustee's right of assumption or rejection, has been criticised as a determination often arrived at after the fact: see National Bankruptcy Review Commission, set up by Congress in 1994, Professor Elizabeth Warren of Harvard University as general reporter. The proposal is to make all contracts subject to this election possibility: see the Commission's Report of 20 Oct 1997.

[223] See n 160 *supra.*

[224] Although other characterisations may also apply, the proprietary consequences may be left even more uncertain. The general rules of bailment as (physical) possession could additionally become applicable: see also nn 156 and 199 *supra* and n 234 *infra* plus accompanying texts for the situation in England and earlier in the USA.

repo (indirectly) outside the narrow ambit of Article 9.[225] The regime for factoring, on the other hand, remains in principle fully incorporated in Article 9 which covers all sales of accounts as we saw (unless for collection purposes only).

Finance leasing, repos and factoring will be further discussed below in sections 2.1, 2.2 and 2.3 also with regard to the American experiences.

1.7   Finance Sales as Distinguished from Secured Transactions in Civil and Common Law: The Recharacterisation Risks

1.7.1   Introduction: Loan and other Types of Funding

The foregoing was a long, but as far as I can see necessary, introduction to finance sales and the distinction between them and secured transactions. We are stuck with the competition between both and must define the legal difference.[226] In line with what I believe is largely the English practice, I have advocated for some time[227] that the true nature of a security interest is that it supports and is accessory to a loan agreement of which an agreed interest rate structure is the true indication.

In other words, if there is no interest agreed, there can be no loan agreement, and if there is no loan agreement there cannot be a security, even if there is some kind of proprietary transfer. On the other hand, when there is an interest rate structure agreed, it must be presumed that there is a loan and any transfer of proprietary interests under it must be considered a security interest. Its creation and execution are then subject to the applicable formalities and safeguards for the creation and execution of security interests.

The requirement of an interest structure is a clear one. It must be specifically agreed and cannot easily be deemed implied (except where there is a pure sham). Without it, there is no loan; there will still be a fee or other reward structure but that is *not* interest and is likely to be indicative of *another* service being provided. In financial or payment matters such services may include proprietary transfers. This is often the situation in repos, finance leases and factoring. Thus in these modern finance sales there is always a proprietary element even though difficult to define as we saw, especially in civil law, but a purely contractual structure is unlikely to reflect reality. Whatever follows then is likely to be a conditional ownership structure.

It may support sales credit, as in the case of a reservation of title, and in many instances of a hire purchase when there is also a purchase money protection arrangement. But there

---

[225] Section 559 of the Bankruptcy Code, which disallows in the case of repurchase agreements the trustee's option to terminate the contracts in certain circumstances, does not go for appropriation instead, probably because of the fungible nature of the investment securities which may affect and undermine the proprietary reclaiming right. It rather adopts a netting approach to all outstanding positions between the same parties, which principle was extended to regular interest rate and foreign exchange swaps by a further amendment of the Code in 1990 (Section 560). This suggests a contractual approach also to repos and avoids in any event any reference to a conditional sale approach, probably to avoid complications under Article 9 UCC.

[226] It is of interest that the recent EBRD Model Law on Secured Transactions does not provide any particular insights into this distinction. According to the Comment on Article 1, the Model Law does not mean to affect any other financing technique besides secured lending, although the expression 'security for a debt' in Article 1 may suggest that the security may also be given for sales credit, which is borne out by the fact that reservation of title, following the UCC, is covered but treated as a security interest (Article 9). Also in the latter case there is therefore a need for an execution sale in the case of default with the return of any overvalue (Article 24(1)) whilst the charge is accessory to the debt (Article 18(1)).

[227] See Dalhuisen, n 37 *supra*.

is also a conditional sale when there is a sale of assets to raise funds if made conditional upon the buyer returning the sale price in due course and paying the fee for this kind of facility, whether or not discounted in the repurchase price. In a finance lease, the condition is the full payment of the instalments which will also include a fee element; in factoring it will be the approval of the receivables and their collectability. Furthermore, in factoring any claims leading to collections in excess of an agreed total may also be returnable, although especially in that case, the borderline with a loan may become thin.

One sees the proprietary element probably more clearly in common law, which is comfortable with split ownership rights and equitable proprietary interests, whilst the party in possession may have additional bailment protections. In countries where on the other hand finance sales continue to be considered purely contractual arrangements, they will be subject to the cherry-picking option of the bankruptcy trustee of either party. It must be admitted that even in common law this possibility sometimes re-emerges in a bankruptcy of either party, as in repos; it is not very logical.

The effect is, as we saw, then countered by close-out netting clauses in standard master agreements — also now common in civil law countries, although the acceptability of the extension of the set-off principle in this manner may still be in doubt. The result is that proprietary protection is substituted for a preference through set-off in bankruptcy, useful only if there are sufficient mutual transactions between the same parties. This relief has not much meaning in factoring, in repurchase agreements concerning inventory, or in situations where one party is always the financier and the other the party being funded (unless the retransfer obligation of the assets concerned can itself be reduced to money).

1.7.2   The Practical Differences between Security- and Ownership-based Funding

To highlight the differences further, it is useful to take the reservation of title as the most obvious example. Of course, there is credit being given by the seller, the sales credit or purchase money — in German, the *Lieferantenkredit*, resulting from the payment deferment clause. That leads in itself only to a (secured) loan agreement if there is also at the same time an agreed interest rate (structure). Normally that is not the case; there is only a concessionary late or postponed payment granted as a competitive incentive. That is not to say that there is no cost to the seller, but that is not usually translated into and recovered through an agreed interest rate.

Thus as long as there is no such rate, there is no loan, and if there is no loan there is no security either and the reservation of title is then merely a conditional or deferred transfer of title. If there were an agreed interest rate, however — and this is by no means impossible — any reservation of title would convert into a security interest. The new Dutch Civil Code,[228] following German law,[229] thus appears to be correct in assuming that a reservation of title in a sale creates a conditional sale and not a security interest. Although it does not say when this assumption is rebutted, it must be when the reservation of title supports a loan rather than a sale credit, and when interest is specifically agreed and charged. It is also rebutted when parties clearly agree otherwise.

The idea that because there must be a cost to the seller, interest is somehow discounted in the sale price, so that there is agreed interest and therefore a loan with a supporting accessory security interest, confuses everything. The sale price is normally set by competitive conditions and is unlikely to allow for an extra charge or component in respect of loss of

---

[228] Article 3. 92 CC; see also text at n 52 *supra*.
[229] Section 449 BGB.

theoretical interest by the seller in the case of sale credit. If it does it is again set by competitive conditions which may have nothing to do with the real interest rate.

Therefore the idea that there is an extra charge, let alone interest, is likely to lack any basis in fact. The seller does not normally have the room unilaterally to impose a mark-up of this sort. His selling point will usually be that he is not doing so, or, if he does, that he is at least competitive. The buyer would not want to hear of any other proposition and would rather go elsewhere. If, on the other hand, there is room for manœuvre as regards the price to be charged, the seller will normally charge the best price he can get so that any mark-up is unlikely to be related to an interest rate for any credit extended. Of course there is a cost, but that is something very different.

This may be even clearer in the repurchase agreement of investment securities. The seller, in order to raise funds, probably to finance the acquisition of the securities in question, will sell them for a certain period (until he wants to resell the securities to third parties). At the end of the agreed period he will refund the sale price and pay the repo rate. This latter rate is not an interest rate. The whole point is that the repo rate, which is in truth a market-dictated fee for this type of service or funding, is likely to be lower. That is the whole point. On the other hand, the amount of funding received may be higher than when a loan against the security of the same assets was agreed as it is the full market value of the underlying asset. As the cost of this type of funding is thus likely to be lower, it makes the repo more attractive to the repo seller than taking out a loan with the relevant investment securities given as a pledge to support the credit.

It thus appears a grave mistake to see all funding as loan financing and all credit as a loan, a mistake nevertheless very common amongst lawyers. Other advantages of ownership-based financing through repos are for the repo seller, therefore for the party requiring funding, in the lack of formalities, the use of existing settlement systems to execute the transactions, the ease and speed that follow from this, and of course the 100 per cent financing. On the other hand, the repo buyer or financier is better protected in the case of the repo seller defaulting in his obligation to tender the purchase price on the appointed date. In a repo characterised as a conditional sale, he will appropriate the full title in the assets and retain any overvalue; that is for him the trade off.

A similar situation presents itself in the finance lease. Here the fee may, however, be higher than the interest rate might have been because there may be other benefits to the lessee besides 100 per cent financing. These could be off-balance sheet financing and better tax treatment. It again underlines the fact that the charge of the lessor is market related for this type of service and not related to the prevailing interest rate. That rate will only be a benchmark for the lessee to determine his extra cost, and for the lessor, his extra profit in providing this kind of service rather than a secured loan.

It brings out a fundamental point: the risk pattern is likely to be entirely different under a conditional or finance sale as compared to a secured loan. Ownership-based and security-based funding are different fund-raising techniques with different cost, risk and reward structures. This is clear enough if there was an outright sale of assets to raise cash rather than entering into a loan arrangement. Everyone would accept that these funding techniques are in no way comparable or related. By making the sale subject to a repurchase duty on the one hand and by securing the loan on the same assets on the other, these two funding possibilities start looking similar but they are not the same.

English law is fully aware of this. Also in French law there are still remnants of this recognition,[230] as there are still symptoms of it in the Dutch reservation of title, but in

---

[230] Note for France the concern, however, about scam secured transactions by using conditional sales, see text at n 87 *supra* and Cour de Cass., 21 Mar 1938, D 2.57 (1938) and earlier 11 Mar. 1879, D 1.401 (1879).

Germany, since its Code of 1900, this perception receded into the background (except for the reservation of title), as it subsequently did on the rest of the European Continent, whilst in the USA, the UCC has tried to ignore the differences altogether.[231] It is submitted, however, that it remains fundamental and of the greatest importance.

1.7.3   Legal Differences between Security- and Ownership-based Funding

The details of ownership-based funding and the conditional sale and transfer inherent in it have remained largely unexplored in civil law but appears fundamental. In conditional finance sales, the position of either party in a dual ownership structure received much attention in the USA but only before the introduction of the UCC. The relevant American case law will be explored in this section. There is no European equivalent, even for the reservation of title. The legal nature of and the relative position of both parties in a finance sale should primarily be contrasted with secured lending and the position of a borrower and lender in a secured loan transaction.

Legally the differences from secured transactions concern largely the necessary formalities, like documentation and publication,[232] the effect of a tender of payment, the appropriation right or execution duty and the entitlement to any overvalue,[233] the qualification of

---

[231] See nn 156, 171, 75, 43, 48, 117 and 200 *supra* and accompanying texts.

[232] See text at n 111 *supra*, n 138 *supra*, and text at n 179 *supra*. In the USA before the UCC, no formalities were imposed on the formation of the contract of conditional sale, even under the Statute of Frauds (which required a document for all contracts to be performed in a period over one year) as long as the goods were delivered to the buyer (in lieu of the requirement that some money was given in credit sales of goods to make the bargain binding) and it concerned chattels that could be paid within the year: see *Barbour Plumbing, Heating & Electric Co v Ewing*, 16 Ala. App. 280 (1917). However, in many states a filing requirement was introduced which also became the system of the Uniform Conditional Sales Act (Section 6, except for railway equipment and other rolling stock that had no permanent place of being).

This was believed necessary to guard against the buyer's apparent ownership whilst the burden on the buyer was deemed slight and the benefit to the public great. The filing was made by the seller at the place the goods were first held after delivery. It made it difficult for subsequent buyers to know where to look. In other states, the reservation of title became treated as a chattel mortgage and was then sometimes registrable as such under applicable chattel mortgage statutes. Where filing was required, a written document normally became necessary, but as between the parties the contract continued to be perfectly valid without it. Even without filing, the reservation of title was also held perfectly valid against earlier security interest holders in the buyer's property with after-acquired property clauses. It was in fact the reason for the popularity conditional sales: see *Babbitt & Co v Carr*, 53 Fla. 480 (1907).

[233] See for details in particular the text at nn 170 and 171 *supra*, and for the appropriation right giving way to the bankruptcy trustee's option under executory contracts also the text at n 225 *supra* and s 2.2.1 *infra*. The execution sale may allow the buyer to acquire the goods free and clear of older charges: see Section 9–618 (9–504(4) old) UCC in the USA. In civil law countries, it might depend on the buyer's *bona fide* acquisition under the normal rules, which in the case of an execution sale might give rise to extra investigation duties, but there may be the exception of the auction sale particularly in Germany.

In the USA before the UCC, the basic rule in conditional sales was that upon full performance by the buyer, title would automatically pass to him and no further acts of transfer would be necessary. One sees here the payment protection nature of many of these sales, which were therefore not in the nature of repos, under which the seller would be the party who had to perform in tendering the repurchase price. Where it was the buyer who had to perform, the nature of his tender and its effect were obvious issues, especially in an intervening bankruptcy of the seller who still had conditional title, although he was (mostly) no longer in possession. It was agreed that the buyer was in sole control of the transfer and could achieve it at any time, even by paying the seller before the maturity of the debt; if interest had been agreed it needed to be added in full: *Cushion v Jewel*, 7 Hun. 525 (1876). The tender of the price had the effect of absolutely vesting title in the buyer: *Day v Basset*, 102 Mass. 445 (1869), even if the tender took place after default on the maturity date: *Hatch v Lamas*, 65 NHS 1 (1888). A third party who had acquired an interest in the goods from the buyer could also make the tender: *Scott v Farnam*, 55 Wash. 336 (1909). A return of possession would not automatically release the buyer from the contract, at least if there was a secured transaction rather than a conditional sale: *Finlay v Ludden & B Southern Music House*, 105 Ga. 264 (1898). The seller had an option to demand the return of the asset if the buyer's conduct in respect of it became unsatisfactory: *Hydraulic Pres Mfg Co v Whetstone*, 63 Kan. 704 (1901).

the interests and the accessory right issues,[234] and the continuing protection of the supporting securities in the case of factoring of receivables.[235]

In the case of default of payment of the purchase price, the seller normally had the option to go for (a) recovery of the price, (b) repossession of the asset or execution of a deemed security interest therein, or (c) damages, or for a combination of these options. All were subject to limitations and the combination more so. They were probably mutually exclusive. It meant that retaking the asset constituted an election by the seller not to sue for the purchase price: *Hanson v Dayton*, 153 Fed. 258 (19070. It excluded a suit for damages at the same time, although the seller might have been able to keep any payments already made as a reward for use of the asset by the buyer, compensation for depreciation in its value or as a normal penalty upon default: *Pfeiffer v Norman*, 22 ND 168 (1911).

It followed that if the seller only demanded the price, the title transfer to the buyer became absolute, therefore even before a collection judgment. Repossession on the other hand was seen as an act of implementation of the contract, and might excuse performance by the buyer who still might have had a redemption right, however: *Fairbanks v Malloy*, 16 Ill. App. 277 (1885). Yet there was much uncertainty on both the right of the buyer to demand a return of his payments and his redemption right. It was conceded that the latter right did not exist at common law for conditional sales: *Franklin Motor Car Co v Hamilton*, 113 Me. 63 (1915). The Uniform Conditional Sales Act in Section 24 allowed the retaking of the asset even after an action for recovery of the price.

If the asset was repossessed, however, the buyer was only liable to the seller upon a resale of the asset for a lower price. Any overvalue on a resale was also for the original buyer. The buyer had a redemption right for 10 days (Section 19), after which a resale had to follow if a buyer had already paid more than 50% of the price. If it had been less, the buyer still had an option to demand such a resale (Section 20) with the same consequences as to under- or over-value.

The right to take repossession was a proprietary right of the seller in replevin, also available in the case of leases: *Ferguson v Lauterstein*, 160 Pa. 427 (1894), therefore good against the buyer's trustee in bankruptcy: *Bryant v Swofford Bros. Dry Goods*, 214 US 279 (1909) and clearly distinguished from the action to obtain possession with a view to a disposition under a secured transaction: *Tufts v Stone*, 70 Miss. 54 (1892). Indeed, Section 16 of the Uniform Conditional Sales Act allowed appropriation by the seller under a conditional sale proper as long as it could be done without breaching the peace. The conditional seller was also protected against earlier mortgagees of the buyer with after-acquired property protection, one of the traditional advantages of this type of sale: *Frank v Denver & RGR Co*, 23 Fed. 123 (1885).

As for damages, these were claimable if the buyer retained and used the asset upon default. The measure of damages was then the reasonable value of this use: *Barton v Mulvane*, 59 Kan. 313 (1898). Where the replevin action could be combined with a demand for the price, the proper measure of damages was deemed the interest on the purchase price: *Winton Motor Carriage Co v Blomberg*, 84 Wash. 451 (1915). If the property had remained unsold by the buyer, the measure of damages was the purchase price plus interest unless the total exceeded the value of the property at the time of the on-sale plus interest until the date of trial: *Hall v Nix*, 156 Ala. 423 (1908).

[234] See more in particular the discussion at nn 4, 53, 100, 124 and 195 *supra*. It shows that in Europe only in France (and probably Belgium) is the conditional interest of a seller in a reservation of title believed accessory to the seller's claim for payment and transfers with it. It is an indication of the right of the seller being seen as a security interest rather as an ownership right. It is well known that the UCC in the USA now characterises the reservation of title as a security interest subject to a duty of disposition in the case of the buyer's default whilst overvalue accrues to the latter. Again French law seems to go the same way, although so far no execution sale is necessary. In the USA before the UCC, the accessory nature of the conditional ownership right was not a big issue but it did not exist except where intended. An assignment by the seller of his right to the purchase price therefore did not automatically include an assignment of his conditional ownership right: *Burch v Pedigo*, 113 Ga. 1157 (1901).

In the USA before the UCC, the qualification issue was not straightforward, however. The conditional sale was mostly defined as a conveyance of personal property which reserved title in the seller until certain conditions were met, usually payment of the purchase price. It was then seen as protecting sellers' credit. The Uniform Conditional Sales Act also included in its Section 1, bailment or leasing of goods, therefore alternative funding techniques under which a bailee or lessee paid total compensation substantially equivalent to the value of the asset upon which he had the right or option to become absolute owner. These structures were thus also seen as conditional sales. Repurchase agreements were not covered, but there was some case law which accepted a seller's option to repay money and demand a reconveyance of the property: *Beck v Blue*, 42 Ala. 32 (1868), which was apparently not uncommon in the slave trade (!), where the buyer might be given a similar option to reclaim the money after deduction of an amount for hire and return the asset: *Reese v Beck*, 24 Ala. 651 (1854).

Although the Uniform Conditional Sales Act also referred to bailments, conditional sales giving possession to the buyer were often seen as creating more than a buyer's bailment, as a bailment itself always implies a return of the asset after the objectives have been met: see *Krause v Com*, 93 Pa. 418 (1880). See for bailments in this connection in Engand, nn 156 and 199 *supra* plus accompanying text. It might have been more appropriate in a repo situation, not normally the objective of these sales, however. Most importantly for this study, even in the USA the conditional sale was sometimes defined as a sale in which the vesting of title in the buyer was subject to a condition *precedent*, the condition being full performance: *Re Columbus Buggy Co*, 143 Fed. 859 (1906) and *Dunlop v*

Then there are the right to capital gains in or the income out of the assets, the risk of loss of the assets and the liability for the harm they may cause.[236] The entirely different

Mercer, 156 Fed. 545 (1907), although depending on the type of condition vesting in the buyer, could also be subject to a condition subsequent and the re-vesting in the seller to a condition precedent: *Re Lutz*, 197 Fed. 492 (1912).

The name and form the parties gave to their contract was irrelevant and their intent decisive: *Adler v Ammerman Furniture Co*, 100 Conn. 223 (1924), but a mere conditional transfer of possession only might not have been enough to create a conditional sale as title could not be substituted for it: *Maxson v Ashland Iron Works*, 85 Ore. 345 (1917). The term 'security' could be indicative of another type of deal. Thus courts had to intervene in the characterisation issue if only to determine the true intent in which connection the circumstances of the case were also taken into account: *Whitsett v Carney*, 124 SW. 443 (1910).

In this connection it was established that inclusion of a power of sale for the buyer did not make the conditional sale a chattel mortgage or lien *per se* as it did not in itself divest seller of his title: *Call v Seymour*, 40 Ohio. St. 670 (1884), but a duty to pay overvalue to the buyer could be indicative of a secured transaction: *Knowles Loom Work v Knowles*, 6 Penn. (Del.) 185 (1906). Especially a conditional sale without an adequate price could be considered a pledge: *Murray v Butte-Monitor Tunnel Min.* Co, 41 Mont. 449 (1910). A present absolute sale to a buyer who mortgaged the goods back to the seller did not result in a conditional sale, however. There was only a security interest (even though the mortgage itself was originally a conditional sale): *Chicago R Equipment Co v Merchant's Nat. Bank*, 136 US 268 (1890).

No fundamental test was, however, developed to distinguish clearly between conditional sales and security interests, but *certain criteria* emerged. There was an assumption of a security interest where there was a sale with a return of overvalue or recovery of a purchase price whilst the interest in the title was also retained. This indicated a mere debt protected by a security interest as there was no reliance on a conditional sale: *Young v Phillips*, 202 Mich. 480 (1918). Thus a conditional sale and an action to recover the price were not truly compatible: see also n 233 *supra*, and if there was emphasis on payment of the price rather than on reclaiming of the goods instead, a secured transaction might be assumed.

Other borderline issues arose between conditional and absolute sales, *intent* always being decisive: *Blackford v Neaves*, 23 Ariz. 501 (1922). In the former case the Uniform Conditional Sales Act was applicable in states that had adopted it and in the latter case the Sale of Goods Act of the relevant state or otherwise the common law of sale of goods: *Ivers & P Piano Co v Allen*, 101 Me. 218 (1906). There could be a difference in the protection of *bona fide* purchasers of the buyer. Again intention decided the issue in principle: *Blackford v Neaves*, *supra*. In the case of doubt the courts were inclined to assume an absolute sale, this being the more normal situation: *Sears, R & Co v Higbee*, 225 Ill. App. 197 (1922). Instalment payments could, however, be indicative of a conditional sale: *Perkins v Metter*, 126 Cal. 100 (1899) and any statement on an invoice that goods were sold was not held conclusive: *HB Claflin Co v Porter*, 34 Atl. 259 (1895).

It was possible for the seller to retain the possession of the assets under a conditional sale. This could raise Statute of Frauds problems, however, if there was no document: see n 232 *supra*. Most importantly, a non-possessory chattel mortgage was then sometimes implied. It was also possible that there would be no more than an executory contract to sell the asset but no sale: *Davis v Giddings*, 30 Neb. 209 (1890). There could be such danger even if the goods had been delivered to the buyer who had not received an interest in the title: *State ex rel. Malin-Yates Co v Justice of the Peace Ct*, 51 Mont. 133 (1915) when a *bona fide* purchaser from the buyer could not obtain title either: *Harkness v Russell & Co*, 118 USA 663 (1886).

[235] It may be argued that in a conditional sale of a receivable any security interest supporting the claim itself is transferred to the new owner and supports his collection activity, whilst this is not automatically the case for a pledgee if the secured receivable is merely pledged. Opinion is divided on the subject.

[236] In a conditional sale, the capital gain or capital depreciation may be for the party who eventually obtains the full ownership which will depend on the fulfilment (or non-fulfilment as the case may be) of the condition and subsequent appropriation, whilst in the case of a security interest the capital gain or loss remains in principle with the owner even if only expressed in terms of overvalue to be returned or undervalue in an execution sale.

Income may be considered to accrue to the owner, who in the case of a conditional sale is probably the person likely to become the ultimate full owner (although under repurchase agreements of investment securities assets paying interest or dividend during the repurchase period are normally not included to avoid any dispute or complication in this regard), and not to the security holder. It may also be that the income is truly for the party that holds the physical possession (the buyer in a repo) at the time it is accrued or is paid out (which need not be the same).

The risk of the loss of the asset for reasons of *force majeure* may, under a conditional sale, also be carried by the person who has the actual possession of the asset. This person may also bear the maintenance and insurance cost and any third party liability for harm caused by the asset. In the case of a security interest, actual possession may have a similar effect but may not render the security holder liable for the loss of the asset due to *force majeure*.

situation under conditional sales, compared to secured transactions, is illustrated in the proprietary protections of each party's interest:[237] in the disposition rights in the goods and of their interests in them, including the protection of *bona fide* buyers;[238] the possibility and

However, in all these cases, contractual arrangements to the contrary may be made except where product liability statutes contain mandatory liability provisions. Voting rights on pledged shares remain normally with the pledgor: see Article 3.247 Dutch CC, whilst the financier may acquire them in a conditional sale to him.

The foregoing means that, barring contractual provisions to the contrary, the person receiving funding through a conditional sale or benefiting from a payment deferment is likely to have the benefits and carry the burdens of the asset, which is by no means always so for the holder of a security interest, although the security agreement may approximate this situation.

If the asset is a receivable, the collection facility and proceeds will normally be with the party providing the funding, although this can only be so upon notification to the debtor in the case of a security interest. Another difference with the collection by a conditional or fiduciary assignee is that the latter, unlike the pledge of receivables, does not need to return any overvalue (except where his rights are equated with those of a pledgee).

In the USA before the UCC, case law elaborated extensively on the benefits and burdens of assets subject to a conditional sale and how they were distributed between seller and buyer. Of course they could be redistributed in the contract itself, but if this had not happened the question was what followed from the conditional sale itself. As the buyer was normally in physical possession of the goods, it followed also in the USA that he was entitled to their enjoyment which carried with it also a *prima facie* responsibility for their burdens. Thus the risk of loss and destruction without fault of either party shifted eventually from the original owner to the person with physical possession and that became the majority view: *Phillips v Hollenburg Music Co*, 82 Ark. 9 (1907), confirmed in Section 27 of the Uniform Conditional Sales Act. But when the goods were still with the carrier, the seller retained the risk, except where under the contract the risk had already passed to the buyer as in a fob sale.

In as far as third party liability was concerned, the seller was not normally thought liable for the negligence of the buyer in the use of the property: *Coonse v Bechold*, 71 Ind. App. 663 (1919). It corresponds with the idea that the physical holder had the risk of the assets and therefore the duty to insure and collect the insurance payments.

Property that remained in the possession of the seller or with an agent at the request of the buyer was at his risk. The right to the capital gain was nevertheless likely to accrue to the ultimate absolute title-holder unless otherwise agreed. It follows that income tax would be for the buyer, capital gains tax for the ultimate owner. Property tax would appear to have been for the buyer's account: *State v White Furniture Co*, 206 Ala. 575 (1921), at least after the delivery of possession was completed.

[237] At least in civil law countries other than Germany, the pledgor as owner may have to defend the rights of the pledgee against third parties who may have divested him. The pledgee may not have the possessory action himself, except in Germany and under common law (like a bailee under a bailment). Conditional owners even if not in physical possession may in this respect have a stronger right, certainly where the *in rem* effect of their expectancy or *Anwartschaft* is accepted.
[238] As regards disposition rights, the pledgee normally has none (except in an execution sale, whilst in England there may be a subpledgee of the possession of the pledgee), but the conditional owners are likely to be able to dispose of their interests even if only an expectancy or option: see also text following nn 60 and 63, see further nn 126 and 139 *supra* plus accompanying text.

It raises the question of delivery of possession in systems like the German and Dutch (and for a pledge also the French) which require it for title transfer. For the conditional owner not holding the asset, the transfer of his conditional proprietary right may be through the mere conclusion of the contract (in Germany, either as an assignment under Section 870 or through a sale and delivery *longa manu* under Section 931 BGB without notice or in the Netherlands with notice) whilst the asset itself remains in the control of the other party. For the latter, the transfer of his proprietary interest will be completed through the physical delivery of the asset or *constituto possessorio* if the asset remains in his control. Both the owner under a resolutive condition and the one under a suspensive condition will thus be able to transfer their respective interests in the title. The *bona fide* purchaser from the conditional owner who acquires physical possession of the asset may thereby even acquire full title, thus title free of any condition. Such uncluttered title cannot be obtained from a conditional owner without physical possession of the goods.

To a purchaser aware of the conditionality, full title can only be transferred by both conditional owners together, except perhaps in some common law countries when disposal is in the nature of the asset or they are disposed of in the ordinary course of business when the *bona fides* of the acquirer may become irrelevant. Also, the inability to dispose of full title might not prevent a financier with conditional title from collecting receivables and using the proceeds for set-off against the purchase price repayment obligation by way of amortisation. Only Dutch law requires for the creation of suspensive ownership the physical transfer of the asset (Article 3.91), particularly relevant for reservations of title.

In the USA before the wide acceptance of the UCC, the possibility for each party to transfer its conditional ownership interest, for the holder to transfer the assets themselves and for *bona fide* purchasers acquiring possession to claim full title, gave rise to much case law. In so far as the protection of *bona fide* purchasers was concerned, the filing requirement in some states also proved relevant.

Although the fact that the seller reserved ownership meant for many that the buyer could not have a proprietary right: see *Re Lyon*, Fed Cas No 8, 644 (1872), it was always clear that the buyer could make himself unilaterally the owner and it was therefore also accepted that the relationship between seller and buyer was not one of merely creditor and debtor: see *Holt Mfg Co v Jaussand*, 132 Wash. 667 (1925), certainly if the seller did not rely on his action to recover the purchase price but on his proprietary protection as a conditional seller only. It was also clear that upon a conditional sale, the position of the seller was never one of absolute unbridled ownership either.

The seller had a lesser interest which he could nevertheless sell. Also the buyer had some interest in the property. Some saw him as a bailee: *Rodgers v Rachman*, 109 Cal. 552 (1895), but it was often thought to be more than that: see *State v Automobile*, 122 Me. 280 (1925). It was sometimes believed that a defeasible title had indeed vested in the buyer: *Peter Water Wheel Co v Oregon Iron & Steel Co*, 87 Or. 248 (1918). Others thought it to be an equitable interest like future interests: *Carolina Co v Unaka Sporings Lumber Co*, 130 Tenn. 354 (1914), whilst the buyer was to all intents and purposes believed the owner in *Kentucky Wagon Mfg Co v Blanton-Curtis Mercantile Co*, 8 Ala. App. 669 (1913). His title was thought to exist in principle, to be ripened by payment into an absolute title in *Newhall v Kingsbury*, 131 Mass. 445 (1881), which the seller could not stop: *Brian v HA Born Packers' Supply Co*, 203 Ill. App. 262 (1917). The buyer was not allowed to divest himself of his interest either through agreement with the seller or through surrender in order to defraud his creditors: *Horn v Georgia Fertilizer & Oil Co*, 18 Ga. App. 35 (1916). A simple return of the property to relieve him from the payment burden was also not accepted: *Appleton v Norwalk Library Corp*, 53 Conn. 4 (1885).

Thus each party had apparently a sufficient interest in the property to be able to defend it independently of the other and had a negligence action against third parties for damage to or destruction of the property, the seller on the basis of a general ownership right and the buyer on the basis of a special ownership right: *Smith v Gufford*, 36 Fla. 481 (1895). Naturally an action of the one was a bar to that of the other: *Louisville & NR Co v Mack*, 2 Tenn. CCA 194 (1911). They needed not to join and the seller needed no permission of the buyer nor did he need possession. A settlement by the buyer did not necessarily bind the seller either, but an action in trespass could only be brought by the seller after default by the buyer: *Fields v Williams*, 91 Ala. 502 (1890).

As for the transfer of each party's interest, it became accepted that both the seller and the buyer could transfer their interest without the consent or involvement of the other party even if this did not transfer full title in the chattels. See for the interest of the seller *Burrier v Cunningham Piano Co*, 135 Md. 135 (1919) and the Uniform Conditional Sales Act was believed to support it: *Van Marel v Watson*, 235 Pac. 144 (1925). The form in which the seller could do this was through assignment, as the seller's right to retake the property was characterised as a chose in action. The assignment was not subject to any formalities in terms of documentation or notification to the conditional buyer in possession: *Swann Davis Co v Stanton*, 7 Ga. App. 688 (1910).

It was necessary to specify the interest transferred; just writing over the contract document that it was assigned was not sufficient. It was also possible to transfer a security interest in the seller's remainder: *Thayer v Yakima Tire Service Co*, 116 Wash. 299 (1921), but there was a question whether in that case the lienee acquired only a collection right for the purchase price or also a security interest in the chattel when it returned to the seller upon default of the buyer: *Bank of California v Danamiller*, 125 Wash. 225 (1923). The assignment of the purchase price itself did not include an assignment of the conditional title except if so intended: see for this ancillarity issue n 234 *supra*. An assignment of the conditional interest itself divested the seller of all his rights in the assets. A subsequent second sale of his interest even if accompanied by delivery of the asset to the new assignee was ineffective even if the latter was *bona fide*: *Newell Bros v Hanson*, 97 Vt. 297 (1924).

A transfer of the buyer's interest in the asset was also possible, and upon the delivery of the asset the full title of the *bona fide* purchaser was more likely to be protected. There could also have been an implied licence of the seller authorising the buyer to do so in the ordinary course of his business which would have protected all purchasers, but the protection for the *bona fide* purchaser remained an exception in line with common law that did not generally accept the principle, but whatever the buyer had in terms of conditional title or future equitable right was normally deemed transferable without consent of the other party: *Re Pittsburgh Industrial Iron Works*, 179 Fed. 151 (1910). As in the case of the seller, the buyer could also sub-encumber his interest either by granting his bank a security interest in his conditional title or by selling-on the interest in a further conditional sale of his own, but case law remained divided as some continued to argue that the buyer had no right in the title at all, but the better view was probably that the sub-vendee acquired a right into the property subject to that of the original seller: *Clinton v Ross*, 108 Ark. 442 (1912).

The protection of *bona fide* purchasers of the assets from a buyer with only limited disposition rights is traditionally exceptional in common law but there are some such exceptions in favour of such purchasers and early US law also dealt with this aspect of conditional sales at some length. It was sometimes held that delivery of possession to the buyer in a conditional sale gave him *indicia of ownership*, but in the majority view this was not truly the case as no title was thought to have passed and possession was no more than *prima facie* evidence of it: see *Blackwell v Walker Bros*, 5 Fed. 419 (1880).

There was as a consequence no entrusting of the asset to the buyer allowing him to at least transfer good title to *bona fide* purchasers. But these purchasers as well as *bona fide* creditors of the buyer were nevertheless protected in some states: see *Beatrice Creamery Co v Sylvester*, 65 Colo. 569 (1919). Where there was a filing requirement, it gave the seller a much better position. On the other hand, its omission tended further to protect

right to (sub)encumber the various interests in the asset;[239] and in the inclusion of future assets and the shifting of the interest into replacement goods.[240] Then there is the difference in the entitlement to the asset in the case of a bankrupt financier in possession: the repurchase option might be merely *in personam*, but the repurchase duty and the tendering of the repurchase price may conceivably give proprietary protection and reclamation rights. Any pledge of a bankrupt financier would, on the other hand, certainly disappear upon repayment of the loan by the debtor which gives him a reclaiming right in the asset. Finally, there are also to be considered the effect of an attachment

the rights of third parties including purchasers and creditors of the buyer, at least if unaware of the seller's interest. The Uniform Conditional Sales Act (Section 3) followed this line.

The seller's title remained, however, protected against after-acquired property clauses in earlier mortgages or security interests granted by the buyer to his creditors. It was one of the main attractions of the conditional sale and one of the main reasons for its popularity as mentioned before: see *Hanesley v Council*, 147 Ga. 27 (1917). This also applied to purchasers in an execution sale conducted against the buyer who could only buy subject to the seller's interest even if *bona fide*. On the other hand, where goods were sold by the buyer in the ordinary course of his business, the purchaser acquired full title even if he was aware of the interests of the original seller. This was a major departure reflected also in the Uniform Conditional Sales Act (Section 9) and was retained in the UCC.

[239] A pledgee normally has no right to re-pledge his interest: see also Article 3.242 Dutch CC. It is only the owner who can do so, although there was authority to the contrary in Roman law and the *ius commune* (C 8.23) and common law in England also accepted the possibility thus viewing the pledgee's interest as a right independent of the claim it insured: see in England *Donald v Suckling* (1866) LR 1, QB 585 subject always to a contractual clause to the contrary when the goods could still be (conditionally) sold however: see nn 4 and 195 *supra*. See in the USA before the UCC, n 238 *supra*.

An interesting complication is whether an encumbrance of his interest by one of the parties in a conditional ownership also affects the other. Under civil law where the *bona fide* pledgee taking possession is often protected he would thus take more than the pledgor may have or can give. This is less likely to be the result under common law, which adopts a more rigorous interpretation of the *nemo dat* rule, certainly outside the law of sales.

[240] See for common law in England, nn 196 and 197 *supra* and accompanying text. In the USA under pre-UCC law, the property conditionally sold had to be specific but could be described generally. Yet the description could be so general as to render the conditional sale invalid, but parole evidence was allowed to describe the property: *Thomas Furniture Co v T&C Furniture Co*, 120 Ga. 879 (1909). Under the Uniform Conditional Sales Act, a reasonable identification was sufficient: *cf also* the present Section 9-108 (9–110 old) UCC. It should be remembered here that a document was not normally necessary for a conditional sale: see n 232 *supra*. Future assets could be included provided they could also be sufficiently identified: *Benner v Puffer*, 114 Mass. 376 (1874), but especially in this context the description could be too general. The general rules of goods *not in esse* were thought applicable and they were at law more restrictive than in equity - and conditional sales were transactions at law (even though where they resulted in future interests in chattels these were equitable).

The inclusion of after-acquired property in the conditional sale was subject to similar specificity requirements, although this inclusion was sometimes explained as creating a security interest in the nature of a floating charge. Such an after-acquired property clause could not affect goods that the seller received under conditional sales. A substitution of property was possible in a conditional sale if specifically so agreed, as in a herd of cows: *Paris v Vail*, 18 Vt. 277 (1846). Sometimes new property was automatically included as in the case of accession (even calf in cattle) or repair (like new tyres on a car). On the other hand, the conditional right in the property could also be lost, e.g. if it was affixed to real estate: see Section 7 of the Uniform Conditional Sales Act.

The conditional sale could also be used to support other debt: *Union Machinery & Supply Co v Thompson*, 98 Wash. 119 (1917), but this had to be agreed and was not automatic: *Smith v Long Cigar & Grocery Co*, 21 Ga. App. 730 (1917). If another debt was to be covered, normally payments were used to extinguish that debt first and the payment of the purchase price which was the true condition of the title transfer would then be deemed to take place last: *Faist v Waldo*, 57 Ark. 270 (1893).

Finally the rights of the seller could shift into proceeds and authorisation did not appear necessary and no general clause to the effect was required in the conditional sale contract. It was not considered a fraud on other creditors: *Prentiss Tool & Supply Co v Schirmer*, 136 NY 305 (1892). However, where the buyer was authorised to sell the property, this could defeat the shift into proceeds: *Re Howland*, 109 Fed. 869 (1901). Where there had been comingling, such proceeds as could be identified to the original conditional sale were reclaimable. If this was not possible, the seller's right was lost which could already be so if the good was irretrievably comingled with others, notably the buyer's own: *Re Agnew*, 178 Fed. 478 (1909).

levied on the interests of either party to a conditional sale, by the creditors of either,[241] or the inclusion of either party's interest in a bankruptcy of the other.[242]

This raises the issue of the ranking of each party's interests in the priority ladder of the other's bankruptcy and their relationship to security holders in the same asset. Thus a

---

[241] Only German law has a statutory rule in the case of reservations of title: see Section 771 CCP, and allows the conditional buyer's creditors to attach the latter's rights. The conditional seller may object to protect his title against a judicial sale and allege unjust attachment. Under German case law, the buyer may similarly object to an attachment of the assets by the seller's creditors. Where the attachment does not itself result in a charge, which is the situation in most West European countries, but not in Germany and in most states of the USA, the measure is a mere order to preserve or execute the asset. As in the case of a conditional sale the attachment does not cover full title but only each conditional owner's limited disposition right and interest in the asset, it might not be very valuable and hardly result in a worthwhile sale, especially in countries where an execution sale is not free and clear of all charges in it: see also n 233 *supra*.

In pre-UCC law in the USA, it was clear that the seller's and buyer's rights in the chattels conditionally sold were both subject to the recovery rights of their creditors, but this did not apply to more than each party to the conditional sale had, although case law remained divided on whether in the case of the buyer, even if in possession, there was a leviable interest. It depended on one's view of the nature of his interest. Where it was considered merely equitable it was sometimes deemed not sufficiently vested to be attachable: *Goodell v Fairbrother*, 12 RI 233 (1878). Yet there was also case law to the contrary: *Savall v Wauful*, 16 NY Supp. 219 (1890).

Another possibility was to give creditors of the buyer the right to tender the purchase price in order to obtain in this manner a leviable interest: *Frank v Batten*, 1 NY Supp. 705 (1888). In any event, creditors of a buyer in possession would normally attempt to attach the whole property, in which case the seller had to defend himself. As a general proposition, the seller's interest was good against the creditors of the buyer, although in recording states this was subject to his proper filing, and in the case of failure to do so, the *bona fide* creditors of the buyer were likely to prevail. Otherwise creditors of the buyer could not interfere with the seller's right on penalty of wrongful attachment and an execution sale would not improve their rights or the title of the buyer in such a sale. Damages would be payable if the seller wrongfully thwarted in regaining physical possession. Yet the attachment was meaningful if it preserved the asset until the maturity date, the payment of the last instalment and the acquisition of absolute title by the buyer.

[242] In a bankruptcy of a seller under a reservation of title, the trustee prevails over a buyer under a reservation of title if the latter does not pay. Only if the contract is still executory, that means that it is not fulfilled in whole or in part by either party, is there a choice for the trustee either to continue or terminate the contract, *cf* e.g. Section 365 of the US Bankruptcy Code and Sections 103 and 107 of the German Insolvency Act 1999. In leasing, the contract is often considered executory even though the lessor has delivered the asset, hence the election right rather than the appropriation in the case of a bankruptcy of the lessee: see also the text at n 225 *supra*.

In the USA, this appears also to be the case in repos. It is important to realise that without the characterisation of the underlying contract as executory with the implied option to terminate the agreement, in a bankruptcy of a financier or buyer of the assets, the bankruptcy trustee may have to wait until the repayment or repayment option date before he can reclaim the purchase price (upon offering the return of the assets), which is in fact no different from a repayment of a secured loan. In a bankruptcy of the conditional vendor, on the other hand, the claim of the financier for the repurchase price will mature immediately so that he may be able to appropriate a full ownership right if there is no payment in full by the trustee. In Germany in a *Sicherungsübereignung*, the original owner always has an *in rem* reclaiming right: see text at n 129 *supra*. It is in fact an *in rem* option.

In the USA in pre-UCC law, as at 1910, the trustee in bankruptcy was given the position of a lien creditor. It meant that the rights of conditional sellers who failed to record or file their interests became inferior to the rights of a trustee in bankruptcy of the buyer. Where there was no need to file, the right of the conditional seller remained superior, however, to the rights of the buyer's trustee. The trustee could of course always pay off the seller in order to acquire full title. As we saw, a conditional seller was no less protected against *bona fide* purchasers from the buyer, except again if he had failed to record his interest in states that required it. There was likely to be an exception if the seller had given the buyer a right to on-sell the asset when *bona fides* of purchasers may also have been irrelevant: see n 238 *supra in fine*. Where the right of the conditional seller was only considered executory, the buyer's trustee in bankruptcy might have had an election to continue or terminate the contract. Repudiation might have allowed the trustee to retain the asset subject to a competing claim for damages, but the more normal solution was to accept the seller's replevin action, except where there had only been an agreement to sell but the buyer was in that case unlikely to have been in possession.

In the case of a bankruptcy of the seller, his right was also likely to pass to his trustee who would have had to respect the buyer's right to acquire full title upon payment. The trustee could not appropriate the asset before there was a default of the buyer. Where the seller still had custody of the assets, it appears that the buyer even in a bankruptcy of the seller was still entitled to them by offering the purchase price on the due date. He could then re-levy the asset. Thus in such cases this right was considered proprietary and superior to the rights of the creditors and the trustee of the seller.

reservation of title may in theory give the highest priority to the seller in a bankruptcy of the buyer but he may be subject to later security interests created by the buyer in the asset. In connection with this, conditional owners may not be competing creditors in the other's bankruptcy at all and may have more the status of co-owners or partners who take subject to the security interest of all others, even if later, although they may sometimes have a facility to resist their creation if they become aware of it. It is likely to affect their revindication right also.[243]

More comparative research will have to be done into the differences between the conditional owners under a funding or payment deferment scheme and the holders of a security interest and between the position of the conditional owners in an asset *inter se*. It is likely to highlight the difference in the overall risk the parties are taking under the various schemes of funding and sales credit.

If we limit ourselves here principally to the appropriation aspect, this may be essential to the party parting with the asset and is particularly indicative of the risk differential between the schemes (which is not limited to the risk of loss of the asset and the liability for any damage caused by it). In an inflationary climate, the seller of an asset under a reservation of title will not be interested in an execution sale and the return of any overvalue to the defaulting buyer. In the case of a default, he would want to resell the asset whenever a good opportunity arises and preserve his store of value until such time rather than incur the extra risk of the delays necessarily attached to an execution sale. Even if technically he might be able to deduct any damages from this overvalue, they will have to be judicially assessed, which is costly and time consuming.

The alternative for him is to agree commercial interest with the buyer from the beginning, the rate of which would have to be very high, a protection which he is unlikely to get for the reasons just stated. Should he nevertheless obtain it, it would then be logical that the reservation would be considered a security interest, with any overvalue accruing to the buyer upon an execution sale. That would then be his bargain. In an environment like that of the USA, not used to high inflation, it may not have occurred to the draftsmen of the UCC that there is a fundamental difference here. In France, where the reservation of title is evolving into a security interest, it is less understandable. In the context of the EBRD Model Law, which is targeted at high inflation countries, the lack of insight into this difference is difficult to explain.

Similarly, in a finance lease, the lessor will not normally be interested in an execution sale upon the default of the lessee. It will be time-consuming and costly, whilst the often valuable asset, like a ship or aeroplane, remains unused; any early cashing in of proceeds

---

[243] If it is true that the *bona fide* pledgee or chargee is protected against the conditionality of the ownership, as is the case for chattels in many civil law countries under the general rules of the protection of *bona fides* (subject to the requirements of proper consideration and actual possession): see also n 239 *supra in fine*, it follows that the conditional owner without possession it postponed even if himself *bona fide* and unaware of any adverse interests created in the property by the other owner in the meantime. Any contractual prohibition concerning the alienability of the asset would not affect him, even if he knew of it: see also Section 9–401 (9–311 old) UCC. Again, it is a general principle in civil law, at least in respect of chattels which cannot be tied down: see for the different civil law attitude in the case of a contractual prohibition of an assignment and for the UCC response, chapter IV, s. 1.7.3. The result is that conditional owners may not be able to disown pledges given by the other party to the conditional sale, at least if the latter has transferred actual possession of the asset to the pledgee, as not both can be protected at the same time.

If the charge is non-possessory, even if registered or published, the situation may well be different and these (later) interests may rank lower than that of the conditional owner not in possession who will have the older right and therefore probably the better title except in systems in which published non-possessory interests have the rank of possessory interests, whilst the interest holder is at least bona fide in respect of the existence of any earlier proprietary interests.

may substantially disrupt funding patterns. Instead, the lessor will normally want to release the asset immediately, if necessary through an operational lease. Or, if the asset was tailor made for the lessee, he may wish to make other arrangements but certainly not conduct an execution sale which may yield very little and destroy everything.

In exchange for this facility and the protection appropriation gives, the rent under the lease could be even lower than the financing cost of an equivalent loan, although it naturally depends on the totality of the arrangement and the risk distribution as well as on market conditions. Banks may be willing to take larger risks in other areas under ownership-based funding for other types of rewards; that is their business and choice. The conditional sales concept allows great flexibility and variety here. That is its attraction and justification, at least amongst professionals.

US law here has been confining in a mandatory manner since the introduction of the unitary functional UCC approach. Apparently it is concerned about abuse — especially appropriation — much as the earlier *lex commissoria* was discouraged in Roman law and in the *ius commune*, with important remnants still left in civil law, especially in the case of securities, although not necessarily when it comes to reclaiming the asset upon default under a sales agreement (at least if there is a clause to the effect in that agreement).[244] The concerns here are likely to be about proportionality of reward, in the sense that the non-defaulting party does not get more than he bargained for through an appropriation windfall. There may also be concerns about the rights of other creditors of the defaulter.

If justified, much of these concerns can be redressed, however, through *in personam* actions including those concerned with the consequences of rescission and unjust enrichment. In other instances, cashing in the overvalue will be a just result as a lower reward structure was balancing this benefit upon default. At least in the professional sphere there does not seem to be any fundamental policy motive against letting participants make their own arrangements in this respect, and therefore also not in the appropriation or execution sale and overvalue aspects. In any event, it is hard to see why a (professional) defaulting party should always be entitled to the overvalue and why he should not be allowed to bargain this value away in advance in conditional ownership arrangements for other benefits.

In modern financial schemes, there may be a combination of all kinds of options or repurchase rights and duties which all raise the question of their *in rem* or proprietary effect. In fact, an option may be clothed in a conditional ownership right which the party may or may not elect to exercise, thus translating it into an *in rem* option. In a conditional sale, the risk-sharing arrangement may be such that the financier who no longer qualifies for the status of creditor proper is as a consequence taken out of the priority ladder of the debtor. This demands other protections or rewards. The financier may end up with an interest in the asset subject to all security interests granted by his counter-party (in possession) to *bona fide* creditors and to which he did not object, if only because he was not aware of their creation.

On the European Continent, where the American functional approach is most certainly not adopted, these issues remain largely unexplored: in France there has been some important case law attempting to distinguish the repurchase option agreement from the secured transaction, but they operate in principle side by side.[245] In Germany the common *Sicherungsübereignung* started as a conditional transfer but has now abandoned many of its features and has, at least in bankruptcy, become more like a preferential right in the sales proceeds of the assets *(Absonderungsrecht)*.[246] In the Netherlands, under its old law, this

---

[244] See section 1.1.6 *supra.*
[245] See n 87 *supra* and accompanying text.
[246] See n 136 *supra* and accompanying text.

structure had acquired the status of a security right *(Aussonderungsrecht)*, as one would expect if supporting a loan agreement.[247]

New Dutch law has attempted to abolish the *in rem* effect of all conditional transfers used to raise money (not for sales credit) if used as a security substitute, but it has failed to introduce either a functional or other workable criterion, and has only increased confusion as a consequence. It remains to be seen how case law will react; the indications so far go in the direction of renewed support for the conditional sales concept in non-loan situations, although the precise consequences for both parties remain unclear.[248]

1.7.4 Concluding Remarks

What does this all add up to? At the very least it means that there is a large area outside secured transactions where major funding operations with some other form of proprietary protection are increasingly situated. By talking about secured transactions all the time, and more so by forcing new funding structures into a unitary system of secured interests, we are making a significant mistake and entering a world of unreality.

The ownership- and security-based systems of funding and protection need to be clearly distinguished. The first normally conform to the pattern of conditional sales of assets, the latter to the traditional secured loan, whilst sale credit protection is likely also to assume the form of the conditional sale. The English mortgage holds some middle ground here as it is a conditional sale in support of a loan. It is right therefore that there is some special debtor's protection, given here in the form of the redemption right rather than an execution sale with the return of overvalue, as is common for secured loans. The conditional transfer inherent in the German *Sicherungsübereignung* has largely been converted into a lien structure for similar reasons.

In all legal systems researched here, these insights are still embryonic, although moving into the direction of greater clarity with English law probably the most sophisticated, and American statutory law (Article 9 UCC) perhaps the least, although American case law is not insensitive to the problems. This conclusion is somewhat surprising as it concerns here two common law countries, whilst academic opinion, shared by many in the UK,[249] often stresses the intellectual and practical superiority of the Article 9 UCC approach.

In the USA, the unavoidable result has been that the modern finance sales, like repos, finance leases and receivable factoring, are difficult to place. Where they must be considered secured transactions, the filing requirements then apply to their ranking, and any omission to file will reduce their rank to just above that of the common creditors. Modern bankruptcy law concepts with their disposition, return of overvalue, stay and dilution possibilities will have a further detrimental impact. Only in England does the law seem to leave ample room for the modern finance sales, including any proprietary effect they may produce for either party, although there is not much discussion of these aspects. Civil law has had little to contribute in the realm of ideas.

Modern Dutch law simply refuses to give security substitutes any proprietary effect. The result is that the modern finance sales are threatened under new Dutch law, which has omitted to give a clear definition of a true security, however. Unlike American law, it does

---

[247] See n 134 *supra*.

[248] See respectively texts at nn 140, 87 and 61*ff supra*: see for an early discussion of ownership based financing also U Drobnig, 'Uncitral Report, Part Two, International payments', in (1977) VIII *Yearbook of the United Nations Commission on International Trade Law (Uncitral)*, who pleads for the functional approach.

[249] See in England the Crowther Report of 1970 and Diamond Report of 1989 and amongst the authors eg MG Bridge, 'Form, Substance and Innovation in Personal Property Security Law' [1994] *J Bus L*, 1.

not even convert conditional sales into secured transactions when threatened. Case law is stepping in to sort matters out.

So in several countries there remains a substantial re-characterisation risk. In the meantime one may ask why ownership-based funding has become so much more popular in the last twenty years, as shown in repos, finance leases and factoring. It may be the possibility of lower cost for the party requiring financing and, particularly, the greater variety of financial products it supports, which are motivated by the need for different risk and reward structures and choice. Certainly the conditional sale and ownership transfer leading to split ownership seems more in tune with the unbundling of risk increasingly practised by banks.

There is another point that may well be particularly relevant in international financing.[250] That is the greater international familiarity with ownership concepts, rather than with securities, which invariably break down into local variants. They normally also invite registration requirements and other formalities which may be meaningful purely domestically, but less so internationally. This is not only because of the difficulties in ascertaining their existence and effect, and in the access to the local registration systems; it is also because their protective relevance may dwindle internationally when assets move across borders, or when their location is altogether uncertain, as in the case of receivables.

Most importantly, opening up the proprietary systems by using the concept of conditional ownership in financing may lead to harmonisation internationally, as it provides a bridge between common and civil law, albeit at a conceptual cost to civil law lawyers. The relative contractualisation of the ownership concept is always subject, however, to the protection of *bona fide* third parties. The concept in the case of tangible movable assets is common to the major civil law jurisdictions as it is to equitable interests in common law. It will require acceptance of the facility contractually to split this ownership with the duality of title this entails. Most importantly, it will show that the split ownership in conditional sales and title transfers also allows for structures in civil law very similar to those of the common law trust, so that some approximation in this important area will occur. Conditional ownership rights and expectancies compare easily to equitable interests in common law. The important difference is the lack of *bona fide* purchaser protection against these interests if in intangibles, especially in receivables.

It is likely that further ratification of the Hague Convention on the Law Applicable to Trusts and on their Recognition of 1985 (since 1992 effective between the UK, Canada, Australia and Italy; to which the Netherlands has now also acceded; and ratification of which is also considered in France: see chapter IV, section 1.4.6) will provide its own stimulus in this approximation process. The development of a more transnationalised concept of ownership, clearly existing in the area of commercial paper and documents of title where it is historically the product of the international law merchant: see chapter I, section 3.2.2, may further facilitate the characterisation, recognition and adjustment of proprietary interests when the assets surface or play a role in other countries. This is very relevant for intangible assets like receivables if their transfer in the nature of negotiable instruments is further encouraged: see chapter IV, section 1.7.7, but it should be so for all types of personal property and the security and particularly conditional ownership interests created therein.

These developments invite discussion on all types of conditional ownership and their operation in the national laws.[251] This is likely to have a similar opening-up effect in the

---

[250] See Dalhuisen, n 35 *supra*, 387.
[251] See for a summary also JH Dalhuisen, 'Conditional Sales and Modern Financial Products' in A Hartkamp et al, *Towards a European Civil Code* (2nd edn, 1998), 525.

civil law of property as the concept of good faith, fairness or reasonableness (*Treu und Glauben*) had in the civil law of contract. Debate in this area is necessary, urgent and greatly to be encouraged. It will lead to an approximation of the different proprietary approaches, at least in international dealings. In fact, in international commerce and financing, there is no real reason or intellectual justification for the fragmentation of the ownership concept along purely domestic lines any longer; it is also illogical. Once this is recognised, it will also be seen that there is no reason or justification for the differences to remain operative at purely domestic levels.

A last observation may be in order here. The equality of creditors is often presented as a justified concern and as an argument against the proprietary effects of all kinds of financial schemes likely to protect the financier, as finance sales also do. However, this equality or the so-called *par conditio creditorum* is not truly the basis of the system of creditors' protection or a fundamental legal principle, although endlessly paraded as such. If it were, it would only be honoured in the breach and it distorts the discussion. In my researches of bankruptcy law I have always found that it is equitable, *not* equal, distribution that is the key, and what is equitable in this respect is now mostly a matter of statutory definition in domestic bankruptcy acts.[252]

It is therefore the *ranking* (and the separation or segregation of assets including reclaiming facilities), and *not* the equality, that is the essence of bankruptcy and of creditors relationships more generally.[253] This cannot be repeated often enough. It is accepted everywhere that, in this context, financiers can negotiate a higher ranking for the liquidity they provide. Whether this is done through a secured loan or through the proprietary effects of conditional sales does not seem to raise any point of principle. Certainly it is not in issue where the latter are sometimes automatically re-characterised and converted into the former, even though this may lead, as we saw, to considerable adverse consequences for the financier under applicable bankruptcy laws.

Nevertheless, the contractualisation of the ownership concept is meant to reinforce the financiers' positions through the introduction of split ownership rights in conditional sales in civil law. Increased reclaiming possibilities of assets, if only to prevent the bankrupt estate from reaping the benefits of unjust enrichment, the shifting of proprietary rights into converted or commingled assets and proceeds, and the widening set-off possibilities through contractual close-out netting are all meant to reinforce the financier's position. This certainly becomes a matter of policy for bankruptcy legislators everywhere, even if the effects are initially mainly seen in case law.

Conceptually, civil law has further to go here, but in the end it is unlikely to hinder the need and tendency to protect the modern funding techniques through some form of proprietary protection in ways different from secured transactions. Putting it like this, the new developments in this area may be no more than re-establishing the balance between financier and fund-raiser in modern ways. Yet civil law may also use the opportunity to broaden the reclaiming, shifting and netting concepts in the process. For the academic observer, this development is of special interest as it may achieve a considerable approximation between common and civil law, besides the one following directly from the acceptance of conditional and split ownership.

Civil law is likely increasingly to incorporate the common law attitudes in this area, although not necessarily the ideas of Article 9 UCC, which has proved a statutory distraction

---

[252] See JH Dalhuisen, *Dalhuisen on International Insolvency and Bankruptcy* (1986), 2–17.
[253] See also the discussion in the text following n 24 *supra*.

inimical to conditional or finance sales. To follow the common law here is logical, as it has traditionally shown better ways and has proved to provide the more imaginative, flexible and efficient support for modern financings, which in any event seem to be largely American-English inspired. It is a positive development that deserves to be guided and encouraged through further study in this important area of the law, and which could lead to a welcome approximation of a number of fundamental common and civil law concepts. It is the reason that so much attention has been given to this subject in this chapter.

1.8 International Aspects of Conditional or Finance Sales and Secured Transactions

1.8.1 *Private International Law Approaches: Uniform Law Attempts of Unidroit and Uncitral*

In chapter IV, section 1.8, the private international law aspects of property were discussed particularly in respect of chattels moving from one country to another when, under the *lex situs* approach,[254] a choice needs to be made between the laws of the country of origin and destination. It is now widely accepted that the law of the country of origin will apply to the creation and perfection of the original proprietary right even if created under the contract law of yet another country, but that the law of the country of destination will impose a recognition regime under which only foreign poprietary rights properly established at the original *situs* and largely equivalent to those in the country of recognition will be accepted. The others might be rejected or, always provided that they were properly created, converted

---

[254] The *lex situs* notion finds general acceptance in proprietary matters, if only because they are often so closely related to enforcement which is also largely a question of the law of the country of location of the asset (although particularly in bankruptcy the proceedings may be opened elsewhere). Indeed Article 16(5) of the EU Convention on Jurisdiction and Enforcement of Judgments in Civil and Commercial Matters of 1968 accepts for enforcement the exclusive jurisdiction of the courts of the *situs* which apply their own law. In proprietary matters, the *lex situs* notion is, however, particularly strained when the assets are intangible or move so frequently, as in the case of aircraft and ships, that the *situs* becomes virtually fortuitous. For intangible claims it is not unreasonable, however, to view them as located at the place of the debtor, again because of the close relationship with enforcement which usually must take place there, or otherwise at the place of the creditor: see also n 297 *infra* and accompanying text.

For ships and aircraft that move internationally, the fortuitous nature of their *situs* does in fact not change the situation dramatically in as far as the creation and recognition of proprietary rights and charges in them are concerned, certainly as to their recognition elsewhere, whilst as for creation and perfection their proper *situs* may be considered the place of their register. It would not avoid the recognition problems in the case of enforcement if ships or aircraft were arrested elsewhere and subjected to a foreign execution, but that seems unavoidable.

There is also a classic *situs* problem when charges shift into manufactured goods or proceeds. In the first case, the *situs* of their manufacture may be considered the place of the conversion: see the Scottish case of *Zahnrad Fabrik Passau GmbH v Terex Ltd*, 1986 SLT 84. For shifting into the proceeds or receivable, an argument can be made that the *situs* is the place of the delivery of the asset or of the payment, the law of which would therefore determine any additional formalities of the continuing charge (which could even be seen as an automatic assignment) or indeed the possibility of such a shift, giving the original seller collection rights. Any continuation of the original charge in the asset backing up any receivable as an ancillary right would then also be covered by this *lex situs*, as would indeed be any rights of *bona fide* successors in the converted property or even of the receivable.

Another *situs* problem arises in respect of registered shares, which are often deemed located at the place of the register. The law of this place then determines the manner of transfer and the way charges may be created in the shares. It does not seem necessary that the law of the place of the register is also the *lex societatis* as companies may choose to maintain registers outside their country of incorporation. A similar approach may obtain for registered bonds, for depositary receipts and indeed also for shares and bonds subject to book entry systems. It may allow internationalisation of these systems under their own transnationalised rules; see chapter IV, s 3.2.

into nearest equivalents: see for the notion of equivalence and the accommodation process chapter IV, section 1.8.2.

For the more limited proprietary rights like secured interests where equivalents might be more difficult to find, this is especially relevant in enforcement in the new country, and more so in bankruptcy when not taking place at the old *situs*. In that case the *lex concursus* may even prevail over the new *lex situs*, at least for the limited purposes of the bankruptcy itself, certainly if the bankruptcy is in a third country. This may create problems if the bankruptcy trustee subsequently seeks to collect the asset from its (new) *situs* where neither the original nor the *lex concursus* attitude to the particular proprietary interest may find favour.

Problems may also arise from disparity in registration and other formation and perfection requirements between the country of origin and destination, even if there is equivalence when some of the equivalent foreign interests are not registered in the recognising country whilst similar local interests may be invalid without it, particularly relevant for secured interests. The fact that the original requirements in this respect are not sufficiently advertised in the country of destination, may be considered an extra impediment for their recognition in that country or anywhere else.

For conditional sales and conditional title, there may be further public policy considerations and impediments to recognition elsewhere when the asset moves or in foreign bankruptcies, although the reservation of title may provide guidance. What interests us here is primarily finance sales like the finance lease, repurchase agreement and factoring. They will be discussed more extensively below. For finance leasing and factoring, some international action is proposed through uniform law as in the Unidroit Leasing Convention of 1988. The international aspects of the factoring technique were discussed more fully in the context of the international assignments of claims: see chapter IV, section 1.9.1. They involve tripartite structures, always of particular difficulty in private international law, hence the effort at unification of some of their more important rules, not only in the Unidroit Factoring Convention of 1988 but now more comprehensively in the 2001 Uncitral Receivable Convention: see also section 2.3.6 below.

No such effort has as yet been made for the international repurchase agreement, which is the prototype of all ownership-based funding. Protection is here usually sought in the technique of netting of all mutual obligations including delivery obligations as we shall see in section 2.2.4 below. In the absence of uniform treaty law, private international law approaches remain particularly relevant for repurchase agreements, although, where affecting eurobonds, transnationalisation tendencies may be expected even in the proprietary aspects.

The Unidroit Conventions on Leasing and Factoring are now effective but have received only a small number of ratifications, The Uncitral Convention only has one signatory and no ratifications. All rely in any event on traditional private international law for aspects outside their scope. They do so even for those aspects within their scope if not specifically covered by the relevant Conventions. In that case, the general principles on which these Conventions are based first prevail, even though it is mostly unclear what these principles may be in the proprietary and enforcement aspects. Also the scope and coverage of these Conventions are often not sharply defined so that one cannot be sure when such general principles may be invoked and relied upon.

In all cases it is helpful to distinguish primarily between the contractual, proprietary and enforcement or bankruptcy aspects and in the case of finance lease also between the derivative or collateral rights of the lessee against the supplier, which are in fact rights exerted against a third party as far as the lessee is concerned.

Further distinctions may have to be made between the types of proceedings in which these issues may arise. Besides enforcement or bankruptcy, the issue of internationality of the legal structures concerned may also be raised in preliminary, provisional or summary proceedings, or in ordinary proceedings on the merits. The recognition of foreign proprietary interests may result differently in these proceedings, even in the country of the new *situs*, in view of their different objectives or the different manner in which the recognition of the interest is invoked, for example as a defence, a collateral issue, or as the main issue.

Whatever the proceedings in which foreign proprietary interests arise, are invoked, or are made the subject of litigation, whether at the *situs* or elsewhere, it remains basic in all of them that international *contractual* issues regarding them arise when the parties to the arrangement are in different countries. The law of the closest connection, often presumed to be the law of the party that must perform the more characteristic obligation, will apply in these contractual aspects (unless parties have chosen another law in areas of contract where they can do so). It does not prevent the contract from creating charges or other types of proprietary interests, which the proper law of the contract may not accept or recognise itself, as long as the asset is in a country or will move to a country where they are accepted. A contract regarding chattels is thus international because the parties are in different countries regardless of whether the chattel being sold or made the object of a charge moves or is intended to move to another country. It will often remain where it is. It does not distract from the internationality of the sales agreement. It only means that in a proprietary sense the transaction is not international.

International *proprietary* issues proper arise only when the asset moves between countries, which may or may not be the consequence of a sale, when there is the need to determine the relative impact between the law of the place of origin and destination on the status of the proprietary right. As mentioned above, whilst the principle of the *lex situs* applies, it means here applicability of the law of the country of origin in matters of creation and of the law of the country of destination in matters of recognition of the foreign interest so created, with or without adjustment of the relevant interest. There is therefore a two-step approach.

International *enforcement* or bankruptcy issues mainly arise when the asset is not located in the country of enforcement at all. In enforcement, which is normally considered an exclusive prerogative of the courts of the *situs*, international issues will thus arise only when the asset moves to the country of enforcement with foreign charges attached to it which are then subject to the recognition and fitting-in process of the *lex executionis* in terms of ranking.

Enforcement issues may more readily present themselves in an international context in the case of a bankruptcy opened at the centre of affairs of a bankrupt with assets in *other* countries. As enforcement proceedings thus take place in a country different from the *situs*, it should still be asked what kind of effect they may have at the *situs* although ultimately this is a matter (of recognition) of the law of the *situs* itself. The enforcement is not international, only the claims to enforcement are.

There are here questions of jurisdiction and of recognition of the result of these proceedings if conducted outside the country of the new *situs*. This recognition should be clearly distinguished from the recognition of a foreign proprietary right when the asset has moved to the country where any of these procedures is initiated. In the bankruptcy itself there arises in that case the question how foreign charges in those assets are treated, even if these assets do not move to the country of the bankruptcy.

For the bankruptcy trustee to collect the various assets, the question of recognition of the bankruptcy decree at the *situs* of the assets will arise and may depend on whether its jurisdiction will be accepted at the *situs* and on the extent to which the bankruptcy court was able to accommodate the foreign proprietary interests. So it goes for the recognition of any other proceedings in which the foreign proprietary rights was an issue, like preliminary, injuctive, pre-judgment attachment proceedings or proceedings on the merits.

It also raises the issue of the proper opening requirements of these procedures, particularly of bankruptcy (with its insolvency requirements and the usual need for more than one creditor), as seen from the perspective of the recognising country. There may be a further difference in treatment between reorganisation and liquidation proceedings. As just mentioned, the recognition may be different in these different types of procedures in view of their different objectives. Thus the collection right under a factoring arrangement or the appropriation right under a conditional or finance sale may receive different recognition at the *situs* if raised in or outside enforcement proceedings, and again may be assessed differently if a provisional measure or injunctive relief is requested or in full proceedings on the merits.

Even if the courts of the *situs* will not surrender the asset under the circumstances, because they do not accept the foreign jurisdiction, foreign procedure or the treatment of the asset and the proprietary or security rights in them, the bankruptcy adjudication in respect of them is not entirely irrelevant, however. This is especially so when a foreign secured interest holder wants to share in the proceeds of the bankruptcy. In that case, he is likely to be asked to account for his foreign interests in the manner imposed by the bankruptcy court, therefore subject to this court's attitude towards the foreign interest and its fitting-in and ranking under the *lex concursus*. This law may itself well be somewhat stretched and adapted to make this possible.

Thus validity, status and rank of or powers under security interests or conditional sales may be differently decided in the various types of proceedings and may be different again for a foreign asset that in the meantime moved to the country of these proceedings and for an asset that remains elsewhere upon recognition and enforcement at the *situs*. In any event, the international status of the ensuing judicial decisions is likely to be very different and subject to different recognition possibilities. In fact, it could even happen that a decision reached on the status of foreign proprietary interests in provisional proceedings or even in proceedings on the merits is not accepted in bankruptcy proceedings in the same country as the ranking and fitting-in process may still require special handling. On the other hand, the bankruptcy findings concerning foreign proprietary interests may not have any further status or impact outside these proceedings, not even in the same country.

1.8.2 Models Laws: The EBRD Attempt

The Unidroit and Uncitral Uniforms Laws will be discussed more in detail below in the context of leasing and factoring. Another approach at harmonisation is the one through model laws. The European Bank for Reconstruction and Development made in 1994 an important attempt at drafting a Model Law on Secured Transactions meant to assist the legislative process in the area of contractually agreed security interests in the former communist countries of Europe and Asia.

The outstanding features of this Model Law are that it applies only to the business sphere (Article 2) and does not attempt to cover conditional or finance sales (Comment Article 1.2).

It does not maintain a functional approach and parties are free to organise their funding activities in the way they deem fit, which at least in the professional sphere appears to be the correct approach. Nevertheless, the reservation of title is characterised as a secured transaction, see Article 9, and requires an execution sale upon default, returning any overvalue to the buyer. Whether this is suitable in high inflation countries or whether this restriction is necessary in the professional sphere must be doubted as the overvalue will go to the defaulting debtor. It should also be realised that this approach applies to reservations of title in other than consumer goods.

Normally, the charges created pursuant to the Model Law are meant to secure loan credit, however, and are therefore seen as ancillary to credit agreements: see Articles 4 and 18.1, but according to the Comment the expression 'secured debt' has a wide meaning and largely depends on what the parties agree in this connection. The debt need not be existing or owing at the time the charge is granted: see Article 4.3.4, provided it can be and is properly identified in the security agreement (Article 4.4), but the maximum amount to be secured must be stated (except in the case of purchaser money security: Article 4.5). The idea is to leave room for further secured credit.

The type of asset that may be encumbered in this connection may be movable, immovable or intangible property: see Articles 1.1 and 5. Again the expression 'charged property' is intended to have a wide meaning and depends largely on what the parties agree. It may cover individualised items or categories of property and cover the fruits: Article 5.9. A charge is valid notwithstanding any agreement not to encumber the asset if it concerns monetary claims (Article 5.4), but the Model Law is not clear whether a charge may cover property that is not transferable by nature. Certain classes of shares may be (without consent or co-operation of the company). The assets must be identified either specifically or generally if they concern a class of assets (Article 5.7). The charge may cover future assets provided they can be and are sufficiently identified in the security agreement (Article 5.8/9), but it cannot be properly created in respect of such goods before the asset is owned by the debtor (Article 6.8), although in that case the charge relates back to the registration (in the case of a non-possessory charge). As regards the inclusion of future receivables, the Model Law takes no position on when they arise and their what/when possible inclusion is, as in the case of debts covered, also left to sufficient identification.

Altogether it may be noted that the Model Law takes a somewhat restrictive view on the debt that can be covered and the assets that may be included in the security. This is a most important deviation from the American model of Article 9 UCC. Another important feature is the reliance on publication or registration of non-possessory interests for their validity (except in the case of purchase money security) which must follow within 30 days from the date of the security agreement: see Article 8. This is an important departure from the practice in most civil law countries for non-possessory security in chattels.

Here the Model Law follows the example of Article 9 UCC in the USA. There is no advance filing or relation back of the charge (see Comment, Article 8.1), however, except that future assets which are sufficiently identified in the security agreement are covered as at the date of registration. The priority therefore normally dates from the date of the creation of the charge, which, if non-possessory, is the date of registration (Article 17), except that purchase money security has the highest priority (Article 17.3). In line with what was said above, the registration in turn is only possible in respect of an identifiable secured debt with an identifiable debtor, ruling out the coverage of unspecific future advances and unspecific future assets. The registration is per debtor and debt and not per secured asset. The Model Law does not enter into the details of the registration system but appears to assume that at least for chattels and intangible assets the most modern computerised systems will be put in place to support its approach. There is only a limited protection for *bona fide* purchasers (Article 21).

Enforcement is by way of execution sale but without the need for a court order: Article 24. Any buyer will receive title free of the charge: Article 26. The beneficiary of an encumbered claim may collect: Article 12.1. Article 28 deals with the distribution of the proceeds of an execution sale giving the debtor any overvalue (Article 28.3.6).

1.8.3   Other Efforts at International Harmonisation: The 2001 Unidroit Convention on International Interests in Mobile Equipment

Unidroit has produced a new convention (with only an aircraft protocol so far) aiming at the creation of an international interest in mobile equipment.[255] The need for internationally supported security has greatly increased through the privatisation of airlines and railways, with the attendant need to raise international financing which can no longer depend on state guarantees whilst the assets have no fixed *lex situs*, so that domestic security interests in them are constantly endangered.

The idea is that a distinct type of international interest is created under the Convention resulting from a security agreement, a reservation of title or a finance lease (Article 2) in mobile equipment as defined in Article 2(3). Realistically, the American functional approach is rejected and the recharacterisation of conditional sales and leases is thus avoided. For purposes of the Convention, mobile equipment concerns categories of equipment that habitually move between states and are identifiable (and not future), like aircraft, aircraft engines, helicopters, ships, oil rigs, containers, railway rolling stock, space property and other categories of uniquely identifiable objects. Parties may derogate from the provisions of the Convention under Article15 whilst the interpretation and supplementation provisions of the Vienna Convention on the International Sale of Goods are followed in Article 5 with an unfortunate ultimate reference to domestic laws.

The interest created under the Convention must result from an agreement in writing and requires registration (Articles 7 and 16). The registration is not debtor- but asset-based (according to the manufacturer's serial number) and Unidroit will designate the registry or registers. Failure to register results in the nullity of the interest. In the case of a default, the beneficiary of the interest has one or more of the following rights in respect of the assets: taking of possession, the selling or granting of a lease, collecting the proceeds or any income or profits arising from the management or use of these assets, applying to the courts for authorisation and direction in any of these remedies (Article 8). Where the interest is a reservation of title or finance lease, the creditor will terminate the arrangement and take possession and appropriate full title under Article 10.

Article 29 deals with priorities of the international interests *inter se* and they conform to the rule 'prior in time prior in right'. The interest is valid against trustees in bankruptcy and other creditors of the debtor (Article 30). *Bona fide* purchasers of an asset with a registered interest are not protected. Ultimately it cannot be avoided that the *lex executionis* or *lex concursus* have the final say on the validity and fitting-in process, especially relevant if the enforcement or bankruptcy and the asset are outside a Contracting State.

---

[255] See for a comment, MJ Stanford, 'Unidroit Convention on International Financial Leasing and the Preliminary Draft Unidroit Convention on International Interests in Mobile Equipment' 27 *International Journal of Legal Information* 188 (1999); see also P Winship, 'International Commercial Transactions', *The Business Journal* 2001 (ABA 1999).

The Convention deals with the problem when it applies (Article 3), in other words what contact with a Contracting State is necessary for the Convention's application to be triggered and therefore for the international interest to emerge. It applies when the debtor (conditional buyer or lessee) is situated in a Contracting State.

1.8.4   Model Laws or Uniform Law: Applicability

The unification effort through a model law is different from the unification through treaty law. Model laws are directed to domestic legislatures and mean to be adopted in national laws, possibly with present or later modifications. The objectives of model laws may differ, however. In the EBRD Model Law, unification is of secondary importance; the aim is rather to provide guidance for new departures in the national laws of countries not used to financing through private capital. There is a clear economic objective. Other model laws, like the Uncitral Model Law on International Commercial Arbitration, also mean to provide guidance but mainly aim at greater international uniformity.

In the uniform laws, common in the USA among the various states, unification is clearly the objective, but they remain *state* laws. Where international or interstate aspects arise, there is, therefore, still a need for a conflicts rule: see also Section 1-301 (1-105 old) UCC (which allows the uniform law to be applied if the transaction bears an appropriate relation to the state concerned), but if there is uniformity between the laws that may so be deemed applicable, the importance of these conflict rules is only to determine that no other law applies. These conflict rules remain of course also of importance where there are still differences in the details because of the different implementation of the model laws. Even in the USA the uniform laws, like the Uniform Commercial Code, are not everywhere similarly enacted and there remain some important differences between the Code as incorporated in the various states.

Uniform *treaty* law on the other hand means introducing the same law in the Contracting States to avoid any conflicts and therefore to eliminate the need for conflict laws further. Once adopted, they are not subject to domestic amendement and are meant to take precedence over national law. Nevertheless, conflict rules cannot always be avoided and a preliminary question remains which law applies if there is an international aspect to the case (whether of a contractual, proprietary or enforcement or bankruptcy nature). In the traditional view, the uniform treaty law is only applicable if the applicable private international law rules point to the law of a Contracting State whilst these private international law rules themselves could still differ. Yet some uniform treaty law introduces here a different rule for Contracting States and renders this law directly applicable in the courts of such states, like the 1980 Vienna Convention does for the international sale of goods.

Indeed, only where the Uniform Treaty Law is applied by the courts *ex officio* as their *lex fori* are conflicts rules avoided (unless residually resort to a local law must still be had under it). In this book it has been submitted over and again that the *lex mercatoria* should apply to the professional sphere at large, independently of the residence of the participants, who must per definition be considered substantially internationalised when involved in commerce. Uniform treaty law has a place within the hierarchy of norms of the *lex mercatoria* in the manner explained in chapter I, Part III without any reference to conflict of laws rules.

Part II   Major Types of Finance Sales

2.1   Finance Leasing

2.1.1   *Rationale of Finance Leasing*

Since the late 1950s, finance leasing has rapidly developed as a means of financing capital goods and has found wide acceptance in most modern economies. Its rationale is to provide the user of assets (usually major types of equipment) with a financing alternative. Instead of the user buying the assets himself either with his own or with borrowed funds (secured on the lease assets themselves), in a lease, a finance company will acquire the assets to the lessee's specifications and will put them at the disposal of the lessee for which the latter will make regular payments to the finance company. It follows that the asset is often only of special use to the lessee and the lease is therefore normally for the useful life of the asset. Lease payments will be made during that time at regular intervals to compensate the lessor for his outlay and to allow him a profit margin.

It is likely that there will be still some use in the assets at the end of the lease period. Any residual rights in them may automatically transfer to the lessee at that time or the lessee may have an option to acquire such rights at such time against a nominal payment. At least that is the continental European model. For reasons that were already mentioned in Part I and will briefly be summarised below, this right or option to acquire the residual value is normally avoided in the UK and the USA.

The idea is always that instead of the user using his own funds (for which he may have a better use) or borrowing them at the prevailing interest rates (probably against the security of the lease assets themselves), there is no such (secured) borrowing under a finance lease, but the user or lessee makes regular payments for the use of the asset bought for him by a financier. As was submitted in section 1.1.2 above, the crucial difference is the absence of a loan agreement of which an agreed interest rate structure is the indication. If such a loan agreement were in existence, the lease would become tantamount to a secured transaction. The finance lease is no interest-bearing device. Naturally, it has a reward structure expressed in the instalments, which have a cost and fee component, but that is neither economically nor legally the same thing although often so confused. There is a choice here. The finance lease is likely to be somewhat more expensive than a loan secured on the same assets would have been for the lessee, but there are other benefits for him. Depending on the competition for this business, the cost could also be lower. The key is to appreciate that there is here a true funding alternative with a different risk and reward structure.

In practice, finance leasing has become an established way of funding all kinds of assets, in particular larger and more costly pieces of equipment, like aircraft or aircraft engines, and sometimes even ships or real estate as in manufacturing plant. The concept is now also used in the consumer sphere, for example for car and household good leasing, probably to avoid legal restrictions on hire purchase, which is a very similar arrangement.

The reason for this arrangement is normally that the user or lessee prefers not to buy the lease assets himself with the attendant need to finance them and carry them on his own balance sheet. As to the latter aspect, in countries like the UK, the USA and the Netherlands, under prevailing accounting rules, the lessee may now have to do so. It is nevertheless the convenience that counts and the availability of a financing alternative leading to another risk and cost structure, to greater liquidity for the lessee and particularly to more room for other acquisitions by him and, in some countries, still to some better tax treatment.

There may be other reasons like the possibility of 100 per cent financing and the saving of legal and mortgage registration costs in real estate leasing. As just mentioned, in exchange, the lessee might accept a somewhat higher charge compared with any interest he might have had to pay if he had borrowed the money (assuming he was in a position to do so on reasonable terms) in order to acquire the asset himself. This is in turn the attraction for the financier. It has led to a specific market for this type of service, which cost is not necessarily comparable to the interest cost in loan financing. In fact, that interest cost will be used as benchmark for determining the financial costs or benefits of the leasing alternative.

2.1.2   Legal Characterisation

As already explained in section 1.1.2. above, the key to the understanding of the finance lease from a legal point of view is that parties in finance leasing take a special kind of risk in terms of ownership and protection against default of the other party, especially if that party is the user of the assets. This risk structure is notably different from that assumed in a loan secured on the same assets and leads as a consequence to a different reward structure also. In a secured loan transaction upon default, there is an execution sale by the creditor (financier) and return of overvalue to the debtor (user), whilst in the finance lease upon default of the lessee there is appropriation of full ownership (including any overvalue) by the lessor. The different recourse and distribution of values in finance leases signify a difference in the risks parties take, which in turn leads to a different reward. From a legal and practical point of view, the (secured) loan and lease structure are therefore not truly comparable and are indeed two different ways of financing, which should not be equated or confounded. There is approximation only if there is a clear loan, signalled by the existence of an agreed interest rate. In that case one would assume a conversion of the lease into full ownership for the lessee subject to a security interest for the lessor. The formalities for the creation of such a security interest will have to be observed. That is the American situation under Article 9 UCC where *all* funding structures using personal property in support are automatically converted into secured transactions whether or not there is a true loan situation, an approach much criticised above: see for a summary section 1.7.4 above.

The fact that there may be an automatic right at the end of the lease for the lessee to acquire full title or that there is an option for him to do so for a nominal price or that the lease itself is for the useful life of the asset should not make any difference here, even if in the USA under Article 9 UCC the conversion into a security interest is based on these features and not on the existence of a loan structure proper. As we already saw in section 1.6.3 above, that has created all kinds of problems with leases, repos and factoring in the USA. Certainly, in finance leases, the lessee has the possession and use of the assets which are still likely to figure as a protection for the lessor upon a default of the lessee but that does not itself make the arrangement a secured loan either. Indeed, the proprietary protection of the lessor may be expressed through conditional ownership rights in the lease assets under which they become subject to appropriation upon default of the lessee. This is just like a seller who has an appropriation right under a reservation of title (in the USA also converted into a security interest, as we saw) or the financier in a hire purchase. The hire purchase is practically the same as a reservation of title except that often special hire purchase companies are involved and these schemes operate especially for consumers, who, under applicable law, may receive special consumer protections (for example, in terms of a return of overvalue upon default even if in consumer goods there seldom is any). What concerns us here is payment protection rather that loan protection. That is the same in finance leases and it follows that only in the case of a true loan situation should these leases be characterised as secured transactions.

Although the finance lease is in essence a simple financial structure, its legal characterisation has nevertheless remained much in doubt. There are here basically three issues:

(a) the contractual aspects of the finance lease which are the simplest, but must include that the assets are provided by the lessor at the lessee's specifications against regular payments of lease instalments,

(b) the proprietary aspects of the lease which are much more complicated as they concern the questions whether and when the lessor or lessee or both have ownership rights in the lease assets and the protection of each lease party in a bankruptcy of the other, and, more recently

(c) the collateral rights of the lessee under the supply agreement between the lessor and the supplier of the lease assets which may lead to third party contractual or derivative rights of the lessee under the supply agreement between supplier and lessor. This is a notable exception to the notion of privity of contract: see for this notion more in particular Chapter II, section 1.5.

The proprietary issue arises as the lessee is economically speaking often considered the owner of the asset and this may also have legal consequences, especially where he has the use of the asset during its entire economic life or is given the residual rights in the lease assets after payment of all lease instalments, either automatically or by way of option. In any event, he has a right to consume the asset whilst in possession. It may even have been built to his specific standards and might as such not be of much use to others. Some division of proprietary rights in the nature of a split between lessor and lessee during the time of the lease suggests itself. It is not a difficult concept under common law, although in the USA now *prima facie* indicative of a security interest under Article 9. In civil law, any duality in ownership outside the accepted number of defined proprietary rights is generally controversial but exists in many countries in the conditional ownership inherent in reservations of title and hire purchases.

In the dual ownership characterisation of the finance lease (unless otherwise agreed), the lessor has in civil law terms the title and possession under the resolutive condition of full payment of the instalments; the lessee under the suspending condition of his full payments. He is in turn the holder under a resolutive condition: see also section 1.1.6 above. Whether this structure can legally also obtain if the lessee is not given residual rights in the asset may be less clear but, as economically he has received all value, his position as conditional owner in the meantime would not need to be in doubt.

In common law, the conditional ownership is not an issue in itself, even if created in chattels when it is equitable, but as we saw in the USA under Article 9 UCC, it is commonly converted (by law) into a security interest if it may be considered to secure payment or performance of an obligation (Section 1-201(a)(35) (1-201(37) old) and Section 9-109(a) (5–6) (9-102(2) old) UCC). This could affect the finance lease, especially if the lease is for the economic life of the asset or is given the residual rights in the assets upon the end of the lease, although not necessarily if the lease allows for a full amortisation of the acquisition costs of the lessor through the lease payments. The borderline is unclear, however, and much litigation results. The consequence of conversion into a secured transaction is full ownership of the lessee subject to a security interest for the lessor. It creates a need to file the interest to safeguard its priority and for a disposition in the case of the lessee's default and a return of any overvalue to him. It thus results in another kind of deal.

To alleviate these problems for at least some type of leases, eventually a new Article 2A UCC was introduced: see also section 1.6.2 above. It concentrates on shorter leases, puts special emphasis on the lessee's involvement in the specifications of the lease assets and gives him collateral rights under the supply agreement. It leaves the proprietary position of both parties under the lease in doubt, although it is clear that the lessee has more than purely contractual rights. So has the lessor, at least in the bankruptcy of his lessee. The exact nature of these respective rights remains unclear, however. Any duality in ownership may be considered to give the lessor no more than a security interest.

The main aim of Article 2A was to clarify that not all finance leases as financing transactions would be converted by law into secured (loan) transactions under Article 9 UCC but the borderline depends in practice still much on the wording of the lease agreement and on the facts of the case. Especially for longer leases the conversion idea is not abandoned.

In the Netherlands, the finance lease became vulnerable as it looked like a substitute security which was deprived of all proprietary or third party effect under Article 84(3) of the new Civil Code of 1992. As we saw in section 1.2.3 above, recent case law has tried to remedy the situation leaving, however, the proprietary position of the lessee much in doubt. The result is the opposite from the one in the USA, where the lessee becomes the owner upon conversion of the lease into a security interest for the lessor.

In the 1960s, some European countries like France also introduced legislation concerning the finance lease, mostly, however, to control leasing companies as lessors but this legislation seldom clarified the proprietary and collateral issues. In fact, the qualification as a conditional sale and transfer also gave rise to some problems in France where as a general rule conditions can no longer mature in a bankruptcy of either party so that title would remain with a bankrupt lessor notwithstanding proper payment by the buyer (or lessee) if due after the bankruptcy date. There is the attendant problem of the status of instalments already paid, a situation only for reservation of title remedied through an amendment of the French Bankruptcy Act in 1980: see also section 1.3.5 above.

Whatever the characterisation problems and consequences, in principle the finance lease can be characterised as a conditional sale, much in the nature of a reservation of title. This is so even in the USA unless the conversion criteria of Article 9 UCC are reached, when it becomes a secured transaction, which, it was submitted, is elsewhere only a proper re-characterisation if there is an underlying loan agreement as evidenced by a interest rate structure. The lease can also be expressed as an outright sale and ownership transfer to the user. On the other end of the scale, it is also possible that the finance lease is expressed in purely contractual terms. It is normal for short term leases under which a mere temporary user right is transferred. In that case the term '*operational lease*' is commonly used in Europe. It is really a rental agreement, for consumers usually referred to as a consumer lease in the USA.

Again the borderline is not always clear. Normally in an operational lease, the lessee has not had the lease assets built or bought to his own specifications. There is no financing aspect either. It means that the lessee in an economic sense can hardly be considered the owner, has normally only minor maintenance duties, no right to acquire full ownership, and has certainly no rights against the original manufacturer or supplier of the assets.

Depending on the circumstances and the wording of the lease, the finance lease may thus be characterised more properly as:

(a) purely contractual (a rental),
(b) a dual, split or conditional ownership arrangement under which the lessee acquires some proprietary rights, much as under a reservation of title or hire purchase,
(c) a secured transaction,

(d)   an outright sale, whilst in the USA there is also the special type of
(e)   the equipment lease in which the proprietary position is in doubt but which is not a secured transaction and gives the lessee collateral rights against the seller of the equipment.

Finance leasing, properly speaking, concerns in truth the variant under (b) with the attendant problem of the precise definition of the proprietary rights of each party. The various other possible characterisations (depending on the wording of the lease document and the facts of the case) fall into well-established other legal categories (except the American equipment lease) and the term 'finance lease' should preferably not be used in those cases (in the USA it is usually equated with the equipment lease). Yet these alternatives have from a legal point of view prevented the finance lease from developing into a single legal structure under most national laws.

Naturally under (b), there is also a contractual aspect to the lease, but even here there is no single contractual structure. Often the lease assets are acquired by the lessor to the lessee's specifications and are then new. This may give rise under modern law to collateral rights for the lessee under the supply agreement. In the USA, it is very much at the heart of the definition of the equipment lease under Article 2A UCC and seems to give rise to yet one more variant under (b). It seems that the more relevant issue is what kind of proprietary right is being transferred. In any event, not all lease assets are built to the specification of the lessee. That is clear in respect of land, although new buildings may be put on it to the lessee's specifications and included in the finance lease. On the other hand, there may also be a 'sale-lease back' of an asset already obtained by the lessee who wants to refinance it through a finance lease and will then more likely continue his direct legal relationship with his supplier or builder.

By way of definition, the only thing that can be said is that under modern law a proper finance lease combines (always) contractual, (often) collateral and (always) proprietary aspects, the latter short of a full transfer of ownership to the lessee.

2.1.3   Comparative Legal Analysis

So far German[256] and French law[257] seem largely uninterested in the proprietary and collateral aspects of the finance lease whilst Dutch law, if not now outlawing the finance

---

[256] In Germany, the finance lease is considered a purely contractual arrangement unless the lessee automatically acquires full title upon payment of the last instalment or (perhaps) if there is at least an option for him to acquire full title without payment of further consideration. See, for the various theories on the nature of the finance lease, PW Heermann, 'Grundprobleme beim Finanzierungsleasing beweglicher Güter in Deutschland und den Vereinigten Staaten von Amerika' [1993] *ZVglRW* 362ff. highlighting in particular the tripartite aspects of many of these arrangements following the American lead. Others see a mere credit agreement, which is also the approach of Section 3(2)(1) of the Consumer Credit Act (VerbraucherKreditGesetz) of 1 Jan 1991. The consequence of a secured transaction is not, however, commonly drawn. The German Supreme Court (BGH) traditionally characterises the finance lease as a rental agreement (which may, however, under German law imply some proprietary protections for the lessee whose lease can in any event not be interrupted by a sale of the title by the lessor), *BGHZ* 71, 189, only more recently with some emphasis on the financial nature of the arrangement, *BGHZ* 95, 39, not considered, however, as a fundamental shift by F von Westphalen, 'Leasing als 'sonstige Finanzierungshilfe' gemäß s 1(2) VerbrKrG', [1991] *ZIP* 640 and by SM Marrinek, *Moderne Vertragstypen, Band I: Leasing und Factoring* (München, 1991), 72. The former author explicitly maintains the BGH interpretation outside the ambit of the VerbrKG, the latter argues for a *sui generis* approach with emphasis on both the financial and user aspects of the lease. Others see a contract of a mixed nature with aspects of financing and purchasing for the lessor and of payment of interest and commission for the lessee: see CW Canaris, *Interessenlage, Grundprinzipien und Rechtsnatur des Finanzierungsleasing* (1990), 450ff.

[257] In France, the finance lease was covered by Law 66–455 of 2 July 1966, now codified in Articles L 313–7 to L 313–111 CMF. It is inconclusive in the proprietary aspects. Some see finance leasing simply as a financing method without characterising it further in terms of secured or ownership based financing, and emphasise the

lease as a pseudo-secured transaction, also seems to characterise the finance lease as a purely contractual arrangement, as we saw.[258]

In Germany the focus of the discussion remains on the characterisation of the finance lease as a rental agreement, which under German law may itself have some proprietary aspects in that it may survive the sale of the asset by the lessor and also his bankruptcy. That may also be the Dutch approach after the recent case law validating finance leases if the conditional sale characterisation or dual ownership concept cannot establish itself for finance leases in that country.

As we saw, the French enacted a special leasing statute in 1966 on the *crédit-bail* mainly from a desire to supervise lease companies, now was superseded in the CMF. It qualifies the lease as a rental agreement but with an option to buy, although not all rules of a rental agreement apply and many contractual and proprietary issues appear to remain unresolved. There is no clear guidance in other countries either. Separate leasing statutes remain on the whole uncommon in Europe with the notable exceptions of Belgium (1967), Spain (1977) and Portugal (1979), all requiring an option to acquire full ownership at the end of the lease.

In that sense, they all suggest conditional ownership, although an automatic right to acquire the full interest upon payment of all the lease instalments would have been a stronger indication. In this connection the characterisation as hire purchase has also been proposed and is often followed in the Netherlands,[259] especially in view of the regular payment aspect. This characterisation is, however, problematic where there is no transfer of ownership at the end and may not be available in the case of immovables and registered chattels, like ships and aircraft. Other drawbacks are that it may make typical consumer protection applicable to what, in a finance lease, is essentially a transaction between professionals. There would notably be an execution sale upon default of the lessee who would also be entitled to any overvalue.

In the UK, where an automatic right or an option of the lessee to acquire full title upon the last lease instalment is also considered indicative of a hire purchase,[260] these rights are for that reason normally avoided in the lease contract as it may subject the arrangement to the mandatory rules of the protection of consumers. Probably to avoid these, there is now also a developing market for car leasing and the leasing of other more common goods with a longer life, like kitchen equipment, in the UK.

In Canada, on the other hand, the borderline between finance leases and secured transactions is the main issue as in the USA. In the Uniform Personal Property Security Act of 1982, this borderline problem has been solved differently, in that every finance lease for a term longer than one year must be published and, although it does not create a security interest with its own proprietary status and execution regime, it makes the lessee the legal owner of the asset but creates a priority right for the lessor in an execution upon the lessee's default It is thus much in the nature of a statutory preference.

---

sui generis nature of the arrangement instead: see P Cordier, Note under Cour de Cass, 9 Jan 1990, Gaz Pal 127 (1990). Others seem to accept some kind of security interest, see G Marty, P Raynaud and P Jestaz, *Les Suretés, La Publicité Foncière* (2nd edn, Sirey, Paris, 1987), 355. There are also those who see a mere rental agreement: see El Mokhtar Bey, Note [1987] *JCP* 20865, later also noting the hybrid character of the finance lease in terms of a sale, a rental or an option: see his 'Des consequénces de la jurisprudence de la chambre mixte de la Cour de Cassation du 25 novembre 1990 sur la symbiotique du crédit bail' [1992] *Gaz Pal* 568.

[258] See n 64 *supra* and accompanying text.
[259] See WM Kleyn, *Leasing*, Paper Netherlands Association 'Handelsrecht' (1989).
[260] R Goode, *Commercial Law* (2nd edn, 1995), 763 and 776; see also n 199 *supra* and accompanying text.

In the UK, a similar approach has been advocated by Professor Diamond in his *Review of Security Interests in Property for the Department of Trade and Industry* of 1989 whilst opting for a three year minimum term, however. This UK document (no 9.7.16) still sees the essence of the finance lease in the circumstance that the aggregate rentals approximate to the full credit price or that the lease is for the full working life of the goods, although shorter term leases may apparently also qualify as finance leases.

As we already saw in the previous section, in the USA since 1988 the finance lease, if an equipment lease under Article 2A and not a secured transaction under Article 9 UCC, is defined in Section 2A-103(l)(g) UCC (not yet accepted in all states) with reference to the active role of the lessee in the selection of the goods. However, the lessor acquires them: see for the resulting tripartite character of the arrangement Section 2A-209(1) but one of the following must occur. The lessee receives the supply contract before signing the lease, the lessee's approval of this contract is made a precondition of the lease, the lessee receives before signing the lease an accurate and complete statement of the major clauses of supply contracts, or (if there is no consumer lease) the lessor informs the lessee to this effect and allows direct contact with the supplier to receive from him directly an accurate and complete statement.

The equipment lease must further conform to the lease definition of Section 2A-103(1)(j) which requires transfer of possession and use and specifies that a sale, including a sale on approval or a sale and return, or retention or creation of a security interest, cannot be an equipment lease. It is the reason why in the USA under Article 2A there is *no* emphasis on amortisation through the rentals and certainly not on the arrangement being for the useful life of the asset, the latter aspect (but not necessarily the former) being an indication of the lease being a security interest instead of an equipment lease. The option to acquire full ownership rights at the end of the lease for a nominal value would be a similar indication of a security interest.

Thus in the USA, in a true finance (equipment) lease, the emphasis is on the *involvement of the lessee* in the supply agreement (and his direct rights against the supplier) and on the limited nature of his user right rather than on any proprietary aspects. They carry the risk of leading to a secured transaction if the lease is accompanied by any future right for the lessee in the full title. Thus, on the one hand, in order to remain within the ambit of the finance or equipment lease, the proprietary rights of the lessee are limited, whereas, on the other hand, his rights against outsiders, like the supplier, are considerably extended.

2.1.4 International Aspects of Finance Leasing

The confusion which may exist locally about the precise legal definition and consequences of the finance lease structure, especially in the proprietary and collateral aspects, may also have international consequences as many assets subject to finance leasing are likely to travel, a situation particularly applying to aircraft and their engines and to ships. With the enormous increase in international trade, many leased objects may increasingly move across borders for other reasons.

In the *proprietary aspects*, the *lex situs* appears usually to be applicable, but this does not provide much of a solution for the rights in assets which are meant to move or which have actually travelled because the proprietary status would then change with the change in location. This is particularly problematic in the area of limited or secured, split or conditional proprietary rights, not known elsewhere.

Often the *lex situs* of the place where a proprietary right first attached is deemed applicable in proprietary aspects subject to recognition by the next country. It largely depends on that country being able to fit the foreign property right into its own proprietary system without too much difficulty or adjustment: see in more detail chapter IV, section 1.8.1. It unavoidably raises the question of the precise meaning of the arrangement under its own law and subsequently of the continued significance of any limitations thereunder in the country of recognition, For example it may be qualified in that country as a reservation of title, even if not accepted under the applicable *lex contractus* or as a hire purchase restricted by mandatory rules of same law. It raises also the question of compliance with the applicable formalities if the arrangement is qualified at the original *situs* as a security and of the relevance of this qualification and these formalities in the country of recognition.

Subsequently, there is the fitting-in process at the new *situs*. This is necessarily a question for the recognising court, particularly important if at the same time it is the execution or bankruptcy court. It is a question of acceptance of acquired rights, in which connection different courts in different countries may well take a substantially different view. Some may be more flexible than others that may only recognise the foreign proprietary rights to the extent that there are clear equivalents under the domestic law. It may also depend on the *purpose* for which and the *procedure* under which these foreign rights are invoked, for example in preliminary or injunctive proceedings, in proceedings on the merits or in enforcement or bankruptcy proceedings. Conflict rules and their precise impact remain obscure in this area and the final result is often unpredictable, all the more so since it may not be clear in advance where the goods may travel or which court may become involved for whatever purpose.

In an international context, there may also be problems in the law applicable to the *contractual aspects*. Here problems are likely to arise when lessor and lessee are in different countries rather than when the asset moves. Further problems may arise if the supplier is elsewhere. There may be conflicts rules more readily available in this area, for example under the EU Rome Convention of 1980 on the Law Applicable to Contractual Obligations, followed by a similar project of the Hague Conference updated in 1986. However, in tripartite structures where each of the three parties (here lessor, lessee and supplier) may be in a different country, there is no clear conflict rule that may bring about the desirable dovetailing of the law applicable to the supply contract and to the lease as the characteristic obligation under either is different and the party performing it in each case different. A contractual choice of the same law in both contracts may help but is not always achievable.

2.1.5   Uniform Substantive Law: The Unidroit Convention

The uncertainty which results both from the confusion that exists with regard to the proper status of leasing under many national laws and the absence of clear conflict rules in the proprietary/enforcement and contractual/collateral aspects of financial leasing if considered a tripartite arrangement, may be particularly undesirable when leasing occurs in an international context. This was the reason the finance lease caught the attention of Unidroit in the early 1970s and this organisation subsequently perceived a need for an international unification of the basic terms by providing for uniform law.

The ensuing Convention of 29 May 1988 came to fruition at a diplomatic conference in Ottawa after fourteen years of preparation, in which at first (until 1985) the approach of uniform rules — each time to be contractually incorporated — rather than of a Convention producing uniform law was favoured. At the end of 2003, there were thirteen signatories to the Convention including three EU countries and the USA as major industrial nations. So far there have been nine ratifications (France in 1991, Italy in 1993, Nigeria in 1994, Hungary in 1996, Latvia in 1997, Panama in 1997, Russian Federation in 1998, Belarus in 1998 and the Republic of Uzbekistan in 2000). The Convention became effective on 1 May 1995, six months after the third ratification.

The Convention is, however, only a partial codification. It is further subordinated to any other present or future treaty law in any of its aspects (Article 17), relevant for example to the Vienna Convention on the International Sale of Goods (1980) in the area of the supply agreement. Even before its entering into force, the Convention created some considerable interest in legal scholarship and contributed to a better understanding of the finance lease as a major modern financial instrument.[261]

The Convention is clearly the product of many different views and various compromises that have not aided its clarity. Particularly in the demarcation with the operational lease and in the proprietary aspects of the finance lease, the Convention has not been able to bring a great deal of clarity and much doubt remains as a consequence, especially on the proprietary position of the lessee, probably because such doubt was not lifted in Article 2A UCC in the USA either. The major innovation of the Convention lies in the collateral rights it gives the lessee against the supplier of the leased assets with whom the lessee normally has no direct contractual relationship. The Convention follows here the American model.

Real estate leasing was excluded from the start as it is less likely to be internationalised; so was any leasing for personal, family or household purposes. Operational leasing was first covered but ultimately deleted. As purely contractual arrangements, operational leases were believed not to give rise to substantial international complications incapable of solution under existing conflict laws, even though, as suggested earlier, the borderline is by no means always clear, even under the Convention, and the deletion is likely to create problems. For this reason it was criticised by the American representatives who probably wanted something even more like their equipment lease.

The Leasing Convention according to its Preamble is only an attempt at formulating 'certain uniform rules relating primarily to the civil and commercial law aspects of international financial leasing'. It concentrates in fact mainly on some contractual and collateral aspects and is incidental in the ownership and enforcement aspects. In these latter aspects it contains some uniform conflict rules, limited, however, to the narrow issues of the law applicable to any publication requirement of the lease (Article 7) and to the question whether the lease asset has become a fixture (Article 4(2)).

Beyond these few instances in which a conflicts rule is given, the rules of the Convention are supplemented by the general principles on which it is based before the normal private international law rules are to be applied (Article 6(2)). This language was borrowed from the Vienna Convention on the International Sale of Goods. The deduction of these general

---

[261] See, MJ Stanford, 'Explanatory Report on the Draft Convention on International Financial Leasing' [1987] *Rev. dr. unif. I*, 169, hereinafter Explanatory Report, and further (amongst many others): RM Goode, 'The Proposed New Factoring and Leasing Conventions' [1987] *JBL* 219, 318, 399 and 'Conclusion of the Leasing and Factoring Conventions' [1988] *JBL* 347; El Mokhtar Bey, 'La Convention d'Ottawa sur le crédit-bail international', in II *Etudes et Commentaires* 15643, 726 (1989); M Reinsma, 'Unidroit Convention on International Financial Leasing' in WM Kleijn and others, *Leasing, Paper Netherlands Association 'Handelsrecht'* (1989), 66; CT Ebenroth, 'Leasing im grenzüberschreitenden Verkehr' in EA Kramer, *Neue Vertragformen der Wirtschaft: Leasing, Factoring, Franchising* (Paul Haupt, Bern/Stuttgart/Wien, 1992), 117, 192; C Dageforde, 'Internationales Finanzierungsleasing in *Europäisches Wirtschaftsrecht, Abteilung A: Monographien Band 2* (Beck, München, 1992), 97, which also contains an extensive bibliography on the subject; D Levy, 'Financial Leasing under the Unidroit Convention and the Uniform Commercial Code, A Comparative Analysis', 5 *Indiana International and Comparative LR* 267 (1995); and F Ferrari, 'General Principles and International Commercial Law Conventions. A Study of the 1980 Vienna Sales Convention and the 1988 Unidroit Conventions on International Factoring and International Leasing', 10 *Pace International Law Rev.* 157 (1998).

principles would be of particular interest in view of the incidental coverage of the Convention, more particularly so in the proprietary and enforcement aspects where contractual provisions including a contractual choice of law may be ineffective. Yet the Convention does not provide much of a framework in these aspects and general principles here appear to be particularly absent. Thus there is heavy reliance on private international law, also it seems in all aspects of doubt on the coverage of the Convention. In view of its rudimentary character, the unity it brings is therefore likely to be very limited.

In matters of interpretation (assuming it can be distinguished from supplementation or gap-filling under Article 6(2)), Article 6(1) refers to consideration of the object and purpose of the Convention as set forth in the Preamble, of its international character, of the need to promote uniformity in its application, and of the observance of good faith in international trade. This language is also derived from the Vienna Convention, although its role and significance in the proprietary and enforcement aspects are unclear and the reference to good faith here in fact wholly inappropriate. In a proper internationalist approach, the reference in respect of both interpretation and supplementation should have been to the international character of the Convention, its general principles, the need for its uniform application, and to international practice and custom, as was already submitted in connection with the Vienna Sales Convention in Chapter II, section 2.3.5. In any event, the application of a convention of this nature should be achieved within the hierarchy of the *lex mercatoria* as a whole, which leaves room for the application of private international law rules only if all else fails.

2.1.6   *The Leasing Convention's Sphere of Application, Its Interpretation and Supplementation*

According to Article 3 of the Convention, the international status of leasing is normally considered to be triggered by the residence or place of business of the lessor and lessee being in different Contracting States rather than by the movement of the lease asset. This is also the approach of the Vienna Sales Convention, with the additional requirement in the Leasing Convention that the supplier is also from a Contracting State or that both the supply and leasing agreement are governed by the law of a Contracting State (which can be so chosen by the parties). The asset itself need not be in a Contracting State at all. This approach is understandable in the *contractual* aspects to which the Vienna Convention was limited, but much less so in the proprietary and enforcement aspects, so important in questions of leasing, in which location and movement are the more essential issues.

As a practical matter, the Convention can in proprietary and enforcement matters only provide solutions if the jurisdictions where the assets are located or move to are Contracting States, notwithstanding the definition of its sphere of application in Article 1. The *lex situs* of third countries cannot be affected by the Convention whatever the latter may pretend in proprietary and enforcement matters in respect of assets elsewhere, although it may still limit the parties in their own dealings concerning the assets amongst themselves.

On the other hand, it follows from the approach of the Convention that the proprietary status of the assets in Contracting States is subject to its regime even if they never move, which may also be somewhat surprising. It was, nonetheless, the reason for excluding real estate leasing from the Convention's scope.

Finally, where the *lex situs* is changed in respect of the proprietary aspects of finance leases as a result of the asset moving between Contracting States, there is under the Convention a curious result, in that finance leases not covered by the Convention may be treated differently in these aspects in the relevant Contracting States. It fractures the proprietary and enforcement regime and makes it dependent on the place of business and the will of the (foreign) participants in the lease rather than on the location of the lease asset.

2.1.7   The Definition of Financial Leasing under the Convention

The definition of financial leasing under the Convention is vague and must be seen as a guideline rather than as a clear legal demarcation circumscribing the Convention's applicability (Article 1). This is immediately clear where (a) the text refers to plant, capital goods or 'other' equipment as the object of the supply agreement in the context of the financial lease, (b) the lessee is not supposed to be 'primarily' dependent on the skill and judgement of the lessor in selecting the lease assets, and (c) the rental payments are supposed to take into account 'in particular' the amortisation of the whole or of a 'substantial' part of the cost of the equipment, whilst (d) there may or may not be an option to buy the equipment whether or not for a nominal price. It is clearer still from the absence of any particular concept of the finance lease, either in its contractual, proprietary or enforcement aspects.

Key elements appear nevertheless that (a) the lessee sets the specifications and approves the supply agreement at least in as far as it concerns his interest (undefined), even though he is not supposed to countersign it, whilst he may still rely on the lessor's skill and judgement and the latter's intervention in the selection of the supplier or the goods, although not primarily so (Article 8), that (b) the lessor acquires the lease assets whilst granting the lessee the right of use and putting him in possession of the assets against payment of rentals, and that (c) the rentals must substantially amortise the acquisition costs. There is no reference to the lessee acquiring the use of the asset for substantially all of its useful life, which, however, seems implied in the amortisation requirement.[262]

As already mentioned, there is neither an automatic transfer of ownership to the lessee at the end of the lease nor an option. Here the Convention appears to recoil from giving legal significance to the notion of economic ownership. It also appears that economic ownership in terms of care for the assets is not fully put on the lessee, although this could of course be agreed in the lease contract, as will normally be the case. In fact, as the risk is usually insured it was believed better to leave the insurance duty to contractual stipulation.[263]

Although it is altogether possible to form some idea of the Convention's notion of finance lease, the Convention gives the impression that it does not want to be pinned down and uses at the beginning of Article 1 advisedly the word 'describe' rather than 'define'. The result of this approach is that no true legal notion of the finance lease emerges, whatever the intent, reinforced by the incidental nature of the provisions, especially in the proprietary aspect. The most notable result is extra doubt on the borderline with the operational lease which is not covered and with bipartite lease situations which are also outside the scope of the Convention.[264] Where the lessee receives the assets directly from the supplier before the lease agreement is signed, there may also be some doubts about the applicability of the Convention. The lease-back appears excluded altogether as the lessee has in that case fully negotiated and signed the supply contract and taken possession and most likely became the owner in the process, although possibly subject to a reservation of title.

---

[262] See also Explanatory report, cited in n 261 *supra*, 40 (no 70).
[263] *Ibid*, 61 (no 114).
[264] *Ibid*, 32 (no 52).

More generally, there must be doubt about the applicability of the Convention when the lessee has co-signed the supply agreement. The Convention requires that the lessee knows of and agrees with the terms of the supply agreement but there is no reference to him (counter)signing it when the provisions concerning his collateral rights would in any event be superfluous. On the other hand, it remains unclear what the minimum level of involvement of the lessee in the supply agreement must be. It is a further indication that the *facts* of the case need to be considered in each instance as regards whether the Convention may apply, not necessarily a happy situation.

The factual approach is also the attitude of the UCC in the USA (Section 1-201(a)(35) 1-201(37) old) but there only in order to distinguish between the finance lease and a secured transaction. As mentioned before, consumer leasing is clearly excluded from the Convention: Article 1(5). From the reference to the parties' place of business in Article 3, it is further clear that the Convention considers leases only amongst businesses or professionals. Real estate leasing is not contemplated either,[265] although the application of the Convention does not cease merely because the equipment has become a fixture to or is incorporated in land: Article 4(1).

The Convention is clearly influenced by the American approach to the equipment lease which puts the emphasis on (a) the active role of the lessee in the selection of the equipment, (b) the tripartite nature of the arrangement, and (c) the transfer of possession and use. There is nothing against this, but it is quite different from the European approach, which is much more likely to look for economic ownership. It is associated with the lease being for the useful life of the asset or with the lessee having the residual rights in the asset or an option to the effect. In the USA, that would lead to the lease being converted into a secured transaction as we saw. It is a difference in approach, which the Convention has not bridged. Instead, it has chosen vagueness in the key aspects and a limited coverage and covers, except for the collateral rights of the lessee under the supply agreement, largely lesser issues.

2.1.8   The Proprietary Aspects

As we have already seen, the Convention notably avoids any clear statement on ownership and possession except in the context of granting quiet possession to the lessee, Article 8(2) and (4), which is a different and, in the context of the Convention, factual concept. As regards the lessor, the Convention states that the lessor 'acquires' the equipment, Article 1(1)(a), whilst Article 7 assumes that the lessor has real rights without defining them (earlier the term 'ownership' was deleted), whilst only Article 8(1)(c) suggests the possibility of ownership in the lessor. The Convention does not exclude the possibility of subleasing (Article 2) and supposedly also not the possibility that the lessor acquires the asset subject to a reservation of title by the supplier depending on the payment terms between them. However, it avoids any consideration of the proprietary relationships also in that case.

The lessee's right is generally expressed in terms of the use of the equipment in return for payment of the rentals, without any reference to a term or to the useful life of the lease assets (Article 1(1)(b)). It might follow from the amortisation reference in Article 1(2)(c) (not necessarily so considered in the USA, however).[266] As there is no need for a lessee's option to buy the equipment (Article 1(3)) or an automatic right to acquire full title upon

---

[265] This follows from the text of Article 1 (1)(a) which refers to equipment, see also Explanatory Report, n 261 *supra*, 36 (no 63).
[266] See s 1.6.3 *supra*.

payment of all the rentals, no proprietary implications (in terms of a conditional ownership) can be deduced from such an option either.

More important is probably that in the case of default by the lessee or upon termination of the lease, there is *no* automatic return of the asset to the lessor: Article 13(2) and Article 9(2).[267] On the other hand, there is no foreclosure in the case of default either; if it is substantial there is a right of termination and repossession for the lessor, the conditions and status of which repossession right are not further defined or described. Respossession suggests nevertheless some proprietary protection of the lessee, perhaps further borne out by the transfer provision of Article 14, under which the lessor cannot thereby alter the nature of the lease. The transferring lessee on the other hand requires the prior consent of the lessor. As his transfer will normally involve the asset itself, the Convention expressly states that such a transfer remains subject to the rights of third parties (Article 14(2)), like presumably reservations of title of suppliers and rights of head lessors, but also to claims to full title by *bona fide* purchasers from the lessee and any repossession right of the lessor upon termination in the case of substantial default by the lessee pursuant to Article 13(2)(a).

2.1.9   The Enforcement Aspects

This leaves us with Article 7, applicable in enforcement situations. It is probably the most interesting Article of the Convention, the subject of much debate and the result of a myriad of compromises. It allows the lessor to maintain his real rights (whatever these may be) against a trustee in bankruptcy of the lessee (without further definition of the type of insolvency or related procedure) or in individual enforcement action of any of the lessee's creditors. It is certainly noteworthy that the Convention, contrary to earlier proposals, gives this facility only in enforcement, *not* therefore in proceedings on the merits or in injunctive proceedings and probably also not in reorganisation proceedings in anticipation of insolvency or in preservation measures. More importantly it does not mention similar rights in terms of ownership, possession or even use of the lessee in enforcement actions against the lessor. One may deduce from Article 14 that in that case ownership may be transferred to third parties without affecting the lease, but one cannot be sure and it would in any event suggest that the lessee has then more than purely contractual rights, as already discussed in the previous section.

If under the applicable domestic law the validity of the lessor's real rights depends on publication, compliance with that requirement is a precondition for the real rights of the lessor to be asserted in enforcement (also if the goods have moved to another country). One must assume that this is relevant only if enforcement is in a Contracting State. In this connection there is also a jurisdictional question which may be differently resolved in preliminary attachment proceedings as a preservation measure (if at all meant to be included in Article 7), execution proceedings, and in bankruptcy. In order to find the applicable law in this connection, a uniform conflicts rule is given in Article 7(3), referring to (a) the law of the place of registration for ships and aircraft, interestingly to (b) the law of the residence of the lessee for other equipment meant to move, and to (c) the *lex situs* for the rest.

These provisions concerning publication are the nearest pointer to the financial lease being also covered by the Convention if considered a type of secured transaction under applicable law. It leaves the question why the Convention insists on publication for such

---

[267] See s 2.1.9 *infra*.

leases under applicable law even when assets have moved to another Contracting State. Nobody outside the country of publication can possibly derive much protection from it except if willing to conduct a costly and (for him) unfamiliar search. It is of interest in this connection that, although the lessee's creditors with proprietary protection are not meant to be affected by this regime in their priorities in the lease assets (Article 7(5)), *bona fide* purchasers are not mentioned or any repossession rights of the lessor or any rights of head-lessors, *cf* also the wider provision of Article 14(2). The Convention clearly did not want to go into these aspects,[268] nor, as we saw, into any ownership claim of lessor or lessee either.

For these interested parties (as for any others) there are at most the general principles on which the Convention is based, which, as suggested above, do not appear much developed, and otherwise the normally applicable conflicts rules, which, as also earlier suggested, may not be very clear when lease assets are moving. The uniform conflict rules for publication set out in Article 7 of the Convention in any event do not appear indicative of general principles on which the Convention is based and can therefore not more universally apply in the proprietary and enforcement aspects of finance leases covered by the Convention. In fact, it is likely that the little uniformity the Convention brings will be overwhelmed by private international law issues.

2.1.10   The Contractual Aspects

The basic assumption of the Convention is that parties will normally make their own arrangements. This notion is supported in Article 5 which allows exclusion of the applicability of the Convention altogether, but only when all parties, including those to the supply agreement, agree. It is a reconfirmation of the tripartite principle underlying the finance lease in the eyes of the Convention, but so rigorously applied it is probably a novel departure.

The likely result of exclusion is that the rights of the lessor are weakened, probably also in respect of third parties, who are therefore not adversely affected, but it should be doubted whether proprietary or other third party or creditors' rights could be impacted by an exclusion of the Convention's applicability by participants in this manner. It would suggest that the proprietary and enforcement aspects of the Convention are in essence contractualised.

Short of full exclusion, the parties may 'in their relations with each other' also derogate from the Convention, therefore without the consent of any other party not part of that relationship. It also allows any individual provisions concerning proprietary rights to be contractually derogated from, like the one of Article 7, presumably, however, only as long as third parties are not adversely affected.[269] Also the interpretation and supplementation provision of Article 6 could thus be varied.

Yet there are three instances in which even then derogation (short of full exclusion) is not possible. These *mandatory* rules concern first any exception to the warranty of quiet possession in the case of gross negligence of the lessor, an exclusion thought in principle to be allowed under common law (Article 8(3)). Secondly, it avoids any agreement requiring a defaulting lessee to pay damages leaving the lessor in a better position than he would have been in if the lessee had fully performed the leasing agreement (Article 13(3)(b)).

---

[268] Explanatory Report, cited in n 261 *supra*, 51 (no 93).
[269] *Ibid*, 78 (no 149).

Finally, where the lessor has terminated the leasing agreement, he is not entitled to acceleration of the rentals except in the context of computing damages (Article 13(4)). Although one can understand the gist of these mandatory rules, one may doubt whether they are appropriate or necessary amongst professionals to whom the Convention is limited.

As for the directory contract rules of the Convention, there is no particular coherent pattern in the provisions. The main obligations of the parties are particularly for the lessor to grant the lessee the right to use the lease assets and for the lessee to pay rentals to the lessor. They are not further detailed and the Convention limits itself in fact to a number of secondary (even though important) issues. Article 8(1) states that the lessor shall not incur liability to the lessee in respect of the equipment, except to the extent that the lessee has suffered loss as a result of his reliance on the lessor's skills (apparently with or without the lessor's knowledge) and to the extent of the latter's intervention in the selection of the supplier.

This limitation is balanced for the lessee by his direct action against the supplier under Article 10. It puts the main burden of performance on the supplier to which Article 8(2) and also Article 12 in the case of non-conform delivery are, however, important exceptions.[270] In his capacity as lessor, the latter will also not be responsible for any third party liability in respect of injury or damage caused by the equipment, but he may be so liable as deemed owner, for example under applicable product liability statutes.

Article 8(2) contains the lessor's warranty of quiet possession (subject to any broader warranty mandatory under the law applicable pursuant to the rules of private international law) except against rights derived from a lessee's act or omission, a provision which, as already mentioned, cannot be varied in respect of any superior rights of third parties derived from an intentional or grossly negligent act or omission of the lessor. To the extent that it implies a warranty beyond the consequences of the lessor's own behaviour, this approach was criticised at the time for putting a responsibility on the lessor not deemed compatible with his passive role in the supply of the lease assets.[271] It is certainly to be noted that in this respect Article 8(2) goes beyond the approach of Article 8(1).

Article 9 requires the lessee to exercise normal care in the use of the equipment, whilst Article 13 finally deals with default of the lessee. The *normal* feature is here that the lessor may recover any *unpaid* rentals together with interest and damages. The *special* feature is that in the case of substantial default (*not*, however, defined) the lessor may *accelerate* future payments if the lease contract so provides, whilst leaving the lessee in possession for the agreed period, or otherwise terminate the agreement and immediately recover possession apparently without further formalities, whilst also claiming damages so as to place him in the same position as would have resulted from full performance. This may include the remaining rentals but would also have to discount the remaining value of the assets for the lessor, who is under a duty to mitigate: see Article 13(6).

It may well mean entering (if possible), into a replacement lease which is then likely to be an operational lease. The contract may liquidate these damages provided they do not result in a figure substantially in excess of those resulting from the Convention, a provision which may not be varied by the parties either. The lessor must make a choice and may not do both: accelerate payment and terminate with recovery of possession and may in any event do neither before he has given the lessee a reasonable opportunity of remedying his default, without the Convention clarifying what this entails.

The right to terminate and immediately recover possession without further proceedings was made explicitly an alternative in order to avoid any doubt on this facility, which

---

[270] See s 2.1.11 *infra*.
[271] See comment by E Gewirtz and J Pote [1988] *International Financial Law Review* 24, 25.

is crucial but might not have existed under common law. The acceleration principle also needed confirmation in the USA in Section 2A-109 UCC which already allows it when the lease contract is substantially endangered.

2.1.11   The Collateral Rights

As mentioned before, the Convention is, at least for Europeans, exceptional in its clear acknowledgement of the tripartite nature of the finance lease, following in this respect the modern American approach, and draws clear consequences from this state of affairs in Articles 10, 11 and 12 by treating the lessee largely as a party to the supply agreement, even though he is not supposed to have signed it.[272] He may still have substantially relied on the guidance of the lessor and is in any event only supposed to have approved the terms in so far as they concern his interests. The manner in which his approval of the supply agreement must be expressed is left open (see respectively Articles 8(1)(a), 1(1)(a) and 1(2)(a)).

Article 10 states that the duties of the supplier to the lessor shall also be owed to the lessee as if he were a party to the supply agreement, as if the equipment was directly supplied to him, but presumably only to the extent that these duties concern him. It is supported by Section 2A-209(1) UCC, which introduced a similar approach, also abandoning the contractual privity notions in this connection. The lessee does not, however, have any right to terminate (or presumably vary) the supply agreement without the consent of the lessor: Article 10(2). On the other hand, Article 11 makes it clear that the lessee is not bound by any later variations in a previously approved supply agreement to which he has not consented. Naturally, the supplier is liable for damages to either the lessor or the lessee and not to both (Article 10(1)), but otherwise the relationship between the lessor and the lessee in their claims against the supplier is not covered.

Whilst Article 10 gives the lessee the direct rights, which the lessor may have against the supplier, it does not appear that he owes the supplier any duties which the lessor may have had under the supply agreement, notably the obligation to pay. However, the lessee will have to accept any exceptions the supplier may derive from his relationship with the lessor, especially when the latter is in default of payment, in which case the lessee can no longer insist upon the performance of the contractual duties by the supplier *vis-à-vis* him. It appears, however, that any exceptions derived from the lessor's behaviour in other contracts with the supplier cannot be used as an excuse for the supplier's duties *vis-à-vis* the lessee under Article 10.

Article 12 finally examines the non-conform delivery, either, it seems, at the time of delivery or surfacing later. Whilst not affecting the lessee's direct rights against the supplier under Article 10 (see also Article 12(6)), for the lessee there is here also an action against the lessor either to reject the equipment or to terminate the lease, with the lessor's right, however, to remedy the default for which no time frame has been set. In either case, the rights of both parties are as if the lessee had agreed to buy the equipment from the lessor on the terms of the supply agreement. The defences of the lessor, including *force majeure*, would then derive from this agreement; bankruptcy of the supplier would not be one of them and also not the inability to obtain similar equipment if, under the law applicable to the contract, the risk had not yet passed and the goods perished or if, after delivery, hidden defects had emerged.

---

[272] Explanatory Report, n 261 *supra*, 62 (no 116).

Because of this particular construction, assuming the direct applicability of the supply agreement between lessor and lessee, one could ask oneself which law applies here as regards the remedies, defences and the passing of the risk. Is it the one of the supply agreement under which the supplier performs the characteristic obligation or should the lessor be substituted for this purpose? If there is a contractual choice of law in the supply agreement, would it also be effective in this case? Similar questions may be asked under Article 10, where, however, the duties of the supplier are the issue which will normally be covered by the law applicable to the supply contract.[273]

There are also some uniform rules in Article 12: the lessee may withhold the rentals until the lessor has remedied the default or the lessee has lost the right to reject the equipment. If he terminates the agreement and claims damages, he has the rights to reclaim any payments less any benefits derived from the equipment. He has, however, no other claims against the lessor except as result from the latter's act or omission. Wherever the Vienna Convention on International Sales applies (which assumes that the supply agreement should be considered a sale) conflict rules are avoided and there will be more clarity, at least in the aspects covered by that Convention. In the case of conflict, it will prevail over the Leasing Convention according to Article 17 of the latter.

Whilst the Convention elaborates on the collateral rights of the lessee under the supply contract in the above manner, it is of interest that there are no provisions at all on the direct relationship between the lessor and supplier. National laws resulting from the applicable conflict rules must provide the answers, which may easily differ. The tripartite nature of the arrangement nevertheless begs the question of what the precise relationship is between the lease, the supply agreement, and the parties thereto. This is particularly important if one of these contracts fails (for example for reasons of *force majeure*). The Convention does not cover this point but it may be assumed that the lease agreement is ancillary to the supply agreement even if the latter is concluded later and is therefore dependent on it and fails with it. It may also be argued that the supply agreement in turn depends on the lease, at least to the extent that the supplier is aware of the situation, which will normally be the case, so that there is *mutual dependence*, which also fits in with the tripartite approach of the Convention.[274]

2.1.12 Concluding Remarks

It is clear that the Convention covers a narrow field. It does not apply to the operational lease, the lease-back, and probably also not to any other arrangement where the lessee receives the goods from the supplier before the lease agreement has been concluded or to situations where the lessee is a co-signatory of the supply agreement or where there is no supplier involvement at all. Consumer and real estate leases are in any event excluded. As especially in relation to the operational lease the demarcation line is unclear, the facts of the case will play an important role in determining the applicability of the Convention, which, in the absence of much guidance, introduces uncertainty limiting its role.

The Convention further requires that the lease contract is concluded between parties having their place of business in different Contracting States, whilst the supplier must also be from a Contracting State *or* both the lease and supply agreement are governed by the

---

[273] Dagefoerde, n 261 *supra*, 153.
[274] Explanatory Report, n 261 *supra*, 109.

law of a Contracting State (which can be so chosen by the parties). Cross-border leasing in this sense is, however, exceptional and is only likely to exist in very major movable capital goods like aircraft and its spare parts and possibly ships. Generally, leasing companies have subsidiaries in the place of the lessee or *vice versa* or are otherwise incorporated in tax havens which are not so likely to become Contracting States.

These factors will limit the impact of the Convention. In proprietary and enforcement matters, notwithstanding the limited coverage of these aspects in the Convention itself, the Convention does not appear to be applicable if the *situs* or place of enforcement is not in a Contracting State. This will also limit the application of the Convention in these important aspects. It raises jurisdiction questions. They may be resolved differently depending on the type of procedure: injunctive, on the merits, or enforcement. In the latter instance, there may be further differences in the case of preliminary attachments as provisional or preservation measures (if at all meant to be covered by Article 7), executions and insolvencies.

On the other hand, one may ask why the Convention should apply in these proprietary and enforcement aspects at all if the assets in Contracting States were never moved or were not destined for movement. Also the difference in proprietary treatment of lease assets covered by the Convention and of other leases within one jurisdiction was noted above. It is probably quite undesirable but unavoidably results as the applicability of the Convention is unrelated to the location or movement of assets but based instead on the place of business of the parties, who may even exclude the application of the Convention in its totality. It appears indirectly to contractualise the ownership and enforcement aspects, an interesting aspect being further that in matters of interpretation in these areas notions of good faith appear to apply (Article 6(1)). One may well wonder what the draftsmen had here in mind.

Finally, the Convention itself contains other limiting provisions. It only requires three ratifications (Article 16), therefore contemplates a narrow area of application. Each Contracting State may limit its field of application further to particular territorial units if it operates different systems of law within its borders (Article 18). States with closely related legal leasing regimes may declare that the Convention will not apply where the supplier, lessor and lessee have their places of business in these states (Article 19). Thus, on the one hand, a country like the USA could limit the application of the Convention to some of its states. On the other hand, those states that already accepted the new Article 2A UCC could be excepted from the application of the Convention on the basis of the closeness of their legal regimes if the parties had their places of business within the territories of those states.

The Convention, moreover, contemplates only a partial codification. It does not present a coherent notion of the finance lease, probably because it was not able to choose between the basic models. It could not bridge the gap between countries like the USA that limit the proprietary rights of the lessee for fear of creating a secured transaction and place emphasis instead on the collateral rights of the lessee under the supply agreement, and those countries, especially from the civil law, that enhance the proprietary rights by assuming or requiring an option for the lessee to acquire full title upon payment of all the instalments or an automatic transfer of full title to the lessee at that time. This being the case, the Convention was also not able substantially to enter into the proprietary aspects which at the same time limits its coverage of enforcement. Here it became distracted by a conflicts rule for the publication of leases in the manner of a security right. Yet it was not able to determine whether there is some security or what the meaning of any publication under a domestic law can be in an international context when the asset has moved elsewhere.

It may well be that in such a context these proprietary status and enforcement aspects of the lease assets are at least as important as the contractual aspects which after all can largely be settled in the contract itself.

The Convention does not in fact manage to spell out the basic contractual rights either and its coverage appears only to be a small collection of contractual incidents which do not greatly bear on the core of the lease. The Convention, following the American lead, is probably most original in its coverage of the collateral rights of the lessee under the supply agreement. Where the Convention does not succeed in formulating uniform law, a uniform conflicts rule is sometimes given, like in the just mentioned aspect of the law applicable to publication or in the question of the lease asset having become a fixture to or incorporated in land (Articles 7 and 4).

The applicable law is otherwise left to be deduced from the general principles underlying the Convention, which, in the absence of a comprehensive notion of the finance lease itself, may hardly exist, certainly in the proprietary aspects. Barring any such principles, the normally applicable (*not* uniformed) domestic conflicts rules remain in force which will therefore continue to be relevant in most instances. Notably the uniform conflicts rule given for publication would not appear to have any further relevance in proprietary matters. However, the uniform substantive rules given for the collateral aspects of the lease may well prove to provide more of a system, based as it is on the tripartite notion of the lease and contractual dependency of the lease and the supply agreement.

Finally, it is to be noted that, with the exception of three incidental mandatory rules meant to protect the lessee against any misbehaviour of the lessor of which the appropriateness may well be questioned in dealings amongst professionals, the Convention contains only directory rules which may be set aside by the parties in their contract. In view of the sophistication of most lease agreements which are greatly standardised, it must be assumed that this normally happens in most aspects. The entire Convention can, on the other hand, only be excluded by the agreement of all three parties to the lease. This would then also affect (any) proprietary and enforcement aspect involving third parties, which is less understandable and presents a further limitation of the effect of the Convention. This is another indication that the Convention's impact, at least in the proprietary and enforcement areas, has not always been fully thought through.

What is altogether left of any real effect that may be anticipated from the present Convention in terms of uniformity across borders in international leasing appears to be modest. That would be so even if the Convention were widely ratified, tripartite cross-border leases were frequent and not normally fully determined in the lease contract itself (except for formation and avoidance, proprietary and enforcement aspects). On the other hand, an effort of this nature unavoidably involves compromise in which conceptual clarity suffers. This shows here in the limited detail of the contractual and particularly of the proprietary and enforcement aspects.

It is in fact not surprising that the end result is fragmentary, avoids difficult questions of demarcation with the operational lease, and seeks to side-step the controversy about the characterisation of the finance lease as a secured transaction, substitute security, reservation of title or hire purchase or any other form of (conditional) proprietary right and the consequences of any such characterisation. There is, however, nothing in the Convention either that would suggest that finance leasing is not a distinct type of arrangement with distinct commercial logic and price that has nothing to do with its being accessory to a credit agreement, if only because there is normally no interest rate related structure of pricing. Yet, where the Convention at least should have been able to decide that a finance lease is not a security, it leaves some serious doubts on the matter in Article 7 where the concern with publication could be seen to point the other way.

Even where the Convention appears to take a view, as in the acceptance of the modern tripartite nature of the scheme and places, as a consequence, emphasis mostly on his collateral rights under the supply agreement (following the American approach in this respect), it cannot clearly say what kind of involvement the lessee is to have in the supply agreement. The Convention may not even apply if there is either too much in the sense that the lessee becomes a signatory, or too little when there may be only an operational lease. Where the Convention insists on the costs of the lease asset being substantially amortised in the rentals, it will not say either that the lease is meant for substantially the useful life of the asset. It proved not even willing or able to spell out that the full economic burden in terms of risks and costs is borne by the lessee. Although from the warranty of quiet possession in Article 8, it appears that the lessor may be less passive in the eyes of the Convention than is normally assumed, one cannot be sure.

Altogether, the Convention is clearly the product of greatly diverging views on its scope and coverage presented at the various drafting stages. Consequently, it may be doubted whether it presents a sufficiently coherent contribution to the subject to be meaningful in terms of legislation and whether in its present limited form it fulfils a true need. It seems that only a more radical and comprehensive approach might do so, although it must be admitted at the same time that such an approach might have prevented any measure of agreement developing in the matter at all.

This international effort must perhaps be seen as a first step but treaty law is not easily adjusted and more comprehensive newer efforts seem far away. The main impact of the Convention may be in the academic interest that it has engendered which has significantly contributed to a better understanding of the finance lease as a modern financial instrument. In introducing and supporting the tripartite nature of the finance lease and the collateral rights of the lessee under the supply agreement, it has, however, also pushed the finance lease forward and introduced significant aspects hitherto unknown in the European leasing laws.

2.2   Repurchase Agreements

2.2.1   *The Repurchase Agreement as Prime Alternative to Secured Lending: Its Legal Characterisation*

The repurchase agreement is the prototype alternative to the secured loan and in its proper form results in a conditional sale of assets subject to a repurchase right and duty, as explained in more detail in section 1.1.1 above. A sale subject to a repurchase facility of the asset and a loan secured on the same assets lead on their face to similar funding alternatives but they are neither legally nor practically the same and must be clearly distinguished. The sale subject to a repurchase facility is likely to have a different risk and reward structure, is subject to different (or no) formalities, and has also a different proprietary structure and enforcement regime.

The repurchase agreement is therefore different from the secured loan. It was submitted earlier that the repurchase agreement would only have to be considered a secured transaction subject to its formalities in its creation (and possible nullity in the absence of them being observed) and enforcement regime if there is a clear loan agreement of which an agreed interest rate structure is the indication. The mere existence of a repurchase price, which will include a mark-up as a reward for this service, is no indication of an interest rate structure. In fact, this excess, in investment securities repos also called the repo rate, will normally be lower than the prevailing interest rate for secured loans. That is (besides the informality) the attraction of the repurchase agreement for the party requiring financing and shows the alternative. The *quid pro quo* is the different rights and obligations of the parties in respect of the assets during the repurchase period and particularly the different remedies in the case of a default.

Thus the repurchase agreement generally allows for greater flexibility in the funding arrangement. There will also be no publicity or other formal requirements in the creation nor an execution sale or other forms of disposition upon the failure of the seller to repurchase the assets. There may also be different arrangements in terms of possession and user rights and liability for the asset and more in particular in the entitlement to any overvalue when no repurchase takes place. Under a true repurchase agreement, the buyer/financier will automatically become full owner upon default if the seller had a right and duty to repurchase.

It would mean that in the seller's bankruptcy, the financier in possession may be able to retain the assets or if possession was left with the seller he may be able to repossess them. If, on the other hand, the buyer cannot deliver the assets on the appointed date, the seller may be able to reclaim the assets in his bankruptcy as the full owner upon his tender of the repurchase price. If he was still in possession he keeps the goods, if the buyer was in possession he may be able to reclaim them as owner. Unlike in the case of a secured loan, there is no sale and return of any overvalue to the original seller. The buyer keeps the assets for their full value. In doing so, he may, however, forfeit any right to damages for undervalue.

As we saw in section 1.1.1 above, in the repurchase agreement, the seller may only have a mere option (instead of a right and duty) to repurchase the asset on an agreed date at an agreed price when it is *unlikely* that there is a conditional sale proper and the financier is in such a case more likely to result immediately as the true owner subject to a contractual or personal retrieval right of the seller. There could also be an option for the financier to retain the asset. In that case he would have a put option, again probably only as a personal right. Normally there is, however, a right and a duty for the seller to repurchase and for the buyer to receive the repurchase price whilst surrendering the assets.

This leads to the conditional transfer with the dual ownership structure just mentioned in which the interest of the buyer/financier could be characterised as ownership subject to a rescinding condition (of the tender of the repurchase price) and of the seller as an ownership under a suspending or acquisitive condition, giving rise in common law terms to a future interest: see also section 1.1.4 above. The right of the buyer could also be characterised as a temporary ownership leading to a return of full title to the seller upon the end of the period, like upon the end of a usufruct in civil law or as a reversionary interest in common law.

It is a question of characterisation of the interest, but it is submitted that the conditional ownership characterisation is the better one: see section 1.1.4 above. Both are easily possible in common law, used to future interests and split ownership forms of this nature. In Dutch law, the problem is that in the case of a conditional sale, the structure may be deprived of any proprietary effect as alternative security interests are ruled out under Article 3.84(3) CC: see for this problem more in particular section 1.2.3 above, whilst as a temporary transfer it is converted into a usufruct under Article 3.85. Either alternative is clearly undesirable. The American unitary functional approach could have an equally adverse effect on repurchase agreements, converting them into secured transactions subject to their formalities but they are generally considered to be outside the reach of Article 9 UCC, at least in the case of the security repo.[275] In fact, the terminology often used by repo users does not help. They may refer to debtors and creditors and the repo fee is often referred to as interest rather than the repo rate. The investment securities are themselves often referred to as collateral. This should not mislead the lawyer.

The characterisation of the repurchase right and duty as a conditional or temporary ownership interest rules out any *cherry-picking option* of the trustee in the bankruptcy of either party under his option to terminate executory contracts (although the applicable bankruptcy law may still dictate this course): see also section 1.1.6 above. It means that the bankruptcy trustee of either party could insist on a return of the asset depending on whether they had either risen or dropped in value. Indeed, if the arrangement was purely contractual, that would be a possibility under normal bankruptcy rules which allow the repudiation of burdensome contracts if still executory, that is not fully performed by either party. In truth, the repurchase agreement is not purely executory, however. Contracts that are followed by a transfer of proprietary rights never are.

The executory contract characterisation is nevertheless common and means that the bankruptcy trustee of either the seller or buyer may be allowed to choose (or cherry pick) to continue or terminate the contract depending on the behaviour of the underlying asset. Thus in a bankruptcy of the buyer, the assets could be retained by his trustee if they had increased in value whilst the repurchase agreement would be repudiated and the seller would only have a competing claim for damages (that is the excess of the value over the repurchase price). If they had fallen in value, the trustee would insist on the performance of the repurchase agreement receiving the repurchase price whilst returning the asset. The trustee for a bankrupt seller would have similar options when the price of the assets had moved. This would only be different for market price related contracts in countries like Germany which are always rescinded in a bankruptcy.

In a conditional (or temporary) sale, on the other hand, upon a proper analysis both parties have a proprietary interest, and the trustee of the bankrupt buyer will have to return the asset when it will become subject to the seller's reclaiming or revindication right as the buyer's title lapses upon the timely tender of the repurchase price by his seller. If the price of the asset has fallen so that the seller may not be interested in it any longer, the trustee of the buyer can still force him to tender the repurchase price as a contractual obligation. In a bankruptcy of the seller, the buyer in possession may retain the asset for the duration of the repurchase agreement and may also have a retention right for the repurchase price. Upon a failure of the bankruptcy trustee of the seller to tender the repurchase price, the buyer becomes full owner, possibly with a competing claim against the seller for any loss in value. If not in possession, this failure to tender the repurchase price may give him reclaiming rights against the trustee.

In this system, there are no special options of either trustee and also no rights to early termination of the arrangement in the nature of an executory contract. Of course, neither party need exercise his proprietary rights in a bankruptcy of the other and claim damages instead as a competing creditor but invoking proprietary protection will often be beneficial. It will not help, however, where the price has fallen and a bankrupt seller's trustee will not retake the asset. In that case, the buyer has at best a competing claim for damages whilst retaining the depreciated asset.

---

[275] See n 201 *supra*.

Especially in investment securities repos, the repurchase agreement is in practice often still characterised as a mere executory contract. There may be a case for it on the basis of the fungible nature of the asset so that only an asset of the same sort must be returned and any ownership right in it becomes tenuous. This will indeed be the case in the repo of investment securities when in any event tracing may not help because the buyer will often on-sell the asset to which under this arrangement he is normally entitled pending the repurchase. In that case, he will buy back assets of the same sort later to be able to deliver upon the repurchase date. When the assets, although fungible, are not on-sold but still with third parties as custodians who must return a similar number of assets on the appointed day, the fungibility issue may not be a bar to the proprietary reclaiming rights, yet the situation is less clear and the executory contract characterisation all the more adopted. It should be borne in mind in this connection, however, that all ownership rights in securities tend to be no more than entitlement rights entered in book entry systems of custodians in which connection fungibility no longer undermines the ownership in them.

The undesirable effects of cherry-picking, which result from the executory contract characterisation, are now commonly balanced by netting agreements in which also delivery obligations are reduced to contractual claims for damages, assuming these netting agreements may be validly made and are effective in bankruptcy, now especially so provided by American and German bankruptcy law amendments (Section 559 of the US Bankruptcy Code and Section 104 of the German Insolvency Act). It is effective only between the same parties with mutually balancing positions, therefore with positions not all one way but has the advantage that it does away with any uncertainty about claims for undervalue, since the non-defaulting party will not claim the full ownership of the securities.

In this connection, for securities repos, frame or master agreements have been devised specifically aiming at facilitating bilateral contractual netting. The best known is the PSA/ISMA Global Master Repurchase Agreement of 1992, amended in 1995, operating in the New York and London repo markets for investment securities. It is in practice particularly relevant for repos concerning eurobonds but through its various Annexes may now also be extended to repos in UK Gilts and US Treasuries, which are the UK and US government bonds: see section 2.2.5 below.

2.2.2 The Development of the Repo in Investment Securities: Securities Lending and the Buy/Sell Back Transaction

It may be useful to elaborate some more on the investment security repo and its various forms, although repos are also common in some agricultural products and commodities. In Europe, they have acquired a special importance in that the new European Central Bank (ECB) commonly provides liquidity to, or takes it away from, banks through repo transactions.[276]

The development of the modern repo in investment securities is related to the lend/borrow activity in these assets. Bond lending, or more generally securities lending, has long existed to meet the needs of a market operator with short positions who is asked to deliver. He can do so by either buying the relevant securities in the market if available or otherwise by borrowing them allowing him more time to close out his overall position.

---

[276] Article 18.1 of the ESCB and ECB Statute mentions the (reverse) repo as one of the monetary policy instruments of the ECB: see also E Uwaifo, 'The Legal Requirements for Securities Lending and Repos and the Legal Effect of EMU' [1997] *European Financial Services Law* 224.

This borrowing is of a special type because it gives the borrower the right to sell the stock. In fact, from a legal point of view it must probably be characterised as a purchase with a sell-back right and duty at the end of the borrowing period. The periods involved vary between a few days and a few weeks. In a proper characterisation, the sale would therefore be conditional or temporary. The price for this service is, however, *not* a sale price followed by a repurchase price, but a fee normally depending on market rates and the financial standing of the borrower and his anticipated ability to return the borrowed securities. Security will normally be asked for and may consist of a portfolio of (other) securities which the borrower puts at the disposal of the securities lender. If he does not return sufficient assets of the same type at the end of the lending period, their full market value will become payable at that moment and upon non-payment will be set off against the realised value of the security. There may also be a margin requirement (see section 2.2.3 below). Normally, the borrower is not entitled to the income on the stock and must make substitute payments to the lender for the relevant amounts (the same goes for the lender in respect of any income he may receive on stocks given to him as security).

Securities lending is not a funding transaction and economically speaking therefore a type of transaction quite different from a repo.[277] This is shown in that the lender or seller who *pays* a repo rate in a funding transaction *receives* a fee in the securities lending transaction. Since there is no funding, no substantial fund transfers are involved (except in case of default) whilst the borrowing of securities may also be a cross-borrowing. There is always a fixed time limit. It can be said, however, that it is the lender in securities borrowing and the buyer in repos (the financier) who are in comparable positions as both receive a fee for their services.

In the true investment securities repos, the objective is funding and to this effect there is an ordinary sale of the securities against what will usually be a normal spot price subject to a repurchase right and duty at a later time against what could be considered a forward price. The repurchase date is normally fixed but could be open ('open repos'), which means that each party can end them at any time, or it may be subject to an option for the one or other party or both to continue ('rolling repos'). The repurchase price, although a forward price, may be quite artificial and will include a fee for the service (the repo rate) which will also allow for the credit risk of the seller and the quality and liquidity of the securities.

Unless there is an agreed loan set-up, the repo rate is not an interest rate but a reward fixed under the competitive conditions of the repo market itself. The result is an immediate payment of a sale price proper and a repurchase price agreed at the same time but payable on the repurchase date. Periods are normally short, from a few days to a few months. The income belongs to the seller and substitute payments must be made by the buyer, but it is more common that the repo period is so chosen that no investment income will be received during it. Substitute payments are therefore normally only of interest in the open or rolling repo.

Repos in marketed securities are usually organised to finance their acquisition themselves. Especially in bonds, they are normally much easier and quicker to arrange than a loan secured on the same assets as the normal channels of trading and settlement of investment securities are used. The documentation (sales note) can also be kept simple, although the repurchase duty, period and price still need to be expressed on it. The arrangement can

---

[277] See C Brown, 'How to Spot the Difference between Repo's and Stock Loans', *International Financial Law Review* 51 (June 1996).

often be made instantaneously for large amounts of money and repo-ing has become a normal extension of the ordinary trading activity of the trading desks in large banks to fund their positions. As a consequence, there is speed and flexibility with low transaction and documentation cost. On the other hand, the form is sometimes dictated by other considerations: many professional fund managers may be allowed to sell securities but not to lend them to others under the terms of the fund management contract. So they may make extra money through repos instead by reinvesting the moneys they so obtain. Tax considerations may also play a role.

In fact, as between the lend/borrow arrangement and the repo proper there has been a change in perspective from pure securities lending with the objective of receiving some extra income on one's securities holdings to a structure through which these holdings are themselves funded in a manner that is cheaper and quicker than would be possible otherwise, for example through a traditional loan secured on the same assets. The repo is now commonly used for the funding of most trading positions in government bonds in the USA and Japan and in eurobonds, with banks being most of the users or fund providers. The repo is also increasingly used for share funding. Where a bank provides the money and is therefore commonly the purchaser, the result is a *reverse repo* if the bank initiates the transaction. It has become important business for many banks.

In this scenario, a bank as securities borrower has become the money provider and the securities lender or the client the one who receives funding. The initiative will normally be with the trading or security house or trading bank, which may take this practice a step further by repo-ing its own securities if it has any excess holdings. In this way it may be able to obtain funding at a discount to the libor rate of a loan in the same amount whilst funding others with this money. This is called *repo matched book trading.*

The use of the securities markets for repos may subject them, however, to price reporting requirements and the need specially to mark off-market transactions upon the repurchase. In the Eurobond market, the repo concerns a transnational negotiable instrument and may well acquire further features in that context. It is in any event clear that within Euroclear and Cedel, the formalities for the creation of secured interests supporting loans are not used for repos. Also there is no physical possession by the buyer/financier but the book entry system for full ownership rights is used in which the buyer is identified as the owner of the securities.

Although the outward form of modern repos, at least of investment securities, is increasingly a conditional sale in which both legs of the transaction are integrated, it can also be a *buy/sell back* transaction, in which there is no such integration. This was the original form, still used on occasion. Under it there are two separate transactions in the same investment securities, one of sale and the other of purchase. There was therefore neither a conditional sale nor margin obligation nor a close-out and netting mechanism. In this structure, the income on the sold securities belonged to the buyer and no substitute payments took place, but the income so received was recompensed in the repurchase price.[278]

In this structure it is all the clearer that there is no substitute secured loan, not even a conditional sale. There is clearly funding and security is likely to be offered separately as in the case of securities lending, usually by offering other assets (mostly investment securities of a different type).

---

[278] See for the differences between a repo and a buy/back also C Brown, 'Similar but Different: Repo's and Buy/Sell Backs Compared', *International Financial Law Review* 45 (March 1996).

2.2.3   Margining

In practice, the funding party in the repo will require protection against the price of the underlying assets going down which would expose him in a bankruptcy of the seller even if he relies here on his possession and ownership rights as his basic protection. Accordingly, he will often request a special *margin* or haircut, that is to say that he may deduct a small percentage, often 2 per cent, of the sale price, and so of the cost at which he acquires the investment securities ('cash margin'). It may also be achieved in the seller providing extra securities ('margin securities'). A variable margin is also conceivable, adjusted daily on the basis of a marking to market of the assets. It may require extra cash or added securities of the same sort (margin securities). Additional margin may be negotiated for any currency mismatch between the denomination of the funds received and the market price of the assets. It requires extra documentation which is time-consuming and costly and destroys one of the attractive features of the repo of investment securities, especially the commodi-tised types thereof, like government securities and eurobonds. A system of daily adjust-ment of margins requires also an administrative infrastructure, which is costly. It may be farmed out to an agent who will also hold the investment securities in question. This is sometimes referred to as a 'tri-party repo'.

Other forms of protection may be provided under a system in which the repurchase price is regularly adjusted. It means on each occasion the termination of the original trans-action and the replacement by a new one ('repriced transaction'). The investment securi-ties, the termination date and the repo rate, as well as the margin, remain the same. The price of the new transaction will be set off against that of the old and the party in a nega-tive position will pay the difference to the other party. This repricing mechanism is partic-ularly suitable in a buy/sell back that has traditionally no margin requirement but may be protected in this manner.

There may also be a replacement under which the old transaction is replaced by one with another number or other type of investment securities. The key is that the replace-ment securities have as market value the amount of the original repurchase price.

2.2.4   The Netting Approach in Repos

Whether repurchase agreements should be considered conditional sales or merely execu-tory contracts is particularly relevant in a bankruptcy of either party, when in the first case the proprietary rights of either in the asset would determine the position and in the latter there would be a cherry-picking option for the trustee in which the market price move-ment in the assets would largely determine whether the trustee would want to honour the contract or repudiate it (except that in countries like Germany contracts in market-related assets are always rescinded in bankruptcy: see Section 104 of the Insolvency Act 1999). The cherry picking between the two sides of what is in essence one transaction of which only the first leg, the sale, is executed creates this possibility.

Given the fact that at least investment securities repos are often characterised as con-tractual in view of the fungibility of the underlying assets and the likelihood that the buyer has on-sold the assets to which he is entitled pending the repurchase, the more common approach is to characterise these repos as executory contracts subject to termi-nation by a bankruptcy trustee of either seller or buyer. As in swaps, where there is considered to be only one contract through the integration of all aspects of the deal, see chapter VI, section 1.4.6 below, there has been an attempt at limiting the implied cherry-picking option in repos by emphasising the close relationship between both legs of the transaction and its integrated nature. The aim is a system of immediate set-offs. This facility is then contractually enhanced with the aim of allowing either the original transaction to be completed as planned once the sale has happened or rather immediately to terminate both sides of the transaction at the same time whilst netting them out through acceleration and the substitution of monetary values for redelivery obligations. The monetary values are then netted out: see for the concept of netting itself, more in particular chapter III, section 1.3.4.

For the seller, the future benefit of cheaper finance is thus lost in a bankruptcy of the buyer/financier as well as any shortfall in the close out because any lowering in the value of the underlying assets will have to be taken into account (whilst any increase may still be for the bankrupt buyer). An extension of this idea is to allow *all* repo transactions between the same parties to be netted out in this (immediate) manner through the principle of aggregation which will also cover these shortfalls, but its success will depend on whether there are sufficient mutual transactions between both parties. This full *bilateral netting* could even be triggered by a default of either party in another relationship under a cross-default clause. Close out is here the aim, rather than replacement which may be more relevant in swaps than in repos because of their short-term nature.

2.2.5 The TBMA/ISMA Global Master Repurchase Agreement

A master agreement with a bilateral accelerated rescission clause through which all repos between the same parties may be considered integrated may help to clarify the situation, especially in respect of close-out netting, and is now in place in the London and New York markets under the TBMA/ISMA (formerly the PSA/ISMA) Global Master Repurchase Agreement of 2000 (GMRA) for repos in investment securities, especially for Eurobonds in the London market but it may be used for other products as well like UK Gilts or for Buy/Sell Back transactions. It was greatly inspired by the earlier American Master Repurchase Agreement (MRA). The TBMA is the Bond Market Association in New York, the successor of the Public Securities Association (PSA), and the ISMA is the Eurobond market's International Securities Market Association. A particular new feature of the 2000 GMRA is the inclusion of conditions precedent allowing parties to withhold further payments or deliveries as soon as a potential event of default occurs.

The Master Agreement is a frame agreement with two principal Annexes (which may be adjusted according to the products) and is subject to English law (which is not necessarily defining in bankruptcy which will be primarily subject to its own bankruptcy laws). The Master Agreement is applicable to all subsequent repos concluded between the parties to the Master. Its main objective is the facilitation of margin payments and of netting in the case of default.

The two Annexes are the most important. The first contains a list of subjects in respect of which parties must make a choice or must make disclosures. Under it, they may also opt for other terms ('Supplemental Terms and Conditions') and will chose the 'base currency' of the agreement, which is particularly relevant for the margin and netting facilities. The base currency may be different from the 'contractual currency' of each deal under Article 7 GMRA. Annex I covers addresses of the parties and possible choices of residence and under it the parties will also specify their 'designated offices' which can only be offices of the parties in jurisdictions that accept the close-out netting of the GMRA. Annex II covers the confirmation ('Form of Confirmation') and the transactional details (like the nature and number of the securities, the purchase and repurchase price and the margin particulars).

The GMRA in Article 1(c) allows for repos other than gross paying bonds (notably Eurobonds) and also covers Net Paying Securities (securities on which income is paid after withholding tax). All securities must be negotiable instruments, however, or at least subject to the book-entry system of Euroclear or Clearstream or another clearing system or be transferable in any other way mutually acceptable to the parties (Article 6(a)). There may also be country Annexes as there are the Belgian, Dutch and Italian (domestic) Annexes for transactions between citizens of the same country in investment securities of that country. All these various optional Annexes are integrated into Annex I.[279]

The Master Agreement addresses a situation in which it is impractical to introduce the necessary clauses on the sale tickets whilst they are as yet unlikely to be deemed implied or customary. It means that regular repo partners in London and New York now normally execute this master agreement amongst themselves.

The Global Master contains a margin system and a close-out system operating on the basis of notional values on the repurchase date resulting in net payments close out after acceleration in the case of a default (as defined in Article 10(a)), in which delivery obligations are also reduced to money (Articles 6(i) and 10(c)) and all are converted into the base currency. There is no cross-default clause but there is aggregation upon default of either partner resulting in a two-way payment, that is to say that even if the defaulting party stands to gain a net benefit it will be turned over. As in swaps, repo netting is not necessarily effective upon bankruptcy under all bankruptcy laws. It depends therefore on the applicable Bankruptcy Act, in which respect the American Bankruptcy Code 1978 as amended in this regard (Section 559) and the German Insolvency Act 1999 (Section 104) are important.

2.2.6   Concluding Remarks

The curious aspect of repurchase agreements in the modern sense is that, at least for investment securities repos, they are commonly considered to be contractual and are in fact characterised as executory contracts for this purpose subject to repudiation by the bankruptcy trustee of either party, the effects of which are, however, sought to be corrected by a bilateral close-out netting agreement. It will mostly bring relief against any cherry picking which follows from the contract characterisation, provided there are a sufficient number of mutual positions between the parties and the close-out netting is supported by the applicable bankruptcy regime. This does not go without saying, and it has for example required amendment to the Bankruptcy Act in the USA, as we saw.

In other countries, there may well be problems if the English law made applicable by the parties to the close-out netting under the GMRA is in result different from that under the applicable bankruptcy law. There may for example be conflict in the conversion of all obligations into the base currency on the day *following* the bankruptcy under the GMRA, which conversion may well have to be on the date of the bankruptcy in some countries. Any subsequently accruing interest may also not be off-settable. The base currency itself, which is unlikely to be the currency of the bankruptcy, may also be questioned. Attachments in respects of moneys subject to the GMRA may also interfere with the set-off, and it must be questioned whether this aspect could also be covered by English law

---

[279] See also G Morton, 'International Coverage of the PSA/ISMA Global Master Repurchase Agreement', (1997) *Butterworth's Journal of International Banking and finanancial Law* 128. like France have their own master agreements for domestic products: see n 92 *supra*.

if the bankruptcy is opened elsewhere, especially sensitive if the attached claim is sought to be set-off against a later arising counterclaim.

The other danger is the one of recharacterisation of the repo as a secured loan transaction or even as a temporary transfer or usufruct. These dangers exist particularly in the USA and under new Dutch law, although modern case law seems to be aware of the risks and may be inclined to support the modern repo practice as a funding arrangement in its own right.

Within the EU, under Article 9(2) of the Finality Directive,[280] the law of the clearing centre in which investment securities are registered in a book entry system covers the security interests that can be created in them. Strictly speaking, this does not cover other types of transfers including repos which are not secured transactions but rather conditional sales. It would be logical, however, to deem the same law applicable also to repos of such book entry securities. In any bankruptcy conducted under a bankruptcy law of a EU country this choice of law rule would have to be respected, but it may not determine the priority the repo may have in relation to other proprietary interests accepted by the *lex concursus* in respect of the same assets, whilst it says nothing about the set-off and close-out netting aspects of modern repo transactions.

The attitude in this book is a different one. It was submitted that the proprietary interests created in internationalised instruments like eurobonds are likely to have a separate regime. This could even extend to the trading of domestic instruments internationally and would also affect repo trading. International clearing, settlement and custody organisations like Euroclear and Clearstream also have their own trans-national regimes, reinforcing this transnationalised proprietary approach. It is true that they are backed by domestic legislation, but this does not appear controlling and domestic case law can, in this view, hardly distract from the prevailing legal regime which has a base in transnational commercial law and practice.[281]

2.3 Factoring or Receivable Financing: The Unidroit Convention and the Uncitral Receivable Financing Convention

2.3.1 Receivable Financing and Factoring: International Attention

What is factoring; what is receivable financing; is there a difference? Factors were traditionally commercial agents who would sell products and collect receivables for their principals (although in their own name and sometimes for their own risk as '*del credere*' agents, which could amount to a collection guarantee for the seller).[282] However, in finance, the term

---

[280] 98/26 EC of 11 June 1998 Directive [1998] OJ L166/45.

[281] It is true that Belgian adverse case law, see n 107 *supra*, prohibiting the *fiducia* as an alternative to secured transactions was remedied for Euroclear by correcting legislation but the applicability of domestic law should be here altogether questioned, see also chapter IV, Part III.

[282] Agents of this sort were common also in the USA. Earlier, common law had denied them much protection, especially a lien on the goods and collections they handled in respect of their commissions. Case law later helped but only the English Factoring Act of 1823, amended in 1842, 1877 and 1889, started to protect them adequately. In commerce, better communication facilities eroded the need for this type of factors. Subsequently, the 'credit factor' or collector and/or guarantor of accounts emerged. This was a type of banker, but was denied the commercial factor's lien in the USA until the NY Factor's Lien Act of 1911 and similar legislation in other states of the USA. This new legislation gave the collecting factor a lien on the receivables and collections amounting together to a floating charge, but separation from commercial activity was not encouraged by the courts which could still deny the lien if no inventory was involved at the same time.

'factoring' acquired a special meaning and developed as a funding tool in the USA in the 1930s on the basis of (collection) guarantees in respect of receivables which could thus be prepaid by factoring companies of this type. This was called 'American Factoring', which therefore included both a guarantee and funding aspect. It was later replaced by the outright buying of receivables by these companies, when insurance companies started to object to the credit insurance aspects of this type of activity. Factors then started to take care of all collection business of their client for a lump sum payment. In the USA, receivable or assignment statutes followed in several states covering both outright sales and security assignments of receivables on the basis of which loans were granted. Under applicable state laws, some required registration as security assignments, others the marking of them in special assignment books of debtors. Sometimes only a written document was required. All these different state statutes were eventually replaced by Article 9 UCC after 1962.

Banks and insurance companies subsequently entered the field in a major way raising the respectability of this business, although some specialised enterprises still remain active in this area. The arrangement is now often one under which the factor gives a revolving credit (to a certain limit) and subsequently collects and reduces the indebtedness. In a typical US arrangement, the factor engages in investigations of the creditworthiness of his client's customers, establishes credit lines for them, does the book-keeping, sends billing statements, and collects. Each receivable is purchased by the factor at the time his client provides its customers with goods or services. Usually there is no recourse and the factor assumes all risk, which is discounted in the price he pays for the receivables.

In the UK, receivable financing or factoring caught on as a separate business only after WW II. In the 1960s and 1970s, it spread to the European Continent, where earlier the practice of invoice discounting had developed. It left a lot of risk with the factors especially in terms of counterclaims and set-off rights of the debtors, an important difference from the discounting of negotiable instruments, which had served as a dangerous and improper example.

In Europe, modern factoring subsequently often tried to minimise these risks, partly through larger portfolios and more turn-over or through forms of recourse, whilst assignment laws became increasingly sympathetic and limited assignment prohibitions but very seldom debtors' defences: see for these developments more generally chapter IV, section 1.7.7. The continental discount business affected the English practice. It developed more quickly when the big commercial banks became involved.

Factoring as a business tends to be cyclical. It is an alternative to secured lending and has its own price structure, under competitive pressures often leading to slimmer margins than in secured financing. That is obviously the attraction to customers or assignors but a lesser incentive for banks. The arrangements may vary greatly in the details. There may be prepayment by the factor amounting to a funding arrangement, normally between 70 and 90 per cent of the total face value of the outstanding receivables. The remainder may then be paid upon collection or partly serve as the factor's reward, which would otherwise be in the region of ½–3 per cent of the portfolio. Where there has been a sale of the receivables and the factor assumes all risk and expense of the collection, there will be an appropriate discount allowing for both a reward and the time factor in the collections. As in the USA, there normally is an ongoing relationship under which the factor acquires his client's debt and funds him on a continuous basis.

If the factor is not taking all risk, an important aspect of the arrangement will be to define the factor's credit exposure, therefore his liability for any shortfall in the collections. In Europe, this has led to forms of so-called *recourse* factoring, that is factoring in which the factor may be able to return non-collected or non-approved receivables to the debtor. It is not unknown in the USA either where this is called a 'charge back' or 'limited recourse' arrangement: see also Section 9-502(2) UCC. If approval of the factor is a precondition, it may be according to the credit line method or order approval method. In the first method, there is a rolling credit limit for each account debtor beyond which claims are not accepted by the factor (alternatively there may be a limit on the total sales of goods to each debtor that will qualify). In the last method each order from prospective buyers needs prior approval, see also chapter IV, section 1.6.5.

Recourse factoring in this manner is then distinguished from the so-called full service, *old line, main line* or *non-recourse* factoring. It leads to a form of conditional assignment under which the debtor retains some exposure and also some interests in the portfolio. This is rare in the USA, where the result would likely be a security assignment subject to a disposition duty and a return of any overvalue in the portfolio. Normally in the USA, there is an outright sale for a price of the whole portfolio with the factor acquiring all the collection risk and cost. This sale is, however, still covered by Article 9 UCC. It is a somewhat curious departure: see also section 1.6.2 above. It subjects the arrangement to filing if involving a substantial part of the receivables portfolio of a debtor seeking financing in this manner in order to bar junior assignees from collecting instead of relying on the more normal common law rule that *bona fide* collecting assignees prevail: see also chapter IV, section 1.7.9. It also subjects the arrangement to the disposition and appropriation rules of Article 9, with a return of any overvalue (not normally however in the case of an outright sale, in which connection the difference between both is maintained: see the special regime of Section 9-607(c) (9-502(2) old).

In modern factoring, the starting point is that a creditor has a large portfolio of receivables. These are contractual claims for payment usually deriving from sales or services. Thus a car manufacturer may sell his cars on credit, say 30, 60, 90 or 120 days or whatever. His administration and collection burden will be considerable and he may require special expertise for this function either in-house or from third parties. The receivables must also be funded as the manufacturer will not normally have the money to advance these credits.

In non-recourse factoring, typically the collection, guarantee and funding elements come together in one of the forms already discussed, under which the manufacturer turns the portfolio over to a collection agent and financier who will relieve him of the administrative and risk burdens and provide him with a form of financing. As in the case of finance leases and repurchase agreements, the type of funding then required is not likely to be in the form of a loan secured by the portfolio of receivables, although it may be. More likely is some form of sale of them, which may still be conditional (in whole or in part) as we just saw.

There is therefore a real alternative to loan financing, which in factoring should only be characterised as secured lending if there is a true loan as evidenced by an agreed interest rate structure (and not a mere reward or fee). Again this may create problems especially in countries like the USA and now even the Netherlands. As we saw, in the USA, the arrangement is automatically equated to a secured loan except where only collection is required (Sections 109(a)(c) (9-102(1)(b) old) and 9-109(d)(4-7) (9-104(f) old) UCC), whilst there may still be a difference in the disposition and return of overvalue (Section 9-502(2)). In the Netherlands, proprietary effect may be withheld altogether (Article 3.84(3) CC) unless the arrangement is set up in the form of a secured transaction (Article 3.239 CC). In all cases, the legal technique used is the one of bulk assignments, although that leaves open the question which type of proprietary right is created thereby: it could be a full, conditional or security transfer.

It follows that, in factoring, there need not always be a funding structure and there could be merely a collection agreement. However, for the arrangement to qualify as factoring proper, therefore as factoring in the more technical sense, there would have to be some transfer of credit risk to the factor. In receivable financing, the accent is more in particular on the funding. It could technically be without collection but both functions are normally combined and receivable financing without a collection agreement is rare. Receivable financing is in this sense the *funding form of factoring* (although it may also take the form of a secured loan or may be equated with it in the USA). The terminology is not stable, however, and more precision is needed in each case properly to describe the role of factoring and receivable financing and their legal characterisation in the contractual and proprietary aspects, as will be attempted below. The terms are in any event often used interchangeably.

There is also the facility of securitisation. It is a bulk assignment of claims to an entity set up for the purpose (the so-called 'SPV' or special purpose vehicle) and is often funded by the issuing of bonds to the public, which bonds are secured upon the cash flow of the new entity. It may lead to a so-called asset-backed security.[283]

Internationally, the subject of factoring and receivable financing has received the attention of Uncitral and earlier of Unidroit. Unidroit produced a Convention on International Factoring at the same time as it produced the Leasing Convention in 1988. It has been signed by fourteen countries and is ratified by six (France, Italy, Nigeria, Germany, Hungary and Latvia). It became effective on 1 May 1995 after six months from the third ratification by Nigeria. Uncitral produced a Receivable Financing Convention in 2001, which by the end of 2003 has only one signtory (Luxembourg). The drafting of these Conventions suggests particular problems with factoring internationally. They derive mainly from the bulk assignment inherent in the transfer of any portfolio of present and future receivables, which may create extra problems when debtors under these receivables are in different countries. What interests us here is mainly the formalities of the assignment so as to be effective *vis-à-vis* foreign creditors (which raises the issues of notification, publication and documentation), the right of the assignee to collect and retain the proceeds, the liquidity of claims, and the liberating payment of the debtor, who may be very differently protected against assignees' claims under his own law.

The Unidroit and Uncitral projects are of particular interest as it was earlier thought that international unification projects in the area of secured and related transactions could not succeed.[284]

2.3.2   Factoring: The Contractual Aspects

As in the case of finance leasing and repurchase agreements, a precise legal definition of (financial) factoring may not be useful or practical, perhaps even less so here, as parties will contractually structure and vary the arrangement considerably and continuously.

---

[283] See for securitisation in more detail, chapter VI s 1.4.7 and SL Schwarcz, 'The Universal Language of Cross-border Finance', 8 *Duke J of Comp & Int'l L* 235 (1998).

[284] See Drobning, n 1 *supra*, 226, stating that 'mere recommendations, even if emanating from an international organisation of the highest repute, will not command sufficient moral or other support for adoption by any sizeable number of States'. Although Uncitral subsequently concluded that unification of the law of security interests in goods was in all likelihood unattainable, after the emergence of the Unidroit Factoring Convention of 1988, it made its own attempt in the area of receivables in 1992.

Indeed, as far as factoring is concerned, there may be very different forms, but there are certain characteristics that recur and lead generally to identifiable types. In this connection, also for factoring (including receivable financing) it is important to distinguish between the contractual and proprietary side.

On the contractual side, there appear broadly three possibilities as we saw: there may only be administration and collection, therefore a *mere collection* agreement. There may also be a credit risk transfer. It means in essence the granting of some form of a *guarantee of payment* by the factor who takes over the risk of non-payment under the receivables, therefore all (in *non-recourse* or old line factoring) or part (in *recourse* factoring) of the credit risk. Instead, there may also be an arrangement under which the assignee must approve the receivables or classes of them before they are covered. Finally, there may also be a *funding* structure, therefore a raising or advancing of capital. It may be and is in fact normally combined with a collection agreement and could be combined also with some guarantee of payment, which may well result from an agreed discount to the nominal value of the portfolio for the credit risk. Funding is at the same time the area of receivable financing.

Indeed, in factoring proper there is normally a cocktail of two, if not of all three, of the contractual possibilities just mentioned, whilst collection seems always part of it. So there is either a guaranteed collection or a funding arrangement under which the financier also collects. Some of this is reflected in Article 1(2) of the Unidroit International Factoring Convention. There is in fact merit in *not* using the term factoring at all when only one of these three possibilities is envisaged, therefore when there is only collection, a guarantee, or mere sale or funding. Uncitral in 2001 Convention on the Assignment of Receivables in International Trade, hardly attempts a definition of receivable financing at all. The reason is that its attention shifted to international bulk assignments, rightly so, it is submitted, as the legal problems are in the assignment and not in the collection, guaranteeing or funding aspects as will be discussed more fully below.

In the first two possibilities of factoring (collection and guaranteeing payments), which can thus be combined, the essence is that the factor pays the creditor/assignor the amounts due from his customers, discounted by a collection fee and, if there is a guarantee, by a further fee for this service. Usually the payments are made by the factor to the assignor on their due date or indeed only upon collection or, in the case of a guarantee, as soon as it becomes clear that collection fails and the factoring agreement will spell out the assumptions and details in this regard.

The funding aspect normally takes the form of immediate payment upon a sale and transfer of the whole portfolio of claims, which will discount the collection cost, the maturity and the risk element in the portfolio. It could also take the form of an advance payment. If the full nominal value of the portfolio is paid (minus collection fee and maturity discount), a guarantee is implied for which there must be some other reward, although sometimes a reimbursement is negotiated if collection fails.

For factoring proper, there must always be a proprietary aspect, therefore a form of transfer of the receivables to the factor, even if there is a mere collection or security agreement. Without this proprietary aspect, again it may be better not to speak of factoring or receivable financing. There are here roughly three possibilities. The transfer can be outright, it can be conditional or fiduciary, or it can be by way of security, although in the last case it would be better not to speak of factoring or receivable financing either. On the proprietary side, there can never be a cocktail, even though there may be much confusion in this aspect, certainly also in the Uncitral draft Convention as we shall see.

2.3.3   Factoring: The Proprietary Aspects

The nature of the transfer is normally an *assignment* (although in France there is also the possibility of subrogation), here more properly a *bulk* assignment, therefore a transfer of a multitude of claims in one assignment. It may also include certain classes of future claims. This is assuming of course that such a bulk transfer facility exists under applicable law and is effective, which is for example not the case if notification to the debtors is a precondition of the validity of assignments, as it is in the Netherlands and was in France. Another problem is the assignability thereunder of future claims. The problems with bulk assignments, at least if covering foreign claims or involving assignments to foreign assignees, is one major reason for a new uniform law. The Uncitral project ultimately perceived this and thus provides a better regime than do many domestic laws for purely local bulk assignments.[285]

In collection agreements, one commonly sees an outright assignment under which a portfolio of present or future receivables is transferred to the factor, often for no other reason than to facilitate his collection activity and status, whilst he will transfer his collections to the assignor whenever received. It exposes the assignor to the creditworthiness of the assignee/factor. It may be different when the collection is guaranteed or when a whole portfolio is transferred for a price in advance, that is funding, obtained at the various discounts already mentioned.

In guaranteed collection or non-recourse financing and in funding arrangements, the transfer of the receivables may be and often is conditional. Thus, although there will normally be one assignment in bulk, often including unspecified future claims or classes of them, especially in non-recourse factoring the transfer of individual claims may still be conditioned. It may be deemed completed only upon *approval* of each of them when they arise, or when *not exceeding* in total a certain amount per debtor. This goes to the assumption of credit risk, therefore to the guarantee, which may thus be conditioned or limited. To put it differently, if these conditions are not fulfilled, the factor retains a right to return the claims. Another condition in this connection may be that the claims are not contested by the debtor.

The key to understanding this mechanism is that the assignment of the relevant claim is avoided when these conditions are not or no longer fulfilled. It leads to the automatic return of the claim to the assignor (unless otherwise agreed), at least in countries that are willing to give this return obligation proprietary effect so that the return becomes automatic. Otherwise there must be a repurchase and retransfer, problematic of course in a bankruptcy of the factor. There is here an obvious problem with this automatic retransfer in the German abstract system of title transfer: see more in particular chapter IV, section 1.7.9, unless one assumes that the condition also affects the real agreement or *dingliche Einigung*, which is indeed often done. However, in Germany, the proprietary effects of factoring seem hardly ever considered and the impression is often created that factoring in a German sense is no more than a *contractual* scheme pursuant to an outright or unconditional transfer, never mind approval requirements or other conditions.[286] It is the *Forderungskauf*.

---

[285] The preparation of rules of (financial) bulk assignments that would operate both at national and international level is from a practical perspective greatly desirable but has always been resisted by the legal experts preparing these conventions for fear that states will not accept such a more general approach outside the realm of international factoring: see eg F Mestre, 'Explanatory Report on the Draft Convention on International Factoring', *Uniform LR*, 45, 53. This was also the worry in Uncitral and no world law of bulk assignments is contemplated.

[286] See for a brief discussion Buelow, *Recht der Kreditsicherheiten* (4th edn, 1997) Rdnr 1452*ff*. See for a discussion in case law, 69 *BGHZ* 257 and 72 *BGHZ* 20. See also 100 *BGHZ* 353 (1987) in which the commercial moral-

That does not conform to international practice. Yet also in the USA and probably in England, an automatic retransfer is little considered. Instead, there may only be a right and duty for the assignor to repurchase the receivable and a right and duty for the factor to retransfer. These transfers would not then be bankruptcy resistant.

When the conditional transfer is used for funding purposes in the sense that a portfolio of present and future receivables is sold and transferred for ready cash, this may be so only up to a certain total of claims or collections. Any excess claims that may accrue under such an assignment are then similarly returned. Again, in this arrangement, the credit risk may be taken over by the factor against a discount but there may still be conditions, which may lead to re-transfers. As just mentioned, for a funding rather than collection arrangement, the form of a secured transaction may also be used. The receivables are then assigned as security.

This is an important difference as more fully explained above in section 1.1.2. It may entail different formalities in terms of notification to the debtor, publication and documentation and there may be a different situation upon default. In a security arrangement, excess collections above the principal and interest must be returned whilst the security interest automatically lapses or is returned. Immature claims may have to be sold off in an execution sale. In a security arrangement, in countries like France (and earlier in the Netherlands), there may, in the case of a security, not be any collection right at all, not even of mature claims. In the USA under Sections 9-607 and 9-608 (9-502 old) UCC, a disposition (often to professional debt collectors) with a return of overvalue is necessary for a security assignment, but in the case of an outright sale as part of a funding transaction, parties are free to determine the conditions and may dispense with a disposition and return of any overvalue.

This approximates to a conditional sale type of funding, regardless of the professed policy of Article 9 UCC converting all conditional sales into security transfers. In pure conditional sales of receivables, upon default of an assignor in repaying the loan or interest, the factor is not only entitled to collect but will also be able to retain excess collections unless there is an agreed maximum. There would be no question of an execution sale. The right to collect was always the advantage of the conditional (or fiduciary) sale of receivables in factoring in France, where, as we saw in section 1.3.5 above, the requirement of notification to the debtor was, however, a great disadvantage. Another point here is that the security assignment creates an accessory right of the beneficiary who can pursue it upon further assignments. That would not be so in the case of a conditional sale of a portfolio of receivables.

When is an assignment a conditional sale and when is it a security transfer in funding situations? We look of course first at the precise terms, but they may not be fully conclusive. Only if there is no true sale but rather a loan as demonstrated by the existence of an agreed interest rate structure, see section 1.1.2 above, may the arrangement, even if structured as a sale, become vulnerable to conversion. It means that for its validity, the interest will be subject to all the formalities of the creation of a security interest.

Neither the Uncitral nor Unidroit Convention has a clear view of the proprietary aspects of bulk assignments and the difference between a conditional sale and secured transaction

---

ity of Section 138 BGB was found not to interfere with the assignment in bulk of future claims in a factoring agreement.

Indeed, recourse financing may in Germany not be characterised as a sale of receivables at all but rather as a way of granting credit. The characterisation of *Sicherungszession* would then logically follow, with the further risk of re-characterisation as an *Absonderungsrecht* in bankruptcy: see also s 1.4.2 *supra*. It seems undesirable and not responding to the nature of recourse financing as commonly understood.

in this connection. The Uncitral Convention, although much more concerned with the proprietary aspects of assignments, only mentions in Article 2 the possibility of a securities transfer besides the outright transfer. It does not go into the conditional transfer and disposition duties at all. The Unidroit Factoring Convention, which is much less concerned with proprietary issues, goes into neither. In view of the confusion on the conditional transfer aspect and the possibility of a conversion into a secured transaction, it would have been better if the Uncitral Convention had at least mentioned the conditional sale as a different way of transferring receivables. It might then also have gone into some bankruptcy aspects.

In the Netherlands, there is the not unrelated problem that all kinds of security substitutes, of which the conditional sale must be considered an important one, are outlawed altogether in their proprietary aspect (Article 3.84(3) CC). In that country under its new Code, bulk assignments are in any event ruled out — except for security purposes — because of the new requirement that all assignments other than security assignments must be notified to the debtor in order to be valid. It is certainly one of several most curious innovations in the new Dutch Civil Code. Both these impediments have led to factoring being conducted entirely as secured transactions in the Netherlands, therefore to a departure from the international norm. An international convention in this area should at least cure *both* these defects.

2.3.4   Bulk Assignments

As we saw, *receivable financing* usually means the funding variety of factoring but all types of factoring have a *bulk assignment* at their centre. Bulk assignments are also conceivable in other types of funding situations. They are therefore not limited to recourse or non-recourse collection agreements and to trade receivables funding proper. When it comes to capital raising, bulk assignments are common in at least two other types of situations. There is project financing against future income, as in the construction of toll roads, and there is securitisation or financing through asset-backed securities where an income stream is transferred to underpin an issue of corporate bonds used by the issuer exactly to fund the acquisition of this cash flow. The term 'factoring' should preferably not be used, nor indeed the term 'receivable financing' for these two types of bulk assignments.

What all these structures have in common is the bulk assignment of present and future claims. To facilitate these nationally and then also internationally is a most important objective, even if not all result in forms of factoring or receivable financing proper. Originally, the Uncitral project was presented as a convention to facilitate the raising of funds on the basis of receivables. Only subsequently did it transpire that the true need was rather for an international facility of bulk assignments of classes of claims, including future claims, with a uniform law particularly in the formalities like notification and documentation and in the proprietary aspects. Hence the struggle to broaden the Uncitral draft into that direction. In its final form it now also means to apply to securitisations, project financing and pure collection agreements.

In the meantime, the economic significance and meaning of these forms of assignments is largely dependent on the assigned claims being unencumbered or subject to liens that do not affect the assignee or factor unless considered to always exist. Notably in Germany, through the *verlängerten Eigentumsvorbehalt* (the extended reservation of title shifting into proceeds), receivables must often be assumed encumbered by hidden liens that survive and take precedence over any bulk assignment of the types just mentioned. They remain therefore effective even *vis-à-vis bona fide* purchasers or assignee/factors. This is a serious impediment to the business of funding through factoring in Germany. It is often given as the reason receivable financing has never acquired great significance and remains less developed in Germany where sub-suppliers must be assumed to be always subject to a reservation of title in whatever they supply whilst their receivables are normally subject to their own supplier's lien. In fact, this is true in most countries. The difference is that in some countries, as in the USA, this will appear more clearly from filing statements but for professional lenders or factors that should not make a difference. They are aware of the situation.

The result is that even if the assignor/sub-supplier gives an undertaking that the assigned claims are free and clear, that would not be of great help if they were not and he went bankrupt in the meantime. Their (presumed) existence makes the receivable portfolio of the factor much less valuable and makes further assignments by him for his own funding much more difficult.[287] The real problem is here not publication or its absence but the shift of the lien into proceeds. It also renders funding assignments less interesting in the USA, even though in that country *bona fide* assignees may be protected against unpublished earlier liens: see also chapter IV, section 1.7.9.

2.3.5   The Liquidity of Claims

As we saw, in all this, the true key focus is the bulk assignment, especially of future claims, also in their proprietary aspects, but maybe the true issue lies even deeper and is in truth the liquidity or easy transferability of monetary claims of whatever nature, and it may be useful in this connection to take a step back and look at the whole scene from that perspective, in American terms therefore from the perspective of Article 2-210 UCC and Article 9-404*ff* (9-318 old) UCC.

In assignments, there are in essence five clusters of problems more fully discussed in chapter IV, section 1.7. They are those concerning:

(a)   the assignability of the claims;
(b)   the validity of the assignment;
(c)   the protection of the debtor in terms of liberating payments, defences and set-off rights, or extra burdens and risks;
(d)   the type of rights that result from the assignment; and
(e)   the position of various assignees of the same claims *inter se*.

Contractual issues should be separated from proprietary issues. They arise in all of these five clusters and it is not always easy to distinguish between them, in fact also not always the five categories themselves, which can overlap, as Dutch case law amply showed.[288] Yet these distinctions have some merit.[289] In bulk assignments they may

---

[287] In Germany there is the further problem whether an earlier factoring agreement may prevail over a later *verlängerten Eigentumsvorbehalt* and a distinction is here often made between recourse and non-recourse factoring: see for the different views, Buelow, n 286 *supra*, Rdnr 1457*ff*.
[288] See n 297 *infra*.
[289] More in particular, the problems of assignments concern (a) the contractual requirements and formalities in terms of notification and documentation with possibly registration or publication for security assignments; (b) the assignability of the claims especially important for unspecific or future claims but also for the impact of contractual assignment restrictions, the extent therefore in which claims may be separated from the legal relationship out of which they arise, and the simultaneous transfer of closely related duties with or without a release of the assignor; (c) the type of interests that can be created and transferred through assignments especially in terms of conditional or security transfers; (d) the effect of the assignment on the underlying contract in terms of

acquire a special importance,[290] particularly the assignability of claims. Indeed, in financing schemes involving receivables, liquidity has become the overriding issue. In this connection, one may also refer to receivable commoditisation. Restrictions of the assignment possibility and overly protective defences against payment requests of assignees are in this approach not favoured. The bankruptcy law impact may here have to be more specifically considered.[291]

The general rule under modern law is that one may freely transfer one's claims (through assignment), but not one's liabilities (through delegation). In its generality, that is now a fairly obvious proposition. A debtor should normally not be interested in the person or entity to whom he must pay, but a creditor is interested in who pays to him. Thus unilateral creditor substitution is possible but not unilateral debtor substitution, that is substitution without consent of the other party in the relationship.

In practice the two are often difficult to separate; rights are often accompanied by obligations. The creditor has indeed a right to payment, but the debtor to a release if he does pay and not to be bothered thereafter. Moreover, he will have the right to pay in a certain place and no duty to do so in others. The creditor on the other hand may have obligations, for example the duty to arbitrate and the duty to release the debtor upon payment

---

amendment or novation, the preservation of any connected securities and the ability of the original parties to continue to amend the underlying agreement at least in the non-assigned aspects; (e) the protection of the debtor against multiple assignments and his facility to make a liberating payment whilst maintaining his defences and set-off rights and avoid extra burdens; (f) the ranking of various assignees in the same property and their entitlement to collect from the debtor or recover from those collecting assignees with lesser rights, the entitlement to the enforcement against the debtor or to initiate alternative enforcement against other assets of the debtor in the case of his default, especially if the assignment was less than a full assignment.

[290] The assignment issues mentioned in the previous footnote all arise in *bulk* assignments but there may be special or additional features. Bulk assignments are unavoidably affected by logistical problems because of the large number of claims that may be included. It may also create legal problems of their own: (a) if under applicable law there is a notification requirement in terms of validity of the assignment, this would require notifications to all debtors for the assignment to be fully effective and impede the bulk transfers greatly; also a documentation requirement may mean that the assignment in respect of each claim needs to be separately documented; (b) the specificity requirement of the claims, also in terms of their adequate description in the assignment document or under the registration or publication requirement in the case of a security assignment, would be a further impediment, as it may make a bulk assignment under which a whole present and future cash flow is intended to be assigned not only difficult to describe, but also ineffective; (c) defences of the debtors and any contractual restrictions on the assignment of individual claims, potentially leading to collection problems, may present other impediments and a substantial degree of abstraction, meaning the facility to cut the receivable out of the relationship out of which it arises whilst making it assignable in isolation and requiring the debtors to accept minor burdens, and a simplified way to allow the debtor to make a liberating payment (without much in terms of verification duties and any checking on multiple assignments or assignments which are not final or full, like security and conditional assignments) may be necessary to ensure prompt payments, essential to make bulk assignment efficient financing tools; (d) to this end there should also be flexibility in the types of the assignments that may be made and in the proprietary status that may be achieved, e.g. in the case of conditional sales or assignments for security purposes.

To elaborate: it is clear that in view of their economic significance and objectives in the financing circuit, it is important that bulk assignments can be achieved in one act or one document of assignment, in such a way therefore that this transfer will be binding on third parties, especially on all debtors under the receivables but also on the creditors of the assignor who will thus lose their ability to recover from the assigned assets as from the date of the bulk assignment. This implies that the assets should leave the assignor's estate as at the date of the assignment (at least in the case of an outright or absolute transfer and not a conditional one or an assignment for security purposes only) and not at the time of individual notifications which would lead to piecemeal treatment. Notification should not be a requirement for the validity of the assignment therefore, but only have a function in the redirection of the payment duty of the debtors. In an effective system of bulk assignments of receivables, a situation must be avoided in which notification of each debtor is necessary for the validity of the bulk assignment (also therefore in respect of future claims). Any doubts on payment rights before or payment duties after notification must also be eliminated.

[291] See also chapter IV, s 1.7.12.

at the intended place and time. There is therefore in an assignment of receivables often the question of the transfer of closely related duties at the same time. Is it automatic, does the assignor remain responsible for their implementation or can the debtor object to the assignment on the basis that he has not consented to their transfer? If he consents, is such a consent tantamount to a novation with loss of the accessory rights?

Neither the Uncitral nor Unidroit Convention goes explicitly into these aspects, although Article 17 of the Uncitral draft requires the debtor's consent if any of his rights or obligations are affected. It seems too strict and implies also a novation danger if this consent is forthcoming. In the USA on the other hand, Section 2-210 UCC envisages under a contract for the sale of goods the possibility of a transfer of duties if the creditor has no substantial interest in having the original promissor perform. The original promisor also remains liable to perform or for breach.

Another important aspect of Section 2-210 UCC is that it allows the monetary obligations under a contract for the sale of goods always to be separated from the underlying agreement and it makes any contractual obligation not to assign them ineffective. This is followed by Sections 9-404*ff* (9-318 old) UCC which allows a security transfer of monetary claims more generally and also favours any contractual limitation of the debtor's defences. This is the concept of the liquidity of claims. Both the Unidroit and Uncitral Conventions have adopted it only to the extent that assignment prohibitions no longer affect the transfer in its proprietary aspects (in respectively Article 6(1) and Article 9), but it would have been better if Sections 2-210 and 9-404*ff* (9-318 old) UCC had been much more fully copied.

Contractually, the assignor remains of course liable for breach of contract *vis-à-vis* the debtor if an assignment prohibition is ignored, but the assignment itself should not be affected, even if the assignee knew or could have known of the restriction and he should not be dependent for the validity of the transfer on his *bona fides* either (which in the case of assignments, at least in civil law, is in any event not a normal protection). Knowledge or connivance may of course still render the assignee subject to a tort action by the debtor.

The liquidity of claims is enormously important. Quite apart from the Conventions, there is as yet no clear parallel in civil law to Section 2-210 UCC, although in many civil law countries bulk assignments are increasingly facilitated. Thus the notification has been deleted in France as a validity requirement under the *Loi Dailly* since 1981 in professional funding arrangements[292] and altogether in Belgium (as far as third parties are concerned), and it is better to forget for the moment the Dutch contrary move in its new Code of 1992, which is inexplicably hostile to the bulk assignment.[293] But nowhere in civil law is the liquidity of monetary claims itself considered a basic principle or a justified requirement of

---

[292] The subrogation approach remains preferred, however, in France: see Lamy, *Droit du Financement, Affacturage* (1996), 1344, 1347 and JP Dumas and R Roblot, 'Cession et Nantissement de Créances Professionelles', *Rep Com Dalloz* 1 (April 1998), but it is not effective in respect of future claims and is in any event individualised per claim and dependent on actual payment of the face amount. It also creates problems with the discounts normally applied for collection, maturity and the taking over of credit risk and the result might not be a sale of receivables in legal terms. See, for older literature on factoring in France, C Gavalda and J Stoufflet, 'Le contrat dit de "factoring"', [1966] *JCP* (ed G), Doctrine nr 2044, Rives-Lange and Contamine-Raynaud, *Droit bancaire* (4th ed. 1986) s. 481, and more recently C Gavalda, 'Perspectives et réalités juridiques de la convention dite d'affacturage' [1989], *Sem Jur* 534; El M Bey, 'Les tiers dans la complexion de l'affacturage' [1994] *RJDA* 207. See for case law Cour de Cass 21 Nov 1972, D jur 213 (1974) and Cour de Cass, 14 Oct 1975, Bull Civ IV, 232 (1975).

[293] See for factoring in the Netherlands especially, CA Knape, 'Factoring', *WPNR* 6141 (1994) and also J Beuving, *Factoring*, Diss, Nijmegen (1996), see also n 69 *supra*. It remains considerably handicapped. In 2003, a proposalo was introduced in Parliament to substitute a registration requirement for the notification requirement (like in the case of security transfers of intangibles), see n 44 *supra*.

commerce and finance, although, in respect of chattels, the law has long been wary of their illiquidity and nowhere favours clauses limiting their transfer. Neither does it automatically include in a transfer any claims in respect of the asset unless expressed as security interests. The Unidroit and Uncitral Conventions do not here make much fundamental progress even if they downgrade transfer restrictions (and also dispense with the notification requirement for the validity of the assignment even if the Unidroit Convention in Article 1(1)(c) is somewhat confusing on the subject).

In a modern system, the assignment should become effective immediately upon the contract of assignment. In German terms, it should effect the *Einigung* or proprietary transfer at the same time (unless explicitly postponed or conditioned by the parties to the assignment). Only then are bulk assignments feasible. That is indeed the system of both Conventions (respectively Articles 1(1)(c), 5(b), 8 and Article 8). Professionalism and commerciality have here an effect and it is perhaps logical that in countries like France any notification requirements were lifted first in professional funding facilities, even though the debtors themselves could still be consumers. That is in fact the system of the Unidroit (Article 1(2)) and Uncitral (Article 4) Conventions, which both aim at covering professional dealings and funding arrangements only.

Also in terms of documentation one does not want to see excessive requirements. German law and English equitable[294] law do not require any. Documentation may in some countries attract stamp duty, which distorts and should be avoided. In France, the documentation requirement remains in force, however. Practically speaking some document is always there, even if as in England often structured as an agreement to assign and not as an assignment itself (in order to avoid stamp duty). The Uncitral Convention (Article 27) after deleting the requirement in earlier drafts finally refered the matter to the law of the place of conclusion of the assignment or, if the assignment is cross-border, to either the law applicable to the assignment or the law of the location of assignor or assignee. This seems unfortunate and seriously damaging. It would make domestic law with all its variations applicable in one of the most important aspects of assignments (as in any other aspect not explicitly settled in the Convention, which includes also the effect of notification, see Article 7(2)).

If only for these four rules: liquidity in principle, inclusion of future claims, abolition of the notification requirement for the validity of the transfer, and limitation or abolition of any document requirement, one should have been grateful for the Conventions. They are the key and international uniformity in these areas is of great importance. Thus the ultimate recourse to domestic laws in the matter of notification was a great blow. More is of course said on the issues of validity, assignability, rights and defences of the debtor and the position of succeeding assignees, especially in the Uncitral text. In both, it must be observed, however, that the defences are not substantially curtailed (*cf* Article 18 Uncitral text)), before notification, they may be curtailed in the contract out of which the receivable arises. The idea that the debtor in a modern society has to accept some transfer burdens does not find any expression here.

---

[294] See for factoring of receivables in England, FR Salinger, *Factoring* (3d edn, 1998) with emphasis on the practical rather than legal aspects of factoring: see for a legal analysis of receivable financing more generally F Oditah, *Aspects of Receivables Financing* (1995). Indeed, under English law, factoring implies a sale of the receivables to the factor, subject to certain defined classes of receivables being returned under certain circumstances: see also R Goode, *Commercial Law* (2nd edn, 802). Whether this return is automatic also in a bankruptcy of the factor remains mostly undiscussed. See for a solid comparative analysis also, B Bjorn, *Factoring, A Comparative Analysis, The Legal and Practical Implications of Factoring as Practised in the United States, England and Denmark* (Diss, Odense, 1995).

On the other hand, in the Uncitral Convention, there is a payment-facilitating provision in Article 17 obliging the debtor to pay the first notifying assignee. Article 8 of the Unidroit Factoring Convention contains an oddity in making the liberating payment of the debtor dependent on his good faith in paying the highest ranking assignee, which ranking he must therefore determine when there are several notifying assignees.[295] This is an undesirable requirement and undue burden on a debtor. If transfer restrictions are no longer upheld, it is all the more necessary that the debtor is here better protected. The proceeds belong, however, to the assignee with the best rights under the law of the assignor (Article 24 Uncitral text) and not therefore as a uniform rule to the *bona fide* assignee who collects (unless the law of the assignor so states). It is a matter to be sorted out amongst the various assignees later.

2.3.6 International Assignments. The Uncitral and Unidroit Conventions. Their Content, Field of Application, Interpretation and Supplementation

In focussing on the efforts of Uncitral and Unidroit in this area,[296] the true issue is international assignments, especially those in bulk. When is an assignment international and what are the concerns? What uniform or other law applies?[297] An assignment imposes a

---

[295] This conforms to the English rule in *Dearle v Hall*, 38 ER 475 (1828).

[296] The Uncitral Convention contains 25 substantive Articles, supplemented by chapters on the Conflict of Laws and on Final Provisions, for a total of 47 Articles, followed by an Annex on Registration. The Unidroit Factoring Convention dates from 1988 and was finalised in the same Ottawa Conference as the Unidroit Leasing Convention. It has 23 Articles. Literature on the Unidroit Factoring Convention is not abundant, but see JC Papeians de Morchoven, 'Unidroit Convention on International Factoring and its Implementation in French Law and Belgian Law', [1996] *International Business Law Journal* 835 and F Ferrari, 'The International Sphere of Application of the 1988 Ottawa Convention on International Factoring' [1997] *The International Lawyer* 41, and earlier F Mestre, 'Explanatory Report on the Draft Convention on International Factoring', [1987] *Uniform LR* 85; RM Goode, 'The Proposed New Factoring and Leasing Conventions', [1987] *JBL* 219, 318, 399 and 'Conclusion of the Leasing and Factoring Conventions', [1988] *JBL* 347; E Rebmann, Das Unidroit-Übereinkommen über das internationale Factoring (Ottawa 1988) *RabelsZ*, 599 (1989) and AF Reisman, ' The Uniform Commercial Code and the Convention on International Factoring', 22 *UCC LJ* 320 (1990). See for a comparative law study, BA Diehl-Leistner, *Internationales Factoring, Eine rechtsvergleichende Darstellung zum Recht der Bundesrepublik Deutschland, Frankreichs under der Vereinigten Staaten unter Einschluß der Unidroit-Konvention über das Internationale Factoring (1988)*, published in 1992.

See, for a discussion (as per 1997) of the Uncitral draft, SV Basinas, 'An International Legal Regime for Receivables Financing: Uncitral's Contribution', 8 *Duke Journal of Comparative and International Law* 313 (1998).

[297] In recent Dutch case law, even in proprietary aspects, sometimes the law of the underlying claim and in other cases the law of the assignment have been upheld applicable following Article 12(1) and (2) of the 1980 Rome Convention on the Law Applicable to Contractual Obligations, rather than on the law of the debtor or that of the assignor: see also chapter IV, s 1.9.2. There are in the Netherlands three Supreme Court cases in this connection, the last two of which have elicited considerable international interest: see HR, 17 Apr 1964 [1965] NJ 23, HR, 11 June 1993 [1993] NJ 776 and HR, 16 May 1997 [1997] RvdW 126. See for a discussion of the first two cases, JH Dalhuisen, 'The Assignment of Claims in Dutch Private International Law' in *Festschrift Kokkini-Iatridou, Comparability and Evaluation* (Asser Institute, 1994), 183 and for the last one THD Struycken, 'The Proprietary Aspects of International Assignment of Debts and the Rome Convention, Article 12' [1998] *LMCLQ* 345 and E-M Kieninger, 'Das Statut der Forderungsabtretung in Verhaltnis zu Dritten' (1998) 62 *RabelsZ* 678.

In 1964, with reference to the never ratified Benelux Uniform Private International Law Statute (Articles 17 and 21), the law governing the underlying claim was deemed applicable to their assignability and to the requirement and formalities of assignment when Indonesian subsidiaries assigned their claims on an Indonesian Bank to their Dutch parents for recovery out of the assets of the bank located in the Netherlands, except that the law of the debtor was considered applicable to his protection (liberating payment) and to the protection of other third parties. In the proprietary aspects proper, as in the position of subsequent assignees, there was some suggestion at the time (in the opinion of the Advocate General) that the law of the assignment applied. In this case, the assignments were deemed properly made under the applicable Indonesian law governing the claims (excluding the expropriation laws which were considered discriminatory) and recovery in the Netherlands was allowed against assets of the Indonesian Bank there, therefore regardless of a nationalisation decree concerning the assignors. (*Note continues overleaf.*)

contractual layer and raises, as we saw, also important transfer or proprietary issues. The proper protection of the debtor is another weighty aspect of assignments.

In 1993, the issue was a German *Globalzession* of future claims by a German supplier to his German Bank. Later sales of the supplier of caravans to a Dutch customer resulted in Dutch terms in claims that under Dutch law could not have been validly assigned as at the time of assignment they were absolutely future and the buyers had as a consequence refused to pay the German assignee bank. The problem was resolved by the Dutch Supreme Court with reference to Article 12 of the Rome Convention (although not yet in force at the time), and ultimately identified as a problem of assignability under Article 12(2), therefore governed by the law of the underlying claim, rather than as an issue of the validity of the assignment (as the lower courts had found), covered by the law of the assignment under Article 12(1), although strictly speaking it did not refer to validity, requirements and formalities of the transfer, where in 1964 the HR had accepted the law of the underlying claim. In the end, the characterisation of the issue in terms of assignability rather than validity determined the issue and alligned the 1993 decision with the one of 1964.

In 1997, the issue was a *verlängerter Eigentumsvorbehalt* (a reservation of title extending into the receivable and its proceeds) under which according to German law the sale of goods to a Dutch manufacturer who onsold them to an end-user resulted in a claim in which the original German supplier had a preferred position. Dutch law does not accept the *verlängerter Eigentumsvorbehalt* and the assignment of absolutely future claims it entails. It now also requires notification for such an assignment to be valid except where a security interest is created according to Dutch law whilst all alternative securities are invalid (Article 3(84)(3)). The Dutch manufacturer went bankrupt and the question was to whom the end-user had to pay. This was resolved in favour of the German supplier with reference to the applicability of the law governing the assignment pursuant to Article 12(1) of the Rome Convention, therefore the law covering the validity rather than the assignability under Article 12(2) which would have been the law of the underlying claim, which, between two Dutch companies, would have been Dutch law.

Who had the collection right was in truth a proprietary issue, according to most authors not covered by the Rome Convention. Not so, or no longer so, in the opinion of the Dutch Supreme Court which applies Article 12 in proprietary matters, probably by way of analogy. Whether these proprietary issues are put under Article 12(1) as a question of validity of the assignment (as the HR did) or under Article 12(2) as a matter of assignability, both solutions seem to allow for party autonomy in the proprietary aspects of an assignment, either as a matter of party choice of law under the assignment agreement (Article 12(1)) or under the contract producing the assigned claim (assuming it was contractual). Dutch case law seems to follow here German law which has always had difficulty in distinguishing between the proprietary and contractual sides of assignments because it does not qualify claims as proper assets. Neither does modern Dutch Law: see s 1.1.3 *supra*.

Yet German law is different in so far as it accepts that the law applicable to the underlying claim applies also to the proprietary aspects of the assignment: see Kegel, *Internationales Privatrecht* (6th ed. 1987), 478. Von Bar, 'Abtretung und Legalzession im neuen deutschen Internationalen Privatrecht' [1989] *RabelsZ* 462 and Reithmann-Martiny, *Internationales Vertragsrecht* (5th ed. 1988), no. 214*ff*.; but *cf* also Kieninger, *supra* There is support for this view also in France: see Loussouarn-Bourel, *Droit International Privé*, (3rd ed., 1988) nrs 424 and 425 and Batiffol-Lagarde, *Droit International Privé*, (7th ed. 1983) nr. 611. In England, see *Dicey Morris on The Conflict of Laws* (13th ed. 2000), Rule 118, (24-054 and 24-061), 981 and 983 also follow this approach. However, the applicability of the law of the assignment in proprietary matters is supported in two German dissertations on the Rome Convention: see Keller, *Zessionsstatut im Lichte des Übereinkommens über das auf vertragliche Schüldverhältnisse anzuwendende Recht* (Munich, 1985) 145 and Kaiser, *Verlängerter Eigentumsvorbehalt und Globalszession im IPR* (1986), 219. On the other hand, the applicability of the law of the underlying claim in the proprietary aspects was defended in a more recent Dutch dissertation: see LFA Steffens, *Overgang van Vorderingen en Schulden in het Nederlandse Internationaal Privaatrecht* (1997) but in the Netherlands, RIVF Bertrams and HLE Verhagen preferred the law of the assignment, 'Goederenrechtelijke Aspecten van de Internationale Cessie en Verpanding van Vorderingen op Naam', *WPNR* 6088, 261 (1993).

See for a more commercially oriented view in England, RM Goode, *Commercial Law* (1995), 1129 and Moshinsky, 'The Assignment of Debts in the Conflict of Laws' (1992) 109 *LQR* 613. In the proprietary aspects, Goode, Moshinsky (except for bulkassignments) and Dalhuisen opt for the law of the debtor, Struycken and Kieninger (and Moshinsky for bulk assignments) for the law of the assignor. In the USA, the UCC in security transfers of claims also opts for the law of the assignor who seeks financing: Section 9–103(3), reinforced in Section 9–301(1) of the 1999 Revision. Note that the 'debtor' is here the person seeking financing and therefore the assignor of the accounts. It is not therefore the 'account debtor'.

The proprietary aspects are often even more hidden in claims than in physical assets. They may surface, however, directly as in questions which subsequent assignee has the better right to collection and proceeds or to whom the debtor must pay, whether as here the seller or rather his buyer. Indirectly proprietary issues may surface in the question of validity of the assignment, as in this case (only by default because the HR thought that Article 12(2) was limitative in its coverage), or even within the context of assignability (can they be transferred and how is it done?, which may directly relate to the validity of assignment also), in terms of their existence (future claims), nature (highly personal claims), transfer (prohibitions of assignments), modalities of transfers (pools and bulk assignments), manner of transfer (notification), type of proprietary right to be created (security or conditional ownership right), protection of the debtor (extra burdens leading to ineffective assignments).

If assignor and assignee are in the same country, the assignment is in its contractual aspects purely domestic even if in respect of foreign claims. They would not in themselves create an international issue and the law of the country of both assignor and assignee applies to the contractual aspects of their assignment, except if they choose another one. Yet if some of the debtors are in other countries, their unavoidable involvement, even though in principle as passive spectators, becomes an issue: when is the assignment valid as regards them, whom do they need to pay and how does payment to an assignee discharge them? Under their own laws they might be very differently protected.

If the assignment is to an assignee in another country, it may on the other hand still be in respect of domestic claims (that is claims between the assignor and debtor located in the same country although even these could be subject to a foreign law). This assignment is in its contractual aspects international and there is a conflict of laws problem. If the parties do not choose otherwise, the law of the assignor will apply as the law of the country where the most characteristic performance takes place except perhaps in pure collections where the assignee may (subsequently) perform the more characteristic obligation (Article 4 of the Rome Convention).

Thus as a general proposition, international contractual problems arise only when the assignor and assignee are in different countries. In the proprietary sense, problems strictly speaking only arise when the asset moves. This is very clear for chattels. In assignments, it poses the question of the location of the claim. Some see it at the place of the creditor/assignor, others at the place of the debtor/payor. The draft European Bankruptcy Convention in Article 2(g) takes the last view. It is submitted that this is the better view: see for a broader discussion chapter IV, section 1.9.2. It means that in a proprietary sense international issues only arise when the debtor moves. That is rare and is not an assignment problem. The situation is here quite different from the international sale of goods requiring delivery elsewhere.

It follows that the law of place of the debtor must normally be considered competent in the proprietary aspects of assignments as the (unchanged) *lex situs*. It will determine who is truly the owner of the claim and therefore to whom the debtor must pay (and his protections in this regard) and who is entitled to enforce the claim against him. The enforcement and ownership law therefore tend to become the same (unless enforcement is sought against the debtor's assets in yet another country). That is logical. In fact, the applicability of the law of the place of the debtor may be justified also, as it is the law of the most likely place of enforcement.

If, on the other hand, one puts the location of the debt at the place of the creditor or assignor, an assignment becomes international in a proprietary sense when the creditor moves, that is when there is an assignment to an assignee in a foreign country. As in the case of chattels that move to another country as a consequence of a sale, one should then ask whether the proprietary law of the country of origin or of destination applies. In the creation of the interest, it would be the law of the assignor but in the recognition of its effect it would be the law of the place of the assignee.

The Conventions seek to overcome most of these problems by imposing a unitary regime for conflict of laws. The Uncitral Convention considers conflict rules in all areas governed by it but not specifically settled in it. Common conflict of laws rules are a sequel of this reference to private international law in areas where the Convention needs supplementation (Article 7), although Contracting States may opt out of these conflict rules.

Unsettling in this connection is the formula on interpretation and supplementation of either Convention, which both use the language of Article 7 of the 1980 Vienna Convention on the International Sale of Goods. In that Convention, the formula applies to *contractual* situations where a distinction was made between interpretation and supplementation. In this contract approach, for interpretation, regard must be had to the international character of the Convention, the need to promote uniformity in its interpretation and the observance of good faith in international trade. For supplementation, regard must be had to the general principles on which the Convention is based and otherwise to the rules of private international law.

In assignments, the issues are rather proprietary than contractual. It was already submitted in connection with similar language in the Unidroit Leasing Convention that the reference to good faith is in its generality entirely inappropriate in proprietary matters and that the reference to private international law is in any event likely to destroy whatever unity the Conventions bring. As in the earlier Hague Sales Conventions, and also in the Unidroit Contract Principles, this reference should be omitted. It creates a search for the applicable national laws in any situation of doubt on the coverage, applicability and meaning of the Convention, whilst the merits of the conflict rules in these areas even if unified as in the Uncitral Convention, may be doubted. Uncertainty and lack of uniformity would result in any instance where conceivably a void in the coverage of the Convention could be construed. That can be done virtually at random. It will destroy the Convention.

Especially in the Uncitral project, there is enough in the Convention itself to accept here a legal regime that can be explained and supplemented through analysis of the Convention itself supplemented by international practices.[298] Interpretation and supplementation need no longer be separated either and the reference should, it is submitted, in both cases be to the international character of the Convention, its general principles, the need for its uniform application and international practice and custom. Both Conventions should in any event be placed in the hierarchy of the *lex mercatoria* as a whole in which conflict of laws rules have only residual significance: see chapter I, section 1.4.4. In the Uncitral Convention a reference is made to practices and custom only in Article 11 determining the rights and obligations of the parties to the assignment where the language of Article 9 of the Vienna Convention is also followed, which looks at custom essentially in terms of implied conditions of the contract. This is also much too limited a view, especially in the proprietary aspect: see further chapter II, section 2.3.6.

In its conflicts provisions, the Uncitral Convention proposes applicability of the law of the assignor for the relations between various assignees (Article 30, rather than protecting the *bona fide* purchaser who collects in good faith as a uniform rule).[299] Assignability (not as such mentioned or defined) seems to be covered by the law applicable to the assigned

---

[298] This is much less true for the Unidroit Factoring Convention, but see for a discussion of the general principles in that Convention also F Ferrari, 'General Principles and International Uniform Law Conventions - A Study of the 1980 Vienna Sales Convention and the 1988 Unidroit Conventions in International Factoring and Leasing', 10 *Pace Intern'l Law Review* 157 (1998). The liquidity of claims regardless of an assignment prohibition in Article 6, the assignability of future claims in Article 5, the abolition of the notification requirement for the validity of the assignment in Articles 1(2)(c) and 8, and the maintenance of the debtor's defences in Article 9, were correctly identified in this connection but do not in themselves provide a coherent assignment regime.

[299] The question of priority amongst succeeding assignees in the same receivables proved one of the most difficult issues. Initially four alternatives were suggested: first in time first in right, first notification to the debtor, first registration in a register to be created, or a private international law rule. Eventually the fourth alternative was adopted and the law of the place of the assignor was chosen. It was a way of avoiding the issue and presents a serious shortcoming in the Convention. As an alternative an optional filing system was introduced at the same time allowing for priority on the basis of the date of filing or registration, a system especially favoured by the US delegates even if of limited impact in the USA under Article 9 UCC in view of its automatic perfection rule for accounts (unless a substantial part of an assignor's receivable portfolio). The solution lies in a better protection of the *bona fide* later assignee who acquires sufficient power in the collection of the receivables and effectively collects.

claim as is the relationship between the assignee and the debtor and also the proper protection of the debtor (Article 29). This is an important impediment to bulk assignments. The particular aspect is here of course the protection of the debtor and the question to whom he should pay and what his defences are. It again seems best covered by his own law, but the Convention takes another view and opts for the law covering the underlying claim. It stays close to Article 12 of the EU Rome Convention on the Law Applicable to Contractual Obligations: see more in particular chapter IV, section 1.9.3.

Whatever the merits of this approach, it is unclear to what extent the proprietary and enforcement issues are covered and to what extent therefore the law of the assignment or the underlying contract applies in these aspect. Assignability itself, made subject to the law of the underlying claim, could have important proprietary aspects in what claims can be transferred and how and what interests may be so created and transferred. Proprietary aspects, like the shift of a reservation of title into proceeds, may also end up under the heading of validity of the assignment, as Dutch case law showed, subject therefore to the law of the assignment.[300]

Although these problems would arise only where the uniform rules of the Convention or its general principles do not suffice, which is itself a matter of interpretation, a further limitation is here its applicability. If one takes the perspective of the bulk assignment, one assumes that the fact that (prospective) debtors are in different countries should kindle the application of the Convention. It still poses some definitional problems as to their location, which gave rise to much discussion, but in the end Uncitral settled for the notion of the place with the closest relationship with the debtor without further definitions or assumptions. More important is perhaps that the Uncitral Convention applies only to international assignments, which are assignments between assignors and assignees in different countries or to the (domestic and other) assignment of international claims (that have a creditor and debtor in different countries): see Article 1. Thus the Convention is not applicable to all bulk assignments.

This is an important limitation. On the other hand, the Uncitral Convention rightly only requires for its application that the assignor is located in a Contracting State (Article 1(a)). Naturally, the Convention would be more effective if as many debtors as possible are also located in a Contraction State and even the assignee but it is not strictly necessary for a Convention of this nature to apply. The Unidroit Convention has in Article 2 a different regime. It requires creditor (assignor) and debtor under the underlying sale agreement out of which the receivable arises to be in different states. *Either* those states and the state of the factor (assignee) must all be Contracting States *or* both the contract of the underlying sale of goods and the factoring contract must be governed by the law of a Contracting State. It greatly narrows the applicability of the Unidroit Factoring Convention.

Under both Conventions, courts in Contracting States would apply the Convention directly if these rules of applicability are met. There is therefore no need first to determine what law is applicable in order then to apply the Convention only if it was adopted by the relevant state, the law of which would be applicable. Although in Uncitral at one stage there was some discussion of this latter approach, it was abandoned. Even a clause similar to Article 1(1)(b) of the Vienna Convention on the International Sale of Goods, which requires the Convention to be applied also if the rules of private international law point to the law of a Contracting State, was not retained. However, the (alternative) reference in the Unidroit Convention (Article 2) to both the sales and factoring contract being governed by the law of a Contracting State has some similar effect.

---

[300] See n 297 *supra*.

2.3.7 Details of the Unidroit Factoring Convention

The Unidroit Convention on International Factoring dates from 1988 and is now effective, having received the minimum number of three ratifications (France, Italy and Nigeria, later joined by Germany). It gives a definition of factoring and describes it as a contract between a supplier and a factor under which the supplier assigns his commercial receivables[301] and performs at least two of the following four functions (Article 1): (a) provide finance for the supplier, (b) maintain the accounts relating to the receivables, (c) collect the receivables, and (d) protect against default in payment by the debtors. It is to be noted in this respect that no clear distinction is made between contractual and proprietary issues nor between an outright sale of the receivables (when the factor takes over all risk at a price), a security transfer (when the factor provides a secured loan), a conditional transfer (when the factor takes over only certain risks in the portfolio), or a mere collection agreement (when the factor does not take over any risks in the portfolio).

As a consequence, the types of risk transferred and the reward structure appear not directly considered by the Convention. This is nevertheless the essence of modern factoring, which, as we saw, is a structure under which financing is provided through a conditional sale of receivables. The conditions concern the risk distribution and reward structure, in the sense that, for example, certain receivables are automatically returned to the supplier if they prove difficult to collect, are not approved, or if an agreed total amount has been recovered by the factor. They are covered, however, assuming there is collection and administration by the factor. Under the definition, pure collection agreements, which normally have an administration function only, seem to be covered as well. So it seems are any outright sales which will always include administration and collection. This is only understandable against the background of the American approach in Article 9 UCC. More logically, secured transactions providing financing are covered if combined with administration and/or collection. So are non-recourse or recourse sales of the portfolio if combined with administration and collection. It is hard to see what is excluded.

For the Unidroit Convention to apply, it is further necessary that the receivables assigned under the factoring agreement arise from sales or service agreements between the supplier and a debtor whose places of business are in different States provided either (a) those States as well as the State in which the factor has its place of business are all Contracting States or (b) both the contract of the sale of goods out of which the receivable arose and the factoring contract are governed by the law of a Contracting State (Article 2). For this purpose the relevant place of business is in each instance the place of business most closely related to the relevant contract and its performance. However, parties may always exclude the application of the Convention either in the factoring agreement or in the underlying sales agreements out of which the receivables arise (Article 3), but only in whole and not in part. This is logical for a Convention that also covers proprietary rights which cannot be amended by the parties.

The Unidroit Factoring Convention provides only a small number of uniform rules. The most important are that the receivables need not be individually specified in the factoring agreement but they must be identifiable at the time of the conclusion of this agreement. Future receivables may thus be included whilst neither need the contract out of which they arise to exist nor need the debtor be known, but they are transferred only

---

[301] Therefore, one assumes, only contractual monetary claims for payment arising out of sales of goods or the supply of services, although this definitional issue may have to be determined on the basis of domestic law pursuant to the applicable conflict rule.

at the moment at which they come into existence (Article 5(b)), although it is stated that there is no need for any new act of transfer. It is therefore automatic. Nevertheless it may still depend on the applicable *lex concursus* what the effect is of an intervening bankruptcy of the assignor. Notably Article 35 of the Dutch Bankruptcy Act requires that claims must have become part of the patrimony of the assignor for the assignment to be effective and that the prior assignment of future claims can not be effective in respect of claims that enter the assignor's estate only after his bankruptcy. This is not a common rule, however.

Notification is not a constitutive requirement of the assignment (even if Article 1(1)(c) is not the clearest in this connection) and becomes relevant only in connection with the payment duty of the debtors (Article 8). It avoids problems of individual notification and specification of the assignment in that connection for purposes of the validity of the agreement. As the Convention does not go into the different types of factoring and especially not into the assignment as a security interest it does not deal with any extra formalities in that connection either, like registration or publication of the interest in respect of any or all receivables.

Assignment restrictions in the underlying agreement are ineffective, although the supplier remains liable to the debtor if he assigns in breach of such a restriction (Article 6). Other defenses of the debtor remain, however, valid against the factor as well as any set-off right (Article 9). Any payments of the debtor to the factor are not recoverable, however, in the case of default of the supplier under the underlying sales agreement as long as the debtor can recover them under applicable law from the supplier, unless the factor has a payment obligation to the debtor in respect of the receivable (and only to that extent) or knew of the supplier's non-performance when he received the payment (Article 10).

Extra burdens for the debtor are not considered in the context of payment excuses. The Convention also does not consider to what extent receivables may be split out, whether closely related duties (or rights) are transfered at the same time, and whether the supplier is then discharged from such obligations. Also the question whether the assigment may amount to an amendment or novation is not considered, except that in Article 7 it is said that the accompanying security interests only transfer with the claims. It would have been more logical to assume an automatic transfer as accessory right unless the assignment agreement had provided otherwise.

Formation, validity or assignability issues are not further considered. Also the Convention does not devote special attention to the debtor's protection, proprietary and enforcement aspects, except that as to the payment duty of debtors, Article 8 imposes a duty for them to pay the factor if, and only if, they have no knowledge of any other's superior right to payment and proper notice in writing is given. What a superior right in this respect is remains notably undefined. As was already pointed out before, this puts a heavy burden on the debtors who would not appear to obtain a liberating payment otherwise.

The likely result is that in case of doubt they will pay neither supplier nor factor. It would have been much better if the notification rules of Article 8 had not left any doubt about the payment duty. Especially notification given by both supplier and factor or by the factor with the clear authority of the supplier should have released the debtor upon payment no matter what other knowledge he might have had. Any dispute should subsequently be a matter between assignees and supplier. The Convention does not go any further into the possibility of double assignments and does not address the various rights assignees may have concurrently under different types of assignments either. The effect of the avoidance or termination of the assignment agreement or the failure of warranties of ownership on any payments made by the debtor to the factor remains also undetermined.

The Convention does not contain any special conflict rules in the areas where no uniform rule is given and therefore also does not address characterisation or the proper *situs* of the claim for proprietary or enforcement issues. It contains in Article 4 the by now usual interpretation and supplementation language in matters covered by the Convention derived from the Vienna Convention on the International Sale of Goods giving preference to the general principles of the Convention before (the normal) conflicts rules are applied. It was criticised in the previous section and is an undesirable addition, although more understandable in the context of the Unidroit Factoring Convention with its more limited uniform regime (which is moreover largely confined to contractual assignment aspects) than in the Uncitral Convention.

2.3.8   Details of the Uncitral Convention

Uncitral has been developing its Convention (rather than a model law) on Receivable Financing since 1992. The final text was completed in the year 2001. It presents a more comprehensive effort than the Unidroit Factoring Convention, in that it covers not only bulk but also individual assignments and deals with many more assignment aspects and provides a much more comprehensive uniform regime. Although the Convention is not limited to bulk assignments, it has particular relevance in the context of the commoditisation of receivables. Success of the Convention could substantially benefit the financial services industry and its practices but could also facilitate international collection.

As for the scope of the Convention, at an early stage it was decided not to define the purposes of the assignment nor to focus mainly on bulk assignments. Unlike in the Unidroit Factoring Convention, there is no attempt to describe the substantive scope or material objective of assignments covered by the Convention. It is clear therefore that this is not exclusively a factoring convention as other types of assignments (but only of contractual monetary claims or 'receivables': see Article 2(a)) are also covered by it. In later texts it became unclear whether the Convention also applies to conditional sales of receivables and mere collection agreements; only the outright sale and a security transfer seem to be considered (Article 2(a)). The true subject became in the meantime international bulk assignments. Whilst no longer limiting the assignments covered to receivable financing, factoring or similar financing techniques, it would have been better, however, also to refer to assignments by way of sale, security or any other type of transfer as earlier texts did. Individual assignments remain covered except for personal family or household purposes. The true focus is, however, bulk assignments of professional receivables for whatever purpose but there remains here still some ambivalence and tension.

Nevertheless, the definitions (in Articles 2, 3 and 5) bear out the bias towards bulk transfers of professional receivables and receivable commoditisation. Article 2(a) separates contractual claims for payment of monetary sums (which are all considered receivables for the purposes of the Convention and could include liquidated claims for damages) from the rest of the contract, whilst any restrictions on the transfer in respect of them are not effective *vis-à-vis* the assignee: see Article 9. As regards the defences and set-off, the debtor may maintain them against the assignee but agreements not to raise them are generally valid (Articles 18 and 19). The coverage of monetary tort claims has been deleted.

It is to be noted that the separation language suggests that closely related obligations do not transfer with the receivable, like accounting or arbitration obligations, or royalty or similar payments related to it. This could, under Article 7(2), remain a matter of applicable domestic law (and also the question whether the assignor was discharged under the circumstances), if not preceded by the application of the general principles on which the Convention is based, whatever these may be in this connection. The questions of delegation of other duties, transfer of the whole agreements and the characterisation as novation or amendment are not or no longer broached in the ultimate text either and could therefore also become a matter of applicable domestic laws, probably the one of the assignment under Article 28. A most undesirable situation.

The commoditisation of receivables does not attain here the level of Sections 2-210 and 9-406(d) (9-318 old) UCC but presents nevertheless an important step forward as compared to the law in many civil law countries. The Convention is also liberal in the identification requirements and therefore favourable to including future receivables as a matter of uniform law (Article 8). The final text deleted the requirement of a document for the assignment, which requirement has now also become subject to domestic law. It is not less unfortunate, all the more as under Article 27 it would not appear immediately clear which local law that could be.

According to the present text of Article 1, the Convention applies to all assignments involving international receivables (with a creditor and debtor in different countries) or to international assignments (with an assignor and assignee in different countries) of all receivables and therefore excludes only domestic assignments of domestic receivables. To connect this kind of international assignment with the Contracting States, Article 1 requires that at least the assignor is located in a Contracting State. For a debtor to become affected he should be located in a Contracting State or the law governing the receivable should be the law of a Contracting State (Article 1(3)).

It follows that for the Convention to have any effect, at least the assignor and one (prospective) debtor must be in different Contracting States or the assignment must be to an assignee in another country which need not be a Contracting State. This does not prevent the assignee in a non-contracting State from invoking the assignment against the assignor and the debtor(s) under the Convention if accepted in their laws. It is of course a bonus if the assignee is also in a Contracting State but it does not appear to be strictly necessary. A requirement to that effect would have been difficult to handle if there were a consortium of assignees in different countries, some of which might not be Contracting States. In fact the assignee will often be a Special Purpose Vehicle as part of an asset securitisation scheme in a tax haven country, not so likely ever to become a Contracting State.

The determination of the status of the rules of the Convention was a delicate matter. The prevailing view was that assignments were basically structures of party autonomy allowing the parties to choose the law applicable to their mutual rights and obligations as well as to derogate from or vary the effect of individual provisions of the Convention but this cannot affect the rights of persons not parties to such an agreement (Article 6). This is a clear indication that *proprietary* issues cannot be so settled. However, there is no clear view of what they are even if upon a proper construction the Convention largely seems to concentrate on them.

On the other hand, the interpretation and supplementation provisions of Article 7, directly derived from the Vienna Convention on the International Sale of Goods and there applicable to only (some of) the contractual aspects of international sales, seems to emphasise coverage of contractual issues only. Its reference to good faith in the interpretation of the Convention is also hardly understandable for proprietary issues. So is the language of Article 11(2) and (3) concerning usage, also derived from the Vienna Convention. There is no appreciation of the role of custom and practices even in the proprietary aspects.

As already pointed out before, this is all undesirable and substantially undermines any positive effect the Convention could have.

But a major other shortcoming of the Convention must be its failure to establish a uniform regime for priorities. Instead, it refers to the matter of the law of the assignor (Article 30), or leaves it to the contracting states to opt for one of the systems set out in the Annex to the Convention (Article 42). Inspired by the UCC filing system, the Annex itself prefers a system based on registration of an assignment (Articles 1*ff* of the Annex). But States may also opt for a *prior tempore* rule based on the time of the contract of assignment (Articles 6*ff* of the Annex), which conforms to the German situation. Finally, they may also opt for priority rule based on the time of the notification of the assignment (Articles 9*ff* of the Annex), which is wholly unconducive to bulk assignments and reflects French law.

2.3.9   Concluding Remarks

To conclude, the Uncitral Convention makes important progress in the areas of the liquidity of claims (although it could have gone further in curtailing the defences and it remains vague in the transfer of connected obligations and the resulting danger of a re-characterisation as novation) and in the inclusion of future claims. It fails to harmonise the notification requirement for the validity of assignments and the documentation requirement. From these perspectives, it provides less than a sound basis for bulk assignments which should have been its proper perspective. But it also fails to harmonise the priority rules allowing states to operate either registration systems or systems that may even require the notification of the debtor. It has therefore found very little acceptance with only one signtory so far.

It is also weak in properly identifying the proprietary aspects that may be established in receivables, particularly in the lack of recognition of conditional ownership transfers inherent in many forms of factoring. It should also have been much more careful with any reference to good faith in the interpretation of proprietary aspects of the Convention, except perhaps if wishing to indicate some greater judicial discretion in explaining the Convention. In this connection there should also have been a reference to international custom and practices.

The reference to private international law in connection with the supplementation of the Convention is an unfortunate mistake. It will prove impossible to draw the line when it comes to interpretation, and this will result in constant reference to domestic laws, whenever the Convention seems incomplete or unclear. This is likely seriously to undermine the impact of its uniform regime and drastically reduce its usefulness. This reference was unnecessary in view of the comprehensive coverage of bulk assignments in the Convention. It led to a set of conflict rules which can only be contentious. Indeed, in view of the experience with Article 12 of the Rome Convention — which they largely track and which proved inadequate in proprietary and enforcement matters — they are much better deleted. Contracting States may opt out of them. The logical sequel would have been also to allow them to opt out of the reference to private international law in the supplementation provision of Article 7.

6

Financial Services, Financial Risk, and Financial Regulation. Internationalisation, Liberalisation, and Re-regulation of Cross-border Financial Services in the EU and WTO/GATS

Part I   Introduction: Financial Services Activities,
Service Providers and Financial Regulation

1.1   Domestic and Cross-border Financial Services. Regulatory Impact

1.1.1   *Financial Services and Financial Regulation*

The financial services sector comprises (a) *banking*, (b) *securities* or investment services and (c) *insurance*. In most countries, *banking* and *insurance* have long been regulated and supervised in view of their impact (a) on customers and, in the case of banks in particular, (b) on the national economies or the public at large.

The aim of this regulation is to avoid, contain, or minimise some of the considerable risks inherent in these businesses, originally especially the *insolvency* risk in order better to protect clients or customers against the adverse consequences of a failure of their banks or insurance companies. This insolvency risk is in fact a composite risk and may derive from other more specific risks like in commercial banking the *credit risk* which concerns the degree of risk in the loans a bank has given or the *market risk* which concerns the risk in investments a bank has made. The clients or customers so protected are, in banking, the depositors. There are *other* risks, especially for investors. They may eg be found in the type of *financial products* on offer and in the way they are *sold* to unsuspecting customers. Particularly in the case of (commercial) banks, there may also be a more modern, broader concern with the protection of the public at large against bank failures as they could have a ripple effect and endanger the whole banking and payment system, thus undermining the entire economy. This is often referred to as *systemic risk*. It is a consequence of banks being normally closely connected through reciprocal lending or in the operation of the payment system and concerns the stability of the financial system.

The regulatory concern with insolvency is then directed not so much to the protection of individual customers or clients, but rather of the public interest more generally. It explains much of the modern regulatory concern with (a) capital standards, (b) proper management and (c) adequate systems. There may also be an important confidence building element in this type of modern regulatory concern: the public is more likely to deposit money in a system which it considers supervised as such and is likely to see this regulation and supervision as some kind of guarantee of the soundness of the system as a whole.

In the 1930s, in the USA, regulation also became important for thes *securities industry* (the issuing of investment securities, securities underwriting, brokerage and advice — activities now often concentrated in so-called investment banks) with emphasis more in particular on (a) investors' protection, (b) transparency in public offerings and trading, and (c) ultimately fair dealing. It concerns here the operations and investment risks in the *capital markets* in which connection reference is also made to *investment services*, a term now more commonly used in Europe where intermediaries like underwriters and brokers are often called *investment firms*.

More recently, this American regulatory example has been widely followed, and the securities industry has as a consequence also become substantially regulated in most countries, although still with very different levels of sophistication per country and per investment function (very differently e.g. for underwriters and brokers). As we shall see, there is here less of a consensus about the risks that need regulatory attention.

Another overriding concern in this area is (d) *market integrity*, which goes back to the issue of the protection of the public at large and of confidence, in this case more in particularly in issuing and trading of investment securities. This concern has acquired added poignancy in connection with the increasing need to create a sound climate for investments to cover the financial needs of an ever ageing population. It means that investments must be carried and be made safe or safer for very long periods. In this vein, regulation is now also becoming important for the pension industry, which is closely related to the life insurance industry.

The discussion in this chapter will especially consider what (a) the industry itself can do about these various types of risks, (b) what the regulators are likely to focus on, and (c) what may reasonably be expected from financial regulation not only in terms of the protection of the public at large but also of depositors and investors more particularly. To anticipate what is to come: it may prove wholly unrealistic to expect a great deal from regulation and the public's expectations in this connection may prove wholly unjustified. To put it another way: the cost of regulation is high and must ultimately be borne by the depositing or investing public whilst bank insolvencies continue unabated and regular financial scandals show that the preventive effect of regulation is often only marginal. Nevertheless, the concern about financial risks and their management is real enough.

In this connection, it is useful from the outset to distinguish clearly between the money recycling function of (a) the (commercial) banks and (b) the capital markets. They give rise to different operations and concerns. Commercial banks take deposits from the public, become owners of these deposits, and issue loans in their own name, say for house-mortgages and business activities or as overdrafts. These deposits function as a major funding vehicle for banks (who may additionally fund themselves by borrowing from other banks in the so-called inter-bank market or may also access the capital markets and issue bonds in that market).

This is one way of recycling money. In the capital market, on the other hand, persons or entities with excess savings meet those who need capital more directly. That could be banks, governments or their agencies, and commercial companies. Instead of depositing their excess funds with commercial banks, investors will then buy shares or bonds issued in that market by these entities. It assumes (a) an *issuer* in (b) the new issues or *primary market*. It further assumes a subsequent trading facility in these instruments in the so-called (c) *secondary* market which provides liquidity, that is the facility to sell these capital market instruments and reduce them to money when needed. Both the primary and secondary markets, are therefore segments of the capital market in operation and may be concentrated in (i) regular stock exchanges or in (ii) Over-the-Counter or OTC or informal markets, as we shall see.

The activities of issuers and investors in the primary and secondary markets (within the capital market) assume *intermediaries* as advisors of issuers, as brokers or investment advisors for investors, or as service providers in exchanges, clearing, settlement and custody.

These are activities in which *investment banks* (rather than commercial banks) or securities houses/investment firms are likely to become involved. In these activities these intermediaries operate for others (their clients) on a service basis for which they receive a fee. Shares or bonds that they hold for clients do *not* become their property as do deposits in commercial banks. It means that they do not share in the risk of the recycling of money (as commercial banks do) e.g. whilst buying or selling shares for their clients. It explains the basic difference in the position of banks and investment firms. The latter may, however, also take positions, especially as *underwriters* in the primary market or *market-makers* in the secondary markets as we shall see. In these cases, they take an own market risk that will be further explained below in section 1.3, but they will *never* be able or be allowed to deal with clients' assets as banks do in the case of deposits, not even when acting as custodians of the investment securities of their clients.

As for regulation, for (commercial) banks it was traditionally at least partly concerned with what they did with the depositor's money after it had become their own. In the securities industry, the concern is here rather about proper segregation of clients' assets. Beyond this, the regulatory concern in the securities industry will be much more about the advice that is being given, but it depends on the different functions. Thus in respect of brokers and investment managers, there is the risk of improper advice. In respect of clearing and settlement systems, there is the risk that trades are not executed. For underwriters and market makers, there is insolvency risk. These risks will all be further discussed below. For the moment, it is only important to distinguish between the functions of commercial and investment banks, their different roles in the recycling of money, and the variations in the regulatory concern depending on the structure, function and risks of these various activities.

Financial regulation of this nature is in modern times likely to imply some *supervisory* function or authority. It is basically of a *domestic* mandatory nature and not internationalised and is therefore diverse, not only because of the different financial functions but also because of differences per country. These latter differences result from differences in the level of regulatory sophistication but also from different views in the evaluations of the various risks. In connection with the details of financial regulation, there is, however, *a general pattern* and it is useful to (a) focus *first* on the *type* of service rendered, like commercial banking, securities or insurance business, which, as just mentioned, may be broken down further into specialised functions like deposit and payment services for commercial banks and underwriting, trading or brokerage, clearing and settlement or investment advice in investment banking. *Subsequently* it is useful to (b) distinguish between the *service provider* and the *service* itself. In respect of both, the regulatory issues can be broken down further.

In the case of the *service provider* (per industry or function), the emphasis commonly is (depending on the type of provider) on (a) *authorisation* and (b) *prudential supervision*. Thus commercial banks as institutions and investment banks per function are likely to need some form of *authorization* or some governmental license. The authorisation itself will depend on (i) *reputation*, (ii) *capital*, (iii) *adequate infrastructure and systems* and (iv) the *business plan* or *profile* of the financial service provider. It will be followed by *prudential supervision* which is based on the ongoing requirement that the basic authorisation requirements remain fulfilled, for commercial banks especially in the aspect of adequate capital and management to prevent insolvency. There are here clear rules to be enforced rather than daily involvement of regulators which would risk making them liable for the consequences. In commercial banking and securities business, concern about the impact of insolvency of financial service providers on their customers may be further alleviated by the organisation of (a) *deposit guarantee schemes* for bank depositors and of (b) *investor protection schemes* for investors in securities. This does not, however, in itself reduce the insolvency risk or eliminate the systemic risk connected in particular with major commercial banking crises, but it allows the regulator to take broader policy considerations into account when deciding on the suitability of action (e.g. to close a bank) in the knowledge that at least the smaller depositors or investors are protected. Broader systemic considerations may thus prevail over the immediate protection of clients.

Commercial banking regulation is largely confined to the supervision of the service provider, therefore to the two regulatory aspects of authorisation and prudential supervision (whilst the activities of deposit taking, providing loans and organising payments are usually covered by the same regulator). In the securities and insurance industries, on the other hand, there is considerable emphasis on the regulation and supervision of the services or activities of these intermediaries themselves. As already noted, in the securities business in particular, these services or functions may vary greatly in terms of underwriting, market making, brokerage, investment advice, information supply, clearing and settlement, and custodial functions and may be differently regulated by different regulators. Concern about service providers may become increasingly relevant also for the more sophisticated banking services, for example in the areas of derivatives and mortgage credit.

As regards these *services*, from a regulatory perspective, a distinction may usefully be made between (a) the *conduct of business* and (b) the type of *products* offered (per function). This focuses on what is sold and how, and the safeguards in these respects for investors or, in the case of banks, borrowers. As just mentioned, these regulatory aspects are so far especially important in investment or securities services, more in particular in respect of the *smaller or retail investor* and the way he is serviced or protected by his service provider who may have some innate duties of care.

In the area of *issuing* new securities (or primary market), there are also likely to be special regulatory requirements. It is best seen as a separate area of financial regulation that concerns more in particular the *issuer or fundraiser*, like its registration with the Securities and Exchange Commission (SEC) in the USA (if the issue is targeted at US investors), which commonly leads to a prospectus requirement. The difference is explained by the distinction between and different roles of issuers and financial intermediaries. The need for issuers to produce at least a prospectus is now also increasingly a common requirement in Europe. It concerns here foremost corporate transparency and identification of corporate risks. This transparency may be all the more required if the issue is at the same time listed and traded on an official stock exchange, therefore targeted to the public at large.

Besides these regulatory requirements in respect of issuers, there may also be company law issues for an issuer if it is a corporate entity (and not a government or governmental agency), for example, the necessary corporate approvals or the nature of the securities that can be offered. In company law, one sees here an important shift in interest from typical organisational or company law matters to capital markets and regulatory concerns, most importantly also in connection with the financial information given and the accounting principles underlying this information. Finally, there may also be tax and stamp duty aspects of new issues and, in international offerings, there may be restrictions on issuers as to the markets in which they may issue or currency restrictions and money transfer problems.

Thus, in the new issue or primary market, financial regulation will foremost affect the *issuer*, therefore the party that needs money and raises it publicly. However, the conduct of the financial service providers or intermediaries, largely underwriters and placement agents, remains important also in the issuing and placement of new securities, their type and advertisement. So may be the involvement of financial service providers as advisors to the issuer on the available funding alternatives and in arranging the documentation, including the prospectus. These are often lawyers but this type of financial regulatory supervision does not usually extend to them (although they will be liable for neglect) and may not itself require authorisation or other forms of supervision for investment banks in this advisory activity either.

In respect of the issuing activity, a whole new area of concern has in the meantime resulted from the emergence of new types of securities (shares or bonds) in terms of book-entry system entitlements. They are replacing the older negotiable instruments, the way investment securities are held and transferred, and *bona fide* purchasers of them are protected. This has been dealt with more in particular in chapter IV, PART III. It is not a regulatory issue proper, rather a question of private law protection that is nevertheless of concern to regulators where it affects investors' rights and remedies, therefore their protection.

The regulatory concerns with proper authorisation and prudential supervision of commercial banks and securities intermediaries or investment banks and with the supervision of the issuing activity itself has, in many countries, resulted in new structures of *administrative* law and in the creation of new supervisory authorities that grant licenses for the various financial functions and supervise the implementation of their conditions. Failure to comply may then lead to a loss or suspension of these licenses subject to some forms of judicial review in the (administrative) courts. For banks, this supervisory function was in first instance mostly exercised by Central Banks and often still is. For the securities industry, it already led in the US in the 1930s to the creation of a specialised regulator, the Securities and Exchange Commission (SEC). The Financial Services Authority (FSA) in the UK is a much more recent creation (since 1997) and is now the *sole* regulator for *all* financial services in the UK. It thus also covers commercial banking supervision that was taken away from the Bank of England. The FSA was preceded by other regulators since 1986 (which did not cover commercial banking). Most other countries still have specialised regulators in the various functions, although, like in the UK (but most notably not in the US), there is some trend in the direction of regulatory consolidation in a *single* regulator. Whether this is a good development will also be discussed later.

On the other hand, concern for conduct of business and products may lead to concern with the reinforcement of *private* law, especially in the area of agency (and duties of care), segregation of assets, and constructive trust. The difference is that even if these rules are further elaborated and expanded in regulatory rule books, the remedies are still likely to be in private law in terms of breach of contract, breach of fiduciary or statutory duties, or tort liability and are as such no regulatory matter, although special ombudsman procedures may be put in place to facilitate proceedings brought on these (reinforced) grounds by small investors against their brokers. Regulatory concern may also cover the (proper) legal characterisation of modern financial products, like security entitlements and custodial arrangements, clearing and settlement, collateralisations, securitisations, derivatives including swaps, and repurchase agreements, set-off and netting, but again primarily as matters of clarification, reinforcement or amplification of *private* law.

In a similar vein, for corporate issuers, modern issuer activity may result in amendments to (private) corporation and commercial law in terms of disclosures, accounting principles, and types of securities on offer. In clearing and settlement, there may be particular concern with safety and proper functioning of these facilities leading to regulatory supervision from that perspective (although less so in Europe), but also to the further development of private law like the evolution of the guarantees of clearing members and of the legal acceptability of close-out netting agreements. It may make more direct regulation of these activities superfluous. In all these instances, the balance between private or administrative law intervention is of considerable interest.

To summarise, the emphasis of modern financial regulation in the area of investment services is particularly on *issuers* in respect of transparency and securities offered and on *intermediaries or service providers* in respect of authorisation and prudential supervision at least for their underwriting, trading, brokerage and advisory activity and sometimes also for support functions like clearing, settlement and custody, and their conduct of business and the products they sell.

It means that modern financial regulation is less likely to relate to the capital, investment, or service *flows* themselves. It does not (or no longer) relate to the organisation and operation of the capital markets either (except in the narrower organisational sense of organised or formal markets like stock exchanges), and even less to the price formation in them. Indeed, the modern trend is to regulate *participants* (intermediaries like brokers and advisors, issuers or sometimes even investors themselves, particularly in taxation and foreign exchange or investment restrictions), *not* therefore markets or issues or the flow of investments, money and the connected services. It leads to a *deregulation* (in principle) of these flows although modern financial regulation will remain concerned with market integrity and as a consequence may cover certain specific market aspects, especially price transparency, proper settlement of transactions, and the prevention of market manipulation and similar abuse like monopolisation and insider dealing.

The way this integrity is promoted is again not only through the traditional means of financial regulation of participants, but also through other sanctions of criminal or private law, like the rules against insider dealing and money laundering.

1.1.2   Financial Intermediaries, their Operations and Regulation. Capital Flows and Monetary Policies

As for the *service providers* in the financial services industries (leaving insurance to one side), they are the entities that provide the basic services to those who need or raise money (like borrowers in the case of commercial banks or issuers in the capital markets) and those who provide it (depositors in the case of commercial banks or investors in the primary or secondary markets).

As already indicated in the previous section, we have here two ways of recycling money, the one through the banking system, the other through the capital markets. For the deposit-taking, loan, and payment activities, the service providers are *commercial* banks. They become the *owners* of the deposits and make a business out of reinvesting that money for their own account in loans to their clients. It was already mentioned that in doing so, they make the depositors mere contractual claimants and competing creditors. In the capital markets this is very different. Here there are *investment* banks/firms or securities houses which in essence act as advisors in the securities broking and investment activities. They may also be active in market functions as underwriters, market makers or matching agents, price and other information providers, clearing and settlement organisers or custodians, all functions that will be discussed in greater detail below. But even if also custodians, they do not take their clients' investment securities as owners; these investors remain in principle the owners of their securities given into custody. Even when brokers are dealing in the markets for their clients in their own name, which is normal, the essence is that the securities they so obtain and the moneys they so handle for their clients do not become their own, although there may still be serious legal problems in terms of segregation especially of fungible securities and client moneys, more in particular in civil law as we shall see, but this is for the moment a detail.

A key difference with commercial banking is therefore that investment banks (or securities houses or investment services providers) do *not* take client assets as their *own* and as a matter of principle there operates here the notion of *segregation*. It would be a very grave matter indeed if they did appropriate these assets which could amount to theft. Instead, investment banking clients will (in principle) hold property rights (rather than contractual or creditors' rights) in respect of these moneys and securities against their brokers or custodians whilst the adequate protection of these proprietary rights is a major legal issue in investment services and its regulation. This is *very different* in commercial banks but in respect of deposits only. (If they operate at the same time as security brokers and custodians, only the money deposited to that effect will be theirs, never the securities they so buy).

It is also important to note that not all financial services are directly related to deposit taking or the selling of banking, investment and insurance products to the public. In commercial banking, there is in this connection especially the *payment function*. In investment services, there are the market-making or order-matching, information supply, clearing, settlement and custody functions. The latter are all market functions, traditionally grouped around the formal or official markets or *stock exchanges* but now often split out and spread over different entities, which have no official status and may compete. This is clear where unofficial or OTC (Over-the-Counter) markets started to operate and compete with the more traditional stock exchanges. They are often markets created by investment banks for their own clients and each other. It is also clear in the information supply and clearing and settlement functions where several private organisations may increasingly compete with the official exchanges for this business. As already mentioned, many of these market functions are now also taken over by investment banks.

It was already noted in the previous section that, as a consequence, the modern financial regulatory objectives and requirements in terms of authorisation, supervision, conduct of business, and product control may be very different in respect of each type of financial service or service provider. As we shall see, there is in modern financial regulation generally a fundamental shift away from the regulation of *institutions*, like the traditional commercial banks and stock exchanges as such, to the regulation of intermediaries according to their different *functions*. It may lead to different regulatory regimes affecting a single financial institution depending on its activities. This is particularly so in the securities business, therefore in the capital markets where this regulation will be adjusted according to the type of service. As a consequence, one service provider may be subject to different regulatory regimes depending on the type of activity or function.

In modern regulation, we not only see a deregulation of the flows of financial services already mentioned in the previous section but also a *deregulation* of institutions even (to some extent) of commercial banks and certainly also of stock exchanges, and a *re-regulation* of the participants according to these functions. If this is less clearly the case in commercial banking, it has largely to do (as we shall see) with the overriding aim to avoid commercial bank insolvencies, insolvency being an institutional phenomenon. The adverse impact of insolvency is in the case of commercial banks enhanced because they own their customers' deposits. Even if the depositors are now often protected through deposit guarantee schemes, the insolvency of commercial banks, if large, may still have a particularly adverse effect on other banks and especially on the smooth functioning of the payment system. To repeat, this concerns systemic risk and affects other banks who are likely to be large creditors of the defaulting bank. Such systemic considerations are much less of an issue for investment banking where insolvencies are not likely to have a similar ripple effect, also because of the key notion of segregation of clients' assets.

The regulation, de-regulation and re-regulation of the financial services (of commercial and investment banks) rendered in connection with the recycling of money or capital should thus be clearly distinguished from the regulation, de-regulation and re-regulation of the *capital flows* themselves, although it is true that the liberalisation of these flows has given an enormous impetus to the liberalisation of the financial services industry world-wide and has greatly encouraged the cross-border delivery of these services. In the EU, the liberalisation of the capital flows after 1988 was indeed the catalyst for the further liberalisation of cross-border financial *services*, even though in principle already freed under the original Rome Treaty of 1958 that created the original EEC, but in practice, the free flow of these services was delayed because of the regulatory complication and the lack of clarity especially on *host* regulator competencies to regulate these incoming services. Only in the second generation of EU Directives in this field, issued in the context of the Single European Act effective in 1992, was there a division of labour achieved between home and host regulator of financial services in this respect (with the emphasis on the former as we shall see), which made the flow of these services to and the right of establishment of the service provider in other EU countries practicable, see more in particular section 2.4 below.

Unlike in the liberalisation of financial services, which, as mentioned before, was meant not any longer to inhibit the financial flows, in the liberalisation of the capital flows we do not primarily think of depositors or investors and their regulatory protection or of borrowers or issuers and the financial services provided to them, but rather of the *free movement* of investments and payments, that is the free export of the own currency, the free import of those of others, and full convertibility. We then also think of the freeing of exchange rates and of interest rates (at least the longer ones), henceforth to be set by market forces, and of the freedom to borrow or raise and invest capital wherever one wants. Another aspect is the freedom to make and accept payments in any currency one wishes.

The deregulation of the capital flows in this sense and their possible re-regulation to prevent financial upheaval or to deal with the international investment and taxation consequences — matters in the 1944 Bretton Woods Agreements essentially left to the government of each currency — raise very different issues that, unlike the regulation of financial services, can hardly be left to (domestic) home/host regulation alone. It must be dealt with at international levels, partly within the IMF, and in Europe for the investment and tax consequences more directly at EU level. In other words, this is not merely a matter of the division of labour between (regulators from) Member States. It will not be considered here in great depth. As just mentioned, in the EU after 1988, these capital flows were fully liberated, see also section 2.4.6 below, whilst the re-regulation possibilities are now very limited (Arts 56-60 EC Treaty). This has left a number of investment and taxation issues that will be discussed in greater detail in section 2.4.7 below.

Finally, regulatory interest, particularly in commercial banks, may be motivated not only by concern for depositors or the public at large (particularly in terms of the functioning of the payment system or in the sense of limiting systemic risk), but also by considerations connected with their *monetary* function, the money supply and (short term) interest rates, inflation control, and the allocation of credit to the various economic sectors. These concerns may also give rise to governmental or rather central bank intervention. This type of money recycling (or flow) through the banking system is therefore traditionally controlled. In England, these matters now come under the Bank of England Act 1998 (whilst the deposit taking function of commercial banks is now regulated under the Financial Services and Markets Act 2000). There are issues here of liquidity and monetary policy rather than of regulation of financial services. They will also be dealt with only incidentally. It should be noted, however, that where it was said in the previous section that in capital market operations, the flows should not be regulated but only the participants, this may thus be different in respect of commercial banks, but again this is *not* then a matter of financial services regulation proper but rather a question of monetary policy. These are not matters of home/host country division of the regulatory burdens either.

Sound functioning of the payment system is another very important issue in commercial banking which will not be covered here in any great detail either except in terms of bank insolvencies and systemic risk. Payments and the operation of payment systems were dealt with in Chapter III.

1.1.3   Objectives of Modern Financial Regulations

Altogether, apart from issuers, the emphasis of *modern* regulation of the financial services industry is foremost on the service and service provider, therefore on the intermediaries in the banking, securities and insurance business, their function, their proper authorisation and supervision, the way they provide these services and the products they offer.

Depending on these services and the way they are provided, the main aims of modern financial regulation may be quite diverse, however. They should be orientated towards the containment or reduction of some clearly defined risks per function, but the clarity of purpose may remain altogether a considerable problem in financial regulation.

Essentially, the major regulatory concerns are the following although their intensity is likely to vary per function or type of institution:

(a)   The *protection of clients*, like bank depositors, securities investors, and insurance policy holders against (i) a bankruptcy of the service provider, (ii) bad selling or advisory practices often caused by a conflict of interests between service provider and client, or (iii) risky products.

As was already mentioned before, insolvency was traditionally a particular concern in respect of commercial banks because they hold client moneys as their own, thus reducing these clients to competing creditors in their bankruptcies. Here an authorisation and prudential supervision regime is normally imposed. It is, from the perspective of deposit protection, less relevant in the investment business as the intermediary is less likely to hold client assets in its own name, although under modern regulation, these intermediaries may now also be subject to licensing and supervision requirements, at least if they deal with the smaller, inexperienced investors. The main problem is here not solvency risk but conflict of interest or poor advice.

This need of protection against risky financial products and the way they are sold, concerns in fact *all* financial services and products, whether they are offered by commercial banks (in terms of deposit taking, lending or payment facilities), investment banks or securities businesses (in terms of investment securities), or insurance companies (in terms of life insurance or pension products), even if more clearly articulated for investment services.

As we already saw, it may lead to private law remedies in terms of clarifying and improving the applicable rules and remedies, e.g. fiduciary and disclosure rules in company law and in the law of agency. It may also lead to clearer segregation obligations in respect of securities brokers and custodians and to greater clarity concerning the nature and status of financial products, like e.g. modern securities entitlements in book-entry systems. In this area, the regulator is often enabled to react through setting further rules (for the future) under *delegated* rule making powers (in a private law manner) and may in this way also be able better to tailor these rules to the different functions of intermediaries and different products and selling techniques as they develop. The remedy is not here normally the termination of authorisation but rather (reinforced) private law remedies normally leading to claims for damages.

These modern concerns about investments and the way they are sold are not necessarily limited to investment securities as transferable instruments, like negotiable shares and bonds. They may also relate to derivatives and deposits or even to life insurance policies or pensions. In fact, the loan business and the proper functioning of payment systems of commercial banks may increasingly become a proper modern regulatory concern in this connection as well. It is appropriate, nevertheless, to distinguish here sharply between the needs of the professional clients and others that have less experience. Only the latter need special protections.

Yet for commercial banks (and also for life insurance companies) the main concern remains insolvency which translates into a special concern for authorisation and supervision, particularly from a point of view of capital adequacy and adequate management and infrastructure. As was already observed before, it still leads here to a more institutional approach. Conduct of business and product concern on the other hand, is mainly associated with securities activities, therefore with the operations of investment banks and securities houses or independent brokers, in a more functional approach.

(b) The creation of a *simplified enforcement regime.*

Another important aspect of financial regulation is that it may introduce a quick and cheap complaint procedure for the smaller customers or investors either through ombudsmen or compulsory arbitration schemes. This may also be extended to commercial bank customers, taking into account, however, that they have a very different legal status vis-à-vis their bank if depositors, whilst in commercial banking the regulatory emphasis generally remains less on conduct of business and product concerns as we already saw.

(c) The creation of a *proper legal framework for financial products and services* generally.

Regulatory concern extends here to the legal characterisation and structure of financial products and services, especially obvious in the case of derivatives (and the ways they are cleared and settled) and other modern types of investments, like book-entry entitlements and custodial services. This also concerns modern set-off and netting facilities. It may also cover insurance products and insurance-related loan or mortgage products. Again this is mostly a private law matter.

This is an important (and often ignored) area of modern regulatory concern which may also go into the transferability or proper unwinding of investments as in the case of the more sophisticated derivatives. Again, regulation will not be here along the traditional lines of authorisation and prudential supervision but may acquire the particular aspect of intervention in private law. It is a question of minimising *legal risk.*

(d) The minimalisation of *contagion or systemic risk* whilst attempting to prevent the collapse of one financial firm affecting others.

As already mentioned several times before, the insolvency risk has also a contagion aspect, which is especially considered in commercial banking where, through the inter-bank market and payment systems, all banks are connected and the failure of one may seriously affect others. It could endanger the whole payment system and liquidity providing function of banks. Although the danger of systemic risk may sometimes be exaggerated, certainly in respect of investment services providers, and may even in respect of commercial banking not in practice be as significant as often claimed, it has become a major incentive for regulation, even of investment banks which are much less exposed to it.

Bank bankruptcies seem to occur, however, unabated whilst it has also become clear that through regulation, especially of the capital adequacy requirements and limitation on large exposures, systemic risk is hardly reduced. Modern regulation would appear therefore largely irrelevant to redress systemic risk.

Proper insulation of problems may require much more radical action leading to some form of narrow banking, as will be discussed more extensively in section 1.2.5 below.

Of interest is here also that limiting systemic risk as regulatory objective is now often implied in older regulatory systems that never meant to combat it. That was so e.g. in the UK where under the Banking Act the objective of banking regulation remained depositors' protection.

(e) The *integrity and smooth operation* of markets.

This is of importance foremost in the investment services industry, more so than in commercial banking. In terms of public policy, it could be seen as the investment services equivalent of systemic risk. It may concern adequate information on issuers (through prospectuses and regular information supply) and adequate price transparency, therefore proper information supply in these markets as well as proper clearing and settlement and custody facilities. It means especially the absence of market abuse or manipulation including insider dealing (although the latter may be more an issue of corporate integrity and credibility, since early disclosure, even through insider dealing, may reinforce market responsiveness itself).

Proper regulation and supervision aims here at encouraging market confidence and liquidity (which means the easy possibility to buy and sell financial products without seriously affecting the price level) and reduces thereby market risk. There may from this perspective be less regulatory insistence on authorisation and conduct of business, but more on issuer and price transparency, fair dealing, and open competition.

Regulatory concern in this connection may be limited to these aspects whilst the result may be self-regulated over-the-counter (OTC) or telephone trading and unregulated information supply, clearing and custody. This has long been the situation in the euromarkets (see for these markets and their operation section 2.4.2 below) with Euroclear and Clearstream (formerly Cedel) as clearers and custodians. In these markets even a prospectus is not compulsory (which appears not to have led to great problems in a market that has become one largely for professionals). Except for concern for proper price information and market abuse, key market functions as well as the issuing activity itself may thus remain entirely unregulated in a modern system.

It shows that full scale regulation of major financial services and activities is not unavoidable, especially in professional dealings of experienced investors (or larger depositors). Even in traditionally heavier regulated domestic markets, deregulation may at least apply to information supply, clearing, settlement and custody activities. Competition may create here the right atmosphere for protection, in the sense that the better capitalised and better managed institutions are likely to attract the most business. This may also hold true for modern derivatives markets with their own counterparty and clearing functions and built-in protections, see in particular section 1.4.4 below.

As the euromarkets show, competition may even deal with issuers in the sense that in the absence of prospectus requirements the market will decide the fate of issues that lack sufficient issuer transparency. Particularly in *professional* markets, as the euromarkets have become, issuer transparency is often much less of a problem as the type of issuers that issue in these markets tends to be well known, is watched by credit agencies and analysts whilst their findings are immediately divulged and discounted in the price for their securities.

Again, in all this, the aim of modern regulation can never be the regulation of the capital flows themselves or of markets in terms of meeting points between supply and demand (they would most likely move elsewhere if regulated in that sense). Regulation has here only a facilitating and safeguarding function as a matter of market efficiency and integrity.

Of course *formal* markets like stock exchanges will be subject to clear operating rules. Even informal or OTC markets will have to enforce some order as do the euro- markets in the International Primary Market Association (IPMA) and International Securities Association (ISMA), therefore through self regulation. As we shall see, these rules are internal and do not mean to regulate the functioning of the market and price formation in them as such or to protect the investors in those markets.

(f)   The concern with *asymmetric markets*.[1]

This is a particular academic concern with the functioning of the markets and with market transparency. The idea is that goods that cannot be properly inspected and valued sell at an average price which may be so low that it induces the sellers of the better goods to withdraw from the market. Thus an un-transparent market may become ever more inferior in the quality of goods offered. It also means that if the better quality of certain goods can be demonstrated, their market price rises. Transposed to securities trading, it suggests that in the offering of investment securities, enforced disclosure requirements might lead to a better quality market and higher prices.

In commercial banking, asymmetry in this sense may result from customers (including other banks) not knowing how strong a particular bank' s position is in terms of liquidity, maturity of its assets and liability, counter-party or position risk, and its asset and liability management. This could in this view lower the quality of the entire banking system whilst leading to an unease or even unwillingness to deal with banks. The same could happen in the insurance and investment brokerage industries. Regulation enforcing proper disclosure or

---

[1] It resulted particularly from the researches of Professor George Akerlof in Berkeley. See his seminal paper, 'The Market for Lemmons', (1970) 84 *Quarterly Journal of Economics*, 488–500. A similar situation was identified in respect of a bank's creditors by J Stiglitz and A Weis, 'Credit rationing in markets with imperfect information', (1981) 71 *American Economic Review*, 393–410, where a bank cannot know whether its borrowers are serious enterpreneurs or gamblers. The idea is here that in the case of increases in interest rates to cover the risk, the category of serious entrepreneurs borrowing money becomes smaller so that (in view of the increased risk) a bank's profit may even decrease. Asking security (rather than regulatory disclosure) may overcome this problem and seek out the better credits. In this view, applicants for credit may order themselves into different classes according to their willingness to give security. To the extent these borrowers are rated, other sources of information will also be available.

suggesting adequate financial supervision would then be the answer and (at least in theory) be likely to upgrade the whole system. This could, however, also derive from the guidance given by rating agencies which might be much more effective and incisive.

This theory also infers that in the investment industry through proper disclosure (forced on by regulation) brokers with better or superior knowledge of the markets could be identified. Whether or not this is a realistic expectation is a different matter entirely.

Regulatory emphasis on proper disclosures and on transparency finds here nevertheless some extra justification but asymmetry considerations were not the original motivation for them and have not so far inspired specific new regulatory measures either.

As for financial markets themselves, there seems to be little proof that they incline towards *lower quality trading*. They have their own *decentralised* ways of information gathering and it is not at all certain whether regulatory insistence on transparency can add a great deal in this connection. Asymmetric information concerns would in any event not appear to justify or provide a proper argument for the centralisation and regulation of the market function as such (in official exchanges), which is sometimes suggested as an additional remedy.

The problem of asymmetrical information is much raised in respect of retail investors who obviously have less information than the professionals. But they have a professional broker to help them. In respect of the choice of a broker, however, similar asymmetric information problems may arise for retail investors. It was just mentioned that it may be doubtful whether in this manner brokers with better knowledge of markets may be spotted. Probably much more important is that retail investors only deal in the market occasionally guided by the prices set by the professional dealers who discount their own superior information. That is their protection and explains why financial markets evolved with strong retail support even in the absence of much regulation of intermediaries and notwithstanding substantial insider dealing and serious conflicts of interests between brokers and their clients, of which churning and front-running are the most obvious examples.

(g) The creation of a *level playing field*, especially between commercial banks.

The idea is here that the more prudent bank should not in the short term be punished for its financial prudence and affected in its competition with other banks. Imposition of similar capital adequacy and infrastructure standards on all is in this connection considered an important regulatory leveler, even if a somewhat odd objective of financial regulation as it does not then seek to protect customers or the system as a whole, but rather financial institutions against each other. It is regulation to protect fair competition.

Fair as the level playing field requirements might be, it may impose extra costs on non-banking business even if operating on a stand alone basis. Although the capital required for this business is likely to be small unless large market positions are taken, it may make a difference for universal banks, which combine commercial banking, non-bank securities business and insurance activity, and would need capital for all of them. To level the playing field, this may lead to similar requirements for non-bank securities intermediaries which engage in investment activities independently, even though, as mentioned before, concern for insolvency and therefore capital adequacy is less strong in relation to them, first because these intermediaries should segregate client assets and moneys and second because their insolvency is less likely to entail systemic risk. Nevertheless, the imposition of an the authorisation requirement with the related capital requirement on this separate business may well have been hastened by level playing field considerations for universal banks.

(h)   The prevention of *monopolies* amongst intermediaries in the financial services.

The risk of monopolisation has always been considerable in financial markets, especially in the securities business. The club atmosphere in stock exchanges that were often given statutory monopoly status is now mostly found objectionable. Informal markets as competitors are therefore often encouraged. At least related services like price and other information supply, clearing and settlement and custody may now mostly be offered in competition. Importantly, modern competition agencies may also force settlement and clearing systems of established exchanges to open to off-exchange dealings by non-members.

The hold of (universal) banks on their smaller customers and on the payment system including the credit card business may here be another matter of competitive concern. On the other hand, another concern in commercial banking is exactly the access of smaller companies to affordable banking services. It is the opposite problem which touches on the public service function of commercial banks. That may also relate to the ability of relatively small account holders to hold on to their account and in this way to their access to the payment system.

These concerns should lead to better access and competition rules, *not* financial regulation in the traditional sense (of authorisation and prudential supervision, conduct of business or product control).

(i)   Concern for the *reputation and soundness of the financial services industry* and financial sectors in the centre(s) from which they operate.

This goes beyond systemic concerns and market integrity and is more properly the issue of *confidence*. Yet the regulator needs to strike a subtle balance between regulation that supports the reputation of its financial community and centre thereby attracting business, and regulation that is so unfocussed or severe as to drive business away. The details are here less important than the general drift and the perceived credibility of the regulator becomes here a major issue.

On the other hand, the survival of national financial centers cannot be the end objective. If other centers can provide the better facilities (in terms of efficiency, reliability and cost), they must prevail. Especially in Europe where each country still aspires to an own stock exchange (like an own airline), this is often a delicate issue.

1.1.4   *Regulatory Objectives and Moral Hazard. Statutory Regulatory Aims*

The true end-objective of financial regulation may well have become the protection of the deposit and investment climate for an ageing population that will be increasingly dependent on their savings and investments. Here confidence is an important element and may be enhanced by regulators who are perceived to help even if on a better analysis the success of this approach may be in serious doubt. Indeed the Parliamentary Ombudsman in the UK showed in June 2003 the fallibility of regulators (the FSA) in this regard and the limited preventive effect this type of regulation can have. New problems emerge all the time and the investor must retain in the end the ultimate responsibility for the choices he made in terms of intermediary and product. Shorter term, there are in particular the concerns with the stability of payment systems which may more properly depend on regulatory acumen and expertise.

At the more theoretical level, regulation has often been defined as governmental intervention through mandatory law in the pursuit of the public interest, more in particular in the pursuit of some social or economic policy. In all this it should be remembered that there are different ways to achieve public policy objectives. As already indicated in the previous sections, it could be done (a) through new governmental agencies which normally operate under administrative law, (b) through self-regulating industry organisations (SROs) which often operate on the basis of contract law vis-à-vis their members, (c) through a strengthening of private law in a mandatory fashion, or more likely (d) through a combination of all three.

Administrative agencies (or regulators) will especially take decisions in terms of authorisation and prudential supervision. To protect the affected intermediary or issuer against an improper refusal or withdrawal of authorisation, there is likely to exist an appeal possibility to the courts (in administrative review proceedings). In respect of the rulebooks that these agencies may impose, there may also be a review procedure to determine whether they acted *intra vires*. The (reinforced) rules of private law are, on the other hand, likely to be used and tested through the ordinary civil courts or in the special complaint procedures (of private law like arbitration or ombudsmen schemes). The latter may allow the customer or investor still an appeal to the ordinary courts (which facility may not be given to the intermediary).

In commercial banking, regulation became universal early on, but even there the true objectives were never fully clear and shifted overtime. First there was the concern with depositors although it became clear that in practice, the resulting concern for banking survival could not be met by merely requiring authorization and the supervision of a minimum capital under an established regulatory framework. In times of crises, *ad hoc* interventions could often not be avoided and there was little proof that modern financial regulation led to fewer such emergencies. The fear of insolvency was more likely to lead to giving banks extra liquidity through Central Banks operating as *banks of last resort*. If they themselves were banking regulators, it could even be a way for them to avoid admitting past regulatory shortcomings or failure.

The existence of this type of informal safety net or even the mere existence of depositor guarantee schemes could in turn lead to adverse effects in terms of the behaviour of bank management. It could make it *less* responsible as it came to rely on public bail-outs of the bank or at least of its depositors either through deposit guarantee schemes or otherwise. This is the issue of *moral hazard*, much highlighted by the Chicago school of economics. It indicates a situation in which the rescuer or even the fact of its existence creates itself the need for rescues. Indeed, modern thinking is much aware of the fact that the more traditional regulators and supervisors may be *captured* by the market which forces their hands. Regulation then suggests an implied guarantee to depositors or investors in a regulatory environment in which the notion of *caveat emptor* is superseded, see for the role of bank regulators as lender of last resort in this connection section 1.2.1 below.

To counter this, lesser regulation could be suggested, including especially a limitation of pay-outs by deposit guarantee schemes. Yet in practice, the regulatory regime has mostly been strengthened, not only in respect of commercial banks, even if its effectiveness may not have been enhanced whilst the cost of regulation is rising dramatically everywhere. This has led to a search for other justifications. Yet some of the newer objectives like systemic risk (now often portrayed as the overriding concern), hardly play a role in investment services and in any event regulation (and modern capital adequacy requirements) may not substantially reduce it. The picture has become further blurred by the existence of so-called universal banks that engage in commercial banking, investment banking and insurance business at the same time. In such banks, at the practical level perfectly appropriate risk taking in one function could endanger all the others.

It must further be realized that in practice, some perfectly valid regulatory objectives may severely conflict. Thus the proper protection of depositors could require an early closure of a bank, which for the functioning of the payment system or for other systemic reasons might not be opportune. Some of this we saw in the BCCI case in London.[2] In a regulatory shift in commercial banking away from depositors concerns (which are now often thought to be better covered by deposit insurance) to systemic risk and concerns for the payment system, supervisors may be perfectly protected if they let the latter concerns prevail, as English case law has shown,[3] even if banking law still puts the main emphasis on the former as was still the case in the UK Banking Act of 1987 now superseded by the Financial Services and Markets Act of 2000 which deals with deposit taking whilst the other functions (like liquidity, monetary policy and function as bank of last resort) of the Bank of England are now covered by the Bank of England Act 1998.

Because of these various complications and the theoretical lack of clarity in the regulatory objectives, the approach to financial regulation has in more recent times become more *pragmatic*. It is largely accepted that *no one single theory* of financial regulation is able to adequately underpin and explain the needs and evolution of modern financial regulatory systems. Hence the emphasis (a) on a more functional approach, (b) on the different application of the authorisation and supervisions requirements, (c) on the conduct of business and product supervision in respect of these different functions and the institutions that carry them out, (d) on the differentiation between wholesale and retail customers when it comes to investors protection, and the emphasis also (e) on more limited and abstract objectives like competition, transparency, level playing field, a sound environment and systemic risk reduction regardless of what more traditional regulation may be able to truly achieve in these areas. Perhaps the true function and impact of regulation, whatever its real effect, is to create greater confidence.[4] It would suggest that the emphasis is (f) on the overall sophistication and bite of the regulator rather than on the precise details of the regulatory regime.

[2] See also TC Baxter and JJ de Saram, 'BCCI: The Lessons for Banking Supervision', in RC Effors (ed), (1997) 4 *Current Legal Issues Affecting Central Banks*, 371.
[3] The House of Lords in *Three Rivers District Council and Others v Governor and Company of the Bank of England,* [2000] 2 WLR 1220, seemed indeed less concerned with depositors but accepted — absent bad faith — the prevailing statutory restrictions on liability for banking supervisors as an adequate defense, even if in the UK more extensively interpreted than elsewhere, like in France, where administrative courts now accept in this connection *faute simple* as sufficient ground for liability, therefore leaving more room for depositors protection, see Cour Administrative d'Appel de Paris, March 30 1999. In *Three Rivers*, reasonable policy objectives and considerations connected with systemic risk or the smooth operation of the financial system did not even seem to figure. They were in any event not weighed against the statutory requirements of depositors' protection as laid down in s 3 of the UK Banking Act 1987. It is assumed in England that the First Banking Directive of 1977 (77/780/EEC), now superseded by the Credit Institution Directive of 2000 (2000/12/EC), even though clearly concerned with depositors, did not give depositors extra rights in this connection. Whatever the objective of that Directive, there was not considered to be any direct effect as the relevant provisions were not deemed sufficiently clear, precise and unconditional. No guidance from the European Court was sought, see also M Andenas, 'Liability for Supervision' [2000] *Euredia*, 379. Protection of regulators appeared here as an objective in itself although not everywhere as widely interpreted as in the UK.
[4] See also C Goodhart et al, *Financial Regulation: Why, How and Where Now?* (London, Routledge 1998), C Ford and J Kay, 'Why Regulate Financial Markets', in F Oditah (ed), *The Future for the Global Securities Market* (Oxford, OUP, 1996), EP Davis, *Debt, Financial Fragility, and Systemic Risk* (1995), J Norton, *Devising International Bank Supervisory Standards* (1995), S Valdez, *Introduction to Global Financial Markets* 2nd ed (1997). See further also, C Goodhart and D Schoenmaker, 'Should the Functions of Monetary Policy and Banking Supervision Be Separated?', (1995) 47 *Oxford Economic Papers* 539, David Llewellyn, *The Economic Rationale for Financial Regulation*, FSA Occasional Paper no 1 (April 1999), M Taylor, *Twin Peaks: A Regulatory Structure for the New Century* (London Centre for the Study of Financial Innovation, 1995).

It suggests that modern up-to-date financial legislation can seldom be fully clear in its goals. Given the very different objectives and levels of regulation and possible contradictions in purpose, this is hardly surprising, yet unsatisfactory. It unavoidably creates *instability* at the core of financial regulation. In all financial regulation, it would seem only normal for the legislator to ask itself at least which financial services functions it wants to regulate, what the precise concerns are, what risks it wants to or can protect against, therefore what the true objectives of such regulation are in each instance, and how it can most effectively be achieved. What is needed therefore is a more extensive *risk analysis* of the financial modern services activities in order to develop a clearer view of (a) what risks must be handled by the industry internally, (b) how its risk management can be enhanced through regulation, and (c) in what manner. This is mostly not forthcoming except in a haphazard way and modern legislation shows this in a lack of clear direction.

In the EU, the Banking Directives, the Investment Services Directive and Third Insurance Directive, which will be discussed later, do not give any unequivocal answer to the objectives of financial regulation at all. Nor do the 2003/2004 Prospectus Directive, Transparency Directive, and the updating of the Investment Services Directive. That is here more understandable as they are primarily concerned with the division of regulatory powers between home and host states, although the Investment Services Directive in its second and forty second Preamble states investor' protection and the stability of the financial system as the aims of the authorisation requirement, but especially in Article 11 it also is concerned with market integrity, its smooth operation and integrity. The 2004 updating of the Investment Services Directive refers more extensively to market integrity.

As already mentioned before, in the UK, the Banking Act 1987 referred especially to the protection of depositors and hence devoted much attention to the deposit protection scheme. Perhaps surprisingly, it did not refer to systemic risk concerns in the context of banking supervision, although the Bank of England in its regular reports started to do so, suggesting an informal shift in regulatory emphasis.[5] The Financial Services Act of 1986 did not make any general statement about its objectives either, except to say that it meant (amongst others) to regulate the carrying on of investment business and to make provisions with respects to the listing of securities, insider dealing and fair trading. Why it did and what the true aims were remained unspecified even if it was clear that it was for the most part investor protection against intermediaries in terms of conflicts of interests, bankruptcy and market manipulation.

The UK Financial Services and Markets Act of 2000, which also covers the commercial banking activity (in which connection 'deposits' are defined and treated as investments), is more specific and refers in Section 2(2) to:

(a) maintaining market confidence which is further defined as confidence in the financial system,
(b) promoting public awareness which is further defined as promoting public understanding of the financial system particularly in assessing benefits and risks of investments through appropriate information supply and advice,

---

[5] Even without a statutory change, the re-focussing of the banking supervision objectives in this direction became clear form the annual reports of the Bank of England on banking supervision before this activity was handed over to the Financial Services Authority (FSA) as from 1997. If managing systemic risk becomes a valid regulatory objective, it may easily be at the expense of depositors' protection. It is in any event clear that this protection objective is less overriding than it once was. It seems that in a modern banking regulation system, they are primarily left to whatever protection depositor guarantee schemes may give them and whatever protection capital adequacy requirements may yield them in a macro sense. See for the concept of systemic risk, R Cranston, *Principles of Banking Law* 2nd ed (Oxford, OUP, 2002), 66.

(c) protectiing consumers to secure an appropriate degree of consumer protection taking into account different degrees of risk, different degrees of experience, the need for advice and accurate information but also their responsibility for their own decisions, and

(d) reducing financial crime by reducing the likelihood that authorised intermediaries become involved in it or are used by criminals.

It is not made clear, however, what the status of these principles is and whether they are meant to be overriding and have therefore a force of their own. That would not be in the nature of the traditional English approach to legislation that avoids purposive interpretation, see also chapter I, section 1.2.11. It might be no more than a list of concerns of the legislator without further relevance for the application of this statute.

According to its title, the new Act also covers markets (Section 3 (2)(a)) but not in the sense of regulating them but rather to promote confidence in them. They may apply for recognition (Section 286). It makes them more official and exempts them from the general prohibition to engage in any regulated activity. This activity is defined in Section 22 and Schedule 2 mainly as dealing in investments, managing investments and giving investment advice. Making or organising markets itself is not as such a regulated activity *per se* and does therefore not need to be authorised in the UK. As for these markets, in the UK the supervisory interest appears to be primarily on the distribution of price information, transparency of corporate information, and proper settlement.

In the meantime, IOSCO (the International Organisation of Securities Commissions: see more in particular section 2.5.1 below), in its 1998 Principles and Objectives of Securities Regulation states as principal objectives (a) the protection of investors, (b) ensuring that markets are fair and transparent, and (c) the reduction of systemic risk. As already noted before, this latter objective would seem a less obvious regulatory objective in the securities intermediaries business.

1.1.5   *Official and Unofficial Financial Markets and the Institutional and Functional Approaches to Regulation. Objective Based Regulation*

In all this, financial markets (in the context of capital markets operations) as places where supply meets demand are, as we already saw, less and less regulated except to create transparency and avoid manipulation. These markets do not denote a specialised concept but cover all financial products and services on offer. They can be divided in essentially five types:

(a) the equity or (corporate) share markets,
(b) the bond or fixed income markets,
(c) the money markets (short term deposits or similar instruments, including interbank operations),
(d) the foreign currency markets, and
(e) the derivative markets (see for the organization of these markets especially section 1.4.4 below).

The markets mentioned under (a) and (b) form the capital market, of which the derivative market is sometimes also considered a part. The instruments of this capital market are called securities and the services therein investment or securities services.

These markets may be institutionalised in certain places, like for shares and bonds in the traditional stock exchanges which are or were regulated (or at least self-regulated) as institutions. Especially in a global economy, they can easily be informalised and move offshore. Because of modern communication facilities, they may in any event become less physical and more abstract and may result in no more than informal telephone markets, like the eurobond market, now the largest capital market in the world, and could establish themselves elsewhere if a domestic set of regulation or other rules start substantially and detrimentally to impinge on them.

As alternatives to formal markets, which remain largely domestic, these informal, often offshore markets have become greatly more important and operate under more flexible rules, mostly self-imposed by the participants. In the capital markets, the eurobond market is the traditional example. Eurobonds issued in that market are often preferred by regular professional issuers and investors for the flexibility and cost savings they bring. Informal markets of this nature have provided useful competition. Helped by paperless trading on the basis of book entry systems (for shares and bonds or securities), they forced substantial change even in the formal domestic markets, which as a minimum had to abandon their monopolistic tendencies and practices.

Originally, in the capital markets or investment services field, regulation being domestic mostly turned around these domestic stock exchanges (for shares and bonds) and their rule books which were often the product of self regulation, therefore meant to bring order amongst members and protect their interests (rather than that of investors). They were therefore less suited for investors protection and to safeguard the public interest more generally. In the securities business, the move to informal markets, required here in any event a re-thinking in which connection the emphasis shifted to investors' protection more generally.

The result was that domestic regulation was increasingly targeted, no longer at the official markets (or exchanges) and their members, but rather at the service providers as intermediaries in the (official or unofficial) stock markets according to (a) what they do (in the security markets mainly as underwriters, specialists or market-makers, clearing and settlement entities, custodians, brokers and investment managers) or (b) whom they serve (in the securities business for example end-investors or other intermediaries, professionals or consumers, who could also include foreign residents especially important for brokers and investment managers who contacted them). As was already noted before, in this approach, *issuers* of securities are regulated separately in terms of prospectus requirements either for accessing the public or more in particular for listing their issues on a particular exchange, or both. In the first case, they may be under the supervision of the regulatory body itself and in the later case under the supervision of the relevant exchange.

This *functional*, rather than institutional approach to regulation was already mentioned several times and became particular clear in the modern securities business, less so in commercial banking, where the emphasis is on the type of risks (rather than the type of activity) and where *institutional* regulation still remains dominant, although strained in universal banking. To repeat, in commercial banking, this institutional approach has to do with the insolvency risk as a composite risk and institutional issue, and with its systemic implications not in the least for the payment system, therefore in modern times to a lesser extent with the effect on depositors (who are now foremost considered protected by deposit guarantee schemes). In the case of commercial banking, the rest of the supervision remains therefore largely subservient to the aim of preventing insolvency, especially in the question of sufficient capital for the entire entity. For this reason, even for universal banks, there remains more of an emphasis on authorisation and prudential supervision, with a predominant concern for capital adequacy for the whole institution. It highlights institutional aspects at the expense of conduct of business and product supervision, which automatically lead to a more functional supervisory approach.

In universal banks, there may be different regulators per activity but it is likely that there will still be one *lead regulator* for capital adequacy of the whole institution. It is normally the banking supervisor. The functional approach itself is much more evident in the securities business when operating on a stand-alone basis. Regulation along these lines is sometimes also referred to as *objective-based* regulation and may then differ for underwriting and trading, for brokerage, clearing, settlement and custody functions, and for investment advice and fund management.

In the securities business where formerly official exchanges regulated themselves and their members (as an institution) for their investment intermediary activities and supervised them by way of a form of self-regulation, the authorisation and supervision (to the extent required per function) are now mostly separated from the trading activity in these exchanges and given to *independent* regulators per activity or function. Modern exchanges now concentrate mainly on the organisation of their trading business, itself often subject to regulation from the outside but this again may vary with the various exchange functions. They may increasingly be taken over by different agencies or service providers, like information supply, clearing and settlement or custody organisations. It may therefore be said that at least in investment services we have deregulated institutionally and re-regulated functionally in relation to participants and their activity, some of which may remain substantially unregulated.

This shift in regulatory approach from institution to function was for the securities business already achieved in the USA under the 1933 Securities and 1934 Securities Exchange Act, which, in the Glass-Steagall Act (which was part of the Securities Exchange Act) at the same time separated the banking and the underwriting business, which could no longer be combined in one institution. This separation endured till 1999. In a country like the UK after the so-called Big Bang in 1986, the functional approach was also favoured and became part of the breaking up of the club atmosphere and monopolising tendencies in the official stock exchange in London. A sequel to this was that, in the UK, market, settlement and custodian facilities may now be freely created, as had already happened in the offshore euromarkets (see for these markets section 2.4.2 below) even to the extent operating from London. They are (unlike in the USA) no longer subject to regulation *per se*, although transparency (and price reporting) was imposed by law on all market participants operating from the UK whilst there is a system of official recognition possible which gives recognised markets, settlement and custody entities that want to operate within the system some advantages in their reporting duties and certainly also more credibility. It also protects them against any charges of engaging in regulated activities without a proper license.

The trend is clear. Formal markets and financial institutions as such are no longer the true focus of regulation but participants are, depending on their function. This is increasingly obvious for the financial service providers, but it may also be so for *issuers*, especially where they must register with regulators, as in the USA. It is even becoming clear for *investors*, especially for their tax obligations, reporting duties in this respect and any foreign exchange and other investment restrictions affecting them (where still obtaining).

It underlines another important shift, already referred to in section 1.1.1 above. The functional approach is directed towards participants per function or service rather than towards the investment flows. This means that the issuing of and trading in financial products itself is increasingly freed from imposts in terms of withholding taxes, foreign exchange restrictions and other limitations except for transparency in price reporting and information supply and the avoidance of market manipulation. As a consequence, in a modern financial environment, the issuing burdens and limitations are shifted from the issue to the issuer and the investment burdens (like taxation and investment or foreign exchange restrictions) from the investments to the end-investors.

This was always the objective of the eurobond market. It was in that market largely achieved through careful selection of the place of the issuer (often a tax haven finance subsidiary), the choice of instrument (usually an anonymous bearer certificate), the type of underwriting and placement syndicate (usually formed by banks from different countries), and the place of payment of principal and interest (where a choice of paying agents in different countries is normally given). National connections with the issue were in this manner minimised and foreign exchange, investment limitations, and tax burdens became a matter for the issuer and investor rather than a restraint on the issuing and trading of eurobonds themselves.

That set the trend already long before the globalisation of the capital markets became a fact, but this globalisation has reinforced the already existing tendency to shift regulation from markets and flows or even institutions as such to participants depending on their functions and position.

1.1.6 Universal Banks, Conglomerate Risks and Supervision

The *universal banking structure* has long been common on the European Continent where commercial banks will engage in many other financial services, especially capital market activities like (typically) investment securities underwriting, trading and brokerage, and fund management. They will also engage in corporate finance activities including mergers and acquisitions. In more recent times, insurance has frequently become a normal activity in banks in which connection the term *bancassurance* is used. The result is *financial conglomaratisation*. In the functional or objective-based approach to regulation, regulators are in principle sector or function specific, as we saw in the previous section, whilst concentrating on the traditional issues of authorisation, prudential supervision, conduct of business and product control, be it in different ways for different sectors or functions. The result is that several regulators are likely to be supervising parts of universal banks and an overview may be lacking.

The risks that are associated with the individual functions and that will be discussed later, like credit-, market-, settlement-, operational-, mismatch-, legal-, liquidity and systemic risk for commercial banks, and especially market-, settlement-, operational- and legal risk for investment services are the same in financial conglomerates. There may, however, be special complications. First, there might be a lack of adequate *centralised* management, corporate and risk control so that there is an insufficient overview also from a management perspective. It is a special aspect of *operational* risk. For conglomerates, there may also be extra solvency risks in mutual loans and guarantees between the different parts (or subsidiaries) and in cross subsidies of the various business activities in other parts of the business (even if organised through a holding company structure) which do no longer operate on a stand alone basis.

In any event, in times of financial stress, the commercial banking activity in a conglomerate may through its access to the inter-bank market avail itself of short term liquidity for the whole group, making that bank extra vulnerable through internal contagion. That bank may thus become a greater danger in terms of systemic risk. It also adds to the burden of banks of last resort (usually Central Banks) or governments in terms of any bail out of such a bank, which may not be easy to separate from the rest of the group. Moral hazard itself might thus increase as implied guarantees for the banking system may (have to) be extended to the entire conglomerate in an institutional sense. In matters of conduct of business, there may arise greater conflicts of interests and greater need for internal information separation through so-called *chinese walls*.

From the perspective of the regulators, in sector specific regulation with functional supervision, there is in the case of financial conglomerates naturally the problem of regulators receiving insufficient information concerning the whole entity. There is also the important question as to which regulator takes the initiative and bears the direct and indirect costs when something goes wrong. Should there be some form of *lead regulator* for the entire entity especially to monitor the capital and enforce compliance at least in this aspect? In practice, that lead regulator would always be the bank regulator as the insolvency risk and its systematic consequences are the most obvious concern in banks.

This situation has led in some countries, notably the UK and Japan, to combining the regulatory functions,[6] especially supervision, into one *conglomerate supervisor* or super-regulator: the Financial Services Authority in the UK (FSA) and the Financial Services Agency (also FSA) in Japan, therefore to the creation of large supervisory agencies. France followed in the French Financial Securities Act of August 2003 which created the French Financial Markets Authority (or *Autorité des Marches Financiers* (AMF) replacing the earlier *Conseil des Marches Financiers* (CMF) and *Commission des Operations de Bourse* (COB)). In France, commercial banking is not included.

At the organisational levels in these agencies, the various financial service functions still tend to be separated. This could even lead to less clarity as to who is primarily responsible. So the problem shifts to the regulator but coordination and the effectiveness of the regulatory supervision and response is in this way often deemed improved (at least on paper) in respect of conglomerate financial institutions. Close relationships with the industry may, however, be lost in conglomerate supervision and respect for the regulator may be lower because of the unavoidable increase in size and bureaucracy of a single regulator. It may also become more arrogant and overbearing. On the other hand, there may be cost savings but large organisations can also be less efficient and more costly. In fact, the rapidly increasing overall cost of regulation has become an important issue everywhere. Regulatory competitiveness is in any even eliminated (which the Americans still favour). For depositors and especially investors there may be a considerable advantage, however, in their access to a unified complaint and appeal structure that is likely to be centralised and more transparent.

A corollary is that the banking supervision and monetary policy in Central Banks, where it was often combined, is now separated in countries that have a single conglomerate regulator who is no longer the Central Bank. Thus in England, the banking supervision was withdrawn from the Bank of England at virtually the same time as it achieved independence in the determination of monetary policy (in 1997). From a regulatory point of view, this separation makes some sense as the function of liquidity provider and of lender of last resort may well be distorted by regulatory failures in the same Central Bank. There was here in any event room for a conflict of interests at that level. On the other hand, for the implementation of their liquidity providing function, Central Banks need some insight into the soundness of the banks to which the liquidity is given. To obtain this information, there is a need for an information exchange between single regulators and Central Banks where Central Banks lost their supervisory role. In the UK this is provided under a special Memorandum of Understanding to the effect.

---

[6] Clive Briault, *The Rationale for a Single Financial Services Regulator*, FSA Occasional Paper No 1 (May 1999).

1.1.7 Market Abuse and Misleading Financial Structures

The incidences of market abuse, like market manipulation, the use of insider dealing, or the use of markets to launder money (see chapter 3, Part III), present a number of externalities which cannot be fought by the traditional tools of financial regulation in terms of authorisation, prudential supervision, conduct of business or product control. They are naturally a public policy concern but must be countered by other means, usually a system of civil and criminal penalties.

The concept of market abuse, especially insider dealing, is not without its complications, however, nor is the question how it is best addressed. Many believe e.g. that insider dealing is not wrong *per se* or might at least be an efficient and therefore beneficial way of distributing information. In any event it should be appreciated that only some forms are outlawed, often quite recently, especially where some insiders might otherwise be able to make large profits, although, except in the case of take-overs, insider information is not always a reliable guide to future price movements. In other words, the markets may react differently to the information than insiders would. It has also been pointed out[7] that this advantage for insiders is truly a matter between the managers (insiders) and shareholders of a company and may be entirely justified if shareholders agree to it as added or substitute compensation for these insiders. It is then no more than distributing by contract the property right to corporate information between managers and shareholders.

More to the point than the size of the reward (although related to it), insider dealing is often said to undermine the confidence in the whole system thereby de-stabling it but there was little evidence of this when insider dealing was more rampant. There is an obvious battle here between greed and envy but less proof of truly harmful effect. Most importantly, many forms of insider dealing remain perfectly accepted. The use of *trade-related* information is not deemed improper (unless derived from a pooling of information). Market-makers thus operate on the basis of the flows they see and the information about sales and purchases they get. As a consequence they are better informed about price formation than others and allowed to trade on it. That does not appear to be reprehensible. In fact, *only* the abuse of *corporate* (not market) information by insiders is the major focus of insider dealing at present and likely now to make the use of it illegal.[8]

As far as market manipulation is concerned, there also seems to be an obvious *prima facie* case against it. On the other hand, it is often thought too undefinable a concept. It may also be self-correcting short of fictitious trading (like acting as buyer and seller at the same time) and fraud (usually making false statements) which can both be easily identified.[9] A market squeeze like ramping (the creation of artificial shortages in supply in such a way that the short sellers cannot meet their delivery obligations except at exorbitant prices exacted by those who hold the securities as part of their scheme) may be an obvious example of abuse, but is quite difficult to distinguish from running large positions in the hope that the short sellers will eventually have to unwind their short positions, whilst a bear squeeze as a defense of a lead underwriter against those in the syndicate or others who short a new issue may be a proper retaliatory tactic.

---

[7] This is a famous Coase insight, see RH Coase, 'Problem of Social Cost', 3 *Journal of Law Economics* 1 (1960).
[8] See DW Carlton and DR Fischel, 'The Regulation of Insider Trading', (1983) 35 *Stanford Law Review*, 857. See for insider dealing in Europe, KJ Hopt, ' The European Insider Dealing Directive', (1990) 27 *CML Rev* 51 (1990).
[9] See DR Fishel and DJ Ross, 'Should the Law Prohibit "Manipulation" in Financial Markets', (1991) 105 *Harvard Law Review* 503. See for the EU Market Abuse Directive which also replaces the earlier Insider Dealings Directive (see s 3.5.7 below). See for the UK, GA Walker, 'Penalties for Market Abuse' in Michael Blair QC et al (eds), *Blackstone's Guide to the Financial Services and Markets Act 2000* (London, 2000) 113.

Stabilisation of new issues, that is managing the supply when a new issue creates a temporary excess is another technique that is often condoned on the grounds that in this way a better market climate is created as excessive price swings are prevented. The buying-in of own shares is usually also believed acceptable. All would appear to depend on the *nature of the intent* to interfere with supply and demand, but this is a very *poor* legal guide as all market intervention including ordinary purchases and sales have a market effect. More objective standards are therefore needed to determine acceptable and unacceptable market behaviour. Except in cases of fictitious sales or misleading disclosures or lack of disclosure, they are not easy to find.

Abuse may also occur through the *structuring* of financial instruments. Enron was a case in point. Its schemes were not unknown nor were they hidden from investors but the details that were given in the company's accounts were not substantial and there was clearly the hope that no further questions would be asked. It could thus be argued that, together with its auditors, Enron sought to mislead the public through incomplete and therefore misleading information. There was further an obvious reliance on legal formalism in the sense that a scheme if legally correct under the positive law, was thought automatically to pass muster also under rules of proper corporate governance and ethics, so that also from that point of view no further questions were to be asked.[10] This is a common problem in financial structuring or engineering which is often reduced to finding new legal and tax structures in the light of a technical reading of the law in order to circumvent or alleviate the (for the relevant party) undesirable consequences of present legal structures and their objectives. Yet again, moral considerations make very difficult legal guidelines unless clear excess becomes obvious.

In the UK, market abuse received a statutory definition in the Financial Services and Markets Act 2000 (Section 118(1)). Market abuse is here considered behaviour that is likely to be regarded by regular users of a market as a failure on the part of the participants concerned to observe standards of behaviour that may reasonably be expected from them (in that market). Three specific behavioural tests are introduced in this connection: the behaviour must (a) be based on information not generally available to others using the same market and would be regarded by them as relevant in their investment decisions, or it must (b) be likely to give the regular user of the market a false or misleading impression as to supply and demand, or it should (c) be regarded by regular market users as behaviour that may distort the market in a particular investment. The FSA has developed these notions further in its Code of Market Conduct. It may impose financial penalties or publish a public censure. It may also apply to the courts for an injunction or restitution or initiate criminal sanctions. Note the obvious difficulties in arriving at more objective standards. Also corporate and trade related insider information is not clearly distinguished. The issue of its apprehensible use is left to the perceptions of participants.

The EU Market Abuse Directive of 2002 (which will replace the Insider Dealing Directive of 1989) defines in Article 1 both inside information and market manipulation. Inside information is information of a precise nature which has not been made public but relates to issuers of financial instruments and which would if made public have a significant effect on the prices of these instruments. This is largely corporate information. For derivatives there is a further provision relating to information of a precise nature not made

---

[10] See WH Widen, 'Enron at the Margin', (2003) 58 *The Business Lawyer* 961, 963 and SL Schwarcz, 'Enron and the Use and Abuse of Special Purpose Entities in Corporate Structures', (2002) 70 *University of Cincinnati Law Review* 1309.

public but which users of these markets on which they are traded would expect to receive under accepted market practices.

Market manipulation means here transacting in such a manner as to give false or misleading signals as to supply and demand for financial instruments or to secure these instruments at abnormal or artificial levels. Acceptable market practices are exempted. Transactions or orders using fictitious devices or any other form of deception or contrivance are also caught. Dissemination of deceptive information is also covered with the proviso that financial journalists may depend on their professional protections unless they use the information to their own benefit (directly or indirectly).

In all these areas: insider dealing, market manipulation and financial structuring, the limits lie in excess. There is reliance on an innate sense of balance on the part of the participants which is often not there. Clear frauds or shams present areas where there may be sufficient legal clarity. Others are where there is a form of conspiracy between participants and their technical advisors, but much must be left to the self-correcting forces within the markets, which may go as far as to accept that Enron situations are necessary occurrences to sanitize the markets (and the practices of participants). With present insights it may not be possible to present an adequate legal regulatory framework that prevents all excess, but improvements can be made.

In the US, in response to the Enron crisis, the *Sarbannes-Oxley* Act of 2002 has tried to tackle corporate frauds and accounting oversights more effectively. It created an independent regulatory board to supervise auditors, requires them to report to corporate audit committees on crucial accounting policies and alternative treatments used in respect of the company in question, introduces new corporate crimes for any one who uses 'scheme and artifice' to defraud investors (with prison terms of up to 25 years), mandates chief executive officers (CEO's) and chief financial officers (CFO's) to certify the company's financial information (with criminal sanctions for knowing or willful violations), broadens the definition of illegal destruction of corporate records, increases the fines for obstruction of justice and mail and wire fraud, reduces the time period for insiders to report trading in the companies shares to two days after the transaction, gives protection to so-called whistleblowers, instructs the SEC to issue new rules regarding disclosure of changes in the financial condition of a company, and prohibits issuers from extending loans to executives and directors that are not available to others.

1.1.8 International Aspects of Financial Regulation. When Are Financial Services International?

It was already said that financial regulation remains in essence domestic. This is largely a result of the mandatory nature of the relevant local legislation. It unavoidably leads to impediments to the free cross-border movement of financial services. Thus, better regulated countries will be wary of allowing lesser regulated foreign service providers to operate on their territories and may bring them and the products they offer under their own regulation and supervision. As a consequence, even in free trade areas or custom unions, like the European Union (EU), and certainly also within the freeing of financial services in the WTO/GATS, regulation by the receiving or host country may result in a form of dual regulation (by both home and host country) and therefore to an important (non-tariff) impediment to the free movement of services and to the right of establishment.

In the EU, this gave rise to important legislation (Directives) in the early 1990s to safeguard these freedoms in a system in which the regulatory tasks were eventually divided between the regulator of the service provider (*home regulation*) and the regulator of the service user (*host regulation*) subject to minimum harmonisation of the applicable rules (in terms of authorisation, prudential supervision and, for securities businesses, in terms of conduct of business and some product supervision) with emphasis firmly on *home* regulation. It will be discussed in much greater detail below and may prove to be an important model also for WTO/GATS.

As for the international aspects of financial services, again it is useful to concentrate on the service provider and the type of service provided. To decide whether there is host country involvement, first it needs to be established *when* a service is cross-border which in an age of telephone or modern electronic communication, is not always easy. Generally, when a service impacts on a country other than that of the service provider, there is a cross-border link, but that may not in itself be sufficient to motivate host country regulation in both authorisation (and prudential supervision) and conduct of business (and product control). In any event, it would be necessary to determine when there is such impact.

It is clear that cross-border services may in principle be provided by a service provider in four ways: (a) *directly but incidentally*, usually per telephone or mail, (b) through more *regular* contacts established on the telephone backed up by visits in the host country, (c) through the creation of an establishment or *branch* there,[11] or (d) through the *incorporation* of a subsidiary.[12]

Where the provider moves to the client and *physically* operates in a host country through a subsidiary, the host country is clearly in control, but there may be doubts if

---

[11] What is an establishment or branch as distinguished from activity which is regular but falls short of it is a question of definition and depends on a degree of permanency. The European Court of Justice (ECJ) in Case C–55/94, (*Reinhard Gebhard v Consiglio dell'Ordine degli Avvocati e Procuratori di Milano* [1995] ECR I–4165, decided the issue under Art 50(3) (ex Art 60(3)) of the EC Treaty in the light of *duration, regularity, periodicity and continuity*. An establishment/branch may therefore be deemed to exist in another country short of the physical appearance of a branch office. From a regulatory point of view the situation may become identical and give rise to (host country) authorisation and supervision requirements as if there were an actual branch office.

It is to be noted in this respect that banks may also operate in other countries through so-called representative offices which do not make loans or take deposits in the host country but only act as originators of business for their head office. In the USA it is also common to use agencies that may make loans but receive only *foreign* deposits. Both agencies and representative offices in the banking sense are normally not considered branches but usually also need some type of authorisation in the countries in which they operate but this authorisation customarily falls well short of a banking licence.

[12] Branches should be understood here in the sense of an office *without* its own legal personality: see further n 142 below. It is true that especially in common law, bank branches have sometimes been given a status of separateness from the head office for withdrawal of deposits or payment instructions. This is often seen as an implied condition in a banking relationship for the convenience of the bank and its organisation, understandable in the days when bank-wide systems did not exist but it makes much less sense now. It does, however, not create a separate legal personality in branches and in the event of liquidity shortages of branches, head offices are normally held responsible, but under federal statutory law in the USA (12 USC 633, 1828(q) 1994) no longer in the case of bankruptcy of foreign branches whose deposits were not guaranteed by the head office. There had always been doubt about a head office's liability in this regard in the case of war or expropriation affecting foreign branches.

Within most countries, bank branching is free from regulatory constraints, but notably not in the USA where under state law traditionally there were states that prohibited all bank branching, limited it to the county of the head office, or only allowed it state-wide. Interstate, the 1927 McFadden Act reflected and enforced the local restrictions at national level. In the USA, there was generally a fear of big banks which fear could not, however, survive the pressures of business. Since the 1994 Riegle-Neal Interstate Banking and Branching Efficiency Act, bank-holding companies may acquire control of a bank in any state subject to some limitations. Banks may now also merge across state borders and create a joint branch network, although states may opt out of this. States may now also authorise new branches for out-of-state banks.

Creating bank branches in other countries has always been subject to the authorisation of the receiving country and usually requires the dedication of some branch capital held in the foreign branch and supervision by the country of the branch. In the EU, the new regime under the Second Banking Directive, effective since 1992, now consolidated in the Credit Institutions Directive of 2000, establishes, however, for EU-incorporated financial legal entities the right freely to branch out into other EU countries subject to the authorisation and supervision of the (head office or home) regulator, as will be discussed in more detail below.

there is merely a branch. Where there is less than a branch, e.g. only some salesmen visits, cross-border contact is still obvious but could merely be the supply of (some) services from abroad in which physical contact could be *de minimis* if staff are sent only occasionally or if there are very few clients and normal contact is per telephone. Yet it could still raise conduct of business concerns in the host country but perhaps less the question of authorisation which may in such cases be more readily left to the home country of the service provider.

Where the client or recipient moves to the provider, there may not be host country activity at all. Thus if a prospective investor contacts a broker in another country, there may not be a cross border services, all the less so if subsequently the investor keeps an account with the broker in the latter's country. More problematic remains, however, the situation where the service is rendered in the host country per telephone or other modern communication methods are used on a more regular basis. In principle, if the service provider initiates the informal contact, it is from this perspective host country business but, if the client does, it is not. This may be problematic in situations in which an investor at his own initiative keeps an account with a broker abroad when this broker subsequently initiates further contacts and tries to sell other products to this client over the telephone at his home. There will thus be the questions of the location of follow-up activity and on the impact of advertising. The *place of the account*, therefore of the place where the client chooses to keep the account, seems to be an important indication for the applicable regulatory regime in such cases.

In the absence of a physical presence in the host country, the place where the *most characteristic obligation* is to be performed under the contract has more recently been suggested in the EU as the proper location. If this place is away from the provider, cross-border activity results and the question of host regulation is activated.[13] It is of interest that a private international law concept, borrowed from the 1980 EU Rome Convention on the Law Applicable to Contractual Obligations, that is not entirely clear and uncontested in itself, is here proposed to be used to determine the applicability of regulatory (mandatory) law. EU legislation or case law will eventually have to decide whether this is the more correct approach. It is to be noted in this connection that the place of the most characteristic performance is normally that of the service provider so that normally no cross-border service would result under this approach and home regulation follows.

Thus *initiative*, *place of account* or of the *characteristic obligation* may be important factors to locate a service, particularly when neither the service provider nor the recipient moves or when the recipient goes to the country of the provider. When the provider goes to the recipient the situation may be more clear cut, but even then incidental contact may not be enough to assume activity in the host state, at least not legally within the EU context. It is an important issue for *only* if there is cross-border activity, however legally defined, is there the question what regulator and regulatory regime will be involved in the authorisation and supervision and subsequently in the conduct of business and product control. There is here a choice between the regulator of the service provider (or the *home*

---

[13] For the preliminary question whether an activity may at all be deemed to be taking place in another country and therefore be cross-border, especially if a foreign client makes contact with brokers elsewhere through modern communication networks: see ss 2.2.2 and 3.1.2 below. The EU Commission takes the view that it depends on where the *most characteristic obligation* must be performed: see its Interpretative Communication referred to in n 14 below. This would at least be so for the purposes of notification of direct cross-border service activity under the Second Banking Dir: see s 3.2.3 below. Naturally, foreign service providers may also use an authorised service provider as agent in the other country and may in this way avoid the authorisation and other requirements of the host country. This could be a subsidiary which takes on also some direct business of the parent.

regulator) and the regulator in the country of the activity (or *host* regulator). Each is subject to its own regulatory regime, although it is in principle conceivable, although not practised, that these regulators act as proxy regulators under the other's regulation.

It is also possible to divide the tasks: for example the home regulator (under his own regime) being in charge of authorisation and prudential supervision and the host regulator being in charge of the activity in terms of conduct of business and product control. The division of labour in this manner may be done differently for different industries, activities or services. This became the EU approach, provided always that there was cross-border service (as defined) in the first place. Thus for banks, home regulation may cover all aspects including conduct of business and product control which is traditionally a lesser regulatory concern in this industry. For securities business the conduct of business and product control is more likely to be a special host country concern, at least in respect of smaller or retail investors.

There may be other foreign aspects to international financial transactions, usually covered by the domestic law most directly concerned. Thus, as far as the issue of new securities is concerned, the rules will be primarily determined by the place where they are issued and underwritten or by the stock exchanges on which they are listed or both, although like under the 2003 EU Prospectus Directive, it may now also be the country of the issuer. As far as their placement and trading are concerned, the rules may be determined by the residence of the investor at whom they are targeted and in whose country there may be selling restrictions or special investor protections and prospectus requirements. But these restrictions may be less relevant in secondary trading and not be a condition of the issue in respect of that type of trading (usually after a certain so-called lock-up period). Even if investments are not meant to flow to certain countries (like the US) that require registration of the issuer for the securities to be sold in that country, investors from those countries may still acquire them in the off-shore markets. That would seem to be their choice and could not be held against foreign brokers or market makers acting at the investors' request.

1.1.9   *International Financial Regulation. The EU Model or Passport and Concept of the General Good*

As explained above, the focus of financial regulation is now mainly on the financial service providers and the type of their cross-border activities in a *functional* way. Especially the EU has had to deal with financial service regulation, which remains in essence domestic, therefore a Member State matter, and its possible restraints on the flow of financial services that may in principle freely move cross-border within the EU. For service providers located within a Member State of the EU and wanting to operate in another EU country, EU case law early confirmed the free movement of *incidental* direct cross-border financial services. It was a consequence of the direct effect of the relevant Articles of the EEC Treaty guaranteeing the free movement of services (Article 49, ex Article 59). Most telephone selling, for example of eurobonds, from London into other EU countries was probably covered by this freedom.

It implied *home* country rule in the aspects of authorisation and prudential supervision of the service provider, that is to say that these aspects were covered by his own home regulator, but even then this was not necessarily so in the aspect of conduct of business and product supervision. Particularly in the retail (consumer) area, there could therefore still be protection under the law of the service receiver, therefore under the law of the host regulator, even for authorisation, on the basis of what became known as the notion of the *general good* as developed in EU case law.

Within the EU and its basic liberalised attitude towards the movement of services, this notion was perceived, however, as being of an *exceptional* nature and therefore restrictively interpreted. There had to be a pressing, imperative and obvious need for host country restrictions, which therefore could not be justified on the mere ground of reasonableness. Even after the liberalisation under EU liberalisation Directives pursuant to the Single European Act of 1992 in which its applicability was much reduced, the general good concept still remains of importance especially in the area of conduct of business and product supervision in respect of retail investors as we shall see in section 3.1.3 below.

In any event, the rendering of *more regular* cross-border services and all the more so the creation of branches in a host country were in the EU at first *always* believed to be subject to host country regulation under this notion of the general good. This was therefore also in the aspects of authorisation and supervision, regardless of the direct effect of Article 43 (ex Article 52) covering the freedom of establishment. Under the concept of the general good, the host country could in such cases even require the establishment of a branch on its territory as a precondition for providing services. It could also deem such a branch to exist, which branch would then be entirely subject to its own rules of authorisation, prudential supervision, conduct of business and product supervision, therefore host regulation.

It became clear, however, that in this manner little progress could be made in the free movement of financial services within the EU short of harmonisation of substantially all the regulatory rules concerning the service providers and their activities. This was attempted at first but proved an unrealistic objective and did not remain the EU's preferred approach.

The alternative was to accept in principle (mutual recognition of) *home* country rule for the authorisation and supervision of *all* types of cross-border financial activity, including branching, but drawing the line at the incorporation of a subsidiary as a new legal entity. This became the accepted EU road to liberalisation under which only subsidiaries in other Member States (and activity from financial services companies from outside the EU) remained subject to host country rule. For all other EU cross-border activity in the financial services field, including branching out, there is now a so-called *European passport*. Under it, it is the home regulator of the service provider (assuming it is incorporated in a EU Member State) that was recognised as solely competent in matters of authorisation and supervision of the activity, therefore also in other EU countries. In this approach, home country regulation extended in principle also to conduct of business and product control, still subject, however, to the general good exception to home country rule as developed by EU case law, especially to protect smaller investors.

The home rule principle required a minimum of harmonisation, however, particularly in the areas of authorisation (as to licensing requirement itself and its basic features), prudential supervision and capital adequacy and the relevant EU Directives provided this so that there were some safeguards in common standards. On the other hand, there were always some agreed exceptions to home country rule especially in the areas of monetary and liquidity policy for banks which in their foreign operations remained subject here to host country rule. The earlier exceptions based on the notion of the general good are now limited in their effects by the various EU Directives as was already done more generally (but also more modestly) in the decisions from the European Court of Justice (ECJ) in Luxembourg. In particular, there can no longer be any requirement to create a branch in the host country under host country rule and the (home country) authorisation and supervision powers can no longer be affected by it.

However, as just mentioned, the concept of the general good is likely to remain particularly relevant for the conduct of financial services and for the sale of products of a more complicated nature, especially when they are rendered or sold to retail or consumer customers in other EU countries. In fact, the relevant securities and insurance Directives shifted the emphasis here more generally to host country rule, see notably Article 11 of the Investment Services Directive. This shift may be amplified by the general good notion, although it is not always clear to what extent host country rule may still be expanded on the basis of this concept. It tends to fracture the common market and is therefore looked upon with unease, all the more so since the concept remains undefined, and is therefore imprecise and easily abused. It is ultimately for the ECJ fully to define its reach from case to case.

So far it is clear that it may not be used to circumvent the liberalisation process itself and it is no longer relevant in areas that are specifically harmonised, like the authorisation, prudential supervision and capital adequacy requirements. On the other hand, there remains room for it particularly in the area of small investors'protection under their own (host country) rules and probably also in the combating of (serious forms of) fraud and other irregularities.[14] The reputation of the own financial center may also be a justified concern for regulators under general good notions, as we shall see, but according to European case law may not be used if it is discriminatory, disproportionate or leads to unnecessary duplication, see for this case law section 2.2.4 below.

1.1.10   The International Capital Market and the EU Project for a Single European Market for Financial Services

Within the EU, we should also consider its call for one Single European Market for financial services. It appeared in the 1998 EU Framework for Action without a roadmap. At the back of it is the idea of the operation of one single European capital market but the concept is somewhat broader and comprises also commercial banking and insurance activities. The idea is obviously a sequel to the appearance of the Euro and it would seem logical that in its wake a single capital market and market for financial services at least for Euro countries should result. Benefits similar to those derived from the large internal market in the US are envisaged. The appropriate level and manner of regulation (of the participants) in that single market would then also have to be (re)considered. Hence the review of all EU Directives in this field.

It is important in this connection to note a number of things. First, there is the euro-market, already several times mentioned before. It has nothing to do with the Euro and operates in any currency. It developed as an off-shore capital market since 1963, is substantially unregulated, and has become the largest capital market in the world. It is mainly a professional market. Although off-shore, it operates substantially from Europe (hence the

---

[14] In 1997, the EU Commission, concerned about the expanding force of the concept of the general good and its effect on the freedom of movement of financial services within the Union, issued an Interpretative Communication on the notion of the general good in the Second Banking Directive see [1997] OJ C209, following an earlier draft of 1995, [1995] OJ C291. This Communication is not a ruling or soft law and not therefore binding on the courts. Yet it is likely to have strong persuasive force. Although it does not have an immediate bearing on the securities and insurance industries, it naturally also contains important clues for the interpretation of the concept of the general good in the Directives concerning these activities. In the meantime, for the insurance industry, the Commission published a Interpretative Communication on the operation of the general good in this industry in 1997: [1997] OJ C365.

name 'euromarket'), see more in particular section 2.4.2 below. Any single European capital market would have to determine its place in relation to that bigger international market in which connection the level of regulation would become an important issue as it would be compared to and have to compete with its bigger off-shore brother. In this connection there is the related drive, either openly or subconsciously, to subject this euromarket to similar regulation. It may drive it away or reduce it to private placements, especially in the equity segment. In other words: it would find other ways to survive and the competition would remain. It is a question of efficiency, liquidity and cost for issuers and investors alike.

The EU inclination implicitly to assume that also for international professional dealings local standards of financial regulation are appropriate is in any event misguided and lacks a sense of reality now markets operate internationally. The EU attitude assumes further that it would not be necessary to (re)test local regulatory standards on their appropriateness if international financial dealings could only be brought within the web of local regulation. The operation of the euromarkets, rather than being the standard, is then seen as an unwelcome aberration. In reality, this narrow perspective is highly detrimental to the development of a proper European financial market and the fact that the dynamics of the international financial markets remain little understood by the EU remains a seriously disturbing element in the present recasting of the Prospectus-, Regular Information or Transparency, and Investment Services Directives, which will be discussed in greater detail below in section 3.5. Unfortunately, the desire to retain local or domestic (stock) markets and to protect them and see financial regulation often in terms of these local markets and their preservation and of the protection of small local investors only, continues to be the horizon of most European politicians.

The result so far has been a tortuous and often disappointing review of the relevant EU Directives and the feeling of many experts that it presents a retrograde step and does nothing to promote a pan-European financial market that is at the same time properly connected with the international or euromarkets.[15] In this view, the present efforts of the EU action plan are a missed opportunity resulting from a lack of understanding of the dynamism of the international financial markets, the autonomic forces working in them, and of the internationalising trends and their opportunities. The bottom line here is that professional markets should in principle be deregulated. In the euromarkets they have shown that they can look after themselves and these markets should therefore be the prime building blocks, not the local exchanges. Special rules should be devised only in respect of market manipulation (even between professionals) and for the protection of smaller investors or depositors.

In all this, the separation between the capital flows and the service flows should also be clearly considered. Both are free in principle in the EU, but, as we already saw, regulation of a domestic nature is accepted for financial services in principle (not for capital flows). Its disturbing effect on the free flow of financial services is well understood and is, in as far as possible, limited in the modern set-up of the European passport through a substantial degree of harmonisation with the prevalence of home regulation as we also saw. In all this, it should be understood that legally the underlying EU perspective is and remains the overriding concern with the free movement of services as a *fundamental* EU objective and *not* with the protection of depositors or investors, although, especially for the smaller ones of

---

[15] See JH Dalhuisen, 'Towards a Single European Capital Market and a Workable System of Regulation', in M Andenas and I Avgerinos (eds), *Financial Markets in Europe* (2003), 35 *et seq.*

them, exceptions must be made, but they are no more than that and may be satisfied by depositors' and investors' guarantee schemes. As already noted before, they now largely translate into host country supervision of conduct of business and products in respect of retail investors under notions of the general good, even though small investors are usually served by foreign intermediaries through subsidiaries in their own countries or otherwise keep accounts with these foreign intermediaries in the latter's countries so that these services do not normally flow across border. As already suggested in the previous section, it follows that small investors are likely to be primarily protected by the regulation of the country of their accounts.

Thus in terms of a Single European Market for financial services, we need — according to the EU's own philosophy of the free movement of services — to think first in terms of liberalisation of at least the *professional* market for financial services and the issuing and trading of securities in them, just as the euromarkets have always done. Regulation is here exceptional and in each instance it should be asked what its proper level should be, therefore why and how the various financial functions should be regulated, what risks are we concerned about, why they can better be dealt with by regulation, and who should be in charge. In the capital markets, this concerns notably the issuing function, underwriting, market making, brokerage, advisory and investment management activities, clearing and settlement, and custody. These are questions that should always be raised but even more so in connection with the rendering of international financial services within the EU, where regulation is likely to be an impediment to the professed free flow of financial services.

With the unregulated euromarket on one side and the fundamental freedom and deregulation ethos of the EU in respect of the basic EU flows on the other, the development of the Single European Market in financial services would suggest as a minimum a narrow margin for regulation and a re-consideration of the need of regulation in all these various functions, particularly those relating to the operation of the capital markets and the investments of professionals. That is *not* at present happening and the small investors' ethos appears to continue to dominate the view of all financial regulation. It is unuseful and in any event unlikely that a European market for its feasibility and vitality could develop merely on the basis of an extrapolation of present *domestic* regulatory attitudes.

In a more rational EU approach, not only the supervisory structures of home/host regulation and issuer disclosure should be constantly reconsidered, but also the regulatory objectives themselves, the need for centralised regulation at EU level, and the feasibility of a single EU regulator. Another important issue is a better private law protection at the micro-level of investors in terms of agency, segregation, collateralisation, netting, and the status of book entry entitlements in international book-entry systems of investment securities. In the dominant approaches to regulation proper, these very important aspects remain mostly overlooked, also in the EU (although in an incidental manner some was done in the Settlement Finality Directive and in the Collateral Directive as we shall see).

In the area of regulatory structures and supervisors, the more direct issue of a single regulatory regime and a single European regulator was considered in a Report of a Committee of Wise Men under the Chairmanship of Mr Lamfalussy, published in March 2001. The idea of a single regulatory framework and regulator was not supported. Emphasis was put instead on a better supervision of the implementation of EU Directives and on a faster method of amendment in the financial area.[16] It is in any event clear that small investors

---

[16] The idea was here to allow for delegated authority in new Investment Services Directives. To that end, a European Securities Committee (ESC) was set up in 2002 with representatives from all Member States which was

would be little served by centralisation of the regulatory function but also the professionals would need regulators operating close to each financial center in the EU short of fuller deregulation. This would certainly also imply a re-consideration of the prospectus and periodic reporting requirements of issuers, and, where such prospectuses would be deemed necessary and are regulated (which in the euromarkets so far they were not), it should lead to their automatic recognition in all formal or informal markets operating in the EU. In 2001, the EU published a first draft of a new Prospectus Directive in this area which was approved in June 2003 and will be discussed later. As already mentioned, a review of all major EU Directives in the investment services area, including the Investment Services Directive will follow, see more in particular section 3.5 below.

Although mutual recognition of authorisation and prospectuses at EU level leading to an *issuer's passport* may be an important step, the internationalisation of capital markets and the services rendered in them also need to involve other major capital markets in the harmonisation process, especially those in the US and the Far East. They should come into a system of the mutual recognition of home country rule worldwide and into the deregulation/re-regulation discussion. That may be more properly a task for WTO/GATS. In any event, within its framework of liberalisation of financial services, the proper level of regulation per function at domestic level, the harmonisation of regulatory principles worldwide, and mutual recognition of home country rule will ultimately also have to be considered, if only to make a freer flow of financial services possible.

1.1.11 The American Regulatory Approach to Issuing Activity and to Financial Services Rendered in the US by Foreign Issuers and Intermediaries

Generally in the USA, securities regulation is now a *federal* matter (although state law also remains competent) and there are a number of federal statutes relevant to the issuance and distribution of investment securities in the USA: the Securities Act of 1933, the Securities Exchange Act of 1934, the Public Utility Holding Company Act of 1935, the Trust Indenture Act of 1939, the Investment Advisers Act of 1940, and the Investment Company Act of 1940. The Securities and Exchange Commission (SEC) administers these acts which, with the exception of the Public Utility Holding Company Act, also apply to foreign securities distributed in the USA or to US investors. The most important innovation of 1933 was that under the Securities Act all securities being distributed in the USA or to US investors (resulting in a *public offering*) must be registered with the SEC, which will decide within five days whether it will review the issue. Most first time offerings are so reviewed, which

intended to function as a regulatory committee in implementation matters. A Committee of European Securities Regulators (CESR) was set up at the same time. It represents the domestic regulators and may be asked to make detailed implementation proposals which in turn may facilitate uniformity in the implementation of the Directives in Member States. The CESR has no decision taking authority. In this connection, it was also suggested that greater use could be made of EU Regulations instead of Directives. They have a direct effect in all Member States and do not depend on local incorporation and achieve therefore speed and uniformity.

In the EU there already existed the Forum of European Securities Commissions (FESCO) as representative of the domestic securities regulators in the EU. It functioned as a pressure group for them and as a think tank at EU level. It was unavoidable that it often presented a domestic perspective of regulation and was inclined to extrapolate domestic approaches. It came nevertheless with important proposals and in its consultation paper of May 2000 on *A European Passport for Issuers* it suggested e.g. an *issuers passport* and later on attempted also a definition of professional and private dealings (in its March 2000 *Report on Categorisation of Investors*). Pursuant to the proposals of the Lamfalussy Report, it became the Committee of European Security Regulators (CESR). The draw back was that domestic regulators were thus moved to the heart of the regulatory process in the EU. One must question the wisdom of this move. See for a further discussion of the Lamfalussy process, section 3.5.2 below.

will take between four and six weeks during which time the securities may be offered but not sold. A preliminary prospectus may even be issued.

It is of interest in this connection to consider what, according to US law, is a prospectus. Under Section 2(a)(10) of the 1933 Act, it is any written offer, offer by radio or television, or conformation of a sale. So the first task is to determine what is an 'offer' in these terms. There is no clear definition but the key appears to be a broad concept that covers any action that conditions the market for the sale of securities. It implies a measure of publicity. Offers (therefore prospectuses) of this nature require a registration statement in which in fact the approval of the prospectus is being sought from the SEC. A satisfactory review will depend on basic conditions of the prospectus having been met. It means that the registration becomes effective only upon such a satisfactory review which operates as an authorisation of the sale. All further distribution of materials must subsequently be accompanied by the registered or official prospectus. The 1934 Act requires in addition ongoing disclosure in respect of issues listed on the US stock exchanges and Nasdaq.

Shelf registration is another way of obtaining this authorisation. In a shelf registration, the authorisation is sought and obtained *in advance* by filing a registration and a prospectus. If the prospectus is satisfactory, the securities may be sold within a two year period. The importance of this facility is that issuers may thus take immediate advantage of good issuing conditions during that period without incurring any registration delays. Any offer during that period must, however, be accompanied by a supplemental prospectus covering the specific terms of the offering and any recent developments in the issuer's business or status.

For *non-public or private* placements, there is a registration exception under Section 4(2) of the 1933 Act, see also Regulation D. It may help foreign issuers desiring only a limited distribution in the US or to US investors. In 1998, the SEC reduced the restrictions on distribution in respect of large seasoned issuers in order not to force them unduly into reliance on private placement exceptions. The necessary information under shelf registrations was expanded. On the other hand, in the area of disclosure, in 2000, the SEC adopted a Regulation FD tightening the rules for selective disclosure of material non-public information. This was meant to reinforce the insider dealing rules.

Except for private placements, in the USA, until 1988, in the securities business, the SEC attitude had always been that all public offerings of securities (foreign or American) using means or instruments of transportation or communication in interstate commerce or the mails would have to be registered with the SEC, unless there was an exemption under Section 5 of the Securities Act of 1933. As for *foreign* issues, issuers would use Forms F-1, F-2 or F-3 for capital raising in the US and F-4 for business combinations. A first time filer would use the well known form F-1 (for ongoing disclosure in respect of listed foreign issues, the form F-20 would be used). Yet it had long been accepted that (other than to prevent or prosecute fraud) this approach did not apply to foreign offerings with only *incidental* contact with the USA. This conclusion was based on a 1964 Securities Act Release 4708 concerning distribution to foreign nationals resulting in securities coming to rest abroad.

On the basis of this Release, practitioners, helped by interpretive letters from the SEC, had developed a number of practices resulting in underwriters (a) not placing directly in the USA, or (b) observing a so-called lock-up period from 90 days to one year during which no secondary sales could be made into the USA or to US persons. To this end, sales restriction statements were inserted into the offering documents and underwriters certified that they had complied with the requirement not to sell in the USA or to US persons. A global note was often used by the issuer to enforce the restrictions on distribution during the lock-up period. There was a (narrow) private placement exception as these placements were not then considered sales to the public.

In 1988, the SEC moved further on three fronts. In Regulation S, it abandoned (in principle) any claim to extraterritoriality of its rules over transactions which properly occurred outside the USA even in US securities or with US persons (except in the case of fraud). This immediately raised the question what was 'outside the USA'. No rule was introduced and the SEC determines this on an *ad hoc* basis, but to clarify the situation Regulation S in Rules 903 and 904 provides two non-exclusive safe harbours, one for issuers and one for re-sales. For either, the offer or sale must be made in an 'off-shore transaction' and no direct placement or selling efforts may be made in the USA. For the issuer, there are further requirements depending on the category of issue, which categorisation is based on the likelihood of the securities flowing back to the USA. A non-reporting issuer of an issue for which no US marketing effort is being made attracts the least restrictions. If the issuer reports to the SEC and there is a substantial US market interest (SUSMI), there will be a lock-up period of 90 days (one year for shares) as from the end of the issuing period (lowered for eurobonds to 40 days). For non-reporting issuers of an issue for which there is substantial US market interest (SUSMI), the requirements are the severest because of lack of information. These requirements will impose on issuers a verification duty and certification requirement that none of the securities issued were purchased by US persons before individual certificates may be issued. The idea behind the lock up period (which in respect of bearer securities requires a global note for the period) is that in the absence of sufficient information the market will have time to discount all eventualities.

The second SEC move was to broaden the private placement option to re-sales under the new Rule 144A. It introduced a further safe harbour for three types of re-sales of *non-fungible* securities, respectively of (a) any privately placed, (b) not listed or (c) privately placed but listed securities. The first type could be resold to qualifying institutional buyers (QIB), which were entities with assets of more than US $100 million, even if residing in the USA; the latter two types could be sold to *all* US or non-US institutions provided that privately placed but listed securities did not filter back into the USA. The aim was not only to attract foreign issuers to the USA but also to facilitate private placements to large US investors and increased liquidity for these investments. After discussion, US securities were excluded as it was felt that qualifying US institutions would be unduly advantaged over the general public in respect of them.

The third change was a new Rule 15a-6 under the Securities Exchange Act of 1934. It elaborated on transactions (giving research and making deals) with US investors from abroad and set out the conditions under which non-US brokers could avoid SEC registration. Here two safe harbours were created for them to deal with US institutions from abroad, but if they had an active business in the USA always through or together with a US-registered broker or with their foreign subsidiary or an international agency based in the USA (generally US institutions may always be approached by foreign brokers if the execution is handled through US registered brokers). Off-shore activities even if involving purchases for US citizens abroad or concerning US securities would no longer require foreign broker registration. Foreign firms providing research reports to major US firms (US $ 100 million minimum assets) may also execute transactions based on such research, if unsolicited. US brokers as well as international agencies in the USA may always be directly solicited by foreign unregistered firms.

An example may be helpful. If the intention is to sell eurobonds in the US, the first question to ask is whether they are meant to be sold in unfungible form to qualifying institutional investors (QIBs) in the US or not. In the first case there would be no problem. If this safe harbour does not obtain (e.g. because the bonds are fungible), the next question is whether there is the more general private placement exception under Section 4(2) of the 1933 Act. For foreign public issues, there is otherwise still the question whether there is, in respect of issues not directly placed or sold in the US, a SUSMI in which case there will be a 40 days lock-up provided there is a global note during that period. If the intention is, however, also to target the issue at the US, a F-1 registration will become necessary.

It should be noted in this connection that the tax aspects are treated quite differently. There are the so-called TEFRA (Tax Equity and Fiscal Responsibility Act) rules for bearer securities. They impose a tax penalty. Eurobonds are exempted (if subject to a global note held by a clearing system so that there is no bearer security proper), provided interest is paid outside the US, there is a legend on the bonds warning of US tax implications for US persons (broadly those subject to American taxation) and there must be reasonable assurances that bonds are not sold to other than US qualifying persons (like financial institutions).

Finally, the situation in respect of commercial banking activities in the US should be briefly considered and is quite different. Generally commercial banks in order to operate need a license or authorisation or, in American terminology, they need to be chartered, which may be done by state or federal authorities (in latter case the Office of the Comptroller of the Currency or OCC) at the option of the bank. If federally chartered, they are called National Banks. State Banks are supervised by states but in addition by the Federal Reserve if they are also members of the Federal Reserve system and otherwise by the Federal Deposit Insurance Corporation if they are federally insured. This supervision will lead to the usual capital adequacy and other prudential measures. Originally this system only applied to American (and not foreign) banks, which were also subject to the federal and state rules restricting their activities. The most important restriction was the Glass-Steagall Act requirement of separation between banking and securities activities, only eliminated in 1999 by the Gramm-Leach-Bliley Act of that year.

Until that time, most banks were subsidiaries of large bank holding companies that were supervised by the Federal Reserve and could do more than banks under Sec.4 (c)(8) of the Bank Holding Companies Act and also engage in activities *closely related to banking,* but generally still not in securities, insurance and commercial activities. They were supervised as main providers of capital to the bank in the holding. Since 1999, under the new section 4(k) of the Bank Holding Companies Act, Bank Holding Companies (BHCs) are allowed to engage through different subsidiaries in the full range of financial activities when a BHC is called a Financial Holding Company (FHC). All larger banking groups are now organised in this manner. Well-capitalised banks may also engage in these activities through subsidiaries.

Another feature of the American system was the limitation on interstate banking under the McFadden Act of 1927, which applied unless a state made an exception. They became more common and the McFadden Act was repealed in 1994. Since then, interstate banking is free (except if a state decides otherwise which has led to reciprocity arrangements between states) although still subject to state rules on competition and community reinvestments.

The situation was originally different for foreign banks opening a *branch* in the US. They were chartered under state law only and had much greater operational flexibility as federal restrictions did not apply to them (unless they acquired a controlling interest in a bank in the US). This flexibility was curtailed, however, by the International Banking Act of 1978 amended in 1991 by the Foreign Bank Supervisory Enhancement Act (FBSEA) and further elaborated in Regulation K of the Federal Reserve Board. It was done foremost to create a better level playing field between foreign and American banks operating in the US. Foreign branches are now authorised at their option by the OCC, the Treasury, or by states. Their activities are determined by the applicable federal or state laws and they are now made subject to all restrictions on non-banking activities (even if charted by a state, as the FBSEA clarified).[17] Foreign bank *subsidiaries* are chartered by either the OCC or a state and operate as any other American bank. These subsidiaries are much less common as banks traditionally prefer to operate through branches which also means protection for deposit holders. A third option is an *agency* of a foreign bank. They are often used and may make loans and attract foreign deposits but no deposits in the US. Again they are either chartered by the OCC or by a state. Representative offices of foreign banks make neither loans nor take deposits in the US but may solicit business for their foreign bank in the US. They are either federally or state chartered.

Branches of foreign banks in the US and their supervision were the most important subject of discussion in this connection. In the next section, the Basle Concordat will be discussed and the amendments thereto in the light of the BCCI case which in the US gave rise to the Foreign Bank Supervision Enhancement Act of 1991. It amended the International Banking Act of 1978. A major concern is federal deposit insurance and the supply of liquidity if an American branch of a foreign bank runs into difficulties (even if this is in principle the business of the lender of last resort of the foreign bank). That may also have an effect on the inter-bank payment system if foreign branches are members. The American approach is to require membership by foreign branches of the deposit insurance scheme and to limit the participation of foreign branches to the electronic payment system (CHIPS). The American regulator will also defer supervision to foreign regulators only if it is satisfied with their capability to do so effectively.

1.1.12 *The Basle Concordat concerning International Banking Regulation and the Efforts to Achieve International Financial Conglomerate Supervision*

Because it serves as an important model, the EU liberalisation efforts in the financial services area will be discussed in greater detail in Part III below. The movement from host to home country rule will be traced whilst the remaining (varying) scope for host government intervention under the EU directives and the concept of the general good will be further explored. It presents a cluster of problems which eventually will also have to be faced within WTO/GATS. It deserves therefore considerable attention.

This discussion within the WTO will have to wait at least until the next negotiation round originally foreseen in 2000. Regulation remains here for the time being an important barrier to the free flow of these services, as it did within the EU. Electronic communication may increasingly cut through this and force the pace in the direction of home country rule, often already accepted if the service provider is not the initiator of the transaction but is accessed by clients directly from abroad, as we saw. This may become the pattern, especially in respect of major investors from less developed countries who may prefer brokers in the main international financial centres even in respect of securities investments made in companies and in government bonds of their own country.[18]

Until such time and except for this direct access, it should be clear, however, that cross-border services outside the EU area, for example between the USA and the EU countries or between them and Japan, remain in essence covered by *host country* regulation in all their aspects. So are financial services between an EU Member State and non-EU members.

---

[17] See also D Gail, J Norton and M O'Neal, 'The Foreign Bank Supervision Enhancement Act of 1991', (1992) 26 *International Lawyer* 993.
[18] See for the distinctions in this respect under EU case law, ss 2.2.3 and 3.1.2 below. See also n 13 above.

However, under the so-called Basle Concordat reached within the Bank of International Settlement (BIS) in 1983 (earlier efforts went back to 1975), following the Herstatt bankruptcy in Germany, certain rules were developed for the *consolidated supervision* of *commercial banks* (only), to the extent they were involved in cross-border banking activities through *foreign branches*.[19] It was in essence based on home country supervision worldwide, especially in terms of capital adequacy.

Following the *BCCI* case, this Concordat was amended in 1992. Although maintaining in principle home country rule if there was adequate home country regulation, foreign branching became subject to the prior approval of both home and host regulator (as we shall see a model not maintained in the EU Second Banking Directive). Under these guidelines, it was suggested that the home regulator also be given powers to gather information on the foreign operations of the bank in question. Host regulators could impose restrictive measures on such operations if basic standards were not maintained by the home regulator or enforced by it in branches of their banks in foreign countries. Although the Basle Concordat is not a binding document, it is, like all BIS policy statements, highly authoritative and generally implemented by banking regulators worldwide.[20]

The issue of international *conglomerate supervision*[21] (as distinguished from consolidated supervision per function) also received attention from the BIS in 1992 when IOSCO produced a paper. It is especially important for international active universal banks. Internationally, there are special conglomerate dangers in regulatory gaps and inconsistencies which may lead to regulatory arbitrage. At that level there arise even more questions than domestically (see the discussion in section 1.1.6 above) concerning the most appropriate regulatory contact point, information exchange and co-operation in and responsibility for crisis management. It is again a matter of proper division of home and host regulation and supervision. The related issues are far away from a satisfactory solution and have been the subject of many studies.

An *ad hoc* Tripartite Group representing the three financial service industries represented by the BIS, IOSCO and IAIS (see sections 1.1.13 and 2.5.1 below for these organisations) reported in 1995. In 1999 there was a further report of an *ad hoc* Joint Forum, more formally set up in 1996, considering some regulatory framework for supervising international financial conglomerates. Major issues were identified like (a) a common measurement technique for regulatory capital, (b) a common fit and proper test for managers, (c) a

---

[19] The first Concordat dates from 1975, see Basle Committee, *Report to the Governors on the Supervision of Banks' Foreign Establishments* (Sept. 1975). See for the revised 1983 Concordat (following an earlier paper of 1978), Basle Committee, *Principles for the Supervision of Banks' Foreign Establishments* (May 1983). There was a mostly technical 1990 Supplement, see Basle Committee, *Report on International Developments in Banking Supervision* ch VI (Sept. 1990). There followed a restatement of minimum standards in 1992 following the BCCI collapse, see Basle Committee, *Report on International Developments in Banking Supervision* ch VI (1992). In 1996, there was a report with 29 recommendations to improve the supervision of cross-border banking more generally, see Basle Committee, *Report on International Developments in Banking Supervision* ch VI (Sept 1996). This was followed in 1997 by 25 Core Principles of banking supervision at national levels prepared with 15 emerging market countries, see Basle Committee, *Core Principles for Effective Bank Supervision* (Sept 1997). It was accompanied by a Compendium that restated all the main Basle policy recommendations since it began issuing them in 1975, see Basle Committee, *Compendium of Documents Produced by the Basle Committee on Banking Supervision* (April 1997).

[20] The EU incorporated the original and the amendments to the Concordat in the First Consolidated Banking Supervision Dir of 1983 superseded by the Second Dir of 1993: see also ss 2.3.2 and 3.4.5 below. In the USA, legislation preceded the revision of the Concordat in 1993 in the Foreign Bank Supervision Enhancement Act of 1991 (FBSEA 1991) which made the establishment of all foreign bank branches, agencies and representative offices in the USA subject to Federal approval and insists that the host country regulators must be confident that the home country regulator is capable of adequate consolidated supervision before they can defer to its supervision.

[21] GA Walker, *Conglomerate Law and International Financial Market Control in International Banking Regulation: Law, Policy and Practice,* (The Hague, Kluwer, 2000), 165.

common exchange of information regime, (d) the concept of the lead regulator. This issue of lead regulator, information co-ordinator or lead co-ordinator and its role presents the most problems.

Is it a mere co-ordinator or also the proper authority to determine the acceptable level of risk on the basis of an own assessment and (pre-) crisis management. This could also affect the position of any lenders of last resort. In these aspects the BIS, IOSCO, the Tripartite Group and the Joint Forum so far failed to give decisive guidance.[22] The Bank of England is traditionally in favour of an international lead regulator or some similar authority to supervise the activities of (conglomerate) international financial institutions. It is a very ambitious position. The US (and within it more in particular the FED) is resisting whilst other countries also have expressed concern on the effect on national regulatory regimes. Pending agreement on these essential points, the effort so far is largely relegated to the collection and dissemination of information.

The EU followed the BIS Concordat in the First Consolidated Banking Directive of 1983 followed by a Second Consolidated Banking Directive in 1992 which also included holding company structures. Another Prudential Supervision Directive was adopted in 1995 following the amended 1992 BIS Concordat. It is now incorporated in the Credit Institution Directive of 2000 which consolidated a number of banking directives. There is also a draft EU Directive in the area of prudential supervision of financial conglomerates operating within the EU, which aims at appropriate capital measures (avoiding any multiple gearing), overall solvency rules, risk exposure rules, intra group transaction rules and rules concerning the professionalism of management. It will be more extensively discussed in section 3.4.5 below.

In the USA, legislation preceded the revision of the Concordat in 1993 in the Foreign Bank Supervision Enhancement Act of 1991 (FBSEA 1991). It made the establishment of all foreign bank branches, agencies and representative offices subject to federal approval whilst insisting that the host country (American) regulators had to be confident that the home country regulator was capable of adequate consolidated supervision before deferring to it.

1.1.13   The Modern International Financial Architecture

In the foregoing, organisations like the Bank of International Settlements (BIS), which is the bank of the central banks located in Basel, and the International Organisation of Securities Commissions (IOSCO), located in Montreal, were already mentioned. The one is, through its Banking Supervision Committee, a think-tank for banking regulation, the other for securities regulation. Neither has regulatory powers of its own. The BIS Committee on Banking Supervision remains the most important as it has the world's most important Central Banks behind it. In the field of insurance, a similar organisation has been formed (the International Association of Insurance Supervisors or IAIS, also in Basel).

---

[22] See for the 1992 BIS paper, Basle Committee, 'Principles for the Supervision of Financial Conglomerates' in *Report on International Developments in Banking Supervision* ch VI (Sept 1992). See for the 1993 IOSCO paper, *Principles for the Supervision of Financial Conglomerates* (Dec 1992). The Tripartite Report of July 1995 was published by the Basle Committee, 'A Report by the Tripartite Group of Bank, Securities, and Insurance Regulators', *Report on the Supervision of Financial Conglomerates* (July 1995). See for the Joint Forum in particular its *Progress Report* of April 9, 1997.

IOSCO and the IAIS are much looser organisations and have not acquired the same reputation as the BIS nor would they seem as effective. As we already saw, all mainly operate through studies although the BIS in its Basle Accord concerning capital adequacy and in its Concordat concerning international banking regulation clearly meant to set industry standards, which have indeed been largely implemented in the major industrialised countries.

There are also the Group of 7 (Industrialised Nations) or G-7 (after the admission of Russia now also referred to as the Group of 8 or G-8), the Group of 10 (Central Banks which in this connection mainly operate through the BIS) or G-10, the Group of 20 or G-20 set up by the G-7 in 1999 between systematically important countries, the Group of 22 (or Williard Group) also set up by the G-7 (in 1998) to study the stability of the international financial system. There is further the Group of 30, which is an informal industry group that produced some important studies in the field of systemic risk and global financial regulation.

IMF, IBRD, Worldbank, and OECD are also involved, the IMF particularly in connection with financial crisis management (like during the last decade the ones in Mexico, Russia, Asia and Argentina), and the OECD on regulatory reform (1997). In the IMF, a relevant recent development in this connection has been the transformation of the IMF Interim Committee, which was an informal ministerial body also in charge of the co-operation with the Worldbank, into the International Monetary and Financial Committee (IMFC) which considers international stability from the monetary and financial perspectives.

It is clear, however, that all these institutions, organisations, committees and groups, together in one form or another concerned with the international financial architecture, do not present more than a patchwork that operates without much co-ordination. At the moment the G-20, in which the IMF and Worldbank also participate, appears to be in the ascendancy. It is often referred to as the Financial Stability Forum (FSF) meant to get a better grip on world wide financial regulation in a broader sense (considering also the capital flows themselves), especially in terms of co-operation and co-ordination. Initially three working groups were set up under it to cover highly leveraged institutions, capital flows, and off-shore financial centres.

More specialist are longer standing bodies like the Committee for Payment and Settlement Systems (CPSS), which delivered important papers on payment systems (1999), and earlier on settlement risk (1996) and real time gross settlement (1977). The Committee on the Global Financial System (CGFS), formerly the Eurocurrency Standing Committee, also acts in a more specialised capacity.[23]

1.2   The Essentials of the (Commercial) Banking Business and its Regulation

1.2.1   Major Aspects of Banking. Supervision and the Role of Banks of Last Resort

The main task of commercial banks is to gather (a) deposits from the public, (b) provide loans, (c) organise payments, and (d) generally provide liquidity to the economies they

---

[23] See M Giovanoli, 'Architecture for the Global Financial Market: Legal Aspects of International Financial Standard Setting', in *International Monetary Law: Issues for the New Millennium* (2000), 1, concentrating on who is involved in the new rule formulation process, what the legal status of the new rules is and how they are being implemented. See also, for an overview GA Walker, *Financial Stability in International Banking Regulation: Law, Policy and Practice*, PART III (The Hague, Kluwer, 2000).

serve. This liquidity providing function is also referred to as the monetary function of banks.

It means that a proper banking system ensures that people and companies not only may safely park their money with banks in the form of deposits but will also have access thereto to retrieve their money or make (bank) payments. They may, if sufficiently creditworthy, also obtain further liquidity facilities from their banks like overdrafts, credit cards and additional loan facilities. As such, banks, if operating properly, fulfill a major economic and social role in providing reasonably cheaply and efficiently liquidity to the public coupled with deposit and payment facilities. In this sense, the banking system offers a vital recycling function. As was already noted in the previous sections, this function should be well distinguished from that of the capital markets which do so in a different manner by providing direct contact between capital providers (or investors) and capital seekers (or issuers) in terms of risk bearing capital (shares) or borrowings (bonds). That is the area of investment securities and investment services or investment banking which will be more extensively covered in section 1.3 below.

From a regulatory point of view, the essential feature of commercial banking is traditionally the public deposit-taking function. That was in fact still the point of departure in the UK banking laws as we saw (section 3 of the Banking Act 1987) now superseded by the Financial Services and Markets Act 2000 which does not define the activity (regardless of the EU definitions in this area) but makes the taking of deposits as a business a licensed activity. In the EU (Article 1 of the First and Second Banking Directives, now replaced by Article 1 of the Credit Institutions Directive) and elsewhere in case law,[24] this deposit-taking function is often seen in combination with, and inseparable from the lending function. In the USA, on the other hand, the National Bank Act (12 USC Section 24) and, in Germany, the Banking Act (Section 1 (1)) rather use a list approach in which common activities of banks are enumerated. This raises the question which activity or minimum of activities makes an entity a bank which would lead to regulation, licencing and supervision.

There may here be a margin of doubt and there are in any event borderline cases: is e.g. deposit-taking for investment purposes outside the banking definition? It will depend on how the money is held. If *segregated* from the investment managers' own funds, there is no deposit. This illustrates a deposit's particular status. Making a deposit in a banking sense means giving up ownership rights and converting these into creditors rights against the deposit taking institution. This is a key distinction and demonstrates the *legal* essence of the bank deposit.[25]

In this connection, commonly requesting deposits as a down payment for the sale of goods or real estate is most certainly not banking activity. Neither is, in the UK, margin call activity under derivative contracts.[26] These moneys belong to clients. It shows that the *context* in which deposit-taking takes place must also be considered.

Banking laws will have to be specific to avoid here problems regarding their applicability and the regulatory jurisdiction of banking regulators. For commercial banks, traditionally the deposit-taking function attracted the most immediate regulatory attention: hence the

---

[24] *Comrs of the State Savings Bank of Victoria v Permewan, Wright Co Ltd* (1915) 19 CLR 457, 470.

[25] The creditor/debtor aspect of the relationship between banks and their clients was established early in common law, see *Foley v Hill* (1848) 2 HCL 28 and *Joachimson v Swiss Bank Corp*, [1921] 3KB 110, 127. In civil law, it follows more directly from its system of proprietary and contractual rights. It allows the bank to deal with client moneys as if they are its own and it need not account for its actions in respect of them to its current account holders and depositors. Although the bank is as a result an ordinary debtor in this situation, its treatment may still be somewhat different on the basis of custom and practicalities. Thus money that is due the client may be retrievable by the latter only upon proper notice at the proper branch, especially if large amounts are involved, but payment instructions can be less easily restricted in amount, although banks usually insist on a number of days for clearing.

[26] *SCF Finance Co Ltd v Masri (No 2)* [1987] QB 1002.

traditional regulatory concern for the safety of the deposits and the protection of depositors. In turn, this created a concern for the banking risks and the continued liquidity and solvency of each bank in the system. But as we saw in section 1.1.3 above, there are now also other regulatory concerns and considerations. One major one is that problems in (major) banks can seldom be seen in isolation. Illiquidity e.g. may easily affect other banks which have lent to the bank in trouble, if only through the inter-bank market, or because payments are expected from such a bank on behalf of their clients, but are not arriving. Thus the inter-bank lending and the payment system, and finally the general system of liquidity and payment, may become affected by illiquidity of one of the banks in the system.

Illiquidity of banks is a situation in which they are short of money to meet their payment obligations. It is important to realise that that does not need to mean that they are also insolvent. Economically, insolvency arises only when their total liabilities exceed their assets. Illiquidity may arise much earlier and is connected with an imbalance between liquid assets and liquid liabilities. It should be realised, however, that in legal terms, depending on the applicable bankruptcy laws, illiquidity of this nature may denote (legal) insolvency leading to bankruptcy proceedings but there could still be an economic surplus. Yet if a bank has long term outstanding loans (which under their own terms cannot be recalled at will but are repayable only on the agreed maturity date) and short term repayment obligations e.g. in respect of demand deposits, it may become squeezed when too many depositors need to have their moneys returned, which could lead to a technical bankruptcy even if the bank is economically not insolvent.

Thus there will be problems if a bank cannot fulfill its payment obligations as they mature, raising the spectre of its liquidation in bankruptcy proceedings. Once this becomes known, other depositors are likely to also want to retrieve their money. It will make the situation only worse and may be the start of a *bank run*. As just mentioned, other banks may then also become involved as they may not be repaid on any inter-bank loans earlier given to the bank in liquidity difficulties. It may engender a liquidity crisis at these banks as well. Here we see the beginning of what is now called *systemic risk*, the contagion of a whole banking system particularly resulting from the inter-bank and payment linkages between the banks in the system. As was already discussed above, one major bank in difficulty may thus destabilise the whole system and a banking system in trouble may destabilise the entire economy. Liquidity dries up altogether and a credit crunch is likely to follow.

The payment system may itself become affected as bankruptcy of one member may create complications in electronic clearing, see also chapter III, section 1.2.4. The result may be that payments may altogether become difficult to make or receive. The inclination for citizens is then to keep their money under the mattress and make and receive payments in cash. It is back to a lower form of economic life. Companies cannot operate in this manner and for private citizens it is likely that there is too little money in circulation to accommodate all their cash needs. Barter may be the next step and the modern economy dissolves. This is not academic. It happened in Russia in the 1990s when a proper banking and payment system failed to develop.

No wonder that Central Banks will often step in. They will not then do so as banking supervisors (which in any event they are no longer in countries like the UK, Germany and Japan). For regulators it is too late and supervision will be shown to have failed. Central Banks will rather enter as so-called *lenders of last resort*. In that capacity, they traditionally provide liquidity to the system. That means that they will lend to banks with temporary liquidity shortages, usually against the security of a bank's bond portfolio or through repos of these bonds. There needs to be nothing sinister in this, as banks may find that on certain days large deposits are withdrawn which may return the next day. This function of lender of last resort is therefore a key function in the operation of a normal banking system.

It may, however, be expanded to help banks that are in more permanent trouble or are even insolvent. In that case, there may not be much security left and it may not be asked. It is strictly speaking a *misuse* of the function of lender of last resort, see also section 1.1.4 above, and it should not be done if only because Central Banks do not have unlimited funds. Central Banks that are also banking supervisors may be particularly tempted, however, to help in this manner to hide their regulatory failure. This is a potent argument in favour of depriving Central Banks from their supervisory role as has been done in the UK and is technically also the situation in Germany. However, systemic concerns are likely to be invoked to justify the practice.

In fact, as depositors will now often be independently insured through deposit insurance or guarantee schemes, their protection may no longer be the prime motivation for support in this manner, although there is mostly a limit on what they can recover under the scheme. As just mentioned, it is systemic risk and also the risks to the payment system that is here the more likely modern justification although banking supervisors and lenders of last resort may also become concerned about the trust in their banking system and its reputation internationally. If banks of last resort ultimately do not have the funds, the survival of the banking system becomes truly a political issue and a matter of tax payers' money.

It was already noted in section 1.1.4 above that (the expectation of) a wholesale bail-out of banks in this manner may make them (even) less prudent in the risks they take and may itself encourage their irresponsible behaviour. This is *moral hazard* or a situation in which the rescuer or the fact of its existence generates itself the need for rescues. It may thus be the regulator or supervisor that may become *captured* by the industry and by its survival at all cost. It turns the table completely. Even banks of last resort or the public purse may be so captured. Deposit guarantee schemes may similarly create *moral hazard*, a reason why they are often so structured as not to give full protection.

Moral hazard is now an important consideration for Central Banks[27] operating as banks of last resort or for politicians in govermental bail-outs. Some Central Banks, like the German Bundesbank, do not accept the role of lenders of last resort in these circumstances as a matter of principle. This is also the position of the European Central Bank. It might not, however, prevent the German government from organising a bail-out in Germany when needed. In fact, in Germany there is a Liquidity Consortium Bank that may do so and in which the Bundesbank takes part. Since 1974 it may grant short-term assistance to banks with temporary problems (it is sometimes described as the lender of next-to-last resort). It may become a model for the Eurozone.

These are situations of danger that proper banking regulation and supervision will try to prevent or minimise, although it may immediately be added that even if modern banking regulation has become more sophisticated and banking supervision more intensive as we shall see, the incidence of bank illiquidity and subsequent bankruptcy seems not to have abated as the savings and loans situation in the early 1990s in the US, the Russian banking crisis after 1998, and the ongoing Japanese and Chinese banking crises show. Especially the capital that modern bank regulation requires in banks, see sections 2.5.2*ff* below, cannot provide an adequate cushion to guard against major macro-economic shocks nor in fact against micro-economic wrong decisions or mismanagement. Also the regulatory limitation on large exposures to single borrowers, which is now common, may not do much in

---

[27] See also RM Lastra, 'Lender of Last Resort: An International Perspective' (1999) 48 *International and Comparative Law Quarterly,* 339.

practice to preserve the health of the banking system. Modern banking regulation can therefore hardly minimise systemic risk. It would require much more drastic action in the direction of imposing much higher capital or narrow banking, see section 1.2.4 below.

As a consequence, in times of crises the protection of the commercial banking system remains largely a matter for banks of last resort and especially for governments. They will (usually) take a decision *after* illiquidity and insolvency has happened. The safeguarding of the banking system remains therefore ultimately a matter of public policy rather than of regulation. It suggests that *de facto* the entire banking industry remains subject to and dependent on an inherent public guarantee. This is the 'too large to fail' philosophy in respect of at least the major financial institutions. Authorisation and supervision could then be seen as the natural *quid pro quo* and an expression of commercial banking being in fact a supervised semi-public industry largely because of its liquidity providing and payment system functions in the public interest. Supervision may at the same time increase the confidence in the system as a whole but is unlikely by itself to save it from disaster.

1.2.2   Types of Banks and their Operations

Deposit taking from the public, lending to the public, or more generally providing liquidity to and organising payments for the public is the traditional remit of what is usually called *commercial* banking but these banks may do much more. Thus they often act as security brokers for account holders and provide in this manner investment services. In this capacity, they will act as buyers and sellers of investment securities in their own name but for the risk and account of their clients. It is a natural extension of their commercial banking role as they will be in a good position to deal with investment transactions for those who hold accounts with them. They may go further and also arrange alternative funding for their corporate clients, especially in the capital markets which for the best borrowers may often prove cheaper than bank loans. It is the issue of des-intermediation to be discussed in section 1.2.7 below. They may in that context even engage in underwriting activities. Subsequently they may actively trade in the securities so issued and even make markets in them.

These underwriting and trading activities are traditionally the remit of *investment banks* and, if combined with commercial banking, they make for so-called *universal banks.* That is the continental European model. It is less common in the UK and was forbidden in the USA under the Glass-Steagall Act of 1933 (Section 20 of the Securities Act) when, during the Great Depression, the combination of commercial banking and underwriting risk in other than government and municipal securities was deemed too risky for commercial banks unless such underwriting was only incidental to their business. It was one way to limit banking risk, therefore through separation.[28] Under pressure of des-intermediation and the resulting reduction in commercial banking income, the Glass-Steagall Act was ultimately repealed in 1999 by the Financial Services Modernisation Act (or Gramm-Leach-Bliley Act). Full affiliation between banks, insurance companies and securities companies is now permitted but only through a bank holding company, see section 1.1.11 above. Straight mergers are therefore still not possible.

---

[28] This concept of incidental business was lately much expanded, whilst so-called Section 20 companies have been authorised since 1989 as subsidiaries of bank holding companies provided their underwriting income (from non-government securities) did not exceed 25 per cent of their gross income. The 1999 Gramm-Leach-Bliley Act does not affect Section 20 companies but diminish the need for them.

Investment banks (in the UK often called merchant banks, which, however, also tend to do some lending to their clients and often also take deposits, at least from companies, and need then to be licenced as deposit taker) may do much more than underwriting and trading investment securities. They may have a corporate finance department giving corporate advice on how best to structure the balance sheet of their client companies or even their activities. Advice on how best to fund is closely related to this activity as is the merger and acquisition advice practice. Investment banks may also engage in brokerage activity and investment management. They usually also take an active view of their own investments and tend to make money out of their own investment portfolio activity in which they may take substantial risk balanced by up-to-date risk management systems and skills. They may also lend money although they normally do not or only incidentally. One thing they cannot do is deposit taking. That would require a (commercial) banking license and turn them into a universal bank.

If commercial banks also acquire an insurance component, again increasingly common in Continental Europe, we often speak of *bancassurance*. In that case, the insurance activity remains, however, usually in a separate legal entity because of its different regulation and capital requirements. Again in the USA, the combination of banking and insurance was precluded by law unless the activity was incidental.[29] They may now be combined through holding companies in which each of these functions still remain distinct at the subsidiaries level, see again section 1.1.11 above.

There are also so-called *non-banks*. These are institutions that provide loans or financing to the public but do not — and are not allowed to — fund themselves through deposits. Finance leasing and factoring companies are examples, but also investment banks if offering loan facilities. Because they are not allowed to take deposits, they create a lesser regulatory concern except as subsidiaries of (universal) banks and are therefore usually unregulated from a banking point of view (investment banks may need authorisation for other activities). They fund themselves through retained earnings, bank loans or through bond issues in the capital markets. Investment funds may also fund themselves additionally in that manner and may in that case become highly leveraged. That is a usual approach in hedge funds, see also section 1.4.9 below. Again, since they are not allowed to take deposits from the public and must keep all client funds segregated, they have remained unregulated except to the extent that they may solicit public participation in the capital of their fund.

Banks extending loans to non-banks (or indeed any other bank in or outside the interbank market) or to more speculative institutions like hedge funds or real estate investment companies, must determine the credit of their borrowers and watch it carefully. This is for them a question of *credit risk*, which is inherent in all their lending activity, all the more so if loans are granted to corporates and individuals. They may try to limit this risk by asking for security (collateral), as in mortgage lending or under floating charges, see section 1.2.3 below. Under applicable secured transactions laws, many other types of collateral lending may be possible. Another way of containing the credit risk is through entering *covenants* in the loan documentation under which loans may be called in under certain circumstances, for example in the case of some act of default in other relationships of the borrower. This is often referred to as *cross-default*.

Banking regulators will particularly watch the credit risk exposure of commercial banks and set limits or more likely require specific capital against each type of lending activity depending on the perceived credit risk of such lending. Secured lending and lending to governments are generally deemed less risky in this sense and may therefore attract lower

---

[29] *Nationsbank of North Carolina v Variable Annuity Life Insurance Co*, 115 Sup Ct. 810 (1995).

regulatory capital requirements. This is the essence of capital adequacy regulation for banks, see sections 2.5.2*ff* below. In this manner, lending to speculative institutions, like hedge funds may also be indirectly curtailed. Trying to regulate these institutions directly, even if considered desirable, would probably only lead to them moving offshore. Of course, commercial and investment banks can also move if they do not like their regulatory regime, but since they must serve a much larger public and depend on much more infrastructure and proper manning levels, they are much less movable. Nevertheless, because of Glass-Steagall it was not unknown for American commercial banks, not able to engage in investment banking in the USA, to incorporate investment subsidiaries elsewhere (notably in London).

1.2.3 Commercial Banking Products, Unsecured and Secured Loans, Leasing, Repos and Receivable Financing, Syndicated Loans, Trade Finance and Project Finance

As we saw, one of the elementary tasks of commercial banks is to gather deposits from the public and to provide loans to their customers. On the funding side, they will also have access to the capital markets and may even borrow short term in the interbank market, therefore from other banks (mostly overnight) if they have such needs. They may also borrow from their own Central Bank, again usually short term to cover liquidity shortfalls. It is part of the bank of last resort function of Central Banks to do so, see also section 1.2.1 above.

On the asset side, they provide loans to the public. They will also invest in investment securities, notably government bonds, which are relatively safe and liquid, that can therefore be sold quickly in the case of liquidity needs and do not, as we shall see, normally attract a large capital adequacy penalty either. Liquidity needs will arise when there is a shortfall in new deposits or when old deposits are withdrawn. They may of course also result from banking losses connected with excessive operating expenses, failures of borrowers to service their debt, foreign exchange trading, swap book or losses or poor investments.

These investments are normally made through a bank's *treasury* operations in which a bank's money might be used for investment or more speculative purposes. In fact, these treasury operations of a bank could amount to hedge fund activities in which a bank may even become a large borrower in respect of these activities themselves. In all events, in large banks these treasury operations are likely to be of enormous proportions as are foreign exchange and swap book dealings. Another source of profits or losses may be in the mismatches between assets and liabilities which will be discussed in the next section together with an analysis of the other risks banks run.

On the loan side (or in the loan book) of a commercial bank, one might find many different types of products. First, loans may be *unsecured* or *secured*. Of the former, credit card, student loans and similar consumer debt are the most obvious categories. Then there are the overdraft facilities in the current or checking accounts. Amongst secured loans, the real estate mortgages are probably the best known. They are loans secured by dwelling houses or commercial property, therefore by specific, fixed assets or *collateral*.

There may also be loans secured by equipment, inventory, or accounts receivable. They are special in so far that they may entail so-called *floating charges* which cover collateral that may vary from day to day as the composition of inventory and accounts receivables of a borrower is subject to constant change, see more in particular chapter IV, section 1.6.7. Under floating charges, the collateral (or security objects) provided will change accordingly so that goods that are sold are freed from the charge but new inventory is automatically subject to it. Thus future assets may be covered in the charge with the security interest relating back to and receiving their rank from the date of the security agreement rather than from the date the goods are produced or the receivables emerge.

Receivables that are paid will in this approach reduce the loans or may be retained as working capital and new receivables will then automatically support what remains outstanding. These various possibilities are best developed in Article 9 of the Uniform Commercial Code (UCC) in the US, see for a comparative study of the collateral laws in the major industrial countries more in particular chapter V.

A bank may also engage in more complicated funding activities like *finance leasing*, *repo financing* and the factoring of receivables or *receivable financing*. They are likely to present conditional sales of assets to the bank, techniques discussed in chapter V and summarised in chapter IV section 1.6.

Another aspect of a bank's activities is *trade financing*. This concerns the issuing of letters of credit or other types of guarantees, arranging collections and discounting bills of exchange. There are often important international legal aspects to consider in this activity, that were discussed in chapter III. Important as they are, these activities do not, however, directly result in loans. Normally a bank is reimbursed immediately for the payments it so makes and paid a fee for these services. Whilst trade financing used to be an important business and included the discounting of bills of exchange, even to the point that there were specialised trade banks, this is now less common and with the improvement of communications worldwide, trade finance activity has relatively declined in banks, even though especially letters of credit continue to constitute an important banking service.

Syndicated loans and *project financing* are other important modern commercial banking (loan) products, normally associated with large scale financings, which, because of their size or the location of the project, often acquire an international flavour.

In *syndicated loans*, banks group together to extend credit to large borrowers who may be corporations, public entities or even states. These loans often have a *standby* function as credit line and may not then be (fully) drawn down. In that sense, they are of interest also to borrowers, corporate or other, who would otherwise access the capital markets directly which would require, however, an immediate draw down. Banks receive a fee for these standby facilities even if not used. An alternative for large borrowers is here the issuance of short term commercial paper or euronotes or even medium term notes.

Syndicated loans may also serve a bridging function and are then of a temporary or short term nature only, e.g. where a take-over has to be immediately financed whilst more permanent financing will be determined later, often by making use of direct access to the capital markets (through the issuing of new bonds or shares).

The advantage of syndicated loans for borrowers is that they constitute one loan package and allow corporate treasurers to deal with only one *agent bank* (for the entire group) rather than with a multitude of banks that each require their own terms and documentation. The group itself may be small and be constituted by the major house banks of a borrower. They may also be large and project oriented like in the case of the original Eurotunnel financing in 1987 which involved around 160 banks in various layers of the syndicate.

The agent or syndicate arranger is usually appointed by the borrower and will approach other banks to form a consortium. In such a structure, there may even be more than one arranger or there may be co-arrangers or sub-arrangers, also called lead, co-lead, managers or co-managers. They are usually the largest contributors in the group who thus become entitled to some of the arranger and management fees. All will share in the participation fee and in the annual facility or commitment fee. Sometimes the treasury department of the borrower retains itself the role of lead manager.

The arranger may undertake the syndication on a best effort basis or may constitute within the syndicate an underwriting group that will guarantee the completion of the facility against a further fee. As just mentioned, there may be different layers of borrowing in terms of length of commitment and maturity of any loans drawn down. Some of them may even be subordinated, especially when syndicated loans are merger or project finance related.

There may be a secondary market in these participations. It means that they can be 'traded', but the legal nature of the commitment or obligation is such that normal trading may not be anticipated. That is commonly reserved for assets and not for liabilities. Stand-by commitments or liabilities can only be transferred through (a form of) novation. If loans have been extended, the right to interest and principal may be assignment but both novation and assignments require various forms of borrower involvement and co-operation depending on the applicable law, see also chapter IV, section 1.7.5. A way around these formalities is granting a *sub-participation* but this means that the original participant is not discharged and his balance sheet not cleaned.

Project finance is often associated with the financing of special capital projects in emerging economies but need not be limited to them. The idea is here that the bank financing is tied to a project and serviced *only* from the project's future cash flow. It could be said that the banks thus acquire an equity interest in the project itself. If there is a short fall in cash flow, the borrower is discharged. Legally, they are likely to receive the assets as collateral and, if possible under applicable law, also the cash flow as a future asset. If there is a specially incorporated company holding these assets, banks may receive a charge over the company's shares as well. Loans under this kind of facility may be syndicated and there may be different currency participants and subordinated debt participants (resulting in so-called *mezzanine* financing).

Besides the vital segregation of the project and its cash flow from the other business of the borrower and the details of the financing itself, the project will also receive considerable attention from the prospective financiers. Depending on the nature of the venture, the project may involve at the same time construction contracts, equipment contracts, labour contracts, independent expert feasibility studies and supervision arrangements, power and water supply agreements and insurance policies during the construction period. Often there is at least some combination of these features. There may also have to be in place relevant governmental licenses and undertakings, as to the applicable foreign exchange and tax regime and consents as to the retention of cash flows abroad. There need be assurances that after completion the necessary supply agreements for the operation of the project and sales or lifting agreements, will be in place and be implemented. Proper management with the necessary operating agreements (and experience) for the construction as well as the operating stage will often be another matter of great interest. They all concern the repayment viability of the project and its eventual completion, start up and continuation. As for the future income streams, they will have to be divided and the amounts to be set aside for the operations and the repayment of the loans will have to be determined in advance. Financiers may even reserve a percentage of net profits after full repayment.

Because of the multifaceted nature of this type of financing, the documentation is likely to be voluminous and complex. From the banks' perspective, risks must be limited in as far as possible. Covenants will normally be entered making loan advances dependent on continuing governmental approval and the successful completion of succeeding stages of the project. Applicable law and jurisdiction/arbitration clauses will also be considered for their effectiveness in eliminating or reducing the various risks (including legal risk) attached to the financing and to the project itself.

1.2.4   Commercial Banking Risks

In the foregoing, we spotted already a number of risks inherent in commercial banking, especially *credit* or *counterparty risk* which concerns the creditworthiness of borrowers. A bank will habitually counter them through diversification (if necessary promoted by securitisations or sub-participations), avoidance of large exposures to any single borrower, collateralisation, guarantees or credit derivatives, and covenants in loan agreements (which would allow a bank to call the loan when the debtors credit deteriorates). Several of these techniques were already discussed or will be discussed later. We also discussed liquidity crises and *systemic risk*, which in a preventive manner will be a more particular regulatory concern, where authorisation and prudential supervision are the more normal responses. As we saw, once a crisis occurs, the problems will shift from regulators to lenders of last resort and governments.

Especially in investment banks there will also be *position risk*. They are *underwriting and trading risks*. These risks are connected with securities positions and may also be referred to as *market risk* as they reflect the effect of market movements (and not of the counterparty's credit) on the value of the positions held. As all (commercial) banks manage large portfolios of securities in their own asset or treasury operations (commercial banks traditionally especially of government bonds and investment banks usually of more risky instruments besides their trading inventory), they also incur considerable position risk from that perspective. It was already mentioned that in modern times these portfolios are often very large and may even be run like highly geared hedge funds, see for these funds section 1.4.10 below. Position risk is managed through hedging especially with derivatives (options, futures and swaps), as will be explained in section 1.4 below, and through diversification. In respect of tradable securities in which there is a market price, these positions are likely to be valued on a daily basis. This is called 'mark to market', so that profits and losses are immediately transparent and realised (in the daily profit and loss account of a bank).

Thus the value of fixed bonds varies according to the prevailing interest rates in the market. If they go up, a fixed rate bond portfolio is worth proportionately less. Even in its loan book a bank incurs position risk. This would be clear if these loans were also marked to market on a daily basis as interests fluctuate in the market, thus affecting the value of the loan book. Lower market interest rates mean a higher value for fixed rate loans and *vice versa*. Marking to market of the loan book would mean regular revaluation on the basis of current interest rate movements. This is uncommon, but it is nevertheless clear that when interest rates go up, a fixed interest rate loan portfolio is worth less and there is a loss which may, however, be temporary (depending on interest rate movements being reversed). It means that (barring credit risk) even though the loan will be repaid in full on the maturity date, a bank would have done better if it had lent for shorter periods.

Another common risk in connection with securities activity is *settlement risk*. It is the risk that arises when market positions are taken and assets are bought or sold or options or futures are acquired in them. These positions may not settle on the agreed day because of a default of the counter party or a hitch in the settlement system, as a consequence of which there may be no delivery of the underlying securities whilst payment has already been made (or *vice versa*). The loss of a deal in this manner may also deprive the bank concerned of the profit in the position or, if used as a hedge, of this protection.

The so-called *Herstatt risk* is a closely connected risk and derives more directly from risks inherent in the payment system. It arose when the Herstatt bank in Cologne went bankrupt in 1972. In its foreign exchange dealings some counter-parties had already provided it with Deutschmarks in Germany whilst they were receiving only later on the same day the countervalue in US dollars from Herstatt in New York. It is a question of *simultaneity*, which is here often disturbed because different currencies are mostly settled through their own Central Banks which may operate in different time zone's. Euro settlement therefore comes before US dollar settlement and yen settlement before Euro settlement. Because of the intervening bankruptcy of Herstatt, foreign exchange creditors were not paid the US dollar amounts and became competing creditors in respect of them.

To limit settlement risk, proper settlement systems centred on payment against documents (CAD) or proper clearing and netting facilities, see for payments Chapter III, section 1.2.4, or central counterparties (CCP) facilities like in derivative trading, see also section 1.4.4, are here possible modern protections.

In respect of the investment portfolio, liquidity risk may acquire a special meaning even for commercial banks. As we saw, liquidity risk is the risk that a bank may not have sufficient cash to meet its repayment obligations in respect of the deposits made with it. Its loan book is by definition illiquid. But even if it has invested some of its money in eg bonds, the further aspect of liquidity risk is that these investments may not be easy to sell or to reduce to money in other ways when needed except at a (substantial) discount. A bank must therefore take care that its investments are readily saleable and will therefore mostly invest in government securities traded on regular official markets.

Regulators will be concerned that commercial banks engaging in their various activities will have sufficient capital to support the different risks they take in this connection and can absorb any resulting losses. They will insist at the same time that the banks will have sufficiently knowledgeable staff to trace these risks (and also conduct a proper asset and liability management) and maintain proper systems. This is *operational risk*. It should at the same time reduce the systemic risk.

A bank should also be aware of the legal ramifications of its business (*legal risk*), eg in the loan business and the products it uses in this connection (like project financing or syndicated loans), the legal effectiveness of the collateral it negotiates (like mortgages or receivable and inventory financing) and of its hedges, including the legal aspects of derivatives trading and swaps and of netting arrangements in clearing and settlement, the legal aspects of its involvement in the payment system, and of its other activities like finance leasing, repo financing, securitisations. The overall banking relationship with its clients through the current account and its rights and obligations in this connection should also be legally clear (see for this aspect more in particular section 1.2.8 below).

As was already observed before, it is a fact that notwithstanding much supervising, greater sophistication in it and tightening of it, commercial bank insolvency remains frequent. The South American crises and the savings and loan situation in the USA greatly affected the banking system there in the 1980s and large government bail-outs became necessary which cost the US tax payer in the region of $200 billion. In Scandinavia, whole banking systems had to be saved in the 1990s. In Japan, the banking sector awaits rescue for which as a start the equivalent $500 billion was set aside but the total may easily rise to $1000 billion or more. Chinese banks are in a similar position in connection with loan burdens derived from a centrally, state run economy. Large bank write-offs were necessary in France during the last few years where Crédit Lyonais had to be saved several times. Even in Switzerland, large write-offs were required in 1996 in connection with real estate lending. And so it goes.

In Russia, the banking system is in permanent crisis and, as at 2003, it still seems impossible to create a modern banking system there. Few deposits are offered as banks were often used by their owners for speculative investment and not for the loan business. Russian banks did not therefore assume their liquidity-providing function whilst their payment function was undermined by the general lack of confidence in them. It holds the whole economy back.

The situation in the Far East since 1997, especially in South Korea, highlights in the meantime another key risk in banking: the *mismatch* between assets and liabilities or between short-term borrowing in foreign currency and longer-term lending in the local currency to local borrowers with doubtful economic projects.

Traditionally, all banks take here a number of risks to make money. Most normal is for banks to fund themselves through short-term deposits at low interest rates and to lend longer at higher interest rates. In fact, this *mismatch* is fundamental to the commercial banking business and the source of its normal profitability. It allows banks to pay their operating expenses and eventually some dividend to their shareholders. It is a form of position risk and there is here a basic exposure of all banks which requires them to take a view on their ability to continue to attract short-term funds against a reasonable price on a continuous basis.

Other mismatches may follow: a bank may borrow in the capital markets or inter-bank markets at floating interest rates but lend in fixed, or *vice versa*. In its *asset and liability management* (ALM), a prudent bank will balance its assets and liabilities as part of its ordinary activity on a daily basis. Its own (government) bond portfolio, through which it is in essence a lender to governments, will allow it to make here rapid adjustments by selling or buying certain classes of bonds in terms of interest rate structures, currencies and maturities. More rapidly still, it may take here the necessary steps through the modern derivatives (option, futures or swap) markets, the operations of which will be explained in sections 1.4.2*ff* below. It will allow it to make instant adjustments in exposure on both the asset and liability sides of the balance sheet.

Thus all commercial banks will have to be and are mismatched to some extent to make money. It is a *normal* banking risk, although in essence a type of position risk. Since at least from the perspective of its shareholders, this is what banking is all about, regulators do not normally control that risk as they do not want to become involved in the bank's business itself. It could make them directly liable for a bank's failings. They focus on credit risk and increasingly on position or portfolio risk and settlement risk instead (and now also on operational risk as we shall see) but again not in order to run the positions themselves but only in terms of setting and implementing general restrictive rules for the entire industry, of which the *capital adequacy* rules are the most obvious, see sections 2.5.2*ff* below. The modern approach is further increasingly to require *disclosure* of large positions and mismatches. Banking regulators will also regularly verify whether banks have sufficient (risk management and other) systems in place at least to measure their positions and mismatches on a constant basis. Again this is a matter of operational risk.

1.2.5   Broad and Narrow Banking. Market Based Monitoring of Banks

All in all, commercial banking has often proved to be a dangerous business. Instances of insolvency remain frequent. It is a f unction of the low capital base with which a bank is allowed to operate. The consequence of this low capital is the possible loss of the liquidity providing function of banks, systemic collapse, and concern about the continuing efficiency of the payment system, without which no modern country can function. It may render regulators, central banks (as lenders of last resort), and even the public purse (when a whole banking system starts collapsing) the effective captives of the banks. As we saw in section 1.2.4 above, moral hazard is effectively built-in to this system. Moreover, the operations of commercial banks may lead, in good times, to an autonomous extra infusion of liquidity in the system that may well prove inflationary whilst, in bad times when the survival of these banks themselves may be at stake, they are likely to restrict liquidity causing an autonomous deflationary effect. Of course, in their monetary policies, central banks may affect the short-term interest rates (or even the longer term by buying government bonds) and thereby try to slow down or accelerate lending activity. Yet banks play here distinctive roles and the short-term interest rate mechanism in which central banks have a major say, may not always be determining or fully effective in providing extra liquidity or in curtailing it. In any event, there are likely to be considerable time lags.

Whatever the reasons, banking regulation either by central banks or other banking supervisors (in Germany and the UK where banking supervision is not or no longer the preserve of the central bank) have, as we saw, never been fully successful in preventing large banking collapses with their potential effect on depositors, liquidity and the payment system. As already suggested before, the banking industry functions in essence as a public utility that operates in a private manner subject to an implied government guarantee, see also section 1.2.1 above *in fine*. It makes liquidity cheaper and easier to obtain and also allows for the operation of a payment system that is often cross-subsidised by other banking activities or considered a function of deposit taking. It may justify a lower deposit interest rate.

It illustrates the innate instability of the commercial banking system which regulation has hardly proved to reduce. This situation has given rise to other ideas. Especially the notion of *narrow banking* has been repeatedly put forward as an alternative. It does not allow consumer deposits and the payment system to be operated by commercial or universal banks in the present manner, therefore as integral parts of their overall business. They would be required to split off their consumer deposit-taking business and put deposits into separate money market funds with limited investment possibilities largely confined to the government bond markets in matching currencies in the nature of a money market fund. Equally, the payment activity would be split out into a separate activity with its own capital through a separate subsidiary. Regulatory supervision would essentially be limited to these two activities and would not have to be heavy.

For the rest, banks would be run as non-banks, fund themselves in the capital markets or through deposits from corporate clients (also called wholesale clients) as some banks that have no private customers, like J.P. Morgan in the USA (before it became part of the Chase Manhattan group) and the former IBJ (now part of Mizuho) in Japan, always did. They would be essentially unregulated and allowed to go under. Present generous capital adequacy requirements (which may be as low as 8 per cent of risk assets as we shall see) would disappear and banks would have to capitalise themselves better as they would otherwise have difficulty in attracting funds (including deposits) in competition with other banks. This in itself would reduce the risk of their failure and moral hazard would disappear although, to preserve liquidity, central banks might still not be indifferent to systemic risk even though the payment system would be separately protected.

Overall, liquidity would probably suffer however, as it may become less easy for small depositors to arrange overdraft facilities and credit cards, which would also become more costly. Even for companies, banks would have to be more careful. Because of the need for extra capital, all bank services would become more expensive. Banks would have to be run as normal businesses and no longer as businesses indirectly guaranteed and therefore subsidised by the public purse as if they were semi-public institutions. Whilst adopting commercial standards of behaviour, the costs of the system would be shifted to customers and shareholders, therefore to those most directly concerned, rather than be borne by taxpayers. This is the key element of this approach.

A variant of the narrow banking approach is the one in which banks would fully back their low interest rate deposits by safe liquid assets such as treasury bills and commercial paper set aside for the purpose and legally ring-fenced.

Another idea is to have banks issue *subordinated public debt*, which is debt ranking lower than deposits and other borrowings but just above share capital. The daily pricing of these securities would provide a market assessment of a bank's risks and regulators could on this basis order banks to reduce risk (or increase capital). There would no longer be dependence on more or less sophisticated risk management systems but the market view would determine regulators' action and the level of the required capital. Lower valuation of these subordinated bonds could soon drive these banks out of business as the cost of more capital would become too high to compete.

As already noted, banking is a dangerous business. History shows that commercial banks in their present operations often take too much risk as measured against their capital. They are allowed to do so in order to provide random liquidity to the whole economic system and provide cheap payment services. The corollary is the implied governmental guarantee and tax payers' exposure. The price for banks is regulation, even if it has proven to be ineffective in preventing financial crises. It seems, however, to be able to create a semblance of order and a façade of respect that underpins the public's confidence in the system. No less important is in this connection the deposit guarantee scheme. Together they make most retail banking customers largely indifferent as to which bank they use.

1.2.6 *Commercial Banking Regulation and Banking Regulators.*
International Aspects

Commercial banking regulation, as all financial regulation, everywhere follows largely the pattern already established above in section 1.1.1: authorisation (with requirements of fitness, reputation, infrastructure and systems, capital adequacy and business plan or profile), and prudential supervision. This pattern will be more fully discussed below. For banking regulators there is traditionally less interest in conduct of business and product supervision and more in institutional regulation as we saw. As already mentioned, another important aspect of modern bank regulation is the creation and operation of deposit guarantee schemes for deposit holders. However, the protection of deposit holders may vary greatly under these schemes. In the USA, it is US $100,000 per depositor, in Germany it is unlimited. In the UK, the covered amount is much smaller.

In Europe, Central Banks are normally also the banking regulators except in Germany where there is a separate agency and in the UK where banking supervision is now brought together with the supervision of the other financial services under the new Financial Services Authority (FSA). The emergence of the European Central Bank (ECB) which issues the Euro and is, within the European System of Central Banks (ESCB), in charge of monetary policy in countries that adopted the new currency on 1 January 1999, does not in itself change the banking supervisory system. Member State Central Banks or alternative national banking supervisors continue to be in charge of bank supervision although arguments have been made for centralising this function also within the EU.[30]

---

[30] See M Andenas and C Hadjiemmanuil, 'Banking Supervision, the Internal Market and European Monetary Union', [1998] *European Business Law Review*, 149. The problem of the decentralised banking regulation after

The present system in the EU only requires co-operation between supervisors: see Articles 28 and 56 of the 2000 Credit Institution Directive that consolidated the earlier Banking Directives, Article 23 of the Investment Services Directive, and Articles 7(3) and 9(4) of the Capital Adequacy Directive. See for these Directives further sections 3.2, 3.3, 3.4 and 3.5 below.

In the USA, there is a more fractured system of banking supervision which has always been characterised by a fear of big banks and big banking regulators. First, there is in the USA the division between state and national banks and further the limitation on branching, see also section 1.1.11 above. There is also a different supervisory regime in respect of them, with further differences depending on whether state banks have deposit insurance or not. In this system, national banks are regulated for safety and soundness by the Office of the Comptroller of the Currency (OCC) while state banks are regulated by the states subject to federal limits, but state banks that have deposit insurance are also regulated by the Federal Reserve Board (Fed) if they are Fed members (like all other banks that are such members),[31] and otherwise by the Federal Deposit Insurance Board (FDIC).

As regards international aspects of banking regulation, the Basle Concordat of the Bank of International Settlements (BIS) was already briefly discussed in section 1.1.12 above. Under it and its 1992 amendments, both the home and host regulator must approve foreign branching and in the supervision of the foreign branch the host regulator will only defer to the home regulator's supervision if it is comfortable with the supervisory capability of the home regulator. The BIS itself is the bank of the central banks, was originally created (in 1930) to manage German reparation payments and is directed by the central bank governors of the Group of Ten. It provides a regular meeting place for central bank governors and is also the think tank of the Group of Ten for banking regulation through its important Committee on Banking Supervision.

Whilst in modern cross-border banking the division of regulatory tasks between home and host country is thus well known, it was considerably tested in the BCCI case, where there was confusion about what was the host country: the country of incorporation of the bank (Luxembourg) or the place where it had its main operations (the UK).

As we shall see, the EU substantially incorporated a system allowing for home country rule: see also section 1.1.9 above. In this regard, both in the Preamble to the Second Banking Directive now superseded by the Credit Institution Directive and to the Investment Services Directive, the desirability of the combination of the registered and head offices within the same jurisdiction was accepted to avoid confusion about who is the home regulator.

---

full implementation of the European Monetary Union (EMU) was early raised by B Eichengreen, *Should the Maastricht Treaty be Saved?* (Princeton Studies in International Finance No. 74, 1992), 42, and later by R Kinsella, 'The European Central Bank and the Emerging EC Regulatory Deficit' in D Currie and JD Whitley (eds), *EMU After Maastricht* (1995), 103. Yet the EU approach is clear and against centralisation of the banking supervisory functions (as it is against creating one EU securities or insurance regulator). There are in any event institutional (jurisdictional) and conceptual (subsidiarity) problems with such centralisation in the present EU set-up. The greatest problems are likely to come not from a lack of centralisation but from any EU-based commercial bank with large non-EU activities facing financial difficulties in those activities and from the problem for any Central Bank in the EU to act as lender of last resort in such circumstances. It is unlikely that the ECB would take over that task. Consolidated supervision on a global scale, either through the BIS or otherwise, is here part of the answer. Within the EU, co-ordination between banking supervisors is, however, an issue and this may itself give rise to the creation of a new level at which supervision of EU-wide banks is exercised.

---

[31] See also above n 12.

1.2.7   Intermediation and Desintermediation of Commercial Banks and the Development of the Securities or Capital Markets

As set out in the previous sections, a major task of commercial banks is to provide loans to the public. It means that they fund private citizens for example through overdrafts or mortgage lending, and businesses mainly through overdrafts and corporate loans. They may in this manner also fund governments or municipal authorities. Of course, businesses are funded also through capital contributions of shareholders and through loans from other sources, often the same shareholders. They may also be funded through direct access to the capital markets in which they may issue bonds to the investing public, as banks always did. If not closely held, they may also issue shares to the public in the capital markets.

Governments and governmental agencies or municipalities traditionally also issue bonds in the capital markets and may avoid in this manner the intervention or intermediation of banks, which is costly. In fact governments and their agencies are traditionally the largest bond issuers, thereafter commercial banks, but they may still choose a banking syndicate to underwrite their bonds as was common for smaller countries when issuing in the eurobond market in other than their own currency. They continue to do so after the introduction of the Euro if they wish to facilitate international placement.

As a result of increasing numbers of corporate issuers accessing the capital markets directly, commercial banks are losing their traditional intermediary role of capturing the flow of investment funds by taking them in as deposits or by borrowing themselves (directly in the inter-bank market or through bond issues in the capital market) and subsequently lending these funds to those requiring them. Naturally banks will borrow at the lowest rates and lend at the highest rates possible to increase their spread and profits, often by offering longer term loans. To avoid the cost of this bank *intermediation*, first class borrowers like governments, banks and good companies have therefore always tried to access the capital markets directly by issuing bonds (or shares) to the investing public in competition with each other and more private companies are now able to follow suit.

This is also attractive for the investors. They are likely to receive in this manner a better return on their money than they could get from banks on their deposits. In addition, they may also obtain instant liquidity by selling their bonds whereas any higher yielding term deposits with banks are basically illiquid and may be held by these banks until maturity. There is for investors also a possibility of making some profits if bonds rise (because interest rates fall) although there is of course also the risk that they may fall (when market interest rates rise), but their full face value will be paid at least at maturity.

More recently, many more large entities requiring capital have been able to turn directly to these investors in the capital markets to obtain the corresponding savings in their funding. Although this facility is still mainly reserved for the better credits, even weak and new corporates are now able to access the capital markets in this manner directly by offering so-called *junk bonds* which have a much higher coupon compensating for the extra risk.

The result is the (partial) side-lining of commercial banks in their deposit-taking and loan activity. This process is usually referred to as bank *disintermediation*. It is cutting into the business of banks that are thus losing their safest and largest borrowers as well as their long term depositors. It not only affects the quantity of the banks' business but also its quality as only lesser credits still need banks, presenting them with a higher average credit risk and greater monitoring costs. Banks have therefore been forced to enter other businesses and the logical sequel for them was the arranging and underwriting of these capital market incursions of their clients. Hence their desire to enter the investment banking business and the pressure that followed in the USA to do away with Glass-Steagall restrictions in this connection.

Yet experience shows that only true investment banks are good at this business. The American investment banks that were precisely the products of Glass-Steagall in the 1930s are the best. Typically they join this underwriting or advising activity in respect of new share and bond issues with market making, brokerage, corporate advice, merger and acquisition expertise and investment management activity as we shall see.

1.2.8   The Banking or Current Account Relationship and Agreement. A Public Function for Banks?

Banks and their regular customers enjoy a contractual relationship. The legal characterisation of that relationship has given rise to problems because it is often multi-faceted. Many different services may pass between a bank and its clients like payment services, deposit services, credit card and overdraft or loan services, if not security brokerage services as well. For corporate customers there may also be standby agreements, receivable finance and inventory financing, and letters of credit or other forms of trade financing. One key question is here whether there is one umbrella relationship to which all present and future transactions of whatever sort (or at least in the payment, deposit and lending sphere) between a client and its bank are legally subordinated or whether each transaction must be considered on its own or may be considered related in other ways, especially in the case of a default or anticipated default in any one of them (short of contractual stipulation to the effect), so that all positions can be promptly netted off.

The preliminary question is who is entitled to open a bank account. Here it is important to realize that without a bank account it is hardly possible to function in the modern world. It is crucial and a key question is therefore whether all members of the public and companies, especially also the smaller ones, are in principle entitled to open banks accounts with whatever commercial bank that is open to the public, what services they may subsequently reasonably request, whether the costs of these services are reasonable, and under what conditions such accounts may be closed by a bank, the practical effect of which may not only be the elimination of the client from the banking system but also from the payment system. Here the public liquidity providing and payment functions of banks may need to be considered, in exchange for which banks *de facto* are receiving some public guarantee against their insolvency as explained above, section 1.2.1 *in fine*. It is a matter of supporting the payment and liquidity providing function of banks and has become a matter of systemic risk and regulatory protection against it.

Indeed, in most modern countries all who wish to do so can open some kind of bank account, at least banks would have to be most careful to refuse them without some good cause. It would allow the customer as a minimum to deposit money in order to make payments to others and receive in their account also payments from others, even if, in the case of private persons, only social security benefits (a particular reason why governments often insist that even the poorest members of society will be allowed to open bank accounts in order to facilitate these payments). It results in a current or checking account, which as such cannot easily be closed by banks either short of the customer starting to run a deficit, which, without an overdraft facility, could be seen as a form of default.[32] It suggests that a

---

[32] In the US there is some long standing case law in this connection, see *Elliott v Capital City State Bank*, 103 NW 777 (Iowa 1905) and *Grants Pass & Josephine Bank v City of Grants Pass*, 28 P 2d 879 (Oregon 1934), which emphasized the freedom of the bank to refuse demand deposits and provide other services unless directed otherwise by banking law. The only obligation of banks was to repay the deposit upon demand. In more modern times, the issue of refusing access may be less straightforward and could even become one of human rights in the case of

bank either refusing the opening of the account or ordering the closing of the account must do so for cause and can no longer act purely at will.

However, the opening of such a current account is likely to allow the customer only minimum services in terms of the withdrawal of any demand deposits and payment services, and both only to the amount of a positive balance in the account, subject further to regular bank charges (assuming that these are reasonable). It might not even allow the customer a cheque book. That at least would appear to be the situation in France. It means that the account is limited to incoming payments and cash withdrawal services only.

At least for customers with regular incomes, the *current account* relationship suggests, however, a framework for other services. Credit card, overdraft services, loan business (especially mortgages) and time deposits may be created. Security or other investment transactions in which the bank acts as broker (or market maker to its clients) are also normally conducted through it. These additional services will all arise under specific agreements to the effect for which, however, the current account is likely to remain the centre. As such it may be seen as the anchor of the entire relationship. This is clear as *de facto*, as all charges accrued under any of the other relationships and all moneys owed under others (like time deposits) are likely to be debited and credited to this account and thus be netted out on a continuous basis. Even where only a mortgage is given, it is not unlikely that a current account is opened at the same time on which the regular payments are reflected and which are settled through that current account.

The key of the current account in this kind of broader relationship is that it is by its very nature *in constant flux* as it nets out the cash side of all the client's transactions on a continuous basis, including payments, new deposits and withdrawals. If there is a positive balance, there will be a deposit aspect; if there is a negative balance, there is an overdraft or loan aspect. One could also say that there results *mutual lending* under it between the bank and its client assuming there is an overdraft facility. It is thus the expressing of a *dynamic* relationship in which the position of net debtor and creditor change all the time between both parties.

The current account framework thus suggests a set of multiple transactions within a single contractual framework, allowing for a netting of all debits and credits and in the case of a default in any transaction for total liquidation, perhaps upon acceleration of all maturities. It is indeed to be considered in how far such a right would follow in the case of default or even a fear of default if no relevant (default or cross default) clauses to the effect were inserted in the various agreements. It would limit the bank's further exposure and in effect terminate the relationship.

However, it can only be repeated that whatever the rights of access to the banking system are, the existence of a current account in itself does not confer any right on the client to additional services beyond cash withdrawals (either at the branch of the account or, at

---

discrimination on the base of sex, religion, colour, disabilities etc., see also the Canadian Charter of Rights 1985, c H-6. On the other hand there may be anti-boycott rules or other public policy considerations.

In fact, in a modern banking system, low income of the prospective client or little anticipated banking volume are unlikely to be accepted as sufficient reason for the refusal or termination of an account, but concern especially for the morality (viz. money laundering) and credit remains legitimate even when accounts are only given in order to make payments against deposited funds.

Especially in France, the Banking Law of Jan. 24 1984 is specific in balancing the contractual approach which gives banks discretion against a more public policy oriented attitude. Under Article 89 banks are exempt from the ant-boycott provisions but under Article 58 anyone refused a bank account may apply to the Bank of France for it to appoint a bank where the petitioner can open an account, but the service may be restricted to cash operations. It is understood that there is no right in such forced accounts to o a cheque book or to credit card facilities.

the bank's option only, also through other branches or cash machines) and payment services *to the extent of* any positive balance of demand deposits. The bank is *not* normally considered obliged to do anything else as a result of the current account relationship, not even to provide a cheque book as we saw. It is therefore not under an inherent duty to provide more services, even to offer (upon request) fixed term deposits for any positive balances (unless saving accounts, which are fixed term deposit against higher interest rates, are offered to the public at large) and certainly not to extend an overdraft facility or credit card or engage in investment securities brokerage or other services for the client. Although smaller companies are often in need of financing that is perfectly legitimate and justified, it cannot be considered the (public) duty of banks to help regardless of the considerable cost of monitoring such clients, although regulators may exert pressure especially in this segment of the loan market or may favour the setting up of special development banks for them.

As far as this current account is concerned and unless otherwise agreed, the bank is moreover *free* to set the interest rate on positive and negative balances and impose its (standard) charges for any movements in the account. It may even change the conditions unilaterally short of effectively closing the account without cause. The remuneration and charges may have to be reasonable in principle and are naturally subject to competitive pressures, but that may still allow for large variations between various banks, even if under applicable law they might not be discriminatory between customers of the same bank unless justifiable from a point of view of increased credit risk and volume of business expectations. The regulatory concern is here often limited to the proper disclosure of such charges beforehand.

A particular aspect of the current account not being terminable at will by the banks is, however, that the entire banking relationship cannot be undermined either by a termination of the current account. Even in respect of a proper termination of the current account, a grace period for the client to make alternative arrangements may still be deemed implied unless in the case of an immediate default or the threat thereof. In any event, regardless of the umbrella function, specific transactions between a bank and its clients in terms of fixed deposits and loans with fixed maturities may not be affected by termination of the current account and they may come to an end only under their own terms which may, however, include a cross default clause or other termination provision predicated upon special events including the termination of the current account for cause.

The client on the other hand has a right to immediate termination of the current account but not thereby of any of the other outstanding facilities either. As mentioned, it is not that simple for the bank, but when there is a current account relationship, it may unilaterally use the balance in it to offset shortfalls or defaults in all special accounts. But the opposite is not necessarily true and a bank may only use special time deposits to cover short falls in the current account if there is a clause to the effect which is likely to be tied to an event of default, or even without such clause to its netting rights upon such an event or activation of the banking lien.

In fact, the agreements for additional services are *not* typical for a true banking relationship, therefore also not a mere time deposit or a mortgage. It would seem that only the current account as centre and anchor of the relationship is, but through the current account arrangement a bank usually also has a set-off or *netting right* and a *lien* on all that it holds for its client in respect of all the client owes it. There is a difference in that the netting affects all the balances automatically whilst the lien reaches assets in custody and will require an execution before proceeds can be added to the set-off and netting. This is likely not only to affect custody accounts but also the contents of safes which may hold client securities and valuables, but for no more than necessary to cover any net deficit.

In respect of the banking lien on the assets, which may thus be rolled into the liquidation, it is possible, however, that there are higher ranking charges in respect of these assets for the benefit of other creditors of the defaulting banking customer. These will have to be respected. It is in this connection to be recalled that bank deposits, as distinguished from the contents of safe deposits or custody accounts, result in the depositor becoming only a creditor of the bank so that there is no need for any lien or charge on the customer in respect of these moneys which the bank has already received in ownership.

In the same vein, if the bank takes out special protection, like mortgages for its housing loans, these mortgages could be structured to cover also any other outstanding debt of the client. If not, the mortgage may stand more alone. In England, there is the special rule that if a particular overdraft is secured, any subsequent overdraft is not automatically covered by the same security whilst any repayment is deemed to be in respect of the oldest overdraft,[33] save of course contrary stipulation. The setting-off and netting principle and banking lien will continue until all is liquidated.

It follows from the foregoing that in the case of a default, there are several lines of defense for a bank. Positive balances in the current account may be used to fill the void. More likely is the trigger of default clauses to effect acceleration and a netting out of all assets and liabilities through the current account, if not implicit in the nature of the relationship itself.

On the European Continent, the connection between the various accounts of a client with its bank and the creation of the bank's lien is usually established under the general banking conditions of a bank which are signed or at least sent to all clients when a client relationship is established. In common law countries, general banking conditions are uncommon and banks will here rely on established practices and case law, itself often relying on implied conditions.[34]

The conclusion is that the banking or current account relationship is one of duration and flexibility, but in the end essentially a conduit resulting in an overall netted creditor/debtor relationship. It suggests an array of banking services of which the payment, deposit and credit supply functions are the most important, the first is always implied.[35] In this manner, through the current account, all financial movements between a bank and its client eventually come together and will be netted out and settled. If there are more current accounts in one relationship, they will ultimately be consolidated. The netted balance in this account leads to either money owed by the bank to its client or to a shortfall when money is owed by the client to the bank.

The debtor/creditor characterisation does not fully explain the banking relationship, however, and seems more the netted result of it. In any event, it should be understood that such a relationship is not static and that the roles may be constantly reversed between the bank and its client in the current account. The rendering of other financial services like the granting of loans may be the more obvious aspect of banking, but was above not found the legal essence of the banking relationship.

Yet, civil law in its legal characterisation puts primary emphasis on the different contract types. There could be an instruction agreement in the case of payments, a deposit agreement in the case of deposits (often not defined, however, in the relevant legal system but distinguished from loan agreements), a loan or overdraft agreement in the case of client

---

[33] Rule in *Clayton's Case*, 35 ER 767 (1816).
[34] The unitary approach follows in England from *Joachimson v Swiss Bank Corp* [1921] KB, 110.
[35] See also R Cranston, *Principles of Banking Law* 1st edn (1997), 137 *et seq.*

borrowing, or a brokerage agreement when securities transactions are executed for clients. In that case there may also be a custody agreement. Greater characterisation difficulties may exist in leasing and factoring which are agreements that in many civil law countries remain undefined.

Looking for and defining special types of contracts is the attitude of civil law. It has as a consequence greater difficulty in defining an overall (banking) relationship when there are different kinds of transactions involved and in establishing the connection between the individual contracts or banking services or products. But also in common law there is here some tension.

Besides the special protections which, in the case of default, the integration notion offers the bank, in practice the true question for the client will be whether it can derive from its established banking relationship some *extra* rights to special services beyond the payment facility and the immediate access to demand deposits. Is this a natural *quid pro quo* for the special protection of the bank being allowed to connect all transactions and client deposits or custody holdings through the current account with the netting facility in the case of (threatened) default? So far, banks would deny the duty to provide more services or make better arrangements even in respect of their regular clients. Yet, they avail themselves of the right to integration regardless, and the law generally supports them. This has come in for criticism and there are some mild variations in attitude in the different countries.

However, the credit risk must be constantly re-evaluated in respect of each banking client and deterioration has, unavoidably, an effect on the continuation of the relationship and types of services and on the rates a bank can offer. On the other hand, if the overall net position of a client with its bank is positive, under more modern law, a bank may have to be careful when refusing special deposits or additional credit facilities, at least if it commonly provides these to other clients. It should also take care in terminating the relationship altogether as we saw, assuming the credit outlook of the client has not substantially deteriorated (it could be justified because of the moral status of a client or when branches are closed in banking re-organisations). Even if it has, longer term contracts of loan or deposit could hardly be affected unless there are acceleration clauses or when there is an immediate default of the expectance of it. But acceleration can only be invoked with care. In the USA, there is some guidance in this connection in Section 1–309 (Section 1–208 old) UCC, which requires good faith in accelerations at will. Even if that is generally a subjective notion under Section 1–201(20) (Section 1–201 (19) old), that cannot be so for the reference to good faith to have any meaning in this context.

It is thus clear that if a bank terminates the current account relationship outside a default situation, individual arrangements and services will continue pursuant to their own terms, although they are unlikely to be renewed, but security brokerage cannot continue and investments held with the bank will be moved immediately (assuming there is a net positive balance). One must assume that other agreements, like those to make and receive all payments through the bank or provide further guarantees or letters of credit also end immediately.

As already mentioned, it is possible that general banking or special provision conditions provide otherwise and that termination of the current account for whatever reason entails immediate termination of all contracts between the bank and its clients under their own terms, at least all deposits and lending facilities. It is not the normal situation, however. It would mean an immediate close-out netting of all positions at the option of a bank regardless of a (threatened) default.

Particularly in Germany, much thought has been given to the banking agreement (*Bankvertrag*). In that country, it is not considered directly connected with the opening of the current account, but rather it seems to be based on the understanding of a longer term credit relationship which does not, however, cover non-credit transactions. Its impact is thus not extended to other than the typical banking relationships in terms of payment, deposit taking, and credit facilities either. All individual deposit and credit agreements may depend on it and are likely to be co-ordinated by it. Thus, if such a relationship is in place, requests for payment, deposit and credit services under it must be seriously considered and can only be refused on good grounds. Termination of the banking agreement by the bank would require proper justification also. No cross-default is implied or simultaneous termination of all deposits and credit agreements upon the end of the banking agreement. As such, its importance may not go beyond what general legal principles of good faith already provide in Germany.[36]

There are other issues that need to concern a lending bank and that are often summed up in terms of *lenders' liability*. They concern the giving of negligent advice to borrowers, pressuring them into accepting loans, failing to warn them against imprudent borrowing, and improperly administering, calling or accelerating a loan, etc.[37] A bank should also be careful not to step in the management's shoes and effectively become involved in the management of its borrowers. It could lead to a postponement of its own loan facility in the case of a bankruptcy of the borrower. In a similar vein, a lending bank own should avoid enabling the borrower to pretend increased creditworthiness *vis-à-vis* third parties whilst the bank itself retains the highest (undisclosed) priority in the case of a default.

1.3 The Essentials of the Securities Business and its Regulation

1.3.1 Major Types of Securities. Negotiable Instruments, Transferable Securities and Investments. Book-entry Systems and Securities Entitlements

Bonds and shares, being the major capital market instruments, are likely to take the form of *transferable securities*. This means that investors may easily dispose of them and acquire shares in other companies or bonds from other governments or corporate borrowers on the relevant formal or informal exchanges on which they trade. Shares (also referred to as stocks or equities) and bonds so issued and traded are commonly referred to as *securities*. Transferability is directly connected with the liquidity of investments and is therefore an important legal issue.

In this connection, it is necessary first to discuss negotiable instruments as they are the traditional form in which securities are made transferable. They are instruments issued to bearer or to order. In the latter case, they are issued to a named person or entity or to its

---

[36] Von Godin, *Kommentar zum Handelsgesetzbuch, Dritter Band* (Berlin, 1963) (ss 343–72), at 365, Anm, 1.2 ziff 2; see also KJ Hopt, *Der Kapitalanlegerschutz im Recht der Banken* (Munich, 1975) 393*ff*. See for dogmatic criticism on the umbrella idea or *Rhamenvertrag*, Canaris, in H Staub, *Handelsgesetzbuch Grosskommentar, Dritter Band, Zweiter Halbband*, ss 352–72 [1978] *Bankvertragrecht*, Rdn 4. See also, Canaris *Grosskommentar HgB, Bank vertragrecht*, I [1988], Rdn. 2 *et seq*. He notes that either party may terminate the relationship at any moment and any mutual obligations depend on the objective law, not on an implied banking relationship agreement. In the context of the good faith requirement of Section 242 BGB similar rights and duties as construed under the banking agreement result. The emphasis on fiduciary duties may make the need for such a contract redundant, see also J Koendgen, 'Neue Entwicklungen im Bankenhaftungsrecht', [1987] *RWS Forum* 1, 138 *et seq*, but might not extend to set-off, proprietary and enforcement issues upon ending a banking relationship.

[37] See also R Cranston, *Principles of Banking Law*, 2nd ed (Oxford, OUP, 2002), 221 and W Blair QC, *Banks, Liability and Risk*, 3rd ed (2001), ch 1.

order or transferee. This type of document has a long history and dates from medieval commercial law, or the international law merchant of those days. In the payment sphere, they led to the development of the bill of exchange and cheque as transferable instruments; in the capital sphere, they led to the development of bonds and shares as transferable investments, and in the goods sphere they led to the development of bills of lading and warehouse receipts. The latter are often called negotiable documents of title. In this vein, negotiable instruments are documents of title concerning money.

The essence is that if they are properly expressed in bearer or order form, they are *negotiable per se*. They are transferred in the case of *bearer* paper by the simple (physical) handing over of the document and in the case of *order* paper by endorsement and handing over to the endorsee. Even the subsequent nationalisation of commercial law through the nineteenth century codifications on the European Continent and much statutory law in common law countries have not changed these basic principles. These documents or instruments in fact continue to enjoy some underlying international status and any tampering with these fundamentals will immediately affect their negotiability. It is true that domestic law in some countries requires the bill of exchange and cheque to be expressed to order only, but by being endorsed in blank they become bearer instruments all the same.

In the case of shares and bonds, being negotiable instruments means that they incorporate the underlying shareholders' claims (or rights to vote, dividends and any net dissolution or winding-up proceeds, and to corporate information) or bondholders' claims (to coupon and principal payments at maturity making them promissory notes). This is at the heart of their easy transferability. It makes possible the simple ownership transfer avoiding the more complicated assignment or novation route which would otherwise be indicated for the transfer of monetary and other claims and would involve the issuer (although less in an assignment than in a novation, see also chapter IV, section 1.7.5).

Another important aspect of this type of securities is that, as negotiable instruments, succeeding owners are likely to take free of any defenses previous owners may have had against them for defective transfers earlier in the chain of ownership. Securities of this type are therefore easy and (legally) relatively safe forms of investments with the added advantage that they may easily be reduced to money by trading them, when needed, in the relevant markets. They are therefore also *liquid* which is an enormous advantage.

Shares and bonds may also take the form of *register(ed) securities* and are not then true negotiable instruments but they might still be transferable. For shares, transfer is in that case pursuant to the approach taken by the applicable company law. It will normally require a change in the shareholders' register held at the seat of the company and a transfer even on a stock exchange would not be perfect without it. This system is common under company laws in common law countries like England where, however, certificates are also issued but they are not transferable by themselves. It allows the company to monitor the identity of its shareholders. For governments there may be tax verification advantages.

Also in this case, transfer is not, however, through assignment or novation, but it is less easy than in the case of negotiable instruments and takes more time. In modern custody systems, transfer of shares and bonds may increasingly be effected through *book-entry* systems kept by the custodians. Custodians like Euroclear and Clearstream (formerly Cedel) in the eurobond market may have the underlying (bearer) instruments as depositories and could deliver them on their clients' behalf, but increasingly pure electronic transfer in a book-entry system is preferred. It may provide for a system of ownership through registration only (although often no longer with the issuer but rather with custodians). It results in securities accounts with intermediaries much like money is held through bank accounts with banks. These are often referred to as *securities entitlements*. The result may be a system of layers of entitlements holders in which investors normally hold their securities entitlement with their broker who in turn have entitlements with other custodians higher up in the chain. Ultimately, the custodians will have an account with a depository who will act as the legal owner as far as the issuer is concerned. This is also referred to as a process of *immobilisation*, see for greater detail chapter IV, section 3.1.1.

At least to protect against assignment or novation requirements in the case of transfer, these newer systems often need the support of the objective law, mostly through legislation, to make an easy transfer possible, which in the case of international transactions may raise the question of the applicable law, also in order to characterise the nature of the entitlement and the rights held thereunder. More generally, the key to the success of these modern systems is, besides the easy transferability and protection of *bona fide* purchasers, the preservation of confidentiality, the protection against earlier defects in the chain of owners (innate in negotiable instruments), and proprietary protection in the case of a bankruptcy of any depository being the registered owner and of any other intermediary/custodian holding securities accounts for clients/investors.

Here it is often best to see the security holder as a beneficial owner in respect of his *pro rata* interest in an underlying pool of fungible securities held by his intermediary (who himself may have no more than a book-entry interest with another custodian or a depository who is registered as owner with the issuer) and to which the end-investor has no direct access, but which are not owned by the intermediary either and are in respect of him *segregated* assets (for which he acts more like a trustee). In the USA, Article 8 of the Uniform Commercial Code presents an advanced example of this approach, which also goes into the transfer of this type of interests and (more indirectly) into its proprietary status, see the discussion in chapter IV, Part III. One sees here a shift from the traditional negotiable instruments to what are now more commonly called *transferable securities* which are a broader class of securities that may therefore have lost the status of negotiable instruments. It should be noted in this connection that negotiability is a term of art, much more than transferability. Transferable securities may also cover specialised types of financial instruments like *derivatives*, therefore futures and options, and, for professionals, swaps.

These so-called derivative products are not securities proper, likes shares or bonds, but are *contracts* with counter-parties which achieve some form of transferability only if they are standardised and dealt in on formal exchanges that allow for dealing in these standard contracts, like modern futures and options exchanges do. Rather than providing a system of transfer, these exchanges offer normally a possibility of closing these contracts for 'sellers' who will be paid the value of these contracts on the moment of 'sale', whilst 'buyers' will be offered similar contracts against a similar price (allowing for market spreads). In formal derivative exchanges, there is mostly a system of a central (single) counter party (CCP), with the exchange functioning as such, which operates through a system of entering opposite positions at current market prices which may be netted out against the old contract, see more in particular section 1.4.4 below. Non-standardised or a-typical OTC futures and options and all swaps can be entered into or unwound or transferred only in co-operation with the counter-party under the relevant contracts (or neutralised through hedges). Major commercial banks may hold themselves out as ready counter-parties in this respect, especially for swaps.

There are thus many different types of transferable securities or derivatives and some may be much less transferable than others. Shares and bonds may themselves be subdivided. Shares may be in the form of ordinary or preferred shares. There are also hybrids like bonds *convertible* into shares and warrants. *Warrants* are a special type of option usually issued by a company at a certain price (or premium) allowing the owners to acquire new shares in the company at a specific issue or striking price during a certain period of time. These warrants are sometimes also issued by financial intermediaries who may hold a portfolio of the underlying company shares.

As far as bonds are concerned, there are fixed and floating interest rate bonds or notes. Notes usually denote a shorter maturity (not more than five years). As far as the maturity is concerned, there is short-term, medium-term and long-term paper and there is likely to be a difference in the manner in which the different types are issued and placed. Consequently there is commercial paper (CPs issued by corporate borrowers) and there are certificates of deposit (CDs issued by banks) as short term or money market paper. Then there are medium term notes (MTNs), usually for no longer than three years and often much shorter.

There may also be a difference in the way these instruments are issued and placed with investors. Bonds and shares when issued are often *underwritten* by investment banks who thereby guarantee the success of the issue (against a fee). It means that to the extent there are no investors at the agreed issue price, these investment banks will buy the issue themselves. Generally, neither short-term paper nor MTNs are underwritten but usually only placed by an intermediary on a best effort basis against prices from time to time indicated by the issuer. Banks may, however, give standby credit lines if not enough money is raised in this manner, which can be a great burden on them when these markets dry up.

Then there are longer term bonds which may even be perpetual. Except for government bonds issued in the domestic currency, they are, as just mentioned, typically underwritten by a consortium of investment banks headed by a lead underwriter. The intermediaries used for placement of these securities tend also to organise a trading facility in them which may be formal through listing on an exchange or informal (OTC) between market makers (whose role will be explained in section 1.3.8 below) willing to act.

Although, historically, negotiable instruments are the classical examples of securities, for regulatory (and investors' protection) purposes, the definition may thus be drawn wider in terms of transferablity. In truth, modern regulators now mostly ignore definitions of this type and aim at covering all *investment* products with a view to best protecting *investors*. Thus the Financial Service and Markets Act 2000 in the UK maintains a list in Schedule 2 to which the Secretary of State has power to add from time to time but there is no definition (bank deposits have become here even 'investments' in this sense). In the USA, Section 2(a) of the Securities Act of 1933, dealing mainly with the public issue of securities, and Section 3(a) of the Securities Exchange Act of 1934, dealing mainly with the listing on and operations of stock exchanges, contain a list of instruments (again the USA uses here the list approach as in banking).

One of them is the so-called 'investment contract'. In the reference to this kind of contract, the US Acts provide for considerable flexibility and this type of contract and its definition holds an important key. The term is undefined, but case law[38] looks for schemes that involve investment money in a *common enterprise* with profits to come solely from the *efforts of others*. The emphasis is thus *not* on the negotiability of the securities *per se* nor even on transferability by some other means, although it would seem to remain an important element, but rather on their *investment* nature.

The American Acts provide in this connection that the *context* is also relevant and may determine that the indicated instruments are not securities. Thus CDs issued by national banks were not considered securities because they were federally insured whilst national

---

[38] *SEC v WJ Howey* Co, 328 USA 293 (1946).

banks are already subject to comprehensive regulation so that further protection through the securities acts was not called for.[39] The same goes all the more for bank deposits (unlike the British approach). For purposes of the Glass-Steagall Act, now superseded, and which required a distinction (and separation) between banking and securities business, swaps were not considered securities either and commercial banks could, as a consequence, freely deal in them, but in other contexts, like that of investor protection, they could be considered securities. Again the context is decisive.

In the UK under the Financial Services and Markets Act, the central theme is the regulation of investment businesses which are businesses conducted by firms dealing in investments (either as principal or agent), arranging deals in investments, managing investments, giving investment advice or operating collective investment schemes. As just mentioned, the term 'investment' is here not defined either, but covers a wide range of products listed in Schedule 2, which also contains a long list of exceptions and explanations. Currency and interest rate swaps are covered, but not pure commodity trading unless there is an investment element. As just mentioned, a peculiarity in the UK is that 'deposits' are now defined as investments with the consequence that banks are now regulated much in the same style and manner as securities intermediaries in respect of their (regulated) activities. It may be doubted whether this was wise. It confuses banking and capital market activities. It also ignores the nature of the deposit which becomes the property of the bank.

On the other hand, in the EU in the 1989 Directive concerning the Public Offer Prospectus, the focus was on *transferable securities*, which are defined in a list approach. Article 3(e) sets them out as being shares in companies, debt securities having a maturity of at least one year, and any other transferable securities giving the right to acquire any such transferable securities by subscription or exchange. In the 1977 European Code of Conduct relating to Transactions in Transferable Securities, they were defined as securities which are or may be the subject of dealings on an organised market, a much narrower definition. In the 1993 Investment Services Directive, transferable securities are defined (Article 1.(4)) as shares in companies and other securities equivalent to shares in companies, bonds or other forms of securitised debt. They are transferable in the capital market and include any other securities normally dealt in giving the right to acquire any such transferable securities by subscription or exchange or giving rise to a cash settlement (excluding instruments of payment).

It is clear that the term 'security' itself here remains undefined and that under EU law the conceptual switch to 'investments' has not yet been fully made. The Investment Services Directive only defines the term 'investment service' and does this also with reference to a list of 'instruments' (neither 'investments' nor 'negotiable' instruments), which contains, besides transferable securities, also financial futures and options, swaps and FRAs, units in collective investment schemes and money market instruments (see Annex, section B). Thus transferability, although important, appears not to be the only or even essential element as some of the mentioned instruments may not always be transferable. Investors' protection is the unspoken aim and that has an effect on the meaning of 'investment' which, even if remaining undefined, generally speaking, acquires significance only in connection with a person who invests his money with a view to receiving a financial reward through the efforts of others.[40]

---

[39] *Marine Bank v Weaver*, 455 US 551 (1982).

[40] It may in this connection be useful to take a closer look at *debt securities*. Under this form of securitisation, indebtedness is incurred by issuing bonds or notes in the capital markets. It makes the issuer a borrower and the investor a lender. This type of securitised lending should be clearly distinguished from the type of lending a bank does which does not normally take the form of a transferable security or note and is therefore not normally

Bank loans are *not* normally deemed investments or investment instruments in this sense and therefore do not benefit from investor protection, that is special protection of the bank as 'investor' in loan products (unlike a bank's investment portfolio which may include considerable numbers of bonds, usually those of governments). Also from an accounting point of view they may be treated differently. At least in commercial banks (it may be different in investment banks), bank loans are not 'marked to market' on a daily basis (that means that they are not revalued daily on the basis of their market value) as bonds and notes usually are. In the loan or banking book, the position or interest rate risk is therefore not immediately discounted, but the credit or counterparty risk are taken into account in that provisions will be made from time to time against this exposure and capital will be held against this risk also. This touches on capital adequacy requirements which will be discussed in greater detail below.

We already saw that in their investment book banks may also buy bonds and notes. It makes them in fact lenders to the issuers of these instruments. Here they are more properly (professional or institutional) investors. The value of bonds and notes in a bank's investment portfolio or trading book are daily adjusted. Under applicable law or practices, banks (at their discretion) may, however, also designate these bonds and notes to their banking rather than to their investment or securities book (see for this distinction and the capital adequacy consequences, section 3.3.7 below) so that their intrinsic loss or profit remains unidentified. It means their value as a banking asset is not daily adjusted on the basis of prevailing interest and foreign exchange rates, because they are seen as long-term banking commitments that are not traded. As banking assets they will then be subject to the capital adequacy requirements of the bank in respect of credit or counter party risk.

1.3.2   Securities Markets and their Organisation. Official Markets

Securities are closely connected with capital markets and their operation. Capital markets suggest trading and therefore transferability of these securities. Conceptually, the capital market works wherever the demand for capital meets the supply. In these markets, savers or investors offer excess funds which those who need capital may want to attract.

The issuing activity in the capital markets is normally referred to as *primary market activity*, the subsequent trading as *secondary market activity*. The primary and secondary markets in this sense can be *formal* or *informal* markets. For shares, they are normally formal markets or stock exchanges on which these instruments are listed, like the NY, London or Tokyo Stock Exchanges. For bonds, the government bond market is also often formal and then usually functions as part of the official domestic stock exchanges in the currency of the country concerned. In these exchanges, there will often also be a section for corporate bonds issued in the domestic currency.

These are therefore instruments that are typically bought and traded in the domestic markets. These markets are mostly also open to *foreign issuers* who are willing to list and qualify for listing. There will be formalities: listing and issuing prospectuses will be

---

transferable in that manner. For the transfer of loans, assignment or novation is required under applicable law of which asset securitisation is one form: see s 1.4.7 below. That is much more difficult and usually requires some involvement of the borrower, who tends to value the banking relationship and may not want to become indebted to another creditor (bank). The two types of securitisation (issuing securities and transferring a portfolio of loans or receivables to create asset-backed securities) mentioned here are very different in nature and should in turn be distinguished from secured lending, which is lending on the basis of collateral.

required and sometimes registration with regulators, like all public issues trading in the USA with the SEC. *Foreign investors* usually also have access to such exchanges (directly or through their own brokers with the help of local brokers). These formal exchanges may also list foreign listed shares which then either trade in their own or local currency depending on the rules of the relevant exchange. Foreign shares may also trade on such exchanges in the form of (American or European) depository receipts (ADRs or EDRs) and are then usually quoted in the currency of the country of the exchange, see also chapter IV, section 3.1.5.

As we saw, there are also informal or OTC (Over-the-Counter) or telephone markets, of which the euro-markets are by far the most important examples, especially for the issuing and trading of eurobonds. Their nature and status will be discussed in section 2.4 below. In the USA, the NASDAQ is often considered such a market as well, although it has obtained a formal structure in the advertisements of quotes and in the price reporting and is regulated as such via the NASD. Here the absence of an official floor and the prevalent telephone interchange between the participants formally leads Americans still to consider the NASDAQ an OTC market, but in all major aspects it is now a formal market. As at 1999, it was seeking official stock market status to compete with the New York Stock Exchange (NYSE).

Other markets, like the euro-markets for eurobonds, the swap markets and the foreign exchange market, are more truly OTC or informal markets. As already mentioned, the derivatives markets are also mostly informal or OTC, even domestically. Only certain standard option and future contracts are traded on more formal option and futures exchanges, see section 1.4.4 below.

When shares are issued in informal markets like the euro-markets this is usually done in tandem with a domestic official listing so that a tranche or several tranches are also quoted on one or various official domestic stock exchanges. It is less common for eurobonds. The interesting aspect of the euro-markets is that they are not merely informal, and thus in essence unregulated, but they also allow for (a) the issue and trading of a special kind of (transnational) negotiable instrument (at least for bonds) expressed in many currencies and for (b) underwriting and trading practices that may also have a transnational legal character: see more in particular section 2.4.4 below. The same may now apply to the more modern securities entitlements held be investors with intermediaries (chiefly their brokers) in modern book-entry systems like those of Euroclear and Clearstream, see chapter IV, Part III.

For bonds, the eurobond market has become the largest bond market in the world, even bigger than the US government bond (or Treasury) market and reached a total new issue amount of US $(equivalent) one trillion worth in 1998 and was at US $(equivalent) 1,2 trillion in 2002 (excluding US $ (equivalent) of 500 billion in privately placed MTNs). It serves large corporates but also governments (who often accept here underwriting) and *supra*-nationals like the World Bank (IBRD) and the European Investment Bank (EIB). Because of the existence of the eurobond market, it has become relatively uncommon for issuers to issue in domestic markets other than their own, although these markets may still present opportunities for lower cost funding at times. Thus a German corporate or international agency may issue in the domestic US (Yankee), UK (Bulldog) or Japanese (Samurai) bond markets in respectively US $, UK sterling and Japanese yen bonds. In practice, these domestic markets cater only for issues in their own currencies.

Informal markets may not lack infrastructure and the euro-markets clearly have one. They have their own standards and practices: see section 2.4.2 below. Most importantly, they also created their own clearing, settlement and custody functions through Euroclear and Cedel (now Clearstream). The distinctive feature is that this has all been organised informally by the most important intermediaries in this market themselves, to great effect. It is true that these intermediaries in the euro-markets (investment banks) are now often (lightly) regulated in the place from which they operate, mostly London. That does not affect the operation of the euro-markets as such, although to avoid cumbersome price reporting requirements recognition was given to ISMA (their trade association) as a reporting centre: see also the next section.

Formal markets or stock exchanges usually have several specific features which one is unlikely to see in informal markets. They require (a) listing of the shares and bonds quoted on them, (b) supervision of the issuers and the setting of rules for the issuing activity, and (c) a regular information supply and the operation of a publication facility in that connection. Like well developed informal markets they will provide (d) secondary trading facilities, determine the type of trading system, maintain a price publication system and set the rules in connection with these trades, and (e) a clearing and settlement system in respect of the trades executed on the market. *Clearing* means here the netting out of positions between the various participants (mostly on a daily basis). In *settlement*, the transaction is effectively executed, first by the matching of the transaction details for both parties and subsequently the transfer of the (netted) securities and (netted) payments per individual client. This is quite apart from the brokers' notifying their clients of their new positions and of the payments made or received for them, which relate to their original instructions but will have to be backed up and implemented by this settlement process. Clearing is not itself settlement either, but only a manner of simplifying it between participants if doing numerous transactions between themselves during the clearing period. The clearing concerns payments but also covers the delivery of fungible securities which are netted per participant per type of security, see more in particular section 1.3.7 below and chapter IV, section 3.1.4.

The functions of clearing and settlement now often go together but that is strictly speaking not necessary. Clearing simplifies the flows of moneys and securities, eliminates funding needs and reduces costs. Official option and futures exchanges have (like informal markets) less concern about issuers and listing particulars, including prospectuses and concentrate instead on the types of contracts that can be offered on it. A facility to close them out, transparency in the quoted and done prices, and reliability in clearing and settlement will be their major focus, where they have often advanced to the central counterparty (CCP) mode of settlement, see sections 1.3.7 and 1.4.4 below.

As already mentioned above, in connection with the listing, official exchanges will require a prospectus in which the issuer presents the major financial and business information about itself. In the case of shares, the listing often coincides with the offering of new shares, although that need not be so. In the case of bonds that is almost always the case. The listing and new issue prospectuses will then be similar and issued simultaneously in one document. For listed shares there may be later increases in capital leading to what is called *secondary* offerings (in the *primary* market!). They will require a new prospectus.

In the USA since 1933, these exchange functions or activities are in the case of public issues preceded by registration of the issuer with the SEC, which requires a prospectus on that occasion. In the EU, this function has largely remained a stock exchange affair and the official exchanges will also deal with the requirement of updating market-relevant information. Prospectuses of this nature give rise to prospectus liability of the issuer if subsequently it proves that wrong or misleading information was given. Advisors and underwriters may here also become affected.

It is to be noted that in the EU, directives have been issued in the area of listing admission and listing prospectus requirements and in the area of interim reporting of listed companies.

They have been implemented for all official exchanges in the EU, see section 2.3.4 below and are now in the process of being updated on the 1998 EU Action Plan concerning a European market for financial services, see also section 1.1 10 above and section 3.5 below.

1.3.3   *Unofficial Markets, Globalisation of Markets, Euromarkets*

As may be gathered from the previous section, informal markets may have less structure than formal markets and may confine themselves to two activities only: (a) issuing activity including underwriting and (b) market-making or other forms of trading. They were already mentioned above in section 1.1.5 and will be discussed further in section 1.3.8 below. In the case of the euro-markets, prospectuses and continuous information on issuers are often of lesser concern for investors as only the best issuers can come to these markets and these investors, who are largely professionals, will be informed through other channels. It means that, for them, prospectuses are less important. Liquidity is their first priority, thereafter cost and effective and safe clearing and settlement. To provide a safe clearing and settlement function, Euroclear and Clearstream (formerly Cedel) were especially created but operate separately from the informal market itself on a purely commercial basis. They are, however, owned and supervised by the major issuers and market makers in the euro-markets.

All official exchanges have a way of advertising quotes or prices and concentrate by their very nature supply and demand. Informal markets here develop their own practices, which, as in the euromarkets, usually mean a *market-making* system with quotations of spreads per market maker to other market makers and selected brokers, see for these secondary market trading systems more in particular section 1.3.5 below. One could say that the whole foreign exchange market is in a similar position. In informal markets, the market makers together form the market and are only informally known and their prices or spreads are traditionally not widely advertised.

In the euro-markets, certain self-regulatory organisations have appeared which have created some order and standards of behaviour. They are the International Primary Market Association (IPMA) for the issuing activity and the International Securities Market Association (ISMA formerly the AIBD) for trading activity. In fact, only the ISMA issues binding rules, the IPMA operates on a system of Recommendations which are, however, always followed and have great authority. It should be clearly understood that these organisations are there primarily to create order amongst their members and *not* to protect investors, although the latter also benefit from the increased dependability and regularity in these markets. See for the operation of the euro-markets more in particular section 2.4.2 below.

The informal euro-markets operate mostly from London and the intermediaries located in London have, since 1986, been subject to UK legislation in terms of authorisation and prudential supervision including a system of price reporting for the members operating from London. In fact, the issues in these markets are often still accompanied by a prospectus, mostly because eurobond issues tend to be listed on a stock exchange (Luxembourg, sometimes also London). Although trading hardly takes place on these exchanges, certain institutional investors may, under their own rules, not be able to invest in bonds that are not officially listed, the reason why this listing takes place. The euro-markets are, however, exempt from the EU Public Offer Prospectus Directive of 1989 (Articles 2(l) and 3(f)) which requires a prospectus to be issued before any public issue is launched. This will be different under the new Prospectus Directive at least in respect of issuers from EU countries for whom a liberalized regime will apply only in respect of bond issues that have denominations in excess of Euro 50, 000, see more in particular section 3.5.3 below.

Under the present regime, in many countries, euro-securities may always be sold without prospectus or other proper forms of advertisement to professional investors or larger companies and investment trusts. This is relevant also where the definition of euro-securities proves too narrow as it requires an international syndicate whilst the securities have to be offered on a significant scale in countries other than that of the issuer and should be acquired only through a credit or other financial institution: see also section 2.4.2 below.

One key advantage of issuing in the euro-markets always was that it could be accessed instantaneously to take advantage of favourable price movements so that the prospectus preceded the closing but not the launch of the issue and it was accepted that that advantage needed to be preserved. In the USA, for SEC registrations, the problems of delay were overcome through the facility of *shelf-registrations* which allows all relevant information including a prospectus to be prepared with the SEC subject to regular updates. This shelf-registration is then valid for two years.

Globalisation has reinforced the operation of the informal markets and they have now often become the favoured venue for the more sophisticated issuer and investor. There is no doubt that especially for institutional investors in the professional circuit, in secondary trading, the move is in the direction of unofficial trading directly with the main investment banks as informal *market makers*. These market makers have long constituted the secondary market in eurobond trading. The question is whether modern regulation within the EU will remain sufficiently supporting of these practices to allow them to continue to be conducted from the EU territory, especially in London as even in large share dealings, official exchanges are increasingly relegated to the smaller deals for private investors, who, as a consequence, must bear the considerable cost of these exchanges. Professional investors will simply go wherever they can get the deal most efficiently and cheaply executed and take the market with them. They normally also avoid the cost of brokers and deal with market makers directly, except if they want to remain anonymous.

Safety in settlement is an important issue for investors in these informal markets, however. As already mentioned, they have the organisations of Euroclear and Cedel (now Clearstream after the merger with the settlement arm of the German Stock Exchange) to help them, and these organisations now also settle domestic (mainly the best known government) bonds traded on the informal secondary euromarkets, and have even started with share transaction settlement. For shares, the domestic clearing and settlement facilities remain important, however, and are often still operated by domestic stock exchanges which have here a kind of monopoly, although they may no longer be able to limit their settlement systems to deals executed on their own exchanges.

The considerable issuing activity in the eurobond markets, the substantial volume of international tranches of new share issues in the euro-markets, and the extraordinary volumes in secondary trading in these markets (much increased through repo transactions) testify to the success of the informal segments of the capital markets. This activity underlines their increasingly international character and integration in one worldwide market of which domestic exchanges now form only one part and they feel the pressure. When communications were slower and more difficult, it was normal for them to carve out their own markets behind their own currencies and governmental or corporate issuers. To this end, they provided and regulated an issuing facility and a centralised physical facility or *floor* for secondary trading on which brokers could meet the matching agents (or specialists) in order-driven and market makers in quote-driven exchanges, see for these systems section 1.3.5 below. Their various functions of regulators, price or other information distributors and settlement organisers came here together.

Competition from informal markets has proved healthy for the regular exchanges and has made them much more efficient whilst forcing them to abandon their monopoly structure. Not only does their market function face severe competition, their other functions, like price and other information distribution and clearing and settlement, may easily be taken over by others too, who may be able to carry them out more cheaply and efficiently. In the USA, as we saw, registration of public issuers and the regular information supply became an SEC rather than an exchange function. It shows that the function of the official exchanges in the primary markets could become merely administrative. Exchanges may also not be able to monopolise their settlement and clearing systems any longer. In option and futures trading, the formal markets may be more essential because of their unwinding and special settlement functions (but only for certain standardized types of contracts).

Larger companies are in any event likely to feel a need to be quoted on the largest stock exchanges in the world so that the smaller exchanges are left not only with smaller investors but also with the smaller domestic companies that generate little turnover in their shares. The emergence of the common currency (Euro) in Europe has created further pressure, especially on the smaller domestic European exchanges. The largest will probably continue to play an important role. During the last few years, the London and Frankfurt exchanges unsuccessfully tried to merge. The exchanges of Paris, Brussels and Amsterdam merged into Euronext to retain their clout and could eventually be joined by other European exchanges. In 2002, Euronext also acquired LIFFE, the derivative market in the UK. The end result may be one or two European exchange systems in the major shares and derivatives contracts, much as the NY Stock Exchange (NYSE) functions in the USA (without, however, a derivatives market). If no consolidation takes place, alternative, largely delocalised, informal markets may be reinforced or newly created. The same goes for the clearing, settlement and custody services in these markets.

In this connection the role of central counterparties in clearing and settlement organizations should not be discounted and it is quite conceivable that they will ultimately become the true informal markets.

1.3.4 The Primary Market and Security Issuers. International Style Offerings

The primary market is the new issue segment of the capital market and concentrates therefore on new issues and the issuers. As we saw, they may issue in either official or unofficial markets, the term 'market' being used here abstractly, as the meeting place or facility (which need not be physical and could e.g. only be on the telephone) between those who require capital and those who are able to provide it and not necessarily as a physical place or a so-called market floor.

As we saw, often the issuing activity requires a prospectus. If the issuing is done in an official market there are also likely to be listing requirements, which again may centre on a prospectus. In such cases the issuing and listing prospectus may be the same. In the previous section, it was already mentioned that in the euro-markets more relaxed rules prevail or under the new EU Prospectus Directive in respect of all issues with large denominations at least for bonds, whether international or domestic. In any event, no listing is required *per se* (even if it is for eurobonds often still done in Luxembourg or sometimes London to accommodate those institutional investors who under their rules may only invest in listed securities) whilst the prospectus may be issued after the initial announcement and informal trading in the so-called *grey market* on the basis of 'if and when issued' may already take place. It is indeed the traditional method in the euromarkets where most trading in any issue is likely to take place in that grey market, therefore before a prospectus is issued and the issue is closed. Under the new Prospectus regime much greater problems may arise in the future in respect of international equity issues, with issuers from the EU, see also section 3.5.3 below.

In so-called International Style Offerings, there are likely to be various tranches of one issue, each targeted at different official or unofficial markets (including the euro-markets). They often concern *share* issues issued across Europe or also into Asia and, to the extent permissible, sometimes even into the US. Outside the country of the issuer, these issues conform to international, more informal market standards and tend not to be subject to any kind of domestic regulation unless the issuer wants to issue in any particular domestic market also.

Most large issues will be underwritten by an underwriting syndicate, which in international offerings will most likely be an international syndicate, see for these underwriting techniques and placement functions more in particular section 1.3.7 below.

1.3.5   Secondary Market and its Trading Systems

Formal and informal markets will determine the types of secondary trading systems they operate. There are here in essence two possibilities: a *quote or price* driven system and an *order or auction* system. In the quote or price driven system, there are *market makers* who quote bid and offer prices for the securities in which they are market makers on a continuous basis during market hours. The difference between their bid and offer quotes is their *spread* or profit margin. They are free to set this spread (unless required by an issuer to make markets in the issue within an agreed, often narrow spread). Yet they must compete with other market makers. Large spreads then mean that they do not want to do serious business, as others offer to buy the securities in question for more and sell them for less.

To get closest to market prices, sophisticated investors in a *quote or price* driven system will not reveal whether they are sellers or buyers whilst asking for the spread, and the market maker has no right to require disclosure of whether the investor is a seller or buyer. It means that he will not be able to move the spread against the investor, who could take advantage by doing the opposite of what the dealer may think and as a consequence either acquire the securities cheaper or sell them for a higher price. The market maker will thus be forced to stay as close as possible to the middle price offered by the rest of the market. This is a vital investors' protection.

An example may clarify this point. Say A wishes to sell a security and sees a market maker's advertised spread at 99 (bid)-101 (offer). It means that the market maker is willing to buy at 99 and to sell at 101. Approaching the market maker for confirmation of this spread, a market maker sensing that A may be a seller may move his spread to 98–100. A can only sell at 98. A's defense is to turn buyer at once and buy for 100. It may allow him to sell higher, make an instant profit and the market maker would be penalised. This system thus protects A against predatory practices. The market maker could widen the spread instead, say to 98–102. But if market prices are near 100 it would mean that no-one would want to sell to or buy from this market maker who in this manner effectively signals or must accept that he is not participating in the market and has or does no business. That is what widening spreads means: market makers place themselves outside the market unless all other market makers do the same. In other words, in a competitive market the need for business will encourage market makers to narrow their spreads which at the same time will protect the customer against market makers' abuses.

Order or auction systems do not have market makers but work on the basis of a *matching* system of offer and bid limits set by prospective sellers and buyers. There are matching agents (or specialists) in this market but they do not take a position (although they may be under a duty to smooth the markets if becoming irregular and may have to determine an openings price and do business at that price). They perform therefore in essence only an administrative function, which in modern times may be taken over by computers. Bids and offers that do not match are returned to the investors for adjustment or withdrawal.

It is clear that the quote or price driven system is more suitable for large orders or for illiquid company stock or corporate bonds since there is much more flexibility in a market making system where the market makers provide liquidity by risking their own capital. In a market-making system the market makers must give quotes for all the issues in which they profess to make a market and there is therefore likely to be always a price, although there may be large swings. An order or auction driven system is most suitable for regular trades in well known shares or bonds with regular quantities of supply and demand. When there are large swings in such markets, there may be little to match and this system is then less effective as no deals will result. But there is a cost to the market-making system and that is in the spreads, which may become large when illiquid positions are involved. On the other hand, particularly in the more liquid eurobonds they may be very small. It may make market making hardly profitable whilst there is a (market or position) risk for market makers who will lay off this risk as fast as possible, either with other clients or other market makers (the street). Spread costs do not exist in an auction system, but a small fee will have to be paid for the matching service.

The London Stock Exchange (LSE) and the euro (bond) markets were typical quote or price driven systems, but as through competition between market-makers the spreads are often driven very low, it is becoming less interesting for market-makers to make markets in regular issues and alternative order driven systems are now set up in these markets. The NASDAQ system in the USA is also quote driven, again logical as it concerns often smaller stocks in which there is no regular supply and demand. The New York SE, Tokyo SE and the continental European exchanges are, on the other hand, all order driven. However, in New York there is a possibility for larger orders to move 'upstairs' to a market-making environment so that they will not disturb the more regular flows in the Exchange. Derivative markets also tend to maintain a quote driven system and so are foreign exchange markets.

Market-makers in regular exchanges are often given more time to report their deals so that they can unwind their positions without the market being informed of them which would make it more difficult to reduce their risk.

1.3.6 Internet or Electronic Trading

Internet, electronic or online securities dealings are a normal consequence of the popularity of modern informal communication facilities. Also here, the issuing and secondary trading should be distinguished. For issuing activity, so far mainly two methods have been developed, the one a more informal one in which sellers and buyers operate more individually and, incidentally, usually on the home page of the issuing company which mainly concerns secondary trading. These pages are often company sponsored to increase the liquidity of their shares. Bids and offers may be freely withdrawn and prices are individually negotiated between the parties. The company will not then become involved and does not receive a fee for the facility but may provide a settlement facility for its shares. This is also called the *bulletin method* of dealing. As to the primary market or issuing activity, it is conceivable that in this manner issuers directly advertise and offer their new issues on their home page together with road show information. They then become direct counterparties to the buyers of their shares.

In the other *crossing method* of dealing, there is more formal centralisation of supply and demand by an agency providing this facility and arranging for a computerised matching system between sellers and buyers. The agent providing this service may or may not be one of the established matching agents or brokers. In this method there could also be issuing activity.

By reducing the involvement of intermediaries, there are of course important timing and cost-saving aspects in electronic trading for investors and issuers alike, but also investor protection and regulatory issues closely connected with practical aspects like the proper advertising and clearing and settlement of these transactions. It should be borne in mind that most of the electronic investors will be small or retail investors, although institutional investors may use similar systems. For the crossing system, there could also be the question of information supply on price and volumes, possibly the question of listing and in any event the question of regular information supply on the affairs of companies whose shares are so traded. Are these crossing systems effectively exchanges and should they be regulated as such? There is certainly also the problem of securities fraud, which again has much to do with the existence of the shares offered and the proper clearing and settlement of the transactions. The trading might also be manipulated and false markets established.[41]

On the other hand, the modern electronic media themselves allow investors real time trade data, company, financial and regulatory news in abundance and an instant insight into official market reactions. These markets may, however, become less liquid and reliable as price indicators when losing business to the informal markets which price-wise they nevertheless indirectly support with their supervision, pricing and anti-fraud mechanisms. This is often seen as a free ride and unfair competition problem. An internet primary offering and secondary trading facility could, however, more properly be seen as only the natural sequel of the easier access to information generally and the need to react more promptly.

In the USA, the bulletin board primary and secondary activity must be approved by the SEC but there is obviously a problem with foreign company home pages accessed from the USA and US investors are likely to be here on their own if not protected by the regulators of those issuers. Regulatory burdens may in any event deter companies from opening their own home page to this activity, an important reason crossing systems are more popular, at least in the USA. Each has its own rules but most execute deals at an indicated time at the mid-point of the highest bid and lowest offer prices within a range set by the participants. In the USA, in most of these schemes only NYSE and NASDAQ shares are involved and they will be settled through these established exchanges with which the on-line trading system will be connected.

Discount brokers are also increasingly accessed on-line especially by day traders. All may be accessed from foreign countries. In that case, from a regulatory point of view, the applicable regime will be foremost that of the accessed party who provides the facility or service. As that party is likely to also make clear the conditions for payment and settlement, it leads in essence to regulation by the country of the service provider (see for the concept of internationality of these services also section 1.1.8 above). This approach is borne out by the 2000 EU E-commerce Directive (although there is still a narrow exception for small

---

[41] See on the regulatory issues in the USA, PD Cohen, 'Securities Trading Via the Internet' [1999] *The Journal of Business Law* 299; see also P Nyquist, 'Failure to Engage: The Regulation of Proprietary Trading Systems', (1995) 13 *Yale Law and Policy Review,* 281. See for securities fraud, JJ Cella III and JR Stark, 'SEC Enforcement and the Internet: Meeting the Challenge of the Next Millennium, A Program for the Eagle and the Internet', (1997) 52 *The Business Lawyer* 815.

investors protection under Article 3 which reminds much of the general good concept, see also section 1.1.9 above).

1.3.7   Modern Clearing, Settlement and Custody

Above in section 1.3.2 clearing and settlement were briefly discussed. Custody in its modern form is closely connected with the book-entry system for investment securities, resulting in security entitlements or security accounts discussed in chapter IV, part III. Settlement is, in this connection, nothing more than the completion of a trade as a consequence of which the seller receives his proceeds and the buyer his securities. It is therefore the method and the occurrence of payment either in cash or kind. Clearing is a technique of simplifying this process amongst intermediaries acting for their clients during a certain time frame, usually one day. Instead of settling each trade with each other they will *net* them out bilaterally or in a more sophisticated set-up multilaterally. This may apply to payments as well as to (fungible) securities.[42] Custody is a resultant service where intermediaries hold the investments for their clients and concern themselves also with the administration of income in the form of dividends or coupons. Formerly, when securities were issued in the form of bearer instruments, it meant holding large amounts of paper which, with the increase in investments of this type, became unmanageable in the 1970s, first in the USA, then also in Europe.

The result was the already mentioned immobilised and dematerialised way of holding investment which became a system of securities entitlements or accounts held with brokers (much in the manner as a bank account held with banks), who would themselves have similar accounts or entitlements with sub custodians and eventually with a depository who would figure as the legal owner of the securities *vis-à-vis* the issuer (and hold them usually by way of a global note or registered security only). The nature of the custody relationship of this kind and the legal characterisation of the securities entitlement were discussed in chapter IV, section 3.1.6. Notions of transfer and possession may acquire here a different legal meaning. It may ever become trans-nationalised in international custody, clearing and settlement systems.

In the meantime, the settlement and clearing techniques were also refined, see also chapter IV, section 3.1.4. Settlement is now normally combined with an information matching in which as a first step buyer and seller will confirm their trades with an independent third party or settlement agent through whom trades are subsequently settled but who would only do so if the information received from both counterparties was identical and even then would only complete the transaction on an exchange of documents and money. This is the so-called DVP system of settlement or documents against payments facility in which no title transfers before these formalities are completed. It suggests a delayed transfer or own type of title transfer in these transactions which ties it to the receipt of funds from the buyer and securities from the seller. In the meantime, there are no more than obligatory rights of both parties against each other in respect of their transaction. The object is here the limitation of settlement risk. Of course, if late settlement or no settlement results under these rules, the party in default will still be liable for damages.

In modern clearing systems, a settlement agent will have bilateral agreements with all participants in the system under which the agent holds sufficient money and securities from each participant in a way that inter-day debits and credits (of fungible securities and moneys) are netted out on a constant basis (which raises the legal nature and status of

---

[42] See also HF Minnerop, 'Clearing Arrangements', (2003) 58 *The Business Lawyer*, 917.

netting agreements, which in international systems may also be trans-nationalised, cf. also chapter III, section 1.3). In book-entry or securities entitlement systems, the physical nature of securities transfers and payments have completely disappeared. The settlement agent is, in such systems, likely to be the sub-custodian of all participants who hold securities as well as bank accounts with the settlement agent and may organize a multilateral settlement system between all of them. That leads into clearing systems.

A modern system of clearing through so-called clearing houses will facilitate this settlement function which is in more advanced systems mostly combined with it. That is the reason why modern clearing and settlement are now mostly referred to together. It works most efficiently in a multi-participants set-up, therefore in a multilateral manner where, like in Euroclear or Clearstream, all brokers in the eurobond market (but not necessarily their clients) are part of the system. Say Broker A owes (for his clients) at the end of the day 50 shares in company Y to B, B owes 50 to C, and C owes 50 to D, whilst C owes 50 to A. In such a situation, it is obviously advantageous that instead of four physical transfers, B simply delivered 50 shares in Y to D. The result would be one physical (net) transfer of securities. Assume that all prices of the transactions were the same, there would also be one physical (net) payment. That would be the *second phase* of this clearing process. There would of course still be adjustments of each and any securities and bank accounts of all four participants with their settlement agent (who in turn would settle with their clients). The number of settlements is not reduced, simply the movement of assets. This simplification through clearing significantly reduces the costs of settlement and also the settlement risk. That makes it of great interest also to regulators.

A modern book-entry system for investment securities and electronic bank transfers for proceeds further facilitates this operation as even net amounts of securities and cash need no longer be transferred, neither between the settlement agent and its members nor between the members as brokers and their clients. Electronic transfers thus become possible for both securities and cash. Normally, in these book-entry systems, clearing and settlement organisations like Euroclear and Clearstream also operate as depositories, therefore as the legal owners of all securities so settled but this is not necessary for the operation of modern clearing. Thus Clearstream might be the depository of securities settled through Euroclear and *vice versa*. These clearing systems furthermore tend to operate as banks to their members to facilitate the payment side of the clearing and settlement.

Another evolution in this system is the appearance of the central counterparty (or CCP). It allows all securities transactions to be conducted with one central counterparty, who acts as buyer or seller in all cases on the basis of back to back agreements with the members of the systems (operating for their clients). Thus if someone long on securities in this system (acquired from the CCP) wants to sell, there will be a sales agreement with the same CCP who will than net both the original purchase contract and the new sales contracts out and pay the seller the difference. At the same time, there will be a new agreement in place with a buyer, who will have paid the CCP for the position. If there is no simultaneous outside buyer for the moment, there may be market-makers in this system (or the CCP may function as such) who will act as buyers from the CCP against a spread which they will quote and at which the CCP will acquire the position of the seller (plus a small fee). This CCP system is practiced in official derivative exchanges but not (yet) at Euroclear or Clearstream or in modern payment systems. It is naturally attractive for end investors who combine here liquidity with a safe execution facility. Of course the CCP could go bankrupt, but is normally guaranteed by the participants in the system.

This CCP facility shows the close modern connection between clearing, settlement and modern securities markets. These markets could disappear in this way in modern clearing and settlements organisations. It may be the way of the future, therefore also for securities trading, and would mean the end of official stock-exchanges as we know them today.

1.3.8   The Role of Investment Banks as Underwriters and Market Makers

New issues of shares and bonds (except government bonds in the domestic currency) are normally underwritten when an underwriting syndicate guarantees placement. Alternatively, placement may occur on a best effort basis. Examples of this are the dealerships in the placement of shorter term interest-bearing paper like CDs, CPs and MTNs. They do not require the intermediary taking any risk but there is also less reward in the fee structure. Another aspect of this latter type of placement is that it is often an ongoing effort in which different prices may be quoted by the dealer on the instruction of the issuer depending on prevailing market conditions from day to day.

The underwriting process on the other hand results in a series of *special agreements*, first between the issuer and the lead underwriter — often called the *subscription agreement* — and subsequently between the lead underwriter and the rest of the consortium or syndicate — the *agreement between underwriters* or the *underwriting agreement*. Then there may be a third layer of agreements between the underwriters and selling groups, the *selling agreements*, which are groups of dealers who will participate in the placement on a best effort basis. They habitually receive some discount on the offer price. Depending on the types of securities offered and services required, there are considerable variations in the substance of these agreements but the essence is always the same.

The key is that on the closing date, the underwriters must provide the issuer with the total amount of the issue (minus fees and agreed costs) whether or not they have been placed with the public. What is not placed is divided amongst the syndicate members according to a distribution formula agreed in the agreement amongst underwriters. Underwriting implies considerable risk and for the underwriting much depends on whether the issue is properly priced. If the price was too high, the risk for underwriters is much greater.

Pricing itself is a matter of agreement between issuer and underwriters in which the issuer sets the pace and underwriters are likely to give expert advice. It cannot always be entirely impartial as a lower price makes placement easier. In the eurobond market there developed also the so-called *bought deal* under which the syndicate would buy the whole issue, place it on their book or the joint book of all the syndicate members according to the agreed formula and subsequently sell it. It is a cleaner way of operating but requires the investment banks to apply more capital to the underwriting function.

As was already mentioned before, an important aspect of this primary market activity and *public placement* is, in the USA, the preparation of the SEC registration which requires disclosure with a prospectus and an on-going information supply. In the EU, there is the public offer prospectus requirement under the Directive of 1989, also already referred to, with an exemption for eurobond issues. It does not mean that eurobond selling in the USA is also exempt from SEC registration (except where it falls into certain categories of foreign investments). If the issuer requires the listing of the issue on an exchange, there will be further formalities and disclosure requirements. This system is now in the process of being reviewed in the EU under the Prospectus Directive, see more in particular section 3.5.3 below.

A new issue even if underwritten need not be publicly placed, either in the formal or informal markets, and *private placements* are also very common. They tend to be more informal, may not need a prospectus (see in the USA section 4 (2) of the 1933 Act and

Regulation D under that Act which exempts from registration some other limited offerings) and are targeted at a small group or at one investor. They may be tailor-made issues but still be in tradable form, although their private placement nature will affect the tradability which may be further curtailed by transfer limitations attached to the issue to preserve the private placement character.

Often it is the investor, who, through an investment bank, makes it known what he requires in terms of investments and the investment bank will then try to find an issuer. These targeted private placements are often still underwritten as a way to reward the investment bank and to qualify for underwriters' league tables, but, as placement is in such cases assured, the underwriting fee is likely to be modest.

In the USA, under SEC Rule 144A, the private placement rules have been considerably widened to allow companies to issue securities in the USA to small groups of large (professional) investors without registration, disclosure, prospectus and continuous reporting requirements. It is particularly important for foreign companies as US companies that issue shares to investors are normally already registered with the SEC and subject to their information updating requirements. A special trading system and settlement system was organised by the NASD for these types of privately placed securities (PORTAL).

Large and frequent issuers could of course attempt to do away with underwriting altogether and save themselves the cost, but they still value advice on the various windows of funding opportunities in the various markets and on pricing. Also, they do not have the specialised staff to organise the placement. They are, however, normally able to negotiate lower underwriting fees.

In bonds, another aspect of the issue is the *paying agent* who pays the coupons and repays the principal to the investor on the appointed payment dates. He may also have some other functions, like notifying investors and keeping contact with them. The situation can be further formalised by making him an (*indenture*) *trustee* of the issue, especially important when a change in conditions may have to be negotiated or when conditions change. Such a trustee will often be given certain powers in this respect in advance (in the trust deed). Because of the cost to the issuer, such a trustee will normally function only in larger more specialised issues. In eurobonds, there are likely to be paying agents only. There will be a number operating in different countries to give investors a choice in their collection of interest and principal. That may be important to them in connection with the confidentiality of their investment or foreign exchange restrictions.

In the new issue or primary market there often obtain special rules on *stabilisation*. Under them, the lead underwriter will intervene in the market to stabilise the price of the new issue if needed to allow for a large flood of new paper to be placed without a price collapse. It is particularly relevant in the case of a secondary offering of new shares. The practice is controversial because there is an element of market manipulation and it is in any event more questionable for an entirely new issue (primary offering). Nevertheless it is usually allowed in Europe on the condition that the activity is disclosed whilst it is going on.

A related way for underwriters to protect themselves, especially if other market participants are trying to short the issue, driving the price down, is to buy up all surplus and subsequently squeeze the shorts (*short squeeze*) who will, in order to cover their position, ultimately have no option but to buy from the underwriters at prices dictated by them. Related to this position is a so-called *ramp* where there are short positions in the secondary market known to a market maker who dominates the supply. He may in fact have induced the market to shorten in order to take subsequent advantage of his position in this manner.

This is likely to be much nearer market manipulation than stabilisation or a defensive squeeze.

A more modern way for the syndicate to defend itself against sudden market movements is the *fixed offer* technique. Under it, the lead manager enforces discipline in the syndicate by obliging members not to offer securities at a price lower than that set by the lead manager until such time as the latter allows the syndicate to be broken, usually when he is satisfied with the degree of placement. This practice has some features of a price cartel but is better considered as an alternative to stabilisation.

In the secondary market, the operations of investment banks are of particular interest when they operate as market-makers. Normally in informal markets like the eurobond markets they will do so either because they accept that obligation *vis-à-vis* issuers for whom they did the underwriting or because they have an interest in providing that liquidity in view of the possibilities of making some money (through their spreads). For the more prominent issues, it may also be a matter of market profile. Such market-making will in principle go on for the life of the issue, which in the case of shares and perpetuals is indefinite, although, as mentioned before, few eurobond issues are actively traded after an initial period and market-makers may drop them from their list. As a consequence, there are many illiquid issues in the eurobond market and most of the new issues only trade actively during and immediately after the launch of the issue. This is trading in the *grey market* on an '*if and when*' issued basis as the securities are not yet issued, which happens only at the closing. If a closing does not follow, all trades are void. Emphasis on trading on the grey market means that after an issue has been closed most investors hold the bonds thereafter until maturity.

As we already saw, market-making is typical for the more informal markets and investment banks as market-makers will form the heart of these informal markets, as they do indeed in the euromarkets. They will often use their screens to advertise their quotes (or spreads), but only to the most important investors or brokers who will know who and where they are. The larger market-makers will also use *sales forces* to access the public and call possible investors. This in-house sales force will also receive the inquiries of the investing public and effectively form the link between market-maker and investor. Market-makers also deal directly with each other (street trading) to adjust their books and lay off their risks. These sales forces are not brokers to the public and not under similar duties to avoid conflicts of interests. They are paid for by the market-makers themselves and contacting them should not give rise to fees.

Investors themselves may either directly approach a market-maker (via its sales forces) or use their broker to do so (in which case they will have to pay a brokerage fee). Market-makers may not, however, be willing to take calls directly from smaller investors because of the extra regulatory burdens this may put on them. It may also present problems in clearing and settlement as small investors are unlikely to be party to the relevant clearing and settlement organisations or systems. The euro-markets are typically markets for professional investors and brokers only.

These brokers may again be investment banks but at least for smaller investors they are more likely to be commercial banks which act as such for their banking customers or independents. An investment or universal bank must be careful to combine the function of market-maker and broker in respect of one client at the same time. If a brokerage fee is demanded, the banker/broker has as a minimum the obligation to test the entire market to obtain the best price for his client, as we shall see in the next section, and that may not be his own. If a broker is forced by the rules of his own organisation to deal solely with his own trading desk (and disclose whether his client is buyer or seller), the broker becomes an extension of it. In that case the broker acts as a mere sales representative and should not charge a brokerage fee on top of the market spread payable to the same organisation, whilst the client should be warned that in this way he is unlikely to get the best spread or price.

1.3.9   *The Role of Security Brokers and Investment Managers. Conflicts of Interests and Duty of Care*

Formal and informal markets need to be accessed by investors and, especially for the latter, that may not be easy, if small. The use of brokers is therefore normal. They make it their business to represent their clients in their investment business and conclude and settle their deals. Especially in quote-driven or market-making systems, their expertise will also be necessary to find the best deal amongst the various market-makers. In the London Stock Exchange before the so-called deregulation through Big Bang in 1986, investors could not directly access the market-makers or jobbers and always needed a broker. That is now no longer so as the monopoly was broken, but in practice brokers are ordinarily used to find the best price and execute the deals.

Brokers deal in their *own name* but for the account of their clients who also take the risk, see for contractual agency chapter II, part III. The broker is thus an agent, usually undisclosed, so that he incurs his own obligation *vis-à-vis* the counterparty to settle the deal (even if the principal or client does not come up with the securities or the money). On the other hand, if the broker defaults or demises, the client by disclosing the agency may be able to establish a direct relationship with the counterparty. In this way, he may collect the price directly from him for sold securities or obtain the securities directly from him by offering the purchase price. If proceeds or securities are already in the hands of the broker, the principal may be able to claim them. At least this is in brief the position at common law. In civil law, the situation is more complicated but it is moving in a similar direction. Under it, an assignment of cash proceeds to the client is sometimes deemed implied (which may create set-off and other problems, however) whilst securities may be directly claimable: see section 1.3.10. below.

The broker in his activities on behalf of the investor will, as his agent, be subject to a number of *fiduciary duties* of which, under common law, the traditional ones are the *duty of care*, *loyalty* and *confidentiality*. The standard of care is here higher than may be acceptable to the broker in his own investments. In securities operations this translates principally into a duty to advise the client concerning product and risk, taking into account his financial situation ('*know your customer*' and '*suitability*' rules). It also requires the broker to obtain best prices for the client ('*best price or best execution*' rule), to avoid aggressive tactics and unjustified turning over of the portfolio to obtain more commissions (*churning*), and to eliminate conflicts of interests by brokers *postponing* their own.

Thus the broker should not compete with his client for similar deals or take first when only a limited number of securities are available at a lower price or can be sold at a better price (no *front-running*). He must transfer to him all direct and indirect benefits of the transaction, including commission rebates, research information (soft commissions), etc. He can deduct only the agreed fees. In modern financial regulation these rules tend to be reinforced, even in civil law countries, and additions are made. Thus an *audit or paper trail* must be kept by the broker identifying in his own records the details of the instructions he received from the client and their timing. Telephone tapes may provide here further proof of client instructions and discussions with them, although they are in most markets not yet obligatory. Orders and transactions should be *time stamped* to show who has the earlier and better right and whether the agreed price corresponds to the market. Proceeds should remain segregated in special client accounts, well separated from the broker's own. This is the principle of *segregation of client funds*. Investment compensation schemes are likely to supplement the system.

On the European Continent, these protections remain often rudimentary mainly because the agency notion is less well developed. Fiduciary duties are not as such a special class of duties under civil law. In modern law, they are often fitted in as disclosure and negotiating duties of good faith but this development is only in its early stages. The EU Investment Service Directive in Article 11 gives expression to some of these protections to effect harmonisation but they are not properly set within the agency structure. Implementation legislation on the Continent often remains elementary, especially in the notion of post-ponement of interests, not charging spreads and brokerage fees at the same time, and segregating client assets. In fact the whole notion of tracing assets under a broker remains underdeveloped in civil law which is a great disadvantage in this area and a substantial handicap in the proper protection of investors.

Investment managers give their clients *advice* on how to handle their portfolios. Such advice is also inherent in the brokerage function, unless the broker acts as an 'execution only' broker, who usually operates against a lower fee. The client normally retains the ulti-mate decision and brokerage accounts are usually *non-discretionary*. Investment or asset managers, on the other hand, are often given discretion by their investing clients to operate for them in the markets in a discretionary manner. It normally requires a contract in which a certain investment strategy is mapped out.

As brokerage *de facto* often means that the broker's investment advice is followed, such an investment policy is mostly also contained in the client agreement between broker and client, at least if the client is a retail client. This fits in with the 'know your customer' and 'suitability' requirements of the brokerage relationship. Where there is formal or *de facto* discretion, the intermediaries' duties *vis-à-vis* their clients are accordingly enhanced. Even if the client retains the last word, the broker is not without duties and must warn against unadvisable investments within the 'know your customer' and 'suitability' rules. But he is discharged from liability if he has done so and the client persists. *Caveat emptor* then remains fully applicable to the client and there is certainly never a general right for small or inexperienced investors to lay off their risks on their brokers if markets turn against them.

In the USA, reference is often made to brokers/dealers. Section 3(a)(4) of the Securities Exchange Act of 1934 defines the broker as any person engaged in the business of effecting transactions in securities for the account of others (but does not include a bank). Under section 3(a)(5) a dealer is defined as any person engaged in the business of buying and sell-ing securities for his own account, through a broker or otherwise. The functions are in the USA normally combined, hence the frequent references to broker/dealers, but should be well distinguished and not give rise to conflict of interests. Under section 15 both must ensure adequate employee supervision, financial responsibility and sufficient capital and fair dealing with customers, including protection of customers' securities and funds and monitoring sales practices.

In turn, these functions should be clearly distinguished from those of exchanges. They are defined in section 3(a)(1) as organisations which constitute, maintain, or provide a market place or facilities for bringing together purchasers and sellers of securities or as otherwise providing the function commonly performed by a stock exchange as that term is generally understood. There is much confusion about this definition and especially infor-mal and now Internet or electronic markets may not always fall within it, especially the bulletin board type. They may, however, fall within the definition of broker/dealer in that they bring buyers and sellers together. It has all to do with registration and its formalities and with supervision: see for the electronic exchanges also section 1.3.5 above. Since 1998 there is a new Rule 3B–12 to cover alternative trading systems giving operators the option between regulation as an exchange or broker dealer, in the latter case with additional requirements depending on their activities and volume. It was a compromise imposed because of the fundamental distinction in American regulatory law between broker, dealers and markets and falls a long way short of devising a regulatory system for a modern electronic market.

1.3.10   Insolvency of Securities Brokers. The Notion of Segregation, Tracing and Constructive Trust in Respect of Client Assets

In the previous section two major risks of engaging a securities broker were identified. One major problem is the duty of care of the broker and the conflicts of interest that there may arise between the broker and his client. The other problem is the insolvency of the broker.

The common law of agency and its fiduciary duties traditionally has a number of solutions for the conflicts of interest. As we saw in the previous section, civil law may be more handicapped and has to develop the necessary investor's protection as far as duties of care and conflicts of interest are concerned within the context of its notion of good faith in contract, which may include certain disclosure and implementation duties. Not all civil law countries are here, however, equally oriented. Especially in Southern Europe, the notion of good faith in contract remains less well developed with a resulting further handicap in developing notions of investors' protection against conflicts of interest: see for the good faith notion more in particular chapter II, section 1.3 and for its operation in the law of agency, chapter II, section 3.1.4.

In the case of a bankruptcy of the intermediary (broker) or agent, civil law also needs to develop further, particularly in the aspect of segregating and tracing (a) client assets (notably client securities and moneys), (b) client assets still in the process of settlement, and (c) claims of the agent against third parties in respect of client assets that have not yet entered settlement. These assets may all be individualised and held as such at the broker's or, much more likely, may be pooled as *fungible assets* at the level of the broker or (again more likely) at third parties with whom the broker has security accounts like a depository (or other type of custodian) in respect of securities or a bank in respect of client money. Money in this sense is always fungible and modern investment securities now normally also are. Fungibility is here an important complicating factor for investors. On the other hand, the simplification through clearing that it allows significantly reduces the costs of settlement and also the settlement risk. That makes it also of great interest to regulators, see section 1.3.7 above.

There is a progression in the investors' protection in this area which resulted in book-entry systems for investment securities as discussed more fully in chapter IV, section 3.1.6. The essence is as follows: if the securities are expressed as book-entry entitlements with a broker, whom in turn has entitlements with depositories or other custodians in an immobilised system of securities holdings, the client has rights against the broker which may be pooled at that level if the broker has more clients who are investing in the same securities, and they in turn may have some rights against the custodian of the broker if he defaults in his duty to give them the rights to the dividends, voting rights, distribution of any winding-up proceeds, and corporate information, which are the essence of their securities' entitlements. At least they will have a right to appoint a replacement intermediary for their entitlements.

What concerns us here are in essence *proprietary* questions, more fully discussed in chapter IV, sections 3.1.3 *et seq.* and in common law largely covered by the equitable notions of disclosure, constructive trust and tracing within agency or custody relationships. Civil law has here no true equivalent or answer and must develop its own property notions in this connection to provide adequate investors' protection against an agent acting on behalf or in the name of clients or against a broker/custodian who operates a book-entry system for his clients. These issues are of particular interest should the broker go bankrupt.

Short of a book-entry system, there are here a number of problems more extensively discussed in chapter II section 3.1.5/6 in connection with the concept of agency proper and in chapter IV, section 3.1.3 *et seq* in the case of custody and book-entry systems. Whilst dealing for his client, the broker is normally an *undisclosed agent* in common law or an indirect agent in civil law, although third parties often realise that the broker mostly does not act for himself. That may make a difference as an agency upon disclosure or a semi-disclosed agency creates under common law *direct* ties between the principal and the third party. In civil law, this type of agency, under which the broker normally acts in his own name (but for the account of his client) excludes, in principle, any direct ties between a third party and the principal or client of the agent, even upon disclosure.

Under modern civil law, this may be different only if the third party has already performed towards the broker. In that case, the client may be able at least to claim title to all identifiable tangible assets (including securities) which the broker acquired for him, but there may still be doubt as to (a) any claims he still has on third parties for performance (on behalf of his principal) or to (b) any moneys or pooled securities that he has so acquired or to (c) any moneys or securities he may have put (in his own name) with third parties, like banks for deposits and depositaries for securities.[43] Again, the problem is more fundamental in respect of assets that by their very nature are fungible.

Thus there are here in principle three possibilities: tangible assets (securities) may still be with a seller, or they are with the broker or a third party in the nature of a client account.

---

[43] In civil law, disclosure of the investors/clients may in law not operate as putting them automatically in the position of the bankrupt brokers *vis-à-vis* counterparties, clearers, bankruptcy trustees, banks or depositaries in the proprietary aspects of the transaction. Specific statutory provisions may now underpin the possibility of clients retrieving specific tangible assets acquired by the agent for them so that title shoots through to them, as under Art 3.110 of the new Dutch Civil Code. However, these statutory provisions may only apply to allocated and individualised securities that physically exist (therefore normally bearer securities) and not to proceeds or residual performance claims against counterparties as many civil law jurisdictions still have problems in characterising proceeds or claims as assets. Also the notion of segregation into client accounts of moneys or pooled assets creating joint property in them may still not be fully accepted.

Without further statutory provisions, like the *Kapitalanlagegesellschaftsgesetz* of 1970 in Germany, it may mean that in civil law countries for securities not yet delivered to the broker, the investor may still be unable to obtain his own position *vis-à-vis* counterparties or in the clearing. Any securities or moneys due upon clearing will in any event always go first into the bankrupt broker even though they may be collected in segregated client accounts, which even then may not provide full protection against the broker's bankruptcy.

In the Netherlands, by special statutory provision (Arts 7.420/421 CC), the claim to securities and proceeds still with the counter-party is now statutorily assigned to the investor upon disclosure of the agency. This still seems to subject it to all complications concerning assignments, including the set-off of any unrelated claims the counterparty may have on the broker. This is undesirable as the investor's assets are used in this manner to pay for the debts of the broker to a counterparty who is generally aware that the broker is unlikely to have dealt for his own account. Already in the beginning of the 19th century the unfairness of this set-off was noted in common law in *Baring v Corrie*, 2 B & Ald 137 (1818). Other possibilities are to assume here, instead of a statutory assignment, some trust structure for which civil law is ill-equipped or to apply the rules of direct agency upon disclosure of the indirect agency in the common law way and trace. It would be the best solution.

The implementation of the EU Investment Services Directive which requires a proper system of segregation, which, it is submitted, must include forms of proprietary tracing to be meaningful, has, from this perspective, mostly been incomplete in most EU countries. The true reason is the underdeveloped notion of (indirect) agency in civil law and of the notions of segregation and tracing or constructive trust. The result is a competitive advantage for common law brokers who by law afford their clients better protection, not only against their own misbehaviour but also against their insolvency.

Therefore, in the case of a securities purchase, shares bought are either still with the counterparty or already delivered to the broker, either physically (individualised or pooled) or more likely pooled through a third party (custodian), whilst the purchase money may still be with the broker, either physically (individualised or pooled) or in a pooled client account with a bank (but in the broker's name) if not already paid out to the seller. Conversely, if there is a sale, the shares may still be in the seller's account, or physically with the broker (either individualized or pooled) or they may already have been delivered to the third party who may have paid for them to the broker who may have the money physically (either individualised or pooled) or may have put it in a pooled client account or already have transferred the money to his client. They may also still be in the clearing, resulting in the transfer of unscrambled net amounts of securities or moneys that remain unallocated between clients even though transferred or at least allocated to the broker or other intermediary who may have gone bankrupt in the meantime.

If, upon a bankruptcy of the broker, performance is not completed between broker and counterparties (either the broker for seller or buyer) as the case may be, there will be intangible claims on these counter-parties to the shares or the money as a matter of performance. Even if there has been performance by the counterparty, the moneys or securities may still be with the broker or his bankers or custodians in the broker's name resulting in corresponding claims of the broker against them. Pooling of assets or moneys at the level of the broker or (in the broker's name) at these third parties may create further complications if respectively these third parties or the broker go bankrupt. Some of these may be resolved in a book-entry system of securities entitlements.

The key is always whether the client has in these circumstances (a) *direct* rights to any uncompleted performance of the counterparty (upon disclosure of his interest), or (b) a proprietary right in any securities and moneys still under the broker (either physically, in an individualised or pooled manner or more likely in a bankrupt broker's pooled, individualized or own account with his bank or custodian). As already mentioned, this is (outside the area of book-entry systems) foremost a matter of agency law and the possibility for the client to *directly* claim his assets in the (constructive) possession of his broker. Closely connected is the question of proper *segregation* of client assets (either under the broker or in client accounts organised and held by him) or otherwise (upon co-mingling) the question of tracing into the broker's own accounts, a concept more controversial in civil than in common law.

At both the level of the bank or custodian and the broker (depending where the assets are), there may be special arrangements which complicate this picture further, although they may also result in better protection for investors if the broker goes bankrupt in the meantime. What concerns us here in particular is the role of clearing and the status of book-entry entitlements, already mentioned above. First, the transaction (delivery of shares or proceeds, not book-entry entitlements) may still be in the clearing. As from a legal point of view, under the common law of agency, the investor may claim all his assets (including the intangible claims for performance) upon disclosure of the agency, he may be able to take the position of the broker in the clearing (if he is a member himself or can timely find a replacement member). Since clearing and settlement are a question of a few days at most, the transaction is likely, however, always to settle in the name of the insolvent broker unless there is an *unwind* or *recast* in the clearing in which case the insolvent broker is eliminented from the system.

If the net number of securities resulting from the clearing is settled in the name of the broker and delivered to him (assuming they are physical securitities), the client may, under common law, still be able to claim them from the broker if the net number of securities the broker receives is subsequently broken out and unscrambled between his clients. In civil law, that would depend on whether in such cases under applicable law title shoots through immediately to the clients. It is easier in the case of identified physical shares or registration than in the case of mere rights or book-entry entitlements (which would only show in the increase of the entitlement of the intermediary with his custodian). If the net number was delivered directly into a client account in the name of the broker, therefore in a segregated account even if held in the name of the broker, the unscrambling would take place through that account and clients are the likely to be protected on the basis of the notion of segregation (assuming that it is also accepted in civil law). It would not then matter whether the assets would be fungible or not. They would be set aside as pools, giving the joint owners the right to segregation against the intermediary (both the broker and the custodian).

If the assets, especially proceeds, are completely commingled with funds or securities in the broker's own accounts, there is, in common law, still the possibility of *tracing* but it may practically speaking come to an end if unscrambling is no longer possible, although the burden of proof of the broker's ownership may still be with the bankruptcy trustee (of the broker) and a joint ownership of the pool (including the broker's interest) might still result. It is in any event the fairer solution. If there is proper segregation through separate client accounts, the clients will now mostly be able to claim their proceeds or securities as common property amongst them. The clients may on the basis of their own data, as confirmed by those of the broker claim their *pro rata* part of the joint client account as interest holders. It assumes further that the client account has not been used for the expenditure of the broker when there will be a shortfall. This will have to be shared *pro rata* by the clients pending resolution of their claim against the broker.

This will usually not be problematic any longer, although it may still take time, require the co-operation of the trustee in bankruptcy and may obstruct for some time the sales possibility for the investors, especially undesirable if markets move adversely. The worst position is here that the investors have no direct claim to divide these assets but depend on the trustee's co-operation and timing to have the securities registered in their own name or rather into the name of a substitute broker appointed by them.

That is particularly important in book-entry systems, where there is no more than an entry of share ownership in the books of the broker (resulting in an entitlement only) underpinned by the broker's own registration in the book's of the custodian in an immobilised system of securities holdings (although there may be more layers). In such cases, one must assume that the bankrupt broker's entitlement reflected in the custodians account will have to be distributed to other brokers according to the end investors' preferences and that their right to choose other intermediaries survives the bankruptcy of a broker with whom entitlements are held by his clients. Statutory law backing up the book-entry systems in most modern countries will now commonly segregate these entitlements out *per se* and protect them in the case of a bankruptcy of the relevant brokers when their clients can simply move their accounts to others without the bankruptcy trustee having any *veto* or delaying power.

As to *unsettled* transactions, the issue of indirect agency and disclosure of the agency to make the title to the shares shoot through to the client, and the issue of segregation may not truly arise in respect of the securities traded in book-entry systems as in that case all is a matter of transfer instructions, much in the manner of modern payment instructions, which the broker implements following his clients sale or purchase order. It is a matter of the crediting or debiting if the relevant client securities accounts. But there are here still the questions concerning the clients' direct rights in respect of any *net* number of securities that result for a broker from the clearing (pending unscrambling of this net number for distribution amongst the clients). There is also the question what client right's are if the brokers own entitlement higher up in the chain was already adjusted for any purchase and there is ultimately the status of any rights to still unsettled transactions and money, which rights are also in the broker's own name. Again these matters are more fully discussed in chapter IV, part III in connection with the operation of book-entry systems of securities entitlements.

1.3.11   *Investment Funds or Collective Investment Schemes*

Vast amounts of money are invested in collective investment schemes, also referred to as investment funds. They are run by investment managers, often investment banks who therefore may (a) advise investors directly in their investments or (b) offer to them instead collective investment schemes which these managers usually organize and market as investment alternatives. They are often investment banking divisions, although they may also be commercial banking subsidiaries or independent companies. Intrinsically, spreading or diversification of investments is guaranteed in these collective schemes that also benefit from professional management. These schemes may be of the *open* or *close-end* type. In the case they are open, new investors can join at all times and may leave the fund also at any moment of their choosing. In principle, they will be entitled to join and leave (or acquire or sell participation certificates) on the basis of the intrinsic value of the fund in respect of which the managers may quote a spread (or bid and offer price). These open-ended investment companies (OEIC) or funds are the more normal type often more suited to the public for their easy exit facilities.

In the UK, collective investment schemes come in several legal forms. They may basically be organised in the form of (a) a trust (or unit trust), (b) an investment company, or (c) a (limited) partnership. In a trust, the investors will operate as beneficial owners, in an investment company as shareholders, and in partnerships as unlimited or limited partners. It may be asked in all these schemes what the true nature of the investor's interest is and in particular whether there are any direct rights of participants to the underlying securities of the fund, an issue briefly discussed in chapter IV, section 3.3.

In the UK, the Financial Services and Markets Act of 2000 (section 235) defines a collective investment scheme as an arrangement with respect to property of any description, including money, the purpose or effect of which is to enable persons taking part in the arrangements (whether becoming owners of the property or any part of it or otherwise) to participate in or receive profits or income from the acquisition, holding, management or disposal of the property or sums paid out of such profits or income. Under Section 237(1), a unit trust scheme means a collective investment scheme under which the property is held in trust for participants. Section 236(1) defines an *investment company* as a collective investment scheme that satisfies two conditions: the property condition and the investment condition.

The implications are similar to those for unit trusts in the sense that the *property condition* allows the scheme's property to beneficially belong to and be managed by a body corporate having as its purpose the investment of its funds with the aim of spreading the investment risk and giving its members the benefit of the results of the management of the funds. The *investment condition* means that an investor may reasonably expect to be able to realise his investment in the scheme after a reasonable period on the basis of the value of the property in respect of which the scheme is set up and makes arrangements. This corporate form of investment schemes was set up in the UK in order to appeal more to foreign investors who might be less familiar and comfortable with the trust concept inherent in unit trusts.[44] Regulation is largely left to special orders of the Treasury which track the situation of unit trusts (Financial Services (Open-ended Investment Companies) Regulations since 1997). In the UK, the property of the open ended investment company must be vested in a different entity (the depository), who acts as trustee of a unit trust and holds the property for the investment company.

In respect of limited partnerships as collective investment schemes, in the UK, a distinction must in this respect be made between limited partnerships and limited liability partnerships. The latter are organised under the Limited Liability Partnership Act 2000 but operate like companies. In the UK, partnerships proper operate under the Partnership Act of 1890. Limited partnerships operate under an Act of 1907. They are still partnerships in the proper sense; the difference is that the limited partners are mere investors and do not become involved in the running of the business. As such, the limited partnership is suitable to be used as a collective investment scheme. Partners are entitled to a share in the profits of the business and to the assets available upon dissolution but it is often assumed that in the meantime no partner has a true proprietary interest in the assets of the partnership itself. Limited liability partnerships (LLPs) under the Act of 2000 were created to protect professionals in professional partnership against negligence claims against other partners. They do not need to have members, are incorporated by registration, need not have capital nor directors. They are here relevant in that they may be used also as open ended investment vehicles (according to Section 21 of the Collective Investment Schemes Order).

Collective investment schemes of the various types are normally subject to strict regulatory supervision. In the EU, for funds of the open type this gave rise to an early division of labour between home and host regulators in the UCITS Directive of 1985, amended in 2001, see also section 2.3.5 below. As part of an EU passport for these funds, the original 1985 Directive set out harmonised rules for authorisation and prudential supervision throughout the EU which subsequently served as a model in all EU countries. There are also some harmonized rules concerning the investments themselves and the spreading of risk. Hence the limitation of these schemes to certain authorised products that have been expanded in the 2001 (Products) Directive. There are also provisions for prospectuses and regular information supply. Host country rule is particularly relevant in the area of investors' protection in terms of cold calling, marketing and advertising.

1.3.12 Other Investment Banking Activities. Corporate Finance, Mergers and Acquisitions, Company Valuations

Another traditional activity of investment banks is the rendering of corporate advice. This is especially relevant to mergers and acquisitions but it may also involve advice on the type of financing that may be the most suitable and obtainable. It may in fact result in advice on the rearrangement of the entire liability side of the balance sheet. It may go further and also

---

[44]The distinction was explained in *Charles v Federal Commission of Taxation* [1954] 90 CLR 598 where it was said that a unit trust is fundamentally different from a share in a company. A share confers upon the holder no legal or equitable interest in the assets of the company; it is a separate piece of property, and if a portion of the company's assets is distributed among the shareholders the question whether it comes to them as income or capital depends in whether the corpus of the property (their shares) remains intact despite the distribution. But a unit confers a proprietary interest in all property which for the time being is subject to the trust of the deed so that the question whether moneys distributed to unit holders under the trust form part of their income or of their capital must be answered by considering the character of those moneys in the hands of the trustees before the distribution is made. It should be noted, however, that by defining the rights of investors in a corporate scheme more precisely (whilst approximating them to that of unit trust holders) the differences here outlined might become much more blurred.

cover corporate activity which may result in a complete re-organisation of the company. The type of advice will of course foremost depend on what the client wants but may also be volunteered by investment banks.

This part of investment banking activity will be done in the corporate finance department. Mergers and acquisitions are the most important slice of this activity. It is cyclical, fashion prone and invariable subject to major disappointments as many mergers ultimately fail to achieve the expected objectives and savings. The figure is sometimes put at 30 per cent of the total, whilst of the rest about half encounter major integration problems. The anticipated added value is often not there. Major redistributions of unwanted assets usually follow in a round of larger or smaller disposals (that may involve investment banks again). At least the agitation surrounding mergers and acquisitions or the threat thereof prevents complacency in corporate life. It may concern here a self-destructing process that may give rise to new life and has a cleansing function. As such it can be seen as an indispensable component of modern business life.

Mergers and acquisitions often have trans-border aspects, as in the larger transactions foreign subsidiaries or assets are invariably involved. There will be corporate and related regulatory complications, especially in unsolicited or contested mergers and acquisitions that may become internationalised. 'Poisoned pills' which are defensive tools triggered when an unwanted take-over is threatened, directors' duties, shareholders' information, veto or consent rights, and minority shareholders protection issues will come to the fore. There are likely to be further complications under securities laws when the target is a publicly quoted company. In international cases, the application of domestic take-over statutes (like the Williams Act in the US) or (informal) codes (like the Take-over Code in the UK) is likely to become an issue also, especially in contested bids.

Other important issues concern the *valuation* of the company to be acquired and, if new shares are issued by the acquiring company in exchange for the shares in that company, also the valuation of the acquiring company itself in relation to the value of the company to be acquired. These valuations are likely to play a big role in contested bids. There are various methods to establish values and this will be one of the most important tasks of investment banks that become involved as advisors. For this activity, they may or may not need to be authorised and supervised; it depends on domestic law. The EU Investment Services Directive does not require it *per se* but to avail themselves of the EU passport for these services, see section 1.1.9 above, they need to be authorised (but that must be part of a broader authorisation, Articles 3 and 14).

Valuation can be done at several levels. One can look at the assets and liabilities of a company or, if its shares are quoted, at the share value. They are of course related but not necessarily directly. A complicating factor is here that the assets and liabilities as presented in the balance sheet may be historical and may have to be revalued in which context off-balance sheet items, like contingent liabilities, will also have to be taken into account. This can be done and the debts and other liabilities will then be deducted from the revalued assets. This gives a value but it is likely to be tantamount to valuing a company at its immediate *liquidation* or *break-up value*. In a merger situation, much more important will be the *going concern* value, therefore the value over and above the break-up value. This is sometimes also called the goodwill. It relates to expertise, positioning in the market, relationships, the effectiveness of patents, and especially future growth prospects. Here the disagreements on proper value may be considerable, especially in contested take-over bids. It concerns the earning potential of a business and its future cash flows (normally understood in terms of net earnings — therefore earnings after expenses, but before interest payments and tax (EBIT) and with a deduction for estimated future investments). These total estimated cash flow streams are then *discounted* to a present day value by using an interest rate which involves a judgment on future interest rate developments and an estimation of the so-called 'equity risk premium'. Here the question is the extra return that shares, which are riskier, should yield over (government) bonds and the volatility (or 'beta') of the specific company's shares within the market.

Yet it allows for a present day value being put on cash flows that may be received a long time from now. In other words, if Swiss Francs 1000 is going to be earned in year ten, its present value can be found after deducting compounded interest over a 10 years period. Modern calculators will give the answer instantaneously, but the two imponderables remain the estimate of the profit in year 10 and the development of interest rates during the 10 years' period. In both cases huge assumptions are likely to be made, especially in the area of anticipated growth rates. This method of valuing is common, however, and assumes that the value of a business is in essence the total of all its cash flows till the end of its existence properly discounted on the basis of a realistic interest rate. Normally a range of outcomes will be produced which may be averaged. The more they differ the greater the risks for the acquirer.

In connection with valuations, the trading multiples of similar companies and the acquisition multiples of precedent transactions are closely scrutinised. Multiples include the classic price/earnings ratios, which divide present share prices by present profits per share, and increasingly EBITDA based multiples which divide the value of a company's shares and its debt by its EBITDA (earnings before tax, interest, depreciation (of assets) and amortisation (of goodwill)). These multiples allow a quick comparison between a proposed purchase price with its implicit multiples and the multiples investors are currently paying in the stock market or were paid in precedent transactions.

Especially for agreed take-overs of publicly quoted companies, valuation issues will focus on the value of the shares. Of course, there is likely to be a daily quote, which should be indicative of real values. Theoretically, they should equal the discounted cash flows per share (or at least the discounted total anticipated dividend stream and any residual liquidation value including retained earnings), but market sentiment may affect the price especially when rumours of an imminent takeover circulate in the market. This explains daily swings which might lead to adjustments in the valuation. It is also said in this connection that 'efficient markets' constantly discount new information which means that share values become subject to a 'random walk'.

In any event, in a take-over situation a premium may be paid. This is often a practical issue (to induce present holders to part with their shareholding) but may be justified on theoretical grounds as a result of the synergies arising from the transaction. Synergies arise from a takeover as the earnings potential of two companies should be greater when they are combined as opposed to when they operate stand alone entities due to basic economies of scale. The likelihood of subsequent disappointment was already signalled above.

All these valuation methods can and have been criticised and are in take-over situations often twisted to obtain the desired result. For the present purpose of showing what investment banks' corporate finance activities involve, it is not necessary to go into them in any greater detail.

1.3.13   *The Risks in the Securities Business. Securities Regulation and its Focus. The European and American Approaches*

What are the typical risks and concerns in the securities business of which the modern securities regulator needs to be aware and which of these risks require regulation? What should be the focus of modern securities regulation and how should it be organised? In investment banking, we take here the functional approach and look therefore at the *type of activity* first, like the issuing activity in respect of issuers, the underwriting activity of investment banks, their market making activity, brokerage activity, investment management activity, clearing and settlement and custody activities. Even stock exchanges as such may still be regulated in this context. How it is done can be chiefly broken down in the manner as set forth in section 1.1.1 in terms of authorisation, prudential supervision, conduct of business and product supervision, except that in as far as issuers are concerned, who are not service providers in this context, the authorisation will translate in prospectus requirements and prudential supervision in regular information supply. As to the objectives of this regulation, they may be very different in respect of each of these functions as we already saw.

Thus in the primary market, there are especially the registration, disclosure or prospectus requirements of the issuer and the prospectus liability connected with the issuing and listing of securities. It is commonly considered a question of investor protection, even though professionals may now have better ways of checking up on issuers whilst the prospectus requirement has never meant much in the euromarkets. As we saw, there was an exemption for these markets in the EU Public Offer Prospectus Directive and under the new EU Prospectus requirements bond issues with large denominations remain also effectively exempt. On the other hand, regulators in domestic markets like the SEC in the US may even have the power to forbid any issues they do not like.

Solvency of the underwriter is another aspect as proceeds of a placement not yet paid over to the issuer may be endangered upon the insolvency of the underwriter. The underwriting obligation itself will then also be affected, but both obligations may devolve on other members of the syndicate. Systemic risk concerns may here also play a role, although probably minor, so may be the concern for the reputation and health of the financial center from which underwriters operate. Investors protection itself would seem here a lesser consideration.

As to the market-making aspect, again there is little risk to investors, except in the potential manipulation of prices and the quoting of spreads. Whatever other concerns there may be, it is likely to be in terms of insolvency and systemic risk only. Again, the systemic risk is unlikely to be great. Nevertheless, in the Investment Services Directive, the EU required authorisation and prudential supervision of *both* the underwriting and market making functions.

In the secondary market, it will be the reliability and expertise of the broker and his solvency that will be major regulatory issues, especially in respect of smaller investors. This insolvency aspect is less important than in banking as the law substantially protects the principal against the insolvency of his broker through segregation duties and tracing possibilities of bought securities or sales proceeds, at least in common law countries. A form of segregation is here implied. In civil law, this area remains much less developed and often requires special statutory intervention which may or may not prove adequate for investors, see section 1.3.10 above.

In all cases, the separation of client assets and funds remains important, as are investor compensation schemes, but the main emphasis of regulation will be the strengthening of investors' rights against an incompetent or unscrupulous broker who prefers his own interests. Hence the elaboration of the fiduciary duties in regulation in common law or of the disclosure and execution duties in regulation in civil law. They allow or should allow for more protection in respect of unsophisticated investors. It means a strenghtening of private law concepts.

In both the primary and secondary markets, another concern may be the monopolisation of particular market functions like those of brokers and market-makers by exchange members whilst limiting the access of outsiders and setting the market-making rules and brokerage fees. This was considered the case in the London Stock Exchange before the Big Bang in 1986. In this connection, there may still be special concern about the accessibility of the clearing and settlement systems of exchanges by outsiders. In respect of them the more common concerns about authorisation, prudential supervision, conduct and products are less relevant. In the EU, there is here no authorisation requirement. As mentioned before, modern regulation, especially in the securities industry, regulates participants according to their function, especially brokers, market makers and, to a lesser extent, market-facilitating institutions like stock exchanges, clearing and settlement systems or custodians, therefore, in principle, all those who are in between investors and users of capital or all those who are involved in the flow of money from savers back to capital users. As was discussed already in section 1.1.4 above, modern regulation will or should no longer attempt primarily to regulate the markets as such.

Whether the market in this abstract sense operates nationally or internationally is in this way no longer greatly relevant for regulators, as business is likely to move to the informal offshore markets if too restricted at home. There is here a form of regulatory competition between countries that wish to maintain a serious venue for financial markets. The key is that investors within each jurisdiction are properly protected, whether they deal in domestic, international or globalised markets and that is a matter of regulation of the activity or service providers and possibly of the products offered, even when coming from abroad. It is not a matter of structures.

For investment banking regulation, the emphasis is therefore more properly on the behaviour of intermediaries for each type of service they provide and on the risk for the investor inherent in their conduct and in the investment products they buy for him. As investment banking activities do not incur the same systemic risk as commercial banking (in terms of liquidity providing and payment systems), there is here less emphasis on adequate capital and sufficient infrastructure from that point of view. In a bankruptcy, even if large, less appears to be at stake in terms of systemic risk. Moreover, investors usually rely on investment compensation schemes and should receive also protection from the segregation of assets in separate client accounts and from their general tracing powers, although still problematic in many civil law countries. In fact the need for the regulation of investment banks for other than conduct of business and product control remains contested for these reasons, therefore especially the need for authorisation and prudential supervision. For the more professional investor there is also less room for concern in the areas of conduct of business and the types of products offered or indeed for transparency in the issuing process through prospectuses. In this vein, corporate finance activity may remain entirely unregulated.

In any event, it follows that, where commercial banks remain largely regulated as deposit-taking *institutions* whilst for regulatory purposes all their other activities are considered substantially subordinated to the deposit-taking function, investment banks (or brokers/dealers) are foremost regulated *per service* they provide, therefore per function, although in the authorisation and supervision there remains for them an institutional element also, but again the type of authorisation they receive and the requirements therefore will be geared to the services they plan to offer. The further consequence is that commercial banks usually have one main supervisor for all their activities, who, even if other activities of a commercial bank like brokerage or investment management are in principle regulated by others, operates as lead regulator at least for capital adequacy purposes.

The result is that investment banks will normally have various regulators. Thus in the USA, broker-dealers and exchanges are subject to SEC registration followed by forms of self-regulation through their own organisations (Self Regulatory Organisations or SROs) per function or activity, like the exchanges for the products they deal in and the NASD for securities operations of their members, although always overseen by the SEC. In the UK, there were the SFA and IMRO as SROs respectively for securities and investment management activities under the oversight of the SIB (with whom intermediaries could also register directly), although in the UK after 1997 the SROs were merged with the SIB into one central supervisory authority also covering commercial banking and insurance (the FSA).

A modern regulatory system concerning financial services should always be considered separately from the regulation of capital flows or monetary control, see also section 1.1.2 above. They should not impede the services flow either. On the other hand, there are in the securities industry other concerns, like the organisation of an investor compensation scheme, an efficient and cheap complaints procedure for smaller investors, civil liability of an intermediary for breach of the rules, and criminal liability for major offences like market manipulation and insider dealing. This civil and criminal liability may be extended from the intermediary firms to their personnel.

Whilst, like in the UK, (official) markets themselves are not or no longer the prime focus of regulation and the emphasis is on the participants and their services and on investor protection needs, it follows that at least organised markets, settlement and custody agencies are increasingly deregulated. They may still obtain some official status through official recognition. That has been the UK system at least since 1986. Official recognition implies conditions but it will reinforce the status of these organisations and may also reduce their (price) reporting and other disclosure burdens. Authorisation itself in the UK system after 1986 has been no prerequisite for the operations of the organised markets, settlement and custody agencies. That was done to avoid monopolies. The clear objective is, nevertheless, for informal structures in the securities markets to become part of the system so as to create a market framework with sufficient resources and reliable facilities.

US law remains here stricter and probably more old-fashioned. Section 5 of the 1934 Act requires that securities exchanges are all registered with the SEC unless exempted under section 6 and they regulate themselves as SROs but always subject to SEC supervision. As already mentioned above, although in the USA the NASDAQ is often presented as an over-the-counter (OTC) or informal market, it is as a registered SRO an officially regulated market and as such quite different from the informal markets like the Euromarket in Europe. The fact that it has no floor and is a telephone market is only an organisational detail.

The American approach remains different from the European, not only in the regulation of official and unofficial markets in the secondary market, but also in what seems excessive emphasis on registration of new issues in the primary market. Neither considers the type and expertise of investors (except under the limited private placement exception of Section 4(a)(2) of the Securities Act). The result is further a suspicion of all foreign securities as regards the way in which they are issued and offered, which seems unwarranted in view of the modern information facilities concerning issuers and international trading facilities: see for the limited American response to the internationalisation of the securities industry sections 1.1.11 above and 3.1. 2 below.

For modern securities regulation, the major underlying aim is not only the protection of investors but more generally also the protection of the reputation of the financial centre from which financial services are offered: see more in particular section 1.1.3 above. Avoidance of monopolies and competition between the market facilitating organisations, like official and informal exchanges, clearing and settlement organisations and custodians may be other aims. Besides, securities legislation may also attempt to provide a better framework for all commercial transactions concerning investments in their various aspects, as was certainly another aim of the 1986 Financial Services Act in the UK, now superseded by the Financial Services and Markets Act 2000.

1.3.14 Securities Regulators

Financial regulation is naturally a political issue, and although the principles are becoming more uniform and therefore to some extent depoliticised, enforcement remains politically sensitive. In the banking area as we saw, the regulator was from early on an organisation separate from government, usually central banks. Although they functioned in Europe often as nationalised entities, they are now mostly given an independent status (at least in Euro countries). Securities regulation to the extent existing often made ministries of finance or economic affairs the ultimate regulator like, until 1986, the Department of Trade and Industry (DTI) in the UK. Most was done by the official exchanges. This system seldom proved successful.

By creating separate agencies like the SIB (now FSA) in the UK and much earlier the SEC in the USA, governments and official exchanges now take mostly a back seat in enforcement. It has become more independent, professional and better equipped, whilst the costs, as in the UK, are often put on the financial services industry, which, however inconvenient for this industry, at least provides adequate funds.

In the new set-up in the UK after 1986, day-to-day regulation was left to self-regulatory organisations (SROs) in the various segments of the securities markets (under the supervision of the SIB now superseded by the SFA). Of these, the SFA (for securities and futures investments) and IMRO (for investment management services) became the most important. They would issue rules following the SIB's guidelines and models.

It was felt, however, that the whole system was not sufficiently transparent and that especially the smaller investor had no proper insight in his recourse possibilities under the various sets of rules and complaints procedures. Thus as at 1997, a new agency was created in the UK, the Financial Services Authority or FSA, into which the SIB and the existing SROs were merged and which acquired at the same time also the banking and insurance supervisory functions, the former from the Bank of England which remained competent for monetary supervision and the overall stability of the financial system. In this connection it also retained its role as lender of last resort, whilst the UK Treasury remains responsible for the institutional framework and regulation and the statutory instruments in this connection but it has no operational role in financial regulation and is also not responsible for the activities of the Bank of England and the FSA in this respect.

In the USA, the SEC is the overall securities regulator assisted by SROs under its oversight and by official (registered) exchange markets. The most important SRO is the National Association of Securities Dealers (NASD) and the most important exchange the NY Stock Exchange. The derivatives markets in the USA have, however, their own supervisory authority.

The SEC, as the oldest securities regulator in the world, is still by far the most experienced and sophisticated. The SEC has broad rule-making powers under the 1933 and 1934 statutes and also issues policy and interpretative releases, staff legal bulletins, interpretative and no-action letters and even telephone interpretations. However, increasing doubts are expressed on the process of its regulation and the piecemeal nature of it, which has resulted in a true patchwork of rules not easy to comprehend for the outsider or even the experienced lawyer. More importantly, it is slow to change when fundamental rethinking is required, sticks to what it has and mostly adds, whilst favouring existing structures and official markets. This has led to criticism.[45] It may well be that the freer UK approach to the development of alternative markets, as explained, has here the edge.

1.3.15   International Aspects of Securities Regulation

Internationally as well as domestically, the modern emphasis on the regulation of investment service providers implies a functional approach: see section 1.1.5 above. Thus the emphasis is not or no longer on markets or institutions as such but principally on the type of service provided by the various intermediaries or market participants and subsequently on the role of the host regulator. However, where freedom of cross-border financial services is promoted, the emphasis may shift to home regulation with (provided it is reasonably sophisticated) a lessening role for the regulator of the investor (host regulator), particularly in commercial banking. This is an important development, which we have seen within the EU and of which we may see more within GATS.

It was already mentioned above that the functional approach to regulation of the type of service provided rather than of the institutions that provide them cannot fulfil a need for institutional capital and infrastructure, and in that sense regulation can never be entirely functional. As capital and infrastructure are particularly important for commercial banks, they remain here subject to a form of institutional regulation, more so than investment banks. The consequence is that the concern for capital and infrastructure is more properly a home country affair and may more easily be centralised in the home regulator. As there is traditionally less concern for conduct of business and product control in commercial banking, home regulation is therefore generally indicated for this type of institution.

It may be different for investment banks in their various functions where the regulatory concern is rather for conduct of business and products, at least for the smaller investors. Host regulation is therefore more likely indicated for investment banks, at least for their cross-border activities and products in the retail area, although not necessarily for their professional dealings, capital and prudential supervision which are in any event lesser regulatory concerns.

The host regulator may be particularly concerned with small investors and the investment products and investment services offered them. On the other hand there is less host country concern with service providers and their duties either as underwriters and placement agents or market makers, and often even less as matching agents or specialists, information suppliers, clearers, custodians, brokers or investment managers. This may, like authorisation, all be left to home regulators if they feel a need to become involved.

---

[45] See MH Wallman, 'Competition, Innovation, and Regulation in the Securities Markets'(1998) 53 *The Business Lawyer*, 341. The applicable legal regime in respect of prospectuses and the possibility to choose has e.g. been much debated in recent times in the US but has not found a response from the SEC. There is an increasing literature on this subject, see HE Jackson and EJ Pan, 'Regulatory Competition in International Securities Markets: Evidence from Europe in 1999-Part I', (2001) *The Business Lawyer*, 653. Their research in Europe points to free markets and competition leading to *higher* voluntary disclosure (and lower) with the prospect of greater proceeds. Regulatory competition and issuers' choice of regulatory alternatives is another approach, see R Romano, 'Empowering Investors: A Market Approach to Securities Regulation' (1998) 107 *Yale Law Journal*, 2359, and S Choi and A Guzman, 'Portable Reciprocity: Rethinking the International Reach of Securities Regulation', (1998) 71 Southern California Law Review 903. See earlier F Easterbrook and O Fischel for serious doubts on the fairness and efficiency of mandatory disclosure systems, 'Mandatory Disclosure and the Protection of Investors', (1984) 70 *Virginia Law Review*, 669 with a response from John C Coffee, 'Market Failure and the Economic Case for a Mandatory Disclosure System', (1984) 70 *Virginia Law Review* 717. The true questioning of the traditional regulatory attitudes in the US goes back to Stigler, 'Public Regulation of the Securities Markets', (1964) 37 *Journal of Business Law*, 117.

The sequel to the internationalisation and the freer rendering of financial services cross-border is thus likely to be some division of tasks between home and host regulators of these intermediaries with emphasis on the home regulators' role. The home regulator would naturally be more interested in licensing requirements and prudential supervision, the host regulator in the services and products foreigners offer in it's territory to retail investors.

To make this division of regulatory tasks work, as in banking, there may be some harmonisation need in the basic concepts and objectives. This is the direction in the EU between the various Member States, see also section 1.1.9 above, after a period in which the EU appeared more interested in the workings of and co-operation between the different existing formal stock exchanges in terms of admission to listing, listing and regular reporting requirements, although it also became concerned with public offerings of securities in general, therefore also those being issued off-exchange in the informal markets.

In the end, the EU understood that it had to focus on the services and the service providers and not on market operations, and divide the regulatory tasks with a bias towards home regulation although with some exceptions for (small) investors' protection: see also sections 1.1.9 above and 2.2.6 below. This is the drift of the EU Investment Services Directive. See for the unilateral US approach to cross-border securities transactions sections 1.1.11 above and 3.1.2 below. Within GATS, host regulation remains for the time being the normal attitude, excepting perhaps some incidental telephone selling. This even applies to the authorisation requirement, as it originally did within the EU.

The host country concern with conduct of business and (small) investors protection should not only extend to the avoidance of conflicts of interests and the formulation of duties of care. It should also extend to the aspects of segregation and tracing. In both areas there is a need for some harmonisation of basic principles. It is to be noted that in the EU Article 11 of the Investment Services Directive does do to some extent for the conflicts of interests and duties of care, but it has not begun to do so in the aspects of segregation and tracing. It would mean a substantial re-evaluation of the principles of agency in both their contractual and proprietary aspects as particularly geared to the securities business. Although in the European Principles of Contract Law there are some provisions on agency (chapter III, see also the discussion on Agency in chapter II), the particular securities trading aspects are hardly addressed.

1.4 Modern Financial Products. Derivatives and Securitisations. Hedge Funds and Their Operation

1.4.1 *Modern Developments in Financial Products*

As part of this general introduction, it may also be useful to say a little on derivatives, securitisations (and asset backed securities), credit derivatives, prime brokerage, and hedge fund operations. They often catch the eye and require some understanding for a better insight into the financial services industry, its operations, the considerable risks it takes, the possibility of the rapid adjustment of these risks, and the regulatory response.

Derivatives in this context are financial products that derive their value from the value of assets traded in other markets. Financial *options* and *futures* are the normal examples. A *call* option gives the buyer or owner of it the *right*, but does *not* impose a duty to buy from the seller or *writer* of the option the underlying asset (often bonds or shares) at the agreed *striking price* during the time of the option. A *put* option gives the option holder the right to sell this asset to the writer of the option at an agreed price (the *striking price*) during the time of the option. By writing a call or a put, the writer exposes himself to the option being exercised against him at the agreed price. He immediately receives a price or *premium* for his willingness to accept that exposure.

The futures contract is an agreement to buy or sell an asset at an agreed future moment for a fixed price, often the present market price (or relevant index). It should be noted in this connection that buying protection against future price movements may mean selling the asset forward at (more or less) current prices. A future of this nature gives a seller the right *and* imposes on him the duty to sell and deliver the underlying asset to the buyer on the agreed date for the agreed price. A buyer under a future has the right *and* duty to acquire the underlying asset (which, in financial futures, may be certain types of bonds but could also be some time-deposit) at that time and price. By entering into a future, both parties acquire rights and obligations in the nature of an ordinary sales contract. The difference is that the delivery of the goods and payment will be delayed until a future date.

In the case of *financial* futures there is another important difference as at the appointed date they may always be settled in money, as we shall see. That is in fact also the case with financial options. In that sense, they are *contracts for differences*. During their period, the positions may be transferred if there are regular exchanges on which this can be done (it is otherwise much more difficult as the contracts may need to be unwound). Thus a profit can be taken at any time or a loss may be fixed by getting out. It is usually done by engaging in an opposite transaction for the same maturity date which transaction is netted out with the original one. Thus if one has sold the underlying asset at a fixed price whilst the market price of that asset is now lower, there is a profit in the future that could be protected by buying that asset back at the lower price in another future (now as buyer), for delivery and payment at the same date of the earlier future.

The financial option and future periods are normally fairly brief (three months, six months or nine months), but could be longer. There may be other particularities. For example, one financial option contract usually covers 100 of the underlying securities. A future is often on an (share) index and may then cover 200 times the difference between the index as it develops and the index at the time of the future contract. It means that if one buys 100 future contracts of this nature one gets 20,000 times the difference.

Swaps are the other traditional example of derivatives. The term 'swap' does not in itself denote any particular legal structure. The common feature is that under a swap either the one or the other party will pay a certain sum if a particular event occurs. Common is an exchange of accruing cash flows, normally resulting from different interest rates (fixed or floating) structures. The result is an *interest rate swap*. They could also be in different currencies (that is a cross-currency or cocktail swap), when there are therefore two possible variables. Their value depends on the relative value of the accruing cash flows that have been temporarily exchanged. The underlying amounts may be purely fictitious and, in modern swaps, there may be no exchange at all. In such swaps there is a new financial instrument created, structured as the difference between two fictitious cash flows in the form of a set-off agreement. This is often referred to as (a form of) novation netting, see also chapter III, section 1.3.3.[46] It provides much greater flexibility in terms of interest rates and maturities, whilst there are no funding needs and physical transfers.

Financial derivatives may be used to make a profit by playing markets in this manner, but they are also important means quickly to incur or change *market* or *position risk* and are therefore of great importance as *hedging* instruments, especially to banks, which

---

[46] Less important for the present discussion are *credit default swaps* under which a sum will be due when a certain party goes bankrupt, see section 1.4.8 infra. In *total return swaps*, payments will be made depending on the market value of a portfolio of shares.

implies the possibility to take positions opposite to the ones they have, thus neutralising this type of risk promptly. These financial derivatives developed rapidly in the fast changing inflation, interest and currency environment in the early 1970s after the end of the fixed exchange rates regime earlier established at Bretton Woods (in 1944). Their development was much helped by the modern computerised calculation and information storage facilities. They are *not* appropriate to change credit risk and are more likely to *add to it* as new relationships are created. To reduce credit risk, so-called *credit derivatives* may now be used which are in fact a type of third party guarantees of credit risk, see section 1.4.8 below. Other ways are the diversification in the loan portfolio, security (collateral), guarantees of third parties (like parent companies), cross default covenants in the loan agreements, and securitisations (which remove the asset from the balance sheet altogether).

Securitisations are both credit and position risk-adjusting mechanisms. Under them, (mostly) a bank with a loan portfolio which it no longer wants, or a company with a lot of outstanding receivables which it no longer wishes to carry, may attempt to clean its balance sheet by moving these assets into a specially created vehicle (a special purpose vehicle or SPV). This is typically done through a bulk assignment for which it receives payment from the newly created entity that usually raises the money in the capital markets on the strength of its newly acquired loan assets or receivables. The result will be asset-backed securities. This process may be much more complicated and, because of legal, tax and regulatory complications, is not always fool proof, see further section 1.4.7 below.

Prime brokerage concerns a facility or service that is typically connected with short selling, therefore the selling of (financial) assets, like shares or bonds, which the seller does not have. If he is required to deliver he may have to borrow the securities. This securities lending/borrowing is a major activity of a prime broker, who may also provide other facilities in this connection like foreign exchange dealing and financing.

Hedge funds operations, finally, are speculative operations normally conducted by funds specialising in high risk or special arbitrage schemes of which the opportunities may become readily apparent in highly volatile markets. A most simple example is a spotted difference between the market value and the theoretical value of a bond which is likely to correct itself. A large position in an undervalued bond may thus be taken. It concerns therefore normally the exploitation of technical market aberrations which can be calculated, and not simply the taking of a large position e.g. in a foreign currency that one hopes will correct. Banks in their treasury functions more and more operate like hedge funds in which positions are constantly changed according to certain risk strategies. The term itself is a misnomer as the idea that these funds hedge risk is often turned on its head: they only seek to manage or harness risk but the resulting exposure may easily prove excessive especially when market behaviour becomes irrational. Unwinding the large positions so taken is then likely to become an extra disturbing market factor.

This has given rise to a call for hedge fund regulation. However, hedge funds are a normal product of free market behaviour and regulating these funds may be of little practical use as they are likely to move offshore. Regulation is relevant, however, in the context of regulatory supervision of the treasury operations of banks and of their lending activity to highly geared hedge funds.

1.4.2   The Use of Derivatives. Hedging

Derivatives are important instruments for parties (particularly banks) to change their *market or position* risk exposure in a relatively quick and cheap manner depending on their view of future market movements in them. This is the essence of *hedging*. Thus buying a put option in certain shares protects the buyer against the shares falling below the striking price. It therefore reduces the risk of holding them. It comes at a cost, however (the price of the option). By selling assets (like foreign exchange) forward into domestic currency at a fixed price under a future, the position risk regarding that asset will be eliminated (but there remains here a credit risk and settlement problem as the hedge assumes that the other party will perform on the future date). By choosing an alternative cash flow under a swap, an uncertain floating rate cash flow may be exchanged for a fixed rate cash flow. In this way, risk on either the asset or liability side of a balance sheet (through an *asset* or *liability* swap) may be reduced, but it could also be increased by going from fixed to floating.

Parties could of course unwind their long or short positions in the underlying assets, but it is more likely that they will use derivatives to hedge their existing positions in the indicated manner by effectively taking (through futures) opposite (short) positions to those which they already have. It is likely to be quicker and cheaper and gives the facility to correct the hedge by undoing it later when the risk position is clearer. Thus if a party is long in a market-sensitive asset, it may go short through a standard futures sales con-tract. That hedge may not exactly mirror its position and may as such not be *perfect* because a contract in the underlying asset may not be readily available in the derivatives market, but a mirror contract may protect sufficiently. In this manner, an underwriter of securities who is long in corporate US $ bonds may try to hedge the position by selling US Treasury futures because these hedge instruments are more readily available and therefore easier, faster and cheaper to obtain. Yet the Treasury and corporate bond mar-ket may not always move in tandem and there may therefore remain an exposure under this *imperfect* hedge.

Similarly, to protect against an interest rate rise in a floating rate outstanding debt or borrowing, the party seeking protection may buy a corresponding floating interest rate (term deposit) future. A swap into a fixed income stream would have the advantage of being able to go out much longer in time than standard futures usually do. It is a more ver-satile instrument. However, it may take somewhat longer to organise, which in a heavily fluctuating market, may prove a considerable disadvantage. The time element will largely determine whether a futures hedge is preferred to a swap.

The difference between protection through a put option or through a futures hedge is more fundamental and the choice will depend on whether the hedging party seeks to become indifferent to market movements altogether or whether it wants to retain upside potential. Thus an investor may seek to protect the value of his portfolio of shares by buy-ing a put which gives him the right to sell that portfolio at the agreed striking price to the writer of the put. Should the price rise, the put does not oblige him to sell anything to the writer and he could sell the assets at a higher price to someone else whilst letting the put expire. The option thus gives him more flexibility than a future (which would likely be a stock index future) but is also more expensive.

The normal use of an option is (a) a speculative instrument, (b) an instrument to create extra income or (c) a hedge to limit exposure in the underlying assets. All kind of plays become possible. A special use is the *straddle* under which an investor buys a put and a call in the same underlying asset at the same time. This may be costly but may serve a purpose in times of extreme volatility as it creates a possibility to make a profit either way. You may do the opposite if you think that the market may not move and cash in on a double pre-mium. It is a very common technique. Common is also the *synthetic future* when an investor buys a call and sells (or writes) a put in the same underlying asset at the same time (thus reducing substantially the net price of the call option), usually but not necessarily at the same striking price. It simulates a long holding in the underlying asset whilst eliminating much of the funding costs (but there is no dividend or coupon income either). The result is that if the market moves up, the investor will exercise the call; if the market moves down, the put will be exercised against him. In either case he will end up with the securities as if he were long, hence the idea of a future. It minimises immediate costs and avoids them altogether if there is no appreciable movement in the market value of the underlying assets so that no option will be exercised.

Rather than as risk-switching instruments or hedges, derivatives may of course also be used as pure investments to enhance income. Thus selling a call option in a share portfolio exercisable at a striking price at or above the market price of the underlying shares gives the writer of the option a premium income. Doing so without such a portfolio (a *naked call option*) will expose the writer to substantial (unlimited) risk when the share price rises above the striking price. Similar risk is incurred when a future contract is sold in assets the seller of the future does not have. This seller will only do so if he believes that the price of the underlying assets will go down. The risk under a put is limited to the striking price and *naked puts* are therefore less risky than naked calls.

In a swap, other kind of plays are possible. A party may enter a swap e.g. without any right to the underlying exchanged cash flow. In fact, as already mentioned, these underlying flows now may be entirely fictitious and parties may agree only to pay or receive the difference in the simulated accruing flows on the appointed payment dates. This makes them better hedge instruments because they can be tailor-made and are more flexible. Except if used as a hedge, the stakes are raised in currency swaps which carry both interest rate and currency differential risk. The stakes may be even higher if the cash flows are actually exchanged. They are higher still if the assets out of which the cash flows arise are also swapped, particularly in (liability) currency swaps, as large amounts of money may have to be returned in a currency that may have increased in value in the meantime. It requires these swaps to be actively managed.

Especially a liability swap may be entered into as an arbitrage or currency play between two different bond issuers who are each better placed to issue bonds in currencies that they do not really need. One party may thus end up with large yen proceeds and the other with US dollar proceeds, although the first one has a need for dollars and the latter for yen. A swap is then the obvious solution, and many international bond issues are swap driven in this manner. Under such an arrangement the relative advantage of each party operating in the, for him, most favourable market will be shared according to an agreed formula.

The result is an exchange of principal as well as the attached interest rate payment obligations. Naked foreign exchange positions for each party will result, as they are short in and must repurchase respectively yen and US dollars on the agreed payment dates of the coupons and on the repayment date of the principal amounts at the then prevailing exchange rates between the currencies or settle the difference between them. As just mentioned, this may mean a great deal of currency risk beside interest rate risk, which risks parties may hedge from time to time during the swap period depending on their view of the development in currency and interest rates.

The swap may thus play at various levels: as an actual exchange at the level of the principal, as an actual exchange at the level of the coupon, or both, or it may simply be a contract for differences between two fictitious accruing or outgoing income streams. The latter type can be freely structured by parties and may incorporate a series of succeeding payment dates during the swap. This type of swap, which has become the most common, avoids at the same time problems with the underlying credit risk when the cash flows and payment dates do not exactly match.

But even in the principal or coupon swaps, the swap parties are unlikely effectively to exchange the amounts or flows involved. In asset swaps, they would each become dependent on the credit risk of third parties. In these principal and coupon swaps, both parties will normally *cross-lend* similar amounts to each other and only assume the credit risk of the other. They will thus continue their normal relationship with the outsiders to whom they may have lent the principal (subject to an asset swap) or from whom they may have borrowed the principal (subject to the liability swap), including the interest payments on these amounts. The swap partner will not become involved in the administration of these loans and payments.

Further developments have led to a number of hybrids like *floors, collars, swap-options or swaptions* and forward rate agreements or FRAs. Caps are instruments under which the seller (of the cap), usually a professional investor or a bank, at a fee payable immediately, guarantees a maximum interest level to a borrower in paying him any excess he may incur in his floating rate obligation during the period in question. Floors do the opposite in guaranteeing a lender with a floating rate a minimum return. Caps and floors can even be introduced in modern floating rate bonds. Collars combine both and will allow the buyer of a cap (the borrower) to function at the same time as a seller of a floor to his lender (the seller of the cap). It reduces the cost of his cap to the extent of the value of the floor, gives him a protection as to the maximum borrowing cost whilst he guarantees a minimum. Swaptions allow the other party, for a fee to be paid immediately, to enter into a pre-agreed swap at a specific later date (usually exchanging a fixed rate bond for a floater). The fee will serve as reward for the risk of the option being exercised and can be used towards the cost. There are some variations: in *extendable* swaps, the party benefiting from the option may extend the swap period to a specified later date; in *callable* swaps, the recipient of the fixed income may shorten the swap period to a specific prior date; in *putable* swaps, the payor of the fixed rate may do so. FRAs, finally, are agreements under which parties agree a swap during an agreed future period leading to a single net payment usually on the first day of the period concerned.

Other types of arbitrage plays may be encouraged by the existence of derivatives. Most of them take advantage of small differences in price between the derivative and the underlying (cash) markets. Thus in *stock index futures*, there may be a fictitious underlying basket of shares and arbitrage between the index future and the basket stocks is a popular activity amongst professionals, facilitated by computer monitoring (*program trading*). It may create large volume flows in the basket assets and has as such been identified as a source of potential instability in stock markets. For the players, there is here a risk of distortion in that the underlying basket assets are quoted at their latest bid and offer prices. In times of high market volatility, they may not reflect the actual values correctly because trade in some of the basket assets may have dried up.

Standard tradable options are likely to exist in major shares and bonds. They may also exist in stock exchange indexes and in some futures and swaps (swaptions, as we saw). Standard futures are less likely in individual shares but do exist in stock exchange indices, as we just saw. They are also common in foreign exchange contracts and likely to exist in major government bonds or bills and in certain standard time-deposits of short duration.

Forward contracts of which financial futures are a further evolution have themselves existed for a long time and were common particularly in agriculture to sell crops (or pork bellies) forward to guarantee a certain income. They subsequently became common also for other types of commodities, particularly crude oil. These forward agreements were intended to lead to delivery and were as such different from the modern financial futures as *contracts for differences* developed as exchange quoted financial instruments since 1974, but the principle is the same.

1.4.3 The Valuation of Derivatives. Contracts for Differences

The value of options or futures depends on the present market value ('cash market') of the underlying assets (or indexes) in which an option is given or which, in futures, are subject to delayed transfer and payment. In futures, there is a direct correlation between the cash and futures value; if the price of the underlying asset rises, so does proportionally the price of the future. In the option, the relationship (or Delta) is usually less than direct and the option price may change less than the price in the underlying assets. This can be demonstrated through a mathematical formula in which not only the cash value of the underlying asset figures but also the diminishing time value of the option and the volatility of the market (this is the famous Black and Scholes model).

Thus in futures, if the market price of the underlying assets rises above the agreed sale price of the asset, the buyer wins and the seller loses. The next day, it could be the other way around. The value of the future (the right and duty for the seller to sell or for the buyer to buy an asset at an agreed price on an agreed future date) rises and falls accordingly. So it happens in term-deposit futures (although it may be affected by the buyer/seller spread and by the interest rates). If interest rates rise, the value of the underlying (future) fixed deposit falls; the future buyer loses and the seller wins. New contracts for the same deposit will be cheaper.

In the option, similarly, the buyer of a call wins when the value of the asset rises above the striking price. The buyer of a put wins when the value of the underlying asset falls below the striking price. As just said, because of the time factor, they may not rise or fall proportionately with the underlying assets. Price fluctuations in the underlying asset will nevertheless have an impact on the call or put price. Accordingly, the option may move *in the money* or *out of the money*.

The price of the option and future thus changes all the time depending on the values of the underlying assets in relation to the agreed striking price in the option or sales price in the future. Options and futures are bought or sold in the markets at a price reflecting this difference. It is important to remember that although the modern financial option (like the future) is often called a contract for differences, when the option is exercised, the underlying assets must still be delivered and paid for. That price (and the commissions payable) is *not* part of the option itself. In reality, modern options and futures, especially when traded as standard contracts on established option and futures exchanges, are unlikely ever to be exercised. As was already mentioned before, normally only the difference (that is the options or futures price prevailing at the time) will be cashed in on the final option or on the final futures date. It is the essence of contracts for differences which modern futures and options normally are.

In the *American* option, the buyer may exercise the option at any time during the period (important when dividend and coupons are going to be paid), not so in the *European* option which can be exercised only on the agreed option date. In the American option, there is therefore a continuous window to exercise the option or claim the difference, not in the European option. It affects the value of the option and the calculation thereof. Note in this connection that the European option exchanges normally use the American option. European options are OTC instruments and much less common.

As already mentioned, under a financial future, the underlying assets can be acquired only on the agreed future date and the party being in the money normally has the right to claim the difference between the market price and the forward price only on the date of settlement. In the meantime, any party in the money may attempt to cash in by transferring his position to others (including his counterparty). As we shall see, this is much facilitated by the modern futures and option exchanges. For some futures contracts, notably those concerning time-deposits, the buyer has in fact *only* an entitlement to the difference on the contract date, as a deposit contract is not normally transferable without the depositors' consent. These deposits exist in fact only nominally. Also in the case of stock index futures, there is an entitlement only to a cash settlement and *never* to the underlying basket assets.

The value of swaps is the difference from time to time between the value of exchanged cash flows as they develop. It determines which party is in the money and for how much: if market interest rates rise, the party entitled to the floating rate cash flow is winning as his (LIBOR or EURIBOR) cash flow rises with the increased interest rate. The party with the fixed rate interest stream loses and would have been better off to stay in floating. In a cross-currency swap the difference may be accentuated or corrected by the development in the exchange rate between the differing currencies of both cash flows.

As already noted, where swaps are structured on the basis of fictitious cash flows, they are contracts for differences. No exchanges and returns of cash flows (or assets out of which they arise like principal loan amounts) are involved. In such a swap, different pay dates during the swap period may be agreed, and this is quite common. Where exchanges of principal amounts and coupon still take place, they are in fact cross-borrowings of the swap partners, as we saw, and also in those cases only the differences in values will normally be settled. Here enters the notion of set-off and netting which will be discussed more extensively below in section 1.4.5.

1.4.4   *Derivatives Markets and their Operations. Clearing and the Notion of Margin*

All three: options, futures and swaps are contracts, not as such negotiable instruments or (transferable) securities, even if for regulatory purposes, they may be considered securities or at least investments. Being contracts, they are not easily transferable and were as a consequence not traditionally traded on exchanges, although in recent times an exception is made for *some* standardised options and futures contracts and options and futures exchanges now operate in many countries. This is not the case for swaps, which have remained typical OTC products.

The most important modern exchanges for financial options and futures are the Chicago Board of Trade (CBOT) and the Chicago Mercantile Exchange (CME). In London there is LIFFE, in Frankfurt the Deutsche Termin Boerse (DTB) and, in Paris, the Matif. Except for the DTB, they traditionally all applied the *open outcry* system, that is that a group of market-makers in a *pit* will shout prices to floor brokers who communicate with them through a set of hand signs. Electronic trading is now taking the upper hand everywhere as it is cheaper whilst doing away with the floor and many of its personnel. The argument for open outcry was always that it was quicker (six seconds) but it became doubtful whether this was really so whilst the communication facilities on the floor remained unavoidably cumbersome. Only the American exchanges remain now wedded to the open outcry.

These future and option exchanges each have their own clearing and settlement systems or may use outside organisations (as LIFFE in London does by using the London Clearing House (LCH)). Official derivative markets are likely to be regulated at least in some of their more essential functions, like the publication of quotes and done prices. Clearing houses may also be regulated, but again probably only lightly. It depends on the country of their location. They may compete and their efficiency and own internal safeguards (for settlement) will determine their success. This may provide better protection of the public at the same time.

Whilst discussing the 'trading' of derivatives, even on formal derivatives markets, it should always be borne in mind that they are *contractual* positions and that in law the transfer of such positions is generally not easy. The simplest way to achieve it would be by assignment, which, without consent of the counterparty, would only be effective for contractual benefits or rights, not for the contractual duties. This may be feasible for options (which by their very nature only confer rights) but may still entail all kind of formalities (in terms of notice) and may not therefore be very suitable. Normally, there are rights and duties under most contracts (certainly in sales contracts like futures and in cash flow exchange contracts like swaps) and consent of the counterparty in the derivative would be necessary for the transfer. This could amount to novation as a tripartite agreement under which the old contract disappears and is replaced by a new one. It gives the original counterparty a very strong position as it can block the transfer. In law, a simple transfer of one's (net) position under a derivative to a third party is thus not a likely facility. This is a great disadvantage in derivative dealing.

Successful futures and option exchanges have to overcome this difficulty. (a) They do this by narrowing the field whilst offering only a limited number of standardised types of derivatives which can be created, 'transferred' and extinguished through the exchange. (b) To facilitate the finding of a 'buyer' or 'seller' as the case may be, these exchanges are likely not only to rely on public demand but also organise market-makers who will take positions if public investors do not do so or do so insufficiently. The idea is here that the party wishing to get out enters the opposite position at present prices. (c) These exchanges become the parties' counterparties in all transactions (or central counterparties (CCPs). They provide a clearing and settlement system at the same time, which is the key to the whole operation and makes *close out* of opposite contractual positions on the exchange possible through the technique of close-out netting, thereby eliminating the transactions, pay out or collect the difference and end the attending counterparty risk. (d) This set-up is supplemented by the concept of margin. (e) The position of the CCP is secured by strong guarantees of the main supporters of the system (often large banks) who operate at the same time as so-called clearing members.

To take the future as an example, it means that instead of there being one contract between a seller and a buyer in the underlying asset in a future, in *exchange-traded* futures, there are in reality two contracts: one sales contract between the seller of the underlying assets and the exchange (which is then the buyer under the future) backed up by one purchase contract for the underlying assets between the buyer and the exchange (which will then be the seller of the same position).

By doing this, the exchange guarantees termination of the future if a party, the original buyer e.g., wanting to 'sell' his long futures position before the expiry date presents a willing 'buyer' (who could be a market-maker) of the same position (but for a different market price) by allowing an opposite chain of two contracts to be organised through it. The 'sale' is therefore no longer at the mercy of the original individual counterparty who has only a contract with the exchange. It will not be affected. In fact, there is no transfer of a futures position at all. A 'buyer' found by the 'seller' of the future (who was the original buyer of the position) on the exchange thus enters into a *new* futures contract with the exchange, and this contract will be backed up by a purchase contract between the exchange and the 'seller' (being the original buyer of the position which he now wants to liquidate).

The consequence is therefore that an original buyer under a future now has a similar sales contract with the exchange, but for a different price. If that party wants a *close out*, both contracts will be netted out by the exchange so that a nil-delivery obligation results under which the exchange either pays or receives payment from the 'seller' depending on whether the latter had a positive or negative position under his original future. That is a form of netting (close-out netting). In practice, the margin requirement system will already have taken care of the payments, as we shall see. The key is that in this system the exchange is committed to co-operate by entering the necessary contracts and, if so required, by closing them out. The arrangement is thus that the exchange cannot refuse to act in this manner and must close out the position if a buyer is found and the seller of the position wants this. The result is that the investor can transfer his position and realise his gain or limit his loss at any time.

The practical steps are as follows. Normally a client wishing to open a futures or option position will do so by approaching his securities broker. This broker will contact a *floor broker* on the exchange and lay in his order. The floor broker will subsequently approach other floor brokers who may have a mirror requirement or otherwise he will approach a *market-maker* who will take positions himself. Subsequently there will have to be a system in which the orders of either party are confirmed and verified. There may even be a form of clearing at this level. Then follows settlement including the close-out netting. Within the clearing there may be a further netting mechanism in the nature of a settlement netting at the end of a given period (usually one day) amongst all participants.

In the official derivative exchanges, this process acquires a typical legal form. The floor broker and market-makers whilst dealing may operate on the exchange only if backed up by a so-called *clearing member* of the exchange. The clearing member so activated by each acting broker/market-maker in the transaction becomes in fact the party to the transaction on behalf of the 'buyer' or 'seller' and enters into the necessary 'purchase' or 'sale' agreement with the clearing organisation itself (which may be outside the exchange as the London Clearing House or LCH is in London). The clearing house thus becomes the *central counter-party* (CCP). This role is the *essence of all modern clearing systems* (although not yet in payment clearing under modern payment systems, as we saw in chapter III, section 1.2.4 or in clearing systems for investment securities in Cedel or Clearstream, where the central party only makes the necessary calculations and arranges the net payments or transfers of securities as the case may be).

In short, in the regular derivatives markets, the central counterparty (CCP) or clearing house operates as seller to the buyer and as buyer to the seller (both represented by clearing members) and nets out the positions on either side if a close out is required. It may be automatic. This system guarantees substantial safety for the 'buyers' and 'sellers' being the end-users (clients) operating through an exchange. This is a key issue as large amounts of money may have to be paid out to investors who would not dare to use the exchange if they cannot be sure of safe settlement.

In such a system, the *clearing members* step into the shoes of 'buyers' and 'sellers' through a series of agency agreements and instructions. The original broker of the 'buyer' or 'seller' has an agency relationship with his client under which he acts in his own name but for the risk and account of the buyer/client. The *floor broker* takes instructions from this house broker of the buyer/client and acts for him under a service contract between them. However, whilst acting with another floor broker or a market-maker to finalise the transaction, he does so in the name of the clearing member supporting him, who, through this chain, ultimately acts in his own name, but on behalf and for the risk and account of the original client, with the clearing organisation or CCP, towards which he also accepts liability for the transaction.

The floor broker and market maker (or trader) have a general power of attorney to commit their clearing member in this way. The clearing member will only at the end of the day find out how many deals are done for which he must accept responsibility (on a netted basis) *vis-à-vis* the CCP, including those of any rogue trader. That is his risk. *Vis-à-vis* the CCP, the clearing member will be responsible for the implementation of all the deals entered into by the floor brokers and market-makers supported by him. Whilst the clearing member is *de facto* bound by the floor broker *vis-à-vis* the counterparty's floor broker or the market-maker who themselves only operate for another clearing member, both clearing members involved in the transaction implement their obligations by entering into a contract with the CCP. It clears, settles and nets out the transaction pursuant to which the necessary payments are made, the seller is released and a new contract is entered into with the buyer.

The details of this system in which the CCP may never know the names of the end users (the 'seller' and 'buyer') may differ between futures markets and option markets and between futures and option markets in different countries, but the principles are similar everywhere. The result of this system is that all futures contracts are split into *two* agreements, with each party having an indirect relationship with the CCP through his own broker and the floor broker acting for a clearing member of the exchange. Thus whilst the own broker contacts the floor broker, he activates at the same time an agency relationship between his client and the clearing member of the floor broker.

There is here neither an assignment nor a novation, but by putting a CCP in between the original parties to a financial future, a mechanism is found in which the one party is not dependent on the other for the transfer of his position under the contract, which takes the form of a close out of his positions once he has been able to organise an opposite position in the manner explained. The clearing organisation is bound at all times to enter into an off-setting contract as soon as a 'buyer' of the original position is found. Through this mechanism, a party can be released whilst he pays to the clearing organisation any negative value of a contract and may claim any positive value from that organisation assuming there is anyone interested in a like position. The result is that his contract is at an end and he is replaced by a new party under a new contract. That result can be achieved by parties to a future at any time of their choosing during the contract period and is an extremely valuable aspect of the operation of regular derivative exchanges.

The objective of the involvement of clearing members standing in for their clients in this manner is that strong intermediaries accept responsibility for the creation, performance and termination of futures and option contracts. They are vetted and supervised by the exchanges for their continued solvency. Bankruptcy of investors in a futures contract is therefore no problem for the exchange. Bankruptcy of a clearing member is a serious matter but they are carefully selected. In fact, this method of clearing and settlement is increasingly adopted also in ordinary stock exchanges to minimise the risk of the system through the operation of well capitalised clearing members who take over the liabilities of individual investors. This system lends itself also to clearing or transfers of foreign exchange transactions and even payment instructions and OTC swaps. In London, the London Clearing House has now started to provide that service for swaps.

In any event, when a futures or options contract turns negative for the party concerned, the CCP will ask *margin* from the relevant clearing house which will debit it to the client. To this end, it will accept a client only via the floor broker if that client has a minimum balance in the account with his own broker, and the floor broker will verify this. *Vis-à-vis* the clearing organisation, this part of the arrangement is irrelevant as the clearing house is first liable for the margin. The margin will go up and down on a daily basis (or will sometimes be assessed intra-day) and gives rise to payment to the client when the contract turns positive. Thus on a close out there is usually nothing to pay either way. This was already referred to above. The system of close out payments is then subsumed in the margin payment system.

For swaps, at first, parties wanting to enter into one had to find a counterparty, which was not easy and banks were often used as brokers. Eventually banks started to operate as counterparties. This is often called *swap warehousing*. It immediately doubled the number of outstanding swaps as, instead of one swap between two end-users, they would now each enter a swap with a bank. Like any market-maker, banks quote a spread between bid and offer prices for their swaps and would also enter into them if they could not immediately find an offsetting swap. This greatly facilitated the operation of the swap market and allowed further development especially towards more specialised swap types based on fictitious cash flows as we saw. Like in futures and options, the trading in swaps normally takes the form of parties entering into mirror swaps to offset their positions, thus locking in certain gains or losses. Warehousing banks are, however, not CCPs subject to close-out netting demands. A bank as counterparty may nevertheless be willing to unwind a swap deal and take or make payment for the accrued differences in cash flow values. No official markets have developed in swaps although there have been calls for it. As just mentioned, clearing houses may now start providing that service as Central Counter Parties in their own right or for others.

A simple example may demonstrate the point: a person entitled to a five-year (fictitious) cash flow at a fixed interest rate of 8 per cent expects a rise in interest rates and swaps into floating for the period. After two years the interest rate is 10 per cent. Now a fall in interest rate is expected and the party concerned may swap back into fixed at 10 per cent through a new swap. The result of both swaps is that this party has locked in a 2 per cent spread for three years whilst having had the benefit of the rising interest rate during the first 2 years.

As the swap market is an informal over-the-counter market, there are no special rules on clearing and settlement and for margin requirements. There is therefore an endless doubling up of counterparty risk. This is all a matter between the client and the swap dealer concerned in which connection bilateral netting becomes important, although, as we saw, modern clearing systems may now start providing a swap clearing service through central counterparties which would logically also entail margin requirements.

1.4.5   Derivatives Risk, Netting and Regulation of Derivatives Activity

Derivatives are off-balance-sheet items. As they may go in and out of the money, they are contingent in value, which value can only be determined from time to time by marking them to market. They may carry substantial risk, especially the naked options and uncovered future sales. In swaps, if principal or cash flows are exchanged, the one party may not receive the return of these amounts in a bankruptcy of the other party, whilst it must still perform its own return duty. If the swap is a question of cross-loans in different currencies, it means that the non-bankrupt party may not receive back its principal, whilst it may still have to repay the bankrupt unless there is a reliable system of set-off or contractual netting (which may allow a set-off between claims in different currencies, which may not otherwise be possible under the applicable law of set-off) acceptable to the bankruptcy court. Equally, it may still have to pay interest to the bankrupt until the end of the loan period whilst it gets nothing in return.

Thus even within one swap, swap risk may be substantially curtailed if the netting principle is fully accepted. For the modern swap based on fictitious amounts and structured as a contract for differences, this may be easy. There is here so-called *novation netting*, netting at the *beginning* of the transaction as the essence of the financial structure in which parties have agreed from the outset a single net payment for two cross-claims. It may be better simply to refer here to a contract for differences and the term novation netting may not add much (see for this concept chapter III, section 1.3.3). It is a financial product in its own right under which the result is that only one amount will be due on the payment date. If cash flows are exchanged or even the underlying bonds out of which they arise, the exposure is much larger. Where such amounts are thus still physically swapped, there may be *settlement netting*, that is netting on the settlement date. This netting may be more contentious when the maturities and currencies are not the same (or non-monetary claims are also involved, for example when bond issues must be returned), see more in particular chapter III, section 1.3 The essence is that the contract might here introduce formulae to deal with different maturities and interest rates. It was already explained above that although we speak here of the exchange of the underlying cash-flows and principal payments, they are in fact more likely to take the form of new cross-loans and the original arrangements remain in place and continue to be served in the ordinary manner. There is thus no exchange of credit risk, but new credit risk is incurred through entering additional transactions.

The situation becomes more acute in the case of an intervening bankruptcy of the parties. If there is merely a contract for differences based on the exchange of fictitious cash flows, the risk is not large and a replacement swap may fill the void if the swap was used as a hedge. If there were cross borrowings, the situation is much more dangerous and a proper set-off becomes here a key facility so that at least the large amounts due the bankrupt are reduced by any counterclaim on the bankrrupt. The key is that whatever is owed the bankrupt is then reduced by whatever was owed by the bankrupt to the non-bankrupt party. That mere competing claim is thus saved for the non-bankrupt party to the extent of his counterclaim.

In this situation, settlement netting may be *contractually* brought forward in a close-out (*close-out netting*) but may then become even more contentious. The most contentious form of close-out netting is, however, the *bilateral (or even multilateral) netting* of *all* outstanding swap positions between two (or more) regular swap partners when one defaults or cross-defaults or goes bankrupt or when other events occur that from a legal or tax point of view may make termination desirable (together called 'close-out events'). To avoid any bankruptcy limitation of the set-off, *contractual novation netting* is often attempted as an alternative, see for the complications chapter III, section 1.3.4. The netting is here a continueous process so that there is only a net balance at any given time.

Bank regulators have had to deal with these aspects. Their normal approach is that for credit risk they mark the off-balance-sheet exposure to market and then apply to the resulting amount their credit conversion factors to arrive at the credit equivalent amounts: see section 2.5.3 below. Since 1993, the BIS allows close-out netting in the manner of novation netting on the basis of its interpretation of the 1988 Basle Accord provided one amount results and this type of netting is accepted (a) under the law of the country of the other party (his residence or corporate seat), (b) under the law of the country of the branch through which that party acted (if not the same), and (c) under the law governing the swap. Legal opinions to the effect must be presented: see also 2.5.5 below. The 'value at risk' approach may eventually lead to further refinement: see for this approach also section 2.5.5 below.

Netting makes an enormous difference. The total netted swap exposure is seldom considered to be more than 2 per cent of the total swap amounts. This means a total exposure for the market as a whole of less than US $ 900 billion on a total of US $ 45 trillion being (nominally) swapped, which was probably the order of the total swap market in 1999.

1.4.6 Legal Aspects of Swaps. Integration and Conditionality, Acceleration and Close Out. The ISDA Swap Master Agreement

As we saw, the swap is an exchange mostly of cash flows, sometimes also of the assets out of which these flows arise, like underlying loans or bond issues (on the asset or especially liability side of the balance sheet). In fact even then, legally they normally amount to *cross-loans* between the partners, as was already mentioned, and the positions under the loan agreements are not themselves swapped. This would have amounted to cross-assignments or cross-delegations depending on whether there was an asset or a liability swap, and would have involved the counterparty, certainly in the latter case, whilst in asset swaps the creditworthiness of the third party debtor would also have become an issue.

The result is that in swaps, even if principal or coupons are in principle exchanged, only the counterparty risk of the swap partner is relevant. In the swap as a contract for differences based on fictitious cash flows, there is (a form of novation) netting from the beginning and there is therefore no exchange of cross claims as explained above. It is a contract or financial product of its own kind. That may not be very relevant. The only characterisation to avoid is that of a speculative or gaming contract which could lead to a void agreement. The law in many countries has now been clarified to prevent this, at least where these products are used for hedging purposes. The other issue is the close-out netting which itself is now mostly cast in a form of (contractual) novation netting to avoid any bankruptcy limitations on the set-off. Whether by contract such a protection can indeed be achieved is another matter and depends on the applicable (bankruptcy) law.

As the legal characterisation of swaps itself is not of the greatest interest, the legal community has been largely concentrating on the close-out netting aspect of swaps. Novation netting is not problematic where netting is the very structure of the contract producing a financial instrument of its own. For other types of netting, it may be different and there could be obstacles particularly if the currencies of the exchanged amounts were not the same or the maturity dates differed, especially important for interest rate payments in cross-currency swaps. For *bilateral* netting there may also be *connexity* problems, see also chapter III, section 1.3. Especially outside bankruptcy, connexity between the obligations being set-off may in some countries (especially of the common law) still be a prerequisite for the set-off. As a consequence there may be a need to bring (as a minimum) all swaps between the same parties within one (master) framework showing dependency. Here the drafting was much helped by the International Swap Dealers Association (ISDA), which since 1985 has produced a swap master agreement.

But there were also the already mentioned bankruptcy complications in a close-out. They are connected with the fact that the counter-party if bankrupt can no longer legally act and that the set-off as a bankruptcy law facility tends to be limited. There is therefore a need to avoid it. In fact, legal drafting concentrates in this connection primarily on the principles of *integration* and *conditionality* to achieve a form of continuous novation netting between regular swap partners. The idea is first (a) to integrate all aspects of each swap within one legal structure and show their interdependence or conditionality so that it is not, or no longer, a two-sided deal. Thus in a bankruptcy situation, there should not be a question of the non-bankrupt party having to return cross-loans or pay interest without receiving anything in return. Interest rate and currency formulae will be inserted to take care of shortened maturities and currency differences between the various amounts so that one total amount either due to or owed by the non-bankrupt party could be easily calculated upon default. But second (b) all mutually outstanding swaps would also be integrated into one single balance payable at all times to the net gaining party (at that moment).

It is the principle of the *running score;* netting could thus follow in respect of each swap without much difficulty. In this manner, also a (bilateral) close-out (settlement) netting could be honoured if envisaged in the swap agreement in the case of a bankruptcy (or other situations of default or in any other close-out event as defined) when it matters most. In this connection it would help of course if the applicable (bankruptcy) law itself were willing to consider some form of integration of contracts to support the economic reality between regular swap parties. It is thus possible that the applicable law itself groups some contracts together and makes them mutually dependent. Naturally, there would still be the potential loss of any net balances due to the non-bankrupt party.

In full bilateral netting of *all* swaps between two partners, the connexity is often less clear, however, no matter the frame contract and may be considered artificial. Moreover, as set-off normally requires notice, it can no longer be legally effective if given after a bankruptcy is opened. Hence the need for an *ipso facto* set-off in most bankruptcies, which is normally a statutory facility. The problem here is that depending on the country of the bankruptcy, any such *ipso facto* (statutory) set-off in a bankruptcy may not go so far as to accept the contractual netting expansions if going beyond it. The danger is then that regardless of the close-out netting clause with full bilateral netting, the *ipso facto* set-off in bankruptcy is not expanded. The result is that such a clause would not give any extra protection.

There may indeed be justified doubt in this aspect and one may not be sure. It is the particular concern of the ISDA approach which is based on one single master agreement between two swap parties in which all their swap deals are considered integrated on a continuous basis (and not only upon a default), see for the master agreement more in particular also chapter II, section 1.3.5. Whether this can overcome the problems of connexity and *ipso facto* bankruptcy law set-off restrictions still depends on national (bankruptcy) laws. In the UK, it is assumed that there is no problem and contractual netting clauses are given much scope. In countries like the USA and France, where there is moreover a reorganisation philosophy in bankruptcy, there was an additional problem in that all close-outs and similar measures were stayed pending a decision on reorganisation or liquidation.[47] It necessitated amendments to save bilateral netting for swaps (and repos). They also recognised the close-out netting. [48]

In bankruptcy, there may be other problems. The non-bankrupt party not only is likely to lose any net balances due him, but may also lose his future (contingent) profits under the swap, including (theoretical netted) cash flows that have already accrued but have not yet been paid. The future profits are, however, impossible to predict and may also turn into losses. They could thus be considered not only contingent but purely speculative. It is only possible to put a present value on them assuming the situation does not itself change.

Instead of losing a future (contingent) profit, the non-bankrupt party may also lose a hedge, when it risks renewed exposure in a neutralised position and incurs the cost of a replacement swap. That may, however, give a clue to the real future loss. To resume the simple example given above in section 1.4.4 *in fine*: if through an off-setting swap at 10 per cent, a spread of 2 per cent for three years was locked in, which lock-in is now endangered, a new offsetting swap at 9 per cent with two years left would present a loss of 1 per cent *per annum* for two years on the amount of the swap. This can be calculated. If now a fixed interest were obtainable at 11 per cent that benefit would likely accrue to the non-defaulting party. It might also induce the trustee in bankruptcy to honour the swap.

As regards the close-out bilateral netting itself, there is a further issue whether the non-bankrupt party needs to pay any amount due from it under the netting clause in view of the fact that it is deprived of its future opportunity. There is the related aspect that a bankrupt should not benefit from its bankruptcy and force (early) payments in this manner. A *one-way payment* by the bankrupt estate only and *walk away* option for the non-bankrupt should it owe a net payment have been advocated in these circumstances

---

[47] See s 365 of the US Bankruptcy Code and Art 37 of the French Bankruptcy Act.
[48] See in the USA, ss 101 and 560 of the Bankruptcy Code, and, in France, Art 8 of Law 93–1444.

but are not always considered fair, may lead to further pressure on the netting principle itself, and have been progressively abandoned. In any event they could not obtain when there is a termination for non-default reasons, for example, where tax or legal reasons required termination when there was always a two-way payment. Two-way payment is now generally the norm.

1.4.7 Asset Securitisation. Legal Aspects and Risks

Asset securitisation is a way of removing assets from a balance sheet. It is particularly relevant for commercial banks which may thus remove classes of loans, like mortgages or credit card advances. It may also be of importance to industrial companies, which may move receivables or car loans in this manner. The reason for banks to use this facility is often concern about capital adequacy. By moving loans they will reduce their capital requirements in respect of all risks connected with the asset (especially counterparty or credit risk, position or market risk, and liquidity risk). Also they may see advantages in acquiring other types of loan assets instead or in simply going liquid. They may even want to pay off some borrowings of their own. For industrial companies, asset securitisation frees up and shortens their balance sheet. It is of course also possible that selling of these assets presents a profit, although that is seldom the prime consideration.

As the assets concern contractual rights, notably receivables or loan assets, they can only be transferred through *assignment* or *novation*. Assignment is a unilateral creditor substitution by the creditor. In the more traditional view, it is limited to the transfer of (impersonal) rights and cannot include a delegation of duties unless these duties are intrinsically connected with the rights (for example a duty to arbitrate any disputes concerning them or the duty to receive payment and give a release under them). The transfer of an entire contractual position is therefore difficult as there are always duties of the creditor or rights of the debtor. There may even be a problem in properly cutting out the receivable or loan repayment obligation from their contractual environment. This is an important modern facility emphasised in the UCC in the US (section 2.210), which also attempts to limit the debtor's defenses. The problems concerning assignments were more fully discussed in chapter IV, section 1.7.

Even a transfer by assignment of a mere right to payment (which may thus require receivables and other monetary claims to be first split out of the underlying contract, which itself remains in place), may impose special burdens on the debtor. It may e.g. force him to pay in another place or involve administrative charges which could be burdensome to him. These extra burdens may give him a right to ignore the assignment when properly notified to him in order to achieve payment to the assignee. That means that he may continue to pay the assignor. This right to continue to pay the assignor becomes much stronger if the claim assigned is subject to adjustment, e.g. in the case of the assignment of interest payments under a floating rate loan pursuant to an adjustment formula introducing the lender-bank's general practices of interests adjustment which may not be adhered to by the assignee-bank.

To commit the debtor fully, a novation may then be necessary. This is a tripartite agreement, which requires the consent of the debtor who holds a veto as a consequence. The consequence is that the old contract disappears and a new contract is created releasing the old creditor. Because of this debtor's consent requirement, it is not a feasible route when a whole portfolio of assets is to be transferred. An important side effect is also that all (accessory) personal and real securities protecting the claim are released at the same time.

In practice, in a securitisation, the assignment route is therefore the only way. It may make the transfer from a legal point of view less than certain as far as the payment to the assignee is concerned and for the assignor there may always remain a question what his residual duties are and how far he is discharged. He may e.g. still be called upon to continue to make advances under credit card agreements and may remain residually involved in often uncertain ways and could therefore retain a risk exposure. This is likely to be a regulatory concern for banks (in the sense that the regulator may not consider the assets fully deleted from the balance sheet for capital adequacy purposes) and will therefore be an extra concern of the assignor. For the assignee, the prime concern is always to *ring fence* the cash flow and separate it sufficiently from that of the assignor/bank as a whole. Adequate legal separation is therefore also crucial for the assignee. Moreover, the assignee also needs to limit the defenses of the debtors under the assigned claims.

For the assignee, one way to avoid problems of payment is for the former creditor/assignor to continue to collect as the *collecting agent* for the assignee under the loans (as agent only). That is common (at a fee to the assignor) and also safeguards established banking relationships of assignor-banks. In fact the loan debtor(s) of a bank may not be informed of the transfer at all. This is possible under assignment laws or practices that do not require notice to them as a prerequisite for the validity of the assignment. That is so in common law under the equitable assignment which became the basis for the assignment law in the USA and is also by far the most practiced method in England. It is also German law, but not the law in France or of the new Dutch Civil Code (although already proposed to be changed): see more in particular chapter IV, section 1.7.

To take a step back: notice to the debtor is *never* a petition for his approval, not even in systems which require it for the validity of the assignment. In systems that do not, it is in essence no more than a direction to the debtor(s) henceforth to pay to the assignee and is therefore part of the implementation of the agreement. It can usually be given by the assignee, but the latter must be able to present proof of the assignment which the debtor may verify with the former creditor (the assignor). In countries that require notice for the assignment to be valid, which remains the old common law (but not equity) and present French approach, this means that before notice the claim is not transferred at all. The significance is that, should in the meantime the assignor go bankrupt, the claims still belong to his estate and not to that of the assignee. Wherever notice is not a precondition of validity, payments made by debtors to the bankrupt assignor belong to the assignee and the proceeds must be turned over to him if they can be identified and traced as such even after the bankruptcy of the assignor.

Like the issue of *adequate separation* of the cash flow and the likelihood of continuing *payments* by the debtors to the assignor (and his defenses against the assignment in this respect), the *notification requirement* as a matter of validity of the transfer itself unavoidably inhibits a transfer of loan assets to a third party (bank) assignee. It notably makes a bulk assignment too cumbersome as all individual debtors have to be notified. The assignee will also be concerned about the *credit risk* in the portfolio (the position or interest rate risk will be discounted in the price paid for these assets). To avoid at least the assignment complications, it is not uncommon that another bank takes some interest in a particular pool of loan assets through a kind of syndicated loan book structure or *sub-participation*. This may take the form of a participation agreement but could also be a trust arrangement under which the investor becomes a beneficiary of the loan portfolio. Yet these alternatives do not remove the loans from the bank's balance sheet.

All these facilities depend on finding a willing partner or counterparty, which is often difficult and always causes delays. In the case of assignments, it is therefore common for an assignor to create its own assignee through the incorporation of a special purpose vehicle (SPV) to which the assets are transferred. This assignment structure presupposes the possibility of an equitable assignment without notice and also assumes that all supporting securities are transferred with the claims as accessory rights (if not, they must be separately transferred, which presents further logistical problems, particularly relevant also for reservations of title which are usually not considered accessory rights). As the situation may be very different here in different countries, normally a class of *debtors* will be chosen in one single country that has a favourable assignment regime. One must assume that *their* law is here controlling (although that is not undisputed in private international law, see more in particular chapter IV, section 1.9).

As we saw, the assignor/bank will normally continue to collect as agent (for a fee payable by the SPV) so that debtors' payment objections may remain remote. It may still raise the question who will set the interest rate policy if there were floating rate loans and, if it is the bank, what should guide it. The SPV needs here to have some say and protection against conflicting interests in the bank. Naturally, this collection structure may expose the assignee in a bankruptcy of the assignor.

The next problem is how the SPV is to pay for the assigned assets. There is no point in the assignor/bank providing it with a loan to make payment possible. It would not reduce the bank's risk assets; it may even increase them if mortgage debt is removed in this manner and a loan to the SPV appears instead (which has a higher risk weighting). It is normal for the SPV to *securitise* the deal, which means raising funds in the (international) capital markets through a bond issue supported by the cash flow to be transferred and that will be used as collateral for bond holders. Hence the term '*asset-backed securities*' (or ABS), which are bonds protected by this cash flow and repaid out of it. These cash flows may derive from mortgages (resulting in mortgage backed securities or MBS) or from bond or other loan portfolios (resulting in Collateral Debt Obligations or CDO's, to be distinguished accordingly in Collateral Bond or Collateral Loan Obligations or CBO's and CLO's). It might sound strange that a bank might want to securitise a portfolio of bonds rather than sell them, but they may be substantially illiquid as in the case of corporate bonds and some (non-OECD) country bonds.

The Servicer in charge of the arrangement will often be the original bank which removed risks assets in this manner. If the Originator was not a bank it may hire an investment bank to be this Servicer, for which a fee is paid. To be able to do a securitisation, the SPV must first show a good, valid and uncomplicated assignment, whilst the new issue of bonds will be secured by the cash flow from the assigned claims, giving rise to another (security) assignment, now of a future cash flow to the bond holders. This leads to a so-called *pass-through securitisation* in which the investors receive pass-though certificates together with their bonds.

The proceeds of the issue will be used to pay off the assignor. The security holders will have recourse in this manner to the cash flow but not to the assignor. To access the capital markets, the SPV must have the highest credit rating and it will normally not be able to obtain this without *enhancement* of its credit standing. The SPV will have to obtain this credit rating from the rating agencies and these have therefore a substantial say in the structuring of the securitisation, which virtually requires their approval.

To *enhance* the SPV's credit, the bank may transfer more loans than the total net face value of the bonds. It means that there may be a balance in the SPV at the end, which the bank somehow must seek to retrieve (probably through a subordinated loan structure). The assets could also be sold at a discount to the SPV with the same possibility of a surplus in the company. Instead or in addition, certain warranties might be given by the assignor/ bank, but it must be careful that it puts enough distance between itself and the SPV to make the removal of the assets effective from a regulatory (for banks, especially from a capital adequacy) point of view. It may be better to organise a guarantee from another bank (at a cost). It is also possible for the SPV to issue several classes of bonds, one of them junk, so that the standing of the others rises.

All has its cost and the SPV must remain capable of servicing all debt and paying all expenses. To this end, it should not incur extra expenditure and will usually be debarred from hiring personnel, and its activities will be very narrowly circumscribed and defined in the founding documents (trust deed or corporate documents). The SPV should also not receive tax bills. It could complicate matters in unexpected ways and the SPV is therefore normally organised in a tax haven (although the debtors may have certain tax advantages that they do not want to loose by paying effectively to a foreign company). A currency mismatch between the underlying cash flows and the denomination of the bonds is another aspect for bond holders to watch.

There are other pitfalls besides the legal and tax complications. As already mentioned, banking supervisors may remain to be convinced that the loans, and particularly all obligations in respect of them, are effectively removed from a bank's balance sheet. The stand-alone nature of the SPV is another major structural hazard. The SPV must stand alone and be *bankruptcy remote* from the assigning bank or other institution. It means that, should the bank or other institution go bankrupt, the SPV is not affected. This requires above all that the assignors should not be seen as the *de facto* shareholder and/or manager of the SPV risking a lifting of the corporate veil of the SPV. Thus the SPV will normally be a charitable trust or company with an outside shareholder. Its liquidation balance should not automatically accrue to the securitising bank either. Also any moneys collected by a securitising bank from the debtors as agent for the SPV should be clearly separated out and be so marked in the bank's book or better still be deposited with another bank. A bank failure should then not impact on the SPV, although debtors are still likely to be disoriented by it and there may result some collection problems for the SPV.

There is always a possibility that for the legal, tax and regulatory reasons mentioned, these schemes may prove not to be fully effective but they have become very popular, particularly in the USA and increasingly also in Western Europe.

1.4.8   *Synthetic Securitisation. Credit Derivatives or Credit Swaps*

Asset securitisation has become a common tool to restructure a balance sheet and is particularly useful for banks to move certain types of loan portfolios, like a cocktail of mortgages, in order to free up capital for other uses or to retire debt. Other financial entities, not subject to stringent capital adequacy requirements, may want to do the same for similar re-balancing reasons. Car finance companies may thus move car loans; credit card companies may move some credit card receivables and commercial companies some trade receivables. But the process is complex and therefore costly and takes some time. It removes (ideally) all risks (credit, market and liquidity risk) in connection with the assets so moved and reduces any applicable capital adequacy requirements accordingly, but where the concern is only credit risk, it may be possible to create a simpler structure that removes only that risk (often to other banks or insurance companies).

This can be done by negotiating a guarantee. That is the traditional way and if the result is a first demand guarantee of a third party, see chapter III, section 2.1.13, it may well be that even bank regulators would accept that, depending on the credit worthiness of the guarantor, the relevant credit risk of the bank in question is removed and the capital adequacy requirement in banks therefore reduced. It cannot, however, be achieved instantaneously and depends very much on finding a willing counterparty.

A modern simpler way of achieving a similar result is through the creation of so-called *synthetic securities* or *credit derivatives* or *credit swaps*. The terminology may be a little confusing. As explained before, a derivative like an option, future or swap is a financial product the value of which is determined by the value of an underlying asset. A credit derivative is rather a financial product the value of which is determined by the creditworthiness of a third party that takes over the credit risk. As stands to reason, these credit derivatives have become particularly popular with banks especially in order to reduce credit risk allowing them to employ their capital more efficiently.

The suggestion is here that a product is sold rather than a guarantee given. Indeed sales language is often used but in truth, only the credit risk is removed or transferred, not by moving any asset (which remains in place), but simply by contract (not therefore by an assignment or novation either, which would involve third parties, or even by a contract of sale which would suggest the transfer of an asset). Yet in an economic sense, risk is perceived here as a tradable commodity or even some kind of investment security in which investors can participate by buying fractions. Terms like 'protection buyer' and 'protection seller' are therefore commonly used in this context.

The most current forms of credit derivatives are *credit default swaps* (CDS) and *credit linked notes* (CLN). In a CDS, in exchange for a one-off or annual premium, the outsider or 'protection seller' will make a payment only upon the occurrence of a previously defined *credit event*, like the down-grading, default or insolvency of the debtor under a *reference asset*, which is the financial asset in respect of which the bank incurs a credit risk that it wants to remove. The ISDA Master Agreement (definitions) may be used in this connection. It may take the form of compensation or the transfer of the reference asset at face value.

Like in the case of a first demand guarantee, the key to the success of the scheme is in the simplicity of the recovery possibility. The difference is that while in first demand guarantees the question is 'pay first argue later', here the scope for further argument is altogether excluded. That has to do with the nature of the liability that is guaranteed which is here pure and simple credit risk. In first demand guarantees like letters of credit, credit risk in respect of payment is the first concern but there may still be quality issues that may have to be argued out later as the underlying transaction is a commodity sale. Here we have credit risk in respect of loan assets where quality risk is not an issue.

Credit Linked Notes (CLN) are securities or notes issued by the 'protection buyer' to the 'protection seller' who pays for them and is repaid the face value of these notes by the 'protection buyer' at the end of the term if no credit event has occurred. If there is such an occurrence, the notes are repaid after deduction of the compensatory amount. Fundraising is here combined with the transfer of credit risk. The CLN structure is so far less common than that of the CDS but more interesting as in the CLN the credit risk may be completely shifted to the capital markets and its investors who are then effectively selling the protection. An SPV may be created in this connection to which the credit risk is transferred by CDS and which issues notes to the public as per CLN.

Here the notion of a *synthetic securitisation* comes in, in which both CDS and CLN play a role. The protection is bought from an SPV to which the risk is transferred and which is paid for this and issues notes to back-up this risk, the proceeds of which will be reinvested. The notes are repaid by the SPV (out of the cash flow of the reinvestments and of the CDS payment) allowing for a deduction for any payments that will be due when a credit event occurs. In the meantime, these notes may trade in the public markets and their market price may become a useful indication of the credit risk of the protection buyer.

The securitisation is considered here 'synthetic' because it does not concern risk assets but only credit risk. It avoids asset transfer problems, like those connected with assignments, and thus leads to simplified documentation. It disperses the underlying obligors and protects therefore also better the confidentiality of the credit protection.

The introduction of a SPV in schemes like these raises all the complication of SPV's and their credit enhancements necessary to make a *public* offer. Where funding is an important part of the scheme, the SPV will have to reassure bondholders that interest and principal (after any deduction for matured credit risk) will be paid on the due dates. This may be done by the originator pledging the loan assets in respect of which the credit risk is transferred as well as their income as security. In this connection reference is also made to Total Return Swaps or TRS.

The credit derivatives have developed quickly during the last few years and that development is not yet at an end. Their impact on the investors has not yet been fully tested but it is already clear that in economic downturns when banks weaken, the transfer of their credit risk to others, especially insurance companies, may have the effect of destabilising these as well. The spread of risk whilst generally to be applauded may thus create greater weakness all around.

1.4.9 *Securities Lending, Short Selling and Prime Brokerage*

Securities lending is an activity already discussed in chapter V section 2.2.2 where the close connection and differences with the repo were also explained. An important aspect of securities lending (like in repos) is that the borrower may sell the securities and only has a re-delivery duty in respect of fungible assets of the same sort. It would therefore appear that the securities borrower obtains some ownership rights in the assets and that there is some kind of sale to him, but this may not be a proper legal characterisation and a *sui generis* structure is often meant under which the borrower pays a fee for the facility and the lender takes the risk that in a bankruptcy of the borrower the securities cannot be located so that he becomes a mere competing creditor, a risk that also affects the repo seller of fungible assets for whom netting may, however, provide some relief, see chapter V, sections 2.2.4 and 2.2.5. The securities lender will often require security to cover the re-delivery risk.

Prime brokerage refers to a number of activities that have to do with the facilitating of *short selling* in which securities lending is likely to play an important role as it is a way for the short seller to meet any delivery requirement in respect of securities that he has sold but does not have. The prime broker may also provide credit, foreign exchange and custody facilities in this connection and normally benefits from a contractual close out facility in respect of a defaulting client that will provide for a bilateral netting facility in respect of all outstanding transactions with that particular client.

1.4.10 *Hedge Funds and their Operations*

Finally, the operation of hedge funds has raised many questions in recent years. They usually spot certain small market irregularities and try to take advantage of the smoothing out process, although there is not one particular investment structure and policy that they follow. They are often risk adverse, but their operations may nevertheless prove highly speculative when markets become irregular. Their problems are then compounded because hedge funds are normally highly geared which means that they operate on large amount of borrowed money.

Market risk is here compounded by management risk in terms of dependence on the ingenuity of (often) only one or two people. From a regulatory point of view, the concern is mainly that banks in their treasury operations do not follow similar speculative policies or lend excessively to these funds. Another concern may be that these funds in fact hold themselves out as deposit takers. Even so they may legally solicit participations but usually address themselves only to experienced investors who understand at least some risk and are able to take a substantial loss.

Regulating these hedge funds is often demanded but is likely to be less successful as they may easily move to other countries. Disclosure may endanger the very schemes that they set up. In any event, it is not possible to regulate all types of speculation which is a normal market function. Although contagion and systemic risk may follow their failure, this will be largely so because such failures affect banks that have lent (too much) money to them. From a regulatory point of view it is this lending that should be scrutinised and if necessary curtailed.

Part II   International Aspects of Financial Services Regulation; Developments in Gatt, The EU and BIS/IOSCO/IAIS

2.1   Free Movement of Goods, Services, Current Payments and Capital after World War II

2.1.1   *Cross-border Movement of Goods. GATT*

Internationalisation or globalisation means in commerce and finance essentially the free movement in goods, payments, capital and services cross-border. Although it substantially prevailing before World War I, this liberalisation is in modern times a relatively new phenomenon. As far as the free movement of goods is concerned, immediately after World War II, import restrictions and other protections were rampant and average tariffs were estimated to be as high as 40 per cent. Some relief was obtained through the General Agreement on Tariffs and Trade (GATT) which entered into force on 1 January 1948 under a Protocol of Provisional Application, therefore as a provisional agreement among States.[49] There were 23 original members, largely developed countries, increased to 146 by 2002 including China and many developing states. Of the main countries, only Russia awaits admission.

It was part of what proved to be an abortive attempt (largely due to US Senate opposition, which had in the meantime turned conservative) at creating an international trade organisation (the ITO pursuant to the Havana Charter of 1948 which resulted from the United Nations Conference on Trade and Development called in 1946 at the initiative of the USA). It was meant to have powers of its own and a decision-making process to stimulate international trade (Articles 75 and 77). The provisional GATT (which had been drafted at the second preparatory meeting for the ITO to deal with a system for tariff reductions) was thereupon continued and assumed to some extent the ITO mantle. It required unanimity in its decision-taking process and provided only a (partial) system to promote international trade in respect of physical goods. It introduced a method for a gradual reduction in protection levels through (a) the standstill agreement, (b) the most favoured nation clause, and (c) a reciprocity notion based on national treatment.

---

[49] From the American point of view, this was not a formal treaty so that a different form of approval could be used, thus avoiding the two-thirds majority rule in the Senate (a procedure later also used for WTO). GATT was subject to the procedure of ratification in most other countries, however. Under international law it has the status of a treaty, as international law does not make a distinction according to the manner in which these international agreements are approved.

This meant in essence that (a) under the standstill agreement no member country could introduce further unilateral restrictions on trade including any increase in tariffs, that (b) under the most favoured nation clause benefits given to any one country had to be extended to all other GATT members, and that (c) under the notion of reciprocity and national treatment internal taxation and other regulation could no longer be used to discriminate against products from other Member States. Production and import subsidies were not deemed illegal *per se,* however, regardless of their trade distorting effects but anti-dumping charges could be imposed at the national level on the importation of dumped products.

It was a system of some checks and balances in which no Member State was required to do anything at all except to make sure that no further tariffs were imposed so as to prevent a race to the bottom and competition in imposing ever higher tariffs that had bedeviled international trade ever since the end of the gold standard regime in the 1930s. It had started an era of nationalism also in currencies and their exchange rates. This allowed for competitive devaluations which subsequently raised the spectre of protection against the consequences through trade barriers in the nature of import restrictions (contingents) or tariffs. With the stand-still agreement in place, it was believed that classical economic theory, which since Adam Smith and Ricardo assumed that liberalisation even if unilateral was in the ultimate best interest of all nations, would work its way. There was no free trade ethos *per se.*

It follows that in this approach, no interdependence or negotiation model was institutionalised, one reason why no need for the ITO was felt in the US. Nevertheless regular multilateral negotiation rounds to reduce tariffs amongst Members became a feature of this system and tended to be propelled by a freer market ethos. The last round was the Uruguay Round which was the eighth, implemented on 1 January 1995. The results of these Rounds were by no means always accepted by or became binding upon all members whilst others remained in default of the objectives which they had agreed to. Nevertheless average tariffs for goods are now estimated to have been reduced to below 5 per cent and they may be as low as 3 per cent after the full implementation of the Uruguay Round. Thus, free movement of goods under GATT had largely been achieved with the exception of agricultural produce and textiles which remain particular stumbling blocks. In these two areas, the Uruguay Round measures intended to phase out quotas, to cut subsidies and replace them with tariffs to be reduced over time, and to eliminate other non-tariff barriers.

The Marshall Plan for Western European was at first a substantial encouragement in the liberalisation process as the US government insisted that recipient nations promised to balance budgets, free prices, halt inflation, stabilise exchange rates, and remove trade barriers. In the 1960s and especially in 1970s (probably connected with the oil crises of those days), there was some lack of interest but in the 1980s the *internationalisation* or *horizontalisation* of the production process worldwide, therefore market-related forces themselves, became another crucial facilitating factor in the liberalisation process feeding upon itself. Yet another part of this process was the progressive globalisation of the market for services and even of capital leading to international capital markets, as examplified by the eurobond market. It made the creation of the World Trade Organisation or WTO possible at the end of the Uruguay Round. It was in fact a more modest version of the organisation originally envisaged by the Havanna Charter. Arguably, it reinforced the focus on the interdependency and negotiation model with free trade as its main objective.

As already mentioned, free movement of goods was as such never the explicit objective of GATT, rather the standstill agreements and other rules at least not to inhibit it. That remains in essence the position. It is an imperfect system that has nevertheless worked. Only in more recent times has it become subject to criticism as some consider it now too producer-driven and free-trade oriented whilst giving insufficient attention to other policy aspects of free trade, like the environmental and labour consequences. The technocratic approach of the modern GATT/WTO is here sometimes also criticized regardless of its achievements and notwithstanding the difficulties in pointing to any adverse effect, even in respect of developing countries. Greater openness and a better political input is advocated but it is not clear who, beyond the member governments which represent so far the political element, could be given a voice (like certain Non Governmental Organisations or NGO's) and whether the result would be any more balanced.

In fact, as the development of the EU has also shown, it is not uncommon for institutions to arise in the international order before a broader input can be achieved at the level of the individual and non-statist organisations and an own democratic legitimacy can be established. In the EU, it was at first left to the processes in Member States to achieve here (indirect) accountability, which in many modern states remains even internally lacking or inefficient. Greater participation by the European Parliament, now directly elected, seems not to have achieved so far a greater sense of participation. This remains a problem in all institutionalised internationalisation efforts including the modern WTO.

2.1.2 Cross-border Payments and Movement of Capital. IMF

Free movement of capital was never itself considered part of the new order after World War II. The Bretton Woods Agreements of 1944, including the IMF (International Monetary Fund) Treaty and the creation of the International Bank for Reconstruction and Development or IRBD ('World Bank') did not mean to liberalise capital movements and accepted that each country could insulate its own capital market. There followed a system of managed exchange rates and exchange rate adjustments with the possibility of emergency liquidity assistance from the IMF to smooth out currency instabilities, again especially to avoid the threat of competitive devaluations and subsequent trade wars. The IMF rules did concern themselves, however, with the liberalisation of payments for trade (except for countries that claimed an exception, see for details chapter III, section 1.1.4). Contrary to the GATT arrangements, these rules were considered to have *direct effect* in the contracting States.

It meant that after the War, the arrangements put in place, concentrated on trade in goods and related current payments only, whilst the capital markets (and services) were allowed to develop in isolation each with their own national practices, interest rate structures and products. It gave governments (a) a strong position in influencing interest rates and indirectly the cost of their borrowings in their own currencies, (b) especially after the final breakdown in 1973 of the fixed exchange rate system agreed at Bretton Woods, a virtually unfettered right to devalue their currency to suit their own purposes, usually under their general foreign policy powers which remained unchecked within their own political systems regardless of the potentially disruptive consequences for others and ultimately for themselves, (c) the possibility of limiting export of capital and checking inward investment, and (d) the facility to control all foreign exchange transactions.

After 1973, in practice, the role of the IMF became itself largely confined to (a) oversee the internationally agreed rules for monetary and liquidity policy and particularly to (b) administer a pool of currencies that could be lent to members suffering from foreign exchange crises. In that context, it now commonly sets conditions for it (governmental) borrowers which in practice often aim at (i) the free convertibility of the currency, (ii) the freeing of capital flows and financial services to keep access to foreign investors, (iii) necessary budgetary restraints and (iv) sound monetary controls and banking practices and supervision.

In this context, it has often been observed that the IMF now operates *de facto* as a bank of last resort to many developing countries. Crises like the Mexican one in 1994, the Asian one in 1997, and the Brazilian one in 1999 seem to bear this out. This has been critisised, but no less the manner in which the IMF fulfills this function through alleged insufficient separation of its early monitoring, support, and execution functions, including the imposition and monitoring of lending conditions. As far as these conditions are concerned, they have in turn been criticised for their strong monetarist and deflationary flavour and limited regard for the social consequences. It is often overlooked in this connection that countries is this position would have been forced to balance budgets and deflate more without international help. The IMF conditions have at least contributed to some sense of international discipline without which the bank of last resort function could hardly be credible or be sustained.

2.1.3   *Cross-border Movement of Services. GATS*

Like capital movements, the free movement of services also had no place in the system that was developed after World War II and neither had the free movement of payments in respect of them and of earnings from labour or capital investments. In the area of services, the emphasis is not normally on tariffs but rather on discriminatory trade barriers of a qualitative and quantitative nature. Thus licenses to provide services may be imposed on foreigners and may simply be refused or market share legally or practically restricted. They might be imposed on all, therefore in a non-discriminatory manner also on local service providers, like in the financial services area, but the requirements may be so difficult or singular to fulfil for foreigners that entry is effectively denied. The applicable regulatory regime may thus become a substantial barrier in this respect, even for service providers coming from the best regulated countries.

As far as services including those in the financial area were concerned, the Uruguay Round planned a beginning of liberalisation subject to further negotiations, in which connection the Final Act of the Uruguay Round made reference to a General Agreement on Trade in Services (GATS). In fact, originally, the inclusion of services, trade-related intellectual property rights (TRIPS) and trade-related investment measures (TRIMS) was a trade-off with developing countries under which the industrial countries agreed to include and liberalise the trade in agricultural products and textiles. In the end, no straightforward trade-off occurred and, in the financial services area, the situation especially with regard to the initial commitments to financial liberalisation and market opening, was not clarified when the negotiations ended and they remained the subject of further discussions.

On the part of the USA, there was a fear of free riders in the financial area. These are countries where did not commit to any substantial liberalisation themselves but, through the most favoured nation clause, would be able to benefit from the liberalisation of others. This fear concerned especially Asian countries including Japan. Pending a resolution, the USA was only willing to preserve the existing activities in its territory of foreign firms coming from these countries, reserved the right to impose limits on their expansion and on new entries short of reciprocity. It exempted itself also from the most favoured nation principle in this area, as it was entitled to do and limited it to countries that were in its view sufficiently open to US service providers, like the EU countries which had obtained most favoured nation treatment from the USA in this area in a separate development in July 1995. These EU countries themselves were more relaxed on the initial commitments as long as financial services were included in the package from the beginning. Helped by an agreement with the Japanese and by the Asian crisis, the USA ultimately obtained the commitments it wanted in December 1997 and 70 countries acceded to the new system. Although only 58 of them had ratified by February 1999, it became effective on 1 March 1999 (Fifth Protocol and Schedules of Commitments).

GATS operates more of an interdependency or negotiation model than the original GATT and provides a framework for further negotiations in the service area on the basis of (a) a negotiation approach per sector based on *effective market access* (equality of competitive opportunities) and national treatment (in the sense of indiscriminatory treatment of foreigners also in terms of access to payments, and, where necessary, to clearing-systems), (b) the introduction of the *most favoured nation clause* in respect of past and future concessions to others, and (c) a compilation of the domestic regulations concerning *market access* to create the necessary transparency and ensure a reasonable, objective and impartial application of domestic laws and regulation.

National treatment in this connection means that the host country may not treat foreign services or service providers less favourably than 'like' domestic services or service providers. It does not mean exactly the same treatment. Here the GATS is more specific than the GATT earlier. The key is that the conditions of competition are not modified in favour of domestic services or service providers. On the other hand, market access and the way in which the service provider chooses to operate in the foreign country (either directly, through a branch or subsidiary) are not defined. In the list of restrictive conditions that should be avoided, the service provider is left free to choose between a branch or a subsidiary. Host country prudential and other regulatory standards must, however, be met and it appears that (like previously in the EU) host countries may insist on the creation of a branch for the foreign activity in their countries subject to their authorisation and other regulatory requirements.

As in trade, a separate Council (for services) was created to monitor the negotiation process and future negotiations. The emphasis on market access besides national treatment meant that national treatment under which foreign service providers could not do more than local ones and were held to the same functional separations (for example between commercial and investment banking or broad and narrow banking), should not result in greater restrictions than those in the major service providing countries.

In this connection, GATS members should apply domestic regulation in a reasonable, objective and impartial manner to avoid undermining commitments to market access. Yet it was always realised that the barriers resulting from regulatory differences in terms of permitted activities, the way they could be conducted, and the financial products that could be offered would take a long time to overcome. It would require deregulation and a minimum of regulatory harmonisation and probably also of competition policy. That is not the present aim of GATS and has only been achieved within the EU.

In fact, the GATS contains a so-called *prudential carve-out* to ensure that the liberalisation under it would not endanger prudential regulation and supervision. A similar precautionary clause may be found in the North American Free Trade Agreement (NAFTA) and in the aborted OECD Multilateral Agreement on Investment (MAI). The regulatory side of the liberalisation of cross-border financial services is likely to receive attention in the next negotiation round. In the meantime, especially within the BIS Group of Ten, the enhancement of co-operation and co-ordination among banking supervisors has become a matter of priority. So has the establishment of strong prudential standards and effective supervision for which the BIS has been issuing guidelines, as will be further discussed below in sections 2.5.1*ff.*

GATT rules never had direct effect and it remains to be seen whether GATS rules will be interpreted any differently.

GATS became part of the Agreement Establishing the World Trade Organisation (WTO) and has two components. The first is the framework agreement that sets the basic rules discussed in the previous section and the second is a schedule giving each country's specific commitments and a list of most favoured nation exemptions.

2.1.4   The WTO

Calls for reinforcements of GATT through conversion into an international or multilateral trade organisation as originally planned in ITO had been frequent and were partly successful in the latter part of the Uruguay Round. As a consequence, as at 1 January 1995, the GATT was transformed into the World Trade Organisation (or WTO) of which the successor GATT and GATS became a part. It has modest administrative powers and, most important, a uniform dispute settlement procedure in all sectors of its activities with an international legal status for the findings. The old GATT had had at least eight different structures for dispute resolution, each depending on the nature of the dispute. All tended to be handled at fairly junior levels with appointments made exclusively by the GATT Secretariat which also made the drafts of the decisions. There was much uncertainty and delay in the procedures. The status of these panels was therefore not high. Their underlying ethos was in fact diplomatic rather than judicial. This is different in the WTO.

The original GATT agreements remain effective between parties not accepting the WTO or refused access thereto because of the lack of agreement on accession. WTO members can technically withdraw from the old GATT 1947 agreement, which the USA did as at 1 January 1996 since it did not wish to be subjected to two different sets of rules with different parties. As the WTO only applies to the future, outstanding GATT disputes lost their legal basis for withdrawing parties, the reason the USA agreed to accept these cases for a period of two years after it ceased to be a member. The USA also instituted a review panel for decisions of the new WTO's dispute mechanism and threatened to leave the WTO if in the view of the panel three consecutive cases went against US trading interests in the first five years.

The Final Act of the Uruguay Round embodying the Agreement Establishing the WTO also contained a set of Annexes and Ministerial Decisions and Declarations. These Annexes cover the various agreements on the trade in goods (the GATT as amended in Annex 1A, the GATT 1994 being legally distinct from the GATT 1947 and bringing all members up to the same level of commitment), in services (the GATS in Annex 1B), and in intellectual property rights (the TRIPS in Annex 1C). They also cover the dispute settlement procedure (in Annex 2), the policy review procedure (in Annex 3), and some special trade agreements like those on civil aircraft and government procurement (in Annex 4 which alone may have a limited membership).[50]

The WTO was accepted by 124 countries and its legal personality is fully recognised. China became its 142nd member in 2001. The WTO as it now functions is sometimes seen as a way to reduce American influence notwithstanding the continuing lack of a majority decision taking process. Yet it established (a) a new legal pattern of conduct, integrating all previous GATT agreements into one system including GATS, TRIPS and even the trade-related movement of persons and investments with the same regime for all. It further instituted (b) a new infrastructure for trade relations with its own Ministerial Conference, General Council, Council for Trade in Goods, Council for Trade in Services, Council for

---

[50] See for the new dispute settlement system in particular E-U Petersman, 'The Dispute Settlements System of the World Trade Organisation and the Evolution of the GATT Dispute Settlement System since 1948' (1994) 31 *Common Market Law Review*, 1157.

Trips, Committee on Trade and Development and its own Secretariate. The WTO finally provides (c) a forum for further negotiations.

The WTO agreement completes in several respects the Bretton Wood Agreements and the structure envisaged in 1945 although itself much changed over time. Together they provide a comprehensive system for the cross-border movements of goods, services and related payments and trade-related movement of persons and investments, although capital movements still remain outside the structure but are increasingly subject to their own market-induced globalisation process (see section 2.4.1 below). In fact, the progressive liberalisation of the capital flows plays an important propelling role also in other areas, not as an issue therefore of agreement between governments but as an autonomous force in tune with classic economic theory in which market forces favour unilateral liberalisation. The new system as a whole was intended as, and may provide, a reasonably effective basis for the international economic order in the first part of the twenty-first century. The Group of Seven (G-7) made up by the most advanced economies informally lords over it. It is therefore not without a political component.

The EU as well as it Members became WTO parties. This duplication was necessary because Member States retain certain powers especially in the area of movement of people and establishments across borders and of intellectual property rights, although the EU has sole power to conclude international agreements covering trade in goods.[51] In the areas where the EU has exclusive powers, Member States must vote as instructed by it.

2.2 The Creation of the EEC and Evolution of the EU

2.2.1 *The Common Market and Monetary Union. The Various Pillars of the EU*

It has not been uncommon for regional trade pacts to emerge that are in essence deviations from the more global GATT approach. From the beginning GATT made allowance for this under certain circumstances. The regional approach to trade of the European Union (EU) when it was first formed (as the European Economic Community or EEC) in 1958 went (for goods) in essence against the global GATT approach and its most favoured nation clause. It was under American influence allowed to develop (as long as trade barriers were not raised in respect of outsiders) because of its overriding political objectives aiming at Western European economic integration. Article XXIV of the GATT now authorises and encourages nations to form such regional trade arrangements as customs unions or free trade areas.

Within these political objectives and as an expression thereof, the trade paragraphs of the EEC Treaty of 1958 aimed higher than the GATT of those days. Amongst its main objectives, it envisaged for its area not only the free movement of goods, Articles 23ff and 28ff (ex Articles 9ff and 30ff),[52] but also of persons, Article 39 (ex Article 48), services,

---

[51] See *EU Opinion* 1/94 [1994] ECR 1–5276.

[52] Art 28 (ex Art 30) concerns quantitative restrictions and all measures having equivalent effect on the free movement of goods which were soon extended by case law to include also qualitative restrictions: see Case 8/74, *Procureur du Roi v Dassonville* [1974] ECR 837 in which all trading rules enacted by Member States which were capable of hindering, actually or potentially, directly or indirectly, intra-Community trade were considered measures having an effect equivalent to quantitative restrictions. It had the effect of potentially evaluating all restrictive domestic rules in terms of legality and proportionality (besides its discriminatory effect), therefore also those applied to national sellers as long as they affected access by sellers of other Member States. Art 28 (ex Art 30) was in that sense considered an access rather than an anti-discrimination rule: see also n 63 below, plus accompanying text. For interpretative guidance see also Dir 70/50 [1970] JO L13/29, Art 3, which deals with the effect of indiscriminatory rules when exerting a restrictive effect on trade that 'exceeds the effects intrinsic to trade rules'.

Article 49 (ex Article 59), including the free right of establishment, Article 43 (ex Article 52), payments, Article 56 (replacing Article 106) and capital, Article 56 (replacing Article 67). These freedoms concern a unitary concept: see Articles 3(3) and 14 (ex Articles 3(3) and 7a). Article 28 (ex Article 30), which removes all non-fiscal barriers to the movement of goods, Article 43 (ex Article 52) which concerns the right of establishment, and Article 49 (ex Article 59) which introduces the free movement of services[53] were promptly given direct effect, although the latter more like an anti-discrimination measure subject to possible limitations if also applying in a non-discriminatory manner to domestic entities, as we shall see below in section 2.2.3.

Article 28 (ex Article 30) prohibiting quantitative restrictions on imports between Member States can also be so explained as we shall see. Also the free movement of persons (workers), established under Article 39 (ex Article 48) and, in support of the free right of establishment and the free movement of services, under Articles 43(2) and 50(3) (ex Articles 52(2) and 60(3)), is cast more in terms of an anti-discrimination measure. Immigration remains a sensitive issue within the EU: see also Articles 18(2) and 95(2) (ex Articles 8a and 100a(2)) which require unanimity for the expansion of citizens' rights in the area of their free movement.

There thus were some differences from the outset between the various freedoms and they were distinguished and differently formulated. The freedom to move capital under old Article 67 was different altogether and *not* considered to be unfettered — in deference to the Bretton Woods agreements and international foreign exchange attitudes at the time. It was also denied direct effect (unlike the Bretton Woods Agreements) and could therefore not directly be invoked by the EU citizens or entities operating on its territory. It remained dependant on further implementation through Directives.

In a similar vein, even after the end of the initial period in 1970, the free movement of *payments* under the original Article 106(1) was considered to be liberalised *only* as a sequel of any ongoing liberalisation in the movement of persons, goods, services and capital and was even then only achieved in the currency of the Member State in which the creditor or the beneficiary resided. This continuing limited direct effect of Article 106(1) was confirmed by the European Court as late as 1981.[54]

In fact, the freedom of movement of capital and payments was only established by the important Directive of 1988 which will be discussed in greater detail in section 2.4.6 *et seq* below. It was virtually also a precondition for the practical liberalisation of financial services, even though in principle already freed as without the free movement of capital and payments cross border financial services remained themselves limited. Yet in this area of the free movement of financial services, there remained also important problems connected with the proper supervision of these services and of the entities rendering them cross-border, which, as we shall see, were solved only through a new generation of Directives of which the Second Banking Directive (consolidated in the Credit Institutions Directive of 2000), the Investment Services Directive, and third generation of Insurance

---

It tends to outlaw local (mandatory) standardisation rules and gave rise to subsequent directives introducing EU standards. A good example is electricity sockets and plugs; the different shapes and sizes may, however, still be maintained on public safety grounds under Art 30 (ex Art 36).

[53] See for Art 28 (ex Art 30) e.g. the fundamental *Dassonville* case, n 52 above. See for Art 43 (ex Art 52), Case 2/74, *Reyners v Belgian State* [1974] ECR 631 and for Art 49 (ex Art 59), Case 33/74, *Van Binsbergen v Bedrijfsvereniging Metaalnijverheid* [1974] ECR 1299.
[54] Case 203/80, *Guerino Cassati* [1981] ECR 3211 and also in Cases 286/82 and 26/83, *Luisi and Carbone* [1984] ECR 377.

Directives were the most important. They will be more extensively discussed below in connection with the so-called European passport for these services.[55]

In the area of the free movement of goods, the EU operates a so-called *customs union*: Articles 23 *et seq* (ex Articles 9 *et seq*). This is an alternative to a free trade area. In the latter, there are no trade barriers, including tariffs and quantitative (and possibly qualitative) restrictions, for goods *originating* in Member States. But there is no common outside customs regime and goods coming from third countries remain subject to the customs restrictions of each member country, even if these goods have been properly imported into one of them. The origin of goods has therefore to be established in any cross-border traffic between these countries and goods from third countries remain subject to each country's own custom regime. Internal border checks thus remain in force.

This problem is eliminated in customs unions. They have a common outside customs' regime and no inside customs' restrictions in respect of any goods properly imported or produced in any of the Member States. That is the EU system: see Articles 23 and 24 (ex Articles 9 and 10) of the Rome Treaty of 1958. It is supplemented by Article 28 (ex Article 30) which eliminates all quantitative restrictions and, under case law interpretation, also all qualitative restrictions except if justified on grounds of public morality, public policy or public security; Article 30 (ex Article 36). Special rules exist here in respect of agriculture where the Common Agricultural Policy (CAP) has traditionally been a social policy device for the re-organisation and modernisation of agriculture within the Union over a longer period of time. In this it has been largely successful although at great cost to taxpayers and consumers. Its progressive dismantling has often been demanded, especially by countries like the UK. There is also an increasing demand for it in the WTO whilst the cost will hardly allow for the expansion of the present agricultural regime eastwards in Europe to new EU Members.

Through the addition of the freedom of movements of persons, services, capital and payments and the addition of the free right of establishment, the EU was from the start meant to be much more than a mere customs union, however. It wanted to be what economists call a true *common market*, supplemented by its own competition, dumping, and state aid rules. It envisaged also a *monetary union*, both to be accomplished by 1970 (Article 2). In the event, it took the Single European Act of 1987 substantially to complete the common market with its basic freedoms of movement (including the financial services) by 1992 and the Maastricht Treaty of 1992 (which entered into force on Nov. 1 1993) to achieve monetary union. In addition, it envisaged a common currency (for most Member States) by 2002.

This common market and monetary union are now often referred to as the First Pillar of the EU. In the Maastricht Treaty, this Pillar was given many new facets in the health, safety, consumer, environment, economic and social policy areas. It also introduced a European citizenship concept. At Maastricht, the First Pillar was joined by a Second and a Third Pillar. The Second Pillar considers co-operation in foreign affairs and security matters and may also lead to the eventual inclusion of defense matters. The Third Pillar concerns co-operation in the fields of justice and home affairs. As just mentioned, citizenship of the Union was introduced through the First Pillar, although the abolition of all border controls on passports was achieved by all Member States except the UK and Ireland, through a separate treaty (of Schengen) and was originally outside the EU set-up (even in

---

[55] See for a good overview of the old and new regimes in the EU, E Lomnicka, 'The Single European Passport in Financial Services', in BAK Rider and M Andenas (eds) *Developments in European Company Law* (1996) I, 181.

the Third Pillar). This was changed in the Treaty of Amsterdam of May 1999 under which the Schengen-acquis was put in the Third Pillar but did not affect all Members. At the same time, the asylum and immigration policies were moved from the Third to the First Pillar (Title IV of the EC Treaty).[56] Neither change affected the UK and Ireland.

The EU further distinguishes itself through its *organisational structure* which centres around the Commission, the Council of Ministers, the European Court of Justice (ECJ) and the European Parliament. Although they operate most specifically in the First Pillar, they have a broader EU function as well (under the conditions and for the purposes provided, Article 5 EU Treaty) but function differently within the other Pillars. The Commission, Council and Parliament operate through a system of decisions, directives and regulations in the areas within their competency (although they may also issue non-binding recommendations and opinions). For the Commission, the promotion of the common market has always been the main objective accompanied by its special powers in agriculture, transportation, competition, dumping, and state aid matters.

Although from the beginning an ever closer union was envisaged by the Member States, as reaffirmed several times in the Maastricht Treaty and which is also at the heart of the Second and Third Pillar, the present EU set-up is not tantamount to the structure of a (federal) state. In fact, the EU itself has as yet no legal personality and is largely a political framework within which the Communities (the Economic Community, Coal and Steel Community and Euratom) in the First Pillar and the other two Pillars operate. Only the three Communities in the First Pillar have legal personality (the Coal and Steel Community having come to an end in 2002). It is in a sense curious that this EU framework itself is less advanced than that of the Communities in the First Pillar. It creates problems, but there is a so-called reflex effect through which common principles for the various Communities are applied to the EU framework as a whole. The own legal order of the European Communities suggests and supports in any event a similar order for all aspects of the EU.

In all this, the Member States remain officially sovereign and the EU and the European Communities can operate only in areas delegated to it by its Members. Its jurisdiction is therefore exceptional and based on the relevant Treaty law, the interpretation of which is left to the European Court of Justice which traditionally takes a flexible and expansive approach to the EU's powers in its various Pillars (especially the First one).

In this connection, it (a) views the legal order of the European Communities, even though only of an exceptional and limited nature, as superior to that of the Member States in the areas covered by the various treaties. It (b) has always been accommodating in its interpretation of the Union's powers in the First Pillar, and (c) has in that Pillar generally accorded citizens direct rights under the various Treaty provisions (unless clearly not intended) and sometimes even under Directives addressed to Member States when remaining unimplemented. The Court's attitudes in these aspects have proved to be of decisive significance in the development of the Union.

Whether the further development of the Union through treaty and case law will eventually lead to a federal structure with its own statehood characterisation remains to be seen. The present limited nature of the EU explains the peculiar structure and powers of the Commission and Council and the modest role of the European Parliament as will be further discussed in section 2.2.2 below. External pressures often led to further reinforcement

---

[56] It means that these policies can now be promoted by the established EU institutions like the Council of Ministers and Commission and may (with limitations especially devised for this area) be tested by the European Court of Justice.

of the community idea, however. Thus globalisation of the international markets finally allowed the completion of the common market through the Single European Act, the creation of the monetary union, and the emergence of the common currency (the EURO) as will be discussed more in detail in section 2.4 below. Common economic, fiscal and taxation policies, the latter especially in the area of VAT, have long been considered and may also be expanded further so that one economic policy structure for the whole Union may emerge eventually, pushed forward by the operation of the single currency. External political and defense pressures, like e.g. those originating in the Balkans or resulting from international terrorism, may reinforce the role of the Union in other Pillars.

Internally, feeling remains divided on further progress along federal lines. The UK and the Scandinavian countries are traditionally more sceptical than the six founding members (Germany, France, Italy, The Netherlands, Belgium and Luxembourg), although the Union (in its various Pillars) is allotted ever greater tasks. Since the Maastricht Treaty, they also extend into the health, safety, consumer, environmental, employment and social areas. According to Article 5 (ex Article 3b) EC Treaty (the former EEC Treaty) in the First Pillar the EU can act only if, under the principle of subsidiarity the objectives cannot be sufficiently achieved at Member State level, but there appears to be a wider remit, although as already mentioned it is vital that for each EU action there is a sufficient basis in underlying treaty provisions, which are, however, by their very nature subject to interpretation and therefore in practice to expansion.

2.2.2 The EU Institutional Framework and Legislation Instruments

At this stage, it may be useful for those who are not immediately familiar with it briefly to summarise how at present the EU works. As already mentioned, the major institution of the Union are the Commission and the Council of Ministers, both operating from Brussels, the European Parliament in Strasbourg (and sometimes Brussels) and the European Court of Justice in Luxembourg. They primarily operate in the First Pillar. There is also the European Council consisting of the Heads of State or government and meeting semi-annually, at first established informally but now recognised in Article D of the Maastricht Treaty of 1992 (after the Treaty of Amsterdam renumbered in Article 4 of the EU Treaty). It is meant to provide the Union with the necessary impetus for its development and determines general policy through political guidelines, therefore not in a formal institutional manner. Yet its meetings are often of the greatest importance for the further development of the Union.

The European Commission can best be seen as the executive branch of the Union but is also responsible for initiating all legislation and for the implementation of this legislation by Member States. Each Member State has one Commissioner, the larger Member States two, appointed by their governments, all at the same time, for four years. They are, however, supposed to act pursuant to their Union mandate and are not representatives of the government which appoints them.

The Council of Ministers represents the Member States' governments, and their ministers sit on it depending on the particular subject at issue. It does therefore not have a fixed membership at personnel level. It is the decision-taking body of the Union and enacts its legislation but only upon the proposals of the Commission as it cannot initiate legislation itself unless specifically given such power under the Union Treaties, originally the European Economic Community or EEC Treaty of 1958 (since 1992 the Treaty Establishing the European Community), the European Coal and Steel Community or

ECSC of 1952, and the European Atomic Energy Community or Euratom dating from 1958, now joined by the Maastricht (1992) and Amsterdam (1997) Treaties which changed the former three and put in place the Treaty on the European Union and the Second and Third Pillar. Chairmanship of the Council of Ministers rotates amongst the Member States every six months according to the alphabet. The country holding the chairmanship of the Council of Ministers also has the presidency of the European Council. The Nice Treaty of 2001 makes further provisions amongst others for the voting system in the context of the enlargement of the EU to cover also many new member countries of Eastern Europe.

The European Parliament is elected directly by the citizens but has a limited legislative function. The idea remains that national parliaments should exercise their basic parliamentary functions through their impact on Member State governments and therefore indirectly on the Council of Ministers. There is here a particular issue of national sovereignty against federalism. The European Parliament has, however, the final say on the EU budget and can also veto the appointment of Commissioners and may dismiss the Commission as a whole, the threat of which was sufficient to make the whole Commission resign in 1999. In most other matters it has a consultative role but its powers are constantly increased as the democratic credibility of the Union is at stake. Often reference is made here to a democratic deficit in the Union which springs foremost from its limited jurisdiction. Broadening the powers of the Parliament and sharpening the use of these powers especially over the Commission suggest the beginnings of statehood for the Union in a federal sense.

As regards its legislative powers, the present set-up in the First Pillar is that in matters that are subject to a qualified majority decision in the Council of Ministers (rather than unanimity which for harmonisation measures was abandoned under the Single European Act of 1987 except in tax, labour and free movement of people matters, see Article 95 (ex Article 100a)), the Parliament has now the right to two readings. The first is when the Commission sends a proposal to the Council. After comments of the Parliament and the Council, the Commission will then proceed to make a revised proposal or a 'common position', which is presented for a second reading to the Parliament. The powers of the Commission and Council in the Second and Third Pillar are much more limited and more incidental.

The European Court of Justice consists of one judge for each country, and the judges are appointed for a period of six years. The Court ensures observance of the EU treaties and generally deals with issues in which the Commission, Council of Ministers or Member States are party. That is mainly so in enforcement actions against Member States concerning their duties under EU law (Articles 226 and 227, ex Articles 169 and 170) or in matters of the legality of EU actions (Article 230, ex Article 173). It is also vested with some special jurisdiction (Article 180). It further deals with referrals from national courts on EU issues (Article 234, ex Article 177). These national courts have a duty to refer these issues to the Court unless they are settled law. It should be realised in this connection that usually individual citizens or legal entities do not have direct recourse to the EU Court except when, as in competition matters, the Commission has decided against them or failed to render a decision (Article 230, ex Article 173). When their rights are curtailed by individual states, their normal recourse is to the competent state courts which then must refer unsettled principles of European law to the European Court of Justice (ECJ). This *supporting role* of the domestic courts in EU matters under the guidance of the ECJ has been of great importance in developing EU law further and securing its impact domestically in each Member State.

As regards the precise legislative instruments at the disposition of the Union, the basic ones are the various Treaties themselves, regulations and directives. The Treaties themselves may in their various provisions be directly applicable (or self-executing) based on their (presumed) underlying intent. If so they do not need further implementation. If not, they will need further measures at EU level. One of the major functions of the Court has been to determine the status in this respect of a great number of Treaty provisions, certainly also in the areas of free movement of services, the right of establishment, and the movement of capital and payments as we already saw in section 2.2.1 above.

A regulation is a piece of legislation of general application that implements the Treaties and is directly applicable throughout the Union. It needs no further implementation by Member States. They are relatively rare but very significant. Regulation 17 was probably one of the most important in setting out the details of the regime for anti-trust enforcement within the EU. By contrast, directives, which must also have their basis in the Treaties themselves, are in principle only directed at Member States and require implementation through domestic legislative channels. Member States usually have two years in which to do so. The details of this implementation in national law are left to the Member States and the results may therefore still vary between Member States, especially in the details. Non- or inadequate implementation may lead to action by the Commission before the ECJ. Under EU case law, a system of direct applicability of directives has resulted for citizens if their State remains deficient in the implementation of these directives and they may in such cases be able to invoke them directly for their protection.

The EU may also operate through recommendations and decisions. Recommendations are not binding but are often the predecessors of directives. In the financial services area, there were a number, like those on Large Exposures (1986), Deposit Guarantee Schemes (1987), and the Code of Conduct for Securities Transactions (1977). Decisions are specific orders of the Commission, like in competition law, and sometimes of the Council (depending on their jurisdiction under European law) binding on the person or entity to which they are addressed. In the financial services area they are not important.

Finally, there may be opinions issued, which, like recommendations, do not have binding force (Article 249, ex Article 189).

2.2.3   Definition of Cross-border Services. Connection with Free Movement of Goods and Persons and with the Right of Establishment

For purposes of the application of EU law, it is often crucial to determine whether there is cross-border activity within the EU, as the four freedoms concern only cross-border movement. Especially for services (which are by their nature immaterial), this may be a difficult issue that will be more fully discussed in section 3.1.2 below. They may be solicited by a client from another country but effectively rendered in the country of the service provider. They may also be merely incidental or temporary. The transfer of goods and rendering of services may also be intimately connected when it may be unclear which EU regime applies e.g. when goods are transported across borders, when the transportation and insurance of them will be a service. Sometimes they can hardly be distinguished, for example when educational books are sent as part of an education course and both Article 28 (ex Article 30) and Article 49 (ex Article 59) could be applied in that case.

As already mentioned, in respect of services, the right to free movement was established by the direct effect of Article 49 (ex Article 59). To better determine whether cross-border services are being rendered and therefore benefit from liberalisation under Article 49 (ex Article 59), a distinction can be made between a situation:

(a) where services are rendered cross-border with movement on the part of the provider. This is considered a clear instance of cross-border movement, whether through a subsidiary, branch or other more than fleeting presence,[57]

(b) where the recipient moves to the provider when the service may not be considered cross-border, especially if the account is held with the foreign provider, and

(c) where there is no movement on the part of either the provider or recipient and the service itself moves.[58] This situation involves telephone, fax or mail communications when the issue of the initiative and the role of advertising may come in to determine the cross-border nature of the service, but it gives problems with the location of follow-up services.

A more recent idea is to determine (in such cases) the location of these services on the basis of the place where (in each instance) the *most characteristic performance* under them must take place,[59] see for this discussion also section 3.1.2 below. It may be that (a) initiative, (b) location of account and (c) place of the most characteristic obligation all play a role depending on the facts of the situation.

Services can thus be rendered by a provider directly from another Member State *or* through an establishment in the host State. Article 43 (ex Article 52) concerns the right of establishment in this connection. As already mentioned before, it is mostly considered a non-discrimination measure and therefore of a somewhat different and less fundamental nature than Article 49 (ex Article 59). In any event, it has more of a support function in respect of the freedom of movement of goods and services, as indeed the movement of persons may also have. It could in any event be argued that it is more normal to subject it to host country rule, just like any other establishment on its territory. Although having direct effect, the freedom of establishment could thus more readily be restricted by a host regulator if locals are similarly limited in their activity, but notably *not* therefore if the limitation is based on nationality or similar considerations.[60]

This is indeed the legal approach in which the ECJ continues to guard also against hidden discrimination amounting to the same thing.[61] Even discrimination on the basis of differing qualifications is sometimes treated as an indirect nationality issue.[62] In other cases, a legitimate objective was required for discrimination in establishment based on urgent reasons of the *general good*: see more in particular section 2.2.4 below,[63] thus

---

[57] See the *Luisi and Carbone* case, in n 54 above. In the case of a subsidiary there is a new entity incorporated in the host state and regulated by it. In the case of a branch or similar arrangement, there is the freedom of establishment to be considered and any limitations that may be put on it in terms of authorisation requirements. More incidental contact without a presence in the host country falls in the category of the freedom to provide services and raises the question also what regulatory constraints the host country may still impose.

[58] Case 76/90, *Saeger v Dennemeyer* [1991] ECR I–4221; see also the Opinion of the Advocate General in Case C–384/93, *Alpine Investment v Minister van Financien*, [1995] ECR I–1141.

[59] See also n 13 above and accompanying text and s 3.1.2 above.

[60] Case 221/85, *Commission v Belgium* [1987] ECR 719 and Case 198/86, *Conradi* [1987] ECR 4469.

[61] Case C–1/93, *Halliburton* [1994] ECR I–1137 and Case C–330/91, *Commerzbank* [1993] ECR I–4017.

[62] Case C–340/89, *Vlassopoulou* [1991] ECR I–2357.

[63] Case C–106/91, *Ramrath* [1992] ECR I–3351, and Case C–19/92, *Kraus* [1993] ECR I–1663. In Case C–55/94, *Reinhard Gebhard v Consiglio dell'Ordine degli Avvocati e Procuratori di Milano* [1995] ECR I–4165, para 35, there may be a more general statement included applying to all four freedoms. It was said that 'national measures liable to hinder or make less attractive the exercise of fundamental freedoms guaranteed by the treaty must fulfill four

subjecting the anti-discrimination provision of Article 43 (ex Article 52), at least in the area of professional qualifications, to the general good excuses with further references to the legitimacy of the objective and the discriminatory measures not going beyond achieving that objective whilst remaining proportionate.

Free movement of persons could be similarly treated, at least if it supports the free movement of services or establishments: Articles 43(2) and 50(3) (ex Articles 52(2) and 60(3)) and is also in Article 39 (ex Article 48) cast in the nature of an anti-discrimination provision whilst under Articles 18(2) and 95(2) (ex Articles 8a(2) and 100a(2)) any expansion of the free movement of persons is subject to unanimity voting. It remains a sensitive area closely related to domestic immigration policies, although the right of EU citizens to move and reside freely within the territories of other Member States is fully recognised in principle (but not for residents that are not EU nationals). The more limited progress that may be expected in this area under the unanimity rule may in the meantime well induce the Court to more judicial action viewing free personal movement increasingly as a human right attached to the EU citizenship notion, which is, however, only a sequel (or additional right) to the nationality of the relevant Member State and does not so far replace it.

On the other hand, originally the free movement of persons was not deemed so critical to the internal market (nor the right of establishment which in Article 58 was compared to that of the movement of persons) except on a temporary basis. The free movement of goods and services was in fact seen as a substitute for the free movement of people who may now produce for export or render services EU-wide from their home base (and were supposed to stay there). However, the free movement of persons may increasingly be considered a natural sequel not only to the EU citizenship but also to the existence of a unitary currency, which requires increased mobility of workers away from depressed regions. In any event, full freedom of movement of people appears a normal ingredient of an ever closer union. This may also affect the right of establishment.

Indeed, it is likely that whilst the EU moves forward, the four freedoms are increasingly seen in parallel as a unitary concept, as already suggested in the 1995 *Gebhard* case just cited. In this approach, anti-discriminative considerations may well become the essence of all newer case law in this area under which selling practices and behaviour are still subject to host country rule, but as a matter of the general good (or public policy) of the host state only and subject to its limitations (which include the anti-discrimination concept: see section 2.2.4 below, although for goods the Court in the decision in *Keck* may have taken a more formal attitude to domestic sales requirements looking at discrimination more legalistically or formally and not necessarily within the context of the general good exception. This may suggest that there may be some more room for domestic regulation concerning goods than may be justified on the basis of the general good only).

In the case of services, on the other hand, the Court seems also interested in effective market access. It could mean that in the case of services, the Court wants in essence domestic deregulation (until re-regulation at EU level) or at least regulatory competition unless

---

conditions: they must be applied in a non-discriminatory manner; they must be justified by imperative requirements in the general interests; they must be suitable for securing the attainment of the objectives which they pursue; and they must not go beyond what is necessary in order to attain it'. One may recognise here the modern attitude of the Court towards the general good exception: see also s 2.2.4 below, which for goods, however, seems not to have been adopted in the earlier Cases C–267/91 and C–268/91, *Criminal Proceedings against Keck and Mithouard* [1995] ECR I–6097 under Art 28 (ex Art 30), possibly restraining its original tenor under *Dassonville*: see n 52 above, but it was adopted in an Art 39 (ex Art 48) case in respect of the free movement of persons: see Case C–415/93, *Union Royale Belge des Sociétés de Football Association ASBL and others v Jean-Marc Bosman* [1995] ECR I–4921.

there are clear grounds against it derived from the concept of the general good (and its limitations). It may be more relaxed on this point for goods where it may now be aiming more in particular at the liberalisation of trade between the Member States rather than at liberalisation *within* these States where domestic regulation would continue to prevail as long as it was not discriminatory. Such could be more in particular justified if domestic regulation were based on considerations that have little to do with intra-Community trade and have only a lateral effect on it.

If domestic restrictions are based on public policy, public security and public health (Article 46, ex Article 56) or on the concept of the general good directly, a test of their legality and proportionality is unavoidable even if the measures are not discriminatory and domestic operators are subject to similar limitations as the effect is still to keep outsiders away and deny them access even if locals are also restricted. That is therefore also relevant for goods. In short, there will still have to be urgent reasons for any domestic regulation that has the effect of keeping others out. Domestic practices may in any event be out-moded, overly paternalistic or simply based on local attitudes that, as in the German beverages cases (*Cassis de Dijon*), indeed worked only to stop imports. It is unlikely that the ECJ will be able to draw here sharp lines as has become clear in the area of the movement of goods. What domestic regulation may or may not survive can therefore not always be clearly predicted although there seems to be less patience with it in the area of the movement of services and the freedom of establishment.

2.2.4 Restrictions on the Basic Freedoms. Regulated Services and the General Good Concept

It should be repeated that in the EU approach, the free movement of persons, goods and services as well as the right of establishment under the direct applicability of the relevant Treaty Articles, although (together with the freedom to move capital and make payments) of a fundamental nature, have always been subject to a limited number of restrictions. They are notably those concerned with public policy, public security, health and safety: see Articles 30, 46 and 55 (ex Articles 36, 56 and 66). Although not especially repeated in the context of the free movement of persons and services, these freedoms are closely connected with the freedom of establishment where they were again spelled out (Article 46, ex Article 56). The general good concept is here an overarching notion, not used in the Treaty but explored and limited in case law.

Within the EU, the free movement of *goods* and the liberalisation of their transportation were substantially achieved by 1992 upon the implementation of the program for the completion of the Common Market set into motion by the Single European Act of 1987 (largely through the introduction of majority voting except in the areas of tax, labour and free movement of persons). It remained always subject to the special rules for agriculture within the Common Agricultural Policy (CAP). The Single European Act also initiated full liberalisation of capital flows and payments completed through the highly important 1988 Directive.[64] Services were liberated under Article 43 (ex Article 52) and the right of establishment under Article 49 (ex Article 59) in the way just explained. So it is largely with the movement of persons where further directives on professional services are still forthcoming. The only true limitation is the general good of the host or importing state if it can be proven to be relevant.

---

[64] See s 2.4.7 below.

In all this, the EU was much helped by the *internationalisation* or *horizontalisation* of production worldwide and globalisation of the capital markets,[65] both autonomous developments which ultimately also facilitated further progress in GATT. In the EU, any remaining restrictions on the freeing of goods (except under the notion of the general good) were eventually reduced to value added tax (VAT) and excise duty problems in the sense of compensatory charges still being levied at each border. Their elimination through harmonisation was finally agreed in 1992 (even though technically outside the 1992 Program).[66]

Historically more difficult proved the elimination of the restrictions on the service industries that were traditionally *regulated* and supervised, therefore on *banks, securities* and *insurance companies*. Article 47(2) (ex Article 57(2)) of the EEC Treaty provided for a system of directives to facilitate the activities of intermediaries generally (self-employed legal or natural persons) in terms of removing legal and administrative impediments. Regulation remained, however, in essence purely domestic in these financial areas and the free movement of these services was under prevailing case law *only* considered liberalised (Articles 43 and 49, ex Articles 52 and 59; see section 2.2.3 above), that is to say not subject to host country regulation, to the extent that this movement was *incidental*. This meant that any other movement was subject to regulation not only in the home country (therefore the country of the service provider) but could also be subjected to that of the host country. The result was double regulation which in practice constituted a serious bar to the free flow of these services. Indeed Article 51 (ex Article 61) explicitly provided that the liberalisation of these services would be effected only in step with the progressive liberalisation of the movement of capital.

In fact, also the *incidental* cross-border financial services coming from other Member States and all the more so more regular provision of cross-border services of these regulated types, even short of establishing branches or agencies (which were all the more vulnerable to dual regulation), could still be and were curtailed in the host country by considerations of the *general good* which played in this area of traditionally regulated services a particularly strong and persistent role. Pursuant to EU case law,[67] it allowed Member States as host regulators even to insist on local branches subject to full authorisation requirements, but only if indispensible as a protection, or apply similar treatment from a regulatory perspective per host state when more direct services where delivered from another Member State. Like in the case of a branch, this could imply a need for full authorisation, but could also be limited to conduct of business or product supervision. It thus continued to provide a strong base for (a) national authorisation and supervision of service providers from other Member States, (b) supervision of their conduct of business, especially in order to protect

---

[65] See s 2.4.3 below.
[66] See for this programme, s 2.2.6 below.
[67] *Cf.* Case 205/84, *Commission v Germany* [1986] ECR 3755, in which a German statutory requirement that a branch be established or implied in Germany to do direct (life) insurance business there was, however, rejected as generally disproportionate but an authorization requirement could still be imposed in relation to the rendering of insurance services from another member State whilst a permanent presence or these services being entirely or principally targeted at Germany could still imply the existence of a branch properly subject to German authorisation). See also, on the notion of the general good, W van Gerven, and J Wouters, 'Free Movement of Financial Services and the European Contracts Convention' in M Andenas and S Kenyon Slade (eds), *EC Financial Market Regulation and Company Law* (London, 1993), 55 *et seq*, and more in particular the Commission Communication referred to in n 14 above. See further also SE Katz, 'The Second Banking Directive' [1992] 12 *Yearbook of European Law* 249, 266; M Tison, 'What is "General Good" in EU Financial Services Law?' [1997] 2 *Legal Issues of European Integration*; and M Bjorkland, 'The Scope of the General Good Notion in the Second EC Banking Directive According to Recent Case Law' [1998] *European Business Law Review*, 227.

national retail customers (consumers), and (c) a review of their products whilst applying their own mandatory (contract) rules to the (foreign) financial or insurance products sold on their territory.

At first, the insurance industry proved here a particularly sensitive industry, especially for the 'mass risks' normally insured by consumers, like fire and theft, the risks connected with the ownership or use of a car, and then also life risk itself. The concept of the general good was subsequently also used for other regulated financial services as in the cross-border banking and securities business.

It became clear, however, that the general good limitations on the free flow of financial services (as in other areas) would not only have to be reasonable but had to be justified by pressing, even imperative, reasons. Restrictive local measures based on it could notably not be *discriminatory* nor lead to unnecessary *duplication* or *disproportionate* action (the principles of equivalency, proportionality and non-discrimination). As already mentioned, non-discrimination in this connection does not mean that a state may simply impose its own condition on any newcomer from another Member State. These measures also had to be objectively necessary and needed to be limited to areas not harmonised by the EU.[68] A public interest had to be served. To avoid home country rule,[69] which became the normal regulatory standard, and the measures taken by host states pursuant to the notion of the general good had to be suitable and capable of achieving the protection objective[70] and should not go beyond it.[71] Nationality could also not enter into it.[72] Nevertheless, the effect of these limitations on the concept of the general good, even though important, was always modest. At least until the new generation of liberalisation directives in the financial service area were enacted after 1988, the general good exception to the free flow of financial services served as a substantial barrier to a common market operating in these services.

2.2.5   The Use of the Notion of the General Good in the EU

As a general background observation, it may be repeated that the general good concept started to operate in the EU in a much broader area than that of the financial services industry. It was first formulated in the EU through case law in 1979,[73] became important in financial services pursuant to the German insurance cases in 1986 and has since been used in the area of consumers' protection,[74] the protection of workers,[75] the protection

---

[68] See for a summary of these criteria in particular Case C–76/90, *Saeger v Dennemeyer* [1991] ECR I–4221. See also the Commission Communication referred to in n 14 above for the observation that the principle of proportionality may lead to greater restrictions where the cross-border service is permanent rather than temporary or incidental. Katz, above n 67, suggests that the purpose of the general good exception to home country rule is to protect the users of financial services from unqualified, unethical, inexperienced or financially irresponsible service providers. After the Second Banking Directive and the Investment Services Directive this must be too broad an approach if service providers are authorised in another EU Member State and would leave too much room for opinion and for host country discretion.

[69] Cf. Case C–55/94, *Reinhard Gebhard v Consiglio dell'Ordine degli Avvocati e Procurati di Milano* [1995] ECR I–4165.

[70] Cf. Case C–362/88, *GB-Inno-BM* [1990] ECR I–667.

[71] Cf. Case C–101/94, *Commission v Italy* [1996] ECR 2691.

[72] Thus Italy was not allowed to require all securities companies operating in Italy to be incorporated on its territory and keep its registered office there which was in truth a nationality requirement: see Case C–101/94, above n 71; cf also M Andenas, 'Italian Nationality Requirement and Community Law' [1996] 17 *Company Lawyer*, 219.

[73] In Joined Cases 110 and 111/78, *Van Wesemael* [1979] ECR 35.

[74] See for the consumer protection aspect, Case 205/84, *Commission v Germany* [1986] ECR 755.

[75] Case 279/80, *Webb* [1981] ECR 3305.

of creditors, and the proper administration of justice.[76] It is also used for social protection,[77] to retain the cohesion of local tax regime,[78] to preserve the good standing of the industry,[79] to prevent fraud,[80] and in certain other areas not directly related to the service industries.[81] In fact, it became in this manner a general and over-arching concept which could also be deemed to include the public policy, security, safety and health exceptions to the free movement of goods and the freedom of establishment.

The concept of the general good itself is not outrageous if it serves to fit the liberalisation measures better into the domestic environments of the various Member States, to avoid undue stress in the liberalisation process, to achieve better co-operation, and to deal promptly with emergencies, market manipulation or fraud. In those situations, the liberalisation could be served and made more effective by the use of the notion of the general good, whilst its credibility would be enhanced.

If used mainly to protect overriding local public interests in the host State, it is reminiscent of the concept and operation of public policy in private international law. However, there should be much more restraint as the relationship between Member States in the areas covered by the EU Treaties and their guaranteed freedoms is subject to Treaty limitations which do not obtain between freely operating sovereign states. Although this still allows the general good concept to be used for host State protection of overriding consumer interests, it follows that its use is mostly unsuitable, especially in the professional area. In financial services, it became in any event a much more limited concept after the generation of liberalisation Directives since 1988, therefore especially after the Second Banking Directive (now consolidated in the Credit Institutions Directive 2000), the Investment Services Directive, and the Third Insurance Directives. As we shall see in section 3.1.3 below, under them even foreign branches became subject to home regulation and no host state authorisation could be imposed any longer. It did not fully eliminate the possibility to impose host state rules of conduct of business or product supervision in respect of retail customers, but again only within the general good concept and its limitations which basically reduced it to small investors' protection.

Nevertheless, even after these Directives, the concept of the general good, which remains undefined, continued as an unsettling element in the provision of cross-border financial services, as will be discussed more extensively below. Even outside the small investors' protection area, it can give rise to abuse through self-serving action of host regulators, see, for example, the text following note 148 below, which action must subsequently be undone by the ECJ, a costly and long-winded procedure. The balance reached in the directives between home and host regulation may thus be easily upset. The European Commission in its 1997 Interpretative Communication on this notion[82] showed its concern and wariness of the general good notion and its operation in the financial services area.

---

[76] Case C–3/95, *Reisebüro Broede v Gerd Sandker* [1996] ECR I–6511.
[77] Case C–272/94, *Guiot* [1996] ECR I–1095.
[78] Case C–204/90, *Bachman* [1992] ECR 249.
[79] Case C–384/93, *Alpine Investments BV v Minister van Financien* [1995] ECR, I–1141.
[80] Case C–275/92, *Schindler* [1995] ECR 1–1039.
[81] See Case 62/70, *Coditel* [1980] ECR 881 in connection with the protection of intellectual property; Case C–180/89, *Commission v Italy* [1991] ECR 709 in connection with the preservation of the national heritage; Case C–353/89, *Mediawet* [1991] ECR I–4069 in connection with cultural policy; Case 55/93, *Van Schaik* [1994] ECR I–4837 in connection with road safety extendable to environmental matters generally.
[82] See n. 14 above.

2.2.6 *Early Failure of Full Harmonisation in Regulated Financial Services*

Before the last generation of liberalisation directives, the liberalisation of cross-border services in the *regulated* services area proved complicated. Regardless of the basic freedoms in the original EEC Treaty, considerations of the general good by the different Member States allowed them, as we saw, to retain specific regulatory protections against financial services coming from other Member States, largely depending on local (host country) circumstances. In this way, even incidental cross-border services could be made subject to host country rule. More regular services could lead the host country to require the creation of a branch of the foreign service provider on its territory subject to its own rules of authorisation, supervision conduct of business and product control.

This was normally motivated by altogether understandable concerns for the protection of (a) smaller deposit holders against bank failures, of (b) smaller investors against brokers' breach of fiduciary duties in the conduct of securities business, of (c) smaller insured parties against abuse by insurers through non-payment, and of (d) similar vulnerable investors to protect their savings by guarding against unfamiliar or over-complicated life insurance and other investment products.

As explained above, these concerns created, however, altogether a major barrier to the free flow of financial services within the EU as it led to *double regulation* (by home and host state). Even though the basic notions of these domestic protections were not always so different, there was nonetheless a great variety in the technical details and sophistication in the various countries. This was so especially in the areas of agency law, as amplified by the local securities and exchange laws to the extent existing, and the protections thereunder of the principal or investor in security dealings, also referred to as conduct of business rules, and of the local mandatory rules applicable to financial products and their sale. It took a long time before it became clear how to promote liberalisation under these circumstances. Another problem was the whole formal structure of domestic supervision usually under central banks, Ministries of Finance, stock exchanges or similar supervisory bodies or insurance supervisory agencies, which was not alway transparent and would have to be reconsidered.

The approach originally chosen was harmonisation of domestic regulation in the financial areas but the progress through harmonisation directives in this area proved modest. This was demonstrated by the 1985 White Paper that led in 1987 to the Single European Act which sought at last fully to implement the internal market also for financial services by the end of 1992 (the 1992 Program). In fact, it was clear by then that the traditional EU approach of harmonisation of basic principles EU-wide (pursuant to Article 94, ex Article 100 of the EEC Treaty) had basically failed in the area of financial regulation or at least had left too much still to be done. A purely *legalistic* attitude proved too complicated, time-consuming and inappropriate to achieve fundamental progress, whilst it became also clear that not all differences needed elimination and that there remained a useful role for local regulation.

Another contributing factor was that in the closely related area of the freedom of capital flows, progress was also slow. By 1988 it was achieved by only three EU countries (Germany, The Netherlands and the UK) and this outside the EU framework. In these countries the freedom of capital movement applied to any and all countries worldwide. In fact, only after the fundamental 1988 Directive freeing the capital movements in the EU by the middle of 1990,[83] did the freeing of the regulated financial services become a true option

---

[83] See s. 2.4.6 below.

(Article 61 of the EEC Treaty had always considered this relationship). For (universal) banking it was achieved on 1 January 1993. For the securities industry it was achieved on 31 December 1995, and for insurance it substantially resulted on 1 July 1994.

It was:

(a)   based on the principle of the mutual recognition of home country rule,

(b)   subjected to a minimum of regulatory harmonisation in key areas, especially in the requirement of authorisation, the capital adequacy requirements, and the prudential supervision regime, and

(c)   made subject to a small number of obvious exceptions where host country rule prevailed, as in banking for monetary and liquidity policy.

It followed nevertheless that considerations of the general good, which remained undefined, could under case law still lead to some (substantial) form of fragmentation of regulation and supervision along national, host country, lines and particularly allow host country interference in sales methods and products, especially to protect consumers and small investors on their territory.[84] The case law limitations to the general good exceptions to home country rule remained, however, applicable and are gradually clarified. In any event (contrary to the original proposals), conduct of business rules were largely left to the host country under the Investment Services Directive and Insurance Directives and the concept of the general good may serve to amplify the host country rules in this respect. On the other hand, the concept could no longer be used for host country intervention where the Directives had provided a clear home country rule. Thus, under the Directives, host countries could no longer require the establishment of a branch subject to their own authorisation and regulation. Where a branch was established by a service provider from another Member State, it was explicitly made subject to home country rule in principle.

The limitations on the concept of the general good introduced by case law[85] could, on the other hand, also become relevant for the small number of instances of host country rule specifically introduced by the directives, as in monetary and liquidity policy for banks, and underline its exceptional character. As was already noted, host country rule, whether based directly on the directives or derived from the concept of the general good, is not without its abuses.[86] The 1997 Commission Interpretative Communication of the subject of the general good[87] testifies to the concerns that exist in this connection and the substantial danger the concept may pose for the common market in financial services if host regulators do not exercise adequate restraint.

2.3   Early EU Achievements in the Regulated Financial Service Industries

2.3.1   *Banking*

Notwithstanding the substantial failure of the full harmonisation approach in the financial services area, some modest early progress was nevertheless made in the EU (formerly

---

[84] See s 3.1.3 below and more in particular for banking s 3.2.1 below, for the securities industry s 3.2.7 below, and for the insurance industry s 3.5.5 below.
[85] See text following n 68 above.
[86] See text at n 148 below for pressing examples.
[87] See for reference n 14 above.

the EEC), especially in the banking field on the basis of a number of Directives, most of them with limited objectives, however. Before discussing the final arrangement under the round of true EU liberalisation Directives in the financial services area, it may be useful briefly to summarise the earlier steps. By 1987, the sum total of EU endeavours in the banking field was largely the First Banking Directive of 1977 aiming at the harmonisation of the conditions for establishing branches or agencies EU-wide, still allowing in this context endowment capital for branches of banks from other EU countries. It did not aim at one single supervisory regime but implicitly continued to accept the concept of market fragmentation under host regulation as we shall see.

It was followed by the Consolidated Supervision Directive of 1983 and the Consolidated Accounts Directive of 1986. Thereafter followed the Large Exposure and Deposit Guarantee Scheme Recommendations of 1986 and 1987. In the field of mortgage credit, an early effort to make a special directive in this area was abandoned. This service was liberalised with other banking services through the Second Banking Directive.

2.3.2 Details of the Early Banking Directives and Recommendations

The First Banking Directive[88] had already been preceded by a Directive of 1973 on the abolition of the restrictions on the freedom of establishment and on the freedom to provide services in respect of self-employed activities of banks and other financial institutions.[89] The aim was for each Member State to create a non-discriminatory authorisation regime for all credit institutions operating on its territory, whether or not based in other Member States. It followed an early 1964 directive concerning the freedom of establishment and the freedom to provide services generally, which, however, had excluded banking and other financial institutions from its coverage.

The Consolidated Supervision Directive of 1983[90] followed the Banco Ambrosiano affair and introduced the notion of consolidated supervision of banking activities by the regulator of the head office of a bank established in the EU (home regulator), although this did not by itself preclude supervision by the host State. It tracked the BIS Basle Concordat: see also section 1.1.12 above. Included in the consolidation were also (more than 50 per cent) controlled companies that granted credits or guarantees, acquired participations or made investments, but not yet other sectors of the financial services industry like insurance.

The Consolidated Accounts Directive[91] harmonised in 1986 the accounting rules for banks, largely following (except for some terminology, layout and valuation aspects) the Fourth Company Law Directive (1978) which had exempted banks and other financial institutions from its accounting and disclosure requirements. Amendments are considered from time to time on the basis of the recommendations of the Accounting Consultative Committee. The Seventh Company Law Directive (1983) on consolidated accounts is also relevant in this respect. Contrary to the principles of these Company Law Directives, the Consolidated Accounts Directive notably allowed prudential undisclosed reserves and eliminated the need for separate accounting for branches of credit institutions incorporated in other EU countries. Branches of non-EU banks are for their annual accounts covered by another directive.[92] Reciprocal arrangements with non-member

---

[88] Council Dir 77/80 EEC [1977] OJ L322 as amended by Council Dir 86/524 EEC [1986] OJ L309.
[89] Council Dir 73/183 EEC [1973] OJ L194.
[90] Council Dir 83/350 EEC [1983] OJ L193.
[91] Council Dir 86/635 EEC [1986] OJ L372.
[92] Council Dir 89/117 EEC [1989] OJ L44.

States were encouraged to achieve a similar result for branches of a non-EU entity on the basis of equivalency.

In the field of large exposures, there followed a Recommendation in 1986,[93] which suggested regular reporting of large exposures of banks to one single client (equivalent to 15 per cent of a bank's capital), which should not exceed 40 per cent of its capital, whilst all large exposures together should not exceed 800 per cent of its capital. It was followed by a Directive in 1992 (see section 3.4.1 below). The Deposit Guarantee Scheme Recommendation of 1987[94] set out some ideas for all Member States in terms of the protection of depositors in the event of bankruptcy of a bank It also covers deposits in branches in other EU countries under host country rule. It was much later followed by a Directive effective in 1995 (see section 3.4.2 below).

2.3.3   Mortgage Credit

An early proposal on the free establishment and supply of services in the area of mortgage credit[95] was meant to supplement the First Banking Directive. It intended to allow mortgage institutions incorporated in a Member State to undertake mortgage business throughout the EU, either through local branches or directly, even using the financial techniques of their home countries. The result would have been that, for example, English endowment mortgages or German mortgage bonds could in this manner be marketed EU-wide, whilst domestic institutions would have been allowed to adopt similar techniques in their own country, even if their own law had not so far allowed them to. The ultimate responsibility for the supervision of intermediaries was split: if there were branches they were subject to host country rule; direct services were subject to home country rule subject to consideration of the general good, especially relevant to the selling methods used and the products offered.

The later Second Banking Directive leading to the European banking passport under home country rule (see section 3.2 below) superseded this approach at least in the areas of authorisation and supervision and also covered mortgage credit: see its Annex 1, footnote 1. Although it did not so specify, under the general rules the question of the mutual recognition of the financial techniques and products in this area could still be subject to the notion of the general good. It may lead to host country intervention especially to protect consumers who are largely the customers of mortgage products. The 1997 Commission Interpretative Communication concerning the general good, mentioned in note 14 above, does not cover the question of mortgage products, or the aspect of conduct of business including the sales techniques concerning these products: but see generally for the approach to the general good section 2.2.5 above and section 3.1.3 below. Further progress in this area of mortgage credit appears not to have a high priority. Because of the very domestic nature of most mortgage products, creating subsidiaries or acquisition of mortgage companies in host Member States still appears the more normal approach for service providers from other Member States in this business.

2.3.4   Details of the Early Securities and Investments Recommendations and Directives

In the securities regulation area proper, there was no early activity of the EU and the subject remained largely overlooked even in the 1987 White Paper leading up the Single

---

[93] Recommendation 87/62 EEC [1987] OJ L33.
[94] Recommendation 87/63 EEC [1987] OJ L33.
[95] COM(84)730 final [1985] OJ C42 and COM(87)255 final [1987] OJ C161.

European Act of 1992. Instead, the EU at first concentrated largely on stock exchange operations and co-operation and only later started to focus on wider areas of investor protection. In 1977 there was agreement, however, on a Recommendation concerning a Code of Conduct for Securities Transactions. Thereafter followed the Admission, Listing, Interim Reporting, Mutual Recognition and Public Offer Prospectus Directives, and finally the important UCITS Directive which introduced the home country supervision approach in the supervision of the cross-border unit trust business.[96] It foreshadowed the system which was to become the prevailing one later in the supervision of all cross-border securities activity in the EU.

Important in this development was thus first the Recommendation concerning a Code of Conduct for Securities Transactions of 1977.[97] It laid down a program of what mainly amounted to harmonisation of some stock exchange practices and some better investor protection but it did not envisage one coherent approach, nor did it present a clear vision. The 1977 Recommendation remains nevertheless of interest and led to the Directives concerning Admission, Listing, Interim Reporting, Mutual Recognition and the Public Offer Prospectus, see the Admission Directive (1979), the Listing Particulars Directive (1980), the Interim Reporting Directive (1982), and the Mutual Recognition Directive (1987).[98] The first four clearly focused on domestic stock exchange operations. Only the Public Offer Prospectus Directive of 1989[99] had a wider scope and applied to all public securities offerings (except euro-securities as defined) on- or off-exchange.

The 1979 Admission Directive was partly directed at a situation in which, especially in Southern Europe, considerable discretion was exercised in the matter of the listing of security issues on the regular exchanges. It continued to allow in Article 5 local restrictions but in a clear legal framework. If investors' protection was the motive, there could be greater flexibility in this respect (Article 10). The Directive only sets a number of minimum conditions for admission of security issuers and their issues to exchanges (which remained undefined). They concern notably the legal formation and operation of the issuer, size of capital (at least ECU 1,000,000 including retained earnings), and the minimum period (at least three years) of existence of the company listing its issues. For shares, it insists on a satisfactory legal framework, their full transferability, the existence of a sufficient number of them, and on their adequate physical form. Bond issues must have a minimum outstanding value of ECU 200,000. Convertible or exchangeable bonds or bonds with warrants may be listed only if the related shares are already listed or are being listed at the same time unless the competent authorities are satisfied that all information necessary to form an opinion concerning their value is available. Refusal of admission to listing must be made subject to proper appeal possibilities (Article 15). Prior issue and listings of shares of the same class or of *pari passu* bonds should have been properly handled.

Subsequent to listing (but always under the Admission Directive), issuers have a number of obligations mainly concerning the publication of annual accounts, of material new developments concerning the company, and of any change in the rights of security holders. In the information supply, there must be equal treatment per class and the information must be made available to all markets on which there is a listing of the relevant issue in

---

[96] See also Lomnicka, above n 55, 191.
[97] Recommendation 77/534 EEC [1977] OJ L212.
[98] Respectively Council Dir 79/279 EEC [1979] OJ L66; Council Dir 80/390 EEC [1980] OJ L100 as amended and Council Dir 90/211 EEC [1990] OJ L112 allowing for mutual recognition and by Council Dir 94/18 EEC [1994] OJ L135; Council Dir 82/121 EEC [1982] OJ L48; Council Dir 87/345 EEC [1987] OJ L185.
[99] Council Dir 89/298 EEC [1989] OJ L124, containing a mutual recognition regime in Art 21.

equivalent form (and supposedly simultaneously). Any amendment to the instrument of incorporation of the company concerned must be disclosed to the competent authorities of the State where the securities are listed. The language of the communications must be that of the relevant exchanges except where the competent authorities accept another language customarily used in financial affairs. The language of the admission prospectus may be decided by the local authorities. It must be published in an official gazette or similar means of communication.

The 1980 Listing Particular Directive concerns especially this prospectus as it covers the initial disclosure requirements for the listing of shares, bonds and certificates representing shares like depositary receipts. The concern of the Directive was the great difference under domestic laws in the lay-out and contents and in the efficacy, method and time of any supervision of the information provided in this connection. The prospectus must provide all information necessary to enable investors and their advisors to make an informed assessment of the financial health of the issuer and of his prospects. It must contain the names and functions of the persons responsible for them, a declaration that to the best of their knowledge the particulars given are in accordance with the facts and contain no material omissions as supported by the findings of the auditors concerning the annual accounts. The basic information concerning the issuer relates to capital structure, principal activities, assets and liabilities, profits and losses and recent developments in the business and its prospects. The prospectus must also contain the relevant information of the issue itself notably concerning their form and conditions, whether they have already been marketed, the rights attached to them, the tax arrangements concerning them (like withholding taxes), date of income payments, name and whereabouts of paying agents, *etc.* It needs approval of the competent authorities as part of the listing process.

This Directive was amended in 1987 (as part of the 1992 EC program) to provide for a system of mutual recognition where listing was requested in more than one Member State. A compulsory recognition regime was provided in the Mutual Recognition Directive of that year under which the recognising State could impose only minimum extra requirements concerning the additional market on which listing was sought, the relevant tax regime, paying agents and the publication method of notices. The mutual recognition of admission prospectuses was further strengthened in a amendment of 1990, following the 1989 Public Offer Prospectus Directive which already contained a better regime in this connection.

The 1982 Regular Financial Reporting of Listed Companies Directive built on the notions of investors' protection and on-going disclosure of financial information to all investors at the same time. It assumes a full report on the listed companies' activities under applicable company law at least once a year pursuant to the Fourth and Seventh Company Law Harmonisation Directives and concentrates therefore particularly on interim reporting after the first six months of each financial year. It sets standards for it aiming only at a disclosure of the essentials of the financial position and the general progress of the business. It does not need to contain an interim balance sheet and profit and loss account (even in un-audited form). Incidental developments must be reported under the Admission Directive itself.

The 1989 Public Offer Directive was meant for all unlisted public offerings (it may at the same time be used for listing subject to an equivalence test under the conditions of Listing Particular Directive). Euro-securities were lifted out of the draft as it was accepted that they were often issued in response to rapidly changing market conditions. They might not always allow for the issue of a prospectus before placement whilst they were generally issued internationally to professionals only (and the definition of euro-securities reflected this). In any event this Directive applies only to issues with denominations smaller than ECU 40,000 and is therefore directed towards the information and protection of the smaller investor.

The Directive seeks a genuine information supply in all public issues, also if no listing is sought, and requires that even in such cases a prospectus is prepared and communicated to the relevant authorities in Member States where the securities will be offered. It must be made public in such States (Articles 14 and 15). There is no need for prior approval of the prospectus by such authorities as there is in the case of the listing prospectus. In that case it is easy to enforce as listing will be withheld without it. The requirements of the prospectus are very similar to those for the listing prospectus. If its information is equivalent to that of a listing prospectus, it may be used as such (within three months) in countries where listing is requested. Upon a first approval of such listing, it must then be recognised in other Member States (subject to proper translations) where additional listings may be required. (Articles 20 and 21): see also Article 24b of the 1982 Listing Particulars Directive as amended.[100] The Public Offer Prospectus itself can be used in other EU countries pursuant to the necessary communication to the competent authorities and publication under Articles 14 and 15.

The Admissions, Listing Particular, and Regular Reporting Directives were consolidated in 2001 into the Consolidated Admissions and Reporting Directive or CARD (2001/34/EC).

2.3.5   UCITS

Separate from this limited program pursuant to the 1977 Recommendation, the EU agreed in 1985 also a Directive on Undertakings for Collective Investments in Transferable Securities (UCITS).[101] A 1993 proposal seeks to include money market funds and funds investing in units of other UCITS and would allow a UCITS freely to choose depositories in other Member States if properly supervised in that State.[102] It also proposes to allow the use of standard derivatives to better manage risk. The proposal was amended in certain aspects on 20 July 1994,[103] but encountered problems. Further amendments were proposed in 1998, the one expanding the number of products in which UCITS could invest which was therefore a follow up to the 1993 proposal, the other concerning management companies and their authorisation and supervision.[104]

The aim of the UCITS Directive was to allow marketing of collective investment schemes of the *open-ended* type or (in UK terminology) unit trusts in all Member States under certain minimum standards as regards structure, activity and disclosure of these funds. The products may be marketed in all EU countries subject to *home country* authorisation and supervision (per individual scheme), although some minimum requirements are laid down in these areas (Article 4), and always provided that the scheme's operator produces a *home regulator certificate* that home rules have been observed before the operations can start in another Member State and has organised payment facilities there.

Host country rule remains effective in the area of *advertising and marketing* and also outside the aspects specifically covered by UCITS (Articles 44 and 45). The general good exceptions are in this way embedded in a more formalised structure. The EU Commission

[100] Council Dir 90/211/EEC of 23 Apr. 1990 [1990] OJ L112/24.
[101] Council Dir 85/611 and 85/612 EEC [1985] OJ L375, as amended by Council Dir 88/220 EEC [1988] OJ L100 increasing the maximum ceiling of investment in a single issuer from 10% to 25%.
[102] COM (93)37 final [1993] OJ C59.
[103] [1994] OJ C242.
[104] COM (98) 0449 final and COM (98) 0451 final.

has not so far directly attempted to erode restrictive sales practices in this area (see third preamble).

In 1998 the EU Commission also professed interest in a similar scheme for collective investment schemes of the closed end type. More importantly, the UCITS Directive was extended in 2001 by two new Directives.[105] The first Directive concentrates on management, giving the same facilities as investment firms under the Investment Services Directive to operate in other EU countries. The second one concentrates on products and expands the range to include money market instruments, units of funds that do not themselves qualify for UCITS status, bank deposits, and financial derivatives.

2.3.6   Early Directives in the Insurance Area

In the insurance sector, there were First Directives in the non-life (1973)[106] and in the life areas (1979).[107] Like the First Banking Directive, they aimed at the harmonisation of the conditions for establishing branches or agencies throughout the EU without establishing one regulatory regime or detracting from host country rule. They also laid down common principles on technical reserves and solvency margins.

These Directives were preceded by a First Motor Insurance Directive in 1972 relating to the compulsory insurance of civil liability, amended in 1984 and 1990,[108] also to cover green cards and agreements between national insurers for green card checks to be abolished. There was also an early 1964 Directive on Reinsurance and Retrocession Activities[109] attempting to create a single reinsurance market.

2.3.7   The System of Branching-Out under the First Banking Directive. Non-discrimination under Host Country Rule. Regulatory Co-operation

The First Banking and Insurance (life and non-life) Directives more in particular considered the right and conditions of establishing branches or agencies in the Member States for EU-based entities on a non-discriminatory basis, whilst branches from entities outside the EU could not be given better treatment. Branch activities remained subject to supervision by the *host* country, however, each with its own authorisation regime. They were subject to a few harmonised rules on prudential supervision (like the requirement of a minimum of two managers of good standing and a proper business plan) and capital protection (designated capital) for banks and for insurance branches on formalities, scheme of operation, technical reserves and solvency margins. Any discrimination in favour of nationals was forbidden. There were notably no single license, shared supervision or even harmonised regulatory standards. The idea remained therefore non-discrimination but host country rule.

Most importantly, the First Banking Directive instituted a system of co-operation between the EU Commission and the supervisory authorities of the Member States. The First Banking Directive, although now substantially superseded, remains of importance

---

[105] 2001/107/EC and 2001/107/EC.
[106] Council Dir 73/239 EEC accompanied by Council Dir 73/240 EEC [1973] OJ L228.
[107] Council Dir 79/267 EEC [1979] OJ L63.
[108] Council Dir 72/166 EEC [1972] OJ L103 and 90/232/EEC [1990] OJ L129, see also Commission Dec 91/323 EEC [1991] OJ L177.
[109] Council Dir 64/225 EEC [1964] OJ 56.

especially in this latter aspect (as the relevant Advisory Committee proved very instrumental in the further progress of liberalisation in the banking sector) and for the *definitions* of financial institutions and their activities.

2.4 The Globalisation of the Financial Markets and the Effect on the Liberalisation of Financial Services

2.4.1 Autonomy of the International Capital Markets

Rather than through the early limited initial EU action in the field of the financial services industry, the liberalisation of the regulated financial services in the EU was more properly propelled by the spontaneous globalisation of the financial markets. It had an autonomous effect on the freeing of capital flows and investments and facilitated eventually also the freeing of related financial services in the EU. The first, early, manifestation of this trend came with the development of the eurobond markets already referred to in the Introduction.[110]

2.4.2 The Early Development of the Eurobond Market and its Main Features. Eurodeposits

At the origin of the liberalisation and internationalisation of the capital markets and the services provided in them was (a) the accumulation of large pools of US dollars outside the USA in the 1960s because of the US trade imbalances, and (b) the virtual closure of the US domestic (Yankee) market for foreign dollar borrowers through tax measures (through the 1963 Interest Equalisation Tax) against the capital export from the USA at the time and the practical need to find alternatives.

This was supported by some inventive legal advice showing ways of tapping these new off-shore pools whilst (a) avoiding local restrictions on bond *issuing* by domestic issuers in a foreign currency through the use of off-shore underwriting facilities, (b) facilitating *placement* through sales predominantly or exclusively outside the country of the issuer or of the currency, (c) avoiding *withholding tax* on the bonds through the use of bearer bonds issued by tax haven finance subsidiaries as issuers (d) safeguarding the *freely convertible and transferable* nature of principal and interest payments by using paying agents in various countries to give the investors a choice, and (e) freeing the use of the proceed *currency* and its conversion into others, ultimately by developing the swap market. The use of tax haven companies had another aspect in that these finance companies would normally lend the proceeds back to the parent so that there had to be some tax treaty that exempted interest payments by the parent to the subsidiary from withholding tax as well. In this connection, particularly the Netherlands Antilles became important for US companies as it had such a tax treaty with the US (through the US/Dutch tax treaty).

With the creation of ever larger offshore pools of funds, also in currencies other than the US $ as a result of large international trade imbalances and the various oil crises, this emerging transnational market subsequently began to cover European currencies as well. It resulted in one of the largest capital markets by the late 1980s and affected more and more the practices of the European domestic bond markets, although in some countries, like

---

[110] See for a description also HS Scott and PA Wellons, *International Finance* 8th ed (New York, 2001), 706.

France, Germany and the Netherlands, euro-issues in national currencies targeted at foreign investors still had to be underwritten in the national financial centre (to support the local banking industry) so that it remained subject to restrictions (a queuing system being sometimes also maintained as a matter of monetary control).

Nevertheless, these various segments of the Euromarkets adapted to uniform rules and practices of a deregulated nature. Domestic and international activity subsequently became more difficult to distinguish to the point that even local government bond issue and placement activity started to conform to the internationalised underwriting and place-ment patterns of the euromarkets. It also had an important effect on withholding taxes on this type of borrowing/investments. Under pressure of internationalisation, they were abolished in the US in 1984 and in Germany in 1989 (in France for foreign investors in the same year). At the same time, it became easier in the US to use domestic finance companies whilst raising funding internationally, but there remained a concern about US investors not paying tax on their holdings of this type of securities. They led to the so-called TEFRA (Tax Equity and Fiscal Responsibility Act 1982) Rules whose purpose was to disadvantage bearer securities. They could not be sold into the US during the issuing period except at a fiscal penalty. Eurobonds were exempted, however, provided three criteria were met: inter-est was to be paid outside the US, the bonds and coupons had to bear a ledger warning US persons of the US tax regime whilst there had to be a reasonable assurance that the bonds would not be sold to other than qualifying US persons (like financial institutions, not therefore private investors).

In many countries, other exemptions emerged especially in terms of registration or prospectus requirements when eurobonds were sold to institutional or professional investors. This was not done in the US but under Regulation S in issues that occurred out-side the US (meaning that there was no direct placement or selling in the US), the issuer would only have to register in the US if there was a 'substantial US market interest' (SUSMI) in the securities offered, see also section 1.1.11 above. This would especially affect American issuers, whose paper was more likely to be bought by US persons. In the case of a SUSMI, there has to be a 40 days seasoning period during which American investors could not buy these securities. The idea is that, barring proper disclosure, they can only do so once the market has priced in all eventualities of the issue. To prevent US investors taking advantage of bearer bonds, the issuers will then only issue a global note so that during the seasoning period all dealings will be known, as investors can only buy and sell their interest in that note by notifying the issuer (or its depositary).

The Euromarkets and the eurobonds have always proved difficult to define because of their multi-faceted aspects which produced bonds which could be less than perfect eurobonds.[111] For the purposes of the exemption to the 1989 Public Offer Prospectus Directive, see also section 1.3.3 above, euro-securities in this sense are defined in Article 3(f) as transferable securities underwritten and distributed by a syndicate of at least two mem-bers from different States and offered on a significant scale in countries other than that of the issuer and that may be subscribed for or initially acquired only through a credit or other financial institution. The Bank of England[112] says that eurobonds are traditionally defined as bonds which are issued, and largely sold, outside the domestic market of the currency in which they are denominated and are typically underwritten by an interna-tional syndicate of banks, are exempt from withholding taxes and are bearer in nature.

---

[111] See for a list of definitions also JH Dalhuisen, *The New UK Securities Legislation and the EC 1992 Program* (Amsterdam, New York/Oxford and Tokyo, 1989), 19.
[112] 1991 31 *BoE Quarterly Bulletin* 521.

There is no one single definition and the description of eurobonds largely depends on the setting in which the definition is used.

The market aspects of this development were substantially strengthened by modern technology with its increase in communication, facilitating cross-border underwriting, placing and trading activity, in which connection the nature of the bond as a bearer instrument was also important. It led to ever greater transparency through instantaneous access to this informal market and to its prices worldwide by way of telephone (although not screen) trading. It also facilitated the creation of more flexible and cost effective capital market products, supported by currency and interest rate swaps, which themselves implied a facility to avoid or circumvent domestic restrictions. Eventually the euromarkets also started to cover equity products. It became a centre of innovation and sophistication with a measure of self-regulation through the International Primary and Securities Market Associations (IPMA and ISMA).

On the other hand, where the syndicates were organised in established financial centres, their participants requiring some presence in these centres could often not escape regulation in terms of authorisation, capital adequacy and prudential supervision. This became clear in the UK after the 1986 Financial Services Act. Syndicate and placement activity itself became also subject to conduct of business rules for example in matters of stabilisation, protection of clients against aggressive sales techniques, and in the price reporting of transactions.

Euromarket activity, at least to the extent operating from London, is therefore no longer entirely unregulated but the art of the UK legislator became to strike a balance and avoid restrictions which would have moved the whole industry to another country. In this partial *re-regulation* it has so far been largely successful, and harmonisation of the rules to the extent pursued under the EU directives has not detrimentally affected the euromarkets which have London as their centre. It may even have been a support for these markets and their credibility. As mentioned before in the Introduction (section 1.1.4 above), the approach taken by the UK since 1986 under the Financial Services Act has been to regulate participants rather than markets, processes and products.

It may be seen from the above that domestic and international markets grew closer, that deregulation took place also domestically and that the market practices became more uniform worldwide. Withholding tax and the use of foreign finance subsidiaries became less important issues, while some domestic regulation was allowed to impinge on the Euromarkets. It has created an environment in which *global offerings* can be used in which an offering is made simultaneously in the international and a number of domestic markets. For large issues this is an important facility as it increases investor interest and liquidity subsequently. The concept dates from a World Bank issue of 1989. There is one currency and one price. Naturally all regulatory and other requirement in each market must be fulfilled but the approximation of the rules and practices in all these markets have made this manageable.[113]

Euro-deposits should be clearly distinguished from the pool of funds used to buy eurobonds, which are offshore funds to which domestic investors can freely add if allowed to by their own foreign exchange regimes. The situation concerning euro-deposits is fundamentally different. The Russians started them after they withdrew their dollar deposits from New York in the wake of the 1962 Cuban Missile Crisis. Subsequently, these deposits,

---

[113] See for more details especially from a US perspective, E Greene, A Beller, G Cohen, M Hudson Jr and E Rosen, *US Regulation of the International Securities Markets* (1999).

at first in US $, were moved by US citizens abroad for them to avail themselves of higher interest rates elsewhere, which were possible outside the USA because of the lack of regulation requiring deposit-taking institutions to maintain mandatory non-interest-bearing reserves in respect of such deposits. They added to the pool of eurodollars already existing but are a separate segment of that pool with its own inter-bank circuit in which these higher interest deposits may also re-lend to other banks and finally to other end users.

These deposits were normally not meant to be paid out (or to be used for payment purposes) outside the USA. If repayment was demanded abroad or cheques drawn against them elsewhere, it was often thought that these were only payable in local currency, although that view was in England abandoned where no implied term to the effect was found.[114] Transfer is thought normally to occur through the clearing facilities in the country of the currency, therefore for US dollars in the USA, as these deposits are usually held through book entries in corresponding banks in the USA. This has raised the further issue whether these deposits remain subject to embargos imposed by the country of the currency, mostly the USA in respect of foreign Arab US $ deposits (held in foreign banks or in foreign branches of American banks mostly in London). There is here even a danger that they may become subject to the mandatory laws of several locations, therefore in the country where the deposit is arranged and in the country of the currency. This problem does not arise in respect of eurobonds.

2.4.3   Further Delocalisation, Competitive Deregulation. Situation in the USA

One major consequence of the eurobond market phenomenon was the progressive breakdown of insulated domestic capital markets. Because there was an alternative, domestic practices and limitations in underwriting and placement were increasingly ignored after the early emergence of the eurobond market in 1963. The essence of this market was and is that it has no clear local ties, as the underwriting syndicate, the placement and trading of the various financial products (of which the eurobond is still by far the most important in volume) are no longer localised. The consequence is an *offshore capital market* largely free of domestic tax, foreign exchange, placement and other restrictions. It also introduced its own type of negotiable instrument, the eurobond as bearer paper probably no longer tied to any local law, and similarly developed its own underwriting practices.[115]

Although participants in this market would still pay considerable lip service to domestic rules and practices, it became clear that whatever could not be done in one country was now often done from another. This could still require the use of (a) a tax haven subsidiary as issuer to avoid withholding tax, (b) paying agents in several countries to avoid foreign exchange restrictions by giving investors a choice where to cash their coupons and principal payments, (c) offshore selling activity to avoid selling restrictions particularly into the country of the currency of a new issue (as used to be the case in Japan) or of certain nationals (notably US citizens) or (d) the use of parallel or back-to-back borrowings now more commonly covered by swap techniques. As a result, it became the investors and *not* the issue, issuer, intermediary or market that bore primarily the brunt of any domestic regulation and taxation, the burden of which largely shifted to the investors' *place of residence.*

Competitive deregulation in the area of capital movements was subsequently forced on national authorities in order for them to retain in their own financial centers (some)

---

[114] See *Libyan Arab Foreign Bank v Bankers Trust* [1988] 1 Lloyds Rep 259.
[115] See JH Dalhuisen (1998 Hart Lecture), 'International Law Aspects of Modern Financial Products', [1998] *European Business Law Review,* 281.

borrowing activity in their own domestic currency by their own issuers and preserve domestic savings. The first result was often the lifting of withholding tax on (government) bonds in order for governments still to compete in borrowing at the best possible rates at home. Subsequently, it led to the opening up of domestic syndicates to foreign management, to the abolition of purely domestic stock exchange listing requirements and stamp duties as well as to the requirement for these types of offerings to be governed by domestic law. it also led to an increasing indifference of the relevant domestic authorities to a system of domestic paying agents (only) and to enforcing local selling restrictions in respect of foreign or eurobonds (even if denominated in their own currency or sold to their own citizens or residents).

Even in the USA, which as one of the largest capital markets remained long immune to these developments, the impact became increasingly clear. This was so for example in the lifting of withholding tax on government (Treasury) bonds in the USA in 1984 as already mentioned in the previous section, and in the exemption of the rules requiring SEC registration under certain circumstances of foreign issues even if sold into the USA. As was noted before, they still require a lock-up period of varying length for the issued securities, now mostly reduced to 40 days after placement, although the possibility thereafter to actively sell in the USA (except to qualifying financial institutions) remains disputed (under Regulation S since 1990), but any flowback will not then affect the registration exemption. The impact of internationalisation is also clear in the relaxation of the registration requirements for private US issues targeted to foreign and certain large US investors (Rule 144A, introduced at the same time). However, the aspect of avoidance of US tax by US citizens, especially in respect of bearer bonds, is still leading to some strict forms of control on sales into the USA or to US citizens elsewhere (under the so-called TEFRA rules, see also section 2.4.2 above).

2.4.4   The Legal Status of Euromarket Instruments and Underwriting Practices

It can be argued that the financial instruments issued in the eurobond market, in particular the eurobond itself as a bearer negotiable instrument, have a transnational property status and derive it from the international law merchant in which originally all negotiable instruments originated, see also chapter I sections 3.2.2 and 3.2.3. This is so regardless of the contractual choice of law clause as, in proprietary matters, the law acquires an autonomous function. English law has always continued to accept that in connection with the negotiability of bearer bonds 'the existence of usage has so often been proved and its convenience is so obvious that it might be taken to be part of the law'.[116] The transfer and protection of *bona fide* purchasers of these bonds is thus also likely to follow internationally saccepted patterns which may well extend to the types of conditional or temporary ownership right and security interests that may be created in them. Prevailing book-entry systems of transfer may underscore the transnational status of the instruments, the interests created in them and the protection of third parties.[117]

The taxation, foreign exchange, underwriting and placement rules may be similarly affected by trans-nationalisation and domestic restrictions or limitations, even if of a mandatory nature, may not or no longer be deemed to impact on the instruments and underwriting and placement practices in this offshore market.

---

[116] *Bechuanaland Exploration Co v London Trading Bank* [1898] 2 QBD 658.
[117] See also JH Dalhuisen, above n 115 and chap IV, s 3.2.1.

2.4.5   Central Bank Involvement

Only the USA, Canada, Australia and New Zealand never attempted to restrict this offshore eurobond issuing activity in their own currencies (although, as just mentioned, notably the USA maintains strict selling restrictions into the USA or to US citizens anywhere for registration and now especially tax reasons). Countries who still do, like Switzerland, can now maintain this attitude only through co-operation of central banks using their combined influence on prospective underwriting banks which they supervise. The same went for countries like Germany, France and The Netherlands, which, although allowing a eurobond market in their currency, long insisted on all underwriting activity being conducted from their own financial centres, through a subsidiary or at least a branch of the underwriting entity in these centres. With further liberalisation within the EU, especially under the Second Banking Directive (as at 1 January 1993) and under the Investment Service Directive (as at 31 December 1995), this restrictive attitude is now illegal. It will be increasingly difficult to maintain at least *vis-à-vis* other EU financial centres, whilst the continuing internationalisation is in any event likely to reinforce further adaptation. With the introduction of the Euro in 1999 the domestic market in most local currencies in any event disappeared.

2.4.6   Effects of the Free Flow of Capital in the EU. The 1988 Directive on the Free Movement of Capital

The effect of the ever freer flows of capital worldwide was a better allocation of resources internationally but it undermined at the same time the Bretton Woods system of insulated capital markets and fixed exchange rates which collapsed in 1973. At times it has also put considerable pressure on other fixed exchange rate (related) regimes like on the EMS in the EU in 1992 and on the Asian and (yet again) South American countries after 1997. The free flow of capital instills an order of its own and compels governments to a more considered borrowing policy as they have lost the monopoly in their own home pool of savings. They must now compete in the international markets where interest rates are easily pushed up and credit ratings easily come down, also for governments, thus increasing the costs. Nevertheless, state borrowings are in aggregate higher than ever before, although substantial declines occasionally occured, especially in the USA and the UK.

The autonomous liberalisation of capital flows in this manner facilitated ever greater offshore capital and money market activity (even though often organised from existing on-shore financial centers, especially London, in the case of the euromarkets). It was eventually supported and reinforced by derivative products like (over-the-counter) swaps (at first parallel loans), futures and options. Domestic capital flow restrictions thus became less and less relevant and could in any event easily be circumvented: see also section 2.4.9 below. It also supported the moves from the original GATT towards WTO, which, like the Bretton Woods Agreements, did never cover the free movement of capital: see section 2.1.2 above.

It also forced the EU to formulate some position towards its own continuing limitations on capital flows and ultimately allowed it to overcome its inability to act more decisively in this field and in the related area of cross-border financial services. The liberalisation of the movement of capital happened mainly through the 1988 Directive on the implementation of Article 67 (old) of the EEC Treaty,[118] effective as at the middle of 1990, the importance of which can hardly be overestimated. It completed the free movement of capital EU wide

---

[118] Council Dir 88/361 EEC [1988] OJ L178.

(although it resulted in fact in worldwide liberalisation of the EU currencies) and superseded in this respect a timid First Directive of 1960, amended in 1962, 1985 and 1986, as well as a 1972 Directive on regulating international capital flows and neutralising their undesirable effects on domestic liquidity. It also laid the ground work for the liberation of the attendant financial services EU wide.

2.4.7   The 1988 Directive and the Redirection of Savings and Tax Avoidance Issues

The 1988 EU Directive liberalised all movements of capital including current payments at the prevailing market rate for the latter (thereby doing away with two-tier foreign exchange rates) and became effective in the richer EU countries in 1990 (1 July). Spain and Ireland had to join by the end of 1992, and Greece and Portugal in 1995. The free movement of capital and money is now assured within the EU, although in the case of severe strain on the conduct of a Member State's monetary and foreign exchange rate policy, temporary protective measures may still be reintroduced by the EU Commission. In case of urgency, this may even be done by Member States themselves subject to the Commission's amendment or withdrawal of the measure. With the emergence of the Euro, these facilities have disappeared for the nine participating Member States. Outside the EU, the informal internationalisation of capital flows continues unabated.

The 1988 Directive created almost immediate anxiety in (some) Member States about the effect on the flow of savings and on the tax avoidance implications, much of which was repeated when the Euro came into force at the beginning of 1999.[119] Great concern had already been expressed in 1989, especially on the tax avoidance subject. It was also clear that the free movement of capital could move scarce savings to the richest EU countries or to those offering the greatest tax incentives, as it became possible for all investors to open bank accounts anywhere in the EU in any currency. A French government report, prepared by Pierre Achard at the beginning of 1988, highlighted in this connection the differences in taxes on investment products, like withholding taxes, stock exchange taxes and stamp duties, which could dramatically affect the place where national savings would be invested.

A request by France and Denmark either to institute a system of reporting of all foreign exchange transactions or to harmonise withholding taxes as a precondition to the free movement of capital was nevertheless defeated. The 1988 Directive (Article 5(6)) requested instead proposals from the Commission aiming at eliminating or reducing the risk of distortion, tax evasion or tax avoidance linked to the diversity of national systems for the taxation of savings. It became clear that possible answers were (a) a uniform withholding tax EU-wide with a possibility of redistributing proceeds to the country of residence of the investor, (b) a reporting system of foreign exchange transactions, or (c) better co-operation between tax authorities by strengthening the 1977 Directive on tax co-operation[120] and stopping Member States from using administrative means to frustrate the effect.

It was followed by a proposal in 1989,[121] requesting Member States to remove administrative obstacles to co-operation if there was considerable suspicion that large amounts of capital were being transferred to other Member States (the proposal was blocked by Luxembourg). There is now also a Council of Europe/OECD Convention on mutual

---

[119] See the Dec 1 1998 Proposal for a Council Dir to ensure a minimum of effective taxation of savings income in the form of interest payments within the Community: Community Preparatory Act 598PC0295. It was ultimately followed by the Directive on Taxation of Savings Income in the Form of Interest Payments: Dir 2003/48/EC of June 3, 2003, see below.

[120] Council Dir 77/799 EEC [1977] OJ L336.

[121] COM (89)60 final [1989] OJ C141.

administrative assistance in this area, effective since 1 April 1995 after the ratification by the USA and the four Nordic countries. The other EU countries did not ratify, although Belgium and the Netherlands signed the Convention. It covers the exchange of foreseeable relevant information in the area of direct and indirect taxation (except inheritance tax and custom duties whilst signatories may opt out of any other tax they wish), but does not extend to assistance in criminal prosecutions. Taxpayers retain the typical protections of their own laws whilst a requested State will respect the due process rights it gives to its own taxpayers.

EU efforts along these lines were abandoned at the time because of:

(a)   technical problems in uniform withholding tax mainly caused by differences in view on the status of eurobonds, euro-deposits and related swaps, and on the position of non-EU debtors generally;
(b)   bank-secrecy problems with regard to reporting duties; and
(c)   the expected avalanche of requests in the co-operation area.

More importantly, it was feared that further elaboration of these measures would result only in severe capital flight from the EU as a whole.

Particularly the harmonisation of withholding taxes regularly reappeared on the EU agenda, however, culminating in a proposal for a Directive in December 1998. It put the burden of collection on paying agents, which would naturally leave the EU under those circumstances as paying agents from outside the EU would not be subject to its jurisdiction. There was no allocation of the taxes collected by Member States. The level of the withholding was put at 20 per cent which was only to be a credit towards any final tax resulting in respect of this kind of income. The UK originally blocked these proposals whilst emphasis was put on an exchange of (tax) information. The alternative thus became disclosure by the paying agents of the investors. Pressure was put on non-EU countries to co-operate in a similar approach. This concerned tax havens but also Switzerland. EU countries like Belgium and Luxembourg on the other hand preferred the withholding tax.

In June 2003, agreement was reached in the sense that EU members were given the option of withholding or disclosure. The withholding was to increase to 35 per cent. Countries of investors were to receive most of this money. The co-operation of Switzerland and many tax havens was in the meantime assured. Elsewhere the dual taxation feature inherent in all taxation of savings is better understood. In the US, the tax on dividend was halved in 2003 and further reductions may follow. They do not yet apply to interest income on bonds. It is clear that an ageing population also needs greater protection of their savings against tax, most certainly also against any double taxation that follows from taxing income out of after-tax savings.

2.4.8   The 1988 Directive and the Movement of Financial Products and Services

The immediate result of the 1988 Directive was freedom of movement of savings, although a further directive in this connection on the management and flow of pension funds ran into serious difficulty in 1994: see section 3.4.4 below. Nevertheless, the idea was freedom for all types of investment products sold cross-border. In this vein, the scope of UCITS was also extended: see section 2.3.5 above, whilst efforts are even made to include funds of the closed type. The problem that sophisticated products from elsewhere might reach an unsuspecting public is largely a general good concern, already noted in sections 2.2.4 and 2.2.5 above and it will be further discussed in section 3.1.3 below in connection with the liberalisation Directives (the Second Banking Directive, the Investment Services Directive and the Third Insurance Directives) concerning the movement of financial services and their supervision. The liberalisation of the capital flows finally allowed a break-through in this area as well.

Under these liberalisation Directives, financial intermediaries may freely operate cross-border subject mainly to home country regulation, as we shall see. However, *insurance* intermediaries, if not themselves banks, securities or insurance companies benefiting from this liberalisation, may still be substantially curtailed in their trans-border operations as a matter of authorisation and supervision. If operating from other EU countries, they may, under the concept of the general good, still be limited under host country rule to inciden-tal activity without any facility of calling or advertising. Their situation is in fact still like that obtaining for banks, securities or insurance companies before the liberalisation Directives: see also section 2.2.4 above and section 3.1.3 below. If from outside the EU, they would be subject to limited liberalisation within GATS; see section 2.1.3 above, but, if they wanted to settle within the EU, they would still be subject to its reciprocity requirements which are now attuned to the GATS approach, see section 3.1.6 below.

2.4.9   The 1988 Directive and Monetary and Exchange Rate Aspects of the Free Flow of Capital. The 1997 Stability Pact

Another concern raised by the 1988 Directive was the conduct of future monetary and exchange rate policies in an open system. It is clear that one of the consequences of the internationalisation of capital flows is that foreign exchange and quantitative restrictions on credit at domestic level may be circumvented by loans denominated in foreign cur-rency, swapped back or hedged into domestic currencies, thus indirectly creating liabilities in the latter. Domestic interest rate policy also runs the risk of becoming ineffectual, as for example an increase in rates to limit the domestic money supply is likely to be neutralised through the free inflow of foreign funds. On the other hand, as governments have long lost the ability to influence long-term interest rates and indirectly the cost of borrowing in their own currency, international monetary discipline appears enhanced but is increasingly exer-cised through the markets and their interest rates rather than through the monetary authorities.

These internationalising tendencies require monetary policies to be more and more conducted at international (EU) levels and possibly even the related economic and fiscal policies. Except for the above-mentioned emergency measures, these subjects were in 1988 left to the future and were notably not part of the 1992 plan to complete the Common Market. Subsequently, they were, however, extensively covered in the 1991 EU Treaty on economic and monetary union (EMU) as part of the Maastricht agreements, which entered into force on 1 November 1993 and introduced the aim of a single unitary cur-rency (Euro) with monetary policy conducted by an independent central bank (ECB) by 1999 at the latest, Member States always retaining, however, a voice in exchange rate policies.

In lieu of a uniform economic and fiscal policy, the EMU Treaty formulated the notion of convergence in inflation and interest rates, government spending and public borrow-ings to support the operation of a single currency. It was supported by a so-called *Stability Pact* as part of the 1997 Amsterdam Treaty allowing for a system of fines for misbehaving Member States. The political coherence on which this framework may ultimately prove to depend can only be expected in a treaty for greater political union. Earlier[122] the

---

[122] Council Dec 90/141 EEC [1990] OJ l78.

convergence of economic policy, including budgetary measures, had been strengthened and supported by another measure[123] on co-operation between the EU central banks giving the Committee of Governors a wider role and allowing its Chairman to participate in the EU Council's deliberations. In the course of 2002 and 2003, the Stability Pact was tested especially in France, Germany and Italy which all exceeded its limits. Many expressed the view that in times of economic decline, its restrictions on government expenditure and borrowing were not suitable. Others noted that the true source of the problems was that in good times government debt had often not been sufficiently reduced to allow more governmental borrowing in bad times.

In the context of the Euro, the emergence of the European Central Bank (ECB) within the European system of central banks (ESCB), composed of the ECB and the European central banks, makes here a great difference, although the old structures remain in place for co-operation with the central banks of non-participating Member States.

2.4.10   The Single European Market for Financial Services and its Relationship to the Euromarkets

The EU project and Action Plan in respect of a Single European Market for Financial Services was already mentioned in section 1.1.10. It refused to take the deregulated euromarket as its basic example but sought instead to depart largely from purely domestic regulatory concepts and needs without a clear appreciation of what internationalisation in this connection had meant and achieved. In fact, under the new Prospectus and Transparency Directives as well as in the amendments of the Investment Services Directive, an unhealthy concern for domestic (regular) markets and their survival and protection seemed to survive. These developments will be further discussed in sections 3.5.3, 3.5.4 and 3.5.5 below.

2.5   Developments in the BIS, IOSCO and IAIS. Capital Adequacy

2.5.1   The Functions of the BIS, IOSCO and IAIS

The origin and role of the Bank of International Settlement (BIS) in Basle, Switzerland, was briefly discussed in sections 1.1.12 and 1.1.13, in connection with the 1983 Basle Concordat concerning supervision of foreign branches of banks. The BIS itself is the bank of Central Banks, originally created in 1930 to manage German reparation payments, and is directed by the Central Bank governors of the Group of Ten, which are (or were) economically speaking the most prominent nations. It now also serves as a think tank to Central Banks in the Group of Ten for banking regulation through the important Committee on Banking Supervision.

This co-ordination is itself motivated by the internationalisation of the banking industry. It concerns here primarily the business and regulation of commercial banks. The most important result has been in the area of capital adequacy for banks, through the 1988 *Capital or Basle Accord, cf.* the BIS Document on Convergence of Capital Measurement and Capital Standards, not to be confused with the 1983 Concordat concerning international

---

[123] Council Dec of the same day, 90/142 EEC [1990] OJ L78.

banking supervision as amended after 1992: see section 1.1.12 above. The *Basle Accord* was based largely on a joint 1986 UK/US initiative which adopted the risk assets methodology. Following the Accord of 1988, the BIS produced a number of further communications in the capital adequacy area, leading to a formal amendment in January 1996, whilst in 1999 it proposed a complete overhaul of the 1988 document which was followed by further proposals in 2001.

These rules are meant to apply to internationally active banks (and therefore not to purely domestic banks, although this changed in the 2001 proposals). None of these rules have any binding force, but through the relevant ten Central Banks they have in practice acquired the form of an international standard, are soft law in that sense, but have been widely implemented also outside the Group of Ten. The EU, in the Solvency and Own Funds Directives (since 2000 consolidated in the Credit Institution Directive), has substantially followed the BIS' lead for the capital adequacy regulation of all its banks and therefore not only for those that are internationally active, which on the other hand motivated some adaptations. The EU rules are naturally close to the BIS Accord as many of its Central Bank governors are part of the BIS Group of Ten.

Apart from in the area of *cross-border* banking supervision and capital adequacy, the BIS is also active in other areas and issued amongst its many communications a Declaration of Principle on Money Laundering in 1988, a Code of Conduct on Large Risks in 1991, and Core Principles for Effective Banking Supervision in 1997. In 1998 there was a paper on Enhancing Bank Transparency and another one on Sound Practices for Loan Accounting, Credit Risk Disclosure and Related Matters. In the same year, the BIS (together with IOSCO, see below) published Recommendations for Public Disclosure of Trading and Derivatives Activities of Banks and Securities Firms.

The securities business misses a similar focus for the international and co-ordination aspects of modern regulation. In the Americas there existed, however, IOSCO, the International Organisation of Securities Commissions as a voluntary organisation of securities regulators based in Montreal. During the 1980s many other securities regulators joined and this organisation now provides through its regular meetings and various committees a focus for international securities regulation although not yet of the same standing as the BIS. It co-operates with the latter particularly in the area of capital adequacy for universal banks. Its most important achievement is probably the 1998 IOSCO Principles and Objectives of Securities Regulation which contain a statement of best practices. It particularly seeks to prevent abuses connected with multi-jurisdiction securities activities.

In the insurance business, there was even less of international co-ordination between supervisors. The International Association of Insurance Supervisors (IAIS) is meant to fill this gap. Like the BIS, it is based in Basle. Its main achievements are in its 1995 Recommendation Concerning Mutual Assistance, Cooperation and Sharing Information and in its 1997 Model Principles for Insurance Supervision.

The BIS, IOSCO and IAIS try to work together. They formed a Joint Forum of Financial Conglomerates in 1996 following the formation of a Tripartite Group in 1995, see more in particular section 1.1.13 above. In the EU in the meantime, there emerged the Forum of European Securities Commissions (FESCO). It represents the domestic securities regulators in the EU and functions as a pressure group for them and as a think tank at EU level. It has now been transformed in an official EU Committee (the Committee of European Securities Regulators or CESR, see also section 1.1.10 above and section 3.5.2 below) meant to advise on the domestic implementation of EU Directives in the securities area. It is unavoidable that it often presents a domestic perspective of regulation. In the context of the 1999 EU Action Plan for a Single Market in Financial Services, it did come with a number of useful proposals, e.g. in the area of the definition of the various types of investors, and also proposed a European passport for issuers. It was always limited to investment services.

2.5.2   The BIS Capital Adequacy Approach for Banks. The Basle Accord. Criticism. Other Regulatory BIS Initiatives

For reasons mentioned in the previous section, on the capital adequacy front, the regulation in most countries became largely based on the BIS model. Thus in the EU its Second Banking Directive (SBC), which was the basis for the completion of the internal market in banking services, was, as we shall see, supplemented by the EU Own Funds and Solvency Directives,[124] both of 1989, following the BIS model closely. They entered into force EU-wide on 1 January 1993 and were consolidated in the Credit Institution Directive in 2000. It resulted in a uniform EU wide regime for banking capital adequacy in respect of all banks incorporated in the EU as part of the harmonisation effort in the area of authorisation and continued banking supervision. In the USA, the Federal Reserve System issued similar Risk Based Capital Guidelines in 1988, updated in 1997, to apply to banks and to be used in the examination and supervisory process of these banks.[125]

As was already pointed out in the previous section, these BIS capital adequacy rules for banks, had no legal force of their own but presented the considered views of the central bank governors of the Group of Ten and were as such implemented by all major countries in the world. In the Capital Adequacy Directive (CAD),[126] the EU has also issued capital rules for investment services as a sequel to its Investment Services Directive (ISD), which form the basis for the completion of the internal market in investment services. In the EU, these rules also apply to the securities operations of banks but are *not* directly derived from the BIS.

The Basle Accord and the bank capital adequacy rules focus in principle on *credit* or counterparty risk. By requiring adequate capital in banks to cover this risk, they did not principally mean to protect depositors (and not at all the owners or shareholders of banks) but primarily to reduce *systemic risk* which, through the payment system and inter-bank market, may result in extra dangers for the whole banking system when one of its major participants fails. They were also meant, however, to create a better playing field between banks internationally by reducing unequal capital adequacy requirements, which gives a competitive advantage to those banks that have a less strict capital adequacy regime. This was in the 1980s notably perceived to be the case in Japan and to a lesser extent in France.

The Basle Accord was extraordinarily successful in that it was widely adopted but its actual effect in preventing bank insolvencies was much less clear whilst its method of requiring capital in respect of *weighted risk assets* (in the manner as discussed below) became widely criticised because of its rough and ready approach as to the weighting which especially did not allow for any differentiation between the credit ratings of non-governmental debt or for any diversification within the loan portfolio. Others felt that the banks were too much encouraged to invest in OECD countries' debt (or bonds) rather than in loans to business because of the nil capital requirements for that type of government debt. The rules could thus easily distort the market. In any event, the overall

---

[124] Respectively Council Dir 89/229 EEC [1989] OJ L124, as amended (in minor ways) by Council Dir 91/633 EEC [1991] OJ L339 and Council Dir 92/16 EEC [1992] OJ L75; and Council Dir 89/647 EEC [1989] OJ L386, as amended (in a minor way) by Commission Dir 91/31 EEC [1991] OJ L17.
[125] 12 Code of Federal Regulations 208 App A.
[126] See s 3.2.2 below.

minimum 8 per centcapital requirement was arbitrary, whilst what was considered qualifying capital was very differently interpreted in different countries. It meant that a level playing field was not always achieved, which was in any event difficult to create in view of the very different emphasis in banks on different activities.

As a consequence, there resulted increasing pressure from the banking community to allow banks' own approaches to capital adequacy to prevail subject to the regulators approval for each individual bank, an attitude first accepted under the 1996 BIS amendment for position risk capital in the *value at risk* or *VAR* approach, see section 2.5.6 below. The key becomes here a form of self-assessment which in the 2001 proposals is now also proposed to be extended to credit risk and operational risk subject to certain conditions as we shall see.

Prior to the 1996 amendments, the BIS already discussed an expansion of its approach in a number of papers (between 1993 and 1996) as will be discussed below. It notably led to the introduction of capital adequacy proposals in respect of some market or position risk in which connection the just mentioned idea of a self-assessment was first introduced (the value at risk approach or VAR). The main drift of the 2001 proposals is indeed that, as an alternative to a standard approach, the internal principles and systems measuring risk and determining the capital needed in qualifying banks will be allowed as an alternative to the (amended) standard BIS approach also for credit risk. It means self-assessment also in the area of credit. In this connection, the individual credit rating of loan debtors may be considered. On the other hand, the valuation of some parts of the loan portfolios may require extra capital. As just mentioned, they also introduce a capital requirement to cover a bank's operational risks, which is the risk connected with a failure of its organisation and systems. Here again some self assessment may take place in lieu of the standard approach.

However, the self assessment does notably *not* go as far as to allow banks to also determine the capital needed which remains based on an 8 per cent minimum of qualifying capital.

The latest proposals will be discussed in greater detail in section 2.5.7 below and some calculations will be presented in section 2.5.9. Implementation is not foreseen before 2005. The move into the direction of more individual capital adequacy assessments which would in fact be determined by the banks themselves acknowledges at the same time that systemic risk concerns cannot be satisfactorily countered by standard capital adequacy rules alone. In any event, we already saw that no bank capital will ever be sufficient to cope with bad banking decisions or adverse macro-economic developments. It would require capital that in normal circumstances could amount to gross over-capitalisation and would therefore undermine the functioning of banks as we know them today. Other set-ups are, however, conceivable like narrow banking as discussed in section 1.2.5 above. It would mean a different style of banking altogether.

In practice, the present capital adequacy rules have not diminished the threat of large bank insolvencies, and when they come it is clear that the intervention of lenders of last resort or policy measures of the most directly affected governments remain the way to cope with (perceived) systemic risk. See for the perceived moral hazard implications, section 1.1.4 above.

As already mentioned in the previous section, the BIS also concerned itself with other regulatory banking concerns. Thus in April 1997, it issued a consultation paper called 'The Core Principles of Effective Banking Supervision' mainly directed at the supervision practice in developing countries in part in response to the Mexican financial crisis of 1994. It contained a set of 25 basic principles of effective banking supervision developed (unusually) in close co-operation with central banks outside the Group of Ten. It requests supervision without political interference within a clear legal framework with operational independence and adequate resources. It went much beyond capital standards and insisted on the need for a proper banking license and details the prudential requirements, including, besides the need for capital standards and minimum capital, an adequate infrastructure and resources, proper record keeping and information supply. The exchange of information between banking supervisors in the various countries was also stressed.

2.5.3   Credit Risk, Position Risk and Settlement Risk. Off-balance Sheet Exposures

As we saw, the Basle Accord was in principle (and certainly at first) based on assessments of *credit* or counterparty risk. It concerned the evaluation of the risk in banking assets and in that connection especially of the creditworthiness of bank debtors and the likelihood of their default. It calculated the minimum capital required in respect of each and all balance sheet *banking* assets, which are assets that are loans or loan-related. The asset approach was taken because their value (depending on the risk of the borrowers and their capability of repaying their loans) tends to fluctuate much more than that of liabilities. The sensitivity to credit risk is also considered in respect of other than typical banking assets, like positions in bonds or other debt instruments in the investment portfolio of a bank. The issue then is the likelihood of default by the bond issuer or the issuer of any other debt instrument. This issue cannot arise in equity holdings, although shares will also reduce in value when the issuer becomes less viable.

In this approach to commercial bank capital adequacy, there was at first no attention given to the *position* or market risk itself or to the *settlement* risk related to the transfer of positions. This concerns especially the bond (and share) portfolio of banks, which attracts both credit and position risk. On the other hand, variations in value of the loan book on the basis of prevailing interest rates (a form therefore of position or market risk) and mismatches (gapping) between assets and funding in terms of maturity, currency or interest rate structures (fixed or floating) were not taken into account either, which may be considered yet another form of position or market risk. Like credit risk, it is considered at the heart of a banks business but is easier to hedge.

So major factors that could influence a bank's financial position and especially its profitability were not considered. As a consequence, the final judgment on a bank's capital adequacy could differ substantially from conclusions that could be drawn merely from its available credit risk capital. In the meantime, certain countries, like the USA, had long required their banks to set some capital against other risks as well. The result was, nevertheless that banks could have quite sufficient capital under the modern capital adequacy test just before they collapsed since many other risks were not taken into account. In any event, the capital could technically still be adequate because banks might not have written down their loan portfolios sufficiently and therefore show more qualifying capital than they really had. This is a very important point and may fatally undermine any capital adequacy test as the capital shown in the balance sheet is in fact not there. In countries like Japan, future tax credits which might not materialise were habitually also taken into account to beef up the qualifying capital.

On the other hand, from the beginning (1988), the Basle guidelines did cover so-called *off-balance* sheet exposures like contingent liabilities, but again in essence only in respect of the counterparty or credit risk of prospective (loan or loan related) assets to be acquired under or resulting from any maturing funding or payment obligation. Examples are a draw-down under a guarantee, or a position gain under a swap. If, however, a simple write-off resulted under a contingent liability, as in a lawsuit pending against the bank, it had to be treated as a loss and valued accordingly rather than as a contingency.

To allow for specific adjustments depending on the particular nature of the contingency, so-called *credit conversion factors* producing *credit equivalent amounts* were introduced. They reflected the likelihood of these potential exposures maturing and were applied to the *nominal* principal amounts of exposure to produce the credit equivalent amount which is risk-weighted according to the category given to the counterparty (for derivatives especially swaps later reduced through bilateral netting). Thus there are here two adjustments to find the risk-weighted asset value. Note that contingent liabilities are not defined by the BIS, although lists of items appeared in the Annexes to the EU Solvency Directive (now incorporated in the Credit Institutions Directive of 2000).[127]

2.5.4 The Risk Assets Ratios, Risk Weightings and Qualifying Capital

The *risk asset ratio* was one of the key notions introduced in the original Basle Accord and is now substantially used everywhere as a means of calculating a bank's overall *credit risk*. Under it, the BIS approach for banks requires a specific amount of capital in respect of credit risk for all banking or similar assets (or for the credit equivalent amounts of contingent liabilities in the above sense) but it also adjusts the total value of the risk assets for this purpose whilst using *risk asset* ratios and defines what may be *qualified* as capital for capital adequacy purposes.

There are different categories of *qualifying capital* which may count either in whole or in part for these purposes: for example, equity and disclosed reserves qualify in full (Tier One). Undisclosed reserves, asset re-valuations, general provisions and subordinated loans (Tier Two) do not qualify in total for more than Tier One capital, whilst within Tier 2 subordinated loans do not qualify if in excess of 50 per cent of Tier One capital. Therefore, there are here *two* limitations. Deductions are made for goodwill and investments in unconsolidated subsidiaries and (at national discretion) for participations in other banks to arrive at the final qualifying capital.

Depending on the nature of the credit risk, four basic scales of *risk weightings* are applied (0, 20, 50, or 100 per cent): these so-called risk asset ratios indicate how much capital is needed in respect of each type of (risk) asset. In this regard, government exposure, especially of OECD members, their agencies, or of international organisations like the World Bank and the EIB, requires as counterparty (borrowers) the least capital (0 per cent); ordinary commercial loans require the most (100 per cent) except for loans to guaranteed or OECD domestic banks which attract 20 per cent risk weighting and cover therefore much of the inter-bank market. Mortgage credit requires only 50 per cent, being secured lending. The values of all risk assets so adjusted are added up to arrive at one total.

The qualifying capital should never be less than 8 per cent of this total of the risk (adjusted) assets. In other words, the total of risk adjusted assets may not exceed twelve and a half times the qualifying capital. It is assumed that Central Banks or other banking

---

[127] In general, contingent liabilities are either *lending-* or *investment*-related: both categories are of interest here. The first (just discussed) broadly covers standby letters of credit, guarantees, commitments to make or purchase loans, or to participate in acceptances. Their nominal values are the basis for the calculation of their credit equivalent amounts. Investment-related contingencies include futures and other forward positions, underwriting and other commitments concerning 'when issued' securities, standby underwriting facilities, securities borrowed or lent, foreign exchange contracts, futures and options, and interest rate and currency swaps. For purposes of deriving the credit equivalent in these investment related cases, the relevant positions are commonly *marked to market*, that means valued at regular intervals, normally daily, on the basis of prevailing market prices or, in the absence of a market, with reference to market prices in related instrument. Any resulting profit will be considered at risk in a counterparty sense. Nominal values are here of no interest.

supervisors could increase the minimum capital ratio required per bank, depending on their assessment of its basic strength and the soundness of its business (this was made explicit in the 2001 proposals). It is an important lever by means of which Central Banks dominate the banking scene besides their regular prudential supervision. See for simple calculation of the necessary capital under the 1988 system, section 2.5.8 below.

2.5.5   1993 BIS Proposals for Netting, Market Risk and Interest Rate Risk. The 1996 Amendment

As we already saw from 1993 the BIS started to propose a number of amendments to the Basle Accord of 1988. They concerned the prudential supervision of *netting* (credit risk), of market risk, and of interest rate risk. In the area of netting, the BIS came with an agreed amendment in 1994 (formally incorporated in January 1996), allowing so-called *bilateral* netting, see also section 1.4.5 above. It particularly concerned the netting of all swap and repo positions between the same parties, but only for capital adequacy purposes. The condition is that the country of the residence of the counterparty (or his place of incorporation) and of the branch through which the bank acted as well as the law applicable to the swap must accept the netting concept.[128] As a consequence, it remains up to each country effectively to incorporate or clarify the notion of netting in its own legal system. In the EU, this capital adequacy aspect required amendment of the relevant Directives, subsequently incorporated into the national laws of each Member State. In April 1996, the BIS released a further paper on 'Interpretation of the Capital Accord for Multilateral Netting of Forward Value Exchange Transactions' which facilitated this type of netting also for *foreign exchange* transactions.

In the area of *market risk* which covers the risk in interest related instruments and equities in the trading book and the foreign exchange and commodity risk within a bank, the BIS proposal of 1993 suggested specific capital charges to cover *open positions* (including derivatives) in debt and equity instruments as part of a bank's trading portfolio and in foreign exchange. It was based on a building block approach, see section 2.5.6 below, under which each identified risk in respect of each position, e.g. in respect of credit or market risk, were seperated and required their own capital. Under it, a separate capital charge would apply to credit risk if not captured otherwise.[129]

Market risk was defined as the risk pertaining to interest rate related instruments and equities in the trading book or investment portfolio and to the foreign exchange and commodity risks in a bank. The standard approach in respect of *interest related* instruments depended on maturity and interest rates, resulting in standard position risk sensitivity, which led to a *haircut* applied to 'mark to market' values, different per type of product (including derivatives but excepting options for which there was a different methodology) and per currency. Offsetting under a hedge was as a matter of right only in identical

---

[128] This became in the meantime a vexed question and could not always be obtained by contractually extending the netting concept of the law of the residence of the counterparty, see e.g. M Affentranger and U Schenker, 'Swiss Law puts Master Agreement in Question' [1995] *International Financial Law Review* 35. Statutory amendements became necessary in various countries: see more in particular the discussion in chapter II, s 1.3.3 *et seq* and s 2.2.1.

[129] If it becomes necessary to cover special risk under market risk, the charges vary from 0.00% for some government bonds to 0.25%. 1%, 1.60% for other 'qualifying' categories, taking into account also maturities and culminating in an 8% charge for 'other' categories.

instruments in the same issuer, coupon, currency and maturity.[130] For imperfect hedges special off-setting rules were devised.

For equities, the capital required was also based on a system of *haircuts* applied to 'mark to market' values. Under it, capital is to be set aside in respect of a certain percentage of loss per type of security based in principle on historical market performance of such securities. Under the Amendment, this charge for general or market risk in equity positions was put at 8 per cent of each net position, irrespective of the type of company or liquidity of the share (and whether or not they were quoted on regular exchanges). For specific or counter party risk, it was also put at 8 per cent unless there was sufficient diversification and liquidity when it was 4 per cent. See for more detailed calculations section 2.5.8 below.

In the calculation of the capital required for credit and market risk, first the bank's capital needs will be determined for credit risk (8 per cent of weighted assets). It will show how much is left in Tier 1 and Tier 2 to cover market risk under the capital adequacy rules pertaining to that risk. A new Tier 3 capital (see below) could only be used in respect of the latter. See for a more detailed calculation, section 2.5.8 below.

In the area of interest rate, maturities and currency risk, the BIS accepted in 1993 that a certain degree of *mismatch* is a normal feature of banking business but proposed to develop a measurement system (rather than an explicit capital charge) so as to identify very large mismatches. It would then be left to national authorities to determine what, if anything, to do. The 1994 BIS Discussion Paper on Public Disclosure of Market and Credit Risk by Financial Intermediaries (Fisher Report) expanded on this idea of disclosure of 1993 and proposed public disclosure rather than disclosure to regulatory bodies only.

In respect of market risk proper, the 1994 Fisher Report accepted for the first time as an *alternative* to the just explained standard approach each bank's own internal risk management system and performance measurement, but for *market risk* only as an alternative to the *building block* approach. Following further proposals of April 1995, it became part of the 1996 Amendment, which therefore allowed as an alternative a measure of self-assessment for market risk ('value at risk' approach or *VAR*). The details will be discussed in section 2.5.9 below. The aim was to require banks to *disclose* quantitative information showing their own estimates of their market risk, their credit exposure and the actual performance of their trading portfolio. It encouraged the use of various modelling techniques such as monte carlo simulations. It was meant to allow a comparison of a bank's own estimates of its exposures (which allowed sensitivity studies calculating the amounts banks were likely to loose by holding certain positions for some time (usually two weeks) against the actual outcome it achieved and thus to gain an insight into the effectiveness of modern risk management and credit control. It held out the promise of lower capital requirements for banks with better risk systems.[131]

In the VAR approach, the required capital would not need to be more than *three times* the predicted average daily value at risk (loss) during the proceeding 60 days or that of the previous day if higher, provided banks could show that they were not likely to loose more than the predicted amount in 99 out of 100 trading days during an obversation period of one year. If it was more, the multiple could go as high as four. Bank supervisors were advised to determine which banks would be allowed to use the new system and limit their

---

[130] Derivatives like forwards, futures and swaps are converted in long and short positions in the underlying instruments. E.g. an interest rate swap under which the bank is receiving floating and paying fixed is treated as a long position in the floating rate instrument (until the date of the next fixing) and a short position in the fixed rate instrument (for the remaining life of the swap).

[131] A problem was, however, how to fit the quantitative risk management information into the traditional accounting principles. This aspect was expressly not covered by the BIS.

capital supervision to an assessment of the reliability of in-house predictions over time. Banks with a less reliable approach could be punished in terms of needing more regulatory capital. The risk management systems could thus become a competitive tool.

In allowing an alternative approach based on self-assessment, the BIS signaled here a fundamental change in attitude, which was followed by the EU and led to a more fundamental reassessment in the EU Capital Adequacy Directive or CAD (see section 3.3 below) also in respect of securities firms (although technically they operate outside the BIS Accord which was only intended for banks).

The resulting 1995 Proposals were adopted in January 1996 (Amendment to the Capital Accord to Incorporate Market Risk) and also allowed for a Tier 3 of capital, representing less permanent and more fluid capital to cover losses on trading activities and other market related risks. As already mentioned, it can only be used to meet capital adequacy requirements in respect of market risk and may not be more than 250 per cent of Tier I capital. The changes were adopted in the EU by amendment to the Own Funds and Solvency Directives now consolidated in the Credit Institutions Directive of 2000, see section 3.3.1 below.

2.5.6   Criticisms. The Building Block Approach. Derivatives Risk

Fundamentally, there resulted no agreed international approach to any other than credit risk, market risks (but only in respect of marketable securities and foreign exchange) and netting in respect of capital needed in commercial banks especially for the swap book and repo financing. But even in its core (its approach to credit risk), the Basle Accord was increasingly criticized for not being sufficiently sensitive to the differentials and to a bank's own measurement and risk management systems and methods. It unduly promoted the investment in OECD government securities, as they did not require any capital, and therefore distracted from the traditional loan business to others. The Accord could even be interpreted as a vehicle to give these governments a substantial borrowing advantage. On the other hand, no rules were provided for *operational risk*. This risk had to do with the possibility that systems or more generally a bank's or investment service provider's infra structure and risk management did not work.

In any event, outside the commercial banking area, all regulators still did their own thing, like the SEC in the USA, and there is no international framework except in the European Union where the Capital Adequacy Directive (CAD) provides a uniform capital framework (but also for only certain types of risk, mainly general and specific risk) for *securities* regulators within the Union (which is important also in universal banking). The CAD deals with credit or counterparty risk in the manner of the risk assets ratios. These different risks may be combined in respect of one particular asset, like bonds. There is also a settlement risk when they are sold or purchased.

More generally, to handle these risks for capital adequacy purposes it is not now uncommon to distinguish between the:

(a) 'building block' approach of the BIS for commercial banks (since its 1993 paper and 1996 amendment) and of the CAD in the EU,
(b) 'comprehensive approach' in the USA, and
(c) 'portfolio approach' used in other countries (and earlier in the UK).

In the *building block* approach, the risk of each position is broken down into its credit risk and market risk, most clearly in a bond portfolio where there is credit risk towards the issuer and interest rate or market risk in holding the bond itself. The risks with regard to the issuer are in financial theory often referred to as *'specific risk'* (or Beta) and the risk derived from market movements or general economic developments as the *'general risk'*, terms now also used in the CAD. The specific risk is less obvious in the case of shares than it is in the case of bonds, as share capital is normally not repaid, but shares do go down if an issuer becomes less viable. They also go down if economic circumstances become less favourable generally or if interest rates rise so that alternative investments become more interesting. That is general risk.

In the CAD building block approach, the specific risk element requires (qualifying) capital of 8 per cent (4 per cent in a well diversified portfolio), much like credit risk in banks. For the true market risk there is the distinction between interest bearing instruments and equities as explained in the previous section. This is now also the BIS approach to banks' position risk but it allows, as we saw, since 1996 an alternative VAR system if the total effect is no less stringent. The CAD and BIS systems also deal with settlement risk (again less important for traditional banks except in their investment book) and there is an additional capital requirement depending on the length of any default.[132]

In the meantime, the SEC was able to stick to its traditional *comprehensive* approach which was too costly to change promptly. It sticks to a straight haircut for all types of risks and requires a minimum of liquid capital in security firms, to protect customers against sudden liquidity shocks. But there is here a different bias as compared to the attitude to banks. They are much less liquid in their loan assets or, to put it differently, security firms can much more quickly liquidate their positions by the very nature of securities holdings. General risk in the securities portfolios should therefore be less worrying than the counterparty risk in a bank's loan book.

In the *portfolio approach* the required capital depends on the balance in the portfolio between long and short positions and on the diversification. It is a more academic approach which was for practical purposes simplified by regulators with some considerable emphasis on a liquidity minimum.[133]

As just mentioned, there is no true international uniformity in the approach to market/ position and settlement risk in investment services except within the BIS (for commercial banks) and CAD (for investment firms in the EU). Efforts since 1989 by the International Organisation of Securities Commissions (IOSCO) to provide a worldwide capital adequacy system for other than commercial banks remained so far unsuccessful. It appeared virtually abandoned by early 1993, although the new BIS approach to netting (1994), see section 2.5.5 above, was announced together with IOSCO and is also recommended for securities business.

In 1995, the BIS also agreed with IOSCO a Framework for Supervisory Information about Derivatives Activity. This document proposed to create a catalogue for regulators in both the banking and securities industries to facilitate the assessment of *derivatives* risk and to provide a minimum common regulatory framework for these products. It focused on credit, liquidity and market or position risk for derivatives.

Credit risk should be measured here according to replacement cost and should be taken care of in the so-called 'add-ons' already foreseen in the original 1988 BIS Accord which allowed for certain factors to be applied to the gross outstanding principal swap amounts

---

[132] *Settlement risk* is the securities operator's type of counterparty risk, the risk therefore that transactions entered into will not settle on the appointed date. Shares are bought but not delivered on the settlement date. Payment may already be sent and be difficult, time-consuming and costly to retrieve. Equally costly and time-consuming may be the enforcement of the claim to the stock. The shares in question may have risen in the meantime so that there is a theoretical loss for the buyer. Alternatively he might have entered into the purchases to hedge some other exposure which now remains unhedged and may show a loss.

[133] See for a description of this system, JH Dalhuisen, *The New UK Securities Legislation and the EC 1992 Program* (Netherlands Academy of Arts and Sciences, 1989), 86 and Scott and Wellons, above n 110, 304.

based on price volatility of the underlying contracts. Collateral could be deducted depending on its quality and marketability. Risk concentrations were to be disclosed and credit ratings used to assess creditworthiness. Liquidity risk was broken down into unwinding and funding risk. For position or market risk, the 'value at risk' approach was suggested as one of the possibilities.

2.5.7   The 1999 BIS Consultation Document and the 2001 BIS Proposals. The American Shadow Committee

In 1999 the BIS came with a proposal for a fundamental revamp of its Accord of 1989. It was after consultation meant to enter into effect in 2002, later extended to 2005. The new BIS scheme was intended to apply to both domestic and international banks, which in fact had already been the case in most countries. The declared aims were:

(a)   improving the safety and soundness in the financial system,
(b)   promoting competitive equality,
(c)   establishing a more comprehensive approach to risk, and especially
(d)   making the system suitable for application to banks of varying levels of complexity and sophistication.

In respect of credit risk and risk assets, the BIS suggested alternatives: the *first* was a continuation of the present approach which was, however, to be refined. Especially the OECD bank and mortgaged loan reductions would disappear (except that the Germans were allowed to retain the mortgage deduction) whilst external credit ratings could be used for all sovereign lending and also for some bank and corporate lending. The required capital would thus vary per borrower depending on these ratings.

To this effect, these borrowers were themselves divided into three classes (sovereigns, banks and corporates), each with different weightings per rated risk. It meant a variation of the risk weighting according to a fixed table in which triple A company debt was to be rated at only 20 per cent and triple A government debt at 0 per cent. On the other hand, some risky assets could be risk weighted at as much as 150 per cent. The peculiar aspect here was that lending to unrated borrowers carried less weight than to the lowest rated (below B-, which carried 150 per cent). It was to accommodate European banks whose clients are less often rated than those in the USA but it has the strange effect that giving up one's rating could make it easier to attract loans.

In this *standard* approach, the original and rigid risk buckets remained otherwise in principle in tact with the extra one of 150 per cent. Interbank lending was to attract the rating either of the borrowing bank's country or of its own. In either option, more capital would be required against these short term loans.

Besides credit risk, in this standard approach, market risk was substantially treated as before, but *operational risk* was also to be covered and a large charge was suggested in this connection although in the original proposals not yet fixed.

The *alternative* approach allowed banks to rely on their own internal ratings in respect of credit risk leading to the *internal ratings based approach* (IRB) besides the already existing *value at risk approach* (VAR) as self-assessment in respect of *market* risks and an *internal measurement approach* (IMA) as a new self-assessment facility in respect of *operational* risk. In these three major risks, there thus appeared a *self-assessment* element as an alternative.

In the original IRB proposals to credit risk, much remained unclear, however, also how and when the choice for this system was to be made and which banks would qualify. As a practical matter, any bank was assumed to operate some form of it in such a way as to maintain its own (desired) credit rating. That was considered the external check on the adopted approach and potentially a most important self-correcting factor.

In the area of *qualifying capital*, there was no fundamental change, therefore no sharper definitions, whilst the Japanese were able to retain their present Tier I capital definition advantages, especially allowing them to include future tax credits. In the new alternative self-assessment approaches, banks continued to be held to a minimum of 8 per cent of risk assets, which was not entirely logical as the consequence of a self-assessment system would be that a bank would also determine the capital it needs. On the other hand, bank regulators could require more than 8 per cent minimum capitals for the weaker ones, a facility that had only been implicit in the 1988 Accord.

This approach (of minimum capital requirements in respect of credit, market and operational risk) was called the *First Pillar*. There were two others. The *Second Pillar* concerned itself with the supervisory review of the capital adequacy and the *Third Pillar* with market discipline. They are meant to underpin the operation of the First Pillar but do not in effect amount to an approach in which the risk management systems of banks opting for self-assessment were tested and given a competitive advantage. In fact, though lower risk weightings would lead to a lesser need for capital in total (although in the proposed system not to a lower percentage of risk assets, as just mentioned), it appeared that the introduction of capital to cover operational risk was meant to counter any substantial reduction in the required total capital for all banks, including the best organised. The use of operational risk in this manner was much criticized from the beginning.

In January 2001, the BIS released a great number of refinements to the 1999 Proposals as a result of the extensive comments and discussions that were received and had taken place in the meantime and issued the text of a new Basle Capital Accord for comments (by the end of May 2001, later extended to 2002). Pending further discussions, the target implementation date was moved to 2005. Implementation in the EU through amendment of the Credit Institutions and Capital Adequacy Directives is likely to take 2 more years. They may not follow the new Accord completely, especially not in the area of consolidation, the treatment of the trading book, and for operational risk.

In essence, the 1999 proposals were maintained. There were the three Pillars, the 8 per cent capital requirement, and the alternative of self-assessment methods for credit risk, market risk and operational risk. However, there was refinement, especially in the self-assessment methods (for the IRB now divided in a foundation and advanced approach). For market risk, a new definition of the trading book was introduced allowing for three different valuation methods covering also illiquid investments that are difficult to mark-to-market. Capital for operational risk continued to be a special problem. The BIS assumed in this connection that in practice banks always kept a buffer of about 20 per cent of their capital to cover systems failures and management mistakes ('risk of direct or indirect losses resulting from inadequate or failed internal processes, people and systems or from external events').

In line with the general approach, both a standard and a self-assessment facility concerning this operational risk continued to be offered. The standard proposal attempted to link the operational risk either to a bank's size, mix of business, or its track record. The major *practical* problem remained, however, the suggested large charge. The final amount was left to local regulators but the committee suggested 15% of the average annual gross income over the previous three years. The major *tactical* problem was that the operational risk charge was seen to have been introduced mainly to maintain capital requirements at more or less the levels under the old accord. The main *conceptual* problem was that it did not here concern an external or business risk nor indeed a rationally quantifiable risk.

If the idea was to check on existing risk management by introducing yet another (operational) rssisk manager who goes into the adequacy of risk management, its methods and systems, it would still not protect against a rogue manager or trader or even against bad management decisions. To immobilise capital against such a risk in a random way seemed to be questionable. In any event, who was to check the operational risk manager?

It could also be said that operational risk is not an independent risk category and is already covered in the accounting for the other risks (credit, market and settlement risk) and the capital set aside for them. Indeed, it could be asked what guarantee there is that operational risk is any better assessed than the other risks with the assessment of which soperational risk is primarily concerned. The layering of risk management through the Board, the Asset and Liability Committee, the Internal Auditor, the External Auditors, the Risk Management Group, and now the Operational Risk Manager, who is supposed to be separated from the other risk managers, not only creates further costs but could also result in a greater lack of co-ordination.

Even apart from the operational risk complication, the overall impression of the new proposals was not entirely positive. Clearly there was a wish to retain the basic structure regardless of the self-assessment which was not to affect the overall requirement of 8 per cent capital. In fact, the internal systems and their sophistication were *not* accepted as a competitive tool (subject to an objective regulatory evaluation). The reason may be that it would have favoured the strongest banks unduly, in itself a justified concern, but the approach is not logical. In any event, the Second Pillar does not function in that manner but suggests a much more superficial checking system. The market discipline and disclosure regime of the Third Pillar — in principle to be greatly welcomed — would not seem to make here a great contribution either. It is so complicated that it is unlikely to be of great help to the untrained eye. On the other hand, the detail of the disclosures may make banks as a whole more vulnerable to non-bank competitors.

The danger is that upon a proper analysis, the capital adequacy system will remain unconvincing in reducing banking risk and might continue to distort banking business. Its contribution to preventing bank insolvencies would hardly seem enhanced. Self-assessment profoundly disturbs any level playing field. In truth, the problem is that no externally imposed capital adequacy system is likely to be here of great help.

The Germans, not withstanding the earlier concession on mortgage credit, remained unconvinced and are worried that in the proposed new system smaller companies will find it increasingly difficult to obtain bank credit as larger companies with better credit ratings will crow them out. In fact, there is here a broader problem as servicing smaller companies is both riskier and more costly for banks. It is often not good business. Yet there is a strong public interest in these companies having access to liquidity.

By the middle of 2003, the US had indicated that only some of its largest banks would be allowed to move to the new system. China opted to stay for the time being with the old system altogether, but encourages its banks to empower its riks management along the lines suggested by Based II. It is clear that (a) regulators, (b) rating agencies and (c) banks themselves hold different views of what is prudent and that the most cautious approach in practice prevails. As that of the rating agencies is likely to be the most conservative, it puts them in a dominant position even though they are merely private companies whose practices remain unsupervised and often un-transparent, whilst their ratings may not always coincide or convince. The consequence is nevertheless that regulatory capital in the standard approaches is likely to become *less relevant* even if they continue to be used. It is an argument to leave all to the rating agencies and avoid the enormous complications of the new capital adequacy proposals which are in any event likely to result in un-transparent capital requirements and will pay lip service only to regulatory level playing fields.

In the US, the entire approach to capital adequacy in banks has been the subject of more fundamental rethinking, (see also section 1.2.5 above).[134] An informal Shadow Committee has been conducting studies for the last 15 years in this area and has proposed an alternative to the 1999 BIS new framework. It is less interested in capital and accepts that debt may be as good, if not better, a cushion against bank failures. It proposes a system in which public subordinated debt is issued and traded so that its holders will become the risk disciplinarians of banks by pricing this type of debt on a continuing basis, thus determining its yield which becomes in this manner the yardstick of a banks safety. It may lead to public discipline: the lower the yield, the better the bank.

Subordinated debt is here debt that ranks lower than the position of common creditors, including depositors. It is therefore extra sensitive to the bank's fate as the position of the subordinated debt creditors is almost as low as that of shareholders. In the proposal, it would cover 2 per cent of non-cash assets. This debt must not be subject to any direct or indirect guarantee, either through deposit insurance schemes or government bailout. For the rest, the present 1988 BIS approach would be maintained except that the capital requirement would be lifted from 8 per cent to 10 per cent of risk assets whilst eliminating the risk buckets and introducing a uniform 100 per cent risk weight for all non-cash items in order to avoid distortions in banking response. The two tiered capital system would also be reformed and made into one. If yields on subordinated debt were rising beyond certain pre-set levels, this would give regulators the right to intervene.

2.5.8   *Capital Adequacy Calculations under Based I. The Level Playing Field for Banks and the Effect of a Change in the Minimum Capital Requirement*

To demonstrate how the *present* capital adequacy regime (under Basle I) works, it may be useful to give some simple examples.

To calculate the *credit risk* capital, it is first necessary to look at the asset side of the balance sheet and determine which balance sheet items are credit risk sensitive, like the loan book and the bond portfolio of a bank. One takes these various balance sheet items and applies to them the risk asset ratios set by regulation that is for example 100 per cent to unsecured corporate and banking loans, 50 per cent to mortgage loans, 0 per cent to OECD government debt. The total of the risk adjusted assets is calculated and measured against the qualifying capital which must not be less than 8 per cent of these risk adjusted assets.

To put it in other words: a bank may have risk assets totaling 12.5 times its qualifying capital. So if it has three asset categories: OECD country loans or bonds, mortgage loans and other loans to corporates or banks, each for US $100 million, its risk adjusted assets are US $150 million and it needs US $12 million qualifying capital. Assume that it has $5 million Tier One capital and $10 million Tier Two capital, it will be US $2 million short as Tier Two capital for this purpose cannot exceed Tier One capital. The bank must therefore attract another US $1 million in Tier One Capital or reduce its loan portfolio in mortgages by US $50 million or in corporate loans by US $25 million.

If there are *off-balance sheet exposures,* they have to be valued and a credit equivalent applied as set by the rules. Thus standby lending commitments may have a credit equivalent

---

[134] See also H P Tarbert, 'Rethinking Capital Adequacy: The Basel Accord and the New Framework', (2001) 56 *The Business Lawyer*, 767, 824.

of 100 per cent applied, standby letters of credit (which are bank guarantees) one of 50 per cent, both of their nominal values, and swaps one of 100 per cent of their 'mark to market' value. Assume that the underlying values are in all three cases US $10 million and that the counterparty for the loan facility and standby letter of credit is a corporate and in the swap an OECD country bank. Applying first the credit equivalents, there result amounts of respectively US $10 million, US $5 million, and US $10 million. Applying the applicable risk weightings of respectively 100 per cent, 100 per cent and 20 per cent to these amounts, the total risk weighted assets resulting from these off-balance sheet exposures is US $17 million, for which the bank needs 8 per cent or another US $1.36 million in qualifying capital.

One of the original ideas (besides generally reducing credit risk in banks) behind this system of capital adequacy for *credit* risk (only) was to create a level playing field for banks especially in setting the minimum capital at 8 per cent. The other was of course to reduce credit risk in banks. But there are other factors that affect the balance so struck. In some countries like the USA mortgage credit may be much more important than in others like Japan. In other countries banks rely much more on off-balance sheet business. The result is that the various risk weightings and credit equivalent amounts may play a very different role in the business of different banks. Also the minimum capital requirement of 8 per cent may mean much less in countries with a strong (implied) governmental guarantee than in others where banks do not have it. Therefore in the latter countries banks would need more capital to compete with banks from the former countries. The uniform 8 per cent may therefore itself be a distorting factor. Tax and accounting rules may further distort.

It has already been said above that the risk buckets themselves may also distort. A 50 per cent risk weighting for mortgage credit might be all right on the basis of the experiences in Western countries but may be far too little in speculative Asian markets where a 150 per cent or even 200 per cent weighting could be much more appropriate in view of past experiences in the movement of real estate prices and the collateral they represent.

On the other hand, within one country, central banks or other banking supervisors may vary the 8 per cent minimum capital standard and increase it for banks that they do not trust or whose business risk they want to reduce. It means that such banks must move into safer assets like OECD government bonds or reduce their loan portfolios. Even a mild increase in capital requirement can thus have a dramatic effect on a commercial bank which in its ordinary banking (loan) business may soon become uncompetitive.

The following calculation may show this for Bank A with a requirement of 8 per cent and bank B with a requirement of 10 per cent (assuming Bank B with a 10 per cent capital requirement can still attract funding at the same average price of 5 per cent as Bank A). For the same loan portfolio of US $100 million at a risk weighting of 100 per cent, Bank A needs US $8 million in qualifying capital and Bank B $10 million. Assume that both banks, in order to cover this need, issue a perpetual bond at 5 per cent. Bank B will have to issue US $2 million more and has an extra cost of US $100,000 per year. In order to recover this cost in full, it has to charge 0.1 per cent more on its loan portfolio of US $100 million. It is unlikely to be able to do so for competitive reasons, makes therefore less profit on the transaction than Bank A and loses out further on this bank. In real life, Bank B can probably also not attract funding at the same cost as Bank A because it is not as good a bank. It has therefore an extra disadvantage. Moreover, Bank A can lend more (12.5 times qualifying capital rather than 10 times by bank B). It shows that banking is not worth it if one does not belong to the league of best banks.

To calculate the required capital to cover market risk after the 1996 amendment, a portfolio of e.g. (a) Euro 500 million German government bonds at 7 per cent with a remaining maturity of 8 years, (b) Euro 75 million corporate bond at 8 per cent and a remaining 3 years maturity, (c) an interest rate swap with a notional value of us $ 100 million where a bank receives floating and pays fixed with a fixing every six months and a residual life of 8 years, (d) a short position in a futures contract of 6 months concerning a Euro 75 million deposit of 3 years maturity (meant to hedge the corporate bond portfolio of Euro 75 million), and (e) a Euro 50 million share portfolio (marked to market) in quoted securities, would be assessed as follows.

For the first position, the risk sensitivity or 'hairant' is deemed to be 3.75 per cent of the 'mark to market' value; for the second position, it is 2.25 per cent (in view of the shorter maturity); for the third position, the position will be broken up in a long and short position, in respect of which the risk sensitivity is 0,70 per cent of 'mark to market' (6 months maturity) on the long position and it is 3.75 per cent on the short position (8 years maturity); for the fourth position, the risk sensitivity is 0.70 per cent of the 'mark to market' value; and for the fifth position it is 8 per cent of the 'mark to market' value.

Assuming that in the above examples the 'mark to market' values in respect of interest sensitive instruments are the nominal values, the risk weighted assets value (before set-off) in (a) is Euro 18.75 million, in (b) it is Euro 1.6875 million, in (c) it is respectively Euro 0.7 million and Euro 3.75 million, in (d) it is Euro 1.6875 million, and in (e) it is Euro 4 million. One of the more important issues is here, however, the treatment of the hedge and of the swap. They both concern the possibility of set-off for capital adequacy purposes. This is foremost a question of maturities. We have therefore a possibility of set-off between (a) and the short position in (c) resulting in a combined charge of Euro 15 million. We also have a possibility between the long position in (c) and the short position in (d), resulting in a combined charge of Euro 0.175 million.[135] However, both set-offs in these imperfect hedges incur an additional charge of 10 per cent of the off-setting amounts, in this case respectively Euro 0.375 million plus Euro 0.0525 million.

It follows that the total capital charge is Euro 17.2895 million against the total qualifying capital in Tiers One, Two and Three after deduction of the capital required in respect of credit risk in Tier One and Two.

The allowed methods of calculations under the VAR alternative will be shown in their simplest form in the next section.

2.5.9 *Capital Adequacy Calculations under Basle II*

The system proposed in Basle II and its impact can, from a calculation point of view, not be summarized in a similarly simple manner because of the self-assessment element. It is in this connection best to concentrate on the three major risks: *credit risk (IRB or Internal Ratings Based approach)*, *market risk (VAR or value at Risk approach)*, and *operational risk (IMA or Internal Measurements Approach*, sometimes also called the Advanced Measurement Approach or *AMA)*.

For the purposes of calculating the capital requirements under the *IRB* approach to credit risk, the banking book is divided into six exposure classes: (a) corporate, (b) sovereigns, (c) banks, (d) retail, (e) project finance, and (f) equity. For each of these exposure classes, the IRB treatment concentrates on *three* so-called 'credit risk components': (a) probability of

---

[135] Note that as to the off-setting possibilities, here we have to set-off long and short positions in different products with the same maturities (or vertically). There are other set-off facilities (horizontal) which will not be further explained here.

default (PD),[136] (b) the loss given default (LGD),[137] and (c) the exposure at default (EAD).[138] The last one is not relevant to the basic calculation and has a meaning only in special situations which will not be here further discussed. So the key is PD and LGD. A risk weight (RW) subsequently uses these risk components to arrive at the risk weighted assets. Maturity (M) affects the risk weight and the BIS proposes here a Benchmark Risk Weight (BRW) assigned to PD grades. [139]

---

[136] PD or default risk is the probability of an event of default. Several events qualify as 'default', like missing a payment obligation for a few days or for more than 90 days, a bankruptcy filing, breaking a covenant, triggering a cross-default, etc. The definition of default is critical for calculating the default probability and measures historical default frequencies.

   The Accord sets the minimum requirements for banks to be allowed to calculate PD on the basis of their own internal ratings. In practice, banks using their internal ratings will frequently use a Moody's or S&P table for the PDs corresponding to each rating: AAA, AA etc. This is the simplest way for them to arrive at the PDs.

   But banks may make their own calculations. There are different ways of calculating the PD. Amongst different techniques, the more popular one in respect of public companies is the *Option theoretic approach to default* (the updated Merton model of default), which considers that equity holders have the option to sell the firm's assets rather than repay the debt if the asset value gets below the debt value. This approach sees equity as a put option on the underlying assets of the firm sold to the lender with a striking price equal to the debt amount. It illustrates the expected default probability since equity prices look forward, as opposed to historical default statistics mostly used by the rating agencies. In this approach, the default is an economic rather than a legal event and probabilities depend on the asset value, the debt value, and the asset volatility.

   To provide a simple example of this calculation of PD, we may assume that the asset value of a borrower over a particular period of time is 100 and the debt value (its borrowings) is 50. We need to take into consideration the volatility of asset prices. Let's assume it is 21.46 (all volatility figures are complex). In the present example, the probability of economic default arises when the asset value drops below the debt value of 50. The PD is in that case $50:21.46=2.33$. This number is subsequently transformed through so-called deviations, which in this case arrives at a figure of 1%. Most PDs are lower, especially of higher rated companies.

   Rating agencies will often use this approach, but for private companies other formulae must be used.

[137] This is the estimated amount at risk at the moment of default less recoveries. In the foundation model, the LGD numbers are imposed by the Accord which also provides that some protections decrease the LGD number such as collateral, third party guarantees, and covenants in the loan agreement. Senior claims on corporate, sovereigns and banks not secured by recognised collateral are assigned a 50% LGD, subordinated claims a 75% LGD, etc. They are standard but based on modeling techniques discussed below. For using a bank's own estimate of LGD in the advanced approach, the estimate must be based on the average economic loss of all observed defaults in its loan book within the data source of the bank and should not be the average of annual loss rates. In its analysis, the bank must consider the extent of any relationship between the risks of the borrower and collateral provider.

   In connection with protections, the Accord adopts a definition of eligible collateral. In general, banks may recognise as collateral cash, a restricted range of debt securities issued by sovereigns, public sector entities, banks, securities firms and corporate, certain equity securities traded on recognized exchanges, and gold. It is necessary to account for the time changes of exposure and collateral values. 'Haircuts' denote here (a) the required excess collateral over exposure to ensure effective credit risk protection, (b) given time periods necessary for readjusting the collateral level (re-margining), (c) recognising the counterparty's failure to pay or to deliver the margin, and (d) the bank's ability to liquidate collateral for cash.

   Two sets of haircuts have been developed for a comprehensive approach for collateral: those established by the Accord (i.e. standard supervisory haircuts), others based on a bank's own estimates of collateral volatility subject to minimum requirements. There is a capital floor, denoted ω, the purpose of which is to encourage banks to focus on the monitoring of credit quality of the borrower in collateralised transactions. To reflect the fact that irrespective of the extent of over-collateralisation a collateralised transaction can never be totally without risk, the normal ω value is 0.15.

   Like for PD estimates, the measurement techniques of LGD are different under various risk modeling methodologies. The option approach mentioned in the previous footnote also provides a facility to calculate the LGD. To reach the LGD number, the Merton model calculates the put and call option value on the assets of the borrower, then calculates the expected recovery under the given PD. LGD=value of the assets minus expected recovery of debt.

[138] EAD for an on-balance sheet or off-balance sheet item is defined as the expected exposure of the facility upon default of the obligor.

[139] RW$=$(LGD/50)$\times$BRW for PD, or 12.5$\times$LGD whichever is smaller, see 'New Accord', Paragraph 173. The result is a percentage that will be applied to the nominal amount of the loan. In this formula, BRW is the benchmark risk weight which derives from the PD figure and catches also the maturity, which should be no more than 3 years. If it is more, there are different formulae. The BRW for PD 0.03% is 14; BRW for PD 0.05% is 19, and so on. See 'New Accord', para 176.

In retail, the notion of 'expected loss' (EL) is used as an alternative to PD and LGD, because there are unlikely to exist credit ratings in respect of retail borrowers. EL is the product of a retail exposure (say us $100) and the PD of a borrower (say 2 per cent) and the LGD, say 50 per cent, in any specific credit risk facility. In this example, EL is us $100×(0.2)×(0.50)=$1.

Thus as the first step for calculating the capital charges in the IRB approach, a bank must normally arrive at the PD estimate. The calculation of PD is the common element of the two approaches under IRB: foundation and advanced. As already mentioned, banks will normally borrow from Moody's or S&P their PDs as corresponding to their credit ratings. The difference starts at the next stage when a bank has to calculate the LGD risk component. Under the advanced approach, the bank is allowed to calculate the LGD number according to its internal methodologies, while under the foundation approach LGD is either given under the rules or has to be calculated according to the regulator's instructions.

To repeat: the calculation formula for risk weighted assets is RW times the nominal value of the loan in which RW=LGD:50×BRW (in respect of the relevant PD), or LGD×12.5 whichever is smaller. The 8 per cent capital requirement is subsequently applied to this number to arrive as the necessary capital charge.[140]

In the foundation IRB approach, a loan portfolio of Euros 500 million AAA government bonds of a remaining 3 years maturity, Euro 100 million AA corporate loans of 2 years maturity, and Euro 300 million of single A inter-bank loans of 6 months maturity is treated as follows. As maturity is less than three years in all cases, we may apply the standard foundation formula which is RW=(LGD:50)×BRW in which LGD is always 50. Assuming that AAA generates a PD of 0,00 per cent, the RW is 1×BRW or 14 per cent, for AA it is 0.01 per cent corresponding with an BRW of also 14 per cent and for single A it will be 0.05 per cent corresponding to a BRW of 19 per cent. The result is therefore a total risk weighted amount of Euro 141 million attracting a minimum capital charge of Euro 11.28 million in terms of qualifying capital under Tier One and Tier Two.

For the self-assessment or *VAR approach to market risk*, the 1996 Basle I amendment will largely continue in force unaltered in Basle II. Its focus is the determination of the maximum loss in a given time period assuming only a 1 per cent probability that it will be larger. That represents a confidence level of 99 per cent. If we say that a position has a 'value at risk' or VAR of Euro 1 million at a 99 per cent confidence level (as imposed by the 1996 Amendement to Basle I), we mean that any daily loss will on average not be higher than Euro 1 million except on only one day in every 100 trading days (therefore only on 2 1/2 days each year, a year having 250 trading days). In the VAR approach to capital adequacy, a bank may use its own value at risk models to determine the value at risk figure in respect of its 'mark to market' positions (in this case resulting in the Euro 1million figure). All value at risk models require (a) the selection of the relevant risk factors and (b) a prediction of their impact. This could be done on the basis of historical data or under more advanced models

---

[140] The IRB approach may be advantageous to banks investing in better credits, see the Quantitative Impact Study (QIS3) of the Accord itself which allows a comparison as follows:

Standard Approach		Foundation IRB	
Rating	Risk Weight	Equivalent PD%	Approx. Risk Weight
AAA	20%	0.00	14.75%
AA	20%	0.01	14.75%
A	50%	0.05	20.03%
BBB	100%	0.26	51.60%
BB	100%	1.20	104.35%
B	150%	5.93	192.70%
CCC	150%	24.64	394.50%

which are here no further discussed.[141] Once the VAR is established, it will be multiplied by 3 (the 'multiplier') to arrive at the capital charge. The regulator may increase this multiplier if it becomes clear that the bank's own risk management systems are unreliable.[142]

In general, the standard approach to market risk is likely to produce a much larger capital charge than any VAR based model, but the saving depends also on the diversification in the portfolio.[143]

Finally, the capital necessary to cover *operational risk* may also cover complicated calculations which can only be summarised here. As we saw, in a first approximation in developing minimum capital charges, the Basle Committee estimates the operational risk at 20 per cent of minimum regulatory capital, but it also proposes three increasingly sophisticated approaches to capital requirements for operational risk: basic indicator; the standard approach, and the internal measurement approach or IMA.

The 'basic indicator approach' links the capital charge for operational risk to a single indicator that serves as a proxy for the bank's overall risk exposure. The indicator is the gross income[144] and each bank should hold capital for operational risk equal to a fixed percentage ('alpha factor') of its gross income (15% is proposed).

The 'standardised approach' builds on the basic indicator approach by dividing a bank's activities into a number of standard business lines (e.g. corporate finance and retail banking). With each business line, the capital charge is a selected indicator of operational risk times a fixed percentage ('beta factor'). Both the indicator and the beta factors may differ across business lines. The beta factor is set by the Committee and serves as a rough proxy for the industry-wide relationship between the operational risk loss experience for a given business line and the indicator for that business line. The total capital charge is calculated as the simple summation of the regulatory capital charges across each of the business lines.

The 'internal measurement approach' finally allows individual banks to rely on internal data for regulatory capital purposes. The technique necessitates three inputs for specific sets of business lines and risk types: an operational risk exposure indicator, the probability that a loss event occurs, and the losses given such events. Together, these components make up a loss distribution for operational risks. The internal measurement approach allows the capital charge to be driven by a bank's own operational loss experience[145] within a supervisory

---

[141] There are commonly three approaches between which banks may choose: the analytical variance-covariance approach, the Monte Carlo approach, and the more traditional historical simulation approach. The last one is the most simple. It involves (a) the selection of the relevant daily risk factors in a given period, say 100 subsequent trading days, (b) the application of them to the values at risk and the revaluation of the current portfolio as many times as the number of days chosen in the sample, (c) the construction of a diagram (histogram) of portfolio values and identification of the value at risk that isolates the first percentile of the distribution compatible with a 99% confidence level.

[142] See for further details M Crouhy, D Galai and R Mark, *Risk Management* (2000), 177 *et seq.*

[143] For example if we consider the portfolio consisting of long US $100m 10 year government bond with 6.50% annual coupon and $US 100m 10 year old swap bank paying fixed against 3 months LIBOR assuming that the counterparty is a corporation, the capital charge under the standardised approach will be US $635,000 and the internal model approach using the VAR method will produce the charge of US $240 000 and the bank will be capable of making the 62% saving. This figure is taken from M Crouhy, above n 142, 165.

On the contrary, if we consider the USD 100 million 10-year swap where bank receives fixed against three-months LIBOR and the counterparty is a corporation, then the capital charge for this position under the VAR model would be higher, viz. US $8,854,294 as against US $3,810,000 under the standard approach. This illustrates the benefits of the Internal Models Approach when the bank's position is well diversified across maturities, countries (i.e. currencies) and products. The more sophisticated the portfolio is, the greater benefit the bank receives from using internal models rather than the standard approach.

[144] 'New Accord', Paragraph 552. Gross income=Net Interest Income + Net Non-interest income. It is intended that this measure should reflect income before deduction of operational losses.

[145] Some studies show that if a bank relies on the available data, then the charge for operational risk under the Basle Accord would exceed the charge for market risk. See, for example, *Using Loss Data to Quantify the Operational Risk* (Federal Reserve Bank of Boston, April 2003).

assessment framework. In the future, a Loss Distribution Approach in which the bank specifies its own loss distributions, business lines and risk types, may be available.

The above was a necessary exercise to show the student some of the very considerable complications in the details of the new regulatory approaches to capital adequacy. In section 2.5.7 above, it was already noted and it should never be forgotten that in practice the credit rating of credit agencies will determine a bank's fate rather than the bank's regulatory capital requirements. The calculations of the rating agencies will therefore be the more important and the final assessment of a bank's solidity will be determined in first instance by these outsiders. Regulatory and internal systems are secondary to their findings. It puts the whole discussion on regulatory capital adequacy in perspective. Caught between the ratings agencies and the banks' internal systems, regulatory capital requirements are probably only of minor importance. They are also loosing their transparency and defying their original objective of creating a level playing field in respect of the necessary capital in banks. The whole exercise of Basel II, its approach, result and use could therefore be seriously questioned. It raises also the important issue whether the considerable extra expense of implementation for the industry is truly justified. In any event, there is no guarantee whatever that banking will become a less dangerous business. This has foremost to do with the obvious fact that, whatever the sophistication of the capital adequacy requirements, the total capital required in banking remains too modest to allow an adequate buffer in the case of serious problems either of a macro-economic or micro-economic nature.

Part III   The Third Generation of EU Directives Completing the Internal Market in Financial Services and the EU Action Plan for a Single Market in Financial Services

3.1   The New EU Approach towards the Regulated Financial Services Industries following the Liberalisation of the Capital Flows in 1988

3.1.1   *The Essence of the New Approach. Mutual Recognition of Home Country Rule. Limited Harmonisation. The European Passport*

In the foregoing, we saw that the liberalisation of capital flows and payments through the 1988 Directive proved of major importance, made the further liberalisation of the financial services sector within the EU possible and urgent, and accelerated the pace. This liberalisation was in fact forced on the EU at the risk of its being overtaken by events which could have affected the viability of the financial services industry in the EU, particularly in countries other than the UK.

The technique chosen was to abandon the idea of progressive harmonisation of regulatory standards. It accepted instead

(a)   mutual recognition of home country rule with only minor exceptions and
(b)   a *small number* of uniform rules as regards
   (i)   the authorisation requirement itself and its basic conditions, notably the required capital,
   (ii)   prudential supervision, and
   (iii)   some aspects of the conduct of business, especially in the securities and insurance sectors.

The key was therefore *regulatory competition* under a system of mutual recognition of home country standards of authorisation, capital and supervision for cross-border activities EU-wide, including any branches elsewhere, which could be freely set up. It resulted in the *European passport* for financial service providers who are *incorporated* in the EU and are subject to proper authorisation and supervision in their home State (state of incorporation and principal business; it is suggested that these places should be the same).

This approach was first formulated in the June 1985 White Paper on the Completion of the Internal Market (p. 27), in partial reliance on the *Cassis de Dijon* case, which, however, concerned the free movement of only (dangerous or unhealthy) *goods* under Article 28 (ex Article 30) EEC Treaty.[146] Through the White Paper this basic approach was extended to services under Article 49(ex Article 59). It was in fact foreshadowed in the First Banking Directive of 1977 (10th Preamble): see also section 2.3.2 above, and already adopted in the 1985 UCITS Directive, see section 2.3.5 above. The First Banking Directive itself, although setting out some common regulatory standards for authorisation and requiring some branch capital, did not yet provide a sufficient basis for home country authorisation and supervision as admitted in its Article 4(1).

Under the embryonic proposals for mortgage credit: see section 2.3.3 above, host country supervision had largely remained the principle (in any event in line with the then prevailing philosophy) in order best to protect local home owners in view of the considerable differences in mortgage products between the EU countries. It was an early elaboration of the idea of the general good, which also in other areas, especially related to investor protection, may still limit the EU-wide licence under home country supervision, as is clear from Article 11 of the Investment Services Directive. This exception to home country rule under European case law continues to operate, although, under case law, generally limited to exceptional situations and in any event curtailed by the liberalisation Directives, as already discussed above in section 2.2.5: see further section 3.1.3 below.

The EU's policy of a market-oriented approach in the regulated services area led to mutual recognition of Member State authorisations for activities EU-wide. It meant in principle home country supervision, subject to only some limited harmonisation principles (in the area of authorisation and required capital with some common prudential rules and principles). The consequence was regulatory competition between various home country rules operating side by side depending on the origin of the service provider involved. Limited areas of host country rule remained, however, in the sectors of conduct of business and product control, particularly under the European case law concerning the general good, but formally accepted under Article 11 of the Investment Services Directive.

For banks, this liberalisation was reflected in the 1988 Second Banking Directive (effective on 1 January 1993), consolidated in the Credit Institutions Directive (CID) in 2000.[147] For the securities industry it was covered in the 1993 Investment Services Directive (effective

---

[146] Case 120/78, *Rewe — Zentral AG v Bundesmonopolverwaltung für Branntwein* [1979] ECR 649, in which it was decided that under Article 28 (ex Article 30), in the absence of common EC rules, Member States still remain competent to regulate the production and use of goods. They may do so even if this results in restrictions on their importation from elsewhere in the EU through the imposition of mandatory rules concerning health, fairness or the protection of the consumer, provided that it can be shown by the relevant authorities that the restrictions were necessary whilst the measures taken were proportionate and did not duplicate. Further limitations may result from Art 30 (ex Art 36) (public morality, safety and health). In the area of regulated services, this amounts to the general good exception: see also s 3.1.3 below. In the *Rewe* case, it was decided, however, that the French (home) regulation of the spirits shipped to Germany was insufficient and that there was in sufficient justification for so the second Banking Directive, duplicatory German regulation, although quite different.

[147] So the second Banking Directive, Council Dir 89/646 EEC [1989] OJ L386, and the Credit Institutions Directive, Directive 2000/12/ EC of the European Parliament and of the Council of March 20, 2000 [2000] OJ L126.

on 31 December 1995)[148] and for the insurance business in the Third Insurance Directives for the life and non-life business, agreed in 1991 and effective since 1 July 1994.[149]

The substantial harmonisation of the capital adequacy standards in these industries (subject to local implementation) as a major part of the authorisation and supervision (prudential) regime was for banks achieved in the Own Funds and Solvency Directives of 1989 (effective on 31 December 1992),[150] also consolidated into the CIDF. For the securities industry (including the securities activities of universal banks) the Capital Adequacy Directive of 1993 (effective on 31 December 1995) covers capital[151] For the insurance industry regulatory capital is covered in the solvency provisions of the Third Insurance Directives. The Insurance Accounts Directive, also agreed in 1991, harmonises the rules on the technical provisions required to cover insurance liabilities.[152]

Although complete harmonisation was no longer the objective, a considerable approximation of regulatory regimes nevertheless resulted within the EU under the new regime. It has not, however led to a single regulator, even on the banking side, where the emergence of the European Central Bank ECB within the framework of the ESCB (European System of Central Banks), that now determines monetary policy and thereby acquires a major say in the provision of liquidity with a natural concern for systemic risk, is going to make much difference in the countries adopting the EURO: see also section 1.2.6 above.

3.1.2   Cross-border Activities through an Establishment or through Direct Services. Different EU and US Approaches

Cross-border services may in principle be rendered by a provider in four different ways: they may be provided (a) direct but incidentally, usually through telephone, fax or mail at the provider's initiative, (b) through more regular established contacts often involving regular travel of representatives of the provider to or the use of local agents by the provider in the host country, (c) through the creation of a branch, and (d) through the creation of a subsidiary in the host country. As was pointed out above in section 2.2.4, only the first mode of operation was freed from the beginning as a result of the direct effect accorded to Article 49 (ex Article 59) of the EEC Treaty. Even then it was subject to exceptions on the basis of the general good, especially as regards the sales methods used and the products sold.[153] This applied all the more so to the second method under which, on the basis of the general good, the host country could infer an establishment and impose its own requirements of authorisation on the foreign provider. This was more naturally also the case when it came to officially establishing a branch[154] and fundamentally when a subsidiary in the host country was being created.

---

[148] Council Dir 93/22 EEC [1993] OJ L141.
[149] Respectively Council Dirs. 92/49 EEC [1992] OJ L228 and 92/96 EEC [1992] OJ L360.
[150] Respectively Council Dirs. 89/229 EEC [1989] OJ L241 and 89/647 EEC [1989] OJ L386.
[151] Council Dir 93/6 EEC [1993] OJ L141.
[152] Council Dir 91/674 EEC [1991] OJ L374.
[153] See also n 67 above for the relevant EU case law.
[154] What constituted a branch was itself not without complication. See in the area of establishing jurisdiction pursuant to the 1968 Brussels Convention on Jurisdiction and the Enforcement of Judgments in Civil and Commercial Matters, Case 14/76, *De Bloos* [1976] ECR 1497 which required head office direction and control, and Case 139/80, *Blanckaert & Willems* [1981] ECR 819 excepting an agent who merely negotiates business whilst basically free to arrange his own work, able to represent several principals and merely transmits orders for others. In Case 33/78, *Somafer* [1978] ECR 2183, the emphasis was on permanence and the possibility of binding the head-office company: see also Case C–439/93, *Lloyd's Register of Shipping v Société Campenon Bernard* [1995]

The Commission in its 1997 Interpretative Communication[155] also considered the role of the provider as active or passive intermediary. If the recipient of financial services in a country other than that of the provider comes to the home country of the provider, a case can be made that *no* cross-border services are being rendered at all, especially if the recipient chooses to keep an account with the provider in his home state. Also in the case of telephone, fax or mail contact, the question of who takes the (original) initiative could determine the trans-border nature of the resulting transaction even if subsequently a two-way traffic in communications develops, but the situation then becomes more complicated. In the case of advertising, the situation is even less clear. It should perhaps not be considered relevant unless there is commercial canvassing in another EU country amounting to an invitation to enter into a contract with the required documentation attached or is followed by a physical journey by the provider and visit. For distance banking through the Internet, the Commission now accepts that no prior notification of cross-border services is required as the supplier cannot be deemed to be pursuing its activities in the customer's territory.

In its 1997 Interpretative Communication, the EU Commission subsequently focused on the *preliminary question* of when there was a direct cross-border service (or an activity within the territory of another Member State) if none of the parties moved in greater detail. It examined in this connection the possibilities of locating the service at the place of the originator of the initiative, the customer's place of residence, or the place where the contracts were signed. It found that none of these could satisfactorily apply to all the activities covered by the Second Banking Directive. After much discussion the Commission in the end took the position that, where modern communication means are being used rather than actual presence of intermediaries, the place of the service should be considered the place where the *characteristic obligation* must be performed. This is so at least *for the purposes of notification* of the trans-border direct service to the home regulator. It may limit the cross-border concept considerably whilst for direct services it separates it from the whereabouts of the parties: see also section 2.2.3 above.

This concept of 'the characteristic obligation' is derived from the 1980 Rome Convention on the Law Applicable to Contractual Obligations (Article 4) and is here used only for the purposes of determining whether the procedure for notification of the home regulator must be used under Article 20 of the Second Banking Directive: see for this notification more in particular section 3.2.3 below, and indirectly whether the host regulators can at all become affected. The reference to the place of characteristic performance of the service seems to take preliminary activity like advertising and cold calling or other ways of seeking clients outside the notification requirement. The notion of the characteristic performance is not used here to establish the law applicable to the service itself. European case law will eventually have to determine whether this approach connecting the service to the place of the most characteristic performance rather than to the place of the customer is the right one and can also be used outside the area of notification. Initiative and place of

---

ECR 1–1961. See above n 11 for the ECJ's attitude under Art 60(3) of the EEC Treaty in the *Reinhard Gebhard* case with the emphasis on duration, regularity, periodicity and continuity. The EU Commission in its Interpretative Communication (above n 14), highlights the existence of an exclusive brief from the head office, the ability to negotiate and commit the company, and the permanence of the arrangement, leading together to a genuine extension of the head office. It always presumes that this type of establishment engages in the head office's activity proper and is not merely a representative office which does often do no more than reconnoitering the market, establish contacts and examine business propositions: see also above n 11.

[155] See the Interpretative Communication referred to in n 14 above.

account may in this connection also remain relevant, depending on the particular facts of the situation.

The question is also of importance in the USA in respect of the registration of securities in the USA and the operation of foreign brokers there, but as the discussion in section 1.1.11 above showed, the question whether a service is rendered within the USA is short-circuited by the definition of certain safe-harbours rather than by defining the place of the transaction. The US approach to foreign investments is generally unilateral and translates in exemptions of the 1933 and 1934 Acts. There is no great interest so far in recognising foreign regulatory regimes or in a division of home and host regulator functions. This might be explained partly because of the absence of regulatory standards in many countries, also in the euromarkets. Yet there is a clear (unilateral) drift in leaving the professional investor (even if American) to his own devices when engaging in foreign investments, increasingly also if these foreign investment are offered directly or indirectly in the US.

3.1.3   Residual Host Country Rules, The Concept of the General Good and its Abuses

The EU liberalisation in the financial services industry meant (in principle) exclusive regulatory jurisdiction of the regulator of the head office of a company in the EU, therefore home regulation. In this approach, the competence of the host regulator (beyond certain specific areas, like monetary and liquidity policy for banks, and a supporting role) is, under a narrowed notion of the *general good*, mainly limited to overriding considerations relating to the protection of the (smaller) depositor, investor or (in insurance) the small injured party, and to the supervision of other types of *consumer* financial activity.

Although the EU liberalisation directives sustain in principle the pre-1986 case law on the general good in the area of the supply of direct cross-border services: see section 2.2.5 above, they substantially amend it as part of the (home) regulation of direct services and branches in other Member States.[156] Thus in the financial services area, the concept of the general good can no longer be used to assume branching under host country rule and to impose authorisation requirements in the case of a more regular supply of direct cross-border services. The concept of the general good remains important, however, in that it may still allow mandatory host country restrictions on the conduct of business and on the nature of the financial products. They thus remain largely marketed *per country* at least in respect of retail customers in as far as his essential protections are concerned.

The main consequence of the liberalisation Directives is that the borderline between operating direct services and using an establishment has become much *less* important except in the formalities of notification which are different in both cases as we shall see in section 3.2.3 below. This is, however, largely a formal issue and not one of substance and the different treatment here may eventually be eliminated. Home country rule is thus extended to regular direct and branch activities of an EU incorporated and regulated financial services provider into another Member State and these activities have become exempt from host country regulation, at least as regards the authorisation, capital adequacy and prudential supervision regime.

Admittedly this is less clear in the conduct of business and product control areas which remain basically a host country affair under the Investment Services and Insurance

---

[156] See Case 205/84, *Commission v Germany*, n 67 above; *cf* the other insurance cases decided at the same time (Dec. 1986) Cases 220/83; 252/83 and 206/84.

Directives, as indeed it is for consumers under Article 5 of the Rome Convention mentioned in the previous section, although under the liberalisation Directives much less clearly so in banking, where it depends on the notion of the general good and may as such be limited to consumer banking cross-border. However, host regulation may in all cases well need to pass the general good test *and* its (case law) limitations, even when the Directives specifically reserve rights to host governments in the area of conduct of business, as under Articles 11 to 19(6) of the Investment Services Directive.[157]

It could mean limitation of host country rule in the areas of the conduct of business and product control to consumer business only. In any event, home country rule in the area of conduct of business and product control seems not to be ousted. The home regulator may certainly set standards in this area for its own service providers when operating at home or abroad, if only to protect the reputation of its own financial system.[158] We are concerned here with market access, with behaviour of service providers in the foreign market, for example their selling (particularly cold calling and advertising) techniques, and with the nature of the products they try to sell in that market, their suitability, for example in the case of insurance products, their legal characteristics, for example in the case of mortgage credit, and their proper settlement or unwinding facility for example in the case of over-the-counter swaps, but also the possibility of their proper protection through segregation between assets of clients and service providers, for example for investment securities bought and held by brokers in their own name but on their clients' behalf.

Clearly there may be here regulatory but also private law concerns, even though the ECJ has so far hardly ever dealt with the latter. What does not seem possible is, however, to keep foreign services and products out on the basis that they have never been offered in host states in the manner proposed by foreign service providers, cannot be accommodated by the host country's legal system or can only be offered in the manner customary in the host state, simply to protect local operators or even wholesale (professional) customers, certainly if these practices and products are normal and currently offered in the home state or more generally in countries with an advanced financial system.

After the last generation of liberalisation directives in the financial services area, therefore after the Second Banking Directive, the Investment Services Directive and the Third Insurance Directives, it may well be proper to conclude as follows. The general good exception to home country rule, although remaining undefined, (a) has no place in matters of authorisation, capital adequacy and prudential supervision or in other matters concerning the establishment and supervision of service providers in other Member States and is therefore limited to the conduct of business and product control; (b) may in these latter areas also be used outside the investment and insurance services particularly in banking but in essence only for pressing retail (or consumer) protection reasons, as Article 11(3) of the Investment Services Directive allows and as the Second Insurance Directives suggest for the application of mandatory host country law to insurance products;[159] and (c) is always subject to the case law restrictions mentioned already in section 2.2.4 above.

---

[157] The principle of subsidiarity has also been mentioned in this context in the wake of Joined Cases C–267 and C–268/91, *Keck and Mithouard* [1993] ECR I–6097, concerning the free movement of goods under Art 30 EEC Treaty after the *Cassis de Dijon* case: see above n146. In *Keck*, the emphasis seemed to switch to equal treatment of national and imported goods. See on this subject also M Andenas, 'Rules of Conduct and the Principle of Subsidiarity' (1994) 15 *The Company Lawyer* 60. Yet in Case C–384/93, *Alpine Investments*, above n 79, this approach was not extended to Art 49 (ex Art 59) EEC Treaty: see further M Andenas, 'Cross-border Cold Calling and the Right to Provide Services', (1995) 16 *The Company Lawyer* 249.

[158] See the *Alpine Investments* case, n 79 above.

[159] See also s 3.5.6 below. Note that the German insurance cases (above n 67), were never applied to co-insurance, which is the EU term for insurance taken out by large undertakings or groups of undertakings which are in a

Thus there must be no discrimination, duplication, or disproportionate action. The protection measures taken by the host regulator under the notion of the general good must be objectively necessary, serve the public interest and be suitable and capable of achieving the protection objective whilst not going beyond it; they should never be used to protect local interests. As far as duplication is concerned, it seems likely that the host country must abstain where the home regulator in banking provides for proper protection of banking clients in the area of conduct of business and banking products. This is all the more likely in countries that have only one financial regulator like now the UK. This could be of importance in the area of banking deposits, overdraft facilities, borrowings and mortgage products in terms of pricing, complication and suitability.

Beyond this, there may also be room for general good action by the host regulator (d) better to fit the liberalisation measures in its own system and to effect the best regulatory co-operation, but this could only lead to marginal adjustments making liberalisation *more* rather than less effective. In (e) emergency situations, the host regulator may also have a role to play but, where he has not been given his own powers of co-operation, only as *ad hoc* representative of the home regulator and until the latter can act especially to prevent market manipulation and fraud.

An example may help. Assume a foreign bank operates or wants to operate a number of ATM machines in another EU country. Regardless of whether the activity was incidental or maintained through an official branch, authorisation and supervision would be home country matters. Even if conduct of business and product supervision have a host country bias under the ISD this is not so under the Banking Directives. Leaving monetary and liquidity policy considerations to one side (and also the question as to which currencies could be distributed in this manner), any intervention of the host state would have to be based on general good considerations. They are severely limited by case law as we saw. The customer's protection would have to be tantamount and require it. The concern ought to be specific, but it could focus on the proper mechanical functioning of these machines (fraud would also be a legitimate host country concern), but probably not much more.

European case law may suggest host country powers on the basis of the general good also to protect more generally the integrity of the host country financial system and its supervision. The coherence of the host country tax system and the effectiveness of tax collection have also been issues. They may become issues more in particular in connection with the free movement of capital and the movement of investments. Short of EU action in these areas, which in its harmonisation and interpretative efforts is motivated by the importance of integrity of the financial system as a whole, host country intervention to protect national financial and tax set-up at the expense of the free flow of financial services hardly seems appropriate.

In one respect, the liberalisation Directives may be more restrictive than the earlier practice: they may also subject the *incidental* trans-border services to the prior notification requirement (to the home regulator), also therefore *minor* cross-border activities. According to the Commission's 1997 Interpretative Communication, the notification of direct cross-border banking services does not, however, apply where there was already activity *before*, provided it was conducted legally, which may not be so simple to establish in view of the earlier restrictive host country regulations. This legality should in any event be judged by EU standards, especially in the light of the direct applicability of Article 49 (ex Article 59) of the EEC Treaty and not by outdated early host country standards and

position to assess and negotiate insurance policies proposed to them: see *Commission v Germany* above n 67, at para 64.

restrictions, the legality of which was often in doubt. It should not be subject to an over-extended interpretation of the general good notion. In any event, the Commission is studying whether the notification requirement for direct services has any useful purpose.

Other specific rights and tasks of host regulators under the liberalisation directives remain the gathering of statistical information, and, in the financial services industry, the conduct of monetary and liquidity policy, at least in countries remaining outside EMU after 1999. Host regulators also monitor large positions in banks, even for branches of banks from other Member States, but always by way of exception. Thus these powers are to be interpreted in a limited way and applied in a non-discriminatory proportionate fashion without leading to regulatory duplication, *much in the way*, it is suggested, as the host regulation under the general good notion. This host regulation and supervision must, therefore, be directed towards clear objectives, may not exceed them and can never extend into areas subject to EU harmonisation like the regime concerning authorisation, capital adequacy and prudential supervision.[160]

In practice, claims to host regulation have given rise to problems mainly in four areas. First, under cover of monetary policy, statistical information-gathering or more generally the general good, host countries have continued to require the issuing of eurobonds in their currencies to take place in their own financial centres. Yet the issuing itself is no monetary matter, statistical information on it can be gathered separately and the general good seems not to be involved (only the interests of local underwriting banks). Another difficulty has been that host regulators have attempted to require foreign service providers to register fully with them to share in their costs (and not only those directly related to conduct of business supervision). For statistical information-gathering, local systems compatible with those of the host regulator have been required, which can be very costly for the foreign service provider. Finally the issue has arisen whether, as part of its conduct of business and product control, a host regulator may insist that its own law applies to these products and that they be dealt in its own local markets. For securities, that last point has been largely resolved by the anti-concentration principle of the Investment Services Directive: see also section 3.2.8 below.

The general good exception to home country rule may also play a role where host regulators continue to insist on prospectus requirements for public issues emanating from other Member States or on some form of local registration of primary issues that may be placed in the host country. This may be especially relevant when they are meant to reach consumer investors. Although eurobonds were exempted from the relevant EU Prospectus Directive at the time: see also section 2.3.4 above, Member States may still take here a more restrictive attitude. The mutual recognition of prospectuses may be a bar to this requirement but does not affect government bonds, which were exempted from the relevant EU directives at the time. The prospectus or registration requirements do not affect secondary trading where, in the consumer area, host country rule may in any event prevail under the relevant Investment Services Directive or under the notion of the general good.

Sales restrictions imposed by the issuer on eurobond sales, particularly into the USA and UK, often reflect host country regulation. Within the EU, such regulation appears to be justified only on the basis of the general good or on the basis of the monetary policy exemption to home country rule. If nevertheless the issuer imposes them also on bondholders, this is another matter and an issue of contract law.

---

[160] See in particular above n 68 and accompanying text.

3.1.4   Division of Tasks. No Single EU Regulator. Regulatory Competition

The end result of the new EU regime is a division of roles between home and host regulator, with emphasis on the predominance of the former although with important residual powers for the latter especially in the area of conduct of business and product control for the more sophisticated products if sold to consumers and in some other limited areas specifically made subject to host country regulation and supervision, like monetary policy and statistical information gathering. The EU notably rejected an approach in which there would be one supranational supervisor with a unitary supervision regime at EU level per industry.

This approach to authorisation and supervision, accepting in essence the idea of one licence on the basis of home country authorisation for the whole EU area in most service sectors, led to the interesting consequence that different regulatory regimes could operate side by side within one EU country depending on the origin of the relevant institution within the EU. This is the essence of the *regulatory competition*, meaning that domestic regulators may be forced to amend their own standards so as to create a level playing field between their own houses and foreign supervised houses on their territory. It shows the *dynamics* of the internationalisation even in regulated areas. It suggests a race to the bottom, but this has not taken place. The minimum of common standards seems so far to have prevented it.

In its harmonisation efforts, albeit limited, the new approach shows the traditional regulatory concerns especially for proper authorisation, capitalisation and prudential supervision to underpin the health of the financial system as a whole, thus reducing *systemic risk*, and in its approach to the general good, concern for the special needs of the consumer and small investors. In the new approach there is less concern, therefore, for professionals and their dealings amongst themselves, even though this differentiation is often still poorly expressed. The filling out of the details and the supervision remain mostly domestic affairs. So does the combating of fraud, although there are now also directives in the area of insider dealing and money laundering,[161] but they function largely outside the above home and host country system of regulation.

3.1.5   Interaction with GATS

In the meantime, internationalisation induced the GATT in its Uruguay Round also to look at services, extending its basic approach to a proposal for a General Agreement on Tariffs and Services (GATS): see section 2.1.3 above. The idea is to give access and rights of establishment to foreign service companies on equal terms with domestic institutions under the national treatment principle, supported by the most favoured nation principle, provided that (depending on the type of service) some basic minimum standards of liberalisation for all are met from the beginning. It is the essence of the negotiation process that is taking place in this area.

As we saw, also under GATS, progress will create a need for a balance between home and host regulation worldwide to make the free supply of cross-border services meaningful for those services that are traditionally regulated, like financial services, probably in ways similar to those already adopted in the EU with emphasis therefore on home regulation, provided there is a minimum standard of regulation amongst members. To bring this standard

---

[161] Respectively Council Dir 89/592 EEC [1989] OJ L334 and Council Dir 91/308 EEC [1991] OJ L166. See for money laundering also chapter III, s 3.1.

up is therefore the more immediate concern. It will have to be followed by co-operation amongst regulators to establish some basic confidence in the effective supervision of home regulators elsewhere in host countries, although it is also conceivable that host regulators will act here as agents for home regulators under the latter's regimes, at least in the areas of prudential supervision.[162]

As things now stand, when a foreign bank comes into the EU, there will be national treatment but still regulatory control by the country of entrance. It is possible that the regulator of the country of entrance may not like the wide activity of the foreign bank and it may still attempt to use regulatory means to undermine national treatment and limit the activity as part of the authorisation process.

3.1.6 The EU Reciprocity Requirements. Relation with Third Countries. National Treatment and Effective Market Access

Pending the further development of GATS, a particular aspect the EU had to face was its relationship with third countries in view of the charge that it was creating a 'Fortress Europe', not only in goods but also in services by excluding non-EU-based institutions from the benefits of its 'passport', even though the EU approach in this area appeared initially mostly inspired by the desire to preserve bargaining power within the Uruguay Round of the GATT.

The solution was found in the introduction of a reciprocity regime based on national treatment, *cf.* Article 9 of the Second Banking Directive and Article 7 of the Investment Services Directive. This is to say that countries which gave EU institutions entry and operation rights on a non-discriminatory basis compared to their own entities (national treatment) would be allowed to incorporate their own subsidiaries in the EU. These could subsequently use the EU passport in order to render services or branch out in other EU countries. The system is that, only failing national treatment, the Commission may intervene with Member States to prevent a foreign entity from gaining access through a subsidiary in the EU (thereby obtaining the passport).

Thus no mirror image reciprocity is necessary aiming at the granting of similar benefits to EU entities in the relevant foreign country as the EU would give to foreign service providers of that country within the EU, although the Southern European countries and the EU Parliament had wanted to go further in this direction. This notably means that the Americans and Japanese may continue to apply a measure of separation between banking, investment and insurance businesses to foreign financial entities as they do to locals without these limitations under the reciprocity requirements impinging on the right of US and Japanese banks to create universal banking subsidiaries in the EU, thus benefiting there from the absence of any such division or limitation.

However, the EU is requiring a certain equivalence in business opportunity (effective market access). If there is a problem in this area, the Council of Ministers may act to start the necessary negotiations, for which it is then likely to instruct the Commission to take the necessary action. In such situations the Commission does not have original powers, however, to request Member States to refuse a licence to a subsidiary of a third country service provider wanting to obtain a passport in this manner. As the matter of effective

---

[162] See for the developments in GATS also HS Scott and PA Mellon, above n 110, 148 *et seq.*

market access is more difficult to establish and a political question, the Council of Ministers reserved the policy to itself.

If American and Japanese (or other third country) service providers wish only to establish a branch in an EU country or wish only to do direct business there, this is a matter entirely for the host country under its own rules. As such a branch is never entitled to a European passport, which can only be given to an entity incorporated in a Member State under its rules of authorisation, EU law does not get involved. Thus such branches may operate in other Member States only to the extent that the national law of such States allows it. In fact, also the creation of a subsidiary is, except for the power of the EU to prevent it if there is no sufficient reciprocity, itself entirely a matter of the host country under its own rules as supplemented by that country's obligations under GATS.

To the extent that GATS succeeds in the area of financial services, the EU will have to abandon the reciprocity policy, which affects primarily the creation of subsidiaries within the EU. This was the effect of the 1 March 1999 GATS Agreement: see section 2.1.3 above.

3.2 The EU Second Bankisng Directive (SBD Consolidated in the Credit Institutions Directive or CID of 2000) and Investment Services Directive (ISD)

3.2.1 SBD/CID: Home Country Rule Reach. Residual Host Country Powers. The General Good

The home country rule in essence concerns itself with (a) authorisation, which is substantially a question of a review of (i) reputation, (ii) capital, and (iii) business profile and activities plan (Articles 4*ff.* CID), and (b) supervision, in which connection there are usually prudential rules (Article 26). It may also concern itself with (c) conduct of business, and (d) product control, but not exclusively. The CID (following the SBD) does not contain substantial rules in these latter two respects (regardless of the heading of Title II) It follows that there is home country rule in principle, but conduct of business and product control may still be of some concern to host States under the notion of the general good.

The CID's essentially home country regulatory approach (Article 26, CID) expressly reserves in Article 27 CID to the *host* regulation matters of liquidity and monetary policy pending further co-ordination, now part of EMU. The host country here remains competent but may not discriminate. Host governments also retain a supporting role in the monitoring of open positions entered into in the pertinent host country. In statistical matters the host country may continue to require reporting (Article 22 CID), which is not defined and may still impose substantial burdens in terms of maintaining adequate systems geared to the accounting principles of the host country.

These powers are not restrained by the limitations attached to the general good exception which is a more limited concept. Preambles 16 and 17 and Articles 20 CID(4), 22(5) and 22(11) CID specifically refer to the host country's power under the general good, without defining the concept. It is, as mentioned before, primarily thought to relate to consumer protection and may have a special meaning in terms of conduct of business or product control, but is in the context of the SBD/CID more likely to relate to the protection of deposits, the sale of foreign mortgage credit products, the preservation of the good reputation of the banking industry as a whole and the prevention of fraud and other irregularities, the latter certainly on an emergency basis (Article 22(7) CID), in that case always subject to the EU Commission's power to amend or abolish these measures.[163]

As noted above, measures taken on the ground of the general good may, according to case law,[164] not duplicate, become disproportionate to the ends to which they are directed nor discriminate, in which connection reference is sometimes made to the principles of *equivalence, proportionality* and *non-discrimination*. They must have a public policy motive and be suitable for the desired end and not overshoot. It is clear however, that under the Second Banking, Investment Services and Third Insurance Directives the general good notion cannot interfere with the authorisation and supervision or prudential process as harmonised areas.

In the product sphere, banking activities, being largely confined to deposit taking, may not be greatly affected by special protections derived from the general good and the Second Banking Directive does not evince a particular concern in this respect, which also goes for local banking acts. The conduct of business equally is not traditionally a particular bank regulator concern and is more typically a concern for the securities and insurance industries. Nevertheless, specialised products like derivatives and mortgage credit may elicit special consumer protection concerns also for banks, and their cross border sale may then give rise to special general good considerations in the recipient country. Mandatory rules of applicable local law in the recipient country may also have their effect.

Within the EU, this applicable law to the extent that it is contractual, which especially concerns investors' obligations under the products bought, will be determined by the Convention on the Law Applicable to Contractual Obligations of 1980 accepted by all EU countries (The Rome Convention). As already mentioned above in another context,[165] it has special consumer protection rules in Article 5 leading mostly to applicability of the (mandatory) law of the country of the habitual residence of the consumer. For others, Article 7 may also allow special protection rules of the host country to prevail if mandatory. As, however, EU law prevails over this Convention (Article 20), any restrictions of these types must still pass the general good tests and limitations.[166] The Second Insurance Directives contained further provisions in this regard for insurance products.

Host governments may take *punitive* action against foreign bank branches violating host country rules issued in accordance with the provisions of the Directives. To facilitate *co-operation*, Memoranda of Understanding are formulated between the various central banks or other banking supervisors on a bilateral basis further to clarify the role of each and the type of assistance to be given. This is so far largely confined to pure banking (prudential) supervision and has often not reached the stage of ancillary activities, like the securities business. This co-ordination awaits the full implementation of the Investment Services Directive for the rest of the securities industry.

3.2.2   SBD/CID: Scope of the Banking Passport. Universal Banking

Under the SBD/CID a bank may receive its passport for all banking activities in a universal banking sense. The passport is tied in principle to the deposit taking and lending activity (covering assimilated financial institutions at the same time: Article 19(2) CID) but may

---

[163] See for the special concerns about long distance selling of banking services to consumers, the proposals discussed in s 3.4.8 below.
[164] See cases cited above in n 68 *et seq.*
[165] See s 3.1.2 above.
[166] See on this aspect also the Commission's Interpretative Communication referred to in n 13 above.

also cover, according to the Annex, mortgage products and securities activities (the original English text erroneously refers only to shares, later corrected), investment management and custody functions, but notably not insurance. The idea is that the scope of the passport basically depends on the scope of the authorisation in the home country.

Yet, since the entering into force of the Investment Services Directive in 1995, the securities business of banks is also covered by that Directive because of its functional rather than institutional approach: see also section 3.2.4 below, and banking supervisors have to take a step back here and must allow for the operation of security supervisors. The relationship between both is a matter of regulatory co-operation and division of tasks according to the details of the local regulatory regime in home and host countries.

3.2.3   SBD/CID: Procedure for Obtaining the Passport. Home and Host Country Communications

As far as the procedure for obtaining the passport is concerned, interested parties must inform their home regulators of their intention to branch out or engage in cross-border services in other EU countries. This must be agreed by the home regulators. In the case of branching out, the home regulator then has a period of three months in which to inform the host regulator concerned. If it does not do so, the petitioning entity may appeal. The host country has two months to make its own (limited) supervisory arrangements and also explain what rules will be applied in respect of the general good. It cannot object to the passport itself and has no blocking powers (Article 20(2) and (3) CID). They are reserved to the home regulator. Explaining the rules concerning the general good is an option of the host regulator and in view of the multi-faceted and undefined nature of the general good exception not a duty, although the foreign service provider should be able to solicit more information.[167]

When only direct cross-border services are considered rather than a branch elsewhere, the procedure is simplified (Article 21 CID) and the home regulator has only one month to send on the file to the host regulator whilst no further period is set for the host regulator to make its own arrangements and give any indication of general good exceptions. The Commission's Interpretative Communication of 1997 makes it clear that the notification itself is not a customer protection measure and its absence has no effect on any contracts concluded. As mentioned above, prior (legal) cross-border activity will excuse a bank from giving notification, although the question of legality of these activities should be determined at EU level and not on the basis of old restrictive domestic regulation.

3.2.4   ISD/CID: Basic Structure. Background and Scope

The Investment Services Directive,[168] covering the passport for intermediaries in the securities industry, was not originally part of the 1992 EU programme as the question of a European passport for securities services was largely overlooked at the time of the Single European Act, whilst progress towards the insurance passport was considered premature at the time. The securities passport was subsequently requested by the securities industry to give it the same facilities as universal banks and denotes true further progress in this field. It is unlikely that the securities industry at the time understood what it was asking for, especially in the area of capital adequacy.

---

[167] See the Commission's Interpretative Communication referred to in n 14 above.
[168] Council Dir 93/22 EEC [1993] OJ L141.

As far as the Investment Services Directive is concerned, the structure of the Second Banking Directive is followed. Yet there is an important difference: the Second Banking Directive in principle adopts an *institutional* approach to the subject and focuses on banks (credit institutions and assimilated financial institutions). The Investment Services Directive takes a more *functional* approach instead and focuses on investment services activity (Article 1(1)) and then defines investment firms in terms of legal (or similar) entities engaged in this activity (Article 1(2)). Most importantly, because of this approach, it also covers the securities business of banks for the prudential and conduct of business aspects, including the capital required for their investment business, but not for the acquisition of the passport (Article 2(1)). It does not apply to insurance undertakings and their various products (Article 2(2)).

As for the scope of the activities covered, according to the Annexes to the Investment Services Directive, it covers underwriting, trading, brokerage and investment management activities in transferable securities, units in unit trusts and money market instrument and futures, options and swaps, to which there may be added certain *non-core* activities, like related lending, foreign exchange activity and advice, mergers and acquisition services and safe custody. These non-core activities need no authorisation but without it there is no passport (Article 14(1)).

Some concern has been expressed about the scope of the Investment Services Directive as defined in the Annexes.[169] The definitional terminology (in all regulated services directives) is not always stable or comprehensive and between the Investment Services Directive and Second Banking Directive not even always compatible. Implementation by the Member States is likely to show some divergences when industry practices, which in any event evolve all the time and are in some EU countries much more advanced than in others, also come into the equation. Certain terms like 'instrument' remain altogether undefined and must then be understood in their common meaning. That probably also goes for many of the semi-defined terms. It is probably unwise to read too much into them but to concentrate on what is *excluded* (see Article 2 of the Investment Services Directive), notably the activities in collective investments, pension funds, insurance products, and investments incidental to professional activity of lawyers and accountants and to commodity trading.

According to the Preamble Member States should not grant a licence if it is requested merely to avoid the stricter conditions of other Member States. The use of a branch solely for spot or forward exchange transactions other than as an investment service would also constitute misuse of the Directive.

3.2.5   ISD: Home Country Rule, Authorisation, Capital, Prudential Rules. Procedure for Obtaining the Passport

Following the Second Banking Directive model, the home country issues the basic authorisation, taking into account the reputation, capital and business profile of the applicant (Article 3(3)). It is of interest that Article 3 does not refer to proper infrastructure and system support. These are mentioned only within the context of prudential supervision in Article 10 (and indirectly in Article 3(7)(e)) which refers to sound administrative and accounting procedures, arrangements for electronic data processing and adequate internal controls.

---

[169] See G Ferranini, 'Towards a European Law of Investment Services and Institutions' (1994) 31 *Common Market Law Review* 1283, 1287 *et seq.*

Strictly speaking there is here still no clear reference to adequate systems support nor to adequate arrangements for settlement and custody, although the Investment Services Directive is more specific in its prudential requirements than the Banking Directive. All Member States must draw up (prudential) rules in this regard based on the limited basic common notions of the Directive (Article 10). They must, as far as capital is concerned, also adhere to the Capital Adequacy Directive.

As for the procedure for obtaining the passport, the system is similar to that for banks (Articles 17(4) and 18(2): see also section 3.2.3 above), with the same doubt about whether incidental services remain fully liberalised or are now also subject to the notification requirement.

3.2.6   ISD: Conduct of Business

Rules of conduct (subject to a list of minimum principles: Article 11) appear to remain mostly a matter for each host country: see Article 11(2). As such they are elaborations of the general good notion and, except where clearly going beyond them, must be considered limited thereby. No specific provisions exist in Article 11 as regards cold calling, more especially relevant if foreign products are on offer, but it may be caught within the general provisions on 'know your customer' or under the residual general good powers especially in the consumer area.[170] Strictly speaking, there are no provisions on suitability either. Confidentiality is also not covered and the audit trail is considered a matter of prudential supervision in Article 10 rather than a matter of investors' protection under Article 11. The question of conflicts of interest is covered both in Articles 10 and 11 in the sense that, from a prudential point of view, a firm must be structured to avoid them whilst under Article 11 conflicts must be avoided and, if impossible, clients must be fairly treated, but there is no question of postponement of the firm's interests itself.

Through Article 10, a firm is subject in this respect to home regulation but in the host country also to the conflict of interest regulation of that country under Article 11. Treatment of client assets and money is also viewed as a prudential matter, as are probably custody and settlement arrangements, where, however, under the third indent of Article 11, the host country could also claim an interest. In any event, in practice, monitoring will be an important host country concern. It may be delegated by the home regulator to the latter under Article 24 and is otherwise likely to be raised with the home regulator under Article 19(4) if the investment firm fails to take the necessary steps. These double (home and host) safeguards may give the foreign firm an advantage when its own home regulation as regards treatment of conflicts and client assets is more precise than that of the host country.

Indeed, classification under either Article 10 or Article 11 makes the difference in regulatory jurisdiction of the home or host State and there may be some doubling up here.

---

[170] In the area of cold calling, the general good notion clearly allows host country restrictions to protect investor-confidence, particularly with regard to more complicated financial products like over-the-counter commodity futures: see Case C–384/93, Alpine Investments BV v Minister van Financiën (1995) ECR I–1141. These products may not be covered by the Investment Services Dir so that their transborder sale may not be further liberalised, especially relevant when the sale is made through establishments in the host country as these remain then subject to host country authorisation and supervision, at least in respect of this activity, which may create some problems where establishments are already operating under the Investment Services Dir in a host country in respect of other products.

On Nov 16, 2000, the Commission issued a communication on the application of Conduct of Business Rules under Art. 11 of the Investment Services Directive (93/22/EEC) asking for greater convergence to make host regulation less of a barrier.

More important is, however, that both Articles are so vague that in the implementation legislation there may be great differences and that modern minimum standards of investor protection, particularly in the area of postponement of brokers' interests and segregation of client assets may still not be met. It would in civil law probably mean a more fundamental adaptation of agency notion in its obligatory and proprietary aspects.

Conduct of business rules are more important in the investment services industry than in banking and are therefore more specifically dealt with in the Investment Services Directive, and somewhat better separated from the prudential rules which are essentially home country matters. The present Articles on conduct of business came in late in the drafting process. There was not much of a harmonisation effort, but Article 11 makes clear that the new standards need not necessarily amount to the standards required to comply with fiduciary duties in a common law sense, although securities houses should try to avoid conflicts of interest besides being professional, honest and fair, knowing their customers and providing adequate disclosure of their dealings. A distinction between types of investors may be made in this regard (Article 11(3)). A further directive in the area of conduct of business is apparently still contemplated to achieve further harmonisation, which at the same time may allow more fully home country rule, at least for wholesale business.

The aspect of product supervision and control by the host country is conditioned by the general good exception without further refinement in the Directive. See for the impact of the Rome Convention on the Law Applicable to Contractual Obligations section 3.1.2 above. In the meantime it must remain doubtful whether foreign firms can be required under this general good exception to submit to membership of host state regulatory bodies like the SFA in the UK and to their registration requirements and rules in respect of direct services from abroad: see also section 3.1.3 above *in fine*.[171]

3.2.7   ISD: Residual Host Country Powers. The General Good

Thus, pending further harmonisation of the conduct of business rules and much more so than in the approach of the Second Banking Directive where it is less relevant (except for specialised banking products), host regulators may retain considerable power in the area of the conduct of business: *cf.* Article 11(3), confirmed by the further elaboration of the principle of the general good, Preambles 33 and 41 and Articles 13, 17(4), 18(2) and 19(6) and (11), which may then also go into the nature of the products sold. The host regulator must further assist the home regulator (Article 24), but may also demand the latter's co-operation (Article 19(4)), especially in areas of supervision reserved to itself (Article 19(2) and (6)). This may also mean enforcing extra (fiduciary) duties to protect small investors in host countries.

It is clear, nevertheless, that in the Investment Services Directive under UK influence more was made of the host regulator role, especially in the area of conduct of business (Article 11(2)).[172] As with banks, host regulators may also request statistical information and remain in charge of monetary policy aspects (if relevant): *cf.* Article 19. They retain in any event an enforcement and investigatory role (Article 19(6)). Powers of host countries

---

[171] In the meantime, the EU also became concerned about long distance selling to consumer investors. What concerns us here is the interface between financial regulation and supervision and the protection of long distance recipients of financial services: see more in particular s 3.4.8 below.

[172] See also M Blair, *Financial Services. The New Rules* (London, 1991), elaborating on the UK core rules and also on the IOSCO Resolution on the International Conduct of Business of Dec, 1990, reproduced in that book.

also continue in the field of unit trusts not covered by the UCITS Directive (Article 14(1)). On the other hand, the home regulator collects all basic information on transactions including prices of all products which are negotiable or standardised, whether or not traded on exchanges (transaction reporting: Article 20).

3.2.8 ISD: Regulated Markets, Concentration Principle, and Stock Exchange Membership. Price Reporting

Within the context of the deliberations on the Investment Services Directive, there arose the question of competition between the formal domestic stock exchanges and the formal or regulated exchanges (as defined in Article 1(13)) in other Member States or the (often offshore) informal markets.

The most important discussions in this connection ultimately centred on the host countries' right to request (a) local transactions in respect of (b) local securities to be exclusively carried out on their own (c) 'regulated' markets (the concentration principle as reflected in principle in Article 14(3)), as against over-the-counter (OTC) or telephone trading in or from other financial centres under their own transparency or price reporting rules (to which Article 21 did not apply). It appeared largely a rearguard action to protect domestic exchanges of the order driven type. The controversies on this subject were resolved in the sense that even habitually resident investors may opt out of such dealing (probably in advance, especially important for euro-securities and large professional trades): see Article 14(4).

Price reporting on *regular* exchanges (Article 21) is for continuous markets in any event only required at the end of each hour in weighted averages over the previous six-hour period, allowing two hours' trading before publication. Every 20 minutes, weighted averages are published and highest and lowest prices for the previous two-hour period allowing one hour's trading before publication. The delays are particularly important to protect market makers in a price-driven system against early disclosure of their positions with any resulting difficulty in unwinding them. The competent authorities may also delay or suspend publication if justified by exceptional market conditions to preserve the anonymity of a trade (for example in small markets), when there are large transactions, or when highly illiquid securities or dealings in bonds or other forms of securitised debt are involved. (Article 21(2)).

Article 20 imposes, however, a more general duty on investment firms to provide the competent authorities with transaction information on or off the regulated markets, but this reporting is then directed towards the home country authorities and only in respect of instruments more commonly dealt with on regulated markets. It is meant to prevent market manipulation and insider dealing.

All securities houses, including universal banks, are allowed under their passport to become members of or have access to domestic regular exchanges (if these have no physical presence) as at the end of 1996 (in Spain, Portugal and Greece by the end of 1999: Article 15). These markets themselves remain domestically regulated subject to mutual recognition EU-wide (Article 16). Article 15(4) is indeed interpreted in the sense that regulated markets benefit from a European passport and access, which allows screen trading in other Member States and Article 15(3) does not apply to this access. There is no rule for OTC markets, their functioning, activities, transactions, participation and price reporting. Market makers may however rely on their passports as service providers. Parties from abroad, with ambitions to bring new trading mechanisms, will not be able to use the ISD, however, but will have to rely on the general principles of 'free movement' and 'non-discrimination' as enshrined in the EC Treaty as such.

3.2.9   ISD: Member States Committee

Finally, the Investment Services Directive, according to its Preamble, aims at setting up a Committee of Representatives of Member States to assist in further progress in this area, in the same manner as the Contact Committee for banking matters under the First Banking Directive. It may become the subject of a further Directive.[173] Although the role of these committees of Member States' representatives and the EU Commission remains largely undefined, they tend to provide an important forum for the discussion of new developments and needs but are not intended to assume the role of EU-wide regulators. They may, however, advise where the Commission is given authority to implement and sometimes change the details of the regulatory regimes. See for the Lamfalussy process and the committees set up thereunder, section 3.5.2 below.

3.3   The EU Approach to Capital Adequacy

3.3.1   *The Own Funds and Solvency Directives for Banks. Differences from BIS Approach*

The BIS capital adequacy guidelines (Basel I) , which had, as we saw, no binding force of their own: see section 2.5.2 above, were generally followed by the Group of Ten countries, six of which were EU members, and are reflected in the EU capital adequacy rules for banks (the Own Funds and Solvency Directives in the meantime consolidated in the Credit Institutions Directive of 2000).[174] Should Basel II become a fact, it must be expected that it will be reflected in amendments to the relevant EU directives then in force.

The Basel I rules were directed only at banks undertaking international business and they assumed consolidation. Individual countries could exclude typical domestic banks or on the other hand adopt a more general and even more severe approach. Thus German banking supervisors always required for their universal banks some capital to cover market and position risk besides counter-party or credit risk. This approach was adopted in the EU as a consequence of the 1993 amendments to the Basle Accord and the entering into force of the Capital Adequacy Directive (CAD) for investment firms at the end of 1995: see section 3.3.2 below. This Directive applies in this aspect also to banks for their securities operations.

The EU capital adequacy rules for banks apply to all banks on EU territory without consolidation and deviate from the BIS approach also in a number of other aspects: they restrict external elements (Second Tier) capital to 50 per cent of Tier One capital; they accept on the other hand undisclosed reserves in Tier One as well as revaluation reserves, general provisions and some subordinated capital; they do not require goodwill to be deducted from qualifying capital or investments in unconsolidated subsidiaries or in other banks. There are also some minor differences in risk weightings and in credit

---

[173] A draft Proposal was presented as an amendment to the Investment Services and Capital Adequacy Directive on 17 July 1995: COM (95)360 final [1995] OJ C253.
[174] See for references n 150 above. Annex 2 to the Insolvency Directive was amended to adopt the policy of netting for capital adequacy purposes as proposed by the BIS: see s 2.5.5 above.

conversion factors. The EU notably accepts all Member States as 0 risks though no OECD countries. Repos are given a 100 per cent weighting (BIS: 50 per cent), whilst the EU, unlike the BIS, does not make reductions in weightings for foreign exchange swaps with non-banks either.

3.3.2 The Capital Adequacy Directive for Investment Services Firms. Market or Position Risk

The Capital Adequacy Directive (CAD)[175] in the meantime covers the required capital for securities firms and for the securities businesses (trading books and portfolios) of banks. It accompanied the Investment Services Directive. The approach to minimum capital requirements is here *essentially different*. The CAD adheres to the building block approach and differentiates essentially between specific risk and general risk. The specific risk is connected with issuer (therefore counterparty risk) and the general risk with market developments. Beyond an absolute minimum and a fixed overhead figure, the specific risk exposure tracks in essence the credit risk regime for banks under the Solvency Directive.

General risk exposure is dealt with through a system of haircuts, varying for example for bonds according to likely interest rate movements and for other products according to their *historical volatility*. On that basis regulation will set various haircuts for different securities depending on type and maturity. Qualifying capital is essentially the same as for the credit risk regime under the Own Funds Directive for banks.

3.3.3 General and Specific Risk. Off-balance-sheet Exposures

Capital protection for securities business may be less relevant since most securities can easily be sold (in other words, they have a high liquidity). In any event, it leads to a more relaxed regulatory approach to risk which can more easily be cut than in banking products. It has led to criticism of the capital adequacy concern of security regulators. Nevertheless the modern trend is to require minimum capital for these operations, and the CAD follows this approach in its building block attitude to capital adequacy. Thus EU regulators deal with general or market risk and specific risk in the instrument and set different standards in respect of them.

Although the specific risk contains a counterparty risk element, counterparty risk is also encountered in settlement, foreign exchange, repos or reverse-repos and swaps for which there are specific rules.

Off-balance-sheet exposures are not so easily divested, and for these exposures the risk weighting approach of the Solvency Directive is used as a matter of specific risk (requiring qualifying capital of 8 per cent of the total). For position or general risk, these derivatives are treated as long or short positions in the underlying instruments and may then be subject to set-offs, for example in swaps.

3.3.4 Settlement and Other Risk. The Treatment of Hedges. Netting

For settlement risk, under the CAD capital needs also to be set aside depending on the length of any default. There was a new counterparty risk rule covering free delivery of

---

[175] Council Dir 93/6 EEC [1993] OJ L141.

securities (that is to say where securities are delivered before payment) and repos, the latter tied to net exposures. Foreign exchange risk coverage is another new item in both the banking and trading books. Hedged positions in interest rate-related instruments like bonds could receive special treatment (depending on the time bands) as they reduce position risk (but may increase counterparty risk) and the need for position risk capital. A further issue was the consolidation of the position of subsidiaries in the process. For counterparty risk, netting of exposures between the same parties follows the 1994 BIS guidance: see section 2.5.5 above. It required amendment of the Solvency and Capital Adequacy Directives. Capital required for specific risk in respect of debt instruments and repos was already calculated on a net exposure basis under the Capital Adequacy Directive.

3.3.5   Qualifying Capital and Capital Adequacy

Qualifying capital needed subsequently to be defined in order to establish whether it was sufficient to cover the various capital requirements resulting under the above principles with the same problems as regards the status of reserves and subordinated loans and the deduction of non-qualifying assets (in this context normally premises and insufficiently secured collectibles) as in the case of banks. Here the approach of the Own Funds Directive for banks was used based on the two-tier capital layers: see section 3.3.1 above. Investments in subsidiaries and connected lending were further deductions. Under the CAD, a Third Tier of capital could be added, however, to cover current profits in trading books (marked to market) if not already included in the other Tiers.

3.3.6   The EU Approach to the Level Playing Field between Banks and Securities Houses

Another objective of the CAD was to create, in as far as possible, a level playing field between banks with securities operations (universal banks) and pure securities houses, at least in the capital adequacy field. This explains the sharp distinction between the *banking* and *investment securities* portfolios (or trading books which need to be identified) of both (except if there are *de minimis* trading books in banks or they concern treasury operations of banks which may thus receive banking treatment at a bank's discretion[176]) and the borrowing from the various Banking Directives in the areas of the funds definition, the large exposure regime (allowing them however to exceed the limits in respect of securities holdings for which extra capital will then be required) and the risk asset ratios (for specific risk and OTC derivatives).

On the other hand, the regime of the various Banking Directives themselves adopts the Capital Adequacy Directive's approach to position and settlement risk for non-banking instruments. It is important to realise that the position risk approach of the CAD is not applied to mismatches (gapping) in the banking book which remain free from capital requirements (although in the nature of position risk) as it is considered the essence of the

---

[176] Bonds included in the banking asset must in principle be held until maturity and a bank cannot easily shift between the banking and investment books but there is traditionally a certain flexibility to redesignate banking assets and take profits on them. The traditional reason was to make the holding of government bonds more attractive by allowing the liquidity facility inherent in them to operate. To hold them as banking assets until profit taking becomes attractive or an early sale desirable for other reasons avoids normal position risk capital for these positions. To shift backwards and forwards is not an option, however.

banking business. Because of the functional approach of the Investment Services Directive, this level playing field is also extended to other areas like the conduct of business rules for the securities businesses of banks, which remained non-specific under the Second Banking Directive. Before the introduction of the Financial Services Directive but after the coming into effect of the Second Banking Directive there was a vacuum in this aspect. Domestic regulation, as in the UK, equalised treatment, although in respect of other EU banks, there was a question how far this was possible and compatible with the approach of the Second Banking Directive.

3.4   Other EU Regulatory Initiatives in the Financial Area

3.4.1   *Large Exposures*

Other EU initiatives in the area of supervised financial services concern primarily the large exposure regime for banks, in which connection there was a 1986 Recommendation (see section 2.3.2 above), of which the conversion into a Directive was accomplished in 1992, effective on 1 January 1994.[177] The Directive provides for certain transitory flexibility until 2001 (Article 6). The 15 per cent notification and 40 per cent prohibition rule of the Recommendation are reduced to respectively 10 and 25 per cent, whilst the allowed total of all large exposures together remains unchanged at 800 per cent. In the Capital Adequacy Directive for securities business there is also a large exposure regime for securities activities as a matter of counterparty risk, in the same manner as foreseen in the Large Exposure Directive, any excesses of the limits in respect of securities activities requiring extra capital. Neither the Large Exposure Directive nor the Capital Adequacy Directive covers as yet large concentrations in (similar) positions notwithstanding the greater difficulty in unwinding these (liquidity risk).

3.4.2   *Deposit Protection and Investor Compensation*

The EU also agreed a Deposit Protection Directive[178] guaranteeing a minimum of protection for depositors EU-wide effective on 1 July 1995 and follows the 1987 Recommendation in this area. It is based on home country schemes, but bank branches elsewhere in the EU may participate in host country schemes to top up the home protection. Until 1999, they could not, however, exceed host country protection. For investors in securities there is envisaged a parallel Investors Compensation Directive,[179] aiming at similar protection for small investors.

---

[177] Council Dir 92/121 EEC [1993] OJ L29.

[178] Council Dir 94/19 EEC [1994] OJ L135; see for the earlier Recommendation s 2.3.2 above. Germany unsuccessfully attacked the new Directive before the ECJ on the ground that the host country limitations on the protection (until 31 Dec 1999) prevented free competition, Germany having the highest level of protection and being willing to extend it to all German bank customers EU-wide, although it objected at the same time to foreign EU institutions having automatic access to membership of the German scheme without necessarily adhering to the strict German preconditions. See on deposit guarantees also D Schoenmaker, 'A Note on the Proposal for a Council Directive on Deposit Guarantee Schemes', Special Paper No 48, *LSE Financial Markets Group*, Aug 1992 and RS Dale, 'Deposit Insurance: Policy Clash over EC and US Reforms', Special Paper No 53, *LSE Financial Markets Group* 1993.

[179] COM (93)381 final [1993] OJ C321 followed by COM (94)585 final [1995] OJ C382 and by Common Position (EC) 26/95 of the Council of 23 Oct 1995 [1995] OJ C320.

3.4.3 Winding-up of Credit Institutions

As regards insolvencies, the Winding-up of Credit Institutions Directive, already proposed in the early 1980s, was revived in 1993.[180] It relies for jurisdiction and applicable law in essence on the home country of the entity, leading to a system of unity and universality, the practical consequences of which remain, however, still a subject of study.

3.4.4 Pension Funds

In the pension area, there was a proposal of 1991 for a directive on the freedom of management and investment of funds.[181] It allowed authorised managers from other Member States to manage funds, guaranteeing in this manner a free choice of professional advice and expertise, and accepted in principle investment freedom subject to a number of general principles concerning liquidity. Member States could no longer request more than 80 per cent matched funding and could also no longer insist on investment in particular assets or localise it in particular Member States. The proposal did not, however, cover cross-border pension fund membership, as earlier there had been much concern about the taxation of pensions earned on the basis of tax relief but paid to beneficiaries who had left the country.[182] Mutual recognition of supervisory systems was therefore less relevant and harmonisation of prudential rules was mainly of interest in the context of any exchange of information. In the meantime, this project ran into considerable difficulty, on the one hand because the 80 per cent limit was thought against the Maastricht provisions (Article 56, ex Article 73(b) and (d) EEC Treaty as amended), whilst other countries wanted greater powers to localise the investments of their own funds. It was as a consequence withdrawn by the Commission which then issued a Communication on the Freedom of Management and Investment of Funds held by Institutions for Retirement Provision.[183]

The Commission especially insisted on proper diversification facilities, also in terms of currency (considering as a first step 60 per cent of matched funding the maximum), and on free access to foreign advice and management expertise to improve income and reduce risk (including also a restriction on investment in connected enterprises). The Commission expressly did not wish to affect the manner of pension funding (or absence thereof), the level of benefit, or the combination of pension protection through private pension, insurance or State schemes, and also excluded cross-border membership from its consideration for the time being (so that there was no question of a pension fund passport at this stage with mutual recognition of regulatory regimes, which created a basic difference from the Life Insurance Directives). Nevertheless the Commission meant to clarify the restrictions that in its view could be imposed on prudential grounds or for reasons of the general good, if only to assist Member States in the interpretation of the EEC Treaty in this area and to provide some uniformity to help service providers when asked to provide information to regulators from other EU countries.

The substitution of the original proposals by a Commission Communication ran into some considerable trouble, however, and the legality of this approach was successfully attacked by France before the ECJ, because it was found to be more than a clarifying document.[184]

---

[180] COM (88)4 final [1988] OJ C36.
[181] COM (91)301 final [1991] OJ C312, amended by COM (93)237 [1993] OJ C171.
[182] GS Zavvos, 'Pension Fund Liberalisation and the Future Retirement Financing in Europe' (1994) 31 *Common Market Law Review*, 609.
[183] [1994] OJ C360.
[184] *France v Commission* [1997] ECR I–1627.

However, a Directive was agreed in May 2003 and covers the operation of employment related pension schemes across-borders in the EU. There is mutual recognition of home state supervision. Investments must meet the standard of a 'prudent person' so that the proper investment policy can be followed for members per country. It must be implemented by 2005.

3.4.5 Consolidated Banking Supervision. Basle Concordat and EU Implementation

Another issue is the consolidation of banking supervision, which, after the 1992 amendment and so-called 1983 revised Basle Concordat of the BIS (pursuant to the original paper of 1975 after the *Herstatt* case) is now the accepted principle worldwide: see also section 1.1.12 above.

The EU followed the original approach of consolidated supervision at the head-office of a bank (home regulator) in its 1983 Directive: see section 2.3.2 above, whilst a second Directive in this area has now been enacted, effective on 1 January 1993,[185] repealing the earlier one and covering also banks' non-banking parents (if holding at least one credit institution as a subsidiary, a concept to be extended to holding one investment services firm as at 1 January 1996: see Article 14) and all its financial subsidiaries in the consolidation (Article 6). They must provide the information requested by the supervisory authorities of the financial entity in the group.

In the meantime, in a 1992 paper (Minimum Standards for the Supervision of International Banking Groups and their Cross-border Establishments), the BIS further elaborated on its approach to consolidated supervision as a consequence of the BCCI affair, applying its rules to the ultimate parent of a banking group but setting out the host country's right and duty to make sure that the home regulator is capable of consolidated supervision, particularly where the group structure is insufficiently transparent. It proposed that the setting up of cross-border banking activities (or branches) needs the approval of both home and host country regulators, whilst host countries may take the necessary action if they do not remain satisfied with the supervisory role of the home regulator.

It may be seen to override to some extent the home regulator principle of the EU directives, which, however, already accepted (in the Preamble to the Second Banking Directive and in the text of the Investment Services Directive) the desirability of combining the registered and head offices within the same jurisdiction so as better to focus supervision and avoid confusion. It is also likely that the EU in the future will ease its strict rules on the passing of confidential information between regulators in this context, whilst insisting on sufficient transparency of the transactions of the group as a whole. In fact, in the summer of 1993 the Commission agreed in principle a new directive on reinforcing prudential supervision along these lines.

In this connection there is the related subject of conglomerate supervision, when a group has activities which are regulated by several different authorities, like banking, securities and insurance operations. Especially in the area of regulated capital supervision, it may be efficient in that case to have a so-called lead regulator, in order to prevent too much capital being tied up separately in different activities. The quality of connected lending may then also be more properly assessed, whilst the lead regulator will supervise the necessary movement of capital within the group and particularly the so-called double gearing

---

[185] Council Dir 92/30 EEC [1992] OJ L110.

(or funding mismatch) under which the parent borrows in the capital markets funds which could not qualify as capital but invests them as equity in its financial subsidiaries which so qualify. Default of the parent in these circumstances would, however, endanger the subsidiaries. A preliminary aspect remains, however, the capital allocation to the different businesses.

It raises more in particular the question whether the same capital may be used twice for very different risks, an issue in fact already arising between banking and securities activities, and under what circumstances. On a daily basis, the simplest approach may be first to calculate the capital needed for securities and insurance activities, deduct this from total capital, and subsequently ascertain whether the remaining capital is sufficient for the banking activities. The situation may become more complicated when the bank is in one country, the insurance or securities company in others or when risks are parked in offshore havens. The lead regulator is then fully dependent on effective information co-ordination which will become the essence of his task.

3.4.6   Lead-regulator Concept. International Co-operation

No lead-regulator concept has emerged as yet in areas other than capital (like supervision of internal operations and the conduct of business of different activities within one group or company).[186] Co-operation between the pertinent regulators will be needed also from this perspective and will primarily depend on an active exchange of information. This is naturally more complicated across borders. International co-operation is itself, however, increasingly achieved through bilateral *ad hoc* arrangements, often by means of so-called Memoranda of Understanding (MOUs) between regulators, not only in the monitoring of capital but also in enforcement. In the banking area this is supported by the BIS.

3.4.7   The E-commerce Directive

In the EU, the 2000 E-commerce Directive[187] deals with information society services generally. Implicitly it also covers security trading on the internet although it is clearly not its main focus, which was to give legitimacy to any type of contract concluded by electronic means (Recital 38). In this connection e-commerce and internet trading are synonymous. Under Article 3, the supervision of the country of origin of the accessed service provider applies to these services. There is an exception only if consumer protection which also includes investors (presumably only the smaller inexperienced ones) is the issue (see Article 3 (4) (a) (iii)) and there is a great risk of impairment, but any host regulator measures (here the regulator of the small investor) must remain proportionate after the regulator of the service provider has been asked to take adequate measures but fails to take them. The EU Commission must be informed and will examine the compatibility of the measures with Community law (which in the case they are not will have to be abandoned).[188]

---

[186] See also CC Lichtenstein, 'International Standards for Consolidated Supervision of Financial Conglomerates: Controlling Systemic Risk' (1993) 19 *Brooklyn Journal of International Law*, 137.
[187] Directive on Certain Legal Aspects of Electronic Commerce in the Internal Market, 2000/31/EC, [2000] OJ L 178, adopted on June 8 2000 to be transported into national laws not later than Jan 17, 2002.
[188] In the insurance area, the service provider's regime will, however, not impact on the regime concerning consumer contracts in particular the limitations on the freedom of parties to choose the applicable law, see the Annex.

It is in fact an indirect expression of the general good notion, which for financial services through e-commerce now falls outside the home/host regulatory system of the ISD. This follows from the location of the service at the place of the service provider which therefore assumes no movement of this service and opts for the regulation of the service provider. A similar result would have been obtained if, whilst accepting the movement of the service, the regulation of the party providing the most characteristic performance would have prevailed.

It conforms to the EU's apprehension for double regulation and suspicion of host country intervention. Yet Article 4 is also an acknowledgement of the fact that the general good notion cannot be entirely suppressed in view of the European Court's case law. Also, whilst cast in terms of consumer protection, there is the general policy of the EC Treaty since the 1992 Maastricht amendments which sees this protection as a major EC objective (Articles 3(t) and 153(3)(b)), a policy never extended as such to (small) investors, however, which are therefore especially mentioned in this Directive and are thus given a similar protection (in language reminiscent of the general good including the reference to proportionality).

Nevertheless, the approach is fundamentally different from that of Article 11 ISD and favours a unitary regulatory regime and chooses in essence that of the service provider. Notification by the service provider to his home regulator, followed by the latter's contact with the host regulator, is here not necessary for this service to be provided. There is no EU passport either, which means that EU branches of non-EU service providers may also be accessed from other EU countries. In this system, the regulator of the customer may remain only relevant in respect of active marketing of the service provider into retail in other member States, in which area a further e-commerce Directive is contemplated.[189]

3.4.8 Long-distance Selling of Financial Products to Consumers

The emphasis is again different in the 1998 EU proposal for long-distance selling of consumer products.[190] It is meant to extend the basic protection of the relevant consumer directive of 1997 also to financial services, but there is also the desire to use modern communication methods in a manner that will further promote the internal market. Consumers are defined in the traditional way as persons acting outside their trade, business or profession. There is no consideration of expertise, as is more normal, at least in respect of the regulatory aspects of investment transactions. The proposal concern itself with the method of selling (particularly through modern electronic equipment like the Internet, telephone, fax or mail) only and *not* with the type of financial service or the financial product involved. They are limited to the opening of the relationship and do not cover follow-up transactions.

The basic protection for consumers is here the right of reflection (upon the supplier's offer) and withdrawal (if the contract was concluded instantaneously at the consumer's request or unfairly induced by the supplier), although other aspects are the confirmation

---

[189] In fact two further measures are being contemplated: one on marketing of financial services online, see Working Document 6 Oct. 2000 and one on liability of service providers. Earlier IOSCO had formulated Principles of Regulation in Securities Activities on the Internet, Report by the Technical Committee (Sept 1998).

[190] The proposal dates from Oct. 1998: see the proposal for a Directive of the European Parliament and of the Council concerning the distance marketing of consumer financial services (COM (1998)468 final), amending Council Dir 90/619/EEC and Dirs 97/7/EC and 98/27/EC: see also the Green Paper: Financial Services — Meeting Consumers' Expectations: COM (96)209 final of 22 May, 1996, and the Commission communication: Financial Services — Enhancing Consumer Confidence: COM (97)309 final of 26 June, 1997.

of the contract terms in writing (or through a durable accessible medium), the impossibility of construing silence as consent, and the outlawing of cold calling (unsolicited communications), although follow-up transactions may be suggested by the supplier. Another concern is a proper complaints and redress procedure.

The idea is that the opening of bank accounts, loan agreements, brokerage relationships and the entering into of insurance contracts are all subject to a possibility of reflection or withdrawal during a certain period. Many of these, like bank and brokerage accounts, may in any event be abandoned at will. Follow-up action is in any event not so protected, therefore the subsequent movement in current accounts or use of credit cards is excluded, as are follow-up transactions in investment services themselves which are in any event *not* covered because of their market-related speculative nature. Customers may have to pay for temporary coverage, for example under an insurance contract which is later rejected. Contracts must be in writing but may, like insurance contracts, be concluded without documentation but subject to written confirmation, important to obtain instant protection. The burden of proof in respect of the supplier's obligations to inform the consumer, obtain his consent and performance is put on the consumer.

The provisions of the Directive are mandatory and cannot be set aside by choosing the law of a third country if the consumer is a resident of a Member State and the contract has a close connection with the EU. The relationship between this Directive and the others existing in connection with the European passport for financial services and aiming at harmonisation, for investment services particularly of the conduct of business in Article 11 of the ISD, is not considered. These are not affected although they may overlap, particularly in the area of unfair inducement and cold calling.

3.5. The Financial Services Action Plan of 1998

3.5.1 The 1998 Action Plan and its Objectives. Initial Lack of a Road Map for Key Issues

A single European market for financial services is not a new idea but was always implicit in the free movement of services. Through the Second Banking Directive and the Investment Services Directive decisive progress was made pursuant to the Single European Act of 1988. Yet more needed to be done and in 1998, the European Council at Cardiff requested the EU Commission to present a framework for action to develop the Single European Market for Financial Services further in the light of the emergence of the Euro and the considerable benefits which further integration in this area was believed to bring.

Consequently, the Commission published a Financial Services Action Plan in 1999, to be implemented by 2005, and saw its task (at first) mainly in the filling in of gaps in the EU measures presented until then and started to present lists of pending Directives or Directives that needed updating. It was clear from the beginning, however, that the Commission could not produce a coherent view of what was needed whilst the European Council had left it without any (political) road map. It had notably omitted to give guidance in important areas like to what extend whole sale services needed regulation, how the international bond market (or euro-market) was to be treated, and what to do about consolidated regulation of trans-border financial activities. Also the important issue of whether or not the EU should move in the direction of a single regulatory regime and a single regulator was not discussed. The unavoidable friction between the key EU freedoms of movement of services and capital and national regulation and the question in how far domestic regulation was still allowed to impede these free flows especially in wholesale or professional dealings were also not revisited. The framework of the Second Banking Directive and the Investment Services Directive with their emphasis on the mutual recognition of home regulation was apparently believed to have been adequate.

The view presented in this book is that in the area of regulation for wholesale business, *de-regulation* needs to proceed any form of (re-)regulation at EU level or through EU harmonization at Member State level. That means that financial regulation in this area must in each case be demonstrated to be justified in the interest of participants or be dictated by systemic risk concerns. This leaves at the same time maximum room for innovation and efficiency considerations (and low cost) and for the freedom of movement of capital and services (including the right of establishment).[191] Thus regulation of underwriting, market-making, clearing and settlement might well prove unhelpful and largely unnecessary. In the EU, often led by countries like France and Germany that have a strong regulation culture, this culture was always likely to spill over at the EU level. Regulation then becomes a purpose in itself. The Action Plan and its implementation have not avoided these pitfalls. There was never much sensitivity to the proper place of financial regulation and its true objectives were never fundamentally re-evaluated. There was no concept of the role of market forces in the area of regulation either. There has never been a proper cost and benefits analysis. The end result is a lack of a coherent view and proper perspective translated in an overly prescriptive regime.[192] This being said, the market may not have allowed itself to be timely and sufficiently alerted to provide a proper forum for consultation. In legal matters it often acts after the fact and then uses financial structuring or moves to more congenial places to get around burdensome or unacceptable impediments.

Indeed, much more important than regulation at every level[193] may be the access given to issuers and investors to all exchanges, formal and informal, and to clearing and settlement institutions subject to the own standards of these institutions in a competitive environment. It may easily improve standards all around as business will go to the institutions that offer better service, lower cost, greater reliability and transparency, and greater liquidity. At least in wholesale, it is in principle for the markets themselves to sort these matters out in a competitive environment. Here the International Debt Markets or euromarkets as the largest capital market in the world that remains largely unregulated offer the key example. It would mean that the proper area for regulation would be largely limited to retail or small investor protection and to market integrity issues and perhaps to better standards and supervision of the issuing activity (although this also could be left to competition

---

[191] See also RS Krozner, 'Can the Financial Markets Privately Regulate Risk? The development of Derivative Clearing Houses and Recent Over-the-Counter Innovations', (Nov. 1999) *Journal of Money, Credit and Banking*; Jonas Niemeyer, 'An Economic Analysis of Securities Market Regulation and Supervision: Where to go after the Lamfalussy Report?' *SSE/EFI Working Paper Series in Economics and Finance*, No 482, Dec 14, 2001; Donald C Langevoort, 'Taming the Animal Spirits of the Stock Markets: A Behavioral Approach to Securities Regulation', *Law and Economics Seminar*, Boalt Hall, UC Berkeley, April 15, 2002; James D Fox, 'The Death of the Securities Regulator', *Globalisation, Law and Economics Seminar*, Boalt Hall, UC Berkeley, April 1, 2002; JH Dalhuisen, 'Towards a Single European Capital Market and a Workable System of Regulation' in M Andenas and Y Avgerinos (eds), *Financial Markets in Europe, Towards a Single Regulator?* (2003) at 35.
[192] This is also the view' of market experts, see e.g. the Wicks Report of November 2003.
[193] Another approach may be that of regulatory competition in which participants (for example issuers) may choose the regulatory regime they prefer. There is an increasing literature on this subject, see HE Jackson and EJ Pan, above n 45, 653. This research points to free markets and competition leading to higher voluntary disclosure (and even increased cost) with the prospect of greater proceeds. See further the literature cited at n 45 above: Romano, 'Empowering Investors: A Market Approach to Securities Regulation'; S Choi and A Guzman, 'Portable Reciprocity: Rethinking the International Reach of Securities Regulation'; F Easterbrook and O Fischel 'Mandatory Disclosure and the Protection of Investors'; John C Coffee, 'Market Failure and the Economic Case for a Mandatory Disclosure System'; and Stigler, 'Public Regulation of the Securities Markets'.

which would give the issuer with the best disclosure probably the greatest benefit in terms of pricing of new issues).

One key would be access of issuers to all formal and informal exchanges and other markets in the EU. This would suggest a separation of prospectus and regular reporting requirements from admission and listing on *regular* exchanges. It may also suggest a separate supervision of the issuing activity in order to make a passport into all markets possible. That would lift this issue out of the competition between markets which would all have to accept the disclosure that took place separately under common rules. It means the abandonment of a competitive element between markets but might be a price worth paying and became the preferred approach in the new Prospectus Directive as we shall see.

In this connection, there was some confusion from the beginning on whether the prime objective of the Action Plan was the creation of a single liquid capital market (following the emergence of the Euro after 1999). It would immediately have posed the question of its relation to the eurobond market and would also have raised the position of domestic stock exchanges or whether the objective was more limited to a Single Market for Financial Services. In the event, the latter became the main focus, but capital market issues were never far below the surface and the issue of regular and OTC markets came to a head in the discussions concerning the redrafting of the Prospectus Directive, see section 3.5.3 below.

In fact, the main objectives identified in the original Action Plan were (a) to create a single wholesale market to enable corporate issues to raise finance on competitive terms on an EU basis and provide investors and intermediaries with access to all markets from a single point of entry, (b) to allow investment service providers to offer their services across border without encountering unnecessary barriers, (c) to achieve an open and secure retail market with information and safeguards to participate in a single financial market, and (d) to formulate state-of-the-art prudential rules and supervision. Eventually it led to an issuing or recasting of 42 EU Directives, although not all were intimately related to financial markets operations, like the Insolvency Directives for banks and insurance companies, the EU Company Statute (introduced by Regulation in October 2001), the Fair Value Accounting Directive of 2001 (concerning valuations other than at purchase price or cost), the Regulation of July 2002 on International Accounting Standards for all listed companies (after 2005), the Accounting Modernisation Directive of 2003 amending the Fourth and Seventh Company Directive (after 2005), proposals for a Tenth and Fourteenth Company Law Directive, the Settlement Finality Directive, and the Collateral Directive (on the cross-border use of collateral).

The Commission flagged two other issues from the start. It did not envisage a single regulatory system but wanted a procedure that would speed up the amendment and implementation of community law in this area into national law. To obtain more of a road map, the EU's Economic and Finance Ministers in Ecofin appointed in 2000 a Committee of Wise Men under the Chairmanship of Mr Lamfalussy which was to focus also on these two issues. It presented its Report in February 2002 (also called the Lamfallusy Report), confirmed the preference for financial regulation at the member State level and suggested a procedure to speed up EU legislation and its incorporation in what came to be called the Lamfalussy Process, which is an example of so-called EU *comitology*. It felt that only if this Process would not adequately function would the idea of a single regulatory framework have to be revisited.

The view presented in this book is that even though a single EU regulatory regime and a single regulator may well be conceivable for commercial banks where the emphasis has always been more on authorisation and prudential supervision, it is likely to create a bureaucratic nightmare that may not work well. It is in any event not feasible for the investment business where the regulatory emphasis is on conduct of business and product supervision. This requires a regulatory presence in all financial centers with rules geared to their markets. Especally in this area the regulator should not be remote from participants. Also complaint procedures for retail should always be available in their own country and language at least to the extent they deal with or through local institutions or intermediaries in domestic markets. These matters cannot be centralised at EU level either.

3.5.2 Lamfalussy Report and the Role of Comitology

The procedure or Process proposed by the Lamfalussy Report to speed up the amendment and implementation of EU legislation in Member States envisages four levels.

In *Level 1* (framework level), primary Community legislation is envisaged based on *framework principles*. It could concern here Directives or Regulations the latter having the advantage of being directly applicable in Member States and achieving speed and uniformity. This is important and the Lamfalussy Report encouraged their use. However, the EU is not entirely free in the choice between Directive and Regulations as it must respect domestic cultures and allow for variations in implementation where dictated by the local legal environment. That is the reason why Directives are often more opportune. Both are adopted through the 'co-decision' procedure between the Council and the European Parliament. The European Securities Committee (ESC) which consists of permanent representatives of Member States fulfills here only an advisory function. It can at this level not exercise any authority and does *not* operate here as a *regulatory committee*.[194]

In *Level 2* (implementation level), the Commission adopts Community legislation concerning the technical details of the framework principles. Here the European Securities Committee (ESC) may be given regulatory powers within new Directives and then operates as a proper regulatory committee[195] but only in *assisting* the Commission in its implementation powers pursuant to Article 202 and Article 211 of the EC Treaty. It takes a vote with a qualified majority where upon the measures will be sent to the European Parliament for approval. At this Level, technical advice will also be given by the

---

[194] This Committee as well as the Committee of European Securities Regulators (CESR) was set up by Decisions of 6 June 2001, 2001/527/EC and 2001/528/EC, OJ L 191, 43 (2001). The CESR is the successor to FESCO.

The European Central Bank may become involved under Art 105(4) of the EC Treaty since it needs to be consulted 'on any proposed Community Act in its field of competence'. Under Council Decision 98/415/EC, OJ L 189/42 (1998) this role is interpreted to include all measures materially influencing the stability of financial institutions and markets. This Decision applies also to national legislation in the field in EMU countries and to Member-states with a derogation under Art 122(3) EC Treaty but not to the UK (Art 5 UK Protocol). Thus the ECB was consulted on the latest UCITS proposals, see OJ L 285/9 (1999). Under Art 105(4) the ECB may also give opinions in the field of its competence. Under Art 105(6) it may even be given special tasks in this connection. There is therefore some basis in the treaty for a supervisory role of the ECB in banking or even more generally where the stability of financial institutions and markets is concerned, see also M Andenas, 'Banking Supervision, the Internal Market and European Economic and Monetary Union', in M Andenas et al (eds), *European Economic and Monetary Union: The Institutional Framework* (1997) at 402. It would seem to be geared, however, to prudential supervision and the operation of the financial system as a whole rather than individual investors' protection and therefore plays a role largely in the area of systemic risk.

There is no equivalent for securities regulators or for an EU committee operating in their stead. The unstable relationship between domestic financial regulators who remain basically in charge and the EU institutions, particularly in the area of investment services had earlier been noted by W Bratton, S Picciotto and J McCahery (eds), *International Regulatory Competition and Coordination* (1996) at 38. If the thesis of this contribution that liberalisation in this area is to precede re-regulation at EU level at least for professional dealings and that retail protection is better exercised at local levels is correct, this state of affairs cannot be considered immediately disturbing or in need of reform. It means, however, that there is little room at present for any real powers for the ESC.

[195] Under the 28 June 1999 Decision on Comitology, Decision 1999/468/EC, OJ L 184/23 (1999).

Committee of European Securities Regulators (CESR) which represents the Regulators of the Member States and which may be further mandated by the ESC. The great danger with the CESR is that it may retain a purely domestic perspective and act as a pressure group of domestic regulators whilst favouring also the position of domestic exchanges at the detriment of the international OTC markets or more rational market evolutions.

In *Level 3*, the implementation or transposition process in Member States is considered in which connection the CESR plays a role in obtaining consistency. It may issue guidelines or common, non-binding, standards. It will also compare and review national regulatory practices.

In *Level 4*, the Commission resumes its normal responsibility for enforcing EU legislation (under Articles 206, 211 and 226 EC Treaty),[196] checking compliance by Member States, and where necessary initiating compliance action before the European Court of Justice.

At both Levels 2 and 3, three other committees function: for commercial banking, for investment business including UCITS, and for insurance including pensions. A fourth committee operates at Level 2 for financial conglomerates.[197] Ecofin has set up a Financial Services Committee of its own (FSC). The whole set-up will be reviewed in 2004.[198] The Prospectus and Market Abuse Directives were the first ones under the new system, now followed by the Transparency Directive and the revision of the Investment Services Directive (ISD).

3.5.3   Implementing Legislation: The New Prospectus Directive. The Issuer's Passport

This Directive[199] is first meant to replace and combine a number of earlier Directives which were discussed in section 2.3.4 being the Admission, Listing Particular, the Mutual Recognition (since 2001 consolidated in the Consolidated Admission and Reporting Directive or CARD) and the Public Offer Directives. The text was adopted in July 2003 and the objective was to provide a single passport for issuers who met the prospectus requirements in one country. The consequence is that the securities may then be placed and sold in any market in the EU. Implementation is expected by 2005.

The new Prospectus Directive became one of the major new measures in the whole Action Plan. It means to create common and enhanced standards for the issuance of securities throughout the EU. It is based on the notion of mutual recognition of prospectuses which acquires here a central importance leading to the issuer's passport. It means that admission to trading is separated from admission and listing and made subject to common rules. In the process, it eliminates an important competitive tool amongst regular and informal markets, limits regulatory competition and the improvement of standards that may flow from it. This point was already raised in section 3.5.1 above.

The key provision is that a prospectus must be published (a) when an offer for securities is made to the public or (b) where they are admitted to a *regulated* market (Article 3).[200]

---

[196] It this connection it was stated at the Stockholm European Council in 2001, which considered the Lamfalussy Report, that the Commission in its enforcement powers in the financial area should not go against 'predominant views' which might emerge in the Council and which as such could derive from national considerations.

[197] See the literature cited above at n 191.

[198] See also Yanis Avgerinos, 'Essential and Non-essential Measures: Delegation of Powers in EU Securities Regulation', (2002) 8 *European Law Journal*, 269.

[199] Directive 2003/71/EEC of the European Parliament and of the Council of Nov. 4, 2003, [2003] OJ 2345/64.

[200] The concept of regulated markets will be redefined in the amendments to the Investment Services Directive (ISD) and removed from CARD, see for CARD section 2.3.4 *in fine*. It is not the same as admission to listing.

The offer to the public is now defined and is any communication presenting sufficient information on the terms of the offer and the securities offered to enable investors to purchase or to subscribe to securities (Article 2(1)(d)). This concept is meant not to constrain unduly the distribution of promotional materials before an offer in these terms which must take the form of a prospectus.

A prospectus in the required form will not be necessary (unless admission on regulated markets is also sought) if the offer is made (a) to qualified investors, or (b) by way of private placement or (c) in denominations of at least Euro 50,000 (Article 3(2)). One may expect that the exemptions will lead to new structures devised around them. The present exemptions for conversion offers, takeovers, and mergers, bonus issuers and employee offers are maintained (Articles 4 (1) and (2)).

The prospectus must contain all information necessary to enable investors to make an informed assessment of the assets and liabilities, financial position, profits and losses and financial prospects of the issuer and of any guarantor. It must also give the necessary information on the rights attached to the securities (Article 5(1)). Much of the details are left to implementation (and CESR guidance). There is no difference between whole sale and retail requirements (except for the exemptions) and not much room for new products that might require a different treatment altogether. Article 7(2)(e) allows some flexibility only in respect of small and medium seized issuers. There must also be a *Summary* (Article 5(2)), considered especially important for retail. This raises the important issue of prospectus liability for inaccurate, inconsistent or incomplete information. Article 5(2)(d) deals with this issue and imposes liability only when these defects appear when the summary is read together with the text of the prospectus itself. Problems may increase when the full prospectus is in another language.

The prospectus may be in three parts (tripartite) consisting of a registration document, a securities note and the Summary (Article 5(3)). It remains valid for 12 months and achieves in this manner the facility of a *shelf registration*. A Supplement is necessary whenever significant new factors arise or a material inaccuracy is noticed between the approval of the prospectus and the closing of the issue (Article 16(1)). A Base prospectus may be presented in respect of MTN programs (Art. 5(4)) In order to avoid time constraints, further terms may be filled out later without approval unless they are inconsistent and form a Supplement (Art. 16(1). Current market practices may bring here also enlightenment.

Approval is through the relevant competent authority of the 'home' Member State (Art. 13(1)). The time limit is 10 days unless the relevant competent authority requires more information. The 'home' Member State is here the Member State where the issuer has its registered office (Art. 2(1)(m)), *except* for non-equity securities with denominations of more than Euro 1,000). A choice is then allowed; it was done to alleviate the problems when the primary listing is in another country. For non-EU issuers of equities or other securities with a denomination below Euro 1,000, the competent authority will be of the member State in which the security is first offered or asked to be admitted to trading. Upon approval the prospectus must be published a reasonable time in advance of the offer (Art. 14(1)). Host competent authorities will have to accept the validity of approved prospectuses for public offers or admission in their state upon simple notification of the approval (Art. 17(1)). In that case, the language must be that acceptable to the host state or any 'customary in the sphere of international finance'. In that case the host country may require the Summary to be translated in its own language (Art. 19(2) and (3)).

Unlike many other Directives in the past, the Prospectus Directives set complete rather than minimum terms which could be exceeded by Member States. A truly uniform regime is foreseen which would perhaps have justified a Regulation, although national competent authorities retain some flexibility in that they may require issuers to include additional information and may also elaborate on listing requirements which are not properly dealt with in the Directive, but the former probably only on an *ad hoc* basis (Art 21(3)(a)).

It will be of interest to see how the euromarkets and especially the international bond market will react. Under the earlier Public Offer Prospectus Directive it was exempt. The key is whether the flexibility and the exemptions the new Directive provides will be sufficient for this market to largely continue to operate within the EU, especially from London. It is likely that it will restructure around the exemptions and other facilities the new Directive present for wholesale market dealings. For large equity placements it may have to go largely offshore. Here one sees the protection by the Directive (supported by CESR) of formal exchanges and similar domestic backwaters. Internationalisation and globalisation appear to come here to an end, even for professional dealings.

3.5.4   Implementing Legislation: The Transparency Directive

This Directive[201] first proposed in March 2003 covers the ground of the earlier Regular Financial Reporting Directive (of Listed Companies) of 1982, see section 2.3.4, and aims at imposing a continuing obligation on all issuers to disclose financial information and new developments. Liability of (outside) directors, lawyers and auditors to the general public throughout the EU for errors in published financial information is here another important issue.

3.5.5   Implementing Legislation: The Amendments to the ISD and Capital
Adequacy Directives

This revision was first proposed in November 2002 and in particular considers new trading environments which go beyond the traditional regulated exchanges.[202] The ideal is that the established exchanges will be exposed to greater competition of each other and of the informal markets. The opposing force is the one of the traditional monopolies in the domestic exchanges. At least brokers may wish to be able to match trades away from exchanges and investment banks may add their market-making facilities. In the US, the rise of electronic communication networks has added to the variety. It has been estimated that in the informal markets, market-makers on Nasdaq now have only 20 per cent of the share dealings in the US. On the other hand, it is estimated that in Europe 70 per cent of share dealings still goes through the official markets. Through mergers they have enforced their market power and may flex their muscle in setting fees for issuers and investors alike.

The battle is fought in the area of the concentration principle, see section 3.2.8 above, and in price disclosure for off-exchange transactions where investment banks are asked to provide greater transparency in trade matching. As between official exchanges, competition is likely to come from fee structures and access to clearing and settlement systems. Any shortfall in competition will have to lead to more supervision by competition authorities.

---

[201] See, for the final unofficial version, Council of the European Union, 22 April 2004, Interinstitutional File: 2003/0045 (COD). See also website www.europa.eu.int.
[202] Directive 2004/39/EC of the European Parliament and of the Council of 21 April 2004 on Markets in Financial Instruments [2004] OJ 2/45/1.

The capital adequacy regimes for banks and investment firms will be amended if and when Basel II is finally agreed.

3.5.6   Implementing Legislation: The Take-over Bids Directive

This Directive[203] was first proposed in Oct. 2002 and replaces an earlier proposal which was rejected by the European Parliament under German pressure. The idea is that a minimum common framework is achieved for the national approval of take-overs including the applicable law, the protection of shareholders and disclosure. A compromise was reached in Nov. 2003 after the EU Commission had wanted to forbid all take over defenses without shareholders backing. The prevailing view remained, however, that it would expose European companies to predatory American practices through contested take-overs. The compromise allows Member States the ultimate say in banning poison pills and multiple voting structures, or allows them to relax any such bans in each instance where the bidding company itself benefits from similar protections. So no harmonisation resulted and this new Directive left a wide-spread feeling of disappointment, although companies may in such cases opt for EU neutrality and break-through rules.

3.5.7   Implementing Legislation: The Market Abuse Directive

The Market Abuse Directive of Jan 2003[204] harmonises the rules on insider dealing and market manipulation in regulated and OTC markets, see also section 1.1.7 above. Its implementation date is Oct. 2004.

3.5.8   Other Parts of the Action Plan: Update UCITS, Distance Selling, Pensions, Electronic Money and Commerce, Money Laundering, Financial Conglomerate Supervision Directive, Insolvency Directives, Clearing and Settlements, Cross-Border Use of Collateral, Taxation of Savings Income

The UCITS Directive of 1985, see also section 2.3.5 above, was updated by two Directives of Jan. 2002. They liberated the types of assets in which UCITS can invest. It regulated also management companies and allowed simplified prospectuses. They must be implemented by Feb. 2004.

The Distance Marketing Directive of Sept. 2002 already discussed in section 3.4.8 covers the conditions of sale for retail products not sold face to face. It must be implemented by 2004. The Pensions Directive discussed in section 3.4.4 above was at last approved in May 2003. It allows cross-border investment but requires a prudent investment policy per country of the members.

In the area of electronic money and commerce, the E-Money Directive of Sept. 2000 defines electronic money and governs capital and authorisation requirements for new electronic money institutions. The implementation date was April 2002. The E-Commerce Directive of June 2000 already discussed in section 3.4.7 above, aims at a legal framework for the free movement of e-commerce including financial services across border. Its implementation date was Jan. 2002.

---

[203] Directive 2004/25/EC of the European Parliament and of the Council of 21 April 2004, [2004] OJ 2/142/12.
[204] Directive 2003/6/EC of the European Parliament and of the Council of 28 Jan 2003 [2003] OJ L96/16; Implementing Directive 2004/72/EC of 29 April 2004, [2004] OJ L 162/70; Implementing Directive 2003/124/EC of 22 Dec 2003.

Money laundering was discussed in chapter III, Part III and the EU measures in section 3.2.2 of that chapter. The Second Money Laundering Directive dates from Dec. 2001, extends the scope of the offenses for reporting purposes and includes professions like those of lawyers and accountants and the activities of casinos. A further Directive is expected by the end of 2004, especially to deal with terrorist financing. It is intended to also consolidate the first two Directives.

In the area of conglomerate supervision, the Directive of 2002 discussed in section 3.4.5 determines who shall be the lead supervisor for financial conglomerates and will be implemented by August 2004.

In corporate insolvency there are now the Insolvency Regulation and the Winding-up Directives of Credit Institutions, already referred to in section 3.4.3 above. An Insurance Winding-up Directive was agreed at the same time (2001).

The Finality Settlement Directive was discussed in chapter III, section 1.2.6 and the Collateral Directive in chapter III, section 1.3.5 and chapter IV, section 3.2.4. For clearing, the key is to make sure that all barriers to cross-border clearing and settlement are eliminated. It will bring costs down. Further measures are foreseen in this direction.[205] It lead to an EU Communication in 2002 in which an overall policy was announced. A further communication is expected in which the facilitation of market-driven improvements in the efficiency of clearing and settlement of cross-border securities transactions will be considered.

The taxation of savings income proved an important issue already discussed in section 2.4.7 above The Taxation of Savings Income Directive was ultimately agreed in June 2003. Under it, Member States must exchange information on interest income payments to non-residents or, in Austria, Belgium and Luxembourg tax that income at source. Switzerland agreed to a similar regime. It will be effective as of Jan 2005.

---

[205] Communication of the Commission to the Council and the European Parliament: *Clearing and Settlement in the European Union — The Way Forward,* Com [2004] 312 final.

Index